# סידור קורן
# עם פירושי הרב אברהם יצחק הכהן קוק
# נוסח אשכנז

The Koren Rav Kook Siddur
Nusaḥ Ashkenaz

ירושלים

# סידור קורן
# עם פירושי הרב אברהם יצחק הכהן קוק
# THE KOREN RAV KOOK SIDDUR

WITH COMMENTARY BASED UPON THE TEACHINGS OF

Rabbi Avraham Yitzḥak haKohen Kook

TRANSLATED AND ADAPTED BY

Rabbi Bezalel Naor

TRANSLATION OF THE TEFILLOT BY

Rabbi Lord Jonathan Sacks

•

KOREN PUBLISHERS JERUSALEM

The Koren Rav Kook Siddur
First Hebrew/English Edition, 2019

Koren Publishers Jerusalem Ltd.
POB 404401, Jerusalem 91040, ISRAEL
POB 8531, New Milford, CT 06776, USA
www.korenpub.com



The English translation in this edition is based on the English translation first published in Great Britain in 2006 in the Authorised Daily Prayer Book of the United Hebrew Congregations of the Commonwealth: New Translation and Commentary by Chief Rabbi Jonathan Sacks, (Fourth Edition, Compilation © United Synagogue) by Collins, a division of HarperCollins Publishers, London.

The image on the front cover is an artistic creation by Eliyahu Misgav adapted from the seal of Rav Kook.



Standard Size, Hardcover, ISBN 978 965 301 754 2

Printed in PRC

Third printing, 2023
KOA03

This Siddur is dedicated
to the memory of our beloved Brother and Uncle

*Aaron Stefansky*

By
David and Estee Stefansky & Children

איש חמודות
רב פעלים לתורה וללומדיה
בר אוריין ובר אבהן

הר"ר **אהרן** ז"ל
בן הרב אליעזר שליט"א
**סטפנסקי**

אהה על שבר, נהי נשמע ברמה
בעל ואב פאר חבר, שוכן באדמה.
התורה חדוותו, שירת הנשמה
הקדיש מכשרונו ושקידתו,
ליל ויממה.
רבנן נשא, קרבתם המה,
צילם חסה, בלב ונשמה.
נפלא בנדבת צדקתו, לסעד והקמה
בהונו ואונו ועזרתו,
ועצתו המחוכמה.
עסקיו באמונה וחרץ, אמרתו מקויימה
חסדו ואמתו במרץ,
נחמד למטה ואהוב ברמה.
הזדכך ביסורי מחלתו, גזירתו קיבל בדממה
על בניו וביתו מליצתו, במורשתו יראו בנחמה.

# CONTENTS


| | | |
|---|---|---|
| תודות | xi | Editor's gratitude |
| קיצורים | xii | Abbreviations |
| המעיין והלב | xiii | The Wellspring and the Heart |
| מבוא לסידור עם פירושי הרב קוק | xvi | Introduction to *The Rav Kook Siddur* |
| מילת פתיחה | xxi | A Word of Introduction |
| הפרדוקס של התפילה | xxii | The Paradox of Prayer |
| שני סוגי תפילה: מיסטי ורציונלי | xxiii | Two Types of Prayer: Mystical and Rational |
| ענייני תפילה | xxv | Matters of Prayer |
| התבוננות לפני (ואחרי) תפילה | xxix | Meditation Before (and After) Prayer |
| דבר המוציא לאור | xxxi | Publisher's Preface |
| **ימי חול** | 3 | **WEEKDAYS** |
| השכמת הבוקר | 5 | On Waking |
| טלית ותפילין | 15 | Tallit and Tefillin |
| הכנה לתפילה | 27 | Preparation for Prayer |
| ברכות השחר | 39 | Morning Blessings |
| קדיש דרבנן | 97 | The Rabbis' Kaddish |
| קדיש יתום | 103 | Mourner's Kaddish |
| פסוקי דזמרה | 105 | Pesukei DeZimra |
| ברכו | 141 | Barekhu |
| קריאת שמע | 153 | The Shema |
| עמידה | 175 | The Amida |
| וידוי | 201 | Viduy |
| אבינו מלכנו | 203 | Avinu Malkenu |
| סדר תחנון | 209 | Taḥanun |
| סדר קריאת התורה | 223 | Reading of the Torah |
| שיר של יום | 249 | The Daily Psalm |
| עשרת הדברות | 273 | The Ten Commandments |
| שלושה עשר עיקרים | 275 | The Thirteen Principles of Jewish Faith |
| מנחה לחול | 279 | Minḥa for Weekdays |
| מעריב לחול | 315 | Ma'ariv for Weekdays |
| סדר ספירת העומר | 357 | Counting of the Omer |
| קריאת שמע על המיטה | 367 | Shema before Sleep at Night |

**שבת 379 SHABBAT**

עירובין 381 Eiruvin

הדלקת נרות 383 Candle Lighting

קבלת שבת 389 Kabbalat Shabbat

מעריב לשבת וליום טוב 415 Ma'ariv for Shabbat and Yom Tov

קידוש וזמירות לליל שבת 451 Kiddush and Zemirot for Shabbat Evening

שחרית לשבת וליום טוב 475 Shaḥarit for Shabbat and Yom Tov

פסוקי דזמרה 479 Pesukei DeZimra

נשמת 521 Nishmat

ברכו 531 Barekhu

קריאת שמע 543 The Shema

עמידה לשבת 553 The Amida for Shabbat

סדר קריאת התורה 571 Reading of the Torah

תפילה לשלום המלכות 591 Prayer for the Welfare of the Government

תפילה לשלום מדינת ישראל 593 Prayer for the State of Israel

ברכת החודש 597 Blessing the New Month

מוסף לשבת 607 Musaf for Shabbat

קידוש וזמירות ליום שבת 647 Kiddush and Zemirot for Shabbat Morning

מנחה לשבת וליום טוב 665 Minḥa For Shabbat and Yom Tov

ברכי נפשי 699 Barekhi Nafshi

פרקי אבות 711 Ethics of the Fathers

סעודה שלישית של שבת 747 Se'uda Shelishit for Shabbat

מעריב למוצאי שבת 751 Ma'ariv for Motza'ei Shabbat

קידוש לבנה 771 Blessing of the New Moon

סדר הבדלה בבית 783 Havdala at Home

**חגים ומועדים 787 FESTIVALS**

סדר נטילת לולב 789 Blessing on Taking the Lulav

סדר הלל 791 Hallel

מוסף לראש חודש 799 Musaf for Rosh Ḥodesh

ביעור חמץ 817 Removal of Ḥametz

עירוב תבשילין 817 Eiruv Tavshilin

| | | |
|---|---|---|
| Kiddush for Yom Tov Evening | 821 | קידוש לליל יום טוב |
| On Entering the Sukka | 825 | תפילה כשנכנסין לסוכה |
| Ushpizin and On Leaving the Sukka | 827 | אושפיזין ותפילה כשיוצאין מן הסוכה |
| Kiddush for Yom Tov Morning | 829 | קידושא רבה ליום טוב |
| Amida for Shaḥarit, Minḥa and Ma'ariv of Yom Tov | 831 | עמידה לשחרית, מנחה ומעריב של יום טוב |
| Hakafot for Simḥat Torah | 847 | סדר הקפות לשמחת תורה |
| Akdamut | 851 | אקדמות |
| Yizkor | 859 | סדר הזכרת נשמות |
| Musaf for Festivals | 869 | מוסף לשלוש רגלים |
| Birkat Kohanim | 895 | ברכת כהנים |
| Prayer for Dew | 905 | תפילת טל |
| Prayer for Rain | 909 | תפילת גשם |
| Hoshanot | 915 | הושענות |
| Hoshanot for Hoshana Raba | 929 | הושענות להושענא רבה |
| Annulment of Vows before Rosh HaShana | 959 | התרת נדרים לערב ראש השנה |
| Kiddush for Rosh HaShana Evening | 963 | קידוש לליל ראש השנה |
| Kiddush for Rosh HaShana Day | 965 | קידושא רבה לראש השנה |
| Tashlikh | 967 | סדר תשליך |
| Kaparot | 969 | סדר כפרות |
| Viduy for Minḥa of Erev Yom Kippur | 971 | וידוי למנחה בערב יום הכיפורים |
| Ḥanukka | 981 | חנוכה |
| Purim | 987 | פורים |
| Shaḥarit for Yom HaZikaron | 991 | שחרית ליום הזיכרון |
| Yom HaAtzma'ut & Yom Yerushalayim | 995 | יום העצמאות ויום ירושלים |
| Seliḥot | 1007 | סליחות |
| GIVING THANKS | 1055 | ברכות |
| Birkat HaMazon / Grace after Meals | 1057 | ברכת המזון |
| Blessings on Mitzvot | 1077 | ברכות המצוות |
| Blessings on Pleasures, Sights and Sounds | 1079 | ברכות הנהנין, הראייה והשמיעה |

| | | |
|---|---|---|
| סדר חנוכת הבית | 1087 | Consecration of a House |
| תפילת הדרך | 1089 | The Traveler's Prayer |
| **מעגל החיים** | **1091** | **THE CYCLE OF LIFE** |
| סדר ברית מילה | 1093 | Brit Mila |
| סדר פדיון הבן | 1105 | Pidyon HaBen |
| סדר תפילה ליולדת | 1109 | Prayer after Childbirth |
| סדר זבד הבת | 1113 | Zeved HaBat |
| סדר קידושין ונישואין | 1117 | Marriage Service |
| שבע ברכות | 1117 | Sheva Berakhot |
| תפילה לחולה | 1123 | Prayer for Recovery from Illness |
| תפילה לעומד מחליו | 1127 | Prayer after Recovery from Illness |
| וידוי שכיב מרע | 1129 | Confession before Death |
| לווית המת | 1131 | Funeral Service |
| תפילה בבית האבל | 1139 | Prayer in a House of Mourning |
| אזכרה | 1141 | Memorial Prayer |
| **קריאת התורה** | **1149** | **TORAH READINGS** |
| לימי שני וחמישי ומנחה בשבת | 1150 | Weekly Portions for Mondays, Thursdays and Shabbat Minḥa |
| לראש חודש, לתעניות ציבור, לחנוכה ולפורים | 1189 | Rosh Ḥodesh, Fast Days, Ḥanukka and Purim |
| לשלוש רגלים | 1201 | Festivals |
| **הלכות תפילה** | **1247** | **GATES TO PRAYER** |
| הלכות למועדי השנה | 1247 | Guide to the Jewish Year |
| הלכות תפילה לימות חול | 1287 | Daily Prayer |
| הלכות תפילות שבת | 1303 | Shabbat Prayer |
| מדריך הלכתי למבקר בישראל | 1309 | Guide for Visitors to Israel |
| חילופי נוסחאות | 1313 | Textual Variants |
| טבלת ההפסקות המותרות בתפילה | 1315 | Table of Permitted Responses |
| ביבליוגרפיה | 1318 | Bibliography |
| קדיש דרבנן באותיות לועזיות | 1319 | Rabbis' Kaddish Transliterated |
| קדיש יתום באותיות לועזיות | 1320 | Mourner's Kaddish Transliterated |

## EDITOR'S GRATITUDE

The Editor wishes to acknowledge his gratitude to David Stefansky for initiating the project of publishing Rav Kook's commentary in English translation and for making the dream a reality; to Matthew Miller of Koren Publishers for undertaking the execution of this noble enterprise; to Lord Rabbi Jonathan Sacks for allowing the use of his fine English translation of the Prayer Book in this edition; to Rabbis Shimon Cohn and Henoch Cohn for acting as facilitators in this process; to Rabbi Moshe Yehiel Halevi Zuriel for being a constant source of inspiration and fount of wisdom in the propagation of Rav Kook's teachings; and to Avrohom Manes, Michael Nagel and Nachman Schneider for acting as "sounding boards" for much of the Torah included in this volume. May Hashem bless them all from the treasury of blessings.

I have based my commentary on the commentary "*'Olat Re'iyah*" with additions from other writings of Rav Kook, as well as some original insights of my own (signed "Editor" to distinguish between my comments and those of Rav Kook). This is the method that I employed previously in *The Rav Kook Hagadah* to great acclaim.

A word about the translations. For the most part, these are not literal word-for-word translations of Rav Kook's comments, but rather paraphrases designed to convey the gist of his meaning. On those occasions where I have translated the Rav's teaching verbatim, the text is set in from the margin to indicate that it is an exact quote.

According to the Talmud (*'Eyn Ya'akov, Ḥagigah* 12b; quoted in *Tosafot, Menaḥot* 110a, s.v. *Michael*), in Heaven there is an altar, and Archangel Michael stands and sacrifices (*makriv*) upon it every day the souls of the righteous. Like Michael, Rav Kook serves to this day as a guardian angel of Israel. And every day – through his spiritual legacy – he brings close (*mekarev*) the souls of the righteous. And in his penetrating "look" (Yiddish, *Kook*), all Israel are "righteous" (*"tsaddikim"*) – even the "sinners of Israel" (*"posh'ei Yisrael"*).

ועמך כלם צדיקים!

BN

3 Ellul, 5777, *Yahrzeit* of Rav Kook

## ABBREVIATIONS

*AT* – *'Arpilei Tohar*
*b.* – *Bavli*
*EA* – *'Eyn Ayah*
*IR* – *Igrot Rayah*
*KMYK* – *Kevatsim mi-Khetav Yad Kodsho*
*m.* – *Mishnah*
*MRIT* – *Me'orot ha-Rayah: 'Inyenei Tefillah*
*MT* – *Mishneh Torah*
*OḤ* – *Oraḥ Ḥayyim*
*OK* – *Orot ha-Kodesh*
*OR* – *'Olat Re'iyah*
RAYH – Rabbi Avraham Yitsḥak Hakohen [Kook]
RZYH – Rabbi Zevi Yehudah Hakohen [Kook]
*SK* – *Shemonah Kevatsim*
*t.* – *Tosefta*
y. – *Yerushalmi*

## KEY TO PRONUNCIATION IN COMMENTARY

*'a* = א
*'a* = ע
*h* = ה
*ḥ* = ח
*ts* = צ

## THE WELLSPRING AND THE HEART

There is a mountain, and on the mountain there stands a stone, and from the stone issues a spring.

Everything has a heart. And the world too in its entirety has a heart…

This mountain – with the stone and the spring – stands at one end of the world, and this heart of the world stands at the other end of the world.

This heart stands opposite the spring and forever longs to come to that spring. It cries out to come to that spring.

And this spring too longs for the heart…

And this spring has no time, for the spring is not within time. (Which is to say, the spring has no time in the world, for it is much higher than the time of the world.)

But the time of the spring is only the one day that the heart bestows upon it.[1]

And when it is the end of the day… close to the end of the day, then the heart and the spring bid farewell to one another (*gezegenen*), and begin to sing wondrous songs (*lieder*) to one another with great love and great longing.

(Rabbi Naḥman of Breslov, "The Seven Beggars," Day Three)

No discussion of prayer from the Jewish perspective would be complete without mention of the famous Maimonides-Naḥmanides controversy.

---

1. Reflecting upon Rabbi Naḥman's story, the thought occurred to the writer (BN) that the Hebrew word for time, *"zeman"* is *notarikon* for *zeh ma"n*. In Lurianic Kabbalah, *ma"n* is shorthand for *mayin nukvin* ("feminine waters"). This coda encapsulates Rabbi Naḥman's philosophy of Time.
For a contemporary interpretation of the trope of the heart and the spring, see Rabbi Adin Steinsaltz, *Beggars and Prayers* (New York: Basic Books, 1985), pp. 179–181. And more recently, Ora Wiskind-Elper, *Tradition and Fantasy in the Tales of Reb Naḥman of Bratslav* (Albany: State University of New York Press, 1998), pp. 209–215.

◂ For Maimonides

For Maimonides, prayer, *"'avodah she-ba-lev"* ("service of the heart") is a Biblical command. It is not bound by time. Naḥmanides took the opposite tack. The obligation of prayer is of rabbinic origin. From its inception, prayer is time-bound, limited by the three prescribed times of "evening, morning, and afternoon."[2] Women (normally exempt from time-bound commandments) were obligated by the rabbis in prayer only because of its exceptional character as *rahamei*, supplication.[3]

Perhaps at the root of the controversy between the two great men of Israel, lie differing perceptions of the essential character of prayer. For Maimonides, prayer is a universal phenomenon. It is not bounded by time; neither is its formula prescribed. It transcends both time and language. Not subject to the exigencies of time, its content remains fluid, undetermined.

In Naḥmanides' reckoning, prayer is a function of time. It comes into being in a specific time, and each time impresses upon prayer its specific stamp; its particular needs; its unique supplication.

Enter Rav Kook. Rav Kook introduces to the conversation a novel insight, a fresh look at prayer. Prayer is an incessant internal monologue. "In truth, the soul constantly prays."[4] In the inner recesses of the soul, there is an uninterrupted flow. What we observe in the formal prayer uttered at the prescribed time is but the eruption of a hidden babbling brook, the surfacing of a subterranean current.[5]

---

2. Psalms 55:18; *b. Berakhot* 20b.
3. See *b. Berakhot* 20b; Maimonides, *Sefer ha-Mitsvot*, positive commandment 5 and Naḥmanides' animadversion there; and positive commandment 10; Maimonides, *MT, Hil. Tefillah* 1:1; Rabbi Aryeh Leib Ginzburg, *Sha'agat Aryeh*, chap. 14; Rabbi Israel Meir Kagan, *Mishnah Berurah* to *Shulhan 'Arukh, OḤ* 106:1.
   When hard-pressed, Nahmanides might be willing to concede that prayer at a time of communal crisis (*"'et tsarah," "tsarat ha-tsibbur"*) is Biblically mandated (loc. cit.).
4. *OR*, vol. 1, *"'Inyenei Tefillah"* 1:2 (p. 11).
5. In this regard, see *Talmidei Rabbenu Yonah, Berakhot*, 11b (pagination of Rav Alfas), s.v. *Tefillah*: "Even though prayer has a set time, since they said, 'If only man would pray the entire day!' [*Berakhot* 21a], we judge it as a commandment that is not time-bound, and therefore women are obligated; or also, because prayer is supplication." (Cf. *Tosafot, Berakhot* 26a, end s.v. *Iba'ya lehu.*) See *"'Inyenei Tefillah"* 1:2 (in previous note).

◂ The foundation

> The foundation of prayer consists of settling within the soul of man the most exalted wants that flow within the interior of his soul from the supernal flow (*shetef*). This flow does not stop for a moment its work.[6]
>
> From the midst of that spring (*ma'yan*) full of natural holiness that is in our hearts, we draw, actualizing its delicate feelings...This is the law of prayer.[7]
>
> Prayer flows from the supernal divine spring (*ma'yan*), in which all that is lofty and sacred is included, and from which they flow.[8]

Rather than being mutually exclusive, Maimonides' and Naḥmanides' perspectives actually complement one another. They describe two dimensions of a single phenomenon. Maimonides addressed the interior process of prayer; Naḥmanides addressed the exterior process of prayer. They call to one another as Rabbi Naḥman's spring and heart yearn for one another.

The wholly transcendent consciousness of the spring longs for immanence in the "heartiness" of the heart; in its trials and tribulations; in its seemingly trivial, mundane, earth-bound and time-bound concerns. The mountain longs for the valley.

By the same token, the heart, time-conditioned as it is, longs for transcendence. It screams for the spring, for the unitive consciousness that is an ongoing, even flow, beyond the vicissitudes of this lowly world. How the heart of the world longs to break out of this world! How it would love to escape the oppressive heat and be cooled by the waters of the wellspring!

And it is this perpetual leave-taking; this ongoing romance; this nightly serenade; these melancholy *Nacht-Lieder* of the Heart and the Spring that constitute the World of Prayer.

BN

6. *MRIT*, p. 345.
7. *SK* 7:144.
8. *'Inyenei Tefillah* 1:5 in *OR*, vol. 1, p. 12.

## INTRODUCTION TO *THE RAV KOOK SIDDUR*

*By Bezalel Naor*

Rav Kook is one of the most important Jewish thinkers of the modern era. If we analyze Rav Kook's thoughts on prayer, we find three major components. I shall list them in order of their historical development.

1. The Spanish Jewish philosopher Rabbi Joseph Albo in his work *Sefer ha-'Ikkarim* raised the following philosophical problem. How is prayer possible? Does not prayer by definition attempt to change God's will? And can *"shinuy ha-ratson"* (change of divine will) be philosophically justified?[1] Albo's solution to the problem is that prayer has the ability to reverse a divine decree by changing the person's circumstance. The decree was directed at a certain type of person; through prayer that person is transformed into a different type altogether, thus rendering the previous decree inapplicable.[2] Rav Kook's response to this challenge is that prayer sets out not to change God but man. In the crucible of prayer, man's will is purified and refined, and ultimately realigned with that of his Maker.[3]
2. East European Hasidism (not to be confused with the medieval

---

1. Rabbi Joseph Albo, *Sefer ha-'Ikkarim* IV, 18; *SK* 1:304; 2:324; 7:98; *OR*, vol. 2, p. 39; Rabbi Moshe Zevi Neriyah, *Orot ha-Tefillah* (Ma'aleh Adumim: Ma'aliyot, 2004), bottom p. 129.
2. See Neriyah, p. 149, quoting Rabbi Ya'akov Moshe Ḥarlap, *Mei Marom* – Passover Haggadah, pp. 89–90. See now *Mei Marom*, vol. 10 [Leviticus] (Jerusalem, 1997), *Aḥarei-Kedoshim, ma'amar* 26 (p. 76).
3. *SK* 7:124, 125; *KMYK*, vol. 1, ed. Boaz Ofen (Jerusaem, 2006), *Pinkas 81 Piska'ot* (Yaffo), par. 52 (p. 181) = *OR*, vol. 1, *'Inyenei Tefillah* 4:14 (p. 31); *EA*, vol. 1, pp. 147–148, par. 71 (*Berakhot* 32a). Cf. Rabbi Judah Löw (Maharal of Prague), *Derekh Ḥayyim* (London: L. Honig and Sons, 1960), *Avot* 2:4; and *MRIT*, p. 544, adjacent to n. 431.
   On the connection of will to prayer, see *SK* 2:350; *OK*, vol. 3, pp. 45–60; *MRIT*, pp. 544–546; *KMYK*, vol. 2, ed. Boaz Ofen (Jerusalem, 2008), *Pinkas ha-Dapim* 1, par. 9 (pp. 54–55), based on *Zohar* II, 133a.

Rhenish pietism of the *Ḥasidei Ashkenaz*), as expounded by Rabbi Dov Baer, the Maggid of Mezritch (eminent disciple of Rabbi Israel Ba'al Shem), taught a quietist form of spirituality.[4] Summed up in a nutshell, the Maggid would have us accept that in reality, all is perfect. This outlook poses a challenge to traditional Jewish Prayer, for if the universe is already the picture of perfection, what room does that leave for *bakashah* or petitionary prayer?[5]

3. Psychoanalysis, the brainchild of the Viennese Jew Sigmund Freud, uncovered the lost continent of the "unconscious." (There are authors who attribute a theory of the unconscious to Rabbi Israel Salanter, founder of the Mussar movement, though it turns out that Rabbi Israel Salanter was actually influenced by Kant.)[6] Rav Kook's theory of the unconscious, if you would have it, is that the soul is constantly praying.[7] This ongoing internal conversation seeks some external expression,

---

4. See Rivkah Schatz-Uffenheimer, *Quietistic Elements in Eighteenth Century Ḥasidic Thought* (Jerusalem, 1968), chap. 6; Rabbi Dov Baer of Mezhirech, *Maggid Devarav le-Ya'akov*, ed. Rivkah Schatz-Uffenheimer (Jerusalem, 1976).

   Here is an example of this dilemma from Rav Kook's journal:

   For the great *tsaddikim*, prayer is exceedingly difficult, as they have no selfish will at all, and their great awareness – bound to their lucid belief in the divine love – sweetens everything for them. So how can they pray to be saved from some trouble, when in reality they haven't any trouble? (*SK* 3:67)

5. See my essay "Two Types of Prayer: Halakhic and Ḥasidic," *Tradition* 25(3), Spring 1991, pp. 26–34; reprinted in Bezalel Naor, *From A Kabbalist's Diary: Collected Essays* (Spring Valley: Orot, 2005), pp. 59–73.

6. See Yitzhak Ahren, quoted in Hillel Goldberg, *Israel Salanter: Text, Structure, Idea* (New York: Ktav, 1982), pp. 170–176.

7. Most instructive in this respect is the passage that occurs as a "comment" published at the end of *Resh Millin* (London, 1917), p. 137, par. 2:

   The activity of the life of the soul is unceasing, just as the general activity of material life never ceases all the days of life. From time to time there is a revelation of intellectual life, when the thinker originates a novel, brilliant thought. We perceive that there is a time lapse between one original thought and the next, but it comes not from the foundational, essential power of life, rather from its mental manifestations. In reality, the essence of life, which is the activity of the soul at its depth, never ceases at all. The thoughts are forever originating and streaming through us. All the toil of our study merely predisposes us – by the revelation that breaks through from the outside to

◀ and it is

and it is this outpouring of the soul, this "catharsis," which is embodied in formal prayer.[8] (It is possible that in this respect Rav Kook was influenced by Rabbi Naḥman of Breslov's notion of *"siḥah beino le-vein kono,"* intimate conversation between man and his Creator.)

These are three of the streams running through Rav Kook's thoughts on prayer: the philosophical, the mystical, and the psychological.

*

The *Siddur 'Olat Re'iyah* first appeared in print in 1939. The editor was Rav Kook's only son, Rabbi Zevi Yehudah Hakohen Kook, who cobbled together the work from three primary sources:

1. An explicit commentary to the Prayer Book;
2. Marginalia to the *Siddur Shelah* (authored by Rabbi Isaiah Halevi Horowitz) from which Rav Kook prayed;
3. Selections from *'Eyn Ayah,* Rav Kook's commentary to the *Agadot* of the Talmud (since published in its entirety by Rabbi Ya'akov Filber).

In at least one instance, Rabbi Zevi Yehudah saw fit to include an entire chapter from *Orot* (*editio princeps* Jerusalem, 1920) in the commentary to the Prayer Book.[9]

The title, which one assumes was chosen by the Editor, is a double entendre. In compliance with the Biblical command, "Three times a year all your males shall be seen by the face of the master, the Lord,"[10] Jews would bring to the Temple in Jerusalem a sacrifice known as the *'olat re'iyah.*[11] *Re'iyah* is also the initials of Rav Kook's name: *R*av *A*vraham *Y*itsḥak *H*akohen.

*

---

the depth of life – to increasingly recognize the stream of thoughts, which is a river that never stops, whose waves churn within us constantly without cease.

8. "Catharsis" is an important concept in modern psychology, specifically in regard to crying. See below Rav Kook's remarks on Psalm 6:7–10, recited in *Taḥanun.* And see now *MRIT,* p. 14.
9. Cf. *OR,* vol. 1, pp. 241–242, s.v. *Ahavah Rabbah* to *Orot, Orot ha-Teḥiyah,* chap. 21.
10. Exodus 23:17; 34:23.
11. See *m. Ḥagigah* 1:1; *b. Ḥagigah* 6a; *MT, Hil. Ḥagigah* 1:1.

◂ According to

According to Rabbi Zevi Yehudah, Rav Kook commenced composition of his work on prayer during his sojourn in London in World War I.[12] The work continued to Rav Kook's last days in Jerusalem, by which time he had reached as far as the verse "Thank the God of gods, His lovingkindness is forever," the beginning of *Hallel ha-Gadol* in *Pesukei de-Zimrah* for Sabbath morning.

Because of the sheer abundance of material, Rabbi Zevi Yehudah decided to divide the prayer book in two volumes: Volume I restricted to the weekday prayer, and Volume II to consist of the prayers for Sabbath and Festivals.[13]

In Volume I, we are informed that the actual commentary *'Olat Re'iyah* extends up to (but does not include) *Yehi Khevod* in *Pesukei de-Zimrah*. The additional material that we find in the volume was supplemented from other writings of the Rav. That goes for the prefatory chapters of *'Inyenei Tefillah* (Matters of Prayer) as well.

Rav Kook (as earlier Rabbi Shneur Zalman of Liadi)[14] used the

---

12. *OR*, vol. 1, Introduction, p. 7. See too RZYH, *Li-Sheloshah be-Ellul*, vol. 1 (Jerusalem, 1938), par. 66 (p. 29).
   In at least one instance, I found that RZYH included in *OR* a piece from an earlier commentary to the Prayer Book penned by his father, the Rav, in his youth. Entitled *"Tselota de-Avraham,"* the commentary covers the beginning of the *Siddur*: *Modeh Ani, Mah Tovu, Adon 'Olam* and *Yigdal*. It first saw the light of print in *Me'orot ha-Rayah: 'Inyenei Tefillah,* pp. 398-411. The commentary on p. 405 has been reworked in *OR*, vol. 2, p. 39, s.v. *ve-aḥarei ki-khelot ha-kol.*
   The editors of the compilation *MRIT* are reticent who titled that earlier commentary *"Tselota de-Avraham."* Was it the youthful author Rav Kook himself? (By the way, this work is not to be confused with the famous *Siddur Tselota de-Avraham* based on the teachings of Rabbi Abraham Landau of Ciechanow [1789–1875].) Rabbi Reuben Margaliot appended to his edition of *Zohar Ḥadash* (Mossad Harav Kook, Jerusalem) marginalia taken from the *Zohar Ḥadash* of Rav Kook's ancestor Rabbi Abraham of Preil and Sebezh. The collection of marginalia is entitled *"Zehiruta de-Avraham."* I speculate that it was Rav Kook who provided the title *"Zehiruta de-Avraham."*
13. Volume One for weekdays was published in 5699/1939. Volume Two for Sabbaths and Festivals was published a decade later in 5709/1949. At the end of Volume 2, RZYH Kook wrote an afterword which sums up the Godly events of the recent War of Independence.
14. Ḥayyim Meir Heilman, *Beit Rabbi* I (Berdichev, 1902), 1b.

*Siddur Shelah* by the kabbalist Rabbi Isaiah Halevi Horowitz, author *Shnei Luḥot ha-Berit.* Rav Kook studied much in that prayer book and penned comments in the margins of his personal copy. An example of these marginalia, mystical in nature, would be that transcribed by Rabbi Zevi Yehudah in the commentary to *Taḥanun*:

> We repeat six times *"YHWH Elohei Yisrael"* because *Tif'eret* is the six cardinal points (*vav ketsavot*).[15]

15. *OR*, vol. 1, p. 304. To the best of my knowledge, generally Rav Kook did not pray with the Lurianic *kavvanot.* A seeming exception to the rule occurred on a trip to Tsefat. In order to compensate for his inability to physically visit the grave of Rabbi Isaac Luria (Ari) buried there – as a *Kohen,* Rav Kook was forbidden by *Halakhah* to enter the cemetery – Rav Kook did the next best thing: He prayed *Minḥah* (the afternoon service) in the local synagogue of Ari according to the lengthy order of the Ari. See RZYH, *Li-Sheloshah be-Ellul,* vol. 1, par. 76 (p. 33), based on the testimony of Rabbi Meir David Schottland, the Karliner Ḥasid who served as Rav Kook's *shamosh* (sexton).

## A WORD OF INTRODUCTION

A student asked his *Rosh Yeshivah,* whether he should study Rav Kook's *Perush* (commentary) to the *Siddur.*

In his inimitable style, the *Rosh Yeshiva* replied: "Ach, it's not a *Perush* (commentary) to the *Siddur.*"

Intrigued, the student asked: "If not a *Perush* (commentary) to the *Siddur,* then what is it?"

"A *neshamah* (soul) on paper."[1]

1. Told to the Editor by Rabbi Elisha Paul, student of Rabbi Shmuel Ya'akov Weinberg, late *Rosh Yeshiva* of Ner Israel, Baltimore.

## THE PARADOX OF PRAYER

When one reaches the realization that in the divine scheme all is perfect, all is present, all is complete, then the very concept of prayer, which is a declaration that something is missing, something is wanting, something is lacking – appears ludicrous. How can we ask for something when we already have everything? But on the other hand, a universe bereft of the dimension of prayer would be lacking a most important ingredient of existence. So existence must encompass prayer.[1]

1. Based on *OR*, vol. 1, p. 150, s.v. *ha-Melekh*.

## TWO TYPES OF PRAYER: MYSTICAL AND RATIONAL

In the following pensée, Rav Kook contrasts the kabbalist's and rationalist's approaches to prayer. The kabbalist believes that owing to the spiritual interconnectivity of all existence, man's every word reverberates throughout the universe. A typical kabblistic *kavvanah* (intention) will include the phrase *"'al-yedei zeh yushpa' shefa' rav be-khol ha-'olamot"* ("through this there will be great influence in all the worlds"). The rationalist, on the other hand, knows of no such invisible threads linking the microcosm to the macrocosm. He would probably view such an outlook as "magical thinking." But the rationalist does acknowledge the effect the moral improvement of even one individual can have upon society as a whole. Inasmuch as prayer can contribute to the ethical refinement of a human being, indirectly it has the ability to impact upon the totality of existence.[1]

> There are two schools of thought regarding the value of prayer: the mystical school and the rationalist school.
>
> The first explains the connection of the universe to man and all his movements, and demonstrates that the expression of man's soulful will, when cleaving to God, truly acts and creates in that spiritual

1. A splendid example of the rationalist philosophy bent on the improvement of society, is Maimonides' interpretation of the first *mishnah* in Tractate *Pe'ah*. Maimonides explains that by performing commandments between man and God (such as *tsitsit*, *tefillin*, Shabbat), one will reap one's due reward in the World to Come. However, by performing commandments between man and man (whose essence is *"gemilut Ḥasadim,"* acts of lovingkindness), one will start to reap the "fruits" or dividends already in this world. "If man performs the commandments that improve relations between men, he will have reward in the World to Come for having performed the commandment, and will derive benefit in this world for having behaved well with people, for if he goes in this way and his fellow goes in this way, he will derive benefit therefrom" (Maimonides, *Perush ha-Mishnah*, ed. Kafaḥ [Jerusalem: Mossad Harav Kook, 1963], *Seder Zera'im*, p. 55).

◀ state

state momentous events in general existence. So automatically, as far as concerns man and his requests, there is a positive effect.

The rationalist school does not recognize these wondrous mysteries. Rather it subsumes prayer within the system of ethics, psychology and poetry. Through prayer, man will be uplifted; his soul will be purified; his character trails will be improved. Ethics certainly plays a part in man's destiny. Through moral betterment, man's lot will be better. All existence aspires to progress, to good. Wickedness is spewed out from existence. The soulful improvement brought about by the poetry of prayer is the end.

According to this school, prayer should not be attached specifically to a desired effect; it comes about through the collective. This school recognizes that if a man does not pray, there will accumulate in his midst many tough traits, lacking perfection and delicacy, and as a result his moral composure will suffer greatly. And the contrary, through prayer, man will be uplifted; spiritually he will be enlightened, so *ipso facto* his wants will be fulfilled.

In general, the idealism of prayer, the expression of the soul, is dearer than the specific end of that which is requested in prayer. It is understood that for this school the ideal state must be more refined in order for prayer to be recognized as an obligation of great value. Truly, the second school is full of an inner idealism – weaving[2] from all of existence in its midst – but it manages to attract hearts to its constancy.[3]

2. Assuming the vocalization is *mozeret*. There is another possibility that the word is vocalized *muzeret* (detached), derived from the root *"huzar,"* "separated" (as in *Nazir*). In that case, it may also mean "strange" or "estranged."

3. *SK* 1:282. Cf. *KMYK*, vol. 2 (Jerusalem, 2008), *Pinkas ha-Dapim* 4, par. 75 (p. 133). There, Rav Kook writes that eventually one graduates from the rationalist understanding of prayer, which yet differentiates between the inner and outer worlds, to the higher outook whereby there is no longer "any difference between these worlds, the outer and the inner, and we find that whatever has been effected for good, has taken effect throughout all of existence."

# ענייני תפילה

## MATTERS OF PRAYER

(*From RZYH Kook's Introduction to* Siddur 'Olat Re'iyah)

### התפילה המתמדת של הנשמה – The Constant Prayer of the Soul

1. The constant prayer of the soul forever strives to come out from concealment to full revelation, to extend over all the life-powers of spirit and soul, and all the life-powers of the entire body. Likewise, the prayer longs to reveal its essence and influence upon the entire environment, the entire world. Toward this end, we need to do some spiritual stock-taking (*Ḥeshbono* shel *'olam*), by way of Torah and wisdom. The outcome will be that the entire service of Torah and her wisdom is the constant revelation of the hidden prayer of the soul. "The soul of all that lives shall bless Your name, Lord our God."[1]

2. Proper prayer results only from the thought that in truth the soul is constantly praying. She longs for and flies to her Beloved without cease; only that during the actual hour of prayer the constant soul-prayer is revealed in deed. This is the delicacy and loveliness of the prayer: She is likened to a rose who opens her beautiful petals to receive the dew or the sun's light rays. Therefore, "Oh, that man would pray the entire day!"[2]

3. Prayer seeks from the soul its function. When days and years go by without meaningful prayer, there gather in the heart many blockages, whereby one feels an inner heaviness. When the good spirit returns and the gift of prayer is granted from on high, with every prayer blocks are removed, and the dams which obstructed the flowing stream of the living soul, disappear. And with the ascent of the soul in each prayer

1. *Nishmat* prayer for Sabbath and Festival.
2. Saying of Rabbi Yoḥanan in *b. Berakhot* 21a.

◂ (for as long

(for as long as it lasts), a certain percentage of lost time is made up for. Certainly not at once can the missing be filled; it is a gradual process. And the window of the prayer increasingly reveals its lights.[3]

4. Prayer brings to light, to life, that which is concealed in the depths of the soul. In direct relation to the degree of inner purity of man, is the impact of prayer as it emerges from the depths of his inner will, as he turns to the Source of all souls and all worlds. Great and wondrous is the effect of man's expression upon life. A great light flows with the word.[4] The word is taken from hidden storehouses of rich life. As great as its inner penetration, so shall be great the luminosity the word reveals and engenders. Clarity of expression clarifies the details of the light, while solidifying existence with a clearly defined will. It is not possible that prayer makes no impression. Whether it brings about the effect according to its specific target, or by a circuitous route – these are wonders of the Perfect Intelligence. Be that as it may, an entire world is revealed in prayer, whether it be the organized prayer that is common to all, or the private prayer flowing from the depths of the heart of every individual and every community, based on its condition and needs. Together with all the preparations for a world order, upper and lower; with all of mankind's advancement – practical, societal, intellectual, artificial – by which the quality of life is improved, by which the world becomes outwardly (and to a degree even inwardly) ordered – there must come at the top of the list *prayer*; prayer which is the inner order, the head of all desires. Prayer will invigorate all the branches of life, all of civilization's improvements. Man will know how to balance out prayer and action; will know how to achieve their integration. "For My house shall be called a House of Prayer for all the peoples."[5]

5. Prayer deepens in us the lofty, holy feeling that is the essence of the light of the Life of the Worlds absorbed in our souls, and prayer inseminates us with holy lights that produce fruits of salvation. Not only

---

3. *KMYK*, vol. 1, *Pinkas "Reshimot mi-London,"* par. 28 (p. 200).
4. Rabbi Israel Ba'al Shem Tov punned on the verse in Genesis 6:16, "Make a light for *the ark*": "Make luminous *the word*!" The Hebrew for *ark*, *"teivah,"* may also signify *word*.
5. Isaiah 56:7; *SK* 6:192.

◂ for us

for us as private individuals; whatever prayer accomplishes, works upon us in relation to all existence and all life, in all their values, past, future and present. How wonderful are the manifestations, how lofty the sparks that are enhanced by every prayer, though it be temporary, solitary and isolated; all the more so, if it be permanent, collective and societal. Prayer flows from the supernal divine spring, in which all that is lofty and sacred is included, and from which they flow. And to that spring, prayer returns with strength and might imbued with holiness, and adds blessing to the Spring of Life, encompassing the Tree of Life and adorning its branches. The underground currents that feed the spring combine together, and many different saps bond together, forming a source of blessing for rivers of eternal love and abundant love, and blessing and peace for all existence. And when the prayer of Israel rises to the holy height, when it is focused in the Land of eternal delight, on the Temple Mount – all the worlds are flooded with light; myriads of souls are renewed by the supernal splendor; and lofty ideals rise in holy pride; and the supernal glory is forever blessed. "Blessed is the LORD's glory from His place."[6]

6. Prayer is for us, and for the entire world, an absolute necessity – and at the same time the most proper of pleasures. The waves of our soul continuously flow. We desire of ourselves and of the world a perfection such that our limited existence cannot provide; as a result, we find ourselves in great trouble, whose misfortune can bring us to utter distraction. But before a long time elapses, before this mass can form in our midst, we come in prayer. We pour out our conversation and rise to a world of perfect existence. Then our inner world truly becomes perfect, our mind is at peace, and that measure of influence that our inner resolve exerts upon existence – of which our interior is one of its components – tilts the entire world to merit on the scales of justice.

7. Prayer is the ideal of all worlds. All existence pines for its source of life. Every plant, every bush; every grain of sand, every clump of earth; all in which life is revealed and all in which life is concealed; all the micro

6. Ezekiel 3:12; *SK* 8:29.

◂ and all the

and all the macro of creation; heavens above and holy seraphs; all the specificity of being, and all its generality; all longs, aspires, pines, thirsts for the pleasant perfection of its highest source – the living, holy, pure and mighty. Man absorbs all of these longings at every hour; he is elevated and ascends by his holy desires. There comes the time that these godly desires be revealed in a prayer that makes waves of light; that goes out in unfettered might, in holy conversation to the divine expanses. With prayer, man uplifts all creation, uniting with him all being; uplifting all to the Source of blessing and the Source of life.[7]

7. *OR*, vol. 1, pp. 11–13

## MEDITATION BEFORE (AND AFTER) PRAYER

> One who prays, needs to pause[1] one hour before the prayer and one hour after the prayer.
>
> Before the prayer, for it says, "Happy are those who dwell in Your House."[2]
>
> After the prayer, for it says, "However the righteous shall give thanks to Your name, the just shall dwell in Your presence."[3]
>
> Our Rabbis taught: The early pious men (*Ḥasidim*) would pause for one hour, and pray for one hour, and once again pause for one hour.
>
> Now since they devoted nine hours a day to prayer, how could their Torah be preserved, and when was their labor done?[4]
>
> But since they were pious men (*Ḥasidim*), their Torah was preserved and their labor was blessed.[5]

In the *Talmud Yerushalmi,* we find a significant variant. In reply to the questions – "When did they engage in Torah? When did they engage in their labor?" – Rabbi Yitsḥak be-Rabbi El'azar replied: "Since they were pious men (*Ḥasidim*), blessing was bestowed upon their Torah and blessing was bestowed upon their labor."[6]

---

1. *Bavli* has "pause" (*sh-h-h*). *Yerushalmi* has "sit" (*y-sh-v*), and so Maimonides, *Hil. Tefillah* 4:16. However, one might counter that *"yashav"* in this context does not mean "sit" but "pause." See Rashi, Leviticus 12:4: "*Yeshivah* is an expression for remaining (*'akavah*)." If that is so, then *shehiyah* of *Bavli* and *yeshivah* of *Yerushalmi* are truly synonymous. The prooftexts from Psalms suggest literal sitting. In practice, some famous Ḥasidic rabbis would deliberately take a seat for a moment before exiting the sanctuary after prayer.
2. Psalms 84:5.
3. Psalms 140:14.
4. "'Nine hours' – for three prayers" (Rashi).
5. *b. Berakhot* 32b.
6. *y. Berakhot* 5:1.

Rav Kook felt that the wording of the *Talmud Yerushalmi* ("blessing was bestowed upon their Torah") as opposed to the wording of the Babylonian Talmud ("their Torah was preserved") lent support to his pet theory that there is an essential difference between the two Talmudim. Rav Kook believed that "because of the influence of the light of prophecy that always appears to some degree in the Land of Israel," the scholars of Israel had an advantage over the scholars of Babylonia. The divine spirit that rested upon those who engaged in Torah in the Land of Israel, aided them in clarifying their doubts and broadening their intellect. This is reflected in the wording of the *Yerushalmi*: "Blessing was bestowed upon their Torah." In Babylonia, *their* Torah was merely "preserved."[7]

7. Letter of Rav Kook to Rabbi Aharon Yitsḥak Zaslansky, datelined "Jerusalem, 14 Shevat 5687 [1927]," responding to Rabbi Zaslansky's *"kuntres"* (booklet) of comments to *Igrot ha-Rayah*. The letter was published in *Eretz Tzvi: Tzvi Menachem Glatt Memorial Volume* (Hebrew) (Jerusalem, 1989), pp. 185–186. Rabbi Zaslansky made the observation concerning the variant in the *Yerushalmi*, and Rav Kook wholeheartedly embraced that finding. Rabbi Zaslansky was commenting on the third letter in the 1922 edition of *Igrot ha-Rayah*. In the later 1962 edition of *Igrot ha-Rayah*, it would be Letter 103 to Rabbi Yitsḥak Isaac Halevi (Rabinowitz), author *Dorot ha-Rishonim* (*IR*, vol. 1, pp. 122–128). For a lengthy discussion of Rav Kook's theory of the *Sitz im Leben* of *Yerushalmi* versus *Bavli*, see Bezalel Naor, *The Limit of Intellectual Freedom: The Letters of Rav Kook* (Spring Valley, NY: Orot, 2011).

## PUBLISHER'S PREFACE

*"One generation will praise Your works to the next..."*

It is with gratitude and pride that we offer the Rav Kook Edition of the Koren Siddur.

This exceptional volume combines the profound thought and analysis of HaRav Avraham Yitzḥak Kook – the great Torah scholar, halakhist, philosopher, and one of the most influential and renowned Jewish leaders of the twentieth century – and the eloquent translation of the *tefillot* by Rabbi Lord Jonathan Sacks, one of the most articulate and original Jewish thinkers of our time.

The creation of this volume owes so much to Rabbi Bezalel Naor, whose incredible scholarship and interpretations of the writings of Rav Kook are evident on the pages of this book. We are grateful for his tireless efforts and admirable dedication to this work.

This unique project would never have come to fruition without the invaluable support of David Stefansky, whose unending enthusiasm for both the importance of Rav Kook's teachings and Rabbi Naor's elucidation have made this essential publication possible. Generations of readers will be forever in your debt.

Since its publication in 1981, The Koren Siddur has been recognized for its textual accuracy and innovative graphic design. It is our hope that through this project we have realized the aim of master typographer Eliyahu Koren, founder of Koren Publishers Jerusalem, "to present to worshipers a means to draw and connect them not only to the words of the prayers, but also to the contents and meaning."

This special edition of the Koren Siddur continues the Koren tradition of making the language of prayer more accessible, thus enhancing the prayer experience. One of the unique features of the Siddur is the use of typesetting to break up a prayer phrase-by-phrase – rather than using a block paragraph format – so that the reader will naturally pause at the correct places. No commas appear in the Hebrew text at the end of lines,

◀ but in the

but in the English translation, where linguistic clarity requires, we have retained the use of commas at the end of lines. Unlike other bilingual siddurim, the Hebrew text is on the left-hand page and the English on the right. This arrangement preserves the distinctive "fanning out" effect of the Koren text and the beauty of the Koren layout.

We thank the small but professional team at Koren for upholding our commitment to enhance the meaning of prayer, in particular typesetter Esther Be'er.

It has been both an honor and a real pleasure for us to collaborate in the publication of this important work. We can only hope that we have extended the teachings of Rav Kook to a new generation and a larger audience, furthering *Avodat HaShem* for Jews everywhere.

Matthew Miller, Publisher
Jerusalem, 5778 (2018)

# סידור קורן
# THE KOREN SIDDUR


| | | |
|---|---|---|
| ימי החול | 5 | WEEKDAYS |
| שבת | 379 | SHABBAT |
| חגים ומועדים | 787 | FESTIVALS |
| ברכות | 1055 | GIVING THANKS |
| מעגל החיים | 1091 | THE CYCLE OF LIFE |
| קריאת התורה | 1149 | TORAH READINGS |
| הלכות תפילה | 1247 | GATES TO PRAYER |

# ימי חול

## WEEKDAYS


| | | |
|---|---|---|
| השכמת הבוקר | 5 | ON WAKING |
| שחרית | 39 | SHAḤARIT |
| מנחה | 279 | MINḤA |
| מעריב | 315 | MA'ARIV |
| ספירת העומר | 357 | COUNTING OF THE OMER |
| קריאת שמע על המיטה | 367 | THE SHEMA BEFORE SLEEP |

# Shaḥarit

*The following order of prayers and blessings, which departs from that of most prayer books, is based on the consensus of recent halakhic authorities. See laws 315–323.*

## ON WAKING

*On waking, our first thought should be that we are in the presence of God. Since we are forbidden to speak God's name until we have washed our hands, the following prayer is said, which, without mentioning God's name, acknowledges His presence and gives thanks for a new day and for the gift of life. See laws 315–323.*

מוֹדֶה I thank You, living and eternal King,
for giving me back my soul in mercy.
Great is Your faithfulness.

*Wash hands and say the following blessings.*
*Some have the custom to say "Wisdom begins" on page 12 at this point.*

בָּרוּךְ Blessed are You, LORD our God, King of the Universe,
who has made us holy through His commandments,
and has commanded us about washing hands.

---

awakens to a glorious universe: a vast, infinite reality. And the wonder is that confronted with the infinite universe, the individual self remains undaunted. And to the contrary, in this limitless vista, the "I" finds divine confirmation and validation.[2]

חַי וְקַיָּם *Living and existing.* In our experience, "life" and "existence" are antithetical. "Life" conjures up images of growth, change, flux. That which "exists," on the other hand, is permanent and unchanging. In the divinity, this apparent contradiction is resolved. In God, there is what mystics refer to as a *"coincidentia oppositorum,"* a coincidence of opposites.[3]

עַל נְטִילַת יָדַיִם / ABOUT WASHING HANDS
The ritual washing of the hands prior to prayer, symbolizes the purity of deeds

2. *OR*, vol. 1, p. 1.
3. *OR*, vol. 1, p. 2, s.v. *ve-kayyam*. Cf. below Rav Kook's commentary to *Barukh she-Amar* (*OR*, vol. 1, pp. 195–196, s.v. *Barukh ḥai la-'ad ve-kayyam la-netsaḥ*).

# שחרית

*The following order of prayers and blessings, which departs from that of most prayer books, is based on the consensus of recent halakhic authorities. See laws 315–323.*

## השכמת הבוקר

*On waking, our first thought should be that we are in the presence of God. Since we are forbidden to speak God's name until we have washed our hands, the following prayer is said, which, without mentioning God's name, acknowledges His presence and gives thanks for a new day and for the gift of life. See laws 315–323.*

מוֹדֶה/ *women* מוֹדָה/ אֲנִי לְפָנֶיךָ מֶלֶךְ חַי וְקַיָּם
שֶׁהֶחֱזַרְתָּ בִּי נִשְׁמָתִי בְּחֶמְלָה
רַבָּה אֱמוּנָתֶךָ.

*Wash hands and say the following blessings.*
*Some have the custom to say* רֵאשִׁית חָכְמָה *on page 13 at this point.*

בָּרוּךְ אַתָּה יהוה אֱלֹהֵינוּ מֶלֶךְ הָעוֹלָם
אֲשֶׁר קִדְּשָׁנוּ בְּמִצְוֹתָיו וְצִוָּנוּ עַל נְטִילַת יָדָיִם.

---

השכמת הבוקר / ON WAKING

*Modeh Ani* is an expression of gratitude to the Almighty for returning my soul to me after its nocturnal journey. We do not wait until we have washed our hands to recite *Modeh Ani*. Gratitude must be expressed immediately. It must not be delayed. There is a lesson to be derived concerning interpersonal relationships. When another human bestows kindness upon us, our expression of gratitude should be forthcoming immediately.[1]

מוֹדֶה אֲנִי *I thank.* The word *"modeh"* has double meaning. Besides conveying thanksgiving, it has another sense of admission or confession. In this particular instance, affirmation of the greater reality is the cause of thanksgiving. Released from the shackles of ordinary, materialist perception, one

---

1. Rabbi Raphael Kook quoting his uncle Rav Kook; in Simḥah Raz, *Mal'akhim ki-B'nei Adam* (Jerusalem, 2002), p. 290.

בָּרוּךְ Blessed are You, Lord our God,
King of the Universe,
who formed man in wisdom
and created in him many orifices and cavities.
It is revealed and known before the throne of Your glory
that were one of them
to be ruptured or blocked,
it would be impossible to survive and stand before You.
Blessed are You, Lord,
Healer of all flesh who does wondrous deeds.

---

In our present state, after the food we eat has been digested, some of it is absorbed and assimilated in our system, while the remainder is eliminated. But it was not always so in the past, and looking into the distance, it will not be this way in the future. Before the Primordial Sin, all of the food ingested remained in the system. It was man's partaking of the Tree of Knowledge (*'Ets ha-Da'at*) that brought about the present state by which some of the nourishment is turned into foul-smelling waste matter. The Sages alluded to this transition when they found support for the *halakhah* (regarding the recitation of *Shema'* and prayer) that one must keep a distance of four cubits from the waste matter of an adult (as opposed to an infant) from the following verse: "He that increases knowledge (*da'at*), increases sorrow."[8] On the other hand, the manna in the Desert, which recaptured the paradisical existence before the Tree of Knowledge, "was absorbed in the two hundred and forty-eight limbs."[9] And in the future, man will once again return to this ideal state. This will be the *tikkun* of the future.[10]

8. Ecclesiastes 1:18; *b. Sukkah* 42b. Rashi explains that the word *"makh'ov"* (sorrow) was understood in this context to mean *"masri'aḥ"* (smell).
9. *b. Yoma* 75b. See Rabbi Zadok Hakohen Rabinowitz of Lublin, *Kedushat Shabbat, ma'amar 7*, in *Peri Zaddik*, vol. 1 (Lublin, 1901), 23b. See also Rashi, Numbers 21:5 and *'Avodah Zarah* 5b, s.v. *ba-leḥem ha-kelokel.*
10. Rabbi Shelomo Elyashev, *Leshem Shevo ve-Aḥlamah: Sefer ha-De'ah (Derushei 'Olam ha-Tohu)* (Piotrków, 1912), Part Two, 3:18 (34b).
*OR*, vol. 2, pp. 204–207.

בָּרוּךְ אַתָּה יהוה אֱלֹהֵינוּ מֶלֶךְ הָעוֹלָם
אֲשֶׁר יָצַר אֶת הָאָדָם בְּחָכְמָה
וּבָרָא בוֹ נְקָבִים נְקָבִים, חֲלוּלִים חֲלוּלִים.
גָּלוּי וְיָדוּעַ לִפְנֵי כִסֵּא כְבוֹדֶךָ
שֶׁאִם יִפָּתֵחַ אֶחָד מֵהֶם
אוֹ יִסָּתֵם אֶחָד מֵהֶם
אִי אֶפְשַׁר לְהִתְקַיֵּם וְלַעֲמֹד לְפָנֶיךָ.
בָּרוּךְ אַתָּה יהוה
רוֹפֵא כָל בָּשָׂר וּמַפְלִיא לַעֲשׂוֹת.

---

which is a prerequisite to the act of prayer. Prayer must not be coupled with unethical deeds. The hands must be free of iniquity.[4]

Perhaps an anecdote concerning Rabbi El'azar is apropos to our discussion. The Talmud relates that it was the custom of Rabbi El'azar to first give a coin to a poor person and (only) afterward pray. He cited the verse: "Through righteousness (*tsedek*) I shall see Your face."[5] The portal to beholding the divine countenance is acting charitably towards one's fellow man.

אֲשֶׁר יָצַר / WHO FORMED MAN IN WISDOM

Man's form, his face, is a manifestation of the divine wisdom. "A man's wisdom lights up his face."[6] Now that divine wisdom ordained that the exalted human form should have bodily needs which it shares with animals. This connection between the spiritual and the material tells us that certainly divine wisdom has some wonderful purpose in impressing a dark material, subject to lowly conditions, with a splendorous stamp.[7]

---

4. *OR*, vol. 1, p. 57.
5. Psalms 17:15; *b. Bava Batra* 10a; Rabbi Shneur Zalman of Liadi, *Tanya* IV, 8 (112b).
6. Ecclesiastes 8:1.
7. *OR*, vol. 1, p. 57. (Cf. Rabbi Moses Isserles' gloss to *Shulḥan 'Arukh, OḤ* 6:1.)

אֱלֹהַי My God,
the soul You placed within me is pure.
You created it, You formed it, You breathed it into me,
and You guard it while it is within me.
One day You will take it from me,
and restore it to me in the time to come.
As long as the soul is within me,
I will thank You, LORD my God and God of my ancestors,
Master of all works, LORD of all souls.
Blessed are You, LORD, who restores souls to lifeless bodies.

### TZITZIT

*The following blessing is said before putting on tzitzit. Neither it nor the subsequent prayer is said by those who wear a tallit. The blessing over the latter exempts the former. See laws 324–330.*

בָּרוּךְ Blessed are You, LORD our God, King of the Universe,
who has made us holy through His commandments,
and has commanded us about the command of tasseled garments.

*After putting on tzitzit, say:*

יְהִי רָצוֹן May it be Your will, LORD my God and God of my ancestors, that the commandment of the tasseled garment be considered before You as if I had fulfilled it in all its specifics, details and intentions, as well as the 613 commandments dependent on it, Amen, Selah.

---

There is no darkness, no shadow of death in that illumination. No obstacle resulting from some corruption or some sin, has the ability to stop up the original light, which penetrates to the interior of every soul.

From that might, comes the first, pure utterance of the morning, spoken with the originality of truth: *My God!*[12]

נְשָׁמָה שֶׁנָּתַתָּ בִּי טְהוֹרָה הִיא *The soul that You placed within me is pure.* There is an ongoing tension between the infinite light *('Or Ein Sof)* which is the source of the soul, and the egoistic, individualistic identity that it must assume for the duration of its bodily sojourn. Despite what one might think to the contrary, the purity of the soul is undiminished, because the soul is forever aspiring to ascend to its lofty source.[13]

וְאַתָּה מְשַׁמְּרָהּ בְּקִרְבִּי *And You guard it while it is within me.* The preservation of

12. *OR*, vol. 1, p. 66.
13. *OR*, vol. 1, p. 67.

אֱלֹהַי
נְשָׁמָה שֶׁנָּתַתָּ בִּי טְהוֹרָה הִיא.
אַתָּה בְרָאתָהּ, אַתָּה יְצַרְתָּהּ, אַתָּה נְפַחְתָּהּ בִּי
וְאַתָּה מְשַׁמְּרָהּ בְּקִרְבִּי, וְאַתָּה עָתִיד לִטְּלָהּ מִמֶּנִּי
וּלְהַחֲזִירָהּ בִּי לֶעָתִיד לָבוֹא.
כָּל זְמַן שֶׁהַנְּשָׁמָה בְקִרְבִּי, מוֹדֶה/ *women* מוֹדָה/ אֲנִי לְפָנֶיךָ
יהוה אֱלֹהַי וֵאלֹהֵי אֲבוֹתַי
רִבּוֹן כָּל הַמַּעֲשִׂים, אֲדוֹן כָּל הַנְּשָׁמוֹת.
בָּרוּךְ אַתָּה יהוה, הַמַּחֲזִיר נְשָׁמוֹת לִפְגָרִים מֵתִים.

### לבישת ציצית

*The following blessing is said before putting on a* טלית קטן. *Neither it nor* יְהִי רָצוֹן *is said by those who wear a* טלית. *The blessing over the latter exempts the former. See laws 324–330.*

בָּרוּךְ אַתָּה יהוה אֱלֹהֵינוּ מֶלֶךְ הָעוֹלָם
אֲשֶׁר קִדְּשָׁנוּ בְּמִצְוֹתָיו וְצִוָּנוּ עַל מִצְוַת צִיצִית.

*After putting on the* טלית קטן, *say:*

יְהִי רָצוֹן מִלְּפָנֶיךָ, יהוה אֱלֹהַי וֵאלֹהֵי אֲבוֹתַי, שֶׁתְּהֵא חֲשׁוּבָה מִצְוַת
צִיצִית לְפָנֶיךָ, כְּאִלּוּ קִיַּמְתִּיהָ בְּכָל פְּרָטֶיהָ וְדִקְדּוּקֶיהָ וְכַוָּנוֹתֶיהָ, וְתַרְיַ״ג
מִצְוֹת הַתְּלוּיוֹת בָּהּ, אָמֵן סֶלָה.

---

אֱלֹהַי / MY GOD

This holy *cri de coeur* whereby each individual confidently addresses the Lord as his personal God, is the expression of the soul at its source. The soul recognizes itself and its strength. It knows that its existence and its vitality are [of] the Living God. It knows that at the hidden height, there is no division of light, and if an innumerable multitude of souls, and creatures and worlds without number, are all drenched with the light (*'or*) of the true God, then the divine vitality (*ḥiyyut*) with unending love penetrates all of them equally – as if there is but one single soul found in all of existence![11]

11. Cf. Judah Halevi, *Kuzari* IV, 1; Maimonides, *Guide of the Perplexed* I, 72.

## BLESSINGS OVER THE TORAH

*Before beginning to pray, we engage in a miniature act of study. So, before beginning to pray, we engage in a miniature act of study, preceded by the appropriate blessings. The blessings are followed by brief selections from Scripture, Mishna and Gemara, the three foundational texts of Judaism.*

בָּרוּךְ Blessed are You, Lord our God, King of the Universe,
who has made us holy through His commandments,
and has commanded us to engage in study of the words of Torah.

וְהַעֲרֶב נָא Please, Lord our God, make the words of Your Torah
sweet in our mouths and in the mouths of Your people,
the house of Israel,
so that we, our descendants (and their descendants)
and the descendants of Your people, the house of Israel,
may all know Your name
and study Your Torah for its own sake.
Blessed are You, Lord,
who teaches Torah to His people Israel.

בָּרוּךְ Blessed are You, Lord our God, King of the Universe,
who has chosen us from all the peoples
and given us His Torah.
Blessed are You, Lord, Giver of the Torah.

יְבָרֶכְךָ May the Lord bless you and protect you. *Num. 6*
May the Lord make His face shine on you and be gracious to you.
May the Lord turn His face toward you and grant you peace.

---

ברכות התורה / BLESSINGS OVER THE TORAH

The blessing recited before studying Torah concludes with the words "Who *gives* the Torah," in the present tense, though the Torah was given on Mount Sinai three thousand years ago. In reality, God is constantly giving the Torah anew. In every age, the Torah flows constantly within the interior of the soul.[1]

1. *OR*, vol. 1, p. 61.

# ברכות התורה

*Before beginning to pray, we engage in a miniature act of study. So, before beginning to pray, we engage in a miniature act of study, preceded by the appropriate blessings. The blessings are followed by brief selections from* תנ״ך, משנה *and* גמרא, *the three foundational texts of Judaism.*

בָּרוּךְ אַתָּה יהוה אֱלֹהֵינוּ מֶלֶךְ הָעוֹלָם
אֲשֶׁר קִדְּשָׁנוּ בְּמִצְוֹתָיו וְצִוָּנוּ לַעֲסֹק בְּדִבְרֵי תוֹרָה.

וְהַעֲרֶב נָא יהוה אֱלֹהֵינוּ אֶת דִּבְרֵי תוֹרָתְךָ
בְּפִינוּ וּבְפִי עַמְּךָ בֵּית יִשְׂרָאֵל
וְנִהְיֶה אֲנַחְנוּ וְצֶאֱצָאֵינוּ (וְצֶאֱצָאֵי צֶאֱצָאֵינוּ)
וְצֶאֱצָאֵי עַמְּךָ בֵּית יִשְׂרָאֵל
כֻּלָּנוּ יוֹדְעֵי שְׁמֶךָ וְלוֹמְדֵי תוֹרָתְךָ לִשְׁמָהּ.
בָּרוּךְ אַתָּה יהוה, הַמְלַמֵּד תּוֹרָה לְעַמּוֹ יִשְׂרָאֵל.

בָּרוּךְ אַתָּה יהוה אֱלֹהֵינוּ מֶלֶךְ הָעוֹלָם
אֲשֶׁר בָּחַר בָּנוּ מִכָּל הָעַמִּים וְנָתַן לָנוּ אֶת תּוֹרָתוֹ.
בָּרוּךְ אַתָּה יהוה, נוֹתֵן הַתּוֹרָה.

יְבָרֶכְךָ יהוה וְיִשְׁמְרֶךָ: במדבר ו
יָאֵר יהוה פָּנָיו אֵלֶיךָ וִיחֻנֶּךָּ:
יִשָּׂא יהוה פָּנָיו אֵלֶיךָ וְיָשֵׂם לְךָ שָׁלוֹם:

---

the soul in the body occurs in two senses: 1) There is the very wonder that there can be this bonding of the spiritual and material realms.[14] 2) The purity of the soul is preserved intact, no matter how low the person may stoop; no matter to what dark depths one may descend.[15]

14. Cf. Rabbi Moses Isserles' gloss to *Shulhan 'Arukh, OḤ* 6:1.
15. *OR*, vol. 1, pp. 67–68.

אֵלּוּ These are the things *Mishna Pe'ah 1:1*
for which there is no fixed measure:
the corner of the field, first-fruits,
appearances before the LORD
[on festivals, with offerings],
acts of kindness
and the study of Torah.

אֵלּוּ These are the things *Shabbat 127a*
whose fruits we eat in this world
but whose full reward awaits us
in the World to Come:
honoring parents;
acts of kindness;
arriving early at the house of study
morning and evening;
hospitality to strangers;
visiting the sick;
helping the needy bride;
attending to the dead;
devotion in prayer;
and bringing peace between people –
but the study of Torah is equal to them all.

*Some say:*

רֵאשִׁית חָכְמָה Wisdom begins in awe of the LORD; *Ps. 111*
all who fulfill [His commandments] gain good understanding;
His praise is ever-lasting.
The Torah Moses commanded us *Deut. 33*
is the heritage of the congregation of Jacob.
Listen, my son, to your father's instruction, *Prov. 1*
and do not forsake your mother's teaching.
May the Torah be my faith and Almighty God my help.
Blessed be the name of His glorious kingdom for ever and all time.

אֵלּוּ דְבָרִים שֶׁאֵין לָהֶם שִׁעוּר משנה פאה א:א
הַפֵּאָה וְהַבִּכּוּרִים וְהָרֵאָיוֹן
וּגְמִילוּת חֲסָדִים
וְתַלְמוּד תּוֹרָה.

אֵלּוּ דְבָרִים שֶׁאָדָם אוֹכֵל פֵּרוֹתֵיהֶם בָּעוֹלָם הַזֶּה שבת קכז.
וְהַקֶּרֶן קַיֶּמֶת לוֹ לָעוֹלָם הַבָּא
וְאֵלּוּ הֵן
כִּבּוּד אָב וָאֵם
וּגְמִילוּת חֲסָדִים
וְהַשְׁכָּמַת בֵּית הַמִּדְרָשׁ שַׁחֲרִית וְעַרְבִית
וְהַכְנָסַת אוֹרְחִים
וּבִקּוּר חוֹלִים
וְהַכְנָסַת כַּלָּה
וּלְוָיַת הַמֵּת
וְעִיּוּן תְּפִלָּה
וַהֲבָאַת שָׁלוֹם בֵּין אָדָם לַחֲבֵרוֹ
וְתַלְמוּד תּוֹרָה כְּנֶגֶד כֻּלָּם.

*Some say:*

רֵאשִׁית חָכְמָה יִרְאַת יהוה תהלים קיא
שֵׂכֶל טוֹב לְכָל־עֹשֵׂיהֶם, תְּהִלָּתוֹ עֹמֶדֶת לָעַד:
תּוֹרָה צִוָּה־לָנוּ מֹשֶׁה, מוֹרָשָׁה קְהִלַּת יַעֲקֹב: דברים לג
שְׁמַע בְּנִי מוּסַר אָבִיךָ וְאַל־תִּטֹּשׁ תּוֹרַת אִמֶּךָ: משלי א
תּוֹרָה תְּהֵא אֱמוּנָתִי, וְאֵל שַׁדַּי בְּעֶזְרָתִי.
בָּרוּךְ שֵׁם כְּבוֹד מַלְכוּתוֹ לְעוֹלָם וָעֶד.

## TALLIT

*Say the following meditation before putting on the tallit. Meditations before the fulfillment of mitzvot are to ensure that we do so with the requisite intention (kavana). This particularly applies to mitzvot whose purpose is to induce in us certain states of mind, as is the case with tallit and tefillin, both of which are external symbols of inward commitment to the life of observance of the mitzvot.*

בָּרְכִי נַפְשִׁי Bless the LORD, my soul. LORD, my God, You are very great, *Ps. 104*
clothed in majesty and splendor, wrapped in a robe of light, spreading out the heavens like a tent.

*Some say:*

For the sake of the unification of the Holy One, blessed be He, and His Divine Presence, in reverence and love, to unify the name *Yod-Heh* with *Vav-Heh* in perfect unity in the name of all Israel.

I am about to wrap myself in this tasseled garment (tallit). So may my soul, my 248 limbs and 365 sinews be wrapped in the light of the tassel (*hatzitzit*) which amounts to 613 [commandments]. And just as I cover myself with a tasseled garment in this world, so may I be worthy of rabbinical dress and a fine garment in the World to Come in the Garden of Eden. Through the commandment of tassels may my life's-breath, spirit, soul and prayer be delivered from external impediments, and may the tallit spread its wings over them like an eagle stirring up its nest, hovering over its *Deut. 32*
young. May the commandment of the tasseled garment be considered before the Holy One, blessed be He, as if I had fulfilled it in all its specifics, details and intentions, as well as the 613 commandments dependent on it, Amen, Selah.

*Before wrapping oneself in the tallit, say:*

בָּרוּךְ Blessed are You, LORD our God, King of the Universe,
who has made us holy through His commandments,
and has commanded us to wrap ourselves in the tasseled garment.

*According to the Shelah (R. Isaiah Horowitz), one should say these verses after wrapping oneself in the tallit:*

מַה־יָּקָר How precious is Your loving-kindness, O God, and the chil- *Ps. 36*
dren of men find refuge under the shadow of Your wings. They are filled with the rich plenty of Your House. You give them drink from Your river of delights. For with You is the fountain of life; in Your light, we see light. Continue Your loving-kindness to those who know You, and Your righteousness to the upright in heart.

---

are comforted by the thought that the darkness presages and will be transformed into light.[1]

1. *OR*, vol. 1, p. 20.

# עטיפת טלית

*Say the following meditation before putting on the* טלית*. Meditations before the fulfillment of* מצוות *are to ensure that we do so with the requisite intention (*כוונה*). This particularly applies to* מצוות *whose purpose is to induce in us certain states of mind, as is the case with* טלית *and* תפילין*, both of which are external symbols of inward commitment to the life of observance of the* מצוות*.*

**בָּרְכִי נַפְשִׁי אֶת־יהוה, יהוה אֱלֹהַי גָּדַלְתָּ מְּאֹד, הוֹד וְהָדָר לָבָשְׁתָּ: עֹטֶה־אוֹר כַּשַּׂלְמָה, נוֹטֶה שָׁמַיִם כַּיְרִיעָה:** תהלים קד

*Some say:*

לְשֵׁם יִחוּד קֻדְשָׁא בְּרִיךְ הוּא וּשְׁכִינְתֵּהּ בִּדְחִילוּ וּרְחִימוּ, לְיַחֵד שֵׁם י״ה בו״ה בְּיִחוּדָא שְׁלִים בְּשֵׁם כָּל יִשְׂרָאֵל.

הֲרֵינִי מִתְעַטֵּף בְּצִיצִית. כֵּן תִּתְעַטֵּף נִשְׁמָתִי וּרְמַ״ח אֵבָרַי וּשְׁסָ״ה גִידַי בְּאוֹר הַצִּיצִית הָעוֹלָה תַּרְיַ״ג. וּכְשֵׁם שֶׁאֲנִי מִתְכַּסֶּה בְּטַלִּית בָּעוֹלָם הַזֶּה, כָּךְ אֶזְכֶּה לַחֲלוּקָא דְרַבָּנָן וּלְטַלִּית נָאָה לָעוֹלָם הַבָּא בְּגַן עֵדֶן. וְעַל יְדֵי מִצְוַת צִיצִית תִּנָּצֵל נַפְשִׁי רוּחִי וְנִשְׁמָתִי וּתְפִלָּתִי מִן הַחִיצוֹנִים. וְהַטַּלִּית תִּפְרֹשׂ כְּנָפֶיהָ עֲלֵיהֶם וְתַצִּילֵם, כְּנֶשֶׁר יָעִיר קִנּוֹ, עַל גּוֹזָלָיו יְרַחֵף: וּתְהֵא חֲשׁוּבָה מִצְוַת צִיצִית לִפְנֵי דברים לב
הַקָּדוֹשׁ בָּרוּךְ הוּא, כְּאִלּוּ קִיַּמְתִּיהָ בְּכָל פְּרָטֶיהָ וְדִקְדּוּקֶיהָ וְכַוָּנוֹתֶיהָ וְתַרְיַ״ג מִצְוֹת הַתְּלוּיוֹת בָּהּ, אָמֵן סֶלָה.

*Before wrapping oneself in the* טלית*, say:*

**בָּרוּךְ אַתָּה יהוה אֱלֹהֵינוּ מֶלֶךְ הָעוֹלָם**
**אֲשֶׁר קִדְּשָׁנוּ בְּמִצְוֹתָיו וְצִוָּנוּ לְהִתְעַטֵּף בַּצִּיצִית.**

*According to the Shelah (R. Isaiah Horowitz), one should say these verses after wrapping oneself in the* טלית*:*

**מַה־יָּקָר חַסְדְּךָ אֱלֹהִים, וּבְנֵי אָדָם בְּצֵל כְּנָפֶיךָ יֶחֱסָיוּן: יִרְוְיֻן מִדֶּשֶׁן בֵּיתֶךָ, וְנַחַל עֲדָנֶיךָ תַשְׁקֵם: כִּי־עִמְּךָ מְקוֹר חַיִּים, בְּאוֹרְךָ נִרְאֶה־אוֹר: מְשֹׁךְ חַסְדְּךָ לְיֹדְעֶיךָ, וְצִדְקָתְךָ לְיִשְׁרֵי־לֵב:** תהלים לו

---

עטיפת טלית / TALLIT

וּבְנֵי אָדָם בְּצֵל כְּנָפֶיךָ יֶחֱסָיוּן *And the children of men find refuge in the shadow of Your wings.* The shadow symbolizes darkness, obscurity, adversity. But this particular shadow is the shadow of wings. Wings symbolize ascent. So we

## TEFILLIN

*Some say the following meditation before putting on the tefillin.*

For the sake of the unification of the Holy One, blessed be He, and His Divine Presence, in reverence and love, to unify the name *Yod-Heh* with *Vav-Heh* in perfect unity in the name of all Israel.

By putting on the tefillin I hereby intend to fulfill the commandment of my Creator who commanded us to wear tefillin, as it is written in His Torah: "Bind them as a sign on your hand, and they shall be an emblem on the center of your head." They contain these four sections of the Torah: one beginning with *Shema* [Deut. 6:4–9]; another with *Vehaya im shamo'a* [ibid. 11:13–21]; the third with *Kadesh Li* [Ex. 13:1–10]; and the fourth with *Vehaya ki yevi'akha* [ibid. 13:11–16]. These proclaim the uniqueness and unity of God, blessed be His name in the world. They also remind us of the miracles and wonders which He did for us when He brought

*Deut. 6*

---

This practice of wearing *tefillin* all or most of the day was maintained by Rav Kook for most of his life.[3] Before Rav Kook's marriage to the daughter of Rabbi Elijah David Rabinowitz-Te'omim (Aderet), his future father-in-law sent him as a Purim gift, three sets of *tefillin*: Rashi; Rabbenu Tam; and a small pair of Rashi to wear under his hat.[4] We read that in 1904, when Rav Kook was in Odessa, from whence he would ship out to Jaffa, he wore small *tefillin* under his hat and cloak.[5] (Out of humility, Rav Kook would hide the fact that he wore the *tefillin* of Rabbenu Tam, which are reserved for the very pious. He practiced this discretion even in later years, by which time he was quite renowned.)[6]

Rav Kook was so strongly committed to the proper observance of the *mitsvah* of *tefillin* that he published in Warsaw in 1891 an anonymous work entitled *Ḥevesh Pe'er* to demonstrate that halakhically the *tefillin* must not be worn on the forehead but rather above the hairline. He traveled from town to town in Lithuania, selling the book (which he pretended not to have authored) and giving edifying talks stressing the importance and significance of *tefillin*.

As recorded by his son, Rabbi Zevi Yehudah, the Rav uttered this intriguing

3. RZYH Kook, *Li-Sheloshah be-Ellul*, vol. 1, p. 47, par. 109.
4. RZYH Kook, *Li-Sheloshah be-Ellul*, vol. 1, p. 6, par. 1.
5. RZYH Kook, *Li-Sheloshah be-Ellul*, vol. 2, p. 11, par. 15.
6. RZYH Kook, *Li-Sheloshah be-Ellul*, vol. 1, pp. 46–47, par. 109.

# הנחת תפילין

*Some say the following meditation before putting on the* תפילין.

לְשֵׁם יִחוּד קֻדְשָׁא בְּרִיךְ הוּא וּשְׁכִינְתֵּהּ בִּדְחִילוּ וּרְחִימוּ, לְיַחֵד שֵׁם י״ה בו״ה בְּיִחוּדָא שְׁלִים בְּשֵׁם כָּל יִשְׂרָאֵל.

הִנְנִי מְכַוֵּן בַּהֲנָחַת תְּפִלִּין לְקַיֵּם מִצְוַת בּוֹרְאִי, שֶׁצִּוָּנוּ לְהָנִיחַ תְּפִלִּין,
כַּכָּתוּב בְּתוֹרָתוֹ: וּקְשַׁרְתָּם לְאוֹת עַל־יָדֶךָ, וְהָיוּ לְטֹטָפֹת בֵּין עֵינֶיךָ: וְהֵן דברים ו
אַרְבַּע פָּרָשִׁיּוֹת אֵלּוּ, שְׁמַע, וְהָיָה אִם שָׁמֹעַ, קַדֶּשׁ לִי, וְהָיָה כִּי יְבִאֲךָ,
שֶׁיֵּשׁ בָּהֶם יִחוּדוֹ וְאַחְדוּתוֹ יִתְבָּרַךְ שְׁמוֹ בָּעוֹלָם, וְשֶׁנִּזְכֹּר נִסִּים וְנִפְלָאוֹת

---

הנחת תפילין / TEFILLIN

During the year that Rav Kook spent studying in the famed Volozhin Yeshivah, he would wear his *tefillin* the entire day, which was a departure from the practice of the *yeshivah*. (Though the Vilna Gaon, who approved the founding of the *yeshivah*, was reputed to have worn *tefillin* all day.) Some fellow students thought this behavior to be "showing off" (*yohara*) and they brought their complaint to the younger Rosh Yeshivah, Rabbi Ḥayyim Soloveitchik. Rabbi Ḥayyim responded that he did not know the student sufficiently to formulate an opinion. Rabbi Ḥayyim referred them to the elder Rosh Yeshivah, Rabbi Naftali Zevi Yehudah Berlin, known as the *"Neziv"* (who was also Rabbi Ḥayyim's grandfather in-law).[1] When confronted with this complaint, the *Neziv* answered: "He is a *gaon* (genius) and a *tsaddik* (righteous man)." Rav Kook's critics were not easily deterred. They pointed around the study hall to two or three other individuals of great spiritual stature. "They are also *ge'onim* and *tsaddikim*, yet they don't have the audacity to wear *tefillin* all day." The *Neziv* came back with this reply: "Leave him alone. He is different. He is a *gaon* and a *tsaddik* – and a *yashar* (just man)."[2]

---

1. Rabbi Ḥayyim Soloveitchik was married to Lifsha, daughter of Rabbi Raphael Shapiro, son-in-law of the Neziv.
2. Told to the Editor (BN) by the grandson of Rabbi Ḥayyim Soloveitchik, Rabbi Ahron Soloveichik of Chicago. For the definition of "*yashar*" in Neziv's lexicon, see the Introduction to his commentary to the Pentateuch, *Ha'amek Davar*. For Rav Kook's own thoughts on the "*yashar*," see *OR*, vol. 1, pp. 333–334, s.v. "However the righteous shall give thanks to Your name, the just (*yesharim*) shall dwell in Your presence"; and *OR*, vol. 2, p. 17, s.v. "Light is sown for the righteous, and joy for the upright in heart" (Psalms 97:11).

us out of Egypt, and that He has the power and the dominion over the highest and the lowest to deal with them as He pleases. He commanded us to place one of the tefillin on the arm in memory of His "outstretched arm" (of redemption), setting it opposite the heart, to subject the desires and designs of our heart to His service, blessed be His name. The other is to be on the head, opposite the brain, so that my mind, whose seat is in the brain, together with my other senses and faculties, may be subjected to His service, blessed be His name. May the spiritual influence of the commandment of the tefillin be with me so that I may have a long life, a flow of holiness, and sacred thoughts, free from any suggestion of sin or iniquity. May the evil inclination neither incite nor entice us, but leave us to serve the LORD, as it is in our hearts to do.

And may it be Your will, LORD our God and God of our ancestors, that the commandment of tefillin be considered before You as if I had fulfilled it in all its specifics, details and intentions, as well as the 613 commandments dependent on it, Amen, Selah.

---

in channeling some of the *"sha'ashu'im ha-'elyonim"* (the supernal delight)[8] from the highest level of divinity into our limited existence.[9]

*

But that is not the final movement in this symphony. After this downward movement, if you would have it, from that which is beyond all will and intent, to a purposeful *kavvanah* or intention, there is an upward movement, whereby one returns once again to that state of the *"sha'ashu'im,"* the spiritual "delight."

---

8. See Proverbs 8:30; Rabbi Moses Cordovero, *Shi'ur Komah* (Warsaw, 1883), s.v. *Torah*, chap. 10 (13b-c); s.v. *Hashgaḥa* (58a); idem, *Elimah* (Lvov, 1881) 1:1:8 (3d); idem, *Derishot be-'Inyenei ha-Mal'akhim*, appended to Rabbi Reuben Margaliot, *Mal'akhei 'Elyon* (Jerusalem, 1945), pp. 28–36; Rabbi Naphtali Bachrach, *'Emek ha-Melekh* (Amsterdam 1648), *Sha'ar Sha'ashu'ei ha-Melekh*, chap. 2 (2c); Rabbi David Cohen, *Kol ha-Nevu'ah* (Jerusalem, 1979), pp. 197–198, 259, 260–261, 264–265.
9. *OR*, vol. 1, pp. 23–24.
   Perhaps this is the key to understanding a curious anecdote in the Talmud (*b. Berakhot* 30b). Various rabbis when questioned why they were in such a very jocular mood (*badaḥ tuva*), responded: "I am wearing *tefillin*" (*"Ana tefillin menaḥna"*). That levity; that divine mirth derived from the unique ability of the *tefillin* to link the finite to the infinite. Cf. Rabbi Shneur Zalman of Liadi, *Torah 'Or* (Vilna, 1899; photo offset Brooklyn, 1972), *Toledot*, s.v. *Mayim rabim* (18a).

שֶׁעָשָׂה עִמָּנוּ בְּהוֹצִיאוֹ אוֹתָנוּ מִמִּצְרָיִם, וַאֲשֶׁר לוֹ הַכֹּחַ וְהַמֶּמְשָׁלָה
בָּעֶלְיוֹנִים וּבַתַּחְתּוֹנִים לַעֲשׂוֹת בָּהֶם כִּרְצוֹנוֹ. וְצִוָּנוּ לְהָנִיחַ עַל הַיָּד
לְזִכְרוֹן זְרוֹעַ הַנְּטוּיָה, וְשֶׁהִיא נֶגֶד הַלֵּב, לְשַׁעְבֵּד בָּזֶה תַּאֲווֹת וּמַחְשְׁבוֹת
לִבֵּנוּ לַעֲבוֹדָתוֹ יִתְבָּרַךְ שְׁמוֹ. וְעַל הָרֹאשׁ נֶגֶד הַמֹּחַ, שֶׁהַנְּשָׁמָה שֶׁבְּמֹחִי
עִם שְׁאָר חוּשַׁי וְכֹחוֹתַי כֻּלָּם יִהְיוּ מְשֻׁעְבָּדִים לַעֲבוֹדָתוֹ, יִתְבָּרַךְ שְׁמוֹ.
וּמִשֶּׁפַע מִצְוַת תְּפִלִּין יִתְמַשֵּׁךְ עָלַי לִהְיוֹת לִי חַיִּים אֲרוּכִים וְשֶׁפַע קֹדֶשׁ
וּמַחֲשָׁבוֹת קְדוֹשׁוֹת בְּלִי הִרְהוּר חֵטְא וְעָוֹן כְּלָל, וְשֶׁלֹּא יְפַתֵּנוּ וְלֹא
יִתְגָּרֶה בָּנוּ יֵצֶר הָרָע, וְיַנִּיחֵנוּ לַעֲבֹד אֶת יהוה כַּאֲשֶׁר עִם לְבָבֵנוּ.

וִיהִי רָצוֹן מִלְּפָנֶיךָ, יהוה אֱלֹהֵינוּ וֵאלֹהֵי אֲבוֹתֵינוּ, שֶׁתְּהֵא חֲשׁוּבָה מִצְוַת
הֲנָחַת תְּפִלִּין לִפְנֵי הַקָּדוֹשׁ בָּרוּךְ הוּא, כְּאִלּוּ קִיַּמְתִּיהָ בְּכָל פְּרָטֶיהָ וְדִקְדּוּקֶיהָ
וְכַוָּנוֹתֶיהָ וְתַרְיַ"ג מִצְוֹת הַתְּלוּיוֹת בָּהּ, אָמֵן סֶלָה.

---

one-liner: "The *tefillin* are the electric batteries of the godly holiness which is the might of Israel."[7]

MEDITATION BEFORE DONNING THE *TEFILLIN*

לְשֵׁם יִחוּד קֻדְשָׁא בְּרִיךְ הוּא וּשְׁכִינְתֵּהּ *For the sake of the unification of the Holy One, blessed be He, and His Divine Presence* (Shekhinah) (*previous page*). In circles influenced by the Kabbalah, it is customary before donning the *tefillin,* to recite this formula. In commenting on this *yiḥud* or mystic unification, Rav Kook launches into a meditation exercise that takes one from the most infinite to the most finite, and specifically to the body of the Israelite about to be wrapped in the *tefillin.*

At the most exalted, infinite level there is yet no will (*ratson*), no direction, no intention. The great Italian kabbalist, Rabbi Menahem Azariah of Fano, wrote that *shemo* (His name) has the same numerical value as *ratson* (will). But on this lofty level, there is yet no name of God, thus no divine will. In donning the *tefillin,* we bring this most abstract, undefined, immaterial level down into the material, mundane plane of existence. We descend from *ayin* (divine no-thingness) to *ani* ("I"), the individual personality

And there is felt a great joy in doing so, for we will thereby have succeeded

---

7. RZYH Kook, *Li-Sheloshah be-Ellul,* vol. 2, p. 18, par. 38.

*Stand and place the hand-tefillin on the biceps of the left arm (or right arm if you are left-handed), angled toward the heart, and before tightening the strap, say:*

בָּרוּךְ Blessed are You, LORD our God, King of the Universe, who has made us holy through His commandments, and has commanded us to put on tefillin.

*Wrap the strap of the hand-tefillin seven times around the arm. Place the head-tefillin above the hairline, centered between the eyes, and say quietly:*

בָּרוּךְ Blessed are You, LORD our God, King of the Universe, who has made us holy through His commandments, and has commanded us about the commandment of tefillin.

*Adjust the head-tefillin and say:*

בָּרוּךְ Blessed be the name of His glorious kingdom for ever and all time.

---

As much as the soul is inflamed by its inner emotion, and from drawing upon the dew of its lights – all is based upon that which is written in the Torah, the supernal mother of all the lights of holiness.[11]

*

The first paragraph of *Shema'* puts us in touch with the absolute unity of God, which is supra-mundane and beyond all words and expression. The second paragraph (*Ve-Hayah 'im shamo'a*) brings to our awareness the workings of God within the world. We transition from a "disembodied" God to an "embodied" God, so to speak. We learn that the world operates with a principle of reward and punishment. Good deeds are rewarded; evil deeds punished. The descent of rain, or the cessation thereof, bespeaks this entire principle of reward and punishment.[12]

ברכות התפילין / BLESSINGS UPON THE *TEFILLIN*

There is a famous controversy between two medieval giants, Rashi and his grandson Rabbenu Tam, how many blessings to pronounce upon "laying" the *tefillin*. According to Rashi, we recite one blessing, *"Le-honi'aḥ tefillin,"* at the time we lay the hand-phylactery, and that suffices for the head-phylactery as well. Rabbenu Tam, on the other hand, held that an additional blessing *"Al mitsvat tefillin"* should be recited upon placing the head-phylactery.[13]

---

11. *OR*, vol. 1, p. 25, end s.v. *ka-katuv.*
12. *OR*, vol. 1, p. 25.
13. Most Ashkenazic Jews follow the ruling of Rabbenu Tam and recite two blessings, one

*Stand and place the* תפילין של יד *on the biceps of the left arm (or right arm if you are left-handed), angled toward the heart, and before tightening the strap, say:*

בָּרוּךְ אַתָּה יהוה אֱלֹהֵינוּ מֶלֶךְ הָעוֹלָם
אֲשֶׁר קִדְּשָׁנוּ בְּמִצְוֹתָיו וְצִוָּנוּ לְהָנִיחַ תְּפִלִּין.

*Wrap the strap of the* תפילין של יד *seven times around the arm.*
*Place the* תפילין של ראש *above the hairline, centered between the eyes, and say quietly:*

בָּרוּךְ אַתָּה יהוה אֱלֹהֵינוּ מֶלֶךְ הָעוֹלָם
אֲשֶׁר קִדְּשָׁנוּ בְּמִצְוֹתָיו וְצִוָּנוּ עַל מִצְוַת תְּפִלִּין.

*Adjust the* תפילין של ראש *and say:*

בָּרוּךְ שֵׁם כְּבוֹד מַלְכוּתוֹ לְעוֹלָם וָעֶד

---

At this point, Rav Kook engages in meticulous textual analysis. He probes the difference between the initial act of *binding* (*keshirah*) the *tefillin* upon the hand, and their subsequent *being* (*havayah*) between the eyes (Deuteronomy 6:8). We are not forever left in a state of binding the spiritual to the material, but go on to simply "be" in that lofty state of bliss, of *"sha'ashu'im,"* which precedes our created reality.

Rav Kook was bothered by the question why we quote in our *kavvanah* the verse from the paragraph of *Shema'* (ibid.) and not the verse from the paragraph of *Ve-Hayah 'im shamo'a* (Deuteronomy 11:18). His solution is that the focus is upon the individual; the goal is to bring Godliness from the loftiest height all the way down to the individual personality.[10] The paragraph of *Shema'*, stated in the singular, is appropriate in this respect. The paragraph of *Ve-Hayah 'im shamo'a,* written in the plural, and referring to the collective (*Kelal Yisrael*), does not serve this specific purpose.

Lest one think that attainment of a state of enlightenment, of divine delight, is the be-all and end-all, we preface our meditation with these words: "By putting on the *tefillin,* I hereby intend to fulfill the commandment of my Creator who commanded us to wear *tefillin, as it is written in His Torah.*" To quote Rav Kook:

---

10. "No one else can reveal the holiness of your individual soul that is nourished by the *Kelal* – but you yourself" (RZYH). See Rabbi Ḥayyim Avihu Schwartz, *Mi-Tokh ha-Torah ha-Go'elet,* vol. 2 (Jerusalem, 1989), p. 78.

*Some say:*

From Your wisdom, God most high, grant me [wisdom], and from Your understanding, give me understanding. May Your loving-kindness be greatly upon me, and in Your might may my enemies and those who rise against me be subdued. Pour Your goodly oil on the seven branches of the menora so that Your good flows down upon Your creatures. You open Your hand, and satisfy every living thing with favor. *Ps. 145*

*Wind the strap of the hand-tefillin three times around the middle finger, saying:*

וְאֵרַשְׂתִּיךְ I will betroth you to Me for ever; *Hos. 2*
I will betroth you to Me in righteousness and justice,
loving-kindness and compassion;
I will betroth you to Me in faithfulness;
and you shall know the Lord.

*After putting on the tefillin, say the following:*

וַיְדַבֵּר The Lord spoke to Moses, saying, "Consecrate to Me every firstborn male. The first offspring of every womb among the Israelites, whether man or beast, belongs to Me." Then Moses said to the people, "Remember this day on which you left Egypt, the slave-house, when the Lord brought you out of it with a mighty hand. No leaven shall be eaten. You are leaving on this day, in the month of Aviv. When the Lord brings you into the land of the Canaanites, Hittites, Amorites, Hivites and Jebusites, the land He swore to your ancestors to give you, a land flowing with milk and honey, you are to observe this service in *Ex. 13*

---

Rashi would have us understand that by the time one has arrived at the donning of the head-phylactery, one is beyond the ability to utter words of blessing. That level of "being" described above, is a world of silence. "To You, silence is praise."[14]

Rabbenu Tam, however, was of the opinion that there is continuity from the world of preparation, connoted by the hand-phylactery. Difficult though it may be, we are able to carry over some of the ability to utter speech, to pronounce words of blessing, from the hand-phylactery to the placement of the head-phylactery.[15]

14. Psalms 65:2.
15. *OR*, vol. 1, pp. 30–31.

*Some say:*

וּמֵחָכְמָתְךָ אֵל עֶלְיוֹן תַּאֲצִיל עָלַי, וּמִבִּינָתְךָ תְּבִינֵנִי, וּבְחַסְדְּךָ תַּגְדִּיל עָלַי, וּבִגְבוּרָתְךָ תַּצְמִית אוֹיְבַי וְקָמַי. וְשֶׁמֶן הַטּוֹב תָּרִיק עַל שִׁבְעָה
תהלים קמה קְנֵי הַמְּנוֹרָה, לְהַשְׁפִּיעַ טוּבְךָ לִבְרִיּוֹתֶיךָ. פּוֹתֵחַ אֶת־יָדֶךָ וּמַשְׂבִּיעַ לְכָל־חַי רָצוֹן:

*Wind the strap of the* תפילין של יד *three times around the middle finger, saying:*

הושע ב וְאֵרַשְׂתִּיךְ לִי לְעוֹלָם
וְאֵרַשְׂתִּיךְ לִי בְּצֶדֶק וּבְמִשְׁפָּט וּבְחֶסֶד וּבְרַחֲמִים:
וְאֵרַשְׂתִּיךְ לִי בֶּאֱמוּנָה, וְיָדַעַתְּ אֶת־יהוה:

*After putting on the* תפילין*, say the following:*

שמות יג וַיְדַבֵּר יהוה אֶל־מֹשֶׁה לֵּאמֹר: קַדֶּשׁ־לִי כָל־בְּכוֹר, פֶּטֶר כָּל־רֶחֶם בִּבְנֵי יִשְׂרָאֵל, בָּאָדָם וּבַבְּהֵמָה, לִי הוּא: וַיֹּאמֶר מֹשֶׁה אֶל־הָעָם, זָכוֹר אֶת־הַיּוֹם הַזֶּה, אֲשֶׁר יְצָאתֶם מִמִּצְרַיִם מִבֵּית עֲבָדִים, כִּי בְּחֹזֶק יָד הוֹצִיא יהוה אֶתְכֶם מִזֶּה, וְלֹא יֵאָכֵל חָמֵץ: הַיּוֹם אַתֶּם יֹצְאִים, בְּחֹדֶשׁ הָאָבִיב: וְהָיָה כִי־יְבִיאֲךָ יהוה אֶל־אֶרֶץ הַכְּנַעֲנִי וְהַחִתִּי וְהָאֱמֹרִי וְהַחִוִּי וְהַיְבוּסִי, אֲשֶׁר נִשְׁבַּע לַאֲבֹתֶיךָ לָתֶת לָךְ, אֶרֶץ זָבַת חָלָב וּדְבָשׁ, וְעָבַדְתָּ אֶת־הָעֲבֹדָה הַזֹּאת בַּחֹדֶשׁ הַזֶּה:

---

Rav Kook explains the halakhic difference between Rashi and Rabbenu Tam in terms of his overall outlook on the commandment of *tefillin*. (See above.)

---

for each phylactery. However, two outstanding Lithuanian halakhic authorities – who had severe ideological differences – both decided in favor of Rashi's opinion (which is also the opinion of Maimonides): Rabbi Elijah, the Gaon of Vilna, and Rabbi Shneur Zalman of Liadi, the author of the *Tanya*. In the latter regard, see Rabbi Abraham Ḥayyim Na'eh, *Piskei ha-Siddur* (Jerusalem, 1937), pp. 12–13, par. 46. The author disagrees with the *Sha'ar ha-Kollel* who assumed a kabbalistic basis for the decision of RSZ. In Rabbi Naeh's reading of the situation, the basis is purely halakhic: "*Safek berakhot le-hakel*." When in doubt, one does not recite a blessing.

this same month. For seven days you shall eat unleavened bread, and make the seventh day a festival to the LORD. Unleavened bread shall be eaten throughout the seven days. No leavened bread may be seen in your possession, and no leaven shall be seen anywhere within your borders. On that day you shall tell your son, 'This is because of what the LORD did for me when I left Egypt.' [These words] shall also be a sign on your hand, and a reminder above your forehead, so that the LORD's Torah may always be in your mouth, because with a mighty hand the LORD brought you out of Egypt. You shall therefore keep this statute at its appointed time from year to year."

וְהָיָה After the LORD has brought you into the land of the Canaanites, as He swore to you and your ancestors, and He has given it to you, you shall set apart for the LORD the first offspring of every womb. All the firstborn males of your cattle belong to the LORD. Every firstling donkey you shall redeem with a lamb. If you do not redeem it, you must break its neck. Every firstborn among your sons you must redeem. If, in time to come, your son asks you, "What does this mean?" you shall say to him, "With a mighty hand the LORD brought us out of Egypt, out of the slave-house. When Pharaoh stubbornly refused to let us leave, the LORD killed all the firstborn in the land of Egypt, both man and beast. That is why I sacrifice to the LORD the first male offspring of every womb, and redeem all the firstborn of my sons." [These words] shall be a sign on your hand and as an emblem above your forehead, that with a mighty hand the LORD brought us out of Egypt.

---

that the most important chapter in the *Book of Tanya* is Chapter 32 (*Lev* or "heart") which is devoted to the subject of *ahavat yisrael* (love of Israel), including those far from the Torah of the LORD and His service.

The Talmud states: "Any [communal] fast in which the sinners of Israel (*posh'ei Yisrael*) do not participate, is not a fast."[3] Rav Kook was wont to illustrate this principle with a mnemonic device. The word *"tsibbur"* (community) is formed by the initials *ts̲addikim* (righteous), *b̲einonim* (average), *u̲-r̲esha'im* (and wicked). A community which is lacking these three diverse elements, is not a community.[4] (Editor)

3. *b. Kereitot* 6b.
4. See *Ma'amrei ha-Rayah* 1 (Jerusalem, 1980), p. 77.

שִׁבְעַת יָמִים תֹּאכַל מַצֹּת, וּבַיּוֹם הַשְּׁבִיעִי חַג לַיהוה: מַצּוֹת יֵאָכֵל אֵת שִׁבְעַת הַיָּמִים, וְלֹא־יֵרָאֶה לְךָ חָמֵץ וְלֹא־יֵרָאֶה לְךָ שְׂאֹר, בְּכָל־גְּבֻלֶךָ: וְהִגַּדְתָּ לְבִנְךָ בַּיּוֹם הַהוּא לֵאמֹר, בַּעֲבוּר זֶה עָשָׂה יהוה לִי בְּצֵאתִי מִמִּצְרָיִם: וְהָיָה לְךָ לְאוֹת עַל־יָדְךָ וּלְזִכָּרוֹן בֵּין עֵינֶיךָ, לְמַעַן תִּהְיֶה תּוֹרַת יהוה בְּפִיךָ, כִּי בְּיָד חֲזָקָה הוֹצִאֲךָ יהוה מִמִּצְרָיִם: וְשָׁמַרְתָּ אֶת־הַחֻקָּה הַזֹּאת לְמוֹעֲדָהּ, מִיָּמִים יָמִימָה:

וְהָיָה כִּי־יְבִאֲךָ יהוה אֶל־אֶרֶץ הַכְּנַעֲנִי כַּאֲשֶׁר נִשְׁבַּע לְךָ וְלַאֲבֹתֶיךָ, וּנְתָנָהּ לָךְ: וְהַעֲבַרְתָּ כָל־פֶּטֶר־רֶחֶם לַיהוה, וְכָל־פֶּטֶר שֶׁגֶר בְּהֵמָה אֲשֶׁר יִהְיֶה לְךָ הַזְּכָרִים, לַיהוה: וְכָל־פֶּטֶר חֲמֹר תִּפְדֶּה בְשֶׂה, וְאִם־לֹא תִפְדֶּה וַעֲרַפְתּוֹ, וְכֹל בְּכוֹר אָדָם בְּבָנֶיךָ תִּפְדֶּה: וְהָיָה כִּי־יִשְׁאָלְךָ בִנְךָ מָחָר, לֵאמֹר מַה־זֹּאת, וְאָמַרְתָּ אֵלָיו, בְּחֹזֶק יָד הוֹצִיאָנוּ יהוה מִמִּצְרַיִם מִבֵּית עֲבָדִים: וַיְהִי כִּי־הִקְשָׁה פַרְעֹה לְשַׁלְּחֵנוּ, וַיַּהֲרֹג יהוה כָּל־בְּכוֹר בְּאֶרֶץ מִצְרַיִם, מִבְּכֹר אָדָם וְעַד־בְּכוֹר בְּהֵמָה, עַל־כֵּן אֲנִי זֹבֵחַ לַיהוה כָּל־פֶּטֶר רֶחֶם הַזְּכָרִים, וְכָל־בְּכוֹר בָּנַי אֶפְדֶּה: וְהָיָה לְאוֹת עַל־יָדְכָה וּלְטוֹטָפֹת בֵּין עֵינֶיךָ, כִּי בְּחֹזֶק יָד הוֹצִיאָנוּ יהוה מִמִּצְרָיִם:

---

הכנה לתפילה / PREPARATION FOR PRAYER *(next page)*

In conjunction with the teaching of the *Ari*, Rabbi Isaac Luria, before beginning the actual prayer, some have the custom to recite, "I hereby accept upon myself the commandment 'You shall love your neighbor as yourself.'"[1] Before embarking upon the journey of prayer, one connects with the entire People of Israel. In this way, one's prayer will be inclusive of all Israel and surely ascend above.[2]

Rabbi Zevi Yehudah Kook, son of the Rav, once pointed out to someone

1. Leviticus 19:18
2. Rabbi Ḥayyim Vital, *Peri 'Ets Ḥayyim, Sha'ar 'Olam ha-'Asiyah*, chap. 1. See the elucidation of Rabbi Ḥayyim of Volozhin, *Nefesh ha-Ḥayyim* II, 18 (conclusion final note).

## PREPARATION FOR PRAYER

*On entering the synagogue:*

# HOW GOODLY

Num. 24

are your tents, Jacob, your dwelling places, Israel.
As for me, in Your great loving-kindness, Ps. 5
I will come into Your House.
I will bow down to Your holy Temple
in awe of You.

---

The placement of these words, "How goodly are your tents, Jacob; your dwelling places, Israel," is not without significance. This verse from the prophecy of Bil'am, provides the *leitmotif* as we begin our journey to the world of prayer. Our prayer, which would soar to the heights of heaven, must not have a destabilizing effect; we must not come unhinged in the process. It is necessary to retain grounding in our earthly reality. Two flows – the one from below to above; the other from above to below – are reflected in the parallelism of the verse.

There are two oppositions: tents/dwelling places; Jacob/Israel. *Jacob* is the more earthly aspect; *Israel,* the more heavenly aspect. The root of the name *Jacob* is *'akev* or heel, which suggests footing. *Israel,* which signifies "that you have striven with God and men, and have succeeded," bespeaks God-wrestling and striving for the divine heights. *Tents* are meant for temporary camping, for being on the move, for journeying. *Dwelling places* are designed for some measure of permanence.

Jacob, grounded as he is, longs to make the ascent; the tent symbolizes his flight, his movement. Israel, on the other hand, from the perspective of the angelic and near-divine, is filled with anxiety and foreboding lest he overstep his mortal bounds. Succor comes to him in the form of "dwelling places" capable of tethering him to mundane reality.

---

with Torah, referred to as *"ḥayyei 'olam"* ("eternal life"). See Rabbi David Kamenetsky, *"Igeret ha-Kodesh shel ha-Gaon Rabbi Ephraim Eliezer Zevi Ḥarlap," Yeshurun,* vol. 26 (Nissan 2012), pp. 829. The manuscript is in the possession of the heirs of Rabbi Ya'akov Moshe Ḥarlap in Jerusalem.

# הכנה לתפילה

*On entering the* בית כנסת:

במדבר כד

מַה־טֹּבוּ

אֹהָלֶיךָ יַעֲקֹב, מִשְׁכְּנֹתֶיךָ יִשְׂרָאֵל:

תהלים ה

וַאֲנִי בְּרֹב חַסְדְּךָ אָבוֹא בֵיתֶךָ

אֶשְׁתַּחֲוֶה אֶל־הֵיכַל־קָדְשְׁךָ

בְּיִרְאָתֶךָ:

---

מַה־טֹּבוּ אֹהָלֶיךָ יַעֲקֹב, מִשְׁכְּנֹתֶיךָ יִשְׂרָאֵל *How goodly are your tents, Jacob; your dwelling places, Israel.* "Jacob" refers to the *ba'alei 'asakim* (business people); "Israel" to the *talmidei ḥakhamim* (professional scholars). Colloquially, they have come to be referred to as "earners" and "learners." For the businessman who must earn his own living rather than be supported by the largesse of the community, the synagogues and houses of study are "tents"; his sojourn therein is perforce temporary. For the Torah scholars, these same structures prove permanent habitations; they are "dwelling places." Both as "tents" and as "dwelling places," they are truly good.[5]

Alternatively, it is possible that the "tents" and the "dwelling places" actually do refer to two different houses. "Tents" refer to synagogues (*batei k'nesset*); "dwelling places" refer to yeshivot (*batei midrash*). The temporary character of the house of worship comes from the fact that we engage there in "temporal life" (*"ḥayyei sha'ah"*); the permanent character of the house of study derives from the fact that there we engage in "eternal life" (*"ḥayyei 'olam"*).[6]

*

5. *MRIT*, pp. 400–401. Elsewhere Rav Kook writes that in the present, the nation is referred to collectively as "Jacob," for we are on a low spiritual level. In the future, the entire nation will rise to the level of "Israel." See *Me'orot ha-Rayah: Yeraḥ ha-Eitanim* (Jerusalem, 1994), pp. 288–289.
6. See *b. Shabbat* 10a; *MRIT*, p. 401. Writing in a kabbalistic vein, Rabbi Ephraim Eliezer Zevi Ḥarlap identified Jacob with *"ḥayyei sha'ah"* ("temporal life") and prayer; and Israel

LORD, I love the habitation of Your House,
the place where Your glory dwells. *Ps. 26*

As for me,
I will bow in worship;
I will bend the knee
before the LORD my Maker.

As for me, *Ps. 69*
may my prayer come to You, LORD,
at a time of favor.
God, in Your great loving-kindness,
answer me with Your faithful salvation.

---

In the summer of 1921, the Rav went to rest in Har Tov. I visited him there and our private conversation extended to the wee hours. The next morning, I noticed that the Rav did not arrive at the prayer. What's more, totally out of character for the Rav (who was punctilious not to engage in any activity before prayer), I saw him approach the innkeeper and begin to discuss with him botanical matters, such as which trees to plant in the vicinity. Only after concluding this conversation, did he proceed to the prayer.

The delay and the incongruous conversation made me wonder, and I plucked up the courage to ask the Rav to explain his curious behavior.

This was his response: "This morning there burnt in my midst such a thirst for the Living God, I feared that in prayer my soul would be consumed (*"kelot ha-nefesh"*).[9] I was forced to dampen my enthusiasm by lowering my thoughts to practical, mundane matters."[10]

יהוה אָהַבְתִּי מְעוֹן בֵּיתֶךָ וּמְקוֹם מִשְׁכַּן כְּבוֹדֶךָ *LORD, I love the habitation of Your House, and the place where Your glory dwells.* As opposed to the preceding two verses where there exists a parallelism of tents/dwelling places (see above) and House/Holy Temple, this third verse is asymmetrical. In the second half

---

9. For the significance of the term *"kelot ha-nefesh"* as a description of a mystical experience, see Rabbi Shneur Zalman of Liadi, *Tanya* 1, 3 (7b).
10. Rabbi Moshe Zevi Neriyah, *Orot ha-Tefillah* (Jerusalem, 2004), p. 19; RZYH Kook, *Li-Sheloshah be-Ellul*, vol. 1, par. 76 (p. 33). Cf. the anecdote concerning Rabbi Moshe Zevi Gutterman of Savran, end *Likkutei Shoshanim* (Lemberg, 1874).

תהלים כו

יהוה אָהַבְתִּי מְעוֹן בֵּיתֶךָ
וּמְקוֹם מִשְׁכַּן כְּבוֹדֶךָ:

וַאֲנִי אֶשְׁתַּחֲוֶה
וְאֶכְרָעָה
אֶבְרְכָה לִפְנֵי יהוה עֹשִׂי.

תהלים סט

וַאֲנִי תְפִלָּתִי־לְךָ יהוה
עֵת רָצוֹן
אֱלֹהִים בְּרָב־חַסְדֶּךָ
עֲנֵנִי בֶּאֱמֶת יִשְׁעֶךָ:

---

The balance of the two movements is certainly *good*.[7]

Episodes in the life of Rav Kook may illustrate the point he wishes to convey.

At the funeral of Rav Kook, held in his Yeshivah Merkaz Harav, his eminent disciple, Rabbi Ya'akov Moshe Ḥarlap, eulogized him. In the course of the *hesped*, Rabbi Ḥarlap related the following incident. In 1914, when Rabbi Ḥarlap traveled with the Rav to the agricultural settlements of the Galilee to bring about a movement of spiritual revival (*"Massa' ha-Teshuvah"*), he was witness to a rare state of ecstasy.

> I was awakened in the middle of the night. I saw the Rav carried as if by a tempest, pacing the length of the room, back and forth. I was frightened and uplifted at the same time. Suddenly, the Rav approached me and took hold of me. His hands were cold as ice, while his face was aflame with fire. From his mouth burst forth words of passion: *"Rav Ya'akov Moshe, Ich ver farbrent fun ahavas Hashem!"* ("Rabbi Ya'akov Moshe, I am being burnt up by love of God!")[8]

On another occasion, Rabbi Ḥarlap related this experience:

---

7. *OR*, vol. 1, pp. 42–43.
8. Rabbi Moshe Zevi Neriyah, *Siḥot ha-Rayah* (Tel-Aviv – Jaffa, 1979), pp. 351–352.

*The following poems, on this page and the next, both from the Middle Ages, are summary statements of Jewish faith, orienting us to the spiritual contours of the world that we actualize in the mind by the act of prayer.*

LORD OF THE UNIVERSE,
who reigned before the birth of any thing –

When by His will all things were made
then was His name proclaimed King.

And when all things shall cease to be
He alone will reign in awe.

He was, He is, and He shall be
glorious for evermore.

---

literal destruction of the world as we know it.[13] Rather, he reads the word *"ki-khelot"* as akin to the intense longing for God of the verse in Psalms 73:26: "My flesh and my heart long; God is the rock of my heart and my portion forever" (*"Kalah she'eri u-levavi, tsur levavi ve-ḥelki Elohim le-'olam"*).[14] And in that connection, he invokes the verse in Isaiah 2:11: "The LORD alone shall be exalted on that day" (*"Ve-Nisgav Hashem levado ba-yom ha-hu"*).[15]

Curiously enough, this very verse is quoted by the Talmud in regard to

---

13. "And when all things cease to be." It is very difficult to reconcile this stanza with the essential promises of our holy prophets, for it seems from this that there will still be a time when all the existents will be absent and there will remain only the Holy One, blessed be He, and His name, as was the case before the creation. This agrees neither with the words of prophecy nor with the opinion of the sages of antiquity and the recent sages of Israel. Neither does it coincide with reason. From the holy words of the prophets we hear on several occasions that the seed of Israel will stand forever. And in the words of the sages: "Just as the Holy One exists forever, so the righteous exist forever" (*b. Sanhedrin* 92a). Demonstrations of the survival of the soul also determine that the soul is corrupted only as divine retribution for sin. So why would "the Judge of all the earth" [Genesis 18:25] do such a thing to His servants, to totally wipe them out? [In our prayers] we say only "all wickedness shall disappear as smoke," but the righteous, their holy souls shall never depart and will forever delight in the pleasantness of the LORD (*"Tselota de-Avraham,"* in *MRIT*, p. 405).
14. In Ḥabad Ḥasidism, the term *"kelot ha-nefesh"* describes a state of extreme ecstasy. See above note 9.
15. *OR*, vol. 1, pp. 46–47.

*The following poems, on this page and the next, both from the Middle Ages, are summary statements of Jewish faith, orienting us to the spiritual contours of the world that we actualize in the mind by the act of prayer.*

# אֲדוֹן עוֹלָם

אֲשֶׁר מָלַךְ בְּטֶרֶם כָּל־יְצִיר נִבְרָא.
לְעֵת נַעֲשָׂה בְחֶפְצוֹ כֹּל אֲזַי מֶלֶךְ שְׁמוֹ נִקְרָא.
וְאַחֲרֵי כִּכְלוֹת הַכֹּל לְבַדּוֹ יִמְלֹךְ נוֹרָא.
וְהוּא הָיָה וְהוּא הֹוֶה וְהוּא יִהְיֶה בְּתִפְאָרָה.

---

of the verse, there is no parallel to the first person pronoun "I" in the first half. Sensing this unbalance, Rav Kook comes up with an explanation derived from the very nature of the mystical experience. When first one happens into a holy place, primacy is given to the "I." It is still all about me. My focus is upon myself; the house of God is peripheral. But as I move into the experience of Godliness; as the experience deepens and becomes more profound, there occurs eventually the total erasure of the "I." There now remains naught but "the place where Your glory dwells."[11]

אֲדוֹן עוֹלָם / LORD OF THE UNIVERSE

Rav Kook's reading of *Adon 'Olam* is extremely mystical – even more than most of his reflections that are informed by Kabbalah. He discusses the Kingship of infinite freedom and unlimited possibility, *Malkhut Ein Sof* (a term from Sarugian Kabbalah),[12] which is beyond name; which precedes the kingship of the created worlds, expressed by the name "King" (*melekh*).

Rav Kook rejects categorically the notion that the other point in time, "when all things shall cease to be" (*ve-aḥarei ki-khelot ha-kol*), refers to the

---

11. *OR*, vol. 1, p. 44.
12. See Rabbi Ḥayyim of Volozhin, *Nefesh ha-Ḥayyim* 3:11, end note; Rabbi Shelomo Elyashev, *Hakdamot u-She'arim* (Piotrków, 1909), *Hakdamah le-Sha'ar ha-Poneh Kadim, "Derekh ha-Kadim"* (59b).

He is One, there is none else,
alone, unique, beyond compare;

Without beginning, without end,
His might, His rule are everywhere.

He is my God; my Redeemer lives.
He is the Rock on whom I rely –

My banner and my safe retreat,
my cup, my portion when I cry.

Into His hand my soul I place,
when I awake and when I sleep.

The LORD is with me, I shall not fear;
body and soul from harm will He keep.

---

totally avoids the negative doomsday prediction of the "end of all," opting instead for a spiritual interpretation. He describes a scenario in which world history will come full circle, the finite returning to its infinite, unbounded state.[21]

Rav Kook points out that it would have been much simpler to write the word *"kelot"* ("cessation") without adding the *"kaf ha-dimyon"* at the beginning. That additional *kaf* indicates similitude: *"like* cessation" ("ki-*khelot*"). To us mortal beings, the experience of *"bittul,"* the erasure of ego, comes across as annihilation, as destruction. But in reality, the holy souls of the prophets and the pious longed for this "end." This is what the sages of old alluded to when they said that the Archangel Michael sacrifices the souls of the righteous on the Altar above.[22] "For this *bittul* (annihilation) is the true *metsi'ut* (existence)."[23]

---

reprinted Mishor Adumim: Aharon Barazani, 2010), *Kelalei Hitpashtut ve-Histalkut* 15:10 (p. 182); 17:5:1 (p. 195); idem, *Sefer ha-De'ah*, Part I (Piotrków, 1912), 5:5:2 (40c-d).

21. *OR*, vol. 1, p. 47.

22. *Tosafot, Menaḥot* 110a, s.v. *u-Michael.* See Rabbi Judah Löw (Maharal) of Prague, *Ḥiddushei Aggadot* there.

23. *"Tselota de-Avraham,"* in *MRIT*, p. 406. Cf. *OR*, vol. 2, p. 39, s.v. *ve-aḥarei ki-khelot ha-kol.*

וְהוּא אֶחָד וְאֵין שֵׁנִי לְהַמְשִׁיל לוֹ לְהַחְבִּירָה.
בְּלִי רֵאשִׁית בְּלִי תַכְלִית וְלוֹ הָעֹז וְהַמִּשְׂרָה.
וְהוּא אֵלִי וְחַי גּוֹאֲלִי וְצוּר חֶבְלִי בְּעֵת צָרָה.
וְהוּא נִסִּי וּמָנוֹס לִי מְנָת כּוֹסִי בְּיוֹם אֶקְרָא.
בְּיָדוֹ אַפְקִיד רוּחִי בְּעֵת אִישַׁן וְאָעִירָה.
וְעִם רוּחִי גְּוִיָּתִי יהוה לִי וְלֹא אִירָא.

---

"the millennium of destruction" (*"ḥad ḥaruv"*) that follows the six millennia of our world.[16] It must be that Rav Kook understood that Talmudic passage as well in a non-literal manner.[17] In fact, the Talmud says that the righteous, the *tsaddikim*, will survive because "the Holy One, blessed be he, will fashion for them wings as eagles and they will hover above the waters" covering the planet.[18] Perhaps in Rav Kook's reading, that hovering action of the righteous is a metaphor for their spiritual ascent.[19] In a recently published manuscript, Rav Kook writes: "The nullification of the vessels will be only those thousand years during which the Holy One, blessed be He, renews His world, but in the future, a new light will be revealed, and through the vessels too there will be known the truth of the light of the LORD."[20]

Whatever the interpretation of that passage in the Talmud, Rav Kook

---

16. *b. Rosh Hashanah* 31a; *Sanhedrin* 97; *'Avodah Zarah* 9a.
17. Rabbi Judah Canpanton (disciple of Ritba) militated against a literalist interpretation of the "destruction" of the seventh millennium. See *Arba'ah Kinyanim*, ed. Blau (Brooklyn, NY, 1997), *ha-ma'amar ha-revi'i* (p. 138).
18. *b. Sanhedrin* 92b.
19. See the anonymous *Ma'arekhet ha-Elohut* (Mantua, 1558), chap. 8 (f.98): "… 'wings' conveys that they will be transformed into spiritual beings." Similarly, Rabbi Judah Canpanton wrote: "Without dout, they refer to wings of the spirit. Those spiritual beings who have no bodily sensations, it appears to them as if they are hovering over the surface of the water" (*Arba'ah Kinyanim*, p. 138). See *SK* 7:31 = *Orot, Yisrael u-Teḥiyato*, chap. 13; and *MRIT*, p. 513.
20. Ibid. p. 514. Cf. Rabbi Shelomo Elyashev, *Sefer ha-De'ah* (Piotrków, 1912), Part One, 5:3:4 (38b); idem, *Leshem Shevo ve-Aḥlamah, Sefer ha-Kelalim* (Jerusalem, 1926;

## GREAT

is the living God and praised.
He exists, and His existence is beyond time.

He is One, and there is no unity like His.
Unfathomable, His Oneness is infinite.

He has neither bodily form nor substance;
His holiness is beyond compare.

---

Rabbi Isaac Hutner once illustrated by way of a parable why most of the medieval authorities (unlike Maimonides, Crescas and Albo) did not attempt to reduce Judaism to principles:

---

> Gabirol, for these later authorities did not know Kabbalah and did not know what they were saying… especially *Yigdal Elohim ḥai* etc., and likewise *Viduy Ashamnu* etc., and likewise on Yom Kippur he would not say the *Viduy* (Confession) of Rabbenu Nissim and Rabbi Shem Tov Ardutiel and Rabbi Isaac ben Israel, each of whom composed a *Viduy*… But he would say prayers and hymns composed by the early authorities, such as the prayer of Rabbi Akiva, and the prayer of Rabbi El'azar ben Arakh, and the prayer of Rabbi Neḥunyah ben Hakaneh. Likewise, he would say all the hymns composed by Rabbi El'azar Kalir that are found in the *Maḥzor* of the Ashkenazim. For all these early authorities composed their words according to the Wisdom of Truth [i.e. Kabbalah] and they knew what they composed. Even if they [i.e. the hymns] occur in the midst of *Birkat Yotser*, he would say them, for they were *Tanna'im* and knew what they were composing, and all their words were based upon the Wisdom of Truth. And I heard in the name of my teacher, of blessed memory, that the Kalir who arranged the *Kerovets* in the *Maḥzor* of the Ashkenazim is Rabbi El'azar ben Rabbi Shim'on… (Rabbi Ḥayyim Vital, *Sha'ar ha-Kavvanot* [Jerusalem, 1902], *'Inyan 'Aleynu leshabe'aḥ ve-nusaḥ ha-tefillah* [50c-d]).

So it is not as if *Yigdal* was singled out for Ari's displeasure. Ari confined himself to prayers and hymns of the *Tanna'im* (or at least those ascribed to *Tanna'im*). Although modern scholarship dates El'azar Kalir in the sixth or early seventh centuries, the *Ba'alei ha*-Tosafot believed him to be the Tanna Rabbi El'azar ben Rabbi Shim'on. See *Tosafot, Ḥagigah* 13a, s.v. *ve-raglei ha-ḥayyot ke-neged kulam*. (The final sentence in *Sha'ar ha-Kavvanot* is practically a direct quote from *Tosafot*.)

See now Ḥannah Kasher and Uri Melamed, "Poetic Versions of Maimonides' Thirteen Principles in Kabbalistic Dress" (Hebrew), *The Flint into a Fountain of Waters* [*Ḥallamish le-Ma'yeno Mayim*]: *Studies in Kabbalah, Jewish Law, Custom and Philosophy Submitted to Prof. Moshe Ḥallamish* (Jerusalem, 2016), pp. 256–264.

# יִגְדַּל

אֱלֹהִים חַי וְיִשְׁתַּבַּח
נִמְצָא וְאֵין עֵת אֶל מְצִיאוּתוֹ.

אֶחָד וְאֵין יָחִיד כְּיִחוּדוֹ
נֶעְלָם וְגַם אֵין סוֹף לְאַחְדוּתוֹ.

אֵין לוֹ דְּמוּת הַגּוּף וְאֵינוֹ גוּף
לֹא נַעֲרֹךְ אֵלָיו קְדֻשָּׁתוֹ.

---

יִגְדַּל / GREAT

As is well known, Rabbi Isaac Luria (Ari) was opposed to reciting the hymn *Yigdal,* a poetic rendition of Maimonides' Thirteen Articles of Faith. Various theories have been offered for Ari's opposition.[24] Rabbi Zevi Yehudah Hakohen Kook was convinced that the Ari was opposed to "favoritism" when it comes to commandments. The Ari was lodging a formal protest against privileging one commandment over the other. Luria's lasting legacy was the formula *"Taryag mitsvot ha-teluyot bah"* ("Six hundred thirteen commandments dependent upon it"). As opposed to the singling out of thirteen principles, Ari taught the total interdependency of the commandments of the Torah.

Parenthetically, Rabbi Zevi Yehudah speculated that Ari's criticism was directed at public recital of the hymn *Yigdal,* for the same reason that the Sages of old abolished the custom of reciting the Ten Commandments in public: "because of the grievance of the sectarians" (i.e. those Jews who would have reduced Judaism to the Decalogue, to the exclusion of the other precepts).[25]

---

24. See recently Rabbi David Cohen, *Ha-Emunah ha-Ne'emanah* (on Maimonides' Thirteen Articles of Faith) (Brooklyn, 2012), pp. 34–37.

25. *b. Berakhot* 12a and Rashi ad loc.; Rabbi Zevi Yehudah Hakohen Kook, *Zemaḥ Zevi: Igrot* (Jerusalem, 5751/1991), Letter 39 (pp. 96–97).

    Actually, there is no mystery concerning Ari's opposition to reciting *Yigdal*:

    > Know that my teacher [i.e. Rabbi Isaac Luria], of blessed memory, would not recite any religious hymn (*piyut*) arranged by later authorities such as Rabbi Solomon ibn

He preceded all that was created.
He was first: there was no beginning to His beginning.

Behold He is Master of the Universe; and every creature
shows His greatness and majesty.

The rich flow of His prophecy He gave
to His treasured people in whom He gloried.

Never in Israel has there arisen another like Moses,
a prophet who beheld God's image.

God gave His people a Torah of truth
by the hand of His prophet, most faithful of His House.

God will not alter or change His law
for any other, for eternity.

He sees and knows our secret thoughts;
as soon as something is begun, He foresees its end.

He rewards people with loving-kindness according to their deeds;
He punishes the wicked according to his wickedness.

At the end of days He will send our Messiah
to redeem those who await His final salvation.

God will revive the dead in His great loving-kindness.
Blessed for evermore is His glorious name!

---

nonetheless in a healthy state, one doesn't feel the difference. But if God forbid, one becomes ill, and is forced to decide between them, then one knows which must be sacrificed for the other.

So in a heathy state, one doesn't pay much attention to *"'ikkarei ha-emunah"* (articles of faith). In a healthy state, one does not feel the difference between commandments. And if one does, then it is a sign that one is sick to one's soul.

For that reason, most of our *Rishonim* did not compose books in the field of *"'ikkarei ha-emunah."*[26] (Editor)

26. Rabbi Leib Ruta, *Reshimot Lev*, vol. 1 (Brooklyn, NY, 2000), *Pesah* 5733 (p. 100).

קַדְמוֹן לְכָל דָּבָר אֲשֶׁר נִבְרָא
רִאשׁוֹן וְאֵין רֵאשִׁית לְרֵאשִׁיתוֹ.

הִנּוֹ אֲדוֹן עוֹלָם
וְכָל נוֹצָר יוֹרֶה גְדֻלָּתוֹ וּמַלְכוּתוֹ.

שֶׁפַע נְבוּאָתוֹ נְתָנוֹ
אֶל־אַנְשֵׁי סְגֻלָּתוֹ וְתִפְאַרְתּוֹ.

לֹא קָם בְּיִשְׂרָאֵל כְּמֹשֶׁה
עוֹד נָבִיא וּמַבִּיט אֶת תְּמוּנָתוֹ.

תּוֹרַת אֱמֶת נָתַן לְעַמּוֹ אֵל
עַל יַד נְבִיאוֹ נֶאֱמַן בֵּיתוֹ.

לֹא יַחֲלִיף הָאֵל וְלֹא יָמִיר דָּתוֹ
לְעוֹלָמִים לְזוּלָתוֹ.

צוֹפֶה וְיוֹדֵעַ סְתָרֵינוּ
מַבִּיט לְסוֹף דָּבָר בְּקַדְמָתוֹ.

גּוֹמֵל לְאִישׁ חֶסֶד כְּמִפְעָלוֹ
נוֹתֵן לְרָשָׁע רָע כְּרִשְׁעָתוֹ.

יִשְׁלַח לְקֵץ יָמִין מְשִׁיחֵנוּ
לִפְדּוֹת מְחַכֵּי קֵץ יְשׁוּעָתוֹ.

מֵתִים יְחַיֶּה אֵל בְּרֹב חַסְדּוֹ
בָּרוּךְ עֲדֵי עַד שֵׁם תְּהִלָּתוֹ.

---

When one is healthy, one doesn't feel a difference between one limb and another. Take for example, the finger and the heart. Though one knows the difference between them and that the heart is more vital than the finger,

## MORNING BLESSINGS

*The following blessings are said aloud by the Leader, but each individual should say them quietly as well. It is our custom to say them standing.*

בָּרוּךְ Blessed are You, LORD our God,
King of the Universe,
who gives the heart understanding
to distinguish day from night.

Blessed are You, LORD our God,
King of the Universe,
who has not made me a heathen.

---

Sanhedrin found *kohanim* properly pedigreed and fit to serve in the Temple, then the *kohanim* would recite this blessing:

> Blessed is the Omnipresent, blessed is He that no disqualification was found in the seed of Aaron; and blessed is He who chose Aaron and his sons to stand to serve in the Holy of Holies.[3]

So why is no such blessing recited on a daily basis? There is a fundamental difference between the chosenness of Israel and the chosenness of the *kohanim* (and the Levites, for that matter). The chosenness of Israel is what Maharal of Prague terms an *"ahavah she-einah teluyah be-davar,"* an unconditional love.[4] This chosenness is not for any specific reason, nor is it contingent on anything. It is an essential chosenness. Therefore it may be invoked on a daily basis with no strings attached. The choseness of Aaron and his sons, on the other hand, is for a specific purpose: to serve in the Temple. By the same token, the Levites were chosen to sing in the Temple. This is a functional, as opposed to an essential chosenness. It makes no sense for a *kohen* to make

---

3. *m. Middot* 5:4. Some versions of the *Mishnah* do not have the final words "and blessed is He Who chose Aaron and his sons, etc."
4. Rabbi Judah Löw, *Netsaḥ Yisrael* (London: L. Honig and Sons, 1960), chap. 11 (pp. 68–69); *Derekh Ḥayyim* (London: L. Honig and Sons, 1960), *Avot* 5:16 (p. 262). This was Maharal's response to the supersessionist theology of Christianity. Had Israel been chosen for a specific reason, then conceivably they could be superseded by another nation, but since the election of Israel was not tied to any reason, they are irreplaceable.

# ברכות השחר

*The following blessings are said aloud by the* שליח ציבור*, but each individual should say them quietly as well. It is our custom to say them standing.*

בָּרוּךְ אַתָּה יהוה אֱלֹהֵינוּ מֶלֶךְ הָעוֹלָם
אֲשֶׁר נָתַן לַשֶּׂכְוִי בִינָה
לְהַבְחִין בֵּין יוֹם וּבֵין לָיְלָה.

בָּרוּךְ אַתָּה יהוה אֱלֹהֵינוּ מֶלֶךְ הָעוֹלָם
שֶׁלֹּא עָשַׂנִי גּוֹי.

---

ברכות השחר / MORNING BLESSINGS

אֲשֶׁר נָתַן לַשֶּׂכְוִי בִינָה *Who gives the heart understanding.* Perhaps inspired by the fact that the Hebrew word *gever* means both a man and a rooster, Rav Kook wrote the following *pensée*:

> We know that all of existence and its life-forms are one unit. Man and the rooster – who crows at dawn, possessing a natural understanding to differentiate between day and night – are truly one creation. A single spirit unites the soul of man and the soul of all living beings, in ways both revealed and occult. Whenever man is uplifted, all the creations are thereby uplifted. This universal vision is revealed to us by the relation of this particular creature, the rooster, calling to awaken the slumbering.[1]

שֶׁלֹּא עָשַׂנִי גּוֹי *Who has not made me a heathen.* Other versions have *"she-'asani Yisrael"* ("who has made me an Israelite").

The Rebbe of Izbica (pronounced Izhbitsa), Rabbi Mordechai Yosef Leiner (author *Mei ha-Shilo'aḥ*) once asked his disciple Rabbi Zadok Hakohen, why a *kohen* (priest) does not recite a daily blessing *"she-'asani kohen"* ("who has made me a priest").[2] The truth is that such a blessing was recited by the *kohanim* (though not on a daily basis). In the days of the Temple, if the

---

1. *OR*, vol. 1, p. 70. Cf. *Orot ha-Emunah*, ed. Rabbi Moshe Gurevitz (Jerusalem, 1998), pp. 158–159. See Rabbi Elijah of Vilna, *Aderet Eliyahu*, ed. Samuel Luria (Warsaw, 1887; photo offset Jerusalem, 1981), Genesis 1:26, s.v. *Na'aseh Adam* (pp. 22–23).
2. Rabbi Zadok Hakohen Rabinowitz, *Peri Zaddik*, vol. 3 (Lublin, 5682/1922), *Emor* (85c).

Blessed are You, LORD our God,
King of the Universe,
who has not made me a slave.

Blessed are You, LORD our God,
King of the Universe,
*men:* who has not made me a woman.
*women:* who has made me according to His will.

Blessed are You, LORD our God,
King of the Universe,
who gives sight to the blind.

Blessed are You, LORD our God,
King of the Universe,
who clothes the naked.

Blessed are You, LORD our God,
King of the Universe,
who sets captives free.

Blessed are You, LORD our God,
King of the Universe,
who raises those bowed down.

---

מַתִּיר אֲסוּרִים *Who sets captives free.* In Rav Kook's literary works, one of the abiding concerns is the subject of freedom.

> The vital desire of the soul is to be free in its movement – material movement and spiritual movement. The desire for ascent and renewal – imprinted in all creatures by their Creator, who constantly goads them by saying, "Ascend! Add strength! Increase light!" – is what spurs them to movement.
>
> In a state of spiritual weakness, the confines become more prodigious, and the passion for life and ascent – bound by the shackles of materialism.
>
> However truthfully, sometimes these blocks and confines come our way in order to make more pleasurable the life of movement; that we may appreciate the advantage of the light *through* the darkness,[7] and

7. Paraphrasing Ecclesiastes 2:13.

בָּרוּךְ אַתָּה יהוה אֱלֹהֵינוּ מֶלֶךְ הָעוֹלָם
שֶׁלֹּא עָשַׂנִי עָבֶד.

בָּרוּךְ אַתָּה יהוה אֱלֹהֵינוּ מֶלֶךְ הָעוֹלָם
*men* שֶׁלֹּא עָשַׂנִי אִשָּׁה. / *women* שֶׁעָשַׂנִי כִּרְצוֹנוֹ.

בָּרוּךְ אַתָּה יהוה אֱלֹהֵינוּ מֶלֶךְ הָעוֹלָם
פּוֹקֵחַ עִוְרִים.

בָּרוּךְ אַתָּה יהוה אֱלֹהֵינוּ מֶלֶךְ הָעוֹלָם
מַלְבִּישׁ עֲרֻמִּים.

בָּרוּךְ אַתָּה יהוה אֱלֹהֵינוּ מֶלֶךְ הָעוֹלָם
מַתִּיר אֲסוּרִים.

בָּרוּךְ אַתָּה יהוה אֱלֹהֵינוּ מֶלֶךְ הָעוֹלָם
זוֹקֵף כְּפוּפִים.

---

the blessing in the abstract, in a vacuum. It must always be within the context of actually serving in the Temple.

And into the distant future, the chosenness of Israel will hold constant. As for the status of the *kohanim* and the Levites, according to Lurianic Kabbalah there will be a reversal of roles in regard to the future service in the Third Temple: The *kohanim* will switch places with the Levites.[5] Rav Kook thought that the distinction of serving in the Temple, which at the time of the sin of the Golden Calf was taken away from the *bekhorim* (firstborn) and transferred to the Levites, will in the future be returned to the firstborn. (According to this scenario, neither will the *kohanim* be disenfranchised.)[6] Again, all this derives from the fact that this is a functional as opposed to an essential chosenness. (Editor)

5. Rabbi Ḥayyim Vital, *Sha'ar ha-Pesukim*, Ezekiel 2:1.
6. *KMYK*, vol. 2, *Maḥberot Ketanot, Boisk 1*, par. 8 (p. 16); *KMYK*, vol. 1, *Pinkas Rishon le-Yaffo*, par. 38a (pp. 95–96).

Blessed are You, Lord our God,
King of the Universe,
who spreads the earth above the waters.

Blessed are You, Lord our God,
King of the Universe,
who has provided me with all I need.

Blessed are You, Lord our God,
King of the Universe,
who makes firm the steps of man.

Blessed are You, Lord our God,
King of the Universe,
who girds Israel with strength.

---

In Kabbalah, *"mitkala,"* the Aramaic word for "balance," is the signature of the *'Olam ha-Tikkun*, the World of Establishment, the fixed, rectified world, as opposed to the *'Olam ha-Tohu*, the World of Chaos, which lacks balance and symmetry. (Editor)

אוֹזֵר יִשְׂרָאֵל בִּגְבוּרָה *Who girds Israel with strength.* While one might rush into explaining this blessing in terms of physical prowess, Rav Kook steers away from this explanation. He writes:

> A special strength is the strength of Israel, a strength that excels not in conquest of others, subjugating them or annihilating them, but a strength which essentially is connected to man's self-conquest; the strength of the godly soul, the noble spirit of man that conquers the animal body and its gross, stormy desires; the strength of forbearance.[12]

This strength is symbolized by the girding of the loins. Traditionally, this blessing is recited at the time of tightening the belt,[13] which placed at the divide between the upper torso and the lower extremities of the body, symbolizes the great divide between the divine and bestial elements of the human composure.[14]

---

12. *OR*, vol. 1, p. 75.
13. *b. Berakhot* 60b.
14. See *Mahzor Vitry* cited in *Tosafot, Shabbat* 10a, s.v. *terihuta*.

בָּרוּךְ אַתָּה יהוה אֱלֹהֵינוּ מֶלֶךְ הָעוֹלָם
רוֹקַע הָאָרֶץ עַל הַמָּיִם.

בָּרוּךְ אַתָּה יהוה אֱלֹהֵינוּ מֶלֶךְ הָעוֹלָם
שֶׁעָשָׂה לִי כָּל צָרְכִּי.

בָּרוּךְ אַתָּה יהוה אֱלֹהֵינוּ מֶלֶךְ הָעוֹלָם
הַמֵּכִין מִצְעֲדֵי גָבֶר.

בָּרוּךְ אַתָּה יהוה אֱלֹהֵינוּ מֶלֶךְ הָעוֹלָם
אוֹזֵר יִשְׂרָאֵל בִּגְבוּרָה.

---

the preciousness of freedom and the blessing of movement *through* the confinement.[8]

רוֹקַע הָאָרֶץ עַל הַמָּיִם *Who spreads the earth above the waters.* Man is not an aquatic creature but rather a terrestrial creature. Nonetheless, going back into hoary antiquity, life emerged from the sea. Thus, man carries within him both elements of earth and sea. The quality of the sea gives liquidity and flexibility to his being; the earth bestows upon him a solid, fixed character.

This balance of the expansive nature of the sea and the constricting nature of the earth, accounts for the rhythm of our lives.[9]

שֶׁעָשָׂה לִי כָּל צָרְכִּי *Who has provided me with all I need.* When a man examines the essence of his life, he finds that God has provided for all of his needs, both material and spiritual. All that is necessary for his true perfection has been sent his way.[10]

הַמֵּכִין מִצְעֲדֵי גָבֶר *Who makes firm the steps of man.* How wondrous it is that man is able to stand erect on two legs, and what's more – walk. What marvelous balance this requires! This equipoise is then a metaphor for the balance that we require in all our affairs. Man is composed of many opposed and conflicting elements, calling for the ability to achieve balance.[11]

---

8. *OR*, vol. 1, pp. 72–73.
9. *OR*, vol. 1, pp. 73–74.
10. *OR*, vol. 1, p. 74.
11. *OR*, vol. 1, p. 74.

Blessed are You, Lord our God,
King of the Universe,
who crowns Israel with glory.

Blessed are You, Lord our God,
King of the Universe,
who gives strength to the weary.

בָּרוּךְ Blessed are You, Lord our God, King of the Universe, who removes sleep from my eyes and slumber from my eyelids. And may it be Your will, Lord our God and God of our ancestors, to accustom us to Your Torah, and make us attached to Your

---

process the input of the previous day. "A man is shown [at night] only that which he thinks [by day]."[17]

Sleep to the eyes – as well as its subsequent removal upon waking – is certainly a great blessing.

We should be attentive to the subtle nuances of language with which the Sages formulated the blessing. The Sages differentiated between *"sheinah"* and *"tenumah."* These two terms refer to two very different sleep modes. While *"sheinah"* is a deep sleep, *"tenumah"* is a light sleep, a sort of "twilight zone" between sleeping and waking consciousness. In a couple of instances, the Mishnah employs the verb form *"mitnamnem,"*[18] which the Talmudic sage Rav Ashi graphically describes: "He sleeps but does not sleep; is awake but is not awake; if called to, he answers; he cannot return an opinion; if reminded, he recalls" (*"Nim ve-lo nim; tir ve-lo tir; de-karu leh ve-'anei; ve-lo yada' le-ahadurei sevara; ve-khi madkeru leh, midkar"*).[19] Analyzing the phraseology of our blessing, one notes that the deep sleep of *"sheinah"* is juxtaposed to the eyes, whereas the light sleep of *"tenumah"* is attached to the eyelids. Evidently, the fluttering of the eyelids is outwardly observable in the state of light sleep termed *"tenumah,"* whereas that activity of the eyelids is absent in the deep sleep of *"sheinah."*[20]

Great strides have been made in modern sleep research utilizing the advanced technology of electroencephalography (EEG) to measure brain

---

17. *b. Berakhot* 55b.
18. *m. Megillah* 2:2; *Pesaḥim* 10:8.
19. *b. Pesaḥim* 120b; *Megillah* 18b.
20. *OR*, vol. 1, p. 76.

בָּרוּךְ אַתָּה יהוה אֱלֹהֵינוּ מֶלֶךְ הָעוֹלָם
עוֹטֵר יִשְׂרָאֵל בְּתִפְאָרָה.

בָּרוּךְ אַתָּה יהוה אֱלֹהֵינוּ מֶלֶךְ הָעוֹלָם
הַנּוֹתֵן לַיָּעֵף כֹּחַ.

בָּרוּךְ אַתָּה יהוה אֱלֹהֵינוּ מֶלֶךְ הָעוֹלָם, הַמַּעֲבִיר שֵׁנָה מֵעֵינַי וּתְנוּמָה מֵעַפְעַפָּי. וִיהִי רָצוֹן מִלְּפָנֶיךָ יהוה אֱלֹהֵינוּ וֵאלֹהֵי אֲבוֹתֵינוּ, שֶׁתַּרְגִּילֵנוּ בְּתוֹרָתֶךָ, וְדַבְּקֵנוּ בְּמִצְוֹתֶיךָ, וְאַל תְּבִיאֵנוּ

---

עוֹטֵר יִשְׂרָאֵל בְּתִפְאָרָה׳ *Who crowns Israel with glory.* For Rav Kook, the crowning glory of Israel is the gift of prophecy. It is safe to assume that he was influenced in this respect by the *Kuzari* of Judah Halevi, who believed that genetically, prophecy is within our DNA. (Maimonides, on the other hand, in his *Epistle to Yemen*, was of the view that prophecy is not the exclusive domain of Israel but rather a universal phenomenon.) As prophecy is engendered in the intellect or head, it befits an Israelite to cover the head, to honor the specialty of the Israelite intellect – which unlike other intellect, is informed by prophetic ability. So at the time of covering the head it is traditional to recite this blessing.[15]

הַנּוֹתֵן לַיָּעֵף כֹּחַ *Who gives strength to the weary.* Beyond the strict sense in which the blessing refers to the rejuvenation from slumber, this blessing is a metaphor for all the times in life when the bodily resources are challenged by obstacles and crises. At such moments, by the love of God there appears a current of spiritual energy from the highest source of the soul, renewing the "spirit of strength" (*ru'aḥ gevurah*) and infusing life with a new power. This is a divine gift.[16]

הַמַּעֲבִיר שֵׁנָה מֵעֵינַי וּתְנוּמָה מֵעַפְעַפָּי *Who removes sleep from my eyes and slumber from my eyelids.* It is primarily through the eyes that we input impressions of the external world. So one of the primary purposes of sleep is – to stop inputting. The closing of the eyes and the sensory deprivation that follows, allow for processing all that input. That is exactly what dreams do. Dreams

15. *b. Berakhot* 60b; *OR*, vol. 1, p. 75.
16. *OR*, vol. 1, pp. 75–76.

commandments. Lead us not into error, transgression, iniquity, temptation or disgrace. Do not let the evil instinct dominate us. Keep us far from a bad man and a bad companion. Help us attach ourselves to the good instinct and to good deeds and bend our instincts to be subservient to You. Grant us, this day and every day, grace, loving-kindness and compassion in Your eyes and in the eyes of all who see us, and bestow loving-kindness upon us. Blessed are You, LORD, who bestows loving-kindness on His people Israel.

יְהִי רָצוֹן May it be Your will, LORD my God and God of my ancestors, to save me today and every day, from the arrogant and from arrogance itself, from a bad man, a bad friend, a bad neighbor, a bad mishap, a destructive adversary, a harsh trial and a harsh opponent, whether or not he is a son of the covenant. *Berakhot 16b*

---

בָּרוּךְ אַתָּה ה׳, גּוֹמֵל חֲסָדִים טוֹבִים לְעַמּוֹ יִשְׂרָאֵל *Blessed are You, LORD, who bestows loving-kindness on His people Israel.* ... יְהִי רָצוֹן מִלְּפָנֶיךָ ה׳ אֱלֹהַי וֵאלֹהֵי אֲבוֹתַי *May it be Your will, LORD my God and God of my ancestors...* The first prayer, which culminates in the blessing, "Blessed are You, LORD, who bestows loving-kindness on His people Israel," is written in the collective form. The import is that the individual Jew, by being included in the collectivity of Israel, will be afforded protection from all evil inclinations that life may bring one's way.

But "at the end of the day," there is the notion of personal responsibility. One is held accountable for one's deeds. So in this second blessing, "May it be Your will, LORD my God and God of my ancestors," written in the singular form, we beseech God for the various challenges that beset us precisely as individuals.[23]

שֶׁתַּצִּילֵנִי הַיּוֹם וּבְכָל יוֹם מֵעַזֵּי פָנִים *Save me today and every day, from the arrogant.* In *Ethics of the Fathers* we find the statement: "An arrogant person [is consigned] to Gehinnom, and a bashful person [is consigned] to the Garden of Eden."[24] This statement gave Rav Kook pause. Why must the arrogant person be doomed to Hell? Why can't the arrogant merely be relegated to an inferior level of Heaven? The answer is that regarding the World to Come it is said: "Each and every one [of the *tsaddikim*] is 'burnt' by the canopy of his companion. Woe to that shame! Woe to that embarrassment!"[25] This is to say, each inhabitant of the Garden of Eden experiences envy of the spiritual attainment

---

23. *OR*, vol. 1, p. 80.
24. *m. Avot* 5:20.
25. *b. Bava Batra* 75a. See also *Numbers Rabbah* 21:22 and *b. Menaḥot* 29b.

לֹא לִידֵי חֵטְא, וְלֹא לִידֵי עֲבֵרָה וְעָוֹן, וְלֹא לִידֵי נִסָּיוֹן וְלֹא לִידֵי בִזָּיוֹן, וְאַל תַּשְׁלֶט בָּנוּ יֵצֶר הָרָע, וְהַרְחִיקֵנוּ מֵאָדָם רָע וּמֵחָבֵר רָע, וְדַבְּקֵנוּ בְּיֵצֶר הַטּוֹב וּבְמַעֲשִׂים טוֹבִים, וְכֹף אֶת יִצְרֵנוּ לְהִשְׁתַּעְבֶּד לָךְ, וּתְנֵנוּ הַיּוֹם וּבְכָל יוֹם לְחֵן וּלְחֶסֶד וּלְרַחֲמִים, בְּעֵינֶיךָ, וּבְעֵינֵי כָל רוֹאֵינוּ, וְתִגְמְלֵנוּ חֲסָדִים טוֹבִים. בָּרוּךְ אַתָּה יהוה, גּוֹמֵל חֲסָדִים טוֹבִים לְעַמּוֹ יִשְׂרָאֵל.

יְהִי רָצוֹן מִלְּפָנֶיךָ יהוה אֱלֹהַי וֵאלֹהֵי אֲבוֹתַי, שֶׁתַּצִּילֵנִי הַיּוֹם וּבְכָל יוֹם ברכות טז:
מֵעַזֵּי פָנִים וּמֵעַזּוּת פָּנִים, מֵאָדָם רָע, וּמֵחָבֵר רָע, וּמִשָּׁכֵן רָע, וּמִפֶּגַע רָע, וּמִשָּׂטָן הַמַּשְׁחִית, מִדִּין קָשֶׁה, וּמִבַּעַל דִּין קָשֶׁה בֵּין שֶׁהוּא בֶן בְּרִית וּבֵין שֶׁאֵינוֹ בֶן בְּרִית.

---

waves. But the fluttering of the eyelids is still some indication (however superficial) of the internal state of the sleeper.

וְהַרְחִיקֵנוּ מֵאָדָם רָע וּמֵחָבֵר רָע *Keep us far from a bad man and a bad companion.* What is the difference between a bad man and a bad companion? There is a man who by all accounts is evil. However there is another man who is not essentially evil. On the contrary, he is essentially good. But for whatever reason, having to do with personal "chemistry," he would not be good for me. This is bad company.[21]

וְדַבְּקֵנוּ בְּיֵצֶר הַטּוֹב וּבְמַעֲשִׂים טוֹבִים *And help us attach ourselves to the good instinct and to good deeds.* Sometimes one has a good inclination, but there is a "disconnect" between the person and his or her good inclination. Good ideas pass through one's mind like images on a screen, but one is but a passive observer, viewing from a remove. The good inclination has not truly penetrated the essence of the personality.

By the same token, there is one who almost accidentally performs good deeds. Here too, the good deeds are not part of the fiber of one's being.

In both these cases, we ask God: "Help us attach ourselves" (*"Ve-dabekenu"*). May we be so connected to good thoughts and to good deeds that they become the very essence of our being.[22]

---

21. *OR*, vol. 1, p. 78.
22. *OR*, vol. 1, pp. 78–79. Cf. the phrase *"medubakim be-yir'atekha"* in *Atah Ḥonantanu* recited at the conclusion of the Sabbath.

## THE BINDING OF ISAAC

*On the basis of Jewish mystical tradition, some have the custom of saying daily the biblical passage recounting the Binding of Isaac, the supreme trial of faith in which Abraham demonstrated his love of God above all other loves. On Shabbat and Yom Tov, most omit the introductory and concluding prayers, "Our God and God of our ancestors" and "Master of the Universe." Others continue with "A person should" on page 56.*

Our God and God of our ancestors, remember us with a favorable memory, and recall us with a remembrance of salvation and compassion from the highest of high heavens. Remember, LORD our God, on our behalf, the love of the ancients, Abraham, Isaac and Yisrael Your servants; the covenant, the loving-kindness, and the oath You swore to Abraham our father on Mount Moriah, and the Binding, when he bound Isaac his son on the altar, as is written in Your Torah:

*The service continues on page 52.*

---

gravitating to the academy of Baron David Günzburg in St. Petersburg, where a select group of talented young men studied medieval Jewish philosophy and Semitic languages. And with all this spiritual baggage – David Cohen was not satisfied. Something gnawed away at his soul, leaving him no respite. He took upon himself extreme ascetic practices. (Eventually, he would be known by the sobriquet "the Nazirite," for as the Nazirites of old, he vowed not to cut his hair nor drink wine.)

In Basel, he heard that temporarily sojourning in St. Gallen was the renowned Rabbi of Jaffa, Rav Kook. In the summer of 1914, Rav Kook had set sail for Europe in order to attend the world conference of the newly formed Agudat Yisrael movement. Rav Kook wished to convey at the conference the centrality of Erets Yisrael and the utmost importance of strengthening the Yishuv. Alas, shortly after his arrival in Europe, World War One broke out. The conference never took place, but what came out of it was that Rav Kook was stranded for the duration of the war in Europe. In these dire circumstances, a kindhearted benefactor by the name of Abraham Kimḥi offered Rav Kook housing in his town of St. Gallen, Switzerland. There, Rav Kook spent a year as the guest of Mr. Kimḥi.

Back to the student David Cohen. As he describes his experience, after having ritually bathed in the Rhine River in anticipation of the meeting, David rode the train to St. Gallen for an audience with the great man.

The discussion between the two men continued long into the night – long enough that David Cohen missed his train back to Basel. He would have to stay overnight and take the train back the next day.

Frankly, the young student of philosophy was somewhat disappointed. While his own knowledge of Greek philosophy came directly from the

# פרשת העקדה

*On the basis of Jewish mystical tradition, some have the custom of saying daily the biblical passage recounting the Binding of Isaac, the supreme trial of faith in which Abraham demonstrated his love of God above all other loves. On* שבת *and* יום טוב*, most omit the introductory and concluding prayers,* אֱלֹהֵינוּ וֵאלֹהֵי אֲבוֹתֵינוּ *and* רִבּוֹנוֹ שֶׁל עוֹלָם*. Others continue with* לְעוֹלָם יְהֵא אָדָם *on page 57.*

אֱלֹהֵינוּ וֵאלֹהֵי אֲבוֹתֵינוּ, זָכְרֵנוּ בְּזִכְרוֹן טוֹב לְפָנֶיךָ, וּפָקְדֵנוּ בִּפְקֻדַּת יְשׁוּעָה וְרַחֲמִים מִשְּׁמֵי שְׁמֵי קֶדֶם, וּזְכָר לָנוּ יהוה אֱלֹהֵינוּ, אַהֲבַת הַקַּדְמוֹנִים אַבְרָהָם יִצְחָק וְיִשְׂרָאֵל עֲבָדֶיךָ, אֶת הַבְּרִית וְאֶת הַחֶסֶד וְאֶת הַשְּׁבוּעָה שֶׁנִּשְׁבַּעְתָּ לְאַבְרָהָם אָבִינוּ בְּהַר הַמּוֹרִיָּה, וְאֶת הָעֲקֵדָה שֶׁעָקַד אֶת יִצְחָק בְּנוֹ עַל גַּבֵּי הַמִּזְבֵּחַ, כַּכָּתוּב בְּתוֹרָתֶךָ:

*The service continues on page 53.*

---

of his peer. So even in Heaven there is a "lesson in humility." And that mild lesson is sufficient to burn away any imperfections that might have crept into the soul. But in the case of the arrogant person, this kind of humility is simply not possible. Even when confronted with another individual's vast superiority, he remains impervious and unabashed. So there is no alternative for the arrogant one but to experience the more radical "re-education" of Gehinnom.[26]

פרשת העקדה / THE BINDING OF ISAAC

וּפָקְדֵנוּ בִּפְקֻדַּת יְשׁוּעָה וְרַחֲמִים מִשְּׁמֵי שְׁמֵי קֶדֶם *And recall us with a remembrance of salvation and compassion from the highest of high heavens.* The story of how one of Rav Kook's greatest disciples and the editor of his magnum opus *Orot ha-Kodesh* (*Lights of Holiness*) met the Rav, was recorded by that disciple in the preface to the book.

In World War One, David Cohen was a young student of philosophy at the University of Basel. His study of ancient Greek philosophy was extremely rigorous. Of course, he studied the ancient sources in the Greek original. He was also attracted to the neo-Kantian philosophy that Hermann Cohen (no relation) was espousing at Marburg.

David Cohen was a Russian Jew. His paternal grandfather, whose home stood opposite that of the renowned *"Ḥafets Ḥayyim,"* served as the Rabbi of Radin. David Cohen attended for a while the Yeshivah of Slabodka before

---

26. According to Rabbi Zevi Yehudah, this was a teaching heard from his father the Rav at the end of his days. See *Siḥot Harav Zevi Yehudah: Shemot*, ed. Shelomo Aviner (Jerusalem, 5758/1997), pp. 47–49. An earlier version of this thought (without the reference to the Talmud, *Bava Batra*) is found in *'Eyn Ayah, Berakhot*, ed. Ya'akov Filber (Jerusalem: Makhon RZYH Kook, 5747/1987), chap. 1, par. 169 (pp. 66–67).

> *salvation,* which is tantamount to the exodus of this holy value from its straits, by virtue of the preciousness of its exalted value in its own right, which makes it worthy of an abundance of *compassion.* Have mercy upon this dear and exalted power, whose root lies in a supernal holiness, but is placed in captivity in the hands of powers that darken its exalted light.
>
> The appearance of *salvation* and arousal of *compassion* must come from the most universal, the most rooted beginning, where the power of the noble soul [once] shone in glory. This is the primordial root of the holy light – not based on its earthly value, already sunk into the crust of the earth, but based on its primordial heavenly value. And not even according to a heavenly value readied for descent to earth, but according to its heavenly value exalted beyond any descent. That value stands eternally exalted, a plenum of light. This is the preciousness of the source: "From the heavens of heavens of yore."[2]

Perhaps such were Rav Kook's thoughts that particular morning in St. Gallen. They might have run along the lines that extraordinary compassion from on high was necessary to extricate the inestimably valuable soul of his young visitor from the powers to which it had been subjugated.

### פרשת העקדה / THE BINDING OF ISAAC

The Binding of Isaac is a Biblical story that has engaged the interest of mankind in general, not only Jews. Kierkegaard, the Danish existentialist philosopher, devoted to the story of the *'Akedah* an entire study, *Fear and Trembling* (1843), devising a philosophical category, "teleological suspension of the ethical," to account for the events described therein.

In a personal letter to his student Moshe Seidel, dated "Rosh Ḥodesh Ellul, 5671 [1911]," Rav Kook proposed an original interpretation of the *nisayon* or trial.

The pagans of old, though certainly misguided, were capable of *"mesirat nefesh"* or self-sacrifice. This found expression in the abominable practice of sacrificing their beloved children to the idol.

Along came Abraham with a new monotheistic faith and a belief in an invisible God. His contemporaries safely assumed that Abraham would never be capable of making the supreme sacrifice to this invisible, intangible deity; would be simply incapable of mustering the same burning passion, the same zeal for this amorphous Creator that they felt – and demonstrated – towards their idol.

The *'Akedah* came to prove them wrong.[3]

In the commentary to the Prayer Book, Rav Kook works his way through

2. *OR,* vol. 1, pp. 82–83.
3. *Igrot ha-Rayah,* vol. 2 (Jerusalem, 1961), p. 43. A translation of the letter is available in

sources, Rav Kook was familiar with the various schools only by reading secondary works or handbooks. That night, the young man slept fitfully in an anxiety-ridden state.

Bright and early the next morning, David was awakened by footsteps. In the room adjacent, Rav Kook was pacing back and forth, melodiously reciting the *Parashat ha-'Akedah*. Precisely when Rav Kook came to the words "And recall us with a remembrance of salvation and compassion from the heavens of heavens of yore," something opened in this gravid heart; a ray of light penetrated to the depths of this soul that had spent so many years desperately searching.

David Cohen had found much more than a professor of philosophy. He found a spiritual teacher. Eventually, Rabbi David would follow his master back to Erets Yisrael, to Jerusalem, and together they would embark on great projects: the founding of a yeshivah unique for its time, Merkaz Harav; and the crystallization of Rav Kook's many spiritual journals into a well-organized work, *Orot ha-Kodesh* (*Lights of Holiness*).

The journey began with the words, "*Zokhrenu be-zikaron tov lefanekha u-fokedenu bi-fekudat yeshu'ah ve-raḥamim mi-shemei shemei kedem*" ("Remember us with a favorable memory, and recall us with a remembrance of salvation and compassion from the heavens of heavens of yore").[1]

What intention did Rav Kook have in mind as he chanted those words on the morning of Erev Rosh Hodesh Ellul, 1915? It is impossible for us to know. But this is Rav Kook's commentary to that phrase in the prayer-book:

> The memory (*zikaron*) proceeds from the great past: the power, the gift of the light in its pristine state before its descent and diminishing in the course of generations. That clarity, from which comes the holy point of the soul (*ha-nekudah ha-nishmatit*) in each and every individual, should be remembered and appear from the ancient source of its existence.
>
> The recall (*pekidah*) is already in relation to the present: The present point [of the soul] – hidden in its existence, and absorbed in the depth of its hiddenness (*hastarah*), so that its light is dimmed, and its salvation be far from it – should ascend. *You should recall us with a remembrance of*

1. The phrase *"shmei shmei kedem"* ("heavens of heavens of yore") first occurs in Psalms 68:34: "To Him that rides upon the heavens of heavens of yore; lo, He utters His voice, a mighty voice." The Targum or Aramaic translation reads: "To Him that sits upon His throne on the heavens of heavens of yore; He with His saying, will give with His voice, the voice of the spirit of prophecy (*kol ru'aḥ nevu'ata*) to the prophets." I have no way of knowing whether the Targum of that verse was known to Rabbi David Cohen. But what is without doubt, is that the acoustic mystical experience in Rav Kook's lodgings that morning contributed to the eventual formulation of Rabbi David Cohen's comprehensive philosophy, published in 1970 as *Kol ha-Nevu'ah* (*The Voice of Prophecy*).

It happened after these things that God tested Abraham. He said to him, "Abraham!" *Gen. 22*
"Here I am," he replied. He said, "Take your son, your only son, Isaac, whom you love, and go to the land of Moriah and offer him there as a burnt-offering on one of the mountains which I shall say to you." Early the next morning Abraham rose and saddled his donkey and took his two lads with him, and Isaac his son, and he cut wood for the burnt offering, and he set out for the place of which God had told him. On the third day Abraham looked up and saw the place from afar. Abraham said to his lads, "Stay here with the donkey while I and the boy go on ahead.

---

of is own institutions, whether it be the Yeshivah Merkaz Harav or the Chief Rabbinate. As the adage states, the shoemaker's children went barefoot.)

Addressing Abraham by name was a means of activating his self-awareness and drawing his attention to his individual, egoic wants. Only after Abraham was put in touch with his "selfishness," with his individuality, could the test obtain its objective.[5]

וַיַּרְא אֶת־הַמָּקוֹם מֵרָחֹק *And [he] saw the place from afar.* We may be a bit perplexed by the phraseology, "He saw the place from afar." Earlier Abraham had been promised that God would tell him upon which mountain the sacrifice should take place. Instead of the promised verbal communication, Abraham "saw the place." In solving the problem, Rav Kook refers to the psychological phenomenon known as "synesthesia," or confusion of the senses, which is recorded in the annals of prophetic or mystical experience. The divine saying came across to Abraham not as an acoustic experience but as a visionary experience.[6] (Rabbi Akiva in the *Mekhilta, Yitro,* posited that this was indeed the collective experience of Israel at Mount Sinai: "'And all the people were seeing the voices' – seeing that which would normally be heard.")[7]

---

individual? All my thoughts are devoted to the collective. But in order to fulfill the request of that Rabbi, I entrust the matter of the prayer to his honor, and the Master of Compassion shall not refrain from answering *his* prayer, uttered with heart and soul."

In his letter, Rabbi Ḥarlap did not divulge the identities of the persons concerned. However in private conversation with his trusted disciple Rabbi Yosef Leib Zussman, Rabbi Ḥarlap revealed that he had been asked by the Rav to pray on behalf of the Rav's only son, Rabbi Zevi Yehudah. Rabbi Zevi Yehudah was not blessed with children, which prompted his father-in-law, Rabbi Yehudah Leib Hutner of Warsaw ("a great rabbi in the Diaspora") to write a letter to Rav Kook, remonstrating with him to intercede on behalf of his beloved son! Ibid. p. 53, note 4.

5. *OR*, vol. 1, p. 85.
6. *OR*, vol. 1, p. 87.
7. See Rashi and Ibn Ezra to Exodus 20:15; Rabbi Ḥayyim Avihu Schwarz, *Mi-Tokh ha-Torah ha-Go'elet*, vol. 2 (Jerusalem, 1989), p. 86.

וַיְהִי אַחַר הַדְּבָרִים הָאֵלֶּה, וְהָאֱלֹהִים נִסָּה אֶת־אַבְרָהָם, וַיֹּאמֶר אֵלָיו בראשית כב
אַבְרָהָם, וַיֹּאמֶר הִנֵּנִי: וַיֹּאמֶר קַח־נָא אֶת־בִּנְךָ אֶת־יְחִידְךָ אֲשֶׁר־אָהַבְתָּ,
אֶת־יִצְחָק, וְלֶךְ־לְךָ אֶל־אֶרֶץ הַמֹּרִיָּה, וְהַעֲלֵהוּ שָׁם לְעֹלָה עַל אַחַד הֶהָרִים
אֲשֶׁר אֹמַר אֵלֶיךָ: וַיַּשְׁכֵּם אַבְרָהָם בַּבֹּקֶר, וַיַּחֲבֹשׁ אֶת־חֲמֹרוֹ, וַיִּקַּח אֶת־
שְׁנֵי נְעָרָיו אִתּוֹ וְאֵת יִצְחָק בְּנוֹ, וַיְבַקַּע עֲצֵי עֹלָה, וַיָּקָם וַיֵּלֶךְ אֶל־הַמָּקוֹם
אֲשֶׁר־אָמַר־לוֹ הָאֱלֹהִים: בַּיּוֹם הַשְּׁלִישִׁי וַיִּשָּׂא אַבְרָהָם אֶת־עֵינָיו וַיַּרְא
אֶת־הַמָּקוֹם מֵרָחֹק: וַיֹּאמֶר אַבְרָהָם אֶל־נְעָרָיו, שְׁבוּ־לָכֶם פֹּה עִם־הַחֲמוֹר,

---

the chapter in the Bible, verse by verse, carefully scrutinizing every nuance of language. Let us examine some of the highlights of the commentary.

וְהָאֱלֹהִים נִסָּה אֶת־אַבְרָהָם, וַיֹּאמֶר אֵלָיו אַבְרָהָם, וַיֹּאמֶר הִנֵּנִי *God tested Abraham. He said to him, "Abraham!" "Here I am," he replied.* Oftentimes we believe that we are free agents, but if we would examine carefully the situation, we would discover that we are conditioned to act in the way that we do. In order for the *nisayon* or trial to be authentic, it would necessitate that Abraham act totally within the limits of his free will. This is borne out by the not insignificant detail that Abraham was addressed by his personal name. Many times the righteous are detached from their personal needs – so consumed are they by the needs of the collective.

(Rav Kook may very well have written this observation in an autobiographical vein. He was notorious for not praying for the members of his own family,[4] and for fund-raising for other men's institutions to the neglect

---

Tzvi Feldman, *Rav A.Y. Kook: Selected Letters* (1986), pp. 153–161. The section pertaining to the *'Akedah* occurs there on pp. 158–160.

4. See Rabbi Moshe Zevi Neriyah, *Siḥot ha-Rayah* (Tel-Aviv – Jaffa, 1979), p. 349. Rabbi Neriyah quoted a passage from a letter of Rabbi Ya'akov Moshe Ḥarlap to Rabbi Shim'on Glitzenstein (who had served as Rav Kook's private secretary in London during World War One). The letter, datelined 16 Tammuz, 5705 [1945], has since been published in its entirety in the journal *Me-Avnei ha-Makom*, vol. 11 (2000). Here is the passage:

   One time, one of Rav Kook's offspring needed salvation, and a great rabbi in the Diaspora who was close to that offspring was very pained by the lack of salvation, and composed a letter to the Rav, saying that he believes with perfect faith that if the Rav would feel the need of salvation for his offspring and would pray for him, certainly his prayer would be answered from Heaven, but on account of his work on behalf of *Kelal Israel*, he is oblivious to the situation and does not focus on praying for his offspring, despite the boundless love he has for his offspring.

   When he received that letter, the Rav sent for me specially and said to me: "I am amazed how that Rabbi hit the mark. What can I do if I do not connect to the

We will worship and we will return to you." Abraham took the wood for the burnt-offering and placed it on Isaac his son, and he took in his hand the fire and the knife, and the two of them went together. Isaac said to Abraham his father, "Father?" and he said "Here I am, my son." And he said, "Here are the fire and the wood, but where is the sheep for the burnt-offering?" Abraham said, "God will see to the sheep for the burnt-offering, my son." And the two of them went together. They came to the place God had told him about, and Abraham built there an altar and arranged the wood and bound Isaac his son and laid him on the altar on top of the wood. He reached out his hand and took the knife to slay his son. Then an angel of the LORD called out to him from heaven, "Abraham! Abraham!" He said, "Here I am." He said, "Do not reach out your hand against the boy; do not do anything to him, for now I know that you fear God, because you have not held back your son, your only son, from Me." Abraham looked up and there he saw a ram caught in a thicket by its horns, and Abraham went and took the ram and offered it as a burnt-offering instead of his son. Abraham called that place "The LORD will see," as is said to this day, "On the mountain of the LORD He will be seen." The angel of the LORD called to Abraham a second time from heaven, and said, "By Myself I swear, declares the LORD, that because you have done this and have not held back your son, your only son, I will greatly bless you and greatly multiply your descendants, as the stars of heaven and the sand of the seashore, and your descendants shall take possession of the gates of their enemies. Through your descendants, all the nations of the earth will be blessed, because you have heeded My voice." Then Abraham returned to his lads, and they rose and went together to Beersheba, and Abraham stayed in Beersheba.

*Most omit this passage on Shabbat and Yom Tov.*

Master of the Universe, just as Abraham our father suppressed his compassion to do Your will wholeheartedly, so may Your compassion suppress Your anger from us and may Your compassion prevail over Your other attributes. Deal with us, LORD our God, with the attributes of loving-kindness and compassion, and in Your great goodness may Your anger be turned away from Your people, Your city, Your land and Your inheritance. Fulfill in us, LORD our God, the promise You made in Your Torah through the hand of Moses Your servant, as it is said: "I will remember My covenant with Jacob, and also My covenant with Isaac, and also My covenant with Abraham I will remember, and the land I will remember." *Lev. 26*

---

would return to their contemporaries; they would bring back with them this exalted experience in order to share it with mankind, to uplift the entire world.[8]

וְיִרַשׁ זַרְעֲךָ אֵת שַׁעַר אֹיְבָיו. וְהִתְבָּרְכוּ בְזַרְעֲךָ כֹּל גּוֹיֵי הָאָרֶץ *And your descendants shall take possession of the gates of their enemies. Through your descendants, all the nations of the earth will be blessed.* There are prophesied two phases in the

8. *OR*, vol. 1, p. 88.

וַאֲנִי וְהַנַּעַר נֵלְכָה עַד־כֹּה, וְנִשְׁתַּחֲוֶה וְנָשׁוּבָה אֲלֵיכֶם: וַיִּקַּח אַבְרָהָם אֶת־עֲצֵי הָעֹלָה וַיָּשֶׂם עַל־יִצְחָק בְּנוֹ, וַיִּקַּח בְּיָדוֹ אֶת־הָאֵשׁ וְאֶת־הַמַּאֲכֶלֶת, וַיֵּלְכוּ שְׁנֵיהֶם יַחְדָּו: וַיֹּאמֶר יִצְחָק אֶל־אַבְרָהָם אָבִיו, וַיֹּאמֶר אָבִי, וַיֹּאמֶר הִנֶּנִּי בְנִי, וַיֹּאמֶר, הִנֵּה הָאֵשׁ וְהָעֵצִים, וְאַיֵּה הַשֶּׂה לְעֹלָה: וַיֹּאמֶר אַבְרָהָם, אֱלֹהִים יִרְאֶה־לּוֹ הַשֶּׂה לְעֹלָה, בְּנִי, וַיֵּלְכוּ שְׁנֵיהֶם יַחְדָּו: וַיָּבֹאוּ אֶל־הַמָּקוֹם אֲשֶׁר אָמַר־לוֹ הָאֱלֹהִים, וַיִּבֶן שָׁם אַבְרָהָם אֶת־הַמִּזְבֵּחַ וַיַּעֲרֹךְ אֶת־הָעֵצִים, וַיַּעֲקֹד אֶת־יִצְחָק בְּנוֹ, וַיָּשֶׂם אֹתוֹ עַל־הַמִּזְבֵּחַ מִמַּעַל לָעֵצִים: וַיִּשְׁלַח אַבְרָהָם אֶת־יָדוֹ, וַיִּקַּח אֶת־הַמַּאֲכֶלֶת, לִשְׁחֹט אֶת־בְּנוֹ: וַיִּקְרָא אֵלָיו מַלְאַךְ יהוה מִן־הַשָּׁמַיִם, וַיֹּאמֶר אַבְרָהָם אַבְרָהָם, וַיֹּאמֶר הִנֵּנִי: וַיֹּאמֶר אַל־תִּשְׁלַח יָדְךָ אֶל־הַנַּעַר, וְאַל־תַּעַשׂ לוֹ מְאוּמָה, כִּי עַתָּה יָדַעְתִּי כִּי־יְרֵא אֱלֹהִים אַתָּה, וְלֹא חָשַׂכְתָּ אֶת־בִּנְךָ אֶת־יְחִידְךָ מִמֶּנִּי: וַיִּשָּׂא אַבְרָהָם אֶת־עֵינָיו, וַיַּרְא וְהִנֵּה־אַיִל, אַחַר נֶאֱחַז בַּסְּבַךְ בְּקַרְנָיו, וַיֵּלֶךְ אַבְרָהָם וַיִּקַּח אֶת־הָאַיִל, וַיַּעֲלֵהוּ לְעֹלָה תַּחַת בְּנוֹ: וַיִּקְרָא אַבְרָהָם שֵׁם־הַמָּקוֹם הַהוּא יהוה יִרְאֶה, אֲשֶׁר יֵאָמֵר הַיּוֹם בְּהַר יהוה יֵרָאֶה: וַיִּקְרָא מַלְאַךְ יהוה אֶל־אַבְרָהָם שֵׁנִית מִן־הַשָּׁמָיִם: וַיֹּאמֶר, בִּי נִשְׁבַּעְתִּי נְאֻם־יהוה, כִּי יַעַן אֲשֶׁר עָשִׂיתָ אֶת־הַדָּבָר הַזֶּה, וְלֹא חָשַׂכְתָּ אֶת־בִּנְךָ אֶת־יְחִידֶךָ: כִּי־בָרֵךְ אֲבָרֶכְךָ, וְהַרְבָּה אַרְבֶּה אֶת־זַרְעֲךָ כְּכוֹכְבֵי הַשָּׁמַיִם, וְכַחוֹל אֲשֶׁר עַל־שְׂפַת הַיָּם, וְיִרַשׁ זַרְעֲךָ אֵת שַׁעַר אֹיְבָיו: וְהִתְבָּרְכוּ בְזַרְעֲךָ כֹּל גּוֹיֵי הָאָרֶץ, עֵקֶב אֲשֶׁר שָׁמַעְתָּ בְּקֹלִי: וַיָּשָׁב אַבְרָהָם אֶל־נְעָרָיו, וַיָּקֻמוּ וַיֵּלְכוּ יַחְדָּו אֶל־בְּאֵר שָׁבַע, וַיֵּשֶׁב אַבְרָהָם בִּבְאֵר שָׁבַע:

*Most omit this passage on* שבת *and* יום טוב.

רִבּוֹנוֹ שֶׁל עוֹלָם, כְּמוֹ שֶׁכָּבַשׁ אַבְרָהָם אָבִינוּ אֶת רַחֲמָיו לַעֲשׂוֹת רְצוֹנְךָ בְּלֵבָב שָׁלֵם, כֵּן יִכְבְּשׁוּ רַחֲמֶיךָ אֶת כַּעַסְךָ מֵעָלֵינוּ וְיִגֹּלּוּ רַחֲמֶיךָ עַל מִדּוֹתֶיךָ. וְתִתְנַהֵג עִמָּנוּ יהוה אֱלֹהֵינוּ בְּמִדַּת הַחֶסֶד וּבְמִדַּת הָרַחֲמִים, וּבְטוּבְךָ הַגָּדוֹל יָשׁוּב חֲרוֹן אַפְּךָ מֵעַמְּךָ וּמֵעִירְךָ וּמֵאַרְצְךָ וּמִנַּחֲלָתֶךָ. וְקַיֶּם לָנוּ יהוה אֱלֹהֵינוּ אֶת הַדָּבָר שֶׁהִבְטַחְתָּנוּ בְּתוֹרָתֶךָ
עַל יְדֵי מֹשֶׁה עַבְדֶּךָ, כָּאָמוּר: וְזָכַרְתִּי אֶת־בְּרִיתִי יַעֲקוֹב וְאַף אֶת־בְּרִיתִי יִצְחָק, וְאַף ויקרא כו
אֶת־בְּרִיתִי אַבְרָהָם אֶזְכֹּר, וְהָאָרֶץ אֶזְכֹּר:

---

וְנִשְׁתַּחֲוֶה וְנָשׁוּבָה אֲלֵיכֶם *"We will worship and we will return to you."* Abraham and his son would not ascend to some spiritual height merely for the sake of self-edification. After paying obeisance, after bowing to the Almighty, they

## ACCEPTING THE SOVEREIGNTY OF HEAVEN

לְעוֹלָם A person should always be God-fearing, privately and publicly, acknowledging the truth and speaking it in his heart. He should rise early and say: *Tanna DeVei Eliyahu, ch. 21*

Master of all worlds,
not because of our righteousness *Dan. 9*
do we lay our pleas before You,
but because of Your great compassion.

What are we? What are our lives?
What is our loving-kindness? What is our righteousness?
What is our salvation? What is our strength?
What is our might? What shall we say before You,
LORD our God and God of our ancestors?
Are not all the mighty like nothing before You,
the men of renown as if they had never been,
the wise as if they know nothing,
and the understanding as if they lack intelligence?
For their many works are in vain,
and the days of their lives like a fleeting breath before You.
The pre-eminence of man over the animals is nothing, *Eccl. 3*
for all is but a fleeting breath.

---

that are not essentially one's own, neither have they arisen originally in one's own thoughts. One must know that together with all the important qualities that come with preservation of one's unique inner truth, one must broaden and ascend to a clear grasp of the absolute truth. And though it comes not from the inwardness of one's consciousness, but from another place – from the influence of realizations more penetrating, more sublime than one's own realizations – let one *acknowledge the truth*![10]

וְדוֹבֵר אֱמֶת בִּלְבָבוֹ *And speaking truth in his heart.*

[Contrariwise] let one not assume that since one has become so dependent upon the great conception of truth that comes from without – from the comments of others greater and better than one – one needn't commune

10. *OR*, vol. 1, pp. 101–102.

# קבלת עול מלכות שמים

תנא דבי אליהו, פרק כא

לְעוֹלָם יְהֵא אָדָם יְרֵא שָׁמַיִם בְּסֵתֶר וּבְגָלוּי
וּמוֹדֶה עַל הָאֱמֶת, וְדוֹבֵר אֱמֶת בִּלְבָבוֹ
וְיַשְׁכֵּם וְיֹאמַר
רִבּוֹן כָּל הָעוֹלָמִים
דניאל ט
לֹא עַל־צִדְקוֹתֵינוּ אֲנַחְנוּ מַפִּילִים תַּחֲנוּנֵינוּ לְפָנֶיךָ
כִּי עַל־רַחֲמֶיךָ הָרַבִּים:

מָה אָנוּ, מֶה חַיֵּינוּ, מֶה חַסְדֵּנוּ, מַה צִּדְקוֹתֵינוּ
מַה יְּשׁוּעָתֵנוּ, מַה כֹּחֵנוּ, מַה גְּבוּרָתֵנוּ
מַה נֹּאמַר לְפָנֶיךָ, יהוה אֱלֹהֵינוּ וֵאלֹהֵי אֲבוֹתֵינוּ
הֲלֹא כָל הַגִּבּוֹרִים כְּאַיִן לְפָנֶיךָ
וְאַנְשֵׁי הַשֵּׁם כְּלֹא הָיוּ
וַחֲכָמִים כִּבְלִי מַדָּע, וּנְבוֹנִים כִּבְלִי הַשְׂכֵּל
כִּי רֹב מַעֲשֵׂיהֶם תֹּהוּ, וִימֵי חַיֵּיהֶם הֶבֶל לְפָנֶיךָ
קהלת ג
וּמוֹתַר הָאָדָם מִן־הַבְּהֵמָה אָיִן
כִּי הַכֹּל הָבֶל:

relations between Israel and the nations. The first phase will be adversarial and combatant. However, this will transition to a second phase in which the nations of the world will come to realize that Israel is no ordinary nation but rather a source of blessing to the entire world.[9]

וּמוֹדֶה עַל הָאֱמֶת *Acknowledging the truth.*

If the truth comes to one as something distant from oneself, because internally one's soul has not yet reached this realization of truth, let one not be so self-contained that one is unwilling to look into the light of a distant truth. Let one not be deluded into thinking that integral to preserving one's unique character is an unwillingness to internalize assets

9. *OR*, vol. 1, p. 96.

אֲבָל Yet we are Your people, the children of Your covenant,
the children of Abraham, Your beloved,
to whom You made a promise on Mount Moriah;
the offspring of Isaac his only one who was bound on the altar;
the congregation of Jacob Your firstborn son
whom – because of the love with which You loved him
and the joy with which You rejoiced in him –
You called Yisrael and Yeshurun.

לְפִיכָךְ Therefore it is our duty to thank You,
and to praise, glorify, bless,
sanctify and give praise and thanks to Your name.
Happy are we, how good is our portion,
how lovely our fate, how beautiful our heritage.

▸ Happy are we who, early and late, evening and morning,
say twice each day –

---

a community. At the end of days, the collective of Israel will have a salutary effect upon all of humanity. This was the vision that Jacob foresaw for his children. This is the destiny of *the congregation of Jacob Your firstborn son.*[12]

אַשְׁרֵינוּ, שֶׁאֲנַחְנוּ מַשְׁכִּימִים וּמַעֲרִיבִים עֶרֶב וָבֹקֶר, וְאוֹמְרִים פַּעֲמַיִם בְּכָל יוֹם *Happy are we who, early and late, evening and morning, say twice each day.* There would seem to be a contradiction here. In the first half of the sentence, morning precedes evening (*mashkimim u-ma'arivim*); in the second half, the order is reversed: first evening, followed by morning.

These two sequences derive from two different events. The first event is Creation. In Genesis, it states, "And it was evening and it was morning." The second event is the Giving of the Torah on Mount Sinai. There was laid down the halakhic principle, "In the realm of the sacred, night follows the day" (*"Ba-Kodashim, laylah holekh aḥar ha-yom"*).[13]

These opposite orders are the fitting preamble to *Shema'* and *Barukh Shem.* In the *Zohar, Shema'* is referred to as the "higher unity" (*yiḥuda 'ila'ah*) and

12. *OR*, vol. 1, pp. 106–107.
13. *b. Ḥullin* 83a.

אֲבָל אֲנַחְנוּ עַמְּךָ בְּנֵי בְרִיתֶךָ
בְּנֵי אַבְרָהָם אֹהַבְךָ שֶׁנִּשְׁבַּעְתָּ לּוֹ בְּהַר הַמּוֹרִיָּה
זֶרַע יִצְחָק יְחִידוֹ שֶׁנֶּעֱקַד עַל גַּבֵּי הַמִּזְבֵּחַ
עֲדַת יַעֲקֹב בִּנְךָ בְּכוֹרֶךָ
שֶׁמֵּאַהֲבָתְךָ שֶׁאָהַבְתָּ אוֹתוֹ, וּמִשִּׂמְחָתְךָ שֶׁשָּׂמַחְתָּ בּוֹ
קָרָאתָ אֶת שְׁמוֹ יִשְׂרָאֵל וִישֻׁרוּן.

לְפִיכָךְ אֲנַחְנוּ חַיָּבִים
לְהוֹדוֹת לְךָ וּלְשַׁבֵּחֲךָ וּלְפָאֶרְךָ
וּלְבָרֵךְ וּלְקַדֵּשׁ וְלָתֵת שֶׁבַח וְהוֹדָיָה לִשְׁמֶךָ.
אַשְׁרֵינוּ, מַה טּוֹב חֶלְקֵנוּ
וּמַה נָּעִים גּוֹרָלֵנוּ, וּמַה יָּפָה יְרֻשָּׁתֵנוּ.

◂ אַשְׁרֵינוּ, שֶׁאֲנַחְנוּ מַשְׁכִּימִים וּמַעֲרִיבִים עֶרֶב וָבֹקֶר
וְאוֹמְרִים פַּעֲמַיִם בְּכָל יוֹם

---

at all with one's soul; one needn't be in touch with what one's inner spirit is uttering within. Not so! Together with acknowledgement of the broad truth that comes to one from distant horizons, one must speak truth in one's heart; one must draw the waters of truth from one's own depths.[11]

עֲדַת יַעֲקֹב בִּנְךָ בְּכוֹרֶךָ *The congregation of Jacob Your firstborn son.* The transference of the primogeniture from Esau to Jacob conferred upon Israel the status of firstborn among the nations. With the primogeniture, comes the responsibility to influence and educate the other sons and daughters who come after; in Israel there was invested the power to influence all the nations to good and to holiness.

This effect, which requires broad dissemination and publicity, cannot be accomplished through an individual acting alone, but requires a *congregation*,

11. *OR*, vol. 1, p. 102.

Listen, Israel: the LORD is our God, the LORD is One. Deut. 6

*Quietly:* Blessed be the name of His glorious kingdom for ever and all time.

*Some congregations say the entire first paragraph of the Shema (below) at this point. If there is a concern that the Shema will not be recited within the prescribed time, then all three paragraphs should be said. See law 340.*

Love the LORD your God with all your heart, with all your soul, and with all your might. These words which I command you today shall be on your heart. Teach them repeatedly to your children, speaking of them when you sit at home and when you travel on the way, when you lie down and when you rise. Bind them as a sign on your hand, and they shall be an emblem between your eyes. Write them on the doorposts of your house and gates.

אַתָּה הוּא It was You who existed before the world was created,
it is You now that the world has been created.
It is You in this world
and You in the World to Come.

---

Rav Kook once again (see above the Rav's comments to the *kavvanah* of *tefillin*) refers to an esoteric kabbalistic concept. There is a level of divinity that is (in Rav Kook's own words) "beyond all direction, beyond all intention, beyond all desire, beyond all will." If one were to say "before You created the world," one would be implying will. But the thought of God that went into the creation is much higher than that. Rav Kook likens it to the divine voice issuing on its own, as it were, from the Tabernacle in the wilderness.[18]

---

before You created the world" (*"Atah hu kodem she-barata ha-'olam"*). Rabbi Isaiah Halevi Horowitz, both in his *Siddur Sha'ar ha-Shamayim* and in his theological tract *Shnei Luḥot ha-Berit* (*Toledot Adam, Ma'amar Hashem*) goes to great lengths to defend the Ashkenazic version of the prayer despite its problematic wording. In his Introduction to *Siddur 'Olat Re'iyah* (p. 8), Rabbi Zevi Yehudah Kook noted that his father "made use of and meditated much in" the prayer book of Rabbi Isaiah Halevi Horowitz, known as *Siddur Shelah*.

18. See Rashi to Numbers 7:89. Rashi explains that *middaber* with a *ḥiriq* rather than a *sheva* under the *mem* is the *hitpa'el* or reflexive form, as if it were written *mitdaber*. Rashi sums up by saying: "[God] speaks to Himself and Moses overhears." Cf. *Orot ha-Emunah*, ed. Rabbi Moshe Gurevitz (Jerusalem, 1998), bottom p. 157, on the difference between *medaber* and *middaber*.

*OR*, vol. 1, pp. 110–111.

דברים ו

# שְׁמַע יִשְׂרָאֵל, יהוה אֱלֹהֵינוּ, יהוה אֶחָד:

*Quietly* בָּרוּךְ שֵׁם כְּבוֹד מַלְכוּתוֹ לְעוֹלָם וָעֶד.

*Some congregations say the entire first paragraph of the שמע (below) at this point. If there is a concern that the שמע will not be recited within the prescribed time, then all three paragraphs should be said. See law 340.*

וְאָהַבְתָּ אֵת יהוה אֱלֹהֶיךָ, בְּכָל־לְבָבְךָ, וּבְכָל־נַפְשְׁךָ, וּבְכָל־מְאֹדֶךָ: וְהָיוּ
הַדְּבָרִים הָאֵלֶּה, אֲשֶׁר אָנֹכִי מְצַוְּךָ הַיּוֹם, עַל־לְבָבֶךָ: וְשִׁנַּנְתָּם לְבָנֶיךָ, וְדִבַּרְתָּ
בָּם, בְּשִׁבְתְּךָ בְּבֵיתֶךָ, וּבְלֶכְתְּךָ בַדֶּרֶךְ, וּבְשָׁכְבְּךָ וּבְקוּמֶךָ: וּקְשַׁרְתָּם לְאוֹת עַל־
יָדֶךָ וְהָיוּ לְטֹטָפֹת בֵּין עֵינֶיךָ: וּכְתַבְתָּם עַל־מְזֻזוֹת בֵּיתֶךָ וּבִשְׁעָרֶיךָ:

אַתָּה הוּא עַד שֶׁלֹּא נִבְרָא הָעוֹלָם
אַתָּה הוּא מִשֶּׁנִּבְרָא הָעוֹלָם.
אַתָּה הוּא בָּעוֹלָם הַזֶּה
וְאַתָּה הוּא לָעוֹלָם הַבָּא.

---

*Barukh Shem* as the "lower unity" (*yiḥuda tata'ah*).[14] The higher unity of *Shema'*, that supernal perception of reality was revealed on Sinai. The lower unity of *Barukh Shem* comes to us through the tangibility of the world of creation.

From below, from Creation, one must work through the darkness to arrive at the light. "In the beginning darkness, and after light" (*"Be-reisha ḥashokha ve-hadar nehora"*).[15] Evening, then morning.

From above, from the revelation at Sinai, comes direct, immediate light. "In the realm of the sacred, night follows the day."[16]

אַתָּה הוּא עַד שֶׁלֹּא נִבְרָא הָעוֹלָם *It was You who existed before the world was created.* Why doesn't it state "It was You who existed before You created the world"? "Before the world was created" sounds as if the creation was not an intentional act, but came about in an almost reflexive manner, as it were.[17]

---

14. *Zohar* 1, 18b; Rabbi Shneur Zalman of Liadi, *Tanya, Sha'ar ha-Yiḥud ve-ha-Emunah*, chap. 1; Rabbi Ḥayyim of Volozhin, *Nefesh ha-Ḥayyim* 3:6, 11; *SK* 7:11.

15. *b. Shabbat* 77b.

16. *OR*, vol. 1, pp. 109–110.

17. In the Sephardic version of the prayer, the wording actually is "It was You who existed

▸ Sanctify Your name through those who sanctify Your name,
and sanctify Your name throughout Your world.
By Your salvation may our pride be exalted; raise high our pride.
Blessed are You, Lord,
who sanctifies His name among the multitudes.

אַתָּה הוּא You are the Lord our God
in heaven and on earth, and in the highest heaven of heavens.
Truly, You are the first and You are the last,
and besides You there is no god.
Gather those who hope in You
from the four quarters of the earth.
May all mankind recognize and know
that You alone are God over all the kingdoms on earth.

---

of darkness and their vanquishing by the light, there be revealed ultimately the indivisible unity of God. This latter form of governance, Luzzatto refers to as the "Secret of Unity" (*Sod ha-Yiḥud*).[19] Rav Kook's formulation, to which we shall return momentarily, may have been influenced by Luzzatto.

When you think about it, Rabbinic Judaism came up with a very strange term for martyrdom: *Kiddush Hashem* (Sanctification of the Name). Truly, how can the seemingly unjust death of a Jew for his belief in his God, be viewed as a sanctification of God's name? If anything, it would appear to be a desecration of that name, raising the spectral problem that God's goodness is

---

19. See Rabbi M.Ḥ. Luzzatto, *Da'at Tevunot*, ed. Friedlander (Tel-Aviv, 1975), Introduction, pp. 19–20 (*"Hanhagat ha-Yiḥud ve-Hanhagat ha-Mishpat"*); Text, par. 166 (pp. 184–187). Cf. Rabbi Aaron Halevi Horowitz of Starosselje, *Sha'arei ha-Yiḥud ve-ha-Emunah* (Shklov, 1820), gate 5 (*Sha'ar Katnut ve-Gadlut*), chap. 5 (f.12r, i.e. f.18v):

> It is His intention, may He be blessed, that there be revealed exactly the opposite, which is the *Sitra Aḥera* (the Other Side), in order that there be revealed His glory, the aspect of His unity, precisely from the opposite side, by overcoming the Other Side and transforming the darkness to light. His intention, may He be blessed … is that there be revelation of His godliness precisely from the opposite side, through its overcoming and transformation.

The author was the eminent disciple of Rabbi Shneur Zalman of Liadi, founder of the Ḥabad school of Ḥasidism.

◂ קַדֵּשׁ אֶת שִׁמְךָ עַל מַקְדִּישֵׁי שְׁמֶךָ
וְקַדֵּשׁ אֶת שִׁמְךָ בְּעוֹלָמֶךָ
וּבִישׁוּעָתְךָ תָּרוּם וְתַגְבִּיהַּ קַרְנֵנוּ.
בָּרוּךְ אַתָּה יהוה, הַמְקַדֵּשׁ אֶת שְׁמוֹ בָּרַבִּים.

אַתָּה הוּא יהוה אֱלֹהֵינוּ
בַּשָּׁמַיִם וּבָאָרֶץ וּבִשְׁמֵי הַשָּׁמַיִם הָעֶלְיוֹנִים.
אֱמֶת, אַתָּה הוּא רִאשׁוֹן וְאַתָּה הוּא אַחֲרוֹן
וּמִבַּלְעָדֶיךָ אֵין אֱלֹהִים.
קַבֵּץ קוֶֹיךָ מֵאַרְבַּע כַּנְפוֹת הָאָרֶץ.
יַכִּירוּ וְיֵדְעוּ כָּל בָּאֵי עוֹלָם
כִּי אַתָּה הוּא הָאֱלֹהִים לְבַדְּךָ לְכֹל מַמְלְכוֹת הָאָרֶץ.

---

קַדֵּשׁ אֶת שִׁמְךָ עַל מַקְדִּישֵׁי שְׁמֶךָ, וְקַדֵּשׁ אֶת שִׁמְךָ בְּעוֹלָמֶךָ *Sanctify Your name through those who sanctify Your name, and sanctify Your name throughout Your world.* One of the supreme challenges to theology is the problem of theodicy, which is to say: How does a merciful God authorize evil in His world? The problem has an especial "bite" to it in our post-Holocaust era, which must come to terms with the stark reality that six million of God's Chosen People were annihilated in unimaginably brutal circumstances within the short span of six years. Some of our greatest religious thinkers have attempted to tackle the problem of theodicy. (The Biblical book of Job is just such an attempt.)

Of note is the philosophic system of the Italian kabbalist, Rabbi Moses Ḥayyim Luzzatto (1707–1746), a short-lived genius whose biography reads like a work of tragedy. Luzzatto developed a theory whereby there are two tracks running through history. One track operates on the rather straightforward principle of reward and punishment. Acts of goodness are rewarded accordingly and acts of wickedness punished. But there is another track, which rather than being bound by the principle of reward and punishment, reflects the overarching divine concern, namely that by the irruption of forces

You made the heavens and the earth,
the sea and all they contain.
Who among all the works of Your hands, above and below,
can tell You what to do?

Heavenly Father, deal kindly with us
for the sake of Your great name
by which we are called,
and fulfill for us, LORD our God,
that which is written:
"At that time I will bring you home, *Zeph. 3*
and at that time I will gather you,
for I will give you renown and praise
among all the peoples of the earth
when I bring back your exiles before your eyes,
says the LORD."

---

collapse these two tracks into one, so that there will not be such a yawning chasm between the absolute goodness of God and the way in which it is perceived (or misperceived) in this world.

Let Your absolute, objective sanctification of Your name appeal to the subjective, relative reason of those who toil so hard in Your vineyard to sanctify Your name, and let the sanctification of Your name be manifest and resound throughout Your world.[22]

בָּעֵת הַהִיא אָבִיא אֶתְכֶם, וּבָעֵת קַבְּצִי אֶתְכֶם, כִּי־אֶתֵּן אֶתְכֶם לְשֵׁם וְלִתְהִלָּה בְּכֹל עַמֵּי הָאָרֶץ, בְּשׁוּבִי אֶת־שְׁבוּתֵיכֶם לְעֵינֵיכֶם, אָמַר יהוה *"At that time I will bring you, and at that time I will gather you, for I will give you renown and praise among all the peoples of the earth when I bring back your exiles before your eyes, said the LORD"* (*Zephaniah 3:20*). All the peoples of the earth will take note of this phenomenon of the ingathering of Israel, but their powers of observation are limited to the external event. Only *your eyes,* likened to "doves,"[23] gifted with pure vision, with insight, have the ability to behold the beauteous spiritual dimension of the Redemption.[24]

---

22. *OR*, vol. 1, pp. 111–112.
23. Song of Songs 4:1.
24. *OR*, vol. 1, p. 116.

אַתָּה עָשִׂיתָ אֶת הַשָּׁמַיִם וְאֶת הָאָרֶץ
אֶת הַיָּם וְאֶת כָּל אֲשֶׁר בָּם
וּמִי בְּכָל מַעֲשֵׂי יָדֶיךָ בָּעֶלְיוֹנִים אוֹ בַתַּחְתּוֹנִים
שֶׁיֹּאמַר לְךָ מַה תַּעֲשֶׂה.

אָבִינוּ שֶׁבַּשָּׁמַיִם עֲשֵׂה עִמָּנוּ חֶסֶד
בַּעֲבוּר שִׁמְךָ הַגָּדוֹל שֶׁנִּקְרָא עָלֵינוּ
וְקַיֶּם לָנוּ יהוה אֱלֹהֵינוּ
מַה שֶּׁכָּתוּב:
בָּעֵת הַהִיא אָבִיא אֶתְכֶם, וּבָעֵת קַבְּצִי אֶתְכֶם צפניה ג
כִּי־אֶתֵּן אֶתְכֶם לְשֵׁם וְלִתְהִלָּה בְּכֹל עַמֵּי הָאָרֶץ
בְּשׁוּבִי אֶת־שְׁבוּתֵיכֶם לְעֵינֵיכֶם
אָמַר יהוה:

not upheld, but rather appears to be subverted in God's world. This "cognitive dissonance" threatens to attack the very core of religious belief.

Rav Kook's only son, Rabbi Zevi Yehudah Hakohen Kook, would oftentimes quote a statement of the Talmud Yerushalmi: "Greater is the sanctification of the name than the desecration of the name." (*"Gadol kiddush hashem me-ḥillul hashem."*)[20] Taken at face value, what a strange statement! Of course, sanctification is greater than desecration. Rabbi Zevi Yehudah gave it a novel twist. Great is the sanctification precisely when it proceeds *from* desecration.[21] I would go so far as to venture that every martyrdom is *ipso facto* precisely a *Kiddush Hashem* that derives from a *Ḥillul Hashem*.

Let us return to Rav Kook's comment on our prayer. He observes that all too often there is a "disconnect" between God's level of *Kiddush Hashem* – understood only to God – and "entry level *Kiddush Hashem*," in other words, what Sanctification of the Name means to human beings toiling "down here below," striving to sanctify God in this lowly world. We are asking God to

20. *y. Kiddushin* 4:1; *Sanhedrin* 6:7.
21. *Siḥot Harav Zevi Yehudah: Shemot*, ed. Rabbi Shelomo Aviner (Jerusalem, 5758/1997), pp. 369–370.

# OFFERINGS

*The sages held that, in the absence of the Temple, studying the laws of sacrifices is the equivalent of offering them. Hence the following texts. There are different customs as to how many passages are to be said, and one should follow the custom of one's congregation. The minimum requirement is to say the verses relating to The Daily Sacrifice on page 70.*

THE BASIN

The LORD spoke to Moses, saying: Make a bronze basin, with its bronze stand for washing, and place it between the Tent of Meeting and the altar, and put water in it. From it, Aaron and his sons are to wash their hands *Ex. 30*

---

daily recitation of the sacrifices before the prayer: the *Parashat ha-Kiyyor* (the Laver), the *Tamid* (the Daily Sacrifice), the *Ketoret* (the Incense). These plant in the depths of the soul the divine greatness of the Great and Holy House, approaching the height that each individual experienced when the nation lived on its soil and in her midst stood the Holy Temple. The seeds of longing for the spiritual completion of the nation, yield their fruits in the furrows of the heart. Those fruits multiply and intertwine with a multitude of good thoughts that are traced back to this center. By the spirit of this mighty building, *Knesset Yisrael* (Ecclesia Israel) ... is built more than by secular insititutions that fortify nations who live only by the flesh and the material. The whole, exalted love of God is aroused and stands erect in the soul of the nation by virtue of her memories of her past, when the candle of God burned brightly within her. The idealism of this exalted memory, draws from the depths every lovely conception, every mighty and holy aspiration, and presents to the eyes of the nation as a whole its great divine value, which in turn, fills with splendor the chambers of the heart of every individual of her children.[3]

פרשת הכיור / THE BASIN

*The Lord spoke to Moses, saying: Make a bronze basin... From it, Aaron and his sons are to wash their hands and feet... When they enter the Tent of Meeting, they shall wash with water so that they will not die. (Exodus 30:17–20)*

The elements are symbolic. Of the three metals utilized in the construction of the *Mishkan* or Tabernacle in the Wilderness – gold, silver and bronze – the last, the least valued of the three, connotes the outer preparation before one enters the inner precincts. (By the same token, the outer altar was of bronze, while the inner altar was of gold.)

---

3. *SK* 1:144.

# סדר הקרבנות

*חז״ל held that, in the absence of the Temple, studying the laws of sacrifices is the equivalent of offering them. Hence the following texts. There are different customs as to how many passages are to be said, and one should follow the custom of one's congregation. The minimum requirement is to say the verses relating to the קרבן התמיד on page 71.*

## פרשת הכיור

שמות ל וַיְדַבֵּר יהוה אֶל־מֹשֶׁה לֵּאמֹר: וְעָשִׂיתָ כִּיּוֹר נְחֹשֶׁת וְכַנּוֹ נְחֹשֶׁת לְרָחְצָה,
וְנָתַתָּ אֹתוֹ בֵּין־אֹהֶל מוֹעֵד וּבֵין הַמִּזְבֵּחַ, וְנָתַתָּ שָׁמָּה מָיִם: וְרָחֲצוּ אַהֲרֹן

---

סדר הקרבנות / OFFERINGS

INTRODUCTION TO *KORBANOT*

With the destruction of the Holy Temple in Jerusalem, we literally pay "lip service" to the actual offering of sacrifices. "We pay for bullocks [the offering of] our lips."[1] "Nonetheless," writes Rav Kook:

> all the logic of our spirit and standing of our soul are founded on the light streaming from days of old and former years; and the life of our prayer, which revives our soul, downtrodden by waves of exile – they are all nourished by the sap of life that remains ours forever, until the day shall come when Israel will be uplifted and return to its tent as in the beginning.
>
> We stand full of pride and brokenness, full of joy and bitterness, full of sorrow and comfort and hope, toward the great vision that opens to us as a living treasury, from which we take the life of [divine] service, the life of prayer… from the greatness of our glorious past, which is the source of the lovely future… treasures of the life of the holy-of-holies, for the nation and its children, for all mankind, and for all the creation.[2]

Rav Kook singles out for mention the recitation of the sacrifices as a means of triggering the memory of the Holy Temple and thus tapping the psychic energies aroused thereby:

> The Holy Temple, as the spiritual center of the nation, and the source of spiritual life of every individual of that nation… must be rebuilt daily by each individual of Israel, in order to infuse into his spirit the inwardness of the nation in its complete state. Then there will return to the individual his fresh soul-powers, in which flourish the life of faith, and the warmth and light of emotion… This goal is accomplished on a practical level by the

---

1. Hosea 14:3.
2. *OR*, vol. 1, p. 118.

and feet. When they enter the Tent of Meeting, they shall wash with water so that they will not die; likewise when they approach the altar to minister, presenting a fire-offering to the LORD. They must wash their hands and feet so that they will not die. This shall be an everlasting ordinance for Aaron and his descendants throughout their generations.

### TAKING OF THE ASHES

The LORD spoke to Moses, saying: Instruct Aaron and his sons, saying, This is the law of the burnt-offering. The burnt-offering shall remain on the altar hearth throughout the night until morning, and the altar fire shall be kept burning on it. The priest shall then put on his linen garments, and linen breeches next to his body, and shall remove the ashes of the burnt-offering that the fire has consumed on the altar and place them beside the altar. Then he shall take off these clothes and put on others, and carry the ashes outside the camp to a clean place. The fire on the altar must be kept burning; it must not go out. Each morning the priest shall burn wood on it, and prepare on it the burnt-offering and burn the fat of the peace-offerings. A perpetual fire must be kept burning on the altar; it must not go out. *Lev. 6*

---

### פרשת תרומת הדשן / TAKING OF THE ASHES

*The priest shall then put on his linen garments, and linen breeches next to his body, and shall remove the ashes of the burnt-offering that the fire has consumed on the altar and place them beside the altar. Then he shall take off these clothes and put on others, and carry the ashes outside the camp to a clean place. (Leviticus 6:3–4)*

The *"terumat ha-deshen"* (taking of the ashes) represents the *"roshem,"* the imprint or afterglow of the holy experience of the sacrifice. These ashes are the residue of the holy fire.

There are two aspects to the *"terumat ha-deshen."* In the first stage, the priest, wearing his finery, places ashes on the side of the altar. This represents the resulting impression upon the soul of the individual. The profound impact upon the psyche is a private affair that cannot be readily communicated to others.

In the second stage of the process, the ashes are taken outside the camp, the purpose being to publicize the holy to broad humanity; to make inroads into secular society. For this task, the fine raiment is removed and other, less costly attire is worn by the priest. As the Rabbis expressed the thought: "In the clothes which he cooked a pot for his master, he should not pour a cup for his master."[10] (Rashi explains the parable. Just as in cooking, the clothing is soiled, so in removing the ashes outside the camp, the clothing is dirtied,

10. *b. Yoma* 23b.

וּבָנָיו מִמֶּנּוּ אֶת־יְדֵיהֶם וְאֶת־רַגְלֵיהֶם: בְּבֹאָם אֶל־אֹהֶל מוֹעֵד יִרְחֲצוּ־מַיִם,
וְלֹא יָמֻתוּ, אוֹ בְגִשְׁתָּם אֶל־הַמִּזְבֵּחַ לְשָׁרֵת, לְהַקְטִיר אִשֶּׁה לַיהוה: וְרָחֲצוּ
יְדֵיהֶם וְרַגְלֵיהֶם וְלֹא יָמֻתוּ, וְהָיְתָה לָהֶם חָק־עוֹלָם, לוֹ וּלְזַרְעוֹ לְדֹרֹתָם:

### פרשת תרומת הדשן

וַיְדַבֵּר יהוה אֶל־מֹשֶׁה לֵּאמֹר: צַו אֶת־אַהֲרֹן וְאֶת־בָּנָיו לֵאמֹר, זֹאת תּוֹרַת ויקרא ו
הָעֹלָה, הִוא הָעֹלָה עַל מוֹקְדָה עַל־הַמִּזְבֵּחַ כָּל־הַלַּיְלָה עַד־הַבֹּקֶר, וְאֵשׁ
הַמִּזְבֵּחַ תּוּקַד בּוֹ: וְלָבַשׁ הַכֹּהֵן מִדּוֹ בַד, וּמִכְנְסֵי־בַד יִלְבַּשׁ עַל־בְּשָׂרוֹ,
וְהֵרִים אֶת־הַדֶּשֶׁן אֲשֶׁר תֹּאכַל הָאֵשׁ אֶת־הָעֹלָה, עַל־הַמִּזְבֵּחַ, וְשָׂמוֹ אֵצֶל
הַמִּזְבֵּחַ: וּפָשַׁט אֶת־בְּגָדָיו, וְלָבַשׁ בְּגָדִים אֲחֵרִים, וְהוֹצִיא אֶת־הַדֶּשֶׁן אֶל־
מִחוּץ לַמַּחֲנֶה, אֶל־מָקוֹם טָהוֹר: וְהָאֵשׁ עַל־הַמִּזְבֵּחַ תּוּקַד־בּוֹ, לֹא תִכְבֶּה,
וּבִעֵר עָלֶיהָ הַכֹּהֵן עֵצִים בַּבֹּקֶר בַּבֹּקֶר, וְעָרַךְ עָלֶיהָ הָעֹלָה, וְהִקְטִיר עָלֶיהָ
חֶלְבֵי הַשְּׁלָמִים: אֵשׁ, תָּמִיד תּוּקַד עַל־הַמִּזְבֵּחַ, לֹא תִכְבֶּה:

---

The purification of the hands represents the sanctification of the intellect, while the purification of the feet, that of the will. The hands work consciously; the feet move instinctively.[4]

If the influx of the light should be greater than the value of the recipient, who is not yet purified to enter into this degree of holiness, then rather than the divine light of Torah enlivening as a "Tree of Life,"[5] it may turn into a destructive force; into a death potion (*sama de-mota*).[6] So, "When they enter the Tent of Meeting, they shall wash with water," symbolizing that the preparation for the revelation must come about through simple, original purification,[7] which consists in the purification of the inner inclination, a return to the "straightness" (*yosher*)[8] which the Creator placed in the soul of man.[9]

---

4. Elsewhere, Rav Kook noted the different circumstances at the birth of the two sets of twins. At the birth of Esau and Jacob, it is Esau's foot that figures prominently. At the birth of Zeraḥ and Peretz, it is Zeraḥ's hand that is front and center. Cf. Genesis 25:24–26 and Genesis 38:27–30. See *Orot ha-Emunah*, ed. Rabbi Moshe Gurevitz (Jerusalem, 1998), *Toledot*, p. 163.
5. Proverbs 3:18; *b. 'Arakhin* 15b.
6. *b. Shabbat* 88b; *Yoma* 72b.
7. Water is the most basic, simple substance.
8. Cf. Ecclesiastes 7:29.
9. *OR*, vol. 1, pp. 119–120.

May it be Your will, LORD our God and God of our ancestors, that You have compassion on us and pardon us all our sins, grant atonement for all our iniquities and forgive all our transgressions. May You rebuild the Temple swiftly in our days so that we may offer You the continual-offering that it may atone for us as You have prescribed for us in Your Torah through Moses Your servant, from the mouthpiece of Your glory, as it is said:

THE DAILY SACRIFICE

וַיְדַבֵּר The LORD said to Moses, "Command the Israelites and tell them: 'Be careful to offer to Me at the appointed time My food-offering consumed by fire, as an aroma pleasing to Me.' Tell them: 'This is the fire-offering you shall offer to the LORD – two lambs a year old without blemish, as a regular burnt-offering each day. Prepare one lamb in the morning and the other toward evening, together with a meal-offering of a tenth of an ephah of fine flour mixed with a quarter of a hin of oil from pressed olives. This is the regular burnt-offering instituted at Mount Sinai as a pleasing aroma, a fire-offering made to the LORD. Its libation is to be a quarter of a hin [of wine] with each lamb, poured in the Sanctuary as a libation of strong drink to the LORD. Prepare the second lamb in the afternoon, along with the same meal-offering and libation as in the morning. This is a fire-offering, an aroma pleasing to the LORD.'" *Num. 28*

וְשָׁחַט He shall slaughter it at the north side of the altar before the LORD, and Aaron's sons the priests shall sprinkle its blood against the altar on all sides. *Lev. 1*

---

There is another crucial difference. The first, morning offering has its source in Sinai.

The explanation is as follows. There were eruptions of holiness before Mount Sinai. "Abraham observed the entire Torah before it was given."[12] But as the Midrash phrased it, "All the commandments that the Patriarchs performed before You, were [but] fragrances (*reiḥot*),"[13] meaning that they were ephemeral in nature. The novelty of Mount Sinai was that for the first time in our history, the sacred assumed a permanent character. Thus, the *tamid*, the permanent offering is sourced in Sinai. The *"rei'aḥ niḥo'aḥ,"* "pleasing aroma," becomes *"isheh la-Hashem,"* "a fire-offering for the LORD."

When it comes to sacrifices (as opposed to the Creation of the World),

12. *b. Yoma* 28b; *Kiddushin* 82a.

13. *Song of Songs Rabbah* 1:3.

יְהִי רָצוֹן מִלְּפָנֶיךָ יהוה אֱלֹהֵינוּ וֵאלֹהֵי אֲבוֹתֵינוּ, שֶׁתְּרַחֵם עָלֵינוּ, וְתִמְחֹל לָנוּ עַל כָּל חַטֹּאתֵינוּ וּתְכַפֵּר לָנוּ עַל כָּל עֲוֹנוֹתֵינוּ וְתִסְלַח לָנוּ עַל כָּל פְּשָׁעֵינוּ, וְתִבְנֶה בֵּית הַמִּקְדָּשׁ בִּמְהֵרָה בְיָמֵינוּ, וְנַקְרִיב לְפָנֶיךָ קָרְבַּן הַתָּמִיד שֶׁיְּכַפֵּר בַּעֲדֵנוּ, כְּמוֹ שֶׁכָּתַבְתָּ עָלֵינוּ בְּתוֹרָתֶךָ עַל יְדֵי מֹשֶׁה עַבְדֶּךָ מִפִּי כְבוֹדֶךָ, כָּאָמוּר

### פרשת קרבן התמיד

וַיְדַבֵּר יהוה אֶל־מֹשֶׁה לֵּאמֹר: צַו אֶת־בְּנֵי יִשְׂרָאֵל וְאָמַרְתָּ אֲלֵהֶם, במדבר כח
אֶת־קָרְבָּנִי לַחְמִי לְאִשַּׁי, רֵיחַ נִיחֹחִי, תִּשְׁמְרוּ לְהַקְרִיב לִי בְּמוֹעֲדוֹ:
וְאָמַרְתָּ לָהֶם, זֶה הָאִשֶּׁה אֲשֶׁר תַּקְרִיבוּ לַיהוה, כְּבָשִׂים בְּנֵי־
שָׁנָה תְמִימִם שְׁנַיִם לַיּוֹם, עֹלָה תָמִיד: אֶת־הַכֶּבֶשׂ אֶחָד תַּעֲשֶׂה
בַבֹּקֶר, וְאֵת הַכֶּבֶשׂ הַשֵּׁנִי תַּעֲשֶׂה בֵּין הָעַרְבָּיִם: וַעֲשִׂירִית הָאֵיפָה
סֹלֶת לְמִנְחָה, בְּלוּלָה בְּשֶׁמֶן כָּתִית רְבִיעִת הַהִין: עֹלַת תָּמִיד,
הָעֲשֻׂיָה בְּהַר סִינַי, לְרֵיחַ נִיחֹחַ אִשֶּׁה לַיהוה: וְנִסְכּוֹ רְבִיעִת הַהִין
לַכֶּבֶשׂ הָאֶחָד, בַּקֹּדֶשׁ הַסֵּךְ נֶסֶךְ שֵׁכָר לַיהוה: וְאֵת הַכֶּבֶשׂ הַשֵּׁנִי
תַּעֲשֶׂה בֵּין הָעַרְבָּיִם, כְּמִנְחַת הַבֹּקֶר וּכְנִסְכּוֹ תַּעֲשֶׂה, אִשֵּׁה רֵיחַ
נִיחֹחַ לַיהוה:

וְשָׁחַט אֹתוֹ עַל יֶרֶךְ הַמִּזְבֵּחַ צָפֹנָה לִפְנֵי יהוה, וְזָרְקוּ בְּנֵי אַהֲרֹן ויקרא א
הַכֹּהֲנִים אֶת־דָּמוֹ עַל־הַמִּזְבֵּחַ, סָבִיב:

---

rendering it unfit for royal service.) Despite this downgrade, both sartorial and geographic, the destination is "to a pure place."[11]

פרשת קרבן התמיד / THE DAILY SACRIFICE

*This is the regular burnt-offering instituted at Mount Sinai as a pleasing aroma, a fire-offering made to the Lord… Prepare the second lamb in the afternoon, along with the same meal-offering and libation as in the morning. This is a fire-offering, an aroma pleasing to the Lord. (Numbers 28:6, 8)*

Note the reversal of language. In the case of the *tamid shel shaḥar*, the morning sacrifice, first it states "a pleasing aroma," and then "a fire-offering made to the Lord." When it comes to the *tamid shel bein ha-'arbayim*, the afternoon sacrifice, the sequence is the opposite: first a "fire-offering," and then "an aroma pleasing to the Lord."

---

11. *OR*, vol. 1, pp. 123–124.

May it be Your will, LORD our God and God of our ancestors,
that this recitation be considered accepted and favored before You
as if we had offered the daily sacrifice at its appointed time and place, according to its laws.

It is You, LORD our God, to whom our ancestors offered fragrant incense when the Temple stood, as You commanded them through Moses Your prophet, as is written in Your Torah:

THE INCENSE

The LORD said to Moses: Take fragrant spices – balsam, onycha, galbanum and pure frankincense, all in equal amounts – and make a fragrant blend of incense, the work of a perfumer, well mixed, pure and holy. Grind it very finely and place it in front of the [Ark of] Testimony in the Tent of Meeting, where I will meet with you. It shall be most holy to you. *Ex. 30*

---

is complete, the challenge is the opposite: to reconnect the practical to the spiritual; to turn "fire" into "fragrance" once again.[20]

פרשת הקטורת / THE INCENSE

The Talmud states that each *Kohen* or priest was given but a single opportunity to offer up the incense, so as to afford every *Kohen* the blessing of wealth. By making sure that each *Kohen* received a chance to offer incense, the wealth would be shared equally. The Talmud derives the fact that the incense bestows wealth from these verses: "They shall place incense in Your nostrils – Bless, LORD, his power."[21]

For Rav Kook, "wealth" in this context symbolizes the entire material plane.

Before Rabbi Ḥarlap attached himself to Rav Kook, he had been a disciple of the Jerusalem saint Rabbi Tsevi Mikhel Shapiro (author *Tsits ha-Kodesh*), from whom the young Rabbi Ya'akov Moshe Ḥarlap learned to practice a strict form of asceticism. (Similarly, it is recorded in the annals of the Ḥasidic movement that before Rabbi Dov Baer of Mezritch was exposed to the teaching of the Ba'al Shem Tov, he was an ascetic. The Ba'al Shem Tov taught the Maggid of Mezritch a new way of serving the LORD with joy.)

In a letter to Rabbi Ḥarlap,[22] Rav Kook pleads with his beloved disciple not to injure his heath by adhering to an abstemious diet, but rather partake of

---

20. *OR*, vol. 1, pp. 130–134.
21. Deuteronomy 33:10, 11; *y. Yoma* 2:3; *b. Yoma* 26a.
22. *IR*, vol. 2, pp. 167–169 (Letter 540). The contents of this particular letter are so esoteric that the editor RZYH commented in a footnote: "See the verso of the title-page of *Resh Millin*." In *Resh Millin* (London, 1917), Rav Kook quoted Maimonides' Introduction

יְהִי רָצוֹן מִלְּפָנֶיךָ, יהוה אֱלֹהֵינוּ וֵאלֹהֵי אֲבוֹתֵינוּ
שֶׁתְּהֵא אֲמִירָה זוֹ חֲשׁוּבָה וּמְקֻבֶּלֶת וּמְרֻצָּה לְפָנֶיךָ
כְּאִלּוּ הִקְרַבְנוּ קָרְבַּן הַתָּמִיד בְּמוֹעֲדוֹ וּבִמְקוֹמוֹ וּכְהִלְכָתוֹ.

אַתָּה הוּא יהוה אֱלֹהֵינוּ שֶׁהִקְטִירוּ אֲבוֹתֵינוּ לְפָנֶיךָ אֶת קְטֹרֶת הַסַּמִּים בִּזְמַן שֶׁבֵּית הַמִּקְדָּשׁ הָיָה קַיָּם, כַּאֲשֶׁר צִוִּיתָ אוֹתָם עַל יְדֵי מֹשֶׁה נְבִיאֶךָ, כַּכָּתוּב בְּתוֹרָתֶךָ:

פרשת הקטורת

שמות ל וַיֹּאמֶר יהוה אֶל־מֹשֶׁה, קַח־לְךָ סַמִּים נָטָף וּשְׁחֵלֶת וְחֶלְבְּנָה, סַמִּים וּלְבֹנָה זַכָּה, בַּד בְּבַד יִהְיֶה: וְעָשִׂיתָ אֹתָהּ קְטֹרֶת, רֹקַח מַעֲשֵׂה רוֹקֵחַ, מְמֻלָּח, טָהוֹר קֹדֶשׁ: וְשָׁחַקְתָּ מִמֶּנָּה הָדֵק, וְנָתַתָּה מִמֶּנָּה לִפְנֵי הָעֵדֻת בְּאֹהֶל מוֹעֵד אֲשֶׁר אִוָּעֵד לְךָ שָׁמָּה, קֹדֶשׁ קָדָשִׁים תִּהְיֶה לָכֶם:

---

"night follows the day.[14] This too is a continuation of the pattern of time established at Sinai.[15] The Torah was given by day: "And it came to pass on the third day when it was morning."[16]

In some sense, the Tabernacle in the Wilderness was a continuation of the Revelation at Sinai.[17] And later, in the Temple in Jerusalem, divine revelation (*giluy Shekhinah*) was bestowed upon the prophets and people of distinction. Jerusalem is referred to by the Prophet Isaiah as the "Valley of Vision" (*gei ḥizayon*).[18] "Rabbi Yoḥanan opened: 'Valley of vision' (*Gei ḥizayon*)… that all the visionaries (*ḥozim*) originate from her. As Rabbi Yoḥanan said: Any prophet whose city [of origin] is not specified, was a Jerusalemite."[19]

The afternoon sacrifice is a copy of the morning sacrifice in every respect except that its description as "a fire-offering" precedes its description as "an aroma pleasing to the Lord." This afternoon sacrifice is just a continuation of the revelation at Sinai. The novelty of converting a mere "fragrance" into a "fire," was revealed already in the morning; the afternoon sacrifice is but the extension of that conceptual breakthrough.

To put things differently, the challenge of the morning is to make the spiritual practical; once the day has gone by and the immersion in the practical

---

14. *b. Ḥullin* 83a.
15. See above commentary to *Ashreinu she-anaḥnu mashkimim u-ma'arivim 'erev va-voker.*
16. Exodus 19:16.
17. See Naḥmanides, Exodus 25:1 (Chavel edition, p. 453); Pseudo-Rashi, *Ta'anit* 21b, s.v. *el mul ha-har ha-hu.*
18. Isaiah 22:1, 5.
19. *Lamentations Rabbah, Petiḥata* 24. Cf. *Otserot ha-Rayah,* ed. Zuriel, vol. 6 (Rishon Lezion, 5776/2016), p. 382.

And it is said:

> Aaron shall burn fragrant incense on the altar every morning when he cleans the lamps. He shall burn incense again when he lights the lamps toward evening so that there will be incense before the LORD at all times, throughout your generations.

The rabbis taught: How was the incense prepared? It weighed 368 manehs, 365 corresponding to the number of days in a solar year, a maneh for each day, half to be offered in the morning and half in the afternoon, and three additional manehs from which the High Priest took two handfuls on Yom Kippur. These were put back into the mortar on the day before Yom Kippur and ground again very thoroughly so as to be extremely fine. The incense contained eleven kinds of spices: balsam, onycha, galbanum and *Keritot 6a*

---

be fragrant with the fear of the LORD."[27] The Rabbis interpreted the verse to mean that the Messiah will be able to judge by the sense of smell.[28] The wisdom of the *menorah* breaks reality down into binary categories of good and evil; into halakhic categories of forbidden and permitted, impure and pure, valid and invalid. But beyond that world of division, there is a world of unity conveyed by the fragrance of the incense. The *ketoret* is the "soul," the inner light of wisdom. Beyond the Tree of Knowledge of Good and Evil, there is the Tree of Life where only good resides.[29] "Evil cannot abide with You."[30] In that world of the holy incense, even the malodorous galbanum (*ḥelbenah*) is converted to a good odor. According to the Talmud, the galbanum symbolizes the "sinners of Israel" (*posh'ei Yisrael*).[31]

There may be another sense in which the light of the wisdom of the Menorah is divisive, and the fragrance of the incense unitive: in the effect that they have upon their students. A wisdom restricted solely to the *menorah* tends to generate envy and enmity among scholars (*kin'at soferim*); the future Messianic wisdom has a unifying, cohesive effect upon those engaged in its study. Hosea prophesied concerning the future state of the People of Israel: "His beauty shall be that of the olive tree and his fragrance that of the Lebanon."[32]

---

27. Isaiah 11:3.
28. *b. Sanhedrin* 93b.
29. See *Ra'aya Mehemna, Nasso* (*Zohar* III, 124b-125a); Rabbi Shneur Zalman of Liadi, *Tanya* IV, 26.
30. Psalms 5:5.
31. *b. Kereitot* 6b.
32. Hosea 14:7. See *Orot, Orot ha-Teḥiyah* (Lights of Renascence), chap. 38 (Maggid edition, pp. 362–363). The verse in Hosea is stated in the singular, yet the *Targum* treats it as if it were written in the plural. Rav Kook solves this conundrum by writing: "The height of soul-attainment, the illumination of the interior life, the spirit of divine life

וְנֶאֱמַר

וְהִקְטִיר עָלָיו אַהֲרֹן קְטֹרֶת סַמִּים, בַּבֹּקֶר בַּבֹּקֶר בְּהֵיטִיבוֹ אֶת־הַנֵּרֹת יַקְטִירֶנָּה: וּבְהַעֲלֹת אַהֲרֹן אֶת־הַנֵּרֹת בֵּין הָעַרְבַּיִם יַקְטִירֶנָּה, קְטֹרֶת תָּמִיד לִפְנֵי יהוה לְדֹרֹתֵיכֶם:

תָּנוּ רַבָּנָן: פִּטּוּם הַקְּטֹרֶת כֵּיצַד, שְׁלֹשׁ מֵאוֹת וְשִׁשִּׁים וּשְׁמוֹנָה מָנִים הָיוּ בָהּ. שְׁלֹשׁ כריתות ו.
מֵאוֹת וְשִׁשִּׁים וַחֲמִשָּׁה כְּמִנְיַן יְמוֹת הַחַמָּה, מָנֶה לְכָל יוֹם, פְּרַס בְּשַׁחֲרִית וּפְרַס בֵּין הָעַרְבַּיִם, וּשְׁלֹשָׁה מָנִים יְתֵרִים שֶׁמֵּהֶם מַכְנִיס כֹּהֵן גָּדוֹל מְלֹא חָפְנָיו בְּיוֹם הַכִּפּוּרִים, וּמַחֲזִירָן לְמַכְתֶּשֶׁת בְּעֶרֶב יוֹם הַכִּפּוּרִים וְשׁוֹחֲקָן יָפֶה יָפֶה, כְּדֵי שֶׁתְּהֵא דַקָּה מִן הַדַּקָּה. וְאַחַד עָשָׂר סַמָּנִים הָיוּ בָהּ, וְאֵלּוּ הֵן: הַצֳּרִי, וְהַצִּפֹּרֶן, וְהַחֶלְבְּנָה,

---

a rich diet (symbolized by the *selav* or quail).[23] While mentioning the incense as bestowing the blessing of wealth, Rav Kook holds up as an example the legendary Rav Hamnuna Saba, who according to the *Zohar* was capable of studying chapters of "words of folly" (*milei di-shtuta*) so as to extract therefrom the mystery of wisdom.[24] Rav Kook concludes the letter by pointing out that on Mount Sinai, the angels who were initially adversarial, ended up befriending Moses. "Even the Angel of Death transmitted to him the secret of the incense."[25]

**וְנֶאֱמַר, וְהִקְטִיר עָלָיו אַהֲרֹן קְטֹרֶת סַמִּים, בַּבֹּקֶר בַּבֹּקֶר בְּהֵיטִיבוֹ אֶת־הַנֵּרֹת יַקְטִירֶנָּה: וּבְהַעֲלֹת אַהֲרֹן אֶת־הַנֵּרֹת בֵּין הָעַרְבַּיִם יַקְטִירֶנָּה, קְטֹרֶת תָּמִיד לִפְנֵי יהוה לְדֹרֹתֵיכֶם:** *And it is said: Aaron shall burn fragrant incense on the altar every morning when he cleans the lamps. Aaron shall burn incense [again] when he lights the lamps toward evening so that there will be incense before the* Lord *at all times, throughout your generations* (*Exodus 30:7–8*). There is an interesting interplay and interaction of the burning of the incense and the lighting of the lamps of the *menorah* or candelabrum. The *menorah* symbolizes wisdom. "He who wishes to become wise, should go south."[26] The candelabrum was located in the South of the Temple. But there is a wisdom higher than earthly wisdom, and that is the unitive wisdom that is symbolized by the *ketoret* or incense. The Messianic wisdom is associated with the olfactory sense: "And he [i.e. the Messiah] shall

---

to *Guide of the Perplexed*: "If the reader finds nothing that will avail him in some way, then he should regard the book as if it had not been composed."

23. Rav Kook's remarks regarding the *selav* or quail in the Desert, recur in *SK* 2:280.
24. *Zohar* III, 47b. Cf. *Orot*, Israel and Its Renascence, chap. 14 (Maggid edition, pp. 190–191); *SK* 2:280.
25. *b. Shabbat* 89a.
26. *b. Bava Batra* 25b.

frankincense, each weighing seventy manehs; myrrh, cassia, spikenard and saffron, each weighing sixteen manehs; twelve manehs of costus, three of aromatic bark; nine of cinnamon; nine kabs of Carsina lye; three seahs and three kabs of Cyprus wine. If Cyprus wine was not available, old white wine might be used. A quarter of a kab of Sodom salt, and a minute amount of a smoke-raising herb. Rabbi Nathan the Babylonian says: also a minute amount of Jordan amber. If one added honey to the mixture, he rendered it unfit for sacred use. If he omitted any one of its ingredients, he is guilty of a capital offense.

Rabban Simeon ben Gamliel says: "Balsam" refers to the sap that drips from the balsam tree. The Carsina lye was used for bleaching the onycha to improve it. The Cyprus wine was used to soak the onycha in it to make it pungent. Though urine is suitable for this purpose, it is not brought into the Temple out of respect.

It was taught, Rabbi Nathan says: While it was being ground, another would say, "Grind well, well grind," because the [rhythmic] sound is good for spices. If it was mixed in half-quantities, it is fit for use, but we have not heard whether this applies to a third or a quarter. Rabbi Judah said: The general rule is that if it was made in the correct proportions, it is fit for use even if made in half-quantity, but if he omitted any one of its ingredients, he is guilty of a capital offense.

It was taught, Bar Kappara says: Once every sixty or seventy years, the accumulated *JT Yoma 4:5*
surpluses amounted to half the yearly quantity. Bar Kappara also taught: If a minute quantity of honey had been mixed into the incense, no one could have resisted the scent. Why did they not put honey into it? Because the Torah says, "For you are not to burn *Lev. 2*
any leaven or honey in a fire-offering made to the LORD."

*The following three verses are each said three times:*

The LORD of hosts is with us; the God of Jacob is our stronghold, Selah. *Ps. 46*
LORD of hosts, happy is the one who trusts in You. *Ps. 84*
LORD, save! May the King answer us on the day we call. *Ps. 20*

---

impacting general society, guaranteeing the continuity and eternity of its influence: *tamid* ("at all times").

The relation between the incense and the lamps is reciprocal. The worldly wisdom of the *menorah* receives its "soul" from the incense; by the same token, it is only through the outer expression of the lamps that the innermost realizations of the incense can be modulated and adjusted to the spiritual condition of every generation: *ledoroteikhem* ("throughout your generations").[33]

הַמֶּלֶךְ יַעֲנֵנוּ בְיוֹם־קָרְאֵנוּ *May the King answer us on the day we call.* When one reaches the realization that in the divine scheme all is perfect, all is present, all is complete, then the very concept of prayer, which is a declaration that something is missing, something is wanting, something is lacking – appears ludicrous.

---

33. *OR*, vol. 1, pp. 138–139.

וְהַלְּבוֹנָה מִשְׁקַל שִׁבְעִים שִׁבְעִים מָנֶה, מוֹר, וּקְצִיעָה, שִׁבֹּלֶת נֵרְדְּ, וְכַרְכֹּם מִשְׁקַל שִׁשָּׁה עָשָׂר שִׁשָּׁה עָשָׂר מָנֶה, הַקֹּשְׁטְ שְׁנֵים עָשָׂר, קִלּוּפָה שְׁלֹשָׁה, קִנָּמוֹן תִּשְׁעָה, בֹּרִית כַּרְשִׁינָה תִּשְׁעָה קַבִּין, יֵין קַפְרִיסִין סְאִין תְּלָת וְקַבִּין תְּלָתָא, וְאִם לֹא מָצָא יֵין קַפְרִיסִין, מֵבִיא חֲמַר חִוַּרְיָן עַתִּיק. מֶלַח סְדוֹמִית רֹבַע, מַעֲלֶה עָשָׁן כָּל שֶׁהוּא. רַבִּי נָתָן הַבַּבְלִי אוֹמֵר: אַף כִּפַּת הַיַּרְדֵּן כָּל שֶׁהוּא, וְאִם נָתַן בָּהּ דְּבַשׁ פְּסָלָהּ, וְאִם חִסַּר אֶחָד מִכָּל סַמָּנֶיהָ, חַיָּב מִיתָה.

רַבָּן שִׁמְעוֹן בֶּן גַּמְלִיאֵל אוֹמֵר: הַצֳּרִי אֵינוֹ אֶלָּא שְׂרָף הַנּוֹטֵף מֵעֲצֵי הַקְּטָף. בֹּרִית כַּרְשִׁינָה שֶׁשָּׁפִין בָּהּ אֶת הַצִּפֹּרֶן כְּדֵי שֶׁתְּהֵא נָאָה, יֵין קַפְרִיסִין שֶׁשּׁוֹרִין בּוֹ אֶת הַצִּפֹּרֶן כְּדֵי שֶׁתְּהֵא עַזָּה, וַהֲלֹא מֵי רַגְלַיִם יָפִין לָהּ, אֶלָּא שֶׁאֵין מַכְנִיסִין מֵי רַגְלַיִם בַּמִּקְדָּשׁ מִפְּנֵי הַכָּבוֹד.

תַּנְיָא, רַבִּי נָתָן אוֹמֵר: כְּשֶׁהוּא שׁוֹחֵק אוֹמֵר, הָדֵק הֵיטֵב הֵיטֵב הָדֵק, מִפְּנֵי שֶׁהַקּוֹל יָפֶה לַבְּשָׂמִים. פִּטְּמָהּ לַחֲצָאִין כְּשֵׁרָה, לִשְׁלִישׁ וְלִרְבִיעַ לֹא שָׁמַעְנוּ. אָמַר רַבִּי יְהוּדָה: זֶה הַכְּלָל, אִם כְּמִדָּתָהּ כְּשֵׁרָה לַחֲצָאִין, וְאִם חִסַּר אֶחָד מִכָּל סַמָּנֶיהָ חַיָּב מִיתָה.

ירושלמי יומא ד, הלכה ה
תַּנְיָא, בַּר קַפָּרָא אוֹמֵר: אַחַת לְשִׁשִּׁים אוֹ לְשִׁבְעִים שָׁנָה הָיְתָה בָאָה שֶׁל שִׁירַיִם לַחֲצָאִין. וְעוֹד תָּנֵי בַּר קַפָּרָא: אִלּוּ הָיָה נוֹתֵן בָּהּ קָרְטוֹב שֶׁל דְּבַשׁ אֵין אָדָם יָכוֹל
ויקרא ב
לַעֲמֹד מִפְּנֵי רֵיחָהּ, וְלָמָּה אֵין מְעָרְבִין בָּהּ דְּבַשׁ, מִפְּנֵי שֶׁהַתּוֹרָה אָמְרָה: כִּי כָל־שְׂאֹר וְכָל־דְּבַשׁ לֹא־תַקְטִירוּ מִמֶּנּוּ אִשֶּׁה לַיהוה:

*The following three verses are each said three times:*

תהלים מו
**יהוה צְבָאוֹת עִמָּנוּ, מִשְׂגָּב לָנוּ אֱלֹהֵי יַעֲקֹב סֶלָה:**

תהלים פד
**יהוה צְבָאוֹת, אַשְׁרֵי אָדָם בֹּטֵחַ בָּךְ:**

תהלים כ
**יהוה הוֹשִׁיעָה, הַמֶּלֶךְ יַעֲנֵנוּ בְיוֹם־קָרְאֵנוּ:**

---

The *Targum* thereto paraphrases: "Their splendor shall be as the splendor of the holy *menorah*, and their fragrance as the fragrance of the incense of spices."

As stated earlier in regard to the afternoon sacrifice (*tamid shel bein ha-'arbayim*), it is necessary that the incense be burnt a second time in the afternoon in order to exert influence upon the mundane sphere of activity. If offered only once in the morning, the *ketoret* would remain in the rarefied atmosphere of the purely spiritual; it is by being burnt again in the afternoon that the incense is capable of making inroads into the workday and of

---

that will be revealed to King Messiah (*Malka Meshiḥa*), will extend to all Israel" (*OR*, vol. 1, p. 141, s.v. *ve-aḥad 'asar samanim hayu bah*).

You are my hiding place; You will protect me from distress and surround me with songs of salvation, Selah. Then the offering of Judah and Jerusalem will be pleasing to the LORD as in the days of old and as in former years. *Ps. 32* *Mal. 3*

THE ORDER OF THE PRIESTLY FUNCTIONS

Abaye related the order of the daily priestly functions in the name of tradition and in accordance with Abba Shaul: The large pile [of wood] comes before the second pile for the incense; the second pile for the incense precedes the laying in order of the two logs of wood; the laying in order of the two logs of wood comes before the removing of ashes from the inner altar; the removing of ashes from the inner altar precedes the cleaning of the five lamps; the cleaning of the five lamps comes before the blood of the daily offering; the blood of the daily offering precedes the cleaning of the [other] two lamps; the cleaning of the two lamps comes before the incense-offering; the incense-offering precedes the burning of the limbs; the burning of the limbs comes before the meal-offering; the meal-offering precedes the pancakes; the pancakes come before the wine-libations; the wine-libations precede the additional offerings; the additional offerings come before the [frankincense] censers; the censers precede the daily afternoon offering; as it is said, "On it he shall arrange burnt-offerings, and on it he shall burn the fat of the peace-offerings" – "on it" [the daily offering] all the offerings were completed. *Yoma 33a* *Lev. 6*

---

In a kabbalistic vein, Rav Kook is struck by the fact that of all persons, it was Abaye who engaged in the activity of imposing order on the otherwise inchoate. On the ultimate level of reality, there is no time sequence (*seder zemanim*); no chronological order. "There is no earlier or later in the Torah." Sequence represents a dramatic descent from the higher reality. In our reduced reality, subject to temporality, we are bereft; we are "orphaned," so to speak, of the luminous, indivisible reality. The historic personality Abaye was an orphan. This tragic circumstance is alluded to in the initials of his name: "***A**sher **B**ekha **Y**eruḥam **Y**atom*" ("For in You an orphan finds mercy").[36] The very act of ordering is in a metaphysical sense, an "orphaning."

By the same token, the initials of the words that characterize Joseph, "*yefeh to'ar vi-yefeh mar'eh*" ("handsome in form and handsome in appearance"), spell out the Hebrew word for orphan: *yatom.*[37] Joseph too was orphaned of his mother (Rachel). And again, the comely, well-groomed appearance

36. Hosea 14:4; Rabbi Ḥayyim Vital, *Sha'ar ha-Gilgulim, hakdamah* 34.
Rabbi Ḥayyim Vital derived this notarikon from the *Sefer ha-Yuḥasin* of Rabbi Abraham Zacuto, who in turn drew on older sources reaching as far back as Rabbi El'azar of Worms (*Roke'aḥ*). See Rabbi Y.A.Z. Miller, "*Bikhdi Safdu Safdaya?*" in: *Ḥitsei Giborim*, vol. 10 (Nissan, 5777/2017), p. 639.

37. Genesis 39:6; Rabbi Ḥayyim Vital, *'Ets Ḥayyim, Sha'ar ha-Kelalim*, end chap. 4. Joseph

אַתָּה סֵתֶר לִי, מִצַּר תִּצְּרֵנִי, רָנֵּי פַלֵּט תְּסוֹבְבֵנִי סֶלָה: וְעָרְבָה לַיהוה מִנְחַת יְהוּדָה תהלים לב מלאכי ג
וִירוּשָׁלָם, כִּימֵי עוֹלָם וּכְשָׁנִים קַדְמֹנִיּוֹת:

## סדר המערכה

אַבַּיֵּי הֲוָה מְסַדֵּר סֵדֶר הַמַּעֲרָכָה מִשְּׁמָא דִּגְמָרָא, וְאַלִּבָּא דְּאַבָּא שָׁאוּל: יומא לג.
מַעֲרָכָה גְּדוֹלָה קוֹדֶמֶת לְמַעֲרָכָה שְׁנִיָּה שֶׁל קְטֹרֶת, וּמַעֲרָכָה שְׁנִיָּה שֶׁל קְטֹרֶת
קוֹדֶמֶת לְסִדּוּר שְׁנֵי גִזְרֵי עֵצִים, וְסִדּוּר שְׁנֵי גִזְרֵי עֵצִים קוֹדֵם לְדִשּׁוּן מִזְבֵּחַ
הַפְּנִימִי, וְדִשּׁוּן מִזְבֵּחַ הַפְּנִימִי קוֹדֵם לַהֲטָבַת חָמֵשׁ נֵרוֹת, וַהֲטָבַת חָמֵשׁ נֵרוֹת
קוֹדֶמֶת לְדַם הַתָּמִיד, וְדַם הַתָּמִיד קוֹדֵם לַהֲטָבַת שְׁתֵּי נֵרוֹת, וַהֲטָבַת שְׁתֵּי
נֵרוֹת קוֹדֶמֶת לִקְטֹרֶת, וּקְטֹרֶת קוֹדֶמֶת לְאֵבָרִים, וְאֵבָרִים לְמִנְחָה, וּמִנְחָה
לַחֲבִתִּין, וַחֲבִתִּין לִנְסָכִין, וּנְסָכִין לְמוּסָפִין, וּמוּסָפִין לְבָזִיכִין, וּבָזִיכִין קוֹדְמִין
לְתָמִיד שֶׁל בֵּין הָעַרְבַּיִם. שֶׁנֶּאֱמַר: וְעָרַךְ עָלֶיהָ הָעֹלָה, וְהִקְטִיר עָלֶיהָ חֶלְבֵי ויקרא ו
הַשְּׁלָמִים: עָלֶיהָ הַשְׁלֵם כָּל הַקָּרְבָּנוֹת כֻּלָּם.

---

How can we ask for something when we already have everything? But on the other hand, a universe bereft of the dimension of prayer would be lacking a most important ingredient of existence. So existence must encompass prayer.[34]

סדר המערכה / THE ORDER OF THE PRIESTLY FUNCTIONS

אַבַּיֵּי הֲוָה מְסַדֵּר סֵדֶר הַמַּעֲרָכָה מִשְּׁמָא דִּגְמָרָא *Abaye related the order of the daily priestly functions in the name of tradition.*[35] More precisely, "Abaye used to arrange the order," or "Abaye used to order the order (*mesader seder*)."

---

34. *OR*, vol. 1, p. 150. This paradox is reminiscent of the comment of the Sages concerning the verse in Genesis 2:2: "God completed on the seventh day His work which He had done." "What was the world lacking? Rest! With the Sabbath there came rest, and the work was completed and finished." (Rashi, ad locum; *Genesis Rabbah* 10:9; Rashi, *Megillah* 9a, s.v. *vayekhal*)

35. Maharal of Prague, in punning fashion, referred to the entire Talmudic enterprise as *"Seder ha-ma'arakha mi-shemeh di-Gemara"*; as an "arrangement of the construct." See Rabbi Judah Löw, *"Derush 'al ha-Mitsvot"* (Prague, 1593), 35b, s.v. *ha-mishmarah ha-tikhonah*; *Derashot Maharal mi-Prag*, appended to *Be'er ha-Golah* (London: L. Honig, 1964), p. 55; Michael Dushinsky, "*'Yayin Nesekh'* (Gentile's Wine) in Maharal's Teachings: Reading His Sermon on the Precepts" (Hebrew), in *Šalom: pocta Bedřichu Noskovi k sedmdesátým narozeninám* [Bedřich Nosek Festschrift], ed. Blažek, Veverková and Biernot (Prague: L. Marek, 2012), p. 391.
    In his journals, Rav Kook often expressed his anxiety over being subjected to the exacting, miniscule study of Talmud, when left to its innate proclivities his soul would soar to the expanses of mysticism.

Please, by the power of Your great right hand, set the captive nation free.
Accept Your people's prayer. Strengthen us, purify us, You who are revered.
Please, Mighty One, guard like the pupil of the eye those who seek Your unity.
Bless them, cleanse them, have compassion on them,
grant them Your righteousness always.

---

אָנָּא, בְּכֹחַ גְּדֻלַּת יְמִינְךָ, תַּתִּיר צְרוּרָה *Please, by the power of Your great right hand, set the captive nation free.* The right hand symbolizes *ḥesed* or love. The purpose of all existence is the expression of God's love: "The world was built by love."[42] Within the realm of love, there is greatness and smallness. A small love bestows kindness only to the extent that the recipient has the ability to absorb the kindness. The large love, rather than limit the kindness to the recipient's reduced circumstances, goes so far as to broaden the recipient's capacity to receive kindness. "The Holy One, blessed be He, gives the righteous strength to receive their good."[43]

The freeing, the loosening of the restriction follows directly from the power of the greatness of the divine right hand. In so doing, the recipient is enabled to receive the most bounteous, unlimited kindness.

קַבֵּל רִנַּת עַמְּךָ, שַׂגְּבֵנוּ, טַהֲרֵנוּ, נוֹרָא *Accept your people's prayer. Strengthen us, purify us, You who are revered.* The term *rinah* denotes song. The song of Israel is an outpouring of the soul of the people. *Knesset Yisrael* (*Ecclesia Israel*) exerts universal influence upon all existence and all the worlds. As the *Tikkunei Zohar* put it, *Yisrael* is *Shir El* (the Song of God).[44] However, in this national outpouring there may be impurities that require cleansing. *Rinah* is external.[45] That process of purification comes about through the aspect of divine awe: *Taharenu, nora.* (Purify us, Awesome One).

נָא גִבּוֹר, דּוֹרְשֵׁי יִחוּדְךָ כְּבָבַת שָׁמְרֵם *Please, Mighty One, guard like the pupil of the eye those who seek Your unity. Knesset Yisrael* (*Ecclesia Israel*) seeks the unity of the Lord in the world, that all creations be unified to do God's will. On account of this idea that forever beats in the heart of Israel, many seek to destroy them, and they require guarding all about. And this guarding requires great might. *Knesset Yisrael* is the eye of the world and its light.

בָּרְכֵם, טַהֲרֵם, רַחֲמֵם, צִדְקָתְךָ תָּמִיד גָּמְלֵם *Bless them, cleanse them, have compassion on them, grant them Your righteousness always.* Rav Kook has recourse to the

---

42. Psalms 89:3.
43. *b. Sanhedrin* 100b.
44. *Tikkunei Zohar, tikkun* 10.
45. Cf. *Zohar* 1, 163a.

אָנָּא, בְּכֹחַ גְּדֻלַּת יְמִינְךָ, תַּתִּיר צְרוּרָה.
קַבֵּל רִנַּת עַמְּךָ, שַׂגְּבֵנוּ, טַהֲרֵנוּ, נוֹרָא.
נָא גִבּוֹר, דּוֹרְשֵׁי יִחוּדְךָ כְּבָבַת שָׁמְרֵם.
בָּרְכֵם, טַהֲרֵם, רַחֲמֵם, צִדְקָתְךָ תָּמִיד גָּמְלֵם.

---

relates to order, to *seder*.[38] Someone who is "put together," is said to be in Hebrew *"mesudar."* But in this very order, in this descent from the infinite light, there is a cosmic tragedy. The sundering from the primal, indivisible, disorderly, disorganized reality produces a *yatom*, an "orphan."[39]

### אָנָּא, בְּכֹחַ / ANA BE-KHO'AḤ

The prayer *Ana be-Kho'aḥ* comes out of the kabbalistic tradition. It was attributed to the *tanna* (sage of the Mishnah) Rabbi Neḥunyah ben ha-Kaneh. Contained therein is a divine name of forty-two letters derived from the first two verses of Genesis.[40]

The name of forty-two letters was employed by the Kabbalists as a meditative technique to achieve ascent of the soul. This is referred to in Kabbalistic literature as the *"sod ha-'afifah"* ("the secret of flying").[41]

---

(*Yesod*) is orphaned of his mother (*Binah*) because the *sefirah* of *Binah* extends downward only as far as *Hod*, stopping short of *Yesod*.

38. According to the Rabbis, Joseph would fix his hair (Rashi, Genesis 39:6; *Genesis Rabbah* 87:3).
39. *OR*, vol. 1, p. 152.
    See Rav Kook's essay "The Souls of the World of Chaos" *("Ha-Neshamot shel 'Olam ha-Tohu")* which first appeared as the third chapter of *"Zer'onim"* in the short-lived journal *Ha-Tarbut ha-Yisraelit* (Jaffa, 1913); subsequently reprinted in the enlarged edition of *Orot* (Jerusalem, 1950).
    Compare this speculation of the modern philosopher John Gray:

    > While it may be the most effective means of explaining how the world works, science cannot explain its own achievements. Scientific inquiry may be successful because everything that exists obeys a few simple laws, which humans have begun to grasp. The order of the human mind may mirror that in the cosmos. Then again, the success of science may come from the fact that its practitioners inhabit a small corner of the universe that is not chaotic. Perhaps it is the disorder of the human mind that is more reflective of reality. (John Gray, *The Soul of the Marionette: A Short Inquiry into Human Freedom* [New York: Farrar, Straus and Giroux, 2015], pp. 149–150)

40. See *b. Kiddushin* 71a; *Tosafot, Ḥagigah* 11b, s.v. *ein doreshin*; Maimonides, *Guide of the Perplexed* 1, 62; Rabbi Moses Cordovero, *Pardess Rimonim* 21:12–13.
41. Rabbi Moses Ḥayyim Luzzatto, *Kin'at Adonai Tseva'ot* 11, in *Ginzei Ramḥal*, ed. Friedlander (B'nei Berak, 5740/1980), p. 124; Rabbi Naphtali Herz Halevi, *Siddur ha-GRA* (Jerusalem, 1895; photo offset Jerusalem, 1971), *Imrei Shefer*, 33b-36a.

Mighty One, Holy One, in Your great goodness guide Your congregation.
Only One, Exalted One, turn to Your people, who proclaim Your holiness.
Accept our plea and heed our cry, You who know all secret thoughts.

Blessed be the name of His glorious kingdom for ever and all time.

Master of the Universe, You have commanded us to offer the daily sacrifice at its appointed time with the priests at their service, the Levites on their platform, and the Israelites at their post. Now, because of our sins, the Temple is destroyed and the daily sacrifice discontinued, and we have no priest at his service, no Levite

---

the thought of whom predates the creation of the world, recall the Only One, the Exalted One who predates the creation of the universe and transcends any desire or ambition of creation. This level of divinity that totally transcends the worlds is encoded in the word *ge'eh* (Exalted One). "His grandeur (*ga'avato*) is more than the world can contain."[47] "The LORD reigned. He is robed in grandeur (*ge'ut*). The LORD is robed, girded with strength. The world is firmly established; it cannot be moved. Your throne stands firm as of old; You are pre-eternal."[48]

> This supernal sanctity is the root of their soul and their being. Despite all the descents that they experienced; all the depths to which they sank; all the material limitation of the World of Making (*'Olam 'Asiyah*), and tumultuous waves that cause one to forget the supreme majesty – they, Israel, retain the memory of the supernal sanctity, the sanctity of the Only One of the Universe (*yeḥido shel 'olam*).

It is fitting then that the Only One turn to the people who are yet conscious of that Only-ness.

שַׁוְעָתֵנוּ קַבֵּל וּשְׁמַע צַעֲקָתֵנוּ, יוֹדֵעַ תַּעֲלוּמוֹת *Accept our plea and heed our cry, You who know all secret thoughts.* The plea (*shav'ah*) relates to the heights; it is the longing for the light. The cry (*tse'akah*) comes from the depths; it arises as a result of the darkness. Only You know the height of the light; only You know the depth of the darkness. From both of these voices – one born of the soul's intense longing for the divine light, and the other conceived in the crucible of suffering brought about by the limitations and confinement of earthly existence – will come the salvation.[49]

---

47. From the hymn *"Eder ve-hod eten be-tsivyon,"* recited in the Ashkenazic rite for the second day of Rosh Hashanah, in the Reader's repetition of the Morning Service.
48. Psalms 93:1, 2.
49. *OR*, vol. 1, pp. 157–160.

חֲסִין קָדוֹשׁ, בְּרֹב טוּבְךָ נַהֵל עֲדָתֶךָ.
יָחִיד גֵּאֶה, לְעַמְּךָ פְּנֵה, זוֹכְרֵי קְדֻשָּׁתֶךָ.
שַׁוְעָתֵנוּ קַבֵּל וּשְׁמַע צַעֲקָתֵנוּ, יוֹדֵעַ תַּעֲלוּמוֹת.
בָּרוּךְ שֵׁם כְּבוֹד מַלְכוּתוֹ לְעוֹלָם וָעֶד.

רִבּוֹן הָעוֹלָמִים, אַתָּה צִוִּיתָנוּ לְהַקְרִיב קָרְבַּן הַתָּמִיד בְּמוֹעֲדוֹ וְלִהְיוֹת כֹּהֲנִים בַּעֲבוֹדָתָם וּלְוִיִּם בְּדוּכָנָם וְיִשְׂרָאֵל בְּמַעֲמָדָם, וְעַתָּה בַּעֲוֹנוֹתֵינוּ חָרַב בֵּית הַמִּקְדָּשׁ וּבְטַל הַתָּמִיד וְאֵין לָנוּ לֹא כֹהֵן בַּעֲבוֹדָתוֹ וְלֹא לֵוִי בְּדוּכָנוֹ וְלֹא יִשְׂרָאֵל

---

kabbalistic scheme of the *sefirot* or divine attributes, whereby *Ḥesed* (Love), *Din* (Law) and *Raḥamim* (Compassion) form a triad, in which the attribute of *Compassion* represents the synthesis of *Love* and *Law*.

*Berakha*, blessing, derives from divine love, from *Ḥesed*. *Toharah*, purity, derives from the restriction of law, of *Din*. The blessing from on high encounters a human being with human limitations and frailties. Thus, purification is required for the blessing to be properly assimilated within the personality. The confluence of these two forces, blessing (*borkhenu*) and purity (*taharenu*) is deemed compassion (*raḥamenu*). Once these components of blessing and purity have come together, they make for a permanent, ongoing arrangement properly modulated to the recipients: Grant them Your righteousness *always*.

חֲסִין קָדוֹשׁ, בְּרֹב טוּבְךָ נַהֵל עֲדָתֶךָ *Mighty One, Holy One, in your great goodness guide Your congregation.* The word *'edah* (congregation) is related to the word *te'udah* (destiny, calling or mission). Israel are Your congregation; they are also Your destiny. They are a people committed to the fulfillment of God's plan, God's ideal for the world. It is Israel's ambition that only the will of the Creator of all worlds shall be at work in all the worlds, and that only the Mighty and Holy shall control and motivate all the systems of nature and all the regimes of existence.

> Mighty One, Holy One, in Your great goodness, the abundant goodness, the absolute goodness – which is the plenitude of life, in all its strength and might – with this great goodness, guide Your congregation, the sanctifiers of Your name, those who fulfill Your destiny in the world.

יָחִיד גֵּאֶה, לְעַמְּךָ פְּנֵה, זוֹכְרֵי קְדֻשָּׁתֶךָ *Only One, Exalted One, turn to Your people, who proclaim Your holiness.* In the previous verse we focused on God's desire in creating the universe; that merely serves as the staging for a climb to a height beyond the very desire of creation. Israel, who "arose in thought,"[46] i.e.,

---

46. *Genesis Rabbah* 1:4.

on his platform, no Israelite at his post. But You said: "We will offer in place of bullocks [the prayer of] our lips." Therefore may it be Your will, LORD our God and God of our ancestors, that the prayer of our lips be considered, accepted and favored before You as if we had offered the daily sacrifice at its appointed time and place, according to its laws. *Hos. 14*

*On Shabbat:*

וּבְיוֹם הַשַּׁבָּת On the Shabbat day, make an offering of two lambs a year old, without blemish, together with two-tenths of an ephah of fine flour mixed with oil as a meal-offering, and its appropriate libation. This is the burnt-offering for every Shabbat, in addition to the regular daily burnt-offering and its libation. *Num. 28*

*On Rosh Ḥodesh:*

וּבְרָאשֵׁי חָדְשֵׁיכֶם On your new moons, present as a burnt-offering to the LORD, two young bulls, one ram, and seven yearling lambs without blemish. There shall be a meal-offering of three-tenths of an ephah of fine flour mixed with oil for each bull, two-tenths of an ephah of fine flour mixed with oil for the ram, and one-tenth of an ephah of fine flour mixed with oil for each lamb. This is the burnt-offering – a fire-offering of pleasing aroma to the LORD. Their libations shall be: half a hin of wine for each bull, a third of a hin for the ram, and a quarter of a hin for each lamb. This is the monthly burnt-offering to be made at each new moon throughout the year. One male goat should be offered as a sin-offering to God, in addition to the regular daily burnt-offering and its libation. *Num. 28*

*The service continues on page 88.*

וּשְׂעִיר עִזִּים אֶחָד לְחַטָּאת לַה׳ *And one male goat, as a sin-offering for the LORD.* The words "a sin-offering for the LORD" suggest boldly enough that the LORD Himself, as it were, is in need of expiation. And in fact, this is the homiletic way in which the Rabbis interpreted the verse: "Bring for me an atonement for my having reduced the moon."[53] According to the Rabbinic legend, originally the sun and the moon, "the two great luminaries,"[54] were equal in size. When the Moon complained to God that "it is impossible for two kings to wear the same crown," God shot back the reply, "Go reduce yourself!"[55] But

53. *b. Ḥullin* 60b; *Genesis Rabbah* 6:3.

54. Genesis 1:16.

55. Either the reduction refers to a reduction in size (the moon being significantly smaller than the sun), or it refers to the fact that the moon has no light of its own but merely reflects the sunlight. (Rabbi Judah Canpanton, *Arba'ah Kinyanim, loc. cit.*)

בְּמַעֲמָדוֹ, וְאַתָּה אָמַרְתָּ: וּנְשַׁלְּמָה פָרִים שְׂפָתֵינוּ: לָכֵן יְהִי רָצוֹן מִלְּפָנֶיךָ יהוה אֱלֹהֵינוּ וֵאלֹהֵי אֲבוֹתֵינוּ, שֶׁיְּהֵא שִׂיחַ שִׂפְתוֹתֵינוּ חָשׁוּב וּמְקֻבָּל וּמְרֻצֶּה לְפָנֶיךָ, כְּאִלּוּ הִקְרַבְנוּ קָרְבַּן הַתָּמִיד בְּמוֹעֲדוֹ וּבִמְקוֹמוֹ וּכְהִלְכָתוֹ. הושע יד

בשבת:

וּבְיוֹם הַשַּׁבָּת שְׁנֵי־כְבָשִׂים בְּנֵי־שָׁנָה תְּמִימִם, וּשְׁנֵי עֶשְׂרֹנִים סֹלֶת מִנְחָה בְּלוּלָה בַשֶּׁמֶן, וְנִסְכּוֹ: עֹלַת שַׁבַּת בְּשַׁבַּתּוֹ, עַל־עֹלַת הַתָּמִיד וְנִסְכָּהּ: במדבר כח

בראש חודש:

וּבְרָאשֵׁי חָדְשֵׁיכֶם תַּקְרִיבוּ עֹלָה לַיהוה, פָּרִים בְּנֵי־בָקָר שְׁנַיִם, וְאַיִל אֶחָד, כְּבָשִׂים בְּנֵי־שָׁנָה שִׁבְעָה, תְּמִימִם: וּשְׁלֹשָׁה עֶשְׂרֹנִים סֹלֶת מִנְחָה בְּלוּלָה בַשֶּׁמֶן לַפָּר הָאֶחָד, וּשְׁנֵי עֶשְׂרֹנִים סֹלֶת מִנְחָה בְּלוּלָה בַשֶּׁמֶן לָאַיִל הָאֶחָד: וְעִשָּׂרֹן עִשָּׂרוֹן סֹלֶת מִנְחָה בְּלוּלָה בַשֶּׁמֶן לַכֶּבֶשׂ הָאֶחָד, עֹלָה רֵיחַ נִיחֹחַ, אִשֶּׁה לַיהוה: וְנִסְכֵּיהֶם, חֲצִי הַהִין יִהְיֶה לַפָּר, וּשְׁלִישִׁת הַהִין לָאַיִל, וּרְבִיעִת הַהִין לַכֶּבֶשׂ, יָיִן, זֹאת עֹלַת חֹדֶשׁ בְּחָדְשׁוֹ לְחָדְשֵׁי הַשָּׁנָה: וּשְׂעִיר עִזִּים אֶחָד לְחַטָּאת לַיהוה, עַל־עֹלַת הַתָּמִיד יֵעָשֶׂה, וְנִסְכּוֹ: במדבר כח

*The service continues on page 89.*

---

זֹאת עֹלַת חֹדֶשׁ בְּחָדְשׁוֹ לְחָדְשֵׁי הַשָּׁנָה *This is the monthly burnt-offering for the months of the year.* The Hebrew word for "month," *ḥodesh,* is an expression of newness, *ḥadash* (new). The word for year, *shanah,* on the other hand, merely indicates "change" (*shinuy*).[50] There is lacking the element of the radically new. As each month comes, one senses a new divine light. However, one graduates from this outlook to a higher consciousness, whereby one realizes that what comes across to us as something essentially new, is in reality but a variation on a theme.[51] Enough of these new moons add up to a year, a *"shanah,"* which again, is not radically new, but merely a "change."[52]

---

50. See Rabbi Judah Canpanton (disciple of Ritba), *Arba'ah Kinyanim,* ed. Blau (Brooklyn, NY, 1997), *Ma'amar ha-Teshuvah,* chap. 4 (p. 89).
51. See Ecclesiastes 1:9–10.
52. *OR,* vol. 1, p. 165.

In our passage, Rav Kook is intrigued by the specific sacrifice brought for atonement: a male goat (*se'ir 'izim*). *Se'ir* can also mean a storm wind, a tempest.[58] Likewise, the word *'ez* is related to *'az*, strong or brazen. Put together, the sense is of a revolt. But this is to be a holy revolt, a *"mered kadosh,"* if you would have it. At times, cataclysmic events are necessary in order for existence to reach its perfection.

The sun represents static, enduring, constant, permanent perfection (*shelemut*); the moon is evocative of the dynamic, innovative, revolutionary, turbulent struggle for open-ended and forever unattainable perfection (*hishtalmut*).[59] This striving required an imperfection in an otherwise perfect creation, symbolized by the imperfection of the moon (*pegimat ha-levanah*). If all were perfect in creation, then there would be no room for improvement.[60] In order to accommodate a creative evolution, there was required a self-diminishing (which according to Lurianic Kabbalah is God's own self-minimization or *Tsimtsum*).

---

his father the Rav wrote *Resh Millin* at a command (*"tsav"*) from above. (According to RZYH, the Rav confided that the same *"tsav"* that prompted him to write *Resh Millin*, prompted him to write the *Halakhah Berurah*. This makes good sense as both works – *Halakhah Berurah* and *Resh Millin* – were conceived in London in World War One. See RZYH, *Li-Sheloshah be-Ellul*, vol. 1 [Jerusalem, 1938; photo offset Jerusalem, 1978], par. 66 [p. 29].)

Inter alia, in *Tikkunei Zohar* the original state in which sun and moon were equal in stature, is related to the original androgynous Janus-faced state of Adam and Eve (*du partsufim*). See ibid. *tikkun* 36.

58. See Deuteronomy 32:2 and Rashi *ad locum*, who explains that since the letters *sin* and *samekh* are interchangeable, *se'ir* with the letter *sin* is the same as *se'arah* with the letter *samekh*. Upon the verse "As storm-winds upon grass" (Deuteronomy 32:2), the Rabbis comment: "This is the east wind that storms the entire world like a male goat" (*Sifré, Ha'azinu*; *b. Bava Batra* 25a).

   In his tale of The Master of Prayer, Rabbi Nahman of Breslov employs the trope of the *"ru'aḥ se'arah."* For the kabbalistic significance of the trope, see Rabbi Nathan Sternhartz, *Likkutei Halakhot, Hil. Tefillah* 4:1, 3; Rabbi Abraham Hazan, *Hokhmah u-Tevunah* (Tel-Aviv: Eshel, n.d.), chap. 14, pars. 8–10, 16 (pp. 111–112, 115); Rabbi Aryeh Kaplan, *Rabbi Nachman's Stories* (n.p.: Breslov Research Institute, 1983), p. 309.

59. See Rabbi David Cohen, *Mishnat ha-Nazir*, ed. Harel Cohen and Yedidyah Cohen (Jerusalem, 2005), p. 60; Yosef Ben-Shelomo, *"Shelemut ve-Hishtalmut be-Torat ha-Elohut shel Harav Kook," Iyyun* 33 (*Tevet-Nissan* 5754/1984), pp. 289–309; idem, *"Shirat ha-Ḥayyim: Perakim be-Mishnato shel Harav Kook* (Universitah Meshuderet – Galei Tsahal, Misrad ha-Bitaḥon [Tel-Aviv, 1989]), pp. 35–40.

60. As the twelfth and thirteenth-century kabbalist Rabbi Azriel of Gerona expressed the thought: "*Ein Sof* is perfection without lack. If you say that He has limitless power but not limited power, then you take away from His perfection." See Rabbi Azriel of Gerona, *Be'ur 'Eser Sefirot*, ed. Moshe Schatz (Jerusalem, 1997), p. 30, no. 3.

afterwards, divine remorse set in, "divine guilt" as it were, prompting this request for exculpation.

Rav Kook was most emphatic that this myth not be taken at face value, because it is inconceivable that the Holy One, blessed be He, should require atonement![56]

What then do the sun and the moon symbolize? What does the diminishing of the moon allude to? What will be the final *tikkun* or rectification of this cosmic flaw? Rav Kook revisits this myth many times in his prodigious literary *oeuvre*.[57]

---

56. *IR*, vol. 2, p. 108. For various medieval interpretations of the myth of the minimization of the moon, see now 'Oded Yisraeli, "'Aren't you going to agree with your companion's opinion?': Studies in the History of the Zoharic Interpretation of the Aggadah" (Hebrew), *The Flint into a Fountain of Waters* [*Ḥallamish le-Ma'yeno Mayim*]: *Studies in Kabbalah, Jewish Law, Custom and Philosophy Submitted to Prof. Moshe Ḥallamish* (Jerusalem, 2016), pp. 305–326 (especially pp. 313–314). See too Emmanuel Elalouf, *Ha-RIF: Bein Sefarad le-Ashkenaz* (Jerusalem, 2016), pp. 347–348. Rabbi Judah Canpanton (loc. cit.) juxtaposed the moon's accusation aganst the sun to Eve's accusation against Adam!

57. See *Orot, Yisrael u-Teḥiyato* (Israel and its Renascence), chap. 10=*SK* 5:51; *"Le-Mahalakh ha-Ide'ot be-Yisrael"* ("To the Process of Ideas in Israel"), beg. chap. 3 (in 1950 ed. Orot, p. 105); *Orot ha-Teshuvah* 16:2; *Orot ha-Kodesh*, vol. 1, pp. 253–254=*SK* 1:279; vol. 2, p. 11=*SK* 1:885; p. 140=*SK* 3:24. See below the commentary to *"'Or Ḥadash"* (*OR*, vol. 1, p. 241), where the Sun symbolizes reality, and the moon reflected reality. (See too the commentary to *Kiddush Levanah*.) In the commentary to *"Emet ve-yatsiv"* (*OR*, vol. 1, pp. 253–254), the sun is equated with reason, and the moon with faith. In the commentary to *Tefillat Rosh Ḥodesh*, the sun symbolizes love of the Lord, and the moon, fear of the Lord (*OR*, vol. 1, pp. 422–423). In *OK*, vol. 1, pp. 253–254, the sun symbolizes intellect and the moon, emotion. See the marginalia of Rabbi Ḥarlap to the piece in *OK*, in *Shirat ha-Yam* (biography of Rabbi Ḥarlap), ed. Yair Ḥarlap (Beit El, 2012), p. 341. Today, one may read that piece in its original sequence in *SK* 1:279. In *SK* 7:136, the Moon in asking for two crowns as opposed to one, adopted a quantitative perspective. Qualitatively, a single crown sufficed for both Sun and Moon. In kind, God's appeasement of the Moon was quantitative: "Since He reduced the Moon, he increased her hosts [i.e. the stars]" (Rashi, Genesis 1:16; *Genesis Rabbah* 6:4). See also the early sermons from manuscript in *Me'orot ha-Rayah: Ḥannukah* (Jerusalem: Makhon RZYH, 1995), pp. 211–212, 301–302. In Boisk, Rav Kook equated the sun with universalism, and the moon with particularism and nationalism; see *Otserot ha-Rayah*, ed. Zuriel, vol. 6 (Rishon Lezion, 5776/2016), p. 98, par. 26.
Finally, in the mystical work, *Resh Millin* (London, 1917), in the meditation upon the vowel *tsereh* (represented by two horizontal points of equal size), Rav Kook throws out tantalizing hints that "the two great luminaries" symbolize the positive and the negative; the visionary and the pragmatic; thought and practice. In that regard, see *Tikkunei Zohar* with commentary of Vilna Gaon (Vilna, 1867), *Hakdamah*, 8b; and *Be'ur ha-GRA*, 147b, s.v. *kamats nekudah*. RZYH confided to the writer (BN) that

## LAWS OF OFFERINGS, MISHNA ZEVAḤIM

Zevaḥim Ch. 5

אֵיזֶהוּ מְקוֹמָן What is the location for sacrifices? The holiest offerings were slaughtered on the north side. The bull and he-goat of Yom Kippur were slaughtered on the north side. Their blood was received in a sacred vessel on the north side, and had to be sprinkled between the poles [of the Ark], toward the veil [screening the Holy of Holies], and on the golden altar. [The omission of] one of these sprinklings invalidated [the atonement ceremony]. The leftover blood was to be poured onto the western base of the outer altar. If this was not done, however, the omission did not invalidate [the ceremony].

The bulls and he-goats that were completely burnt were slaughtered on the north side, their blood was received in a sacred vessel on the north side, and had to be sprinkled toward the veil and on the golden altar. [The omission of] one of these sprinklings invalidated [the ceremony]. The leftover blood was to be poured onto the western base of the outer altar. If this was not done, however, the omission did not invalidate [the ceremony]. All these offerings were burnt where the altar ashes were deposited.

The communal and individual sin-offerings – these are the communal sin-offerings: the he-goats offered on Rosh Ḥodesh and Festivals were slaughtered on the north side, their blood was received in a sacred vessel on the north side, and required four sprinklings, one on each of the four corners of the altar. How was this done? The priest ascended the ramp and turned [right] onto the surrounding ledge. He came to the southeast corner, then went to the northeast, then to the northwest, then to the southwest. The leftover blood he poured onto the southern base. [The meat of these offerings], prepared in any manner, was eaten within the [courtyard] curtains, by males of the priest-hood, on that day and the following night, until midnight.

The burnt-offering was among the holiest of sacrifices. It was slaughtered on the north side, its blood was received in a sacred vessel on the north side, and

---

The destructive element within revolution is cause for dismay; it can be overwhelming. What is required ultimately is to view this breakdown as a painful, yet necessary phase within an ongoing creative process.[63] Thus, *kaparah* or atonement is achieved.[64]

63. See Rav Kook's essay, "The Souls of the World of Chaos" (*"Ha-Neshamot shel 'Olam ha-Tohu"*) in the expanded version of *Orot* (Jerusalem, 1950), pp. 121–123; *Li-Nevukhei ha-Dor*, ed. Rabbi Shahar Raḥmani (Tel-Aviv, 2014), chap. 29 (pp. 152, 154).

64. *OR*, vol. 1, pp. 165–166.

דיני זבחים

זבחים פרק ה

אֵיזֶהוּ מְקוֹמָן שֶׁל זְבָחִים. קָדְשֵׁי קָדָשִׁים שְׁחִיטָתָן בַּצָּפוֹן. פַּר וְשָׂעִיר שֶׁל יוֹם הַכִּפּוּרִים, שְׁחִיטָתָן בַּצָּפוֹן, וְקִבּוּל דָּמָן בִּכְלִי שָׁרֵת בַּצָּפוֹן, וְדָמָן טָעוּן הַזָּיָה עַל בֵּין הַבַּדִּים, וְעַל הַפָּרֹכֶת, וְעַל מִזְבַּח הַזָּהָב. מַתָּנָה אַחַת מֵהֶן מְעַכָּבֶת. שְׁיָרֵי הַדָּם הָיָה שׁוֹפֵךְ עַל יְסוֹד מַעֲרָבִי שֶׁל מִזְבֵּחַ הַחִיצוֹן, אִם לֹא נָתַן לֹא עִכֵּב.

פָּרִים הַנִּשְׂרָפִים וּשְׂעִירִים הַנִּשְׂרָפִים, שְׁחִיטָתָן בַּצָּפוֹן, וְקִבּוּל דָּמָן בִּכְלִי שָׁרֵת בַּצָּפוֹן, וְדָמָן טָעוּן הַזָּיָה עַל הַפָּרֹכֶת וְעַל מִזְבַּח הַזָּהָב. מַתָּנָה אַחַת מֵהֶן מְעַכָּבֶת. שְׁיָרֵי הַדָּם הָיָה שׁוֹפֵךְ עַל יְסוֹד מַעֲרָבִי שֶׁל מִזְבֵּחַ הַחִיצוֹן, אִם לֹא נָתַן לֹא עִכֵּב. אֵלּוּ וָאֵלּוּ נִשְׂרָפִין בְּבֵית הַדֶּשֶׁן.

חַטֹּאת הַצִּבּוּר וְהַיָּחִיד. אֵלּוּ הֵן חַטֹּאת הַצִּבּוּר: שְׂעִירֵי רָאשֵׁי חֳדָשִׁים וְשֶׁל מוֹעֲדוֹת. שְׁחִיטָתָן בַּצָּפוֹן, וְקִבּוּל דָּמָן בִּכְלִי שָׁרֵת בַּצָּפוֹן, וְדָמָן טָעוּן אַרְבַּע מַתָּנוֹת עַל אַרְבַּע קְרָנוֹת. כֵּיצַד, עָלָה בַכֶּבֶשׁ, וּפָנָה לַסּוֹבֵב, וּבָא לוֹ לְקֶרֶן דְּרוֹמִית מִזְרָחִית, מִזְרָחִית צְפוֹנִית, צְפוֹנִית מַעֲרָבִית, מַעֲרָבִית דְּרוֹמִית. שְׁיָרֵי הַדָּם הָיָה שׁוֹפֵךְ עַל יְסוֹד דְּרוֹמִי. וְנֶאֱכָלִין לִפְנִים מִן הַקְּלָעִים, לְזִכְרֵי כְהֻנָּה, בְּכָל מַאֲכָל, לְיוֹם וָלַיְלָה עַד חֲצוֹת.

הָעוֹלָה קֹדֶשׁ קָדָשִׁים. שְׁחִיטָתָהּ בַּצָּפוֹן, וְקִבּוּל דָּמָהּ בִּכְלִי שָׁרֵת

---

There are times in history that call for drastic measures. "A king may break down a fence to make his way."[61] "A time to do for the Lord, they voided Your Torah."[62]

---

61. *m. Sanhedrin* 2:4; *b. Sanhedrin* 20b; Maimonides, *Hil. Melakhim* 5:3. In *b. Pesaḥim* 110a, the word *"geder"* (*"porets geder"*) or "fence" is included.
In English Law, this is known as "the right of eminent domain."
62. Psalms 119:126.

required two sprinklings [at opposite corners of the altar], making four in all. The offering had to be flayed, dismembered and wholly consumed by fire.

The communal peace-offerings and the guilt-offerings – these are the guilt-offerings: the guilt-offering for robbery; the guilt-offering for profane use of a sacred object; the guilt-offering [for violating] a betrothed maidservant; the guilt-offering of a Nazirite [who had become defiled by a corpse]; the guilt-offering of a leper [at his cleansing]; and the guilt-offering in case of doubt. All these were slaughtered on the north side, their blood was received in a sacred vessel on the north side, and required two sprinklings [at opposite corners of the altar], making four in all. [The meat of these offerings], prepared in any manner, was eaten within the [courtyard] curtains, by males of the priesthood, on that day and the following night, until midnight.

The thanksgiving-offering and the ram of a Nazirite were offerings of lesser holiness. They could be slaughtered anywhere in the Temple court, and their blood required two sprinklings [at opposite corners of the altar], making four in all. The meat of these offerings, prepared in any manner, was eaten anywhere within the city [Jerusalem], by anyone during that day and the following night until midnight. This also applied to the portion of these sacrifices [given to the priests], except that the priests' portion was only to be eaten by the priests, their wives, children and servants.

Peace-offerings were [also] of lesser holiness. They could be slaughtered anywhere in the Temple court, and their blood required two sprinklings [at opposite corners of the altar], making four in all. The meat of these offerings, prepared in any manner, was eaten anywhere within the city [Jerusalem], by anyone, for two days and one night. This also applied to the portion of these sacrifices [given to the priests], except that the priests' portion was only to be eaten by the priests, their wives, children and servants.

The firstborn and tithe of cattle and the Pesaḥ lamb were sacrifices of lesser holiness. They could be slaughtered anywhere in the Temple court, and their blood required only one sprinkling, which had to be done at the base of the altar. They differed in their consumption: the firstborn was eaten only by priests, while the tithe could be eaten by anyone. Both could be eaten anywhere within the city, prepared in any manner, during two days and one night. The Pesaḥ lamb had to be eaten that night until midnight. It could only be eaten by those who had been numbered for it, and eaten only roasted.

בַּצָּפוֹן, וְדָמָהּ טָעוּן שְׁתֵּי מַתָּנוֹת שֶׁהֵן אַרְבַּע, וּטְעוּנָה הֶפְשֵׁט וְנִתּוּחַ, וְכָלִיל לָאִשִּׁים.

זִבְחֵי שַׁלְמֵי צִבּוּר וַאֲשָׁמוֹת. אֵלּוּ הֵן אֲשָׁמוֹת: אֲשַׁם גְּזֵלוֹת, אֲשַׁם מְעִילוֹת, אֲשַׁם שִׁפְחָה חֲרוּפָה, אֲשַׁם נָזִיר, אֲשַׁם מְצֹרָע, אָשָׁם תָּלוּי. שְׁחִיטָתָן בַּצָּפוֹן, וְקִבּוּל דָּמָן בִּכְלִי שָׁרֵת בַּצָּפוֹן, וְדָמָן טָעוּן שְׁתֵּי מַתָּנוֹת שֶׁהֵן אַרְבַּע. וְנֶאֱכָלִין לִפְנִים מִן הַקְּלָעִים, לְזִכְרֵי כְהֻנָּה, בְּכָל מַאֲכָל, לְיוֹם וָלַיְלָה עַד חֲצוֹת.

הַתּוֹדָה וְאֵיל נָזִיר קָדָשִׁים קַלִּים. שְׁחִיטָתָן בְּכָל מָקוֹם בָּעֲזָרָה, וְדָמָן טָעוּן שְׁתֵּי מַתָּנוֹת שֶׁהֵן אַרְבַּע, וְנֶאֱכָלִין בְּכָל הָעִיר, לְכָל אָדָם, בְּכָל מַאֲכָל, לְיוֹם וָלַיְלָה עַד חֲצוֹת. הַמּוּרָם מֵהֶם כַּיּוֹצֵא בָהֶם, אֶלָּא שֶׁהַמּוּרָם נֶאֱכָל לַכֹּהֲנִים, לִנְשֵׁיהֶם, וְלִבְנֵיהֶם וּלְעַבְדֵיהֶם.

שְׁלָמִים קָדָשִׁים קַלִּים. שְׁחִיטָתָן בְּכָל מָקוֹם בָּעֲזָרָה, וְדָמָן טָעוּן שְׁתֵּי מַתָּנוֹת שֶׁהֵן אַרְבַּע, וְנֶאֱכָלִין בְּכָל הָעִיר, לְכָל אָדָם, בְּכָל מַאֲכָל, לִשְׁנֵי יָמִים וְלַיְלָה אֶחָד. הַמּוּרָם מֵהֶם כַּיּוֹצֵא בָהֶם, אֶלָּא שֶׁהַמּוּרָם נֶאֱכָל לַכֹּהֲנִים, לִנְשֵׁיהֶם, וְלִבְנֵיהֶם וּלְעַבְדֵיהֶם.

הַבְּכוֹר וְהַמַּעֲשֵׂר וְהַפֶּסַח קָדָשִׁים קַלִּים. שְׁחִיטָתָן בְּכָל מָקוֹם בָּעֲזָרָה, וְדָמָן טָעוּן מַתָּנָה אֶחָת, וּבִלְבָד שֶׁיִּתֵּן כְּנֶגֶד הַיְסוֹד. שִׁנָּה בַאֲכִילָתָן, הַבְּכוֹר נֶאֱכָל לַכֹּהֲנִים וְהַמַּעֲשֵׂר לְכָל אָדָם, וְנֶאֱכָלִין בְּכָל הָעִיר, בְּכָל מַאֲכָל, לִשְׁנֵי יָמִים וְלַיְלָה אֶחָד. הַפֶּסַח אֵינוֹ נֶאֱכָל אֶלָּא בַלַּיְלָה, וְאֵינוֹ נֶאֱכָל אֶלָּא עַד חֲצוֹת, וְאֵינוֹ נֶאֱכָל אֶלָּא לִמְנוּיָו, וְאֵינוֹ נֶאֱכָל אֶלָּא צָלִי.

THE INTERPRETIVE PRINCIPLES OF RABBI YISHMAEL

רַבִּי יִשְׁמָעֵאל Rabbi Yishmael says:

The Torah is expounded by thirteen principles:

1. An inference from a lenient law to a strict one, and vice versa.
2. An inference drawn from identical words in two passages.
3. A general principle derived from one text or two related texts.
4. A general law followed by specific examples [where the law applies exclusively to those examples].
5. A specific example followed by a general law [where the law applies to everything implied in the general statement].
6. A general law followed by specific examples and concluding with a general law: here you may infer only cases similar to the examples.
7. When a general statement requires clarification by a specific example, or a specific example requires clarification by a general statement [then rules 4 and 5 do not apply].
8. When a particular case, already included in the general statement, is expressly mentioned to teach something new, that special provision applies to all other cases included in the general statement.
9. When a particular case, though included in the general statement, is expressly mentioned with a provision similar to the general law, such a case is singled out to lessen the severity of the law, not to increase it.
10. When a particular case, though included in the general statement, is explicitly mentioned with a provision differing from the general law, it is singled out to lessen in some respects, and in others to increase, the severity of the law.
11. When a particular case, though included in the general statement, is explicitly mentioned with a new provision, the terms of the general statement no longer apply to it, unless Scripture indicates explicitly that they do apply.

---

which Rabbi David taught perrsonally.[1] Some of that material eventually found its way into the *Nazir*'s own magnum opus *Kol ha-Nevu'ah* (*The Voice of Prophecy*). Rabbi Cohen noted that in the manuscript of the *Sifra* in the Library of the Vatican (Codex Assemani 66), probably written in the ninth or tenth century C.E. (making it one of the oldest Rabbinic manuscripts in

1. Rabbi David Cohen, *Mishnat ha-Nazir*, p. 50, par. 2; p. 55.

בריייתא דרבי ישמעאל

רַבִּי יִשְׁמָעֵאל אוֹמֵר: בִּשְׁלֹשׁ עֶשְׂרֵה מִדּוֹת הַתּוֹרָה נִדְרֶשֶׁת

א מִקַּל וָחֹמֶר

ב וּמִגְּזֵרָה שָׁוָה

ג מִבִּנְיַן אָב מִכָּתוּב אֶחָד, וּמִבִּנְיַן אָב מִשְּׁנֵי כְתוּבִים

ד מִכְּלָל וּפְרָט

ה מִפְּרָט וּכְלָל

ו כְּלָל וּפְרָט וּכְלָל, אִי אַתָּה דָן אֶלָּא כְּעֵין הַפְּרָט

ז מִכְּלָל שֶׁהוּא צָרִיךְ לִפְרָט, וּמִפְּרָט שֶׁהוּא צָרִיךְ לִכְלָל

ח כָּל דָּבָר שֶׁהָיָה בִּכְלָל, וְיָצָא מִן הַכְּלָל לְלַמֵּד
לֹא לְלַמֵּד עַל עַצְמוֹ יָצָא, אֶלָּא לְלַמֵּד עַל הַכְּלָל כֻּלּוֹ יָצָא

ט כָּל דָּבָר שֶׁהָיָה בִּכְלָל, וְיָצָא לִטְעֹן טֹעַן אֶחָד שֶׁהוּא כְעִנְיָנוֹ
יָצָא לְהָקֵל וְלֹא לְהַחֲמִיר

י כָּל דָּבָר שֶׁהָיָה בִּכְלָל, וְיָצָא לִטְעֹן טֹעַן אַחֵר שֶׁלֹּא כְעִנְיָנוֹ
יָצָא לְהָקֵל וּלְהַחֲמִיר

יא כָּל דָּבָר שֶׁהָיָה בִּכְלָל, וְיָצָא לִדּוֹן בַּדָּבָר הֶחָדָשׁ
אִי אַתָּה יָכוֹל לְהַחֲזִירוֹ לִכְלָלוֹ
עַד שֶׁיַּחֲזִירֶנּוּ הַכָּתוּב לִכְלָלוֹ בְּפֵרוּשׁ

---

רַבִּי יִשְׁמָעֵאל אוֹמֵר: בִּשְׁלֹשׁ עֶשְׂרֵה מִדּוֹת הַתּוֹרָה נִדְרֶשֶׁת, מִקַּל וָחֹמֶר *Rabbi Yishmael says: The Torah is expounded by thirteen principles: from argumentum a fiori.* This piece is the preamble to the *Sifra* or *Torat Kohanim*, the Midrash Halakhah to the Book of Leviticus, one of the oldest works of Rabbinic literature.

Rabbi David Cohen (the Nazirite) was a very organized, systematic thinker. (It was this talent which enabled him to arrange Rav Kook's *Shemonah Kevatsim* or *Eight Journals* into the magnificent edifice of *Orot ha-Kodesh, Lights of Holiness.*) At Rav Kook's behest, he drew up a curriculum for Yeshivat Merkaz Harav at the time of its founding in 1921. Included in the curriculum was a course in the Thirteen Hermeneutic Principles,

12. A matter elucidated from its context, or from the following passage.
▸ 13. Also, when two passages [seem to] contradict each other,
[they are to be elucidated by] a third passage that reconciles them.

May it be Your will, LORD our God and God of our ancestors, that the Temple be speedily rebuilt in our days, and grant us our share in Your Torah. And may we serve You there in reverence, as in the days of old and as in former years.

---

This is not merely a matter of which direction one must face during the *'Amidah* prayer. Rather, a visualization is called for. In one's mind's eye, one must imagine that one is actually facing the Temple. Rav Kook's eminent disciple, Rabbi Ya'akov Moshe Ḥarlap wrote to his son in America that through meditative prayer one actually extends the "airspace of the Land of Israel" (*"avira de-Erets Israel"*)![5] Earlier, Rabbi Nahman of Breslov taught that by clapping one's hands during prayer, one is able to purify the contaminated air outside the Land of Israel. "And then the air of the place where the Israelite prays is purified, and he draws the holy air as in the Land of Israel."[6]

Rav Kook takes pause at the unusual grammatical form *she-yibaneh* ("that it be built"). It would have been much simpler and more direct to state *she-tivneh* ("that You build").[7] What then does the reflexive form of the verb come to signify?

Not only in this connection but on several other occasions in his commentary to the *Siddur*, Rav Kook writes that the creation itself is beyond any

---

5. Rabbi Ya'akov Moshe Ḥarlap, *Mikhtevei Marom*, ed. Ze'ev Wolf Charlop (Jerusalem, 1988), Letter 1 (p. 9). Cf. *IR*, vol. 2, p. 154; and the letter of Rabbi Ḥarlap to Rabbi Zevi Yehudah Kook concerning his father's mystical work *Resh Millin* (London, 1917), published as the preface to the new edition of *Resh Millin* (Jerusalem: Yeshivat ha-Ḥayyim ve-ha-Shalom, 1972): "We cannot say other than that from the height of the Temple, the Holy of Holies, until the dwelling place of his greatness, may he live, in London, a space is cleared of the impure air of the Diaspora, and a holy pipeline of pure, holy air flows upon him constantly ..."
Cf. Rabbi Joseph Baer Soloveitchik of Brisk, *She'elot u-Teshuvot Beit Halevi*, Part Two (Warsaw, 1874), *Derush* 15 (15c).
6. Rabbi Naḥman of Breslov, *Likkutei Moharan* 1, 44.
7. Rabbi Menaḥem di Lonzano advocated saying "*she-tivneh*" ("that You build") in consideration of the Midrash that the third Temple will be constructed by God, not man. (Cited by Rabbi Ḥ.Y.D. Azulai in *Nitsutsei Orot* to *Zohar* III, 221a and in *Birkei Yosef* to *Shulḥan 'Arukh, OḤ* 123:1; see *Sha'arei Teshuvah* there.) See Rashi, *Sukkah* 41a, s.v. *i nami*; *Rosh Hashanah* 30a, s.v. *i nami de-ibnei ba-laylah*; and *Tosafot*, *Shavu'ot* 15b, s.v. *Ein binyan beit ha-mikdash ba-laylah*.
However, as clearly outlined by Maimonides (*MT, Hil. Beit ha-Beḥirah*), the future Temple will be the work of human beings laboring by physical means.

יב דָּבָר הַלָּמֵד מֵעִנְיָנוֹ, וְדָבָר הַלָּמֵד מִסּוֹפוֹ

◂ יג וְכֵן שְׁנֵי כְתוּבִים הַמַּכְחִישִׁים זֶה אֶת זֶה
עַד שֶׁיָּבוֹא הַכָּתוּב הַשְּׁלִישִׁי וְיַכְרִיעַ בֵּינֵיהֶם.

יְהִי רָצוֹן מִלְּפָנֶיךָ, יהוה אֱלֹהֵינוּ וֵאלֹהֵי אֲבוֹתֵינוּ, שֶׁיִּבָּנֶה בֵּית הַמִּקְדָּשׁ בִּמְהֵרָה בְיָמֵינוּ, וְתֵן חֶלְקֵנוּ בְּתוֹרָתֶךָ, וְשָׁם נַעֲבָדְךָ בְּיִרְאָה כִּימֵי עוֹלָם וּכְשָׁנִים קַדְמוֹנִיּוֹת.

---

existence), this first principle is not *kal va-ḥomer* but *kol va-ḥomer*. (The word *kol* has a *ḥolam* over the *vav*.)[2]

שֶׁיִּבָּנֶה בֵּית הַמִּקְדָּשׁ *That the Temple be rebuilt.* Before we enter the inner sanctum of prayer, we connect to our Holy Temple on the mountain in Jerusalem. "Let him direct his heart to the Holy of Holies."[3] Our Rabbis taught:

> If he was standing outside the Land [of Israel], he should direct his heart to the Land of Israel;
> if he was standing in the Land of Israel, he should direct his heart to Jerusalem;
> if he was standing in Jerusalem, he should direct his heart to the Holy Temple;
> if he was standing in the Holy Temple, he should direct his heart to the Holy of Holies;
> if he was standing in the Holy of Holies, he should direct his heart to the Holy Ark;
> if he was standing behind the Holy Ark, he should envision himself as if he is standing before the Holy Ark.
> Thus, we find that one standing in the East, faces West; in the West, faces East; in the South, faces North; in the North, faces South. The result being that all Israel direct their heart to one place.[4]

---

2. See Rabbi David Cohen, *Kol ha-Nevu'ah* (Jerusalem: Mossad Harav Kook, 1970), p. 92, n. 52.
3. *m. Berakhot* 4:5, 6; *b. Berakhot* 28b.
4. *t. Berakhot* 3:16; *b. Berakhot* 30a. In Talmud Yerushalmi, the point is made that not only while the Temple stands but even after its destruction, our prayers are directed there. See *y. Berakhot* 4:5; *Song of Songs Rabbah* 4 (to Song of Songs 4:4). See also *b. Berakhot* 31a: "Perhaps a man might pray to which ever direction he pleases? Scripture says: '[windows in his attic opened] opposite Jerusalem' [Daniel 6:11]."

## THE RABBIS' KADDISH

*The following prayer requires the presence of a minyan.*
*A transliteration can be found on page 1319.*

*Mourner:* יִתְגַּדַּל Magnified and sanctified may His great name be,
in the world He created by His will.
May He establish His kingdom
in your lifetime and in your days,
and in the lifetime of all the house of Israel,
swiftly and soon – and say: Amen.

---

because the imagination is satiated by the light of the intellect, but within a short time the imagination topples, because the light of the intellect departs from its midst, and the person feels a spiritual weariness. One must renew the light of knowledge from the highest, holiest source of intellect. And if no opposition arises on account of physical fatigue, afterward the lovely imagination will return to dress up the new illumination, and one will be able to start a new service in joy and gladness of heart.

Especially are we in need of a renewed intellectual enlightenment between the sections of prayer. This is the foundation of the *Kaddish* between the four famous sections of prayer: *'Asiyah, Yetsirah, Beri'ah, Atsilut.*[1] Except that during the day, between *Beri'ah* and *Atsilut* there is not required an interruption, and it is precisely the juxtaposition [of the two] that is praiseworthy.[2]

---

1. Rabbi Ḥayyim Vital, *Peri 'Ets Ḥayyim, Sha'ar ha-Kaddishim,* chap. 1. See below the commentary to the Conclusion of *Pesukei de-Zimrah.*
In the Kabbalistic scheme, the Morning Blessings (*Birkhot ha-Shaḥar*) correspond to the lowest of the four worlds, the World of Making (*'Asiyah*); the Verses of Song (*Pesukei de-Zimrah*) to the World of Formation (*Yetsirah*); *Shema'* and its blessings to the World of Creation (*Beri'ah*); and finally the *'Amidah* or *Shemoneh 'Esreh* to the highest World of Emanation (*Atsilut*).
2. See *y. Berakhot* 1:1; *b. Berakhot* 42a. See *b. Berakhot* 4b: "Who is a citizen of the World to Come? This is one who juxtaposes 'Redemption' (*Ge'ulah*) to Prayer (*Tefillah,* i.e. *Shemoneh 'Esreh*)." And *MT, Hil. Tefillah* 7:17. The juxtaposition of *Ge'ulah* to *Tefillah* is explained kabbalistically in *Sha'ar ha-Kaddishim,* ibid.
SK 1:679–680. In RZYH's transcription of this *pensée* found in the Rivkah Schatz collection (Scholem MS RS 11), there occurs at top the word *"La-Siddur"* ("To the Prayer Book"). The obvious intent was that this piece should be published in Rav Kook's commentary to the Prayer Book.

## קדיש דרבנן

*The following prayer requires the presence of a* מנין.
*A transliteration can be found on page 1319.*

אבל: יִתְגַּדַּל וְיִתְקַדַּשׁ שְׁמֵהּ רַבָּא (קהל: אָמֵן)
בְּעָלְמָא דִּי בְרָא כִרְעוּתֵהּ
וְיַמְלִיךְ מַלְכוּתֵהּ
בְּחַיֵּיכוֹן וּבְיוֹמֵיכוֹן וּבְחַיֵּי דְכָל בֵּית יִשְׂרָאֵל
בַּעֲגָלָא וּבִזְמַן קָרִיב, וְאִמְרוּ אָמֵן. (קהל: אָמֵן)

---

definable intention, "above any limitation, even a content that would delimit some purpose or intention." Which is not to say that the universe is random happenstance. Rather, the highest truth reveals "the purpose of all purposes and intention of all intentions."

Our Holy Temple precedes the creation of the world: "A throne of glory, exalted from the beginning, is the place of our Temple."[8] Thus, the Temple is rooted in that reality which surpasses intentionality. And for that reason, talk of its building is lifted out of the normal consciousness of causality; of linear cause-and-effect. Instead, the language is reflexive, as if the building is automatic, unrelated to any specific goal or objective.

At the same time that we invoke this will-beyond-wills that comes across to us in a reflexive form of verbalization, we beseech God: "And grant us our share in Your Torah." For it is only through the Torah that we shall have the ability to convey the divine light that defies all definition into the finite world which is the stuff of purpose and intention. It is the Torah that penetrates from the loftiest heights to the deepest abyss. We ask that "our portion," limited and circumscribed as it is, be joined to the higher source, the Source of all life – by virtue of the Torah.[9]

קדיש / KADDISH

In the Kabbalistic understanding of the service, this *Kaddish* separates between the World of Making (*'Olam ha-Asiyah*) and the World of Formation (*'Olam ha-Yetsirah*).

Sometimes we begin the service with joy and the light of knowledge,

---

8. Jeremiah 17:12; *b. Pesaḥim* 54a.
9. *OR*, vol. 1, pp. 184–186.

*All:* May His great name be blessed
for ever and all time.

*Mourner:* Blessed and praised,
glorified and exalted,
raised and honored,
uplifted and lauded
be the name of the Holy One,
blessed be He,
beyond any blessing,
song, praise and consolation
uttered in the world –
and say: Amen.

To Israel, to the teachers, their disciples
and their disciples' disciples,
and to all who engage in the study of Torah,
in this (*in Israel add:* holy) place or elsewhere,
may there come to them and you great peace,
grace, kindness and compassion,
long life, ample sustenance and deliverance,
from their Father in Heaven –
and say: Amen.

May there be great peace from heaven,
and (good) life for us and all Israel –
and say: Amen.

*Bow, take three steps back, as if taking leave of the Divine Presence, then bow, first left, then right, then center, while saying:*
May He who makes peace in His high places,
in His compassion make peace for us and all Israel –
and say: Amen.

*On Shabbat, Yom Tov, and Hoshana Raba, continue Shaḥarit on page 474.*

קהל ואבל: יְהֵא שְׁמֵהּ רַבָּא מְבָרַךְ לְעָלַם וּלְעָלְמֵי עָלְמַיָּא.

אבל: יִתְבָּרַךְ וְיִשְׁתַּבַּח וְיִתְפָּאַר וְיִתְרוֹמַם וְיִתְנַשֵּׂא
וְיִתְהַדָּר וְיִתְעַלֶּה וְיִתְהַלָּל
שְׁמֵהּ דְּקֻדְשָׁא בְּרִיךְ הוּא (קהל: בְּרִיךְ הוּא)
לְעֵלָּא מִן כָּל בִּרְכָתָא
/בעשרת ימי תשובה: לְעֵלָּא לְעֵלָּא מִכָּל בִּרְכָתָא/
וְשִׁירָתָא, תֻּשְׁבְּחָתָא וְנֶחֱמָתָא
דַּאֲמִירָן בְּעָלְמָא, וְאִמְרוּ אָמֵן. (קהל: אָמֵן)

עַל יִשְׂרָאֵל וְעַל רַבָּנָן, וְעַל תַּלְמִידֵיהוֹן
וְעַל כָּל תַּלְמִידֵי תַלְמִידֵיהוֹן
וְעַל כָּל מָאן דְּעָסְקִין בְּאוֹרַיְתָא
דִּי בְּאַתְרָא (בארץ ישראל: קַדִּישָׁא) הָדֵין, וְדִי בְּכָל אֲתַר וַאֲתַר
יְהֵא לְהוֹן וּלְכוֹן שְׁלָמָא רַבָּא
חִנָּא וְחִסְדָּא, וְרַחֲמֵי, וְחַיֵּי אֲרִיכֵי, וּמְזוֹנֵי רְוִיחֵי
וּפֻרְקָנָא מִן קֳדָם אֲבוּהוֹן דִּי בִשְׁמַיָּא, וְאִמְרוּ אָמֵן. (קהל: אָמֵן)

יְהֵא שְׁלָמָא רַבָּא מִן שְׁמַיָּא
וְחַיִּים (טוֹבִים) עָלֵינוּ וְעַל כָּל יִשְׂרָאֵל, וְאִמְרוּ אָמֵן. (קהל: אָמֵן)

*Bow, take three steps back, as if taking leave of the Divine Presence, then bow, first left, then right, then center, while saying:*

עֹשֶׂה שָׁלוֹם/ בעשרת ימי תשובה: הַשָּׁלוֹם/ בִּמְרוֹמָיו
הוּא יַעֲשֶׂה בְרַחֲמָיו שָׁלוֹם
עָלֵינוּ וְעַל כָּל יִשְׂרָאֵל, וְאִמְרוּ אָמֵן. (קהל: אָמֵן)

*On* שבת*,* יום טוב*, and* הושענא רבה*, continue* שחרית *on page 475.*

## A PSALM BEFORE VERSES OF PRAISE

מִזְמוֹר שִׁיר A psalm of David. A song for the dedication of the House. *Ps. 30*
I will exalt You, LORD, for You have lifted me up, and not let my enemies rejoice over me. LORD, my God, I cried to You for help and You healed me. LORD, You lifted my soul from the grave; You spared me from going down to the pit. Sing to the LORD, you His devoted ones, and give thanks to His holy name. For His anger is for a moment, but His favor for a lifetime. At night there may be weeping, but in the morning there is joy. When I felt secure, I said, "I shall never be shaken." LORD, when You favored me, You made me stand firm as a mountain, but when You hid Your face, I was terrified. To You, LORD, I called; I pleaded with my LORD: "What gain would there be if I died and went down to the grave? Can dust thank You? Can it declare Your truth? Hear, LORD, and be gracious to me; LORD, be my help." ▸ You have turned my sorrow into dancing. You have removed my sackcloth and clothed me with joy, so that my soul may sing to You and not be silent. LORD my God, for ever will I thank You.

---

כִּי רֶגַע בְּאַפּוֹ, חַיִּים בִּרְצוֹנוֹ *For His anger is for a moment, but His will for a lifetime.*

The general observation of the LORD's love which fills the world, teaches us that good and the love of life are the presiding principle in existence. If we find that evil – anger and wrath – is revealed in the world, then in contrast to the overall good, it is a temporary phenomenon, an exception to the rule. The evil comes to establish the good, to deepen it and broaden it.[3] There can be no doubt that the general objective is revealed in the foundation, in the permanent content constantly flowing in the entire world. When we examine the foundations of the world and all of existence, we recognize that life conforms to His permanent will, which is the foundation of the general governance (*hanhagah kelalit*), and the anger is but a moment – fleeting, passing, transitory – designed to make shine even brighter the foundation of life and existence in the plenitude of their goodness.[4]

3. Cf. *Sefer Yetsirah* 6:4: "The evil distinguishes (*mavḥin*) the good."
4. *OR*, vol. 1, p. 188. Cf. Maimonides, *Guide of the Perplexed* III, 10–12. See especially Maimonides' refutation of al-Razi, ibid. (Pines edition, p. 441).

# מזמור לפני פסוקי דזמרה

מִזְמוֹר שִׁיר־חֲנֻכַּת הַבַּיִת לְדָוִד: אֲרוֹמִמְךָ יהוה כִּי דִלִּיתָנִי, וְלֹא־ תהלים ל
שִׂמַּחְתָּ אֹיְבַי לִי: יהוה אֱלֹהָי, שִׁוַּעְתִּי אֵלֶיךָ וַתִּרְפָּאֵנִי: יהוה, הֶעֱלִיתָ
מִן־שְׁאוֹל נַפְשִׁי, חִיִּיתַנִי מִיָּרְדִי־בוֹר: זַמְּרוּ לַיהוה חֲסִידָיו, וְהוֹדוּ
לְזֵכֶר קָדְשׁוֹ: כִּי רֶגַע בְּאַפּוֹ, חַיִּים בִּרְצוֹנוֹ, בָּעֶרֶב יָלִין בֶּכִי וְלַבֹּקֶר
רִנָּה: וַאֲנִי אָמַרְתִּי בְשַׁלְוִי, בַּל־אֶמּוֹט לְעוֹלָם: יהוה, בִּרְצוֹנְךָ
הֶעֱמַדְתָּה לְהַרְרִי עֹז, הִסְתַּרְתָּ פָנֶיךָ הָיִיתִי נִבְהָל: אֵלֶיךָ יהוה
אֶקְרָא, וְאֶל־אֲדֹנָי אֶתְחַנָּן: מַה־בֶּצַע בְּדָמִי, בְּרִדְתִּי אֶל שָׁחַת,
הֲיוֹדְךָ עָפָר, הֲיַגִּיד אֲמִתֶּךָ: שְׁמַע־יהוה וְחָנֵּנִי, יהוה הֱיֵה־עֹזֵר לִי:
› הָפַכְתָּ מִסְפְּדִי לְמָחוֹל לִי, פִּתַּחְתָּ שַׂקִּי, וַתְּאַזְּרֵנִי שִׂמְחָה: לְמַעַן
יְזַמֶּרְךָ כָבוֹד וְלֹא יִדֹּם, יהוה אֱלֹהַי, לְעוֹלָם אוֹדֶךָּ:

---

יהוה, הֶעֱלִיתָ מִן־שְׁאוֹל נַפְשִׁי, חִיִּיתַנִי מִיָּרְדִי־בוֹר *Lord, You lifted my soul from the grave* (She'ol)*; You spared* (literally, vivified) *me from going down to the pit. She'ol,* the Biblical term for the underworld, is related to the root *she'ol,* "to ask." In this vision, not so different from the Myth of Tantalus, the suffering consists of a constant asking or wishing which is forever unrequited and unfilled. True, *She'ol* is torture, but at least one is still alive. In the very wish, there is evidenced a spark of life. One wants, and ultimately what one wants is life itself.

Worse even than the state of *She'ol* is the state of *"bor,"* the pit. *Bor* is related to *boor,* a state of being so primitive, so unevolved and undeveloped that it predates life. In the agricultural realm, *"sdeh boor"* is a field which is totally inarable, without any potential for growth. In the intellectual sphere, a *"boor"* is even less than an "*'am ha-arets*" (ignoramus, literally "people of the earth"). The *'am ha-arets* is raw, but his intellect can be cultivated; the *boor* lacks any promise whatsoever.[1]

The Lord merely lifts the soul up from *She'ol;* the rescue from descent into the boorish state requires a divine infusion of life (*ḥiyyitani*).[2]

---

1. See *m. Avot* 2:5: "A *boor* is not fearful of sin, neither is an ignoramus pious." See Maimonides, *Commentary to Mishnah, Avot* 5:6 (Kafaḥ ed., p. 298); *Tosafot, Kiddushin* 32b, s.v. *zaken ashmai.*
2. *OR,* vol. 1, p. 187.

## MOURNER'S KADDISH

*The following prayer, said by mourners, requires the presence of a minyan. A transliteration can be found on page 1320.*

*Mourner:* יִתְגַּדַּל Magnified and sanctified may His great name be,
in the world He created by His will.
May He establish His kingdom
in your lifetime and in your days,
and in the lifetime of all the house of Israel,
swiftly and soon –
and say: Amen.

*All:* May His great name be blessed
for ever and all time.

*Mourner:* Blessed and praised,
glorified and exalted,
raised and honored,
uplifted and lauded
be the name of the Holy One,
blessed be He,
beyond any blessing,
song, praise and consolation
uttered in the world –
and say: Amen.

May there be great peace from heaven,
and life for us and all Israel –
and say: Amen.

*Bow, take three steps back, as if taking leave of the Divine Presence, then bow, first left, then right, then center, while saying:*

May He who makes peace in His high places,
make peace for us and all Israel –
and say: Amen.

## קדיש יתום

*The following prayer, said by mourners, requires the presence of a* מנין.
*A transliteration can be found on page 1320.*

אבל: יִתְגַּדַּל וְיִתְקַדַּשׁ שְׁמֵהּ רַבָּא (קהל: אָמֵן)
בְּעָלְמָא דִּי בְרָא כִרְעוּתֵהּ
וְיַמְלִיךְ מַלְכוּתֵהּ
בְּחַיֵּיכוֹן וּבְיוֹמֵיכוֹן וּבְחַיֵּי דְכָל בֵּית יִשְׂרָאֵל
בַּעֲגָלָא וּבִזְמַן קָרִיב, וְאִמְרוּ אָמֵן. (קהל: אָמֵן)

קהל ואבל: יְהֵא שְׁמֵהּ רַבָּא מְבָרַךְ לְעָלַם וּלְעָלְמֵי עָלְמַיָּא.

אבל: יִתְבָּרַךְ וְיִשְׁתַּבַּח וְיִתְפָּאַר
וְיִתְרוֹמַם וְיִתְנַשֵּׂא וְיִתְהַדָּר וְיִתְעַלֶּה וְיִתְהַלָּל
שְׁמֵהּ דְּקֻדְשָׁא בְּרִיךְ הוּא (קהל: בְּרִיךְ הוּא)
לְעֵלָּא מִן כָּל בִּרְכָתָא
/בעשרת ימי תשובה: לְעֵלָּא לְעֵלָּא מִכָּל בִּרְכָתָא/
וְשִׁירָתָא, תֻּשְׁבְּחָתָא וְנֶחֱמָתָא
דַּאֲמִירָן בְּעָלְמָא, וְאִמְרוּ אָמֵן. (קהל: אָמֵן)

יְהֵא שְׁלָמָא רַבָּא מִן שְׁמַיָּא
וְחַיִּים, עָלֵינוּ וְעַל כָּל יִשְׂרָאֵל, וְאִמְרוּ אָמֵן. (קהל: אָמֵן)

*Bow, take three steps back, as if taking leave of the Divine Presence, then bow, first left, then right, then center, while saying:*

עֹשֶׂה שָׁלוֹם/בעשרת ימי תשובה: הַשָּׁלוֹם/ בִּמְרוֹמָיו
הוּא יַעֲשֶׂה שָׁלוֹם
עָלֵינוּ וְעַל כָּל יִשְׂרָאֵל, וְאִמְרוּ אָמֵן. (קהל: אָמֵן)

## PESUKEI DEZIMRA

*The introductory blessing to the Pesukei DeZimra (Verses of Praise) is said standing, while holding the two front tzitziot of the tallit. They are kissed and released at the end of the blessing at "songs of praise" (on next page). From the beginning of this prayer to the end of the Amida, conversation is forbidden. See table on pages 1315–1317 for permitted congregational responses.*

*Some say:*

I hereby prepare my mouth to thank, praise and laud my Creator, for the sake of the unification of the Holy One, blessed be He, and His Divine Presence, through that which is hidden and concealed, in the name of all Israel.

BLESSED IS HE WHO SPOKE
and the world came into being, blessed is He.
Blessed is He who creates the universe.
Blessed is He who speaks and acts.
Blessed is He who decrees and fulfills.
Blessed is He who shows compassion to the earth.
Blessed is He who shows compassion to all creatures.
Blessed is He who gives a good reward to those who fear Him.
Blessed is He who lives for ever and exists to eternity.
Blessed is He who redeems and saves.
Blessed is His name.

---

Into them penetrates the divine light which transcends every limitation. Whence comes the power to unite the transcendent aspect of divinity (*Kudsha Berikh Hu*) and the immanent aspect, His *Shekhinah* or indwelling? This is a hidden, recondite power that belongs not to the individual but to the collective of Israel. Israel, by virtue of the fact that they predate the Creation,[2] which is to say that they are anterior to the division into transcendence and immanence, have the ability to unite the two aspects into one.[3]

בָּרוּךְ מְרַחֵם עַל הָאָרֶץ, בָּרוּךְ מְרַחֵם עַל הַבְּרִיּוֹת *Blessed is He who shows compassion to the earth. Blessed is He who shows compassion to all creatures.* These are two

---

he terms *kedushah*. See *Zohar* III, 61a, 93a, 94b; and Rabbi David Cohen (the Nazirite), *OK*, vol. 1, Introduction, pp. 18–19; beginning vol. 2.

2. See above Rav Kook's comments on *Ana Be-Kho'aḥ*, s.v. *yaḥid ge'eh le-'amekha feneh zokherei kedushatekha.*

3. *OR*, vol. 1, p. 193.

# פסוקי דזמרה

*The introductory blessing to the* פסוקי דזמרה *is said standing, while holding the two front* ציציות *of the* טלית*. They are kissed and released at the end of the blessing at* בַּתִּשְׁבָּחוֹת *(on next page). From the beginning of this prayer to the end of the* עמידה*, conversation is forbidden. See table on pages 1315–1317 for permitted congregational responses.*

*Some say:*

הֲרֵינִי מְזַמֵּן אֶת פִּי לְהוֹדוֹת וּלְהַלֵּל וּלְשַׁבֵּחַ אֶת בּוֹרְאִי, לְשֵׁם יִחוּד קֻדְשָׁא בְּרִיךְ הוּא וּשְׁכִינְתֵּהּ עַל יְדֵי הַהוּא טָמִיר וְנֶעְלָם בְּשֵׁם כָּל יִשְׂרָאֵל.

## בָּרוּךְ שֶׁאָמַר

וְהָיָה הָעוֹלָם, בָּרוּךְ הוּא.

בָּרוּךְ עוֹשֶׂה בְרֵאשִׁית
בָּרוּךְ אוֹמֵר וְעוֹשֶׂה
בָּרוּךְ גּוֹזֵר וּמְקַיֵּם
בָּרוּךְ מְרַחֵם עַל הָאָרֶץ
בָּרוּךְ מְרַחֵם עַל הַבְּרִיּוֹת
בָּרוּךְ מְשַׁלֵּם שָׂכָר טוֹב לִירֵאָיו
בָּרוּךְ חַי לָעַד וְקַיָּם לָנֶצַח
בָּרוּךְ פּוֹדֶה וּמַצִּיל
בָּרוּךְ שְׁמוֹ

---

פסוקי דזמרה / VERSES OF SONG

לְשֵׁם יִחוּד קֻדְשָׁא בְּרִיךְ הוּא וּשְׁכִינְתֵּהּ עַל יְדֵי הַהוּא טָמִיר וְנֶעְלָם בְּשֵׁם כָּל יִשְׂרָאֵל *For the sake of the unification of the Holy One, blessed be He, and His Shekhinah (Divine Presence), through that which is hidden and concealed, in the name of all Israel.* Prayer reaches to the lofty level of holiness that transcends all borders and limitations. Yet that limitless holiness is united with the holiness that signifies borders, finite times and spaces, deeds and thoughts, ambitions and desires.[1]

1. For the limitless holiness, Rav Kook uses the term *kodesh,* whereas the limited holiness

Blessed are You, LORD our God, King of the Universe,
God, compassionate Father,
extolled by the mouth of His people,
praised and glorified
by the tongue of His devoted ones
and those who serve Him.
With the songs of Your servant David
we will praise You, O LORD our God.
With praises and psalms
we will magnify and praise You, glorify You,
Speak Your name and proclaim Your kingship,
our King, our God, ▸ the only One, Giver of life to the worlds,
the King whose great name
is praised and glorified to all eternity.
Blessed are You, LORD,
the King extolled with songs of praise.

הוֹדוּ Thank the LORD, call on His name, make His acts known *1 Chr. 16*
among the peoples. Sing to Him, make music to Him, tell of all His wonders. Glory in His holy name; let the hearts of those who seek the LORD rejoice. Search out the LORD and His strength; seek His presence at all times. Remember the wonders He has done, His miracles, and the judgments He pronounced. Descendants of

---

human being lives; a mathematical truth exists. To say that a human "exists" or that a mathematical equation "lives" would be absurd. A human who exists rather than lives, has been stripped of his humanity. To endow mathematics with "life," would be a joke.

Only in the deity is such a reconciliation, such a *coincidentia oppositorum* (coincidence of opposites) conceivable. God at once "lives" and "exists."[5]

Likewise, the Hebrew *'ad* conveys a monotonous perpetuity. *Netsaḥ*, on the other hand, suggests variation, changing scenery and pageantry throughout eternity. By coupling *'ad* with *ḥai* and *netsaḥ* with *kayyam*, we have a

5. Cf. above Rav Kook's commentary to *Modeh Ani*.

בָּרוּךְ אַתָּה יהוה אֱלֹהֵינוּ מֶלֶךְ הָעוֹלָם
הָאֵל הָאָב הָרַחֲמָן הַמְהֻלָּל בְּפִי עַמּוֹ
מְשֻׁבָּח וּמְפֹאָר בִּלְשׁוֹן חֲסִידָיו וַעֲבָדָיו
וּבְשִׁירֵי דָוִד עַבְדֶּךָ, נְהַלֶּלְךָ יהוה אֱלֹהֵינוּ.
בִּשְׁבָחוֹת וּבִזְמִירוֹת נְגַדֶּלְךָ וּנְשַׁבֵּחֲךָ וּנְפָאֶרְךָ
וְנַזְכִּיר שִׁמְךָ וְנַמְלִיכְךָ
מַלְכֵּנוּ אֱלֹהֵינוּ, ◂ יָחִיד חֵי הָעוֹלָמִים
מֶלֶךְ, מְשֻׁבָּח וּמְפֹאָר עֲדֵי עַד שְׁמוֹ הַגָּדוֹל
בָּרוּךְ אַתָּה יהוה, מֶלֶךְ מְהֻלָּל בַּתִּשְׁבָּחוֹת.

הוֹדוּ לַיהוה קִרְאוּ בִשְׁמוֹ, הוֹדִיעוּ בָעַמִּים עֲלִילֹתָיו: שִׁירוּ לוֹ, דברי הימים א, טז
זַמְּרוּ־לוֹ, שִׂיחוּ בְּכָל־נִפְלְאוֹתָיו: הִתְהַלְלוּ בְּשֵׁם קָדְשׁוֹ, יִשְׂמַח
לֵב מְבַקְשֵׁי יהוה: דִּרְשׁוּ יהוה וְעֻזּוֹ, בַּקְּשׁוּ פָנָיו תָּמִיד: זִכְרוּ
נִפְלְאֹתָיו אֲשֶׁר עָשָׂה, מֹפְתָיו וּמִשְׁפְּטֵי־פִיהוּ: זֶרַע יִשְׂרָאֵל עַבְדּוֹ,

distinct entities: the earth and the creations. And each is deserving of compassion. This observation of Rav Kook sounds prescient of much ecological thinking which in its most extreme form has been propounded as the "Gaia" theory. At any rate, not always do the larger global concerns and the narrow interests of mankind coincide; at times they conflict. We acknowledge divine compassion upon both: the earth and humanity.[4]

בָּרוּךְ חַי לָעַד וְקַיָּם לָנֶצַח *Blessed is He who lives for ever and exists to eternity (pevious page).* There are two oppositions here: lives (*ḥai*)/exists (*kayyam*); ever (*'ad*)/eternity (*netsaḥ*). While in English translation the opposition is dulled to the point that the terms might appear as synonyms rather than antonyms, in the Hebrew original the distinction is felt with full force.

In our human realm of experience, "life" and "existence" are totally incompatible. That which lives, does not exist; that which exists, does not live. A

4. *OR*, vol. 1, p. 195.

Yisrael His servant, sons of Jacob His chosen ones: He is the LORD our God. His judgments are throughout the earth. Remember His covenant for ever, the word He commanded for a thousand generations. He made it with Abraham, vowed it to Isaac, and confirmed it to Jacob as a statute and to Israel as an everlasting covenant, saying, "To you I will give the land of Canaan as your allotted heritage." You were then small in number, few, strangers there, wandering from nation to nation, from one kingdom to another, but He let no man oppress them, and for their sake He rebuked kings: "Do not touch My anointed ones, and do My prophets no harm." Sing to the LORD, all the earth; proclaim His salvation daily. Declare His glory among the nations, His marvels among all the peoples. For great is the LORD and greatly to be praised; He is awesome beyond all heavenly powers. ▸ For all the gods of the peoples are mere idols; it was the LORD who made the heavens.

---

Our ancestors wandered through both nations and regimes. They brought with them the "nuclei of holiness" (*gar'inei kodesh*), which inevitably had impact on both the host nation and its form of government. At the same time, they extracted from those nations nuggets of holiness—"the good and the beautiful rooted in holiness"—and took away from those regimes valuable lessons in statecraft. So it was a two-way relation.[8]

לֹא־הִנִּיחַ לְאִישׁ לְעָשְׁקָם, וַיּוֹכַח עֲלֵיהֶם מְלָכִים: אַל־תִּגְּעוּ בִּמְשִׁיחָי, וּבִנְבִיאַי אַל־תָּרֵעוּ: *He let no man oppress them, and for their sake He rebuked kings: "Do not touch my anointed ones, and do My prophets no harm!"* Narrowly, the reference is to the patriarchs who founded our nation. Both Pharaoh and Abimelech were chastised when they thought to bed Abraham's wife Sarah.[9] Likewise, Laban was castigated by God when he pursued Jacob.[10]

The divine admonishment was twofold, reflecting the double role our ancestors played in history. They were both "anointed ones," "messiahs" (*meshiḥim*)

---

8. *OR*, vol. 1, p. 204.
9. Genesis 12:17; 20:3. After the divine visitation, Abimelech in fact refers to Abraham as a *"navi"* or prophet (Genesis 20:7).
10. Genesis 31:24.

בְּנֵי יַעֲקֹב בְּחִירָיו: הוּא יהוה אֱלֹהֵינוּ בְּכָל־הָאָרֶץ מִשְׁפָּטָיו:
זִכְרוּ לְעוֹלָם בְּרִיתוֹ, דָּבָר צִוָּה לְאֶלֶף דּוֹר: אֲשֶׁר כָּרַת אֶת־
אַבְרָהָם, וּשְׁבוּעָתוֹ לְיִצְחָק: וַיַּעֲמִידֶהָ לְיַעֲקֹב לְחֹק, לְיִשְׂרָאֵל
בְּרִית עוֹלָם: לֵאמֹר, לְךָ אֶתֵּן אֶרֶץ־כְּנָעַן, חֶבֶל נַחֲלַתְכֶם:
בִּהְיוֹתְכֶם מְתֵי מִסְפָּר, כִּמְעַט וְגָרִים בָּהּ: וַיִּתְהַלְּכוּ מִגּוֹי אֶל־
גּוֹי, וּמִמַּמְלָכָה אֶל־עַם אַחֵר: לֹא־הִנִּיחַ לְאִישׁ לְעָשְׁקָם, וַיּוֹכַח
עֲלֵיהֶם מְלָכִים: אַל־תִּגְּעוּ בִּמְשִׁיחָי, וּבִנְבִיאַי אַל־תָּרֵעוּ: שִׁירוּ
לַיהוה כָּל־הָאָרֶץ, בַּשְּׂרוּ מִיּוֹם־אֶל־יוֹם יְשׁוּעָתוֹ: סַפְּרוּ בַגּוֹיִם
אֶת־כְּבוֹדוֹ, בְּכָל־הָעַמִּים נִפְלְאֹתָיו: כִּי גָדוֹל יהוה וּמְהֻלָּל מְאֹד,
וְנוֹרָא הוּא עַל־כָּל־אֱלֹהִים: ▸ כִּי כָּל־אֱלֹהֵי הָעַמִּים אֱלִילִים,
וַיהוה שָׁמַיִם עָשָׂה:

---

heightened sense of how the deity defies our mortal definitions and categories. God lives, but His "life" is constant and unswerving. He exists, but his "existence" is not drab, rather colorful in the extreme.[6]

בִּהְיוֹתְכֶם מְתֵי מִסְפָּר, כִּמְעַט וְגָרִים בָּהּ *You were then small in number, few, strangers there [i.e. in the Land of Canaan].* Normally, it takes a protracted amount of time for a people to develop an attachment to a land. It is a gradual historic process over several generations. In your case – because of the divine covenant – you bonded to the land almost immediately, though numerically you were insignificant and your status was but that of aliens.[7]

וַיִּתְהַלְּכוּ מִגּוֹי אֶל־גּוֹי, וּמִמַּמְלָכָה אֶל־עַם אַחֵר *Wandering from nation to nation, from one kingdom to another.* There is a difference between a *goy* (nation) and a *mamlakhah* (kingdom). Each *nation* has a distinct spiritual content which is the culmination of both its nature and its nurturing; its genetic makeup and its environment. A kingdom, on the other hand, is an artificial, man-made convention, a social contract.

---

6. *OR*, vol. 1, pp. 195–196.
7. *OR*, vol. 1, pp. 203–204.

Before Him are majesty and splendor; there is strength and beauty in His holy place. Render to the LORD, families of the peoples, render to the LORD honor and might. Render to the LORD the glory due to His name; bring an offering and come before Him; bow down to the LORD in the splendor of holiness. Tremble before Him, all the earth; the world stands firm, it will not be shaken. Let the heavens rejoice and the earth be glad; let them declare among the nations, "The LORD is King." Let the sea roar, and all that is in it; let the fields be jubilant, and all they contain. Then the trees of the forest will sing for joy before the LORD, for He is coming to judge the earth. Thank the LORD for He is good; His loving-kindness is for ever. Say: "Save us, God of our salvation; gather us and rescue us from the nations, to acknowledge Your holy name and glory in Your praise. Blessed is the LORD, God of Israel, from this world to eternity." And let all the people say "Amen" and "Praise the LORD."

▸ Exalt the LORD our God and bow before His footstool: He is *Ps. 99*
holy. Exalt the LORD our God and bow at His holy mountain; for holy is the LORD our God.

He is compassionate. He forgives iniquity and does not destroy. *Ps. 78*
Repeatedly He suppresses His anger, not rousing His full wrath.
You, LORD: do not withhold Your compassion from me. May Your *Ps. 40*
loving-kindness and truth always guard me. Remember, LORD, *Ps. 25*

---

אָז יְרַנְּנוּ עֲצֵי הַיָּעַר *Then the trees of the forest will sing for joy.* When the world is chaotic and unjust, the forest witnesses this injustice. The "law of the jungle" is the rule. The strong tears apart the weak. The trees which protect the wildlife in their midst, bemoan their fate that they must harbor "criminals," an entire world of wickedness and savagery. When human society becomes just, then that justice will spread to all of existence. *Then the trees of the forest will sing for joy before the LORD, for He is coming to judge the earth.*[12]

12. *OR*, vol. 1, p. 210.

הוֹד וְהָדָר לְפָנָיו, עֹז וְחֶדְוָה בִּמְקֹמוֹ: הָבוּ לַיהוה מִשְׁפְּחוֹת
עַמִּים, הָבוּ לַיהוה כָּבוֹד וָעֹז: הָבוּ לַיהוה כְּבוֹד שְׁמוֹ, שְׂאוּ
מִנְחָה וּבֹאוּ לְפָנָיו, הִשְׁתַּחֲווּ לַיהוה בְּהַדְרַת־קֹדֶשׁ: חִילוּ מִלְּפָנָיו
כָּל־הָאָרֶץ, אַף־תִּכּוֹן תֵּבֵל בַּל־תִּמּוֹט: יִשְׂמְחוּ הַשָּׁמַיִם וְתָגֵל
הָאָרֶץ, וְיֹאמְרוּ בַגּוֹיִם יהוה מָלָךְ: יִרְעַם הַיָּם וּמְלוֹאוֹ, יַעֲלֹץ
הַשָּׂדֶה וְכָל־אֲשֶׁר־בּוֹ: אָז יְרַנְּנוּ עֲצֵי הַיָּעַר, מִלִּפְנֵי יהוה, כִּי־בָא
לִשְׁפּוֹט אֶת־הָאָרֶץ: הוֹדוּ לַיהוה כִּי טוֹב, כִּי לְעוֹלָם חַסְדּוֹ:
וְאִמְרוּ, הוֹשִׁיעֵנוּ אֱלֹהֵי יִשְׁעֵנוּ, וְקַבְּצֵנוּ וְהַצִּילֵנוּ מִן־הַגּוֹיִם,
לְהֹדוֹת לְשֵׁם קָדְשֶׁךָ, לְהִשְׁתַּבֵּחַ בִּתְהִלָּתֶךָ: בָּרוּךְ יהוה אֱלֹהֵי
יִשְׂרָאֵל מִן־הָעוֹלָם וְעַד־הָעֹלָם, וַיֹּאמְרוּ כָל־הָעָם אָמֵן, וְהַלֵּל
לַיהוה:

‣ רוֹמְמוּ יהוה אֱלֹהֵינוּ וְהִשְׁתַּחֲווּ לַהֲדֹם רַגְלָיו, קָדוֹשׁ הוּא: תהלים צט
רוֹמְמוּ יהוה אֱלֹהֵינוּ וְהִשְׁתַּחֲווּ לְהַר קָדְשׁוֹ, כִּי־קָדוֹשׁ יהוה
אֱלֹהֵינוּ:

וְהוּא רַחוּם, יְכַפֵּר עָוֹן וְלֹא־יַשְׁחִית, וְהִרְבָּה לְהָשִׁיב אַפּוֹ, תהלים עח
וְלֹא־יָעִיר כָּל־חֲמָתוֹ: אַתָּה יהוה לֹא־תִכְלָא רַחֲמֶיךָ מִמֶּנִּי, חַסְדְּךָ תהלים מ

---

and "prophets" (*nevi'im*). "Messiahs," inasmuch as they were the standard-bearers of a Messianic ideal that involves the eventual redemption of all mankind; and "prophets" who provided mankind with the toolkit, the practical knowhow to bring about the longed-for redemption. "Messiahs" are utopian visionaries; "prophets" are social critics.[11]

---

11. *OR*, vol. 1, pp. 204–205. In his essay "A Sage is Superior to a Prophet" ("*Ḥakham 'adif mi-navi*") Rav Kook writes that prophets give only general guidelines how to improve society, whereas the sage, the halakhist, deals with the specific details, the "nuts and bolts" necessary to bring about that amelioration. Published in the enlarged edition of *Orot* (1950), pp. 120–121.

Your acts of compassion and love, for they have existed for ever.
Ascribe power to God, whose majesty is over Israel and whose Ps. 68
might is in the skies. You are awesome, God, in Your holy places.
It is the God of Israel who gives might and strength to the people,
may God be blessed. God of retribution, LORD, God of retribu- Ps. 94
tion, appear. Arise, Judge of the earth, to repay the arrogant their
just deserts. Salvation belongs to the LORD; may Your blessing rest Ps. 3
upon Your people, Selah! ▸ The LORD of hosts is with us, the God Ps. 46
of Jacob is our stronghold, Selah! LORD of hosts, happy is the one Ps. 84
who trusts in You. LORD, save! May the King answer us on the day Ps. 20
we call.

Save Your people and bless Your heritage; tend them and carry Ps. 28
them for ever. Our soul longs for the LORD; He is our Help and Ps. 33

---

*the day we call.* There are two levels of awareness. The higher level is *devekut*, communing with the Creator. On this level, there is no need for calling, for prayer. One is totally attuned to the LORD. "All my bones shall say: 'LORD, who is like You?'"[15] But not always is man capable of being so in touch with the divine; not at all times is his awareness heightened to the degree that there is no lack, and thus no need for asking and for being answered. One's realization is no longer that of the essential name (*shem ha-meforash ha-'atsmi*), but of the King. In such reduced circumstances, the soul petitions the King, and the King does respond. Here, on this lowly level subject to descent and ascent, is the place of prayer.[16]

הוֹשִׁיעָה אֶת־עַמֶּךָ, וּבָרֵךְ אֶת־נַחֲלָתֶךָ, וּרְעֵם וְנַשְּׂאֵם עַד־הָעוֹלָם *Save Your people and bless Your heritage; tend them and carry them for ever.* Salvation comes to extricate man from some trouble. Blessing, on the other hand, is an additional uplift. Corresponding to "salvation" and "blessing," come the verbs "shepherd" and "uplift." Israel are in need of both the shepherding that accompanies salvation, and the uplift that accrues from blessing.[17]

---

15. Psalms 35:10.
16. *OR*, vol. 1, p. 216. Cf. Rav Kook's remarks on this same verse above p. 53, at the conclusion of the Incense (*Ha-Ketoret*), s.v. *ha-Melekh* (the King).
17. *OR*, vol. 1, pp. 216–217.

וְאֲמִתְּךָ תָּמִיד יִצְּרוּנִי: זְכֹר־רַחֲמֶיךָ יהוה וַחֲסָדֶיךָ, כִּי מֵעוֹלָם תהלים כה
הֵמָּה: תְּנוּ עֹז לֵאלֹהִים, עַל־יִשְׂרָאֵל גַּאֲוָתוֹ, וְעֻזּוֹ בַּשְּׁחָקִים: תהלים סח
נוֹרָא אֱלֹהִים מִמִּקְדָּשֶׁיךָ, אֵל יִשְׂרָאֵל הוּא נֹתֵן עֹז וְתַעֲצֻמוֹת
לָעָם, בָּרוּךְ אֱלֹהִים: אֵל־נְקָמוֹת יהוה, אֵל נְקָמוֹת הוֹפִיעַ: תהלים צד
הִנָּשֵׂא שֹׁפֵט הָאָרֶץ, הָשֵׁב גְּמוּל עַל־גֵּאִים: לַיהוה הַיְשׁוּעָה, תהלים ג
עַל־עַמְּךָ בִרְכָתֶךָ סֶּלָה: ‹ יהוה צְבָאוֹת עִמָּנוּ, מִשְׂגָּב לָנוּ אֱלֹהֵי תהלים מו
יַעֲקֹב סֶלָה: יהוה צְבָאוֹת, אַשְׁרֵי אָדָם בֹּטֵחַ בָּךְ: יהוה הוֹשִׁיעָה, תהלים פד תהלים כ
הַמֶּלֶךְ יַעֲנֵנוּ בְיוֹם־קָרְאֵנוּ:

הוֹשִׁיעָה אֶת־עַמֶּךָ, וּבָרֵךְ אֶת־נַחֲלָתֶךָ, וּרְעֵם וְנַשְּׂאֵם תהלים כח
עַד־הָעוֹלָם: נַפְשֵׁנוּ חִכְּתָה לַיהוה, עֶזְרֵנוּ וּמָגִנֵּנוּ הוּא: כִּי־ תהלים לג

---

יהוה צְבָאוֹת, אַשְׁרֵי אָדָם בֹּטֵחַ בָּךְ *Lord of hosts, happy is the one who trusts in You.* In contrast to the dim awareness that comes from the secular outlook on the totality of existence, that produces in the individual a profound despair, given the thought that he is but a speck of dust drowning in a vast ocean of the universe – the holy awareness looks out at the overall vastness from the perspective of *Elohei Yisrael*, the God of Israel, Lord of hosts. From this very creation – with its infinite breadth and depth and might – may be viewed the quality that affirms the existence of every individual.[13]

The good fortune of existence in its totality is individuated, so that each unique personality shares in the fortune associated with the name *Hashem Tseva'ot* (Lord of hosts), signifying the hosts upon hosts of the universe, but also referencing Israel, who are the *Tsiv'ot Hashem*, the army of the Lord in His world.[14]

יהוה הוֹשִׁיעָה, הַמֶּלֶךְ יַעֲנֵנוּ בְיוֹם־קָרְאֵנוּ *Lord, save! May the King answer us on*

---

13. Rav Kook plays on the word *"ashrei,"* which besides meaning "happy" and "fortunate," also conveys the sense of "affirmed." In Modern Hebrew, an *"ishur"* is an affirmation or confirmation (usually in writing).
14. *OR*, vol. 1, p. 216.

Shield. For in Him our hearts rejoice, for in His holy name we have
trusted. May Your loving-kindness, LORD, be upon us, as we have
put our hope in You. Show us, LORD, Your loving-kindness and *Ps. 85*
grant us Your salvation. Arise, help us and redeem us for the sake *Ps. 44*
of Your love. I am the LORD your God who brought you up from *Ps. 81*
the land of Egypt: open your mouth wide and I will fill it. Happy *Ps. 144*
is the people for whom this is so; happy is the people whose God
is the LORD. ▸ As for me, I trust in Your loving-kindness; my heart *Ps. 13*
rejoices in Your salvation. I will sing to the LORD for He has been
good to me.

---

ongoing event.[20] It continues for all the souls who belong to it. The ascent is unbounded; the ambition is limitless. The only thing that can prevent this ascent, is the soul imposing limitations on its quest. But once you know this secret that you are ready for unceasing ascent, widen your requests, rise up beyond every limitation, transcend every smallness! *Open your mouth wide and I will fill it.*[21]

The great Yiddish storyteller Isaac Leib Peretz (1852–1915) wrote a famous tale entitled *"Bontche Schweig"* ("Bontche the Silent") about a man who led a miserable life, suffering indescribable abuse all along the way, yet never once complained, bearing the brunt of his pain in silence. After his passing, his soul was summoned to the Celestial Court. In this world, Bontche had been but an insignificant speck of dust. However in the other world, he was regarded with awe. Never had there been such a righteous man. When he appeared before the Celestial Court, he was told that he could have whatever he asked for. "Just state your wish and it will be granted." The ministering angels eagerly awaited the righteous man's reply. Bontche looked around sheepishly and in a meek voice asked: "Could I please have a hot roll with butter?"

Most of us resemble Bontche in this respect. We think small and therefore our requests are small. Rav Kook calls upon us to think big and widen our wishes.[22]

---

20. Cf. *Orot, Orot me-Ofel* (Lights from Darkness), chap. 28; Rabbi Shneur Zalman of Liadi, *Tanya* 1, 31, 47.
21. *OR*, vol. 1, pp. 219–220.
22. Cf. *EA*, vol. 1, p. 44, par. 114 (*Berakhot* 9).

בוֹ יִשְׂמַח לִבֵּנוּ, כִּי בְשֵׁם קָדְשׁוֹ בָטָחְנוּ: יְהִי־חַסְדְּךָ יהוה עָלֵינוּ,
כַּאֲשֶׁר יִחַלְנוּ לָךְ: הַרְאֵנוּ יהוה חַסְדֶּךָ, וְיֶשְׁעֲךָ תִּתֶּן־לָנוּ: קוּמָה תהלים פה תהלים מד
עֶזְרָתָה לָּנוּ, וּפְדֵנוּ לְמַעַן חַסְדֶּךָ: אָנֹכִי יהוה אֱלֹהֶיךָ הַמַּעַלְךָ תהלים פא
מֵאֶרֶץ מִצְרָיִם, הַרְחֶב־פִּיךָ וַאֲמַלְאֵהוּ: אַשְׁרֵי הָעָם שֶׁכָּכָה לּוֹ, תהלים קמד
אַשְׁרֵי הָעָם שֶׁיהוה אֱלֹהָיו: ‹ וַאֲנִי בְּחַסְדְּךָ בָטַחְתִּי, יָגֵל לִבִּי תהלים יג
בִּישׁוּעָתֶךָ, אָשִׁירָה לַיהוה, כִּי גָמַל עָלָי:

---

כִּי־בוֹ יִשְׂמַח לִבֵּנוּ, כִּי בְשֵׁם קָדְשׁוֹ בָטָחְנוּ *For in Him our hearts rejoice, for in His holy name we have trusted.* There is a difference between "Him" and "His holy name." When we are in touch with "Him," and we are able to transcend all limitations, all worries brought on by calamities that may be crushing – then our soul experiences limitless joy. But there are other times that we are not able to rise to that pure conception of the divinity. Our relation is not to "Him," but only to "His holy name." At such times, "joy" (*simḥah*) is not the word to describe our experience, but rather "trust" (*bitaḥon*). Even in this diminished state, there remain with us impressions (*reshamim*) of the lofty holiness that is essential to our souls, and they will tide us over through the time of travail.[18]

הַרְאֵנוּ יהוה חַסְדֶּךָ, וְיֶשְׁעֲךָ תִּתֶּן־לָנוּ *Show us, Lord, Your loving-kindness, and grant us Your salvation.* There are two oppositions here: loving-kindness/salvation; show/grant or give.

The divine love (*ḥesed Hashem*) is infinite, thereby transcending the grasp of mortal man. We can have only a glimpse of the love of the Lord. The salvation of the Lord (*yeshu'at Hashem*), on the other hand, is something that comes into our orbit; as it is modulated to our human understanding, we may, so to speak, "possess" it. Your love can only be shown to us, but Your salvation can actually be given over to us.[19]

אָנֹכִי יהוה אֱלֹהֶיךָ הַמַּעַלְךָ מֵאֶרֶץ מִצְרָיִם, הַרְחֶב־פִּיךָ וַאֲמַלְאֵהוּ *I am the Lord your God who raises you up from the Land of Egypt: Open your mouth wide and I will fill it.* The divine raising up from Egypt is unlimited in time; it is an

---

18. *OR*, vol. 1, p. 218.
19. *OR*, vol. 1, p. 219.

*The following psalm recalls the thanksgiving-offering in Temple times. It is not said on Erev Pesaḥ, on Ḥol HaMo'ed Pesaḥ, or Erev Yom Kippur since no thanksgiving-offerings were brought on these days. To emphasize its sacrificial nature, the custom is to say it standing.*

מִזְמוֹר A psalm of thanksgiving. Shout joyously to the LORD, all *Ps. 100*
the earth. Serve the LORD with joy. Come before Him with jubilation. Know that the LORD is God. He made us and we are His.

---

refers to the recitation of *Mizmor le-Todah* at the time of the future expansion of the city of Jerusalem.[25] The Halakhah mandates that in the event the limits of the city of Jerusalem or of the Temple precints are expanded, thanksgiving sacrifices must be offered up and the psalm *Mizmor le-Todah* recited as well.[26] According to the Talmud: "In the future the Holy One, blessed be He, will add to Jerusalem."[27]

> Behold, days are coming, says the LORD, that the city shall be built to the LORD from the Tower of Ḥananel unto the Gate of the Corner. And the measuring line shall yet go out straight forward unto the hill Gareb, and shall turn about unto Goah. And the whole valley of the dead bodies, and of the ashes, and all the fields unto the brook Kidron, unto the corner of the Horse Gate toward the east, shall be holy unto the LORD.[28] (Editor)

---

*Adam*. (The quote from Rashi in *Ḥayyei Adam* is actually a conflation of Rashi and Targum to Psalms 100:1.) Also Rabbi Abraham Azulai, *'Or ha-Ḥammah* to *Zohar* III, 8a, s.v. *be-kohanei ve-leiva'ei.*

25. Rabbi Moshe Greenwald, *Minḥat ha-Tamid*, notes to Rabbi Moshe ben Amram Greenwald, *'Olat ha-Tamid* (Brooklyn, 1979), end Tractate *Tamid* (pp. 100–101); Rabbi Judah Aryeh Alter, *Emet li-Yehudah* (n.p., 1989), *Shavu'ot* 15b; idem, *Ari be-Mistarim 'al ha-Torah* (n.p., 1996), *Likkutim*, s.v. *kol ha-shirot beteilot* (p. 226).
26. Rashi, *Shavu'ot* 15b. Maimonides however, omits mention of *Mizmor le-Todah*. See *MT, Hil. Beit ha-Beḥirah* 6:12 and *Mishneh le-Melekh* there; and the gloss of Rabbi Samuel Strashun to *Shavu'ot* 15b.
    Rabbi David Rapaport wrote that the song recited on this special occasion of the expansion of the city and the Temple precints, does not belong to the category proper of the song of a sacrifice (*shir shel korban*), but rather comes under the rubric of a general song of happiness (*shir shel simḥa*), such as sung at the bringing of the first fruits (*bikkurim*) and the Festivity of Drawing the Water (*simḥat beit ha-sho'evah*). See *Mikdash David: Kodashim* (Piotrków, 1928), chap. 10 ("*Nesakhim*"), p. 66.
27. *b. Bava Batra* 75b.
28. Jeremiah 31:37–39. See Rashi, Rabbi David Kimḥi and *Metsudat David* there. See further *Sifré, Devarim*; *Yalkut Shim'oni, Devarim, remez* 792; Zechariah, *remez* 575; Rashi, Zechariah 9:1; Rashi, Song of Songs 7:5.

*The following psalm recalls the* קרבן תודה *in Temple times. It is not said on* ערב פסח, חול המועד פסח *or* ערב יום כיפור, *since no* קורבנות תודה *were brought on these days. To emphasize its sacrificial nature, the custom is to say it standing.*

מִזְמוֹר לְתוֹדָה, הָרִיעוּ לַיהוה כָּל־הָאָרֶץ: עִבְדוּ אֶת־יהוה בְּשִׂמְחָה, בֹּאוּ לְפָנָיו בִּרְנָנָה: דְּעוּ כִּי־יהוה הוּא אֱלֹהִים, תהלים ק

---

מִזְמוֹר לְתוֹדָה *A Psalm of Thanksgiving* (*Psalm 100*). In *Shulhan 'Arukh, OḤ* 51:9, the author states that *Mizmor le-Todah* should be sung, "for in the future, all the songs shall cease to exist, except for *Mizmor le-Todah*."[23] Many great authorities have agonized over this statement.[24] A plausible explanation is that it

---

23. The source for that statement is Rabbi Aaron Hakohen of Lunel, *Orḥot Ḥayyim* (Firenze, 1750), *Hil. Me'ah Berakhot*, par. 26 (6a), citing Rabbi Nathan. (Quoted by Rabbi Joseph Karo, *Beit Yosef* to *Tur, OḤ*, chap. 51.) See also the anonymous *Kol Bo*, chap. 4.

It is generally assumed that this is a variation of the *Midrash Leviticus Rabbah* (9:7): "In the future all the sacrifices shall cease to exist and the thanksgiving sacrifice shall not cease to exist. All the prayers shall cease to exist; the thanksgiving (*hoda'ah*) shall not cease to exist." *Midrash Tanḥuma, Emor*, 14 reads: "In the future all the sacrifices shall cease to exist and the thanksgiving sacrifice shall never cease to exist. All the thanksgivings (*hodayot*) shall cease to exist and the thanksgiving of the thanksgiving sacrifice (*hodayat todah*) shall never cease to exist." See *EA*, vol. 1, pp. 33–34, par. 78 (*Berakhot* 7b); *Orot, Orot ha-Teḥiyah*, chap. 49 = *SK* 2:344; *SK* 3:176; *Li-Nevukhei ha-Dor*, ed. Rabbi Shaḥar Raḥmani (Tel-Aviv, 2014), chap. 10 (p. 72); Rabbi Ya'akov Moshe Ḥarlap, *Mei Marom*, vol. 8 [Bereshit] (Jerusalem, 1994), *ma'amar* 88:3; *Mikets*, p. 290.

24. See the explanation of Rabbi Moshe Schreiber (*Ḥatam Sofer*) published at the conclusion of Rabbenu Menaḥem ha-Me'iri, *Beit ha-Beḥirah*, Tractate *Tamid*, ed. Abraham Schreiber (Vienna, 1934). In his notes, the editor, a grandson of *Ḥatam Sofer*, objected to his explanation because Maimonides (*Hil. Klei ha-Mikdash* 3:2; *Hil. Temidin u-Mussafin* 6:8) is of the opinion that no song was recited on the individual's offering. (See also *Tosafot, 'Arakhin* 11b, s.v. *'olat*, and Ri quoted in *Shitah Mekubetset*, s.v. *o einah te'unah shir*.) However, the *Sefer ha-Manhig* by Rabbi Abraham ben Nathan HaYarḥi (of Lunel) is explicit: "In France they are accustomed to skip *Mizmor le-Todah* on Sabbaths and Festivals. And so by law, for at the time of the Temple they would recite it upon the thanksgiving offering brought by the 'four [categories] who must offer thanks,' and it was not sacrificed on the Sabbath or on a festival, for vows and voluntary sacrifices are not sacrificed on those days" (*Sefer ha-Manhig*, Warsaw 1885, *Dinei Tefillah*, par. 21 [9a]). (Even more explicit is Rabbi Mordechai Jaffe, *Levush ha-Ḥur, OḤ*, chap. 604.) See also Rabbenu Gershom, *'Arakhin* 11b. Rabbi Meir Simḥa Hakohen of Dvinsk opined that for Maimonides, rather than constituting *"shir"* (song) per se, *Mizmor le-Todah* would come under the rubric of *"divrei shevaḥ"* (words of praise). See *'Or Sameah, Hil. Ma'aseh ha-Korbanot* 3:15; Rabbi Abraham Danzig, conclusion to *Ḥayyei*

We are His people and the flock He tends. Enter His gates with thanksgiving, His courts with praise. Thank Him and bless His name. ▸ For the LORD is good, His loving-kindness is everlasting, and His faithfulness is for every generation.

יְהִי כְבוֹד May the LORD's glory be for ever; may the LORD rejoice *Ps. 104*
in His works. May the LORD's name be blessed, now and for ever. *Ps. 113*
From the rising of the sun to its setting, may the LORD's name be
praised. The LORD is high above all nations; His glory is above the
heavens. LORD, Your name is for ever. Your renown, LORD, is for all *Ps. 135*
generations. The LORD has established His throne in heaven; His *Ps. 103*
kingdom rules all. Let the heavens rejoice and the earth be glad. Let *I Chr. 16*
them say among the nations, "The LORD is King." The LORD is King,
the LORD was King, the LORD will be King for ever and all time. The *Ps. 10*
LORD is King for ever and all time; nations will perish from His land.
The LORD foils the plans of nations; He frustrates the intentions of *Ps. 33*
peoples. Many are the intentions in a person's mind, but the LORD's *Prov. 19*
plan prevails. The LORD's plan shall stand for ever, His mind's intent *Ps. 33*
for all generations. For He spoke and it was; He commanded and
it stood firm. For the LORD has chosen Zion; He desired it for His *Ps. 132*
dwelling. For the LORD has chosen Jacob as His own, Israel as His *Ps. 135*
special treasure. For the LORD will not abandon His people; nor *Ps. 94*
will He forsake His heritage. ▸ He is compassionate. He forgives *Ps. 78*
iniquity and does not destroy. Repeatedly He suppresses His anger,
not rousing His full wrath. LORD, save! May the King answer us on *Ps. 20*
the day we call.

---

But even this assurance is insufficient. Man might assume that the connection was severed at the moment of the creation *ex nihilo* and that now man is alone, left to fend for himself in an inhospitable universe. So we reiterate that not only did God make us once upon a time, but the relation between God and man continues to this very day: "He made us and we are His."

Furthermore, His caring and compassion is not restricted to the collective; it extends to each and every individual: "His people and the flock of sheep he tends." A pastor cares for each sheep individually.[29]

---

29. *OR*, vol. 1, pp. 221–222.

הוּא עָשָׂנוּ וְלוֹ אֲנַחְנוּ, עַמּוֹ וְצֹאן מַרְעִיתוֹ: בֹּאוּ שְׁעָרָיו
בְּתוֹדָה, חֲצֵרֹתָיו בִּתְהִלָּה, הוֹדוּ לוֹ, בָּרְכוּ שְׁמוֹ: ‹ כִּי־טוֹב
יהוה, לְעוֹלָם חַסְדּוֹ, וְעַד־דֹּר וָדֹר אֱמוּנָתוֹ:

יְהִי כְבוֹד יהוה לְעוֹלָם, יִשְׂמַח יהוה בְּמַעֲשָׂיו: יְהִי שֵׁם יהוה תהלים קד / תהלים קיג
מְבֹרָךְ, מֵעַתָּה וְעַד־עוֹלָם: מִמִּזְרַח־שֶׁמֶשׁ עַד־מְבוֹאוֹ, מְהֻלָּל
שֵׁם יהוה: רָם עַל־כָּל־גּוֹיִם יהוה, עַל הַשָּׁמַיִם כְּבוֹדוֹ: יהוה תהלים קלה
שִׁמְךָ לְעוֹלָם, יהוה זִכְרְךָ לְדֹר־וָדֹר: יהוה בַּשָּׁמַיִם הֵכִין כִּסְאוֹ, תהלים קג
וּמַלְכוּתוֹ בַּכֹּל מָשָׁלָה: יִשְׂמְחוּ הַשָּׁמַיִם וְתָגֵל הָאָרֶץ, וְיֹאמְרוּ דברי הימים א׳ טז
בַגּוֹיִם יהוה מָלָךְ: יהוה מֶלֶךְ, יהוה מָלָךְ, יהוה יִמְלֹךְ לְעוֹלָם וָעֶד.
יהוה מֶלֶךְ עוֹלָם וָעֶד, אָבְדוּ גוֹיִם מֵאַרְצוֹ: יהוה הֵפִיר עֲצַת־גּוֹיִם, תהלים י / תהלים לג
הֵנִיא מַחְשְׁבוֹת עַמִּים: רַבּוֹת מַחֲשָׁבוֹת בְּלֶב־אִישׁ, וַעֲצַת יהוה משלי יט
הִיא תָקוּם: עֲצַת יהוה לְעוֹלָם תַּעֲמֹד, מַחְשְׁבוֹת לִבּוֹ לְדֹר וָדֹר: תהלים לג
כִּי הוּא אָמַר וַיֶּהִי, הוּא־צִוָּה וַיַּעֲמֹד: כִּי־בָחַר יהוה בְּצִיּוֹן, אִוָּהּ תהלים קלב
לְמוֹשָׁב לוֹ: כִּי־יַעֲקֹב בָּחַר לוֹ יָהּ, יִשְׂרָאֵל לִסְגֻלָּתוֹ: כִּי לֹא־יִטֹּשׁ תהלים קלה / תהלים צד
יהוה עַמּוֹ, וְנַחֲלָתוֹ לֹא יַעֲזֹב: ‹ וְהוּא רַחוּם, יְכַפֵּר עָוֹן וְלֹא־יַשְׁחִית, תהלים עח
וְהִרְבָּה לְהָשִׁיב אַפּוֹ, וְלֹא־יָעִיר כָּל־חֲמָתוֹ: יהוה הוֹשִׁיעָה, הַמֶּלֶךְ תהלים כ
יַעֲנֵנוּ בְיוֹם־קָרְאֵנוּ:

---

דְּעוּ כִּי־יהוה הוּא אֱלֹהִים, הוּא עָשָׂנוּ וְלוֹ אֲנַחְנוּ, עַמּוֹ וְצֹאן מַרְעִיתוֹ *Know that the Lord is God; He made us and we are His, His people and the flock of sheep He tends.* (*previous page*). The Tetragrammaton (God's ineffable name, hereafter "*Havayah*") signifies the utter transcendence of the deity, who is beyond every law of nature; beyond every limitation. This transcendence might cause man to despair of ever connecting to the deity. Therefore it is imperative that we know that this very transcendent deity is *Elohim* (God), signifying immanence and intimate relation to the creations. Implicit in the name *Elohim* is *hashgaḥa* (divine supervision).

*The line beginning with "You open Your hand" should be said with special concentration, representing as it does the key idea of this psalm, and of Pesukei DeZimra as a whole, that God is the creator and sustainer of all. Some have the custom to touch the hand-tefillin at °, and the head-tefillin at °°.*

אַשְׁרֵי Happy are those who dwell in Your House; *Ps. 84*
they shall continue to praise You, Selah!

Happy are the people for whom this is so; *Ps. 144*
happy are the people whose God is the LORD.

A song of praise by David. *Ps. 145*

I will exalt You, my God, the King, and bless Your name for ever and all time. Every day I will bless You, and praise Your name for

---

study Torah, and that tranquility and equanimity is possible only if there is a modicum of income.[33]

תְּהִלָּה לְדָוִד / A SONG OF PRAISE BY DAVID (PSALM 145)
*Pesukei de-Zimra* proper, the "Verses of Song," consist of the last six Psalms (Psalms 145–150). Their recitation on a daily basis originates in a statement in the Talmud:

> Said Rabbi Yosé: May my portion be with those who recite Hallel every day.[34]

The Talmud clarifies that the statement refers to *"Pesukei de-Zimra."* In Rabbi Isaac Alfasi's transcription of the Talmud, there is further clarification:

> And which are they? From *Tehillah le-David* through *Kol ha-Neshamah Tehallel Yah.*[35]

---

33. *OR*, vol. 1, pp. 225–226; *EA*, vol. 1, *Berakhot*, chap. 1, par. 21 (p. 12).
34. *b. Shabbat* 118b.
35. *Shabbat*, chap. 16 (44a in foliation of Alfasi). See also *Tractate Soferim* 17:11; in the critical edition of M. Higger (New York, 1937) 18:1. Aptowitzer conjectured that both the author of *Tractate Soferim* and Alfasi did not read thus in their texts of the Talmud but simply added their own explanatory gloss in conformity with the prevailing custom of their own periods. See Avigdor Aptowitzer in *Ha-Tsofeh me-Erets Hager*, 1, p.85ff; quoted in Richard S. Sarason, "On the Use of Method in the Modern Study of Jewish Liturgy," in *Approaches to Ancient Judaism: Theory and Practice*, ed. William Scott Green (Brown University, 1978), p. 164, n. 242.

*The line beginning with* פּוֹתֵחַ אֶת יָדֶךָ *should be said with special concentration, representing as it does the key idea of this psalm, and of* פסוקי דזמרה *as a whole, that God is the creator and sustainer of all. Some have the custom to touch the* תפילין של יד *at* °, *and the* תפילין של ראש *at* °°.

אַשְׁרֵי יוֹשְׁבֵי בֵיתֶךָ, עוֹד יְהַלְלוּךָ סֶּלָה: תהלים פד

אַשְׁרֵי הָעָם שֶׁכָּכָה לּוֹ, אַשְׁרֵי הָעָם שֶׁיהוה אֱלֹהָיו: תהלים קמד

תְּהִלָּה לְדָוִד תהלים קמה

אֲרוֹמִמְךָ אֱלוֹהַי הַמֶּלֶךְ, וַאֲבָרְכָה שִׁמְךָ לְעוֹלָם וָעֶד:

בְּכָל־יוֹם אֲבָרְכֶךָּ, וַאֲהַלְלָה שִׁמְךָ לְעוֹלָם וָעֶד:

אַשְׁרֵי / HAPPY ARE THOSE

> Said Rabbi Yoḥanan: "Why is the letter *nun* omitted from *Ashrei*? Because it contains the downfall of Israel, for it is written, 'The virgin of Israel has fallen, she shall no longer rise.'"[30]

What is most difficult about Exile is that within the Exile itself there is absolutely no power of redemption. The redemption can come only from a power that is not inherent in the Exile, a higher, divine power. So in our reality, in our realm of experience, there honestly can be no getting up from that fall. Though there can be no rising up from within, there can be a support from without. And that is the next verse: "The Lord supports all who fall."[31]

> Said Rabbi El'azar bar Avina: "Whoever recites *Ashrei* three times a day is assured the World to Come … because it contains both the Aleph Bet and 'You open Your hand.'"[32]

What is unique about *Ashrei* and what makes the one who recites it eligible for the World to Come is 1)its alphabetical arrangement, and 2)its invoking livelihood.

The Aleph Bet is symbolic of the Torah which is expressed in the letters of the Hebrew alphabet. But the letters of Torah alone will not convey one to the World to Come. There is required the peace of mind to properly

30. Amos 5:2; *b. Berakhot* 4b.
31. *OR*, vol. 1, p. 224; *EA*, Vol. 1, chap. 1, par. 22 (p. 12).
32. *b. Berakhot* 4b.

ever and all time. Great is the LORD and greatly to be praised; His greatness is unfathomable. One generation will praise Your works to the next, and tell of Your mighty deeds. On the glorious splendor of Your majesty I will meditate, and on the acts of Your wonders. They shall talk of the power of Your awesome deeds, and I will tell of Your greatness. They shall recite the record of Your great goodness, and sing with joy of Your righteousness. The LORD is gracious and compassionate, slow to anger and great in loving-kindness. The LORD is good to all, and His compassion extends to all His works. All Your works shall thank You, LORD, and Your devoted ones shall bless You. They shall talk of the glory of Your kingship, and speak of Your might. To make known to mankind His mighty deeds and the glorious majesty of His kingship. Your kingdom is an everlasting kingdom, and Your reign is for all generations. The LORD supports all who fall, and raises all who are bowed down. All raise their eyes to You in hope, and You give them their food in due season. °You open Your hand, °°and satisfy every living thing with favor. The LORD is righteous in all His ways, and kind in all He does. The LORD is close to all who call on Him, to all who call on Him in truth. He fulfills the will of those who revere Him; He hears their cry and saves them. The LORD guards all who love Him, but all the wicked He will destroy. ▸ My mouth shall speak the praise of the LORD, and all creatures shall bless His holy name for ever and all time.

We will bless the LORD now and for ever. Halleluya! *Ps. 115*

---

Rav Amram Gaon explained that these Psalms commence with *"Halleluyah"* and conclude with *"Halleluyah,"* and in order to complete the chain, we conclude *Tehillah le-David* with a verse imported from Psalms 115:18 because it supplies the missing *"Halleluyah."*[37]

These six Psalms are the core of *Pesukei de-Zimra*. Other readings from the Tanakh were added later.[38] (Editor)

37. Quoted in *Tur, OḤ*, chap. 51.
38. Maimonides, *Hil. Tefillah* 7:12.

גָּדוֹל יהוה וּמְהֻלָּל מְאֹד, וְלִגְדֻלָּתוֹ אֵין חֵקֶר:
דּוֹר לְדוֹר יְשַׁבַּח מַעֲשֶׂיךָ, וּגְבוּרֹתֶיךָ יַגִּידוּ:
הֲדַר כְּבוֹד הוֹדֶךָ, וְדִבְרֵי נִפְלְאֹתֶיךָ אָשִׂיחָה:
וֶעֱזוּז נוֹרְאֹתֶיךָ יֹאמֵרוּ, וּגְדוּלָּתְךָ אֲסַפְּרֶנָּה:
זֵכֶר רַב־טוּבְךָ יַבִּיעוּ, וְצִדְקָתְךָ יְרַנֵּנוּ:
חַנּוּן וְרַחוּם יהוה, אֶרֶךְ אַפַּיִם וּגְדָל־חָסֶד:
טוֹב־יהוה לַכֹּל, וְרַחֲמָיו עַל־כָּל־מַעֲשָׂיו:
יוֹדוּךָ יהוה כָּל־מַעֲשֶׂיךָ, וַחֲסִידֶיךָ יְבָרְכוּכָה:
כְּבוֹד מַלְכוּתְךָ יֹאמֵרוּ, וּגְבוּרָתְךָ יְדַבֵּרוּ:
לְהוֹדִיעַ לִבְנֵי הָאָדָם גְּבוּרֹתָיו, וּכְבוֹד הֲדַר מַלְכוּתוֹ:
מַלְכוּתְךָ מַלְכוּת כָּל־עֹלָמִים, וּמֶמְשַׁלְתְּךָ בְּכָל־דּוֹר וָדֹר:
סוֹמֵךְ יהוה לְכָל־הַנֹּפְלִים, וְזוֹקֵף לְכָל־הַכְּפוּפִים:
עֵינֵי־כֹל אֵלֶיךָ יְשַׂבֵּרוּ, וְאַתָּה נוֹתֵן־לָהֶם אֶת־אָכְלָם בְּעִתּוֹ:
°פּוֹתֵחַ אֶת־יָדֶךָ, °°וּמַשְׂבִּיעַ לְכָל־חַי רָצוֹן:
צַדִּיק יהוה בְּכָל־דְּרָכָיו, וְחָסִיד בְּכָל־מַעֲשָׂיו:
קָרוֹב יהוה לְכָל־קֹרְאָיו, לְכֹל אֲשֶׁר יִקְרָאֻהוּ בֶאֱמֶת:
רְצוֹן־יְרֵאָיו יַעֲשֶׂה, וְאֶת־שַׁוְעָתָם יִשְׁמַע, וְיוֹשִׁיעֵם:
שׁוֹמֵר יהוה אֶת־כָּל־אֹהֲבָיו, וְאֵת כָּל־הָרְשָׁעִים יַשְׁמִיד:
◂ תְּהִלַּת יהוה יְדַבֶּר פִּי, וִיבָרֵךְ כָּל־בָּשָׂר שֵׁם קָדְשׁוֹ לְעוֹלָם וָעֶד:
תהלים קטו וַאֲנַחְנוּ נְבָרֵךְ יָהּ מֵעַתָּה וְעַד־עוֹלָם, הַלְלוּיָהּ:

---

Elsewhere Alfasi elaborates:

> And the Rabbis instituted to say a blessing before and a blessing after, and what are they? *Barukh she-Amar* and *Yishtabaḥ*.[36]

---

36. *Berakhot*, chap. 5 (23a in foliation of Alfasi).

הַלְלוּיָהּ Halleluya! Praise the LORD, my soul. I will praise the LORD all my life; I will sing to my God as long as I live. Put not your trust in princes, or in mortal man who cannot save. His breath expires, he returns to the earth; on that day his plans come to an end. Happy is he whose help is the God of Jacob, whose hope is in the LORD his God who made heaven and earth, the sea and all they contain; He who keeps faith for ever. He secures justice for the oppressed. He gives food to the hungry. The LORD sets captives free. The LORD gives sight to the blind. The LORD raises those bowed down. The LORD loves the righteous. The LORD protects the stranger. He gives courage to the orphan and widow. He thwarts the way of the wicked. ▸ The LORD shall reign for ever. He is your God, Zion, for all generations. Halleluya! *Ps. 146*

הַלְלוּיָהּ Halleluya! How good it is to sing songs to our God; how pleasant and fitting to praise Him. The LORD rebuilds Jerusalem. He gathers the scattered exiles of Israel. He heals the brokenhearted and binds up their wounds. He counts the number of the stars, calling each by name. Great is our LORD and mighty in power; His understanding has no limit. The LORD gives courage to the humble, but casts the wicked to the ground. Sing to the LORD in thanks; make music to our God on the harp. He covers the sky with clouds. He provides the earth with rain and makes grass grow on the hills. He gives food to the cattle and to the ravens when they cry. He does not take delight in the strength of horses nor pleasure in the fleetness of man. The LORD takes pleasure in those who fear Him, who put their hope in His loving care. Praise the LORD, Jerusalem; sing to your God, Zion, for He has strengthened the bars of your gates and blessed your children in your midst. He has brought peace to your borders, and satisfied you with the finest wheat. He sends His commandment to earth; swiftly runs His word. He spreads snow like fleece, sprinkles frost like ashes, scatters hail like crumbs. Who can stand His cold? He sends His word and melts them; He makes the wind blow and the waters flow. ▸ He has declared His words to Jacob, His statutes and laws to Israel. He has done this for no other nation; such laws they do not know. Halleluya! *Ps. 147*

תהלים קמו

הַלְלוּיָהּ, הַלְלִי נַפְשִׁי אֶת־יהוה: אֲהַלְלָה יהוה בְּחַיָּי, אֲזַמְּרָה לֵאלֹהַי בְּעוֹדִי: אַל־תִּבְטְחוּ בִנְדִיבִים, בְּבֶן־אָדָם שֶׁאֵין לוֹ תְשׁוּעָה: תֵּצֵא רוּחוֹ, יָשֻׁב לְאַדְמָתוֹ, בַּיּוֹם הַהוּא אָבְדוּ עֶשְׁתֹּנוֹתָיו: אַשְׁרֵי שֶׁאֵל יַעֲקֹב בְּעֶזְרוֹ, שִׂבְרוֹ עַל־יהוה אֱלֹהָיו: עֹשֶׂה שָׁמַיִם וָאָרֶץ, אֶת־הַיָּם וְאֶת־כָּל־אֲשֶׁר־בָּם, הַשֹּׁמֵר אֱמֶת לְעוֹלָם: עֹשֶׂה מִשְׁפָּט לַעֲשׁוּקִים, נֹתֵן לֶחֶם לָרְעֵבִים, יהוה מַתִּיר אֲסוּרִים: יהוה פֹּקֵחַ עִוְרִים, יהוה זֹקֵף כְּפוּפִים, יהוה אֹהֵב צַדִּיקִים: יהוה שֹׁמֵר אֶת־גֵּרִים, יָתוֹם וְאַלְמָנָה יְעוֹדֵד, וְדֶרֶךְ רְשָׁעִים יְעַוֵּת: ‹ יִמְלֹךְ יהוה לְעוֹלָם, אֱלֹהַיִךְ צִיּוֹן לְדֹר וָדֹר, הַלְלוּיָהּ:

תהלים קמז

הַלְלוּיָהּ, כִּי־טוֹב זַמְּרָה אֱלֹהֵינוּ, כִּי־נָעִים נָאוָה תְהִלָּה: בּוֹנֵה יְרוּשָׁלַםִ יהוה, נִדְחֵי יִשְׂרָאֵל יְכַנֵּס: הָרוֹפֵא לִשְׁבוּרֵי לֵב, וּמְחַבֵּשׁ לְעַצְּבוֹתָם: מוֹנֶה מִסְפָּר לַכּוֹכָבִים, לְכֻלָּם שֵׁמוֹת יִקְרָא: גָּדוֹל אֲדוֹנֵינוּ וְרַב־כֹּחַ, לִתְבוּנָתוֹ אֵין מִסְפָּר: מְעוֹדֵד עֲנָוִים יהוה, מַשְׁפִּיל רְשָׁעִים עֲדֵי־אָרֶץ: עֱנוּ לַיהוה בְּתוֹדָה, זַמְּרוּ לֵאלֹהֵינוּ בְכִנּוֹר: הַמְכַסֶּה שָׁמַיִם בְּעָבִים, הַמֵּכִין לָאָרֶץ מָטָר, הַמַּצְמִיחַ הָרִים חָצִיר: נוֹתֵן לִבְהֵמָה לַחְמָהּ, לִבְנֵי עֹרֵב אֲשֶׁר יִקְרָאוּ: לֹא בִגְבוּרַת הַסּוּס יֶחְפָּץ, לֹא־בְשׁוֹקֵי הָאִישׁ יִרְצֶה: רוֹצֶה יהוה אֶת־יְרֵאָיו, אֶת־הַמְיַחֲלִים לְחַסְדּוֹ: שַׁבְּחִי יְרוּשָׁלַםִ אֶת־יהוה, הַלְלִי אֱלֹהַיִךְ צִיּוֹן: כִּי־חִזַּק בְּרִיחֵי שְׁעָרָיִךְ, בֵּרַךְ בָּנַיִךְ בְּקִרְבֵּךְ: הַשָּׂם־גְּבוּלֵךְ שָׁלוֹם, חֵלֶב חִטִּים יַשְׂבִּיעֵךְ: הַשֹּׁלֵחַ אִמְרָתוֹ אָרֶץ, עַד־מְהֵרָה יָרוּץ דְּבָרוֹ: הַנֹּתֵן שֶׁלֶג כַּצָּמֶר, כְּפוֹר כָּאֵפֶר יְפַזֵּר: מַשְׁלִיךְ קַרְחוֹ כְפִתִּים, לִפְנֵי קָרָתוֹ מִי יַעֲמֹד: יִשְׁלַח דְּבָרוֹ וְיַמְסֵם, יַשֵּׁב רוּחוֹ יִזְּלוּ־מָיִם: ‹ מַגִּיד דְּבָרָו לְיַעֲקֹב, חֻקָּיו וּמִשְׁפָּטָיו לְיִשְׂרָאֵל: לֹא עָשָׂה כֵן לְכָל־גּוֹי, וּמִשְׁפָּטִים בַּל־יְדָעוּם, הַלְלוּיָהּ:

הַלְלוּיָהּ Halleluya! Praise the LORD from the heavens, praise Him in the heights. Praise Him, all His angels; praise Him, all His hosts. Praise Him, sun and moon; praise Him, all shining stars. Praise Him, highest heavens and the waters above the heavens. Let them praise the name of the LORD, for He commanded and they were created. He established them for ever and all time, issuing a decree that will never change. Praise the LORD from the earth: sea monsters and all the deep seas; fire and hail, snow and mist, storm winds that obey His word; mountains and all hills, fruit trees and all cedars; wild animals and all cattle, creeping things and winged birds; kings of the earth and all nations, princes and all judges on earth; youths and maidens, old and young. ▸ Let them praise the name of the LORD, for His name alone is sublime; His majesty is above earth and heaven. He has raised the pride of His people, for the glory of all His devoted ones, the children of Israel, the people close to Him. Halleluya! *Ps. 148*

הַלְלוּיָהּ Halleluya! Sing to the LORD a new song, His praise in the assembly of the devoted. Let Israel rejoice in its Maker; let the children of Zion exult in their King. Let them praise His name with dancing; sing praises to Him with timbrel and harp. For the LORD delights in His people; He adorns the humble with salvation. Let the devoted revel in glory; let them sing for joy on their beds. Let high praises of God be in their throats, and a two-edged sword in their hand: to impose retribution on the nations, punishment on the peoples, ▸ binding their kings with chains, their nobles with iron fetters, carrying out the judgment written against them. This is the glory of all His devoted ones. Halleluya! *Ps. 149*

הַלְלוּיָהּ Halleluya! Praise God in His holy place; praise Him in the heavens of His power. Praise Him for His mighty deeds; praise Him for His surpassing greatness. Praise Him with blasts of the shofar; praise Him with the harp and lyre. Praise Him with timbrel and dance; praise Him with strings and flute. Praise Him with clashing cymbals; praise Him with resounding cymbals. ▸ Let all that breathes praise the LORD. Halleluya! Let all that breathes praise the LORD. Halleluya! *Ps. 150*

תהלים קמח
הַלְלוּיָהּ, הַלְלוּ אֶת־יהוה מִן־הַשָּׁמַיִם, הַלְלוּהוּ בַּמְּרוֹמִים: הַלְלוּהוּ כָל־מַלְאָכָיו, הַלְלוּהוּ כָּל־צְבָאָו: הַלְלוּהוּ שֶׁמֶשׁ וְיָרֵחַ, הַלְלוּהוּ כָּל־כּוֹכְבֵי אוֹר: הַלְלוּהוּ שְׁמֵי הַשָּׁמָיִם, וְהַמַּיִם אֲשֶׁר מֵעַל הַשָּׁמָיִם: יְהַלְלוּ אֶת־שֵׁם יהוה, כִּי הוּא צִוָּה וְנִבְרָאוּ: וַיַּעֲמִידֵם לָעַד לְעוֹלָם, חָק־נָתַן וְלֹא יַעֲבוֹר: הַלְלוּ אֶת־יהוה מִן־הָאָרֶץ, תַּנִּינִים וְכָל־תְּהֹמוֹת: אֵשׁ וּבָרָד שֶׁלֶג וְקִיטוֹר, רוּחַ סְעָרָה עֹשָׂה דְבָרוֹ: הֶהָרִים וְכָל־גְּבָעוֹת, עֵץ פְּרִי וְכָל־אֲרָזִים: הַחַיָּה וְכָל־בְּהֵמָה, רֶמֶשׂ וְצִפּוֹר כָּנָף: מַלְכֵי־אֶרֶץ וְכָל־לְאֻמִּים, שָׂרִים וְכָל־שֹׁפְטֵי אָרֶץ: בַּחוּרִים וְגַם־בְּתוּלוֹת, זְקֵנִים עִם־נְעָרִים: › יְהַלְלוּ אֶת־שֵׁם יהוה, כִּי־נִשְׂגָּב שְׁמוֹ לְבַדּוֹ, הוֹדוֹ עַל־אֶרֶץ וְשָׁמָיִם: וַיָּרֶם קֶרֶן לְעַמּוֹ, תְּהִלָּה לְכָל־חֲסִידָיו, לִבְנֵי יִשְׂרָאֵל עַם קְרֹבוֹ, הַלְלוּיָהּ:

תהלים קמט
הַלְלוּיָהּ, שִׁירוּ לַיהוה שִׁיר חָדָשׁ, תְּהִלָּתוֹ בִּקְהַל חֲסִידִים: יִשְׂמַח יִשְׂרָאֵל בְּעֹשָׂיו, בְּנֵי־צִיּוֹן יָגִילוּ בְמַלְכָּם: יְהַלְלוּ שְׁמוֹ בְמָחוֹל, בְּתֹף וְכִנּוֹר יְזַמְּרוּ־לוֹ: כִּי־רוֹצֶה יהוה בְּעַמּוֹ, יְפָאֵר עֲנָוִים בִּישׁוּעָה: יַעְלְזוּ חֲסִידִים בְּכָבוֹד, יְרַנְּנוּ עַל־מִשְׁכְּבוֹתָם: רוֹמְמוֹת אֵל בִּגְרוֹנָם, וְחֶרֶב פִּיפִיּוֹת בְּיָדָם: לַעֲשׂוֹת נְקָמָה בַּגּוֹיִם, תּוֹכֵחוֹת בַּלְאֻמִּים: › לֶאְסֹר מַלְכֵיהֶם בְּזִקִּים, וְנִכְבְּדֵיהֶם בְּכַבְלֵי בַרְזֶל: לַעֲשׂוֹת בָּהֶם מִשְׁפָּט כָּתוּב, הָדָר הוּא לְכָל־חֲסִידָיו, הַלְלוּיָהּ:

תהלים קנ
הַלְלוּיָהּ, הַלְלוּ־אֵל בְּקָדְשׁוֹ, הַלְלוּהוּ בִּרְקִיעַ עֻזּוֹ: הַלְלוּהוּ בִגְבוּרֹתָיו, הַלְלוּהוּ כְּרֹב גֻּדְלוֹ: הַלְלוּהוּ בְּתֵקַע שׁוֹפָר, הַלְלוּהוּ בְּנֵבֶל וְכִנּוֹר: הַלְלוּהוּ בְתֹף וּמָחוֹל, הַלְלוּהוּ בְּמִנִּים וְעוּגָב: הַלְלוּהוּ בְצִלְצְלֵי־שָׁמַע, הַלְלוּהוּ בְּצִלְצְלֵי תְרוּעָה: › כֹּל הַנְּשָׁמָה תְּהַלֵּל יָהּ, הַלְלוּיָהּ: כֹּל הַנְּשָׁמָה תְּהַלֵּל יָהּ, הַלְלוּיָהּ:

בָּרוּךְ Blessed be the Lord for ever. Amen and Amen. Ps. 89
Blessed from Zion be the Lord Ps. 135
who dwells in Jerusalem. Halleluya!
Blessed be the Lord, God of Israel, who alone does wonders. Ps. 72
▸ Blessed be His glorious name for ever,
and may all the earth be filled with His glory.
Amen and Amen.

*Stand until after "Bless the Lord" on page 140.*

וַיְבָרֶךְ David blessed the Lord in front of the entire assembly. *1 Chr. 29*
David said, "Blessed are You, Lord, God of our father Yisrael, for ever and ever. Yours, Lord, are the greatness and the power, the glory, majesty and splendor, for everything in heaven and earth is Yours. Yours, Lord, is the kingdom; You are exalted as Head over

---

by a complete understanding of its totality, for it is but one entity, and this is beyond any thinker or theoretician...

We go from wonder to wonder... to a higher awareness. Those things that initially appeared to us as disjoint and disparate – before we knew their interrelation – will stand before us as "great things" *(gedolot).*

But just when we imagine that we have before us a complete work of the Master of the Universe; just when we think that our investigations have brought us to know the laws of this existence and that we have solved some of the great riddle – even more astonishing wonders pile up, until we decide: "We have not arrived at a complete picture; we have witnessed but a small portion of the works of the Master of all, and are incapable of revealing all the laws of existence." So the "great things" are – "beyond inquiry."[41]

וְהַנֵּצַח וְהַהוֹד *And the eternity and the splendor.*

"*And the eternity*" – this is Jerusalem;
"*And the splendor*" – this is the Holy Temple.[42]

The word *netsaḥ* is related to *nitsu'aḥ*, victory in war. Jerusalem must be battled for in order to wrest it from the control of the nations. But the Temple itself will not be cause for battle; the nations will willingly, voluntarily seek to

---

41. *OR*, vol. 1, pp. 229–230 = *EA*, vol. 2, *Berakhot*, chap. 9, par. 304 (pp. 377–378).
42. *b. Berakhot* 58a.

בָּרוּךְ יהוה לְעוֹלָם, אָמֵן וְאָמֵן: תהלים פט

בָּרוּךְ יהוה מִצִּיּוֹן, שֹׁכֵן יְרוּשָׁלָםִ, הַלְלוּיָהּ: תהלים קלה

בָּרוּךְ יהוה אֱלֹהִים אֱלֹהֵי יִשְׂרָאֵל, עֹשֵׂה נִפְלָאוֹת לְבַדּוֹ: תהלים עב

◂ וּבָרוּךְ שֵׁם כְּבוֹדוֹ לְעוֹלָם
וְיִמָּלֵא כְבוֹדוֹ אֶת־כָּל־הָאָרֶץ, אָמֵן וְאָמֵן:

*Stand until after* בָּרְכוּ *on page 141.*

דברי הימים א, כט
וַיְבָרֶךְ דָּוִיד אֶת־יהוה לְעֵינֵי כָּל־הַקָּהָל, וַיֹּאמֶר דָּוִיד, בָּרוּךְ
אַתָּה יהוה, אֱלֹהֵי יִשְׂרָאֵל אָבִינוּ, מֵעוֹלָם וְעַד־עוֹלָם: לְךָ יהוה
הַגְּדֻלָּה וְהַגְּבוּרָה וְהַתִּפְאֶרֶת וְהַנֵּצַח וְהַהוֹד, כִּי־כֹל בַּשָּׁמַיִם
וּבָאָרֶץ, לְךָ יהוה הַמַּמְלָכָה וְהַמִּתְנַשֵּׂא לְכֹל לְרֹאשׁ: וְהָעֹשֶׁר

---

לְךָ יהוה הַגְּדֻלָּה *Yours, Lord, (are) the greatness.*

"Yours, Lord (are) the greatness" – This refers to the act of creation (*ma'aseh bereshit*), and so it says, "He does great things beyond inquiry."[39]

The works of creation lead us to the discovery that all of existence is one act, whose details are myriads of physical worlds without number, and a multitude of spiritual creations without end. With all their causes, conditions and aspects, they all bond together as one. If we were able to behold the big picture of all existence, there would be revealed to us a single *macroanthropus*.[40] And so it is fitting for the single Lord that all of His deeds should amount – not to disjoint, disparate sparks, but rather – to a braided torch of light… All these manifold details, each one of which amazes us with its awesomeness, bond together as limbs of a body, or as an awe-inspiring machine made up of infinitely many parts…

Even if man should be able to gather in to his intellect a great portion of existence, and should grasp the bond that holds together its specifics and forces – he would still be at a loss to solve the many riddles that would appear to him in the wisdom of creation, for as much as he will increase knowledge, so will he increase wonders upon wonders.

The reason for this fact is that the solution to existence can be had only

---

39. Job 9:10; *b. Berakhot* 58a.
40. Cf. Moses Maimonides, *Guide of the Perplexed* 1, 72.

all. Both riches and honor are in Your gift and You reign over all things. In Your hand are strength and might. It is in Your power to make great and give strength to all. Therefore, our God, we thank You and praise Your glorious name." You alone are *Neh. 9*
the LORD. You made the heavens, even the highest heavens, and all their hosts, the earth and all that is on it, the seas and all they contain. You give life to them all, and the hosts of heaven worship You. ▸ You are the LORD God who chose Abram and brought him out of Ur of the Chaldees, changing his name to Abraham. You found his heart faithful toward You, ◂ and You made a covenant with him to give to his descendants the land of the Canaanites, Hittites, Amorites, Perizzites, Jebusites and Girgashites. You fulfilled Your promise for You are righteous. You saw the suffering of our ancestors in Egypt. You heard their cry at the Sea of Reeds. You sent signs and wonders against Pharaoh, all his servants and all the people of his land, because You knew how arrogantly the Egyptians treated them. You created for Yourself renown that remains to this day. ▸ You divided the sea before them, so that they passed through the sea on dry land, but You cast their pursuers into the depths, like a stone into mighty waters.

---

proper to employ it in the service of the LORD, in Torah and *mitsvot* (commandments). Therefore the Prophet invoked the original name of Abram, who was a man imbued with the righteousness and justice of national love (*ahavah le'umit*). The LORD chose him to lift him up to the universal love of Abraham, "a father of a multitude of nations."[44] And so, the entire value of nationalism serves a lofty purpose.[45]

---

44. Genesis 17:5.
45. *OR*, vol. 1, p. 234. Cf. *EA*, vol. 1, *Berakhot*, chap. 1, par. 177 (pp. 69–70). Though *b. Berakhot* 13a refers to Nehemiah as the *"Navi"* ("Prophet"), this is untenable. (Nehemiah was not a prophet.) The words were uttered by the Levites Yeshu'a, Kadmiel, et al (Nehemiah 9:5). In the parallel *y. Berakhot* 1:6, for *"Navi,"* we have *"Anshei K'nesset ha-Gedolah"* ("the Men of the Great Assembly"). See *Maharats Ḥayyot, Berakhot* 13a. However, Rabbi Joseph Rosen (the Rogatchover Gaon) upholds the reading "the Prophet," based on the words of Maimonides (*Guide of the Perplexed* II, 45, end 2nd Degree): "Also all these are called, in a general way, prophets." See *Tsafnat Pa'ne'aḥ* on the Pentateuch, vol. 6 (Jerusalem, 1964), p. 403.

וְהַכָּבוֹד מִלְּפָנֶיךָ, וְאַתָּה מוֹשֵׁל בַּכֹּל, וּבְיָדְךָ כֹּחַ וּגְבוּרָה, וּבְיָדְךָ
לְגַדֵּל וּלְחַזֵּק לַכֹּל: וְעַתָּה אֱלֹהֵינוּ מוֹדִים אֲנַחְנוּ לָךְ, וּמְהַלְלִים
לְשֵׁם תִּפְאַרְתֶּךָ: אַתָּה־הוּא יהוה לְבַדֶּךָ, אַתָּ עָשִׂיתָ נחמיה ט
אֶת־הַשָּׁמַיִם, שְׁמֵי הַשָּׁמַיִם וְכָל־צְבָאָם, הָאָרֶץ וְכָל־אֲשֶׁר
עָלֶיהָ, הַיַּמִּים וְכָל־אֲשֶׁר בָּהֶם, וְאַתָּה מְחַיֶּה אֶת־כֻּלָּם, וּצְבָא
הַשָּׁמַיִם לְךָ מִשְׁתַּחֲוִים: ‹ אַתָּה הוּא יהוה הָאֱלֹהִים אֲשֶׁר
בָּחַרְתָּ בְּאַבְרָם, וְהוֹצֵאתוֹ מֵאוּר כַּשְׂדִּים, וְשַׂמְתָּ שְׁמוֹ אַבְרָהָם:
וּמָצָאתָ אֶת־לְבָבוֹ נֶאֱמָן לְפָנֶיךָ, ‹ וְכָרוֹת עִמּוֹ הַבְּרִית לָתֵת
אֶת־אֶרֶץ הַכְּנַעֲנִי הַחִתִּי הָאֱמֹרִי וְהַפְּרִזִּי וְהַיְבוּסִי וְהַגִּרְגָּשִׁי,
לָתֵת לְזַרְעוֹ, וַתָּקֶם אֶת־דְּבָרֶיךָ, כִּי צַדִּיק אָתָּה: וַתֵּרֶא אֶת־
עֳנִי אֲבֹתֵינוּ בְּמִצְרָיִם, וְאֶת־זַעֲקָתָם שָׁמַעְתָּ עַל־יַם־סוּף: וַתִּתֵּן
אֹתֹת וּמֹפְתִים בְּפַרְעֹה וּבְכָל־עֲבָדָיו וּבְכָל־עַם אַרְצוֹ, כִּי יָדַעְתָּ
כִּי הֵזִידוּ עֲלֵיהֶם, וַתַּעַשׂ־לְךָ שֵׁם כְּהַיּוֹם הַזֶּה: ‹ וְהַיָּם בָּקַעְתָּ
לִפְנֵיהֶם, וַיַּעַבְרוּ בְתוֹךְ־הַיָּם בַּיַּבָּשָׁה, וְאֶת־רֹדְפֵיהֶם הִשְׁלַכְתָּ
בִמְצוֹלֹת כְּמוֹ־אֶבֶן, בְּמַיִם עַזִּים:

---

bask in the splendor of the Holy Temple and learn from the wise ways of the Lord. "Like the majesty (*hod malkhut*) displayed on a just and wise king, that inspires such love and uplift, that all run to enter under his banner."[43]

אַתָּה הוּא יהוה הָאֱלֹהִים אֲשֶׁר בָּחַרְתָּ בְּאַבְרָם, וְהוֹצֵאתוֹ מֵאוּר כַּשְׂדִּים, וְשַׂמְתָּ שְׁמוֹ אַבְרָהָם *You are the Lord God Who chose Abram and brought him out of Ur of the Chaldees, adjusting his name to Abraham.*

The nationalist feeling is an exalted feeling in its right nature, but if it is not directed to a higher goal of universal perfection, in the end it will break down the fences of justice, overstepping its bounds to inherit dwellings that are not its own – without justice or any sacred purpose. But since the nationalist sentiment *per se* is just and exalted, it must not be abandoned or negated; like all character traits – even the lowliest among them – it is

43. *OR*, vol. 1, pp. 233–234 = *EA*, vol. 2, *Berakhot*, chap. 9, par. 314 (p. 380).

וַיּוֹשַׁע That day the LORD saved Israel from the hands of the Egyptians, and Israel saw the Egyptians lying dead on the seashore. ▸ When Israel saw the great power the LORD had displayed against the Egyptians, the people feared the LORD, and believed in the LORD and in His servant, Moses. *Ex. 14*

אָז יָשִׁיר־מֹשֶׁה Then Moses and the Israelites sang this song to the LORD, saying: *Ex. 15*

I will sing to the LORD, for He has triumphed gloriously;
horse and rider He has hurled into the sea.
The LORD is my strength and song; He has become my salvation.
This is my God, and I will beautify Him,
my father's God, and I will exalt Him.
The LORD is a Master of war; LORD is His name.
Pharaoh's chariots and army He cast into the sea;
the best of his officers drowned in the Sea of Reeds.
The deep waters covered them;
they went down to the depths like a stone.
Your right hand, LORD, is majestic in power.
Your right hand, LORD, shatters the enemy.
In the greatness of Your majesty, You overthrew those who rose against You.
You sent out Your fury; it consumed them like stubble.
By the blast of Your nostrils the waters piled up.
The surging waters stood straight like a wall;
the deeps congealed in the heart of the sea.
The enemy said, "I will pursue. I will overtake. I will divide the spoil.
My desire shall have its fill of them.
I will draw my sword. My hand will destroy them."
You blew with Your wind; the sea covered them.
They sank in the mighty waters like lead.
Who is like You, LORD, among the mighty?
Who is like You – majestic in holiness, awesome in glory, working wonders?
You stretched out Your right hand,
the earth swallowed them.
In Your loving-kindness, You led the people You redeemed.
In Your strength, You guided them to Your holy abode.

וַיּֽוֹשַׁע יהוה בַּיּוֹם הַהוּא אֶת־יִשְׂרָאֵל מִיַּד מִצְרָֽיִם, וַיַּרְא יִשְׂרָאֵל שמות יד
אֶת־מִצְרַֽיִם מֵת עַל־שְׂפַת הַיָּם: › וַיַּרְא יִשְׂרָאֵל אֶת־הַיָּד הַגְּדֹלָה
אֲשֶׁר עָשָׂה יהוה בְּמִצְרַֽיִם, וַיִּירְאוּ הָעָם אֶת־יהוה, וַיַּאֲמִֽינוּ
בַּיהוה וּבְמֹשֶׁה עַבְדּוֹ:

אָז יָשִׁיר־מֹשֶׁה וּבְנֵי יִשְׂרָאֵל אֶת־הַשִּׁירָה הַזֹּאת לַיהוה, וַיֹּאמְרוּ שמות טו
לֵאמֹר, אָשִֽׁירָה לַיהוה כִּי־גָאֹה גָּאָה, סוּס
וְרֹכְבוֹ רָמָה בַיָּם: עָזִּי וְזִמְרָת יָהּ וַיְהִי־לִי
לִישׁוּעָה, זֶה אֵלִי וְאַנְוֵֽהוּ, אֱלֹהֵי
אָבִי וַאֲרֹמְמֶֽנְהוּ: יהוה אִישׁ מִלְחָמָה, יהוה
שְׁמוֹ: מַרְכְּבֹת פַּרְעֹה וְחֵילוֹ יָרָה בַיָּם, וּמִבְחַר
שָׁלִשָׁיו טֻבְּעוּ בְיַם־סוּף: תְּהֹמֹת יְכַסְיֻֽמוּ, יָרְדוּ בִמְצוֹלֹת כְּמוֹ־
אָֽבֶן: יְמִינְךָ יהוה נֶאְדָּרִי בַּכֹּֽחַ, יְמִינְךָ
יהוה תִּרְעַץ אוֹיֵב: וּבְרֹב גְּאוֹנְךָ תַּהֲרֹס
קָמֶֽיךָ, תְּשַׁלַּח חֲרֹנְךָ יֹאכְלֵֽמוֹ כַּקַּשׁ: וּבְרֽוּחַ
אַפֶּֽיךָ נֶֽעֶרְמוּ מַֽיִם, נִצְּבוּ כְמוֹ־נֵד
נֹזְלִים, קָפְאוּ תְהֹמֹת בְּלֶב־יָם: אָמַר
אוֹיֵב אֶרְדֹּף, אַשִּׂיג, אֲחַלֵּק שָׁלָל, תִּמְלָאֵֽמוֹ
נַפְשִׁי, אָרִיק חַרְבִּי תּוֹרִישֵֽׁמוֹ יָדִי: נָשַֽׁפְתָּ
בְרוּחֲךָ כִּסָּֽמוֹ יָם, צָֽלְלוּ כַּעוֹפֶֽרֶת בְּמַֽיִם
אַדִּירִים: מִי־כָמֹֽכָה בָּאֵלִם יהוה, מִי
כָּמֹֽכָה נֶאְדָּר בַּקֹּֽדֶשׁ, נוֹרָא תְהִלֹּת עֹֽשֵׂה
פֶֽלֶא: נָטִֽיתָ יְמִינְךָ תִּבְלָעֵֽמוֹ אָֽרֶץ: נָחִֽיתָ
בְחַסְדְּךָ עַם־זוּ גָּאָֽלְתָּ, נֵהַֽלְתָּ בְעָזְּךָ אֶל־נְוֵה

Nations heard and trembled;
terror gripped Philistia's inhabitants.
The chiefs of Edom were dismayed,
Moab's leaders were seized with trembling,
the people of Canaan melted away.
Fear and dread fell upon them.
By the power of Your arm, they were still as stone –
until Your people crossed, LORD,
until the people You acquired crossed over.
You will bring them and plant them
on the mountain of Your heritage –
the place, LORD, You made for Your dwelling,
the Sanctuary, LORD, Your hands established.
The LORD will reign for ever and all time.

The LORD will reign for ever and all time.
The LORD's kingship is established
for ever and to all eternity.

When Pharaoh's horses, chariots and riders went into the sea,
the LORD brought the waters of the sea back over them,
but the Israelites walked on dry land through
the sea.

▸ For kingship is the LORD's *Ps. 22*
and He rules over the nations.
Saviors shall go up to Mount Zion *Ob. 1*
to judge Mount Esau,
and the LORD's shall be the kingdom.

Then the LORD shall be King over all the earth; *Zech. 14*
on that day the LORD shall be One and His name One,

(as it is written in Your Torah, saying:
Listen, Israel: the LORD is our God, the LORD is One.) *Deut. 6*

קָדְשֶׁךָ: שָׁמְעוּ עַמִּים יִרְגָּזוּן, חִיל
אָחַז יֹשְׁבֵי פְּלָשֶׁת: אָז נִבְהֲלוּ אַלּוּפֵי
אֱדוֹם, אֵילֵי מוֹאָב יֹאחֲזֵמוֹ רָעַד, נָמֹגוּ
כֹּל יֹשְׁבֵי כְנָעַן: תִּפֹּל עֲלֵיהֶם אֵימָתָה
וָפַחַד, בִּגְדֹל זְרוֹעֲךָ יִדְּמוּ כָּאָבֶן, עַד־
יַעֲבֹר עַמְּךָ יהוה, עַד־יַעֲבֹר עַם־זוּ
קָנִיתָ: תְּבִאֵמוֹ וְתִטָּעֵמוֹ בְּהַר נַחֲלָתְךָ, מָכוֹן
לְשִׁבְתְּךָ פָּעַלְתָּ יהוה, מִקְּדָשׁ אֲדֹנָי כּוֹנְנוּ
יָדֶיךָ: יהוה יִמְלֹךְ לְעֹלָם וָעֶד:

יהוה יִמְלֹךְ לְעֹלָם וָעֶד.
יהוה מַלְכוּתֵהּ קָאֵם לְעָלַם וּלְעָלְמֵי עָלְמַיָּא.

כִּי
בָא סוּס פַּרְעֹה בְּרִכְבּוֹ וּבְפָרָשָׁיו בַּיָּם, וַיָּשֶׁב יהוה עֲלֵהֶם אֶת־מֵי
הַיָּם, וּבְנֵי יִשְׂרָאֵל הָלְכוּ בַיַּבָּשָׁה בְּתוֹךְ הַיָּם:

◂ כִּי לַיהוה הַמְּלוּכָה וּמֹשֵׁל בַּגּוֹיִם: תהלים כב
וְעָלוּ מוֹשִׁעִים בְּהַר צִיּוֹן עובדיה א
לִשְׁפֹּט אֶת־הַר עֵשָׂו
וְהָיְתָה לַיהוה הַמְּלוּכָה:

וְהָיָה יהוה לְמֶלֶךְ עַל־כָּל־הָאָרֶץ זכריה יד
בַּיּוֹם הַהוּא יִהְיֶה יהוה אֶחָד וּשְׁמוֹ אֶחָד:

(וּבְתוֹרָתְךָ כָּתוּב לֵאמֹר
שְׁמַע יִשְׂרָאֵל, יהוה אֱלֹהֵינוּ יהוה אֶחָד:) דברים ו

ישְׁתַּבַּח May Your name be praised for ever, our King,
the great and holy God, King in heaven and on earth.
For to You, LORD our God and God of our ancestors,
it is right to offer song and praise, hymn and psalm,
strength and dominion, eternity, greatness and power,
song of praise and glory, holiness and kingship,
▸ blessings and thanks, from now and for ever.
Blessed are You, LORD,
God and King, exalted in praises,
God of thanksgivings, Master of wonders,
who delights in hymns of song,
King, God, Giver of life to the worlds.

---

Did we succeed in what we set out to achieve? Were we able to complete the task of offering praise to the LORD?

We are now reciting the concluding blessing of *Yishtabaḥ*. At the end of the journey, we know that we have failed to accomplish our mission. We are unequal to the challenge of singing all God's praises. There creeps in a feeling of insufficiency, perhaps even of defeat.[48] The last line of the blessing, according to the Ḥasidic master, jolts us out of our despondency:

> If a man should say songs and praises to the very best of his ability, and yet his heart burns with love and it is yet his will to praise and glorify – this love is called *"shirei zimrah,"* that is, the remainder (*shirayim*) of the song that remains behind in the heart. And it is this that the LORD chooses (*boḥer*), for this is more essential than the praise itself.[49] (Editor)

---

48. According to the Midrash, King David himself received a lesson in humility:

> When he completed the Book of Psalms, he became swell-headed and said to the Holy One, blessed be He: "Master of the Universe, is there a creation that You created in Your world that outdoes me in uttering songs and praises?"
> Precisely then, there happened along a frog and said to him: "David, don't be swell-headed, for I outdo you in uttering songs and praises." (*Yalkut Shim'oni*, Psalms 150, *remez* 889; *Perek Shirah*)

49. Rabbi Simḥa Bunim of Przysucha, quoted in Rabbi Samuel Bornstein of Sochaczew, *Shem mi-Shmuel*, Rosh Hashanah 5672. The author, Rebbe of Sochaczew, added that the "voice of the *shofar*" issuing from the interior of the heart is such an undifferentiated expression. Cf. Rabbi Joseph Baer Soloveitchik, *Shi'urim le-Zekher Abba Mari* (Jerusalem: Mossad Harav Kook, 2002), vol. 2, pp. 83–84 (*"Teki'ah ve-Shirah ba-Mikdash"*); pp. 27–28 (*"Pesukei de-Zimrah"*); idem, *Yemei Zikaron* (Jerusalem: WZO, 1986), p. 140; Rabbi Hershel Schachter, *Nefesh Harav* (Jerusalem, 1994), pp. 112–113.

יִשְׁתַּבַּח שִׁמְךָ לָעַד, מַלְכֵּנוּ
הָאֵל הַמֶּלֶךְ הַגָּדוֹל וְהַקָּדוֹשׁ בַּשָּׁמַיִם וּבָאָרֶץ
כִּי לְךָ נָאֶה, יהוה אֱלֹהֵינוּ וֵאלֹהֵי אֲבוֹתֵינוּ
שִׁיר וּשְׁבָחָה, הַלֵּל וְזִמְרָה, עֹז וּמֶמְשָׁלָה, נֶצַח
גְּדֻלָּה וּגְבוּרָה, תְּהִלָּה וְתִפְאֶרֶת, קְדֻשָּׁה וּמַלְכוּת
◂ בְּרָכוֹת וְהוֹדָאוֹת, מֵעַתָּה וְעַד עוֹלָם.
בָּרוּךְ אַתָּה יהוה, אֵל מֶלֶךְ גָּדוֹל בַּתִּשְׁבָּחוֹת
אֵל הַהוֹדָאוֹת, אֲדוֹן הַנִּפְלָאוֹת
הַבּוֹחֵר בְּשִׁירֵי זִמְרָה, מֶלֶךְ, אֵל, חֵי הָעוֹלָמִים.

---

יִשְׁתַּבַּח / MAY YOUR NAME BE PRAISED

הַבּוֹחֵר בְּשִׁירֵי זִמְרָה *Who delights in hymns of song.* There appears to be a redundancy here. *Shir* and *zemer* are synonyms for song.[46]

The great Polish Ḥasidic master Rabbi Simḥa Bunim of Pshiskha (Polish *Przysucha*) interpreted the word *"shirei"* in this context to be the *nismakh* form of the word *"shirayim"* (leftover or remainder).[47]

We commenced *Pesukei de-Zimrah* with the blessing of *Barukh she-Amar*. In that blessing we expressed our ambition:

> With the songs of Your servant David we will praise you, O Lord our God. With praises and psalms we will magnify You, and praise You, and glorify You.

---

46. Seligman Baer sought to alleviate the redundancy by writing that *zimrah* means praise. (Cf. Onkelos to Genesis 43:11.) *"Shirei zimrah"* thus yields "songs of praise." See *Seder 'Avodat Yisrael* (Roedelheim, 1868; photo offset Tel-Aviv, 1957), p. 75.
    Rabbi Isaac Hutner taught that *shir* and *zimrah* are actually antonyms. *Shir* evokes an expansive mood; a sensation of survival, of continuity. *Zimrah* evokes a sense of shrinking; what's more, of self-nullification (*bittul*) before one who is greater. Rabbi Hutner explained that in the Tanakh, the root *zmr* can mean "to cut." (See e.g. Lev. 25:3–4; Isaiah 18:15.) Thus, in the act of offering praise to another, one's own ego is cut down. How Rabbi Hutner arrived at the notion that *shir* is about preservation of ego and self-validation, is left to the reader's imagination. See Rabbi Isaac Hutner, *Paḥad Yitsḥak: Sha'ar u-be-Yom ha-Shabbat* (New York, NY, 2003), *ma'amar* 2:8 (pp. 40–41). (I thank Rabbi Nachman Schneider for bringing this passage in *Paḥad Yitsḥak* to my attention.)
47. Cf. Rabbi Isaac Dov Baer Schneerson of Liadi, *Seder Tefillah 'im Peirush Maharid* (Berdichev, 1913; photo offset Kefar Ḥabad, 1991), vol. 1, 69a, s.v. *ha-boḥer be-shirei zimrah.*

*Between Rosh HaShana and Yom Kippur, and on Hoshana Raba, many congregations open the Ark and say this psalm responsively, verse by verse.*

שִׁיר הַמַּעֲלוֹת A song of ascents. From the depths I have called to You, LORD. *Ps. 130*
LORD, hear my voice; let Your ears be attentive to my plea. If You, LORD, should keep account of sins, O LORD, who could stand? But with You there is forgiveness, that You may be held in awe. I wait for the LORD, my soul waits, and in His word I put my hope. My soul waits for the LORD more than watchmen wait for the morning, more than watchmen wait for the morning. Israel, put your hope in the LORD, for with the LORD there is loving-kindness, and great is His power to redeem. It is He who will redeem Israel from all their sins.

HALF KADDISH

*Leader:* יִתְגַּדַּל Magnified and sanctified
may His great name be,
in the world He created by His will.
May He establish His kingdom
in your lifetime and in your days,
and in the lifetime of all the house of Israel,
swiftly and soon –
and say: Amen.

*All:* May His great name be blessed
for ever and all time.

*Leader:* Blessed and praised,
glorified and exalted,
raised and honored,
uplifted and lauded
be the name of the Holy One,
blessed be He,
beyond any blessing,
song, praise and consolation
uttered in the world –
and say: Amen.

*During the* עשרת ימי תשובה*, and on* הושענא רבה*,*
*many congregations open the* ארון קודש *and say this psalm responsively, verse by verse.*

שִׁיר הַמַּעֲלוֹת, מִמַּעֲמַקִּים קְרָאתִֽיךָ יהוה: אֲדֹנָי שִׁמְעָה בְקוֹלִי, תהלים קל
תִּהְיֶֽינָה אָזְנֶֽיךָ קַשֻּׁבוֹת לְקוֹל תַּחֲנוּנָי: אִם־עֲוֹנוֹת תִּשְׁמָר־יָהּ, אֲדֹנָי
מִי יַעֲמֹד: כִּי־עִמְּךָ הַסְּלִיחָה, לְמַעַן תִּוָּרֵא: קִוִּֽיתִי יהוה קִוְּתָה נַפְשִׁי,
וְלִדְבָרוֹ הוֹחָֽלְתִּי: נַפְשִׁי לַאדֹנָי, מִשֹּׁמְרִים לַבֹּֽקֶר, שֹׁמְרִים לַבֹּֽקֶר:
יַחֵל יִשְׂרָאֵל אֶל יהוה, כִּי־עִם־יהוה הַחֶֽסֶד, וְהַרְבֵּה עִמּוֹ פְדוּת:
וְהוּא יִפְדֶּה אֶת־יִשְׂרָאֵל, מִכֹּל עֲוֹנוֹתָיו:

## חצי קדיש

ש״ץ: יִתְגַּדַּל וְיִתְקַדַּשׁ שְׁמֵהּ רַבָּא (קהל: אָמֵן)
בְּעָלְמָא דִּי בְרָא כִרְעוּתֵהּ
וְיַמְלִיךְ מַלְכוּתֵהּ
בְּחַיֵּיכוֹן וּבְיוֹמֵיכוֹן וּבְחַיֵּי דְכָל בֵּית יִשְׂרָאֵל
בַּעֲגָלָא וּבִזְמַן קָרִיב
וְאִמְרוּ אָמֵן. (קהל: אָמֵן)

קהל וש״ץ: יְהֵא שְׁמֵהּ רַבָּא מְבָרַךְ לְעָלַם וּלְעָלְמֵי עָלְמַיָּא.

ש״ץ: יִתְבָּרַךְ וְיִשְׁתַּבַּח וְיִתְפָּאַר וְיִתְרוֹמַם וְיִתְנַשֵּׂא
וְיִתְהַדָּר וְיִתְעַלֶּה וְיִתְהַלָּל
שְׁמֵהּ דְּקֻדְשָׁא בְּרִיךְ הוּא (קהל: בְּרִיךְ הוּא)
לְעֵֽלָּא מִן כָּל בִּרְכָתָא
/בעשרת ימי תשובה: לְעֵֽלָּא לְעֵֽלָּא מִכָּל בִּרְכָתָא/
וְשִׁירָתָא, תֻּשְׁבְּחָתָא וְנֶחֱמָתָא
דַּאֲמִירָן בְּעָלְמָא
וְאִמְרוּ אָמֵן. (קהל: אָמֵן)

## BLESSINGS OF THE SHEMA

*The following blessing and response are said only in the presence of a minyan. They represent a formal summons to the congregation to engage in an act of collective prayer. The custom of bowing at this point is based on 1 Chronicles 29:20, "David said to the whole assembly, 'Now bless the LORD your God.' All the assembly blessed the LORD God of their fathers and bowed their heads low to the LORD and the King."*

*The Leader says the following, bowing at "Bless," standing straight at "the LORD." The congregation, followed by the Leader, responds, bowing at "Bless," standing straight at "the LORD."*

*Leader:* **BLESS**
the LORD, the blessed One.

*Congregation:* Bless the LORD, the blessed One,
for ever and all time.

*Leader:* Bless the LORD, the blessed One,
for ever and all time.

*The custom is to sit from this point until the Amida, since the predominant emotion of this section of the prayers is love rather than awe.*

---

the soul has been affected by the outer impressions it has received from the poetry, the lyric quality of the world surrounding us all about. We now leave behind this world with its spatio-temporal coordinates and ascend into inner space. Upon our arrival in this world of the infinite we intone this blessing:

בָּרוּךְ יהוה הַמְבֹרָךְ לְעוֹלָם וָעֶד
Bless the LORD, the blessed One, for ever and all time.[2]

---

Rabbi Immanuel Ḥai Ricchi, *Mishnat Ḥasidim, Masekhet Tefillat ha-Beri'ah* 1:2; *Be'ur ha-Gra* to *Tikkunim mi-Zohar Ḥadash*, appended to *Tikkunei Zohar* (Vilna, 1867), s.v. *u-be-Yishtabaḥ* (13b); Rabbi N.H. Halevi Weidenbaum, *Sha'ar Naftali* to *Siddur ha-Gra* (Jerusalem, 1895–1898; photo offset Jerusalem, 1971), 76a.

2. *OR*, vol. 1, pp. 237–238.

# קריאת שמע וברכותיה

*The following blessing and response are said only in the presence of a* מנין.
*They represent a formal summons to the* קהל *to engage in an act of collective prayer.*
*The custom of bowing at this point is based on* דברי הימים א׳ כט: כ, *"David said to the whole assembly, 'Now bless the* Lord *your God.' All the assembly blessed the* Lord *God of their fathers and bowed their heads low to the* Lord *and the King."*

*The* שליח ציבור *says the following,*
*bowing at* בָּרְכוּ, *standing straight at* ה׳. *The* קהל, *followed by*
*the* שליח ציבור, *responds, bowing at* בָּרוּךְ, *standing straight at* ה׳.

ש״ץ: **בָּרְכוּ**

**אֶת יהוה הַמְבֹרָךְ.**

קהל: **בָּרוּךְ יהוה הַמְבֹרָךְ לְעוֹלָם וָעֶד.**

ש״ץ: **בָּרוּךְ יהוה הַמְבֹרָךְ לְעוֹלָם וָעֶד.**

*The custom is to sit from this point until the* עמידה, *since the predominant emotion of this section of the prayers is love rather than awe.*

---

CONCLUSION OF *PESUKEI DE-ZIMRAH*

As we transition from *Pesukei de-Zimrah* (Verses of Song) to the *Birkhot Keri'at Shema'* (Blessings of *Shema'*), we move from one world to another, from the World of Formation (*'Olam ha-Yetsirah*) to the World of Creation (*'Olam ha-Beri'ah*), to employ the terminology of the Kabbalists.[1] Until now,

1. According to Rabbi Isaac Luria, the *Kaddish* is the pillar by which one ascends from the lower World of *Yetsirah* to the higher World of *Beri'ah*. Rabbi Naftali Hertz Halevi (who immediately preceded Rav Kook as Rabbi of Jaffa) understood from the Gaon of Vilna that the transition takes place in *Yishtabaḥ* itself. See Rabbi Ḥayyim Vital, *Peri 'Ets Ḥayyim*, beg. *Sha'ar ha-Kaddishim*; *Sha'ar ha-Zemirot – 'Olam ha-Yetsirah*, chap. 6;

*Conversation is forbidden until after the Amida. See table on pages 1315–1317.*

בָּרוּךְ Blessed are You, LORD our God, King of the Universe,
who forms light and creates darkness, *Is. 45*
makes peace and creates all.

---

Isaiah was describing the "facts on the ground," so to speak. One cannot deny the facticity of evil in our world. Unfortunately, the world abounds in evil.

The Prophet described the reality of our plane of existence. The Sages understood that on a higher level of reality (referred to as "the All"), the seemingly discrete, disparate, disjoint elements bond together in a simple unicity:

> The prophecy, which is intended to inculcate a moral lesson in opposition to philosophies that would undermine monotheism, is stated in terms of human perception: "creates darkness," "creates evil"... But we in our prayer, inasmuch as it our objective to tell the truth of the honor of the LORD, are correct in saying "creates the all"... But in order "to mention the attribute of day by night, and the attribute of night by day,"[6] i.e., the principle of the singularity of divine rule throughout all the opposite manners in which existence is governed – both general and specific – we mention too that which is our common perception: "creates darkness."
>
> However, since the purpose of the blessing is also to bless the LORD for His lovingkindness – *"Ki amarti 'olam ḥesed yibaneh"* ("For I said, the world is established with lovingkindness")[7] – it is worthy to conclude the blessing with the acknowledgment of the truth, that the LORD created no evil, and there is in existence no absolute evil, and the perceived evil is joined to the totality to perfect the good, so that evil is subsumed under the term "the All."[8]

---

6. *b. Berakhot* 11b.
7. Psalms 89:3. See also *Genesis Rabbah* 8:5: "Lovingkindness says, 'He [i.e., Adam] should be created.'" It should be noted however that the words *"asher amar 'olam yibaneh"* ("which said the world should be created") are lacking in the original of *EA*, and would therefore appear to be a gloss of RZYH to his father's work. (See next note.)
8. *OR*, vol. 1, p. 239; *EA*, vol. 1, *Berakhot*, chap. 1, par. 160 (pp. 63-64). The text of *'Olat Re'iyah* differs from that of *'Eyn Ayah* (Rav Kook's commentary to *'Eyn Ya'akov*). Rav Kook's son, Rabbi Zevi Yehudah Hakohen Kook (1891-1982) adapted the section from *'Eyn Ayah* to the *Siddur*.

*Conversation is forbidden until after the* עמידה*. See table on pages 1315–1317.*

בָּרוּךְ אַתָּה יהוה אֱלֹהֵינוּ מֶלֶךְ הָעוֹלָם

יוֹצֵר אוֹר וּבוֹרֵא חֹשֶׁךְ

עֹשֶׂה שָׁלוֹם וּבוֹרֵא אֶת הַכֹּל.

ישעיה מה

---

יוֹצֵר אוֹר וּבוֹרֵא חֹשֶׁךְ, עֹשֶׂה שָׁלוֹם וּבוֹרֵא אֶת הַכֹּל *Who forms light and creates darkness, makes peace and creates all.* All philosophic systems must ultimately come to terms with the problem of evil. If God is good, then how does evil arise in this universe? The ancient Persian religion of Zoroastrianism was conveniently able to posit two opposite forces at work in the world: Ahura Mazda (or Hormazd, Hormuz),[3] the god of good and light, versus Ahriman, the god of evil and darkness. However, the Israelite prophet Isaiah railed against this dualistic perception of reality, upholding a strict monotheism, a single deity who "forms light and creates darkness, makes peace and creates evil; I am the Lord who does all this" (*"yotser 'or u-boré ḥoshekh, 'oseh shalom u-boré ra', ani Havayah 'oseh kol eleh"*).[4]

Evil has no existence independent of God. Ultimately, the evil in the world is authored by God. Judaism could not afford the dualism of the Persian prophet Zoroaster (or Zarathustra). In the simple, yet eloquent words of the Prophet Isaiah: "[The Lord] creates evil" (*"boré ra'"*).

In the morning prayer established by our Sages who postdated Isaiah, the Prophet's stark, shocking statement has been emended to read: "[The Lord] creates *all*" (*"boré et ha-kol"*).[5]

Rav Kook explains the difference between the Prophet Isaiah's formula and that instituted by the Sages in our prayer.

---

3. See *b. Gittin* 11a and *Tosafot* ad locum, s.v. *Hormin*; *b. Sanhedrin* 39a and *Tosafot* ad loc., s.v. *Hormiz*.
4. Isaiah 45:7. The passage occurs within the context of a prophecy to Cyrus, King of Persia.
5. Rabbi Reuben Margaliot suggested that the reason the Sages changed the formula of the verse by a single word from *"ra'"* to *"ha-kol,"* was to thereby circumvent the principle enunciated in the Talmud Yerushalmi that a blessing must not conclude with a verse from the Bible. *"Ein omrin berakha pasuk"* (*y. Berakhot* 1:5; *Ta'anit* 2:3 and *P'nei Moshe* there). See R. Margaliot, *Ha-Mikra ve-ha-Mesorah* (Jerusalem: Mossad Harav Kook, 1964), p. 49, n. 7. Cf. B. Naor, *Be-Mayim 'Azim Netivah* (n.p., 1988), *b. Yoma* 53b (pp. 9–10).

הַמֵּאִיר In compassion He gives light to the earth and its inhabitants,
and in His goodness continually renews the work of creation,
day after day.
How numerous are Your works, O LORD. Ps. 104
You made them all in wisdom.
The earth is full of Your creations.
He is the King exalted alone since the beginning of time –
praised, glorified and elevated since the world began.
Eternal God,
in Your great compassion, have compassion on us,
LORD of our strength, Rock of our refuge,
Shield of our salvation, You are our stronghold.

---

is superior to a prophet.")[9] Based on their theodicy, the Men of the Great Assembly actually surpassed the Prophets.[10]

הַמֵּאִיר לָאָרֶץ וְלַדָּרִים עָלֶיהָ בְּרַחֲמִים *In compassion He gives light to the Earth and its inhabitants.* The word *"be-raḥamim"* ("in compassion") seems strange in this context. What does it mean to illumine the Earth with compassion? What would it mean to illumine the earth without compassion?

Rabbi Joseph David Epstein, one of the great *Ba'alei ha-Mussar*, a disciple of Rabbi Yeruḥam Levovitz of Mir, explained this passage based on the latest findings of science. We now know that surrounding the earth is a layer of ozone that protects the Earth and Earth-dwellers from the rays of the sun. When there are tears in the ozone layer, allowing too much of the sun's rays to penetrate to the earth, there are deleterious results. For one, the incidence of skin cancer rises. Beyond that, there results the phenomenon of "global warming," with the concomitant "climate change."

---

9. *b. Bava Batra* 12b; Rabbi Judah Löw (Maharal) of Prague, *Gevurot Hashem*, First Introduction.

10. See *y. Berakhot* 7:3; *b. Yoma* 69b; Rabbi Isaac Hutner, *Paḥad Yitsḥak: Kuntres ve-Zot Ḥannukah, ma'amar 8.*
Rabbi Isaac Hutner was a disciple of Rav Kook during Rabbi Hutner's early years in Jerusalem. (However, Rabbi Ahron Soloveichik once communicated to this writer in private conversation that he felt it an inexactitude to use the term *"talmid"* [disciple] to describe Rabbi Hutner's relation to Rav Kook. Rabbi Hutner was the private teacher of Rabbi Ahron Soloveichik during the latter's youth in Warsaw.)

הַמֵּאִיר לָאָרֶץ וְלַדָּרִים עָלֶיהָ בְּרַחֲמִים
וּבְטוּבוֹ מְחַדֵּשׁ בְּכָל יוֹם תָּמִיד מַעֲשֵׂה בְרֵאשִׁית.
מָה־רַבּוּ מַעֲשֶׂיךָ יהוה תהלים קד
כֻּלָּם בְּחָכְמָה עָשִׂיתָ
מָלְאָה הָאָרֶץ קִנְיָנֶךָ:
הַמֶּלֶךְ הַמְרוֹמָם לְבַדּוֹ מֵאָז
הַמְשֻׁבָּח וְהַמְפֹאָר וְהַמִּתְנַשֵּׂא מִימוֹת עוֹלָם.
אֱלֹהֵי עוֹלָם
בְּרַחֲמֶיךָ הָרַבִּים רַחֵם עָלֵינוּ
אֲדוֹן עֻזֵּנוּ, צוּר מִשְׂגַּבֵּנוּ
מָגֵן יִשְׁעֵנוּ, מִשְׂגָּב בַּעֲדֵנוּ.

---

According to Rav Kook, the relation of the text of the prayer to that of the prophecy is exactly the reverse of what we have generally been led to believe. Most of us assume that Isaiah spoke truth itself and that the Rabbis, in formulating the prayer, "toned down," ameliorated or even censored that truth, substituting a euphemism "all" for Isaiah's unflinching "evil." Comes Rav Kook and tells us the exact opposite. The ultimate truth is that formulated by the Sages, the Men of the Great Assembly: In reality there is no evil. Once evil has been grasped as part of the totality of existence, it disappears from our vision. It was the Prophet Isaiah, who for the purposes of moral exhortation in combating philosophies that would deny pure monotheism, overstated the case for evil, couching reality in terms convenient to the common perception of man.

Although Rav Kook chalks the difference of the prophecy and the prayer to their varying objectives – moral exhortation versus singing the praises of God, who is ultimately a loving God – one is tempted to explain the difference in terms of the prophet's and sage's differing perceptions of reality. When confronted with the problem of evil, the purview of the Prophet is circumscribed; the Sages' grasp of reality is more comprehensive. At this point, one might invoke the famous maxim: *"Ḥakham 'adif mi-navi."* ("A sage

The blessed God, great in knowledge,
prepared and made the rays of the sun.
He who is good formed glory for His name,
surrounding His power with radiant stars.
The leaders of His hosts, the holy ones,
exalt the Almighty,
constantly proclaiming God's glory and holiness.
Be blessed, LORD our God,
for the magnificence of Your handiwork
and for the radiant lights You have made.
May they glorify You, Selah!

תִּתְבָּרַךְ May You be blessed,
our Rock, King and Redeemer, Creator of holy beings.
May Your name be praised for ever,
our King, Creator of the ministering angels,
all of whom stand in the universe's heights,
proclaiming together, in awe, aloud,
the words of the living God, the eternal King.
They are all beloved, all pure, all mighty,
and all perform in awe and reverence the will of their Maker.
▸ All open their mouths in holiness and purity,
with song and psalm,
and bless, praise, glorify,
revere, sanctify and declare the sovereignty of – ◂
the name of the great, mighty
and awesome God and King,
holy is He.

---

The divine "compassion" (*raḥamim*) in our context is an allusion to the protective sheath of ozone provided by the Creator to surround our planet.[11] (Editor)

11. Communicated by Rabbi Epstein zt"l to the Editor (BN) in private conversation.

אֵל בָּרוּךְ גְּדוֹל דֵּעָה, הֵכִין וּפָעַל זָהֳרֵי חַמָּה
טוֹב יָצַר כָּבוֹד לִשְׁמוֹ, מְאוֹרוֹת נָתַן סְבִיבוֹת עֻזּוֹ
פִּנּוֹת צְבָאָיו קְדוֹשִׁים, רוֹמְמֵי שַׁדַּי
תָּמִיד מְסַפְּרִים כְּבוֹד אֵל וּקְדֻשָּׁתוֹ.
תִּתְבָּרַךְ יהוה אֱלֹהֵינוּ
עַל שֶׁבַח מַעֲשֵׂה יָדֶיךָ.
וְעַל מְאוֹרֵי אוֹר שֶׁעָשִׂיתָ
יְפָאֲרוּךָ סֶּלָה.

תִּתְבָּרַךְ
צוּרֵנוּ מַלְכֵּנוּ וְגוֹאֲלֵנוּ, בּוֹרֵא קְדוֹשִׁים
יִשְׁתַּבַּח שִׁמְךָ לָעַד
מַלְכֵּנוּ, יוֹצֵר מְשָׁרְתִים
וַאֲשֶׁר מְשָׁרְתָיו כֻּלָּם עוֹמְדִים בְּרוּם עוֹלָם
וּמַשְׁמִיעִים בְּיִרְאָה יַחַד בְּקוֹל
דִּבְרֵי אֱלֹהִים חַיִּים וּמֶלֶךְ עוֹלָם.
כֻּלָּם אֲהוּבִים, כֻּלָּם בְּרוּרִים, כֻּלָּם גִּבּוֹרִים
וְכֻלָּם עוֹשִׂים בְּאֵימָה וּבְיִרְאָה רְצוֹן קוֹנָם
◄ וְכֻלָּם פּוֹתְחִים אֶת פִּיהֶם בִּקְדֻשָּׁה וּבְטָהֳרָה
בְּשִׁירָה וּבְזִמְרָה
וּמְבָרְכִים וּמְשַׁבְּחִים וּמְפָאֲרִים
◄ וּמַעֲרִיצִים וּמַקְדִּישִׁים וּמַמְלִיכִים
אֶת שֵׁם הָאֵל הַמֶּלֶךְ הַגָּדוֹל, הַגִּבּוֹר וְהַנּוֹרָא
קָדוֹשׁ הוּא.

▸ All accept on themselves, one from another,
the yoke of the kingdom of heaven,
granting permission to one another
to sanctify the One who formed them,
in serene spirit, pure speech and sweet melody.
All, as one, proclaim His holiness,
saying in awe:

*All say aloud:* Holy, holy, holy is the LORD of hosts; *Is. 6*
the whole world is filled with His glory.

▸ Then the Ophanim and the Holy Ḥayyot,
with a roar of noise,
raise themselves toward the Seraphim and,
facing them, give praise, saying:

*All say aloud:* Blessed is the LORD's glory from His place. *Ezek. 3*

לָאֵל To the blessed God they offer melodies.
To the King, living and eternal God,
they say psalms and proclaim praises.
For it is He alone
who does mighty deeds
and creates new things,
who is Master of battles,
and sows righteousness,
who makes salvation grow
and creates cures,
who is revered in praises,
LORD of wonders,
who in His goodness,
continually renews the work of creation, day after day,
as it is said,
"[Praise] Him who made the great lights, *Ps. 136*
for His love endures for ever."

◂ וְכֻלָּם מְקַבְּלִים עֲלֵיהֶם עֹל מַלְכוּת שָׁמַיִם זֶה מִזֶּה
וְנוֹתְנִים רְשׁוּת זֶה לָזֶה
לְהַקְדִּישׁ לְיוֹצְרָם בְּנַחַת רוּחַ
בְּשָׂפָה בְרוּרָה וּבִנְעִימָה
קְדֻשָּׁה כֻּלָּם כְּאֶחָד
עוֹנִים וְאוֹמְרִים בְּיִרְאָה

*All say aloud* קָדוֹשׁ, קָדוֹשׁ, קָדוֹשׁ יהוה צְבָאוֹת ישעיה ו
מְלֹא כָל־הָאָרֶץ כְּבוֹדוֹ:

◂ וְהָאוֹפַנִּים וְחַיּוֹת הַקֹּדֶשׁ
בְּרַעַשׁ גָּדוֹל מִתְנַשְּׂאִים לְעֻמַּת שְׂרָפִים
לְעֻמָּתָם מְשַׁבְּחִים וְאוֹמְרִים

*All say aloud* בָּרוּךְ כְּבוֹד־יהוה מִמְּקוֹמוֹ: יחזקאל ג

לָאֵל בָּרוּךְ נְעִימוֹת יִתֵּנוּ
לַמֶּלֶךְ אֵל חַי וְקַיָּם
זְמִירוֹת יֹאמֵרוּ וְתִשְׁבָּחוֹת יַשְׁמִיעוּ
כִּי הוּא לְבַדּוֹ
פּוֹעֵל גְּבוּרוֹת, עוֹשֶׂה חֲדָשׁוֹת
בַּעַל מִלְחָמוֹת, זוֹרֵעַ צְדָקוֹת
מַצְמִיחַ יְשׁוּעוֹת, בּוֹרֵא רְפוּאוֹת
נוֹרָא תְהִלּוֹת, אֲדוֹן הַנִּפְלָאוֹת
הַמְחַדֵּשׁ בְּטוּבוֹ בְּכָל יוֹם תָּמִיד מַעֲשֵׂה בְרֵאשִׁית
כָּאָמוּר
לְעֹשֵׂה אוֹרִים גְּדֹלִים, כִּי לְעוֹלָם חַסְדּוֹ: תהלים קלו

▸ May You make a new light shine over Zion,
and may we all soon be worthy of its light.
Blessed are You, Lord, who forms the radiant lights.

אַהֲבָה You have loved us with great love, Lord our God,
and with surpassing compassion
have You had compassion on us.
Our Father, our King,
for the sake of our ancestors who trusted in You,
and to whom You taught the laws of life,
be gracious also to us and teach us.
Our Father, compassionate Father, ever compassionate,
have compassion on us.
Instill in our hearts
the desire to understand and discern,
to listen, learn and teach,
to observe, perform and fulfill
all the teachings of Your Torah in love.
Enlighten our eyes in Your Torah
and let our hearts cling to Your commandments.
Unite our hearts to love and revere Your name,
so that we may never be ashamed.
And because we have trusted in Your holy, great and revered name,
may we be glad and rejoice in Your salvation.

---

through the receptacle, through the "vessels" (*kelim*) and the worlds, is but a reflection of the true reality. We are longing for the revelation of a new light, at which time the moon will be equal to the sun in spiritual stature, and the vessels of this world, rather than distort the light, will be able to manifest it in its fullness. Then, "all of us" (*"khulanu"*) – even those of us who, bereft of *ru'aḥ ha-kodesh* (divine inspiration), apprehend the divinity only through the worlds – will merit to see the light.[13]

---

13. *OR*, vol. 1, p. 241; *MRIT*, p. 514.

אוֹר חָדָשׁ עַל צִיּוֹן תָּאִיר וְנִזְכֶּה כֻלָּנוּ מְהֵרָה לְאוֹרוֹ.
בָּרוּךְ אַתָּה יהוה, יוֹצֵר הַמְּאוֹרוֹת.

אַהֲבָה רַבָּה אֲהַבְתָּנוּ, יהוה אֱלֹהֵינוּ
חֶמְלָה גְדוֹלָה וִיתֵרָה חָמַלְתָּ עָלֵינוּ.
אָבִינוּ מַלְכֵּנוּ
בַּעֲבוּר אֲבוֹתֵינוּ שֶׁבָּטְחוּ בְךָ, וַתְּלַמְּדֵם חֻקֵּי חַיִּים
כֵּן תְּחָנֵּנוּ וּתְלַמְּדֵנוּ.
אָבִינוּ, הָאָב הָרַחֲמָן, הַמְרַחֵם
רַחֵם עָלֵינוּ
וְתֵן בְּלִבֵּנוּ לְהָבִין וּלְהַשְׂכִּיל
לִשְׁמֹעַ, לִלְמֹד וּלְלַמֵּד, לִשְׁמֹר וְלַעֲשׂוֹת, וּלְקַיֵּם
אֶת כָּל דִּבְרֵי תַלְמוּד תּוֹרָתֶךָ בְּאַהֲבָה.
וְהָאֵר עֵינֵינוּ בְּתוֹרָתֶךָ, וְדַבֵּק לִבֵּנוּ בְּמִצְוֹתֶיךָ
וְיַחֵד לְבָבֵנוּ לְאַהֲבָה וּלְיִרְאָה אֶת שְׁמֶךָ
וְלֹא נֵבוֹשׁ לְעוֹלָם וָעֶד.
כִּי בְשֵׁם קָדְשְׁךָ הַגָּדוֹל וְהַנּוֹרָא בָּטָחְנוּ
נָגִילָה וְנִשְׂמְחָה בִּישׁוּעָתֶךָ.

---

אוֹר חָדָשׁ עַל צִיּוֹן תָּאִיר וְנִזְכֶּה כֻלָּנוּ מְהֵרָה לְאוֹרוֹ. בָּרוּךְ אַתָּה יהוה, יוֹצֵר הַמְּאוֹרוֹת *May You make a new light shine over Zion, and may we all soon be worthy of its light. Blessed are You, Lord, who forms the radiant lights* (ha-me'orot). *"Ha-Me'orot,"* the two luminaries, refer to the sun and the moon.[12] The sun represents the true reality. The moon, which has no light of its own but merely reflects the light of the sun, represents our diminished reality. Reality as perceived

---

12. Rav Kook references Rabbi Moses Cordovero, *Shi'ur Komah* (Warsaw, 1883), chap. 3 (*"Me'orot"*), 5b.

*At this point, gather the four tzitziot of the tallit, holding them in the left hand.*

Bring us back in peace from the four quarters of the earth
and lead us upright to our land.
▸ For You are a God who performs acts of salvation,
and You chose us from all peoples and tongues,
bringing us close to Your great name for ever in truth,
that we may thank You and proclaim Your Oneness in love.
Blessed are You, Lord, who chooses His people Israel in love.

*The Shema must be said with intense concentration. In the first paragraph one should accept, with love, the sovereignty of God; in the second, the mitzvot as the will of God. The end of the third paragraph constitutes fulfillment of the mitzva to remember, morning and evening, the exodus from Egypt. See laws 346–355.*

*When not praying with a minyan, say:*

God, faithful King!

*The following verse should be said aloud, while covering the eyes with the right hand:*

**Listen, Israel: the Lord is our God, the Lord is One.** *Deut. 6*

*Quietly:* Blessed be the name of His glorious kingdom for ever and all time.

---

*is one.* We stretch out the *dalet*, the final letter of the word *Eḥad.*[15] But in doing so, we are cautioned not to elide the preceding letter *ḥet.*[16]

In the Talmud there is an anecdote:

> Rabbi Jeremiah was sitting before Rabbi Ḥiyya bar Abba. He saw that he was lengthening overly much [the word *Eḥad*]. He said to him: "Once you've established Him as King above and below and to the four directions, you needn't more." [17]

---

15. *b. Berakhot* 13b.
    This is possible only if one pronounces the letter properly as a *dalet rafah* or soft consonant, whereby it sounds like *th* in the English word "the." If one pronounces it improperly as a *dalet degushah* or hard consonant, with the sound "d," it is of course impossible to draw out the sound. In phonetics "th" would be termed a continuant; "d," an oral stop or plosive consonant. Thus, properly pronounced the word is *Eḥadh*, not *Eḥad.*
16. *b. Berakhot* 13b.
17. *Ibid.*

*At this point, gather the four* ציציות *of the* טלית*, holding them in the left hand.*

וַהֲבִיאֵנוּ לְשָׁלוֹם מֵאַרְבַּע כַּנְפוֹת הָאָרֶץ
וְתוֹלִיכֵנוּ קוֹמְמִיּוּת לְאַרְצֵנוּ.
◂ כִּי אֵל פּוֹעֵל יְשׁוּעוֹת אָתָּה
וּבָנוּ בָחַרְתָּ מִכָּל עַם וְלָשׁוֹן
וְקֵרַבְתָּנוּ לְשִׁמְךָ הַגָּדוֹל סֶלָה, בֶּאֱמֶת
לְהוֹדוֹת לְךָ וּלְיַחֶדְךָ בְּאַהֲבָה.
בָּרוּךְ אַתָּה יהוה, הַבּוֹחֵר בְּעַמּוֹ יִשְׂרָאֵל בְּאַהֲבָה.

*The* שמע *must be said with intense concentration. In the first paragraph one should accept, with love, the sovereignty of God; in the second, the* מצוות *as the will of God. The end of the third paragraph constitutes fulfillment of the* מצווה *to remember, morning and evening, the exodus from Egypt. See laws 346–355.*

*When not praying with a* מנין*, say:*

אֵל מֶלֶךְ נֶאֱמָן

*The following verse should be said aloud, while covering the eyes with the right hand:*

דברים ו **שְׁמַע יִשְׂרָאֵל, יהוה אֱלֹהֵינוּ, יהוה ׀ אֶחָד:**

*Quietly* בָּרוּךְ שֵׁם כְּבוֹד מַלְכוּתוֹ לְעוֹלָם וָעֶד.

---

וְתוֹלִיכֵנוּ קוֹמְמִיּוּת לְאַרְצֵנוּ *And lead us upright to our Land.* Rabbi Ḥayyim Uri Lipschitz, a native of Jerusalem who lived most of his mature life as an exile in America, returning to Jerusalem in old age, used to interpret this prayer with reference to the saying of the Sages that the righteous who are buried outside the Land of Israel, "the Holy One, blessed be He, makes for them underground tunnels (*meḥilot*)," and their bones roll through them until they arrive in the Land of Israel.[14] Rabbi Lipschitz understood this prayer to be a request that we merit to go to the Land of Israel while yet we live, standing upright (*komemiyut*), rather than lying down, going through *gilgul meḥilot*.

שְׁמַע יִשְׂרָאֵל, יהוה אֱלֹהֵינוּ, יהוה אֶחָד *Listen, Israel: The Lord is our God, the Lord*

---

14. *y. Kil'ayim* 9:3; *Genesis Rabbah* 96:5. Cf. *b. Ketubot* 111a.

children, speaking of them when you sit at home and when you travel on the way, when you lie down and when you rise. °Bind them as a sign on your hand, and °°they shall be an emblem between your eyes. Write them on the doorposts of your house and gates.

---

a vessel and be limited thereby. Neither could the vessel support the light. Therefore, the *neshamah* is referred to by the appellation *"me'od"* ("very"), which indicates its superabundance.[29]

Associated with these three levels of our personality are three levels of love, from the most basic to the most supreme. That which *nefesh* cannot abide, *ru'aḥ* can abide; and that which even *ru'aḥ* cannot tolerate, *neshamah* can tolerate.

Rav Kook provides a medical example. If a person must undergo a physically painful medical procedure, the *nefesh*, the body, instinctively resists. But this resistance can be overcome by the *ru'aḥ* (or *lev*) which is synonymous with free will (*ratson*).[30] The *ru'aḥ* decides that it is in the best interest of the person to have the procedure done, painful though it be, and overrules the immediate "knee jerk response" of the *nefesh*.

But what happens when the events befalling a person appeal to neither body (*nefesh*) nor rational choice (*ru'aḥ*)? How is a person to accept

---

29. *OR*, vol. 1, p. 250. Rav Kook's description of the level of *neshamah* as being extracorporeal is in line with the teachings of Rabbi Ḥayyim of Volozhin (and of his master the Vilna Gaon). See Rabbi Ḥayyim of Volozhin, *Nefesh ha-Ḥayyim* I, 15:

> The *neshamah*... Its essence does not flow and is not revealed within man, for it dwells on high, within His mouth, as it were. Except that it bestows understanding in sparks of light upon him; to enlighten him with the depths of the mysteries of the holy Torah. And that which is written in the *Zohar* and the Kabbalists, of blessed memory, that the residence of the *neshamah* is in the brain of man – their intention is the sparks of light that enlighten his brain and intellect, not the real essence of the *neshamah*.

This teaching was received from the Vilna Gaon, who writes that the *neshamah* is outside the body. See the sources quoted in Yosef Avivi, *Kabbalat ha-Gra* (Jerusalem, 1993), pp. 42–44; and Esther Eisenman, "The Structure and Content of Rabbi Ḥayyim Volozhin's *Nefesh ha-Ḥayyim*" (Hebrew), in *The Vilna Gaon and his Disciples*, eds. Ḥallamish, Rivlin and Shuchat (Ramat-Gan: Bar-Ilan University Press, 2003), pp. 192–193.

See now Rabbi Ḥayyim Ya'akov Levene (a disciple of Rav Kook), *Yeshurun*, vol. 30 (Nissan 5774/2014), p. 521, s.v. *ha-neshamah – tagin*.

30. For *ru'aḥ* (spirit) as a synonym of *ratson* (will), see Maimonides, *Guide of the Perplexed* I, 40.

וְשִׁנַּנְתָּם לְבָנֶיךָ וְדִבַּרְתָּ בָּם, בְּשִׁבְתְּךָ בְּבֵיתֶךָ וּבְלֶכְתְּךָ בַדֶּרֶךְ, וּבְשָׁכְבְּךָ וּבְקוּמֶךָ: °וּקְשַׁרְתָּם לְאוֹת עַל־יָדֶךָ °°וְהָיוּ לְטֹטָפֹת בֵּין עֵינֶיךָ: וּכְתַבְתָּם עַל־מְזֻזוֹת בֵּיתֶךָ וּבִשְׁעָרֶיךָ:

---

וְאָהַבְתָּ אֵת יהוה אֱלֹהֶיךָ, בְּכָל־לְבָבְךָ וּבְכָל־נַפְשְׁךָ וּבְכָל־מְאֹדֶךָ *Love the* Lord *your God with all your heart* (lev)*, with all your soul* (nefesh)*, and with all your might* (me'od) *(previous page)*. Based on the tripartite psychology of the Kabbalah, the soul of man is divided into three levels: *nefesh* (body or basic biology), *ru'aḥ* (spirit) and *neshamah* (soul).[24] Traditionally, the *nefesh* resides in the liver which is composed of blood. As Scripture says, "For the blood is the *nefesh*."[25] The *ru'aḥ* or spirit, which is the centerpiece of our personality, the essence of our humanity, resides in the heart.[26] (Inasmuch as the *ru'aḥ* is central, "through it the *nefesh* is uplifted, and the light of the *neshamah* is drawn down.")[27] The two lower levels of *nefesh* and *ru'aḥ* reside within man's body and are limited thereby.

As for the highest of the three levels, *neshamah* or soul (generally associated with the brain),[28] Rav Kook adopts the position that the *neshamah* is truly out-of-body.

> The *neshamah* cannot possibly enter entirely into the body, but from the *neshamah* is illuminated the intellect (*sekhel*), which is felt in the body. On account of its magnitude, it is not possible for the *neshamah* to enter into

---

See further Rabbi Shneur Zalman of Liadi, *Tanya* II, 1, 7; Rabbi Ḥayyim of Volozhin, *Nefesh ha-Ḥayyim* III, 6, 11 (note); *SK* 7:11.

24. See Rabbi Ḥayyim of Volozhin, *Nefesh ha-Ḥayyim* I, 14.
25. Deuteronomy 12:23.
26. Rav Kook writes:

    > The heart is the dwelling place of the *ru'aḥ*, and the root of free will and the beginning of its foundation is the aspect of *ru'aḥ*, which is the level of man (*she-hu madregat ha-adam*). (*OR*, vol. 1, p. 249)

    For the centrality of the *ru'aḥ* in human psychology, see *Likkutei ha-Gra* published at the conclusion to *Be'ur ha-Gra* to *Sifra di-Tseni'uta*, s.v. *'inyan ha-levushim she-na'asim mi-yemei ha-adam*: "Just as the heart is the main part of man, so too the *ru'aḥ*." There, man is advised to live in the present (the *ru'aḥ*), and not dwell on the past (the *neshamah*) or obsess over the future (the *nefesh*). See also Rabbi David Tevel of Minsk (disciple of Rabbi Ḥayyim of Volozhin), *Derashot Beit David*, ed. Rabbi David Naḥman Rubinstein (Jerusalem: Mossad Harav Kook, 2015), *derush* 1 (pp. 11–13).
27. Evidently, Rav Kook reasons that because of the centrality of *ru'aḥ* to the personality, *lev* precedes in the verse both the lower *nefesh* and the higher *me'od* (*neshamah*).
28. See e.g. the Long Commentary of Abraham ibn Ezra to Exodus 23:25.

*Touch the hand-tefillin at ° and the head-tefillin at °°.*

וְהָיָה If you indeed heed My commandments with which I charge you today, to love the LORD your God and worship Him with all your heart and with all your soul, I will give rain in your land in its season, the early and late rain; and you shall gather in your grain, wine and oil. I will give grass in your field for your cattle, and you shall eat and be satisfied. Be careful lest your heart be tempted and you go astray and worship other gods, bowing down to them. Then the LORD's anger will flare against you and He will close the heavens so that there will be no rain. The land will not yield its crops, and you will perish swiftly from the good land that the LORD is giving you. Therefore, set these, My words, on your heart and soul. °Bind them as a sign on your hand, °°and they shall be an emblem between your eyes. Teach them to your children, speaking of them when you sit at home and when you travel on the way, when you lie down and when you rise. Write them on the doorposts of your house and gates, so that you and your children may live long in the land that the LORD swore to your ancestors to give them, for as long as the heavens are above the earth. *Deut. 11*

*Hold the tzitziot in the right hand also (some transfer to the right hand), kissing them at °.*

וַיֹּאמֶר The LORD spoke to Moses, saying: Speak to the Israelites and tell them to make °tassels on the corners of their garments for all generations. They shall attach to the °tassel at each corner a thread of blue. This shall be your °tassel, and you shall see it and remember all of the LORD's commandments and keep them, not straying after your heart and after your eyes, following your own sinful desires. Thus you will be reminded to keep all My *Num. 15*

---

The love of God must confront things whose final good is inconceivable… and this cannot be processed by the level of will or *ru'aḥ*. Only by *me'od*, which is the *neshamah*, can this love come about… by virtue of the higher intellect.[32]

32. *OR*, vol. 1, p. 250.

*Touch the* תפילין של יד *at* ° *and the* תפילין של ראש *at* °°.

וְהָיָה אִם־שָׁמֹעַ תִּשְׁמְעוּ אֶל־מִצְוֺתַי אֲשֶׁר אָנֹכִי מְצַוֶּה אֶתְכֶם דברים יא
הַיּוֹם, לְאַהֲבָה אֶת־יהוה אֱלֹהֵיכֶם וּלְעָבְדוֹ, בְּכָל־לְבַבְכֶם וּבְכָל־
נַפְשְׁכֶם: וְנָתַתִּי מְטַר־אַרְצְכֶם בְּעִתּוֹ, יוֹרֶה וּמַלְקוֹשׁ, וְאָסַפְתָּ
דְגָנֶךָ וְתִירֹשְׁךָ וְיִצְהָרֶךָ: וְנָתַתִּי עֵשֶׂב בְּשָׂדְךָ לִבְהֶמְתֶּךָ, וְאָכַלְתָּ
וְשָׂבָעְתָּ: הִשָּׁמְרוּ לָכֶם פֶּן־יִפְתֶּה לְבַבְכֶם, וְסַרְתֶּם וַעֲבַדְתֶּם
אֱלֹהִים אֲחֵרִים וְהִשְׁתַּחֲוִיתֶם לָהֶם: וְחָרָה אַף־יהוה בָּכֶם, וְעָצַר
אֶת־הַשָּׁמַיִם וְלֹא־יִהְיֶה מָטָר, וְהָאֲדָמָה לֹא תִתֵּן אֶת־יְבוּלָהּ,
וַאֲבַדְתֶּם מְהֵרָה מֵעַל הָאָרֶץ הַטֹּבָה אֲשֶׁר יהוה נֹתֵן לָכֶם:
וְשַׂמְתֶּם אֶת־דְּבָרַי אֵלֶּה עַל־לְבַבְכֶם וְעַל־נַפְשְׁכֶם, °וּקְשַׁרְתֶּם
אֹתָם לְאוֹת עַל־יֶדְכֶם, °°וְהָיוּ לְטוֹטָפֹת בֵּין עֵינֵיכֶם: וְלִמַּדְתֶּם
אֹתָם אֶת־בְּנֵיכֶם לְדַבֵּר בָּם, בְּשִׁבְתְּךָ בְּבֵיתֶךָ וּבְלֶכְתְּךָ בַדֶּרֶךְ,
וּבְשָׁכְבְּךָ וּבְקוּמֶךָ: וּכְתַבְתָּם עַל־מְזוּזוֹת בֵּיתֶךָ וּבִשְׁעָרֶיךָ: לְמַעַן
יִרְבּוּ יְמֵיכֶם וִימֵי בְנֵיכֶם עַל הָאֲדָמָה אֲשֶׁר נִשְׁבַּע יהוה לַאֲבֹתֵיכֶם
לָתֵת לָהֶם, כִּימֵי הַשָּׁמַיִם עַל־הָאָרֶץ:

*Hold the* ציציות *in the right hand also (some transfer to the right hand), kissing them at* °.

וַיֹּאמֶר יהוה אֶל־מֹשֶׁה לֵּאמֹר: דַּבֵּר אֶל־בְּנֵי יִשְׂרָאֵל וְאָמַרְתָּ במדבר טו
אֲלֵהֶם, וְעָשׂוּ לָהֶם °צִיצִת עַל־כַּנְפֵי בִגְדֵיהֶם לְדֹרֹתָם, וְנָתְנוּ
°עַל־צִיצִת הַכָּנָף פְּתִיל תְּכֵלֶת: וְהָיָה לָכֶם °לְצִיצִת, וּרְאִיתֶם
אֹתוֹ וּזְכַרְתֶּם אֶת־כָּל־מִצְוֺת יהוה וַעֲשִׂיתֶם אֹתָם, וְלֹא תָתֻרוּ
אַחֲרֵי לְבַבְכֶם וְאַחֲרֵי עֵינֵיכֶם, אֲשֶׁר־אַתֶּם זֹנִים אַחֲרֵיהֶם: לְמַעַן

---

adversity; to lovingly embrace vicissitudes? That is where the highest level of *neshamah* comes in. This is the rabbinic reading of *"Be-khol me'odekha"* – *"be-khol middah u-middah she-moded lekha."* "With every measure that He measures out to you."[31]

---

31. *m. Berakhot* 9:5; *b. Berakhot* 54a.

commandments, and be holy to your God. I am the LORD your God, who brought you out of the land of Egypt to be your God. I am the LORD your God.

°True –

*The Leader repeats:*

▸ The LORD your God is true –

וְיַצִּיב And firm, established and enduring, right, faithful,
beloved, cherished, delightful, pleasant,
awesome, mighty, perfect, accepted,
good and beautiful
is this faith for us for ever.

True is the eternal God, our King,
Rock of Jacob, Shield of our salvation.
He exists and His name exists
through all generations.
His throne is established,
His kingship and faithfulness endure for ever.

*At °, kiss the tzitziot and release them.*

His words live and persist, faithful and desirable
°for ever and all time.
▸ So they were for our ancestors, so they are for us,
and so they will be for our children
and all our generations and for all future generations
of the seed of Israel, Your servants. ◂

---

flashes of lightning. By night, with its murkiness, we must rely upon faith. The truth be told, not only during the night, but sometimes even during the day, the domain of reason, we must be guided by faith. This is alluded to by the fact that the moon, symbol of faith, is sometimes visible by day. As the Holy One, blessed be He, instructed the Moon: "Go rule by day and by night."[34]

34. *b. Ḥullin* 60b. See above commentary to "*U-se'ir 'izim eḥad, le-ḥat'at la-Hashem*" (*OR*, vol. 1, pp. 165–166).
*OR*, vol. 1, pp. 253–254 = *EA*, vol. 1, chap. 1, par. 164 (p. 65).

תִּזְכְּרוּ וַעֲשִׂיתֶם אֶת־כָּל־מִצְוֺתָי, וִהְיִיתֶם קְדֹשִׁים לֵאלֹהֵיכֶם: אֲנִי יהוה אֱלֹהֵיכֶם, אֲשֶׁר הוֹצֵאתִי אֶתְכֶם מֵאֶרֶץ מִצְרַיִם, לִהְיוֹת לָכֶם לֵאלֹהִים, אֲנִי יהוה אֱלֹהֵיכֶם:

אֱמֶת°

*The* שליח ציבור *repeats:*

◂ יהוה אֱלֹהֵיכֶם אֱמֶת

וְיַצִּיב, וְנָכוֹן וְקַיָּם, וְיָשָׁר וְנֶאֱמָן
וְאָהוּב וְחָבִיב, וְנֶחְמָד וְנָעִים
וְנוֹרָא וְאַדִּיר, וּמְתֻקָּן וּמְקֻבָּל, וְטוֹב וְיָפֶה
הַדָּבָר הַזֶּה עָלֵינוּ לְעוֹלָם וָעֶד.
אֱמֶת אֱלֹהֵי עוֹלָם מַלְכֵּנוּ
צוּר יַעֲקֹב מָגֵן יִשְׁעֵנוּ
לְדוֹר וָדוֹר הוּא קַיָּם וּשְׁמוֹ קַיָּם
וְכִסְאוֹ נָכוֹן
וּמַלְכוּתוֹ וֶאֱמוּנָתוֹ לָעַד קַיָּמֶת.

*At °, kiss the* ציציות *and release them.*

וּדְבָרָיו חָיִים וְקַיָּמִים, נֶאֱמָנִים וְנֶחֱמָדִים
°לָעַד וּלְעוֹלְמֵי עוֹלָמִים
◂ עַל אֲבוֹתֵינוּ וְעָלֵינוּ, עַל בָּנֵינוּ וְעַל דּוֹרוֹתֵינוּ
וְעַל כָּל דּוֹרוֹת זֶרַע יִשְׂרָאֵל עֲבָדֶיךָ. ◂

---

**אֱמֶת וְיַצִּיב** *True and firm.* By day we say *"Emet ve-yatsiv"* ("True and firm") and by night we say *"Emet ve-emunah"* ("True and faithful").[33] The day, with its clarity, symbolizes those rare moments when we humans are privileged to know the truth by rational means. But as Maimonides illustrated in the Introduction to the *Guide,* those moments of lucidity might be likened to fleeting

---

33. *b. Berakhot* 12a.

For the early and the later generations
this faith has proved good and enduring for ever –

True and faithful, an irrevocable law.

True You are the LORD: our God and God of our ancestors,
▸ our King and King of our ancestors,
our Redeemer and Redeemer of our ancestors,
our Maker, Rock of our salvation,
our Deliverer and Rescuer:
this has ever been Your name.
There is no God but You.

עֶזְרַת You have always been the help of our ancestors,
Shield and Savior of their children after them
in every generation.
Your dwelling is in the heights of the universe,
and Your judgments and righteousness
reach to the ends of the earth.

Happy is the one who obeys Your commandments
and takes to heart Your teaching and Your word.

True You are the Master of Your people
and a mighty King who pleads their cause.

True You are the first and You are the last.
Besides You, we have no king, redeemer or savior.
From Egypt You redeemed us,
LORD our God,
and from the slave-house You delivered us.
All their firstborn You killed,
but Your firstborn You redeemed.
You split the Sea of Reeds
and drowned the arrogant.
You brought Your beloved ones across.
The water covered their foes; *Ps. 106*
not one of them was left.

עַל הָרִאשׁוֹנִים וְעַל הָאַחֲרוֹנִים
דָּבָר טוֹב וְקַיָּם לְעוֹלָם וָעֶד

אֱמֶת וֶאֱמוּנָה, חֹק וְלֹא יַעֲבֹר.

אֱמֶת שָׁאַתָּה הוּא יהוה אֱלֹהֵינוּ וֵאלֹהֵי אֲבוֹתֵינוּ
◂ מַלְכֵּנוּ מֶלֶךְ אֲבוֹתֵינוּ
גּוֹאֲלֵנוּ גּוֹאֵל אֲבוֹתֵינוּ
יוֹצְרֵנוּ צוּר יְשׁוּעָתֵנוּ
פּוֹדֵנוּ וּמַצִּילֵנוּ מֵעוֹלָם שְׁמֶךָ
אֵין אֱלֹהִים זוּלָתֶךָ.

עֶזְרַת אֲבוֹתֵינוּ אַתָּה הוּא מֵעוֹלָם
מָגֵן וּמוֹשִׁיעַ לִבְנֵיהֶם אַחֲרֵיהֶם בְּכָל דּוֹר וָדוֹר.
בְּרוּם עוֹלָם מוֹשָׁבֶךָ, וּמִשְׁפָּטֶיךָ וְצִדְקָתְךָ עַד אַפְסֵי אָרֶץ.
אַשְׁרֵי אִישׁ שֶׁיִּשְׁמַע לְמִצְוֹתֶיךָ
וְתוֹרָתְךָ וּדְבָרְךָ יָשִׂים עַל לִבּוֹ.

אֱמֶת אַתָּה הוּא אָדוֹן לְעַמֶּךָ
וּמֶלֶךְ גִּבּוֹר לָרִיב רִיבָם.

אֱמֶת אַתָּה הוּא רִאשׁוֹן וְאַתָּה הוּא אַחֲרוֹן
וּמִבַּלְעָדֶיךָ אֵין לָנוּ מֶלֶךְ גּוֹאֵל וּמוֹשִׁיעַ.
מִמִּצְרַיִם גְּאַלְתָּנוּ, יהוה אֱלֹהֵינוּ
וּמִבֵּית עֲבָדִים פְּדִיתָנוּ
כָּל בְּכוֹרֵיהֶם הָרָגְתָּ, וּבְכוֹרְךָ גָּאָלְתָּ
וְיַם סוּף בָּקַעְתָּ, וְזֵדִים טִבַּעְתָּ, וִידִידִים הֶעֱבַרְתָּ
וַיְכַסּוּ־מַיִם צָרֵיהֶם, אֶחָד מֵהֶם לֹא נוֹתָר: תהלים קו

For this, the beloved ones praised and exalted God,
the cherished ones sang psalms, songs and praises,
blessings and thanksgivings to the King,
the living and enduring God.
High and exalted, great and awesome,
He humbles the haughty
and raises the lowly,
freeing captives
and redeeming those in need,
helping the poor
and answering His people when they cry out to Him.

*Stand in preparation for the Amida.*
*Take three steps back before beginning the Amida.*

▸ Praises to God Most High, the Blessed One who is blessed.
Moses and the children of Israel
recited to You a song with great joy,
and they all exclaimed:
"Who is like You, LORD, among the mighty? *Ex. 15*
Who is like You, majestic in holiness,
awesome in praises, doing wonders?"
▸ With a new song, the redeemed people praised
Your name at the seashore.
Together they all gave thanks,
proclaimed Your kingship,
and declared:
"The LORD shall reign for ever and ever." *Ibid.*

*Congregants should end the following blessing together with the Leader so as to be able to move directly from the words "redeemed Israel" to the Amida, without the interruption of saying Amen.*

▸ צוּר יִשְׂרָאֵל Rock of Israel! Arise to the help of Israel.
Deliver, as You promised, Judah and Israel.
Our Redeemer, the LORD of hosts is His name, *Is. 47*
the Holy One of Israel.
Blessed are You, LORD, who redeemed Israel.

*The service continues on page 174.*

עַל זֹאת שִׁבְּחוּ אֲהוּבִים, וְרוֹמְמוּ אֵל
וְנָתְנוּ יְדִידִים זְמִירוֹת, שִׁירוֹת וְתִשְׁבָּחוֹת
בְּרָכוֹת וְהוֹדָאוֹת לַמֶּלֶךְ אֵל חַי וְקַיָּם
רָם וְנִשָּׂא, גָּדוֹל וְנוֹרָא
מַשְׁפִּיל גֵּאִים וּמַגְבִּיהַּ שְׁפָלִים
מוֹצִיא אֲסִירִים, וּפוֹדֶה עֲנָוִים וְעוֹזֵר דַּלִּים
וְעוֹנֶה לְעַמּוֹ בְּעֵת שַׁוְּעָם אֵלָיו.

*Stand in preparation for the* עמידה. *Take three steps back before beginning the* עמידה.

◂ תְּהִלּוֹת לְאֵל עֶלְיוֹן, בָּרוּךְ הוּא וּמְבֹרָךְ
מֹשֶׁה וּבְנֵי יִשְׂרָאֵל
לְךָ עָנוּ שִׁירָה בְּשִׂמְחָה רַבָּה
וְאָמְרוּ כֻלָּם
שמות טו מִי־כָמֹכָה בָּאֵלִם, יהוה
מִי כָּמֹכָה נֶאְדָּר בַּקֹּדֶשׁ, נוֹרָא תְהִלֹּת, עֹשֵׂה פֶלֶא:
◂ שִׁירָה חֲדָשָׁה שִׁבְּחוּ גְאוּלִים
לְשִׁמְךָ עַל שְׂפַת הַיָּם
יַחַד כֻּלָּם הוֹדוּ וְהִמְלִיכוּ
וְאָמְרוּ
שם יהוה יִמְלֹךְ לְעֹלָם וָעֶד:

*The* קהל *should end the following blessing together with the* שליח ציבור *so as to be able to move directly from the words* גָּאַל יִשְׂרָאֵל *to the* עמידה, *without the interruption of saying* אמן.

◂ צוּר יִשְׂרָאֵל, קוּמָה בְּעֶזְרַת יִשְׂרָאֵל
וּפְדֵה כִנְאֻמֶךָ יְהוּדָה וְיִשְׂרָאֵל.
ישעיה מז גֹּאֲלֵנוּ יהוה צְבָאוֹת שְׁמוֹ, קְדוֹשׁ יִשְׂרָאֵל:
בָּרוּךְ אַתָּה יהוה, גָּאַל יִשְׂרָאֵל.

*The service continues on page 175.*

need-awareness. On the higher niveau there is no feeling of lack and thus prayer is inappropriate. One must go down to the depths, which are also the depths of understanding, much deeper than surface understanding. Since lacks exist, and mankind – collective and individual – suffer so from them, one must deepen one's understanding beyond that feeling that causes one to be oblivious to all deficiencies.[5]

*

> And said Rabbi Yosé bar Ḥanina in the name of Rabbi Eliezer ben Ya'akov: "One who prays must adjust his feet [i.e. put his feet together], for it says, 'Their feet were a straight foot.'"[6]

The feet serve two functions: walking and standing. In order to walk, the legs must part from one another; standing, one's legs may very well be joined. In walking, one advances to a new destination; in standing, one solidifies one's attainments. These two very different activities – the dynamic of walking and the holding pattern of standing – are alluded to by the Psalmist: "Who shall ascend the mountain of the LORD and who shall stand in His holy place?"[7]

Torah is synonymous with walking.[8] In the pursuit of Torah knowledge, one must constantly advance; if not, one stultifies. "He who does not add, shall perish."[9]

Prayer, on the other hand, is synonymous with standing. The prayer posture of standing with feet together is derived from the angels, whose "feet are a straight foot." The angels are referred to as "standing": "I shall give you places to walk among these who are standing."[10]

Prayer is an activity vastly different from learning Torah. In the course of Torah study, the thoughts race ahead; in prayer, the thoughts are settled. (One could almost say that they are stationary.)[11]

> Torah will forever give man intellectual apprehensions that constantly flow anew... Prayer engages not in dispensing new information and enrichment of man's intellect, but rather in the utilization of old, established information, and in deepening – through emotion – the effect of those ethics upon the soul-powers.[12]

5. *OR*, vol. 1, p. 259 = *EA*, vol. 1, *Berakhot*, chap. 1, par. 152 (p. 61).
6. Ezekiel 1:7; *b. Berakhot* 10b.
7. Psalms 24:3.
8. The very term for Jewish Law, *"Halakhah,"* means literally "walking."
9. *m. Avot* 1:13.
10 . Zechariah 3:7.
11. *OR*, vol. 1, p. 262 = *EA*, vol. 1, *Berakhot*, chap. 1, par. 153 (p. 61).
12. *'Eyn Ayah* to *Shabbat* 10a (*EA*, vol. 3, chap. 1, par. 6; p. 3); transcribed in RZYH's preface to the Prayer Book, "*'Inyenei Tefillah*" 3:3 (*OR*, vol. 1, p. 20).

INTRODUCTION TO THE AMIDA

> How much time should one wait between one prayer and another?
>
> Rav Huna and Rav Ḥisda disagreed. One said: Enough time that one's mind will be settled (*titḥonen*). And the other said: Enough time that one's mind will be settled (*titḥolel*). (Rashi explains that both words refer to settling of the mind, and their disagreement is mere semantics.)
>
> The one who opined *"titḥonen,"* based his opinion on *"Va-etḥanan"* [Deuteronomy 3:23]. And the one who opined "*titḥolel*," based his opinion on *"Vayeḥal"* [Exodus 32:11].[1]

The root of *titḥonen* is *ḥn*, which may mean "to encamp."[2] The root of *titḥolel* is *ḥll*, which conjures up the exact opposite image of a *"ḥalal panuy,"* an empty space, a forbidden zone off-limits to human habitation.

There are times when man's mind is permitted to wander and explore in prayer. Other times, his natural curiosity must be reined in. If the prayer is of the lower variety, one may safely explore in the spiritual realm. If one's prayer is on a higher niveau, then exploration carries with it a risk and is discouraged.

A prayer which allows for "encampment," is that of the individual on his own behalf (*tefillat ha-yaḥid*), such as when Moses beseeched the Lord to be allowed to enter the Promised Land. A prayer which requires limits, is the prayer uttered on behalf of the collective (*tefillat ha-rabbim*), such as Moses' prayer that the Lord not annihilate the People of Israel after the sin of the Golden Calf.[3]

*

Before one commences prayer, one must situate oneself in the proper place to pray.

> Rabbi Yosé bar Ḥanina said in the name of Rabbi Eliezer ben Ya'akov: "A man should not stand in a high place and pray, rather he should pray in a low place, for it says, 'From the depths I called to you, O Lord.'"[4]

When a man is in an exalted state of divine ecstasy, the needs of the world have no reality for him. In such a lofty state, one has no ability to empathize with the plight of the individual and the collective that are in need.

So for the sake of prayer, one must lower one's station that one might feel

---

1. *b. Berakhot* 30b.
2. See *b. 'Avodah Zarah* 20a.
3. *OR*, vol. 1, pp. 256–257. This is a reworking of the manuscript now made available in *MRIT*, pp. 58–61. It is complemented by the piece in *EA*, vol. 1, *Berakhot*, chap. 4, par. 57 (p. 126). It seems that the version of *OR* is the older of the two, for in *EA* Rav Kook refers to a previous rendition: "Some days ago I explained with the help of God…"
4. Psalms 130:1; *b. Berakhot* 10b. Cf. *t. Berakhot* 3:17.

*bittul*: Fathers and Thanksgiving. When we assess our stature opposite that of our Patriarchs, Abraham, Isaac and Jacob, we should be overcome with humility. These role models surpass us by so much. And the same goes for God's manifold miracles and wonders performed on our behalf. Words alone can never express our gratitude to the Almighty. Body language can.

But one must not take *"bittul"* to an extreme. One must not develop an "inferiority complex." Man must be taught not to bow at every blessing.

> But the purpose of surrender, the foundation of its consciousness, is that man should find within himself the strength to ascend to the mighty levels that are rightfully his by virtue of his godly soul... So man must not engage overly much in self-abasement, for he must recognize as well his own excellence, bestowed upon him by divine love. "His heart must be lifted up in the ways of the LORD."[18]
>
> Surrender in the proper place is a beautiful trait, but its real service is in rendering assistance to the elevation of the soul in the great ways of the LORD. One mustn't be left only with the feeling of lowliness but rather know all the different feelings that shine from the true light.[19]

*

> When one bows, one bows at *"Barukh"* ("Blessed").
> And when one straightens up, one straightens up at the Name [of God].
> What is the reason?
> For it is written, "The LORD straightens those bowed down."[20]
> [But is it not written] "Before My name he is prostrate"?[21]
> Is it written "At My name"? It is written "Before My name"![22]

On the journey to the LORD, which is the final destination, the knight of faith must engage in self-conquest. One must conquer the negative aspects of one's personality. This self-conquest is embodied in the act of bowing. But once one has arrived at the great Name, the body bespeaks another language altogether. The posture is now erect. The negative personality traits have been sublimated. "I shall uplift him for he has known My name."[23] How mistaken are those who would equate fear of the LORD with a broken spirit. Once one gets past the preliminary stages ("before my name") and arrives at the Name itself, the

18. Adapted from 2 Chronicles 17:6.
19. *OR*, vol. 1, p. 266 = *EA*, vol. 1, *Berakhot*, chap. 5, par. 112 (pp. 163–164).
20. Psalms 146:8.
21. Malachi 2:5.
22. *b. Berakhot* 12a.
23. Psalms 91:14.

This crucial difference between prayer and Torah study comes to bear in another regard as well: Torah study can entertain doubts and speculation. Prayer suffers no ambiguity; it acknowledges only certainties. "He whose name is certain; so His praise."[13]

Thus did Rav Kook reconcile the fact that the same Maimonides who wrote in his Code that "one who says in supplication, 'He who had mercy upon the bird's nest, that we not take away the mother bird together with the fledglings ... should have mercy upon us,' is to be silenced, for these commandments are a decree of the Scripture (*gezerat ha-katuv*) and not [signs of] compassion"[14] – later wrote in his *Guide* that compassion is precisely the reason for the command to send away the mother bird.[15] For Rav Kook the solution is elementary. In the *Guide,* there is ample room to speculate and theorize about the rationales for the various commandments. Prayer will have none of that. What is certain beyond a shadow of doubt is that the commandment is a *gezerah,* a divine decree, and with that prayer must suffice.[16]

*

> Our Rabbis taught, "These are the blessings [of *Shemoneh 'Esreh*] in which a man bows: In *Avot* (Fathers), beginning and end, [and] in *Hoda'ah* (Thanksgiving), beginning and end. If he is about to bow at the end of every blessing and the beginning of every blessing, we instruct him not to bow."[17]

Bowing is a recognition of one's insufficiency; it is an expression of self-nullification (*bittul 'atsmi*). This acknowledgment of one's inferiority may take two forms: emotional and intellectual. A bow at the onset of the blessing, which is immediate and without delay, stems from a gush of emotion. Prostration at the end of the blessing, a delayed reaction, is the product of intellectual deliberation.

There are two blessings which should by right evoke an outer display of

---

13. *"Ve-khol ma'aminim."* From the High Holy Day liturgy according to the Ashkenazic rite.
14. *MT, Hil. Tefillah* 9:7. See *m. Berakhot* 5:3; *Megillah* 4:9; *b. Berakhot* 33b; *Megillah* 25a. Rabbi Jacob ben Asher observed that for Maimonides (unlike the *Mishnah*), the prohibition of reciting this formula is not limited to a public prayer leader but extends to the private individual as well. See *Tur, OḤ,* chap. 113.
15. *Guide of the Perplexed* III, 48.
16. See the Introduction to the Prayer Book where RZYH recorded the version that he received "from the holy mouth" of his father; and the written version in *EA,* vol. 1, chap. 5, par. 104 (p. 160). Cf. Rabbi Mordechai Joseph Leiner of Izbica, *Mei ha-Shilo'aḥ,* Part 1, *Emor,* s.v. *ve-shor o seh;* Rabbi Jacob Leiner of Izbica-Radzyn, *Beit Ya'akov,* vol. 3 (Lublin, 1937), *Shemini,* par. 21, s.v. *va-tetse esh* (45d).
17. *b. Berakhot* 34a.

blessings.[29] The beginning and the end are clearly defined and intentional; as for the interim, the historical process, we muddle through.

Second, if one committed an error in one of the first three blessings or the final three, one must go back to the beginning of that order. However, if one was confused during the middle blessings, one may restart from wherever one went wrong.[30] The process is not as orderly as the beginning or the end. It is perforce somewhat inchoate and jumbled. Stated bluntly, "The middle blessings have no order."[31] The first three blessings are an indivisible unit; the same goes for the final three benedictions. The middle blessings come apart. Our mission is oftentimes interrupted. Plans are waylaid and we pick them up again from where we left off before the distraction.

And thirdly, the formula of both the first three and last blessings is fixed; improvisations are impermissible. The various *bakashot,* on the other hand, allow latitude for impromptu petitions – for health, wealth, etc.[32] In our collective search, surprises and exigencies constantly arise, and we script our reality as we go along. (Editor)

EIGHTEEN OR SEVENTEEN BENEDICTIONS IN THE *'AMIDAH* PRAYER?

We are familiar with the formulation of the *Talmud Bavli,* whereby originally there were eighteen benedictions in the *'Amidah,* and later in the days of Rabban Gamliel in Yavneh, a nineteenth benediction (or perhaps *malediction* is the better word) was added, known as *"birkat ha-minim"* (the blessing of the sectarians).[33] We are less familiar with the formula of the *Talmud Yerushalmi* whereby originally there were but seventeen benedictions (the Midrash notes that seventeen is the numerical value of the word *"tov"* or good),[34]

29. According to Maimonides (*Hil. Tefillah* 10:1), only the first blessing absolutely requires intention. Rabbis Isaac of Corbeil and Alexander Suslin wrote that *Modim* as well requires intention. See *Mishnah Berurah* to *OḤ* 101:1(3) citing *Semak and Sefer ha-Agudah.*
30. Maimonides, *Hil. Tefillah* 10:1 and *Kesef Mishneh* there; *Tosafot, Megillah* 17b, s.v. *hisdir.*
31. Statement of Rav Asi in *b. Berakhot* 34a.
32. Maimonides, *MT, Hil. Tefillah* 6:2, 3.
33. *b. Berakhot* 28b-29a; *Megillah* 17b-18a; Maimonides, *MT, Hil. Tefillah* 2:1.
34. See *Midrash Tanḥuma, Korah* 12; and *Numbers Rabbah* 18:21. The Midrash reads:

    "Pardon all iniquity, and accept good (*tov*), and let us pay bullocks with our lips" [Hosea 14:3].

    Israel said: Master of the Universe, when the Temple stood, we would offer a sacrifice and achieve atonement. And now there is nothing in our hands but prayer. *Tov* has the numerical value (*gematria*) of seventeen [prayers].

    And Rabbi Simon says: *Tov* (good) by the permutation of letters known as Atbash becomes *nefesh* (soul). Israel said: When the Temple stood, we would burn fats and innards, and achieve atonement. And now, here are our fat and blood and souls.

personality is strengthened and emboldened. The soul of man is essentially good[24]; whatever negative aspects exist, are accidents. Why vitiate the soul?[25]

*

Rav Sheshet, when he would bow down, he would bow down like a stick; when he would straighten up, he would straighten up like a snake.[26]

The prostration symbolizes subjugation of the negative qualities within the personality; they are best dealt a quick, decisive blow, like the snap of a stick. Elevation, spiritual ascent, on the other hand, is gradual. This growth is an arduous, at times serpentine process that requires time and patience.[27]

### OVERVIEW OF *SHEMONEH 'ESREH*

The Eighteen Benedictions are divided into three discrete units. The first three blessings come under the rubric of *"Shevaḥ"* (Praise). The final three blessings are epitomized as *"Hodayah"* (Thanksgiving). The middle twelve blessings constitute *"Bakashah"* (Petition).[28]

Encapsulated in these Eighteen Blessings is all of Jewish history. The first three blessings correspond to the three Patriarchs Abraham, Isaac and Jacob. They are our past, our origin. The last three blessings are our future, our destiny. They speak of the restoration of the *Shekhinah* to Zion, the reestablishment of the service in the Temple, and the ultimate blessing of peace. The intervening blessings are our present, which is fluid and uncertain. Our past and future have already been scripted and are clearly laid out before us. As for the present, it is being written this very moment. Our foundation was laid by our forefathers; our future is the handiwork of the Almighty. It is the present which we craft with our own hands. The first three blessings are "prehistoric"; the last three blessings are "post-historic." The twelve blessings in the interim are "history." And it is this ongoing historic process, with its doubts and uncertainties, and even bouts of amnesia that is referred to as *"bakashah."* It is one great *"bikush,"* a collective "search."

The different natures of the first and last blessings as opposed to the middle blessings is reflected in several *halakhot* or laws of prayer:

First, in regard to *kavvanah* or intention. The first blessing and the blessing of *Modim* are invalid without intention, which is not the case for the middle

24. The Midrash (*Tanḥuma, Koraḥ* 12; *Numbers Rabbah* 18:21) notes that in the code of Atbash, the Hebrew word for good, *tov*, is permutated to *nefesh*, soul.
25. *OR*, vol. 1, p. 267 = *EA*, vol. 1, *Berakhot*, chap. 1, par. 165 (p. 65).
26. *b. Berakhot* 12b.
27. *OR*, vol. 1, pp. 267–268 = *EA*, vol. 1, *Berakhot*, chap. 1, par. 166 (pp. 65–66).
28. *y. Berakhot* 2:4; Maimonides, *MT*, *Hil. Tefillah* 1:2, 4.

> Rav arrived in Babylonia. He saw that they were reciting *Hallel* on *Rosh Ḥodesh* (the first of the month). He thought to stop them. Once he saw that they were skipping [some chapters of *Hallel*], he understood that this was the custom that they received from their fathers.[39]
>
> Rav arrived in Babylonia on a communal fast day... All fell on their faces (for the *Taḥanun* prayer), and Rav did not fall on his face... Let him [i.e. Rav] fall on his face... He was not willing to change his custom.[40]

It is possible that in our case, we have the opposite scenario. Rav actually approved of the Babylonian custom of dividing the rebuilding of Jerusalem and the reestablishment of David's kingdom into two separate blessings, and strongly disapproved of the formula "God of David" then in vogue in *Erets Israel.* Rav's *agadah* concerning King David's failure to withstand the test presented him, was in fact a thinly veiled protest against this particular custom of *Erets Israel.*[41] (Editor)

39. *b. Ta'anit* 28b.
40. *b. Megillah* 22b.
41. In *b. Shabbat* 56a we find this statement of Rav: "Rabbi [Judah the Prince] who comes from David, turns over [the verse] and preaches the merit of David." The discussion there concerns whether King David committed a sin in cohabiting with Bathsheba. Rav, though a disciple of Rabbi Judah, might have found Rabbi Judah's exegesis a bit too resourceful. Also, Rav's pedigree was considered inferior to that of Rabbi Judah. Rabbi Judah was descended from the royal House of David; his ancestor Shefatyah was the son of David and his wife Avital. Rav, on the other hand, was descended not from David, but from David's brother Shim'i. See *b. Ketubot* 62b concerning Rabbi Ḥiyya. (Rabbi Hiyya was the uncle of Rav; see *b. Pesaḥim* 4a, *Sanhedrin* 5a.) *Inter alia,* despicable persons attempted to cast aspersions on the legitimacy of the children of both Rabbi Judah and Rabbi Ḥiyya, whereby they would have the status of *mamzerim.* See *b. Shabbat* 30b. (In the version of *'Eyn Ya'akov,* there is no mention of Rabbi Ḥiyya.)

    The later interpolation in the Midrash (cited above note #34), after puzzling over the shift from seventeen to nineteen benedictions, chalks the change up to the institution of *Birkat ha-Minim* in Yavneh, and to the emergence of *"Tsemaḥ David"* as a distinct benediction on account of David's failure to pass the test of Bathsheba. (See commentaries of Rabbi David Luria and Rabbi Samuel Strashun to *Numbers Rabbah* 18:21. Rabbi Ze'ev Wolf Einhorn's interpretation of the Midrash that David passed the test as the Patriarchs, flies in the face of the *agadah* in *Sanhedrin* 107!)

    What is novel about our reading of the situation is that Rav actually intended the *agadah* of David and Bathsheba to contribute to the reformation of the *Nusaḥ Erets Israel.* A most comprehensive weighing of the sources that militates for the rite of the *Talmud Bavli* as opposed to that of the *Talmud Yerushalmi,* is to be found in Rabbi Isaiah di Trani, *Tosafot Rid, Ta'anit* 13b (first published as an appendix to *Sefer ha-Makhri'a,* Livorno 1779).

and the addition of the blessing of the sectarians brought the total up to eighteen.

In the *nusah* or rite of *Erets Israel,* our blessings for the rebuilding of Jerusalem (*"Boneh Yerushalayim"*) and the reestablishment of the Kingdom of David were collapsed into a single blessing, which concluded with the words *"Elohei David u-boneh Yerushalayim"* ("God of David and Builder of Jerusalem").[35] It seems that this practice continued in *Erets Israel* as late as the sixth or even early seventh century, for the Erets-Israeli religious poet El'azar Kalir wrote *piyyutim* that conform to this rite.

Why was this custom of *Erets Israel* discontinued? It has been speculated that for one, there was theological opposition to the formula "God of David." As a general matter of policy, the Talmud Bavli states emphatically, "We call 'fathers' only three; we call 'mothers' only four."[36] The three Patriarchs are of course Abraham, Isaac and Jacob; the four Matriarchs are Sarah, Rebekah, Rachel and Leah.[37] More specifically there is recorded in *Perek Ḥelek* an *agadah* or legend that has King David complaining to the Master of the Universe:

> Why do we say "God of Abraham, God of Isaac and God of Jacob," and do not say "God of David"?[38]

The divine reply was that Abraham, Isaac and Jacob were tested, while David was untested. Thereupon, David requested that he too be tested. Immediately, David was tempted by the beauty of Bathsheba, a test that he failed. The moral to be derived from the story is that a man should not bring himself to be tested.

But it is possible that there was another point to the story, a veiled criticism of the Erets-Israeli rite. The author of this *agadah* was Rav. The great sage Rav (honorific title of Abba Arikha) was an Amora of the first generation, who studied in *Erets Israel* and later "descended" to Babylonia, where he exerted a profound influence upon Jewish religious life. In Babylonia, Rav would encounter various customs with which he was unacquainted. The *Bavli* records a couple of these instances where Rav was confronted for the first time with a custom that he found problematic.

---

May it be Your will that that be atonement for us, "and let us pay bullocks with our lips."

35. *t. Berakhot* 3:25 (Zuckermandel ed., p. 8); *y. Berakhot* 2:4, 4:3; *Rosh Hashanah* 4:6; *Ta'anit* 2:2.

36. *b. Berakhot* 16b.

37. Rashi *ad locum.* See Rabbi Isaac of Vienna, *'Or Zaru'a, Hil. Tefillah,* chap. 106, citing Rabbenu Ḥananel. Based on Rabbenu Ḥananel, Rabbi Isaac 'Or Zaru'a understood the statement in the Talmud to mean that in our prayer we do not call on the merits of men later than Jacob.

38. *b. Sanhedrin* 107a. See the parallel *Midrash Tehillim,* chap. 18.

He sustains the living with loving-kindness,
and with great compassion revives the dead.
He supports the fallen, heals the sick, sets captives free,
and keeps His faith with those who sleep in the dust.
Who is like You, Master of might, and who can compare to You,
O King who brings death and gives life,
and makes salvation grow?

*Between Rosh HaShana & Yom Kippur:* Who is like You, compassionate Father,
who remembers His creatures in compassion, for life?

Faithful are You to revive the dead.
Blessed are You, LORD, who revives the dead.

*When saying the Amida silently, continue with "You are holy" on the next page.*

---

KEDUSHA

*During the Leader's Repetition, the following is said standing with feet together, rising on the toes at the words indicated by* ▲.

*Cong. then Leader:* נְקַדֵּשׁ We will sanctify Your name on earth,
as they sanctify it in the highest heavens,
as is written by Your prophet,
"And they [the angels] call to one another saying: Is. 6

*Cong. then Leader:* ▲Holy, ▲holy, ▲holy is the LORD of hosts;
the whole world is filled with His glory."
Those facing them say "Blessed –"

*Cong. then Leader:* ▲"Blessed is the LORD's glory from His place." Ezek. 3
And in Your holy Writings it is written thus:

*Cong. then Leader:* ▲"The LORD shall reign for ever. He is your God, Zion, Ps. 146
from generation to generation, Halleluya!"

*Leader:* From generation to generation we will declare Your greatness,
and we will proclaim Your holiness for evermore.
Your praise, our God, shall not leave our mouth forever,
for You, God, are a great and holy King.
Blessed are You, LORD, the holy God. /
*Between Rosh HaShana & Yom Kippur:* the holy King./

*The Leader continues with "You grace humanity" on the next page.*

מְכַלְכֵּל חַיִּים בְּחֶסֶד, מְחַיֵּה מֵתִים בְּרַחֲמִים רַבִּים
סוֹמֵךְ נוֹפְלִים, וְרוֹפֵא חוֹלִים, וּמַתִּיר אֲסוּרִים
וּמְקַיֵּם אֱמוּנָתוֹ לִישֵׁנֵי עָפָר.
מִי כָמְוֹךָ, בַּעַל גְּבוּרוֹת, וּמִי דְּוֹמֶה לָּךְ
מֶלֶךְ, מֵמִית וּמְחַיֶּה וּמַצְמִיחַ יְשׁוּעָה.

בעשרת ימי תשובה: מִי כָמְוֹךָ אַב הָרַחֲמִים
זוֹכֵר יְצוּרָיו לְחַיִּים בְּרַחֲמִים.

וְנֶאֱמָן אַתָּה לְהַחֲיוֹת מֵתִים.
בָּרוּךְ אַתָּה יהוה, מְחַיֵּה הַמֵּתִים.

*When saying the* עמידה *silently, continue with* אַתָּה קָדוֹשׁ *on the next page.*

---

## קדושה

*During* חזרת הש״ץ*, the following is said standing with feet together, rising on the toes at the words indicated by* ˄.

then קהל ש״ץ: נְקַדֵּשׁ אֶת שִׁמְךָ בָּעוֹלָם, כְּשֵׁם שֶׁמַּקְדִּישִׁים אוֹתוֹ בִּשְׁמֵי מָרוֹם
כַּכָּתוּב עַל יַד נְבִיאֶךָ, וְקָרָא זֶה אֶל־זֶה וְאָמַר — ישעיה ו

then קהל ש״ץ: ˄קָדוֹשׁ, ˄קָדוֹשׁ, ˄קָדוֹשׁ, יהוה צְבָאוֹת, מְלֹא כָל־הָאָרֶץ כְּבוֹדוֹ:
לְעֻמָּתָם בָּרוּךְ יֹאמֵרוּ

then קהל ש״ץ: ˄בָּרוּךְ כְּבוֹד־יהוה מִמְּקוֹמוֹ: — יחזקאל ג
וּבְדִבְרֵי קָדְשְׁךָ כָּתוּב לֵאמֹר

then קהל ש״ץ: ˄יִמְלֹךְ יהוה לְעוֹלָם, אֱלֹהַיִךְ צִיּוֹן לְדֹר וָדֹר, הַלְלוּיָהּ: — תהלים קמו

ש״ץ: לְדוֹר וָדוֹר נַגִּיד גָּדְלֶךָ, וּלְנֵצַח נְצָחִים קְדֻשָּׁתְךָ נַקְדִּישׁ
וְשִׁבְחֲךָ אֱלֹהֵינוּ מִפִּינוּ לֹא יָמוּשׁ לְעוֹלָם וָעֶד
כִּי אֵל מֶלֶךְ גָּדוֹל וְקָדוֹשׁ אָתָּה.
בָּרוּךְ אַתָּה יהוה, הָאֵל הַקָּדוֹשׁ./ בעשרת ימי תשובה: הַמֶּלֶךְ הַקָּדוֹשׁ./

*The* שליח ציבור *continues with* אַתָּה חוֹנֵן *on the next page.*

HOLINESS

אַתָּה קָדוֹשׁ You are holy and Your name is holy,
and holy ones praise You daily, Selah!
Blessed are You, Lord,
the holy God. / *Between Rosh HaShana & Yom Kippur:* the holy King./
(*If forgotten, repeat the Amida.*)

KNOWLEDGE

אַתָּה חוֹנֵן You grace humanity with knowledge
and teach mortals understanding.
Grace us with the knowledge, understanding
and discernment that come from You.
Blessed are You, Lord,
who graciously grants knowledge.

REPENTANCE

הֲשִׁיבֵנוּ Bring us back, our Father, to Your Torah.
Draw us near, our King, to Your service.
Lead us back to You in perfect repentance.
Blessed are You, Lord,
who desires repentance.

---

and commandments by superstition. Service of the Lord should issue from enlightenment and love.[43]

Then there is the passage in the Talmud which contrasts *"teshuvah mi-yir'ah"* (return from fear) and *"teshuvah me-ahavah"* (return from love).[44] While the former succeeds only in repression, the latter achieves sublimation, or to adopt Mordechai Rotenberg's term, "rebiography." There is the final chapter of Maimonides' *Hilkhot Teshuvah*, which opposes one who serves the Lord from fear and base motives (*"'oved mi-yir'ah"*) to one who serves the Lord from love and altruistic motives (*"'oved me-ahavah"*). And the *Zohar* which speaks of *"teshuvah tata'ah,"* the lower return (corresponding to the bottom-

43. *Li-Nevukhei ha-Dor*, ed. Rabbi Shaḥar Raḥmani (Tel-Aviv, 2014), chap. 38 (p. 190).
44. *b. Yoma* 86b.

קדושת השם

אַתָּה קָדוֹשׁ וְשִׁמְךָ קָדוֹשׁ
וּקְדוֹשִׁים בְּכָל יוֹם יְהַלְלוּךָ סֶּלָה.
בָּרוּךְ אַתָּה יהוה, הָאֵל הַקָּדוֹשׁ./ בעשרת ימי תשובה: הַמֶּלֶךְ הַקָּדוֹשׁ./
(*If forgotten, repeat the* עמידה.)

דעת

אַתָּה חוֹנֵן לְאָדָם דַּעַת
וּמְלַמֵּד לֶאֱנוֹשׁ בִּינָה.
חָנֵּנוּ מֵאִתְּךָ דֵּעָה בִּינָה וְהַשְׂכֵּל.
בָּרוּךְ אַתָּה יהוה, חוֹנֵן הַדָּעַת.

תשובה

הֲשִׁיבֵנוּ אָבִינוּ לְתוֹרָתֶךָ
וְקָרְבֵנוּ מַלְכֵּנוּ לַעֲבוֹדָתֶךָ
וְהַחֲזִירֵנוּ בִּתְשׁוּבָה שְׁלֵמָה לְפָנֶיךָ.
בָּרוּךְ אַתָּה יהוה, הָרוֹצֶה בִּתְשׁוּבָה.

---

תשובה / REPENTANCE

One of the great innovations of Rav Kook in Jewish life was the splendid way in which he taught that *teshuvah* (repentance) can and must be a positive, ennobling experience, informed by understanding and predicated on love – not fear. The sources upon which he based his philosophy of *Teshuvah* are unimpeachable.

It all starts with the explanation of the Talmud as to the juxtaposition of these two blessings of Knowledge and Repentance. The verse states: "And his heart shall understand and he shall return and be healed."[42] Proper *teshuvah* is based on knowledge and understanding, not ignorance and fear. Especially in the modern world, people should not be cowed into acceptance of Torah

---

42. Isaiah 6:10; *b. Megillah* 17b.

### FORGIVENESS

*Strike the left side of the chest at °.*

סְלַח לָנוּ Forgive us, our Father, for we have °sinned.
Pardon us, our King, for we have °transgressed;
for You pardon and forgive.
Blessed are You, LORD,
the gracious One who repeatedly forgives.

### REDEMPTION

רְאֵה Look on our affliction, plead our cause,
and redeem us soon for Your name's sake,
for You are a powerful Redeemer.
Blessed are You, LORD,
the Redeemer of Israel.

---

*On Fast Days the Leader adds:*

עֲנֵנוּ Answer us, LORD, answer us on our Fast Day, for we are in great distress. Look not at our wickedness. Do not hide Your face from us and do not ignore our plea. Be near to our cry; please let Your loving-kindness comfort us. Even before we call to You, answer us, as is said, "Before they call, I will answer. While they are still speaking, I will hear." *Is. 65* For You, LORD, are the One who answers in time of distress, redeems and rescues in all times of trouble and anguish. Blessed are You, LORD, who answers in time of distress.

---

The Rav was able to plumb new depths in psychology, expressing his thoughts in breathtakingly poetic language, spiritually uplifting in and of itself.

In 1924, while Rav Kook was away on a fund-raising mission in America, his son Rabbi Zevi Yehudah issued the work *Orot ha-Teshuvah* (Lights of Return), a collection of the Rav's many pensées on the subject. The book has remained a classic of Jewish thought ever since. Whereas in past presentations, *teshuvah* took on melancholic, lugubrious notes, and was painted in somber hues, in the deft hands of the Master, *teshuvah* sounds an upbeat note and is streaming *orot* (lights). During the month of Ellul, Rav Kook himself would study *Orot ha-Teshuvah* in preparation for the High Holy Days.

סליחה

*Strike the left side of the chest at °.*

סְלַח לָנוּ אָבִינוּ כִּי °חָטָאנוּ
מְחַל לָנוּ מַלְכֵּנוּ כִּי °פָשָׁעְנוּ
כִּי מוֹחֵל וְסוֹלֵחַ אָתָּה.
בָּרוּךְ אַתָּה יהוה, חַנּוּן הַמַּרְבֶּה לִסְלֹחַ.

גאולה

רְאֵה בְעָנְיֵנוּ, וְרִיבָה רִיבֵנוּ
וּגְאָלֵנוּ מְהֵרָה לְמַעַן שְׁמֶךָ
כִּי גּוֹאֵל חָזָק אָתָּה.
בָּרוּךְ אַתָּה יהוה, גּוֹאֵל יִשְׂרָאֵל.

---

*On Fast Days the* שליח ציבור *adds:*

עֲנֵנוּ יהוה עֲנֵנוּ בְּיוֹם צוֹם תַּעֲנִיתֵנוּ, כִּי בְצָרָה גְדוֹלָה אֲנָחְנוּ. אַל תֵּפֶן אֶל רִשְׁעֵנוּ, וְאַל תַּסְתֵּר פָּנֶיךָ מִמֶּנּוּ, וְאַל תִּתְעַלַּם מִתְּחִנָּתֵנוּ. הֱיֵה נָא קָרוֹב לְשַׁוְעָתֵנוּ, יְהִי נָא חַסְדְּךָ לְנַחֲמֵנוּ, טֶרֶם נִקְרָא אֵלֶיךָ עֲנֵנוּ, כַּדָּבָר שֶׁנֶּאֱמַר: וְהָיָה טֶרֶם יִקְרָאוּ וַאֲנִי אֶעֱנֶה, עוֹד הֵם מְדַבְּרִים וַאֲנִי אֶשְׁמָע: כִּי אַתָּה יהוה ישעיה סה הָעוֹנֶה בְּעֵת צָרָה, פּוֹדֶה וּמַצִּיל בְּכָל עֵת צָרָה וְצוּקָה. בָּרוּךְ אַתָּה יהוה, הָעוֹנֶה בְּעֵת צָרָה.

---

most *sefirah* of *Malkhut* or Kingship), as opposed to *teshuvah 'ila'ah,* the higher return (corresponding to the superior *sefirah* of *Binah* or Understanding).[45]

With these texts in hand, Rav Kook embarked on an exploration of the varieties of religious experience that captures the imagination of modern man.

45. *Ra'aya Mehemna* in *Zohar* III, 122; Rabbi Shneur Zalman of Liadi, *Tanya,* Part III (*Igeret ha-Teshuvah*), chaps. 4–11. Though the *Tanya* (93b) ascribes the terms *"teshuvah tata'ah"* and *"teshuvah 'ila'ah"* to the *Zohar,* to the very best of my knowledge (BN) nowhere do those exact terms show up in *Zohar*. Regarding the terms *"hé tata'ah"* and *"hé 'ila'ah,"* see Rabbi Meir Popper's *Me'orei 'Or,* s.v. *teshuvah.*

HEALING

רְפָאֵנוּ Heal us, Lord, and we shall be healed.
Save us and we shall be saved,
for You are our praise.
Bring complete recovery for all our ailments,

---

*The following prayer for a sick person may be said here:*
May it be Your will, O Lord my God and God of my ancestors, that You speedily send a complete recovery from heaven, a healing of both soul and body, to the patient (*name*), son/daughter of (*mother's name*) among the other afflicted of Israel.

---

for You, God, King, are a faithful and compassionate Healer.
Blessed are You, Lord, Healer of the sick of His people Israel.

PROSPERITY

*The phrase "Grant dew and rain as a blessing" is said from December 5th (in the year before a civil leap year, December 6th) until Pesaḥ. In Israel, it is said from the 7th of Marḥeshvan. The phrase "Grant blessing" is said from Ḥol HaMo'ed Pesaḥ until December 4th (in the year before a civil leap year, December 5th). In Israel it is said through the 6th of Marḥeshvan. See laws 147–149.*

בָּרֵךְ Bless this year for us, Lord our God,
and all its types of produce for good.

*In winter:* Grant dew and rain as a blessing
*In other seasons:* Grant blessing

on the face of the earth,
and from its goodness satisfy us,
blessing our year as the best of years.
Blessed are You, Lord, who blesses the years.

INGATHERING OF EXILES

תְּקַע Sound the great shofar for our freedom,
raise high the banner to gather our exiles,
and gather us together from the four quarters of the earth.
Blessed are You, Lord,
who gathers the dispersed of His people Israel.

רפואה

**רְפָאֵנוּ יהוה וְנֵרָפֵא**
**הוֹשִׁיעֵנוּ וְנִוָּשֵׁעָה, כִּי תְהִלָּתֵנוּ אָתָּה**
**וְהַעֲלֵה רְפוּאָה שְׁלֵמָה לְכָל מַכּוֹתֵינוּ**

---

*The following prayer for a sick person may be said here:*

יְהִי רָצוֹן מִלְּפָנֶיךָ יהוה אֱלֹהַי וֵאלֹהֵי אֲבוֹתַי, שֶׁתִּשְׁלַח מְהֵרָה רְפוּאָה שְׁלֵמָה מִן הַשָּׁמַיִם רְפוּאַת הַנֶּפֶשׁ וּרְפוּאַת הַגּוּף לַחוֹלֶה/לַחוֹלָה *name of patient* בֶּן/בַּת *mother's name* בְּתוֹךְ שְׁאָר חוֹלֵי יִשְׂרָאֵל.

---

**כִּי אֵל מֶלֶךְ רוֹפֵא נֶאֱמָן וְרַחֲמָן אָתָּה.**
**בָּרוּךְ אַתָּה יהוה, רוֹפֵא חוֹלֵי עַמּוֹ יִשְׂרָאֵל.**

ברכת השנים

*The phrase* וְתֵן טַל וּמָטָר לִבְרָכָה *is said from December 5th (in the year before a civil leap year, December 6th) until* פסח*. In* ארץ ישראל*, it is said from* ז׳ מרחשון*. The phrase* וְתֵן בְּרָכָה *is said from* חול המועד פסח *until December 4th (in the year before a civil leap year, December 5th). In* ארץ ישראל *it is said through* ו׳ מרחשון*. See laws 147–149.*

**בָּרֵךְ עָלֵינוּ יהוה אֱלֹהֵינוּ אֶת הַשָּׁנָה הַזֹּאת**
**וְאֶת כָּל מִינֵי תְבוּאָתָהּ, לְטוֹבָה**
בחורף: **וְתֵן טַל וּמָטָר לִבְרָכָה** / בקיץ: **וְתֵן בְּרָכָה**
**עַל פְּנֵי הָאֲדָמָה, וְשַׂבְּעֵנוּ מִטּוּבָהּ**
**וּבָרֵךְ שְׁנָתֵנוּ כַּשָּׁנִים הַטּוֹבוֹת.**
**בָּרוּךְ אַתָּה יהוה, מְבָרֵךְ הַשָּׁנִים.**

קבוץ גלויות

**תְּקַע בְּשׁוֹפָר גָּדוֹל לְחֵרוּתֵנוּ, וְשָׂא נֵס לְקַבֵּץ גָּלֻיּוֹתֵינוּ**
**וְקַבְּצֵנוּ יַחַד מֵאַרְבַּע כַּנְפוֹת הָאָרֶץ.**
**בָּרוּךְ אַתָּה יהוה, מְקַבֵּץ נִדְחֵי עַמּוֹ יִשְׂרָאֵל.**

JUSTICE

הָשִׁיבָה Restore our judges as at first,
and our counselors as at the beginning,
and remove from us sorrow and sighing.
May You alone, LORD,
reign over us with loving-kindness and compassion,
and vindicate us in justice.
Blessed are You, LORD,
the King who loves righteousness and justice.
/ *Between Rosh HaShana & Yom Kippur, end the blessing:* the King of justice./

AGAINST INFORMERS

וְלַמַּלְשִׁינִים For the slanderers let there be no hope,
and may all wickedness perish in an instant.
May all Your people's enemies swiftly be cut down.
May You swiftly uproot, crush, cast down
and humble the arrogant swiftly in our days.
Blessed are You, LORD,
who destroys enemies and humbles the arrogant.

THE RIGHTEOUS

עַל הַצַּדִּיקִים To the righteous, the pious,
the elders of Your people the house of Israel,
the remnant of their scholars, the righteous converts, and to us,
may Your compassion be aroused, LORD our God.
Grant a good reward to all who sincerely trust in Your name.
Set our lot with them, so that we may never be ashamed,
for in You we trust.
Blessed are You, LORD,
who is the support and trust of the righteous.

---

the Fathers 4:24) is the verse "If your enemy falls, do not rejoice" (Proverbs 24:17). Only one totally free of malice toward Israel's internal enemies is worthy of instituting a prayer to the Almighty that they be uprooted.[46]

---

46. *b. Berakhot* 28b; *EA*, vol. 1, *Berakhot*, chap. 4, par. 40 (p. 121) = *OR*, vol. 1, pp. 277–278; *IR*, vol. 2, p. 187 (Letter 555).

השבת המשפט

הָשִׁיבָה שׁוֹפְטֵינוּ כְּבָרִאשׁוֹנָה וְיוֹעֲצֵינוּ כְּבַתְּחִלָּה
וְהָסֵר מִמֶּנּוּ יָגוֹן וַאֲנָחָה
וּמְלֹךְ עָלֵינוּ אַתָּה יהוה לְבַדְּךָ בְּחֶסֶד וּבְרַחֲמִים
וְצַדְּקֵנוּ בַּמִּשְׁפָּט.
בָּרוּךְ אַתָּה יהוה
מֶלֶךְ אוֹהֵב צְדָקָה וּמִשְׁפָּט. / בעשרת ימי תשובה: הַמֶּלֶךְ הַמִּשְׁפָּט./

ברכת המינים

וְלַמַּלְשִׁינִים אַל תְּהִי תִקְוָה, וְכָל הָרִשְׁעָה כְּרֶגַע תֹּאבֵד
וְכָל אוֹיְבֵי עַמְּךָ מְהֵרָה יִכָּרֵתוּ
וְהַזֵּדִים מְהֵרָה תְעַקֵּר וּתְשַׁבֵּר וּתְמַגֵּר וְתַכְנִיעַ בִּמְהֵרָה בְיָמֵינוּ.
בָּרוּךְ אַתָּה יהוה, שׁוֹבֵר אוֹיְבִים וּמַכְנִיעַ זֵדִים.

על הצדיקים

עַל הַצַּדִּיקִים וְעַל הַחֲסִידִים, וְעַל זִקְנֵי עַמְּךָ בֵּית יִשְׂרָאֵל
וְעַל פְּלֵיטַת סוֹפְרֵיהֶם, וְעַל גֵּרֵי הַצֶּדֶק, וְעָלֵינוּ
יֶהֱמוּ רַחֲמֶיךָ יהוה אֱלֹהֵינוּ
וְתֵן שָׂכָר טוֹב לְכָל הַבּוֹטְחִים בְּשִׁמְךָ בֶּאֱמֶת
וְשִׂים חֶלְקֵנוּ עִמָּהֶם
וּלְעוֹלָם לֹא נֵבוֹשׁ כִּי בְךָ בָּטָחְנוּ.
בָּרוּךְ אַתָּה יהוה, מִשְׁעָן וּמִבְטָח לַצַּדִּיקִים.

---

ברכת המינים / AGAINST INFORMERS
This additional blessing (perhaps a euphemism) directed against sectarians, brings up the number of blessings in the *'Amidah* prayer from the original eighteen to nineteen. (Today, *"Shmoneh 'Esreh"* or "Eighteen" is an anachronism.) It was composed by Shmuel HaKatan ("Samuel the Small"). It is surely no coincidence that the maxim attributed to him in *Pirket Avot* (Ethics of

REBUILDING JERUSALEM

וְלִירוּשָׁלַיִם To Jerusalem, Your city, may You return in compassion,
and may You dwell in it as You promised.
May You rebuild it rapidly in our days as an everlasting structure,
and install within it soon the throne of David.
Blessed are You, LORD, who builds Jerusalem.

KINGDOM OF DAVID

אֶת צֶמַח May the offshoot of Your servant David soon flower,
and may his pride be raised high by Your salvation,
for we wait for Your salvation all day.
Blessed are You, LORD, who makes the glory of salvation flourish.

RESPONSE TO PRAYER

שְׁמַע קוֹלֵנוּ Listen to our voice, LORD our God.
Spare us and have compassion on us,
and in compassion and favor accept our prayer,
for You, God, listen to prayers and pleas.
Do not turn us away, O our King,
empty-handed from Your presence,*
for You listen with compassion to the prayer of Your people Israel.
Blessed are You, LORD, who listens to prayer.

---

**In times of drought in Israel, add:*

וַעֲנֵנוּ And answer us through the attribute of compassion, Creator of the universe who chooses His people Israel to make known His greatness and majestic glory. You who listen to prayer, grant dew and rain on the face of the earth, satisfying the whole universe from Your goodness. Fill our hands from Your blessings and Your hand's rich gift. Guard and deliver this year from all evil, all kinds of destruction and punishment, and give it hope and a peaceful end. Spare us and have compassion on us and on all our produce and fruit, blessing us with bounteous rain. May we merit life, plenty and peace as in the good years. Remove from us plague, sword and famine, wild animals, captivity and plunder, the evil instinct and serious and dangerous illnesses and events. Decree for us goodly decrees, and may Your compassion prevail over Your other attributes, that You may act toward Your children through the attribute of compassion, and in compassion and favor accept our prayer.

*Continue with "for You listen" above.*

בניין ירושלים

וְלִירוּשָׁלַיִם עִירְךָ בְּרַחֲמִים תָּשׁוּב, וְתִשְׁכֹּן בְּתוֹכָהּ כַּאֲשֶׁר דִּבַּרְתָּ
וּבְנֵה אוֹתָהּ בְּקָרוֹב בְּיָמֵינוּ בִּנְיַן עוֹלָם
וְכִסֵּא דָוִד מְהֵרָה לְתוֹכָהּ תָּכִין.
בָּרוּךְ אַתָּה יהוה, בּוֹנֵה יְרוּשָׁלָיִם.

מלכות בית דוד

אֶת צֶמַח דָּוִד עַבְדְּךָ מְהֵרָה תַצְמִיחַ, וְקַרְנוֹ תָּרוּם בִּישׁוּעָתֶךָ
כִּי לִישׁוּעָתְךָ קִוִּינוּ כָּל הַיּוֹם.
בָּרוּךְ אַתָּה יהוה, מַצְמִיחַ קֶרֶן יְשׁוּעָה.

שומע תפילה

שְׁמַע קוֹלֵנוּ יהוה אֱלֹהֵינוּ
חוּס וְרַחֵם עָלֵינוּ, וְקַבֵּל בְּרַחֲמִים וּבְרָצוֹן אֶת תְּפִלָּתֵנוּ
כִּי אֵל שׁוֹמֵעַ תְּפִלּוֹת וְתַחֲנוּנִים אָתָּה
וּמִלְּפָנֶיךָ מַלְכֵּנוּ רֵיקָם אַל תְּשִׁיבֵנוּ*
כִּי אַתָּה שׁוֹמֵעַ תְּפִלַּת עַמְּךָ יִשְׂרָאֵל בְּרַחֲמִים.
בָּרוּךְ אַתָּה יהוה, שׁוֹמֵעַ תְּפִלָּה.

---

**In times of drought in* ארץ ישראל*, add:*

וַעֲנֵנוּ בּוֹרֵא עוֹלָם בְּמִדַּת הָרַחֲמִים, בּוֹחֵר בְּעַמּוֹ יִשְׂרָאֵל לְהוֹדִיעַ גָּדְלוֹ וְהַדְרַת כְּבוֹדוֹ. שׁוֹמֵעַ תְּפִלָּה, תֵּן טַל וּמָטָר עַל פְּנֵי הָאֲדָמָה, וְתַשְׂבִּיעַ אֶת הָעוֹלָם כֻּלּוֹ מִטּוּבֶךָ, וּמַלֵּא יָדֵינוּ מִבִּרְכוֹתֶיךָ וּמֵעֹשֶׁר מַתְּנַת יָדֶךָ. שְׁמֹר וְהַצֵּל שָׁנָה זוֹ מִכָּל דָּבָר רָע, וּמִכָּל מִינֵי מַשְׁחִית וּמִכָּל מִינֵי פֻרְעָנִיּוֹת, וַעֲשֵׂה לָהּ תִּקְוָה וְאַחֲרִית שָׁלוֹם. חוּס וְרַחֵם עָלֵינוּ וְעַל כָּל תְּבוּאָתֵנוּ וּפֵרוֹתֵינוּ, וּבָרְכֵנוּ בְּגִשְׁמֵי בְרָכָה, וְנִזְכֶּה לְחַיִּים וְשֹׂבַע וְשָׁלוֹם כַּשָּׁנִים הַטּוֹבוֹת. וְהָסֵר מִמֶּנּוּ דֶּבֶר וְחֶרֶב וְרָעָב, וְחַיָּה רָעָה וּשְׁבִי וּבִזָּה, וְיֵצֶר הָרָע וָחֳלָיִים רָעִים וְקָשִׁים וּמְאֹרָעוֹת רָעִים וְקָשִׁים. וּגְזֹר עָלֵינוּ גְּזֵרוֹת טוֹבוֹת מִלְּפָנֶיךָ, וְיִגֹּלּוּ רַחֲמֶיךָ עַל מִדּוֹתֶיךָ, וְתִתְנַהֵג עִם בָּנֶיךָ בְּמִדַּת הָרַחֲמִים, וְקַבֵּל בְּרַחֲמִים וּבְרָצוֹן אֶת תְּפִלָּתֵנוּ.

*Continue with* כִּי אַתָּה שׁוֹמֵעַ *above.*

TEMPLE SERVICE

רְצֵה Find favor, LORD our God, in Your people Israel and their prayer. Restore the service to Your most holy House, and accept in love and favor the fire-offerings of Israel and their prayer. May the service of Your people Israel always find favor with You.

---

*On Rosh Ḥodesh and Ḥol HaMo'ed, say:*

אֱלֹהֵינוּ Our God and God of our ancestors, may there rise, come, reach, appear, be favored, heard, regarded and remembered before You, our recollection and remembrance, as well as the remembrance of our ancestors, and of the Messiah, son of David Your servant, and of Jerusalem Your holy city, and of all Your people the house of Israel – for deliverance and well-being, grace, loving-kindness and compassion, life and peace, on this day of:

*On Rosh Ḥodesh:* Rosh Ḥodesh.
*On Pesaḥ:* the Festival of Matzot.
*On Sukkot:* the Festival of Sukkot.

On it remember us, LORD our God, for good; recollect us for blessing, and deliver us for life. In accord with Your promise of salvation and compassion, spare us and be gracious to us; have compassion on us and deliver us, for our eyes are turned to You because You, God, are a gracious and compassionate King.

---

וְתֶחֱזֶינָה And may our eyes witness Your return to Zion in compassion. Blessed are You, LORD, who restores His Presence to Zion.

---

In his famous eulogy *"Ha-Misped bi-Yerushalayim"* (1904), Rav Kook likened our era to that of Messiah son of Joseph.[50] (Editor)

50. See "The Lamentation in Jerusalem" (*"Ha-Misped bi-Yerushalayim"*) in our collection *When God Becomes History: Historical Essays of Rabbi Abraham Isaac Hakohen Kook* (Spring Valley, NY: Orot, 2003).
Rabbi Isaac Luria instructed his disciples that when one recites the words in the *'Amidah,* "And install within it soon the throne of David" (*"ve-khise David 'avdekha meherah le-tokhah takhin"*) one should pray that Messiah son of Joseph not be killed by the wicked Armilus. (Scholars speculate that Armilus is a corruption of Romulus, the legendary founder of Rome.) Rabbi Ḥayyim Vital believed that his master Rabbi Isaac Luria (who died an untimely death at age thirty-eight) was Messiah son of Joseph. A later kabbalist, Rabbi Nathan Spira Yerushalmi conceived the notion that Messiah son of Joseph reincarnates in every generation. See Rabbi Ḥayyim Vital, *Peri 'Ets Hayyim* (Dubrovna, 1804), *Sha'ar ha-'Amidah,* chap. 19, s.v. *tishkon* (58c). Rav Kook saw Herzl (who died at the young age of forty-four) as falling into the tradition of Messiah son of Joseph. While these men did not die violent deaths, they were premature.

עבודה

רְצֵה יהוה אֱלֹהֵינוּ בְּעַמְּךָ יִשְׂרָאֵל וּבִתְפִלָּתָם
וְהָשֵׁב אֶת הָעֲבוֹדָה לִדְבִיר בֵּיתֶךָ
וְאִשֵּׁי יִשְׂרָאֵל וּתְפִלָּתָם בְּאַהֲבָה תְקַבֵּל בְּרָצוֹן
וּתְהִי לְרָצוֹן תָּמִיד עֲבוֹדַת יִשְׂרָאֵל עַמֶּךָ.

*On* ראש חודש *and* חול המועד*, say:*

אֱלֹהֵינוּ וֵאלֹהֵי אֲבוֹתֵינוּ, יַעֲלֶה וְיָבוֹא וְיַגִּיעַ, וְיֵרָאֶה וְיֵרָצֶה וְיִשָּׁמַע, וְיִפָּקֵד וְיִזָּכֵר זִכְרוֹנֵנוּ וּפִקְדוֹנֵנוּ וְזִכְרוֹן אֲבוֹתֵינוּ, וְזִכְרוֹן מָשִׁיחַ בֶּן דָּוִד עַבְדֶּךָ, וְזִכְרוֹן יְרוּשָׁלַיִם עִיר קָדְשֶׁךָ, וְזִכְרוֹן כָּל עַמְּךָ בֵּית יִשְׂרָאֵל, לְפָנֶיךָ, לִפְלֵיטָה לְטוֹבָה, לְחֵן וּלְחֶסֶד וּלְרַחֲמִים, לְחַיִּים וּלְשָׁלוֹם בְּיוֹם
בראש חודש: רֹאשׁ הַחֹדֶשׁ / בפסח: חַג הַמַּצּוֹת / בסוכות: חַג הַסֻּכּוֹת
הַזֶּה. זָכְרֵנוּ יהוה אֱלֹהֵינוּ בּוֹ לְטוֹבָה, וּפָקְדֵנוּ בוֹ לִבְרָכָה, וְהוֹשִׁיעֵנוּ בוֹ לְחַיִּים. וּבִדְבַר יְשׁוּעָה וְרַחֲמִים, חוּס וְחָנֵּנוּ וְרַחֵם עָלֵינוּ וְהוֹשִׁיעֵנוּ, כִּי אֵלֶיךָ עֵינֵינוּ, כִּי אֵל מֶלֶךְ חַנּוּן וְרַחוּם אָתָּה.

וְתֶחֱזֶינָה עֵינֵינוּ בְּשׁוּבְךָ לְצִיּוֹן בְּרַחֲמִים.
בָּרוּךְ אַתָּה יהוה, הַמַּחֲזִיר שְׁכִינָתוֹ לְצִיּוֹן.

ON *ROSH ḤODESH* AND *ḤOL HAMOʿED*

וְזִכְרוֹן מָשִׁיחַ בֶּן דָּוִד עַבְדֶּךָ *And the remembrance of the Messiah, son of David Your servant.* In the medieval work *Sefer ha-Tamid* of Rabbi Reuben ben Ḥayyim (teacher of Rabbi Menaḥem Ha-Me'iri) we find the variant *"Meshiḥenu"* ("our Messiah"), which the author interprets as

> Messiah son of Joseph. Remember the promise made to us by Your prophets that You will send him to us, and even though he will be killed,[47] it is the beginning of the redemption (*athalta di-ge'ulah*), and in his days, "many will be purified,"[48] and the gold will emerge from the refinery.[49]

47. *b. Sukkah* 52a.
48. Daniel 12:10. Cf. Saʿadyah Gaon, *Emunot ve-Deʿot,* ed. Kafaḥ (Jerusalem, 1970), 8:5 (p. 246); Maimonides, *MT, Hil. Melakhim* 11:4 (in uncensored editions).
49. *Sefer ha-Tamid,* ed. Rabbis Yaʿakov Moshe Toledano and Ḥayyim Yehudah Ehrenreich (Homna, 1935; photo offset Jerusalem, 1977), p. 38.

THANKSGIVING

*Bow at the first nine words.*

מוֹדִים* We give thanks to You,
for You are the LORD our God
and God of our ancestors
for ever and all time.
You are the Rock of our lives,
Shield of our salvation
from generation to generation.
We will thank You and
declare Your praise for our lives,
which are entrusted into Your hand;
for our souls,
which are placed in Your charge;
for Your miracles
which are with us every day;
and for Your wonders and favors
at all times,
evening, morning and midday.
You are good –
for Your compassion never fails.
You are compassionate –
for Your loving-
kindnesses never cease.
We have always
placed our hope in You.

*During the Leader's Repetition, the congregation says quietly:*

מוֹדִים* We give thanks to You,
for You are the LORD
our God
and God of our ancestors,
God of all flesh,
who formed us
and formed the universe.
Blessings and thanks are due
to Your great and holy name
for giving us life
and sustaining us.
May You continue
to give us life and sustain us;
and may You gather
our exiles
to Your holy courts,
to keep Your decrees,
do Your will and serve You
with a perfect heart,
for it is for us
to give You thanks.
Blessed be God
to whom thanksgiving is due.

---

*On Ḥanukka:*

עַל הַנִּסִּים [We thank You also] for the miracles, the redemption, the mighty deeds, the salvations, and the victories in battle which You performed for our ancestors in those days, at this time.

בִּימֵי מַתִּתְיָהוּ In the days of Mattityahu, son of Yoḥanan, the High Priest, the Hasmonean, and his sons, the wicked Greek kingdom rose up against Your people Israel to make them forget Your Torah and to force them to transgress the statutes of Your will. It was then that You in Your great compassion stood by them in the time of their distress. You championed their cause, judged their claim, and avenged their wrong. You delivered the strong into the hands of the weak, the many into the hands of the few, the impure into the hands of the pure, the wicked

**הודאה**

*Bow at the first five words.*

ˈמוֹדִים אֲנַחְנוּ לָךְ
שָׁאַתָּה הוּא יהוה אֱלֹהֵינוּ
וֵאלֹהֵי אֲבוֹתֵינוּ לְעוֹלָם וָעֶד.
צוּר חַיֵּינוּ
מָגֵן יִשְׁעֵנוּ
אַתָּה הוּא לְדוֹר וָדוֹר.
נוֹדֶה לְּךָ וּנְסַפֵּר תְּהִלָּתֶךָ
עַל חַיֵּינוּ הַמְּסוּרִים בְּיָדֶךָ
וְעַל נִשְׁמוֹתֵינוּ הַפְּקוּדוֹת לָךְ
וְעַל נִסֶּיךָ שֶׁבְּכָל יוֹם עִמָּנוּ
וְעַל נִפְלְאוֹתֶיךָ וְטוֹבוֹתֶיךָ
שֶׁבְּכָל עֵת
עֶרֶב וָבֹקֶר וְצָהֳרָיִם.
הַטּוֹב, כִּי לֹא כָלוּ רַחֲמֶיךָ
וְהַמְרַחֵם, כִּי לֹא תַמּוּ חֲסָדֶיךָ
מֵעוֹלָם קִוִּינוּ לָךְ.

*During* חזרת הש״ץ, *the* קהל *says quietly:*

ˈמוֹדִים אֲנַחְנוּ לָךְ
שָׁאַתָּה הוּא
יהוה אֱלֹהֵינוּ
וֵאלֹהֵי אֲבוֹתֵינוּ
אֱלֹהֵי כָל בָּשָׂר
יוֹצְרֵנוּ, יוֹצֵר בְּרֵאשִׁית.
בְּרָכוֹת וְהוֹדָאוֹת
לְשִׁמְךָ הַגָּדוֹל וְהַקָּדוֹשׁ
עַל שֶׁהֶחֱיִיתָנוּ וְקִיַּמְתָּנוּ.
כֵּן תְּחַיֵּנוּ וּתְקַיְּמֵנוּ
וְתֶאֱסֹף גָּלֻיּוֹתֵינוּ
לְחַצְרוֹת קָדְשֶׁךָ
לִשְׁמֹר חֻקֶּיךָ
וְלַעֲשׂוֹת רְצוֹנֶךָ וּלְעָבְדְּךָ
בְּלֵבָב שָׁלֵם
עַל שֶׁאֲנַחְנוּ מוֹדִים לָךְ.
בָּרוּךְ אֵל הַהוֹדָאוֹת.

---

בחנוכה:

עַל הַנִּסִּים וְעַל הַפֻּרְקָן וְעַל הַגְּבוּרוֹת וְעַל הַתְּשׁוּעוֹת וְעַל הַמִּלְחָמוֹת שֶׁעָשִׂיתָ לַאֲבוֹתֵינוּ בַּיָּמִים הָהֵם בַּזְּמַן הַזֶּה.

בִּימֵי מַתִּתְיָהוּ בֶּן יוֹחָנָן כֹּהֵן גָּדוֹל חַשְׁמוֹנַאי וּבָנָיו, כְּשֶׁעָמְדָה מַלְכוּת יָוָן הָרְשָׁעָה עַל עַמְּךָ יִשְׂרָאֵל לְהַשְׁכִּיחָם תּוֹרָתֶךָ וּלְהַעֲבִירָם מֵחֻקֵּי רְצוֹנֶךָ, וְאַתָּה בְּרַחֲמֶיךָ הָרַבִּים עָמַדְתָּ לָהֶם בְּעֵת צָרָתָם, רַבְתָּ אֶת רִיבָם, דַּנְתָּ אֶת דִּינָם, נָקַמְתָּ אֶת נִקְמָתָם, מָסַרְתָּ גִבּוֹרִים בְּיַד חַלָּשִׁים, וְרַבִּים בְּיַד

into the hands of the righteous, and the arrogant into the hands of those who were engaged in the study of Your Torah. You made for Yourself great and holy renown in Your world, and for Your people Israel You performed a great salvation and redemption as of this very day. Your children then entered the holiest part of Your House, cleansed Your Temple, purified Your Sanctuary, kindled lights in Your holy courts, and designated these eight days of Ḥanukka for giving thanks and praise to Your great name. *Continue with "For all these things."*

*On Purim:*

עַל הַנִּסִּים [We thank You also] for the miracles, the redemption, the mighty deeds, the salvations, and the victories in battle which You performed for our ancestors in those days, at this time.

בִּימֵי מָרְדְּכַי In the days of Mordekhai and Esther, in Shushan the capital, the wicked Haman rose up against them and sought to destroy, slay and exterminate *Esther 3*
all the Jews, young and old, children and women, on one day, the thirteenth day of the twelfth month, which is the month of Adar, and to plunder their possessions. Then You in Your great compassion thwarted his counsel, frustrated his plans, and caused his scheme to recoil on his own head, so that they hanged him and his sons on the gallows. *Continue with "For all these things."*

---

וְעַל כֻּלָּם For all these things may Your name be blessed and exalted, our King, continually, for ever and all time.

*Between Rosh HaShana & Yom Kippur:* And write, for a good life, all the children of Your covenant.

Let all that lives thank You, Selah! and praise Your name in truth, God, our Savior and Help, Selah!

▾Blessed are You, LORD, whose name is "the Good" and to whom thanks are due.

---

*The following is said by the Leader during the Repetition of the Amida, except in a house of mourning and on Tisha B'Av. In Israel, if Kohanim bless the congregation, turn to page 902. See laws 370–377.*

Our God and God of our fathers, bless us with the threefold blessing in the Torah, written by the hand of Moses Your servant and pronounced by Aaron and his sons the priests, Your holy people, as it is said:

May the LORD bless you and protect you. *Cong:* May it be Your will. *Num. 6*
May the LORD make His face shine on you and be gracious to you. *Cong:* May it be Your will.
May the LORD turn His face toward you, and grant you peace. *Cong:* May it be Your will.

---

מְעַטִּים, וּטְמֵאִים בְּיַד טְהוֹרִים, וּרְשָׁעִים בְּיַד צַדִּיקִים, וְזֵדִים בְּיַד עוֹסְקֵי תוֹרָתֶךָ, וּלְךָ עָשִׂיתָ שֵׁם גָּדוֹל וְקָדוֹשׁ בְּעוֹלָמֶךָ, וּלְעַמְּךָ יִשְׂרָאֵל עָשִׂיתָ תְּשׁוּעָה גְדוֹלָה וּפֻרְקָן כְּהַיּוֹם הַזֶּה. וְאַחַר כֵּן בָּאוּ בָנֶיךָ לִדְבִיר בֵּיתֶךָ, וּפִנּוּ אֶת הֵיכָלֶךָ, וְטִהֲרוּ אֶת מִקְדָּשֶׁךָ, וְהִדְלִיקוּ נֵרוֹת בְּחַצְרוֹת קָדְשֶׁךָ, וְקָבְעוּ שְׁמוֹנַת יְמֵי חֲנֻכָּה אֵלּוּ, לְהוֹדוֹת וּלְהַלֵּל לְשִׁמְךָ הַגָּדוֹל.

*Continue with* וְעַל כֻּלָּם.

בפורים:

עַל הַנִּסִּים וְעַל הַפֻּרְקָן וְעַל הַגְּבוּרוֹת וְעַל הַתְּשׁוּעוֹת וְעַל הַמִּלְחָמוֹת שֶׁעָשִׂיתָ לַאֲבוֹתֵינוּ בַּיָּמִים הָהֵם בַּזְּמַן הַזֶּה.

בִּימֵי מָרְדְּכַי וְאֶסְתֵּר בְּשׁוּשַׁן הַבִּירָה, כְּשֶׁעָמַד עֲלֵיהֶם הָמָן הָרָשָׁע, בִּקֵּשׁ לְהַשְׁמִיד לַהֲרֹג וּלְאַבֵּד אֶת־כָּל־הַיְּהוּדִים מִנַּעַר וְעַד־זָקֵן טַף וְנָשִׁים בְּיוֹם אֶחָד, בִּשְׁלוֹשָׁה עָשָׂר לְחֹדֶשׁ שְׁנֵים־עָשָׂר, הוּא־חֹדֶשׁ אֲדָר, וּשְׁלָלָם לָבוֹז: וְאַתָּה בְּרַחֲמֶיךָ הָרַבִּים הֵפַרְתָּ אֶת עֲצָתוֹ, וְקִלְקַלְתָּ אֶת מַחֲשַׁבְתּוֹ, וַהֲשֵׁבוֹתָ לּוֹ גְּמוּלוֹ בְּרֹאשׁוֹ, וְתָלוּ אוֹתוֹ וְאֶת בָּנָיו עַל הָעֵץ. אסתר ג

*Continue with* וְעַל כֻּלָּם.

---

וְעַל כֻּלָּם יִתְבָּרַךְ וְיִתְרוֹמַם שִׁמְךָ מַלְכֵּנוּ תָּמִיד לְעוֹלָם וָעֶד.

בעשרת ימי תשובה: וּכְתֹב לְחַיִּים טוֹבִים כָּל בְּנֵי בְרִיתֶךָ.

וְכֹל הַחַיִּים יוֹדְוּךָ סֶּלָה, וִיהַלְלוּ אֶת שִׁמְךָ בֶּאֱמֶת הָאֵל יְשׁוּעָתֵנוּ וְעֶזְרָתֵנוּ סֶלָה.

ׂבָּרוּךְ אַתָּה יהוה, הַטּוֹב שִׁמְךָ וּלְךָ נָאֶה לְהוֹדוֹת.

---

*The following is said by the* שליח ציבור *during* חזרת הש״ץ *except in a house of mourning and on* תשעה באב. *In* ארץ ישראל *if* כהנים *say* ברכת כהנים *turn to page 903. See laws 370–377.*

אֱלֹהֵינוּ וֵאלֹהֵי אֲבוֹתֵינוּ, בָּרְכֵנוּ בַּבְּרָכָה הַמְשֻׁלֶּשֶׁת בַּתּוֹרָה, הַכְּתוּבָה עַל יְדֵי מֹשֶׁה עַבְדֶּךָ, הָאֲמוּרָה מִפִּי אַהֲרֹן וּבָנָיו כֹּהֲנִים עַם קְדוֹשֶׁיךָ, כָּאָמוּר

יְבָרֶכְךָ יהוה וְיִשְׁמְרֶךָ: קהל: כֵּן יְהִי רָצוֹן במדבר ו

יָאֵר יהוה פָּנָיו אֵלֶיךָ וִיחֻנֶּךָּ: קהל: כֵּן יְהִי רָצוֹן

יִשָּׂא יהוה פָּנָיו אֵלֶיךָ וְיָשֵׂם לְךָ שָׁלוֹם: קהל: כֵּן יְהִי רָצוֹן

PEACE

שִׂים שָׁלוֹם Grant peace, goodness and blessing,
grace, loving-kindness and compassion
to us and all Israel Your people.
Bless us, our Father, all as one, with the light of Your face,
for by the light of Your face You have given us, LORD our God,
the Torah of life and love of kindness,
righteousness, blessing, compassion, life and peace.
May it be good in Your eyes to bless Your people Israel
at every time, in every hour, with Your peace.

*Between Rosh HaShana & Yom Kippur:* In the book of life, blessing, peace and prosperity,
may we and all Your people the house of Israel
be remembered and written before You
for a good life, and for peace.*

Blessed are You, LORD, who blesses His people Israel with peace.

**Between Rosh HaShana and Yom Kippur in the Diaspora, many end the blessing:*
Blessed are You, LORD, who makes peace.

*The following verse concludes the Leader's Repetition of the Amida. Some also say it here as part of the silent Amida. See law 368.*

May the words of my mouth and the meditation of my heart *Ps. 19*
find favor before You, LORD, my Rock and Redeemer.

---

chaos, of disintegration.[51] Through "the light of Your face" was given the Torah, which is the divine plan for integrating and unifying all creation. It is a *"Torat Ḥayyim,"* a life-giving Torah, which goes hand in hand with the "love of kindness." It is after all the divine will to bestow goodness which is responsible for the creation of the world. "The world was built upon kindness (*ḥesed*)."[52] And for this reason, Rabbi Akiva was able to sum up the entire Torah in the single verse "You shall love your neighbor as yourself."[53] "Rabbi Akiva says: 'You shall love your neighbor as yourself.' This is a great principle in the Torah."[54]

51. *b. Sanhedrin* 97a; *'Avodah Zarah* 9a.
52. Psalms 89:3.
53. Leviticus 19:18.
54. *Sifra, Kedoshim*; *y. Nedarim* 9:4; *Genesis Rabbah* 24:7. Cf. *b. Shabbat* 31a. *OR*, vol. 1, pp. 289–291.

שלום

**שִׂים שָׁלוֹם טוֹבָה וּבְרָכָה**
**חֵן וָחֶסֶד וְרַחֲמִים עָלֵינוּ וְעַל כָּל יִשְׂרָאֵל עַמֶּךָ.**
**בָּרְכֵנוּ אָבִינוּ כֻּלָּנוּ כְּאֶחָד בְּאוֹר פָּנֶיךָ**
**כִּי בְאוֹר פָּנֶיךָ נָתַתָּ לָּנוּ יהוה אֱלֹהֵינוּ**
**תּוֹרַת חַיִּים וְאַהֲבַת חֶסֶד**
**וּצְדָקָה וּבְרָכָה וְרַחֲמִים וְחַיִּים וְשָׁלוֹם.**
**וְטוֹב בְּעֵינֶיךָ לְבָרֵךְ אֶת עַמְּךָ יִשְׂרָאֵל**
**בְּכָל עֵת וּבְכָל שָׁעָה בִּשְׁלוֹמֶךָ.**

בעשרת ימי תשובה: **בְּסֵפֶר חַיִּים, בְּרָכָה וְשָׁלוֹם, וּפַרְנָסָה טוֹבָה נִזָּכֵר וְנִכָּתֵב לְפָנֶיךָ, אֲנַחְנוּ וְכָל עַמְּךָ בֵּית יִשְׂרָאֵל לְחַיִּים טוֹבִים וּלְשָׁלוֹם.***

**בָּרוּךְ אַתָּה יהוה, הַמְבָרֵךְ אֶת עַמּוֹ יִשְׂרָאֵל בַּשָּׁלוֹם.**

**During the* עשרת ימי תשובה *in* חוץ לארץ*, many end the blessing:*

**בָּרוּךְ אַתָּה יהוה, עוֹשֶׂה הַשָּׁלוֹם.**

*The following verse concludes the* חזרת הש״ץ.
*Some also say it here as part of the silent* עמידה*. See law 368.*

תהלים יט **יִהְיוּ לְרָצוֹן אִמְרֵי־פִי וְהֶגְיוֹן לִבִּי לְפָנֶיךָ, יהוה צוּרִי וְגֹאֲלִי:**

---

**בָּרְכֵנוּ אָבִינוּ כֻּלָּנוּ כְּאֶחָד בְּאוֹר פָּנֶיךָ, כִּי בְאוֹר פָּנֶיךָ נָתַתָּ לָּנוּ יהוה אֱלֹהֵינוּ, תּוֹרַת חַיִּים וְאַהֲבַת חֶסֶד** *Bless us, our Father, all as one, with the light of Your face, for by the light of Your face You have given us, Lord our God, the Torah of life and love of kindness.* The designation "our Father," as opposed to "our King," indicates an intimacy beyond the formalities, beyond the role of King. We address a level of godliness that transcends all that. This utter transcendence is further enforced by the words "the light of Your face." We are striving for a unity of all existence ("all as one") not readily available in the worlds. This unity can come about only through the Torah. The Torah was preceded by two millennia of *"Tohu,"* of

אֱלֹהַי My God, *Berakhot 17a*
guard my tongue from evil and my lips from deceitful speech.
To those who curse me, let my soul be silent;
may my soul be to all like the dust.
Open my heart to Your Torah
and let my soul pursue Your commandments.
As for all who plan evil against me,
swiftly thwart their counsel and frustrate their plans.
Act for the sake of Your name; act for the sake of Your right hand;
act for the sake of Your holiness; act for the sake of Your Torah.
That Your beloved ones may be delivered, *Ps. 60*
save with Your right hand and answer me.
May the words of my mouth and the meditation of my heart *Ps. 19*
find favor before You, Lord, my Rock and Redeemer.

*Bow, take three steps back, then bow, first left, then right, then center, while saying:*

May He who makes peace in His high places,
make peace for us and all Israel – and say: Amen.

---

"And I am in the midst of the exile."[57] The internal, essential "I."

Adam sinned for he was alienated from his essence; he turned to the opinion of the Serpent, and lost himself. He did not how to respond clearly to the [divine] question "Where are you?"[58] because he did know his self; because the true "I" was lost from him.[59]

And so goes the world, drowning in the loss of the "I" of each one, individual and collective. There come along learned educators. They gaze at the externals. They too lose sight of the "I," and add straw to the fire, slaking thirst with vinegar, and stuffing brains and hearts with all that is external. The "I" is increasingly forgotten. And once there is no "I," there is no "he," and of course, there is no "you."

"The breath of our nostrils, the Messiah of the Lord."[60] This is Messiah's

57. Ezekiel 1:1.
58. Genesis 3:9.
59. According to Rabbi Shneur Zalman of Liadi, this question *"Ayeka?"* ("Where are you?") resounds throughout time. God is forever asking man, "Where are you in the world?" "What have you accomplished in your lifetime?" "Have you benefited mankind?" (H.M. Heilman, *Beit Rabbi* [Berdichev 1902], Part 1, chap. 15; f. 29)
60. Lamentations 4:20.

אֱלֹהַי ברכות יז.

נְצֹר לְשׁוֹנִי מֵרָע וּשְׂפָתַי מִדַּבֵּר מִרְמָה

וְלִמְקַלְלַי נַפְשִׁי תִדֹּם, וְנַפְשִׁי כֶּעָפָר לַכֹּל תִּהְיֶה.

פְּתַח לִבִּי בְּתוֹרָתֶךָ, וּבְמִצְוֹתֶיךָ תִּרְדֹּף נַפְשִׁי.

וְכָל הַחוֹשְׁבִים עָלַי רָעָה

מְהֵרָה הָפֵר עֲצָתָם וְקַלְקֵל מַחֲשַׁבְתָּם.

עֲשֵׂה לְמַעַן שְׁמֶךָ, עֲשֵׂה לְמַעַן יְמִינֶךָ

עֲשֵׂה לְמַעַן קְדֻשָּׁתֶךָ, עֲשֵׂה לְמַעַן תּוֹרָתֶךָ.

לְמַעַן יֵחָלְצוּן יְדִידֶיךָ, הוֹשִׁיעָה יְמִינְךָ וַעֲנֵנִי: תהלים ס

יִהְיוּ לְרָצוֹן אִמְרֵי־פִי וְהֶגְיוֹן לִבִּי לְפָנֶיךָ, יהוה צוּרִי וְגֹאֲלִי: תהלים יט

*Bow, take three steps back, then bow, first left, then right, then center, while saying:*

עֹשֶׂה שָׁלוֹם/ בעשרת ימי תשובה: הַשָּׁלוֹם/ בִּמְרוֹמָיו

הוּא יַעֲשֶׂה שָׁלוֹם עָלֵינוּ וְעַל כָּל יִשְׂרָאֵל

וְאִמְרוּ אָמֵן.

---

יִהְיוּ לְרָצוֹן אִמְרֵי־פִי וְהֶגְיוֹן לִבִּי לְפָנֶיךָ *May the words of my mouth…find favor.* There is a kabbalistic custom to recite at this point a verse from the *Tanakh* (Bible) containing either outright mention of one's name, or an allusion thereto, inasmuch as the verse begins with the first letter of the name and ends with the last letter of the name.[55] In this way, after death one will be spared Gehinnom. (One who cannot remember his or her name on Judgment Day, will be sentenced by the Celestial Court to Gehinnom.)[56]

Without belittling the kabbalistic custom, the truth is, some of us experience "Gehinnom" while yet we live. The name is the essence of the self; one who is alienated from self, from the source of being, is sentenced to a living Hell.

---

55. *OR*, vol. 1 p. 292.
56. See Naftali Herz Treves, *Siddur Dikduk Tefillah* (Tihingen, 1560); Rabbi Yeḥiel Mikhel Epstein, *Kitsur Shelah: Mahadura Batra* (Amsterdam, 1701), *"Tikkun Ḥibbut ha-Kever,"* f.115; parenthetical remarks of "Rabbi Obadiah the Prophet" inserted in Rashi, Micah 6:9; Rabbi Baruch Katz, *"Le-Khulam Shemot Yikra,"* in Rabbi Yosef Aryeh Katz, *Divrei Yosef* (B'nei Berak, 1987), pp. 137–162.

יְהִי רָצוֹן May it be Your will, Lord our God and God of our ancestors,
that the Temple be rebuilt speedily in our days,
and grant us a share in Your Torah.
And there we will serve You with reverence,
as in the days of old and as in former years.
Then the offering of Judah and Jerusalem will be pleasing to the Lord *Mal. 3*
as in the days of old and as in former years.

*When praying with a minyan, the Amida is repeated aloud by the Leader.*

*On days when Taḥanun is said (see page 208), start Taḥanun on page 208.*
*On Mondays and Thursdays start Taḥanun on page 208.*
*In Israel, on days on which Taḥanun is said, some say Viduy and the Thirteen Attributes of Divine Compassion on page 200. See law 478a.*

*On fast days (except Tisha B'Av) most congregations say Seliḥot on page 1006 before Avinu Malkenu on page 202.*

*Between Rosh HaShana and Yom Kippur (but not on Erev Yom Kippur, unless it falls on Friday), say Avinu Malkenu on page 202.*

*On Rosh Ḥodesh, Ḥanukka, Ḥol HaMo'ed, Yom HaAtzma'ut and Yom Yerushalayim, say Hallel on page 790.*

*On other days when Taḥanun is not said (see page 208), the Leader says Half Kaddish on page 222.*

---

In the future, "as in the days of old and as in former years," the animals will once again be most intelligent, and it would be unseemly to slaughter them, just as it is morally unjustifiable to slaughter humans today. At that time, sacrifices from the vegetable kingdom – not the animal kingdom – will be pleasing to the Lord.[66]

---

Ḥayyim Luzzatto, *Adir ba-Marom*, vol. 1, ed. Spinner (Jerusalem, 1990), pp. 30–33; Rabbi Shneur Zalman of Liadi, *Likkutei Torah, Tsav*, s.v. *va-akhaltem akhol ve-savo'a* (7c).

66. *OR*, vol. 1, p. 292. Cf. *SK* 1:763; *"Afikim ba-Negev"* in *Otserot ha-Rayah*, ed. Zuriel, vol. 2 (Tel-Aviv, 1988), p. 756; Rav Kook's commentary to *Hagadah shel Pesah* (Jerusalem, 1994), p. 225; *OR*, vol. 2, p. 49, s.v. *u-shnei 'esronim solet*; *KMYK*, vol. 2, *Maḥberot Ketanot, Boisk* 1, par. 8 (p. 15); *Li-Nevukhei ha-Dor*, ed. Rabbi Shaḥar Raḥmani (Tel-Aviv, 2014), chap. 10 (p. 72).
Concerning Rav Kook's view on vegetarianism in general, see Bezalel Naor, *"Ha-Tsimḥonut bi-re'i ha-Yahadut"* ("Vegetarianism in the View of Judaism") in idem, *Ben Shanah Shaul* (Saul Nyer Memorial Volume) (Jerusalem, 5755/1995), pp. 291–298; and Avinoam Rosenak, *The Prophetic Halakhah: Rabbi A.I.H. Kook's Philosophy of Halakhah* (Hebrew) (Jerusalem: Magnes, 2007), pp. 358–364.

יְהִי רָצוֹן מִלְּפָנֶיךָ יהוה אֱלֹהֵינוּ וֵאלֹהֵי אֲבוֹתֵינוּ
שֶׁיִּבָּנֶה בֵּית הַמִּקְדָּשׁ בִּמְהֵרָה בְיָמֵינוּ, וְתֵן חֶלְקֵנוּ בְּתוֹרָתֶךָ
וְשָׁם נַעֲבָדְךָ בְּיִרְאָה כִּימֵי עוֹלָם וּכְשָׁנִים קַדְמֹנִיּוֹת.
מלאכי ג וְעָרְבָה לַיהוה מִנְחַת יְהוּדָה וִירוּשָׁלָםִ כִּימֵי עוֹלָם וּכְשָׁנִים קַדְמֹנִיּוֹת:

*When praying with a* מנין*, the* עמידה *is repeated aloud by the* שליח ציבור*.*

*On days when* תחנון *is said (see page 209), start* תחנון *on page 209.*
*On Mondays and Thursdays start* תחנון *on page 209.*
*In* ארץ ישראל*, on days on which* תחנון *is said,*
*some say* וידוי *and the* י״ג מדות *on page 201. See law 478a.*

*On fast days (except* תשעה באב*) most congregations say* סליחות
*on page 1007 before* אבינו מלכנו *on page 203.*

*During the* עשרת ימי תשובה *(but not on* ערב יום כיפור*,*
*unless it falls on Friday), say* אבינו מלכנו *on page 203.*

*On* ראש חודש*,* חנוכה*,* חול המועד*,* יום העצמאות *and* יום ירושלים*,*
*say* הלל *on page 791.*

*On other days when* תחנון *is not said (see page 209),*
*the* שליח ציבור *says* חצי קדיש *on page 223.*

---

strength, the majesty of his greatness. The Messiah is not outside of us; he is the very breath of our nostrils.

The Lord our God and David our King we shall seek …[61] Our "I" we shall seek; our self we shall seek and we shall find.[62] (Editor)

**וְעָרְבָה לַיהוה מִנְחַת יְהוּדָה וִירוּשָׁלָםִ כִּימֵי עוֹלָם וּכְשָׁנִים קַדְמֹנִיּוֹת** *The offering* (minḥat) *of Judah and Jerusalem will be pleasing to the Lord as in the days of old and as in former years.*[63] Rav Kook subscribed to the belief that in the future the *minḥah*, a meal offering, will be the sacrifice brought in the Holy Temple, replacing animal sacrifices. This belief is rooted in a Lurianic teaching that before the Primordial Sin, the animals were possessed of an intelligence on a par with our own human intelligence today. (The donkey of Rabbi Pinḥas ben Yair, legendary for its extreme intelligence,[64] was a "throwback" to that bygone era.)[65]

---

61. Adapted from Hosea 3:5.
62. *OK*, vol. 3, pp. 140–141 = *SK* 3:24. Cf. *SK* 6:198.
63. Malachi 3:4.
64. *b. Shabbat* 112b; *Ḥullin* 7; *y. Demai* 1:3; *Shekalim* 5:1; *Genesis Rabbah* 60:8.
65. Rabbi Ḥayyim Vital, *Likkutei Torah* (Vilna, 1880), *'Ekev* (97b-c). See also Rabbi Moses

# VIDUY

*In Israel on days on which Taḥanun is said (see page 208), some say Viduy and the Thirteen Attributes of Divine Compassion. See law 478a. The congregation stands and says:*

אֱלֹהֵינוּ Our God and God of our fathers, let our prayer come before You, and do not hide Yourself from our plea, for we are not so arrogant or obstinate as to say before You, LORD, our God and God of our fathers, we are righteous and have not sinned, for in truth, we and our fathers have sinned.

*At each expression, strike the chest on the left side:*

אָשַׁמְנוּ We have been guilty, we have acted treacherously, we have robbed, we have spoken slander. We have acted perversely, we have acted wickedly, we have acted presumptuously, we have been violent, we have framed lies. We have given bad advice, we have deceived, we have scorned, we have rebelled, we have provoked, we have turned away, we have committed iniquity, we have transgressed, we have persecuted, we have been obstinate. We have acted wickedly, we have corrupted, we have acted abominably, we have strayed, we have led others astray.

We have turned away from Your commandments and good laws, to no avail, for You are just in all that has befallen us, for You have acted faithfully while we have done wickedly. *Neh. 9*

*When praying without a minyan continue with "He is compassionate" on page 208.*

## THIRTEEN ATTRIBUTES OF DIVINE COMPASSION

אֵל אֶרֶךְ You are a God slow to anger, You are called Master of Compassion, and You have taught the way of repentance. May You remember today and every day the greatness of Your compassion and loving-kindness for the sake of the descendants of Your beloved ones. Turn toward us in compassion, for You are the Master of Compassion. We come before You in plea and prayer, as You in ancient times showed the humble one [Moses]. Turn from Your fierce anger, as is written in Your Torah. In the shadow of Your wings may we shelter and abide, as on the day when the LORD descended in the cloud. ▸ Disregard transgression and erase guilt as on the day You stood with him [Moses] there. Hear our cry and heed our word, as on the day You proclaimed in the name of the LORD, and there it is written:

*All say aloud:*

וַיַּעֲבֹר And the LORD passed by before him and proclaimed: *Ex. 34*

The LORD, the LORD, compassionate and gracious God, slow to anger, abounding in loving-kindness and truth, extending loving-kindness to a thousand generations, forgiving iniquity, rebellion and sin,
and absolving [the guilty who repent]. Forgive us our iniquity and our sin, and take us as Your inheritance. Forgive us, our Father, for we have sinned. Pardon us, our King, for we have transgressed. For You, LORD, are good and forgiving, abounding in loving-kindness to all who call on You. *Ps. 86*

*On Mondays and Thursdays continue with "He is compassionate" on page 208; on other days with "David said" on page 216.*

# וידוי

*In* ארץ ישראל *on days on which* תחנון *is said* (*see page 209*), *some say* וידוי *and the* י״ג מדות. *See law 478a. The* קהל *stands and says:*

אֱלֹהֵינוּ וֵאלֹהֵי אֲבוֹתֵינוּ, תָּבוֹא לְפָנֶיךָ תְּפִלָּתֵנוּ, וְאַל תִּתְעַלַּם מִתְּחִנָּתֵנוּ, שֶׁאֵין אֲנַחְנוּ עַזֵּי פָנִים וּקְשֵׁי עֹרֶף לוֹמַר לְפָנֶיךָ, יהוה אֱלֹהֵינוּ וֵאלֹהֵי אֲבוֹתֵינוּ, צַדִּיקִים אֲנַחְנוּ וְלֹא חָטָאנוּ, אֲבָל אֲנַחְנוּ וַאֲבוֹתֵינוּ חָטָאנוּ.

*At each expression, strike the chest on the left side:*

אָשַׁמְנוּ, בָּגַדְנוּ, גָּזַלְנוּ, דִּבַּרְנוּ דֹפִי, הֶעֱוִינוּ, וְהִרְשַׁעְנוּ, זַדְנוּ, חָמַסְנוּ, טָפַלְנוּ שֶׁקֶר, יָעַצְנוּ רָע, כִּזַּבְנוּ, לַצְנוּ, מָרַדְנוּ, נִאַצְנוּ, סָרַרְנוּ, עָוִינוּ, פָּשַׁעְנוּ, צָרַרְנוּ, קִשִּׁינוּ עֹרֶף, רָשַׁעְנוּ, שִׁחַתְנוּ, תִּעַבְנוּ, תָּעִינוּ, תִּעְתָּעְנוּ.

סַרְנוּ מִמִּצְוֹתֶיךָ וּמִמִּשְׁפָּטֶיךָ הַטּוֹבִים, וְלֹא שָׁוָה לָנוּ. וְאַתָּה צַדִּיק עַל כָּל־הַבָּא עָלֵינוּ, כִּי־אֱמֶת עָשִׂיתָ, וַאֲנַחְנוּ הִרְשָׁעְנוּ: נחמיה ט

*When praying without a* מנין *continue with* וְהוּא רַחוּם *on page 209.*

י״ג מדות

אֵל אֶרֶךְ אַפַּיִם אַתָּה, וּבַעַל הָרַחֲמִים נִקְרֵאתָ, וְדֶרֶךְ תְּשׁוּבָה הוֹרֵיתָ. גְּדֻלַּת רַחֲמֶיךָ וַחֲסָדֶיךָ, תִּזְכֹּר הַיּוֹם וּבְכָל יוֹם לְזֶרַע יְדִידֶיךָ. תֵּפֶן אֵלֵינוּ בְּרַחֲמִים, כִּי אַתָּה הוּא בַּעַל הָרַחֲמִים. בְּתַחֲנוּן וּבִתְפִלָּה פָּנֶיךָ נְקַדֵּם, כְּהוֹדַעְתָּ לֶעָנָו מִקֶּדֶם. מֵחֲרוֹן אַפְּךָ שׁוּב, כְּמוֹ בְּתוֹרָתְךָ כָּתוּב. וּבְצֵל כְּנָפֶיךָ נֶחֱסֶה וְנִתְלוֹנָן, כְּיוֹם וַיֵּרֶד יהוה בֶּעָנָן. ‹ תַּעֲבֹר עַל פֶּשַׁע וְתִמְחֶה אָשָׁם, כְּיוֹם וַיִּתְיַצֵּב עִמּוֹ שָׁם. תַּאֲזִין שַׁוְעָתֵנוּ וְתַקְשִׁיב מֶנּוּ מַאֲמַר, כְּיוֹם וַיִּקְרָא בְשֵׁם יהוה, וְשָׁם נֶאֱמַר:

*All say aloud:*

וַיַּעֲבֹר יהוה עַל־פָּנָיו וַיִּקְרָא שמות לד

יהוה, יהוה, אֵל רַחוּם וְחַנּוּן, אֶרֶךְ אַפַּיִם וְרַב־חֶסֶד וֶאֱמֶת:
נֹצֵר חֶסֶד לָאֲלָפִים, נֹשֵׂא עָוֹן וָפֶשַׁע וְחַטָּאָה, וְנַקֵּה:
וְסָלַחְתָּ לַעֲוֹנֵנוּ וּלְחַטָּאתֵנוּ, וּנְחַלְתָּנוּ:
סְלַח לָנוּ אָבִינוּ כִּי חָטָאנוּ, מְחַל לָנוּ מַלְכֵּנוּ כִּי פָשָׁעְנוּ
כִּי־אַתָּה אֲדֹנָי טוֹב וְסַלָּח וְרַב־חֶסֶד לְכָל־קֹרְאֶיךָ: תהלים פו

*On Mondays and Thursdays continue with* וְהוּא רַחוּם *on page 209; on other days with* וַיֹּאמֶר דָּוִד *on page 217.*

*The following nine verses are said responsively, first by the Leader, then by the congregation:*

Our Father, our King, bring us back to You in perfect repentance.

Our Father, our King, send a complete healing to the sick of Your people.

Our Father, our King, tear up the evil decree against us.

Our Father, our King, remember us with a memory of favorable deeds before You.

*Between Rosh HaShana and Yom Kippur:*

Our Father, our King, write us in the book of good life.

Our Father, our King, write us in the book of redemption and salvation.

Our Father, our King, write us in the book of livelihood and sustenance.

Our Father, our King, write us in the book of merit.

Our Father, our King, write us in the book of pardon and forgiveness.

*On Fast Days:*

Our Father, our King, remember us for a good life.

Our Father, our King, remember us for redemption and salvation.

Our Father, our King, remember us for livelihood and sustenance.

Our Father, our King, remember us for merit.

Our Father, our King, remember us for pardon and forgiveness.

*End of responsive reading.*

Our Father, our King, let salvation soon flourish for us.

Our Father, our King, raise the honor of Your people Israel.

Our Father, our King, raise the honor of Your anointed.

*The following nine verses are said responsively, first by the* שליח ציבור*, then by the* קהל*:*

אָבִינוּ מַלְכֵּנוּ, הַחֲזִירֵנוּ בִּתְשׁוּבָה שְׁלֵמָה לְפָנֶיךָ.
אָבִינוּ מַלְכֵּנוּ, שְׁלַח רְפוּאָה שְׁלֵמָה לְחוֹלֵי עַמֶּךָ.
אָבִינוּ מַלְכֵּנוּ, קְרַע רֹעַ גְּזַר דִּינֵנוּ.
אָבִינוּ מַלְכֵּנוּ, זָכְרֵנוּ בְּזִכְרוֹן טוֹב לְפָנֶיךָ.

*During the* עשרת ימי תשובה*:*

אָבִינוּ מַלְכֵּנוּ, כָּתְבֵנוּ בְּסֵפֶר חַיִּים טוֹבִים.
אָבִינוּ מַלְכֵּנוּ, כָּתְבֵנוּ בְּסֵפֶר גְּאֻלָּה וִישׁוּעָה.
אָבִינוּ מַלְכֵּנוּ, כָּתְבֵנוּ בְּסֵפֶר פַּרְנָסָה וְכַלְכָּלָה.
אָבִינוּ מַלְכֵּנוּ, כָּתְבֵנוּ בְּסֵפֶר זְכֻיּוֹת.
אָבִינוּ מַלְכֵּנוּ, כָּתְבֵנוּ בְּסֵפֶר סְלִיחָה וּמְחִילָה.

*On Fast Days:*

אָבִינוּ מַלְכֵּנוּ, זָכְרֵנוּ לְחַיִּים טוֹבִים.
אָבִינוּ מַלְכֵּנוּ, זָכְרֵנוּ לִגְאֻלָּה וִישׁוּעָה.
אָבִינוּ מַלְכֵּנוּ, זָכְרֵנוּ לְפַרְנָסָה וְכַלְכָּלָה.
אָבִינוּ מַלְכֵּנוּ, זָכְרֵנוּ לִזְכֻיּוֹת.
אָבִינוּ מַלְכֵּנוּ, זָכְרֵנוּ לִסְלִיחָה וּמְחִילָה.

*End of responsive reading.*

אָבִינוּ מַלְכֵּנוּ, הַצְמַח לָנוּ יְשׁוּעָה בְּקָרוֹב.
אָבִינוּ מַלְכֵּנוּ, הָרֵם קֶרֶן יִשְׂרָאֵל עַמֶּךָ.
אָבִינוּ מַלְכֵּנוּ, הָרֵם קֶרֶן מְשִׁיחֶךָ.

Our Father, our King, fill our hands with Your blessings.

Our Father, our King, fill our storehouses with abundance.

Our Father, our King, hear our voice, pity and be compassionate to us.

Our Father, our King, accept, with compassion and favor, our prayer.

Our Father, our King, open the gates of heaven to our prayer.

Our Father, our King, remember that we are dust.

Our Father, our King, please do not turn us away from You empty-handed.

Our Father, our King, may this moment be a moment of compassion and a time of favor before You.

Our Father, our King, have pity on us, our children and our infants.

Our Father, our King, act for the sake of those who were killed for Your holy name.

Our Father, our King, act for the sake of those who were slaughtered for proclaiming Your Unity.

Our Father, our King, act for the sake of those
who went through fire and water
to sanctify Your name.

Our Father, our King, avenge before our eyes
the spilt blood of Your servants.

Our Father, our King, act for Your sake, if not for ours.

Our Father, our King, act for Your sake, and save us.

Our Father, our King, act for the sake of Your abundant compassion.

Our Father, our King, act for the sake of Your great, mighty and awesome name by which we are called.

▸ Our Father, our King, be gracious to us and answer us, though we have no worthy deeds; act with us in charity and loving-kindness and save us.

*The Ark is closed.*

אָבִינוּ מַלְכֵּנוּ, מַלֵּא יָדֵינוּ מִבִּרְכוֹתֶיךָ.
אָבִינוּ מַלְכֵּנוּ, מַלֵּא אֲסָמֵינוּ שָׂבָע.
אָבִינוּ מַלְכֵּנוּ, שְׁמַע קוֹלֵנוּ, חוּס וְרַחֵם עָלֵינוּ.
אָבִינוּ מַלְכֵּנוּ, קַבֵּל בְּרַחֲמִים וּבְרָצוֹן אֶת תְּפִלָּתֵנוּ.
אָבִינוּ מַלְכֵּנוּ, פְּתַח שַׁעֲרֵי שָׁמַיִם לִתְפִלָּתֵנוּ.
אָבִינוּ מַלְכֵּנוּ, זְכֹר כִּי עָפָר אֲנָחְנוּ.
אָבִינוּ מַלְכֵּנוּ, נָא אַל תְּשִׁיבֵנוּ רֵיקָם מִלְּפָנֶיךָ.
אָבִינוּ מַלְכֵּנוּ, תְּהֵא הַשָּׁעָה הַזֹּאת שְׁעַת רַחֲמִים וְעֵת רָצוֹן מִלְּפָנֶיךָ.
אָבִינוּ מַלְכֵּנוּ, חֲמֹל עָלֵינוּ וְעַל עוֹלָלֵינוּ וְטַפֵּנוּ.
אָבִינוּ מַלְכֵּנוּ, עֲשֵׂה לְמַעַן הֲרוּגִים עַל שֵׁם קָדְשֶׁךָ.
אָבִינוּ מַלְכֵּנוּ, עֲשֵׂה לְמַעַן טְבוּחִים עַל יִחוּדֶךָ.
אָבִינוּ מַלְכֵּנוּ, עֲשֵׂה לְמַעַן בָּאֵי בָאֵשׁ וּבַמַּיִם עַל קִדּוּשׁ שְׁמֶךָ.
אָבִינוּ מַלְכֵּנוּ, נְקֹם לְעֵינֵינוּ נִקְמַת דַּם עֲבָדֶיךָ הַשָּׁפוּךְ.
אָבִינוּ מַלְכֵּנוּ, עֲשֵׂה לְמַעַנְךָ אִם לֹא לְמַעֲנֵנוּ.
אָבִינוּ מַלְכֵּנוּ, עֲשֵׂה לְמַעַנְךָ וְהוֹשִׁיעֵנוּ.
אָבִינוּ מַלְכֵּנוּ, עֲשֵׂה לְמַעַן רַחֲמֶיךָ הָרַבִּים.
אָבִינוּ מַלְכֵּנוּ, עֲשֵׂה לְמַעַן שִׁמְךָ הַגָּדוֹל הַגִּבּוֹר וְהַנּוֹרָא שֶׁנִּקְרָא עָלֵינוּ.
◄ אָבִינוּ מַלְכֵּנוּ, חָנֵּנוּ וַעֲנֵנוּ, כִּי אֵין בָּנוּ מַעֲשִׂים עֲשֵׂה עִמָּנוּ צְדָקָה וָחֶסֶד וְהוֹשִׁיעֵנוּ.

*The* ארון קודש *is closed.*

# TAḤANUN

*On Mondays and Thursdays, when Taḥanun is said, begin with "He is compassionate" below. On other days when Taḥanun is said, begin with "David said" on page 216.*

*Taḥanun is not said on: Rosh Ḥodesh, Ḥanukka, Tu BiShvat, the 14th and 15th of Adar I, Purim and Shushan Purim, in the month of Nisan, Yom HaAtzma'ut, the 14th of Iyar (Pesaḥ Sheni), Lag BaOmer, Yom Yerushalayim, from Rosh Ḥodesh Sivan through the day after Shavuot (in Israel through 12th of Sivan), Tisha B'Av, Tu B'Av, Erev Rosh HaShana, and from Erev Yom Kippur through the day after Simḥat Torah (in Israel through Rosh Ḥodesh Marḥeshvan).*

*Taḥanun is also not said: on the morning of a Brit Mila, either where the brit will take place or where the father, Sandak or Mohel are present; if a groom is present (and some say a bride) on the day of his wedding or during the week of Sheva Berakhot; in a house of mourning.*

*In Israel on days on which Taḥanun is said, say Viduy and the Thirteen Attributes of Divine Compassion on page 200. See law 478a.*

*The following until "David said" on page 216 is said standing.*

וְהוּא רַחוּם He is compassionate. He forgives iniquity and does not destroy. *Ps. 78*
Repeatedly He suppresses His anger, not rousing His full wrath. LORD, do
not withhold Your compassion from us. May Your loving-kindness and
truth always protect us. Save us, LORD our God, and gather us from among *Ps. 106*
the nations, that we may give thanks to Your holy name and glory in Your
praise. If You, LORD, should keep account of sins, O LORD, who could stand? *Ps. 130*
But with You is forgiveness, that You may be revered. Do not deal with us
according to our sins; do not repay us according to our iniquities. Though *Jer. 14*
our iniquities testify against us, LORD, act for Your name's sake. Remember, *Ps. 25*
LORD, Your compassion and loving-kindness, for they are everlasting. May *Ps. 20*
the LORD answer us when we are in distress; may the name of Jacob's God
protect us. LORD, save! May the King answer us when we call. Our Father,
our King, be gracious to us and answer us, though we have no worthy deeds;
act charitably with us for Your name's sake. LORD our God, hear the sound
of our pleas. Remember for us the covenant of our ancestors, and save us for
Your name's sake.

---

Two *halakhot* (laws) emerge from this passage: One should not fall upon one's face unless one is assured that God will answer him as he did Joshua, telling him to rise.[2] And falling upon the face is appropriate only in the presence of the ark, i.e. a Torah scroll.[3] The exception to this rule is Jerusalem. In the city of Jerusalem, it is customary to fall on the face even in the absence

2. *y. Ta'anit* 2:6; *'Avodah Zarah* 4:1; *b. Megillah* 22b; Maimonides, *MT, Hil. Tefillah* 5:14; *Shulḥan 'Arukh, OḤ* 131:8.
3. Rabbi El'azar of Worms, *Roke'aḥ*, chap. 324 (cited in Rabbi Joseph Karo, *Beit Yosef, OḤ* 131); *Shulḥan 'Arukh, OḤ* 131:2 (gloss of Rabbi Moses Isserles).

# סדר תחנון

*On Mondays and Thursdays, when* תחנון *is said, begin with* וְהוּא רַחוּם *below.*
*On other days when* תחנון *is said, begin with* וַיֹּאמֶר דָּוִד *on page 217.*

תחנון *is not said on:* ראש חודש, חנוכה, ט״ו בשבט*, the 14th and 15th of* אדר א׳, פורים *and* שושן פורים, *in the month of* ניסן, יום העצמאות, *the 14th of* אייר (פסח שני), ל״ג בעומר, יום ירושלים, *from* ראש חודש סיון *through the day after* שבועות (*in* ארץ ישראל *through* י״ב סיון), תשעה באב, ט״ו באב, ערב ראש השנה, *and from* ערב יום כיפור *through the day after* שמחת תורה (*in* ארץ ישראל *through* ראש חודש מרחשון).

תחנון *is also not said: on the morning of a* ברית מילה*, either where the* ברית *will take place or where the father,* סנדק *or* מוהל *are present; if a* חתן *is present (and some say a* כלה*) on the day of his wedding or during the week of* שבע ברכות*; in a house of mourning.*

*In* ארץ ישראל *on days on which* תחנון *is said, say* וידוי *and the* י״ג מדות *on page 201. See law 478a.*

*The following until* וַיֹּאמֶר דָּוִד *on page 217 is said standing.*

וְהוּא רַחוּם, יְכַפֵּר עָוֹן וְלֹא־יַשְׁחִית, וְהִרְבָּה לְהָשִׁיב אַפּוֹ וְלֹא־יָעִיר כָּל־ תהלים עח
חֲמָתוֹ: אַתָּה יהוה לֹא־תִכְלָא רַחֲמֶיךָ מִמֶּנּוּ, חַסְדְּךָ וַאֲמִתְּךָ תָּמִיד יִצְּרוּנוּ.
הוֹשִׁיעֵנוּ יהוה אֱלֹהֵינוּ וְקַבְּצֵנוּ מִן־הַגּוֹיִם, לְהוֹדוֹת לְשֵׁם קָדְשֶׁךָ, לְהִשְׁתַּבֵּחַ תהלים קו
בִּתְהִלָּתֶךָ: אִם־עֲוֹנוֹת תִּשְׁמָר־יָהּ, אֲדֹנָי מִי יַעֲמֹד: כִּי־עִמְּךָ הַסְּלִיחָה לְמַעַן תהלים קל
תִּוָּרֵא: לֹא כַחֲטָאֵינוּ תַּעֲשֶׂה לָּנוּ, וְלֹא כַעֲוֹנוֹתֵינוּ תִּגְמֹל עָלֵינוּ. אִם־עֲוֹנֵינוּ ירמיה יד
עָנוּ בָנוּ, יהוה עֲשֵׂה לְמַעַן שְׁמֶךָ: זְכֹר־רַחֲמֶיךָ יהוה וַחֲסָדֶיךָ, כִּי מֵעוֹלָם תהלים כה
הֵמָּה: יַעַנְנוּ יהוה בְּיוֹם צָרָה, יְשַׂגְּבֵנוּ שֵׁם אֱלֹהֵי יַעֲקֹב. יהוה הוֹשִׁיעָה, תהלים כ
הַמֶּלֶךְ יַעֲנֵנוּ בְיוֹם־קָרְאֵנוּ: אָבִינוּ מַלְכֵּנוּ, חָנֵּנוּ וַעֲנֵנוּ, כִּי אֵין בָּנוּ מַעֲשִׂים,
צְדָקָה עֲשֵׂה עִמָּנוּ לְמַעַן שְׁמֶךָ. אֲדוֹנֵינוּ אֱלֹהֵינוּ, שְׁמַע קוֹל תַּחֲנוּנֵינוּ,
וּזְכָר לָנוּ אֶת בְּרִית אֲבוֹתֵינוּ וְהוֹשִׁיעֵנוּ לְמַעַן שְׁמֶךָ.

---

סדר תחנון / TAḤANUN

The paradigm for this supplicatory prayer accompanied by *"nefilat apayim"* (falling on the face) is the story in the Book of Judges concerning the first, failed attempt to conquer the city of 'Ai, which resulted in the death of thirty-six of the Children of Israel. There we read:

> And Joshua rent his clothes and fell upon his face to the earth before the ark of the Lord…
>
> And the Lord said to Joshua: Get up! Why are you falling upon your face?[1]

1. Joshua 7:6, 10.

וְעַתָּה And now, My LORD, our God, who took Your people out of the land Dan. 9
of Egypt with a mighty hand, creating for Yourself renown to this day: we have sinned and acted wrongly. LORD, in keeping with all Your righteousness, please turn Your wrath and anger away from Jerusalem, Your holy mountain. Because of our sins and the iniquities of our ancestors, Jerusalem and Your people have become the scorn of all those around us. And now, our God, heed Your servant's prayer and pleas, and let Your face shine on Your desolate Sanctuary, for Your sake, O LORD. Incline Your ear, my God, and hear. Open Your eyes and see our desolation and that of the city called by Your name. Not because of our righteousness do we lay our pleas before You, but because of Your great compassion. LORD, hear! LORD, forgive! LORD, listen and act! Do not delay – for Your sake, my God, because Your city and Your people are called by Your name.

אָבִינוּ Our Father, compassionate Father, show us a sign for good, and gather our scattered ones from the four quarters of the earth. Let all the nations rec-
ognize and know that You are the LORD our God. And now, LORD, You are our Is. 64
Father. We are the clay and You are our Potter; we are all the work of Your hand. Save us for the sake of Your name, our Rock, our King and our Redeemer. Pity
Your people, LORD. Let not Your heritage become an object of scorn, a byword Joel 2
among nations. Why should they say among the peoples, "Where is their God?" We know we have sinned and that there is no one to stand up for us. Let Your great name stand up for us in time of trouble. We know we have no merits of

---

king fretted that he might lose it. So he put the key on a chain which would prevent its loss.

> So said the Holy One, blessed be He: "If I leave Israel the way they are, they will be swallowed up among the nations, so I'm associating my name with them, and thereby they'll survive. As it is written: 'And what shall You do for Your great name' – that is associated with us?"[7]

Joshua was able to turn around the defeat and transform the *"ḥillul ha-shem"* into a *"kiddush ha-shem,"* a sanctification of the name. Rabbi Zevi Yehudah Hakohen Kook was fond of quoting the Talmud Yerushalmi: "Great is the Kiddush Hashem *from* Ḥillul Hashem."[8] Great is the sanctification of the name that proceeds from desecration of the name. This was the rare achieve-

7. *y. Ta'anit* 2:6; *Yalkut Shim'oni, remez* 17; quoted in Rabbi Ḥayyim of Volozhin, *Nefesh ha-Ḥayyim* I, 19.
8. *y. Kiddushin* 4:1; *Sanhedrin* 6:7. *Siḥot Harav Zevi Yehudah: Shemot*, ed. Rabbi Shelomo Aviner (Jerusalem, 5758), pp. 369-370.

וְעַתָּה אֲדֹנָי אֱלֹהֵינוּ, אֲשֶׁר הוֹצֵאתָ אֶת־עַמְּךָ מֵאֶרֶץ מִצְרַיִם בְּיָד חֲזָקָה דניאל ט
וַתַּעַשׂ־לְךָ שֵׁם כַּיּוֹם הַזֶּה, חָטָאנוּ רָשָׁעְנוּ: אֲדֹנָי, כְּכָל־צִדְקֹתֶךָ יָשָׁב־נָא
אַפְּךָ וַחֲמָתְךָ, מֵעִירְךָ יְרוּשָׁלִַם הַר־קָדְשֶׁךָ, כִּי בַחֲטָאֵינוּ וּבַעֲוֹנוֹת אֲבֹתֵינוּ,
יְרוּשָׁלִַם וְעַמְּךָ לְחֶרְפָּה לְכָל־סְבִיבֹתֵינוּ: וְעַתָּה שְׁמַע אֱלֹהֵינוּ אֶל־תְּפִלַּת
עַבְדְּךָ וְאֶל־תַּחֲנוּנָיו, וְהָאֵר פָּנֶיךָ עַל־מִקְדָּשְׁךָ הַשָּׁמֵם, לְמַעַן אֲדֹנָי: הַטֵּה
אֱלֹהַי אָזְנְךָ וּשֲׁמָע, פְּקַח עֵינֶיךָ וּרְאֵה שֹׁמְמֹתֵינוּ וְהָעִיר אֲשֶׁר־נִקְרָא שִׁמְךָ
עָלֶיהָ, כִּי לֹא עַל־צִדְקֹתֵינוּ אֲנַחְנוּ מַפִּילִים תַּחֲנוּנֵינוּ לְפָנֶיךָ, כִּי עַל־רַחֲמֶיךָ
הָרַבִּים: אֲדֹנָי שְׁמָעָה, אֲדֹנָי סְלָחָה, אֲדֹנָי הַקְשִׁיבָה וַעֲשֵׂה אַל־תְּאַחַר,
לְמַעַנְךָ אֱלֹהַי, כִּי־שִׁמְךָ נִקְרָא עַל־עִירְךָ וְעַל־עַמֶּךָ:

אָבִינוּ הָאָב הָרַחֲמָן, הַרְאֵנוּ אוֹת לְטוֹבָה וְקַבֵּץ נְפוּצוֹתֵינוּ מֵאַרְבַּע כַּנְפוֹת
הָאָרֶץ. יַכִּירוּ וְיֵדְעוּ כָּל הַגּוֹיִם כִּי אַתָּה יהוה אֱלֹהֵינוּ. וְעַתָּה יהוה אָבִינוּ ישעיה סד
אָתָּה, אֲנַחְנוּ הַחֹמֶר וְאַתָּה יֹצְרֵנוּ וּמַעֲשֵׂה יָדְךָ כֻּלָּנוּ: הוֹשִׁיעֵנוּ לְמַעַן
שְׁמֶךָ, צוּרֵנוּ מַלְכֵּנוּ וְגוֹאֲלֵנוּ. חוּסָה יהוה עַל־עַמֶּךָ, וְאַל־תִּתֵּן נַחֲלָתְךָ יואל ב
לְחֶרְפָּה לִמְשָׁל־בָּם גּוֹיִם, לָמָּה יֹאמְרוּ בָעַמִּים אַיֵּה אֱלֹהֵיהֶם: יָדַעְנוּ כִּי
חָטָאנוּ וְאֵין מִי יַעֲמֹד בַּעֲדֵנוּ, שִׁמְךָ הַגָּדוֹל יַעֲמָד לָנוּ בְּעֵת צָרָה. יָדַעְנוּ

---

of a *Sefer Torah*. "All of the holy city of Jerusalem is considered in this respect as a place containing an ark."[4]

*

From the kabbalistic perspective, the act of *nefilat apayim* (falling on the face) symbolizes sacrificing oneself.[5]

While prostrate with grief, Joshua cries out impassionedly: "And what shall You do for Your great name?[6] The implication being that the outcome of the defeat of the People of Israel will surely be a *"Ḥillul Hashem,"* a desecration of the great name of God. The Talmud Yerushalmi tells a parable of a king who was concerned about the key to the palace. As the key was so small, the

---

4. RZYH, *OR*, Vol. 1, p. 302, par. 4. Rabbi Ben-Shim'on wrote that Jerusalem, due to its exalted sanctity, is superior to a house containing sacred books. See Rabbi Raphael Aaron Ben-Shim'on, *Nehar Mitsrayim*, vol. 1 (Alexandria, 1908), 7a, par. 9; quoted in Rabbi Shemtob Gaguine, *Keter Shem Tov*, vol. 1 (Keidan, 1934), p. 78, n. 121. (The latter work contains the lengthy, substantial *haskamah* of Rav Kook.)
5. See *Siddur Shelah*.
6. Joshua 7:9.

our own: therefore deal with us charitably for Your name's sake. As a father has compassion on his children, so, LORD, have compassion on us, and save us for the sake of Your name. Have mercy on Your people; have compassion for Your heritage; take pity in Your great compassion. Be gracious to us and answer us, for righteousness is Yours, LORD. Always You do wondrous things.

הַבֶּט נָא Please look, please swiftly have compassion for Your people for Your name's sake. In Your great compassion, LORD our God, have pity and compassion, and rescue the flock You tend. Let us not be ruled by wrath, for our eyes are turned toward You. Save us for Your name's sake. Have compassion on us for the sake of Your covenant. Look and answer us in time of trouble, for Yours, LORD, is the power to save. Our hope is in You, God of forgiveness. Please forgive, good and forgiving God, for You are a gracious, compassionate God and King.

אָנָּא מֶלֶךְ Please, gracious and compassionate King, remember and call to mind the Covenant between the Pieces [with Abraham] and let the binding of his only son [Isaac] appear before You for Israel's sake. Our Father, our King, be gracious to us and answer us, for we are called by Your great name. You who work miracles at all times, deal with us according to Your loving-kindness. Gracious and compassionate One, look and answer us in time of trouble, for salvation is Yours, LORD. Our Father, our King, our Refuge, do not act with us according to our evil deeds. Remember, LORD, Your tender mercies and Your love. Save us in Your great goodness, and have mercy on us, for we have no other god but You, our Rock. Do not abandon us, LORD our God, do not be distant from us, for we are worn out by the sword and captivity, pestilence and plague, and by every trouble and sorrow. Rescue us, for in You lies our hope. Put us not to shame, LORD our God. Let Your face shine upon us. Remember for us the covenant of our ancestors and save us for Your name's sake. See our troubles and heed the voice of our prayer, for You heed the prayer of every mouth.

אֵל רַחוּם וְחַנּוּן O Compassionate and gracious God, have compassion on us and on all Your works, for there is none like You, LORD our God. Please, we beg You, forgive our sins, our Father, our King, our Rock, our Redeemer, living and eternal God, mighty in strength, loving and good to all Your works, for You are the LORD our God. O God, slow to anger and full of compassion, act with us according to Your great compassion and save us for Your name's sake. Hear our prayer, our King, and save us from our enemies' hands. Heed our prayer, our King, and save us from all distress and sorrow. You are our

כִּי אֵין בָּנוּ מַעֲשִׂים, צְדָקָה עֲשֵׂה עִמָּנוּ לְמַעַן שְׁמֶךָ. כְּרַחֵם אָב עַל בָּנִים כֵּן תְּרַחֵם יהוה עָלֵינוּ, וְהוֹשִׁיעֵנוּ לְמַעַן שְׁמֶךָ. חֲמֹל עַל עַמֶּךָ, רַחֵם עַל נַחֲלָתֶךָ, חוּסָה נָּא כְּרֹב רַחֲמֶיךָ, חָנֵּנוּ וַעֲנֵנוּ. כִּי לְךָ יהוה הַצְּדָקָה, עֹשֵׂה נִפְלָאוֹת בְּכָל עֵת.

הַבֶּט נָא, רַחֶם נָא עַל עַמְּךָ מְהֵרָה לְמַעַן שְׁמֶךָ בְּרַחֲמֶיךָ הָרַבִּים יהוה אֱלֹהֵינוּ. חוּס וְרַחֵם וְהוֹשִׁיעָה צֹאן מַרְעִיתֶךָ, וְאַל יִמְשָׁל בָּנוּ קֶצֶף, כִּי לְךָ עֵינֵינוּ תְלוּיוֹת. הוֹשִׁיעֵנוּ לְמַעַן שְׁמֶךָ. רַחֵם עָלֵינוּ לְמַעַן בְּרִיתֶךָ. הַבִּיטָה וַעֲנֵנוּ בְּעֵת צָרָה, כִּי לְךָ יהוה הַיְשׁוּעָה. בְּךָ תוֹחַלְתֵּנוּ אֱלוֹהַּ סְלִיחוֹת, אָנָּא סְלַח נָא אֵל טוֹב וְסַלָּח, כִּי אֵל מֶלֶךְ חַנּוּן וְרַחוּם אָתָּה.

אָנָּא מֶלֶךְ חַנּוּן וְרַחוּם, זְכֹר וְהַבֵּט לִבְרִית בֵּין הַבְּתָרִים, וְתֵרָאֶה לְפָנֶיךָ עֲקֵדַת יָחִיד לְמַעַן יִשְׂרָאֵל. אָבִינוּ מַלְכֵּנוּ, חָנֵּנוּ וַעֲנֵנוּ, כִּי שִׁמְךָ הַגָּדוֹל נִקְרָא עָלֵינוּ. עֹשֵׂה נִפְלָאוֹת בְּכָל עֵת, עֲשֵׂה עִמָּנוּ כְּחַסְדֶּךָ. חַנּוּן וְרַחוּם, הַבִּיטָה וַעֲנֵנוּ בְּעֵת צָרָה, כִּי לְךָ יהוה הַיְשׁוּעָה. אָבִינוּ מַלְכֵּנוּ מַחֲסֵנוּ, אַל תַּעַשׂ עִמָּנוּ כְּרֹעַ מַעֲלָלֵינוּ. זְכֹר רַחֲמֶיךָ יהוה וַחֲסָדֶיךָ, וּכְרֹב טוּבְךָ הוֹשִׁיעֵנוּ, וַחֲמָל נָא עָלֵינוּ, כִּי אֵין לָנוּ אֱלוֹהַּ אַחֵר מִבַּלְעָדֶיךָ צוּרֵנוּ. אַל תַּעַזְבֵנוּ יהוה אֱלֹהֵינוּ אַל תִּרְחַק מִמֶּנּוּ. כִּי נַפְשֵׁנוּ קְצָרָה, מֵחֶרֶב וּמִשְּׁבִי וּמִדֶּבֶר וּמִמַּגֵּפָה. וּמִכָּל צָרָה וְיָגוֹן הַצִּילֵנוּ, כִּי לְךָ קִוִּינוּ. וְאַל תַּכְלִימֵנוּ יהוה אֱלֹהֵינוּ, וְהָאֵר פָּנֶיךָ בָּנוּ, וּזְכָר לָנוּ אֶת בְּרִית אֲבוֹתֵינוּ וְהוֹשִׁיעֵנוּ לְמַעַן שְׁמֶךָ. רְאֵה בְצָרוֹתֵינוּ, וּשְׁמַע קוֹל תְּפִלָּתֵנוּ, כִּי אַתָּה שׁוֹמֵעַ תְּפִלַּת כָּל פֶּה.

אֵל רַחוּם וְחַנּוּן, רַחֵם עָלֵינוּ וְעַל כָּל מַעֲשֶׂיךָ, כִּי אֵין כָּמוֹךָ יהוה אֱלֹהֵינוּ. אָנָּא שָׂא נָא פְשָׁעֵינוּ, אָבִינוּ מַלְכֵּנוּ צוּרֵנוּ וְגוֹאֲלֵנוּ, אֵל חַי וְקַיָּם הַחֲסִין בַּכֹּחַ, חָסִיד וָטוֹב עַל כָּל מַעֲשֶׂיךָ, כִּי אַתָּה הוּא יהוה אֱלֹהֵינוּ. אֵל אֶרֶךְ אַפַּיִם וּמָלֵא רַחֲמִים, עֲשֵׂה עִמָּנוּ כְּרֹב רַחֲמֶיךָ, וְהוֹשִׁיעֵנוּ לְמַעַן שְׁמֶךָ. שְׁמַע מַלְכֵּנוּ תְּפִלָּתֵנוּ, וּמִיַּד אוֹיְבֵינוּ הַצִּילֵנוּ. שְׁמַע מַלְכֵּנוּ תְּפִלָּתֵנוּ, וּמִכָּל

---

ment of Joshua, but again, not everyone is a *tsaddik* (righteous man) on a par with Joshua, and not everyone has this remarkable ability. (Editor)

Father, our King. We are called by Your name. Do not desert us. Do not abandon us, our Father. Do not cast us away, our Creator. Do not forget us, our Maker – for You are a gracious and compassionate God and King.

אֵין כָּמְוֹךָ There is none like You in grace and compassion, LORD our God. There is none like You, God, slow to anger and abounding in loving-kindness and truth. Save us in Your great compassion; rescue us from storm and turmoil. Remember Your servants Abraham, Isaac and Jacob; do not attend to our stubbornness, wickedness and sinfulness. Turn from Your fierce anger, *Ex. 32*
and relent from the evil meant for Your people. Remove from us the scourge of death, for You are compassionate. This is Your way, to show unearned loving-kindness to every generation. Have pity on Your people, LORD, and save us from Your wrath. Remove from us the scourge of plague and the harsh decree, for You are the Guardian of Israel. You are right, my LORD, and we are *Dan. 9*
shamefaced. How can we complain? What can we say? What can we plead? How can we justify ourselves? Let us search our ways and examine them and return to You, for Your right hand is outstretched to receive those who return. Please, LORD, please save. Please, LORD, please send success. Please, LORD, *Ps. 118*
answer us when we call. For You, LORD, we wait. For You, LORD, we hope. For You, LORD, we long. Do not be silent while we suffer, for the nations are saying, "Their hope is lost." To You alone every knee must bend, and those who hold themselves high bow down.

הַפּוֹתֵחַ יָד You who hold out an open hand of repentance to receive transgressors and sinners – our soul is overwhelmed by our great sorrow. Do not forget us for ever. Arise and save us, for we seek refuge in You. Our Father, our King, though we lack righteousness and good deeds, remember for us the covenant of our fathers, and our testimonies daily that "The LORD is One." Look on our affliction, for many are our sufferings and heartaches. Have pity on us, LORD, in the land of our captivity. Do not pour out Your wrath on us, for we are Your people, the children of Your covenant. God, see how low our glory has sunk among the nations. They abhor us as if we were impure. How long will Your strength be captive, and Your glory in the hand of the foe? Arouse Your strength and zeal against Your enemies. Let them be shamed and deprived of power. Let not our hardships seem small to You. Swiftly may Your compassion reach us in the day of our distress. If not for our sake, act for Yours, so that the memory of our survivors be not destroyed. Be gracious to the nation who, in constant love, proclaim twice daily the unity of Your name, saying, "Listen, Israel, the LORD is our God, the LORD is One." *Deut. 6*

צָרָה וְיָגוֹן הַצִּילֵנוּ. אָבִינוּ מַלְכֵּנוּ אַתָּה, וְשִׁמְךָ עָלֵינוּ נִקְרָא. אַל תַּנִּחֵנוּ, אַל תַּעַזְבֵנוּ אָבִינוּ וְאַל תִּטְּשֵׁנוּ בּוֹרְאֵנוּ וְאַל תִּשְׁכָּחֵנוּ יוֹצְרֵנוּ, כִּי אֵל מֶלֶךְ חַנּוּן וְרַחוּם אָתָּה.

אֵין כָּמְוֹךָ חַנּוּן וְרַחוּם יהוה אֱלֹהֵינוּ, אֵין כָּמְוֹךָ אֵל אֶרֶךְ אַפַּיִם וְרַב חֶסֶד
וֶאֱמֶת. הוֹשִׁיעֵנוּ בְּרַחֲמֶיךָ הָרַבִּים, מֵרַעַשׁ וּמֵרֹגֶז הַצִּילֵנוּ. זְכֹר לַעֲבָדֶיךָ
לְאַבְרָהָם לְיִצְחָק וּלְיַעֲקֹב, אַל תֵּפֶן אֶל קְשְׁיֵנוּ וְאֶל רִשְׁעֵנוּ וְאֶל חַטָּאתֵנוּ.
שׁוּב מֵחֲרוֹן אַפֶּךָ, וְהִנָּחֵם עַל־הָרָעָה לְעַמֶּךָ: וְהָסֵר מִמֶּנּוּ מַכַּת הַמָּוֶת כִּי שמות לב
רַחוּם אָתָּה, כִּי כֵן דַּרְכֶּךָ, עוֹשֶׂה חֶסֶד חִנָּם בְּכָל דּוֹר וָדוֹר. חְוּסָה יהוה עַל
עַמֶּךָ וְהַצִּילֵנוּ מִזַּעְמֶךָ, וְהָסֵר מִמֶּנּוּ מַכַּת הַמַּגֵּפָה וּגְזֵרָה קָשָׁה, כִּי אַתָּה
שׁוֹמֵר יִשְׂרָאֵל. לְךָ אֲדֹנָי הַצְּדָקָה וְלָנוּ בֹּשֶׁת הַפָּנִים: מַה נִּתְאוֹנֵן, מַה נֹּאמַר, דניאל ט
מַה נְּדַבֵּר וּמַה נִּצְטַדָּק. נַחְפְּשָׂה דְרָכֵינוּ וְנַחְקְרָה וְנָשׁוּבָה אֵלֶיךָ, כִּי יְמִינְךָ
פְשׁוּטָה לְקַבֵּל שָׁבִים. אָנָּא יהוה הוֹשִׁיעָה נָּא, אָנָּא יהוה הַצְלִיחָה נָא: תהלים קיח
אָנָּא יהוה עֲנֵנוּ בְּיוֹם קָרְאֵנוּ. לְךָ יהוה חִכִּינוּ, לְךָ יהוה קִוִּינוּ, לְךָ יהוה
נְיַחֵל. אַל תֶּחֱשֶׁה וּתְעַנֵּנוּ, כִּי נָאֲמוּ גוֹיִם, אָבְדָה תִקְוָתָם. כָּל בֶּרֶךְ וְכָל
קוֹמָה, לְךָ לְבַד תִּשְׁתַּחֲוֶה.

הַפּוֹתֵחַ יָד בִּתְשׁוּבָה לְקַבֵּל פּוֹשְׁעִים וְחַטָּאִים, נִבְהֲלָה נַפְשֵׁנוּ מֵרֹב עִצְּבוֹנֵנוּ. אַל תִּשְׁכָּחֵנוּ נֶצַח, קוּמָה וְהוֹשִׁיעֵנוּ כִּי חָסִינוּ בָךְ. אָבִינוּ מַלְכֵּנוּ, אִם אֵין בָּנוּ צְדָקָה וּמַעֲשִׂים טוֹבִים, זְכָר לָנוּ אֶת בְּרִית אֲבוֹתֵינוּ וְעֵדוּתֵנוּ בְּכָל יוֹם יהוה אֶחָד. הַבִּיטָה בְעָנְיֵנוּ, כִּי רַבּוּ מַכְאוֹבֵינוּ וְצָרוֹת לְבָבֵנוּ. חְוּסָה יהוה עָלֵינוּ בְּאֶרֶץ שִׁבְיֵנוּ, וְאַל תִּשְׁפֹּךְ חֲרוֹנְךָ עָלֵינוּ, כִּי אֲנַחְנוּ עַמְּךָ בְּנֵי בְרִיתֶךָ. אֵל, הַבִּיטָה, דַּל כְּבוֹדֵנוּ בַּגּוֹיִם וְשִׁקְּצְוּנוּ כְּטֻמְאַת הַנִּדָּה. עַד מָתַי עֻזְּךָ בַּשְּׁבִי, וְתִפְאַרְתְּךָ בְּיַד צָר. עוֹרְרָה גְבוּרָתְךָ וְקִנְאָתְךָ עַל אוֹיְבֶיךָ. הֵם יֵבְוֹשׁוּ וְיֵחַתּוּ מִגְּבוּרָתָם. וְאַל יִמְעֲטוּ לְפָנֶיךָ תְּלָאוֹתֵינוּ. מַהֵר יְקַדְּמְוּנוּ רַחֲמֶיךָ בְּיוֹם צָרָתֵנוּ. וְאִם לֹא לְמַעֲנֵנוּ, לְמַעַנְךָ פְעַל, וְאַל תַּשְׁחִית זֵכֶר שְׁאֵרִיתֵנוּ, וְחֹן אֹם הַמְיַחֲדִים שִׁמְךָ פַּעֲמַיִם בְּכָל יוֹם תָּמִיד בְּאַהֲבָה,
וְאוֹמְרִים, שְׁמַע יִשְׂרָאֵל, יהוה אֱלֹהֵינוּ, יהוה אֶחָד: דברים ו

## LOWERING THE HEAD

*On Sundays, Tuesdays, Wednesdays and Fridays, begin Taḥanun here. The following, until "We do not know" on page 220, is said sitting. When praying in a place where there is a Torah scroll, one should lean forward, resting one's head on the arm on which the tefillin are not worn, until "in sudden shame."*

וַיֹּאמֶר דָּוִד David said to Gad, "I am in great distress. Let us fall into God's hand, for His *II Sam. 24*
mercy is great; but do not let me fall into the hand of man."

Compassionate and gracious One, I have sinned before You. LORD, full of compassion, have compassion on me and accept my pleas.

LORD, do not rebuke me in Your anger or chastise me in Your wrath. Be gra- *Ps. 6*
cious to me, LORD, for I am weak. Heal me, LORD, for my bones are in agony. My soul is in anguish, and You, O LORD – how long? Turn, LORD, set my soul free; save me for the sake of Your love. For no one remembers You when he is dead. Who can praise You from the grave? I am weary with my sighing. Every night I drench my bed, I soak my couch with my tears. My eye grows dim from grief, worn out because of all my foes. Leave me, all you evildoers, for the LORD has heard the sound of my weeping. The LORD has heard my pleas. The LORD will accept my prayer. All my enemies will be shamed and utterly dismayed. They will turn back in sudden shame.

*Sit upright. On Mondays and Thursdays, say the following.* *On other days, continue with "Guardian of Israel" on page 220.*

---

יָגַעְתִּי בְּאַנְחָתִי, אַשְׂחֶה בְכָל־לַיְלָה מִטָּתִי, בְּדִמְעָתִי עַרְשִׂי אַמְסֶה: עָשְׁשָׁה מִכַּעַס עֵינִי עָתְקָה בְּכָל־צוֹרְרָי: סוּרוּ מִמֶּנִּי כָּל־פֹּעֲלֵי אָוֶן, כִּי שָׁמַע יהוה קוֹל בִּכְיִי: שָׁמַע יהוה תְּחִנָּתִי, יהוה תְּפִלָּתִי יִקָּח: *I am weary with my sighing; every night I drench my bed, I soak my couch with my tears. My eye grows dim from grief, worn out because of all my foes. Leave me, all evildoers, for the Lord has heard the sound of my weeping. The Lord has heard my plea, the Lord will accept my prayer.* Rav Kook describes a situation in which one is blocked from shedding tears. If one could purge oneself through the outpour of tears, this would provide the necessary catharsis and purification. But even in the present state, the Holy One, blessed be He, to whom are revealed all things hidden, accepts the internal, tearless crying.

The first part of the verse "I am weary with my sighing" is a statement of fact. Then, the Psalmist engages in wishful thinking: "Would that I could soak my couch with tears!" But the sigh never quite finds expression in tears. The reason being: "My eye is grown strong from anger, annealed by all my foes" (*'Asheshah mi-ka'as 'eyni, 'atkah be-khol tsorerai*).[10] This hardening and

---

10. Rav Kook explains that like many Hebrew verbs, the word *'ashash* has two opposite meanings: to grow weak or to grow strong. A classic example is the word *shorash*, which can mean either "rooted" or "uprooted."

## נפילת אפיים

*On Sundays, Tuesdays, Wednesdays and Fridays, begin* תחנון *here.*
*The following, until* וַאֲנַחְנוּ לֹא נֵדַע *on page 221, is said sitting. When praying in a place where there is a* ספר תורה*, one should lean forward, resting one's head on the arm on which the* תפילין *are not worn, until* יֵבֹשׁוּ רָגַע.

וַיֹּאמֶר דָּוִד אֶל־גָּד, צַר־לִי מְאֹד, נִפְּלָה־נָּא בְּיַד־יהוה, כִּי רַבִּים רַחֲמָו, וּבְיַד־ שמואל ב, כד
אָדָם אַל־אֶפֹּלָה:

רַחוּם וְחַנּוּן, חָטָאתִי לְפָנֶיךָ. יהוה מָלֵא רַחֲמִים, רַחֵם עָלַי וְקַבֵּל תַּחֲנוּנָי.

יהוה, אַל־בְּאַפְּךָ תוֹכִיחֵנִי, וְאַל־בַּחֲמָתְךָ תְיַסְּרֵנִי: חָנֵּנִי יהוה, כִּי אֻמְלַל תהלים ו
אָנִי, רְפָאֵנִי יהוה, כִּי נִבְהֲלוּ עֲצָמָי: וְנַפְשִׁי נִבְהֲלָה מְאֹד, וְאַתְּ יהוה,
עַד־מָתָי: שׁוּבָה יהוה, חַלְּצָה נַפְשִׁי, הוֹשִׁיעֵנִי לְמַעַן חַסְדֶּךָ: כִּי אֵין
בַּמָּוֶת זִכְרֶךָ, בִּשְׁאוֹל מִי יוֹדֶה־לָּךְ: יָגַעְתִּי בְּאַנְחָתִי, אַשְׂחֶה בְכָל־
לַיְלָה מִטָּתִי, בְּדִמְעָתִי עַרְשִׂי אַמְסֶה: עָשְׁשָׁה מִכַּעַס עֵינִי, עָתְקָה
בְּכָל־צוֹרְרָי: סוּרוּ מִמֶּנִּי כָּל־פֹּעֲלֵי אָוֶן, כִּי שָׁמַע יהוה קוֹל בִּכְיִי:
שָׁמַע יהוה תְּחִנָּתִי, יהוה תְּפִלָּתִי יִקָּח: יֵבֹשׁוּ וְיִבָּהֲלוּ מְאֹד כָּל־אֹיְבָי,
יָשֻׁבוּ יֵבֹשׁוּ רָגַע:

*Sit upright. On Mondays and Thursdays, say the following.*
*On other days, continue with* שׁוֹמֵר יִשְׂרָאֵל *on page 221.*

---

THE MYSTERY OF *NEFILAT APAYIM*

After man's consciousness has been expanded by the light of the highest spirituality and his heart is full of vim and vigor, what results is that the good in his soul is strengthened and magnified – but the evil as well, "the yeast in the dough" [*b. Berakhot* 17a], the base instincts, are also strengthened by this pronounced strength and vitality. So man must now direct his attention – after this time of joy – to that which is lowly and ugly within him. He will be disgusted with his life on account of its deficiency, the negative character traits, the inane actions. In so doing, he will be divested of the imperfections and their power will wane. What will remain in its purity is the soulful might absorbed from the sanctity of the prayer. And the insights and emotions derived from the prayer will go on to be integrated in daily life through *Kedusha de-Sidra* [i.e. *U-Va le-Zion*].[9]

---

9. *OR*, vol. 1, p. 443, *Hashmatah*.

Lord, God of Israel, turn away from Your fierce anger,
and relent from the evil against Your people.

Look down from heaven and see how we have become an object of scorn and derision among the nations. We are regarded as sheep led to the slaughter, to be killed, destroyed, beaten and humiliated. Yet, despite all this, we have not forgotten Your name. Please do not forget us.

Lord, God of Israel, turn away from Your fierce anger,
and relent from the evil against Your people.

Strangers say, "You have no hope or expectation." Be gracious to the nation whose hope is in Your name. O Pure One, bring our deliverance close. We are exhausted. We are given no rest. May Your compassion suppress Your anger against us. Please turn away from Your fierce anger, and have compassion on the people You chose as Your own.

Lord, God of Israel, turn away from Your fierce anger,
and relent from the evil against Your people.

Have pity on us, Lord, in Your compassion, and do not hand us over to cruel oppressors. Why should the nations say, "Where is their God now?" For Your own sake, deal kindly with us, and do not delay. Please turn away from Your fierce anger, and have compassion on the people You chose as Your own.

Lord, God of Israel, turn away from Your fierce anger,
and relent from the evil against Your people.

Heed our voice and be gracious. Do not abandon us into the hand of our enemies to blot out our name. Remember what You promised our fathers: "I will make your descendants as many as the stars of heaven" – yet now we are only a few left from many. Yet, despite all this, we have not forgotten Your name. Please do not forget us.

Lord, God of Israel, turn away from Your fierce anger,
and relent from the evil against Your people.

---

יהוה אֱלֹהֵי יִשְׂרָאֵל, שׁוּב מֵחֲרוֹן אַפֶּךָ וְהִנָּחֵם עַל הָרָעָה לְעַמֶּךָ *Lord, God of Israel* (Havayah Elohei Yisrael), *turn away from Your fierce anger, and relent from the evil against Your people.*

We repeat six times *"Havayah Elohei Yisrael"* because *Tif'eret* is the six cardinal points (*vav ketsavot*).[12]

---

12. *OR*, vol. 1, p. 304.
I.e. the cognomen *"Havayah Elohei Yisrael"* corresponds to the *sefirah* of *Tif'eret*, which in turn symbolizes in Lurianic Kabbalah the *vav kestavot*, the six *sefirot* of *Ḥesed, Gevurah, Tif'eret, Netsaḥ, Hod, Yesod.*
RZYH records that this note was written in his father's hand in the *Siddur Sha'ar ha-Shamayim* of the *Shelah* (initials of *Shnei Luḥot ha-Berit*, the famous work by Rabbi Isaiah Halevi Horowitz).

יהוה אֱלֹהֵי יִשְׂרָאֵל, שׁוּב מֵחֲרוֹן אַפֶּךָ וְהִנָּחֵם עַל הָרָעָה לְעַמֶּךָ.

הַבֵּט מִשָּׁמַיִם וּרְאֵה כִּי הָיִינוּ לַעַג וָקֶלֶס בַּגּוֹיִם
נֶחְשַׁבְנוּ כַּצֹּאן לַטֶּבַח יוּבָל, לַהֲרֹג וּלְאַבֵּד וּלְמַכָּה וּלְחֶרְפָּה.
וּבְכָל זֹאת שִׁמְךָ לֹא שָׁכָחְנוּ, נָא אַל תִּשְׁכָּחֵנוּ.

יהוה אֱלֹהֵי יִשְׂרָאֵל, שׁוּב מֵחֲרוֹן אַפֶּךָ וְהִנָּחֵם עַל הָרָעָה לְעַמֶּךָ.

זָרִים אוֹמְרִים אֵין תּוֹחֶלֶת וְתִקְוָה, חֹן אֹם לְשִׁמְךָ מְקַוֶּה
טָהוֹר יְשׁוּעָתֵנוּ קָרְבָה, יָגַעְנוּ וְלֹא הוּנַח לָנוּ
רַחֲמֶיךָ יִכְבְּשׁוּ אֶת כַּעַסְךָ מֵעָלֵינוּ.
אָנָּא שׁוּב מֵחֲרוֹנְךָ וְרַחֵם סְגֻלָּה אֲשֶׁר בָּחָרְתָּ.

יהוה אֱלֹהֵי יִשְׂרָאֵל, שׁוּב מֵחֲרוֹן אַפֶּךָ וְהִנָּחֵם עַל הָרָעָה לְעַמֶּךָ.

חוּסָה יהוה עָלֵינוּ בְּרַחֲמֶיךָ, וְאַל תִּתְּנֵנוּ בִּידֵי אַכְזָרִים.
לָמָּה יֹאמְרוּ הַגּוֹיִם אַיֵּה נָא אֱלֹהֵיהֶם
לְמַעַנְךָ עֲשֵׂה עִמָּנוּ חֶסֶד וְאַל תְּאַחַר.
אָנָּא שׁוּב מֵחֲרוֹנְךָ וְרַחֵם סְגֻלָּה אֲשֶׁר בָּחָרְתָּ.

יהוה אֱלֹהֵי יִשְׂרָאֵל, שׁוּב מֵחֲרוֹן אַפֶּךָ וְהִנָּחֵם עַל הָרָעָה לְעַמֶּךָ.

קוֹלֵנוּ תִשְׁמַע וְתָחֹן, וְאַל תִּטְּשֵׁנוּ בְּיַד אֹיְבֵינוּ לִמְחוֹת אֶת שְׁמֵנוּ.
זְכֹר אֲשֶׁר נִשְׁבַּעְתָּ לַאֲבוֹתֵינוּ כְּכוֹכְבֵי הַשָּׁמַיִם אַרְבֶּה אֶת זַרְעֲכֶם
וְעַתָּה נִשְׁאַרְנוּ מְעַט מֵהַרְבֵּה.
וּבְכָל זֹאת שִׁמְךָ לֹא שָׁכָחְנוּ, נָא אַל תִּשְׁכָּחֵנוּ.

יהוה אֱלֹהֵי יִשְׂרָאֵל, שׁוּב מֵחֲרוֹן אַפֶּךָ וְהִנָּחֵם עַל הָרָעָה לְעַמֶּךָ.

---

coarsening of the eye prevents it from shedding tears. And nonetheless, "the LORD has heard the sound of my weeping," which is certainly without tears and perhaps inaudible to humans. So the evildoers, who were the ones who brought on this tragic situation – where the hurt is so deep, the pain of the wound so intense that the soul is blocked and the tear ducts dammed up – would do well to take off. "Leave me, all evildoers."[11]

---

11. *OR*, vol. 1, pp. 303–304.

Help us, God of our salvation, for the sake of the glory of Your name. Save us and pardon our sins for Your name's sake. Ps. 79

LORD, God of Israel, turn away from Your fierce anger,
and relent from the evil against Your people.

*On all days continue here:*

שׁוֹמֵר יִשְׂרָאֵל Guardian of Israel, guard the remnant of Israel,
and let not Israel perish, who declare, "Listen, Israel."
Guardian of a unique nation, guard the remnant of a unique people,
and let not that unique nation perish, who proclaim the unity
of Your name [saying], "The LORD is our God, the LORD is One."
Guardian of a holy nation, guard the remnant of that holy people,
and let not the holy nation perish, who three times repeat
the threefold declaration of holiness to the Holy One.
You who are conciliated by calls for compassion and placated by pleas,
be conciliated and placated toward an afflicted generation,
for there is no other help.
Our Father, our King, be gracious to us and answer us,
though we have no worthy deeds;
act with us in charity and loving-kindness and save us.

*Stand at ▴.*

וַאֲנַחְנוּ We do not know ▴what to do, but our eyes are turned to You. II Chr. 12
Remember, LORD, Your compassion and loving-kindness, Ps. 25
for they are everlasting.
May Your loving-kindness, LORD, be with us, Ps. 33
for we have put our hope in You.
Do not hold against us the sins of those who came before us. Ps. 79
May Your mercies meet us swiftly,
for we have been brought very low.
Be gracious to us, LORD, be gracious to us, Ps. 123
for we are sated with contempt.
In wrath, remember mercy. Hab. 3
He knows our nature; He remembers that we are dust. Ps. 103
▸ Help us, God of our salvation, Ps. 79
for the sake of the glory of Your name.
Save us and grant atonement for our sins for Your name's sake.

עָזְרֵנוּ אֱלֹהֵי יִשְׁעֵנוּ עַל־דְּבַר כְּבוֹד־שְׁמֶךָ, תהלים עט
וְהַצִּילֵנוּ וְכַפֵּר עַל־חַטֹּאתֵינוּ לְמַעַן שְׁמֶךָ:

יהוה אֱלֹהֵי יִשְׂרָאֵל, שׁוּב מֵחֲרוֹן אַפֶּךָ וְהִנָּחֵם עַל הָרָעָה לְעַמֶּךָ.

*On all days continue here:*

שׁוֹמֵר יִשְׂרָאֵל, שְׁמֹר שְׁאֵרִית יִשְׂרָאֵל, וְאַל יֹאבַד יִשְׂרָאֵל
הָאוֹמְרִים שְׁמַע יִשְׂרָאֵל.

שׁוֹמֵר גּוֹי אֶחָד, שְׁמֹר שְׁאֵרִית עַם אֶחָד, וְאַל יֹאבַד גּוֹי אֶחָד
הַמְיַחֲדִים שִׁמְךָ, יהוה אֱלֹהֵינוּ יהוה אֶחָד.

שׁוֹמֵר גּוֹי קָדוֹשׁ, שְׁמֹר שְׁאֵרִית עַם קָדוֹשׁ, וְאַל יֹאבַד גּוֹי קָדוֹשׁ
הַמְשַׁלְּשִׁים בְּשָׁלֹשׁ קְדֻשּׁוֹת לְקָדוֹשׁ.

מִתְרַצֶּה בְרַחֲמִים וּמִתְפַּיֵּס בְּתַחֲנוּנִים, הִתְרַצֵּה וְהִתְפַּיֵּס לְדוֹר עָנִי
כִּי אֵין עוֹזֵר.

אָבִינוּ מַלְכֵּנוּ, חָנֵּנוּ וַעֲנֵנוּ, כִּי אֵין בָּנוּ מַעֲשִׂים
עֲשֵׂה עִמָּנוּ צְדָקָה וָחֶסֶד וְהוֹשִׁיעֵנוּ.

*Stand at ▴.*

וַאֲנַחְנוּ לֹא נֵדַע ▴מַה־נַּעֲשֶׂה, כִּי עָלֶיךָ עֵינֵינוּ: דברי הימים ב׳ יב
זְכֹר־רַחֲמֶיךָ יהוה וַחֲסָדֶיךָ, כִּי מֵעוֹלָם הֵמָּה: תהלים כה
יְהִי־חַסְדְּךָ יהוה עָלֵינוּ, כַּאֲשֶׁר יִחַלְנוּ לָךְ: תהלים לג
אַל־תִּזְכָּר־לָנוּ עֲוֹנֹת רִאשֹׁנִים תהלים עט
מַהֵר יְקַדְּמוּנוּ רַחֲמֶיךָ, כִּי דַלּוֹנוּ מְאֹד:
חָנֵּנוּ יהוה חָנֵּנוּ, כִּי־רַב שָׂבַעְנוּ בוּז: תהלים קכג
בְּרֹגֶז רַחֵם תִּזְכּוֹר: חבקוק ג
כִּי־הוּא יָדַע יִצְרֵנוּ, זָכוּר כִּי־עָפָר אֲנָחְנוּ: תהלים קג
◂ עָזְרֵנוּ אֱלֹהֵי יִשְׁעֵנוּ עַל־דְּבַר כְּבוֹד־שְׁמֶךָ תהלים עט
וְהַצִּילֵנוּ וְכַפֵּר עַל־חַטֹּאתֵינוּ לְמַעַן שְׁמֶךָ:

HALF KADDISH

*Leader:* יִתְגַּדַּל Magnified and sanctified may His great name be,
in the world He created by His will.
May He establish His kingdom
in your lifetime and in your days,
and in the lifetime of all the house of Israel,
swiftly and soon –
and say: Amen.

*All:* May His great name be blessed for ever and all time.

*Leader:* Blessed and praised, glorified and exalted,
raised and honored, uplifted and lauded
be the name of the Holy One,
blessed be He,
beyond any blessing,
song, praise and consolation
uttered in the world –
and say: Amen.

## REMOVING THE TORAH FROM THE ARK

*On Mondays and Thursdays, Rosh Ḥodesh, Ḥol HaMo'ed, Ḥanukka, Purim and Fast Days, the Torah is read when a minyan is present.* *On all other days, continue with "Happy are those" on page 234.*

*Before taking the Torah out of the Ark, on Mondays and Thursdays, stand while reciting "God, slow to anger." It is not said on Rosh Ḥodesh, Ḥol HaMo'ed, Erev Pesaḥ, Ḥanukka, the 14th and 15th of Adar I, Purim and Shushan Purim, Tisha B'Av or in a house of mourning, and in Israel on Isru Ḥag and, according to the Chief Rabbinate of Israel, on Yom HaAtzma'ut and Yom Yerushalayim. Most people say both paragraphs; some say only the first.*

God, slow to anger, abounding
in loving-kindness and truth,
do not rebuke us in Your anger.
Have pity on Your people, LORD,
and save us from all evil.
We have sinned against You, LORD.
Please forgive in accordance with
Your great compassion, God.

God, slow to anger, full of compassion,
do not hide Your face from us.
Have pity on the remnant of Israel
Your people, LORD,
and deliver us from all evil.
We have sinned against You, LORD.
Please forgive in accordance with
Your great compassion, God.

### חצי קדיש

ש״ץ: יִתְגַּדַּל וְיִתְקַדַּשׁ שְׁמֵהּ רַבָּא (קהל: אָמֵן)
בְּעָלְמָא דִּי בְרָא כִרְעוּתֵהּ
וְיַמְלִיךְ מַלְכוּתֵהּ
בְּחַיֵּיכוֹן וּבְיוֹמֵיכוֹן וּבְחַיֵּי דְכָל בֵּית יִשְׂרָאֵל
בַּעֲגָלָא וּבִזְמַן קָרִיב, וְאִמְרוּ אָמֵן. (קהל: אָמֵן)

קהל וש״ץ: יְהֵא שְׁמֵהּ רַבָּא מְבָרַךְ לְעָלַם וּלְעָלְמֵי עָלְמַיָּא.

ש״ץ: יִתְבָּרַךְ וְיִשְׁתַּבַּח וְיִתְפָּאַר וְיִתְרוֹמַם וְיִתְנַשֵּׂא
וְיִתְהַדָּר וְיִתְעַלֶּה וְיִתְהַלָּל
שְׁמֵהּ דְּקֻדְשָׁא בְּרִיךְ הוּא (קהל: בְּרִיךְ הוּא)
לְעֵלָּא מִן כָּל בִּרְכָתָא
/בעשרת ימי תשובה: לְעֵלָּא לְעֵלָּא מִכָּל בִּרְכָתָא/
וְשִׁירָתָא, תֻּשְׁבְּחָתָא וְנֶחֱמָתָא
דַּאֲמִירָן בְּעָלְמָא, וְאִמְרוּ אָמֵן. (קהל: אָמֵן)

## הוצאת ספר תורה

*On Mondays and Thursdays,* ראש חודש, חול המועד, חנוכה, פורים *and Fast Days, the* תורה *is read when a* מנין *is present. On all other days, continue with* אשרי *on page 235.*

*Before taking the* תורה *out of the* ארון קודש*, on Mondays and Thursdays, stand while reciting* אֵל אֶרֶךְ אַפַּיִם*. It is not said on:* ראש חודש, חול המועד, ערב פסח, חנוכה*, the 14th and 15th of* אדר א׳, פורים *and* שושן פורים, תשעה באב *or in a house of mourning, and in* ארץ ישראל *on* אסרו חג *and, according to the Chief Rabbinate of Israel, on* יום העצמאות *and* יום ירושלים*. Most people say both paragraphs, some say only the first.*

אֵל אֶרֶךְ אַפַּיִם וְרַב חֶסֶד וֶאֱמֶת
אַל בְּאַפְּךָ תוֹכִיחֵנוּ.
חוּסָה יהוה עַל עַמֶּךָ
וְהוֹשִׁיעֵנוּ מִכָּל רָע.
חָטָאנוּ לְךָ אָדוֹן
סְלַח נָא כְּרֹב רַחֲמֶיךָ אֵל.

אֵל אֶרֶךְ אַפַּיִם וּמָלֵא רַחֲמִים
אַל תַּסְתֵּר פָּנֶיךָ מִמֶּנּוּ.
חוּסָה יהוה עַל שְׁאֵרִית יִשְׂרָאֵל עַמֶּךָ
וְהַצִּילֵנוּ מִכָּל רָע.
חָטָאנוּ לְךָ אָדוֹן
סְלַח נָא כְּרֹב רַחֲמֶיךָ אֵל.

*The Ark is opened and the congregation stands. All say:*

וַיְהִי בִּנְסֹעַ Whenever the Ark set out, Moses would say, "Arise, LORD, and may Your enemies be scattered. May those who hate You flee before You." For the Torah shall come forth from Zion, and the word of the LORD from Jerusalem. Blessed is He who, in His holiness, gave the Torah to His people Israel. *Num. 10* *Is. 2*

Blessed is the name of the Master of the Universe. Blessed is Your crown and Your place. May Your favor always be with Your people Israel. Show Your people the salvation of Your right hand in Your Temple. Grant us the gift of Your good light, and accept our prayers in mercy. May it be Your will to prolong our life in goodness. May I be counted among the righteous, so that You will have compassion on me and protect me and all that is mine and all that is Your people Israel's. You feed all; You sustain all; You rule over all; You rule over kings, for sovereignty is Yours. I am a servant of the Holy One, blessed be He, before whom and before whose glorious Torah I bow at all times. Not in man do I trust, nor on any angel do I rely, but on the God of heaven who is the God of truth, whose Torah is truth, whose prophets speak truth, and who abounds in acts of love and truth. ▸ In Him I trust, and to His holy and glorious name I offer praises. May it be Your will to open my heart to the Torah, and to fulfill the wishes of my heart and of the hearts of all Your people Israel for good, for life, and for peace. *Zohar, Vayak-hel*

*The Leader takes the Torah scroll in his right arm, bows toward the Ark and says:*

Magnify the LORD with me, and let us exalt His name together. *Ps. 34*

*The Ark is closed. The Leader carries the Torah scroll to the bima and the congregation says:*

לְךָ Yours, LORD, are the greatness and the power, the glory and the majesty and splendor, for everything in heaven and earth is Yours. Yours, LORD, is the kingdom; You are exalted as Head over all. *1 Chr. 29*

רוֹמְמוּ Exalt the LORD our God and bow to His footstool; He is holy. Exalt the LORD our God, and bow at His holy mountain, for holy is the LORD our God. *Ps. 99*

אַב הָרַחֲמִים May the Father of compassion have compassion on the people borne by Him. May He remember the covenant with the mighty [patriarchs], and deliver us from evil times. May He

*The* ארון קודש *is opened and the* קהל *stands. All say:*

במדבר י וַיְהִי בִּנְסֹעַ הָאָרֹן וַיֹּאמֶר מֹשֶׁה, קוּמָה יהוה וְיָפֻצוּ אֹיְבֶיךָ וְיָנֻסוּ מְשַׂנְאֶיךָ מִפָּנֶיךָ: כִּי מִצִּיּוֹן תֵּצֵא תוֹרָה וּדְבַר־יהוה מִירוּשָׁלָםִ: ישעיה ב
בָּרוּךְ שֶׁנָּתַן תּוֹרָה לְעַמּוֹ יִשְׂרָאֵל בִּקְדֻשָּׁתוֹ.

זוהר ויקהל בְּרִיךְ שְׁמֵהּ דְּמָרֵא עָלְמָא, בְּרִיךְ כִּתְרָךְ וְאַתְרָךְ. יְהֵא רְעוּתָךְ עִם עַמָּךְ יִשְׂרָאֵל לְעָלַם, וּפֻרְקַן יְמִינָךְ אַחֲזִי לְעַמָּךְ בְּבֵית מַקְדְּשָׁךְ, וּלְאַמְטוּיֵי לָנָא מִטּוּב נְהוֹרָךְ, וּלְקַבֵּל צְלוֹתַנָא בְּרַחֲמִין. יְהֵא רַעֲוָא קֳדָמָךְ דְּתוֹרִיךְ לַן חַיִּין בְּטִיבוּ, וְלֶהֱוֵי אֲנָא פְקִידָא בְּגוֹ צַדִּיקַיָּא, לְמִרְחַם עָלַי וּלְמִנְטַר יָתִי וְיָת כָּל דִּי לִי וְדִי לְעַמָּךְ יִשְׂרָאֵל. אַנְתְּ הוּא זָן לְכֹלָּא וּמְפַרְנֵס לְכֹלָּא, אַנְתְּ הוּא שַׁלִּיט עַל כֹּלָּא, אַנְתְּ הוּא דְּשַׁלִּיט עַל מַלְכַיָּא, וּמַלְכוּתָא דִּילָךְ הִיא. אֲנָא עַבְדָּא דְקֻדְשָׁא בְּרִיךְ הוּא, דְּסָגֵדְנָא קַמֵּהּ וּמִקַּמֵּי דִּיקַר אוֹרַיְתֵהּ בְּכָל עִדָּן וְעִדָּן. לָא עַל אֱנָשׁ רָחִיצְנָא וְלָא עַל בַּר אֱלָהִין סָמִיכְנָא, אֶלָּא בֶּאֱלָהָא דִשְׁמַיָּא, דְּהוּא אֱלָהָא קְשׁוֹט, וְאוֹרַיְתֵהּ קְשׁוֹט, וּנְבִיאוֹהִי קְשׁוֹט, וּמַסְגֵּא לְמֶעְבַּד טַבְוָן וּקְשׁוֹט. ◄ בֵּהּ אֲנָא רָחִיץ, וְלִשְׁמֵהּ קַדִּישָׁא יַקִּירָא אֲנָא אֵמַר תֻּשְׁבְּחָן. יְהֵא רַעֲוָא קֳדָמָךְ דְּתִפְתַּח לִבַּאי בְּאוֹרַיְתָא, וְתַשְׁלִים מִשְׁאֲלִין דְּלִבַּאי וְלִבָּא דְכָל עַמָּךְ יִשְׂרָאֵל לְטָב וּלְחַיִּין וְלִשְׁלָם.

*The* שליח ציבור *takes the* ספר תורה *in his right arm, bows toward the* ארון קודש *and says:*

תהלים לד גַּדְּלוּ לַיהוה אִתִּי וּנְרוֹמְמָה שְׁמוֹ יַחְדָּו:

*The* ארון קודש *is closed. The* שליח ציבור *carries the* ספר תורה *to the* בימה *and the* קהל *says:*

דברי הימים א, כט לְךָ יהוה הַגְּדֻלָּה וְהַגְּבוּרָה וְהַתִּפְאֶרֶת וְהַנֵּצַח וְהַהוֹד, כִּי־כֹל בַּשָּׁמַיִם וּבָאָרֶץ, לְךָ יהוה הַמַּמְלָכָה וְהַמִּתְנַשֵּׂא לְכֹל לְרֹאשׁ:

תהלים צט רוֹמְמוּ יהוה אֱלֹהֵינוּ וְהִשְׁתַּחֲווּ לַהֲדֹם רַגְלָיו, קָדוֹשׁ הוּא: רוֹמְמוּ יהוה אֱלֹהֵינוּ וְהִשְׁתַּחֲווּ לְהַר קָדְשׁוֹ, כִּי־קָדוֹשׁ יהוה אֱלֹהֵינוּ:

אַב הָרַחֲמִים הוּא יְרַחֵם עַם עֲמוּסִים, וְיִזְכֹּר בְּרִית אֵיתָנִים, וְיַצִּיל נַפְשׁוֹתֵינוּ מִן הַשָּׁעוֹת הָרָעוֹת, וְיִגְעַר בְּיֵצֶר הָרָע מִן הַנְּשׂוּאִים,

reproach the evil instinct in the people carried by Him, and graciously grant that we be an everlasting remnant. May He fulfill in good measure our requests for salvation and compassion.

*The Torah scroll is placed on the bima and the Gabbai calls a Kohen to the Torah.*
*See laws 383–397.*

May His kingship over us be soon revealed and made manifest. May He be gracious to our surviving remnant, the remnant of His people the house of Israel in grace, loving-kindness, compassion and favor, and let us say: Amen. Let us all render greatness to our God and give honor to the Torah. *Let the Kohen come forward. Arise (*name* son of *father's name*), the Kohen.

**If no Kohen is present, a Levi or Yisrael is called up as follows:*

/As there is no Kohen, arise (*name* son of *father's name*) in place of a Kohen./

Blessed is He who, in His holiness, gave the Torah to His people Israel.

*Congregation followed by the Gabbai:*

You who cling to the LORD your God are all alive today. *Deut. 4*

*The appropriate Torah portions are to be found from page 1150.*

*The Reader shows the oleh the section to be read.*
*The oleh touches the scroll at that place with the tzitzit of his tallit,*
*which he then kisses. Holding the handles of the scroll, he says:*

*Oleh:* Bless the LORD, the blessed One.

*Cong:* Bless the LORD, the blessed One, for ever and all time.

*Oleh:* Bless the LORD, the blessed One, for ever and all time.

Blessed are You, LORD our God, King of the Universe,
who has chosen us from all peoples
and has given us His Torah.
Blessed are You, LORD, Giver of the Torah.

*After the reading, the oleh says:*

*Oleh:* Blessed are You, LORD our God, King of the Universe,
who has given us the Torah of truth,
planting everlasting life in our midst.
Blessed are You, LORD, Giver of the Torah.

וְיָחֹן אוֹתָנוּ לִפְלֵיטַת עוֹלָמִים, וִימַלֵּא מִשְׁאֲלוֹתֵינוּ בְּמִדָּה טוֹבָה יְשׁוּעָה וְרַחֲמִים.

*The* ספר תורה *is placed on the* שולחן *and the* גבאי *calls a* כהן *to the* תורה*. See laws 383–397.*

וְתִגָּלֶה וְתֵרָאֶה מַלְכוּתוֹ עָלֵינוּ בִּזְמַן קָרוֹב, וְיָחֹן פְּלֵיטָתֵנוּ וּפְלֵיטַת עַמּוֹ בֵּית יִשְׂרָאֵל לְחֵן וּלְחֶסֶד וּלְרַחֲמִים וּלְרָצוֹן וְנֹאמַר אָמֵן. הַכֹּל הָבוּ גֹדֶל לֵאלֹהֵינוּ וּתְנוּ כָבוֹד לַתּוֹרָה. *כֹּהֵן קְרַב, יַעֲמֹד (פלוני בֶּן פלוני) הַכֹּהֵן.

**If no* כהן *is present, a* לוי *or* ישראל *is called up as follows:*

/אֵין כָּאן כֹּהֵן, יַעֲמֹד (פלוני בֶּן פלוני) בִּמְקוֹם כֹּהֵן./

בָּרוּךְ שֶׁנָּתַן תּוֹרָה לְעַמּוֹ יִשְׂרָאֵל בִּקְדֻשָּׁתוֹ.

קהל *followed by the* גבאי*:*

וְאַתֶּם הַדְּבֵקִים בַּיהוה אֱלֹהֵיכֶם חַיִּים כֻּלְּכֶם הַיּוֹם: דברים ד

*The appropriate* תורה *portions are to be found from page 1150.*

*The* קורא *shows the* עולה *the section to be read. The* עולה *touches the* ספר תורה *at that place with the* ציצית *of his* טלית*, which he then kisses. Holding the handles of the* ספר תורה*, he says:*

עולה: בָּרְכוּ אֶת יהוה הַמְבֹרָךְ.

קהל: בָּרוּךְ יהוה הַמְבֹרָךְ לְעוֹלָם וָעֶד.

עולה: בָּרוּךְ יהוה הַמְבֹרָךְ לְעוֹלָם וָעֶד.
בָּרוּךְ אַתָּה יהוה, אֱלֹהֵינוּ מֶלֶךְ הָעוֹלָם
אֲשֶׁר בָּחַר בָּנוּ מִכָּל הָעַמִּים
וְנָתַן לָנוּ אֶת תּוֹרָתוֹ.
בָּרוּךְ אַתָּה יהוה, נוֹתֵן הַתּוֹרָה.

*After the* קריאת התורה*, the* עולה *says:*

עולה: בָּרוּךְ אַתָּה יהוה אֱלֹהֵינוּ מֶלֶךְ הָעוֹלָם
אֲשֶׁר נָתַן לָנוּ תּוֹרַת אֱמֶת
וְחַיֵּי עוֹלָם נָטַע בְּתוֹכֵנוּ.
בָּרוּךְ אַתָּה יהוה, נוֹתֵן הַתּוֹרָה.

*One who has survived a situation of danger (see laws 398–399) says:*

Blessed are You, Lord our God, King of the Universe, who bestows good on the unworthy, who has bestowed on me much good.

*The congregation responds:*

Amen. May He who bestowed much good on you continue to bestow on you much good, Selah.

*Special blessings and memorial prayers may be said at this point.* *See pages 580–582 and 860.*

*After a Bar Mitzva boy has finished the Torah blessing, his father says aloud:*

Blessed is He who has released me
from the responsibility for this child.

HALF KADDISH

*After the Reading of the Torah, the Reader says Half Kaddish:*

*Reader:* יִתְגַּדַּל Magnified and sanctified may His great name be,
in the world He created by His will.
May He establish His kingdom in your lifetime and in your days,
and in the lifetime of all the house of Israel,
swiftly and soon – and say: Amen.

*All:* May His great name be blessed for ever and all time.

*Reader:* Blessed and praised, glorified and exalted,
raised and honored, uplifted and lauded
be the name of the Holy One, blessed be He,
beyond any blessing, song, praise and consolation
uttered in the world – and say: Amen.

---

uplifts their spirits, so that upon arriving in civilization they will feel good about the journey itself. But in the case of the sick and the prisoners, the main good they experience is being healed or set free. Thus in the latter two cases, the words "healed" and "went out" are inserted.

By the same token, in regard to voyaging by sea and by land, entire classes of people who fit into a socio-economic bracket are indicated: "those who go down to sea," "those who walk in the deserts" (plural). This is not the case in regard to the sick and the imprisoned. These are individual incapacitations, so they are referred to in the singular: "whoever was sick," "whoever was locked up."[2]

2. *OR*, vol. 1, p. 312 = *EA*, vol. 2, *Berakhot*, chap. 9, par. 15 (p. 253).

*One who has survived a situation of danger (see laws 398–399) says:*

בָּרוּךְ אַתָּה יהוה אֱלֹהֵינוּ מֶלֶךְ הָעוֹלָם, הַגּוֹמֵל לְחַיָּבִים טוֹבוֹת שֶׁגְּמָלַנִי כָּל טוֹב.

*The* קהל *responds:*

אָמֵן. מִי שֶׁגְּמָלְךָ כָּל טוֹב הוּא יִגְמָלְךָ כָּל טוֹב, סֶלָה.

*Special* מי שברך *and memorial prayers may be said at this point.* *See pages 581–583 and 861.*

*After a* בר מצווה *has finished the* תורה *blessing, his father says aloud:*

בָּרוּךְ שֶׁפְּטָרַנִי מֵעָנְשׁוֹ שֶׁלָּזֶה.

## חצי קדיש

*After the* קריאת התורה*, the* קורא *says* חצי קדיש*:*

קורא: יִתְגַּדַּל וְיִתְקַדַּשׁ שְׁמֵהּ רַבָּא (קהל: אָמֵן)
בְּעָלְמָא דִּי בְרָא כִרְעוּתֵהּ, וְיַמְלִיךְ מַלְכוּתֵהּ
בְּחַיֵּיכוֹן וּבְיוֹמֵיכוֹן וּבְחַיֵּי דְכָל בֵּית יִשְׂרָאֵל
בַּעֲגָלָא וּבִזְמַן קָרִיב, וְאִמְרוּ אָמֵן. (קהל: אָמֵן)

קורא וקהל: יְהֵא שְׁמֵהּ רַבָּא מְבָרַךְ לְעָלַם וּלְעָלְמֵי עָלְמַיָּא.

קורא: יִתְבָּרַךְ וְיִשְׁתַּבַּח וְיִתְפָּאַר וְיִתְרוֹמַם וְיִתְנַשֵּׂא
וְיִתְהַדָּר וְיִתְעַלֶּה וְיִתְהַלָּל
שְׁמֵהּ דְּקֻדְשָׁא בְּרִיךְ הוּא (קהל: בְּרִיךְ הוּא)
לְעֵלָּא מִן כָּל בִּרְכָתָא / בעשרת ימי תשובה: לְעֵלָּא לְעֵלָּא מִכָּל בִּרְכָתָא/
וְשִׁירָתָא, תֻּשְׁבְּחָתָא וְנֶחֱמָתָא
דַּאֲמִירָן בְּעָלְמָא, וְאִמְרוּ אָמֵן. (קהל: אָמֵן)

---

**ברכת הגומל / BIRKAT HA-GOMEL**

> Four must give thanks: those who go down to sea; those who walk in the deserts; and whoever was sick and healed; and whoever was locked up in prison and went out.[1]

In the case of the seafarers and those who travel the deserts, the additional knowledge that they obtain in the course of their journey enriches them and

---

1. *b. Berakhot* 54b.

*The Torah scroll is lifted and the congregation says:*

וְזֹאת הַתּוֹרָה This is the Torah Deut. 4
that Moses placed before the children of Israel,
at the LORD's commandment, by the hand of Moses. Num. 9

*Some add:*

It is a tree of life to those who grasp it, and those who uphold it are happy. Prov. 3
Its ways are ways of pleasantness, and all its paths are peace.
Long life is at its right hand; at its left, riches and honor.
It pleased the LORD for the sake of [Israel's] righteousness, Is. 42
to make the Torah great and glorious.

*On those Mondays and Thursdays when Taḥanun is said,*
*the Leader says the following while the Torah scroll is being bound:*

יְהִי רָצוֹן May it be the will of our Father in heaven to establish
(the Temple), home of our life,
and to restore His Presence to our midst,
swiftly in our days – and let us say: Amen.

יְהִי רָצוֹן May it be the will of our Father in heaven
to have compassion on us and our remnant,
and to keep destruction and plague away from us
and from all His people the house of Israel –
and let us say: Amen.

יְהִי רָצוֹן May it be the will of our Father in heaven
to preserve among us the sages of Israel:
them, their wives, their sons and daughters,
their disciples and their disciples' disciples,
in all their dwelling places – and let us say: Amen.

יְהִי רָצוֹן May it be the will of our Father in heaven
that we may hear and be given good tidings
of salvation and consolation,
and that our dispersed be gathered
from the four quarters of the earth – and let us say: Amen.

*All:*

אַחֵינוּ As for our brothers of the whole house of Israel who are in distress or captivity, on sea or land, may the All-Present have compassion on them and lead them from distress to relief, from darkness to light, and from oppression to freedom, now, swiftly and soon – and let us say: Amen.

*The* ספר תורה *is lifted and the* קהל *says:*

וְזֹאת הַתּוֹרָה אֲשֶׁר־שָׂם מֹשֶׁה לִפְנֵי בְּנֵי יִשְׂרָאֵל: דברים ד

עַל־פִּי יהוה בְּיַד־מֹשֶׁה: במדבר ט

*Some add:*

עֵץ־חַיִּים הִיא לַמַּחֲזִיקִים בָּהּ וְתֹמְכֶיהָ מְאֻשָּׁר: משלי ג
דְּרָכֶיהָ דַרְכֵי־נֹעַם וְכָל־נְתִיבֹתֶיהָ שָׁלוֹם:
אֹרֶךְ יָמִים בִּימִינָהּ, בִּשְׂמֹאולָהּ עֹשֶׁר וְכָבוֹד:
יהוה חָפֵץ לְמַעַן צִדְקוֹ יַגְדִּיל תּוֹרָה וְיַאְדִּיר: ישעיה מב

*On those Mondays and Thursdays when* תחנון *is said, the* שליח ציבור *says the following while the* ספר תורה *is being bound:*

יְהִי רָצוֹן מִלִּפְנֵי אָבִינוּ שֶׁבַּשָּׁמַיִם, לְכוֹנֵן אֶת בֵּית חַיֵּינוּ
וּלְהָשִׁיב אֶת שְׁכִינָתוֹ בְּתוֹכֵנוּ
בִּמְהֵרָה בְיָמֵינוּ, וְנֹאמַר אָמֵן.

יְהִי רָצוֹן מִלִּפְנֵי אָבִינוּ שֶׁבַּשָּׁמַיִם, לְרַחֵם עָלֵינוּ וְעַל פְּלֵיטָתֵנוּ
וְלִמְנֹעַ מַשְׁחִית וּמַגֵּפָה מֵעָלֵינוּ
וּמֵעַל כָּל עַמּוֹ בֵּית יִשְׂרָאֵל, וְנֹאמַר אָמֵן.

יְהִי רָצוֹן מִלִּפְנֵי אָבִינוּ שֶׁבַּשָּׁמַיִם, לְקַיֶּם בָּנוּ חַכְמֵי יִשְׂרָאֵל
הֵם וּנְשֵׁיהֶם וּבְנֵיהֶם וּבְנוֹתֵיהֶם
וְתַלְמִידֵיהֶם וְתַלְמִידֵי תַלְמִידֵיהֶם
בְּכָל מְקוֹמוֹת מוֹשְׁבוֹתֵיהֶם, וְנֹאמַר אָמֵן.

יְהִי רָצוֹן מִלִּפְנֵי אָבִינוּ שֶׁבַּשָּׁמַיִם
שֶׁנִּשְׁמַע וְנִתְבַּשֵּׂר בְּשׂוֹרוֹת טוֹבוֹת, יְשׁוּעוֹת וְנֶחָמוֹת
וִיקַבֵּץ נִדָּחֵינוּ מֵאַרְבַּע כַּנְפוֹת הָאָרֶץ, וְנֹאמַר אָמֵן.

*All:*

אַחֵינוּ כָּל בֵּית יִשְׂרָאֵל, הַנְּתוּנִים בַּצָּרָה וּבַשִּׁבְיָה, הָעוֹמְדִים בֵּין בַּיָּם וּבֵין בַּיַּבָּשָׁה, הַמָּקוֹם יְרַחֵם עֲלֵיהֶם וְיוֹצִיאֵם מִצָּרָה לִרְוָחָה, וּמֵאֲפֵלָה לְאוֹרָה, וּמִשִּׁעְבּוּד לִגְאֻלָּה, הַשְׁתָּא בַּעֲגָלָא וּבִזְמַן קָרִיב, וְנֹאמַר אָמֵן.

## RETURNING THE TORAH TO THE ARK

*The Ark is opened. The Leader takes the Torah scroll and says:*

יְהַלְלוּ Let them praise the name of the LORD, *Ps. 148*
for His name alone is sublime.

*The congregation responds:*

הוֹדוֹ His majesty is above earth and heaven.
He has raised the horn of His people,
for the glory of all His devoted ones,
the children of Israel, the people close to Him.
Halleluya!

*As the Torah scroll is returned to the Ark, say:*

לְדָוִד מִזְמוֹר A psalm of David. The earth is the LORD's and all it contains, *Ps. 24* the world and all who live in it. For He founded it on the seas and established it on the streams. Who may climb the mountain of the LORD? Who may stand in His holy place? He who has clean hands and a pure heart, who has not taken My name in vain, or sworn deceitfully. He shall receive blessing from the LORD, and just reward from God, his salvation. This is a generation of those who seek Him, the descendants of Jacob who seek Your presence, Selah! Lift up your heads, O gates; be uplifted, eternal doors, so that the King of glory may enter. Who is the King of glory? It is the LORD, strong and mighty, the LORD mighty in battle. ▸ Lift up your heads, O gates; lift them up, eternal doors, so that the King of glory may enter. Who is He, the King of glory? The LORD of hosts, He is the King of glory, Selah!

*As the Torah scroll is placed into the Ark, say:*

וּבְנֻחֹה יֹאמַר When the Ark came to rest, Moses would say: "Return, O *Num. 10*
LORD, to the myriad thousands of Israel." Advance, LORD, to Your resting *Ps. 132*
place, You and Your mighty Ark. Your priests are clothed in righteousness,
and Your devoted ones sing in joy. For the sake of Your servant David,
do not reject Your anointed one. For I give you good instruction; do not *Prov. 4*
forsake My Torah. It is a tree of life to those who grasp it, and those who *Prov. 3*
uphold it are happy. Its ways are ways of pleasantness, and all its paths *Prov. 3*
are peace. ▸ Turn us back, O LORD, to You, and we will return. Renew *Lam. 5*
our days as of old.

*The Ark is closed.*

# הכנסת ספר תורה

*The* ארון קודש *is opened. The* שליח ציבור *takes the* ספר תורה *and says:*

תהלים קמח
יְהַלְלוּ אֶת־שֵׁם יהוה, כִּי נִשְׂגָּב־שְׁמוֹ, לְבַדּוֹ

*The* קהל *responds:*

הוֹדוֹ עַל־אֶרֶץ וְשָׁמָיִם:
וַיָּרֶם קֶרֶן לְעַמּוֹ
תְּהִלָּה לְכָל־חֲסִידָיו
לִבְנֵי יִשְׂרָאֵל עַם קְרֹבוֹ, הַלְלוּיָהּ:

*As the* ספר תורה *is returned to the* ארון קודש*, say:*

תהלים כד
לְדָוִד מִזְמוֹר, לַיהוה הָאָרֶץ וּמְלוֹאָהּ, תֵּבֵל וְיֹשְׁבֵי בָהּ: כִּי־הוּא עַל־יַמִּים יְסָדָהּ, וְעַל־נְהָרוֹת יְכוֹנְנֶהָ: מִי־יַעֲלֶה בְהַר־יהוה, וּמִי־יָקוּם בִּמְקוֹם קָדְשׁוֹ: נְקִי כַפַּיִם וּבַר־לֵבָב, אֲשֶׁר לֹא־נָשָׂא לַשָּׁוְא נַפְשִׁי וְלֹא נִשְׁבַּע לְמִרְמָה: יִשָּׂא בְרָכָה מֵאֵת יהוה, וּצְדָקָה מֵאֱלֹהֵי יִשְׁעוֹ: זֶה דּוֹר דֹּרְשָׁו, מְבַקְשֵׁי פָנֶיךָ, יַעֲקֹב, סֶלָה: שְׂאוּ שְׁעָרִים רָאשֵׁיכֶם, וְהִנָּשְׂאוּ פִּתְחֵי עוֹלָם, וְיָבוֹא מֶלֶךְ הַכָּבוֹד: מִי זֶה מֶלֶךְ הַכָּבוֹד, יהוה עִזּוּז וְגִבּוֹר, יהוה גִּבּוֹר מִלְחָמָה: ‹ שְׂאוּ שְׁעָרִים רָאשֵׁיכֶם, וּשְׂאוּ פִּתְחֵי עוֹלָם, וְיָבֹא מֶלֶךְ הַכָּבוֹד: מִי הוּא זֶה מֶלֶךְ הַכָּבוֹד, יהוה צְבָאוֹת הוּא מֶלֶךְ הַכָּבוֹד, סֶלָה:

*As the* ספר תורה *is placed into the* ארון קודש*, say:*

במדבר י / תהלים קלב
וּבְנֻחֹה יֹאמַר, שׁוּבָה יהוה רִבְבוֹת אַלְפֵי יִשְׂרָאֵל: קוּמָה יהוה לִמְנוּחָתֶךָ, אַתָּה וַאֲרוֹן עֻזֶּךָ: כֹּהֲנֶיךָ יִלְבְּשׁוּ־צֶדֶק, וַחֲסִידֶיךָ יְרַנֵּנוּ:

משלי ד
בַּעֲבוּר דָּוִד עַבְדֶּךָ אַל־תָּשֵׁב פְּנֵי מְשִׁיחֶךָ: כִּי לֶקַח טוֹב נָתַתִּי לָכֶם, תּוֹרָתִי אַל־תַּעֲזֹבוּ:

משלי ג
עֵץ־חַיִּים הִיא לַמַּחֲזִיקִים בָּהּ, וְתֹמְכֶיהָ מְאֻשָּׁר:

משלי ג / איכה ה
דְּרָכֶיהָ דַרְכֵי־נֹעַם וְכָל־נְתִיבֹתֶיהָ שָׁלוֹם: ‹ הֲשִׁיבֵנוּ יהוה אֵלֶיךָ וְנָשׁוּבָ, חַדֵּשׁ יָמֵינוּ כְּקֶדֶם:

*The* ארון קודש *is closed.*

## CONCLUSION OF THE SERVICE

*Some have the custom to touch the hand-tefillin at °, and the head-tefillin at °°.*

אַשְׁרֵי Happy are those who dwell in Your House; Ps. 84
they shall continue to praise You, Selah!

Happy are the people for whom this is so; Ps. 144
happy are the people whose God is the LORD.

A song of praise by David. Ps. 145

I will exalt You, my God, the King, and bless Your name for ever and all time. Every day I will bless You, and praise Your name for ever and all time. Great is the LORD and greatly to be praised; His greatness is unfathomable. One generation will praise Your works to the next, and tell of Your mighty deeds. On the glorious splendor of Your majesty I will meditate, and on the acts of Your wonders. They shall talk of the power of Your awesome deeds, and I will tell of Your greatness. They shall recite the record of Your great goodness, and sing with joy of Your righteousness. The LORD is gracious and compassionate, slow to anger and great in loving-kindness. The LORD is good to all, and His compassion extends to all His works. All Your works shall thank You, LORD, and Your devoted ones shall bless You. They shall talk of the glory of Your kingship, and speak of Your might. To make known to mankind His mighty deeds and the glorious majesty of His kingship. Your kingdom is an everlasting kingdom, and Your reign is for all generations. The LORD supports all who fall, and raises all who are bowed down. All raise their eyes to You in hope, and You give them their food in due season. °You open Your hand, °°and satisfy every living thing with favor. The LORD is righteous in all His ways, and kind in all He does. The LORD is close to all who call on Him, to all who call on Him in truth. He fulfills the will of those who revere Him; He hears their cry and saves them. The LORD guards all who love Him, but all the wicked He will destroy. ▸ My mouth shall speak the praise of the LORD, and all creatures shall bless His holy name for ever and all time.

We will bless the LORD now and for ever. Halleluya! Ps. 115

# סיום התפילה

*Some have the custom to touch the* תפילין של יד *at* °, *and the* תפילין של ראש *at* °°.

אַשְׁרֵי יוֹשְׁבֵי בֵיתֶךָ, עוֹד יְהַלְלוּךָ סֶּלָה: תהלים פד

אַשְׁרֵי הָעָם שֶׁכָּכָה לּוֹ, אַשְׁרֵי הָעָם שֶׁיהוה אֱלֹהָיו: תהלים קמד

תְּהִלָּה לְדָוִד תהלים קמה

אֲרוֹמִמְךָ אֱלוֹהַי הַמֶּלֶךְ, וַאֲבָרְכָה שִׁמְךָ לְעוֹלָם וָעֶד:

בְּכָל־יוֹם אֲבָרְכֶךָּ, וַאֲהַלְלָה שִׁמְךָ לְעוֹלָם וָעֶד:

גָּדוֹל יהוה וּמְהֻלָּל מְאֹד, וְלִגְדֻלָּתוֹ אֵין חֵקֶר:

דּוֹר לְדוֹר יְשַׁבַּח מַעֲשֶׂיךָ, וּגְבוּרֹתֶיךָ יַגִּידוּ:

הֲדַר כְּבוֹד הוֹדֶךָ, וְדִבְרֵי נִפְלְאֹתֶיךָ אָשִׂיחָה:

וֶעֱזוּז נוֹרְאֹתֶיךָ יֹאמֵרוּ, וּגְדוּלָּתְךָ אֲסַפְּרֶנָּה:

זֵכֶר רַב־טוּבְךָ יַבִּיעוּ, וְצִדְקָתְךָ יְרַנֵּנוּ:

חַנּוּן וְרַחוּם יהוה, אֶרֶךְ אַפַּיִם וּגְדָל־חָסֶד:

טוֹב־יהוה לַכֹּל, וְרַחֲמָיו עַל־כָּל־מַעֲשָׂיו:

יוֹדוּךָ יהוה כָּל־מַעֲשֶׂיךָ, וַחֲסִידֶיךָ יְבָרְכוּכָה:

כְּבוֹד מַלְכוּתְךָ יֹאמֵרוּ, וּגְבוּרָתְךָ יְדַבֵּרוּ:

לְהוֹדִיעַ לִבְנֵי הָאָדָם גְּבוּרֹתָיו, וּכְבוֹד הֲדַר מַלְכוּתוֹ:

מַלְכוּתְךָ מַלְכוּת כָּל־עֹלָמִים, וּמֶמְשַׁלְתְּךָ בְּכָל־דּוֹר וָדֹר:

סוֹמֵךְ יהוה לְכָל־הַנֹּפְלִים, וְזוֹקֵף לְכָל־הַכְּפוּפִים:

עֵינֵי־כֹל אֵלֶיךָ יְשַׂבֵּרוּ, וְאַתָּה נוֹתֵן־לָהֶם אֶת־אָכְלָם בְּעִתּוֹ:

°פּוֹתֵחַ אֶת־יָדֶךָ, °°וּמַשְׂבִּיעַ לְכָל־חַי רָצוֹן:

צַדִּיק יהוה בְּכָל־דְּרָכָיו, וְחָסִיד בְּכָל־מַעֲשָׂיו:

קָרוֹב יהוה לְכָל־קֹרְאָיו, לְכֹל אֲשֶׁר יִקְרָאֻהוּ בֶאֱמֶת:

רְצוֹן־יְרֵאָיו יַעֲשֶׂה, וְאֶת־שַׁוְעָתָם יִשְׁמַע, וְיוֹשִׁיעֵם:

שׁוֹמֵר יהוה אֶת־כָּל־אֹהֲבָיו, וְאֵת כָּל־הָרְשָׁעִים יַשְׁמִיד:

◂ תְּהִלַּת יהוה יְדַבֶּר פִּי, וִיבָרֵךְ כָּל־בָּשָׂר שֵׁם קָדְשׁוֹ לְעוֹלָם וָעֶד:

וַאֲנַחְנוּ נְבָרֵךְ יָהּ מֵעַתָּה וְעַד־עוֹלָם, הַלְלוּיָהּ: תהלים קטו

*Omit on Rosh Ḥodesh, Ḥol HaMo'ed, Erev Pesaḥ, Erev Yom Kippur, Ḥanukka, the 14th and 15th of Adar I, Purim and Shushan Purim, Tisha B'Av, or in a house of mourning, and in Israel on Isru Ḥag and, according to the Chief Rabbinate of Israel, on Yom HaAtzma'ut and Yom Yerushalayim.*

לַמְנַצֵּחַ For the conductor of music. A psalm of David. May the LORD *Ps. 20*
answer you when you are in distress; may the name of Jacob's God protect you. May He send you help from the Sanctuary and support from Zion. May He remember all your meal-offerings and accept your burnt-offerings, Selah! May He give you your heart's desire and make all your plans succeed. We will shout for joy at Your salvation and lift a banner in the name of our God. May the LORD grant all your requests. Now I know that the LORD saves His anointed; He answers him from His holy heaven with the saving power of His right hand. Some trust in chariots, others in horses, but we call on the name of the LORD our God. They were brought to their knees and fell, but we rose up and stood firm. ▸ LORD, save! May the King answer us on the day we call.

*In a house of mourning and on Tisha B'Av omit the verse beginning "As for Me" and continue with "You are the Holy One."*

וּבָא לְצִיּוֹן גּוֹאֵל "A redeemer will come to Zion, *Is. 59*
to those in Jacob who repent of their sins," declares the LORD.
"As for Me, this is My covenant with them," says the LORD.
"My spirit, that is on you,
and My words I have placed in your mouth
will not depart from your mouth,
or from the mouth of your children,
or from the mouth of their descendants
from this time on and for ever," says the LORD.

---

The Rav believed that the long exile had produced an overly cerebral Judaism to the detriment of the body. To this effect, the Rav wrote:

> Great is our bodily demand. We need a healthy body. We dealt much in soulfulness; we forgot the holiness of the body (*kedushat ha-guf*). We neglected bodily health and strength. We forgot that we have holy flesh no less than we have holy spirit.[2]

2. *Orot, Orot ha-Teḥiyah* (Lights of Renascence), chap. 33; Maggid edition, p. 353.

*Omit on* ראש חודש, חול המועד, ערב פסח, ערב יום כיפור, חנוכה, *the 14th and 15th of* אדר *on* א׳, פורים *and* שושן פורים, תשעה באב, *or in a house of mourning, and in* ארץ ישראל *on* יום ירושלים *and* יום העצמאות *and, according to the Chief Rabbinate of Israel, on* אסרו חג.

תהלים כ
לַמְנַצֵּחַ מִזְמוֹר לְדָוִד: יַעַנְךָ יהוה בְּיוֹם צָרָה, יְשַׂגֶּבְךָ שֵׁם אֱלֹהֵי יַעֲקֹב: יִשְׁלַח־עֶזְרְךָ מִקֹּדֶשׁ, וּמִצִּיּוֹן יִסְעָדֶךָּ: יִזְכֹּר כָּל־מִנְחֹתֶיךָ, וְעוֹלָתְךָ יְדַשְּׁנֶה סֶלָה: יִתֶּן־לְךָ כִלְבָבֶךָ וְכָל־עֲצָתְךָ יְמַלֵּא: נְרַנְּנָה בִּישׁוּעָתֶךָ, וּבְשֵׁם־אֱלֹהֵינוּ נִדְגֹּל, יְמַלֵּא יהוה כָּל־מִשְׁאֲלוֹתֶיךָ: עַתָּה יָדַעְתִּי כִּי הוֹשִׁיעַ יהוה מְשִׁיחוֹ, יַעֲנֵהוּ מִשְּׁמֵי קָדְשׁוֹ, בִּגְבֻרוֹת יֵשַׁע יְמִינוֹ: אֵלֶּה בָרֶכֶב וְאֵלֶּה בַסּוּסִים, וַאֲנַחְנוּ בְּשֵׁם־יהוה אֱלֹהֵינוּ נַזְכִּיר: הֵמָּה כָּרְעוּ וְנָפָלוּ, וַאֲנַחְנוּ קַּמְנוּ וַנִּתְעוֹדָד: ‹ יהוה הוֹשִׁיעָה, הַמֶּלֶךְ יַעֲנֵנוּ בְיוֹם־קָרְאֵנוּ:

*In a house of mourning and on* תשעה באב *omit the verse beginning* וַאֲנִי זֹאת בְּרִיתִי *and continue with* וְאַתָּה קָדוֹשׁ.

ישעיה נט
וּבָא לְצִיּוֹן גּוֹאֵל, וּלְשָׁבֵי פֶשַׁע בְּיַעֲקֹב, נְאֻם יהוה:
וַאֲנִי זֹאת בְּרִיתִי אוֹתָם, אָמַר יהוה
רוּחִי אֲשֶׁר עָלֶיךָ וּדְבָרַי אֲשֶׁר־שַׂמְתִּי בְּפִיךָ
לֹא־יָמוּשׁוּ מִפִּיךָ וּמִפִּי זַרְעֲךָ וּמִפִּי זֶרַע זַרְעֲךָ
אָמַר יהוה, מֵעַתָּה וְעַד־עוֹלָם:

---

וּבָא לְצִיּוֹן גּוֹאֵל, וּלְשָׁבֵי פֶשַׁע בְּיַעֲקֹב *U-Va le-Tsiyon go'el u-le-shavei fesha' be-Ya'akov.* A redeemer will come to Zion, and to those in Jacob who repent of sin.

Rav Kook was of the firm conviction that in the future all the Children of Israel – even those visibly straying and lost – shall return to their source. In this regard, he would quote our verse from Isaiah 59:20: "A redeemer will come to Zion, and to those in Jacob who repent of sin."[1]

*

One of the revolutions that Rav Kook sought to bring about in Jewish life, was reclaiming what he called *"kedushat ha-guf"* ("the holiness of the body").

1. See *IR*, vol. 1, p. 369 (Letter 332); vol. 2, p. 37 (Letter 378).

▸ You are the Holy One, enthroned on the praises of Israel. *Ps. 22*
And (the angels) call to one another, saying,
"Holy, holy, holy is the LORD of hosts; *Is. 6*
the whole world is filled with His glory."

And they receive permission from one another, saying: *Targum Yonatan Is. 6*
"Holy in the highest heavens, home of His Presence;
holy on earth, the work of His strength;
holy for ever and all time is the LORD of hosts;
the whole earth is full of His radiant glory."

▸ Then a wind lifted me up and I heard behind me *Ezek. 3*
the sound of a great noise, saying,
"Blessed is the LORD's glory from His place."

Then a wind lifted me up and I heard behind me *Targum Yonatan Ezek. 3*
the sound of a great tempest of those who uttered praise, saying,
"Blessed is the LORD's glory from the place of the home of His Presence."

The LORD shall reign for ever and all time. *Ex. 15*

The LORD's kingdom is established for ever and all time. *Targum Onkelos Ex. 15*

---

is indicated that the initials of the three words "*go'el u-le-shavei fesha'*" spell out the word "*guf*" (body).[4] Perhaps Rav Kook heard in this comment of the great kabbalist an intimation that part and parcel of the "*tahalikh ha-go'el*" (the redemptive process) and of the collective *teshuvah* of the People dwelling in Zion, would be a return to the body.[5]

Rav Kook may also have been inspired by this striking passage in the writings of that genius of Ḥasidism, Rabbi Naḥman of Breslov:

> And these great souls need a body that will be "fruit of the Land,"[6] of the "air of the Land of Israel." When the air is sanctified, of "the air of the Land of Israel," then all the fruits and grain that grow there, by which the person is nourished… all is of the Land of Israel. And from there comes the semen, and from there the body is formed, "I was formed in the lowest parts of the Land,"[7] the Land of Israel, and then the body is "fruit of the Land."

---

4. Rabbi Ḥayyim Vital, *Peri 'Ets Ḥayyim, Sha'ar Keri'at ha-Torah*, chap. 5.
5. *Orot ha-Teshuvah* opens with the concept that integral to *Teshuvah* (Return) is return to the body and restoration of physical heath.
6. Isaiah 4:2.
7. Palms 139:15.

◂ וְאַתָּה קָדוֹשׁ יוֹשֵׁב תְּהִלּוֹת יִשְׂרָאֵל: תהלים כב
וְקָרָא זֶה אֶל־זֶה וְאָמַר ישעיה ו
קָדוֹשׁ, קָדוֹשׁ, קָדוֹשׁ, יהוה צְבָאוֹת, מְלֹא כָל־הָאָרֶץ כְּבוֹדוֹ:
וּמְקַבְּלִין דֵּין מִן דֵּין וְאָמְרִין תרגום יונתן ישעיה ו
קַדִּישׁ בִּשְׁמֵי מְרוֹמָא עִלָּאָה בֵּית שְׁכִינְתֵּהּ
קַדִּישׁ עַל אַרְעָא עוֹבַד גְּבוּרְתֵּהּ
קַדִּישׁ לְעָלַם וּלְעָלְמֵי עָלְמַיָּא
יהוה צְבָאוֹת, מַלְיָא כָל אַרְעָא זִיו יְקָרֵהּ.

◂ וַתִּשָּׂאֵנִי רוּחַ, וָאֶשְׁמַע אַחֲרַי קוֹל רַעַשׁ גָּדוֹל יחזקאל ג
בָּרוּךְ כְּבוֹד־יהוה מִמְּקוֹמוֹ:
וּנְטָלַתְנִי רוּחָא, וּשְׁמָעִית בַּתְרַי קָל זִיעַ סַגִּיא, דִּמְשַׁבְּחִין וְאָמְרִין תרגום יונתן יחזקאל ג
בְּרִיךְ יְקָרָא דַיהוה מֵאֲתַר בֵּית שְׁכִינְתֵּהּ.

יהוה יִמְלֹךְ לְעֹלָם וָעֶד: שמות טו
יהוה מַלְכוּתֵהּ קָאֵם לְעָלַם וּלְעָלְמֵי עָלְמַיָּא. תרגום אונקלוס שמות טו

---

Rav Kook even had the audacity to sing the praises of physical exercise (*hit'amlut*):

> The exercise that the youths of Israel engage in *Erets Yisrael* to strengthen their bodies in order to be powerful sons to the nation, enhances the spiritual prowess of the exalted righteous who engage in *yiḥudim* (mystical unifications) of the divine names, to increase the accentuation of the divine light in the world. One revelation of light cannot stand without the other.[3]

In 1920, when these passages first appeared in print, in Rav Kook's seminal work *Orot,* they caused quite a stir in the rabbinic world. That a rabbi of Rav Kook's stature would so strongly endorse such a *bouleversement* of the traditional, time-honored educational system, was indeed found shocking. Today, from the distance of time, we can view these passages in his writing more dispassionately.

One may find of interest that in the Lurianic intentions to the prayers, it

3. *Orot, Orot ha-Teḥiyah* (Lights of Renascence), chap. 34; Maggid edition, p. 355.

יהוה LORD, God of Abraham, Isaac and Yisrael, our ancestors, may You keep this for ever so that it forms the thoughts in Your people's heart, and directs their heart toward You. He is compassionate. He forgives iniquity and does not destroy. Repeatedly He suppresses His anger, not rousing His full wrath. For You, my LORD, are good and forgiving, abundantly kind to all who call on You. Your righteousness is eternally righteous, and Your Torah is truth. Grant truth to Jacob, loving-kindness to Abraham, as You promised our ancestors in ancient times. Blessed is my LORD for day after day He burdens us [with His blessings]; God is our salvation, Selah! The LORD of hosts is with us; the God of Jacob is our refuge, Selah! LORD of hosts, happy is the one who trusts in You. LORD, save! May the King answer us on the day we call.

*1 Chr. 29; Ps. 78; Ps. 86; Ps. 119; Mic. 7; Ps. 68; Ps. 46; Ps. 84; Ps. 20*

בָּרוּךְ Blessed is He, our God, who created us for His glory, separating us from those who go astray; who gave us the Torah of truth, planting within us eternal life. May He open our heart to His Torah, imbuing our heart with the love and awe of Him, that we may do His will and serve Him with a perfect heart, so that we neither toil in vain nor give birth to confusion.

יְהִי רָצוֹן May it be Your will, O LORD our God and God of our ancestors, that we keep Your laws in this world, and thus be worthy to live, see and inherit goodness and blessing in the Messianic Age and in the life of the World to Come. So that my soul may sing to You and not be silent. LORD, my God, for ever I will thank You. Blessed is the man who trusts in the LORD, whose trust is in the LORD alone. Trust in the LORD for evermore, for God, the LORD, is an everlasting Rock. ▸ Those who know Your name trust in You, for You, LORD, do not forsake those who seek You. The LORD desired, for the sake of Israel's merit, to make the Torah great and glorious.

*Ps. 30; Jer. 17; Is. 26; Ps. 9; Is. 42*

*On Rosh Ḥodesh and Ḥol HaMo'ed, the Leader says Half Kaddish, page 228. The service then continues with Musaf for Rosh Ḥodesh on page 798, for Ḥol HaMo'ed on page 868.*

*On other days, the Leader continues with Full Kaddish on the next page.*

---

receive a great soul, and vice versa. Therefore, there are countries where the intellect is thick and corpulent, and likewise, there are countries where the intellect is pure and refined. All depends on the country, on the food that comes out of it. So when we are driven from the "air of the Land of Israel," we cannot receive a great soul.[9]

9. Rabbi Naḥman of Breslov, *Likkutei Moharan* 1, 61:3.

יהוה אֱלֹהֵי אַבְרָהָם יִצְחָק וְיִשְׂרָאֵל אֲבֹתֵינוּ, שָׁמְרָה־זֹּאת לְעוֹלָם דברי הימים א׳ כט
לְיֵצֶר מַחְשְׁבוֹת לְבַב עַמֶּךָ, וְהָכֵן לְבָבָם אֵלֶיךָ: וְהוּא רַחוּם יְכַפֵּר עָוֹן תהלים עח
וְלֹא־יַשְׁחִית, וְהִרְבָּה לְהָשִׁיב אַפּוֹ, וְלֹא־יָעִיר כָּל־חֲמָתוֹ: כִּי־אַתָּה תהלים פו
אֲדֹנָי טוֹב וְסַלָּח, וְרַב־חֶסֶד לְכָל־קֹרְאֶיךָ: צִדְקָתְךָ צֶדֶק לְעוֹלָם תהלים קיט
וְתוֹרָתְךָ אֱמֶת: תִּתֵּן אֱמֶת לְיַעֲקֹב, חֶסֶד לְאַבְרָהָם, אֲשֶׁר־נִשְׁבַּעְתָּ מיכה ז
לַאֲבֹתֵינוּ מִימֵי קֶדֶם: בָּרוּךְ אֲדֹנָי יוֹם יוֹם יַעֲמָס־לָנוּ, הָאֵל יְשׁוּעָתֵנוּ תהלים סח
סֶלָה: יהוה צְבָאוֹת עִמָּנוּ, מִשְׂגָּב לָנוּ אֱלֹהֵי יַעֲקֹב סֶלָה: יהוה צְבָאוֹת, תהלים מו תהלים פד
אַשְׁרֵי אָדָם בֹּטֵחַ בָּךְ: יהוה הוֹשִׁיעָה, הַמֶּלֶךְ יַעֲנֵנוּ בְיוֹם־קָרְאֵנוּ: תהלים כ

בָּרוּךְ הוּא אֱלֹהֵינוּ שֶׁבְּרָאָנוּ לִכְבוֹדוֹ, וְהִבְדִּילָנוּ מִן הַתּוֹעִים, וְנָתַן לָנוּ תּוֹרַת אֱמֶת, וְחַיֵּי עוֹלָם נָטַע בְּתוֹכֵנוּ. הוּא יִפְתַּח לִבֵּנוּ בְּתוֹרָתוֹ, וְיָשֵׂם בְּלִבֵּנוּ אַהֲבָתוֹ וְיִרְאָתוֹ וְלַעֲשׂוֹת רְצוֹנוֹ וּלְעָבְדוֹ בְּלֵבָב שָׁלֵם, לְמַעַן לֹא נִיגַע לָרִיק וְלֹא נֵלֵד לַבֶּהָלָה.

יְהִי רָצוֹן מִלְּפָנֶיךָ יהוה אֱלֹהֵינוּ וֵאלֹהֵי אֲבוֹתֵינוּ, שֶׁנִּשְׁמֹר חֻקֶּיךָ
בָּעוֹלָם הַזֶּה, וְנִזְכֶּה וְנִחְיֶה וְנִרְאֶה וְנִירַשׁ טוֹבָה וּבְרָכָה, לִשְׁנֵי יְמוֹת
הַמָּשִׁיחַ וּלְחַיֵּי הָעוֹלָם הַבָּא. לְמַעַן יְזַמֶּרְךָ כָבוֹד וְלֹא יִדֹּם, יהוה תהלים ל
אֱלֹהַי, לְעוֹלָם אוֹדֶךָּ: בָּרוּךְ הַגֶּבֶר אֲשֶׁר יִבְטַח בַּיהוה, וְהָיָה יהוה ירמיה יז
מִבְטַחוֹ: בִּטְחוּ בַיהוה עֲדֵי־עַד, כִּי בְּיָהּ יהוה צוּר עוֹלָמִים: ‹ וְיִבְטְחוּ ישעיה כו תהלים ט
בְךָ יוֹדְעֵי שְׁמֶךָ, כִּי לֹא־עָזַבְתָּ דֹרְשֶׁיךָ, יהוה: יהוה חָפֵץ לְמַעַן צִדְקוֹ, ישעיה מב
יַגְדִּיל תּוֹרָה וְיַאְדִּיר:

*On* ראש חודש *and* חול המועד*, the* שליח ציבור *says* חצי קדיש*, page 229. The service then continues with* מוסף *for* ראש חודש *on page 799, for* חול המועד *on page 869.*

*On other days the* שליח ציבור *continues with* קדיש שלם *on the next page.*

---

And then it is worthy of receiving a great soul: "'He calls to the heavens above' – this is the soul; 'and to the earth' – this is the body."[8] Because the soul is according to the body. When the body is pure and clean, it can

---

8. Psalms 50:4; *b. Sanhedrin* 91b.

## FULL KADDISH

*Leader:* יִתְגַּדַּל Magnified and sanctified may His great name be,
in the world He created by His will.
May He establish His kingdom in your lifetime
and in your days,
and in the lifetime of all the house of Israel,
swiftly and soon –
and say: Amen.

*All:* May His great name be blessed
for ever and all time.

*Leader:* Blessed and praised,
glorified and exalted,
raised and honored,
uplifted and lauded be
the name of the Holy One,
blessed be He,
beyond any blessing,
song, praise and consolation
uttered in the world –
and say: Amen.

*On Tisha B'Av, omit the next verse and continue with "May there be great peace."*

May the prayers and pleas of all Israel
be accepted by their Father in heaven –
and say: Amen.

May there be great peace from heaven,
and life for us and all Israel –
and say: Amen.

*Bow, take three steps back, as if taking leave of the Divine Presence, then bow, first left, then right, then center, while saying:*

May He who makes peace in His high places,
make peace for us and all Israel –
and say: Amen.

## קדיש שלם

ש״ץ: יִתְגַּדַּל וְיִתְקַדַּשׁ שְׁמֵהּ רַבָּא (קהל: אָמֵן)
בְּעָלְמָא דִּי בְרָא כִרְעוּתֵהּ
וְיַמְלִיךְ מַלְכוּתֵהּ
בְּחַיֵּיכוֹן וּבְיוֹמֵיכוֹן וּבְחַיֵּי דְכָל בֵּית יִשְׂרָאֵל
בַּעֲגָלָא וּבִזְמַן קָרִיב
וְאִמְרוּ אָמֵן. (קהל: אָמֵן)

קהל וש״ץ: יְהֵא שְׁמֵהּ רַבָּא מְבָרַךְ לְעָלַם וּלְעָלְמֵי עָלְמַיָּא.

ש״ץ: יִתְבָּרַךְ וְיִשְׁתַּבַּח וְיִתְפָּאַר
וְיִתְרוֹמַם וְיִתְנַשֵּׂא וְיִתְהַדָּר וְיִתְעַלֶּה וְיִתְהַלָּל
שְׁמֵהּ דְּקֻדְשָׁא בְּרִיךְ הוּא (קהל: בְּרִיךְ הוּא)
לְעֵלָּא מִן כָּל בִּרְכָתָא / בעשרת ימי תשובה: לְעֵלָּא לְעֵלָּא מִכָּל בִּרְכָתָא/
וְשִׁירָתָא, תֻּשְׁבְּחָתָא וְנֶחֱמָתָא
דַּאֲמִירָן בְּעָלְמָא
וְאִמְרוּ אָמֵן. (קהל: אָמֵן)

*On* תשעה באב*, omit the next verse and continue with* יְהֵא שְׁלָמָא.

תִּתְקַבַּל צְלוֹתְהוֹן וּבָעוּתְהוֹן דְּכָל יִשְׂרָאֵל
קֳדָם אֲבוּהוֹן דִּי בִשְׁמַיָּא
וְאִמְרוּ אָמֵן. (קהל: אָמֵן)

יְהֵא שְׁלָמָא רַבָּא מִן שְׁמַיָּא
וְחַיִּים, עָלֵינוּ וְעַל כָּל יִשְׂרָאֵל
וְאִמְרוּ אָמֵן. (קהל: אָמֵן)

*Bow, take three steps back, as if taking leave of the Divine Presence, then bow, first left, then right, then center, while saying:*

עֹשֶׂה שָׁלוֹם/ בעשרת ימי תשובה: הַשָּׁלוֹם/ בִּמְרוֹמָיו
הוּא יַעֲשֶׂה שָׁלוֹם עָלֵינוּ וְעַל כָּל יִשְׂרָאֵל
וְאִמְרוּ אָמֵן. (קהל: אָמֵן)

*Stand while saying Aleinu. Bow at* ▾.

עָלֵינוּ It is our duty to praise the Master of all,
and ascribe greatness to the Author of creation,
who has not made us like the nations of the lands
nor placed us like the families of the earth;
who has not made our portion like theirs,
nor our destiny like all their multitudes.
(For they worship vanity and emptiness,
and pray to a god who cannot save.)
▾But we bow in worship and thank the Supreme King of kings,
the Holy One, blessed be He,
who extends the heavens and establishes the earth,
whose throne of glory is in the heavens above,
and whose power's Presence is in the highest of heights.
He is our God; there is no other.
Truly He is our King, there is none else,
as it is written in His Torah:
"You shall know and take to heart this day that the LORD is God, *Deut. 4*
in heaven above and on earth below. There is no other."

Therefore, we place our hope in You, LORD our God,
that we may soon see the glory of Your power,
when You will remove abominations from the earth,
and idols will be utterly destroyed,
when the world will be perfected
under the sovereignty of the Almighty,
when all humanity will call on Your name,
to turn all the earth's wicked toward You.
All the world's inhabitants will realize and know
that to You every knee must bow and every tongue swear loyalty.
Before You, LORD our God, they will kneel and bow down
and give honor to Your glorious name.
They will all accept the yoke of Your kingdom,
and You will reign over them soon and for ever.
For the kingdom is Yours, and to all eternity You will reign in glory,
as it is written in Your Torah: "The LORD will reign for ever and ever." *Ex. 15*
▸ And it is said: "Then the LORD shall be King over all the earth; *Zech. 14*
on that day the LORD shall be One and His name One."

*Stand while saying* עָלֵינוּ*. Bow at* ▼.

עָלֵינוּ לְשַׁבֵּחַ לַאֲדוֹן הַכֹּל, לָתֵת גְּדֻלָּה לְיוֹצֵר בְּרֵאשִׁית
שֶׁלֹּא עָשָׂנוּ כְּגוֹיֵי הָאֲרָצוֹת, וְלֹא שָׂמָנוּ כְּמִשְׁפְּחוֹת הָאֲדָמָה
שֶׁלֹּא שָׂם חֶלְקֵנוּ כָּהֶם וְגוֹרָלֵנוּ כְּכָל הֲמוֹנָם.
(שֶׁהֵם מִשְׁתַּחֲוִים לְהֶבֶל וָרִיק וּמִתְפַּלְּלִים אֶל אֵל לֹא יוֹשִׁיעַ.)
▼וַאֲנַחְנוּ כּוֹרְעִים וּמִשְׁתַּחֲוִים וּמוֹדִים
לִפְנֵי מֶלֶךְ מַלְכֵי הַמְּלָכִים, הַקָּדוֹשׁ בָּרוּךְ הוּא
שֶׁהוּא נוֹטֶה שָׁמַיִם וְיוֹסֵד אָרֶץ, וּמוֹשַׁב יְקָרוֹ בַּשָּׁמַיִם מִמַּעַל
וּשְׁכִינַת עֻזּוֹ בְּגָבְהֵי מְרוֹמִים.
הוּא אֱלֹהֵינוּ, אֵין עוֹד.
אֱמֶת מַלְכֵּנוּ, אֶפֶס זוּלָתוֹ
כַּכָּתוּב בְּתוֹרָתוֹ
וְיָדַעְתָּ הַיּוֹם וַהֲשֵׁבֹתָ אֶל־לְבָבֶךָ דברים ד
כִּי יהוה הוּא הָאֱלֹהִים בַּשָּׁמַיִם מִמַּעַל וְעַל־הָאָרֶץ מִתָּחַת, אֵין עוֹד:

עַל כֵּן נְקַוֶּה לְּךָ יהוה אֱלֹהֵינוּ, לִרְאוֹת מְהֵרָה בְּתִפְאֶרֶת עֻזֶּךָ
לְהַעֲבִיר גִּלּוּלִים מִן הָאָרֶץ, וְהָאֱלִילִים כָּרוֹת יִכָּרֵתוּן
לְתַקֵּן עוֹלָם בְּמַלְכוּת שַׁדַּי.
וְכָל בְּנֵי בָשָׂר יִקְרְאוּ בִשְׁמֶךָ לְהַפְנוֹת אֵלֶיךָ כָּל רִשְׁעֵי אָרֶץ.
יַכִּירוּ וְיֵדְעוּ כָּל יוֹשְׁבֵי תֵבֵל
כִּי לְךָ תִּכְרַע כָּל בֶּרֶךְ, תִּשָּׁבַע כָּל לָשׁוֹן.
לְפָנֶיךָ יהוה אֱלֹהֵינוּ יִכְרְעוּ וְיִפֹּלוּ, וְלִכְבוֹד שִׁמְךָ יְקָר יִתֵּנוּ
וִיקַבְּלוּ כֻלָּם אֶת עֹל מַלְכוּתֶךָ
וְתִמְלֹךְ עֲלֵיהֶם מְהֵרָה לְעוֹלָם וָעֶד.
כִּי הַמַּלְכוּת שֶׁלְּךָ הִיא וּלְעוֹלְמֵי עַד תִּמְלֹךְ בְּכָבוֹד
כַּכָּתוּב בְּתוֹרָתֶךָ, יהוה יִמְלֹךְ לְעֹלָם וָעֶד: שמות טו
◄ וְנֶאֱמַר, וְהָיָה יהוה לְמֶלֶךְ עַל־כָּל־הָאָרֶץ זכריה יד
בַּיּוֹם הַהוּא יִהְיֶה יהוה אֶחָד וּשְׁמוֹ אֶחָד:

*Some add:*

Have no fear of sudden terror or of the ruin when it overtakes the wicked. *Prov. 3*
Devise your strategy, but it will be thwarted; propose your plan, *Is. 8*
but it will not stand, for God is with us.
When you grow old, I will still be the same. *Is. 46*
When your hair turns gray, I will still carry you.
I made you, I will bear you, I will carry you, and I will rescue you.

## MOURNER'S KADDISH

*The following prayer, said by mourners, requires the presence of a minyan.*
*A transliteration can be found on page 1320.*

*Mourner:* יִתְגַּדַּל Magnified and sanctified
may His great name be,
in the world He created by His will.
May He establish His kingdom
in your lifetime and in your days,
and in the lifetime of all the house of Israel,
swiftly and soon –
and say: Amen.

*All:* May His great name be blessed for ever and all time.

*Mourner:* Blessed and praised, glorified and exalted,
raised and honored, uplifted and lauded
be the name of the Holy One,
blessed be He,
beyond any blessing,
song, praise and consolation
uttered in the world –
and say: Amen.

May there be great peace from heaven,
and life for us and all Israel –
and say: Amen.

*Bow, take three steps back, as if taking leave of the Divine Presence,*
*then bow, first left, then right, then center, while saying:*

May He who makes peace in His high places,
make peace for us and all Israel –
and say: Amen.

*Some add:*

אַל־תִּירָא מִפַּחַד פִּתְאֹם וּמִשֹּׁאַת רְשָׁעִים כִּי תָבֹא: משלי ג

עֻצוּ עֵצָה וְתֻפָר, דַּבְּרוּ דָבָר וְלֹא יָקוּם, כִּי עִמָּנוּ אֵל: ישעיה ח

וְעַד־זִקְנָה אֲנִי הוּא, וְעַד־שֵׂיבָה אֲנִי אֶסְבֹּל ישעיה מו

אֲנִי עָשִׂיתִי וַאֲנִי אֶשָּׂא וַאֲנִי אֶסְבֹּל וַאֲמַלֵּט:

## קדיש יתום

*The following prayer, said by mourners, requires the presence of a* מנין*.*
*A transliteration can be found on page 1320.*

אבל: יִתְגַּדַּל וְיִתְקַדַּשׁ שְׁמֵהּ רַבָּא (קהל: אָמֵן)

בְּעָלְמָא דִּי בְרָא כִרְעוּתֵהּ

וְיַמְלִיךְ מַלְכוּתֵהּ

בְּחַיֵּיכוֹן וּבְיוֹמֵיכוֹן וּבְחַיֵּי דְכָל בֵּית יִשְׂרָאֵל

בַּעֲגָלָא וּבִזְמַן קָרִיב, וְאִמְרוּ אָמֵן. (קהל: אָמֵן)

קהל ואבל: יְהֵא שְׁמֵהּ רַבָּא מְבָרַךְ לְעָלַם וּלְעָלְמֵי עָלְמַיָּא.

אבל: יִתְבָּרַךְ וְיִשְׁתַּבַּח וְיִתְפָּאַר

וְיִתְרוֹמַם וְיִתְנַשֵּׂא וְיִתְהַדָּר וְיִתְעַלֶּה וְיִתְהַלָּל

שְׁמֵהּ דְּקֻדְשָׁא בְּרִיךְ הוּא (קהל: בְּרִיךְ הוּא)

לְעֵלָּא מִן כָּל בִּרְכָתָא / בעשרת ימי תשובה: לְעֵלָּא לְעֵלָּא מִכָּל בִּרְכָתָא/

וְשִׁירָתָא, תֻּשְׁבְּחָתָא וְנֶחֱמָתָא

דַּאֲמִירָן בְּעָלְמָא, וְאִמְרוּ אָמֵן. (קהל: אָמֵן)

יְהֵא שְׁלָמָא רַבָּא מִן שְׁמַיָּא

וְחַיִּים, עָלֵינוּ וְעַל כָּל יִשְׂרָאֵל, וְאִמְרוּ אָמֵן. (קהל: אָמֵן)

*Bow, take three steps back, as if taking leave of the Divine Presence, then bow, first left, then right, then center, while saying:*

עֹשֶׂה שָׁלוֹם/ בעשרת ימי תשובה: הַשָּׁלוֹם/ בִּמְרוֹמָיו

הוּא יַעֲשֶׂה שָׁלוֹם

עָלֵינוּ וְעַל כָּל יִשְׂרָאֵל, וְאִמְרוּ אָמֵן. (קהל: אָמֵן)

THE DAILY PSALM

*One of the following psalms is said on the appropriate day of the week as indicated. After the psalm, the Mourner's Kaddish on page 246 is said.*

*After the Daily Psalm, on Rosh Ḥodesh, add Barekhi Nafshi, page 260 (in Israel, some only say Barekhi Nafshi). On Ḥanukka, add Psalm 30, page 100, followed by Mourner's Kaddish. From the second day of Rosh Ḥodesh Elul through Shemini Atzeret (in Israel, through Hoshana Raba), add Psalm 27 on page 262. In a house of mourning the service concludes on page 1138.*

*Sunday:* Today is the first day of the week,
on which the Levites used to say this psalm in the Temple:

לְדָוִד מִזְמוֹר A psalm of David. The earth is the LORD's and all it contains, the world and all who live in it. For He founded it on the seas and established it on the streams. Who may climb the mountain of the LORD? Who may stand *Ps. 24*

---

kabbalistic explanation for the number of Levites appointed by King David to sing in the Temple. We read in the Book of Chronicles that at the time David established the twenty-four watches of Levites,[15] there were twelve Levites in each watch, for a grand total of 288 Levites![16]

This work of isolating and separating the sparks from the matrix in which they are embedded, is referred to as *"'avodat ha-birurim"* (the work of selection).[17] Not only are the Levites *"mevarerim"*; not only are the Levites engaged in the work of selection, but they themselves are referred to in Chronicles as *"ha-berurim"* ("the select," "the chosen").[18] (Editor)

15. *Seder 'Olam*, chap. 20; *t. Ta'anit* 3:2; *y. Ta'anit* 4:2; *b. Ta'anit* 27a; Maimonides, *MT, Hil. Klei ha-Mikdash* 3:9.
16. 1 Chronicles 25:7. See Pseudo-Rashi to verse 9.
17. The term gained currency in the Ḥabad school of Ḥasidism. Whereas in the present reality our process is *"'avodat ha-birurim,"* our future focus will be *"yiḥudim"* (unifications). See Rabbi Shneur Zalman of Liadi, *Tanya* IV, 26 (145a); V, 5 (160a).
18. 1 Chronicles 16:41. Parenthetically, this precise terminology persists much later in Maimonides' code of law: "The one in charge of the singers, chooses (*borer*) every day the singers who stand on the platform to say song by mouth" (*MT, Hil. Klei ha-Mikdash* 7:5). See *Ḥiddushei Maran Riz Halevi* ad loc. (For an example of this usage of *borer* in Mishnaic Hebrew, see *m. Ta'anit* 4:8.) In the Middle Ages, in communities as diverse as Gerona in the West and Prague in the East, officials of the Jewish community were referred to as *"berurim."*
    Cf. Rabbi Menaḥem Mendel Schneersohn of Lubavitch (*"Tsemaḥ Tsedek"*), *Derekh Mitsvotekha – Ta'amei ha-Mitsvot* (Poltava, 1911), 114a (*"Igeret ha-Kodesh,"* Holy Epistle); in new edition Brooklyn, 2006, 198a. At the conclusion of the Holy Epistle, there is a play on the word *"barah"* ("the choice one") in Song of Songs 6:9: "This refers to his making selections (*mevarer birurim*) by this power of Torah and *mitsvot* the entire day."

## שיר של יום

*One of the following psalms is said on the appropriate day of the week as indicated. After the psalm,* קדיש יתום *on page 247 is said.*

*After* שיר של יום*, on* ראש חודש*, add* בָּרְכִי נַפְשִׁי*, page 261 (in* ארץ ישראל*, some only say* בָּרְכִי נַפְשִׁי*). On* חנוכה*, add* מִזְמוֹר שִׁיר־חֲנֻכַּת הַבַּיִת*, page 101, followed by* קדיש יתום*. From the second day of* ראש חודש אלול *through* שמיני עצרת *(in* ארץ ישראל*, through* הושענא רבה*), add* לְדָוִד, יהוה אוֹרִי *on page 263. In a house of mourning the service concludes on page 1139.*

*Sunday* **הַיּוֹם יוֹם רִאשׁוֹן בְּשַׁבָּת, שֶׁבּוֹ הָיוּ הַלְוִיִּם אוֹמְרִים בְּבֵית הַמִּקְדָּשׁ:**

תהלים כד לְדָוִד מִזְמוֹר, לַיהוה הָאָרֶץ וּמְלוֹאָהּ, תֵּבֵל וְיֹשְׁבֵי בָהּ: כִּי־הוּא עַל־
יַמִּים יְסָדָהּ, וְעַל־נְהָרוֹת יְכוֹנְנֶהָ: מִי־יַעֲלֶה בְהַר־יהוה, וּמִי־יָקוּם

---

**שיר של יום / THE DAILY PSALM**

**הָיוּ הַלְוִיִּם אוֹמְרִים בְּבֵית הַמִּקְדָּשׁ** *The Levites used to say this psalm in the Temple.* According to Lurianic Kabbalah, at the time of the creation of the world, there occurred the cataclysmic event of the "shattering of the vessels" (*Shevirat ha-Kelim*), whereupon 288 sparks (*rapa"h nitsotsin*) fell below and were dispersed throughout existence.[10] It is our work to isolate these sparks and uplift them through our Torah and *mitsvot* (commandments), and especially through our prayers.[11] These 288 sparks are alluded to in the second verse of the Torah: "And the spirit of God was hovering (*meraḥefet*) over the surface of the waters." By metathesis, "*meraḥefet*" ("hovering") yields the words *met rapa"h* (288 dead), which is to say 288 sparks were among the dead. ("Whoever goes down from his original level, is referred to as having died.")[12]

Specifically the Levites, through their song, separate these sparks from their surroundings.[13] (This service was assigned to the Levites who personify *gevurot*, "strengths" or "stringencies," as opposed to the *kohanim*, the priests, who are the personification of *ḥasadim* or love.)[14] This would be the

---

10. Rabbi Ḥayyim Vital, *'Ets Ḥayyim*, Gate 18 (*Sha'ar Rapa"ḥ Nitsotsin*), chap. 1.
11. Rabbi Ḥayyim Vital, Gate 49 (*Sha'ar Kelipat Nogah*), chap 3; idem, *Peri 'Ets Ḥayyim, Sha'ar ha-Tefillah*, chap. 7; Rabbi Shneur Zalman of Liadi, *Tanya, Kuntres Aḥaron* (155a).
12. *Zohar*, III, 135b (*Idra Rabba*).
13. See Rabbi Nathan Sternhartz, *Likkutei Halakhot, Hil. Periyah u-Reviyah* 3:4, 18, 30; *Hil. Ḥakirut ve-Kablanut* 1:5; Rabbi Isaac of Komarno, *Heikhal ha-Berakha* (Lemberg, 1869), *Tetsaveh*, 238c, s.v. *ketefot* (Exodus 28:7).
14. See *Zohar* III, 8a. Also *Zohar* I, 148b; 242a and 244 (*Ra'aya Mehemna*), all commenting on Psalms 132:9; Rabbi Nathan Sternhartz, *Likkutei Halakhot, Hil. Periyah u-Reviyah* 3:30; *Orot, Orot ha-Teḥiyah* (Lights of Renascence), end chap. 43. And see Rabbi Ḥayyim Vital, *Likkutei Torah* (Vilna, 1880), Psalms 89:10 (132a); idem, *Sefer ha-Likkutim*, Psalms 89:10.

in His holy place? He who has clean hands and a pure heart, who has not taken My name in vain or sworn deceitfully. He shall receive a blessing from the LORD, and just reward from the God of his salvation. This is a generation of those who seek Him, the descendants of Jacob who seek Your presence, Selah! Lift up your heads, O gates; be uplifted, eternal doors, so that the King of glory may enter. Who is the King of glory? It is the LORD, strong and mighty, the LORD mighty in battle. Lift up your heads, O gates; lift them up, eternal doors, that the King of glory may enter. ‣ Who is He, the King of glory? The LORD of hosts, He is the King of glory, Selah!

*Mourner's Kaddish (page 246)*

---

appeals to nationalistic sentiments that the Jewish People entertain, beyond that, the Temple is universal in significance.

> And also to the stranger who is not of Your people Israel but comes from a far-off land for the sake of Your name. For they will hear of Your name and of Your strong hand and of Your outstretched arm; and he will come and pray at this house. You will listen in heaven, the place of Your dwelling, and do according to all that the stranger will call on You for; in order that all the peoples of the earth may know Your name, to fear You, as (do) Your people Israel; and in order to know that this house that I have built is called by Your name.[21]

Thus in the Temple there is an interplay of two forces: the peculiar, singular role that the People of Israel play in history; and global concern for the spiritual evolution of mankind in general. It was this delicate balance that wise King Solomon wished to convey to the gates of the Holy of Holies. First he addressed them as "gates" (*she'arim*), the insular gates of the People of Israel. But beyond that, he addressed them as "doors of the world" (*pitḥei 'olam*).

The gates were not satisfied with the epithet "the King of glory." They needed to hear that Israel would be militarily strong and able to protect its sovereignty from threatening foes: "It is the LORD, strong and mighty, the LORD mighty in battle."

Solomon in his proverbial wisdom understood that this parochial strain had to be balanced by a universal vision, whereby all faith communities are bands on a spiritual spectrum; whereby all nations chime in a marvelous symphony of religious ideas. This time around, Solomon refers to the LORD not as a man of war but as "the LORD of hosts." The hosts are the "seventy nations of the world."

---

21. 1 Kings 8:41–43. Cf. 2 Chron. 6:32, 33.

בִּמְקוֹם קׇדְשׁוֹ: נְקִי כַפַּיִם וּבַר־לֵבָב, אֲשֶׁר לֹא־נָשָׂא לַשָּׁוְא נַפְשִׁי,
וְלֹא נִשְׁבַּע לְמִרְמָה: יִשָּׂא בְרָכָה מֵאֵת יהוה, וּצְדָקָה מֵאֱלֹהֵי יִשְׁעוֹ:
זֶה דּוֹר דֹּרְשָׁו, מְבַקְשֵׁי פָנֶיךָ יַעֲקֹב סֶלָה: שְׂאוּ שְׁעָרִים רָאשֵׁיכֶם,
וְהִנָּשְׂאוּ פִּתְחֵי עוֹלָם, וְיָבוֹא מֶלֶךְ הַכָּבוֹד: מִי זֶה מֶלֶךְ הַכָּבוֹד, יהוה
עִזּוּז וְגִבּוֹר, יהוה גִּבּוֹר מִלְחָמָה: שְׂאוּ שְׁעָרִים רָאשֵׁיכֶם, וּשְׂאוּ פִּתְחֵי
עוֹלָם, וְיָבֹא מֶלֶךְ הַכָּבוֹד: ‹ מִי הוּא זֶה מֶלֶךְ הַכָּבוֹד, יהוה צְבָאוֹת
הוּא מֶלֶךְ הַכָּבוֹד סֶלָה:

קדיש יתום (*page 247*)

---

SUNDAY (PSALM 24)

*Lift up your heads, O gates; be uplifted, eternal doors,*
*so that the King of glory may enter. Who is the King of glory?*
*It is the* LORD, *strong and mighty, the* LORD *mighty in battle.*
*Lift up your heads, O gates; lift them up, eternal doors,*
*that the King of glory may enter. Who is He, the King of glory?*
*The* LORD *of hosts, He is the King of glory, Selah!*

The Talmud recounts that at the time King Solomon completed building the Temple in Jerusalem, he attempted to bring the Ark of the Covenant into the Holy of Holies, but the gates to the Holy of Holies were firmly stuck together and would not give way, despite Solomon's twenty-four prayers.[19]

Solomon began to implore the gates, saying "Lift up your heads, O gates; be uplifted, eternal doors, so that the King of glory may enter." The gates mistakenly assumed that by "the King of glory," Solomon intended himself, and were about to swallow him up. Luckily for King Solomon, they first demanded clarification: "Who is the King of glory?" Once the gates received assurance that Solomon was not referring to himself but rather to the LORD, they were placated. Solomon then tried a second time: "Lift up your heads, O gates; be uplifted, eternal doors, that the King of glory may enter." And yet the gates would not budge. Finally, Solomon invoked the name of his father David: "LORD God, turn not away the face of Your anointed; remember the pious deeds of David Your servant."[20] Immediately, the gates opened wide.

Rav Kook sees in this charming legend a deep philosophic teaching concerning the *raison d'etre* of the Temple in Jerusalem. While the Temple

---

19. *b. Shabbat* 30a. See too *b. Berakhot* 29a.
20. 2 Chronicles 6:42.

*Monday:* Today is the second day of the week,
on which the Levites used to say this psalm in the Temple:

שִׁיר מִזְמוֹר A song. A psalm of the sons of Koraḥ. Great is the LORD and greatly to be praised in the city of God, on His holy mountain – beautiful in its heights, joy of all the earth, Mount Zion on its northern side, city of the great King. In its citadels God is known as a stronghold. See how the kings joined forces, advancing together. They saw, they were astounded, they panicked, they fled. There fear seized them, like the pains of a woman giving birth, like ships of Tarshish wrecked by an eastern wind. What we had heard, now we have seen, in the city of the LORD of hosts, in the city of our God. May God preserve it for ever, Selah! In the midst of Your Temple, God, we meditate on Your love. As is Your name, God, so is Your praise: it reaches to *Ps. 48*

---

Mendel of Shklov (d. 1827), a primary disciple of the Vilna Gaon, who settled in Jerusalem, where he was responsible for the establishment of the Ashkenazic community of "Perushim," writes: "And there, the imagination (*dimyon*) is right, in Zion."[26] And so wrote Rabbi Zadok Hakohen of Lublin: "In *Erets Yisrael*, the imagination (*dimyon*) too is clean, as it states, 'The air of the Land of Israel makes wise.'"[27] And finally, Rav Kook wrote in his masterpiece

---

26. Rabbi Menaḥem Mendel of Shklov, *Mayim Adirim* (Jerusalem, 1987), pp. 171–172. Rabbi Menaḥem Mendel is most famous for composing the Vilna Gaon's commentary to the Book of Proverbs (*Mishlei*), although he was certainly a distinguished kabbalist in his own right. For his theory of imagination, see Moshe Idel, "*Bein ha-Kabbalah ha-Nevu'it le-Kabbalat Rabbi Menaḥem Mendel mi-Shklov*" (English title, "*R. Menaḥem Mendel of Shklov and R. Avraham Abulafia*") in *Ha-Gra u-Beit Midrasho* (*The Vilna Gaon and his Disciples*), ed. Ḥallamish, Rivlin and Shuchat (Ramat Gan: Bar-Ilan Universty, 2003), pp. 176–179.
27. *b. Bava Batra* 158b; Rabbi Zadok Hakohen Rabinowitz, *Dover Zedek* (Piotrków, 1911), 25c; idem, *Siḥat Mal'akhei ha-Sharet* (Lublin, 1927), 4d. Rabbi Zadok Hakohen's point of departure is the statement in *b. Ketubot* 110b: "Whoever dwells in Erets Israel, it is like (*domeh*) he has a God; and whoever dwells outside the Land, it is like (*domeh*) he has no God." The word *domeh* is related to *dimyon* (imagination). Independently, Rav Kook arrived at the same *jeu de mots*. See *KMYK*, vol. 1, *Pinkas "Rishon le-Yaffo,"* par. 17 (p. 84). There, Rav Kook invokes the authority of Maimonides' *Guide of the Perplexed* regarding the part imagination plays in prophecy. The *pensée* concludes with Judah Halevi's famous line: "The life of souls is the air of your land" (from the elegy "*Zion, ha-lo tish'ali*").
   This is but one of many instances where there is a meeting of these two great minds, Rabbi Zadok Hakohen and Rabbi Abraham Isaac Hakohen. See Rabbi Yeshayahu Hadari, "*Shnei Kohanim Gedolim*" ("Two High Priests"), anthologized in *Me'at*

*Monday* הַיּוֹם יוֹם שֵׁנִי בְּשַׁבָּת, שֶׁבּוֹ הָיוּ הַלְוִיִּם אוֹמְרִים בְּבֵית הַמִּקְדָּשׁ:

שִׁיר מִזְמוֹר לִבְנֵי־קֹרַח: גָּדוֹל יהוה וּמְהֻלָּל מְאֹד, בְּעִיר אֱלֹהֵינוּ, הַר־ תהלים מח
קָדְשׁוֹ: יְפֵה נוֹף מְשׂוֹשׂ כָּל־הָאָרֶץ, הַר־צִיּוֹן יַרְכְּתֵי צָפוֹן, קִרְיַת מֶלֶךְ
רָב: אֱלֹהִים בְּאַרְמְנוֹתֶיהָ נוֹדַע לְמִשְׂגָּב: כִּי־הִנֵּה הַמְּלָכִים נוֹעֲדוּ,
עָבְרוּ יַחְדָּו: הֵמָּה רָאוּ כֵּן תָּמָהוּ, נִבְהֲלוּ נֶחְפָּזוּ: רְעָדָה אֲחָזָתַם שָׁם,
חִיל כַּיּוֹלֵדָה: בְּרוּחַ קָדִים תְּשַׁבֵּר אֳנִיּוֹת תַּרְשִׁישׁ: כַּאֲשֶׁר שָׁמַעְנוּ
כֵּן רָאִינוּ, בְּעִיר־יהוה צְבָאוֹת, בְּעִיר אֱלֹהֵינוּ, אֱלֹהִים יְכוֹנְנֶהָ עַד־
עוֹלָם סֶלָה: דִּמִּינוּ אֱלֹהִים חַסְדֶּךָ, בְּקֶרֶב הֵיכָלֶךָ: כְּשִׁמְךָ אֱלֹהִים כֵּן

---

Said Rabbi Yoḥanan: What is written, "The Lord gives a word; the women that proclaim the tidings are a great host"?

Every word that left the divine mouth was divided into seventy languages.[22]

Rav Kook notes a significant difference between the two petitions of King Solomon. In the first petition, where Israel as a distinct entity is the point of reference, the Lord is *zeh* (this), as in "This is my God, and I will beautify Him," upon which the Rabbis comment that at the Splitting of the Reed Sea, each and every one was able to point to Him with the finger.[23] There is a directness in the way that the Lord is revealed to the People of the Covenant.

In the second petition to the gates of the Holy of Holies, in which the Lord of hosts – the hosts of nations – is invoked, the Lord is referred to obliquely in the third person as *hu* (he). ("Who is He?") Immediacy has been replaced by intermediacy; directness by indirectness. Certainly the Sinaitic revelation has been broadcast to the seventy nations of the world, but "this-ness" has been lost in translation.[24]

MONDAY (PSALM 48)

דִּמִּינוּ אֱלֹהִים חַסְדֶּךָ, בְּקֶרֶב הֵיכָלֶךָ *In the midst of Your Temple, God, we meditate on Your love.*[25] The key word here is *"diminu"* from *dimyon* (imagination). "We imagined, God, Your love in the midst of Your Temple." Rabbi Menaḥem

---

22. Psalms 68:12; *b. Shabbat* 88b.
23. Exodus 15:2; Rashi ad locum; *Exodus Rabbah* 23:15.
24. *OR*, vol. 1, pp. 314–318 = *EA*, vol. 3, *Shabbat*, chap. 2, par. 40–45 (pp. 83–86).
25. Psalms 48:10.

the ends of the earth. Your right hand is filled with righteousness. Let Mount Zion rejoice, let the towns of Judah be glad, because of Your judgments. Walk around Zion and encircle it. Count its towers, note its strong walls, view its citadels, so that you may tell a future generation ▸ that this is God, our God, for ever and ever. He will guide us for evermore.

*Mourner's Kaddish (page 246)*

*Tuesday:* Today is the third day of the week,
on which the Levites used to say this psalm in the Temple:

מִזְמוֹר לְאָסָף A psalm of Asaph. God stands in the divine assembly. Among the judges He delivers judgment. How long will you judge unjustly, showing favor to the wicked? Selah. Do justice to the weak and the orphaned. Vindicate the poor and destitute. Rescue the weak and needy. Save them from the hand of the wicked. They do not know nor do they understand. They walk about in darkness while all the earth's foundations shake. I once said, "You *Ps. 82*

---

imagination [the individual] will stray from the way of reason, and be driven off course by emotion.[31]

There may be alluded to in our verse a meditation upon the manifestation of God's love in the Holy Temple in Jerusalem. (Cf. above page 94 Rabbi Ḥarlap's advice that in prayer, one must avail oneself of the "airspace of the Land of Israel" [*"avira de-Erets Israel"*].)

In prayer it is of paramount importance to engage and harness the power of imagination.[32] (Editor)

31. *"'Inyenei Tefillah"* 3:7 in *OR*, vol. 1, pp. 23–24 = *EA*, vol. 1, *Berakhot*, chap. 5, par. 75 (p. 149).
32. See Rabbi Naḥman of Breslov:

> By clapping hands we are able to see the "similitude of the Lord" [Numbers 12:8], for the "similitude of the Lord" consists of the similes by which we call him: "Merciful," "Compassionate," et cetera. All these similes were revealed by the Prophets. The word *"navi"* refers to speech, from the word *"niv"* or expression, as in *"niv sefatayim,"* "the expression of the lips" [Isaiah 57:19]. [See Rashi, Exodus 7:1.] The prophets are the speech of prayer. And when we speak with our lips the similes, and clap hands, then there is fulfilled the verse "In the hand of the prophets I shall stir imagination" [Hosea 12:11], for the prophets are the speech, and the palms are the hand of the prophets. And then imagination (*dimyon*) is revealed, "In the hand of the prophets I shall stir imagination," and there is fulfilled the verse "And the similitude of the Lord he shall behold" [Numbers 12:8]. (*Likkutei Moharan* I, 212)

Cf. Rabbi Joseph Dov Halevi Soloveitchik, *Shi'urim le-Zekher Abba Mari* (Jerusalem: Mossad Harav Kook, 2002), vol. 2, pp. 188–189.

תְּהִלָּתְךָ עַל־קַצְוֵי־אֶרֶץ, צֶדֶק מָלְאָה יְמִינֶךָ: יִשְׂמַח הַר־צִיּוֹן, תָּגֵלְנָה
בְּנוֹת יְהוּדָה, לְמַעַן מִשְׁפָּטֶיךָ: סֹבּוּ צִיּוֹן וְהַקִּיפוּהָ, סִפְרוּ מִגְדָּלֶיהָ:
שִׁיתוּ לִבְּכֶם לְחֵילָה, פַּסְּגוּ אַרְמְנוֹתֶיהָ, לְמַעַן תְּסַפְּרוּ לְדוֹר אַחֲרוֹן:
◂ כִּי זֶה אֱלֹהִים אֱלֹהֵינוּ עוֹלָם וָעֶד, הוּא יְנַהֲגֵנוּ עַל־מוּת:

קדיש יתום (*page 247*)

*Tuesday* הַיּוֹם יוֹם שְׁלִישִׁי בְּשַׁבָּת, שֶׁבּוֹ הָיוּ הַלְוִיִּם אוֹמְרִים בְּבֵית הַמִּקְדָּשׁ:

תהלים פב
מִזְמוֹר לְאָסָף, אֱלֹהִים נִצָּב בַּעֲדַת־אֵל, בְּקֶרֶב אֱלֹהִים יִשְׁפֹּט: עַד־
מָתַי תִּשְׁפְּטוּ־עָוֶל, וּפְנֵי רְשָׁעִים תִּשְׂאוּ־סֶלָה: שִׁפְטוּ־דַל וְיָתוֹם,
עָנִי וָרָשׁ הַצְדִּיקוּ: פַּלְּטוּ־דַל וְאֶבְיוֹן, מִיַּד רְשָׁעִים הַצִּילוּ: לֹא יָדְעוּ
וְלֹא יָבִינוּ, בַּחֲשֵׁכָה יִתְהַלָּכוּ, יִמּוֹטוּ כָּל־מוֹסְדֵי אָרֶץ: אֲנִי־אָמַרְתִּי

---

*Orot*: "The imagination (d*imyon*) of the Land of Israel is lucid and clear, clean and pure."[28] Specifically in regard to the Temple, Rav Kook wrote:

> The Temple is called "the beauty of the world"[29] and "a House of Prayer for all the peoples."[30] The true beauty is the perfection of the [power of] imagination in accordance with the dictates of reason… and the cornerstone of prayer is built upon this perfection. Verily, as long as the center of perfection of all humanity – representing equilibrium of reason and imagination – existed in the world, it was easy for each individual to maintain a balance of visions and the laws of reason; and with the ascendance of the power of imagination, man was prepared to do great things. But "from the day the Temple was destroyed," and there was nullified the center of humanity's ability to connect the imaginative powers to the light of reason, "the gates of prayer were locked." Left to one's own resources, it became exceedingly difficult for the individual to lift imagination to the heights of reason. And sometimes with the strengthening of the power of

---

*la-Tzadik*, ed. Rabbi Gershon Kitzis (Jerusalem, 2000), pp. 77–95; *Siḥot Harav Zevi Yehudah: Segulat Yisrael*, ed. Rabbi Shelomo Aviner (Jerusalem, 2015), pp. 140, 158, 177–178.

28. Rabbi Abraham Isaac Hakohen Kook, *Orot* (Jerusalem: Maggid, 2015), *Erets Yisrael*, chap. 5 (pp. 120–121).
29. *b. Zevaḥim* 54b.
30. Isaiah 56:7.

are like gods, all of you are sons of the Most High." But you shall die like mere men, you will fall like any prince. ▸ Arise, O LORD, judge the earth, for all the nations are Your possession.

*Mourner's Kaddish (page 246)*

*Wednesday:* Today is the fourth day of the week,
on which the Levites used to say this psalm in the Temple:

אֵל־נְקָמוֹת God of retribution, LORD, God of retribution, appear! Rise up, *Ps. 94*
Judge of the earth. Repay to the arrogant what they deserve. How long shall the wicked, LORD, how long shall the wicked triumph? They pour out insolent words. All the evildoers are full of boasting. They crush Your people, LORD, and oppress Your inheritance. They kill the widow and the stranger. They murder the orphaned. They say, "The LORD does not see. The God of Jacob pays no heed." Take heed, you most brutish people. You fools, when will you grow wise? Will He who implants the ear not hear? Will He who formed the eye not see? Will He who disciplines nations – He who teaches man knowledge – not punish? The LORD knows that the thoughts of man are a mere fleeting breath. Happy is the man whom You discipline, LORD, the one You instruct in Your Torah, giving him tranquility in days of trouble, until a pit is dug for the wicked. For the LORD will not forsake His people, nor abandon His heritage. Judgment shall again accord with justice, and all the upright in heart will follow it. Who will rise up for me against the wicked? Who will stand up for me against wrongdoers? Had the LORD not been my help, I would soon have dwelt in death's silence. When I thought my foot was slipping, Your loving-kindness, LORD, gave me support. When I was filled with anxiety, Your consolations soothed my soul. Can a corrupt throne be allied with You? Can injustice be framed into law? They join forces against the life of the righteous, and condemn the innocent to death. But the LORD is my stronghold, my God is the Rock of my refuge. He will bring back on them their wickedness, and destroy them for their evil deeds. The LORD our God will destroy them.

▸ Come, let us sing for joy to the LORD; let us shout aloud to the Rock of *Ps. 95*
our salvation. Let us greet Him with thanksgiving, shout aloud to Him with songs of praise. For the LORD is the great God, the King great above all powers.

*Mourner's Kaddish (page 246)*

**אֱלֹהִים אַתֶּם, וּבְנֵי עֶלְיוֹן כֻּלְּכֶם: אָכֵן כְּאָדָם תְּמוּתוּן, וּכְאַחַד הַשָּׂרִים**
**תִּפֹּלוּ: ‹ קוּמָה אֱלֹהִים שָׁפְטָה הָאָרֶץ, כִּי־אַתָּה תִנְחַל בְּכָל־הַגּוֹיִם:**

קדיש יתום (*page 247*)

*Wednesday* הַיּוֹם יוֹם רְבִיעִי בְּשַׁבָּת, שֶׁבּוֹ הָיוּ הַלְוִיִּם אוֹמְרִים בְּבֵית הַמִּקְדָּשׁ:

תהלים צד **אֵל־נְקָמוֹת יהוה, אֵל נְקָמוֹת הוֹפִיעַ: הִנָּשֵׂא שֹׁפֵט הָאָרֶץ, הָשֵׁב גְּמוּל**
**עַל־גֵּאִים: עַד־מָתַי רְשָׁעִים, יהוה, עַד־מָתַי רְשָׁעִים יַעֲלֹזוּ: יַבִּיעוּ**
**יְדַבְּרוּ עָתָק, יִתְאַמְּרוּ כָּל־פֹּעֲלֵי אָוֶן: עַמְּךָ יהוה יְדַכְּאוּ, וְנַחֲלָתְךָ**
**יְעַנּוּ: אַלְמָנָה וְגֵר יַהֲרֹגוּ, וִיתוֹמִים יְרַצֵּחוּ: וַיֹּאמְרוּ לֹא יִרְאֶה־יָּהּ,**
**וְלֹא־יָבִין אֱלֹהֵי יַעֲקֹב: בִּינוּ בֹּעֲרִים בָּעָם, וּכְסִילִים מָתַי תַּשְׂכִּילוּ:**
**הֲנֹטַע אֹזֶן הֲלֹא יִשְׁמָע, אִם־יֹצֵר עַיִן הֲלֹא יַבִּיט: הֲיֹסֵר גּוֹיִם הֲלֹא**
**יוֹכִיחַ, הַמְלַמֵּד אָדָם דָּעַת: יהוה יֹדֵעַ מַחְשְׁבוֹת אָדָם, כִּי־הֵמָּה**
**הָבֶל: אַשְׁרֵי הַגֶּבֶר אֲשֶׁר־תְּיַסְּרֶנּוּ יָּהּ, וּמִתּוֹרָתְךָ תְלַמְּדֶנּוּ: לְהַשְׁקִיט**
**לוֹ מִימֵי רָע, עַד יִכָּרֶה לָרָשָׁע שָׁחַת: כִּי לֹא־יִטֹּשׁ יהוה עַמּוֹ, וְנַחֲלָתוֹ**
**לֹא יַעֲזֹב: כִּי־עַד־צֶדֶק יָשׁוּב מִשְׁפָּט, וְאַחֲרָיו כָּל־יִשְׁרֵי־לֵב: מִי־**
**יָקוּם לִי עִם־מְרֵעִים, מִי־יִתְיַצֵּב לִי עִם־פֹּעֲלֵי אָוֶן: לוּלֵי יהוה עֶזְרָתָה**
**לִּי, כִּמְעַט שָׁכְנָה דוּמָה נַפְשִׁי: אִם־אָמַרְתִּי מָטָה רַגְלִי, חַסְדְּךָ יהוה**
**יִסְעָדֵנִי: בְּרֹב שַׂרְעַפַּי בְּקִרְבִּי, תַּנְחוּמֶיךָ יְשַׁעַשְׁעוּ נַפְשִׁי: הַיְחָבְרְךָ**
**כִּסֵּא הַוּוֹת, יֹצֵר עָמָל עֲלֵי־חֹק: יָגוֹדּוּ עַל־נֶפֶשׁ צַדִּיק, וְדָם נָקִי יַרְשִׁיעוּ:**
**וַיְהִי יהוה לִי לְמִשְׂגָּב, וֵאלֹהַי לְצוּר מַחְסִי: וַיָּשֶׁב עֲלֵיהֶם אֶת־אוֹנָם,**
**וּבְרָעָתָם יַצְמִיתֵם, יַצְמִיתֵם יהוה אֱלֹהֵינוּ:**

תהלים צה **‹ לְכוּ נְרַנְּנָה לַיהוה, נָרִיעָה לְצוּר יִשְׁעֵנוּ: נְקַדְּמָה פָנָיו בְּתוֹדָה,**
**בִּזְמִרוֹת נָרִיעַ לוֹ: כִּי אֵל גָּדוֹל יהוה, וּמֶלֶךְ גָּדוֹל עַל־כָּל־אֱלֹהִים:**

קדיש יתום (*page 247*)

*Thursday:* Today is the fifth day of the week,
on which the Levites used to say this psalm in the Temple:

לַמְנַצֵּחַ For the conductor of music. On the Gittit. By Asaph. Sing for joy *Ps. 81*
to God, our strength. Shout aloud to the God of Jacob. Raise a song, beat
the drum, play the sweet harp and lyre. Sound the shofar on the new moon,
on our feast day when the moon is hidden. For it is a statute for Israel, an
ordinance of the God of Jacob. He established it as a testimony for Joseph
when He went forth against the land of Egypt, where I heard a language
that I did not know. I relieved his shoulder of the burden. His hands were
freed from the builder's basket. In distress you called and I rescued you.

---

That *hé* added to Joseph's name by Gabriel, enabling him to master the seventy languages of antiquity, is absorbed in Joshua's being and empowers him to clarify the imagination, which takes in the entire esthetic dimension.[38]

Eventually, in the days of Ezra, the Men of the Great Assembly would stop up the *yitsra de-'avodah zarah* in a "lead pot" (*duda de-avara*), and quite predictably, that would in turn bring about the cessation of prophecy in Israel. But in Rav Kook's reverie, *"kapav mi-dud ta'avornah,"* "his palms will be set free from the pot."[39] (Rav Kook finds additional "support" for his interpretation

---

did not *kill* the *yester ha-ra'* [evil inclination] in a manner of *bittul* [total nullification]," but rather "slaughtered it." Rabbi Kasher's footnote references a teaching of the Ba'al Shem Tov whereby after its future slaughter, the *"Yetser ha-Ra'"* will remain a holy angel.

38. Concerning the esthetic dimension of Joseph's personality, see Rashi, Gen. 39:6 and *Genesis Rabbah* 87:3.

39. The Talmud (*b. Rosh Hashanah* 11) derives from the verse "I relieved his shoulder of the burden, etc." that Joseph left prison on Rosh Hashanah. See also *y. Rosh Hashanah* 4:4 (and *P'nei Moshe* ad loc.).
It is possible that for Rav Kook the word *"kapav"* alludes to the *"kaph ha-dimyon,"* the comparative *kaph*. Cf. Rabbi Zadok Hakohen, who writes at the beginning of *Maḥshevot Ḥaruts* (Piotrków, 1912), that the root of imagination lies in the Serpent's temptation to Adam and Eve: "You shall be as God (*ke-Elohim*)."
[Each month of the year corresponds to one of the twelve tribes of Israel. Rabbi Zadok adheres to the notion that the month of Adar corresponds to Joseph. (Rabbi Zadok references Rabbi Levi Isaac of Berdichev, *Kedushat Levi*. See ibid. *Parashat Shekalim*, s.v. *ta'am 'al Adar*.) In *Sefer Yetsirah*, the letter assigned to the month of Adar is *koph*, the ape. To ape someone is to imitate that person. *Maḥshevot Ḥaruts*, chap. 4 (6c-d).]
Rav Kook may also have associated the hand with prophecy as in the verses *"Haytah 'alai yad Hashem"* ("The hand of the LORD was upon me") in Ezekiel 37:1, and *"U-be-yad ha-nevi'im adameh"* ("And in the hand of the prophets I shall stir imagination") in Hosea 12:11. See Rabbi Naḥman of Breslov, *Likkutei Moharan* I, 212 (quoted above note #32). More directly to the point, the *"kaph"* or palm itself may be a metaphor for prophetic inspiration, as in Exodus 33:22–23. See Onkelos and Rashi there.

*Thursday* הַיּוֹם יוֹם חֲמִישִׁי בְּשַׁבָּת, שֶׁבּוֹ הָיוּ הַלְוִיִּם אוֹמְרִים בְּבֵית הַמִּקְדָּשׁ:

**לַמְנַצֵּחַ עַל־הַגִּתִּית לְאָסָף: הַרְנִינוּ לֵאלֹהִים עוּזֵּנוּ, הָרִיעוּ לֵאלֹהֵי** תהלים פא
**יַעֲקֹב: שְׂאוּ־זִמְרָה וּתְנוּ־תֹף, כִּנּוֹר נָעִים עִם־נָבֶל: תִּקְעוּ בַחֹדֶשׁ**
**שׁוֹפָר, בַּכֵּסֶה לְיוֹם חַגֵּנוּ: כִּי חֹק לְיִשְׂרָאֵל הוּא, מִשְׁפָּט לֵאלֹהֵי יַעֲקֹב:**
**עֵדוּת בִּיהוֹסֵף שָׂמוֹ, בְּצֵאתוֹ עַל־אֶרֶץ מִצְרָיִם, שְׂפַת לֹא־יָדַעְתִּי**
**אֶשְׁמָע: הֲסִירוֹתִי מִסֵּבֶל שִׁכְמוֹ, כַּפָּיו מִדּוּד תַּעֲבֹרְנָה: בַּצָּרָה קָרָאתָ**

THURSDAY (PSALM 81)

עֵדוּת בִּיהוֹסֵף שָׂמוֹ, בְּצֵאתוֹ עַל־אֶרֶץ מִצְרָיִם, שְׂפַת לֹא־יָדַעְתִּי אֶשְׁמָע: הֲסִירוֹתִי מִסֵּבֶל שִׁכְמוֹ, כַּפָּיו מִדּוּד תַּעֲבֹרְנָה: *He established it as a testimony for Jehoseph when he went forth against the Land of Egypt, where I heard a language that I did not know. I relieved his shoulder of the burden, his hands were freed from the builder's basket.*[33] According to Talmudic legend, the Psalmist alludes to the fact that Joseph, being tutored for his role as Viceroy of Egypt, was taught the seventy languages by Archangel Gabriel.[34] Rav Kook sees in the Biblical passage yet another dimension; yet another facet of Joseph's fascinating personality. Besides his linguistic ability, we are given a peek at Joseph's mastery over the power of imagination. (Actually, as we shall see, the two may very well be linked to one another.)

In the Talmudic reading, Joshua was censured in a verse in Nehemiah, stripped of the letter *hé* in his name, and reduced from Yehoshua to Yeshua, because he failed to abolish the drive for idolatry (*yitsra de-'avodah zarah*), despite the merit of *Erets Yisrael* that would have enabled him to do so.[35]

Rav Kook, as it were, rises to the defense of Joshua and restores the *hé* to his name. The reason that Joshua did not abolish the hankering for idolatry, which is a function of the imaginative faculty, is because Joshua as a descendant of Joseph, was of the firm conviction that this power of imagination – crucial for prophetic ability – need not be abolished.[36] "The *yitsra de-'avodah zarah* shall be converted to a holy light, instrumental in fanning the flame of holiness."[37]

---

33. Psalms 81:6, 7.
34. *b. Sotah* 36b.
35. Neḥemiah 8:17; *b. 'Arakhin* 32b.
36. See RAYH, *Orot* (Jerusalem: Maggid, 2015), Israel and its Renascence, chap. 18 (pp. 204–207); Bezalel Naor, *Orot ha-Nevu'ah/Lights of Prophecy* (New York: Orthodox Union, 1990).
37. *SK* 1:867.
Cf. Rabbi Joseph Rosen (the Gaon of Rogatchov), *Tsafnat Pa'ne'aḥ*, ed. Kasher (Jerusalem, 1967), Genesis 39:2 (p. 144, n. 56). The Rogatchover writes "that Joseph

I answered you from the secret place of thunder; I tested you at the waters of Meribah, Selah! Hear, My people, and I will warn you. Israel, if you would only listen to Me! Let there be no strange god among you. Do not bow down to an alien god. I am the LORD your God who brought you out of the land of Egypt. Open your mouth wide and I will fill it. But My people would not listen to Me. Israel would have none of Me. So I left them to their stubborn hearts, letting them follow their own devices. If only My people would listen to Me, if Israel would walk in My ways, I would soon subdue their enemies, and turn My hand against their foes. Those who hate the LORD would cower before Him and their doom would last for ever. ▸ He would feed Israel with the finest wheat – with honey from the rock I would satisfy you.

*Mourner's Kaddish* *(page 246)*

*Friday:* Today is the sixth day of the week,
on which the Levites used to say this psalm in the Temple:

יהוה מָלָךְ The LORD reigns. He is robed in majesty. The LORD is robed, girded *Ps. 93*
with strength. The world is firmly established; it cannot be moved. Your throne stands firm as of old; You are eternal. Rivers lift up, LORD, rivers lift up their voice, rivers lift up their crashing waves. Mightier than the noise of many waters, than the mighty waves of the sea is the LORD on high. ▸ Your testimonies are very sure; holiness adorns Your House, LORD, for evermore.

*Mourner's Kaddish* *(page 246)*

*On Rosh Ḥodesh, the following psalm is said:*

בָּרְכִי נַפְשִׁי Bless the LORD, my soul. LORD, my God, You are very great, *Ps. 104*
clothed in majesty and splendor, wrapped in a robe of light. You have spread out the heavens like a tent. He has laid the beams of His lofts in the waters. He makes the clouds His chariot, riding on the wings of the wind. He makes the winds His messengers, flames of fire His ministers. He has fixed the earth on its foundations so that it will never be shaken. You covered it with the deep like a cloak; the waters stood above the mountains. At Your rebuke they fled; at the sound of Your thunder they rushed away, flowing over the hills, pouring down into the valleys to the place You appointed for them. You fixed a boundary they were not to pass, so that they would never cover the earth again. He makes springs flow in the valleys; they make their way between the hills, giving drink to all the beasts of

---

in the words of the next verse, *"E'enkha be-seter ra'am evḥonkha,"* whose initials spell out *"avara"* [lead].) Imagination will be liberated and prophecy restored.

וָאֲחַלֶּצְךָ, אֶעֶנְךָ בְּסֵתֶר רַעַם, אֶבְחָנְךָ עַל־מֵי מְרִיבָה סֶלָה: שְׁמַע עַמִּי וְאָעִידָה בָּךְ, יִשְׂרָאֵל אִם־תִּשְׁמַע־לִי: לֹא־יִהְיֶה בְךָ אֵל זָר, וְלֹא תִשְׁתַּחֲוֶה לְאֵל נֵכָר: אָנֹכִי יהוה אֱלֹהֶיךָ, הַמַּעַלְךָ מֵאֶרֶץ מִצְרָיִם, הַרְחֶב־פִּיךָ וַאֲמַלְאֵהוּ: וְלֹא־שָׁמַע עַמִּי לְקוֹלִי, וְיִשְׂרָאֵל לֹא־אָבָה לִי: וָאֲשַׁלְּחֵהוּ בִּשְׁרִירוּת לִבָּם, יֵלְכוּ בְּמוֹעֲצוֹתֵיהֶם: לוּ עַמִּי שֹׁמֵעַ לִי, יִשְׂרָאֵל בִּדְרָכַי יְהַלֵּכוּ: כִּמְעַט אוֹיְבֵיהֶם אַכְנִיעַ, וְעַל־צָרֵיהֶם אָשִׁיב יָדִי: מְשַׂנְאֵי יהוה יְכַחֲשׁוּ־לוֹ, וִיהִי עִתָּם לְעוֹלָם: ‹ וַיַּאֲכִילֵהוּ מֵחֵלֶב חִטָּה, וּמִצּוּר, דְּבַשׁ אַשְׂבִּיעֶךָ:

קדיש יתום (*page 247*)

*Friday* הַיּוֹם יוֹם שִׁשִּׁי בְּשַׁבָּת, שֶׁבּוֹ הָיוּ הַלְוִיִּם אוֹמְרִים בְּבֵית הַמִּקְדָּשׁ

תהלים צג
יהוה מָלָךְ, גֵּאוּת לָבֵשׁ, לָבֵשׁ יהוה עֹז הִתְאַזָּר, אַף־תִּכּוֹן תֵּבֵל בַּל־תִּמּוֹט: נָכוֹן כִּסְאֲךָ מֵאָז, מֵעוֹלָם אָתָּה: נָשְׂאוּ נְהָרוֹת יהוה, נָשְׂאוּ נְהָרוֹת קוֹלָם, יִשְׂאוּ נְהָרוֹת דָּכְיָם: מִקֹּלוֹת מַיִם רַבִּים, אַדִּירִים מִשְׁבְּרֵי־יָם, אַדִּיר בַּמָּרוֹם יהוה: ‹ עֵדֹתֶיךָ נֶאֶמְנוּ מְאֹד, לְבֵיתְךָ נַאֲוָה־קֹדֶשׁ, יהוה לְאֹרֶךְ יָמִים:

קדיש יתום (*page 247*)

*On* ראש חודש*, the following psalm is said:*

תהלים קד
בָּרְכִי נַפְשִׁי אֶת־יהוה, יהוה אֱלֹהַי גָּדַלְתָּ מְּאֹד, הוֹד וְהָדָר לָבָשְׁתָּ: עֹטֶה־אוֹר כַּשַּׂלְמָה, נוֹטֶה שָׁמַיִם כַּיְרִיעָה: הַמְקָרֶה בַמַּיִם עֲלִיּוֹתָיו, הַשָּׂם־עָבִים רְכוּבוֹ, הַמְהַלֵּךְ עַל־כַּנְפֵי־רוּחַ: עֹשֶׂה מַלְאָכָיו רוּחוֹת, מְשָׁרְתָיו אֵשׁ לֹהֵט: יָסַד־אֶרֶץ עַל־מְכוֹנֶיהָ, בַּל־תִּמּוֹט עוֹלָם וָעֶד: תְּהוֹם כַּלְּבוּשׁ כִּסִּיתוֹ, עַל־הָרִים יַעַמְדוּ־מָיִם: מִן־גַּעֲרָתְךָ יְנוּסוּן, מִן־קוֹל רַעַמְךָ יֵחָפֵזוּן: יַעֲלוּ הָרִים, יֵרְדוּ בְקָעוֹת, אֶל־מְקוֹם זֶה יָסַדְתָּ לָהֶם: גְּבוּל־שַׂמְתָּ בַּל־יַעֲבֹרוּן, בַּל־יְשׁוּבוּן לְכַסּוֹת הָאָרֶץ: הַמְשַׁלֵּחַ מַעְיָנִים בַּנְּחָלִים, בֵּין הָרִים יְהַלֵּכוּן: יַשְׁקוּ כָּל־חַיְתוֹ שָׂדָי, יִשְׁבְּרוּ

the field; the wild donkeys quench their thirst. The birds of the sky dwell beside them, singing among the foliage. He waters the mountains from His lofts: the earth is sated with the fruit of Your work. He makes grass grow for the cattle, and plants for the use of man, that he may produce bread from the earth, wine to cheer the heart of man, oil to make the face shine, and bread to sustain man's heart. The trees of the LORD drink their fill, the cedars of Lebanon which He planted. There, birds build their nests; the stork makes its home in the cypresses. High hills are for the wild goats; crags are shelter for the badgers. He made the moon to mark the seasons, and makes the sun know when to set. You bring darkness and it is night; then all the beasts of the forests stir. The young lions roar for prey, seeking their food from God. When the sun rises, they slink away and seek rest in their lairs. Man goes out to his work and his labor until evening. How numerous are Your works, LORD; You made them all with wisdom; the earth is full of Your creations. There is the vast, immeasurable sea with its countless swarming creatures, living things great and small. There ships sail. There is Leviathan You formed to sport there. All of them look to You in hope, to give them their food when it is due. What You give them, they gather up. When You open Your hand, they are sated with good. When You hide Your face, they are dismayed. When You take away their breath, they die and return to dust. When You send back Your breath, they are created, giving new life to the earth. May the glory of the LORD be for ever; may the LORD rejoice in His works. When He looks at the earth, it trembles. When He touches the mountains, they pour forth smoke. I will sing to the LORD as long as I live; I will sing psalms to my God all my life. ▸ May my meditation be pleasing to Him; I shall rejoice in the LORD. May sinners vanish from the earth, and the wicked be no more. Bless the LORD, my soul. Halleluya!

*Mourner's Kaddish (page 246)*

*During the month of Elul (except Erev Rosh HaShana), the shofar is sounded (some sound the shofar after the psalm below). From the second day of Rosh Ḥodesh Elul through Shemini Atzeret (in Israel through Hoshana Raba), the following psalm is said:*

לְדָוִד By David. The LORD is my light and my salvation – whom then shall I fear? The LORD is the stronghold of my life – of whom shall I be afraid? When evil men close in on me to devour my flesh, it is they, my enemies and foes, who stumble and fall. Should an army besiege me, my heart would not fear. Should war break out against me, still I would be confident. One thing I ask of the LORD, only this do I seek: to live in the House of the LORD all the days of my life, to gaze on the beauty of the LORD and worship in His Temple. For *Ps. 27*

פְּרָאִים צְמָאָם: עֲלֵיהֶם עוֹף־הַשָּׁמַיִם יִשְׁכּוֹן, מִבֵּין עֳפָאיִם יִתְּנוּ־קוֹל: מַשְׁקֶה הָרִים מֵעֲלִיּוֹתָיו, מִפְּרִי מַעֲשֶׂיךָ תִּשְׂבַּע הָאָרֶץ: מַצְמִיחַ חָצִיר לַבְּהֵמָה, וְעֵשֶׂב לַעֲבֹדַת הָאָדָם, לְהוֹצִיא לֶחֶם מִן־הָאָרֶץ: וְיַיִן יְשַׂמַּח לְבַב־אֱנוֹשׁ, לְהַצְהִיל פָּנִים מִשָּׁמֶן, וְלֶחֶם לְבַב־אֱנוֹשׁ יִסְעָד: יִשְׂבְּעוּ עֲצֵי יהוה, אַרְזֵי לְבָנוֹן אֲשֶׁר נָטָע: אֲשֶׁר־שָׁם צִפֳּרִים יְקַנֵּנוּ, חֲסִידָה בְּרוֹשִׁים בֵּיתָהּ: הָרִים הַגְּבֹהִים לַיְּעֵלִים, סְלָעִים מַחְסֶה לַשְׁפַנִּים: עָשָׂה יָרֵחַ לְמוֹעֲדִים, שֶׁמֶשׁ יָדַע מְבוֹאוֹ: תָּשֶׁת־חֹשֶׁךְ וִיהִי לָיְלָה, בּוֹ־תִרְמֹשׂ כָּל־חַיְתוֹ־יָעַר: הַכְּפִירִים שֹׁאֲגִים לַטָּרֶף, וּלְבַקֵּשׁ מֵאֵל אָכְלָם: תִּזְרַח הַשֶּׁמֶשׁ יֵאָסֵפוּן, וְאֶל־מְעוֹנֹתָם יִרְבָּצוּן: יֵצֵא אָדָם לְפָעֳלוֹ, וְלַעֲבֹדָתוֹ עֲדֵי־עָרֶב: מָה־רַבּוּ מַעֲשֶׂיךָ יהוה, כֻּלָּם בְּחָכְמָה עָשִׂיתָ, מָלְאָה הָאָרֶץ קִנְיָנֶךָ: זֶה הַיָּם גָּדוֹל וּרְחַב יָדָיִם, שָׁם־רֶמֶשׂ וְאֵין מִסְפָּר, חַיּוֹת קְטַנּוֹת עִם־גְּדֹלוֹת: שָׁם אֳנִיּוֹת יְהַלֵּכוּן, לִוְיָתָן זֶה־יָצַרְתָּ לְשַׂחֶק־בּוֹ: כֻּלָּם אֵלֶיךָ יְשַׂבֵּרוּן, לָתֵת אָכְלָם בְּעִתּוֹ: תִּתֵּן לָהֶם יִלְקֹטוּן, תִּפְתַּח יָדְךָ יִשְׂבְּעוּן טוֹב: תַּסְתִּיר פָּנֶיךָ יִבָּהֵלוּן, תֹּסֵף רוּחָם יִגְוָעוּן, וְאֶל־עֲפָרָם יְשׁוּבוּן: תְּשַׁלַּח רוּחֲךָ יִבָּרֵאוּן, וּתְחַדֵּשׁ פְּנֵי אֲדָמָה: יְהִי כְבוֹד יהוה לְעוֹלָם, יִשְׂמַח יהוה בְּמַעֲשָׂיו: הַמַּבִּיט לָאָרֶץ וַתִּרְעָד, יִגַּע בֶּהָרִים וְיֶעֱשָׁנוּ: אָשִׁירָה לַיהוה בְּחַיָּי, אֲזַמְּרָה לֵאלֹהַי בְּעוֹדִי: ◂ יֶעֱרַב עָלָיו שִׂיחִי, אָנֹכִי אֶשְׂמַח בַּיהוה: יִתַּמּוּ חַטָּאִים מִן־הָאָרֶץ, וּרְשָׁעִים עוֹד אֵינָם, בָּרְכִי נַפְשִׁי אֶת־יהוה, הַלְלוּיָהּ:

קדיש יתום (page 247)

*During the month of* אלול *(except* ערב ראש השנה*), the* שופר *is sounded (some sound the* שופר *after the psalm below). From the second day of* ראש חודש אלול *through* הושענא רבה *(*שמיני עצרת *in* ארץ ישראל*), the following psalm is said:*

תהלים כז
לְדָוִד, יהוה אוֹרִי וְיִשְׁעִי, מִמִּי אִירָא, יהוה מָעוֹז־חַיַּי, מִמִּי אֶפְחָד: בִּקְרֹב עָלַי מְרֵעִים לֶאֱכֹל אֶת־בְּשָׂרִי, צָרַי וְאֹיְבַי לִי, הֵמָּה כָשְׁלוּ וְנָפָלוּ: אִם־תַּחֲנֶה עָלַי מַחֲנֶה, לֹא־יִירָא לִבִּי, אִם־תָּקוּם עָלַי מִלְחָמָה, בְּזֹאת אֲנִי בוֹטֵחַ: אַחַת שָׁאַלְתִּי מֵאֵת־יהוה, אוֹתָהּ אֲבַקֵּשׁ, שִׁבְתִּי בְּבֵית־

He will keep me safe in His pavilion on the day of trouble. He will hide me under the cover of His tent. He will set me high upon a rock. Now my head is high above my enemies who surround me. I will sacrifice in His tent with shouts of joy. I will sing and chant praises to the LORD. LORD, hear my voice when I call. Be gracious to me and answer me. On Your behalf my heart says, "Seek My face." Your face, LORD, will I seek. Do not hide Your face from me. Do not turn Your servant away in anger. You have been my help. Do not reject or forsake me, God, my Savior. Were my father and my mother to forsake me, the LORD would take me in. Teach me Your way, LORD, and lead me on a level path, because of my oppressors. Do not abandon me to the will of my foes, for false witnesses have risen against me, breathing violence. ▸ Were it not for my faith that I shall see the LORD's goodness in the land of the living. Hope in the LORD. Be strong and of good courage, and hope in the LORD!

*Mourner's Kaddish (page 246)*

*In Israel the following through "Bless the LORD," on page 268, is said:*

אֵין כֵּאלֹהֵינוּ There is none like our God, none like our LORD,
none like our King, none like our Savior.
Who is like our God? Like our LORD?
Like our King? Like our Savior?
We will thank our God, thank our LORD,
thank our King, thank our Savior.
Blessed is our God, blessed our LORD,
blessed our King, blessed our Savior.
You are our God, You are our LORD,
You are our King, You are our Savior.
You are He to whom our ancestors offered the fragrant incense.

פִּטּוּם הַקְּטֹרֶת The incense mixture consisted of balsam, onycha, galbanum and frankincense, each weighing seventy manehs; myrrh, cassia, spikenard and saffron, each weighing sixteen manehs; twelve manehs of costus, three of aromatic bark; nine of cinnamon; nine kabs of Carsina lye; three seahs and three kabs of Cyprus wine. If Cyprus wine was not available, old white wine might be used. A quarter of a kab of Sodom salt, and a minute amount of a smoke-raising herb. Rabbi Nathan says: Also a minute amount of Jordan amber. If one added honey to the mixture, he rendered it unfit for sacred use. If he omitted any one of its ingredients, he is guilty of a capital offense. *Keritot 6a*

יהוה כָּל־יְמֵי חַיַּי, לַחֲזוֹת בְּנֹעַם־יהוה, וּלְבַקֵּר בְּהֵיכָלוֹ: כִּי יִצְפְּנֵנִי בְּסֻכֹּה בְּיוֹם רָעָה, יַסְתִּרֵנִי בְּסֵתֶר אָהֳלוֹ, בְּצוּר יְרוֹמְמֵנִי: וְעַתָּה יָרוּם רֹאשִׁי עַל אֹיְבַי סְבִיבוֹתַי, וְאֶזְבְּחָה בְאָהֳלוֹ זִבְחֵי תְרוּעָה, אָשִׁירָה וַאֲזַמְּרָה לַיהוה: שְׁמַע־יהוה קוֹלִי אֶקְרָא, וְחָנֵּנִי וַעֲנֵנִי: לְךָ אָמַר לִבִּי בַּקְּשׁוּ פָנָי, אֶת־פָּנֶיךָ יהוה אֲבַקֵּשׁ: אַל־תַּסְתֵּר פָּנֶיךָ מִמֶּנִּי, אַל תַּט־בְּאַף עַבְדֶּךָ, עֶזְרָתִי הָיִיתָ, אַל־תִּטְּשֵׁנִי וְאַל־תַּעַזְבֵנִי, אֱלֹהֵי יִשְׁעִי: כִּי־אָבִי וְאִמִּי עֲזָבוּנִי, וַיהוה יַאַסְפֵנִי: הוֹרֵנִי יהוה דַּרְכֶּךָ, וּנְחֵנִי בְּאֹרַח מִישׁוֹר, לְמַעַן שׁוֹרְרָי: אַל־תִּתְּנֵנִי בְּנֶפֶשׁ צָרָי, כִּי קָמוּ־בִי עֵדֵי־שֶׁקֶר, וִיפֵחַ חָמָס: › לוּלֵא הֶאֱמַנְתִּי לִרְאוֹת בְּטוּב־יהוה בְּאֶרֶץ חַיִּים: קַוֵּה אֶל־יהוה, חֲזַק וְיַאֲמֵץ לִבֶּךָ, וְקַוֵּה אֶל־יהוה:

קדיש יתום (*page 247*)

*In* ארץ ישראל *the following through* בָּרְכוּ*, on page 269, is said:*

אֵין כֵּאלֹהֵינוּ, אֵין כַּאדוֹנֵינוּ, אֵין כְּמַלְכֵּנוּ, אֵין כְּמוֹשִׁיעֵנוּ.
מִי כֵאלֹהֵינוּ, מִי כַאדוֹנֵינוּ, מִי כְמַלְכֵּנוּ, מִי כְמוֹשִׁיעֵנוּ.
נוֹדֶה לֵאלֹהֵינוּ, נוֹדֶה לַאדוֹנֵינוּ, נוֹדֶה לְמַלְכֵּנוּ, נוֹדֶה לְמוֹשִׁיעֵנוּ.
בָּרוּךְ אֱלֹהֵינוּ, בָּרוּךְ אֲדוֹנֵינוּ, בָּרוּךְ מַלְכֵּנוּ, בָּרוּךְ מוֹשִׁיעֵנוּ.
אַתָּה הוּא אֱלֹהֵינוּ, אַתָּה הוּא אֲדוֹנֵינוּ,
אַתָּה הוּא מַלְכֵּנוּ, אַתָּה הוּא מוֹשִׁיעֵנוּ.
אַתָּה הוּא שֶׁהִקְטִירוּ אֲבוֹתֵינוּ לְפָנֶיךָ אֶת קְטֹרֶת הַסַּמִּים.

פִּטּוּם הַקְּטֹרֶת: הַצֳּרִי, וְהַצִּפֹּרֶן, וְהַחֶלְבְּנָה, וְהַלְּבוֹנָה מִשְׁקַל שִׁבְעִים שִׁבְעִים מָנֶה, מֹר, וּקְצִיעָה, שִׁבֹּלֶת נֵרְדְּ, וְכַרְכֹּם מִשְׁקַל שִׁשָּׁה עָשָׂר שִׁשָּׁה עָשָׂר מָנֶה, הַקֹּשְׁטְ שְׁנֵים עָשָׂר, קִלּוּפָה שְׁלֹשָׁה, קִנָּמוֹן תִּשְׁעָה, בֹּרִית כַּרְשִׁינָה תִּשְׁעָה קַבִּין, יֵין קַפְרִיסִין סְאִין תְּלָת וְקַבִּין תְּלָתָא, וְאִם לֹא מָצָא יֵין קַפְרִיסִין, מֵבִיא חֲמַר חִוַּרְיָן עַתִּיק. מֶלַח סְדוֹמִית רֹבַע, מַעֲלֶה עָשָׁן כָּל שֶׁהוּא. רַבִּי נָתָן הַבַּבְלִי אוֹמֵר: אַף כִּפַּת הַיַּרְדֵּן כָּל שֶׁהוּא, וְאִם נָתַן בָּהּ דְּבַשׁ פְּסָלָהּ, וְאִם חִסַּר אֶחָד מִכָּל סַמָּנֶיהָ, חַיָּב מִיתָה. כריתות ו.

Rabban Shimon ben Gamliel says: "Balsam" refers to the sap that drips from the balsam tree. The Carsina lye was used for bleaching the onycha to improve it. The Cyprus wine was used to soak the onycha in it to make it pungent. Though urine is suitable for this purpose, it is not brought into the Temple out of respect.

It was taught in the Academy of Elijah: Whoever studies [Torah] laws every day is assured that he will be destined for the World to Come, as it is said, "The ways of the world are His" – read not, "ways" [*halikhot*] but "laws" [*halakhot*]. *Megilla 28b* *Hab. 3*

Rabbi Elazar said in the name of Rabbi Ḥanina: The disciples of the sages increase peace in the world, as it is said, "And all your children shall be taught of the Lord, and great shall be the peace of your children [*banayikh*]." Read not *banayikh*, "your children," but *bonayikh*, "your builders." Those who love Your Torah have great peace; there is no stumbling block for them. May there be peace within your ramparts, prosperity in your palaces. For the sake of my brothers and friends, I shall say, "Peace be within you." For the sake of the House of the Lord our God, I will seek your good. ▸ May the Lord grant strength to His people; may the Lord bless His people with peace. *Berakhot 64a* *Is. 54* *Ps. 119* *Ps. 122* *Ps. 29*

---

shall recognize that all of them, even those who hold opinions opposite their own, are "taught of the Lord." Through each of them is revealed the knowledge of the Lord.

"And great shall be the peace of your children." The word used for "great" is not *"gadol,"* rather *"rav." "Gadol"* would have implied uniformity; *"rav,"* on the other hand, suggests multiplicity.

"Read not 'your children' but 'your builders.'" The building is constructed of different parts. Truth is constructed of different sides and opinions, different ways of [divine] service and pedagogical methods. Each has its place and its value. "These and those are the words of the Living God."[40] We must not lose any talent but rather develop it and find a place for it. If you see a contradiction between concepts, study them closely to discover the inner law whereby they no longer contradict one another. The panoply of opinions brought about by the difference of souls and upbringing, enriches and broadens wisdom. Eventually it will be understood that the peace cannot be built other than through those influences that appear mutually antagonistic.[41]

40. *b. 'Eruvin* 13b.

41. *OR*, vol. 1, pp. 330–331.

רַבָּן שִׁמְעוֹן בֶּן גַּמְלִיאֵל אוֹמֵר: הַצֳּרִי אֵינוֹ אֶלָּא שְׂרָף הַנּוֹטֵף מֵעֲצֵי הַקְּטָף. בֹּרִית כַּרְשִׁינָה שֶׁשָּׁפִין בָּהּ אֶת הַצִּפֹּרֶן כְּדֵי שֶׁתְּהֵא נָאָה, יֵין קַפְרִיסִין שֶׁשּׁוֹרִין בּוֹ אֶת הַצִּפֹּרֶן כְּדֵי שֶׁתְּהֵא עַזָּה, וַהֲלֹא מֵי רַגְלַיִם יָפִין לָהּ, אֶלָּא שֶׁאֵין מַכְנִיסִין מֵי רַגְלַיִם בַּמִּקְדָּשׁ מִפְּנֵי הַכָּבוֹד.

תָּנָא דְבֵי אֵלִיָּהוּ: כָּל הַשּׁוֹנֶה הֲלָכוֹת בְּכָל יוֹם, מֻבְטָח לוֹ שֶׁהוּא בֶּן עוֹלָם מגילה כח:
הַבָּא, שֶׁנֶּאֱמַר הֲלִיכוֹת עוֹלָם לוֹ: אַל תִּקְרֵי הֲלִיכוֹת אֶלָּא הֲלָכוֹת. חבקוק ג

אָמַר רַבִּי אֶלְעָזָר, אָמַר רַבִּי חֲנִינָא: תַּלְמִידֵי חֲכָמִים מַרְבִּים שָׁלוֹם בָּעוֹלָם, ברכות סד.
שֶׁנֶּאֱמַר וְכָל־בָּנַיִךְ לִמּוּדֵי יהוה, וְרַב שְׁלוֹם בָּנָיִךְ: אַל תִּקְרֵי בָּנָיִךְ, אֶלָּא ישעיה נד
בּוֹנָיִךְ. שָׁלוֹם רָב לְאֹהֲבֵי תוֹרָתֶךָ, וְאֵין־לָמוֹ מִכְשׁוֹל: יְהִי־שָׁלוֹם בְּחֵילֵךְ, תהלים קיט
שַׁלְוָה בְּאַרְמְנוֹתָיִךְ: לְמַעַן אַחַי וְרֵעָי אֲדַבְּרָה־נָּא שָׁלוֹם בָּךְ: לְמַעַן בֵּית־יהוה תהלים קכב
אֱלֹהֵינוּ אֲבַקְשָׁה טוֹב לָךְ: ‹ יהוה עֹז לְעַמּוֹ יִתֵּן, יהוה יְבָרֵךְ אֶת־עַמּוֹ בַשָּׁלוֹם: תהלים כט

---

אָמַר רַבִּי אֶלְעָזָר, אָמַר רַבִּי חֲנִינָא: תַּלְמִידֵי חֲכָמִים מַרְבִּים שָׁלוֹם בָּעוֹלָם, שֶׁנֶּאֱמַר וְכָל־בָּנַיִךְ לִמּוּדֵי יהוה, וְרַב שְׁלוֹם בָּנָיִךְ: אַל תִּקְרֵי בָּנָיִךְ, אֶלָּא בּוֹנָיִךְ *Rabbi Elazar said in the name of Rabbi Ḥanina: The disciples of the sages increase peace in the world, as it is said, "And all your children shall be taught of the Lord, and great shall be the peace of your children [banayikh]." Read not banayikh, "your children," but bonayikh, "your builders."*

Some mistakenly think that world peace will come about only through uniformity of opinions and characteristics, and for that reason, when they behold sages investigating the Torah, and thereby multiplying the sides and opinions, they assume that the sages bring about controversy, which is the opposite of peace. In truth, this is not so. True peace cannot come to the world other than by diversification. There must be made visible all the sides and opinions, and it must be clarified how all have their place, each according to its value – even those things which appear mutually contradictory. Only through the collection of all the parts and specifics, all the opinions that appear dissimilar, and all the divided disciplines – will there become manifest the light of truth, the light of the Torah of Truth. So "the sages increase peace," because by broadening and expanding upon the concepts, and generating new wisdom in diverse forms – they actually increase peace.

"As it is said, 'And all your children shall be taught of the Lord.'" All

## THE RABBIS' KADDISH

*The following prayer requires the presence of a minyan.*
*A transliteration can be found on page 1319.*

*Mourner:* יִתְגַּדַּל Magnified and sanctified may His great name be,
in the world He created by His will.
May He establish His kingdom in your lifetime
and in your days, and in the lifetime of all the house of Israel,
swiftly and soon – and say: Amen.

*All:* May His great name be blessed for ever and all time.

*Mourner:* Blessed and praised, glorified and exalted,
raised and honored, uplifted and lauded be
the name of the Holy One, blessed be He,
beyond any blessing,
song, praise and consolation
uttered in the world – and say: Amen.

To Israel, to the teachers,
their disciples and their disciples' disciples,
and to all who engage in the study of Torah,
in this (*in Israel add:* holy) place or elsewhere,
may there come to them and you great peace,
grace, kindness and compassion,
long life, ample sustenance and deliverance,
from their Father in Heaven – and say: Amen.

May there be great peace from heaven,
and (good) life for us and all Israel – and say: Amen.

*Bow, take three steps back, as if taking leave of the Divine Presence,*
*then bow, first left, then right, then center, while saying:*
May He who makes peace in His high places,
in His compassion make peace for us
and all Israel – and say: Amen.

*In Israel, on days when the Torah is not read,*
*the person saying Kaddish adds:*
Bless the LORD, the blessed One.

*and the congregation responds:*
Bless the LORD, the blessed One, for ever and all time.

*In Israel during Elul, some congregations blow shofar and say Psalm 27 (page 262) at this point. In a house of mourning the service continues on page 1138.*

## קדיש דרבנן

*The following prayer requires the presence of a* מנין.
*A transliteration can be found on page 1319.*

אבל: יִתְגַּדַּל וְיִתְקַדַּשׁ שְׁמֵהּ רַבָּא (קהל: אָמֵן)
בְּעָלְמָא דִּי בְרָא כִרְעוּתֵהּ, וְיַמְלִיךְ מַלְכוּתֵהּ
בְּחַיֵּיכוֹן וּבְיוֹמֵיכוֹן וּבְחַיֵּי דְכָל בֵּית יִשְׂרָאֵל
בַּעֲגָלָא וּבִזְמַן קָרִיב, וְאִמְרוּ אָמֵן. (קהל: אָמֵן)

קהל ואבל: יְהֵא שְׁמֵהּ רַבָּא מְבָרַךְ לְעָלַם וּלְעָלְמֵי עָלְמַיָּא.

אבל: יִתְבָּרַךְ וְיִשְׁתַּבַּח וְיִתְפָּאַר וְיִתְרוֹמַם וְיִתְנַשֵּׂא
וְיִתְהַדָּר וְיִתְעַלֶּה וְיִתְהַלָּל, שְׁמֵהּ דְּקֻדְשָׁא בְּרִיךְ הוּא (קהל: בְּרִיךְ הוּא)
לְעֵלָּא מִן כָּל בִּרְכָתָא / בעשרת ימי תשובה: לְעֵלָּא לְעֵלָּא מִכָּל בִּרְכָתָא /
וְשִׁירָתָא, תֻּשְׁבְּחָתָא וְנֶחֱמָתָא
דַּאֲמִירָן בְּעָלְמָא, וְאִמְרוּ אָמֵן. (קהל: אָמֵן)

עַל יִשְׂרָאֵל וְעַל רַבָּנָן, וְעַל תַּלְמִידֵיהוֹן וְעַל כָּל תַּלְמִידֵי תַלְמִידֵיהוֹן
וְעַל כָּל מָאן דְּעָסְקִין בְּאוֹרַיְתָא
דִּי בְאַתְרָא (בארץ ישראל: קַדִּישָׁא) הָדֵין וְדִי בְכָל אֲתַר וַאֲתַר
יְהֵא לְהוֹן וּלְכוֹן שְׁלָמָא רַבָּא, חִנָּא וְחִסְדָּא, וְרַחֲמֵי, וְחַיֵּי אֲרִיכֵי
וּמְזוֹנֵי רְוִיחֵי, וּפֻרְקָנָא מִן קֳדָם אֲבוּהוֹן דִּי בִשְׁמַיָּא, וְאִמְרוּ אָמֵן. (קהל: אָמֵן)

יְהֵא שְׁלָמָא רַבָּא מִן שְׁמַיָּא
וְחַיִּים (טוֹבִים) עָלֵינוּ וְעַל כָּל יִשְׂרָאֵל, וְאִמְרוּ אָמֵן. (קהל: אָמֵן)

*Bow, take three steps back, as if taking leave of the Divine Presence,*
*then bow, first left, then right, then center, while saying:*

עֹשֶׂה שָׁלוֹם/ בעשרת ימי תשובה: הַשָּׁלוֹם/ בִּמְרוֹמָיו
הוּא יַעֲשֶׂה בְרַחֲמָיו שָׁלוֹם, עָלֵינוּ וְעַל כָּל יִשְׂרָאֵל, וְאִמְרוּ אָמֵן. (קהל: אָמֵן)

*In* ארץ ישראל*, on days when the* תורה *is not read, the person saying* קדיש *adds:*

בָּרְכוּ אֶת יהוה הַמְבֹרָךְ.

*and the* קהל *responds:*

בָּרוּךְ יהוה הַמְבֹרָךְ לְעוֹלָם וָעֶד.

*In* ארץ ישראל *during* אלול*, some congregations blow* שופר *and say* לְדָוִד, יהוה אוֹרִי
*(page 261) at this point. In a house of mourning the service continues on page 1139.*

# READINGS AFTER THE SERVICE

*Some say the following daily after morning prayers:*

THE SIX REMEMBRANCES

*The Exodus from Egypt*

That you may remember the day you left the land of Egypt all the days of your life. *Deut. 16*

*The Revelation at Mount Sinai*

Only be careful and watch yourself very closely lest you forget the things your eyes have seen or let them slip from your heart all the days of your life. You shall make them known to your children and your children's children – the day you stood before the LORD your God at Horeb when the LORD said to me, "Assemble the people before Me and I will let them hear My words, so that they may learn to be in awe of Me as long as they live on earth, and they will teach them to their children." *Deut. 4*

*Amalek*

Remember what Amalek did to you on your way out of Egypt, how he met you on the way, cutting off those who were lagging behind, when you were tired and exhausted, and he did not fear God. So, when the LORD your God grants you rest from all your enemies around you in the land the LORD your God is about to give you to possess as an inheritance, you shall wipe out the memory of Amalek from under the heavens: you shall not forget. *Deut. 25*

*The Golden Calf*

Remember, and do not forget, how you provoked the LORD your God in the wilderness. *Deut. 9*

*Miriam*

Remember what the LORD your God did to Miriam on the way when you came out of Egypt. *Deut. 24*

*The Shabbat*

Remember the Shabbat day to hallow it. *Ex. 20*

---

The effect of the prayer should not extend only to the actual duration of the prayer. Rather, through the exaltation and sanctification of the soul in prayer, all avenues of life should be sanctified and proceed to the goal of truth and righteousness. "In all your ways know Him."[2] Sitting for a while after the prayer serves to bind the conceptions, the lofty feelings of the hour of prayer, with all one's material ways of life. This is the level of the *"yashar"* (the just man), who does not foreswear the affairs of this world

2. Proverbs 3:6; *b. Berakhot* 63a; *MT, Hil. De'ot* 3:3; *Shulḥan 'Arukh, OḤ*, chap. 231.

# אמירות לאחר התפילה

*Some say the following daily after morning prayers:*

## שש זכירות

יציאת מצרים

לְמַעַן תִּזְכֹּר אֶת־יוֹם צֵאתְךָ מֵאֶרֶץ מִצְרַיִם כֹּל יְמֵי חַיֶּיךָ׃ דברים טז

מעמד הר סיני

רַק הִשָּׁמֶר לְךָ וּשְׁמֹר נַפְשְׁךָ מְאֹד פֶּן־תִּשְׁכַּח אֶת־הַדְּבָרִים אֲשֶׁר־רָאוּ עֵינֶיךָ דברים ד
וּפֶן־יָסוּרוּ מִלְּבָבְךָ כֹּל יְמֵי חַיֶּיךָ וְהוֹדַעְתָּם לְבָנֶיךָ וְלִבְנֵי בָנֶיךָ׃ יוֹם אֲשֶׁר עָמַדְתָּ
לִפְנֵי יהוה אֱלֹהֶיךָ בְּחֹרֵב בֶּאֱמֹר יהוה אֵלַי הַקְהֶל־לִי אֶת־הָעָם וְאַשְׁמִעֵם
אֶת־דְּבָרָי אֲשֶׁר יִלְמְדוּן לְיִרְאָה אֹתִי כָּל־הַיָּמִים אֲשֶׁר הֵם חַיִּים עַל־הָאֲדָמָה
וְאֶת־בְּנֵיהֶם יְלַמֵּדוּן׃

מעשה עמלק ומחייתו

זָכוֹר אֵת אֲשֶׁר־עָשָׂה לְךָ עֲמָלֵק בַּדֶּרֶךְ בְּצֵאתְכֶם מִמִּצְרָיִם׃ אֲשֶׁר קָרְךָ בַּדֶּרֶךְ דברים כה
וַיְזַנֵּב בְּךָ כָּל־הַנֶּחֱשָׁלִים אַחֲרֶיךָ וְאַתָּה עָיֵף וְיָגֵעַ וְלֹא יָרֵא אֱלֹהִים׃ וְהָיָה
בְּהָנִיחַ יהוה אֱלֹהֶיךָ ׀ לְךָ מִכָּל־אֹיְבֶיךָ מִסָּבִיב בָּאָרֶץ אֲשֶׁר־יהוה אֱלֹהֶיךָ
נֹתֵן לְךָ נַחֲלָה לְרִשְׁתָּהּ תִּמְחֶה אֶת־זֵכֶר עֲמָלֵק מִתַּחַת הַשָּׁמָיִם לֹא תִּשְׁכָּח׃

מעשי אבותינו במדבר

זְכֹר אַל־תִּשְׁכַּח אֵת אֲשֶׁר־הִקְצַפְתָּ אֶת־יהוה אֱלֹהֶיךָ בַּמִּדְבָּר דברים ט

מעשה מרים

זָכוֹר אֵת אֲשֶׁר־עָשָׂה יהוה אֱלֹהֶיךָ לְמִרְיָם בַּדֶּרֶךְ בְּצֵאתְכֶם מִמִּצְרָיִם׃ דברים כד

שבת

זָכוֹר אֶת־יוֹם הַשַּׁבָּת לְקַדְּשׁוֹ׃ שמות כ

---

It is customary upon the conclusion of the prayer to sit a while and say this verse: "However the righteous shall give thanks to Your name, the just (*yesharim*) shall dwell in Your presence."[1]

---

1. Psalms 140:14; *y. Berakhot* 5:1; *b. Berakhot* 32b; Rabbi Solomon Luria, *Responsa Maharshal*, no. 64; Rabbi Abraham David Lavut, *Sha'ar ha-Kollel*, chap. 11, par. 37. See our discussion above "Meditation Before (and After) Prayer."

THE TEN COMMANDMENTS

God spoke all these words, saying: *Ex. 20*

1. אָנֹכִי I am the LORD your God who brought you out of the land of Egypt, from the slave-house.
2. לֹא־יִהְיֶה Have no other gods besides Me. Do not make a sculptured image for yourself, or any likeness of what is in the heavens above, or on the earth below, or in the waters under the earth. Do not bow down to them or worship them, for I am the LORD your God, a zealous God, visiting the guilt of the parents on the children to the third and fourth generation, if they also reject Me; but showing kindness to thousands of generations of those who love Me and keep My commandments.
3. לֹא תִשָּׂא Do not take the name of the LORD your God in vain. The LORD will not leave unpunished one who utters His name in vain.
4. זָכוֹר Remember the Sabbath and keep it holy. Six days you shall labor and do all your work, but the seventh day is a Sabbath of the LORD your God; on it you shall not do any work – you, your son or daughter, your male or female slaves, your cattle, or the stranger within your gates. For in six days the LORD made heaven and earth and sea, and all that is in them, and rested on the seventh day; therefore the LORD blessed the Sabbath day and made it holy.
5. כַּבֵּד Honor your father and your mother, so that you may live long in the land that the LORD your God is giving you.
6. לֹא תִרְצַח Do not murder.
7. לֹא תִנְאָף Do not commit adultery.
8. לֹא תִגְנֹב Do not steal.
9. לֹא־תַעֲנֶה Do not testify as a false witness against your neighbor.
10. לֹא תַחְמֹד Do not be envious of your neighbor's house. Do not be envious of your neighbor's wife, his male or female slave, his ox, his ass, or anything else that is your neighbor's.

---

*"yesharim."*[3] This is also touched upon in *Ḥovot ha-Levavot* (*Duties of the Heart*), *Sha'ar ha-Perishut* (Gate of Asceticism) [chap. 7].[4]

---

3. *b. 'Avodah Zarah* 25b.
4. See Baḥya ibn Pakuda, *The Book of Direction to the Duties of the Heart*, trans. and ed. Menaḥem Mansoor (London: Routledge and Kegan Paul, 1973), p. 422.
*OR*, vol. 1, pp. 333–334 = *EA*, vol. 1, *Berakhot*, chap. 5, par. 87 (pp. 154–155). On the Patriarchs as *"yesharim,"* see now *Shemu'ot Rayah*, ed. Rabbi Ḥayyim Yeshayah Hadari (Jerusalem: World Zionist Organization, 2015), *Shemot*, pp. 219–221.

## עשרת הדברות

שמות כ
וַיְדַבֵּר אֱלֹהִים אֵת כָּל־הַדְּבָרִים הָאֵלֶּה לֵאמֹר:

א אָנֹכִי יהוה אֱלֹהֶיךָ אֲשֶׁר הוֹצֵאתִיךָ מֵאֶרֶץ מִצְרַיִם מִבֵּית עֲבָדִים:

ב לֹא־יִהְיֶה לְךָ אֱלֹהִים אֲחֵרִים עַל־פָּנָי: לֹא־תַעֲשֶׂה לְךָ פֶסֶל וְכָל־תְּמוּנָה
אֲשֶׁר בַּשָּׁמַיִם מִמַּעַל וַאֲשֶׁר בָּאָרֶץ מִתָּחַת וַאֲשֶׁר בַּמַּיִם מִתַּחַת לָאָרֶץ:
לֹא־תִשְׁתַּחֲוֶה לָהֶם וְלֹא תָעָבְדֵם כִּי אָנֹכִי יהוה אֱלֹהֶיךָ אֵל קַנָּא פֹּקֵד עֲוֹן
אָבֹת עַל־בָּנִים עַל־שִׁלֵּשִׁים וְעַל־רִבֵּעִים לְשֹׂנְאָי: וְעֹשֶׂה חֶסֶד לַאֲלָפִים
לְאֹהֲבַי וּלְשֹׁמְרֵי מִצְוֹתָי:

ג לֹא תִשָּׂא אֶת־שֵׁם־יהוה אֱלֹהֶיךָ לַשָּׁוְא כִּי לֹא יְנַקֶּה יהוה אֵת אֲשֶׁר־
יִשָּׂא אֶת־שְׁמוֹ לַשָּׁוְא:

ד זָכוֹר אֶת־יוֹם הַשַּׁבָּת לְקַדְּשׁוֹ: שֵׁשֶׁת יָמִים תַּעֲבֹד וְעָשִׂיתָ כָּל־מְלַאכְתֶּךָ:
וְיוֹם הַשְּׁבִיעִי שַׁבָּת לַיהוה אֱלֹהֶיךָ לֹא־תַעֲשֶׂה כָל־מְלָאכָה אַתָּה ׀ וּבִנְךָ
וּבִתֶּךָ עַבְדְּךָ וַאֲמָתְךָ וּבְהֶמְתֶּךָ וְגֵרְךָ אֲשֶׁר בִּשְׁעָרֶיךָ: כִּי שֵׁשֶׁת־יָמִים עָשָׂה
יהוה אֶת־הַשָּׁמַיִם וְאֶת־הָאָרֶץ אֶת־הַיָּם וְאֶת־כָּל־אֲשֶׁר־בָּם וַיָּנַח בַּיּוֹם
הַשְּׁבִיעִי עַל־כֵּן בֵּרַךְ יהוה אֶת־יוֹם הַשַּׁבָּת וַיְקַדְּשֵׁהוּ:

ה כַּבֵּד אֶת־אָבִיךָ וְאֶת־אִמֶּךָ לְמַעַן יַאֲרִכוּן יָמֶיךָ עַל הָאֲדָמָה אֲשֶׁר־יהוה
אֱלֹהֶיךָ נֹתֵן לָךְ:

ו לֹא תִרְצָח

ז לֹא תִנְאָף

ח לֹא תִגְנֹב

ט לֹא־תַעֲנֶה בְרֵעֲךָ עֵד שָׁקֶר:

י לֹא תַחְמֹד בֵּית רֵעֶךָ לֹא־תַחְמֹד אֵשֶׁת רֵעֶךָ וְעַבְדּוֹ וַאֲמָתוֹ וְשׁוֹרוֹ וַחֲמֹרוֹ
וְכֹל אֲשֶׁר לְרֵעֶךָ:

---

but expands them and strengthens them for the purpose of true success. This was the character of the Patriarchs. The Torah tells of their mundane affairs, and the Rabbis stated that Abraham, Isaac and Jacob are called

THE THIRTEEN PRINCIPLES OF JEWISH FAITH

1. I believe with perfect faith
that the Creator,
blessed be His name,
creates and rules all creatures,
and that He alone made, makes, and will make, all things.

2. I believe with perfect faith
that the Creator,
blessed be His name, is One;
that there is no Oneness like His in any way;
and that He alone is our God who was, is, and ever will be.

3. I believe with perfect faith
that the Creator,
blessed be His name, is not physical,
that no physical attributes can apply to Him,
and that there is nothing whatsoever to compare to Him.

4. I believe with perfect faith
that the Creator,
blessed be His name, is first and last.

5. I believe with perfect faith
that the Creator,
blessed be His name,
is the only one to whom it is proper to pray,
and that it is improper to pray to anyone else.

6. I believe with perfect faith
that all the words of the prophets are true.

7. I believe with perfect faith
that the prophecy of Moses our teacher,
peace be to him, was true,
and that he was the father of the prophets –
those who preceded him and those who followed him.

8. I believe with perfect faith
that the entire Torah now in our hands
is the same one that was given to Moses our teacher,
peace be upon him.

## שלושה עשר עיקרים

א אֲנִי מַאֲמִין בֶּאֱמוּנָה שְׁלֵמָה
שֶׁהַבּוֹרֵא יִתְבָּרַךְ שְׁמוֹ הוּא בּוֹרֵא וּמַנְהִיג לְכָל הַבְּרוּאִים
וְהוּא לְבַדּוֹ עָשָׂה וְעוֹשֶׂה וְיַעֲשֶׂה לְכָל הַמַּעֲשִׂים.

ב אֲנִי מַאֲמִין בֶּאֱמוּנָה שְׁלֵמָה
שֶׁהַבּוֹרֵא יִתְבָּרַךְ שְׁמוֹ הוּא יָחִיד
וְאֵין יְחִידוּת כָּמְוֹהוּ בְּשׁוּם פָּנִים
וְהוּא לְבַדּוֹ אֱלֹהֵינוּ, הָיָה הֹוֶה וְיִהְיֶה.

ג אֲנִי מַאֲמִין בֶּאֱמוּנָה שְׁלֵמָה
שֶׁהַבּוֹרֵא יִתְבָּרַךְ שְׁמוֹ אֵינוֹ גוּף
וְלֹא יַשִּׂיגְוּהוּ מַשִּׂיגֵי הַגּוּף
וְאֵין לוֹ שׁוּם דִּמְיוֹן כְּלָל.

ד אֲנִי מַאֲמִין בֶּאֱמוּנָה שְׁלֵמָה
שֶׁהַבּוֹרֵא יִתְבָּרַךְ שְׁמוֹ הוּא רִאשׁוֹן וְהוּא אַחֲרוֹן.

ה אֲנִי מַאֲמִין בֶּאֱמוּנָה שְׁלֵמָה
שֶׁהַבּוֹרֵא יִתְבָּרַךְ שְׁמוֹ לוֹ לְבַדּוֹ רָאוּי לְהִתְפַּלֵּל
וְאֵין רָאוּי לְהִתְפַּלֵּל לְזוּלָתוֹ.

ו אֲנִי מַאֲמִין בֶּאֱמוּנָה שְׁלֵמָה
שֶׁכָּל דִּבְרֵי נְבִיאִים אֱמֶת.

ז אֲנִי מַאֲמִין בֶּאֱמוּנָה שְׁלֵמָה
שֶׁנְּבוּאַת מֹשֶׁה רַבֵּנוּ עָלָיו הַשָּׁלוֹם הָיְתָה אֲמִתִּית
וְשֶׁהוּא הָיָה אָב לַנְּבִיאִים, לַקּוֹדְמִים לְפָנָיו וְלַבָּאִים אַחֲרָיו.

ח אֲנִי מַאֲמִין בֶּאֱמוּנָה שְׁלֵמָה
שֶׁכָּל הַתּוֹרָה הַמְּצוּיָה עַתָּה בְּיָדֵינוּ
הִיא הַנְּתוּנָה לְמֹשֶׁה רַבֵּנוּ עָלָיו הַשָּׁלוֹם.

9. I believe with perfect faith
   that this Torah will not be changed,
   nor will there be any other Torah from the Creator,
   blessed be His name.

10. I believe with perfect faith
   that the Creator, blessed be His name,
   knows all the deeds and thoughts of humanity,
   as it is said, "He fashions the hearts of them all, *Ps. 33*
   comprehending all their deeds."

11. I believe with perfect faith
   that the Creator, blessed be His name,
   rewards those who keep His commandments,
   and punishes those who transgress them.

12. I believe with perfect faith
   in the coming of the Messiah,
   and though he may delay,
   I wait daily for his coming.

13. I believe with perfect faith
   that the dead will live again
   at a time of the Creator's choosing:
   blessed be His name and exalted be His mention
   for ever and all time.

ט אֲנִי מַאֲמִין בֶּאֱמוּנָה שְׁלֵמָה
שֶׁזֹּאת הַתּוֹרָה לֹא תְהֵא מֻחְלֶפֶת
וְלֹא תְהֵא תּוֹרָה אַחֶרֶת מֵאֵת הַבּוֹרֵא יִתְבָּרַךְ שְׁמוֹ.

י אֲנִי מַאֲמִין בֶּאֱמוּנָה שְׁלֵמָה
שֶׁהַבּוֹרֵא יִתְבָּרַךְ שְׁמוֹ
יוֹדֵעַ כָּל מַעֲשֵׂה בְנֵי אָדָם וְכָל מַחְשְׁבוֹתָם.
שֶׁנֶּאֱמַר: הַיֹּצֵר יַחַד לִבָּם, הַמֵּבִין אֶל־כָּל־מַעֲשֵׂיהֶם: תהלים לג

יא אֲנִי מַאֲמִין בֶּאֱמוּנָה שְׁלֵמָה
שֶׁהַבּוֹרֵא יִתְבָּרַךְ שְׁמוֹ גּוֹמֵל טוֹב לְשׁוֹמְרֵי מִצְוֹתָיו
וּמַעֲנִישׁ לְעוֹבְרֵי מִצְוֹתָיו.

יב אֲנִי מַאֲמִין בֶּאֱמוּנָה שְׁלֵמָה
בְּבִיאַת הַמָּשִׁיחַ
וְאַף עַל פִּי שֶׁיִּתְמַהְמֵהַּ עִם כָּל זֶה אֲחַכֶּה לּוֹ
בְּכָל יוֹם שֶׁיָּבוֹא.

יג אֲנִי מַאֲמִין בֶּאֱמוּנָה שְׁלֵמָה
שֶׁתִּהְיֶה תְּחִיַּת הַמֵּתִים
בְּעֵת שֶׁיַּעֲלֶה רָצוֹן מֵאֵת הַבּוֹרֵא
יִתְבָּרַךְ שְׁמוֹ וְיִתְעַלֶּה זִכְרוֹ לָעַד וּלְנֵצַח נְצָחִים.

# Minḥa for Weekdays

אַשְׁרֵי Happy are those who dwell in Your House; *Ps. 84*
they shall continue to praise You, Selah!
Happy are the people for whom this is so; *Ps. 144*
happy are the people whose God is the Lord.
A song of praise by David. *Ps. 145*

I will exalt You, my God, the King, and bless Your name for ever and all time. Every day I will bless You, and praise Your name for ever and all time. Great is the Lord and greatly to be praised; His greatness is unfathomable. One generation will praise Your works to the next, and tell of Your mighty deeds. On the glorious splendor of Your majesty I will meditate, and on the acts of Your wonders. They shall talk of the power of Your awesome deeds, and I will tell of Your greatness. They shall recite the record of Your great goodness, and sing with joy of Your righteousness. The Lord is gracious and compassionate, slow to anger and great in loving-kindness. The Lord is good to all, and His compassion extends to all His works. All Your works shall thank You,

---

has another connotation of gathering grain or some form of edible vegetation. *"La-su'aḥ"* is derived from the word *"si'aḥ"* (vegetation), as in *"Ve-khol si'aḥ ha-sadeh terem yihyeh ba-arets"* ("And all the vegetation of the field had yet to be on the earth").[4] Based on this word association, the great Ḥasidic master, Rabbi Naḥman of Breslov developed the idea that incorporated in Isaac's prayer, inspiring and invigorating it, was all the grass of the field.[5] Rabbi Naḥman finds a hint to this thought in the initials of the words "V*ayyetse* Y*itsḥak* l*a-su'aḥ* b*a-sadeh*": *Yevul* (produce, crop or yield).

It seems this uniquely "vegetative" character of the Afternoon Prayer instituted by Father Isaac is preserved for posterity in the appellation *"Minḥah,"* which was that sacrifice in the Temple brought from the vegetable kingdom.[6] (Editor)

---

4. Genesis 2:5. See Ibn Ezra and Rashbam *ad locum*; [Talmidei] Rabbenu Yonah, *Berakhot*, 22b (in pagination of *Hilkhot Rav Alfas*), s.v. *ve-ein siḥah ela tefillah she-ne'emar "Vayyetse Yitsḥak la-su'aḥ ba-sadeh,"* quoting Rabbenu Yitsḥak Hazaken (i.e. Rabbi Isaac of Dampierre); Rabbenu Ḥananel, *Sukkah* 21b.
5. Rabbi Naḥman of Breslov, *Likkutei Moharan* II, 11. Cf. *LM* II, 63.
6. Cf. Rav Kook's interpretation above, s.v. *Ve-'Arevah la-Hashem minḥat Yehudah vi-Yerushalayim.*

# מנחה לחול

אַשְׁרֵי יוֹשְׁבֵי בֵיתֶךָ, עוֹד יְהַלְלוּךָ סֶּלָה: תהלים פד

אַשְׁרֵי הָעָם שֶׁכָּכָה לּוֹ, אַשְׁרֵי הָעָם שֶׁיהוה אֱלֹהָיו: תהלים קמד

תְּהִלָּה לְדָוִד תהלים קמה

אֲרוֹמִמְךָ אֱלוֹהַי הַמֶּלֶךְ, וַאֲבָרְכָה שִׁמְךָ לְעוֹלָם וָעֶד:
בְּכָל־יוֹם אֲבָרְכֶךָּ, וַאֲהַלְלָה שִׁמְךָ לְעוֹלָם וָעֶד:
גָּדוֹל יהוה וּמְהֻלָּל מְאֹד, וְלִגְדֻלָּתוֹ אֵין חֵקֶר:
דּוֹר לְדוֹר יְשַׁבַּח מַעֲשֶׂיךָ, וּגְבוּרֹתֶיךָ יַגִּידוּ:
הֲדַר כְּבוֹד הוֹדֶךָ, וְדִבְרֵי נִפְלְאֹתֶיךָ אָשִׂיחָה:
וֶעֱזוּז נוֹרְאֹתֶיךָ יֹאמֵרוּ, וּגְדוּלָּתְךָ אֲסַפְּרֶנָּה:
זֵכֶר רַב־טוּבְךָ יַבִּיעוּ, וְצִדְקָתְךָ יְרַנֵּנוּ:
חַנּוּן וְרַחוּם יהוה, אֶרֶךְ אַפַּיִם וּגְדָל־חָסֶד:
טוֹב־יהוה לַכֹּל, וְרַחֲמָיו עַל־כָּל־מַעֲשָׂיו:
יוֹדוּךָ יהוה כָּל־מַעֲשֶׂיךָ, וַחֲסִידֶיךָ יְבָרְכוּכָה:

---

INTRODUCTION TO *MINḤAH* / AFTERNOON SERVICE

In regard to this prayer, a very basic question arises: Why is it called *Minḥah*? *Shaḥarit* refers to *"shaḥar"* or morning. *"'Arvit"* too refers to *"'erev"* or evening. Logic would dictate that the afternoon prayer be called *"Tsoharit"* after *"tsoharayim"* (afternoon). Simply, *"minḥah"* does not refer to any specific time of day. Rather, the *minḥah* was a meal-offering in the Temple. And in fact, the *minḥah* was offered twice daily, once in the morning and once in the afternoon.[1]

Perhaps the answer lies in the source of the prayer. According to our tradition, it was our forefather Isaac who instituted the afternoon prayer. *"Vayyetse Yitsḥak la-su'aḥ ba-sadeh lifnot 'arev."* "Isaac went out to converse in the field toward evening."[2] "And *siḥah* cannot mean other than prayer."[3] But *"la-suaḥ"*

---

1. *Tosafot, Pesaḥim* 107a, s.v. *samukh le-minḥah.* Rabbi David Abudarham attempts to solve the difficulty by referencing Targum Onkelos to Genesis 3:8: *"li-menaḥ yoma."* (Earlier this was suggested by Nahmanides, Exodus 12:6.) But *Minḥah* appears to be a Hebrew, not Aramaic word.
2. Genesis 24:63.
3. *b. Berakhot* 26b.

LORD, and Your devoted ones shall bless You. They shall talk of the glory of Your kingship, and speak of Your might. To make known to mankind His mighty deeds and the glorious majesty of His kingship. Your kingdom is an everlasting kingdom, and Your reign is for all generations. The LORD supports all who fall, and raises all who are bowed down. All raise their eyes to You in hope, and You give them their food in due season. You open Your hand, and satisfy every living thing with favor. The LORD is righteous in all His ways, and kind in all He does. The LORD is close to all who call on Him, to all who call on Him in truth. He fulfills the will of those who revere Him; He hears their cry and saves them. The LORD guards all who love Him, but all the wicked He will destroy. ▸ My mouth shall speak the praise of the LORD, and all creatures shall bless His holy name for ever and all time.

We will bless the LORD now and for ever. Halleluya! *Ps. 115*

HALF KADDISH

*Leader:* יִתְגַּדַּל Magnified and sanctified may His great name be,
in the world He created by His will.
May He establish His kingdom
in your lifetime and in your days,
and in the lifetime of all the house of Israel,
swiftly and soon –
and say: Amen.

*All:* May His great name be blessed for ever and all time.

*Leader:* Blessed and praised, glorified and exalted,
raised and honored, uplifted and lauded
be the name of the Holy One, blessed be He,
beyond any blessing,
song, praise and consolation
uttered in the world –
and say: Amen.

*On fast days, turn to Removing the Torah from the Ark on page 222. The Torah reading and Haftara for fast days are on page 1190. After the Torah is returned to the Ark, the Leader says Half Kaddish.*

כְּבוֹד מַלְכוּתְךָ יֹאמֵרוּ, וּגְבוּרָתְךָ יְדַבֵּרוּ:
לְהוֹדִיעַ לִבְנֵי הָאָדָם גְּבוּרֹתָיו, וּכְבוֹד הֲדַר מַלְכוּתוֹ:
מַלְכוּתְךָ מַלְכוּת כָּל־עֹלָמִים, וּמֶמְשַׁלְתְּךָ בְּכָל־דּוֹר וָדֹר:
סוֹמֵךְ יהוה לְכָל־הַנֹּפְלִים, וְזוֹקֵף לְכָל־הַכְּפוּפִים:
עֵינֵי־כֹל אֵלֶיךָ יְשַׂבֵּרוּ, וְאַתָּה נוֹתֵן־לָהֶם אֶת־אָכְלָם בְּעִתּוֹ:
פּוֹתֵחַ אֶת־יָדֶךָ, וּמַשְׂבִּיעַ לְכָל־חַי רָצוֹן:
צַדִּיק יהוה בְּכָל־דְּרָכָיו, וְחָסִיד בְּכָל־מַעֲשָׂיו:
קָרוֹב יהוה לְכָל־קֹרְאָיו, לְכֹל אֲשֶׁר יִקְרָאֻהוּ בֶאֱמֶת:
רְצוֹן־יְרֵאָיו יַעֲשֶׂה, וְאֶת־שַׁוְעָתָם יִשְׁמַע, וְיוֹשִׁיעֵם:
שׁוֹמֵר יהוה אֶת־כָּל־אֹהֲבָיו, וְאֵת כָּל־הָרְשָׁעִים יַשְׁמִיד:
◂ תְּהִלַּת יהוה יְדַבֶּר פִּי, וִיבָרֵךְ כָּל־בָּשָׂר שֵׁם קָדְשׁוֹ לְעוֹלָם וָעֶד:
וַאֲנַחְנוּ נְבָרֵךְ יָהּ מֵעַתָּה וְעַד־עוֹלָם, הַלְלוּיָהּ: תהלים קטו

חצי קדיש

ש״ץ: יִתְגַּדַּל וְיִתְקַדַּשׁ שְׁמֵהּ רַבָּא (קהל: אָמֵן)
בְּעָלְמָא דִּי בְרָא כִרְעוּתֵהּ, וְיַמְלִיךְ מַלְכוּתֵהּ
בְּחַיֵּיכוֹן וּבְיוֹמֵיכוֹן וּבְחַיֵּי דְכָל בֵּית יִשְׂרָאֵל
בַּעֲגָלָא וּבִזְמַן קָרִיב, וְאִמְרוּ אָמֵן. (קהל: אָמֵן)

קהל וש״ץ: יְהֵא שְׁמֵהּ רַבָּא מְבָרַךְ לְעָלַם וּלְעָלְמֵי עָלְמַיָּא.

ש״ץ: יִתְבָּרַךְ וְיִשְׁתַּבַּח וְיִתְפָּאַר וְיִתְרוֹמַם וְיִתְנַשֵּׂא
וְיִתְהַדָּר וְיִתְעַלֶּה וְיִתְהַלָּל
שְׁמֵהּ דְּקֻדְשָׁא בְּרִיךְ הוּא (קהל: בְּרִיךְ הוּא)
לְעֵלָּא מִן כָּל בִּרְכָתָא / בעשרת ימי תשובה: לְעֵלָּא לְעֵלָּא מִכָּל בִּרְכָתָא/
וְשִׁירָתָא, תֻּשְׁבְּחָתָא וְנֶחֱמָתָא
דַּאֲמִירָן בְּעָלְמָא, וְאִמְרוּ אָמֵן. (קהל: אָמֵן)

*On fast days, turn to* הוצאת ספר תורה *on page 223. The* תורה *reading and* הפטרה *for fast days are on page 1190. After the* תורה *is returned to the* ארון קודש*, the* שליח ציבור *says* חצי קדיש.

## THE AMIDA

*The following prayer, until "in former years" on page 302, is said silently, standing with feet together. If there is a minyan, the Amida is repeated aloud by the Leader. Take three steps forward and at the points indicated by ▾, bend the knees at the first word, bow at the second, and stand straight before saying God's name.*

When I proclaim the LORD's name, give glory to our God. *Deut. 32*
O LORD, open my lips, so that my mouth may declare Your praise. *Ps. 51*

PATRIARCHS

▾בָּרוּךְ▾ Blessed are You, LORD our God and God of our fathers,
God of Abraham, God of Isaac and God of Jacob;
the great, mighty and awesome God, God Most High,
who bestows acts of loving-kindness and creates all,
who remembers the loving-kindness of the fathers
and will bring a Redeemer to their children's children
for the sake of His name, in love.

*Between Rosh HaShana & Yom Kippur:* Remember us for life, O King who desires life,
and write us in the book of life –
for Your sake, O God of life.

King, Helper, Savior, Shield:
▾Blessed are You, LORD, Shield of Abraham.

DIVINE MIGHT

אַתָּה גִּבּוֹר You are eternally mighty, LORD.
You give life to the dead and have great power to save.

*The phrase "He makes the wind blow and the rain fall" is added from Simḥat Torah until Pesaḥ. In Israel the phrase "He causes the dew to fall" is added from Pesaḥ until Shemini Atzeret. See laws 129–131.*

*In fall & winter:* He makes the wind blow and the rain fall.

*In Israel, in spring & summer:* He causes the dew to fall.

He sustains the living with loving-kindness,
and with great compassion revives the dead.
He supports the fallen, heals the sick, sets captives free,
and keeps His faith with those who sleep in the dust.

# עמידה

*The following prayer, until* קַדְמֹנִיּוֹת *on page 303, is said silently, standing with feet together. If there is a* מנין*, the* עמידה *is repeated aloud by the* שליח ציבור*. Take three steps forward and at the points indicated by* ▾*, bend the knees at the first word, bow at the second, and stand straight before saying God's name.*

כִּי שֵׁם יהוה אֶקְרָא, הָבוּ גֹדֶל לֵאלֹהֵינוּ: דברים לב
אֲדֹנָי, שְׂפָתַי תִּפְתָּח, וּפִי יַגִּיד תְּהִלָּתֶךָ: תהלים נא

אבות

▾בָּרוּךְ אַתָּה יהוה, אֱלֹהֵינוּ וֵאלֹהֵי אֲבוֹתֵינוּ
אֱלֹהֵי אַבְרָהָם, אֱלֹהֵי יִצְחָק, וֵאלֹהֵי יַעֲקֹב
הָאֵל הַגָּדוֹל הַגִּבּוֹר וְהַנּוֹרָא, אֵל עֶלְיוֹן
גּוֹמֵל חֲסָדִים טוֹבִים, וְקוֹנֵה הַכֹּל
וְזוֹכֵר חַסְדֵי אָבוֹת
וּמֵבִיא גוֹאֵל לִבְנֵי בְנֵיהֶם לְמַעַן שְׁמוֹ בְּאַהֲבָה.

בעשרת ימי תשובה: זָכְרֵנוּ לְחַיִּים, מֶלֶךְ חָפֵץ בַּחַיִּים
וְכָתְבֵנוּ בְּסֵפֶר הַחַיִּים, לְמַעַנְךָ אֱלֹהִים חַיִּים.

מֶלֶךְ עוֹזֵר וּמוֹשִׁיעַ וּמָגֵן.
▾בָּרוּךְ אַתָּה יהוה, מָגֵן אַבְרָהָם.

גבורות

אַתָּה גִּבּוֹר לְעוֹלָם, אֲדֹנָי
מְחַיֵּה מֵתִים אַתָּה, רַב לְהוֹשִׁיעַ

*The phrase* מַשִּׁיב הָרְוּחַ *is added from* שמחת תורה *until* פסח*.*
*In* ארץ ישראל *the phrase* מוֹרִיד הַטָּל *is added from* פסח *until* שמיני עצרת*. See laws 129–131.*

בחורף: מַשִּׁיב הָרְוּחַ וּמוֹרִיד הַגֶּשֶׁם / בארץ ישראל בקיץ: מוֹרִיד הַטָּל

מְכַלְכֵּל חַיִּים בְּחֶסֶד, מְחַיֵּה מֵתִים בְּרַחֲמִים רַבִּים
סוֹמֵךְ נוֹפְלִים, וְרוֹפֵא חוֹלִים, וּמַתִּיר אֲסוּרִים
וּמְקַיֵּם אֱמוּנָתוֹ לִישֵׁנֵי עָפָר.

Who is like You, Master of might, and who can compare to You,
O King who brings death and gives life,
and makes salvation grow?

*Between Rosh HaShana & Yom Kippur:* Who is like You, compassionate Father,
who remembers His creatures in compassion, for life?

Faithful are You to revive the dead.
Blessed are You, Lord, who revives the dead.

*When saying the Amida silently, continue with "You are holy" below.*

---

KEDUSHA

*During the Leader's Repetition, the following is said standing with feet together, rising on the toes at the words indicated by ▴.*

*Cong. then Leader:* נְקַדֵּשׁ We will sanctify Your name on earth,
as they sanctify it in the highest heavens,
as is written by Your prophet,
"And they [the angels] call to one another saying: *Is. 6*

*Cong. then Leader:* ▴Holy, ▴holy, ▴holy is the Lord of hosts;
the whole world is filled with His glory."
Those facing them say "Blessed –"

*Cong. then Leader:* ▴"Blessed is the Lord's glory from His place." *Ezek. 3*
And in Your holy Writings it is written thus:

*Cong. then Leader:* ▴"The Lord shall reign for ever. He is your God, Zion, *Ps. 146*
from generation to generation, Halleluya!"

*Leader:* From generation to generation we will declare Your greatness,
and we will proclaim Your holiness for evermore.
Your praise, our God, shall not leave our mouth forever,
for You, God, are a great and holy King. Blessed are You, Lord,
the holy God. / *Between Rosh HaShana & Yom Kippur:* the holy King./

*The Leader continues with "You grace humanity" on the next page.*

---

HOLINESS

אַתָּה קָדוֹשׁ You are holy and Your name is holy,
and holy ones praise You daily, Selah!
Blessed are You, Lord,
the holy God. / *Between Rosh HaShana & Yom Kippur:* the holy King./

*(If forgotten, repeat the Amida.)*

מִי כָמְוֹךָ, בַּעַל גְּבוּרוֹת, וּמִי דּוֹמֶה לָּךְ
מֶלֶךְ, מֵמִית וּמְחַיֶּה וּמַצְמִיחַ יְשׁוּעָה.

בעשרת ימי תשובה: מִי כָמְוֹךָ אַב הָרַחֲמִים
זוֹכֵר יְצוּרָיו לְחַיִּים בְּרַחֲמִים.

וְנֶאֱמָן אַתָּה לְהַחֲיוֹת מֵתִים.
בָּרוּךְ אַתָּה יהוה, מְחַיֵּה הַמֵּתִים.

*When saying the* עמידה *silently, continue with* אַתָּה קָדוֹשׁ *below.*

---

קדושה

*During the* חזרת הש״ץ*, the following is said standing with feet together, rising on the toes at the words indicated by* ˄.

קהל *then* ש״ץ: נְקַדֵּשׁ אֶת שִׁמְךָ בָּעוֹלָם, כְּשֵׁם שֶׁמַּקְדִּישִׁים אוֹתוֹ בִּשְׁמֵי מָרוֹם
כַּכָּתוּב עַל יַד נְבִיאֶךָ: וְקָרָא זֶה אֶל־זֶה וְאָמַר ישעיה ו

קהל *then* ש״ץ: ˄קָדוֹשׁ, ˄קָדוֹשׁ, ˄קָדוֹשׁ, יהוה צְבָאוֹת, מְלֹא כָל־הָאָרֶץ כְּבוֹדוֹ:
לְעֻמָּתָם בָּרוּךְ יֹאמֵרוּ

קהל *then* ש״ץ: ˄בָּרוּךְ כְּבוֹד־יהוה מִמְּקוֹמוֹ: יחזקאל ג
וּבְדִבְרֵי קָדְשְׁךָ כָּתוּב לֵאמֹר

קהל *then* ש״ץ: ˄יִמְלֹךְ יהוה לְעוֹלָם, אֱלֹהַיִךְ צִיּוֹן לְדֹר וָדֹר, הַלְלוּיָהּ: תהלים קמו

ש״ץ: לְדוֹר וָדוֹר נַגִּיד גָּדְלֶךָ, וּלְנֵצַח נְצָחִים קְדֻשָּׁתְךָ נַקְדִּישׁ
וְשִׁבְחֲךָ אֱלֹהֵינוּ מִפִּינוּ לֹא יָמוּשׁ לְעוֹלָם וָעֶד
כִּי אֵל מֶלֶךְ גָּדוֹל וְקָדוֹשׁ אָתָּה.
בָּרוּךְ אַתָּה יהוה, הָאֵל הַקָּדוֹשׁ./ בעשרת ימי תשובה: הַמֶּלֶךְ הַקָּדוֹשׁ./

*The* שליח ציבור *continues with* אַתָּה חוֹנֵן *on the next page.*

---

קדושת השם

אַתָּה קָדוֹשׁ וְשִׁמְךָ קָדוֹשׁ, וּקְדוֹשִׁים בְּכָל יוֹם יְהַלְלְוּךָ סֶּלָה.
בָּרוּךְ אַתָּה יהוה, הָאֵל הַקָּדוֹשׁ./ בעשרת ימי תשובה: הַמֶּלֶךְ הַקָּדוֹשׁ./
(*If forgotten, repeat the* עמידה*.*)

### KNOWLEDGE

אַתָּה חוֹנֵן You grace humanity with knowledge
and teach mortals understanding.
Grace us with the knowledge, understanding
and discernment that come from You.
Blessed are You, LORD, who graciously grants knowledge.

### REPENTANCE

הֲשִׁיבֵנוּ Bring us back, our Father, to Your Torah.
Draw us near, our King, to Your service.
Lead us back to You in perfect repentance.
Blessed are You, LORD, who desires repentance.

### FORGIVENESS

*Strike the left side of the chest at °.*

סְלַח לָנוּ Forgive us, our Father, for we have °sinned.
Pardon us, our King, for we have °transgressed;
for You pardon and forgive.
Blessed are You, LORD, the gracious One who repeatedly forgives.

### REDEMPTION

רְאֵה Look on our affliction, plead our cause,
and redeem us soon for Your name's sake,
for You are a powerful Redeemer.
Blessed are You, LORD, the Redeemer of Israel.

---

*On fast days the Leader adds:*

עֲנֵנוּ Answer us, LORD, answer us on our Fast Day, for we are in great distress. Look not at our wickedness. Do not hide Your face from us and do not ignore our plea. Be near to our cry; please let Your loving-kindness comfort us. Even before we call to You, answer us, as it is said,
"Before they call, I will answer. While they are still speaking, I will hear." *Is. 65*
For You, LORD, are the One who answers in time of distress, redeems and rescues in all times of trouble and anguish. Blessed are You, LORD, who answers in time of distress.

---

דעת

אַתָּה חוֹנֵן לְאָדָם דַּעַת, וּמְלַמֵּד לֶאֱנוֹשׁ בִּינָה.
חָנֵּנוּ מֵאִתְּךָ דֵּעָה בִּינָה וְהַשְׂכֵּל.
בָּרוּךְ אַתָּה יהוה, חוֹנֵן הַדָּעַת.

תשובה

הֲשִׁיבֵנוּ אָבִינוּ לְתוֹרָתֶךָ, וְקָרְבֵנוּ מַלְכֵּנוּ לַעֲבוֹדָתֶךָ
וְהַחֲזִירֵנוּ בִּתְשׁוּבָה שְׁלֵמָה לְפָנֶיךָ.
בָּרוּךְ אַתָּה יהוה, הָרוֹצֶה בִּתְשׁוּבָה.

סליחה

*Strike the left side of the chest at °.*

סְלַח לָנוּ אָבִינוּ כִּי °חָטָאנוּ
מְחַל לָנוּ מַלְכֵּנוּ כִּי °פָשָׁעְנוּ
כִּי מוֹחֵל וְסוֹלֵחַ אָתָּה.
בָּרוּךְ אַתָּה יהוה, חַנּוּן הַמַּרְבֶּה לִסְלֹחַ.

גאולה

רְאֵה בְעָנְיֵנוּ, וְרִיבָה רִיבֵנוּ
וּגְאָלֵנוּ מְהֵרָה לְמַעַן שְׁמֶךָ, כִּי גּוֹאֵל חָזָק אָתָּה.
בָּרוּךְ אַתָּה יהוה, גּוֹאֵל יִשְׂרָאֵל.

---

*On fast days the* שליח ציבור *adds:*

עֲנֵנוּ יהוה עֲנֵנוּ בְּיוֹם צוֹם תַּעֲנִיתֵנוּ, כִּי בְצָרָה גְדוֹלָה אֲנָחְנוּ. אַל תֵּפֶן אֶל רִשְׁעֵנוּ, וְאַל תַּסְתֵּר פָּנֶיךָ מִמֶּנּוּ, וְאַל תִּתְעַלַּם מִתְּחִנָּתֵנוּ. הֱיֵה נָא קָרוֹב לְשַׁוְעָתֵנוּ, יְהִי נָא חַסְדְּךָ לְנַחֲמֵנוּ, טֶרֶם נִקְרָא אֵלֶיךָ עֲנֵנוּ, כַּדָּבָר שֶׁנֶּאֱמַר:
ישעיה סה וְהָיָה טֶרֶם יִקְרָאוּ וַאֲנִי אֶעֱנֶה, עוֹד הֵם מְדַבְּרִים וַאֲנִי אֶשְׁמָע: כִּי אַתָּה יהוה הָעוֹנֶה בְּעֵת צָרָה, פּוֹדֶה וּמַצִּיל בְּכָל עֵת צָרָה וְצוּקָה. בָּרוּךְ אַתָּה יהוה, הָעוֹנֶה בְּעֵת צָרָה.

### HEALING

רְפָאֵנוּ Heal us, LORD, and we shall be healed.
Save us and we shall be saved,
for You are our praise.
Bring complete recovery
for all our ailments,

---

*The following prayer for a sick person may be said here:*
May it be Your will, O LORD my God and God of my ancestors, that You speedily send a complete recovery from heaven, a healing of both soul and body, to the patient (*name*), son/daughter of (*mother's name*) among the other afflicted of Israel.

---

for You, God, King,
are a faithful and compassionate Healer.
Blessed are You, LORD,
Healer of the sick of His people Israel.

### PROSPERITY

*The phrase "Grant dew and rain as a blessing" is said from December 5th (in the year before a civil leap year, December 6th) until Pesaḥ. In Israel, it is said from the 7th of Marḥeshvan. The phrase "Grant blessing" is said from Ḥol HaMo'ed Pesaḥ until December 4th (in the year before a civil leap year, December 5th). In Israel it is said through the 6th of Marḥeshvan. See laws 147–149.*

בָּרֵךְ Bless this year for us, LORD our God,
and all its types of produce for good.

*In winter:* Grant dew and rain as a blessing
*In other seasons:* Grant blessing

on the face of the earth,
and from its goodness satisfy us,
blessing our year as the best of years.
Blessed are You, LORD,
who blesses the years.

רפואה

**רְפָאֵנוּ יהוה וְנֵרָפֵא**
**הוֹשִׁיעֵנוּ וְנִוָּשֵׁעָה**
**כִּי תְהִלָּתֵנוּ אָתָּה**
**וְהַעֲלֵה רְפוּאָה שְׁלֵמָה לְכָל מַכּוֹתֵינוּ**

---

*The following prayer for a sick person may be said here:*

יְהִי רָצוֹן מִלְּפָנֶיךָ יהוה אֱלֹהַי וֵאלֹהֵי אֲבוֹתַי, שֶׁתִּשְׁלַח מְהֵרָה רְפוּאָה שְׁלֵמָה
מִן הַשָּׁמַיִם רְפוּאַת הַנֶּפֶשׁ וּרְפוּאַת הַגּוּף לַחוֹלֶה/לַחוֹלָה *name of patient*
בֶּן/בַּת *mother's name* בְּתוֹךְ שְׁאָר חוֹלֵי יִשְׂרָאֵל.

---

**כִּי אֵל מֶלֶךְ רוֹפֵא נֶאֱמָן וְרַחֲמָן אָתָּה.**
**בָּרוּךְ אַתָּה יהוה, רוֹפֵא חוֹלֵי עַמּוֹ יִשְׂרָאֵל.**

ברכת השנים

*The phrase* וְתֵן טַל וּמָטָר לִבְרָכָה *is said from December 5th (in the year before a civil leap year, December 6th) until* פסח*. In* ארץ ישראל*, it is said from* ז׳ מרחשון*. The phrase* וְתֵן בְּרָכָה *is said from* חול המועד פסח *until December 4th (in the year before a civil leap year, December 5th). In* ארץ ישראל *it is said through* ו׳ מרחשון*.*
*See laws 147–149.*

**בָּרֵךְ עָלֵינוּ יהוה אֱלֹהֵינוּ אֶת הַשָּׁנָה הַזֹּאת**
**וְאֶת כָּל מִינֵי תְבוּאָתָהּ, לְטוֹבָה**
בחורף: **וְתֵן טַל וּמָטָר לִבְרָכָה** / בקיץ: **וְתֵן בְּרָכָה**
**עַל פְּנֵי הָאֲדָמָה**
**וְשַׂבְּעֵנוּ מִטּוּבָהּ**
**וּבָרֵךְ שְׁנָתֵנוּ כַּשָּׁנִים הַטּוֹבוֹת.**
**בָּרוּךְ אַתָּה יהוה, מְבָרֵךְ הַשָּׁנִים.**

### INGATHERING OF EXILES

תְּקַע Sound the great shofar for our freedom,
raise high the banner to gather our exiles,
and gather us together from the four quarters of the earth.
Blessed are You, Lord,
who gathers the dispersed of His people Israel.

### JUSTICE

הָשִׁיבָה Restore our judges as at first,
and our counselors as at the beginning,
and remove from us sorrow and sighing.
May You alone, Lord,
reign over us with loving-kindness and compassion,
and vindicate us in justice.
Blessed are You, Lord,
the King who loves righteousness and justice.
/*Between Rosh HaShana & Yom Kippur, end the blessing:* the King of justice./

### AGAINST INFORMERS

וְלַמַּלְשִׁינִים For the slanderers let there be no hope,
and may all wickedness perish in an instant.
May all Your people's enemies swiftly be cut down.
May You swiftly uproot, crush, cast down
and humble the arrogant swiftly in our days.
Blessed are You, Lord,
who destroys enemies and humbles the arrogant.

### THE RIGHTEOUS

עַל הַצַּדִּיקִים To the righteous, the pious,
the elders of Your people the house of Israel,
the remnant of their scholars,
the righteous converts, and to us,
may Your compassion be aroused, Lord our God.

קבוץ גלויות

תְּקַע בְּשׁוֹפָר גָּדוֹל לְחֵרוּתֵנוּ
וְשָׂא נֵס לְקַבֵּץ גָּלֻיּוֹתֵינוּ
וְקַבְּצֵנוּ יַחַד מֵאַרְבַּע כַּנְפוֹת הָאָרֶץ.
בָּרוּךְ אַתָּה יהוה, מְקַבֵּץ נִדְחֵי עַמּוֹ יִשְׂרָאֵל.

השבת המשפט

הָשִׁיבָה שׁוֹפְטֵינוּ כְּבָרִאשׁוֹנָה וְיוֹעֲצֵינוּ כְּבַתְּחִלָּה
וְהָסֵר מִמֶּנּוּ יָגוֹן וַאֲנָחָה
וּמְלֹךְ עָלֵינוּ אַתָּה יהוה לְבַדְּךָ בְּחֶסֶד וּבְרַחֲמִים
וְצַדְּקֵנוּ בַּמִּשְׁפָּט.
בָּרוּךְ אַתָּה יהוה
מֶלֶךְ אוֹהֵב צְדָקָה וּמִשְׁפָּט. / בעשרת ימי תשובה: הַמֶּלֶךְ הַמִּשְׁפָּט./

ברכת המינים

וְלַמַּלְשִׁינִים אַל תְּהִי תִקְוָה, וְכָל הָרִשְׁעָה כְּרֶגַע תֹּאבֵד
וְכָל אוֹיְבֵי עַמְּךָ מְהֵרָה יִכָּרֵתוּ
וְהַזֵּדִים מְהֵרָה תְעַקֵּר וּתְשַׁבֵּר וּתְמַגֵּר וְתַכְנִיעַ בִּמְהֵרָה בְיָמֵינוּ.
בָּרוּךְ אַתָּה יהוה, שׁוֹבֵר אוֹיְבִים וּמַכְנִיעַ זֵדִים.

על הצדיקים

עַל הַצַּדִּיקִים וְעַל הַחֲסִידִים
וְעַל זִקְנֵי עַמְּךָ בֵּית יִשְׂרָאֵל
וְעַל פְּלֵיטַת סוֹפְרֵיהֶם
וְעַל גֵּרֵי הַצֶּדֶק, וְעָלֵינוּ
יֶהֱמוּ רַחֲמֶיךָ יהוה אֱלֹהֵינוּ

Grant a good reward to all who sincerely trust in Your name.
Set our lot with them,
so that we may never be ashamed, for in You we trust.
Blessed are You, LORD,
who is the support and trust of the righteous.

REBUILDING JERUSALEM

וְלִירוּשָׁלַיִם To Jerusalem, Your city, may You return in compassion,
and may You dwell in it as You promised.
May You rebuild it rapidly in our days
as an everlasting structure,
and install within it soon the throne of David.
*Blessed are You, LORD,
who builds Jerusalem.

---

**On Tisha B'Av all conclude as follows:*

נַחֵם Console, O LORD our God, the mourners of Zion and the mourners of Jerusalem, and the city that is in sorrow, laid waste, scorned and desolate; that grieves for the loss of its children, that is laid waste of its dwellings, robbed of its glory, desolate without inhabitants. She sits with her head covered like a barren childless woman. Legions have devoured her; idolaters have taken possession of her; they have put Your people Israel to the sword and deliberately killed the devoted followers of the Most High. Therefore Zion weeps bitterly, and Jerusalem raises her voice. My heart, my heart grieves for those they killed; I am in anguish, I am in anguish for those they killed. For You, O LORD, consumed it with fire, and with fire You will rebuild it in the future, as is said, "And I Myself will be a wall of fire around it, says the LORD, *Zech. 2* and I will be its glory within." Blessed are You, LORD, who consoles Zion and rebuilds Jerusalem.

*Continue with "May the offshoot" below.*

---

KINGDOM OF DAVID

אֶת צֶמַח May the offshoot of Your servant David soon flower,
and may his pride be raised high by Your salvation,
for we wait for Your salvation all day.
Blessed are You, LORD,
who makes the glory of salvation flourish.

וְתֵן שָׂכָר טוֹב לְכָל הַבּוֹטְחִים בְּשִׁמְךָ בֶּאֱמֶת
וְשִׂים חֶלְקֵנוּ עִמָּהֶם
וּלְעוֹלָם לֹא נֵבוֹשׁ כִּי בְךָ בָּטָחְנוּ.
בָּרוּךְ אַתָּה יהוה, מִשְׁעָן וּמִבְטָח לַצַּדִּיקִים.

בניין ירושלים

וְלִירוּשָׁלַיִם עִירְךָ בְּרַחֲמִים תָּשׁוּב
וְתִשְׁכֹּן בְּתוֹכָהּ כַּאֲשֶׁר דִּבַּרְתָּ
וּבְנֵה אוֹתָהּ בְּקָרוֹב בְּיָמֵינוּ בִּנְיַן עוֹלָם
וְכִסֵּא דָוִד מְהֵרָה לְתוֹכָהּ תָּכִין.
*בָּרוּךְ אַתָּה יהוה, בּוֹנֵה יְרוּשָׁלָיִם.

---

**On תשעה באב, all conclude as follows:*

נַחֵם יהוה אֱלֹהֵינוּ אֶת אֲבֵלֵי צִיּוֹן וְאֶת אֲבֵלֵי יְרוּשָׁלַיִם, וְאֶת הָעִיר הָאֲבֵלָה
וְהַחֲרֵבָה וְהַבְּזוּיָה וְהַשּׁוֹמֵמָה. הָאֲבֵלָה מִבְּלִי בָנֶיהָ, וְהַחֲרֵבָה מִמְּעוֹנוֹתֶיהָ,
וְהַבְּזוּיָה מִכְּבוֹדָהּ, וְהַשּׁוֹמֵמָה מֵאֵין יוֹשֵׁב. וְהִיא יוֹשֶׁבֶת וְרֹאשָׁהּ חָפוּי,
כְּאִשָּׁה עֲקָרָה שֶׁלֹּא יָלָדָה. וַיְבַלְּעוּהָ לִגְיוֹנוֹת, וַיִּירָשׁוּהָ עוֹבְדֵי פְסִילִים, וַיָּטִילוּ
אֶת עַמְּךָ יִשְׂרָאֵל לֶחָרֶב, וַיַּהַרְגוּ בְזָדוֹן חֲסִידֵי עֶלְיוֹן. עַל כֵּן צִיּוֹן בְּמַר תִּבְכֶּה,
וִירוּשָׁלַיִם תִּתֵּן קוֹלָהּ. לִבִּי לִבִּי עַל חַלְלֵיהֶם, מֵעַי מֵעַי עַל חַלְלֵיהֶם, כִּי אַתָּה
יהוה בָּאֵשׁ הִצַּתָּהּ, וּבָאֵשׁ אַתָּה עָתִיד לִבְנוֹתָהּ. כָּאָמוּר: וַאֲנִי אֶהְיֶה־לָּהּ, זכריה ב
נְאֻם־יהוה, חוֹמַת אֵשׁ סָבִיב, וּלְכָבוֹד אֶהְיֶה בְתוֹכָהּ: בָּרוּךְ אַתָּה יהוה,
מְנַחֵם צִיּוֹן וּבוֹנֵה יְרוּשָׁלָיִם.

*Continue with* אֶת צֶמַח *below.*

---

משיח בן דוד

אֶת צֶמַח דָּוִד עַבְדְּךָ מְהֵרָה תַצְמִיחַ
וְקַרְנוֹ תָּרוּם בִּישׁוּעָתֶךָ
כִּי לִישׁוּעָתְךָ קִוִּינוּ כָּל הַיּוֹם.
בָּרוּךְ אַתָּה יהוה, מַצְמִיחַ קֶרֶן יְשׁוּעָה.

RESPONSE TO PRAYER

שְׁמַע קוֹלֵנוּ Listen to our voice, LORD our God.
Spare us and have compassion on us,
and in compassion and favor accept our prayer,
for You, God, listen to prayers and pleas.
Do not turn us away, O our King,
empty-handed from Your presence,*
for You listen with compassion
to the prayer of Your people Israel.
Blessed are You, LORD, who listens to prayer.

---

**At this point on fast days, the congregation adds "Answer us" below.*
*In times of drought in Israel, say "And answer us" on page 186.*

עֲנֵנוּ Answer us, LORD, answer us on our Fast Day, for we are in great distress. Look not at our wickedness. Do not hide Your face from us and do not ignore our plea. Be near to our cry; please let Your loving-kindness comfort us. Even before we call to You, answer us, as is said,
"Before they call, I will answer. While they are still speaking, I will *Is. 65*
hear." For You, LORD, are the One who answers in time of distress, redeems and rescues in all times of trouble and anguish.

*Continue with "for You listen" above.*

---

TEMPLE SERVICE

רְצֵה Find favor, LORD our God,
in Your people Israel and their prayer.
Restore the service to Your most holy House,
and accept in love and favor
the fire-offerings of Israel and their prayer.
May the service of Your people Israel always find favor with You.

---

*On Rosh Ḥodesh and Ḥol HaMo'ed, say:*

אֱלֹהֵינוּ Our God and God of our ancestors, may there rise, come, reach, appear, be favored, heard, regarded and remembered before You, our recollection and remembrance, as well as the remembrance of our ancestors, and of the Messiah, son of David Your servant, and of Jerusalem Your holy city, and of all Your people the house of

שומע תפילה

שְׁמַע קוֹלֵנוּ יהוה אֱלֹהֵינוּ
חוּס וְרַחֵם עָלֵינוּ
וְקַבֵּל בְּרַחֲמִים וּבְרָצוֹן אֶת תְּפִלָּתֵנוּ
כִּי אֵל שׁוֹמֵעַ תְּפִלּוֹת וְתַחֲנוּנִים אָתָּה
וּמִלְּפָנֶיךָ מַלְכֵּנוּ רֵיקָם אַל תְּשִׁיבֵנוּ*
כִּי אַתָּה שׁוֹמֵעַ תְּפִלַּת עַמְּךָ יִשְׂרָאֵל בְּרַחֲמִים.
בָּרוּךְ אַתָּה יהוה, שׁוֹמֵעַ תְּפִלָּה.

---

**At this point on fast days, the* קהל *adds* עֲנֵנוּ *below.*
*In times of drought in* ארץ ישראל, *say* וַעֲנֵנוּ *on page 187.*

עֲנֵנוּ יהוה עֲנֵנוּ בְּיוֹם צוֹם תַּעֲנִיתֵנוּ, כִּי בְצָרָה גְדוֹלָה אֲנָחְנוּ. אַל תֵּפֶן אֶל רִשְׁעֵנוּ, וְאַל תַּסְתֵּר פָּנֶיךָ מִמֶּנּוּ, וְאַל תִּתְעַלַּם מִתְּחִנָּתֵנוּ. הֱיֵה נָא קָרוֹב לְשַׁוְעָתֵנוּ, יְהִי נָא חַסְדְּךָ לְנַחֲמֵנוּ, טֶרֶם נִקְרָא אֵלֶיךָ עֲנֵנוּ, כַּדָּבָר
שֶׁנֶּאֱמַר: וְהָיָה טֶרֶם יִקְרָאוּ וַאֲנִי אֶעֱנֶה, עוֹד הֵם מְדַבְּרִים וַאֲנִי אֶשְׁמָע: ישעיה סה
כִּי אַתָּה יהוה הָעוֹנֶה בְּעֵת צָרָה, פּוֹדֶה וּמַצִּיל בְּכָל עֵת צָרָה וְצוּקָה.

*Continue with* כִּי אַתָּה שׁוֹמֵעַ *above.*

---

עבודה

רְצֵה יהוה אֱלֹהֵינוּ בְּעַמְּךָ יִשְׂרָאֵל וּבִתְפִלָּתָם
וְהָשֵׁב אֶת הָעֲבוֹדָה לִדְבִיר בֵּיתֶךָ
וְאִשֵּׁי יִשְׂרָאֵל וּתְפִלָּתָם בְּאַהֲבָה תְקַבֵּל בְּרָצוֹן
וּתְהִי לְרָצוֹן תָּמִיד עֲבוֹדַת יִשְׂרָאֵל עַמֶּךָ.

---

*On* ראש חודש *and* חול המועד, *say:*

אֱלֹהֵינוּ וֵאלֹהֵי אֲבוֹתֵינוּ, יַעֲלֶה וְיָבוֹא וְיַגִּיעַ, וְיֵרָאֶה וְיֵרָצֶה וְיִשָּׁמַע, וְיִפָּקֵד וְיִזָּכֵר זִכְרוֹנֵנוּ וּפִקְדוֹנֵנוּ וְזִכְרוֹן אֲבוֹתֵינוּ, וְזִכְרוֹן מָשִׁיחַ בֶּן דָּוִד עַבְדֶּךָ, וְזִכְרוֹן יְרוּשָׁלַיִם עִיר קָדְשֶׁךָ, וְזִכְרוֹן כָּל עַמְּךָ בֵּית

Israel – for deliverance and well-being, grace, loving-kindness and compassion, life and peace, on this day of:

*On Rosh Ḥodesh:* Rosh Ḥodesh.
*On Pesaḥ:* the Festival of Matzot.
*On Sukkot:* the Festival of Sukkot.

On it remember us, LORD our God, for good; recollect us for blessing, and deliver us for life. In accord with Your promise of salvation and compassion, spare us and be gracious to us; have compassion on us and deliver us, for our eyes are turned to You because You, God, are a gracious and compassionate King.

---

וְתֶחֱזֶינָה And may our eyes witness Your return to Zion in compassion. Blessed are You, LORD, who restores His Presence to Zion.

THANKSGIVING

*Bow at the first nine words.*

מוֹדִים We give thanks to You,
for You are the LORD our God
and God of our ancestors
for ever and all time.
You are the Rock of our lives,
Shield of our salvation
from generation to generation.
We will thank You and
declare Your praise for our lives,
which are entrusted into Your hand;
for our souls,
which are placed in Your charge;
for Your miracles
which are with us every day;
and for Your wonders and favors
at all times, evening, morning and midday.
You are good –
for Your compassion never fails.
You are compassionate –
for Your loving-kindnesses never cease.
We have always placed our hope in You.

*During the Leader's Repetition, the congregation says quietly:*

מוֹדִים We give thanks to You,
for You are the LORD our God
and God of our ancestors,
God of all flesh,
who formed us
and formed the universe.
Blessings and thanks
are due to Your great
and holy name for giving us
life and sustaining us.
May You continue
to give us life
and sustain us;
and may You gather our
exiles to Your holy courts,
to keep Your decrees,
do Your will
and serve You
with a perfect heart,
for it is for us
to give You thanks.
Blessed be God to whom
thanksgiving is due.

יִשְׂרָאֵל, לְפָנֶיךָ, לִפְלֵיטָה לְטוֹבָה, לְחֵן וּלְחֶסֶד וּלְרַחֲמִים, לְחַיִּים וּלְשָׁלוֹם בְּיוֹם

בראש חודש: רֹאשׁ הַחֹדֶשׁ / בפסח: חַג הַמַּצּוֹת / בסוכות: חַג הַסֻּכּוֹת הַזֶּה. זָכְרֵנוּ יהוה אֱלֹהֵינוּ בּוֹ לְטוֹבָה, וּפָקְדֵנוּ בוֹ לִבְרָכָה, וְהוֹשִׁיעֵנוּ בוֹ לְחַיִּים. וּבִדְבַר יְשׁוּעָה וְרַחֲמִים, חוּס וְחָנֵּנוּ וְרַחֵם עָלֵינוּ וְהוֹשִׁיעֵנוּ, כִּי אֵלֶיךָ עֵינֵינוּ, כִּי אֵל מֶלֶךְ חַנּוּן וְרַחוּם אָתָּה.

---

וְתֶחֱזֶינָה עֵינֵינוּ בְּשׁוּבְךָ לְצִיּוֹן בְּרַחֲמִים.
בָּרוּךְ אַתָּה יהוה, הַמַּחֲזִיר שְׁכִינָתוֹ לְצִיּוֹן.

הודאה

*Bow at the first five words.*

מוֹדִים אֲנַחְנוּ לָךְ
שָׁאַתָּה הוּא יהוה אֱלֹהֵינוּ
וֵאלֹהֵי אֲבוֹתֵינוּ לְעוֹלָם וָעֶד.
צוּר חַיֵּינוּ, מָגֵן יִשְׁעֵנוּ
אַתָּה הוּא לְדוֹר וָדוֹר.
נוֹדֶה לְּךָ וּנְסַפֵּר תְּהִלָּתֶךָ
עַל חַיֵּינוּ הַמְּסוּרִים בְּיָדֶךָ
וְעַל נִשְׁמוֹתֵינוּ הַפְּקוּדוֹת לָךְ
וְעַל נִסֶּיךָ שֶׁבְּכָל יוֹם עִמָּנוּ
וְעַל נִפְלְאוֹתֶיךָ וְטוֹבוֹתֶיךָ
שֶׁבְּכָל עֵת
עֶרֶב וָבֹקֶר וְצָהֳרָיִם.
הַטּוֹב, כִּי לֹא כָלוּ רַחֲמֶיךָ
וְהַמְרַחֵם, כִּי לֹא תַמּוּ חֲסָדֶיךָ
מֵעוֹלָם קִוִּינוּ לָךְ.

*During the* חזרת הש״ץ*, the* קהל *says quietly:*

מוֹדִים אֲנַחְנוּ לָךְ
שָׁאַתָּה הוּא יהוה אֱלֹהֵינוּ
וֵאלֹהֵי אֲבוֹתֵינוּ
אֱלֹהֵי כָל בָּשָׂר
יוֹצְרֵנוּ, יוֹצֵר בְּרֵאשִׁית.
בְּרָכוֹת וְהוֹדָאוֹת
לְשִׁמְךָ הַגָּדוֹל וְהַקָּדוֹשׁ
עַל שֶׁהֶחֱיִיתָנוּ וְקִיַּמְתָּנוּ.
כֵּן תְּחַיֵּנוּ וּתְקַיְּמֵנוּ
וְתֶאֱסֹף גָּלֻיּוֹתֵינוּ
לְחַצְרוֹת קָדְשֶׁךָ
לִשְׁמֹר חֻקֶּיךָ
וְלַעֲשׂוֹת רְצוֹנֶךָ וּלְעָבְדְּךָ
בְּלֵבָב שָׁלֵם
עַל שֶׁאֲנַחְנוּ מוֹדִים לָךְ.
בָּרוּךְ אֵל הַהוֹדָאוֹת.

*On Hanukka:*

עַל הַנִּסִּים [We thank You also] for the miracles, the redemption, the mighty deeds, the salvations, and the victories in battle which You performed for our ancestors in those days, at this time.

בִּימֵי מַתִּתְיָהוּ In the days of Mattityahu, son of Yohanan, the High Priest, the Hasmonean, and his sons, the wicked Greek kingdom rose up against Your people Israel to make them forget Your Torah and to force them to transgress the statutes of Your will. It was then that You in Your great compassion stood by them in the time of their distress. You championed their cause, judged their claim, and avenged their wrong. You delivered the strong into the hands of the weak, the many into the hands of the few, the impure into the hands of the pure, the wicked into the hands of the righteous, and the arrogant into the hands of those who were engaged in the study of Your Torah. You made for Yourself great and holy renown in Your world, and for Your people Israel You performed a great salvation and redemption as of this very day. Your children then entered the holiest part of Your House, cleansed Your Temple, purified Your Sanctuary, kindled lights in Your holy courts, and designated these eight days of Hanukka for giving thanks and praise to Your great name.

*Continue with "For all these things" below.*

*On Purim:*

עַל הַנִּסִּים [We thank You also] for the miracles, the redemption, the mighty deeds, the salvations, and the victories in battle which You performed for our ancestors in those days, at this time.

בִּימֵי מָרְדְּכַי In the days of Mordekhai and Esther, in Shushan the capital, the wicked Haman rose up against them and sought to destroy, slay and exterminate all the Jews, young and old, children and women, on one day, the thirteenth day of the twelfth month, which is the month of Adar, and to plunder their possessions. Then You in Your great compassion thwarted his counsel, frustrated his plans, and caused his scheme to recoil on his own head, so that they hanged him and his sons on the gallows. *Esther 3*

*Continue with "For all these things" below.*

וְעַל כֻּלָּם For all these things may Your name be blessed and exalted, our King, continually, for ever and all time.

*Between Rosh HaShana & Yom Kippur:* And write, for a good life, all the children of Your covenant.

Let all that lives thank You, Selah! and praise Your name in truth, God, our Savior and Help, Selah!

▾Blessed are You, LORD, whose name is "the Good" and to whom thanks are due.

בחנוכה:

עַל הַנִּסִּים וְעַל הַפֻּרְקָן וְעַל הַגְּבוּרוֹת וְעַל הַתְּשׁוּעוֹת וְעַל הַמִּלְחָמוֹת שֶׁעָשִׂיתָ לַאֲבוֹתֵינוּ בַּיָּמִים הָהֵם בַּזְּמַן הַזֶּה.

בִּימֵי מַתִּתְיָהוּ בֶּן יוֹחָנָן כֹּהֵן גָּדוֹל חַשְׁמוֹנַאי וּבָנָיו, כְּשֶׁעָמְדָה מַלְכוּת יָוָן הָרְשָׁעָה עַל עַמְּךָ יִשְׂרָאֵל לְהַשְׁכִּיחָם תּוֹרָתֶךָ וּלְהַעֲבִירָם מֵחֻקֵּי רְצוֹנֶךָ, וְאַתָּה בְּרַחֲמֶיךָ הָרַבִּים עָמַדְתָּ לָהֶם בְּעֵת צָרָתָם, רַבְתָּ אֶת רִיבָם, דַּנְתָּ אֶת דִּינָם, נָקַמְתָּ אֶת נִקְמָתָם, מָסַרְתָּ גִבּוֹרִים בְּיַד חַלָּשִׁים, וְרַבִּים בְּיַד מְעַטִּים, וּטְמֵאִים בְּיַד טְהוֹרִים, וּרְשָׁעִים בְּיַד צַדִּיקִים, וְזֵדִים בְּיַד עוֹסְקֵי תוֹרָתֶךָ, וּלְךָ עָשִׂיתָ שֵׁם גָּדוֹל וְקָדוֹשׁ בְּעוֹלָמֶךָ, וּלְעַמְּךָ יִשְׂרָאֵל עָשִׂיתָ תְּשׁוּעָה גְדוֹלָה וּפֻרְקָן כְּהַיּוֹם הַזֶּה. וְאַחַר כֵּן בָּאוּ בָנֶיךָ לִדְבִיר בֵּיתֶךָ, וּפִנּוּ אֶת הֵיכָלֶךָ, וְטִהֲרוּ אֶת מִקְדָּשֶׁךָ, וְהִדְלִיקוּ נֵרוֹת בְּחַצְרוֹת קָדְשֶׁךָ, וְקָבְעוּ שְׁמוֹנַת יְמֵי חֲנֻכָּה אֵלּוּ, לְהוֹדוֹת וּלְהַלֵּל לְשִׁמְךָ הַגָּדוֹל.

*Continue with* וְעַל כֻּלָּם *below.*

בפורים:

עַל הַנִּסִּים וְעַל הַפֻּרְקָן וְעַל הַגְּבוּרוֹת וְעַל הַתְּשׁוּעוֹת וְעַל הַמִּלְחָמוֹת שֶׁעָשִׂיתָ לַאֲבוֹתֵינוּ בַּיָּמִים הָהֵם בַּזְּמַן הַזֶּה.

בִּימֵי מָרְדְּכַי וְאֶסְתֵּר בְּשׁוּשַׁן הַבִּירָה, כְּשֶׁעָמַד עֲלֵיהֶם הָמָן הָרָשָׁע,
בִּקֵּשׁ לְהַשְׁמִיד לַהֲרֹג וּלְאַבֵּד אֶת־כָּל־הַיְּהוּדִים מִנַּעַר וְעַד־זָקֵן טַף אסתר ג
וְנָשִׁים בְּיוֹם אֶחָד, בִּשְׁלוֹשָׁה עָשָׂר לְחֹדֶשׁ שְׁנֵים־עָשָׂר, הוּא־חֹדֶשׁ אֲדָר,
וּשְׁלָלָם לָבוֹז: וְאַתָּה בְּרַחֲמֶיךָ הָרַבִּים הֵפַרְתָּ אֶת עֲצָתוֹ, וְקִלְקַלְתָּ אֶת
מַחֲשַׁבְתּוֹ, וַהֲשֵׁבוֹתָ לּוֹ גְּמוּלוֹ בְּרֹאשׁוֹ, וְתָלוּ אוֹתוֹ וְאֶת בָּנָיו עַל הָעֵץ.

*Continue with* וְעַל כֻּלָּם *below.*

וְעַל כֻּלָּם יִתְבָּרַךְ וְיִתְרוֹמַם שִׁמְךָ מַלְכֵּנוּ תָּמִיד לְעוֹלָם וָעֶד.

בעשרת ימי תשובה: וּכְתֹב לְחַיִּים טוֹבִים כָּל בְּנֵי בְרִיתֶךָ.

וְכֹל הַחַיִּים יוֹדוּךָ סֶּלָה, וִיהַלְלוּ אֶת שִׁמְךָ בֶּאֱמֶת הָאֵל יְשׁוּעָתֵנוּ וְעֶזְרָתֵנוּ סֶלָה.

בָּרוּךְ אַתָּה יהוה, הַטּוֹב שִׁמְךָ וּלְךָ נָאֶה לְהוֹדוֹת.

*On public fast days only, the following is said by the Leader during the Repetition of the Amida, except in a house of mourning. In Israel, on Fast Days, if Kohanim bless the congregation,* *turn to page 902. See laws 370–377.*

Our God and God of our fathers, bless us with the threefold blessing in the Torah, written by the hand of Moses Your servant and pronounced by Aaron and his sons the priests, Your holy people, as it is said:

May the LORD bless you and protect you. *Cong:* May it be Your will. *Num. 6*
May the LORD make His face shine on you and be gracious to you.
*Cong:* May it be Your will.
May the LORD turn His face toward you, and grant you peace.
*Cong:* May it be Your will.

שָׁלוֹם רָב Grant great peace to Your people Israel for ever, for You are the sovereign LORD of all peace; and may it be good in Your eyes to bless Your people Israel at every time, at every hour, with Your peace.

*On fast days:*
שִׂים שָׁלוֹם Grant peace,
goodness and blessing,
grace, loving-kindness and compassion
to us and all Israel Your people.
Bless us, our Father, all as one,
with the light of Your face,
for by the light of Your face
You have given us, LORD our God,
the Torah of life and love of kindness,
righteousness, blessing, compassion,
life and peace.
May it be good in Your eyes
to bless Your people Israel
at every time, in every hour,
with Your peace.

*Between Rosh HaShana & Yom Kippur:* In the book of life, blessing, peace and prosperity,
may we and all Your people the house of Israel
be remembered and written before You
for a good life, and for peace.*

Blessed are You, LORD, who blesses His people Israel with peace.

**Between Rosh HaShana and Yom Kippur in the Diaspora, many end the blessing:*
Blessed are You, LORD, who makes peace.

*The following verse concludes the Leader's Repetition of the Amida. Some also say it here as part of the silent Amida.* *See law 368.*

May the words of my mouth and the meditation of my heart *Ps. 19*
find favor before You, LORD, my Rock and Redeemer.

*On public fast days only, the following is said by the* שליח ציבור *during the* חזרת הש״ץ *except in a house of mourning. In* ארץ ישראל*, on Fast Days, if* כהנים *say* ברכת כהנים *turn to page 903. See laws 370–377.*

אֱלֹהֵינוּ וֵאלֹהֵי אֲבוֹתֵינוּ, בָּרְכֵנוּ בַּבְּרָכָה הַמְשֻׁלֶּשֶׁת בַּתּוֹרָה, הַכְּתוּבָה עַל יְדֵי מֹשֶׁה עַבְדֶּךָ, הָאֲמוּרָה מִפִּי אַהֲרֹן וּבָנָיו כֹּהֲנִים עַם קְדוֹשֶׁיךָ, כָּאָמוּר

יְבָרֶכְךָ יהוה וְיִשְׁמְרֶךָ: קהל: כֵּן יְהִי רָצוֹן במדבר ו

יָאֵר יהוה פָּנָיו אֵלֶיךָ וִיחֻנֶּךָּ: קהל: כֵּן יְהִי רָצוֹן

יִשָּׂא יהוה פָּנָיו אֵלֶיךָ וְיָשֵׂם לְךָ שָׁלוֹם: קהל: כֵּן יְהִי רָצוֹן

ברכת שלום

שָׁלוֹם רָב עַל יִשְׂרָאֵל
עַמְּךָ תָּשִׂים לְעוֹלָם
כִּי אַתָּה הוּא
מֶלֶךְ אָדוֹן לְכָל הַשָּׁלוֹם.
וְטוֹב בְּעֵינֶיךָ
לְבָרֵךְ אֶת עַמְּךָ יִשְׂרָאֵל
בְּכָל עֵת וּבְכָל שָׁעָה
בִּשְׁלוֹמֶךָ.

*On fast days:*

שִׂים שָׁלוֹם טוֹבָה וּבְרָכָה
חֵן וָחֶסֶד וְרַחֲמִים
עָלֵינוּ וְעַל כָּל יִשְׂרָאֵל עַמֶּךָ.
בָּרְכֵנוּ אָבִינוּ כֻּלָּנוּ כְּאֶחָד בְּאוֹר פָּנֶיךָ
כִּי בְאוֹר פָּנֶיךָ נָתַתָּ לָּנוּ יהוה אֱלֹהֵינוּ
תּוֹרַת חַיִּים וְאַהֲבַת חֶסֶד
וּצְדָקָה וּבְרָכָה וְרַחֲמִים וְחַיִּים וְשָׁלוֹם.
וְטוֹב בְּעֵינֶיךָ לְבָרֵךְ אֶת עַמְּךָ יִשְׂרָאֵל
בְּכָל עֵת וּבְכָל שָׁעָה בִּשְׁלוֹמֶךָ.

בעשרת ימי תשובה: בְּסֵפֶר חַיִּים, בְּרָכָה וְשָׁלוֹם, וּפַרְנָסָה טוֹבָה
נִזָּכֵר וְנִכָּתֵב לְפָנֶיךָ, אֲנַחְנוּ וְכָל עַמְּךָ בֵּית יִשְׂרָאֵל
לְחַיִּים טוֹבִים וּלְשָׁלוֹם.*

בָּרוּךְ אַתָּה יהוה, הַמְבָרֵךְ אֶת עַמּוֹ יִשְׂרָאֵל בַּשָּׁלוֹם.

**During the* עשרת ימי תשובה *in* חוץ לארץ*, many end the blessing:*

בָּרוּךְ אַתָּה יהוה, עוֹשֵׂה הַשָּׁלוֹם.

*The following verse concludes the* חזרת הש״ץ.
*Some also say it here as part of the silent* עמידה. *See law 368.*

יִהְיוּ לְרָצוֹן אִמְרֵי־פִי וְהֶגְיוֹן לִבִּי לְפָנֶיךָ, יהוה צוּרִי וְגֹאֲלִי: תהלים יט

אֱלֹהַי My God, Berakhot 17a
guard my tongue from evil and my lips from deceitful speech.
To those who curse me, let my soul be silent;
may my soul be to all like the dust.
Open my heart to Your Torah and let my soul
pursue Your commandments. As for all who plan evil against me,
swiftly thwart their counsel and frustrate their plans.
Act for the sake of Your name; act for the sake of Your right hand;
act for the sake of Your holiness; act for the sake of Your Torah.
That Your beloved ones may be delivered, Ps. 60
save with Your right hand and answer me.
*May the words of my mouth and the meditation of my heart Ps. 19
find favor before You, Lord, my Rock and Redeemer.

*Bow, take three steps back, then bow, first left, then right, then center, while saying:*

May He who makes peace in His high places,
make peace for us and all Israel – and say: Amen.

יְהִי רָצוֹן May it be Your will, Lord our God and God of our ancestors,
that the Temple be rebuilt speedily in our days,
and grant us a share in Your Torah.
And there we will serve You with reverence,
as in the days of old and as in former years.
Then the offering of Judah and Jerusalem will be pleasing to the Lord Mal. 3
as in the days of old and as in former years.

*On days when Taḥanun is not said, the Leader says Full Kaddish on page 308.*

---

**A person undertaking a personal fast says the following at Minḥa before the fast:*

Master of all worlds, I hereby take upon myself before You a voluntary fast tomorrow. May it be Your will, Lord my God and God of my ancestors, that You accept me in love and favor, that my prayer may come before You, and that You may answer my entreaty in Your great compassion, for You hear the prayer of every mouth.

*On the afternoon of the fast, the following is said:*

Master of all worlds, it is revealed and known to You that when the Temple stood, a person who sinned would offer a sacrifice, of which were offered only the fat and blood, yet You in Your great compassion granted atonement. Now I have fasted, and my fat and blood have been diminished. May it be Your will that this diminution today of my fat and blood be as if I had offered them before You on the altar, and may You show me favor.

ברכות יז.

אֱלֹהַי
נְצֹר לְשׁוֹנִי מֵרָע וּשְׂפָתַי מִדַּבֵּר מִרְמָה
וְלִמְקַלְלַי נַפְשִׁי תִדֹּם, וְנַפְשִׁי כֶּעָפָר לַכֹּל תִּהְיֶה.
פְּתַח לִבִּי בְּתוֹרָתֶךָ, וּבְמִצְוֹתֶיךָ תִּרְדֹּף נַפְשִׁי.
וְכָל הַחוֹשְׁבִים עָלַי רָעָה, מְהֵרָה הָפֵר עֲצָתָם וְקַלְקֵל מַחֲשַׁבְתָּם.
עֲשֵׂה לְמַעַן שְׁמֶךָ, עֲשֵׂה לְמַעַן יְמִינֶךָ
עֲשֵׂה לְמַעַן קְדֻשָּׁתֶךָ, עֲשֵׂה לְמַעַן תּוֹרָתֶךָ.
לְמַעַן יֵחָלְצוּן יְדִידֶיךָ, הוֹשִׁיעָה יְמִינְךָ וַעֲנֵנִי: תהלים ס
*יִהְיוּ לְרָצוֹן אִמְרֵי־פִי וְהֶגְיוֹן לִבִּי לְפָנֶיךָ, יהוה צוּרִי וְגֹאֲלִי: תהלים יט

*Bow, take three steps back, then bow, first left, then right, then center, while saying:*

עֹשֶׂה שָׁלוֹם/ בעשרת ימי תשובה: הַשָּׁלוֹם/ בִּמְרוֹמָיו
הוּא יַעֲשֶׂה שָׁלוֹם עָלֵינוּ וְעַל כָּל יִשְׂרָאֵל, וְאִמְרוּ אָמֵן.

יְהִי רָצוֹן מִלְּפָנֶיךָ יהוה אֱלֹהֵינוּ וֵאלֹהֵי אֲבוֹתֵינוּ
שֶׁיִּבָּנֶה בֵּית הַמִּקְדָּשׁ בִּמְהֵרָה בְיָמֵינוּ, וְתֵן חֶלְקֵנוּ בְּתוֹרָתֶךָ
וְשָׁם נַעֲבָדְךָ בְּיִרְאָה כִּימֵי עוֹלָם וּכְשָׁנִים קַדְמֹנִיּוֹת.
וְעָרְבָה לַיהוה מִנְחַת יְהוּדָה וִירוּשָׁלָםִ כִּימֵי עוֹלָם וּכְשָׁנִים קַדְמֹנִיּוֹת: מלאכי ג

*On days when* תחנון *is not said, the* שליח ציבור *says* קדיש שלם *on page 309.*

---

**A person undertaking a personal fast says the following at* מנחה *before the fast:*

רִבּוֹן כָּל הָעוֹלָמִים, הֲרֵי אֲנִי לְפָנֶיךָ בְּתַעֲנִית נְדָבָה לְמָחָר. יְהִי רָצוֹן מִלְּפָנֶיךָ יהוה אֱלֹהַי וֵאלֹהֵי אֲבוֹתַי, שֶׁתְּקַבְּלֵנִי בְּאַהֲבָה וּבְרָצוֹן, וְתָבֹא לְפָנֶיךָ תְּפִלָּתִי, וְתַעֲנֶה עֲתִירָתִי בְּרַחֲמֶיךָ הָרַבִּים, כִּי אַתָּה שׁוֹמֵעַ תְּפִלַּת כָּל־פֶּה.

*On the afternoon of the fast, the following is said:*

רִבּוֹן כָּל הָעוֹלָמִים, גָּלוּי וְיָדוּעַ לְפָנֶיךָ, בִּזְמַן שֶׁבֵּית הַמִּקְדָּשׁ קַיָּם, אָדָם חוֹטֵא וּמַקְרִיב קָרְבָּן, וְאֵין מַקְרִיבִין מִמֶּנּוּ אֶלָּא חֶלְבּוֹ וְדָמוֹ, וְאַתָּה בְּרַחֲמֶיךָ הָרַבִּים מְכַפֵּר. וְעַכְשָׁו יָשַׁבְתִּי בְּתַעֲנִית, וְנִתְמַעֵט חֶלְבִּי וְדָמִי. יְהִי רָצוֹן מִלְּפָנֶיךָ, שֶׁיְּהֵא מִעוּט חֶלְבִּי וְדָמִי שֶׁנִּתְמַעֵט הַיּוֹם, כְּאִלּוּ הִקְרַבְתִּיו עַל־גַּבֵּי הַמִּזְבֵּחַ, וְתִרְצֵנִי.

---

*Between Rosh HaShana and Yom Kippur and on fast days, except days when Taḥanun is not said (see list below), Avinu Malkenu (on page 202) is said here.*

## TAḤANUN

*Taḥanun is not said on Erev Shabbat and Erev Yom Tov. It is also not said on the following days: Rosh Ḥodesh, Ḥanukka, Tu BiShvat, the 14th and 15th of Adar I, Purim and Shushan Purim, Yom HaAtzma'ut, Lag BaOmer, Yom Yerushalayim, Tisha B'Av, Tu B'Av, and the preceding afternoons, the month of Nisan, the 14th of Iyar (Pesaḥ Sheni), from Rosh Ḥodesh Sivan through the day after Shavuot (in Israel through 12th of Sivan), and from Erev Yom Kippur through the day after Simḥat Torah (in Israel through Rosh Ḥodesh Marḥeshvan). Taḥanun is also not said: on the occasion of a Brit Mila, either where the brit will take place or where the father, Sandak or Mohel are present; if a groom is present (and some say, a bride) on the day of his wedding or during the week of Sheva Berakhot; in a house of mourning.*

### LOWERING THE HEAD

*Say while sitting; in the presence of a Torah scroll say until "in sudden shame," leaning forward and resting one's head on the left arm.*

וַיֹּאמֶר דָּוִד David said to Gad, "I am in great distress. *II Sam. 24*
Let us fall into God's hand, for His mercy is great;
but do not let me fall into the hand of man."

Compassionate and gracious One, I have sinned before You.
Lord, full of compassion,
have compassion on me and accept my pleas.

Lord, do not rebuke me in Your anger or chastise me in Your wrath. *Ps. 6*
Be gracious to me, Lord, for I am weak.
Heal me, Lord, for my bones are in agony.
My soul is in anguish, and You, O Lord – how long?
Turn, Lord, set my soul free; save me for the sake of Your love.
For no one remembers You when he is dead.
Who can praise You from the grave? I am weary with my sighing.
Every night I drench my bed, I soak my couch with my tears.
My eye grows dim from grief, worn out because of all my foes.
Leave me, all you evildoers,
for the Lord has heard the sound of my weeping.
The Lord has heard my pleas. The Lord will accept my prayer.
All my enemies will be shamed and utterly dismayed.
They will turn back in sudden shame.

*Sit upright.*

*During the* עשרת ימי תשובה *and on fast days, except days when* תחנון *is not said (see list below),* אבינו מלכנו *(on page 203) is said here.*

# סדר תחנון

תחנון *is not said on* ערב שבת *and* ערב יום טוב*. It is also not said on the following days:* ראש חודש, חנוכה, ט״ו בשבט*, the 14th and 15th of* אדר א׳, פורים *and* שושן פורים, יום העצמאות, ל״ג בעומר, יום ירושלים, תשעה באב, ט״ו באב*, and the preceding afternoons, the month of* ניסן*, the 14th of* אייר *(*פסח שני*), from* ראש חודש סיון *through the day after* שבועות *(in* ארץ ישראל *through* י״ב סיון*), and from* ערב יום כיפור *through the day after* שמחת תורה *(in* ארץ ישראל *through* ראש חודש מרחשון*).* תחנון *is also not said: on the occasion of a* ברית מילה*, either where the* ברית *will take place or where the father,* סנדק *or* מוהל *are present; if a* חתן *is present (and some say, a* כלה*) on the day of his wedding or during the week of* שבע ברכות*; in a house of mourning.*

## נפילת אפיים

*Say while sitting; in the presence of a* ספר תורה *say until* יֵבֹשׁוּ רָגַע*, leaning forward and resting one's head on the left arm.*

וַיֹּאמֶר דָּוִד אֶל־גָּד, צַר־לִי מְאֹד שמואל ב׳ כד
נִפְּלָה־נָּא בְיַד־יהוה, כִּי רַבִּים רַחֲמָו, וּבְיַד־אָדָם אַל־אֶפֹּלָה:

רַחוּם וְחַנּוּן, חָטָאתִי לְפָנֶיךָ.
יהוה מָלֵא רַחֲמִים, רַחֵם עָלַי וְקַבֵּל תַּחֲנוּנָי.

יהוה, אַל־בְּאַפְּךָ תוֹכִיחֵנִי, וְאַל־בַּחֲמָתְךָ תְיַסְּרֵנִי: תהלים ו
חָנֵּנִי יהוה, כִּי אֻמְלַל אָנִי, רְפָאֵנִי יהוה, כִּי נִבְהֲלוּ עֲצָמָי:
וְנַפְשִׁי נִבְהֲלָה מְאֹד, וְאַתָּ יהוה, עַד־מָתָי:
שׁוּבָה יהוה, חַלְּצָה נַפְשִׁי, הוֹשִׁיעֵנִי לְמַעַן חַסְדֶּךָ:
כִּי אֵין בַּמָּוֶת זִכְרֶךָ, בִּשְׁאוֹל מִי יוֹדֶה־לָּךְ:
יָגַעְתִּי בְּאַנְחָתִי, אַשְׂחֶה בְכָל־לַיְלָה מִטָּתִי, בְּדִמְעָתִי עַרְשִׂי אַמְסֶה:
עָשְׁשָׁה מִכַּעַס עֵינִי, עָתְקָה בְּכָל־צוֹרְרָי:
סוּרוּ מִמֶּנִּי כָּל־פֹּעֲלֵי אָוֶן, כִּי־שָׁמַע יהוה קוֹל בִּכְיִי:
שָׁמַע יהוה תְּחִנָּתִי, יהוה תְּפִלָּתִי יִקָּח:
יֵבֹשׁוּ וְיִבָּהֲלוּ מְאֹד כָּל־אֹיְבָי, יָשֻׁבוּ יֵבֹשׁוּ רָגַע:

*Sit upright.*

שׁוֹמֵר יִשְׂרָאֵל Guardian of Israel,
guard the remnant of Israel,
and let not Israel perish, who declare, "Listen, Israel."

Guardian of a unique nation, guard the remnant of a unique people,
and let not that unique nation perish, who proclaim the unity of
Your name [saying], "The LORD is our God, the LORD is One."

Guardian of a holy nation, guard the remnant of that holy people,
and let not the holy nation perish, who three times repeat
the threefold declaration of holiness to the Holy One.

You who are conciliated by calls for compassion and placated by pleas,
be conciliated and placated toward an afflicted generation,
for there is no other help.

Our Father, our King, be gracious to us and answer us,
though we have no worthy deeds;
act with us in charity and loving-kindness and save us.

*Stand at ▲.*

וַאֲנַחְנוּ We do not know ▲what to do, but our eyes are turned to You. *II Chr. 12*
Remember, LORD, Your compassion and loving-kindness, *Ps. 25*
for they are everlasting.
May Your loving-kindness, LORD, be with us, *Ps. 33*
for we have put our hope in You.
Do not hold against us the sins of those who came before us. *Ps. 79*
May Your mercies meet us swiftly,
for we have been brought very low.
Be gracious to us, LORD, be gracious to us, *Ps. 123*
for we are sated with contempt.
In wrath, remember mercy. *Hab. 3*
He knows our nature; He remembers that we are dust. *Ps. 103*
► Help us, God of our salvation, *Ps. 79*
for the sake of the glory of Your name.
Save us and grant atonement
for our sins for Your name's sake.

שׁוֹמֵר יִשְׂרָאֵל, שְׁמֹר שְׁאֵרִית יִשְׂרָאֵל, וְאַל יֹאבַד יִשְׂרָאֵל
הָאוֹמְרִים שְׁמַע יִשְׂרָאֵל.

שׁוֹמֵר גּוֹי אֶחָד, שְׁמֹר שְׁאֵרִית עַם אֶחָד, וְאַל יֹאבַד גּוֹי אֶחָד
הַמְיַחֲדִים שִׁמְךָ, יהוה אֱלֹהֵינוּ יהוה אֶחָד.

שׁוֹמֵר גּוֹי קָדוֹשׁ, שְׁמֹר שְׁאֵרִית עַם קָדוֹשׁ, וְאַל יֹאבַד גּוֹי קָדוֹשׁ
הַמְשַׁלְּשִׁים בְּשָׁלֹשׁ קְדֻשּׁוֹת לְקָדוֹשׁ.

מִתְרַצֶּה בְּרַחֲמִים וּמִתְפַּיֵּס בְּתַחֲנוּנִים, הִתְרַצֵּה וְהִתְפַּיֵּס לְדוֹר עָנִי
כִּי אֵין עוֹזֵר.

אָבִינוּ מַלְכֵּנוּ, חָנֵּנוּ וַעֲנֵנוּ, כִּי אֵין בָּנוּ מַעֲשִׂים
עֲשֵׂה עִמָּנוּ צְדָקָה וָחֶסֶד וְהוֹשִׁיעֵנוּ.

*Stand at* ▸.

דברי הימים ב׳ יב — וַאֲנַחְנוּ לֹא נֵדַע ׳מַה־נַּעֲשֶׂה, כִּי עָלֶיךָ עֵינֵינוּ:
תהלים כה — זְכֹר־רַחֲמֶיךָ יהוה וַחֲסָדֶיךָ, כִּי מֵעוֹלָם הֵמָּה:
תהלים לג — יְהִי־חַסְדְּךָ יהוה עָלֵינוּ, כַּאֲשֶׁר יִחַלְנוּ לָךְ:
תהלים עט — אַל־תִּזְכָּר־לָנוּ עֲוֹנֹת רִאשֹׁנִים
מַהֵר יְקַדְּמוּנוּ רַחֲמֶיךָ, כִּי דַלּוֹנוּ מְאֹד:
תהלים קכג — חָנֵּנוּ יהוה חָנֵּנוּ, כִּי־רַב שָׂבַעְנוּ בוּז:
חבקוק ג — בְּרֹגֶז רַחֵם תִּזְכּוֹר:
תהלים קג — כִּי־הוּא יָדַע יִצְרֵנוּ, זָכוּר כִּי־עָפָר אֲנָחְנוּ:
תהלים עט — ◂ עָזְרֵנוּ אֱלֹהֵי יִשְׁעֵנוּ עַל־דְּבַר כְּבוֹד־שְׁמֶךָ
וְהַצִּילֵנוּ וְכַפֵּר עַל־חַטֹּאתֵינוּ לְמַעַן שְׁמֶךָ:

FULL KADDISH

*Leader:* יִתְגַּדַּל Magnified and sanctified
may His great name be,
in the world He created by His will.
May He establish His kingdom
in your lifetime and in your days,
and in the lifetime of all the house of Israel,
swiftly and soon –
and say: Amen.

*All:* May His great name be blessed
for ever and all time.

*Leader:* Blessed and praised,
glorified and exalted,
raised and honored,
uplifted and lauded be
the name of the Holy One,
blessed be He,
beyond any blessing,
song, praise and consolation
uttered in the world –
and say: Amen.

May the prayers and pleas of all Israel
be accepted by their Father in heaven –
and say: Amen.

May there be great peace from heaven,
and life for us and all Israel –
and say: Amen.

*Bow, take three steps back, as if taking leave of the Divine Presence, then bow, first left, then right, then center, while saying:*

May He who makes peace in His high places,
make peace for us and all Israel –
and say: Amen.

## קדיש שלם

ש״ץ: יִתְגַּדַּל וְיִתְקַדַּשׁ שְׁמֵהּ רַבָּא (קהל: אָמֵן)
בְּעָלְמָא דִּי בְרָא כִרְעוּתֵהּ
וְיַמְלִיךְ מַלְכוּתֵהּ
בְּחַיֵּיכוֹן וּבְיוֹמֵיכוֹן וּבְחַיֵּי דְכָל בֵּית יִשְׂרָאֵל
בַּעֲגָלָא וּבִזְמַן קָרִיב
וְאִמְרוּ אָמֵן. (קהל: אָמֵן)

קהל וש״ץ: יְהֵא שְׁמֵהּ רַבָּא מְבָרַךְ לְעָלַם וּלְעָלְמֵי עָלְמַיָּא.

ש״ץ: יִתְבָּרַךְ וְיִשְׁתַּבַּח וְיִתְפָּאַר
וְיִתְרוֹמַם וְיִתְנַשֵּׂא וְיִתְהַדָּר וְיִתְעַלֶּה וְיִתְהַלָּל
שְׁמֵהּ דְּקֻדְשָׁא בְּרִיךְ הוּא (קהל: בְּרִיךְ הוּא)
לְעֵלָּא מִן כָּל בִּרְכָתָא/ בעשרת ימי תשובה: לְעֵלָּא לְעֵלָּא מִכָּל בִּרְכָתָא/
וְשִׁירָתָא, תֻּשְׁבְּחָתָא וְנֶחֱמָתָא
דַּאֲמִירָן בְּעָלְמָא
וְאִמְרוּ אָמֵן. (קהל: אָמֵן)

תִּתְקַבַּל צְלוֹתְהוֹן וּבָעוּתְהוֹן דְּכָל יִשְׂרָאֵל
קֳדָם אֲבוּהוֹן דִּי בִשְׁמַיָּא
וְאִמְרוּ אָמֵן. (קהל: אָמֵן)

יְהֵא שְׁלָמָא רַבָּא מִן שְׁמַיָּא
וְחַיִּים, עָלֵינוּ וְעַל כָּל יִשְׂרָאֵל
וְאִמְרוּ אָמֵן. (קהל: אָמֵן)

*Bow, take three steps back, as if taking leave of the Divine Presence, then bow, first left, then right, then center, while saying:*

עֹשֶׂה שָׁלוֹם/ בעשרת ימי תשובה: הַשָּׁלוֹם/ בִּמְרוֹמָיו
הוּא יַעֲשֶׂה שָׁלוֹם עָלֵינוּ וְעַל כָּל יִשְׂרָאֵל
וְאִמְרוּ אָמֵן. (קהל: אָמֵן)

*Stand while saying Aleinu. Bow at* ▾.

עָלֵינוּ It is our duty to praise the Master of all,
and ascribe greatness to the Author of creation,
who has not made us like the nations of the lands
nor placed us like the families of the earth;
who has not made our portion like theirs,
nor our destiny like all their multitudes.
(For they worship vanity and emptiness,
and pray to a god who cannot save.)
▾But we bow in worship and thank the Supreme King of kings,
the Holy One, blessed be He,
who extends the heavens and establishes the earth,
whose throne of glory is in the heavens above,
and whose power's Presence is in the highest of heights.
He is our God; there is no other.
Truly He is our King, there is none else,
as it is written in His Torah:
"You shall know and take to heart this day that the LORD is God, *Deut. 4*
in heaven above and on earth below. There is no other."

Therefore, we place our hope in You, LORD our God,
that we may soon see the glory of Your power,
when You will remove abominations from the earth,
and idols will be utterly destroyed,
when the world will be perfected under the sovereignty of the Almighty,
when all humanity will call on Your name,
to turn all the earth's wicked toward You.
All the world's inhabitants will realize and know
that to You every knee must bow and every tongue swear loyalty.
Before You, LORD our God, they will kneel and bow down
and give honor to Your glorious name.
They will all accept the yoke of Your kingdom,
and You will reign over them soon and for ever.
For the kingdom is Yours, and to all eternity You will reign in glory,
as it is written in Your Torah: "The LORD will reign for ever and ever." *Ex. 15*
▸ And it is said: "Then the LORD shall be King over all the earth; *Zech. 14*
on that day the LORD shall be One and His name One."

*Stand while saying* עָלֵינוּ*. Bow at* ▾.

עָלֵינוּ לְשַׁבֵּחַ לַאֲדוֹן הַכֹּל, לָתֵת גְּדֻלָּה לְיוֹצֵר בְּרֵאשִׁית
שֶׁלֹּא עָשָׂנוּ כְּגוֹיֵי הָאֲרָצוֹת, וְלֹא שָׂמָנוּ כְּמִשְׁפְּחוֹת הָאֲדָמָה
שֶׁלֹּא שָׂם חֶלְקֵנוּ כָּהֶם וְגוֹרָלֵנוּ כְּכָל הֲמוֹנָם.
(שֶׁהֵם מִשְׁתַּחֲוִים לְהֶבֶל וָרִיק וּמִתְפַּלְלִים אֶל אֵל לֹא יוֹשִׁיעַ.)
▾וַאֲנַחְנוּ כּוֹרְעִים וּמִשְׁתַּחֲוִים וּמוֹדִים
לִפְנֵי מֶלֶךְ מַלְכֵי הַמְּלָכִים, הַקָּדוֹשׁ בָּרוּךְ הוּא
שֶׁהוּא נוֹטֶה שָׁמַיִם וְיוֹסֵד אָרֶץ
וּמוֹשַׁב יְקָרוֹ בַּשָּׁמַיִם מִמַּעַל, וּשְׁכִינַת עֻזּוֹ בְּגָבְהֵי מְרוֹמִים.
הוּא אֱלֹהֵינוּ, אֵין עוֹד.
אֱמֶת מַלְכֵּנוּ, אֶפֶס זוּלָתוֹ
כַּכָּתוּב בְּתוֹרָתוֹ, וְיָדַעְתָּ הַיּוֹם וַהֲשֵׁבֹתָ אֶל־לְבָבֶךָ דברים ד
כִּי יהוה הוּא הָאֱלֹהִים בַּשָּׁמַיִם מִמַּעַל וְעַל־הָאָרֶץ מִתָּחַת, אֵין עוֹד:

עַל כֵּן נְקַוֶּה לְּךָ יהוה אֱלֹהֵינוּ, לִרְאוֹת מְהֵרָה בְּתִפְאֶרֶת עֻזֶּךָ
לְהַעֲבִיר גִּלּוּלִים מִן הָאָרֶץ, וְהָאֱלִילִים כָּרוֹת יִכָּרֵתוּן
לְתַקֵּן עוֹלָם בְּמַלְכוּת שַׁדַּי.
וְכָל בְּנֵי בָשָׂר יִקְרְאוּ בִשְׁמֶךָ לְהַפְנוֹת אֵלֶיךָ כָּל רִשְׁעֵי אָרֶץ.
יַכִּירוּ וְיֵדְעוּ כָּל יוֹשְׁבֵי תֵבֵל
כִּי לְךָ תִּכְרַע כָּל בֶּרֶךְ, תִּשָּׁבַע כָּל לָשׁוֹן.
לְפָנֶיךָ יהוה אֱלֹהֵינוּ יִכְרְעוּ וְיִפֹּלוּ, וְלִכְבוֹד שִׁמְךָ יְקָר יִתֵּנוּ
וִיקַבְּלוּ כֻלָּם אֶת עֹל מַלְכוּתֶךָ
וְתִמְלֹךְ עֲלֵיהֶם מְהֵרָה לְעוֹלָם וָעֶד.
כִּי הַמַּלְכוּת שֶׁלְּךָ הִיא וּלְעוֹלְמֵי עַד תִּמְלֹךְ בְּכָבוֹד
כַּכָּתוּב בְּתוֹרָתֶךָ, יהוה יִמְלֹךְ לְעֹלָם וָעֶד: שמות טו
◂ וְנֶאֱמַר, וְהָיָה יהוה לְמֶלֶךְ עַל־כָּל־הָאָרֶץ זכריה יד
בַּיּוֹם הַהוּא יִהְיֶה יהוה אֶחָד וּשְׁמוֹ אֶחָד:

*Some add:*

Have no fear of sudden terror or of the ruin when it overtakes the wicked. *Prov. 3*
Devise your strategy, but it will be thwarted; propose your plan, *Is. 8*
but it will not stand, for God is with us.
When you grow old, I will still be the same. *Is. 46*
When your hair turns gray, I will still carry you.
I made you, I will bear you, I will carry you, and I will rescue you.

## MOURNER'S KADDISH

*The following prayer, said by mourners, requires the presence of a minyan. A transliteration can be found on page 1320.*

*Mourner:* יִתְגַּדַּל Magnified and sanctified may His great name be,
in the world He created by His will.
May He establish His kingdom
in your lifetime and in your days,
and in the lifetime of all the house of Israel,
swiftly and soon –
and say: Amen.

*All:* May His great name be blessed for ever and all time.

*Mourner:* Blessed and praised, glorified and exalted,
raised and honored, uplifted and lauded
be the name of the Holy One,
blessed be He,
beyond any blessing,
song, praise and consolation
uttered in the world –
and say: Amen.

May there be great peace from heaven,
and life for us and all Israel –
and say: Amen.

*Bow, take three steps back, as if taking leave of the Divine Presence, then bow, first left, then right, then center, while saying:*

May He who makes peace in His high places,
make peace for us and all Israel –
and say: Amen.

*Some add:*

אַל־תִּירָא מִפַּחַד פִּתְאֹם וּמִשֹּׁאַת רְשָׁעִים כִּי תָבֹא: משלי ג

עֻצוּ עֵצָה וְתֻפָר, דַּבְּרוּ דָבָר וְלֹא יָקוּם, כִּי עִמָּנוּ אֵל: ישעיה ח

וְעַד־זִקְנָה אֲנִי הוּא, וְעַד־שֵׂיבָה אֲנִי אֶסְבֹּל ישעיה מו

אֲנִי עָשִׂיתִי וַאֲנִי אֶשָּׂא וַאֲנִי אֶסְבֹּל וַאֲמַלֵּט:

## קדיש יתום

*The following prayer, said by mourners, requires the presence of a* מנין*.*
*A transliteration can be found on page 1320.*

אבל: יִתְגַּדַּל וְיִתְקַדַּשׁ שְׁמֵהּ רַבָּא (קהל: אָמֵן)
בְּעָלְמָא דִּי בְרָא כִרְעוּתֵהּ
וְיַמְלִיךְ מַלְכוּתֵהּ
בְּחַיֵּיכוֹן וּבְיוֹמֵיכוֹן וּבְחַיֵּי דְכָל בֵּית יִשְׂרָאֵל
בַּעֲגָלָא וּבִזְמַן קָרִיב, וְאִמְרוּ אָמֵן. (קהל: אָמֵן)

קהל ואבל: יְהֵא שְׁמֵהּ רַבָּא מְבָרַךְ לְעָלַם וּלְעָלְמֵי עָלְמַיָּא.

אבל: יִתְבָּרַךְ וְיִשְׁתַּבַּח וְיִתְפָּאַר
וְיִתְרוֹמַם וְיִתְנַשֵּׂא וְיִתְהַדָּר וְיִתְעַלֶּה וְיִתְהַלָּל
שְׁמֵהּ דְּקֻדְשָׁא בְּרִיךְ הוּא (קהל: בְּרִיךְ הוּא)
לְעֵלָּא מִן כָּל בִּרְכָתָא / בעשרת ימי תשובה: לְעֵלָּא לְעֵלָּא מִכָּל בִּרְכָתָא/
וְשִׁירָתָא, תֻּשְׁבְּחָתָא וְנֶחֱמָתָא
דַּאֲמִירָן בְּעָלְמָא, וְאִמְרוּ אָמֵן. (קהל: אָמֵן)

יְהֵא שְׁלָמָא רַבָּא מִן שְׁמַיָּא
וְחַיִּים, עָלֵינוּ וְעַל כָּל יִשְׂרָאֵל, וְאִמְרוּ אָמֵן. (קהל: אָמֵן)

*Bow, take three steps back, as if taking leave of the Divine Presence, then bow, first left, then right, then center, while saying:*

עֹשֶׂה שָׁלוֹם/ בעשרת ימי תשובה: הַשָּׁלוֹם/ בִּמְרוֹמָיו
הוּא יַעֲשֶׂה שָׁלוֹם
עָלֵינוּ וְעַל כָּל יִשְׂרָאֵל, וְאִמְרוּ אָמֵן. (קהל: אָמֵן)

# Ma'ariv for Weekdays

*On Motza'ei Shabbat some have the custom to sing Psalm 144 and Psalm 67 before the Ma'ariv Service (page 750).*

וְהוּא רַחוּם He is compassionate. *Ps. 78*
He forgives iniquity and does not destroy.
Repeatedly He suppresses His anger, not rousing His full wrath.
Lord, save! May the King, answer us on the day we call. *Ps. 20*

## BLESSINGS OF THE SHEMA

*The Leader says the following, bowing at "Bless," standing straight at "the Lord"; the congregation, followed by the Leader, responds, bowing at "Bless," standing straight at "the Lord":*

*Leader:* BLESS
the Lord, the blessed One.

*Congregation:* Bless the Lord, the blessed One,
for ever and all time.

*Leader:* Bless the Lord, the blessed One,
for ever and all time.

---

spontaneously from the walls of the heart. Obligation threatens spontaneity. Prayer that is free of all imposition is referred to as *"pegi'ah,"* "a happening." The verse in the Torah which recounts how Jacob our Father initiated the evening prayer reads, "He happened upon the place" (*"Vayifga' ba-makom"*).[3]

There is an additional reason that the keyword *"pegi'ah"* is appropriate for the evening prayer. The evening prayer is conducive to sudden, unexpected incursions of *ru'aḥ ha-kodesh* (divine inspiration) and even *nevu'ah*

---

evening prayer with its voluntary character (*nedavah*) is a throwback to the period of the Patriarchs before the giving of the Torah on Mount Sinai, when worship was strictly voluntary. Specifically Abraham is referred to as *"nadiv,"* a volunteer; see *b. Hagigah* 3a. (Ibid., p. 328.)

3. Genesis 28:11; *b. Berakhot* 26b. *OR*, vol. 1, p. 409.

# מעריב לחול

*On* מוצאי שבת *some have the custom to sing* לְדָוִד, בָּרוּךְ יהוה צוּרִי
*and* לַמְנַצֵּחַ בִּנְגִינֹת מִזְמוֹר שִׁיר *before* תפילת מעריב *(page 751).*

(page 751)

וְהוּא רַחוּם, יְכַפֵּר עָוֹן וְלֹא־יַשְׁחִית תהלים עח
וְהִרְבָּה לְהָשִׁיב אַפּוֹ, וְלֹא־יָעִיר כָּל־חֲמָתוֹ:
יהוה הוֹשִׁיעָה, הַמֶּלֶךְ יַעֲנֵנוּ בְיוֹם־קָרְאֵנוּ: תהלים כ

## קריאת שמע וברכותיה

*The* שליח ציבור *says the following, bowing at* בָּרְכוּ*, standing straight at* ה'*; the* קהל*,*
*followed by the* שליח ציבור*, responds, bowing at* בָּרוּךְ*, standing straight at* ה'*:*

ש״ץ: בָּרְכוּ
אֶת יהוה הַמְבֹרָךְ.

קהל: בָּרוּךְ יהוה הַמְבֹרָךְ לְעוֹלָם וָעֶד.

ש״ץ: בָּרוּךְ יהוה הַמְבֹרָךְ לְעוֹלָם וָעֶד.

---

INTRODUCTION TO *MA'ARIV* / EVENING SERVICE

On the one hand, the evening prayer is placed at a disadvantage. The Halakhah decided that *"Tefillat 'arvit – reshut"*; the evening prayer (as opposed to the morning and afternoon prayers) is optional not obligatory.[1] On the other hand, precisely its optional character gives the evening prayer an advantage over the other two prayers.[2] Essentially, prayer must flow

1. *y. Berakhot* 4:1; *Ta'anit* 4:1; *b. Berakhot* 27b; Maimonides, *MT, Hil. Tefillah* 1:6; 3:6, 9:9; *Shulhan 'Arukh, OḤ*, chaps. 235–237.
2. See now *Shemu'ot Rayah*, ed. Rabbi Ḥayyim Yeshayah Hadari (Jerusalem: World Zionist Organization, 2015), *Terumah*, pp. 321–322. There the point is made that the

בָּרוּךְ Blessed are You, Lord our God, King of the Universe,
who by His word brings on evenings,
by His wisdom opens the gates of heaven,
with understanding makes time change and the seasons rotate,
and by His will
orders the stars in their constellations in the sky.
He creates day and night,
rolling away the light before the darkness,
and darkness before the light.
▸ He makes the day pass and brings on night,
distinguishing day from night:
the Lord of hosts is His name.
May the living and forever enduring God rule over us for all time.
Blessed are You, Lord, who brings on evenings.

---

sanctity of the Festival. This custom was instituted in his Yeshivat Merkaz Harav.[8]

בּוֹרֵא יוֹם וָלָיְלָה, גּוֹלֵל אוֹר מִפְּנֵי חֹשֶׁךְ וְחֹשֶׁךְ מִפְּנֵי אוֹר *He creates day and night, rolling away the light before the darkness, and darkness before the light.* Spiritually, we are constantly growing, advancing, ascending. If there were no darkness in the world, we would stagnate and level off. Come night, the darkness challenges and provokes us to probe deeper. And with the light of the new day, comes a new outlook, a fresh perspective. And by this new day's standard, the previous day would not be reckoned day at all, but rather night! And then the ongoing process resumes once more; the creative interplay of darkness and light starts all over again, and the cycle repeats itself – upon the next level. The *tikkunim* are a constant process, whereby good is forever ascending higher and higher.[9]

---

8. RZYH explained that his father adopted this custom when he served in the rabbinate of Boisk. The custom originated with Rabbi Ya'akov of Boisk, author Responsa *Zikhron Ya'akov* (Vilna, 1874). (Rabbi Ya'akov of Boisk was a grandson of the famed kabbalist Rabbi Samuel Ḥasid of Rassein.) See Rabbi Ḥayyim Avihu Schwartz, *Mi-Tokh ha-Torah ha-Go'elet*, vol. 1 (Jerusalem, 1989), p. 118.

9. *OR*, vol. 1, pp. 410–411. Cf. Rabbi Dov Baer Shneuri of Lubavitch, *Sha'arei 'Orah* (Johannisberg, n.d.; photo offset Brooklyn, 1979), chap. 55 (22b-23a).

בָּרוּךְ אַתָּה יהוה אֱלֹהֵינוּ מֶלֶךְ הָעוֹלָם
אֲשֶׁר בִּדְבָרוֹ מַעֲרִיב עֲרָבִים
בְּחָכְמָה פּוֹתֵחַ שְׁעָרִים
וּבִתְבוּנָה מְשַׁנֶּה עִתִּים וּמַחֲלִיף אֶת הַזְּמַנִּים
וּמְסַדֵּר אֶת הַכּוֹכָבִים בְּמִשְׁמְרוֹתֵיהֶם בָּרָקִיעַ כִּרְצוֹנוֹ.
בּוֹרֵא יוֹם וָלַיְלָה
גּוֹלֵל אוֹר מִפְּנֵי חֹשֶׁךְ וְחֹשֶׁךְ מִפְּנֵי אוֹר
◂ וּמַעֲבִיר יוֹם וּמֵבִיא לַיְלָה
וּמַבְדִּיל בֵּין יוֹם וּבֵין לַיְלָה
יהוה צְבָאוֹת שְׁמוֹ.
אֵל חַי וְקַיָּם תָּמִיד, יִמְלֹךְ עָלֵינוּ לְעוֹלָם וָעֶד.
בָּרוּךְ אַתָּה יהוה, הַמַּעֲרִיב עֲרָבִים.

---

(prayer).[4] These fleeting moments of illumination were likened by Maimonides to lightning flashes.[5] Baḥya ibn Pakuda enumerated the many spiritual advantages of the evening prayer over daytime prayer, chief among them being isolation from the madding crowd.[6] And indeed, after his evening prayer, Jacob our Father merited the exalted prophetic vision of the Ladder.[7]

וְהוּא רַחוּם / HE IS COMPASSIONATE (*PREVIOUS PAGE*)

It was Rav Kook's custom not to recite *Ve-Hu Raḥum* at the Evening Service of the Intermediate Days of a Festival (*Ḥol ha-Mo'ed*) in recognition of the

---

4. In *Tur* and *Shulhan 'Arukh, OḤ,* chap. 98 it is written that the pious would meditate in prayer until they reached a state of divestment of the corporeal (*hitpashtut ha-gashmiyut*) and intellectual vigor approaching the level of prophecy (*karov le-ma'alat ha-nevu'ah*). (However, the evening prayer is not singled out in that context.)
5. See the Introduction to Maimonides' *Guide of the Perplexed.*
6. Baḥya ibn Pakuda, *Ḥovot ha-Levavot* (*Duties of the Heart*), *Sha'ar Ahavat Hashem,* chap. 6.
7. "'*Inyenei Tefillah*" 2:6, in *OR*, vol. 1, p. 17 = *EA*, vol. 1, *Berakhot,* chap. 4, par. 2 (pp. 109–110).

אַהֲבַת עוֹלָם With everlasting love
have You loved Your people, the house of Israel.
You have taught us Torah and commandments,
decrees and laws of justice.
Therefore, LORD our God, when we lie down and when we rise up
we will speak of Your decrees, rejoicing in the words of Your Torah
and Your commandments for ever.
► For they are our life and the length of our days;
on them will we meditate day and night.
May You never take away Your love from us.
Blessed are You, LORD, who loves His people Israel.

*The Shema must be said with intense concentration. See laws 349–355.*
*When not with a minyan, say:*
God, faithful King!

*The following verse should be said aloud, while covering the eyes with the right hand:*

## Listen, Israel: the LORD is our God, the LORD is One. *Deut. 6*

*Quietly:* Blessed be the name of His glorious kingdom for ever and all time.

וְאָהַבְתָּ Love the LORD your God with all your heart, with all your soul, and with all your might. These words which I command you today shall be on your heart. Teach them repeatedly to your children, speaking of them when you sit at home and when you travel on the way, when you lie down and when you rise. Bind them as a sign on your hand, and they shall be an emblem between your eyes. Write them on the doorposts of your house and gates. *Deut. 6*

וְהָיָה If you indeed heed My commandments with which I charge you today, to love the LORD your God and worship Him with all your heart and with all your soul, I will give rain in your land in its season, the early and late rain; and you shall gather in your grain, wine and oil. I will give grass in your field for your cattle, and you shall eat and be satisfied. Be careful lest your heart be tempted and you go astray and worship other gods, bowing down *Deut. 11*

אַהֲבַת עוֹלָם בֵּית יִשְׂרָאֵל עַמְּךָ אָהָבְתָּ
תּוֹרָה וּמִצְוֹת, חֻקִּים וּמִשְׁפָּטִים, אוֹתָנוּ לִמַּדְתָּ
עַל כֵּן יהוה אֱלֹהֵינוּ בְּשָׁכְבֵנוּ וּבְקוּמֵנוּ נָשִׂיחַ בְּחֻקֶּיךָ
וְנִשְׂמַח בְּדִבְרֵי תוֹרָתֶךָ וּבְמִצְוֹתֶיךָ לְעוֹלָם וָעֶד
◂ כִּי הֵם חַיֵּינוּ וְאֹרֶךְ יָמֵינוּ, וּבָהֶם נֶהְגֶּה יוֹמָם וָלָיְלָה.
וְאַהֲבָתְךָ אַל תָּסִיר מִמֶּנּוּ לְעוֹלָמִים.
בָּרוּךְ אַתָּה יהוה, אוֹהֵב עַמּוֹ יִשְׂרָאֵל.

*The שמע must be said with intense concentration. See laws 349–355.*

*When not with a מנין, say:*

אֵל מֶלֶךְ נֶאֱמָן

*The following verse should be said aloud, while covering the eyes with the right hand:*

**שְׁמַע יִשְׂרָאֵל, יהוה אֱלֹהֵינוּ, יהוה ׀ אֶחָד׃** דברים ו

*Quietly* בָּרוּךְ שֵׁם כְּבוֹד מַלְכוּתוֹ לְעוֹלָם וָעֶד.

וְאָהַבְתָּ אֵת יהוה אֱלֹהֶיךָ, בְּכָל־לְבָבְךָ וּבְכָל־נַפְשְׁךָ וּבְכָל־ דברים ו
מְאֹדֶךָ׃ וְהָיוּ הַדְּבָרִים הָאֵלֶּה, אֲשֶׁר אָנֹכִי מְצַוְּךָ הַיּוֹם, עַל־לְבָבֶךָ׃
וְשִׁנַּנְתָּם לְבָנֶיךָ וְדִבַּרְתָּ בָּם, בְּשִׁבְתְּךָ בְּבֵיתֶךָ וּבְלֶכְתְּךָ בַדֶּרֶךְ,
וּבְשָׁכְבְּךָ וּבְקוּמֶךָ׃ וּקְשַׁרְתָּם לְאוֹת עַל־יָדֶךָ וְהָיוּ לְטֹטָפֹת בֵּין
עֵינֶיךָ׃ וּכְתַבְתָּם עַל־מְזֻזוֹת בֵּיתֶךָ וּבִשְׁעָרֶיךָ׃

וְהָיָה אִם־שָׁמֹעַ תִּשְׁמְעוּ אֶל־מִצְוֹתַי אֲשֶׁר אָנֹכִי מְצַוֶּה אֶתְכֶם דברים יא
הַיּוֹם, לְאַהֲבָה אֶת־יהוה אֱלֹהֵיכֶם וּלְעָבְדוֹ, בְּכָל־לְבַבְכֶם וּבְכָל־
נַפְשְׁכֶם׃ וְנָתַתִּי מְטַר־אַרְצְכֶם בְּעִתּוֹ, יוֹרֶה וּמַלְקוֹשׁ, וְאָסַפְתָּ
דְגָנֶךָ וְתִירֹשְׁךָ וְיִצְהָרֶךָ׃ וְנָתַתִּי עֵשֶׂב בְּשָׂדְךָ לִבְהֶמְתֶּךָ, וְאָכַלְתָּ
וְשָׂבָעְתָּ׃ הִשָּׁמְרוּ לָכֶם פֶּן־יִפְתֶּה לְבַבְכֶם, וְסַרְתֶּם וַעֲבַדְתֶּם
אֱלֹהִים אֲחֵרִים וְהִשְׁתַּחֲוִיתֶם לָהֶם׃ וְחָרָה אַף־יהוה בָּכֶם, וְעָצַר

to them. Then the LORD's anger will flare against you and He will close the heavens so that there will be no rain. The land will not yield its crops, and you will perish swiftly from the good land that the LORD is giving you. Therefore, set these, My words, on your heart and soul. Bind them as a sign on your hand, and they shall be an emblem between your eyes. Teach them to your children, speaking of them when you sit at home and when you travel on the way, when you lie down and when you rise. Write them on the doorposts of your house and gates, so that you and your children may live long in the land that the LORD swore to your ancestors to give them, for as long as the heavens are above the earth.

וַיֹּאמֶר The LORD spoke to Moses, saying: Speak to the Israelites and tell them to make tassels on the corners of their garments for all generations. They shall attach to the tassel at each corner a thread of blue. This shall be your tassel, and you shall see it and remember all of the LORD's commandments and keep them, not straying after your heart and after your eyes, following your own sinful desires. Thus you will be reminded to keep all My commandments, and be holy to your God. I am the LORD your God, who brought you out of the land of Egypt to be your God. I am the LORD your God. *Num. 15*

## True –

*The Leader repeats:*

▸ The LORD your God is true –

וֶאֱמוּנָה – and faithful is all this,
and firmly established for us
that He is the LORD our God,
and there is none besides Him,
and that we, Israel, are His people.
He is our King, who redeems us from the hand of kings
and delivers us from the grasp of all tyrants.

אֶת־הַשָּׁמַ֗יִם וְלֹא־יִהְיֶ֣ה מָטָ֔ר, וְהָ֣אֲדָמָ֔ה לֹ֥א תִתֵּ֖ן אֶת־יְבוּלָ֑הּ, וַאֲבַדְתֶּ֣ם מְהֵרָ֗ה מֵעַל֙ הָאָ֣רֶץ הַטֹּבָ֔ה אֲשֶׁ֥ר יהו֖ה נֹתֵ֥ן לָכֶֽם: וְשַׂמְתֶּם֙ אֶת־דְּבָרַ֣י אֵ֔לֶּה עַל־לְבַבְכֶ֖ם וְעַֽל־נַפְשְׁכֶ֑ם, וּקְשַׁרְתֶּ֨ם אֹתָ֤ם לְאוֹת֙ עַל־יֶדְכֶ֔ם, וְהָי֥וּ לְטוֹטָפֹ֖ת בֵּ֥ין עֵינֵיכֶֽם: וְלִמַּדְתֶּ֥ם אֹתָ֛ם אֶת־בְּנֵיכֶ֖ם לְדַבֵּ֣ר בָּ֑ם, בְּשִׁבְתְּךָ֤ בְּבֵיתֶ֙ךָ֙ וּבְלֶכְתְּךָ֣ בַדֶּ֔רֶךְ, וּֽבְשָׁכְבְּךָ֖ וּבְקוּמֶֽךָ: וּכְתַבְתָּ֛ם עַל־מְזוּז֥וֹת בֵּיתֶ֖ךָ וּבִשְׁעָרֶֽיךָ: לְמַ֨עַן יִרְבּ֤וּ יְמֵיכֶם֙ וִימֵ֣י בְנֵיכֶ֔ם עַ֚ל הָֽאֲדָמָ֔ה אֲשֶׁ֨ר נִשְׁבַּ֧ע יהו֛ה לַאֲבֹתֵיכֶ֖ם לָתֵ֣ת לָהֶ֑ם, כִּימֵ֥י הַשָּׁמַ֖יִם עַל־הָאָֽרֶץ:

וַיֹּ֥אמֶר יהו֖ה אֶל־מֹשֶׁ֥ה לֵּאמֹֽר: דַּבֵּ֞ר אֶל־בְּנֵ֤י יִשְׂרָאֵל֙ וְאָמַרְתָּ֣ אֲלֵהֶ֔ם, וְעָשׂ֨וּ לָהֶ֥ם צִיצִ֛ת עַל־כַּנְפֵ֥י בִגְדֵיהֶ֖ם לְדֹרֹתָ֑ם, וְנָֽתְנ֛וּ עַל־צִיצִ֥ת הַכָּנָ֖ף פְּתִ֥יל תְּכֵֽלֶת: וְהָיָ֣ה לָכֶם֮ לְצִיצִת֒, וּרְאִיתֶ֣ם אֹת֗וֹ וּזְכַרְתֶּם֙ אֶת־כׇּל־מִצְוֺ֣ת יהו֔ה וַעֲשִׂיתֶ֖ם אֹתָ֑ם, וְלֹֽא־תָת֜וּרוּ אַחֲרֵ֤י לְבַבְכֶם֙ וְאַחֲרֵ֣י עֵֽינֵיכֶ֔ם, אֲשֶׁר־אַתֶּ֥ם זֹנִ֖ים אַחֲרֵיהֶֽם: לְמַ֣עַן תִּזְכְּר֔וּ וַעֲשִׂיתֶ֖ם אֶת־כׇּל־מִצְוֺתָ֑י, וִהְיִיתֶ֥ם קְדֹשִׁ֖ים לֵאלֹהֵיכֶֽם: אֲנִ֞י יהו֣ה אֱלֹֽהֵיכֶ֗ם, אֲשֶׁ֨ר הוֹצֵ֤אתִי אֶתְכֶם֙ מֵאֶ֣רֶץ מִצְרַ֔יִם, לִהְי֥וֹת לָכֶ֖ם לֵאלֹהִ֑ים, אֲנִ֖י יהו֥ה אֱלֹהֵיכֶֽם: במדבר טו

## אֱמֶת

*The* שליח ציבור *repeats:*

◂ יהוה אֱלֹהֵיכֶם אֱמֶת

וֶאֱמוּנָה כׇּל זֹאת וְקַיָּם עָלֵינוּ
כִּי הוּא יהוה אֱלֹהֵינוּ וְאֵין זוּלָתוֹ
וַאֲנַחְנוּ יִשְׂרָאֵל עַמּוֹ.
הַפּוֹדֵנוּ מִיַּד מְלָכִים
מַלְכֵּנוּ הַגּוֹאֲלֵנוּ מִכַּף כׇּל הֶעָרִיצִים.

He is our God, who on our behalf repays our foes
and brings just retribution on our mortal enemies;
who performs great deeds beyond understanding
and wonders beyond number;
who kept us alive, not letting our foot slip;
who led us on the high places of our enemies,
raising our pride above all our foes;
who did miracles for us
and brought vengeance against Pharaoh;
who performed signs and wonders
in the land of Ham's children;
who smote in His wrath all the firstborn of Egypt,
and brought out His people Israel from their midst
into everlasting freedom;
who led His children through the divided Reed Sea,
plunging their pursuers and enemies into the depths.
When His children saw His might,
they gave praise and thanks to His name,
▸ and willingly accepted His Sovereignty.
Moses and the children of Israel
then sang a song to You with great joy,
and they all exclaimed:

מִי־כָמֹכָה "Who is like You, LORD, among the mighty? *Ex. 15*
Who is like You, majestic in holiness,
awesome in praises, doing wonders?"

▸ Your children beheld Your majesty
as You parted the sea before Moses.
"This is my God!" they responded, and then said:
"The LORD shall reign for ever and ever." *Ex. 15*

▸ And it is said,
"For the LORD has redeemed Jacob and rescued him *Jer. 31*
from a power stronger than his own."
Blessed are You, LORD, who redeemed Israel.

הָאֵל הַנִּפְרָע לָנוּ מִצָּרֵינוּ
וְהַמְשַׁלֵּם גְּמוּל לְכָל אוֹיְבֵי נַפְשֵׁנוּ.
הָעוֹשֶׂה גְדוֹלוֹת עַד אֵין חֵקֶר, וְנִפְלָאוֹת עַד אֵין מִסְפָּר
הַשָּׂם נַפְשֵׁנוּ בַּחַיִּים, וְלֹא נָתַן לַמּוֹט רַגְלֵנוּ
הַמַּדְרִיכֵנוּ עַל בָּמוֹת אוֹיְבֵינוּ
וַיָּרֶם קַרְנֵנוּ עַל כָּל שׂוֹנְאֵינוּ.
הָעוֹשֶׂה לָּנוּ נִסִּים וּנְקָמָה בְּפַרְעֹה
אוֹתוֹת וּמוֹפְתִים בְּאַדְמַת בְּנֵי חָם.
הַמַּכֶּה בְעֶבְרָתוֹ כָּל בְּכוֹרֵי מִצְרָיִם
וַיּוֹצֵא אֶת עַמּוֹ יִשְׂרָאֵל מִתּוֹכָם לְחֵרוּת עוֹלָם.
הַמַּעֲבִיר בָּנָיו בֵּין גִּזְרֵי יַם סוּף
אֶת רוֹדְפֵיהֶם וְאֶת שׂוֹנְאֵיהֶם בִּתְהוֹמוֹת טִבַּע
וְרָאוּ בָנָיו גְּבוּרָתוֹ, שִׁבְּחוּ וְהוֹדוּ לִשְׁמוֹ
◂ וּמַלְכוּתוֹ בְּרָצוֹן קִבְּלוּ עֲלֵיהֶם.
מֹשֶׁה וּבְנֵי יִשְׂרָאֵל, לְךָ עָנוּ שִׁירָה בְּשִׂמְחָה רַבָּה
וְאָמְרוּ כֻלָּם

מִי־כָמֹכָה בָּאֵלִם יהוה שמות טו
מִי כָּמֹכָה נֶאְדָּר בַּקֹּדֶשׁ
נוֹרָא תְהִלֹּת עֹשֵׂה פֶלֶא:

◂ מַלְכוּתְךָ רָאוּ בָנֶיךָ, בּוֹקֵעַ יָם לִפְנֵי מֹשֶׁה
זֶה אֵלִי עָנוּ, וְאָמְרוּ
יהוה יִמְלֹךְ לְעֹלָם וָעֶד: שמות טו

◂ וְנֶאֱמַר
כִּי־פָדָה יהוה אֶת־יַעֲקֹב, וּגְאָלוֹ מִיַּד חָזָק מִמֶּנּוּ: ירמיהו לא
בָּרוּךְ אַתָּה יהוה, גָּאַל יִשְׂרָאֵל.

הַשְׁכִּיבֵנוּ Help us lie down, O LORD our God, in peace,
and rise up, O our King, to life.
Spread over us Your canopy of peace.
Direct us with Your good counsel,
and save us for the sake of Your name.
Shield us and remove from us every enemy,
plague, sword, famine and sorrow.
Remove the adversary from before and behind us.
Shelter us in the shadow of Your wings,
for You, God, are our Guardian and Deliverer;
You, God, are a gracious and compassionate King.
▸ Guard our going out and our coming in,
for life and peace, from now and for ever.
Blessed are You, LORD, who guards His people Israel for ever.

*In Israel the service continues with Half Kaddish on page 328.*

בָּרוּךְ Blessed be the LORD for ever. Amen and Amen. *Ps. 89*
Blessed from Zion be the LORD *Ps. 135*
who dwells in Jerusalem. Halleluya.
Blessed be the LORD, God of Israel, *Ps. 72*
who alone does wondrous things.
Blessed be His glorious name for ever,
and may the whole earth be filled with His glory. Amen and Amen.
May the glory of the LORD endure for ever; *Ps. 104*
may the LORD rejoice in His works.
May the name of the LORD be blessed now and for all time. *Ps. 113*
For the sake of His great name *1 Sam. 12*
the LORD will not abandon His people,
for the LORD vowed to make you a people of His own.
When all the people saw [God's wonders] they fell on their faces *1 Kings 18*
and said: "The LORD, He is God; the LORD, He is God."
Then the LORD shall be King over all the earth; *Zech. 14*
on that day the LORD shall be One and His name One.
May Your love, LORD, be upon us, as we have put our hope in You. *Ps. 33*

הַשְׁכִּיבֵנוּ יהוה אֱלֹהֵינוּ לְשָׁלוֹם
וְהַעֲמִידֵנוּ מַלְכֵּנוּ לְחַיִּים
וּפְרֹשׂ עָלֵינוּ סֻכַּת שְׁלוֹמֶךָ, וְתַקְּנֵנוּ בְּעֵצָה טוֹבָה מִלְּפָנֶיךָ
וְהוֹשִׁיעֵנוּ לְמַעַן שְׁמֶךָ.
וְהָגֵן בַּעֲדֵנוּ, וְהָסֵר מֵעָלֵינוּ אוֹיֵב, דֶּבֶר וְחֶרֶב וְרָעָב וְיָגוֹן
וְהָסֵר שָׂטָן מִלְּפָנֵינוּ וּמֵאַחֲרֵינוּ, וּבְצֵל כְּנָפֶיךָ תַּסְתִּירֵנוּ
כִּי אֵל שׁוֹמְרֵנוּ וּמַצִּילֵנוּ אָתָּה
כִּי אֵל מֶלֶךְ חַנּוּן וְרַחוּם אָתָּה.
◂ וּשְׁמֹר צֵאתֵנוּ וּבוֹאֵנוּ לְחַיִּים וּלְשָׁלוֹם מֵעַתָּה וְעַד עוֹלָם.
בָּרוּךְ אַתָּה יהוה, שׁוֹמֵר עַמּוֹ יִשְׂרָאֵל לָעַד.

*In* ארץ ישראל *the service continues with* חצי קדיש *on page 329.*

בָּרוּךְ יהוה לְעוֹלָם, אָמֵן וְאָמֵן: תהלים פט
בָּרוּךְ יהוה מִצִּיּוֹן, שֹׁכֵן יְרוּשָׁלָםִ, הַלְלוּיָהּ: תהלים קלה
בָּרוּךְ יהוה אֱלֹהִים אֱלֹהֵי יִשְׂרָאֵל, עֹשֵׂה נִפְלָאוֹת לְבַדּוֹ: תהלים עב
וּבָרוּךְ שֵׁם כְּבוֹדוֹ לְעוֹלָם
וְיִמָּלֵא כְבוֹדוֹ אֶת־כָּל־הָאָרֶץ, אָמֵן וְאָמֵן:
יְהִי כְבוֹד יהוה לְעוֹלָם, יִשְׂמַח יהוה בְּמַעֲשָׂיו: תהלים קד
יְהִי שֵׁם יהוה מְבֹרָךְ מֵעַתָּה וְעַד־עוֹלָם: תהלים קיג
כִּי לֹא־יִטֹּשׁ יהוה אֶת־עַמּוֹ בַּעֲבוּר שְׁמוֹ הַגָּדוֹל שמואל א, יב
כִּי הוֹאִיל יהוה לַעֲשׂוֹת אֶתְכֶם לוֹ לְעָם:
וַיַּרְא כָּל־הָעָם וַיִּפְּלוּ עַל־פְּנֵיהֶם מלכים א, יח
וַיֹּאמְרוּ, יהוה הוּא הָאֱלֹהִים, יהוה הוּא הָאֱלֹהִים:
וְהָיָה יהוה לְמֶלֶךְ עַל־כָּל־הָאָרֶץ זכריה יד
בַּיּוֹם הַהוּא יִהְיֶה יהוה אֶחָד וּשְׁמוֹ אֶחָד:
יְהִי־חַסְדְּךָ יהוה עָלֵינוּ, כַּאֲשֶׁר יִחַלְנוּ לָךְ: תהלים לג

הוֹשִׁיעֵנוּ Save us, LORD our God, gather us Ps. 106
and deliver us from the nations,
to thank Your holy name, and glory in Your praise.
All the nations You made shall come and bow before You, LORD, Ps. 86
and pay honor to Your name,
for You are great and You perform wonders: You alone are God.
We, Your people, the flock of Your pasture, Ps. 79
will praise You for ever.
For all generations we will relate Your praise.

בָּרוּךְ Blessed is the LORD by day, blessed is the LORD by night.
Blessed is the LORD when we lie down;
blessed is the LORD when we rise.
For in Your hand are the souls of the living and the dead,
[as it is written:] "In His hand is every living soul, Job 12
and the breath of all mankind."
Into Your hand I entrust my spirit: Ps. 31
You redeemed me, LORD, God of truth.
Our God in heaven, bring unity to Your name,
establish Your kingdom constantly
and reign over us for ever and all time.

יִרְאוּ May our eyes see, our hearts rejoice,
and our souls be glad in Your true salvation,
when Zion is told, "Your God reigns."
The LORD is King, the LORD was King,
the LORD will be King for ever and all time.
▸ For sovereignty is Yours,
and to all eternity You will reign in glory,
for we have no king but You.
Blessed are You, LORD,
the King who in His constant glory will reign over us
and all His creation for ever and all time.

הוֹשִׁיעֵנוּ יהוה אֱלֹהֵינוּ, וְקַבְּצֵנוּ מִן־הַגּוֹיִם לְהוֹדוֹת לְשֵׁם קָדְשֶׁךָ, לְהִשְׁתַּבֵּחַ בִּתְהִלָּתֶךָ: תהלים קו

כָּל־גּוֹיִם אֲשֶׁר עָשִׂיתָ, יָבוֹאוּ וְיִשְׁתַּחֲווּ לְפָנֶיךָ, אֲדֹנָי וִיכַבְּדוּ לִשְׁמֶךָ: תהלים פו

כִּי־גָדוֹל אַתָּה וְעֹשֵׂה נִפְלָאוֹת, אַתָּה אֱלֹהִים לְבַדֶּךָ:

וַאֲנַחְנוּ עַמְּךָ וְצֹאן מַרְעִיתֶךָ, נוֹדֶה לְּךָ לְעוֹלָם לְדוֹר וָדֹר נְסַפֵּר תְּהִלָּתֶךָ: תהלים עט

בָּרוּךְ יהוה בַּיּוֹם, בָּרוּךְ יהוה בַּלָּיְלָה
בָּרוּךְ יהוה בְּשָׁכְבֵנוּ, בָּרוּךְ יהוה בְּקוּמֵנוּ.
כִּי בְיָדְךָ נַפְשׁוֹת הַחַיִּים וְהַמֵּתִים.
אֲשֶׁר בְּיָדוֹ נֶפֶשׁ כָּל־חָי, וְרוּחַ כָּל־בְּשַׂר־אִישׁ: איוב יב
בְּיָדְךָ אַפְקִיד רוּחִי, פָּדִיתָה אוֹתִי יהוה אֵל אֱמֶת: תהלים לא
אֱלֹהֵינוּ שֶׁבַּשָּׁמַיִם, יַחֵד שִׁמְךָ וְקַיֵּם מַלְכוּתְךָ תָּמִיד וּמְלֹךְ עָלֵינוּ לְעוֹלָם וָעֶד.

יִרְאוּ עֵינֵינוּ וְיִשְׂמַח לִבֵּנוּ
וְתָגֵל נַפְשֵׁנוּ בִּישׁוּעָתְךָ בֶּאֱמֶת
בֶּאֱמֹר לְצִיּוֹן מָלַךְ אֱלֹהָיִךְ.
יהוה מֶלֶךְ, יהוה מָלָךְ, יהוה יִמְלֹךְ לְעֹלָם וָעֶד.
◄ כִּי הַמַּלְכוּת שֶׁלְּךָ הִיא, וּלְעוֹלְמֵי עַד תִּמְלֹךְ בְּכָבוֹד
כִּי אֵין לָנוּ מֶלֶךְ אֶלָּא אָתָּה.
בָּרוּךְ אַתָּה יהוה
הַמֶּלֶךְ בִּכְבוֹדוֹ תָּמִיד, יִמְלֹךְ עָלֵינוּ לְעוֹלָם וָעֶד
וְעַל כָּל מַעֲשָׂיו.

HALF KADDISH

*Leader:* יִתְגַּדַּל Magnified and sanctified
may His great name be,
in the world He created by His will.
May He establish His kingdom
in your lifetime and in your days,
and in the lifetime
of all the house of Israel,
swiftly and soon –
and say: Amen.

*All:* May His great name be blessed
for ever and all time.

*Leader:* Blessed and praised, glorified and exalted,
raised and honored, uplifted and lauded
be the name of the Holy One,
blessed be He,
beyond any blessing,
song, praise and consolation
uttered in the world –
and say: Amen.

## THE AMIDA

*The following prayer, until "in former years" on page 346, is said silently, standing with feet together. Take three steps forward and at the points indicated by ▾, bend the knees at the first word, bow at the second, and stand straight before saying God's name.*

O Lord, open my lips,
so that my mouth may declare Your praise. *Ps. 51*

PATRIARCHS

▾בָּרוּךְ Blessed are You, Lord our God and God of our fathers,
God of Abraham, God of Isaac and God of Jacob;
the great, mighty and awesome God, God Most High,

## חצי קדיש

ש״ץ: יִתְגַּדַּל וְיִתְקַדַּשׁ שְׁמֵהּ רַבָּא (קהל: אָמֵן)
בְּעָלְמָא דִּי בְרָא כִרְעוּתֵהּ
וְיַמְלִיךְ מַלְכוּתֵהּ
בְּחַיֵּיכוֹן וּבְיוֹמֵיכוֹן וּבְחַיֵּי דְכָל בֵּית יִשְׂרָאֵל
בַּעֲגָלָא וּבִזְמַן קָרִיב
וְאִמְרוּ אָמֵן. (קהל: אָמֵן)

קהל וש״ץ: יְהֵא שְׁמֵהּ רַבָּא מְבָרַךְ לְעָלַם וּלְעָלְמֵי עָלְמַיָּא.

ש״ץ: יִתְבָּרַךְ וְיִשְׁתַּבַּח וְיִתְפָּאַר וְיִתְרוֹמַם וְיִתְנַשֵּׂא
וְיִתְהַדָּר וְיִתְעַלֶּה וְיִתְהַלָּל
שְׁמֵהּ דְּקֻדְשָׁא בְּרִיךְ הוּא (קהל: בְּרִיךְ הוּא)
לְעֵלָּא מִן כָּל בִּרְכָתָא
/בעשרת ימי תשובה: לְעֵלָּא לְעֵלָּא מִכָּל בִּרְכָתָא/
וְשִׁירָתָא, תֻּשְׁבְּחָתָא וְנֶחֱמָתָא
דַּאֲמִירָן בְּעָלְמָא
וְאִמְרוּ אָמֵן. (קהל: אָמֵן)

# עמידה

*The following prayer, until* קַדְמֹנִיּוֹת *on page 347, is said silently, standing with feet together. Take three steps forward and at the points indicated by* ׳*, bend the knees at the first word, bow at the second, and stand straight before saying God's name.*

תהלים נא אֲדֹנָי, שְׂפָתַי תִּפְתָּח, וּפִי יַגִּיד תְּהִלָּתֶךָ:

## אבות

׳בָּרוּךְ אַתָּה יהוה, אֱלֹהֵינוּ וֵאלֹהֵי אֲבוֹתֵינוּ
אֱלֹהֵי אַבְרָהָם, אֱלֹהֵי יִצְחָק, וֵאלֹהֵי יַעֲקֹב
הָאֵל הַגָּדוֹל הַגִּבּוֹר וְהַנּוֹרָא, אֵל עֶלְיוֹן

who bestows acts of loving-kindness and creates all,
who remembers the loving-kindness of the fathers
and will bring a Redeemer to their children's children
for the sake of His name, in love.

*Between Rosh HaShana & Yom Kippur:* Remember us for life, O King who desires life,
and write us in the book of life –
for Your sake, O God of life.

King, Helper, Savior, Shield:
▾Blessed are You, LORD, Shield of Abraham.

DIVINE MIGHT

אַתָּה גִּבּוֹר You are eternally mighty, LORD.
You give life to the dead
and have great power to save.

*The phrase "He makes the wind blow and the rain fall" is added from Simḥat Torah until Pesaḥ. In Israel the phrase "He causes the dew to fall" is added from Pesaḥ until Shemini Atzeret. See laws 129–131.*

*In fall & winter:* He makes the wind blow and the rain fall.
*In Israel, in spring & summer:* He causes the dew to fall.

He sustains the living with loving-kindness,
and with great compassion revives the dead.
He supports the fallen, heals the sick,
sets captives free,
and keeps His faith with those who sleep in the dust.
Who is like You, Master of might,
and who can compare to You,
O King who brings death and gives life,
and makes salvation grow?

*Between Rosh HaShana & Yom Kippur:* Who is like You, compassionate Father,
who remembers His creatures
in compassion, for life?

Faithful are You to revive the dead.
Blessed are You, LORD, who revives the dead.

גּוֹמֵל חֲסָדִים טוֹבִים, וְקֹנֵה הַכֹּל
וְזוֹכֵר חַסְדֵי אָבוֹת
וּמֵבִיא גוֹאֵל לִבְנֵי בְנֵיהֶם לְמַעַן שְׁמוֹ בְּאַהֲבָה.

בעשרת ימי תשובה: זָכְרֵנוּ לְחַיִּים, מֶלֶךְ חָפֵץ בַּחַיִּים
וְכָתְבֵנוּ בְּסֵפֶר הַחַיִּים
לְמַעַנְךָ אֱלֹהִים חַיִּים.

מֶלֶךְ עוֹזֵר וּמוֹשִׁיעַ וּמָגֵן.
ּבָּרוּךְ אַתָּה יהוה, מָגֵן אַבְרָהָם.

גבורות

אַתָּה גִּבּוֹר לְעוֹלָם, אֲדֹנָי
מְחַיֵּה מֵתִים אַתָּה, רַב לְהוֹשִׁיעַ

*The phrase* מַשִּׁיב הָרְוּחַ *is added from* שמחת תורה *until* פסח. *In* ארץ ישראל *the phrase* מוֹרִיד הַטָּל *is added from* פסח *until* שמיני עצרת. *See laws 129–131.*

בחורף: מַשִּׁיב הָרְוּחַ וּמוֹרִיד הַגֶּשֶׁם / בארץ ישראל בקיץ: מוֹרִיד הַטָּל

מְכַלְכֵּל חַיִּים בְּחֶסֶד, מְחַיֵּה מֵתִים בְּרַחֲמִים רַבִּים
סוֹמֵךְ נוֹפְלִים, וְרוֹפֵא חוֹלִים, וּמַתִּיר אֲסוּרִים
וּמְקַיֵּם אֱמוּנָתוֹ לִישֵׁנֵי עָפָר.
מִי כָמְוֹךָ, בַּעַל גְּבוּרוֹת
וּמִי דּוֹמֶה לָּךְ
מֶלֶךְ, מֵמִית וּמְחַיֶּה וּמַצְמִיחַ יְשׁוּעָה.

בעשרת ימי תשובה: מִי כָמְוֹךָ אַב הָרַחֲמִים
זוֹכֵר יְצוּרָיו לְחַיִּים בְּרַחֲמִים.

וְנֶאֱמָן אַתָּה לְהַחֲיוֹת מֵתִים.
בָּרוּךְ אַתָּה יהוה, מְחַיֵּה הַמֵּתִים.

HOLINESS

אַתָּה קָדוֹשׁ You are holy and Your name is holy,
and holy ones praise You daily, Selah!
Blessed are You, LORD,
the holy God. / *Between Rosh HaShana & Yom Kippur:* the holy King./
*(If forgotten, repeat the Amida.)*

KNOWLEDGE

אַתָּה חוֹנֵן You grace humanity with knowledge
and teach mortals understanding.

---

*On Motza'ei Shabbat and Motza'ei Yom Tov add:*

אַתָּה חוֹנַנְתָּנוּ You have graced us with the knowledge of Your Torah, and taught us to perform the statutes of Your will. You have distinguished, LORD our God, between sacred and profane, light and darkness, Israel and the nations, and between the seventh day and the six days of work. Our Father, our King, may the days approaching us bring peace; may we be free from all sin, cleansed from all iniquity, holding fast to our reverence of You. And

---

Grace us with the knowledge, understanding
and discernment that come from You.
Blessed are You, LORD,
who graciously grants knowledge.

---

(*tehar yoma*); perhaps "*ve-taher*" means that the man is pure (*tehar gavra*)?[11] There are days that are pure and days that are impure; days imprinted with purity and days imprinted with impurity (*roshem tum'ah*).[12] This is the homiletic interpretation of the words "Abraham was old, come in days."[13] He came to the end of life's journey with all his days intact.[14] (Editor)

11. *b. Berakhot* 2.
12. Rabbi Abraham Bornstein of Sochaczew, *Eglei Tal* (Piotrków, 1931; photo offset New York, 1968), end Introduction, quoting the author's father, Rabbi Ze'ev Naḥum Bornstein of Biala (author *Agudat Ezov*).
13. Genesis 24:1.
14. *EA*, vol. 1, *Berakhot*, chap. 1, par. 3 (pp. 1–2).

קדושת השם

אַתָּה קָדוֹשׁ וְשִׁמְךָ קָדוֹשׁ
וּקְדוֹשִׁים בְּכָל יוֹם יְהַלְלוּךָ סֶּלָה.
בָּרוּךְ אַתָּה יהוה
הָאֵל הַקָּדוֹשׁ./ בעשרת ימי תשובה: הַמֶּלֶךְ הַקָּדוֹשׁ./

(*If forgotten, repeat the* עמידה.)

דעת

אַתָּה חוֹנֵן לְאָדָם דַּעַת
וּמְלַמֵּד לֶאֱנוֹשׁ בִּינָה.

---

*On* מוצאי שבת *and* מוצאי יום טוב *add:*

אַתָּה חוֹנַנְתָּנוּ לְמַדַּע תּוֹרָתֶךָ, וַתְּלַמְּדֵנוּ לַעֲשׂוֹת חֻקֵּי רְצוֹנֶךָ, וַתַּבְדֵּל יהוה אֱלֹהֵינוּ בֵּין קֹדֶשׁ לְחֹל, בֵּין אוֹר לְחֹשֶׁךְ, בֵּין יִשְׂרָאֵל לָעַמִּים, בֵּין יוֹם הַשְּׁבִיעִי לְשֵׁשֶׁת יְמֵי הַמַּעֲשֶׂה. אָבִינוּ מַלְכֵּנוּ, הָחֵל עָלֵינוּ הַיָּמִים הַבָּאִים לִקְרָאתֵנוּ לְשָׁלוֹם, חֲשׂוּכִים מִכָּל חֵטְא וּמְנֻקִּים מִכָּל עָוֹן וּמְדֻבָּקִים בְּיִרְאָתֶךָ. וְ

---

חָנֵּנוּ מֵאִתְּךָ דֵּעָה בִּינָה וְהַשְׂכֵּל.
בָּרוּךְ אַתָּה יהוה, חוֹנֵן הַדָּעַת.

---

ON MOTZA'EI SHABBAT

הָחֵל עָלֵינוּ הַיָּמִים הַבָּאִים לִקְרָאתֵנוּ לְשָׁלוֹם, חֲשׂוּכִים מִכָּל חֵטְא וּמְנֻקִּים מִכָּל עָוֹן וּמְדֻבָּקִים בְּיִרְאָתֶךָ *May the days approaching us bring peace; free from all sin, cleansed from all iniquity, holding fast to our reverence of You.* In truth, the language is ambiguous. What is the referent: the days or we humans?[10] The same ambiguity exists in regard to the verse in Leviticus 22:7: *"U-va ha-shemesh ve-taher."* The Talmud asks: How can one be sure that *"ve-taher"* means that the day is pure

---

10. RZYH understood that the referent is "the days." See Ḥayyim Avihu Schwartz, *Mi-Tokh ha-Torah ha-Go'elet*, vol. 2 (Jerusalem, 1989), p. 232.

REPENTANCE

הֲשִׁיבֵנוּ Bring us back, our Father, to Your Torah.
Draw us near, our King, to Your service.
Lead us back to You in perfect repentance.
Blessed are You, LORD,
who desires repentance.

FORGIVENESS

*Strike the left side of the chest at °.*

סְלַח לָנוּ Forgive us, our Father, for we have °sinned.
Pardon us, our King, for we have °transgressed;
for You pardon and forgive.
Blessed are You, LORD,
the gracious One who repeatedly forgives.

REDEMPTION

רְאֵה Look on our affliction, plead our cause,
and redeem us soon for Your name's sake,
for You are a powerful Redeemer.
Blessed are You, LORD,
the Redeemer of Israel.

HEALING

רְפָאֵנוּ Heal us, LORD, and we shall be healed.
Save us and we shall be saved,
for You are our praise.
Bring complete recovery for all our ailments,

---

*The following prayer for a sick person may be said here:*
May it be Your will, O LORD my God and God of my ancestors, that You speedily send a complete recovery from heaven, a healing of both soul and body, to the patient (*name*), son/daughter of (*mother's name*) among the other afflicted of Israel.

---

for You, God, King, are a faithful and compassionate Healer.
Blessed are You, LORD,
Healer of the sick of His people Israel.

תשובה

הֲשִׁיבֵנוּ אָבִינוּ לְתוֹרָתֶךָ, וְקָרְבֵנוּ מַלְכֵּנוּ לַעֲבוֹדָתֶךָ
וְהַחֲזִירֵנוּ בִּתְשׁוּבָה שְׁלֵמָה לְפָנֶיךָ.
בָּרוּךְ אַתָּה יהוה, הָרוֹצֶה בִּתְשׁוּבָה.

סליחה

*Strike the left side of the chest at °.*

סְלַח לָנוּ אָבִינוּ כִּי °חָטָאנוּ
מְחַל לָנוּ מַלְכֵּנוּ כִּי °פָשָׁעְנוּ
כִּי מוֹחֵל וְסוֹלֵחַ אָתָּה.
בָּרוּךְ אַתָּה יהוה, חַנּוּן הַמַּרְבֶּה לִסְלֹחַ.

גאולה

רְאֵה בְעָנְיֵנוּ, וְרִיבָה רִיבֵנוּ
וּגְאָלֵנוּ מְהֵרָה לְמַעַן שְׁמֶךָ
כִּי גּוֹאֵל חָזָק אָתָּה.
בָּרוּךְ אַתָּה יהוה, גּוֹאֵל יִשְׂרָאֵל.

רפואה

רְפָאֵנוּ יהוה וְנֵרָפֵא
הוֹשִׁיעֵנוּ וְנִוָּשֵׁעָה, כִּי תְהִלָּתֵנוּ אָתָּה
וְהַעֲלֵה רְפוּאָה שְׁלֵמָה לְכָל מַכּוֹתֵינוּ

---

*The following prayer for a sick person may be said here:*

יְהִי רָצוֹן מִלְּפָנֶיךָ יהוה אֱלֹהַי וֵאלֹהֵי אֲבוֹתַי, שֶׁתִּשְׁלַח מְהֵרָה רְפוּאָה שְׁלֵמָה מִן הַשָּׁמַיִם רְפוּאַת הַנֶּפֶשׁ וּרְפוּאַת הַגּוּף לַחוֹלֶה/לַחוֹלָה *name of patient* בֶּן/בַּת *mother's name* בְּתוֹךְ שְׁאָר חוֹלֵי יִשְׂרָאֵל.

---

כִּי אֵל מֶלֶךְ רוֹפֵא נֶאֱמָן וְרַחֲמָן אָתָּה.
בָּרוּךְ אַתָּה יהוה, רוֹפֵא חוֹלֵי עַמּוֹ יִשְׂרָאֵל.

PROSPERITY

*The phrase "Grant dew and rain as a blessing" is said from December 5th (in the year before a civil leap year, December 6th) until Pesaḥ. In Israel, it is said from the 7th of Marḥeshvan. The phrase "Grant blessing" is said from Ḥol HaMo'ed Pesaḥ until December 4th (in the year before a civil leap year, December 5th). In Israel it is said through the 6th of Marḥeshvan. See laws 147–149.*

בָּרֵךְ Bless this year for us, LORD our God,
and all its types of produce for good.

*In winter:* Grant dew and rain as a blessing
*In other seasons:* Grant blessing

on the face of the earth,
and from its goodness satisfy us,
blessing our year as the best of years.
Blessed are You, LORD,
who blesses the years.

INGATHERING OF EXILES

תְּקַע Sound the great shofar for our freedom,
raise high the banner to gather our exiles,
and gather us together
from the four quarters of the earth.
Blessed are You, LORD,
who gathers the dispersed of His people Israel.

JUSTICE

הָשִׁיבָה Restore our judges as at first,
and our counselors as at the beginning,
and remove from us sorrow and sighing.
May You alone, LORD,
reign over us with loving-kindness and compassion,
and vindicate us in justice.
Blessed are You, LORD,
the King who loves righteousness and justice.
/*Between Rosh HaShana & Yom Kippur, end the blessing:* the King of justice./

ברכת השנים

*The phrase* וְתֵן טַל וּמָטָר לִבְרָכָה *is said from December 5th (in the year before a civil leap year, December 6th) until* פסח. *In* ארץ ישראל*, it is said from* ז׳ מרחשון.
*The phrase* וְתֵן בְּרָכָה *is said from* חול המועד פסח *until December 4th (in the year before a civil leap year, December 5th). In* ארץ ישראל *it is said through* ו׳ מרחשון. *See laws 147–149.*

בָּרֵךְ עָלֵינוּ יהוה אֱלֹהֵינוּ אֶת הַשָּׁנָה הַזֹּאת
וְאֶת כָּל מִינֵי תְבוּאָתָהּ, לְטוֹבָה
בחורף: וְתֵן טַל וּמָטָר לִבְרָכָה / בקיץ: וְתֵן בְּרָכָה
עַל פְּנֵי הָאֲדָמָה
וְשַׂבְּעֵנוּ מִטּוּבָהּ
וּבָרֵךְ שְׁנָתֵנוּ כַּשָּׁנִים הַטּוֹבוֹת.
בָּרוּךְ אַתָּה יהוה, מְבָרֵךְ הַשָּׁנִים.

קבוץ גלויות

תְּקַע בְּשׁוֹפָר גָּדוֹל לְחֵרוּתֵנוּ
וְשָׂא נֵס לְקַבֵּץ גָּלֻיּוֹתֵינוּ
וְקַבְּצֵנוּ יַחַד מֵאַרְבַּע כַּנְפוֹת הָאָרֶץ.
בָּרוּךְ אַתָּה יהוה, מְקַבֵּץ נִדְחֵי עַמּוֹ יִשְׂרָאֵל.

השבת המשפט

הָשִׁיבָה שׁוֹפְטֵינוּ כְּבָרִאשׁוֹנָה
וְיוֹעֲצֵינוּ כְּבַתְּחִלָּה
וְהָסֵר מִמֶּנּוּ יָגוֹן וַאֲנָחָה
וּמְלֹךְ עָלֵינוּ אַתָּה יהוה לְבַדְּךָ בְּחֶסֶד וּבְרַחֲמִים
וְצַדְּקֵנוּ בַּמִּשְׁפָּט.
בָּרוּךְ אַתָּה יהוה
מֶלֶךְ אוֹהֵב צְדָקָה וּמִשְׁפָּט. / בעשרת ימי תשובה: הַמֶּלֶךְ הַמִּשְׁפָּט./

### AGAINST INFORMERS

וְלַמַּלְשִׁינִים For the slanderers let there be no hope,
and may all wickedness perish in an instant.
May all Your people's enemies swiftly be cut down.
May You swiftly uproot, crush, cast down
and humble the arrogant swiftly in our days.
Blessed are You, Lord,
who destroys enemies and humbles the arrogant.

### THE RIGHTEOUS

עַל הַצַּדִּיקִים To the righteous, the pious,
the elders of Your people the house of Israel,
the remnant of their scholars,
the righteous converts, and to us,
may Your compassion be aroused, Lord our God.
Grant a good reward to all who sincerely trust in Your name.
Set our lot with them, so that we may never be ashamed,
for in You we trust.
Blessed are You, Lord,
who is the support and trust of the righteous.

### REBUILDING JERUSALEM

וְלִירוּשָׁלַיִם To Jerusalem, Your city, may You return in compassion,
and may You dwell in it as You promised.
May You rebuild it rapidly in our days as an everlasting structure,
and install within it soon the throne of David.
Blessed are You, Lord,
who builds Jerusalem.

### KINGDOM OF DAVID

אֶת צֶמַח May the offshoot of Your servant David soon flower,
and may his pride be raised high by Your salvation,
for we wait for Your salvation all day.
Blessed are You, Lord,
who makes the glory of salvation flourish.

ברכת המינים

וְלַמַּלְשִׁינִים אַל תְּהִי תִקְוָה, וְכָל הָרִשְׁעָה כְּרֶגַע תֹּאבֵד
וְכָל אוֹיְבֵי עַמְּךָ מְהֵרָה יִכָּרֵתוּ
וְהַזֵּדִים מְהֵרָה תְעַקֵּר וּתְשַׁבֵּר וּתְמַגֵּר וְתַכְנִיעַ בִּמְהֵרָה בְיָמֵינוּ.
בָּרוּךְ אַתָּה יהוה, שׁוֹבֵר אוֹיְבִים וּמַכְנִיעַ זֵדִים.

על הצדיקים

עַל הַצַּדִּיקִים וְעַל הַחֲסִידִים
וְעַל זִקְנֵי עַמְּךָ בֵּית יִשְׂרָאֵל
וְעַל פְּלֵיטַת סוֹפְרֵיהֶם
וְעַל גֵּרֵי הַצֶּדֶק, וְעָלֵינוּ
יֶהֱמוּ רַחֲמֶיךָ יהוה אֱלֹהֵינוּ
וְתֵן שָׂכָר טוֹב לְכָל הַבּוֹטְחִים בְּשִׁמְךָ בֶּאֱמֶת
וְשִׂים חֶלְקֵנוּ עִמָּהֶם, וּלְעוֹלָם לֹא נֵבוֹשׁ כִּי בְךָ בָטָחְנוּ.
בָּרוּךְ אַתָּה יהוה, מִשְׁעָן וּמִבְטָח לַצַּדִּיקִים.

בניין ירושלים

וְלִירוּשָׁלַיִם עִירְךָ בְּרַחֲמִים תָּשׁוּב
וְתִשְׁכֹּן בְּתוֹכָהּ כַּאֲשֶׁר דִּבַּרְתָּ
וּבְנֵה אוֹתָהּ בְּקָרוֹב בְּיָמֵינוּ בִּנְיַן עוֹלָם
וְכִסֵּא דָוִד מְהֵרָה לְתוֹכָהּ תָּכִין.
בָּרוּךְ אַתָּה יהוה, בּוֹנֵה יְרוּשָׁלָיִם.

משיח בן דוד

אֶת צֶמַח דָּוִד עַבְדְּךָ מְהֵרָה תַצְמִיחַ, וְקַרְנוֹ תָּרוּם בִּישׁוּעָתֶךָ
כִּי לִישׁוּעָתְךָ קִוִּינוּ כָּל הַיּוֹם.
בָּרוּךְ אַתָּה יהוה, מַצְמִיחַ קֶרֶן יְשׁוּעָה.

RESPONSE TO PRAYER

שְׁמַע קוֹלֵנוּ Listen to our voice, LORD our God.
Spare us and have compassion on us,
and in compassion and favor accept our prayer,
for You, God, listen to prayers and pleas.
Do not turn us away, O our King,
empty-handed from Your presence,*
for You listen with compassion to the prayer of Your people Israel.
Blessed are You, LORD, who listens to prayer.

*At this point, in times of drought in Israel, say "And answer us" on page 186.

TEMPLE SERVICE

רְצֵה Find favor, LORD our God,
in Your people Israel and their prayer.
Restore the service to Your most holy House,
and accept in love and favor
the fire-offerings of Israel and their prayer.
May the service of Your people Israel always find favor with You.

---

*On Rosh Ḥodesh and Ḥol HaMo'ed, say:*

אֱלֹהֵינוּ Our God and God of our ancestors, may there rise, come, reach, appear, be favored, heard, regarded and remembered before You, our recollection and remembrance, as well as the remembrance of our ancestors, and of the Messiah, son of David Your servant, and of Jerusalem Your holy city, and of all Your people the house of Israel – for deliverance and well-being, grace, loving-kindness and compassion, life and peace, on this day of:

*On Rosh Ḥodesh:* Rosh Ḥodesh.
*On Pesaḥ:* the Festival of Matzot.
*On Sukkot:* the Festival of Sukkot.

On it remember us, LORD our God, for good; recollect us for blessing, and deliver us for life. In accord with Your promise of salvation and compassion, spare us and be gracious to us; have compassion on us and deliver us, for our eyes are turned to You because You, God, are a gracious and compassionate King.

---

שומע תפילה

שְׁמַע קוֹלֵנוּ יהוה אֱלֹהֵינוּ
חוּס וְרַחֵם עָלֵינוּ
וְקַבֵּל בְּרַחֲמִים וּבְרָצוֹן אֶת תְּפִלָּתֵנוּ
כִּי אֵל שׁוֹמֵעַ תְּפִלּוֹת וְתַחֲנוּנִים אָתָּה
וּמִלְּפָנֶיךָ מַלְכֵּנוּ רֵיקָם אַל תְּשִׁיבֵנוּ*
כִּי אַתָּה שׁוֹמֵעַ תְּפִלַּת עַמְּךָ יִשְׂרָאֵל בְּרַחֲמִים.
בָּרוּךְ אַתָּה יהוה, שׁוֹמֵעַ תְּפִלָּה.

*At this point, in times of drought in ארץ ישראל, say וַעֲנֵנוּ on page 187.

עבודה

רְצֵה יהוה אֱלֹהֵינוּ בְּעַמְּךָ יִשְׂרָאֵל וּבִתְפִלָּתָם
וְהָשֵׁב אֶת הָעֲבוֹדָה לִדְבִיר בֵּיתֶךָ
וְאִשֵּׁי יִשְׂרָאֵל וּתְפִלָּתָם בְּאַהֲבָה תְקַבֵּל בְּרָצוֹן
וּתְהִי לְרָצוֹן תָּמִיד עֲבוֹדַת יִשְׂרָאֵל עַמֶּךָ.

---

*On* ראש חודש *and* חול המועד, *say:*

אֱלֹהֵינוּ וֵאלֹהֵי אֲבוֹתֵינוּ, יַעֲלֶה וְיָבוֹא וְיַגִּיעַ, וְיֵרָאֶה וְיֵרָצֶה וְיִשָּׁמַע, וְיִפָּקֵד וְיִזָּכֵר זִכְרוֹנֵנוּ וּפִקְדוֹנֵנוּ וְזִכְרוֹן אֲבוֹתֵינוּ, וְזִכְרוֹן מָשִׁיחַ בֶּן דָּוִד עַבְדֶּךָ, וְזִכְרוֹן יְרוּשָׁלַיִם עִיר קָדְשֶׁךָ, וְזִכְרוֹן כָּל עַמְּךָ בֵּית יִשְׂרָאֵל, לְפָנֶיךָ, לִפְלֵיטָה לְטוֹבָה, לְחֵן וּלְחֶסֶד וּלְרַחֲמִים, לְחַיִּים וּלְשָׁלוֹם בְּיוֹם

בראש חודש: רֹאשׁ הַחֹדֶשׁ / בפסח: חַג הַמַּצּוֹת / בסוכות: חַג הַסֻּכּוֹת

הַזֶּה. זָכְרֵנוּ יהוה אֱלֹהֵינוּ בּוֹ לְטוֹבָה, וּפָקְדֵנוּ בוֹ לִבְרָכָה, וְהוֹשִׁיעֵנוּ בוֹ לְחַיִּים. וּבִדְבַר יְשׁוּעָה וְרַחֲמִים, חוּס וְחָנֵּנוּ וְרַחֵם עָלֵינוּ וְהוֹשִׁיעֵנוּ, כִּי אֵלֶיךָ עֵינֵינוּ, כִּי אֵל מֶלֶךְ חַנּוּן וְרַחוּם אָתָּה.

וְתֶחֱזֶינָה And may our eyes witness Your return to Zion in compassion.
Blessed are You, LORD, who restores His Presence to Zion.

THANKSGIVING

*Bow at the first nine words.*

מוֹדִים We give thanks to You,
for You are the LORD our God and God of our ancestors
for ever and all time.
You are the Rock of our lives,
Shield of our salvation from generation to generation.
We will thank You and declare Your praise for our lives,
which are entrusted into Your hand;
for our souls, which are placed in Your charge;
for Your miracles which are with us every day;
and for Your wonders and favors at all times,
evening, morning and midday.
You are good – for Your compassion never fails.
You are compassionate – for Your loving-kindnesses never cease.
We have always placed our hope in You.

---

*On Ḥanukka:*

עַל הַנִּסִּים [We thank You also] for the miracles, the redemption, the mighty deeds, the salvations, and the victories in battle which You performed for our ancestors in those days, at this time.

בִּימֵי מַתִּתְיָהוּ In the days of Mattityahu, son of Yoḥanan, the High Priest, the Hasmonean, and his sons, the wicked Greek kingdom rose up against Your people Israel to make them forget Your Torah and to force them to transgress the statutes of Your will. It was then that You in Your great compassion stood by them in the time of their distress. You championed their cause, judged their claim, and avenged their wrong. You delivered the strong into the hands of the weak, the many into the hands of the few, the impure into the hands of the pure, the wicked into the hands of the righteous, and the arrogant into the hands of those who were engaged in the study of Your Torah. You made for Yourself great and holy renown in Your world, and for Your people Israel You performed a great salvation and redemption as of this very day. Your children then entered the holiest part of Your House, cleansed Your Temple, purified Your Sanctuary, kindled lights in Your holy courts, and designated these eight days of Ḥanukka for giving thanks and praise to Your great name.

*Continue with "For all these things" on the next page.*

וְתֶחֱזֶינָה עֵינֵינוּ בְּשׁוּבְךָ לְצִיּוֹן בְּרַחֲמִים.
בָּרוּךְ אַתָּה יהוה, הַמַּחֲזִיר שְׁכִינָתוֹ לְצִיּוֹן.

הודאה

*Bow at the first five words.*

מוֹדִים אֲנַחְנוּ לָךְ
שָׁאַתָּה הוּא יהוה אֱלֹהֵינוּ וֵאלֹהֵי אֲבוֹתֵינוּ לְעוֹלָם וָעֶד.
צוּר חַיֵּינוּ, מָגֵן יִשְׁעֵנוּ אַתָּה הוּא לְדוֹר וָדוֹר.
נוֹדֶה לְּךָ וּנְסַפֵּר תְּהִלָּתֶךָ
עַל חַיֵּינוּ הַמְּסוּרִים בְּיָדֶךָ, וְעַל נִשְׁמוֹתֵינוּ הַפְּקוּדוֹת לָךְ
וְעַל נִסֶּיךָ שֶׁבְּכָל יוֹם עִמָּנוּ, וְעַל נִפְלְאוֹתֶיךָ וְטוֹבוֹתֶיךָ
שֶׁבְּכָל עֵת, עֶרֶב וָבֹקֶר וְצָהֳרָיִם.
הַטּוֹב, כִּי לֹא כָלוּ רַחֲמֶיךָ
וְהַמְרַחֵם, כִּי לֹא תַמּוּ חֲסָדֶיךָ
מֵעוֹלָם קִוִּינוּ לָךְ.

---

בחנוכה:
עַל הַנִּסִּים וְעַל הַפֻּרְקָן וְעַל הַגְּבוּרוֹת וְעַל הַתְּשׁוּעוֹת וְעַל הַמִּלְחָמוֹת שֶׁעָשִׂיתָ לַאֲבוֹתֵינוּ בַּיָּמִים הָהֵם בַּזְּמַן הַזֶּה.

בִּימֵי מַתִּתְיָהוּ בֶּן יוֹחָנָן כֹּהֵן גָּדוֹל חַשְׁמוֹנַאי וּבָנָיו, כְּשֶׁעָמְדָה מַלְכוּת יָוָן הָרְשָׁעָה עַל עַמְּךָ יִשְׂרָאֵל לְהַשְׁכִּיחָם תּוֹרָתֶךָ וּלְהַעֲבִירָם מֵחֻקֵּי רְצוֹנֶךָ, וְאַתָּה בְּרַחֲמֶיךָ הָרַבִּים עָמַדְתָּ לָהֶם בְּעֵת צָרָתָם, רַבְתָּ אֶת רִיבָם, דַּנְתָּ אֶת דִּינָם, נָקַמְתָּ אֶת נִקְמָתָם, מָסַרְתָּ גִבּוֹרִים בְּיַד חַלָּשִׁים, וְרַבִּים בְּיַד מְעַטִּים, וּטְמֵאִים בְּיַד טְהוֹרִים, וּרְשָׁעִים בְּיַד צַדִּיקִים, וְזֵדִים בְּיַד עוֹסְקֵי תוֹרָתֶךָ, וּלְךָ עָשִׂיתָ שֵׁם גָּדוֹל וְקָדוֹשׁ בְּעוֹלָמֶךָ, וּלְעַמְּךָ יִשְׂרָאֵל עָשִׂיתָ תְּשׁוּעָה גְדוֹלָה וּפֻרְקָן כְּהַיּוֹם הַזֶּה. וְאַחַר כֵּן בָּאוּ בָנֶיךָ לִדְבִיר בֵּיתֶךָ, וּפִנּוּ אֶת הֵיכָלֶךָ, וְטִהֲרוּ אֶת מִקְדָּשֶׁךָ, וְהִדְלִיקוּ נֵרוֹת בְּחַצְרוֹת קָדְשֶׁךָ, וְקָבְעוּ שְׁמוֹנַת יְמֵי חֲנֻכָּה אֵלּוּ, לְהוֹדוֹת וּלְהַלֵּל לְשִׁמְךָ הַגָּדוֹל.

*Continue with* וְעַל כֻּלָּם *on the next page.*

*On Purim:*

עַל הַנִּסִּים [We thank You also] for the miracles, the redemption, the mighty deeds, the salvations, and the victories in battle which You performed for our ancestors in those days at this time.

בִּימֵי מָרְדְּכַי In the days of Mordekhai and Esther, in Shushan the capital, the wicked Haman rose up against them and sought to destroy, slay and exterminate all the Jews, young and old, children and women, on one day, the thirteenth day of the twelfth month, which is the month of Adar, and to plunder their possessions. Then You in Your great compassion thwarted his counsel, frustrated his plans, and caused his scheme to recoil on his own head, so that they hanged him and his sons on the gallows. *Esther 3*

*Continue with "For all these things".*

---

וְעַל כֻּלָּם For all these things may Your name be blessed and exalted, our King, continually, for ever and all time.

*Between Rosh HaShana & Yom Kippur:* And write, for a good life, all the children of Your covenant.

Let all that lives thank You, Selah! and praise Your name in truth, God, our Savior and Help, Selah!
▾Blessed are You, Lord, whose name is "the Good" and to whom thanks are due.

PEACE

שָׁלוֹם רָב Grant great peace to Your people Israel for ever,
for You are the sovereign Lord of all peace;
and may it be good in Your eyes
to bless Your people Israel
at every time, at every hour, with Your peace.

*Between Rosh HaShana & Yom Kippur:* In the book of life, blessing, peace and prosperity,
may we and all Your people the house of Israel
be remembered and written before You
for a good life, and for peace.*

Blessed are You, Lord, who blesses His people Israel with peace.

**Between Rosh HaShana and Yom Kippur in the Diaspora, many end the blessing:*
Blessed are You, Lord, who makes peace.

בפורים:

עַל הַנִּסִּים וְעַל הַפֻּרְקָן וְעַל הַגְּבוּרוֹת וְעַל הַתְּשׁוּעוֹת וְעַל הַמִּלְחָמוֹת שֶׁעָשִׂיתָ לַאֲבוֹתֵינוּ בַּיָּמִים הָהֵם בַּזְּמַן הַזֶּה.

בִּימֵי מָרְדְּכַי וְאֶסְתֵּר בְּשׁוּשַׁן הַבִּירָה, כְּשֶׁעָמַד עֲלֵיהֶם הָמָן הָרָשָׁע, בִּקֵּשׁ
לְהַשְׁמִיד לַהֲרֹג וּלְאַבֵּד אֶת־כָּל־הַיְּהוּדִים מִנַּעַר וְעַד־זָקֵן טַף וְנָשִׁים בְּיוֹם אסתר ג
אֶחָד, בִּשְׁלוֹשָׁה עָשָׂר לְחֹדֶשׁ שְׁנֵים־עָשָׂר, הוּא־חֹדֶשׁ אֲדָר, וּשְׁלָלָם
לָבוֹז: וְאַתָּה בְּרַחֲמֶיךָ הָרַבִּים הֵפַרְתָּ אֶת עֲצָתוֹ, וְקִלְקַלְתָּ אֶת מַחֲשַׁבְתּוֹ,
וַהֲשֵׁבוֹתָ לּוֹ גְּמוּלוֹ בְּרֹאשׁוֹ, וְתָלוּ אוֹתוֹ וְאֶת בָּנָיו עַל הָעֵץ.

*Continue with* וְעַל כֻּלָּם.

---

וְעַל כֻּלָּם יִתְבָּרַךְ וְיִתְרוֹמַם שִׁמְךָ מַלְכֵּנוּ תָּמִיד לְעוֹלָם וָעֶד.

בעשרת ימי תשובה: וּכְתֹב לְחַיִּים טוֹבִים כָּל בְּנֵי בְרִיתֶךָ.

וְכֹל הַחַיִּים יוֹדוּךָ סֶּלָה, וִיהַלְלוּ אֶת שִׁמְךָ בֶּאֱמֶת
הָאֵל יְשׁוּעָתֵנוּ וְעֶזְרָתֵנוּ סֶלָה.
בָּרוּךְ אַתָּה יהוה, הַטּוֹב שִׁמְךָ וּלְךָ נָאֶה לְהוֹדוֹת.

ברכת שלום

שָׁלוֹם רָב עַל יִשְׂרָאֵל עַמְּךָ תָּשִׂים לְעוֹלָם
כִּי אַתָּה הוּא מֶלֶךְ אָדוֹן לְכָל הַשָּׁלוֹם.
וְטוֹב בְּעֵינֶיךָ לְבָרֵךְ אֶת עַמְּךָ יִשְׂרָאֵל
בְּכָל עֵת וּבְכָל שָׁעָה בִּשְׁלוֹמֶךָ.

בעשרת ימי תשובה: בְּסֵפֶר חַיִּים, בְּרָכָה וְשָׁלוֹם, וּפַרְנָסָה טוֹבָה
נִזָּכֵר וְנִכָּתֵב לְפָנֶיךָ, אֲנַחְנוּ וְכָל עַמְּךָ בֵּית יִשְׂרָאֵל
לְחַיִּים טוֹבִים וּלְשָׁלוֹם.*

בָּרוּךְ אַתָּה יהוה, הַמְבָרֵךְ אֶת עַמּוֹ יִשְׂרָאֵל בַּשָּׁלוֹם.

**During the* עשרת ימי תשובה *in* חוץ לארץ, *many end the blessing:*

בָּרוּךְ אַתָּה יהוה, עוֹשֵׂה הַשָּׁלוֹם.

*Some say the following verse (see law 368):*

May the words of my mouth and the meditation of my heart find favor before You, LORD, my Rock and Redeemer. Ps. 19

אֱלֹהַי My God, Berakhot 17a
guard my tongue from evil and my lips from deceitful speech.
To those who curse me, let my soul be silent;
may my soul be to all like the dust.
Open my heart to Your Torah
and let my soul pursue Your commandments.
As for all who plan evil against me,
swiftly thwart their counsel and frustrate their plans.
Act for the sake of Your name; act for the sake of Your right hand;
act for the sake of Your holiness; act for the sake of Your Torah.
That Your beloved ones may be delivered, Ps. 60
save with Your right hand and answer me.
May the words of my mouth Ps. 19
and the meditation of my heart find favor before You,
LORD, my Rock and Redeemer.

*Bow, take three steps back, then bow, first left, then right, then center, while saying:*

May He who makes peace in His high places,
make peace for us and all Israel – and say: Amen.

יְהִי רָצוֹן May it be Your will, LORD our God and God of our ancestors,
that the Temple be rebuilt speedily in our days,
and grant us a share in Your Torah.
And there we will serve You with reverence,
as in the days of old and as in former years.
Then the offering of Judah and Jerusalem Mal. 3
will be pleasing to the LORD as in the days of old and as in former years.

*On Motza'ei Shabbat (except when Yom Tov or Erev Pesaḥ falls in the following week), the Leader continues with Half Kaddish on page 328, then "May the pleasantness" on page 752.*

*On Motza'ei Shabbat when Yom Tov falls in the following week, the service continues on page 756.*

*On other evenings the Leader says Full Kaddish on the next page.*

*Some say the following verse (see law 368):*

יִהְיוּ לְרָצוֹן אִמְרֵי־פִי וְהֶגְיוֹן לִבִּי לְפָנֶיךָ, יהוה צוּרִי וְגֹאֲלִי: תהלים יט

אֱלֹהַי ברכות יז.

נְצֹר לְשׁוֹנִי מֵרָע וּשְׂפָתַי מִדַּבֵּר מִרְמָה

וְלִמְקַלְלַי נַפְשִׁי תִדֹּם, וְנַפְשִׁי כֶּעָפָר לַכֹּל תִּהְיֶה.

פְּתַח לִבִּי בְּתוֹרָתֶךָ, וּבְמִצְוֺתֶיךָ תִּרְדֹּף נַפְשִׁי.

וְכָל הַחוֹשְׁבִים עָלַי רָעָה

מְהֵרָה הָפֵר עֲצָתָם וְקַלְקֵל מַחֲשַׁבְתָּם.

עֲשֵׂה לְמַעַן שְׁמֶךָ, עֲשֵׂה לְמַעַן יְמִינֶךָ

עֲשֵׂה לְמַעַן קְדֻשָּׁתֶךָ, עֲשֵׂה לְמַעַן תּוֹרָתֶךָ.

לְמַעַן יֵחָלְצוּן יְדִידֶיךָ, הוֹשִׁיעָה יְמִינְךָ וַעֲנֵנִי: תהלים ס

יִהְיוּ לְרָצוֹן אִמְרֵי־פִי וְהֶגְיוֹן לִבִּי לְפָנֶיךָ, יהוה צוּרִי וְגֹאֲלִי: תהלים יט

*Bow, take three steps back, then bow, first left, then right, then center, while saying:*

עֹשֶׂה שָׁלוֹם/ בעשרת ימי תשובה: הַשָּׁלוֹם/ בִּמְרוֹמָיו

הוּא יַעֲשֶׂה שָׁלוֹם עָלֵינוּ וְעַל כָּל יִשְׂרָאֵל

וְאִמְרוּ אָמֵן.

יְהִי רָצוֹן מִלְּפָנֶיךָ יהוה אֱלֹהֵינוּ וֵאלֹהֵי אֲבוֹתֵינוּ

שֶׁיִּבָּנֶה בֵּית הַמִּקְדָּשׁ בִּמְהֵרָה בְיָמֵינוּ, וְתֵן חֶלְקֵנוּ בְּתוֹרָתֶךָ

וְשָׁם נַעֲבָדְךָ בְּיִרְאָה כִּימֵי עוֹלָם וּכְשָׁנִים קַדְמֹנִיּוֹת.

וְעָרְבָה לַיהוה מִנְחַת יְהוּדָה וִירוּשָׁלָםִ כִּימֵי עוֹלָם וּכְשָׁנִים קַדְמֹנִיּוֹת: מלאכי ג

*On* מוצאי שבת *(except when* יום טוב *or* ערב פסח *falls in the following week),*
*the* שליח ציבור *continues with* חצי קדיש *on page 329, then* וִיהִי נֹעַם *on page 753.*

*On* מוצאי שבת *when* יום טוב *falls in the following week,*
*the service continues on page 757.*

*On other evenings the* שליח ציבור *says* קדיש שלם *on the next page.*

## FULL KADDISH

*Leader:* יִתְגַּדַּל Magnified and sanctified
may His great name be,
in the world He created by His will.
May He establish His kingdom
in your lifetime and in your days,
and in the lifetime of all the house of Israel,
swiftly and soon –
and say: Amen.

*All:* May His great name be blessed for ever and all time.

*Leader:* Blessed and praised, glorified and exalted,
raised and honored, uplifted and lauded be
the name of the Holy One,
blessed be He,
beyond any blessing,
song, praise and consolation
uttered in the world –
and say: Amen.

May the prayers and pleas of all Israel
be accepted by their Father in heaven –
and say: Amen.

May there be great peace from heaven,
and life for us and all Israel –
and say: Amen.

*Bow, take three steps back, as if taking leave of the Divine Presence, then bow, first left, then right, then center, while saying:*

May He who makes peace in His high places,
make peace for us and all Israel –
and say: Amen.

*From the second night of Pesaḥ until the night before Shavuot, the Omer is counted here* *(page 356)**.*

*On Purim, Megillat Esther is read; on Tisha B'Av, Megillat Eikha is read.*

## קדיש שלם

ש״ץ: יִתְגַּדַּל וְיִתְקַדַּשׁ שְׁמֵהּ רַבָּא (קהל: אָמֵן)
בְּעָלְמָא דִּי בְרָא כִרְעוּתֵהּ
וְיַמְלִיךְ מַלְכוּתֵהּ
בְּחַיֵּיכוֹן וּבְיוֹמֵיכוֹן וּבְחַיֵּי דְכָל בֵּית יִשְׂרָאֵל
בַּעֲגָלָא וּבִזְמַן קָרִיב, וְאִמְרוּ אָמֵן. (קהל: אָמֵן)

קהל וש״ץ: יְהֵא שְׁמֵהּ רַבָּא מְבָרַךְ לְעָלַם וּלְעָלְמֵי עָלְמַיָּא.

ש״ץ: יִתְבָּרַךְ וְיִשְׁתַּבַּח וְיִתְפָּאַר וְיִתְרוֹמַם וְיִתְנַשֵּׂא
וְיִתְהַדָּר וְיִתְעַלֶּה וְיִתְהַלָּל
שְׁמֵהּ דְּקֻדְשָׁא בְּרִיךְ הוּא (קהל: בְּרִיךְ הוּא)
לְעֵלָּא מִן כָּל בִּרְכָתָא
/בעשרת ימי תשובה: לְעֵלָּא לְעֵלָּא מִכָּל בִּרְכָתָא/
וְשִׁירָתָא, תֻּשְׁבְּחָתָא וְנֶחָמָתָא
דַּאֲמִירָן בְּעָלְמָא, וְאִמְרוּ אָמֵן. (קהל: אָמֵן)

תִּתְקַבַּל צְלוֹתְהוֹן וּבָעוּתְהוֹן דְּכָל יִשְׂרָאֵל
קֳדָם אֲבוּהוֹן דִּי בִשְׁמַיָּא, וְאִמְרוּ אָמֵן. (קהל: אָמֵן)

יְהֵא שְׁלָמָא רַבָּא מִן שְׁמַיָּא
וְחַיִּים, עָלֵינוּ וְעַל כָּל יִשְׂרָאֵל, וְאִמְרוּ אָמֵן. (קהל: אָמֵן)

*Bow, take three steps back, as if taking leave of the Divine Presence, then bow, first left, then right, then center, while saying:*

עֹשֶׂה שָׁלוֹם/בעשרת ימי תשובה: הַשָּׁלוֹם/ בִּמְרוֹמָיו
הוּא יַעֲשֶׂה שָׁלוֹם
עָלֵינוּ וְעַל כָּל יִשְׂרָאֵל, וְאִמְרוּ אָמֵן. (קהל: אָמֵן)

*From the second night of* פסח *until the night before* שבועות*, the* עומר *is counted here* *(page 357)*.

*On* פורים*,* מגילת אסתר *is read; on* תשעה באב*,* מגילת איכה *is read.*

*Stand while saying Aleinu. Bow at* ▾.

עָלֵינוּ It is our duty to praise the Master of all,
and ascribe greatness to the Author of creation,
who has not made us like the nations of the lands
nor placed us like the families of the earth;
who has not made our portion like theirs,
nor our destiny like all their multitudes.
(For they worship vanity and emptiness,
and pray to a god who cannot save.)
▾But we bow in worship and thank the Supreme King of kings,
the Holy One, blessed be He,
who extends the heavens and establishes the earth,
whose throne of glory is in the heavens above,
and whose power's Presence is in the highest of heights.
He is our God; there is no other.
Truly He is our King, there is none else,
as it is written in His Torah:
"You shall know and take to heart this day *Deut. 4*
that the LORD is God,
in heaven above and on earth below. There is no other."

Therefore, we place our hope in You, LORD our God,
that we may soon see the glory of Your power,
when You will remove abominations from the earth,
and idols will be utterly destroyed,
when the world will be perfected
under the sovereignty of the Almighty,
when all humanity will call on Your name,
to turn all the earth's wicked toward You.
All the world's inhabitants will realize and know
that to You every knee must bow and every tongue swear loyalty.
Before You, LORD our God, they will kneel and bow down
and give honor to Your glorious name.
They will all accept the yoke of Your kingdom,
and You will reign over them soon and for ever.

כִּי הַמַּלְכוּת שֶׁלְּךָ הִיא וּלְעוֹלְמֵי עַד תִּמְלֹךְ בְּכָבוֹד
כַּכָּתוּב בְּתוֹרָתֶךָ, יהוה יִמְלֹךְ לְעֹלָם וָעֶד: שמות טו
◂ וְנֶאֱמַר, וְהָיָה יהוה לְמֶלֶךְ עַל־כָּל־הָאָרֶץ זכריה יד
בַּיּוֹם הַהוּא יִהְיֶה יהוה אֶחָד וּשְׁמוֹ אֶחָד:

*Some add:*

אַל־תִּירָא מִפַּחַד פִּתְאֹם וּמִשֹּׁאַת רְשָׁעִים כִּי תָבֹא: משלי ג
עֻצוּ עֵצָה וְתֻפָר, דַּבְּרוּ דָבָר וְלֹא יָקוּם, כִּי עִמָּנוּ אֵל: ישעיה ח
וְעַד־זִקְנָה אֲנִי הוּא, וְעַד־שֵׂיבָה אֲנִי אֶסְבֹּל ישעיה מו
אֲנִי עָשִׂיתִי וַאֲנִי אֶשָּׂא וַאֲנִי אֶסְבֹּל וַאֲמַלֵּט:

## קדיש יתום

*The following prayer requires the presence of a* מנין*.*
*A transliteration can be found on page 1320.*

אבל: יִתְגַּדַּל וְיִתְקַדַּשׁ שְׁמֵהּ רַבָּא (קהל: אָמֵן)
בְּעָלְמָא דִּי בְרָא כִרְעוּתֵהּ
וְיַמְלִיךְ מַלְכוּתֵהּ
בְּחַיֵּיכוֹן וּבְיוֹמֵיכוֹן וּבְחַיֵּי דְכָל בֵּית יִשְׂרָאֵל
בַּעֲגָלָא וּבִזְמַן קָרִיב, וְאִמְרוּ אָמֵן. (קהל: אָמֵן)

קהל ואבל: יְהֵא שְׁמֵהּ רַבָּא מְבָרַךְ לְעָלַם וּלְעָלְמֵי עָלְמַיָּא.

אבל: יִתְבָּרַךְ וְיִשְׁתַּבַּח וְיִתְפָּאַר
וְיִתְרוֹמַם וְיִתְנַשֵּׂא וְיִתְהַדָּר וְיִתְעַלֶּה וְיִתְהַלָּל
שְׁמֵהּ דְּקֻדְשָׁא בְּרִיךְ הוּא (קהל: בְּרִיךְ הוּא)
לְעֵלָּא מִן כָּל בִּרְכָתָא
/בעשרת ימי תשובה: לְעֵלָּא לְעֵלָּא מִכָּל בִּרְכָתָא/
וְשִׁירָתָא, תֻּשְׁבְּחָתָא וְנֶחֱמָתָא
דַּאֲמִירָן בְּעָלְמָא, וְאִמְרוּ אָמֵן. (קהל: אָמֵן)

May there be great peace from heaven,
and life for us and all Israel –
and say: Amen.

*Bow, take three steps back, as if taking leave of the Divine Presence, then bow, first left, then right, then center, while saying:*

May He who makes peace in His high places,
make peace for us and all Israel –
and say: Amen.

*From the second day of Rosh Ḥodesh Elul through Shemini Atzeret (in Israel through Hoshana Raba), the following psalm is said:*

לְדָוִד By David. The Lord is my light and my salvation – whom then shall I fear? The Lord is the stronghold of my life – of whom shall I be afraid? When evil men close in on me to devour my flesh, it is they, my enemies and foes, who stumble and fall. Should an army besiege me, my heart would not fear. Should war break out against me, still I would be confident. One thing I ask of the Lord, only this do I seek: to live in the House of the Lord all the days of my life, to gaze on the beauty of the Lord and worship in His Temple. For He will keep me safe in His pavilion on the day of trouble. He will hide me under the cover of His tent. He will set me high upon a rock. Now my head is high above my enemies who surround me. I will sacrifice in His tent with shouts of joy. I will sing and chant praises to the Lord. Lord, hear my voice when I call. Be gracious to me and answer me. On Your behalf my heart says, "Seek My face." Your face, Lord, will I seek. Do not hide Your face from me. Do not turn Your servant away in anger. You have been my help. Do not reject or forsake me, God, my Savior. Were my father and my mother to forsake me, the Lord would take me in. Teach me Your way, Lord, and lead me on a level path, because of my oppressors. Do not abandon me to the will of my foes, for false witnesses have risen against me, breathing violence. ▸ Were it not for my faith that I shall see the Lord's goodness in the land of the living. Hope in the Lord. Be strong and of good courage, and hope in the Lord! *Ps. 27*

*Mourner's Kaddish* *(on previous page)*

*In a house of mourning the service continues on page 1138.*

יְהֵא שְׁלָמָא רַבָּא מִן שְׁמַיָּא
וְחַיִּים, עָלֵינוּ וְעַל כָּל יִשְׂרָאֵל
וְאִמְרוּ אָמֵן. (קהל: אָמֵן)

*Bow, take three steps back, as if taking leave of the Divine Presence, then bow, first left, then right, then center, while saying:*

עֹשֶׂה שָׁלוֹם/ בעשרת ימי תשובה: הַשָּׁלוֹם/ בִּמְרוֹמָיו
הוּא יַעֲשֶׂה שָׁלוֹם עָלֵינוּ וְעַל כָּל יִשְׂרָאֵל
וְאִמְרוּ אָמֵן. (קהל: אָמֵן)

*From the second day of* ראש חודש אלול *through* שמיני עצרת (*in* ארץ ישראל *through* הושענא רבה), *the following psalm is said:*

לְדָוִד, יהוה אוֹרִי וְיִשְׁעִי, מִמִּי אִירָא, יהוה מָעוֹז־חַיַּי, מִמִּי אֶפְחָד: בִּקְרֹב עָלַי מְרֵעִים לֶאֱכֹל אֶת־בְּשָׂרִי, צָרַי וְאֹיְבַי לִי, הֵמָּה כָשְׁלוּ וְנָפָלוּ: אִם־תַּחֲנֶה עָלַי מַחֲנֶה, לֹא־יִירָא לִבִּי, אִם־תָּקוּם עָלַי מִלְחָמָה, בְּזֹאת אֲנִי בוֹטֵחַ: אַחַת שָׁאַלְתִּי מֵאֵת־יהוה, אוֹתָהּ אֲבַקֵּשׁ, שִׁבְתִּי בְּבֵית־יהוה כָּל־יְמֵי חַיַּי, לַחֲזוֹת בְּנֹעַם־יהוה, וּלְבַקֵּר בְּהֵיכָלוֹ: כִּי יִצְפְּנֵנִי בְּסֻכֹּה בְּיוֹם רָעָה, יַסְתִּרֵנִי בְּסֵתֶר אָהֳלוֹ, בְּצוּר יְרוֹמְמֵנִי: וְעַתָּה יָרוּם רֹאשִׁי עַל אֹיְבַי סְבִיבוֹתַי, וְאֶזְבְּחָה בְאָהֳלוֹ זִבְחֵי תְרוּעָה, אָשִׁירָה וַאֲזַמְּרָה לַיהוה: שְׁמַע־יהוה קוֹלִי אֶקְרָא, וְחָנֵּנִי וַעֲנֵנִי: לְךָ אָמַר לִבִּי בַּקְּשׁוּ פָנָי, אֶת־פָּנֶיךָ יהוה אֲבַקֵּשׁ: אַל־תַּסְתֵּר פָּנֶיךָ מִמֶּנִּי, אַל תַּט־בְּאַף עַבְדֶּךָ, עֶזְרָתִי הָיִיתָ, אַל־תִּטְּשֵׁנִי וְאַל־תַּעַזְבֵנִי, אֱלֹהֵי יִשְׁעִי: כִּי־אָבִי וְאִמִּי עֲזָבוּנִי, וַיהוה יַאַסְפֵנִי: הוֹרֵנִי יהוה דַּרְכֶּךָ, וּנְחֵנִי בְּאֹרַח מִישׁוֹר, לְמַעַן שׁוֹרְרָי: אַל־תִּתְּנֵנִי בְּנֶפֶשׁ צָרָי, כִּי קָמוּ־בִי עֵדֵי־שֶׁקֶר, וִיפֵחַ חָמָס: ‹ לוּלֵא הֶאֱמַנְתִּי לִרְאוֹת בְּטוּב־יהוה בְּאֶרֶץ חַיִּים: קַוֵּה אֶל־יהוה, חֲזַק וְיַאֲמֵץ לִבֶּךָ, וְקַוֵּה אֶל־יהוה: תהלים כז

קדיש יתום (*on previous page*)

*In a house of mourning the service continues on page 1139.*

## COUNTING OF THE OMER

*The Omer is counted each night from the second night of Pesaḥ until the night before Shavuot. See laws 221–224.*

*Some say the following meditation before the blessing:*

For the sake of the unification of the Holy One, blessed be He,
and His Divine Presence, in reverence and love,
to unify the name *Yod-Heh* with *Vav-Heh*
in perfect unity in the name of all Israel.

הִנְנִי I am prepared and ready to fulfill the positive commandment of Counting the Omer, as is written in the Torah, "You shall count seven complete weeks from the day following the [Pesaḥ] rest day, when you brought the Omer as a wave-offering. To the day after the seventh week you shall count fifty days. Then you shall present a meal-offering of new grain to the LORD." May the pleasantness of the LORD our God be upon us. Establish for us the work of our hands, O establish the work of our hands. *Lev. 23* *Ps. 90*

בָּרוּךְ Blessed are You, LORD our God, King of the Universe,
who has made us holy through His commandments,
and has commanded us about counting the Omer.

16 Nisan

1. Today is the first day of the Omer.

17 Nisan

2. Today is the second day of the Omer.

18 Nisan

3. Today is the third day of the Omer.

19 Nisan

4. Today is the fourth day of the Omer.

20 Nisan

5. Today is the fifth day of the Omer.

21 Nisan

6. Today is the sixth day of the Omer.

22 Nisan

7. Today is the seventh day, making one week of the Omer.

---

same token, when the collective nation sacrifices its material abilities, consecrating them to the LORD, the nation is united in its will with the will of the LORD, God of the Universe.[15]

15. *OR*, vol. 1, p. 417 = *SK* 1:383.

# סדר ספירת העומר

*The* עומר *is counted each night from the second night of* פסח
*until the night before* שבועות*. See laws 221–224.*

*Some say the following meditation before the blessing:*

לְשֵׁם יִחוּד קֻדְשָׁא בְּרִיךְ הוּא וּשְׁכִינְתֵּהּ בִּדְחִילוּ וּרְחִימוּ
לְיַחֵד שֵׁם י״ה בו״ה בְּיִחוּדָא שְׁלִים בְּשֵׁם כָּל יִשְׂרָאֵל.

הִנְנִי מוּכָן וּמְזֻמָּן לְקַיֵּם מִצְוַת עֲשֵׂה שֶׁל סְפִירַת הָעֹמֶר. כְּמוֹ שֶׁכָּתוּב
בַּתּוֹרָה, וּסְפַרְתֶּם לָכֶם מִמָּחֳרַת הַשַּׁבָּת, מִיּוֹם הֲבִיאֲכֶם אֶת־עֹמֶר הַתְּנוּפָה, ויקרא כג
שֶׁבַע שַׁבָּתוֹת תְּמִימֹת תִּהְיֶינָה: עַד מִמָּחֳרַת הַשַּׁבָּת הַשְּׁבִיעִת תִּסְפְּרוּ
חֲמִשִּׁים יוֹם, וְהִקְרַבְתֶּם מִנְחָה חֲדָשָׁה לַיהוה: וִיהִי נֹעַם אֲדֹנָי אֱלֹהֵינוּ תהלים צ
עָלֵינוּ, וּמַעֲשֵׂה יָדֵינוּ כּוֹנְנָה עָלֵינוּ, וּמַעֲשֵׂה יָדֵינוּ כּוֹנְנֵהוּ:

**בָּרוּךְ אַתָּה יהוה אֱלֹהֵינוּ מֶלֶךְ הָעוֹלָם**
**אֲשֶׁר קִדְּשָׁנוּ בְּמִצְוֹתָיו, וְצִוָּנוּ עַל סְפִירַת הָעֹמֶר.**

טז בניסן
1. **הַיּוֹם יוֹם אֶחָד בָּעֹמֶר.**
חסד שבחסד

יז בניסן
2. **הַיּוֹם שְׁנֵי יָמִים בָּעֹמֶר.**
גבורה שבחסד

יח בניסן
3. **הַיּוֹם שְׁלֹשָׁה יָמִים בָּעֹמֶר.**
תפארת שבחסד

יט בניסן
4. **הַיּוֹם אַרְבָּעָה יָמִים בָּעֹמֶר.**
נצח שבחסד

כ בניסן
5. **הַיּוֹם חֲמִשָּׁה יָמִים בָּעֹמֶר.**
הוד שבחסד

כא בניסן
6. **הַיּוֹם שִׁשָּׁה יָמִים בָּעֹמֶר.**
יסוד שבחסד

כב בניסן
7. **הַיּוֹם שִׁבְעָה יָמִים**
**שֶׁהֵם שָׁבוּעַ אֶחָד בָּעֹמֶר.**
מלכות שבחסד

---

**סדר ספירת העומר / COUNTING OF THE OMER**

The sacrifice of the *'Omer* comes from barley, which is the food of animals. [Thus, the *'Omer* symbolizes the *"nefesh behemit,"* the animal soul within man.] When the animal soul ascends to its lofty source, and with its mighty strength inclines to holiness, the mighty love of God celebrates. By the

23 Nisan

8. Today is the eighth day,
making one week
and one day
of the Omer.

24 Nisan

9. Today is the ninth day,
making one week
and two days
of the Omer.

25 Nisan

10. Today is the tenth day,
making one week
and three days
of the Omer.

26 Nisan

11. Today is the eleventh day,
making one week
and four days
of the Omer.

27 Nisan

12. Today is the twelfth day,
making one week
and five days
of the Omer.

28 Nisan

13. Today is the thirteenth day,
making one week
and six days of the Omer.

29 Nisan

14. Today is the fourteenth day,
making two weeks
of the Omer.

30 Nisan, 1st day Rosh Ḥodesh

15. Today is the fifteenth day,
making two weeks
and one day
of the Omer.

1 Iyar, 2nd day Rosh Ḥodesh

16. Today is the sixteenth day,
making two weeks
and two days
of the Omer.

2 Iyar

17. Today is the seventeenth day,
making two weeks
and three days
of the Omer.

3 Iyar

18. Today is the eighteenth day,
making two weeks
and four days
of the Omer.

4 Iyar

19. Today is the nineteenth day,
making two weeks
and five days
of the Omer.

5 Iyar, Yom HaAtzma'ut

20. Today is the twentieth day,
making two weeks
and six days
of the Omer.

6 Iyar

21. Today is the twenty-first day,
making three weeks
of the Omer.

כג בניסן

8. הַיּוֹם שְׁמוֹנָה יָמִים
שֶׁהֵם שָׁבוּעַ אֶחָד וְיוֹם אֶחָד
בָּעֹמֶר. חסד שבגבורה

כד בניסן

9. הַיּוֹם תִּשְׁעָה יָמִים
שֶׁהֵם שָׁבוּעַ אֶחָד וּשְׁנֵי יָמִים
בָּעֹמֶר. גבורה שבגבורה

כה בניסן

10. הַיּוֹם עֲשָׂרָה יָמִים
שֶׁהֵם שָׁבוּעַ אֶחָד וּשְׁלֹשָׁה
יָמִים בָּעֹמֶר. תפארת שבגבורה

כו בניסן

11. הַיּוֹם אַחַד עָשָׂר יוֹם
שֶׁהֵם שָׁבוּעַ אֶחָד וְאַרְבָּעָה
יָמִים בָּעֹמֶר. נצח שבגבורה

כז בניסן

12. הַיּוֹם שְׁנֵים עָשָׂר יוֹם
שֶׁהֵם שָׁבוּעַ אֶחָד וַחֲמִשָּׁה
יָמִים בָּעֹמֶר. הוד שבגבורה

כח בניסן

13. הַיּוֹם שְׁלֹשָׁה עָשָׂר יוֹם
שֶׁהֵם שָׁבוּעַ אֶחָד וְשִׁשָּׁה יָמִים
בָּעֹמֶר. יסוד שבגבורה

כט בניסן

14. הַיּוֹם אַרְבָּעָה עָשָׂר יוֹם
שֶׁהֵם שְׁנֵי שָׁבוּעוֹת
בָּעֹמֶר. מלכות שבגבורה

ל בניסן, א׳ דראש חודש

15. הַיּוֹם חֲמִשָּׁה עָשָׂר יוֹם
שֶׁהֵם שְׁנֵי שָׁבוּעוֹת וְיוֹם אֶחָד
בָּעֹמֶר. חסד שבתפארת

א באייר, ב׳ דראש חודש

16. הַיּוֹם שִׁשָּׁה עָשָׂר יוֹם
שֶׁהֵם שְׁנֵי שָׁבוּעוֹת וּשְׁנֵי יָמִים
בָּעֹמֶר. גבורה שבתפארת

ב באייר

17. הַיּוֹם שִׁבְעָה עָשָׂר יוֹם
שֶׁהֵם שְׁנֵי שָׁבוּעוֹת וּשְׁלֹשָׁה
יָמִים בָּעֹמֶר. תפארת שבתפארת

ג באייר

18. הַיּוֹם שְׁמוֹנָה עָשָׂר יוֹם
שֶׁהֵם שְׁנֵי שָׁבוּעוֹת וְאַרְבָּעָה
יָמִים בָּעֹמֶר. נצח שבתפארת

ד באייר

19. הַיּוֹם תִּשְׁעָה עָשָׂר יוֹם
שֶׁהֵם שְׁנֵי שָׁבוּעוֹת וַחֲמִשָּׁה
יָמִים בָּעֹמֶר. הוד שבתפארת

ה באייר, יום העצמאות

20. הַיּוֹם עֶשְׂרִים יוֹם
שֶׁהֵם שְׁנֵי שָׁבוּעוֹת וְשִׁשָּׁה
יָמִים בָּעֹמֶר. יסוד שבתפארת

ו באייר

21. הַיּוֹם אֶחָד וְעֶשְׂרִים יוֹם
שֶׁהֵם שְׁלֹשָׁה שָׁבוּעוֹת בָּעֹמֶר.
מלכות שבתפארת

7 Iyar

22. Today is the twenty-second day,
making three weeks
and one day
of the Omer.

8 Iyar

23. Today is the twenty-third day,
making three weeks
and two days
of the Omer.

9 Iyar

24. Today is the twenty-fourth day,
making three weeks
and three days
of the Omer.

10 Iyar

25. Today is the twenty-fifth day,
making three weeks
and four days
of the Omer.

11 Iyar

26. Today is the twenty-sixth day,
making three weeks
and five days
of the Omer.

12 Iyar

27. Today is the twenty-seventh day,
making three weeks
and six days
of the Omer.

13 Iyar

28. Today is the twenty-eighth day,
making four weeks
of the Omer.

14 Iyar, Pesaḥ Sheni

29. Today is the twenty-ninth day,
making four weeks
and one day
of the Omer.

15 Iyar

30. Today is the thirtieth day,
making four weeks
and two days
of the Omer.

16 Iyar

31. Today is the thirty-first day,
making four weeks
and three days
of the Omer.

17 Iyar

32. Today is the thirty-second day,
making four weeks
and four days
of the Omer.

18 Iyar, Lag BaOmer

33. Today is the thirty-third day,
making four weeks
and five days
of the Omer.

19 Iyar

34. Today is the thirty-fourth day,
making four weeks
and six days
of the Omer.

20 Iyar

35. Today is the thirty-fifth day,
making five weeks
of the Omer.

ז באייר

22. הַיּוֹם שְׁנַיִם וְעֶשְׂרִים יוֹם
שֶׁהֵם שְׁלֹשָׁה שָׁבוּעוֹת
וְיוֹם אֶחָד בָּעֹמֶר. חסד שבנצח

ח באייר

23. הַיּוֹם שְׁלֹשָׁה וְעֶשְׂרִים יוֹם
שֶׁהֵם שְׁלֹשָׁה שָׁבוּעוֹת
וּשְׁנֵי יָמִים בָּעֹמֶר. גבורה שבנצח

ט באייר

24. הַיּוֹם אַרְבָּעָה וְעֶשְׂרִים יוֹם
שֶׁהֵם שְׁלֹשָׁה שָׁבוּעוֹת וּשְׁלֹשָׁה
יָמִים בָּעֹמֶר. תפארת שבנצח

י באייר

25. הַיּוֹם חֲמִשָּׁה וְעֶשְׂרִים יוֹם
שֶׁהֵם שְׁלֹשָׁה שָׁבוּעוֹת
וְאַרְבָּעָה יָמִים בָּעֹמֶר. נצח שבנצח

יא באייר

26. הַיּוֹם שִׁשָּׁה וְעֶשְׂרִים יוֹם
שֶׁהֵם שְׁלֹשָׁה שָׁבוּעוֹת
וַחֲמִשָּׁה יָמִים בָּעֹמֶר. הוד שבנצח

יב באייר

27. הַיּוֹם שִׁבְעָה וְעֶשְׂרִים יוֹם
שֶׁהֵם שְׁלֹשָׁה שָׁבוּעוֹת
וְשִׁשָּׁה יָמִים בָּעֹמֶר. יסוד שבנצח

יג באייר

28. הַיּוֹם שְׁמוֹנָה וְעֶשְׂרִים יוֹם
שֶׁהֵם אַרְבָּעָה שָׁבוּעוֹת
בָּעֹמֶר. מלכות שבנצח

יד באייר, פסח שני

29. הַיּוֹם תִּשְׁעָה וְעֶשְׂרִים יוֹם
שֶׁהֵם אַרְבָּעָה שָׁבוּעוֹת
וְיוֹם אֶחָד בָּעֹמֶר. חסד שבהוד

טו באייר

30. הַיּוֹם שְׁלֹשִׁים יוֹם
שֶׁהֵם אַרְבָּעָה שָׁבוּעוֹת
וּשְׁנֵי יָמִים בָּעֹמֶר. גבורה שבהוד

טז באייר

31. הַיּוֹם אֶחָד וּשְׁלֹשִׁים יוֹם
שֶׁהֵם אַרְבָּעָה שָׁבוּעוֹת
וּשְׁלֹשָׁה יָמִים בָּעֹמֶר.
תפארת שבהוד

יז באייר

32. הַיּוֹם שְׁנַיִם וּשְׁלֹשִׁים יוֹם
שֶׁהֵם אַרְבָּעָה שָׁבוּעוֹת
וְאַרְבָּעָה יָמִים בָּעֹמֶר. נצח שבהוד

יח באייר, לג בעומר

33. הַיּוֹם שְׁלֹשָׁה וּשְׁלֹשִׁים יוֹם
שֶׁהֵם אַרְבָּעָה שָׁבוּעוֹת וַחֲמִשָּׁה
יָמִים בָּעֹמֶר. הוד שבהוד

יט באייר

34. הַיּוֹם אַרְבָּעָה וּשְׁלֹשִׁים יוֹם
שֶׁהֵם אַרְבָּעָה שָׁבוּעוֹת
וְשִׁשָּׁה יָמִים בָּעֹמֶר. יסוד שבהוד

כ באייר

35. הַיּוֹם חֲמִשָּׁה וּשְׁלֹשִׁים יוֹם
שֶׁהֵם חֲמִשָּׁה שָׁבוּעוֹת
בָּעֹמֶר. מלכות שבהוד

21 Iyar

36. Today is the thirty-sixth day,
making five weeks
and one day
of the Omer.

22 Iyar

37. Today is the thirty-seventh day,
making five weeks
and two days
of the Omer.

23 Iyar

38. Today is the thirty-eighth day,
making five weeks
and three days
of the Omer.

24 Iyar

39. Today is the thirty-ninth day,
making five weeks
and four days
of the Omer.

25 Iyar

40. Today is the fortieth day,
making five weeks
and five days
of the Omer.

26 Iyar

41. Today is the forty-first day,
making five weeks
and six days
of the Omer.

27 Iyar

42. Today is the forty-second day,
making six weeks
of the Omer.

28 Iyar, Yom Yerushalayim

43. Today is the forty-third day,
making six weeks
and one day
of the Omer.

29 Iyar

44. Today is the forty-fourth day,
making six weeks
and two days
of the Omer.

1 Sivan, Rosh Ḥodesh

45. Today is the forty-fifth day,
making six weeks
and three days
of the Omer.

2 Sivan

46. Today is the forty-sixth day,
making six weeks
and four days
of the Omer.

3 Sivan

47. Today is the forty-seventh day,
making six weeks
and five days
of the Omer.

4 Sivan

48. Today is the forty-eighth day,
making six weeks
and six days
of the Omer.

5 Sivan, Erev Shavuot

49. Today is the forty-ninth day,
making seven weeks
of the Omer.

כא באייר

36. הַיּוֹם שִׁשָּׁה וּשְׁלֹשִׁים יוֹם
שֶׁהֵם חֲמִשָּׁה שָׁבוּעוֹת
וְיוֹם אֶחָד בָּעְֹמֶר. חסד שביסוד

כב באייר

37. הַיּוֹם שִׁבְעָה וּשְׁלֹשִׁים יוֹם
שֶׁהֵם חֲמִשָּׁה שָׁבוּעוֹת
וּשְׁנֵי יָמִים בָּעְֹמֶר. גבורה שביסוד

כג באייר

38. הַיּוֹם שְׁמוֹנָה וּשְׁלֹשִׁים יוֹם
שֶׁהֵם חֲמִשָּׁה שָׁבוּעוֹת
וּשְׁלֹשָׁה יָמִים בָּעְֹמֶר.
תפארת שביסוד

כד באייר

39. הַיּוֹם תִּשְׁעָה וּשְׁלֹשִׁים יוֹם
שֶׁהֵם חֲמִשָּׁה שָׁבוּעוֹת וְאַרְבָּעָה
יָמִים בָּעְֹמֶר. נצח שביסוד

כה באייר

40. הַיּוֹם אַרְבָּעִים יוֹם
שֶׁהֵם חֲמִשָּׁה שָׁבוּעוֹת
וַחֲמִשָּׁה יָמִים בָּעְֹמֶר. הוד שביסוד

כו באייר

41. הַיּוֹם אֶחָד וְאַרְבָּעִים יוֹם
שֶׁהֵם חֲמִשָּׁה שָׁבוּעוֹת
וְשִׁשָּׁה יָמִים בָּעְֹמֶר. יסוד שביסוד

כז באייר

42. הַיּוֹם שְׁנַיִם וְאַרְבָּעִים יוֹם
שֶׁהֵם שִׁשָּׁה שָׁבוּעוֹת
בָּעְֹמֶר. מלכות שביסוד

כח באייר, יום ירושלים

43. הַיּוֹם שְׁלֹשָׁה וְאַרְבָּעִים יוֹם
שֶׁהֵם שִׁשָּׁה שָׁבוּעוֹת
וְיוֹם אֶחָד בָּעְֹמֶר. חסד שבמלכות

כט באייר

44. הַיּוֹם אַרְבָּעָה וְאַרְבָּעִים יוֹם
שֶׁהֵם שִׁשָּׁה שָׁבוּעוֹת
וּשְׁנֵי יָמִים בָּעְֹמֶר. גבורה שבמלכות

א בסיון, ראש חודש

45. הַיּוֹם חֲמִשָּׁה וְאַרְבָּעִים יוֹם
שֶׁהֵם שִׁשָּׁה שָׁבוּעוֹת וּשְׁלֹשָׁה
יָמִים בָּעְֹמֶר. תפארת שבמלכות

ב בסיון

46. הַיּוֹם שִׁשָּׁה וְאַרְבָּעִים יוֹם
שֶׁהֵם שִׁשָּׁה שָׁבוּעוֹת וְאַרְבָּעָה
יָמִים בָּעְֹמֶר. נצח שבמלכות

ג בסיון

47. הַיּוֹם שִׁבְעָה וְאַרְבָּעִים יוֹם
שֶׁהֵם שִׁשָּׁה שָׁבוּעוֹת וַחֲמִשָּׁה
יָמִים בָּעְֹמֶר. הוד שבמלכות

ד בסיון

48. הַיּוֹם שְׁמוֹנָה וְאַרְבָּעִים יוֹם
שֶׁהֵם שִׁשָּׁה שָׁבוּעוֹת וְשִׁשָּׁה
יָמִים בָּעְֹמֶר. יסוד שבמלכות

ה בסיון, ערב שבועות

49. הַיּוֹם תִּשְׁעָה וְאַרְבָּעִים יוֹם
שֶׁהֵם שִׁבְעָה שָׁבוּעוֹת בָּעְֹמֶר.
מלכות שבמלכות

הָרַחֲמָן May the Compassionate One
restore the Temple service to its place speedily in our days.
Amen, Selah.

*Some add:*

לַמְנַצֵּחַ For the conductor of music. With stringed instruments. A psalm, a song. *Ps. 67*
May God be gracious to us and bless us. May He make His face shine on us, Selah. Then will Your way be known on earth, Your salvation among all the nations. Let the peoples praise You, God; let all peoples praise You. Let nations rejoice and sing for joy, for You judge the peoples with equity, and guide the nations of the earth, Selah. Let the peoples praise You, God; let all peoples praise You. The earth has yielded its harvest. May God, our God, bless us. God will bless us, and all the ends of the earth will fear Him.

אָנָּא Please, by the power of Your great right hand, set the captive nation free.
Accept Your people's prayer. Strengthen us, purify us, You who are revered.
Please, Mighty One, guard like the pupil of the eye those who seek
Your unity.
Bless them, cleanse them, have compassion on them, grant them Your
righteousness always.
Mighty One, Holy One, in Your great goodness guide Your congregation.
Only One, Exalted One, turn to Your people, who proclaim Your holiness.
Accept our plea and heed our cry, You who know all secret thoughts.
Blessed be the name of His glorious kingdom for ever and all time.

רִבּוֹנוֹ שֶׁל עוֹלָם Master of the Universe, You commanded us through Your servant Moses to count the Omer, to cleanse our carapaces and impurities, as You have
written in Your Torah: "You shall count seven complete weeks from the day *Lev. 23*
following the [Pesaḥ] rest day, when you brought the Omer as a wave-offering. To the day after the seventh week, you shall count fifty days." This is so that the souls of Your people Israel may be purified from their uncleanliness. May it also be Your will, Lord our God and God of our ancestors, that in the merit of the Omer count that I have counted today, there may be rectified any defect on my part in the counting of (*insert appropriate sefira for each day*). May I be cleansed and sanctified with Your holiness on high, and through this may there flow a rich stream through all worlds, to rectify our lives, spirits and souls from any dross and defect, purifying and sanctifying us with Your sublime holiness. Amen, Selah.

*The service continues with Aleinu on page 350.*

## הָרַחֲמָן הוּא יַחֲזִיר לָנוּ עֲבוֹדַת בֵּית הַמִּקְדָּשׁ לִמְקוֹמָהּ בִּמְהֵרָה בְּיָמֵינוּ, אָמֵן סֶלָה.

*Some add:*

תהלים סז לַמְנַצֵּחַ בִּנְגִינֹת, מִזְמוֹר שִׁיר: אֱלֹהִים יְחָנֵּנוּ וִיבָרְכֵנוּ, יָאֵר פָּנָיו אִתָּנוּ סֶלָה:
לָדַעַת בָּאָרֶץ דַּרְכֶּךָ, בְּכָל־גּוֹיִם יְשׁוּעָתֶךָ: יוֹדוּךָ עַמִּים אֱלֹהִים, יוֹדוּךָ עַמִּים
כֻּלָּם: יִשְׂמְחוּ וִירַנְּנוּ לְאֻמִּים, כִּי־תִשְׁפֹּט עַמִּים מִישֹׁר, וּלְאֻמִּים בָּאָרֶץ תַּנְחֵם
סֶלָה: יוֹדוּךָ עַמִּים אֱלֹהִים, יוֹדוּךָ עַמִּים כֻּלָּם: אֶרֶץ נָתְנָה יְבוּלָהּ, יְבָרְכֵנוּ
אֱלֹהִים אֱלֹהֵינוּ: יְבָרְכֵנוּ אֱלֹהִים, וְיִירְאוּ אוֹתוֹ כָּל־אַפְסֵי־אָרֶץ:

אָנָּא, בְּכֹחַ גְּדֻלַּת יְמִינְךָ, תַּתִּיר צְרוּרָה.
קַבֵּל רִנַּת עַמְּךָ, שַׂגְּבֵנוּ, טַהֲרֵנוּ, נוֹרָא.
נָא גִבּוֹר, דּוֹרְשֵׁי יִחוּדְךָ כְּבָבַת שָׁמְרֵם.
בָּרְכֵם, טַהֲרֵם, רַחֲמֵם, צִדְקָתְךָ תָּמִיד גָּמְלֵם.
חֲסִין קָדוֹשׁ, בְּרֹב טוּבְךָ נַהֵל עֲדָתֶךָ.
יָחִיד גֵּאֶה, לְעַמְּךָ פְּנֵה, זוֹכְרֵי קְדֻשָּׁתֶךָ.
שַׁוְעָתֵנוּ קַבֵּל וּשְׁמַע צַעֲקָתֵנוּ, יוֹדֵעַ תַּעֲלוּמוֹת.
בָּרוּךְ שֵׁם כְּבוֹד מַלְכוּתוֹ לְעוֹלָם וָעֶד.

רִבּוֹנוֹ שֶׁל עוֹלָם, אַתָּה צִוִּיתָנוּ עַל יְדֵי מֹשֶׁה עַבְדֶּךָ לִסְפֹּר סְפִירַת הָעֹמֶר, כְּדֵי
ויקרא כג לְטַהֲרֵנוּ מִקְּלִפּוֹתֵינוּ וּמִטֻּמְאוֹתֵינוּ. כְּמוֹ שֶׁכָּתַבְתָּ בְּתוֹרָתֶךָ: וּסְפַרְתֶּם לָכֶם
מִמָּחֳרַת הַשַּׁבָּת, מִיּוֹם הֲבִיאֲכֶם אֶת־עֹמֶר הַתְּנוּפָה, שֶׁבַע שַׁבָּתוֹת תְּמִימֹת
תִּהְיֶינָה: עַד מִמָּחֳרַת הַשַּׁבָּת הַשְּׁבִיעִת תִּסְפְּרוּ חֲמִשִּׁים יוֹם: כְּדֵי שֶׁיִּטָּהֲרוּ
נַפְשׁוֹת עַמְּךָ יִשְׂרָאֵל מִזֻּהֲמָתָם. וּבְכֵן יְהִי רָצוֹן מִלְּפָנֶיךָ יהוה אֱלֹהֵינוּ וֵאלֹהֵי
אֲבוֹתֵינוּ, שֶׁבִּזְכוּת סְפִירַת הָעֹמֶר שֶׁסָּפַרְתִּי הַיּוֹם, יְתֻקַּן מַה שֶּׁפָּגַמְתִּי בִּסְפִירָה
(*insert appropriate* ספירה *for each day*) וְאֶטָּהֵר וְאֶתְקַדֵּשׁ בִּקְדֻשָּׁה שֶׁל מַעְלָה, וְעַל יְדֵי
זֶה יֻשְׁפַּע שֶׁפַע רַב בְּכָל הָעוֹלָמוֹת, לְתַקֵּן אֶת נַפְשׁוֹתֵינוּ וְרוּחוֹתֵינוּ וְנִשְׁמוֹתֵינוּ
מִכָּל סִיג וּפְגָם, וּלְטַהֲרֵנוּ וּלְקַדְּשֵׁנוּ בִּקְדֻשָּׁתְךָ הָעֶלְיוֹנָה, אָמֵן סֶלָה.

*The service continues with* עָלֵינוּ *on page 351.*

## SHEMA BEFORE SLEEP AT NIGHT

הֲרֵינִי I hereby forgive anyone who has angered or provoked me or sinned against me, physically or financially or by failing to give me due respect, or in any other matter relating to me, involuntarily or willingly, inadvertently or deliberately, whether in word or deed: let no one incur punishment because of me.

בָּרוּךְ Blessed are You, LORD our God, King of the Universe, who makes the bonds of sleep fall on my eyes, and slumber on my eye-lids. May it be Your will, LORD my God and God of my fathers, that You make me lie down in peace and arise in peace. Let not my imagination, bad dreams

---

Rav Kook taught that in the future all Jews will be on the level of King David: "The feeblest among them on that day shall be as David."[4] According to Rabbi Moses Ḥayyim Luzzatto, sleep resulted from the corruption of the world. In the ideal state of *Tikkun*, man will have no further need of sleep.[5]

The sons of the Vilna Gaon attested that the Gaon slept but two hours per day.[6]

The rest of us might do well to hearken to Maimonides' advice to sleep eight hours per day.[7] (Editor)

---

4. Zechariah 12:8.
5. *Me'orot ha-Rayah: Yeraḥ ha-Eitanim* (Jerusalem, 1994), pp. 293, 321 (Rav Kook as quoted by his son-in-law Rabbi Shalom Nathan Ra'anan). Cf. Rabbi Nathan Sternhartz, *Likkutei Halakhot, Hil. Tefillin* 5:18–19.

   David never slept sixty breaths because he lived "long life," new life each hour. He could not sleep, just the minimum necessary for "long life." Therefore the kingdom of David is compared to the moon that is renewed every time. (*Likkutei Halakhot, Hil. Tefillin* 5:19)

6. He accepted upon himself all his days not to sleep more than two hours in a twenty-four hour day. All his days he never slept more than a half hour at a time. During that half hour, his lips were mumbling *halakhot* and *agadot*. At the conclusion of the half hour, he would rise up as a lion, wash his hands and start learning in a loud voice. After, he would sleep for another half hour. Thus, the span of his sleep was three half hours by night, and one half hour by day. (Introduction of Rabbi Abraham and Rabbi Judah Leib, the sons of the Gaon Rabbi Elijah of Vilna, to *Be'ur ha-Gra* to *Shulhan 'Arukh, OḤ*, Shklov, 1803)

   See also Rabbi Isaac Haver, *Binyan 'Olam* (Warsaw, 1851), *OḤ*, no. 1.
7. *MT, Hil. De'ot* 4:4.

# קריאת שמע על המיטה

הֲרֵינִי מוֹחֵל לְכָל מִי שֶׁהִכְעִיס וְהִקְנִיט אוֹתִי אוֹ שֶׁחָטָא כְּנֶגְדִּי, בֵּין בְּגוּפִי בֵּין בְּמָמוֹנִי בֵּין בִּכְבוֹדִי בֵּין בְּכָל אֲשֶׁר לִי, בֵּין בְּאֹנֶס בֵּין בְּרָצוֹן, בֵּין בְּשׁוֹגֵג בֵּין בְּמֵזִיד, בֵּין בְּדִבּוּר בֵּין בְּמַעֲשֶׂה, וְלֹא יֵעָנֵשׁ שׁוּם אָדָם בְּסִבָּתִי.

בָּרוּךְ אַתָּה יהוה אֱלֹהֵינוּ מֶלֶךְ הָעוֹלָם, הַמַּפִּיל חֶבְלֵי שֵׁנָה עַל עֵינַי וּתְנוּמָה עַל עַפְעַפָּי. וִיהִי רָצוֹן מִלְּפָנֶיךָ, יהוה אֱלֹהַי וֵאלֹהֵי אֲבוֹתַי, שֶׁתַּשְׁכִּיבֵנִי לְשָׁלוֹם וְתַעֲמִידֵנִי לְשָׁלוֹם, וְאַל יְבַהֲלוּנִי רַעְיוֹנַי

---

קריאת שמע על המיטה / SHEMA BEFORE SLEEP AT NIGHT

It is said of King David that his sleep was as brief as that of a horse, sixty breaths.[1]

> Said Rav: It is prohibited for man to sleep by day more than the sleep of the horse.[2] And how long is the sleep of the horse? Sixty breaths.
>
> Said Abaye: The sleep of [Rabbah bar Naḥmani] is as that of Rav, and that of Rav as that of Rabbi [Judah the Prince], and that of Rabbi [Judah the Prince] as that of David, and that of David as that of a horse, and that of a horse – sixty breaths.[3]

---

1. According to the latest findings, horses require approximately two and a half hours of sleep, on average, in a 24-hour period. Most of this sleep occurs in many short intervals of about 15 minutes each.
2. "Because of the loss of Torah learning" (Rashi). See *Shulhan 'Arukh, OḤ* 4:16 and 231, and commentaries.
3. *b. Sukkah* 26b. Rabbi Judah the Prince was descended from King David (*b. Shabbat* 56a; *Ketubot* 62b; *Sanhedrin* 5a; *y. Kil'ayim* 9:3), so this was ancestral tradition; see Rashi, *Sukkah* 26b.
   On Tuesday night, 5 Adar Rishon, 5649/1889, Rav Kook dreamt the passage in the *Zohar* (I, 207a) that David would not sleep sixty breaths at a stretch so as not to taste the taste of death, for "sleep is one sixtieth of death" (*b. Berakhot* 57b). Rav Kook then dreamt an original kabbalistic symbolism of the number sixty in this context. Rav Kook saw fit to record the contents of the dream because, in his words, "I never merited to see such a veridical and logical dream" (*MRIT*, p. 520).
   There seems to be a discrepancy between the Talmudic and Zoharic accounts. In the Talmud, David sleeps sixty breaths; in the *Zohar*, David sleeps sixty breaths minus one. However, see Malbim's ingenious solution whereby the final statement of the *Zohar* (1, 207b) is in agreement with the Talmud; *Malbim, Artsot ha-Ḥayyim, Erets Yehudah* to *OḤ* 4:16.

or troubling thoughts disturb me. May my bed be flawless before You. Enlighten my eyes lest I sleep the sleep of death, for it is You who illuminates the pupil of the eye. Blessed are You, LORD, who gives light to the whole world in His glory.

*When saying all three paragraphs of Shema, say:*

God, faithful King!

*The following verse should be said aloud, while covering the eyes with the right hand:*

**Listen, Israel: the LORD is our God, the LORD is One.** *Deut. 6*

*Quietly:* Blessed be the name of His glorious kingdom for ever and all time.

וְאָהַבְתָּ Love the LORD your God with all your heart, with all your soul, and with all your might. These words which I command you today shall be on your heart. Teach them repeatedly to your children, speaking of them when you sit at home and when you travel on the way, when you lie down and when you rise. Bind them as a sign on your hand, and they shall be an emblem between your eyes. Write them on the doorposts of your house and gates. *Deut. 6*

וִיהִי May the pleasantness of the LORD our God be upon us. Establish for us the work of our hands, O establish the work of our hands. *Ps. 90*

יֹשֵׁב He who lives in the shelter of the Most High dwells in the shadow of the Almighty. I say of God, my Refuge and Stronghold, my LORD in whom I trust, that He will save you from the fowler's snare and the deadly pestilence. With His pinions He will cover you, and beneath His wings you will find *Ps. 91*

---

The purpose of this additional recitation is to ward off *mazikin* (evil spirits).[9] We find elsewhere in the Talmud that Rabbi Joshua ben Levi himself would recite the verses of the *Shir shel Pega'im* when he would go to sleep at night.[10] What is the *Shir shel Pega'im*? Literally, it means the Song of Demons. The reference is to our own Psalm 91. In order to better appreciate its significance,

9. *Tosafot, Berakhot* 2a, s.v. *me-eimatai korin.* For this reason, on the night of Passover, which is *"Leil Shimurim,"* a night guarded from demons, it is customary not to recite the full-length *Keri'at Shema' 'al ha-Mitah* (gloss of Rabbi Moses Isserles to *OḤ* 481:2).

10. *b. Shavu'ot* 15b; Rav Alfas, *Berakhot*, 3a; Rabbenu Asher, *Berakhot* 1:6; *Shulhan 'Arukh, OḤ* 239:1.

וַחֲלוֹמוֹת רָעִים וְהִרְהוּרִים רָעִים, וּתְהֵא מִטָּתִי שְׁלֵמָה לְפָנֶיךָ, וְהָאֵר עֵינַי פֶּן אִישַׁן הַמָּוֶת, כִּי אַתָּה הַמֵּאִיר לְאִישׁוֹן בַּת עָיִן. בָּרוּךְ אַתָּה יהוה, הַמֵּאִיר לָעוֹלָם כֻּלּוֹ בִּכְבוֹדוֹ.

*When saying all three paragraphs of* שמע*, say:*

אֵל מֶלֶךְ נֶאֱמָן

*The following verse should be said aloud, while covering the eyes with the right hand:*

דברים ו **שְׁמַע יִשְׂרָאֵל, יהוה אֱלֹהֵינוּ, יהוה ׀ אֶחָד:**

*Quietly* בָּרוּךְ שֵׁם כְּבוֹד מַלְכוּתוֹ לְעוֹלָם וָעֶד.

דברים ו וְאָהַבְתָּ אֵת יהוה אֱלֹהֶיךָ, בְּכָל־לְבָבְךָ וּבְכָל־נַפְשְׁךָ וּבְכָל־מְאֹדֶךָ: וְהָיוּ הַדְּבָרִים הָאֵלֶּה, אֲשֶׁר אָנֹכִי מְצַוְּךָ הַיּוֹם, עַל־לְבָבֶךָ: וְשִׁנַּנְתָּם לְבָנֶיךָ וְדִבַּרְתָּ בָּם, בְּשִׁבְתְּךָ בְּבֵיתֶךָ וּבְלֶכְתְּךָ בַדֶּרֶךְ, וּבְשָׁכְבְּךָ וּבְקוּמֶךָ: וּקְשַׁרְתָּם לְאוֹת עַל־יָדֶךָ וְהָיוּ לְטֹטָפֹת בֵּין עֵינֶיךָ: וּכְתַבְתָּם עַל־מְזֻזוֹת בֵּיתֶךָ וּבִשְׁעָרֶיךָ:

תהלים צ וִיהִי נֹעַם אֲדֹנָי אֱלֹהֵינוּ עָלֵינוּ וּמַעֲשֵׂה יָדֵינוּ כּוֹנְנָה עָלֵינוּ וּמַעֲשֵׂה יָדֵינוּ כּוֹנְנֵהוּ:

תהלים צא יֹשֵׁב בְּסֵתֶר עֶלְיוֹן, בְּצֵל שַׁדַּי יִתְלוֹנָן: אֹמַר לַיהוה מַחְסִי וּמְצוּדָתִי, אֱלֹהַי אֶבְטַח־בּוֹ: כִּי הוּא יַצִּילְךָ מִפַּח יָקוּשׁ, מִדֶּבֶר הַוּוֹת: בְּאֶבְרָתוֹ יָסֶךְ לָךְ,

---

וִיהִי נֹעַם אֲדֹנָי אֱלֹהֵינוּ עָלֵינוּ וּמַעֲשֵׂה יָדֵינוּ כּוֹנְנָה עָלֵינוּ וּמַעֲשֵׂה יָדֵינוּ כּוֹנְנֵהוּ *May the pleasantness of the Lord our God be upon us. Establish for us the work of our hands, O establish the work of our hands* (Psalms 90:17).

יֹשֵׁב בְּסֵתֶר עֶלְיוֹן, בְּצֵל שַׁדַּי יִתְלוֹנָן *He who lives in the shelter of the Most High dwells in the shadow of the Almighty (Psalms 91:1).*

Embodiment versus Disembodiment

Said Rabbi Joshua ben Levi: Even though a man has read *Keri'at Shema'* in the synagogue, it is a *mitsvah* (commandment) to read it on his bed.[8]

---

8. *b. Berakhot* 4b.

shelter; His faithfulness is an encircling shield. You need not fear terror by night, nor the arrow that flies by day; not the pestilence that stalks in darkness, nor the plague that ravages at noon. A thousand may fall at your side, ten

---

And it is one of eleven psalms in the Book of Psalms composed by Moses.[16]

One asks what necessitated reciting the *Shir shel Pega'im* (Song of Demons) specifically at the time of erecting the Tabernacle (or in later Jewish history, when adding on to the city of Jerusalem or the Temple precincts)?[17]

---

16. Rashi, *Shavu'ot* 15b, s.v. *ve-shir shel pega'im.* (See also Rashi, *Zevaḥim* 24a.) There are many unanswered questions in this regard. Rashi seems to convey that Moses recited the *Shir shel Pega'im* at the time he blessed the people. But according to the Midrash, Moses recited it when he ascended the mountain. See *Numbers Rabbah* 12:3; *Midrash Tehillim* 91:1; *Tanḥuma, Nasso* 23. And conversely, it is not readily comprehensible why we recite the verse of *Viyhi No'am* as a preamble to the *Shir shel Pega'im* before retiring for the night. We are not constructing the Tabernacle! (In truth, *Shelah Hakadosh* and Rabbi Shneur Zalman of Liadi omit that verse from their version of *Keri'at Shema' 'al ha-Mitah.*) See Rabbi Ya'akov Werdiger's *Sheruta di-Tselota*, commentary to Rabbi Abraham Landau of Tchechanow, *Siddur Tselota de-Avraham*, vol. 2 (Tel-Aviv, 1961), pp. 826–827.

17. Various explanations have been offered why Maimonides omits mention of the *Shir shel Pega'im*. Some speculate that Maimonides understood that the psalm is recited only when there are mortal enemies who oppose the addition, such as was the case at the time of Ezra and Neḥemiah when Sanballat and his party opposed the building of the wall of Jerusalem (referenced in Rashi, *Shavu'ot* 15b, s.v. *ve-omer Hashem mah rabu tsarai*). See Maimonides, *MT, Hil. Beit ha-Beḥirah* 6:12; and *Kesef Mishneh* and *Mishneh le-Melekh* there (based on *Tosafot, Shavu'ot* 15b, s.v. *'ad ki atah Hashem maḥsi*). Rabbi Joseph Kafaḥ thought that the *Shir shel Pega'im* might have been missing in Maimonides' copy of the Talmud. See Kafaḥ ed. *Perush ha-Mishnah, Shavu'ot* 2:2 (p. 169, n. 17). The thought occurs to this writer that the significant omission might be attributed to Maimonides' rationalist mindset, from which stems his general avoidance of the topic of demons (along with other superstitions). See *Be'ur ha-Gra, Yoreh De'ah* 179:13; Malbim, *Artsot ha-Ḥayyim, Erets Yehudah* to *Shulḥan 'Arukh, OḤ* 4:4; and *Hasagot ha-Rabad le-Mishneh Torah*, ed. Bezalel Naor (Jerusalem: Zur-Ot, 1985), *Hil. Tefillah* 7:8 (p. 85). See also Rabbi El'azar Landau, *Yad ha-Melekh* (Lvov, 1826), *Hil. Tefillah* 14:12, and Rabbi Isaac Arieli, *'Eynayim le-Mishpat* (Jerusalem, 1952), *Berakhot* 55b. Maimonides treats the *Shir shel Pega'im* at length in the *Guide* (III, 51) within a discussion of divine providence (*hashgaḥa peratit*). He omits there any mention of the demonic realm, giving the psalm a naturalistic bent. See Pines ed. *Guide of the Peplexed*, pp. 626–627. (Pines translates *Shir shel Pega'im* as "song on mishaps.") In a responsum, Maimonides wrote: "Here in Egypt we saw them taking tablets of gold or silver, engraving upon them the *Shir shel Pega'im*, and hanging them on the necks of the lads. We protested against this most vehemently" (*Teshuvot ha-Rambam*, ed. Blau, vol. 2, no. 268 [p. 512]).

וְתַֽחַת־כְּנָפָיו תֶּחְסֶה, צִנָּה וְסֹחֵרָה אֲמִתּוֹ: לֹא־תִירָא מִפַּֽחַד לָֽיְלָה, מֵחֵץ יָעוּף יוֹמָם: מִדֶּֽבֶר בָּאֹֽפֶל יַהֲלֹךְ, מִקֶּֽטֶב יָשׁוּד צָהֳרָֽיִם: יִפֹּל מִצִּדְּךָ אֶֽלֶף,

---

we need to see it in the context in which it appears in the Talmud. That context is the consecration of the Temple.[11]

An addition to the city of Jerusalem or to the Temple precints requires special halakhic clearance as well as a formal procession through the city:

> We do not add to the city [of Jerusalem] or to the Temple precincts except by [authorization of] a king, a prophet, the Urim and Thummim, a Sanhedrin of seventy-one [members], two thankgiving offerings and song. The *Beit Din* walk and the two thanksgiving offerings after them, and all Israel after them.[12]

The *Beraita* elaborates on the "song":

> A song of thanksgiving with harps and lyres and cymbals at every corner and every stone in Jerusalem, and says, "[A psalm of David. A song for the dedication of the House.] I will exalt You, LORD, for You have lifted me up, etc."[13] and the Song of Demons (*Shir sel Pega'im*) – "He who lives in the shelter of the Most High dwells in the shadow of the Almighty" – until "Because you said, 'The LORD is my Refuge,' taking the Most High as Your shelter."[14]

This recitation has its origin in the consecration by Moses of the *Mishkan* or Tabernacle in the wilderness:

> Moses recited it at the erection of the Tabernacle, for it says, "And Moses blessed them."[15] With what did he bless them? "May it be the [divine] will that the *Shekhinah* (divine presence) rest upon the work of your hands. 'May the pleasantness of the LORD our God be upon us [and establish for us the work of our hands].'" So it states in *Torat Kohanim*.

---

11. There are two alternate names for Psalm 91: *Shir shel Pega'im* and *Shir shel Nega'im* (*b. Shavu'ot* 15b). According to the Talmud, the latter name is derived from the word *nega'* in verse 10. Though unstated in the Talmud, the former name may refer to the term *pega' ra'* in 1 Kings 5:18.
12. *m. Shavu'ot* 2:2. The Talmud (*b. Shavu'ot* 15b) clarifies that the actual practice was the opposite: The two thanksgiving offerings would lead, followed by the *Beit Din*, followed by all Israel. See Neḥemiah 12:31–34.
13. Psalms 30:1–2.
14. Psalms 91:9; *b. Shavu'ot* 15b. Cf. *y. Shabbat* 6:2 (*Shir shel Pigu'im*); *'Eruvin* 10:11.
15. Exodus 39:43.

thousand at your right hand, but it will not come near you. You will only look with your eyes and see the punishment of the wicked. Because you said, "The LORD is my Refuge," taking the Most High as your shelter, no harm will befall you, no plague come near your tent, for He will command His angels about you, to guard you in all your ways. They will lift you in their hands, lest your foot stumble on a stone. You will tread on lions and vipers; you will trample on young lions and snakes. [God says:] "Because he loves Me, I will rescue him; I will protect him, because he acknowledges My name. When he calls on Me, I will answer him; I will be with him in distress, I will deliver him and bring him honor. With long life I will satisfy him and show him My salvation.
With long life I will satisfy him and show him My salvation.

---

This explains the mystery of why the *Shir shel Pega'im* was recited by Moses at the completion of the Tabernacle, and why we continue to recite it whenever we desire to expand the city of Jerusalem or the Temple precincts. And by extension, it would explain why it is recited *Motsa'ei Shabbat* as we are about to embark on a new week. The entire Sabbath we were prohibited from engaging in the thirty-nine categories of labor that went into the work of the *Mishkan* or Tabernacle. With the conclusion of the Sabbath, we are about to go out to the work week, to engage once again in the thirty-nine labors, which is our construction of the *Mishkan*, our contribution to the world. As Moses of old, we ask that the *Shekhinah* rest on the work of our hands, and at the same time, we ask the Almighty to intercede on our behalf that forces of negativity, destructive elements, not oppose and impede our creation.

There remains to explain the custom of Rabbi Joshua ben Levi who would recite the *Shir shel Pega'im* before retiring for the night. In sleep, there is a "disconnect" between soul and body. There is a certain allure, a certain enticement of the disembodied state. Reciting the *Shir shel Pega'im*, designed to distance disembodied spirits (*mazikin*), was a way of resisting the temptation, the siren call of disembodiment. As wonderful as the visions seen during sleep may be, Rabbi Joshua ben Levi was sending a message to his unconscious not to fall into the trap. As a Jew, he knew that for the time allotted him on this earth, he is dutybound to serve God in the body, not out of body. Before retiring for the night, Rabbi Joshua ben Levi left internal instruction that he was to receive a "wake up call" in the morning. (Editor)

---

to Solomon the whereabouts of the *shamir* worm necessary for the construction of the Temple.

וּרְבָבָה מִימִינֶךָ, אֵלֶיךָ לֹא יִגָּשׁ: רַק בְּעֵינֶיךָ תַבִּיט, וְשִׁלֻּמַת רְשָׁעִים תִּרְאֶה:
כִּי־אַתָּה יהוה מַחְסִי, עֶלְיוֹן שַׂמְתָּ מְעוֹנֶךָ: לֹא־תְאֻנֶּה אֵלֶיךָ רָעָה, וְנֶגַע
לֹא־יִקְרַב בְּאָהֳלֶךָ: כִּי מַלְאָכָיו יְצַוֶּה־לָּךְ, לִשְׁמָרְךָ בְּכָל־דְּרָכֶיךָ: עַל־כַּפַּיִם
יִשָּׂאוּנְךָ, פֶּן־תִּגֹּף בָּאֶבֶן רַגְלֶךָ: עַל־שַׁחַל וָפֶתֶן תִּדְרֹךְ, תִּרְמֹס כְּפִיר וְתַנִּין:
כִּי בִי חָשַׁק וַאֲפַלְּטֵהוּ, אֲשַׂגְּבֵהוּ כִּי־יָדַע שְׁמִי: יִקְרָאֵנִי וְאֶעֱנֵהוּ, עִמּוֹ־אָנֹכִי
בְצָרָה, אֲחַלְּצֵהוּ וַאֲכַבְּדֵהוּ: אֹרֶךְ יָמִים אַשְׂבִּיעֵהוּ, וְאַרְאֵהוּ בִּישׁוּעָתִי:
אֹרֶךְ יָמִים אַשְׂבִּיעֵהוּ, וְאַרְאֵהוּ בִּישׁוּעָתִי:

---

Immediately following the *beraita,* we are told by the Talmud that Rabbi Joshua ben Levi would recite the verses of the *Shir shel Pega'im* when he would go to sleep at night.

It is also our custom to recite the *Shir shel Pega'im* Saturday night at the conclusion of the Sabbath after the *'Amidah* prayer. There too, there appears a connection to the work of the Tabernacle. (For that reason, if a festival falls out during the following week we omit saying *Viyhi No'am.*)[18]

Rav Kook is able to provide some much needed perspective. He writes that the *"mazikin"* or demons are disembodied spirits.[19] Not only are they themselves disembodied, but they oppose the embodiment of *kedushah* (holiness). The very essence of the embodiment of the *Shekhinah* in this world is the Tabernacle. (At the time of the dedication of the First Temple, Solomon boldly declared, "But will God in very truth dwell on the earth?)[20] Therefore, specifically at the time that the Tabernacle reached completion and the *Shekhinah* was about ready to descend upon it, it was necessary to ward off these negative, opposing elements.[21]

---

18. Zedekiah ben Abraham Anav of Rome, *Shibbolei ha-Leket ha-Shalem,* ed. Samuel K. Mirsky (Brooklyn, NY: Sura, 1966), chap. 129 (pp. 424–427); *Tanya Rabbati,* chap. 21; *Tur* and *Shulḥan 'Arukh, OḤ,* chap. 295 (gloss of Rabbi Moses Isserles there); *Turei Zahav* ad loc.
19. See *OR,* vol. 2, pp. 178–179 (to *m. Avot* 5:6).
20. 1 Kings 8:27.
21. *SK* 7:8 = *OK,* vol. 2, p. 321. Rav Kook writes: "And all assisted in the construction of the Temple" (ibid.) The Editor of *OK,* Rabbi David Cohen (the Nazirite) sources the statement in the Midrash *Numbers Rabbah* 14:3 and *Song of Songs Rabbah* 1:5: "All assist the King... even spirits; even demons; even angels." See *OK,* vol. 2, p. 601 (25). (See *Yedei Moshe* to *Numbers Rabbah* 14:3.) There is also the famous fable in *b. Gittin* 68 that eventually Ashmedai (Asmodeus), King of the Demons, revealed

יהוה LORD, how numerous are my enemies, how many rise against me. Many *Ps. 3* say of me: "There is no help for him in God," Selah. But You, LORD, are a shield around me. You are my glory; You raise my head high. I cry aloud to the LORD, and He answers me from His holy mountain, Selah. I lie down to sleep and I wake again, for the LORD supports me. I will not fear the myriad forces ranged against me on all sides. Arise, LORD, save me, O my God; strike all my enemies across the cheek; break the teeth of the wicked. From the LORD comes deliverance; may Your blessing rest upon Your people, Selah.

הַשְׁכִּיבֵנוּ Help us lie down, O LORD our God, in peace, and rise up, O our King, to life. Spread over us Your canopy of peace. Direct us with Your good counsel, and save us for the sake of Your name. Shield us and remove from us every enemy, plague, sword, famine and sorrow. Remove the adversary from before and behind us. Shelter us in the shadow of Your wings, for You, God, are our Guardian and Deliverer; You, God, are a gracious and compassionate King. Guard our going out and our coming in, for life and peace, from now and for ever.

בָּרוּךְ Blessed is the LORD by day, blessed is the LORD by night. Blessed is the LORD when we lie down; blessed is the LORD when we rise. For in Your hand are the souls of the living and the dead, [as it is written:] "In His hand is every *Job 12* living soul, and the breath of all mankind." Into Your hand I entrust my spirit: *Ps. 31* You redeemed me, LORD, God of truth. Our God in heaven, bring unity to Your name, establish Your kingdom constantly and reign over us for ever and all time.

יִרְאוּ May our eyes see, our hearts rejoice, and our souls be glad in Your true salvation, when Zion is told, "Your God reigns." The LORD is King, the LORD was King, and the LORD will be King for ever and all time. For sovereignty is Yours, and to all eternity You will reign in glory, for we have no king but You.

הַמַּלְאָךְ May the angel who rescued me from all harm, bless these boys. May *Gen. 48* they be called by my name and the names of my fathers Abraham and Isaac, and may they increase greatly on the earth.

וַיֹּאמֶר He said, "If you listen carefully to the voice of the LORD your God and *Ex. 15* do what is right in His eyes, if you pay attention to His commandments and keep all His statutes, I will not bring on you any of the diseases I brought on the Egyptians, for I am the LORD who heals you." The LORD said to the accuser, *Zech. 3* "The LORD shall rebuke you, accuser. The LORD who has chosen Jerusalem shall rebuke you! Is not this man a burning stick snatched from the fire?" Look! It *Song. 3* is Solomon's bed, escorted by sixty warriors, the noblest of Israel, all of them wearing the sword, experienced in battle, each with his sword at his side, prepared for the terror of the nights.

יהוה מָה־רַבּוּ צָרָי, רַבִּים קָמִים עָלָי: רַבִּים אֹמְרִים לְנַפְשִׁי, אֵין יְשׁוּעָֽתָה תהלים ג
לּוֹ בֵאלֹהִים, סֶלָה: וְאַתָּה יהוה מָגֵן בַּעֲדִי, כְּבוֹדִי וּמֵרִים רֹאשִׁי: קוֹלִי
אֶל־יהוה אֶקְרָא, וַיַּעֲנֵנִי מֵהַר קָדְשׁוֹ, סֶלָה: אֲנִי שָׁכַבְתִּי וָאִישָׁנָה, הֱקִיצוֹתִי
כִּי יהוה יִסְמְכֵנִי: לֹא־אִירָא מֵרִבְבוֹת עָם, אֲשֶׁר סָבִיב שָׁתוּ עָלָי: קוּמָה
יהוה, הוֹשִׁיעֵנִי אֱלֹהַי, כִּי־הִכִּיתָ אֶת־כָּל־אֹיְבַי לֶחִי, שִׁנֵּי רְשָׁעִים שִׁבַּרְתָּ:
לַיהוה הַיְשׁוּעָה, עַל־עַמְּךָ בִרְכָתֶךָ סֶּלָה:

הַשְׁכִּיבֵנוּ, יהוה אֱלֹהֵינוּ, לְשָׁלוֹם. וְהַעֲמִידֵנוּ, מַלְכֵּנוּ, לְחַיִּים. וּפְרֹשׂ עָלֵינוּ סֻכַּת שְׁלוֹמֶךָ, וְתַקְּנֵנוּ בְּעֵצָה טוֹבָה מִלְּפָנֶיךָ, וְהוֹשִׁיעֵנוּ לְמַעַן שְׁמֶךָ. וְהָגֵן בַּעֲדֵנוּ, וְהָסֵר מֵעָלֵינוּ אוֹיֵב, דֶּבֶר וְחֶרֶב וְרָעָב וְיָגוֹן. וְהָסֵר שָׂטָן מִלְּפָנֵינוּ וּמֵאַחֲרֵינוּ, וּבְצֵל כְּנָפֶיךָ תַּסְתִּירֵנוּ, כִּי אֵל שׁוֹמְרֵנוּ וּמַצִּילֵנוּ אָתָּה, כִּי אֵל מֶלֶךְ חַנּוּן וְרַחוּם אָתָּה. וּשְׁמֹר צֵאתֵנוּ וּבוֹאֵנוּ לְחַיִּים וּלְשָׁלוֹם מֵעַתָּה וְעַד עוֹלָם.

בָּרוּךְ יהוה בַּיּוֹם, בָּרוּךְ יהוה בַּלָּיְלָה, בָּרוּךְ יהוה בְּשָׁכְבֵנוּ, בָּרוּךְ יהוה
בְּקוּמֵנוּ. כִּי בְיָדְךָ נַפְשׁוֹת הַחַיִּים וְהַמֵּתִים. אֲשֶׁר בְּיָדוֹ נֶפֶשׁ כָּל־חָי, וְרוּחַ איוב יב
כָּל־בְּשַׂר־אִישׁ: בְּיָדְךָ אַפְקִיד רוּחִי, פָּדִיתָה אוֹתִי יהוה אֵל אֱמֶת: אֱלֹהֵינוּ תהלים לא
שֶׁבַּשָּׁמַיִם, יַחֵד שִׁמְךָ וְקַיֵּם מַלְכוּתְךָ תָּמִיד, וּמְלֹךְ עָלֵינוּ לְעוֹלָם וָעֶד.

יִרְאוּ עֵינֵינוּ וְיִשְׂמַח לִבֵּנוּ, וְתָגֵל נַפְשֵׁנוּ בִּישׁוּעָתְךָ בֶּאֱמֶת, בֶּאֱמֹר לְצִיּוֹן מָלַךְ אֱלֹהָיִךְ. יהוה מֶלֶךְ, יהוה מָלָךְ, יהוה יִמְלֹךְ לְעוֹלָם וָעֶד. כִּי הַמַּלְכוּת שֶׁלְּךָ הִיא, וּלְעוֹלְמֵי עַד תִּמְלֹךְ בְּכָבוֹד, כִּי אֵין לָנוּ מֶלֶךְ אֶלָּא אָתָּה.

הַמַּלְאָךְ הַגֹּאֵל אֹתִי מִכָּל־רָע יְבָרֵךְ אֶת־הַנְּעָרִים, וְיִקָּרֵא בָהֶם שְׁמִי וְשֵׁם בראשית מח
אֲבֹתַי אַבְרָהָם וְיִצְחָק, וְיִדְגּוּ לָרֹב בְּקֶרֶב הָאָרֶץ:

וַיֹּאמֶר אִם־שָׁמוֹעַ תִּשְׁמַע לְקוֹל יהוה אֱלֹהֶיךָ, וְהַיָּשָׁר בְּעֵינָיו תַּעֲשֶׂה, שמות טו
וְהַאֲזַנְתָּ לְמִצְוֹתָיו וְשָׁמַרְתָּ כָּל־חֻקָּיו, כָּל־הַמַּחֲלָה אֲשֶׁר־שַׂמְתִּי בְמִצְרַיִם
לֹא־אָשִׂים עָלֶיךָ, כִּי אֲנִי יהוה רֹפְאֶךָ: וַיֹּאמֶר יהוה אֶל־הַשָּׂטָן, יִגְעַר יהוה זכריה ג
בְּךָ הַשָּׂטָן, וְיִגְעַר יהוה בְּךָ הַבֹּחֵר בִּירוּשָׁלָםִ, הֲלוֹא זֶה אוּד מֻצָּל מֵאֵשׁ:
הִנֵּה מִטָּתוֹ שֶׁלִּשְׁלֹמֹה, שִׁשִּׁים גִּבֹּרִים סָבִיב לָהּ, מִגִּבֹּרֵי יִשְׂרָאֵל: כֻּלָּם שיר השירים ג
אֲחֻזֵי חֶרֶב, מְלֻמְּדֵי מִלְחָמָה, אִישׁ חַרְבּוֹ עַל־יְרֵכוֹ מִפַּחַד בַּלֵּילוֹת:

*Say three times:*

יְבָרֶכְךָ May the LORD bless you and protect you. *Num. 6*
May the LORD make His face shine on you and be gracious to you.
May the LORD turn His face toward you and grant you peace.

*Say three times:*

הִנֵּה See – the Guardian of Israel neither slumbers nor sleeps. *Ps. 121*

*Say three times:*

לִישׁוּעָתְךָ For Your salvation I hope, LORD. *Gen. 49*
I hope, LORD, for Your salvation.
LORD, for Your salvation I hope.

*Say three times:*

בְּשֵׁם In the name of the LORD, God of Israel:
may Michael be at my right hand,
Gabriel, at my left;
in front of me, Uriel,
behind me, Raphael;
and above my head the Presence of God.

שִׁיר הַמַּעֲלוֹת A song of ascents. Happy are all who fear the LORD, who walk in His ways. When you eat the fruit of your labor, happy and fortunate are you. Your wife shall be like a fruitful vine within your house; your sons like olive saplings around your table. So shall the man who fears the LORD be blessed. May the LORD bless you from Zion; may you see the good of Jerusalem all the days of your life; and may you live to see your children's children. Peace be on Israel! *Ps. 128*

*Say three times:*

רִגְזוּ Tremble, and do not sin. *Ps. 4*
Search your heart as you lie on your bed, and be silent. Selah.

אֲדוֹן עוֹלָם LORD of the Universe, who reigned before the birth of any thing; when by His will all things were made, then was His name proclaimed King. And when all things shall cease to be, He alone will reign in awe. He was, He is, and He shall be glorious for evermore. He is One, there is none else, alone, unique, beyond compare; Without beginning, without end, His might, His rule are everywhere. He is my God; my Redeemer lives. He is the Rock on whom I rely – my banner and my safe retreat, my cup, my portion when I cry. Into His hand my soul I place, when I awake and when I sleep. The LORD is with me, I shall not fear; body and soul from harm will He keep.

*Say three times:*

יְבָרֶכְךָ יהוה וְיִשְׁמְרֶךָ׃ במדבר ו
יָאֵר יהוה פָּנָיו אֵלֶיךָ וִיחֻנֶּךָּ׃
יִשָּׂא יהוה פָּנָיו אֵלֶיךָ וְיָשֵׂם לְךָ שָׁלוֹם׃

*Say three times:*

הִנֵּה לֹא־יָנוּם וְלֹא יִישָׁן שׁוֹמֵר יִשְׂרָאֵל׃ תהלים קכא

*Say three times:*

לִישׁוּעָתְךָ קִוִּיתִי יהוה׃ בראשית מט
קִוִּיתִי יהוה לִישׁוּעָתְךָ, יהוה לִישׁוּעָתְךָ קִוִּיתִי

*Say three times:*

בְּשֵׁם יהוה אֱלֹהֵי יִשְׂרָאֵל
מִימִינִי מִיכָאֵל, וּמִשְּׂמֹאלִי גַּבְרִיאֵל
וּמִלְּפָנַי אוּרִיאֵל, וּמֵאֲחוֹרַי רְפָאֵל
וְעַל רֹאשִׁי שְׁכִינַת אֵל.

שִׁיר הַמַּעֲלוֹת, אַשְׁרֵי כָּל־יְרֵא יהוה, הַהֹלֵךְ בִּדְרָכָיו: יְגִיעַ כַּפֶּיךָ כִּי תֹאכֵל, תהלים קכח
אַשְׁרֶיךָ וְטוֹב לָךְ: אֶשְׁתְּךָ כְּגֶפֶן פֹּרִיָּה בְּיַרְכְּתֵי בֵיתֶךָ, בָּנֶיךָ כִּשְׁתִלֵי זֵיתִים,
סָבִיב לְשֻׁלְחָנֶךָ: הִנֵּה כִי־כֵן יְבֹרַךְ גָּבֶר יְרֵא יהוה: יְבָרֶכְךָ יהוה מִצִּיּוֹן,
וּרְאֵה בְּטוּב יְרוּשָׁלָםִ, כֹּל יְמֵי חַיֶּיךָ: וּרְאֵה־בָנִים לְבָנֶיךָ, שָׁלוֹם עַל־יִשְׂרָאֵל:

*Say three times:*

רִגְזוּ וְאַל־תֶּחֱטָאוּ, אִמְרוּ בִלְבַבְכֶם עַל־מִשְׁכַּבְכֶם, וְדֹמּוּ סֶלָה: תהלים ד

אֲדוֹן עוֹלָם אֲשֶׁר מָלַךְ בְּטֶרֶם כָּל־יְצִיר נִבְרָא. לְעֵת נַעֲשָׂה בְחֶפְצוֹ כֹּל אֲזַי מֶלֶךְ שְׁמוֹ נִקְרָא. וְאַחֲרֵי כִּכְלוֹת הַכֹּל לְבַדּוֹ יִמְלֹךְ נוֹרָא. וְהוּא הָיָה וְהוּא הֹוֶה וְהוּא יִהְיֶה בְּתִפְאָרָה. וְהוּא אֶחָד וְאֵין שֵׁנִי לְהַמְשִׁיל לוֹ לְהַחְבִּירָה. בְּלִי רֵאשִׁית בְּלִי תַכְלִית וְלוֹ הָעֹז וְהַמִּשְׂרָה. וְהוּא אֵלִי וְחַי גֹּאֲלִי וְצוּר חֶבְלִי בְּעֵת צָרָה. וְהוּא נִסִּי וּמָנוֹס לִי מְנָת כּוֹסִי בְּיוֹם אֶקְרָא. בְּיָדוֹ אַפְקִיד רוּחִי בְּעֵת אִישַׁן וְאָעִירָה. וְעִם רוּחִי גְּוִיָּתִי יהוה לִי וְלֹא אִירָא.

# שבת
## SHABBAT


| | | |
|---|---|---|
| עירובין | 381 | EIRUVIN |
| קבלת שבת | 389 | KABBALAT SHABBAT |
| מעריב לשבת וליום טוב | 415 | MA'ARIV FOR SHABBAT AND YOM TOV |
| קידוש וזמירות לליל שבת | 451 | KIDDUSH AND ZEMIROT FOR SHABBAT EVENING |
| שחרית לשבת וליום טוב | 475 | SHAḤARIT FOR SHABBAT AND YOM TOV |
| מוסף לשבת | 607 | MUSAF FOR SHABBAT |
| קידוש וזמירות ליום שבת | 647 | KIDDUSH AND ZEMIROT FOR SHABBAT MORNING |
| מנחה לשבת וליום טוב | 665 | MINḤA FOR SHABBAT AND YOM TOV |
| ברכי נפשי | 699 | BAREKHI NAFSHI |
| פרקי אבות | 711 | ETHICS OF THE FATHERS |
| מעריב למוצאי שבת | 751 | MA'ARIV FOR MOTZA'EI SHABBAT |

# Erev Shabbat and Yom Tov

## EIRUV TEḤUMIN

*On Shabbat and Yom Tov it is forbidden to walk more than 2000 cubits (about 3000 feet) beyond the boundary (teḥum) of the town where you live or are staying when the day begins. By placing food sufficient for two meals, before nightfall, at a point within 2000 cubits from the town limits, you confer on that place the status of a dwelling for the next day, and are then permitted to walk 2000 cubits from there.*

בָּרוּךְ Blessed are You, LORD our God, King of the Universe,
who has made us holy through His commandments,
and has commanded us about the mitzva of Eiruv.

By this Eiruv may we be permitted to walk from this place, 2000 cubits in any direction.

## EIRUV ḤATZEROT

*On Shabbat it is forbidden to carry objects from one private domain to another, or from a private domain into space shared by others, such as a communal staircase, corridor or courtyard. An Eiruv Ḥatzerot is created when each of the Jewish households in a court or apartment block, before Shabbat, places a loaf of bread or matza in one of the homes. The entire court or block then becomes a single private domain within which it is permitted to carry.*

בָּרוּךְ Blessed are You, LORD our God, King of the Universe,
who has made us holy through His commandments,
and has commanded us about the mitzva of Eiruv.

By this Eiruv may we be permitted to move, carry out and carry in from the houses to the courtyard, or from the courtyard to the houses, or from house to house, for all the houses within the courtyard.

## EIRUV TAVSHILIN

*It is not permitted to cook for Shabbat when a Yom Tov falls on Thursday or Friday unless an Eiruv Tavshilin has been made prior to the Yom Tov. This is done by taking a loaf or piece of matza together with a boiled egg, or a piece of cooked fish or meat to be used on Shabbat. While holding them, say the following:*

בָּרוּךְ Blessed are You, LORD our God, King of the Universe,
who has made us holy through His commandments,
and has commanded us about the mitzva of Eiruv.

By this Eiruv may we be permitted to bake, cook, insulate food, light a flame and do everything necessary on the festival for the sake of Shabbat, for us and for all Jews living in this city.

# ערב שבת ויום טוב

## עירוב תחומין

*On* שבת *and* יום טוב *it is forbidden to walk more than 2000 cubits (about 3000 feet) beyond the boundary (*תחום*) of the town where you live or are staying when the day begins. By placing food sufficient for two meals, before nightfall, at a point within 2000 cubits from the town limits, you confer on that place the status of a dwelling for the next day, and are then permitted to walk 2000 cubits from there.*

בָּרוּךְ אַתָּה יהוה אֱלֹהֵינוּ מֶלֶךְ הָעוֹלָם
אֲשֶׁר קִדְּשָׁנוּ בְּמִצְוֹתָיו וְצִוָּנוּ עַל מִצְוַת עֵרוּב.

בְּדֵין עֵרוּבָא יְהֵא שְׁרֵא לִי לְמֵיזַל מֵאַתְרָא הָדֵין תְּרֵין אַלְפִין אַמִּין לְכָל רוּחָא.

## עירוב חצרות

*On* שבת *it is forbidden to carry objects from one private domain to another, or from a private domain into space shared by others, such as a communal staircase, corridor or courtyard. An* עירוב חצרות *is created when each of the Jewish households in a court or apartment block, before* שבת*, places a loaf of bread or matza in one of the homes. The entire court or block then becomes a single private domain within which it is permitted to carry.*

בָּרוּךְ אַתָּה יהוה אֱלֹהֵינוּ מֶלֶךְ הָעוֹלָם
אֲשֶׁר קִדְּשָׁנוּ בְּמִצְוֹתָיו וְצִוָּנוּ עַל מִצְוַת עֵרוּב.

בְּדֵין עֵרוּבָא יְהֵא שְׁרֵא לַנָא לְטַלְטוּלֵי וּלְאַפּוּקֵי וּלְעַיּוּלֵי מִן הַבָּתִּים לֶחָצֵר וּמִן הֶחָצֵר לַבָּתִּים וּמִבַּיִת לְבַיִת לְכָל הַבָּתִּים שֶׁבֶּחָצֵר.

## עירוב תבשילין

*It is not permitted to cook for* שבת *when a* יום טוב *falls on Thursday or Friday unless an* עירוב תבשלין *has been made prior to the* יום טוב*. This is done by taking a loaf or piece of matza together with a boiled egg, or a piece of cooked fish or meat to be used on* שבת*. While holding them, say the following:*

בָּרוּךְ אַתָּה יהוה אֱלֹהֵינוּ מֶלֶךְ הָעוֹלָם
אֲשֶׁר קִדְּשָׁנוּ בְּמִצְוֹתָיו וְצִוָּנוּ עַל מִצְוַת עֵרוּב.

בְּדֵין עֵרוּבָא יְהֵא שְׁרֵא לַנָא לְמֵיפֵא וּלְבַשָּׁלָא וּלְאַטְמָנָא וּלְאַדְלָקָא שְׁרָגָא וּלְמֶעְבַּד כָּל צָרְכָנָא מִיּוֹמָא טָבָא לְשַׁבַּתָּא, לָנוּ וּלְכָל יִשְׂרָאֵל הַדָּרִים בָּעִיר הַזֹּאת.

## CANDLE LIGHTING

*On Erev Shabbat that is not a Yom Tov, cover the eyes with the hands after lighting the candles, and say:*

בָּרוּךְ Blessed are You, LORD our God, King of the Universe, who has made us holy through His commandments, and has commanded us to light the Sabbath light.

*On Erev Yom Tov, say the following blessing and then light the candles from an existing flame. If also Shabbat, cover the eyes with the hands after lighting the candles and say the following blessing, adding the words in parentheses.*

בָּרוּךְ Blessed are You, LORD our God, King of the Universe, who has made us holy through His commandments, and has commanded us to light (the Sabbath light and) the festival light.

*The blessing "Sheheḥeyanu" ("Who has given us life") is said on Yom Tov evenings, except on the last evenings of Pesaḥ. (In Israel, it is not said on the last evening of Pesaḥ.)*

בָּרוּךְ Blessed are You, LORD our God, King of the Universe, who has given us life, sustained us, and brought us to this time.

---

In this regard, perfect timing is of the essence. The Great Sabbath, the Messianic Era, must not be ushered in prematurely. This would prove disastrous for an unprepared mankind. We must recognize that the opposites are intertwined and both sets serve the divine scheme. "And they are turned round about by His guidance that they may do."[4] Thus, the period preceding the light relates to the light and prepares the light – through the cloud. The darkness of the pillar of cloud prepares the way for the light of the pillar of fire. The interplay of darkness and light is the fine arrangement of the Almighty.

The workday and the Sabbath are also interrelated. One must not light too early in the day; a premature incursion of the Sabbath would encroach upon the territory of the secular. "When the light is late, it is meant to be late." "Everything He has made beautiful in its (proper) time."[5]

4. Job 37:12. This verse figures prominently in the theology of Rabbi Moses Ḥayyim Luzzatto. See Yosef Avivi, *Zohar Ramḥal* (Jerusalem, 1997), 95ff.

5. Ecclesiastes 3:11.

# הדלקת נרות

*On* ערב שבת *that is not a* יום טוב, *cover the eyes with the hands after lighting the candles, and say:*

בָּרוּךְ אַתָּה יהוה אֱלֹהֵינוּ מֶלֶךְ הָעוֹלָם
אֲשֶׁר קִדְּשָׁנוּ בְּמִצְוֹתָיו, וְצִוָּנוּ לְהַדְלִיק נֵר שֶׁל שַׁבָּת.

*On* ערב יום טוב, *say the following blessing and then light the candles from an existing flame. If also* שבת, *cover the eyes with the hands after lighting the candles and say the following blessing, adding the words in parentheses.*

בָּרוּךְ אַתָּה יהוה אֱלֹהֵינוּ מֶלֶךְ הָעוֹלָם
אֲשֶׁר קִדְּשָׁנוּ בְּמִצְוֹתָיו
וְצִוָּנוּ לְהַדְלִיק נֵר שֶׁל (שַׁבָּת וְשֶׁל) יוֹם טוֹב.

*The blessing* שֶׁהֶחֱיָנוּ *is said on* יום טוב *evenings, except on the last evenings of* פסח. (*In* ארץ ישראל, *it is not said on the last evening of* פסח.)

בָּרוּךְ אַתָּה יהוה אֱלֹהֵינוּ מֶלֶךְ הָעוֹלָם
שֶׁהֶחֱיָנוּ וְקִיְּמָנוּ וְהִגִּיעָנוּ לַזְּמַן הַזֶּה.

---

הדלקת נרות / CANDLE LIGHTING

The wife of Rav Yosef would kindle the Sabbath lamp late in the day approaching night.

Rav Yosef said to her: I interpret the verse "He did not take away the pillar of cloud by day, nor the pillar of fire by night"[1] to mean that the pillar of fire overlapped with the pillar of cloud at the conclusion of the day, and the pillar of cloud overlapped with the pillar of fire at the conclusion of the night. [The inference was that the fire should be lit in broad daylight.]

She then thought to light the Sabbath lamp very early in the day.

An elder said to her: It should be kindled neither too early nor too late.[2]

The Sabbath lights, whose purpose is to enhance domestic harmony (*shalom bayit*),[3] symbolize the light of the Messianic Era which will bring peace to this strife-torn planet.

1. Exodus 13:22.
2. *b. Shabbat* 23b.
3. *b. Shabbat* 23b, 25b; Maimonides, *MT, Hil. Ḥannukah* 4:14.

*On Erev Yom Kippur, cover the eyes with the hands after lighting the candles, and say (on Shabbat add the words in parentheses):*

בָּרוּךְ Blessed are You, LORD our God, King of the Universe,
who has made us holy through His commandments,
and has commanded us to light (the Sabbath light and)
the light of the Day of Atonement.

בָּרוּךְ Blessed are You, LORD our God, King of the Universe,
who has given us life, sustained us,
and brought us to this time.

*Some add:*

יְהִי May it be Your will, LORD our God and God of our ancestors, that the Temple be speedily rebuilt in our days, and grant us our share in Your Torah. And may we serve You there in reverence, as in the days of old and as in former years.

*Prayer after candlelighting*
*(add the words in parentheses as appropriate):*

יְהִי May it be Your will, LORD my God and God of my forebears, that You give me grace – me (and my husband/and my father/and my mother/and my sons and my daughters) and all those close to me, and give us and all Israel good and long lives. And remember us with a memory that brings goodness and blessing; come to us with compassion and bless us with great blessings. Build our homes until they are complete, and allow Your Presence to live among us. And may I merit to raise children and grandchildren, each one wise and understanding, loving the LORD and in awe of God, people of truth, holy children, who will cling on to the LORD and light up the world with Torah and with good actions, and with all the kinds of work that serve the Creator. Please, hear my pleading at this time, by the merit of Sarah and Rebecca, Rachel and Leah our mothers, and light our candle that it should never go out, and light up Your face, so that we shall be saved, Amen.

---

and the sacred. Without that all-important point of contact between the workday and the Day of Rest, we would be deprived an appreciation of the divine micromanagement of history.[6]

6. *OR*, vol. 2, pp. 14–15 = *EA*, vol. 3, *Shabbat*, chap. 2, par. 31 (p. 77).

*On ערב יום כיפור, cover the eyes with the hands after lighting the candles, and say (on שבת add the words in parentheses):*

בָּרוּךְ אַתָּה יהוה אֱלֹהֵינוּ מֶלֶךְ הָעוֹלָם
אֲשֶׁר קִדְּשָׁנוּ בְּמִצְוֹתָיו
וְצִוָּנוּ לְהַדְלִיק נֵר שֶׁל (שַׁבָּת וְשֶׁל) יוֹם הַכִּפּוּרִים.

בָּרוּךְ אַתָּה יהוה אֱלֹהֵינוּ מֶלֶךְ הָעוֹלָם
שֶׁהֶחֱיָנוּ וְקִיְּמָנוּ, וְהִגִּיעָנוּ לַזְּמַן הַזֶּה.

*Some add:*

יְהִי רָצוֹן מִלְּפָנֶיךָ יהוה אֱלֹהֵינוּ וֵאלֹהֵי אֲבוֹתֵינוּ, שֶׁיִּבָּנֶה בֵּית הַמִּקְדָּשׁ בִּמְהֵרָה בְיָמֵינוּ, וְתֵן חֶלְקֵנוּ בְּתוֹרָתֶךָ, וְשָׁם נַעֲבָדְךָ בְּיִרְאָה כִּימֵי עוֹלָם
מלאכי ג וּכְשָׁנִים קַדְמֹנִיּוֹת. וְעָרְבָה לַיהוה מִנְחַת יְהוּדָה וִירוּשָׁלָםִ כִּימֵי עוֹלָם וּכְשָׁנִים קַדְמֹנִיּוֹת:

*Prayer after candlelighting (add the words in parentheses as appropriate):*

יְהִי רָצוֹן מִלְּפָנֶיךָ יהוה אֱלֹהַי וֵאלֹהֵי אֲבוֹתַי, שֶׁתְּחוֹנֵן אוֹתִי (וְאֶת אִישִׁי/ וְאֶת אָבִי/ וְאֶת אִמִּי/ וְאֶת בָּנַי וְאֶת בְּנוֹתַי) וְאֶת כָּל קְרוֹבַי, וְתִתֶּן לָנוּ וּלְכָל יִשְׂרָאֵל חַיִּים טוֹבִים וַאֲרֻכִּים, וְתִזְכְּרֵנוּ בְּזִכְרוֹן טוֹבָה וּבְרָכָה, וְתִפְקְדֵנוּ בִּפְקֻדַּת יְשׁוּעָה וְרַחֲמִים, וּתְבָרְכֵנוּ בְּרָכוֹת גְּדוֹלוֹת, וְתַשְׁלִים בָּתֵּינוּ וְתַשְׁכֵּן שְׁכִינָתְךָ בֵּינֵינוּ. וְזַכֵּנִי לְגַדֵּל בָּנִים וּבְנֵי בָנִים חֲכָמִים וּנְבוֹנִים, אוֹהֲבֵי יהוה יִרְאֵי אֱלֹהִים, אַנְשֵׁי אֱמֶת זֶרַע קֹדֶשׁ, בַּיהוה דְּבֵקִים וּמְאִירִים אֶת הָעוֹלָם בַּתּוֹרָה וּבְמַעֲשִׂים טוֹבִים וּבְכָל מְלֶאכֶת עֲבוֹדַת הַבּוֹרֵא. אָנָּא שְׁמַע אֶת תְּחִנָּתִי בָּעֵת הַזֹּאת בִּזְכוּת שָׂרָה וְרִבְקָה וְרָחֵל וְלֵאָה אִמּוֹתֵינוּ, וְהָאֵר נֵרֵנוּ שֶׁלֹּא יִכְבֶּה לְעוֹלָם וָעֶד, וְהָאֵר פָּנֶיךָ וְנִוָּשֵׁעָה. אָמֵן.

---

At the other extreme, kindling the light too late in the day, would remove the overlap of cloud and fire. It would eliminate the contiguity of the secular

*The service starts with Minḥa for Weekdays on page 278.*
*Most congregations sing "Beloved of the soul" before the Kabbalat Shabbat service.*

*On Yom Tov or Motza'ei Yom Tov falling on Shabbat, or on Shabbat Ḥol HaMo'ed, the service begins with Psalm 92 on page 404.*

*On Yom Tov falling on a weekday, the service begins with "Bless" on page 414.*

יְדִיד Beloved of the soul, Father of compassion,
draw Your servant close to Your will.
Like a deer will Your servant run
and fall prostrate before Your beauty.
To him Your love is sweeter
than honey from the comb, than any taste.

הָדוּר Glorious, beautiful, radiance of the world,
my soul is sick with love for You.
Please, God, heal her now by showing her Your tender radiance.
Then she will recover her strength and be healed,
Be Your servant for eternity.

וָתִיק Ancient of Days, let Your mercy be aroused;
please have pity on Your beloved child.
How long have I yearned to see the glory
of Your strength.
Please, my God, my heart's desire – hasten; do not hide Yourself.

הִגָּלֵה Reveal Yourself, beloved, and spread over me
the tabernacle of Your peace.
Let the earth shine with Your glory,
let us be overjoyed and rejoice in You.
Hurry, beloved, for the appointed time has come,
and be gracious to me as in the times of old.

*The service starts with* מנחה לחול *on page 279.*
*Most congregations sing* יְדִיד נֶפֶשׁ *at this point before* קבלת שבת*.*

*On* שבת חול המועד*, or on* שבת *falling on* מוצאי יום טוב *or* יום טוב *On*
*the service begins with* מִזְמוֹר שִׁיר *on page 405.*

*On* יום טוב *falling on a weekday, the service begins with* בָּרְכוּ *on page 415.*

יְדִיד נֶפֶשׁ, אָב הָרַחֲמָן, מְשֹׁךְ עַבְדְּךָ אֶל רְצוֹנֶךָ
יָרוּץ עַבְדְּךָ כְּמוֹ אַיָּל, יִשְׁתַּחֲוֶה מוּל הֲדָרֶךָ
כִּי יֶעֱרַב לוֹ יְדִידוּתָךְ, מִנֹּפֶת צוּף וְכָל טָעַם.

הָדוּר, נָאֶה, זִיו הָעוֹלָם, נַפְשִׁי חוֹלַת אַהֲבָתֶךָ
אָנָּא, אֵל נָא, רְפָא נָא לָהּ, בְּהַרְאוֹת לָהּ נֹעַם זִיוֶךָ
אָז תִּתְחַזֵּק וְתִתְרַפֵּא, וְהָיְתָה לָךְ שִׁפְחַת עוֹלָם.

וָתִיק, יֶהֱמוּ רַחֲמֶיךָ, וְחוּס נָא עַל בֵּן אוֹהֲבָךְ
כִּי זֶה כַּמֶּה נִכְסֹף נִכְסַף לִרְאוֹת בְּתִפְאֶרֶת עֻזָּךְ
אָנָּא, אֵלִי, מַחְמַד לִבִּי, חוּשָׁה נָּא, וְאַל תִּתְעַלָּם.

הִגָּלֶה נָא וּפְרֹשׂ, חָבִיב, עָלַי אֶת סֻכַּת שְׁלוֹמָךְ
תָּאִיר אֶרֶץ מִכְּבוֹדָךְ, נָגִילָה וְנִשְׂמְחָה בָךְ.
מַהֵר, אָהוּב, כִּי בָא מוֹעֵד, וְחָנֵּנִי כִּימֵי עוֹלָם.

# Kabbalat Shabbat

*Mourners during the week of Shiva leave the synagogue at this point, returning after "Come, my Beloved" on page 402.*

לְכוּ נְרַנְּנָה Come, let us sing for joy to the Lord, let us shout aloud to the Rock of our salvation. Let us greet Him with thanksgiving, shout aloud to Him with songs of praise. For the Lord is the great God, the King great above all powers. In His hand are the depths of the earth, and the mountain peaks are His. The sea is His, for He made it; the dry land too, for His hands formed it. Come, let us bow in worship and bend the knee before the Lord our Maker. For He is our God, and we are the people of His pasture, the flock He tends – today, if you would heed His voice. Do not harden your hearts as you did at Meribah, as you did that day at Massah in the desert, when your ancestors tested and tried Me though they had seen My deeds. ▸ For forty years I strove with that generation. I said, "They are a people whose hearts go astray, who have not understood My ways." So I swore in My anger, "They shall not enter My place of rest." *Ps. 95*

שִׁירוּ Sing to the Lord a new song; sing to the Lord all the earth. Sing to the Lord, bless His name; proclaim his deliverance day after day. Declare His glory among the nations, His marvels among all peoples. For great is the Lord and greatly to be praised; He is awesome beyond all heavenly powers. For all the gods of the peoples are mere idols: it was the Lord who made the heavens. Before Him are majesty and splendor; there are strength and beauty in His holy place. Render to the Lord, O families of the peoples; render to the Lord glory and might. Render to the Lord the glory due to His name; bring an offering and come into His courts. Bow down to the Lord in the splendor of holiness. Tremble before Him, all the earth. Say among the nations, "The Lord is King." The world stands firm, it will not be shaken. He will judge the peoples with equity. ▸ Let the heavens rejoice and the earth be glad. Let the sea roar, and all that is in it; let the fields be jubilant, and all they contain. Then the trees of the forest will sing for joy before the Lord, for He is coming to judge the earth. He will judge the world with justice, and the peoples with His faithfulness. *Ps. 96*

# קבלת שבת

*Mourners during the week of* שבעה *leave the* בית כנסת *at this point, returning after* לְכָה דוֹדִי *on page 403.*

תהלים צה

לְכוּ נְרַנְּנָה לַיהוה, נָרִיעָה לְצוּר יִשְׁעֵנוּ: נְקַדְּמָה פָנָיו בְּתוֹדָה, בִּזְמִרוֹת נָרִיעַ לוֹ: כִּי אֵל גָּדוֹל יהוה, וּמֶלֶךְ גָּדוֹל עַל־כָּל־אֱלֹהִים: אֲשֶׁר בְּיָדוֹ מֶחְקְרֵי־אָרֶץ, וְתוֹעֲפוֹת הָרִים לוֹ: אֲשֶׁר־לוֹ הַיָּם וְהוּא עָשָׂהוּ, וְיַבֶּשֶׁת יָדָיו יָצָרוּ: בֹּאוּ נִשְׁתַּחֲוֶה וְנִכְרָעָה, נִבְרְכָה לִפְנֵי־יהוה עֹשֵׂנוּ: כִּי הוּא אֱלֹהֵינוּ, וַאֲנַחְנוּ עַם מַרְעִיתוֹ וְצֹאן יָדוֹ, הַיּוֹם אִם־בְּקֹלוֹ תִשְׁמָעוּ: אַל־תַּקְשׁוּ לְבַבְכֶם כִּמְרִיבָה, כְּיוֹם מַסָּה בַּמִּדְבָּר: אֲשֶׁר נִסּוּנִי אֲבוֹתֵיכֶם, בְּחָנוּנִי גַּם רָאוּ פָעֳלִי: ◂ אַרְבָּעִים שָׁנָה אָקוּט בְּדוֹר, וָאֹמַר עַם תֹּעֵי לֵבָב הֵם, וְהֵם לֹא־יָדְעוּ דְרָכָי: אֲשֶׁר־נִשְׁבַּעְתִּי בְאַפִּי, אִם־יְבֹאוּן אֶל מְנוּחָתִי:

תהלים צו

שִׁירוּ לַיהוה שִׁיר חָדָשׁ, שִׁירוּ לַיהוה כָּל־הָאָרֶץ: שִׁירוּ לַיהוה, בָּרְכוּ שְׁמוֹ, בַּשְּׂרוּ מִיּוֹם־לְיוֹם יְשׁוּעָתוֹ: סַפְּרוּ בַגּוֹיִם כְּבוֹדוֹ, בְּכָל־הָעַמִּים נִפְלְאוֹתָיו: כִּי גָדוֹל יהוה וּמְהֻלָּל מְאֹד, נוֹרָא הוּא עַל־כָּל־אֱלֹהִים: כִּי כָּל־אֱלֹהֵי הָעַמִּים אֱלִילִים, וַיהוה שָׁמַיִם עָשָׂה: הוֹד־וְהָדָר לְפָנָיו, עֹז וְתִפְאֶרֶת בְּמִקְדָּשׁוֹ: הָבוּ לַיהוה מִשְׁפְּחוֹת עַמִּים, הָבוּ לַיהוה כָּבוֹד וָעֹז: הָבוּ לַיהוה כְּבוֹד שְׁמוֹ, שְׂאוּ־מִנְחָה וּבֹאוּ לְחַצְרוֹתָיו: הִשְׁתַּחֲווּ לַיהוה בְּהַדְרַת־קֹדֶשׁ, חִילוּ מִפָּנָיו כָּל־הָאָרֶץ: אִמְרוּ בַגּוֹיִם יהוה מָלָךְ, אַף־תִּכּוֹן תֵּבֵל בַּל־תִּמּוֹט, יָדִין עַמִּים בְּמֵישָׁרִים: ◂ יִשְׂמְחוּ הַשָּׁמַיִם וְתָגֵל הָאָרֶץ, יִרְעַם הַיָּם וּמְלֹאוֹ: יַעֲלֹז שָׂדַי וְכָל־אֲשֶׁר־בּוֹ, אָז יְרַנְּנוּ כָּל־עֲצֵי־יָעַר: לִפְנֵי יהוה כִּי בָא, כִּי בָא לִשְׁפֹּט הָאָרֶץ, יִשְׁפֹּט־תֵּבֵל בְּצֶדֶק, וְעַמִּים בֶּאֱמוּנָתוֹ:

יהוה מָלָךְ The Lord reigns, let the earth be glad. Let the many islands rejoice. Clouds and thick darkness surround Him; righteousness and justice are the foundation of His throne. Fire goes ahead of Him, consuming His enemies on every side. His lightning lights up the world; the earth sees and trembles. Mountains melt like wax before the Lord, before the Lord of all the earth. The heavens proclaim His righteousness, and all the peoples see His glory. All who worship images and boast in idols are put to shame. Bow down to Him, all you heavenly powers. Zion hears and rejoices, and the towns of Judah are glad because of your judgments, Lord. For You, Lord, are supreme over all the earth; You are exalted far above all heavenly powers. ▸ Let those who love the Lord hate evil, for He protects the lives of his devoted ones, delivering them from the hand of the wicked. Light is sown for the righteous, and joy for the upright in heart. Rejoice in the Lord, you who are righteous, and give thanks to His holy name. *Ps. 97*

מִזְמוֹר A Psalm. Sing a new song to the Lord, for He has done wondrous things; He has saved by His right hand and His holy arm. The Lord has made His salvation known; He has displayed His righteousness in the sight of the nations. He remembered His *Ps. 98*

---

of God.[8] For the present time, he must struggle with darkness; the light is reserved for him in the future as an eternal reward. Thus, it is a light sown like a seedling. The "straight of heart" experiences joy in the present rather than as some delayed gratification. Inasmuch as his will is identical with the will of God,[9] he beholds eternity while yet he lives.[10]

8. Cf. Rabbi Zadok Hakohen Rabinowitz, *Peri Zaddik*, vol. 3 (Lublin, 1922), *Shemini*, par. 2 (45b-c), citing *Zohar* 1, 202a: "There is nothing to break the evil inclination but Torah."
9. See Rabbi Judah Löw (Maharal) of Prague, *Derekh Ḥayyim* (London: L. Honig and Sons, 1960), commentary to *Avot* 2:4 (p. 75, col. 1): "the connection of the will of man to the will of God until it is considered one will." (RZYH Kook)
10. *OR*, vol. 2, p. 17. Writing in a kabbalistic vein, Rav Kook observes that the initials of *"u-le-yishrei lev simḥah"* form the word *"selav,"* the quail that the Children of Israel ate in the Desert. The Rav's point is that the *"yashar"* is able to consume meat, a symbol of material pleasures, without in the least compromising his spiritual integrity. See *SK* 2:280 and *IR*, vol. 2, pp. 168-169 (Letter 540 to Rabbi Y.M. Ḥarlap).

יהוה מָלָךְ תָּגֵל הָאָרֶץ, יִשְׂמְחוּ אִיִּים רַבִּים: עָנָן וַעֲרָפֶל סְבִיבָיו, תהלים צז
צֶדֶק וּמִשְׁפָּט מְכוֹן כִּסְאוֹ: אֵשׁ לְפָנָיו תֵּלֵךְ, וּתְלַהֵט סָבִיב צָרָיו:
הֵאִירוּ בְרָקָיו תֵּבֵל, רָאֲתָה וַתָּחֵל הָאָרֶץ: הָרִים כַּדּוֹנַג נָמַסּוּ
מִלִּפְנֵי יהוה, מִלִּפְנֵי אֲדוֹן כָּל־הָאָרֶץ: הִגִּידוּ הַשָּׁמַיִם צִדְקוֹ, וְרָאוּ
כָל־הָעַמִּים כְּבוֹדוֹ: יֵבֹשׁוּ כָּל־עֹבְדֵי פֶסֶל הַמִּתְהַלְלִים בָּאֱלִילִים,
הִשְׁתַּחֲווּ־לוֹ כָּל־אֱלֹהִים: שָׁמְעָה וַתִּשְׂמַח צִיּוֹן, וַתָּגֵלְנָה בְּנוֹת
יְהוּדָה, לְמַעַן מִשְׁפָּטֶיךָ יהוה: כִּי־אַתָּה יהוה עֶלְיוֹן עַל־כָּל־
הָאָרֶץ, מְאֹד נַעֲלֵיתָ עַל־כָּל־אֱלֹהִים: › אֹהֲבֵי יהוה שִׂנְאוּ רָע, שֹׁמֵר
נַפְשׁוֹת חֲסִידָיו, מִיַּד רְשָׁעִים יַצִּילֵם: אוֹר זָרֻעַ לַצַּדִּיק, וּלְיִשְׁרֵי־
לֵב שִׂמְחָה: שִׂמְחוּ צַדִּיקִים בַּיהוה, וְהוֹדוּ לְזֵכֶר קָדְשׁוֹ:

מִזְמוֹר, שִׁירוּ לַיהוה שִׁיר חָדָשׁ כִּי־נִפְלָאוֹת עָשָׂה, הוֹשִׁיעָה־לּוֹ תהלים צח
יְמִינוֹ וּזְרוֹעַ קָדְשׁוֹ: הוֹדִיעַ יהוה יְשׁוּעָתוֹ, לְעֵינֵי הַגּוֹיִם גִּלָּה
צִדְקָתוֹ: זָכַר חַסְדּוֹ וֶאֱמוּנָתוֹ לְבֵית יִשְׂרָאֵל, רָאוּ כָל־אַפְסֵי־אָרֶץ

---

אוֹר זָרֻעַ לַצַּדִּיק, וּלְיִשְׁרֵי־לֵב שִׂמְחָה *Light is sown for the righteous, and joy for the upright in heart.* (Psalm 97)

> For the righteous (*tsaddikim*) light,
> And for the straight (*yesharim*) joy. (*b. Ta'anit* 15a)
> The straight are superior to the righteous. (Pseudo-Rashi)

What is the difference between the "righteous" and the "straight"? In the *Eight Chapters*, Maimonides contrasts two types: the one who conquers his evil inclination (*kovesh et yitsro*) versus the one who is naturally pious (*ḥasid*). The will of the *ḥasid* is naturally aligned with the divine will; he cleaves to God in an unmediated manner.[7] The *kovesh et yitsro*, on the other hand, does not come to God naturally. By nature, his will is independent of the will of God, and only through the intervention of the Torah – which is not essentially him – is he able to bend his will to the will

7. Maimonides, *Eight Chapters* (Introduction to Commentary to Mishnah, *Avot*), chap. 6.

loving-kindness and faithfulness to the house of Israel; all the ends of the earth have seen the victory of our LORD. Shout for joy to the LORD, all the earth; burst into song, sing with joy, play music. Play music to the LORD on the harp – on the harp with the sound of singing. With trumpets and the sound of the shofar, shout for joy before the LORD, the King. ▸ Let the sea and all that is in it thunder, the world and all who live in it. Let the rivers clap their hands, the mountains sing together for joy – before the LORD, for He is coming to judge the earth. He will judge the world with justice, and the peoples with equity.

יהוה מָלָךְ The LORD reigns, let the peoples tremble. He sits enthroned on the Cherubim, let the earth quake. Great is the LORD in Zion, He is exalted over all the peoples. Let them praise Your name, O great and awesome One: He is holy! The King in His might loves justice. You have established equity. The justice and righteousness in Jacob is Your doing. Exalt the LORD our God, and bow at His footstool: He is holy! Moses and Aaron were among His priests; Samuel was among those who called on His name. They called on the LORD and He answered them. ▸ He spoke to them in a pillar of cloud; they observed His testimonies and the statute He gave them. LORD our God, You answered them. You were for them a forgiving God, though You punished their misdeeds. Exalt the LORD our God and bow at His holy mountain, for the LORD our God is holy. *Ps. 99*

*The following psalm is said standing:*

מִזְמוֹר לְדָוִד A psalm of David. Render to the LORD, you angelic powers, render to the LORD glory and might. Render to the LORD the glory due to His name. Bow to the LORD in the beauty of holiness. The LORD's voice echoes over the waters; the God of glory *Ps. 29*

---

(*binyan*) to the exclusion of the destruction (*ḥurban*). However, the destructive side plays an integral part in the overall divine scheme. "Go see the deeds of the LORD, Who has made desolations on the earth."[12] In our psalm, David gives expression to these cataclysmic events. His ears are attuned to the voice of

12. Psalms 46:9.

אֶת יְשׁוּעַת אֱלֹהֵינוּ: הָרִיעוּ לַיהוה כָּל־הָאָרֶץ, פִּצְחוּ וְרַנְּנוּ וְזַמֵּרוּ: זַמְּרוּ לַיהוה בְּכִנּוֹר, בְּכִנּוֹר וְקוֹל זִמְרָה: בַּחֲצֹצְרוֹת וְקוֹל שׁוֹפָר, הָרִיעוּ לִפְנֵי הַמֶּלֶךְ יהוה: ׀ יִרְעַם הַיָּם וּמְלֹאוֹ, תֵּבֵל וְיֹשְׁבֵי בָהּ: נְהָרוֹת יִמְחֲאוּ־כָף, יַחַד הָרִים יְרַנֵּנוּ: לִפְנֵי יהוה כִּי בָא לִשְׁפֹּט הָאָרֶץ, יִשְׁפֹּט־תֵּבֵל בְּצֶדֶק, וְעַמִּים בְּמֵישָׁרִים:

תהלים צט יהוה מָלָךְ יִרְגְּזוּ עַמִּים, יֹשֵׁב כְּרוּבִים תָּנוּט הָאָרֶץ: יהוה בְּצִיּוֹן גָּדוֹל, וְרָם הוּא עַל־כָּל־הָעַמִּים: יוֹדוּ שִׁמְךָ גָּדוֹל וְנוֹרָא קָדוֹשׁ הוּא: וְעֹז מֶלֶךְ מִשְׁפָּט אָהֵב, אַתָּה כּוֹנַנְתָּ מֵישָׁרִים, מִשְׁפָּט וּצְדָקָה בְּיַעֲקֹב אַתָּה עָשִׂיתָ: רוֹמְמוּ יהוה אֱלֹהֵינוּ, וְהִשְׁתַּחֲווּ לַהֲדֹם רַגְלָיו, קָדוֹשׁ הוּא: מֹשֶׁה וְאַהֲרֹן בְּכֹהֲנָיו, וּשְׁמוּאֵל בְּקֹרְאֵי שְׁמוֹ, קֹרְאִים אֶל־יהוה וְהוּא יַעֲנֵם: ׀ בְּעַמּוּד עָנָן יְדַבֵּר אֲלֵיהֶם, שָׁמְרוּ עֵדֹתָיו וְחֹק נָתַן־לָמוֹ: יהוה אֱלֹהֵינוּ אַתָּה עֲנִיתָם, אֵל נֹשֵׂא הָיִיתָ לָהֶם, וְנֹקֵם עַל־עֲלִילוֹתָם: רוֹמְמוּ יהוה אֱלֹהֵינוּ, וְהִשְׁתַּחֲווּ לְהַר קָדְשׁוֹ, כִּי־קָדוֹשׁ יהוה אֱלֹהֵינוּ:

*The following psalm is said standing:*

תהלים כט מִזְמוֹר לְדָוִד, הָבוּ לַיהוה בְּנֵי אֵלִים, הָבוּ לַיהוה כָּבוֹד וָעֹז: הָבוּ לַיהוה כְּבוֹד שְׁמוֹ, הִשְׁתַּחֲווּ לַיהוה בְּהַדְרַת־קֹדֶשׁ: קוֹל יהוה עַל הַמָּיִם, אֵל־הַכָּבוֹד הִרְעִים, יהוה עַל־מַיִם רַבִּים: קוֹל־יהוה

---

מִזְמוֹר לְדָוִד ... קוֹל יהוה עַל הַמָּיִם *A psalm of David... The LORD's voice echoes over the waters.* (*Psalm 29*)

These seven blessings of the Sabbath, to what do they correspond?

Said Rabbi Ḥalafta ben Shaul: They correspond to the seven "voices" David said, starting with the waters.[11]

Our view of existence is one-sided and partial. We focus on the construction

11. *b. Berakhot* 29a.

thunders; the LORD is over the mighty waters. The LORD's voice in power, the LORD's voice in beauty, the LORD's voice breaks cedars, the LORD shatters the cedars of Lebanon. He makes Lebanon skip like a calf, Sirion like a young wild ox. The LORD's voice cleaves flames of fire. The LORD's voice makes the desert quake, the LORD shakes the desert of Kadesh. ▸ The LORD's voice makes hinds calve and strips the forests bare, and in His temple all say: "Glory!" The LORD sat enthroned at the Flood, the LORD sits enthroned as King for ever. The LORD will give strength to His people; the LORD will bless His people with peace.

*The following is said in some congregations:*

Please, by the power of Your great right hand, set the captive nation free.
Accept Your people's prayer. Strengthen us, purify us, You who are revered.
Please, Mighty One, guard like the pupil of the eye those who seek
Your unity.
Bless them, cleanse them, have compassion on them,
grant them Your righteousness always.
Mighty One, Holy One, in Your great goodness guide Your congregation.
Only One, Exalted One, turn to Your people, who proclaim Your holiness.
Accept our plea and heed our cry, You who know all secret thoughts.

Blessed be the name of His glorious kingdom for ever and all time.

---

> The drive for the destruction of the world is in existence, in all of its values; just as there is the drive for the construction of the world, its uplifting and its perfection.[14]

The Sabbath is a statement, an acknowledgment that creation is not the be-all and end-all. The Sabbath takes us beyond "the usual rationalist view that deems the general evil and its many specifics just a collection of random affairs, whose constancy is not but the natural necessity of matter."[15]

For the "workaholic" who measures his self-worth in terms of output and productivity, *Shabbat* can be a challenge, forcing him to come to terms with other aspects of being that he has likely repressed. By getting in touch with these "uncreative" regions of his internal universe, he may glimpse a horizon broader than he could ever have imagined.

---

14. *SK* 5:45.
15. *SK* 7:130. It appears the reference is to Maimonides, *Guide of the Perplexed* III, 10, 12. *OR*, vol. 2, pp. 19–20 = *EA*, vol. 1, *Berakhot*, chap. 4, par. 43 (p. 122).

בַּכֹּחַ, קוֹל יהוה בֶּהָדָר: קוֹל יהוה שֹׁבֵר אֲרָזִים, וַיְשַׁבֵּר יהוה אֶת־
אַרְזֵי הַלְּבָנוֹן: וַיַּרְקִידֵם כְּמוֹ־עֵגֶל, לְבָנוֹן וְשִׂרְיוֹן כְּמוֹ בֶן־רְאֵמִים:
קוֹל־יהוה חֹצֵב לַהֲבוֹת אֵשׁ: קוֹל יהוה יָחִיל מִדְבָּר, יָחִיל יהוה
מִדְבַּר קָדֵשׁ: ▸ קוֹל יהוה יְחוֹלֵל אַיָּלוֹת וַיֶּחֱשֹׂף יְעָרוֹת, וּבְהֵיכָלוֹ,
כֻּלּוֹ אֹמֵר כָּבוֹד: יהוה לַמַּבּוּל יָשָׁב, וַיֵּשֶׁב יהוה מֶלֶךְ לְעוֹלָם:
יהוה עֹז לְעַמּוֹ יִתֵּן, יהוה יְבָרֵךְ אֶת־עַמּוֹ בַשָּׁלוֹם:

*The following is said in some congregations:*

אָנָּא, בְּכֹחַ גְּדֻלַּת יְמִינְךָ, תַּתִּיר צְרוּרָה.
קַבֵּל רִנַּת עַמְּךָ, שַׂגְּבֵנוּ, טַהֲרֵנוּ, נוֹרָא.
נָא גִבּוֹר, דּוֹרְשֵׁי יִחוּדְךָ כְּבָבַת שָׁמְרֵם.
בָּרְכֵם, טַהֲרֵם, רַחֲמֵם, צִדְקָתְךָ תָּמִיד גָּמְלֵם.
חֲסִין קָדוֹשׁ, בְּרֹב טוּבְךָ נַהֵל עֲדָתֶךָ.
יָחִיד גֵּאֶה, לְעַמְּךָ פְּנֵה, זוֹכְרֵי קְדֻשָּׁתֶךָ.
שַׁוְעָתֵנוּ קַבֵּל וּשְׁמַע צַעֲקָתֵנוּ, יוֹדֵעַ תַּעֲלוּמוֹת.
בָּרוּךְ שֵׁם כְּבוֹד מַלְכוּתוֹ לְעוֹלָם וָעֶד.

---

the Lord resounding in natural catastrophes that threaten human habitation on this planet. We hear the voice of the Lord in the destruction, in flames of fire issuing from a volcanic eruption, in earthquakes, in flood waters that engulf the earth. And through all of that "the Lord sits enthroned as King for ever."

What does this destructive side of existence have to do with the Sabbath? The Sabbath is the day when there is cessation of creation. Creation goes on for six days; on the seventh it grinds to a halt. The Sabbath enlightens us that there is more to the divine plan than just creation. The Sabbath is "the culmination (*takhlit*) of the work of heaven and earth."[13] The Hebrew word *takhlit* has two meanings: "cessation" and "purpose." The Sabbath is both. On that day creation ceases, but on that day too we are privileged to glimpse "the purpose of the work of heaven and earth." And in that grand scheme, there is room not only for creation, but for destruction as well.

The Sabbath puts us in touch with these mythic forces of destruction. They too are part and parcel of the macrocosm and of the microcosm.

---

13. *'Amidah* for Sabbath night.

לְכָה דוֹדִי Come, my Beloved, to greet the bride;
let us welcome the Sabbath.

Come, my Beloved, to greet the bride;
let us welcome the Sabbath.

שָׁמוֹר "Observe" and "Remember" in one act of speech,
the One and Only God made us hear.
The Lord is One and His name is One,
for renown, for splendor, and for praise.

Come, my Beloved, to greet the bride;
let us welcome the Sabbath.

לִקְרַאת To greet the Sabbath, come let us go,
for of blessing, she is the source.
From the outset, as of old, ordained:
last in deed, first in thought.

Come, my Beloved, to greet the bride;
let us welcome the Sabbath.

מִקְדַּשׁ Sanctuary of the King, royal city,
arise, go forth from your ruined state.
Too long have you dwelt in the valley of tears.
He will shower compassion on you.

Come, my Beloved, to greet the bride;
let us welcome the Sabbath.

הִתְנַעֲרִי Shake yourself off, arise from the dust!
Put on your clothes of glory, My people.
Through the son of Jesse the Bethlehemite,
draw near to my soul and redeem it.

Come, my Beloved, to greet the bride;
let us welcome the Sabbath.

---

לְכָה דוֹדִי / LEKHA DODI

הִתְנַעֲרִי, מֵעָפָר קוּמִי, לִבְשִׁי בִּגְדֵי תִפְאַרְתֵּךְ עַמִּי *Shake yourself off from the dust, arise! Put on your clothes of glory, My people.* One of the literati in Erets Israel

לְכָה דוֹדִי לִקְרַאת כַּלָּה, פְּנֵי שַׁבָּת נְקַבְּלָה.
לְכָה דוֹדִי לִקְרַאת כַּלָּה, פְּנֵי שַׁבָּת נְקַבְּלָה.

שָׁמוֹר וְזָכוֹר בְּדִבּוּר אֶחָד
הִשְׁמִיעָנוּ אֵל הַמְיֻחָד
יהוה אֶחָד וּשְׁמוֹ אֶחָד
לְשֵׁם וּלְתִפְאֶרֶת וְלִתְהִלָּה.
לְכָה דוֹדִי לִקְרַאת כַּלָּה, פְּנֵי שַׁבָּת נְקַבְּלָה.

לִקְרַאת שַׁבָּת לְכוּ וְנֵלְכָה
כִּי הִיא מְקוֹר הַבְּרָכָה
מֵרֹאשׁ מִקֶּדֶם נְסוּכָה
סוֹף מַעֲשֶׂה בְּמַחֲשָׁבָה תְּחִלָּה.
לְכָה דוֹדִי לִקְרַאת כַּלָּה, פְּנֵי שַׁבָּת נְקַבְּלָה.

מִקְדַּשׁ מֶלֶךְ עִיר מְלוּכָה
קוּמִי צְאִי מִתּוֹךְ הַהֲפֵכָה
רַב לָךְ שֶׁבֶת בְּעֵמֶק הַבָּכָא
וְהוּא יַחֲמֹל עָלַיִךְ חֶמְלָה.
לְכָה דוֹדִי לִקְרַאת כַּלָּה, פְּנֵי שַׁבָּת נְקַבְּלָה.

הִתְנַעֲרִי, מֵעָפָר קוּמִי
לִבְשִׁי בִּגְדֵי תִפְאַרְתֵּךְ עַמִּי
עַל יַד בֶּן יִשַׁי בֵּית הַלַּחְמִי
קָרְבָה אֶל נַפְשִׁי, גְּאָלָהּ.
לְכָה דוֹדִי לִקְרַאת כַּלָּה, פְּנֵי שַׁבָּת נְקַבְּלָה.

הִתְעוֹרְרִי Wake up, wake up,
for your light has come: rise, shine!
Awake, awake, break out in song,
for the LORD's glory is revealed on you.
Come, my Beloved, to greet the bride;
let us welcome the Sabbath.

לֹא תֵבֹשִׁי Do not be ashamed, do not be confounded.
Why be downcast? Why do you mourn?
In you the needy of My people find shelter,
and the city shall be rebuilt on its hill.
Come, my Beloved, to greet the bride;
let us welcome the Sabbath.

וְהָיוּ Those who despoiled you shall be despoiled,
and all who devoured you shall be far away.
Your God will rejoice over you
as a bridegroom rejoices over his bride.
Come, my Beloved, to greet the bride;
let us welcome the Sabbath.

---

> Awake, awake, put on your strength, O Zion; put on your clothes of glory, O Jerusalem, the holy city; for henceforth there shall no more come into you the uncircumcised and the unclean.
> Shake yourself off from the dust; arise, sit down, O Jerusalem ...[16]

The subject to which the verb "put on" refers, is not "My people," but rather Jerusalem, which, as a city, is truly feminine. When God commands, "Shake yourself off from the dust, arise! Put on your clothes of glory," He is addressing the city of Jerusalem. As for the word *'ami*, "My people," at the end of the line (not found in Isaiah), this is an insertion on the part of the poet. Rabbi Shelomo Alkabetz is sharing with us his own interpretation of the verse in Isaiah. What are the "clothes of glory" that Jerusalem is to put on? "My people" (*'ami*)![17]

16. Isaiah 52:1, 2.
17. Rabbi Ze'ev Aryeh Rabiner, *Ha-Shabbat, Ha-'Am ve-ha-Arets* (Tel-Aviv, 1948), p. 212, citing Rabbi Shmuel Barukh Werner (son-in-law of Rabbi Ya'akov Moshe Ḥarlap).

הִתְעוֹרְרִי הִתְעוֹרְרִי
כִּי בָא אוֹרֵךְ קוּמִי אוֹרִי
עוּרִי עוּרִי, שִׁיר דַּבֵּרִי
כְּבוֹד יהוה עָלַיִךְ נִגְלָה.
לְכָה דוֹדִי לִקְרַאת כַּלָּה, פְּנֵי שַׁבָּת נְקַבְּלָה.

לֹא תֵבֹשִׁי וְלֹא תִכָּלְמִי
מַה תִּשְׁתּוֹחֲחִי וּמַה תֶּהֱמִי
בָּךְ יֶחֱסוּ עֲנִיֵּי עַמִּי
וְנִבְנְתָה עִיר עַל תִּלָּהּ.
לְכָה דוֹדִי לִקְרַאת כַּלָּה, פְּנֵי שַׁבָּת נְקַבְּלָה.

וְהָיוּ לִמְשִׁסָּה שֹׁאסָיִךְ
וְרָחֲקוּ כָּל מְבַלְּעָיִךְ
יָשִׂישׂ עָלַיִךְ אֱלֹהָיִךְ
כִּמְשׂוֹשׂ חָתָן עַל כַּלָּה.
לְכָה דוֹדִי לִקְרַאת כַּלָּה, פְּנֵי שַׁבָּת נְקַבְּלָה.

---

published an article asserting that our version of *Lekha Dodi* violates the laws of grammar and called for its emendation. The writer contended that since the word *'am* (people) is masculine, the words *livshi* (put on) and *tif'artekh* (your glory), which are feminine, must be changed to *levosh* and *tif'artekha,* to conform to masculine gender.

Rav Kook responded that emendation is uncalled for. He explained that Rabbi Shelomo Alkabetz, the composer of the poem *Lekha Dodi,* based that line on the verses in Isaiah:

יָמִין Right and left you shall spread out,
and the LORD you will revere.
Through the descendant of Peretz,
we shall rejoice and we shall be glad.

Come, my Beloved, to greet the bride;
let us welcome the Sabbath.

---

*ha-go'el*). Mind-boggling as it might sound, this breakdown of traditional Jewish society will eventuate a breakthrough to hitherto undreamed of spiritual vistas.

The malaise of our contemporary scene ("the discontents of society") is summed up most aptly by Rav Kook's faithful disciple Rabbi Ya'akov Moshe Ḥarlap:

> In the "footsteps of Messiah," the generation of Ben Partzi, all the components, all the opinions break out, and seek their *tikkun*, their correction, their perfection. They seek to come out of their status of *peratim*, of specific details, and be accorded the status of *kelalim*, of generalities, of universals. At that time, all seek to fill that which is lacking in them…
>
> The midwife screams: "Why have you breached?"[20] Nevertheless, out of this comes the Son of David.
>
> God-fearing Torah scholars who increase peace in the world,[21] are called upon… to bring about the perfection of every good portion of Israel and the establishment of every opinion on a firm basis, by the isolation of the weeds that have grown up in them.
>
> This is a "difficult service in the Temple," "one must neither exclude nor include,"[22] and its final completion will come about only through the Son of David himself. Yet one must not shirk this holy service, for through it shines the light of Messiah.[23]

---

20. Genesis 38:29.
21. *b. Berakhot* 64a.
22. *b. Yoma* 47b; *Menaḥot* 11a.
23. Rabbi Ya'akov Moshe Ḥarlap, *Mei Marom*, vol. 13 [on the Prayer Book] (Jerusalem: Beit Zevul, 1998), p. 165.

יָמִין וּשְׂמֹאל תִּפְרֹצִי
וְאֶת יהוה תַּעֲרִיצִי
עַל יַד אִישׁ בֶּן פַּרְצִי
וְנִשְׂמְחָה וְנָגִילָה.
לְכָה דוֹדִי לִקְרַאת כַּלָּה, פְּנֵי שַׁבָּת נְקַבְּלָה.

---

יָמִין וּשְׂמֹאל תִּפְרֹצִי, וְאֶת יהוה תַּעֲרִיצִי, עַל יַד אִישׁ בֶּן פַּרְצִי, וְנִשְׂמְחָה וְנָגִילָה *Right and left you shall spread out, and God you will revere. Through the descendant of Peretz, we shall rejoice and we shall be glad.* The long-awaited Messiah is referred to as "Ben Partzi." Simply, this is on account of the fact that the Messiah is descended from David, who in turn is descended from Peretz, son of Judah.[18] But the name "Ben Partzi" is pregnant with meaning. It is related to *peritzut*, "breaking down" fences, "breaching" accepted codes and standards of behavior.[19]

Rav Kook devoted much thought to the breakdown of traditional values that he witnessed during his career as Rabbi of Jaffa and later Jerusalem. To say that it pained him deeply, would be an understatement. Yet the Rav firmly believed that out of this terrible breakdown of Halakhic law and order, there would one day emerge a Judaism much stronger and higher than that of previous generations. And this breakdown – heart-wrenching, tragic though it be – is in fact part of the redemptive process (*ha-tahalikh*

---

18. Genesis 38:29; Ruth 4:18–22.

19. See *SK* 5:192:

> And such a lofty luminary of *teshuvah* (return) that repairs the entire world precisely after its rupture and its fall into the lowliest depths, is the light of Messiah, who comes from Peretz. "Right and left you shall spread out/And God you will revere/Through the descendant of Peretz/We shall rejoice and we shall be glad."

In *SK* 5:180 and *Orot ha-Teshuvah* 4:8, rather than referencing the stanza from *Lekhah Dodi* by Rabbi Shelomo Alkabetz, Rav Kook builds upon the line from Rabbi Shelomo ibn Gabirol's composition *"She'eh Ne'esar,"* recited in the *Seliḥot* for the Seventeenth of Tammuz: *"Gedor pirtzi be-Ben Partzi"* ("Fence in my breach by the Son of Peretz").

*Stand and turn to face the door or the rear (usually western side) of the synagogue, as if to greet the incoming bride, bowing at the words "Enter, O bride!," then turn back.*

בּוֹאִי Come in peace, O crown of her husband;
come with joy and jubilation,
among the faithful of the treasured people.
Enter, O bride! Enter, O bride!

Come, my Beloved, to greet the bride;
let us welcome the Sabbath.

*Mourners during the week of Shiva return to the synagogue at this point. They are greeted with the following words of consolation:*

הַמָּקוֹם May the Almighty comfort you
among the other mourners of Zion and Jerusalem.

---

Rabbi Yannai would wrap himself [in finery], *stand*, and say: "Enter, O Bride! Enter, O Bride![25]

---

There may be a further connection of the Sabbath to Jacob. The attribute of Jacob is truth (*emet*): "Truth to Jacob" (Micah 7:20). According to the *Talmud Yerushalmi*, people are disinclined to tell a lie on the Sabbath:

> If one purchased fruits from an individual who is unreliable in regard to tithes, and forgot to tithe the fruit [before the Sabbath], he may ask him [i.e. the vendor] on the Sabbath and eat on his say-so… Rabbi Bibai said in the name of Rabbi Ḥanina, "The awe of the Sabbath is upon him and he says the truth." (*y. Demai* 4:1)

The Sabbath, like Father Jacob, who established it, is the personification of truth.

25. *b. Bava Kamma* 32. Comment of Rabbi Elijah David Rabinowitz-Te'omim (Aderet), father-in-law of Rav Kook, from his work *Tefillah le-David*; *OR*, vol. 2, p. 396, par. 15; p. 15, par. 2. In *b. Shabbat* 119a, it is Rabbi Ḥanina who stands to receive the Sabbath, not Rabbi Yannai. (In the celestial academy, Rabbi Yannai sits adjacent to Rabbi Ḥanina; *b. Bava Metsi'a* 85b. This may suggest that Rabbi Yannai had received from Rabbi Ḥanina. Rabbi Yoḥanan who is seated adjacent to Rabbi Yannai, was Rabbi Yannai's student; ibid. See Maimonides' Introduction to *Mishneh Torah*.)
In Maimonides' version, the word *ha-Melekh* (the King) replaces *ha-Malkah* (the Queen) in Rabbi Ḥanina's statement (*b. Shabbat* 119a): "Come, let us go out to greet the Sabbath, the Queen." According to Don Vidal of Tolosa, this was based on an alternate recension of the Talmud which had *Malka* (King) instead of our *Malketa* (Queen). See *Maggid Mishneh* to Maimonides, *MT, Hil. Shabbat* 30:2; and *Nimmukei Maharai* ad loc. It is possible that Rashi shared this variant with Maimonides; see Rashi's comment in *Bava Kamma* 32b, s.v. *bo'u ve-netse*.

*Stand and turn to face the door or the rear (usually western side) of the* בית כנסת*, as if to greet the incoming bride, bowing at the words* בּוֹאִי כַלָּה*, then turn back.*

בּוֹאִי בְשָׁלוֹם עֲטֶרֶת בַּעְלָהּ
גַּם בְּשִׂמְחָה וּבְצָהֳלָה
תּוֹךְ אֱמוּנֵי עַם סְגֻלָּה
בּוֹאִי כַלָּה, בּוֹאִי כַלָּה.
לְכָה דוֹדִי לִקְרַאת כַּלָּה, פְּנֵי שַׁבָּת נְקַבְּלָה.

*Mourners during the week of* שבעה *return to the* בית כנסת *at this point. They are greeted with the following words of consolation:*

הַמָּקוֹם יְנַחֵם אֶתְכֶם בְּתוֹךְ שְׁאָר אֲבֵלֵי צִיּוֹן וִירוּשָׁלָיִם.

---

בּוֹאִי כַלָּה, בּוֹאִי כַלָּה *Enter, O bride!* Enter, O bride! It is customary to stand for these words. Evidently the custom is based upon the anecdote in the Talmud:

> Rabbi Ḥanina said: "Come, let us go out to greet the Bride, the Queen." Some say: "To greet the Sabbath, the Bride, the Queen."[24]

---

24. The initials of the words *Shabbat Kallah Malketa* form the word "Shechem." It was in Shechem that we find Father Jacob observing the Sabbath. See Genesis 33:18: "And Jacob came in peace to the city of Shechem ... and encamped before the city." "He entered [the city] on the Eve of the Sabbath with the approach of sunset, while it was yet day, and established the Sabbath limits (*teḥumin*). This is what is said that Jacob kept the Sabbath before it was given" (*Genesis Rabbah* 79:6). Elsewhere, the Midrash juxtaposes Abraham, of whom there is no written record that he kept the Sabbath, to Jacob, of whom it is written that he kept the Sabbath (*Gen. Rabbah* 11:7). The commentaries to the Midrash explain that *"vayiḥan"* ("he encamped") is interpreted as an expression of Sabbath rest (*menuḥah*). (Rabbi Abraham Zevi Margaliyot, *Keren Orah* [Jerusalem, 1986], *Vayeḥi*, pp. 78–79)
The author, known in Jerusalem as the "Rav of Glusk," was the eminent disciple of Rabbi Zadok Hakohen of Lublin. *Keren Orah* is prefaced by *haskamot* of Rabbis Sonnenfeld and Kook from the year 1928. (The *haskamot* refer to *Ḥemdat Yerushalayim*, Rabbi Margaliyot's work on *Talmud Yerushalmi, Zera'im*.)
The intrinsic connection of the Sabbath to Father Jacob is borne out in this dictum:

> Said Rabbi Yoḥanan in the name of Rabbi Yosé: "Whoever delights in the Sabbath is given an inheritance without borders, for it says, 'Then you will delight in the LORD, and I will cause you to ride on the heights of the earth, and to feast on the inheritance of Jacob your father' [Isaiah 58:14]." (*b. Shabbat* 118; *MT*, end *Hil. Shabbat*)

*On Yom Tov, Motza'ei Yom Tov or Shabbat Ḥol HaMo'ed, Kabbalat Shabbat begins here.*

מִזְמוֹר A psalm. A song for the Sabbath day. It is good to thank the LORD and sing psalms to Your name, Most High – to tell of Your loving-kindness in the morning and Your faithfulness at night, to the music of the ten-stringed lyre and the melody of the harp. For You have made me rejoice by Your work, O LORD; I sing for joy at the deeds of Your hands. How great are Your deeds, LORD, and how very deep Your thoughts. A boor cannot know, nor can a fool understand, that though the wicked spring up like grass and all evildoers flourish, it is only that they may be destroyed for ever. But You, LORD, are eternally exalted. For behold Your enemies, LORD, behold Your enemies will perish; all evildoers will be scattered. You have raised my pride like that of a wild ox; I am anointed with fresh oil. My eyes shall look in triumph on my adversaries, my ears shall hear the downfall of the wicked who rise against me. ▸ The righteous will flourish like a palm tree and grow tall like a cedar in Lebanon. Planted in the LORD's House, blossoming in our God's courtyards, they will still bear fruit in old age, and stay vigorous and fresh, proclaiming that the LORD is upright: He is my Rock, in whom there is no wrong. *Ps. 92*

---

> and sits in a serious state of mind, anticipating receiving the face of the Sabbath, as if he is going out to receive the King.[28]

Maimonides has added to the anecdote a psychological depth. We are enlightened as to the interior state that accompanies "sitting": "a serious state of mind (*koved rosh*),[29] anticipating receiving the face of the Sabbath, as if he is going out to receive the King." (Editor)

---

28. Maimonides, *MT, Hil. Shabbat* 30:2.
29. Cf. Maimonides, *MT, Hil. Sefer Torah* 10:11 (*yeshev be-koved rosh*).
    The anecdote recorded by Rabbi Raphael Hakohen Kook whereby the Rav of Brisk, Rabbi Isaac Ze'ev Halevi Soloveitchik, stood for *Mizmor Shir* and sourced his behavior in Maimonides' ruling above – has probably lost something in transmission. Maimonides is clear that the posture for accepting into one's heart the presence of the Sabbath is sitting, not standing. See *Reshimot Talmidim mi-Maran ha-GRIZ Halevi* (Reḥovot: Da'at Sofrim, n.d. [5776]), *"Hakdamat ha-Ge'onim B'nei ha-GRRHK."*

*On* קבלת שבת, שבת חול המועד *or* מוצאי יום טוב, יום טוב *begins here.*

מִזְמוֹר שִׁיר לְיוֹם הַשַּׁבָּת: טוֹב לְהֹדוֹת לַיהוה, וּלְזַמֵּר לְשִׁמְךָ תהלים צב
עֶלְיוֹן: לְהַגִּיד בַּבֹּקֶר חַסְדֶּךָ, וֶאֱמוּנָתְךָ בַּלֵּילוֹת: עֲלֵי־עָשׂוֹר
וַעֲלֵי־נָבֶל, עֲלֵי הִגָּיוֹן בְּכִנּוֹר: כִּי שִׂמַּחְתַּנִי יהוה בְּפָעֳלֶךָ, בְּמַעֲשֵׂי
יָדֶיךָ אֲרַנֵּן: מַה־גָּדְלוּ מַעֲשֶׂיךָ יהוה, מְאֹד עָמְקוּ מַחְשְׁבֹתֶיךָ:
אִישׁ־בַּעַר לֹא יֵדָע, וּכְסִיל לֹא־יָבִין אֶת־זֹאת: בִּפְרֹחַ רְשָׁעִים
כְּמוֹ עֵשֶׂב, וַיָּצִיצוּ כָּל־פֹּעֲלֵי אָוֶן, לְהִשָּׁמְדָם עֲדֵי־עַד: וְאַתָּה
מָרוֹם לְעֹלָם יהוה: כִּי הִנֵּה אֹיְבֶיךָ יהוה, כִּי־הִנֵּה אֹיְבֶיךָ יֹאבֵדוּ,
יִתְפָּרְדוּ כָּל־פֹּעֲלֵי אָוֶן: וַתָּרֶם כִּרְאֵים קַרְנִי, בַּלֹּתִי בְּשֶׁמֶן רַעֲנָן:
וַתַּבֵּט עֵינִי בְּשׁוּרָי, בַּקָּמִים עָלַי מְרֵעִים תִּשְׁמַעְנָה אָזְנָי: ◂ צַדִּיק
כַּתָּמָר יִפְרָח, כְּאֶרֶז בַּלְּבָנוֹן יִשְׂגֶּה: שְׁתוּלִים בְּבֵית יהוה, בְּחַצְרוֹת
אֱלֹהֵינוּ יַפְרִיחוּ: עוֹד יְנוּבוּן בְּשֵׂיבָה, דְּשֵׁנִים וְרַעֲנַנִּים יִהְיוּ: לְהַגִּיד
כִּי־יָשָׁר יהוה, צוּרִי, וְלֹא־עַוְלָתָה בּוֹ:

---

מִזְמוֹר שִׁיר לְיוֹם הַשַּׁבָּת *A psalm. A song for the Sabbath day. (Psalm 92)* With these words, one formally accepts the sanctity of the Sabbath and is henceforth prohibited from doing labor.[26]

The Talmud relates:

> Such was the custom of Rabbi Judah bar Ila'i: On the Eve of the Sabbath they would bring him a tub full of hot water. He would wash his face, hands and feet, and wrap himself in linen robes with fringes (*tsitsit*) and sit; whereupon he resembled an angel of the LORD of Hosts.[27]

Maimonides incorporates this anecdote in his work of Halakhah:

> What is honor (*kavod*)? This is what the sages said that it is incumbent upon man to wash his face, hands and feet in hot water on the Eve of the Sabbath out of honor of the Sabbath. He [then] wraps himself in the *tsitsit*

---

26. See *Shulhan 'Arukh, OḤ* 261:4 (and *Mishnah Berurah* there); 263:10 and 15 (*Mishnah Berurah*).
27. *b. Shabbat* 25b.

יהוה מָלָךְ The LORD reigns. He is robed in majesty. The LORD is robed, girded with strength. The world is firmly established; it cannot be moved. Your throne stands firm as of old; You are eternal. Rivers lift up, LORD, rivers lift up their voice, rivers lift up their crashing waves. ▸ Mightier than the noise of many waters, than the mighty waves of the sea is the LORD on high. Your testimonies are very sure; holiness adorns Your House, LORD, for evermore. *Ps. 93*

## MOURNER'S KADDISH

*The following prayer requires the presence of a minyan.*
*A transliteration can be found on page 1320.*

*Mourner:* יִתְגַּדַּל Magnified and sanctified may His great name be,
in the world He created by His will.
May He establish His kingdom
in your lifetime and in your days,
and in the lifetime of all the house of Israel,
swiftly and soon –
and say: Amen.

*All:* May His great name be blessed for ever and all time.

*Mourner:* Blessed and praised, glorified and exalted,
raised and honored, uplifted and lauded
be the name of the Holy One,
blessed be He,
beyond any blessing, song, praise and consolation
uttered in the world –
and say: Amen.

May there be great peace from heaven,
and life for us and all Israel –
and say: Amen.

*Bow, take three steps back, as if taking leave of the Divine Presence,*
*then bow, first left, then right, then center, while saying:*

May He who makes peace in His high places,
make peace for us and all Israel –
and say: Amen.

תהלים צג
יהוה מָלָךְ, גֵּאוּת לָבֵשׁ, לָבֵשׁ יהוה עֹז הִתְאַזָּר, אַף־תִּכּוֹן תֵּבֵל
בַּל־תִּמּוֹט: נָכוֹן כִּסְאֲךָ מֵאָז, מֵעוֹלָם אָתָּה: נָשְׂאוּ נְהָרוֹת יהוה,
נָשְׂאוּ נְהָרוֹת קוֹלָם, יִשְׂאוּ נְהָרוֹת דָּכְיָם: ◂ מִקֹּלוֹת מַיִם רַבִּים,
אַדִּירִים מִשְׁבְּרֵי־יָם, אַדִּיר בַּמָּרוֹם יהוה: עֵדֹתֶיךָ נֶאֶמְנוּ מְאֹד,
לְבֵיתְךָ נַאֲוָה־קֹּדֶשׁ, יהוה לְאֹרֶךְ יָמִים:

## קדיש יתום

*The following prayer requires the presence of a* מנין.
*A transliteration can be found on page 1320.*

אבל: יִתְגַּדַּל וְיִתְקַדַּשׁ שְׁמֵהּ רַבָּא (קהל: אָמֵן)
בְּעָלְמָא דִּי בְרָא כִרְעוּתֵהּ, וְיַמְלִיךְ מַלְכוּתֵהּ
בְּחַיֵּיכוֹן וּבְיוֹמֵיכוֹן וּבְחַיֵּי דְכָל בֵּית יִשְׂרָאֵל
בַּעֲגָלָא וּבִזְמַן קָרִיב, וְאִמְרוּ אָמֵן. (קהל: אָמֵן)

קהל ואבל: יְהֵא שְׁמֵהּ רַבָּא מְבָרַךְ לְעָלַם וּלְעָלְמֵי עָלְמַיָּא.

אבל: יִתְבָּרַךְ וְיִשְׁתַּבַּח וְיִתְפָּאַר
וְיִתְרוֹמַם וְיִתְנַשֵּׂא וְיִתְהַדָּר וְיִתְעַלֶּה וְיִתְהַלָּל
שְׁמֵהּ דְּקֻדְשָׁא בְּרִיךְ הוּא (קהל: בְּרִיךְ הוּא)
לְעֵלָּא מִן כָּל בִּרְכָתָא / בשבת שובה: לְעֵלָּא לְעֵלָּא מִכָּל בִּרְכָתָא/
וְשִׁירָתָא, תֻּשְׁבְּחָתָא וְנֶחֱמָתָא
דַּאֲמִירָן בְּעָלְמָא, וְאִמְרוּ אָמֵן. (קהל: אָמֵן)

יְהֵא שְׁלָמָא רַבָּא מִן שְׁמַיָּא
וְחַיִּים, עָלֵינוּ וְעַל כָּל יִשְׂרָאֵל, וְאִמְרוּ אָמֵן. (קהל: אָמֵן)

*Bow, take three steps back, as if taking leave of the Divine Presence,*
*then bow, first left, then right, then center, while saying:*

עֹשֶׂה שָׁלוֹם/ בשבת שובה: הַשָּׁלוֹם/ בִּמְרוֹמָיו
הוּא יַעֲשֶׂה שָׁלוֹם
עָלֵינוּ וְעַל כָּל יִשְׂרָאֵל, וְאִמְרוּ אָמֵן. (קהל: אָמֵן)

*The following is not said on Yom Tov, Shabbat Ḥol HaMo'ed or Motza'ei Yom Tov.*

1. בַּמֶּה מַדְלִיקִין With what wicks may we light the Sabbath lamp and with what may we not light? We may not use a wick of cedar bast, or uncombed flax, or raw silk, or a wick made of willow bast or desert weed, or seaweed. [For oil] we may not use pitch, or wax, or cotton-seed oil or [contaminated consecrated] oil that must be destroyed by burning, or fat from sheeps' tails, or tallow. Naḥum the Mede says: We may use boiled tallow. But the sages say: Whether boiled or not boiled, we may not use it. *Mishna Shabbat, chapter 2*

2. [Contaminated consecrated] oil that must be destroyed by burning may not be used for a festival lamp. Rabbi Yishmael says: We may not use tar out of respect for the honor due to the Sabbath. But the sages permit all these oils: sesame oil, nut oil, radish oil, fish oil, gourd oil, tar or naphtha. Rabbi Tarfon, however, says: We may use only olive oil.

3. No product from a tree may be used as a wick for the Sabbath lamp, except flax. Also no product of a tree can contract "tent" uncleanness, except flax. If a wick was made from a cloth that has been twisted but not singed, Rabbi Eliezer declares, it is susceptible to contamination and may not be used for a Sabbath lamp; but Rabbi Akiva says, it is not susceptible to contamination, and may be used for the Sabbath lamp.

4. One may not pierce an eggshell, fill it with oil, and put it over the mouth of a lamp so that the oil may drip from it into the lamp, even if the vessel is of earthenware, but Rabbi Judah permits it. If, however, the potter had originally attached it to the lamp, it is permitted because it constitutes a single vessel. One may not fill a bowl with oil, put it beside a lamp, and put the end of the wick in it so that it draws oil from the bowl; but Rabbi Judah permits this.

5. One who extinguishes a lamp because he is afraid of heathens, robbers, or depression, or to enable a sick person to sleep, is not liable [for violating the Sabbath]. If he did it to spare the lamp, or the oil, or the wick, he is liable. Rabbi Yose absolves him in all these cases except that of sparing the wick, because he thereby turns it into charcoal.

*The following is not said on* שבת חול המועד ,יום טוב *or* .מוצאי יום טוב

משנה שבת פרק שני

א בַּמֶּה מַדְלִיקִין וּבַמָּה אֵין מַדְלִיקִין. אֵין מַדְלִיקִין לֹא בְּלֶכֶשׁ, וְלֹא בְּחֹסֶן, וְלֹא בְּכַלָּךְ, וְלֹא בִּפְתִילַת הָאִידָן, וְלֹא בִּפְתִילַת הַמִּדְבָּר, וְלֹא בִירוֹקָה שֶׁעַל פְּנֵי הַמָּיִם. וְלֹא בְזֶפֶת וְלֹא בְשַׁעֲוָה וְלֹא בְשֶׁמֶן קִיק וְלֹא בְשֶׁמֶן שְׂרֵפָה וְלֹא בְאַלְיָה וְלֹא בְחֵלֶב. נַחוּם הַמָּדִי אוֹמֵר: מַדְלִיקִין בְּחֵלֶב מְבֻשָּׁל, וַחֲכָמִים אוֹמְרִים: אֶחָד מְבֻשָּׁל וְאֶחָד שֶׁאֵינוֹ מְבֻשָּׁל, אֵין מַדְלִיקִין בּוֹ.

ב אֵין מַדְלִיקִין בְּשֶׁמֶן שְׂרֵפָה בְּיוֹם טוֹב. רַבִּי יִשְׁמָעֵאל אוֹמֵר: אֵין מַדְלִיקִין בְּעִטְרָן מִפְּנֵי כְּבוֹד הַשַּׁבָּת. וַחֲכָמִים מַתִּירִין בְּכָל הַשְּׁמָנִים, בְּשֶׁמֶן שֻׁמְשְׁמִין, בְּשֶׁמֶן אֱגוֹזִים, בְּשֶׁמֶן צְנוֹנוֹת, בְּשֶׁמֶן דָּגִים, בְּשֶׁמֶן פַּקּוּעוֹת, בְּעִטְרָן וּבְנֵפְטְ. רַבִּי טַרְפוֹן אוֹמֵר: אֵין מַדְלִיקִין אֶלָּא בְּשֶׁמֶן זַיִת בִּלְבָד.

ג כָּל הַיּוֹצֵא מִן הָעֵץ אֵין מַדְלִיקִין בּוֹ, אֶלָּא פִשְׁתָּן. וְכָל הַיּוֹצֵא מִן הָעֵץ אֵינוֹ מִטַּמֵּא טֻמְאַת אֹהָלִים, אֶלָּא פִשְׁתָּן. פְּתִילַת הַבֶּגֶד שֶׁקִּפְּלָהּ וְלֹא הִבְהֲבָהּ, רַבִּי אֱלִיעֶזֶר אוֹמֵר: טְמֵאָה הִיא, וְאֵין מַדְלִיקִין בָּהּ. רַבִּי עֲקִיבָא אוֹמֵר: טְהוֹרָה הִיא, וּמַדְלִיקִין בָּהּ.

ד לֹא יִקֹּב אָדָם שְׁפוֹפֶרֶת שֶׁל בֵּיצָה וִימַלְּאֶנָּה שֶׁמֶן וְיִתְּנֶנָּה עַל פִּי הַנֵּר, בִּשְׁבִיל שֶׁתְּהֵא מְנַטֶּפֶת, וַאֲפִילוּ הִיא שֶׁל חֶרֶס. וְרַבִּי יְהוּדָה מַתִּיר. אֲבָל אִם חִבְּרָהּ הַיּוֹצֵר מִתְּחִלָּה מֻתָּר, מִפְּנֵי שֶׁהוּא כְּלִי אֶחָד. לֹא יְמַלֵּא אָדָם אֶת הַקְּעָרָה שֶׁמֶן וְיִתְּנֶנָּה בְּצַד הַנֵּר וְיִתֵּן רֹאשׁ הַפְּתִילָה בְּתוֹכָהּ, בִּשְׁבִיל שֶׁתְּהֵא שׁוֹאֶבֶת. וְרַבִּי יְהוּדָה מַתִּיר.

ה הַמְכַבֶּה אֶת הַנֵּר מִפְּנֵי שֶׁהוּא מִתְיָרֵא מִפְּנֵי גוֹיִם, מִפְּנֵי לִסְטִים, מִפְּנֵי רוּחַ רָעָה, אוֹ בִשְׁבִיל הַחוֹלֶה שֶׁיִּישָׁן, פָּטוּר. כְּחָס עַל הַנֵּר, כְּחָס עַל הַשֶּׁמֶן, כְּחָס עַל הַפְּתִילָה, חַיָּב. רַבִּי יוֹסֵי פּוֹטֵר בְּכֻלָּן חוּץ מִן הַפְּתִילָה, מִפְּנֵי שֶׁהוּא עוֹשָׂהּ פֶּחָם.

6. For three transgressions women may die in childbirth: for being careless in observing the laws of menstruation, separating challah [dough-offering], and lighting the Sabbath light.

7. One should say three things at home on the eve of the Sabbath just before dark: Have you tithed? Have you prepared the Eiruv? Light the Sabbath lamp. If there is doubt whether or not darkness has fallen, we may not tithe definitely untithed produce, nor immerse [unclean] vessels, nor light the Sabbath lamp. We may tithe produce about which there is a doubt whether it has been tithed or not, we may prepare an Eiruv, and insulate hot food.

It was taught, Rabbi Ḥanina said: One should examine his clothing on the eve of the Sabbath before nightfall [to ensure that one is not carrying anything], for one may forget and go out. Rabbi Yosef said: This is an important law about the Sabbath [for it is easy to forget, and thus inadvertently violate the holiness of the day]. *Shabbat 12a*

Rabbi Elazar said in the name of Rabbi Ḥanina: The disciples of the sages increase peace in the world, as it is said, "And all your children shall be taught of the Lord, and great shall be the peace of your children [*banayikh*]." Read not *banayikh*, "your children," but *bonayikh*, "your builders." Those who love Your Torah have great peace; there is no stumbling block for them. May there be peace within your ramparts, prosperity in your palaces. For the sake of my brothers and friends, I shall say, "Peace be within you." For the sake of the House of the Lord our God, I will seek your good. ▸ May the Lord grant strength to His people; may the Lord bless His people with peace. *Berakhot 64a* *Is. 54* *Ps. 119* *Ps. 122* *Ps. 29*

## THE RABBIS' KADDISH

*The following prayer requires the presence of a minyan.*
*A transliteration can be found on page 1319.*

*Mourner:* יִתְגַּדַּל Magnified and sanctified may His great name be,
in the world He created by His will.
May He establish His kingdom in your lifetime
and in your days, and in the lifetime
of all the house of Israel,
swiftly and soon – and say: Amen.

ו עַל שָׁלֹשׁ עֲבֵרוֹת נָשִׁים מֵתוֹת בִּשְׁעַת לֵדָתָן, עַל שֶׁאֵינָן זְהִירוֹת בַּנִּדָּה, בַּחַלָּה וּבְהַדְלָקַת הַנֵּר.

ז שְׁלֹשָׁה דְבָרִים צָרִיךְ אָדָם לוֹמַר בְּתוֹךְ בֵּיתוֹ עֶרֶב שַׁבָּת עִם חֲשֵׁכָה: עִשַּׂרְתֶּם, עֵרַבְתֶּם, הַדְלִיקוּ אֶת הַנֵּר. סָפֵק חֲשֵׁכָה סָפֵק אֵינָהּ חֲשֵׁכָה, אֵין מְעַשְּׂרִין אֶת הַוַּדַּאי, וְאֵין מַטְבִּילִין אֶת הַכֵּלִים, וְאֵין מַדְלִיקִין אֶת הַנֵּרוֹת. אֲבָל מְעַשְּׂרִין אֶת הַדְּמַאי, וּמְעָרְבִין וְטוֹמְנִין אֶת הַחַמִּין.

תַּנְיָא, אָמַר רַבִּי חֲנִינָא: חַיָּב אָדָם לְמַשְׁמֵשׁ בְּגָדָיו בְּעֶרֶב שַׁבָּת עִם חֲשֵׁכָה, שֶׁמָּא יִשְׁכַּח וְיֵצֵא. אָמַר רַב יוֹסֵף: הִלְכְתָא רַבְּתָא לְשַׁבַּתָּא. שבת יב.

אָמַר רַבִּי אֶלְעָזָר, אָמַר רַבִּי חֲנִינָא: תַּלְמִידֵי חֲכָמִים מַרְבִּים שָׁלוֹם ברכות סד.
בָּעוֹלָם, שֶׁנֶּאֱמַר: וְכָל־בָּנַיִךְ לִמּוּדֵי יהוה, וְרַב שְׁלוֹם בָּנָיִךְ: אַל תִּקְרֵי ישעיה נד
בָּנָיִךְ, אֶלָּא בּוֹנָיִךְ. שָׁלוֹם רָב לְאֹהֲבֵי תוֹרָתֶךָ, וְאֵין־לָמוֹ מִכְשׁוֹל: תהלים קיט
יְהִי־שָׁלוֹם בְּחֵילֵךְ, שַׁלְוָה בְּאַרְמְנוֹתָיִךְ: לְמַעַן אַחַי וְרֵעָי אֲדַבְּרָה־נָּא תהלים קכב
שָׁלוֹם בָּךְ: לְמַעַן בֵּית־יהוה אֱלֹהֵינוּ אֲבַקְשָׁה טוֹב לָךְ: ◂ יהוה עֹז תהלים כט
לְעַמּוֹ יִתֵּן, יהוה יְבָרֵךְ אֶת־עַמּוֹ בַשָּׁלוֹם:

### קדיש דרבנן

*The following prayer requires the presence of a* מנין*.*
*A transliteration can be found on page 1319.*

אבל: יִתְגַּדַּל וְיִתְקַדַּשׁ שְׁמֵהּ רַבָּא (קהל: אָמֵן)
בְּעָלְמָא דִּי בְרָא כִרְעוּתֵהּ
וְיַמְלִיךְ מַלְכוּתֵהּ
בְּחַיֵּיכוֹן וּבְיוֹמֵיכוֹן וּבְחַיֵּי דְכָל בֵּית יִשְׂרָאֵל
בַּעֲגָלָא וּבִזְמַן קָרִיב
וְאִמְרוּ אָמֵן. (קהל: אָמֵן)

*All:* May His great name be blessed
for ever and all time.

*Mourner:* Blessed and praised,
glorified and exalted,
raised and honored,
uplifted and lauded
be the name of the Holy One,
blessed be He,
beyond any blessing,
song, praise and consolation
uttered in the world –
and say: Amen.

To Israel, to the teachers,
their disciples and their disciples' disciples,
and to all who engage in the study of Torah,
in this (*In Israel add:* holy) place or elsewhere,
may there come to them
and you great peace,
grace, kindness and compassion,
long life, ample sustenance and deliverance,
from their Father in Heaven –
and say: Amen.

May there be great peace from heaven,
and (good) life for us and all Israel –
and say: Amen.

*Bow, take three steps back, as if taking leave of the Divine Presence, then bow, first left, then right, then center, while saying:*
May He who makes peace in His high places,
in His compassion make peace
for us and all Israel –
and say: Amen.

קהל ואבל: יְהֵא שְׁמֵהּ רַבָּא מְבָרַךְ לְעָלַם וּלְעָלְמֵי עָלְמַיָּא.

אבל: יִתְבָּרַךְ וְיִשְׁתַּבַּח וְיִתְפָּאַר וְיִתְרוֹמַם וְיִתְנַשֵּׂא
וְיִתְהַדָּר וְיִתְעַלֶּה וְיִתְהַלָּל
שְׁמֵהּ דְּקֻדְשָׁא בְּרִיךְ הוּא (קהל: בְּרִיךְ הוּא)
לְעֵלָּא מִן כָּל בִּרְכָתָא
/בשבת שובה: לְעֵלָּא לְעֵלָּא מִכָּל בִּרְכָתָא/
וְשִׁירָתָא, תֻּשְׁבְּחָתָא וְנֶחֱמָתָא
דַּאֲמִירָן בְּעָלְמָא
וְאִמְרוּ אָמֵן. (קהל: אָמֵן)

עַל יִשְׂרָאֵל וְעַל רַבָּנָן
וְעַל תַּלְמִידֵיהוֹן וְעַל כָּל תַּלְמִידֵי תַלְמִידֵיהוֹן
וְעַל כָּל מָאן דְּעָסְקִין בְּאוֹרַיְתָא
דִּי בְּאַתְרָא (בארץ ישראל: קַדִּישָׁא) הָדֵין, וְדִי בְּכָל אֲתַר וַאֲתַר
יְהֵא לְהוֹן וּלְכוֹן שְׁלָמָא רַבָּא
חִנָּא וְחִסְדָּא, וְרַחֲמֵי, וְחַיֵּי אֲרִיכֵי, וּמְזוֹנֵי רְוִיחֵי
וּפֻרְקָנָא מִן קֳדָם אֲבוּהוֹן דִּי בִשְׁמַיָּא
וְאִמְרוּ אָמֵן. (קהל: אָמֵן)

יְהֵא שְׁלָמָא רַבָּא מִן שְׁמַיָּא
וְחַיִּים (טוֹבִים) עָלֵינוּ וְעַל כָּל יִשְׂרָאֵל
וְאִמְרוּ אָמֵן. (קהל: אָמֵן)

*Bow, take three steps back, as if taking leave of the Divine Presence, then bow, first left, then right, then center, while saying:*

עֹשֶׂה שָׁלוֹם/ בשבת שובה: הַשָּׁלוֹם/ בִּמְרוֹמָיו
הוּא יַעֲשֶׂה בְרַחֲמָיו שָׁלוֹם עָלֵינוּ וְעַל כָּל יִשְׂרָאֵל
וְאִמְרוּ אָמֵן. (קהל: אָמֵן)

# Ma'ariv for Shabbat and Yom Tov

## BLESSINGS OF THE SHEMA

*The Leader says the following, bowing at "Bless," standing straight at "the Lord." The congregation, followed by the Leader, responds, bowing at "Bless," standing straight at "the Lord."*

*Leader:* BLESS
the Lord, the blessed One.

*Congregation:* Bless the Lord, the blessed One,
for ever and all time.

*Leader:* Bless the Lord, the blessed One,
for ever and all time.

בָּרוּךְ Blessed are You, Lord our God, King of the Universe,
who by His word brings on evenings,
by His wisdom opens the gates of heaven,
with understanding makes time change and the seasons rotate,
and by His will orders the stars in their constellations in the sky.
He creates day and night,
rolling away the light before the darkness,
and darkness before the light.
▸ He makes the day pass and brings on night,
distinguishing day from night:
the Lord of hosts is His name.
May the living and forever enduring God
rule over us for all time.
Blessed are You, Lord,
who brings on evenings.

# מעריב לשבת וליום טוב

## קריאת שמע וברכותיה

*The* שליח ציבור *says the following, bowing at* בָּרְכוּ*, standing straight at* ה׳.
*The* קהל*, followed by the* שליח ציבור*, responds, bowing at* בָּרוּךְ*, standing straight at* ה׳.

ש״ץ: **בָּרְכוּ**
אֶת יהוה הַמְבֹרָךְ.

קהל: בָּרוּךְ יהוה הַמְבֹרָךְ לְעוֹלָם וָעֶד.

ש״ץ: בָּרוּךְ יהוה הַמְבֹרָךְ לְעוֹלָם וָעֶד.

בָּרוּךְ אַתָּה יהוה אֱלֹהֵינוּ מֶלֶךְ הָעוֹלָם
אֲשֶׁר בִּדְבָרוֹ מַעֲרִיב עֲרָבִים
בְּחָכְמָה פּוֹתֵחַ שְׁעָרִים
וּבִתְבוּנָה מְשַׁנֶּה עִתִּים וּמַחֲלִיף אֶת הַזְּמַנִּים
וּמְסַדֵּר אֶת הַכּוֹכָבִים בְּמִשְׁמְרוֹתֵיהֶם בָּרָקִיעַ כִּרְצוֹנוֹ.
בּוֹרֵא יוֹם וָלָיְלָה, גּוֹלֵל אוֹר מִפְּנֵי חֹשֶׁךְ וְחֹשֶׁךְ מִפְּנֵי אוֹר
◄ וּמַעֲבִיר יוֹם וּמֵבִיא לָיְלָה
וּמַבְדִּיל בֵּין יוֹם וּבֵין לָיְלָה
יהוה צְבָאוֹת שְׁמוֹ.
אֵל חַי וְקַיָּם תָּמִיד, יִמְלֹךְ עָלֵינוּ לְעוֹלָם וָעֶד.
בָּרוּךְ אַתָּה יהוה, הַמַּעֲרִיב עֲרָבִים.

אַהֲבַת עוֹלָם With everlasting love
have You loved Your people, the house of Israel.
You have taught us Torah and commandments,
decrees and laws of justice.
Therefore, LORD our God, when we lie down and when we rise up
we will speak of Your decrees, rejoicing in the words of Your Torah
and Your commandments for ever.
► For they are our life and the length of our days;
on them will we meditate day and night.
May You never take away Your love from us.
Blessed are You, LORD, who loves His people Israel.

*The Shema must be said with intense concentration. See laws 349–355.*
*When not with a minyan, say:*
God, faithful King!

*The following verse should be said aloud, while covering the eyes with the right hand:*

## Listen, Israel: the LORD is our God, the LORD is One. *Deut. 6*

*Quietly:* Blessed be the name of His glorious kingdom for ever and all time.

וְאָהַבְתָּ Love the LORD your God with all your heart, with all your soul, and with all your might. These words which I command you today shall be on your heart. Teach them repeatedly to your children, speaking of them when you sit at home and when you travel on the way, when you lie down and when you rise. Bind them as a sign on your hand, and they shall be an emblem between your eyes. Write them on the doorposts of your house and gates. *Deut. 6*

וְהָיָה If you indeed heed My commandments with which I charge you today, to love the LORD your God and worship Him with all your heart and with all your soul, I will give rain in your land in its season, the early and late rain; and you shall gather in your grain, wine and oil. I will give grass in your field for your cattle, and you shall eat and be satisfied. Be careful lest your heart be tempted and *Deut. 11*

אַהֲבַת עוֹלָם בֵּית יִשְׂרָאֵל עַמְּךָ אָהָבְתָּ
תּוֹרָה וּמִצְוֹת, חֻקִּים וּמִשְׁפָּטִים, אוֹתָנוּ לִמַּדְתָּ
עַל כֵּן יהוה אֱלֹהֵינוּ בְּשָׁכְבֵנוּ וּבְקוּמֵנוּ נָשִׂיחַ בְּחֻקֶּיךָ
וְנִשְׂמַח בְּדִבְרֵי תוֹרָתֶךָ וּבְמִצְוֹתֶיךָ לְעוֹלָם וָעֶד
◂ כִּי הֵם חַיֵּינוּ וְאֹרֶךְ יָמֵינוּ, וּבָהֶם נֶהְגֶּה יוֹמָם וָלָיְלָה.
וְאַהֲבָתְךָ אַל תָּסִיר מִמֶּנּוּ לְעוֹלָמִים.
בָּרוּךְ אַתָּה יהוה, אוֹהֵב עַמּוֹ יִשְׂרָאֵל.

*The* שמע *must be said with intense concentration. See laws 349–355.*

*When not with a* מנין*, say:*

אֵל מֶלֶךְ נֶאֱמָן

*The following verse should be said aloud, while covering the eyes with the right hand:*

**שְׁמַע יִשְׂרָאֵל, יהוה אֱלֹהֵינוּ, יהוה ׀ אֶחָד:** דברים ו

*Quietly* בָּרוּךְ שֵׁם כְּבוֹד מַלְכוּתוֹ לְעוֹלָם וָעֶד.

וְאָהַבְתָּ אֵת יהוה אֱלֹהֶיךָ, בְּכָל־לְבָבְךָ וּבְכָל־נַפְשְׁךָ וּבְכָל־מְאֹדֶךָ: דברים ו
וְהָיוּ הַדְּבָרִים הָאֵלֶּה, אֲשֶׁר אָנֹכִי מְצַוְּךָ הַיּוֹם, עַל־לְבָבֶךָ: וְשִׁנַּנְתָּם
לְבָנֶיךָ וְדִבַּרְתָּ בָּם, בְּשִׁבְתְּךָ בְּבֵיתֶךָ וּבְלֶכְתְּךָ בַדֶּרֶךְ, וּבְשָׁכְבְּךָ
וּבְקוּמֶךָ: וּקְשַׁרְתָּם לְאוֹת עַל־יָדֶךָ וְהָיוּ לְטֹטָפֹת בֵּין עֵינֶיךָ:
וּכְתַבְתָּם עַל־מְזֻזוֹת בֵּיתֶךָ וּבִשְׁעָרֶיךָ:

וְהָיָה אִם־שָׁמֹעַ תִּשְׁמְעוּ אֶל־מִצְוֹתַי אֲשֶׁר אָנֹכִי מְצַוֶּה אֶתְכֶם דברים יא
הַיּוֹם, לְאַהֲבָה אֶת־יהוה אֱלֹהֵיכֶם וּלְעָבְדוֹ, בְּכָל־לְבַבְכֶם וּבְכָל־
נַפְשְׁכֶם: וְנָתַתִּי מְטַר־אַרְצְכֶם בְּעִתּוֹ, יוֹרֶה וּמַלְקוֹשׁ, וְאָסַפְתָּ דְגָנֶךָ
וְתִירֹשְׁךָ וְיִצְהָרֶךָ: וְנָתַתִּי עֵשֶׂב בְּשָׂדְךָ לִבְהֶמְתֶּךָ, וְאָכַלְתָּ וְשָׂבָעְתָּ:
הִשָּׁמְרוּ לָכֶם פֶּן־יִפְתֶּה לְבַבְכֶם, וְסַרְתֶּם וַעֲבַדְתֶּם אֱלֹהִים אֲחֵרִים

you go astray and worship other gods, bowing down to them. Then the Lord's anger will flare against you and He will close the heavens so that there will be no rain. The land will not yield its crops, and you will perish swiftly from the good land that the Lord is giving you. Therefore, set these, My words, on your heart and soul. Bind them as a sign on your hand, and they shall be an emblem between your eyes. Teach them to your children, speaking of them when you sit at home and when you travel on the way, when you lie down and when you rise. Write them on the doorposts of your house and gates, so that you and your children may live long in the land that the Lord swore to your ancestors to give them, for as long as the heavens are above the earth.

וַיֹּאמֶר The Lord spoke to Moses, saying: Speak to the Israelites and tell them to make tassels on the corners of their garments for all generations. They shall attach to the tassel at each corner a thread of blue. This shall be your tassel, and you shall see it and remember all of the Lord's commandments and keep them, not straying after your heart and after your eyes, following your own sinful desires. Thus you will be reminded to keep all My commandments, and be holy to your God. I am the Lord your God, who brought you out of the land of Egypt to be your God. I am the Lord your God. *Num. 15*

## True –

*The Leader repeats:*

▸ The Lord your God is true –

וֶאֱמוּנָה – and faithful is all this,
and firmly established for us
that He is the Lord our God,
and there is none besides Him,
and that we, Israel, are His people.
He is our King, who redeems us from the hand of kings
and delivers us from the grasp of all tyrants.

וְהִשְׁתַּחֲוִיתֶם לָהֶם: וְחָרָה אַף־יְהוָה בָּכֶם, וְעָצַר אֶת־הַשָּׁמַיִם וְלֹא־יִהְיֶה מָטָר, וְהָאֲדָמָה לֹא תִתֵּן אֶת־יְבוּלָהּ, וַאֲבַדְתֶּם מְהֵרָה מֵעַל הָאָרֶץ הַטֹּבָה אֲשֶׁר יְהוָה נֹתֵן לָכֶם: וְשַׂמְתֶּם אֶת־דְּבָרַי אֵלֶּה עַל־לְבַבְכֶם וְעַל־נַפְשְׁכֶם, וּקְשַׁרְתֶּם אֹתָם לְאוֹת עַל־יֶדְכֶם, וְהָיוּ לְטוֹטָפֹת בֵּין עֵינֵיכֶם: וְלִמַּדְתֶּם אֹתָם אֶת־בְּנֵיכֶם לְדַבֵּר בָּם, בְּשִׁבְתְּךָ בְּבֵיתֶךָ וּבְלֶכְתְּךָ בַדֶּרֶךְ, וּבְשָׁכְבְּךָ וּבְקוּמֶךָ: וּכְתַבְתָּם עַל־מְזוּזוֹת בֵּיתֶךָ וּבִשְׁעָרֶיךָ: לְמַעַן יִרְבּוּ יְמֵיכֶם וִימֵי בְנֵיכֶם עַל הָאֲדָמָה אֲשֶׁר נִשְׁבַּע יְהוָה לַאֲבֹתֵיכֶם לָתֵת לָהֶם, כִּימֵי הַשָּׁמַיִם עַל־הָאָרֶץ:

במדבר טו
וַיֹּאמֶר יְהוָה אֶל־מֹשֶׁה לֵּאמֹר: דַּבֵּר אֶל־בְּנֵי יִשְׂרָאֵל וְאָמַרְתָּ אֲלֵהֶם, וְעָשׂוּ לָהֶם צִיצִת עַל־כַּנְפֵי בִגְדֵיהֶם לְדֹרֹתָם, וְנָתְנוּ עַל־צִיצִת הַכָּנָף פְּתִיל תְּכֵלֶת: וְהָיָה לָכֶם לְצִיצִת, וּרְאִיתֶם אֹתוֹ וּזְכַרְתֶּם אֶת־כָּל־מִצְוֹת יְהוָה וַעֲשִׂיתֶם אֹתָם, וְלֹא תָתוּרוּ אַחֲרֵי לְבַבְכֶם וְאַחֲרֵי עֵינֵיכֶם, אֲשֶׁר־אַתֶּם זֹנִים אַחֲרֵיהֶם: לְמַעַן תִּזְכְּרוּ וַעֲשִׂיתֶם אֶת־כָּל־מִצְוֹתָי, וִהְיִיתֶם קְדֹשִׁים לֵאלֹהֵיכֶם: אֲנִי יְהוָה אֱלֹהֵיכֶם, אֲשֶׁר הוֹצֵאתִי אֶתְכֶם מֵאֶרֶץ מִצְרַיִם, לִהְיוֹת לָכֶם לֵאלֹהִים, אֲנִי יְהוָה אֱלֹהֵיכֶם:

## אֱמֶת

*The* שליח ציבור *repeats:*

◂ יְהוָה אֱלֹהֵיכֶם אֱמֶת

וֶאֱמוּנָה כָּל זֹאת וְקַיָּם עָלֵינוּ
כִּי הוּא יְהוָה אֱלֹהֵינוּ וְאֵין זוּלָתוֹ
וַאֲנַחְנוּ יִשְׂרָאֵל עַמּוֹ.
הַפּוֹדֵנוּ מִיַּד מְלָכִים
מַלְכֵּנוּ הַגּוֹאֲלֵנוּ מִכַּף כָּל הֶעָרִיצִים.

He is our God, who on our behalf repays our foes
and brings just retribution on our mortal enemies;
who performs great deeds beyond understanding
and wonders beyond number;
who kept us alive, not letting our foot slip;
who led us on the high places of our enemies,
raising our pride above all our foes;
who did miracles for us
and brought vengeance against Pharaoh;
who performed signs and wonders
in the land of Ham's children;
who smote in His wrath all the firstborn of Egypt,
and brought out His people Israel from their midst
into everlasting freedom;
who led His children through the divided Reed Sea,
plunging their pursuers and enemies into the depths.
When His children saw His might,
they gave praise and thanks to His name,
▸ and willingly accepted His Sovereignty.
Moses and the children of Israel
then sang a song to You with great joy,
and they all exclaimed:

"Who is like You, LORD, among the mighty? *Ex. 15*
Who is like You, majestic in holiness,
awesome in praises, doing wonders?"

▸ Your children beheld Your majesty
as You parted the sea before Moses.
"This is my God!" they responded, and then said:

"The LORD shall reign for ever and ever." *Ex. 15*

▸ And it is said,

"For the LORD has redeemed Jacob *Jer. 31*
and rescued him from a power stronger than his own."

Blessed are You, LORD, who redeemed Israel.

הָאֵל הַנִּפְרָע לָנוּ מִצָּרֵינוּ
וְהַמְשַׁלֵּם גְּמוּל לְכָל אוֹיְבֵי נַפְשֵׁנוּ.
הָעוֹשֶׂה גְדוֹלוֹת עַד אֵין חֵקֶר, וְנִפְלָאוֹת עַד אֵין מִסְפָּר
הַשָּׂם נַפְשֵׁנוּ בַּחַיִּים, וְלֹא נָתַן לַמּוֹט רַגְלֵנוּ
הַמַּדְרִיכֵנוּ עַל בָּמוֹת אוֹיְבֵינוּ
וַיָּרֶם קַרְנֵנוּ עַל כָּל שׂוֹנְאֵינוּ.
הָעוֹשֶׂה לָּנוּ נִסִּים וּנְקָמָה בְּפַרְעֹה
אוֹתוֹת וּמוֹפְתִים בְּאַדְמַת בְּנֵי חָם.
הַמַּכֶּה בְעֶבְרָתוֹ כָּל בְּכוֹרֵי מִצְרָיִם
וַיּוֹצֵא אֶת עַמּוֹ יִשְׂרָאֵל מִתּוֹכָם לְחֵרוּת עוֹלָם.
הַמַּעֲבִיר בָּנָיו בֵּין גִּזְרֵי יַם סוּף
אֶת רוֹדְפֵיהֶם וְאֶת שׂוֹנְאֵיהֶם בִּתְהוֹמוֹת טִבַּע
וְרָאוּ בָנָיו גְּבוּרָתוֹ, שִׁבְּחוּ וְהוֹדוּ לִשְׁמוֹ
◂ וּמַלְכוּתוֹ בְּרָצוֹן קִבְּלוּ עֲלֵיהֶם.
מֹשֶׁה וּבְנֵי יִשְׂרָאֵל, לְךָ עָנוּ שִׁירָה בְּשִׂמְחָה רַבָּה
וְאָמְרוּ כֻלָּם

מִי־כָמֹכָה בָּאֵלִם יהוה — שמות טו
מִי כָּמֹכָה נֶאְדָּר בַּקֹּדֶשׁ
נוֹרָא תְהִלֹּת עֹשֵׂה פֶלֶא:

◂ מַלְכוּתְךָ רָאוּ בָנֶיךָ, בּוֹקֵעַ יָם לִפְנֵי מֹשֶׁה
זֶה אֵלִי עָנוּ, וְאָמְרוּ
יהוה יִמְלֹךְ לְעֹלָם וָעֶד: — שמות טו

◂ וְנֶאֱמַר
כִּי־פָדָה יהוה אֶת־יַעֲקֹב, וּגְאָלוֹ מִיַּד חָזָק מִמֶּנּוּ: — ירמיהו לא
בָּרוּךְ אַתָּה יהוה, גָּאַל יִשְׂרָאֵל.

הַשְׁכִּיבֵנוּ Help us lie down, O LORD our God, in peace,
and rise up, O our King, to life.
Spread over us Your canopy of peace.
Direct us with Your good counsel,
and save us for the sake of Your name.
Shield us and remove from us every enemy,
plague, sword, famine and sorrow.
Remove the adversary from before and behind us.
Shelter us in the shadow of Your wings,
for You, God, are our Guardian and Deliverer;
You, God, are a gracious and compassionate King.
▸ Guard our going out and our coming in,
for life and peace,
from now and for ever.
Spread over us Your canopy of peace.
Blessed are You, LORD,
who spreads a canopy of peace over us,
over all His people Israel,
and over Jerusalem.

*On Shabbat, the congregation stands and, together with the Leader, says:*

וְשָׁמְרוּ The children of Israel must keep the Sabbath, *Ex. 31*
observing the Sabbath in every generation
as an everlasting covenant.
It is a sign between Me and the children of Israel for ever,
for in six days the LORD made the heavens and the earth,
but on the seventh day He ceased work
and refreshed Himself.

*On Yom Tov of the Three Festivals, say:*

וַיְדַבֵּר Thus Moses announced the LORD's appointed seasons *Lev. 23*
to the children of Israel.

הַשְׁכִּיבֵנוּ יהוה אֱלֹהֵינוּ לְשָׁלוֹם
וְהַעֲמִידֵנוּ מַלְכֵּנוּ לְחַיִּים
וּפְרֹשׂ עָלֵינוּ סֻכַּת שְׁלוֹמֶךָ
וְתַקְּנֵנוּ בְּעֵצָה טוֹבָה מִלְּפָנֶיךָ
וְהוֹשִׁיעֵנוּ לְמַעַן שְׁמֶךָ.
וְהָגֵן בַּעֲדֵנוּ,
וְהָסֵר מֵעָלֵינוּ אוֹיֵב, דֶּבֶר וְחֶרֶב וְרָעָב וְיָגוֹן
וְהָסֵר שָׂטָן מִלְּפָנֵינוּ וּמֵאַחֲרֵינוּ, וּבְצֵל כְּנָפֶיךָ תַּסְתִּירֵנוּ
כִּי אֵל שׁוֹמְרֵנוּ וּמַצִּילֵנוּ אָתָּה
כִּי אֵל מֶלֶךְ חַנּוּן וְרַחוּם אָתָּה.
◂ וּשְׁמֹר צֵאתֵנוּ וּבוֹאֵנוּ לְחַיִּים וּלְשָׁלוֹם
מֵעַתָּה וְעַד עוֹלָם.
וּפְרֹשׂ עָלֵינוּ סֻכַּת שְׁלוֹמֶךָ.
בָּרוּךְ אַתָּה יהוה
הַפּוֹרֵשׂ סֻכַּת שָׁלוֹם עָלֵינוּ וְעַל כָּל עַמּוֹ יִשְׂרָאֵל וְעַל יְרוּשָׁלָיִם.

*On* שבת*, the* קהל *stands and,*
*together with the* שליח ציבור*, says:*

שמות לא וְשָׁמְרוּ בְנֵי־יִשְׂרָאֵל אֶת־הַשַּׁבָּת
לַעֲשׂוֹת אֶת־הַשַּׁבָּת לְדֹרֹתָם בְּרִית עוֹלָם:
בֵּינִי וּבֵין בְּנֵי יִשְׂרָאֵל, אוֹת הִוא לְעֹלָם
כִּי־שֵׁשֶׁת יָמִים עָשָׂה יהוה אֶת־הַשָּׁמַיִם וְאֶת־הָאָרֶץ
וּבַיּוֹם הַשְּׁבִיעִי שָׁבַת וַיִּנָּפַשׁ:

*On* יום טוב *of the* שלוש רגלים*, say:*

ויקרא כג וַיְדַבֵּר מֹשֶׁה אֶת־מֹעֲדֵי יהוה אֶל־בְּנֵי יִשְׂרָאֵל:

HALF KADDISH

*Leader:* יִתְגַּדַּל Magnified and sanctified may His great name be,
in the world He created by His will.
May He establish His kingdom
in your lifetime and in your days,
and in the lifetime of all the house of Israel,
swiftly and soon – and say: Amen.

*All:* May His great name be blessed for ever and all time.

*Leader:* Blessed and praised,
glorified and exalted,
raised and honored,
uplifted and lauded
be the name of the Holy One,
blessed be He,
beyond any blessing,
song, praise and consolation
uttered in the world – and say: Amen.

*On Yom Tov (including one that falls on Shabbat) say the appropriate Amida on page 830.*

## THE AMIDA

*The following prayer, until "in former years" on page 434, is said silently, standing with feet together. Take three steps forward and at the points indicated by ˅, bend the knees at the first word, bow at the second, and stand straight before saying God's name.*

O Lord, open my lips, *Ps. 51*
so that my mouth may declare Your praise.

PATRIARCHS

˅בָּרוּךְ Blessed are You, Lord our God and God of our fathers,
God of Abraham, God of Isaac and God of Jacob;
the great, mighty and awesome God, God Most High,
who bestows acts of loving-kindness and creates all,
who remembers the loving-kindness of the fathers
and will bring a Redeemer to their children's children
for the sake of His name, in love.

חצי קדיש

ש״ץ: יִתְגַּדַּל וְיִתְקַדַּשׁ שְׁמֵהּ רַבָּא (קהל: אָמֵן)
בְּעָלְמָא דִּי בְרָא כִרְעוּתֵהּ
וְיַמְלִיךְ מַלְכוּתֵהּ
בְּחַיֵּיכוֹן וּבְיוֹמֵיכוֹן וּבְחַיֵּי דְכָל בֵּית יִשְׂרָאֵל
בַּעֲגָלָא וּבִזְמַן קָרִיב, וְאִמְרוּ אָמֵן. (קהל: אָמֵן)

קהל וש״ץ: יְהֵא שְׁמֵהּ רַבָּא מְבָרַךְ לְעָלַם וּלְעָלְמֵי עָלְמַיָּא.

ש״ץ: יִתְבָּרַךְ וְיִשְׁתַּבַּח וְיִתְפָּאַר וְיִתְרוֹמַם וְיִתְנַשֵּׂא
וְיִתְהַדָּר וְיִתְעַלֶּה וְיִתְהַלָּל
שְׁמֵהּ דְּקֻדְשָׁא בְּרִיךְ הוּא (קהל: בְּרִיךְ הוּא)
לְעֵלָּא מִן כָּל בִּרְכָתָא / בשבת שובה: לְעֵלָּא לְעֵלָּא מִכָּל בִּרְכָתָא/
וְשִׁירָתָא, תֻּשְׁבְּחָתָא וְנֶחֱמָתָא
דַּאֲמִירָן בְּעָלְמָא, וְאִמְרוּ אָמֵן. (קהל: אָמֵן)

*On* יום טוב *(including one that falls on* שבת*) say the appropriate* עמידה *on page 831.*

## עמידה

*The following prayer, until* קַדְמֹנִיּוֹת *on page 435, is said silently, standing with feet together. Take three steps forward and at the points indicated by* ᵛ*, bend the knees at the first word, bow at the second, and stand straight before saying God's name.*

אֲדֹנָי, שְׂפָתַי תִּפְתָּח, וּפִי יַגִּיד תְּהִלָּתֶךָ: תהלים נא

אבות

ᵛבָּרוּךְ אַתָּה יהוה, אֱלֹהֵינוּ וֵאלֹהֵי אֲבוֹתֵינוּ
אֱלֹהֵי אַבְרָהָם, אֱלֹהֵי יִצְחָק, וֵאלֹהֵי יַעֲקֹב
הָאֵל הַגָּדוֹל הַגִּבּוֹר וְהַנּוֹרָא, אֵל עֶלְיוֹן
גּוֹמֵל חֲסָדִים טוֹבִים, וְקוֹנֵה הַכֹּל
וְזוֹכֵר חַסְדֵי אָבוֹת
וּמֵבִיא גוֹאֵל לִבְנֵי בְנֵיהֶם לְמַעַן שְׁמוֹ בְּאַהֲבָה.

*On Shabbat Shuva:* Remember us for life, O King who desires life,
and write us in the book of life –
for Your sake, O God of life.

King, Helper, Savior, Shield:
▾Blessed are You, Lord, Shield of Abraham.

DIVINE MIGHT

אַתָּה גִּבּוֹר You are eternally mighty, Lord.
You give life to the dead and have great power to save.

*The phrase "He makes the wind blow and the rain fall" is added from Simḥat Torah until Pesaḥ. In Israel, the phrase "He causes the dew to fall" is added from Pesaḥ until Shemini Atzeret. See laws 129–131.*

*In fall & winter:* He makes the wind blow and the rain fall.
*In Israel, in spring & summer:* He causes the dew to fall.

He sustains the living with loving-kindness,
and with great compassion revives the dead.
He supports the fallen, heals the sick, sets captives free,
and keeps His faith with those who sleep in the dust.
Who is like You, Master of might, and who can compare to You,
O King who brings death and gives life,
and makes salvation grow?

*On Shabbat Shuva:* Who is like You, compassionate Father,
who remembers His creatures
in compassion, for life?

Faithful are You to revive the dead.
Blessed are You, Lord, who revives the dead.

HOLINESS

אַתָּה קָדוֹשׁ You are holy and Your name is holy,
and holy ones praise You daily, Selah!
Blessed are You, Lord,
the holy God. / *On Shabbat Shuva:* the holy King./
*(If forgotten, repeat the Amida.)*

בשבת שובה: זָכְרֵנוּ לְחַיִּים, מֶלֶךְ חָפֵץ בַּחַיִּים
וְכָתְבֵנוּ בְּסֵפֶר הַחַיִּים, לְמַעַנְךָ אֱלֹהִים חַיִּים.

מֶלֶךְ עוֹזֵר וּמוֹשִׁיעַ וּמָגֵן.
ּבָּרוּךְ אַתָּה יהוה, מָגֵן אַבְרָהָם.

גבורות

אַתָּה גִּבּוֹר לְעוֹלָם, אֲדֹנָי
מְחַיֵּה מֵתִים אַתָּה, רַב לְהוֹשִׁיעַ

*The phrase* מַשִּׁיב הָרְוּחַ *is added from* שמחת תורה *until* פסח.
*In* ארץ ישראל *the phrase* מוֹרִיד הַטָּל *is added from* פסח *until* שמיני עצרת. *See laws 129–131.*

בחורף: מַשִּׁיב הָרְוּחַ וּמוֹרִיד הַגֶּשֶׁם / בארץ ישראל בקיץ: מוֹרִיד הַטָּל

מְכַלְכֵּל חַיִּים בְּחֶסֶד, מְחַיֵּה מֵתִים בְּרַחֲמִים רַבִּים
סוֹמֵךְ נוֹפְלִים, וְרוֹפֵא חוֹלִים, וּמַתִּיר אֲסוּרִים
וּמְקַיֵּם אֱמוּנָתוֹ לִישֵׁנֵי עָפָר.
מִי כָמְוֹךָ, בַּעַל גְּבוּרוֹת, וּמִי דּוֹמֶה לָּךְ
מֶלֶךְ, מֵמִית וּמְחַיֶּה וּמַצְמִיחַ יְשׁוּעָה.

בשבת שובה: מִי כָמְוֹךָ אַב הָרַחֲמִים
זוֹכֵר יְצוּרָיו לְחַיִּים בְּרַחֲמִים.

וְנֶאֱמָן אַתָּה לְהַחֲיוֹת מֵתִים.
בָּרוּךְ אַתָּה יהוה, מְחַיֵּה הַמֵּתִים.

קדושת השם

אַתָּה קָדוֹשׁ וְשִׁמְךָ קָדוֹשׁ
וּקְדוֹשִׁים בְּכָל יוֹם יְהַלְלְוּךָ סֶּלָה.
בָּרוּךְ אַתָּה יהוה, הָאֵל הַקָּדוֹשׁ. / בשבת שובה: הַמֶּלֶךְ הַקָּדוֹשׁ./
(*If forgotten, repeat the* עמידה.)

HOLINESS OF THE DAY

אַתָּה קִדַּשְׁתָּ You sanctified the seventh day for Your name's sake,
as the culmination of the creation of heaven and earth.
Of all days, You blessed it; of all seasons You sanctified it –
and so it is written in Your Torah:

וַיְכֻלּוּ Then the heavens and the earth were completed, *Gen. 2*
and all their array.
With the seventh day, God completed the work He had done.
He ceased on the seventh day from all the work He had done.
God blessed the seventh day and declared it holy,
because on it He ceased from all His work He had created to do.

אֱלֹהֵינוּ Our God and God of our ancestors,
may You find favor in our rest.
Make us holy through Your commandments
and grant us our share in Your Torah.
Satisfy us with Your goodness, grant us joy in Your salvation,
and purify our hearts to serve You in truth.
In love and favor, O Lord our God,
grant us as our heritage Your holy Shabbat,
so that Israel, who sanctify Your name, may find rest on it.
Blessed are You, Lord, who sanctifies the Sabbath.

TEMPLE SERVICE

רְצֵה Find favor, Lord our God, in Your people Israel
and their prayer.
Restore the service to Your most holy House,
and accept in love and favor the fire-offerings of Israel
and their prayer.
May the service of Your people Israel always find favor with You.

---

*On Rosh Ḥodesh and Ḥol HaMo'ed, say:*

אֱלֹהֵינוּ Our God and God of our ancestors, may there rise, come, reach, appear, be favored, heard, regarded and remembered before You, our recollection and remembrance, as well as the remembrance of our ancestors, and of the Messiah, son of David Your servant, and of

קדושת היום

אַתָּה קִדַּשְׁתָּ אֶת יוֹם הַשְּׁבִיעִי לִשְׁמֶךָ
תַּכְלִית מַעֲשֵׂה שָׁמַיִם וָאָרֶץ
וּבֵרַכְתּוֹ מִכָּל הַיָּמִים, וְקִדַּשְׁתּוֹ מִכָּל הַזְּמַנִּים
וְכֵן כָּתוּב בְּתוֹרָתֶךָ

וַיְכֻלּוּ הַשָּׁמַיִם וְהָאָרֶץ וְכָל־צְבָאָם׃ בראשית ב
וַיְכַל אֱלֹהִים בַּיּוֹם הַשְּׁבִיעִי מְלַאכְתּוֹ אֲשֶׁר עָשָׂה
וַיִּשְׁבֹּת בַּיּוֹם הַשְּׁבִיעִי מִכָּל־מְלַאכְתּוֹ אֲשֶׁר עָשָׂה׃
וַיְבָרֶךְ אֱלֹהִים אֶת־יוֹם הַשְּׁבִיעִי, וַיְקַדֵּשׁ אֹתוֹ
כִּי בוֹ שָׁבַת מִכָּל־מְלַאכְתּוֹ, אֲשֶׁר־בָּרָא אֱלֹהִים לַעֲשׂוֹת׃

אֱלֹהֵינוּ וֵאלֹהֵי אֲבוֹתֵינוּ, רְצֵה בִמְנוּחָתֵנוּ.
קַדְּשֵׁנוּ בְּמִצְוֹתֶיךָ, וְתֵן חֶלְקֵנוּ בְּתוֹרָתֶךָ
שַׂבְּעֵנוּ מִטּוּבֶךָ, וְשַׂמְּחֵנוּ בִּישׁוּעָתֶךָ
וְטַהֵר לִבֵּנוּ לְעָבְדְּךָ בֶּאֱמֶת.
וְהַנְחִילֵנוּ, יהוה אֱלֹהֵינוּ, בְּאַהֲבָה וּבְרָצוֹן שַׁבַּת קָדְשֶׁךָ
וְיָנוּחוּ בָהּ יִשְׂרָאֵל מְקַדְּשֵׁי שְׁמֶךָ.
בָּרוּךְ אַתָּה יהוה, מְקַדֵּשׁ הַשַּׁבָּת.

עבודה

רְצֵה יהוה אֱלֹהֵינוּ בְּעַמְּךָ יִשְׂרָאֵל וּבִתְפִלָּתָם
וְהָשֵׁב אֶת הָעֲבוֹדָה לִדְבִיר בֵּיתֶךָ
וְאִשֵּׁי יִשְׂרָאֵל וּתְפִלָּתָם בְּאַהֲבָה תְקַבֵּל בְּרָצוֹן
וּתְהִי לְרָצוֹן תָּמִיד עֲבוֹדַת יִשְׂרָאֵל עַמֶּךָ.

---

*On* ראש חודש *and* חול המועד*, say:*

אֱלֹהֵינוּ וֵאלֹהֵי אֲבוֹתֵינוּ, יַעֲלֶה וְיָבוֹא וְיַגִּיעַ, וְיֵרָאֶה וְיֵרָצֶה וְיִשָּׁמַע,
וְיִפָּקֵד וְיִזָּכֵר זִכְרוֹנֵנוּ וּפִקְדוֹנֵנוּ וְזִכְרוֹן אֲבוֹתֵינוּ, וְזִכְרוֹן מָשִׁיחַ בֶּן דָּוִד

Jerusalem Your holy city, and of all Your people the house of Israel – for deliverance and well-being, grace, loving-kindness and compassion, life and peace, on this day of:

*On Rosh Ḥodesh:* Rosh Ḥodesh.
*On Pesaḥ:* the Festival of Matzot.
*On Sukkot:* the Festival of Sukkot.

On it remember us, Lord our God, for good; recollect us for blessing, and deliver us for life. In accord with Your promise of salvation and compassion, spare us and be gracious to us; have compassion on us and deliver us, for our eyes are turned to You because You, God, are a gracious and compassionate King.

---

וְתֶחֱזֶינָה And may our eyes witness Your return to Zion in compassion. Blessed are You, Lord, who restores His Presence to Zion.

THANKSGIVING

*Bow at the first nine words.*

מוֹדִים We give thanks to You,
for You are the Lord our God and God of our ancestors
for ever and all time.
You are the Rock of our lives,
Shield of our salvation from generation to generation.
We will thank You and declare Your praise for our lives,
which are entrusted into Your hand;
for our souls, which are placed in Your charge;
for Your miracles which are with us every day;
and for Your wonders and favors
at all times, evening, morning and midday.
You are good – for Your compassion never fails.
You are compassionate – for Your loving-kindnesses never cease.
We have always placed our hope in You.

---

*On Ḥanukka:*

עַל הַנִּסִּים [We thank You also] for the miracles, the redemption, the mighty deeds, the salvations, and the victories in battle which You performed for our ancestors in those days, at this time.

בִּימֵי מַתִּתְיָהוּ In the days of Mattityahu, son of Yoḥanan, the High Priest, the Hasmonean, and his sons, the wicked Greek kingdom rose up against Your

עַבְדֶּךָ, וְזִכְרוֹן יְרוּשָׁלַיִם עִיר קָדְשֶׁךָ, וְזִכְרוֹן כָּל עַמְּךָ בֵּית יִשְׂרָאֵל, לְפָנֶיךָ, לִפְלֵיטָה לְטוֹבָה, לְחֵן וּלְחֶסֶד וּלְרַחֲמִים, לְחַיִּים וּלְשָׁלוֹם בְּיוֹם

בראש חודש: רֹאשׁ הַחֹדֶשׁ / בפסח: חַג הַמַּצּוֹת / בסוכות: חַג הַסֻּכּוֹת

הַזֶּה. זָכְרֵנוּ יהוה אֱלֹהֵינוּ בּוֹ לְטוֹבָה, וּפָקְדֵנוּ בוֹ לִבְרָכָה, וְהוֹשִׁיעֵנוּ בוֹ לְחַיִּים. וּבִדְבַר יְשׁוּעָה וְרַחֲמִים, חוּס וְחָנֵּנוּ וְרַחֵם עָלֵינוּ וְהוֹשִׁיעֵנוּ, כִּי אֵלֶיךָ עֵינֵינוּ, כִּי אֵל מֶלֶךְ חַנּוּן וְרַחוּם אָתָּה.

---

וְתֶחֱזֶינָה עֵינֵינוּ בְּשׁוּבְךָ לְצִיּוֹן בְּרַחֲמִים.
בָּרוּךְ אַתָּה יהוה, הַמַּחֲזִיר שְׁכִינָתוֹ לְצִיּוֹן.

הודאה

*Bow at the first five words.*

מוֹדִים אֲנַחְנוּ לָךְ
שָׁאַתָּה הוּא יהוה אֱלֹהֵינוּ וֵאלֹהֵי אֲבוֹתֵינוּ לְעוֹלָם וָעֶד.
צוּר חַיֵּינוּ, מָגֵן יִשְׁעֵנוּ, אַתָּה הוּא לְדוֹר וָדוֹר.
נוֹדֶה לְּךָ וּנְסַפֵּר תְּהִלָּתֶךָ
עַל חַיֵּינוּ הַמְּסוּרִים בְּיָדֶךָ, וְעַל נִשְׁמוֹתֵינוּ הַפְּקוּדוֹת לָךְ
וְעַל נִסֶּיךָ שֶׁבְּכָל יוֹם עִמָּנוּ, וְעַל נִפְלְאוֹתֶיךָ וְטוֹבוֹתֶיךָ
שֶׁבְּכָל עֵת, עֶרֶב וָבֹקֶר וְצָהֳרָיִם.
הַטּוֹב, כִּי לֹא כָלוּ רַחֲמֶיךָ
וְהַמְרַחֵם, כִּי לֹא תַמּוּ חֲסָדֶיךָ
מֵעוֹלָם קִוִּינוּ לָךְ.

---

בחנוכה:

עַל הַנִּסִּים וְעַל הַפֻּרְקָן וְעַל הַגְּבוּרוֹת וְעַל הַתְּשׁוּעוֹת וְעַל הַמִּלְחָמוֹת שֶׁעָשִׂיתָ לַאֲבוֹתֵינוּ בַּיָּמִים הָהֵם בַּזְּמַן הַזֶּה.

בִּימֵי מַתִּתְיָהוּ בֶּן יוֹחָנָן כֹּהֵן גָּדוֹל חַשְׁמוֹנַאי וּבָנָיו, כְּשֶׁעָמְדָה מַלְכוּת יָוָן הָרְשָׁעָה עַל עַמְּךָ יִשְׂרָאֵל לְהַשְׁכִּיחָם תּוֹרָתֶךָ וּלְהַעֲבִירָם מֵחֻקֵּי רְצוֹנֶךָ,

people Israel to make them forget Your Torah and to force them to transgress the statutes of Your will. It was then that You in Your great compassion stood by them in the time of their distress. You championed their cause, judged their claim, and avenged their wrong. You delivered the strong into the hands of the weak, the many into the hands of the few, the impure into the hands of the pure, the wicked into the hands of the righteous, and the arrogant into the hands of those who were engaged in the study of Your Torah. You made for Yourself great and holy renown in Your world, and for Your people Israel You performed a great salvation and redemption as of this very day. Your children then entered the holiest part of Your House, cleansed Your Temple, purified Your Sanctuary, kindled lights in Your holy courts, and designated these eight days of Ḥanukka for giving thanks and praise to Your great name.

*Continue with "For all these things".*

*On Purim:*

עַל הַנִּסִּים [We thank You also] for the miracles, the redemption, the mighty deeds, the salvations, and the victories in battle which You performed for our ancestors in those days at this time.

בִּימֵי מָרְדְּכַי In the days of Mordekhai and Esther, in Shushan the capital, the wicked Haman rose up against them and sought to destroy, slay and exterminate *Esther 3* all the Jews, young and old, children and women, on one day, the thirteenth day of the twelfth month, which is the month of Adar, and to plunder their possessions. Then You in Your great compassion thwarted his counsel, frustrated his plans, and caused his scheme to recoil on his own head, so that they hanged him and his sons on the gallows.

*Continue with "For all these things".*

---

וְעַל כֻּלָּם For all these things may Your name be blessed and exalted, our King, continually, for ever and all time.

*On Shabbat Shuva:* And write, for a good life, all the children of Your covenant.

Let all that lives thank You, Selah! and praise Your name in truth, God, our Savior and Help, Selah!
▾Blessed are You, LORD, whose name is "the Good"
and to whom thanks are due.

PEACE

שָׁלוֹם רָב Grant great peace to Your people Israel for ever,
for You are the sovereign LORD of all peace;
and may it be good in Your eyes to bless Your people Israel
at every time, at every hour, with Your peace.

וְאַתָּה בְּרַחֲמֶיךָ הָרַבִּים עָמַדְתָּ לָהֶם בְּעֵת צָרָתָם, רַבְתָּ אֶת רִיבָם, דַּנְתָּ אֶת דִּינָם, נָקַמְתָּ אֶת נִקְמָתָם, מָסַרְתָּ גִבּוֹרִים בְּיַד חַלָּשִׁים, וְרַבִּים בְּיַד מְעַטִּים, וּטְמֵאִים בְּיַד טְהוֹרִים, וּרְשָׁעִים בְּיַד צַדִּיקִים, וְזֵדִים בְּיַד עוֹסְקֵי תוֹרָתֶךָ, וּלְךָ עָשִׂיתָ שֵׁם גָּדוֹל וְקָדוֹשׁ בְּעוֹלָמֶךָ, וּלְעַמְּךָ יִשְׂרָאֵל עָשִׂיתָ תְּשׁוּעָה גְדוֹלָה וּפֻרְקָן כְּהַיּוֹם הַזֶּה. וְאַחַר כֵּן בָּאוּ בָנֶיךָ לִדְבִיר בֵּיתֶךָ, וּפִנּוּ אֶת הֵיכָלֶךָ, וְטִהֲרוּ אֶת מִקְדָּשֶׁךָ, וְהִדְלִיקוּ נֵרוֹת בְּחַצְרוֹת קָדְשֶׁךָ, וְקָבְעוּ שְׁמוֹנַת יְמֵי חֲנֻכָּה אֵלּוּ, לְהוֹדוֹת וּלְהַלֵּל לְשִׁמְךָ הַגָּדוֹל.

*Continue with* וְעַל כֻּלָּם.

בפורים:

עַל הַנִּסִּים וְעַל הַפֻּרְקָן וְעַל הַגְּבוּרוֹת וְעַל הַתְּשׁוּעוֹת וְעַל הַמִּלְחָמוֹת שֶׁעָשִׂיתָ לַאֲבוֹתֵינוּ בַּיָּמִים הָהֵם בַּזְּמַן הַזֶּה.

בִּימֵי מָרְדְּכַי וְאֶסְתֵּר בְּשׁוּשַׁן הַבִּירָה, כְּשֶׁעָמַד עֲלֵיהֶם הָמָן הָרָשָׁע, בִּקֵּשׁ
לְהַשְׁמִיד לַהֲרֹג וּלְאַבֵּד אֶת־כָּל־הַיְּהוּדִים מִנַּעַר וְעַד־זָקֵן טַף וְנָשִׁים בְּיוֹם אסתר ג
אֶחָד, בִּשְׁלוֹשָׁה עָשָׂר לְחֹדֶשׁ שְׁנֵים־עָשָׂר, הוּא־חֹדֶשׁ אֲדָר, וּשְׁלָלָם
לָבוֹז: וְאַתָּה בְּרַחֲמֶיךָ הָרַבִּים הֵפַרְתָּ אֶת עֲצָתוֹ, וְקִלְקַלְתָּ אֶת מַחֲשַׁבְתּוֹ,
וַהֲשֵׁבוֹתָ לּוֹ גְּמוּלוֹ בְּרֹאשׁוֹ, וְתָלוּ אוֹתוֹ וְאֶת בָּנָיו עַל הָעֵץ.

*Continue with* וְעַל כֻּלָּם.

---

וְעַל כֻּלָּם יִתְבָּרַךְ וְיִתְרוֹמַם שִׁמְךָ מַלְכֵּנוּ תָּמִיד לְעוֹלָם וָעֶד.

בשבת שובה: וּכְתֹב לְחַיִּים טוֹבִים כָּל בְּנֵי בְרִיתֶךָ.

וְכֹל הַחַיִּים יוֹדוּךָ סֶּלָה, וִיהַלְלוּ אֶת שִׁמְךָ בֶּאֱמֶת
הָאֵל יְשׁוּעָתֵנוּ וְעֶזְרָתֵנוּ סֶלָה.
בָּרוּךְ אַתָּה יהוה, הַטּוֹב שִׁמְךָ וּלְךָ נָאֶה לְהוֹדוֹת.

ברכת שלום

שָׁלוֹם רָב עַל יִשְׂרָאֵל עַמְּךָ תָּשִׂים לְעוֹלָם
כִּי אַתָּה הוּא מֶלֶךְ אָדוֹן לְכָל הַשָּׁלוֹם.
וְטוֹב בְּעֵינֶיךָ לְבָרֵךְ אֶת עַמְּךָ יִשְׂרָאֵל
בְּכָל עֵת וּבְכָל שָׁעָה בִּשְׁלוֹמֶךָ.

*On Shabbat Shuva:* In the book of life, blessing, peace and prosperity,
may we and all Your people the house of Israel
be remembered and written before You
for a good life, and for peace.*

Blessed are You, LORD, who blesses His people Israel with peace.

**On Shabbat Shuva in the Diaspora, many end the blessing:*
Blessed are You, LORD, who makes peace.

*Some say the following verse (see law 368):*
May the words of my mouth and the meditation of my heart — *Ps. 19*
find favor before You, LORD, my Rock and Redeemer.

אֱלֹהַי My God, — *Berakhot 17a*
guard my tongue from evil and my lips from deceitful speech.
To those who curse me, let my soul be silent;
may my soul be to all like the dust.
Open my heart to Your Torah
and let my soul pursue Your commandments.
As for all who plan evil against me,
swiftly thwart their counsel and frustrate their plans.
Act for the sake of Your name; act for the sake of Your right hand;
act for the sake of Your holiness; act for the sake of Your Torah.
That Your beloved ones may be delivered, — *Ps. 60*
save with Your right hand and answer me.
May the words of my mouth — *Ps. 19*
and the meditation of my heart find favor before You,
LORD, my Rock and Redeemer.

*Bow, take three steps back, then bow, first left, then right, then center, while saying:*
May He who makes peace in His high places,
make peace for us and all Israel – and say: Amen.

יְהִי רָצוֹן May it be Your will, LORD our God and God of our ancestors,
that the Temple be rebuilt speedily in our days, and grant us a share in Your Torah.
And there we will serve You with reverence,
as in the days of old and as in former years.
Then the offering of Judah and Jerusalem — *Mal. 3*
will be pleasing to the LORD as in the days of old and as in former years.

בשבת שובה: בְּסֵפֶר חַיִּים, בְּרָכָה וְשָׁלוֹם, וּפַרְנָסָה טוֹבָה
נִזָּכֵר וְנִכָּתֵב לְפָנֶיךָ, אֲנַחְנוּ וְכָל עַמְּךָ בֵּית יִשְׂרָאֵל
לְחַיִּים טוֹבִים וּלְשָׁלוֹם.*

**בָּרוּךְ אַתָּה יהוה, הַמְבָרֵךְ אֶת עַמּוֹ יִשְׂרָאֵל בַּשָּׁלוֹם.**

**On שבת שובה in חוץ לארץ, many end the blessing:*

**בָּרוּךְ אַתָּה יהוה, עוֹשֶׂה הַשָּׁלוֹם.**

*Some say the following verse (see law 368):*

יִהְיוּ לְרָצוֹן אִמְרֵי־פִי וְהֶגְיוֹן לִבִּי לְפָנֶיךָ, יהוה צוּרִי וְגֹאֲלִי: תהלים יט

ברכות יז.

**אֱלֹהַי**

נְצֹר לְשׁוֹנִי מֵרָע וּשְׂפָתַי מִדַּבֵּר מִרְמָה
וְלִמְקַלְלַי נַפְשִׁי תִדֹּם, וְנַפְשִׁי כֶּעָפָר לַכֹּל תִּהְיֶה.
פְּתַח לִבִּי בְּתוֹרָתֶךָ, וּבְמִצְוֹתֶיךָ תִּרְדֹּף נַפְשִׁי.
וְכָל הַחוֹשְׁבִים עָלַי רָעָה
מְהֵרָה הָפֵר עֲצָתָם וְקַלְקֵל מַחֲשַׁבְתָּם.
עֲשֵׂה לְמַעַן שְׁמֶךָ, עֲשֵׂה לְמַעַן יְמִינֶךָ
עֲשֵׂה לְמַעַן קְדֻשָּׁתֶךָ, עֲשֵׂה לְמַעַן תּוֹרָתֶךָ.
לְמַעַן יֵחָלְצוּן יְדִידֶיךָ, הוֹשִׁיעָה יְמִינְךָ וַעֲנֵנִי: תהלים ס
יִהְיוּ לְרָצוֹן אִמְרֵי־פִי וְהֶגְיוֹן לִבִּי לְפָנֶיךָ, יהוה צוּרִי וְגֹאֲלִי: תהלים יט

*Bow, take three steps back, then bow, first left, then right, then center, while saying:*

עֹשֶׂה שָׁלוֹם/ בשבת שובה: הַשָּׁלוֹם/ בִּמְרוֹמָיו
הוּא יַעֲשֶׂה שָׁלוֹם עָלֵינוּ וְעַל כָּל יִשְׂרָאֵל, וְאִמְרוּ אָמֵן.

יְהִי רָצוֹן מִלְּפָנֶיךָ יהוה אֱלֹהֵינוּ וֵאלֹהֵי אֲבוֹתֵינוּ
שֶׁיִּבָּנֶה בֵּית הַמִּקְדָּשׁ בִּמְהֵרָה בְיָמֵינוּ, וְתֵן חֶלְקֵנוּ בְּתוֹרָתֶךָ
וְשָׁם נַעֲבָדְךָ בְּיִרְאָה כִּימֵי עוֹלָם וּכְשָׁנִים קַדְמֹנִיּוֹת.
וְעָרְבָה לַיהוה מִנְחַת יְהוּדָה וִירוּשָׁלָםִ כִּימֵי עוֹלָם וּכְשָׁנִים קַדְמֹנִיּוֹת: מלאכי ג

*All stand and say:*

וַיְכֻלּוּ Then the heavens and the earth were completed, Gen. 2
and all their array.
With the seventh day, God completed the work He had done.
He ceased on the seventh day from all the work He had done. God
blessed the seventh day and declared it holy,
because on it He ceased from all His work He had created to do.

*On the first two nights of Pesaḥ (first night in Israel), some congregations recite Hallel (page 790) at this point. The following until "who sanctifies the Sabbath" below, is omitted when praying with an occasional minyan or alone. See law 453. It is also omitted when the first day of Pesaḥ falls on Shabbat.*

*The Leader continues:*

בָּרוּךְ Blessed are You, LORD our God and God of our fathers,
God of Abraham, God of Isaac and God of Jacob,
the great, mighty and awesome God,
God Most High, Creator of heaven and earth.

*The congregation then the Leader:*

מָגֵן אָבוֹת By His word, He was the Shield of our ancestors.
By His promise, He will revive the dead.
There is none like the holy God /*On Shabbat Shuva:* the holy King/
who gives rest to His people on His holy Sabbath day,
for He found them worthy of His favor to give them rest.
Before Him we will come in worship with reverence and awe,
giving thanks to His name daily, continually, with due blessings.
He is God to whom thanks are due, the LORD of peace
who sanctifies the Sabbath and blesses the seventh day,
and in holiness gives rest to a people filled with delight,
in remembrance of the work of creation.

*The Leader continues:*

אֱלֹהֵינוּ Our God and God of our ancestors,
may You find favor in our rest.
Make us holy through Your commandments
and grant us our share in Your Torah.
Satisfy us with Your goodness, grant us joy in Your salvation,
and purify our hearts to serve You in truth.

*All stand and say:*

וַיְכֻלּוּ הַשָּׁמַיִם וְהָאָרֶץ וְכָל־צְבָאָם: בראשית ב
וַיְכַל אֱלֹהִים בַּיּוֹם הַשְּׁבִיעִי מְלַאכְתּוֹ אֲשֶׁר עָשָׂה
וַיִּשְׁבֹּת בַּיּוֹם הַשְּׁבִיעִי מִכָּל־מְלַאכְתּוֹ אֲשֶׁר עָשָׂה:
וַיְבָרֶךְ אֱלֹהִים אֶת־יוֹם הַשְּׁבִיעִי, וַיְקַדֵּשׁ אֹתוֹ
כִּי בוֹ שָׁבַת מִכָּל־מְלַאכְתּוֹ, אֲשֶׁר־בָּרָא אֱלֹהִים, לַעֲשׂוֹת:

*On the first two nights of* פסח *(first night in* ארץ ישראל*), some congregations recite* הלל *(page 791) at this point. The following until* מְקַדֵּשׁ הַשַּׁבָּת *below, is omitted when praying with an occasional* מנין *or alone. See law 453. It is also omitted when the first day of* פסח *falls on* שבת.

*The* שליח ציבור *continues:*

בָּרוּךְ אַתָּה יהוה, אֱלֹהֵינוּ וֵאלֹהֵי אֲבוֹתֵינוּ
אֱלֹהֵי אַבְרָהָם, אֱלֹהֵי יִצְחָק, וֵאלֹהֵי יַעֲקֹב
הָאֵל הַגָּדוֹל הַגִּבּוֹר וְהַנּוֹרָא, אֵל עֶלְיוֹן, קֹנֵה שָׁמַיִם וָאָרֶץ.

*The* קהל *then the* שליח ציבור*:*

מָגֵן אָבוֹת בִּדְבָרוֹ, מְחַיֵּה מֵתִים בְּמַאֲמָרוֹ
הָאֵל / בשבת שובה: הַמֶּלֶךְ / הַקָּדוֹשׁ שֶׁאֵין כָּמוֹהוּ
הַמֵּנִיחַ לְעַמּוֹ בְּיוֹם שַׁבַּת קָדְשׁוֹ
כִּי בָם רָצָה לְהָנִיחַ לָהֶם, לְפָנָיו נַעֲבֹד בְּיִרְאָה וָפַחַד
וְנוֹדֶה לִשְׁמוֹ בְּכָל יוֹם תָּמִיד, מֵעֵין הַבְּרָכוֹת
אֵל הַהוֹדָאוֹת, אֲדוֹן הַשָּׁלוֹם
מְקַדֵּשׁ הַשַּׁבָּת וּמְבָרֵךְ שְׁבִיעִי
וּמֵנִיחַ בִּקְדֻשָּׁה לְעַם מְדֻשְּׁנֵי עֹנֶג, זֵכֶר לְמַעֲשֵׂה בְרֵאשִׁית.

*The* שליח ציבור *continues:*

אֱלֹהֵינוּ וֵאלֹהֵי אֲבוֹתֵינוּ, רְצֵה בִמְנוּחָתֵנוּ.
קַדְּשֵׁנוּ בְּמִצְוֹתֶיךָ וְתֵן חֶלְקֵנוּ בְּתוֹרָתֶךָ
שַׂבְּעֵנוּ מִטּוּבֶךָ וְשַׂמְּחֵנוּ בִּישׁוּעָתֶךָ
וְטַהֵר לִבֵּנוּ לְעָבְדְּךָ בֶּאֱמֶת.

In love and favor, LORD our God,
grant us as our heritage Your holy Sabbath,
so that Israel who sanctify Your name may find rest on it.
Blessed are You, LORD, who sanctifies the Sabbath.

## FULL KADDISH

*Leader:* יִתְגַּדַּל Magnified and sanctified
may His great name be,
in the world He created by His will.
May He establish His kingdom
in your lifetime and in your days,
and in the lifetime of all the house of Israel,
swiftly and soon –
and say: Amen.

*All:* May His great name be blessed for ever and all time.

*Leader:* Blessed and praised, glorified and exalted,
raised and honored, uplifted and lauded be
the name of the Holy One,
blessed be He, beyond any blessing,
song, praise and consolation uttered in the world –
and say: Amen.

May the prayers and pleas of all Israel
be accepted by their Father in heaven –
and say: Amen.

May there be great peace from heaven,
and life for us and all Israel –
and say: Amen.

*Bow, take three steps back, as if taking leave of the Divine Presence, then bow, first left, then right, then center, while saying:*

May He who makes peace in His high places,
make peace for us and all Israel –
and say: Amen.

וְהַנְחִילֵנוּ יהוה אֱלֹהֵינוּ בְּאַהֲבָה וּבְרָצוֹן שַׁבַּת קָדְשֶׁךָ
וְיָנוּחוּ בָהּ יִשְׂרָאֵל מְקַדְּשֵׁי שְׁמֶךָ.
בָּרוּךְ אַתָּה יהוה, מְקַדֵּשׁ הַשַּׁבָּת.

## קדיש שלם

ש״ץ: יִתְגַּדַּל וְיִתְקַדַּשׁ שְׁמֵהּ רַבָּא (קהל: אָמֵן)
בְּעָלְמָא דִּי בְרָא כִרְעוּתֵהּ
וְיַמְלִיךְ מַלְכוּתֵהּ
בְּחַיֵּיכוֹן וּבְיוֹמֵיכוֹן וּבְחַיֵּי דְכָל בֵּית יִשְׂרָאֵל
בַּעֲגָלָא וּבִזְמַן קָרִיב, וְאִמְרוּ אָמֵן. (קהל: אָמֵן)

קהל וש״ץ: יְהֵא שְׁמֵהּ רַבָּא מְבָרַךְ לְעָלַם וּלְעָלְמֵי עָלְמַיָּא.

ש״ץ: יִתְבָּרַךְ וְיִשְׁתַּבַּח וְיִתְפָּאַר
וְיִתְרוֹמַם וְיִתְנַשֵּׂא וְיִתְהַדָּר וְיִתְעַלֶּה וְיִתְהַלָּל
שְׁמֵהּ דְּקֻדְשָׁא בְּרִיךְ הוּא (קהל: בְּרִיךְ הוּא)
לְעֵלָּא מִן כָּל בִּרְכָתָא / בשבת שובה: לְעֵלָּא לְעֵלָּא מִכָּל בִּרְכָתָא/
וְשִׁירָתָא, תֻּשְׁבְּחָתָא וְנֶחֱמָתָא
דַּאֲמִירָן בְּעָלְמָא, וְאִמְרוּ אָמֵן. (קהל: אָמֵן)

תִּתְקַבַּל צְלוֹתְהוֹן וּבָעוּתְהוֹן דְּכָל יִשְׂרָאֵל
קֳדָם אֲבוּהוֹן דִּי בִשְׁמַיָּא, וְאִמְרוּ אָמֵן. (קהל: אָמֵן)

יְהֵא שְׁלָמָא רַבָּא מִן שְׁמַיָּא
וְחַיִּים, עָלֵינוּ וְעַל כָּל יִשְׂרָאֵל, וְאִמְרוּ אָמֵן. (קהל: אָמֵן)

*Bow, take three steps back, as if taking leave of the Divine Presence, then bow, first left, then right, then center, while saying:*

עֹשֶׂה שָׁלוֹם/ בשבת שובה: הַשָּׁלוֹם/ בִּמְרוֹמָיו
הוּא יַעֲשֶׂה שָׁלוֹם
עָלֵינוּ וְעַל כָּל יִשְׂרָאֵל, וְאִמְרוּ אָמֵן. (קהל: אָמֵן)

*On Yom Tov, say the Kiddush on page 820.*

## KIDDUSH IN THE SYNAGOGUE

*The Leader raises a cup of wine and says:*

Please pay attention, my masters.

בָּרוּךְ Blessed are You, LORD our God, King of the Universe,
who creates the fruit of the vine.

בָּרוּךְ Blessed are You, LORD our God, King of the Universe, who has made us holy with His commandments, has favored us, and in love and favor given us His holy Sabbath as a heritage, a remembrance of the work of creation. It is the first among the holy days of assembly, a remembrance of the exodus from Egypt. For You chose us and sanctified us from all the peoples, and in love and favor gave us Your holy Sabbath as a heritage. Blessed are You, LORD, who sanctifies the Sabbath.

*The wine should be drunk by children under the age of Bar/Bat Mitzva*
*or, if there are none, by the Leader.*
*From the second night of Pesaḥ until the night before Shavuot,*
*the Omer is counted here (page 356).*

*Stand while saying Aleinu. Bow at* ▾.

עָלֵינוּ It is our duty to praise the Master of all,
and ascribe greatness to the Author of creation,
who has not made us like the nations of the lands
nor placed us like the families of the earth;
who has not made our portion like theirs,
nor our destiny like all their multitudes.
(For they worship vanity and emptiness,
and pray to a god who cannot save.)
▾But we bow in worship
and thank the Supreme King of kings, the Holy One, blessed be He,
who extends the heavens and establishes the earth,
whose throne of glory is in the heavens above,
and whose power's Presence is in the highest of heights.
He is our God; there is no other.
Truly He is our King, there is none else,
as it is written in His Torah: "You shall know and take to heart this day *Deut. 4*
that the LORD is God, in heaven above and on earth below.
There is no other."

*On* יום טוב*, say the* קידוש *on page 821.*

# קידוש בבית הכנסת

*The* שליח ציבור *raises a cup of wine and says:*

סַבְרִי מָרָנָן

בָּרוּךְ אַתָּה יהוה אֱלֹהֵינוּ מֶלֶךְ הָעוֹלָם בּוֹרֵא פְּרִי הַגָּפֶן.

בָּרוּךְ אַתָּה יהוה אֱלֹהֵינוּ מֶלֶךְ הָעוֹלָם, אֲשֶׁר קִדְּשָׁנוּ בְּמִצְוֹתָיו, וְרָצָה בָנוּ וְשַׁבַּת קָדְשׁוֹ בְּאַהֲבָה וּבְרָצוֹן הִנְחִילָנוּ, זִכָּרוֹן לְמַעֲשֵׂה בְרֵאשִׁית, כִּי הוּא יוֹם תְּחִלָּה לְמִקְרָאֵי קֹדֶשׁ, זֵכֶר לִיצִיאַת מִצְרָיִם, כִּי בָנוּ בָחַרְתָּ וְאוֹתָנוּ קִדַּשְׁתָּ מִכָּל הָעַמִּים וְשַׁבַּת קָדְשְׁךָ בְּאַהֲבָה וּבְרָצוֹן הִנְחַלְתָּנוּ. בָּרוּךְ אַתָּה יהוה, מְקַדֵּשׁ הַשַּׁבָּת.

*The wine should be drunk by children under the age of* בר מצווה *or* בת מצווה *or, if there are none, by the* שליח ציבור.

*From the second night of* פסח *until the night before* שבועות*, the* עומר *is counted here* (*page 357*).

*Stand while saying* עָלֵינוּ*. Bow at* ׳.

עָלֵינוּ לְשַׁבֵּחַ לַאֲדוֹן הַכֹּל, לָתֵת גְּדֻלָּה לְיוֹצֵר בְּרֵאשִׁית\
שֶׁלֹּא עָשָׂנוּ כְּגוֹיֵי הָאֲרָצוֹת, וְלֹא שָׂמָנוּ כְּמִשְׁפְּחוֹת הָאֲדָמָה\
שֶׁלֹּא שָׂם חֶלְקֵנוּ כָּהֶם וְגוֹרָלֵנוּ כְּכָל הֲמוֹנָם.\
(שֶׁהֵם מִשְׁתַּחֲוִים לְהֶבֶל וָרִיק וּמִתְפַּלְלִים אֶל אֵל לֹא יוֹשִׁיעַ.)\
׳וַאֲנַחְנוּ כּוֹרְעִים וּמִשְׁתַּחֲוִים וּמוֹדִים\
לִפְנֵי מֶלֶךְ מַלְכֵי הַמְּלָכִים, הַקָּדוֹשׁ בָּרוּךְ הוּא\
שֶׁהוּא נוֹטֶה שָׁמַיִם וְיוֹסֵד אָרֶץ\
וּמוֹשַׁב יְקָרוֹ בַּשָּׁמַיִם מִמַּעַל, וּשְׁכִינַת עֻזּוֹ בְּגָבְהֵי מְרוֹמִים.\
הוּא אֱלֹהֵינוּ, אֵין עוֹד.\
אֱמֶת מַלְכֵּנוּ, אֶפֶס זוּלָתוֹ\
כַּכָּתוּב בְּתוֹרָתוֹ\
וְיָדַעְתָּ הַיּוֹם וַהֲשֵׁבֹתָ אֶל־לְבָבֶךָ דברים ד\
כִּי יהוה הוּא הָאֱלֹהִים בַּשָּׁמַיִם מִמַּעַל וְעַל־הָאָרֶץ מִתָּחַת, אֵין עוֹד:

Therefore, we place our hope in You, LORD our God,
that we may soon see the glory of Your power,
when You will remove abominations from the earth,
and idols will be utterly destroyed,
when the world will be perfected under the sovereignty of the Almighty,
when all humanity will call on Your name,
to turn all the earth's wicked toward You.
All the world's inhabitants will realize and know
that to You every knee must bow and every tongue swear loyalty.
Before You, LORD our God, they will kneel and bow down
and give honor to Your glorious name.
They will all accept the yoke of Your kingdom,
and You will reign over them soon and for ever.
For the kingdom is Yours,
and to all eternity You will reign in glory,
as it is written in Your Torah: "The LORD will reign for ever and ever." *Ex. 15*
▸ And it is said: "Then the LORD shall be King over all the earth; *Zech. 14*
on that day the LORD shall be One and His name One."

*Some add:*

Have no fear of sudden terror or of the ruin when it overtakes the wicked. *Prov. 3*
Devise your strategy, but it will be thwarted; *Is. 8*
propose your plan, but it will not stand, for God is with us.
When you grow old, I will still be the same. *Is. 46*
When your hair turns gray, I will still carry you.
I made you, I will bear you, I will carry you, and I will rescue you.

## MOURNER'S KADDISH

*The following prayer, said by mourners, requires the presence of a minyan.*
*A transliteration can be found on page 1320.*

*Mourner:* יִתְגַּדַּל Magnified and sanctified
may His great name be, in the world He created by His will.
May He establish His kingdom
in your lifetime and in your days,
and in the lifetime of all the house of Israel,
swiftly and soon – and say: Amen.

*All:* May His great name be blessed for ever and all time.

עַל כֵּן נְקַוֶּה לְּךָ יהוה אֱלֹהֵינוּ, לִרְאוֹת מְהֵרָה בְּתִפְאֶרֶת עֻזֶּךָ
לְהַעֲבִיר גִּלּוּלִים מִן הָאָרֶץ, וְהָאֱלִילִים כָּרוֹת יִכָּרֵתוּן
לְתַקֵּן עוֹלָם בְּמַלְכוּת שַׁדַּי.
וְכָל בְּנֵי בָשָׂר יִקְרְאוּ בִשְׁמֶךָ לְהַפְנוֹת אֵלֶיךָ כָּל רִשְׁעֵי אָרֶץ.
יַכִּירוּ וְיֵדְעוּ כָּל יוֹשְׁבֵי תֵבֵל
כִּי לְךָ תִּכְרַע כָּל בֶּרֶךְ, תִּשָּׁבַע כָּל לָשׁוֹן.
לְפָנֶיךָ יהוה אֱלֹהֵינוּ יִכְרְעוּ וְיִפֹּלוּ, וְלִכְבוֹד שִׁמְךָ יְקָר יִתֵּנוּ
וִיקַבְּלוּ כֻלָּם אֶת עֹל מַלְכוּתֶךָ
וְתִמְלֹךְ עֲלֵיהֶם מְהֵרָה לְעוֹלָם וָעֶד.
כִּי הַמַּלְכוּת שֶׁלְּךָ הִיא וּלְעוֹלְמֵי עַד תִּמְלֹךְ בְּכָבוֹד
כַּכָּתוּב בְּתוֹרָתֶךָ, יהוה יִמְלֹךְ לְעֹלָם וָעֶד: שמות טו
◄ וְנֶאֱמַר, וְהָיָה יהוה לְמֶלֶךְ עַל־כָּל־הָאָרֶץ זכריה יד
בַּיּוֹם הַהוּא יִהְיֶה יהוה אֶחָד וּשְׁמוֹ אֶחָד:

*Some add:*

אַל־תִּירָא מִפַּחַד פִּתְאֹם וּמִשֹּׁאַת רְשָׁעִים כִּי תָבֹא: משלי ג
עֻצוּ עֵצָה וְתֻפָר, דַּבְּרוּ דָבָר וְלֹא יָקוּם, כִּי עִמָּנוּ אֵל: ישעיה ח
וְעַד־זִקְנָה אֲנִי הוּא, וְעַד־שֵׂיבָה אֲנִי אֶסְבֹּל, אֲנִי עָשִׂיתִי וַאֲנִי אֶשָּׂא וַאֲנִי אֶסְבֹּל וַאֲמַלֵּט: ישעיה מו

## קדיש יתום

*The following prayer, said by mourners, requires the presence of a* מנין*.*
*A transliteration can be found on page 1320.*

אבל: יִתְגַּדַּל וְיִתְקַדַּשׁ שְׁמֵהּ רַבָּא (קהל: אָמֵן)
בְּעָלְמָא דִּי בְרָא כִרְעוּתֵהּ
וְיַמְלִיךְ מַלְכוּתֵהּ
בְּחַיֵּיכוֹן וּבְיוֹמֵיכוֹן וּבְחַיֵּי דְכָל בֵּית יִשְׂרָאֵל
בַּעֲגָלָא וּבִזְמַן קָרִיב, וְאִמְרוּ אָמֵן. (קהל: אָמֵן)

קהל ואבל: יְהֵא שְׁמֵהּ רַבָּא מְבָרַךְ לְעָלַם וּלְעָלְמֵי עָלְמַיָּא.

*Mourner:* Blessed and praised, glorified and exalted,
raised and honored, uplifted and lauded
be the name of the Holy One,
blessed be He, beyond any blessing,
song, praise and consolation
uttered in the world –
and say: Amen.

May there be great peace from heaven,
and life for us and all Israel –
and say: Amen.

*Bow, take three steps back, as if taking leave of the Divine Presence, then bow, first left, then right, then center, while saying:*

May He who makes peace in His high places,
make peace for us and all Israel –
and say: Amen.

*From the second day of Rosh Ḥodesh Elul until and including Shemini Atzeret (in Israel until and including Hoshana Raba), the following psalm is said:*

לְדָוִד A psalm of David. The LORD is my light and my salvation – *Ps. 27*
whom then shall I fear? The LORD is the stronghold of my life – of whom shall I be afraid? When evil men close in on me to devour my flesh, it is they, my enemies and foes, who stumble and fall. Should an army besiege me, my heart would not fear. Should war break out against me, still I would be confident. One thing I ask of the LORD, only this do I seek: to live in the House of the LORD all the days of my life, to gaze on the beauty of the LORD and worship in His Temple. For He will keep me safe in His pavilion on the day of trouble. He will hide me under the cover of His tent. He will set me high upon a rock. Now my head is high above my enemies who surround me. I will sacrifice in His tent with shouts of joy. I will sing and chant praises to the LORD. LORD, hear my voice when I call. Be gracious to me and answer me. On Your behalf my heart says, "Seek My face." Your face, LORD, will I seek. Do not hide Your face from me. Do not turn Your servant away in anger. You have been my help.

אבל: יִתְבָּרַךְ וְיִשְׁתַּבַּח וְיִתְפָּאַר
וְיִתְרוֹמַם וְיִתְנַשֵּׂא וְיִתְהַדָּר וְיִתְעַלֶּה וְיִתְהַלָּל
שְׁמֵהּ דְּקֻדְשָׁא בְּרִיךְ הוּא (קהל: בְּרִיךְ הוּא)
לְעֵלָּא מִן כָּל בִּרְכָתָא / בשבת שובה: לְעֵלָּא לְעֵלָּא מִכָּל בִּרְכָתָא/
וְשִׁירָתָא, תֻּשְׁבְּחָתָא וְנֶחֱמָתָא
דַּאֲמִירָן בְּעָלְמָא, וְאִמְרוּ אָמֵן. (קהל: אָמֵן)

יְהֵא שְׁלָמָא רַבָּא מִן שְׁמַיָּא
וְחַיִּים, עָלֵינוּ וְעַל כָּל יִשְׂרָאֵל, וְאִמְרוּ אָמֵן. (קהל: אָמֵן)

*Bow, take three steps back, as if taking leave of the Divine Presence, then bow, first left, then right, then center, while saying:*

עֹשֶׂה שָׁלוֹם/ בשבת שובה: הַשָּׁלוֹם/ בִּמְרוֹמָיו
הוּא יַעֲשֶׂה שָׁלוֹם
עָלֵינוּ וְעַל כָּל יִשְׂרָאֵל, וְאִמְרוּ אָמֵן. (קהל: אָמֵן)

*From the second day of* ראש חודש אלול *until and including* שמיני עצרת *(in* ארץ ישראל *until and including* הושענא רבה*), the following psalm is said:*

תהלים כז

לְדָוִד, יהוה אוֹרִי וְיִשְׁעִי, מִמִּי אִירָא, יהוה מָעוֹז־חַיַּי, מִמִּי אֶפְחָד: בִּקְרֹב עָלַי מְרֵעִים לֶאֱכֹל אֶת־בְּשָׂרִי, צָרַי וְאֹיְבַי לִי, הֵמָּה כָשְׁלוּ וְנָפָלוּ: אִם־תַּחֲנֶה עָלַי מַחֲנֶה, לֹא־יִירָא לִבִּי, אִם־תָּקוּם עָלַי מִלְחָמָה, בְּזֹאת אֲנִי בוֹטֵחַ: אַחַת שָׁאַלְתִּי מֵאֵת־יהוה, אוֹתָהּ אֲבַקֵּשׁ, שִׁבְתִּי בְּבֵית־יהוה כָּל־יְמֵי חַיַּי, לַחֲזוֹת בְּנֹעַם־יהוה, וּלְבַקֵּר בְּהֵיכָלוֹ: כִּי יִצְפְּנֵנִי בְּסֻכֹּה בְּיוֹם רָעָה, יַסְתִּרֵנִי בְּסֵתֶר אָהֳלוֹ, בְּצוּר יְרוֹמְמֵנִי: וְעַתָּה יָרוּם רֹאשִׁי עַל אֹיְבַי סְבִיבוֹתַי, וְאֶזְבְּחָה בְאָהֳלוֹ זִבְחֵי תְרוּעָה, אָשִׁירָה וַאֲזַמְּרָה לַיהוה: שְׁמַע־יהוה קוֹלִי אֶקְרָא, וְחָנֵּנִי וַעֲנֵנִי: לְךָ אָמַר לִבִּי בַּקְּשׁוּ פָנָי, אֶת־פָּנֶיךָ יהוה אֲבַקֵּשׁ: אַל־תַּסְתֵּר פָּנֶיךָ מִמֶּנִּי, אַל תַּט־בְּאַף עַבְדֶּךָ, עֶזְרָתִי הָיִיתָ, אַל־

Do not reject or forsake me, God, my Savior. Were my father and my mother to forsake me, the LORD would take me in. Teach me Your way, LORD, and lead me on a level path, because of my oppressors. Do not abandon me to the will of my foes, for false witnesses have risen against me, breathing violence. ▸ Were it not for my faith that I shall see the LORD's goodness in the land of the living. Hope in the LORD. Be strong and of good courage, and hope in the LORD!

MOURNER'S KADDISH

*The following prayer, said by mourners, requires the presence of a minyan.*
*A transliteration can be found on page 1320.*

*Mourner:* יִתְגַּדַּל Magnified and sanctified
may His great name be,
in the world He created by His will.
May He establish His kingdom
in your lifetime and in your days,
and in the lifetime of all the house of Israel,
swiftly and soon –
and say: Amen.

*All:* May His great name be blessed for ever and all time.

*Mourner:* Blessed and praised, glorified and exalted,
raised and honored, uplifted and lauded
be the name of the Holy One,
blessed be He, beyond any blessing,
song, praise and consolation
uttered in the world –
and say: Amen.

May there be great peace from heaven,
and life for us and all Israel –
and say: Amen.

*Bow, take three steps back, as if taking leave of the Divine Presence,*
*then bow, first left, then right, then center, while saying:*

May He who makes peace in His high places,
make peace for us and all Israel –
and say: Amen.

תִּטְּשֵׁנִי וְאַל־תַּעַזְבֵנִי, אֱלֹהֵי יִשְׁעִי: כִּי־אָבִי וְאִמִּי עֲזָבוּנִי, וַיהוה יַאַסְפֵנִי: הוֹרֵנִי יהוה דַּרְכֶּךָ, וּנְחֵנִי בְּאֹרַח מִישׁוֹר, לְמַעַן שׁוֹרְרָי: אַל־תִּתְּנֵנִי בְּנֶפֶשׁ צָרָי, כִּי קָמוּ־בִי עֵדֵי־שֶׁקֶר, וִיפֵחַ חָמָס: ‹ לוּלֵא הֶאֱמַנְתִּי לִרְאוֹת בְּטוּב־יהוה בְּאֶרֶץ חַיִּים: קַוֵּה אֶל־יהוה, חֲזַק וְיַאֲמֵץ לִבֶּךָ, וְקַוֵּה אֶל־יהוה:

## קדיש יתום

*The following prayer, said by mourners, requires the presence of a* מנין.
*A transliteration can be found on page 1320.*

אבל: יִתְגַּדַּל וְיִתְקַדַּשׁ שְׁמֵהּ רַבָּא (קהל: אָמֵן)
בְּעָלְמָא דִּי בְרָא כִרְעוּתֵהּ, וְיַמְלִיךְ מַלְכוּתֵהּ
בְּחַיֵּיכוֹן וּבְיוֹמֵיכוֹן וּבְחַיֵּי דְכָל בֵּית יִשְׂרָאֵל
בַּעֲגָלָא וּבִזְמַן קָרִיב, וְאִמְרוּ אָמֵן. (קהל: אָמֵן)

קהל ואבל: יְהֵא שְׁמֵהּ רַבָּא מְבָרַךְ לְעָלַם וּלְעָלְמֵי עָלְמַיָּא.

אבל: יִתְבָּרַךְ וְיִשְׁתַּבַּח וְיִתְפָּאַר
וְיִתְרוֹמַם וְיִתְנַשֵּׂא וְיִתְהַדָּר וְיִתְעַלֶּה וְיִתְהַלָּל
שְׁמֵהּ דְּקֻדְשָׁא בְּרִיךְ הוּא (קהל: בְּרִיךְ הוּא)
לְעֵלָּא מִן כָּל בִּרְכָתָא / בשבת שובה: לְעֵלָּא לְעֵלָּא מִכָּל בִּרְכָתָא/
וְשִׁירָתָא, תֻּשְׁבְּחָתָא וְנֶחֱמָתָא
דַּאֲמִירָן בְּעָלְמָא, וְאִמְרוּ אָמֵן. (קהל: אָמֵן)

יְהֵא שְׁלָמָא רַבָּא מִן שְׁמַיָּא
וְחַיִּים, עָלֵינוּ וְעַל כָּל יִשְׂרָאֵל, וְאִמְרוּ אָמֵן. (קהל: אָמֵן)

*Bow, take three steps back, as if taking leave of the Divine Presence, then bow, first left, then right, then center, while saying:*

עֹשֶׂה שָׁלוֹם/ בשבת שובה: הַשָּׁלוֹם/ בִּמְרוֹמָיו
הוּא יַעֲשֶׂה שָׁלוֹם
עָלֵינוּ וְעַל כָּל יִשְׂרָאֵל, וְאִמְרוּ אָמֵן. (קהל: אָמֵן)

*Most congregations sing Yigdal at this point.*
*In Israel, most congregations sing Adon Olam (page 30).*

GREAT
is the living God and praised.
He exists, and His existence is beyond time.

He is One, and there is no unity like His.
Unfathomable, His Oneness is infinite.

He has neither bodily form nor substance;
His holiness is beyond compare.

He preceded all that was created.
He was first: there was no beginning to His beginning.

Behold He is Master of the Universe; every creature
shows His greatness and majesty.

The rich flow of His prophecy He gave
to His treasured people in whom He gloried.

Never in Israel has there arisen another like Moses,
a prophet who beheld God's image.

God gave His people a Torah of truth
by the hand of His prophet, most faithful of His House.

God will not alter or change His law
for any other, for eternity.

He sees and knows our secret thoughts;
as soon as something is begun, He foresees its end.

He rewards people with loving-kindness according to their deeds;
He punishes the wicked according to his wickedness.

At the end of days He will send our Messiah,
to redeem those who await His final salvation.

God will revive the dead in His great loving-kindness.
Blessed for evermore is His glorious name!

*Most congregations sing* יגדל *at this point.*
*In* ארץ ישראל*, most congregations sing* אדון עולם (*page 31*).

# יִגְדַּל

אֱלֹהִים חַי וְיִשְׁתַּבַּח, נִמְצָא וְאֵין עֵת אֶל מְצִיאוּתוֹ.
אֶחָד וְאֵין יָחִיד כְּיִחוּדוֹ, נֶעְלָם וְגַם אֵין סוֹף לְאַחְדוּתוֹ.
אֵין לוֹ דְּמוּת הַגּוּף וְאֵינוֹ גוּף, לֹא נַעֲרֹךְ אֵלָיו קְדֻשָּׁתוֹ.
קַדְמוֹן לְכָל דָּבָר אֲשֶׁר נִבְרָא, רִאשׁוֹן וְאֵין רֵאשִׁית לְרֵאשִׁיתוֹ.
הִנּוֹ אֲדוֹן עוֹלָם, וְכָל נוֹצָר יוֹרֶה גְדֻלָּתוֹ וּמַלְכוּתוֹ.
שֶׁפַע נְבוּאָתוֹ נְתָנוֹ אֶל־אַנְשֵׁי סְגֻלָּתוֹ וְתִפְאַרְתּוֹ.
לֹא קָם בְּיִשְׂרָאֵל כְּמֹשֶׁה עוֹד נָבִיא וּמַבִּיט אֶת תְּמוּנָתוֹ.
תּוֹרַת אֱמֶת נָתַן לְעַמּוֹ אֵל עַל יַד נְבִיאוֹ נֶאֱמַן בֵּיתוֹ.
לֹא יַחֲלִיף הָאֵל וְלֹא יָמִיר דָּתוֹ לְעוֹלָמִים לְזוּלָתוֹ.
צוֹפֶה וְיוֹדֵעַ סְתָרֵינוּ, מַבִּיט לְסוֹף דָּבָר בְּקַדְמָתוֹ.
גּוֹמֵל לְאִישׁ חֶסֶד כְּמִפְעָלוֹ, נוֹתֵן לְרָשָׁע רָע כְּרִשְׁעָתוֹ.
יִשְׁלַח לְקֵץ יָמִין מְשִׁיחֵנוּ לִפְדּוֹת מְחַכֵּי קֵץ יְשׁוּעָתוֹ.
מֵתִים יְחַיֶּה אֵל בְּרֹב חַסְדּוֹ, בָּרוּךְ עֲדֵי עַד שֵׁם תְּהִלָּתוֹ.

# Kiddush and Zemirot for Shabbat Evening

## BLESSING THE CHILDREN

*On the evenings of Shabbat and Yom Tov, many have the custom to bless their children.*

*To sons, say:*

יְשִׂמְךָ May God
make you like Ephraim
and Manasseh.

*To daughters, say:*

יְשִׂימֵךְ May God
make you like Sarah, Rebecca,
Rachel and Leah.

*Gen. 48*

יְבָרֶכְךָ May the LORD bless you and protect you.
May the LORD make His face shine on you and be gracious to you.
May the LORD turn His face toward you and grant you peace.

*Num. 6*

*Many people sing each of the four verses of the following song three times:*

שָׁלוֹם עֲלֵיכֶם Welcome, ministering angels, angels of the Most High,
from the Supreme King of kings,
the Holy One, blessed be He.

Enter in peace, angels of peace, angels of the Most High,
from the Supreme King of kings,
the Holy One, blessed be He.

Bless me with peace, angels of peace, angels of the Most High,
from the Supreme King of kings,
the Holy One, blessed be He.

Go in peace, angels of peace, angels of the Most High,
from the Supreme King of kings,
the Holy One, blessed be He.

כִּי מַלְאָכָיו He will command His angels about you, *Ps. 91*
to guard you in all your ways.
May the LORD guard your going out and your return, *Ps. 121*
from now and for all time.

# קידוש וזמירות לליל שבת

## ברכת הבנים

*On* ליל שבת *and* ערב יום טוב, *many have the custom to bless their children.*

*To sons, say:*

בראשית מח יְשִׂמְךָ אֱלֹהִים
כְּאֶפְרַיִם וְכִמְנַשֶּׁה:

*To daughters, say:*

יְשִׂימֵךְ אֱלֹהִים
כְּשָׂרָה רִבְקָה רָחֵל וְלֵאָה.

במדבר ו יְבָרֶכְךָ יהוה וְיִשְׁמְרֶךָ:
יָאֵר יהוה פָּנָיו אֵלֶיךָ וִיחֻנֶּךָּ:
יִשָּׂא יהוה פָּנָיו אֵלֶיךָ וְיָשֵׂם לְךָ שָׁלוֹם:

*Many people sing each of the four verses of the following song three times:*

שָׁלוֹם עֲלֵיכֶם, מַלְאֲכֵי הַשָּׁרֵת, מַלְאֲכֵי עֶלְיוֹן
מִמֶּלֶךְ מַלְכֵי הַמְּלָכִים, הַקָּדוֹשׁ בָּרוּךְ הוּא.

בּוֹאֲכֶם לְשָׁלוֹם, מַלְאֲכֵי הַשָּׁלוֹם, מַלְאֲכֵי עֶלְיוֹן
מִמֶּלֶךְ מַלְכֵי הַמְּלָכִים, הַקָּדוֹשׁ בָּרוּךְ הוּא.

בָּרְכוּנִי לְשָׁלוֹם, מַלְאֲכֵי הַשָּׁלוֹם, מַלְאֲכֵי עֶלְיוֹן
מִמֶּלֶךְ מַלְכֵי הַמְּלָכִים, הַקָּדוֹשׁ בָּרוּךְ הוּא.

צֵאתְכֶם לְשָׁלוֹם, מַלְאֲכֵי הַשָּׁלוֹם, מַלְאֲכֵי עֶלְיוֹן
מִמֶּלֶךְ מַלְכֵי הַמְּלָכִים, הַקָּדוֹשׁ בָּרוּךְ הוּא.

תהלים צא כִּי מַלְאָכָיו יְצַוֶּה־לָּךְ, לִשְׁמָרְךָ בְּכָל־דְּרָכֶיךָ:
תהלים קכא יהוה יִשְׁמָר־צֵאתְךָ וּבוֹאֶךָ, מֵעַתָּה וְעַד־עוֹלָם:

*Some say:*

רִבּוֹן כָּל הָעוֹלָמִים Master of all worlds, LORD of all souls, LORD of peace, mighty, blessed and great King, King who speaks peace, King who is glorious, enduring and pure, King who gives life to worlds, King who is good and does good, King alone and unique, great King who robes Himself in compassion, King who reigns over all kings, who is exalted and supports those who fall, King who is Author of creation, who redeems and rescues, who is radiant and ruddy, King who is holy, high and exalted, King who hears prayer, King whose way is just: I thank You, LORD my God and God of my ancestors, for all the loving-kindness You have done and will do for me, and all the members of my household and all my fellow creatures. Blessed are Your angels, holy and pure, who do Your will. LORD of peace, King to whom peace belongs, bless me with peace, and grant me and the members of my household, and all Your people the house of Israel, a good and peaceful life. King exalted over all the heavenly array, who formed me and who formed creation, I entreat Your radiant presence, that You find me and all the members of my household worthy of grace and good favor in Your eyes and the eyes of all people and all who see us, that we may serve You. May we be worthy to receive Sabbaths amidst great joy, wealth and honor, and few sins. May You remove from me and all the members of my household and all Your people the house of Israel all sickness and disease, all poverty, hardship and destitution. Grant us a virtuous desire to serve You in truth, awe and love. May we find honor in Your eyes and the eyes of all who see us, for You are the King of honor: to You it belongs, to You it accords. Please, King who reigns over all kings, command Your angels, ministering angels who minister to the Most High, to act compassionately toward me when they enter my house on our holy day, for I have lit my lights, spread my couch and changed my clothes in honor of the Sabbath; I have come to Your House to lay my pleas before You that You remove my sighs; I have testified that in six days You created all things, and said it a second time, and will testify to it a third time over my cup, in joy, as You commanded me to remember it, delighting in the extra soul You have given me. On it [the Sabbath] I shall rest as You have commanded me, thereby to serve You. So too I will declare Your greatness in joyful song, for I have set the LORD before me, that You may have compassion upon me in my exile, redeeming me and awakening my heart to Your love. Then I will keep Your commands and statutes without sadness, praying correctly as is right and fitting. Angels of peace, come in peace and bless me with peace; declare blessed the table I have prepared, and go in peace, now and forever. Amen, Selah.

*Some say:*

רִבּוֹן כָּל הָעוֹלָמִים, אֲדוֹן כָּל הַנְּשָׁמוֹת, אֲדוֹן הַשָּׁלוֹם. מֶלֶךְ אַבִּיר, מֶלֶךְ בָּרוּךְ, מֶלֶךְ גָּדוֹל, מֶלֶךְ דּוֹבֵר שָׁלוֹם, מֶלֶךְ הָדוּר, מֶלֶךְ וָתִיק, מֶלֶךְ זַךְ, מֶלֶךְ חֵי הָעוֹלָמִים, מֶלֶךְ טוֹב וּמֵטִיב, מֶלֶךְ יָחִיד וּמְיֻחָד, מֶלֶךְ כַּבִּיר, מֶלֶךְ לוֹבֵשׁ רַחֲמִים, מֶלֶךְ מַלְכֵי הַמְּלָכִים, מֶלֶךְ נִשְׂגָּב, מֶלֶךְ סוֹמֵךְ נוֹפְלִים, מֶלֶךְ עֹשֶׂה מַעֲשֵׂה בְרֵאשִׁית, מֶלֶךְ פּוֹדֶה וּמַצִּיל, מֶלֶךְ צַח וְאָדֹם, מֶלֶךְ קָדוֹשׁ, מֶלֶךְ רָם וְנִשָּׂא, מֶלֶךְ שׁוֹמֵעַ תְּפִלָּה, מֶלֶךְ תָּמִים דַּרְכּוֹ. מוֹדֶה אֲנִי לְפָנֶיךָ, יהוה אֱלֹהַי וֵאלֹהֵי אֲבוֹתַי, עַל כָּל הַחֶסֶד אֲשֶׁר עָשִׂיתָ עִמָּדִי וַאֲשֶׁר אַתָּה עָתִיד לַעֲשׂוֹת עִמִּי וְעִם כָּל בְּנֵי בֵיתִי וְעִם כָּל בְּרִיּוֹתֶיךָ, בְּנֵי בְרִיתִי. וּבְרוּכִים הֵם מַלְאָכֶיךָ הַקְּדוֹשִׁים וְהַטְּהוֹרִים שֶׁעוֹשִׂים רְצוֹנֶךָ. אֲדוֹן הַשָּׁלוֹם, מֶלֶךְ שֶׁהַשָּׁלוֹם שֶׁלּוֹ, בָּרְכֵנִי בַשָּׁלוֹם, וְתִפְקֹד אוֹתִי וְאֶת כָּל בְּנֵי בֵיתִי וְכָל עַמְּךָ בֵּית יִשְׂרָאֵל לְחַיִּים טוֹבִים וּלְשָׁלוֹם. מֶלֶךְ עֶלְיוֹן עַל כָּל צְבָא מָרוֹם, יוֹצְרֵנוּ, יוֹצֵר בְּרֵאשִׁית, אֲחַלֶּה פָנֶיךָ הַמְּאִירִים, שֶׁתְּזַכֶּה אוֹתִי וְאֶת כָּל בְּנֵי בֵיתִי לִמְצֹא חֵן וְשֵׂכֶל טוֹב בְּעֵינֶיךָ וּבְעֵינֵי כָל בְּנֵי אָדָם וּבְעֵינֵי כָל רוֹאֵינוּ לַעֲבוֹדָתֶךָ. וְזַכֵּנוּ לְקַבֵּל שַׁבָּתוֹת מִתּוֹךְ רֹב שִׂמְחָה וּמִתּוֹךְ עֹשֶׁר וְכָבוֹד וּמִתּוֹךְ מִעוּט עֲוֹנוֹת. וְהָסֵר מִמֶּנִּי וּמִכָּל בְּנֵי בֵיתִי וּמִכָּל עַמְּךָ בֵּית יִשְׂרָאֵל כָּל מִינֵי חֹלִי וְכָל מִינֵי מַדְוֶה וְכָל מִינֵי דַלּוּת וַעֲנִיּוּת וְאֶבְיוֹנוּת. וְתֵן בָּנוּ יֵצֶר טוֹב לְעָבְדְּךָ בֶּאֱמֶת וּבְיִרְאָה וּבְאַהֲבָה. וְנִהְיֶה מְכֻבָּדִים בְּעֵינֶיךָ וּבְעֵינֵי כָל רוֹאֵינוּ, כִּי אַתָּה הוּא מֶלֶךְ הַכָּבוֹד, כִּי לְךָ נָאֶה, כִּי לְךָ יָאֶה. אָנָּא, מֶלֶךְ מַלְכֵי הַמְּלָכִים, צַוֵּה לְמַלְאָכֶיךָ, מַלְאֲכֵי הַשָּׁרֵת, מְשָׁרְתֵי עֶלְיוֹן, שֶׁיִּפְקְדוּנִי בְּרַחֲמִים וִיבָרְכוּנִי בְּבוֹאָם לְבֵיתִי בְּיוֹם קָדְשֵׁנוּ, כִּי הִדְלַקְתִּי נֵרוֹתַי וְהִצַּעְתִּי מִטָּתִי וְהֶחֱלַפְתִּי שִׂמְלוֹתַי לִכְבוֹד יוֹם הַשַּׁבָּת וּבָאתִי לְבֵיתְךָ לְהַפִּיל תְּחִנָּתִי לְפָנֶיךָ, שֶׁתַּעֲבִיר אַנְחָתִי, וָאָעִיד אֲשֶׁר בָּרָאתָ בְשִׁשָּׁה יָמִים כָּל הַיְצוּר, וָאֶשְׁנֶה וַאֲשַׁלֵּשׁ עוֹד לְהָעִיד עַל כּוֹסִי בְּתוֹךְ שִׂמְחָתִי, כַּאֲשֶׁר צִוִּיתַנִי לְזָכְרוֹ וּלְהִתְעַנֵּג בְּיֶתֶר נִשְׁמָתִי אֲשֶׁר נָתַתָּ בִּי. בּוֹ אֶשְׁבֹּת כַּאֲשֶׁר צִוִּיתַנִי לְשָׁרְתֶךָ, וְכֵן אַגִּיד גְּדֻלָּתְךָ בְּרִנָּה, וְשִׁוִּיתִי יהוה לִקְרָאתִי שֶׁתְּרַחֲמֵנִי עוֹד בְּגָלוּתִי לְגָאֳלֵנִי לְעוֹרֵר לִבִּי לְאַהֲבָתֶךָ. וְאָז אֶשְׁמֹר פִּקּוּדֶיךָ וְחֻקֶּיךָ בְּלִי עֶצֶב, וְאֶתְפַּלֵּל כַּדָּת כָּרָאוּי וְכַנָּכוֹן. מַלְאֲכֵי הַשָּׁלוֹם, בּוֹאֲכֶם לְשָׁלוֹם, בָּרְכוּנִי לְשָׁלוֹם, וְאִמְרוּ בָּרוּךְ לְשֻׁלְחָנִי הֶעָרוּךְ, וְצֵאתְכֶם לְשָׁלוֹם מֵעַתָּה וְעַד עוֹלָם, אָמֵן סֶלָה.

אֵשֶׁת־חַיִל A woman of strength, who can find? *Prov. 31*
Her worth is far beyond pearls.
Her husband's heart trusts in her, and he has no lack of gain.
She brings him good, not harm, all the days of her life.
She seeks wool and linen, and works with willing hands.
She is like a ship laden with merchandise, bringing her food from afar.
She rises while it is still night, providing food for her household,
portions for her maids.
She considers a field and buys it; from her earnings she plants a vineyard.
She girds herself with strength, and braces her arms for her tasks.
She sees that her business goes well; her lamp does not go out at night.
She holds the distaff in her hand, and grasps the spindle with her palms.
She reaches out her palm to the poor, and extends her hand to the needy.
She has no fear for her family when it snows,
for all her household is clothed in crimson wool.
She makes elegant coverings; her clothing is fine linen and purple wool.
Her husband is well known in the gates,
where he sits with the elders of the land.
She makes linen garments and sells them, and supplies merchants with sashes.
She is clothed with strength and dignity; she can laugh at the days to come.
She opens her mouth with wisdom,
and the law of kindness is on her tongue.
She watches over the ways of her household,
and never eats the bread of idleness.
Her children rise and call her happy; her husband also praises her:
"Many women have excelled, but you surpass them all."
Charm is deceptive and beauty vain:
it is the God-fearing woman who deserves praise.
Give her the reward she has earned;
let her deeds bring her praise in the gates.

---

they do so as an aggregate of individuals. The holy collective of *Knesset Yisrael*, in the true sense of *Kelal Yisrael* – a concept that only the very lofty can possibly understand – never sinned all the days of her life. Throughout the millennia of her history, *Knesset Yisrael* has bestowed only goodness upon her Beloved.[31]

---

31. Rabbi Ya'akov Moshe Ḥarlap, *Mei Marom*, vol. 13 [on the Prayer Book] (Jerusalem: Beit Zevul, 1998), p. 171. Cf. Rabbi Y.M. Ḥarlap, *"Hitnagdut ve-Ḥasidut," 'Itturei Kohanim* 100 (Sivan 5753); reprinted in Rabbi Reuven Raz, *Harav Kuk bein Ḥasidim u-Mitnagdim* (Jerusalem: Mosad Harav Kook, 2016), p. 178.

משלי לא

אֵֽשֶׁת־חַֽיִל מִי יִמְצָא, וְרָחֹק מִפְּנִינִים מִכְרָהּ:
בָּֽטַח בָּהּ לֵב בַּעְלָהּ, וְשָׁלָל לֹא יֶחְסָר:
גְּמָלַֽתְהוּ טוֹב וְלֹא־רָע, כֹּל יְמֵי חַיֶּֽיהָ:
דָּֽרְשָׁה צֶֽמֶר וּפִשְׁתִּים, וַתַּֽעַשׂ בְּחֵֽפֶץ כַּפֶּֽיהָ:
הָיְתָה כָּאֳנִיּוֹת סוֹחֵר, מִמֶּרְחָק תָּבִיא לַחְמָהּ:
וַתָּֽקָם בְּעוֹד לַֽיְלָה, וַתִּתֵּן טֶֽרֶף לְבֵיתָהּ, וְחֹק לְנַעֲרֹתֶֽיהָ:
זָמְמָה שָׂדֶה וַתִּקָּחֵֽהוּ, מִפְּרִי כַפֶּֽיהָ נָֽטַע כָּֽרֶם:
חָגְרָה בְעוֹז מָתְנֶֽיהָ, וַתְּאַמֵּץ זְרוֹעֹתֶֽיהָ:
טָֽעֲמָה כִּי־טוֹב סַחְרָהּ, לֹא־יִכְבֶּה בַלַּֽיִל נֵרָהּ:
יָדֶֽיהָ שִׁלְּחָה בַכִּישׁוֹר, וְכַפֶּֽיהָ תָּֽמְכוּ פָֽלֶךְ:
כַּפָּהּ פָּֽרְשָׂה לֶעָנִי, וְיָדֶֽיהָ שִׁלְּחָה לָאֶבְיוֹן:
לֹא־תִירָא לְבֵיתָהּ מִשָּֽׁלֶג, כִּי כָל־בֵּיתָהּ לָבֻשׁ שָׁנִים:
מַרְבַדִּים עָֽשְׂתָה־לָּהּ, שֵׁשׁ וְאַרְגָּמָן לְבוּשָׁהּ:
נוֹדָע בַּשְּׁעָרִים בַּעְלָהּ, בְּשִׁבְתּוֹ עִם־זִקְנֵי־אָֽרֶץ:
סָדִין עָֽשְׂתָה וַתִּמְכֹּר, וַחֲגוֹר נָֽתְנָה לַכְּנַעֲנִי:
עֹז־וְהָדָר לְבוּשָׁהּ, וַתִּשְׂחַק לְיוֹם אַחֲרוֹן:
פִּֽיהָ פָּֽתְחָה בְחָכְמָה, וְתֽוֹרַת־חֶֽסֶד עַל־לְשׁוֹנָהּ:
צוֹפִיָּה הֲלִיכוֹת בֵּיתָהּ, וְלֶֽחֶם עַצְלוּת לֹא תֹאכֵל:
קָֽמוּ בָנֶֽיהָ וַֽיְאַשְּׁרֽוּהָ, בַּעְלָהּ וַיְהַֽלְלָהּ:
רַבּוֹת בָּנוֹת עָֽשׂוּ חָֽיִל, וְאַתְּ עָלִית עַל־כֻּלָּֽנָה:
שֶֽׁקֶר הַחֵן וְהֶֽבֶל הַיֹּֽפִי, אִשָּׁה יִרְאַת־יהוה הִיא תִתְהַלָּל:
תְּנוּ־לָהּ מִפְּרִי יָדֶֽיהָ, וִֽיהַלְלֽוּהָ בַשְּׁעָרִים מַעֲשֶֽׂיהָ:

---

אֵֽשֶׁת־חַֽיִל / A WOMAN OF STRENGTH *(Proverbs 31)*

גְּמָלַֽתְהוּ טוֹב וְלֹא־רָע, כֹּל יְמֵי חַיֶּֽיהָ *She brings him good, not harm, all the days of her life.* The *eshet ḥayil*, the "woman of strength," is *Knesset Yisrael* (*Ecclesia Israel*).[30] The sanctity of Israel as a collective entity was never impaired. All the sins, all the flaws are of individual Jews. Should even an entire community of Jews stray,

---

30. *Zohar* III, 42b.

*Some say:*

Prepare the feast of perfect faith, joy of the holy King.
Prepare the royal feast.

This is the feast [mystically known as] "the Field of Holy Apples" –
and "the Small Face" and "the Holy Ancient One"
[mystical terms for aspects of the Divine] come to partake in the feast with it.

With songs of praise I will cut away [evil forces],
to enter the holy gates of "the Field of Apples."
We now invite Her [the Divine Presence] with a newly prepared table
and a fine candelabrum spreading light upon our heads.
Between right and left is the bride, decked with jewelry, adorned and robed.
Her husband embraces her, and in the joy of their togetherness
[evil forces] are crushed.
Cries and suffering stop and cease; a new face comes upon spirits and souls.
She will have great and doubled joy; light will come, and bounteous blessing.
Come near, dear friends, and prepare delicacies of many kinds, and fish and fowl.
Renewing souls and spirits through the thirty-two [paths of wisdom]
and the three branches [of Scripture].
She [the Divine Presence] has seventy crowns, and above,
the King is crowned with all in the Holy of Holies.
Engraved and hidden with her are all worlds,
but the pestle of the Ancient of Days releases all that is hidden.
May it be His will that the Divine Presence rest on His people who,
for His name's sake, delight in sweet foods and honey.
To the south, I will arrange the candelabrum of hidden [wisdom],
to the north I will set the table with bread.
With wine in the cup, and myrtle clusters for bridegroom and bride,
the weak will be given strength.
Let us make them crowns of precious words, seventy crowns beyond the fifty.
May the Divine Presence be crowned with six loaves on each side, like
the two sets of six loaves [of showbread] and other articles [in the Temple].
[On the Sabbath] impure powers and afflicting angels cease and desist; and
those who are confined have respite.
To break bread the size of an olive or an egg, for there are two ways of
interpreting the *Yod* [of the divine name], restrictively or expansively.
It is like pure olive oil, pressed in a mill, flowing like rivers, whispering secrets.
Let us speak of mysteries, secrets unrevealed, hidden and concealed.
To crown the bride with mysteries above, at this,
the holy angels' wedding celebration.

*Some say:*

אַתְקִֽינוּ סְעוּדָתָא דִמְהֵימְנוּתָא שְׁלִימְתָא
חֶדְוָתָא דְמַלְכָּא קַדִּישָׁא.
אַתְקִֽינוּ סְעוּדָתָא דְמַלְכָּא.

דָּא הִיא סְעוּדָתָא דַּחֲקַל תַּפּוּחִין קַדִּישִׁין
וּזְעֵיר אַנְפִּין וְעַתִּיקָא קַדִּישָׁא אַתְיָן לְסַעֲדָה בַּהֲדַהּ.

אֲזַמֵּר בִּשְׁבָחִין / לְמֶעַל גּוֹ פִתְחִין / דִּבַחֲקַל תַּפּוּחִין / דְּאִנּוּן קַדִּישִׁין.
נְזַמֵּן לַהּ הַשְׁתָּא / בְּפָתוֹרָא חַדְתָּא / וּבִמְנָרְתָא טָבְתָא / דְּנָהֲרָה עַל רֵישִׁין.
יְמִינָא וּשְׂמָאלָא / וּבֵינַיְהוּ כַלָּה / בְּקִשּׁוּטִין אָזְלָא / וּמָנִין וּלְבוּשִׁין.
יְחַבֵּק לַהּ בַּעְלָהּ / וּבִיסוֹדָא דִי לַהּ / דְּעָבֵד נַיְחָא לַהּ / יְהֵא כָתֵשׁ כְּתִישִׁין.
צְוָחִין אוּף עָקְתִין / בְּטִילִין וּשְׁבִיתִין / בְּרַם אַנְפִּין חַדְתִּין / וְרוּחִין עִם נַפְשִׁין.
חֲדוּ סַגִּי יֵיתֵי / וְעַל חֲדָה תַרְתֵּי / נְהוֹרָא לַהּ יַמְטֵי / וּבִרְכָן דִּנְפִישִׁין.
קְרִֽיבוּ שׁוֹשְׁבִינִין / עֲבִֽידוּ תִקּוּנִין / לְאַפָּשָׁה זֵינִין / וְנוּנִין עִם רַחְשִׁין.
לְמֶעְבַּד נִשְׁמָתִין / וְרוּחִין חַדְתִּין / בְּתַרְתֵּי וּתְלָתִין / וּבִתְלָתָא שִׁבְשִׁין.
וְעִטְרִין שַׁבְעִין לַהּ / וּמַלְכָּא דִּלְעֵלָּא / דְּיִתְעַטַּר כֹּלָּא / בְּקַדִּישׁ קַדִּישִׁין.
רְשִׁימִין וּסְתִימִין / בְּגַוַּהּ כָּל עָלְמִין / בְּרַם עַתִּיק יוֹמִין / הֲלָא בָטֵשׁ בְּטִישִׁין.
יְהֵא רַעֲוָה קַמֵּהּ / דְּתִשְׁרֵי עַל עַמֵּהּ / דְּיִתְעַנַּג לִשְׁמֵהּ / בְּמִתְקִין וְדֻבְשִׁין.
אֲסַדֵּר לִדְרוֹמָא / מְנָרְתָא דִסְתִימָא / וְשֻׁלְחָן עִם נַהֲמָא / בִּצְפוֹנָא אַדְשִׁין.
בְּחַמְרָא גוֹ כָסָא / וּמַדָּנֵי אָסָא / לְאָרוּס וַאֲרוּסָה / לְאַתְקָפָא חַלָּשִׁין.
נְעַבֵּד לוֹן כִּתְרִין / בְּמִלִּין יַקִּירִין / בְּשַׁבְעִין עִטּוּרִין / דְּעַל גַּבֵּי חַמְשִׁין.
שְׁכִינְתָא תִתְעַטַּר / בְּשִׁית נַהֲמֵי לִסְטַר / בְּוָוִין תִּתְקַטַּר / וְזֵינִין דִּכְנִישִׁין.
(שְׁבִיתִין וּשְׁבִיקִין / מְסָאֲבִין דְּדָחֲקִין / חֲבִילִין דִּמְעִיקִין / וְכָל זֵינֵי חַרְשִׁין.)
לְמִבְצַע עַל רִיפְתָּא / כְּזֵיתָא וּכְבֵיעְתָא / תְּרֵין יוּדִין נָקְטָא / סְתִימִין וּפְרִישִׁין.
מְשַׁח זֵיתָא דָכְיָא / דְּטָחֲנִין רֵיחַיָּא / וְנָגְדִין נַחְלַיָּא / בְּגַוַּהּ בִּלְחִישִׁין.
הֲלָא נֵימָא רָזִין / וּמִלִּין דִּגְנִיזִין / דְּלֵיתֵיהוֹן מִתְחֲזִין / טְמִירִין וּכְבִישִׁין.
לְאַעְטָרָה כַלָּה / בְּרָזִין דִּלְעֵלָּא / בְּגוֹ הַאי הִלּוּלָה / דְּעִירִין קַדִּישִׁין.

# KIDDUSH FOR SHABBAT EVENING

*For Kiddush on Yom Tov see page 8[illegible], and on Rosh HaShana, see page 962.*

*Quietly:* And it was evening, and there was morning – Gen. 1
יוֹם הַשִּׁשִּׁי the sixth day.

Then the heavens and the earth were completed, Gen. 2
and all their array.
With the seventh day, God completed the work He had done.
He ceased on the seventh day from all the work He had done.
God blessed the seventh day and declared it holy,
because on it He ceased from all His work He had created to do.

*When saying Kiddush for others, add:*
Please pay attention, my masters.

Blessed are You, LORD our God, King of the Universe,
who creates the fruit of the vine.

Blessed are You, LORD our God, King of the Universe,
who has made us holy through His commandments,
who has favored us,
and in love and favor gave us His holy Sabbath as a heritage,
a remembrance of the work of creation.
It is the first among the holy days of assembly,
a remembrance of the exodus from Egypt.
For You chose us and sanctified us
from all the peoples,
and in love and favor gave us Your holy Sabbath as a heritage.
Blessed are You, LORD, who sanctifies the Sabbath.

*On Shabbat Ḥol HaMo'ed Sukkot, if Kiddush is made in the sukka, add:*
Blessed are You, LORD our God, King of the Universe,
who has made us holy through his commandments
and has commanded us to dwell in the sukka.

*It is customary for all present to drink of the wine.*

# קידוש לליל שבת

*For* קידוש *on* יום טוב *see page 821, and on* ראש השנה*, see page 963.*

*Quietly* וַיְהִי־עֶרֶב וַיְהִי־בֹקֶר בראשית א

יוֹם הַשִּׁשִּׁי:

וַיְכֻלּוּ הַשָּׁמַיִם וְהָאָרֶץ וְכָל־צְבָאָם: בראשית ב

וַיְכַל אֱלֹהִים בַּיּוֹם הַשְּׁבִיעִי מְלַאכְתּוֹ אֲשֶׁר עָשָׂה

וַיִּשְׁבֹּת בַּיּוֹם הַשְּׁבִיעִי מִכָּל־מְלַאכְתּוֹ אֲשֶׁר עָשָׂה:

וַיְבָרֶךְ אֱלֹהִים אֶת־יוֹם הַשְּׁבִיעִי, וַיְקַדֵּשׁ אֹתוֹ

כִּי בוֹ שָׁבַת מִכָּל־מְלַאכְתּוֹ, אֲשֶׁר־בָּרָא אֱלֹהִים, לַעֲשׂוֹת:

*When saying* קידוש *for others, add:*

סַבְרִי מָרָנָן

בָּרוּךְ אַתָּה יהוה אֱלֹהֵינוּ מֶלֶךְ הָעוֹלָם, בּוֹרֵא פְּרִי הַגָּפֶן.

בָּרוּךְ אַתָּה יהוה אֱלֹהֵינוּ מֶלֶךְ הָעוֹלָם

אֲשֶׁר קִדְּשָׁנוּ בְּמִצְוֹתָיו, וְרָצָה בָנוּ

וְשַׁבַּת קָדְשׁוֹ בְּאַהֲבָה וּבְרָצוֹן הִנְחִילָנוּ

זִכָּרוֹן לְמַעֲשֵׂה בְרֵאשִׁית

כִּי הוּא יוֹם תְּחִלָּה לְמִקְרָאֵי קֹדֶשׁ, זֵכֶר לִיצִיאַת מִצְרָיִם

כִּי בָנוּ בָחַרְתָּ וְאוֹתָנוּ קִדַּשְׁתָּ מִכָּל הָעַמִּים

וְשַׁבַּת קָדְשְׁךָ בְּאַהֲבָה וּבְרָצוֹן הִנְחַלְתָּנוּ.

בָּרוּךְ אַתָּה יהוה, מְקַדֵּשׁ הַשַּׁבָּת.

*On* שבת חול המועד סוכות*, if* קידוש *is made in the* סוכה*, add:*

בָּרוּךְ אַתָּה יהוה אֱלֹהֵינוּ מֶלֶךְ הָעוֹלָם

אֲשֶׁר קִדְּשָׁנוּ בְּמִצְוֹתָיו, וְצִוָּנוּ לֵישֵׁב בַּסֻּכָּה.

*It is customary for all present to drink of the wine.*

# ZEMIROT FOR SHABBAT EVENING

כָּל מְקַדֵּשׁ All who fittingly sanctify the seventh day,
All who protect the Sabbath properly from desecration,
Will have great reward in accord with their deed.
"Each in his own camp, each under his own banner." *Num. 1*

Lovers of the LORD, who await the building of the Temple,
Be glad and joyful on the Sabbath as if receiving the gift of God's inheritance,
Raise your hands in holiness and say to God:
"Blessed is the LORD who has given rest to His people Israel." *1 Kings 8*

Seekers of the LORD, offspring of His beloved Abraham,
Who are slow to leave the Sabbath but hasten to enter it,
Who rejoice to keep it and make its Eiruv –
"This is the day the LORD has made, let us rejoice and be glad in it." *Ps. 118*

Remember Moses' Torah, from which the laws of Sabbath are learned,
Engraved is the seventh day like a bedecked bride between her companions,
The pure inherit it and sanctify it with the words: "All that He had made."
"With the seventh day God completed the work He had done." *Gen. 2*

It is a sacred day from beginning to end,
All Jacob's offspring will honor it as the King's word and decree,
Resting on it and rejoicing with delights of food and drink.
"All the congregation of Israel will observe it." *Ex. 12*

Extend Your loving-kindness to those who know You, zealous and retributive God,
Those who keep the seventh day, fulfilling "Remember" and "Observe,"
Grant them the joy of Jerusalem rebuilt, make them shine with the light of Your face.
"Fill them with the rich plenty of Your House, give them drink from Your river of delights." *Ps. 36*

Help those who, on the seventh day, rest from plow and harvest,
Who walk slowly, and eat three meals to bless You.
May their righteousness shine like the light of the seven days,
LORD God of Israel, grant completion. *1 Sam. 14*

# זמירות לליל שבת

כָּל מְקַדֵּשׁ שְׁבִיעִי כָּרָאוּי לוֹ
כָּל שׁוֹמֵר שַׁבָּת כַּדָּת, מֵחַלְּלוֹ
שְׂכָרוֹ הַרְבֵּה מְאֹד עַל פִּי פָעֳלוֹ
אִישׁ עַל־מַחֲנֵהוּ וְאִישׁ עַל־דִּגְלוֹ: במדבר א

אוֹהֲבֵי יהוה הַמְחַכִּים לְבִנְיַן אֲרִיאֵל
בְּיוֹם הַשַּׁבָּת שִׂישׂוּ וְשִׂמְחוּ כִּמְקַבְּלֵי מַתַּן נַחֲלִיאֵל
גַּם שְׂאוּ יְדֵיכֶם קֹדֶשׁ וְאִמְרוּ לָאֵל
בָּרוּךְ יהוה אֲשֶׁר נָתַן מְנוּחָה לְעַמּוֹ יִשְׂרָאֵל: מלכים א, ח

דּוֹרְשֵׁי יהוה זֶרַע אַבְרָהָם אוֹהֲבוֹ
הַמְאַחֲרִים לָצֵאת מִן הַשַּׁבָּת וּמְמַהֲרִים לָבוֹא
וּשְׂמֵחִים לְשָׁמְרוֹ וּלְעָרֵב עֵרוּבוֹ
זֶה־הַיּוֹם עָשָׂה יהוה, נָגִילָה וְנִשְׂמְחָה בוֹ: תהלים קיח

זִכְרוּ תּוֹרַת מֹשֶׁה בְּמִצְוַת שַׁבָּת גְּרוּסָה
חֲרוּתָה לַיּוֹם הַשְּׁבִיעִי, כְּכַלָּה בֵּין רֵעוֹתֶיהָ מְשֻׁבָּצָה
טְהוֹרִים יִירָשׁוּהָ, וִיקַדְּשׁוּהָ בְּמַאֲמַר כָּל אֲשֶׁר עָשָׂה
וַיְכַל אֱלֹהִים בַּיּוֹם הַשְּׁבִיעִי מְלַאכְתּוֹ אֲשֶׁר עָשָׂה: בראשית ב

יוֹם קָדוֹשׁ הוּא, מִבּוֹאוֹ וְעַד צֵאתוֹ
כָּל זֶרַע יַעֲקֹב יְכַבְּדוּהוּ, כִּדְבַר הַמֶּלֶךְ וְדָתוֹ
לָנוּחַ בּוֹ וְלִשְׂמֹחַ בְּתַעֲנוּג אָכוֹל וְשָׁתֹה
כָּל־עֲדַת יִשְׂרָאֵל יַעֲשׂוּ אֹתוֹ: שמות יב

מְשֹׁךְ חַסְדְּךָ לְיוֹדְעֶיךָ, אֵל קַנּוֹא וְנוֹקֵם
נוֹטְרֵי יוֹם הַשְּׁבִיעִי זָכוֹר וְשָׁמוֹר לְהָקֵם
שַׂמְּחֵם בְּבִנְיַן שָׁלֵם, בְּאוֹר פָּנֶיךָ תַּבְהִיקֵם
יִרְוְיֻן מִדֶּשֶׁן בֵּיתֶךָ, וְנַחַל עֲדָנֶיךָ תַשְׁקֵם: תהלים לו

עֲזֹר לַשּׁוֹבְתִים בַּשְּׁבִיעִי, בֶּחָרִישׁ וּבַקָּצִיר עוֹלָמִים
פּוֹסְעִים בּוֹ פְּסִיעָה קְטַנָּה, סוֹעֲדִים בּוֹ, לְבָרֵךְ שָׁלֹשׁ פְּעָמִים
צִדְקָתָם תַּצְהִיר כְּאוֹר שִׁבְעַת הַיָּמִים
יהוה אֱלֹהֵי יִשְׂרָאֵל, הָבָה תָמִים: שמואל א, יד

מְנוּחָה וְשִׂמְחָה Rest and joy, light for all Jews,
Is the Sabbath day, day of delights;
Those who keep and recall it bear witness
That in six days all creation was made.

The highest heavens, land and seas,
The hosts of heaven, high and sublime;
Sea monsters, humans and all wild beasts,
Were created by God, the LORD, who formed all worlds.

It was He who spoke to His treasured people:
"Keep it to make it holy from beginning to end."
The holy Sabbath is His day of delight,
For on it God rested from all His work.

Through the Sabbath commandment
God will give you strength,
Rise, pray to Him, and He will invigorate you.
Recite the Nishmat prayer, and the Kedusha,
Then eat with joy, for He is pleased with you.

With twin loaves, and wine for the Kiddush,
With many delicacies and a willing spirit;
Those who delight in it shall merit great reward:
The coming of the redeemer, and life in the World to Come.

מְנוּחָה וְשִׂמְחָה אוֹר לַיְּהוּדִים
יוֹם שַׁבָּתוֹן, יוֹם מַחֲמַדִּים
שׁוֹמְרָיו וְזוֹכְרָיו הֵמָּה מְעִידִים
כִּי לְשִׁשָּׁה כֹּל בְּרוּאִים וְעוֹמְדִים.

שְׁמֵי שָׁמַיִם, אֶרֶץ וְיַמִּים
כָּל צְבָא מָרוֹם גְּבוֹהִים וְרָמִים
תַּנִּין וְאָדָם וְחַיַּת רְאֵמִים
כִּי בְּיָהּ יהוה צוּר עוֹלָמִים.

הוּא אֲשֶׁר דִּבֶּר לְעַם סְגֻלָּתוֹ
שָׁמוֹר לְקַדְּשׁוֹ מִבּוֹאוֹ עַד צֵאתוֹ
שַׁבַּת קֹדֶשׁ יוֹם חֶמְדָּתוֹ
כִּי בוֹ שָׁבַת אֵל מִכָּל מְלַאכְתּוֹ.

בְּמִצְוַת שַׁבָּת אֵל יַחֲלִיצָךְ
קוּם קְרָא אֵלָיו, יָחִישׁ לְאַמְּצָךְ
נִשְׁמַת כָּל חַי וְגַם נַעֲרִיצָךְ
אֱכֹל בְּשִׂמְחָה כִּי כְבָר רָצָךְ.

בְּמִשְׁנֶה לֶחֶם וְקִדּוּשׁ רַבָּה
בְּרֹב מַטְעַמִּים וְרוּחַ נְדִיבָה
יִזְכּוּ לְרַב טוּב הַמִּתְעַנְּגִים בָּהּ
בְּבִיאַת גּוֹאֵל לְחַיֵּי הָעוֹלָם הַבָּא.

מַה־יְּדִידוּת How beloved is your rest, Sabbath Queen,
We run to greet you: Come, royal bride,
Dressed in fine robes. We light the light with blessing.
All labors end [as is said:] "You shall do no work."
To savor the delights of fowl, quail and fish.

In advance all kinds of tasty food have been prepared,
Fattened chickens made ready while it was still day.
Varied dishes set out, and fragrant wines to drink,
And special delicacies all three times.
To savor the delights of fowl, quail and fish.

They shall inherit Jacob's heritage, a heritage unbounded,
Rich and poor will honor [the Sabbath] and be worthy of redemption,
If you keep the Sabbath day you will be My special treasure,
Six days shall you labor – and on the seventh let us rejoice.
To savor the delights of fowl, quail and fish.

Your secular concerns are forbidden; so too are calculations.
Reflections are permitted, and arranging matches for girls,
And teaching a child a book, and singing songs of praise,
And meditating on fine words at every place and gathering.
To savor the delights of fowl, quail and fish.

Your walk shall be unhurried; you shall call the Sabbath a delight.
Sleep too is praiseworthy, for it refreshes the spirit.
Therefore my soul yearns for you, to rest in you in love,
As if within a fence of roses: on it son and daughter rest.
To savor the delights of fowl, quail and fish.

A foretaste of the World to Come is the day of Sabbath rest.
All who take delight in it will be worthy of great joy.
They will be delivered with relief from the birthpangs of the Messiah,
May our redemption spring forth, and sadness and sighing flee away.
To savor the delights of fowl, quail and fish.

מַה־יְּדִידוּת מְנוּחָתֵךְ, אַתְּ שַׁבָּת הַמַּלְכָּה
בְּכֵן נָרוּץ לִקְרָאתֵךְ, בּוֹאִי כַלָּה נְסוּכָה
לְבוּשׁ בִּגְדֵי חֲמוּדוֹת, לְהַדְלִיק נֵר בִּבְרָכָה
וַתֵּכֶל כָּל הָעֲבוֹדוֹת, לֹא תַעֲשׂוּ מְלָאכָה.
לְהִתְעַנֵּג בְּתַעֲנוּגִים בַּרְבּוּרִים וּשְׂלָו וְדָגִים.

מֵעֶרֶב מַזְמִינִים כָּל מִינֵי מַטְעַמִּים
מִבְּעוֹד יוֹם מוּכָנִים תַּרְנְגוֹלִים מְפֻטָּמִים
וְלַעֲרֹךְ כַּמָּה מִינִים, שְׁתוֹת יֵינוֹת מְבֻשָּׂמִים
וְתַפְנוּקֵי מַעֲדַנִּים בְּכָל שָׁלֹשׁ פְּעָמִים.
לְהִתְעַנֵּג בְּתַעֲנוּגִים בַּרְבּוּרִים וּשְׂלָו וְדָגִים.

נַחֲלַת יַעֲקֹב יִירָשׁ, בְּלִי מְצָרִים נַחֲלָה
וִיכַבְּדוּהוּ עָשִׁיר וָרָשׁ, וְתִזְכּוּ לִגְאֻלָּה
יוֹם שַׁבָּת אִם תְּכַבֵּדוּ וִהְיִיתֶם לִי סְגֻלָּה
שֵׁשֶׁת יָמִים תַּעֲבֹדוּ וּבַשְּׁבִיעִי נָגִילָה.
לְהִתְעַנֵּג בְּתַעֲנוּגִים בַּרְבּוּרִים וּשְׂלָו וְדָגִים.

חֲפָצֶיךָ אֲסוּרִים וְגַם לַחֲשֹׁב חֶשְׁבּוֹנוֹת
הִרְהוּרִים מֻתָּרִים וּלְשַׁדֵּךְ הַבָּנוֹת
וְתִינוֹק לְלַמְּדוֹ סֵפֶר, לַמְנַצֵּחַ בִּנְגִינוֹת
וְלַהֲגוֹת בְּאִמְרֵי שֶׁפֶר בְּכָל פִּנּוֹת וּמַחֲנוֹת.
לְהִתְעַנֵּג בְּתַעֲנוּגִים בַּרְבּוּרִים וּשְׂלָו וְדָגִים.

הִלּוּכָךְ יְהֵא בְנַחַת, עֹנֶג קְרָא לַשַּׁבָּת
וְהַשֵּׁנָה מְשֻׁבַּחַת כַּדָּת נֶפֶשׁ מְשִׁיבַת
בְּכֵן נַפְשִׁי לְךָ עָרְגָה וְלָנוּחַ בְּחִבַּת
כְּשׁוֹשַׁנִּים סוּגָה, בּוֹ יָנוּחוּ בֵּן וּבַת.
לְהִתְעַנֵּג בְּתַעֲנוּגִים בַּרְבּוּרִים וּשְׂלָו וְדָגִים.

מֵעֵין עוֹלָם הַבָּא יוֹם שַׁבָּת מְנוּחָה
כָּל הַמִּתְעַנְּגִים בָּהּ יִזְכּוּ לְרֹב שִׂמְחָה
מֵחֶבְלֵי מָשִׁיחַ יֻצָּלוּ לִרְוָחָה
פְּדוּתֵנוּ תַצְמִיחַ, וְנָס יָגוֹן וַאֲנָחָה.
לְהִתְעַנֵּג בְּתַעֲנוּגִים בַּרְבּוּרִים וּשְׂלָו וְדָגִים.

יוֹם זֶה לְיִשְׂרָאֵל This day for Israel is light and joy,
a Sabbath of serenity.
At the assembly at Sinai You decreed the laws,
Sabbath and the festivals – to keep them all my years;
Setting a table before me with courses of fine food –
A Sabbath of serenity.

This day, for Israel, is light and joy, a Sabbath of serenity.

Heart's delight to a shattered people,
To suffering spirits, an extra soul.
From troubled hearts may it banish sighs –
A Sabbath of serenity.

This day, for Israel, is light and joy, a Sabbath of serenity.

You sanctified and blessed it above all other days.
In six days You finished the making of all worlds.
On it sad souls find quiet and safety –
A Sabbath of serenity.

This day, for Israel, is light and joy, a Sabbath of serenity.

All work is forbidden by the revered One's commandment,
I will merit royal glory if I keep the Sabbath day,
Bringing the awesome One a sweetly scented gift –
A Sabbath of serenity.

This day, for Israel, is light and joy, a Sabbath of serenity.

Renew our Sanctuary, remember the ruined city.
Bestow Your goodness, Savior, on one who is sad,
Yet still she spends the Sabbath in song and praise –
A Sabbath of serenity.

This day, for Israel, is light and joy, a Sabbath of serenity.

יוֹם זֶה לְיִשְׂרָאֵל אוֹרָה וְשִׂמְחָה, שַׁבַּת מְנוּחָה.
צִוִּיתָ פִּקּוּדִים בְּמַעֲמַד סִינַי
שַׁבָּת וּמוֹעֲדִים לִשְׁמֹר בְּכָל שָׁנַי
לַעֲרֹךְ לְפָנַי מַשְׂאֵת וַאֲרוּחָה שַׁבַּת מְנוּחָה.
יוֹם זֶה לְיִשְׂרָאֵל אוֹרָה וְשִׂמְחָה, שַׁבַּת מְנוּחָה.

חֶמְדַּת הַלְּבָבוֹת לְאֻמָּה שְׁבוּרָה
לִנְפָשׁוֹת נִכְאָבוֹת נְשָׁמָה יְתֵרָה
לְנֶפֶשׁ מְצֵרָה יָסִיר אֲנָחָה שַׁבַּת מְנוּחָה.
יוֹם זֶה לְיִשְׂרָאֵל אוֹרָה וְשִׂמְחָה, שַׁבַּת מְנוּחָה.

קִדַּשְׁתָּ בֵּרַכְתָּ אוֹתוֹ מִכָּל יָמִים
בְּשֵׁשֶׁת כִּלִּיתָ מְלֶאכֶת עוֹלָמִים
בּוֹ מָצְאוּ עֲגוּמִים הַשְׁקֵט וּבִטְחָה שַׁבַּת מְנוּחָה.
יוֹם זֶה לְיִשְׂרָאֵל אוֹרָה וְשִׂמְחָה, שַׁבַּת מְנוּחָה.

לְאִסּוּר מְלָאכָה צִוִּיתָנוּ נוֹרָא
אֶזְכֶּה הוֹד מְלוּכָה אִם שַׁבָּת אֶשְׁמְרָה
אַקְרִיב שַׁי לַמּוֹרָא, מִנְחָה מֶרְקָחָה שַׁבַּת מְנוּחָה.
יוֹם זֶה לְיִשְׂרָאֵל אוֹרָה וְשִׂמְחָה, שַׁבַּת מְנוּחָה.

חַדֵּשׁ מִקְדָּשֵׁנוּ, זָכְרָה נֶחֱרֶבֶת
טוּבְךָ, מוֹשִׁיעֵנוּ, תְּנָה לַנֶּעֱצֶבֶת
בְּשַׁבָּת יוֹשֶׁבֶת בְּזֶמֶר וּשְׁבָחָה שַׁבַּת מְנוּחָה.
יוֹם זֶה לְיִשְׂרָאֵל אוֹרָה וְשִׂמְחָה, שַׁבַּת מְנוּחָה.

יָהּ רִבּוֹן Master of all worlds, our God, adored,
King of kings, over all the Lord:
Your wondrous deeds to applaud
We sing to You with one accord.

God of all worlds, our God, adored;
King of kings, over all, the Lord.

Early and late my praise shall ring,
To You, holy Author of every thing:
Beasts of the field, birds that take wing.
Angels and mortals to You shall sing.

God of all worlds, our God, adored;
King of kings, over all, the Lord.

Your great good deeds are vast in scale,
You humble the proud, You lift the frail.
A thousand years would not avail
Of Your works to tell the tale.

God of all worlds, our God, adored;
King of kings, over all, the Lord.

Yours is the glory, the greatness too,
From the lion's jaw, Your flock rescue.
Bring Your exiles home to You:
The people You chose, deliver anew.

God of all worlds, our God, adored;
King of kings, over all, the Lord.

Come back to Your Temple, Your sacred shrine,
That there in joy our souls may entwine.
In song our voices to combine,
When Jerusalem's beauty again will shine.

God of all worlds, our God, adored;
King of kings, over all, the Lord.

יָהּ רִבּוֹן עָלַם וְעָלְמַיָּא
אַנְתְּ הוּא מַלְכָּא מֶלֶךְ מַלְכַיָּא
עוֹבַד גְּבוּרְתָךְ וְתִמְהַיָּא
שְׁפַר קֳדָמָךְ לְהַחֲוָיָא.
יָהּ רִבּוֹן עָלַם וְעָלְמַיָּא, אַנְתְּ הוּא מַלְכָּא מֶלֶךְ מַלְכַיָּא.

שְׁבָחִין אֲסַדֵּר צַפְרָא וְרַמְשָׁא
לָךְ אֱלָהָא קַדִּישָׁא דִּי בְרָא כָּל נַפְשָׁא
עִירִין קַדִּישִׁין וּבְנֵי אֱנָשָׁא
חֵיוַת בָּרָא וְעוֹפֵי שְׁמַיָּא.
יָהּ רִבּוֹן עָלַם וְעָלְמַיָּא, אַנְתְּ הוּא מַלְכָּא מֶלֶךְ מַלְכַיָּא.

רַבְרְבִין עוֹבְדָיךְ וְתַקִּיפִין
מָכֵךְ רָמַיָּא וְזָקֵף כְּפִיפִין
לוּ יְחֵי גְבַר שְׁנִין אַלְפִין
לָא יֵעוֹל גְּבוּרְתָּךְ בְּחֻשְׁבְּנַיָּא.
יָהּ רִבּוֹן עָלַם וְעָלְמַיָּא, אַנְתְּ הוּא מַלְכָּא מֶלֶךְ מַלְכַיָּא.

אֱלָהָא דִּי לֵהּ יְקָר וּרְבוּתָא
פְּרֹק יָת עָנָךְ מִפֻּם אַרְיָוָתָא
וְאַפֵּק יָת עַמָּךְ מִגּוֹ גָלוּתָא
עַמָּא דִּי בְחַרְתְּ מִכָּל אֻמַּיָּא.
יָהּ רִבּוֹן עָלַם וְעָלְמַיָּא, אַנְתְּ הוּא מַלְכָּא מֶלֶךְ מַלְכַיָּא.

לְמַקְדְּשָׁךְ תּוּב וּלְקֹדֶשׁ קֻדְשִׁין
אֲתַר דִּי בֵהּ יֶחֱדוּן רוּחִין וְנַפְשִׁין
וִיזַמְּרוּן לָךְ שִׁירִין וְרַחֲשִׁין
בִּירוּשְׁלֵם קַרְתָּא דְשֻׁפְרַיָּא.
יָהּ רִבּוֹן עָלַם וְעָלְמַיָּא, אַנְתְּ הוּא מַלְכָּא מֶלֶךְ מַלְכַיָּא.

צָמְאָה נַפְשִׁי My soul thirsts for God, the living God *Ps. 42*
My heart and flesh will sing joyfully to the living God. *Ps. 84*
The One God created me, and said "As I live,
No one shall see Me and live."
My soul thirsts for God, the living God
My heart and flesh will sing joyfully to the living God.

He created all with wisdom, design and deliberation,
Deeply hidden though it is from the eyes of all that live.
His glory is high above all, every mouth makes known His splendor,
Blessed is He in whose hands is the life-force of all that lives.
My soul thirsts for God, the living God
My heart and flesh will sing joyfully to the living God.

He set apart the quiet one's offspring, to teach them decrees,
Which if one performs them, thereby he shall live.
Who can vindicate himself? We are like specks of dust,
Truly none can vindicate itself before You, nothing that lives.
My soul thirsts for God, the living God
My heart and flesh will sing joyfully to the living God.

In the heart, the inclination is like a viper's poison,
How then can we return, and be like flesh that lives?
Those who have gone astray, if they wished, could turn from their way,
Before they go to their rest in the place destined for all that lives.
My soul thirsts for God, the living God
My heart and flesh will sing joyfully to the living God.

For everything, I shall thank You, every mouth shall declare Your Oneness,
You who open Your hand and satisfy all that lives.
Recall the love of ancient times, and revive those who slumber,
Bring near the days when the Messiah shall live.
My soul thirsts for God, the living God
My heart and flesh will sing joyfully to the living God.

See who is the true mistress, when the handmaid says,
"No, your son is dead while my son lives."
I will bow face down and spread my hands toward you,
When I open my mouth to say: "The soul of all that lives."
My soul thirsts for God, the living God
My heart and flesh will sing joyfully to the living God.

צָמְאָה נַפְשִׁי לֵאלֹהִים לָאֵל חָי: לִבִּי וּבְשָׂרִי יְרַנְּנוּ אֶל אֵל־חָי: תהלים מב תהלים פד
אֵל אֶחָד בְּרָאַנִי, וְאָמַר חַי אָנִי כִּי לֹא יִרְאַנִי הָאָדָם וָחָי.
צָמְאָה נַפְשִׁי לֵאלֹהִים לָאֵל חָי, לִבִּי וּבְשָׂרִי יְרַנְּנוּ אֶל אֵל־חָי.

בָּרָא כֹל בְּחָכְמָה, בְּעֵצָה וּבִמְזִמָּה מְאֹד נֶעֶלָמָה מֵעֵינֵי כָּל חָי.
רָם עַל כֹּל כְּבוֹדוֹ, כָּל פֶּה יְחַוֶּה הוֹדוֹ בָּרוּךְ אֲשֶׁר בְּיָדוֹ נֶפֶשׁ כָּל חָי.
צָמְאָה נַפְשִׁי לֵאלֹהִים לָאֵל חָי, לִבִּי וּבְשָׂרִי יְרַנְּנוּ אֶל אֵל־חָי.

הִבְדִּיל נִינֵי תָם, חֻקִּים לְהוֹרוֹתָם אֲשֶׁר יַעֲשֶׂה אוֹתָם הָאָדָם וָחָי.
מִי זֶה יִצְטַדָּק, נִמְשַׁל לְאָבָק דָּק אֱמֶת, כִּי לֹא יִצְדַּק לְפָנֶיךָ כָּל חָי.
צָמְאָה נַפְשִׁי לֵאלֹהִים לָאֵל חָי, לִבִּי וּבְשָׂרִי יְרַנְּנוּ אֶל אֵל־חָי.

בְּלֵב יֵצֶר חָשׁוּב כִּדְמוּת חֲמַת עַכְשׁוּב וְאֵיכָכָה יָשׁוּב הַבָּשָׂר הֶחָי.
נְסוֹגִים אִם אָבוּ, וּמִדַּרְכָּם שָׁבוּ טֶרֶם יִשְׁכָּבוּ בֵּית מוֹעֵד לְכָל חָי.
צָמְאָה נַפְשִׁי לֵאלֹהִים לָאֵל חָי, לִבִּי וּבְשָׂרִי יְרַנְּנוּ אֶל אֵל־חָי.

עַל כֹּל אֲהוֹדֶךָ, כָּל פֶּה תְּיַחֲדֶךָ פּוֹתֵחַ אֶת יָדֶךָ וּמַשְׂבִּיעַ לְכָל חָי.
זְכֹר אַהֲבַת קְדוּמִים, וְהַחֲיֵה נִרְדָּמִים וְקָרֵב הַיָּמִים אֲשֶׁר בֶּן יִשַׁי חָי.
צָמְאָה נַפְשִׁי לֵאלֹהִים לָאֵל חָי, לִבִּי וּבְשָׂרִי יְרַנְּנוּ אֶל אֵל־חָי.

רְאֵה לִגְבֶרֶת אֱמֶת, שִׁפְחָה נוֹאֱמֶת לֹא כִי, בְּנֵךְ הַמֵּת וּבְנִי הֶחָי.
אֶקֹּד עַל אַפִּי, וְאֶפְרֹשׁ לְךָ כַּפִּי עֵת אֶפְתַּח פִּי בְּנִשְׁמַת כָּל חָי.
צָמְאָה נַפְשִׁי לֵאלֹהִים לָאֵל חָי, לִבִּי וּבְשָׂרִי יְרַנְּנוּ אֶל אֵל־חָי.

צוּר מִשֶּׁלּוֹ The Rock from whom we have eaten:
Bless Him, my faithful friends;
we have sufficed, we have left over,
just as the LORD said.

He feeds His world – our Shepherd, our Father,
we have eaten of His bread, His wine we have drunk.
So let us thank His name, let us praise Him with our mouths,
saying, singing: None is holy like the LORD.

The Rock from whom we have eaten: Bless Him, my faithful friends;
we have sufficed, we have left over, just as the LORD said.

With song and sound of thanks, we shall bless our God,
for the gift He gave our fathers: A lovely land.
With food and sustenance He has satisfied our souls.
His kindness overwhelms us: True is the LORD.

The Rock from whom we have eaten: Bless Him, my faithful friends;
we have sufficed, we have left over, just as the LORD said.

Have compassion in Your love for Your people, our Rock,
for Zion, Your home of glory, Temple of our splendor.
The son of David Your servant: may he come and redeem us,
breath of our life, anointed of the LORD.

The Rock from whom we have eaten: Bless Him, my faithful friends;
we have sufficed, we have left over, just as the LORD said.

May the Temple be rebuilt, Zion's city full again;
there we will sing a new song as we go up in joy,
to the Compassionate, the Holy One –
may He be blessed and raised on high –
with a full cup of wine, sign of the blessing of the LORD.

The Rock from whom we have eaten: Bless Him, my faithful friends;
we have sufficed, we have left over, just as the LORD said.

צוּר מִשֶּׁלּוֹ אָכַלְנוּ בָּרְכוּ אֱמוּנַי
שָׂבַעְנוּ וְהוֹתַרְנוּ כִּדְבַר יהוה.

הַזָּן אֶת עוֹלָמוֹ רוֹעֵנוּ אָבִינוּ
אָכַלְנוּ אֶת לַחְמוֹ וְיֵינוֹ שָׁתִינוּ
עַל כֵּן נוֹדֶה לִשְׁמוֹ וּנְהַלְּלוֹ בְּפִינוּ
אָמַרְנוּ וְעָנִינוּ אֵין קָדוֹשׁ כַּיהוה.

צוּר מִשֶּׁלּוֹ אָכַלְנוּ, בָּרְכוּ אֱמוּנַי, שָׂבַעְנוּ וְהוֹתַרְנוּ כִּדְבַר יהוה.

בְּשִׁיר וְקוֹל תּוֹדָה נְבָרֵךְ אֱלֹהֵינוּ
עַל אֶרֶץ חֶמְדָּה שֶׁהִנְחִיל לַאֲבוֹתֵינוּ
מָזוֹן וְצֵידָה הִשְׂבִּיעַ לְנַפְשֵׁנוּ
חַסְדּוֹ גָּבַר עָלֵינוּ וֶאֱמֶת יהוה.

צוּר מִשֶּׁלּוֹ אָכַלְנוּ, בָּרְכוּ אֱמוּנַי, שָׂבַעְנוּ וְהוֹתַרְנוּ כִּדְבַר יהוה.

רַחֵם בְּחַסְדֶּךָ עַל עַמְּךָ צוּרֵנוּ
עַל צִיּוֹן מִשְׁכַּן כְּבוֹדֶךָ זְבוּל בֵּית תִּפְאַרְתֵּנוּ
בֶּן דָּוִד עַבְדֶּךָ יָבוֹא וְיִגְאָלֵנוּ
רוּחַ אַפֵּינוּ מְשִׁיחַ יהוה.

צוּר מִשֶּׁלּוֹ אָכַלְנוּ, בָּרְכוּ אֱמוּנַי, שָׂבַעְנוּ וְהוֹתַרְנוּ כִּדְבַר יהוה.

יִבָּנֶה הַמִּקְדָּשׁ עִיר צִיּוֹן תְּמַלֵּא
וְשָׁם נָשִׁיר שִׁיר חָדָשׁ וּבִרְנָנָה נַעֲלֶה
הָרַחֲמָן הַנִּקְדָּשׁ יִתְבָּרַךְ וְיִתְעַלֶּה
עַל כּוֹס יַיִן מָלֵא כְּבִרְכַּת יהוה.

צוּר מִשֶּׁלּוֹ אָכַלְנוּ, בָּרְכוּ אֱמוּנַי, שָׂבַעְנוּ וְהוֹתַרְנוּ כִּדְבַר יהוה.

# Shaḥarit for Shabbat and Yom Tov

*Begin as on weekdays, from pages 4–98.*

## A PSALM BEFORE VERSES OF PRAISE

מִזְמוֹר שִׁיר A psalm of David. *Ps. 30*
A song for the dedication of the House.
I will exalt You, LORD, for You have lifted me up,
and not let my enemies rejoice over me.
LORD, my God, I cried to You for help and You healed me.
LORD, You lifted my soul from the grave;
You spared me from going down to the pit.
Sing to the LORD, you His devoted ones,
and give thanks to His holy name.
For His anger is for a moment,
but His favor for a lifetime.
At night there may be weeping,
but in the morning there is joy.
When I felt secure, I said, "I shall never be shaken."
LORD, when You favored me,
You made me stand firm as a mountain,
but when You hid Your face, I was terrified.
To You, LORD, I called; I pleaded with my LORD:
"What gain would there be if I died and went down to the grave?
Can dust thank You? Can it declare Your truth?
Hear, LORD, and be gracious to me; LORD, be my help."
You have turned my sorrow into dancing.
▸ You have removed my sackcloth and clothed me with joy,
so that my soul may sing to You and not be silent.
LORD my God, for ever will I thank You.

# שחרית לשבת וליום טוב

*Begin as on weekdays, from pages 5–99.*

## מזמור לפני פסוקי דזמרה

תהלים ל

מִזְמוֹר שִׁיר־חֲנֻכַּת הַבַּיִת לְדָוִד:
אֲרוֹמִמְךָ יהוה כִּי דִלִּיתָנִי, וְלֹא־שִׂמַּחְתָּ אֹיְבַי לִי:
יהוה אֱלֹהָי, שִׁוַּעְתִּי אֵלֶיךָ וַתִּרְפָּאֵנִי:
יהוה, הֶעֱלִיתָ מִן־שְׁאוֹל נַפְשִׁי, חִיִּיתַנִי מִיָּרְדִי־בוֹר:
זַמְּרוּ לַיהוה חֲסִידָיו, וְהוֹדוּ לְזֵכֶר קָדְשׁוֹ:
כִּי רֶגַע בְּאַפּוֹ, חַיִּים בִּרְצוֹנוֹ
בָּעֶרֶב יָלִין בֶּכִי וְלַבֹּקֶר רִנָּה:
וַאֲנִי אָמַרְתִּי בְשַׁלְוִי, בַּל־אֶמּוֹט לְעוֹלָם:
יהוה, בִּרְצוֹנְךָ הֶעֱמַדְתָּה לְהַרְרִי עֹז,
הִסְתַּרְתָּ פָנֶיךָ הָיִיתִי נִבְהָל:
אֵלֶיךָ יהוה אֶקְרָא, וְאֶל־אֲדֹנָי אֶתְחַנָּן:
מַה־בֶּצַע בְּדָמִי, בְּרִדְתִּי אֶל שָׁחַת
הֲיוֹדְךָ עָפָר, הֲיַגִּיד אֲמִתֶּךָ:
שְׁמַע־יהוה וְחָנֵּנִי, יהוה הֱיֵה־עֹזֵר לִי:
◂ הָפַכְתָּ מִסְפְּדִי לְמָחוֹל לִי
פִּתַּחְתָּ שַׂקִּי, וַתְּאַזְּרֵנִי שִׂמְחָה:
לְמַעַן יְזַמֶּרְךָ כָבוֹד וְלֹא יִדֹּם
יהוה אֱלֹהַי, לְעוֹלָם אוֹדֶךָּ:

## MOURNER'S KADDISH

*The following prayer, said by mourners, requires the presence of a minyan. A transliteration can be found on page 1320.*

*Mourner:* יִתְגַּדַּל Magnified and sanctified
may His great name be,
in the world He created by His will.
May He establish His kingdom
in your lifetime and in your days,
and in the lifetime
of all the house of Israel,
swiftly and soon –
and say: Amen.

*All:* May His great name be blessed
for ever and all time.

*Mourner:* Blessed and praised,
glorified and exalted,
raised and honored,
uplifted and lauded
be the name of the Holy One,
blessed be He,
beyond any blessing,
song, praise and consolation
uttered in the world –
and say: Amen.

May there be great peace from heaven,
and life for us and all Israel –
and say: Amen.

*Bow, take three steps back, as if taking leave of the Divine Presence, then bow, first left, then right, then center, while saying:*

May He who makes peace in His high places,
make peace for us and all Israel –
and say: Amen.

## קדיש יתום

*The following prayer, said by mourners, requires the presence of a* מנין*.*
*A transliteration can be found on page 1320.*

אבל: יִתְגַּדַּל וְיִתְקַדַּשׁ שְׁמֵהּ רַבָּא (קהל: אָמֵן)
בְּעָלְמָא דִּי בְרָא כִרְעוּתֵהּ
וְיַמְלִיךְ מַלְכוּתֵהּ
בְּחַיֵּיכוֹן וּבְיוֹמֵיכוֹן וּבְחַיֵּי דְכָל בֵּית יִשְׂרָאֵל
בַּעֲגָלָא וּבִזְמַן קָרִיב
וְאִמְרוּ אָמֵן. (קהל: אָמֵן)

קהל ואבל: יְהֵא שְׁמֵהּ רַבָּא מְבָרַךְ לְעָלַם וּלְעָלְמֵי עָלְמַיָּא.

אבל: יִתְבָּרַךְ וְיִשְׁתַּבַּח וְיִתְפָּאַר
וְיִתְרוֹמַם וְיִתְנַשֵּׂא וְיִתְהַדָּר וְיִתְעַלֶּה וְיִתְהַלָּל
שְׁמֵהּ דְּקֻדְשָׁא בְּרִיךְ הוּא (קהל: בְּרִיךְ הוּא)
לְעֵלָּא מִן כָּל בִּרְכָתָא
/בשבת שובה: לְעֵלָּא לְעֵלָּא מִכָּל בִּרְכָתָא/
וְשִׁירָתָא, תֻּשְׁבְּחָתָא וְנֶחֱמָתָא
דַּאֲמִירָן בְּעָלְמָא
וְאִמְרוּ אָמֵן. (קהל: אָמֵן)

יְהֵא שְׁלָמָא רַבָּא מִן שְׁמַיָּא
וְחַיִּים, עָלֵינוּ וְעַל כָּל יִשְׂרָאֵל
וְאִמְרוּ אָמֵן. (קהל: אָמֵן)

*Bow, take three steps back, as if taking leave of the Divine Presence, then bow, first left, then right, then center, while saying:*

עֹשֶׂה שָׁלוֹם/בשבת שובה: הַשָּׁלוֹם/ בִּמְרוֹמָיו
הוּא יַעֲשֶׂה שָׁלוֹם עָלֵינוּ וְעַל כָּל יִשְׂרָאֵל
וְאִמְרוּ אָמֵן. (קהל: אָמֵן)

## PESUKEI DEZIMRA

*The following introductory blessing to the Pesukei DeZimra (Verses of Praise) is said standing, while holding the two front tzitziot of the tallit. They are kissed and released at the end of the blessing at "songs of praise" (below). From the beginning of this prayer to the end of the Amida, conversation is forbidden.* *See table on pages 1315–1317 for permitted congregational responses.*

*Some say:*

I hereby prepare my mouth to thank, praise and laud my Creator, for the sake of the unification of the Holy One, blessed be He, and His Divine Presence, through that which is hidden and concealed, in the name of all Israel.

# BLESSED IS HE WHO SPOKE

and the world came into being, blessed is He.

Blessed is He who creates the universe.
Blessed is He who speaks and acts.
Blessed is He who decrees and fulfills.
Blessed is He who shows compassion
to the earth.
Blessed is He who shows compassion
to all creatures.
Blessed is He who gives a good reward
to those who fear Him.
Blessed is He who lives for ever
and exists to eternity.
Blessed is He who redeems and saves.
Blessed is His name.

Blessed are You, LORD our God, King of the Universe, God, compassionate Father, extolled by the mouth of His people, praised and glorified by the tongue of His devoted ones and those who serve Him. With the songs of Your servant David we will praise You, O LORD our God. With praises and psalms we will magnify and praise You, glorify You, Speak Your name and proclaim Your kingship, our King, our God, ▸ the only One, Giver of life to the worlds, the King whose great name is praised and glorified to all eternity. Blessed are You, LORD, the King extolled with songs of praise.

## פסוקי דזמרה

*The following introductory blessing to the* פסוקי דזמרה *is said standing, while holding the two front* ציציות *of the* טלית*. They are kissed and released at the end of the blessing at* בַּתִּשְׁבָּחוֹת *(below). From the beginning of this prayer to the end of the* עמידה*, conversation is forbidden. See table on pages 1315–1317 for permitted congregational responses.*

*Some say:*

הֲרֵינִי מְזַמֵּן אֶת פִּי לְהוֹדוֹת וּלְהַלֵּל וּלְשַׁבֵּחַ אֶת בּוֹרְאִי, לְשֵׁם יִחוּד קֻדְשָׁא בְּרִיךְ הוּא וּשְׁכִינְתֵּהּ עַל יְדֵי הַהוּא טָמִיר וְנֶעְלָם בְּשֵׁם כָּל יִשְׂרָאֵל.

**בָּרוּךְ שֶׁאָמַר** וְהָיָה הָעוֹלָם, בָּרוּךְ הוּא.

בָּרוּךְ עוֹשֶׂה בְרֵאשִׁית

בָּרוּךְ אוֹמֵר וְעוֹשֶׂה

בָּרוּךְ גּוֹזֵר וּמְקַיֵּם

בָּרוּךְ מְרַחֵם עַל הָאָרֶץ

בָּרוּךְ מְרַחֵם עַל הַבְּרִיּוֹת

בָּרוּךְ מְשַׁלֵּם שָׂכָר טוֹב לִירֵאָיו

בָּרוּךְ חַי לָעַד וְקַיָּם לָנֶצַח

בָּרוּךְ פּוֹדֶה וּמַצִּיל

בָּרוּךְ שְׁמוֹ

בָּרוּךְ אַתָּה יהוה אֱלֹהֵינוּ מֶלֶךְ הָעוֹלָם, הָאֵל הָאָב הָרַחֲמָן הַמְהֻלָּל בְּפִי עַמּוֹ, מְשֻׁבָּח וּמְפֹאָר בִּלְשׁוֹן חֲסִידָיו וַעֲבָדָיו, וּבְשִׁירֵי דָוִד עַבְדֶּךָ, נְהַלֶּלְךָ יהוה אֱלֹהֵינוּ. בִּשְׁבָחוֹת וּבִזְמִירוֹת נְגַדֶּלְךָ וּנְשַׁבֵּחֲךָ וּנְפָאֶרְךָ, וְנַזְכִּיר שִׁמְךָ וְנַמְלִיכְךָ מַלְכֵּנוּ אֱלֹהֵינוּ. ‹ יָחִיד חֵי הָעוֹלָמִים, מֶלֶךְ, מְשֻׁבָּח וּמְפֹאָר עֲדֵי עַד שְׁמוֹ הַגָּדוֹל. בָּרוּךְ אַתָּה יהוה, מֶלֶךְ מְהֻלָּל בַּתִּשְׁבָּחוֹת.

הוֹדוּ Thank the Lord, call on His name, make His acts known among the peoples. Sing to Him, make music to Him, tell of all His wonders. Glory in His holy name; let the hearts of those who seek the Lord rejoice. Search out the Lord and His strength; seek His presence at all times. Remember the wonders He has done, His miracles, and the judgments He pronounced. Descendants of Yisrael His servant, sons of Jacob His chosen ones: He is the Lord our God. His judgments are throughout the earth. Remember His covenant for ever, the word He commanded for a thousand generations. He made it with Abraham, vowed it to Isaac, and confirmed it to Jacob as a statute and to Israel as an everlasting covenant, saying, "To you I will give the land of Canaan as your allotted heritage." You were then small in number, few, strangers there, wandering from nation to nation, from one kingdom to another, but He let no man oppress them, and for their sake He rebuked kings: "Do not touch My anointed ones, and do My prophets no harm." Sing to the Lord, all the earth; proclaim His salvation daily. Declare His glory among the nations, His marvels among all the peoples. For great is the Lord and greatly to be praised; He is awesome beyond all heavenly powers. ▸ For all the gods of the peoples are mere idols; it was the Lord who made the heavens. *1 Chr. 16*

Before Him are majesty and splendor; there is strength and beauty in His holy place. Render to the Lord, families of the peoples, render to the Lord honor and might. Render to the Lord the glory due to His name; bring an offering and come before Him; bow down to the Lord in the splendor of holiness. Tremble before Him, all the earth; the world stands firm, it will not be shaken. Let the heavens rejoice and the earth be glad; let them declare among the nations, "The Lord is King." Let the sea roar, and all that is in it; let the fields be jubilant, and all they contain. Then the trees of the forest will sing for joy before the Lord, for He is coming to judge the earth. Thank the Lord for He is good; His loving-kindness is for ever. Say: "Save us, God of our salvation; gather us and rescue us from the nations, to acknowledge Your holy name and glory in Your praise. Blessed is the Lord, God of Israel, from this world to eternity." And let all the people say "Amen" and "Praise the Lord."

דברי הימים א׳ טז

הוֹדוּ לַיהוה קִרְאוּ בִשְׁמוֹ, הוֹדִיעוּ בָעַמִּים עֲלִילֹתָיו: שִׁירוּ לוֹ,
זַמְּרוּ־לוֹ, שִׂיחוּ בְּכָל־נִפְלְאֹתָיו: הִתְהַלְלוּ בְּשֵׁם קָדְשׁוֹ, יִשְׂמַח לֵב
מְבַקְשֵׁי יהוה: דִּרְשׁוּ יהוה וְעֻזּוֹ, בַּקְּשׁוּ פָנָיו תָּמִיד: זִכְרוּ נִפְלְאֹתָיו
אֲשֶׁר עָשָׂה, מֹפְתָיו וּמִשְׁפְּטֵי־פִיהוּ: זֶרַע יִשְׂרָאֵל עַבְדּוֹ, בְּנֵי יַעֲקֹב
בְּחִירָיו: הוּא יהוה אֱלֹהֵינוּ בְּכָל־הָאָרֶץ מִשְׁפָּטָיו: זִכְרוּ לְעוֹלָם
בְּרִיתוֹ, דָּבָר צִוָּה לְאֶלֶף דּוֹר: אֲשֶׁר כָּרַת אֶת־אַבְרָהָם, וּשְׁבוּעָתוֹ
לְיִצְחָק: וַיַּעֲמִידֶהָ לְיַעֲקֹב לְחֹק, לְיִשְׂרָאֵל בְּרִית עוֹלָם: לֵאמֹר, לְךָ
אֶתֵּן אֶרֶץ־כְּנָעַן, חֶבֶל נַחֲלַתְכֶם: בִּהְיוֹתְכֶם מְתֵי מִסְפָּר, כִּמְעַט
וְגָרִים בָּהּ: וַיִּתְהַלְּכוּ מִגּוֹי אֶל־גּוֹי, וּמִמַּמְלָכָה אֶל־עַם אַחֵר: לֹא־
הִנִּיחַ לְאִישׁ לְעָשְׁקָם, וַיּוֹכַח עֲלֵיהֶם מְלָכִים: אַל־תִּגְּעוּ בִּמְשִׁיחָי,
וּבִנְבִיאַי אַל־תָּרֵעוּ: שִׁירוּ לַיהוה כָּל־הָאָרֶץ, בַּשְּׂרוּ מִיּוֹם־אֶל־
יוֹם יְשׁוּעָתוֹ: סַפְּרוּ בַגּוֹיִם אֶת־כְּבוֹדוֹ, בְּכָל־הָעַמִּים נִפְלְאֹתָיו:
כִּי גָדוֹל יהוה וּמְהֻלָּל מְאֹד, וְנוֹרָא הוּא עַל־כָּל־אֱלֹהִים: › כִּי
כָּל־אֱלֹהֵי הָעַמִּים אֱלִילִים, וַיהוה שָׁמַיִם עָשָׂה:

הוֹד וְהָדָר לְפָנָיו, עֹז וְחֶדְוָה בִּמְקֹמוֹ: הָבוּ לַיהוה מִשְׁפְּחוֹת
עַמִּים, הָבוּ לַיהוה כָּבוֹד וָעֹז: הָבוּ לַיהוה כְּבוֹד שְׁמוֹ, שְׂאוּ מִנְחָה
וּבֹאוּ לְפָנָיו, הִשְׁתַּחֲווּ לַיהוה בְּהַדְרַת־קֹדֶשׁ: חִילוּ מִלְּפָנָיו כָּל־
הָאָרֶץ, אַף־תִּכּוֹן תֵּבֵל בַּל־תִּמּוֹט: יִשְׂמְחוּ הַשָּׁמַיִם וְתָגֵל הָאָרֶץ,
וְיֹאמְרוּ בַגּוֹיִם יהוה מָלָךְ: יִרְעַם הַיָּם וּמְלוֹאוֹ, יַעֲלֹץ הַשָּׂדֶה
וְכָל־אֲשֶׁר־בּוֹ: אָז יְרַנְּנוּ עֲצֵי הַיָּעַר, מִלִּפְנֵי יהוה, כִּי־בָא לִשְׁפּוֹט
אֶת־הָאָרֶץ: הוֹדוּ לַיהוה כִּי טוֹב, כִּי לְעוֹלָם חַסְדּוֹ: וְאִמְרוּ,
הוֹשִׁיעֵנוּ אֱלֹהֵי יִשְׁעֵנוּ, וְקַבְּצֵנוּ וְהַצִּילֵנוּ מִן־הַגּוֹיִם, לְהֹדוֹת
לְשֵׁם קָדְשֶׁךָ, לְהִשְׁתַּבֵּחַ בִּתְהִלָּתֶךָ: בָּרוּךְ יהוה אֱלֹהֵי יִשְׂרָאֵל
מִן־הָעוֹלָם וְעַד־הָעֹלָם, וַיֹּאמְרוּ כָל־הָעָם אָמֵן, וְהַלֵּל לַיהוה:

‣ Exalt the LORD our God and bow before His footstool: He is holy. Exalt the LORD our God and bow at His holy mountain; for holy is the LORD our God. Ps. 99

He is compassionate. He forgives iniquity and does not destroy. Ps. 78
Repeatedly He suppresses His anger, not rousing His full wrath. You, Ps. 40
LORD: do not withhold Your compassion from me. May Your loving-
kindness and truth always guard me. Remember, LORD, Your acts of Ps. 25
compassion and love, for they have existed for ever. Ascribe power Ps. 68
to God, whose majesty is over Israel and whose might is in the skies.
You are awesome, God, in Your holy places. It is the God of Israel
who gives might and strength to the people, may God be blessed.
God of retribution, LORD, God of retribution, appear. Arise, Judge of Ps. 94
the earth, to repay the arrogant their just deserts. Salvation belongs Ps. 3
to the LORD; may Your blessing rest upon Your people, Selah! ‣ The Ps. 46
LORD of hosts is with us, the God of Jacob is our stronghold, Selah!
LORD of hosts, happy is the one who trusts in You. LORD, save! May Ps. 84 Ps. 20
the King answer us on the day we call.

Save Your people and bless Your heritage; tend them and carry Ps. 28
them for ever. Our soul longs for the LORD; He is our Help and Shield. Ps. 33
For in Him our hearts rejoice, for in His holy name we have trusted.
May Your loving-kindness, LORD, be upon us, as we have put our hope
in You. Show us, LORD, Your loving-kindness and grant us Your salva- Ps. 85
tion. Arise, help us and redeem us for the sake of Your love. I am the Ps. 44 Ps. 81
LORD your God who brought you up from the land of Egypt: open
your mouth wide and I will fill it. Happy is the people for whom this Ps. 144
is so; happy is the people whose God is the LORD. ‣ As for me, I trust Ps. 13
in Your loving-kindness; my heart rejoices in Your salvation. I will sing
to the LORD for He has been good to me.

*On Hoshana Raba, the following psalm is said. The custom is to say it standing.*

מִזְמוֹר A psalm of thanksgiving. Shout joyously to the LORD, all the earth. Ps. 100
Serve the LORD with joy. Come before Him with jubilation. Know that the LORD is God. He made us and we are His. We are His people and the flock He tends. Enter His gates with thanksgiving, His courts with praise. Thank Him and bless His name. ‣ For the LORD is good, His loving-kindness is everlasting, and His faithfulness is for every generation.

◂ רוֹמְמוּ יהוה אֱלֹהֵינוּ וְהִשְׁתַּחֲווּ לַהֲדֹם רַגְלָיו, קָדוֹשׁ הוּא: תהלים צט
רוֹמְמוּ יהוה אֱלֹהֵינוּ וְהִשְׁתַּחֲווּ לְהַר קָדְשׁוֹ, כִּי־קָדוֹשׁ יהוה אֱלֹהֵינוּ:

וְהוּא רַחוּם, יְכַפֵּר עָוֹן וְלֹא־יַשְׁחִית, וְהִרְבָּה לְהָשִׁיב אַפּוֹ, תהלים עח
וְלֹא־יָעִיר כָּל־חֲמָתוֹ: אַתָּה יהוה לֹא־תִכְלָא רַחֲמֶיךָ מִמֶּנִּי, חַסְדְּךָ תהלים מ
וַאֲמִתְּךָ תָּמִיד יִצְּרוּנִי: זְכֹר־רַחֲמֶיךָ יהוה וַחֲסָדֶיךָ, כִּי מֵעוֹלָם תהלים כה
הֵמָּה: תְּנוּ עֹז לֵאלֹהִים, עַל־יִשְׂרָאֵל גַּאֲוָתוֹ, וְעֻזּוֹ בַּשְּׁחָקִים: תהלים סח
נוֹרָא אֱלֹהִים מִמִּקְדָּשֶׁיךָ, אֵל יִשְׂרָאֵל הוּא נֹתֵן עֹז וְתַעֲצֻמוֹת
לָעָם, בָּרוּךְ אֱלֹהִים: אֵל־נְקָמוֹת יהוה, אֵל נְקָמוֹת הוֹפִיעַ: הִנָּשֵׂא תהלים צד
שֹׁפֵט הָאָרֶץ, הָשֵׁב גְּמוּל עַל־גֵּאִים: לַיהוה הַיְשׁוּעָה, עַל־עַמְּךָ תהלים ג
בִרְכָתֶךָ סֶּלָה: ◂ יהוה צְבָאוֹת עִמָּנוּ, מִשְׂגָּב לָנוּ אֱלֹהֵי יַעֲקֹב תהלים מו
סֶלָה: יהוה צְבָאוֹת, אַשְׁרֵי אָדָם בֹּטֵחַ בָּךְ: יהוה הוֹשִׁיעָה, הַמֶּלֶךְ תהלים פד תהלים כ
יַעֲנֵנוּ בְיוֹם־קָרְאֵנוּ:

הוֹשִׁיעָה אֶת־עַמֶּךָ, וּבָרֵךְ אֶת־נַחֲלָתֶךָ, וּרְעֵם וְנַשְּׂאֵם עַד־ תהלים כח
הָעוֹלָם: נַפְשֵׁנוּ חִכְּתָה לַיהוה, עֶזְרֵנוּ וּמָגִנֵּנוּ הוּא: כִּי־בוֹ יִשְׂמַח תהלים לג
לִבֵּנוּ, כִּי בְשֵׁם קָדְשׁוֹ בָטָחְנוּ: יְהִי־חַסְדְּךָ יהוה עָלֵינוּ, כַּאֲשֶׁר
יִחַלְנוּ לָךְ: הַרְאֵנוּ יהוה חַסְדֶּךָ, וְיֶשְׁעֲךָ תִּתֶּן־לָנוּ: קוּמָה עֶזְרָתָה תהלים פה תהלים מד
לָּנוּ, וּפְדֵנוּ לְמַעַן חַסְדֶּךָ: אָנֹכִי יהוה אֱלֹהֶיךָ הַמַּעַלְךָ מֵאֶרֶץ תהלים פא
מִצְרָיִם, הַרְחֶב־פִּיךָ וַאֲמַלְאֵהוּ: אַשְׁרֵי הָעָם שֶׁכָּכָה לּוֹ, אַשְׁרֵי תהלים קמד
הָעָם שֶׁיהוה אֱלֹהָיו: ◂ וַאֲנִי בְּחַסְדְּךָ בָטַחְתִּי, יָגֵל לִבִּי בִּישׁוּעָתֶךָ, תהלים יג
אָשִׁירָה לַיהוה, כִּי גָמַל עָלָי:

*On הושענא רבה, the following psalm is said. The custom is to say it standing.*

מִזְמוֹר לְתוֹדָה, הָרִיעוּ לַיהוה כָּל־הָאָרֶץ: עִבְדוּ אֶת־יהוה בְּשִׂמְחָה, תהלים ק
בֹּאוּ לְפָנָיו בִּרְנָנָה: דְּעוּ כִּי־יהוה הוּא אֱלֹהִים, הוּא עָשָׂנוּ וְלוֹ אֲנַחְנוּ,
עַמּוֹ וְצֹאן מַרְעִיתוֹ: בֹּאוּ שְׁעָרָיו בְּתוֹדָה, חֲצֵרֹתָיו בִּתְהִלָּה, הוֹדוּ לוֹ,
בָּרְכוּ שְׁמוֹ: ◂ כִּי־טוֹב יהוה, לְעוֹלָם חַסְדּוֹ, וְעַד־דֹּר וָדֹר אֱמוּנָתוֹ:

לַמְנַצֵּחַ For the conductor of music. A psalm of David. The heavens declare the glory of God; the skies proclaim the work of His hands. Day to day they pour forth speech; night to night they communicate knowledge. There is no speech, there are no words, their voice is not heard. Yet their music carries throughout the earth, their words to the end of the world. In them He has set a tent for the sun. It emerges like a groom from his marriage chamber, rejoicing like a champion about to run a race. It rises at one end of the heaven and makes its circuit to the other: nothing is hidden from its heat. The LORD's Torah is perfect, refreshing the soul. The LORD's testimony is faithful, making the simple wise. The LORD's precepts are just, gladdening the heart. The LORD's commandment is radiant, giving light to the eyes. The fear of the LORD is pure, enduring for ever. The LORD's judgments are true, altogether righteous. More precious than gold, than much fine gold. They are sweeter than honey, than honey from the comb.Your servant, too, is careful of them, for in observing them there is great reward. Yet who can discern his errors? Cleanse me of hidden faults. Keep Your servant also from willful sins; let them not have dominion over me. Then shall I be blameless, and innocent of grave sin. ▸ May the words of my mouth and the meditation of my heart find favor before You, LORD, my Rock and my Redeemer. *Ps. 19*

---

מִקְצֵה הַשָּׁמַיִם מוֹצָאוֹ, וּתְקוּפָתוֹ עַל־קְצוֹתָם וְאֵין נִסְתָּר מֵחַמָּתוֹ: *It rises at one end of the heaven and makes its circuit to the other; nothing is hidden from its heat.* The power contained in the sun evokes for us the majesty of the entire creation. The Sun, a star, raises our consciousness to the level of all the stars in the universe. By fixing our awareness on our star, the star of our Solar System, we begin to grasp the infinity of the universe.

But this macro-awareness does not diminish in the least from our micro-awareness. The surprise, the punch of the verse, is that with all of the Sun's magnitude, "nothing is hidden from its heat." The Psalmist is attentive to the impact that the Sun has upon every aspect of terrestrial existence and upon every living creature on the face of the Earth. And all of this is a metaphor for the divine macro- and micro-management of the world (*hashgaḥah kelalit* and *hashgaḥah peratit*).[2]

---

2. *OR*, vol. 2, pp. 55–56.

לַמְנַצֵּחַ מִזְמוֹר לְדָוִד: הַשָּׁמַיִם מְסַפְּרִים כְּבוֹד־אֵל, וּמַעֲשֵׂה יָדָיו מַגִּיד הָרָקִיעַ: יוֹם לְיוֹם יַבִּיעַ אֹמֶר, וְלַיְלָה לְּלַיְלָה יְחַוֶּה־דָּעַת: אֵין־אֹמֶר וְאֵין דְּבָרִים, בְּלִי נִשְׁמָע קוֹלָם: בְּכָל־הָאָרֶץ יָצָא קַוָּם, וּבִקְצֵה תֵבֵל מִלֵּיהֶם לַשֶּׁמֶשׁ שָׂם־אֹהֶל בָּהֶם: וְהוּא כְּחָתָן יֹצֵא מֵחֻפָּתוֹ, יָשִׂישׂ כְּגִבּוֹר לָרוּץ אֹרַח: מִקְצֵה הַשָּׁמַיִם מוֹצָאוֹ, וּתְקוּפָתוֹ עַל־קְצוֹתָם וְאֵין נִסְתָּר מֵחַמָּתוֹ: תּוֹרַת יהוה תְּמִימָה, מְשִׁיבַת נָפֶשׁ עֵדוּת יהוה נֶאֱמָנָה, מַחְכִּימַת פֶּתִי: פִּקּוּדֵי יהוה יְשָׁרִים, מְשַׂמְּחֵי־לֵב מִצְוַת יהוה בָּרָה, מְאִירַת עֵינָיִם: יִרְאַת יהוה טְהוֹרָה, עוֹמֶדֶת לָעַד מִשְׁפְּטֵי־יהוה אֱמֶת, צָדְקוּ יַחְדָּו: הַנֶּחֱמָדִים מִזָּהָב וּמִפַּז רָב, וּמְתוּקִים מִדְּבַשׁ וְנֹפֶת צוּפִים: גַּם־עַבְדְּךָ נִזְהָר בָּהֶם, בְּשָׁמְרָם עֵקֶב רָב: שְׁגִיאוֹת מִי־יָבִין, מִנִּסְתָּרוֹת נַקֵּנִי: גַּם מִזֵּדִים חֲשֹׂךְ עַבְדֶּךָ, אַל־יִמְשְׁלוּ־בִי אָז אֵיתָם, וְנִקֵּיתִי מִפֶּשַׁע רָב: ◂ יִהְיוּ לְרָצוֹן אִמְרֵי־פִי וְהֶגְיוֹן לִבִּי לְפָנֶיךָ, יהוה, צוּרִי וְגֹאֲלִי: תהלים יט

הַשָּׁמַיִם מְסַפְּרִים כְּבוֹד־אֵל, וּמַעֲשֵׂה יָדָיו מַגִּיד הָרָקִיעַ: יוֹם לְיוֹם יַבִּיעַ אֹמֶר, וְלַיְלָה לְּלַיְלָה יְחַוֶּה־דָּעַת: *The heavens declare the glory of God; The skies proclaim the work of His hands. Day to day they pour forth speech; Night to night they communicate knowledge* (*Psalm 19*). That which man beholds by day may be expressed in language, but that which man beholds by night is inexpressible, and must remain an inner knowledge. With the setting of the sun, the stars become visible, and man is privy to a glimpse of infinite space.

This contrast between day and night is a metaphor for our intellectual endeavors. That which is apprehended by our intellect is communicable by language. But beyond that, there is that which cannot be apprehended by intellect. Only the soul, with its inner logic, knows that which is "above the sun."[1]

1. Statement of Rabbi Yudan in *Ecclesiastes Rabbah* 1:3.

*OR*, vol. 2, pp. 53–54.

לְדָוִד Of David. When he pretended to be insane before Abimelech, Ps. 34
who drove him away, and he left. I will bless the LORD at all times;
His praise will be always on my lips. My soul will glory in the LORD;
let the lowly hear this and rejoice. Magnify the LORD with me; let
us exalt His name together. I sought the LORD, and He answered
me; He saved me from all my fears. Those who look to Him are
radiant; their faces are never downcast. This poor man called, and

(*tamid*). Perhaps *tehillah* is related etymologically to *"yahel 'or,"* the shining of light,[7] in which case it refers to a state of illumination, of higher consciousness. Whatever the etymology,

> "*tehillah* is the inner awareness that the good influx and the source of life flows eternal without break; and all that is lofty, exalted and beautiful, all the good and love is truly unabated, constant (*tamid*), unbroken by time (*'et*)."[8]

בַּיהוה תִּתְהַלֵּל נַפְשִׁי, יִשְׁמְעוּ עֲנָוִים וְיִשְׂמָחוּ *My soul will glory (tit-hallel) in the LORD; let the lowly hear this and rejoice.* Initially, *'anavah* (humility), awareness of one's insufficiency, is devastating. Being reduced to "ground zero," can have a negative effect; it can prove debilitating and nerve-shattering. But this personality trait was designed on high to reinforce in man the awareness that all strength, all perfection comes only from the light of the LORD imbuing and illuminating all. If there be even one point in his soul where man yet holds in high regard his private, egoistic essence – the light of the LORD cannot penetrate there. It is only when the soul is thoroughly illuminated (*tit-hallel*) by the LORD,[9] totally, without reservation, that the previously negative experience of humility is transformed into joy. Then the humble, the lowly may rejoice.[10]

7. Cf. Job 31:26. The same etymology occurs in *MRIT*, p. 518. See Rabbi Isaiah Halevi Horowitz, *Siddur Shelah, "Sha'ar ha-Shamayim,"* ed. Rabbi Ya'akov Moshe Hillel, vol. 1 (Jerusalem: Ahavat Shalom, 1998), p. 247, s.v. *Tehillah le-David,* quoting Rabbi Moses Cordovero; Rabbi Shneur Zalman of Liadi, *Torah 'Or* (Brooklyn: Kehot, 1972), *Vayyeshev,* 30a; Rabbi Dov Baer Shneuri of Lubavitch, *Sha'arei Orah* (Johannisberg, n.d.; photo offset Brooklyn, 1979), *Sha'ar ha-Ḥanukkah,* chap. 43 (18a); Rabbi Menaḥem Mendel Schneersohn of Lubavitch (*Tsemaḥ Tsedek*), *Derekh Mitsvotekha* (Poltava, 1911; photo offset Brooklyn: Kehot, 1953), *Hallel* (148a); idem, *Yahel 'Or* [commentary to Psalms] (Brooklyn: Kehot, 1984), pp. 558, 693.
8. *OR,* vol. 2, pp. 61–62.
9. See the preceding verse for the relation of *tehillah* (and thus *hallel*) to *yahel 'or.*
10. *OR,* vol. 2, p. 62.

לְדָוִד, בְּשַׁנּוֹתוֹ אֶת־טַעְמוֹ לִפְנֵי אֲבִימֶלֶךְ, וַיְגָרְשֵׁהוּ וַיֵּלַךְ: אֲבָרְכָה תהלים לד
אֶת־יהוה בְּכָל־עֵת, תָּמִיד תְּהִלָּתוֹ בְּפִי: בַּיהוה תִּתְהַלֵּל נַפְשִׁי,
יִשְׁמְעוּ עֲנָוִים וְיִשְׂמָחוּ: גַּדְּלוּ לַיהוה אִתִּי, וּנְרוֹמְמָה שְׁמוֹ יַחְדָּו:
דָּרַשְׁתִּי אֶת־יהוה וְעָנָנִי, וּמִכָּל־מְגוּרוֹתַי הִצִּילָנִי: הִבִּיטוּ אֵלָיו
וְנָהָרוּ, וּפְנֵיהֶם אַל־יֶחְפָּרוּ: זֶה עָנִי קָרָא, וַיהוה שָׁמֵעַ, וּמִכָּל־

---

לְדָוִד, בְּשַׁנּוֹתוֹ אֶת־טַעְמוֹ לִפְנֵי אֲבִימֶלֶךְ, וַיְגָרְשֵׁהוּ וַיֵּלַךְ *Of David. When he pretended to be insane before Abimelech, who drove him away, and he left* (*Psalm* 34). There was a time when David, hunted by King Saul, sought refuge in the Philistine city of Gath. Brought before Achish, King of Gath, David feigned madness, drooling into his beard.[3] Achish's reaction was: "Am I lacking madmen (*meshuga'im*) that you have brought this one to go crazy on me?"[4] This ruse spared David's life, and he hastily departed from Gath.

The divine wisdom is beyond what we humans deem "wisdom" or "logic." In fact, from the vantage point of the divine wisdom there is truly no difference between the rational and the irrational or even outright madness. We see that sometimes the divine plan is brought about by the irrational and illogical. "With Him are strength and wise counsel; the misled and the misleader."[5]

The same applies to the values of good and evil. From the vantage of absolute reality, it is impossible to say that what we call "good" is good, and that what we call "bad" is bad. From the perspective of the supernal wisdom, all is good.

David's rescue by "temporary insanity" gives pause to think about the values that we mortals have assigned to "reason" and to "good."[6]

אֲבָרְכָה אֶת־יהוה בְּכָל־עֵת, תָּמִיד תְּהִלָּתוֹ בְּפִי *I will bless the* Lord *at all times; His praise will be always on my lips.* Note the parallelism of the verse. A "blessing" (*berakha*) is pinned to a "time" (*'et*), to a specific occasion. One does not utter a benediction unless it is warranted by a special event. "Praise" (*tehillah*) on the other hand, requires no novel occasion to trigger it; it is ongoing, "eternal"

---

3. The Bible commentators point out that "Abimelech" was the title of the kings of Philistia, just as "Pharaoh" was the title of the kings of Egypt. The man's proper name was "Achish." See Rashi, Psalms 34:1; Rashbam, Genesis 41:10; Numbers 24:7.
4. 1 Samuel 21:15.
5. Job 12:16. One of the greatest rationalist thinkers of all time, Moses Maimonides, quoted approvingly the maxim, "Without madmen, the world would remain a wasteland" (Maimonides, Introduction to *Commentary to the Mishnah*, ed. Kafaḥ, p. 23).
6. *OR*, vol. 2, p. 61.

the LORD heard; He saved him from all his troubles.The LORD's angel encamps around those who fear Him, and He rescues them. Taste and see that the LORD is good; happy is the man who takes refuge in Him. Fear the LORD, you His holy ones, for those who fear Him lack nothing. Young lions may grow weak and hungry, but those who seek the LORD lack no good thing. Come, my children, listen to me; I will teach you the fear of the LORD. Who desires life, loving each day to see good? Then guard your tongue from evil and your lips from speaking deceit. Turn from evil and do good; seek peace and pursue it. The eyes of the LORD are on the righteous and His ears attentive to their cry; The LORD's face is set against those who do evil, to erase their memory from the earth. The righteous cry out, and the LORD hears them; delivering them from all their troubles. The LORD is close to the brokenhearted, and saves those who are crushed in spirit. Many troubles may befall the righteous, but the LORD delivers him from them all; He protects all his bones, so that none of them will be broken. Evil will slay the wicked; the enemies of the righteous will be condemned. ▸ The LORD redeems His servants; none who take refuge in Him shall be condemned.

---

which he strives. The *tsaddik* must realize that through these very troubles that pierce his spirit as thorns, he evolves, he is sanctified and purified. To wit, his salvation comes about *from* all of these trials and tribulations.[12]

שֹׁמֵר כָּל־עַצְמוֹתָיו, אַחַת מֵהֵנָּה לֹא נִשְׁבָּרָה *He protects all his bones, so that none of them will be broken.* In the course of the spiritual journey toward self-perfection, many changes must be effected in the personality of the *tsaddik*. The transformations may be so drastic that one is tempted to think that the essence itself has undergone change. But no! The changes are external, superficial. The essence of the *tsaddik*, his "bones," have not been broken. The inner essence has been preserved intact.[13]

---

12. *OR*, vol. 2, p. 68.
13. *OR*, vol. 2, p. 68.

צָרוֹתָיו הוֹשִׁיעוֹ: חֹנֶה מַלְאַךְ־יהוה סָבִיב לִירֵאָיו, וַיְחַלְּצֵם: טַעֲמוּ
וּרְאוּ כִּי־טוֹב יהוה, אַשְׁרֵי הַגֶּבֶר יֶחֱסֶה־בּוֹ: יְראוּ אֶת־יהוה
קְדֹשָׁיו, כִּי־אֵין מַחְסוֹר לִירֵאָיו: כְּפִירִים רָשׁוּ וְרָעֵבוּ, וְדֹרְשֵׁי יהוה
לֹא־יַחְסְרוּ כָל־טוֹב: לְכוּ־בָנִים שִׁמְעוּ־לִי, יִרְאַת יהוה אֲלַמֶּדְכֶם:
מִי־הָאִישׁ הֶחָפֵץ חַיִּים, אֹהֵב יָמִים לִרְאוֹת טוֹב: נְצֹר לְשׁוֹנְךָ
מֵרָע, וּשְׂפָתֶיךָ מִדַּבֵּר מִרְמָה: סוּר מֵרָע וַעֲשֵׂה־טוֹב, בַּקֵּשׁ שָׁלוֹם
וְרָדְפֵהוּ: עֵינֵי יהוה אֶל־צַדִּיקִים, וְאָזְנָיו אֶל־שַׁוְעָתָם: פְּנֵי יהוה
בְּעֹשֵׂי רָע, לְהַכְרִית מֵאֶרֶץ זִכְרָם: צָעֲקוּ וַיהוה שָׁמֵעַ, וּמִכָּל־
צָרוֹתָם הִצִּילָם: קָרוֹב יהוה לְנִשְׁבְּרֵי־לֵב, וְאֶת־דַּכְּאֵי־רוּחַ יוֹשִׁיעַ:
רַבּוֹת רָעוֹת צַדִּיק, וּמִכֻּלָּם יַצִּילֶנּוּ יהוה: שֹׁמֵר כָּל־עַצְמֹתָיו, אַחַת
מֵהֵנָּה לֹא נִשְׁבָּרָה: תְּמוֹתֵת רָשָׁע רָעָה, וְשֹׂנְאֵי צַדִּיק יֶאְשָׁמוּ:
◂ פּוֹדֶה יהוה נֶפֶשׁ עֲבָדָיו, וְלֹא יֶאְשְׁמוּ כָּל־הַחֹסִים בּוֹ:

---

**טַעֲמוּ וּרְאוּ כִּי־טוֹב יהוה, אַשְׁרֵי הַגֶּבֶר יֶחֱסֶה־בּוֹ** *Taste and see that the Lord is good; happy is the man who takes refuge in Him.* There are two pipelines to God: one internal, the other external. The internal pipeline is referred to as "tasting." Within us, there stir feelings of longing for closeness to God. We can almost taste these feelings. The external pipeline consists of all the manifestations of the hand of God in the creation that surrounds us all about. This external conduit is referred to as "seeing." Both conduits nudge us to the awareness that we must find our fortress in the Rock of Worlds. Only in the Lord will we ever find complete happiness.[11]

**רַבּוֹת רָעוֹת צַדִּיק, וּמִכֻּלָּם יַצִּילֶנּוּ יהוה** *Many troubles may befall the righteous, but the Lord delivers him from them all.* The *tsaddik* (righteous) is dismayed by the many imperfections, the many "evils" (*ra'ot*) that he finds in himself, whether they be the result of bodily makeup, the influence of the surrounding society, or his own personality traits. As a result, he becomes frustrated with himself; he regards all these as impediments to the attainment of self-perfection for

11. *OR*, vol. 2, p. 64.

תְּפִלָּה לְמֹשֶׁה A prayer of Moses, the man of God. LORD, You have been our shelter in every generation. Before the mountains were born, before You brought forth the earth and the world, from everlasting to everlasting You are God. You turn men back to dust, saying, "Return, you children of men." For a thousand years in Your sight are like yesterday when it has passed, like a watch in the night. You sweep men away; they sleep. In the morning they are like grass newly grown: in the morning it flourishes and is new, but by evening it withers and dries up. For we are consumed by Your anger, terrified by Your fury. You have set our iniquities before You, our secret sins in the light of Your presence. All our days pass away in Your wrath, we spend our years like a sigh. The span of our life is seventy years, or if we are strong, eighty years; but the best of them is trouble and sorrow, for they quickly pass, and we fly away. Who can know the force of Your anger? Your wrath matches the fear due to You. Teach us rightly to number our days, that we may gain a heart of wisdom. Relent, O LORD! How much longer? Be sorry for Your servants. Satisfy us in the morning with Your loving-kindness, *Ps. 90*

---

According to the later Lurianic Kabbalah, with its theory of transmigration of souls, in a previous lifetime Moses had been Noah. (The obvious parallel is that both men's lives were spared by residing for a while in a *teivah* or ark floating on the water.)[18]

Rav Kook resorts to neither Kabbalistic tradition in order to explain Moses' ability to transcend the limitations of time and take mankind back to the very source of existence. Rather it is by dint of the fact that Moses is "the prophet of the Torah." And for Rav Kook,

> The prophecy of Moses our Teacher is not part of the spiritual nature of existence, as is other prophecy… whose appearance is natural. The prophecy of the Master of Prophets is a miracle, just like the creation of the world *ex nihilo*. And just as the moment of the origin of existence passes through all the times that flow onward, and the foundation of this process undergoes no change, so the Torah undergoes no change.[19]

---

18. Rabbi Ḥayyim Vital, *Sha'ar ha-Pesukim*, Gen. 6:3. See *Ba'alei ha-Tosafot* there and *b. Ḥullin* 139b.
19. *SK* 2:54; *AT* (Jerusalem, 1983), p. 22.

תְּפִלָּה לְמֹשֶׁה אִישׁ־הָאֱלֹהִים, אֲדֹנָי, מָעוֹן אַתָּה הָיִיתָ לָּנוּ בְּדֹר וָדֹר: בְּטֶרֶם הָרִים יֻלָּדוּ, וַתְּחוֹלֵל אֶרֶץ וְתֵבֵל, וּמֵעוֹלָם עַד־עוֹלָם אַתָּה אֵל: תָּשֵׁב אֱנוֹשׁ עַד־דַּכָּא, וַתֹּאמֶר שׁוּבוּ בְנֵי־אָדָם: כִּי אֶלֶף שָׁנִים בְּעֵינֶיךָ, כְּיוֹם אֶתְמוֹל כִּי יַעֲבֹר, וְאַשְׁמוּרָה בַלָּיְלָה: זְרַמְתָּם, שֵׁנָה יִהְיוּ, בַּבֹּקֶר כֶּחָצִיר יַחֲלֹף: בַּבֹּקֶר יָצִיץ וְחָלָף, לָעֶרֶב יְמוֹלֵל וְיָבֵשׁ: כִּי־כָלִינוּ בְאַפֶּךָ, וּבַחֲמָתְךָ נִבְהָלְנוּ: שַׁתָּ עֲוֹנֹתֵינוּ לְנֶגְדֶּךָ, עֲלֻמֵנוּ לִמְאוֹר פָּנֶיךָ: כִּי כָל־יָמֵינוּ פָּנוּ בְעֶבְרָתֶךָ, כִּלִּינוּ שָׁנֵינוּ כְמוֹ־הֶגֶה: יְמֵי־שְׁנוֹתֵינוּ בָהֶם שִׁבְעִים שָׁנָה, וְאִם בִּגְבוּרֹת שְׁמוֹנִים שָׁנָה, וְרָהְבָּם עָמָל וָאָוֶן, כִּי־גָז חִישׁ וַנָּעֻפָה: מִי־יוֹדֵעַ עֹז אַפֶּךָ, וּכְיִרְאָתְךָ עֶבְרָתֶךָ, לִמְנוֹת יָמֵינוּ כֵּן הוֹדַע, וְנָבִא לְבַב חָכְמָה: שׁוּבָה יהוה עַד־מָתָי, וְהִנָּחֵם עַל־עֲבָדֶיךָ: שַׂבְּעֵנוּ בַבֹּקֶר תהלים צ

---

תְּפִלָּה לְמֹשֶׁה אִישׁ־הָאֱלֹהִים, אֲדֹנָי, מָעוֹן אַתָּה הָיִיתָ לָּנוּ בְּדֹר וָדֹר: בְּטֶרֶם הָרִים יֻלָּדוּ, וַתְּחוֹלֵל אֶרֶץ וְתֵבֵל, וּמֵעוֹלָם עַד־עוֹלָם אַתָּה אֵל: *A prayer of Moses, the man of God. Lord, You have been our shelter in every generation. Before the mountains were born, before You brought forth the earth and the world, from everlasting to everlasting You are God.* (*Psalm 90*)

Only the prayer of the man of God, Moses – the foundation of whose soul is cleaving to God, the Bundle of Life of all the worlds – only such a prayer could express the connection of man and his life, and of all existence to their Creator, going back all the way in time.

Only the prophet of the Torah, to whom the Lord spoke face to face[14]; who sees through a shining speculum,[15] commences from the beginning of the creation, while all flows from the supernal source, from the source of life.[16]

According to a medieval Kabbalistic tradition, Moses was from the previous *shemitah* or aeon of *Ḥesed* (Love), which preceded our present *shemitah* or aeon of *Paḥad* (Fear).[17]

---

14. Exodus 33:11.
15. *b. Yevamot* 49b.
16. *OR*, vol. 2, p. 69.
17. See Rabbi Shneur Zalman of Liadi, *Torah 'Or* (Brooklyn: Kehot, 1972), *Shemot*, 51d, citing the anonymous *Sefer ha-Temunah.*

that we may sing and rejoice all our days. Grant us joy for as many days as You have afflicted us, for as many years as we saw trouble. Let Your deeds be seen by Your servants, and Your glory by their children. ▸ May the pleasantness of the Lord our God be upon us. Establish for us the work of our hands, O establish the work of our hands.

יֹשֵׁב בְּסֵתֶר He who lives in the shelter of the Most High dwells in the shadow of the Almighty. I say of the Lord, my Refuge and Stronghold, my God in whom I trust, that He will save you from the fowler's snare and the deadly pestilence. With His pinions He will cover you, and beneath His wings you will find shelter; His faithfulness is an encircling shield. You need not fear terror by night, nor the arrow that flies by day; not the pestilence that stalks in darkness, nor the plague that ravages at noon. A thousand may fall at your side, ten thousand at your right hand, but it will not come near you. You will only look with your eyes and see the punishment of the wicked. Because you said "The Lord is my Refuge," Ps. 91

From the interplay of these two lights [i.e. the hidden and the revealed], we shall be uplifted and sanctified.[22]

רַק בְּעֵינֶיךָ תַבִּיט, וְשִׁלֻּמַת רְשָׁעִים תִּרְאֶה *You will only look with your eyes and see the punishment of the wicked.*

In this look, there is a benevolence that may save one who is worthy of being saved by your power, though his own merit is insufficient. As for the absolutely wicked, who are totally wayward and worthy only of punishment – in this regard too, there is an inner content of the Lord's abundant compassion, a far-reaching counsel, whereby there may be saved of the wicked whatever can possibly be saved: a root, a branch, a spark. All this comes about by power of the remaining connection of the trusting *tsaddik* (righteous) – who transcends all the material bounds – to the world and its finite creations.[23]

In 1913, Rav Kook exchanged letters with the Rabbi of Tsefat (formerly of

very moment" (*Genesis Rabbah* 46:3). The divine name *Shaddai* is interpreted as *She-Dai* (That-Enough).

22. *OR*, vol. 2, p. 74.

23. *OR*, vol. 2, p. 76.

חַסְדֶּךָ, וּנְרַנְּנָה וְנִשְׂמְחָה בְּכָל־יָמֵינוּ: שַׂמְּחֵנוּ כִּימוֹת עִנִּיתָנוּ,
שְׁנוֹת רָאִינוּ רָעָה: יֵרָאֶה אֶל־עֲבָדֶיךָ פָעֳלֶךָ, וַהֲדָרְךָ עַל־בְּנֵיהֶם:
▸ וִיהִי נֹעַם אֲדֹנָי אֱלֹהֵינוּ עָלֵינוּ, וּמַעֲשֵׂה יָדֵינוּ כּוֹנְנָה עָלֵינוּ,
וּמַעֲשֵׂה יָדֵינוּ כּוֹנְנֵהוּ:

יֹשֵׁב בְּסֵתֶר עֶלְיוֹן, בְּצֵל שַׁדַּי יִתְלוֹנָן: אֹמַר לַיהוה מַחְסִי וּמְצוּדָתִי, תהלים צא
אֱלֹהַי אֶבְטַח־בּוֹ: כִּי הוּא יַצִּילְךָ מִפַּח יָקוּשׁ, מִדֶּבֶר הַוּוֹת:
בְּאֶבְרָתוֹ יָסֶךְ לָךְ, וְתַחַת־כְּנָפָיו תֶּחְסֶה, צִנָּה וְסֹחֵרָה אֲמִתּוֹ:
לֹא־תִירָא מִפַּחַד לָיְלָה, מֵחֵץ יָעוּף יוֹמָם: מִדֶּבֶר בָּאֹפֶל יַהֲלֹךְ,
מִקֶּטֶב יָשׁוּד צָהֳרָיִם: יִפֹּל מִצִּדְּךָ אֶלֶף, וּרְבָבָה מִימִינֶךָ, אֵלֶיךָ
לֹא יִגָּשׁ: רַק בְּעֵינֶיךָ תַבִּיט, וְשִׁלֻּמַת רְשָׁעִים תִּרְאֶה: כִּי־אַתָּה

---

יֹשֵׁב בְּסֵתֶר עֶלְיוֹן, בְּצֵל שַׁדַּי יִתְלוֹנָן *The Most High dwells in hiding; Shaddai rests in shadow.* (*Psalm 91*)

The divine manifestation comes to us from the midst of the supernal mystery of a hiding God, *Deus absconditus*. In truth, there is no possibility of limited thought [such as ours] grasping the limitless supernal light. We know that it is forever hidden and sealed because of the might of its holiness. But even this knowledge, of not knowing, partakes of supernal hues, at once awful and wonderful; they are the source of our lives; the splendor, the essence of our eternity.[20]

What is closer to us, grasped already by the power of our intellect (when it is lucid), is the knowledge that comes after the limitation that the Eternal Source engraved upon His worlds, concrete and ethereal; after He spread a *shadow* upon the infinite light, and said *"Dai!"* ("Enough!") to his supernal worlds,[21] inducing them to tow a line; to be revealed in proportion, so as to illumine His creations and creatures.

---

20. "The end of knowledge is that we not know" is an expression that derives from Maimonides' *via negativa*. It is invoked a couple of times in *Likkutei Moharan* by Rabbi Nahman of Breslov (who as much as he opposed Maimonides' philosophy, was much indebted to it). Rav Kook's point is that though the *Deus absconditus* (*"El mistater"*) is intellectually inapprehensible, nonetheless, our souls are nourished thereby.
21. "I am the one that said to my world, to the heaven and to the earth, 'Enough' (*'Dai'*), for if I had not said to them 'Enough,' they would continue to expand right up to this

taking the Most High as your shelter, no harm will befall you, no plague will come near your tent, for He will command His angels about you, to guard you in all your ways. They will lift you in their hands, lest your foot stumble on a stone. You will tread on lions and vipers, you will trample on young lions and snakes. [God says] "Because he loves Me, I will rescue him; I will protect him, because he acknowledges My name. When he calls on Me, I will answer him, I will be with him in distress, I will deliver him and bring him honor.
▸ With long life I will satisfy him, and show him My salvation.
With long life I will satisfy him, and show him My salvation."

הַלְלוּיָהּ Halleluya! Praise the name of the LORD. Praise Him, you servants of the LORD who stand in the LORD's House, in the courtyards of the House of our God. Praise the LORD, for the LORD is *Ps. 135*

---

"captivate souls,"[26] is never futile. At times the effects are visible, inasmuch as those brought close improve their deeds and straighten their opinions. Sometimes but an inner seed enters into them, ensuring that they shall not leave this world without returning. And even if, God forbid, the person reached is so bad that he himself is beyond return, this seed will work on the nature of his soul, and there will come out of him a good son who will return; and he in turn will fix the soul of his father.[27] The LORD knows that I do not bring close all the sinners – only those that I feel have a great "treasure" tucked away inside them. There are many ways to know this and great books should be written to explain if only a smattering of this great thing.[28]

הַלְלוּיָהּ, הַלְלוּ אֶת־שֵׁם יהוה, הַלְלוּ עַבְדֵי יהוה: שֶׁעֹמְדִים בְּבֵית יהוה, בְּחַצְרוֹת בֵּית אֱלֹהֵינוּ: *Halleluyah! Praise the name of the LORD. Praise Him, you servants of the LORD who stand in the LORD's House, in the courtyards of the House of our God.* The service of the LORD assumes two forms. One, takes place inside the very Temple. It is devoted solely to the thought of the LORD (*Havayah*)

---

26. *Ḥakhamim lokḥei nefashot*. Cf. Proverbs 11:30. In *b. Bava Metsi'a* 85a, the epithet *"loke'aḥ nefashot ḥakham"* was applied to Rabbi Shim'on ben Isi ben Lakonia, who by teaching Torah to Rabbi Yosé, a wayward son of Rabbi El'azar ben Rabbi Shim'on, was able to return him to the fold. See further Rabbi Zadok Hakohen Rabinowitz, *Zidkat ha-Zaddik* (Lublin, 1913), chap. 114 (17b-c).
27. See *SK* 7:51–52: *"bera mezakeh abba."* The quote comes from *b. Sanhedrin* 104a.
28. *IR*, vol. 2, pp. 187–188.

יהוה מַחְסִי, עֶלְיוֹן שַׂמְתָּ מְעוֹנֶךָ: לֹא־תְאֻנֶּה אֵלֶיךָ רָעָה, וְנֶגַע
לֹא־יִקְרַב בְּאׇהֳלֶךָ: כִּי מַלְאָכָיו יְצַוֶּה־לָּךְ, לִשְׁמׇרְךָ בְּכׇל־דְּרָכֶיךָ:
עַל־כַּפַּיִם יִשָּׂאוּנְךָ, פֶּן־תִּגֹּף בָּאֶבֶן רַגְלֶךָ: עַל־שַׁחַל וָפֶתֶן תִּדְרֹךְ,
תִּרְמֹס כְּפִיר וְתַנִּין: כִּי בִי חָשַׁק וַאֲפַלְּטֵהוּ, אֲשַׂגְּבֵהוּ כִּי־יָדַע
שְׁמִי: יִקְרָאֵנִי וְאֶעֱנֵהוּ, עִמּוֹ אָנֹכִי בְצָרָה, אֲחַלְּצֵהוּ וַאֲכַבְּדֵהוּ:
◂ אֹרֶךְ יָמִים אַשְׂבִּיעֵהוּ, וְאַרְאֵהוּ בִּישׁוּעָתִי:
אֹרֶךְ יָמִים אַשְׂבִּיעֵהוּ, וְאַרְאֵהוּ בִּישׁוּעָתִי:

הַלְלוּיָהּ, הַלְלוּ אֶת־שֵׁם יהוה, הַלְלוּ עַבְדֵי יהוה: שֶׁעֹמְדִים בְּבֵית תהלים קלה
יהוה, בְּחַצְרוֹת בֵּית אֱלֹהֵינוּ: הַלְלוּיָהּ כִּי־טוֹב יהוה, זַמְּרוּ לִשְׁמוֹ

Slutsk), Jacob David Wilovski, (1845–1914), known by the acronym "Ridbaz."[24] Ridbaz criticized Rav Kook for what he viewed as the excessive overtures he made toward the wicked. In a lengthy response, Rav Kook laid out his philosophy of *"kiruv reḥokim"* or outreach to disaffected Jews. Here are a few snippets:

> He is amazed that I draw all close, even "sinners of Israel," in order to return them. I hinted to my intention: Whoever is worthy to delve into the inner mysteries of the Torah, is filled with the light of love of the "Torah of love," and there devolves upon him the obligation to engage in the *"tikkun"* (fixing) of the fallen, and in bringing close the alienated. (In the language of the masters of the esoteric lore, this is also referred to as gathering the sparks of holiness from the midst of the *"kelipot"* or husks.)[25]
>
> Such Torah scholars naturally recognize the inner *"segulah"* (treasure), and know how to separate from it the volitional *"kelipah."* They are obligated to bring close such sinners who possess an inner treasure, in order to arouse the power of good hidden within them, until it totally overcomes the volitional evil and vanquishes it. The activity of such wise men, who

24. Ridbaz once remarked to Rav Kook that his philosophy is beyond his ken and that he would prefer the simple Judaism of his grandmother, of blessed memory. Rav Kook responded that though Ridbaz's grandmother was certainly a pious woman, it is inconceivable that the Jewish People be conducted by the simple faith of his grandmother. For that leadership, there are required the lofty thoughts of the Torah. See RZYH, *Li-Sheloshah be-Ellul*, vol. 1 (Jerusalem, 1938; photo offset Jerusalem, 1978), par. 42 (p. 20).

25. *IR*, vol. 2, p. 186.

good; sing praises to His name, for it is lovely. For the LORD has chosen Jacob as His own, Israel as His treasure. For I know that the LORD is great, that our LORD is above all heavenly powers. Whatever pleases the LORD, He does, in heaven and on earth, in the seas and all the depths. He raises clouds from the ends of the earth; He sends lightning with the rain; He brings out the wind from His storehouses. He struck down the firstborn of Egypt, of both man and animals. He sent signs and wonders into your midst, Egypt – against Pharaoh and all his servants. He struck down many nations and slew mighty kings: Siḥon, King of the Amorites, Og, King of Bashan, and all the kingdoms of Canaan, giving their land as a heritage, a heritage for His people Israel. Your name, LORD, endures for ever; Your renown, LORD, for all generations. For the

---

כִּי אֲנִי יָדַעְתִּי כִּי־גָדוֹל יהוה, וַאֲדֹנֵינוּ מִכָּל־אֱלֹהִים *For I know that the LORD is great, that our LORD (Adonenu) is above all heavenly powers.* These are two different realizations. The first is realization of the LORD's greatness, transcending and unrelated to His creation. On this level, our thought is of the essence of the divinity. The Kabbalists would term it *Ein Sof* (the Infinite).

This thought can sustain us as long as we do not descend into the worlds and life with its limitations. But then an involvement with mundane affairs, with the various forces that dominate our plane of existence, evokes another realization, that our Master (*Adonenu*) surpasses all these mighty forces (*elohim*).

These two realizations reinforce one another: the knowledge of God as absolute, and the knowledge of God relative to the world.[32] The latter "fastens in our midst *devekut* (cleaving) to the Master of all the worlds, the Source of

---

32. In the latter regard, Rav Kook throws in the term *"legabei didan"* (relative to us). The opposite term (which does not occur in our passage but may be implicit) is *"legabei dideh"* (relative to Himself). Cf. *EA*, vol. 1, *Berakhot*, chap. 1, par. 132 (p. 53): "As for our talk of His relation to the creations – that is all from our side (*mi-tsidenu*), but relative to Himself, may He be blessed (*legabeh, yitbarakh*), there is not any relation, since there is nothing beside Him in reality. As Maimonides wrote in *Hil. Yesodei ha-Torah* [1:4], this is what is written 'The LORD God is truth' [Jeremiah 10:10], i.e. there is no true existent beside Him."
For the distinction between the two perspectives, the divine perspective versus the human perspective – *"mi-tsido/mi-tsidenu"* ("from His side/from our side") – see Rabbi Ḥayyim of Volozhin, *Nefesh ha-Ḥayyim* III, 4–7.

כִּי נָעִים: כִּי־יַעֲקֹב בָּחַר לוֹ יָהּ, יִשְׂרָאֵל לִסְגֻלָּתוֹ: כִּי אֲנִי יָדַעְתִּי
כִּי־גָדוֹל יהוה, וַאֲדֹנֵינוּ מִכָּל־אֱלֹהִים: כֹּל אֲשֶׁר־חָפֵץ יהוה עָשָׂה,
בַּשָּׁמַיִם וּבָאָרֶץ, בַּיַּמִּים וְכָל־תְּהֹמוֹת: מַעֲלֶה נְשִׂאִים מִקְצֵה
הָאָרֶץ, בְּרָקִים לַמָּטָר עָשָׂה, מוֹצֵא־רוּחַ מֵאוֹצְרוֹתָיו: שֶׁהִכָּה
בְּכוֹרֵי מִצְרָיִם, מֵאָדָם עַד־בְּהֵמָה: שָׁלַח אוֹתֹת וּמֹפְתִים בְּתוֹכֵכִי
מִצְרָיִם, בְּפַרְעֹה וּבְכָל־עֲבָדָיו: שֶׁהִכָּה גּוֹיִם רַבִּים, וְהָרַג מְלָכִים
עֲצוּמִים: לְסִיחוֹן מֶלֶךְ הָאֱמֹרִי, וּלְעוֹג מֶלֶךְ הַבָּשָׁן, וּלְכֹל מַמְלְכוֹת
כְּנָעַן: וְנָתַן אַרְצָם נַחֲלָה, נַחֲלָה לְיִשְׂרָאֵל עַמּוֹ: יהוה שִׁמְךָ
לְעוֹלָם, יהוה זִכְרְךָ לְדֹר־וָדֹר: כִּי־יָדִין יהוה עַמּוֹ, וְעַל־עֲבָדָיו

---

alone and unrelated to the creation. The second form of service, takes place "in the courtyards," in the outer chambers. This second set of servants strives to assure the continued relation of God (*Elohim*) to His creations, that He extend His divine love, His goodness to all His minions.[29]

כִּי־יַעֲקֹב בָּחַר לוֹ יָהּ, יִשְׂרָאֵל לִסְגֻלָּתוֹ *For the Lord (Yah) has chosen Jacob as His own, Israel as His treasure.* The difference between the concept of *beḥirah*, "choice" (or in its more modern form, *nivharut,* chosenness), and *segulah* ("treasure") is the difference between *giluyyim* (manifestations) and *'etsem* (essence).

Chosenness implies that there exists an alternative. This is the level of *giluyyim*, the outer manifestations, the worlds symbolized by the name *Yah*. As the Rabbis said: "'For with *Yah*, the Lord formed worlds.' These are two worlds that the Holy One, blessed be He, created, one with the letter *hé*, and one with the letter *yod*. This world with the letter *hé*, and the World to Come with the letter *yod*."[30] And it is Jacob who is chosen. Jacob – as opposed to Israel – connotes the more worldly aspect of our nation. But then there is the essence, the "treasure," which is to say that no alternative was ever entertained. And this, the essence, is reserved for "Israel," our spiritual essence.[31]

---

29. *OR*, vol. 2, p. 79.
30. *b. Menaḥot* 29b.
31. *OR*, vol. 2, pp. 79–80. Cf. Rabbi Ya'akov Moshe Ḥarlap, *Mei Marom*, vol. 13 (on the Prayer Book) (Jerusalem: Beit Zevul, 1998), pp. 42–43, commenting on the verse in 1 Chronicles 16:13: "Seed of Israel, His servant; sons of Jacob, His chosen."

Lord will bring justice to His people, and have compassion on His servants. The idols of the nations are silver and gold, the work of human hands. They have mouths, but cannot speak; eyes, but cannot see; ears, but cannot hear; there is no breath in their mouths. Those who make them will become like them: so will all who trust in them. ▸ House of Israel, bless the Lord. House of Aaron, bless the Lord. House of Levi, bless the Lord. You who fear the Lord, bless the Lord. Blessed is the Lord from Zion, He who dwells in Jerusalem. Halleluya!

*The custom is to stand for the following psalm.*

הודו Thank the Lord for He is good; His loving-kindness is for ever. *Ps. 136*
Thank the God of gods, His loving-kindness is for ever.

---

and we all wear different hats ("kings" and "priests"), collectively, as a nation, we are that singular "kingdom of priests," "top teachers and instructors to the entire world,"[36] destined to enlighten mankind about God.[37]

INTRODUCTION TO *HALLEL HA-GADOL*

הודו לַיהוה כִּי־טוֹב, כִּי לְעוֹלָם חַסְדּוֹ *Thank the Lord for He is good; His loving-kindness is for ever.* (*Psalm 136*)

> Said Rabbi Joshua ben Levi: These twenty-six [stanzas of] *Hodu* correspond to twenty-six generations that the Holy One, blessed be He, created in His world – before He gave the Torah – and supported by His love.[38]

The reckoning of the twenty-six generations is as follows. From Adam to Noah were ten generations, from Noah to Abraham were another ten generations,[39] and from Abraham to Amram (Moses' father) were yet six more generations. Moses the Lawgiver was the seventh generation from Abraham.

Once the Torah has been given, the world can be sustained on a basis of merit; observance of Torah justifies the continued existence of the world. But

36. *EA*, vol. 4, *Shabbat*, chap. 9, par. 23 (p. 171).
37. *OR*, vol. 2, p. 87.
38. *b. Pesaḥim* 118a.
39. *m. Avot* 5:2.

יִתְנֶחָם: עֲצַבֵּי הַגּוֹיִם כֶּסֶף וְזָהָב, מַעֲשֵׂה יְדֵי אָדָם: פֶּה־לָהֶם וְלֹא יְדַבֵּרוּ, עֵינַיִם לָהֶם וְלֹא יִרְאוּ: אָזְנַיִם לָהֶם וְלֹא יַאֲזִינוּ, אַף אֵין־יֶשׁ־רוּחַ בְּפִיהֶם: כְּמוֹהֶם יִהְיוּ עֹשֵׂיהֶם, כֹּל אֲשֶׁר־בֹּטֵחַ בָּהֶם: › בֵּית יִשְׂרָאֵל בָּרְכוּ אֶת־יהוה, בֵּית אַהֲרֹן בָּרְכוּ אֶת־יהוה: בֵּית הַלֵּוִי בָּרְכוּ אֶת־יהוה, יִרְאֵי יהוה בָּרְכוּ אֶת־יהוה: בָּרוּךְ יהוה מִצִּיּוֹן, שֹׁכֵן יְרוּשָׁלָםִ, הַלְלוּיָהּ:

*The custom is to stand for the following psalm.*

תהלים קלו

הוֹדוּ לַיהוה כִּי־טוֹב כִּי לְעוֹלָם חַסְדּוֹ:
הוֹדוּ לֵאלֹהֵי הָאֱלֹהִים כִּי לְעוֹלָם חַסְדּוֹ:

---

all existence, *also* through the limited light that shines in all the expanses of the worlds and life's narrow highways."[33]

בָּרוּךְ יהוה מִצִּיּוֹן, שֹׁכֵן יְרוּשָׁלָםִ, הַלְלוּיָהּ *Blessed is the* L*ORD from Zion, He who dwells in Jerusalem. Halleluyah!* The People of Israel was destined to be "a kingdom of priests and a holy nation."[34] The two names of our capital city symbolize different dimensions of our polity. "Zion," the city of David, represents the temporal aspect of "kingdom" (*mamlakhah*). "Jerusalem" corresponds to the *kehunah,* the priestly aspect that revolves around the service in the Temple. But these two "crowns" that the People of Israel wear, are inseparable.[35] Though different roles have been assigned to various members of our nation,

---

33. *OR*, vol. 2, p. 80.
34. Exodus 19:6.
35. See *Seder Eliyahu Zuta,* ed. M. Friedmann (Vienna, 1904), chap. 4 (p. 179), that the two crowns the angels bestowed upon the Children of Israel at the time they received the Torah on Mount Sinai, correspond to the two promises of "Kingdom of Priests" and "Holy Nation." Cited in note to *Be'ur ha-Gra* to *Sifra di-Tseni'uta,* ed. Samuel Luria (Vilna, 1882), chap. 1 (3a). The unification of the two crowns is borne out by the fact that a single angel bestowed both crowns, totaling sixty myriads of angels for the sixty myriads of Israelites. At the time of their divestment, subsequent to the worship of the Golden Calf, one hundred and twenty myriad angels were required for the task of removing the crowns (two angels for each of the sixty myriads of Israelites), symbolizing that the bond between the two crowns had been broken. See *b. Shabbat* 88a.

Thank the LORD of lords, His loving-kindness is for ever.
To the One who alone works great wonders, His loving-kindness is for ever.
Who made the heavens with wisdom, His loving-kindness is for ever.
Who spread the earth upon the waters, His loving-kindness is for ever.
Who made the great lights, His loving-kindness is for ever.
The sun to rule by day, His loving-kindness is for ever.
The moon and the stars to rule by night, His loving-kindness is for ever.
Who struck Egypt through their firstborn, His loving-kindness is for ever.
And brought out Israel from their midst, His loving-kindness is for ever.
With a strong hand and outstretched arm, His loving-kindness is for ever.
Who split the Reed Sea into parts, His loving-kindness is for ever.
And made Israel pass through it, His loving-kindness is for ever.
Casting Pharaoh and his army into the Reed Sea; His loving-kindness is for ever.
Who led His people through the wilderness; His loving-kindness is for ever.
Who struck down great kings, His loving-kindness is for ever.

---

or "proper name" (*shem ha-'etsem*) of God,[41] is the name that sustains all existents.[42]

In some kabbalistically-oriented prayer books, the four letters of the divine name are inserted at the appropriate intervals: *yod* at the tenth verse; *hé* at the fifteenth verse; *vav* at the twenty-first verse; and *hé* at the twenty-sixth verse.

**הוֹדוּ לַיהוה כִּי־טוֹב, כִּי לְעוֹלָם חַסְדּוֹ** *Thank the LORD, for He is good; His loving-kindness is forever (previous page).* The main thing that triggers in all human beings the emotion of gratitude is the recognition of God's absolute goodness. This essential good transcends time and every limitation. It is a universal love that "is forever."[43]

41. See Maimonides, *MT, Hil. Yesodei ha-Torah* 6:2; *Hil. Nesi'at Kapayim* 14:10; idem, *Guide of the Perplexed* I, 61–63; Rabbi Judah Halevi, *Kuzari* IV, 1.
42. Rabbi Judah Löw (Maharal) of Prague, *Gevurot Hashem* (London: L. Honig, 1954), chap. 65 (p. 302).
43. *OR*, vol. 2, p. 88.

הוֹדוּ לַאֲדֹנֵי הָאֲדֹנִים | כִּי לְעוֹלָם חַסְדּוֹ:
לְעֹשֵׂה נִפְלָאוֹת גְּדֹלוֹת לְבַדּוֹ | כִּי לְעוֹלָם חַסְדּוֹ:
לְעֹשֵׂה הַשָּׁמַיִם בִּתְבוּנָה | כִּי לְעוֹלָם חַסְדּוֹ:
לְרֹקַע הָאָרֶץ עַל־הַמָּיִם | כִּי לְעוֹלָם חַסְדּוֹ:
לְעֹשֵׂה אוֹרִים גְּדֹלִים | כִּי לְעוֹלָם חַסְדּוֹ:
אֶת־הַשֶּׁמֶשׁ לְמֶמְשֶׁלֶת בַּיּוֹם | כִּי לְעוֹלָם חַסְדּוֹ:
אֶת־הַיָּרֵחַ וְכוֹכָבִים לְמֶמְשְׁלוֹת בַּלָּיְלָה | כִּי לְעוֹלָם חַסְדּוֹ:
לְמַכֵּה מִצְרַיִם בִּבְכוֹרֵיהֶם | כִּי לְעוֹלָם חַסְדּוֹ:
וַיּוֹצֵא יִשְׂרָאֵל מִתּוֹכָם | כִּי לְעוֹלָם חַסְדּוֹ:
בְּיָד חֲזָקָה וּבִזְרוֹעַ נְטוּיָה | כִּי לְעוֹלָם חַסְדּוֹ:
לְגֹזֵר יַם־סוּף לִגְזָרִים | כִּי לְעוֹלָם חַסְדּוֹ:
וְהֶעֱבִיר יִשְׂרָאֵל בְּתוֹכוֹ | כִּי לְעוֹלָם חַסְדּוֹ:
וְנִעֵר פַּרְעֹה וְחֵילוֹ בְיַם־סוּף | כִּי לְעוֹלָם חַסְדּוֹ:
לְמוֹלִיךְ עַמּוֹ בַּמִּדְבָּר | כִּי לְעוֹלָם חַסְדּוֹ:
לְמַכֵּה מְלָכִים גְּדֹלִים | כִּי לְעוֹלָם חַסְדּוֹ:

---

before the Torah was given; before the merit system was in place, it was the pure love of God that sustained the world.

Rav Kook adds the observation that the greatest *ḥesed* (love) of all is Torah:

> Is not the good fortune of man's moral purity a great love? Is it not the highest love? ...The light of Torah is the highest, absolute love, which was revealed in the world after twenty-six generations.[40]

Twenty-six is the numerical value of the four-letter name of God, the Tetragrammaton: *Havayah*. This name, which is called the *nomen proprium*

---

40. *OR*, vol. 2, p. 88. RZYH (*OR*, vol. 2, p. 489, par. 56) references the Zoharic literature whereby "Torah emanates from *Ḥokhmah* (Wisdom)," and *Ḥokhmah* is synonymous with *Ḥesed* (Love). See *Zohar* II, 81; III, 65; and *Hakdamat Tikkunei Zohar*. Cf. Rabbi Isaac Hutner, *Paḥad Yitsḥak: Rosh Hashanah* (New York, NY, 2003), 4:4 (pp. 48–49).

| | |
|---|---|
| And slew mighty kings, | His loving-kindness is for ever. |
| Siḥon, King of the Amorites, | His loving-kindness is for ever. |
| And Og, King of Bashan, | His loving-kindness is for ever. |
| And gave their land as a heritage, | His loving-kindness is for ever. |
| A heritage for His servant Israel; | His loving-kindness is for ever. |
| Who remembered us in our lowly state, | His loving-kindness is for ever. |
| And rescued us from our tormentors, | His loving-kindness is for ever. |
| ▸ Who gives food to all flesh, | His loving-kindness is for ever. |
| Give thanks to the God of heaven. | His loving-kindness is for ever. |

רַנְּנוּ Sing joyfully to the LORD, you righteous, for praise from the upright is seemly. Give thanks to the LORD with the harp; make music to Him on the ten-stringed lute. Sing Him a new song, play skillfully with shouts of joy. For the LORD's word is right, and all His deeds are done in faith. He loves righteousness and justice; the earth is full of the LORD's loving-kindness. By the LORD's word the heavens were made, and all their starry host by the breath of His mouth. He gathers the sea waters as a heap, and places the deep in storehouses. Let all the earth fear the LORD, and all the world's inhabitants stand in awe of Him. For He spoke, and it was; He commanded, and it stood firm. The LORD foils the plans of nations; He thwarts the intentions of peoples. The LORD's plans stand for ever, His heart's intents for all generations. Happy is the nation whose God is the LORD, the people He has chosen as His own. From heaven the LORD looks down and sees all mankind; from His dwelling place He oversees all who live on earth. He forms the hearts of all, and discerns all their deeds. No king is saved by the size of his army; no warrior is delivered by great strength. A horse is a vain hope for deliverance; despite its great strength, it cannot save. The eye of the LORD is on those who fear Him, on those who place their hope in His unfailing love, to rescue their soul from death, and keep them alive in famine. Our

*Ps. 33*

וַיַּהֲרֹג מְלָכִים אַדִּירִים | כִּי לְעוֹלָם חַסְדּוֹ:
לְסִיחוֹן מֶלֶךְ הָאֱמֹרִי | כִּי לְעוֹלָם חַסְדּוֹ:
וּלְעוֹג מֶלֶךְ הַבָּשָׁן | כִּי לְעוֹלָם חַסְדּוֹ:
וְנָתַן אַרְצָם לְנַחֲלָה | כִּי לְעוֹלָם חַסְדּוֹ:
נַחֲלָה לְיִשְׂרָאֵל עַבְדּוֹ | כִּי לְעוֹלָם חַסְדּוֹ:
שֶׁבְּשִׁפְלֵנוּ זָכַר לָנוּ | כִּי לְעוֹלָם חַסְדּוֹ:
וַיִּפְרְקֵנוּ מִצָּרֵינוּ | כִּי לְעוֹלָם חַסְדּוֹ:
◂ נֹתֵן לֶחֶם לְכָל־בָּשָׂר | כִּי לְעוֹלָם חַסְדּוֹ:
הוֹדוּ לְאֵל הַשָּׁמָיִם | כִּי לְעוֹלָם חַסְדּוֹ:

רַנְּנוּ צַדִּיקִים בַּיהוה, לַיְשָׁרִים נָאוָה תְהִלָּה: הוֹדוּ לַיהוה בְּכִנּוֹר, תהלים לג
בְּנֵבֶל עָשׂוֹר זַמְּרוּ־לוֹ: שִׁירוּ־לוֹ שִׁיר חָדָשׁ, הֵיטִיבוּ נַגֵּן בִּתְרוּעָה:
כִּי־יָשָׁר דְּבַר־יהוה, וְכָל־מַעֲשֵׂהוּ בֶּאֱמוּנָה: אֹהֵב צְדָקָה וּמִשְׁפָּט,
חֶסֶד יהוה מָלְאָה הָאָרֶץ: בִּדְבַר יהוה שָׁמַיִם נַעֲשׂוּ, וּבְרוּחַ פִּיו
כָּל־צְבָאָם: כֹּנֵס כַּנֵּד מֵי הַיָּם, נֹתֵן בְּאוֹצָרוֹת תְּהוֹמוֹת: יִירְאוּ
מֵיהוה כָּל־הָאָרֶץ, מִמֶּנּוּ יָגוּרוּ כָּל־יֹשְׁבֵי תֵבֵל: כִּי הוּא אָמַר
וַיֶּהִי, הוּא־צִוָּה וַיַּעֲמֹד: יהוה הֵפִיר עֲצַת־גּוֹיִם, הֵנִיא מַחְשְׁבוֹת
עַמִּים: עֲצַת יהוה לְעוֹלָם תַּעֲמֹד, מַחְשְׁבוֹת לִבּוֹ לְדֹר וָדֹר:
אַשְׁרֵי הַגּוֹי אֲשֶׁר־יהוה אֱלֹהָיו, הָעָם בָּחַר לְנַחֲלָה לוֹ: מִשָּׁמַיִם
הִבִּיט יהוה, רָאָה אֶת־כָּל־בְּנֵי הָאָדָם: מִמְּכוֹן־שִׁבְתּוֹ הִשְׁגִּיחַ,
אֶל כָּל־יֹשְׁבֵי הָאָרֶץ: הַיֹּצֵר יַחַד לִבָּם, הַמֵּבִין אֶל־כָּל־מַעֲשֵׂיהֶם:
אֵין־הַמֶּלֶךְ נוֹשָׁע בְּרָב־חָיִל, גִּבּוֹר לֹא־יִנָּצֵל בְּרָב־כֹּחַ: שֶׁקֶר
הַסּוּס לִתְשׁוּעָה, וּבְרֹב חֵילוֹ לֹא יְמַלֵּט: הִנֵּה עֵין יהוה אֶל־יְרֵאָיו,
לַמְיַחֲלִים לְחַסְדּוֹ: לְהַצִּיל מִמָּוֶת נַפְשָׁם, וּלְחַיּוֹתָם בָּרָעָב: נַפְשֵׁנוּ

soul waits for the LORD; He is our Help and Shield. ▸ In Him our hearts rejoice, for we trust in His holy name. Let Your unfailing love be upon us, LORD, as we have put our hope in You.

מִזְמוֹר שִׁיר A psalm. A song for the Sabbath day. It is good to thank *Ps. 92* the LORD and sing psalms to Your name, Most High – to tell of Your loving-kindness in the morning and Your faithfulness at night, to the music of the ten-stringed lyre and the melody of the harp. For You have made me rejoice by Your work, O LORD; I sing for joy at the deeds of Your hands. How great are Your deeds, LORD, and how very deep Your thoughts. A boor cannot know, nor can a fool understand, that though the wicked spring up like grass and all evildoers flourish, it is only that they may be destroyed for ever. But You, LORD, are eternally exalted. For behold Your enemies, LORD, behold Your enemies will perish; all evildoers will be scattered. You have raised my pride like that of a wild ox; I am anointed with fresh oil. My eyes shall look in triumph on my adversaries, my ears shall hear the downfall of the wicked who rise against me. ▸ The righteous will flourish like a palm tree and grow tall like a cedar in Lebanon. Planted in the LORD's House, blossoming in our God's courtyards, they will still bear fruit in old age, and stay vigorous and fresh, proclaiming that the LORD is upright: He is my Rock, in whom there is no wrong.

יהוה מָלָךְ The LORD reigns. He is robed in majesty. The LORD is robed, *Ps. 93* girded with strength. The world is firmly established; it cannot be moved. Your throne stands firm as of old; You are eternal. Rivers lift up, LORD, rivers lift up their voice, rivers lift up their crashing waves. ▸ Mightier than the noise of many waters, than the mighty waves of the sea is the LORD on high. Your testimonies are very sure; holiness adorns Your House, LORD, for evermore.

יְהִי כְבוֹד May the LORD's glory be for ever; may the LORD rejoice *Ps. 104*
in His works. May the LORD's name be blessed, now and for ever. *Ps. 113*
From the rising of the sun to its setting, may the LORD's name be praised. The LORD is high above all nations; His glory is above the heavens. LORD, Your name is for ever. Your renown, LORD, is for all *Ps. 135*

חִכְּתָה לַיהוה, עֶזְרֵנוּ וּמָגִנֵּנוּ הוּא: ‹ כִּי־בוֹ יִשְׂמַח לִבֵּנוּ, כִּי בְשֵׁם
קָדְשׁוֹ בָטָחְנוּ: יְהִי־חַסְדְּךָ יהוה עָלֵינוּ, כַּאֲשֶׁר יִחַלְנוּ לָךְ:

מִזְמוֹר שִׁיר לְיוֹם הַשַּׁבָּת: טוֹב לְהֹדוֹת לַיהוה, וּלְזַמֵּר לְשִׁמְךָ תהלים צב
עֶלְיוֹן: לְהַגִּיד בַּבֹּקֶר חַסְדֶּךָ, וֶאֱמוּנָתְךָ בַּלֵּילוֹת: עֲלֵי־עָשׂוֹר
וַעֲלֵי־נָבֶל, עֲלֵי הִגָּיוֹן בְּכִנּוֹר: כִּי שִׂמַּחְתַּנִי יהוה בְּפָעֳלֶךָ, בְּמַעֲשֵׂי
יָדֶיךָ אֲרַנֵּן: מַה־גָּדְלוּ מַעֲשֶׂיךָ יהוה, מְאֹד עָמְקוּ מַחְשְׁבֹתֶיךָ:
אִישׁ־בַּעַר לֹא יֵדָע, וּכְסִיל לֹא־יָבִין אֶת־זֹאת: בִּפְרֹחַ רְשָׁעִים
כְּמוֹ עֵשֶׂב, וַיָּצִיצוּ כָּל־פֹּעֲלֵי אָוֶן, לְהִשָּׁמְדָם עֲדֵי־עַד: וְאַתָּה
מָרוֹם לְעֹלָם יהוה: כִּי הִנֵּה אֹיְבֶיךָ יהוה, כִּי־הִנֵּה אֹיְבֶיךָ יֹאבֵדוּ,
יִתְפָּרְדוּ כָּל־פֹּעֲלֵי אָוֶן: וַתָּרֶם כִּרְאֵים קַרְנִי, בַּלֹּתִי בְּשֶׁמֶן רַעֲנָן:
וַתַּבֵּט עֵינִי בְּשׁוּרָי, בַּקָּמִים עָלַי מְרֵעִים תִּשְׁמַעְנָה אָזְנָי: ‹ צַדִּיק
כַּתָּמָר יִפְרָח, כְּאֶרֶז בַּלְּבָנוֹן יִשְׂגֶּה: שְׁתוּלִים בְּבֵית יהוה, בְּחַצְרוֹת
אֱלֹהֵינוּ יַפְרִיחוּ: עוֹד יְנוּבוּן בְּשֵׂיבָה, דְּשֵׁנִים וְרַעֲנַנִּים יִהְיוּ: לְהַגִּיד
כִּי־יָשָׁר יהוה, צוּרִי, וְלֹא־עַוְלָתָה בּוֹ:

יהוה מָלָךְ, גֵּאוּת לָבֵשׁ, לָבֵשׁ יהוה עֹז הִתְאַזָּר, אַף־תִּכּוֹן תֵּבֵל תהלים צג
בַּל־תִּמּוֹט: נָכוֹן כִּסְאֲךָ מֵאָז, מֵעוֹלָם אָתָּה: נָשְׂאוּ נְהָרוֹת יהוה,
נָשְׂאוּ נְהָרוֹת קוֹלָם, יִשְׂאוּ נְהָרוֹת דָּכְיָם: ‹ מִקֹּלוֹת מַיִם רַבִּים,
אַדִּירִים מִשְׁבְּרֵי־יָם, אַדִּיר בַּמָּרוֹם יהוה: עֵדֹתֶיךָ נֶאֶמְנוּ מְאֹד
לְבֵיתְךָ נַאֲוָה־קֹדֶשׁ, יהוה לְאֹרֶךְ יָמִים:

יְהִי כְבוֹד יהוה לְעוֹלָם, יִשְׂמַח יהוה בְּמַעֲשָׂיו: יְהִי שֵׁם יהוה תהלים קד תהלים קיג
מְבֹרָךְ, מֵעַתָּה וְעַד־עוֹלָם: מִמִּזְרַח־שֶׁמֶשׁ עַד־מְבוֹאוֹ, מְהֻלָּל
שֵׁם יהוה: רָם עַל־כָּל־גּוֹיִם יהוה, עַל הַשָּׁמַיִם כְּבוֹדוֹ: יהוה תהלים קלה

generations. The LORD has established His throne in heaven; His kingdom rules all. Let the heavens rejoice and the earth be glad. Let them say among the nations, "The LORD is King." The LORD is King, the LORD was King, the LORD will be King for ever and all time. The LORD is King for ever and all time; nations will perish from His land. The LORD foils the plans of nations; He frustrates the intentions of peoples. Many are the intentions in a person's mind, but the LORD's plan prevails. The LORD's plan shall stand for ever, His mind's intent for all generations. For He spoke and it was; He commanded and it stood firm. For the LORD has chosen Zion; He desired it for His dwelling. For the LORD has chosen Jacob, Israel as His special treasure. For the LORD will not abandon His people; nor will He forsake His heritage. ▸ He is compassionate. He forgives iniquity and does not destroy. Repeatedly He suppresses His anger, not rousing His full wrath. LORD, save! May the King answer us on the day we call.

*Ps. 103* · *1 Chr. 16* · *Ps. 10* · *Ps. 33* · *Prov. 19* · *Ps. 33* · *Ps. 132* · *Ps. 135* · *Ps. 94* · *Ps. 78* · *Ps. 20*

*The line beginning with "You open Your hand" should be said with special concentration, representing as it does the key idea of this psalm, and of Pesukei DeZimra as a whole, that God is the creator and sustainer of all.*

אַשְׁרֵי Happy are those who dwell in Your House; *Ps. 84*
they shall continue to praise You, Selah!
Happy are the people for whom this is so; *Ps. 144*
happy are the people whose God is the LORD.
A song of praise by David. *Ps. 145*

I will exalt You, my God, the King, and bless Your name for ever and all time. Every day I will bless You, and praise Your name for ever and all time. Great is the LORD and greatly to be praised; His greatness is unfathomable. One generation will praise Your works to the next, and tell of Your mighty deeds. On the glorious splendor of Your majesty I will meditate, and on the acts of Your wonders. They shall talk of the power of Your awesome deeds, and I will tell of Your greatness. They shall recite the record of Your great goodness, and sing with

שִׁמְךָ לְעוֹלָם, יהוה זִכְרְךָ לְדֹר־וָדֹר: יהוה בַּשָּׁמַיִם הֵכִין כִּסְאוֹ, תהלים קג
וּמַלְכוּתוֹ בַּכֹּל מָשָׁלָה: יִשְׂמְחוּ הַשָּׁמַיִם וְתָגֵל הָאָרֶץ, וְיֹאמְרוּ דברי הימים א׳ טז
בַגּוֹיִם יהוה מָלָךְ: יהוה מֶלֶךְ, יהוה מָלָךְ, יהוה יִמְלֹךְ לְעוֹלָם וָעֶד.
יהוה מֶלֶךְ עוֹלָם וָעֶד, אָבְדוּ גוֹיִם מֵאַרְצוֹ: יהוה הֵפִיר עֲצַת־גּוֹיִם, תהלים י תהלים לג
הֵנִיא מַחְשְׁבוֹת עַמִּים: רַבּוֹת מַחֲשָׁבוֹת בְּלֶב־אִישׁ, וַעֲצַת יהוה משלי יט
הִיא תָקוּם: עֲצַת יהוה לְעוֹלָם תַּעֲמֹד, מַחְשְׁבוֹת לִבּוֹ לְדֹר וָדֹר: תהלים לג
כִּי הוּא אָמַר וַיֶּהִי, הוּא־צִוָּה וַיַּעֲמֹד: כִּי־בָחַר יהוה בְּצִיּוֹן, אִוָּהּ תהלים קלב
לְמוֹשָׁב לוֹ: כִּי־יַעֲקֹב בָּחַר לוֹ יָהּ, יִשְׂרָאֵל לִסְגֻלָּתוֹ: כִּי לֹא־יִטֹּשׁ תהלים קלה תהלים צד
יהוה עַמּוֹ, וְנַחֲלָתוֹ לֹא יַעֲזֹב: ◄ וְהוּא רַחוּם, יְכַפֵּר עָוֹן וְלֹא־יַשְׁחִית, תהלים עח
וְהִרְבָּה לְהָשִׁיב אַפּוֹ, וְלֹא־יָעִיר כָּל־חֲמָתוֹ: יהוה הוֹשִׁיעָה, הַמֶּלֶךְ תהלים כ
יַעֲנֵנוּ בְיוֹם־קָרְאֵנוּ:

*The line beginning with* פּוֹתֵחַ אֶת יָדֶךָ *should be said with special concentration, representing as it does the key idea of this psalm, and of* פסוקי דזמרה *as a whole, that God is the creator and sustainer of all.*

אַשְׁרֵי יוֹשְׁבֵי בֵיתֶךָ, עוֹד יְהַלְלוּךָ סֶּלָה: תהלים פד
אַשְׁרֵי הָעָם שֶׁכָּכָה לּוֹ, אַשְׁרֵי הָעָם שֶׁיהוה אֱלֹהָיו: תהלים קמד
תְּהִלָּה לְדָוִד תהלים קמה

אֲרוֹמִמְךָ אֱלוֹהַי הַמֶּלֶךְ, וַאֲבָרְכָה שִׁמְךָ לְעוֹלָם וָעֶד:
בְּכָל־יוֹם אֲבָרְכֶךָּ, וַאֲהַלְלָה שִׁמְךָ לְעוֹלָם וָעֶד:
גָּדוֹל יהוה וּמְהֻלָּל מְאֹד, וְלִגְדֻלָּתוֹ אֵין חֵקֶר:
דּוֹר לְדוֹר יְשַׁבַּח מַעֲשֶׂיךָ, וּגְבוּרֹתֶיךָ יַגִּידוּ:
הֲדַר כְּבוֹד הוֹדֶךָ, וְדִבְרֵי נִפְלְאֹתֶיךָ אָשִׂיחָה:
וֶעֱזוּז נוֹרְאֹתֶיךָ יֹאמֵרוּ, וּגְדוּלָּתְךָ אֲסַפְּרֶנָּה:
זֵכֶר רַב־טוּבְךָ יַבִּיעוּ, וְצִדְקָתְךָ יְרַנֵּנוּ:

joy of Your righteousness. The LORD is gracious and compassionate, slow to anger and great in loving-kindness. The LORD is good to all, and His compassion extends to all His works. All Your works shall thank You, LORD, and Your devoted ones shall bless You. They shall talk of the glory of Your kingship, and speak of Your might. To make known to mankind His mighty deeds and the glorious majesty of His kingship. Your kingdom is an everlasting kingdom, and Your reign is for all generations. The LORD supports all who fall, and raises all who are bowed down. All raise their eyes to You in hope, and You give them their food in due season. You open Your hand, and satisfy every living thing with favor. The LORD is righteous in all His ways, and kind in all He does. The LORD is close to all who call on Him, to all who call on Him in truth. He fulfills the will of those who revere Him; He hears their cry and saves them. The LORD guards all who love Him, but all the wicked He will destroy. ▸ My mouth shall speak the praise of the LORD, and all creatures shall bless His holy name for ever and all time.

We will bless the LORD now and for ever. Halleluya! *Ps. 115*

הַלְלוּיָהּ Halleluya! Praise the LORD, my soul. I will praise the LORD all my life; I will sing to my God as long as I live. Put not your trust in princes, or in mortal man who cannot save. His breath expires, he returns to the earth; on that day his plans come to an end. Happy is he whose help is the God of Jacob, whose hope is in the LORD his God who made heaven and earth, the sea and all they contain; He who keeps faith for ever. He secures justice for the oppressed. He gives food to the hungry. The LORD sets captives free. The LORD gives sight to the blind. The LORD raises those bowed down. The LORD loves the righteous. The LORD protects the stranger. He gives courage to the orphan and widow. He thwarts the way of the wicked. ▸ The LORD shall reign for ever. He is your God, Zion, for all generations. Halleluya! *Ps. 146*

חַנּוּן וְרַחוּם יהוה, אֶרֶךְ אַפַּיִם וּגְדָל־חָסֶד:
טוֹב־יהוה לַכֹּל, וְרַחֲמָיו עַל־כָּל־מַעֲשָׂיו:
יוֹדוּךָ יהוה כָּל־מַעֲשֶׂיךָ, וַחֲסִידֶיךָ יְבָרְכוּכָה:
כְּבוֹד מַלְכוּתְךָ יֹאמֵרוּ, וּגְבוּרָתְךָ יְדַבֵּרוּ:
לְהוֹדִיעַ לִבְנֵי הָאָדָם גְּבוּרֹתָיו, וּכְבוֹד הֲדַר מַלְכוּתוֹ:
מַלְכוּתְךָ מַלְכוּת כָּל־עֹלָמִים, וּמֶמְשַׁלְתְּךָ בְּכָל־דּוֹר וָדֹר:
סוֹמֵךְ יהוה לְכָל־הַנֹּפְלִים, וְזוֹקֵף לְכָל־הַכְּפוּפִים:
עֵינֵי־כֹל אֵלֶיךָ יְשַׂבֵּרוּ, וְאַתָּה נוֹתֵן־לָהֶם אֶת־אָכְלָם בְּעִתּוֹ:
פּוֹתֵחַ אֶת־יָדֶךָ, וּמַשְׂבִּיעַ לְכָל־חַי רָצוֹן:
צַדִּיק יהוה בְּכָל־דְּרָכָיו, וְחָסִיד בְּכָל־מַעֲשָׂיו:
קָרוֹב יהוה לְכָל־קֹרְאָיו, לְכֹל אֲשֶׁר יִקְרָאֻהוּ בֶאֱמֶת:
רְצוֹן־יְרֵאָיו יַעֲשֶׂה, וְאֶת־שַׁוְעָתָם יִשְׁמַע, וְיוֹשִׁיעֵם:
שׁוֹמֵר יהוה אֶת־כָּל־אֹהֲבָיו, וְאֵת כָּל־הָרְשָׁעִים יַשְׁמִיד:
› תְּהִלַּת יהוה יְדַבֶּר פִּי, וִיבָרֵךְ כָּל־בָּשָׂר שֵׁם קָדְשׁוֹ לְעוֹלָם וָעֶד:
וַאֲנַחְנוּ נְבָרֵךְ יָהּ מֵעַתָּה וְעַד־עוֹלָם, הַלְלוּיָהּ: תהלים קטו

תהלים קמו הַלְלוּיָהּ, הַלְלִי נַפְשִׁי אֶת־יהוה: אֲהַלְלָה יהוה בְּחַיָּי, אֲזַמְּרָה לֵאלֹהַי בְּעוֹדִי: אַל־תִּבְטְחוּ בִנְדִיבִים, בְּבֶן־אָדָם שֶׁאֵין לוֹ תְשׁוּעָה: תֵּצֵא רוּחוֹ, יָשֻׁב לְאַדְמָתוֹ, בַּיּוֹם הַהוּא אָבְדוּ עֶשְׁתֹּנֹתָיו: אַשְׁרֵי שֶׁאֵל יַעֲקֹב בְּעֶזְרוֹ, שִׂבְרוֹ עַל־יהוה אֱלֹהָיו: עֹשֶׂה שָׁמַיִם וָאָרֶץ, אֶת־הַיָּם וְאֶת־כָּל־אֲשֶׁר־בָּם, הַשֹּׁמֵר אֱמֶת לְעוֹלָם: עֹשֶׂה מִשְׁפָּט לָעֲשׁוּקִים, נֹתֵן לֶחֶם לָרְעֵבִים, יהוה מַתִּיר אֲסוּרִים: יהוה פֹּקֵחַ עִוְרִים, יהוה זֹקֵף כְּפוּפִים, יהוה אֹהֵב צַדִּיקִים: יהוה שֹׁמֵר אֶת־גֵּרִים, יָתוֹם וְאַלְמָנָה יְעוֹדֵד, וְדֶרֶךְ רְשָׁעִים יְעַוֵּת: › יִמְלֹךְ יהוה לְעוֹלָם, אֱלֹהַיִךְ צִיּוֹן לְדֹר וָדֹר, הַלְלוּיָהּ:

הַלְלוּיָהּ Halleluya! How good it is to sing songs to our God; how pleasant and fitting to praise Him. The LORD rebuilds Jerusalem. He gathers the scattered exiles of Israel. He heals the broken-hearted and binds up their wounds. He counts the number of the stars, calling each by name. Great is our LORD and mighty in power; His understanding has no limit. The LORD gives courage to the humble, but casts the wicked to the ground. Sing to the LORD in thanks; make music to our God on the harp. He covers the sky with clouds. He provides the earth with rain and makes grass grow on the hills. He gives food to the cattle and to the ravens when they cry. He does not take delight in the strength of horses nor pleasure in the fleetness of man. The LORD takes pleasure in those who fear Him, who put their hope in His loving care. Praise the LORD, Jerusalem; sing to your God, Zion, for He has strengthened the bars of your gates and blessed your children in your midst. He has brought peace to your borders, and satisfied you with the finest wheat. He sends His commandment to earth; swiftly runs His word. He spreads snow like fleece, sprinkles frost like ashes, scatters hail like crumbs. Who can stand His cold? He sends His word and melts them; He makes the wind blow and the waters flow. ▸ He has declared His words to Jacob, His statutes and laws to Israel. He has done this for no other nation; such laws they do not know. Halleluya! *Ps. 147*

הַלְלוּיָהּ Halleluya! Praise the LORD from the heavens, praise Him in the heights. Praise Him, all His angels; praise Him, all His hosts. Praise Him, sun and moon; praise Him, all shining stars. Praise Him, highest heavens and the waters above the heavens. Let them praise the name of the LORD, for He commanded and they were created. He established them for ever and all time, issuing a decree that will never change. Praise the LORD from the earth: sea monsters and all the deep seas; fire and hail, snow and mist, storm winds that obey His word; mountains and all hills, fruit trees and *Ps. 148*

תהלים קמז

הַלְלוּיָהּ, כִּי־טוֹב זַמְּרָה אֱלֹהֵינוּ, כִּי־נָעִים נָאוָה תְהִלָּה: בּוֹנֵה יְרוּשָׁלַםִ יהוה, נִדְחֵי יִשְׂרָאֵל יְכַנֵּס: הָרוֹפֵא לִשְׁבוּרֵי לֵב, וּמְחַבֵּשׁ לְעַצְּבוֹתָם: מוֹנֶה מִסְפָּר לַכּוֹכָבִים, לְכֻלָּם שֵׁמוֹת יִקְרָא: גָּדוֹל אֲדוֹנֵינוּ וְרַב־כֹּחַ, לִתְבוּנָתוֹ אֵין מִסְפָּר: מְעוֹדֵד עֲנָוִים יהוה, מַשְׁפִּיל רְשָׁעִים עֲדֵי־אָרֶץ: עֱנוּ לַיהוה בְּתוֹדָה, זַמְּרוּ לֵאלֹהֵינוּ בְכִנּוֹר: הַמְכַסֶּה שָׁמַיִם בְּעָבִים, הַמֵּכִין לָאָרֶץ מָטָר, הַמַּצְמִיחַ הָרִים חָצִיר: נוֹתֵן לִבְהֵמָה לַחְמָהּ, לִבְנֵי עֹרֵב אֲשֶׁר יִקְרָאוּ: לֹא בִגְבוּרַת הַסּוּס יֶחְפָּץ, לֹא־בְשׁוֹקֵי הָאִישׁ יִרְצֶה: רוֹצֶה יהוה אֶת־יְרֵאָיו, אֶת־הַמְיַחֲלִים לְחַסְדּוֹ: שַׁבְּחִי יְרוּשָׁלַםִ אֶת־יהוה, הַלְלִי אֱלֹהַיִךְ צִיּוֹן: כִּי־חִזַּק בְּרִיחֵי שְׁעָרָיִךְ, בֵּרַךְ בָּנַיִךְ בְּקִרְבֵּךְ: הַשָּׂם־גְּבוּלֵךְ שָׁלוֹם, חֵלֶב חִטִּים יַשְׂבִּיעֵךְ: הַשֹּׁלֵחַ אִמְרָתוֹ אָרֶץ, עַד־מְהֵרָה יָרוּץ דְּבָרוֹ: הַנֹּתֵן שֶׁלֶג כַּצָּמֶר, כְּפוֹר כָּאֵפֶר יְפַזֵּר: מַשְׁלִיךְ קַרְחוֹ כְפִתִּים, לִפְנֵי קָרָתוֹ מִי יַעֲמֹד: יִשְׁלַח דְּבָרוֹ וְיַמְסֵם, יַשֵּׁב רוּחוֹ יִזְּלוּ־מָיִם: ‹ מַגִּיד דְּבָרָו לְיַעֲקֹב, חֻקָּיו וּמִשְׁפָּטָיו לְיִשְׂרָאֵל: לֹא עָשָׂה כֵן לְכָל־גּוֹי, וּמִשְׁפָּטִים בַּל־יְדָעוּם, הַלְלוּיָהּ:

תהלים קמח

הַלְלוּיָהּ, הַלְלוּ אֶת־יהוה מִן־הַשָּׁמַיִם, הַלְלוּהוּ בַּמְּרוֹמִים: הַלְלוּהוּ כָל־מַלְאָכָיו, הַלְלוּהוּ כָּל־צְבָאָו: הַלְלוּהוּ שֶׁמֶשׁ וְיָרֵחַ, הַלְלוּהוּ כָּל־כּוֹכְבֵי אוֹר: הַלְלוּהוּ שְׁמֵי הַשָּׁמָיִם, וְהַמַּיִם אֲשֶׁר מֵעַל הַשָּׁמָיִם: יְהַלְלוּ אֶת־שֵׁם יהוה, כִּי הוּא צִוָּה וְנִבְרָאוּ: וַיַּעֲמִידֵם לָעַד לְעוֹלָם, חָק־נָתַן וְלֹא יַעֲבוֹר: הַלְלוּ אֶת־יהוה מִן־הָאָרֶץ, תַּנִּינִים וְכָל־תְּהֹמוֹת: אֵשׁ וּבָרָד שֶׁלֶג וְקִיטוֹר, רוּחַ סְעָרָה עֹשָׂה דְבָרוֹ: הֶהָרִים וְכָל־גְּבָעוֹת, עֵץ פְּרִי וְכָל־אֲרָזִים:

all cedars; wild animals and all cattle, creeping things and winged birds; kings of the earth and all nations, princes and all judges on earth; youths and maidens, old and young. ▸ Let them praise the name of the LORD, for His name alone is sublime; His majesty is above earth and heaven. He has raised the pride of His people, for the glory of all His devoted ones, the children of Israel, the people close to Him. Halleluya!

הַלְלוּיָהּ Halleluya! Sing to the LORD a new song, His praise in the assembly of the devoted. Let Israel rejoice in its Maker; let the children of Zion exult in their King. Let them praise His name with dancing; sing praises to Him with timbrel and harp. For the LORD delights in His people; He adorns the humble with salvation. Let the devoted revel in glory; let them sing for joy on their beds. Let high praises of God be in their throats, and a two-edged sword in their hand: to impose retribution on the nations, punishment on the peoples, ▸ binding their kings with chains, their nobles with iron fetters, carrying out the judgment written against them. This is the glory of all His devoted ones. Halleluya! *Ps. 149*

הַלְלוּיָהּ Halleluya! Praise God in His holy place; *Ps. 150*
praise Him in the heavens of His power.
Praise Him for His mighty deeds;
praise Him for His surpassing greatness.
Praise Him with blasts of the shofar;
praise Him with the harp and lyre.
Praise Him with timbrel and dance;
praise Him with strings and flute.
▸ Praise Him with clashing cymbals;
praise Him with resounding cymbals.
Let all that breathes
praise the LORD. Halleluya!
Let all that breathes
praise the LORD. Halleluya!

הַחַיָּה וְכָל־בְּהֵמָה, רֶמֶשׂ וְצִפּוֹר כָּנָף: מַלְכֵי־אֶרֶץ וְכָל־לְאֻמִּים, שָׂרִים וְכָל־שֹׁפְטֵי אָרֶץ: בַּחוּרִים וְגַם־בְּתוּלוֹת, זְקֵנִים עִם־נְעָרִים: ◂ יְהַלְלוּ אֶת־שֵׁם יהוה, כִּי־נִשְׂגָּב שְׁמוֹ לְבַדּוֹ, הוֹדוֹ עַל־אֶרֶץ וְשָׁמָיִם: וַיָּרֶם קֶרֶן לְעַמּוֹ, תְּהִלָּה לְכָל־חֲסִידָיו, לִבְנֵי יִשְׂרָאֵל עַם קְרֹבוֹ, הַלְלוּיָהּ:

תהלים קמט
הַלְלוּיָהּ, שִׁירוּ לַיהוה שִׁיר חָדָשׁ, תְּהִלָּתוֹ בִּקְהַל חֲסִידִים: יִשְׂמַח יִשְׂרָאֵל בְּעֹשָׂיו, בְּנֵי־צִיּוֹן יָגִילוּ בְמַלְכָּם: יְהַלְלוּ שְׁמוֹ בְמָחוֹל, בְּתֹף וְכִנּוֹר יְזַמְּרוּ־לוֹ: כִּי־רוֹצֶה יהוה בְּעַמּוֹ, יְפָאֵר עֲנָוִים בִּישׁוּעָה: יַעְלְזוּ חֲסִידִים בְּכָבוֹד, יְרַנְּנוּ עַל־מִשְׁכְּבוֹתָם: רוֹמְמוֹת אֵל בִּגְרוֹנָם, וְחֶרֶב פִּיפִיּוֹת בְּיָדָם: לַעֲשׂוֹת נְקָמָה בַּגּוֹיִם, תּוֹכֵחוֹת בַּלְאֻמִּים: ◂ לֶאְסֹר מַלְכֵיהֶם בְּזִקִּים, וְנִכְבְּדֵיהֶם בְּכַבְלֵי בַרְזֶל: לַעֲשׂוֹת בָּהֶם מִשְׁפָּט כָּתוּב, הָדָר הוּא לְכָל־חֲסִידָיו, הַלְלוּיָהּ:

תהלים קנ
הַלְלוּיָהּ, הַלְלוּ־אֵל בְּקָדְשׁוֹ
הַלְלוּהוּ בִּרְקִיעַ עֻזּוֹ:
הַלְלוּהוּ בִגְבוּרֹתָיו
הַלְלוּהוּ כְּרֹב גֻּדְלוֹ:
הַלְלוּהוּ בְּתֵקַע שׁוֹפָר
הַלְלוּהוּ בְּנֵבֶל וְכִנּוֹר:
הַלְלוּהוּ בְתֹף וּמָחוֹל
הַלְלוּהוּ בְּמִנִּים וְעוּגָב:
◂ הַלְלוּהוּ בְצִלְצְלֵי־שָׁמַע
הַלְלוּהוּ בְּצִלְצְלֵי תְרוּעָה:
כֹּל הַנְּשָׁמָה תְּהַלֵּל יָהּ, הַלְלוּיָהּ:
כֹּל הַנְּשָׁמָה תְּהַלֵּל יָהּ, הַלְלוּיָהּ:

בָּרוּךְ Blessed be the Lord for ever. Amen and Amen. *Ps. 89*
Blessed from Zion be the Lord *Ps. 135*
who dwells in Jerusalem. Halleluya!
Blessed be the Lord, God of Israel, who alone does wonders. *Ps. 72*
▸ Blessed be His glorious name for ever,
and may all the earth be filled with His glory.
Amen and Amen.

*Stand until "The soul" on page 520.*

וַיְבָרֶךְ דָּוִיד David blessed the Lord in front of the entire assembly. *1 Chr. 29*
David said, "Blessed are You, Lord, God of our father Yisrael, for ever and ever. Yours, Lord, are the greatness and the power, the glory, majesty and splendor, for everything in heaven and earth is Yours. Yours, Lord, is the kingdom; You are exalted as Head over all. Both riches and honor are in Your gift and You reign over all things. In Your hand are strength and might. It is in Your power to make great and give strength to all. Therefore, our God, we thank You and praise Your glorious name." You alone are the *Neh. 9*
Lord. You made the heavens, even the highest heavens, and all their hosts, the earth and all that is on it, the seas and all they contain. You give life to them all, and the hosts of heaven worship You. ▸ You are the Lord God who chose Abram and brought him out of Ur of the Chaldees, changing his name to Abraham. You found his heart faithful toward You, ◂ and You made a covenant with him to give to his descendants the land of the Canaanites, Hittites, Amorites, Perizzites, Jebusites and Girgashites. You fulfilled Your promise for You are righteous. You saw the suffering of our ancestors in Egypt. You heard their cry at the Sea of Reeds. You sent signs and wonders against Pharaoh, all his servants and all the people of his land, because You knew how arrogantly the Egyptians treated them. You created for Yourself renown that remains to this day. ▸ You divided the sea before them, so that they passed through the sea on dry land, but You cast their pursuers into the depths, like a stone into mighty waters.

בָּרוּךְ יהוה לְעוֹלָם, אָמֵן וְאָמֵן: תהלים פט

בָּרוּךְ יהוה מִצִּיּוֹן, שֹׁכֵן יְרוּשָׁלָםִ, הַלְלוּיָהּ: תהלים קלה

בָּרוּךְ יהוה אֱלֹהִים אֱלֹהֵי יִשְׂרָאֵל, עֹשֵׂה נִפְלָאוֹת לְבַדּוֹ: תהלים עב

◂ וּבָרוּךְ שֵׁם כְּבוֹדוֹ לְעוֹלָם
וְיִמָּלֵא כְבוֹדוֹ אֶת־כָּל־הָאָרֶץ, אָמֵן וְאָמֵן:

*Stand until* נִשְׁמַת *on page 521.*

דברי הימים א׳ כט
וַיְבָרֶךְ דָּוִיד אֶת־יהוה לְעֵינֵי כָּל־הַקָּהָל, וַיֹּאמֶר דָּוִיד, בָּרוּךְ אַתָּה יהוה, אֱלֹהֵי יִשְׂרָאֵל אָבִינוּ, מֵעוֹלָם וְעַד־עוֹלָם: לְךָ יהוה הַגְּדֻלָּה וְהַגְּבוּרָה וְהַתִּפְאֶרֶת וְהַנֵּצַח וְהַהוֹד, כִּי־כֹל בַּשָּׁמַיִם וּבָאָרֶץ, לְךָ יהוה הַמַּמְלָכָה וְהַמִּתְנַשֵּׂא לְכֹל לְרֹאשׁ: וְהָעֹשֶׁר וְהַכָּבוֹד מִלְּפָנֶיךָ, וְאַתָּה מוֹשֵׁל בַּכֹּל, וּבְיָדְךָ כֹּחַ וּגְבוּרָה, וּבְיָדְךָ לְגַדֵּל וּלְחַזֵּק לַכֹּל: וְעַתָּה אֱלֹהֵינוּ מוֹדִים אֲנַחְנוּ לָךְ, וּמְהַלְלִים לְשֵׁם תִּפְאַרְתֶּךָ:

נחמיה ט
אַתָּה־הוּא יהוה לְבַדֶּךָ, אַתְּ עָשִׂיתָ אֶת־הַשָּׁמַיִם, שְׁמֵי הַשָּׁמַיִם וְכָל־צְבָאָם, הָאָרֶץ וְכָל־אֲשֶׁר עָלֶיהָ, הַיַּמִּים וְכָל־אֲשֶׁר בָּהֶם, וְאַתָּה מְחַיֶּה אֶת־כֻּלָּם, וּצְבָא הַשָּׁמַיִם לְךָ מִשְׁתַּחֲוִים: ◂ אַתָּה הוּא יהוה הָאֱלֹהִים אֲשֶׁר בָּחַרְתָּ בְּאַבְרָם, וְהוֹצֵאתוֹ מֵאוּר כַּשְׂדִּים, וְשַׂמְתָּ שְּׁמוֹ אַבְרָהָם: וּמָצָאתָ אֶת־לְבָבוֹ נֶאֱמָן לְפָנֶיךָ, ◂ וְכָרוֹת עִמּוֹ הַבְּרִית לָתֵת אֶת־אֶרֶץ הַכְּנַעֲנִי הַחִתִּי הָאֱמֹרִי וְהַפְּרִזִּי וְהַיְבוּסִי וְהַגִּרְגָּשִׁי, לָתֵת לְזַרְעוֹ, וַתָּקֶם אֶת־דְּבָרֶיךָ, כִּי צַדִּיק אָתָּה: וַתֵּרֶא אֶת־עֳנִי אֲבֹתֵינוּ בְּמִצְרָיִם, וְאֶת־זַעֲקָתָם שָׁמַעְתָּ עַל־יַם־סוּף: וַתִּתֵּן אֹתֹת וּמֹפְתִים בְּפַרְעֹה וּבְכָל־עֲבָדָיו וּבְכָל־עַם אַרְצוֹ, כִּי יָדַעְתָּ כִּי הֵזִידוּ עֲלֵיהֶם, וַתַּעַשׂ־לְךָ שֵׁם כְּהַיּוֹם הַזֶּה: ◂ וְהַיָּם בָּקַעְתָּ לִפְנֵיהֶם, וַיַּעַבְרוּ בְתוֹךְ־הַיָּם בַּיַּבָּשָׁה, וְאֶת־רֹדְפֵיהֶם הִשְׁלַכְתָּ בִמְצוֹלֹת כְּמוֹ־אֶבֶן, בְּמַיִם עַזִּים:

וַיּוֹשַׁע That day the LORD saved Israel from the hands of the Egyptians, and Israel saw the Egyptians lying dead on the seashore. ▸ When Israel saw the great power the LORD had displayed against the Egyptians, the people feared the LORD, and believed in the LORD and in His servant, Moses. *Ex. 14*

אָז יָשִׁיר־מֹשֶׁה Then Moses and the Israelites sang this song to the LORD, saying: *Ex. 15*

I will sing to the LORD, for He has triumphed gloriously;
horse and rider He has hurled into the sea.
The LORD is my strength and song; He has become my salvation.
This is my God, and I will beautify Him,
my father's God, and I will exalt Him.
The LORD is a Master of war; LORD is His name.
Pharaoh's chariots and army He cast into the sea;
the best of his officers drowned in the Sea of Reeds.
The deep waters covered them;
they went down to the depths like a stone.
Your right hand, LORD, is majestic in power.
Your right hand, LORD, shatters the enemy.
In the greatness of Your majesty, You overthrew those who rose against You.
You sent out Your fury; it consumed them like stubble.
By the blast of Your nostrils the waters piled up.
The surging waters stood straight like a wall;
the deeps congealed in the heart of the sea.
The enemy said, "I will pursue. I will overtake. I will divide the spoil.
My desire shall have its fill of them.
I will draw my sword. My hand will destroy them."
You blew with Your wind; the sea covered them.
They sank in the mighty waters like lead.
Who is like You, LORD, among the mighty?
Who is like You – majestic in holiness, awesome in glory, working wonders?
You stretched out Your right hand, the earth swallowed them.

שמות יד וַיּֽוֹשַׁע יהוה בַּיּוֹם הַהוּא אֶת־יִשְׂרָאֵל מִיַּד מִצְרָֽיִם, וַיַּרְא יִשְׂרָאֵל
אֶת־מִצְרַֽיִם מֵת עַל־שְׂפַת הַיָּם: › וַיַּרְא יִשְׂרָאֵל אֶת־הַיָּד הַגְּדֹלָה
אֲשֶׁר עָשָׂה יהוה בְּמִצְרַֽיִם, וַיִּירְאוּ הָעָם אֶת־יהוה, וַיַּאֲמִֽינוּ
בַּיהוה וּבְמֹשֶׁה עַבְדּוֹ:

שמות טו אָז יָשִׁיר־מֹשֶׁה וּבְנֵי יִשְׂרָאֵל אֶת־הַשִּׁירָה הַזֹּאת לַיהוה, וַיֹּאמְרוּ
לֵאמֹר, אָשִֽׁירָה לַיהוה כִּי־גָאֹה גָּאָה, סוּס
וְרֹכְבוֹ רָמָה בַיָּם: עָזִּי וְזִמְרָת יָהּ וַיְהִי־לִי
לִישׁוּעָה, זֶה אֵלִי וְאַנְוֵֽהוּ, אֱלֹהֵי
אָבִי וַאֲרֹמְמֶֽנְהוּ: יהוה אִישׁ מִלְחָמָה, יהוה
שְׁמוֹ: מַרְכְּבֹת פַּרְעֹה וְחֵילוֹ יָרָה בַיָּם, וּמִבְחַר
שָׁלִשָׁיו טֻבְּעוּ בְיַם־סוּף: תְּהֹמֹת יְכַסְיֻֽמוּ, יָרְדוּ בִמְצוֹלֹת כְּמוֹ־
אָֽבֶן: יְמִינְךָ יהוה נֶאְדָּרִי בַּכֹּֽחַ, יְמִינְךָ
יהוה תִּרְעַץ אוֹיֵב: וּבְרֹב גְּאוֹנְךָ תַּהֲרֹס
קָמֶֽיךָ, תְּשַׁלַּח חֲרֹנְךָ יֹאכְלֵֽמוֹ כַּקַּשׁ: וּבְרֽוּחַ
אַפֶּֽיךָ נֶֽעֶרְמוּ מַֽיִם, נִצְּבוּ כְמוֹ־נֵד
נֹזְלִים, קָפְאוּ תְהֹמֹת בְּלֶב־יָם: אָמַר
אוֹיֵב אֶרְדֹּף, אַשִּׂיג, אֲחַלֵּק שָׁלָל, תִּמְלָאֵֽמוֹ
נַפְשִׁי, אָרִיק חַרְבִּי תּוֹרִישֵֽׁמוֹ יָדִי: נָשַֽׁפְתָּ
בְרוּחֲךָ כִּסָּֽמוֹ יָם, צָלְלוּ כַּעוֹפֶֽרֶת בְּמַֽיִם
אַדִּירִים: מִי־כָמֹֽכָה בָּאֵלִם יהוה, מִי
כָּמֹֽכָה נֶאְדָּר בַּקֹּֽדֶשׁ, נוֹרָא תְהִלֹּת עֹֽשֵׂה
פֶֽלֶא: נָטִֽיתָ יְמִינְךָ תִּבְלָעֵֽמוֹ אָֽרֶץ: נָחִֽיתָ
בְחַסְדְּךָ עַם־זוּ גָּאָֽלְתָּ, נֵהַֽלְתָּ בְעָזְּךָ אֶל־נְוֵה

In Your loving-kindness, You led the people You redeemed.
In Your strength, You guided them to Your holy abode.
Nations heard and trembled;
terror gripped Philistia's inhabitants.
The chiefs of Edom were dismayed,
Moab's leaders were seized with trembling,
the people of Canaan melted away.
Fear and dread fell upon them.
By the power of Your arm, they were still as stone –
until Your people crossed, LORD,
until the people You acquired crossed over.
You will bring them and plant them on the mountain of Your heritage –
the place, LORD, You made for Your dwelling,
the Sanctuary, LORD, Your hands established.
The LORD will reign for ever and all time.

The LORD will reign for ever and all time.
The LORD's kingship is established for ever and to all eternity.

When Pharaoh's horses, chariots and riders went into the sea,
the LORD brought the waters of the sea back over them, but the Israelites walked on dry land through the sea.

▸ For kingship is the LORD's *Ps. 22*
and He rules over the nations.
Saviors shall go up to Mount Zion *Ob. 1*
to judge Mount Esau,
and the LORD's shall be the kingdom.
Then the LORD shall be King over all the earth; *Zech. 14*
on that day the LORD shall be One and His name One,

(as it is written in Your Torah, saying:
Listen, Israel: the LORD is our God, the LORD is One.) *Deut. 6*

*On Hoshana Raba, continue with the weekday service*
*from "May Your name be praised" on page 136.*

קָדְשֶׁךָ: שָׁמְעוּ עַמִּים יִרְגָּזוּן, חִיל
אָחַז יֹשְׁבֵי פְּלָשֶׁת: אָז נִבְהֲלוּ אַלּוּפֵי
אֱדוֹם, אֵילֵי מוֹאָב יֹאחֲזֵמוֹ רָעַד, נָמֹגוּ
כֹּל יֹשְׁבֵי כְנָעַן: תִּפֹּל עֲלֵיהֶם אֵימָתָה
וָפַחַד, בִּגְדֹל זְרוֹעֲךָ יִדְּמוּ כָּאָבֶן, עַד־
יַעֲבֹר עַמְּךָ יהוה, עַד־יַעֲבֹר עַם־זוּ
קָנִיתָ: תְּבִאֵמוֹ וְתִטָּעֵמוֹ בְּהַר נַחֲלָתְךָ, מָכוֹן
לְשִׁבְתְּךָ פָּעַלְתָּ יהוה, מִקְּדָשׁ אֲדֹנָי כּוֹנְנוּ
יָדֶיךָ: יהוה יִמְלֹךְ לְעֹלָם וָעֶד:

יהוה יִמְלֹךְ לְעֹלָם וָעֶד.
יהוה מַלְכוּתֵהּ קָאֵם לְעָלַם וּלְעָלְמֵי עָלְמַיָּא.

כִּי
בָא סוּס פַּרְעֹה בְּרִכְבּוֹ וּבְפָרָשָׁיו בַּיָּם, וַיָּשֶׁב יהוה עֲלֵהֶם אֶת־מֵי
הַיָּם, וּבְנֵי יִשְׂרָאֵל הָלְכוּ בַיַּבָּשָׁה בְּתוֹךְ הַיָּם:

◂ כִּי לַיהוה הַמְּלוּכָה וּמֹשֵׁל בַּגּוֹיִם: תהלים כב
וְעָלוּ מוֹשִׁעִים בְּהַר צִיּוֹן לִשְׁפֹּט אֶת־הַר עֵשָׂו עובדיה א
וְהָיְתָה לַיהוה הַמְּלוּכָה:
וְהָיָה יהוה לְמֶלֶךְ עַל־כָּל־הָאָרֶץ זכריה יד
בַּיּוֹם הַהוּא יִהְיֶה יהוה אֶחָד וּשְׁמוֹ אֶחָד:

(וּבְתוֹרָתְךָ כָּתוּב לֵאמֹר, שְׁמַע יִשְׂרָאֵל, יהוה אֱלֹהֵינוּ יהוה אֶחָד:) דברים ו

*On* הושענא רבה, *continue with the weekday service from* יִשְׁתַּבַּח *on page 137.*

# THE SOUL

of all that lives shall bless Your name, LORD our God,
and the spirit of all flesh shall always glorify
and exalt Your remembrance, our King.
From eternity to eternity You are God.
Without You, we have no King, Redeemer or Savior,
who liberates, rescues, sustains
and shows compassion in every time of trouble and distress.
We have no King but You, God of the first and last,
God of all creatures, Master of all ages,
extolled by a multitude of praises,
who guides His world with loving-kindness
and His creatures with compassion.
The LORD neither slumbers nor sleeps.
He rouses the sleepers and wakens the slumberers.
He makes the dumb speak, sets the bound free,
supports the fallen, and raises those bowed down.
To You alone we give thanks:
If our mouths were as full of song as the sea,
and our tongue with jubilation as its myriad waves,
if our lips were full of praise like the spacious heavens,
and our eyes shone like the sun and moon,
if our hands were outstretched like eagles of the sky,
and our feet as swift as hinds –
still we could not thank You enough,
LORD our God and God of our ancestors,
or bless Your name for even one of the thousand thousands
and myriad myriads of favors You did for our ancestors and for us.
You redeemed us from Egypt, LORD our God,
and freed us from the house of bondage.
In famine You nourished us; in times of plenty You sustained us.
You delivered us from the sword, saved us from the plague,
and spared us from serious and lasting illness.

# נִשְׁמַת

כָּל חַי תְּבָרֵךְ אֶת שִׁמְךָ, יהוה אֱלֹהֵינוּ
וְרוּחַ כָּל בָּשָׂר תְּפָאֵר וּתְרוֹמֵם זִכְרְךָ מַלְכֵּנוּ תָּמִיד.
מִן הָעוֹלָם וְעַד הָעוֹלָם אַתָּה אֵל
וּמִבַּלְעָדֶיךָ אֵין לָנוּ מֶלֶךְ גּוֹאֵל וּמוֹשִׁיעַ
פּוֹדֶה וּמַצִּיל וּמְפַרְנֵס וּמְרַחֵם
בְּכָל עֵת צָרָה וְצוּקָה אֵין לָנוּ מֶלֶךְ אֶלָּא אָתָּה.
אֱלֹהֵי הָרִאשׁוֹנִים וְהָאַחֲרוֹנִים, אֱלוֹהַּ כָּל בְּרִיּוֹת
אֲדוֹן כָּל תּוֹלָדוֹת, הַמְהֻלָּל בְּרֹב הַתִּשְׁבָּחוֹת
הַמְנַהֵג עוֹלָמוֹ בְּחֶסֶד וּבְרִיּוֹתָיו בְּרַחֲמִים.
וַיהוה לֹא יָנוּם וְלֹא יִישָׁן
הַמְעוֹרֵר יְשֵׁנִים וְהַמֵּקִיץ נִרְדָּמִים
וְהַמֵּשִׂיחַ אִלְּמִים וְהַמַּתִּיר אֲסוּרִים
וְהַסּוֹמֵךְ נוֹפְלִים וְהַזּוֹקֵף כְּפוּפִים.
לְךָ לְבַדְּךָ אֲנַחְנוּ מוֹדִים.
אִלּוּ פִינוּ מָלֵא שִׁירָה כַּיָּם, וּלְשׁוֹנֵנוּ רִנָּה כַּהֲמוֹן גַּלָּיו
וְשִׂפְתוֹתֵינוּ שֶׁבַח כְּמֶרְחֲבֵי רָקִיעַ, וְעֵינֵינוּ מְאִירוֹת כַּשֶּׁמֶשׁ וְכַיָּרֵחַ
וְיָדֵינוּ פְרוּשׂוֹת כְּנִשְׁרֵי שָׁמָיִם, וְרַגְלֵינוּ קַלּוֹת כָּאַיָּלוֹת
אֵין אֲנַחְנוּ מַסְפִּיקִים לְהוֹדוֹת לְךָ, יהוה אֱלֹהֵינוּ וֵאלֹהֵי אֲבוֹתֵינוּ
וּלְבָרֵךְ אֶת שְׁמֶךָ, עַל אַחַת מֵאָלֶף אֶלֶף אַלְפֵי אֲלָפִים
וְרִבֵּי רְבָבוֹת פְּעָמִים הַטּוֹבוֹת, שֶׁעָשִׂיתָ עִם אֲבוֹתֵינוּ וְעִמָּנוּ.
מִמִּצְרַיִם גְּאַלְתָּנוּ, יהוה אֱלֹהֵינוּ, וּמִבֵּית עֲבָדִים פְּדִיתָנוּ
בְּרָעָב זַנְתָּנוּ וּבְשָׂבָע כִּלְכַּלְתָּנוּ, מֵחֶרֶב הִצַּלְתָּנוּ וּמִדֶּבֶר מִלַּטְתָּנוּ
וּמֵחֳלָיִים רָעִים וְנֶאֱמָנִים דִּלִּיתָנוּ.

Until now Your mercies have helped us.
Your love has not forsaken us.
May You, LORD our God, never abandon us.
Therefore the limbs You formed within us,
the spirit and soul You breathed into our nostrils,
and the tongue You placed in our mouth –
they will thank and bless, praise and glorify, exalt and esteem,
hallow and do homage to Your name, O our King.
For every mouth shall give thanks to You,
every tongue vow allegiance to You,
every knee shall bend to You, every upright body shall bow to You,
all hearts shall fear You,
and our innermost being sing praises to Your name,
as is written:

"All my bones shall say: LORD, who is like You? *Ps. 35*
You save the poor from one stronger than him,
the poor and needy from one who would rob him."

Who is like You? Who is equal to You?
Who can be compared to You?
O great, mighty and awesome God, God Most High,
Maker of heaven and earth.
▸ We will laud, praise and glorify You and bless Your holy name,
as it is said:

"Of David. Bless the LORD, O my soul, *Ps. 103*
and all that is within me bless His holy name."

---

But as we know, based on "words of truth" [i.e. Kabbalah], the soul extends throughout the bodily organs, which means that even the simple vitality comes from a high place, and that very soul that dispatches to the brain towards the end of intellection, dispatches to the organs that do gross work. The "dew of vitality" (*tal teḥiyah*) descends upon all of man's body.[44]

---

44. See *b. Berakhot* 10a.
*OR*, vol. 2, p. 97.

עַד הֵנָּה עֲזָרוּנוּ רַחֲמֶיךָ, וְלֹא עֲזָבוּנוּ חֲסָדֶיךָ
וְאַל תִּטְּשֵׁנוּ, יהוה אֱלֹהֵינוּ, לָנֶצַח.
עַל כֵּן אֵבָרִים שֶׁפִּלַּגְתָּ בָּנוּ
וְרוּחַ וּנְשָׁמָה שֶׁנָּפַחְתָּ בְּאַפֵּנוּ, וְלָשׁוֹן אֲשֶׁר שַׂמְתָּ בְּפִינוּ
הֵן הֵם יוֹדוּ וִיבָרְכוּ וִישַׁבְּחוּ וִיפָאֲרוּ
וִירוֹמְמוּ וְיַעֲרִיצוּ וְיַקְדִּישׁוּ וְיַמְלִיכוּ אֶת שִׁמְךָ מַלְכֵּנוּ
כִּי כָל פֶּה לְךָ יוֹדֶה וְכָל לָשׁוֹן לְךָ תִשָּׁבַע
וְכָל בֶּרֶךְ לְךָ תִכְרַע וְכָל קוֹמָה לְפָנֶיךָ תִשְׁתַּחֲוֶה
וְכָל לְבָבוֹת יִירָאוּךָ וְכָל קֶרֶב וּכְלָיוֹת יְזַמְּרוּ לִשְׁמֶךָ
כַּדָּבָר שֶׁכָּתוּב

תהלים לה
כָּל עַצְמֹתַי תֹּאמַרְנָה יהוה מִי כָמוֹךָ
מַצִּיל עָנִי מֵחָזָק מִמֶּנּוּ, וְעָנִי וְאֶבְיוֹן מִגֹּזְלוֹ:

מִי יִדְמֶה לָּךְ וּמִי יִשְׁוֶה לָּךְ וּמִי יַעֲרָךְ לָךְ
הָאֵל הַגָּדוֹל, הַגִּבּוֹר וְהַנּוֹרָא
אֵל עֶלְיוֹן, קֹנֵה שָׁמַיִם וָאָרֶץ.
◂ נְהַלֶּלְךָ וּנְשַׁבֵּחֲךָ וּנְפָאֶרְךָ וּנְבָרֵךְ אֶת שֵׁם קָדְשֶׁךָ
כָּאָמוּר

תהלים קג
לְדָוִד, בָּרְכִי נַפְשִׁי אֶת־יהוה
וְכָל־קְרָבַי אֶת־שֵׁם קָדְשׁוֹ:

---

לְדָוִד, בָּרְכִי נַפְשִׁי אֶת־יהוה, וְכָל־קְרָבַי אֶת־שֵׁם קָדְשׁוֹ *"Of David. Bless the Lord, O my soul, and all that is within me* (ve-khol keravai) *bless His holy name"* (*Psalm 103:1*). One of the perennial problems in philosophy is the Mind-Body problem. If we adhere to Cartesian dualism, these are two separate entities. If that is the case, then there is a total "disconnect" between mind and body. And if so, praise for the Lord must proceed purely from the intellect, with the corporeal barred from "standing before the King."

*On Yom Tov the Leader begins here:*

הָאֵל God – in Your absolute power,
Great – in the glory of Your name,
Mighty – for ever,
Awesome – in Your awe-inspiring deeds,
The King – who sits on a throne.
High and lofty

*On Shabbat the Leader begins here:*

HE INHABITS ETERNITY;
exalted and holy is His name.
And it is written:
"Sing joyfully to the LORD, you righteous, *Ps. 33*
for praise from the upright is seemly."

▸ By the mouth of the upright You shall be praised.
By the words of the righteous You shall be blessed.
By the tongue of the devout You shall be extolled,
And in the midst of the holy You shall be sanctified.

וּבְמַקְהֲלוֹת And in the assemblies
of tens of thousands of Your people, the house of Israel,
with joyous song shall Your name, our King,
be glorified in every generation.
▸ For this is the duty of all creatures before You,
LORD our God and God of our ancestors:
to thank, praise, laud, glorify, exalt,
honor, bless, raise high and acclaim –
even beyond all the words of song and praise
of David, son of Jesse, Your servant, Your anointed.

---

עַל כָּל דִּבְרֵי שִׁירוֹת וְתִשְׁבְּחוֹת דָּוִד בֶּן יִשַׁי, עַבְדְּךָ מְשִׁיחֶךָ *Even beyond all the words of song and praise of David, son of Jesse, Your servant, Your anointed.* One might ask: How can we be so bold as to assert that we shall utter praise to the LORD

*On* יום טוב *the* שליח ציבור *begins here:*

הָאֵל בְּתַעֲצוּמוֹת עֻזֶּךָ
הַגָּדוֹל בִּכְבוֹד שְׁמֶךָ
הַגִּבּוֹר לָנֶצַח וְהַנּוֹרָא בְּנוֹרְאוֹתֶיךָ
הַמֶּלֶךְ הַיּוֹשֵׁב עַל כִּסֵּא
רָם וְנִשָּׂא

*On* שבת *the* שליח ציבור *begins here:*

# שׁוֹכֵן עַד

מָרוֹם וְקָדוֹשׁ שְׁמוֹ
וְכָתוּב
רַנְּנוּ צַדִּיקִים בַּיהוה, לַיְשָׁרִים נָאוָה תְהִלָּה: תהלים לג
◂ בְּפִי יְשָׁרִים תִּתְהַלָּל
וּבְדִבְרֵי צַדִּיקִים תִּתְבָּרַךְ
וּבִלְשׁוֹן חֲסִידִים תִּתְרוֹמָם
וּבְקֶרֶב קְדוֹשִׁים תִּתְקַדָּשׁ

וּבְמַקְהֲלוֹת רִבְבוֹת עַמְּךָ בֵּית יִשְׂרָאֵל
בְּרִנָּה יִתְפָּאַר שִׁמְךָ מַלְכֵּנוּ בְּכָל דּוֹר וָדוֹר
◂ שֶׁכֵּן חוֹבַת כָּל הַיְצוּרִים
לְפָנֶיךָ יהוה אֱלֹהֵינוּ וֵאלֹהֵי אֲבוֹתֵינוּ
לְהוֹדוֹת, לְהַלֵּל, לְשַׁבֵּחַ, לְפָאֵר, לְרוֹמֵם
לְהַדֵּר, לְבָרֵךְ, לְעַלֵּה וּלְקַלֵּס
עַל כָּל דִּבְרֵי שִׁירוֹת וְתִשְׁבְּחוֹת
דָּוִד בֶּן יִשַׁי, עַבְדְּךָ מְשִׁיחֶךָ.

*Stand until after "Barekhu" on page 530.*

יִשְׁתַּבַּח May Your name be praised for ever, our King,
the great and holy God, King in heaven and on earth.
For to You, LORD our God and God of our ancestors,
it is right to offer song and praise,
hymn and psalm, strength and dominion,
eternity, greatness and power,
song of praise and glory,
holiness and kingship,
▸ blessings and thanks,
from now and for ever.
Blessed are You, LORD,
God and King, exalted in praises,
God of thanksgivings, Master of wonders,
who delights in hymns of song,
King, God, Giver of life to the worlds.

---

Narbonne (teacher of Rabbi Menaḥem ha-Me'iri of Perpignan) comments on this line in the prayer book:

> One must add and innovate words of praise and song beyond the songs of David.[47]

Elsewhere he comments:

> "Halleluyah! Sing to the LORD a new song."[48]
>
> Beyond the written songs, you, innovate new songs, for the entire day the LORD innovates for you wonders.[49]

Rav Kook encouraged original spiritual poetry. He was especially supportive of his protégé, the poet Yosef Zevi Rimon, whom he envisioned as the first

---

47. *Sefer ha-Tamid*, ed. Rabbis Ya'akov Moshe Toledano and Ḥayyim Yehudah Ehrenreich (Homna, 1935; photo offset Jerusalem, 1977), p. 31. For biographical details of the author, see ibid., pp. 39–40; Rabbi Menaḥem ha-Me'iri, *Seder ha-Kabbalah*, ed. S.Z. Havlin (Jerusalem-Cleveland: Ofeq Institute, 1995), pp. 138–139.
48. Psalm 149:1.
49. *Sefer ha-Tamid*, p. 23.

*Stand until after* בָּרְכוּ *on page 531.*

יִשְׁתַּבַּח שִׁמְךָ לָעַד, מַלְכֵּנוּ
הָאֵל הַמֶּלֶךְ הַגָּדוֹל וְהַקָּדוֹשׁ בַּשָּׁמַיִם וּבָאָרֶץ
כִּי לְךָ נָאֶה, יהוה אֱלֹהֵינוּ וֵאלֹהֵי אֲבוֹתֵינוּ
שִׁיר וּשְׁבָחָה, הַלֵּל וְזִמְרָה
עֹז וּמֶמְשָׁלָה, נֶצַח, גְּדֻלָּה וּגְבוּרָה
תְּהִלָּה וְתִפְאֶרֶת, קְדֻשָּׁה וּמַלְכוּת
◂ בְּרָכוֹת וְהוֹדָאוֹת, מֵעַתָּה וְעַד עוֹלָם.
בָּרוּךְ אַתָּה יהוה
אֵל מֶלֶךְ גָּדוֹל בַּתִּשְׁבָּחוֹת
אֵל הַהוֹדָאוֹת, אֲדוֹן הַנִּפְלָאוֹת
הַבּוֹחֵר בְּשִׁירֵי זִמְרָה
מֶלֶךְ, אֵל, חֵי הָעוֹלָמִים.

---

beyond or in addition to the Psalms of David? Is that not overstepping the bounds? Can one improve upon perfection?[45]

According to the Midrash,

> When King David completed the Book of Psalms, he became swell-headed and said to the Holy One, blessed be He: "Master of the Universe, is there a creation that You created in Your world that outdoes me in uttering songs and praises?"
>
> Precisely then, there happened along a frog and said to him: "David, don't be swell-headed, for I outdo you in uttering songs and praises."[46]

One of the great medieval authorities, Rabbi Reuben ben Ḥayyim of

45. See Rabbi David Cohen, *Mas'at Kapai*, vol. 2 (Brooklyn, NY, 1986), pp. 41–42. One of the accusations leveled against Rabbi Moses Ḥayyim Luzzatto (1707–1746) by his bitter enemies, was that he had authored his own book of psalms containing 150 psalms, the exact number in King David's Book of Psalms!

46. *Yalkut Shim'oni*, Psalm 150 (*remez* 889); *Perek Shirah.*

*On Shabbat Shuva, many congregations open the Ark and say this psalm responsively, verse by verse.*

שִׁיר הַמַּעֲלוֹת A song of ascents. From the depths I have called to You, LORD. *Ps. 130*
LORD, hear my voice; let Your ears be attentive to my plea. If You, LORD, should keep account of sins, O LORD, who could stand? But with You there is forgiveness, that You may be held in awe. I wait for the LORD, my soul waits, and in His word I put my hope. My soul waits for the LORD more than watchmen wait for the morning, more than watchmen wait for the morning. Israel, put your hope in the LORD, for with the LORD there is loving-kindness, and great is His power to redeem. It is He who will redeem Israel from all their sins.

HALF KADDISH

*Leader:* יִתְגַּדַּל Magnified and sanctified may His great name be,
in the world He created by His will.
May He establish His kingdom
in your lifetime and in your days,
and in the lifetime of all the house of Israel,
swiftly and soon – and say: Amen.

*All:* May His great name be blessed for ever and all time.

*Leader:* Blessed and praised, glorified and exalted,
raised and honored, uplifted and lauded
be the name of the Holy One, blessed be He,
beyond any blessing, song, praise and consolation
uttered in the world – and say: Amen.

---

unique in our time, for all his thoughts and the flight of his song flow from the living spring of Israel, its eternity, its might, and the holiness of its soul.

It may be that he is the one who is likely to open the way of holiness in the new poetry of Israel. After a silence of hundreds of years, she has opened her mouth to speak great things.

Let us hope that in days to come, he will not be just one of the poets, but an example to the future poets of Judah, who will proudly celebrate the name of the LORD, Rock of Israel.

See Dror Eydar, *Aḥaron Meshorerei ha-Elohim: Mitos, Etos u-Misṭiḳah bi-Yetsirato shel Yosef Tsevi Rimon* [*The Last of the Poets of God: Mythos, Ethos and Mysticism in the Creation of Yosef Tsevi Rimon*] (Jerusalem: Magnes, 2009).

*On* שבת שובה*, many congregations open the* ארון קודש
*and say this psalm responsively, verse by verse.*

תהלים קל
שִׁיר הַמַּעֲלוֹת, מִמַּעֲמַקִּים קְרָאתִיךָ יהוה: אֲדֹנָי שִׁמְעָה בְקוֹלִי,
תִּהְיֶינָה אָזְנֶיךָ קַשֻּׁבוֹת לְקוֹל תַּחֲנוּנָי: אִם־עֲוֹנוֹת תִּשְׁמָר־יָהּ, אֲדֹנָי
מִי יַעֲמֹד: כִּי־עִמְּךָ הַסְּלִיחָה, לְמַעַן תִּוָּרֵא: קִוִּיתִי יהוה קִוְּתָה נַפְשִׁי,
וְלִדְבָרוֹ הוֹחָלְתִּי: נַפְשִׁי לַאדֹנָי, מִשֹּׁמְרִים לַבֹּקֶר, שֹׁמְרִים לַבֹּקֶר: יַחֵל
יִשְׂרָאֵל אֶל יהוה, כִּי־עִם־יהוה הַחֶסֶד, וְהַרְבֵּה עִמּוֹ פְדוּת: וְהוּא
יִפְדֶּה אֶת־יִשְׂרָאֵל, מִכֹּל עֲוֹנוֹתָיו:

### חצי קדיש

ש״ץ: יִתְגַּדַּל וְיִתְקַדַּשׁ שְׁמֵהּ רַבָּא (קהל: אָמֵן)
בְּעָלְמָא דִּי בְרָא כִרְעוּתֵהּ, וְיַמְלִיךְ מַלְכוּתֵהּ
בְּחַיֵּיכוֹן וּבְיוֹמֵיכוֹן וּבְחַיֵּי דְכָל בֵּית יִשְׂרָאֵל
בַּעֲגָלָא וּבִזְמַן קָרִיב, וְאִמְרוּ אָמֵן. (קהל: אָמֵן)

קהל וש״ץ: יְהֵא שְׁמֵהּ רַבָּא מְבָרַךְ לְעָלַם וּלְעָלְמֵי עָלְמַיָּא.

ש״ץ: יִתְבָּרַךְ וְיִשְׁתַּבַּח וְיִתְפָּאַר וְיִתְרוֹמַם וְיִתְנַשֵּׂא
וְיִתְהַדָּר וְיִתְעַלֶּה וְיִתְהַלָּל
שְׁמֵהּ דְּקֻדְשָׁא בְּרִיךְ הוּא (קהל: בְּרִיךְ הוּא)
לְעֵלָּא מִן כָּל בִּרְכָתָא / בשבת שובה: לְעֵלָּא לְעֵלָּא מִכָּל בִּרְכָתָא/
וְשִׁירָתָא, תֻּשְׁבְּחָתָא וְנֶחֱמָתָא
דַּאֲמִירָן בְּעָלְמָא, וְאִמְרוּ אָמֵן. (קהל: אָמֵן)

---

in a line of poets in reborn Erets Yisrael who would produce works suffused with Godliness.[50] Rav Kook himself was a gifted poet. (Editor)

50. In 1932, on the twenty-fifth anniversary of Rimon's literary activity, there was issued in his honor *Ḥoveret ha-Yovel… Yosef Tsevi Rimon,* edited by Pinhas Grayevsky. The booklet opens with a letter of blessing from Rav Kook, who writes:

    The time has come to wake up, to give honor and strength to the poet who is

## BLESSINGS OF THE SHEMA

*The following blessing and response are said only in the presence of a minyan. They represent a formal summons to the congregation to engage in an act of collective prayer. The custom of bowing at this point is based on 1 Chronicles 29:20, "David said to the whole assembly, 'Now bless the Lord your God.' All the assembly blessed the Lord God of their fathers and bowed their heads low to the Lord and the King."*

*The Leader says the following, bowing at "Bless," standing straight at "the Lord." The congregation, followed by the Leader, responds, bowing at "Bless," standing straight at "the Lord."*

*Leader:* BLESS
the Lord, the blessed One.

*Congregation:* Bless the Lord, the blessed One,
for ever and all time.

*Leader:* Bless the Lord, the blessed One,
for ever and all time.

*The custom is to sit from this point until the Amida, since the predominant emotion of this section of the prayers is love rather than awe. Conversation is forbidden until after the Amida. See table on pages 1315–1317*

בָּרוּךְ Blessed are You, Lord our God, King of the Universe,
who forms light and creates darkness, *Is. 45*
makes peace and creates all.

*If Yom Tov falls on a weekday continue with "In compassion" on the next page below the line.*

All will thank You. All will praise You.
All will declare: Nothing is as holy as the Lord.
All will exalt You, Selah, You who form all –
the God who daily opens the doors of the gates of the East
and cleaves the windows of the sky,
who brings out the sun from its place
and the moon from its abode,
giving light to the whole world and its inhabitants
whom He created by the attribute of compassion.

# קריאת שמע וברכותיה

*The following blessing and response are said only in the presence of a* מנין. *They represent a formal summons to the* קהל *to engage in an act of collective prayer. The custom of bowing at this point is based on* דברי הימים א׳ כט: כ, *"David said to the whole assembly, 'Now bless the Lord your God.' All the assembly blessed the Lord God of their fathers and bowed their heads low to the Lord and the King."*

*The* שליח ציבור *says the following, bowing at* בָּרְכוּ, *standing straight at* ה׳.
*The* קהל, *followed by the* שליח ציבור, *responds, bowing at* בָּרוּךְ, *standing straight at* ה׳.

ש״ץ: בָּרְכוּ

אֶת יהוה הַמְבֹרָךְ.

קהל: בָּרוּךְ יהוה הַמְבֹרָךְ לְעוֹלָם וָעֶד.

ש״ץ: בָּרוּךְ יהוה הַמְבֹרָךְ לְעוֹלָם וָעֶד.

*The custom is to sit from this point until the* עמידה, *since the predominant emotion of this section of the prayers is love rather than awe.*
*Conversation is forbidden until after the* עמידה. *See table on pages 1315–1317.*

בָּרוּךְ אַתָּה יהוה אֱלֹהֵינוּ מֶלֶךְ הָעוֹלָם
יוֹצֵר אוֹר וּבוֹרֵא חֹשֶׁךְ ישעיה מה
עֹשֶׂה שָׁלוֹם וּבוֹרֵא אֶת הַכֹּל.

*If* יום טוב *falls on a weekday continue with* הַמֵּאִיר לָאָרֶץ *on the next page below the line.*

הַכֹּל יוֹדוּךָ וְהַכֹּל יְשַׁבְּחוּךָ
וְהַכֹּל יֹאמְרוּ אֵין קָדוֹשׁ כַּיהוה
הַכֹּל יְרוֹמְמוּךָ סֶּלָה, יוֹצֵר הַכֹּל.
הָאֵל הַפּוֹתֵחַ בְּכָל יוֹם דַּלְתוֹת שַׁעֲרֵי מִזְרָח, וּבוֹקֵעַ חַלּוֹנֵי רָקִיעַ
מוֹצִיא חַמָּה מִמְּקוֹמָהּ וּלְבָנָה מִמְּכוֹן שִׁבְתָּהּ
וּמֵאִיר לָעוֹלָם כֻּלּוֹ וּלְיוֹשְׁבָיו, שֶׁבָּרָא בְּמִדַּת הָרַחֲמִים.

*On Shabbat continue here:*

In compassion He gives light to the earth and its inhabitants,
and in His goodness daily, continually, renews the work of creation.
He is the King who alone was exalted since time began,
praised, glorified and raised high from days of old.
Eternal God, in Your great compassion, have compassion on us,
Lord of our strength, Rock of our refuge,
Shield of our salvation, Stronghold of our safety.

אֵין כְּעֶרְכְּךָ None can be compared to You,
there is none besides You;
None without You.
Who is like You?

▸ None can be compared to You, Lord our God –
in this world.
There is none besides You, our King –
in the life of the World to Come.
There is none but You, our Redeemer –
in the days of the Messiah.
There is none like You, our Savior –
at the resurrection of the dead.

---

*If Yom Tov falls on a weekday continue here:*

הַמֵּאִיר In compassion He gives light to the earth and its inhabitants, and in His goodness continually renews the work of creation, day after day. How numerous are Your works, O Lord. You made them all in wisdom. The earth is full of Your creations. He is the King exalted alone since the beginning of time – praised, glorified and elevated since the world began. Eternal God, in Your great compassion, have compassion on us, Lord of our strength, Rock of our refuge, Shield of our salvation, You are our stronghold. The blessed God, great in knowledge, prepared and made the rays of the sun. He who is good formed glory for His name, surrounding His power with radiant stars. The leaders of His hosts, the holy ones, exalt the Almighty, constantly proclaiming God's glory and holiness. ▸ Be blessed, Lord our God, for the magnificence of Your handiwork and for the radiant lights You have made. May they glorify You, Selah! *Ps. 104*

*Continue with "May You be blessed, our Rock" on page 538.*

*On שבת continue here:*

הַמֵּאִיר לָאָֽרֶץ וְלַדָּרִים עָלֶֽיהָ בְּרַחֲמִים
וּבְטוּבוֹ מְחַדֵּשׁ בְּכָל יוֹם תָּמִיד מַעֲשֵׂה בְרֵאשִׁית.
הַמֶּֽלֶךְ הַמְרוֹמָם לְבַדּוֹ מֵאָז
הַמְשֻׁבָּח וְהַמְפֹאָר וְהַמִּתְנַשֵּׂא מִימוֹת עוֹלָם.
אֱלֹהֵי עוֹלָם, בְּרַחֲמֶֽיךָ הָרַבִּים רַחֵם עָלֵֽינוּ
אֲדוֹן עֻזֵּֽנוּ, צוּר מִשְׂגַּבֵּֽנוּ, מָגֵן יִשְׁעֵֽנוּ, מִשְׂגָּב בַּעֲדֵֽנוּ.

אֵין כְּעֶרְכֶּֽךָ
וְאֵין זוּלָתֶֽךָ
אֶֽפֶס בִּלְתֶּֽךָ
וּמִי דּֽוֹמֶה לָּךְ.

► אֵין כְּעֶרְכְּךָ, יהוה אֱלֹהֵֽינוּ, בָּעוֹלָם הַזֶּה
וְאֵין זוּלָתְךָ, מַלְכֵּֽנוּ, לְחַיֵּי הָעוֹלָם הַבָּא
אֶֽפֶס בִּלְתְּךָ, גּוֹאֲלֵֽנוּ, לִימוֹת הַמָּשִֽׁיחַ
וְאֵין דּֽוֹמֶה לְּךָ, מוֹשִׁיעֵֽנוּ, לִתְחִיַּת הַמֵּתִים.

---

*If יום טוב falls on a weekday continue here:*

הַמֵּאִיר לָאָֽרֶץ וְלַדָּרִים עָלֶֽיהָ בְּרַחֲמִים, וּבְטוּבוֹ מְחַדֵּשׁ בְּכָל יוֹם תָּמִיד מַעֲשֵׂה בְרֵאשִׁית. מָה רַבּוּ מַעֲשֶֽׂיךָ יהוה, כֻּלָּם בְּחָכְמָה עָשִֽׂיתָ, מָלְאָה הָאָֽרֶץ קִנְיָנֶֽךָ: הַמֶּֽלֶךְ הַמְרוֹמָם לְבַדּוֹ מֵאָז, הַמְשֻׁבָּח וְהַמְפֹאָר וְהַמִּתְנַשֵּׂא מִימוֹת עוֹלָם. אֱלֹהֵי עוֹלָם, בְּרַחֲמֶֽיךָ הָרַבִּים רַחֵם עָלֵֽינוּ, אֲדוֹן עֻזֵּֽנוּ, צוּר מִשְׂגַּבֵּֽנוּ, מָגֵן יִשְׁעֵֽנוּ, מִשְׂגָּב בַּעֲדֵֽנוּ. אֵל בָּרוּךְ גְּדוֹל דֵּעָה, הֵכִין וּפָעַל זָהֳרֵי חַמָּה, טוֹב יָצַר כָּבוֹד לִשְׁמוֹ, מְאוֹרוֹת נָתַן סְבִיבוֹת עֻזּוֹ, פִּנּוֹת צְבָאָיו קְדוֹשִׁים, רוֹמְמֵי שַׁדַּי, תָּמִיד מְסַפְּרִים כְּבוֹד אֵל וּקְדֻשָּׁתוֹ. ► תִּתְבָּרַךְ יהוה אֱלֹהֵֽינוּ עַל שֶֽׁבַח מַעֲשֵׂה יָדֶֽיךָ, וְעַל מְאוֹרֵי אוֹר שֶׁעָשִֽׂיתָ יְפָאֲרֽוּךָ סֶּֽלָה.

תהלים קד

*Continue with תִּתְבָּרַךְ, צוּרֵֽנוּ on page 539.*

אֵל אָדוֹן God, Lord of all creation,
the Blessed, is blessed by every soul.
His greatness and goodness fill the world;
knowledge and wisdom surround Him.

Exalted above the holy Ḥayyot,
adorned in glory on the Chariot;
merit and right are before His throne,
kindness and compassion before His glory.

Good are the radiant stars our God created;
He formed them with knowledge,
understanding and deliberation.
He gave them strength and might
to rule throughout the world.

Full of splendor, radiating light,
beautiful is their splendor throughout the world.
Glad as they go forth, joyous as they return,
they fulfill with awe their Creator's will.

Glory and honor they give to His name,
jubilation and song at the mention of His majesty.
He called the sun into being and it shone with light.
He looked and fashioned the form of the moon.

All the hosts on high give Him praise;
the Seraphim, Ophanim and holy Ḥayyot
ascribe glory and greatness –

---

noted the interesting difference between the formula recited in *Birkat ha-Levanah* and that of *Birkat Yotser* of Shabbat.[1] When we recite the Blessing of the New Moon, we say:

שָׂשִׂים וּשְׂמֵחִים לַעֲשׂוֹת רְצוֹן קוֹנָם
They are *joyous and glad* to fulfill the will of their Creator.

Why the shift in terminology Sabbath morning? Would it not have been more appropriate to continue the theme of joy? Why must we inject an

1. Rabbi Judah Löw, *Netivot 'Olam, Netiv ha-'Avodah*, chap. 13.

אֵל אָדוֹן עַל כָּל הַמַּעֲשִׂים
בָּרוּךְ וּמְבֹרָךְ בְּפִי כָּל נְשָׁמָה
גָּדְלוֹ וְטוּבוֹ מָלֵא עוֹלָם
דַּעַת וּתְבוּנָה סוֹבְבִים אוֹתוֹ.

הַמִּתְגָּאֶה עַל חַיּוֹת הַקֹּדֶשׁ
וְנֶהְדָּר בְּכָבוֹד עַל הַמֶּרְכָּבָה
זְכוּת וּמִישׁוֹר לִפְנֵי כִסְאוֹ
חֶסֶד וְרַחֲמִים לִפְנֵי כְבוֹדוֹ.

טוֹבִים מְאוֹרוֹת שֶׁבָּרָא אֱלֹהֵינוּ
יְצָרָם בְּדַעַת בְּבִינָה וּבְהַשְׂכֵּל
כֹּחַ וּגְבוּרָה נָתַן בָּהֶם
לִהְיוֹת מוֹשְׁלִים בְּקֶרֶב תֵּבֵל.

מְלֵאִים זִיו וּמְפִיקִים נֹגַהּ
נָאֶה זִיוָם בְּכָל הָעוֹלָם
שְׂמֵחִים בְּצֵאתָם וְשָׂשִׂים בְּבוֹאָם
עוֹשִׂים בְּאֵימָה רְצוֹן קוֹנָם.

פְּאֵר וְכָבוֹד נוֹתְנִים לִשְׁמוֹ
צָהֳלָה וְרִנָּה לְזֵכֶר מַלְכוּתוֹ
קָרָא לַשֶּׁמֶשׁ וַיִּזְרַח אוֹר
רָאָה וְהִתְקִין צוּרַת הַלְּבָנָה.

שֶׁבַח נוֹתְנִים לוֹ כָּל צְבָא מָרוֹם
תִּפְאֶרֶת וּגְדֻלָּה, שְׂרָפִים וְאוֹפַנִּים וְחַיּוֹת הַקֹּדֶשׁ.

---

שְׂמֵחִים בְּצֵאתָם וְשָׂשִׂים בְּבוֹאָם, עוֹשִׂים בְּאֵימָה רְצוֹן קוֹנָם *Glad as they go forth, joyous as they return, they fulfill with awe their Creator's will.* Maharal of Prague

לָאֵל To God who rested from all works,
and on the seventh day
ascended and sat on His throne of glory.
He robed the day of rest in glory
and called the Sabbath day a delight.
This is the praise of the seventh day,
that on it God rested from all His work.
The seventh day itself gives praise, saying,
"A psalm, a song for the Sabbath day. *Ps. 92*
It is good to give thanks to the Lord."
Therefore let all He has formed glorify and bless God.
Let them give praise, honor and grandeur to God,
the King, who formed all things,
and in His holiness gave a heritage of rest
to His people Israel on the holy Sabbath day.
May Your name, O Lord our God, be sanctified,
and Your renown, O our King, be glorified
in the heavens above and on earth below.
May You be blessed, our Deliverer,
by the praises of Your handiwork,
and by the radiant lights You have made:
may they glorify You. Selah!

---

hesitation. The *Yerushalmi's* explanation? "The awe of the Sabbath (*eimat Shabbat*) is upon him and he says the truth."[2] Evidently, this attitude of awe is reflected in the peculiar phraseology of the blessing recited Sabbath morning.[3] (Editor)

---

2. *y. Demai* 4:1.
3. Whether the halakhic concept of "*simḥah*" or joy applies to the Sabbath, is a point of contention among the authorities. See Zedekiah Harofe, *Shibbolei ha-Leket ha-Shalem*, ed. S.K. Mirsky (Brooklyn, NY: Sura, 1966), chap. 82 (p. 314), quoting Rabbi Avigdor Kohen Tsedek; Rabbi David Cohen, *Mas'at Kapai*, vol. 3 (Brooklyn, NY, 1990), p. 85; and Rabbi Elchanan Hakohen Adler, *'Et le-Ḥenenah: Be'urim bi-Tefillat Mussaf shel Shabbat* (n.p., 2016), pp. 108–110.

לָאֵל אֲשֶׁר שָׁבַת מִכׇּל הַמַּעֲשִׂים
בַּיּוֹם הַשְּׁבִיעִי נִתְעַלָּה וְיָשַׁב עַל כִּסֵּא כְבוֹדוֹ.
תִּפְאֶרֶת עָטָה לְיוֹם הַמְּנוּחָה
עֹנֶג קָרָא לְיוֹם הַשַּׁבָּת.
זֶה שֶׁבַח שֶׁלַּיּוֹם הַשְּׁבִיעִי
שֶׁבּוֹ שָׁבַת אֵל מִכׇּל מְלַאכְתּוֹ
וְיוֹם הַשְּׁבִיעִי מְשַׁבֵּחַ וְאוֹמֵר
מִזְמוֹר שִׁיר לְיוֹם הַשַּׁבָּת תהלים צב
טוֹב לְהֹדוֹת לַיהוה:
לְפִיכָךְ יְפָאֲרוּ וִיבָרְכוּ לָאֵל כׇּל יְצוּרָיו
שֶׁבַח יְקָר וּגְדֻלָּה יִתְּנוּ לָאֵל מֶלֶךְ יוֹצֵר כֹּל
הַמַּנְחִיל מְנוּחָה לְעַמּוֹ יִשְׂרָאֵל בִּקְדֻשָּׁתוֹ בְּיוֹם שַׁבַּת קֹדֶשׁ.
שִׁמְךָ יהוה אֱלֹהֵינוּ יִתְקַדַּשׁ
וְזִכְרְךָ מַלְכֵּנוּ יִתְפָּאַר
בַּשָּׁמַיִם מִמַּעַל וְעַל הָאָרֶץ מִתָּחַת.
תִּתְבָּרַךְ מוֹשִׁיעֵנוּ עַל שֶׁבַח מַעֲשֵׂה יָדֶיךָ
וְעַל מְאוֹרֵי אוֹר שֶׁעָשִׂיתָ
יְפָאֲרוּךָ סֶּלָה.

---

element of awe? The thought occurs to this writer (BN) that on the Sabbath there is indeed an aura of awe. The *Talmud Yerushalmi* explains a perplexing *halakhah*. The Mishnah states that if one purchased fruits from a party who is not generally trustworthy regarding the removal of tithes from produce, and one forgot to tithe the fruits himself before the Sabbath arrived, the law is that one may inquire of the seller whether they were tithed, and if the answer is in the affirmative, one may eat the fruits without

תִּתְבָּרַךְ May You be blessed,
our Rock, King and Redeemer,
Creator of holy beings.
May Your name be praised for ever,
our King, Creator of the ministering angels,
all of whom stand in the universe's heights,
proclaiming together, in awe, aloud,
the words of the living God, the eternal King.
They are all beloved, all pure, all mighty,
and all perform in awe and reverence
the will of their Maker.
▸ All open their mouths in holiness and purity,
with song and psalm,
and bless, praise, glorify,
revere, sanctify and declare the sovereignty of –
the name of the great, mighty and awesome God and King,
holy is He.
▸ All accept on themselves, one from another,
the yoke of the kingdom of heaven,
granting permission to one another
to sanctify the One who formed them, in serene spirit,
pure speech and sweet melody.
All, as one, proclaim His holiness,
saying in awe:

*All say aloud:*
Holy, holy, holy is the Lord of hosts; *Is. 6*
the whole world is filled with His glory.

▸ Then the Ophanim and the Holy Ḥayyot,
with a roar of noise,
raise themselves toward the Seraphim and,
facing them, give praise, saying:

*All say aloud:*
Blessed is the Lord's glory from His place. *Ezek. 3*

תִּתְבָּרַךְ
צוּרֵנוּ מַלְכֵּנוּ וְגוֹאֲלֵנוּ, בּוֹרֵא קְדוֹשִׁים
יִשְׁתַּבַּח שִׁמְךָ לָעַד
מַלְכֵּנוּ, יוֹצֵר מְשָׁרְתִים
וַאֲשֶׁר מְשָׁרְתָיו כֻּלָּם עוֹמְדִים בְּרוּם עוֹלָם
וּמַשְׁמִיעִים בְּיִרְאָה יַחַד בְּקוֹל דִּבְרֵי אֱלֹהִים חַיִּים וּמֶלֶךְ עוֹלָם.
כֻּלָּם אֲהוּבִים, כֻּלָּם בְּרוּרִים, כֻּלָּם גִּבּוֹרִים
וְכֻלָּם עוֹשִׂים בְּאֵימָה וּבְיִרְאָה רְצוֹן קוֹנָם
◂ וְכֻלָּם פּוֹתְחִים אֶת פִּיהֶם בִּקְדֻשָּׁה וּבְטָהֳרָה
בְּשִׁירָה וּבְזִמְרָה
וּמְבָרְכִים וּמְשַׁבְּחִים וּמְפָאֲרִים
וּמַעֲרִיצִים וּמַקְדִּישִׁים וּמַמְלִיכִים ◂
אֶת שֵׁם הָאֵל הַמֶּלֶךְ הַגָּדוֹל, הַגִּבּוֹר וְהַנּוֹרָא
קָדוֹשׁ הוּא.
◂ וְכֻלָּם מְקַבְּלִים עֲלֵיהֶם עֹל מַלְכוּת שָׁמַיִם זֶה מִזֶּה
וְנוֹתְנִים רְשׁוּת זֶה לָזֶה
לְהַקְדִּישׁ לְיוֹצְרָם בְּנַחַת רוּחַ, בְּשָׂפָה בְרוּרָה וּבִנְעִימָה
קְדֻשָּׁה כֻּלָּם כְּאֶחָד, עוֹנִים וְאוֹמְרִים בְּיִרְאָה

*All say aloud:*

ישעיה ו
קָדוֹשׁ, קָדוֹשׁ, קָדוֹשׁ יהוה צְבָאוֹת
מְלֹא כָל־הָאָרֶץ כְּבוֹדוֹ:

◂ וְהָאוֹפַנִּים וְחַיּוֹת הַקֹּדֶשׁ, בְּרַעַשׁ גָּדוֹל מִתְנַשְּׂאִים לְעֻמַּת שְׂרָפִים
לְעֻמָּתָם מְשַׁבְּחִים וְאוֹמְרִים

*All say aloud:*

יחזקאל ג
בָּרוּךְ כְּבוֹד־יהוה מִמְּקוֹמוֹ:

לָאֵל To the blessed God they offer melodies.
To the King, living and eternal God,
they say psalms and proclaim praises.
For it is He alone
who does mighty deeds
and creates new things,
who is Master of battles
and sows righteousness,
who makes salvation grow
and creates cures,
who is is revered in praises,
the LORD of wonders,
who in His goodness, continually renews the work of creation,
day after day, as it is said,
"[Praise] Him who made the great lights, *Ps. 136*
for His love endures for ever."
▸ May You make a new light shine over Zion,
and may we all soon be worthy of its light.
Blessed are You, LORD,
who forms the radiant lights.

אַהֲבָה You have loved us with great love, LORD our God,
and with surpassing compassion
have You had compassion on us.
Our Father, our King,
for the sake of our ancestors who trusted in You,
and to whom You taught the laws of life,
be gracious also to us and teach us.
Our Father, compassionate Father, ever compassionate,
have compassion on us.
Instill in our hearts the desire to understand and discern,
to listen, learn and teach, to observe, perform and fulfill
all the teachings of Your Torah in love.

לָאֵל בָּרוּךְ נְעִימוֹת יִתֵּנוּ
לַמֶּלֶךְ אֵל חַי וְקַיָּם
זְמִירוֹת יֹאמֵרוּ וְתִשְׁבָּחוֹת יַשְׁמִיעוּ
כִּי הוּא לְבַדּוֹ
פּוֹעֵל גְּבוּרוֹת, עוֹשֶׂה חֲדָשׁוֹת
בַּעַל מִלְחָמוֹת, זוֹרֵעַ צְדָקוֹת
מַצְמִיחַ יְשׁוּעוֹת, בּוֹרֵא רְפוּאוֹת
נוֹרָא תְהִלּוֹת, אֲדוֹן הַנִּפְלָאוֹת
הַמְחַדֵּשׁ בְּטוּבוֹ בְּכָל יוֹם תָּמִיד מַעֲשֵׂה בְרֵאשִׁית
כָּאָמוּר
תהלים קלו לְעֹשֵׂה אוֹרִים גְּדֹלִים, כִּי לְעוֹלָם חַסְדּוֹ:
◂ אוֹר חָדָשׁ עַל צִיּוֹן תָּאִיר וְנִזְכֶּה כֻלָּנוּ מְהֵרָה לְאוֹרוֹ.
בָּרוּךְ אַתָּה יהוה, יוֹצֵר הַמְּאוֹרוֹת.

אַהֲבָה רַבָּה אֲהַבְתָּנוּ, יהוה אֱלֹהֵינוּ
חֶמְלָה גְדוֹלָה וִיתֵרָה חָמַלְתָּ עָלֵינוּ.
אָבִינוּ מַלְכֵּנוּ
בַּעֲבוּר אֲבוֹתֵינוּ שֶׁבָּטְחוּ בְךָ, וַתְּלַמְּדֵם חֻקֵּי חַיִּים
כֵּן תְּחָנֵּנוּ וּתְלַמְּדֵנוּ.
אָבִינוּ, הָאָב הָרַחֲמָן, הַמְרַחֵם
רַחֵם עָלֵינוּ
וְתֵן בְּלִבֵּנוּ לְהָבִין וּלְהַשְׂכִּיל
לִשְׁמֹעַ, לִלְמֹד וּלְלַמֵּד, לִשְׁמֹר וְלַעֲשׂוֹת, וּלְקַיֵּם
אֶת כָּל דִּבְרֵי תַלְמוּד תּוֹרָתֶךָ בְּאַהֲבָה.

Enlighten our eyes in Your Torah
and let our hearts cling to Your commandments.
Unite our hearts to love and revere Your name,
so that we may never be ashamed.
And because we have trusted in Your holy, great and revered name,
may we be glad and rejoice in Your salvation.

*At this point, gather the four tzitziot of the tallit, holding them in the left hand.*

Bring us back in peace from the four quarters of the earth
and lead us upright to our land.
▸ For You are a God who performs acts of salvation,
and You chose us from all peoples and tongues,
bringing us close to Your great name for ever in truth,
that we may thank You and proclaim Your Oneness in love.
Blessed are You, LORD,
who chooses His people Israel in love.

*The Shema must be said with intense concentration. In the first paragraph one should accept, with love, the sovereignty of God; in the second, the mitzvot as the will of God. The end of the third paragraph constitutes fulfillment of the mitzva to remember, morning and evening, the exodus from Egypt. See laws 346–355.*

*When not praying with a minyan, say:*

God, faithful King!

*The following verse should be said aloud, while covering the eyes with the right hand:*

**Listen, Israel: the LORD is our God, the LORD is One.** Deut. 6

*Quietly:* Blessed be the name of His glorious kingdom for ever and all time.

וְאָהַבְתָּ Love the LORD your God with all your heart, with all your soul, and with all your might. These words which I command you today shall be on your heart. Teach them repeatedly to your children, speaking of them when you sit at home and when you travel on the way, when you lie down and when you rise. Deut. 6

וְהָאֵר עֵינֵינוּ בְּתוֹרָתֶךָ, וְדַבֵּק לִבֵּנוּ בְּמִצְוֹתֶיךָ
וְיַחֵד לְבָבֵנוּ לְאַהֲבָה וּלְיִרְאָה אֶת שְׁמֶךָ
וְלֹא נֵבוֹשׁ לְעוֹלָם וָעֶד.
כִּי בְשֵׁם קָדְשְׁךָ הַגָּדוֹל וְהַנּוֹרָא בָּטָחְנוּ
נָגִילָה וְנִשְׂמְחָה בִּישׁוּעָתֶךָ.

*At this point, gather the four* ציציות *of the* טלית*, holding them in the left hand.*

וַהֲבִיאֵנוּ לְשָׁלוֹם מֵאַרְבַּע כַּנְפוֹת הָאָרֶץ
וְתוֹלִיכֵנוּ קוֹמְמִיּוּת לְאַרְצֵנוּ.
◂ כִּי אֵל פּוֹעֵל יְשׁוּעוֹת אָתָּה, וּבָנוּ בָחַרְתָּ מִכָּל עַם וְלָשׁוֹן
וְקֵרַבְתָּנוּ לְשִׁמְךָ הַגָּדוֹל סֶלָה, בֶּאֱמֶת
לְהוֹדוֹת לְךָ וּלְיַחֶדְךָ בְּאַהֲבָה.
בָּרוּךְ אַתָּה יהוה, הַבּוֹחֵר בְּעַמּוֹ יִשְׂרָאֵל בְּאַהֲבָה.

*The* שמע *must be said with intense concentration. In the first paragraph one should accept, with love, the sovereignty of God; in the second, the* מצוות *as the will of God. The end of the third paragraph constitutes fulfillment of the* מצווה *to remember, morning and evening, the exodus from Egypt. See laws 346–355.*

*When not praying with a* מנין*, say:*

אֵל מֶלֶךְ נֶאֱמָן

*The following verse should be said aloud, while covering the eyes with the right hand:*

## שְׁמַע יִשְׂרָאֵל, יהוה אֱלֹהֵינוּ, יהוה ׀ אֶחָד׃ דברים ו

*Quietly* בָּרוּךְ שֵׁם כְּבוֹד מַלְכוּתוֹ לְעוֹלָם וָעֶד.

וְאָהַבְתָּ אֵת יהוה אֱלֹהֶיךָ, בְּכָל־לְבָבְךָ וּבְכָל־נַפְשְׁךָ וּבְכָל־ דברים ו
מְאֹדֶךָ׃ וְהָיוּ הַדְּבָרִים הָאֵלֶּה, אֲשֶׁר אָנֹכִי מְצַוְּךָ הַיּוֹם, עַל־לְבָבֶךָ׃
וְשִׁנַּנְתָּם לְבָנֶיךָ וְדִבַּרְתָּ בָּם, בְּשִׁבְתְּךָ בְּבֵיתֶךָ וּבְלֶכְתְּךָ בַדֶּרֶךְ,

Bind them as a sign on your hand, and they shall be an emblem between your eyes. Write them on the doorposts of your house and gates.

וְהָיָה If you indeed heed My commandments with which I charge you today, to love the LORD your God and worship Him with all your heart and with all your soul, I will give rain in your land in its season, the early and late rain; and you shall gather in your grain, wine and oil. I will give grass in your field for your cattle, and you shall eat and be satisfied. Be careful lest your heart be tempted and you go astray and worship other gods, bowing down to them. Then the LORD's anger will flare against you and He will close the heavens so that there will be no rain. The land will not yield its crops, and you will perish swiftly from the good land that the LORD is giving you. Therefore, set these, My words, on your heart and soul. Bind them as a sign on your hand, and they shall be an emblem between your eyes. Teach them to your children, speaking of them when you sit at home and when you travel on the way, when you lie down and when you rise. Write them on the doorposts of your house and gates, so that you and your children may live long in the land that the LORD swore to your ancestors to give them, for as long as the heavens are above the earth. *Deut. 11*

*Hold the tzitziot in the right hand also (some transfer to the right hand), kissing them at °.*

וַיֹּאמֶר The LORD spoke to Moses, saying: Speak to the Israelites and tell them to make °tassels on the corners of their garments for all generations. They shall attach to the °tassel at each corner a thread of blue. This shall be your °tassel, and you shall see it and remember all of the LORD's commandments and keep them, not straying after your heart and after your eyes, following your own sinful desires. Thus you will be reminded to keep all My commandments, and be holy to your God. I am the LORD your *Num. 15*

וּבְשָׁכְבְּךָ וּבְקוּמֶךָ: וּקְשַׁרְתָּם לְאוֹת עַל־יָדֶךָ וְהָיוּ לְטֹטָפֹת בֵּין
עֵינֶיךָ: וּכְתַבְתָּם עַל־מְזֻזוֹת בֵּיתֶךָ וּבִשְׁעָרֶיךָ:

דברים יא וְהָיָה אִם־שָׁמֹעַ תִּשְׁמְעוּ אֶל־מִצְוֺתַי אֲשֶׁר אָנֹכִי מְצַוֶּה אֶתְכֶם
הַיּוֹם, לְאַהֲבָה אֶת־יהוה אֱלֹהֵיכֶם וּלְעָבְדוֹ, בְּכָל־לְבַבְכֶם וּבְכָל־
נַפְשְׁכֶם: וְנָתַתִּי מְטַר־אַרְצְכֶם בְּעִתּוֹ, יוֹרֶה וּמַלְקוֹשׁ, וְאָסַפְתָּ
דְגָנֶךָ וְתִירֹשְׁךָ וְיִצְהָרֶךָ: וְנָתַתִּי עֵשֶׂב בְּשָׂדְךָ לִבְהֶמְתֶּךָ, וְאָכַלְתָּ
וְשָׂבָעְתָּ: הִשָּׁמְרוּ לָכֶם פֶּן־יִפְתֶּה לְבַבְכֶם, וְסַרְתֶּם וַעֲבַדְתֶּם
אֱלֹהִים אֲחֵרִים וְהִשְׁתַּחֲוִיתֶם לָהֶם: וְחָרָה אַף־יהוה בָּכֶם, וְעָצַר
אֶת־הַשָּׁמַיִם וְלֹא־יִהְיֶה מָטָר, וְהָאֲדָמָה לֹא תִתֵּן אֶת־יְבוּלָהּ,
וַאֲבַדְתֶּם מְהֵרָה מֵעַל הָאָרֶץ הַטֹּבָה אֲשֶׁר יהוה נֹתֵן לָכֶם:
וְשַׂמְתֶּם אֶת־דְּבָרַי אֵלֶּה עַל־לְבַבְכֶם וְעַל־נַפְשְׁכֶם, וּקְשַׁרְתֶּם
אֹתָם לְאוֹת עַל־יֶדְכֶם, וְהָיוּ לְטוֹטָפֹת בֵּין עֵינֵיכֶם: וְלִמַּדְתֶּם
אֹתָם אֶת־בְּנֵיכֶם לְדַבֵּר בָּם, בְּשִׁבְתְּךָ בְּבֵיתֶךָ וּבְלֶכְתְּךָ בַדֶּרֶךְ,
וּבְשָׁכְבְּךָ וּבְקוּמֶךָ: וּכְתַבְתָּם עַל־מְזוּזוֹת בֵּיתֶךָ וּבִשְׁעָרֶיךָ: לְמַעַן
יִרְבּוּ יְמֵיכֶם וִימֵי בְנֵיכֶם עַל הָאֲדָמָה אֲשֶׁר נִשְׁבַּע יהוה לַאֲבֹתֵיכֶם
לָתֵת לָהֶם, כִּימֵי הַשָּׁמַיִם עַל־הָאָרֶץ:

*Hold the* ציציות *in the right hand also (some transfer to the right hand), kissing them at °.*

במדבר טו וַיֹּאמֶר יהוה אֶל־מֹשֶׁה לֵּאמֹר: דַּבֵּר אֶל־בְּנֵי יִשְׂרָאֵל וְאָמַרְתָּ
אֲלֵהֶם, וְעָשׂוּ לָהֶם °צִיצִת עַל־כַּנְפֵי בִגְדֵיהֶם לְדֹרֹתָם, וְנָתְנוּ
°עַל־צִיצִת הַכָּנָף פְּתִיל תְּכֵלֶת: וְהָיָה לָכֶם °לְצִיצִת, וּרְאִיתֶם
אֹתוֹ וּזְכַרְתֶּם אֶת־כָּל־מִצְוֺת יהוה וַעֲשִׂיתֶם אֹתָם, וְלֹא תָתוּרוּ
אַחֲרֵי לְבַבְכֶם וְאַחֲרֵי עֵינֵיכֶם, אֲשֶׁר־אַתֶּם זֹנִים אַחֲרֵיהֶם: לְמַעַן
תִּזְכְּרוּ וַעֲשִׂיתֶם אֶת־כָּל־מִצְוֺתָי, וִהְיִיתֶם קְדֹשִׁים לֵאלֹהֵיכֶם: אֲנִי

For the early and the later generations
this faith has proved good and enduring for ever –

True and faithful, an irrevocable law.

True You are the LORD: our God and God of our ancestors,
▸ our King and King of our ancestors,
our Redeemer and Redeemer of our ancestors,
our Maker, Rock of our salvation,
our Deliverer and Rescuer:
this has ever been Your name.
There is no God but You.

עֶזְרַת You have always been the help of our ancestors,
Shield and Savior of their children
after them in every generation.
Your dwelling is in the heights of the universe,
and Your judgments and righteousness
reach to the ends of the earth.

Happy is the one who obeys Your commandments
and takes to heart Your teaching and Your word.

True You are the Master of Your people
and a mighty King who pleads their cause.

True You are the first and You are the last.
Besides You, we have no king, redeemer or savior.
From Egypt You redeemed us, LORD our God,
and from the slave-house You delivered us.
All their firstborn You killed,
but Your firstborn You redeemed.
You split the Sea of Reeds
and drowned the arrogant.
You brought Your beloved ones across.
The water covered their foes; *Ps. 106*
not one of them was left.

עַל הָרִאשׁוֹנִים וְעַל הָאַחֲרוֹנִים
דָּבָר טוֹב וְקַיָּם לְעוֹלָם וָעֶד

אֱמֶת וֶאֱמוּנָה, חֹק וְלֹא יַעֲבֹר.

אֱמֶת שָׁאַתָּה הוּא יהוה אֱלֹהֵינוּ וֵאלֹהֵי אֲבוֹתֵינוּ
◂ מַלְכֵּנוּ מֶלֶךְ אֲבוֹתֵינוּ
גּוֹאֲלֵנוּ גּוֹאֵל אֲבוֹתֵינוּ
יוֹצְרֵנוּ צוּר יְשׁוּעָתֵנוּ
פּוֹדֵנוּ וּמַצִּילֵנוּ מֵעוֹלָם שְׁמֶךָ
אֵין אֱלֹהִים זוּלָתֶךָ.

עֶזְרַת אֲבוֹתֵינוּ אַתָּה הוּא מֵעוֹלָם
מָגֵן וּמוֹשִׁיעַ לִבְנֵיהֶם אַחֲרֵיהֶם בְּכָל דּוֹר וָדוֹר.
בְּרוּם עוֹלָם מוֹשָׁבֶךָ
וּמִשְׁפָּטֶיךָ וְצִדְקָתְךָ עַד אַפְסֵי אָרֶץ.
אַשְׁרֵי אִישׁ שֶׁיִּשְׁמַע לְמִצְוֹתֶיךָ
וְתוֹרָתְךָ וּדְבָרְךָ יָשִׂים עַל לִבּוֹ.

אֱמֶת אַתָּה הוּא אָדוֹן לְעַמֶּךָ
וּמֶלֶךְ גִּבּוֹר לָרִיב רִיבָם.

אֱמֶת אַתָּה הוּא רִאשׁוֹן וְאַתָּה הוּא אַחֲרוֹן
וּמִבַּלְעָדֶיךָ אֵין לָנוּ מֶלֶךְ גּוֹאֵל וּמוֹשִׁיעַ.
מִמִּצְרַיִם גְּאַלְתָּנוּ, יהוה אֱלֹהֵינוּ
וּמִבֵּית עֲבָדִים פְּדִיתָנוּ
כָּל בְּכוֹרֵיהֶם הָרַגְתָּ, וּבְכוֹרְךָ גָּאָלְתָּ
וְיַם סוּף בָּקַעְתָּ, וְזֵדִים טִבַּעְתָּ, וִידִידִים הֶעֱבַרְתָּ
וַיְכַסּוּ־מַיִם צָרֵיהֶם, אֶחָד מֵהֶם לֹא נוֹתָר: תהלים קו

For this, the beloved ones praised and exalted God,
the cherished ones sang psalms, songs and praises,
blessings and thanksgivings to the King,
the living and enduring God.
High and exalted, great and awesome,
He humbles the haughty and raises the lowly,
freeing captives and redeeming those in need,
helping the poor
and answering His people when they cry out to Him.

*Stand in preparation for the Amida. Take three steps back before beginning the Amida.*

▸ Praises to God Most High,
the Blessed One who is blessed.
Moses and the children of Israel
recited to You a song with great joy,
and they all exclaimed:
"Who is like You, LORD, among the mighty? *Ex. 15*
Who is like You, majestic in holiness,
awesome in praises, doing wonders?"

▸ With a new song, the redeemed people praised
Your name at the seashore.
Together they all gave thanks,
proclaimed Your kingship,
and declared:
"The LORD shall reign for ever and ever." *Ibid.*

*Congregants should end the following blessing together with the Leader so as to be able to move directly from the words "redeemed Israel" to the Amida, without the interruption of saying Amen.*

▸ צוּר יִשְׂרָאֵל Rock of Israel! Arise to the help of Israel.
Deliver, as You promised, Judah and Israel.
Our Redeemer, the LORD of hosts is His name, *Is. 47*
the Holy One of Israel.
Blessed are You, LORD,
who redeemed Israel.

עַל זֹאת שִׁבְּחוּ אֲהוּבִים, וְרוֹמְמוּ אֵל
וְנָתְנוּ יְדִידִים זְמִירוֹת, שִׁירוֹת וְתִשְׁבָּחוֹת
בְּרָכוֹת וְהוֹדָאוֹת לַמֶּלֶךְ אֵל חַי וְקַיָּם
רָם וְנִשָּׂא, גָּדוֹל וְנוֹרָא
מַשְׁפִּיל גֵּאִים וּמַגְבִּיהַּ שְׁפָלִים
מוֹצִיא אֲסִירִים, וּפוֹדֶה עֲנָוִים וְעוֹזֵר דַּלִּים
וְעוֹנֶה לְעַמּוֹ בְּעֵת שַׁוְּעָם אֵלָיו.

*Stand in preparation for the* עמידה*. Take three steps back before beginning the* עמידה*.*

◂ תְּהִלּוֹת לְאֵל עֶלְיוֹן
בָּרוּךְ הוּא וּמְבֹרָךְ
מֹשֶׁה וּבְנֵי יִשְׂרָאֵל
לְךָ עָנוּ שִׁירָה בְּשִׂמְחָה רַבָּה
וְאָמְרוּ כֻלָּם

מִי־כָמֹכָה בָּאֵלִם, יהוה — שמות טו
מִי כָּמֹכָה נֶאְדָּר בַּקֹּדֶשׁ, נוֹרָא תְהִלֹּת, עֹשֵׂה פֶלֶא:

◂ שִׁירָה חֲדָשָׁה שִׁבְּחוּ גְאוּלִים
לְשִׁמְךָ עַל שְׂפַת הַיָּם
יַחַד כֻּלָּם הוֹדוּ וְהִמְלִיכוּ
וְאָמְרוּ

יהוה יִמְלֹךְ לְעֹלָם וָעֶד: — שם

*The* קהל *should end the following blessing together with the* שליח ציבור *so as to be able to move directly from the words* גָּאַל יִשְׂרָאֵל *to the* עמידה*, without the interruption of saying* אמן*.*

◂ צוּר יִשְׂרָאֵל, קוּמָה בְּעֶזְרַת יִשְׂרָאֵל
וּפְדֵה כִנְאֻמֶךָ יְהוּדָה וְיִשְׂרָאֵל.

גֹּאֲלֵנוּ יהוה צְבָאוֹת שְׁמוֹ, קְדוֹשׁ יִשְׂרָאֵל: — ישעיה מז

בָּרוּךְ אַתָּה יהוה, גָּאַל יִשְׂרָאֵל.

*On Yom Tov (including one that falls on Shabbat) say the appropriate Amida on page 830.*

## THE AMIDA

*The following prayer, until "in former years" on page 566, is said silently, standing with feet together. If there is a minyan, the Amida is repeated aloud by the Leader. Take three steps forward and at the points indicated by ▾, bend the knees at the first word, bow at the second, and stand straight before saying God's name.*

O Lord, open my lips, so that my mouth may declare Your praise. *Ps. 51*

### PATRIARCHS

▾בָּרוּךְ Blessed are You, Lord our God and God of our fathers,
God of Abraham, God of Isaac and God of Jacob;
the great, mighty and awesome God, God Most High,
who bestows acts of loving-kindness and creates all,
who remembers the loving-kindness of the fathers
and will bring a Redeemer to their children's children
for the sake of His name, in love.

*On Shabbat Shuva:* Remember us for life, O King who desires life,
and write us in the book of life –
for Your sake, O God of life.

King, Helper, Savior, Shield:
▾Blessed are You, Lord, Shield of Abraham.

### DIVINE MIGHT

אַתָּה גִּבּוֹר You are eternally mighty, Lord.
You give life to the dead and have great power to save.

*The phrase "He makes the wind blow and the rain fall" is added from Simhat Torah until Pesah. In Israel the phrase "He causes the dew to fall" is added from Pesah until Shemini Atzeret. See laws 129–131.*

*In fall & winter:* He makes the wind blow and the rain fall.
*In Israel, in spring & summer:* He causes the dew to fall.

He sustains the living with loving-kindness,
and with great compassion revives the dead.
He supports the fallen, heals the sick, sets captives free,
and keeps His faith with those who sleep in the dust.

*On* יום טוב *(including one that falls on* שבת*) say the appropriate* עמידה *on page 831.*

# עמידה

*The following prayer, until* קַדְמֹנִיּוֹת *on page 567, is said silently, standing with feet together. If there is a* מנין*, the* עמידה *is repeated aloud by the* שליח ציבור*. Take three steps forward and at the points indicated by* ▾*, bend the knees at the first word, bow at the second, and stand straight before saying God's name.*

אֲדֹנָי, שְׂפָתַי תִּפְתָּח, וּפִי יַגִּיד תְּהִלָּתֶךָ: תהלים נא

### אבות

▾בָּרוּךְ אַתָּה יהוה, אֱלֹהֵינוּ וֵאלֹהֵי אֲבוֹתֵינוּ
אֱלֹהֵי אַבְרָהָם, אֱלֹהֵי יִצְחָק, וֵאלֹהֵי יַעֲקֹב
הָאֵל הַגָּדוֹל הַגִּבּוֹר וְהַנּוֹרָא, אֵל עֶלְיוֹן
גּוֹמֵל חֲסָדִים טוֹבִים, וְקוֹנֵה הַכֹּל
וְזוֹכֵר חַסְדֵי אָבוֹת
וּמֵבִיא גוֹאֵל לִבְנֵי בְנֵיהֶם לְמַעַן שְׁמוֹ בְּאַהֲבָה.

בשבת שובה: זָכְרֵנוּ לְחַיִּים, מֶלֶךְ חָפֵץ בַּחַיִּים
וְכָתְבֵנוּ בְּסֵפֶר הַחַיִּים, לְמַעַנְךָ אֱלֹהִים חַיִּים.

מֶלֶךְ עוֹזֵר וּמוֹשִׁיעַ וּמָגֵן.
▾בָּרוּךְ אַתָּה יהוה, מָגֵן אַבְרָהָם.

### גבורות

אַתָּה גִּבּוֹר לְעוֹלָם, אֲדֹנָי, מְחַיֵּה מֵתִים אַתָּה, רַב לְהוֹשִׁיעַ

*The phrase* מַשִּׁיב הָרְוּחַ *is added from* שמחת תורה *until* פסח*.*
*In* ארץ ישראל *the phrase* מוֹרִיד הַטָּל *is added from* פסח *until* שמיני עצרת*. See laws 129–131.*

בחורף: מַשִּׁיב הָרְוּחַ וּמוֹרִיד הַגֶּשֶׁם / בארץ ישראל בקיץ: מוֹרִיד הַטָּל

מְכַלְכֵּל חַיִּים בְּחֶסֶד, מְחַיֵּה מֵתִים בְּרַחֲמִים רַבִּים
סוֹמֵךְ נוֹפְלִים, וְרוֹפֵא חוֹלִים, וּמַתִּיר אֲסוּרִים
וּמְקַיֵּם אֱמוּנָתוֹ לִישֵׁנֵי עָפָר.

Who is like You, Master of might, and who can compare to You,
O King who brings death and gives life, and makes salvation grow?

*On Shabbat Shuva:* Who is like You, compassionate Father,
who remembers His creatures in compassion, for life?

Faithful are You to revive the dead.
Blessed are You, LORD, who revives the dead.

*When saying the Amida silently, continue with "You are holy" on the next page.*

---

KEDUSHA

*During the Leader's Repetition, the following is said standing with feet together, rising on the toes at the words indicated by* ▲.

*Cong. then Leader:* נְקַדֵּשׁ We will sanctify Your name on earth,
as they sanctify it in the highest heavens,
as is written by Your prophet,
"And they [the angels] call to one another saying: *Is. 6*

*Cong. then Leader:* ▲Holy, ▲holy, ▲holy is the LORD of hosts;
the whole world is filled with His glory."
Then with a sound of mighty noise, majestic and strong,
they make their voice heard, raising themselves
toward the Seraphim, and facing them say: "Blessed…

*Cong. then Leader:* ▲"Blessed is the LORD's glory from His place." *Ezek. 3*
Reveal Yourself from Your place, O our King, and reign over us,
for we are waiting for You. When will You reign in Zion?
May it be soon in our days, and may You dwell there for ever
and all time. May You be exalted and sanctified in the midst of
Jerusalem, Your city, from generation to generation for evermore.
May our eyes see Your kingdom, as is said in the songs of Your
splendor, written by David Your righteous anointed one:

*Cong. then Leader:* ▲"The LORD shall reign for ever. He is your God, Zion, *Ps. 146*
from generation to generation, Halleluya!"

*Leader:* From generation to generation we will declare Your greatness,
and we will proclaim Your holiness for evermore.
Your praise, our God, shall not leave our mouth forever,
for You, God, are a great and holy King. Blessed are You, LORD,
the holy God. / *On Shabbat Shuva:* the holy King./

*The Leader continues with "Moses rejoiced" on the next page.*

מִי כָמְוֹךָ, בַּעַל גְּבוּרוֹת, וּמִי דְּוֹמֶה לָּךְ
מֶלֶךְ, מֵמִית וּמְחַיֶּה וּמַצְמִיחַ יְשׁוּעָה.

בשבת שובה: מִי כָמְוֹךָ אַב הָרַחֲמִים, זוֹכֵר יְצוּרָיו לְחַיִּים בְּרַחֲמִים.

וְנֶאֱמָן אַתָּה לְהַחֲיוֹת מֵתִים.
בָּרוּךְ אַתָּה יהוה, מְחַיֵּה הַמֵּתִים.

*When saying the* עמידה *silently, continue with* אַתָּה קָדוֹשׁ *on the next page.*

---

קדושה

*During the* חזרת הש״ץ*, the following is said standing with feet together, rising on the toes at the words indicated by* ˄.

then קהל ש״ץ: נְקַדֵּשׁ אֶת שִׁמְךָ בָּעוֹלָם, כְּשֵׁם שֶׁמַּקְדִּישִׁים אוֹתוֹ בִּשְׁמֵי מָרוֹם
כַּכָּתוּב עַל יַד נְבִיאֶךָ: וְקָרָא זֶה אֶל־זֶה וְאָמַר — ישעיה ו

then קהל ש״ץ: ˄קָדוֹשׁ, ˄קָדוֹשׁ, ˄קָדוֹשׁ, יהוה צְבָאוֹת, מְלֹא כָל־הָאָרֶץ כְּבוֹדוֹ:
אָז בְּקוֹל רַעַשׁ גָּדוֹל אַדִּיר וְחָזָק, מַשְׁמִיעִים קוֹל
מִתְנַשְּׂאִים לְעֻמַּת שְׂרָפִים, לְעֻמָּתָם בָּרוּךְ יֹאמֵרוּ

then קהל ש״ץ: ˄בָּרוּךְ כְּבוֹד־יהוה מִמְּקוֹמוֹ: — יחזקאל ג
מִמְּקוֹמְךָ מַלְכֵּנוּ תוֹפִיעַ וְתִמְלֹךְ עָלֵינוּ, כִּי מְחַכִּים אֲנַחְנוּ לָךְ
מָתַי תִּמְלֹךְ בְּצִיּוֹן, בְּקָרוֹב בְּיָמֵינוּ לְעוֹלָם וָעֶד תִּשְׁכֹּן
תִּתְגַּדַּל וְתִתְקַדַּשׁ בְּתוֹךְ יְרוּשָׁלַיִם עִירְךָ, לְדוֹר וָדוֹר וּלְנֵצַח נְצָחִים.
וְעֵינֵינוּ תִרְאֶינָה מַלְכוּתֶךָ
כַּדָּבָר הָאָמוּר בְּשִׁירֵי עֻזֶּךָ, עַל יְדֵי דָוִד מְשִׁיחַ צִדְקֶךָ

then קהל ש״ץ: ˄יִמְלֹךְ יהוה לְעוֹלָם, אֱלֹהַיִךְ צִיּוֹן לְדֹר וָדֹר, הַלְלוּיָהּ: — תהלים קמו

ש״ץ: לְדוֹר וָדוֹר נַגִּיד גָּדְלֶךָ, וּלְנֵצַח נְצָחִים קְדֻשָּׁתְךָ נַקְדִּישׁ
וְשִׁבְחֲךָ אֱלֹהֵינוּ מִפִּינוּ לֹא יָמוּשׁ לְעוֹלָם וָעֶד
כִּי אֵל מֶלֶךְ גָּדוֹל וְקָדוֹשׁ אָתָּה.
בָּרוּךְ אַתָּה יהוה הָאֵל הַקָּדוֹשׁ./ בשבת שובה: הַמֶּלֶךְ הַקָּדוֹשׁ./

*The* שליח ציבור *continues with* יִשְׂמַח מֹשֶׁה *on the next page.*

HOLINESS

אַתָּה קָדוֹשׁ You are holy and Your name is holy,
and holy ones praise You daily, Selah!
Blessed are You, Lord,
the holy God. / *On Shabbat Shuva:* the holy King./
*(If forgotten, repeat the Amida.)*

HOLINESS OF THE DAY

יִשְׂמַח Moses rejoiced at the gift of his portion
when You called him "faithful servant."
A crown of glory You placed on his head
when he stood before You on Mount Sinai.
He brought down in his hands two tablets of stone
on which was engraved the observance of the Sabbath.
So it is written in Your Torah:

וְשָׁמְרוּ The children of Israel must keep the Sabbath, *Ex. 31*
observing the Sabbath in every generation
as an everlasting covenant.
It is a sign between Me and the children of Israel for ever,
for in six days the Lord made the heavens and the earth,
but on the seventh day He ceased work
and refreshed Himself.

וְלֹא You, O Lord our God,
did not give it to the other nations of the world,
nor did You, our King,
give it as a heritage
to those who worship idols.
In its rest the uncircumcised do not dwell,
for You gave it in love to Israel Your people,
to the descendants of Jacob whom You chose.

קדושת השם

אַתָּה קָדוֹשׁ וְשִׁמְךָ קָדוֹשׁ,
וּקְדוֹשִׁים בְּכָל יוֹם יְהַלְלְוּךָ סֶּלָה.
בָּרוּךְ אַתָּה יהוה, הָאֵל הַקָּדוֹשׁ. / בשבת שובה: הַמֶּלֶךְ הַקָּדוֹשׁ./

(*If forgotten, repeat the* עמידה.)

קדושת היום

יִשְׂמַח מֹשֶׁה בְּמַתְּנַת חֶלְקוֹ
כִּי עֶבֶד נֶאֱמָן קָרָאתָ לּוֹ
כְּלִיל תִּפְאֶרֶת בְּרֹאשׁוֹ נָתַתָּ לּוֹ
בְּעָמְדוֹ לְפָנֶיךָ עַל הַר סִינַי
וּשְׁנֵי לוּחוֹת אֲבָנִים הוֹרִיד בְּיָדוֹ
וְכָתוּב בָּהֶם שְׁמִירַת שַׁבָּת
וְכֵן כָּתוּב בְּתוֹרָתֶךָ

וְשָׁמְרוּ בְנֵי־יִשְׂרָאֵל אֶת־הַשַּׁבָּת שמות לא
לַעֲשׂוֹת אֶת־הַשַּׁבָּת לְדֹרֹתָם בְּרִית עוֹלָם:
בֵּינִי וּבֵין בְּנֵי יִשְׂרָאֵל אוֹת הִוא לְעֹלָם
כִּי־שֵׁשֶׁת יָמִים עָשָׂה יהוה אֶת־הַשָּׁמַיִם וְאֶת־הָאָרֶץ
וּבַיּוֹם הַשְּׁבִיעִי שָׁבַת וַיִּנָּפַשׁ:

וְלֹא נְתַתּוֹ, יהוה אֱלֹהֵינוּ, לְגוֹיֵי הָאֲרָצוֹת
וְלֹא הִנְחַלְתּוֹ, מַלְכֵּנוּ, לְעוֹבְדֵי פְסִילִים
וְגַם בִּמְנוּחָתוֹ לֹא יִשְׁכְּנוּ עֲרֵלִים
כִּי לְיִשְׂרָאֵל עַמְּךָ נְתַתּוֹ בְּאַהֲבָה
לְזֶרַע יַעֲקֹב אֲשֶׁר בָּם בָּחָרְתָּ.

May the people who sanctify the seventh day
all find satisfaction and delight in Your goodness,
for You favored the seventh day and made it holy,
calling it the most cherished of days,
a remembrance of the act of creation.

אֱלֹהֵינוּ Our God and God of our ancestors,
find favor in our rest.
Make us holy through Your commandments
and grant us our share in Your Torah.
Satisfy us with Your goodness,
grant us joy in Your salvation,
and purify our hearts to serve You in truth.
In love and favor, LORD our God,
grant us as our heritage Your holy Sabbath,
so that Israel who sanctify Your name may find rest on it.
Blessed are You, LORD,
who sanctifies the Sabbath.

TEMPLE SERVICE

רְצֵה Find favor, LORD our God, in Your people Israel
and their prayer.
Restore the service to Your most holy House,
and accept in love and favor the fire-offerings of Israel
and their prayer.
May the service of Your people Israel
always find favor with You.

---

*On Rosh Ḥodesh and Ḥol HaMo'ed, say:*

אֱלֹהֵינוּ Our God and God of our ancestors, may there rise, come, reach, appear, be favored, heard, regarded and remembered before You, our recollection and remembrance, as well as the remembrance of our ancestors, and of the Messiah, son of David Your servant, and of Jerusalem Your holy city, and of all Your people the house of Israel – for deliverance

עַם מְקַדְּשֵׁי שְׁבִיעִי
כֻּלָּם יִשְׂבְּעוּ וְיִתְעַנְּגוּ מִטּוּבֶךָ
וּבַשְּׁבִיעִי רָצִיתָ בּוֹ וְקִדַּשְׁתּוֹ
חֶמְדַּת יָמִים אוֹתוֹ קָרָאתָ
זֵכֶר לְמַעֲשֵׂה בְרֵאשִׁית.

אֱלֹהֵינוּ וֵאלֹהֵי אֲבוֹתֵינוּ, רְצֵה בִמְנוּחָתֵנוּ
קַדְּשֵׁנוּ בְּמִצְוֹתֶיךָ וְתֵן חֶלְקֵנוּ בְּתוֹרָתֶךָ
שַׂבְּעֵנוּ מִטּוּבֶךָ וְשַׂמְּחֵנוּ בִּישׁוּעָתֶךָ
וְטַהֵר לִבֵּנוּ לְעָבְדְּךָ בֶּאֱמֶת
וְהַנְחִילֵנוּ, יהוה אֱלֹהֵינוּ, בְּאַהֲבָה וּבְרָצוֹן שַׁבַּת קָדְשֶׁךָ
וְיָנוּחוּ בוֹ יִשְׂרָאֵל מְקַדְּשֵׁי שְׁמֶךָ.
בָּרוּךְ אַתָּה יהוה
מְקַדֵּשׁ הַשַּׁבָּת.

עבודה

רְצֵה יהוה אֱלֹהֵינוּ בְּעַמְּךָ יִשְׂרָאֵל וּבִתְפִלָּתָם
וְהָשֵׁב אֶת הָעֲבוֹדָה לִדְבִיר בֵּיתֶךָ
וְאִשֵּׁי יִשְׂרָאֵל וּתְפִלָּתָם בְּאַהֲבָה תְקַבֵּל בְּרָצוֹן
וּתְהִי לְרָצוֹן תָּמִיד עֲבוֹדַת יִשְׂרָאֵל עַמֶּךָ.

---

*On* ראש חודש *and* חול המועד, *say:*

אֱלֹהֵינוּ וֵאלֹהֵי אֲבוֹתֵינוּ, יַעֲלֶה וְיָבוֹא וְיַגִּיעַ, וְיֵרָאֶה וְיֵרָצֶה וְיִשָּׁמַע, וְיִפָּקֵד וְיִזָּכֵר זִכְרוֹנֵנוּ וּפִקְדּוֹנֵנוּ וְזִכְרוֹן אֲבוֹתֵינוּ, וְזִכְרוֹן מָשִׁיחַ בֶּן דָּוִד עַבְדֶּךָ, וְזִכְרוֹן יְרוּשָׁלַיִם עִיר קָדְשֶׁךָ, וְזִכְרוֹן כָּל עַמְּךָ בֵּית יִשְׂרָאֵל,

and well-being, grace, loving-kindness and compassion, life and peace, on this day of:

*On Rosh Ḥodesh:* Rosh Ḥodesh.
*On Pesaḥ:* the Festival of Matzot.
*On Sukkot:* the Festival of Sukkot.

On it remember us, LORD our God, for good; recollect us for blessing, and deliver us for life. In accord with Your promise of salvation and compassion, spare us and be gracious to us; have compassion on us and deliver us, for our eyes are turned to You because You, God, are a gracious and compassionate King.

וְתֶחֱזֶינָה And may our eyes witness Your return to Zion in compassion. Blessed are You, LORD, who restores His Presence to Zion.

THANKSGIVING

*Bow at the first nine words.*

מוֹדִים We give thanks to You,
for You are the LORD our God
and God of our ancestors
for ever and all time.
You are the Rock of our lives,
Shield of our salvation
from generation to generation.
We will thank You and
declare Your praise for our lives,
which are entrusted into Your hand;
for our souls,
which are placed in Your charge;
for Your miracles
which are with us every day;
and for Your wonders and favors
at all times, evening,
morning and midday.
You are good –
for Your compassion never fails.
You are compassionate –
for Your loving-kindnesses never cease.
We have always placed our hope in You.

*During the Leader's Repetition, the congregation says quietly:*

מוֹדִים We give thanks to You,
for You are the LORD our God
and God of our ancestors,
God of all flesh,
who formed us
and formed the universe.
Blessings and thanks
are due to Your great
and holy name for giving us
life and sustaining us.
May You continue
to give us life and sustain us;
and may You gather our
exiles to Your holy courts,
to keep Your decrees,
do Your will and serve You
with a perfect heart,
for it is for us
to give You thanks.
Blessed be God to whom
thanksgiving is due.

לְפָנֶיךָ, לִפְלֵיטָה לְטוֹבָה, לְחֵן וּלְחֶסֶד וּלְרַחֲמִים, לְחַיִּים וּלְשָׁלוֹם בְּיוֹם

בראש חודש: רֹאשׁ הַחֹדֶשׁ / בפסח: חַג הַמַּצּוֹת / בסוכות: חַג הַסֻּכּוֹת

הַזֶּה. זָכְרֵנוּ יהוה אֱלֹהֵינוּ בּוֹ לְטוֹבָה, וּפָקְדֵנוּ בוֹ לִבְרָכָה, וְהוֹשִׁיעֵנוּ בוֹ לְחַיִּים. וּבִדְבַר יְשׁוּעָה וְרַחֲמִים, חוּס וְחָנֵּנוּ וְרַחֵם עָלֵינוּ וְהוֹשִׁיעֵנוּ, כִּי אֵלֶיךָ עֵינֵינוּ, כִּי אֵל מֶלֶךְ חַנּוּן וְרַחוּם אָתָּה.

---

וְתֶחֱזֶינָה עֵינֵינוּ בְּשׁוּבְךָ לְצִיּוֹן בְּרַחֲמִים.
בָּרוּךְ אַתָּה יהוה, הַמַּחֲזִיר שְׁכִינָתוֹ לְצִיּוֹן.

הודאה

*Bow at the first five words.*

מוֹדִים אֲנַחְנוּ לָךְ
שָׁאַתָּה הוּא יהוה אֱלֹהֵינוּ
וֵאלֹהֵי אֲבוֹתֵינוּ לְעוֹלָם וָעֶד.
צוּר חַיֵּינוּ, מָגֵן יִשְׁעֵנוּ
אַתָּה הוּא לְדוֹר וָדוֹר.
נוֹדֶה לְּךָ וּנְסַפֵּר תְּהִלָּתֶךָ
עַל חַיֵּינוּ הַמְּסוּרִים בְּיָדֶךָ
וְעַל נִשְׁמוֹתֵינוּ הַפְּקוּדוֹת לָךְ
וְעַל נִסֶּיךָ שֶׁבְּכָל יוֹם עִמָּנוּ
וְעַל נִפְלְאוֹתֶיךָ וְטוֹבוֹתֶיךָ
שֶׁבְּכָל עֵת
עֶרֶב וָבֹקֶר וְצָהֳרָיִם.
הַטּוֹב, כִּי לֹא כָלוּ רַחֲמֶיךָ
וְהַמְרַחֵם, כִּי לֹא תַמּוּ חֲסָדֶיךָ
מֵעוֹלָם קִוִּינוּ לָךְ.

*During the* חזרת הש״ץ, *the* קהל *says quietly:*

מוֹדִים אֲנַחְנוּ לָךְ
שָׁאַתָּה הוּא יהוה אֱלֹהֵינוּ
וֵאלֹהֵי אֲבוֹתֵינוּ
אֱלֹהֵי כָל בָּשָׂר
יוֹצְרֵנוּ, יוֹצֵר בְּרֵאשִׁית.
בְּרָכוֹת וְהוֹדָאוֹת
לְשִׁמְךָ הַגָּדוֹל וְהַקָּדוֹשׁ
עַל שֶׁהֶחֱיִיתָנוּ וְקִיַּמְתָּנוּ.
כֵּן תְּחַיֵּנוּ וּתְקַיְּמֵנוּ
וְתֶאֱסֹף גָּלֻיּוֹתֵינוּ
לְחַצְרוֹת קָדְשֶׁךָ
לִשְׁמֹר חֻקֶּיךָ
וְלַעֲשׂוֹת רְצוֹנֶךָ וּלְעָבְדְּךָ
בְּלֵבָב שָׁלֵם
עַל שֶׁאֲנַחְנוּ מוֹדִים לָךְ.
בָּרוּךְ אֵל הַהוֹדָאוֹת.

*On Ḥanukka:*

עַל הַנִּסִּים [We thank You also] for the miracles, the redemption, the mighty deeds, the salvations, and the victories in battle which You performed for our ancestors in those days, at this time.

בִּימֵי מַתִּתְיָהוּ In the days of Mattityahu, son of Yoḥanan, the High Priest, the Hasmonean, and his sons, the wicked Greek kingdom rose up against Your people Israel to make them forget Your Torah and to force them to transgress the statutes of Your will. It was then that You in Your great compassion stood by them in the time of their distress. You championed their cause, judged their claim, and avenged their wrong. You delivered the strong into the hands of the weak, the many into the hands of the few, the impure into the hands of the pure, the wicked into the hands of the righteous, and the arrogant into the hands of those who were engaged in the study of Your Torah. You made for Yourself great and holy renown in Your world, and for Your people Israel You performed a great salvation and redemption as of this very day. Your children then entered the holiest part of Your House, cleansed Your Temple, purified Your Sanctuary, kindled lights in Your holy courts, and designated these eight days of Ḥanukka for giving thanks and praise to Your great name.

*Continue with "For all these things."*

*On Shushan Purim in Jerusalem:*

עַל הַנִּסִּים [We thank You also] for the miracles, the redemption, the mighty deeds, the salvations, and the victories in battle which You performed for our ancestors in those days, at this time.

בִּימֵי מָרְדְּכַי In the days of Mordekhai and Esther, in Shushan the capital, the wicked Haman rose up against them and sought to destroy, slay and exterminate *Esther 3*
all the Jews, young and old, children and women, on one day, the thirteenth day of the twelfth month, which is the month of Adar, and to plunder their possessions. Then You in Your great compassion thwarted his counsel, frustrated his plans, and caused his scheme to recoil on his own head, so that they hanged him and his sons on the gallows.

*Continue with "For all these things."*

וְעַל כֻּלָּם For all these things may Your name be blessed and exalted, our King, continually, for ever and all time.

*On Shabbat Shuva:* And write, for a good life, all the children of Your covenant.

Let all that lives thank You, Selah! and praise Your name in truth,
God, our Savior and Help, Selah!
▾Blessed are You, Lord, whose name is "the Good"
and to whom thanks are due.

בחנוכה:

עַל הַנִּסִּים וְעַל הַפֻּרְקָן וְעַל הַגְּבוּרוֹת וְעַל הַתְּשׁוּעוֹת וְעַל הַמִּלְחָמוֹת שֶׁעָשִׂיתָ לַאֲבוֹתֵינוּ בַּיָּמִים הָהֵם בַּזְּמַן הַזֶּה.

בִּימֵי מַתִּתְיָהוּ בֶּן יוֹחָנָן כֹּהֵן גָּדוֹל חַשְׁמוֹנַאי וּבָנָיו, כְּשֶׁעָמְדָה מַלְכוּת יָוָן הָרְשָׁעָה עַל עַמְּךָ יִשְׂרָאֵל לְהַשְׁכִּיחָם תּוֹרָתֶךָ וּלְהַעֲבִירָם מֵחֻקֵּי רְצוֹנֶךָ, וְאַתָּה בְּרַחֲמֶיךָ הָרַבִּים עָמַדְתָּ לָהֶם בְּעֵת צָרָתָם, רַבְתָּ אֶת רִיבָם, דַּנְתָּ אֶת דִּינָם, נָקַמְתָּ אֶת נִקְמָתָם, מָסַרְתָּ גִבּוֹרִים בְּיַד חַלָּשִׁים, וְרַבִּים בְּיַד מְעַטִּים, וּטְמֵאִים בְּיַד טְהוֹרִים, וּרְשָׁעִים בְּיַד צַדִּיקִים, וְזֵדִים בְּיַד עוֹסְקֵי תוֹרָתֶךָ, וּלְךָ עָשִׂיתָ שֵׁם גָּדוֹל וְקָדוֹשׁ בְּעוֹלָמֶךָ, וּלְעַמְּךָ יִשְׂרָאֵל עָשִׂיתָ תְּשׁוּעָה גְדוֹלָה וּפֻרְקָן כְּהַיּוֹם הַזֶּה. וְאַחַר כֵּן בָּאוּ בָנֶיךָ לִדְבִיר בֵּיתֶךָ, וּפִנּוּ אֶת הֵיכָלֶךָ, וְטִהֲרוּ אֶת מִקְדָּשֶׁךָ, וְהִדְלִיקוּ נֵרוֹת בְּחַצְרוֹת קָדְשֶׁךָ, וְקָבְעוּ שְׁמוֹנַת יְמֵי חֲנֻכָּה אֵלּוּ, לְהוֹדוֹת וּלְהַלֵּל לְשִׁמְךָ הַגָּדוֹל.

*Continue with* וְעַל כֻּלָּם.

בשושן פורים בירושלים:

עַל הַנִּסִּים וְעַל הַפֻּרְקָן וְעַל הַגְּבוּרוֹת וְעַל הַתְּשׁוּעוֹת וְעַל הַמִּלְחָמוֹת שֶׁעָשִׂיתָ לַאֲבוֹתֵינוּ בַּיָּמִים הָהֵם בַּזְּמַן הַזֶּה.

בִּימֵי מָרְדְּכַי וְאֶסְתֵּר בְּשׁוּשַׁן הַבִּירָה, כְּשֶׁעָמַד עֲלֵיהֶם הָמָן הָרָשָׁע, בִּקֵּשׁ לְהַשְׁמִיד לַהֲרֹג וּלְאַבֵּד אֶת־כָּל־הַיְּהוּדִים מִנַּעַר וְעַד־זָקֵן טַף וְנָשִׁים בְּיוֹם אֶחָד, בִּשְׁלוֹשָׁה עָשָׂר לְחֹדֶשׁ שְׁנֵים־עָשָׂר, הוּא־חֹדֶשׁ אֲדָר, וּשְׁלָלָם לָבוֹז: אסתר ג
וְאַתָּה בְּרַחֲמֶיךָ הָרַבִּים הֵפַרְתָּ אֶת עֲצָתוֹ, וְקִלְקַלְתָּ אֶת מַחֲשַׁבְתּוֹ, וַהֲשֵׁבוֹתָ לּוֹ גְּמוּלוֹ בְּרֹאשׁוֹ, וְתָלוּ אוֹתוֹ וְאֶת בָּנָיו עַל הָעֵץ.

*Continue with* וְעַל כֻּלָּם.

וְעַל כֻּלָּם יִתְבָּרַךְ וְיִתְרוֹמַם שִׁמְךָ מַלְכֵּנוּ תָּמִיד לְעוֹלָם וָעֶד.

בשבת שובה: וּכְתֹב לְחַיִּים טוֹבִים כָּל בְּנֵי בְרִיתֶךָ.

וְכֹל הַחַיִּים יוֹדוּךָ סֶּלָה, וִיהַלְלוּ אֶת שִׁמְךָ בֶּאֱמֶת הָאֵל יְשׁוּעָתֵנוּ וְעֶזְרָתֵנוּ סֶלָה.

ּבָּרוּךְ אַתָּה יהוה, הַטּוֹב שִׁמְךָ וּלְךָ נָאֶה לְהוֹדוֹת.

*The following is said by the Leader during the Repetition of the Amida, except in a house of mourning and on Tisha B'Av. In Israel, if Kohanim bless the congregation,* *turn to page 902.* *See laws 370–377.*

Our God and God of our fathers, bless us with the threefold blessing in the Torah, written by the hand of Moses Your servant and pronounced by Aaron and his sons the priests, Your holy people, as it is said:

May the Lord bless you and protect you. *Cong:* May it be Your will. *Num. 6*
May the Lord make His face shine on you
and be gracious to you. *Cong:* May it be Your will.
May the Lord turn His face toward you,
and grant you peace. *Cong:* May it be Your will.

PEACE

שִׂים שָׁלוֹם Grant peace, goodness and blessing,
grace, loving-kindness and compassion
to us and all Israel Your people.
Bless us, our Father, all as one,
with the light of Your face,
for by the light of Your face You have given us, Lord our God,
the Torah of life and love of kindness,
righteousness, blessing, compassion, life and peace.
May it be good in Your eyes to bless Your people Israel
at every time, in every hour, with Your peace.

*On Shabbat Shuva:* In the book of life, blessing, peace and prosperity,
may we and all Your people
the house of Israel be remembered and written
before You for a good life, and for peace.*

Blessed are You, Lord, who blesses His people Israel with peace.

**On Shabbat Shuva in the Diaspora, many end the blessing:*
Blessed are You, Lord, who makes peace.

*The following verse concludes the Leader's Repetition of the Amida. Some also say it here as part of the silent Amida. See law 368.*

May the words of my mouth and the meditation of my heart *Ps. 19*
find favor before You, Lord, my Rock and Redeemer.

*The following is said by the* שליח ציבור *during* חזרת הש״ץ.
*In* ארץ ישראל, *if* כהנים *say* ברכת כהנים, *turn to page 903. See laws 370–377.*

אֱלֹהֵינוּ וֵאלֹהֵי אֲבוֹתֵינוּ, בָּרְכֵנוּ בַבְּרָכָה הַמְשֻׁלֶּשֶׁת בַּתּוֹרָה, הַכְּתוּבָה עַל יְדֵי מֹשֶׁה עַבְדֶּךָ, הָאֲמוּרָה מִפִּי אַהֲרֹן וּבָנָיו כֹּהֲנִים עַם קְדוֹשֶׁיךָ, כָּאָמוּר

יְבָרֶכְךָ יהוה וְיִשְׁמְרֶךָ: קהל: כֵּן יְהִי רָצוֹן במדבר ו
יָאֵר יהוה פָּנָיו אֵלֶיךָ וִיחֻנֶּךָּ: קהל: כֵּן יְהִי רָצוֹן
יִשָּׂא יהוה פָּנָיו אֵלֶיךָ וְיָשֵׂם לְךָ שָׁלוֹם: קהל: כֵּן יְהִי רָצוֹן

ברכת שלום

שִׂים שָׁלוֹם טוֹבָה וּבְרָכָה
חֵן וָחֶסֶד וְרַחֲמִים עָלֵינוּ וְעַל כָּל יִשְׂרָאֵל עַמֶּךָ.
בָּרְכֵנוּ אָבִינוּ כֻּלָּנוּ כְּאֶחָד בְּאוֹר פָּנֶיךָ
כִּי בְאוֹר פָּנֶיךָ נָתַתָּ לָּנוּ, יהוה אֱלֹהֵינוּ
תּוֹרַת חַיִּים וְאַהֲבַת חֶסֶד
וּצְדָקָה וּבְרָכָה וְרַחֲמִים וְחַיִּים וְשָׁלוֹם.
וְטוֹב בְּעֵינֶיךָ לְבָרֵךְ אֶת עַמְּךָ יִשְׂרָאֵל
בְּכָל עֵת וּבְכָל שָׁעָה בִּשְׁלוֹמֶךָ.

בשבת שובה: בְּסֵפֶר חַיִּים, בְּרָכָה וְשָׁלוֹם, וּפַרְנָסָה טוֹבָה נִזָּכֵר וְנִכָּתֵב לְפָנֶיךָ, אֲנַחְנוּ וְכָל עַמְּךָ בֵּית יִשְׂרָאֵל לְחַיִּים טוֹבִים וּלְשָׁלוֹם.*

בָּרוּךְ אַתָּה יהוה, הַמְבָרֵךְ אֶת עַמּוֹ יִשְׂרָאֵל בַּשָּׁלוֹם.

**On* שבת שובה *in* חוץ לארץ, *many end the blessing:*

בָּרוּךְ אַתָּה יהוה, עוֹשֶׂה הַשָּׁלוֹם.

*The following verse concludes the* חזרת הש״ץ.
*Some also say it here as part of the silent* עמידה. *See law 368.*

יִהְיוּ לְרָצוֹן אִמְרֵי־פִי וְהֶגְיוֹן לִבִּי לְפָנֶיךָ, יהוה צוּרִי וְגֹאֲלִי: תהלים יט

אֱלֹהַי My God, Berakhot 17a
guard my tongue from evil
and my lips from deceitful speech.
To those who curse me, let my soul be silent;
may my soul be to all like the dust.
Open my heart to Your Torah
and let my soul pursue Your commandments.
As for all who plan evil against me,
swiftly thwart their counsel and frustrate their plans.

Act for the sake of Your name;
act for the sake of Your right hand;
act for the sake of Your holiness;
act for the sake of Your Torah.

That Your beloved ones may be delivered, Ps. 60
save with Your right hand and answer me.
May the words of my mouth and the meditation of my heart Ps. 19
find favor before You, LORD, my Rock and Redeemer.

*Bow, take three steps back, then bow, first left, then right, then center, while saying:*

May He who makes peace in His high places,
make peace for us and all Israel –
and say: Amen.

יְהִי רָצוֹן May it be Your will, LORD our God and God of our ancestors,
that the Temple be rebuilt speedily in our days,
and grant us a share in Your Torah.
And there we will serve You with reverence,
as in the days of old and as in former years.
Then the offering of Judah and Jerusalem Mal. 3
will be pleasing to the LORD as in the days of old and as in former years.

*On Rosh Ḥodesh, Ḥol HaMo'ed and Ḥanukka,*
*the service continues with Hallel on page 790.*

אֱלֹהַי ברכות יז.

נְצֹר לְשׁוֹנִי מֵרָע, וּשְׂפָתַי מִדַּבֵּר מִרְמָה

וְלִמְקַלְלַי נַפְשִׁי תִדֹּם, וְנַפְשִׁי כֶּעָפָר לַכֹּל תִּהְיֶה.

פְּתַח לִבִּי בְּתוֹרָתֶךָ, וּבְמִצְוֹתֶיךָ תִּרְדֹּף נַפְשִׁי.

וְכָל הַחוֹשְׁבִים עָלַי רָעָה

מְהֵרָה הָפֵר עֲצָתָם וְקַלְקֵל מַחֲשַׁבְתָּם.

עֲשֵׂה לְמַעַן שְׁמֶךָ

עֲשֵׂה לְמַעַן יְמִינֶךָ

עֲשֵׂה לְמַעַן קְדֻשָּׁתֶךָ

עֲשֵׂה לְמַעַן תּוֹרָתֶךָ.

לְמַעַן יֵחָלְצוּן יְדִידֶיךָ, הוֹשִׁיעָה יְמִינְךָ וַעֲנֵנִי: תהלים ס

יִהְיוּ לְרָצוֹן אִמְרֵי־פִי וְהֶגְיוֹן לִבִּי לְפָנֶיךָ, יהוה צוּרִי וְגוֹאֲלִי: תהלים יט

*Bow, take three steps back, then bow, first left, then right, then center, while saying:*

עֹשֶׂה שָׁלוֹם/ בשבת שובה: הַשָּׁלוֹם/ בִּמְרוֹמָיו

הוּא יַעֲשֶׂה שָׁלוֹם עָלֵינוּ וְעַל כָּל יִשְׂרָאֵל

וְאִמְרוּ אָמֵן.

יְהִי רָצוֹן מִלְּפָנֶיךָ יהוה אֱלֹהֵינוּ וֵאלֹהֵי אֲבוֹתֵינוּ

שֶׁיִּבָּנֶה בֵּית הַמִּקְדָּשׁ בִּמְהֵרָה בְיָמֵינוּ, וְתֵן חֶלְקֵנוּ בְּתוֹרָתֶךָ

וְשָׁם נַעֲבָדְךָ בְּיִרְאָה כִּימֵי עוֹלָם וּכְשָׁנִים קַדְמֹנִיּוֹת.

וְעָרְבָה לַיהוה מִנְחַת יְהוּדָה וִירוּשָׁלָםִ כִּימֵי עוֹלָם וּכְשָׁנִים קַדְמֹנִיּוֹת: מלאכי ג

*On* ראש חודש, חול המועד *and* חנוכה,
*the service continues with* הלל *on page 791.*

## FULL KADDISH

*Leader:* יִתְגַּדַּל Magnified and sanctified
may His great name be,
in the world He created by His will.
May He establish His kingdom
in your lifetime and in your days,
and in the lifetime of all the house of Israel,
swiftly and soon –
and say: Amen.

*All:* May His great name be blessed
for ever and all time.

*Leader:* Blessed and praised, glorified and exalted,
raised and honored, uplifted and lauded
be the name of the Holy One,
blessed be He,
beyond any blessing,
song, praise and consolation
uttered in the world –
and say: Amen.

May the prayers and pleas of all Israel
be accepted by their Father in heaven –
and say: Amen.

May there be great peace from heaven,
and life for us and all Israel –
and say: Amen.

*Bow, take three steps back, as if taking leave of the Divine Presence, then bow, first left, then right, then center, while saying:*

May He who makes peace in His high places,
make peace for us and all Israel –
and say: Amen.

## קדיש שלם

ש״ץ: יִתְגַּדַּל וְיִתְקַדַּשׁ שְׁמֵהּ רַבָּא (קהל: אָמֵן)
בְּעָלְמָא דִּי בְרָא כִרְעוּתֵהּ
וְיַמְלִיךְ מַלְכוּתֵהּ
בְּחַיֵּיכוֹן וּבְיוֹמֵיכוֹן וּבְחַיֵּי דְכָל בֵּית יִשְׂרָאֵל
בַּעֲגָלָא וּבִזְמַן קָרִיב, וְאִמְרוּ אָמֵן. (קהל: אָמֵן)

קהל וש״ץ: יְהֵא שְׁמֵהּ רַבָּא מְבָרַךְ לְעָלַם וּלְעָלְמֵי עָלְמַיָּא.

ש״ץ: יִתְבָּרַךְ וְיִשְׁתַּבַּח וְיִתְפָּאַר
וְיִתְרוֹמַם וְיִתְנַשֵּׂא וְיִתְהַדָּר וְיִתְעַלֶּה וְיִתְהַלָּל
שְׁמֵהּ דְּקֻדְשָׁא בְּרִיךְ הוּא (קהל: בְּרִיךְ הוּא)
לְעֵלָּא מִן כָּל בִּרְכָתָא
/בשבת שובה: לְעֵלָּא לְעֵלָּא מִכָּל בִּרְכָתָא/
וְשִׁירָתָא, תֻּשְׁבְּחָתָא וְנֶחֱמָתָא
דַּאֲמִירָן בְּעָלְמָא, וְאִמְרוּ אָמֵן. (קהל: אָמֵן)

תִּתְקַבַּל צְלוֹתְהוֹן וּבָעוּתְהוֹן דְּכָל יִשְׂרָאֵל
קֳדָם אֲבוּהוֹן דִּי בִשְׁמַיָּא, וְאִמְרוּ אָמֵן. (קהל: אָמֵן)

יְהֵא שְׁלָמָא רַבָּא מִן שְׁמַיָּא
וְחַיִּים, עָלֵינוּ וְעַל כָּל יִשְׂרָאֵל, וְאִמְרוּ אָמֵן. (קהל: אָמֵן)

*Bow, take three steps back, as if taking leave of the Divine Presence, then bow, first left, then right, then center, while saying:*

עֹשֶׂה שָׁלוֹם/ בשבת שובה: הַשָּׁלוֹם/ בִּמְרוֹמָיו
הוּא יַעֲשֶׂה שָׁלוֹם
עָלֵינוּ וְעַל כָּל יִשְׂרָאֵל, וְאִמְרוּ אָמֵן. (קהל: אָמֵן)

*On Hoshana Raba continue:*

Master of the Universe, fulfill my requests for good. Satisfy my desire, grant my request, and pardon me for all my iniquities and all iniquities of the members of my household, with the pardon of loving-kindness and compassion. Purify us from our sins, our iniquities and our transgressions; remember us with a memory of favorable deeds before You and be mindful of us in salvation and compassion. Remember us for a good life, for peace, for livelihood and sustenance, for bread to eat and clothes to wear, for wealth, honor and length of days dedicated to Your Torah and its commandments. Grant us discernment and understanding that we may understand and discern its deep secrets. Send healing for all our pain, and bless all the work of our hands. Ordain for us decrees of good, salvation and consolation, and nullify all hard and harsh decrees against us. And may the hearts of the government, its advisers and ministers / *in Israel:* And may the hearts of our ministers and their advisers, / be favorable toward us. Amen. May this be Your will.

*On Yom Tov (except on Shabbat) continue, inserting appropriate phrase/s in parentheses:*

Master of the Universe, fulfill my heart's requests for good. Satisfy my desire, grant my request, and enable me (*name*, son/daughter of *father's name*), (and my wife/ husband, and my sons/daughters) and all the members of my household to do Your will with a perfect heart. Deliver us from the evil impulse, grant us our share in Your Torah, and make us worthy that Your Presence may rest upon us. Confer on us a spirit of wisdom and understanding, and may there be fulfilled in us the verse: "The spirit *Is. 11*
of the LORD will rest upon him – a spirit of wisdom and understanding, a spirit of counsel and strength, a spirit of knowledge and reverence for the LORD." So too may it be Your will, LORD our God and God of our ancestors, that we be worthy to do deeds that are good in Your sight, and to walk before You in the ways of the upright. Make us holy through Your holiness, so that we may be worthy of a good and long life, and of the World to Come. Guard us from evil deeds and bad times that threaten to bring turmoil to the world. May loving-kindness sur- *Ps. 32*
round one who trusts in the LORD. Amen.

יִהְיוּ May the words of my mouth and the meditation of my heart find favor before You, LORD, my Rock and Redeemer. *Ps. 19*

*Say the following verse three times:*

וַאֲנִי As for me, may my prayer come to You, LORD, at a time of favor. O God, in Your great love, answer me with Your faithful salvation. *Ps. 69*

*On Shabbat, Yom Tov and Hoshana Raba:*

*Zohar, Vayak-hel*

Blessed is the name of the Master of the Universe. Blessed is Your crown and Your place. May Your favor always be with Your people Israel. Show Your people the salvation of Your right hand in Your Temple. Grant us the gift of Your good light, and accept our prayers in mercy. May it be Your will to prolong our life in goodness. May I be counted among the righteous, so that You will have compassion on me and protect me and all that is mine and all that is Your people Israel's. You feed all; You sustain all; You rule over all; You rule over kings, for sovereignty is Yours. I am a servant of the Holy One, blessed be He, before whom and before

*On* הושענא רבה *continue:*

רִבּוֹנוֹ שֶׁל עוֹלָם, מַלֵּא מִשְׁאֲלוֹתַי לְטוֹבָה, וְהָפֵק רְצוֹנִי וְתֵן שְׁאֵלָתִי, וּמְחֹל לִי עַל כָּל עֲוֹנוֹתַי וְעַל כָּל עֲוֹנוֹת אַנְשֵׁי בֵיתִי, מְחִילָה בְּחֶסֶד מְחִילָה בְּרַחֲמִים, וְטַהֲרֵנוּ מֵחֲטָאֵינוּ וּמֵעֲוֹנוֹתֵינוּ וּמִפְּשָׁעֵינוּ, וְזָכְרֵנוּ בְּזִכָּרוֹן טוֹב לְפָנֶיךָ, וּפָקְדֵנוּ בִּפְקֻדַּת יְשׁוּעָה וְרַחֲמִים. וְזָכְרֵנוּ לְחַיִּים טוֹבִים וּלְשָׁלוֹם, וּפַרְנָסָה וְכַלְכָּלָה, וְלֶחֶם לֶאֱכֹל וּבֶגֶד לִלְבֹּשׁ, וְעֹשֶׁר וְכָבוֹד, וְאֹרֶךְ יָמִים לַהֲגוֹת בְּתוֹרָתֶךָ וּלְקַיֵּם מִצְוֹתֶיהָ, וְשֵׂכֶל וּבִינָה לְהָבִין וּלְהַשְׂכִּיל עִמְקֵי סוֹדוֹתֶיהָ. וְהָפֵק רְפוּאָה לְכָל מַכְאוֹבֵינוּ, וּבָרֵךְ כָּל מַעֲשֵׂה יָדֵינוּ, וּגְזֹר עָלֵינוּ גְּזֵרוֹת טוֹבוֹת יְשׁוּעוֹת וְנֶחָמוֹת, וּבַטֵּל מֵעָלֵינוּ כָּל גְּזֵרוֹת קָשׁוֹת וְרָעוֹת, וְתֵן בְּלֵב הַמַּלְכוּת וְיוֹעֲצֶיהָ וְשָׂרֶיהָ / בארץ ישראל: וְתֵן בְּלֵב שָׂרֵינוּ וְיוֹעֲצֵיהֶם/ עָלֵינוּ לְטוֹבָה. אָמֵן וְכֵן יְהִי רָצוֹן.

*On* יום טוב *(except on* שבת*) continue, inserting appropriate phrase/s in parentheses:*

רִבּוֹנוֹ שֶׁל עוֹלָם, מַלֵּא מִשְׁאֲלוֹת לִבִּי לְטוֹבָה, וְהָפֵק רְצוֹנִי וְתֵן שְׁאֵלָתִי, וְזַכֵּה לִי (פלוני(ת) בֶּן/בַּת פלוני) (וְאִשְׁתִּי/בַּעֲלִי וּבָנַי וּבְנוֹתַי) וְכָל בְּנֵי בֵיתִי, לַעֲשׂוֹת רְצוֹנְךָ בְּלֵבָב שָׁלֵם, וּמַלְּטֵנוּ מִיֵּצֶר הָרָע, וְתֵן חֶלְקֵנוּ בְּתוֹרָתֶךָ, וְזַכֵּנוּ שֶׁתַּשְׁרֶה שְׁכִינָתְךָ עָלֵינוּ, וְהוֹפַע עָלֵינוּ רוּחַ חָכְמָה וּבִינָה. וְיִתְקַיֵּם
ישעיה יא בָּנוּ מִקְרָא שֶׁכָּתוּב: וְנָחָה עָלָיו רוּחַ יהוה, רוּחַ חָכְמָה וּבִינָה, רוּחַ עֵצָה וּגְבוּרָה, רוּחַ דַּעַת וְיִרְאַת יהוה: וּבְכֵן יְהִי רָצוֹן מִלְּפָנֶיךָ יהוה אֱלֹהֵינוּ וֵאלֹהֵי אֲבוֹתֵינוּ, שֶׁתְּזַכֵּנוּ לַעֲשׂוֹת מַעֲשִׂים טוֹבִים בְּעֵינֶיךָ וְלָלֶכֶת בְּדַרְכֵי יְשָׁרִים לְפָנֶיךָ, וְקַדְּשֵׁנוּ בִּקְדֻשָּׁתֶךָ כְּדֵי שֶׁנִּזְכֶּה לְחַיִּים טוֹבִים וַאֲרוּכִים וּלְחַיֵּי הָעוֹלָם הַבָּא, וְתִשְׁמְרֵנוּ מִמַּעֲשִׂים רָעִים וּמִשָּׁעוֹת רָעוֹת הַמִּתְרַגְּשׁוֹת לָבוֹא לָעוֹלָם,
תהלים לב וְהַבּוֹטֵחַ בַּיהוה חֶסֶד יְסוֹבְבֶנּוּ: אָמֵן.

תהלים יט יִהְיוּ לְרָצוֹן אִמְרֵי־פִי וְהֶגְיוֹן לִבִּי לְפָנֶיךָ, יהוה צוּרִי וְגֹאֲלִי:

*Say the following verse three times:*

תהלים סט וַאֲנִי תְפִלָּתִי־לְךָ יהוה, עֵת רָצוֹן, אֱלֹהִים בְּרָב־חַסְדֶּךָ
עֲנֵנִי בֶּאֱמֶת יִשְׁעֶךָ:

*On* יום טוב, שבת *and on* הושענא רבה*:*

זוהר ויקהל בְּרִיךְ שְׁמֵהּ דְּמָרֵא עָלְמָא, בְּרִיךְ כִּתְרָךְ וְאַתְרָךְ. יְהֵא רְעוּתָךְ עִם עַמָּךְ יִשְׂרָאֵל לְעָלַם, וּפֻרְקַן יְמִינָךְ אַחֲזִי לְעַמָּךְ בְּבֵית מַקְדְּשָׁךְ, וּלְאַמְטוּיֵי לָנָא מִטּוּב נְהוֹרָךְ, וּלְקַבֵּל צְלוֹתָנָא בְּרַחֲמִין. יְהֵא רַעֲוָא קֳדָמָךְ דְּתוֹרִיךְ לַן חַיִּין בְּטִיבוּ, וְלֶהֱוֵי אֲנָא פְקִידָא בְּגוֹ צַדִּיקַיָּא, לְמִרְחַם עָלַי וּלְמִנְטַר יָתִי וְיַת כָּל דִּי לִי וְדִי לְעַמָּךְ יִשְׂרָאֵל. אַנְתְּ הוּא זָן לְכֹלָּא וּמְפַרְנֵס לְכֹלָּא, אַנְתְּ הוּא שַׁלִּיט עַל כֹּלָּא, אַנְתְּ הוּא דְשַׁלִּיט עַל מַלְכַיָּא, וּמַלְכוּתָא דִּילָךְ הִיא. אֲנָא עַבְדָּא דְקֻדְשָׁא בְּרִיךְ הוּא, דְּסָגֵדְנָא

whose glorious Torah I bow at all times. Not in man do I trust, nor on any angel do I rely, but on the God of heaven who is the God of truth, whose Torah is truth, whose prophets speak truth, and who abounds in acts of love and truth. ▸ In Him I trust, and to His holy and glorious name I offer praises. May it be Your will to open my heart to the Torah, and to fulfill the wishes of my heart and of the hearts of all Your people Israel for good, for life, and for peace.

*The Leader takes the Torah scroll in his right arm. Leader then congregation:*

Listen, Israel: the LORD is our God, the LORD is One. *Deut. 6*

*Leader then congregation:*

One is our God; great is our Master;
holy (*On Hoshana Raba:* and awesome) is His name.

*The Leader turns to face the Ark, bows and says:*

Magnify the LORD with me,
and let us exalt His name together. *Ps. 34*

*The Ark is closed. The Leader carries the Torah scroll to the bima and the congregation says:*

לְךָ Yours, LORD, are the greatness and the power, the glory and the majesty and splendor, for everything in heaven and earth is Yours. Yours, LORD, is the kingdom; You are exalted as Head over all. *1 Chr. 29*

רוֹמְמוּ Exalt the LORD our God and bow to His footstool; He is holy. Exalt the LORD our God, and bow at His holy mountain, for holy is the LORD our God. *Ps. 99*

Over all may the name of the Supreme King of kings, the Holy One blessed be He, be magnified and sanctified, praised and glorified, exalted and extolled, in the worlds that He has created – this world and the World to Come – in accordance with His will, and the will of those who fear Him, and the will of the whole house of Israel. He is the Rock of worlds, LORD of all creatures, God of all souls, who dwells in the spacious heights and inhabits the high heavens of old. His holiness is over the Ḥayyot and over the throne of glory. Therefore may Your name, LORD our God, be sanctified among us in the sight of all that lives. Let us sing before Him a new song, as it is written: "Sing to God, make music for His name, extol Him who rides the clouds – the LORD is His name – and exult before Him." And may we see Him eye to eye when He returns to His abode as it is written: "For they shall see eye to eye when the LORD returns to *Ps. 68* *Is. 52*

קַמֵּהּ וּמִקַּמֵּי דִּיקַר אוֹרַיְתֵהּ בְּכָל עִדָּן וְעִדָּן. לָא עַל אֱנָשׁ רָחִיצְנָא וְלָא עַל בַּר אֱלָהִין סָמִיכְנָא, אֶלָּא בֶּאֱלָהָא דִשְׁמַיָּא, דְּהוּא אֱלָהָא קְשׁוֹט, וְאוֹרַיְתֵהּ קְשׁוֹט, וּנְבִיאוֹהִי קְשׁוֹט, וּמַסְגֵּא לְמֶעְבַּד טַבְוָן וּקְשׁוֹט. › בֵּהּ אֲנָא רָחִיץ, וְלִשְׁמֵהּ קַדִּישָׁא יַקִּירָא אֲנָא אֵמַר תֻּשְׁבְּחָן. יְהֵא רַעֲוָא קֳדָמָךְ דְּתִפְתַּח לִבַּאי בְּאוֹרַיְתָא, וְתַשְׁלִים מִשְׁאֲלִין דְּלִבַּאי וְלִבָּא דְכָל עַמָּךְ יִשְׂרָאֵל לְטָב וּלְחַיִּין וְלִשְׁלָם.

*The* שליח ציבור *takes the* ספר תורה *in his right arm.* קהל *then* שליח ציבור*:*

דברים ו **שְׁמַע יִשְׂרָאֵל, יהוה אֱלֹהֵינוּ, יהוה אֶחָד:**

קהל *then* שליח ציבור*:*

**אֶחָד אֱלֹהֵינוּ, גָּדוֹל אֲדוֹנֵינוּ, קָדוֹשׁ** (בהושענא רבה: **וְנוֹרָא**) **שְׁמוֹ.**

*The* שליח ציבור *turns to face the* ארון קודש*, bows and says:*

תהלים לד **גַּדְּלוּ לַיהוה אִתִּי וּנְרוֹמְמָה שְׁמוֹ יַחְדָּו:**

*The* ארון קודש *is closed.*
*The* שליח ציבור *carries the* ספר תורה *to the* בימה *and the* קהל *says:*

דברי הימים א׳ כט **לְךָ יהוה הַגְּדֻלָּה וְהַגְּבוּרָה וְהַתִּפְאֶרֶת וְהַנֵּצַח וְהַהוֹד, כִּי־כֹל בַּשָּׁמַיִם וּבָאָרֶץ, לְךָ יהוה הַמַּמְלָכָה וְהַמִּתְנַשֵּׂא לְכֹל לְרֹאשׁ:**

תהלים צט **רוֹמְמוּ יהוה אֱלֹהֵינוּ וְהִשְׁתַּחֲווּ לַהֲדֹם רַגְלָיו, קָדוֹשׁ הוּא: רוֹמְמוּ יהוה אֱלֹהֵינוּ וְהִשְׁתַּחֲווּ לְהַר קָדְשׁוֹ, כִּי־קָדוֹשׁ יהוה אֱלֹהֵינוּ:**

עַל הַכֹּל יִתְגַּדַּל וְיִתְקַדַּשׁ וְיִשְׁתַּבַּח וְיִתְפָּאַר וְיִתְרוֹמַם וְיִתְנַשֵּׂא שְׁמוֹ שֶׁל מֶלֶךְ מַלְכֵי הַמְּלָכִים הַקָּדוֹשׁ בָּרוּךְ הוּא בָּעוֹלָמוֹת שֶׁבָּרָא, הָעוֹלָם הַזֶּה וְהָעוֹלָם הַבָּא, כִּרְצוֹנוֹ וְכִרְצוֹן יְרֵאָיו וְכִרְצוֹן כָּל בֵּית יִשְׂרָאֵל. צוּר הָעוֹלָמִים, אֲדוֹן כָּל הַבְּרִיּוֹת, אֱלוֹהַּ כָּל הַנְּפָשׁוֹת, הַיּוֹשֵׁב בְּמֶרְחֲבֵי מָרוֹם, הַשּׁוֹכֵן בִּשְׁמֵי שְׁמֵי קֶדֶם, קְדֻשָּׁתוֹ עַל הַחַיּוֹת, וּקְדֻשָּׁתוֹ עַל כִּסֵּא הַכָּבוֹד. וּבְכֵן יִתְקַדַּשׁ שִׁמְךָ בָּנוּ יהוה אֱלֹהֵינוּ לְעֵינֵי
תהלים סח כָּל חָי, וְנֹאמַר לְפָנָיו שִׁיר חָדָשׁ, כַּכָּתוּב: שִׁירוּ לֵאלֹהִים זַמְּרוּ שְׁמוֹ, סֹלּוּ לָרֹכֵב
ישעיה נב בָּעֲרָבוֹת, בְּיָהּ שְׁמוֹ, וְעִלְזוּ לְפָנָיו: וְנִרְאֵהוּ עַיִן בְּעַיִן בְּשׁוּבוֹ אֶל נָוֵהוּ, כַּכָּתוּב: כִּי

Zion." And it is said: "Then will the glory of the Lord be revealed, and all mankind together shall see that the mouth of the Lord has spoken." *Is. 40*

Father of mercy, have compassion on the people borne by Him. May He remember the covenant with the mighty (patriarchs), and deliver us from evil times. May He reproach the evil instinct in the people by Him, and graciously grant that we be an eternal remnant. May He fulfill in good measure our requests for salvation and compassion.

*The Torah scroll is placed on the bima and the Gabbai calls a Kohen to the Torah. See laws 383–397.*

וְיַעֲזֹר May He help, shield and save all who seek refuge in Him, and let us say: Amen. Let us all render greatness to our God and give honor to the Torah. *Let the Kohen come forward. Arise (*name* son of *father's name*), the Kohen.

**If no Kohen is present, a Levi or Yisrael is called up as follows:*

/As there is no Kohen, arise (*name* son of *father's name*) in place of a Kohen./

Blessed is He who, in His holiness, gave the Torah to His people Israel.

*The congregation followed by the Gabbai:*

You who cling to the Lord your God are all alive today. *Deut. 4*

*The appropriate Torah portion is read. The Torah portions for Yom Tov are to be found from page 1201. On the first day of Shavuot, turn to Akdamut on page 850.*

---

For Rav Kook, the revelation of the future will bring a lesson in humility. We will know how little we truly know:

> They will see and know that all the supposed attainment – after all the investigations and in-depth studies – is but a shadow of an image that is instructive of the glory of the Lord, as much as permission is granted and there is the capacity to receive. All will recognize that what we see is but the shadow of the supernal glory. All mankind together shall see that what is attainable is only what was permitted to be revealed. Of *Ein Sof* (the Infinite) one must not think.[4] All [divine] speech, all revelations proceed from the "mouth of the Lord," i.e. [the *sefirah* of] *Malkhut*.[5]

4. Cf. *Likkutei ha-Gra* appended to *Be'ur ha-Gra* to *Sifra di-Tseni'uta*, s.v. *Sod ha-Tsimtsum*: "Know that one must not think into *Ein Sof* at all."
5. *Tikkunei Zohar*, Second Introduction (*Pataḥ Eliyahu*), "*Malkhut* is the mouth." *OR*, vol. 2, p. 113.
RZYH (ibid. p. 490, p. 58) references *Peri Yitsḥak*, the commentary of Rabbi Isaac Ḥaver to *Sefer Yetsirah* 1:9: "*Malkhut* is speech, for *Malkhut* is called 'the word of the Lord' (*devar Hashem*); it is the revelation of *Ze'ir Anpin*, which is called 'the Lord' (*Hashem*)."

עַיִן בְּעַיִן יִרְאוּ בְּשׁוּב יהוה צִיּוֹן: וְנֶאֱמַר: וְנִגְלָה כְּבוֹד יהוה, וְרָאוּ כָל־בָּשָׂר יַחְדָּו כִּי פִּי יהוה דִּבֵּר: ישעיה מ

אַב הָרַחֲמִים הוּא יְרַחֵם עַם עֲמוּסִים, וְיִזְכֹּר בְּרִית אֵיתָנִים, וְיַצִּיל נַפְשׁוֹתֵינוּ מִן הַשָּׁעוֹת הָרָעוֹת, וְיִגְעַר בְּיֵצֶר הָרָע מִן הַנְּשׂוּאִים, וְיָחֹן אוֹתָנוּ לִפְלֵיטַת עוֹלָמִים, וִימַלֵּא מִשְׁאֲלוֹתֵינוּ בְּמִדָּה טוֹבָה יְשׁוּעָה וְרַחֲמִים.

*The* ספר תורה *is placed on the* שולחן *and the* גבאי *calls a* כהן *to the* תורה. *See laws 383–397.*

וְיַעֲזֹר וְיָגֵן וְיוֹשִׁיעַ לְכָל הַחוֹסִים בּוֹ, וְנֹאמַר אָמֵן. הַכֹּל הָבוּ גֹדֶל לֵאלֹהֵינוּ וּתְנוּ כָבוֹד לַתּוֹרָה. *כֹּהֵן קְרַב, יַעֲמֹד (פלוני בֶּן פלוני) הַכֹּהֵן.

**If no* כהן *is present, a* לוי *or* ישראל *is called up as follows:*

/אֵין כָּאן כֹּהֵן, יַעֲמֹד (פלוני בֶּן פלוני) בִּמְקוֹם כֹּהֵן./

בָּרוּךְ שֶׁנָּתַן תּוֹרָה לְעַמּוֹ יִשְׂרָאֵל בִּקְדֻשָּׁתוֹ.

*The* קהל *followed by the* גבאי:

וְאַתֶּם הַדְּבֵקִים בַּיהוה אֱלֹהֵיכֶם חַיִּים כֻּלְּכֶם הַיּוֹם: דברים ד

*The appropriate* תורה *portion is read. The* תורה *portions for* יום טוב *are to be found from page 1201. On the first day of* שבועות, *turn to* אקדמות *on page 851.*

---

**וְנִגְלָה כְּבוֹד יהוה, וְרָאוּ כָל־בָּשָׂר יַחְדָּו כִּי פִּי יהוה דִּבֵּר** *Then will the glory of the Lord be revealed, and all mankind together shall see that the mouth of the Lord has spoken (Isaiah 40:5)*. This verse is problematic. Taken at face value, it presents a contradiction in terms. How does one see speech? Rabbi Ḥayyim of Volozhin understood that in the future we shall once again assume the spiritual level that we enjoyed on Mount Sinai, of which it is said, "and all the people were seeing the sounds."[1] According to Rabbi Ḥayyim, at that time we were privileged to see with "eyes of flesh" the divine speech that permeates all existence.[2]

A beautiful story is told concerning the last days on earth of Rabbi Shneur Zalman of Liadi. As he lay dying, he asked his beloved grandson Menaḥem Mendel (author *"Tsemaḥ Tsedek"*): "Do you see the beams of the ceiling?" The grandson was taken aback by this question. The Rabbi said to him: "Believe me. All that I see now is the divine 'nothingness' (*ayin*) that vivifies all."[3]

---

1. Exodus 20:15.
2. Rabbi Ḥayyim of Volozhin, *Nefesh ha-Ḥayyim* III, 11.
3. Ḥayyim Meir Heilman, *Beit Rabbi* (Berdichev, 1902), Part I, chap. 28 (46a, n. 1).

*The Reader shows the oleh the section to be read.*
*The oleh touches the scroll at that place with the tzitzit of his tallit,*
*which he then kisses. Holding the handles of the scroll, he says:*

*Oleh:* Bless the LORD, the blessed One.

*Cong:* Bless the LORD, the blessed One,
for ever and all time.

*Oleh:* Bless the LORD, the blessed One,
for ever and all time.

Blessed are You, LORD our God, King of the Universe,
who has chosen us from all peoples
and has given us His Torah.
Blessed are You, LORD, Giver of the Torah.

*After the reading, the oleh says:*

*Oleh:* Blessed are You, LORD our God, King of the Universe,
who has given us the Torah of truth,
planting everlasting life in our midst.
Blessed are You, LORD, Giver of the Torah.

*One who has survived a situation of danger says:*

Blessed are You, LORD our God, King of the Universe,
who bestows good on the unworthy,
who has bestowed on me much good.

*The congregation responds:*

Amen. May He who bestowed much good on you
continue to bestow on you much good, Selah.

*After a Bar Mitzva boy has finished the Torah blessing, his father says aloud:*

Blessed is He who has released me
from the responsibility for this child.

*In some congregations, during the week before a*
*yahrzeit, "God, full of mercy" on page 860 is said.*

*The* קורא *shows the* עולה *the section to be read.*
*The* עולה *touches the scroll at that place with the* ציצית *of his* טלית*,*
*which he then kisses. Holding the handles of the scroll, he says:*

עולה: **בָּרְכוּ אֶת יהוה הַמְבֹרָךְ.**

קהל: בָּרוּךְ יהוה הַמְבֹרָךְ לְעוֹלָם וָעֶד.

עולה: **בָּרוּךְ יהוה הַמְבֹרָךְ לְעוֹלָם וָעֶד.**

**בָּרוּךְ אַתָּה יהוה, אֱלֹהֵינוּ מֶלֶךְ הָעוֹלָם**
**אֲשֶׁר בָּחַר בָּנוּ מִכָּל הָעַמִּים**
**וְנָתַן לָנוּ אֶת תּוֹרָתוֹ.**
**בָּרוּךְ אַתָּה יהוה, נוֹתֵן הַתּוֹרָה.**

*After the* קריאת התורה*, the* עולה *says:*

עולה: **בָּרוּךְ אַתָּה יהוה אֱלֹהֵינוּ מֶלֶךְ הָעוֹלָם**
**אֲשֶׁר נָתַן לָנוּ תּוֹרַת אֱמֶת**
**וְחַיֵּי עוֹלָם נָטַע בְּתוֹכֵנוּ.**
**בָּרוּךְ אַתָּה יהוה, נוֹתֵן הַתּוֹרָה.**

*One who has survived a situation of danger says:*

**בָּרוּךְ אַתָּה יהוה אֱלֹהֵינוּ מֶלֶךְ הָעוֹלָם הַגּוֹמֵל לְחַיָּבִים טוֹבוֹת שֶׁגְּמָלַנִי כָּל טוֹב.**

*The* קהל *responds:*

**אָמֵן. מִי שֶׁגְּמָלְךָ כָּל טוֹב הוּא יִגְמָלְךָ כָּל טוֹב, סֶלָה.**

*After a* בר מצווה *has finished the* תורה *blessing, his father says aloud:*

**בָּרוּךְ שֶׁפְּטָרַנִי מֵעָנְשׁוֹ שֶׁלָּזֶה.**

*In some congregations, during the week before a yahrzeit,*
אֵל מָלֵא רַחֲמִים *on page 861 is said.*

### FOR AN OLEH

May He who blessed our fathers, Abraham, Isaac and Jacob, bless (*name*, son of *father's name*) who has been called up in honor of the All-Present, in honor of the Torah, and in honor of the Sabbath (*On Yom Tov:* and in honor of the festival). As a reward for this, may the Holy One, blessed be He, protect and deliver him from all trouble and distress, all infection and illness, and send blessing and success to all the work of his hands (*On Yom Tov:* and may he merit to go up to Jerusalem for the festivals), together with all Israel, his brethren, and let us say: Amen.

### FOR A SICK MAN

May He who blessed our fathers, Abraham, Isaac and Jacob, Moses and Aaron, David and Solomon, bless and heal one who is ill, (*sick person's name*, son of *mother's name*), on whose behalf (*name of the one making the offering*) is making a contribution to charity. As a reward for this, may the Holy One, blessed be He, be filled with compassion for him, to restore his health, cure him, strengthen and revive him, sending him a swift and full recovery from heaven to all his 248 organs and 365 sinews, amongst the other sick ones in Israel, a healing of the spirit and a healing of the body – though on Shabbat (*On Yom Tov:* on festivals) it is forbidden to cry out, may healing be quick to come – now, swiftly and soon, and let us say: Amen.

### FOR A SICK WOMAN

May He who blessed our fathers, Abraham, Isaac and Jacob, Moses and Aaron, David and Solomon, bless and heal one who is ill, (*sick person's name*, daughter of *mother's name*), on whose behalf (*name of the one making the offering*) is making a contribution to charity. As a reward for this, may the Holy One, blessed be He, be filled with compassion for her, to restore her health, cure her, strengthen and revive her, sending her a swift and full recovery from heaven to all her organs and sinews, amongst the other sick ones in Israel, a healing of the spirit and a healing of the body – though on the Sabbath (*On Yom Tov:* on festivals) it is forbidden to cry out, may healing be quick to come – now, swiftly and soon, and let us say: Amen.

מי שברך לעולה לתורה

מִי שֶׁבֵּרַךְ אֲבוֹתֵינוּ אַבְרָהָם יִצְחָק וְיַעֲקֹב, הוּא יְבָרֵךְ אֶת (פלוני בֶּן פלוני), בַּעֲבוּר שֶׁעָלָה לִכְבוֹד הַמָּקוֹם וְלִכְבוֹד הַתּוֹרָה וְלִכְבוֹד הַשַּׁבָּת (ביום טוב: וְלִכְבוֹד הָרֶגֶל). בִּשְׂכַר זֶה הַקָּדוֹשׁ בָּרוּךְ הוּא יִשְׁמְרֵהוּ וְיַצִּילֵהוּ מִכָּל צָרָה וְצוּקָה וּמִכָּל נֶגַע וּמַחֲלָה, וְיִשְׁלַח בְּרָכָה וְהַצְלָחָה בְּכָל מַעֲשֵׂה יָדָיו (ביום טוב: וְיִזְכֶּה לַעֲלוֹת לָרֶגֶל) עִם כָּל יִשְׂרָאֵל אֶחָיו, וְנֹאמַר אָמֵן.

מי שברך לחולֶה

מִי שֶׁבֵּרַךְ אֲבוֹתֵינוּ אַבְרָהָם יִצְחָק וְיַעֲקֹב, מֹשֶׁה וְאַהֲרֹן דָּוִד וּשְׁלֹמֹה הוּא יְבָרֵךְ וִירַפֵּא אֶת הַחוֹלֶה (פלוני בֶּן פלונית) בַּעֲבוּר שֶׁ(פלוני בֶּן פלוני) נוֹדֵר צְדָקָה בַּעֲבוּרוֹ. בִּשְׂכַר זֶה הַקָּדוֹשׁ בָּרוּךְ הוּא יִמָּלֵא רַחֲמִים עָלָיו לְהַחֲלִימוֹ וּלְרַפְּאתוֹ וּלְהַחֲזִיקוֹ וּלְהַחֲיוֹתוֹ וְיִשְׁלַח לוֹ מְהֵרָה רְפוּאָה שְׁלֵמָה מִן הַשָּׁמַיִם לִרְמַ״ח אֵבָרָיו וּשְׁסָ״ה גִּידָיו בְּתוֹךְ שְׁאָר חוֹלֵי יִשְׂרָאֵל, רְפוּאַת הַנֶּפֶשׁ וּרְפוּאַת הַגּוּף. שַׁבָּת הִיא מִלִּזְעֹק / ביום טוב: יוֹם טוֹב הוּא מִלִּזְעֹק/ וּרְפוּאָה קְרוֹבָה לָבוֹא, הַשְׁתָּא בַּעֲגָלָא וּבִזְמַן קָרִיב, וְנֹאמַר אָמֵן.

מי שברך לחולָה

מִי שֶׁבֵּרַךְ אֲבוֹתֵינוּ אַבְרָהָם יִצְחָק וְיַעֲקֹב, מֹשֶׁה וְאַהֲרֹן דָּוִד וּשְׁלֹמֹה הוּא יְבָרֵךְ וִירַפֵּא אֶת הַחוֹלָה (פלונית בַּת פלונית) בַּעֲבוּר שֶׁ(פלוני בֶּן פלוני) נוֹדֵר צְדָקָה בַּעֲבוּרָהּ. בִּשְׂכַר זֶה הַקָּדוֹשׁ בָּרוּךְ הוּא יִמָּלֵא רַחֲמִים עָלֶיהָ לְהַחֲלִימָהּ וּלְרַפְּאתָהּ וּלְהַחֲזִיקָהּ וּלְהַחֲיוֹתָהּ וְיִשְׁלַח לָהּ מְהֵרָה רְפוּאָה שְׁלֵמָה מִן הַשָּׁמַיִם לְכָל אֵבָרֶיהָ וּלְכָל גִּידֶיהָ בְּתוֹךְ שְׁאָר חוֹלֵי יִשְׂרָאֵל, רְפוּאַת הַנֶּפֶשׁ וּרְפוּאַת הַגּוּף. שַׁבָּת הִיא מִלִּזְעֹק / ביום טוב: יוֹם טוֹב הוּא מִלִּזְעֹק/ וּרְפוּאָה קְרוֹבָה לָבוֹא, הַשְׁתָּא בַּעֲגָלָא וּבִזְמַן קָרִיב, וְנֹאמַר אָמֵן.

ON THE BIRTH OF A SON

May He who blessed our fathers, Abraham, Isaac and Jacob, Moses and Aaron, David and Solomon, Sarah, Rebecca, Rachel and Leah, bless the woman who has given birth (*name,* daughter of *father's name*), and her son who has been born to her as an auspicious sign. Her husband, the child's father, is making a contribution to charity. As a reward for this, may father and mother merit to bring the child into the covenant of Abraham and to a life of Torah, to the marriage canopy and to good deeds, and let us say: Amen.

ON THE BIRTH OF A DAUGHTER

May He who blessed our fathers, Abraham, Isaac and Jacob, Moses and Aaron, David and Solomon, Sarah, Rebecca, Rachel and Leah, bless the woman who has given birth (*name,* daughter of *father's name*), and her daughter who has been born to her as an auspicious sign; and may her name be called in Israel (*baby's name,* daughter of *father's name*). Her husband, the child's father, is making a contribution to charity. As a reward for this, may father and mother merit to raise her to a life of Torah, to the marriage canopy, and to good deeds, and let us say: Amen.

FOR A BAR MITZVA

May He who blessed our fathers, Abraham, Isaac and Jacob, bless (*name,* son of *father's name*) who has completed thirteen years and attained the age of the commandments, who has been called to the Torah to give praise and thanks to God, may His name be blessed, for all the good He has bestowed on him. May the Holy One, blessed be He, protect and sustain him and direct his heart to be perfect with God, to walk in His ways and keep the commandments all the days of his life, and let us say: Amen.

FOR A BAT MITZVA

May He who blessed our fathers, Abraham, Isaac and Jacob, Sarah, Rebecca, Rachel and Leah, bless (*name,* daughter of *father's name*) who has completed twelve years and attained the age of the commandments, and gives praise and thanks to God, may His name be blessed, for all the good He has bestowed on her. May the Holy One, blessed be He, protect and sustain her and direct her heart to be perfect with God, to walk in His ways and keep the commandments all the days of her life, and let us say: Amen.

### מי שברך ליולדת בן

מִי שֶׁבֵּרַךְ אֲבוֹתֵינוּ אַבְרָהָם יִצְחָק וְיַעֲקֹב, מֹשֶׁה וְאַהֲרֹן דָּוִד וּשְׁלֹמֹה, שָׂרָה רִבְקָה רָחֵל וְלֵאָה הוּא יְבָרֵךְ אֶת הָאִשָּׁה הַיּוֹלֶדֶת (פלונית בַּת פלוני) וְאֶת בְּנָהּ שֶׁנּוֹלַד לָהּ לְמַזָּל טוֹב בַּעֲבוּר שֶׁבַּעְלָהּ וְאָבִיו נוֹדֵר צְדָקָה בַּעֲדָם. בִּשְׂכַר זֶה יִזְכּוּ אָבִיו וְאִמּוֹ לְהַכְנִיסוֹ בִּבְרִיתוֹ שֶׁל אַבְרָהָם אָבִינוּ וּלְגַדְּלוֹ לְתוֹרָה וּלְחֻפָּה וּלְמַעֲשִׂים טוֹבִים, וְנֹאמַר אָמֵן.

### מי שברך ליולדת בת

מִי שֶׁבֵּרַךְ אֲבוֹתֵינוּ אַבְרָהָם יִצְחָק וְיַעֲקֹב, מֹשֶׁה וְאַהֲרֹן דָּוִד וּשְׁלֹמֹה, שָׂרָה רִבְקָה רָחֵל וְלֵאָה הוּא יְבָרֵךְ אֶת הָאִשָּׁה הַיּוֹלֶדֶת (פלונית בַּת פלוני) וְאֶת בִּתָּהּ שֶׁנּוֹלְדָה לָהּ לְמַזָּל טוֹב וְיִקָּרֵא שְׁמָהּ בְּיִשְׂרָאֵל (פלונית בַּת פלוני), בַּעֲבוּר שֶׁבַּעְלָהּ וְאָבִיהָ נוֹדֵר צְדָקָה בַּעֲדָן. בִּשְׂכַר זֶה יִזְכּוּ אָבִיהָ וְאִמָּהּ לְגַדְּלָהּ לְתוֹרָה וּלְחֻפָּה וּלְמַעֲשִׂים טוֹבִים, וְנֹאמַר אָמֵן.

### מי שברך לבר מצווה

מִי שֶׁבֵּרַךְ אֲבוֹתֵינוּ אַבְרָהָם יִצְחָק וְיַעֲקֹב הוּא יְבָרֵךְ אֶת (פלוני בֶּן פלוני) שֶׁמָּלְאוּ לוֹ שְׁלֹשׁ עֶשְׂרֵה שָׁנָה וְהִגִּיעַ לְמִצְוֹת, וְעָלָה לַתּוֹרָה, לָתֵת שֶׁבַח וְהוֹדָיָה לְהַשֵּׁם יִתְבָּרַךְ עַל כָּל הַטּוֹבָה שֶׁגָּמַל אִתּוֹ. יִשְׁמְרֵהוּ הַקָּדוֹשׁ בָּרוּךְ הוּא וִיחַיֵּהוּ, וִיכוֹנֵן אֶת לִבּוֹ לִהְיוֹת שָׁלֵם עִם יהוה וְלָלֶכֶת בִּדְרָכָיו וְלִשְׁמֹר מִצְוֹתָיו כָּל הַיָּמִים, וְנֹאמַר אָמֵן.

### מי שברך לבת מצווה

מִי שֶׁבֵּרַךְ אֲבוֹתֵינוּ אַבְרָהָם יִצְחָק וְיַעֲקֹב, שָׂרָה רִבְקָה רָחֵל וְלֵאָה, הוּא יְבָרֵךְ אֶת (פלונית בַּת פלוני) שֶׁמָּלְאוּ לָהּ שְׁתֵּים עֶשְׂרֵה שָׁנָה וְהִגִּיעָה לְמִצְוֹת, וְנוֹתֶנֶת שֶׁבַח וְהוֹדָיָה לְהַשֵּׁם יִתְבָּרַךְ עַל כָּל הַטּוֹבָה שֶׁגָּמַל אִתָּהּ. יִשְׁמְרֶהָ הַקָּדוֹשׁ בָּרוּךְ הוּא וִיחַיֶּהָ, וִיכוֹנֵן אֶת לִבָּהּ לִהְיוֹת שָׁלֵם עִם יהוה וְלָלֶכֶת בִּדְרָכָיו וְלִשְׁמֹר מִצְוֹתָיו כָּל הַיָּמִים, וְנֹאמַר אָמֵן.

## HALF KADDISH

*Before Maftir is read, the Reader says Half Kaddish:*

*Reader:* יִתְגַּדַּל Magnified and sanctified may His great name be,
in the world He created by His will.
May He establish His kingdom
in your lifetime and in your days,
and in the lifetime of all the house of Israel,
swiftly and soon – and say: Amen.

*All:* May His great name be blessed for ever and all time.

*Reader:* Blessed and praised, glorified and exalted,
raised and honored, uplifted and lauded
be the name of the Holy One, blessed be He,
beyond any blessing, song, praise and consolation
uttered in the world – and say: Amen.

## HAGBAHA AND GELILA

*The Torah scroll is lifted and the congregation says:*

וְזֹאת הַתּוֹרָה This is the Torah *Deut. 4*
that Moses placed before the children of Israel,
at the LORD's commandment, by the hand of Moses. *Num. 9*

*Some add:* It is a tree of life to those who grasp it, *Prov. 3*
and those who uphold it are happy.
Its ways are ways of pleasantness, and all its paths are peace.
Long life is in its right hand; in its left, riches and honor.
It pleased the LORD for the sake of [Israel's] righteousness, *Is. 42*
to make the Torah great and glorious.

*The Torah scroll is bound and covered.*

## BLESSINGS BEFORE AND AFTER READING THE HAFTARA

*Before reading the Haftara, the person called up for Maftir says:*

בָּרוּךְ Blessed are You, LORD our God, King of the Universe, who chose good prophets and was pleased with their words, spoken in truth. Blessed are You, LORD, who chose the Torah, His servant Moses, His people Israel, and the prophets of truth and righteousness.

## חצי קדיש

*Before* מפטיר *is read, the* קורא *says* חצי קדיש:

קורא: יִתְגַּדַּל וְיִתְקַדַּשׁ שְׁמֵהּ רַבָּא (קהל: אָמֵן)
בְּעָלְמָא דִּי בְרָא כִרְעוּתֵהּ, וְיַמְלִיךְ מַלְכוּתֵהּ
בְּחַיֵּיכוֹן וּבְיוֹמֵיכוֹן וּבְחַיֵּי דְכָל בֵּית יִשְׂרָאֵל
בַּעֲגָלָא וּבִזְמַן קָרִיב, וְאִמְרוּ אָמֵן. (קהל: אָמֵן)

קהל וקורא: יְהֵא שְׁמֵהּ רַבָּא מְבָרַךְ לְעָלַם וּלְעָלְמֵי עָלְמַיָּא.

קורא: יִתְבָּרַךְ וְיִשְׁתַּבַּח וְיִתְפָּאַר וְיִתְרוֹמַם וְיִתְנַשֵּׂא
וְיִתְהַדָּר וְיִתְעַלֶּה וְיִתְהַלָּל
שְׁמֵהּ דְּקֻדְשָׁא בְּרִיךְ הוּא (קהל: בְּרִיךְ הוּא)
לְעֵלָּא מִן כָּל בִּרְכָתָא / בשבת שובה: לְעֵלָּא לְעֵלָּא מִכָּל בִּרְכָתָא/
וְשִׁירָתָא, תֻּשְׁבְּחָתָא וְנֶחֱמָתָא
דַּאֲמִירָן בְּעָלְמָא, וְאִמְרוּ אָמֵן. (קהל: אָמֵן)

## הגבהה וגלילה

*The* ספר תורה *is lifted and the* קהל *says:*

וְזֹאת הַתּוֹרָה אֲשֶׁר־שָׂם מֹשֶׁה לִפְנֵי בְּנֵי יִשְׂרָאֵל: דברים ד
עַל־פִּי יהוה בְּיַד מֹשֶׁה: במדבר ט

*Some add* עֵץ־חַיִּים הִיא לַמַּחֲזִיקִים בָּהּ וְתֹמְכֶיהָ מְאֻשָּׁר: משלי ג
דְּרָכֶיהָ דַרְכֵי־נֹעַם וְכָל־נְתִיבוֹתֶיהָ שָׁלוֹם:
אֹרֶךְ יָמִים בִּימִינָהּ, בִּשְׂמֹאולָהּ עֹשֶׁר וְכָבוֹד:
יהוה חָפֵץ לְמַעַן צִדְקוֹ יַגְדִּיל תּוֹרָה וְיַאְדִּיר: ישעיה מב

*The* ספר תורה *is bound and covered.*

## ברכות ההפטרה

*Before reading the* הפטרה*, the person called up for* מפטיר *says:*

בָּרוּךְ אַתָּה יהוה אֱלֹהֵינוּ מֶלֶךְ הָעוֹלָם אֲשֶׁר בָּחַר בִּנְבִיאִים טוֹבִים, וְרָצָה בְדִבְרֵיהֶם הַנֶּאֱמָרִים בֶּאֱמֶת. בָּרוּךְ אַתָּה יהוה, הַבּוֹחֵר בַּתּוֹרָה וּבְמֹשֶׁה עַבְדּוֹ וּבְיִשְׂרָאֵל עַמּוֹ וּבִנְבִיאֵי הָאֱמֶת וָצֶדֶק.

*After the Haftara, the person called up for Maftir says the following blessings:*

בָּרוּךְ Blessed are You, LORD our God, King of the Universe, Rock of all worlds, righteous for all generations, the faithful God who says and does, speaks and fulfills, all of whose words are truth and righteousness. You are faithful, LORD our God, and faithful are Your words, not one of which returns unfulfilled, for You, God, are a faithful (and compassionate) King. Blessed are You, LORD, faithful in all His words.

רַחֵם Have compassion on Zion for it is the source of our life, and save the one grieved in spirit swiftly in our days. Blessed are You, LORD, who makes Zion rejoice in her children.

שַׂמְּחֵנוּ Grant us joy, LORD our God, through Elijah the prophet Your servant, and through the kingdom of the house of David Your anointed – may he soon come and make our hearts glad. May no stranger sit on his throne, and may others not continue to inherit his glory, for You promised him by Your holy name that his light would never be extinguished. Blessed are You, LORD, Shield of David.

*On a regular Shabbat, as well as Shabbat Ḥol HaMo'ed Pesaḥ, say:*

עַל הַתּוֹרָה For the Torah, for divine worship, for the prophets, and for this Sabbath day which You, LORD our God, have given us for holiness and rest, honor and glory – for all these we thank and bless You, LORD our God, and may Your name be blessed by the mouth of all that lives, continually, for ever and all time. Blessed are You, LORD, who sanctifies the Sabbath.

*On Yom Tov and on Shabbat Ḥol HaMo'ed Sukkot, say*
*(adding on Shabbat the words in parentheses):*

For the Torah, for divine worship, for the prophets, (for this Sabbath day) and for this day of

*On Pesaḥ:* the Festival of Matzot
*On Shavuot:* the Festival of Shavuot
*On Sukkot:* the Festival of Sukkot
*On Shemini Atzeret and Simḥat Torah:* the Festival of Shemini Atzeret

which You, LORD our God, have given us (for holiness and rest), for joy and gladness, honor and glory – for all these we thank and bless You, LORD our God, and may Your name be blessed by the mouth of all that lives, continually, for ever and all time. Blessed are You, LORD, who sanctifies (the Sabbath and) Israel and the festivals.

*After the הפטרה, the person called up for מפטיר says the following blessings:*

בָּרוּךְ אַתָּה יהוה אֱלֹהֵינוּ מֶלֶךְ הָעוֹלָם, צוּר כָּל הָעוֹלָמִים, צַדִּיק בְּכָל הַדּוֹרוֹת, הָאֵל הַנֶּאֱמָן, הָאוֹמֵר וְעוֹשֶׂה, הַמְדַבֵּר וּמְקַיֵּם, שֶׁכָּל דְּבָרָיו אֱמֶת וָצֶדֶק. נֶאֱמָן אַתָּה הוּא יהוה אֱלֹהֵינוּ וְנֶאֱמָנִים דְּבָרֶיךָ, וְדָבָר אֶחָד מִדְּבָרֶיךָ אָחוֹר לֹא יָשׁוּב רֵיקָם, כִּי אֵל מֶלֶךְ נֶאֱמָן (וְרַחֲמָן) אָתָּה. בָּרוּךְ אַתָּה יהוה, הָאֵל הַנֶּאֱמָן בְּכָל דְּבָרָיו.

רַחֵם עַל צִיּוֹן כִּי הִיא בֵּית חַיֵּינוּ, וְלַעֲלוּבַת נֶפֶשׁ תּוֹשִׁיעַ בִּמְהֵרָה בְיָמֵינוּ. בָּרוּךְ אַתָּה יהוה, מְשַׂמֵּחַ צִיּוֹן בְּבָנֶיהָ.

שַׂמְּחֵנוּ יהוה אֱלֹהֵינוּ בְּאֵלִיָּהוּ הַנָּבִיא עַבְדֶּךָ, וּבְמַלְכוּת בֵּית דָּוִד מְשִׁיחֶךָ, בִּמְהֵרָה יָבוֹא וְיָגֵל לִבֵּנוּ. עַל כִּסְאוֹ לֹא יֵשֶׁב זָר, וְלֹא יִנְחֲלוּ עוֹד אֲחֵרִים אֶת כְּבוֹדוֹ, כִּי בְשֵׁם קָדְשְׁךָ נִשְׁבַּעְתָּ לּוֹ שֶׁלֹּא יִכְבֶּה נֵרוֹ לְעוֹלָם וָעֶד. בָּרוּךְ אַתָּה יהוה, מָגֵן דָּוִד.

*On a regular שבת, as well as שבת חול המועד פסח, say:*

עַל הַתּוֹרָה וְעַל הָעֲבוֹדָה וְעַל הַנְּבִיאִים וְעַל יוֹם הַשַּׁבָּת הַזֶּה, שֶׁנָּתַתָּ לָּנוּ יהוה אֱלֹהֵינוּ לִקְדֻשָּׁה וְלִמְנוּחָה, לְכָבוֹד וּלְתִפְאָרֶת. עַל הַכֹּל יהוה אֱלֹהֵינוּ אֲנַחְנוּ מוֹדִים לָךְ וּמְבָרְכִים אוֹתָךְ, יִתְבָּרַךְ שִׁמְךָ בְּפִי כָּל חַי תָּמִיד לְעוֹלָם וָעֶד. בָּרוּךְ אַתָּה יהוה, מְקַדֵּשׁ הַשַּׁבָּת.

*On יום טוב and on שבת חול המועד סוכות, say (adding on שבת the words in parentheses):*

עַל הַתּוֹרָה וְעַל הָעֲבוֹדָה וְעַל הַנְּבִיאִים (בשבת: וְעַל יוֹם הַשַּׁבָּת הַזֶּה), וְעַל יוֹם

בפסח: חַג הַמַּצּוֹת הַזֶּה / בשבועות: חַג הַשָּׁבוּעוֹת הַזֶּה

בסוכות: חַג הַסֻּכּוֹת הַזֶּה / בשמיני עצרת ובש״ת: הַשְּׁמִינִי חַג הָעֲצֶרֶת הַזֶּה

שֶׁנָּתַתָּ לָּנוּ, יהוה אֱלֹהֵינוּ (בשבת: לִקְדֻשָּׁה וְלִמְנוּחָה) לְשָׂשׂוֹן וּלְשִׂמְחָה, לְכָבוֹד וּלְתִפְאָרֶת. עַל הַכֹּל יהוה אֱלֹהֵינוּ אֲנַחְנוּ מוֹדִים לָךְ וּמְבָרְכִים אוֹתָךְ. יִתְבָּרַךְ שִׁמְךָ בְּפִי כָּל חַי תָּמִיד לְעוֹלָם וָעֶד. בָּרוּךְ אַתָּה יהוה, מְקַדֵּשׁ (בשבת: הַשַּׁבָּת וְ)יִשְׂרָאֵל וְהַזְּמַנִּים.

*The following three paragraphs are not said on a Yom Tov occurring on a weekday. They are only said when praying with a minyan (some say the first paragraph without a minyan).*

יְקוּם פֻּרְקָן May deliverance arise from heaven, bringing grace, love and compassion, long life, ample sustenance and heavenly help, physical health and enlightenment of mind, living and thriving children who will neither interrupt nor cease from the words of the Torah – to our masters and teachers of the holy communities in the land of Israel and Babylon; to the leaders of assemblies and the leaders of communities in exile; to the heads of academies and to the judges in the gates; to all their disciples and their disciples' disciples, and to all who occupy themselves in study of the Torah. May the King of the Universe bless them, prolonging their lives, increasing their days, and adding to their years. May they be redeemed and delivered from all distress and illness. May our Master in heaven be their help at all times and seasons; and let us say: Amen.

יְקוּם פֻּרְקָן May deliverance arise from heaven, bringing grace, love and compassion, long life, ample sustenance and heavenly help, physical health and enlightenment of mind, living and thriving children who will neither interrupt nor cease from the words of the Torah – to all this holy congregation, great and small, women and children. May the King of the Universe bless you, prolonging your lives, increasing your days, and adding to your years. May you be redeemed and delivered from all distress and illness. May our Master in heaven be your help at all times and seasons; and let us say: Amen.

מִי שֶׁבֵּרַךְ May He who blessed our fathers, Abraham, Isaac and Jacob, bless all this holy congregation, together with all other holy congregations: them, their wives, their sons and daughters, and all that is theirs. May He bless those who unite to form synagogues for prayer and those who come there to pray; those who provide lamps for light and wine for Kiddush and Havdala, food for visitors and charity for the poor, and all who faithfully occupy themselves with the needs of the community. May the Holy One, blessed be He, give them their reward; may He remove from them all illness, grant them complete healing, and forgive all their sins. May He send blessing and success to all the work of their hands, together with all Israel their brethren; and let us say: Amen.

*The following three paragraphs are not said on a יום טוב occurring on a weekday. They are only said when praying with a מנין (some say the first paragraph without a מנין).*

יְקוּם פֻּרְקָן מִן שְׁמַיָּא, חִנָּא וְחִסְדָּא וְרַחֲמֵי וְחַיֵּי אֲרִיכֵי וּמְזוֹנֵי רְוִיחֵי, וְסִיַּעְתָּא דִשְׁמַיָּא, וּבַרְיוּת גּוּפָא וּנְהוֹרָא מְעַלְּיָא, זַרְעָא חַיָּא וְקַיָּמָא, זַרְעָא דִּי לָא יִפְסֻק וְדִי לָא יִבְטֻל מִפִּתְגָמֵי אוֹרַיְתָא, לְמָרָנָן וְרַבָּנָן חֲבוּרָתָא קַדִּישָׁתָא דִּי בְאַרְעָא דְיִשְׂרָאֵל וְדִי בְּבָבֶל, לְרֵישֵׁי כַלָּה, וּלְרֵישֵׁי גַלְוָתָא, וּלְרֵישֵׁי מְתִיבָתָא, וּלְדַיָּנֵי דְבָבָא, לְכָל תַּלְמִידֵיהוֹן, וּלְכָל תַּלְמִידֵי תַלְמִידֵיהוֹן, וּלְכָל מָאן דְּעָסְקִין בְּאוֹרַיְתָא. מַלְכָּא דְעָלְמָא יְבָרֵךְ יָתְהוֹן, יַפֵּשׁ חַיֵּיהוֹן וְיַסְגֵּא יוֹמֵיהוֹן, וְיִתֵּן אַרְכָא לִשְׁנֵיהוֹן, וְיִתְפָּרְקוּן וְיִשְׁתֵּיזְבוּן מִן כָּל עָקָא וּמִן כָּל מַרְעִין בִּישִׁין. מָרַן דִּי בִשְׁמַיָּא יְהֵא בְסַעְדְּהוֹן כָּל זְמַן וְעִדָּן, וְנֹאמַר אָמֵן.

יְקוּם פֻּרְקָן מִן שְׁמַיָּא, חִנָּא וְחִסְדָּא וְרַחֲמֵי וְחַיֵּי אֲרִיכֵי וּמְזוֹנֵי רְוִיחֵי, וְסִיַּעְתָּא דִשְׁמַיָּא, וּבַרְיוּת גּוּפָא וּנְהוֹרָא מְעַלְּיָא, זַרְעָא חַיָּא וְקַיָּמָא, זַרְעָא דִּי לָא יִפְסֻק וְדִי לָא יִבְטֻל מִפִּתְגָמֵי אוֹרַיְתָא, לְכָל קְהָלָא קַדִּישָׁא הָדֵין, רַבְרְבַיָּא עִם זְעֵרַיָּא, טַפְלָא וּנְשַׁיָּא. מַלְכָּא דְעָלְמָא יְבָרֵךְ יָתְכוֹן, יַפֵּשׁ חַיֵּיכוֹן וְיַסְגֵּא יוֹמֵיכוֹן, וְיִתֵּן אַרְכָא לִשְׁנֵיכוֹן, וְתִתְפָּרְקוּן וְתִשְׁתֵּיזְבוּן מִן כָּל עָקָא וּמִן כָּל מַרְעִין בִּישִׁין. מָרַן דִּי בִשְׁמַיָּא יְהֵא בְסַעְדְּכוֹן כָּל זְמַן וְעִדָּן, וְנֹאמַר אָמֵן.

מִי שֶׁבֵּרַךְ אֲבוֹתֵינוּ אַבְרָהָם יִצְחָק וְיַעֲקֹב, הוּא יְבָרֵךְ אֶת כָּל הַקָּהָל הַקָּדוֹשׁ הַזֶּה עִם כָּל קְהִלּוֹת הַקֹּדֶשׁ, הֵם וּנְשֵׁיהֶם וּבְנֵיהֶם וּבְנוֹתֵיהֶם וְכָל אֲשֶׁר לָהֶם, וּמִי שֶׁמְּיַחֲדִים בָּתֵּי כְנֵסִיּוֹת לִתְפִלָּה, וּמִי שֶׁבָּאִים בְּתוֹכָם לְהִתְפַּלֵּל, וּמִי שֶׁנּוֹתְנִים נֵר לַמָּאוֹר וְיַיִן לְקִדּוּשׁ וּלְהַבְדָּלָה וּפַת לָאוֹרְחִים וּצְדָקָה לָעֲנִיִּים, וְכָל מִי שֶׁעוֹסְקִים בְּצָרְכֵי צִבּוּר בֶּאֱמוּנָה. הַקָּדוֹשׁ בָּרוּךְ הוּא יְשַׁלֵּם שְׂכָרָם, וְיָסִיר מֵהֶם כָּל מַחֲלָה, וְיִרְפָּא לְכָל גּוּפָם, וְיִסְלַח לְכָל עֲוֹנָם, וְיִשְׁלַח בְּרָכָה וְהַצְלָחָה בְּכָל מַעֲשֵׂי יְדֵיהֶם עִם כָּל יִשְׂרָאֵל אֲחֵיהֶם, וְנֹאמַר אָמֵן.

## PRAYER FOR THE STATE OF ISRAEL

*The Leader says the following prayer:*

אָבִינוּ שֶׁבַּשָּׁמַיִם Heavenly Father, Israel's Rock and Redeemer, bless the State of Israel, the first flowering of our redemption. Shield it under the wings of Your loving-kindness and spread over it the Tabernacle of Your peace. Send Your light and truth to its leaders, ministers and counselors, and direct them with good counsel before You.

Strengthen the hands of the defenders of our Holy Land; grant them deliverance, our God, and crown them with the crown of victory. Grant peace in the land and everlasting joy to its inhabitants.

As for our brothers, the whole house of Israel, remember them in all the lands of our (*In Israel say:* their) dispersion, and swiftly lead us (*In Israel say:* them) upright to Zion Your city, and Jerusalem Your dwelling place, as is written in the Torah of Moses Your servant: "Even if you are scattered to the furthermost lands under the heavens, from there the LORD your God will gather you and take you back. The LORD your God will bring you to the land your ancestors possessed and you will possess it; and He will make you more prosperous and numerous than your ancestors. Then the LORD your God will open up your heart and the heart of your descendants, to love the LORD your God with all your heart and with all your soul, that you may live." *Deut. 30*

Unite our hearts to love and revere Your name and observe all the words of Your Torah, and swiftly send us Your righteous anointed one of the house of David, to redeem those who long for Your salvation.

Appear in Your glorious majesty over all the dwellers on earth, and let all who breathe declare: The LORD God of Israel is King and His kingship has dominion over all. Amen, Selah.

## תפילה לשלום מדינת ישראל

*The* שליח ציבור *says the following prayer:*

אָבִינוּ שֶׁבַּשָּׁמַיִם, צוּר יִשְׂרָאֵל וְגוֹאֲלוֹ, בָּרֵךְ אֶת מְדִינַת יִשְׂרָאֵל, רֵאשִׁית צְמִיחַת גְּאֻלָּתֵנוּ. הָגֵן עָלֶיהָ בְּאֶבְרַת חַסְדֶּךָ וּפְרֹשׂ עָלֶיהָ סֻכַּת שְׁלוֹמֶךָ, וּשְׁלַח אוֹרְךָ וַאֲמִתְּךָ לְרָאשֶׁיהָ, שָׂרֶיהָ וְיוֹעֲצֶיהָ, וְתַקְּנֵם בְּעֵצָה טוֹבָה מִלְּפָנֶיךָ.

חַזֵּק אֶת יְדֵי מְגִנֵּי אֶרֶץ קָדְשֵׁנוּ, וְהַנְחִילֵם אֱלֹהֵינוּ יְשׁוּעָה וַעֲטֶרֶת נִצָּחוֹן תְּעַטְּרֵם, וְנָתַתָּ שָׁלוֹם בָּאָרֶץ וְשִׂמְחַת עוֹלָם לְיוֹשְׁבֶיהָ.

וְאֶת אַחֵינוּ כָּל בֵּית יִשְׂרָאֵל, פְּקָד נָא בְּכָל אַרְצוֹת פְּזוּרֵינוּ,
וְתוֹלִיכֵנוּ / בארץ ישראל: פְּזוּרֵיהֶם, וְתוֹלִיכֵם/ מְהֵרָה קוֹמְמִיּוּת לְצִיּוֹן
עִירֶךָ וְלִירוּשָׁלַיִם מִשְׁכַּן שְׁמֶךָ, כַּכָּתוּב בְּתוֹרַת מֹשֶׁה עַבְדֶּךָ:
אִם־יִהְיֶה נִדַּחֲךָ בִּקְצֵה הַשָּׁמָיִם, מִשָּׁם יְקַבֶּצְךָ יהוה אֱלֹהֶיךָ דברים ל
וּמִשָּׁם יִקָּחֶךָ: וֶהֱבִיאֲךָ יהוה אֱלֹהֶיךָ אֶל־הָאָרֶץ אֲשֶׁר־יָרְשׁוּ
אֲבֹתֶיךָ וִירִשְׁתָּהּ, וְהֵיטִבְךָ וְהִרְבְּךָ מֵאֲבֹתֶיךָ: וּמָל יהוה אֱלֹהֶיךָ
אֶת־לְבָבְךָ וְאֶת־לְבַב זַרְעֶךָ, לְאַהֲבָה אֶת־יהוה אֱלֹהֶיךָ בְּכָל־
לְבָבְךָ וּבְכָל־נַפְשְׁךָ, לְמַעַן חַיֶּיךָ:

וְיַחֵד לְבָבֵנוּ לְאַהֲבָה וּלְיִרְאָה אֶת שְׁמֶךָ, וְלִשְׁמֹר אֶת כָּל דִּבְרֵי תוֹרָתֶךָ, וּשְׁלַח לָנוּ מְהֵרָה בֶּן דָּוִד מְשִׁיחַ צִדְקֶךָ, לִפְדּוֹת מְחַכֵּי קֵץ יְשׁוּעָתֶךָ.

וְהוֹפַע בַּהֲדַר גְּאוֹן עֻזֶּךָ עַל כָּל יוֹשְׁבֵי תֵּבֵל אַרְצֶךָ וְיֹאמַר כֹּל אֲשֶׁר נְשָׁמָה בְאַפּוֹ, יהוה אֱלֹהֵי יִשְׂרָאֵל מֶלֶךְ וּמַלְכוּתוֹ בַּכֹּל מָשָׁלָה, אָמֵן סֶלָה.

## PRAYER FOR ISRAEL'S DEFENSE FORCES

*The Leader says the following prayer:*

מִי שֶׁבֵּרַךְ May He who blessed our ancestors, Abraham, Isaac and Jacob, bless the members of Israel's Defense Forces and its security services who stand guard over our land and the cities of our God from the Lebanese border to the Egyptian desert, from the Mediterranean sea to the approach of the Aravah, and wherever else they are, on land, in air and at sea. May the LORD make the enemies who rise against us be struck down before them. May the Holy One, blessed be He, protect and deliver them from all trouble and distress, affliction and illness, and send blessing and success to all the work of their hands. May He subdue our enemies under them and crown them with deliverance and victory. And may there be fulfilled in them the verse, "It is the LORD your God who goes with you to fight *Deut. 20*
for you against your enemies, to deliver you." And let us say: Amen.

## PRAYER FOR THOSE BEING HELD IN CAPTIVITY

*If Israeli soldiers or civilians are being held in captivity, the Leader says the following:*

מִי שֶׁבֵּרַךְ May He who blessed our ancestors, Abraham, Isaac and Jacob, Joseph, Moses and Aaron, David and Solomon, bless, protect and guard the members of Israel's Defense Forces missing in action or held captive, and other captives among our brethren, the whole house of Israel, who are in distress or captivity, as we, the members of this holy congregation, pray on their behalf. May the Holy One, blessed be He, have compassion on them and bring them out from darkness and the shadow of death; may He break their bonds, deliver them from their distress, and bring them swiftly back to their families' embrace. Give thanks to the LORD for His loving-kindness *Ps. 107*
and for the wonders He does for the children of men; and may there be fulfilled in them the verse: "Those redeemed by the LORD will *Is. 35*
return; they will enter Zion with singing, and everlasting joy will crown their heads. Gladness and joy will overtake them, and sorrow and sighing will flee away." And let us say: Amen.

## מי שברך לחיילי צה״ל

*The* שליח ציבור *says the following prayer:*

מִי שֶׁבֵּרַךְ אֲבוֹתֵינוּ אַבְרָהָם יִצְחָק וְיַעֲקֹב הוּא יְבָרֵךְ אֶת חַיָּלֵי צְבָא הַהֲגָנָה לְיִשְׂרָאֵל וְאַנְשֵׁי כֹּחוֹת הַבִּטָּחוֹן, הָעוֹמְדִים עַל מִשְׁמַר אַרְצֵנוּ וְעָרֵי אֱלֹהֵינוּ, מִגְּבוּל הַלְּבָנוֹן וְעַד מִדְבַּר מִצְרַיִם וּמִן הַיָּם הַגָּדוֹל עַד לְבוֹא הָעֲרָבָה וּבְכָל מָקוֹם שֶׁהֵם, בַּיַּבָּשָׁה, בָּאֲוִיר וּבַיָּם. יִתֵּן יהוה אֶת אוֹיְבֵינוּ הַקָּמִים עָלֵינוּ נִגָּפִים לִפְנֵיהֶם. הַקָּדוֹשׁ בָּרוּךְ הוּא יִשְׁמֹר וְיַצִּיל אֶת חַיָּלֵינוּ מִכָּל צָרָה וְצוּקָה וּמִכָּל נֶגַע וּמַחֲלָה, וְיִשְׁלַח בְּרָכָה וְהַצְלָחָה בְּכָל מַעֲשֵׂי יְדֵיהֶם. יַדְבֵּר שׂוֹנְאֵינוּ תַּחְתֵּיהֶם וִיעַטְּרֵם בְּכֶתֶר יְשׁוּעָה וּבַעֲטֶרֶת נִצָּחוֹן.
וִיקֻיַּם בָּהֶם הַכָּתוּב: כִּי יהוה אֱלֹהֵיכֶם הַהֹלֵךְ עִמָּכֶם לְהִלָּחֵם לָכֶם עִם־אֹיְבֵיכֶם לְהוֹשִׁיעַ אֶתְכֶם: וְנֹאמַר אָמֵן. דברים כ

## מי שברך לשבויים

*If Israeli soldiers or civilians are being held in captivity, the* שליח ציבור *says the following:*

מִי שֶׁבֵּרַךְ אֲבוֹתֵינוּ אַבְרָהָם יִצְחָק וְיַעֲקֹב, יוֹסֵף מֹשֶׁה וְאַהֲרֹן, דָּוִד וּשְׁלֹמֹה, הוּא יְבָרֵךְ וְיִשְׁמֹר וְיִנְצֹר אֶת נֶעְדְּרֵי צְבָא הַהֲגָנָה לְיִשְׂרָאֵל וּשְׁבוּיָו, וְאֶת כָּל אַחֵינוּ הַנְּתוּנִים בְּצָרָה וּבְשִׁבְיָה, בַּעֲבוּר שֶׁכָּל הַקָּהָל הַקָּדוֹשׁ הַזֶּה מִתְפַּלֵּל בַּעֲבוּרָם. הַקָּדוֹשׁ בָּרוּךְ הוּא יִמָּלֵא רַחֲמִים עֲלֵיהֶם, וְיוֹצִיאֵם מֵחֹשֶׁךְ וְצַלְמָוֶת, וּמוֹסְרוֹתֵיהֶם יְנַתֵּק, וּמִמְּצוּקוֹתֵיהֶם יוֹשִׁיעֵם, וִישִׁיבֵם מְהֵרָה
לְחֵיק מִשְׁפְּחוֹתֵיהֶם. יוֹדוּ לַיהוה חַסְדּוֹ וְנִפְלְאוֹתָיו לִבְנֵי אָדָם: תהלים קז
וִיקֻיַּם בָּהֶם מִקְרָא שֶׁכָּתוּב: וּפְדוּיֵי יהוה יְשֻׁבוּן, וּבָאוּ צִיּוֹן ישעיה לה
בְּרִנָּה, וְשִׂמְחַת עוֹלָם עַל־רֹאשָׁם, שָׂשׂוֹן וְשִׂמְחָה יַשִּׂיגוּ, וְנָסוּ יָגוֹן וַאֲנָחָה: וְנֹאמַר אָמֵן.

## BLESSING THE NEW MONTH

*On the Shabbat before Rosh Ḥodesh, the following is said by the congregation, and repeated by the Leader:*

יְהִי רָצוֹן May it be Your will, Lord our God and God of our fathers, to renew for us this coming month for good and blessing. Grant us long life, a life of peace, a life of goodness, a life of blessing, a life of sustenance, a life of physical health, a life marked by reverence for heaven and dread of sin, a life without shame or disgrace, a life of wealth and honor, a life in which we have love for the Torah and reverence for heaven, a life in which our hearts' desires are fulfilled for good. Amen, Selah. *Berakhot 16b*

*The new moon is announced, then the Leader takes the Torah scroll in his right arm and says:*

מִי שֶׁעָשָׂה May He who performed miracles for our ancestors
and redeemed them from slavery to freedom, redeem us soon,
and gather in our dispersed people from the four quarters of the earth,
so that all Israel may be united in friendship, and let us say: Amen.

*The Leader, then the congregation:*

The new month of (*Hebrew month*) will occur on (*day of week*).
May it come to us and all Israel for good.

---

never properly integrated into their lives. So we are asking for such a life that includes *within it* dread of sin. As the sages said: "'I shall walk in the presence of the Lord in the land of the living' – this is the marketplace."[6]

חַיִּים... חַיִּים... חַיִּים *Life... life... life...* A Midrash that evidently grabbed Rav Kook's attention (for he quotes it on numerous occasions) goes:

> Said the Holy One, blessed be He, to Israel: In the past, I gave you Torah; in the future, I am going to give you life (*ḥayyim*).[7]
>
> Instead of a "Torah of life" ("*Torat Ḥayyim*"), with a side name (*shem levai*), there will be revealed the essential light of life.[8]
>
> The soul of Israel – the source of Torah – will find herself, and once

---

6. Psalms 116:9; *b. Yoma* 71a.
   *OR*, vol. 2, p. 122.
7. The closest Midrash we have to Rav Kook's rendition is *Exodus Rabbah* 48:4: "Said the Holy One, blessed be He, to Israel: In this world, My spirit would bestow upon you wisdom, but in the future, My spirit will enliven you, for it says, 'I will put breath in you and you shall live' [Ezekiel 37:6]." (Rabbi Eliezer Waldman)
8. *SK* 1:777.

## ברכת החודש

*On the* שבת *before* ראש חודש*, the following is said by the* קהל*, and repeated by the* שליח ציבור*:*

יְהִי רָצוֹן מִלְּפָנֶיךָ, יהוה אֱלֹהֵינוּ וֵאלֹהֵי אֲבוֹתֵינוּ, שֶׁתְּחַדֵּשׁ עָלֵינוּ אֶת הַחֹדֶשׁ הַזֶּה לְטוֹבָה וְלִבְרָכָה. וְתִתֶּן לָנוּ חַיִּים אֲרוּכִים, חַיִּים שֶׁל שָׁלוֹם, חַיִּים שֶׁל טוֹבָה, חַיִּים שֶׁל בְּרָכָה, חַיִּים שֶׁל פַּרְנָסָה, חַיִּים שֶׁל חִלּוּץ עֲצָמוֹת, חַיִּים שֶׁיֵּשׁ בָּהֶם יִרְאַת שָׁמַיִם וְיִרְאַת חֵטְא, חַיִּים שֶׁאֵין בָּהֶם בּוּשָׁה וּכְלִמָּה, חַיִּים שֶׁל עֹשֶׁר וְכָבוֹד, חַיִּים שֶׁתְּהֵא בָנוּ אַהֲבַת תּוֹרָה וְיִרְאַת שָׁמַיִם, חַיִּים שֶׁיְּמַלְּאוּ מִשְׁאֲלוֹת לִבֵּנוּ לְטוֹבָה, אָמֵן סֶלָה. ברכות טז:

*The* מולד *is announced, then the* שליח ציבור *takes the* ספר תורה *in his right arm and says:*

מִי שֶׁעָשָׂה נִסִּים לַאֲבוֹתֵינוּ
וְגָאַל אוֹתָם מֵעַבְדוּת לְחֵרוּת
הוּא יִגְאַל אוֹתָנוּ בְּקָרוֹב
וִיקַבֵּץ נִדָּחֵינוּ מֵאַרְבַּע כַּנְפוֹת הָאָרֶץ
חֲבֵרִים כָּל יִשְׂרָאֵל וְנֹאמַר אָמֵן.

*The* שליח ציבור*, then the* קהל*:*

רֹאשׁ חֹדֶשׁ *month* יִהְיֶה בְּיוֹם *day* (*וּבְיוֹם *day* )
הַבָּא עָלֵינוּ וְעַל כָּל יִשְׂרָאֵל לְטוֹבָה.

**if the second day falls on Sunday, then substitute:* וּלְמָחֳרָתוֹ בְּיוֹם

---

ברכת החודש / BLESSING THE NEW MONTH

**חַיִּים שֶׁיֵּשׁ בָּהֶם יִרְאַת שָׁמַיִם וְיִרְאַת חֵטְא** *A life marked by reverence for heaven and dread of sin.*

We are asking that *yir'at shamayim* (reverence for heaven) be mixed together with life. There are people who have reverence for heaven, but it is not integral to their being. Therefore, when they are removed from the hustle and bustle of everyday life, they are God-fearing, but as soon as they enter society and immerse themselves in their business and professional life, their dread of sin flies out the window, so to speak – because it was

*The congregation and Leader continue:*

*In the Diaspora:*
May the Holy One, blessed be He, renew this new month for us and for all His people, the house of Israel, for life and peace, gladness and joy, salvation and consolation; and let us say: Amen.

*In Israel:*
May the Holy One, blessed be He,
renew this month for us
and for all His people the house of Israel,
wherever they are, for good and blessing,
gladness and joy, for salvation and consolation,
livelihood and sustenance, for life and peace,
good tidings and good news,
(*In winter:* for rain in its due season,)
for complete healing and imminent redemption,
and let us say: Amen.

*The following is omitted on days when Taḥanun is not said (see page 208). It is also omitted on a Shabbat before Rosh Ḥodesh (except for the Shabbat before Rosh Ḥodesh Iyar and Rosh Ḥodesh Sivan) and on Shabbat Shekalim, Zakhor, Para and HaḤodesh.*

*On the last day of Pesaḥ, the second day of Shavuot (first day in Israel) and Shemini Atzeret, Yizkor is said, page 858.*

*On other Festivals continue with "Lord my God," page 866.*

אַב הָרַחֲמִים Father of compassion, who dwells on high: may He remember in His compassion the pious, the upright and the blameless – holy communities who sacrificed their lives for the sanctification of God's name. Lovely and pleasant in their lives, in death they were not parted. They were swifter than eagles and stronger than lions to do the will of their Maker and the desire of their Creator. O our God, remember them for good with the other righteous of the world, and may He exact retribution for the shed blood of His servants, as it is written in the Torah of Moses, the man of
God: "O nations, acclaim His people, for He will avenge the blood of His servants, wreak vengeance on His foes, and make clean His people's land." *Deut. 32*
And by Your servants, the prophets, it is written: "I shall cleanse their blood which I have not yet cleansed, says the Lord who dwells in Zion." And in *Joel 4*
the holy Writings it says: "Why should the nations say: Where is their God? Before our eyes, may those nations know that You avenge the shed blood *Ps. 79*

all the secular will be uplifted to the sacred; all the inane to the sublime and exalted.[10]

10. *SK* 8:81 = *OK*, vol. 3, p. 106. The Editor of *Orot ha-Kodesh*, Rabbi David Cohen (the Nazirite) transcribed the last words of the sentence *"ve-ha-meromam me'od"* ("very sublime"). The editors of *Shemonah Kevatsim* transcribed the last words *"ve-ha-meromam me-'az"* ("exalted since time began"). Cf. *Birkat Yotser* for Sabbath: *"Ha-Melekh ha-meromam levado me-'az"* ("the King who alone was exalted since time began").

*The* קהל *and* שליח ציבור *continue:*

*In* חוץ לארץ *say:*

יְחַדְּשֵׁהוּ
הַקָּדוֹשׁ בָּרוּךְ הוּא
עָלֵינוּ
וְעַל כָּל עַמּוֹ בֵּית יִשְׂרָאֵל
לְחַיִּים וּלְשָׁלוֹם
לְשָׂשׂוֹן וּלְשִׂמְחָה
לִישׁוּעָה וּלְנֶחָמָה
וְנֹאמַר אָמֵן.

*in* ארץ ישראל *say:*

יְחַדְּשֵׁהוּ הַקָּדוֹשׁ בָּרוּךְ הוּא
עָלֵינוּ וְעַל כָּל עַמּוֹ בֵּית יִשְׂרָאֵל בְּכָל מָקוֹם שֶׁהֵם
לְטוֹבָה וְלִבְרָכָה, לְשָׂשׂוֹן וּלְשִׂמְחָה
לִישׁוּעָה וּלְנֶחָמָה
לְפַרְנָסָה וּלְכַלְכָּלָה
לְחַיִּים וּלְשָׁלוֹם
לִשְׁמוּעוֹת טוֹבוֹת וְלִבְשׂוֹרוֹת טוֹבוֹת
(בחורף: וְלִגְשָׁמִים בְּעִתָּם)
וְלִרְפוּאָה שְׁלֵמָה, וְלִגְאֻלָּה קְרוֹבָה, וְנֹאמַר אָמֵן.

*The following is omitted on days when* תחנון *is not said (see page 209). It is also omitted on* שבת מברכים *(except for the* שבת *before* ראש חודש אייר *and* ראש חודש סיון*) and on the "*ארבע פרשיות*",* שקלים*,* זכור*,* פרה *and* החודש*.*

*On the last day of* פסח*, the second day of* שבועות *(first day in* ארץ ישראל*) and* שמיני עצרת*,* יזכור *is said, page 859.*

*On other* חגים *continue with* יָהּ אֵלִי*, page 867.*

אַב הָרַחֲמִים שׁוֹכֵן מְרוֹמִים, בְּרַחֲמָיו הָעֲצוּמִים הוּא יִפְקֹד בְּרַחֲמִים
הַחֲסִידִים וְהַיְשָׁרִים וְהַתְּמִימִים, קְהִלּוֹת הַקֹּדֶשׁ שֶׁמָּסְרוּ נַפְשָׁם עַל קְדֻשַּׁת
הַשֵּׁם, הַנֶּאֱהָבִים וְהַנְּעִימִים בְּחַיֵּיהֶם, וּבְמוֹתָם לֹא נִפְרָדוּ, מִנְּשָׁרִים קַלּוּ
וּמֵאֲרָיוֹת גָּבֵרוּ לַעֲשׂוֹת רְצוֹן קוֹנָם וְחֵפֶץ צוּרָם. יִזְכְּרֵם אֱלֹהֵינוּ לְטוֹבָה
עִם שְׁאָר צַדִּיקֵי עוֹלָם, וְיִנְקֹם לְעֵינֵינוּ נִקְמַת דַּם עֲבָדָיו הַשָּׁפוּךְ, כַּכָּתוּב
דברים לב בְּתוֹרַת מֹשֶׁה אִישׁ הָאֱלֹהִים: הַרְנִינוּ גוֹיִם עַמּוֹ, כִּי דַם־עֲבָדָיו יִקּוֹם,
וְנָקָם יָשִׁיב לְצָרָיו, וְכִפֶּר אַדְמָתוֹ עַמּוֹ: וְעַל יְדֵי עֲבָדֶיךָ הַנְּבִיאִים כָּתוּב
יואל ד לֵאמֹר: וְנִקֵּיתִי, דָּמָם לֹא־נִקֵּיתִי, וַיהוה שֹׁכֵן בְּצִיּוֹן: וּבְכִתְבֵי הַקֹּדֶשׁ
תהלים עט נֶאֱמַר: לָמָּה יֹאמְרוּ הַגּוֹיִם אַיֵּה אֱלֹהֵיהֶם, יִוָּדַע בַּגּוֹיִם לְעֵינֵינוּ נִקְמַת

she has found herself, there will shine before her all the letters of Torah with their glorious splendor of life, and there will be called upon Israel an eternal name, "a new name which the mouth of the Lord shall name."[9]

But even the will is but a small branch of the total Tree of Life, and the future strides towards the coming into being of life in its fullness, when

9. Isaiah 62:2; *SK* 6:198 = *OK*, vol. 3, p. 138.

of Your servants." And it also says: "For the Avenger of blood remembers *Ps. 9*
them and does not forget the cry of the afflicted." And it further says: "He *Ps. 110*
will execute judgment among the nations, filled with the dead, crushing
rulers far and wide. From the brook by the wayside he will drink, then he
will hold his head high."

אַשְׁרֵי Happy are those who dwell in Your House; *Ps. 84*
they shall continue to praise You, Selah!
Happy are the people for whom this is so; *Ps. 144*
happy are the people whose God is the LORD.
A song of praise by David. *Ps. 145*

I will exalt You, my God, the King, and bless Your name for ever and all time. Every day I will bless You, and praise Your name for ever and all time. Great is the LORD and greatly to be praised; His greatness is unfathomable. One generation will praise Your works to the next, and tell of Your mighty deeds. On the glorious splendor of Your majesty I will meditate, and on the acts of Your wonders. They shall talk of the power of Your awesome deeds, and I will tell of Your greatness. They shall recite the record of Your great goodness, and sing with joy of Your righteousness. The LORD is gracious and compassionate, slow to anger and great in loving-kindness. The LORD is good to all, and His compassion extends to all His works. All Your works shall thank You, LORD, and Your devoted ones shall bless You. They shall talk of the glory of Your kingship, and speak of Your might. To make known to mankind His mighty deeds and the glorious majesty of His kingship. Your kingdom is an everlasting kingdom, and Your reign is for all generations. The LORD supports all who fall, and raises all who are bowed down. All raise their eyes to You in hope, and You give them their food in due season. You open Your hand, and satisfy every living thing with favor. The LORD is righteous in all His ways, and kind in all He does. The LORD is close to all who call on Him, to all who call on Him in truth. He fulfills the will of those who revere Him; He hears their cry and saves them. The LORD guards all

דַּם־עֲבָדֶיךָ הַשָּׁפוּךְ: וְאוֹמֵר: כִּי־דֹרֵשׁ דָּמִים אוֹתָם זָכָר, לֹא־שָׁכַח צַעֲקַת תהלים ט
עֲנָוִים: וְאוֹמֵר: יָדִין בַּגּוֹיִם מָלֵא גְוִיּוֹת, מָחַץ רֹאשׁ עַל־אֶרֶץ רַבָּה: מִנַּחַל תהלים קי
בַּדֶּרֶךְ יִשְׁתֶּה, עַל־כֵּן יָרִים רֹאשׁ:

אַשְׁרֵי יוֹשְׁבֵי בֵיתֶךָ, עוֹד יְהַלְלוּךָ סֶּלָה: תהלים פד
אַשְׁרֵי הָעָם שֶׁכָּכָה לּוֹ, אַשְׁרֵי הָעָם שֶׁיהוה אֱלֹהָיו: תהלים קמד
תְּהִלָּה לְדָוִד תהלים קמה

אֲרוֹמִמְךָ אֱלוֹהַי הַמֶּלֶךְ, וַאֲבָרְכָה שִׁמְךָ לְעוֹלָם וָעֶד:
בְּכָל־יוֹם אֲבָרְכֶךָּ, וַאֲהַלְלָה שִׁמְךָ לְעוֹלָם וָעֶד:
גָּדוֹל יהוה וּמְהֻלָּל מְאֹד, וְלִגְדֻלָּתוֹ אֵין חֵקֶר:
דּוֹר לְדוֹר יְשַׁבַּח מַעֲשֶׂיךָ, וּגְבוּרֹתֶיךָ יַגִּידוּ:
הֲדַר כְּבוֹד הוֹדֶךָ, וְדִבְרֵי נִפְלְאֹתֶיךָ אָשִׂיחָה:
וֶעֱזוּז נוֹרְאֹתֶיךָ יֹאמֵרוּ, וּגְדוּלָּתְךָ אֲסַפְּרֶנָּה:
זֵכֶר רַב־טוּבְךָ יַבִּיעוּ, וְצִדְקָתְךָ יְרַנֵּנוּ:
חַנּוּן וְרַחוּם יהוה, אֶרֶךְ אַפַּיִם וּגְדָל־חָסֶד:
טוֹב־יהוה לַכֹּל, וְרַחֲמָיו עַל־כָּל־מַעֲשָׂיו:
יוֹדוּךָ יהוה כָּל־מַעֲשֶׂיךָ, וַחֲסִידֶיךָ יְבָרְכוּכָה:
כְּבוֹד מַלְכוּתְךָ יֹאמֵרוּ, וּגְבוּרָתְךָ יְדַבֵּרוּ:
לְהוֹדִיעַ לִבְנֵי הָאָדָם גְּבוּרֹתָיו, וּכְבוֹד הֲדַר מַלְכוּתוֹ:
מַלְכוּתְךָ מַלְכוּת כָּל־עֹלָמִים, וּמֶמְשַׁלְתְּךָ בְּכָל־דּוֹר וָדֹר:
סוֹמֵךְ יהוה לְכָל־הַנֹּפְלִים, וְזוֹקֵף לְכָל־הַכְּפוּפִים:
עֵינֵי־כֹל אֵלֶיךָ יְשַׂבֵּרוּ, וְאַתָּה נוֹתֵן־לָהֶם אֶת־אָכְלָם בְּעִתּוֹ:
פּוֹתֵחַ אֶת־יָדֶךָ, וּמַשְׂבִּיעַ לְכָל־חַי רָצוֹן:
צַדִּיק יהוה בְּכָל־דְּרָכָיו, וְחָסִיד בְּכָל־מַעֲשָׂיו:
קָרוֹב יהוה לְכָל־קֹרְאָיו, לְכֹל אֲשֶׁר יִקְרָאֻהוּ בֶאֱמֶת:
רְצוֹן־יְרֵאָיו יַעֲשֶׂה, וְאֶת־שַׁוְעָתָם יִשְׁמַע, וְיוֹשִׁיעֵם:

who love Him, but all the wicked He will destroy. ▸ My mouth shall speak the praise of the LORD, and all creatures shall bless His holy name for ever and all time.

We will bless the LORD now and for ever. Halleluya! Ps. 115

## RETURNING THE TORAH TO THE ARK

*The Ark is opened. All stand. The Leader takes the Torah scroll and says:*

יְהַלְלוּ Let them praise the name of the LORD, Ps. 148
for His name alone is sublime.

*The congregation responds:*

הוֹדוֹ His majesty is above earth and heaven.
He has raised the horn of His people,
for the glory of all His devoted ones,
the children of Israel, the people close to Him. Halleluya!

*While the Torah scroll is being returned to the Ark, on Shabbat say:*

מִזְמוֹר לְדָוִד A psalm of David. Render to the LORD, you angelic powers, Ps. 29
render to the LORD glory and might. Render to the LORD the glory due to His name. Bow to the LORD in the beauty of holiness. The LORD's voice echoes over the waters; the God of glory thunders; the LORD is over the mighty waters. The LORD's voice in power, the LORD's voice in beauty, the LORD's voice breaks cedars, the LORD shatters the cedars of Lebanon. He makes Lebanon skip like a calf, Sirion like a young wild ox. The LORD's voice cleaves flames of fire. ▸ The LORD's voice makes the desert quake, the LORD shakes the desert of Kadesh. The LORD's voice makes hinds calve and strips the forests bare, and in His temple all say: "Glory!" The LORD sat enthroned at the Flood, the LORD sits enthroned as King for ever. The LORD will give strength to His people; the LORD will bless His people with peace.

*On a Yom Tov occurring on a weekday say:*

לְדָוִד מִזְמוֹר A psalm of David. The earth is the LORD's and all it contains, the Ps. 24
world and all who live in it. For He founded it on the seas and established it on the streams. Who may climb the mountain of the LORD? Who may stand in His holy place? He who has clean hands and a pure heart, who has not taken My name in vain, or sworn deceitfully. He shall receive blessing

שׁוֹמֵר יהוה אֶת־כָּל־אֹהֲבָיו, וְאֵת כָּל־הָרְשָׁעִים יַשְׁמִיד:
› תְּהִלַּת יהוה יְדַבֶּר פִּי, וִיבָרֵךְ כָּל־בָּשָׂר שֵׁם קָדְשׁוֹ לְעוֹלָם וָעֶד:
וַאֲנַחְנוּ נְבָרֵךְ יָהּ מֵעַתָּה וְעַד־עוֹלָם, הַלְלוּיָהּ: תהלים קטו

# הכנסת ספר תורה

*The* ארון קודש *is opened. All stand. The* שליח ציבור *takes the* ספר תורה *and says:*

יְהַלְלוּ אֶת־שֵׁם יהוה, כִּי־נִשְׂגָּב שְׁמוֹ, לְבַדּוֹ תהלים קמח

*The* קהל *responds:*

הוֹדוֹ עַל־אֶרֶץ וְשָׁמָיִם:
וַיָּרֶם קֶרֶן לְעַמּוֹ, תְּהִלָּה לְכָל־חֲסִידָיו
לִבְנֵי יִשְׂרָאֵל עַם קְרֹבוֹ, הַלְלוּיָהּ:

*While the* ספר תורה *is being returned to the* ארון קודש*, on* שבת *say:*

מִזְמוֹר לְדָוִד, הָבוּ לַיהוה בְּנֵי אֵלִים, הָבוּ לַיהוה כָּבוֹד וָעֹז: הָבוּ תהלים כט
לַיהוה כְּבוֹד שְׁמוֹ, הִשְׁתַּחֲווּ לַיהוה בְּהַדְרַת־קֹדֶשׁ: קוֹל יהוה
עַל־הַמָּיִם, אֵל־הַכָּבוֹד הִרְעִים, יהוה עַל־מַיִם רַבִּים: קוֹל־יהוה
בַּכֹּחַ, קוֹל יהוה בֶּהָדָר: קוֹל יהוה שֹׁבֵר אֲרָזִים, וַיְשַׁבֵּר יהוה אֶת־
אַרְזֵי הַלְּבָנוֹן: וַיַּרְקִידֵם כְּמוֹ־עֵגֶל, לְבָנוֹן וְשִׂרְיוֹן כְּמוֹ בֶן־רְאֵמִים:
קוֹל־יהוה חֹצֵב לַהֲבוֹת אֵשׁ: › קוֹל יהוה יָחִיל מִדְבָּר, יָחִיל יהוה
מִדְבַּר קָדֵשׁ: קוֹל יהוה יְחוֹלֵל אַיָּלוֹת וַיֶּחֱשֹׂף יְעָרוֹת, וּבְהֵיכָלוֹ, כֻּלּוֹ
אֹמֵר כָּבוֹד: יהוה לַמַּבּוּל יָשָׁב, וַיֵּשֶׁב יהוה מֶלֶךְ לְעוֹלָם: יהוה עֹז
לְעַמּוֹ יִתֵּן, יהוה יְבָרֵךְ אֶת־עַמּוֹ בַשָּׁלוֹם:

*On a* יום טוב *occurring on a weekday say:*

לְדָוִד מִזְמוֹר, לַיהוה הָאָרֶץ וּמְלוֹאָהּ, תֵּבֵל וְיֹשְׁבֵי בָהּ: כִּי־הוּא עַל־ תהלים כד
יַמִּים יְסָדָהּ, וְעַל־נְהָרוֹת יְכוֹנְנֶהָ: מִי־יַעֲלֶה בְהַר־יהוה, וּמִי־יָקוּם
בִּמְקוֹם קָדְשׁוֹ: נְקִי כַפַּיִם וּבַר־לֵבָב, אֲשֶׁר לֹא־נָשָׂא לַשָּׁוְא נַפְשִׁי וְלֹא
נִשְׁבַּע לְמִרְמָה: יִשָּׂא בְרָכָה מֵאֵת יהוה, וּצְדָקָה מֵאֱלֹהֵי יִשְׁעוֹ:

from the Lord, and just reward from God, his salvation. This is a generation of those who seek Him, the descendants of Jacob who seek Your presence, Selah! Lift up your heads, O gates; be uplifted, eternal doors, so that the King of glory may enter. Who is the King of glory? It is the Lord, strong and mighty, the Lord mighty in battle. Lift up your heads, O gates; lift them up, eternal doors, so that the King of glory may enter. ▸ Who is He, the King of glory? The Lord of hosts, He is the King of glory, Selah!

*As the Torah scroll is placed into the Ark, all say:*

וּבְנֻחֹה יֹאמַר When the Ark came to rest, Moses would say: "Return, *Num. 10*
O Lord, to the myriad thousands of Israel." Advance, Lord, to Your *Ps. 132*
resting place, You and Your mighty Ark. Your priests are clothed
in righteousness, and Your devoted ones sing in joy. For the sake
of Your servant David, do not reject Your anointed one. For I give *Prov. 4*
you good instruction; do not forsake My Torah. It is a tree of life *Prov. 3*
to those who grasp it, and those who uphold it are happy. Its ways
are ways of pleasantness, and all its paths are peace. ▸ Turn us back, *Lam. 5*
O Lord, to You, and we will return. Renew our days as of old.

*The Ark is closed.*

## HALF KADDISH

*Leader:* יִתְגַּדַּל Magnified and sanctified may His great name be,
in the world He created by His will.
May He establish His kingdom
in your lifetime and in your days,
and in the lifetime of all the house of Israel,
swiftly and soon –
and say: Amen.

*All:* May His great name be blessed for ever and all time.

*Leader:* Blessed and praised, glorified and exalted,
raised and honored, uplifted and lauded
be the name of the Holy One, blessed be He,
beyond any blessing,
song, praise and consolation uttered in the world –
and say: Amen.

זֶה דּוֹר דֹּרְשָׁו, מְבַקְשֵׁי פָנֶיךָ, יַעֲקֹב, סֶלָה: שְׂאוּ שְׁעָרִים רָאשֵׁיכֶם, וְהִנָּשְׂאוּ פִּתְחֵי עוֹלָם, וְיָבוֹא מֶלֶךְ הַכָּבוֹד: מִי זֶה מֶלֶךְ הַכָּבוֹד, יהוה עִזּוּז וְגִבּוֹר, יהוה גִּבּוֹר מִלְחָמָה: שְׂאוּ שְׁעָרִים רָאשֵׁיכֶם, וּשְׂאוּ פִּתְחֵי עוֹלָם, וְיָבֹא מֶלֶךְ הַכָּבוֹד: ‹ מִי הוּא זֶה מֶלֶךְ הַכָּבוֹד, יהוה צְבָאוֹת הוּא מֶלֶךְ הַכָּבוֹד, סֶלָה:

*As the* ספר תורה *is placed into the* ארון קודש*, all say:*

וּבְנֻחֹה יֹאמַר, שׁוּבָה יהוה רִבְבוֹת אַלְפֵי יִשְׂרָאֵל: קוּמָה יהוה במדבר י תהלים קלב
לִמְנוּחָתֶךָ, אַתָּה וַאֲרוֹן עֻזֶּךָ: כֹּהֲנֶיךָ יִלְבְּשׁוּ־צֶדֶק, וַחֲסִידֶיךָ יְרַנֵּנוּ:
בַּעֲבוּר דָּוִד עַבְדֶּךָ אַל־תָּשֵׁב פְּנֵי מְשִׁיחֶךָ: כִּי לֶקַח טוֹב נָתַתִּי משלי ד
לָכֶם, תּוֹרָתִי אַל־תַּעֲזֹבוּ: עֵץ־חַיִּים הִיא לַמַּחֲזִיקִים בָּהּ, וְתֹמְכֶיהָ משלי ג
מְאֻשָּׁר: דְּרָכֶיהָ דַרְכֵי־נֹעַם וְכָל־נְתִיבֹתֶיהָ שָׁלוֹם: ‹ הֲשִׁיבֵנוּ יהוה איכה ה
אֵלֶיךָ וְנָשׁוּבָה, חַדֵּשׁ יָמֵינוּ כְּקֶדֶם:

*The* ארון קודש *is closed.*

### חצי קדיש

ש״ץ: יִתְגַּדַּל וְיִתְקַדַּשׁ שְׁמֵהּ רַבָּא (קהל: אָמֵן)
בְּעָלְמָא דִּי בְרָא כִרְעוּתֵהּ, וְיַמְלִיךְ מַלְכוּתֵהּ
בְּחַיֵּיכוֹן וּבְיוֹמֵיכוֹן וּבְחַיֵּי דְכָל בֵּית יִשְׂרָאֵל
בַּעֲגָלָא וּבִזְמַן קָרִיב, וְאִמְרוּ אָמֵן. (קהל: אָמֵן)

קהל וש״ץ: יְהֵא שְׁמֵהּ רַבָּא מְבָרַךְ לְעָלַם וּלְעָלְמֵי עָלְמַיָּא.

ש״ץ: יִתְבָּרַךְ וְיִשְׁתַּבַּח וְיִתְפָּאַר וְיִתְרוֹמַם וְיִתְנַשֵּׂא
וְיִתְהַדָּר וְיִתְעַלֶּה וְיִתְהַלָּל
שְׁמֵהּ דְּקֻדְשָׁא בְּרִיךְ הוּא (קהל: בְּרִיךְ הוּא)
לְעֵלָּא מִן כָּל בִּרְכָתָא / בשבת שובה: לְעֵלָּא לְעֵלָּא מִכָּל בִּרְכָתָא/
וְשִׁירָתָא, תֻּשְׁבְּחָתָא וְנֶחֱמָתָא
דַּאֲמִירָן בְּעָלְמָא, וְאִמְרוּ אָמֵן. (קהל: אָמֵן)

# Musaf for Shabbat

*On Yom Tov (including Shabbat Ḥol HaMo'ed) say the Musaf for Festivals on page 868.*

## THE AMIDA

*The following prayer, until "in former years" on page 622, is said silently, standing with feet together. If there is a minyan, the Amida is repeated aloud by the Leader. Take three steps forward and at the points indicated by ▾, bend the knees at the first word, bow at the second, and stand straight before saying God's name.*

When I proclaim the LORD's name, give glory to our God. *Deut. 32*
O LORD, open my lips, so that my mouth may declare Your praise. *Ps. 51*

### PATRIARCHS

▾בָּרוּךְ▾ Blessed are You, LORD our God and God of our fathers,
God of Abraham, God of Isaac and God of Jacob;
the great, mighty and awesome God, God Most High,
who bestows acts of loving-kindness and creates all,
who remembers the loving-kindness of the fathers
and will bring a Redeemer to their children's children
for the sake of His name, in love.

*On Shabbat Shuva:* Remember us for life, O King who desires life,
and write us in the book of life – for Your sake, O God of life.

King, Helper, Savior, Shield:
▾Blessed are You, LORD, Shield of Abraham.

### DIVINE MIGHT

אַתָּה גִּבּוֹר You are eternally mighty, LORD.
You give life to the dead and have great power to save.

*The phrase "He makes the wind blow and the rain fall" is added from Simḥat Torah until Pesaḥ. In Israel the phrase "He causes the dew to fall" is added from Pesaḥ until Shemini Atzeret. See laws 129–131.*

*In fall & winter:* He makes the wind blow and the rain fall.
*In Israel, in spring & summer:* He causes the dew to fall.

He sustains the living with loving-kindness,
and with great compassion revives the dead.
He supports the fallen, heals the sick, sets captives free,
and keeps His faith with those who sleep in the dust.

# מוסף לשבת

*On* יום טוב *(including* שבת חול המועד*) say the* מוסף לשלוש רגלים *on page 869.*

## עמידה

*The following prayer, until* קַדְמֹנִיּוֹת *on page 623, is said standing with feet together. If there is a* מנין*, the* עמידה *is repeated aloud by the* שליח ציבור*. Take three steps forward and at the points indicated by* ˺*, bend the knees at the first word, bow at the second, and stand straight before saying God's name.*

כִּי שֵׁם יהוה אֶקְרָא, הָבוּ גֹדֶל לֵאלֹהֵינוּ: דברים לב

אֲדֹנָי, שְׂפָתַי תִּפְתָּח, וּפִי יַגִּיד תְּהִלָּתֶךָ: תהלים נא

### אבות

˺בָּרוּךְ ˺אַתָּה יהוה, אֱלֹהֵינוּ וֵאלֹהֵי אֲבוֹתֵינוּ
אֱלֹהֵי אַבְרָהָם, אֱלֹהֵי יִצְחָק, וֵאלֹהֵי יַעֲקֹב
הָאֵל הַגָּדוֹל הַגִּבּוֹר וְהַנּוֹרָא, אֵל עֶלְיוֹן
גּוֹמֵל חֲסָדִים טוֹבִים, וְקוֹנֵה הַכֹּל, וְזוֹכֵר חַסְדֵי אָבוֹת
וּמֵבִיא גוֹאֵל לִבְנֵי בְנֵיהֶם לְמַעַן שְׁמוֹ בְּאַהֲבָה.

בשבת שובה: זָכְרֵנוּ לְחַיִּים, מֶלֶךְ חָפֵץ בַּחַיִּים
וְכָתְבֵנוּ בְּסֵפֶר הַחַיִּים, לְמַעַנְךָ אֱלֹהִים חַיִּים.

מֶלֶךְ עוֹזֵר וּמוֹשִׁיעַ וּמָגֵן.
˺בָּרוּךְ ˺אַתָּה יהוה, מָגֵן אַבְרָהָם.

### גבורות

אַתָּה גִּבּוֹר לְעוֹלָם, אֲדֹנָי
מְחַיֵּה מֵתִים אַתָּה, רַב לְהוֹשִׁיעַ

*The phrase* מַשִּׁיב הָרוּחַ *is added from* שמחת תורה *until* פסח*.*
*In* ארץ ישראל *the phrase* מוֹרִיד הַטָּל *is added from* פסח *until* שמיני עצרת*. See laws 129–131.*

בחורף: מַשִּׁיב הָרוּחַ וּמוֹרִיד הַגֶּשֶׁם / בארץ ישראל בקיץ: מוֹרִיד הַטָּל

מְכַלְכֵּל חַיִּים בְּחֶסֶד, מְחַיֵּה מֵתִים בְּרַחֲמִים רַבִּים
סוֹמֵךְ נוֹפְלִים, וְרוֹפֵא חוֹלִים, וּמַתִּיר אֲסוּרִים
וּמְקַיֵּם אֱמוּנָתוֹ לִישֵׁנֵי עָפָר.

Who is like You, Master of might, and who can compare to You,
O King who brings death and gives life, and makes salvation grow?

*On Shabbat Shuva:* Who is like You, compassionate Father,
who remembers His creatures in compassion, for life?

Faithful are You to revive the dead.
Blessed are You, Lord, who revives the dead.

*When saying the Amida silently, continue with "You are holy" on the next page.*

---

KEDUSHA *During the Leader's Repetition, the following is said standing with feet together, rising on the toes at the words indicated by ▴.*

*Cong. then Leader:* נַעֲרִיצְךָ We will revere and sanctify You with the words uttered by the holy Seraphim who sanctify Your name in the Sanctuary; as is written by Your prophet: "They call out to one another, saying: *Is. 6*

*Cong. then Leader:* ▴Holy, ▴holy, ▴holy is the Lord of hosts; the whole world is filled with His glory."
His glory fills the universe. His ministering angels ask each other, "Where is the place of His glory?" Those facing them reply "Blessed –"

*Cong. then Leader:* ▴"Blessed is the Lord's glory from His place." *Ezek. 3*
From His place may He turn with compassion and be gracious to the people who proclaim the unity of His name, morning and evening, every day, continually, twice each day reciting in love the Shema:

*Cong. then Leader:* "Listen, Israel, the Lord is our God, the Lord is One." *Deut. 6*
He is our God, He is our Father, He is our King, He is our Savior – and He, in His compassion, will let us hear a second time in the presence of all that lives, His promise to be "Your God." "I am the Lord your God." *Num. 15*

*Leader:* And in Your holy Writings it is written:
*Cong. then Leader:* ▴"The Lord shall reign for ever. He is your God, Zion, from generation to generation, Halleluya!" *Ps. 146*

*Leader:* From generation to generation we will declare Your greatness, and we will proclaim Your holiness for evermore. Your praise, our God, shall not leave our mouth forever, for You, God, are a great and holy King. Blessed are You, Lord, the holy God.
/ *On Shabbat Shuva:* the holy King./

*The Leader continues on the next page with "You instituted the Sabbath" on Shabbat, and "Long ago You formed" on Rosh Ḥodesh.*

מִי כָמְוֹךָ, בַּעַל גְּבוּרוֹת, וּמִי דּוֹמֶה לָּךְ
מֶלֶךְ, מֵמִית וּמְחַיֶּה וּמַצְמִיחַ יְשׁוּעָה.

בשבת שובה: מִי כָמְוֹךָ אַב הָרַחֲמִים, זוֹכֵר יְצוּרָיו לְחַיִּים בְּרַחֲמִים.

וְנֶאֱמָן אַתָּה לְהַחֲיוֹת מֵתִים.
בָּרוּךְ אַתָּה יהוה, מְחַיֵּה הַמֵּתִים.

*When saying the* עמידה *silently, continue with* אַתָּה קָדוֹשׁ *on the next page.*

---

קדושה

*During the* חזרת הש״ץ*, the following is said standing with feet together, rising on the toes at the words indicated by* ▲.

קהל *then* ש״ץ: נַעֲרִיצְךָ וְנַקְדִּישְׁךָ כְּסוֹד שִׂיחַ שַׂרְפֵי קֹדֶשׁ, הַמַּקְדִּישִׁים שִׁמְךָ בַּקֹּדֶשׁ,
כַּכָּתוּב עַל יַד נְבִיאֶךָ: וְקָרָא זֶה אֶל־זֶה וְאָמַר ישעיה ו

קהל *then* ש״ץ: ▲קָדוֹשׁ, ▲קָדוֹשׁ, ▲קָדוֹשׁ, יהוה צְבָאוֹת, מְלֹא כָל הָאָרֶץ כְּבוֹדוֹ:
כְּבוֹדוֹ מָלֵא עוֹלָם, מְשָׁרְתָיו שׁוֹאֲלִים זֶה לָזֶה, אַיֵּה מְקוֹם כְּבוֹדוֹ
לְעֻמָּתָם בָּרוּךְ יֹאמֵרוּ

קהל *then* ש״ץ: ▲בָּרוּךְ כְּבוֹד־יהוה מִמְּקוֹמוֹ: יחזקאל ג
מִמְּקוֹמוֹ הוּא יִפֶן בְּרַחֲמִים, וְיָחֹן עַם הַמְיַחֲדִים שְׁמוֹ, עֶרֶב וָבְקֶר
בְּכָל יוֹם תָּמִיד, פַּעֲמַיִם בְּאַהֲבָה שְׁמַע אוֹמְרִים

קהל *then* ש״ץ: שְׁמַע יִשְׂרָאֵל, יהוה אֱלֹהֵינוּ, יהוה אֶחָד: דברים ו
הוּא אֱלֹהֵינוּ, הוּא אָבִינוּ, הוּא מַלְכֵּנוּ, הוּא מוֹשִׁיעֵנוּ, וְהוּא
יַשְׁמִיעֵנוּ בְּרַחֲמָיו שֵׁנִית לְעֵינֵי כָּל חָי, לִהְיוֹת לָכֶם לֵאלֹהִים, אֲנִי במדבר טו
יהוה אֱלֹהֵיכֶם:

ש״ץ: וּבְדִבְרֵי קָדְשְׁךָ כָּתוּב לֵאמֹר

קהל *then* ש״ץ: ▲יִמְלֹךְ יהוה לְעוֹלָם, אֱלֹהַיִךְ צִיּוֹן לְדֹר וָדֹר, הַלְלוּיָהּ: תהלים קמו

ש״ץ: לְדוֹר וָדוֹר נַגִּיד גָּדְלֶךָ, וּלְנֵצַח נְצָחִים קְדֻשָּׁתְךָ נַקְדִּישׁ, וְשִׁבְחֲךָ
אֱלֹהֵינוּ מִפִּינוּ לֹא יָמוּשׁ לְעוֹלָם וָעֶד, כִּי אֵל מֶלֶךְ גָּדוֹל וְקָדוֹשׁ
אָתָּה. בָּרוּךְ אַתָּה יהוה, הָאֵל הַקָּדוֹשׁ./ בשבת שובה: הַמֶּלֶךְ הַקָּדוֹשׁ./

*The* שליח ציבור *continues on the next page with* תִּכַּנְתָּ שַׁבָּת *on* שבת*, and* אַתָּה יָצַרְתָּ *on* ראש חודש.

HOLINESS

אַתָּה קָדוֹשׁ You are holy and Your name is holy,
and holy ones praise You daily, Selah!
Blessed are You, Lord,
the holy God. / *On Shabbat Shuva:* the holy King./

*(If forgotten, repeat the Amida.)*

*On Shabbat Rosh Ḥodesh say "Long ago You formed" below the line.*

HOLINESS OF THE DAY

תִּכַּנְתָּ שַׁבָּת You instituted the Sabbath, You favored its offerings.
You commanded its specific laws
along with the order of its libations.
Those who delight in it inherit eternal glory,
those who relish it merit life,
and those who love its teachings have chosen greatness.
Even before Sinai they were commanded about it.
Then You, Lord our God, commanded us to offer on it
the additional offering of the Sabbath in the proper way.

---

*On Shabbat Rosh Ḥodesh:*

אַתָּה יָצַרְתָּ Long ago You formed Your world,
completing Your work on the seventh day.
You loved us. You favored us,
raising us above all languages.
You made us holy through Your commandments,
brought us near, O our King, to Your service,
and called us by Your great and holy name.
You also gave us in love, Lord our God,
Sabbaths for rest and New Moons for atonement.
But because we and our ancestors sinned against You,
our city was laid waste, our Sanctuary made desolate,
our splendor exiled, and the glory gone from our House of life.
We can no longer fulfill our obligations in Your chosen House,
the great and holy Temple called by Your name,
because of the hand that was stretched out against Your Sanctuary.

*Continue below the line on the next page.*

קדושת השם

אַתָּה קָדוֹשׁ וְשִׁמְךָ קָדוֹשׁ
וּקְדוֹשִׁים בְּכָל יוֹם יְהַלְלוּךָ סֶּלָה.
בָּרוּךְ אַתָּה יהוה, הָאֵל הַקָּדוֹשׁ. / בשבת שובה: הַמֶּלֶךְ הַקָּדוֹשׁ./

(*If forgotten, repeat the* עמידה.)

*On* שבת ראש חודש *say* אַתָּה יָצַרְתָּ *below the line.*

קדושת היום

תִּכַּנְתָּ שַׁבָּת, רָצִיתָ קָרְבְּנוֹתֶיהָ
צִוִּיתָ פֵּרוּשֶׁיהָ עִם סִדּוּרֵי נְסָכֶיהָ
מְעַנְּגֶיהָ לְעוֹלָם כָּבוֹד יִנְחָלוּ, טוֹעֲמֶיהָ חַיִּים זָכוּ
וְגַם הָאוֹהֲבִים דְּבָרֶיהָ גְּדֻלָּה בָּחָרוּ.
אָז מִסִּינַי נִצְטַוּוּ עָלֶיהָ
וַתְּצַוֵּנוּ יהוה אֱלֹהֵינוּ לְהַקְרִיב בָּהּ קָרְבַּן מוּסַף שַׁבָּת כָּרָאוּי.

---

בשבת ראש חודש:

אַתָּה יָצַרְתָּ עוֹלָמְךָ מִקֶּדֶם, כִּלִּיתָ מְלַאכְתְּךָ בַּיּוֹם הַשְּׁבִיעִי
אָהַבְתָּ אוֹתָנוּ וְרָצִיתָ בָּנוּ, וְרוֹמַמְתָּנוּ מִכָּל הַלְּשׁוֹנוֹת
וְקִדַּשְׁתָּנוּ בְּמִצְוֹתֶיךָ, וְקֵרַבְתָּנוּ מַלְכֵּנוּ לַעֲבוֹדָתֶךָ
וְשִׁמְךָ הַגָּדוֹל וְהַקָּדוֹשׁ עָלֵינוּ קָרָאתָ.
וַתִּתֶּן לָנוּ יהוה אֱלֹהֵינוּ בְּאַהֲבָה
שַׁבָּתוֹת לִמְנוּחָה וְרָאשֵׁי חֳדָשִׁים לְכַפָּרָה.
וּלְפִי שֶׁחָטָאנוּ לְפָנֶיךָ אֲנַחְנוּ וַאֲבוֹתֵינוּ
חָרְבָה עִירֵנוּ, וְשָׁמֵם בֵּית מִקְדָּשֵׁנוּ, וְגָלָה יְקָרֵנוּ, וְנֻטַּל כָּבוֹד מִבֵּית חַיֵּינוּ
וְאֵין אֲנַחְנוּ יְכוֹלִים לַעֲשׂוֹת חוֹבוֹתֵינוּ בְּבֵית בְּחִירָתֶךָ
בַּבַּיִת הַגָּדוֹל וְהַקָּדוֹשׁ שֶׁנִּקְרָא שִׁמְךָ עָלָיו
מִפְּנֵי הַיָּד שֶׁנִּשְׁתַּלְּחָה בְּמִקְדָּשֶׁךָ.

*Continue below the line on the next page.*

יְהִי רָצוֹן May it be Your will,
Lord our God and God of our ancestors, to lead us back in joy
to our land and to plant us within our borders.
There we will prepare for You our obligatory offerings:
the regular daily offerings in their order,
and the additional offerings according to their laws.

וְאֶת מוּסַף And the additional offering of this Sabbath day
we will prepare and offer before You in love,
in accord with Your will's commandment,
as You wrote for us in Your Torah
through Your servant Moses, by Your own word,
as it is said:

"On the Sabbath day, *Num. 28*
make an offering of two lambs a year old, without blemish,
together with two-tenths of an ephah of fine flour
mixed with oil as a meal-offering, and its appropriate libation.
This is the burnt-offering for every Sabbath,
in addition to the regular daily burnt-offering and its libation."

---

May it be Your will, Lord our God and God of our ancestors,
to lead us back in joy to our land, and to plant us within our borders.
There we will prepare for You our obligatory offerings:
the regular daily offerings in their order,
and the additional offerings according to their laws.
And the additional offerings of this Sabbath day, and of this New Moon day,
we will prepare and offer before You in love,
in accord with Your will's commandment,
as You wrote for us in Your Torah through Your servant Moses,
by Your own word, as it is said:

"On the Sabbath day, make an offering of two lambs a year old, without blemish, *Num. 28*
together with two-tenths of an ephah of fine flour mixed with oil as a meal-offering, and its appropriate libation. This is the burnt-offering for every Sabbath, in addition to the regular daily burnt-offering and its libation."

"And on your new moons, present as a burnt-offering to the Lord two young bulls, *Num. 28*
one ram, and seven yearling lambs without blemish."

*Continue below the line on the next page.*

יְהִי רָצוֹן מִלְּפָנֶיךָ, יהוה אֱלֹהֵינוּ וֵאלֹהֵי אֲבוֹתֵינוּ
שֶׁתַּעֲלֵנוּ בְשִׂמְחָה לְאַרְצֵנוּ וְתִטָּעֵנוּ בִּגְבוּלֵנוּ
וְשָׁם נַעֲשֶׂה לְפָנֶיךָ אֶת קָרְבְּנוֹת חוֹבוֹתֵינוּ
תְּמִידִים כְּסִדְרָם וּמוּסָפִים כְּהִלְכָתָם.

וְאֶת מוּסַף יוֹם הַשַּׁבָּת הַזֶּה
נַעֲשֶׂה וְנַקְרִיב לְפָנֶיךָ בְּאַהֲבָה כְּמִצְוַת רְצוֹנֶךָ
כְּמוֹ שֶׁכָּתַבְתָּ עָלֵינוּ בְּתוֹרָתֶךָ
עַל יְדֵי מֹשֶׁה עַבְדֶּךָ מִפִּי כְבוֹדֶךָ
כָּאָמוּר

וּבְיוֹם הַשַּׁבָּת שְׁנֵי־כְבָשִׂים בְּנֵי־שָׁנָה תְּמִימִם במדבר כח
וּשְׁנֵי עֶשְׂרֹנִים סֹלֶת מִנְחָה בְּלוּלָה בַשֶּׁמֶן וְנִסְכּוֹ:
עֹלַת שַׁבַּת בְּשַׁבַּתּוֹ, עַל־עֹלַת הַתָּמִיד וְנִסְכָּהּ:

---

יְהִי רָצוֹן מִלְּפָנֶיךָ, יהוה אֱלֹהֵינוּ וֵאלֹהֵי אֲבוֹתֵינוּ
שֶׁתַּעֲלֵנוּ בְשִׂמְחָה לְאַרְצֵנוּ וְתִטָּעֵנוּ בִּגְבוּלֵנוּ
וְשָׁם נַעֲשֶׂה לְפָנֶיךָ אֶת קָרְבְּנוֹת חוֹבוֹתֵינוּ
תְּמִידִים כְּסִדְרָם וּמוּסָפִים כְּהִלְכָתָם.
וְאֶת מוּסְפֵי יוֹם הַשַּׁבָּת הַזֶּה וְיוֹם רֹאשׁ הַחֹדֶשׁ הַזֶּה
נַעֲשֶׂה וְנַקְרִיב לְפָנֶיךָ בְּאַהֲבָה כְּמִצְוַת רְצוֹנֶךָ
כְּמוֹ שֶׁכָּתַבְתָּ עָלֵינוּ בְּתוֹרָתֶךָ עַל יְדֵי מֹשֶׁה עַבְדֶּךָ
מִפִּי כְבוֹדֶךָ, כָּאָמוּר

וּבְיוֹם הַשַּׁבָּת שְׁנֵי־כְבָשִׂים בְּנֵי־שָׁנָה תְּמִימִם, וּשְׁנֵי עֶשְׂרֹנִים סֹלֶת מִנְחָה במדבר כח
בְּלוּלָה בַשֶּׁמֶן וְנִסְכּוֹ: עֹלַת שַׁבַּת בְּשַׁבַּתּוֹ, עַל־עֹלַת הַתָּמִיד וְנִסְכָּהּ:

וּבְרָאשֵׁי חָדְשֵׁיכֶם תַּקְרִיבוּ עֹלָה לַיהוה, פָּרִים בְּנֵי־בָקָר שְׁנַיִם, וְאַיִל אֶחָד, במדבר כח
כְּבָשִׂים בְּנֵי־שָׁנָה שִׁבְעָה, תְּמִימִם:

*Continue below the line on the next page.*

יִשְׂמְחוּ Those who keep the Sabbath and call it a delight
shall rejoice in Your kingship.
The people who sanctify the seventh day shall all be satisfied
and take delight in Your goodness,
for You favored the seventh day and declared it holy.
You called it "most desirable of days"
in remembrance of Creation.

אֱלֹהֵינוּ Our God and God of our ancestors,
find favor in our rest.
Make us holy through Your commandments
and grant us our share in Your Torah.
Satisfy us with Your goodness, grant us joy in Your salvation,
and purify our hearts to serve You in truth.
In love and favor, LORD our God,
grant us as our heritage Your holy Sabbath,
so that Israel who sanctify Your name may find rest on it.
Blessed are You, LORD, who sanctifies the Sabbath.

---

And their meal-offerings and wine-libations as ordained: three-tenths of an ephah for each bull, two-tenths of an ephah for the ram, one-tenth of an ephah for each lamb, wine for the libations, a male goat for atonement, and two regular daily offerings according to their law.

Those who keep the Sabbath and call it a delight shall rejoice in Your kingship. The people who sanctify the seventh day shall all be satisfied and take delight in Your goodness, for You favored the seventh day and declared it holy. You called it "most desirable of days" in remembrance of Creation.

Our God and God of our ancestors, find favor in our rest, and on this Sabbath day renew for us the coming month for good and blessing, joy and gladness, deliverance and consolation, sustenance and support, life and peace, pardon of sin and forgiveness of iniquity (*From Marḥeshvan to Adar II in a Jewish leap year:* and atonement of transgression). For You have chosen Your people Israel from all nations; You have made known to them Your holy Sabbath, and instituted for them rules for the New Moon. Blessed are You, LORD, who sanctifies the Sabbath, Israel and the New Moons.

*Continue with "Find favor" on the next page.*

יִשְׂמְחוּ בְמַלְכוּתְךָ שׁוֹמְרֵי שַׁבָּת וְקוֹרְאֵי עֹנֶג
עַם מְקַדְּשֵׁי שְׁבִיעִי
כֻּלָּם יִשְׂבְּעוּ וְיִתְעַנְּגוּ מִטּוּבֶךָ
וּבַשְּׁבִיעִי רָצִיתָ בּוֹ וְקִדַּשְׁתּוֹ
חֶמְדַּת יָמִים אוֹתוֹ קָרָאתָ, זֵכֶר לְמַעֲשֵׂה בְרֵאשִׁית.

אֱלֹהֵינוּ וֵאלֹהֵי אֲבוֹתֵינוּ, רְצֵה בִמְנוּחָתֵנוּ
קַדְּשֵׁנוּ בְּמִצְוֹתֶיךָ וְתֵן חֶלְקֵנוּ בְּתוֹרָתֶךָ
שַׂבְּעֵנוּ מִטּוּבֶךָ, וְשַׂמְּחֵנוּ בִּישׁוּעָתֶךָ
וְטַהֵר לִבֵּנוּ לְעָבְדְּךָ בֶּאֱמֶת
וְהַנְחִילֵנוּ יהוה אֱלֹהֵינוּ בְּאַהֲבָה וּבְרָצוֹן שַׁבַּת קָדְשֶׁךָ
וְיָנוּחוּ בוֹ יִשְׂרָאֵל מְקַדְּשֵׁי שְׁמֶךָ.
בָּרוּךְ אַתָּה יהוה, מְקַדֵּשׁ הַשַּׁבָּת.

---

וּמִנְחָתָם וְנִסְכֵּיהֶם כִּמְדֻבָּר, שְׁלֹשָׁה עֶשְׂרֹנִים לַפָּר, וּשְׁנֵי עֶשְׂרֹנִים לָאָיִל, וְעִשָּׂרוֹן לַכֶּבֶשׂ, וְיַיִן כְּנִסְכּוֹ, וְשָׂעִיר לְכַפֵּר, וּשְׁנֵי תְמִידִים כְּהִלְכָתָם.

יִשְׂמְחוּ בְמַלְכוּתְךָ שׁוֹמְרֵי שַׁבָּת וְקוֹרְאֵי עֹנֶג, עַם מְקַדְּשֵׁי שְׁבִיעִי, כֻּלָּם יִשְׂבְּעוּ וְיִתְעַנְּגוּ מִטּוּבֶךָ, וּבַשְּׁבִיעִי רָצִיתָ בּוֹ וְקִדַּשְׁתּוֹ, חֶמְדַּת יָמִים אוֹתוֹ קָרָאתָ, זֵכֶר לְמַעֲשֵׂה בְרֵאשִׁית.

אֱלֹהֵינוּ וֵאלֹהֵי אֲבוֹתֵינוּ, רְצֵה בִמְנוּחָתֵנוּ, וְחַדֵּשׁ עָלֵינוּ בְּיוֹם הַשַּׁבָּת הַזֶּה אֶת הַחֹדֶשׁ הַזֶּה, לְטוֹבָה וְלִבְרָכָה, לְשָׂשׂוֹן וּלְשִׂמְחָה, לִישׁוּעָה וּלְנֶחָמָה, לְפַרְנָסָה וּלְכַלְכָּלָה, לְחַיִּים וּלְשָׁלוֹם, לִמְחִילַת חֵטְא וְלִסְלִיחַת עָוֹן (*From* מרחשון *to* אדר שני *in a Jewish leap year* וּלְכַפָּרַת פָּשַׁע), כִּי בְעַמְּךָ יִשְׂרָאֵל בָּחַרְתָּ מִכָּל הָאֻמּוֹת, וְשַׁבַּת קָדְשְׁךָ לָהֶם הוֹדַעְתָּ וְחֻקֵּי רָאשֵׁי חֳדָשִׁים לָהֶם קָבָעְתָּ. בָּרוּךְ אַתָּה יהוה, מְקַדֵּשׁ הַשַּׁבָּת וְיִשְׂרָאֵל וְרָאשֵׁי חֳדָשִׁים.

*Continue with* רְצֵה *on the next page.*

## TEMPLE SERVICE

רְצֵה Find favor, Lord our God, in Your people Israel
and their prayer.
Restore the service to Your most holy House,
and accept in love and favor the fire-offerings of Israel
and their prayer.
May the service of Your people Israel always find favor with You.
And may our eyes witness Your return to Zion in compassion.
Blessed are You, Lord, who restores His Presence to Zion.

## THANKSGIVING

*Bow at the first nine words.*

מוֹדִים We give thanks to You,
for You are the Lord our God
and God of our ancestors
for ever and all time.
You are the Rock of our lives,
Shield of our salvation
from generation to generation.
We will thank You and
declare Your praise for our lives,
which are entrusted into Your hand;
for our souls,
which are placed in Your charge;
for Your miracles
which are with us every day;
and for Your wonders and favors
at all times,
evening, morning and midday.
You are good –
for Your compassion never fails.
You are compassionate –
for Your loving-kindnesses never cease.
We have always placed our hope in You.

*During the Leader's Repetition, the congregation says quietly:*

מוֹדִים We give thanks to You,
for You are the Lord our God
and God of our ancestors,
God of all flesh,
who formed us
and formed the universe.
Blessings and thanks
are due to Your great
and holy name for giving us
life and sustaining us.
May You continue
to give us life
and sustain us;
and may You gather our
exiles to Your holy courts,
to keep Your decrees,
do Your will and serve You
with a perfect heart,
for it is for us
to give You thanks.
Blessed be God to whom
thanksgiving is due.

עבודה

רְצֵה יהוה אֱלֹהֵינוּ בְּעַמְּךָ יִשְׂרָאֵל וּבִתְפִלָּתָם
וְהָשֵׁב אֶת הָעֲבוֹדָה לִדְבִיר בֵּיתֶךָ
וְאִשֵּׁי יִשְׂרָאֵל וּתְפִלָּתָם בְּאַהֲבָה תְקַבֵּל בְּרָצוֹן
וּתְהִי לְרָצוֹן תָּמִיד עֲבוֹדַת יִשְׂרָאֵל עַמֶּךָ.
וְתֶחֱזֶינָה עֵינֵינוּ בְּשׁוּבְךָ לְצִיּוֹן בְּרַחֲמִים.
בָּרוּךְ אַתָּה יהוה, הַמַּחֲזִיר שְׁכִינָתוֹ לְצִיּוֹן.

הודאה

*Bow at the first five words.*

מוֹדִים אֲנַחְנוּ לָךְ
שָׁאַתָּה הוּא יהוה אֱלֹהֵינוּ
וֵאלֹהֵי אֲבוֹתֵינוּ לְעוֹלָם וָעֶד.
צוּר חַיֵּינוּ, מָגֵן יִשְׁעֵנוּ
אַתָּה הוּא לְדוֹר וָדוֹר.
נוֹדֶה לְּךָ וּנְסַפֵּר תְּהִלָּתֶךָ
עַל חַיֵּינוּ הַמְּסוּרִים בְּיָדֶךָ
וְעַל נִשְׁמוֹתֵינוּ הַפְּקוּדוֹת לָךְ
וְעַל נִסֶּיךָ שֶׁבְּכָל יוֹם עִמָּנוּ
וְעַל נִפְלְאוֹתֶיךָ וְטוֹבוֹתֶיךָ
שֶׁבְּכָל עֵת
עֶרֶב וָבֹקֶר וְצָהֳרָיִם.
הַטּוֹב, כִּי לֹא כָלוּ רַחֲמֶיךָ
וְהַמְרַחֵם, כִּי לֹא תַמּוּ חֲסָדֶיךָ
מֵעוֹלָם קִוִּינוּ לָךְ.

*During the* חזרת הש״ץ*, the* קהל *says quietly:*

מוֹדִים אֲנַחְנוּ לָךְ
שָׁאַתָּה הוּא יהוה אֱלֹהֵינוּ
וֵאלֹהֵי אֲבוֹתֵינוּ
אֱלֹהֵי כָל בָּשָׂר
יוֹצְרֵנוּ, יוֹצֵר בְּרֵאשִׁית.
בְּרָכוֹת וְהוֹדָאוֹת
לְשִׁמְךָ הַגָּדוֹל וְהַקָּדוֹשׁ
עַל שֶׁהֶחֱיִיתָנוּ וְקִיַּמְתָּנוּ.
כֵּן תְּחַיֵּנוּ וּתְקַיְּמֵנוּ
וְתֶאֱסֹף גָּלֻיּוֹתֵינוּ
לְחַצְרוֹת קָדְשֶׁךָ
לִשְׁמֹר חֻקֶּיךָ
וְלַעֲשׂוֹת רְצוֹנֶךָ וּלְעָבְדְּךָ
בְּלֵבָב שָׁלֵם
עַל שֶׁאֲנַחְנוּ מוֹדִים לָךְ.
בָּרוּךְ אֵל הַהוֹדָאוֹת.

*On Ḥanukka:*

עַל הַנִּסִּים [We thank You also] for the miracles, the redemption, the mighty deeds, the salvations, and the victories in battle which You performed for our ancestors in those days, at this time.

בִּימֵי מַתִּתְיָהוּ In the days of Mattityahu, son of Yoḥanan, the High Priest, the Hasmonean, and his sons, the wicked Greek kingdom rose up against Your people Israel to make them forget Your Torah and to force them to transgress the statutes of Your will. It was then that You in Your great compassion stood by them in the time of their distress. You championed their cause, judged their claim, and avenged their wrong. You delivered the strong into the hands of the weak, the many into the hands of the few, the impure into the hands of the pure, the wicked into the hands of the righteous, and the arrogant into the hands of those who were engaged in the study of Your Torah. You made for Yourself great and holy renown in Your world, and for Your people Israel You performed a great salvation and redemption as of this very day. Your children then entered the holiest part of Your House, cleansed Your Temple, purified Your Sanctuary, kindled lights in Your holy courts, and designated these eight days of Ḥanukka for giving thanks and praise to Your great name.

*Continue with "For all these things."*

*On Shushan Purim in Jerusalem:*

עַל הַנִּסִּים [We thank You also] for the miracles, the redemption, the mighty deeds, the salvations, and the victories in battle which You performed for our ancestors in those days at this time.

בִּימֵי מָרְדְּכַי In the days of Mordekhai and Esther, in Shushan the capital, the wicked Haman rose up against them and sought to destroy, slay and exterminate *Esther 3* all the Jews, young and old, children and women, on one day, the thirteenth day of the twelfth month, which is the month of Adar, and to plunder their possessions. Then You in Your great compassion thwarted his counsel, frustrated his plans, and caused his scheme to recoil on his own head, so that they hanged him and his sons on the gallows.

*Continue with "For all these things."*

וְעַל כֻּלָּם For all these things may Your name be blessed and exalted, our King, continually, for ever and all time.

*On Shabbat Shuva:* And write, for a good life, all the children of Your covenant.

Let all that lives thank You, Selah! and praise Your name in truth, God, our Savior and Help, Selah!

▾Blessed are You, Lord, whose name is "the Good" and to whom thanks are due.

בחנוכה:

עַל הַנִּסִּים וְעַל הַפֻּרְקָן וְעַל הַגְּבוּרוֹת וְעַל הַתְּשׁוּעוֹת וְעַל הַמִּלְחָמוֹת שֶׁעָשִׂיתָ לַאֲבוֹתֵינוּ בַּיָּמִים הָהֵם בַּזְּמַן הַזֶּה.

בִּימֵי מַתִּתְיָהוּ בֶּן יוֹחָנָן כֹּהֵן גָּדוֹל חַשְׁמוֹנַאי וּבָנָיו, כְּשֶׁעָמְדָה מַלְכוּת יָוָן הָרְשָׁעָה עַל עַמְּךָ יִשְׂרָאֵל לְהַשְׁכִּיחָם תּוֹרָתֶךָ וּלְהַעֲבִירָם מֵחֻקֵּי רְצוֹנֶךָ, וְאַתָּה בְּרַחֲמֶיךָ הָרַבִּים עָמַדְתָּ לָהֶם בְּעֵת צָרָתָם, רַבְתָּ אֶת רִיבָם, דַּנְתָּ אֶת דִּינָם, נָקַמְתָּ אֶת נִקְמָתָם, מָסַרְתָּ גִבּוֹרִים בְּיַד חַלָּשִׁים, וְרַבִּים בְּיַד מְעַטִּים, וּטְמֵאִים בְּיַד טְהוֹרִים, וּרְשָׁעִים בְּיַד צַדִּיקִים, וְזֵדִים בְּיַד עוֹסְקֵי תוֹרָתֶךָ, וּלְךָ עָשִׂיתָ שֵׁם גָּדוֹל וְקָדוֹשׁ בְּעוֹלָמֶךָ, וּלְעַמְּךָ יִשְׂרָאֵל עָשִׂיתָ תְּשׁוּעָה גְדוֹלָה וּפֻרְקָן כְּהַיּוֹם הַזֶּה. וְאַחַר כֵּן בָּאוּ בָנֶיךָ לִדְבִיר בֵּיתֶךָ, וּפִנּוּ אֶת הֵיכָלֶךָ, וְטִהֲרוּ אֶת מִקְדָּשֶׁךָ, וְהִדְלִיקוּ נֵרוֹת בְּחַצְרוֹת קָדְשֶׁךָ, וְקָבְעוּ שְׁמוֹנַת יְמֵי חֲנֻכָּה אֵלּוּ, לְהוֹדוֹת וּלְהַלֵּל לְשִׁמְךָ הַגָּדוֹל.

*Continue with* וְעַל כֻּלָּם.

בשושן פורים בירושלים:

עַל הַנִּסִּים וְעַל הַפֻּרְקָן וְעַל הַגְּבוּרוֹת וְעַל הַתְּשׁוּעוֹת וְעַל הַמִּלְחָמוֹת שֶׁעָשִׂיתָ לַאֲבוֹתֵינוּ בַּיָּמִים הָהֵם בַּזְּמַן הַזֶּה.

בִּימֵי מָרְדְּכַי וְאֶסְתֵּר בְּשׁוּשַׁן הַבִּירָה, כְּשֶׁעָמַד עֲלֵיהֶם הָמָן הָרָשָׁע, בִּקֵּשׁ לְהַשְׁמִיד לַהֲרֹג וּלְאַבֵּד אֶת־כָּל־הַיְּהוּדִים מִנַּעַר וְעַד־זָקֵן טַף וְנָשִׁים בְּיוֹם אסתר ג
אֶחָד, בִּשְׁלוֹשָׁה עָשָׂר לְחֹדֶשׁ שְׁנֵים־עָשָׂר, הוּא־חֹדֶשׁ אֲדָר, וּשְׁלָלָם לָבוֹז: וְאַתָּה בְּרַחֲמֶיךָ הָרַבִּים הֵפַרְתָּ אֶת עֲצָתוֹ, וְקִלְקַלְתָּ אֶת מַחֲשַׁבְתּוֹ, וַהֲשֵׁבוֹתָ לּוֹ גְּמוּלוֹ בְּרֹאשׁוֹ, וְתָלוּ אוֹתוֹ וְאֶת בָּנָיו עַל הָעֵץ.

*Continue with* וְעַל כֻּלָּם.

וְעַל כֻּלָּם יִתְבָּרַךְ וְיִתְרוֹמַם שִׁמְךָ מַלְכֵּנוּ תָּמִיד לְעוֹלָם וָעֶד.

בשבת שובה: וּכְתֹב לְחַיִּים טוֹבִים כָּל בְּנֵי בְרִיתֶךָ.

וְכֹל הַחַיִּים יוֹדוּךָ סֶּלָה, וִיהַלְלוּ אֶת שִׁמְךָ בֶּאֱמֶת הָאֵל יְשׁוּעָתֵנוּ וְעֶזְרָתֵנוּ סֶלָה.

בָּרוּךְ אַתָּה יהוה, הַטּוֹב שִׁמְךָ וּלְךָ נָאֶה לְהוֹדוֹת.

*The following is said by the Leader during the Repetition of the Amida.*
*In Israel, if Kohanim bless the congregation,* *turn to page 902. See laws 370–377.*

Our God and God of our fathers, bless us with the threefold blessing in the Torah, written by the hand of Moses Your servant and pronounced by Aaron and his sons the priests, Your holy people, as it is said:

May the LORD bless you and protect you. *Num. 6*
*Cong:* May it be Your will.
May the LORD make His face shine on you and be gracious to you.
*Cong:* May it be Your will.
May the LORD turn His face toward you, and grant you peace.
*Cong:* May it be Your will.

PEACE

שִׂים שָׁלוֹם Grant peace, goodness and blessing, grace,
loving-kindness and compassion to us
and all Israel Your people.
Bless us, our Father, all as one,
with the light of Your face,
for by the light of Your face You have given us,
LORD our God, the Torah of life and love of kindness,
righteousness, blessing, compassion, life and peace.
May it be good in Your eyes to bless Your people Israel
at every time, in every hour, with Your peace.

*On Shabbat Shuva:* In the book of life, blessing, peace and prosperity,
may we and all Your people the house of Israel
be remembered and written before You for a good life,
and for peace.*

Blessed are You, LORD, who blesses His people Israel with peace.

**On Shabbat Shuva in the Diaspora, many end the blessing:*
Blessed are You, LORD, who makes peace.

*The following verse concludes the Leader's Repetition of the Amida.*
*Some also say it here as part of the silent Amida. See law 368.*

May the words of my mouth and the meditation of my heart *Ps. 19*
find favor before You, LORD, my Rock and Redeemer.

*The following is said by the* שליח ציבור *during* חורת הש״ץ.
*In* ארץ ישראל *if* כהנים *say* ברכת כהנים *turn to page 903. See laws 370–377.*

אֱלֹהֵינוּ וֵאלֹהֵי אֲבוֹתֵינוּ, בָּרְכֵנוּ בַּבְּרָכָה הַמְשֻׁלֶּשֶׁת בַּתּוֹרָה, הַכְּתוּבָה עַל יְדֵי מֹשֶׁה עַבְדֶּךָ, הָאֲמוּרָה מִפִּי אַהֲרֹן וּבָנָיו כֹּהֲנִים עַם קְדוֹשֶׁיךָ, כָּאָמוּר

יְבָרֶכְךָ יהוה וְיִשְׁמְרֶךָ: קהל: כֵּן יְהִי רָצוֹן במדבר ו

יָאֵר יהוה פָּנָיו אֵלֶיךָ וִיחֻנֶּךָּ: קהל: כֵּן יְהִי רָצוֹן

יִשָּׂא יהוה פָּנָיו אֵלֶיךָ וְיָשֵׂם לְךָ שָׁלוֹם: קהל: כֵּן יְהִי רָצוֹן

ברכת שלום

**שִׂים שָׁלוֹם טוֹבָה וּבְרָכָה**
**חֵן וָחֶסֶד וְרַחֲמִים עָלֵינוּ וְעַל כָּל יִשְׂרָאֵל עַמֶּךָ.**
**בָּרְכֵנוּ אָבִינוּ כֻּלָּנוּ כְּאֶחָד בְּאוֹר פָּנֶיךָ**
**כִּי בְאוֹר פָּנֶיךָ נָתַתָּ לָּנוּ, יהוה אֱלֹהֵינוּ**
**תּוֹרַת חַיִּים וְאַהֲבַת חֶסֶד**
**וּצְדָקָה וּבְרָכָה וְרַחֲמִים וְחַיִּים וְשָׁלוֹם.**
**וְטוֹב בְּעֵינֶיךָ לְבָרֵךְ אֶת עַמְּךָ יִשְׂרָאֵל**
**בְּכָל עֵת וּבְכָל שָׁעָה בִּשְׁלוֹמֶךָ.**

בשבת שובה: בְּסֵפֶר חַיִּים, בְּרָכָה וְשָׁלוֹם, וּפַרְנָסָה טוֹבָה
נִזָּכֵר וְנִכָּתֵב לְפָנֶיךָ, אֲנַחְנוּ וְכָל עַמְּךָ בֵּית יִשְׂרָאֵל
לְחַיִּים טוֹבִים וּלְשָׁלוֹם.*

**בָּרוּךְ אַתָּה יהוה, הַמְבָרֵךְ אֶת עַמּוֹ יִשְׂרָאֵל בַּשָּׁלוֹם.**

**On* שבת שובה *in* חוץ לארץ*, many end the blessing:*

בָּרוּךְ אַתָּה יהוה, עוֹשֶׂה הַשָּׁלוֹם.

*The following verse concludes the* חזרת הש״ץ.
*Some also say it here as part of the silent* עמידה. *See law 368.*

יִהְיוּ לְרָצוֹן אִמְרֵי־פִי וְהֶגְיוֹן לִבִּי לְפָנֶיךָ, יהוה צוּרִי וְגֹאֲלִי: תהלים יט

אֱלֹהַי My God, *Berakhot 17a*
guard my tongue from evil
and my lips from deceitful speech.
To those who curse me,
let my soul be silent;
may my soul be to all like the dust.
Open my heart to Your Torah
and let my soul pursue Your commandments.
As for all who plan evil against me,
swiftly thwart their counsel and frustrate their plans.
Act for the sake of Your name;
act for the sake of Your right hand;
act for the sake of Your holiness;
act for the sake of Your Torah.
That Your beloved ones may be delivered, *Ps. 60*
save with Your right hand and answer me.
May the words of my mouth and the meditation of my heart *Ps. 19*
find favor before You, LORD, my Rock and Redeemer.

*Bow, take three steps back, then bow, first left, then right, then center, while saying:*

May He who makes peace in His high places,
make peace for us and all Israel –
and say: Amen.

יְהִי רָצוֹן May it be Your will, LORD our God and God of our ancestors,
that the Temple be rebuilt speedily in our days,
and grant us a share in Your Torah.
And there we will serve You with reverence,
as in the days of old and as in former years.
Then the offering of Judah and Jerusalem *Mal. 3*
will be pleasing to the LORD as in the days of old and as in former years.

אֱלֹהַי ברכות יז.

נְצֹר לְשׁוֹנִי מֵרָע וּשְׂפָתַי מִדַּבֵּר מִרְמָה
וְלִמְקַלְלַי נַפְשִׁי תִדֹּם, וְנַפְשִׁי כֶּעָפָר לַכֹּל תִּהְיֶה.
פְּתַח לִבִּי בְּתוֹרָתֶךָ, וּבְמִצְוֹתֶיךָ תִּרְדֹּף נַפְשִׁי.
וְכָל הַחוֹשְׁבִים עָלַי רָעָה
מְהֵרָה הָפֵר עֲצָתָם וְקַלְקֵל מַחֲשַׁבְתָּם.
עֲשֵׂה לְמַעַן שְׁמֶךָ
עֲשֵׂה לְמַעַן יְמִינֶךָ
עֲשֵׂה לְמַעַן קְדֻשָּׁתֶךָ
עֲשֵׂה לְמַעַן תּוֹרָתֶךָ.
לְמַעַן יֵחָלְצוּן יְדִידֶיךָ, הוֹשִׁיעָה יְמִינְךָ וַעֲנֵנִי: תהלים ס
יִהְיוּ לְרָצוֹן אִמְרֵי־פִי וְהֶגְיוֹן לִבִּי לְפָנֶיךָ, יהוה צוּרִי וְגֹאֲלִי: תהלים יט

*Bow, take three steps back, then bow, first left, then right, then center, while saying:*

עֹשֶׂה שָׁלוֹם/ בשבת שובה: הַשָּׁלוֹם/ בִּמְרוֹמָיו
הוּא יַעֲשֶׂה שָׁלוֹם עָלֵינוּ וְעַל כָּל יִשְׂרָאֵל
וְאִמְרוּ אָמֵן.

יְהִי רָצוֹן מִלְּפָנֶיךָ יהוה אֱלֹהֵינוּ וֵאלֹהֵי אֲבוֹתֵינוּ
שֶׁיִּבָּנֶה בֵּית הַמִּקְדָּשׁ בִּמְהֵרָה בְיָמֵינוּ,
וְתֵן חֶלְקֵנוּ בְּתוֹרָתֶךָ
וְשָׁם נַעֲבָדְךָ בְּיִרְאָה כִּימֵי עוֹלָם וּכְשָׁנִים קַדְמֹנִיּוֹת.
וְעָרְבָה לַיהוה מִנְחַת יְהוּדָה וִירוּשָׁלָםִ כִּימֵי עוֹלָם וּכְשָׁנִים קַדְמֹנִיּוֹת: מלאכי ג

FULL KADDISH

*Leader:* יִתְגַּדַּל Magnified and sanctified may His great name be,
in the world He created by His will.
May He establish His kingdom
in your lifetime and in your days,
and in the lifetime of all the house of Israel,
swiftly and soon – and say: Amen.

*All:* May His great name be blessed for ever and all time.

*Leader:* Blessed and praised, glorified and exalted,
raised and honored, uplifted and lauded
be the name of the Holy One, blessed be He,
beyond any blessing, song, praise and consolation
uttered in the world – and say: Amen.

May the prayers and pleas of all Israel
be accepted by their Father in heaven – and say: Amen.

May there be great peace from heaven,
and life for us and all Israel – and say: Amen.

*Bow, take three steps back, as if taking leave of the Divine Presence, then bow, first left, then right, then center, while saying:*

May He who makes peace in His high places,
make peace for us and all Israel – and say: Amen.

אֵין כֵּאלֹהֵינוּ There is none like our God, none like our Lord,
none like our King, none like our Savior.
Who is like our God? Who is like our Lord?
Who is like our King? Who is like our Savior?
We will thank our God, we will thank our Lord,
we will thank our King, we will thank our Savior.
Blessed is our God, blessed is our Lord,
blessed is our King, blessed is our Savior.
You are our God, You are our Lord,
You are our King, You are our Savior.
You are He to whom our ancestors offered the fragrant incense.

## קדיש שלם

ש״ץ: יִתְגַּדַּל וְיִתְקַדַּשׁ שְׁמֵהּ רַבָּא (קהל: אָמֵן)
בְּעָלְמָא דִּי בְרָא כִרְעוּתֵהּ, וְיַמְלִיךְ מַלְכוּתֵהּ
בְּחַיֵּיכוֹן וּבְיוֹמֵיכוֹן וּבְחַיֵּי דְכָל בֵּית יִשְׂרָאֵל
בַּעֲגָלָא וּבִזְמַן קָרִיב, וְאִמְרוּ אָמֵן. (קהל: אָמֵן)

קהל וש״ץ: יְהֵא שְׁמֵהּ רַבָּא מְבָרַךְ לְעָלַם וּלְעָלְמֵי עָלְמַיָּא.

ש״ץ: יִתְבָּרַךְ וְיִשְׁתַּבַּח וְיִתְפָּאַר וְיִתְרוֹמַם וְיִתְנַשֵּׂא
וְיִתְהַדָּר וְיִתְעַלֶּה וְיִתְהַלָּל, שְׁמֵהּ דְּקֻדְשָׁא בְּרִיךְ הוּא (קהל: בְּרִיךְ הוּא)
לְעֵלָּא מִן כָּל בִּרְכָתָא / בשבת שובה: לְעֵלָּא לְעֵלָּא מִכָּל בִּרְכָתָא/
וְשִׁירָתָא, תֻּשְׁבְּחָתָא וְנֶחֱמָתָא
דַּאֲמִירָן בְּעָלְמָא, וְאִמְרוּ אָמֵן. (קהל: אָמֵן)

תִּתְקַבַּל צְלוֹתְהוֹן וּבָעוּתְהוֹן דְּכָל יִשְׂרָאֵל
קֳדָם אֲבוּהוֹן דִּי בִשְׁמַיָּא, וְאִמְרוּ אָמֵן. (קהל: אָמֵן)

יְהֵא שְׁלָמָא רַבָּא מִן שְׁמַיָּא
וְחַיִּים, עָלֵינוּ וְעַל כָּל יִשְׂרָאֵל, וְאִמְרוּ אָמֵן. (קהל: אָמֵן)

*Bow, take three steps back, as if taking leave of the Divine Presence, then bow, first left, then right, then center, while saying:*

עֹשֶׂה שָׁלוֹם/ בשבת שובה: הַשָּׁלוֹם/ בִּמְרוֹמָיו
הוּא יַעֲשֶׂה שָׁלוֹם עָלֵינוּ וְעַל כָּל יִשְׂרָאֵל, וְאִמְרוּ אָמֵן. (קהל: אָמֵן)

אֵין כֵּאלֹהֵינוּ, אֵין כַּאדוֹנֵינוּ, אֵין כְּמַלְכֵּנוּ, אֵין כְּמוֹשִׁיעֵנוּ.
מִי כֵאלֹהֵינוּ, מִי כַאדוֹנֵינוּ, מִי כְמַלְכֵּנוּ, מִי כְמוֹשִׁיעֵנוּ.
נוֹדֶה לֵאלֹהֵינוּ, נוֹדֶה לַאדוֹנֵינוּ, נוֹדֶה לְמַלְכֵּנוּ, נוֹדֶה לְמוֹשִׁיעֵנוּ.
בָּרוּךְ אֱלֹהֵינוּ, בָּרוּךְ אֲדוֹנֵינוּ, בָּרוּךְ מַלְכֵּנוּ, בָּרוּךְ מוֹשִׁיעֵנוּ.
אַתָּה הוּא אֱלֹהֵינוּ, אַתָּה הוּא אֲדוֹנֵינוּ,
אַתָּה הוּא מַלְכֵּנוּ, אַתָּה הוּא מוֹשִׁיעֵנוּ.
אַתָּה הוּא שֶׁהִקְטִירוּ אֲבוֹתֵינוּ לְפָנֶיךָ אֶת קְטֹרֶת הַסַּמִּים.

פִּטּוּם הַקְּטֹרֶת The incense mixture consisted of balsam, onycha, galbanum and frankincense, each weighing seventy manehs; myrrh, cassia, spikenard and saffron, each weighing sixteen manehs; twelve manehs of costus, three of aromatic bark; nine of cinnamon; nine kabs of Carsina lye; three seahs and three kabs of Cyprus wine. If Cyprus wine was not available, old white wine might be used. A quarter of a kab of Sodom salt, and a minute amount of a smoke-raising herb. Rabbi Nathan says: Also a minute amount of Jordan amber. If one added honey to the mixture, he rendered it unfit for sacred use. If he omitted any one of its ingredients, he is guilty of a capital offense. *Keritot 6a*

Rabban Shimon ben Gamliel says: "Balsam" refers to the sap that drips from the balsam tree. The Carsina lye was used for bleaching the onycha to improve it. The Cyprus wine was used to soak the onycha in it to make it pungent. Though urine is suitable for this purpose, it is not brought into the Temple out of respect.

These were the Psalms which the Levites used to recite in the Temple: *Mishna, Tamid 7*
On the first day of the week they used to say: "The earth is the Lord's and all *Ps. 24*
it contains, the world and all who live in it." On the second day they used to
say: "Great is the Lord and greatly to be praised in the city of God, on His *Ps. 48*
holy mountain." On the third day they used to say: "God stands in the divine *Ps. 82*
assembly. Among the judges He delivers judgment." On the fourth day they
used to say: "God of retribution, Lord, God of retribution, appear." On the *Ps. 94*
fifth day they used to say: "Sing for joy to God, our strength. Shout aloud to *Ps. 81*
the God of Jacob." On the sixth day they used to say: "The Lord reigns: He is *Ps. 93*
robed in majesty; the Lord is robed, girded with strength; the world is firmly
established; it cannot be moved." On the Sabbath they used to say: "A psalm, *Ps. 92*
a song for the Sabbath day" – [meaning] a psalm and song for the time to
come, for the day which will be entirely Sabbath and rest for life everlasting.

It was taught in the Academy of Elijah: Whoever studies [Torah] laws every *Megilla 28b*
day is assured that he will be destined for the World to Come, as it is said, "The *Hab. 3*
ways of the world are His" – read not, "ways" [*halikhot*] but "laws" [*halakhot*].

Rabbi Elazar said in the name of Rabbi Ḥanina: The disciples of the sages *Berakhot 64a*
increase peace in the world, as it is said, "And all your children shall be taught *Is. 54*
of the Lord, and great shall be the peace of your children [*banayikh*]." Read
not *banayikh*, "your children," but *bonayikh*, "your builders." Those who love *Ps. 119*
Your Torah have great peace; there is no stumbling block for them. May there *Ps. 122*
be peace within your ramparts, prosperity in your palaces. For the sake of my
brothers and friends, I shall say, "Peace be within you." For the sake of the
House of the Lord our God, I will seek your good. ▸ May the Lord grant *Ps. 29*
strength to His people; may the Lord bless His people with peace.

פִּטּוּם הַקְּטֹרֶת. הַצְּרִי, וְהַצִּפֹּרֶן, וְהַחֶלְבְּנָה, וְהַלְּבוֹנָה מִשְׁקַל שִׁבְעִים שִׁבְעִים מָנֶה, מֹר, וּקְצִיעָה, שִׁבֹּלֶת נֵרְדְּ, וְכַרְכֹּם מִשְׁקַל שִׁשָּׁה עָשָׂר שִׁשָּׁה עָשָׂר מָנֶה, הַקֹּשְׁטְ שְׁנֵים עָשָׂר, קִלּוּפָה שְׁלֹשָׁה, קִנָּמוֹן תִּשְׁעָה, בֹּרִית כַּרְשִׁינָה תִּשְׁעָה קַבִּין, יֵין קַפְרִיסִין סְאִין תְּלָת וְקַבִּין תְּלָתָא, וְאִם לֹא מָצָא יֵין קַפְרִיסִין, מֵבִיא חֲמַר חִוַּרְיָן עַתִּיק. מֶלַח סְדוֹמִית רֹבַע, מַעֲלֶה עָשָׁן כָּל שֶׁהוּא. רַבִּי נָתָן הַבַּבְלִי אוֹמֵר: אַף כִּפַּת הַיַּרְדֵּן כָּל שֶׁהוּא, וְאִם נָתַן בָּהּ דְּבַשׁ פְּסָלָהּ, וְאִם חִסַּר אֶחָד מִכָּל סַמָּנֶיהָ, חַיָּב מִיתָה. כריתות ו.

רַבָּן שִׁמְעוֹן בֶּן גַּמְלִיאֵל אוֹמֵר: הַצְּרִי אֵינוֹ אֶלָּא שְׂרָף הַנּוֹטֵף מֵעֲצֵי הַקְּטָף. בֹּרִית כַּרְשִׁינָה שֶׁשָּׁפִין בָּהּ אֶת הַצִּפֹּרֶן כְּדֵי שֶׁתְּהֵא נָאָה, יֵין קַפְרִיסִין שֶׁשּׁוֹרִין בּוֹ אֶת הַצִּפֹּרֶן כְּדֵי שֶׁתְּהֵא עַזָּה, וַהֲלֹא מֵי רַגְלַיִם יָפִין לָהּ, אֶלָּא שֶׁאֵין מַכְנִיסִין מֵי רַגְלַיִם בַּמִּקְדָּשׁ מִפְּנֵי הַכָּבוֹד.

הַשִּׁיר שֶׁהַלְוִיִּם הָיוּ אוֹמְרִים בְּבֵית הַמִּקְדָּשׁ: משנה תמיד ז

בַּיּוֹם הָרִאשׁוֹן הָיוּ אוֹמְרִים, לַיהוה הָאָרֶץ וּמְלוֹאָהּ, תֵּבֵל וְיֽשְׁבֵי בָהּ: תהלים כד

בַּשֵּׁנִי הָיוּ אוֹמְרִים, גָּדוֹל יהוה וּמְהֻלָּל מְאֹד, בְּעִיר אֱלֹהֵינוּ הַר־קָדְשׁוֹ: תהלים מח

בַּשְּׁלִישִׁי הָיוּ אוֹמְרִים, אֱלֹהִים נִצָּב בַּעֲדַת־אֵל, בְּקֶרֶב אֱלֹהִים יִשְׁפֹּט: תהלים פב

בָּרְבִיעִי הָיוּ אוֹמְרִים, אֵל־נְקָמוֹת יהוה, אֵל נְקָמוֹת הוֹפִיעַ: תהלים צד

בַּחֲמִישִׁי הָיוּ אוֹמְרִים, הַרְנִינוּ לֵאלֹהִים עוּזֵּנוּ, הָרִיעוּ לֵאלֹהֵי יַעֲקֹב: תהלים פא

בַּשִּׁשִּׁי הָיוּ אוֹמְרִים, יהוה מָלָךְ גֵּאוּת לָבֵשׁ תהלים צג

לָבֵשׁ יהוה עֹז הִתְאַזָּר, אַף־תִּכּוֹן תֵּבֵל בַּל־תִּמּוֹט:

בַּשַּׁבָּת הָיוּ אוֹמְרִים, מִזְמוֹר שִׁיר לְיוֹם הַשַּׁבָּת: תהלים צב

מִזְמוֹר שִׁיר לֶעָתִיד לָבוֹא, לְיוֹם שֶׁכֻּלּוֹ שַׁבָּת וּמְנוּחָה לְחַיֵּי הָעוֹלָמִים.

תָּנָא דְבֵי אֵלִיָּהוּ: כָּל הַשּׁוֹנֶה הֲלָכוֹת בְּכָל יוֹם, מֻבְטָח לוֹ שֶׁהוּא בֶּן עוֹלָם הַבָּא, שֶׁנֶּאֱמַר: הֲלִיכוֹת עוֹלָם לוֹ: אַל תִּקְרֵי הֲלִיכוֹת אֶלָּא הֲלָכוֹת. מגילה כח: חבקוק ג

אָמַר רַבִּי אֶלְעָזָר, אָמַר רַבִּי חֲנִינָא: תַּלְמִידֵי חֲכָמִים מַרְבִּים שָׁלוֹם בָּעוֹלָם, ברכות סד.
שֶׁנֶּאֱמַר, וְכָל־בָּנַיִךְ לִמּוּדֵי יהוה, וְרַב שְׁלוֹם בָּנָיִךְ: אַל תִּקְרֵי בָּנָיִךְ, אֶלָּא ישעיה נד
בּוֹנָיִךְ. שָׁלוֹם רָב לְאֹהֲבֵי תוֹרָתֶךָ, וְאֵין־לָמוֹ מִכְשׁוֹל: יְהִי־שָׁלוֹם בְּחֵילֵךְ, תהלים קיט תהלים קכב
שַׁלְוָה בְּאַרְמְנוֹתָיִךְ: לְמַעַן אַחַי וְרֵעָי אֲדַבְּרָה־נָּא שָׁלוֹם בָּךְ: לְמַעַן בֵּית־יהוה
אֱלֹהֵינוּ אֲבַקְשָׁה טוֹב לָךְ: · יהוה עֹז לְעַמּוֹ יִתֵּן, יהוה יְבָרֵךְ אֶת־עַמּוֹ בַשָּׁלוֹם: תהלים כט

## THE RABBIS' KADDISH

*The following prayer requires the presence of a minyan.*
*A transliteration can be found on page 1319.*

*Mourner:* יִתְגַּדַּל Magnified and sanctified may His great name be,
in the world He created by His will.
May He establish His kingdom
in your lifetime and in your days,
and in the lifetime of all the house of Israel,
swiftly and soon –
and say: Amen.

*All:* May His great name be blessed for ever and all time.

*Mourner:* Blessed and praised, glorified and exalted,
raised and honored, uplifted and lauded
be the name of the Holy One, blessed be He,
beyond any blessing,
song, praise and consolation
uttered in the world –
and say: Amen.

To Israel, to the teachers,
their disciples and their disciples' disciples,
and to all who engage in the study of Torah,
in this (*in Israel add:* holy) place or elsewhere,
may there come to them and you great peace,
grace, kindness and compassion,
long life, ample sustenance and deliverance,
from their Father in Heaven –
and say: Amen.

May there be great peace from heaven,
and (good) life for us and all Israel –
and say: Amen.

*Bow, take three steps back, as if taking leave of the Divine Presence,*
*then bow, first left, then right, then center, while saying:*
May He who makes peace in His high places,
in His compassion make peace for us and all Israel –
and say: Amen.

## קדיש דרבנן

*The following prayer requires the presence of a* מנין.
*A transliteration can be found on page 1319.*

אבל: יִתְגַּדַּל וְיִתְקַדַּשׁ שְׁמֵהּ רַבָּא (קהל: אָמֵן)
בְּעָלְמָא דִּי בְרָא כִרְעוּתֵהּ, וְיַמְלִיךְ מַלְכוּתֵהּ
בְּחַיֵּיכוֹן וּבְיוֹמֵיכוֹן וּבְחַיֵּי דְכָל בֵּית יִשְׂרָאֵל
בַּעֲגָלָא וּבִזְמַן קָרִיב, וְאִמְרוּ אָמֵן. (קהל: אָמֵן)

קהל ואבל: יְהֵא שְׁמֵהּ רַבָּא מְבָרַךְ לְעָלַם וּלְעָלְמֵי עָלְמַיָּא.

אבל: יִתְבָּרַךְ וְיִשְׁתַּבַּח וְיִתְפָּאַר וְיִתְרוֹמַם וְיִתְנַשֵּׂא
וְיִתְהַדָּר וְיִתְעַלֶּה וְיִתְהַלָּל
שְׁמֵהּ דְּקֻדְשָׁא בְּרִיךְ הוּא (קהל: בְּרִיךְ הוּא)
לְעֵלָּא מִן כָּל בִּרְכָתָא / בשבת שובה: לְעֵלָּא לְעֵלָּא מִכָּל בִּרְכָתָא/
וְשִׁירָתָא, תֻּשְׁבְּחָתָא וְנֶחֱמָתָא
דַּאֲמִירָן בְּעָלְמָא, וְאִמְרוּ אָמֵן. (קהל: אָמֵן)

עַל יִשְׂרָאֵל וְעַל רַבָּנָן
וְעַל תַּלְמִידֵיהוֹן וְעַל כָּל תַּלְמִידֵי תַלְמִידֵיהוֹן
וְעַל כָּל מָאן דְּעָסְקִין בְּאוֹרַיְתָא
דִּי בְּאַתְרָא (בארץ ישראל: קַדִּישָׁא) הָדֵין, וְדִי בְּכָל אֲתַר וַאֲתַר
יְהֵא לְהוֹן וּלְכוֹן שְׁלָמָא רַבָּא
חִנָּא וְחִסְדָּא, וְרַחֲמֵי, וְחַיֵּי אֲרִיכֵי, וּמְזוֹנֵי רְוִיחֵי
וּפֻרְקָנָא מִן קֳדָם אֲבוּהוֹן דִּי בִשְׁמַיָּא, וְאִמְרוּ אָמֵן. (קהל: אָמֵן)

יְהֵא שְׁלָמָא רַבָּא מִן שְׁמַיָּא
וְחַיִּים (טוֹבִים) עָלֵינוּ וְעַל כָּל יִשְׂרָאֵל, וְאִמְרוּ אָמֵן. (קהל: אָמֵן)

*Bow, take three steps back, as if taking leave of the Divine Presence, then bow, first left, then right, then center, while saying:*

עֹשֶׂה שָׁלוֹם/ בשבת שובה: הַשָּׁלוֹם/ בִּמְרוֹמָיו
הוּא יַעֲשֶׂה בְרַחֲמָיו שָׁלוֹם
עָלֵינוּ וְעַל כָּל יִשְׂרָאֵל, וְאִמְרוּ אָמֵן. (קהל: אָמֵן)

*Stand while saying Aleinu. Bow at* ▾.

עָלֵינוּ It is our duty to praise the Master of all,
and ascribe greatness to the Author of creation,
who has not made us like the nations of the lands
nor placed us like the families of the earth;
who has not made our portion like theirs,
nor our destiny like all their multitudes.
(For they worship vanity and emptiness,
and pray to a god who cannot save.)
▾But we bow in worship
and thank the Supreme King of kings, the Holy One,
blessed be He,
who extends the heavens and establishes the earth,
whose throne of glory is in the heavens above,
and whose power's Presence is in the highest of heights.
He is our God; there is no other.
Truly He is our King, there is none else,
as it is written in His Torah:
"You shall know and take to heart this day *Deut. 4*
that the LORD is God, in heaven above and on earth below.
There is no other."

Therefore, we place our hope in You, LORD our God,
that we may soon see the glory of Your power,
when You will remove abominations from the earth,
and idols will be utterly destroyed,
when the world will be perfected
under the sovereignty of the Almighty,
when all humanity will call on Your name,
to turn all the earth's wicked toward You.
All the world's inhabitants will realize and know
that to You every knee must bow
and every tongue swear loyalty.

*Stand while saying* עָלֵינוּ. *Bow at* ▼.

עָלֵינוּ לְשַׁבֵּחַ לַאֲדוֹן הַכֹּל, לָתֵת גְּדֻלָּה לְיוֹצֵר בְּרֵאשִׁית
שֶׁלֹּא עָשָׂנוּ כְּגוֹיֵי הָאֲרָצוֹת, וְלֹא שָׂמָנוּ כְּמִשְׁפְּחוֹת הָאֲדָמָה
שֶׁלֹּא שָׂם חֶלְקֵנוּ כָּהֶם וְגוֹרָלֵנוּ כְּכָל הֲמוֹנָם.
(שֶׁהֵם מִשְׁתַּחֲוִים לְהֶבֶל וָרִיק וּמִתְפַּלְּלִים אֶל אֵל לֹא יוֹשִׁיעַ.)
▼וַאֲנַחְנוּ כּוֹרְעִים וּמִשְׁתַּחֲוִים וּמוֹדִים
לִפְנֵי מֶלֶךְ מַלְכֵי הַמְּלָכִים, הַקָּדוֹשׁ בָּרוּךְ הוּא
שֶׁהוּא נוֹטֶה שָׁמַיִם וְיוֹסֵד אָרֶץ
וּמוֹשַׁב יְקָרוֹ בַּשָּׁמַיִם מִמַּעַל
וּשְׁכִינַת עֻזּוֹ בְּגָבְהֵי מְרוֹמִים.
הוּא אֱלֹהֵינוּ, אֵין עוֹד.
אֱמֶת מַלְכֵּנוּ, אֶפֶס זוּלָתוֹ
כַּכָּתוּב בְּתוֹרָתוֹ
וְיָדַעְתָּ הַיּוֹם וַהֲשֵׁבֹתָ אֶל־לְבָבֶךָ דברים ד
כִּי יהוה הוּא הָאֱלֹהִים בַּשָּׁמַיִם מִמַּעַל וְעַל־הָאָרֶץ מִתָּחַת,
אֵין עוֹד:

עַל כֵּן נְקַוֶּה לְּךָ יהוה אֱלֹהֵינוּ, לִרְאוֹת מְהֵרָה בְּתִפְאֶרֶת עֻזֶּךָ
לְהַעֲבִיר גִּלּוּלִים מִן הָאָרֶץ
וְהָאֱלִילִים כָּרוֹת יִכָּרֵתוּן
לְתַקֵּן עוֹלָם בְּמַלְכוּת שַׁדַּי.
וְכָל בְּנֵי בָשָׂר יִקְרְאוּ בִשְׁמֶךָ
לְהַפְנוֹת אֵלֶיךָ כָּל רִשְׁעֵי אָרֶץ.
יַכִּירוּ וְיֵדְעוּ כָּל יוֹשְׁבֵי תֵבֵל
כִּי לְךָ תִּכְרַע כָּל בֶּרֶךְ, תִּשָּׁבַע כָּל לָשׁוֹן.

Before You, LORD our God, they will kneel and bow down
and give honor to Your glorious name.
They will all accept the yoke of Your kingdom,
and You will reign over them soon and for ever.
For the kingdom is Yours,
and to all eternity You will reign in glory,
as it is written in Your Torah:
"The LORD will reign for ever and ever." *Ex. 15*
▸ And it is said:
"Then the LORD shall be King over all the earth; *Zech. 14*
on that day the LORD shall be One and His name One."

*Some add:*

Have no fear of sudden terror or of the ruin when it overtakes the wicked. *Prov. 3*
Devise your strategy, but it will be thwarted; *Is. 8*
propose your plan, but it will not stand, for God is with us.
When you grow old, I will still be the same. *Is. 46*
When your hair turns gray, I will still carry you.
I made you, I will bear you, I will carry you, and I will rescue you.

## MOURNER'S KADDISH

*The following prayer, said by mourners, requires the presence of a minyan.*
*A transliteration can be found on page 1320.*

*Mourner:* יִתְגַּדַּל Magnified and sanctified may His great name be,
in the world He created by His will.
May He establish His kingdom
in your lifetime and in your days,
and in the lifetime of all the house of Israel,
swiftly and soon –
and say: Amen.

*All:* May His great name be blessed for ever and all time.

*Mourner:* Blessed and praised, glorified and exalted,
raised and honored, uplifted and lauded
be the name of the Holy One,
blessed be He,

לְפָנֶיךָ יהוה אֱלֹהֵינוּ יִכְרְעוּ וְיִפֹּלוּ
וְלִכְבוֹד שִׁמְךָ יְקָר יִתֵּנוּ
וִיקַבְּלוּ כֻלָּם אֶת עֹל מַלְכוּתֶךָ
וְתִמְלֹךְ עֲלֵיהֶם מְהֵרָה לְעוֹלָם וָעֶד.
כִּי הַמַּלְכוּת שֶׁלְּךָ הִיא וּלְעוֹלְמֵי עַד תִּמְלֹךְ בְּכָבוֹד
כַּכָּתוּב בְּתוֹרָתֶךָ, יהוה יִמְלֹךְ לְעֹלָם וָעֶד: שמות טו
◄ וְנֶאֱמַר, וְהָיָה יהוה לְמֶלֶךְ עַל־כָּל־הָאָרֶץ זכריה יד
בַּיּוֹם הַהוּא יִהְיֶה יהוה אֶחָד וּשְׁמוֹ אֶחָד:

*Some add:*

אַל־תִּירָא מִפַּחַד פִּתְאֹם וּמִשֹּׁאַת רְשָׁעִים כִּי תָבֹא: משלי ג
עֻצוּ עֵצָה וְתֻפָר, דַּבְּרוּ דָבָר וְלֹא יָקוּם, כִּי עִמָּנוּ אֵל: ישעיה ח
וְעַד־זִקְנָה אֲנִי הוּא, וְעַד־שֵׂיבָה אֲנִי אֶסְבֹּל ישעיה מו
אֲנִי עָשִׂיתִי וַאֲנִי אֶשָּׂא וַאֲנִי אֶסְבֹּל וַאֲמַלֵּט:

## קדיש יתום

*The following prayer, said by mourners, requires the presence of a* מנין*.*
*A transliteration can be found on page 1320.*

אבל: יִתְגַּדַּל וְיִתְקַדַּשׁ שְׁמֵהּ רַבָּא (קהל: אָמֵן)
בְּעָלְמָא דִּי בְרָא כִרְעוּתֵהּ
וְיַמְלִיךְ מַלְכוּתֵהּ
בְּחַיֵּיכוֹן וּבְיוֹמֵיכוֹן וּבְחַיֵּי דְכָל בֵּית יִשְׂרָאֵל
בַּעֲגָלָא וּבִזְמַן קָרִיב, וְאִמְרוּ אָמֵן. (קהל: אָמֵן)

קהל ואבל: יְהֵא שְׁמֵהּ רַבָּא מְבָרַךְ לְעָלַם וּלְעָלְמֵי עָלְמַיָּא.

אבל: יִתְבָּרַךְ וְיִשְׁתַּבַּח וְיִתְפָּאַר
וְיִתְרוֹמַם וְיִתְנַשֵּׂא וְיִתְהַדָּר וְיִתְעַלֶּה וְיִתְהַלָּל
שְׁמֵהּ דְּקֻדְשָׁא בְּרִיךְ הוּא (קהל: בְּרִיךְ הוּא)

beyond any blessing,
song, praise and consolation
uttered in the world –
and say: Amen.

May there be great peace from heaven,
and life for us and all Israel –
and say: Amen.

*Bow, take three steps back, as if taking leave of the Divine Presence, then bow, first left, then right, then center, while saying:*

May He who makes peace in His high places,
make peace for us and all Israel –
and say: Amen.

*On Yom Tov that falls on a weekday, say the appropriate Daily Psalm (page 248).*
*On Shabbat continue with the Daily Psalm below.*
*Many congregations say the Daily Psalm after the Song of Glory, page 638.*
*(In Israel on Shabbat Rosh Ḥodesh, some say Barekhi Nafshi, page 698, as the Daily Psalm.)*

Today is the holy Sabbath,
on which the Levites used to say this psalm in the Temple:

מִזְמוֹר A psalm. A song for the Sabbath day. It is good to thank the *Ps. 92*
Lord and sing psalms to Your name, Most High – to tell of Your loving-kindness in the morning and Your faithfulness at night, to the music of the ten-stringed lyre and the melody of the harp. For You have made me rejoice by Your work, O Lord; I sing for joy at the deeds of Your hands. How great are Your deeds, Lord, and how very deep Your thoughts. A boor cannot know, nor can a fool understand, that though the wicked spring up like grass and all evildoers flourish, it is only that they may be destroyed for ever. But You, Lord, are eternally exalted. For behold Your enemies, Lord, behold Your enemies will perish; all evildoers will be scattered. You have raised my pride like that of a wild ox; I am anointed with fresh oil. My eyes shall look in triumph on my adversaries; my ears shall hear the downfall of the wicked who rise against me. The righteous will flourish like a palm

לְעֵלָּא מִן כָּל בִּרְכָתָא
/בשבת שובה: לְעֵלָּא לְעֵלָּא מִכָּל בִּרְכָתָא/
וְשִׁירָתָא, תֻּשְׁבְּחָתָא וְנֶחֱמָתָא
דַּאֲמִירָן בְּעָלְמָא, וְאִמְרוּ אָמֵן. (קהל: אָמֵן)

יְהֵא שְׁלָמָא רַבָּא מִן שְׁמַיָּא
וְחַיִּים, עָלֵינוּ וְעַל כָּל יִשְׂרָאֵל, וְאִמְרוּ אָמֵן. (קהל: אָמֵן)

*Bow, take three steps back, as if taking leave of the Divine Presence, then bow, first left, then right, then center, while saying:*

עֹשֶׂה שָׁלוֹם/ בשבת שובה: הַשָּׁלוֹם/ בִּמְרוֹמָיו
הוּא יַעֲשֶׂה שָׁלוֹם
עָלֵינוּ וְעַל כָּל יִשְׂרָאֵל, וְאִמְרוּ אָמֵן. (קהל: אָמֵן)

*On* יום טוב *that falls on a weekday, say the appropriate* שיר של יום *(page 249).*

*On* שבת *continue with the* שיר של יום *below. Many congregations say the* שיר של יום *after the* שיר הכבוד*, page 639.*

*(In* ארץ ישראל *on* שבת ראש חודש*, some say* בָּרְכִי נַפְשִׁי*, page 699, as the* שיר של יום*.)*

הַיּוֹם יוֹם שַׁבַּת קֹדֶשׁ, שֶׁבּוֹ הָיוּ הַלְוִיִּם אוֹמְרִים בְּבֵית הַמִּקְדָּשׁ:

מִזְמוֹר שִׁיר לְיוֹם הַשַּׁבָּת: טוֹב לְהֹדוֹת לַיהוה, וּלְזַמֵּר לְשִׁמְךָ תהלים צב
עֶלְיוֹן: לְהַגִּיד בַּבֹּקֶר חַסְדֶּךָ, וֶאֱמוּנָתְךָ בַּלֵּילוֹת: עֲלֵי־עָשׂוֹר
וַעֲלֵי־נָבֶל, עֲלֵי הִגָּיוֹן בְּכִנּוֹר: כִּי שִׂמַּחְתַּנִי יהוה בְּפָעֳלֶךָ, בְּמַעֲשֵׂי
יָדֶיךָ אֲרַנֵּן: מַה־גָּדְלוּ מַעֲשֶׂיךָ יהוה, מְאֹד עָמְקוּ מַחְשְׁבֹתֶיךָ:
אִישׁ־בַּעַר לֹא יֵדָע, וּכְסִיל לֹא־יָבִין אֶת־זֹאת: בִּפְרֹחַ רְשָׁעִים
כְּמוֹ־עֵשֶׂב, וַיָּצִיצוּ כָּל־פֹּעֲלֵי אָוֶן, לְהִשָּׁמְדָם עֲדֵי־עַד: וְאַתָּה
מָרוֹם לְעֹלָם יהוה: כִּי הִנֵּה אֹיְבֶיךָ יהוה, כִּי־הִנֵּה אֹיְבֶיךָ יֹאבֵדוּ,
יִתְפָּרְדוּ כָּל־פֹּעֲלֵי אָוֶן: וַתָּרֶם כִּרְאֵים קַרְנִי, בַּלֹּתִי בְּשֶׁמֶן רַעֲנָן:
וַתַּבֵּט עֵינִי בְּשׁוּרָי, בַּקָּמִים עָלַי מְרֵעִים תִּשְׁמַעְנָה אָזְנָי: צַדִּיק

tree and grow tall like a cedar in Lebanon. Planted in the LORD's House, blossoming in our God's courtyards, ▸ they will still bear fruit in old age, and stay vigorous and fresh, proclaiming that the LORD is upright: He is my Rock, in whom there is no wrong.

*Mourner's Kaddish (page 632)*

*On Rosh Ḥodesh, say Barekhi Nafshi on page 698 followed by Mourner's Kaddish. On Ḥanukka, many congregations add Psalm 30 on page 474, followed by Mourner's Kaddish.*

*From the second day of Rosh Ḥodesh Elul through Shemini Atzeret (in Israel through Hoshana Raba), the following psalm is said:*

לְדָוִד A psalm of David. The LORD is my light and my salvation – Ps. 27
whom then shall I fear? The LORD is the stronghold of my life – of whom shall I be afraid? When evil men close in on me to devour my flesh, it is they, my enemies and foes, who stumble and fall. Should an army besiege me, my heart would not fear. Should war break out against me, still I would be confident. One thing I ask of the LORD, only this do I seek: to live in the House of the LORD all the days of my life, to gaze on the beauty of the LORD and worship in His Temple. For He will keep me safe in His pavilion on the day of trouble. He will hide me under the cover of His tent. He will set me high upon a rock. Now my head is high above my enemies who surround me. I will sacrifice in His tent with shouts of joy. I will sing and chant praises to the LORD. LORD, hear my voice when I call. Be gracious to me and answer me. On Your behalf my heart says, "Seek My face." Your face, LORD, will I seek. Do not hide Your face from me. Do not turn Your servant away in anger. You have been my help. Do not reject or forsake me, God, my Savior. Were my father and my mother to forsake me, the LORD would take me in. Teach me Your way, LORD, and lead me on a level path, because of my oppressors. Do not abandon me to the will of my foes, for false witnesses have risen against me, breathing violence. ▸ Were it not for my faith that I shall see the LORD's goodness in the land of the living. Hope in the LORD. Be strong and of good courage, and hope in the LORD!

*Mourner's Kaddish (page 632)*

כַּתָּמָר יִפְרָח, כְּאֶרֶז בַּלְּבָנוֹן יִשְׂגֶּה: שְׁתוּלִים בְּבֵית יהוה, בְּחַצְרוֹת אֱלֹהֵינוּ יַפְרִיחוּ: ‹ עוֹד יְנוּבוּן בְּשֵׂיבָה, דְּשֵׁנִים וְרַעֲנַנִּים יִהְיוּ: לְהַגִּיד כִּי־יָשָׁר יהוה, צוּרִי, וְלֹא־עַוְלָתָה בּוֹ:

קדיש יתום (*page 633*)

*On* ראש חודש*, say* בָּרְכִי נַפְשִׁי *on page 699 followed by* קדיש יתום*.*
*On* חנוכה*, many congregations add* מִזְמוֹר שִׁיר־חֲנֻכַּת הַבַּיִת *on page 475, followed by* קדיש יתום*.*

*From the second day of* ראש חודש אלול *through* שמיני עצרת *(in* ארץ ישראל *through* הושענא רבה*), the following psalm is said:*

לְדָוִד, יהוה אוֹרִי וְיִשְׁעִי, מִמִּי אִירָא, יהוה מָעוֹז־חַיַּי, מִמִּי אֶפְחָד: בִּקְרֹב עָלַי מְרֵעִים לֶאֱכֹל אֶת־בְּשָׂרִי, צָרַי וְאֹיְבַי לִי, הֵמָּה כָשְׁלוּ וְנָפָלוּ: אִם־תַּחֲנֶה עָלַי מַחֲנֶה, לֹא־יִירָא לִבִּי, אִם־תָּקוּם עָלַי מִלְחָמָה, בְּזֹאת אֲנִי בוֹטֵחַ: אַחַת שָׁאַלְתִּי מֵאֵת־יהוה, אוֹתָהּ אֲבַקֵּשׁ, שִׁבְתִּי בְּבֵית־יהוה כָּל־יְמֵי חַיַּי, לַחֲזוֹת בְּנֹעַם־יהוה, וּלְבַקֵּר בְּהֵיכָלוֹ: כִּי יִצְפְּנֵנִי בְּסֻכֹּה בְּיוֹם רָעָה, יַסְתִּרֵנִי בְּסֵתֶר אָהֳלוֹ, בְּצוּר יְרוֹמְמֵנִי: וְעַתָּה יָרוּם רֹאשִׁי עַל אֹיְבַי סְבִיבוֹתַי, וְאֶזְבְּחָה בְאָהֳלוֹ זִבְחֵי תְרוּעָה, אָשִׁירָה וַאֲזַמְּרָה לַיהוה: שְׁמַע־יהוה קוֹלִי אֶקְרָא, וְחָנֵּנִי וַעֲנֵנִי: לְךָ אָמַר לִבִּי בַּקְּשׁוּ פָנָי, אֶת־פָּנֶיךָ יהוה אֲבַקֵּשׁ: אַל־תַּסְתֵּר פָּנֶיךָ מִמֶּנִּי, אַל תַּט־בְּאַף עַבְדֶּךָ, עֶזְרָתִי הָיִיתָ, אַל־תִּטְּשֵׁנִי וְאַל־תַּעַזְבֵנִי, אֱלֹהֵי יִשְׁעִי: כִּי־אָבִי וְאִמִּי עֲזָבוּנִי, וַיהוה יַאַסְפֵנִי: הוֹרֵנִי יהוה דַּרְכֶּךָ, וּנְחֵנִי בְּאֹרַח מִישׁוֹר, לְמַעַן שׁוֹרְרָי: אַל־תִּתְּנֵנִי בְּנֶפֶשׁ צָרָי, כִּי קָמוּ־בִי עֵדֵי־שֶׁקֶר, וִיפֵחַ חָמָס: ‹ לוּלֵא הֶאֱמַנְתִּי לִרְאוֹת בְּטוּב־יהוה בְּאֶרֶץ חַיִּים: קַוֵּה אֶל־יהוה, חֲזַק וְיַאֲמֵץ לִבֶּךָ, וְקַוֵּה אֶל־יהוה: תהלים כז

קדיש יתום (*page 633*)

## SONG OF GLORY

*The Ark is opened and all stand.*

*Leader:* I will sing sweet psalms and I will weave songs,
to You for whom my soul longs.

*Cong:* My soul yearns for the shelter of Your hand,
that all Your mystic secrets I might understand.

*Leader:* Whenever I speak of Your glory above,
my heart is yearning for Your love.

*Cong:* So Your glories I will proclaim,
and in songs of love give honor to Your name.

*Leader:* I will tell of Your glory though I have not seen You;
imagine and describe You, though I have not known You.

*Cong:* By the hand of Your prophets, through Your servants' mystery,
You gave a glimpse of Your wondrous majesty.

*Leader:* Recounting Your grandeur and Your glory,
of Your great deeds they told the story.

*Cong:* They depicted You, though not as You are,
but as You do: Your acts, Your power.

*Leader:* They represented You in many visions;
through them all You are One without divisions.

*Cong:* They saw You, now old, then young,
Your head with gray, with black hair hung.

*Leader:* Aged on the day of judgment, yet on the day of war,
a young warrior with mighty hands they saw.

*Cong:* Triumph like a helmet He wore on His head;
His right hand and holy arm to victory have led.

*Leader:* His curls are filled with dew-drops of light,
His locks with fragments of the night.

*Cong:* He will glory in me, for He delights in me;
My diadem of beauty He shall be.

*Leader:* His head is like pure beaten gold;
Engraved on His brow, His sacred name behold.

*Cong:* For grace and glory, beauty and renown,
His people have adorned Him with a crown.

# שיר הכבוד

*The* ארון קודש *is opened and all stand.*

שׁ״ץ: אַנְעִים זְמִירוֹת וְשִׁירִים אֶאֱרֹג, כִּי אֵלֶיךָ נַפְשִׁי תַעֲרֹג.
קהל: נַפְשִׁי חָמְדָה בְּצֵל יָדֶךָ, לָדַעַת כָּל רָז סוֹדֶךָ.

שׁ״ץ: מִדֵּי דַבְּרִי בִּכְבוֹדֶךָ, הוֹמֶה לִבִּי אֶל דּוֹדֶיךָ.
קהל: עַל כֵּן אֲדַבֵּר בְּךָ נִכְבָּדוֹת, וְשִׁמְךָ אֲכַבֵּד בְּשִׁירֵי יְדִידוֹת.

שׁ״ץ: אֲסַפְּרָה כְבוֹדְךָ וְלֹא רְאִיתִיךָ, אֲדַמְּךָ אֲכַנְּךָ וְלֹא יְדַעְתִּיךָ.
קהל: בְּיַד נְבִיאֶיךָ בְּסוֹד עֲבָדֶיךָ, דִּמִּיתָ הֲדַר כְּבוֹד הוֹדֶךָ.

שׁ״ץ: גְּדֻלָּתְךָ וּגְבוּרָתֶךָ, כִּנּוּ לְתֹקֶף פְּעֻלָּתֶךָ.
קהל: דִּמּוּ אוֹתְךָ וְלֹא כְּפִי יֶשְׁךָ, וַיְשַׁוּוּךָ לְפִי מַעֲשֶׂיךָ.

שׁ״ץ: הִמְשִׁילְוּךָ בְּרֹב חֶזְיוֹנוֹת, הִנְּךָ אֶחָד בְּכָל דִּמְיוֹנוֹת.
קהל: וַיֶּחֱזוּ בְךָ זִקְנָה וּבַחֲרוּת, וּשְׂעַר רֹאשְׁךָ בְּשֵׂיבָה וְשַׁחֲרוּת.

שׁ״ץ: זִקְנָה בְּיוֹם דִּין וּבַחֲרוּת בְּיוֹם קְרָב, כְּאִישׁ מִלְחָמוֹת יָדָיו לוֹ רָב.
קהל: חָבַשׁ כּוֹבַע יְשׁוּעָה בְּרֹאשׁוֹ, הוֹשִׁיעָה לּוֹ יְמִינוֹ וּזְרוֹעַ קָדְשׁוֹ.

שׁ״ץ: טַלְלֵי אוֹרוֹת רֹאשׁוֹ נִמְלָא, קְוֻצּוֹתָיו רְסִיסֵי לָיְלָה.
קהל: יִתְפָּאֵר בִּי כִּי חָפֵץ בִּי, וְהוּא יִהְיֶה לִּי לַעֲטֶרֶת צְבִי.

שׁ״ץ: כֶּתֶם טָהוֹר פָּז דְּמוּת רֹאשׁוֹ, וְחַק עַל מֵצַח כְּבוֹד שֵׁם קָדְשׁוֹ.
קהל: לְחֵן וּלְכָבוֹד צְבִי תִפְאָרָה, אֻמָּתוֹ לוֹ עִטְּרָה עֲטָרָה.

*Leader:* Like a youth's, His hair in locks unfurls;
Its black tresses flowing in curls.

*Cong:* Jerusalem, His splendor, is the dwelling place of right;
may He prize it as His highest delight.

*Leader:* Like a crown in His hand may His treasured people be,
a turban of beauty and of majesty.

*Cong:* He bore them, carried them, with a crown He adorned them.
They were precious in His sight, and He honored them.

*Leader:* His glory is on me; my glory is on Him.
He is near to me when I call to Him.

*Cong:* He is bright and rosy; red will be His dress,
when He comes from Edom, treading the winepress.

*Leader:* He showed the tefillin-knot to Moses, humble, wise,
when the LORD's likeness was before his eyes.

*Cong:* He delights in His people; the humble He does raise –
He glories in them; He sits enthroned upon their praise.

*Leader:* Your first word, Your call to every age, is true:
O seek the people who seek You.

*Cong:* My many songs please take and hear
and may my hymn of joy to You come near.

*Leader:* May my praise be a crown for Your head,
and like incense before You, the prayers I have said.

*Cong:* May a poor man's song be precious in Your eyes,
like a song sung over sacrifice.

*Leader:* To the One who sustains all, may my blessing take flight:
Creator, Life-Giver, God of right and might.

*Cong:* And when I offer blessing, to me Your head incline:
accepting it as spice, fragrant and fine.

*Leader:* May my prayer be to You sweet song.
For You my soul will always long.

*The Ark is closed.*

Yours, LORD, are the greatness and the power, the glory, the majesty *I Chr. 29*
and splendor, for everything in heaven and earth is Yours. Yours, LORD,
is the kingdom; You are exalted as Head over all. ▸ Who can tell of the *Ps. 106*
mighty acts of the LORD and make all His praise be heard?

ש״ץ: מַחְלְפוֹת רֹאשׁוֹ כְּבִימֵי בְחוּרוֹת, קְוֻצּוֹתָיו תַּלְתַּלִּים שְׁחוֹרוֹת.
קהל: נְוֵה הַצֶּדֶק צְבִי תִפְאַרְתּוֹ, יַעֲלֶה נָּא עַל רֹאשׁ שִׂמְחָתוֹ.

ש״ץ: סְגֻלָּתוֹ תְּהִי בְיָדוֹ עֲטֶרֶת, וּצְנִיף מְלוּכָה צְבִי תִפְאֶרֶת.
קהל: עֲמוּסִים נְשָׂאָם, עֲטֶרֶת עִנְּדָם, מֵאֲשֶׁר יָקְרוּ בְעֵינָיו כִּבְּדָם.

ש״ץ: פְּאֵרוֹ עָלַי וּפְאֵרִי עָלָיו, וְקָרוֹב אֵלַי בְּקָרְאִי אֵלָיו.
קהל: צַח וְאָדֹם לִלְבוּשׁוֹ אָדֹם, פּוּרָה בְדָרְכוֹ בְּבוֹאוֹ מֵאֱדוֹם.

ש״ץ: קֶשֶׁר תְּפִלִּין הֶרְאָה לֶעָנָו, תְּמוּנַת יהוה לְנֶגֶד עֵינָיו.
קהל: רוֹצֶה בְעַמּוֹ עֲנָוִים יְפָאֵר, יוֹשֵׁב תְּהִלּוֹת בָּם לְהִתְפָּאֵר.

ש״ץ: רֹאשׁ דְּבָרְךָ אֱמֶת קוֹרֵא מֵרֹאשׁ דּוֹר וָדוֹר, עַם דּוֹרֶשְׁךָ דְּרֹשׁ.
קהל: שִׁית הֲמוֹן שִׁירַי נָא עָלֶיךָ, וְרִנָּתִי תִּקְרַב אֵלֶיךָ.

ש״ץ: תְּהִלָּתִי תְּהִי לְרֹאשְׁךָ עֲטֶרֶת, וּתְפִלָּתִי תִּכּוֹן קְטֹרֶת.
קהל: תִּיקַר שִׁירַת רָשׁ בְּעֵינֶיךָ, כַּשִּׁיר יוּשַׁר עַל קָרְבָּנֶיךָ.

ש״ץ: בִּרְכָתִי תַעֲלֶה לְרֹאשׁ מַשְׁבִּיר, מְחוֹלֵל וּמוֹלִיד, צַדִּיק כַּבִּיר.
קהל: וּבְבִרְכָתִי תְנַעֲנַע לִי רֹאשׁ, וְאוֹתָהּ קַח לְךָ כִּבְשָׂמִים רֹאשׁ.

ש״ץ: יֶעֱרַב נָא שִׂיחִי עָלֶיךָ, כִּי נַפְשִׁי תַעֲרֹג אֵלֶיךָ.

*The* ארון קודש *is closed.*

לְךָ יהוה הַגְּדֻלָּה וְהַגְּבוּרָה וְהַתִּפְאֶרֶת וְהַנֵּצַח וְהַהוֹד — דברי הימים א׳ כט
כִּי־כֹל בַּשָּׁמַיִם וּבָאָרֶץ
לְךָ יהוה הַמַּמְלָכָה וְהַמִּתְנַשֵּׂא לְכֹל לְרֹאשׁ:

◂ מִי יְמַלֵּל גְּבוּרוֹת יהוה, יַשְׁמִיעַ כָּל־תְּהִלָּתוֹ: — תהלים קו

## MOURNER'S KADDISH

*The following prayer, said by mourners, requires the presence of a minyan.*
*A transliteration can be found on page 1320.*

*Mourner:* יִתְגַּדַּל Magnified and sanctified
may His great name be,
in the world He created by His will.
May He establish His kingdom
in your lifetime and in your days,
and in the lifetime of all the house of Israel,
swiftly and soon –
and say: Amen.

*All:* May His great name
be blessed for ever and all time.

*Mourner:* Blessed and praised,
glorified and exalted,
raised and honored,
uplifted and lauded
be the name of the Holy One,
blessed be He,
beyond any blessing,
song, praise and consolation
uttered in the world –
and say: Amen.

May there be great peace from heaven,
and life for us and all Israel –
and say: Amen.

*Bow, take three steps back, as if taking leave of the Divine Presence,*
*then bow, first left, then right, then center, while saying:*

May He who makes peace in His high places,
make peace for us and all Israel –
and say: Amen.

## קדיש יתום

*The following prayer, said by mourners, requires the presence of a* מנין.
*A transliteration can be found on page 1320.*

אבל: יִתְגַּדַּל וְיִתְקַדַּשׁ שְׁמֵהּ רַבָּא (קהל: אָמֵן)
בְּעָלְמָא דִּי בְרָא כִרְעוּתֵהּ
וְיַמְלִיךְ מַלְכוּתֵהּ
בְּחַיֵּיכוֹן וּבְיוֹמֵיכוֹן וּבְחַיֵּי דְכָל בֵּית יִשְׂרָאֵל
בַּעֲגָלָא וּבִזְמַן קָרִיב
וְאִמְרוּ אָמֵן. (קהל: אָמֵן)

קהל ואבל: יְהֵא שְׁמֵהּ רַבָּא מְבָרַךְ לְעָלַם וּלְעָלְמֵי עָלְמַיָּא.

אבל: יִתְבָּרַךְ וְיִשְׁתַּבַּח וְיִתְפָּאַר
וְיִתְרוֹמַם וְיִתְנַשֵּׂא וְיִתְהַדָּר וְיִתְעַלֶּה וְיִתְהַלָּל
שְׁמֵהּ דְּקֻדְשָׁא בְּרִיךְ הוּא (קהל: בְּרִיךְ הוּא)
לְעֵלָּא מִן כָּל בִּרְכָתָא / בשבת שובה: לְעֵלָּא לְעֵלָּא מִכָּל בִּרְכָתָא/
וְשִׁירָתָא, תֻּשְׁבְּחָתָא וְנֶחֱמָתָא
דַּאֲמִירָן בְּעָלְמָא
וְאִמְרוּ אָמֵן. (קהל: אָמֵן)

יְהֵא שְׁלָמָא רַבָּא מִן שְׁמַיָּא
וְחַיִּים, עָלֵינוּ וְעַל כָּל יִשְׂרָאֵל
וְאִמְרוּ אָמֵן. (קהל: אָמֵן)

*Bow, take three steps back, as if taking leave of the Divine Presence, then bow, first left, then right, then center, while saying:*

עֹשֶׂה שָׁלוֹם/ בשבת שובה: הַשָּׁלוֹם/ בִּמְרוֹמָיו
הוּא יַעֲשֶׂה שָׁלוֹם עָלֵינוּ וְעַל כָּל יִשְׂרָאֵל
וְאִמְרוּ אָמֵן. (קהל: אָמֵן)

LORD OF THE UNIVERSE,
who reigned before the birth of any thing –

When by His will all things were made
then was His name proclaimed King.

And when all things shall cease to be
He alone will reign in awe.

He was, He is, and He shall be
glorious for evermore.

He is One, there is none else,
alone, unique, beyond compare;

Without beginning, without end,
His might, His rule are everywhere.

He is my God; my Redeemer lives.
He is the Rock on whom I rely –

My banner and my safe retreat,
my cup, my portion when I cry.

Into His hand my soul I place,
when I awake and when I sleep.

The LORD is with me, I shall not fear;
body and soul from harm will He keep.

# אֲדוֹן עוֹלָם

אֲשֶׁר מָלַךְ בְּטֶרֶם כָּל־יְצִיר נִבְרָא.
לְעֵת נַעֲשָׂה בְחֶפְצוֹ כֹּל אֲזַי מֶלֶךְ שְׁמוֹ נִקְרָא.
וְאַחֲרֵי כִּכְלוֹת הַכֹּל לְבַדּוֹ יִמְלֹךְ נוֹרָא.
וְהוּא הָיָה וְהוּא הֹוֶה וְהוּא יִהְיֶה בְּתִפְאָרָה.
וְהוּא אֶחָד וְאֵין שֵׁנִי לְהַמְשִׁיל לוֹ לְהַחְבִּירָה.
בְּלִי רֵאשִׁית בְּלִי תַכְלִית וְלוֹ הָעֹז וְהַמִּשְׂרָה.
וְהוּא אֵלִי וְחַי גּוֹאֲלִי וְצוּר חֶבְלִי בְּעֵת צָרָה.
וְהוּא נִסִּי וּמָנוֹס לִי מְנָת כּוֹסִי בְּיוֹם אֶקְרָא.
בְּיָדוֹ אַפְקִיד רוּחִי בְּעֵת אִישַׁן וְאָעִירָה.
וְעִם רוּחִי גְּוִיָּתִי יהוה לִי וְלֹא אִירָא.

# Kiddush and Zemirot for Shabbat Morning

*Some say:*

אַתְקִינוּ Prepare the feast of perfect faith, joy of the holy King. Prepare the royal feast, this is the feast [mystically known as] "the Holy Ancient One" – and "the Small Face" and "the Field of Holy Apples" [mystical terms for aspects of the Divine] come to partake in the feast with it.

אֲסַדֵּר I will prepare the Sabbath morning feast,
and invite to it "the Holy Ancient One."
May His radiance shine on it, on the great Kiddush
and goodly wine that gladdens the soul.
May He send us His splendor; may we see His glory;
may He reveal to us His whispered secrets.
May He disclose to us the reason for the twelve loaves of bread,
which are [the twelve combinations of the letters of] His name,
and [the twelve sons of Jacob] the youngest patriarch.
May we be united with the One above, who gives life to all;
may our strength increase and [our prayers] reach [God's] head.
Laborers in the field [of Torah] rejoice with speech
and voice, speaking words sweet as honey.
Before the Master of the Universe,
reveal the meaning of, and give new interpretations to, matters veiled in mystery.
To adorn the table with precious secrets, deep, esoteric, not widely to be shared.
These words become sky; new heavens, and the sun then is the same.
He will be lifted to a higher level, and [God] will take [Israel],
from whom He had been separated, as His bride.

חַי יהוה The LORD lives; my Rock is blessed. My soul glories in the LORD.
For the LORD gives light to my lamp; His radiance shines on my head.
The LORD is my Shepherd, I shall not want. He leads me beside the still waters.
He gives food to all flesh; He feeds me my daily bread.
May it be Your will, You, my holy God, To prepare a table before me,
to anoint my head with oil.
Who will lay my rest before the LORD of peace,
and grant that my children stay faithful, [blessed with] life and peace?
May He send His angel before me, to accompany me on the way.
I lift my face with a cup of salvation; my cup is filled to overflowing.
My soul thirsts for the LORD; may He fill my store with plenty.
I lift my eyes to the sages, [celebrating Shabbat] like Hillel, not Shammai.
Most delightful of days and eternity's years; awake, my soul, awake.
Above my head let there shine as one,
the lamp of the commandments and the Torah's light.
Advance, LORD, to where I rest; You and Your mighty Ark.
Please, God, take my blessing and strengthen the shield of Your seer.

# קידוש וזמירות ליום שבת

*Some say:*

אַתְקִֽינוּ סְעוּדָתָא דִמְהֵימְנוּתָא שְׁלִימְתָא, חֶדְוָתָא דְמַלְכָּא קַדִּישָׁא. אַתְקִֽינוּ סְעוּדָתָא דְמַלְכָּא. דָּא הִיא סְעוּדָתָא דְעַתִּיקָא קַדִּישָׁא, וּזְעֵיר אַנְפִּין וַחֲקַל תַּפּוּחִין קַדִּישִׁין אָתַיִן לְסַעֲדָה בַּהֲדֵהּ.

אֲסַדֵּר לִסְעוּדָתָא בְּצַפְרָא דְשַׁבַּתָּא     וְאַזְמִין בַּהּ הַשְׁתָּא עַתִּיקָא קַדִּישָׁא.
נְהוֹרֵהּ יִשְׁרֵי בַהּ בְּקִדּוּשָׁא רַבָּה     וּמֵחַמְרָא טָבָא דְּבֵהּ תֶּחְדֵּי נַפְשָׁא.
יְשַׁדַּר לַן שׁוּפְרֵהּ וְנֶחֱזֵי בִּיקָרֵהּ     וְיַחֲזֵי לַן סִתְרֵהּ דְּמִתְאֲמַר בִּלְחִישָׁה.
יְגַלֵּה לַן טַעְמֵי דְּבִתְרֵיסַר נַהֲמֵי     דְּאִנּוּן אָת בִּשְׁמֵהּ כְּפִילָה וּקְלִישָׁא.
צְרוֹרָא דִלְעֵלָּא דְּבֵהּ חַיֵּי כֹלָּא     וְיִתְרַבֵּי חֵילָא וְתִסַּק עַד רֵישָׁא.
חֲדוּ חַצְּדֵי חַקְלָא בְּדִבּוּר וּבְקָלָא     וּמַלִּלוּ מִלָּה מְתִיקָא כְּדֻבְשָׁא.
קֳדָם רִבּוֹן עָלְמִין בְּמִלִּין סְתִימִין     תְּגַלּוֹן פִּתְגָּמִין וְתֵימְרוּן חִדּוּשָׁא.
לְעַטֵּר פָּתוֹרָא בְּרָזָא יַקִּירָא     עֲמִיקָא וּטְמִירָא וְלָאו מִלְּתָא אֲוְשָׁא.
וְאִלֵּין מִלַּיָּא יְהוֹן לִרְקִיעַיָּא     חֲדְתִין וּשְׁמַיָּא בְּכֵן הַהוּא שִׁמְשָׁא.
רְבוּ יַתִּיר יִסְגֵּי לְעֵילָא מִן דַּרְגֵּהּ     וְיִסַּב בַּת זוּגֵהּ דְּהֲוָת פְּרִישָׁא.

חַי יהוה וּבָרוּךְ צוּרִי, בַּיהוה תִּתְהַלֵּל נַפְשִׁי
כִּי יהוה יָאִיר נֵרִי, בְּהִלּוֹ נֵרוֹ עֲלֵי רֹאשִׁי.
יהוה רֹעִי לֹא אֶחְסָר, עַל מֵי מְנוּחוֹת יְנַהֲלֵנִי
נוֹתֵן לֶחֶם לְכָל בָּשָׂר, לֶחֶם חֻקִּי הַטְרִיפֵנִי.
יְהִי רָצוֹן מִלְּפָנֶיךָ, אַתָּה אֱלֹהַי קְדוֹשִׁי
תַּעֲרֹךְ לְפָנַי שֻׁלְחָנֶךָ, תְּדַשֵּׁן בַּשֶּׁמֶן רֹאשִׁי.
מִי יִתֵּן מְנוּחָתִי, לִפְנֵי אֲדוֹן הַשָּׁלוֹם
וְהָיְתָה שְׁלֵמָה מִטָּתִי, הַחַיִּים וְהַשָּׁלוֹם.
יִשְׁלַח מַלְאָכוֹ לְפָנַי, לְלַוּוֹתִי לִוְיָה
בְּכוֹס יְשׁוּעוֹת אֶשָּׂא פָנַי, מְנָת כּוֹסִי רְוָיָה.
צָמְאָה נַפְשִׁי אֶל יהוה, יְמַלֵּא שֹׂבַע אֲסָמַי
אֶל הֶהָרִים אֶשָּׂא עֵינַי, כְּהִלֵּל וְלֹא כְשַׁמַּאי.
חֶדְוַת יָמִים וּשְׁנוֹת עוֹלָמִים, עוּרָה כְבוֹדִי עוּרָה
וְעַל רֹאשִׁי יִהְיוּ תַמִּים, נֵר מִצְוָה וְאוֹר תּוֹרָה.
קוּמָה יהוה לִמְנוּחָתִי, אַתָּה וַאֲרוֹן עֻזֶּךָ
קַח נָא אֵל אֶת בִּרְכָתִי, וְהַחֲזֵק מָגֵן חוֹזֶךָ.

מִזְמוֹר לְדָוִד A psalm of David. The Lord is my Shepherd, I shall not want. *Ps. 23*
He makes me lie down in green pastures. He leads me beside the still waters.
He refreshes my soul.
He guides me in the paths of righteousness for His name's sake.
Though I walk through the valley of the shadow of death,
I will fear no evil, for You are with me;
Your rod and Your staff, they comfort me.
You set a table before me in the presence of my enemies;
You anoint my head with oil; my cup is filled to overflowing.
May goodness and kindness follow me all the days of my life,
and may I live in the House of the Lord for evermore.

## SHABBAT MORNING KIDDUSH

*Some say:*

אִם־תָּשִׁיב If you keep your feet from breaking the Sabbath, *Is. 58*
and from pursuing your affairs on My holy day,
if you call the Sabbath a delight, and the Lord's holy day honorable,
and if you honor it by not going your own way
or attending to your own affairs, or speaking idle words,
then you will find joy in the Lord,
and I will cause you to ride on the heights of the earth
and to feast on the inheritance of your father Jacob,
for the mouth of the Lord has spoken.

---

(delight) refers to. [But] when it says, 'Call the Sabbath a delight,'[2] one may assume this refers to the delight of the Sabbath (*'Oneg Shabbat*)."[3]

From *'Oneg Shabbat* (delight of the Sabbath) proceed two blessings – which are in reality intertwined – an inheritance without borders, and the fulfilment of one's fondest wishes. By nature, man, who is finite, does not wish for that which is infinite. This unique gift – which comes from having delighted in the Sabbath; from having tasted of infinity – consists in man wishing for that which is truly infinite. That very longing for the infinite will then create the "vessel" to receive "an inheritance without borders."[4]

2. Isaiah 58:13.
3. *b. Shabbat* 118.
4. *OR*, vol. 2, p. 138. Cf. above Rav Kook's comment on the verse "Open your mouth wide and I will fill it" (Psalms 81:11).

תהלים כג

מִזְמוֹר לְדָוִד, יהוה רֹעִי לֹא אֶחְסָר:
בִּנְאוֹת דֶּשֶׁא יַרְבִּיצֵנִי, עַל־מֵי מְנוּחוֹת יְנַהֲלֵנִי:
נַפְשִׁי יְשׁוֹבֵב, יַנְחֵנִי בְמַעְגְּלֵי־צֶדֶק לְמַעַן שְׁמוֹ:
גַּם כִּי־אֵלֵךְ בְּגֵיא צַלְמָוֶת לֹא־אִירָא רָע, כִּי־אַתָּה עִמָּדִי
שִׁבְטְךָ וּמִשְׁעַנְתֶּךָ הֵמָּה יְנַחֲמֻנִי:
תַּעֲרֹךְ לְפָנַי שֻׁלְחָן נֶגֶד צֹרְרָי, דִּשַּׁנְתָּ בַשֶּׁמֶן רֹאשִׁי, כּוֹסִי רְוָיָה:
אַךְ טוֹב וָחֶסֶד יִרְדְּפוּנִי כָּל־יְמֵי חַיָּי, וְשַׁבְתִּי בְּבֵית־יהוה לְאֹרֶךְ יָמִים:

## קידושא רבה

*Some say:*

ישעיה נח

אִם־תָּשִׁיב מִשַּׁבָּת רַגְלֶךָ עֲשׂוֹת חֲפָצֶךָ בְּיוֹם קָדְשִׁי
וְקָרָאתָ לַשַּׁבָּת עֹנֶג לִקְדוֹשׁ יהוה מְכֻבָּד
וְכִבַּדְתּוֹ מֵעֲשׂוֹת דְּרָכֶיךָ מִמְּצוֹא חֶפְצְךָ וְדַבֵּר דָּבָר:
אָז תִּתְעַנַּג עַל־יהוה
וְהִרְכַּבְתִּיךָ עַל־בָּמֳתֵי אָרֶץ, וְהַאֲכַלְתִּיךָ נַחֲלַת יַעֲקֹב אָבִיךָ
כִּי פִּי יהוה דִּבֵּר:

---

**קידושא רבה / SHABBAT MORNING KIDDUSH**

**אָז תִּתְעַנַּג עַל־יהוה, וְהִרְכַּבְתִּיךָ עַל־בָּמֳתֵי אָרֶץ, וְהַאֲכַלְתִּיךָ נַחֲלַת יַעֲקֹב אָבִיךָ, כִּי פִּי יהוה דִּבֵּר** *Then you will find joy in the Lord, and I will cause you to ride on the heights of the earth and to feast on the inheritance of your father Jacob, for the mouth of the Lord has spoken.* (*Isaiah 58:14*)

Said Rabbi Yoḥanan in the name of Rabbi Yosé: "Whoever delights in the Sabbath is given an inheritance without borders, for it says, 'Then you will delight in the Lord, and I will cause you to ride on the heights of the earth, and to feast on the inheritance of Jacob your father.'"

Said Rav Yehudah in the name of Rav: "Whoever delights in the Sabbath is given the wishes of his heart, for it says: 'So delight in the Lord; and He shall give you the wishes of your heart.'[1] I don't know what this *'oneg*

---

1. Psalms 37:4

*Most begin Kiddush here.*
*On Yom Tov that falls on Shabbat, say the Kiddush on page 828.*

וְשָׁמְרוּ The children of Israel must keep the Sabbath, *Ex. 31*
observing the Sabbath in every generation
as an everlasting covenant.
It is a sign between Me and the children of Israel for ever,
for in six days the LORD made the heavens and the earth,
but on the seventh day He ceased work
and refreshed Himself.

זָכוֹר Remember the Sabbath day to keep it holy. *Ex. 20*
Six days you shall labor and do all your work,
but the seventh day is a Sabbath of the LORD your God;
on it you shall not do any work –
you, your son or daughter,
your male or female slave, or your cattle,
or the stranger within your gates.
For in six days the LORD made heaven and earth
and sea and all that is in them,
and rested on the seventh day;
therefore the LORD blessed the Sabbath day
and declared it holy.

*When saying Kiddush for others, add:*
Please pay attention, my masters.

בָּרוּךְ Blessed are You, LORD our God,
King of the Universe,
who creates the fruit of the vine.

*On Shabbat Ḥol HaMo'ed Sukkot, if Kiddush is made in the sukka, add:*
Blessed are You, LORD our God,
King of the Universe,
who has made us holy through His commandments,
and has commanded us to dwell in the sukka.

*Most begin* קידוש *here.*
*On* יום טוב *that falls on* שבת *say the* קידוש *on page 829.*

On יום טוב that falls on שבת say the קידוש on page 829.

שמות לא

וְשָׁמְרוּ בְנֵי־יִשְׂרָאֵל אֶת־הַשַּׁבָּת
לַעֲשׂוֹת אֶת־הַשַּׁבָּת לְדֹרֹתָם בְּרִית עוֹלָם:
בֵּינִי וּבֵין בְּנֵי יִשְׂרָאֵל אוֹת הִוא לְעֹלָם
כִּי־שֵׁשֶׁת יָמִים עָשָׂה יהוה אֶת־הַשָּׁמַיִם וְאֶת־הָאָרֶץ
וּבַיּוֹם הַשְּׁבִיעִי שָׁבַת וַיִּנָּפַשׁ:

שמות כ

זָכוֹר אֶת־יוֹם הַשַּׁבָּת לְקַדְּשׁוֹ:
שֵׁשֶׁת יָמִים תַּעֲבֹד, וְעָשִׂיתָ כָּל־מְלַאכְתֶּךָ:
וְיוֹם הַשְּׁבִיעִי שַׁבָּת לַיהוה אֱלֹהֶיךָ
לֹא־תַעֲשֶׂה כָל־מְלָאכָה אַתָּה וּבִנְךָ וּבִתֶּךָ
עַבְדְּךָ וַאֲמָתְךָ וּבְהֶמְתֶּךָ, וְגֵרְךָ אֲשֶׁר בִּשְׁעָרֶיךָ:
כִּי שֵׁשֶׁת־יָמִים עָשָׂה יהוה אֶת־הַשָּׁמַיִם וְאֶת־הָאָרֶץ
אֶת־הַיָּם וְאֶת־כָּל־אֲשֶׁר־בָּם
וַיָּנַח בַּיּוֹם הַשְּׁבִיעִי
עַל־כֵּן בֵּרַךְ יהוה אֶת־יוֹם הַשַּׁבָּת וַיְקַדְּשֵׁהוּ:

*When saying* קידוש *for others, add:*

סַבְרִי מָרָנָן

בָּרוּךְ אַתָּה יהוה אֱלֹהֵינוּ מֶלֶךְ הָעוֹלָם בּוֹרֵא פְּרִי הַגָּפֶן.

*On* שבת חול המועד סוכות *if* קידוש *is made in the* סוכה *add:*

בָּרוּךְ אַתָּה יהוה אֱלֹהֵינוּ מֶלֶךְ הָעוֹלָם
אֲשֶׁר קִדְּשָׁנוּ בְּמִצְוֹתָיו, וְצִוָּנוּ לֵישֵׁב בַּסֻּכָּה.

# ZEMIROT FOR SHABBAT DAY

בָּרוּךְ Blessed be the LORD who, day by day, carries our burden with salvation and redemption. We will rejoice in His name all day long, and raise our head high in His salvation. For He is a stronghold for the poor and a refuge for the needy.

The LORD's tribes are Israel's testimony: He was distressed in their distress, in their suffering and slavery. Through a pavement of sapphire He showed them the strength of His love, He revealed Himself, lifting them from the depths of the pit. For with the LORD is loving-kindness; He abounds in redemption. *Ps. 130*

How precious is His loving-kindness; He shelters them under His shade. For their sake He went with them into exile in Babylon. When they went down in ships, He was counted among them. He ensured that they were treated mercifully by those who took them captive. For the LORD will not forsake His people, for the sake of His great name.

In Eilam He placed His throne, to rescue His beloved, to remove from them the stronghold of His rebels. He redeemed His servants from passing under the sword. He raised the pride of His people, for the glory of all His devoted ones. For though He afflicts, He also shows compassion and loving-kindness. *Lam. 3*

When the he-goat [Greece] extended its power, and the vision of the four ascended to the heights, And in their hearts they intended to destroy those He loved, through His priests He laid low those who rose against Him: The LORD's kindness has not ended nor His compassion ceased. *Lam. 3*

I was handed over to Edom [Rome] by my quarrelsome friends, who daily sated their appetite with my treasures. His help was with me, supporting my foundations, He will not forsake me all the days of my age. For the LORD does not reject forever. *Lam. 3*

When He comes from Edom with garments stained crimson, there will be slaughter in Botzra, and an execution of traitors, their blood will turn His garments red, in His great strength He will bring the leaders low. With His mighty blast like a day of the east wind. *Is. 27*

When the oppressor from Edom sees how it will be, He will think Botzra to be a refuge like Betzer, giving protection to angels and men, willful and accidental sinners alike. Love the LORD, all His devoted ones: all His faithful ones He will guard. *Ps. 31*

The Rock in His kindness will command His communities to gather, coming together from the four winds, He will settle them upon the high mountains, He will return with us, gathering the dispersed, for it does not say, "He will bring back" but "He will return" and gather.

Blessed is our God who has bestowed good upon us. In His compassion and abundant kindness, He has done great things for us. Like these and those, may He do yet more for us, to magnify His great, mighty and awesome name, by which we are called.

Blessed is our God who created us for His glory, To praise and laud Him and tell of His majesty, His loving-kindness is greater to us than to any other nation. Therefore with all our heart and soul and might, let us proclaim His kingship and His unity.

May He to whom peace belongs, send us blessing and peace. From left and right, may Israel have peace. May the Compassionate One bless His people with peace, and may they merit to see children and children's children, occupied with Torah and the commandments, bringing Israel peace. Wondrous Counselor, mighty God, everlasting Father, Prince of peace. *Is. 9*

# זמירות ליום שבת

בָּרוּךְ אֲדֹנָי יוֹם יוֹם, יַעֲמָס לָנוּ יֶשַׁע וּפִדְיוֹם, וּבִשְׁמוֹ נָגִיל כָּל הַיּוֹם, וּבִישׁוּעָתוֹ נָרִים רֹאשׁ עֶלְיוֹן. כִּי הוּא מָעוֹז לַדָּל וּמַחְסֶה לָאֶבְיוֹן.

שִׁבְטֵי יָהּ לְיִשְׂרָאֵל עֵדוּת, בְּצָרָתָם לוֹ צָר בְּסִבְלוּת וּבְעַבְדוּת, בְּלִבְנַת הַסַּפִּיר הֶרְאָם עֹז יְדִידוּת, וְנִגְלָה לְהַעֲלוֹתָם מֵעֹמֶק בּוֹר וָדוּת. כִּי־עִם־יהוה הַחֶסֶד, וְהַרְבֵּה עִמּוֹ פְדוּת: תהלים קל

מַה יָּקָר חַסְדּוֹ בְּצִלּוֹ לְגוֹנְנֵמוֹ, בְּגָלוּת בָּבֶלָה שֻׁלַּח לְמַעֲנֵמוֹ, לְהוֹרִיד בָּרִיחִים נִמְנָה בֵינֵימוֹ, וַיִּתְּנֵם לְרַחֲמִים לִפְנֵי שׁוֹבֵימוֹ. כִּי לֹא יִטֹּשׁ יהוה אֶת עַמּוֹ, בַּעֲבוּר הַגָּדוֹל שְׁמוֹ.

עֵילָם שָׁת כִּסְאוֹ לְהַצִּיל יְדִידָיו, לְהַאֲבִיד מִשָּׁם מָעֻזְנֵי מוֹרְדָיו, מֵעֲבֹר בַּשֶּׁלַח פָּדָה אֶת עֲבָדָיו, קֶרֶן לְעַמּוֹ יָרִים, תְּהִלָּה לְכָל חֲסִידָיו. כִּי אִם־הוֹגָה, וְרִחַם כְּרֹב חֲסָדָו: איכה ג

וּצְפִיר הָעִזִּים הִגְדִּיל עֲצוּמָיו, וְגַם חָזוּת אַרְבַּע עָלוּ לִמְרוֹמָיו, וּבְלִבָּם דִּמּוּ לְהַשְׁחִית אֶת רְחוּמָיו, עַל יְדֵי כֹהֲנָיו מִגֵּר מִתְקוֹמְמָיו. חַסְדֵי יהוה כִּי לֹא־תָמְנוּ, כִּי לֹא כָלוּ רַחֲמָיו: איכה ג

נִסְגַּרְתִּי לֶאֱדוֹם בְּיַד רֵעַי מְדָנַי, שֶׁבְּכָל יוֹם מְמַלְּאִים כְּרֵסָם מֵעֲדָנַי, עֶזְרָתוֹ עִמִּי לִסְמֹךְ אֶת אֲדָנַי, וְלֹא נְטַשְׁתַּנִי כָּל יְמֵי עִדָּנַי. כִּי לֹא יִזְנַח לְעוֹלָם אֲדֹנָי: איכה ג

בְּבוֹאוֹ מֵאֱדוֹם חֲמוּץ בְּגָדִים, זֶבַח לוֹ בְּבָצְרָה וְטֶבַח לוֹ בְּבוֹגְדִים, וְיֵז נִצְחָם מַלְבּוּשָׁיו לְהַאְדִּים, בְּכֹחוֹ הַגָּדוֹל יִבְצֹר רוּחַ נְגִידִים. הָגָה בְּרוּחוֹ הַקָּשָׁה בְּיוֹם קָדִים: ישעיה כז

רְאוֹתוֹ כִּי כֵן אֲדוֹמִי הָעוֹצֵר, יַחְשֹׁב לוֹ בָּצְרָה תִּקְלֹט כְּבֶצֶר, וּמַלְאָךְ כְּאָדָם בְּתוֹכָהּ יִנָּצֵר, וּמֵזִיד כַּשּׁוֹגֵג בְּמִקְלָט יֵעָצֵר. אֶהֱבוּ אֶת־יהוה כָּל־חֲסִידָיו, אֱמוּנִים נֹצֵר: תהלים לא

יְצַוֶּה צוּר חַסְדּוֹ קְהִלּוֹתָיו לְקַבֵּץ, מֵאַרְבַּע רוּחוֹת עָדָיו לְהִקָּבֵץ, וּבְהַר מְרוֹם הָרִים אוֹתָנוּ לְהַרְבֵּץ, וְאִתָּנוּ יָשׁוּב נִדָּחִים קוֹבֵץ. יָשִׁיב לֹא נֶאֱמַר, כִּי אִם וְשָׁב וְקִבֵּץ.

בָּרוּךְ הוּא אֱלֹהֵינוּ אֲשֶׁר טוֹב גְּמָלָנוּ, כְּרַחֲמָיו וּכְרֹב חֲסָדָיו הִגְדִּיל לָנוּ, אֵלֶּה וְכָאֵלֶּה יוֹסֵף עִמָּנוּ, לְהַגְדִּיל שְׁמוֹ הַגָּדוֹל הַגִּבּוֹר וְהַנּוֹרָא, שֶׁנִּקְרָא עָלֵינוּ.

בָּרוּךְ הוּא אֱלֹהֵינוּ שֶׁבְּרָאָנוּ לִכְבוֹדוֹ, לְהַלְלוֹ וּלְשַׁבְּחוֹ וּלְסַפֵּר הוֹדוֹ, מִכָּל אֹם גָּבַר עָלֵינוּ חַסְדּוֹ, לָכֵן בְּכָל לֵב וּבְכָל נֶפֶשׁ וּבְכָל מְאוֹדוֹ, נַמְלִיכוֹ וּנְיַחֲדוֹ.

שֶׁהַשָּׁלוֹם שֶׁלּוֹ יָשִׂים עָלֵינוּ בְּרָכָה וְשָׁלוֹם, מִשְּׂמֹאל וּמִיָּמִין עַל יִשְׂרָאֵל שָׁלוֹם, הָרַחֲמָן הוּא יְבָרֵךְ אֶת עַמּוֹ בַשָּׁלוֹם, וְיִזְכּוּ לִרְאוֹת בָּנִים וּבְנֵי בָנִים, עוֹסְקִים, בַּתּוֹרָה וּבְמִצְוֹת, עַל יִשְׂרָאֵל שָׁלוֹם. פֶּלֶא יוֹעֵץ אֵל גִּבּוֹר אֲבִי־עַד שַׂר־שָׁלוֹם: ישעיה ט

בָּרוּךְ אֵל עֶלְיוֹן Blessed is God Most High who has given us rest,
To relieve our souls from distress and pain.
May He seek the good of Zion, the outcast city.
How long must she grieve, her spirits downcast?
All who keep the Sabbath, man and woman alike, find favor like an offering made to God.

He who rides the heavens, King of worlds,
Gently told His people to rest,
With tasty food and delicacies of all kinds,
With elegant dress, as at a family feast.
All who keep the Sabbath, man and woman alike, find favor like an offering made to God.

Happy are all who await a double reward
From the One who sees all, though He dwells in dense dark.
He will grant him a heritage in hill and valley,
A heritage and resting place like [Jacob] on whom the sun shone.
All who keep the Sabbath, man and woman alike, find favor like an offering made to God.

Whoever keeps the Sabbath fully, not profaning it,
Shows that he is worthy; holy is his lot.
Happy is he who fulfills the day's duty;
It is like a gift presented to God who fashioned him.
All who keep the Sabbath, man and woman alike, find favor like an offering made to God.

The Rock, my God, called it "Beloved of days."
Happy are the faithful if it is kept intact.
He will set on their head a close-fitting crown.
On them the Rock of Eternity will make His spirit rest.
All who keep the Sabbath, man and woman alike, find favor like an offering made to God.

He who remembers the Sabbath day to keep it holy
Will gain high honor like a diadem on his head.
Therefore let each give to his soul
Delight and joy with which to be exalted.
All who keep the Sabbath, man and woman alike, find favor like an offering made to God.

Let her be holy to you – Sabbath the queen –
Placing a blessing in your home.
In all your dwellings, do no work,
Nor your sons and daughters, your servant or maid.
All who keep the Sabbath, man and woman alike, find favor like an offering made to God.

# בָּרוּךְ אֵל עֶלְיוֹן

אֲשֶׁר נָתַן מְנוּחָה, לְנַפְשֵׁנוּ פִּדְיוֹן מִשֵּׁאת וַאֲנָחָה
וְהוּא יִדְרשׁ לְצִיּוֹן, עִיר הַנִּדָּחָה, עַד אָנָה תּוּגְיוֹן נֶפֶשׁ נֶאֱנָחָה.

הַשּׁוֹמֵר שַׁבָּת הַבֵּן עִם הַבַּת, לָאֵל יֵרָצוּ כְּמִנְחָה עַל מַחֲבַת.

רוֹכֵב בָּעֲרָבוֹת, מֶלֶךְ עוֹלָמִים, אֶת עַמּוֹ לִשְׁבֹּת אִזֵּן בַּנְּעִימִים
בְּמַאֲכָלוֹת עֲרֵבוֹת בְּמִינֵי מַטְעַמִּים, בְּמַלְבּוּשֵׁי כָבוֹד זֶבַח מִשְׁפָּחָה.

הַשּׁוֹמֵר שַׁבָּת הַבֵּן עִם הַבַּת, לָאֵל יֵרָצוּ כְּמִנְחָה עַל מַחֲבַת.

וְאַשְׁרֵי כָּל חוֹכֶה לְתַשְׁלוּמֵי כֵפֶל, מֵאֵת כָּל סוֹכֶה, שׁוֹכֵן בָּעֲרָפֶל
נַחֲלָה לוֹ יִזְכֶּה בָּהָר וּבַשָּׁפֶל, נַחֲלָה וּמְנוּחָה כַּשֶּׁמֶשׁ לוֹ זָרְחָה.

הַשּׁוֹמֵר שַׁבָּת הַבֵּן עִם הַבַּת, לָאֵל יֵרָצוּ כְּמִנְחָה עַל מַחֲבַת.

כָּל שׁוֹמֵר שַׁבָּת כַּדָּת מֵחַלְּלוֹ, הֵן הֶכְשַׁר חִבַּת קֹדֶשׁ גּוֹרָלוֹ
וְאִם יֵצֵא חוֹבַת הַיּוֹם, אַשְׁרֵי לוֹ, אֶל אֵל אָדוֹן מְחוֹלְלוֹ מִנְחָה הִיא שְׁלוּחָה.

הַשּׁוֹמֵר שַׁבָּת הַבֵּן עִם הַבַּת, לָאֵל יֵרָצוּ כְּמִנְחָה עַל מַחֲבַת.

חֶמְדַּת הַיָּמִים קְרָאוֹ אֵלִי צוּר, וְאַשְׁרֵי לִתְמִימִים אִם יִהְיֶה נָצוּר
כֶּתֶר הִלּוּמִים עַל רֹאשָׁם יָצוּר, צוּר הָעוֹלָמִים, רוּחוֹ בָּם נָחָה.

הַשּׁוֹמֵר שַׁבָּת הַבֵּן עִם הַבַּת, לָאֵל יֵרָצוּ כְּמִנְחָה עַל מַחֲבַת.

זָכוֹר אֶת יוֹם הַשַּׁבָּת לְקַדְּשׁוֹ, קַרְנוֹ כִּי גָבְהָה נֵזֶר עַל רֹאשׁוֹ
עַל כֵּן יִתֵּן הָאָדָם לְנַפְשׁוֹ, עֹנֶג וְגַם שִׂמְחָה בָּהֶם לְמָשְׁחָה.

הַשּׁוֹמֵר שַׁבָּת הַבֵּן עִם הַבַּת, לָאֵל יֵרָצוּ כְּמִנְחָה עַל מַחֲבַת.

קֹדֶשׁ הִיא לָכֶם שַׁבָּת הַמַּלְכָּה, אֶל תּוֹךְ בָּתֵּיכֶם לְהָנִיחַ בְּרָכָה
בְּכָל מוֹשְׁבוֹתֵיכֶם לֹא תַעֲשׂוּ מְלָאכָה, בְּנֵיכֶם וּבְנוֹתֵיכֶם עֶבֶד וְגַם שִׁפְחָה.

הַשּׁוֹמֵר שַׁבָּת הַבֵּן עִם הַבַּת, לָאֵל יֵרָצוּ כְּמִנְחָה עַל מַחֲבַת.

יוֹם זֶה מְכֻבָּד This day is honored above all others,
For on it He who formed worlds found rest.

For six days, do your work
But the seventh day is God's:
On the Sabbath you shall do no work,
For in six days He made all.

This day is honored above all others,
for on it He who formed worlds found rest.

Foremost among sacred days
Is this day of rest, this holy Sabbath.
So let each say Kiddush over wine,
And break bread over two complete loaves.

This day is honored above all others,
for on it He who formed worlds found rest.

Eat choice food, drink sweet wine,
For God will give to those who cleave to Him
Clothes to wear, due portions of bread,
Meat and fish, and all tasty foods.

This day is honored above all others,
for on it He who formed worlds found rest.

On it you shall lack nothing – so eat,
Be satisfied and bless
The LORD your God, whom you love,
For He has blessed you from all peoples.

This day is honored above all others,
for on it He who formed worlds found rest.

The heavens declare His glory
And the earth is full of His loving-kindness.
See all these things His hand has made
For He is the Rock, His work is perfect.

This day is honored above all others,
for on it He who formed worlds found rest.

יוֹם זֶה מְּכֻבָּד מִכָּל יָמִים, כִּי בוֹ שָׁבַת צוּר עוֹלָמִים.

שֵׁשֶׁת יָמִים תַּעֲשֶׂה מְּלַאכְתֶּךָ
וְיוֹם הַשְּׁבִיעִי לֵאלֹהֶיךָ
שַׁבָּת לֹא תַעֲשֶׂה בוֹ מְּלָאכָה
כִּי כֹל עָשָׂה שֵׁשֶׁת יָמִים.

יוֹם זֶה מְּכֻבָּד מִכָּל יָמִים, כִּי בוֹ שָׁבַת צוּר עוֹלָמִים.

רִאשׁוֹן הוּא לְמִקְרָאֵי קֹדֶשׁ
יוֹם שַׁבָּתוֹן יוֹם שַׁבַּת קֹדֶשׁ
עַל כֵּן כָּל אִישׁ בְּיֵינוֹ יְקַדֵּשׁ
עַל שְׁתֵּי לֶחֶם יִבְצְעוּ תְמִימִים.

יוֹם זֶה מְּכֻבָּד מִכָּל יָמִים, כִּי בוֹ שָׁבַת צוּר עוֹלָמִים.

אֱכֹל מַשְׁמַנִּים, שְׁתֵה מַמְתַּקִּים
כִּי אֵל יִתֵּן לְכֹל בּוֹ דְּבֵקִים
בֶּגֶד לִלְבֹּשׁ, לֶחֶם חֻקִּים
בָּשָׂר וְדָגִים וְכָל מַטְעַמִּים.

יוֹם זֶה מְּכֻבָּד מִכָּל יָמִים, כִּי בוֹ שָׁבַת צוּר עוֹלָמִים.

לֹא תֶחְסַר כֹּל בּוֹ, וְאָכַלְתָּ
וְשָׂבָעְתָּ וּבֵרַכְתָּ
אֶת יהוה אֱלֹהֶיךָ אֲשֶׁר אָהַבְתָּ
כִּי בֵרַכְךָ מִכָּל הָעַמִּים.

יוֹם זֶה מְּכֻבָּד מִכָּל יָמִים, כִּי בוֹ שָׁבַת צוּר עוֹלָמִים.

הַשָּׁמַיִם מְסַפְּרִים כְּבוֹדוֹ
וְגַם הָאָרֶץ מָלְאָה חַסְדּוֹ
רְאוּ כָּל אֵלֶּה עָשְׂתָה יָדוֹ
כִּי הוּא הַצּוּר פָּעֳלוֹ תָמִים.

יוֹם זֶה מְּכֻבָּד מִכָּל יָמִים, כִּי בוֹ שָׁבַת צוּר עוֹלָמִים.

יוֹם שַׁבָּתוֹן The day of rest should not be forgotten, Its memory is like sweet fragrance,
On it the dove found rest, And in it the exhausted rest.

This day is honored by the people of faith. Parents and children guard it with care.
It was engraved on two tablets of stone,
By the greatness of His power and His unfailing strength.

On it the dove found rest, And in it the exhausted rest.

All came together in a covenant: "We will do and we will obey," they said as one.
Then they responded, saying, "The LORD is One" –
Blessed is He who gives the weary strength.

On it the dove found rest, And in it the exhausted rest.

He spoke in His holiness on the Mount of Myrrh [Sinai]:
"Remember and observe the seventh day."
And learn together all His commands: Gird your loins and muster strength.

On it the dove found rest, And in it the exhausted rest.

The people who have wandered like a straying flock –
May He remember the covenant and the oath,
So that no harm should happen to them, As You swore at the end of Noah's flood.

On it the dove found rest, And in it the exhausted rest.

שַׁבָּת הַיּוֹם Today is the Sabbath of the LORD. Celebrate greatly with my songs,
Multiply my delicacies, Keep it like the LORD's command.

Today is the Sabbath of the LORD.

Do not travel beyond boundaries, Do not labor on this day:
Eat, drink, make merry. This is the day the LORD has made.

Today is the Sabbath of the LORD.

If you keep it God will guard you like the pupil of His eye,
You, your son and daughter too. If you call the Sabbath a delight
Then you will find delight before the LORD.

Today is the Sabbath of the LORD.

Eat rich foods and delicacies, Tasty dishes of many kinds,
Soft-shelled nuts and pomegranates: Eat, be satisfied and bless the LORD.

Today is the Sabbath of the LORD.

Make ready on the table delicious bread, And make, this day, three meals.
Bless and thank His glorious name. Take care, observe and do, my sons.

Today is the Sabbath of the LORD.

יוֹם שַׁבָּתוֹן אֵין לִשְׁכֹּחַ, זִכְרוֹ כְּרֵיחַ הַנִּיחֹחַ
יוֹנָה מָצְאָה בוֹ מָנוֹחַ וְשָׁם יָנוּחוּ יְגִיעֵי כֹחַ.

הַיּוֹם נִכְבָּד לִבְנֵי אֱמוּנִים, זְהִירִים לְשָׁמְרוֹ אָבוֹת וּבָנִים
חָקוּק בִּשְׁנֵי לוּחוֹת אֲבָנִים, מֵרֹב אוֹנִים וְאַמִּיץ כֹּחַ.

יוֹנָה מָצְאָה בוֹ מָנוֹחַ וְשָׁם יָנוּחוּ יְגִיעֵי כֹחַ.

וּבָאוּ כֻלָּם בִּבְרִית יַחַד, נַעֲשֶׂה וְנִשְׁמַע אָמְרוּ כְּאֶחָד
וּפָתְחוּ וְעָנוּ יהוה אֶחָד, בָּרוּךְ נֹתֵן לַיָּעֵף כֹּחַ.

יוֹנָה מָצְאָה בוֹ מָנוֹחַ וְשָׁם יָנוּחוּ יְגִיעֵי כֹחַ.

דִּבֶּר בְּקָדְשׁוֹ בְּהַר הַמֹּר, יוֹם הַשְּׁבִיעִי זָכוֹר וְשָׁמוֹר
וְכָל פִּקּוּדָיו יַחַד לִגְמֹר, חַזֵּק מָתְנַיִם וְאַמֵּץ כֹּחַ.

יוֹנָה מָצְאָה בוֹ מָנוֹחַ וְשָׁם יָנוּחוּ יְגִיעֵי כֹחַ.

הָעָם אֲשֶׁר נָע, כַּצֹּאן תָּעָה, יִזְכֹּר לְפָקְדוֹ בְּרִית וּשְׁבוּעָה
לְבַל יַעֲבָר בָּם מִקְרֵה רָעָה, כַּאֲשֶׁר נִשְׁבַּעְתָּ עַל מֵי נֹחַ.

יוֹנָה מָצְאָה בוֹ מָנוֹחַ וְשָׁם יָנוּחוּ יְגִיעֵי כֹחַ.

שַׁבָּת הַיּוֹם לַיהוה, מְאֹד צַהֲלוּ בְּרִנּוּנַי
וְגַם הַרְבּוּ מַעֲדָנַי, אוֹתוֹ לִשְׁמֹר כְּמִצְוַת יהוה. שַׁבָּת הַיּוֹם לַיהוה.

מֵעֲבֹר דֶּרֶךְ וּגְבוּלִים, מֵעֲשׂוֹת הַיּוֹם פְּעָלִים
לֶאֱכֹל וְלִשְׁתּוֹת בְּהִלּוּלִים, זֶה הַיּוֹם עָשָׂה יהוה. שַׁבָּת הַיּוֹם לַיהוה.

וְאִם תִּשְׁמְרֶנּוּ, יָהּ יִנְצָרְךָ כְּבָבַת, אַתָּה וּבִנְךָ וְגַם הַבַּת
וְקָרָאתָ עֹנֶג לַשַּׁבָּת, אָז תִּתְעַנַּג עַל יהוה. שַׁבָּת הַיּוֹם לַיהוה.

אֱכֹל מַשְׁמַנִּים וּמַעֲדַנִּים, וּמַטְעַמִּים הַרְבֵּה מִינִים
אֱגוֹזֵי פֶרֶךְ וְרִמּוֹנִים, וְאָכַלְתָּ וְשָׂבָעְתָּ וּבֵרַכְתָּ אֶת יהוה. שַׁבָּת הַיּוֹם לַיהוה.

לַעֲרֹךְ בְּשֻׁלְחָן לֶחֶם חֲמוּדוֹת, לַעֲשׂוֹת הַיּוֹם שָׁלֹשׁ סְעוּדוֹת
אֶת הַשֵּׁם הַנִּכְבָּד לְבָרֵךְ וּלְהוֹדוֹת, שִׁקְדוּ וְשִׁמְרוּ וַעֲשׂוּ בָנָי. שַׁבָּת הַיּוֹם לַיהוה.

שִׁמְרוּ שַׁבְּתוֹתַי Observe My Sabbaths, so that you are nourished and sated,
From the radiance of My blessings,
when you come to rest. Borrow on My account, My children,
Delight in My pleasures: Today is the Sabbath of the Lord.

Borrow on My account, My children,
Delight in My pleasures: Today is the Sabbath of the Lord.

Proclaim freedom from toil, then I will grant My blessing,
joining one to the next,
bringing gladness on My day of joy. Wear clothes of fine linen and wool.
And learn from My elders: Today is the Sabbath of the Lord.

Borrow on My account, My children,
Delight in My pleasures: Today is the Sabbath of the Lord.

Quickly bring the portion, obey Esther's command.
Make a reckoning with the Creator,
He will repay you for the food, and more. Trust in Me, My faithful ones,
And drink wine from My plentiful supply. Today is the Sabbath of the Lord.

Borrow on My account, My children,
Delight in My pleasures: Today is the Sabbath of the Lord.

Today is a day of redemption, if you observe the Sabbath;
Then you will be My special treasure.
Stay [for the night of exile], then pass on. Then you will live before Me.
And be filled from My hidden store. Today is the Sabbath of the Lord.

Borrow on My account, My children,
Delight in My pleasures: Today is the Sabbath of the Lord.

Make my city strong, God, the God most high.
Bring back my Temple,
With joy and words of song. There may my singers chant,
My Levites and my priests.
Then you will delight in the Lord. Today is the Sabbath of the Lord.

Borrow on My account, My children,
Delight in My pleasures: Today is the Sabbath of the Lord.

שִׁמְרוּ שַׁבְּתוֹתַי, לְמַעַן תִּינְקוּ וּשְׂבַעְתֶּם, מִזִּיו בִּרְכוֹתַי
אֶל הַמְּנוּחָה כִּי בָאתֶם, וּלְווּ עָלַי בָּנַי, וְעִדְנוּ מַעֲדָנַי
שַׁבָּת הַיּוֹם לַיהוה.
וּלְווּ עָלַי בָּנַי, וְעִדְנוּ מַעֲדָנַי, שַׁבָּת הַיּוֹם לַיהוה.

לְעָמֵל קִרְאוּ דְּרוֹר, וְנָתַתִּי אֶת בִּרְכָתִי, אִשָּׁה אֶל אֲחוֹתָהּ לִצְרוֹר
לְגַלּוֹת עַל יוֹם שִׂמְחָתִי, בִּגְדֵי שֵׁשׁ עִם שָׁנִי, וְהִתְבּוֹנְנוּ מִזְּקֵנַי
שַׁבָּת הַיּוֹם לַיהוה.
וּלְווּ עָלַי בָּנַי, וְעִדְנוּ מַעֲדָנַי, שַׁבָּת הַיּוֹם לַיהוה.

מַהֲרוּ אֶת הַמָּנֶה, לַעֲשׂוֹת אֶת דְּבַר אֶסְתֵּר, וְחִשְׁבוּ עִם הַקּוֹנֶה
לְשַׁלֵּם אָכוֹל וְהוֹתֵר, בִּטְחוּ בִי אֱמוּנַי, וּשְׁתוּ יֵין מִשְׁמַנַּי
שַׁבָּת הַיּוֹם לַיהוה.
וּלְווּ עָלַי בָּנַי, וְעִדְנוּ מַעֲדָנַי, שַׁבָּת הַיּוֹם לַיהוה.

הִנֵּה יוֹם גְּאֻלָּה, יוֹם שַׁבָּת אִם תִּשְׁמֹרוּ, וִהְיִיתֶם לִי סְגֻלָּה
לִינוּ וְאַחַר תַּעֲבֹרוּ, וְאָז תִּחְיוּ לְפָנַי, וּתְמַלְּאוּ צְפוּנַי
שַׁבָּת הַיּוֹם לַיהוה.
וּלְווּ עָלַי בָּנַי, וְעִדְנוּ מַעֲדָנַי, שַׁבָּת הַיּוֹם לַיהוה.

חַזֵּק קִרְיָתִי, אֵל אֱלֹהִים עֶלְיוֹן, וְהָשֵׁב אֶת נָוָתִי
בְּשִׂמְחָה וּבְהִגָּיוֹן, יְשׁוֹרְרוּ שָׁם רְנָנַי, לְוִיַּי וְכֹהֲנַי, אָז תִּתְעַנַּג עַל יהוה
שַׁבָּת הַיּוֹם לַיהוה.
וּלְווּ עָלַי בָּנַי, וְעִדְנוּ מַעֲדָנַי, שַׁבָּת הַיּוֹם לַיהוה.

כִּי אֶשְׁמְרָה If I keep the Sabbath, God will keep me,
It is an eternal sign between God and me.
It is an eternal sign between God and me.

It is forbidden to engage in business or to travel,
Even to speak about the things we need, or about matters of trade or state.
Instead I will study God's Torah and it will make me wise.
It is an eternal sign between God and me.

On it I always find refreshment for my soul.
See: My Holy One gave the first generation,
A sign, by giving them a double portion on the sixth day.
So may my food be doubled every sixth day!
It is an eternal sign between God and me.

Engraved in God's law is His priests' decree,
To prepare the Show-Bread in His presence.
So, His sages ruled, on it fasting is forbidden, except on sins' Atonement Day.
It is an eternal sign between God and me.

It is a day of honor, a day of delight, with bread and fine wine, meat and fish.
On it those who mourn are turned around,
For it is a joyous day and it will bring me joy.
It is an eternal sign between God and me.

Those who desecrate it by working will, in the end, be cut off.
Therefore I cleanse my heart with it as if with soap.
Evening and morning I will pray to God,
Additional and afternoon prayer also, and He will answer me.
It is an eternal sign between God and me.

דְּרוֹר יִקְרָא God proclaims freedom to boy and girl,
And guards you like the pupil of His eye.
Your name is pleasant, never will it cease. Rest and be at ease on the Sabbath day.

Seek my Temple and my hall, And show me a sign of salvation.
Plant a shoot in my vineyard. Hear the cry of my people.

Tread the winepress in Botzra, And in Babylon which overpowered.
Crush my foes in anger and wrath, Hear my voice on the day I cry.

God, let there be on the desert mountain, Myrtle, acacia, cypress and box tree.
To one who warns and one who is warned, Let peace flow like river waters.

Crush those who rise against me, zealous God, Melting their heart with grief.
Then we will open and fill our mouths, And tongues with songs of joy to You.

Know what is wisdom for your soul, And it will be a crown for your head.
Keep your Holy One's command, Observe your holy Sabbath day.

כִּי אֶשְׁמְרָה שַׁבָּת אֵל יִשְׁמְרֵנִי. אוֹת הִיא לְעוֹלְמֵי עַד בֵּינוֹ וּבֵינִי.
אוֹת הִיא לְעוֹלְמֵי עַד בֵּינוֹ וּבֵינִי.

אָסוּר מְצֹא חֵפֶץ, עֲשׂוֹת דְּרָכִים, גַּם מִלְּדַבֵּר בּוֹ דִּבְרֵי צְרָכִים
דִּבְרֵי סְחוֹרָה אַף דִּבְרֵי מְלָכִים, אֶהְגֶּה בְּתוֹרַת אֵל וּתְחַכְּמֵנִי.
אוֹת הִיא לְעוֹלְמֵי עַד בֵּינוֹ וּבֵינִי.

בּוֹ אֶמְצָא תָמִיד נֹפֶשׁ לְנַפְשִׁי, הִנֵּה לְדוֹר רִאשׁוֹן נָתַן קְדוֹשִׁי
מוֹפֵת, בְּתֵת לֶחֶם מִשְׁנֶה בַּשִּׁשִּׁי, כָּכָה בְּכָל שִׁשִּׁי יַכְפִּיל מְזוֹנִי.
אוֹת הִיא לְעוֹלְמֵי עַד בֵּינוֹ וּבֵינִי.

רָשַׁם בְּדַת הָאֵל חֹק אֶל סְגָנָיו, בּוֹ לַעֲרֹךְ לֶחֶם פָּנִים בְּפָנָיו
עַל כֵּן לְהִתְעַנּוֹת בּוֹ עַל פִּי נְבוֹנָיו, אָסוּר, לְבַד מִיּוֹם כִּפּוּר עֲוֹנִי.
אוֹת הִיא לְעוֹלְמֵי עַד בֵּינוֹ וּבֵינִי.

הוּא יוֹם מְכֻבָּד, הוּא יוֹם תַּעֲנוּגִים, לֶחֶם וְיַיִן טוֹב, בָּשָׂר וְדָגִים
הַמִּתְאַבְּלִים בּוֹ אָחוֹר נְסוֹגִים, כִּי יוֹם שְׂמָחוֹת הוּא וּתְשַׂמְּחֵנִי.
אוֹת הִיא לְעוֹלְמֵי עַד בֵּינוֹ וּבֵינִי.

מֵחֵל מְלָאכָה בּוֹ סוֹפוֹ לְהַכְרִית, עַל כֵּן אֲכַבֵּס בּוֹ לִבִּי כְּבוֹרִית
וְאֶתְפַּלְּלָה אֶל אֵל עַרְבִית וְשַׁחְרִית, מוּסָף וְגַם מִנְחָה הוּא יַעֲנֵנִי.
אוֹת הִיא לְעוֹלְמֵי עַד בֵּינוֹ וּבֵינִי.

דְּרוֹר יִקְרָא לְבֵן עִם בַּת, וְיִנְצָרְכֶם כְּמוֹ בָבַת
נְעִים שִׁמְכֶם וְלֹא יֻשְׁבַּת, שְׁבוּ נוּחוּ בְּיוֹם שַׁבָּת

דְּרֹשׁ נָוִי וְאוּלַמִּי, וְאוֹת יֶשַׁע עֲשֵׂה עִמִּי
נְטַע שׂוֹרֵק בְּתוֹךְ כַּרְמִי, שְׁעֵה שַׁוְעַת בְּנֵי עַמִּי.

דְּרֹךְ פּוּרָה בְּתוֹךְ בָּצְרָה, וְגַם בָּבֶל אֲשֶׁר גָּבְרָה
נְתֹץ צָרַי בְּאַף עֶבְרָה, שְׁמַע קוֹלִי בְּיוֹם אֶקְרָא.

אֱלֹהִים תֵּן בַּמִּדְבָּר הַר, הֲדַס שִׁטָּה בְּרוֹשׁ תִּדְהָר
וְלַמַּזְהִיר וְלַנִּזְהָר, שְׁלוֹמִים תֵּן כְּמֵי נָהָר.

הֲדֹךְ קָמַי, אֵל קַנָּא, בְּמוֹג לֵבָב וּבִמְגִנָּה
וְנַרְחִיב פֶּה וּנְמַלְאֶנָּה, לְשׁוֹנֵנוּ לְךָ רִנָּה.

דְּעֵה חָכְמָה לְנַפְשֶׁךָ, וְהִיא כֶתֶר לְרֹאשֶׁךָ
נְצֹר מִצְוַת קְדוֹשֶׁךָ, שְׁמֹר שַׁבַּת קָדְשֶׁךָ.

# Minḥa for Shabbat and Yom Tov

אַשְׁרֵי Happy are those who dwell in Your House; *Ps. 84*
they shall continue to praise You, Selah!
Happy are the people for whom this is so; *Ps. 144*
happy are the people whose God is the Lord.
A song of praise by David. *Ps. 145*

I will exalt You, my God, the King, and bless Your name for ever and all time. Every day I will bless You, and praise Your name for ever and all time. Great is the Lord and greatly to be praised; His greatness is unfathomable. One generation will praise Your works to the next, and tell of Your mighty deeds. On the glorious splendor of Your majesty I will meditate, and on the acts of Your wonders. They shall talk of the power of Your awesome deeds, and I will tell of Your greatness. They shall recite the record of Your great goodness, and sing with joy of Your righteousness. The Lord is gracious and compassionate, slow to anger and great in loving-kindness. The Lord is good to all, and His compassion extends to all His works. All Your works shall thank You, Lord, and Your devoted ones shall bless You. They shall talk of the glory of Your kingship, and speak of Your might. To make known to mankind His mighty deeds and the glorious majesty of His kingship. Your kingdom is an everlasting kingdom, and Your reign is for all generations. The Lord supports all who fall, and raises all who are bowed down. All raise their eyes to You in hope, and You give them their food in due season. You open Your hand, and satisfy every living thing with favor. The Lord is righteous in all His ways, and kind in all He does. The Lord is close to all who call on Him, to all who call on Him in truth. He fulfills the will of those who revere Him; He hears their cry and saves them. The Lord guards all who love Him, but all the wicked He will destroy. ▸ My mouth shall speak the praise of the Lord, and all creatures shall bless His holy name for ever and all time.

We will bless the Lord now and for ever. Halleluya! *Ps. 115*

# מנחה לשבת וליום טוב

אַשְׁרֵי יוֹשְׁבֵי בֵיתֶךָ, עוֹד יְהַלְלְוּךָ סֶּלָה: תהלים פד

אַשְׁרֵי הָעָם שֶׁכָּכָה לּוֹ, אַשְׁרֵי הָעָם שֶׁיהוה אֱלֹהָיו: תהלים קמד

תְּהִלָּה לְדָוִד תהלים קמה

אֲרוֹמִמְךָ אֱלוֹהַי הַמֶּלֶךְ, וַאֲבָרְכָה שִׁמְךָ לְעוֹלָם וָעֶד:

בְּכָל־יוֹם אֲבָרְכֶךָּ, וַאֲהַלְלָה שִׁמְךָ לְעוֹלָם וָעֶד:

גָּדוֹל יהוה וּמְהֻלָּל מְאֹד, וְלִגְדֻלָּתוֹ אֵין חֵקֶר:

דּוֹר לְדוֹר יְשַׁבַּח מַעֲשֶׂיךָ, וּגְבוּרֹתֶיךָ יַגִּידוּ:

הֲדַר כְּבוֹד הוֹדֶךָ, וְדִבְרֵי נִפְלְאֹתֶיךָ אָשִׂיחָה:

וֶעֱזוּז נוֹרְאֹתֶיךָ יֹאמֵרוּ, וּגְדוּלָּתְךָ אֲסַפְּרֶנָּה:

זֵכֶר רַב־טוּבְךָ יַבִּיעוּ, וְצִדְקָתְךָ יְרַנֵּנוּ:

חַנּוּן וְרַחוּם יהוה, אֶרֶךְ אַפַּיִם וּגְדָל־חָסֶד:

טוֹב־יהוה לַכֹּל, וְרַחֲמָיו עַל־כָּל־מַעֲשָׂיו:

יוֹדְוּךָ יהוה כָּל־מַעֲשֶׂיךָ, וַחֲסִידֶיךָ יְבָרְכוּכָה:

כְּבוֹד מַלְכוּתְךָ יֹאמֵרוּ, וּגְבוּרָתְךָ יְדַבֵּרוּ:

לְהוֹדִיעַ לִבְנֵי הָאָדָם גְּבוּרֹתָיו, וּכְבוֹד הֲדַר מַלְכוּתוֹ:

מַלְכוּתְךָ מַלְכוּת כָּל־עֹלָמִים, וּמֶמְשַׁלְתְּךָ בְּכָל־דּוֹר וָדֹר:

סוֹמֵךְ יהוה לְכָל־הַנֹּפְלִים, וְזוֹקֵף לְכָל־הַכְּפוּפִים:

עֵינֵי־כֹל אֵלֶיךָ יְשַׂבֵּרוּ, וְאַתָּה נוֹתֵן־לָהֶם אֶת־אָכְלָם בְּעִתּוֹ:

פּוֹתֵחַ אֶת־יָדֶךָ, וּמַשְׂבִּיעַ לְכָל־חַי רָצוֹן:

צַדִּיק יהוה בְּכָל־דְּרָכָיו, וְחָסִיד בְּכָל־מַעֲשָׂיו:

קָרוֹב יהוה לְכָל־קֹרְאָיו, לְכֹל אֲשֶׁר יִקְרָאֻהוּ בֶאֱמֶת:

רְצוֹן־יְרֵאָיו יַעֲשֶׂה, וְאֶת־שַׁוְעָתָם יִשְׁמַע, וְיוֹשִׁיעֵם:

שׁוֹמֵר יהוה אֶת־כָּל־אֹהֲבָיו, וְאֵת כָּל־הָרְשָׁעִים יַשְׁמִיד:

◂ תְּהִלַּת יהוה יְדַבֶּר פִּי, וִיבָרֵךְ כָּל־בָּשָׂר שֵׁם קָדְשׁוֹ לְעוֹלָם וָעֶד:

וַאֲנַחְנוּ נְבָרֵךְ יָהּ מֵעַתָּה וְעַד־עוֹלָם, הַלְלוּיָהּ: תהלים קטו

וּבָא לְצִיּוֹן גּוֹאֵל "A redeemer will come to Zion, *Is. 59*
to those of Jacob who repent of their sins," declares the LORD.
"As for Me, this is My covenant with them," says the LORD.
"My spirit, that is on you, and My words I have placed in your mouth will not depart from your mouth, or from the mouth of your children, or from the mouth of their descendants from this time on and for ever," says the LORD.

▸ You are the Holy One, enthroned on the praises of Israel. *Ps. 22*
And [the angels] call to one another, saying, ◂ "Holy, holy, holy is the LORD of hosts; the whole world is filled with His glory." *Is. 6*
And they receive permission from one another, saying:
"Holy in the highest heavens, home of His Presence; holy on earth, the work of His strength; holy for ever and all time is the LORD of hosts; the whole earth is full of His radiant glory." *Targum Yonatan Is. 6*

▸ Then a wind lifted me up and I heard behind me the sound of a great noise, saying, ◂ "Blessed is the LORD's glory from His place." *Ezek. 3*
Then a wind lifted me up and I heard behind me
the sound of a great tempest of those who uttered praise, saying,
"Blessed is the LORD's glory from the place of the home of His Presence." *Targum Yonatan Ezek. 3*

The LORD shall reign for ever and all time. *Ex. 15*
The LORD's kingdom is established for ever and all time. *Targum Onkelos Ex. 15*

יהוה LORD, God of Abraham, Isaac and Yisrael, our ancestors, may You keep this for ever so that it forms the thoughts in Your people's heart, and directs their heart toward You. He is compassionate. He forgives iniquity and does not destroy. Repeatedly He suppresses His anger, not rousing His full wrath. For You, my LORD, are good and forgiving, abundantly kind to all who call on You. Your righteousness is eternally righteous, and Your Torah is truth. Grant truth to Jacob, loving-kindness to Abraham, as You promised our ancestors in ancient times. Blessed is my LORD for day after day He burdens us [with His blessings]; is our salvation, Selah! The LORD of hosts is with us; the God of Jacob is our refuge, Selah! LORD of hosts, happy is the one who trusts in You. LORD, save. May the King answer us on the day we call. *1 Chr. 29, Ps. 78, Ps. 86, Ps. 119, Mic. 7, Ps. 68, Ps. 46, Ps. 84, Ps. 20*

ישעיה נט
וּבָא לְצִיּוֹן גּוֹאֵל, וּלְשָׁבֵי פֶשַׁע בְּיַעֲקֹב, נְאֻם יהוה:
וַאֲנִי זֹאת בְּרִיתִי אוֹתָם, אָמַר יהוה
רוּחִי אֲשֶׁר עָלֶיךָ וּדְבָרַי אֲשֶׁר־שַׂמְתִּי בְּפִיךָ
לֹא־יָמְוּשׁוּ מִפִּיךָ וּמִפִּי זַרְעֲךָ וּמִפִּי זֶרַע זַרְעֲךָ
אָמַר יהוה, מֵעַתָּה וְעַד־עוֹלָם:

תהלים כב / ישעיה ו
◂ וְאַתָּה קָדוֹשׁ יוֹשֵׁב תְּהִלּוֹת יִשְׂרָאֵל: וְקָרָא זֶה אֶל־זֶה וְאָמַר ◂
קָדוֹשׁ, קָדוֹשׁ, קָדוֹשׁ, יהוה צְבָאוֹת, מְלֹא כָל־הָאָרֶץ כְּבוֹדוֹ:

תרגום יונתן ישעיה ו
וּמְקַבְּלִין דֵּין מִן דֵּין וְאָמְרִין, קַדִּישׁ בִּשְׁמֵי מְרוֹמָא עִלָּאָה בֵּית שְׁכִינְתֵּהּ
קַדִּישׁ עַל אַרְעָא עוֹבַד גְּבוּרְתֵּהּ, קַדִּישׁ לְעָלַם וּלְעָלְמֵי עָלְמַיָּא
יהוה צְבָאוֹת, מַלְיָא כָל אַרְעָא זִיו יְקָרֵהּ.

יחזקאל ג
◂ וַתִּשָּׂאֵנִי רוּחַ, וָאֶשְׁמַע אַחֲרַי קוֹל רַעַשׁ גָּדוֹל ◂
בָּרוּךְ כְּבוֹד־יהוה מִמְּקוֹמוֹ:

תרגום יונתן יחזקאל ג
וּנְטָלַתְנִי רוּחָא, וּשְׁמָעִית בַּתְרַי קָל זִיעַ סַגִּיא, דִּמְשַׁבְּחִין וְאָמְרִין
בְּרִיךְ יְקָרָא דַיהוה מֵאֲתַר בֵּית שְׁכִינְתֵּהּ.

שמות טו
יהוה יִמְלֹךְ לְעֹלָם וָעֶד:

תרגום אונקלוס שמות טו
יהוה מַלְכוּתֵהּ קָאֵם לְעָלַם וּלְעָלְמֵי עָלְמַיָּא.

דברי הימים א, כט
יהוה אֱלֹהֵי אַבְרָהָם יִצְחָק וְיִשְׂרָאֵל אֲבֹתֵינוּ, שָׁמְרָה־זֹּאת לְעוֹלָם
תהלים עח
לְיֵצֶר מַחְשְׁבוֹת לְבַב עַמֶּךָ, וְהָכֵן לְבָבָם אֵלֶיךָ: וְהוּא רַחוּם יְכַפֵּר
עָוֹן וְלֹא־יַשְׁחִית, וְהִרְבָּה לְהָשִׁיב אַפּוֹ, וְלֹא־יָעִיר כָּל־חֲמָתוֹ:
תהלים פו / תהלים קיט
כִּי־אַתָּה אֲדֹנָי טוֹב וְסַלָּח, וְרַב־חֶסֶד לְכָל־קֹרְאֶיךָ: צִדְקָתְךָ צֶדֶק
מיכה ז
לְעוֹלָם וְתוֹרָתְךָ אֱמֶת: תִּתֵּן אֱמֶת לְיַעֲקֹב, חֶסֶד לְאַבְרָהָם, אֲשֶׁר־
תהלים סח
נִשְׁבַּעְתָּ לַאֲבֹתֵינוּ מִימֵי קֶדֶם: בָּרוּךְ אֲדֹנָי יוֹם יוֹם יַעֲמָס־לָנוּ,
תהלים מו
הָאֵל יְשׁוּעָתֵנוּ סֶלָה: יהוה צְבָאוֹת עִמָּנוּ, מִשְׂגָּב לָנוּ אֱלֹהֵי יַעֲקֹב
תהלים פד / תהלים כ
סֶלָה: יהוה צְבָאוֹת, אַשְׁרֵי אָדָם בֹּטֵחַ בָּךְ: יהוה הוֹשִׁיעָה, הַמֶּלֶךְ
יַעֲנֵנוּ בְיוֹם־קָרְאֵנוּ:

בָּרוּךְ Blessed is He, our God, who created us for His glory, separating us from those who go astray; who gave us the Torah of truth, planting within us eternal life. May He open our heart to His Torah, imbuing our heart with the love and awe of Him, that we may do His will and serve Him with a perfect heart, so that we neither toil in vain nor give birth to confusion.

יְהִי רָצוֹן May it be Your will, O LORD our God and God of our ancestors, that we keep Your laws in this world, and thus be worthy to live, see and inherit goodness and blessing in the Messianic Age and in
the life of the World to Come. So that my soul may sing to You and *Ps. 30*
not be silent. LORD, my God, for ever I will thank You. Blessed is *Jer. 17*
the man who trusts in the LORD, whose trust is in the LORD alone.
Trust in the LORD for evermore, for God, the LORD, is an everlast- *Is. 26*
ing Rock. ▸ Those who know Your name trust in You, for You, LORD, *Ps. 9*
do not forsake those who seek You. The LORD desired, for the sake *Is. 42*
of Israel's merit, to make the Torah great and glorious.

HALF KADDISH

*Leader:* יִתְגַּדַּל Magnified and sanctified
may His great name be,
in the world He created by His will.
May He establish His kingdom
in your lifetime and in your days,
and in the lifetime of all the house of Israel,
swiftly and soon – and say: Amen.

*All:* May His great name be blessed for ever and all time.

*Leader:* Blessed and praised, glorified and exalted,
raised and honored, uplifted and lauded
be the name of the Holy One,
blessed be He,
beyond any blessing,
song, praise and consolation
uttered in the world – and say: Amen.

בָּרוּךְ הוּא אֱלֹהֵינוּ שֶׁבְּרָאָנוּ לִכְבוֹדוֹ, וְהִבְדִּילָנוּ מִן הַתּוֹעִים, וְנָתַן לָנוּ תּוֹרַת אֱמֶת, וְחַיֵּי עוֹלָם נָטַע בְּתוֹכֵנוּ. הוּא יִפְתַּח לִבֵּנוּ בְּתוֹרָתוֹ, וְיָשֵׂם בְּלִבֵּנוּ אַהֲבָתוֹ וְיִרְאָתוֹ וְלַעֲשׂוֹת רְצוֹנוֹ וּלְעָבְדוֹ בְּלֵבָב שָׁלֵם, לְמַעַן לֹא נִיגַע לָרִיק וְלֹא נֵלֵד לַבֶּהָלָה.

יְהִי רָצוֹן מִלְּפָנֶיךָ יהוה אֱלֹהֵינוּ וֵאלֹהֵי אֲבוֹתֵינוּ, שֶׁנִּשְׁמֹר חֻקֶּיךָ
בָּעוֹלָם הַזֶּה, וְנִזְכֶּה וְנִחְיֶה וְנִרְאֶה וְנִירַשׁ טוֹבָה וּבְרָכָה, לִשְׁנֵי
יְמוֹת הַמָּשִׁיחַ וּלְחַיֵּי הָעוֹלָם הַבָּא. לְמַעַן יְזַמֶּרְךָ כָבוֹד וְלֹא יִדֹּם, תהלים ל
יהוה אֱלֹהַי, לְעוֹלָם אוֹדֶךָּ: בָּרוּךְ הַגֶּבֶר אֲשֶׁר יִבְטַח בַּיהוה, ירמיה יז
וְהָיָה יהוה מִבְטַחוֹ: בִּטְחוּ בַיהוה עֲדֵי־עַד, כִּי בְּיָהּ יהוה צוּר ישעיה כו
עוֹלָמִים: ◂ וְיִבְטְחוּ בְךָ יוֹדְעֵי שְׁמֶךָ, כִּי לֹא־עָזַבְתָּ דֹרְשֶׁיךָ, יהוה: תהלים ט
יהוה חָפֵץ לְמַעַן צִדְקוֹ, יַגְדִּיל תּוֹרָה וְיַאְדִּיר: ישעיה מב

חצי קדיש

ש״ץ: יִתְגַּדַּל וְיִתְקַדַּשׁ שְׁמֵהּ רַבָּא (קהל: אָמֵן)
בְּעָלְמָא דִּי בְרָא כִרְעוּתֵהּ
וְיַמְלִיךְ מַלְכוּתֵהּ
בְּחַיֵּיכוֹן וּבְיוֹמֵיכוֹן וּבְחַיֵּי דְכָל בֵּית יִשְׂרָאֵל
בַּעֲגָלָא וּבִזְמַן קָרִיב, וְאִמְרוּ אָמֵן. (קהל: אָמֵן)

קהל וש״ץ: יְהֵא שְׁמֵהּ רַבָּא מְבָרַךְ לְעָלַם וּלְעָלְמֵי עָלְמַיָּא.

ש״ץ: יִתְבָּרַךְ וְיִשְׁתַּבַּח וְיִתְפָּאַר וְיִתְרוֹמַם וְיִתְנַשֵּׂא
וְיִתְהַדָּר וְיִתְעַלֶּה וְיִתְהַלָּל
שְׁמֵהּ דְּקֻדְשָׁא בְּרִיךְ הוּא (קהל: בְּרִיךְ הוּא)
לְעֵלָּא מִן כָּל בִּרְכָתָא / בשבת שובה: לְעֵלָּא לְעֵלָּא מִכָּל בִּרְכָתָא/
וְשִׁירָתָא, תֻּשְׁבְּחָתָא וְנֶחֱמָתָא
דַּאֲמִירָן בְּעָלְמָא, וְאִמְרוּ אָמֵן. (קהל: אָמֵן)

*On Shabbat continue below. On Yom Tov falling on a weekday, say the Amida on page 678.*

וַאֲנִי As for me, may my prayer come to You, LORD, *Ps. 69*
at a time of favor. O God, in Your great love,
answer me with Your faithful salvation.

*The Ark is opened and the congregation stands. All say:*

וַיְהִי בִּנְסֹעַ Whenever the Ark set out, Moses would say, *Num. 10*
"Arise, LORD, and may Your enemies be scattered.
May those who hate You flee before You."
For the Torah shall come forth from Zion, *Is. 2*
and the word of the LORD from Jerusalem.
Blessed is He who, in His holiness,
gave the Torah to His people Israel.

Blessed is the name of the Master of the Universe. Blessed is Your crown and Your place. May Your favor always be with Your people Israel. Show Your people the salvation of Your right hand in Your Temple. Grant us the gift of Your good light, and accept our prayers in mercy. May it be Your will to prolong our life in goodness. May I be counted among the righteous, so that You will have compassion on me and protect me and all that is mine and all that is Your people Israel's. You feed all; You sustain all; You rule over all; You rule over kings, for sovereignty is Yours. I am a servant of the Holy One, blessed be He, before whom and before whose glorious Torah I bow at all times. Not in man do I trust, nor on any angel do I rely, but on the God of heaven who is the God of truth, whose Torah is truth, whose prophets speak truth, and who abounds in acts of love and truth. ▸ In Him I trust, and to His holy and glorious name I offer praises. May it be Your will to open my heart to the Torah, and to fulfill the wishes of my heart and of the hearts of all Your people Israel for good, for life, and for peace. *Zohar, Vayak-hel*

*The Leader takes the Torah scroll in his right arm, bows toward the Ark and says:*

Magnify the LORD with me, and let us exalt His name together. *Ps. 34*

*The Ark is closed. The Leader carries the Torah scroll to the bima and the congregation says:*

לְךָ Yours, LORD, are the greatness and the power, the glory and the majesty and splendor, for everything in heaven and earth is Yours. Yours, LORD, is the kingdom; You are exalted as Head over all. *1 Chr. 29*

רוֹמְמוּ Exalt the LORD our God and bow to His footstool; He is holy. Exalt the LORD our God, and bow at His holy mountain, for holy is the LORD our God. *Ps. 99*

*On* שבת *continue below. On* יום טוב *falling on a weekday, say the* עמידה *on page 679.*

תהלים סט

וַאֲנִי תְפִלָּתִי־לְךָ יהוה, עֵת רָצוֹן, אֱלֹהִים בְּרָב־חַסְדֶּךָ
עֲנֵנִי בֶּאֱמֶת יִשְׁעֶךָ:

*The* ארון קודש *is opened and the* קהל *stands. All say:*

במדבר י

וַיְהִי בִּנְסֹעַ הָאָרֹן וַיֹּאמֶר מֹשֶׁה
קוּמָה יהוה וְיָפֻצוּ אֹיְבֶיךָ וְיָנֻסוּ מְשַׂנְאֶיךָ מִפָּנֶיךָ:

ישעיה ב

כִּי מִצִּיּוֹן תֵּצֵא תוֹרָה וּדְבַר־יהוה מִירוּשָׁלָםִ:
בָּרוּךְ שֶׁנָּתַן תּוֹרָה לְעַמּוֹ יִשְׂרָאֵל בִּקְדֻשָּׁתוֹ.

זוהר ויקהל

בְּרִיךְ שְׁמֵהּ דְּמָרֵא עָלְמָא, בְּרִיךְ כִּתְרָךְ וְאַתְרָךְ. יְהֵא רְעוּתָךְ עִם עַמָּךְ יִשְׂרָאֵל לְעָלַם, וּפֻרְקַן יְמִינָךְ אַחֲזִי לְעַמָּךְ בְּבֵית מַקְדְּשָׁךְ, וּלְאַמְטוּיֵי לַנָא מִטּוּב נְהוֹרָךְ, וּלְקַבֵּל צְלוֹתַנָא בְּרַחֲמִין. יְהֵא רַעֲוָא קֳדָמָךְ דְּתוֹרִיךְ לַן חַיִּין בְּטִיבוּ, וְלֶהֱוֵי אֲנָא פְקִידָא בְּגוֹ צַדִּיקַיָּא, לְמִרְחַם עָלַי וּלְמִנְטַר יָתִי וְיַת כָּל דִּי לִי וְדִי לְעַמָּךְ יִשְׂרָאֵל. אַנְתְּ הוּא זָן לְכֹלָּא וּמְפַרְנֵס לְכֹלָּא, אַנְתְּ הוּא שַׁלִּיט עַל כֹּלָּא, אַנְתְּ הוּא דְּשַׁלִּיט עַל מַלְכַיָּא, וּמַלְכוּתָא דִּילָךְ הִיא. אֲנָא עַבְדָּא דְקֻדְשָׁא בְּרִיךְ הוּא, דְּסָגֵדְנָא קַמֵּהּ וּמִקַּמֵּי דִּיקַר אוֹרַיְתֵהּ בְּכָל עִדָּן וְעִדָּן. לָא עַל אֱנָשׁ רָחִיצְנָא וְלָא עַל בַּר אֱלָהִין סָמִיכְנָא, אֶלָּא בֶּאֱלָהָא דִשְׁמַיָּא, דְּהוּא אֱלָהָא קְשׁוֹט, וְאוֹרַיְתֵהּ קְשׁוֹט, וּנְבִיאוֹהִי קְשׁוֹט, וּמַסְגֵּא לְמֶעְבַּד טַבְוָן וּקְשׁוֹט. ‹ בֵּהּ אֲנָא רָחִיץ, וְלִשְׁמֵהּ קַדִּישָׁא יַקִּירָא אֲנָא אֵמַר תֻּשְׁבְּחָן. יְהֵא רַעֲוָא קֳדָמָךְ דְּתִפְתַּח לִבַּאי בְּאוֹרַיְתָא, וְתַשְׁלִים מִשְׁאֲלִין דְּלִבַּאי וְלִבָּא דְכָל עַמָּךְ יִשְׂרָאֵל לְטָב וּלְחַיִּין וְלִשְׁלָם.

*The* שליח ציבור *takes the* ספר תורה *in his right arm, bows toward the* ארון קודש *and says:*

תהלים לד

גַּדְּלוּ לַיהוה אִתִּי וּנְרוֹמְמָה שְׁמוֹ יַחְדָּו:

*The* ארון קודש *is closed. The* שליח ציבור *carries the* ספר תורה *to the* בימה *and the* קהל *says:*

דברי הימים א׳ כט

לְךָ יהוה הַגְּדֻלָּה וְהַגְּבוּרָה וְהַתִּפְאֶרֶת וְהַנֵּצַח וְהַהוֹד, כִּי־כֹל בַּשָּׁמַיִם וּבָאָרֶץ: לְךָ יהוה הַמַּמְלָכָה וְהַמִּתְנַשֵּׂא לְכֹל לְרֹאשׁ:

תהלים צט

רוֹמְמוּ יהוה אֱלֹהֵינוּ וְהִשְׁתַּחֲווּ לַהֲדֹם רַגְלָיו, קָדוֹשׁ הוּא: רוֹמְמוּ יהוה אֱלֹהֵינוּ וְהִשְׁתַּחֲווּ לְהַר קָדְשׁוֹ, כִּי־קָדוֹשׁ יהוה אֱלֹהֵינוּ:

אַב הָרַחֲמִים May the Father of compassion have compassion on the people borne by Him. May He remember the covenant with the mighty [patriarchs], and deliver us from evil times. May He reproach the evil instinct in the people carried by Him, and graciously grant that we be an everlasting remnant. May He fulfill in good measure our requests for salvation and compassion.

*The Torah scroll is placed on the bima and the Gabbai calls a Kohen to the Torah.*
*See laws 383–397.*

וְתִגָּלֶה May His kingship over us be soon revealed and made manifest. May He be gracious to our surviving remnant, the remnant of His people the house of Israel in grace, loving-kindness, compassion and favor, and let us say: Amen. Let us all render greatness to our God and give honor to the Torah. *Let the Kohen come forward. Arise (*name* son of *father's name*), the Kohen.

**If no Kohen is present, a Levi or Yisrael is called up as follows:*

/As there is no Kohen, arise (*name* son of *father's name*)
in place of a Kohen./

Blessed is He who, in His holiness, gave the Torah to His people Israel.

*The congregation followed by the Gabbai:*

You who cling to the LORD your God are all alive today. *Deut. 4*

*The appropriate Torah portions are to be found from page 1150.*

*The Reader shows the oleh the section to be read. The oleh touches the scroll at that place with the tzitzit of his tallit or the fabric belt of the Torah scroll, which he then kisses. Holding the handles of the scroll, he says:*

*Oleh:* Bless the LORD, the blessed One.

*Cong:* Bless the LORD, the blessed One, for ever and all time.

*Oleh:* Bless the LORD, the blessed One, for ever and all time.

Blessed are You, LORD our God, King of the Universe,
who has chosen us from all peoples
and has given us His Torah.
Blessed are You, LORD, Giver of the Torah.

*After the reading, the oleh says:*

*Oleh:* Blessed are You, LORD our God, King of the Universe,
who has given us the Torah of truth,
planting everlasting life in our midst.
Blessed are You, LORD, Giver of the Torah.

אַב הָרַחֲמִים הוּא יְרַחֵם עַם עֲמוּסִים, וְיִזְכֹּר בְּרִית אֵיתָנִים, וְיַצִּיל נַפְשׁוֹתֵינוּ מִן הַשָּׁעוֹת הָרָעוֹת, וְיִגְעַר בְּיֵצֶר הָרָע מִן הַנְּשׂוּאִים, וְיָחֹן אוֹתָנוּ לִפְלֵיטַת עוֹלָמִים, וִימַלֵּא מִשְׁאֲלוֹתֵינוּ בְּמִדָּה טוֹבָה יְשׁוּעָה וְרַחֲמִים.

*The* ספר תורה *is placed on the* שולחן *and the* גבאי *calls a* כהן *to the* תורה.
*See laws 383–397.*

וְתִגָּלֶה וְתֵרָאֶה מַלְכוּתוֹ עָלֵינוּ בִּזְמַן קָרוֹב, וְיָחֹן פְּלֵיטָתֵנוּ וּפְלֵיטַת עַמּוֹ בֵּית יִשְׂרָאֵל לְחֵן וּלְחֶסֶד וּלְרַחֲמִים וּלְרָצוֹן וְנֹאמַר אָמֵן. הַכֹּל הָבוּ גֹדֶל לֵאלֹהֵינוּ וּתְנוּ כָבוֹד לַתּוֹרָה. *כֹּהֵן קְרָב, יַעֲמֹד (פלוני בֶּן פלוני) הַכֹּהֵן.

**If no* כהן *is present, a* לוי *or* ישראל *is called up as follows:*

/אֵין כָּאן כֹּהֵן, יַעֲמֹד (פלוני בֶּן פלוני) בִּמְקוֹם כֹּהֵן./

בָּרוּךְ שֶׁנָּתַן תּוֹרָה לְעַמּוֹ יִשְׂרָאֵל בִּקְדֻשָּׁתוֹ.

*The* קהל *followed by the* גבאי:

וְאַתֶּם הַדְּבֵקִים בַּיהוה אֱלֹהֵיכֶם חַיִּים כֻּלְּכֶם הַיּוֹם: דברים ד

*The appropriate* תורה *portions are to be found from page 1150.*
*The* קורא *shows the* עולה *the section to be read. The* עולה *touches the scroll at that place with the* ציצית *of his* טלית *or the gartel of the* ספר תורה, *which he then kisses. Holding the handles of the scroll, he says:*

עולה: בָּרְכוּ אֶת יהוה הַמְבֹרָךְ.

קהל: בָּרוּךְ יהוה הַמְבֹרָךְ לְעוֹלָם וָעֶד.

עולה: בָּרוּךְ יהוה הַמְבֹרָךְ לְעוֹלָם וָעֶד.

בָּרוּךְ אַתָּה יהוה, אֱלֹהֵינוּ מֶלֶךְ הָעוֹלָם
אֲשֶׁר בָּחַר בָּנוּ מִכָּל הָעַמִּים, וְנָתַן לָנוּ אֶת תּוֹרָתוֹ.
בָּרוּךְ אַתָּה יהוה, נוֹתֵן הַתּוֹרָה.

*After the* קריאת התורה, *the* עולה *says:*

עולה: בָּרוּךְ אַתָּה יהוה אֱלֹהֵינוּ מֶלֶךְ הָעוֹלָם
אֲשֶׁר נָתַן לָנוּ תּוֹרַת אֱמֶת, וְחַיֵּי עוֹלָם נָטַע בְּתוֹכֵנוּ.
בָּרוּךְ אַתָּה יהוה, נוֹתֵן הַתּוֹרָה.

*The Torah scroll is lifted and the congregation says:*

וְזֹאת הַתּוֹרָה This is the Torah that Deut. 4
Moses placed before the children of Israel,
at the LORD's commandment, by the hand of Moses. Num. 9

*Some add:* It is a tree of life to those who grasp it, and those who uphold it are happy. Its ways are ways of pleasantness, and all its paths are peace. Long life is in its right hand; in its left, riches and honor. It pleased the LORD for the sake of [Israel's] righteousness, to make the Torah great and glorious. Prov. 3 Is. 42

*The Torah scroll is bound and covered.*

*In some congregations, during the week before a yahrzeit, "God, full of mercy" on page 860 is said.*

*The Ark is opened. The Leader takes the Torah scroll and says:*

יְהַלְלוּ Let them praise the name of the LORD, Ps. 148
for His name alone is sublime.

*The congregation responds:*

הוֹדוֹ His majesty is above earth and heaven.
He has raised the horn of His people,
for the glory of all His devoted ones,
the children of Israel, the people close to Him.
Halleluya!

*As the Torah scroll is returned to the Ark say:*

לְדָוִד מִזְמוֹר A psalm of David. The earth is the LORD's and all it contains, the world and all who live in it. For He founded it on the seas and established it on the streams. Who may climb the mountain of the LORD? Who may stand in His holy place? He who has clean hands and a pure heart, who has not taken My name in vain, or sworn deceitfully. He shall receive blessing from the LORD, and just reward from God, his salvation. This is a generation of those who seek Him, the descendants of Jacob who seek Your presence, Selah! Lift up your heads, O gates; be uplifted, eternal doors, so that the King of glory may enter. Who is the King of glory? It is the LORD, strong and mighty, the LORD mighty in battle. ▸ Lift up your Ps. 24

*The* ספר תורה *is lifted and the* קהל *says:*

וְזֹאת הַתּוֹרָה אֲשֶׁר־שָׂם מֹשֶׁה לִפְנֵי בְּנֵי יִשְׂרָאֵל: דברים ד

עַל־פִּי יהוה בְּיַד מֹשֶׁה: במדבר ט

*Some add* עֵץ־חַיִּים הִיא לַמַּחֲזִיקִים בָּהּ וְתֹמְכֶיהָ מְאֻשָּׁר: משלי ג
דְּרָכֶיהָ דַרְכֵי־נֹעַם וְכָל־נְתִיבֹתֶיהָ שָׁלוֹם: אֹרֶךְ יָמִים
בִּימִינָהּ, בִּשְׂמֹאולָהּ עֹשֶׁר וְכָבוֹד: יהוה חָפֵץ לְמַעַן ישעיה מב
צִדְקוֹ יַגְדִּיל תּוֹרָה וְיַאְדִּיר:

*The* ספר תורה *is bound and covered.*

*In some congregations, during the week before a yahrzeit,*
אֵל מָלֵא רַחֲמִים *on page 861 is said.*

*The* ארון קודש *is opened. The* שליח ציבור *takes the* ספר תורה *and says:*

יְהַלְלוּ אֶת־שֵׁם יהוה, כִּי־נִשְׂגָּב שְׁמוֹ, לְבַדּוֹ תהלים קמח

*The* קהל *responds:*

הוֹדוֹ עַל־אֶרֶץ וְשָׁמָיִם:
וַיָּרֶם קֶרֶן לְעַמּוֹ
תְּהִלָּה לְכָל־חֲסִידָיו
לִבְנֵי יִשְׂרָאֵל עַם קְרֹבוֹ
הַלְלוּיָהּ:

*As the* ספר תורה *is returned to the* ארון קודש*, say:*

לְדָוִד מִזְמוֹר, לַיהוה הָאָרֶץ וּמְלוֹאָהּ, תֵּבֵל וְיֹשְׁבֵי בָהּ: כִּי־הוּא תהלים כד
עַל־יַמִּים יְסָדָהּ, וְעַל־נְהָרוֹת יְכוֹנְנֶהָ: מִי־יַעֲלֶה בְהַר־יהוה,
וּמִי־יָקוּם בִּמְקוֹם קָדְשׁוֹ: נְקִי כַפַּיִם וּבַר־לֵבָב, אֲשֶׁר לֹא־נָשָׂא
לַשָּׁוְא נַפְשִׁי וְלֹא נִשְׁבַּע לְמִרְמָה: יִשָּׂא בְרָכָה מֵאֵת יהוה, וּצְדָקָה
מֵאֱלֹהֵי יִשְׁעוֹ: זֶה דּוֹר דֹּרְשָׁו, מְבַקְשֵׁי פָנֶיךָ, יַעֲקֹב, סֶלָה: שְׂאוּ
שְׁעָרִים רָאשֵׁיכֶם, וְהִנָּשְׂאוּ פִּתְחֵי עוֹלָם, וְיָבוֹא מֶלֶךְ הַכָּבוֹד: מִי
זֶה מֶלֶךְ הַכָּבוֹד, יהוה עִזּוּז וְגִבּוֹר, יהוה גִּבּוֹר מִלְחָמָה: ‹ שְׂאוּ

heads, O gates; lift them up, eternal doors, so that the King of glory may enter. Who is He, the King of glory? The LORD of hosts, He is the King of glory, Selah!

*As the Torah scroll is placed into the Ark, say:*

וּבְנֻחֹה יֹאמַר When the Ark came to rest, Moses would say: "Return, *Num. 10*
O LORD, to the myriad thousands of Israel." Advance, LORD, to Your *Ps. 132*
resting place, You and Your mighty Ark. Your priests are clothed
in righteousness, and Your devoted ones sing in joy. For the sake
of Your servant David, do not reject Your anointed one. For I give *Prov. 4*
you good instruction; do not forsake My Torah. It is a tree of life *Prov. 3*
to those who grasp it, and those who uphold it are happy. Its ways
are ways of pleasantness, and all its paths are peace. ▸ Turn us back, *Lam. 5*
O LORD, to You, and we will return. Renew our days as of old.

*The Ark is closed.*

HALF KADDISH

*Leader:* יִתְגַּדַּל Magnified and sanctified
may His great name be,
in the world He created by His will.
May He establish His kingdom
in your lifetime and in your days,
and in the lifetime of all the house of Israel,
swiftly and soon –
and say: Amen.

*All:* May His great name be blessed for ever and all time.

*Leader:* Blessed and praised, glorified and exalted,
raised and honored, uplifted and lauded
be the name of the Holy One, blessed be He,
beyond any blessing,
song, praise and consolation
uttered in the world –
and say: Amen.

שְׂעָרִים רָאשֵׁיכֶם, וּשְׂאוּ פִּתְחֵי עוֹלָם, וְיָבֹא מֶלֶךְ הַכָּבוֹד: מִי הוּא זֶה מֶלֶךְ הַכָּבוֹד, יהוה צְבָאוֹת הוּא מֶלֶךְ הַכָּבוֹד, סֶלָה:

*As the* ספר תורה *is placed into the* ארון קודש*, say:*

וּבְנֻחֹה יֹאמַר, שׁוּבָה יהוה רִבְבוֹת אַלְפֵי יִשְׂרָאֵל: קוּמָה יהוה במדבר י
לִמְנוּחָתֶךָ, אַתָּה וַאֲרוֹן עֻזֶּךָ: כֹּהֲנֶיךָ יִלְבְּשׁוּ־צֶדֶק, וַחֲסִידֶיךָ יְרַנֵּנוּ: תהלים קלב
בַּעֲבוּר דָּוִד עַבְדֶּךָ אַל־תָּשֵׁב פְּנֵי מְשִׁיחֶךָ: כִּי לֶקַח טוֹב נָתַתִּי משלי ד
לָכֶם, תּוֹרָתִי אַל־תַּעֲזֹבוּ: עֵץ־חַיִּים הִיא לַמַּחֲזִיקִים בָּהּ, וְתֹמְכֶיהָ משלי ג
מְאֻשָּׁר: דְּרָכֶיהָ דַרְכֵי־נֹעַם וְכָל־נְתִיבֹתֶיהָ שָׁלוֹם: ◂ הֲשִׁיבֵנוּ יהוה איכה ה
אֵלֶיךָ וְנָשׁוּבָה, חַדֵּשׁ יָמֵינוּ כְּקֶדֶם:

*The* ארון קודש *is closed.*

## חצי קדיש

ש״ץ: יִתְגַּדַּל וְיִתְקַדַּשׁ שְׁמֵהּ רַבָּא (קהל: אָמֵן)
בְּעָלְמָא דִּי בְרָא כִרְעוּתֵהּ
וְיַמְלִיךְ מַלְכוּתֵהּ
בְּחַיֵּיכוֹן וּבְיוֹמֵיכוֹן, וּבְחַיֵּי דְכָל בֵּית יִשְׂרָאֵל
בַּעֲגָלָא וּבִזְמַן קָרִיב, וְאִמְרוּ אָמֵן. (קהל: אָמֵן)

קהל וש״ץ: יְהֵא שְׁמֵהּ רַבָּא מְבָרַךְ לְעָלַם וּלְעָלְמֵי עָלְמַיָּא.

ש״ץ: יִתְבָּרַךְ וְיִשְׁתַּבַּח וְיִתְפָּאַר וְיִתְרוֹמַם וְיִתְנַשֵּׂא
וְיִתְהַדָּר וְיִתְעַלֶּה וְיִתְהַלָּל
שְׁמֵהּ דְּקֻדְשָׁא בְּרִיךְ הוּא (קהל: בְּרִיךְ הוּא)
לְעֵלָּא מִן כָּל בִּרְכָתָא / בשבת שובה: לְעֵלָּא לְעֵלָּא מִכָּל בִּרְכָתָא/
וְשִׁירָתָא, תֻּשְׁבְּחָתָא וְנֶחֱמָתָא
דַּאֲמִירָן בְּעָלְמָא, וְאִמְרוּ אָמֵן. (קהל: אָמֵן)

*On Yom Tov (including one that falls on Shabbat) say the appropriate Amida on page 830.*

## THE AMIDA

*The following prayer, until "in former years" on page 690, is said silently, standing with feet together. If there is a minyan, the Amida is repeated aloud by the Leader. Take three steps forward and at the points indicated by ▾, bend the knees at the first word, bow at the second, and stand straight before saying God's name.*

When I proclaim the LORD's name, give glory to our God. *Deut. 32*
O LORD, open my lips, so that my mouth may declare Your praise. *Ps. 51*

### PATRIARCHS

▾בָּרוּךְ Blessed are You, LORD our God and God of our fathers,
God of Abraham, God of Isaac and God of Jacob;
the great, mighty and awesome God, God Most High,
who bestows acts of loving-kindness and creates all,
who remembers the loving-kindness of the fathers
and will bring a Redeemer to their children's children
for the sake of His name, in love.

*On Shabbat Shuva:* Remember us for life, O King who desires life,
and write us in the book of life –
for Your sake, O God of life.

King, Helper, Savior, Shield:
▾Blessed are You, LORD, Shield of Abraham.

### DIVINE MIGHT

אַתָּה גִּבּוֹר You are eternally mighty, LORD.
You give life to the dead and have great power to save.

*The phrase "He makes the wind blow and the rain fall" is added from Simḥat Torah until Pesaḥ. In Israel, the phrase "He causes the dew to fall" is added from Pesaḥ until Shemini Atzeret. See laws 129–131.*

*In fall & winter:* He makes the wind blow and the rain fall.
*In Israel, in spring & summer:* He causes the dew to fall.

He sustains the living with loving-kindness,
and with great compassion revives the dead.
He supports the fallen, heals the sick, sets captives free,
and keeps His faith with those who sleep in the dust.

*On* יום טוב *(including one that falls on* שבת*) say the appropriate* עמידה *on page 831.*

# עמידה

*The following prayer, until* קַדְמֹנִיּוֹת *on page 691, is said silently, standing with feet together. If there is a* מנין*, the* עמידה *is repeated aloud by the* שליח ציבור*. Take three steps forward and at the points indicated by* ▾*, bend the knees at the first word, bow at the second, and stand straight before saying God's name.*

כִּי שֵׁם יהוה אֶקְרָא, הָבוּ גֹדֶל לֵאלֹהֵינוּ: דברים לב

אֲדֹנָי, שְׂפָתַי תִּפְתָּח, וּפִי יַגִּיד תְּהִלָּתֶךָ: תהלים נא

אבות

▾בָּרוּךְ אַתָּה יהוה, אֱלֹהֵינוּ וֵאלֹהֵי אֲבוֹתֵינוּ
אֱלֹהֵי אַבְרָהָם, אֱלֹהֵי יִצְחָק, וֵאלֹהֵי יַעֲקֹב
הָאֵל הַגָּדוֹל הַגִּבּוֹר וְהַנּוֹרָא, אֵל עֶלְיוֹן
גּוֹמֵל חֲסָדִים טוֹבִים, וְקוֹנֵה הַכֹּל, וְזוֹכֵר חַסְדֵי אָבוֹת
וּמֵבִיא גוֹאֵל לִבְנֵי בְנֵיהֶם לְמַעַן שְׁמוֹ בְּאַהֲבָה.

בשבת שובה: זָכְרֵנוּ לְחַיִּים, מֶלֶךְ חָפֵץ בַּחַיִּים
וְכָתְבֵנוּ בְּסֵפֶר הַחַיִּים, לְמַעַנְךָ אֱלֹהִים חַיִּים.

מֶלֶךְ עוֹזֵר וּמוֹשִׁיעַ וּמָגֵן.
▾בָּרוּךְ אַתָּה יהוה, מָגֵן אַבְרָהָם.

גבורות

אַתָּה גִּבּוֹר לְעוֹלָם, אֲדֹנָי
מְחַיֵּה מֵתִים אַתָּה, רַב לְהוֹשִׁיעַ

*The phrase* מַשִּׁיב הָרְוּחַ *is added from* שמחת תורה *until* פסח*.*
*In* ארץ ישראל*, the phrase* מוֹרִיד הַטָּל *is added from* פסח *until* שמיני עצרת*. See laws 129–131.*

בחורף: מַשִּׁיב הָרְוּחַ וּמוֹרִיד הַגֶּשֶׁם / בארץ ישראל בקיץ: מוֹרִיד הַטָּל

מְכַלְכֵּל חַיִּים בְּחֶסֶד, מְחַיֵּה מֵתִים בְּרַחֲמִים רַבִּים
סוֹמֵךְ נוֹפְלִים, וְרוֹפֵא חוֹלִים, וּמַתִּיר אֲסוּרִים
וּמְקַיֵּם אֱמוּנָתוֹ לִישֵׁנֵי עָפָר.

Who is like You, Master of might,
and who can compare to You,
O King who brings death and gives life, and makes salvation grow?

*On Shabbat Shuva:* Who is like You, compassionate Father,
who remembers His creatures in compassion, for life?

Faithful are You to revive the dead.
Blessed are You, LORD, who revives the dead.

*When saying the Amida silently, continue with "You are holy" below.*

---

KEDUSHA

*During the Leader's Repetition, the following is said standing with feet together, rising on the toes at the words indicated by ▴.*

*Cong. then Leader:* נְקַדֵּשׁ We will sanctify Your name on earth,
as they sanctify it in the highest heavens,
as is written by Your prophet,
"And they [the angels] call to one another saying: *Is. 6*

*Cong. then Leader:* ▴Holy, ▴holy, ▴holy is the LORD of hosts;
the whole world is filled with His glory."
Those facing them say "Blessed –"

*Cong. then Leader:* ▴"Blessed is the LORD's glory from His place." *Ezek. 3*
And in Your holy Writings it is written thus:

*Cong. then Leader:* ▴"The LORD shall reign for ever. He is your God, Zion, *Ps. 146*
from generation to generation, Halleluya!"

*Leader:* From generation to generation we will declare Your greatness,
and we will proclaim Your holiness for evermore.
Your praise, our God, shall not leave our mouth forever,
for You, God, are a great and holy King. Blessed are You, LORD,
the holy God. / *On Shabbat Shuva:* the holy King./

*The Leader continues with "You are One" on the next page.*

---

HOLINESS

אַתָּה קָדוֹשׁ You are holy and Your name is holy,
and holy ones praise You daily, Selah!
Blessed are You, LORD,
the holy God. / *On Shabbat Shuva:* the holy King./
(*If forgotten, repeat the Amida.*)

מִי כָמְוֹךָ, בַּֽעַל גְּבוּרוֹת, וּמִי דּֽוֹמֶה לָּךְ
מֶֽלֶךְ, מֵמִית וּמְחַיֶּה וּמַצְמִֽיחַ יְשׁוּעָה.

בשבת שובה: מִי כָמְוֹךָ אַב הָרַחֲמִים, זוֹכֵר יְצוּרָיו לְחַיִּים בְּרַחֲמִים.

וְנֶאֱמָן אַתָּה לְהַחֲיוֹת מֵתִים.
בָּרוּךְ אַתָּה יהוה, מְחַיֵּה הַמֵּתִים.

*When saying the* עמידה *silently, continue with* אַתָּה קָדוֹשׁ *below.*

---

קדושה

*During the* חזרת הש״ץ*, the following is said standing with feet together, rising on the toes at the words indicated by* ˄.

קהל *then* ש״ץ: נְקַדֵּשׁ אֶת שִׁמְךָ בָּעוֹלָם, כְּשֵׁם שֶׁמַּקְדִּישִׁים אוֹתוֹ בִּשְׁמֵי מָרוֹם
כַּכָּתוּב עַל יַד נְבִיאֶךָ: וְקָרָא זֶה אֶל־זֶה וְאָמַר ישעיה ו

קהל *then* ש״ץ: ˄קָדוֹשׁ, ˄קָדוֹשׁ, ˄קָדוֹשׁ, יהוה צְבָאוֹת, מְלֹא כָל־הָאָֽרֶץ כְּבוֹדוֹ:
לְעֻמָּתָם בָּרוּךְ יֹאמֵֽרוּ

קהל *then* ש״ץ: ˄בָּרוּךְ כְּבוֹד־יהוה מִמְּקוֹמוֹ: יחזקאל ג
וּבְדִבְרֵי קָדְשְׁךָ כָּתוּב לֵאמֹר

קהל *then* ש״ץ: ˄יִמְלֹךְ יהוה לְעוֹלָם, אֱלֹהַֽיִךְ צִיּוֹן לְדֹר וָדֹר, הַלְלוּיָהּ: תהלים קמו

ש״ץ: לְדוֹר וָדוֹר נַגִּיד גָּדְלֶֽךָ, וּלְנֵֽצַח נְצָחִים קְדֻשָּׁתְךָ נַקְדִּישׁ
וְשִׁבְחֲךָ אֱלֹהֵֽינוּ מִפִּֽינוּ לֹא יָמוּשׁ לְעוֹלָם וָעֶד
כִּי אֵל מֶֽלֶךְ גָּדוֹל וְקָדוֹשׁ אָֽתָּה. בָּרוּךְ אַתָּה יהוה
הָאֵל הַקָּדוֹשׁ. / בשבת שובה: הַמֶּֽלֶךְ הַקָּדוֹשׁ./

*The* שליח ציבור *continues with* אַתָּה אֶחָד *on the next page.*

---

קדושת השם

אַתָּה קָדוֹשׁ וְשִׁמְךָ קָדוֹשׁ
וּקְדוֹשִׁים בְּכָל יוֹם יְהַלְלֽוּךָ סֶּֽלָה.
בָּרוּךְ אַתָּה יהוה, הָאֵל הַקָּדוֹשׁ. / בשבת שובה: הַמֶּֽלֶךְ הַקָּדוֹשׁ./
(*If forgotten, repeat the* עמידה.)

HOLINESS OF THE DAY

אַתָּה You are One, Your name is One;
and who is like Your people Israel, a nation unique on earth?
Splendor of greatness and a crown of salvation
is the day of rest and holiness You have given Your people.
Abraham will rejoice, Isaac will sing for joy,
Jacob and his children will find rest in it –
a rest of love and generosity, a rest of truth and faith,
a rest of peace and tranquility, calm and trust;
a complete rest in which You find favor.
May Your children recognize and know
that their rest comes from You,
and that by their rest they sanctify Your name.

אֱלֹהֵינוּ Our God and God of our ancestors, find favor in our rest.
Make us holy through Your commandments
and grant us our share in Your Torah.
Satisfy us with Your goodness, grant us joy in Your salvation,
and purify our hearts to serve You in truth.
In love and favor, Lord our God,
grant us as our heritage Your holy Sabbaths,
so that Israel who sanctify Your name may find rest on them.
Blessed are You, Lord, who sanctifies the Sabbath.

TEMPLE SERVICE

רְצֵה Find favor, Lord our God,
in Your people Israel and their prayer.
Restore the service to Your most holy House,
and accept in love and favor
the fire-offerings of Israel and their prayer.
May the service of Your people Israel always find favor with You.

---

*On Rosh Hodesh and Hol HaMo'ed, say:*

אֱלֹהֵינוּ Our God and God of our ancestors, may there rise, come, reach, appear, be favored, heard, regarded and remembered before You, our recollection and remembrance, as well as the remembrance of our ancestors, and of the Messiah,

קדושת היום

אַתָּה אֶחָד וְשִׁמְךָ אֶחָד, וּמִי כְּעַמְּךָ יִשְׂרָאֵל גּוֹי אֶחָד בָּאָרֶץ.
תִּפְאֶרֶת גְּדֻלָּה וַעֲטֶרֶת יְשׁוּעָה, יוֹם מְנוּחָה וּקְדֻשָּׁה לְעַמְּךָ נָתָתָּ.
אַבְרָהָם יָגֵל, יִצְחָק יְרַנֵּן, יַעֲקֹב וּבָנָיו יָנוּחוּ בוֹ
מְנוּחַת אַהֲבָה וּנְדָבָה, מְנוּחַת אֱמֶת וֶאֱמוּנָה
מְנוּחַת שָׁלוֹם וְשַׁלְוָה וְהַשְׁקֵט וָבֶטַח
מְנוּחָה שְׁלֵמָה שֶׁאַתָּה רוֹצֶה בָּהּ.
יַכִּירוּ בָנֶיךָ וְיֵדְעוּ, כִּי מֵאִתְּךָ הִיא מְנוּחָתָם
וְעַל מְנוּחָתָם יַקְדִּישׁוּ אֶת שְׁמֶךָ.

אֱלֹהֵינוּ וֵאלֹהֵי אֲבוֹתֵינוּ, רְצֵה בִמְנוּחָתֵנוּ
קַדְּשֵׁנוּ בְּמִצְוֹתֶיךָ וְתֵן חֶלְקֵנוּ בְּתוֹרָתֶךָ
שַׂבְּעֵנוּ מִטּוּבֶךָ וְשַׂמְּחֵנוּ בִּישׁוּעָתֶךָ
וְטַהֵר לִבֵּנוּ לְעָבְדְּךָ בֶּאֱמֶת.
וְהַנְחִילֵנוּ יהוה אֱלֹהֵינוּ בְּאַהֲבָה וּבְרָצוֹן שַׁבְּתוֹת קָדְשֶׁךָ
וְיָנוּחוּ בָם יִשְׂרָאֵל מְקַדְּשֵׁי שְׁמֶךָ.
בָּרוּךְ אַתָּה יהוה, מְקַדֵּשׁ הַשַּׁבָּת.

עבודה

רְצֵה יהוה אֱלֹהֵינוּ בְּעַמְּךָ יִשְׂרָאֵל וּבִתְפִלָּתָם
וְהָשֵׁב אֶת הָעֲבוֹדָה לִדְבִיר בֵּיתֶךָ
וְאִשֵּׁי יִשְׂרָאֵל וּתְפִלָּתָם בְּאַהֲבָה תְקַבֵּל בְּרָצוֹן
וּתְהִי לְרָצוֹן תָּמִיד עֲבוֹדַת יִשְׂרָאֵל עַמֶּךָ.

---

*On* ראש חודש *and* חול המועד*, say:*

אֱלֹהֵינוּ וֵאלֹהֵי אֲבוֹתֵינוּ, יַעֲלֶה וְיָבוֹא וְיַגִּיעַ, וְיֵרָאֶה וְיֵרָצֶה וְיִשָּׁמַע,
וְיִפָּקֵד וְיִזָּכֵר זִכְרוֹנֵנוּ וּפִקְדוֹנֵנוּ וְזִכְרוֹן אֲבוֹתֵינוּ, וְזִכְרוֹן מָשִׁיחַ בֶּן דָּוִד

son of David Your servant, and of Jerusalem Your holy city, and of all Your people the house of Israel – for deliverance and well-being, grace, loving-kindness and compassion, life and peace, on this day of:

*On Rosh Ḥodesh:* Rosh Ḥodesh.
*On Pesaḥ:* the Festival of Matzot.
*On Sukkot:* the Festival of Sukkot.

On it remember us, LORD our God, for good; recollect us for blessing, and deliver us for life. In accord with Your promise of salvation and compassion, spare us and be gracious to us; have compassion on us and deliver us, for our eyes are turned to You because You, God, are a gracious and compassionate King.

---

וְתֶחֱזֶינָה And may our eyes witness Your return to Zion in compassion. Blessed are You, LORD, who restores His Presence to Zion.

THANKSGIVING

*Bow at the first nine words.*

מוֹדִים We give thanks to You,
for You are the LORD our God
and God of our ancestors
for ever and all time.
You are the Rock of our lives,
Shield of our salvation
from generation to generation.
We will thank You and
declare Your praise for our lives,
which are entrusted into Your hand;
for our souls,
which are placed in Your charge;
for Your miracles
which are with us every day;
and for Your wonders and favors
at all times, evening, morning and
midday.
You are good –
for Your compassion never fails.
You are compassionate –
for Your loving-kindnesses never cease.
We have always placed our hope in You.

*During the Leader's Repetition, the congregation says quietly:*

מוֹדִים We give thanks to You,
for You are the LORD our God
and God of our ancestors,
God of all flesh,
who formed us
and formed the universe.
Blessings and thanks
are due to Your great
and holy name for giving us
life and sustaining us.
May You continue
to give us life and sustain us;
and may You gather our
exiles to Your holy courts,
to keep Your decrees,
do Your will and serve You
with a perfect heart,
for it is for us
to give You thanks.
Blessed be God to whom
thanksgiving is due.

עַבְדֶּךָ, וְזִכְרוֹן יְרוּשָׁלַיִם עִיר קָדְשֶׁךָ, וְזִכְרוֹן כָּל עַמְּךָ בֵּית יִשְׂרָאֵל, לְפָנֶיךָ, לִפְלֵיטָה לְטוֹבָה, לְחֵן וּלְחֶסֶד וּלְרַחֲמִים, לְחַיִּים וּלְשָׁלוֹם בְּיוֹם

בראש חודש: רֹאשׁ הַחֹדֶשׁ / בפסח: חַג הַמַּצּוֹת / בסוכות: חַג הַסֻּכּוֹת

הַזֶּה. זָכְרֵנוּ יהוה אֱלֹהֵינוּ בּוֹ לְטוֹבָה, וּפָקְדֵנוּ בוֹ לִבְרָכָה, וְהוֹשִׁיעֵנוּ בוֹ לְחַיִּים. וּבִדְבַר יְשׁוּעָה וְרַחֲמִים, חוּס וְחָנֵּנוּ וְרַחֵם עָלֵינוּ וְהוֹשִׁיעֵנוּ, כִּי אֵלֶיךָ עֵינֵינוּ, כִּי אֵל מֶלֶךְ חַנּוּן וְרַחוּם אָתָּה.

---

וְתֶחֱזֶינָה עֵינֵינוּ בְּשׁוּבְךָ לְצִיּוֹן בְּרַחֲמִים.
בָּרוּךְ אַתָּה יהוה, הַמַּחֲזִיר שְׁכִינָתוֹ לְצִיּוֹן.

הודאה

*Bow at the first five words.*

מוֹדִים אֲנַחְנוּ לָךְ
שָׁאַתָּה הוּא יהוה אֱלֹהֵינוּ
וֵאלֹהֵי אֲבוֹתֵינוּ לְעוֹלָם וָעֶד.
צוּר חַיֵּינוּ, מָגֵן יִשְׁעֵנוּ
אַתָּה הוּא לְדוֹר וָדוֹר.
נוֹדֶה לְּךָ וּנְסַפֵּר תְּהִלָּתֶךָ
עַל חַיֵּינוּ הַמְּסוּרִים בְּיָדֶךָ
וְעַל נִשְׁמוֹתֵינוּ הַפְּקוּדוֹת לָךְ
וְעַל נִסֶּיךָ שֶׁבְּכָל יוֹם עִמָּנוּ
וְעַל נִפְלְאוֹתֶיךָ וְטוֹבוֹתֶיךָ
שֶׁבְּכָל עֵת, עֶרֶב וָבֹקֶר וְצָהֳרָיִם.
הַטּוֹב, כִּי לֹא כָלוּ רַחֲמֶיךָ
וְהַמְרַחֵם, כִּי לֹא תַמּוּ חֲסָדֶיךָ
מֵעוֹלָם קִוִּינוּ לָךְ.

*During the* חזרת הש״ץ, *the* קהל *says quietly:*

מוֹדִים אֲנַחְנוּ לָךְ
שָׁאַתָּה הוּא יהוה אֱלֹהֵינוּ
וֵאלֹהֵי אֲבוֹתֵינוּ
אֱלֹהֵי כָל בָּשָׂר
יוֹצְרֵנוּ, יוֹצֵר בְּרֵאשִׁית.
בְּרָכוֹת וְהוֹדָאוֹת
לְשִׁמְךָ הַגָּדוֹל וְהַקָּדוֹשׁ
עַל שֶׁהֶחֱיִיתָנוּ וְקִיַּמְתָּנוּ.
כֵּן תְּחַיֵּנוּ וּתְקַיְּמֵנוּ
וְתֶאֱסֹף גָּלֻיּוֹתֵינוּ
לְחַצְרוֹת קָדְשֶׁךָ
לִשְׁמֹר חֻקֶּיךָ וְלַעֲשׂוֹת רְצוֹנֶךָ
וּלְעָבְדְּךָ בְּלֵבָב שָׁלֵם
עַל שֶׁאֲנַחְנוּ מוֹדִים לָךְ.
בָּרוּךְ אֵל הַהוֹדָאוֹת.

*On Ḥanukka:*

עַל הַנִּסִּים [We thank You also] for the miracles, the redemption, the mighty deeds, the salvations, and the victories in battle which You performed for our ancestors in those days, at this time.

בִּימֵי מַתִּתְיָהוּ In the days of Mattityahu, son of Yoḥanan, the High Priest, the Hasmonean, and his sons, the wicked Greek kingdom rose up against Your people Israel to make them forget Your Torah and to force them to transgress the statutes of Your will. It was then that You in Your great compassion stood by them in the time of their distress. You championed their cause, judged their claim, and avenged their wrong. You delivered the strong into the hands of the weak, the many into the hands of the few, the impure into the hands of the pure, the wicked into the hands of the righteous, and the arrogant into the hands of those who were engaged in the study of Your Torah. You made for Yourself great and holy renown in Your world, and for Your people Israel You performed a great salvation and redemption as of this very day. Your children then entered the holiest part of Your House, cleansed Your Temple, purified Your Sanctuary, kindled lights in Your holy courts, and designated these eight days of Ḥanukka for giving thanks and praise to Your great name.

*Continue with "For all these things."*

*On Shushan Purim in Jerusalem:*

עַל הַנִּסִּים [We thank You also] for the miracles, the redemption, the mighty deeds, the salvations, and the victories in battle which You performed for our ancestors in those days, at this time.

בִּימֵי מָרְדְּכַי In the days of Mordekhai and Esther, in Shushan the capital, the
wicked Haman rose up against them and sought to destroy, slay and exterminate *Esther 3*
all the Jews, young and old, children and women, on one day, the thirteenth day of the twelfth month, which is the month of Adar, and to plunder their possessions. Then You in Your great compassion thwarted his counsel, frustrated his plans, and caused his scheme to recoil on his own head, so that they hanged him and his sons on the gallows.

*Continue with "For all these things."*

וְעַל כֻּלָּם For all these things may Your name be blessed and exalted, our King, continually, for ever and all time.

*On Shabbat Shuva:* And write, for a good life,
all the children of Your covenant.

Let all that lives thank You, Selah! and praise Your name in truth, God, our Savior and Help, Selah!

▾Blessed are You, Lord, whose name is "the Good" and to whom thanks are due.

בחנוכה:

עַל הַנִּסִּים וְעַל הַפֻּרְקָן וְעַל הַגְּבוּרוֹת וְעַל הַתְּשׁוּעוֹת וְעַל הַמִּלְחָמוֹת שֶׁעָשִׂיתָ לַאֲבוֹתֵינוּ בַּיָּמִים הָהֵם בַּזְּמַן הַזֶּה.

בִּימֵי מַתִּתְיָהוּ בֶּן יוֹחָנָן כֹּהֵן גָּדוֹל חַשְׁמוֹנַאי וּבָנָיו, כְּשֶׁעָמְדָה מַלְכוּת יָוָן הָרְשָׁעָה עַל עַמְּךָ יִשְׂרָאֵל לְהַשְׁכִּיחָם תּוֹרָתֶךָ וּלְהַעֲבִירָם מֵחֻקֵּי רְצוֹנֶךָ, וְאַתָּה בְּרַחֲמֶיךָ הָרַבִּים עָמַדְתָּ לָהֶם בְּעֵת צָרָתָם, רַבְתָּ אֶת רִיבָם, דַּנְתָּ אֶת דִּינָם, נָקַמְתָּ אֶת נִקְמָתָם, מָסַרְתָּ גִבּוֹרִים בְּיַד חַלָּשִׁים, וְרַבִּים בְּיַד מְעַטִּים, וּטְמֵאִים בְּיַד טְהוֹרִים, וּרְשָׁעִים בְּיַד צַדִּיקִים, וְזֵדִים בְּיַד עוֹסְקֵי תוֹרָתֶךָ, וּלְךָ עָשִׂיתָ שֵׁם גָּדוֹל וְקָדוֹשׁ בְּעוֹלָמֶךָ, וּלְעַמְּךָ יִשְׂרָאֵל עָשִׂיתָ תְּשׁוּעָה גְדוֹלָה וּפֻרְקָן כְּהַיּוֹם הַזֶּה. וְאַחַר כֵּן בָּאוּ בָנֶיךָ לִדְבִיר בֵּיתֶךָ, וּפִנּוּ אֶת הֵיכָלֶךָ, וְטִהֲרוּ אֶת מִקְדָּשֶׁךָ, וְהִדְלִיקוּ נֵרוֹת בְּחַצְרוֹת קָדְשֶׁךָ, וְקָבְעוּ שְׁמוֹנַת יְמֵי חֲנֻכָּה אֵלּוּ, לְהוֹדוֹת וּלְהַלֵּל לְשִׁמְךָ הַגָּדוֹל.

*Continue with* וְעַל כֻּלָּם.

בשושן פורים בירושלים:

עַל הַנִּסִּים וְעַל הַפֻּרְקָן וְעַל הַגְּבוּרוֹת וְעַל הַתְּשׁוּעוֹת וְעַל הַמִּלְחָמוֹת שֶׁעָשִׂיתָ לַאֲבוֹתֵינוּ בַּיָּמִים הָהֵם בַּזְּמַן הַזֶּה.

בִּימֵי מָרְדְּכַי וְאֶסְתֵּר בְּשׁוּשַׁן הַבִּירָה, כְּשֶׁעָמַד עֲלֵיהֶם הָמָן הָרָשָׁע, בִּקֵּשׁ לְהַשְׁמִיד לַהֲרֹג וּלְאַבֵּד אֶת־כָּל־הַיְּהוּדִים מִנַּעַר וְעַד־זָקֵן טַף וְנָשִׁים בְּיוֹם אסתר ג
אֶחָד, בִּשְׁלוֹשָׁה עָשָׂר לְחֹדֶשׁ שְׁנֵים־עָשָׂר, הוּא־חֹדֶשׁ אֲדָר, וּשְׁלָלָם לָבוֹז: וְאַתָּה בְּרַחֲמֶיךָ הָרַבִּים הֵפַרְתָּ אֶת עֲצָתוֹ, וְקִלְקַלְתָּ אֶת מַחֲשַׁבְתּוֹ, וַהֲשֵׁבוֹתָ לּוֹ גְּמוּלוֹ בְּרֹאשׁוֹ, וְתָלוּ אוֹתוֹ וְאֶת בָּנָיו עַל הָעֵץ.

*Continue with* וְעַל כֻּלָּם.

וְעַל כֻּלָּם יִתְבָּרַךְ וְיִתְרוֹמַם שִׁמְךָ מַלְכֵּנוּ תָּמִיד לְעוֹלָם וָעֶד.

בשבת שובה: וּכְתֹב לְחַיִּים טוֹבִים כָּל בְּנֵי בְרִיתֶךָ.

וְכֹל הַחַיִּים יוֹדוּךָ סֶּלָה, וִיהַלְלוּ אֶת שִׁמְךָ בֶּאֱמֶת הָאֵל יְשׁוּעָתֵנוּ וְעֶזְרָתֵנוּ סֶלָה.

בָּרוּךְ אַתָּה יהוה, הַטּוֹב שִׁמְךָ וּלְךָ נָאֶה לְהוֹדוֹת.

PEACE

שָׁלוֹם רָב Grant
great peace
to Your people Israel
for ever,
for You are
the sovereign LORD
of all peace;
and may it be good
in Your eyes
to bless Your people Israel
at every time,
at every hour,
with Your peace.

*In Israel:*

שִׂים שָׁלוֹם Grant peace,
goodness and blessing,
grace, loving-kindness and compassion
to us and all Israel Your people.
Bless us, our Father, all as one,
with the light of Your face,
for by the light of Your face
You have given us, LORD our God,
the Torah of life and love of kindness,
righteousness, blessing, compassion,
life and peace.
May it be good in Your eyes
to bless Your people Israel
at every time, in every hour,
with Your peace.

*On Shabbat Shuva:* In the book of life, blessing, peace and prosperity,
may we and all Your people the house of Israel be
remembered and written before You for a good life,
and for peace.*

Blessed are You, LORD, who blesses His people Israel with peace.

**On Shabbat Shuva in the Diaspora, many end the blessing:*
Blessed are You, LORD, who makes peace.

*The following verse concludes the Leader's Repetition of the Amida. Some also say it here as part of the silent Amida. See law 368.*

May the words of my mouth and the meditation of my heart *Ps. 19*
find favor before You, LORD, my Rock and Redeemer.

אֱלֹהַי My God, *Berakhot 17a*
guard my tongue from evil and my lips from deceitful speech.
To those who curse me, let my soul be silent;
may my soul be to all like the dust.
Open my heart to Your Torah
and let my soul pursue Your commandments.
As for all who plan evil against me,
swiftly thwart their counsel and frustrate their plans.

ברכת שלום

שָׁלוֹם רָב עַל יִשְׂרָאֵל עַמְּךָ
תָּשִׂים לְעוֹלָם
כִּי אַתָּה הוּא
מֶלֶךְ אָדוֹן לְכָל הַשָּׁלוֹם.
וְטוֹב בְּעֵינֶיךָ
לְבָרֵךְ אֶת עַמְּךָ יִשְׂרָאֵל
בְּכָל עֵת וּבְכָל שָׁעָה
בִּשְׁלוֹמֶךָ.

*In* ארץ ישראל:

שִׂים שָׁלוֹם טוֹבָה וּבְרָכָה
חֵן וָחֶסֶד וְרַחֲמִים
עָלֵינוּ וְעַל כָּל יִשְׂרָאֵל עַמֶּךָ.
בָּרְכֵנוּ אָבִינוּ כֻּלָּנוּ כְּאֶחָד בְּאוֹר פָּנֶיךָ
כִּי בְאוֹר פָּנֶיךָ נָתַתָּ לָּנוּ יהוה אֱלֹהֵינוּ
תּוֹרַת חַיִּים וְאַהֲבַת חֶסֶד
וּצְדָקָה וּבְרָכָה וְרַחֲמִים וְחַיִּים וְשָׁלוֹם.
וְטוֹב בְּעֵינֶיךָ לְבָרֵךְ אֶת עַמְּךָ יִשְׂרָאֵל
בְּכָל עֵת וּבְכָל שָׁעָה בִּשְׁלוֹמֶךָ.

בשבת שובה: בְּסֵפֶר חַיִּים, בְּרָכָה וְשָׁלוֹם, וּפַרְנָסָה טוֹבָה
נִזָּכֵר וְנִכָּתֵב לְפָנֶיךָ, אֲנַחְנוּ וְכָל עַמְּךָ בֵּית יִשְׂרָאֵל
לְחַיִּים טוֹבִים וּלְשָׁלוֹם.*

**בָּרוּךְ אַתָּה יהוה, הַמְבָרֵךְ אֶת עַמּוֹ יִשְׂרָאֵל בַּשָּׁלוֹם.**

**On* שבת שובה *in* חוץ לארץ *many end the blessing:*

בָּרוּךְ אַתָּה יהוה, עוֹשֶׂה הַשָּׁלוֹם.

*The following verse concludes the* חזרת הש״ץ.
*Some also say it here as part of the silent* עמידה. *See law 368.*

יִהְיוּ לְרָצוֹן אִמְרֵי־פִי וְהֶגְיוֹן לִבִּי לְפָנֶיךָ, יהוה צוּרִי וְגֹאֲלִי: תהלים יט

אֱלֹהַי ברכות יז.
נְצֹר לְשׁוֹנִי מֵרָע וּשְׂפָתַי מִדַּבֵּר מִרְמָה
וְלִמְקַלְלַי נַפְשִׁי תִדֹּם, וְנַפְשִׁי כֶּעָפָר לַכֹּל תִּהְיֶה.
פְּתַח לִבִּי בְּתוֹרָתֶךָ, וּבְמִצְוֹתֶיךָ תִּרְדֹּף נַפְשִׁי.
וְכָל הַחוֹשְׁבִים עָלַי רָעָה
מְהֵרָה הָפֵר עֲצָתָם וְקַלְקֵל מַחֲשַׁבְתָּם.

Act for the sake of Your name;
act for the sake of Your right hand;
act for the sake of Your holiness;
act for the sake of Your Torah.
That Your beloved ones may be delivered, *Ps. 60*
save with Your right hand and answer me.
May the words of my mouth *Ps. 19*
and the meditation of my heart find favor before You,
Lord, my Rock and Redeemer.

*Bow, take three steps back, then bow, first left, then right, then center, while saying:*

May He who makes peace in His high places,
make peace for us and all Israel –
and say: Amen.

יְהִי רָצוֹן May it be Your will, Lord our God and God of our ancestors,
that the Temple be rebuilt speedily in our days,
and grant us a share in Your Torah.
And there we will serve You with reverence,
as in the days of old and as in former years.
Then the offering of Judah and Jerusalem *Mal. 3*
will be pleasing to the Lord
as in the days of old and as in former years.

*The following is omitted on days when Taḥanun is not said (see page 208).*

צִדְקָתְךָ Your righteousness is an everlasting righteousness, *Ps. 119*
and Your Torah is truth.

Your righteousness, O God, reaches to the highest heights, *Ps. 71*
for You have done great things.
O God, who is like You?

Your righteousness is like the mighty mountains; *Ps. 36*
Your judgments like the great depths.
O Lord, You save both man and beast.

עֲשֵׂה לְמַעַן שְׁמֶךָ
עֲשֵׂה לְמַעַן יְמִינֶךָ
עֲשֵׂה לְמַעַן קְדֻשָּׁתֶךָ
עֲשֵׂה לְמַעַן תּוֹרָתֶךָ.

לְמַעַן יֵחָלְצוּן יְדִידֶיךָ, הוֹשִׁיעָה יְמִינְךָ וַעֲנֵנִי: תהלים ס

יִהְיוּ לְרָצוֹן אִמְרֵי־פִי וְהֶגְיוֹן לִבִּי לְפָנֶיךָ, יהוה צוּרִי וְגֹאֲלִי: תהלים יט

*Bow, take three steps back, then bow, first left, then right, then center, while saying:*

עֹשֶׂה שָׁלוֹם/ בשבת שובה: הַשָּׁלוֹם/ בִּמְרוֹמָיו
הוּא יַעֲשֶׂה שָׁלוֹם עָלֵינוּ וְעַל כָּל יִשְׂרָאֵל
וְאִמְרוּ אָמֵן.

יְהִי רָצוֹן מִלְּפָנֶיךָ יהוה אֱלֹהֵינוּ וֵאלֹהֵי אֲבוֹתֵינוּ
שֶׁיִּבָּנֶה בֵּית הַמִּקְדָּשׁ בִּמְהֵרָה בְיָמֵינוּ
וְתֵן חֶלְקֵנוּ בְּתוֹרָתֶךָ
וְשָׁם נַעֲבָדְךָ בְּיִרְאָה כִּימֵי עוֹלָם וּכְשָׁנִים קַדְמֹנִיּוֹת.
וְעָרְבָה לַיהוה מִנְחַת יְהוּדָה וִירוּשָׁלָםִ מלאכי ג
כִּימֵי עוֹלָם וּכְשָׁנִים קַדְמֹנִיּוֹת:

*The following is omitted on days when* תחנון *is not said* *(see page 209)*.

צִדְקָתְךָ צֶדֶק לְעוֹלָם תהלים קיט
וְתוֹרָתְךָ אֱמֶת:

וְצִדְקָתְךָ אֱלֹהִים עַד־מָרוֹם, אֲשֶׁר־עָשִׂיתָ גְדֹלוֹת תהלים עא
אֱלֹהִים, מִי כָמוֹךָ:

צִדְקָתְךָ כְּהַרְרֵי־אֵל, מִשְׁפָּטֶיךָ תְּהוֹם רַבָּה תהלים לו
אָדָם וּבְהֵמָה תוֹשִׁיעַ יהוה:

## FULL KADDISH

*Leader:* יִתְגַּדַּל Magnified and sanctified may His great name be,
in the world He created by His will.
May He establish His kingdom
in your lifetime and in your days,
and in the lifetime of all the house of Israel,
swiftly and soon –
and say: Amen.

*All:* May His great name be blessed for ever and all time.

*Leader:* Blessed and praised, glorified and exalted,
raised and honored,
uplifted and lauded
be the name of the Holy One,
blessed be He,
beyond any blessing,
song, praise and consolation
uttered in the world –
and say: Amen.

May the prayers and pleas of all Israel
be accepted by their Father in heaven –
and say: Amen.

May there be great peace from heaven,
and life for us and all Israel –
and say: Amen.

*Bow, take three steps back, as if taking leave of the Divine Presence, then bow, first left, then right, then center, while saying:*

May He who makes peace in His high places,
make peace for us and all Israel –
and say: Amen.

*Between Sukkot and Pesaḥ, some recite Barekhi Nafshi, page 698, at this point.*
*Between Pesaḥ and Rosh HaShana some recite Ethics of the Fathers, page 710, at this point.*

## קדיש שלם

ש״ץ: יִתְגַּדַּל וְיִתְקַדַּשׁ שְׁמֵהּ רַבָּא (קהל: אָמֵן)
בְּעָלְמָא דִּי בְרָא כִרְעוּתֵהּ
וְיַמְלִיךְ מַלְכוּתֵהּ
בְּחַיֵּיכוֹן וּבְיוֹמֵיכוֹן וּבְחַיֵּי דְכָל בֵּית יִשְׂרָאֵל
בַּעֲגָלָא וּבִזְמַן קָרִיב, וְאִמְרוּ אָמֵן. (קהל: אָמֵן)

קהל וש״ץ: יְהֵא שְׁמֵהּ רַבָּא מְבָרַךְ לְעָלַם וּלְעָלְמֵי עָלְמַיָּא.

ש״ץ: יִתְבָּרַךְ וְיִשְׁתַּבַּח וְיִתְפָּאַר
וְיִתְרוֹמַם וְיִתְנַשֵּׂא וְיִתְהַדָּר וְיִתְעַלֶּה וְיִתְהַלָּל
שְׁמֵהּ דְּקֻדְשָׁא בְּרִיךְ הוּא (קהל: בְּרִיךְ הוּא)
לְעֵלָּא מִן כָּל בִּרְכָתָא
/ בשבת שובה: לְעֵלָּא לְעֵלָּא מִכָּל בִּרְכָתָא/
וְשִׁירָתָא, תֻּשְׁבְּחָתָא וְנֶחֱמָתָא
דַּאֲמִירָן בְּעָלְמָא, וְאִמְרוּ אָמֵן. (קהל: אָמֵן)

תִּתְקַבַּל צְלוֹתְהוֹן וּבָעוּתְהוֹן דְּכָל יִשְׂרָאֵל
קֳדָם אֲבוּהוֹן דִּי בִשְׁמַיָּא, וְאִמְרוּ אָמֵן. (קהל: אָמֵן)

יְהֵא שְׁלָמָא רַבָּא מִן שְׁמַיָּא
וְחַיִּים, עָלֵינוּ וְעַל כָּל יִשְׂרָאֵל, וְאִמְרוּ אָמֵן. (קהל: אָמֵן)

*Bow, take three steps back, as if taking leave of the Divine Presence, then bow, first left, then right, then center, while saying:*

עֹשֶׂה שָׁלוֹם/ בשבת שובה: הַשָּׁלוֹם/ בִּמְרוֹמָיו
הוּא יַעֲשֶׂה שָׁלוֹם עָלֵינוּ וְעַל כָּל יִשְׂרָאֵל
וְאִמְרוּ אָמֵן. (קהל: אָמֵן)

*Between* סוכות *and* פסח*, some recite* ברכי נפשי*, page 699, at this point.*
*Between* פסח *and* ראש השנה *some recite* פרקי אבות*, page 711, at this point.*

*Stand while saying Aleinu. Bow at* ▾.

עָלֵינוּ It is our duty to praise the Master of all,
and ascribe greatness to the Author of creation,
who has not made us like the nations of the lands
nor placed us like the families of the earth;
who has not made our portion like theirs,
nor our destiny like all their multitudes.
(For they worship vanity and emptiness,
and pray to a god who cannot save.)
▾But we bow in worship
and thank the Supreme King of kings,
the Holy One, blessed be He,
who extends the heavens and establishes the earth,
whose throne of glory is in the heavens above,
and whose power's Presence is in the highest of heights.
He is our God; there is no other.
Truly He is our King, there is none else,
as it is written in His Torah:
"You shall know and take to heart this day *Deut. 4*
that the LORD is God, in heaven above and on earth below.
There is no other."

Therefore, we place our hope in You, LORD our God,
that we may soon see the glory of Your power,
when You will remove abominations from the earth,
and idols will be utterly destroyed,
when the world will be perfected under the sovereignty of the Almighty,
when all humanity will call on Your name,
to turn all the earth's wicked toward You.
All the world's inhabitants will realize and know
that to You every knee must bow and every tongue swear loyalty.
Before You, LORD our God, they will kneel and bow down
and give honor to Your glorious name.
They will all accept the yoke of Your kingdom,
and You will reign over them soon and for ever.
For the kingdom is Yours, and to all eternity You will reign in glory,
as it is written in Your Torah: "The LORD will reign for ever and ever." *Ex. 15*

*Stand while saying* עָלֵינוּ*. Bow at* ״.

עָלֵינוּ לְשַׁבֵּחַ לַאֲדוֹן הַכֹּל, לָתֵת גְּדֻלָּה לְיוֹצֵר בְּרֵאשִׁית
שֶׁלֹּא עָשָׂנוּ כְּגוֹיֵי הָאֲרָצוֹת, וְלֹא שָׂמָנוּ כְּמִשְׁפְּחוֹת הָאֲדָמָה
שֶׁלֹּא שָׂם חֶלְקֵנוּ כָּהֶם וְגוֹרָלֵנוּ כְּכָל הֲמוֹנָם.
(שֶׁהֵם מִשְׁתַּחֲוִים לְהֶבֶל וָרִיק וּמִתְפַּלְלִים אֶל אֵל לֹא יוֹשִׁיעַ.)
״וַאֲנַחְנוּ כּוֹרְעִים וּמִשְׁתַּחֲוִים וּמוֹדִים
לִפְנֵי מֶלֶךְ מַלְכֵי הַמְּלָכִים, הַקָּדוֹשׁ בָּרוּךְ הוּא
שֶׁהוּא נוֹטֶה שָׁמַיִם וְיוֹסֵד אָרֶץ
וּמוֹשַׁב יְקָרוֹ בַּשָּׁמַיִם מִמַּעַל
וּשְׁכִינַת עֻזּוֹ בְּגָבְהֵי מְרוֹמִים.
הוּא אֱלֹהֵינוּ, אֵין עוֹד.
אֱמֶת מַלְכֵּנוּ, אֶפֶס זוּלָתוֹ
כַּכָּתוּב בְּתוֹרָתוֹ
דברים ד וְיָדַעְתָּ הַיּוֹם וַהֲשֵׁבֹתָ אֶל־לְבָבֶךָ
כִּי יהוה הוּא הָאֱלֹהִים בַּשָּׁמַיִם מִמַּעַל וְעַל־הָאָרֶץ מִתָּחַת, אֵין עוֹד:

עַל כֵּן נְקַוֶּה לְּךָ יהוה אֱלֹהֵינוּ, לִרְאוֹת מְהֵרָה בְּתִפְאֶרֶת עֻזֶּךָ
לְהַעֲבִיר גִּלּוּלִים מִן הָאָרֶץ, וְהָאֱלִילִים כָּרוֹת יִכָּרֵתוּן
לְתַקֵּן עוֹלָם בְּמַלְכוּת שַׁדַּי.
וְכָל בְּנֵי בָשָׂר יִקְרְאוּ בִשְׁמֶךָ לְהַפְנוֹת אֵלֶיךָ כָּל רִשְׁעֵי אָרֶץ.
יַכִּירוּ וְיֵדְעוּ כָּל יוֹשְׁבֵי תֵבֵל
כִּי לְךָ תִּכְרַע כָּל בֶּרֶךְ, תִּשָּׁבַע כָּל לָשׁוֹן.
לְפָנֶיךָ יהוה אֱלֹהֵינוּ יִכְרְעוּ וְיִפֹּלוּ, וְלִכְבוֹד שִׁמְךָ יְקָר יִתֵּנוּ
וִיקַבְּלוּ כֻלָּם אֶת עֹל מַלְכוּתֶךָ
וְתִמְלֹךְ עֲלֵיהֶם מְהֵרָה לְעוֹלָם וָעֶד.
כִּי הַמַּלְכוּת שֶׁלְּךָ הִיא וּלְעוֹלְמֵי עַד תִּמְלֹךְ בְּכָבוֹד
שמות טו כַּכָּתוּב בְּתוֹרָתֶךָ, יהוה יִמְלֹךְ לְעֹלָם וָעֶד:

▸ And it is said: "Then the Lord shall be King over all the earth; *Zech. 14*
on that day the Lord shall be One and His name One."

*Some add:*

Have no fear of sudden terror or of the ruin when it overtakes the wicked. *Prov. 3*
Devise your strategy, but it will be thwarted; propose your plan, *Is. 8*
but it will not stand, for God is with us. When you grow old, I will still be the same. *Is. 46*
When your hair turns gray, I will still carry you. I made you, I will bear you,
I will carry you, and I will rescue you.

## MOURNER'S KADDISH

*The following prayer, said by mourners, requires the presence of a minyan.*
*A transliteration can be found on page 1320.*

*Mourner:* יִתְגַּדַּל Magnified and sanctified may His great name be,
in the world He created by His will.
May He establish His kingdom in your lifetime
and in your days,
and in the lifetime of all the house of Israel,
swiftly and soon – and say: Amen.

*All:* May His great name be blessed for ever and all time.

*Mourner:* Blessed and praised,
glorified and exalted,
raised and honored,
uplifted and lauded
be the name of the Holy One, blessed be He,
beyond any blessing,
song, praise and consolation
uttered in the world –
and say: Amen.

May there be great peace from heaven,
and life for us and all Israel –
and say: Amen.

*Bow, take three steps back, as if taking leave of the Divine Presence,*
*then bow, first left, then right, then center, while saying:*

May He who makes peace in His high places,
make peace for us and all Israel – and say: Amen.

◂ וְנֶאֱמַר, וְהָיָה יהוה לְמֶלֶךְ עַל־כָּל־הָאָרֶץ זכריה יד
בַּיּוֹם הַהוּא יִהְיֶה יהוה אֶחָד וּשְׁמוֹ אֶחָד:

*Some add:*

אַל־תִּירָא מִפַּחַד פִּתְאֹם וּמִשֹּׁאַת רְשָׁעִים כִּי תָבֹא: משלי ג
עֻצוּ עֵצָה וְתֻפָר, דַּבְּרוּ דָבָר וְלֹא יָקוּם, כִּי עִמָּנוּ אֵל: ישעיה ח
וְעַד־זִקְנָה אֲנִי הוּא, וְעַד־שֵׂיבָה אֲנִי אֶסְבֹּל, אֲנִי עָשִׂיתִי וַאֲנִי אֶשָּׂא וַאֲנִי אֶסְבֹּל וַאֲמַלֵּט: ישעיה מו

## קדיש יתום

*The following prayer, said by mourners, requires the presence of a* מנין*.*
*A transliteration can be found on page 1320.*

אבל: יִתְגַּדַּל וְיִתְקַדַּשׁ שְׁמֵהּ רַבָּא (קהל: אָמֵן)
בְּעָלְמָא דִּי בְרָא כִרְעוּתֵהּ
וְיַמְלִיךְ מַלְכוּתֵהּ
בְּחַיֵּיכוֹן וּבְיוֹמֵיכוֹן וּבְחַיֵּי דְכָל בֵּית יִשְׂרָאֵל
בַּעֲגָלָא וּבִזְמַן קָרִיב, וְאִמְרוּ אָמֵן. (קהל: אָמֵן)

קהל ואבל: יְהֵא שְׁמֵהּ רַבָּא מְבָרַךְ לְעָלַם וּלְעָלְמֵי עָלְמַיָּא.

אבל: יִתְבָּרַךְ וְיִשְׁתַּבַּח וְיִתְפָּאַר
וְיִתְרוֹמַם וְיִתְנַשֵּׂא וְיִתְהַדָּר וְיִתְעַלֶּה וְיִתְהַלָּל
שְׁמֵהּ דְּקֻדְשָׁא בְּרִיךְ הוּא (קהל: בְּרִיךְ הוּא)
לְעֵלָּא מִן כָּל בִּרְכָתָא / בשבת שובה: לְעֵלָּא לְעֵלָּא מִכָּל בִּרְכָתָא/
וְשִׁירָתָא, תֻּשְׁבְּחָתָא וְנֶחֱמָתָא
דַּאֲמִירָן בְּעָלְמָא, וְאִמְרוּ אָמֵן. (קהל: אָמֵן)

יְהֵא שְׁלָמָא רַבָּא מִן שְׁמַיָּא
וְחַיִּים, עָלֵינוּ וְעַל כָּל יִשְׂרָאֵל, וְאִמְרוּ אָמֵן. (קהל: אָמֵן)

*Bow, take three steps back, as if taking leave of the Divine Presence, then bow, first left, then right, then center, while saying:*

עֹשֶׂה שָׁלוֹם/ בשבת שובה: הַשָּׁלוֹם/ בִּמְרוֹמָיו
הוּא יַעֲשֶׂה שָׁלוֹם עָלֵינוּ וְעַל כָּל יִשְׂרָאֵל, וְאִמְרוּ אָמֵן. (קהל: אָמֵן)

## BAREKHI NAFSHI

*The following psalms are said from the Shabbat after Simḥat Torah until (but not including) the Shabbat before Pesaḥ.*

בָּרְכִי נַפְשִׁי Bless the Lord, my soul. Lord, my God, You are very great, clothed in majesty and splendor, wrapped in a robe of light. You have spread out the heavens like a tent. He has laid the beams of His lofts in the waters. He makes the clouds His chariot, riding on the wings of the wind. He makes the winds His messengers, flames of fire His ministers. He has fixed the earth on its foundations so that it will never be shaken. You covered it with the deep like a cloak; the waters stood above the mountains. At Your rebuke they fled; at the sound of Your thunder they rushed away, flowing over the hills, pouring down into the valleys to the place You appointed for them. You fixed a boundary they were not to pass, so that they would never cover the earth again. He makes springs flow in the valleys; they make their way between the hills, giving drink to all the beasts of the field; the wild donkeys quench their thirst. The birds of the sky dwell beside them, singing among the foliage. He waters the mountains from His lofts: the earth is sated with the fruit of Your work. *Ps. 104*

---

There is a subtle difference between a *mal'akh* (messenger) and a *mesharet* (minister). The messenger is dispatched on a distant mission; the minister remains within the confines of the palace and attends to the king's immediate desires. The *mal'akhim* (messengers) are the Masters of Torah (*ba'alei Torah*); the *mesharetim* (ministers) are the Masters of Prayer (*ba'alei tefillah*).

The teacher of Torah is likened to a messenger: "For the lips of the priest shall keep knowledge and Torah they shall seek from his mouth; for he is the messenger of the Lord of hosts."[3] The Torah which he transmits is compared to fire: "Is not My word like fire? says the Lord."[4] By such angelic beings, the torch of Torah is carried; through such holy teachers, the message of Torah is transmitted abroad.

The *mesharetim* (ministers), the *ba'alei tefillah* (masters of prayer) focus on another element: *ru'aḥ* (wind). *Ru'aḥ* (wind) is synonymous with *ratson*

---

3. Malachi 2:7; *b. Mo'ed Katan* 17a; *Ḥagigah* 15b; Maimonides, *Commentary to Mishnah, Avot* 5:13 (Kafaḥ ed., p. 302); idem, *MT, Hil. Talmud* Torah 4:1.
4. Jeremiah 23:29.

# ברכי נפשי

*The following psalms are said from* שבת בראשית *until (but not including)* שבת הגדול.

בָּרְכִי נַפְשִׁי אֶת־יהוה, יהוה אֱלֹהַי גָּדַלְתָּ מְּאֹד, הוֹד וְהָדָר לָבָשְׁתָּ: תהלים קד
עֹטֶה־אוֹר כַּשַּׂלְמָה, נוֹטֶה שָׁמַיִם כַּיְרִיעָה: הַמְקָרֶה בַמַּיִם עֲלִיּוֹתָיו,
הַשָּׂם־עָבִים רְכוּבוֹ, הַמְהַלֵּךְ עַל־כַּנְפֵי־רוּחַ: עֹשֶׂה מַלְאָכָיו רוּחוֹת,
מְשָׁרְתָיו אֵשׁ לֹהֵט: יָסַד־אֶרֶץ עַל־מְכוֹנֶיהָ, בַּל־תִּמּוֹט עוֹלָם וָעֶד:
תְּהוֹם כַּלְּבוּשׁ כִּסִּיתוֹ, עַל־הָרִים יַעַמְדוּ־מָיִם: מִן־גַּעֲרָתְךָ יְנוּסוּן,
מִן־קוֹל רַעַמְךָ יֵחָפֵזוּן: יַעֲלוּ הָרִים, יֵרְדוּ בְקָעוֹת, אֶל־מְקוֹם זֶה
יָסַדְתָּ לָהֶם: גְּבוּל־שַׂמְתָּ בַּל־יַעֲבֹרוּן, בַּל־יְשׁוּבוּן לְכַסּוֹת הָאָרֶץ:
הַמְשַׁלֵּחַ מַעְיָנִים בַּנְּחָלִים, בֵּין הָרִים יְהַלֵּכוּן: יַשְׁקוּ כָּל־חַיְתוֹ שָׂדָי,
יִשְׁבְּרוּ פְרָאִים צְמָאָם: עֲלֵיהֶם עוֹף־הַשָּׁמַיִם יִשְׁכּוֹן, מִבֵּין עֳפָאיִם
יִתְּנוּ־קוֹל: מַשְׁקֶה הָרִים מֵעֲלִיּוֹתָיו, מִפְּרִי מַעֲשֶׂיךָ תִּשְׂבַּע הָאָרֶץ:

---

עֹשֶׂה מַלְאָכָיו רוּחוֹת, מְשָׁרְתָיו אֵשׁ לֹהֵט *He makes the winds His messengers, flames of fire His ministers (Psalms 104:4).* There is a beautiful interplay of Torah study and prayer; of intellect (*sekhel*) and will (*ratson*).

Rabbi Naḥman of Breslov said that we must turn our Torah into *tefillah* (prayer).[1] In fulfilment of this command, Rabbi Naḥman's faithful disciple Rabbi Nathan of Nemirov converted the *torot*, the teachings in his master's *Likkutei Moharan* into a collection of prayers, *Likkutei Tefillot*.[2]

But the reverse is also true: The *tefillot* (prayers) must be turned into *torot* (study).

---

1. *Likkutei Moharan* II, 25; *Siḥot ha-Ran*, par. 145.
2. Both Rav Kook and his son Rabbi Zevi Yehudah were extremely fond of the volume *Likkutei Tefillot* composed by Rabbi Nathan. Rabbi Israel Porath, a major disciple of Rav Kook (and later Rabbi of Cleveland, Ohio), attested that in the Jaffa era, *Likkutei Tefillot* never left Rav Kook's *shtender* or prayer stand. See also RZYH, *Tsemaḥ Tsevi* (Jerusalem, 1991), p. 26 (Letter 9, datelined "16 Av, 5670/1910, Jaffa" to Rabbi Y.M. Ḥarlap), and p. 45 (Letter 15, datelined "Jaffa, 22 Sivan, 5673/1913" to Rabbi Y.M. Ḥarlap).

He makes grass grow for the cattle, and plants for the use of man, that he may produce bread from the earth, wine to cheer the heart of man, oil to make the face shine, and bread to sustain man's heart. The trees of the LORD drink their fill, the cedars of Lebanon which He planted. There, birds build their nests; the stork makes its home in the cypresses. High hills are for the wild goats; crags are shelter for the badgers. He made the moon to mark the seasons, and makes the sun know when to set. You bring darkness and it is night; then all the beasts of the forests stir. The young lions roar for prey, seeking their food from God. When the sun rises, they slink away and seek rest in their lairs. Man goes out to his work and his labor until evening. How numerous are Your works, LORD; You made them all with wisdom; the earth is full of Your creations. There is the vast, immeasurable sea with its countless swarming creatures, living

---

And prayer must be in sync with the "fire of Torah." In this regard, there is an important apercu of Rav Kook to a passage in the Talmud:

> Rabbi Jeremiah was sitting before Rabbi Zeira and they were involved in study. It was late to pray and Rabbi Jeremiah abruptly stood up. Rabbi Zeira commented: "He who turns his ear away from hearing Torah – even his prayer is an abomination (*to'evah*)."[8]

Rav Kook explained that one might mistakenly assume that only man's corporeal urges are in need of guidance from the Torah, but certainly his lofty, spiritual aspirations, which take the form of prayer, should be given free rein. Surely, these noble sentiments have no need of instruction from the Torah. The verse in Proverbs cautions how simpleminded is this assumption. One must not be too hasty to abandon Torah learning for the sake of prayer. Even the holy feeling which results in prayer, must draw proper guidance from the wellsprings of Torah. Without the guidance provided by divine intellect, prayer has the potential for corruption. It is likely to run riot.[9]

"The closer prayer comes to Torah, the less it is an abomination (*to'evah*). The perfect prayer is one with Torah."[10]

---

8. Proverbs 28:9; *b. Shabbat* 10a.
9. "'*Inyenei Tefillah*" 3:4 in *OR*, vol. 1, p. 21 = *EA*, vol. 3, *Shabbat*, chap. 1, par. 7 (pp. 3–4). See also *OR*, vol. 1, p. 256.
10. RZYH, *Tsemaḥ Tsevi*, p. 26.

מַצְמִיחַ חָצִיר לַבְּהֵמָה, וְעֵשֶׂב לַעֲבֹדַת הָאָדָם, לְהוֹצִיא לֶחֶם מִן־
הָאָרֶץ: וְיַיִן יְשַׂמַּח לְבַב־אֱנוֹשׁ, לְהַצְהִיל פָּנִים מִשָּׁמֶן, וְלֶחֶם לְבַב־
אֱנוֹשׁ יִסְעָד: יִשְׂבְּעוּ עֲצֵי יהוה, אַרְזֵי לְבָנוֹן אֲשֶׁר נָטָע: אֲשֶׁר־שָׁם
צִפֳּרִים יְקַנֵּנוּ, חֲסִידָה בְּרוֹשִׁים בֵּיתָהּ: הָרִים הַגְּבֹהִים לַיְּעֵלִים,
סְלָעִים מַחְסֶה לַשְׁפַנִּים: עָשָׂה יָרֵחַ לְמוֹעֲדִים, שֶׁמֶשׁ יָדַע מְבוֹאוֹ:
תָּשֶׁת־חֹשֶׁךְ וִיהִי לָיְלָה, בּוֹ־תִרְמֹשׂ כָּל־חַיְתוֹ־יָעַר: הַכְּפִירִים שֹׁאֲגִים
לַטָּרֶף, וּלְבַקֵּשׁ מֵאֵל אָכְלָם: תִּזְרַח הַשֶּׁמֶשׁ יֵאָסֵפוּן, וְאֶל־מְעוֹנֹתָם
יִרְבָּצוּן: יֵצֵא אָדָם לְפָעֳלוֹ, וְלַעֲבֹדָתוֹ עֲדֵי־עָרֶב: מָה־רַבּוּ מַעֲשֶׂיךָ
יהוה, כֻּלָּם בְּחָכְמָה עָשִׂיתָ, מָלְאָה הָאָרֶץ קִנְיָנֶךָ: זֶה הַיָּם גָּדוֹל
וּרְחַב יָדָיִם, שָׁם־רֶמֶשׂ וְאֵין מִסְפָּר, חַיּוֹת קְטַנּוֹת עִם־גְּדֹלוֹת: שָׁם

(will).[5] The Master of Prayer expresses the divine will. What comes out of his mouth is the will of the Almighty.

Given their natural proclivities, the Psalmist should have assigned fire (Torah) to the messengers (teachers), and tagged the winds (will) to the ministers (prayer leaders). Instead, surprise! We find the reverse. The *mal'akhim* or teachers of Torah are identified with *ruḥot* or the divine will, and the *mesharetim* or prayer leaders are linked to fire, the symbol of Torah. This crisscrossing of Torah and *Tefillah,* of learning and prayer, is essential. The Master of Torah must be attuned to the will of God, and the Master of Prayer must bear the torch of Torah.[6]

The purpose of studying Torah is to grasp thereby the will of the Creator. According to our sages, the reason that the Land was lost, was because they did not recite the appropriate blessing before engaging in the study of Torah. In other words, though they studied Torah, their study of Torah was disconnected from the Giver of the Torah.[7]

5. See Maimonides, *Guide of the Perplexed* I, 40.
6. *OR,* vol. 2, pp. 149–151. The version in *OR* is a reworking of the manuscript just published in *MRIT* (Jerusalem: Makhon RZYH, 2016), pp. 148–150.
7. *b. Nedarim* 81; *Bava Metsi'a* 85; Rabbbi Judah Löw (Maharal) of Prague, Introduction to *Tif'eret Yisrael.* Maharal is bold enough to suggest that the scholars' extreme love of Torah displaced the love of God.

things great and small. There ships sail. There is Leviathan You formed to sport there. All of them look to You in hope, to give them their food when it is due. What You give them, they gather up. When You open Your hand, they are sated with good. When You hide Your face, they are dismayed. When You take away their breath, they die and return to dust. When You send back Your breath, they are created, giving new life to the earth. May the glory of the LORD be for ever; may the LORD rejoice in His works. When He looks at the earth, it trembles. When He touches the mountains, they pour forth smoke. I will sing to the LORD as long as I live; I will sing psalms to my God all my life. May my meditation be pleasing to Him; I shall rejoice in the LORD. May sinners vanish from the earth, and the wicked be no more. Bless the LORD, my soul. Halleluya!

A song of ascents. I called to the LORD in my distress and He answered *Ps. 120*
me. "LORD, save my soul from lying lips, from a deceitful tongue." What will a deceitful tongue profit you? What will you gain? Only a warrior's sharp arrows, and hot coals of broom-wood. Woe to me that I dwell in Meshekh, that I live among the tents of Kedar. I have lived too long among those who hate peace. I am for peace, but whenever I speak of it, they are for war.

A song of ascents. I lift my eyes up to the hills; from where will my help *Ps. 121*
come? My help comes from the LORD, Maker of heaven and earth. He will not let your foot stumble; He who guards you does not slumber. See: the Guardian of Israel neither slumbers nor sleeps. The LORD is your Guardian; the LORD is your Shade at your right hand. The sun will not strike you by day, nor the moon by night. The LORD will guard you from all harm; He will guard your life. The LORD will guard your going and coming, now and for evermore.

A song of ascents. Of David. I rejoiced when they said to me, "Let us go *Ps. 122*
to the House of the LORD." Our feet stood within your gates, Jerusalem: Jerusalem built as a city joined together. There the tribes went up, the tribes of the LORD – as a testimony to Israel – to give thanks to the name of the LORD. For there the thrones of justice are set, the thrones of the house of David. Pray for the peace of Jerusalem: "May those who love you prosper. May there be peace within your ramparts, tranquility in your

בְּאַרְמְנוֹתָיִךְ: לְמַעַן אַחַי וְרֵעָי, אֲדַבְּרָה־נָּא שָׁלוֹם בָּךְ: לְמַעַן בֵּית־יהוה אֱלֹהֵינוּ, אֲבַקְשָׁה טוֹב לָךְ:

תהלים קכג שִׁיר הַמַּעֲלוֹת, אֵלֶיךָ נָשָׂאתִי אֶת־עֵינַי, הַיֹּשְׁבִי בַּשָּׁמָיִם: הִנֵּה כְעֵינֵי עֲבָדִים אֶל־יַד אֲדוֹנֵיהֶם, כְּעֵינֵי שִׁפְחָה אֶל־יַד גְּבִרְתָּהּ, כֵּן עֵינֵינוּ אֶל־יהוה אֱלֹהֵינוּ, עַד שֶׁיְּחָנֵּנוּ: חָנֵּנוּ יהוה חָנֵּנוּ, כִּי־רַב שָׂבַעְנוּ בוּז: רַבַּת שָׂבְעָה־לָּהּ נַפְשֵׁנוּ, הַלַּעַג הַשַּׁאֲנַנִּים, הַבּוּז לִגְאֵי יוֹנִים:

תהלים קכד שִׁיר הַמַּעֲלוֹת לְדָוִד, לוּלֵי יהוה שֶׁהָיָה לָנוּ, יֹאמַר־נָא יִשְׂרָאֵל: לוּלֵי יהוה שֶׁהָיָה לָנוּ, בְּקוּם עָלֵינוּ אָדָם: אֲזַי חַיִּים בְּלָעוּנוּ, בַּחֲרוֹת אַפָּם בָּנוּ: אֲזַי הַמַּיִם שְׁטָפוּנוּ, נַחְלָה עָבַר עַל־נַפְשֵׁנוּ: אֲזַי עָבַר עַל־נַפְשֵׁנוּ, הַמַּיִם הַזֵּידוֹנִים: בָּרוּךְ יהוה, שֶׁלֹּא נְתָנָנוּ טֶרֶף לְשִׁנֵּיהֶם: נַפְשֵׁנוּ כְּצִפּוֹר נִמְלְטָה מִפַּח יוֹקְשִׁים, הַפַּח נִשְׁבָּר וַאֲנַחְנוּ נִמְלָטְנוּ: עֶזְרֵנוּ בְּשֵׁם יהוה, עֹשֵׂה שָׁמַיִם וָאָרֶץ:

תהלים קכה שִׁיר הַמַּעֲלוֹת, הַבֹּטְחִים בַּיהוה, כְּהַר־צִיּוֹן לֹא־יִמּוֹט, לְעוֹלָם יֵשֵׁב: יְרוּשָׁלַםִ, הָרִים סָבִיב לָהּ, וַיהוה סָבִיב לְעַמּוֹ, מֵעַתָּה וְעַד־עוֹלָם: כִּי לֹא יָנוּחַ שֵׁבֶט הָרֶשַׁע עַל גּוֹרַל הַצַּדִּיקִים, לְמַעַן לֹא־יִשְׁלְחוּ הַצַּדִּיקִים בְּעַוְלָתָה יְדֵיהֶם: הֵיטִיבָה יהוה לַטּוֹבִים, וְלִישָׁרִים בְּלִבּוֹתָם: וְהַמַּטִּים עֲקַלְקַלּוֹתָם יוֹלִיכֵם יהוה אֶת־פֹּעֲלֵי הָאָוֶן, שָׁלוֹם עַל־יִשְׂרָאֵל:

תהלים קכו שִׁיר הַמַּעֲלוֹת, בְּשׁוּב יהוה אֶת־שִׁיבַת צִיּוֹן, הָיִינוּ כְּחֹלְמִים: אָז יִמָּלֵא שְׂחוֹק פִּינוּ וּלְשׁוֹנֵנוּ רִנָּה, אָז יֹאמְרוּ בַגּוֹיִם הִגְדִּיל יהוה לַעֲשׂוֹת עִם־אֵלֶּה: הִגְדִּיל יהוה לַעֲשׂוֹת עִמָּנוּ, הָיִינוּ שְׂמֵחִים: שׁוּבָה יהוה אֶת־שְׁבִיתֵנוּ, כַּאֲפִיקִים בַּנֶּגֶב: הַזֹּרְעִים בְּדִמְעָה בְּרִנָּה יִקְצֹרוּ: הָלוֹךְ יֵלֵךְ וּבָכֹה נֹשֵׂא מֶשֶׁךְ־הַזָּרַע, בֹּא־יָבֹא בְרִנָּה נֹשֵׂא אֲלֻמֹּתָיו:

A song of ascents. Of Solomon. Unless the LORD builds the house, its builders labor in vain. Unless the LORD guards the city, in vain does the guard keep watch. In vain do you rise early and go late to rest, toiling for the bread you eat. He provides for His loved ones while they sleep. Children are a heritage from the LORD; the fruit of the womb, His reward. Like arrows in the hand of a warrior are the sons of one's youth. Happy is the man who fills his quiver with them; they shall not be put to shame when they contend with the enemy at the gate. *Ps. 127*

A song of ascents. Happy are all who fear the LORD, who walk in His ways. When you eat the fruit of your labor, happy and fortunate are you. Your wife shall be like a fruitful vine within your house; your sons like olive saplings around your table. So shall the man who fears the LORD be blessed. May the LORD bless you from Zion; may you see the good of Jerusalem all the days of your life; and may you live to see your children's children. Peace be on Israel! *Ps. 128*

A song of ascents. Often since I was young I have been attacked – let Israel now say – often since I was young I have been attacked, but never have my attackers prevailed. Plowmen plowed across my back, making long furrows. But the LORD is just; He has cut the bonds of the wicked. Let all who hate Zion be driven back in shame. Let them be like the grass on roofs that fades before it can be pulled up. It will never fill a reaper's hand nor yield an armful for the gatherer of sheaves. No passersby will say to them: "The LORD's blessing be upon you. We bless you in the name of the LORD." *Ps. 129*

A song of ascents. From the depths I have called to You, O LORD. LORD, hear my voice; let Your ears be attentive to my plea. If You, LORD, should keep account of sins, O LORD, who could stand? But with You there is forgiveness, that You may be held in awe. I wait for the LORD, my soul waits, and in His word I put my hope. My soul waits for the LORD more than watchmen wait for the morning, more than watchmen wait for the morning. Israel, put your hope in the LORD, for with the LORD there is loving-kindness, and great is His power to redeem. It is He who will redeem Israel from all their sins. *Ps. 130*

תהלים קכז שִׁיר הַמַּעֲלוֹת לִשְׁלֹמֹה, אִם־יהוה לֹא־יִבְנֶה בַיִת, שָׁוְא עָמְלוּ בוֹנָיו בּוֹ, אִם־יהוה לֹא־יִשְׁמָר־עִיר, שָׁוְא שָׁקַד שׁוֹמֵר: שָׁוְא לָכֶם מַשְׁכִּימֵי קוּם מְאַחֲרֵי־שֶׁבֶת, אֹכְלֵי לֶחֶם הָעֲצָבִים, כֵּן יִתֵּן לִידִידוֹ שֵׁנָא: הִנֵּה נַחֲלַת יהוה בָּנִים, שָׂכָר פְּרִי הַבָּטֶן: כְּחִצִּים בְּיַד־גִּבּוֹר כֵּן בְּנֵי הַנְּעוּרִים: אַשְׁרֵי הַגֶּבֶר אֲשֶׁר מִלֵּא אֶת־אַשְׁפָּתוֹ מֵהֶם, לֹא־יֵבֹשׁוּ כִּי־יְדַבְּרוּ אֶת־אוֹיְבִים בַּשָּׁעַר:

תהלים קכח שִׁיר הַמַּעֲלוֹת, אַשְׁרֵי כָּל־יְרֵא יהוה, הַהֹלֵךְ בִּדְרָכָיו: יְגִיעַ כַּפֶּיךָ כִּי תֹאכֵל, אַשְׁרֶיךָ וְטוֹב לָךְ: אֶשְׁתְּךָ כְּגֶפֶן פֹּרִיָּה בְּיַרְכְּתֵי בֵיתֶךָ, בָּנֶיךָ כִּשְׁתִלֵי זֵיתִים, סָבִיב לְשֻׁלְחָנֶךָ: הִנֵּה כִי־כֵן יְבֹרַךְ גָּבֶר יְרֵא יהוה: יְבָרֶכְךָ יהוה מִצִּיּוֹן, וּרְאֵה בְּטוּב יְרוּשָׁלָםִ, כֹּל יְמֵי חַיֶּיךָ: וּרְאֵה־בָנִים לְבָנֶיךָ, שָׁלוֹם עַל־יִשְׂרָאֵל:

תהלים קכט שִׁיר הַמַּעֲלוֹת, רַבַּת צְרָרוּנִי מִנְּעוּרָי, יֹאמַר־נָא יִשְׂרָאֵל: רַבַּת צְרָרוּנִי מִנְּעוּרָי, גַּם לֹא־יָכְלוּ לִי: עַל־גַּבִּי חָרְשׁוּ חֹרְשִׁים, הֶאֱרִיכוּ לְמַעֲנִיתָם: יהוה צַדִּיק, קִצֵּץ עֲבוֹת רְשָׁעִים: יֵבֹשׁוּ וְיִסֹּגוּ אָחוֹר כֹּל שֹׂנְאֵי צִיּוֹן: יִהְיוּ כַּחֲצִיר גַּגּוֹת שֶׁקַּדְמַת שָׁלַף יָבֵשׁ: שֶׁלֹּא מִלֵּא כַפּוֹ קוֹצֵר, וְחִצְנוֹ מְעַמֵּר: וְלֹא אָמְרוּ הָעֹבְרִים, בִּרְכַּת־יהוה אֲלֵיכֶם, בֵּרַכְנוּ אֶתְכֶם בְּשֵׁם יהוה:

תהלים קל שִׁיר הַמַּעֲלוֹת, מִמַּעֲמַקִּים קְרָאתִיךָ יהוה: אֲדֹנָי שִׁמְעָה בְקוֹלִי, תִּהְיֶינָה אָזְנֶיךָ קַשֻּׁבוֹת לְקוֹל תַּחֲנוּנָי: אִם־עֲוֺנוֹת תִּשְׁמָר־יָהּ, אֲדֹנָי מִי יַעֲמֹד: כִּי־עִמְּךָ הַסְּלִיחָה, לְמַעַן תִּוָּרֵא: קִוִּיתִי יהוה קִוְּתָה נַפְשִׁי, וְלִדְבָרוֹ הוֹחָלְתִּי: נַפְשִׁי לַאדֹנָי, מִשֹּׁמְרִים לַבֹּקֶר, שֹׁמְרִים לַבֹּקֶר: יַחֵל יִשְׂרָאֵל אֶל־יהוה, כִּי־עִם־יהוה הַחֶסֶד, וְהַרְבֵּה עִמּוֹ פְדוּת: וְהוּא יִפְדֶּה אֶת־יִשְׂרָאֵל, מִכֹּל עֲוֺנֹתָיו:

A song of ascents. By David. LORD, my heart is not proud, nor are my eyes haughty. I do not busy myself with great affairs or with things beyond me. But I have made my soul still and quiet, like a weaned child with its mother; like a weaned child is my soul within me. Israel, put your hope in the LORD, now and for evermore. *Ps. 131*

A song of ascents. LORD, remember David and all the hardship he endured. He swore an oath to the LORD and made a vow to the Mighty One of Jacob: "I will not enter my house, nor go to bed; I will not give sleep to my eyes or slumber to my eyelids, until I find a place for the LORD, a dwelling for the Mighty One of Jacob." We heard of it in Efrat, we found it in the fields of Yaar. Let us enter His dwelling, worship at His footstool. Advance, LORD, to Your resting place, You and Your mighty Ark. Your priests are robed in righteousness; Your devoted ones sing for joy. For the sake of Your servant David, do not reject Your anointed one. The LORD swore to David a firm oath that He will not revoke: "One of your own descendants I will set upon your throne. If your sons keep My covenant and My decrees that I teach them, then their sons shall sit upon your throne for all time." For the LORD has chosen Zion; He desired it for His home. This is My resting place for all time; here I will dwell, for that is My desire. I will amply bless its store of food; its poor I will satisfy with bread. I will clothe its priests with salvation; its loyal ones shall sing for joy. There I will make David's dynasty flourish; I will prepare a lamp for My anointed one. I will clothe his enemies with shame, but on him will be a shining crown. *Ps. 132*

A song of ascents. By David. How good and pleasant it is when brothers dwell together. It is like fragrant oil on the head, running down onto the beard, Aaron's beard, that runs down over the collar of his robes. It is like the dew of Hermon that falls on the mountains of Zion. There the LORD bestows His blessing, life for evermore. *Ps. 133*

A song of ascents. Come, bless the LORD, all you servants of the LORD, who nightly stand in the House of the LORD. Lift up your hands toward the Sanctuary and bless the LORD. May the LORD, Maker of heaven and earth, bless you from Zion! *Ps. 134*

תהלים קלא
שִׁיר הַמַּעֲלוֹת לְדָוִד, יהוה לֹא־גָבַהּ לִבִּי, וְלֹא־רָמוּ עֵינַי, וְלֹא־הִלַּכְתִּי בִּגְדֹלוֹת וּבְנִפְלָאוֹת מִמֶּנִּי: אִם־לֹא שִׁוִּיתִי וְדוֹמַמְתִּי נַפְשִׁי, כְּגָמֻל עֲלֵי אִמּוֹ, כַּגָּמֻל עָלַי נַפְשִׁי: יַחֵל יִשְׂרָאֵל אֶל־יהוה, מֵעַתָּה וְעַד־עוֹלָם:

תהלים קלב
שִׁיר הַמַּעֲלוֹת, זְכוֹר־יהוה לְדָוִד אֵת כָּל־עֻנּוֹתוֹ: אֲשֶׁר נִשְׁבַּע לַיהוה, נָדַר לַאֲבִיר יַעֲקֹב: אִם־אָבֹא בְּאֹהֶל בֵּיתִי, אִם־אֶעֱלֶה עַל־עֶרֶשׂ יְצוּעָי: אִם־אֶתֵּן שְׁנָת לְעֵינָי, לְעַפְעַפַּי תְּנוּמָה: עַד־אֶמְצָא מָקוֹם לַיהוה, מִשְׁכָּנוֹת לַאֲבִיר יַעֲקֹב: הִנֵּה־שְׁמַעֲנוּהָ בְאֶפְרָתָה, מְצָאנוּהָ בִּשְׂדֵי־יָעַר: נָבוֹאָה לְמִשְׁכְּנוֹתָיו, נִשְׁתַּחֲוֶה לַהֲדֹם רַגְלָיו: קוּמָה יהוה לִמְנוּחָתֶךָ, אַתָּה וַאֲרוֹן עֻזֶּךָ: כֹּהֲנֶיךָ יִלְבְּשׁוּ־צֶדֶק, וַחֲסִידֶיךָ יְרַנֵּנוּ: בַּעֲבוּר דָּוִד עַבְדֶּךָ, אַל־תָּשֵׁב פְּנֵי מְשִׁיחֶךָ: נִשְׁבַּע־יהוה לְדָוִד, אֱמֶת לֹא־יָשׁוּב מִמֶּנָּה, מִפְּרִי בִטְנְךָ אָשִׁית לְכִסֵּא־לָךְ: אִם־יִשְׁמְרוּ בָנֶיךָ בְּרִיתִי, וְעֵדֹתִי זוֹ אֲלַמְּדֵם, גַּם־בְּנֵיהֶם עֲדֵי־עַד, יֵשְׁבוּ לְכִסֵּא־לָךְ: כִּי־בָחַר יהוה בְּצִיּוֹן, אִוָּהּ לְמוֹשָׁב לוֹ: זֹאת־מְנוּחָתִי עֲדֵי־עַד, פֹּה אֵשֵׁב כִּי אִוִּתִיהָ: צֵידָהּ בָּרֵךְ אֲבָרֵךְ, אֶבְיוֹנֶיהָ אַשְׂבִּיעַ לָחֶם: וְכֹהֲנֶיהָ אַלְבִּישׁ יֶשַׁע, וַחֲסִידֶיהָ רַנֵּן יְרַנֵּנוּ: שָׁם אַצְמִיחַ קֶרֶן לְדָוִד, עָרַכְתִּי נֵר לִמְשִׁיחִי: אוֹיְבָיו אַלְבִּישׁ בֹּשֶׁת, וְעָלָיו יָצִיץ נִזְרוֹ:

תהלים קלג
שִׁיר הַמַּעֲלוֹת לְדָוִד, הִנֵּה מַה־טּוֹב וּמַה־נָּעִים, שֶׁבֶת אַחִים גַּם־יָחַד: כַּשֶּׁמֶן הַטּוֹב עַל־הָרֹאשׁ, יֹרֵד עַל־הַזָּקָן, זְקַן־אַהֲרֹן שֶׁיֹּרֵד עַל־פִּי מִדּוֹתָיו: כְּטַל־חֶרְמוֹן שֶׁיֹּרֵד עַל־הַרְרֵי צִיּוֹן, כִּי שָׁם צִוָּה יהוה אֶת־הַבְּרָכָה, חַיִּים עַד־הָעוֹלָם:

תהלים קלד
שִׁיר הַמַּעֲלוֹת, הִנֵּה בָּרְכוּ אֶת־יהוה כָּל־עַבְדֵי יהוה, הָעֹמְדִים בְּבֵית־יהוה בַּלֵּילוֹת: שְׂאוּ־יְדֵכֶם קֹדֶשׁ, וּבָרְכוּ אֶת־יהוה: יְבָרֶכְךָ יהוה מִצִּיּוֹן, עֹשֵׂה שָׁמַיִם וָאָרֶץ:

# ETHICS OF THE FATHERS

*One of the following chapters is read each Shabbat after Pesaḥ until the Shabbat before Rosh HaShana. On the last three Shabbatot before Rosh HaShana, two chapters are read.*

All Israel have a share in the World to Come, as it is said: *Sanhedrin 90a*
"Your people are all righteous; they shall inherit the land for ever; *Is. 60*
they are a shoot of My own planting,
a work of My own hands, that I may be glorified."

## CHAPTER I

1. Moses received the Torah at Sinai and handed it on to Yehoshua; Yehoshua to the elders; the elders to the prophets; and the prophets handed it on to the men of the Great Assembly. They (the men of the Great Assembly) said three things: Be careful in judgment; raise up many disciples; and make a fence for the Torah.
2. Shimon the Just was one of the last survivors of the Great Assembly. He used to say: On three things the world stands: on the Torah, on divine worship, and on acts of loving-kindness.
3. Antigonos of Sokho received [the Torah tradition] from Shimon the Just. He used to say: Do not be like servants who serve their master on condition of receiving a reward, but be like servants who serve their master not on condition of receiving a reward; and let the fear of Heaven be upon you.
4. Yose ben Yo'ezer of Zereda and Yose ben Yoḥanan of Jerusalem received [the tradition] from them. Yose ben Yo'ezer of Zereda used to say: Let your house be a meeting place for sages; sit in the dust at their feet, and with thirst, drink in their words.
5. Yose ben Yoḥanan of Jerusalem used to say: Let your house be open wide; let the poor join the members of your household; and do not gossip inordinately with women. This was said about one's own wife; all the more so does it apply to another man's wife. Hence the sages say: a man who talks too much with a woman brings trouble on himself, neglects the study of Torah, and in the end will inherit Gehinnom.
6. Yehoshua ben Peraḥya and Nittai the Arbelite received [the tradition] from them. Yehoshua ben Peraḥya used to say: Get yourself a teacher, acquire a companion, and give everyone the benefit of the doubt.
7. Nittai the Arbelite used to say: Keep far from a bad neighbor, do not associate with a bad person, and do not despair of divine retribution.
8. Yehuda ben Tabbai and Shimon ben Shataḥ received [the tradition] from them. Yehuda ben Tabbai used to say: [When sitting as a judge] do not act

# פרקי אבות

*One of the following chapters is read each* שבת *after* פסח *until the* שבת *before* ראש השנה*. On the last three* שבתות *before* ראש השנה*, two chapters are read.*

כָּל יִשְׂרָאֵל יֵשׁ לָהֶם חֵלֶק לָעוֹלָם הַבָּא. שֶׁנֶּאֱמַר: סנהדרין צ.
וְעַמֵּךְ כֻּלָּם צַדִּיקִים, לְעוֹלָם יִירְשׁוּ אָרֶץ ישעיה ס
נֵצֶר מַטָּעַי, מַעֲשֵׂה יָדַי לְהִתְפָּאֵר:

## פרק ראשון

א מֹשֶׁה קִבֵּל תּוֹרָה מִסִּינַי וּמְסָרָהּ לִיהוֹשֻׁעַ, וִיהוֹשֻׁעַ לִזְקֵנִים, וּזְקֵנִים לִנְבִיאִים, וּנְבִיאִים מְסָרוּהָ לְאַנְשֵׁי כְנֶסֶת הַגְּדוֹלָה. הֵם אָמְרוּ שְׁלֹשָׁה דְבָרִים: הֱווּ מְתוּנִים בַּדִּין, וְהַעֲמִידוּ תַלְמִידִים הַרְבֵּה, וַעֲשׂוּ סְיָג לַתּוֹרָה.

ב שִׁמְעוֹן הַצַּדִּיק הָיָה מִשְּׁיָרֵי כְנֶסֶת הַגְּדוֹלָה. הוּא הָיָה אוֹמֵר: עַל שְׁלֹשָׁה דְבָרִים הָעוֹלָם עוֹמֵד, עַל הַתּוֹרָה, וְעַל הָעֲבוֹדָה, וְעַל גְּמִילוּת חֲסָדִים.

ג אַנְטִיגְנוֹס אִישׁ סוֹכוֹ קִבֵּל מִשִּׁמְעוֹן הַצַּדִּיק. הוּא הָיָה אוֹמֵר: אַל תִּהְיוּ כַּעֲבָדִים הַמְשַׁמְּשִׁים אֶת הָרַב עַל מְנָת לְקַבֵּל פְּרָס, אֶלָּא הֱווּ כַּעֲבָדִים הַמְשַׁמְּשִׁים אֶת הָרַב שֶׁלֹּא עַל מְנָת לְקַבֵּל פְּרָס, וִיהִי מוֹרָא שָׁמַיִם עֲלֵיכֶם.

ד יוֹסֵי בֶּן יוֹעֶזֶר אִישׁ צְרֵדָה וְיוֹסֵי בֶּן יוֹחָנָן אִישׁ יְרוּשָׁלַיִם קִבְּלוּ מֵהֶם. יוֹסֵי בֶּן יוֹעֶזֶר אִישׁ צְרֵדָה אוֹמֵר: יְהִי בֵיתְךָ בֵּית וַעַד לַחֲכָמִים, וֶהֱוֵי מִתְאַבֵּק בַּעֲפַר רַגְלֵיהֶם, וֶהֱוֵי שׁוֹתֶה בַצָּמָא אֶת דִּבְרֵיהֶם.

ה יוֹסֵי בֶּן יוֹחָנָן אִישׁ יְרוּשָׁלַיִם אוֹמֵר: יְהִי בֵיתְךָ פָּתוּחַ לִרְוָחָה, וְיִהְיוּ עֲנִיִּים בְּנֵי בֵיתֶךָ, וְאַל תַּרְבֶּה שִׂיחָה עִם הָאִשָּׁה. בְּאִשְׁתּוֹ אָמְרוּ, קַל וָחֹמֶר בְּאֵשֶׁת חֲבֵרוֹ. מִכָּאן אָמְרוּ חֲכָמִים: כָּל הַמַּרְבֶּה שִׂיחָה עִם הָאִשָּׁה, גּוֹרֵם רָעָה לְעַצְמוֹ, וּבוֹטֵל מִדִּבְרֵי תוֹרָה, וְסוֹפוֹ יוֹרֵשׁ גֵּיהִנָּם.

ו יְהוֹשֻׁעַ בֶּן פְּרַחְיָה וְנִתַּאי הָאַרְבֵּלִי קִבְּלוּ מֵהֶם. יְהוֹשֻׁעַ בֶּן פְּרַחְיָה אוֹמֵר: עֲשֵׂה לְךָ רַב, וּקְנֵה לְךָ חָבֵר, וֶהֱוֵי דָן אֶת כָּל הָאָדָם לְכַף זְכוּת.

ז נִתַּאי הָאַרְבֵּלִי אוֹמֵר: הַרְחֵק מִשָּׁכֵן רָע, וְאַל תִּתְחַבֵּר לָרָשָׁע, וְאַל תִּתְיָאֵשׁ מִן הַפֻּרְעָנוּת.

ח יְהוּדָה בֶּן טַבַּאי וְשִׁמְעוֹן בֶּן שָׁטָח קִבְּלוּ מֵהֶם. יְהוּדָה בֶּן טַבַּאי אוֹמֵר: אַל תַּעַשׂ עַצְמְךָ כְּעוֹרְכֵי הַדַּיָּנִין, וּכְשֶׁיִּהְיוּ בַּעֲלֵי הַדִּין עוֹמְדִים לְפָנֶיךָ יִהְיוּ בְעֵינֶיךָ

as an advocate; when the parties to a lawsuit appear before you, regard them both as guilty; but when they leave you, having accepted the verdict, regard them both as innocent.

9. Shimon ben Shataḥ used to say: Examine the witnesses thoroughly, and be careful in your words, lest through them they learn how to lie.

10. Shemaya and Avtalyon received [the tradition] from them. Shemaya used to say: Love work, hate public office, and do not become too intimate with the ruling power.

11. Avtalyon used to say: Sages, be careful in what you say, lest you incur the penalty of exile and find yourself banished to a place of evil waters, where your disciples who follow you may drink from them and die, with the result that the name of Heaven will be profaned.

12. Hillel and Shammai received [the tradition] from them. Hillel said: Be among the disciples of Aaron, loving peace and pursuing peace, loving people and drawing them close to the Torah.

13. He used to say: A name made great is a name destroyed. He who does not increase [his knowledge] loses it. He who does not study deserves to die, and he who makes worldly use of the crown [of Torah] passes away.

14. He used to say: If I am not for myself, who will be for me? And if I am only for myself, what am I? And if not now, when?

15. Shammai used to say: Make your Torah study a fixed habit. Say little and do much; and greet everyone cheerfully.

16. Rabban Gamliel used to say: Get yourself a teacher, avoid doubt, and do not make a habit of giving tithes by guessing.

17. Shimon, his son, used to say: All my life I grew up among sages and I found that nothing is better for a person than silence. Not learning but doing is the main thing; and one who talks too much causes sin.

18. Rabban Shimon ben Gamliel used to say: On three things does the world stand – on truth, justice and peace, as it is said, "Administer truth and the judgment of peace in your gates." *Zech. 8*

Rabbi Ḥananya ben Akashya said: The Holy One, blessed be He, wanted to confer merit on Israel. That is why He gave them a copious Torah and many commandments, as it is said, "It pleased the LORD, for the sake of [Israel's] righteousness, to make the Torah great and glorious." *Makkot 23b* *Is. 42*

*If there is a minyan, mourners say the Rabbis' Kaddish (page 628).*

* * *

כִּרְשָׁעִים, וּכְשֶׁנִּפְטָרִים מִלְּפָנֶיךָ יִהְיוּ בְעֵינֶיךָ כְּזַכָּאִין, כְּשֶׁקִּבְּלוּ עֲלֵיהֶם אֶת הַדִּין.

ט שִׁמְעוֹן בֶּן שָׁטָח אוֹמֵר: הֱוֵי מַרְבֶּה לַחֲקֹר אֶת הָעֵדִים, וֶהֱוֵי זָהִיר בִּדְבָרֶיךָ, שֶׁמָּא מִתּוֹכָם יִלְמְדוּ לְשַׁקֵּר.

י שְׁמַעְיָה וְאַבְטַלְיוֹן קִבְּלוּ מֵהֶם. שְׁמַעְיָה אוֹמֵר: אֱהֹב אֶת הַמְּלָאכָה, וּשְׂנָא אֶת הָרַבָּנוּת, וְאַל תִּתְוַדַּע לָרָשׁוּת.

יא אַבְטַלְיוֹן אוֹמֵר: חֲכָמִים הִזָּהֲרוּ בְּדִבְרֵיכֶם, שֶׁמָּא תָחוּבוּ חוֹבַת גָּלוּת, וְתִגְלוּ לִמְקוֹם מַיִם הָרָעִים, וְיִשְׁתּוּ הַתַּלְמִידִים הַבָּאִים אַחֲרֵיכֶם וְיָמוּתוּ, וְנִמְצָא שֵׁם שָׁמַיִם מִתְחַלֵּל.

יב הִלֵּל וְשַׁמַּאי קִבְּלוּ מֵהֶם. הִלֵּל אוֹמֵר: הֱוֵי מִתַּלְמִידָיו שֶׁל אַהֲרֹן, אוֹהֵב שָׁלוֹם וְרוֹדֵף שָׁלוֹם, אוֹהֵב אֶת הַבְּרִיּוֹת וּמְקָרְבָן לַתּוֹרָה.

יג הוּא הָיָה אוֹמֵר: נְגַד שְׁמָא אֲבַד שְׁמֵהּ, וּדְלָא מוֹסִיף יָסוּף, וּדְלָא יָלֵף קְטָלָא חַיָּב, וּדְאִשְׁתַּמַּשׁ בְּתָגָא חֲלָף.

יד הוּא הָיָה אוֹמֵר: אִם אֵין אֲנִי לִי מִי לִי, וּכְשֶׁאֲנִי לְעַצְמִי מָה אֲנִי, וְאִם לֹא עַכְשָׁו אֵימָתָי.

טו שַׁמַּאי אוֹמֵר: עֲשֵׂה תוֹרָתְךָ קֶבַע, אֱמֹר מְעַט וַעֲשֵׂה הַרְבֵּה, וֶהֱוֵי מְקַבֵּל אֶת כָּל הָאָדָם בְּסֵבֶר פָּנִים יָפוֹת.

טז רַבָּן גַּמְלִיאֵל אוֹמֵר: עֲשֵׂה לְךָ רַב, וְהִסְתַּלֵּק מִן הַסָּפֵק, וְאַל תַּרְבֶּה לְעַשֵּׂר אֻמָּדוֹת.

יז שִׁמְעוֹן בְּנוֹ אוֹמֵר: כָּל יָמַי גָּדַלְתִּי בֵּין הַחֲכָמִים, וְלֹא מָצָאתִי לַגּוּף טוֹב מִשְּׁתִיקָה, וְלֹא הַמִּדְרָשׁ עִקָּר אֶלָּא הַמַּעֲשֶׂה, וְכָל הַמַּרְבֶּה דְבָרִים מֵבִיא חֵטְא.

יח רַבָּן שִׁמְעוֹן בֶּן גַּמְלִיאֵל אוֹמֵר: עַל שְׁלֹשָׁה דְבָרִים הָעוֹלָם קַיָּם, עַל הַדִּין, וְעַל הָאֱמֶת, וְעַל הַשָּׁלוֹם. שֶׁנֶּאֱמַר: אֱמֶת וּמִשְׁפַּט שָׁלוֹם שִׁפְטוּ בְּשַׁעֲרֵיכֶם: זכריה ח

רַבִּי חֲנַנְיָא בֶּן עֲקַשְׁיָא אוֹמֵר: רָצָה הַקָּדוֹשׁ בָּרוּךְ הוּא לְזַכּוֹת אֶת יִשְׂרָאֵל, לְפִיכָךְ הִרְבָּה לָהֶם תּוֹרָה וּמִצְוֹת. שֶׁנֶּאֱמַר: יהוה חָפֵץ לְמַעַן צִדְקוֹ, יַגְדִּיל תּוֹרָה וְיַאְדִּיר: מכות כג: ישעיה מב

*If there is a* מנין*, mourners say the* קדיש דרבנן *(page 629).*

* * *

All Israel have a share in the World to Come, as it is said: *Sanhedrin 90a*
"Your people are all righteous; they shall inherit the land for ever; *Is. 60*
they are a shoot of My own planting,
a work of My own hands, that I may be glorified."

CHAPTER 2

1. Rabbi [Judah the Prince] said: What is the right path a person should choose for himself? Whatever is honorable to one who chooses it and honorable in the eyes of others. Be as meticulous in the observance of a minor mitzva as a major one, for you do not know the reward for each mitzva. Against the loss that fulfilling a mitzva may entail, reckon its reward, and against the benefit a transgression may bring, reckon the loss it involves. Reflect on three things and you will not fall into transgression: know what is above you – a seeing eye, a hearing ear, and a book in which all your deeds are written.
2. Rabban Gamliel, son of Rabbi Judah the Prince, said: It is good to combine Torah study with a worldly occupation, for the effort involved in both makes one forget sin. Torah study without an occupation will in the end fail and lead to sin. And all who work for the community should do so for the sake of Heaven, for their ancestral merit will support them and their righteousness endures for ever. And as for you [God will say], I count you worthy of great reward as though you yourselves had accomplished it all.
3. Be wary in your dealings with the ruling power, for they only befriend a man when it serves their needs. When it is to their advantage, they appear as friends, but they do not stand by a person in his hour of need.
4. He used to say: Do His will as if it were yours, so that He may do your will as if it were His. Set aside your will for the sake of His, that He may set aside the will of others before yours.
5. Hillel said: Do not separate yourself from the community. Do not be sure of yourself until the day you die. Do not judge your fellow until you have stood in his place. Do not say anything that cannot be understood [at once] in the hope that it will eventually be understood. And do not say, I will study when I have the time, for you may never have the time.
6. He used to say: An uncouth person cannot be sin-fearing, nor can an ignoramus be pious. A shy person cannot learn, nor can an impatient one teach. A person over-occupied in business does not always become wise. In a place where there are no worthy people, strive to be worthy.
7. Seeing a skull floating on the water, he said: "Because you drowned others, they drowned you, and those who drowned you will themselves eventually be drowned."
8. He used to say: The more flesh, the more worms. The more possessions, the more worries. The more wives, the more witchcraft. The more maidservants,

כָּל יִשְׂרָאֵל יֵשׁ לָהֶם חֵלֶק לָעוֹלָם הַבָּא. שֶׁנֶּאֱמַר: סנהדרין צ.
וְעַמֵּךְ כֻּלָּם צַדִּיקִים, לְעוֹלָם יִירְשׁוּ אָרֶץ ישעיה ס
נֵצֶר מַטָּעַי, מַעֲשֵׂה יָדַי לְהִתְפָּאֵר:

## פרק שני

א רַבִּי אוֹמֵר: אֵיזוֹ הִיא דֶרֶךְ יְשָׁרָה שֶׁיָּבֹר לוֹ הָאָדָם, כָּל שֶׁהִיא תִּפְאֶרֶת לְעֹשֶׂיהָ וְתִפְאֶרֶת לוֹ מִן הָאָדָם. וֶהֱוֵי זָהִיר בְּמִצְוָה קַלָּה כְּבַחֲמוּרָה, שֶׁאֵין אַתָּה יוֹדֵעַ מַתַּן שְׂכָרָן שֶׁל מִצְוֹת. וֶהֱוֵי מְחַשֵּׁב הֶפְסֵד מִצְוָה כְּנֶגֶד שְׂכָרָהּ, וּשְׂכַר עֲבֵרָה כְּנֶגֶד הֶפְסֵדָהּ. הִסְתַּכֵּל בִּשְׁלֹשָׁה דְבָרִים, וְאֵין אַתָּה בָא לִידֵי עֲבֵרָה. דַּע מַה לְּמַעְלָה מִמְּךָ, עַיִן רוֹאָה, וְאֹזֶן שׁוֹמַעַת, וְכָל מַעֲשֶׂיךָ בַּסֵּפֶר נִכְתָּבִים.

ב רַבָּן גַּמְלִיאֵל בְּנוֹ שֶׁל רַבִּי יְהוּדָה הַנָּשִׂיא אוֹמֵר: יָפֶה תַּלְמוּד תּוֹרָה עִם דֶּרֶךְ אֶרֶץ, שֶׁיְּגִיעַת שְׁנֵיהֶם מְשַׁכַּחַת עָוֹן. וְכָל תּוֹרָה שֶׁאֵין עִמָּהּ מְלָאכָה, סוֹפָהּ בְּטֵלָה וְגוֹרֶרֶת עָוֹן. וְכָל הָעוֹסְקִים עִם הַצִּבּוּר, יִהְיוּ עוֹסְקִים עִמָּהֶם לְשֵׁם שָׁמַיִם, שֶׁזְּכוּת אֲבוֹתָם מְסַיַּעְתָּם, וְצִדְקָתָם עוֹמֶדֶת לָעַד. וְאַתֶּם, מַעֲלֶה אֲנִי עֲלֵיכֶם שָׂכָר הַרְבֵּה כְּאִלּוּ עֲשִׂיתֶם.

ג הֱווּ זְהִירִין בָּרָשׁוּת, שֶׁאֵין מְקָרְבִין לוֹ לָאָדָם אֶלָּא לְצֹרֶךְ עַצְמָן. נִרְאִין כְּאוֹהֲבִין בִּשְׁעַת הֲנָאָתָן, וְאֵין עוֹמְדִין לוֹ לָאָדָם בִּשְׁעַת דָּחְקוֹ.

ד הוּא הָיָה אוֹמֵר: עֲשֵׂה רְצוֹנוֹ כִּרְצוֹנְךָ, כְּדֵי שֶׁיַּעֲשֶׂה רְצוֹנְךָ כִּרְצוֹנוֹ. בַּטֵּל רְצוֹנְךָ מִפְּנֵי רְצוֹנוֹ, כְּדֵי שֶׁיְּבַטֵּל רְצוֹן אֲחֵרִים מִפְּנֵי רְצוֹנֶךָ.

ה הִלֵּל אוֹמֵר: אַל תִּפְרֹשׁ מִן הַצִּבּוּר, וְאַל תַּאֲמִין בְּעַצְמְךָ עַד יוֹם מוֹתְךָ, וְאַל תָּדִין אֶת חֲבֵרְךָ עַד שֶׁתַּגִּיעַ לִמְקוֹמוֹ. וְאַל תֹּאמַר דָּבָר שֶׁאִי אֶפְשָׁר לִשְׁמֹעַ, שֶׁסּוֹפוֹ לְהִשָּׁמַע. וְאַל תֹּאמַר לִכְשֶׁאֶפָּנֶה אֶשְׁנֶה, שֶׁמָּא לֹא תִפָּנֶה.

ו הוּא הָיָה אוֹמֵר: אֵין בּוּר יְרֵא חֵטְא, וְלֹא עַם הָאָרֶץ חָסִיד, וְלֹא הַבַּיְשָׁן לָמֵד, וְלֹא הַקַּפְּדָן מְלַמֵּד, וְלֹא כָל הַמַּרְבֶּה בִסְחוֹרָה מַחְכִּים. וּבְמָקוֹם שֶׁאֵין אֲנָשִׁים, הִשְׁתַּדֵּל לִהְיוֹת אִישׁ.

ז אַף הוּא רָאָה גֻּלְגֹּלֶת אַחַת שֶׁצָּפָה עַל פְּנֵי הַמָּיִם. אָמַר לָהּ: עַל דַּאֲטֵפְתְּ אַטְפוּךְ, וְסוֹף מְטִיפַיִךְ יְטוּפוּן.

ח הוּא הָיָה אוֹמֵר: מַרְבֶּה בָשָׂר, מַרְבֶּה רִמָּה. מַרְבֶּה נְכָסִים, מַרְבֶּה דְאָגָה. מַרְבֶּה נָשִׁים, מַרְבֶּה כְשָׁפִים. מַרְבֶּה שְׁפָחוֹת, מַרְבֶּה זִמָּה. מַרְבֶּה עֲבָדִים,

the more lewdness. The more menservants, the more robbery. The more Torah, the more life. The more study, the more wisdom. The more counsel, the more understanding. The more charity, the more peace. Whoever acquires a good name acquires something for himself. Whoever acquires for himself words of Torah acquires for himself life in the World to Come.

9. Rabban Yoḥanan ben Zakkai received [the tradition] from Hillel and Shammai. He used to say: If you have learnt much Torah, take no special credit for yourself, for it was for this that you were created.

10. Rabban Yoḥanan ben Zakkai had five [pre-eminent] disciples, namely: Rabbi Eliezer ben Hyrcanus, Rabbi Yehoshua ben Ḥananya, Rabbi Yose the Priest, Rabbi Shimon ben Netanel and Rabbi Elazar ben Arakh.

11. He used to recount their praise: Eliezer ben Hyrcanus: a plastered well that never loses a drop. Yehoshua ben Ḥananya: happy the one who gave him birth. Yose the Priest: a pious man. Shimon ben Netanel: a man who fears sin. Elazar ben Arakh: an ever-flowing spring.

12. He used to say: If all the sages of Israel were in one scale of a balance and Eliezer ben Hyrcanus in the other, he would outweigh them all. However, Abba Saul said in his name: If all the sages of Israel, including Eliezer ben Hyrcanus, were in one scale of a balance, and Elazar ben Arakh in the other, he would outweigh them all.

13. He said to them: Go and see which is the right way to which one should cling. Rabbi Eliezer said: a good eye [generosity of spirit]. Rabbi Yehoshua said: a good companion. Rabbi Yose said: a good neighbor. Rabbi Shimon said: one who considers the consequences. Rabbi Elazar said: a good heart. Then he said to them: I prefer the answer of Elazar ben Arakh, for his view includes all of yours.

14. He said to them: Go and see which is the wrong way one should avoid. Rabbi Eliezer said: an evil eye [envy]. Rabbi Yehoshua said: an evil companion. Rabbi Yose said: an evil neighbor. Rabbi Shimon said: one who borrows and does not repay, for borrowing from a person is like borrowing from God, as
it is said, "The wicked borrows and does not repay, but the Righteous One is *Ps. 37*
gracious and repays." Rabbi Elazar said: an evil heart. Then he said to them: I prefer the answer of Elazar ben Arakh, for his view includes all of yours.

15. Each of the disciples said three things. Rabbi Eliezer said: Let the honor of your fellow be as precious to you as your own. Do not be easily provoked to anger. Repent one day before you die. [He also said:] Warm yourself by the fire of the sages, but be careful of their glowing coals lest you be burnt; for their bite is the bite of a fox, their sting is the sting of a scorpion, their hiss is the hiss of a serpent, and all their words are like fiery coals.

מַרְבֶּה גָזֵל. מַרְבֶּה תוֹרָה, מַרְבֶּה חַיִּים. מַרְבֶּה יְשִׁיבָה, מַרְבֶּה חָכְמָה. מַרְבֶּה עֵצָה, מַרְבֶּה תְבוּנָה. מַרְבֶּה צְדָקָה, מַרְבֶּה שָׁלוֹם. קָנָה שֵׁם טוֹב, קָנָה לְעַצְמוֹ. קָנָה לוֹ דִבְרֵי תוֹרָה, קָנָה לוֹ חַיֵּי הָעוֹלָם הַבָּא.

ט רַבָּן יוֹחָנָן בֶּן זַכַּאי קִבֵּל מֵהִלֵּל וּמִשַּׁמַּאי. הוּא הָיָה אוֹמֵר: אִם לָמַדְתָּ תּוֹרָה הַרְבֵּה, אַל תַּחֲזִיק טוֹבָה לְעַצְמְךָ, כִּי לְכָךְ נוֹצָרְתָּ.

י חֲמִשָּׁה תַלְמִידִים הָיוּ לְרַבָּן יוֹחָנָן בֶּן זַכַּאי. וְאֵלּוּ הֵן: רַבִּי אֱלִיעֶזֶר בֶּן הוּרְקְנוֹס, רַבִּי יְהוֹשֻׁעַ בֶּן חֲנַנְיָה, רַבִּי יוֹסֵי הַכֹּהֵן, רַבִּי שִׁמְעוֹן בֶּן נְתַנְאֵל, רַבִּי אֶלְעָזָר בֶּן עֲרָךְ.

יא הוּא הָיָה מוֹנֶה שִׁבְחָם: אֱלִיעֶזֶר בֶּן הוּרְקְנוֹס, בּוֹר סוּד שֶׁאֵינוֹ מְאַבֵּד טִפָּה. יְהוֹשֻׁעַ בֶּן חֲנַנְיָה, אַשְׁרֵי יוֹלַדְתּוֹ. יוֹסֵי הַכֹּהֵן, חָסִיד. שִׁמְעוֹן בֶּן נְתַנְאֵל, יְרֵא חֵטְא. אֶלְעָזָר בֶּן עֲרָךְ, כְּמַעְיָן הַמִּתְגַּבֵּר.

יב הוּא הָיָה אוֹמֵר: אִם יִהְיוּ כָּל חַכְמֵי יִשְׂרָאֵל בְּכַף מֹאזְנַיִם, וֶאֱלִיעֶזֶר בֶּן הוּרְקְנוֹס בְּכַף שְׁנִיָּה, מַכְרִיעַ אֶת כֻּלָּם. אַבָּא שָׁאוּל אוֹמֵר מִשְּׁמוֹ: אִם יִהְיוּ כָּל חַכְמֵי יִשְׂרָאֵל בְּכַף מֹאזְנַיִם, וֶאֱלִיעֶזֶר בֶּן הוּרְקְנוֹס אַף עִמָּהֶם, וְאֶלְעָזָר בֶּן עֲרָךְ בְּכַף שְׁנִיָּה, מַכְרִיעַ אֶת כֻּלָּם.

יג אָמַר לָהֶם: צְאוּ וּרְאוּ אֵיזוֹ הִיא דֶּרֶךְ טוֹבָה, שֶׁיִּדְבַּק בָּהּ הָאָדָם. רַבִּי אֱלִיעֶזֶר אוֹמֵר: עַיִן טוֹבָה. רַבִּי יְהוֹשֻׁעַ אוֹמֵר: חָבֵר טוֹב. רַבִּי יוֹסֵי אוֹמֵר: שָׁכֵן טוֹב. רַבִּי שִׁמְעוֹן אוֹמֵר: הָרוֹאֶה אֶת הַנּוֹלָד. רַבִּי אֶלְעָזָר אוֹמֵר: לֵב טוֹב. אָמַר לָהֶם, רוֹאֶה אֲנִי אֶת דִּבְרֵי אֶלְעָזָר בֶּן עֲרָךְ מִדִּבְרֵיכֶם, שֶׁבִּכְלָל דְּבָרָיו דִּבְרֵיכֶם.

יד אָמַר לָהֶם: צְאוּ וּרְאוּ, אֵיזוֹ הִיא דֶּרֶךְ רָעָה, שֶׁיִּתְרַחֵק מִמֶּנָּה הָאָדָם. רַבִּי אֱלִיעֶזֶר אוֹמֵר: עַיִן רָעָה. רַבִּי יְהוֹשֻׁעַ אוֹמֵר: חָבֵר רָע. רַבִּי יוֹסֵי אוֹמֵר: שָׁכֵן רָע. רַבִּי שִׁמְעוֹן אוֹמֵר: הַלֹּוֶה וְאֵינוֹ מְשַׁלֵּם, אֶחָד הַלֹּוֶה מִן הָאָדָם כְּלֹוֶה מִן הַמָּקוֹם, שֶׁנֶּאֱמַר: לֹוֶה רָשָׁע וְלֹא יְשַׁלֵּם, וְצַדִּיק חוֹנֵן וְנוֹתֵן: רַבִּי אֶלְעָזָר תהלים לז
אוֹמֵר: לֵב רָע. אָמַר לָהֶם: רוֹאֶה אֲנִי אֶת דִּבְרֵי אֶלְעָזָר בֶּן עֲרָךְ מִדִּבְרֵיכֶם, שֶׁבִּכְלָל דְּבָרָיו דִּבְרֵיכֶם.

טו הֵם אָמְרוּ שְׁלֹשָׁה דְבָרִים. רַבִּי אֱלִיעֶזֶר אוֹמֵר: יְהִי כְבוֹד חֲבֵרְךָ חָבִיב עָלֶיךָ כְּשֶׁלָּךְ, וְאַל תְּהִי נוֹחַ לִכְעֹס. וְשׁוּב יוֹם אֶחָד לִפְנֵי מִיתָתְךָ. וֶהֱוֵי מִתְחַמֵּם כְּנֶגֶד אוּרָן שֶׁל חֲכָמִים, וֶהֱוֵי זָהִיר בְּגַחַלְתָּן שֶׁלֹּא תִכָּוֶה, שֶׁנְּשִׁיכָתָן נְשִׁיכַת שׁוּעָל, וַעֲקִיצָתָן עֲקִיצַת עַקְרָב, וּלְחִישָׁתָן לְחִישַׁת שָׂרָף, וְכָל דִּבְרֵיהֶם כְּגַחֲלֵי אֵשׁ.

16. Rabbi Yehoshua said: The evil eye [envy], the evil impulse, and hatred of humankind drive a person out of the world.
17. Rabbi Yose said: Let the property of your fellow be as precious to you as your own. Prepare yourself to study Torah, for it does not come to you as an inheritance. And let all your deeds be for the sake of Heaven.
18. Rabbi Shimon said: Be meticulous in reciting the Shema and the [Amida] prayer. When you pray, do not do so as a fixed routine, but as a plea for mercy and grace before God, as it is said, "For He is gracious and compassionate, *Joel 2* slow to anger, abounding in kindness, and renouncing punishment." Do not be evil in your own eyes.
19. Rabbi Elazar said: Be diligent in the study of Torah. Know how to answer a heretic. Know for whom you labor and who is your Employer who will pay you the reward of your work.
20. Rabbi Tarfon said: The day is short, the task is great, the laborers are lazy, the reward is much, and the Master insistent.
21. He used to say: It is not for you to complete the task, but neither are you free to stand aside from it. If you have studied much Torah, you will be given great reward, for your Employer will faithfully reward your work. Know, though, that the reward of the righteous is granted in the time to come.

Rabbi Ḥananya ben Akashya said: The Holy One, blessed be He, wanted to confer *Makkot 23b* merit on Israel. That is why He gave them a copious Torah and many commandments, as it is said, "It pleased the LORD, for the sake of [Israel's] righteousness, *Is. 42* to make the Torah great and glorious."

*If there is a minyan, mourners say the Rabbis' Kaddish (page 628).*

* * *

All Israel have a share in the World to Come, as it is said, *Sanhedrin 90a*
"Your people are all righteous; they shall inherit the land for ever; *Is. 60*
they are a shoot of My own planting,
a work of My own hands, that I may be glorified."

## CHAPTER 3

1. Akavya ben Mahalalel said: Reflect on three things and you will avoid transgression: Know where you came from, where you are going, and before whom you will have to give an account and reckoning. "Where you came from" – from a putrid drop. "Where you are going" – to a place of dust, worms and maggots. "And before whom you will have to give an account and reckoning" – before the Supreme King of kings, the Holy One, blessed be He.

טו רַבִּי יְהוֹשֻׁעַ אוֹמֵר: עַיִן הָרָע וְיֵצֶר הָרָע וְשִׂנְאַת הַבְּרִיּוֹת, מוֹצִיאִין אֶת הָאָדָם
מִן הָעוֹלָם.

יז רַבִּי יוֹסֵי אוֹמֵר: יְהִי מָמוֹן חֲבֵרְךָ חָבִיב עָלֶיךָ כְּשֶׁלָּךְ. וְהַתְקֵן עַצְמְךָ לִלְמֹד
תּוֹרָה, שֶׁאֵינָהּ יְרֻשָּׁה לָךְ. וְכָל מַעֲשֶׂיךָ יִהְיוּ לְשֵׁם שָׁמָיִם.

יח רַבִּי שִׁמְעוֹן אוֹמֵר: הֱוֵי זָהִיר בִּקְרִיאַת שְׁמַע וּבִתְפִלָּה. וּכְשֶׁאַתָּה מִתְפַּלֵּל
אַל תַּעַשׂ תְּפִלָּתְךָ קֶבַע, אֶלָּא רַחֲמִים וְתַחֲנוּנִים לִפְנֵי הַמָּקוֹם, שֶׁנֶּאֱמַר: כִּי יואל ב
חַנּוּן וְרַחוּם הוּא, אֶרֶךְ אַפַּיִם וְרַב־חֶסֶד וְנִחָם עַל־הָרָעָה: וְאַל תְּהִי רָשָׁע
בִּפְנֵי עַצְמֶךָ.

יט רַבִּי אֶלְעָזָר אוֹמֵר: הֱוֵי שָׁקוּד לִלְמֹד תּוֹרָה. וְדַע מַה שֶּׁתָּשִׁיב לְאֶפִּיקוֹרוֹס.
וְדַע לִפְנֵי מִי אַתָּה עָמֵל, וּמִי הוּא בַּעַל מְלַאכְתְּךָ, שֶׁיְּשַׁלֶּם לְךָ שְׂכַר פְּעֻלָּתֶךָ.

כ רַבִּי טַרְפוֹן אוֹמֵר: הַיּוֹם קָצָר, וְהַמְּלָאכָה מְרֻבָּה, וְהַפּוֹעֲלִים עֲצֵלִים, וְהַשָּׂכָר
הַרְבֵּה, וּבַעַל הַבַּיִת דּוֹחֵק.

כא הוּא הָיָה אוֹמֵר: לֹא עָלֶיךָ הַמְּלָאכָה לִגְמֹר, וְלֹא אַתָּה בֶן חוֹרִין לִבָּטֵל מִמֶּנָּה.
אִם לָמַדְתָּ תּוֹרָה הַרְבֵּה, נוֹתְנִין לְךָ שָׂכָר הַרְבֵּה. וְנֶאֱמָן הוּא בַּעַל מְלַאכְתְּךָ,
שֶׁיְּשַׁלֶּם לְךָ שְׂכַר פְּעֻלָּתֶךָ. וְדַע, שֶׁמַּתַּן שְׂכָרָן שֶׁל צַדִּיקִים לֶעָתִיד לָבוֹא.

מכות כג: רַבִּי חֲנַנְיָא בֶּן עֲקַשְׁיָא אוֹמֵר: רָצָה הַקָּדוֹשׁ בָּרוּךְ הוּא לְזַכּוֹת אֶת יִשְׂרָאֵל, לְפִיכָךְ
ישעיה מב הִרְבָּה לָהֶם תּוֹרָה וּמִצְוֹת. שֶׁנֶּאֱמַר: יהוה חָפֵץ לְמַעַן צִדְקוֹ, יַגְדִּיל תּוֹרָה וְיַאְדִּיר:

*If there is a* מנין*, mourners say the* קדיש דרבנן *(page 629).*

(page 629)

* * *

סנהדרין צ. כָּל יִשְׂרָאֵל יֵשׁ לָהֶם חֵלֶק לָעוֹלָם הַבָּא. שֶׁנֶּאֱמַר:
ישעיה ס וְעַמֵּךְ כֻּלָּם צַדִּיקִים, לְעוֹלָם יִירְשׁוּ אָרֶץ
נֵצֶר מַטָּעַי, מַעֲשֵׂה יָדַי לְהִתְפָּאֵר:

## פרק שלישי

א עֲקַבְיָא בֶּן מַהֲלַלְאֵל אוֹמֵר: הִסְתַּכֵּל בִּשְׁלֹשָׁה דְבָרִים, וְאֵין אַתָּה בָא לִידֵי
עֲבֵרָה. דַּע מֵאַיִן בָּאתָ, וּלְאָן אַתָּה הוֹלֵךְ, וְלִפְנֵי מִי אַתָּה עָתִיד לִתֵּן דִּין
וְחֶשְׁבּוֹן. מֵאַיִן בָּאתָ, מִטִּפָּה סְרוּחָה. וּלְאָן אַתָּה הוֹלֵךְ, לִמְקוֹם עָפָר, רִמָּה
וְתוֹלֵעָה. וְלִפְנֵי מִי אַתָּה עָתִיד לִתֵּן דִּין וְחֶשְׁבּוֹן, לִפְנֵי מֶלֶךְ מַלְכֵי הַמְּלָכִים,
הַקָּדוֹשׁ בָּרוּךְ הוּא.

2. Rabbi Ḥanina, the deputy High Priest, said: Pray for the welfare of the government, for were it not for fear of it, people would swallow one another alive.

3. Rabbi Ḥanina ben Teradyon said: When two people sit together and no words of Torah pass between them, they are regarded as a company of scoffers, as it is said, "He does not sit in the company of scoffers." But when two people *Ps. 1* sit together and words of Torah do pass between them, the Divine Presence rests with them, as it is said, "Then those who feared the LORD talked together, *Mal. 3* and the LORD listened and heard, and a scroll of remembrance was written before Him concerning those who feared the LORD and cherished His name." This verse tells me about two people; from where can I learn that even one person who sits alone and studies Torah, the Holy One, blessed be He, grants him a reward? From the verse, "Though he sits alone and meditates quietly, *Lam. 3* He will grant him a reward."

4. Rabbi Shimon said: Three who eat at one table, and do not speak words of Torah, are as if they had eaten of sacrifices of dead idols, as it is said, "For all *Is. 28* the tables are full of vomit and filth, when God is absent." However, three who eat at one table and speak words of Torah, it is as if they had eaten at God's table, as it is said, "And He spoke to me: This is the table before the LORD." *Ezek. 41*

5. Rabbi Ḥanina ben Ḥakhinai said: One who stays awake at night, travels alone, or turns his mind to idle thoughts, endangers his soul.

6. Rabbi Neḥunya ben HaKanna said: One who takes on himself the yoke of Torah will be spared the yoke of government and the yoke of worldly responsibilities, but one who throws off the yoke of the Torah will bear the yoke of government and the yoke of worldly responsibilities.

7. Rabbi Ḥalafta ben Dosa of Kfar Ḥananya said: When ten people sit together and study Torah, the Divine Presence rests among them, as it is said, "God *Ps. 82* stands in the divine assembly." How do we know that the same applies to five? From the verse, "He has founded His group on the earth." And how do *Amos 9* we know that it applies even to three? From the verse, "He judges among the *Ps. 82* judges." How do we know that the same applies even to two? From the verse, "Then those who feared the LORD talked together, and the LORD listened *Mal. 3* and heard." And how do we know that it applies even to one? From the verse, "In every place where I cause My name to be mentioned, I will come to you *Ex. 20* and bless you."

8. Rabbi Elazar of Bartota said: Give Him what is His, for you and yours are His. This was also said by David: "For all things come from You, and we have *1 Chr. 29* given You only what is Yours."

9. Rabbi Jacob said: One who is reviewing his Torah study while walking on the way, and interrupts his study to say, "What a beautiful tree" or "What a beautiful field," is regarded by Scripture as if he had endangered his soul.

ב רַבִּי חֲנִינָא סְגַן הַכֹּהֲנִים אוֹמֵר: הֱוֵי מִתְפַּלֵּל בִּשְׁלוֹמָהּ שֶׁל מַלְכוּת, שֶׁאִלְמָלֵא מוֹרָאָהּ, אִישׁ אֶת רֵעֵהוּ חַיִּים בְּלָעוֹ.

ג רַבִּי חֲנִינָא בֶּן תְּרַדְיוֹן אוֹמֵר: שְׁנַיִם שֶׁיּוֹשְׁבִין, וְאֵין בֵּינֵיהֶם דִּבְרֵי תוֹרָה, הֲרֵי
זֶה מוֹשַׁב לֵצִים, שֶׁנֶּאֱמַר: וּבְמוֹשַׁב לֵצִים לֹא יָשָׁב: אֲבָל שְׁנַיִם שֶׁיּוֹשְׁבִין, תהלים א
וְיֵשׁ בֵּינֵיהֶם דִּבְרֵי תוֹרָה, שְׁכִינָה שְׁרוּיָה בֵינֵיהֶם, שֶׁנֶּאֱמַר: אָז נִדְבְּרוּ יִרְאֵי מלאכי ג
יהוה אִישׁ אֶל־רֵעֵהוּ, וַיַּקְשֵׁב יהוה וַיִּשְׁמָע, וַיִּכָּתֵב סֵפֶר זִכָּרוֹן לְפָנָיו לְיִרְאֵי
יהוה וּלְחֹשְׁבֵי שְׁמוֹ: אֵין לִי אֶלָּא שְׁנַיִם, מִנַּיִן אֲפִלּוּ אֶחָד שֶׁיּוֹשֵׁב וְעוֹסֵק
בַּתּוֹרָה שֶׁהַקָּדוֹשׁ בָּרוּךְ הוּא קוֹבֵעַ לוֹ שָׂכָר, שֶׁנֶּאֱמַר: יֵשֵׁב בָּדָד וְיִדֹּם כִּי נָטַל איכה ג
עָלָיו:

ד רַבִּי שִׁמְעוֹן אוֹמֵר: שְׁלֹשָׁה שֶׁאָכְלוּ עַל שֻׁלְחָן אֶחָד וְלֹא אָמְרוּ עָלָיו דִּבְרֵי
תוֹרָה, כְּאִלּוּ אָכְלוּ מִזִּבְחֵי מֵתִים, שֶׁנֶּאֱמַר: כִּי כָּל־שֻׁלְחָנוֹת מָלְאוּ קִיא ישעיה כח
צֹאָה בְּלִי מָקוֹם: אֲבָל שְׁלֹשָׁה שֶׁאָכְלוּ עַל שֻׁלְחָן אֶחָד, וְאָמְרוּ עָלָיו דִּבְרֵי
תוֹרָה, כְּאִלּוּ אָכְלוּ מִשֻּׁלְחָנוֹ שֶׁל מָקוֹם, שֶׁנֶּאֱמַר: וַיְדַבֵּר אֵלַי, זֶה הַשֻּׁלְחָן יחזקאל מא
אֲשֶׁר לִפְנֵי יהוה:

ה רַבִּי חֲנִינָא בֶּן חֲכִינַאי אוֹמֵר: הַנֵּעוֹר בַּלַּיְלָה, וְהַמְהַלֵּךְ בַּדֶּרֶךְ יְחִידִי, וְהַמְפַנֶּה לִבּוֹ לְבַטָּלָה, הֲרֵי זֶה מִתְחַיֵּב בְּנַפְשׁוֹ.

ו רַבִּי נְחוּנְיָא בֶּן הַקָּנָה אוֹמֵר: כָּל הַמְקַבֵּל עָלָיו עֹל תּוֹרָה, מַעֲבִירִין מִמֶּנּוּ עֹל מַלְכוּת וְעֹל דֶּרֶךְ אֶרֶץ. וְכָל הַפּוֹרֵק מִמֶּנּוּ עֹל תּוֹרָה, נוֹתְנִין עָלָיו עֹל מַלְכוּת וְעֹל דֶּרֶךְ אֶרֶץ.

ז רַבִּי חֲלַפְתָּא בֶּן דּוֹסָא אִישׁ כְּפַר חֲנַנְיָה אוֹמֵר: עֲשָׂרָה שֶׁיּוֹשְׁבִין וְעוֹסְקִין
בַּתּוֹרָה שְׁכִינָה שְׁרוּיָה בֵינֵיהֶם, שֶׁנֶּאֱמַר: אֱלֹהִים נִצָּב בַּעֲדַת־אֵל: וּמִנַּיִן אֲפִלּוּ תהלים פב
חֲמִשָּׁה, שֶׁנֶּאֱמַר: וַאֲגֻדָּתוֹ עַל־אֶרֶץ יְסָדָהּ: וּמִנַּיִן אֲפִלּוּ שְׁלֹשָׁה, שֶׁנֶּאֱמַר: עמוס ט
בְּקֶרֶב אֱלֹהִים יִשְׁפֹּט: וּמִנַּיִן אֲפִלּוּ שְׁנַיִם, שֶׁנֶּאֱמַר: אָז נִדְבְּרוּ יִרְאֵי יהוה אִישׁ תהלים פב מלאכי ג
אֶל־רֵעֵהוּ, וַיַּקְשֵׁב יהוה וַיִּשְׁמָע: וּמִנַּיִן אֲפִלּוּ אֶחָד, שֶׁנֶּאֱמַר: בְּכָל־הַמָּקוֹם שמות כ
אֲשֶׁר אַזְכִּיר אֶת־שְׁמִי, אָבוֹא אֵלֶיךָ וּבֵרַכְתִּיךָ:

ח רַבִּי אֶלְעָזָר אִישׁ בַּרְתּוֹתָא אוֹמֵר: תֶּן לוֹ מִשֶּׁלּוֹ, שֶׁאַתָּה וְשֶׁלְּךָ שֶׁלּוֹ. וְכֵן בְּדָוִד
הוּא אוֹמֵר: כִּי־מִמְּךָ הַכֹּל, וּמִיָּדְךָ נָתַנּוּ לָךְ: דברי הימים א׳ כט

ט רַבִּי יַעֲקֹב אוֹמֵר: הַמְהַלֵּךְ בַּדֶּרֶךְ וְשׁוֹנֶה, וּמַפְסִיק מִמִּשְׁנָתוֹ וְאוֹמֵר, מַה נָּאֶה אִילָן זֶה, מַה נָּאֶה נִיר זֶה, מַעֲלֶה עָלָיו הַכָּתוּב כְּאִלּוּ מִתְחַיֵּב בְּנַפְשׁוֹ.

10. Rabbi Dostai of Rabbi Yannai said in the name of Rabbi Meir: One who forgets even one thing of his Torah learning, Scripture regards him as if he had endangered his soul, for it is said, "Only take heed and guard your soul very carefully so that you do not forget the things that your eyes saw." One might think that this applies even to one who finds his studies too hard to remember. Therefore the verse adds, "Lest they be removed from your heart all the days of your life." Thus, one does not endanger his soul unless he deliberately removes teachings from his heart. *Deut. 4* *Deut. 4*

11. Rabbi Ḥanina ben Dosa said: For one who puts fear of sin before wisdom, wisdom endures. For one who puts wisdom before fear of sin, wisdom does not endure.

12. He also used to say: For one whose good deeds exceed his wisdom, wisdom endures. For one whose wisdom exceeds his good deeds, wisdom does not endure.

13. He also used to say: In one in whom people delight, God delights. In one in whom people do not delight, God does not delight.

14. Rabbi Dosa ben Harkinas said: Sleeping late in the morning, drinking wine at midday, chattering with children and sitting in gatherings of the ignorant – these drive a person from the world.

15. Rabbi Elazar of Modin said: One who desecrates sacred things, despises the festivals, shames his fellow in public, nullifies the covenant of our father Abraham, or attributes meanings to the Torah contrary to normative law, even though he has to his credit Torah and good deeds, has no share in the World to Come.

16. Rabbi Yishmael said: Be yielding to a superior, pleasing to the young, and receive everyone cheerfully.

17. Rabbi Akiva said: Mocking and frivolity lead to immorality. The oral tradition (*Mesora*) is a fence protecting the Torah; tithes are a fence protecting wealth; vows are a fence protecting abstinence. The fence protecting wisdom is silence.

18. He used to say: Beloved is man, for he was created in the image of God. As a gesture of special love, it was made known to him that he was created in the image of God, as it is said, "For in the image of God He made man." Beloved are Israel for they are called God's children. As a gesture of special love, it was made known to them that they are called God's children, as it is said, "You are the children of the Lord your God." Beloved are Israel, for they were given a precious vessel [the Torah]. As a gesture of special love, it was made known to them that they were given the precious vessel through which the world was created, as it is said, "I have given you good instruction; do not forsake My Torah." *Gen. 9* *Deut. 14* *Prov. 4*

י רַבִּי דוֹסְתָּאִי בְּרַבִּי יַנַּאי מִשּׁוּם רַבִּי מֵאִיר אוֹמֵר: כָּל הַשּׁוֹכֵחַ דָּבָר אֶחָד
מִמִּשְׁנָתוֹ, מַעֲלֶה עָלָיו הַכָּתוּב כְּאִלּוּ מִתְחַיֵּב בְּנַפְשׁוֹ, שֶׁנֶּאֱמַר: רַק הִשָּׁמֶר דברים ד
לְךָ וּשְׁמֹר נַפְשְׁךָ מְאֹד, פֶּן־תִּשְׁכַּח אֶת־הַדְּבָרִים אֲשֶׁר־רָאוּ עֵינֶיךָ: יָכוֹל אֲפִלּוּ
תָּקְפָה עָלָיו מִשְׁנָתוֹ, תַּלְמוּד לוֹמַר: וּפֶן יָסוּרוּ מִלְּבָבְךָ כֹּל יְמֵי חַיֶּיךָ: הָא אֵינוֹ דברים ד
מִתְחַיֵּב בְּנַפְשׁוֹ, עַד שֶׁיֵּשֵׁב וִיסִירֵם מִלִּבּוֹ.

יא רַבִּי חֲנִינָא בֶּן דּוֹסָא אוֹמֵר: כָּל שֶׁיִּרְאַת חֶטְאוֹ קוֹדֶמֶת לְחָכְמָתוֹ, חָכְמָתוֹ
מִתְקַיֶּמֶת. וְכָל שֶׁחָכְמָתוֹ קוֹדֶמֶת לְיִרְאַת חֶטְאוֹ, אֵין חָכְמָתוֹ מִתְקַיֶּמֶת.

יב הוּא הָיָה אוֹמֵר: כָּל שֶׁמַּעֲשָׂיו מְרֻבִּין מֵחָכְמָתוֹ, חָכְמָתוֹ מִתְקַיֶּמֶת. וְכָל
שֶׁחָכְמָתוֹ מְרֻבָּה מִמַּעֲשָׂיו, אֵין חָכְמָתוֹ מִתְקַיֶּמֶת.

יג הוּא הָיָה אוֹמֵר: כָּל שֶׁרוּחַ הַבְּרִיּוֹת נוֹחָה הֵימֶנּוּ, רוּחַ הַמָּקוֹם נוֹחָה הֵימֶנּוּ.
וְכָל שֶׁאֵין רוּחַ הַבְּרִיּוֹת נוֹחָה הֵימֶנּוּ, אֵין רוּחַ הַמָּקוֹם נוֹחָה הֵימֶנּוּ.

יד רַבִּי דוֹסָא בֶּן הַרְכִּינַס אוֹמֵר: שֵׁנָה שֶׁל שַׁחֲרִית, וְיַיִן שֶׁל צָהֳרַיִם, וְשִׂיחַת
הַיְלָדִים, וִישִׁיבַת בָּתֵּי כְנֵסִיּוֹת שֶׁל עַמֵּי הָאָרֶץ, מוֹצִיאִין אֶת הָאָדָם מִן
הָעוֹלָם.

טו רַבִּי אֶלְעָזָר הַמּוֹדָעִי אוֹמֵר: הַמְחַלֵּל אֶת הַקֳּדָשִׁים, וְהַמְבַזֶּה אֶת הַמּוֹעֲדוֹת,
וְהַמַּלְבִּין פְּנֵי חֲבֵרוֹ בָּרַבִּים, וְהַמֵּפֵר בְּרִיתוֹ שֶׁל אַבְרָהָם אָבִינוּ, וְהַמְגַלֶּה פָנִים
בַּתּוֹרָה שֶׁלֹּא כַהֲלָכָה, אַף עַל פִּי שֶׁיֵּשׁ בְּיָדוֹ תּוֹרָה וּמַעֲשִׂים טוֹבִים, אֵין לוֹ
חֵלֶק לָעוֹלָם הַבָּא.

טז רַבִּי יִשְׁמָעֵאל אוֹמֵר: הֱוֵי קַל לְרֹאשׁ וְנוֹחַ לְתִשְׁחֹרֶת, וֶהֱוֵי מְקַבֵּל אֶת כָּל
הָאָדָם בְּשִׂמְחָה.

יז רַבִּי עֲקִיבָא אוֹמֵר: שְׂחוֹק וְקַלּוּת רֹאשׁ מַרְגִּילִין אֶת הָאָדָם לְעֶרְוָה. מַסֹּרֶת
סְיָג לַתּוֹרָה, מַעְשְׂרוֹת סְיָג לָעֹשֶׁר, נְדָרִים סְיָג לַפְּרִישׁוּת, סְיָג לַחָכְמָה שְׁתִיקָה.

יח הוּא הָיָה אוֹמֵר, חָבִיב אָדָם שֶׁנִּבְרָא בְצֶלֶם, חִבָּה יְתֵרָה נוֹדַעַת לוֹ שֶׁנִּבְרָא
בְּצֶלֶם, שֶׁנֶּאֱמַר: כִּי בְּצֶלֶם אֱלֹהִים עָשָׂה אֶת־הָאָדָם: חֲבִיבִין יִשְׂרָאֵל בראשית ט
שֶׁנִּקְרְאוּ בָנִים לַמָּקוֹם, חִבָּה יְתֵרָה נוֹדַעַת לָהֶם שֶׁנִּקְרְאוּ בָנִים לַמָּקוֹם,
שֶׁנֶּאֱמַר: בָּנִים אַתֶּם לַיהוה אֱלֹהֵיכֶם: חֲבִיבִין יִשְׂרָאֵל שֶׁנִּתַּן לָהֶם כְּלִי דברים יד
חֶמְדָּה, חִבָּה יְתֵרָה נוֹדַעַת לָהֶם שֶׁנִּתַּן לָהֶם כְּלִי חֶמְדָּה שֶׁבּוֹ נִבְרָא הָעוֹלָם,
שֶׁנֶּאֱמַר: כִּי לֶקַח טוֹב נָתַתִּי לָכֶם, תּוֹרָתִי אַל־תַּעֲזֹבוּ: משלי ד

19. All is foreseen, yet freedom of choice is given. The world is judged with goodness, but all depends on the majority of one's deeds.
20. He used to say: All is given on collateral, and a net is spread over all the living. The shop is open, the shopkeeper extends credit, the ledger is open, and the hand records. Whoever wishes to borrow may come and borrow. The collectors regularly make their daily rounds and collect payment from a person, whether he realizes it or not. They have [a record] on which they can rely; the judgment is just; and all is prepared for the banquet.
21. Rabbi Elazar ben Azariah said: If there is no Torah, there is no respect; if there is no respect, there is no Torah. If there is no wisdom, there is no reverence; if there is no reverence, there is no wisdom. If there is no knowledge, there is no understanding; if there is no understanding, there is no knowledge. If there is no flour [sustenance], there is no Torah; if there is no Torah, there is no flour.
22. He used to say: To what may one whose wisdom exceeds his deeds be compared? To a tree with many branches but few roots. When a wind comes, it uproots and overturns it, as it is said, "He shall be like a juniper tree in the desert, *Jer. 17*
which does not sense the coming of good: it is set in the scorched places of the wilderness in a barren, uninhabited land." To what may one whose deeds exceed his wisdom be compared? To a tree with few branches but many roots. Even if all the winds of the world come and blow against it, they cannot dislodge it from its place, as it is said, "He shall be like a tree planted by waters, sending forth its *Jer. 17*
roots by a stream: it does not sense the coming of heat; its leaves are ever fresh; it has no care in a year of drought; it does not cease to bear fruit."
23. Rabbi Elazar ben Ḥisma said: The laws of bird offerings and the calculation of menstrual periods are essential laws; astronomy and mathematics are adjuncts to wisdom.

Rabbi Ḥananya ben Akashya said: The Holy One, blessed be He, wanted to confer *Makkot 23b*
merit on Israel. That is why He gave them a copious Torah and many commandments, as it is said, "It pleased the LORD, for the sake of [Israel's] righteousness, *Is. 42*
to make the Torah great and glorious."

*If there is a minyan, mourners say the Rabbis' Kaddish (page 628).*

* * *

All Israel have a share in the World to Come, as it is said: *Sanhedrin 90a*
"Your people are all righteous; they shall inherit the land for ever; *Is. 60*
they are a shoot of My own planting,
a work of My own hands, that I may be glorified."

## CHAPTER 4

1. Ben Zoma said: Who is wise? One who learns from everyone, as it is said, "From all my teachers I have learned, for Your testimonies are my meditation." Who is *Ps. 119*
strong? One who masters his evil impulse, as it is said, "He who is slow to anger is *Prov. 16*

יט הַכֹּל צָפוּי, וְהָרְשׁוּת נְתוּנָה, וּבְטוֹב הָעוֹלָם נִדּוֹן, וְהַכֹּל לְפִי רֹב הַמַּעֲשֶׂה.

כ הוּא הָיָה אוֹמֵר: הַכֹּל נָתוּן בְּעֵרָבוֹן, וּמְצוּדָה פְּרוּסָה עַל כָּל הַחַיִּים. הֶחָנוּת פְּתוּחָה, וְהַחֶנְוָנִי מַקִּיף, וְהַפִּנְקָס פָּתְוּחַ, וְהַיָּד כּוֹתֶבֶת, וְכָל הָרוֹצֶה לִלְווֹת יָבֹא וְיִלְוֶה. וְהַגַּבָּאִין מַחֲזִירִין תָּדִיר בְּכָל יוֹם, וְנִפְרָעִין מִן הָאָדָם מִדַּעְתּוֹ וְשֶׁלֹּא מִדַּעְתּוֹ, וְיֵשׁ לָהֶם עַל מַה שֶּׁיִּסְמְכוּ. וְהַדִּין, דִּין אֱמֶת. וְהַכֹּל מְתֻקָּן לִסְעוּדָה.

כא רַבִּי אֶלְעָזָר בֶּן עֲזַרְיָה אוֹמֵר: אִם אֵין תּוֹרָה אֵין דֶּרֶךְ אֶרֶץ, אִם אֵין דֶּרֶךְ אֶרֶץ אֵין תּוֹרָה. אִם אֵין חָכְמָה אֵין יִרְאָה, אִם אֵין יִרְאָה אֵין חָכְמָה. אִם אֵין דַּעַת אֵין בִּינָה, אִם אֵין בִּינָה אֵין דַּעַת. אִם אֵין קֶמַח אֵין תּוֹרָה, אִם אֵין תּוֹרָה אֵין קֶמַח.

כב הוּא הָיָה אוֹמֵר: כָּל שֶׁחָכְמָתוֹ מְרֻבָּה מִמַּעֲשָׂיו, לְמָה הוּא דוֹמֶה, לְאִילָן שֶׁעֲנָפָיו מְרֻבִּין וְשָׁרָשָׁיו מֻעָטִין, וְהָרְוּחַ בָּאָה וְעוֹקַרְתּוֹ וְהוֹפַכְתּוֹ עַל פָּנָיו.
שֶׁנֶּאֱמַר, וְהָיָה כְּעַרְעָר בָּעֲרָבָה, וְלֹא יִרְאֶה כִּי־יָבוֹא טוֹב, וְשָׁכַן חֲרֵרִים ירמיה יז
בַּמִּדְבָּר, אֶרֶץ מְלֵחָה וְלֹא תֵשֵׁב: אֲבָל כָּל שֶׁמַּעֲשָׂיו מְרֻבִּין מֵחָכְמָתוֹ, לְמָה
הוּא דוֹמֶה, לְאִילָן שֶׁעֲנָפָיו מֻעָטִין וְשָׁרָשָׁיו מְרֻבִּין, שֶׁאֲפִלּוּ כָּל הָרוּחוֹת
שֶׁבָּעוֹלָם בָּאוֹת וְנוֹשְׁבוֹת בּוֹ, אֵין מְזִיזִין אוֹתוֹ מִמְּקוֹמוֹ. שֶׁנֶּאֱמַר: וְהָיָה כְּעֵץ ירמיה יז
שָׁתוּל עַל־מַיִם, וְעַל־יוּבַל יְשַׁלַּח שָׁרָשָׁיו, וְלֹא יִרְאֶ כִּי־יָבֹא חֹם, וְהָיָה עָלֵהוּ
רַעֲנָן, וּבִשְׁנַת בַּצֹּרֶת לֹא יִדְאָג, וְלֹא יָמִישׁ מֵעֲשׂוֹת פֶּרִי:

כג רַבִּי אֶלְעָזָר בֶּן חִסְמָא אוֹמֵר: קִנִּין וּפִתְחֵי נִדָּה הֵן הֵן גּוּפֵי הֲלָכוֹת, תְּקוּפוֹת וְגִימַטְרִיָּאוֹת פַּרְפְּרָאוֹת לַחָכְמָה.

רַבִּי חֲנַנְיָא בֶּן עֲקַשְׁיָא אוֹמֵר: רָצָה הַקָּדוֹשׁ בָּרוּךְ הוּא לְזַכּוֹת אֶת יִשְׂרָאֵל, לְפִיכָךְ מכות כג:
הִרְבָּה לָהֶם תּוֹרָה וּמִצְוֹת. שֶׁנֶּאֱמַר: יהוה חָפֵץ לְמַעַן צִדְקוֹ, יַגְדִּיל תּוֹרָה וְיַאְדִּיר: ישעיה מב

*If there is a* מנין*, mourners say the* קדיש דרבנן *(page 629).*

* * *

כָּל יִשְׂרָאֵל יֵשׁ לָהֶם חֵלֶק לָעוֹלָם הַבָּא. שֶׁנֶּאֱמַר: סנהדרין צ.
וְעַמֵּךְ כֻּלָּם צַדִּיקִים, לְעוֹלָם יִירְשׁוּ אָרֶץ ישעיה ס
נֵצֶר מַטָּעַי, מַעֲשֵׂה יָדַי לְהִתְפָּאֵר:

## פרק רביעי

א בֶּן זוֹמָא אוֹמֵר: אֵיזֶהוּ חָכָם, הַלּוֹמֵד מִכָּל אָדָם, שֶׁנֶּאֱמַר: מִכָּל־מְלַמְּדַי תהלים קיט
הִשְׂכַּלְתִּי, כִּי עֵדְוֹתֶיךָ שִׂיחָה לִּי: אֵיזֶהוּ גִבּוֹר, הַכּוֹבֵשׁ אֶת יִצְרוֹ, שֶׁנֶּאֱמַר: טוֹב משלי טז

better than the mighty, and he who rules over his spirit is better than he who conquers a city." Who is rich? One who rejoices in what he has, as it is said, "When you eat from the labor of your hands, you will be happy and all will be well with you." "You will be happy" – in this world, "and all will be well with you" – in the World to Come. Who is honored? One who honors others, as it is said, "Those who honor Me, I will honor; but those who scorn Me will be despised." *Ps. 128* *1 Sam. 2*

2. Ben Azzai said: Run to do even a minor mitzva, and flee from sin, for one mitzva leads to another, and one sin leads to another – for the reward of a mitzva is another mitzva, and the recompense of a sin is another sin.

3. He used to say: Despise no one and disdain nothing, for there is no one who does not have his hour and there is nothing that does not have its place.

4. Rabbi Levitas of Yavne said: Have extreme humility of spirit, for the end of mortal man is the worm [the grave].

5. Rabbi Yoḥanan ben Beroka said: Whoever profanes God's name in secret will be punished in public. Profaning the name is the same whether done inadvertently or deliberately.

6. Rabbi Yishmael his son said: One who learns in order to teach will be given the opportunity to learn and teach. One who learns in order to do will be given the opportunity to learn, teach, keep and do.

7. Rabbi Tzaddok said: Do not separate yourself from the community. [When sitting as a judge] do not act as a lawyer. Do not use [the Torah] as a crown for self-glorification, or as a spade with which to dig. Likewise Hillel used to say: One who makes worldly use of the crown [of the Torah] shall fade away. From this you learn that one who seeks personal benefit from the words of Torah risks destroying his life.

8. Rabbi Yose said: One who honors the Torah will be honored by mankind. One who disgraces the Torah will be disgraced by mankind.

9. Rabbi Yishmael his son said: One who avoids serving as a judge spares himself enmity, robbery and false swearing. One who is over-confident in giving decisions is foolish, wicked and arrogant.

10. He used to say: Do not act as a judge alone, for none may judge alone except the One. Do not say "Accept my view"; for they are permitted, not you.

11. Rabbi Yonatan said: Whoever keeps the Torah when poor will eventually keep it in wealth. Whoever neglects the Torah when wealthy will eventually neglect it in poverty.

12. Rabbi Meir said: Limit your business activities and occupy yourself with Torah. Have humility before everyone. If you neglect the Torah, you will have many excuses to neglect it, but if you labor in the Torah, He has great reward to give you.

אֶרֶךְ אַפַּיִם מִגִּבּוֹר וּמֹשֵׁל בְּרוּחוֹ מִלֹּכֵד עִיר: אֵיזֶהוּ עָשִׁיר, הַשָּׂמֵחַ בְּחֶלְקוֹ,
שֶׁנֶּאֱמַר: יְגִיעַ כַּפֶּיךָ כִּי תֹאכֵל אַשְׁרֶיךָ וְטוֹב לָךְ: אַשְׁרֶיךָ בָּעוֹלָם הַזֶּה וְטוֹב תהלים קכח
לָךְ לָעוֹלָם הַבָּא. אֵיזֶהוּ מְכֻבָּד, הַמְכַבֵּד אֶת הַבְּרִיּוֹת, שֶׁנֶּאֱמַר: כִּי־מְכַבְּדַי שמואל א׳ ב
אֲכַבֵּד, וּבֹזַי יֵקָלּוּ:

ב בֶּן עַזַּאי אוֹמֵר: הֱוֵי רָץ לְמִצְוָה קַלָּה וּבוֹרֵחַ מִן הָעֲבֵרָה. שֶׁמִּצְוָה גּוֹרֶרֶת מִצְוָה, וַעֲבֵרָה גּוֹרֶרֶת עֲבֵרָה. שֶׁשְּׂכַר מִצְוָה מִצְוָה, וּשְׂכַר עֲבֵרָה עֲבֵרָה.

ג הוּא הָיָה אוֹמֵר: אַל תְּהִי בָז לְכָל אָדָם, וְאַל תְּהִי מַפְלִיג לְכָל דָּבָר. שֶׁאֵין לְךָ אָדָם שֶׁאֵין לוֹ שָׁעָה, וְאֵין לְךָ דָבָר שֶׁאֵין לוֹ מָקוֹם.

ד רַבִּי לְוִיטַס אִישׁ יַבְנֶה אוֹמֵר: מְאֹד מְאֹד הֱוֵי שְׁפַל רוּחַ, שֶׁתִּקְוַת אֱנוֹשׁ רִמָּה.

ה רַבִּי יוֹחָנָן בֶּן בְּרוֹקָא אוֹמֵר: כָּל הַמְחַלֵּל שֵׁם שָׁמַיִם בַּסֵּתֶר, נִפְרָעִין מִמֶּנּוּ בַּגָּלוּי. אֶחָד שׁוֹגֵג וְאֶחָד מֵזִיד בְּחִלּוּל הַשֵּׁם.

ו רַבִּי יִשְׁמָעֵאל בְּנוֹ אוֹמֵר: הַלּוֹמֵד עַל מְנָת לְלַמֵּד, מַסְפִּיקִין בְּיָדוֹ לִלְמֹד וּלְלַמֵּד. וְהַלּוֹמֵד עַל מְנָת לַעֲשׂוֹת, מַסְפִּיקִין בְּיָדוֹ לִלְמֹד וּלְלַמֵּד, לִשְׁמֹר וְלַעֲשׂוֹת.

ז רַבִּי צָדוֹק אוֹמֵר: אַל תִּפְרֹשׁ מִן הַצִּבּוּר, וְאַל תַּעַשׂ עַצְמְךָ כְּעוֹרְכֵי הַדַּיָּנִין, וְאַל תַּעֲשֶׂהָ עֲטָרָה לְהִתְגַּדֵּל בָּהּ, וְלֹא קַרְדֹּם לַחְפֹּר בָּהּ. וְכָךְ הָיָה הִלֵּל אוֹמֵר: וּדְאִשְׁתַּמֵּשׁ בְּתָגָא חֲלָף. הָא לָמַדְתָּ, כָּל הַנֶּהֱנֶה מִדִּבְרֵי תוֹרָה, נוֹטֵל חַיָּיו מִן הָעוֹלָם.

ח רַבִּי יוֹסֵי אוֹמֵר: כָּל הַמְכַבֵּד אֶת הַתּוֹרָה, גּוּפוֹ מְכֻבָּד עַל הַבְּרִיּוֹת. וְכָל הַמְחַלֵּל אֶת הַתּוֹרָה, גּוּפוֹ מְחֻלָּל עַל הַבְּרִיּוֹת.

ט רַבִּי יִשְׁמָעֵאל בְּנוֹ אוֹמֵר: הַחוֹשֵׂךְ עַצְמוֹ מִן הַדִּין, פּוֹרֵק מִמֶּנּוּ אֵיבָה וְגָזֵל וּשְׁבוּעַת שָׁוְא. וְהַגַּס לִבּוֹ בְּהוֹרָאָה, שׁוֹטֶה, רָשָׁע וְגַס רוּחַ.

י הוּא הָיָה אוֹמֵר: אַל תְּהִי דָן יְחִידִי, שֶׁאֵין דָּן יְחִידִי אֶלָּא אֶחָד. וְאַל תֹּאמַר קַבְּלוּ דַעְתִּי, שֶׁהֵן רַשָּׁאִין וְלֹא אָתָּה.

יא רַבִּי יוֹנָתָן אוֹמֵר: כָּל הַמְקַיֵּם אֶת הַתּוֹרָה מֵעֹנִי, סוֹפוֹ לְקַיְּמָהּ מֵעֹשֶׁר. וְכָל הַמְבַטֵּל אֶת הַתּוֹרָה מֵעֹשֶׁר, סוֹפוֹ לְבַטְּלָהּ מֵעֹנִי.

יב רַבִּי מֵאִיר אוֹמֵר: הֱוֵי מְמַעֵט בְּעֵסֶק וַעֲסֹק בַּתּוֹרָה, וֶהֱוֵי שְׁפַל רוּחַ בִּפְנֵי כָל אָדָם. וְאִם בָּטַלְתָּ מִן הַתּוֹרָה, יֶשׁ לְךָ בְּטֵלִים הַרְבֵּה כְּנֶגְדְּךָ. וְאִם עָמַלְתָּ בַּתּוֹרָה, יֶשׁ לוֹ שָׂכָר הַרְבֵּה לִתֶּן לָךְ.

13. Rabbi Eliezer ben Jacob said: One who performs a single mitzva acquires for himself an advocate. One who commits a single transgression acquires for himself an accuser. Repentance and good deeds are a shield against punishment.

14. Rabbi Yoḥanan the sandal maker said: Every gathering that meets for the sake of heaven will have an enduring effect. One that is not for the sake of heaven will not have an enduring effect.

15. Rabbi Elazar ben Shammua said: Let your student's honor be as precious to you as your own; let your colleague's honor be like the reverence due to your teacher; and let the reverence you have for your teacher be like the reverence due to Heaven.

16. Rabbi Judah said: Be careful when you study, for an inadvertent error in study is tantamount to an intentional sin.

17. Rabbi Shimon said: There are three crowns: the crown of Torah, the crown of priesthood, and the crown of kingship – but the crown of a good name surpasses them all.

18. Rabbi Nehorai said: Exile yourself to a place of Torah, and do not assume that it will come after you, for your fellow students will ensure that it will remain with you. "Do not rely on your own understanding." *Prov. 3*

19. Rabbi Yannai said: It is not in our power to explain either the peace of the wicked or the suffering of the righteous.

20. Rabbi Matya ben Ḥarash said: Be first in greeting everyone. Be a tail to lions rather than a head to foxes.

21. Rabbi Jacob said: This world is like an antechamber before the World to Come. Prepare yourself in the antechamber so that you may enter the banqueting hall.

22. He used to say: Better one hour of repentance and good deeds in this world than all the life in the World to Come. Better one hour of bliss in the World to Come than the whole life of this world.

23. Rabbi Shimon ben Elazar said: Do not try to placate your fellow in his hour of anger. Do not try to comfort him while his dead lies before him. Do not question him about his vow at the time he is making it. Do not try to see him in his hour of disgrace.

24. Samuel the Younger used to quote: "If your enemy falls, do not rejoice; if he stumbles, let not your heart be glad; lest the LORD see it and be displeased, and divert His wrath from him to you." *Prov. 24*

25. Elisha ben Abuya said: When you learn as a child, what is it like? Like ink written on clean paper. When you learn in old age, what is it like? Like ink written on blotted paper.

יג רַבִּי אֱלִיעֶזֶר בֶּן יַעֲקֹב אוֹמֵר: הָעוֹשֶׂה מִצְוָה אַחַת, קוֹנֶה לּוֹ פְּרַקְלִיט אֶחָד. וְהָעוֹבֵר עֲבֵרָה אַחַת, קוֹנֶה לּוֹ קַטֵּגוֹר אֶחָד. תְּשׁוּבָה וּמַעֲשִׂים טוֹבִים, כִּתְרִיס בִּפְנֵי הַפֻּרְעָנוּת.

יד רַבִּי יוֹחָנָן הַסַּנְדְּלָר אוֹמֵר: כָּל כְּנֵסִיָּה שֶׁהִיא לְשֵׁם שָׁמַיִם, סוֹפָהּ לְהִתְקַיֵּם. וְשֶׁאֵינָהּ לְשֵׁם שָׁמַיִם, אֵין סוֹפָהּ לְהִתְקַיֵּם.

טו רַבִּי אֶלְעָזָר בֶּן שַׁמּוּעַ אוֹמֵר: יְהִי כְבוֹד תַּלְמִידְךָ חָבִיב עָלֶיךָ כְּשֶׁלָּךְ, וּכְבוֹד חֲבֵרְךָ כְּמוֹרָא רַבָּךְ, וּמוֹרָא רַבָּךְ כְּמוֹרָא שָׁמָיִם.

טז רַבִּי יְהוּדָה אוֹמֵר: הֱוֵי זָהִיר בְּתַלְמוּד, שֶׁשִּׁגְגַת תַּלְמוּד עוֹלָה זָדוֹן.

יז רַבִּי שִׁמְעוֹן אוֹמֵר: שְׁלֹשָׁה כְתָרִים הֵן, כֶּתֶר תּוֹרָה וְכֶתֶר כְּהֻנָּה וְכֶתֶר מַלְכוּת, וְכֶתֶר שֵׁם טוֹב עוֹלֶה עַל גַּבֵּיהֶן.

יח רַבִּי נְהוֹרַאי אוֹמֵר: הֱוֵי גוֹלֶה לִמְקוֹם תּוֹרָה. וְאַל תֹּאמַר שֶׁהִיא תָבוֹא אַחֲרֶיךָ,
שֶׁחֲבֵרֶיךָ יְקַיְּמוּהָ בְיָדֶךָ. וְאֶל־בִּינָתְךָ אַל־תִּשָּׁעֵן: משלי ג

יט רַבִּי יַנַּאי אוֹמֵר: אֵין בְּיָדֵינוּ לֹא מִשַּׁלְוַת הָרְשָׁעִים וְאַף לֹא מִיִּסּוּרֵי הַצַּדִּיקִים.

כ רַבִּי מַתְיָא בֶּן חָרָשׁ אוֹמֵר: הֱוֵי מַקְדִּים בִּשְׁלוֹם כָּל אָדָם, וֶהֱוֵי זָנָב לָאֲרָיוֹת, וְאַל תְּהִי רֹאשׁ לַשּׁוּעָלִים.

כא רַבִּי יַעֲקֹב אוֹמֵר: הָעוֹלָם הַזֶּה דּוֹמֶה לִפְרוֹזְדוֹר בִּפְנֵי הָעוֹלָם הַבָּא. הַתְקֵן עַצְמְךָ בַפְּרוֹזְדוֹר, כְּדֵי שֶׁתִּכָּנֵס לַטְּרַקְלִין.

כב הוּא הָיָה אוֹמֵר: יָפָה שָׁעָה אַחַת בִּתְשׁוּבָה וּמַעֲשִׂים טוֹבִים בָּעוֹלָם הַזֶּה, מִכָּל חַיֵּי הָעוֹלָם הַבָּא. וְיָפָה שָׁעָה אַחַת שֶׁל קוֹרַת רוּחַ בָּעוֹלָם הַבָּא, מִכָּל חַיֵּי הָעוֹלָם הַזֶּה.

כג רַבִּי שִׁמְעוֹן בֶּן אֶלְעָזָר אוֹמֵר: אַל תְּרַצֶּה אֶת חֲבֵרְךָ בִּשְׁעַת כַּעְסוֹ, וְאַל תְּנַחֲמֵהוּ בְּשָׁעָה שֶׁמֵּתוֹ מֻטָּל לְפָנָיו, וְאַל תִּשְׁאַל לוֹ בִּשְׁעַת נִדְרוֹ, וְאַל תִּשְׁתַּדֵּל לִרְאוֹתוֹ בִּשְׁעַת קַלְקָלָתוֹ.

כד שְׁמוּאֵל הַקָּטָן אוֹמֵר: בִּנְפֹל אוֹיִבְךָ אַל־תִּשְׂמָח, וּבִכָּשְׁלוֹ אַל־יָגֵל לִבֶּךָ: פֶּן־ משלי כד
יִרְאֶה יהוה וְרַע בְּעֵינָיו, וְהֵשִׁיב מֵעָלָיו אַפּוֹ:

כה אֱלִישָׁע בֶּן אֲבוּיָה אוֹמֵר: הַלּוֹמֵד יֶלֶד, לְמָה הוּא דוֹמֶה, לִדְיוֹ כְתוּבָה עַל נְיָר חָדָשׁ. וְהַלּוֹמֵד זָקֵן, לְמָה הוּא דוֹמֶה, לִדְיוֹ כְתוּבָה עַל נְיָר מָחוּק.

26. Rabbi Yose bar Judah of Kfar Bavli said: When you learn from the young, what is it like? Like eating unripe grapes or drinking wine straight from the vat. When you learn from the old, what is it like? Like eating ripe grapes and drinking old wine.
27. Rabbi Meir said: Do not look at the container but at what it contains, for a new flask may contain old wine, and an old flask may not contain anything, even new wine.
28. Rabbi Elazar HaKappar said: Envy, lust, and the seeking of honor, drive a person out of the world.
29. He used to say: Those who are born will one day die, those who die will live again, and the living will be judged. It is for us to know, make known, and confirm that He is God, He is the Maker; He is the Creator; He is the Discerner; He is the Judge; He is the Witness; He is the Plaintiff; and He will deliver the judgment. Blessed is He before whom there is no unrighteousness, no forgetfulness, no favoritism and no taking of bribes; and know that all is according to a strict reckoning. Do not let your evil impulse persuade you that the grave is, for you, a place of refuge: for without your consent you were formed, without your consent you were born, without your consent you live, without your consent you will die, and without your consent you will in the future have to give an account and reckoning before the Supreme King of kings, the Holy One, blessed be He.

Rabbi Ḥananya ben Akashya said: The Holy One, blessed be He, wanted to confer merit on Israel. That is why He gave them a copious Torah and many commandments, as it is said, "It pleased the Lord, for the sake of [Israel's] righteousness, to make the Torah great and glorious." *Makkot 23b* *Is. 42*

*If there is a minyan, mourners say the Rabbis' Kaddish (page 628).*

* * *

All Israel have a share in the World to Come, as it is said, *Sanhedrin 90a*
"Your people are all righteous; they shall inherit the land for ever; *Is. 60*
they are a shoot of My own planting,
a work of My own hands, that I may be glorified."

## CHAPTER 5

1. By ten acts of speech the world was created. What does this teach us? Could not the world have been created by a single act of speech? It is to exact punishment from the wicked who destroy a world created by ten acts of speech, and richly to reward the righteous who sustain the world created by ten acts of speech.

כו רַבִּי יוֹסֵי בַּר יְהוּדָה אִישׁ כְּפַר הַבַּבְלִי אוֹמֵר: הַלּוֹמֵד מִן הַקְּטַנִּים, לְמָה הוּא דוֹמֶה, לְאוֹכֵל עֲנָבִים קֵהוֹת וְשׁוֹתֶה יַיִן מִגִּתּוֹ. וְהַלּוֹמֵד מִן הַזְּקֵנִים, לְמָה הוּא דוֹמֶה, לְאוֹכֵל עֲנָבִים בְּשׁוּלוֹת וְשׁוֹתֶה יַיִן יָשָׁן.

כז רַבִּי מֵאִיר אוֹמֵר: אַל תִּסְתַּכֵּל בַּקַּנְקַן, אֶלָּא בְּמַה שֶּׁיֵּשׁ בּוֹ. יֵשׁ קַנְקַן חָדָשׁ מָלֵא יָשָׁן, וְיָשָׁן שֶׁאֲפִלּוּ חָדָשׁ אֵין בּוֹ.

כח רַבִּי אֶלְעָזָר הַקַּפָּר אוֹמֵר: הַקִּנְאָה וְהַתַּאֲוָה וְהַכָּבוֹד, מוֹצִיאִין אֶת הָאָדָם מִן הָעוֹלָם.

כט הוּא הָיָה אוֹמֵר: הַיִּלּוֹדִים לָמוּת, וְהַמֵּתִים לִחְיוֹת, וְהַחַיִּים לִדּוֹן, לֵידַע וּלְהוֹדִיעַ וּלְהִוָּדַע, שֶׁהוּא אֵל, הוּא הַיּוֹצֵר, הוּא הַבּוֹרֵא, הוּא הַמֵּבִין, הוּא הַדַּיָּן, הוּא הָעֵד, הוּא בַּעַל דִּין, הוּא עָתִיד לָדוּן. בָּרוּךְ הוּא, שֶׁאֵין לְפָנָיו לֹא עַוְלָה וְלֹא שִׁכְחָה, וְלֹא מַשּׂוֹא פָנִים וְלֹא מִקַּח שֹׁחַד, שֶׁהַכֹּל שֶׁלּוֹ. וְדַע, שֶׁהַכֹּל לְפִי הַחֶשְׁבּוֹן. וְאַל יַבְטִיחֲךָ יִצְרְךָ שֶׁהַשְּׁאוֹל בֵּית מָנוֹס לָךְ, שֶׁעַל כָּרְחֲךָ אַתָּה נוֹצָר, וְעַל כָּרְחֲךָ אַתָּה נוֹלָד, וְעַל כָּרְחֲךָ אַתָּה חַי, וְעַל כָּרְחֲךָ אַתָּה מֵת, וְעַל כָּרְחֲךָ אַתָּה עָתִיד לִתֵּן דִּין וְחֶשְׁבּוֹן לִפְנֵי מֶלֶךְ מַלְכֵי הַמְּלָכִים הַקָּדוֹשׁ בָּרוּךְ הוּא.

רַבִּי חֲנַנְיָא בֶּן עֲקַשְׁיָא אוֹמֵר: רָצָה הַקָּדוֹשׁ בָּרוּךְ הוּא לְזַכּוֹת אֶת יִשְׂרָאֵל, מכות כג:
לְפִיכָךְ הִרְבָּה לָהֶם תּוֹרָה וּמִצְוֹת. שֶׁנֶּאֱמַר: יהוה חָפֵץ לְמַעַן צִדְקוֹ, יַגְדִּיל תּוֹרָה וְיַאְדִּיר: ישעיה מב

*If there is a* מנין*, mourners say the* קדיש דרבנן *(page 629).*

* * *

כָּל יִשְׂרָאֵל יֵשׁ לָהֶם חֵלֶק לָעוֹלָם הַבָּא. שֶׁנֶּאֱמַר: סנהדרין צ.
וְעַמֵּךְ כֻּלָּם צַדִּיקִים, לְעוֹלָם יִירְשׁוּ אָרֶץ ישעיה ס
נֵצֶר מַטָּעַי, מַעֲשֵׂה יָדַי לְהִתְפָּאֵר:

## פרק חמישי

א בַּעֲשָׂרָה מַאֲמָרוֹת נִבְרָא הָעוֹלָם. וּמַה תַּלְמוּד לוֹמַר, וַהֲלֹא בְּמַאֲמָר אֶחָד יָכוֹל לְהִבָּרְאוֹת, אֶלָּא לְהִפָּרַע מִן הָרְשָׁעִים, שֶׁמְּאַבְּדִין אֶת הָעוֹלָם שֶׁנִּבְרָא בַּעֲשָׂרָה מַאֲמָרוֹת, וְלִתֵּן שָׂכָר טוֹב לַצַּדִּיקִים, שֶׁמְּקַיְּמִין אֶת הָעוֹלָם שֶׁנִּבְרָא בַּעֲשָׂרָה מַאֲמָרוֹת.

2. There were ten generations from Adam to Noah, to make known how patient God is, for all those generations increasingly provoked Him until He brought on them the waters of the Flood.

3. There were ten generations from Noah to Abraham, to make known how patient God is, for all those generations increasingly provoked Him until Abraham our father came and received the reward which could have been theirs.

4. Abraham our father was tested with ten trials and he withstood all of them, to make known how deep was our father Abraham's love of God.

5. Ten miracles were performed for our ancestors in Egypt, and ten at the Sea. The Holy One, blessed be He, brought ten plagues against the Egyptians in Egypt, and ten at the Sea.

6. With ten trials our ancestors tried the patience of the Holy One, blessed be He, in the wilderness, as it is written, "They have tested Me these ten times, *Num. 14* and did not listen to My voice."

7. Ten miracles were performed for our ancestors in the Temple: (1) No woman miscarried from the aroma of the sacrificial meat; (2) the sacrificial meat never became putrid; (3) no fly was seen in the slaughterhouse; (4) the High Priest never suffered ritual pollution on Yom Kippur; (5) rain never extinguished the fire of the wood-pile on the altar; (6) the wind never blew away the column of smoke that rose from the altar; (7) no defect was ever found in the Omer, the Two Loaves, or the Showbread; (8) the people stood crowded together, yet there was ample space when they prostrated themselves; (9) no serpent or scorpion ever harmed anyone in Jerusalem; and (10) no one ever said to his fellow, "There is no room for me to stay overnight in Jerusalem."

8. Ten things were created on the eve of the Sabbath at twilight. They were: (1) the mouth of the earth; (2) the mouth of the well; (3) the mouth of [Balaam's] ass; (4) the rainbow; (5) the manna; (6) the staff; (7) the Shamir; (8) the writing [on the Tablets]; (9) the inscription; and (10) the Tablets. Some say: also the demons, Moses' burial place, and the ram of our father Abraham. And some say: also tongs made with tongs.

9. Seven traits characterize an uncultured person, and seven a sage. A sage: (1) does not speak before one who is wiser than he; (2) does not interrupt the words of his fellow; (3) does not answer impetuously; (4) asks relevant questions and gives appropriate answers; (5) deals with first things first, and last things last; (6) about something he has not heard he says, "I have not heard"; and (7) he acknowledges the truth. The opposites of these characterize an uncultured person.

10. Seven types of punishment come into the world for seven kinds of transgression: (1) If some tithe and others do not, a famine caused by drought occurs, so that some go hungry while others have sufficient. (2) If all decide not to

ב עֲשָׂרָה דוֹרוֹת מֵאָדָם וְעַד נֹחַ, לְהוֹדִיעַ כַּמָּה אֶרֶךְ אַפַּיִם לְפָנָיו, שֶׁכָּל הַדּוֹרוֹת הָיוּ מַכְעִיסִין וּבָאִין, עַד שֶׁהֵבִיא עֲלֵיהֶם אֶת מֵי הַמַּבּוּל.

ג עֲשָׂרָה דוֹרוֹת מִנֹּחַ וְעַד אַבְרָהָם, לְהוֹדִיעַ כַּמָּה אֶרֶךְ אַפַּיִם לְפָנָיו, שֶׁכָּל הַדּוֹרוֹת הָיוּ מַכְעִיסִין וּבָאִין, עַד שֶׁבָּא אַבְרָהָם אָבִינוּ וְקִבֵּל שְׂכַר כֻּלָּם.

ד עֲשָׂרָה נִסְיוֹנוֹת נִתְנַסָּה אַבְרָהָם אָבִינוּ וְעָמַד בְּכֻלָּם, לְהוֹדִיעַ כַּמָּה חִבָּתוֹ שֶׁל אַבְרָהָם אָבִינוּ.

ה עֲשָׂרָה נִסִּים נַעֲשׂוּ לַאֲבוֹתֵינוּ בְּמִצְרַיִם, וַעֲשָׂרָה עַל הַיָּם. עֶשֶׂר מַכּוֹת הֵבִיא הַקָּדוֹשׁ בָּרוּךְ הוּא עַל הַמִּצְרִיִּים בְּמִצְרַיִם, וְעֶשֶׂר עַל הַיָּם.

ו עֲשָׂרָה נִסְיוֹנוֹת נִסּוּ אֲבוֹתֵינוּ אֶת הַקָּדוֹשׁ בָּרוּךְ הוּא בַּמִּדְבָּר, שֶׁנֶּאֱמַר: וַיְנַסּוּ במדבר יד
אֹתִי זֶה עֶשֶׂר פְּעָמִים, וְלֹא שָׁמְעוּ בְּקוֹלִי:

ז עֲשָׂרָה נִסִּים נַעֲשׂוּ לַאֲבוֹתֵינוּ בְּבֵית הַמִּקְדָּשׁ. לֹא הִפִּילָה אִשָּׁה מֵרֵיחַ בְּשַׂר הַקֹּדֶשׁ, וְלֹא הִסְרִיחַ בְּשַׂר הַקֹּדֶשׁ מֵעוֹלָם, וְלֹא נִרְאָה זְבוּב בְּבֵית הַמִּטְבְּחַיִם, וְלֹא אֵרַע קֶרִי לְכֹהֵן גָּדוֹל בְּיוֹם הַכִּפּוּרִים, וְלֹא כִבּוּ הַגְּשָׁמִים אֵשׁ שֶׁל עֲצֵי הַמַּעֲרָכָה, וְלֹא נִצְּחָה הָרוּחַ אֶת עַמּוּד הֶעָשָׁן, וְלֹא נִמְצָא פְסוּל בָּעֹמֶר וּבִשְׁתֵּי הַלֶּחֶם וּבְלֶחֶם הַפָּנִים, עוֹמְדִים צְפוּפִים וּמִשְׁתַּחֲוִים רְוָחִים, וְלֹא הִזִּיק נָחָשׁ וְעַקְרָב בִּירוּשָׁלַיִם מֵעוֹלָם, וְלֹא אָמַר אָדָם לַחֲבֵרוֹ: צַר לִי הַמָּקוֹם שֶׁאָלִין בִּירוּשָׁלָיִם.

ח עֲשָׂרָה דְבָרִים נִבְרְאוּ בְּעֶרֶב שַׁבָּת בֵּין הַשְּׁמָשׁוֹת. וְאֵלּוּ הֵן, פִּי הָאָרֶץ, פִּי הַבְּאֵר, פִּי הָאָתוֹן, הַקֶּשֶׁת, וְהַמָּן, וְהַמַּטֶּה, וְהַשָּׁמִיר, הַכְּתָב, וְהַמִּכְתָּב, וְהַלּוּחוֹת. וְיֵשׁ אוֹמְרִים, אַף הַמַּזִּיקִין, וּקְבוּרָתוֹ שֶׁל מֹשֶׁה, וְאֵילוֹ שֶׁל אַבְרָהָם אָבִינוּ. וְיֵשׁ אוֹמְרִים, אַף צְבָת בִּצְבָת עֲשׂוּיָה.

ט שִׁבְעָה דְבָרִים בַּגֹּלֶם, וְשִׁבְעָה בֶּחָכָם. חָכָם אֵינוֹ מְדַבֵּר לִפְנֵי מִי שֶׁגָּדוֹל מִמֶּנּוּ בְּחָכְמָה, וְאֵינוֹ נִכְנָס לְתוֹךְ דִּבְרֵי חֲבֵרוֹ, וְאֵינוֹ נִבְהָל לְהָשִׁיב, שׁוֹאֵל כָּעִנְיָן וּמֵשִׁיב כַּהֲלָכָה, וְאוֹמֵר עַל רִאשׁוֹן רִאשׁוֹן וְעַל אַחֲרוֹן אַחֲרוֹן, וְעַל מַה שֶּׁלֹּא שָׁמַע אוֹמֵר לֹא שָׁמַעְתִּי, וּמוֹדֶה עַל הָאֱמֶת. וְחִלּוּפֵיהֶן בַּגֹּלֶם.

י שִׁבְעָה מִינֵי פֻרְעָנִיּוֹת בָּאִין לָעוֹלָם עַל שִׁבְעָה גוּפֵי עֲבֵרָה. מִקְצָתָן מְעַשְּׂרִין וּמִקְצָתָן אֵינָן מְעַשְּׂרִין, רָעָב שֶׁל בַּצֹּרֶת בָּא, מִקְצָתָן רְעֵבִים וּמִקְצָתָן שְׂבֵעִים.

tithe, a famine comes through tumult [of war] as well as drought. (3) If they also decide not to set apart ḥalla, a fatal famine ensues.

11. (4) Pestilence comes to the world for crimes that, according to the Torah, carry the death penalty, but are not the preserve of a human tribunal, and also for violation of the laws relating to produce of the seventh year. (5) The sword comes to the world for delay of justice, the perversion of justice, and for those who give a legal decision in violation of normative Torah law.

12. (6) Wild beasts come to the world because of perjury and the desecration of God's name. (7) Exile comes to the world for idolatry, sexual immorality and bloodshed, and for violating the sabbatical year of the land.

13. At four periods [of the seven-year sabbatical cycle] pestilence increases: in the fourth year, the seventh year, the year following the sabbatical year, and annually at the conclusion of the Festival of Sukkot. In the fourth year, [pestilence increases] because of neglect of the tithe for the poor in the third year; in the seventh year, because of neglect of the tithe for the poor in the sixth year; in the year following the sabbatical year, because of the violation of the laws of the seventh-year produce; and at the conclusion of the Festival of Sukkot, for robbing the poor of their gifts.

14. There are four types of human character: (1) One who says, "What is mine is mine, and what is yours is yours," is an average person, though some say this is a Sodom type. (2) One who says, "What is mine is yours and what is yours is mine," is an ignoramus. (3) One who says, "What is mine is yours and what is yours is yours," is pious. (4) One who says, "What is yours is mine and what is mine is mine," is wicked.

15. There are four types of temperament: (1) One who is easily angered and easily pacified – his loss is canceled by his gain. (2) One who is hard to anger and hard to pacify – his gain is canceled by his loss. (3) One who is hard to anger and easily pacified is pious. (4) One who is easily angered and hard to pacify is wicked.

16. There are four types of student: (1) One who learns quickly and forgets quickly – his gain is canceled by his loss. (2) One who learns slowly and forgets slowly – his loss is canceled by his gain. (3) One who learns quickly and forgets slowly – his is a happy lot. (4) One who learns slowly and forgets quickly – his is a sad lot.

17. There are four types of donor to charity: (1) One who wishes to give but does not want others to give, begrudges others. (2) One who wants others to give, but does not himself give, begrudges himself. (3) One who gives and wants others to give is pious. (4) One who does not himself give and does not want others to give is wicked.

18. There are four types among those who attend the House of Study: (1) One who goes but does not practice [what he learns] receives a reward for

גָּמְרוּ שֶׁלֹּא לְעַשֵּׂר, רָעָב שֶׁל מְהוּמָה וְשֶׁל בַּצֹּרֶת בָּא. וְשֶׁלֹּא לִטּוֹל אֶת הַחַלָּה, רָעָב שֶׁל כְּלָיָה בָּא.

יא דֶּבֶר בָּא לָעוֹלָם עַל מִיתוֹת הָאֲמוּרוֹת בַּתּוֹרָה שֶׁלֹּא נִמְסְרוּ לְבֵית דִּין, וְעַל פֵּרוֹת שְׁבִיעִית. חֶרֶב בָּאָה לָעוֹלָם עַל עִנּוּי הַדִּין, וְעַל עִוּוּת הַדִּין, וְעַל הַמּוֹרִים בַּתּוֹרָה שֶׁלֹּא כַהֲלָכָה.

יב חַיָּה רָעָה בָּאָה לָעוֹלָם עַל שְׁבוּעַת שָׁוְא וְעַל חִלּוּל הַשֵּׁם. גָּלוּת בָּאָה לָעוֹלָם עַל עֲבוֹדָה זָרָה, וְעַל גִּלּוּי עֲרָיוֹת, וְעַל שְׁפִיכוּת דָּמִים, וְעַל שְׁמִטַּת הָאָרֶץ.

יג בְּאַרְבָּעָה פְרָקִים הַדֶּבֶר מִתְרַבֶּה, בָּרְבִיעִית, וּבַשְּׁבִיעִית, וּבְמוֹצָאֵי שְׁבִיעִית, וּבְמוֹצָאֵי הֶחָג שֶׁבְּכָל שָׁנָה וְשָׁנָה. בָּרְבִיעִית, מִפְּנֵי מַעְשַׂר עָנִי שֶׁבַּשְּׁלִישִׁית. בַּשְּׁבִיעִית, מִפְּנֵי מַעְשַׂר עָנִי שֶׁבַּשִּׁשִּׁית. בְּמוֹצָאֵי שְׁבִיעִית, מִפְּנֵי פֵּרוֹת שְׁבִיעִית. בְּמוֹצָאֵי הֶחָג שֶׁבְּכָל שָׁנָה וְשָׁנָה, מִפְּנֵי גֶזֶל מַתְּנוֹת עֲנִיִּים.

יד אַרְבַּע מִדּוֹת בָּאָדָם. הָאוֹמֵר שֶׁלִּי שֶׁלִּי וְשֶׁלְּךָ שֶׁלָּךְ, זוֹ מִדָּה בֵינוֹנִית, וְיֵשׁ אוֹמְרִים, זוֹ מִדַּת סְדוֹם. שֶׁלִּי שֶׁלָּךְ וְשֶׁלְּךָ שֶׁלִּי, עַם הָאָרֶץ. שֶׁלִּי שֶׁלָּךְ וְשֶׁלְּךָ שֶׁלָּךְ, חָסִיד. שֶׁלְּךָ שֶׁלִּי וְשֶׁלִּי שֶׁלִּי, רָשָׁע.

טו אַרְבַּע מִדּוֹת בַּדֵּעוֹת. נוֹחַ לִכְעֹס וְנוֹחַ לִרְצוֹת, יָצָא הֶפְסֵדוֹ בִשְׂכָרוֹ. קָשֶׁה לִכְעֹס וְקָשֶׁה לִרְצוֹת, יָצָא שְׂכָרוֹ בְּהֶפְסֵדוֹ. קָשֶׁה לִכְעֹס וְנוֹחַ לִרְצוֹת, חָסִיד. נוֹחַ לִכְעֹס וְקָשֶׁה לִרְצוֹת, רָשָׁע.

טז אַרְבַּע מִדּוֹת בַּתַּלְמִידִים. מָהִיר לִשְׁמֹעַ וּמָהִיר לְאַבֵּד, יָצָא שְׂכָרוֹ בְּהֶפְסֵדוֹ. קָשֶׁה לִשְׁמֹעַ וְקָשֶׁה לְאַבֵּד, יָצָא הֶפְסֵדוֹ בִשְׂכָרוֹ. מָהִיר לִשְׁמֹעַ וְקָשֶׁה לְאַבֵּד, זֶה חֵלֶק טוֹב. קָשֶׁה לִשְׁמֹעַ וּמָהִיר לְאַבֵּד, זֶה חֵלֶק רָע.

יז אַרְבַּע מִדּוֹת בְּנוֹתְנֵי צְדָקָה. הָרוֹצֶה שֶׁיִּתֵּן וְלֹא יִתְּנוּ אֲחֵרִים, עֵינוֹ רָעָה בְּשֶׁל אֲחֵרִים. יִתְּנוּ אֲחֵרִים וְהוּא לֹא יִתֵּן, עֵינוֹ רָעָה בְּשֶׁלּוֹ. יִתֵּן וְיִתְּנוּ אֲחֵרִים, חָסִיד. לֹא יִתֵּן וְלֹא יִתְּנוּ אֲחֵרִים, רָשָׁע.

יח אַרְבַּע מִדּוֹת בְּהוֹלְכֵי בֵית הַמִּדְרָשׁ. הוֹלֵךְ וְאֵינוֹ עוֹשֶׂה, שְׂכַר הֲלִיכָה בְּיָדוֹ.

going. (2) One who practices but does not go receives a reward for practicing. (3) One who goes and also practices is pious. (4) One who neither goes nor practices is wicked.

19. There are four types among those who sit before the sages: the sponge, the funnel, the strainer and the sieve. The sponge absorbs everything. The funnel takes in at one end and lets out at the other. The strainer lets out the wine and retains the sediment. The sieve allows the flour dust to pass through and retains the fine flour.

20. If love depends on a specific cause, when the cause ends, so does the love. If love does not depend on a specific cause, then it never ends. What is an example of love depending on a specific cause? The love of Amnon for Tamar. What is an example of love not dependent on a specific cause? The love of David and Jonathan.

21. Any dispute for the sake of Heaven will have enduring value, but any dispute not for the sake of Heaven will not have enduring value. What is an example of a dispute for the sake of heaven? The dispute between Hillel and Shammai. What is an example of one not for the sake of heaven? The dispute of Koraḥ and all his company.

22. One who brings merit to the many will not be the cause of sin. One who causes the many to sin will be denied the means to repent. Moses attained merit and brought merit to the many; therefore the merit of the many was attributed to him, as it is said, "He carried out the LORD's righteousness and His *Deut. 33*
ordinances with Israel." Jeroboam, son of Nebat, sinned and caused the many to sin; therefore the sin of the many was attributed to him, as it is said, "For *1 Kings 15*
the sins of Jeroboam that he committed and that he caused Israel to commit."

23. Whoever possesses these three traits is one of the disciples of our father Abraham; whoever possesses the three opposite traits is one of the disciples of the wicked Balaam. A generous eye, a modest demeanor and a humble soul are the traits of the disciples of our father Abraham. An evil eye, an arrogant demeanor and an insatiable soul are attributes of the disciples of the wicked Balaam. What is the difference between our father Abraham's disciples and those of the wicked Balaam? Our father Abraham's disciples enjoy this world and inherit the World to Come, as it is said, "That I may cause those who *Prov. 8*
love me to inherit substance and so that I may fill their treasures." The wicked Balaam's disciples inherit Gehinnom and go down to the pit of destruction, as it is said, "But You, God, will bring them down to the pit of destruction; blood- *Ps. 55*
thirsty and deceitful men shall not live out half their days; but I trust in You."

24. Judah ben Tema said: Be strong as a leopard, light as an eagle, swift as a gazelle, and brave as a lion, to do the will of your Father in heaven. He used to say: The

עוֹשֶׂה וְאֵינוֹ הוֹלֵךְ, שְׂכַר מַעֲשֶׂה בְּיָדוֹ. הוֹלֵךְ וְעוֹשֶׂה, חָסִיד. לֹא הוֹלֵךְ וְלֹא עוֹשֶׂה, רָשָׁע.

יט אַרְבַּע מִדּוֹת בְּיוֹשְׁבִים לִפְנֵי חֲכָמִים, סְפוֹג, וּמַשְׁפֵּךְ, מְשַׁמֶּרֶת, וְנָפָה. סְפוֹג, שֶׁהוּא סוֹפֵג אֶת הַכֹּל. וּמַשְׁפֵּךְ, שֶׁמַּכְנִיס בְּזוֹ וּמוֹצִיא בְזוֹ. מְשַׁמֶּרֶת, שֶׁמּוֹצִיאָה אֶת הַיַּיִן וְקוֹלֶטֶת אֶת הַשְּׁמָרִים. וְנָפָה, שֶׁמּוֹצִיאָה אֶת הַקֶּמַח וְקוֹלֶטֶת אֶת הַסֹּלֶת.

כ כָּל אַהֲבָה שֶׁהִיא תְלוּיָה בְדָבָר, בָּטֵל דָּבָר, בְּטֵלָה אַהֲבָה. וְשֶׁאֵינָהּ תְּלוּיָה בְדָבָר, אֵינָהּ בְּטֵלָה לְעוֹלָם. אֵיזוֹ הִיא אַהֲבָה שֶׁהִיא תְלוּיָה בְדָבָר, זוֹ אַהֲבַת אַמְנוֹן וְתָמָר. וְשֶׁאֵינָהּ תְּלוּיָה בְדָבָר, זוֹ אַהֲבַת דָּוִד וִיהוֹנָתָן.

כא כָּל מַחֲלֹקֶת שֶׁהִיא לְשֵׁם שָׁמַיִם, סוֹפָהּ לְהִתְקַיֵּם. וְשֶׁאֵינָהּ לְשֵׁם שָׁמַיִם, אֵין סוֹפָהּ לְהִתְקַיֵּם. אֵיזוֹ הִיא מַחֲלֹקֶת שֶׁהִיא לְשֵׁם שָׁמַיִם, זוֹ מַחֲלֹקֶת הִלֵּל וְשַׁמַּאי. וְשֶׁאֵינָהּ לְשֵׁם שָׁמַיִם, זוֹ מַחֲלֹקֶת קֹרַח וְכָל עֲדָתוֹ.

כב כָּל הַמְזַכֶּה אֶת הָרַבִּים, אֵין חֵטְא בָּא עַל יָדוֹ. וְכָל הַמַּחֲטִיא אֶת הָרַבִּים, אֵין מַסְפִּיקִין בְּיָדוֹ לַעֲשׂוֹת תְּשׁוּבָה. מֹשֶׁה זָכָה וְזִכָּה אֶת הָרַבִּים, זְכוּת
הָרַבִּים תָּלוּי בּוֹ, שֶׁנֶּאֱמַר: צִדְקַת יהוה עָשָׂה וּמִשְׁפָּטָיו עִם־יִשְׂרָאֵל: יָרָבְעָם דברים לג
בֶּן נְבָט, חָטָא וְהֶחֱטִיא אֶת הָרַבִּים, חֵטְא הָרַבִּים תָּלוּי בּוֹ, שֶׁנֶּאֱמַר: עַל־ מלכים א׳ טו
חַטֹּאות יָרָבְעָם אֲשֶׁר חָטָא וַאֲשֶׁר הֶחֱטִיא אֶת־יִשְׂרָאֵל:

כג כָּל מִי שֶׁיֵּשׁ בּוֹ שְׁלֹשָׁה דְּבָרִים הַלָּלוּ, הוּא מִתַּלְמִידָיו שֶׁל אַבְרָהָם אָבִינוּ, וּשְׁלֹשָׁה דְּבָרִים אֲחֵרִים, הוּא מִתַּלְמִידָיו שֶׁל בִּלְעָם הָרָשָׁע. עַיִן טוֹבָה, וְרוּחַ נְמוּכָה, וְנֶפֶשׁ שְׁפָלָה, תַּלְמִידָיו שֶׁל אַבְרָהָם אָבִינוּ. עַיִן רָעָה, וְרוּחַ גְּבוֹהָה וְנֶפֶשׁ רְחָבָה, תַּלְמִידָיו שֶׁל בִּלְעָם הָרָשָׁע. מַה בֵּין תַּלְמִידָיו שֶׁל אַבְרָהָם אָבִינוּ לְתַלְמִידָיו שֶׁל בִּלְעָם הָרָשָׁע. תַּלְמִידָיו שֶׁל אַבְרָהָם אָבִינוּ
אוֹכְלִין בָּעוֹלָם הַזֶּה וְנוֹחֲלִין הָעוֹלָם הַבָּא, שֶׁנֶּאֱמַר: לְהַנְחִיל אֹהֲבַי יֵשׁ משלי ח
וְאֹצְרֹתֵיהֶם אֲמַלֵּא: אֲבָל תַּלְמִידָיו שֶׁל בִּלְעָם הָרָשָׁע יוֹרְשִׁין גֵּיהִנֹּם וְיוֹרְדִין
לִבְאֵר שַׁחַת, שֶׁנֶּאֱמַר: וְאַתָּה אֱלֹהִים תּוֹרִדֵם לִבְאֵר שַׁחַת, אַנְשֵׁי דָמִים תהלים נה
וּמִרְמָה לֹא־יֶחֱצוּ יְמֵיהֶם, וַאֲנִי אֶבְטַח־בָּךְ:

כד יְהוּדָה בֶן תֵּימָא אוֹמֵר: הֱוֵי עַז כַּנָּמֵר וְקַל כַּנֶּשֶׁר, רָץ כַּצְּבִי וְגִבּוֹר כָּאֲרִי,

shameless go to Gehinnom; those who have a sense of shame are destined for the Garden of Eden. May it be Your will, O Lord our God and God of our ancestors that the Temple be speedily rebuilt in our days; and grant us our portion in Your Torah.

25. He used to say: Five years old is the age to begin studying Scripture; ten for Mishna; thirteen for the obligation of the commandments; fifteen for the study of Talmud; eighteen for marriage; twenty for seeking a livelihood; thirty for full strength; forty for understanding; fifty for giving counsel; sixty for old age; seventy for ripe old age; eighty for exceptional strength; and ninety for a bent back; at a hundred, one is as if he were dead and had left and gone from the world.

26. Ben Bag-Bag said: Turn it [the Torah] over and over, for everything is in it. Reflect on it, grow old and gray in it and do not stir from it, for there is no better portion for you than this. Ben Heh-Heh said: According to the effort is the reward.

Rabbi Ḥananya ben Akashya said: The Holy One, blessed be He, wanted to confer merit on Israel. That is why He gave them a copious Torah and many commandments, as it is said, "It pleased the Lord, for the sake of [Israel's] righteousness, to make the Torah great and glorious." *Makkot 23b* *Is. 42*

*If there is a minyan, mourners say the Rabbis' Kaddish (page 628).*

* * *

All Israel have a share in the World to Come, as it is said, *Sanhedrin 90a*
"Your people are all righteous; they shall inherit the land for ever; *Is. 60*
they are a shoot of My own planting,
a work of My own hands, that I may be glorified."

## CHAPTER 6

The sages taught the following in the style of the Mishna – blessed be He who chose them and their teaching.

1. Rabbi Meir said: Whoever engages in Torah study for its own sake merits many things; moreover, the whole world is worthwhile for his sake alone. He is called friend, beloved, a lover of God and a lover of mankind. . He brings joy to God; he brings joy to mankind. [The Torah] clothes him with humility and reverence. It prepares him to be righteous, pious, upright and faithful. It keeps him far from sin and near to virtue. People benefit from his advice and wisdom, understanding and courage, as it is said, "Mine are counsel and wisdom; I am understanding, courage is mine." It gives him sovereignty, dominion and discerning judgment. To him the secrets of the Torah are revealed. He becomes like a never-failing fountain, like a river that never runs dry. He becomes modest and patient; he forgives insults. It makes him great, exalting him above all things. *Prov. 8*

לַעֲשׂוֹת רְצוֹן אָבִיךָ שֶׁבַּשָּׁמָיִם. הוּא הָיָה אוֹמֵר: עַז פָּנִים לְגֵיהִנֹּם, וּבֹשֶׁת פָּנִים לְגַן עֵדֶן. יְהִי רָצוֹן מִלְּפָנֶיךָ, יהוה אֱלֹהֵינוּ וֵאלֹהֵי אֲבוֹתֵינוּ, שֶׁיִּבָּנֶה בֵּית הַמִּקְדָּשׁ בִּמְהֵרָה בְיָמֵינוּ, וְתֵן חֶלְקֵנוּ בְּתוֹרָתֶךָ.

כה הוּא הָיָה אוֹמֵר: בֶּן חָמֵשׁ שָׁנִים לַמִּקְרָא, בֶּן עֶשֶׂר שָׁנִים לַמִּשְׁנָה, בֶּן שְׁלֹשׁ עֶשְׂרֵה לַמִּצְוֹת, בֶּן חֲמֵשׁ עֶשְׂרֵה לַגְּמָרָא, בֶּן שְׁמוֹנֶה עֶשְׂרֵה לַחֻפָּה, בֶּן עֶשְׂרִים לִרְדֹּף, בֶּן שְׁלֹשִׁים לַכֹּחַ, בֶּן אַרְבָּעִים לַבִּינָה, בֶּן חֲמִשִּׁים לָעֵצָה, בֶּן שִׁשִּׁים לַזִּקְנָה, בֶּן שִׁבְעִים לַשֵּׂיבָה, בֶּן שְׁמוֹנִים לַגְּבוּרָה, בֶּן תִּשְׁעִים לָשׁוּחַ, בֶּן מֵאָה כְּאִלּוּ מֵת וְעָבַר וּבָטֵל מִן הָעוֹלָם.

כו בֶּן בַּג בַּג אוֹמֵר: הֲפָךְ בָּהּ וַהֲפָךְ בָּהּ דְּכֹלָּא בַהּ, וּבַהּ תֶּחֱזֵי, וְסִיב וּבְלֵה בַהּ, וּמִנַּהּ לָא תְזוּעַ, שֶׁאֵין לְךָ מִדָּה טוֹבָה הֵימֶנָּה. בֶּן הֵא הֵא אוֹמֵר: לְפוּם צַעֲרָא אַגְרָא.

רַבִּי חֲנַנְיָא בֶּן עֲקַשְׁיָא אוֹמֵר: רָצָה הַקָּדוֹשׁ בָּרוּךְ הוּא לְזַכּוֹת אֶת יִשְׂרָאֵל, לְפִיכָךְ הִרְבָּה לָהֶם תּוֹרָה וּמִצְוֹת. שֶׁנֶּאֱמַר: יהוה חָפֵץ לְמַעַן צִדְקוֹ, יַגְדִּיל תּוֹרָה וְיַאְדִּיר: מכות כג: / ישעיה מב

*If there is a* מנין, *mourners say the* קדיש דרבנן *(page 629).*

* * *

כָּל יִשְׂרָאֵל יֵשׁ לָהֶם חֵלֶק לָעוֹלָם הַבָּא. שֶׁנֶּאֱמַר: סנהדרין צ.
וְעַמֵּךְ כֻּלָּם צַדִּיקִים, לְעוֹלָם יִירְשׁוּ אָרֶץ ישעיה ס
נֵצֶר מַטָּעַי, מַעֲשֵׂה יָדַי לְהִתְפָּאֵר:

## פרק ששי

שָׁנוּ חֲכָמִים בִּלְשׁוֹן הַמִּשְׁנָה, בָּרוּךְ שֶׁבָּחַר בָּהֶם וּבְמִשְׁנָתָם.

א רַבִּי מֵאִיר אוֹמֵר: כָּל הָעוֹסֵק בַּתּוֹרָה לִשְׁמָהּ, זוֹכֶה לִדְבָרִים הַרְבֵּה. וְלֹא עוֹד, אֶלָּא שֶׁכָּל הָעוֹלָם כֻּלּוֹ כְּדַאי הוּא לוֹ. נִקְרָא רֵעַ, אָהוּב, אוֹהֵב אֶת הַמָּקוֹם, אוֹהֵב אֶת הַבְּרִיּוֹת, מְשַׂמֵּחַ אֶת הַמָּקוֹם, מְשַׂמֵּחַ אֶת הַבְּרִיּוֹת, וּמַלְבַּשְׁתּוֹ עֲנָוָה וְיִרְאָה, וּמַכְשַׁרְתּוֹ לִהְיוֹת צַדִּיק, חָסִיד, יָשָׁר, וְנֶאֱמָן, וּמְרַחַקְתּוֹ מִן הַחֵטְא, וּמְקָרַבְתּוֹ לִידֵי זְכוּת, וְנֶהֱנִין מִמֶּנּוּ עֵצָה וְתוּשִׁיָּה, בִּינָה וּגְבוּרָה, שֶׁנֶּאֱמַר: לִי־עֵצָה וְתוּשִׁיָּה, אֲנִי בִינָה, לִי גְבוּרָה: וְנוֹתֶנֶת לוֹ מַלְכוּת וּמֶמְשָׁלָה, וְחִקּוּר דִּין, וּמְגַלִּין לוֹ רָזֵי תוֹרָה, וְנַעֲשֶׂה כְּמַעְיָן הַמִּתְגַּבֵּר וּכְנָהָר שֶׁאֵינוֹ פּוֹסֵק, וְהֹוֶה צָנוּעַ, וְאֶרֶךְ רוּחַ, וּמוֹחֵל עַל עֶלְבּוֹנוֹ, וּמְגַדַּלְתּוֹ וּמְרוֹמַמְתּוֹ עַל כָּל הַמַּעֲשִׂים. משלי ח

2. Rabbi Yehoshua ben Levi said: Every day a heavenly voice resounds from Mount Horeb, proclaiming and saying: "Woe to mankind for their contempt of the Torah!" For whoever does not occupy himself with the Torah is called reprehensible, as it is said, "Like a gold ring in the snout of a pig is a beautiful woman bereft of sense." It also says, "The tablets were the work of God, and the writing was the writing of God, engraved (*ḥarut*) on the tablets." Read not *ḥarut* ("engraved") but *ḥerut* ("freedom"), for the only person who is truly free is one who occupies himself with Torah study; and whoever occupies himself with Torah study will be exalted, as it is said, "And from Mattana to Naḥaliel, and from Naḥaliel to Bamot." *Prov. 11* *Ex. 32* *Num. 21*

3. Whoever learns from someone else a single chapter, a single law, a single verse, a single word, even a single letter, must treat him with honor, for so we find in the case of David, King of Israel, who learned only two things from Aḥitophel, yet he called him his teacher, his guide, and his close friend, for so it says, "But it is you, my equal, my guide, my close friend." The following inference can be derived: If David, King of Israel, who learned only two things from Aḥitophel, called him his teacher, guide and close friend, how much more must one who learns from someone else a chapter, a law, a verse, a word or even a single letter, treat him with honor! And honor is due only to Torah, as it is written, "The wise shall inherit honor," and "The wholehearted shall attain good," and "good" signifies Torah, as it is said, "I have given you good instruction; do not forsake My Torah." *Ps. 55* *Prov. 3* *Prov. 28* *Prov. 4*

4. This is the way of Torah: Eat bread with salt, drink water by measure, sleep on the ground, live a life of hardship, but toil in the Torah! If you do so, "You will be happy and it will be well with you": "You will be happy" in this world, "and it shall be well with you" in the World to Come.

5. Do not seek greatness for yourself, and do not long for honor. Let your deeds exceed your learning. Do not crave the table of kings, for your table is greater than theirs, your crown is greater than their crown, and your Employer can be relied upon to pay you your labor's reward.

6. The Torah is greater than priesthood and kingship, for kingship is acquired with thirty attainments, and priesthood is endowed with twenty-four [gifts], but the Torah is acquired by forty-eight virtues. They are: study, attentive listening, well-ordered speech, intuitive understanding, awe, reverence, humility, joy, purity, serving the wise, association with colleagues, debate with students, serenity, knowledge of Scripture and Mishna; minimizing time spent on business, worldly matters, pleasure, sleep, small talk or laughter; patience, a kindly heart, faith in the sages, and acceptance of suffering; knowing one's place, being happy with one's lot, restraining one's words, and claiming

ב אָמַר רַבִּי יְהוֹשֻׁעַ בֶּן לֵוִי: בְּכָל יוֹם וָיוֹם, בַּת קוֹל יוֹצֵאת מֵהַר חוֹרֵב וּמַכְרֶזֶת
וְאוֹמֶרֶת, אוֹי לָהֶם לַבְּרִיּוֹת מֵעֶלְבּוֹנָהּ שֶׁל תּוֹרָה, שֶׁכָּל מִי שֶׁאֵינוֹ עוֹסֵק
בַּתּוֹרָה נִקְרָא נָזוּף, שֶׁנֶּאֱמַר: נֶזֶם זָהָב בְּאַף חֲזִיר, אִשָּׁה יָפָה וְסָרַת טָעַם: משלי יא
וְאוֹמֵר: וְהַלֻּחֹת מַעֲשֵׂה אֱלֹהִים הֵמָּה, וְהַמִּכְתָּב מִכְתַּב אֱלֹהִים הוּא, חָרוּת שמות לב
עַל־הַלֻּחֹת: אַל תִּקְרָא חָרוּת אֶלָּא חֵרוּת, שֶׁאֵין לְךָ בֶּן חוֹרִין אֶלָּא מִי שֶׁעוֹסֵק
בְּתַלְמוּד תּוֹרָה. וְכָל מִי שֶׁעוֹסֵק בְּתַלְמוּד תּוֹרָה, הֲרֵי זֶה מִתְעַלֶּה, שֶׁנֶּאֱמַר:
וּמִמַּתָּנָה נַחֲלִיאֵל, וּמִנַּחֲלִיאֵל בָּמוֹת: במדבר כא

ג הַלּוֹמֵד מֵחֲבֵרוֹ פֶּרֶק אֶחָד, אוֹ הֲלָכָה אַחַת, אוֹ פָּסוּק אֶחָד, אוֹ דִבּוּר אֶחָד,
אוֹ אֲפִלּוּ אוֹת אַחַת, צָרִיךְ לִנְהָג בּוֹ כָּבוֹד. שֶׁכֵּן מָצִינוּ בְּדָוִד מֶלֶךְ יִשְׂרָאֵל,
שֶׁלֹּא לָמַד מֵאֲחִיתֹפֶל אֶלָּא שְׁנֵי דְבָרִים בִּלְבָד, קְרָאוֹ רַבּוֹ אַלּוּפוֹ וּמְיֻדָּעוֹ,
שֶׁנֶּאֱמַר: וְאַתָּה אֱנוֹשׁ כְּעֶרְכִּי, אַלּוּפִי וּמְיֻדָּעִי: וַהֲלֹא דְבָרִים קַל וָחֹמֶר. וּמַה תהלים נה
דָּוִד מֶלֶךְ יִשְׂרָאֵל, שֶׁלֹּא לָמַד מֵאֲחִיתֹפֶל אֶלָּא שְׁנֵי דְבָרִים בִּלְבָד, קְרָאוֹ
רַבּוֹ אַלּוּפוֹ וּמְיֻדָּעוֹ, הַלּוֹמֵד מֵחֲבֵרוֹ פֶּרֶק אֶחָד, אוֹ הֲלָכָה אַחַת, אוֹ פָּסוּק
אֶחָד, אוֹ דִבּוּר אֶחָד, אוֹ אֲפִלּוּ אוֹת אַחַת, עַל אַחַת כַּמָּה וְכַמָּה שֶׁצָּרִיךְ
לִנְהָג בּוֹ כָּבוֹד. וְאֵין כָּבוֹד אֶלָּא תוֹרָה, שֶׁנֶּאֱמַר: כָּבוֹד חֲכָמִים יִנְחָלוּ: משלי ג
וּתְמִימִים יִנְחֲלוּ־טוֹב: וְאֵין טוֹב אֶלָּא תוֹרָה, שֶׁנֶּאֱמַר: כִּי לֶקַח טוֹב נָתַתִּי משלי כח משלי ד
לָכֶם, תּוֹרָתִי אַל־תַּעֲזֹבוּ:

ד כָּךְ הִיא דַּרְכָּהּ שֶׁל תּוֹרָה. פַּת בַּמֶּלַח תֹּאכֵל, וּמַיִם בַּמְּשׂוּרָה תִּשְׁתֶּה, וְעַל
הָאָרֶץ תִּישַׁן, וְחַיֵּי צַעַר תִּחְיֶה, וּבַתּוֹרָה אַתָּה עָמֵל. אִם אַתָּה עוֹשֶׂה כֵּן,
אַשְׁרֶיךָ וְטוֹב לָךְ, אַשְׁרֶיךָ בָּעוֹלָם הַזֶּה, וְטוֹב לָךְ לָעוֹלָם הַבָּא.

ה אַל תְּבַקֵּשׁ גְּדֻלָּה לְעַצְמְךָ, וְאַל תַּחְמֹד כָּבוֹד. יוֹתֵר מִלִּמּוּדְךָ עֲשֵׂה. וְאַל
תִּתְאַוֶּה לְשֻׁלְחָנָם שֶׁל מְלָכִים, שֶׁשֻּׁלְחָנְךָ גָּדוֹל מִשֻּׁלְחָנָם, וְכִתְרְךָ גָּדוֹל
מִכִּתְרָם. וְנֶאֱמָן הוּא בַּעַל מְלַאכְתְּךָ, שֶׁיְּשַׁלֶּם לְךָ שְׂכַר פְּעֻלָּתֶךָ.

ו גְּדוֹלָה תוֹרָה יוֹתֵר מִן הַכְּהֻנָּה וּמִן הַמַּלְכוּת. שֶׁהַמַּלְכוּת נִקְנֵית בִּשְׁלֹשִׁים
מַעֲלוֹת, וְהַכְּהֻנָּה בְּעֶשְׂרִים וְאַרְבַּע, וְהַתּוֹרָה נִקְנֵית בְּאַרְבָּעִים וּשְׁמוֹנָה
דְבָרִים. וְאֵלּוּ הֵן, בְּתַלְמוּד, בִּשְׁמִיעַת הָאֹזֶן, בַּעֲרִיכַת שְׂפָתַיִם, בְּבִינַת
הַלֵּב, בְּאֵימָה, בְּיִרְאָה, בַּעֲנָוָה, בְּשִׂמְחָה, בְּטָהֳרָה, בְּשִׁמּוּשׁ חֲכָמִים, בְּדִקְדּוּק
חֲבֵרִים, בְּפִלְפּוּל הַתַּלְמִידִים, בְּיִשּׁוּב, בְּמִקְרָא, בְּמִשְׁנָה, בְּמִעוּט סְחוֹרָה,
בְּמִעוּט דֶּרֶךְ אֶרֶץ, בְּמִעוּט תַּעֲנוּג, בְּמִעוּט שֵׁנָה, בְּמִעוּט שִׂיחָה, בְּמִעוּט

no credit for oneself; being loved, loving God, loving mankind and loving righteousness, justice and admonishment; shunning honors, avoiding arrogance in one's learning or delight in giving decisions; sharing someone else's burden, giving him the benefit of the doubt, guiding him to truth and peace; concentrating on one's study, asking and answering questions, listening and adding to one's knowledge; learning in order to teach, learning in order to do, making one's teacher wiser, being precise in one's studies, and reporting a saying in the name of the one who said it. For you have learned: Whoever reports a saying in the name of the one who said it brings deliverance to the world, as it is said, "And Esther told the king in the name of Mordekhai." *Esther 2*

7. Great is Torah for it gives life to its practitioners in both this world and the World to Come, as it is said, "For they are life to those that find them, and *Prov. 4* healing to all their flesh"; and it says, "It shall be healing for your body and *Prov. 3* marrow for your bones"; and it says, "It is a tree of life to those who grasp it, and those who support it shall be happy"; and it says, "They shall be a garland *Prov. 1* of grace on your head, and pendants for your neck"; and it says, "It will adorn *Prov. 4* your head with a garland of grace, and bestow on you a crown of glory"; and it says, "Through me shall your days increase, and years of life shall be added *Prov. 9* to you"; and it says, "At its right hand is length of days; in its left, riches and *Prov. 3* honor"; and it says, "For length of days and years of life and peace shall they *Ibid.* add to you."

8. Rabbi Shimon ben Menasya said in the name of Rabbi Shimon ben Yoḥai: Beauty, strength, wealth, honor, wisdom, old age, gray hair, and children are fitting for the righteous and for the world, as it is said: "Gray hair is a crown *Prov. 16* of glory; it is attained by the way of righteousness"; and it says, "The crown *Prov. 14* of the wise is their wealth"; and it says, "Grandchildren are the crown of *Prov. 17* their elders; the glory of children is their parents"; and it says, "The glory of *Prov. 20* the young is their strength; the majesty of the old is their gray hair"; and it says, "Then the moon shall be ashamed and the sun shall be abashed, for the *Is. 24* Lord of hosts will reign on Mount Zion and in Jerusalem, and glory shall be before His elders." Rabbi Shimon ben Menasya said: These seven qualities which the sages attributed to the righteous were all present in Rabbi [Judah the Prince] and his sons.

9. Rabbi Yose ben Kisma said: Once I was walking along the road when a man met and greeted me, and I returned his greeting. He said to me, "Rabbi, where do you come from?" I replied, "I come from a great city of sages and scribes." He said to me, "Rabbi, if you are willing to live with us in our place I will give you a million gold dinars, as well as precious stones and pearls." I replied, "Were you to give me all the silver and gold and precious stones and pearls

שְׂחוֹק, בְּאֶרֶךְ אַפַּיִם, בְּלֵב טוֹב, בֶּאֱמוּנַת חֲכָמִים, בְּקַבָּלַת הַיִּסּוּרִין, הַמַּכִּיר
אֶת מְקוֹמוֹ, וְהַשָּׂמֵחַ בְּחֶלְקוֹ, וְהָעוֹשֶׂה סְיָג לִדְבָרָיו, וְאֵינוֹ מַחֲזִיק טוֹבָה
לְעַצְמוֹ, אָהוּב, אוֹהֵב אֶת הַמָּקוֹם, אוֹהֵב אֶת הַבְּרִיּוֹת, אוֹהֵב אֶת הַצְּדָקוֹת,
אוֹהֵב אֶת הַמֵּישָׁרִים, אוֹהֵב אֶת הַתּוֹכָחוֹת, וּמִתְרַחֵק מִן הַכָּבוֹד, וְלֹא מֵגִיס
לִבּוֹ בְּתַלְמוּדוֹ, וְאֵינוֹ שָׂמֵחַ בְּהוֹרָאָה, נוֹשֵׂא בְעֹל עִם חֲבֵרוֹ, וּמַכְרִיעוֹ לְכַף
זְכוּת, וּמַעֲמִידוֹ עַל הָאֱמֶת, וּמַעֲמִידוֹ עַל הַשָּׁלוֹם, וּמִתְיַשֵּׁב לִבּוֹ בְּתַלְמוּדוֹ,
שׁוֹאֵל וּמֵשִׁיב, שׁוֹמֵעַ וּמוֹסִיף, הַלּוֹמֵד עַל מְנָת לְלַמֵּד, וְהַלּוֹמֵד עַל מְנָת
לַעֲשׂוֹת, הַמַּחְכִּים אֶת רַבּוֹ, וְהַמְכַוֵּן אֶת שְׁמוּעָתוֹ, וְהָאוֹמֵר דָּבָר בְּשֵׁם אוֹמְרוֹ.
הָא לָמַדְתָּ, כָּל הָאוֹמֵר דָּבָר בְּשֵׁם אוֹמְרוֹ, מֵבִיא גְאֻלָּה לָעוֹלָם, שֶׁנֶּאֱמַר:
וַתֹּאמֶר אֶסְתֵּר לַמֶּלֶךְ בְּשֵׁם מָרְדֳּכָי: אסתר ב

ז גְּדוֹלָה תוֹרָה, שֶׁהִיא נוֹתֶנֶת חַיִּים לְעוֹשֶׂיהָ בָּעוֹלָם הַזֶּה וּבָעוֹלָם הַבָּא,
שֶׁנֶּאֱמַר: כִּי־חַיִּים הֵם לְמֹצְאֵיהֶם, וּלְכָל־בְּשָׂרוֹ מַרְפֵּא: וְאוֹמֵר: רִפְאוּת תְּהִי משלי ד משלי ג
לְשָׁרֶּךָ, וְשִׁקּוּי לְעַצְמוֹתֶיךָ: וְאוֹמֵר: עֵץ־חַיִּים הִיא לַמַּחֲזִיקִים בָּהּ, וְתֹמְכֶיהָ
מְאֻשָּׁר: וְאוֹמֵר: כִּי לִוְיַת חֵן הֵם לְרֹאשֶׁךָ, וַעֲנָקִים לְגַרְגְּרֹתֶיךָ: וְאוֹמֵר: תִּתֵּן משלי א משלי ד
לְרֹאשְׁךָ לִוְיַת־חֵן, עֲטֶרֶת תִּפְאֶרֶת תְּמַגְּנֶךָּ: וְאוֹמֵר: כִּי־בִי יִרְבּוּ יָמֶיךָ, וְיוֹסִיפוּ משלי ט
לְךָ שְׁנוֹת חַיִּים: וְאוֹמֵר: אֹרֶךְ יָמִים בִּימִינָהּ, בִּשְׂמֹאולָהּ עֹשֶׁר וְכָבוֹד: משלי ג
וְאוֹמֵר: כִּי אֹרֶךְ יָמִים וּשְׁנוֹת חַיִּים וְשָׁלוֹם יוֹסִיפוּ לָךְ: שם

ח רַבִּי שִׁמְעוֹן בֶּן מְנַסְיָא מִשּׁוּם רַבִּי שִׁמְעוֹן בֶּן יוֹחַאי אוֹמֵר: הַנּוֹי, וְהַכֹּחַ,
וְהָעֹשֶׁר, וְהַכָּבוֹד, וְהַחָכְמָה, וְהַזִּקְנָה, וְהַשֵּׂיבָה, וְהַבָּנִים, נָאֶה לַצַּדִּיקִים
וְנָאֶה לָעוֹלָם, שֶׁנֶּאֱמַר: עֲטֶרֶת תִּפְאֶרֶת שֵׂיבָה, בְּדֶרֶךְ צְדָקָה תִּמָּצֵא: וְאוֹמֵר: משלי טז
עֲטֶרֶת חֲכָמִים עָשְׁרָם: וְאוֹמֵר: עֲטֶרֶת זְקֵנִים בְּנֵי בָנִים, וְתִפְאֶרֶת בָּנִים משלי יד משלי יז
אֲבוֹתָם: וְאוֹמֵר: תִּפְאֶרֶת בַּחוּרִים כֹּחָם, וַהֲדַר זְקֵנִים שֵׂיבָה: וְאוֹמֵר: וְחָפְרָה משלי כ ישעיה כד
הַלְּבָנָה וּבוֹשָׁה הַחַמָּה, כִּי־מָלַךְ יהוה צְבָאוֹת בְּהַר צִיּוֹן וּבִירוּשָׁלַיִם, וְנֶגֶד
זְקֵנָיו כָּבוֹד: רַבִּי שִׁמְעוֹן בֶּן מְנַסְיָא אוֹמֵר: אֵלּוּ שֶׁבַע מִדּוֹת שֶׁמָּנוּ חֲכָמִים
לַצַּדִּיקִים, כֻּלָּם נִתְקַיְּמוּ בְּרַבִּי וּבְבָנָיו.

ט אָמַר רַבִּי יוֹסֵי בֶּן קִסְמָא: פַּעַם אַחַת הָיִיתִי מְהַלֵּךְ בַּדֶּרֶךְ, וּפָגַע בִּי אָדָם
אֶחָד, וְנָתַן לִי שָׁלוֹם וְהֶחֱזַרְתִּי לוֹ שָׁלוֹם. אָמַר לִי, רַבִּי, מֵאֵיזֶה מָקוֹם אָתָּה.
אָמַרְתִּי לוֹ, מֵעִיר גְּדוֹלָה שֶׁל חֲכָמִים וְשֶׁל סוֹפְרִים אָנִי. אָמַר לִי, רַבִּי, רְצוֹנְךָ
שֶׁתָּדוּר עִמָּנוּ בִּמְקוֹמֵנוּ, וַאֲנִי אֶתֵּן לָךְ אֶלֶף אֲלָפִים דִּינְרֵי זָהָב וַאֲבָנִים

in the world, I would not live anywhere except in a place of Torah, for so it is written in the book of Psalms by David, King of Israel, 'I prefer the Torah of your mouth to thousands of gold and silver pieces.' Furthermore, when a person departs from this world, neither silver nor gold nor precious stones nor pearls accompany him, but only Torah and good deeds, as it is said, 'When you walk, it will lead you; when you lie down, it will watch over you; and when you awake, it will talk with you.' 'When you walk, it will lead you' – in this world; 'when you lie down, it will watch over you' – in the grave; 'and when you awake, it will speak for you' – in the World to Come. And it says, 'Mine is the silver, and Mine is the gold, says the LORD of hosts.'" *Ps. 119* *Prov. 6* *Hag. 2*

10. Five possessions did the Holy One, blessed be He, declare as His own in His world, and they are: the Torah, heaven and earth, Abraham, Israel and the Temple. How do we know this about the Torah? Because it is written, "The LORD created me at the beginning of His way, as the first of His works in days of old." How do we know it about heaven and earth? Because it is written, "So says the LORD: the heaven is My throne, and the earth is My footstool; what house can you build for Me, and where is the place for My rest?"; and it also says, "How numerous are Your works, O LORD! You made them all in wisdom; the earth is full of Your possessions." How do we know it about Abraham? Because it is written, "And He blessed him and said, Blessed be Abram of God the Most High, owner of heaven and earth." How do we know it about Israel? Because it is written, "Until Your people pass over, O LORD, until this people You acquired pass over"; and it also says, "As for the holy ones who are on earth and for the mighty, all My delight is in them." How do we know it about the Temple? Because it is written, "Your dwelling place which You, LORD, have made; the Temple, O LORD, which Your hands established"; and it also says, "He brought them to His holy realm, the mountain His right hand had acquired." *Prov. 8* *Is. 66* *Ps. 104* *Gen. 14* *Ex. 15* *Ps. 16* *Ex. 15* *Ps. 78*

11. All that the Holy One, blessed be He, created in His world, He created solely for His glory, as it is said, "All that is called by My name, it is for My glory that I created it, formed it and made it"; and it also says, "The LORD shall reign for ever and ever." *Is. 43* *Ex. 15*

Rabbi Ḥananya ben Akashya said: The Holy One, blessed be He, wanted to confer merit on Israel. That is why He gave them a copious Torah and many commandments, as it is said, "It pleased the LORD, for the sake of [Israel's] righteousness, to make the Torah great and glorious." *Makkot 23b* *Is. 42*

*If there is a minyan, mourners say the Rabbis' Kaddish* (*page 628*).

טוֹבוֹת וּמַרְגָּלִיּוֹת. אָמַרְתִּי לוֹ, אִם אַתָּה נוֹתֵן לִי כָּל כֶּסֶף וְזָהָב וַאֲבָנִים
טוֹבוֹת וּמַרְגָּלִיּוֹת שֶׁבָּעוֹלָם, אֵינִי דָר אֶלָּא בִּמְקוֹם תּוֹרָה, וְכֵן כָּתוּב בְּסֵפֶר
תְּהִלִּים עַל יְדֵי דָוִד מֶלֶךְ יִשְׂרָאֵל: טוֹב־לִי תוֹרַת־פִּיךָ מֵאַלְפֵי זָהָב וָכָסֶף: תהלים קיט
וְלֹא עוֹד, אֶלָּא שֶׁבִּשְׁעַת פְּטִירָתוֹ שֶׁל אָדָם, אֵין מְלַוִּין לוֹ לְאָדָם לֹא כֶסֶף
וְלֹא זָהָב וְלֹא אֲבָנִים טוֹבוֹת וּמַרְגָּלִיּוֹת, אֶלָּא תּוֹרָה וּמַעֲשִׂים טוֹבִים בִּלְבָד,
שֶׁנֶּאֱמַר: בְּהִתְהַלֶּכְךָ תַּנְחֶה אֹתָךְ, בְּשָׁכְבְּךָ תִּשְׁמֹר עָלֶיךָ, וַהֲקִיצוֹתָ הִיא משלי ו
תְשִׂיחֶךָ: בְּהִתְהַלֶּכְךָ תַּנְחֶה אֹתָךְ, בָּעוֹלָם הַזֶּה. בְּשָׁכְבְּךָ תִּשְׁמֹר עָלֶיךָ,
בַּקֶּבֶר. וַהֲקִיצוֹתָ הִיא תְשִׂיחֶךָ, לָעוֹלָם הַבָּא. וְאוֹמֵר: לִי הַכֶּסֶף וְלִי הַזָּהָב, חגי ב
נְאֻם יהוה צְבָאוֹת:

י חֲמִשָּׁה קִנְיָנִים קָנָה הַקָּדוֹשׁ בָּרוּךְ הוּא בְּעוֹלָמוֹ. וְאֵלּוּ הֵן, תּוֹרָה קִנְיָן אֶחָד,
שָׁמַיִם וָאָרֶץ קִנְיָן אֶחָד, אַבְרָהָם קִנְיָן אֶחָד, יִשְׂרָאֵל קִנְיָן אֶחָד, בֵּית הַמִּקְדָּשׁ
קִנְיָן אֶחָד. תּוֹרָה מִנַּיִן, דִּכְתִיב: יהוה קָנָנִי רֵאשִׁית דַּרְכּוֹ, קֶדֶם מִפְעָלָיו משלי ח
מֵאָז: שָׁמַיִם וָאָרֶץ מִנַּיִן, דִּכְתִיב: כֹּה אָמַר יהוה הַשָּׁמַיִם כִּסְאִי וְהָאָרֶץ ישעיה סו
הֲדֹם רַגְלָי, אֵי־זֶה בַיִת אֲשֶׁר תִּבְנוּ־לִי, וְאֵי־זֶה מָקוֹם מְנוּחָתִי: וְאוֹמֵר: מָה־ תהלים קד
רַבּוּ מַעֲשֶׂיךָ יהוה, כֻּלָּם בְּחָכְמָה עָשִׂיתָ, מָלְאָה הָאָרֶץ קִנְיָנֶךָ: אַבְרָהָם
מִנַּיִן, דִּכְתִיב: וַיְבָרְכֵהוּ וַיֹּאמַר, בָּרוּךְ אַבְרָם לְאֵל עֶלְיוֹן, קֹנֵה שָׁמַיִם וָאָרֶץ: בראשית יד
יִשְׂרָאֵל מִנַּיִן, דִּכְתִיב: עַד־יַעֲבֹר עַמְּךָ יהוה, עַד־יַעֲבֹר עַם־זוּ קָנִיתָ: וְאוֹמֵר: שמות טו
לִקְדוֹשִׁים אֲשֶׁר־בָּאָרֶץ הֵמָּה, וְאַדִּירֵי כָּל־חֶפְצִי־בָם: בֵּית הַמִּקְדָּשׁ מִנַּיִן, תהלים טז
דִּכְתִיב: מָכוֹן לְשִׁבְתְּךָ פָּעַלְתָּ יהוה, מִקְּדָשׁ אֲדֹנָי כּוֹנְנוּ יָדֶיךָ: וְאוֹמֵר: וַיְבִיאֵם שמות טו / תהלים עח
אֶל־גְּבוּל קָדְשׁוֹ, הַר־זֶה קָנְתָה יְמִינוֹ:

יא כָּל מַה שֶּׁבָּרָא הַקָּדוֹשׁ בָּרוּךְ הוּא בְּעוֹלָמוֹ, לֹא בְרָאוֹ אֶלָּא לִכְבוֹדוֹ, שֶׁנֶּאֱמַר:
כֹּל הַנִּקְרָא בִשְׁמִי וְלִכְבוֹדִי בְּרָאתִיו, יְצַרְתִּיו אַף־עֲשִׂיתִיו: וְאוֹמֵר: יהוה ישעיה מג / שמות טו
יִמְלֹךְ לְעֹלָם וָעֶד:

רַבִּי חֲנַנְיָא בֶּן עֲקַשְׁיָא אוֹמֵר: רָצָה הַקָּדוֹשׁ בָּרוּךְ הוּא לְזַכּוֹת אֶת יִשְׂרָאֵל, מכות כג.
לְפִיכָךְ הִרְבָּה לָהֶם תּוֹרָה וּמִצְוֹת. שֶׁנֶּאֱמַר: יהוה חָפֵץ לְמַעַן צִדְקוֹ, יַגְדִּיל תּוֹרָה ישעיה מב
וְיַאְדִּיר:

*If there is a* מנין*, mourners say the* קדיש דרבנן *(page 629).*

# Se'uda Shelishit for Shabbat

אַתְקִינוּ Prepare the feast of perfect faith, joy of the holy King.
Prepare the Royal feast,
this is the feast [mystically known as] "the Small Face,"
and "the Holy Ancient One" and "the Field of Holy Apples"
[mystical terms for aspects of the Divine]
come to partake in the feast with it.

Children of the palace
who yearn to see the radiance of "the Small Face,"
be here at this table in which the King is engraved.
Long to join this gathering together with the winged angels.
Rejoice now at this time of favor when there is no displeasure.
Come close to me, see my strength, for there are no harsh judgments:
Those brazen dogs are outside, unable to enter.
So I invite the holy Ancient of Days,
His brow of desire as the moment fades,
And His will is revealed, to annul all forces of impurity.
Hurl them into the abyss, hide them in the clefts of rocks,
For now, at Minḥa-time, is a time of joy for "the Small Face."

מִזְמוֹר לְדָוִד A psalm of David. *Ps. 23*
The Lord is my Shepherd, I shall not want.
He makes me lie down in green pastures.
He leads me beside the still waters.
He refreshes my soul.
He guides me in the paths of righteousness for His name's sake.
Though I walk through the valley of the shadow of death,
I will fear no evil, for You are with me;
Your rod and Your staff, they comfort me.
You set a table before me in the presence of my enemies;
You anoint my head with oil; my cup is filled to overflowing.
May goodness and kindness follow me all the days of my life,
and may I live in the House of the Lord for evermore.

# סעודה שלישית של שבת

אַתְקִינוּ סְעוּדָתָא דִמְהֵימְנוּתָא שְׁלִימְתָא, חֶדְוְתָא דְמַלְכָּא קַדִּישָׁא.
אַתְקִינוּ סְעוּדָתָא דְמַלְכָּא.
דָא הִיא סְעוּדָתָא דִזְעֵיר אַנְפִּין
וְעַתִּיקָא קַדִּישָׁא וַחֲקַל תַּפּוּחִין קַדִּישִׁין אָתַיִן לְסַעֲדָה בַּהֲדֵהּ.

בְּנֵי הֵיכְלָא, דִּכְסִיפִין לְמֶחֱזֵי זִיו זְעֵיר אַנְפִּין
יְהוֹן הָכָא, בְּהַאי תַּכָּא, דְּבֵהּ מַלְכָּא בְּגִלּוּפִין.
צְבוּ לַחְדָא, בְּהַאי וַעְדָא, בְּגוֹ עִירִין וְכָל גַּדְפִין.
חֲדוּ הַשְׁתָא, בְּהַאי שַׁעְתָא, דְּבֵהּ רַעֲוָא וְלֵית זַעְפִין.
קְרִיבוּ לִי, חֲזוּ חֵילִי, דְּלֵית דִּינִין דְּתַקִּיפִין.
לְבַר נַטְלִין, וְלָא עַלִּין, הָנֵי כַלְבִין דַּחֲצִיפִין.
וְהָא אַזְמִין עַתִּיק יוֹמִין, לְמִצְחֵהּ עַד יְהוֹן חַלְפִין.
רְעוּ דִי לֵהּ, דְּגַלֵּי לֵהּ, לְבַטָּלָה בְּכָל קְלִיפִין.
יְשַׁוֵּי לוֹן, בְּנִקְבֵּיהוֹן, וְיִטַּמְרוּן בְּגוֹ כֵפִין.
אֲרֵי הַשְׁתָא, בְּמִנְחֲתָא, בְּחֶדְוְתָא דִזְעֵיר אַנְפִּין.

מִזְמוֹר לְדָוִד, יהוה רֹעִי לֹא אֶחְסָר: תהלים כג
בִּנְאוֹת דֶּשֶׁא יַרְבִּיצֵנִי, עַל־מֵי מְנֻחוֹת יְנַהֲלֵנִי:
נַפְשִׁי יְשׁוֹבֵב, יַנְחֵנִי בְמַעְגְּלֵי־צֶדֶק לְמַעַן שְׁמוֹ:
גַּם כִּי־אֵלֵךְ בְּגֵיא צַלְמָוֶת לֹא־אִירָא רָע, כִּי־אַתָּה עִמָּדִי
שִׁבְטְךָ וּמִשְׁעַנְתֶּךָ הֵמָּה יְנַחֲמֻנִי:
תַּעֲרֹךְ לְפָנַי שֻׁלְחָן נֶגֶד צֹרְרָי, דִּשַּׁנְתָּ בַשֶּׁמֶן רֹאשִׁי, כּוֹסִי רְוָיָה:
אַךְ טוֹב וָחֶסֶד יִרְדְּפוּנִי כָּל־יְמֵי חַיָּי
וְשַׁבְתִּי בְּבֵית־יהוה לְאֹרֶךְ יָמִים:

יְדִיד Beloved of the soul, Father of compassion, draw Your servant close to Your will. Like a deer will Your servant run and fall prostrate before Your beauty. To him Your love is sweeter than honey from the comb, than any taste.

הָדוּר Glorious, beautiful, radiance of the world, my soul is sick with love for You. Please, God, heal her now by showing her Your tender radiance. Then she will recover her strength and be healed, Be Your servant for eternity.

וָתִיק Ancient of days, let Your mercy be aroused; please have pity on Your beloved child. How long have I yearned to see the glory of Your strength. Please, my God, my heart's desire – hasten; do not hide Yourself.

הִגָּלֶה Reveal Yourself, beloved, and spread over me the tabernacle of Your peace. Let the earth shine with Your glory, let us be overjoyed and rejoice in You. Hurry, beloved, for the appointed time has come, and be gracious to me as in the times of old.

אֵל מִסְתַּתֵּר God hides Himself in the beauty of concealment, His wisdom opaque to all human thought; Cause of causes, adorned with the highest crown, they [the angels] give You, Lord, a crown. In the beginning was Your primordial Torah, inscribed with Your hermetic wisdom. Where can it be found? It is hidden. Wisdom begins in awe of the Lord. Wider than a river, like never-ending streams, deep waters, that only an understanding man can draw, its outcomes are the fifty gates of understanding. The faithful are guarded by the Lord. Great God, all eyes are turned toward You. Your great kindness is higher than the heavens. God of Abraham, remember Your servant, I will tell of the Lord's kindness, sing praises to the Lord. Sublime, majestic in strength and might, who brings forth unparalleled light, "Awe of Isaac," make our judgment light. Forever, Lord, is Your might. Who is like You, God, doing great deeds, Mighty One of Jacob, awesome in praise, Splendor of Israel, who listens to prayers, Lord who listens to those in need. God, may the merit of the fathers be our shield. Eternal One of Israel, redeem us from distress. Draw us, raise us, from the pit of exile, that we may loudly sing in service at the House of the Lord. From right and left the prophets were inspired, finding within them Eternity and Glory, known by the names of Yakhin and Boaz, and all your children shall be learned of the Lord. Foundation, the Righteous, is hidden in Seven, the sign of the covenant to the world. Source of blessing, Righteous, Foundation of the world, righteous are You, Lord. Restore, please, David and Solomon's kingdom, with the crown with which his mother crowned it. The congregation of Israel is sweetly called a bride, a crown of splendor in the hand of the Lord. Mighty One, unite the ten Sefirot as one. Those who divide them from the Lord will see no light. Together they shine like sapphire. Bring my song close to You, the Lord.

*Birkat HaMazon can be found on page 1056.*

יְדִיד נֶפֶשׁ, אָב הָרַחֲמָן, מְשֹׁךְ עַבְדְּךָ אֶל רְצוֹנָךְ
יָרוּץ עַבְדְּךָ כְּמוֹ אַיָּל, יִשְׁתַּחֲוֶה מוּל הֲדָרָךְ
כִּי יֶעֱרַב לוֹ יְדִידוּתָךְ, מִנֹּפֶת צוּף וְכָל טָעַם.

הָדוּר, נָאֶה, זִיו הָעוֹלָם, נַפְשִׁי חוֹלַת אַהֲבָתָךְ
אָנָּא, אֵל נָא, רְפָא נָא לָהּ, בְּהַרְאוֹת לָהּ נֹעַם זִיוָךְ
אָז תִּתְחַזֵּק וְתִתְרַפֵּא, וְהָיְתָה לָךְ שִׁפְחַת עוֹלָם.

וָתִיק, יֶהֱמוּ רַחֲמֶיךָ, וְחוּס נָא עַל בֵּן אוֹהֲבָךְ
כִּי זֶה כַּמָּה נִכְסֹף נִכְסַף לִרְאוֹת בְּתִפְאֶרֶת עֻזָּךְ
אָנָּא, אֵלִי, מַחְמַד לִבִּי, חוּשָׁה נָּא, וְאַל תִּתְעַלָּם.

הִגָּלֶה נָא וּפְרֹשׂ, חָבִיב, עָלַי אֶת סֻכַּת שְׁלוֹמָךְ
תָּאִיר אֶרֶץ מִכְּבוֹדָךְ, נָגִילָה וְנִשְׂמְחָה בָךְ.
מַהֵר, אָהוּב, כִּי בָא מוֹעֵד, וְחָנֵּנִי כִּימֵי עוֹלָם.

אֵל מִסְתַּתֵּר בְּשַׁפְרִיר חֶבְיוֹן, הַשֵּׂכֶל הַנֶּעְלָם מִכָּל רַעְיוֹן, עִלַּת הָעִלּוֹת מֻכְתָּר בְּכֶתֶר עֶלְיוֹן, כֶּתֶר יִתְּנוּ לְךָ יהוה. בְּרֵאשִׁית תּוֹרָתְךָ הַקְּדוּמָה, רְשׁוּמָה חָכְמָתְךָ הַסְּתוּמָה, מֵאַיִן תִּמָּצֵא וְהִיא נֶעְלָמָה, רֵאשִׁית חָכְמָה יִרְאַת יהוה. רְחוֹבוֹת הַנָּהָר נַחֲלֵי אֱמוּנָה, מַיִם עֲמֻקִּים יִדְלֵם אִישׁ תְּבוּנָה, תּוֹצְאוֹתֶיהָ חֲמִשִּׁים שַׁעֲרֵי בִינָה, אֱמוּנִים נוֹצֵר יהוה. הָאֵל הַגָּדוֹל עֵינֵי כֹל נֶגְדֶּךָ, רַב חֶסֶד גָּדוֹל עַל הַשָּׁמַיִם חַסְדֶּךָ, אֱלֹהֵי אַבְרָהָם זְכֹר לְעַבְדֶּךָ, חַסְדֵי יהוה אַזְכִּיר תְּהִלּוֹת יהוה. מָרוֹם נֶאְדָּר בְּכֹחַ וּגְבוּרָה, מוֹצִיא אוֹרָה מֵאֵין תְּמוּרָה, פַּחַד יִצְחָק מִשְׁפָּטֵנוּ הָאִירָה, אַתָּה גִּבּוֹר לְעוֹלָם יהוה. מִי אֵל כָּמוֹךָ עוֹשֶׂה גְדוֹלוֹת, אֲבִיר יַעֲקֹב נוֹרָא תְהִלּוֹת, תִּפְאֶרֶת יִשְׂרָאֵל שׁוֹמֵעַ תְּפִלּוֹת, כִּי שׁוֹמֵעַ אֶל אֶבְיוֹנִים יהוה. יָהּ, זְכוּת אָבוֹת יָגֵן עָלֵינוּ, נֶצַח יִשְׂרָאֵל, מִצָּרוֹתֵינוּ גְּאָלֵנוּ, וּמִבּוֹר גָּלוּת דְּלֵנוּ וְהַעֲלֵנוּ, לְנַצֵּחַ עַל מְלֶאכֶת בֵּית יהוה. מִיָּמִין וּמִשְּׂמֹאל יְנִיקַת הַנְּבִיאִים, נֶצַח וָהוֹד מֵהֶם נִמְצָאִים, יָכִין וּבֹעַז בְּשֵׁם נִקְרָאִים, וְכָל בָּנַיִךְ לִמּוּדֵי יהוה. יְסוֹד צַדִּיק בְּשִׁבְעָה נֶעְלָם, אוֹת בְּרִית הוּא לְעוֹלָם, מַעְיַן הַבְּרָכָה צַדִּיק יְסוֹד עוֹלָם, צַדִּיק אַתָּה יהוה. נָא הָקֵם מַלְכוּת דָּוִד וּשְׁלֹמֹה, בָּעֲטָרָה שֶׁעִטְּרָה לוֹ אִמּוֹ, כְּנֶסֶת יִשְׂרָאֵל כַּלָּה קְרוּאָה בִּנְעִימָה, עֲטֶרֶת תִּפְאֶרֶת בְּיַד יהוה. חָזָק מְיַחֵד כְּאֶחָד עֶשֶׂר סְפִירוֹת, וּמַפְרִיד אַלּוּף לֹא יִרְאֶה מְאוֹרוֹת, סַפִּיר גִּזְרָתָם יַחַד מְאִירוֹת, תִּקְרַב רִנָּתִי לְפָנֶיךָ יהוה.

ברכת המזון *can be found on page 1057.*

# Ma'ariv for Motza'ei Shabbat

*In many congregations, the following two psalms are sung before Ma'ariv at the end of Shabbat.*

לְדָוִד Of David. Blessed is the LORD, my Rock, who trains my hands for war, my fingers for battle. He is my Benefactor, my Fortress, my Stronghold and my Refuge, my Shield in whom I trust, He who subdues nations under me. LORD, what is man that You care for him, what are mortals that You think of them? Man is no more than a breath, his days like a fleeting shadow. LORD, part Your heavens and come down; touch the mountains so that they pour forth smoke. Flash forth lightning and scatter them; shoot Your arrows and panic them. Reach out Your hand from on high; deliver me and rescue me from the mighty waters, from the hands of strangers, whose every word is worthless, whose right hands are raised in falsehood. To You, God, I will sing a new song; to You I will play music on a ten-stringed harp. He who gives salvation to kings, who saved His servant David from the cruel sword: may He deliver me and rescue me from the hands of strangers, whose every word is worthless, whose right hands are raised in falsehood. Then our sons will be like saplings, well nurtured in their youth. Our daughters will be like pillars carved for a palace. Our barns will be filled with every kind of provision. Our sheep will increase by thousands, even tens of thousands in our fields. Our oxen will draw heavy loads. There will be no breach in the walls, no going into captivity, no cries of distress in our streets. Happy are the people for whom this is so; happy are the people whose God is the LORD. *Ps. 144*

לַמְנַצֵּחַ For the conductor of music. With stringed instruments. A psalm, a song. May God be gracious to us and bless us. May He make His face shine on us, Selah. Then will Your way be known on earth, Your salvation among all the nations. Let the peoples praise You, God; let all peoples praise You. Let nations rejoice and sing for joy, for You judge the peoples with equity, and guide the nations of the earth, Selah. Let the peoples praise You, God; let all peoples praise You. The earth has yielded its harvest. May God, our God, bless us. God will bless us, and all the ends of the earth will fear Him. *Ps. 67*

*The service continues with Ma'ariv for Weekdays on page 314. After the Amida, the Leader says Half Kaddish and the congregation continues on the next page.*

# מעריב למוצאי שבת

*In many congregations, the following two psalms are sung before* מעריב *on* מוצאי שבת.

תהלים קמד
לְדָוִד, בָּרוּךְ יהוה צוּרִי, הַמְלַמֵּד יָדַי לַקְרָב, אֶצְבְּעוֹתַי לַמִּלְחָמָה:
חַסְדִּי וּמְצוּדָתִי מִשְׂגַּבִּי וּמְפַלְטִי לִי, מָגִנִּי וּבוֹ חָסִיתִי, הָרוֹדֵד
עַמִּי תַחְתָּי: יהוה מָה־אָדָם וַתֵּדָעֵהוּ, בֶּן־אֱנוֹשׁ וַתְּחַשְּׁבֵהוּ:
אָדָם לַהֶבֶל דָּמָה, יָמָיו כְּצֵל עוֹבֵר: יהוה הַט־שָׁמֶיךָ וְתֵרֵד,
גַּע בֶּהָרִים וְיֶעֱשָׁנוּ: בְּרוֹק בָּרָק וּתְפִיצֵם, שְׁלַח חִצֶּיךָ וּתְהֻמֵּם:
שְׁלַח יָדֶיךָ מִמָּרוֹם, פְּצֵנִי וְהַצִּילֵנִי מִמַּיִם רַבִּים, מִיַּד בְּנֵי נֵכָר:
אֲשֶׁר פִּיהֶם דִּבֶּר־שָׁוְא, וִימִינָם יְמִין שָׁקֶר: אֱלֹהִים שִׁיר חָדָשׁ
אָשִׁירָה לָּךְ, בְּנֵבֶל עָשׂוֹר אֲזַמְּרָה־לָּךְ: הַנּוֹתֵן תְּשׁוּעָה לַמְּלָכִים,
הַפּוֹצֶה אֶת־דָּוִד עַבְדּוֹ מֵחֶרֶב רָעָה: פְּצֵנִי וְהַצִּילֵנִי מִיַּד בְּנֵי נֵכָר,
אֲשֶׁר פִּיהֶם דִּבֶּר־שָׁוְא, וִימִינָם יְמִין שָׁקֶר: אֲשֶׁר בָּנֵינוּ כִּנְטִעִים,
מְגֻדָּלִים בִּנְעוּרֵיהֶם, בְּנוֹתֵינוּ כְזָוִיּוֹת, מְחֻטָּבוֹת תַּבְנִית הֵיכָל:
מְזָוֵינוּ מְלֵאִים, מְפִיקִים מִזַּן אֶל־זַן, צֹאונֵנוּ מַאֲלִיפוֹת מְרֻבָּבוֹת
בְּחוּצוֹתֵינוּ: אַלּוּפֵינוּ מְסֻבָּלִים, אֵין פֶּרֶץ וְאֵין יוֹצֵאת, וְאֵין צְוָחָה
בִּרְחֹבֹתֵינוּ: אַשְׁרֵי הָעָם שֶׁכָּכָה לּוֹ, אַשְׁרֵי הָעָם שֶׁיהוה אֱלֹהָיו:

תהלים סז
לַמְנַצֵּחַ בִּנְגִינֹת, מִזְמוֹר שִׁיר: אֱלֹהִים יְחָנֵּנוּ וִיבָרְכֵנוּ, יָאֵר פָּנָיו
אִתָּנוּ סֶלָה: לָדַעַת בָּאָרֶץ דַּרְכֶּךָ, בְּכָל־גּוֹיִם יְשׁוּעָתֶךָ: יוֹדוּךָ עַמִּים
אֱלֹהִים, יוֹדוּךָ עַמִּים כֻּלָּם: יִשְׂמְחוּ וִירַנְּנוּ לְאֻמִּים, כִּי־תִשְׁפֹּט
עַמִּים מִישֹׁר, וּלְאֻמִּים בָּאָרֶץ תַּנְחֵם סֶלָה: יוֹדוּךָ עַמִּים אֱלֹהִים,
יוֹדוּךָ עַמִּים כֻּלָּם: אֶרֶץ נָתְנָה יְבוּלָהּ, יְבָרְכֵנוּ אֱלֹהִים אֱלֹהֵינוּ:
יְבָרְכֵנוּ אֱלֹהִים, וְיִירְאוּ אוֹתוֹ כָּל־אַפְסֵי־אָרֶץ:

*The service continues with* מעריב לחול *on page 315. After the* עמידה, *the* שליח ציבור *says* חצי קדיש *and the* קהל *continues on the next page.*

וִיהִי נֹעַם May the pleasantness of the LORD our God be upon us. *Ps. 90*
Establish for us the work of our hands, O establish the work of our hands.

יֹשֵׁב He who lives in the shelter of the Most High dwells in the shadow *Ps. 91*
of the Almighty. I say of the LORD, my Refuge and Stronghold, my God in whom I trust, that He will save you from the fowler's snare and the deadly pestilence. With His pinions He will cover you, and beneath His wings you will find shelter; His faithfulness is an encircling shield. You need not fear terror by night, nor the arrow that flies by day; not the pestilence that stalks in darkness, nor the plague that ravages at noon. A thousand may fall at your side, ten thousand at your right hand, but it will not come near you. You will only look with your eyes and see the punishment of the wicked. Because you said, "The LORD is my Refuge," taking the Most High as your shelter, no harm will befall you, no plague come near your tent, for He will command His angels about you, to guard you in all your ways. They will lift you in their hands, lest your foot stumble on a stone. You will tread on lions and vipers; you will trample on young lions and snakes. [God says:] "Because he loves Me, I will rescue him; I will protect him, because he acknowledges My name. When he calls on Me, I will answer him; I will be with him in distress, I will deliver him and bring him honor.
▸ With long life I will satisfy him and show him My salvation.
With long life I will satisfy him and show him My salvation.

▸ You are the Holy One, enthroned on the praises of Israel. *Ps. 22*
And [the angels] call to one another, saying, "Holy, holy, holy *Is. 6*
is the LORD of hosts; the whole world is filled with His glory."
And they receive permission from one another, saying: *Targum Yonatan Is. 6*
"Holy in the highest heavens, home of His Presence; holy on earth, the work of His strength; holy for ever and all time is the LORD of hosts; the whole earth is full of His radiant glory."

---

hands,[1] and at the same time, we ask the Almighty to intercede on our behalf that forces of negativity, destructive elements, not oppose and impede our creation. (See above commentary to *Keri'at Shema' 'al ha-Mitah.*) (Editor)

1. Cf. Zedekiah ben Abraham Anav of Rome, *Shibbolei ha-Leket ha-Shalem*, ed. Samuel K. Mirsky (Brooklyn, NY: Sura, 1966), chap. 129 (pp. 424–427); *Tanya Rabbati*, chap. 21.

וִיהִי נֹעַם אֲדֹנָי אֱלֹהֵינוּ עָלֵינוּ וּמַעֲשֵׂה יָדֵינוּ כּוֹנְנָה עָלֵינוּ וּמַעֲשֵׂה יָדֵינוּ כּוֹנְנֵהוּ: תהלים צ

יֹשֵׁב בְּסֵתֶר עֶלְיוֹן, בְּצֵל שַׁדַּי יִתְלוֹנָן: אֹמַר לַיהוה מַחְסִי וּמְצוּדָתִי, תהלים צא
אֱלֹהַי אֶבְטַח־בּוֹ: כִּי הוּא יַצִּילְךָ מִפַּח יָקוּשׁ, מִדֶּבֶר הַוּוֹת:
בְּאֶבְרָתוֹ יָסֶךְ לָךְ, וְתַחַת־כְּנָפָיו תֶּחְסֶה, צִנָּה וְסֹחֵרָה אֲמִתּוֹ:
לֹא־תִירָא מִפַּחַד לָיְלָה, מֵחֵץ יָעוּף יוֹמָם: מִדֶּבֶר בָּאֹפֶל יַהֲלֹךְ,
מִקֶּטֶב יָשׁוּד צָהֳרָיִם: יִפֹּל מִצִּדְּךָ אֶלֶף, וּרְבָבָה מִימִינֶךָ, אֵלֶיךָ
לֹא יִגָּשׁ: רַק בְּעֵינֶיךָ תַבִּיט, וְשִׁלֻּמַת רְשָׁעִים תִּרְאֶה: כִּי־אַתָּה
יהוה מַחְסִי, עֶלְיוֹן שַׂמְתָּ מְעוֹנֶךָ: לֹא־תְאֻנֶּה אֵלֶיךָ רָעָה, וְנֶגַע
לֹא־יִקְרַב בְּאָהֳלֶךָ: כִּי מַלְאָכָיו יְצַוֶּה־לָּךְ, לִשְׁמָרְךָ בְּכָל־דְּרָכֶיךָ:
עַל־כַּפַּיִם יִשָּׂאוּנְךָ, פֶּן־תִּגֹּף בָּאֶבֶן רַגְלֶךָ: עַל־שַׁחַל וָפֶתֶן תִּדְרֹךְ,
תִּרְמֹס כְּפִיר וְתַנִּין: כִּי בִי חָשַׁק וַאֲפַלְּטֵהוּ, אֲשַׂגְּבֵהוּ כִּי־יָדַע
שְׁמִי: יִקְרָאֵנִי וְאֶעֱנֵהוּ, עִמּוֹ אָנֹכִי בְצָרָה, אֲחַלְּצֵהוּ וַאֲכַבְּדֵהוּ:
◂ אֹרֶךְ יָמִים אַשְׂבִּיעֵהוּ, וְאַרְאֵהוּ בִּישׁוּעָתִי:
אֹרֶךְ יָמִים אַשְׂבִּיעֵהוּ, וְאַרְאֵהוּ בִּישׁוּעָתִי:

◂ וְאַתָּה קָדוֹשׁ יוֹשֵׁב תְּהִלּוֹת יִשְׂרָאֵל: וְקָרָא זֶה אֶל־זֶה וְאָמַר תהלים כב
קָדוֹשׁ, קָדוֹשׁ, קָדוֹשׁ, יהוה צְבָאוֹת, מְלֹא כָל־הָאָרֶץ כְּבוֹדוֹ: ישעיה ו
וּמְקַבְּלִין דֵּין מִן דֵּין וְאָמְרִין, קַדִּישׁ בִּשְׁמֵי מְרוֹמָא עִלָּאָה בֵּית שְׁכִינְתֵּהּ תרגום יונתן ישעיה ו
קַדִּישׁ עַל אַרְעָא עוֹבַד גְּבוּרְתֵּהּ, קַדִּישׁ לְעָלַם וּלְעָלְמֵי עָלְמַיָּא
יהוה צְבָאוֹת, מַלְיָא כָל אַרְעָא זִיו יְקָרֵהּ.

---

וִיהִי נֹעַם *May the pleasantness.* The entire Sabbath we were prohibited from engaging in the thirty-nine categories of labor that went into the formation of the *Mishkan* or Tabernacle. With the conclusion of the Sabbath, we are about to go out to the work week to engage once again in the thirty-nine labors, which are our construction of the *Mishkan,* our contribution to the world. As Moses of old, we ask that the *Shekhinah* rest on the work of our

▸ Then a wind lifted me up and I heard behind me the sound of a great noise, saying, "Blessed is the LORD's glory from His place." *Ezek. 3*

Then a wind lifted me up and I heard behind me
the sound of a great tempest of those who uttered praise, saying,
"Blessed is the LORD's glory from the place of the home of His Presence." *Targum Yonatan Ezek. 3*

The LORD shall reign for ever and all time. *Ex. 15*
The LORD's kingdom is established for ever and all time. *Targum Onkelos Ex. 15*

יהוה LORD, God of Abraham, Isaac and Yisrael, our ancestors, may *1 Chr. 29*
You keep this for ever so that it forms the thoughts in Your people's
heart, and directs their heart toward You. He is compassionate. He *Ps. 78*
forgives iniquity and does not destroy. Repeatedly He suppresses His
anger, not rousing His full wrath. For You, my LORD, are good and *Ps. 86*
forgiving, abundantly kind to all who call on You. Your righteousness *Ps. 119*
is eternally righteous, and Your Torah is truth. Grant truth to Jacob, *Mic. 7*
loving-kindness to Abraham, as You promised our ancestors in ancient
times. Blessed is my LORD for day after day He burdens us [with His *Ps. 68*
blessings]; God is our salvation, Selah! The LORD of hosts is with us; the *Ps. 46*
God of Jacob is our refuge, Selah! LORD of hosts, happy is the one who *Ps. 84*
trusts in You. LORD, save! May the King answer us on the day we call. *Ps. 20*

בָּרוּךְ Blessed is He, our God, who created us for His glory, separating us from those who go astray; who gave us the Torah of truth, planting within us eternal life. May He open our heart to His Torah, imbuing our heart with the love and awe of Him, that we may do His will and serve Him with a perfect heart, so that we neither toil in vain nor give birth to confusion.

יְהִי רָצוֹן May it be Your will, O LORD our God and God of our ancestors, that we keep Your laws in this world, and thus be worthy to live,
see and inherit goodness and blessing in the Messianic Age and in the
life of the World to Come. So that my soul may sing to You and not *Ps. 30*
be silent. LORD, my God, for ever I will thank You. Blessed is the man *Jer. 17*
who trusts in the LORD, whose trust is in the LORD alone. Trust in the *Is. 26*
LORD for evermore, for God, the LORD, is an everlasting Rock. ▸ Those *Ps. 9*
who know Your name trust in You, for You, LORD, do not forsake those
who seek You. The LORD desired, for the sake of Israel's merit, to make *Is. 42*
the Torah great and glorious.

‹ וַתִּשָּׂאֵנִי רוּחַ, וָאֶשְׁמַע אַחֲרַי קוֹל רַעַשׁ גָּדוֹל  יחזקאל ג
בָּרוּךְ כְּבוֹד־יהוה מִמְּקוֹמוֹ:

וּנְטָלַתְנִי רוּחָא, וּשְׁמָעִית בַּתְרַי קָל זִיעַ סַגִּיא, דִּמְשַׁבְּחִין וְאָמְרִין  תרגום יונתן יחזקאל ג
בְּרִיךְ יְקָרָא דַיהוה מֵאֲתַר בֵּית שְׁכִינְתֵהּ.

יהוה יִמְלֹךְ לְעֹלָם וָעֶד:  שמות טו

יהוה מַלְכוּתֵהּ קָאֵם לְעָלַם וּלְעָלְמֵי עָלְמַיָּא.  תרגום אונקלוס שמות טו

יהוה אֱלֹהֵי אַבְרָהָם יִצְחָק וְיִשְׂרָאֵל אֲבֹתֵינוּ, שָׁמְרָה־זֹּאת לְעוֹלָם  דברי הימים א׳ כט
לְיֵצֶר מַחְשְׁבוֹת לְבַב עַמֶּךָ, וְהָכֵן לְבָבָם אֵלֶיךָ: וְהוּא רַחוּם יְכַפֵּר עָוֺן  תהלים עח
וְלֹא־יַשְׁחִית, וְהִרְבָּה לְהָשִׁיב אַפּוֹ, וְלֹא־יָעִיר כָּל־חֲמָתוֹ: כִּי־אַתָּה  תהלים פו
אֲדֹנָי טוֹב וְסַלָּח, וְרַב־חֶסֶד לְכָל־קֹרְאֶיךָ: צִדְקָתְךָ צֶדֶק לְעוֹלָם  תהלים קיט
וְתוֹרָתְךָ אֱמֶת: תִּתֵּן אֱמֶת לְיַעֲקֹב, חֶסֶד לְאַבְרָהָם, אֲשֶׁר־נִשְׁבַּעְתָּ  מיכה ז
לַאֲבֹתֵינוּ מִימֵי קֶדֶם: בָּרוּךְ אֲדֹנָי יוֹם יוֹם יַעֲמָס־לָנוּ, הָאֵל יְשׁוּעָתֵנוּ  תהלים סח
סֶלָה: יהוה צְבָאוֹת עִמָּנוּ, מִשְׂגָּב לָנוּ אֱלֹהֵי יַעֲקֹב סֶלָה: יהוה צְבָאוֹת,  תהלים מו תהלים פד
אַשְׁרֵי אָדָם בֹּטֵחַ בָּךְ: יהוה הוֹשִׁיעָה, הַמֶּלֶךְ יַעֲנֵנוּ בְיוֹם־קָרְאֵנוּ:  תהלים כ

בָּרוּךְ הוּא אֱלֹהֵינוּ שֶׁבְּרָאָנוּ לִכְבוֹדוֹ, וְהִבְדִּילָנוּ מִן הַתּוֹעִים, וְנָתַן לָנוּ תּוֹרַת אֱמֶת, וְחַיֵּי עוֹלָם נָטַע בְּתוֹכֵנוּ. הוּא יִפְתַּח לִבֵּנוּ בְּתוֹרָתוֹ, וְיָשֵׂם בְּלִבֵּנוּ אַהֲבָתוֹ וְיִרְאָתוֹ וְלַעֲשׂוֹת רְצוֹנוֹ וּלְעָבְדוֹ בְּלֵבָב שָׁלֵם, לְמַעַן לֹא נִיגַע לָרִיק וְלֹא נֵלֵד לַבֶּהָלָה.

יְהִי רָצוֹן מִלְּפָנֶיךָ יהוה אֱלֹהֵינוּ וֵאלֹהֵי אֲבוֹתֵינוּ, שֶׁנִּשְׁמֹר חֻקֶּיךָ
בָּעוֹלָם הַזֶּה, וְנִזְכֶּה וְנִחְיֶה וְנִרְאֶה וְנִירַשׁ טוֹבָה וּבְרָכָה, לִשְׁנֵי יְמוֹת
הַמָּשִׁיחַ וּלְחַיֵּי הָעוֹלָם הַבָּא. לְמַעַן יְזַמֶּרְךָ כָבוֹד וְלֹא יִדֹּם, יהוה  תהלים ל
אֱלֹהַי, לְעוֹלָם אוֹדֶךָּ: בָּרוּךְ הַגֶּבֶר אֲשֶׁר יִבְטַח בַּיהוה, וְהָיָה יהוה  ירמיה יז
מִבְטַחוֹ: בִּטְחוּ בַיהוה עֲדֵי־עַד, כִּי בְּיָהּ יהוה צוּר עוֹלָמִים: ‹ וְיִבְטְחוּ  ישעיה כו תהלים ט
בְךָ יוֹדְעֵי שְׁמֶךָ, כִּי לֹא־עָזַבְתָּ דֹרְשֶׁיךָ, יהוה: יהוה חָפֵץ לְמַעַן צִדְקוֹ,  ישעיה מב
יַגְדִּיל תּוֹרָה וְיַאְדִּיר:

FULL KADDISH

*Leader:* יִתְגַּדַּל Magnified and sanctified may His great name be,
in the world He created by His will.
May He establish His kingdom
in your lifetime and in your days,
and in the lifetime of all the house of Israel,
swiftly and soon –
and say: Amen.

*All:* May His great name be blessed for ever and all time.

*Leader:* Blessed and praised, glorified and exalted,
raised and honored, uplifted and lauded be
the name of the Holy One,
blessed be He,
beyond any blessing,
song, praise and consolation uttered in the world –
and say: Amen.

*On Purim and Tisha B'Av, omit the next verse*
*and continue with "May there be great peace."*

May the prayers and pleas of all Israel
be accepted by their Father in heaven –
and say: Amen.

May there be great peace from heaven,
and life for us and all Israel –
and say: Amen.

*Bow, take three steps back, as if taking leave of the Divine Presence,*
*then bow, first left, then right, then center, while saying:*

May He who makes peace in His high places,
make peace for us and all Israel –
and say: Amen.

*Between Pesaḥ and Shavuot the Omer is counted at this point on page 356.*

*On Ḥanukka, the candles are lit at this point, page 980.*

*On Tisha B'Av, the following prayers are omitted*
*and the service continues with Aleinu on page 764.*

## קדיש שלם

ש״ץ: יִתְגַּדַּל וְיִתְקַדַּשׁ שְׁמֵהּ רַבָּא (קהל: אָמֵן)
בְּעָלְמָא דִּי בְרָא כִרְעוּתֵהּ
וְיַמְלִיךְ מַלְכוּתֵהּ
בְּחַיֵּיכוֹן וּבְיוֹמֵיכוֹן וּבְחַיֵּי דְכָל בֵּית יִשְׂרָאֵל
בַּעֲגָלָא וּבִזְמַן קָרִיב, וְאִמְרוּ אָמֵן. (קהל: אָמֵן)

קהל וש״ץ: יְהֵא שְׁמֵהּ רַבָּא מְבָרַךְ לְעָלַם וּלְעָלְמֵי עָלְמַיָּא.

ש״ץ: יִתְבָּרַךְ וְיִשְׁתַּבַּח וְיִתְפָּאַר
וְיִתְרוֹמַם וְיִתְנַשֵּׂא וְיִתְהַדָּר וְיִתְעַלֶּה וְיִתְהַלָּל
שְׁמֵהּ דְּקֻדְשָׁא בְּרִיךְ הוּא (קהל: בְּרִיךְ הוּא)
לְעֵלָּא מִן כָּל בִּרְכָתָא / בעשרת ימי תשובה: לְעֵלָּא לְעֵלָּא מִכָּל בִּרְכָתָא/
וְשִׁירָתָא, תֻּשְׁבְּחָתָא וְנֶחֱמָתָא
דַּאֲמִירָן בְּעָלְמָא, וְאִמְרוּ אָמֵן. (קהל: אָמֵן)

*On* פורים *and* תשעה באב*, omit the next verse and continue with* יְהֵא שְׁלָמָא.

תִּתְקַבַּל צְלוֹתְהוֹן וּבָעוּתְהוֹן דְּכָל יִשְׂרָאֵל
קֳדָם אֲבוּהוֹן דִּי בִשְׁמַיָּא, וְאִמְרוּ אָמֵן. (קהל: אָמֵן)

יְהֵא שְׁלָמָא רַבָּא מִן שְׁמַיָּא
וְחַיִּים, עָלֵינוּ וְעַל כָּל יִשְׂרָאֵל, וְאִמְרוּ אָמֵן. (קהל: אָמֵן)

*Bow, take three steps back, as if taking leave of the Divine Presence, then bow, first left, then right, then center, while saying:*

עֹשֶׂה שָׁלוֹם/ בעשרת ימי תשובה: הַשָּׁלוֹם/ בִּמְרוֹמָיו
הוּא יַעֲשֶׂה שָׁלוֹם עָלֵינוּ וְעַל כָּל יִשְׂרָאֵל, וְאִמְרוּ אָמֵן. (קהל: אָמֵן)

*Between* פסח *and* שבועות *the* עומר *is counted at this point on page 357.*

*On* חנוכה*, the candles are lit at this point, page 981.*

*On* תשעה באב*, the following prayers are omitted and the service continues with* עָלֵינוּ *on page 765.*

## BIBLICAL VERSES OF BLESSING

וְיִתֶּן־לְךָ May God give you dew from heaven and the richness of the earth, and *Gen. 27*
corn and wine in plenty. May peoples serve you and nations bow down to you.
Be lord over your brothers, and may your mother's sons bow down to you.
A curse on those who curse you, but a blessing on those who bless you.

וְאֵל שַׁדַּי May God Almighty bless you; may He make you fruitful and numer- *Gen. 28*
ous until you become an assembly of peoples. May He give you and your
descendants the blessing of Abraham, that you may possess the land where
you are now staying, the land God gave to Abraham. This comes from the God *Gen. 49*
of your father – may He help you – and from the Almighty – may He bless
you with blessings of the heaven above and the blessings of the deep that lies
below, the blessings of breast and womb. The blessings of your father surpass
the blessings of my fathers to the bounds of the endless hills. May they rest on
the head of Joseph, on the brow of the prince among his brothers. He will love *Deut. 7*
you and bless you and increase your numbers. He will bless the fruit of your
womb and the fruit of your land: your corn, your wine and oil, the calves of
your herds and the lambs of your flocks, in the land He swore to your fathers to
give you. You will be blessed more than any other people. None of your men or
women will be childless, nor any of your livestock without young. The LORD
will keep you free from any disease. He will not inflict on you the terrible
diseases you knew in Egypt, but He will inflict them on those who hate you.

הַמַּלְאָךְ May the angel who rescued me from all harm, bless these boys. May they *Gen. 48*
be called by my name and the names of my fathers Abraham and Isaac, and may
they increase greatly on the earth. The LORD your God has increased your num- *Deut. 1*
bers so that today you are as many as the stars in the sky. May the LORD, God of
your fathers, increase you a thousand times, and bless you as He promised you.

בָּרוּךְ You will be blessed in the city, and blessed in the field. You will be blessed *Deut. 28*
when you come in, and blessed when you go out. Your basket and your knead-
ing trough will be blessed. The fruit of your womb will be blessed, and the
crops of your land, and the young of your livestock, the calves of your herds
and the lambs of your flocks. The LORD will send a blessing on your barns,
and on everything you put your hand to. The LORD your God will bless you
in the land He is giving you. The LORD will open for you the heavens, the
storehouse of His bounty, to send rain on your land in season, and to bless all
the work of your hands. You will lend to many nations but will borrow from
none. For the LORD your God will bless you as He has promised: you will lend *Deut. 15*
to many nations but will borrow from none. You will rule over many nations,
but none will rule over you. Happy are you, Israel! Who is like you, a people *Deut. 33*

פסוקי ברכה

בראשית כז וְיִתֶּן־לְךָ הָאֱלֹהִים מִטַּל הַשָּׁמַיִם וּמִשְׁמַנֵּי הָאָרֶץ, וְרֹב דָּגָן וְתִירשׁ: יַעַבְדוּךָ
עַמִּים וְיִשְׁתַּחֲוּ לְךָ לְאֻמִּים, הֱוֵה גְבִיר לְאַחֶיךָ וְיִשְׁתַּחֲווּ לְךָ בְּנֵי אִמֶּךָ,
אֹרְרֶיךָ אָרוּר וּמְבָרְכֶיךָ בָּרוּךְ:

בראשית כח וְאֵל שַׁדַּי יְבָרֵךְ אֹתְךָ וְיַפְרְךָ וְיַרְבֶּךָ, וְהָיִיתָ לִקְהַל עַמִּים: וְיִתֶּן־לְךָ אֶת־
בִּרְכַּת אַבְרָהָם, לְךָ וּלְזַרְעֲךָ אִתָּךְ, לְרִשְׁתְּךָ אֶת־אֶרֶץ מְגֻרֶיךָ אֲשֶׁר־נָתַן
בראשית מט אֱלֹהִים לְאַבְרָהָם: מֵאֵל אָבִיךָ וְיַעְזְרֶךָּ וְאֵת שַׁדַּי וִיבָרְכֶךָּ, בִּרְכֹת שָׁמַיִם
מֵעָל בִּרְכֹת תְּהוֹם רֹבֶצֶת תָּחַת, בִּרְכֹת שָׁדַיִם וָרָחַם: בִּרְכֹת אָבִיךָ גָּבְרוּ
עַל־בִּרְכֹת הוֹרַי עַד־תַּאֲוַת גִּבְעֹת עוֹלָם, תִּהְיֶיןָ לְרֹאשׁ יוֹסֵף וּלְקָדְקֹד
דברים ז נְזִיר אֶחָיו: וַאֲהֵבְךָ וּבֵרַכְךָ וְהִרְבֶּךָ, וּבֵרַךְ פְּרִי־בִטְנְךָ וּפְרִי־אַדְמָתֶךָ, דְּגָנְךָ
וְתִירשְׁךָ וְיִצְהָרֶךָ, שְׁגַר־אֲלָפֶיךָ וְעַשְׁתְּרֹת צֹאנֶךָ, עַל הָאֲדָמָה אֲשֶׁר־
נִשְׁבַּע לַאֲבֹתֶיךָ לָתֶת לָךְ: בָּרוּךְ תִּהְיֶה מִכָּל־הָעַמִּים, לֹא־יִהְיֶה בְךָ
עָקָר וַעֲקָרָה וּבִבְהֶמְתֶּךָ: וְהֵסִיר יהוה מִמְּךָ כָּל־חֹלִי, וְכָל־מַדְוֵי מִצְרַיִם
הָרָעִים אֲשֶׁר יָדַעְתָּ, לֹא יְשִׂימָם בָּךְ, וּנְתָנָם בְּכָל־שֹׂנְאֶיךָ:

בראשית מח הַמַּלְאָךְ הַגֹּאֵל אֹתִי מִכָּל־רָע יְבָרֵךְ אֶת־הַנְּעָרִים, וְיִקָּרֵא בָהֶם שְׁמִי
דברים א וְשֵׁם אֲבֹתַי אַבְרָהָם וְיִצְחָק, וְיִדְגּוּ לָרֹב בְּקֶרֶב הָאָרֶץ: יהוה אֱלֹהֵיכֶם
הִרְבָּה אֶתְכֶם, וְהִנְּכֶם הַיּוֹם כְּכוֹכְבֵי הַשָּׁמַיִם לָרֹב: יהוה אֱלֹהֵי אֲבוֹתֵיכֶם
יֹסֵף עֲלֵיכֶם כָּכֶם אֶלֶף פְּעָמִים, וִיבָרֵךְ אֶתְכֶם כַּאֲשֶׁר דִּבֶּר לָכֶם:

דברים כח בָּרוּךְ אַתָּה בָּעִיר, וּבָרוּךְ אַתָּה בַּשָּׂדֶה: בָּרוּךְ אַתָּה בְּבֹאֶךָ, וּבָרוּךְ אַתָּה
בְּצֵאתֶךָ: בָּרוּךְ טַנְאֲךָ וּמִשְׁאַרְתֶּךָ: בָּרוּךְ פְּרִי־בִטְנְךָ וּפְרִי אַדְמָתְךָ וּפְרִי
בְהֶמְתֶּךָ, שְׁגַר אֲלָפֶיךָ וְעַשְׁתְּרוֹת צֹאנֶךָ: יְצַו יהוה אִתְּךָ אֶת־הַבְּרָכָה
בַּאֲסָמֶיךָ וּבְכֹל מִשְׁלַח יָדֶךָ, וּבֵרַכְךָ בָּאָרֶץ אֲשֶׁר־יהוה אֱלֹהֶיךָ נֹתֵן לָךְ:
יִפְתַּח יהוה לְךָ אֶת־אוֹצָרוֹ הַטּוֹב אֶת־הַשָּׁמַיִם, לָתֵת מְטַר־אַרְצְךָ בְּעִתּוֹ,
דברים טו וּלְבָרֵךְ אֵת כָּל־מַעֲשֵׂה יָדֶךָ, וְהִלְוִיתָ גּוֹיִם רַבִּים וְאַתָּה לֹא תִלְוֶה: כִּי־יהוה
אֱלֹהֶיךָ בֵּרַכְךָ כַּאֲשֶׁר דִּבֶּר־לָךְ, וְהַעֲבַטְתָּ גּוֹיִם רַבִּים וְאַתָּה לֹא תַעֲבֹט,
דברים לג וּמָשַׁלְתָּ בְּגוֹיִם רַבִּים וּבְךָ לֹא יִמְשֹׁלוּ: אַשְׁרֶיךָ יִשְׂרָאֵל, מִי כָמוֹךָ, עַם

saved by the LORD? He is your Shield and Helper and your glorious Sword. Your enemies will cower before you, and you will tread on their high places.

מָחִיתִי I have wiped away your transgressions like a cloud, your sins like the morning mist. Return to Me for I have redeemed you. Sing for joy, O heavens, for the LORD has done this; shout aloud, you depths of the earth; burst into song, you mountains, you forests and all your trees, for the LORD has redeemed Jacob, and will glory in Israel. Our Redeemer, the LORD of hosts is His name, the Holy One of Israel. *Is. 44* *Is. 47*

יִשְׂרָאֵל Israel is saved by the LORD with everlasting salvation. You will never be ashamed or disgraced to time everlasting. You will eat your fill and praise the name of the LORD your God, who has worked wonders for you. Never again shall My people be shamed. Then you will know that I am in the midst of Israel, that I am the LORD your God, and there is no other. Never again will My people be shamed. You will go out in joy and be led out in peace. The mountains and hills will burst into song before you, and all the trees of the field will clap their hands. Behold, God is my salvation, I will trust and not be afraid. The LORD, the LORD, is my strength and my song. He has become my salvation. With joy you will draw water from the springs of salvation. On that day you will say, "Thank the LORD, proclaim His name, make His deeds known among the nations." Declare that His name is exalted. Sing to the LORD, for He has done glorious things; let this be known throughout the world. Shout aloud and sing for joy, you who dwell in Zion, for great in your midst is the Holy One of Israel. On that day they will say, "See, this is our God; we set our hope in Him and He saved us. This is the LORD in whom we hoped; let us rejoice and be glad in His salvation." *Is. 45* *Joel 2* *Is. 55* *Is. 12* *Is. 25*

בֵּית Come, house of Jacob: let us walk in the light of the LORD. He will be the sure foundation of your times; a rich store of salvation, wisdom and knowledge – the fear of the LORD is a person's treasure. In everything he did, David was successful, for the LORD was with him. *Is. 2* *Is. 32* *1 Sam. 18*

פָּדָה He redeemed my soul in peace from the battle waged against me, for the sake of the many who were with me. The people said to Saul, "Shall Jonathan die – he who has brought about this great deliverance in Israel? Heaven forbid! As surely as the LORD lives, not a hair of his head shall fall to the ground, for he did this today with God's help." So the people rescued Jonathan and he did not die. Those redeemed by the LORD shall return; they will enter Zion singing; everlasting joy will crown their heads. Gladness and joy will overtake them, and sorrow and sighing will flee away. *Ps. 55* *1 Sam. 14* *Is. 35*

נוֹשַׁע בַּיהוה, מָגֵן עֶזְרֶךָ וַאֲשֶׁר־חֶרֶב גַּאֲוָתֶךָ, וְיִכָּחֲשׁוּ אֹיְבֶיךָ לָךְ, וְאַתָּה
עַל־בָּמוֹתֵימוֹ תִדְרֹךְ:

מָחִיתִי כָעָב פְּשָׁעֶיךָ וְכֶעָנָן חַטֹּאותֶיךָ, שׁוּבָה אֵלַי כִּי גְאַלְתִּיךָ: רָנּוּ שָׁמַיִם ישעיה מד
כִּי־עָשָׂה יהוה, הָרִיעוּ תַּחְתִּיּוֹת אָרֶץ, פִּצְחוּ הָרִים רִנָּה, יַעַר וְכָל־עֵץ
בּוֹ, כִּי־גָאַל יהוה יַעֲקֹב וּבְיִשְׂרָאֵל יִתְפָּאָר: גֹּאֲלֵנוּ, יהוה צְבָאוֹת שְׁמוֹ, ישעיה מז
קְדוֹשׁ יִשְׂרָאֵל:

יִשְׂרָאֵל נוֹשַׁע בַּיהוה תְּשׁוּעַת עוֹלָמִים, לֹא־תֵבֹשׁוּ וְלֹא־תִכָּלְמוּ עַד־ ישעיה מה
עוֹלְמֵי עַד: וַאֲכַלְתֶּם אָכוֹל וְשָׂבוֹעַ, וְהִלַּלְתֶּם אֶת־שֵׁם יהוה אֱלֹהֵיכֶם יואל ב
אֲשֶׁר־עָשָׂה עִמָּכֶם לְהַפְלִיא, וְלֹא־יֵבֹשׁוּ עַמִּי לְעוֹלָם: וִידַעְתֶּם כִּי בְקֶרֶב
יִשְׂרָאֵל אָנִי, וַאֲנִי יהוה אֱלֹהֵיכֶם וְאֵין עוֹד, וְלֹא־יֵבֹשׁוּ עַמִּי לְעוֹלָם: כִּי־ ישעיה נה
בְשִׂמְחָה תֵצֵאוּ וּבְשָׁלוֹם תּוּבָלוּן, הֶהָרִים וְהַגְּבָעוֹת יִפְצְחוּ לִפְנֵיכֶם רִנָּה,
וְכָל־עֲצֵי הַשָּׂדֶה יִמְחֲאוּ־כָף: הִנֵּה אֵל יְשׁוּעָתִי אֶבְטַח, וְלֹא אֶפְחָד, כִּי־ ישעיה יב
עָזִּי וְזִמְרָת יָהּ יהוה, וַיְהִי־לִי לִישׁוּעָה: וּשְׁאַבְתֶּם־מַיִם בְּשָׂשׂוֹן, מִמַּעַיְנֵי
הַיְשׁוּעָה: וַאֲמַרְתֶּם בַּיּוֹם הַהוּא, הוֹדוּ לַיהוה קִרְאוּ בִשְׁמוֹ, הוֹדִיעוּ בָעַמִּים
עֲלִילֹתָיו, הַזְכִּירוּ כִּי נִשְׂגָּב שְׁמוֹ: זַמְּרוּ יהוה כִּי גֵאוּת עָשָׂה, מוּדַעַת זֹאת
בְּכָל־הָאָרֶץ: צַהֲלִי וָרֹנִּי יוֹשֶׁבֶת צִיּוֹן, כִּי־גָדוֹל בְּקִרְבֵּךְ קְדוֹשׁ יִשְׂרָאֵל:
וְאָמַר בַּיּוֹם הַהוּא, הִנֵּה אֱלֹהֵינוּ זֶה קִוִּינוּ לוֹ וְיוֹשִׁיעֵנוּ, זֶה יהוה קִוִּינוּ לוֹ, ישעיה כה
נָגִילָה וְנִשְׂמְחָה בִּישׁוּעָתוֹ:

בֵּית יַעֲקֹב לְכוּ וְנֵלְכָה בְּאוֹר יהוה: וְהָיָה אֱמוּנַת עִתֶּיךָ, חֹסֶן יְשׁוּעֹת ישעיה ב / ישעיה לג
חָכְמַת וָדָעַת, יִרְאַת יהוה הִיא אוֹצָרוֹ: וַיְהִי דָוִד לְכָל־דְּרָכָו מַשְׂכִּיל, שמואל א׳ יח
וַיהוה עִמּוֹ:

פָּדָה בְשָׁלוֹם נַפְשִׁי מִקְּרָב־לִי, כִּי־בְרַבִּים הָיוּ עִמָּדִי: וַיֹּאמֶר הָעָם אֶל־שָׁאוּל, תהלים נה / שמואל א׳ יד
הֲיוֹנָתָן יָמוּת אֲשֶׁר עָשָׂה הַיְשׁוּעָה הַגְּדוֹלָה הַזֹּאת בְּיִשְׂרָאֵל, חָלִילָה, חַי־
יהוה אִם־יִפֹּל מִשַּׂעֲרַת רֹאשׁוֹ אַרְצָה, כִּי־עִם־אֱלֹהִים עָשָׂה הַיּוֹם הַזֶּה,
וַיִּפְדּוּ הָעָם אֶת־יוֹנָתָן וְלֹא־מֵת: וּפְדוּיֵי יהוה יְשֻׁבוּן וּבָאוּ צִיּוֹן בְּרִנָּה, ישעיה לה
וְשִׂמְחַת עוֹלָם עַל־רֹאשָׁם, שָׂשׂוֹן וְשִׂמְחָה יַשִּׂיגוּ, וְנָסוּ יָגוֹן וַאֲנָחָה:

הָפַכְתָּ You have turned my sorrow into dancing. You have removed my sackcloth *Ps. 30*
and clothed me with joy. The LORD your God refused to listen to Balaam; in- *Deut. 23*
stead the LORD your God turned the curse into a blessing, for the LORD your
God loves you. Then maidens will dance and be glad; so too will young men and *Jer. 31*
old together; I will turn their mourning into gladness; I will give them comfort
and joy instead of sorrow.

בּוֹרֵא I create the speech of lips: Peace, peace to those far and near, says the LORD, *Is. 57*
and I will heal them. Then the spirit came upon Amasai, chief of the captains, *1 Chr. 12*
and he said: "We are yours, David! We are with you, son of Jesse! Peace, peace to
you, and peace to those who help you; for your God will help you." Then David
received them and made them leaders of his troop. And you shall say: "To life! *1 Sam. 25*
Peace be to you, peace to your household, and peace to all that is yours!" The *Ps. 29*
LORD will give strength to His people; the LORD will bless His people with peace.

אָמַר Rabbi Yoḥanan said: Wherever you find the greatness of the Holy One, *Megilla 31a*
blessed be He, there you find His humility. This is written in the Torah, repeated
in the Prophets, and stated a third time in the Writings. It is written in the
Torah: "For the LORD your God is God of gods and LORD of lords, the great, *Deut. 10*
mighty and awe-inspiring God, who shows no favoritism and accepts no bribe."
Immediately afterwards it is written, "He upholds the cause of the orphan and
widow, and loves the stranger, giving him food and clothing." It is repeated in
the Prophets, as it says: "So says the High and Exalted One, who lives for ever *Is. 57*
and whose name is Holy: I live in a high and holy place, but also with the con-
trite and lowly in spirit, to revive the spirit of the lowly, and to revive the heart of
the contrite." It is stated a third time in the Writings: "Sing to God, make music *Ps. 68*
for His name, extol Him who rides the clouds – the LORD is His name – and
exult before Him." Immediately afterwards it is written: "Father of the orphans
and Justice of widows, is God in His holy habitation."

יְהִי May the LORD our God be with us, as He was with our ancestors. May He *1 Kings 8*
never abandon us or forsake us. You who cleave to the LORD your God are all alive *Deut. 4*
this day. For the LORD will comfort Zion, He will comfort all her ruins; He will *Is. 51*
make her wilderness like Eden, and her desert like a garden of the LORD. Joy and
gladness will be found there, thanksgiving and the sound of singing. It pleased the *Is. 42*
LORD for the sake of [Israel's] righteousness to make the Torah great and glorious.

שִׁיר הַמַּעֲלוֹת A song of ascents. Happy are all who fear the LORD, who walk in *Ps. 128*
His ways. When you eat the fruit of your labor, happy and fortunate are you.
Your wife shall be like a fruitful vine within your house; your sons like olive sap-
lings around your table. So shall the man who fears the LORD be blessed. May
the LORD bless you from Zion; may you see the good of Jerusalem all the days
of your life; and may you live to see your children's children. Peace be on Israel!

הָפַכְתָּ מִסְפְּדִי לְמָחוֹל לִי, פִּתַּחְתָּ שַׂקִּי, וַתְּאַזְּרֵנִי שִׂמְחָה: וְלֹא־אָבָה יהוה תהלים ל / דברים כג
אֱלֹהֶיךָ לִשְׁמֹעַ אֶל־בִּלְעָם, וַיַּהֲפֹךְ יהוה אֱלֹהֶיךָ לְּךָ אֶת־הַקְּלָלָה לִבְרָכָה,
כִּי אֲהֵבְךָ יהוה אֱלֹהֶיךָ: אָז תִּשְׂמַח בְּתוּלָה בְּמָחוֹל, וּבַחֻרִים וּזְקֵנִים יַחְדָּו, ירמיה לא
וְהָפַכְתִּי אֶבְלָם לְשָׂשׂוֹן, וְנִחַמְתִּים, וְשִׂמַּחְתִּים מִיגוֹנָם:

בּוֹרֵא נִיב שְׂפָתָיִם, שָׁלוֹם שָׁלוֹם לָרָחוֹק וְלַקָּרוֹב אָמַר יהוה, וּרְפָאתִיו: וְרוּחַ ישעיה נז / דברי הימים א׳ יב
לָבְשָׁה אֶת־עֲמָשַׂי רֹאשׁ הַשָּׁלִישִׁים, לְךָ דָוִיד וְעִמְּךָ בֶן־יִשַׁי, שָׁלוֹם שָׁלוֹם
לְךָ וְשָׁלוֹם לְעֹזְרֶךָ, כִּי עֲזָרְךָ אֱלֹהֶיךָ, וַיְקַבְּלֵם דָּוִיד וַיִּתְּנֵם בְּרָאשֵׁי הַגְּדוּד:
וַאֲמַרְתֶּם כֹּה לֶחָי, וְאַתָּה שָׁלוֹם וּבֵיתְךָ שָׁלוֹם וְכֹל אֲשֶׁר־לְךָ שָׁלוֹם: יהוה שמואל א׳ כה / תהלים כט
עֹז לְעַמּוֹ יִתֵּן, יהוה יְבָרֵךְ אֶת־עַמּוֹ בַשָּׁלוֹם:

אָמַר רַבִּי יוֹחָנָן: בְּכָל מָקוֹם שֶׁאַתָּה מוֹצֵא גְּדֻלָּתוֹ שֶׁל הַקָּדוֹשׁ בָּרוּךְ מגילה לא.
הוּא, שָׁם אַתָּה מוֹצֵא עַנְוְתָנוּתוֹ. דָּבָר זֶה כָּתוּב בַּתּוֹרָה, וְשָׁנוּי בַּנְּבִיאִים,
וּמְשֻׁלָּשׁ בַּכְּתוּבִים. כָּתוּב בַּתּוֹרָה: כִּי יהוה אֱלֹהֵיכֶם הוּא אֱלֹהֵי הָאֱלֹהִים דברים י
וַאֲדֹנֵי הָאֲדֹנִים, הָאֵל הַגָּדֹל הַגִּבֹּר וְהַנּוֹרָא, אֲשֶׁר לֹא־יִשָּׂא פָנִים וְלֹא יִקַּח
שֹׁחַד: וּכְתִיב בַּתְרֵהּ: עֹשֶׂה מִשְׁפַּט יָתוֹם וְאַלְמָנָה, וְאֹהֵב גֵּר לָתֶת לוֹ לֶחֶם
וְשִׂמְלָה: שָׁנוּי בַּנְּבִיאִים, דִּכְתִיב: כִּי כֹה אָמַר רָם וְנִשָּׂא שֹׁכֵן עַד וְקָדוֹשׁ ישעיה נז
שְׁמוֹ, מָרוֹם וְקָדוֹשׁ אֶשְׁכּוֹן, וְאֶת־דַּכָּא וּשְׁפַל־רוּחַ, לְהַחֲיוֹת רוּחַ שְׁפָלִים
וּלְהַחֲיוֹת לֵב נִדְכָּאִים: מְשֻׁלָּשׁ בַּכְּתוּבִים, דִּכְתִיב: שִׁירוּ לֵאלֹהִים, זַמְּרוּ תהלים סח
שְׁמוֹ, סֹלּוּ לָרֹכֵב בָּעֲרָבוֹת בְּיָהּ שְׁמוֹ, וְעִלְזוּ לְפָנָיו: וּכְתִיב בַּתְרֵהּ: אֲבִי
יְתוֹמִים וְדַיַּן אַלְמָנוֹת, אֱלֹהִים בִּמְעוֹן קָדְשׁוֹ:

יְהִי יהוה אֱלֹהֵינוּ עִמָּנוּ כַּאֲשֶׁר הָיָה עִם־אֲבֹתֵינוּ, אַל־יַעַזְבֵנוּ וְאַל־יִטְּשֵׁנוּ: מלכים א׳ ח
וְאַתֶּם הַדְּבֵקִים בַּיהוה אֱלֹהֵיכֶם, חַיִּים כֻּלְּכֶם הַיּוֹם: כִּי־נִחַם יהוה צִיּוֹן, נִחַם דברים ד / ישעיה נא
כָּל־חָרְבֹתֶיהָ, וַיָּשֶׂם מִדְבָּרָהּ כְּעֵדֶן וְעַרְבָתָהּ כְּגַן־יהוה, שָׂשׂוֹן וְשִׂמְחָה יִמָּצֵא
בָהּ, תּוֹדָה וְקוֹל זִמְרָה: יהוה חָפֵץ לְמַעַן צִדְקוֹ, יַגְדִּיל תּוֹרָה וְיַאְדִּיר: ישעיה מב

שִׁיר הַמַּעֲלוֹת, אַשְׁרֵי כָּל־יְרֵא יהוה, הַהֹלֵךְ בִּדְרָכָיו: יְגִיעַ כַּפֶּיךָ כִּי תֹאכֵל, תהלים קכח
אַשְׁרֶיךָ וְטוֹב לָךְ: אֶשְׁתְּךָ כְּגֶפֶן פֹּרִיָּה בְּיַרְכְּתֵי בֵיתֶךָ, בָּנֶיךָ כִּשְׁתִלֵי זֵיתִים,
סָבִיב לְשֻׁלְחָנֶךָ: הִנֵּה כִי־כֵן יְבֹרַךְ גָּבֶר יְרֵא יהוה: יְבָרֶכְךָ יהוה מִצִּיּוֹן, וּרְאֵה
בְּטוּב יְרוּשָׁלָיִם, כֹּל יְמֵי חַיֶּיךָ: וּרְאֵה־בָנִים לְבָנֶיךָ, שָׁלוֹם עַל־יִשְׂרָאֵל:

## HAVDALA IN THE SYNAGOGUE

*Some say the full Havdala on page 782.*

*On Motza'ei Yom Tov that is not a Motza'ei Shabbat, the blessings for the spices and flame are omitted. At the end of Yom Kippur, only the blessing for the spices is omitted. See laws 468, 469, 471.*

*The Leader takes the cup of wine in his right hand, and says:*

Please pay attention, my masters.

Blessed are You, LORD our God, King of the Universe, who creates the fruit of the vine.

*Holding the spice box, the Leader says:*

Blessed are You, LORD our God, King of the Universe, who creates the various spices.

*The Leader smells the spices and puts the spice box down.*

*He lifts his hands toward the flame of the Havdala candle, and says:*

Blessed are You, LORD our God, King of the Universe, who creates the lights of fire.

*He lifts the cup of wine in his right hand, and says:*

Blessed are You, LORD our God, King of the Universe, who distinguishes between sacred and secular, between light and darkness, between Israel and the nations, between the seventh day and the six days of work. Blessed are You, LORD, who distinguishes between sacred and secular.

*Stand while saying Aleinu. Bow at ▾.*

עָלֵינוּ It is our duty to praise the Master of all,
and ascribe greatness to the Author of creation,
who has not made us like the nations of the lands
nor placed us like the families of the earth;
who has not made our portion like theirs,
nor our destiny like all their multitudes.
(For they worship vanity and emptiness,
and pray to a god who cannot save.)
▾But we bow in worship and thank the Supreme King of kings,
the Holy One, blessed be He,
who extends the heavens and establishes the earth,
whose throne of glory is in the heavens above,
and whose power's Presence is in the highest of heights.
He is our God; there is no other.
Truly He is our King, there is none else, as it is written in His Torah:
"You shall know and take to heart this day that the LORD is God, *Deut. 4*
in heaven above and on earth below. There is no other."

# הבדלה בבית הכנסת

*Some say the full* הבדלה *on page 783.*

*Some say the full* הבדלה *on page 783.*

*On* מוצאי יום טוב *that is not a* מוצאי שבת*, the blessings for the spices and flame are omitted. At the end of* יום כפור*, only the blessing for the spices is omitted. See laws 468, 469, 471.*

*The* שליח ציבור *takes the cup of wine in his right hand, and says:*

סַבְרִי מָרָנָן

בָּרוּךְ אַתָּה יהוה אֱלֹהֵינוּ מֶלֶךְ הָעוֹלָם, בּוֹרֵא פְּרִי הַגָּפֶן.

*Holding the spice box, the* שליח ציבור *says:*

בָּרוּךְ אַתָּה יהוה אֱלֹהֵינוּ מֶלֶךְ הָעוֹלָם, בּוֹרֵא מִינֵי בְשָׂמִים.

*The* שליח ציבור *smells the spices and puts the spice box down.*

*He lifts his hands toward the flame of the* הבדלה *candle, and says:*

בָּרוּךְ אַתָּה יהוה אֱלֹהֵינוּ מֶלֶךְ הָעוֹלָם, בּוֹרֵא מְאוֹרֵי הָאֵשׁ.

*He lifts the cup of wine in his right hand, and says:*

בָּרוּךְ אַתָּה יהוה אֱלֹהֵינוּ מֶלֶךְ הָעוֹלָם, הַמַּבְדִּיל בֵּין קֹדֶשׁ לְחֹל, בֵּין אוֹר לְחֹשֶׁךְ, בֵּין יִשְׂרָאֵל לָעַמִּים, בֵּין יוֹם הַשְּׁבִיעִי לְשֵׁשֶׁת יְמֵי הַמַּעֲשֶׂה. בָּרוּךְ אַתָּה יהוה, הַמַּבְדִּיל בֵּין קֹדֶשׁ לְחֹל.

*Stand while saying* עָלֵינוּ*. Bow at* ▾*.*

עָלֵינוּ לְשַׁבֵּחַ לַאֲדוֹן הַכֹּל, לָתֵת גְּדֻלָּה לְיוֹצֵר בְּרֵאשִׁית\
שֶׁלֹּא עָשָׂנוּ כְּגוֹיֵי הָאֲרָצוֹת, וְלֹא שָׂמָנוּ כְּמִשְׁפְּחוֹת הָאֲדָמָה\
שֶׁלֹּא שָׂם חֶלְקֵנוּ כָּהֶם וְגוֹרָלֵנוּ כְּכָל הֲמוֹנָם.\
(שֶׁהֵם מִשְׁתַּחֲוִים לְהֶבֶל וָרִיק וּמִתְפַּלְלִים אֶל אֵל לֹא יוֹשִׁיעַ.)\
▾וַאֲנַחְנוּ כּוֹרְעִים וּמִשְׁתַּחֲוִים וּמוֹדִים\
לִפְנֵי מֶלֶךְ מַלְכֵי הַמְּלָכִים, הַקָּדוֹשׁ בָּרוּךְ הוּא\
שֶׁהוּא נוֹטֶה שָׁמַיִם וְיוֹסֵד אָרֶץ\
וּמוֹשַׁב יְקָרוֹ בַּשָּׁמַיִם מִמַּעַל, וּשְׁכִינַת עֻזּוֹ בְּגָבְהֵי מְרוֹמִים.\
הוּא אֱלֹהֵינוּ, אֵין עוֹד.\
אֱמֶת מַלְכֵּנוּ, אֶפֶס זוּלָתוֹ, כַּכָּתוּב בְּתוֹרָתוֹ\
דברים ד וְיָדַעְתָּ הַיּוֹם וַהֲשֵׁבֹתָ אֶל־לְבָבֶךָ\
כִּי יהוה הוּא הָאֱלֹהִים בַּשָּׁמַיִם מִמַּעַל וְעַל־הָאָרֶץ מִתָּחַת, אֵין עוֹד:

Therefore, we place our hope in You, LORD our God,
that we may soon see the glory of Your power,
when You will remove abominations from the earth,
and idols will be utterly destroyed,
when the world will be perfected under the sovereignty of the Almighty,
when all humanity will call on Your name,
to turn all the earth's wicked toward You.
All the world's inhabitants will realize and know
that to You every knee must bow and every tongue swear loyalty.
Before You, LORD our God, they will kneel and bow down
and give honor to Your glorious name.
They will all accept the yoke of Your kingdom,
and You will reign over them soon and for ever.
For the kingdom is Yours, and to all eternity You will reign in glory,
as it is written in Your Torah: "The LORD will reign for ever and ever." *Ex. 15*
▸ And it is said: "Then the LORD shall be King over all the earth; *Zech. 14*
on that day the LORD shall be One and His name One."

*Some add:*

Have no fear of sudden terror or of the ruin when it overtakes the wicked. *Prov. 3*
Devise your strategy, but it will be thwarted; propose your plan, *Is. 8*
but it will not stand, for God is with us. When you grow old, I will still be the same. *Is. 46*
When your hair turns gray, I will still carry you. I made you, I will bear you,
I will carry you, and I will rescue you.

## MOURNER'S KADDISH

*The following prayer, said by mourners, requires the presence of a minyan.*
*A transliteration can be found on page 1320.*

*Mourner:* יִתְגַּדַּל Magnified and sanctified may His great name be,
in the world He created by His will.
May He establish His kingdom
in your lifetime and in your days,
and in the lifetime of all the house of Israel,
swiftly and soon – and say: Amen.

*All:* May His great name be blessed for ever and all time.

*Mourner:* Blessed and praised, glorified and exalted,
raised and honored, uplifted and lauded
be the name of the Holy One, blessed be He,

עַל כֵּן נְקַוֶּה לְּךָ יהוה אֱלֹהֵינוּ, לִרְאוֹת מְהֵרָה בְּתִפְאֶרֶת עֻזֶּךָ
לְהַעֲבִיר גִּלּוּלִים מִן הָאָרֶץ, וְהָאֱלִילִים כָּרוֹת יִכָּרֵתוּן
לְתַקֵּן עוֹלָם בְּמַלְכוּת שַׁדַּי.
וְכָל בְּנֵי בָשָׂר יִקְרְאוּ בִשְׁמֶךָ לְהַפְנוֹת אֵלֶיךָ כָּל רִשְׁעֵי אָרֶץ.
יַכִּירוּ וְיֵדְעוּ כָּל יוֹשְׁבֵי תֵבֵל, כִּי לְךָ תִּכְרַע כָּל בֶּרֶךְ, תִּשָּׁבַע כָּל לָשׁוֹן.
לְפָנֶיךָ יהוה אֱלֹהֵינוּ יִכְרְעוּ וְיִפֹּלוּ, וְלִכְבוֹד שִׁמְךָ יְקָר יִתֵּנוּ
וִיקַבְּלוּ כֻלָּם אֶת עֹל מַלְכוּתֶךָ וְתִמְלֹךְ עֲלֵיהֶם מְהֵרָה לְעוֹלָם וָעֶד.
כִּי הַמַּלְכוּת שֶׁלְּךָ הִיא וּלְעוֹלְמֵי עַד תִּמְלֹךְ בְּכָבוֹד
כַּכָּתוּב בְּתוֹרָתֶךָ, יהוה יִמְלֹךְ לְעֹלָם וָעֶד: שמות טו
◂ וְנֶאֱמַר, וְהָיָה יהוה לְמֶלֶךְ עַל־כָּל־הָאָרֶץ זכריה יד
בַּיּוֹם הַהוּא יִהְיֶה יהוה אֶחָד וּשְׁמוֹ אֶחָד:

*Some add:*

אַל־תִּירָא מִפַּחַד פִּתְאֹם וּמִשֹּׁאַת רְשָׁעִים כִּי תָבֹא: משלי ג
עֻצוּ עֵצָה וְתֻפָר, דַּבְּרוּ דָבָר וְלֹא יָקוּם, כִּי עִמָּנוּ אֵל: ישעיה ח
וְעַד־זִקְנָה אֲנִי הוּא, וְעַד־שֵׂיבָה אֲנִי אֶסְבֹּל, אֲנִי עָשִׂיתִי וַאֲנִי אֶשָּׂא וַאֲנִי אֶסְבֹּל וַאֲמַלֵּט: ישעיה מו

## קדיש יתום

*The following prayer, said by mourners, requires the presence of a* מנין*.*
*A transliteration can be found on page 1320.*

אבל: יִתְגַּדַּל וְיִתְקַדַּשׁ שְׁמֵהּ רַבָּא (קהל: אָמֵן)
בְּעָלְמָא דִּי בְרָא כִרְעוּתֵהּ
וְיַמְלִיךְ מַלְכוּתֵהּ
בְּחַיֵּיכוֹן וּבְיוֹמֵיכוֹן וּבְחַיֵּי דְכָל בֵּית יִשְׂרָאֵל
בַּעֲגָלָא וּבִזְמַן קָרִיב, וְאִמְרוּ אָמֵן. (קהל: אָמֵן)

קהל ואבל: יְהֵא שְׁמֵהּ רַבָּא מְבָרַךְ לְעָלַם וּלְעָלְמֵי עָלְמַיָּא.

אבל: יִתְבָּרַךְ וְיִשְׁתַּבַּח וְיִתְפָּאַר
וְיִתְרוֹמַם וְיִתְנַשֵּׂא וְיִתְהַדָּר וְיִתְעַלֶּה וְיִתְהַלָּל
שְׁמֵהּ דְּקֻדְשָׁא בְּרִיךְ הוּא (קהל: בְּרִיךְ הוּא)

beyond any blessing,
song, praise and consolation
uttered in the world –
and say: Amen.

May there be great peace from heaven,
and life for us and all Israel –
and say: Amen.

*Bow, take three steps back, as if taking leave of the Divine Presence, then bow, first left, then right, then center, while saying:*

May He who makes peace in His high places,
make peace for us and all Israel –
and say: Amen.

*From the second day of Rosh Ḥodesh Elul through Shemini Atzeret (in Israel through Hoshana Raba), the following psalm is said:*

לְדָוִד By David. The LORD is my light and my salvation – whom then shall Ps. 27
I fear? The LORD is the stronghold of my life – of whom shall I be afraid? When evil men close in on me to devour my flesh, it is they, my enemies and foes, who stumble and fall. Should an army besiege me, my heart would not fear. Should war break out against me, still I would be confident. One thing I ask of the LORD, only this do I seek: to live in the House of the LORD all the days of my life, to gaze on the beauty of the LORD and worship in His Temple. For He will keep me safe in His pavilion on the day of trouble. He will hide me under the cover of His tent. He will set me high upon a rock. Now my head is high above my enemies who surround me. I will sacrifice in His tent with shouts of joy. I will sing and chant praises to the LORD. LORD, hear my voice when I call. Be gracious to me and answer me. On Your behalf my heart says, "Seek My face." Your face, LORD, will I seek. Do not hide Your face from me. Do not turn Your servant away in anger. You have been my help. Do not reject or forsake me, God, my Savior. Were my father and my mother to forsake me, the LORD would take me in. Teach me Your way, LORD, and lead me on a level path, because of my oppressors. Do not abandon me to the will of my foes, for false witnesses have risen against me, breathing violence. ▸ Were it not for my faith that I shall see the LORD's goodness in the land of the living. Hope in the LORD. Be strong and of good courage, and hope in the LORD!

*Mourner's Kaddish* (*previous page*)

*In a house of mourning the service continues on page 1138.*

לְעֵלָּא מִן כָּל בִּרְכָתָא / בעשרת ימי תשובה: לְעֵלָּא לְעֵלָּא מִכָּל בִּרְכָתָא/
וְשִׁירָתָא, תֻּשְׁבְּחָתָא וְנֶחֱמָתָא
דַּאֲמִירָן בְּעָלְמָא, וְאִמְרוּ אָמֵן. (קהל: אָמֵן)

יְהֵא שְׁלָמָא רַבָּא מִן שְׁמַיָּא
וְחַיִּים, עָלֵינוּ וְעַל כָּל יִשְׂרָאֵל, וְאִמְרוּ אָמֵן. (קהל: אָמֵן)

*Bow, take three steps back, as if taking leave of the Divine Presence, then bow, first left, then right, then center, while saying:*

עֹשֶׂה שָׁלוֹם/ בעשרת ימי תשובה: הַשָּׁלוֹם / בִּמְרוֹמָיו
הוּא יַעֲשֶׂה שָׁלוֹם עָלֵינוּ וְעַל כָּל יִשְׂרָאֵל, וְאִמְרוּ אָמֵן. (קהל: אָמֵן)

*From the second day of* ראש חודש אלול *through* שמיני עצרת
*(in* ארץ ישראל *through* הושענא רבה*), the following psalm is said:*

תהלים כז
לְדָוִד, יהוה אוֹרִי וְיִשְׁעִי, מִמִּי אִירָא, יהוה מָעוֹז־חַיַּי, מִמִּי אֶפְחָד: בִּקְרֹב עָלַי מְרֵעִים לֶאֱכֹל אֶת־בְּשָׂרִי, צָרַי וְאֹיְבַי לִי, הֵמָּה כָשְׁלוּ וְנָפָלוּ: אִם־תַּחֲנֶה עָלַי מַחֲנֶה, לֹא־יִירָא לִבִּי, אִם־תָּקוּם עָלַי מִלְחָמָה, בְּזֹאת אֲנִי בוֹטֵחַ: אַחַת שָׁאַלְתִּי מֵאֵת־יהוה, אוֹתָהּ אֲבַקֵּשׁ, שִׁבְתִּי בְּבֵית־יהוה כָּל־יְמֵי חַיַּי, לַחֲזוֹת בְּנֹעַם־יהוה, וּלְבַקֵּר בְּהֵיכָלוֹ: כִּי יִצְפְּנֵנִי בְּסֻכֹּה בְּיוֹם רָעָה, יַסְתִּרֵנִי בְּסֵתֶר אָהֳלוֹ, בְּצוּר יְרוֹמְמֵנִי: וְעַתָּה יָרוּם רֹאשִׁי עַל אֹיְבַי סְבִיבוֹתַי, וְאֶזְבְּחָה בְאָהֳלוֹ זִבְחֵי תְרוּעָה, אָשִׁירָה וַאֲזַמְּרָה לַיהוה: שְׁמַע־יהוה קוֹלִי אֶקְרָא, וְחָנֵּנִי וַעֲנֵנִי: לְךָ אָמַר לִבִּי בַּקְּשׁוּ פָנָי, אֶת־פָּנֶיךָ יהוה אֲבַקֵּשׁ: אַל־תַּסְתֵּר פָּנֶיךָ מִמֶּנִּי, אַל תַּט־בְּאַף עַבְדֶּךָ, עֶזְרָתִי הָיִיתָ, אַל־תִּטְּשֵׁנִי וְאַל־תַּעַזְבֵנִי, אֱלֹהֵי יִשְׁעִי: כִּי־אָבִי וְאִמִּי עֲזָבוּנִי, וַיהוה יַאַסְפֵנִי: הוֹרֵנִי יהוה דַּרְכֶּךָ, וּנְחֵנִי בְּאֹרַח מִישׁוֹר, לְמַעַן שׁוֹרְרָי: אַל־תִּתְּנֵנִי בְּנֶפֶשׁ צָרָי, כִּי קָמוּ־בִי עֵדֵי־שֶׁקֶר, וִיפֵחַ חָמָס: › לוּלֵא הֶאֱמַנְתִּי לִרְאוֹת בְּטוּב־יהוה בְּאֶרֶץ חַיִּים: קַוֵּה אֶל־יהוה, חֲזַק וְיַאֲמֵץ לִבֶּךָ, וְקַוֵּה אֶל־יהוה:

קדיש יתום *(previous page)*

*In a house of mourning the service continues on page 1139.*

## BLESSING OF THE NEW MOON

*Kiddush Levana, the Blessing of the New Moon, is said between the third day and the middle day of each month. If possible, it should be said at the end of Shabbat, under the open sky, and in the presence of a minyan. See law 470.*

הַלְלוּיָהּ Halleluya! Praise the LORD from the heavens, praise Him in the heights. Praise Him, all His angels; praise Him, all His hosts. Praise Him, sun and moon; praise Him, all shining stars. Praise Him, highest heavens and the waters above the heavens. Let them praise the name of the LORD, for He commanded and they were created. He established them for ever and all time, issuing a decree that will never change. *Ps. 148*

כִּי־אֶרְאֶה When I see Your heavens, the work of Your fingers, *Ps. 8*
the moon and the stars which You have set in place:
What is man that You are mindful of him,
the son of man that You care for him?

*Look at the moon, then say:*

בָּרוּךְ Blessed are You, LORD our God, King of the Universe
who by His word created the heavens,
and by His breath all their host.
He set for them laws and times,
so that they should not deviate from their appointed task.
They are joyous and glad to perform the will of their Owner,
the Worker of truth whose work is truth.

---

Holy One, blessed be He, who diminished her [i.e. the Moon] by truth and by law."[2] (Editor)

2. *Tosafot's* interpretation is fascinating because earlier in the discussion, the Talmud rejected the idea of blessing *"Dayyan ha-emet"* ("Truthful Judge") on the waning of the moon, as if we experience evil thereby. We do not recite *"Barukh dayyan ha-emet"* on our own behalf, but acting as surrogates for the Moon, so to speak, we recite the blessing *"Po'el emet"* on her behalf. A lunar eclipse was considered an evil omen for Israel, who reckon time according to the moon (*b. Sukkah* 29a), but the monthly waning of the moon is insufficient grounds for uttering the blessing *"Dayyan ha-emet."* So much for our own subjective experience. As for the Moon herself, her diminishing warrants the blessing *"Po'el emet."*

# קידוש לבנה

*קידוש לבנה, the Blessing of the New Moon, is said between the third day and the middle day of each month. If possible, it should be said at the end of שבת, under the open sky, and in the presence of a מנין. See law 470.*

הַלְלוּיָהּ, הַלְלוּ אֶת־יהוה מִן־הַשָּׁמַיִם, הַלְלוּהוּ בַּמְּרוֹמִים: הַלְלוּהוּ כָל־מַלְאָכָיו, הַלְלוּהוּ כָּל־צְבָאָו: הַלְלוּהוּ שֶׁמֶשׁ וְיָרֵחַ, הַלְלוּהוּ כָּל־כּוֹכְבֵי אוֹר: הַלְלוּהוּ שְׁמֵי הַשָּׁמָיִם, וְהַמַּיִם אֲשֶׁר מֵעַל הַשָּׁמָיִם: יְהַלְלוּ אֶת־שֵׁם יהוה, כִּי הוּא צִוָּה וְנִבְרָאוּ: וַיַּעֲמִידֵם לָעַד לְעוֹלָם, חָק־נָתַן וְלֹא יַעֲבוֹר: תהלים קמח

כִּי־אֶרְאֶה שָׁמֶיךָ מַעֲשֵׂה אֶצְבְּעֹתֶיךָ, יָרֵחַ וְכוֹכָבִים אֲשֶׁר כּוֹנָנְתָּה: מָה־אֱנוֹשׁ כִּי־תִזְכְּרֶנּוּ, וּבֶן־אָדָם כִּי תִפְקְדֶנּוּ: תהלים ח

*Look at the moon, then say:*

בָּרוּךְ אַתָּה יהוה אֱלֹהֵינוּ מֶלֶךְ הָעוֹלָם,
אֲשֶׁר בְּמַאֲמָרוֹ בָּרָא שְׁחָקִים, וּבְרוּחַ פִּיו כָּל צְבָאָם
חֹק וּזְמַן נָתַן לָהֶם שֶׁלֹּא יְשַׁנּוּ אֶת תַּפְקִידָם.
שָׂשִׂים וּשְׂמֵחִים לַעֲשׂוֹת רְצוֹן קוֹנָם
פּוֹעֵל אֱמֶת שֶׁפְּעֻלָּתוֹ אֱמֶת.

---

קידוש לבנה / BLESSING OF THE NEW MOON

פּוֹעֵל אֱמֶת שֶׁפְּעֻלָּתוֹ אֱמֶת *Worker of truth whose work is truth.* In the text of the Talmud there are two readings. Rashi and Maimonides read *"po'alei emet she-pe'ulatan emet"* ("workers of truth whose work is truth") in the plural. The reference is to the heavenly bodies. We follow the reading of the *Tosafot*: *"Po'el"* ("Worker") in the singular.[1] *Tosafot* explain that this "refers to the

---

1. *b. Sanhedrin* 42a; Rashi and *Tosafot*, s.v *po'alei emet*; and Maimonides, *MT*, *Hil. Berakhot* 10:16. The Vilna Gaon adopted the reading of Rashi and Maimonides, as attested to by the Gaon's disciple Rabbi Benjamin of Shklov and as witnessed by the Gaon's version of Tractate *Soferim* 20:1. See *Ma'aseh Rav*.

To the moon He said that it should renew itself as a crown of beauty
for those He carried from the womb [Israel],
for they are destined to be renewed like it,
and to praise their Creator for the sake of His glorious majesty.
Blessed are You, Lord, who renews the months.

---

In the primordial myth, the Moon complained to the Holy One, blessed be He: "Is it possible for two kings to wear the same crown?" (In other words, the Moon was not satisfied that she and the Sun were of equal grandeur.) God's response was: "Go, diminish yourself!"[8] But in the future, the Moon's "crown" will once again be equal to that of the Sun. She will wear the crown of the Sun. This promise is reflected in the two words *"'ateret Tif'eret"* ("crown of *Tif'eret*"). In Kabbalah, *Tif'eret* is code for the Sun.[9] (Editor)

---

the six sides of the cube, or the four cardinal directions and up and down. In Kabbalah, the six sefirot of *Ḥesed, Gevurah, Tif'eret, Netsaḥ, Hod* and *Yesod* are referred to as the *"shesh ketsavot"* ("six edges"). The truth is that this symbolism goes back to *Sefer Yetsirah*, the Book of Creation (4:4): "Up and down, East and West, North and South, and the Holy Palace precisely in the center, and it supports them all" (trans. Aryeh Kaplan). See Rabbi Joseph Gikatilia, *Ginat Egoz* (Jerusalem: Ha-Ḥayyim ve-ha-Shalom, 1989), Part Two, pp. 228–229.

It was precisely in Egypt, when Israel assumed the "full belly," the sixness that comes under the general rubric of *"Tif'eret,"* that they were commanded their very first *mitsvah* of sanctifying the Moon, symbolized by the seventh *sefirah* of *Malkhut*: "This month shall be to you the head of months" (Exodus 12:2; Rashi, Genesis 1:1).

> To the moon He said that it should renew itself as a crown of beauty (*tif'eret*) for the full-bellied (*'amusei vaten*) [Israel], for they are destined to be renewed like it, and to praise their Creator for the sake of His glorious majesty (*malkhut*).

This would explain the juxtaposition of *Tif'eret* to *"'amusei vaten."* (*Tif'eret* itself is synonymous with Israel as in the verse in Lamentations 2:1: *"Tif'eret Yisrael."* See *Zohar* II, 216a. Maharal titled one of his works *"Tif'eret Yisrael."*) The final *tikkun* or cosmic correction, consists in the union of *Tif'eret* (which comprises six *sefirot*) with *Malkhut*, the seventh *sefirah*. See Rabbi Joseph Engel, *Ma'amar Levanah*, par. 2, in *Otserot Yosef* (Warsaw, 1929). See also Rabbi Moses Sofer (Schreiber), *Ḥatam Sofer: Derashot*, ed. Yosef Naftali Stern, vol. 2 (Nissan-Tishri) (Grosswardein, 1929; photo offset New York, 1961), *Derush le-Zakh Ellul [5]589*, s.v. *Hashem elohei avoteikhem yosef 'aleikem kakhem* (363d): "The root of the sun is above in *Atsilut, Tif'eret Yisrael*, as is known..."

8. *b. Ḥullin* 60b.
9. See Rabbi Isaiah Halevi Horowitz, *Siddur Sha'ar ha-Shamayim, Yotser* for Shabbat, s.v. *Shevaḥ notenim lo kol tseva marom.* (See *Ra'aya Mehemna* in *Zohar* II, 116a.) Also Rabbi Joseph Engel, *Ma'amar Levanah*, par. 8.

# וְלַלְּבָנָה אָמַר שֶׁתִּתְחַדֵּשׁ
# עֲטֶרֶת תִּפְאֶרֶת לַעֲמוּסֵי בָטֶן
# שֶׁהֵם עֲתִידִים לְהִתְחַדֵּשׁ כְּמוֹתָהּ
# וּלְפָאֵר לְיוֹצְרָם עַל שֵׁם כְּבוֹד מַלְכוּתוֹ.
# בָּרוּךְ אַתָּה יהוה, מְחַדֵּשׁ חֳדָשִׁים.

---

**וְלַלְּבָנָה אָמַר שֶׁתִּתְחַדֵּשׁ, עֲטֶרֶת תִּפְאֶרֶת לַעֲמוּסֵי בָטֶן, שֶׁהֵם עֲתִידִים לְהִתְחַדֵּשׁ כְּמוֹתָהּ, וּלְפָאֵר לְיוֹצְרָם עַל שֵׁם כְּבוֹד מַלְכוּתוֹ** *To the moon He said that it should renew itself as a crown of beauty for those He carried from the womb* (la-'amusei vaten) *[Israel],*[3] *for they are destined to be renewed like it, and to praise their Creator for the sake of His glorious majesty* (malkhut). *"La-'Amusei vaten"* refers to "pregnancy" (*'ibbur*). *"'Ibbur"* is a term out of Lurianic Kabbalah.[4] The People of Israel – as the Moon, to which we are likened[5] – is yet in an embryonic state. Our God-consciousness is not yet fully developed. In the future, the *sefirah* of *Malkhut* (Majesty), which symbolizes both the Moon and *K'nesset Yisrael,* will be revealed in its full light. At that time, the "the two great luminaries"[6] will be equal; the light of the moon shall be as the light of the sun. The Sun symbolizes the reality of God *per se*; the Moon symbolizes God as reflected through the reality of the worlds. On that day, the two realities shall be as one.[7]

*

3. See Psalms 46:3.
4. The terminology that the Sages employed in regard to the month, invokes the imagery of gestation and birth. If the *Beit Din* (Court) declared it a thirty-day (as opposed to a twenty-nine day) month, they "impregnated" (*"'ibberu"*) the month. By the same token, if they declared the year a leap year (with an extra thirteenth month), they "impregnated" (*"'ibberu"*) the year. And the first appearance of the New Moon is referred to as the *"molad,"* the "birth" of the new month.
5. See *Exodus Rabbah* 15:26; *Song of Songs Rabbah* 6:10.
6. Genesis 1:16.
7. *MRIT*, pp. 513–514. A reworked version is found in *OR*, vol. 1, p. 430.
   It is possible that *"'amusei vaten"* ("full-bellied," "gravid") refers to the Midrashic tradition (*Exodus Rabbah* 1:8) that in Egypt the Hebrew women would give birth to sextuplets: *"shishah be-keress ehad"* ("six in one belly"). Rabbi Judah Löw (Maharal) of Prague explains at great length the symbolism of the number six. It is not coincidence that the number of Hebrews who left Egypt was six hundred thousand. See Rabbi Judah Löw, *Gevurot Hashem*, chap. 12; idem, *Gur Aryeh*, supercommentary to Rashi, Exodus 1:7. Maharal gives geometrical expression to this symbolism when he speaks of

*The following five verses are each said three times:*

Blessed is He who formed you; blessed is He who made you;
blessed is He who owns you; blessed is He who created you.

*The following verse is said rising on the toes.*

Just as I leap toward you but cannot touch you,
so may none of my enemies be able to touch me to do me harm.

May fear and dread fall upon them; *Ex. 15*
by the power of Your arm may they be still as stone.

May they be still as stone through the power of Your arm,
when dread and fear fall upon them.

David, King of Israel, lives and endures.

*Turn to three people and say to each:*

Peace upon you.

*They respond:*

Upon you, peace.

*Say three times:*

May it be a good sign and a good omen for us and all Israel. Amen.

קוֹל Hark! My beloved! Here he comes, leaping over the mountains, *Song. 2*
bounding over the hills. My beloved is like a gazelle, like a young deer. There he stands outside our wall, peering in through the windows, gazing through the lattice.

---

name is invoked while blessing the new moon. In the famous legend of the dimunition of the Moon, whereby the Moon was reduced from a *"ma'or gadol"* ("large luminary") to a *"ma'or katan"* ("small luminary"), as consolation it was pointed out to her that in the future several men would be called "small" after her, one of them being – *"Ya'akov ha-Katan"* ("Jacob the Small").[12] (Editor)

---

fragmentation. All this – the destruction and construction – is apropos to the *tikkun*, the cosmic rectification of the flawed state of the moon. It would be impossible to effect the *tikkun* if one were not understanding of and empathic to the fragmentation. Cf. Rav Kook's commentary to the *Birkat ha-Minim* regarding Shmuel HaKatan ("Samuel the Small"). Shmuel HaKatan can call for the destruction of the destroyers because he does not rejoice in their downfall. He too is offered to the Moon as a sort of consolation; *b. Ḥullin* 60b.

12. Amos 7:2; *b. Ḥullin* 60b.

*The following five verses are each said three times:*

בָּרוּךְ יוֹצְרֵךְ, בָּרוּךְ עוֹשֵׂךְ, בָּרוּךְ קוֹנֵךְ, בָּרוּךְ בּוֹרְאֵךְ.

*The following verse is said rising on the toes.*

כְּשֵׁם שֶׁאֲנִי רוֹקֵד כְּנֶגְדֵּךְ וְאֵינִי יָכוֹל לִנְגֹּעַ בָּךְ
כָּךְ לֹא יוּכְלוּ כָּל אוֹיְבַי לִנְגֹּעַ בִּי לְרָעָה.

שמות טו תִּפֹּל עֲלֵיהֶם אֵימָתָה וָפַחַד, בִּגְדֹל זְרוֹעֲךָ יִדְּמוּ כָּאָבֶן:
כָּאָבֶן יִדְּמוּ זְרוֹעֲךָ בִּגְדֹל, וָפַחַד אֵימָתָה עֲלֵיהֶם תִּפֹּל.
דָּוִד מֶלֶךְ יִשְׂרָאֵל חַי וְקַיָּם.

*Turn to three people and say to each:*

שָׁלוֹם עֲלֵיכֶם.

*They respond:*

עֲלֵיכֶם שָׁלוֹם.

*Say three times:*

סִימָן טוֹב וּמַזָּל טוֹב יְהֵא לָנוּ וּלְכָל יִשְׂרָאֵל, אָמֵן.

שיר השירים ב קוֹל דּוֹדִי הִנֵּה־זֶה בָּא, מְדַלֵּג עַל־הֶהָרִים, מְקַפֵּץ עַל־הַגְּבָעוֹת: דּוֹמֶה דוֹדִי לִצְבִי אוֹ לְעֹפֶר הָאַיָּלִים, הִנֵּה־זֶה עוֹמֵד אַחַר כָּתְלֵנוּ, מַשְׁגִּיחַ מִן־הַחַלֹּנוֹת, מֵצִיץ מִן־הַחֲרַכִּים:

---

בָּרוּךְ יוֹצְרֵךְ, בָּרוּךְ עוֹשֵׂךְ, בָּרוּךְ קוֹנֵךְ, בָּרוּךְ בּוֹרְאֵךְ *Blessed is He who formed you. Blessed is He who made you. Blessed is He who owns you. Blessed is He who created you.* The initials of the four words *Yotsrekh, 'Osekh, Konekh, Borekh* form the word *Ya'akov* or Jacob.[10] The Midrash refers to Jacob (in imitation of God) as a *"bore 'olamot,"* a "creator of worlds."[11] There is another reason that Jacob's

---

10. Anonymous, *Kol Bo* (Venice, 1567), chap. 43 (*Rosh Ḥodesh*), 43b; Rabbi Jacob ben Asher, *Arba'ah Turim, OḤ*, chap. 426.

11. *Genesis Rabbah* 98:3; *Leviticus Rabbah* 36:4. The prooftext is Isaiah 43:1. See S. Baer, *'Avodat Yisrael* (Roedelheim, 1868), p. 338. In *Gen. Rabbah* 98:3, Jacob (again in imitation of God) is also referred to as a *"meḥalek 'olamot"* ("fragmenter of worlds"). Cf. Genesis 49:7. Jacob is called after the moon because he has undergone the experience of

שִׁיר לַמַּעֲלוֹת A song of ascents. I lift my eyes up to the hills; from where will my help come? My help comes from the LORD, Maker of heaven and earth. He will not let your foot stumble; He who guards you does not slumber. See: the Guardian of Israel neither slumbers nor sleeps. The LORD is your Guardian; the LORD is your Shade at your right hand. The sun will not strike you by day, nor the moon by night. The LORD will guard you from all harm; He will guard your life. The LORD will guard your going and coming, now and for evermore. *Ps. 121*

הַלְלוּיָהּ Halleluya! Praise God in His holy place; praise Him in the heavens of His power. Praise Him for His mighty deeds; praise Him for His surpassing greatness. Praise Him with blasts of the ram's horn; praise Him with the harp and lyre. Praise Him with timbrel and dance; praise Him with strings and flute. Praise Him with clashing cymbals; praise Him with resounding cymbals. Let all that breathes praise the LORD. Halleluya! *Ps. 150*

תָּנָא In the academy of Rabbi Yishma'el it was taught: Were the people of Israel privileged to greet the presence of their heavenly Father only once a month, it would have been sufficient for them. Abaye said: Therefore it [the blessing of the moon] should be said standing. Who is this coming up from the desert, leaning on her beloved? *Sanhedrin 42a* *Song. 8*

וִיהִי May it be Your will, LORD my God and God of my ancestors, to make good the deficiency of the moon, so that it is no longer in its diminished state. May the light of the moon be like the light of the sun and like the light of the seven days of creation as it was before it was diminished, as it says, "The two great luminaries." And may there be fulfilled for us the verse: "They shall seek the LORD their God, and David their king." Amen. *Gen. 1* *Hos. 3*

לַמְנַצֵּחַ For the conductor of music. With stringed instruments, a psalm. A song. May God be gracious to us and bless us. May He make His face shine on us, Selah. Then will Your way be known on earth, Your salvation among all the nations. Let the peoples praise You, God; let all peoples praise You. Let nations rejoice and sing for joy, for You judge the peoples with equity, and guide the nations of the earth, Selah. Let the peoples praise You, God; let all peoples praise You. The earth has yielded its harvest. May God, our God, bless us. God will bless us, and all the ends of the earth will fear Him. *Ps. 67*

שִׁיר לַמַּעֲלוֹת, אֶשָּׂא עֵינַי אֶל־הֶהָרִים, מֵאַיִן יָבֹא עֶזְרִי: עֶזְרִי מֵעִם תהלים קכא
יהוה, עֹשֵׂה שָׁמַיִם וָאָרֶץ: אַל־יִתֵּן לַמּוֹט רַגְלֶךָ, אַל־יָנוּם שֹׁמְרֶךָ:
הִנֵּה לֹא־יָנוּם וְלֹא יִישָׁן, שׁוֹמֵר יִשְׂרָאֵל: יהוה שֹׁמְרֶךָ, יהוה צִלְּךָ
עַל־יַד יְמִינֶךָ: יוֹמָם הַשֶּׁמֶשׁ לֹא־יַכֶּכָּה, וְיָרֵחַ בַּלָּיְלָה: יהוה יִשְׁמָרְךָ
מִכָּל־רָע, יִשְׁמֹר אֶת־נַפְשֶׁךָ: יהוה יִשְׁמָר־צֵאתְךָ וּבוֹאֶךָ, מֵעַתָּה
וְעַד־עוֹלָם:

הַלְלוּיָהּ, הַלְלוּ־אֵל בְּקָדְשׁוֹ, הַלְלוּהוּ בִּרְקִיעַ עֻזּוֹ: הַלְלוּהוּ בִגְבוּרֹתָיו, תהלים קנ
הַלְלוּהוּ כְּרֹב גֻּדְלוֹ: הַלְלוּהוּ בְּתֵקַע שׁוֹפָר, הַלְלוּהוּ בְּנֵבֶל וְכִנּוֹר:
הַלְלוּהוּ בְּתֹף וּמָחוֹל, הַלְלוּהוּ בְּמִנִּים וְעֻגָב: הַלְלוּהוּ בְצִלְצְלֵי־
שָׁמַע, הַלְלוּהוּ בְּצִלְצְלֵי תְרוּעָה: כֹּל הַנְּשָׁמָה תְּהַלֵּל יָהּ, הַלְלוּיָהּ:

תָּנָא דְּבֵי רַבִּי יִשְׁמָעֵאל: אִלְמָלֵי לֹא זָכוּ יִשְׂרָאֵל אֶלָּא לְהַקְבִּיל פְּנֵי סנהדרין מב.
אֲבִיהֶם שֶׁבַּשָּׁמַיִם פַּעַם אַחַת בַּחֹדֶשׁ, דַּיָּם. אָמַר אַבַּיֵּי: הִלְכָּךְ צָרִיךְ
לְמֵימְרָא מְעֻמָּד. מִי זֹאת עֹלָה מִן־הַמִּדְבָּר, מִתְרַפֶּקֶת עַל־דּוֹדָהּ: שיר השירים ח

וִיהִי רָצוֹן מִלְּפָנֶיךָ יהוה אֱלֹהַי וֵאלֹהֵי אֲבוֹתַי, לְמַלֹּאת פְּגִימַת
הַלְּבָנָה וְלֹא יִהְיֶה בָּהּ שׁוּם מִעוּט. וִיהִי אוֹר הַלְּבָנָה כְּאוֹר הַחַמָּה
וּכְאוֹר שִׁבְעַת יְמֵי בְרֵאשִׁית, כְּמוֹ שֶׁהָיְתָה קֹדֶם מִעוּטָהּ, שֶׁנֶּאֱמַר:
אֶת־שְׁנֵי הַמְּאֹרֹת הַגְּדֹלִים: וְיִתְקַיֵּם בָּנוּ מִקְרָא שֶׁכָּתוּב: וּבִקְשׁוּ בראשית א הושע ג
אֶת־יהוה אֱלֹהֵיהֶם וְאֵת דָּוִיד מַלְכָּם: אָמֵן.

לַמְנַצֵּחַ בִּנְגִינֹת, מִזְמוֹר שִׁיר: אֱלֹהִים יְחָנֵּנוּ וִיבָרְכֵנוּ, יָאֵר פָּנָיו תהלים סז
אִתָּנוּ סֶלָה: לָדַעַת בָּאָרֶץ דַּרְכֶּךָ, בְּכָל־גּוֹיִם יְשׁוּעָתֶךָ: יוֹדוּךָ עַמִּים
אֱלֹהִים, יוֹדוּךָ עַמִּים כֻּלָּם: יִשְׂמְחוּ וִירַנְּנוּ לְאֻמִּים, כִּי־תִשְׁפֹּט עַמִּים
מִישֹׁר, וּלְאֻמִּים בָּאָרֶץ תַּנְחֵם סֶלָה: יוֹדוּךָ עַמִּים אֱלֹהִים, יוֹדוּךָ
עַמִּים כֻּלָּם: אֶרֶץ נָתְנָה יְבוּלָהּ, יְבָרְכֵנוּ אֱלֹהִים אֱלֹהֵינוּ: יְבָרְכֵנוּ
אֱלֹהִים, וְיִירְאוּ אוֹתוֹ כָּל־אַפְסֵי־אָרֶץ:

*Stand while saying Aleinu. Bow at* ▾.

עָלֵינוּ It is our duty to praise the Master of all,
and ascribe greatness to the Author of creation,
who has not made us like the nations of the lands
nor placed us like the families of the earth;
who has not made our portion like theirs,
nor our destiny like all their multitudes.
(For they worship vanity and emptiness, and pray to a god who cannot save.)
▾But we bow in worship and thank the Supreme King of kings,
the Holy One, blessed be He,
who extends the heavens and establishes the earth,
whose throne of glory is in the heavens above,
and whose power's Presence is in the highest of heights.
He is our God; there is no other.
Truly He is our King, there is none else,
as it is written in His Torah: "You shall know and take to heart this day *Deut. 4*
that the LORD is God, in heaven above and on earth below. There is no other."

Therefore, we place our hope in You, LORD our God,
that we may soon see the glory of Your power,
when You will remove abominations from the earth,
and idols will be utterly destroyed,
when the world will be perfected under the sovereignty of the Almighty,
when all humanity will call on Your name,
to turn all the earth's wicked toward You.
All the world's inhabitants will realize and know
that to You every knee must bow and every tongue swear loyalty.
Before You, LORD our God, they will kneel and bow down
and give honor to Your glorious name.
They will all accept the yoke of Your kingdom,
and You will reign over them soon and for ever.
For the kingdom is Yours, and to all eternity You will reign in glory,
as it is written in Your Torah: "The LORD will reign for ever and ever." *Ex. 15*
▸ And it is said: "Then the LORD shall be King over all the earth; *Zech. 14*
on that day the LORD shall be One and His name One."

*Some add:*

Have no fear of sudden terror or of the ruin when it overtakes the wicked. Devise *Prov. 3* *Is. 8*
your strategy, but it will be thwarted; propose your plan, but it will not stand, for God
is with us. When you grow old, I will still be the same. When your hair turns gray, I *Is. 46*
will still carry you. I made you, I will bear you, I will carry you, and I will rescue you.

*Stand while saying* עָלֵינוּ. *Bow at* ▾.

עָלֵינוּ לְשַׁבֵּחַ לַאֲדוֹן הַכֹּל, לָתֵת גְּדֻלָּה לְיוֹצֵר בְּרֵאשִׁית
שֶׁלֹּא עָשָׂנוּ כְּגוֹיֵי הָאֲרָצוֹת, וְלֹא שָׂמָנוּ כְּמִשְׁפְּחוֹת הָאֲדָמָה
שֶׁלֹּא שָׂם חֶלְקֵנוּ כָּהֶם וְגוֹרָלֵנוּ כְּכָל הֲמוֹנָם.
(שֶׁהֵם מִשְׁתַּחֲוִים לְהֶבֶל וָרִיק וּמִתְפַּלְלִים אֶל אֵל לֹא יוֹשִׁיעַ.)
▾וַאֲנַחְנוּ כּוֹרְעִים וּמִשְׁתַּחֲוִים וּמוֹדִים
לִפְנֵי מֶלֶךְ מַלְכֵי הַמְּלָכִים, הַקָּדוֹשׁ בָּרוּךְ הוּא
שֶׁהוּא נוֹטֶה שָׁמַיִם וְיוֹסֵד אָרֶץ
וּמוֹשַׁב יְקָרוֹ בַּשָּׁמַיִם מִמַּעַל, וּשְׁכִינַת עֻזּוֹ בְּגָבְהֵי מְרוֹמִים.
הוּא אֱלֹהֵינוּ, אֵין עוֹד.
אֱמֶת מַלְכֵּנוּ, אֶפֶס זוּלָתוֹ
דברים ד כַּכָּתוּב בְּתוֹרָתוֹ, וְיָדַעְתָּ הַיּוֹם וַהֲשֵׁבֹתָ אֶל־לְבָבֶךָ
כִּי יהוה הוּא הָאֱלֹהִים בַּשָּׁמַיִם מִמַּעַל וְעַל־הָאָרֶץ מִתָּחַת, אֵין עוֹד:

עַל כֵּן נְקַוֶּה לְּךָ יהוה אֱלֹהֵינוּ, לִרְאוֹת מְהֵרָה בְּתִפְאֶרֶת עֻזֶּךָ
לְהַעֲבִיר גִּלּוּלִים מִן הָאָרֶץ, וְהָאֱלִילִים כָּרוֹת יִכָּרֵתוּן
לְתַקֵּן עוֹלָם בְּמַלְכוּת שַׁדַּי.
וְכָל בְּנֵי בָשָׂר יִקְרְאוּ בִשְׁמֶךָ לְהַפְנוֹת אֵלֶיךָ כָּל רִשְׁעֵי אָרֶץ.
יַכִּירוּ וְיֵדְעוּ כָּל יוֹשְׁבֵי תֵבֵל, כִּי לְךָ תִּכְרַע כָּל בֶּרֶךְ, תִּשָּׁבַע כָּל לָשׁוֹן.
לְפָנֶיךָ יהוה אֱלֹהֵינוּ יִכְרְעוּ וְיִפֹּלוּ, וְלִכְבוֹד שִׁמְךָ יְקָר יִתֵּנוּ
וִיקַבְּלוּ כֻלָּם אֶת עֹל מַלְכוּתֶךָ וְתִמְלֹךְ עֲלֵיהֶם מְהֵרָה לְעוֹלָם וָעֶד.
כִּי הַמַּלְכוּת שֶׁלְּךָ הִיא וּלְעוֹלְמֵי עַד תִּמְלֹךְ בְּכָבוֹד
שמות טו כַּכָּתוּב בְּתוֹרָתֶךָ, יהוה יִמְלֹךְ לְעֹלָם וָעֶד:
זכריה יד ◂ וְנֶאֱמַר, וְהָיָה יהוה לְמֶלֶךְ עַל־כָּל־הָאָרֶץ
בַּיּוֹם הַהוּא יִהְיֶה יהוה אֶחָד וּשְׁמוֹ אֶחָד:

*Some add:*

משלי ג אַל־תִּירָא מִפַּחַד פִּתְאֹם וּמִשֹּׁאַת רְשָׁעִים כִּי תָבֹא:
ישעיה ח עֻצוּ עֵצָה וְתֻפָר, דַּבְּרוּ דָבָר וְלֹא יָקוּם, כִּי עִמָּנוּ אֵל:
ישעיה מו וְעַד־זִקְנָה אֲנִי הוּא, וְעַד־שֵׂיבָה אֲנִי אֶסְבֹּל, אֲנִי עָשִׂיתִי וַאֲנִי אֶשָּׂא וַאֲנִי אֶסְבֹּל וַאֲמַלֵּט:

## MOURNER'S KADDISH

*The following prayer, said by mourners, requires the presence of a minyan.*
*A transliteration can be found on page 1320.*

*Mourner:* יִתְגַּדַּל Magnified and sanctified may His great name be,
in the world He created by His will.
May He establish His kingdom
in your lifetime and in your days,
and in the lifetime of all the house of Israel,
swiftly and soon – and say: Amen.

*All:* May His great name be blessed for ever and all time.

*Mourner:* Blessed and praised, glorified and exalted,
raised and honored, uplifted and lauded
be the name of the Holy One, blessed be He,
beyond any blessing, song, praise and consolation
uttered in the world – and say: Amen.

May there be great peace from heaven,
and life for us and all Israel – and say: Amen.

*Bow, take three steps back, as if taking leave of the Divine Presence,*
*then bow, first left, then right, then center, while saying:*

May He who makes peace in His high places,
make peace for us and all Israel – and say: Amen.

*All sing:*

טוֹבִים Good are the radiant stars our God created;
He formed them with knowledge,
understanding and deliberation.
He gave them strength and might
to rule throughout the world.

Full of splendor, radiating light,
beautiful is their splendor throughout the world.
Glad as they go forth, joyous as they return,
they fulfill with awe their Creator's will.

Glory and honor they give to His name,
jubilation and song at the mention of His majesty.
He called the sun into being and it shone with light.
He looked and fashioned the form of the moon.

## קדיש יתום

*The following prayer, said by mourners, requires the presence of a* מנין*.*
*A transliteration can be found on page 1320.*

אבל: יִתְגַּדַּל וְיִתְקַדַּשׁ שְׁמֵהּ רַבָּא (קהל: אָמֵן)
בְּעָלְמָא דִּי בְרָא כִרְעוּתֵהּ, וְיַמְלִיךְ מַלְכוּתֵהּ
בְּחַיֵּיכוֹן וּבְיוֹמֵיכוֹן וּבְחַיֵּי דְכָל בֵּית יִשְׂרָאֵל
בַּעֲגָלָא וּבִזְמַן קָרִיב, וְאִמְרוּ אָמֵן. (קהל: אָמֵן)

קהל ואבל: יְהֵא שְׁמֵהּ רַבָּא מְבָרַךְ לְעָלַם וּלְעָלְמֵי עָלְמַיָּא.

אבל: יִתְבָּרַךְ וְיִשְׁתַּבַּח וְיִתְפָּאַר
וְיִתְרוֹמַם וְיִתְנַשֵּׂא וְיִתְהַדָּר וְיִתְעַלֶּה וְיִתְהַלָּל
שְׁמֵהּ דְּקֻדְשָׁא בְּרִיךְ הוּא (קהל: בְּרִיךְ הוּא)
לְעֵלָּא מִן כָּל בִּרְכָתָא /בעשרת ימי תשובה: לְעֵלָּא לְעֵלָּא מִכָּל בִּרְכָתָא/
וְשִׁירָתָא, תֻּשְׁבְּחָתָא וְנֶחֱמָתָא
דַּאֲמִירָן בְּעָלְמָא, וְאִמְרוּ אָמֵן. (קהל: אָמֵן)

יְהֵא שְׁלָמָא רַבָּא מִן שְׁמַיָּא
וְחַיִּים, עָלֵינוּ וְעַל כָּל יִשְׂרָאֵל, וְאִמְרוּ אָמֵן. (קהל: אָמֵן)

*Bow, take three steps back, as if taking leave of the Divine Presence, then bow, first left, then right, then center, while saying:*

עֹשֶׂה שָׁלוֹם/בעשרת ימי תשובה: הַשָּׁלוֹם/ בִּמְרוֹמָיו
הוּא יַעֲשֶׂה שָׁלוֹם עָלֵינוּ וְעַל כָּל יִשְׂרָאֵל, וְאִמְרוּ אָמֵן. (קהל: אָמֵן)

*All sing:*

טוֹבִים מְאוֹרוֹת שֶׁבָּרָא אֱלֹהֵינוּ, יְצָרָם בְּדַעַת בְּבִינָה וּבְהַשְׂכֵּל
כֹּחַ וּגְבוּרָה נָתַן בָּהֶם, לִהְיוֹת מוֹשְׁלִים בְּקֶרֶב תֵּבֵל.

מְלֵאִים זִיו וּמְפִיקִים נֹגַהּ, נָאֶה זִיוָם בְּכָל הָעוֹלָם
שְׂמֵחִים בְּצֵאתָם וְשָׂשִׂים בְּבוֹאָם, עוֹשִׂים בְּאֵימָה רְצוֹן קוֹנָם.

פְּאֵר וְכָבוֹד נוֹתְנִים לִשְׁמוֹ, צָהֳלָה וְרִנָּה לְזֵכֶר מַלְכוּתוֹ
קָרָא לַשֶּׁמֶשׁ וַיִּזְרַח אוֹר, רָאָה וְהִתְקִין צוּרַת הַלְּבָנָה.

## HAVDALA AT HOME

*On Motza'ei Yom Tov that is not a Motza'ei Shabbat, the blessings for the spices and flame are omitted. At the end of Yom Kippur, only the blessing for the spices is omitted. See law 471.*

*Taking a cup of wine in the right hand, say:*

הִנֵּה Behold, God is my salvation. I will trust and not be afraid. The LORD, the *Is. 12*
LORD, is my strength and my song. He has become my salvation. With joy
you will draw water from the springs of salvation. Salvation is the LORD's; on *Ps. 3*
Your people is Your blessing, Selah. The LORD of hosts is with us, the God of *Ps. 46*
Jacob is our stronghold, Selah. LORD of hosts: happy is the one who trusts *Ps. 84*
in You. LORD, save! May the King answer us on the day we call. For the Jews *Esther 8*
there was light and gladness, joy and honor – so may it be for us. I will lift *Ps. 116*
the cup of salvation and call on the name of the LORD.

*When making Havdala for others, add:*
Please pay attention, my masters.

Blessed are You, LORD our God, King of the Universe,
who creates the fruit of the vine.

*Hold the spice box and say:*

Blessed are You, LORD our God, King of the Universe,
who creates the various spices.

*Smell the spices and put the spice box down.*

*Lift the hands toward the flame of the Havdala candle and say:*

Blessed are You, LORD our God, King of the Universe,
who creates the lights of fire.

*Holding the cup of wine again in the right hand, say:*

בָּרוּךְ Blessed are You, LORD our God, King of the Universe, who distinguishes between sacred and secular, between light and darkness, between Israel and the nations, between the seventh day and the six days of work. Blessed are You, LORD, who distinguishes between sacred and secular.

*On Sukkot, if Kiddush is made in the sukka, add:*
Blessed are You, LORD our God, King of the Universe,
who has made us holy through his commandments
and has commanded us to dwell in the sukka.

---

In 1914, Rav Kook together with his disciple Rabbi Ḥarlap and other illustrious rabbis (including Rabbi Yosef Ḥayyim Sonnenfeld of the Old Yishuv of

---

*Sha'ar ha-Shabbat*, chap. 24. (RZYH, "Supplements," unnumbered pages at the end of vol. 2 of *OR*). See too Rabbi Joseph Karo, *Maggid Meisharim* (Vilna, 1875), *Vayyeshev*, *'Or le-Yom Shabbat, Yom Rishon la-Ḥanukkah* (12c).

# סדר הבדלה בבית

*On* מוצאי יום טוב *that is not a* מוצאי שבת*, the first paragraph and the blessings for the spices and flame are omitted. At the end of* יום כפור*, only the blessing for the spices is omitted. See law 471.*

*Taking a cup of wine in the right hand, say:*

הִנֵּה אֵל יְשׁוּעָתִי אֶבְטַח, וְלֹא אֶפְחָד, כִּי־עָזִּי וְזִמְרָת יָהּ יהוה, וַיְהִי־ ישעיה יב
לִי לִישׁוּעָה: וּשְׁאַבְתֶּם־מַיִם בְּשָׂשׂוֹן, מִמַּעַיְנֵי הַיְשׁוּעָה: לַיהוה תהלים ג
הַיְשׁוּעָה, עַל־עַמְּךָ בִרְכָתֶךָ סֶּלָה: יהוה צְבָאוֹת עִמָּנוּ, מִשְׂגָּב לָנוּ תהלים מו
אֱלֹהֵי יַעֲקֹב סֶלָה: יהוה צְבָאוֹת, אַשְׁרֵי אָדָם בֹּטֵחַ בָּךְ: יהוה תהלים פד / תהלים כ
הוֹשִׁיעָה, הַמֶּלֶךְ יַעֲנֵנוּ בְיוֹם־קָרְאֵנוּ: לַיְּהוּדִים הָיְתָה אוֹרָה וְשִׂמְחָה אסתר ח
וְשָׂשֹׂן וִיקָר: כֵּן תִּהְיֶה לָּנוּ. כּוֹס־יְשׁוּעוֹת אֶשָּׂא, וּבְשֵׁם יהוה אֶקְרָא: תהלים קטז

*When making* הבדלה *for others, add:*

סַבְרִי מָרָנָן

בָּרוּךְ אַתָּה יהוה אֱלֹהֵינוּ מֶלֶךְ הָעוֹלָם, בּוֹרֵא פְּרִי הַגָּפֶן.

*Hold the spice box and say:*

בָּרוּךְ אַתָּה יהוה אֱלֹהֵינוּ מֶלֶךְ הָעוֹלָם, בּוֹרֵא מִינֵי בְשָׂמִים.

*Smell the spices and put the spice box down.*

*Lift the hands toward the flame of the* הבדלה *candle and say:*

בָּרוּךְ אַתָּה יהוה אֱלֹהֵינוּ מֶלֶךְ הָעוֹלָם, בּוֹרֵא מְאוֹרֵי הָאֵשׁ.

*Holding the cup of wine again in the right hand, say:*

בָּרוּךְ אַתָּה יהוה אֱלֹהֵינוּ מֶלֶךְ הָעוֹלָם, הַמַּבְדִּיל בֵּין קֹדֶשׁ לְחֹל, בֵּין אוֹר לְחֹשֶׁךְ, בֵּין יִשְׂרָאֵל לָעַמִּים, בֵּין יוֹם הַשְּׁבִיעִי לְשֵׁשֶׁת יְמֵי הַמַּעֲשֶׂה. בָּרוּךְ אַתָּה יהוה, הַמַּבְדִּיל בֵּין קֹדֶשׁ לְחֹל.

*On* סוכות*, if* קידוש *is made in the* סוכה*, add:*

בָּרוּךְ אַתָּה יהוה אֱלֹהֵינוּ מֶלֶךְ הָעוֹלָם
אֲשֶׁר קִדְּשָׁנוּ בְּמִצְוֹתָיו, וְצִוָּנוּ לֵישֵׁב בַּסֻּכָּה.

---

הבדלה / HAVDALAH

Rav Kook was punctilious to pour a bit of water into the beaker of wine upon which he would recite the *Kiddush* for Sabbath and festivals. When it came to *Havdalah* though, he would not mix any water into the wine.[1]

1. See *y. Berakhot* 7:5 (regarding the *Kiddush* cup); Rabbi Ḥayyim Vital, *Peri 'Ets Ḥayyim*,

הַמַּבְדִּיל He who distinguishes between sacred and secular, may He forgive our sins. May He multiply our offspring and wealth like the sand, and like the stars at night. The day has passed like a palm tree's shadow; I call on God to fulfill what the watchman said: "Morning comes, though now it is night." Your righteousness is as high as Mount Tabor. May You pass high over my sins. [Let them be] like yesterday when it has passed, like a watch in the night. The time of offerings has passed. Would that I might rest. I am weary with my sighing, every night I drench [with tears]. Hear my voice; let it not be cast aside. Open for me the lofty gate. My head is filled with the dew of dawn, my hair with raindrops of the night. Heed my prayer, revered and awesome God. When I cry, grant me deliverance at twilight, as the day fades, or in the darkness of the night. I call to You, Lord: Save me. Make known to me the path of life. Rescue me from misery before day turns to night. Cleanse the defilement of my deeds, lest those who torment me say, "Where is the God who made me, who gives cause for songs in the night?" We are in Your hands like clay: please forgive our sins, light and grave. Day to day they pour forth speech, and night to night [they communicate knowledge].

*Is. 21*
*Ps. 90*
*Ps. 6*
*Song. 5*
*Prov. 7*
*Job 35*
*Ps. 19*

---

He sought to unify the nation of Israel in the Land and to bring about a rapprochement between the *Ḥaredim* and the *Ḥilonim*; the Orthodox and the secularists. To achieve this lofty ideal, it would be necessary to break down the barrier between the two sectors by "sweetening" or softening the harsh judgment. The extraordinary historical circumstances justified this *"hora'at sha'ah"* (ad hoc decision). And without further ado, Rav Kook poured a bit of water into the cup of *Havdalah*, as he was about to recite the blessing *"Ha-Mavdil bein kodesh le-ḥol"* ("Who distinguishes between sacred and secular").[2]

2. RZYH Kook, *Li-Sheloshah be-Ellul*, vol. 1 (Jerusalem, 1938), par. 48 (p. 23). In oral conversation to his students, RZYH recounted that on that extraordinary occasion in Zikhron Ya'akov, Rabbi Ḥayyim Sonnenfeld followed suit and also added a drop of water to his beaker of wine for *Havdalah*. See Rabbi Ḥayyim Avihu Schwartz, *Mi-Tokh ha-Torah ha-Go'elet*, vol. 1 (Jerusalem, 1989), pp. 113–114.
Wine symbolizes *gevurot* (rigors) and water symbolizes *ḥasadim* (love). This is the kabbalistic significance of the water libation (*nisukh ha-mayim*) in addition to the wine libation (*nisukh ha-yayin*) on Sukkot. See Rabbi Shneur Zalman of Liadi, *Ma'amrei Admor Hazaken: Et-halekh Liozhna* (Brooklyn: Kehot, 2012), s.v. *Lehavin 'inyan nisukh ha-mayim ba-ḥag* (pp. 47–49); idem, *Siddur 'im Daḥ* (Brooklyn: Kehot, 1971), *Sha'ar ha-Sukkot*, s.v. *U-She'avtem mayim be-sasson mi-ma'yenei ha-yeshu'ah* (268a-269b); idem, *Likkutei Torah* (Brooklyn, Kehot, 1972), *Derushim le-Sukkot*, s.v. *U-She'avtem mayim be-sasson mi-ma'yenei ha-yeshu'ah* (79d-80d).

הַמַּבְדִּיל בֵּין קֹדֶשׁ לְחֹל, חַטֹּאתֵינוּ הוּא יִמְחֹל
זַרְעֵנוּ וְכַסְפֵּנוּ יַרְבֶּה כַּחוֹל וְכַכּוֹכָבִים בַּלָּיְלָה.

יוֹם פָּנָה כְּצֵל תֹּמֶר, אֶקְרָא לָאֵל עָלַי גּוֹמֵר
אָמַר שֹׁמֵר, אָתָא בֹקֶר וְגַם־לָיְלָה: ישעיה כא

צִדְקָתְךָ כְּהַר תָּבוֹר, עַל חֲטָאַי עָבוֹר תַּעֲבֹר
כְּיוֹם אֶתְמוֹל כִּי יַעֲבֹר, וְאַשְׁמוּרָה בַלָּיְלָה: תהלים צ

חָלְפָה עוֹנַת מִנְחָתִי, מִי יִתֵּן מְנוּחָתִי
יָגַעְתִּי בְּאַנְחָתִי, אַשְׂחֶה בְכָל־לָיְלָה: תהלים ו

קוֹלִי בַּל יֻנְטַל, פְּתַח לִי שַׁעַר הַמְנֻטָּל
שֶׁרֹּאשִׁי נִמְלָא טָל, קְוֻצּוֹתַי רְסִיסֵי לָיְלָה: שיר השירים ה

הֵעָתֵר נוֹרָא וְאָיֹם, אֲשַׁוֵּעַ, תְּנָה פִדְיוֹם
בְּנֶשֶׁף־בְּעֶרֶב יוֹם, בְּאִישׁוֹן לָיְלָה: משלי ז

קְרָאתִיךָ יָהּ, הוֹשִׁיעֵנִי, אֹרַח חַיִּים תּוֹדִיעֵנִי
מִדַּלָּה תְבַצְּעֵנִי, מִיּוֹם עַד לָיְלָה.

טַהֵר טִנּוּף מַעֲשַׂי, פֶּן יֹאמְרוּ מַכְעִיסַי
אַיֵּה אֱלוֹהַּ עֹשָׂי, נֹתֵן זְמִרוֹת בַּלָּיְלָה: איוב לה

נַחְנוּ בְיָדְךָ כַּחֹמֶר, סְלַח נָא עַל קַל וָחֹמֶר
יוֹם לְיוֹם יַבִּיעַ אֹמֶר, וְלַיְלָה לְּלָיְלָה: תהלים יט

---

Jerusalem) toured the newly established settlements of the Galilee to inspire religious observance. Many of the *ḥalutsim* or pioneers were notorious for their laxity in regard to Judaic practice, if not outright abandonment of the traditional lifestyle. This tour was known as the *"Massa' ha-Teshuvah"* (Journey of Return).

Before reciting *Havdalah* for the settlers Saturday night, Rav Kook remarked that generally his custom was not to pour water into the cup of *Havdalah*, but this time he would make an exception to the rule. He explained that according to Kabbalistic teaching the wine symbolizes stern judgment.

# חגים ומועדים

## FESTIVALS


| | | |
|---|---|---|
| נטילת לולב | 789 | BLESSING ON THE LULAV |
| הלל | 791 | HALLEL |
| מוסף לראש חודש | 799 | MUSAF FOR ROSH ḤODESH |
| קידוש לשלוש רגלים | 821 | KIDDUSH FOR YOM TOV |
| אושפיזין | 827 | USHPIZIN |
| עמידה לשלוש רגלים | 831 | AMIDA FOR YOM TOV |
| יזכור | 859 | YIZKOR |
| מוסף לשלוש רגלים | 869 | MUSAF FOR FESTIVALS |
| הושענות | 915 | HOSHANOT |
| התרת נדרים | 959 | ANNULMENT OF VOWS |
| קידוש לראש השנה | 963 | KIDDUSH FOR ROSH HASHANA |
| תשליך | 967 | TASHLIKH |
| וידוי לערב יום הכפורים | 971 | VIDUY BEFORE YOM KIPPUR |
| חנוכה | 981 | ḤANUKKA |
| פורים | 987 | PURIM |
| יום הזיכרון | 991 | YOM HAZIKARON |
| יום העצמאות | 995 | YOM HAATZMA'UT |
| סליחות | 1007 | SELIḤOT |

# Blessing on Taking the Lulav

*On Sukkot, except on Shabbat, the lulav and etrog are taken before Hallel.*

*Some say the following:*

יְהִי רָצוֹן May it be Your will, LORD my God and God of my fathers, that through the fruit of the citron tree, the palm frond, the myrtle branches and willows of the brook, the letters of Your unique name draw close to one another and become united in my hand. Make it known I am called by Your name, so that [evil] will fear to come close to me. When I wave them, may a rich flow of blessings flow from the supreme Source of wisdom to the place of the Tabernacle and the site of the House of our God. May the command of these four species be considered by You as if I had fulfilled it in all its details and roots, as well as the 613 commandments dependent on it, for it is my intention to unify the name of the Holy One, blessed be He, and His Divine Presence, in reverence and love, to unify the name *Yod-Heh* with *Vav-*
*Heh*, in perfect unity in the name of all Israel, Amen. Blessed is the *Ps. 89*
LORD forever, Amen and Amen.

*The lulav is taken in the right hand, with the myrtle leaves on the right, willow leaves on the left. The etrog is taken in the left hand, with its pointed end toward the floor. Then say the following blessing:*

בָּרוּךְ Blessed are You, LORD our God, King of the Universe,
who has made us holy through His commandments,
and has commanded us about taking the lulav.

*On the first day the lulav is taken, add:*

בָּרוּךְ Blessed are You, LORD our God, King of the Universe,
who has given us life, sustained us and brought us to this time.

*Invert the etrog, so that its pointed end is facing up.*
*Face the front of the synagogue and wave the lulav and etrog i*
*n the following sequence, three times in each direction:*
*ahead, right, back, left, up, down.*
*Continue to hold the lulav and etrog during Hallel.*

# סדר נטילת לולב

*On סוכות, except on שבת, the לולב and אתרוג are taken before הלל.*

*Some say the following:*

יְהִי רָצוֹן מִלְּפָנֶיךָ יהוה אֱלֹהַי וֵאלֹהֵי אֲבוֹתַי, בִּפְרִי עֵץ הָדָר וְכַפֹּת תְּמָרִים וַעֲנַף עֵץ עָבוֹת וְעַרְבֵי נַחַל, אוֹתִיּוֹת שִׁמְךָ הַמְיֻחָד תְּקָרֵב אֶחָד אֶל אֶחָד וְהָיוּ לַאֲחָדִים בְּיָדִי, וְלֵידַע אֵיךְ שִׁמְךָ נִקְרָא עָלַי וְיִירְאוּ מִגֶּשֶׁת אֵלַי. וּבְנַעֲנוּעִי אוֹתָם תַּשְׁפִּיעַ שֶׁפַע בְּרָכוֹת מִדֵּעַת עֶלְיוֹן לִנְוֵה אַפִּרְיוֹן לִמְכוֹן בֵּית אֱלֹהֵינוּ, וּתְהֵא חֲשׁוּבָה לְפָנֶיךָ מִצְוַת אַרְבָּעָה מִינִים אֵלּוּ כְּאִלּוּ קִיַּמְתִּיהָ בְּכָל פְּרָטוֹתֶיהָ וְשָׁרָשֶׁיהָ וְתַרְיַ״ג מִצְוֹת הַתְּלוּיוֹת בָּהּ, כִּי כַוָּנָתִי לְיַחֲדָא שְׁמָא דְקֻדְשָׁא בְּרִיךְ הוּא וּשְׁכִינְתֵהּ בִּדְחִילוּ וּרְחִימוּ, לְיַחֵד שֵׁם י״ה בו״ה בְּיִחוּדָא שְׁלִים בְּשֵׁם כָּל יִשְׂרָאֵל, אָמֵן. בָּרוּךְ יהוה לְעוֹלָם, אָמֵן וְאָמֵן: תהלים פט

*The לולב is taken in the right hand, with the הדסים on the right, ערבות on the left. The אתרוג is taken in the left hand, with its pointed end toward the floor. Then say the following blessing:*

בָּרוּךְ אַתָּה יהוה אֱלֹהֵינוּ מֶלֶךְ הָעוֹלָם
אֲשֶׁר קִדְּשָׁנוּ בְּמִצְוֹתָיו, וְצִוָּנוּ עַל נְטִילַת לוּלָב.

*On the first day the לולב is taken, add:*

בָּרוּךְ אַתָּה יהוה אֱלֹהֵינוּ מֶלֶךְ הָעוֹלָם
שֶׁהֶחֱיָנוּ וְקִיְּמָנוּ וְהִגִּיעָנוּ לַזְּמַן הַזֶּה.

*Invert the אתרוג, so that its pointed end is facing up.*
*Face the front of the בית כנסת and wave the לולב and אתרוג*
*in the following sequence, three times in each direction:*
*ahead, right, back, left, up, down.*
*Continue to hold the לולב and אתרוג during הלל.*

# Hallel

*On the first two days of Pesaḥ (in Israel on the first evening and day); Shavuot; the entire festival of Sukkot, Shemini Atzeret and Simḥat Torah, Ḥanukka, Full Hallel is said. Customs vary regarding the recitation of Hallel on Yom HaAtzma'ut and Yom Yerushalayim. On Rosh Ḥodesh and the last six days of Pesaḥ, Half Hallel is said. See laws 438–439.*

בָּרוּךְ Blessed are You, LORD our God, King of the Universe,
who has made us holy through His commandments
and has commanded us to recite the Hallel.

הַלְלוּיָהּ Halleluya! Servants of the LORD, give praise; praise the name Ps. 113
of the LORD. Blessed be the name of the LORD now and for evermore. From the rising of the sun to its setting, may the LORD's name be praised. High is the LORD above all nations; His glory is above the heavens. Who is like the LORD our God, who sits enthroned so high, yet turns so low to see the heavens and the earth? ▸ He raises the poor from the dust and the needy from the refuse heap, giving them a place alongside princes, the princes of His people. He makes the woman in a childless house a happy mother of children. Halleluya!

בְּצֵאת When Israel came out of Egypt, the house of Jacob from a Ps. 114
people of foreign tongue, Judah became His sanctuary, Israel His dominion. The sea saw and fled; the Jordan turned back. The mountains skipped like rams, the hills like lambs. ▸ Why was it, sea, that you fled? Jordan, why did you turn back? Why, mountains, did you skip like rams, and you, hills, like lambs? It was at the presence of the LORD, Creator of the earth, at the presence of the God of Jacob, who turned the rock into a pool of water, flint into a flowing spring.

*Omit on Rosh Ḥodesh (except on Ḥanukka) and the last six days of Pesaḥ:*

לֹא לָנוּ Not to us, LORD, not to us, but to Your name give glory, for Your Ps. 115
love, for Your faithfulness. Why should the nations say, "Where now is their God?" Our God is in heaven; whatever He wills He does. Their idols are silver and gold, made by human hands. They have mouths but cannot speak; eyes but cannot see. They have ears but cannot hear; noses but cannot smell. They have hands but cannot feel; feet but cannot walk. No sound comes from their throat. Those who make them become like them; so will all who

# סדר הלל

*On the first two days of* פסח *(in* ארץ ישראל *on the first evening and day);* שבועות*;*
*the entire festival of* סוכות*,* שמיני עצרת *and* שמחת תורה*,* חנוכה*, and,* הלל שלם *is said.*
*Customs vary regarding the recitation of* הלל *on* יום העצמאות *and* יום ירושלים*.*
*On* ראש חודש *and the last six days of* פסח*,* הלל בדילוג *is said. See laws 438–439.*

**בָּרוּךְ אַתָּה יהוה אֱלֹהֵינוּ מֶלֶךְ הָעוֹלָם**
**אֲשֶׁר קִדְּשָׁנוּ בְּמִצְוֹתָיו, וְצִוָּנוּ לִקְרֹא אֶת הַהַלֵּל.**

הַלְלוּיָהּ, הַלְלוּ עַבְדֵי יהוה, הַלְלוּ אֶת־שֵׁם יהוה: יְהִי שֵׁם יהוה תהלים קיג
מְבֹרָךְ, מֵעַתָּה וְעַד־עוֹלָם: מִמִּזְרַח־שֶׁמֶשׁ עַד־מְבוֹאוֹ, מְהֻלָּל שֵׁם
יהוה: רָם עַל־כָּל־גּוֹיִם יהוה, עַל הַשָּׁמַיִם כְּבוֹדוֹ: מִי כַּיהוה אֱלֹהֵינוּ,
הַמַּגְבִּיהִי לָשָׁבֶת: הַמַּשְׁפִּילִי לִרְאוֹת, בַּשָּׁמַיִם וּבָאָרֶץ: ‹ מְקִימִי
מֵעָפָר דָּל, מֵאַשְׁפֹּת יָרִים אֶבְיוֹן: לְהוֹשִׁיבִי עִם־נְדִיבִים, עִם נְדִיבֵי
עַמּוֹ: מוֹשִׁיבִי עֲקֶרֶת הַבַּיִת, אֵם־הַבָּנִים שְׂמֵחָה, הַלְלוּיָהּ:

בְּצֵאת יִשְׂרָאֵל מִמִּצְרָיִם, בֵּית יַעֲקֹב מֵעַם לֹעֵז: הָיְתָה יְהוּדָה תהלים קיד
לְקָדְשׁוֹ, יִשְׂרָאֵל מַמְשְׁלוֹתָיו: הַיָּם רָאָה וַיָּנֹס, הַיַּרְדֵּן יִסֹּב לְאָחוֹר:
הֶהָרִים רָקְדוּ כְאֵילִים, גְּבָעוֹת כִּבְנֵי־צֹאן: ‹ מַה־לְּךָ הַיָּם כִּי תָנוּס,
הַיַּרְדֵּן תִּסֹּב לְאָחוֹר: הֶהָרִים תִּרְקְדוּ כְאֵילִים, גְּבָעוֹת כִּבְנֵי־צֹאן:
מִלִּפְנֵי אָדוֹן חוּלִי אָרֶץ, מִלִּפְנֵי אֱלוֹהַּ יַעֲקֹב: הַהֹפְכִי הַצּוּר אֲגַם־
מָיִם, חַלָּמִישׁ לְמַעְיְנוֹ־מָיִם:

*Omit on* ראש חודש *(except on* חנוכה*) and the last six days of* פסח*:*

לֹא לָנוּ יהוה לֹא לָנוּ, כִּי־לְשִׁמְךָ תֵּן כָּבוֹד, עַל־חַסְדְּךָ עַל־אֲמִתֶּךָ: לָמָּה תהלים קטו
יֹאמְרוּ הַגּוֹיִם אַיֵּה־נָא אֱלֹהֵיהֶם: וֵאלֹהֵינוּ בַשָּׁמָיִם, כֹּל אֲשֶׁר־חָפֵץ
עָשָׂה: עֲצַבֵּיהֶם כֶּסֶף וְזָהָב, מַעֲשֵׂה יְדֵי אָדָם: פֶּה־לָהֶם וְלֹא יְדַבֵּרוּ,
עֵינַיִם לָהֶם וְלֹא יִרְאוּ: אָזְנַיִם לָהֶם וְלֹא יִשְׁמָעוּ, אַף לָהֶם וְלֹא יְרִיחוּן:
יְדֵיהֶם וְלֹא יְמִישׁוּן, רַגְלֵיהֶם וְלֹא יְהַלֵּכוּ, לֹא־יֶהְגּוּ בִּגְרוֹנָם: כְּמוֹהֶם יִהְיוּ

trust in them. ▸ Israel, trust in the LORD – He is their Help and their Shield. House of Aaron, trust in the LORD – He is their Help and their Shield. You who fear the LORD, trust in the LORD – He is their Help and their Shield.

יהוה זְכָרָנוּ The LORD remembers us and will bless us. He will bless the house of Israel. He will bless the house of Aaron. He will bless those who fear the LORD, small and great alike. May the LORD give you increase: you and your children. May you be blessed by the LORD, Maker of heaven and earth. ▸ The heavens are the LORD's, but the earth He has given over to mankind. It is not the dead who praise the LORD, nor those who go down to the silent grave. But we will bless the LORD, now and for ever. Halleluya!

*Omit on Rosh Ḥodesh (except on Ḥanukka) and the last six days of Pesaḥ:*

אָהַבְתִּי I love the LORD, for He hears my voice, my pleas. He turns His ear to me whenever I call. The bonds of death encompassed me, the anguish of the grave came upon me, I was overcome by trouble and sorrow. Then I called on the name of the LORD: "LORD, I pray, save my life." Gracious is the LORD, and righteous; our God is full of compassion. The LORD protects the simple-hearted. When I was brought low, He saved me. My soul, be at peace once more, for the LORD has been good to you. For You have rescued me from death, my eyes from weeping, my feet from stumbling. ▸ I shall walk in the presence of the LORD in the land of the living. I had faith, even when I said, "I am greatly afflicted," even when I said rashly, "All men are liars." *Ps. 116*

מָה־אָשִׁיב How can I repay the LORD for all His goodness to me? I will lift the cup of salvation and call on the name of the LORD. I will fulfill my vows to the LORD in the presence of all His people. Grievous in the LORD's sight is the death of His devoted ones. Truly, LORD, I am Your servant; I am Your servant, the son of Your maidservant. You set me free from my chains. ▸ To You I shall bring a thanksgiving-offering and call on the LORD by name. I will fulfill my vows to the LORD in the presence of all His people, in the courts of the House of the LORD, in your midst, Jerusalem. Halleluya.

הַלְלוּ Praise the LORD, all nations; acclaim Him, all you peoples; *Ps. 117*
for His loving-kindness to us is strong,
and the LORD's faithfulness is everlasting.
Halleluya.

עֹשֵׂיהֶם, כֹּל אֲשֶׁר־בֹּטֵחַ בָּהֶם: ◂ יִשְׂרָאֵל בְּטַח בַּיהוה, עֶזְרָם וּמָגִנָּם הוּא: בֵּית אַהֲרֹן בִּטְחוּ בַיהוה, עֶזְרָם וּמָגִנָּם הוּא: יִרְאֵי יהוה בִּטְחוּ בַיהוה, עֶזְרָם וּמָגִנָּם הוּא:

יהוה זְכָרָנוּ יְבָרֵךְ, יְבָרֵךְ אֶת־בֵּית יִשְׂרָאֵל, יְבָרֵךְ אֶת־בֵּית אַהֲרֹן: יְבָרֵךְ יִרְאֵי יהוה, הַקְּטַנִּים עִם־הַגְּדֹלִים: יֹסֵף יהוה עֲלֵיכֶם, עֲלֵיכֶם וְעַל־בְּנֵיכֶם: בְּרוּכִים אַתֶּם לַיהוה, עֹשֵׂה שָׁמַיִם וָאָרֶץ: ◂ הַשָּׁמַיִם שָׁמַיִם לַיהוה, וְהָאָרֶץ נָתַן לִבְנֵי־אָדָם: לֹא הַמֵּתִים יְהַלְלוּ־יָהּ, וְלֹא כָּל־יֹרְדֵי דוּמָה: וַאֲנַחְנוּ נְבָרֵךְ יָהּ, מֵעַתָּה וְעַד־עוֹלָם, הַלְלוּיָהּ:

*Omit on* ראש חודש *(except on* חנוכה*) and the last six days of* פסח*:*

תהלים קטז

אָהַבְתִּי, כִּי־יִשְׁמַע יהוה, אֶת־קוֹלִי תַּחֲנוּנָי: כִּי־הִטָּה אָזְנוֹ לִי, וּבְיָמַי אֶקְרָא: אֲפָפוּנִי חֶבְלֵי־מָוֶת, וּמְצָרֵי שְׁאוֹל מְצָאוּנִי, צָרָה וְיָגוֹן אֶמְצָא: וּבְשֵׁם־יהוה אֶקְרָא, אָנָּה יהוה מַלְּטָה נַפְשִׁי: חַנּוּן יהוה וְצַדִּיק, וֵאלֹהֵינוּ מְרַחֵם: שֹׁמֵר פְּתָאיִם יהוה, דַּלּוֹתִי וְלִי יְהוֹשִׁיעַ: שׁוּבִי נַפְשִׁי לִמְנוּחָיְכִי, כִּי־יהוה גָּמַל עָלָיְכִי: כִּי חִלַּצְתָּ נַפְשִׁי מִמָּוֶת, אֶת־עֵינִי מִן־דִּמְעָה, אֶת־רַגְלִי מִדֶּחִי: ◂ אֶתְהַלֵּךְ לִפְנֵי יהוה, בְּאַרְצוֹת הַחַיִּים: הֶאֱמַנְתִּי כִּי אֲדַבֵּר, אֲנִי עָנִיתִי מְאֹד: אֲנִי אָמַרְתִּי בְחָפְזִי, כָּל־הָאָדָם כֹּזֵב:

מָה־אָשִׁיב לַיהוה, כָּל־תַּגְמוּלוֹהִי עָלָי: כּוֹס־יְשׁוּעוֹת אֶשָּׂא, וּבְשֵׁם יהוה אֶקְרָא: נְדָרַי לַיהוה אֲשַׁלֵּם, נֶגְדָה־נָּא לְכָל־עַמּוֹ: יָקָר בְּעֵינֵי יהוה, הַמָּוְתָה לַחֲסִידָיו: אָנָּה יהוה כִּי־אֲנִי עַבְדֶּךָ, אֲנִי־עַבְדְּךָ בֶּן־אֲמָתֶךָ, פִּתַּחְתָּ לְמוֹסֵרָי: ◂ לְךָ־אֶזְבַּח זֶבַח תּוֹדָה, וּבְשֵׁם יהוה אֶקְרָא: נְדָרַי לַיהוה אֲשַׁלֵּם, נֶגְדָה־נָּא לְכָל־עַמּוֹ: בְּחַצְרוֹת בֵּית יהוה, בְּתוֹכֵכִי יְרוּשָׁלָםִ, הַלְלוּיָהּ:

תהלים קיז

הַלְלוּ אֶת־יהוה כָּל־גּוֹיִם, שַׁבְּחוּהוּ כָּל־הָאֻמִּים:
כִּי גָבַר עָלֵינוּ חַסְדּוֹ, וֶאֱמֶת־יהוה לְעוֹלָם
הַלְלוּיָהּ:

*The following verses are chanted by the Leader.*
*At the end of each verse, the congregation responds, "Thank the LORD for He is good; His loving-kindness is for ever." See law 439.*
*On Sukkot, the lulav and etrog are waved, three waves for each word of the verse (except God's name). On the first word, wave forward, then, on subsequent words, wave right, back, left, up and down respectively. The Leader waves only for the first two verses. The congregation waves each time the first verse is said in response.*

הוֹדוּ Thank the LORD for He is good; His loving-kindness is for ever. Ps. 118
Let Israel say His loving-kindness is for ever.
Let the house of Aaron say His loving-kindness is for ever.
Let those who fear the LORD say His loving-kindness is for ever.

מִן־הַמֵּצַר In my distress I called on the LORD. The LORD answered me and set me free. The LORD is with me; I will not be afraid. What can man do to me? The LORD is with me. He is my Helper. I will see the downfall of my enemies. It is better to take refuge in the LORD than to trust in man. It is better to take refuge in the LORD than to trust in princes. The nations all surrounded me, but in the LORD's name I drove them off. They surrounded me on every side, but in the LORD's name I drove them off. They surrounded me like bees, they attacked me as fire attacks brushwood, but in the LORD's name I drove them off. They thrust so hard against me, I nearly fell, but the LORD came to my help. The LORD is my strength and my song; He has become my salvation. Sounds of song and salvation resound in the tents of the righteous: "The LORD's right hand has done mighty deeds. The LORD's right hand is lifted high. The LORD's right hand has done mighty deeds." I will not die but live, and tell what the LORD has done. The LORD has chastened me severely, but He has not given me over to death. ▸ Open for me the gates of righteousness that I may enter them and thank the LORD. This is the gateway to the LORD; through it, the righteous shall enter.

אוֹדְךָ I will thank You, for You answered me, and became my salvation.
I will thank You, for You answered me, and became my salvation.

The stone the builders rejected has become the main cornerstone.
The stone the builders rejected has become the main cornerstone.

This is the LORD's doing. It is wondrous in our eyes.
This is the LORD's doing. It is wondrous in our eyes.

This is the day the LORD has made. Let us rejoice and be glad in it.
This is the day the LORD has made. Let us rejoice and be glad in it.

*The following verses are chanted by the* שליח ציבור.
*At the end of each verse, the* קהל *responds:* הוֹדוּ לַיהוה כִּי־טוֹב, כִּי לְעוֹלָם חַסְדּוֹ. *See law 439.*
*On* סוכות, *the* לולב *and* אתרוג *are waved, three waves for each word of the verse (except God's name). On the first word, wave forward, then, on subsequent words, wave right, back, left, up and down respectively. The* שליח ציבור *waves only for the first two verses. The* קהל *waves each time the first verse is said in response.*

תהלים קיח

הוֹדוּ לַיהוה כִּי־טוֹב כִּי לְעוֹלָם חַסְדּוֹ:
יֹאמַר־נָא יִשְׂרָאֵל כִּי לְעוֹלָם חַסְדּוֹ:
יֹאמְרוּ־נָא בֵית־אַהֲרֹן כִּי לְעוֹלָם חַסְדּוֹ:
יֹאמְרוּ־נָא יִרְאֵי יהוה כִּי לְעוֹלָם חַסְדּוֹ:

מִן־הַמֵּצַר קָרָאתִי יָּהּ, עָנָנִי בַמֶּרְחָב יָהּ: יהוה לִי לֹא אִירָא, מַה־יַּעֲשֶׂה לִי אָדָם: יהוה לִי בְּעֹזְרָי, וַאֲנִי אֶרְאֶה בְשֹׂנְאָי: טוֹב לַחֲסוֹת בַּיהוה, מִבְּטֹחַ בָּאָדָם: טוֹב לַחֲסוֹת בַּיהוה, מִבְּטֹחַ בִּנְדִיבִים: כָּל־גּוֹיִם סְבָבוּנִי, בְּשֵׁם יהוה כִּי אֲמִילַם: סַבּוּנִי גַם־סְבָבוּנִי, בְּשֵׁם יהוה כִּי אֲמִילַם: סַבּוּנִי כִדְבֹרִים, דֹּעֲכוּ כְּאֵשׁ קוֹצִים, בְּשֵׁם יהוה כִּי אֲמִילַם: דָּחֹה דְחִיתַנִי לִנְפֹּל, וַיהוה עֲזָרָנִי: עָזִּי וְזִמְרָת יָהּ, וַיְהִי־לִי לִישׁוּעָה: קוֹל רִנָּה וִישׁוּעָה בְּאָהֳלֵי צַדִּיקִים, יְמִין יהוה עֹשָׂה חָיִל: יְמִין יהוה רוֹמֵמָה, יְמִין יהוה עֹשָׂה חָיִל: לֹא־אָמוּת כִּי־אֶחְיֶה, וַאֲסַפֵּר מַעֲשֵׂי יָהּ: יַסֹּר יִסְּרַנִּי יָּהּ, וְלַמָּוֶת לֹא נְתָנָנִי: ‹ פִּתְחוּ־לִי שַׁעֲרֵי־צֶדֶק, אָבֹא־בָם אוֹדֶה יָהּ: זֶה־הַשַּׁעַר לַיהוה, צַדִּיקִים יָבֹאוּ בוֹ:

אוֹדְךָ כִּי עֲנִיתָנִי, וַתְּהִי־לִי לִישׁוּעָה:
אוֹדְךָ כִּי עֲנִיתָנִי, וַתְּהִי־לִי לִישׁוּעָה:

אֶבֶן מָאֲסוּ הַבּוֹנִים, הָיְתָה לְרֹאשׁ פִּנָּה:
אֶבֶן מָאֲסוּ הַבּוֹנִים, הָיְתָה לְרֹאשׁ פִּנָּה:

מֵאֵת יהוה הָיְתָה זֹּאת, הִיא נִפְלָאת בְּעֵינֵינוּ:
מֵאֵת יהוה הָיְתָה זֹּאת, הִיא נִפְלָאת בְּעֵינֵינוּ:

זֶה־הַיּוֹם עָשָׂה יהוה, נָגִילָה וְנִשְׂמְחָה בוֹ:
זֶה־הַיּוֹם עָשָׂה יהוה, נָגִילָה וְנִשְׂמְחָה בוֹ:

*On Sukkot, the lulav and etrog are waved while saying "LORD, please, save us," three waves for each word of the verse (except God's name). On the first word, wave forward and right; third word: back and left; fourth word: up and down.*

*Leader followed by congregation:*

אָנָּא LORD, please, save us.
LORD, please, save us.
LORD, please, grant us success.
LORD, please, grant us success.

*On Sukkot, the lulav and etrog are waved while saying "Thank the LORD…," three waves for each word of the verse (except God's name). On the first word, wave forward, then, on subsequent words, wave right, back, left, up and down respectively.*

בָּרוּךְ Blessed is one who comes in the name of the LORD;
we bless you from the House of the LORD.
Blessed is one who comes in the name of the LORD;
we bless you from the House of the LORD.

The LORD is God; He has given us light. Bind the festival offering with thick cords [and bring it] to the horns of the altar.
The LORD is God; He has given us light. Bind the festival offering with thick cords [and bring it] to the horns of the altar.

You are my God and I will thank You; You are my God, I will exalt You.
You are my God and I will thank You; You are my God, I will exalt You.

Thank the LORD for He is good; His loving-kindness is for ever.
Thank the LORD for He is good; His loving-kindness is for ever.

יְהַלְלוּךָ All Your works will praise You, LORD our God, and Your devoted ones – the righteous who do Your will, together with all Your people the house of Israel – will joyously thank, bless, praise, glorify, exalt, revere, sanctify, and proclaim the sovereignty of Your name, our King. ▸ For it is good to thank You and fitting to sing psalms to Your name, for from eternity to eternity You are God. Blessed are You, LORD, King who is extolled with praises.

*On Rosh Ḥodesh and Ḥol HaMo'ed, say Full Kaddish on page 242 and continue the service with the Reading of the Torah on page 222 (on Hoshana Raba on page 570).*

*On Sukkot some say at this point Hoshanot on page 914, then Full Kaddish on page 242.*

*On Shabbat and Yom Tov, the service continues with Full Kaddish on page 568.*

*On weekday Ḥanukka (except Rosh Ḥodesh Tevet), Yom HaAtzma'ut and Yom Yerushalayim, the service continues with Half Kaddish on page 222.*

*On* סוכות*, the* לולב *and* אתרוג *are waved while saying* אָנָּא יהוה הוֹשִׁיעָה נָּא*, three waves for each word of the verse (except God's name). On the first word, wave forward and right; third word: back and left; fourth word: up and down.*
שליח ציבור *followed by* קהל*:*

**אָנָּא יהוה הוֹשִׁיעָה נָּא:**
**אָנָּא יהוה הוֹשִׁיעָה נָּא:**
**אָנָּא יהוה הַצְלִיחָה נָא:**
**אָנָּא יהוה הַצְלִיחָה נָא:**

*On* סוכות*, the* לולב *and* אתרוג *are waved while saying* הוֹדוּ לַיהוה כִּי־טוֹב, כִּי לְעוֹלָם חַסְדּוֹ*, three waves for each word of the verse (except God's name). On the first word, wave forward, then, on subsequent words, wave right, back, left, up and down respectively.*

**בָּרוּךְ הַבָּא בְּשֵׁם יהוה, בֵּרַכְנוּכֶם מִבֵּית יהוה:**
בָּרוּךְ הַבָּא בְּשֵׁם יהוה, בֵּרַכְנוּכֶם מִבֵּית יהוה:

**אֵל יהוה וַיָּאֶר לָנוּ, אִסְרוּ־חַג בַּעֲבֹתִים עַד־קַרְנוֹת הַמִּזְבֵּחַ:**
אֵל יהוה וַיָּאֶר לָנוּ, אִסְרוּ־חַג בַּעֲבֹתִים עַד־קַרְנוֹת הַמִּזְבֵּחַ:

**אֵלִי אַתָּה וְאוֹדֶךָּ, אֱלֹהַי אֲרוֹמְמֶךָּ:**
אֵלִי אַתָּה וְאוֹדֶךָּ, אֱלֹהַי אֲרוֹמְמֶךָּ:

**הוֹדוּ לַיהוה כִּי־טוֹב, כִּי לְעוֹלָם חַסְדּוֹ:**
הוֹדוּ לַיהוה כִּי־טוֹב, כִּי לְעוֹלָם חַסְדּוֹ:

**יְהַלְלְוּךָ יהוה אֱלֹהֵינוּ כָּל מַעֲשֶׂיךָ, וַחֲסִידֶיךָ צַדִּיקִים עוֹשֵׂי רְצוֹנֶךָ, וְכָל עַמְּךָ בֵּית יִשְׂרָאֵל בְּרִנָּה יוֹדוּ וִיבָרְכוּ וִישַׁבְּחוּ וִיפָאֲרוּ וִירוֹמְמוּ וְיַעֲרִיצוּ וְיַקְדִּישׁוּ וְיַמְלִיכוּ אֶת שִׁמְךָ מַלְכֵּנוּ. • כִּי לְךָ טוֹב לְהוֹדוֹת וּלְשִׁמְךָ נָאֶה לְזַמֵּר, כִּי מֵעוֹלָם וְעַד עוֹלָם אַתָּה אֵל. בָּרוּךְ אַתָּה יהוה, מֶלֶךְ מְהֻלָּל בַּתִּשְׁבָּחוֹת.**

*On* ראש חודש *and* חול המועד*, say* קדיש שלם *on page 243 and continue the service with* קריאת התורה *on page 223 (on* הושענא רבה *on page 571).*

*On* סוכות *some say at this point* הושענות *on page 915, then* קדיש שלם *on page 243.*

*On* שבת *and* יום טוב*, the service continues with* קדיש שלם *on page 569.*

*On weekday* חנוכה *(except* ראש חודש טבת*),* יום העצמאות *and* יום ירושלים*, the service continues with* חצי קדיש *on page 223.*

# Musaf for Rosh Ḥodesh

## THE AMIDA

*The following prayer, until "in former years" on page 814, is said silently, standing with feet together. If there is a minyan, the Amida is repeated aloud by the Leader. Take three steps forward and at the points indicated by ▾, bend the knees at the first word, bow at the second, and stand straight before saying God's name.*

When I proclaim the LORD's name, give glory to our God. *Deut. 32*
O LORD, open my lips, so that my mouth may declare Your praise. *Ps. 51*

### PATRIARCHS

▾בָּרוּךְ▾ Blessed are You, LORD our God and God of our fathers,
God of Abraham, God of Isaac and God of Jacob;
the great, mighty and awesome God, God Most High,
who bestows acts of loving-kindness and creates all,
who remembers the loving-kindness
of the fathers and will bring a Redeemer
to their children's children for the sake of His name, in love.
King, Helper, Savior, Shield:
▾Blessed are You, LORD,
Shield of Abraham.

### DIVINE MIGHT

אַתָּה גִּבּוֹר You are eternally mighty, LORD.
You give life to the dead and have great power to save.

*The phrase "He makes the wind blow and the rain fall" is added from Simḥat Torah until Pesaḥ. In Israel the phrase "He causes the dew to fall" is added from Pesaḥ until Shemini Atzeret. See laws 129–131.*

*In fall & winter:* He makes the wind blow and the rain fall.
*In Israel, in spring & summer:* He causes the dew to fall.

He sustains the living with loving-kindness,
and with great compassion revives the dead.
He supports the fallen, heals the sick, sets captives free,
and keeps His faith with those who sleep in the dust.

מִי כָמְוֹךָ, בַּעַל גְּבוּרוֹת, וּמִי דְּוֹמֶה לָּךְ
מֶלֶךְ, מֵמִית וּמְחַיֶּה וּמַצְמִיחַ יְשׁוּעָה.
וְנֶאֱמָן אַתָּה לְהַחֲיוֹת מֵתִים.
בָּרוּךְ אַתָּה יהוה, מְחַיֵּה הַמֵּתִים.

*When saying the* עמידה *silently, continue with* אַתָּה קָדוֹשׁ *below.*

---

קדושה

*During the* חזרת הש״ץ*, the following is said standing with feet together, rising on the toes at the words indicated by* ^.

then קהל ש״ץ: נְקַדֵּשׁ אֶת שִׁמְךָ בָּעוֹלָם, כְּשֵׁם שֶׁמַּקְדִּישִׁים אוֹתוֹ בִּשְׁמֵי מָרוֹם
כַּכָּתוּב עַל יַד נְבִיאֶךָ: וְקָרָא זֶה אֶל־זֶה וְאָמַר — ישעיה ו

then קהל ש״ץ: ^קָדוֹשׁ, ^קָדוֹשׁ, ^קָדוֹשׁ, יהוה צְבָאוֹת, מְלֹא כָל־הָאָרֶץ כְּבוֹדוֹ:
לְעֻמָּתָם בָּרוּךְ יֹאמֵרוּ

then קהל ש״ץ: ^בָּרוּךְ כְּבוֹד־יהוה מִמְּקוֹמוֹ: — יחזקאל ג
וּבְדִבְרֵי קָדְשְׁךָ כָּתוּב לֵאמֹר

then קהל ש״ץ: ^יִמְלֹךְ יהוה לְעוֹלָם, אֱלֹהַיִךְ צִיּוֹן לְדֹר וָדֹר, הַלְלוּיָהּ: — תהלים קמו

ש״ץ: לְדוֹר וָדוֹר נַגִּיד גָּדְלֶךָ, וּלְנֵצַח נְצָחִים קְדֻשָּׁתְךָ נַקְדִּישׁ
וְשִׁבְחֲךָ אֱלֹהֵינוּ מִפִּינוּ לֹא יָמוּשׁ לְעוֹלָם וָעֶד
כִּי אֵל מֶלֶךְ גָּדוֹל וְקָדוֹשׁ אָתָּה.
בָּרוּךְ אַתָּה יהוה הָאֵל הַקָּדוֹשׁ.

*The* שליח ציבור *continues with* רָאשֵׁי חֳדָשִׁים *on the next page.*

---

קדושת השם

אַתָּה קָדוֹשׁ וְשִׁמְךָ קָדוֹשׁ
וּקְדוֹשִׁים בְּכָל יוֹם יְהַלְלוּךָ סֶּלָה.
בָּרוּךְ אַתָּה יהוה, הָאֵל הַקָּדוֹשׁ.

HOLINESS OF THE DAY

רָאשֵׁי חֳדָשִׁים You have given New Moons to Your people as a time of atonement for all their offspring.

---

Rachel stole *the teraphim* (idols) of her father Laban.[5] According to the Rabbis, she did so in order to separate her father from worshipping idolatry.[6] She then hid the *teraphim* in the saddle of the camel and sat upon them. And when Laban searched high and low for his missing *teraphim*, Rachel excused herself from dismounting from the saddle because she was experiencing, in her own words, the "way of women."[7] Rachel's husband Jacob, on the other hand, was not determined to keep his father-in-law from the worship of idolatry. He was willing to accommodate Laban by returning the stolen "gods."[8]

Thus in the final analysis, it was Rachel's menstrual cycle, her internal lunar rhythm, which kept her father from his pagan "gods." And for the women of Israel's refusal to cooperate with their menfolk in the fashioning of pagan "gods," they were rewarded forever after with the joyous celebration of the New Moon.

There is Judaism of the sun and of intellect, and there is Judaism of the moon and of intuition. The latter is as basic as the tides of the ocean and the flow of women. There were times in our history when the Judaism of the sun, of reason, of the men, succumbed to idolatry in forms subtle or not so subtle, and then it was the power of the women, of stubborn, obstinate women, who refused to capitulate to outside, foreign influences, that guarded our faith. Such was the case in two classic communities of *anussim* (Jews forcibly converted to the dominant religion): the *anussim* or *Marranos* of Belmonte, Portugal, and the *anussim* of Meshed, Persia. In Portugal, the Jews were forcibly converted to Roman Catholicism; in Persia, to Shi'ite Islam. In both communities, it was the women who managed over generations to keep the spark of Judaism alive underground, in a form that has come to be termed "crypto-Judaism."

In those times of communal crisis, it was the healthy, unimpaired instinct of "Mother Rachel" that preserved our religious identity. In recognition of their outstanding accomplishments – against all odds and against the "voice of reason" of their moderate menfolk – Jewish women were rewarded with the festival of *Rosh Ḥodesh*. (Editor)

---

5. Genesis 31:20.
6. Rashi ad loc; *Genesis Rabbah* 74:5.
7. Genesis 31:34, 35.
8. Genesis 31:32.

קדושת היום

# רָאשֵׁי חֳדָשִׁים לְעַמְּךָ נָתַתָּ
# זְמַן כַּפָּרָה לְכָל תּוֹלְדוֹתָם

---

רָאשֵׁי חֳדָשִׁים לְעַמְּךָ נָתַתָּ *You have given New Moons to Your people.* The initials of the words *Rashei ḥodashim le-ʿamekha* spell out the name of our Matriarch *Raḥel.*[1]

In the Torah, we find Rachel making mention of the fact that she was menstruating (in order to excuse herself for not dismounting from the camel to greet her father Laban, as proper etiquette would have dictated).[2] The connection of woman to the moon is biological; the monthly period is related to the lunar cycle.

It is customary that women observe *Rosh Ḥodesh* as a minor festival, some going so far as to refrain from labor on that day.[3] According to *Pirkei de-Rabbi Eliezer,* this festival was granted to the women by the Almighty as their due reward for refusing their husband's request to contribute their gold earrings to the fashioning of the Golden Calf.[4]

The cause and effect are well-nigh incomprehensible. By what stretch of the imagination is the observance of *Rosh Ḥodesh* a commensurate reward for not contributing to idolatry? The answer would appear to lie in the story of Rachel referred to above.

---

1. Rabbi Ḥayyim Vital, *Peri ʿEts Ḥayyim, Shaʿar Rosh Ḥodesh,* chap. 3. Rabbi Ḥayyim Yosef David Azulai (Ḥida) records the following tradition:

   > Rachel our Matriarch – In her merit the New Moons were given to Israel and so *Roshei Ḥodashim Le-ʿamekha* initials *Raḥel.* And the Additional Service of the New Moon (*Mussaf Rosh Ḥodesh*) was instituted by Rachel our Matriarch for she foresaw with divine inspiration that the women in the desert would not succumb to the Calf, and she hinted her name in the initials *Roshei Ḥodashim Le-ʿamekha.* (Rabbi Ḥ.Y.D. Azulai, *Midbar Kedemot, Reish,* no. 5)

2. Genesis 31:35. Traditionally *"derekh nashim"* is understood as menstruation, although there is a minority opinion among Bible commentators that in this context it refers to pregnancy.
3. Targum and Radak to 1 Samuel 20:19; *y. Pesaḥim* 4:1 and *Taʿanit* 1:6; *Tur* and *Shulḥan ʿArukh, OḤ,* chap. 417. See *Be'ur Halakhah* there.
4. *Pirkei de-Rabbi Eliezer,* chap. 45; Rashi and *Tosafot, Megillah* 22b; *Tosafot, Ḥagigah* 18a, s.v. *Rosh Ḥodesh,* and *Rosh Hashanah* 23a, s.v. *mi-shum.* For the women's refusal to fork over their jewelry to their husbands, see Pseudo-Jonathan to Exodus 32:3.

They would bring You offerings of goodwill,
and goats as sin-offerings for atonement.
May it serve as a remembrance for them all,
and a deliverance of their lives from the hand of the enemy.
May You establish a new altar in Zion,
and may we offer on it the New Moon burnt-offering,
and prepare goats in favor.
May we all rejoice in the Temple service,
and may the songs of David Your servant,
be heard in Your city, chanted before Your altar.
Bestow on them everlasting love,
and remember the covenant of the fathers for their children.

---

Rav Kook portrays the Sun as *"ahavah"* (love of the Lord) and the Moon as *"yir'ah"* (fear of the Lord). At the present time, worship of God out of fear is certainly inferior to service out of love.[11] But there will come a day when the two will once again be on a par. We strive for that *tikkun 'olam,* that cosmic correction.[9]

How can fear take its rightful place alongside love? There are two types of *yir'ah*. In medieval Jewish philosophy, they are known as *"yir'at ha-'onesh"* (fear of punishment) and *yir'at ha-romemut* (awe).[12] (In *Tikkunei Zohar,* the first word of the Torah, *"Bereshit,"* is permutated to two words, *"Yare-boshet,"* "fear-shame," which is to say a fear coupled with embarassment. Today we might say "shock and awe.")[13] Maimonides describes a to-and-fro movement whereby initially one experiences love and attraction to the Almighty, only to be taken aback, humbled and devastated in the presence of the Lord.[14]

---

11. Maimonides, *MT, Hil. Teshuvah* 10:1, 2.
12. See Baḥya ibn Pakuda, *Ḥovot ha-Levavot, Sha'ar Ahavat Hashem,* chap. 6; anonymous *Peirush* to *MT, Hil. Yesodei ha-Torah* 2:1; Rabbi Moses Ḥayyim Luzzatto, *Mesillat Yesharim,* chap. 24; Rabbi Israel Salanter, *'Or Yisrael,* ed. Rabbi Isaac Blaser (Vilna, 1900), 5c. See also *Zohar* I, 11b; *Tikkunei Zohar, tikkun* 30 (Vilna edition, 81b).
In the *Tanya,* they are referred to as *yir'ah tata'ah* (the lower fear) and *yir'ah 'ila'ah* (the higher fear). See Rabbi Shneur Zalman of Liadi, *Tanya* I, 41 (57a).
13. *Tikkunei Zohar, tikkunim* 7, 58; *Ra'aya Mehemna* in *Zohar* III, 257a. See *Tanya* I, 41 (57a) where *"yare boshet"* is equated with the higher fear (*yir'ah 'ila'ah*). And ibid. chap. 3 (7b) for the equation of *"yir'at ha-romemut"* with *"yare-boshet."*
14. Maimonides, *MT, Hil. Yesodei ha-Torah* 2:2. Many years ago, the Editor (BN) suggested

בִּהְיוֹתָם מַקְרִיבִים לְפָנֶיךָ זִבְחֵי רָצוֹן
וּשְׂעִירֵי חַטָּאת לְכַפֵּר בַּעֲדָם.
זִכָּרוֹן לְכֻלָּם יִהְיוּ, וּתְשׁוּעַת נַפְשָׁם מִיַּד שׂוֹנֵא.
מִזְבֵּחַ חָדָשׁ בְּצִיּוֹן תָּכִין, וְעוֹלַת רֹאשׁ חֹדֶשׁ נַעֲלֶה עָלָיו
וּשְׂעִירֵי עִזִּים נַעֲשֶׂה בְרָצוֹן
וּבַעֲבוֹדַת בֵּית הַמִּקְדָּשׁ נִשְׂמַח כֻּלָּנוּ
וּבְשִׁירֵי דָוִד עַבְדְּךָ הַנִּשְׁמָעִים בְּעִירֶךָ, הָאֲמוּרִים לִפְנֵי מִזְבְּחֶךָ.
אַהֲבַת עוֹלָם תָּבִיא לָהֶם, וּבְרִית אָבוֹת לַבָּנִים תִּזְכֹּר.

---

זְמַן כַּפָּרָה לְכָל תּוֹלְדוֹתָם *As a time of atonement for all their offspring* (*previous page*). There is an early custom to fast on the eve of *Rosh Ḥodesh*. It is referred to as *"Yom Kippur Katan"* ("Minor Day of Atonement"). One is struck by the anomaly. When it comes to the actual Day of Atonement, we are commanded to eat on *Erev Yom Kippur* and to fast on *Yom Kippur* itself. In regard to *Rosh Ḥodesh* though, we have the opposite scenario. We fast on the day preceding, and eat a *se'udah* or festive meal on the actual day of *Rosh Ḥodesh*. Rav Kook explains that fasting symbolizes "return from fear" (*"teshuvah mi-yir'ah"*), whereas feasting symbolizes "return from love" (*"teshuvah me-ahavah"*). Now on a superficial level (*ḥitsoniyut*), love is higher than fear. So on *Rosh Ḥodesh*, fast precedes feast. From fear we ascend to love. But on a level of inwardness (*penimiyut*), fear (or perhaps the better word is *awe*) is actually higher than love, for thereby one reaches a state where there is no selfish motive. One's motivation is purely to cleave to the Lord. From this perspective, one ascends from love to fear. So on Yom Kippur, feast precedes fast.[9] (See the following Excursus.)

EXCURSUS ON THE MYTH OF THE MINIMIZATION OF THE MOON

In the myth of the dimunition of the Moon, the Moon complained to the Holy One, blessed be He, that it is impossible for two kings (Sun and Moon) to wear the same crown. To which came the divine response: "Go reduce yourself."[10]

---

9. *OR*, vol. 1, pp. 422–423.
10. *b. Ḥullin 60b*.

וַהֲבִיאֵנוּ Bring us back, with song, to Zion Your city,
and to Jerusalem Your Sanctuary with everlasting joy.
There we will prepare for You our obligatory offerings:
the regular daily offerings in their order,
and the additional offerings according to their law.

---

The *kitrug*, the accusation of the Moon, stemmed from "scarcity mentality," from anxiety and insecurity. That mentality itself became the platform for an entire *seder ha-'avodah* (service) predicated on lower-level primal fear. (One might say that the *"yir'ah ra'ah"* or "evil fear" stemming from *"katnut"* or small-mindedness was the very onset of the *"mi'ut 'atsmi"* or self-reduction.)[20] The *tikkun*, the repair lies in taking that fear up to the higher level, whereby it is no longer a fear of extinction but rather, to use a Ḥasidic term, *"bittul bi-metsi'ut"* (self-annihilation or dissolution of the ego).[21]

In Kabbalistic jargon, in the future it will still be said of the moon that it has nothing of its own (*"de-leit lah mi-garmah kelum"*), but this will no longer

---

his father Rabbi Perets Ḥen, who heard from the *Tsemaḥ Tsedek*; Moshe Charitin in *Heikhal ha-Besht, Tishrei* 5766 (2005), pp. 167–168; Rabbi Moshe Zevi Neriyah, *Siḥot ha-Rayah* (Tel-Aviv – Jaffa, 1979), p. 258. The Alter Rebbe's paraphrase of the verse in Psalms occurs in *Torah 'Or, Noaḥ*, 9a, and *Toledot*, 17d.

Rabbi Neriyah recounted how on Simḥat Torah at the afternoon repast, Rav Kook abruptly rose from the table and paced the length of the room while singing enthusiastically Rabbi Shneur Zalman's melody to those words. (Subsequent to the publication of *Siḥot ha-Rayah*, Rabbi Neriyah was challenged by Ḥabad Ḥasidim who never heard a *niggun* to those words. Undaunted, Rabbi Neriyah maintained that Rav Kook did not originate the tune but evidently received it in his youth from the Kopyster Ḥasidim in his birthplace of Grieva, including Rav Kook's maternal grandfather Rabbi Raphael and the famed *mashpi'a* of the Kopyster Rebbe, Rabbi Yeḥezkel Yanover. See Rabbi Moshe Tsevi Neriyah, *Bi-Sdeh ha-Rayah* [Tel-Aviv, 1991], p. 127.)

20. See Rav Kook's advice to his dearly beloved disciple Rabbi Y.M. Ḥarlap not to subject his soul to "'evil fears' (*yir'ot ra'ot*) that come out of 'shufflings of God of smallness' (*tserufei Elohim de-katnut*)"; *IR*, vol. 2, p. 38 (Letter 378).

21. In Ḥabad Ḥasidism, *"bittul bi-metsi'ut"* has become a *terminus technicus*, but the words themselves occur earlier in Maharal. Cf. Rabbi Judah Löw (Maharal) of Prague, *Tif'eret Yisrael*, chap. 10, and Rabbi Menaḥem Mendel Schneersohn of Lubavitch, *Derekh Mitsvotekha, Mitsvat Tum'at Metsora'*, 100b-101a.

Bezalel Safran observed similarities between the thought of Maharal and that of Rabbi Menaḥem Mendel of (Horodok and) Vitebsk, Rabbi Shneur Zalman's superior. See B. Safran, "Maharal and Early Ḥasidism," in *Ḥasidism: Continuity or Innovation* (Cambridge, Mass: Harvard University Press, 1988), pp. 47–144.

וַהֲבִיאֵנוּ לְצִיּוֹן עִירְךָ בְּרִנָּה
וְלִירוּשָׁלַיִם בֵּית מִקְדָּשְׁךָ בְּשִׂמְחַת עוֹלָם
וְשָׁם נַעֲשֶׂה לְפָנֶיךָ אֶת קָרְבְּנוֹת חוֹבוֹתֵינוּ
תְּמִידִים כְּסִדְרָם וּמוּסָפִים כְּהִלְכָתָם.

Love of the Lord is a wonderful thing, but it may be eclipsed by awe of the Lord. Love is pleasurable and comes with ego.[15] Upon closer examination, it may be revealed as self-love.[16] "And after there appears the higher fear, whereby one desires for one's self nothing but to cleave to the Lord."[17]

Rav Kook was fond of singing a few lines that Rabbi Shneur Zalman of Liadi (referred to as the "*Alter Rebbe*" or "Old Rabbi") was reputed to utter in a state of *devekut* or ecstasy: *"Mi li ba-shamayim ve-'imekha lo ḥafatsti ba-arets."* "Who is there for me in heaven, and beside You I desire none on earth."[18] *"Ich vill zhe gornisht. Ich vill nit dein Gan 'Eden. Ich vill nit dein 'Olam Habo. Ich vill mehr nit az dich alein."* "I desire nothing. I desire not Your Paradise. I desire not Your World to Come. I desire but You alone."[19]

---

that Maimonides might have been influenced by the reading of the verse from Ezekiel 1:14 (*"ve-ha-ḥayyot ratso va-shov"*) in *Sefer Yetsirah* 1:8, whereby it is lifted from its angelological context and given an anthropological interpretation. *Sefer Yetsirah* merited commentaries by illustrious medieval authors such as Sa'adyah Gaon, Rabbi Judah ben Barzilai Albargeloni and Judah Halevi, yet is never mentioned explicitly by Maimonides.

15. Rabbi Judah Löw (Maharal) of Prague, *Tif'eret Yisrael,* chap. 10; Rabbi Shneur Zalman of Liadi, *Torah 'Or, Vayakhel,* 114d (*"Yesh mi she-ohev,"* "There is someone who loves"); Rabbi Menaḥem Mendel Schneersohn of Lubavitch, *Derekh Mitsvotekha* (Poltava, 1911; photo offset Brooklyn: Kehot, 1953), *Mitsvat Tum'at Metsora',* 100b; *Sefer ha-'Arakhim Ḥabad* (*Ḥabad Encyclopedia*), vol. 1 (Brooklyn, NY: Kehot, 1970), s.v. *Ahavat Hashem,* p. 279, n. 138.
    In *Netivot 'Olam* (London: L. Honig & Sons, 1960), *Netiv ha-'Avodah,* chap. 13 (p. 120), Maharal describes *ahavah* and *yir'ah* as having the exact opposite effect. Love creates fusion with the loved one, whereas fear results in alienation. The two passages in Maharal's *oeuvre* (*TY* and *NO*) must be reconciled somehow.
16. *Sefer ha-'Arakhim Ḥabad,* vol. 1, s.v. *Ahavah,* p. 231.
17. *OR,* vol. 1, p. 423.
18. Psalms 73:25.
19. Rabbi Menaḥem Mendel Schneersohn of Lubavitch, *Derekh Mitsvotekha, Shoresh Mitsvat ha-Tefillah,* chap 41 (138a). There are several versions of the Alter Rebbe's meditation. See *Ha-Mashpi'a* (Biography of Rabbi Shelomo Zalman Havlin) (Jerusalem, 1982), pp. 126–127, quoting Rabbi David Tsevi Ḥen of Chernigov, who heard from

וְאֶת מוּסַף The additional offering of this New Moon day
we will prepare and offer to You
with love according to Your will's commandment,
as You have written for us in Your Torah
by Your own word, through Your servant Moses,
as it is said:

"On your new moons, present as a burnt-offering to the Lord, *Num. 28*
two young bulls, one ram,
and seven yearling lambs without blemish."

וּמִנְחָתָם And their meal-offerings and wine-libations as ordained:
three-tenths of an ephah for each bull,
two-tenths of an ephah for the ram,
one-tenth of an ephah for each lamb,
wine for the libations,
a male goat for atonement,
and two regular daily offerings according to their law.

אֱלֹהֵינוּ O God and God of our ancestors,
renew for us the coming month for good and blessing,
joy and gladness, deliverance and consolation,
sustenance and support, life and peace,
pardon of sin and forgiveness of iniquity
(*From Marḥeshvan to Adar II in a Jewish leap year* and atonement of transgression).
For You have chosen Your people Israel from all nations,
and have instituted for them rules for the New Moon.
Blessed are You, Lord, who sanctifies Israel and the New Moons.

---

Ultimately the Sun and the Moon will share a single crown; the love and fear will come together in a *selfless* love, the element of selflessness being the Moon's unique contribution, as it injects an element of *yir'ah 'ila'ah*, the higher fear. The warm light of the Sun will provide the positive affect, the *via positiva*; and the cool light of the Moon will temper that with *bittul*, the *via negativa*. (Editor)

וְאֶת מוּסַף יוֹם רֹאשׁ הַחֹדֶשׁ הַזֶּה
נַעֲשֶׂה וְנַקְרִיב לְפָנֶיךָ בְּאַהֲבָה כְּמִצְוַת רְצוֹנֶךָ
כְּמוֹ שֶׁכָּתַבְתָּ עָלֵינוּ בְּתוֹרָתֶךָ
עַל יְדֵי מֹשֶׁה עַבְדֶּךָ מִפִּי כְבוֹדֶךָ
כָּאָמוּר
וּבְרָאשֵׁי חָדְשֵׁיכֶם תַּקְרִיבוּ עֹלָה לַיהוה במדבר כח
פָּרִים בְּנֵי־בָקָר שְׁנַיִם וְאַיִל אֶחָד
כְּבָשִׂים בְּנֵי־שָׁנָה שִׁבְעָה, תְּמִימִם:

וּמִנְחָתָם וְנִסְכֵּיהֶם כִּמְדֻבָּר
שְׁלֹשָׁה עֶשְׂרֹנִים לַפָּר, וּשְׁנֵי עֶשְׂרֹנִים לָאָיִל
וְעִשָּׂרוֹן לַכֶּבֶשׂ, וְיַיִן כְּנִסְכּוֹ, וְשָׂעִיר לְכַפֵּר
וּשְׁנֵי תְמִידִים כְּהִלְכָתָם.

אֱלֹהֵינוּ וֵאלֹהֵי אֲבוֹתֵינוּ
חַדֵּשׁ עָלֵינוּ אֶת הַחֹדֶשׁ הַזֶּה לְטוֹבָה וְלִבְרָכָה
לְשָׂשׂוֹן וּלְשִׂמְחָה, לִישׁוּעָה וּלְנֶחָמָה
לְפַרְנָסָה וּלְכַלְכָּלָה, לְחַיִּים וּלְשָׁלוֹם
לִמְחִילַת חֵטְא וְלִסְלִיחַת עָוֹן
(*From* מרחשון *to* אדר שני *in a Jewish leap year* וּלְכַפָּרַת פָּשַׁע)
כִּי בְעַמְּךָ יִשְׂרָאֵל בָּחַרְתָּ מִכָּל הָאֻמּוֹת
וְחֻקֵּי רָאשֵׁי חֳדָשִׁים לָהֶם קָבָעְתָּ.
בָּרוּךְ אַתָּה יהוה, מְקַדֵּשׁ יִשְׂרָאֵל וְרָאשֵׁי חֳדָשִׁים.

---

produce the lower variety of *yir'ah*, but rather the higher *yir'ah*: *yare boshet*. *Yir'ah* out of selfishness will be transmuted to *yir'ah* out of selflessness.

TEMPLE SERVICE

רְצֵה Find favor, LORD our God, in Your people Israel
and their prayer.
Restore the service to Your most holy House,
and accept in love and favor the fire-offerings of Israel
and their prayer.
May the service of Your people Israel always find favor with You
And may our eyes witness Your return to Zion in compassion.
Blessed are You, LORD,
who restores His Presence to Zion.

THANKSGIVING

*Bow at the first nine words.*

מוֹדִים* We give thanks to You,
for You are the LORD our God
and God of our ancestors
for ever and all time.
You are the Rock of our lives,
Shield of our salvation
from generation to generation.
We will thank You and
declare Your praise for our lives,
which are entrusted into Your hand;
for our souls,
which are placed in Your charge;
for Your miracles
which are with us every day;
and for Your wonders and favors
at all times, evening,
morning and midday.
You are good –
for Your compassion never fails.
You are compassionate –
for Your loving-kindnesses never cease.
We have always placed our hope in You.

*During the Leader's Repetition, the congregation says quietly:*

מוֹדִים* We give thanks to You,
for You are the
LORD our God
and God of our ancestors,
God of all flesh,
who formed us
and formed the universe.
Blessings and thanks
are due to Your great
and holy name for giving us
life and sustaining us.
May You continue
to give us life
and sustain us;
and may You gather our
exiles to Your holy courts,
to keep Your decrees,
do Your will and serve You
with a perfect heart,
for it is for us
to give You thanks.
Blessed be God to whom
thanksgiving is due.

עבודה

רְצֵה יהוה אֱלֹהֵינוּ בְּעַמְּךָ יִשְׂרָאֵל וּבִתְפִלָּתָם
וְהָשֵׁב אֶת הָעֲבוֹדָה לִדְבִיר בֵּיתֶךָ
וְאִשֵּׁי יִשְׂרָאֵל וּתְפִלָּתָם בְּאַהֲבָה תְקַבֵּל בְּרָצוֹן
וּתְהִי לְרָצוֹן תָּמִיד עֲבוֹדַת יִשְׂרָאֵל עַמֶּךָ.
וְתֶחֱזֶינָה עֵינֵינוּ בְּשׁוּבְךָ לְצִיּוֹן בְּרַחֲמִים.
בָּרוּךְ אַתָּה יהוה, הַמַּחֲזִיר שְׁכִינָתוֹ לְצִיּוֹן.

הודאה

*Bow at the first five words.*

מוֹדִים אֲנַחְנוּ לָךְ
שָׁאַתָּה הוּא יהוה אֱלֹהֵינוּ
וֵאלֹהֵי אֲבוֹתֵינוּ לְעוֹלָם וָעֶד.
צוּר חַיֵּינוּ, מָגֵן יִשְׁעֵנוּ
אַתָּה הוּא לְדוֹר וָדוֹר.
נוֹדֶה לְּךָ וּנְסַפֵּר תְּהִלָּתֶךָ
עַל חַיֵּינוּ הַמְּסוּרִים בְּיָדֶךָ
וְעַל נִשְׁמוֹתֵינוּ הַפְּקוּדוֹת לָךְ
וְעַל נִסֶּיךָ שֶׁבְּכָל יוֹם עִמָּנוּ
וְעַל נִפְלְאוֹתֶיךָ וְטוֹבוֹתֶיךָ
שֶׁבְּכָל עֵת
עֶרֶב וָבֹקֶר וְצָהֳרָיִם.
הַטּוֹב, כִּי לֹא כָלוּ רַחֲמֶיךָ
וְהַמְרַחֵם, כִּי לֹא תַמּוּ חֲסָדֶיךָ
מֵעוֹלָם קִוִּינוּ לָךְ.

*During the* חזרת הש״ץ*, the* קהל *says quietly:*

מוֹדִים אֲנַחְנוּ לָךְ
שָׁאַתָּה הוּא יהוה אֱלֹהֵינוּ
וֵאלֹהֵי אֲבוֹתֵינוּ
אֱלֹהֵי כָל בָּשָׂר
יוֹצְרֵנוּ, יוֹצֵר בְּרֵאשִׁית.
בְּרָכוֹת וְהוֹדָאוֹת
לְשִׁמְךָ הַגָּדוֹל וְהַקָּדוֹשׁ
עַל שֶׁהֶחֱיִיתָנוּ וְקִיַּמְתָּנוּ.
כֵּן תְּחַיֵּנוּ וּתְקַיְּמֵנוּ
וְתֶאֱסֹף גָּלֻיּוֹתֵינוּ
לְחַצְרוֹת קָדְשֶׁךָ
לִשְׁמֹר חֻקֶּיךָ
וְלַעֲשׂוֹת רְצוֹנֶךָ וּלְעָבְדְּךָ
בְּלֵבָב שָׁלֵם
עַל שֶׁאֲנַחְנוּ מוֹדִים לָךְ.
בָּרוּךְ אֵל הַהוֹדָאוֹת.

*On Hanukka:*

עַל הַנִּסִּים [We thank You also] for the miracles, the redemption, the mighty deeds, the salvations, and the victories in battle which You performed for our ancestors in those days, at this time.

בִּימֵי מַתִּתְיָהוּ In the days of Mattityahu, son of Yohanan, the High Priest, the Hasmonean, and his sons, the wicked Greek kingdom rose up against Your people Israel to make them forget Your Torah and to force them to transgress the statutes of Your will. It was then that You in Your great compassion stood by them in the time of their distress. You championed their cause, judged their claim, and avenged their wrong. You delivered the strong into the hands of the weak, the many into the hands of the few, the impure into the hands of the pure, the wicked into the hands of the righteous, and the arrogant into the hands of those who were engaged in the study of Your Torah. You made for Yourself great and holy renown in Your world, and for Your people Israel You performed a great salvation and redemption as of this very day. Your children then entered the holiest part of Your House, cleansed Your Temple, purified Your Sanctuary, kindled lights in Your holy courts, and designated these eight days of Hanukka for giving thanks and praise to Your great name.

*Continue with "For all these things."*

וְעַל כֻּלָּם For all these things may Your name be blessed
and exalted, our King, continually, for ever and all time.
Let all that lives thank You, Selah! and praise Your name in truth,
God, our Savior and Help, Selah!
▾Blessed are You, Lord, whose name is "the Good"
and to whom thanks are due.

*When saying the Amida silently, continue with "Grant peace" on the next page.*

*The following is said by the Leader during the Repetition of the Amida.*
*In Israel, if Kohanim bless the congregation, turn to page 902. See laws 370–377.*

Our God and God of our fathers, bless us with the threefold blessing in the Torah, written by the hand of Moses Your servant and pronounced by Aaron and his sons the priests, Your holy people, as it is said:

May the Lord bless you and protect you. *Cong:* May it be Your will. *Num. 6*
May the Lord make His face shine on you and be gracious to you.
*Cong:* May it be Your will.
May the Lord turn His face toward you, and grant you peace.
*Cong:* May it be Your will.

*The Leader continues with "Grant peace" on the next page.*

בחנוכה:

עַל הַנִּסִּים וְעַל הַפֻּרְקָן וְעַל הַגְּבוּרוֹת וְעַל הַתְּשׁוּעוֹת וְעַל הַמִּלְחָמוֹת שֶׁעָשִׂיתָ לַאֲבוֹתֵינוּ בַּיָּמִים הָהֵם בַּזְּמַן הַזֶּה.

בִּימֵי מַתִּתְיָהוּ בֶּן יוֹחָנָן כֹּהֵן גָּדוֹל חַשְׁמוֹנַאי וּבָנָיו, כְּשֶׁעָמְדָה מַלְכוּת יָוָן הָרְשָׁעָה עַל עַמְּךָ יִשְׂרָאֵל לְהַשְׁכִּיחָם תּוֹרָתֶךָ וּלְהַעֲבִירָם מֵחֻקֵּי רְצוֹנֶךָ, וְאַתָּה בְּרַחֲמֶיךָ הָרַבִּים עָמַדְתָּ לָהֶם בְּעֵת צָרָתָם, רַבְתָּ אֶת רִיבָם, דַּנְתָּ אֶת דִּינָם, נָקַמְתָּ אֶת נִקְמָתָם, מָסַרְתָּ גִבּוֹרִים בְּיַד חַלָּשִׁים, וְרַבִּים בְּיַד מְעַטִּים, וּטְמֵאִים בְּיַד טְהוֹרִים, וּרְשָׁעִים בְּיַד צַדִּיקִים, וְזֵדִים בְּיַד עוֹסְקֵי תוֹרָתֶךָ, וּלְךָ עָשִׂיתָ שֵׁם גָּדוֹל וְקָדוֹשׁ בְּעוֹלָמֶךָ, וּלְעַמְּךָ יִשְׂרָאֵל עָשִׂיתָ תְּשׁוּעָה גְדוֹלָה וּפֻרְקָן כְּהַיּוֹם הַזֶּה. וְאַחַר כֵּן בָּאוּ בָנֶיךָ לִדְבִיר בֵּיתֶךָ, וּפִנּוּ אֶת הֵיכָלֶךָ, וְטִהֲרוּ אֶת מִקְדָּשֶׁךָ, וְהִדְלִיקוּ נֵרוֹת בְּחַצְרוֹת קָדְשֶׁךָ, וְקָבְעוּ שְׁמוֹנַת יְמֵי חֲנֻכָּה אֵלּוּ, לְהוֹדוֹת וּלְהַלֵּל לְשִׁמְךָ הַגָּדוֹל.

*Continue with* וְעַל כֻּלָּם.

וְעַל כֻּלָּם יִתְבָּרַךְ וְיִתְרוֹמַם שִׁמְךָ מַלְכֵּנוּ תָּמִיד לְעוֹלָם וָעֶד.
וְכֹל הַחַיִּים יוֹדְוּךָ סֶּלָה, וִיהַלְלוּ אֶת שִׁמְךָ בֶּאֱמֶת
הָאֵל יְשׁוּעָתֵנוּ וְעֶזְרָתֵנוּ סֶלָה.
בָּרוּךְ אַתָּה יהוה, הַטּוֹב שִׁמְךָ וּלְךָ נָאֶה לְהוֹדוֹת.

*When saying the* עמידה *silently, continue with* שִׂים שָׁלוֹם *on the next page.*

*The following is said by the* שליח ציבור *during the* חזרת הש״ץ.
*In* ארץ ישראל, *if* כהנים *say* ברכת כהנים, *turn to page 903. See laws 370–377.*

אֱלֹהֵינוּ וֵאלֹהֵי אֲבוֹתֵינוּ, בָּרְכֵנוּ בַּבְּרָכָה הַמְשֻׁלֶּשֶׁת בַּתּוֹרָה, הַכְּתוּבָה עַל יְדֵי מֹשֶׁה עַבְדֶּךָ, הָאֲמוּרָה מִפִּי אַהֲרֹן וּבָנָיו כֹּהֲנִים עַם קְדוֹשֶׁךָ, כָּאָמוּר

יְבָרֶכְךָ יהוה וְיִשְׁמְרֶךָ: קהל: כֵּן יְהִי רָצוֹן — במדבר ו
יָאֵר יהוה פָּנָיו אֵלֶיךָ וִיחֻנֶּךָּ: קהל: כֵּן יְהִי רָצוֹן
יִשָּׂא יהוה פָּנָיו אֵלֶיךָ וְיָשֵׂם לְךָ שָׁלוֹם: קהל: כֵּן יְהִי רָצוֹן

*The* שליח ציבור *continues with* שִׂים שָׁלוֹם *on the next page.*

PEACE

שִׂים שָׁלוֹם Grant peace, goodness and blessing,
grace, loving-kindness and compassion
to us and all Israel Your people.
Bless us, our Father, all as one, with the light of Your face,
for by the light of Your face You have given us, LORD our God,
the Torah of life and love of kindness,
righteousness, blessing, compassion, life and peace.
May it be good in Your eyes to bless Your people Israel
at every time, in every hour, with Your peace.
Blessed are You, LORD, who blesses His people Israel with peace.

*The following verse concludes the Leader's Repetition of the Amida. Some also say it here as part of the silent Amida. See law 368.*

May the words of my mouth and the meditation of my heart *Ps. 19*
find favor before You, LORD, my Rock and Redeemer.

אֱלֹהַי My God, guard my tongue from evil and my lips from deceitful speech. *Berakhot 17a*
To those who curse me, let my soul be silent;
may my soul be to all like the dust.
Open my heart to Your Torah and let my soul pursue Your commandments.
As for all who plan evil against me,
swiftly thwart their counsel and frustrate their plans.
Act for the sake of Your name; act for the sake of Your right hand;
act for the sake of Your holiness; act for the sake of Your Torah.
That Your beloved ones may be delivered, *Ps. 60*
save with Your right hand and answer me.
May the words of my mouth and the meditation of my heart *Ps. 19*
find favor before You, LORD, my Rock and Redeemer.

*Bow, take three steps back, then bow, first left, then right, then center, while saying:*

May He who makes peace in His high places,
make peace for us and all Israel – and say: Amen.

יְהִי רָצוֹן May it be Your will, LORD our God and God of our ancestors, that the Temple be rebuilt speedily in our days, and grant us a share in Your Torah. And there we will serve You with reverence, as in the days of old and as in former years. Then the offering of Judah and Jerusalem will be pleasing to the LORD as in the days of old and as in former years. *Mal. 3*

*After the Leader's Repetition, the service continues with Full Kaddish (page 242), followed by Aleinu (page 244), the Daily Psalm (page 248) and Barekhi Nafshi (page 260).*

ברכת שלום

שִׂים שָׁלוֹם טוֹבָה וּבְרָכָה
חֵן וָחֶסֶד וְרַחֲמִים עָלֵינוּ וְעַל כָּל יִשְׂרָאֵל עַמֶּךָ.
בָּרְכֵנוּ אָבִינוּ כֻּלָּנוּ כְּאֶחָד בְּאוֹר פָּנֶיךָ
כִּי בְאוֹר פָּנֶיךָ נָתַתָּ לָּנוּ יהוה אֱלֹהֵינוּ
תּוֹרַת חַיִּים וְאַהֲבַת חֶסֶד, וּצְדָקָה וּבְרָכָה וְרַחֲמִים וְחַיִּים וְשָׁלוֹם.
וְטוֹב בְּעֵינֶיךָ לְבָרֵךְ אֶת עַמְּךָ יִשְׂרָאֵל
בְּכָל עֵת וּבְכָל שָׁעָה בִּשְׁלוֹמֶךָ.
בָּרוּךְ אַתָּה יהוה, הַמְבָרֵךְ אֶת עַמּוֹ יִשְׂרָאֵל בַּשָּׁלוֹם.

*The following verse concludes the* חזרת הש״ץ.
*Some also say it here as part of the silent* עמידה. *See law 368.*

תהלים יט יִהְיוּ לְרָצוֹן אִמְרֵי־פִי וְהֶגְיוֹן לִבִּי לְפָנֶיךָ, יהוה צוּרִי וְגוֹאֲלִי:

ברכות יז. אֱלֹהַי, נְצֹר לְשׁוֹנִי מֵרָע וּשְׂפָתַי מִדַּבֵּר מִרְמָה
וְלִמְקַלְלַי נַפְשִׁי תִדֹּם, וְנַפְשִׁי כֶּעָפָר לַכֹּל תִּהְיֶה.
פְּתַח לִבִּי בְּתוֹרָתֶךָ, וּבְמִצְוֹתֶיךָ תִּרְדֹּף נַפְשִׁי.
וְכָל הַחוֹשְׁבִים עָלַי רָעָה, מְהֵרָה הָפֵר עֲצָתָם וְקַלְקֵל מַחֲשַׁבְתָּם.
עֲשֵׂה לְמַעַן שְׁמֶךָ, עֲשֵׂה לְמַעַן יְמִינֶךָ
עֲשֵׂה לְמַעַן קְדֻשָּׁתֶךָ, עֲשֵׂה לְמַעַן תּוֹרָתֶךָ.
תהלים ס לְמַעַן יֵחָלְצוּן יְדִידֶיךָ, הוֹשִׁיעָה יְמִינְךָ וַעֲנֵנִי:
תהלים יט יִהְיוּ לְרָצוֹן אִמְרֵי־פִי וְהֶגְיוֹן לִבִּי לְפָנֶיךָ, יהוה צוּרִי וְגוֹאֲלִי:

*Bow, take three steps back, then bow, first left, then right, then center, while saying:*

עֹשֶׂה שָׁלוֹם בִּמְרוֹמָיו
הוּא יַעֲשֶׂה שָׁלוֹם עָלֵינוּ וְעַל כָּל יִשְׂרָאֵל, וְאִמְרוּ אָמֵן.

יְהִי רָצוֹן מִלְּפָנֶיךָ יהוה אֱלֹהֵינוּ וֵאלֹהֵי אֲבוֹתֵינוּ, שֶׁיִּבָּנֶה בֵּית הַמִּקְדָּשׁ בִּמְהֵרָה
בְיָמֵינוּ, וְתֵן חֶלְקֵנוּ בְּתוֹרָתֶךָ, וְשָׁם נַעֲבָדְךָ בְּיִרְאָה כִּימֵי עוֹלָם וּכְשָׁנִים קַדְמֹנִיּוֹת.
מלאכי ג וְעָרְבָה לַיהוה מִנְחַת יְהוּדָה וִירוּשָׁלָיִם כִּימֵי עוֹלָם וּכְשָׁנִים קַדְמֹנִיּוֹת:

*After the* חזרת הש״ץ, *the service continues with* קדיש שלם *(page 243),*
*followed by* עָלֵינוּ *(page 245),* שיר של יום *(page 249) and* בָּרְכִי נַפְשִׁי *(page 261).*

## REMOVAL OF ḤAMETZ

*On the night before Pesaḥ, a search for ḥametz, such as breadcrumbs, products containing leaven and grain alcohol, is made in the house. The custom is to do so at night by the light of a candle, but a flashlight may also be used. If Pesaḥ falls on Motza'ei Shabbat, the search is made on Thursday night. Those who plan to be away on Pesaḥ should conduct the search the night before their departure, but without making a blessing. Before the search, make the following blessing:*

בָּרוּךְ Blessed are You, Lord our God, King of the Universe,
who has made us holy through His commandments,
and has commanded us about the removal of leaven.

*After the search, say:*

כָּל חֲמִירָא May all ḥametz or leaven that is in my possession which I have not seen or removed be annulled and deemed like the dust of the earth.

*On the following morning after burning the ḥametz, say:*

כָּל חֲמִירָא May all ḥametz or leaven that is in my possession, whether I have seen it or not, whether I have removed it or not, be annulled and deemed like the dust of the earth.

## EIRUV TAVSHILIN

*It is not permitted to cook for Shabbat when a Yom Tov falls on Thursday or Friday unless an Eiruv Tavshilin has been made prior to the Yom Tov. This is done by taking a loaf or piece of matza together with a boiled egg, or a piece of cooked fish or meat to be used on Shabbat. While holding them, say the following:*

בָּרוּךְ Blessed are You, Lord our God, King of the Universe,
who has made us holy through His commandments,
and has commanded us about the mitzva of Eiruv.

By this Eiruv may we be permitted to bake, cook, insulate food, light a flame and do everything necessary on the festival for the sake of Shabbat, for us and for all Jews living in this city.

*For Eiruv Teḥumin see page 380.*

---

that one is faithful to one's essential being, one is free. To the degree that one is alienated from one's essential being, one is enslaved. The free man feels that his life is endowed with purpose. In the world of freedom, life is of intrinsic value. The spirit of the slave inhabits a different universe altogether. In the world of slavery, life has no essential worth. A life's worth is determined by its value to another who exerts dominion and control over it – whether that rule be formal and contractual, or purely by moral exhortation, to the effect that one is conditioned by what another deems "beautiful" and "good."

# ביעור חמץ

*On the night before פסח, a search for חמץ, such as breadcrumbs, products containing leaven and grain alcohol, is made in the house. The custom is to do so at night by the light of a candle, but a flashlight may also be used. If פסח falls on מוצאי שבת, the search is made on Thursday night. Those who plan to be away on פסח should conduct the search the night before their departure, but without making a blessing. Before the search, make the following blessing:*

**בָּרוּךְ אַתָּה יהוה אֱלֹהֵינוּ מֶלֶךְ הָעוֹלָם
אֲשֶׁר קִדְּשָׁנוּ בְּמִצְוֹתָיו וְצִוָּנוּ עַל בִּעוּר חָמֵץ.**

*After the search, say:*

**כָּל חֲמִירָא וַחֲמִיעָא דְּאִכָּא בִרְשׁוּתִי, דְּלָא חֲמִתֵּהּ וּדְלָא בִעַרְתֵּהּ, לִבְטִיל וְלֶהֱוֵי הֶפְקֵר כְּעַפְרָא דְאַרְעָא.**

*On the following morning after burning the חמץ, say:*

**כָּל חֲמִירָא וַחֲמִיעָא דְּאִכָּא בִרְשׁוּתִי, דַּחֲמִתֵּהּ וּדְלָא חֲמִתֵּהּ, דְּבִעַרְתֵּהּ וּדְלָא בִעַרְתֵּהּ, לִבְטִיל וְלֶהֱוֵי הֶפְקֵר כְּעַפְרָא דְאַרְעָא.**

# עירוב תבשילין

*It is not permitted to cook for שבת when a יום טוב falls on Thursday or Friday unless an עירוב תבשלין has been made prior to the יום טוב. This is done by taking a loaf or piece of matza together with a boiled egg, or a piece of cooked fish or meat to be used on שבת. While holding them, say the following:*

**בָּרוּךְ אַתָּה יהוה אֱלֹהֵינוּ מֶלֶךְ הָעוֹלָם
אֲשֶׁר קִדְּשָׁנוּ בְּמִצְוֹתָיו וְצִוָּנוּ עַל מִצְוַת עֵרוּב.**

**בַּהֲדֵין עֵרוּבָא יְהֵא שְׁרֵא לָנָא לַאֲפּוֹיֵי וּלְבַשּׁוּלֵי וּלְאַטְמוּנֵי וּלְאַדְלוּקֵי שְׁרָגָא, וּלְמֶעְבַּד כָּל צָרְכָּנָא מִיּוֹמָא טָבָא לְשַׁבַּתָּא, לָנוּ וּלְכָל יִשְׂרָאֵל הַדָּרִים בָּעִיר הַזֹּאת.**

*For עירוב תחומין see page 381.*

---

ביעור חמץ / REMOVAL OF ḤAMETZ

Passover is called the "Time of Our Freedom" (*"zeman ḥerutenu"*). How does one define freedom? The obvious answer is in terms of physical freedom. By breaking the shackles of bondage, one is emancipated. But there is a more subtle form of freedom: spiritual freedom.

The truth is that the difference between the freedman and the slave is not simply a matter of class. Paradoxically, there is a physical slave who is free in spirit; and a physically free man who suffers spiritual bondage. To the degree

## CANDLE LIGHTING

*On Erev Yom Tov, say the following blessing and then light the candles from an existing flame. If also Shabbat, cover the eyes with the hands after lighting the candles and say the following blessing, adding the words in parentheses.*

בָּרוּךְ Blessed are You, Lord our God, King of the Universe, who has made us holy through His commandments, and has commanded us to light (the Sabbath light and) the festival light.

*The blessing "Sheheḥeyanu" ("Who has given us life") is said on Yom Tov evenings, except on the last evenings of Pesaḥ. (In Israel, it is not said on the last evening of Pesaḥ.)*

בָּרוּךְ Blessed are You, Lord our God, King of the Universe, who has given us life, sustained us, and brought us to this time.

*Some add:*

יְהִי May it be Your will, Lord our God and God of our ancestors, that the Temple be speedily rebuilt in our days, and grant us our share in Your Torah.
And may we serve You there in reverence, as in the days of old and as in *Mal. 3*
former years.

*Prayer after candlelighting (add the words in parentheses as appropriate):*

יְהִי May it be Your will, Lord my God and God of my forebears, that You give me grace – me (and my husband/and my father/and my mother/and my sons and my daughters) and all those close to me, and give us and all Israel good and long lives. And remember us with a memory that brings goodness and blessing; come to us with compassion and bless us with great blessings. Build our homes until they are complete, and allow Your Presence to live among us. And may I merit to raise children and grandchildren, each one wise and understanding, loving the Lord and in awe of God, people of truth, holy children, who will cling on to the Lord and light up the world with Torah and with good actions, and with all the kinds of work that serve the Creator. Please, hear my pleading at this time, by the merit of Sarah and Rebecca, Rachel and Leah our mothers, and light our candle that it should never go out, and light up Your face, so that we shall be saved, Amen.

---

or collective freedom – can be won only by "eliminating the leaven" (*bi'ur ḥamets*). It requires purging the "yeast in the dough" (*"se'or she-ba-'isah"*),[2] the foreign, extraneous influence that keeps us from our inner essence.[3]

2. See *b. Berakhot* 17a and Rashi there.
3. *OR*, vol. 2, pp. 244–245.

# הדלקת נרות

*On* ערב יום טוב*, say the following blessing and then light the candles from an existing flame. If also* שבת*, cover the eyes with the hands after lighting the candles and say the following blessing, adding the words in parentheses.*

בָּרוּךְ אַתָּה יהוה אֱלֹהֵינוּ מֶלֶךְ הָעוֹלָם
אֲשֶׁר קִדְּשָׁנוּ בְּמִצְוֹתָיו
וְצִוָּנוּ לְהַדְלִיק נֵר שֶׁל (שַׁבָּת וְשֶׁל) יוֹם טוֹב.

*The blessing* שֶׁהֶחֱיָנוּ *is said on* יום טוב *evenings, except on the last evenings of* פסח*.*
*(In* ארץ ישראל*, it is not said on the last evening of* פסח*.)*

בָּרוּךְ אַתָּה יהוה אֱלֹהֵינוּ מֶלֶךְ הָעוֹלָם
שֶׁהֶחֱיָנוּ וְקִיְּמָנוּ וְהִגִּיעָנוּ לַזְּמַן הַזֶּה.

*Some add:*

יְהִי רָצוֹן מִלְּפָנֶיךָ יהוה אֱלֹהֵינוּ וֵאלֹהֵי אֲבוֹתֵינוּ, שֶׁיִּבָּנֶה בֵּית הַמִּקְדָּשׁ בִּמְהֵרָה בְיָמֵינוּ, וְתֵן חֶלְקֵנוּ בְּתוֹרָתֶךָ, וְשָׁם נַעֲבָדְךָ בְּיִרְאָה כִּימֵי עוֹלָם וּכְשָׁנִים קַדְמֹנִיּוֹת.
וְעָרְבָה לַיהוה מִנְחַת יְהוּדָה וִירוּשָׁלָםִ כִּימֵי עוֹלָם וּכְשָׁנִים קַדְמֹנִיּוֹת: מלאכי ג

*Prayer after candlelighting (add the words in parentheses as appropriate):*

יְהִי רָצוֹן מִלְּפָנֶיךָ יהוה אֱלֹהַי וֵאלֹהֵי אֲבוֹתַי, שֶׁתְּחוֹנֵן אוֹתִי (וְאֶת אִישִׁי/ וְאֶת אָבִי/ וְאֶת אִמִּי/ וְאֶת בָּנַי וְאֶת בְּנוֹתַי) וְאֶת כָּל קְרוֹבַי, וְתִתֶּן לָנוּ וּלְכָל יִשְׂרָאֵל חַיִּים טוֹבִים וַאֲרֻכִּים, וְתִזְכְּרֵנוּ בְּזִכְרוֹן טוֹבָה וּבְרָכָה, וְתִפְקְדֵנוּ בִּפְקֻדַּת יְשׁוּעָה וְרַחֲמִים, וּתְבָרְכֵנוּ בְּרָכוֹת גְּדוֹלוֹת, וְתַשְׁלִים בָּתֵּינוּ וְתַשְׁכֵּן שְׁכִינָתְךָ בֵּינֵינוּ. וְזַכֵּנִי לְגַדֵּל בָּנִים וּבְנֵי בָנִים חֲכָמִים וּנְבוֹנִים, אוֹהֲבֵי יהוה יִרְאֵי אֱלֹהִים, אַנְשֵׁי אֱמֶת זֶרַע קֹדֶשׁ, בַּיהוה דְּבֵקִים וּמְאִירִים אֶת הָעוֹלָם בַּתּוֹרָה וּבְמַעֲשִׂים טוֹבִים וּבְכָל מְלֶאכֶת עֲבוֹדַת הַבּוֹרֵא. אָנָּא שְׁמַע אֶת תְּחִנָּתִי בָּעֵת הַזֹּאת בִּזְכוּת שָׂרָה וְרִבְקָה וְרָחֵל וְלֵאָה אִמּוֹתֵינוּ, וְהָאֵר נֵרֵנוּ שֶׁלֹּא יִכְבֶּה לְעוֹלָם וָעֶד, וְהָאֵר פָּנֶיךָ וְנִוָּשֵׁעָה. אָמֵן.

---

Our freedom from Egypt was not purely physical emancipation. At its core, it consisted of the "revelation of the divine presence" (*"Giluy Shekhinah"*).[1]

Brothers, freedom, essential freedom – whether it be individual freedom

---

1. "'And with great terror' [Deuteronomy 26:8] – This refers to the revelation of the divine presence" (*Passover Hagadah*).

# Kiddush for Festival Evening

*On Shabbat add:*

*quietly:* And it was evening, and it was morning – *Gen. 1*
יוֹם הַשִּׁשִּׁי the sixth day.

Then the heavens and the earth were completed, *Gen. 2*
and all their array.
With the seventh day, God completed the work He had done.
He ceased on the seventh day from all the work He had done.
God blessed the seventh day and declared it holy,
because on it He ceased from all His work He had created to do.

*On other evenings Kiddush starts here:*

*When saying Kiddush for others, add:*
Please pay attention, my masters.

Blessed are You, Lord our God, King of the Universe,
who creates the fruit of the vine.

*On Shabbat, add the words in parentheses.*

בָּרוּךְ Blessed are You, Lord our God,
King of the Universe,
who has chosen us from among all peoples,
raised us above all tongues,
and made us holy through His commandments.
You have given us, Lord our God, in love
(Sabbaths for rest), festivals for rejoicing,
holy days and seasons for joy, (this Sabbath day and) this day of:

*On Pesaḥ:* the festival of Matzot,
the time of our freedom

*On Shavuot:* the festival of Shavuot,
the time of the giving of our Torah

*On Sukkot:* the festival of Sukkot,
our time of rejoicing

*On Shemini Atzeret & Simḥat Torah:* the festival of the eighth day, Shemini Atzeret,
our time of rejoicing

# קידוש לליל שלוש רגלים

*On* שבת *add:*

*quietly* וַיְהִי־עֶרֶב וַיְהִי־בֹקֶר בראשית א

יוֹם הַשִּׁשִּׁי:

וַיְכֻלּוּ הַשָּׁמַיִם וְהָאָרֶץ וְכָל־צְבָאָם: בראשית ב

וַיְכַל אֱלֹהִים בַּיּוֹם הַשְּׁבִיעִי מְלַאכְתּוֹ אֲשֶׁר עָשָׂה

וַיִּשְׁבֹּת בַּיּוֹם הַשְּׁבִיעִי מִכָּל־מְלַאכְתּוֹ אֲשֶׁר עָשָׂה:

וַיְבָרֶךְ אֱלֹהִים אֶת־יוֹם הַשְּׁבִיעִי, וַיְקַדֵּשׁ אֹתוֹ

כִּי בוֹ שָׁבַת מִכָּל־מְלַאכְתּוֹ, אֲשֶׁר־בָּרָא אֱלֹהִים, לַעֲשׂוֹת:

*On other evenings the* קידוש *starts here:*

*When saying* קידוש *for others, add:*

סַבְרִי מָרָנָן

בָּרוּךְ אַתָּה יהוה אֱלֹהֵינוּ מֶלֶךְ הָעוֹלָם, בּוֹרֵא פְּרִי הַגָּפֶן.

*On* שבת*, add the words in parentheses.*

בָּרוּךְ אַתָּה יהוה אֱלֹהֵינוּ מֶלֶךְ הָעוֹלָם

אֲשֶׁר בָּחַר בָּנוּ מִכָּל עָם

וְרוֹמְמָנוּ מִכָּל לָשׁוֹן, וְקִדְּשָׁנוּ בְּמִצְוֹתָיו

וַתִּתֶּן לָנוּ יהוה אֱלֹהֵינוּ בְּאַהֲבָה

(שַׁבָּתוֹת לִמְנוּחָה וּ) מוֹעֲדִים לְשִׂמְחָה

חַגִּים וּזְמַנִּים לְשָׂשׂוֹן, אֶת יוֹם (הַשַּׁבָּת הַזֶּה וְאֶת יוֹם)

בפסח: חַג הַמַּצּוֹת הַזֶּה, זְמַן חֵרוּתֵנוּ

בשבועות: חַג הַשָּׁבוּעוֹת הַזֶּה, זְמַן מַתַּן תּוֹרָתֵנוּ

בסוכות: חַג הַסֻּכּוֹת הַזֶּה, זְמַן שִׂמְחָתֵנוּ

בשמע״צ ובש״ת: הַשְּׁמִינִי חַג הָעֲצֶרֶת הַזֶּה, זְמַן שִׂמְחָתֵנוּ

(with love), a holy assembly in memory of the exodus from Egypt.
For You have chosen us and sanctified us above all peoples,
and given us as our heritage (Your holy Sabbath in love and favor and)
Your holy festivals for joy and gladness.
Blessed are you, LORD,
who sanctifies (the Sabbath and) Israel and the festivals.

*On Motza'ei Shabbat, the following Havdala is added:*

בָּרוּךְ Blessed are You, LORD our God,
King of the Universe,
who creates the lights of fire.

Blessed are You, LORD our God, King of the Universe, who distinguishes between sacred and secular, between light and darkness, between Israel and the nations, between the seventh day and the six days of work. You have made a distinction between the holiness of the Sabbath and the holiness of festivals, and have sanctified the seventh day above the six days of work. You have distinguished and sanctified Your people Israel with Your holiness. Blessed are You, LORD, who distinguishes between sacred and sacred.

*On Sukkot, say the following blessing. On the first night it is said before the blessing "Who has given us life"; on the second night, after it (some say it before on both nights).*

בָּרוּךְ Blessed are You, LORD our God,
King of the Universe,
who has made us holy though His commandments,
and has commanded us to dwell in the sukka.

*The following blessing is omitted on the last two nights of Pesaḥ (in Israel, the last night).*

בָּרוּךְ Blessed are You, LORD our God,
King of the Universe,
who has given us life, sustained us,
and brought us to this time.

*It is customary for all present to drink of the wine.*

(בְּאַהֲבָה) מִקְרָא קֹדֶשׁ, זֵכֶר לִיצִיאַת מִצְרָיִם
כִּי בָנוּ בָחַרְתָּ וְאוֹתָנוּ קִדַּשְׁתָּ מִכָּל הָעַמִּים (וְשַׁבָּת)
וּמוֹעֲדֵי קָדְשֶׁךָ (בְּאַהֲבָה וּבְרָצוֹן)
בְּשִׂמְחָה וּבְשָׂשׂוֹן הִנְחַלְתָּנוּ.
בָּרוּךְ אַתָּה יהוה
מְקַדֵּשׁ (הַשַּׁבָּת וְ) יִשְׂרָאֵל וְהַזְּמַנִּים.

*On מוצאי שבת, the following הבדלה is added:*

בָּרוּךְ אַתָּה יהוה אֱלֹהֵינוּ מֶלֶךְ הָעוֹלָם
בּוֹרֵא מְאוֹרֵי הָאֵשׁ.

בָּרוּךְ אַתָּה יהוה אֱלֹהֵינוּ מֶלֶךְ הָעוֹלָם, הַמַּבְדִּיל בֵּין קֹדֶשׁ לְחֹל, בֵּין אוֹר לְחֹשֶׁךְ, בֵּין יִשְׂרָאֵל לָעַמִּים, בֵּין יוֹם הַשְּׁבִיעִי לְשֵׁשֶׁת יְמֵי הַמַּעֲשֶׂה. בֵּין קְדֻשַּׁת שַׁבָּת לִקְדֻשַּׁת יוֹם טוֹב הִבְדַּלְתָּ, וְאֶת יוֹם הַשְּׁבִיעִי מִשֵּׁשֶׁת יְמֵי הַמַּעֲשֶׂה קִדַּשְׁתָּ, הִבְדַּלְתָּ וְקִדַּשְׁתָּ אֶת עַמְּךָ יִשְׂרָאֵל בִּקְדֻשָּׁתֶךָ. בָּרוּךְ אַתָּה יהוה, הַמַּבְדִּיל בֵּין קֹדֶשׁ לְקֹדֶשׁ.

*On סוכות, say the following blessing. On the first night it is said before the blessing שֶׁהֶחֱיָנוּ; on the second night, after it (some say it before on both nights).*

בָּרוּךְ אַתָּה יהוה אֱלֹהֵינוּ מֶלֶךְ הָעוֹלָם
אֲשֶׁר קִדְּשָׁנוּ בְּמִצְוֹתָיו, וְצִוָּנוּ לֵישֵׁב בַּסֻּכָּה.

*The following blessing is omitted on the last two nights of פסח (in ארץ ישראל, the last night).*

בָּרוּךְ אַתָּה יהוה אֱלֹהֵינוּ מֶלֶךְ הָעוֹלָם
שֶׁהֶחֱיָנוּ וְקִיְּמָנוּ וְהִגִּיעָנוּ לַזְּמַן הַזֶּה.

*It is customary for all present to drink of the wine.*

# Meditation in the Sukka

הֲרֵינִי I am hereby prepared and ready to fulfill the commandment of Sukka, as the Creator, blessed be His name has commanded me: "You shall live in booths for seven days; every citizen in Israel shall live in booths so that future generations will know that I made the Israelites live in booths when I brought them out of Egypt. I am the LORD your God." *Lev. 23*

Sit, sit, exalted guests. Sit, sit, holy guests. Sit, sit, guests in faith. Sit in the shade of the Holy One, blessed be He. Worthy is the portion of Israel, as is written, "For the LORD's portion is His people, Jacob His allotted inheritance." *Deut. 32*

May it be Your will, LORD my God and God of my fathers, that You cause Your Divine Presence to rest among us and that You spread over us the tabernacle of Your peace, in the merit of the commandment of Sukka which we are fulfilling to unify the name of the Holy One, blessed be He, and His Divine Presence, in reverence and love, to unify the name *Yod-Heh* with *Vav-Heh,* in perfect unity in the name of all Israel. May You surround it with the radiance of Your holy and pure glory, spread above their heads like an eagle that stirs up its nest, and from there may a rich flow of life stream down on your servant (*name* son of *mother's name,* Your servant). In the merit of leaving my house to go outside, running in the way of Your commandments, may I be considered as if I had wandered far. Cleanse me thoroughly from my iniquity and purify me from my sin. From the exalted guests, the guests in faith, may Your ears attend to much blessing. To the hungry and thirsty grant unfailing food and drink. Grant me the privilege of sitting and taking refuge under the shadow of Your wings when I take leave of this world, taking refuge from stream and rain when You rain fiery coals on the wicked. May this command of Sukka that I am fulfilling be considered by You as if I had fulfilled it in all its specifics, details and conditions, as well as all the commandments dependent on it. May the sealing of our fate be for good, and grant us the merit of living for many years on the soil of the Holy Land, serving You and revering You. Blessed is the LORD forever, Amen and Amen. *Ps. 89*

# תפילה כשנכנסין לסוכה

הֲרֵינִי מוּכָן וּמְזֻמָּן לְקַיֵּם מִצְוַת סֻכָּה, כַּאֲשֶׁר צִוַּנִי הַבּוֹרֵא יִתְבָּרַךְ
שְׁמוֹ: בַּסֻּכֹּת תֵּשְׁבוּ שִׁבְעַת יָמִים, כָּל־הָאֶזְרָח בְּיִשְׂרָאֵל יֵשְׁבוּ בַּסֻּכֹּת: ויקרא כג
לְמַעַן יֵדְעוּ דֹרֹתֵיכֶם, כִּי בַסֻּכּוֹת הוֹשַׁבְתִּי אֶת־בְּנֵי יִשְׂרָאֵל, בְּהוֹצִיאִי
אוֹתָם מֵאֶרֶץ מִצְרָיִם:

תִּיבוּ תִּיבוּ אֻשְׁפִּיזִין עִלָּאִין, תִּיבוּ תִּיבוּ אֻשְׁפִּיזִין קַדִּישִׁין, תִּיבוּ תִּיבוּ
אֻשְׁפִּיזִין דִּמְהֵימְנוּתָא. זַכָּאָה חֻלְקְהוֹן דְּיִשְׂרָאֵל, דִּכְתִיב: כִּי חֵלֶק דברים לב
יהוה עַמּוֹ, יַעֲקֹב חֶבֶל נַחֲלָתוֹ:

יְהִי רָצוֹן מִלְּפָנֶיךָ יהוה אֱלֹהַי וֵאלֹהֵי אֲבוֹתַי, שֶׁתַּשְׁרֶה שְׁכִינָתְךָ
בֵּינֵינוּ, וְתִפְרֹס עָלֵינוּ סֻכַּת שְׁלוֹמֶךָ, בִּזְכוּת מִצְוַת סֻכָּה שֶׁאֲנַחְנוּ
מְקַיְּמִין לְיַחֲדָא שְׁמָא דְקֻדְשָׁא בְּרִיךְ הוּא וּשְׁכִינְתֵּהּ בִּדְחִילוּ וּרְחִימוּ,
לְיַחֲדָא שֵׁם י״ה בו״ה בְּיִחוּדָא שְׁלִים בְּשֵׁם כָּל יִשְׂרָאֵל, וּלְהַקִּיף
אוֹתָהּ מִזִּיו כְּבוֹדְךָ הַקָּדוֹשׁ וְהַטָּהוֹר, נָטוּי עַל רָאשֵׁיהֶם מִלְמַעְלָה
כַּנֶּשֶׁר יָעִיר קִנּוֹ, וּמִשָּׁם יַשְׁפַּע שֶׁפַע הַחַיִּים לְעַבְדְּךָ (פְּלוֹנִי בֶּן פְּלוֹנִית
אֲמָתֶךָ). וּבִזְכוּת צֵאתִי מִבֵּיתִי הַחוּצָה וְדֶרֶךְ מִצְוֹתֶיךָ אָרוּצָה, יֵחָשֵׁב
לִי זֹאת כְּאִלּוּ הִרְחַקְתִּי נְדוֹד, וְהֶרֶב כַּבְּסֵנִי מֵעֲוֹנִי וּמֵחַטָּאתִי טַהֲרֵנִי,
וּמֵאֻשְׁפִּיזִין עִלָּאִין אֻשְׁפִּיזִין דִּמְהֵימְנוּתָא תִּהְיֶינָה אָזְנֶיךָ קַשֻּׁבוֹת רַב
בְּרָכוֹת, וְלָרְעֵבִים גַּם צְמֵאִים תֶּן לַחְמָם וּמֵימָם הַנֶּאֱמָנִים, וְתִתֶּן לִי
זְכוּת לָשֶׁבֶת וְלַחֲסוֹת בְּסֵתֶר צֵל כְּנָפֶיךָ בְּעֵת פְּטִירָתִי מִן הָעוֹלָם,
וְלַחֲסוֹת מִזֶּרֶם וּמִמָּטָר, כִּי תַמְטִיר עַל רְשָׁעִים פַּחִים. וּתְהֵא חֲשׁוּבָה
מִצְוַת סֻכָּה זוֹ שֶׁאֲנִי מְקַיֵּם, כְּאִלּוּ קִיַּמְתִּיהָ בְּכָל פְּרָטֶיהָ וְדִקְדּוּקֶיהָ
וּתְנָאֶיהָ וְכָל מִצְוֹת הַתְּלוּיוֹת בָּהּ. וְתֵיטִיב לָנוּ הַחֲתִימָה, וּתְזַכֵּנוּ לֵישֵׁב
יָמִים רַבִּים עַל הָאֲדָמָה אַדְמַת קֹדֶשׁ, בַּעֲבוֹדָתְךָ וּבְיִרְאָתֶךָ. בָּרוּךְ תהלים פט
יהוה לְעוֹלָם אָמֵן וְאָמֵן:

*On entering the sukka and before saying Kiddush, many have the custom to welcome "guests" from the biblical past, who are said to join us as we sit in the sukka:*

אֻזְמִין I invite to my meal the exalted guests,
Abraham, Isaac, Jacob, Joseph, Moses, Aaron, and David.

*On the first day*

I pray you, Abraham, exalted guest,
that all the other exalted guests may sit here with me and you:
Isaac, Jacob, Joseph, Moses, Aaron, and David.

*On the second day*

I pray you, Isaac, exalted guest,
that all the other exalted guests may sit here with me and you:
Abraham, Jacob, Joseph, Moses, Aaron, and David.

*On the third day*

I pray you, Jacob, exalted guest,
that all the other exalted guests may sit here with me and you:
Abraham, Isaac, Joseph, Moses, Aaron, and David.

*On the fourth day*

I pray you, Joseph, exalted guest,
that all the other exalted guests may sit here with me and you:
Abraham, Isaac, Jacob, Moses, Aaron, and David.

*On the fifth day*

I pray you, Moses, exalted guest,
that all the other exalted guests may sit here with me and you:
Abraham, Isaac, Jacob, Joseph, Aaron, and David.

*On the sixth day*

I pray you, Aaron, exalted guest,
that all the other exalted guests may sit here with me and you:
Abraham, Isaac, Jacob, Joseph, Moses, and David.

*On Hoshana Raba*

I pray you, David, exalted guest,
that all the other exalted guests may sit here with me and you:
Abraham, Isaac, Jacob, Joseph, Moses and Aaron.

*On the last day of Sukkot, on leaving the sukka:*

May it be Your will, Lord our God and God of our fathers, that as I have fulfilled [Your commandment] and sat in this sukka, so next year may I have the privilege of sitting in the sukka made of the skin of Leviathan.

*On entering the* סוכה *and before saying* קידוש*, many have the custom to welcome "guests" from the biblical past, who are said to join us as we sit in the* סוכה*:*

אֲזַמִּין לִסְעוּדָתִי אֻשְׁפִּיזִין עִלָּאִין
אַבְרָהָם יִצְחָק יַעֲקֹב יוֹסֵף מֹשֶׁה אַהֲרֹן וְדָוִד.

*On the first day*

בְּמָטוּ מִנָּךְ אַבְרָהָם אֻשְׁפִּיזִי עִלָּאִי דְּתֵיתֵב עִמִּי
וְעִמָּךְ כָּל אֻשְׁפִּיזֵי עִלָּאֵי: יִצְחָק יַעֲקֹב יוֹסֵף מֹשֶׁה אַהֲרֹן וְדָוִד.

*On the second day*

בְּמָטוּ מִנָּךְ יִצְחָק אֻשְׁפִּיזִי עִלָּאִי דְּתֵיתֵב עִמִּי
וְעִמָּךְ כָּל אֻשְׁפִּיזֵי עִלָּאֵי: אַבְרָהָם יַעֲקֹב יוֹסֵף מֹשֶׁה אַהֲרֹן וְדָוִד.

*On the third day*

בְּמָטוּ מִנָּךְ יַעֲקֹב אֻשְׁפִּיזִי עִלָּאִי דְּתֵיתֵב עִמִּי
וְעִמָּךְ כָּל אֻשְׁפִּיזֵי עִלָּאֵי: אַבְרָהָם יִצְחָק יוֹסֵף מֹשֶׁה אַהֲרֹן וְדָוִד.

*On the fourth day*

בְּמָטוּ מִנָּךְ יוֹסֵף אֻשְׁפִּיזִי עִלָּאִי דְּתֵיתֵב עִמִּי
וְעִמָּךְ כָּל אֻשְׁפִּיזֵי עִלָּאֵי: אַבְרָהָם יִצְחָק יַעֲקֹב מֹשֶׁה אַהֲרֹן וְדָוִד.

*On the fifth day*

בְּמָטוּ מִנָּךְ מֹשֶׁה אֻשְׁפִּיזִי עִלָּאִי דְּתֵיתֵב עִמִּי
וְעִמָּךְ כָּל אֻשְׁפִּיזֵי עִלָּאֵי: אַבְרָהָם יִצְחָק יַעֲקֹב יוֹסֵף אַהֲרֹן וְדָוִד.

*On the sixth day*

בְּמָטוּ מִנָּךְ אַהֲרֹן אֻשְׁפִּיזִי עִלָּאִי דְּתֵיתֵב עִמִּי
וְעִמָּךְ כָּל אֻשְׁפִּיזֵי עִלָּאֵי: אַבְרָהָם יִצְחָק יַעֲקֹב יוֹסֵף מֹשֶׁה וְדָוִד.

*On* הושענא רבה

בְּמָטוּ מִנָּךְ דָּוִד אֻשְׁפִּיזִי עִלָּאִי דְּתֵיתֵב עִמִּי
וְעִמָּךְ כָּל אֻשְׁפִּיזֵי עִלָּאֵי: אַבְרָהָם יִצְחָק יַעֲקֹב יוֹסֵף מֹשֶׁה וְאַהֲרֹן.

*On the last day of* סוכות *on leaving the* סוכה*:*

יְהִי רָצוֹן מִלְּפָנֶיךָ יהוה אֱלֹהֵינוּ וֵאלֹהֵי אֲבוֹתֵינוּ
כְּשֵׁם שֶׁקִּיַּמְתִּי וְיָשַׁבְתִּי בְּסֻכָּה זוֹ
כֵּן אֶזְכֶּה לְשָׁנָה הַבָּאָה לֵישֵׁב בְּסֻכַּת עוֹרוֹ שֶׁל לִוְיָתָן.

# Kiddush for Yom Tov Morning

*On Shabbat Ḥol HaMo'ed turn to page 646.*
*On a Yom Tov that falls on Shabbat, start Kiddush here:*

וְשָׁמְרוּ The children of Israel must keep the Sabbath, observing the Sabbath in every generation as an everlasting covenant. It is a sign between Me and the children of Israel for ever, for in six days the LORD made the heavens and the earth, but on the seventh day He ceased work and refreshed Himself. *Ex. 31*

זָכוֹר Remember the Sabbath day to keep it holy. Six days you shall labor and do all your work, but the seventh day is a Sabbath of the LORD your God; on it you shall not do any work – you, your son or daughter, your male or female slave, or your cattle, or the stranger within your gates. For in six days the LORD made heaven and earth and sea and all that is in them, and rested on the seventh day; *Ex. 20*

*On a Yom Tov that falls on Shabbat, some start Kiddush here instead:*
Therefore the LORD blessed the Sabbath day and declared it holy.

*On a Yom Tov that falls on a weekday, start here:*

אֵלֶּה These are the appointed times of the LORD, *Lev. 23*
sacred assemblies,
which you shall announce in their due season.
Thus Moses announced the LORD's appointed seasons
to the children of Israel.

*When saying Kiddush for others, add:*
Please pay attention, my masters.

בָּרוּךְ Blessed are You, LORD our God, King of the Universe, who creates the fruit of the vine.

*On Sukkot:* בָּרוּךְ Blessed are You, LORD our God, King of the Universe,
who has made us holy through His commandments
and has commanded us to dwell in the sukka.

# קידושא רבה לשלוש רגלים

*On* שבת חול המועד *turn to page 649.*
*On* יום טוב *that falls on* שבת*, start* קידוש *here:*

וְשָׁמְרוּ בְנֵי־יִשְׂרָאֵל אֶת־הַשַּׁבָּת, לַעֲשׂוֹת אֶת־הַשַּׁבָּת לְדֹרֹתָם שמות לא
בְּרִית עוֹלָם: בֵּינִי וּבֵין בְּנֵי יִשְׂרָאֵל אוֹת הִוא לְעֹלָם, כִּי־שֵׁשֶׁת
יָמִים עָשָׂה יהוה אֶת־הַשָּׁמַיִם וְאֶת־הָאָרֶץ וּבַיּוֹם הַשְּׁבִיעִי שָׁבַת
וַיִּנָּפַשׁ:

זָכוֹר אֶת־יוֹם הַשַּׁבָּת לְקַדְּשׁוֹ: שֵׁשֶׁת יָמִים תַּעֲבֹד, וְעָשִׂיתָ כָּל־ שמות כ
מְלַאכְתֶּךָ: וְיוֹם הַשְּׁבִיעִי שַׁבָּת לַיהוה אֱלֹהֶיךָ, לֹא־תַעֲשֶׂה כָל־
מְלָאכָה אַתָּה וּבִנְךָ וּבִתֶּךָ, עַבְדְּךָ וַאֲמָתְךָ וּבְהֶמְתֶּךָ, וְגֵרְךָ אֲשֶׁר
בִּשְׁעָרֶיךָ: כִּי שֵׁשֶׁת־יָמִים עָשָׂה יהוה אֶת־הַשָּׁמַיִם וְאֶת־הָאָרֶץ
אֶת־הַיָּם וְאֶת־כָּל־אֲשֶׁר־בָּם, וַיָּנַח בַּיּוֹם הַשְּׁבִיעִי

*On* יום טוב *that falls on* שבת*, some start* קידוש *here instead:*

עַל־כֵּן בֵּרַךְ יהוה אֶת־יוֹם הַשַּׁבָּת וַיְקַדְּשֵׁהוּ:

*On* יום טוב *that falls on a weekday, start here:*

אֵלֶּה מוֹעֲדֵי יהוה מִקְרָאֵי קֹדֶשׁ ויקרא כג
אֲשֶׁר־תִּקְרְאוּ אֹתָם בְּמוֹעֲדָם:
וַיְדַבֵּר מֹשֶׁה אֶת־מֹעֲדֵי יהוה אֶל־בְּנֵי יִשְׂרָאֵל:

*When saying* קידוש *for others, add:*

סַבְרִי מָרָנָן
בָּרוּךְ אַתָּה יהוה אֱלֹהֵינוּ מֶלֶךְ הָעוֹלָם
בּוֹרֵא פְּרִי הַגָּפֶן.

בסוכות: בָּרוּךְ אַתָּה יהוה אֱלֹהֵינוּ מֶלֶךְ הָעוֹלָם
אֲשֶׁר קִדְּשָׁנוּ בְּמִצְוֹתָיו, וְצִוָּנוּ לֵישֵׁב בַּסֻּכָּה.

# Service for Festivals

*On Erev Yom Tov, Minḥa begins on page 278. On Shabbat Ḥol HaMo'ed, or when Yom Tov falls on Shabbat, Ma'ariv begins with Psalm 92 on page 404.*

*When Yom Tov falls on a weekday, Ma'ariv begins with Barekhu on page 414; when Ḥol HaMo'ed falls on a weekday, Ma'ariv begins with "He is compassionate" on page 314.*

*The following Amida is said at Shaḥarit, Minḥa and Ma'ariv on Yom Tov Pesaḥ, Shavuot, Sukkot, Shemini Atzeret and Simḥat Torah, but not on Ḥol HaMo'ed.*

## AMIDA FOR SHAḤARIT, MINḤA AND MA'ARIV

*The following prayer, until "in former years" on page 844, is said silently, standing with feet together. If there is a minyan, the Amida is repeated aloud by the Leader, except during Ma'ariv. Take three steps forward and at the points indicated by ▾, bend the knees at the first word, bow at the second, and stand straight before saying God's name.*

*At Minḥa:* When I proclaim the LORD's name, give glory to our God. *Deut. 32*
O LORD, open my lips, so that my mouth may declare Your praise. *Ps. 51*

PATRIARCHS

▾בָּרוּךְ▾ Blessed are You, LORD our God and God of our fathers,
God of Abraham, God of Isaac and God of Jacob;
the great, mighty and awesome God, God Most High,
who bestows acts of loving-kindness and creates all,
who remembers the loving-kindness of the fathers
and will bring a Redeemer to their children's children
for the sake of His name, in love.
King, Helper, Savior, Shield:
▾Blessed are You, LORD, Shield of Abraham.

DIVINE MIGHT

אַתָּה גִּבּוֹר You are eternally mighty, LORD.
You give life to the dead
and have great power to save.

*From Minḥa of Shemini Atzeret, through Shaḥarit on the first day of Pesaḥ (see laws 129–131):*
He makes the wind blow and the rain fall.

*In Israel, on other Festivals:*
He causes the dew to fall.

# שלוש רגלים

*On ערב יום טוב, מנחה begins on page 279. On שבת חול המועד or when*
*יום טוב falls on שבת, מעריב begins with מִזְמוֹר שִׁיר on page 405.*

*When יום טוב falls on a weekday, מעריב begins with בָּרְכוּ on page 415;*
*when חול המועד falls on a weekday, מעריב begins with וְהוּא רַחוּם on page 315.*

*The following עמידה is said at שחרית, מנחה and מעריב of פסח, שבועות,*
*סוכות, שמיני עצרת and שמחת תורה, but not on חול המועד.*

## עמידה לשחרית, מנחה ומעריב

*The following prayer, until קַדְמֹנִיּוֹת on page 845, is said silently, standing with feet together. If there is a מנין, the עמידה is repeated aloud by the שליח ציבור, except during מעריב. Take three steps forward and at the points indicated by ˙, bend the knees at the first word, bow at the second, and stand straight before saying God's name.*

למנחה: כִּי שֵׁם יהוה אֶקְרָא, הָבוּ גֹדֶל לֵאלֹהֵינוּ: דברים לב

אֲדֹנָי, שְׂפָתַי תִּפְתָּח, וּפִי יַגִּיד תְּהִלָּתֶךָ: תהלים נא

### אבות

˙בָּרוּךְ אַתָּה יהוה, אֱלֹהֵינוּ וֵאלֹהֵי אֲבוֹתֵינוּ
אֱלֹהֵי אַבְרָהָם, אֱלֹהֵי יִצְחָק, וֵאלֹהֵי יַעֲקֹב
הָאֵל הַגָּדוֹל הַגִּבּוֹר וְהַנּוֹרָא, אֵל עֶלְיוֹן
גּוֹמֵל חֲסָדִים טוֹבִים, וְקוֹנֵה הַכֹּל, וְזוֹכֵר חַסְדֵי אָבוֹת
וּמֵבִיא גוֹאֵל לִבְנֵי בְנֵיהֶם לְמַעַן שְׁמוֹ בְּאַהֲבָה.
מֶלֶךְ עוֹזֵר וּמוֹשִׁיעַ וּמָגֵן.
˙בָּרוּךְ אַתָּה יהוה, מָגֵן אַבְרָהָם.

### גבורות

אַתָּה גִּבּוֹר לְעוֹלָם, אֲדֹנָי
מְחַיֵּה מֵתִים אַתָּה, רַב לְהוֹשִׁיעַ

*From שמיני עצרת of מנחה*
*through שחרית on the first day of פסח (see laws 129–131):*

מַשִּׁיב הָרְוּחַ וּמוֹרִיד הַגֶּשֶׁם

*In ארץ ישראל on other חגים:*

מוֹרִיד הַטָּל

He sustains the living with loving-kindness,
and with great compassion revives the dead.
He supports the fallen, heals the sick, sets captives free,
and keeps His faith with those who sleep in the dust.
Who is like You, Master of might,
and who can compare to You,
O King who brings death and gives life, and makes salvation grow?
Faithful are You to revive the dead.
Blessed are You, LORD, who revives the dead.

*When saying the Amida silently, continue with "You are holy" on the next page.*
*During the Leader's Repetition of Minḥa, turn to the Kedusha on the next page.*

---

### KEDUSHA FOR SHAḤARIT

*During the Leader's Repetition, the following is said standing with feet together, rising on the toes at the words indicated by ▲.*

*Cong. then Leader:* נְקַדֵּשׁ We will sanctify Your name on earth, as they sanctify it in the highest heavens, as is written by Your prophet, "And they [the angels] call to one another saying: *Is. 6*

*Cong. then Leader:* ▲Holy, ▲holy, ▲holy is the LORD of hosts; the whole world is filled with His glory."
Then with a sound of mighty noise, majestic and strong, they make their voice heard, raising themselves toward the Seraphim, and facing them say: "Blessed…

*Cong. then Leader:* ▲"Blessed is the LORD's glory from His place." *Ezek. 3*
Reveal Yourself from Your place, O our King, and reign over us, for we are waiting for You. When will You reign in Zion? May it be soon in our days, and may You dwell there for ever and all time. May You be exalted and sanctified in the midst of Jerusalem, Your city, from generation to generation for evermore. May our eyes see Your kingdom, as is said in the songs of Your splendor, written by David Your righteous anointed one:

*Cong. then Leader:* ▲"The LORD shall reign for ever. He is your God, Zion, from generation to generation, Halleluya!" *Ps. 146*

*Leader:* From generation to generation we will declare Your greatness, and we will proclaim Your holiness for evermore. Your praise, our God, shall not leave our mouth forever, for You, God, are a great and holy King. Blessed are You, LORD, the holy God.

*The Leader continues with "You have chosen us" on the next page.*

מְכַלְכֵּל חַיִּים בְּחֶסֶד, מְחַיֵּה מֵתִים בְּרַחֲמִים רַבִּים
סוֹמֵךְ נוֹפְלִים, וְרוֹפֵא חוֹלִים, וּמַתִּיר אֲסוּרִים
וּמְקַיֵּם אֱמוּנָתוֹ לִישֵׁנֵי עָפָר.
מִי כָמְוֹךָ, בַּעַל גְּבוּרוֹת, וּמִי דּוֹמֶה לָּךְ
מֶלֶךְ, מֵמִית וּמְחַיֶּה וּמַצְמִיחַ יְשׁוּעָה.
וְנֶאֱמָן אַתָּה לְהַחֲיוֹת מֵתִים.
בָּרוּךְ אַתָּה יהוה, מְחַיֵּה הַמֵּתִים.

*When saying the עמידה silently, continue with אַתָּה קָדוֹשׁ on the next page.*
*During the חזרת הש״ץ of מנחה, turn to the קדושה on the next page.*

---

## קדושה לשחרית

*During the חזרת הש״ץ, the following is said standing with feet together, rising on the toes at the words indicated by ▲.*

קהל then ש״ץ: נְקַדֵּשׁ אֶת שִׁמְךָ בָּעוֹלָם, כְּשֵׁם שֶׁמַּקְדִּישִׁים אוֹתוֹ בִּשְׁמֵי מָרוֹם
כַּכָּתוּב עַל יַד נְבִיאֶךָ: וְקָרָא זֶה אֶל־זֶה וְאָמַר ישעיה ו

קהל then ש״ץ: ▲קָדוֹשׁ, ▲קָדוֹשׁ, ▲קָדוֹשׁ, יהוה צְבָאוֹת, מְלֹא כָל־הָאָרֶץ כְּבוֹדוֹ:
אָז בְּקוֹל רַעַשׁ גָּדוֹל אַדִּיר וְחָזָק, מַשְׁמִיעִים קוֹל
מִתְנַשְּׂאִים לְעֻמַּת שְׂרָפִים, לְעֻמָּתָם בָּרוּךְ יֹאמֵרוּ

קהל then ש״ץ: ▲בָּרוּךְ כְּבוֹד־יהוה מִמְּקוֹמוֹ: יחזקאל ג
מִמְּקוֹמְךָ מַלְכֵּנוּ תוֹפִיעַ וְתִמְלֹךְ עָלֵינוּ, כִּי מְחַכִּים אֲנַחְנוּ לָךְ
מָתַי תִּמְלֹךְ בְּצִיּוֹן, בְּקָרוֹב בְּיָמֵינוּ לְעוֹלָם וָעֶד תִּשְׁכֹּן
תִּתְגַּדַּל וְתִתְקַדַּשׁ בְּתוֹךְ יְרוּשָׁלַיִם עִירְךָ לְדוֹר וָדוֹר וּלְנֵצַח נְצָחִים.
וְעֵינֵינוּ תִרְאֶינָה מַלְכוּתֶךָ
כַּדָּבָר הָאָמוּר בְּשִׁירֵי עֻזֶּךָ עַל יְדֵי דָוִד מְשִׁיחַ צִדְקֶךָ

קהל then ש״ץ: ▲יִמְלֹךְ יהוה לְעוֹלָם, אֱלֹהַיִךְ צִיּוֹן לְדֹר וָדֹר, הַלְלוּיָהּ: תהלים קמו

ש״ץ: לְדוֹר וָדוֹר נַגִּיד גָּדְלֶךָ, וּלְנֵצַח נְצָחִים קְדֻשָּׁתְךָ נַקְדִּישׁ
וְשִׁבְחֲךָ אֱלֹהֵינוּ מִפִּינוּ לֹא יָמוּשׁ לְעוֹלָם וָעֶד
כִּי אֵל מֶלֶךְ גָּדוֹל וְקָדוֹשׁ אָתָּה. בָּרוּךְ אַתָּה יהוה הָאֵל הַקָּדוֹשׁ.

*The שליח ציבור continues with אַתָּה בְחַרְתָּנוּ on the next page.*

## KEDUSHA FOR MINHA

*During the Leader's Repetition, the following is said standing with feet together, rising on the toes at the words indicated by ▴.*

*Cong. then Leader:* נְקַדֵּשׁ We will sanctify Your name on earth,
as they sanctify it in the highest heavens,
as is written by Your prophet,
"And they [the angels] call to one another saying: *Is. 6*

*Cong. then Leader:* ▴Holy, ▴holy, ▴holy is the LORD of hosts;
the whole world is filled with His glory."
Those facing them say "Blessed –"

*Cong. then Leader:* ▴"Blessed is the LORD's glory from His place." *Ezek. 3*
And in Your holy Writings it is written thus:

*Cong. then Leader:* ▴"The LORD shall reign for ever. He is your God, Zion, *Ps. 146*
from generation to generation, Halleluya!"

*Leader:* From generation to generation we will declare Your greatness,
and we will proclaim Your holiness for evermore.
Your praise, our God, shall not leave our mouth forever,
for You, God, are a great and holy King.
Blessed are You, LORD, the holy God.

*The Leader continues with "You have chosen us" below.*

---

*When saying the Amida silently, continue here:*

## HOLINESS

אַתָּה קָדוֹשׁ You are holy
and Your name is holy,
and holy ones praise You daily, Selah!
Blessed are You, LORD, the holy God.

## HOLINESS OF THE DAY

אַתָּה בְחַרְתָּנוּ You have chosen us from among all peoples.
You have loved and favored us.
You have raised us above all tongues.
You have made us holy through Your commandments.
You have brought us near, our King, to Your service,
and have called us by Your great and holy name.

## קדושה למנחה

*During the* חזרת הש״ץ, *the following is said standing with feet together, rising on the toes at the words indicated by* ▲.

*then* קהל ש״ץ: נְקַדֵּשׁ אֶת שִׁמְךָ בָּעוֹלָם, כְּשֵׁם שֶׁמַּקְדִּישִׁים אוֹתוֹ בִּשְׁמֵי מָרוֹם
כַּכָּתוּב עַל יַד נְבִיאֶךָ: וְקָרָא זֶה אֶל־זֶה וְאָמַר ישעיה ו

*then* קהל ש״ץ: ▲קָדוֹשׁ, ▲קָדוֹשׁ, ▲קָדוֹשׁ, יהוה צְבָאוֹת, מְלֹא כָל־הָאָרֶץ כְּבוֹדוֹ:
לְעֻמָּתָם בָּרוּךְ יֹאמֵרוּ

*then* קהל ש״ץ: ▲בָּרוּךְ כְּבוֹד־יהוה מִמְּקוֹמוֹ: יחזקאל ג
וּבְדִבְרֵי קָדְשְׁךָ כָּתוּב לֵאמֹר

*then* קהל ש״ץ: ▲יִמְלֹךְ יהוה לְעוֹלָם, אֱלֹהַיִךְ צִיּוֹן לְדֹר וָדֹר, הַלְלוּיָהּ: תהלים קמו

ש״ץ: לְדוֹר וָדוֹר נַגִּיד גָּדְלֶךָ, וּלְנֵצַח נְצָחִים קְדֻשָּׁתְךָ נַקְדִּישׁ
וְשִׁבְחֲךָ אֱלֹהֵינוּ מִפִּינוּ לֹא יָמוּשׁ לְעוֹלָם וָעֶד
כִּי אֵל מֶלֶךְ גָּדוֹל וְקָדוֹשׁ אָתָּה.
בָּרוּךְ אַתָּה יהוה הָאֵל הַקָּדוֹשׁ.

*The* שליח ציבור *continues with* אַתָּה בְחַרְתָּנוּ *below.*

---

*When saying the* עמידה *silently, continue here:*

## קדושת השם

אַתָּה קָדוֹשׁ וְשִׁמְךָ קָדוֹשׁ
וּקְדוֹשִׁים בְּכָל יוֹם יְהַלְלוּךָ סֶּלָה.
בָּרוּךְ אַתָּה יהוה, הָאֵל הַקָּדוֹשׁ.

## קדושת היום

אַתָּה בְחַרְתָּנוּ מִכָּל הָעַמִּים
אָהַבְתָּ אוֹתָנוּ וְרָצִיתָ בָּנוּ
וְרוֹמַמְתָּנוּ מִכָּל הַלְּשׁוֹנוֹת
וְקִדַּשְׁתָּנוּ בְּמִצְוֹתֶיךָ
וְקֵרַבְתָּנוּ מַלְכֵּנוּ לַעֲבוֹדָתֶךָ
וְשִׁמְךָ הַגָּדוֹל וְהַקָּדוֹשׁ עָלֵינוּ קָרָאתָ.

*On Motza'ei Shabbat:*

וַתּוֹדִיעֵנוּ You have made known to us, LORD our God, Your righteous laws, and have taught us to perform Your will's decrees. You have given us, LORD our God, just laws and true teachings, good precepts and commandments. You have given us as our heritage seasons of joy, holy festivals, and occasions for presenting our freewill offerings. You have given us as our heritage the holiness of the Sabbath, the glory of the festival, and the festive offerings of the pilgrimage days. You have distinguished, LORD our God, between sacred and secular, between light and darkness, between Israel and the nations, between the seventh day and the six days of work. You have distinguished between the holiness of the Sabbath and the holiness of the festival, and have made the seventh day holy above the six days of work. You have distinguished and sanctified Your people Israel with Your holiness.

*On Shabbat, add the words in parentheses:*

וַתִּתֶּן לָנוּ And You, LORD our God, have given us in love
(Sabbaths for rest and) festivals for rejoicing,
holy days and seasons for joy, (this Sabbath day and) this day of:
*On Pesaḥ:* the festival of Matzot, the time of our freedom
*On Shavuot:* the festival of Shavuot,
the time of the giving of our Torah
*On Sukkot:* the festival of Sukkot, our time of rejoicing
*On Shemini Atzeret & Simḥat Torah:* the festival of the eighth day, Shemini Atzeret,
our time of rejoicing
(with love), a holy assembly in memory of the exodus from Egypt.

אֱלֹהֵינוּ Our God and God of our ancestors,
may there rise, come, reach, appear, be favored, heard,
regarded and remembered before You,
our recollection and remembrance,
as well as the remembrance of our ancestors,
and of the Messiah, son of David Your servant,
and of Jerusalem Your holy city,
and of all Your people the house of Israel –

*On* מוצאי שבת:

וַתּוֹדִיעֵנוּ יהוה אֱלֹהֵינוּ אֶת מִשְׁפְּטֵי צִדְקֶךָ, וַתְּלַמְּדֵנוּ לַעֲשׂוֹת חֻקֵּי רְצוֹנֶךָ, וַתִּתֶּן לָנוּ יהוה אֱלֹהֵינוּ מִשְׁפָּטִים יְשָׁרִים וְתוֹרוֹת אֱמֶת, חֻקִּים וּמִצְוֹת טוֹבִים, וַתַּנְחִילֵנוּ זְמַנֵּי שָׂשׂוֹן וּמוֹעֲדֵי קֹדֶשׁ וְחַגֵּי נְדָבָה, וַתּוֹרִישֵׁנוּ קְדֻשַּׁת שַׁבָּת וּכְבוֹד מוֹעֵד וַחֲגִיגַת הָרֶגֶל. וַתַּבְדֵּל יהוה אֱלֹהֵינוּ בֵּין קֹדֶשׁ לְחֹל, בֵּין אוֹר לְחֹשֶׁךְ, בֵּין יִשְׂרָאֵל לָעַמִּים, בֵּין יוֹם הַשְּׁבִיעִי לְשֵׁשֶׁת יְמֵי הַמַּעֲשֶׂה. בֵּין קְדֻשַּׁת שַׁבָּת לִקְדֻשַּׁת יוֹם טוֹב הִבְדַּלְתָּ, וְאֶת יוֹם הַשְּׁבִיעִי מִשֵּׁשֶׁת יְמֵי הַמַּעֲשֶׂה קִדַּשְׁתָּ, הִבְדַּלְתָּ וְקִדַּשְׁתָּ אֶת עַמְּךָ יִשְׂרָאֵל בִּקְדֻשָּׁתֶךָ.

*On* שבת*, add the words in parentheses:*

וַתִּתֶּן לָנוּ יהוה אֱלֹהֵינוּ בְּאַהֲבָה
(שַׁבָּתוֹת לִמְנוּחָה וּ) מוֹעֲדִים לְשִׂמְחָה
חַגִּים וּזְמַנִּים לְשָׂשׂוֹן
אֶת יוֹם (הַשַּׁבָּת הַזֶּה וְאֶת יוֹם)

בפסח: חַג הַמַּצּוֹת הַזֶּה, זְמַן חֵרוּתֵנוּ

בשבועות: חַג הַשָּׁבוּעוֹת הַזֶּה, זְמַן מַתַּן תּוֹרָתֵנוּ

בסוכות: חַג הַסֻּכּוֹת הַזֶּה, זְמַן שִׂמְחָתֵנוּ

בשמע״צ ובש״ת: הַשְּׁמִינִי חַג הָעֲצֶרֶת הַזֶּה, זְמַן שִׂמְחָתֵנוּ

(בְּאַהֲבָה) מִקְרָא קֹדֶשׁ, זֵכֶר לִיצִיאַת מִצְרָיִם.

אֱלֹהֵינוּ וֵאלֹהֵי אֲבוֹתֵינוּ
יַעֲלֶה וְיָבוֹא וְיַגִּיעַ, וְיֵרָאֶה וְיֵרָצֶה וְיִשָּׁמַע
וְיִפָּקֵד וְיִזָּכֵר זִכְרוֹנֵנוּ וּפִקְדוֹנֵנוּ וְזִכְרוֹן אֲבוֹתֵינוּ
וְזִכְרוֹן מָשִׁיחַ בֶּן דָּוִד עַבְדֶּךָ, וְזִכְרוֹן יְרוּשָׁלַיִם עִיר קָדְשֶׁךָ
וְזִכְרוֹן כָּל עַמְּךָ בֵּית יִשְׂרָאֵל, לְפָנֶיךָ

for deliverance and well-being, grace,
loving-kindness and compassion,
life and peace, on this day of:

*On Pesaḥ:* the festival of Matzot.
*On Shavuot:* the festival of Shavuot.
*On Sukkot:* the festival of Sukkot.
*On Shemini Atzeret & Simḥat Torah:* the festival of Shemini Atzeret.

On it remember us, LORD our God, for good;
recollect us for blessing, and deliver us for life.
In accord with Your promise of salvation and compassion,
spare us and be gracious to us;
have compassion on us and deliver us,
for our eyes are turned to You
because You, God, are a gracious and compassionate King.

*On Shabbat, add the words in parentheses:*

וְהַשִּׂיאֵנוּ Bestow on us, LORD our God,
the blessings of Your festivals
for good life and peace, joy and gladness,
as You desired and promised to bless us.
(Our God and God of our fathers, find favor in our rest.)
Make us holy through Your commandments
and grant us a share in Your Torah.
Satisfy us with Your goodness,
gladden us with Your salvation,
and purify our hearts to serve You in truth.
Grant us as our heritage,
LORD our God (with love and favor,) with joy and gladness,
Your holy (Sabbath and) festivals,
and may Israel, who sanctify Your name, rejoice in You.
Blessed are You, LORD,
who sanctifies (the Sabbath and) Israel
and the festive seasons.

לִפְלֵיטָה, לְטוֹבָה, לְחֵן וּלְחֶסֶד וּלְרַחֲמִים
לְחַיִּים וּלְשָׁלוֹם בְּיוֹם

בפסח: חַג הַמַּצּוֹת הַזֶּה.

בשבועות: חַג הַשָּׁבוּעוֹת הַזֶּה.

בסוכות: חַג הַסֻּכּוֹת הַזֶּה.

בשמע״צ ובש״ת: הַשְּׁמִינִי חַג הָעֲצֶרֶת הַזֶּה.

זָכְרֵנוּ יהוה אֱלֹהֵינוּ בּוֹ לְטוֹבָה, וּפָקְדֵנוּ בוֹ לִבְרָכָה
וְהוֹשִׁיעֵנוּ בוֹ לְחַיִּים.
וּבִדְבַר יְשׁוּעָה וְרַחֲמִים, חוּס וְחָנֵּנוּ
וְרַחֵם עָלֵינוּ וְהוֹשִׁיעֵנוּ
כִּי אֵלֶיךָ עֵינֵינוּ, כִּי אֵל מֶלֶךְ חַנּוּן וְרַחוּם אָתָּה.

*On שבת, add the words in parentheses:*

וְהַשִּׂיאֵנוּ יהוה אֱלֹהֵינוּ אֶת בִּרְכַּת מוֹעֲדֶיךָ
לְחַיִּים וּלְשָׁלוֹם, לְשִׂמְחָה וּלְשָׂשׂוֹן
כַּאֲשֶׁר רָצִיתָ וְאָמַרְתָּ לְבָרְכֵנוּ.
(אֱלֹהֵינוּ וֵאלֹהֵי אֲבוֹתֵינוּ, רְצֵה בִמְנוּחָתֵנוּ)
קַדְּשֵׁנוּ בְּמִצְוֹתֶיךָ
וְתֵן חֶלְקֵנוּ בְּתוֹרָתֶךָ
שַׂבְּעֵנוּ מִטּוּבֶךָ, וְשַׂמְּחֵנוּ בִּישׁוּעָתֶךָ
וְטַהֵר לִבֵּנוּ לְעָבְדְּךָ בֶּאֱמֶת.
וְהַנְחִילֵנוּ יהוה אֱלֹהֵינוּ (בְּאַהֲבָה וּבְרָצוֹן)
בְּשִׂמְחָה וּבְשָׂשׂוֹן (שַׁבָּת וּ) מוֹעֲדֵי קָדְשֶׁךָ
וְיִשְׂמְחוּ בְךָ יִשְׂרָאֵל מְקַדְּשֵׁי שְׁמֶךָ.
בָּרוּךְ אַתָּה יהוה, מְקַדֵּשׁ (הַשַּׁבָּת וְ) יִשְׂרָאֵל וְהַזְּמַנִּים.

TEMPLE SERVICE

רְצֵה Find favor, LORD our God, in Your people Israel
and their prayer.
Restore the service to Your most holy House,
and accept in love and favor the fire-offerings of Israel
and their prayer.
May the service of Your people Israel
always find favor with You.
And may our eyes witness Your return to Zion in compassion.
Blessed are You, LORD, who restores His Presence to Zion.

THANKSGIVING

*Bow at the first nine words.*

מוֹדִים We give thanks to You,
for You are the LORD our God
and God of our ancestors
for ever and all time.
You are the Rock of our lives,
Shield of our salvation
from generation to generation.
We will thank You and
declare Your praise for our lives,
which are entrusted into Your hand;
for our souls,
which are placed in Your charge;
for Your miracles
which are with us every day;
and for Your wonders and favors
at all times, evening,
morning and midday.
You are good –
for Your compassion never fails.
You are compassionate –
for Your loving-kindnesses never cease.
We have always placed our hope in You.

*During the Leader's Repetition, the congregation says quietly:*

מוֹדִים We give thanks to You,
for You are the LORD our God
and God of our ancestors,
God of all flesh,
who formed us
and formed the universe.
Blessings and thanks
are due to Your great
and holy name for giving us
life and sustaining us.
May You continue
to give us life and sustain us;
and may You gather our
exiles to Your holy courts,
to keep Your decrees,
do Your will and serve You
with a perfect heart,
for it is for us
to give You thanks.
Blessed be God to whom
thanksgiving is due.

עבודה

רְצֵה יהוה אֱלֹהֵינוּ בְּעַמְּךָ יִשְׂרָאֵל וּבִתְפִלָּתָם
וְהָשֵׁב אֶת הָעֲבוֹדָה לִדְבִיר בֵּיתֶךָ
וְאִשֵּׁי יִשְׂרָאֵל וּתְפִלָּתָם בְּאַהֲבָה תְקַבֵּל בְּרָצוֹן
וּתְהִי לְרָצוֹן תָּמִיד עֲבוֹדַת יִשְׂרָאֵל עַמֶּךָ.
וְתֶחֱזֶינָה עֵינֵינוּ בְּשׁוּבְךָ לְצִיּוֹן בְּרַחֲמִים.
בָּרוּךְ אַתָּה יהוה, הַמַּחֲזִיר שְׁכִינָתוֹ לְצִיּוֹן.

הודאה

*Bow at the first five words.*

מוֹדִים אֲנַחְנוּ לָךְ
שָׁאַתָּה הוּא יהוה אֱלֹהֵינוּ
וֵאלֹהֵי אֲבוֹתֵינוּ לְעוֹלָם וָעֶד.
צוּר חַיֵּינוּ, מָגֵן יִשְׁעֵנוּ
אַתָּה הוּא לְדוֹר וָדוֹר.
נוֹדֶה לְּךָ וּנְסַפֵּר תְּהִלָּתֶךָ
עַל חַיֵּינוּ הַמְּסוּרִים בְּיָדֶךָ
וְעַל נִשְׁמוֹתֵינוּ הַפְּקוּדוֹת לָךְ
וְעַל נִסֶּיךָ שֶׁבְּכָל יוֹם עִמָּנוּ
וְעַל נִפְלְאוֹתֶיךָ וְטוֹבוֹתֶיךָ
שֶׁבְּכָל עֵת
עֶרֶב וָבֹקֶר וְצָהֳרָיִם.
הַטּוֹב, כִּי לֹא כָלוּ רַחֲמֶיךָ
וְהַמְרַחֵם, כִּי לֹא תַמּוּ חֲסָדֶיךָ
מֵעוֹלָם קִוִּינוּ לָךְ.

*During the* חזרת הש״ץ, *the* קהל *says quietly:*

מוֹדִים אֲנַחְנוּ לָךְ
שָׁאַתָּה הוּא יהוה אֱלֹהֵינוּ
וֵאלֹהֵי אֲבוֹתֵינוּ
אֱלֹהֵי כָל בָּשָׂר
יוֹצְרֵנוּ, יוֹצֵר בְּרֵאשִׁית.
בְּרָכוֹת וְהוֹדָאוֹת
לְשִׁמְךָ הַגָּדוֹל וְהַקָּדוֹשׁ
עַל שֶׁהֶחֱיִיתָנוּ וְקִיַּמְתָּנוּ.
כֵּן תְּחַיֵּנוּ וּתְקַיְּמֵנוּ
וְתֶאֱסֹף גָּלֻיּוֹתֵינוּ
לְחַצְרוֹת קָדְשֶׁךָ
לִשְׁמֹר חֻקֶּיךָ
וְלַעֲשׂוֹת רְצוֹנֶךָ וּלְעָבְדְּךָ
בְּלֵבָב שָׁלֵם
עַל שֶׁאֲנַחְנוּ מוֹדִים לָךְ.
בָּרוּךְ אֵל הַהוֹדָאוֹת.

וְעַל כֻּלָּם For all these things may Your name be blessed and exalted, our King, continually, for ever and all time.
Let all that lives thank You, Selah!
and praise Your name in truth, God, our Savior and Help, Selah!
▾Blessed are You, LORD, whose name is "the Good"
and to whom thanks are due.

---

*For the blessing of the Kohanim in Israel, see page 902.*
*The Leader says the following during the Repetition of the Shaharit Amida.*
*It is also said in Israel when no Kohanim bless the congregation. See laws 370–377.*

Our God and God of our fathers, bless us with the threefold blessing in the Torah, written by the hand of Moses Your servant and pronounced by Aaron and his sons the priests, Your holy people, as it is said:

May the LORD bless you and protect you. *Cong:* May it be Your will. *Num. 6*
May the LORD make His face shine on you and be gracious to you.
*Cong:* May it be Your will.
May the LORD turn His face toward you, and grant you peace.
*Cong:* May it be Your will.

---

PEACE

| *At Minha and Ma'ariv:* | *At Shaharit and in Israel at Shabbat Minha:* |
|---|---|
| שָׁלוֹם רָב Grant great peace to Your people Israel for ever, for You are the sovereign LORD of all peace; and may it be good in Your eyes to bless Your people Israel at every time, at every hour, with Your peace. | שִׂים שָׁלוֹם Grant peace, goodness and blessing, grace, loving-kindness and compassion to us and all Israel Your people. Bless us, our Father, all as one, with the light of Your face, for by the light of Your face You have given us, LORD our God, the Torah of life and love of kindness, righteousness, blessing, compassion, life and peace. May it be good in Your eyes to bless Your people Israel at every time, in every hour, with Your peace. |

Blessed are You, LORD, who blesses His people Israel with peace.

*The following verse concludes the Leader's Repetition of the Amida.*
*Some also say it here as part of the silent Amida. See law 368.*

May the words of my mouth and the meditation of my heart *Ps. 19*
find favor before You, LORD, my Rock and Redeemer.

וְעַל כֻּלָּם יִתְבָּרַךְ וְיִתְרוֹמַם שִׁמְךָ מַלְכֵּנוּ תָּמִיד לְעוֹלָם וָעֶד.
וְכֹל הַחַיִּים יוֹדְוּךָ סֶּלָה
וִיהַלְלוּ אֶת שִׁמְךָ בֶּאֱמֶת, הָאֵל יְשׁוּעָתֵנוּ וְעֶזְרָתֵנוּ סֶלָה.
•בָּרוּךְ אַתָּה יהוה, הַטּוֹב שִׁמְךָ וּלְךָ נָאֶה לְהוֹדוֹת.

---

*For the blessing of the* כהנים *in* ארץ ישראל *see page 903.*
*The* שליח ציבור *says the following during the* חורת הש״ץ *of* שחרית*.*
*It is also said in* ארץ ישראל *when no* כהנים *bless the congregation. See laws 370–377.*

אֱלֹהֵינוּ וֵאלֹהֵי אֲבוֹתֵינוּ, בָּרְכֵנוּ בַּבְּרָכָה הַמְשֻׁלֶּשֶׁת בַּתּוֹרָה, הַכְּתוּבָה עַל יְדֵי מֹשֶׁה עַבְדֶּךָ, הָאֲמוּרָה מִפִּי אַהֲרֹן וּבָנָיו כֹּהֲנִים עַם קְדוֹשֶׁיךָ, כָּאָמוּר

במדבר ו יְבָרֶכְךָ יהוה וְיִשְׁמְרֶךָ: קהל: כֵּן יְהִי רָצוֹן
יָאֵר יהוה פָּנָיו אֵלֶיךָ וִיחֻנֶּךָּ: קהל: כֵּן יְהִי רָצוֹן
יִשָּׂא יהוה פָּנָיו אֵלֶיךָ וְיָשֵׂם לְךָ שָׁלוֹם: קהל: כֵּן יְהִי רָצוֹן

---

## ברכת שלום

במנחה ובמעריב:

שָׁלוֹם רָב
עַל יִשְׂרָאֵל עַמְּךָ
תָּשִׂים לְעוֹלָם
כִּי אַתָּה הוּא
מֶלֶךְ אָדוֹן לְכָל הַשָּׁלוֹם.
וְטוֹב בְּעֵינֶיךָ לְבָרֵךְ
אֶת עַמְּךָ יִשְׂרָאֵל
בְּכָל עֵת וּבְכָל שָׁעָה
בִּשְׁלוֹמֶךָ.

בשחרית ובארץ ישראל במנחה בשבת:

שִׂים שָׁלוֹם טוֹבָה וּבְרָכָה
חֵן וָחֶסֶד וְרַחֲמִים
עָלֵינוּ וְעַל כָּל יִשְׂרָאֵל עַמֶּךָ.
בָּרְכֵנוּ אָבִינוּ כֻּלָּנוּ כְּאֶחָד בְּאוֹר פָּנֶיךָ
כִּי בְאוֹר פָּנֶיךָ נָתַתָּ לָּנוּ יהוה אֱלֹהֵינוּ
תּוֹרַת חַיִּים וְאַהֲבַת חֶסֶד
וּצְדָקָה וּבְרָכָה וְרַחֲמִים וְחַיִּים וְשָׁלוֹם.
וְטוֹב בְּעֵינֶיךָ לְבָרֵךְ אֶת עַמְּךָ יִשְׂרָאֵל
בְּכָל עֵת וּבְכָל שָׁעָה בִּשְׁלוֹמֶךָ.

בָּרוּךְ אַתָּה יהוה, הַמְבָרֵךְ אֶת עַמּוֹ יִשְׂרָאֵל בַּשָּׁלוֹם.

*The following verse concludes the* חורת הש״ץ*.*
*Some also say it here as part of the silent* עמידה*. See law 368.*

תהלים יט יִהְיוּ לְרָצוֹן אִמְרֵי־פִי וְהֶגְיוֹן לִבִּי לְפָנֶיךָ, יהוה צוּרִי וְגֹאֲלִי:

אֱלֹהַי My God, *Berakhot 17a*
guard my tongue from evil and my lips from deceitful speech.
To those who curse me, let my soul be silent;
may my soul be to all like the dust.
Open my heart to Your Torah
and let my soul pursue Your commandments.
As for all who plan evil against me,
swiftly thwart their counsel and frustrate their plans.
Act for the sake of Your name; act for the sake of Your right hand;
act for the sake of Your holiness; act for the sake of Your Torah.
That Your beloved ones may be delivered, *Ps. 60*
save with Your right hand and answer me.
May the words of my mouth and the meditation of my heart *Ps. 19*
find favor before You, LORD, my Rock and Redeemer.

*Bow, take three steps back, then bow, first left, then right, then center, while saying:*

May He who makes peace in His high places,
make peace for us and all Israel – and say: Amen.

יְהִי רָצוֹן May it be Your will, LORD our God and God of our ancestors,
that the Temple be rebuilt speedily in our days, and grant us a share in Your Torah.
And there we will serve You with reverence,
as in the days of old and as in former years.
Then the offering of Judah and Jerusalem *Mal. 3*
will be pleasing to the LORD as in the days of old and as in former years.

*On Friday night, the service continues with "Then the heavens and the earth" on pages 436–438.*
*If the first night of Pesaḥ falls on Shabbat, only the first paragraph is said.*
*On the Seder night many say Full Hallel (page 790) followed by Full Kaddish (page 438).*
*On the other Yamim Tovim, both at Minḥa and Ma'ariv, Full Kaddish (page 438) is said.*
*On the last nights of Pesaḥ, the Omer (page 356) is counted after Full Kaddish (page 438).*
*On Simḥat Torah, both at Ma'ariv and Shaḥarit say Full Kaddish (page 438), then continue with "You have been shown" and Hakafot on the next page.*
*At Shaḥarit, continue with Full Hallel (page 790), Full Kaddish (page 568), Torah Reading (page 570) and Musaf (page 868).*
*If the first day of Pesaḥ falls on Shabbat, then Shir HaShirim is read before the Torah reading at Shaḥarit on the last day (in Israel, on the first day). Otherwise it is read on Shabbat Ḥol HaMo'ed.*
*On the second day of Shavuot, Megillat Rut is read before the Torah reading at Shaḥarit (in Israel, on the first day).*
*If the first day of Sukkot falls on Shabbat, then Kohelet is read before the Torah reading at Shaḥarit on Shemini Atzeret (in Israel, on the first day of Sukkot). Otherwise it is read on Shabbat Ḥol HaMo'ed.*

אֱלֹהַי ברכות יז.

נְצֹר לְשׁוֹנִי מֵרָע וּשְׂפָתַי מִדַּבֵּר מִרְמָה

וְלִמְקַלְלַי נַפְשִׁי תִדֹּם, וְנַפְשִׁי כֶּעָפָר לַכֹּל תִּהְיֶה.

פְּתַח לִבִּי בְּתוֹרָתֶךָ, וּבְמִצְוֹתֶיךָ תִּרְדֹּף נַפְשִׁי.

וְכָל הַחוֹשְׁבִים עָלַי רָעָה

מְהֵרָה הָפֵר עֲצָתָם וְקַלְקֵל מַחֲשַׁבְתָּם.

עֲשֵׂה לְמַעַן שְׁמֶךָ, עֲשֵׂה לְמַעַן יְמִינֶךָ

עֲשֵׂה לְמַעַן קְדֻשָּׁתֶךָ, עֲשֵׂה לְמַעַן תּוֹרָתֶךָ.

לְמַעַן יֵחָלְצוּן יְדִידֶיךָ, הוֹשִׁיעָה יְמִינְךָ וַעֲנֵנִי: תהלים ס

יִהְיוּ לְרָצוֹן אִמְרֵי־פִי וְהֶגְיוֹן לִבִּי לְפָנֶיךָ, יהוה צוּרִי וְגֹאֲלִי: תהלים יט

*Bow, take three steps back, then bow, first left, then right, then center, while saying:*

עֹשֶׂה שָׁלוֹם בִּמְרוֹמָיו

הוּא יַעֲשֶׂה שָׁלוֹם עָלֵינוּ וְעַל כָּל יִשְׂרָאֵל, וְאִמְרוּ אָמֵן.

יְהִי רָצוֹן מִלְּפָנֶיךָ יהוה אֱלֹהֵינוּ וֵאלֹהֵי אֲבוֹתֵינוּ

שֶׁיִּבָּנֶה בֵּית הַמִּקְדָּשׁ בִּמְהֵרָה בְיָמֵינוּ, וְתֵן חֶלְקֵנוּ בְּתוֹרָתֶךָ

וְשָׁם נַעֲבָדְךָ בְּיִרְאָה כִּימֵי עוֹלָם וּכְשָׁנִים קַדְמוֹנִיּוֹת.

וְעָרְבָה לַיהוה מִנְחַת יְהוּדָה וִירוּשָׁלָיִם כִּימֵי עוֹלָם וּכְשָׁנִים קַדְמֹנִיּוֹת: מלאכי ג

*On Friday night, the service continues with* וַיְכֻלּוּ *and* מעין שבע *on pages 437–439.*
*If the first night of* פסח *falls on* שבת*,* מעין שבע *is omitted.*

*On* ליל הסדר *many say* הלל שלם *(page 791) followed by* קדיש שלם *(page 439).*

*On the other* ימים טובים*, both at* מנחה *and* מעריב*,* קדיש שלם *(page 439) is said.*

*On the last nights of* פסח*, the* עומר *(page 357) is counted after* קדיש שלם *(page 439).*

*On* שמחת תורה*, both at* מעריב *and* שחרית *say* קדיש שלם *(page 439),*
*then continue with* אַתָּה הָרְאֵתָ *and* הקפות *on the next page.*

*At* שחרית*, continue with* הלל שלם *(page 791),* קדיש שלם
*(page 569),* קריאת התורה *(page 571) and* מוסף *(page 869).*

*If the first day of* פסח *falls on* שבת*, then* שיר השירים *is read before* קריאת התורה *at* שחרית
*on the last day (in* ארץ ישראל*, on the first day). Otherwise it is read on* שבת חול המועד*.*

*On the second day of* שבועות*,* רות *is read before* קריאת התורה
*at* שחרית *(in* ארץ ישראל*, on the first day).*

*If the first day of* סוכות *falls on* שבת*, then* קהלת *is read before* קריאת התורה *at* שחרית *on*
שמיני עצרת *(in* ארץ ישראל*, on the first day of* סוכות*). Otherwise it is read on* שבת חול המועד*.*

## HAKAFOT

*At Ma'ariv and Shaḥarit of Simḥat Torah the following is said after Full Kaddish (page 568).*

אַתָּה הָרְאֵתָ You have been shown [these things] so that you may know that the LORD is God; besides Him there is no other. *Deut. 4*

To the One who alone does great wonders, His loving-kindness is forever. *Ps. 136*

There is none like You among the heavenly powers, my LORD, and there are no works like Yours. *Ps. 86*

May the LORD's glory be forever; may the LORD rejoice in His works. *Ps. 104*

May the LORD's name be blessed from now and forever. *Ps. 113*

May the LORD our God be with us as He was with our ancestors; may He never leave us or forsake us. *1 Kings 8*

Say, "Save us, God our Savior; gather and deliver us from the nations, that we may give thanks to Your holy name, that we may glory in Your praise." *1 Chr. 16*

The LORD is King, the LORD was King, the LORD will be King for ever and all time.

The LORD will give strength to His people; the LORD will bless His people with peace. *Ps. 29*

May our words find favor before the LORD of all.

*The Ark is opened.*

Whenever the Ark set out, Moses would say, "Arise, LORD, and may Your enemies be scattered; may those who hate You flee before You." *Num. 10*

Advance, LORD, to Your resting place, You and Your mighty Ark. *Ps. 132*

Your priests are clothed in righteousness, and Your devoted ones sing for joy.

For the sake of Your servant David, do not reject Your anointed one.

In that day they will say, "This is our God; we trusted in Him, and He saved us. This is the LORD, we trusted in Him; let us rejoice and be glad in His salvation." *Is. 25*

Your kingdom is an eternal kingdom, and Your dominion is for all generations. *Ps. 145*

For the Torah shall come forth from Zion and the word of the LORD from Jerusalem. *Is. 2*

Father of compassion, favor Zion with Your goodness; rebuild the walls of Jerusalem. *Ps. 51*
For we trust in You alone, King, God, high and exalted, Master of worlds.

# סדר הקפות

*At* מעריב *and* שחרית *of* שמחת תורה, *the following is said after* קדיש שלם *(page 569).*

אַתָּה הָרְאֵתָ לָדַעַת, כִּי יהוה הוּא הָאֱלֹהִים, אֵין עוֹד מִלְּבַדּוֹ: דברים ד
לְעֹשֵׂה נִפְלָאוֹת גְּדֹלוֹת לְבַדּוֹ, כִּי לְעוֹלָם חַסְדּוֹ: תהלים קלו
אֵין־כָּמְוֹךָ בָאֱלֹהִים, אֲדֹנָי, וְאֵין כְּמַעֲשֶׂיךָ: תהלים פו
יְהִי כְבוֹד יהוה לְעוֹלָם, יִשְׂמַח יהוה בְּמַעֲשָׂיו: תהלים קד
יְהִי שֵׁם יהוה מְבֹרָךְ, מֵעַתָּה וְעַד־עוֹלָם: תהלים קיג
יְהִי יהוה אֱלֹהֵינוּ עִמָּנוּ, כַּאֲשֶׁר הָיָה עִם־אֲבֹתֵינוּ מלכים א׳ ח
אַל־יַעַזְבֵנוּ וְאַל־יִטְּשֵׁנוּ:
וְאִמְרוּ, הוֹשִׁיעֵנוּ אֱלֹהֵי יִשְׁעֵנוּ, וְקַבְּצֵנוּ וְהַצִּילֵנוּ מִן־הַגּוֹיִם דברי הימים א׳ טז
לְהֹדוֹת לְשֵׁם קָדְשֶׁךָ, לְהִשְׁתַּבֵּחַ בִּתְהִלָּתֶךָ:
יהוה מֶלֶךְ, יהוה מָלָךְ, יהוה יִמְלֹךְ לְעֹלָם וָעֶד.
יהוה עֹז לְעַמּוֹ יִתֵּן, יהוה יְבָרֵךְ אֶת־עַמּוֹ בַשָּׁלוֹם: תהלים כט
וְיִהְיוּ נָא אֲמָרֵינוּ לְרָצוֹן, לִפְנֵי אֲדוֹן כֹּל.

*The* ארון קודש *is opened.*

וַיְהִי בִּנְסֹעַ הָאָרֹן וַיֹּאמֶר מֹשֶׁה במדבר י
קוּמָה יהוה וְיָפֻצוּ אֹיְבֶיךָ, וְיָנֻסוּ מְשַׂנְאֶיךָ מִפָּנֶיךָ:
קוּמָה יהוה לִמְנוּחָתֶךָ, אַתָּה וַאֲרוֹן עֻזֶּךָ: תהלים קלב
כֹּהֲנֶיךָ יִלְבְּשׁוּ־צֶדֶק, וַחֲסִידֶיךָ יְרַנֵּנוּ:
בַּעֲבוּר דָּוִד עַבְדֶּךָ, אַל־תָּשֵׁב פְּנֵי מְשִׁיחֶךָ:
וְאָמַר בַּיּוֹם הַהוּא ישעיה כה
הִנֵּה אֱלֹהֵינוּ זֶה קִוִּינוּ לוֹ, וְיוֹשִׁיעֵנוּ
זֶה יהוה קִוִּינוּ לוֹ, נָגִילָה וְנִשְׂמְחָה בִּישׁוּעָתוֹ:
מַלְכוּתְךָ מַלְכוּת כָּל־עֹלָמִים, וּמֶמְשַׁלְתְּךָ בְּכָל־דּוֹר וָדֹר: תהלים קמה
כִּי מִצִּיּוֹן תֵּצֵא תוֹרָה, וּדְבַר־יהוה מִירוּשָׁלָםִ: ישעיה ב

אַב הָרַחֲמִים, הֵיטִיבָה בִרְצוֹנְךָ אֶת־צִיּוֹן, תִּבְנֶה חוֹמוֹת יְרוּשָׁלָםִ: תהלים נא
כִּי בְךָ לְבַד בָּטָחְנוּ, מֶלֶךְ אֵל רָם וְנִשָּׂא, אֲדוֹן עוֹלָמִים.

*All the Torah scrolls are taken from the Ark.*

*First Hakafa*

LORD, please save us. *Ps. 118*
LORD, please grant us success.
LORD, please answer us on the day we cry.

God of spirits, please save us.
Searcher of hearts, please grant us success.
Mighty Redeemer, answer us on the day we cry.

*Second Hakafa*

Speaker of righteousness, please save us.
Robed in majesty, please grant us success.
Ancient and loving One, answer us on the day we cry.

*Third Hakafa*

Pure and right, please save us.
Gracious and compassionate, please grant us success.
He who is good and does good, answer us on the day we cry.

*Fourth Hakafa*

He who knows thoughts, please save us.
Mighty and resplendent, please grant us success.
Robed in righteousness, answer us on the day we cry.

*Fifth Hakafa*

Eternal King, please save us.
Resplendent and mighty, please grant us success.
Supporter of the fallen, answer us on the day we cry.

*Sixth Hakafa*

Helper of the poor, please save us.
Redeemer and Rescuer, please grant us success.
Eternal Rock, answer us on the day we cry.

*Seventh Hakafa*

Holy and awesome, please save us.
Compassionate and gracious, please grant us success.
Dweller in the heavens, answer us on the day we cry.

Supporter of the innocent, please save us.
Eternally powerful, please grant us success.
Perfect in His deeds, answer us on the day we cry.

*The Torah scrolls are returned to the Ark except for those used in the Torah Reading. The service continues with Removing the Torah from the Ark, beginning with "Listen, Israel" on page 574. At Ma'ariv, three (in some congregations, five) are called up and the "VeZot HaBerakha" Torah portion (pages 1239–1240) is read. See law 136. During Shaḥarit, the prevalent custom is to call up every adult male in the congregation. See law 139.*

*All the* ספרי תורה *are taken from the* ארון קודש.

*First* הקפה

אָנָּא יהוה הוֹשִׁיעָה נָּא, אָנָּא יהוה הַצְלִיחָה נָא: תהלים קיח

אָנָּא יהוה עֲנֵנוּ בְיוֹם קָרְאֵנוּ.

אֱלֹהֵי הָרוּחוֹת הוֹשִׁיעָה נָּא, בּוֹחֵן לְבָבוֹת הַצְלִיחָה נָא

גּוֹאֵל חָזָק עֲנֵנוּ בְיוֹם קָרְאֵנוּ.

*Second* הקפה

דּוֹבֵר צְדָקוֹת הוֹשִׁיעָה נָּא, הָדוּר בִּלְבוּשׁוֹ הַצְלִיחָה נָא

וָתִיק וְחָסִיד עֲנֵנוּ בְיוֹם קָרְאֵנוּ.

*Third* הקפה

זַךְ וְיָשָׁר הוֹשִׁיעָה נָּא, חַנּוּן וְרַחוּם הַצְלִיחָה נָא

טוֹב וּמֵטִיב עֲנֵנוּ בְיוֹם קָרְאֵנוּ.

*Fourth* הקפה

יוֹדֵעַ מַחֲשָׁבוֹת הוֹשִׁיעָה נָּא, כַּבִּיר כֹּחַ הַצְלִיחָה נָא

לוֹבֵשׁ צְדָקוֹת עֲנֵנוּ בְיוֹם קָרְאֵנוּ.

*Fifth* הקפה

מֶלֶךְ עוֹלָמִים הוֹשִׁיעָה נָּא, נָאוֹר וְאַדִּיר הַצְלִיחָה נָא

סוֹמֵךְ וְסוֹעֵד עֲנֵנוּ בְיוֹם קָרְאֵנוּ.

*Sixth* הקפה

עוֹזֵר דַּלִּים הוֹשִׁיעָה נָּא, פּוֹדֶה וּמַצִּיל הַצְלִיחָה נָא

צוּר עוֹלָמִים עֲנֵנוּ בְיוֹם קָרְאֵנוּ.

*Seventh* הקפה

קָדוֹשׁ וְנוֹרָא הוֹשִׁיעָה נָּא, רַחוּם וְחַנּוּן הַצְלִיחָה נָא

שׁוֹכֵן שְׁחָקִים עֲנֵנוּ בְיוֹם קָרְאֵנוּ.

תּוֹמֵךְ תְּמִימִים הוֹשִׁיעָה נָּא, תַּקִּיף לָעַד הַצְלִיחָה נָא

תָּמִים בְּמַעֲשָׂיו עֲנֵנוּ בְיוֹם קָרְאֵנוּ.

*The* ספרי תורה *are returned to the* ארון קודש *except for those used in the* קריאת התורה. *The service continues with* הוצאת ספר תורה, *beginning with "*שמע ישראל*" on page 575. At* מעריב, *three (in some congregations, five) are called up and the* קריאה *of* וְזֹאת הַבְּרָכָה *(pages 1239–1240) is read. See law 136. During* שחרית, *the prevalent custom is to call up every adult male in the congregation. See law 139.*

# AKDAMUT

*On the first day of Shavuot, after the Kohen is called up to the Torah and before he makes the blessing, the following is said responsively by the Reader and the congregation.*

*Leader:* The beginning of words – the opening of speech:
I shall ask permission and leave to begin.

*Cong:* Trembling I open my mouth with two matters and three,
by leave of the One who bears us through to old age.

*Leader:* His are eternal mighty acts,
which could not be laid out in words,
even were all the skies parchment, and all the forests reeds;

*Cong:* if all the seas were ink, and all the lakes,
and the all people, scribes and clerks.

*Leader:* The glorious Master of Heaven, Ruler of the land,
founded His world alone, and took control of it.

*Cong:* Without weariness He perfected it, without tiring at all;
by the lightest of letters, something without substance.

*Leader:* He summoned forth all creation in those six days;
and then His shining glory rose, to sit upon His throne of fire.

*Cong:* A heavenly host of a thousand thousands
and myriads serve Him –
created each morning anew, so great is His faithfulness.

*Leader:* Seraphim, covered with six wings, bow many times over,
and stand in utter silence until they have leave.

*Cong:* They receive leave from each other –
and at once, without pause,
His glory fills all the world, at their threefold sanctifying.

# אקדמות

*On the first day of* שבועות*, after the* כהן *is called up to the* תורה *and before he makes the* ברכה*, the following is said responsively by the* שליח ציבור *and the* קהל*.*

ש״ץ: אַקְדָּמוּת מִלִּין וְשָׁרָיוּת שׁוּתָא
אַוְלָא שָׁקֵלְנָא הַרְמָן וּרְשׁוּתָא.

קהל: בְּבָבֵי תְּרֵי וּתְלָת דְּאֶפְתַּח בְּנַקְשׁוּתָא
בְּבָרֵי דְּבָרֵי וְטָרֵי עֲדֵי לְקַשִּׁישׁוּתָא.

ש״ץ: גְּבוּרָן עָלְמִין לֵהּ, וְלָא סָפֵק פְּרִישׁוּתָא
גְּוִיל אִלּוּ רְקִיעֵי, קְנֵי כָּל חֻרְשָׁתָא.

קהל: דְּיוֹ אִלּוּ יַמֵּי וְכָל מֵי כְנִישׁוּתָא
דָּיְרֵי אַרְעָא סָפְרֵי וְרָשְׁמֵי רַשְׁוָתָא.

ש״ץ: הֲדַר מָרֵי שְׁמַיָּא וְשַׁלִּיט בְּיַבֶּשְׁתָּא
הֲקֵים עָלְמָא יְחִידָאי, וְכַבְּשֵׁהּ בְּכַבְּשׁוּתָא.

קהל: וּבְלָא לֵאוּ שַׁכְלְלֵהּ, וּבְלָא תְשָׁשׁוּתָא
וּבְאָתָא קַלִּילָא דְּלֵית בַּהּ מְשָׁשׁוּתָא.

ש״ץ: זַמֵּן כָּל עֲבִידְתֵּהּ בְּהַךְ יוֹמֵי שִׁתָּא
זְהוֹר יְקָרֵהּ עֲלִי, עֲלֵי כָרְסְיֵהּ דְּאֶשָּׁתָא.

קהל: חֵיל אֶלֶף אַלְפִין וְרִבּוֹא לְשַׁמָּשׁוּתָא
חַדְתִּין נְבוֹט לְצַפְרִין, סַגִּיאָה טָרְשׁוּתָא.

ש״ץ: טְפֵי יְקִידִין שְׂרָפִין, כְּלוּל גַּפֵּי שִׁתָּא
טְעֵם עַד יִתְיְהֵב לְהוֹן, שְׁתִיקִין בְּאַדִּישְׁתָּא.

קהל: יְקַבְּלוּן דֵּין מִן דֵּין שָׁוֵי דְּלָא בְשַׁשְׁתָּא
יְקָר מְלֵי כָל אַרְעָא לְתַלּוֹתֵי קְדֻשְּׁתָא.

*Leader:* Like a voice from the Almighty, like the noise of many waters –
Cherubim raise themselves towards the Ophanim
in a roar of noise,

*Cong:* to see face to face what looks like sparks of the rainbow flying,
and wherever they are sent, they arrive in a flash of motion.

*Leader:* They bless His glory in every secret term,
from the place of the home of His Presence,
which cannot even be sought.

*Cong:* And all the hosts of heaven give praises in great fear,
of the sovereignty that will last through all ages, forever.

*Leader:* They each lay out His holiness in praise,
and when their moment has passed
it is gone forever; seven years will go by and it will not return.

*Cong:* His precious estate, Israel – they are more fortunate, for always
may they praise Him, dawn and dusk.

*Leader:* They are set apart, His portion, to perform His will,
and they will tell the wonders of His praise in speech.

*Cong:* He desires and values and yearns for them
to labor for Him to weariness,
and so He accepts their prayers; it is their pleas that are fulfilled.

*Leader:* And those pleas are joined, with a crown and an oath,
to the One who lives forever,
and worn with the phylacteries He binds to Himself always,

*Cong:* which are inscribed inside with wisdom and with insight,
with the greatness of Israel, who read the Shema.

*Leader:* And I, in the same way, praise the Master of the Universe,
and it befits me to speak of Him to those of other nations,

*Cong:* who come and form crowds, like waves all around,
doubting, asking about Him, about the signs He performs –

ש״ץ: כְּקָל מִן קֳדָם שַׁדַּי, כְּקָל מֵי נְפִישׁוּתָא
כְּרוּבִין קֳבֵל גַּלְגִּלִּין מְרוֹמְמִין בְּאַוְשָׁתָא.

קהל: לְמֶחֱזֵי בְּאַנְפָּא עֵין כְּוַת גִּירֵי קַשְׁתָּא
לְכָל אֲתַר דְּמִשְׁתַּלְּחִין, זְרִיזִין בְּאַשְׁוָתָא.

ש״ץ: מְבָרְכִין בְּרִיךְ יְקָרֵהּ בְּכָל לִשַּׁן לְחִישׁוּתָא
מֵאֲתַר בֵּית שְׁכִינְתֵּהּ, דְּלָא צְרִיךְ בְּחִישׁוּתָא.

קהל: נְהֵם כָּל חֵיל מְרוֹמָא, מְקַלְּסִין בַּחֲשַׁשְׁתָּא
נְהִירָא מַלְכוּתֵהּ לְדָר וְדָר לְאַפְרַשְׁתָּא.

ש״ץ: סְדִירָא בְּהוֹן קְדֻשְׁתָּא, וְכַד חָלְפָא שַׁעְתָּא
סִיּוּמָא דִלְעָלַם, וְאוֹף לָא לְשָׁבוּעֲתָא.

קהל: עֲדַב יְקַר אַחְסַנְתֵּהּ חֲבִיבִין, דִּבְקַבַּעְתָּא
עֲבִידִין לֵהּ חֲטִיבָא בִּדְנַח וּשְׁקַעְתָּא.

ש״ץ: פְּרִישָׁן לְמָנָתֵהּ לְמֶעְבַּד לֵהּ רְעוּתָא
פְּרִישָׁתֵי שְׁבָחֵהּ יְחַוּוֹן בְּשָׁעוּתָא.

קהל: צְבִי וְחָמֵד וְרָגֵג דְּיִלְאוֹן בְּלָעוּתָא
צְלוֹתְהוֹן בְּכֵן מְקַבֵּל, וְהָנְיָא בָעוּתָא.

ש״ץ: קְטִירָא לְחַי עָלְמָא בְּתָגָא בִשְׁבוּעֲתָא
קֳבֵל יְקַר טוֹטֶפְתָּא יְתִיבָא בִקְבִיעֲתָא.

קהל: רְשִׁימָא הִיא גּוּפָא בְּחָכְמְתָא וּבְדַעְתָּא
רְבוּתְהוֹן דְּיִשְׂרָאֵל, קָרְאֵי בִשְׁמַעְתָּא.

ש״ץ: שְׁבַח רִבּוֹן עָלְמָא, אֲמִירָא דַכְוָתָא
שְׁפַר עֲלַי לְחַוּוֹיֵהּ בְּאַפֵּי מַלְכְּוָתָא.

קהל: תָּאִין וּמִתְכַּנְּשִׁין כְּחֵזוּ אַדְוָתָא
תְּמֵהִין וְשָׁיְלִין לֵהּ בְּעֵסֶק אָתְוָתָא.

*Leader:* "Where is your Beloved from, yes who is He, who is so beautiful,
that you let yourselves be killed for Him in the lions' den?

*Cong:* "You would be more respected, lovelier,
if you bent yourselves to our rule:
your will would be done then wherever you would be."

*Leader:* With wisdom I reply to them, telling them of the end –
"If you only knew, if you only truly knew Him,

*Cong:* "and what your greatness is worth when compared to that glory,
or the greatness
I will be granted when my salvation comes...

*Leader:* "When light comes to me, and shame covers you over;
when His presence is revealed to me in might and in great pride."

*Cong:* He shall pay His enemies back in kind, the aggressors
of the distant isles,
and perform justice for the beloved people, rich in merit,

*Leader:* when He brings perfect happiness, and us as pure vessels;
when He brings the exiles back into the city of Jerusalem.

*Cong:* He shall cast His glory over them day and night,
as a canopy where they shall voice the splendor in
joyful songs,

*Leader:* for the shining of those clouds will make each canopy fine
as the actions of the one who sits in it; so will each shelter
be made.

*Cong:* On seats of finest gold, in seven tiers, sit the righteous
in their places before the One whose acts are manifold.

*Leader:* And they appear as seven tiers of joy,
like the dome of the sky in its brilliance, like stars of light.

*Cong:* This is a glory no mouth can express,
glory that the prophets never heard or saw in their visions.

ש״ץ: מְנָן וּמַאן הוּא רְחִימָךְ, שַׁפִּירָא בְּרֵוָתָא
אֲרוּם בְּגִינֵהּ סְפֵית מְדוֹר אַרְיָוָתָא.

קהל: יְקָרָא וְיָאָה אַתְּ, אִין תְּעָרְבִי לְמָרְוָתָא
רְעוּתֵךְ נַעֲבֵד לִיךְ בְּכָל אַתְרְוָתָא.

ש״ץ: בְּחָכְמְתָא מְתִיבְתָא לְהוֹן, קְצָת לְהוֹדָעוּתָא
יְדַעְתּוּן חַכְּמִין לֵהּ בְּאִשְׁתְּמוֹדָעוּתָא.

קהל: רְבוּתְכוֹן מָה חֲשִׁיבָא קֳבֵל הַהִיא שְׁבַחְתָּא
רְבוּתָא דְּיַעֲבֵד לִי, כַּד מָטְיָא יְשׁוּעָתָא.

ש״ץ: בְּמֵיתֵי לִי נְהוֹרָא, וְתַחֲפֵי לְכוֹן בַּהֲתָא
יְקָרֵהּ כַּד אִתְגְּלֵי בְּתָקְפָּא וּבְגֵיוְתָא.

קהל: יְשַׁלֵּם גְּמָלַיָּא לְשָׂנְאֵי וְנַגְוָתָא
צִדְקָתָא לְעַם חָבִיב וְסַגֵּי זַכְוָתָא.

ש״ץ: חֲדוּ שְׁלֵמָא בְּמֵיתֵי, וּמָנָא דַכְוָתָא
קִרְיְתָא דִירוּשְׁלֵם כַּד יְכַנֵּשׁ גָּלְוָתָא.

קהל: יְקָרֵהּ מַטֵּל עֲלֵהּ בְּיוֹמֵי וְלֵילְוָתָא
גְּנוּנֵהּ לְמֶעְבַּד בַּהּ בְּתֻשְׁבְּחָן כְּלִילָתָא.

ש״ץ: דְּזֵהוֹר עֲנָנַיָּא לְמִשְׁפַּר כִּילָתָא
לְפֻמֵּהּ דַּעֲבִידְתָּא עֲבִידָן מְטַלַּלְתָּא.

קהל: בְּתַכְתְּקֵי דְהַב פִּזָא, וְשִׁבְעָא מַעֲלָתָא
תְּחִימִין צַדִּיקֵי קֳדָם רַב פָּעֳלָתָא.

ש״ץ: וְרֵוֵיהוֹן דָּמֵי לְשָׂבְעָא חֶדְוָתָא
רְקִיעָא בְּזֵהוֹרֵהּ וְכוֹכְבֵי זִיוָתָא.

קהל: הֲדָרָא דְּלָא אֶפְשָׁר לְמִפְרַט שִׂפְוָתָא
וְלָא אִשְׁתְּמַע וַחֲמֵי נְבִיאָן חֶזְוָתָא.

*Leader:* For no eye has ever overseen the Garden of Eden,
where the righteous circle the place of the dance, and the holy
Presence among them.

*Cong:* And they point to Him, saying with awe, "It is He!
"The One for whom we longed when we were captives, in our
powerful faith.

*Leader:* "And He will lead us in both worlds; and He will lead us dancing,
as if we were young again;
lead us to our land, set aside from the beginning of the world
for us."

*Cong:* He plays with the Leviathan, with the Behemoth of the
high mountain,
and when they wrestle one another in their great duel,

*Leader:* the horns of the great Behemoth will gore,
and the mighty Leviathan will leap out at him with his fins,

*Cong:* and finally, his Creator will step forward with His great sword,
and prepare a meal, a feast, of that meat, for all the righteous.

*Leader:* And they shall sit at tables of rubies and gems,
with rivers of balsam flowing before them,

*Cong:* and quench their thirst in luxury with overflowing cups
of the wondrous wine stored up for them since the first days
of creation.

*Leader:* My righteous listeners, as you have heard the praises in this song,
so may you be promised a place in those joyous circles.

*Cong:* And may you merit to sit in those heavenly rows,
for heeding God's words, which come forth in splendor.

*Leader:* Our God is in the highest heights, the first and the last,
desiring us and cherishing us, and giving us the Torah.

*The service continues with the reading of the Torah on page 1224.*

ש״ץ: בְּלָא שָׁלְטָא בֵהּ עֵין, בְּגוֹ עֵדֶן גִּנְּתָא
מְטַיְּלֵי בֵהּ חִנְגָּא לְבַהֲדֵי דִשְׁכִינְתָּא.

קהל: עֲלֵהּ רָמְזֵי דֵּין הוּא, בְּרַם בְּאֵימְתָנוּתָא
שְׁבַרְנָא לֵהּ בְּשִׁבְיַן, תְּקוֹף הֵמָנוּתָא.

ש״ץ: יְדַבֵּר לַן עָלְמִין, עָלְמִין מְדַמּוּתָא
מְנָת דִּילַן דְּמִלְּקַדְמִין פָּרֵשׁ בַּאֲרָמוּתָא.

קהל: טְלוּלָא דְלִוְיָתָן וְתוֹר טוּר רָמוּתָא
וְחַד בְּחַד כִּי סָבֵךְ וְעָבֵד קְרָבוּתָא.

ש״ץ: בְּקַרְנוֹהִי מְנַגַּח בְּהֵמוֹת בִּרְבוּתָא
יְקַרְטַע נוּן לְקִבְלֵהּ בְּצִיצוֹי בִּגְבוּרְתָא.

קהל: מְקָרֵב לֵהּ בָּרְיֵהּ בְּחַרְבֵּהּ בְּרַבְרְבוּתָא
אֲרִסְטוֹן לְצַדִּיקֵי יְתַקֵּן, וְשֵׁרוּתָא.

ש״ץ: מְסַחֲרִין עֲלֵי תַכֵּי דְּכַדְכֹּד וְגוּמַרְתָּא
נְגִידִין קָמֵיהוֹן אֲפַרְסְמוֹן נַהֲרָתָא.

קהל: וּמִתְפַּנְּקִין וְרָווּ בְּכָסֵי רְוָיָתָא
חֲמַר מְרַת דְּמִבְּרֵאשִׁית נְטִיר בֵּי נַעֲוָתָא.

ש״ץ: זַכָּאִין, כַּד שְׁמַעְתּוּן שְׁבַח דָּא שִׁירָתָא
קְבִיעִין כֵּן תֶּהֱווֹן בְּהַנְהוּ חֲבוּרָתָא.

קהל: וְתִזְכּוּן דִּי תֵיתְּבוּן בְּעֵלָּא דָרָתָא
אֲרֵי תְצִיתוּן לְמִלּוֹי, דְּנָפְקִין בְּהַדְרָתָא.

ש״ץ: מְרוֹמַם הוּא אֱלָהִין בְּקַדְמְתָא וּבַתְרַיְתָא
צְבִי וְאִתְרְעִי בַן, וּמְסַר לַן אוֹרַיְתָא.

*The service continues with* קריאת התורה *on page 1224.*

# YIZKOR

*The Yizkor service is said on the last day of Pesaḥ, the second day of Shavuot (first day in Israel), Yom Kippur and Shemini Atzeret. In some communities, those who have not been bereaved of a parent or close relative do not participate in the service, but leave the synagogue and return at the end of Yizkor.*

יהוה Lord, what is man that You care for him, *Ps. 144*
a mortal that You notice him?
Man is like a fleeting breath, his days like a passing shadow.
In the morning he flourishes and grows; *Ps. 90*
in the evening he withers and dries up.
Teach us to number our days, that we may get a heart of wisdom.
Mark the blameless, note the upright, for the end of such a person is peace. *Ps. 37*
God will redeem my soul from the grave, for He will receive me, Selah. *Ps. 49*
My flesh and my heart may fail, *Ps. 73*
but God is the strength of my heart and my portion for ever.
The dust returns to the earth as it was, *Eccl. 12*
but the spirit returns to God who gave it.

יֹשֵׁב He who lives in the shelter of the Most High dwells in the shadow of *Ps. 91*
the Almighty. I say of the Lord, my Refuge and Stronghold, my God in whom I trust, that He will save you from the fowler's snare and the deadly pestilence. With His pinions He will cover you, and beneath His wings you will find shelter; His faithfulness is an encircling shield. You need not fear terror by night, nor the arrow that flies by day; not the pestilence that stalks in darkness, nor the plague that ravages at noon. A thousand may fall at your side, ten thousand at your right hand, but it will not come near you. You will only look with your eyes and see the punishment of the wicked. Because you said, "the Lord is my Refuge," taking the Most High as your shelter, no harm will befall you, no plague will come near your tent, for He will command His angels about you, to guard you in all your ways. They will lift you in their hands, lest your foot stumble on a stone. You will tread on lions and vipers; you will trample on young lions and snakes. [God says:] "Because he loves Me, I will rescue him; I will protect him, because he acknowledges My name. When he calls on Me, I will answer him; I will be with him in distress, I will deliver him and bring him honor.
With long life I will satisfy him and show him My salvation.
With long life I will satisfy him and show him My salvation.

# סדר הזכרת נשמות

*The* יזכור *service is said on the last day of* פסח*, the second day of* שבועות *(first day in* ארץ ישראל*),* יום כיפור *and* שמיני עצרת*. In some communities, those who have not been bereaved of a parent or close relative do not participate in the service, but leave the* בית כנסת *and return at the end of* סדר הזכרת נשמות*.*

תהלים קמד יהוה מָה־אָדָם וַתֵּדָעֵהוּ, בֶּן־אֱנוֹשׁ וַתְּחַשְּׁבֵהוּ:
אָדָם לַהֶבֶל דָּמָה, יָמָיו כְּצֵל עוֹבֵר:
תהלים צ בַּבֹּקֶר יָצִיץ וְחָלָף, לָעֶרֶב יְמוֹלֵל וְיָבֵשׁ:
לִמְנוֹת יָמֵינוּ כֵּן הוֹדַע, וְנָבִא לְבַב חָכְמָה:
תהלים לז שְׁמָר־תָּם וּרְאֵה יָשָׁר, כִּי־אַחֲרִית לְאִישׁ שָׁלוֹם:
תהלים מט אַךְ־אֱלֹהִים יִפְדֶּה נַפְשִׁי מִיַּד שְׁאוֹל, כִּי יִקָּחֵנִי סֶלָה:
תהלים עג כָּלָה שְׁאֵרִי וּלְבָבִי, צוּר־לְבָבִי וְחֶלְקִי אֱלֹהִים לְעוֹלָם:
קהלת יב וְיָשֹׁב הֶעָפָר עַל־הָאָרֶץ כְּשֶׁהָיָה
וְהָרוּחַ תָּשׁוּב אֶל־הָאֱלֹהִים אֲשֶׁר נְתָנָהּ:

תהלים צא יֹשֵׁב בְּסֵתֶר עֶלְיוֹן, בְּצֵל שַׁדַּי יִתְלוֹנָן: אֹמַר לַיהוה מַחְסִי וּמְצוּדָתִי,
אֱלֹהַי אֶבְטַח־בּוֹ: כִּי הוּא יַצִּילְךָ מִפַּח יָקוּשׁ, מִדֶּבֶר הַוּוֹת: בְּאֶבְרָתוֹ
יָסֶךְ לָךְ, וְתַחַת־כְּנָפָיו תֶּחְסֶה, צִנָּה וְסֹחֵרָה אֲמִתּוֹ: לֹא־תִירָא מִפַּחַד
לָיְלָה, מֵחֵץ יָעוּף יוֹמָם: מִדֶּבֶר בָּאֹפֶל יַהֲלֹךְ, מִקֶּטֶב יָשׁוּד צָהֳרָיִם:
יִפֹּל מִצִּדְּךָ אֶלֶף, וּרְבָבָה מִימִינֶךָ, אֵלֶיךָ לֹא יִגָּשׁ: רַק בְּעֵינֶיךָ תַבִּיט,
וְשִׁלֻּמַת רְשָׁעִים תִּרְאֶה: כִּי־אַתָּה יהוה מַחְסִי, עֶלְיוֹן שַׂמְתָּ מְעוֹנֶךָ:
לֹא־תְאֻנֶּה אֵלֶיךָ רָעָה, וְנֶגַע לֹא־יִקְרַב בְּאָהֳלֶךָ: כִּי מַלְאָכָיו יְצַוֶּה־לָּךְ,
לִשְׁמָרְךָ בְּכָל־דְּרָכֶיךָ: עַל־כַּפַּיִם יִשָּׂאוּנְךָ, פֶּן־תִּגֹּף בָּאֶבֶן רַגְלֶךָ: עַל־
שַׁחַל וָפֶתֶן תִּדְרֹךְ, תִּרְמֹס כְּפִיר וְתַנִּין: כִּי בִי חָשַׁק וַאֲפַלְּטֵהוּ, אֲשַׂגְּבֵהוּ
כִּי־יָדַע שְׁמִי: יִקְרָאֵנִי וְאֶעֱנֵהוּ, עִמּוֹ־אָנֹכִי בְצָרָה, אֲחַלְּצֵהוּ וַאֲכַבְּדֵהוּ:
אֹרֶךְ יָמִים אַשְׂבִּיעֵהוּ, וְאַרְאֵהוּ בִּישׁוּעָתִי:
אֹרֶךְ יָמִים אַשְׂבִּיעֵהוּ, וְאַרְאֵהוּ בִּישׁוּעָתִי:

*For one's father:*

יִזְכֹּר May God remember the soul of my father, my teacher (*name* son of *father's name*) who has gone to his eternal home, and to this I pledge (without formal vow) to give charity on his behalf, that his soul may be bound in the bond of everlasting life together with the souls of Abraham, Isaac and Jacob, Sarah, Rebecca, Rachel and Leah, and all the other righteous men and women in the Garden of Eden, and let us say: Amen.

*For one's mother:*

יִזְכֹּר May God remember the soul of my mother, my teacher (*name* daughter of *father's name*) who has gone to her eternal home, and to this I pledge (without formal vow) to give charity on her behalf, that her soul may be bound in the bond of everlasting life together with the souls of Abraham, Isaac and Jacob, Sarah, Rebecca, Rachel and Leah, and all the other righteous men and women in the Garden of Eden, and let us say: Amen.

*For a male close relative:*

יִזְכֹּר May God remember the soul of (my grandfather / my uncle / my brother / my son / my husband) (*name* son of *father's name*) who has gone to his eternal home, and to this I pledge (without formal vow) to give charity on his behalf, that his soul may be bound in the bond of everlasting life together with the souls of Abraham, Isaac and Jacob, Sarah, Rebecca, Rachel and Leah, and all the other righteous men and women in the Garden of Eden, and let us say: Amen.

*For a female close relative:*

יִזְכֹּר May God remember the soul of (my grandmother / my aunt / my sister / my daughter / my wife) (*name* daughter of *father's name*) who has gone to her eternal home, and to this I pledge (without formal vow) to give charity on her behalf, that her soul may be bound in the bond of everlasting life together with the souls of Abraham, Isaac and Jacob, Sarah, Rebecca, Rachel and Leah, and all the other righteous men and women in the Garden of Eden, and let us say: Amen.

*For a male close relative:*

אֵל מָלֵא רַחֲמִים God, full of mercy, who dwells on high, grant fitting rest on the wings of the Divine Presence, in the heights of the holy and the pure who shine like the radiance of heaven, to the soul of (*name* son of *father's name*) who has gone to his eternal home, and to this I pledge

*For one's father:*

יִזְכֹּר אֱלֹהִים נִשְׁמַת אָבִי מוֹרִי (פלוני בֶּן פלוני) שֶׁהָלַךְ לְעוֹלָמוֹ, בַּעֲבוּר שֶׁבְּלִי נֶדֶר אֶתֵּן צְדָקָה בַּעֲדוֹ. בִּשְׂכַר זֶה תְּהֵא נַפְשׁוֹ צְרוּרָה בִּצְרוֹר הַחַיִּים עִם נִשְׁמוֹת אַבְרָהָם יִצְחָק וְיַעֲקֹב, שָׂרָה רִבְקָה רָחֵל וְלֵאָה, וְעִם שְׁאָר צַדִּיקִים וְצִדְקָנִיּוֹת שֶׁבְּגַן עֵדֶן, וְנֹאמַר אָמֵן.

*For one's mother:*

יִזְכֹּר אֱלֹהִים נִשְׁמַת אִמִּי מוֹרָתִי (פלונית בַּת פלוני) שֶׁהָלְכָה לְעוֹלָמָהּ, בַּעֲבוּר שֶׁבְּלִי נֶדֶר אֶתֵּן צְדָקָה בַּעֲדָהּ. בִּשְׂכַר זֶה תְּהֵא נַפְשָׁהּ צְרוּרָה בִּצְרוֹר הַחַיִּים עִם נִשְׁמוֹת אַבְרָהָם יִצְחָק וְיַעֲקֹב, שָׂרָה רִבְקָה רָחֵל וְלֵאָה, וְעִם שְׁאָר צַדִּיקִים וְצִדְקָנִיּוֹת שֶׁבְּגַן עֵדֶן, וְנֹאמַר אָמֵן.

*For a male close relative:*

יִזְכֹּר אֱלֹהִים נִשְׁמַת (*my grandfather* זְקֵנִי / *my uncle* דּוֹדִי / *my brother* אָחִי / *my son* בְּנִי / *my husband* בַּעְלִי) (פלוני בֶּן פלוני) שֶׁהָלַךְ לְעוֹלָמוֹ, בַּעֲבוּר שֶׁבְּלִי נֶדֶר אֶתֵּן צְדָקָה בַּעֲדוֹ. בִּשְׂכַר זֶה תְּהֵא נַפְשׁוֹ צְרוּרָה בִּצְרוֹר הַחַיִּים עִם נִשְׁמוֹת אַבְרָהָם יִצְחָק וְיַעֲקֹב, שָׂרָה רִבְקָה רָחֵל וְלֵאָה, וְעִם שְׁאָר צַדִּיקִים וְצִדְקָנִיּוֹת שֶׁבְּגַן עֵדֶן, וְנֹאמַר אָמֵן.

*For a female close relative:*

יִזְכֹּר אֱלֹהִים נִשְׁמַת (*my grandmother* זְקֶנְתִּי / *my aunt* דּוֹדָתִי / *my sister* אֲחוֹתִי / *my daughter* בִּתִּי / *my wife* אִשְׁתִּי) (פלונית בַּת פלוני) שֶׁהָלְכָה לְעוֹלָמָהּ, בַּעֲבוּר שֶׁבְּלִי נֶדֶר אֶתֵּן צְדָקָה בַּעֲדָהּ. בִּשְׂכַר זֶה תְּהֵא נַפְשָׁהּ צְרוּרָה בִּצְרוֹר הַחַיִּים עִם נִשְׁמוֹת אַבְרָהָם יִצְחָק וְיַעֲקֹב, שָׂרָה רִבְקָה רָחֵל וְלֵאָה, וְעִם שְׁאָר צַדִּיקִים וְצִדְקָנִיּוֹת שֶׁבְּגַן עֵדֶן, וְנֹאמַר אָמֵן.

*For a male close relative:*

אֵל מָלֵא רַחֲמִים, שׁוֹכֵן בַּמְּרוֹמִים, הַמְצֵא מְנוּחָה נְכוֹנָה עַל כַּנְפֵי הַשְּׁכִינָה, בְּמַעֲלוֹת קְדוֹשִׁים וּטְהוֹרִים, כְּזֹהַר הָרָקִיעַ מַזְהִירִים, לְנִשְׁמַת (פלוני בֶּן פלוני) שֶׁהָלַךְ לְעוֹלָמוֹ, בַּעֲבוּר שֶׁבְּלִי נֶדֶר אֶתֵּן צְדָקָה

(without formal vow) to give charity in his memory, may his resting place be in the Garden of Eden. Therefore, Master of compassion, shelter him in the shadow of Your wings forever and bind his soul in the bond of everlasting life. The Lord is his heritage; may he rest in peace, and let us say: Amen.

*For a female close relative:*

אֵל מָלֵא רַחֲמִים God, full of mercy, who dwells on high, grant fitting rest on the wings of the Divine Presence, in the heights of the holy and the pure who shine like the radiance of heaven, to the soul of (*name* daughter of *father's name*) who has gone to her eternal home, and to this I pledge (without formal vow) to give charity in her memory, may her resting place be in the Garden of Eden. Therefore, Master of compassion, shelter her in the shadow of Your wings forever and bind her soul in the bond of everlasting life. The Lord is her heritage; may she rest in peace, and let us say: Amen.

*For martyrs:*

יִזְכֹּר May God remember the soul of (*name*, son/daughter of *father's name*), and the souls of all my relatives, on my father's or mother's side, who were killed, murdered, slaughtered, burned, drowned or strangled for the sanctification of God's name, and to this I pledge (without formal vow) to give charity in their memory. May their souls be bound in the bond of everlasting life together with the souls of Abraham, Isaac and Jacob, Sarah, Rebecca, Rachel and Leah, and all the other righteous men and women in the Garden of Eden, and let us say: Amen.

*For the Israeli soldiers:*

אֵל מָלֵא רַחֲמִים God, full of mercy, who dwells on high, grant fitting rest on the wings of the Divine Presence, in the heights of the holy, the pure and the brave, who shine like the radiance of heaven, to the souls of the holy ones who fought in any of Israel's battles, in clandestine operations and in Israel's Defense Forces, who fell in battle and sacrificed their lives for the consecration of God's name, for the people and the land, and for this we pray for the ascent of their souls. Therefore, Master of compassion, shelter them in the shadow of Your wings forever, and bind their souls in the bond of everlasting life. The Lord is their heritage; may the Garden of Eden be their resting place, may they rest in peace, may their

בַּעַד הַזְכָּרַת נִשְׁמָתוֹ, בְּגַן עֵדֶן תְּהֵא מְנוּחָתוֹ. לָכֵן, בַּעַל הָרַחֲמִים יַסְתִּירֵהוּ בְּסֵתֶר כְּנָפָיו לְעוֹלָמִים, וְיִצְרֹר בִּצְרוֹר הַחַיִּים אֶת נִשְׁמָתוֹ, יהוה הוּא נַחֲלָתוֹ, וְיָנְוּחַ בְּשָׁלוֹם עַל מִשְׁכָּבוֹ, וְנֹאמַר אָמֵן.

*For a female close relative:*

אֵל מָלֵא רַחֲמִים, שׁוֹכֵן בַּמְּרוֹמִים, הַמְצֵא מְנוּחָה נְכוֹנָה עַל כַּנְפֵי הַשְּׁכִינָה, בְּמַעֲלוֹת קְדוֹשִׁים וּטְהוֹרִים, כְּזְהַר הָרָקִיעַ מַזְהִירִים, לְנִשְׁמַת (פלונית בַּת פלוני) שֶׁהָלְכָה לְעוֹלָמָהּ, בַּעֲבוּר שֶׁבְּלִי נֶדֶר אֶתֵּן צְדָקָה בְּעַד הַזְכָּרַת נִשְׁמָתָהּ, בְּגַן עֵדֶן תְּהֵא מְנוּחָתָהּ. לָכֵן, בַּעַל הָרַחֲמִים יַסְתִּירֶהָ בְּסֵתֶר כְּנָפָיו לְעוֹלָמִים, וְיִצְרֹר בִּצְרוֹר הַחַיִּים אֶת נִשְׁמָתָהּ, יהוה הוּא נַחֲלָתָהּ, וְתָנְוּחַ בְּשָׁלוֹם עַל מִשְׁכָּבָהּ, וְנֹאמַר אָמֵן.

*For martyrs:*

יִזְכֹּר אֱלֹהִים נִשְׁמַת (*male* פלוני בֶּן פלוני / *female* פלונית בַּת פלוני) וְנִשְׁמוֹת כָּל קְרוֹבַי וּקְרוֹבוֹתַי, הֵן מִצַּד אָבִי הֵן מִצַּד אִמִּי, שֶׁהוּמְתוּ וְשֶׁנֶּהֶרְגוּ וְשֶׁנִּשְׁחֲטוּ וְשֶׁנִּשְׂרְפוּ וְשֶׁנִּטְבְּעוּ וְשֶׁנֶּחְנְקוּ עַל קִדּוּשׁ הַשֵּׁם, בַּעֲבוּר שֶׁבְּלִי נֶדֶר אֶתֵּן צְדָקָה בְּעַד הַזְכָּרַת נִשְׁמוֹתֵיהֶם. בִּשְׂכַר זֶה תִּהְיֶינָה נַפְשׁוֹתֵיהֶם צְרוּרוֹת בִּצְרוֹר הַחַיִּים עִם נִשְׁמוֹת אַבְרָהָם יִצְחָק וְיַעֲקֹב, שָׂרָה רִבְקָה רָחֵל וְלֵאָה, וְעִם שְׁאָר צַדִּיקִים וְצִדְקָנִיּוֹת שֶׁבְּגַן עֵדֶן, וְנֹאמַר אָמֵן.

*For the Israeli soldiers:*

אֵל מָלֵא רַחֲמִים, שׁוֹכֵן בַּמְּרוֹמִים, הַמְצֵא מְנוּחָה נְכוֹנָה עַל כַּנְפֵי הַשְּׁכִינָה, בְּמַעֲלוֹת קְדוֹשִׁים טְהוֹרִים וְגִבּוֹרִים, כְּזְהַר הָרָקִיעַ מַזְהִירִים, לְנִשְׁמוֹת הַקְּדוֹשִׁים שֶׁנִּלְחֲמוּ בְּכָל מַעַרְכוֹת יִשְׂרָאֵל, בַּמַּחְתֶּרֶת וּבִצְבָא הַהֲגָנָה לְיִשְׂרָאֵל, וְשֶׁנָּפְלוּ בְּמִלְחַמְתָּם וּמָסְרוּ נַפְשָׁם עַל קְדֻשַּׁת הַשֵּׁם, הָעָם וְהָאָרֶץ, בַּעֲבוּר שֶׁאָנוּ מִתְפַּלְלִים לְעִלּוּי נִשְׁמוֹתֵיהֶם. לָכֵן, בַּעַל הָרַחֲמִים יַסְתִּירֵם בְּסֵתֶר כְּנָפָיו לְעוֹלָמִים, וְיִצְרֹר בִּצְרוֹר הַחַיִּים אֶת נִשְׁמוֹתֵיהֶם, יהוה הוּא נַחֲלָתָם, בְּגַן עֵדֶן

merit stand for all Israel, and may they receive their reward at the End of Days, and let us say: Amen.

*For the Holocaust victims:*

אֵל מָלֵא רַחֲמִים God, full of mercy, Justice of widows and Father of orphans, please do not be silent and hold Your peace for the blood of Israel that was shed like water. Grant fitting rest on the wings of the Divine Presence, in the heights of the holy and the pure who shine and radiate light like the radiance of heaven, to the souls of the millions of Jews, men, women and children, who were murdered, slaughtered, burned, strangled, and buried alive, in the lands touched by the German enemy and its followers. They were all holy and pure; among them were great scholars and righteous individuals, cedars of Lebanon and noble masters of Torah, may the Garden of Eden be their resting place. Therefore, Master of compassion, shelter them in the shadow of Your wings forever, and bind their souls in the bond of everlasting life. The Lord is their heritage; may they rest in peace, and let us say: Amen.

*Congregation and Leader:*

אַב הָרַחֲמִים Father of compassion, who dwells on high: may He remember in His compassion the pious, the upright and the blameless – holy communities who sacrificed their lives for the sanctification of God's name. Lovely and pleasant in their lives, in death they were not parted. They were swifter than eagles and stronger than lions to do the will of their Maker and the desire of their Creator. O our God, remember them for good with the other righteous of the world, and may He exact retribution for the shed blood of His servants, as it is written in the Torah
of Moses, the man of God: "O nations, acclaim His people, for He will *Deut. 32*
avenge the blood of His servants, wreak vengeance on His foes, and make clean His people's land." And by Your servants, the prophets, it is written:
"I shall cleanse their blood which I have not yet cleansed, says the Lord *Joel 4*
who dwells in Zion." And in the holy Writings it says: "Why should the *Ps. 79*
nations say: Where is their God? Before our eyes, may those nations know that You avenge the shed blood of Your servants." And it also says:
"For the Avenger of blood remembers them and does not forget the cry *Ps. 9*
of the afflicted." And it further says: "He will execute judgment among *Ps. 110*
the nations, filled with the dead, crushing rulers far and wide. From the brook by the wayside he will drink, then he will hold his head high."

תְּהֵא מְנוּחָתָם, וְיָנוּחוּ בְּשָׁלוֹם עַל מִשְׁכְּבוֹתֵיהֶם וְתַעֲמֹד לְכָל יִשְׂרָאֵל זְכוּתָם, וְיַעַמְדוּ לְגוֹרָלָם לְקֵץ הַיָּמִין, וְנֹאמַר אָמֵן.

*For the Holocaust victims:*

אֵל מָלֵא רַחֲמִים, דַּיַּן אַלְמָנוֹת וַאֲבִי יְתוֹמִים, אַל נָא תֶּחֱשֶׁה וְתִתְאַפַּק לְדַם יִשְׂרָאֵל שֶׁנִּשְׁפַּךְ כַּמַּיִם. הַמְצֵא מְנוּחָה נְכוֹנָה עַל כַּנְפֵי הַשְּׁכִינָה, בְּמַעֲלוֹת קְדוֹשִׁים וּטְהוֹרִים, כְּזֹהַר הָרָקִיעַ מְאִירִים וּמַזְהִירִים, לְנִשְׁמוֹתֵיהֶם שֶׁל רִבְבוֹת אַלְפֵי יִשְׂרָאֵל, אֲנָשִׁים וְנָשִׁים, יְלָדִים וִילָדוֹת, שֶׁנֶּהֶרְגוּ וְנִשְׁחֲטוּ וְנִשְׂרְפוּ וְנֶחְנְקוּ וְנִקְבְּרוּ חַיִּים, בָּאֲרָצוֹת אֲשֶׁר נָגְעָה בָּהֶן יַד הַצּוֹרֵר הַגֶּרְמָנִי וּגְרוּרָיו. כֻּלָּם קְדוֹשִׁים וּטְהוֹרִים, וּבָהֶם גְּאוֹנִים וְצַדִּיקִים, אַרְזֵי הַלְּבָנוֹן אַדִּירֵי הַתּוֹרָה. בְּגַן עֵדֶן תְּהֵא מְנוּחָתָם. לָכֵן, בַּעַל הָרַחֲמִים יַסְתִּירֵם בְּסֵתֶר כְּנָפָיו לְעוֹלָמִים, וְיִצְרֹר בִּצְרוֹר הַחַיִּים אֶת נִשְׁמָתָם, יהוה הוּא נַחֲלָתָם, וְיָנוּחוּ בְּשָׁלוֹם עַל מִשְׁכָּבָם, וְנֹאמַר אָמֵן.

קהל ושליח ציבור:

אַב הָרַחֲמִים שׁוֹכֵן מְרוֹמִים, בְּרַחֲמָיו הָעֲצוּמִים הוּא יִפְקֹד בְּרַחֲמִים הַחֲסִידִים וְהַיְשָׁרִים וְהַתְּמִימִים, קְהִלּוֹת הַקֹּדֶשׁ שֶׁמָּסְרוּ נַפְשָׁם עַל קְדֻשַּׁת הַשֵּׁם, הַנֶּאֱהָבִים וְהַנְּעִימִים בְּחַיֵּיהֶם, וּבְמוֹתָם לֹא נִפְרָדוּ, מִנְּשָׁרִים קַלּוּ וּמֵאֲרָיוֹת גָּבֵרוּ לַעֲשׂוֹת רְצוֹן קוֹנָם וְחֵפֶץ צוּרָם. יִזְכְּרֵם אֱלֹהֵינוּ לְטוֹבָה עִם שְׁאָר צַדִּיקֵי עוֹלָם, וְיִנְקֹם לְעֵינֵינוּ נִקְמַת דַּם
עֲבָדָיו הַשָּׁפוּךְ, כַּכָּתוּב בְּתוֹרַת מֹשֶׁה אִישׁ הָאֱלֹהִים, הַרְנִינוּ גוֹיִם דברים לב
עַמּוֹ, כִּי דַם־עֲבָדָיו יִקּוֹם, וְנָקָם יָשִׁיב לְצָרָיו, וְכִפֶּר אַדְמָתוֹ עַמּוֹ: וְעַל
יְדֵי עֲבָדֶיךָ הַנְּבִיאִים כָּתוּב לֵאמֹר, וְנִקֵּיתִי, דָּמָם לֹא־נִקֵּיתִי, וַיהוה יואל ד
שֹׁכֵן בְּצִיּוֹן: וּבְכִתְבֵי הַקֹּדֶשׁ נֶאֱמַר, לָמָּה יֹאמְרוּ הַגּוֹיִם אַיֵּה אֱלֹהֵיהֶם, תהלים עט
יִוָּדַע בַּגּוֹיִם לְעֵינֵינוּ נִקְמַת דַּם־עֲבָדֶיךָ הַשָּׁפוּךְ: וְאוֹמֵר, כִּי־דֹרֵשׁ דָּמִים תהלים ט
אוֹתָם זָכָר, לֹא־שָׁכַח צַעֲקַת עֲנָוִים: וְאוֹמֵר, יָדִין בַּגּוֹיִם מָלֵא גְוִיּוֹת, תהלים קי
מָחַץ רֹאשׁ עַל־אֶרֶץ רַבָּה: מִנַּחַל בַּדֶּרֶךְ יִשְׁתֶּה, עַל־כֵּן יָרִים רֹאשׁ:

*Most congregations omit the following on days that Yizkor is said.*
*Some also omit on Shabbat.*

יָהּ אֵלִי Lord my God and Redeemer,
I will stand to greet You,
[God] who was and will be, was and is,
the land of every nation is Yours.

The thanksgiving-offering, burnt-offering, meal-offering, sin-offering, guilt-offering, peace-offering and inauguration-offering are all offerings to You.
Remember the weary nation that has borne much, and bring it back to Your land. I will always praise You with
"Happy are those who dwell in Your House."

Fine beyond fine, undecipherable,
His understanding is unfathomable,
Awesome God who distinguishes between
good and evil with a single glance.

The thanksgiving-offering, burnt-offering, meal-offering, sin-offering, guilt-offering, peace-offering and inauguration-offering are all offerings to You.
Remember the weary nation that has borne much, and bring it back to Your land. I will always praise You with
"Happy are those who dwell in Your House."

Lord of hosts, with many wonders,
He joined all His tent,
making all blossom in the ways of the heart:
the Rock, perfect is His work.

The thanksgiving-offering, burnt-offering, meal-offering, sin-offering, guilt-offering, peace-offering and inauguration-offering are all offerings to You.
Remember the weary nation that has borne much, and bring it back to Your land. I will always praise You with
"Happy are those who dwell in Your House."

*Most congregations omit the following on days that* יזכור *is said. Some also omit on* שבת*.*

יָהּ אֵלִי וְגוֹאֲלִי, אֶתְיַצְּבָה לִקְרָאתֶךָ
הָיָה וְיִהְיֶה, הָיָה וְהֹוֶה, כָּל גּוֹי אַדְמָתֶךָ.

וְתוֹדָה וְלָעוֹלָה וְלַמִּנְחָה וְלַחַטָּאת וְלָאָשָׁם
וְלַשְּׁלָמִים וְלַמִּלּוּאִים כָּל קָרְבָּנֶךָ.
זְכֹר נִלְאָה אֲשֶׁר נָשְׂאָה וְהָשִׁיבָה לְאַדְמָתֶךָ
סֶלָה אֲהַלֶּלְךָ בְּאַשְׁרֵי יוֹשְׁבֵי בֵיתֶךָ.

דַּק עַל דַּק, עַד אֵין נִבְדַּק, וְלִתְבוּנָתוֹ אֵין חֵקֶר
הָאֵל נוֹרָא, בְּאַחַת סְקִירָה, בֵּין טוֹב לָרַע יְבַקֵּר.

וְתוֹדָה וְלָעוֹלָה וְלַמִּנְחָה וְלַחַטָּאת וְלָאָשָׁם
וְלַשְּׁלָמִים וְלַמִּלּוּאִים כָּל קָרְבָּנֶךָ.
זְכֹר נִלְאָה אֲשֶׁר נָשְׂאָה וְהָשִׁיבָה לְאַדְמָתֶךָ
סֶלָה אֲהַלֶּלְךָ בְּאַשְׁרֵי יוֹשְׁבֵי בֵיתֶךָ.

אֲדוֹן צְבָאוֹת, בְּרֹב פְּלָאוֹת, חִבֵּר כָּל אָהֳלוֹ
בִּנְתִיבוֹת לֵב לִבְלֵב, הַצּוּר תָּמִים פָּעֳלוֹ.

וְתוֹדָה וְלָעוֹלָה וְלַמִּנְחָה וְלַחַטָּאת וְלָאָשָׁם
וְלַשְּׁלָמִים וְלַמִּלּוּאִים כָּל קָרְבָּנֶךָ.
זְכֹר נִלְאָה אֲשֶׁר נָשְׂאָה וְהָשִׁיבָה לְאַדְמָתֶךָ
סֶלָה אֲהַלֶּלְךָ בְּאַשְׁרֵי יוֹשְׁבֵי בֵיתֶךָ.

# Musaf for Festivals

*The following Amida is said on Yom Tov and Ḥol HaMo'ed (including Shabbat Ḥol HaMo'ed).*
*On the first day of Pesaḥ, the Leader begins the Repetition with "Prayer for Dew" on page 904;*
*on Shemini Atzeret, with "Prayer for Rain" on page 908.*
*In Israel, these prayers are said before the silent recitation of the Amida.*

*The following prayer, until "in former years" on page 892, is said silently, standing with feet together. If there is a minyan, the Amida is repeated aloud by the Leader. Take three steps forward and at the points indicated by ▾, bend the knees at the first word, bow at the second, and stand straight before saying God's name.*

When I proclaim the LORD's name, give glory to our God. *Deut. 32*
O LORD, open my lips, so that my mouth may declare Your praise. *Ps. 51*

PATRIARCHS

▾בָּרוּךְ Blessed are You, LORD our God and God of our fathers,
God of Abraham, God of Isaac and God of Jacob;
the great, mighty and awesome God, God Most High,
who bestows acts of loving-kindness and creates all,
who remembers the loving-kindness of the fathers
and will bring a Redeemer to their children's children
for the sake of His name, in love.
King, Helper, Savior, Shield:
▾Blessed are You, LORD, Shield of Abraham.

DIVINE MIGHT

אַתָּה גִּבּוֹר You are eternally mighty, LORD.
You give life to the dead and have great power to save.

*On Shemini Atzeret if announced (see law 128 and commentary on Tefillat Geshem, pages 908–912), Simḥat Torah and the first day of Pesaḥ (see laws 129–131):*
He makes the wind blow and the rain fall.

*In Israel, on other Festivals:*
He causes the dew to fall.

He sustains the living with loving-kindness,
and with great compassion revives the dead.
He supports the fallen, heals the sick, sets captives free,
and keeps His faith with those who sleep in the dust.
Who is like You, Master of might, and who can compare to You,
O King who brings death and gives life, and makes salvation grow?

# מוסף לשלוש רגלים

*The following* עמידה *is said on* יום טוב *and* חול המועד *(including* שבת חול המועד*).*
*On the first day of* פסח*, the* שליח ציבור *begins the* חזרת הש״ץ *with* תפילת טל *on page 905;*
*on* שמיני עצרת*, with* תפילת גשם *on page 909.*
*In* ארץ ישראל*, these prayers are said before the silent recitation of the* עמידה*.*

*The following prayer, until* קַדְמֹנִיּוֹת *on page 893, is said silently, standing with feet together. If there is a* מנין*, the* עמידה *is repeated aloud by the* שליח ציבור*.*
*Take three steps forward and at the points indicated by* ˅*, bend the knees at the first word, bow at the second, and stand straight before saying God's name.*

כִּי שֵׁם יהוה אֶקְרָא, הָבוּ גֹדֶל לֵאלֹהֵינוּ: דברים לב
אֲדֹנָי, שְׂפָתַי תִּפְתָּח, וּפִי יַגִּיד תְּהִלָּתֶךָ: תהלים נא

אבות

˅בָּרוּךְ אַתָּה יהוה, אֱלֹהֵינוּ וֵאלֹהֵי אֲבוֹתֵינוּ
אֱלֹהֵי אַבְרָהָם, אֱלֹהֵי יִצְחָק, וֵאלֹהֵי יַעֲקֹב
הָאֵל הַגָּדוֹל הַגִּבּוֹר וְהַנּוֹרָא, אֵל עֶלְיוֹן
גּוֹמֵל חֲסָדִים טוֹבִים, וְקוֹנֵה הַכֹּל, וְזוֹכֵר חַסְדֵי אָבוֹת
וּמֵבִיא גוֹאֵל לִבְנֵי בְנֵיהֶם לְמַעַן שְׁמוֹ בְּאַהֲבָה.
מֶלֶךְ עוֹזֵר וּמוֹשִׁיעַ וּמָגֵן.
˅בָּרוּךְ אַתָּה יהוה, מָגֵן אַבְרָהָם.

גבורות

אַתָּה גִּבּוֹר לְעוֹלָם, אֲדֹנָי, מְחַיֵּה מֵתִים אַתָּה, רַב לְהוֹשִׁיעַ

*On* שמיני עצרת *if announced (see law 128 and commentary on* תפילת גשם*, pages 909–913),* שמחת תורה *and the first day of* פסח *(see laws 129–131):*

מַשִּׁיב הָרוּחַ וּמוֹרִיד הַגֶּשֶׁם

*In* ארץ ישראל*, on other* חגים*:*

מוֹרִיד הַטָּל

מְכַלְכֵּל חַיִּים בְּחֶסֶד, מְחַיֵּה מֵתִים בְּרַחֲמִים רַבִּים
סוֹמֵךְ נוֹפְלִים, וְרוֹפֵא חוֹלִים, וּמַתִּיר אֲסוּרִים
וּמְקַיֵּם אֱמוּנָתוֹ לִישֵׁנֵי עָפָר.
מִי כָמוֹךָ, בַּעַל גְּבוּרוֹת, וּמִי דּוֹמֶה לָּךְ
מֶלֶךְ, מֵמִית וּמְחַיֶּה וּמַצְמִיחַ יְשׁוּעָה.

Faithful are You to revive the dead.
Blessed are You, Lord, who revives the dead.

*When saying the Amida silently, continue with "You are holy" on the next page.*

---

KEDUSHA

*On Ḥol HaMo'ed, turn to the Kedusha on the next page. On Yom Tov, Shabbat Ḥol HaMo'ed and Hoshana Raba, during the Repetition, the following is said standing with feet together, rising on the toes at the words indicated by ▲.*

*Cong. then Leader:* נַעֲרִיצְךָ We will revere and sanctify You with the words uttered by the holy Seraphim who sanctify Your name in the Sanctuary; as is written by Your prophet: "They call out to one another, saying: *Is. 6*

*Cong. then Leader:* ▲Holy, ▲holy, ▲holy is the Lord of hosts; the whole world is filled with His glory."
His glory fills the universe. His ministering angels ask each other, "Where is the place of His glory?" Those facing them reply "Blessed –"

*Cong. then Leader:* ▲"Blessed is the Lord's glory from His place." *Ezek. 3*
From His place may He turn with compassion and be gracious to the people who proclaim the unity of His name, morning and evening, every day, continually, twice each day reciting in love the Shema:

*Cong. then Leader:* "Listen, Israel, the Lord is our God, the Lord is One." *Deut. 6*
He is our God, He is our Father, He is our King, He is our Savior – and He, in His compassion, will let us hear a second time in the presence of all that lives, His promise "to be Your God. *Num. 15*
I am the Lord your God."

*On Shabbat Ḥol HaMo'ed, the following paragraph is omitted:*

*Cong. then Leader:* Glorious is our Glorious One, Lord our Master, and glorious is Your name throughout the earth. Then the Lord shall be King over all the earth; on that day the Lord shall be One and His name One. *Ps. 8* *Zech. 14*

*Leader:* And in Your holy Writings it is written:

*Cong. then Leader:* ▲"The Lord shall reign for ever. He is your God, Zion, from generation to generation, Halleluya!" *Ps. 146*

*Leader:* From generation to generation we will declare Your greatness, and we will proclaim Your holiness for evermore. Your praise, our God, shall not leave our mouth forever, for You, God, are a great and holy King. Blessed are You, Lord, the holy God.

*The Leader continues with "You have chosen us" on the next page.*

# וְנֶאֱמָן אַתָּה לְהַחֲיוֹת מֵתִים.
# בָּרוּךְ אַתָּה יהוה, מְחַיֵּה הַמֵּתִים.

*When saying the עמידה silently, continue with אַתָּה קָדוֹשׁ on the next page.*

---

## קדושה

*On חול המועד, שבת חול המועד, turn to the קדושה on the next page. On יום טוב and הושענא רבה, during the חזרת הש״ץ, the following is said standing with feet together, rising on the toes at the words indicated by ▲.*

קהל then ש״ץ: נַעֲרִיצְךָ וְנַקְדִּישְׁךָ כְּסוֹד שִׂיחַ שַׂרְפֵי קֹדֶשׁ, הַמַּקְדִּישִׁים שִׁמְךָ בַּקֹּדֶשׁ,
כַּכָּתוּב עַל יַד נְבִיאֶךָ: וְקָרָא זֶה אֶל־זֶה וְאָמַר ישעיה ו

קהל then ש״ץ: ▲קָדוֹשׁ, ▲קָדוֹשׁ, ▲קָדוֹשׁ, יהוה צְבָאוֹת, מְלֹא כָל הָאָרֶץ כְּבוֹדוֹ:
כְּבוֹדוֹ מָלֵא עוֹלָם, מְשָׁרְתָיו שׁוֹאֲלִים זֶה לָזֶה, אַיֵּה מְקוֹם כְּבוֹדוֹ,
לְעֻמָּתָם בָּרוּךְ יֹאמֵרוּ

קהל then ש״ץ: ▲בָּרוּךְ כְּבוֹד־יהוה מִמְּקוֹמוֹ: יחזקאל ג
מִמְּקוֹמוֹ הוּא יִפֶן בְּרַחֲמִים, וְיָחֹן עַם הַמְיַחֲדִים שְׁמוֹ, עֶרֶב וָבֹקֶר
בְּכָל יוֹם תָּמִיד, פַּעֲמַיִם בְּאַהֲבָה שְׁמַע אוֹמְרִים

קהל then ש״ץ: שְׁמַע יִשְׂרָאֵל, יהוה אֱלֹהֵינוּ, יהוה אֶחָד: דברים ו
הוּא אֱלֹהֵינוּ, הוּא אָבִינוּ, הוּא מַלְכֵּנוּ, הוּא מוֹשִׁיעֵנוּ, וְהוּא
יַשְׁמִיעֵנוּ בְּרַחֲמָיו שֵׁנִית לְעֵינֵי כָּל חָי, לִהְיוֹת לָכֶם לֵאלֹהִים, אֲנִי במדבר טו
יהוה אֱלֹהֵיכֶם:

*On שבת חול המועד, the following paragraph is omitted:*

קהל then ש״ץ: אַדִּיר אַדִּירֵנוּ, יהוה אֲדֹנֵינוּ, מָה־אַדִּיר שִׁמְךָ בְּכָל־הָאָרֶץ: תהלים ח
וְהָיָה יהוה לְמֶלֶךְ עַל־כָּל־הָאָרֶץ, בַּיּוֹם הַהוּא יִהְיֶה יהוה אֶחָד זכריה יד
וּשְׁמוֹ אֶחָד:

ש״ץ: וּבְדִבְרֵי קָדְשְׁךָ כָּתוּב לֵאמֹר

קהל then ש״ץ: ▲יִמְלֹךְ יהוה לְעוֹלָם, אֱלֹהַיִךְ צִיּוֹן לְדֹר וָדֹר, הַלְלוּיָהּ: תהלים קמו

ש״ץ: לְדוֹר וָדוֹר נַגִּיד גָּדְלֶךָ, וּלְנֵצַח נְצָחִים קְדֻשָּׁתְךָ נַקְדִּישׁ, וְשִׁבְחֲךָ אֱלֹהֵינוּ מִפִּינוּ לֹא יָמוּשׁ לְעוֹלָם וָעֶד, כִּי אֵל מֶלֶךְ גָּדוֹל וְקָדוֹשׁ אָתָּה. בָּרוּךְ אַתָּה יהוה, הָאֵל הַקָּדוֹשׁ.

*The שליח ציבור continues with אַתָּה בְחַרְתָּנוּ on the next page.*

## KEDUSHA FOR ḤOL HAMO'ED

*During the Leader's Repetition, the following is said standing with feet together, rising on the toes at the words indicated by* ▲.

*Cong. then Leader:* נְקַדֵּשׁ We will sanctify Your name on earth, as they sanctify it in the highest heavens, as is written by Your prophet, "And they [the angels] call to one another saying: *Is. 6*

*Cong. then Leader:* ▲Holy, ▲holy, ▲holy is the LORD of hosts; the whole world is filled with His glory."
Those facing them say "Blessed –"

*Cong. then Leader:* ▲"Blessed is the LORD's glory from His place." *Ezek. 3*
And in Your holy Writings it is written thus:

*Cong. then Leader:* ▲"The LORD shall reign for ever. He is your God, Zion, from generation to generation, Halleluya!" *Ps. 146*

*Leader:* From generation to generation we will declare Your greatness, and we will proclaim Your holiness for evermore. Your praise, our God, shall not leave our mouth forever, for You, God, are a great and holy King. Blessed are You, LORD, the holy God.

*The Leader continues with "You have chosen us" below.*

---

*When saying the Amida silently, continue here with "You are holy":*

### HOLINESS

אַתָּה קָדוֹשׁ You are holy
and Your name is holy,
and holy ones praise You daily, Selah!
Blessed are You, LORD,
the holy God.

### HOLINESS OF THE DAY

אַתָּה בְחַרְתָּנוּ You have chosen us from among all peoples.
You have loved and favored us.
You have raised us above all tongues.
You have made us holy through Your commandments.
You have brought us near, our King, to Your service,
and have called us by Your great and holy name.

קדושה בחול המועד

*During the* חזרת הש״ץ*, the following is said standing with feet together, rising on the toes at the words indicated by* ˄.

קהל *then* ש״ץ: נְקַדֵּשׁ אֶת שִׁמְךָ בָּעוֹלָם, כְּשֵׁם שֶׁמַּקְדִּישִׁים אוֹתוֹ בִּשְׁמֵי מָרוֹם
כַּכָּתוּב עַל יַד נְבִיאֶךָ: וְקָרָא זֶה אֶל־זֶה וְאָמַר ישעיה ו

קהל *then* ש״ץ: ˄קָדוֹשׁ, ˄קָדוֹשׁ, ˄קָדוֹשׁ, יהוה צְבָאוֹת, מְלֹא כָל־הָאָרֶץ כְּבוֹדוֹ:
לְעֻמָּתָם בָּרוּךְ יֹאמֵרוּ

קהל *then* ש״ץ: ˄בָּרוּךְ כְּבוֹד־יהוה מִמְּקוֹמוֹ: יחזקאל ג
וּבְדִבְרֵי קָדְשְׁךָ כָּתוּב לֵאמֹר

קהל *then* ש״ץ: ˄יִמְלֹךְ יהוה לְעוֹלָם, אֱלֹהַיִךְ צִיּוֹן לְדֹר וָדֹר, הַלְלוּיָהּ: תהלים קמו

ש״ץ: לְדוֹר וָדוֹר נַגִּיד גָּדְלֶךָ, וּלְנֵצַח נְצָחִים קְדֻשָּׁתְךָ נַקְדִּישׁ, וְשִׁבְחֲךָ
אֱלֹהֵינוּ מִפִּינוּ לֹא יָמוּשׁ לְעוֹלָם וָעֶד, כִּי אֵל מֶלֶךְ גָּדוֹל וְקָדוֹשׁ
אָתָּה. בָּרוּךְ אַתָּה יהוה, הָאֵל הַקָּדוֹשׁ.

*The* שליח ציבור *continues with* אַתָּה בְחַרְתָּנוּ *below.*

---

*When saying the* עמידה *silently, continue here with* אַתָּה קָדוֹשׁ:

קדושת השם

אַתָּה קָדוֹשׁ וְשִׁמְךָ קָדוֹשׁ, וּקְדוֹשִׁים בְּכָל יוֹם יְהַלְלוּךָ סֶּלָה.
בָּרוּךְ אַתָּה יהוה, הָאֵל הַקָּדוֹשׁ.

קדושת היום

אַתָּה בְחַרְתָּנוּ מִכָּל הָעַמִּים
אָהַבְתָּ אוֹתָנוּ וְרָצִיתָ בָּנוּ
וְרוֹמַמְתָּנוּ מִכָּל הַלְּשׁוֹנוֹת
וְקִדַּשְׁתָּנוּ בְּמִצְוֹתֶיךָ
וְקֵרַבְתָּנוּ מַלְכֵּנוּ לַעֲבוֹדָתֶךָ
וְשִׁמְךָ הַגָּדוֹל וְהַקָּדוֹשׁ עָלֵינוּ קָרָאתָ.

*On Shabbat, add the words in parentheses:*

וַתִּתֶּן לָנוּ And You, LORD our God, have given us in love
(Sabbaths for rest and) festivals for rejoicing,
holy days and seasons for joy,
(this Sabbath day and) this day of:

*On Pesaḥ:* the festival of Matzot,
the time of our freedom

*On Shavuot:* the festival of Shavuot,
the time of the giving of our Torah

*On Sukkot:* the festival of Sukkot,
our time of rejoicing

*On Shemini Atzeret & Simḥat Torah:* the festival of eighth day, Shemini Atzeret,
our time of rejoicing

(with love), a holy assembly in memory of the exodus from Egypt.

וּמִפְּנֵי חֲטָאֵינוּ But because of our sins
we were exiled from our land
and driven far from our country.
We cannot go up to appear and bow before You,
and to perform our duties in Your chosen House,
the great and holy Temple that was called by Your name,
because of the hand that was stretched out
against Your Sanctuary.
May it be Your will,
LORD our God and God of our ancestors, merciful King,
that You in Your abounding compassion may once more
have mercy on us and on Your Sanctuary,
rebuilding it swiftly and adding to its glory.
Our Father, our King,
reveal the glory of Your kingdom to us swiftly.
Appear and be exalted over us in the sight of all that lives.
Bring back our scattered ones from among the nations,
and gather our dispersed people from the ends of the earth.

*On* שבת*, add the words in parentheses:*

וַתִּתֶּן לָֽנוּ יהוה אֱלֹהֵֽינוּ בְּאַהֲבָה
(שַׁבָּתוֹת לִמְנוּחָה וּ) מוֹעֲדִים לְשִׂמְחָה
חַגִּים וּזְמַנִּים לְשָׂשׂוֹן
אֶת יוֹם (הַשַּׁבָּת הַזֶּה וְאֶת יוֹם)

בפסח: חַג הַמַּצּוֹת הַזֶּה, זְמַן חֵרוּתֵֽנוּ
בשבועות: חַג הַשָּׁבוּעוֹת הַזֶּה, זְמַן מַתַּן תּוֹרָתֵֽנוּ
בסוכות: חַג הַסֻּכּוֹת הַזֶּה, זְמַן שִׂמְחָתֵֽנוּ
בשמע״צ ובש״ת: הַשְּׁמִינִי חַג הָעֲצֶֽרֶת הַזֶּה, זְמַן שִׂמְחָתֵֽנוּ

(בְּאַהֲבָה) מִקְרָא קֹֽדֶשׁ, זֵֽכֶר לִיצִיאַת מִצְרָֽיִם.

וּמִפְּנֵי חֲטָאֵֽינוּ גָּלִֽינוּ מֵאַרְצֵֽנוּ, וְנִתְרַחַֽקְנוּ מֵעַל אַדְמָתֵֽנוּ
וְאֵין אֲנַֽחְנוּ יְכוֹלִים לַעֲלוֹת וְלֵרָאוֹת וּלְהִשְׁתַּחֲווֹת לְפָנֶֽיךָ
וְלַעֲשׂוֹת חוֹבוֹתֵֽינוּ בְּבֵית בְּחִירָתֶֽךָ
בַּבַּֽיִת הַגָּדוֹל וְהַקָּדוֹשׁ שֶׁנִּקְרָא שִׁמְךָ עָלָיו
מִפְּנֵי הַיָּד שֶׁנִּשְׁתַּלְּחָה בְּמִקְדָּשֶֽׁךָ.
יְהִי רָצוֹן מִלְּפָנֶֽיךָ יהוה אֱלֹהֵֽינוּ וֵאלֹהֵי אֲבוֹתֵֽינוּ
מֶֽלֶךְ רַחֲמָן
שֶׁתָּשׁוּב וּתְרַחֵם עָלֵֽינוּ וְעַל מִקְדָּשְׁךָ בְּרַחֲמֶֽיךָ הָרַבִּים
וְתִבְנֵֽהוּ מְהֵרָה וּתְגַדֵּל כְּבוֹדוֹ.
אָבִֽינוּ מַלְכֵּֽנוּ, גַּלֵּה כְּבוֹד מַלְכוּתְךָ עָלֵֽינוּ מְהֵרָה
וְהוֹפַע וְהִנָּשֵׂא עָלֵֽינוּ לְעֵינֵי כָּל חָי
וְקָרֵב פְּזוּרֵֽינוּ מִבֵּין הַגּוֹיִם
וּנְפוּצוֹתֵֽינוּ כַּנֵּס מִיַּרְכְּתֵי אָֽרֶץ.

Lead us to Zion, Your city, in jubilation,
and to Jerusalem, home of Your Temple, with everlasting joy.
There we will prepare for You our obligatory offerings:
the regular daily offerings in their order
and the additional offerings according to their law.
And the additional offering(s of this Sabbath day and) of this day of:

*On Pesaḥ:* the festival of Matzot.

*On Shavuot:* the festival of Shavuot.

*On Sukkot:* the festival of Sukkot.

*On Shemini Atzeret & Simḥat Torah:* the festival of Shemini Atzeret.

we will prepare and offer before You in love,
in accord with Your will's commandment,
as You wrote for us in Your Torah
through Your servant Moses, by Your own word,
as it is said:

---

*On Shabbat add:*

וּבְיוֹם הַשַּׁבָּת On the Sabbath day, make an offering of two lambs a year old, without blemish, together with two-tenths of an ephah of fine flour mixed with oil as a meal-offering, and its appropriate libation. This is the burnt-offering for every Sabbath, in addition to the regular daily burnt-offering and its libation. *Num. 28*

---

*On the first two days of Pesaḥ say (in Israel, on the first day only):*

וּבַחֹדֶשׁ הָרִאשׁוֹן On the fourteenth day of the first month there shall be a Pesaḥ offering to the Lord. And on the fifteenth day of this month there shall be a festival: seven days unleavened bread shall be eaten. On the first day there shall be a sacred assembly: you shall do no laborious work. And you shall bring an offering consumed by fire, a burnt-offering to the Lord: two young bullocks, one ram, and seven yearling male lambs; they shall be to you unblemished. And their meal-offerings and wine-libations as ordained: three-tenths of an ephah for each bull, two-tenths of an ephah for the ram, one-tenth of an ephah for each lamb, wine for the libations, a male goat for atonement, and two regular daily offerings according to their law. *Num. 28*

*On weekdays, continue with "Our God and God of our ancestors" on page 884.*
*On Shabbat, continue with "Those who keep the Sabbath" at the top of page 884.*

וַהֲבִיאֵנוּ לְצִיּוֹן עִירְךָ בְּרִנָּה
וְלִירוּשָׁלַיִם בֵּית מִקְדָּשְׁךָ בְּשִׂמְחַת עוֹלָם
וְשָׁם נַעֲשֶׂה לְפָנֶיךָ אֶת קָרְבְּנוֹת חוֹבוֹתֵינוּ
תְּמִידִים כְּסִדְרָם וּמוּסָפִים כְּהִלְכָתָם
וְאֶת מוּסַף יוֹם / שבת: וְאֶת מוּסְפֵי יוֹם הַשַּׁבָּת הַזֶּה וְיוֹם/

בפסח: חַג הַמַּצּוֹת הַזֶּה

בשבועות: חַג הַשָּׁבוּעוֹת הַזֶּה

בסוכות: חַג הַסֻּכּוֹת הַזֶּה

בשמע״צ ובש״ת: הַשְּׁמִינִי חַג הָעֲצֶרֶת הַזֶּה

נַעֲשֶׂה וְנַקְרִיב לְפָנֶיךָ בְּאַהֲבָה כְּמִצְוַת רְצוֹנֶךָ
כְּמוֹ שֶׁכָּתַבְתָּ עָלֵינוּ בְּתוֹרָתֶךָ
עַל יְדֵי מֹשֶׁה עַבְדֶּךָ מִפִּי כְבוֹדֶךָ, כָּאָמוּר

---

*On* שבת *add:*

וּבְיוֹם הַשַּׁבָּת, שְׁנֵי־כְבָשִׂים בְּנֵי־שָׁנָה תְּמִימִם, וּשְׁנֵי עֶשְׂרֹנִים סֹלֶת מִנְחָה בְּלוּלָה בַשֶּׁמֶן וְנִסְכּוֹ: עֹלַת שַׁבַּת בְּשַׁבַּתּוֹ, עַל־עֹלַת הַתָּמִיד וְנִסְכָּהּ: במדבר כח

---

*On the first two days of* פסח *say (in* ארץ ישראל*, on the first day only):*

וּבַחֹדֶשׁ הָרִאשׁוֹן בְּאַרְבָּעָה עָשָׂר יוֹם לַחֹדֶשׁ, פֶּסַח לַיהוה: וּבַחֲמִשָּׁה עָשָׂר במדבר כח
יוֹם לַחֹדֶשׁ הַזֶּה חָג, שִׁבְעַת יָמִים מַצּוֹת יֵאָכֵל: בַּיּוֹם הָרִאשׁוֹן מִקְרָא־
קֹדֶשׁ, כָּל־מְלֶאכֶת עֲבֹדָה לֹא תַעֲשׂוּ: וְהִקְרַבְתֶּם אִשֶּׁה עֹלָה לַיהוה, פָּרִים
בְּנֵי־בָקָר שְׁנַיִם וְאַיִל אֶחָד, וְשִׁבְעָה כְבָשִׂים בְּנֵי שָׁנָה תְּמִימִם יִהְיוּ לָכֶם:
וּמִנְחָתָם וְנִסְכֵּיהֶם כִּמְדֻבָּר, שְׁלֹשָׁה עֶשְׂרֹנִים לַפָּר וּשְׁנֵי עֶשְׂרֹנִים לָאָיִל,
וְעִשָּׂרוֹן לַכֶּבֶשׂ, וְיַיִן כְּנִסְכּוֹ, וְשָׂעִיר לְכַפֵּר, וּשְׁנֵי תְמִידִים כְּהִלְכָתָם.

*On weekdays, continue with* אֱלֹהֵינוּ וֵאלֹהֵי אֲבוֹתֵינוּ *on page 885.*
*On* שבת*, continue with* יִשְׂמְחוּ בְמַלְכוּתְךָ *at the top of page 885.*

---

*On the last six days of Pesaḥ say:*

וְהִקְרַבְתֶּם And you shall bring an offering consumed by fire, a burnt-offering to the LORD: two young bullocks, one ram, and seven yearling male lambs; they shall be to you unblemished. And their meal-offerings and wine-libations as ordained: three-tenths of an ephah for each bull, two-tenths of an ephah for the ram, one-tenth of an ephah for each lamb, wine for the libations, a male goat for atonement, and two regular daily offerings according to their law. *Num. 28*

*On weekdays, continue with "Our God and God of our ancestors" on page 884.*
*On Shabbat, continue with "Those who keep the Sabbath" at the top of page 884.*

*On Shavuot say:*

וּבְיוֹם הַבִּכּוּרִים On the day of the first fruits, when you bring an offering of new grain to the LORD, on your Festival of Weeks, there shall be a sacred assembly: you shall do no laborious work. You shall offer a burnt-offering of pleasing aroma to the LORD: two young bullocks, one ram, and seven yearling male lambs. And their meal-offerings and wine-libations as ordained: three-tenths of an ephah for each bull, two-tenths of an ephah for the ram, one-tenth of an ephah for each lamb, wine for the libations, a male goat for atonement, and two regular daily offerings according to their law. *Num. 28*

*On weekdays, continue with "Our God and God of our ancestors" on page 884.*
*On Shabbat, continue with "Those who keep the Sabbath" at the top of page 884.*

*On the first two days of Sukkot say (in Israel, the first day only):*

וּבַחֲמִשָּׁה עָשָׂר On the fifteenth day of the seventh month you shall hold a sacred assembly. You shall do no laborious work, and you shall celebrate a festival to the LORD for seven days. You shall offer a burnt-offering, a fire-offering of pleasing aroma to the LORD: thirteen young bullocks, two rams, and fourteen yearling male lambs; they shall be without blemish. And their meal-offerings and wine-libations as ordained: three-tenths of an ephah for each bull, two-tenths of an ephah for each ram, one-tenth of an ephah for each lamb, wine for the libations, a male goat for atonement, and two regular daily offerings according to their law. *Num. 29*

*On weekdays, continue with "Our God and God of our ancestors" on page 884.*
*On Shabbat, continue with "Those who keep the Sabbath" at the top of page 884.*

*On the first day of Ḥol HaMo'ed Sukkot,*
*say the following two paragraphs (in Israel say only the first):*

וּבַיּוֹם הַשֵּׁנִי On the second day you shall offer twelve young bullocks, two rams, fourteen yearling male lambs without blemish. And their meal-offerings and wine-libations as ordained: three-tenths of an ephah for each bull, two-tenths of an ephah for each ram, one-tenth of an ephah for each lamb, wine for the libations, a male goat for atonement, and two regular daily offerings according to their law. *Num. 29*

*Continue with "On the third day" at the top of the next page.*

*On the last six days of פסח say:*

במדבר כח

וְהִקְרַבְתֶּם אִשֶּׁה עֹלָה לַיהוה, פָּרִים בְּנֵי־בָקָר שְׁנַיִם וְאַיִל אֶחָד, וְשִׁבְעָה כְבָשִׂים בְּנֵי שָׁנָה, תְּמִימִם יִהְיוּ לָכֶם: וּמִנְחָתָם וְנִסְכֵּיהֶם כִּמְדֻבָּר, שְׁלֹשָׁה עֶשְׂרֹנִים לַפָּר וּשְׁנֵי עֶשְׂרֹנִים לָאָיִל, וְעִשָּׂרוֹן לַכֶּבֶשׂ, וְיַיִן כְּנִסְכּוֹ, וְשָׂעִיר לְכַפֵּר, וּשְׁנֵי תְמִידִים כְּהִלְכָתָם.

*On weekdays, continue with* אֱלֹהֵינוּ וֵאלֹהֵי אֲבוֹתֵינוּ *on page 885.*
*On* שבת*, continue with* יִשְׂמְחוּ בְמַלְכוּתְךָ *at the top of page 885.*

---

*On* שבועות *say:*

במדבר כח

וּבְיוֹם הַבִּכּוּרִים, בְּהַקְרִיבְכֶם מִנְחָה חֲדָשָׁה לַיהוה בְּשָׁבֻעֹתֵיכֶם, מִקְרָא־קֹדֶשׁ יִהְיֶה לָכֶם, כָּל־מְלֶאכֶת עֲבֹדָה לֹא תַעֲשׂוּ: וְהִקְרַבְתֶּם עוֹלָה לְרֵיחַ נִיחֹחַ לַיהוה, פָּרִים בְּנֵי־בָקָר שְׁנַיִם, אַיִל אֶחָד, שִׁבְעָה כְבָשִׂים בְּנֵי שָׁנָה: וּמִנְחָתָם וְנִסְכֵּיהֶם כִּמְדֻבָּר, שְׁלֹשָׁה עֶשְׂרֹנִים לַפָּר וּשְׁנֵי עֶשְׂרֹנִים לָאָיִל, וְעִשָּׂרוֹן לַכֶּבֶשׂ, וְיַיִן כְּנִסְכּוֹ, וְשָׂעִיר לְכַפֵּר, וּשְׁנֵי תְמִידִים כְּהִלְכָתָם.

*On weekdays, continue with* אֱלֹהֵינוּ וֵאלֹהֵי אֲבוֹתֵינוּ *on page 885.*
*On* שבת*, continue with* יִשְׂמְחוּ בְמַלְכוּתְךָ *at the top of page 885.*

---

*On the first two days of* סוכות *say (in* ארץ ישראל*, the first day only):*

במדבר כט

וּבַחֲמִשָּׁה עָשָׂר יוֹם לַחֹדֶשׁ הַשְּׁבִיעִי, מִקְרָא־קֹדֶשׁ יִהְיֶה לָכֶם, כָּל־מְלֶאכֶת עֲבֹדָה לֹא תַעֲשׂוּ, וְחַגֹּתֶם חַג לַיהוה שִׁבְעַת יָמִים: וְהִקְרַבְתֶּם עֹלָה אִשֵּׁה רֵיחַ נִיחֹחַ לַיהוה, פָּרִים בְּנֵי־בָקָר שְׁלֹשָׁה עָשָׂר, אֵילִם שְׁנָיִם, כְּבָשִׂים בְּנֵי־שָׁנָה אַרְבָּעָה עָשָׂר, תְּמִימִם יִהְיוּ: וּמִנְחָתָם וְנִסְכֵּיהֶם כִּמְדֻבָּר, שְׁלֹשָׁה עֶשְׂרֹנִים לַפָּר וּשְׁנֵי עֶשְׂרֹנִים לָאָיִל, וְעִשָּׂרוֹן לַכֶּבֶשׂ, וְיַיִן כְּנִסְכּוֹ, וְשָׂעִיר לְכַפֵּר, וּשְׁנֵי תְמִידִים כְּהִלְכָתָם.

*On weekdays, continue with* אֱלֹהֵינוּ וֵאלֹהֵי אֲבוֹתֵינוּ *on page 885.*
*On* שבת*, continue with* יִשְׂמְחוּ בְמַלְכוּתְךָ *at the top of page 885.*

---

*On the first day of* חול המועד סוכות*,*
*say the following two paragraphs (in* ארץ ישראל *say only the first):*

במדבר כט

וּבַיּוֹם הַשֵּׁנִי, פָּרִים בְּנֵי־בָקָר שְׁנֵים עָשָׂר, אֵילִם שְׁנָיִם, כְּבָשִׂים בְּנֵי־שָׁנָה אַרְבָּעָה עָשָׂר, תְּמִימִם: וּמִנְחָתָם וְנִסְכֵּיהֶם כִּמְדֻבָּר, שְׁלֹשָׁה עֶשְׂרֹנִים לַפָּר, וּשְׁנֵי עֶשְׂרֹנִים לָאָיִל, וְעִשָּׂרוֹן לַכֶּבֶשׂ, וְיַיִן כְּנִסְכּוֹ, וְשָׂעִיר לְכַפֵּר, וּשְׁנֵי תְמִידִים כְּהִלְכָתָם.

*Continue with* וּבַיּוֹם הַשְּׁלִישִׁי *at the top of the next page.*

וּבַיּוֹם הַשְּׁלִישִׁי On the third day you shall offer eleven bullocks, two rams, fourteen yearling male lambs without blemish. And their meal-offerings and wine-libations as ordained: three-tenths of an ephah for each bull, two-tenths of an ephah for the ram, one-tenth of an ephah for each lamb, wine for the libations, a male goat for atonement, and two regular daily offerings according to their law. *Num. 29*

*On weekdays, continue with "Our God and God of our ancestors" on page 884.*
*On Shabbat, continue with "Those who keep the Sabbath" at the top of page 884.*

---

*On the second day of Ḥol HaMo'ed Sukkot,*
*say the following two paragraphs (in Israel say only the first):*

וּבַיּוֹם הַשְּׁלִישִׁי On the third day you shall offer eleven bullocks, two rams, fourteen yearling male lambs without blemish. And their meal-offerings and wine-libations as ordained: three-tenths of an ephah for each bull, two-tenths of an ephah for each ram, one-tenth of an ephah for each lamb, wine for the libations, a male goat for atonement, and two regular daily offerings according to their law. *Num. 29*

וּבַיּוֹם הָרְבִיעִי On the fourth day you shall offer ten bullocks, two rams, fourteen yearling male lambs without blemish. And their meal-offerings and wine-libations as ordained: three-tenths of an ephah for each bull, two-tenths of an ephah for each ram, one-tenth of an ephah for each lamb, wine for the libations, a male goat for atonement, and two regular daily offerings according to their law. *Num. 29*

*On weekdays, continue with "Our God and God of our ancestors" on page 884.*
*On Shabbat, continue with "Those who keep the Sabbath" at the top of page 884.*

---

*On the third day of Ḥol HaMo'ed Sukkot,*
*say the following two paragraphs (in Israel say only the first):*

וּבַיּוֹם הָרְבִיעִי On the fourth day you shall offer ten bullocks, two rams, fourteen yearling male lambs without blemish. And their meal-offerings and wine-libations as ordained: three-tenths of an ephah for each bull, two-tenths of an ephah for each ram, one-tenth of an ephah for each lamb, wine for the libations, a male goat for atonement, and two regular daily offerings according to their law. *Num. 29*

וּבַיּוֹם הַחֲמִישִׁי On the fifth day you shall offer nine bullocks, two rams, fourteen yearling male lambs without blemish. And their meal-offerings and wine-libations as ordained: three-tenths of an ephah for each bull, two-tenths of an ephah for each ram, one-tenth of an ephah for each lamb, wine for the libations, a male goat for atonement, and two regular daily offerings according to their law. *Num. 29*

*On weekdays, continue with "Our God and God of our ancestors" on page 884.*
*On Shabbat, continue with "Those who keep the Sabbath" at the top of page 884.*

---

וּבַיּוֹם הַשְּׁלִישִׁי, פָּרִים עַשְׁתֵּי־עָשָׂר, אֵילִם שְׁנָיִם, כְּבָשִׂים בְּנֵי־שָׁנָה אַרְבָּעָה עָשָׂר, תְּמִימִם: וּמִנְחָתָם וְנִסְכֵּיהֶם כִּמְדֻבָּר, שְׁלֹשָׁה עֶשְׂרֹנִים לַפָּר, וּשְׁנֵי עֶשְׂרֹנִים לָאָיִל, וְעִשָּׂרוֹן לַכֶּבֶשׂ, וְיַיִן כְּנִסְכּוֹ, וְשָׂעִיר לְכַפֵּר, וּשְׁנֵי תְמִידִים כְּהִלְכָתָם. במדבר כט

*On weekdays, continue with* אֱלֹהֵינוּ וֵאלֹהֵי אֲבוֹתֵינוּ *on page 885.*
*On* שבת*, continue with* יִשְׂמְחוּ בְמַלְכוּתְךָ *at the top of page 885.*

---

*On the second day of* חול המועד סוכות*,*
*say the following two paragraphs (in* ארץ ישראל *say only the first):*

וּבַיּוֹם הַשְּׁלִישִׁי, פָּרִים עַשְׁתֵּי־עָשָׂר, אֵילִם שְׁנָיִם, כְּבָשִׂים בְּנֵי־שָׁנָה אַרְבָּעָה עָשָׂר, תְּמִימִם: וּמִנְחָתָם וְנִסְכֵּיהֶם כִּמְדֻבָּר, שְׁלֹשָׁה עֶשְׂרֹנִים לַפָּר, וּשְׁנֵי עֶשְׂרֹנִים לָאָיִל, וְעִשָּׂרוֹן לַכֶּבֶשׂ, וְיַיִן כְּנִסְכּוֹ, וְשָׂעִיר לְכַפֵּר, וּשְׁנֵי תְמִידִים כְּהִלְכָתָם. במדבר כט

וּבַיּוֹם הָרְבִיעִי, פָּרִים עֲשָׂרָה, אֵילִם שְׁנָיִם, כְּבָשִׂים בְּנֵי־שָׁנָה אַרְבָּעָה עָשָׂר, תְּמִימִם: וּמִנְחָתָם וְנִסְכֵּיהֶם כִּמְדֻבָּר, שְׁלֹשָׁה עֶשְׂרֹנִים לַפָּר, וּשְׁנֵי עֶשְׂרֹנִים לָאָיִל, וְעִשָּׂרוֹן לַכֶּבֶשׂ, וְיַיִן כְּנִסְכּוֹ, וְשָׂעִיר לְכַפֵּר, וּשְׁנֵי תְמִידִים כְּהִלְכָתָם. במדבר כט

*On weekdays, continue with* אֱלֹהֵינוּ וֵאלֹהֵי אֲבוֹתֵינוּ *on page 885.*
*On* שבת*, continue with* יִשְׂמְחוּ בְמַלְכוּתְךָ *at the top of page 885.*

---

*On the third day of* חול המועד סוכות*,*
*say the following two paragraphs (in* ארץ ישראל *say only the first):*

וּבַיּוֹם הָרְבִיעִי, פָּרִים עֲשָׂרָה, אֵילִם שְׁנָיִם, כְּבָשִׂים בְּנֵי־שָׁנָה אַרְבָּעָה עָשָׂר, תְּמִימִם: וּמִנְחָתָם וְנִסְכֵּיהֶם כִּמְדֻבָּר, שְׁלֹשָׁה עֶשְׂרֹנִים לַפָּר, וּשְׁנֵי עֶשְׂרֹנִים לָאָיִל, וְעִשָּׂרוֹן לַכֶּבֶשׂ, וְיַיִן כְּנִסְכּוֹ, וְשָׂעִיר לְכַפֵּר, וּשְׁנֵי תְמִידִים כְּהִלְכָתָם. במדבר כט

וּבַיּוֹם הַחֲמִישִׁי, פָּרִים תִּשְׁעָה, אֵילִם שְׁנָיִם, כְּבָשִׂים בְּנֵי־שָׁנָה אַרְבָּעָה עָשָׂר, תְּמִימִם: וּמִנְחָתָם וְנִסְכֵּיהֶם כִּמְדֻבָּר, שְׁלֹשָׁה עֶשְׂרֹנִים לַפָּר, וּשְׁנֵי עֶשְׂרֹנִים לָאָיִל, וְעִשָּׂרוֹן לַכֶּבֶשׂ, וְיַיִן כְּנִסְכּוֹ, וְשָׂעִיר לְכַפֵּר, וּשְׁנֵי תְמִידִים כְּהִלְכָתָם. במדבר כט

*On weekdays, continue with* אֱלֹהֵינוּ וֵאלֹהֵי אֲבוֹתֵינוּ *on page 885.*
*On* שבת*, continue with* יִשְׂמְחוּ בְמַלְכוּתְךָ *at the top of page 885.*

---

*On the fourth day of Ḥol HaMo'ed Sukkot, say the following two paragraphs (in Israel say only the first):*

וּבַיּוֹם הַחֲמִישִׁי On the fifth day you shall offer nine bullocks, two rams, fourteen yearling male lambs without blemish. And their meal-offerings and wine-libations as ordained: three-tenths of an ephah for each bull, two-tenths of an ephah for each ram, one-tenth of an ephah for each lamb, wine for the libations, a male goat for atonement, and two regular daily offerings according to their law. *Num. 29*

וּבַיּוֹם הַשִּׁשִּׁי On the sixth day you shall offer eight bullocks, two rams, fourteen yearling male lambs without blemish. And their meal-offerings and wine-libations as ordained: three-tenths of an ephah for each bull, two-tenths of an ephah for each ram, one-tenth of an ephah for each lamb, wine for the libations, a male goat for atonement, and two regular daily offerings according to their law. *Num. 29*

*On weekdays, continue with "Our God and God of our ancestors" on the next page. On Shabbat, continue with "Those who keep the Sabbath" at the top of the next page.*

---

*On Hoshana Raba, say the following two paragraphs. In Israel, say the first paragraph on the fifth day of Ḥol HaMo'ed and the second on Hoshana Raba.*

וּבַיּוֹם הַשִּׁשִּׁי On the sixth day you shall offer eight bullocks, two rams, fourteen yearling male lambs without blemish. And their meal-offerings and wine-libations as ordained: three-tenths of an ephah for each bull, two-tenths of an ephah for each ram, one-tenth of an ephah for each lamb, wine for the libations, a male goat for atonement, and two regular daily offerings according to their law. *Num. 29*

וּבַיּוֹם הַשְּׁבִיעִי On the seventh day you shall offer seven bullocks, two rams, fourteen yearling male lambs without blemish. And their meal-offerings and wine-libations as ordained: three-tenths of an ephah for each bull, two-tenths of an ephah for each ram, one-tenth of an ephah for each lamb, wine for the libations, a male goat for atonement, and two regular daily offerings according to their law. *Num. 29*

*Continue with "Our God and God of our ancestors" on the next page.*

---

*On Shemini Atzeret and Simḥat Torah, say:*

בַּיּוֹם הַשְּׁמִינִי On the eighth day you shall hold an assembly; you shall do no laborious work. And you shall offer a burnt-offering, a fire-offering of pleasing odor to the Lord: one bullock, one ram, seven yearling male lambs without blemish. And their meal-offerings and wine-libations as ordained: three-tenths of an ephah for each bull, two-tenths of an ephah for the ram, one-tenth of an ephah for each lamb, wine for the libations, a male goat for atonement, and two regular daily offerings according to their law. *Num. 29*

*On weekdays, continue with "Our God and God of our ancestors" on the next page. On Shabbat, continue with "Those who keep the Sabbath" at the top of the next page.*

*On the fourth day of* חול המועד סוכות*, say the following two paragraphs (in* ארץ ישראל *say only the first):*

במדבר כט וּבַיּוֹם הַחֲמִישִׁי, פָּרִים תִּשְׁעָה, אֵילִם שְׁנָיִם, כְּבָשִׂים בְּנֵי־שָׁנָה אַרְבָּעָה עָשָׂר, תְּמִימִם: וּמִנְחָתָם וְנִסְכֵּיהֶם כִּמְדֻבָּר, שְׁלֹשָׁה עֶשְׂרֹנִים לַפָּר, וּשְׁנֵי עֶשְׂרֹנִים לָאָיִל, וְעִשָּׂרוֹן לַכֶּבֶשׂ, וְיַיִן כְּנִסְכּוֹ, וְשָׂעִיר לְכַפֵּר, וּשְׁנֵי תְמִידִים כְּהִלְכָתָם.

במדבר כט וּבַיּוֹם הַשִּׁשִּׁי, פָּרִים שְׁמֹנָה, אֵילִם שְׁנָיִם, כְּבָשִׂים בְּנֵי־שָׁנָה אַרְבָּעָה עָשָׂר, תְּמִימִם: וּמִנְחָתָם וְנִסְכֵּיהֶם כִּמְדֻבָּר, שְׁלֹשָׁה עֶשְׂרֹנִים לַפָּר, וּשְׁנֵי עֶשְׂרֹנִים לָאָיִל, וְעִשָּׂרוֹן לַכֶּבֶשׂ, וְיַיִן כְּנִסְכּוֹ, וְשָׂעִיר לְכַפֵּר, וּשְׁנֵי תְמִידִים כְּהִלְכָתָם.

*On weekdays, continue with* אֱלֹהֵינוּ וֵאלֹהֵי אֲבוֹתֵינוּ *on the next page.*
*On* שבת*, continue with* יִשְׂמְחוּ בְמַלְכוּתְךָ *at the top of the next page.*

*On* הושענא רבה*, say the following two paragraphs.*
*In* ארץ ישראל*, say the first paragraph on the fifth day of* חול המועד *and the second on* הושענא רבה*:*

במדבר כט וּבַיּוֹם הַשִּׁשִּׁי, פָּרִים שְׁמֹנָה, אֵילִם שְׁנָיִם, כְּבָשִׂים בְּנֵי־שָׁנָה אַרְבָּעָה עָשָׂר, תְּמִימִם: וּמִנְחָתָם וְנִסְכֵּיהֶם כִּמְדֻבָּר, שְׁלֹשָׁה עֶשְׂרֹנִים לַפָּר, וּשְׁנֵי עֶשְׂרֹנִים לָאָיִל, וְעִשָּׂרוֹן לַכֶּבֶשׂ, וְיַיִן כְּנִסְכּוֹ, וְשָׂעִיר לְכַפֵּר, וּשְׁנֵי תְמִידִים כְּהִלְכָתָם.

במדבר כט וּבַיּוֹם הַשְּׁבִיעִי, פָּרִים שִׁבְעָה, אֵילִם שְׁנָיִם, כְּבָשִׂים בְּנֵי־שָׁנָה אַרְבָּעָה עָשָׂר, תְּמִימִם: וּמִנְחָתָם וְנִסְכֵּיהֶם כִּמְדֻבָּר, שְׁלֹשָׁה עֶשְׂרֹנִים לַפָּר, וּשְׁנֵי עֶשְׂרֹנִים לָאָיִל, וְעִשָּׂרוֹן לַכֶּבֶשׂ, וְיַיִן כְּנִסְכּוֹ, וְשָׂעִיר לְכַפֵּר, וּשְׁנֵי תְמִידִים כְּהִלְכָתָם.

*Continue with* אֱלֹהֵינוּ וֵאלֹהֵי אֲבוֹתֵינוּ *on the next page.*

*On* שמיני עצרת *and* שמחת תורה*, say:*

במדבר כט בַּיּוֹם הַשְּׁמִינִי, עֲצֶרֶת תִּהְיֶה לָכֶם, כָּל־מְלֶאכֶת עֲבֹדָה לֹא תַעֲשׂוּ: וְהִקְרַבְתֶּם עֹלָה אִשֵּׁה רֵיחַ נִיחֹחַ לַיהוה, פַּר אֶחָד, אַיִל אֶחָד, כְּבָשִׂים בְּנֵי־שָׁנָה שִׁבְעָה, תְּמִימִם: וּמִנְחָתָם וְנִסְכֵּיהֶם כִּמְדֻבָּר, שְׁלֹשָׁה עֶשְׂרֹנִים לַפָּר וּשְׁנֵי עֶשְׂרֹנִים לָאָיִל, וְעִשָּׂרוֹן לַכֶּבֶשׂ, וְיַיִן כְּנִסְכּוֹ, וְשָׂעִיר לְכַפֵּר, וּשְׁנֵי תְמִידִים כְּהִלְכָתָם.

*On weekdays, continue with* אֱלֹהֵינוּ וֵאלֹהֵי אֲבוֹתֵינוּ *on the next page.*
*On* שבת*, continue with* יִשְׂמְחוּ בְמַלְכוּתְךָ *at the top of the next page.*

*On Shabbat say:*

יִשְׂמְחוּ Those who keep the Sabbath and call it a delight shall rejoice in Your kingship. The people who sanctify the seventh day shall all be satisfied and take delight in Your goodness, for You favored the seventh day and declared it holy. You called it "most desirable of days" in remembrance of Creation.

אֱלֹהֵינוּ Our God and God of our ancestors,
merciful King, have compassion upon us.
You who are good and do good, respond to our call.
Return to us in Your abounding mercy
for the sake of our fathers who did Your will.
Rebuild Your Temple as at the beginning,
and establish Your Sanctuary on its site.
Let us witness its rebuilding
and gladden us by its restoration.
Bring the priests back to their service,
the Levites to their song and music,
and the Israelites to their homes.

וְשָׁם נַעֲלֶה There we will go up and appear and bow before You
on the three pilgrimage festivals,
as is written in Your Torah:
"Three times in the year all your males shall appear *Deut. 16*
before the LORD your God
at the place He will choose:
on Pesaḥ, Shavuot and Sukkot.
They shall not appear before the LORD empty-handed.
Each shall bring such a gift as he can,
in proportion to the blessing
that the LORD your God grants you."

*On Shabbat add the words in parentheses:*

וְהַשִּׂיאֵנוּ Bestow on us, LORD our God,
the blessing of Your festivals
for life and peace, joy and gladness,
as You desired and promised to bless us.

*On* שבת *say:*

יִשְׂמְחוּ בְמַלְכוּתְךָ שׁוֹמְרֵי שַׁבָּת וְקוֹרְאֵי עֹנֶג. עַם מְקַדְּשֵׁי שְׁבִיעִי כֻּלָּם יִשְׂבְּעוּ וְיִתְעַנְּגוּ מִטּוּבֶךָ, וּבַשְּׁבִיעִי רָצִיתָ בּוֹ וְקִדַּשְׁתּוֹ, חֶמְדַּת יָמִים אוֹתוֹ קָרָאתָ, זֵכֶר לְמַעֲשֵׂה בְרֵאשִׁית.

אֱלֹהֵינוּ וֵאלֹהֵי אֲבוֹתֵינוּ
מֶלֶךְ רַחֲמָן רַחֵם עָלֵינוּ, טוֹב וּמֵטִיב הִדָּרֶשׁ לָנוּ
שׁוּבָה אֵלֵינוּ בַּהֲמוֹן רַחֲמֶיךָ
בִּגְלַל אָבוֹת שֶׁעָשׂוּ רְצוֹנֶךָ.
בְּנֵה בֵיתְךָ כְּבַתְּחִלָּה, וְכוֹנֵן מִקְדָּשְׁךָ עַל מְכוֹנוֹ
וְהַרְאֵנוּ בְּבִנְיָנוֹ, וְשַׂמְּחֵנוּ בְּתִקּוּנוֹ
וְהָשֵׁב כֹּהֲנִים לַעֲבוֹדָתָם, וּלְוִיִּם לְשִׁירָם וּלְזִמְרָם
וְהָשֵׁב יִשְׂרָאֵל לִנְוֵיהֶם.

וְשָׁם נַעֲלֶה וְנֵרָאֶה וְנִשְׁתַּחֲוֶה לְפָנֶיךָ בְּשָׁלֹשׁ פַּעֲמֵי רְגָלֵינוּ
כַּכָּתוּב בְּתוֹרָתֶךָ
דברים טז
שָׁלוֹשׁ פְּעָמִים בַּשָּׁנָה יֵרָאֶה כָל־זְכוּרְךָ
אֶת־פְּנֵי יהוה אֱלֹהֶיךָ
בַּמָּקוֹם אֲשֶׁר יִבְחָר
בְּחַג הַמַּצּוֹת, וּבְחַג הַשָּׁבֻעוֹת, וּבְחַג הַסֻּכּוֹת
וְלֹא יֵרָאֶה אֶת־פְּנֵי יהוה רֵיקָם:
אִישׁ כְּמַתְּנַת יָדוֹ, כְּבִרְכַּת יהוה אֱלֹהֶיךָ אֲשֶׁר נָתַן־לָךְ:

*On* שבת *add the words in parentheses:*

וְהַשִּׂיאֵנוּ יהוה אֱלֹהֵינוּ אֶת בִּרְכַּת מוֹעֲדֶיךָ
לְחַיִּים וּלְשָׁלוֹם, לְשִׂמְחָה וּלְשָׂשׂוֹן
כַּאֲשֶׁר רָצִיתָ וְאָמַרְתָּ לְבָרְכֵנוּ.

(Our God and God of our ancestors, be pleased with our rest.)
Make us holy through Your commandments
and grant us a share in Your Torah;
satisfy us with Your goodness, gladden us with Your salvation,
and purify our hearts to serve You in truth.
And grant us a heritage, LORD our God, (with love and favor,)
with joy and gladness Your holy (Sabbath and) festivals.
May Israel, who sanctify Your name, rejoice in You.
Blessed are You, LORD,
who sanctifies (the Sabbath and) Israel, and the festive seasons.

TEMPLE SERVICE

רְצֵה Find favor, LORD our God, in Your people Israel
and their prayer.
Restore the service to Your most holy House,
and accept in love and favor the fire-offerings of Israel
and their prayer.
May the service of Your people Israel
always find favor with You.
And may our eyes witness Your return to Zion in compassion.
Blessed are You, LORD, who restores His Presence to Zion.

---

*If Kohanim bless the congregation during the Leader's Repetition, the following is said. It is not said on Ḥol HaMo'ed or Shabbat Ḥol HaMo'ed.*

*All:* וְתֶעֱרַב May our entreaty be as pleasing to You as a burnt-offering and sacrifice. Please, Compassionate One, in Your abounding mercy restore Your Presence to Zion, Your city, and the order of the Temple service to Jerusalem. May our eyes witness Your return in compassion to Zion, that there we may serve You with reverence as in the days of old and as in former years.

*Leader:* Blessed are You, LORD, for You alone do we serve with reverence.

*Continue with "We give thanks" on the next page.*

*In Israel:*

*All:* וְתֶעֱרַב May our entreaty be as pleasing to You as a burnt-offering and sacrifice. Please, Compassionate One, in Your abounding mercy restore Your Presence to Zion, Your city, and the order of the Temple service to Jerusalem. That there we may serve You with reverence as in the days of old and as in former years.

*Continue with "And may our eyes" on the next page.*

---

(אֱלֹהֵינוּ וֵאלֹהֵי אֲבוֹתֵינוּ, רְצֵה בִמְנוּחָתֵנוּ)
קַדְּשֵׁנוּ בְּמִצְוֹתֶיךָ
וְתֵן חֶלְקֵנוּ בְּתוֹרָתֶךָ
שַׂבְּעֵנוּ מִטּוּבֶךָ
וְשַׂמְּחֵנוּ בִּישׁוּעָתֶךָ
וְטַהֵר לִבֵּנוּ לְעָבְדְּךָ בֶּאֱמֶת
וְהַנְחִילֵנוּ יהוה אֱלֹהֵינוּ (בְּאַהֲבָה וּבְרָצוֹן)
בְּשִׂמְחָה וּבְשָׂשׂוֹן (שַׁבָּת וּ) מוֹעֲדֵי קָדְשֶׁךָ
וְיִשְׂמְחוּ בְךָ יִשְׂרָאֵל מְקַדְּשֵׁי שְׁמֶךָ.
בָּרוּךְ אַתָּה יהוה, מְקַדֵּשׁ (הַשַּׁבָּת וְ) יִשְׂרָאֵל וְהַזְּמַנִּים.

עבודה
רְצֵה יהוה אֱלֹהֵינוּ בְּעַמְּךָ יִשְׂרָאֵל וּבִתְפִלָּתָם
וְהָשֵׁב אֶת הָעֲבוֹדָה לִדְבִיר בֵּיתֶךָ
וְאִשֵּׁי יִשְׂרָאֵל וּתְפִלָּתָם בְּאַהֲבָה תְקַבֵּל בְּרָצוֹן
וּתְהִי לְרָצוֹן תָּמִיד עֲבוֹדַת יִשְׂרָאֵל עַמֶּךָ.

---

*If* כהנים *say* ברכת כהנים *during* חזרת הש״ץ*, the following is said. It is not said on* שבת חול המועד *or* חול המועד*.*

קהל וש״ץ: וְתֶעֱרַב עָלֶיךָ עֲתִירָתֵנוּ כְּעוֹלָה וּכְקָרְבָּן. אָנָּא רַחוּם, בְּרַחֲמֶיךָ הָרַבִּים הָשֵׁב שְׁכִינָתְךָ לְצִיּוֹן עִירֶךָ, וְסֵדֶר הָעֲבוֹדָה לִירוּשָׁלָיִם. וְתֶחֱזֶינָה עֵינֵינוּ בְּשׁוּבְךָ לְצִיּוֹן בְּרַחֲמִים. וְשָׁם נַעֲבָדְךָ בְּיִרְאָה כִּימֵי עוֹלָם וּכְשָׁנִים קַדְמוֹנִיּוֹת.

ש״ץ: בָּרוּךְ אַתָּה יהוה שֶׁאוֹתְךָ לְבַדְּךָ בְּיִרְאָה נַעֲבֹד.

*Continue with* מודים *on the next page.*

בארץ ישראל:

קהל וש״ץ: וְתֶעֱרַב עָלֶיךָ עֲתִירָתֵנוּ כְּעוֹלָה וּכְקָרְבָּן. אָנָּא רַחוּם, בְּרַחֲמֶיךָ הָרַבִּים הָשֵׁב שְׁכִינָתְךָ לְצִיּוֹן עִירֶךָ, וְסֵדֶר הָעֲבוֹדָה לִירוּשָׁלָיִם. וְשָׁם נַעֲבָדְךָ בְּיִרְאָה כִּימֵי עוֹלָם וּכְשָׁנִים קַדְמוֹנִיּוֹת.

*Continue with* וְתֶחֱזֶינָה *on the next page.*

---

And may our eyes witness Your return to Zion in compassion.
Blessed are You, LORD, who restores His Presence to Zion.

THANKSGIVING

*Bow at the first nine words.*

▾מוֹדִים We give thanks to You,
for You are the LORD our God
and God of our ancestors
for ever and all time.
You are the Rock of our lives,
Shield of our salvation
from generation to generation.
We will thank You and
declare Your praise for our lives,
which are entrusted into Your hand;
for our souls,
which are placed in Your charge;
for Your miracles
which are with us every day;
and for Your wonders and favors
at all times, evening,
morning and midday.
You are good –
for Your compassion never fails.
You are compassionate –
for Your loving-kindnesses never cease.
We have always placed our hope in You.

*During the Leader's Repetition, the congregation says quietly:*
▾מוֹדִים We give thanks to You,
for You are the LORD our God
and God of our ancestors,
God of all flesh,
who formed us
and formed the universe.
Blessings and thanks
are due to Your great
and holy name for giving us
life and sustaining us.
May You continue
to give us life
and sustain us;
and may You gather our
exiles to Your holy courts,
to keep Your decrees,
do Your will and serve You
with a perfect heart,
for it is for us
to give You thanks.
Blessed be God to whom
thanksgiving is due.

וְעַל כֻּלָּם For all these things may Your name be blessed
and exalted, our King, continually, for ever and all time.
Let all that lives thank You, Selah!
and praise Your name in truth, God, our Savior and Help, Selah!
▾Blessed are You, LORD, whose name is "the Good"
and to whom thanks are due.

וְתֶחֱזֶינָה עֵינֵינוּ בְּשׁוּבְךָ לְצִיּוֹן בְּרַחֲמִים.
בָּרוּךְ אַתָּה יהוה, הַמַּחֲזִיר שְׁכִינָתוֹ לְצִיּוֹן.

הודאה

*Bow at the first five words.*

<table>
<tr><td>

מוֹדִים אֲנַחְנוּ לָךְ<br>
שָׁאַתָּה הוּא יהוה אֱלֹהֵינוּ<br>
וֵאלֹהֵי אֲבוֹתֵינוּ לְעוֹלָם וָעֶד.<br>
צוּר חַיֵּינוּ, מָגֵן יִשְׁעֵנוּ<br>
אַתָּה הוּא לְדוֹר וָדוֹר.<br>
נוֹדֶה לְּךָ וּנְסַפֵּר תְּהִלָּתֶךָ<br>
עַל חַיֵּינוּ הַמְּסוּרִים בְּיָדֶךָ<br>
וְעַל נִשְׁמוֹתֵינוּ הַפְּקוּדוֹת לָךְ<br>
וְעַל נִסֶּיךָ שֶׁבְּכָל יוֹם עִמָּנוּ<br>
וְעַל נִפְלְאוֹתֶיךָ וְטוֹבוֹתֶיךָ<br>
שֶׁבְּכָל עֵת<br>
עֶרֶב וָבֹקֶר וְצָהֳרָיִם.<br>
הַטּוֹב, כִּי לֹא כָלוּ רַחֲמֶיךָ<br>
וְהַמְרַחֵם, כִּי לֹא תַמּוּ חֲסָדֶיךָ<br>
מֵעוֹלָם קִוִּינוּ לָךְ.

</td><td>

*During the* חזרת הש״ץ, *the* קהל *says quietly:*<br>
מוֹדִים אֲנַחְנוּ לָךְ<br>
שָׁאַתָּה הוּא יהוה אֱלֹהֵינוּ<br>
וֵאלֹהֵי אֲבוֹתֵינוּ<br>
אֱלֹהֵי כָל בָּשָׂר<br>
יוֹצְרֵנוּ, יוֹצֵר בְּרֵאשִׁית.<br>
בְּרָכוֹת וְהוֹדָאוֹת<br>
לְשִׁמְךָ הַגָּדוֹל וְהַקָּדוֹשׁ<br>
עַל שֶׁהֶחֱיִיתָנוּ וְקִיַּמְתָּנוּ.<br>
כֵּן תְּחַיֵּנוּ וּתְקַיְּמֵנוּ<br>
וְתֶאֱסֹף גָּלֻיּוֹתֵינוּ<br>
לְחַצְרוֹת קָדְשֶׁךָ<br>
לִשְׁמֹר חֻקֶּיךָ<br>
וְלַעֲשׂוֹת רְצוֹנֶךָ וּלְעָבְדְּךָ<br>
בְּלֵבָב שָׁלֵם<br>
עַל שֶׁאֲנַחְנוּ מוֹדִים לָךְ.<br>
בָּרוּךְ אֵל הַהוֹדָאוֹת.

</td></tr>
</table>

וְעַל כֻּלָּם יִתְבָּרַךְ וְיִתְרוֹמַם שִׁמְךָ מַלְכֵּנוּ תָּמִיד לְעוֹלָם וָעֶד.
וְכֹל הַחַיִּים יוֹדְוּךָ סֶּלָה
וִיהַלְלוּ אֶת שִׁמְךָ בֶּאֱמֶת, הָאֵל יְשׁוּעָתֵנוּ וְעֶזְרָתֵנוּ סֶלָה.
בָּרוּךְ אַתָּה יהוה, הַטּוֹב שִׁמְךָ וּלְךָ נָאֶה לְהוֹדוֹת.

*In the Diaspora, if Kohanim bless the congregation during the Leader's Repetition, the service continues on page 894. In Israel, the regular Priestly Blessing on page 902 is said. If Kohanim do not ascend, the following is said. See laws 370–377.*

Our God and God of our fathers, bless us with the threefold blessing in the Torah, written by the hand of Moses Your servant and pronounced by Aaron and his sons the priests, Your holy people, as it is said:

May the LORD bless you and protect you. (*Cong:* May it be Your will.) *Num. 6*
May the LORD make His face shine on you and be gracious to you.
(*Cong:* May it be Your will.)
May the LORD turn His face toward you, and grant you peace.
(*Cong:* May it be Your will.)

PEACE

שִׂים שָׁלוֹם Grant peace, goodness and blessing,
grace, loving-kindness and compassion to us
and all Israel Your people.
Bless us, our Father, all as one, with the light of Your face,
for by the light of Your face You have given us, LORD our God,
the Torah of life and love of kindness,
righteousness, blessing, compassion, life and peace.
May it be good in Your eyes to bless Your people Israel
at every time, in every hour, with Your peace.
Blessed are You, LORD,
who blesses His people Israel with peace.

*The following verse concludes the Leader's Repetition of the Amida. Some also say it here as part of the silent Amida. See law 368.*

May the words of my mouth and the meditation of my heart *Ps. 19*
find favor before You, LORD, my Rock and Redeemer.

אֱלֹהַי My God, *Berakhot 17a*
guard my tongue from evil
and my lips from deceitful speech.
To those who curse me, let my soul be silent;
may my soul be to all like the dust.
Open my heart to Your Torah
and let my soul pursue Your commandments.
As for all who plan evil against me,
swiftly thwart their counsel and frustrate their plans.

*In* חוץ לארץ*, if* כהנים *say* ברכת כהנים*, during* חזרת הש״ץ *the service continues on page 895.*
*In* ארץ ישראל*, the regular* ברכת כהנים *on page 903 is said.*
*If* כהנים *do not ascend, the following is said. See laws 370–377.*

אֱלֹהֵינוּ וֵאלֹהֵי אֲבוֹתֵינוּ, בָּרְכֵנוּ בַּבְּרָכָה הַמְשֻׁלֶּשֶׁת בַּתּוֹרָה, הַכְּתוּבָה עַל יְדֵי מֹשֶׁה עַבְדֶּךָ, הָאֲמוּרָה מִפִּי אַהֲרֹן וּבָנָיו כֹּהֲנִים עַם קְדוֹשֶׁיךָ, כָּאָמוּר

יְבָרֶכְךָ יהוה וְיִשְׁמְרֶךָ: קהל: כֵּן יְהִי רָצוֹן במדבר ו
יָאֵר יהוה פָּנָיו אֵלֶיךָ וִיחֻנֶּךָּ: קהל: כֵּן יְהִי רָצוֹן
יִשָּׂא יהוה פָּנָיו אֵלֶיךָ וְיָשֵׂם לְךָ שָׁלוֹם: קהל: כֵּן יְהִי רָצוֹן

שלום

שִׂים שָׁלוֹם טוֹבָה וּבְרָכָה
חֵן וָחֶסֶד וְרַחֲמִים עָלֵינוּ וְעַל כָּל יִשְׂרָאֵל עַמֶּךָ.
בָּרְכֵנוּ אָבִינוּ כֻּלָּנוּ כְּאֶחָד בְּאוֹר פָּנֶיךָ
כִּי בְאוֹר פָּנֶיךָ נָתַתָּ לָּנוּ יהוה אֱלֹהֵינוּ
תּוֹרַת חַיִּים וְאַהֲבַת חֶסֶד
וּצְדָקָה וּבְרָכָה וְרַחֲמִים וְחַיִּים וְשָׁלוֹם.
וְטוֹב בְּעֵינֶיךָ לְבָרֵךְ אֶת עַמְּךָ יִשְׂרָאֵל
בְּכָל עֵת וּבְכָל שָׁעָה בִּשְׁלוֹמֶךָ.
בָּרוּךְ אַתָּה יהוה, הַמְבָרֵךְ אֶת עַמּוֹ יִשְׂרָאֵל בַּשָּׁלוֹם.

*The following verse concludes the* חזרת הש״ץ.
*Some also say it here as part of the silent* עמידה*. See law 368.*

יִהְיוּ לְרָצוֹן אִמְרֵי־פִי וְהֶגְיוֹן לִבִּי לְפָנֶיךָ, יהוה צוּרִי וְגֹאֲלִי: תהלים יט

אֱלֹהַי ברכות יז.
נְצֹר לְשׁוֹנִי מֵרָע וּשְׂפָתַי מִדַּבֵּר מִרְמָה
וְלִמְקַלְלַי נַפְשִׁי תִדֹּם, וְנַפְשִׁי כֶּעָפָר לַכֹּל תִּהְיֶה.
פְּתַח לִבִּי בְּתוֹרָתֶךָ, וּבְמִצְוֹתֶיךָ תִּרְדֹּף נַפְשִׁי.
וְכָל הַחוֹשְׁבִים עָלַי רָעָה
מְהֵרָה הָפֵר עֲצָתָם וְקַלְקֵל מַחֲשַׁבְתָּם.

Act for the sake of Your name;
act for the sake of Your right hand;
act for the sake of Your holiness;
act for the sake of Your Torah.

That Your beloved ones may be delivered, *Ps. 60*
save with Your right hand and answer me.
May the words of my mouth and the meditation of my heart *Ps. 19*
find favor before You, Lord, my Rock and Redeemer.

*Bow, take three steps back, then bow, first left, then right, then center, while saying:*

May He who makes peace in His high places,
make peace for us and all Israel –
and say: Amen.

יְהִי רָצוֹן May it be Your will, Lord our God and God of our ancestors,
that the Temple be rebuilt speedily in our days,
and grant us a share in Your Torah.
And there we will serve You with reverence,
as in the days of old and as in former years.
Then the offering of Judah and Jerusalem will be pleasing to the Lord *Mal. 3*
as in the days of old and as in former years.

*On Sukkot, Hoshanot (page 914) are said at this point.*

*On other days of Yom Tov and Shabbat Ḥol HaMo'ed, Full Kaddish (page 624) is said and the service continues with "There is none like our God" on page 625.*

*On Ḥol HaMo'ed Pesaḥ, Full Kaddish (page 242) is said and the service continues with Aleinu (page 244).*

עֲשֵׂה לְמַֽעַן שְׁמֶֽךָ
עֲשֵׂה לְמַֽעַן יְמִינֶֽךָ
עֲשֵׂה לְמַֽעַן קְדֻשָּׁתֶֽךָ
עֲשֵׂה לְמַֽעַן תּוֹרָתֶֽךָ.

לְמַֽעַן יֵחָלְצוּן יְדִידֶֽיךָ, הוֹשִֽׁיעָה יְמִינְךָ וַעֲנֵֽנִי: תהלים ס

יִהְיוּ לְרָצוֹן אִמְרֵי־פִי וְהֶגְיוֹן לִבִּי לְפָנֶֽיךָ, יהוה צוּרִי וְגֹאֲלִי: תהלים יט

*Bow, take three steps back, then bow, first left, then right, then center, while saying:*

עֹשֶׂה שָׁלוֹם בִּמְרוֹמָיו
הוּא יַעֲשֶׂה שָׁלוֹם עָלֵֽינוּ וְעַל כָּל יִשְׂרָאֵל, וְאִמְרוּ אָמֵן.

יְהִי רָצוֹן מִלְּפָנֶֽיךָ יהוה אֱלֹהֵֽינוּ וֵאלֹהֵי אֲבוֹתֵֽינוּ
שֶׁיִּבָּנֶה בֵּית הַמִּקְדָּשׁ בִּמְהֵרָה בְיָמֵֽינוּ
וְתֵן חֶלְקֵֽנוּ בְּתוֹרָתֶֽךָ
וְשָׁם נַעֲבָדְךָ בְּיִרְאָה כִּימֵי עוֹלָם וּכְשָׁנִים קַדְמֹנִיּוֹת.
וְעָרְבָה לַיהוה מִנְחַת יְהוּדָה וִירוּשָׁלָֽםִ כִּימֵי עוֹלָם וּכְשָׁנִים קַדְמֹנִיּוֹת: מלאכי ג

*On* סוכות, הושענות *(page 915) are said at this point.*

*On other days of* יום טוב *and* שבת חול המועד, קדיש שלם *(page 625) is said and the service continues with* אֵין כֵּאלֹהֵֽינוּ *on page 625.*

*On* חול המועד פסח, קדיש שלם *(page 243) is said and the service continues with* עָלֵֽינוּ *(page 245).*

# Birkat Kohanim

*The following supplication is recited quietly while the Leader says "Let all that lives"* *(page 888)**:*

*In some communities, the congregation says:*

יְהִי רָצוֹן May it be Your will, LORD our God and God of our ancestors, that this blessing with which You have commanded to bless Your people Israel should be a complete blessing, with neither hindrance nor sin, now and forever.

*The Kohanim say:*

יְהִי רָצוֹן May it be Your will, LORD our God and God of our ancestors, that this blessing with which You have commanded us to bless Your people Israel should be a complete blessing, with neither hindrance nor sin, now and forever.

*The following is recited quietly by the Leader:*

אֱלֹהֵינוּ Our God and God of our fathers,
bless us with the threefold blessing in the Torah,
written by the hand of Moses Your servant
and pronounced by Aaron and his sons:

*The Leader says aloud:*

Kohanim!

*In most places, the congregation responds:*

Your holy people, as it said:

*The Kohanim say the following blessing in unison:*

בָּרוּךְ Blessed are You, LORD our God, King of the Universe,
who has made us holy with the holiness of Aaron,
and has commanded us to bless His people Israel with love.

*The first word in each sentence is said by the Leader, followed by the Kohanim. Some read silently the accompanying verses. One should remain silent and not look at the Kohanim while the blessings are being said.*

| | | |
|---|---|---|
| May [He] bless you | May the LORD, Maker of heaven and earth, bless you from Zion. | *Ps. 134* |
| The LORD | LORD, our LORD, how majestic is Your name throughout the earth. | *Ps. 8* |
| And protect you. | Protect me, God, for in You I take refuge. | *Ps. 16* |

# ברכת כהנים

*The following supplication is recited quietly while the* שליח ציבור *says* וְכֹל הַחַיִּים *(page 889):*

*In some communities, the* קהל *says:*

יְהִי רָצוֹן מִלְּפָנֶיךָ, יהוה אֱלֹהֵינוּ וֵאלֹהֵי אֲבוֹתֵינוּ, שֶׁתְּהֵא הַבְּרָכָה הַזֹּאת שֶׁצִּוִּיתָ לְבָרֵךְ אֶת עַמְּךָ יִשְׂרָאֵל בְּרָכָה שְׁלֵמָה, וְלֹא יִהְיֶה בָּהּ שׁוּם מִכְשׁוֹל וְעָוֹן מֵעַתָּה וְעַד עוֹלָם.

*The* כהנים *say:*

יְהִי רָצוֹן מִלְּפָנֶיךָ, יהוה אֱלֹהֵינוּ וֵאלֹהֵי אֲבוֹתֵינוּ, שֶׁתְּהֵא הַבְּרָכָה הַזֹּאת שֶׁצִּוִּיתָנוּ לְבָרֵךְ אֶת עַמְּךָ יִשְׂרָאֵל בְּרָכָה שְׁלֵמָה, וְלֹא יִהְיֶה בָּהּ שׁוּם מִכְשׁוֹל וְעָוֹן מֵעַתָּה וְעַד עוֹלָם.

*The following is recited quietly by the* שליח ציבור*:*

אֱלֹהֵינוּ וֵאלֹהֵי אֲבוֹתֵינוּ, בָּרְכֵנוּ בַּבְּרָכָה הַמְשֻׁלֶּשֶׁת בַּתּוֹרָה הַכְּתוּבָה עַל יְדֵי מֹשֶׁה עַבְדֶּךָ, הָאֲמוּרָה מִפִּי אַהֲרֹן וּבָנָיו

*The* שליח ציבור *says aloud:*

כֹּהֲנִים

*In most places, the* קהל *responds:*

עַם קְדוֹשֶׁךָ, כָּאָמוּר:

*The* כהנים *say the following blessing in unison:*

בָּרוּךְ אַתָּה יהוה אֱלֹהֵינוּ מֶלֶךְ הָעוֹלָם
אֲשֶׁר קִדְּשָׁנוּ בִּקְדֻשָּׁתוֹ שֶׁל אַהֲרֹן
וְצִוָּנוּ לְבָרֵךְ אֶת עַמּוֹ יִשְׂרָאֵל בְּאַהֲבָה.

*The first word in each sentence is said by the* שליח ציבור*, followed by the* כהנים*. Some read silently the accompanying verses. One should remain silent and not look at the* כהנים *while the blessings are being said.*

**יְבָרֶכְךָ** יְבָרֶכְךָ יהוה מִצִּיּוֹן, עֹשֵׂה שָׁמַיִם וָאָרֶץ: תהלים קלד

**יהוה** יהוה אֲדֹנֵינוּ, מָה־אַדִּיר שִׁמְךָ בְּכָל־הָאָרֶץ: תהלים ח

**וְיִשְׁמְרֶךָ:** שָׁמְרֵנִי אֵל, כִּי־חָסִיתִי בָךְ: תהלים טז

*Read the following silently while the Kohanim chant. Omit on Shabbat.*

Master of the Universe, I am Yours and my dreams are Yours. I have dreamt a dream and I do not know what it means. May it be Your will, Lord my God and God of my fathers, that all my dreams be, for me and all Israel, for good, whether I have dreamt about myself, or about others, or others have dreamt about me. If they are good, strengthen and reinforce them, and may they be fulfilled in me and them like the dreams of the righteous Joseph. If, though, they need healing, heal them as You healed Hezekiah King of Judah from his illness, like Miriam the prophetess from her leprosy, like Na'aman from his leprosy, like the waters of Mara by Moses our teacher, and like the waters of Jericho by Elisha. And just as You turned the curses of Balaam the wicked from curse to blessing, so turn all my dreams about me and all Israel to good; protect me, be gracious to me and accept me. Amen.

| | | |
|---|---|---|
| May [He] make shine | May God be gracious to us and bless us; may He make His face shine upon us, Selah. | *Ps. 67* |
| The Lord | The Lord, the Lord, compassionate and gracious God, slow to anger, abounding in kindness and truth. | *Ex. 34* |
| His face | Turn to me and be gracious to me, for I am alone and afflicted. | *Ps. 25* |
| On you | To You, Lord, I lift up my soul. | *Ps. 25* |
| And be gracious to you. | As the eyes of slaves turn to their master's hand, or the eyes of a slave-girl to the hand of her mistress, so our eyes are turned to the Lord our God, awaiting His favor. | *Ps. 123* |

*Read the following silently while the Kohanim chant. Omit on Shabbat.*

Master of the Universe, I am Yours and my dreams are Yours. I have dreamt a dream and I do not know what it means. May it be Your will, Lord my God and God of my fathers, that all my dreams be, for me and all Israel, for good, whether I have dreamt about myself, or about others, or others have dreamt about me. If they are good, strengthen and reinforce them, and may they be fulfilled in me and them like the dreams of the righteous Joseph. If, though, they need healing, heal them as You healed Hezekiah King of Judah from his illness, like Miriam the prophetess from her leprosy, like Na'aman from his leprosy, like the waters of Mara by Moses our teacher, and like the waters of Jericho by Elisha. And just as You turned the curses of Balaam the wicked from curse to blessing, so turn all my dreams about me and all Israel to good; protect me, be gracious to me and accept me. Amen.

*Read the following silently while the* כהנים *chant. Omit on* שבת.

רִבּוֹנוֹ שֶׁל עוֹלָם, אֲנִי שֶׁלָּךְ וַחֲלוֹמוֹתַי שֶׁלָּךְ. חֲלוֹם חָלַמְתִּי וְאֵינִי יוֹדֵעַ מַה הוּא. יְהִי רָצוֹן מִלְּפָנֶיךָ, יהוה אֱלֹהַי וֵאלֹהֵי אֲבוֹתַי, שֶׁיִּהְיוּ כָּל חֲלוֹמוֹתַי עָלַי וְעַל כָּל יִשְׂרָאֵל לְטוֹבָה, בֵּין שֶׁחָלַמְתִּי עַל עַצְמִי, וּבֵין שֶׁחָלַמְתִּי עַל אֲחֵרִים, וּבֵין שֶׁחָלְמוּ אֲחֵרִים עָלָי. אִם טוֹבִים הֵם, חַזְּקֵם וְאַמְּצֵם, וְיִתְקַיְּמוּ בִי וּבָהֶם, כַּחֲלוֹמוֹתָיו שֶׁל יוֹסֵף הַצַּדִּיק. וְאִם צְרִיכִים רְפוּאָה, רְפָאֵם כְּחִזְקִיָּהוּ מֶלֶךְ יְהוּדָה מֵחָלְיוֹ, וּכְמִרְיָם הַנְּבִיאָה מִצָּרַעְתָּהּ, וּכְנַעֲמָן מִצָּרַעְתּוֹ, וּכְמֵי מָרָה עַל יְדֵי מֹשֶׁה רַבֵּנוּ, וּכְמֵי יְרִיחוֹ עַל יְדֵי אֱלִישָׁע. וּכְשֵׁם שֶׁהָפַכְתָּ אֶת קִלְלַת בִּלְעָם הָרָשָׁע מִקְּלָלָה לִבְרָכָה, כֵּן תַּהֲפֹךְ כָּל חֲלוֹמוֹתַי עָלַי וְעַל כָּל יִשְׂרָאֵל לְטוֹבָה, וְתִשְׁמְרֵנִי וּתְחָנֵּנִי וְתִרְצֵנִי. אָמֵן.

**יָאֵר** אֱלֹהִים יְחָנֵּנוּ וִיבָרְכֵנוּ, יָאֵר פָּנָיו אִתָּנוּ סֶלָה: תהלים סז

**יהוה** יהוה, יהוה, אֵל רַחוּם וְחַנּוּן, אֶרֶךְ אַפַּיִם וְרַב־חֶסֶד וֶאֱמֶת: שמות לד

**פָּנָיו** פְּנֵה־אֵלַי וְחָנֵּנִי, כִּי־יָחִיד וְעָנִי אָנִי: תהלים כה

**אֵלֶיךָ** אֵלֶיךָ יהוה נַפְשִׁי אֶשָּׂא: תהלים כה

**וִיחֻנֶּךָּ:** הִנֵּה כְעֵינֵי עֲבָדִים אֶל־יַד אֲדוֹנֵיהֶם תהלים קכג
כְּעֵינֵי שִׁפְחָה אֶל־יַד גְּבִרְתָּהּ, כֵּן עֵינֵינוּ אֶל־יהוה אֱלֹהֵינוּ
עַד שֶׁיְּחָנֵּנוּ:

*Read the following silently while the* כהנים *chant. Omit on* שבת.

רִבּוֹנוֹ שֶׁל עוֹלָם, אֲנִי שֶׁלָּךְ וַחֲלוֹמוֹתַי שֶׁלָּךְ. חֲלוֹם חָלַמְתִּי וְאֵינִי יוֹדֵעַ מַה הוּא. יְהִי רָצוֹן מִלְּפָנֶיךָ, יהוה אֱלֹהַי וֵאלֹהֵי אֲבוֹתַי, שֶׁיִּהְיוּ כָּל חֲלוֹמוֹתַי עָלַי וְעַל כָּל יִשְׂרָאֵל לְטוֹבָה, בֵּין שֶׁחָלַמְתִּי עַל עַצְמִי, וּבֵין שֶׁחָלַמְתִּי עַל אֲחֵרִים, וּבֵין שֶׁחָלְמוּ אֲחֵרִים עָלָי. אִם טוֹבִים הֵם, חַזְּקֵם וְאַמְּצֵם, וְיִתְקַיְּמוּ בִי וּבָהֶם, כַּחֲלוֹמוֹתָיו שֶׁל יוֹסֵף הַצַּדִּיק. וְאִם צְרִיכִים רְפוּאָה, רְפָאֵם כְּחִזְקִיָּהוּ מֶלֶךְ יְהוּדָה מֵחָלְיוֹ, וּכְמִרְיָם הַנְּבִיאָה מִצָּרַעְתָּהּ, וּכְנַעֲמָן מִצָּרַעְתּוֹ, וּכְמֵי מָרָה עַל יְדֵי מֹשֶׁה רַבֵּנוּ, וּכְמֵי יְרִיחוֹ עַל יְדֵי אֱלִישָׁע. וּכְשֵׁם שֶׁהָפַכְתָּ אֶת קִלְלַת בִּלְעָם הָרָשָׁע מִקְּלָלָה לִבְרָכָה, כֵּן תַּהֲפֹךְ כָּל חֲלוֹמוֹתַי עָלַי וְעַל כָּל יִשְׂרָאֵל לְטוֹבָה, וְתִשְׁמְרֵנִי וּתְחָנֵּנִי וְתִרְצֵנִי. אָמֵן.

| | | |
|---|---|---|
| May [He] turn | May he receive a blessing from the LORD<br>and a just reward from the God of his salvation.<br>And he will win grace and good favor<br>in the eyes of God and man. | *Ps. 24*<br><br>*Prov. 3* |
| The LORD | LORD, be gracious to us; we yearn for You.<br>Be their strength every morning,<br>our salvation in time of distress. | *Is. 33* |
| His face | Do not hide Your face from me in the day of my distress.<br>Turn Your ear to me; on the day I call, swiftly answer me. | *Ps. 102* |
| Toward you | To You, enthroned in heaven, I lift my eyes. | *Ps. 123* |
| And give | They shall place My name on the children of Israel,<br>and I will bless them. | *Num. 6* |
| You | Yours, LORD, are the greatness and the power,<br>the glory, majesty and splendor, for everything<br>in heaven and earth is Yours. Yours, LORD, is the kingdom;<br>You are exalted as Head over all. | *1 Chr. 29* |
| Peace. | "Peace, peace, to those far and near," says the LORD,<br>"and I will heal him." | *Is. 57* |

*Read the following silently while the Kohanim chant. Omit on Shabbat.*

May it be Your will, LORD my God and God of my fathers, that You act for the sake of Your simple, sacred kindness and great compassion, and for the purity of Your great, mighty and awesome name of twenty-two letters derived from the verses of the priestly blessing spoken by Aaron and his sons, Your holy people. May You be close to me when I call to You. May You hear my prayer, plea and cry as You did the cry of Jacob Your perfect one who was called "a plain man." May You grant me and all the members of my household our food and sustenance, generously not meagerly, honestly not otherwise, with satisfaction not pain, from Your generous hand, just as You gave a portion of bread to eat and clothes to wear to Jacob our father who was called "a plain man." May we find love, grace, kindness and compassion in Your sight and in the eyes of all who see us. May my words in service to You be heard, as You granted Joseph Your righteous one, at the time when he was robed by his father in a cloak of fine wool, that he find grace, kindness and compassion in Your sight and in the eyes of all who saw him. May You do wonders and miracles with me, and a sign for good. Grant me success in my paths, and set in my heart understanding that I may

**יִשָּׂא** יִשָּׂא בְרָכָה מֵאֵת יהוה, וּצְדָקָה מֵאֱלֹהֵי יִשְׁעוֹ: תהלים כד
וּמְצָא־חֵן וְשֵׂכֶל־טוֹב בְּעֵינֵי אֱלֹהִים וְאָדָם: משלי ג

**יהוה** יהוה חָנֵּנוּ, לְךָ קִוִּינוּ, הֱיֵה זְרֹעָם לַבְּקָרִים ישעיה לג
אַף־יְשׁוּעָתֵנוּ בְּעֵת צָרָה:

**פָּנָיו** אַל־תַּסְתֵּר פָּנֶיךָ מִמֶּנִּי בְּיוֹם צַר לִי תהלים קב
הַטֵּה־אֵלַי אָזְנֶךָ
בְּיוֹם אֶקְרָא מַהֵר עֲנֵנִי:

**אֵלֶיךָ** אֵלֶיךָ נָשָׂאתִי אֶת־עֵינַי, הַיֹּשְׁבִי בַּשָּׁמָיִם: תהלים קכג

**וְיָשֵׂם** וְשָׂמוּ אֶת־שְׁמִי עַל־בְּנֵי יִשְׂרָאֵל, וַאֲנִי אֲבָרְכֵם: במדבר ו

**לְךָ** לְךָ יהוה הַגְּדֻלָּה וְהַגְּבוּרָה וְהַתִּפְאֶרֶת וְהַנֵּצַח וְהַהוֹד דברי הימים א׳ כט
כִּי־כֹל בַּשָּׁמַיִם וּבָאָרֶץ, לְךָ יהוה הַמַּמְלָכָה
וְהַמִּתְנַשֵּׂא לְכֹל לְרֹאשׁ:

**שָׁלוֹם:** שָׁלוֹם שָׁלוֹם לָרָחוֹק וְלַקָּרוֹב, אָמַר יהוה, וּרְפָאתִיו: ישעיה נז

*Read the following silently while the* כהנים *chant. Omit on* שבת*.*

יְהִי רָצוֹן מִלְּפָנֶיךָ, יהוה אֱלֹהַי וֵאלֹהֵי אֲבוֹתַי, שֶׁתַּעֲשֶׂה לְמַעַן קְדֻשַּׁת חֲסָדֶיךָ וְגֹדֶל רַחֲמֶיךָ הַפְּשׁוּטִים, וּלְמַעַן טָהֳרַת שִׁמְךָ הַגָּדוֹל הַגִּבּוֹר וְהַנּוֹרָא, בֶּן עֶשְׂרִים וּשְׁתַּיִם אוֹתִיּוֹת הַיּוֹצֵא מִפְּסוּקִים שֶׁל בִּרְכַּת כֹּהֲנִים הָאֲמוּרָה מִפִּי אַהֲרֹן וּבָנָיו עַם קְדוֹשֶׁךָ, שֶׁתִּהְיֶה קָרוֹב לִי בְּקָרְאִי לָךְ, וְתִשְׁמַע תְּפִלָּתִי נַאֲקָתִי וְאֶנְקָתִי תָּמִיד, כְּשֵׁם שֶׁשָּׁמַעְתָּ אֶנְקַת יַעֲקֹב תְּמִימֶךָ הַנִּקְרָא אִישׁ תָּם. וְתִתֶּן לִי וּלְכָל נַפְשׁוֹת בֵּיתִי מְזוֹנוֹתֵינוּ וּפַרְנָסָתֵנוּ בְּרֶוַח וְלֹא בְצִמְצוּם, בְּהֶתֵּר וְלֹא בְאִסּוּר, בְּנַחַת וְלֹא בְצַעַר, מִתַּחַת יָדְךָ הָרְחָבָה, כְּשֵׁם שֶׁנָּתַתָּ פִּסַּת לֶחֶם לֶאֱכֹל וּבֶגֶד לִלְבֹּשׁ לְיַעֲקֹב אָבִינוּ הַנִּקְרָא אִישׁ תָּם. וְתִתְּנֵנוּ לְאַהֲבָה, לְחֵן וּלְחֶסֶד וּלְרַחֲמִים בְּעֵינֶיךָ וּבְעֵינֵי כָל רוֹאֵינוּ, וְיִהְיוּ דְבָרַי נִשְׁמָעִים לַעֲבוֹדָתֶךָ, כְּשֵׁם שֶׁנָּתַתָּ אֶת יוֹסֵף צַדִּיקֶךָ בְּשָׁעָה שֶׁהִלְבִּישׁוֹ אָבִיו כְּתֹנֶת פַּסִּים לְחֵן וּלְחֶסֶד וּלְרַחֲמִים בְּעֵינֶיךָ וּבְעֵינֵי כָל רוֹאָיו. וְתַעֲשֶׂה עִמִּי נִפְלָאוֹת וְנִסִּים, וּלְטוֹבָה אוֹת, וְתַצְלִיחֵנִי בִּדְרָכַי, וְתֵן בְּלִבִּי בִּינָה לְהָבִין וּלְהַשְׂכִּיל

understand, discern and fulfill all the words of Your Torah's teachings and mysteries. Save me from errors and purify my thoughts and my heart to serve You and be in awe of You. Prolong my days (*add, where appropriate:* and those of my father, mother, wife, husband, son/s, and daughter/s) in joy and happiness, with much strength and peace. Amen, Selah.

*The Leader continues with "Grant peace" below.*

*The congregation says:*
אַדִּיר Majestic One on high who dwells in power: You are peace and Your name is peace. May it be Your will to bestow on us and on Your people the house of Israel, life and blessing as a safeguard for peace.

*The Kohanim say:*
רִבּוֹנוֹ Master of the Universe: we have done what You have decreed for us. So too may You deal with us as You have promised us. Look down from Your holy dwelling place, from heaven, and bless Your people Israel and the land You have given us as You promised on oath to our ancestors, a land flowing with milk and honey. *Deut. 26*

*The Leader continues:*

שִׂים שָׁלוֹם Grant peace, goodness and blessing,
grace, loving-kindness and compassion to us
and all Israel Your people.
Bless us, our Father, all as one,
with the light of Your face,
for by the light of Your face You have given us, Lord our God,
the Torah of life and love of kindness,
righteousness, blessing, compassion, life and peace.
May it be good in Your eyes to bless Your people Israel
at every time, in every hour, with Your peace.
Blessed are You, Lord,
who blesses His people Israel with peace.

*The following verse concludes the Leader's Repetition of the Amida (see law 368).*
May the words of my mouth and the meditation of my heart *Ps. 19*
find favor before You, Lord, my Rock and Redeemer.

וּלְקַיֵּם אֶת כָּל דִּבְרֵי תַלְמוּד תּוֹרָתֶךָ וְסוֹדוֹתֶיהָ, וְתַצִּילֵנִי מִשְּׁגִיאוֹת, וּתְטַהֵר רַעְיוֹנַי וְלִבִּי לַעֲבוֹדָתֶךָ, וְתַאֲרִיךְ יָמַי (וִימֵי אָבִי וְאִמִּי / וְאִשְׁתִּי / וּבַעְלִי / וּבָנַי וּבְנוֹתַי) בְּטוֹב וּבִנְעִימוֹת, בְּרֹב עֹז וְשָׁלוֹם, אָמֵן סֶלָה.

*The* שליח ציבור *continues with* שִׂים שָׁלוֹם *below.*

*The* קהל *says:*

אַדִּיר בַּמָּרוֹם שׁוֹכֵן בִּגְבוּרָה, אַתָּה שָׁלוֹם וְשִׁמְךָ שָׁלוֹם. יְהִי רָצוֹן שֶׁתָּשִׂים עָלֵינוּ וְעַל כָּל עַמְּךָ בֵּית יִשְׂרָאֵל חַיִּים וּבְרָכָה לְמִשְׁמֶרֶת שָׁלוֹם.

*The* כהנים *say:*

רִבּוֹנוֹ שֶׁל עוֹלָם, עָשִׂינוּ מַה שֶּׁגָּזַרְתָּ עָלֵינוּ, אַף אַתָּה עֲשֵׂה עִמָּנוּ כְּמוֹ שֶׁהִבְטַחְתָּנוּ. הַשְׁקִיפָה מִמְּעוֹן קָדְשְׁךָ מִן־הַשָּׁמַיִם, וּבָרֵךְ אֶת־עַמְּךָ אֶת־יִשְׂרָאֵל, וְאֵת הָאֲדָמָה אֲשֶׁר נָתַתָּה לָנוּ, כַּאֲשֶׁר נִשְׁבַּעְתָּ לַאֲבֹתֵינוּ, אֶרֶץ זָבַת חָלָב וּדְבָשׁ: דברים כו

*The* שליח ציבור *continues:*

שִׂים שָׁלוֹם טוֹבָה וּבְרָכָה
חֵן וָחֶסֶד וְרַחֲמִים עָלֵינוּ וְעַל כָּל יִשְׂרָאֵל עַמֶּךָ.
בָּרְכֵנוּ אָבִינוּ כֻּלָּנוּ כְּאֶחָד בְּאוֹר פָּנֶיךָ
כִּי בְאוֹר פָּנֶיךָ נָתַתָּ לָּנוּ יהוה אֱלֹהֵינוּ
תּוֹרַת חַיִּים וְאַהֲבַת חֶסֶד
וּצְדָקָה וּבְרָכָה וְרַחֲמִים וְחַיִּים וְשָׁלוֹם.
וְטוֹב בְּעֵינֶיךָ לְבָרֵךְ אֶת עַמְּךָ יִשְׂרָאֵל
בְּכָל עֵת וּבְכָל שָׁעָה בִּשְׁלוֹמֶךָ.
בָּרוּךְ אַתָּה יהוה, הַמְבָרֵךְ אֶת עַמּוֹ יִשְׂרָאֵל בַּשָּׁלוֹם.

*The following verse concludes the* חזרת הש״ץ *(see law 368).*

יִהְיוּ לְרָצוֹן אִמְרֵי־פִי וְהֶגְיוֹן לִבִּי לְפָנֶיךָ, יהוה צוּרִי וְגֹאֲלִי: תהלים יט

# BIRKAT KOHANIM IN ISRAEL

*In Israel, the following is said by the Leader during the Repetition of the Amida when Kohanim bless the congregation. If there is more than one Kohen, a member of the congregation calls: (See laws 370–377.)*

Kohanim!

*The Kohanim respond:*

Blessed are You, LORD our God, King of the Universe,
who has made us holy with the holiness of Aaron,
and has commanded us to bless His people Israel with love.

*The Leader calls word by word, followed by the Kohanim:*

יְבָרֶכְךָ May the LORD bless you and protect you. (*Cong:* Amen.) *Num. 6*
May the LORD make His face shine on you and be gracious to you.
(*Cong:* Amen.)
May the LORD turn His face toward you, and grant you peace. (*Cong:* Amen.)

*The Leader continues with "Grant peace" below.*

*The congregation says:*
אַדִּיר Majestic One on high who dwells in power: You are peace and Your name is peace. May it be Your will to bestow on us and on Your people the house of Israel, life and blessing as a safeguard for peace.

*The Kohanim say:*
רִבּוֹנוֹ Master of the Universe: we have done what You have decreed for us. So too may You deal with us as You have promised us. Look down from Your holy dwelling place, from heaven, and bless Your people Israel and the land You have given us as You promised on oath to our ancestors, a land flowing with milk and honey. *Deut. 26*

*The Leader continues:*

שִׂים שָׁלוֹם Grant peace, goodness and blessing, grace, loving-kindness and compassion to us and all Israel Your people. Bless us, our Father, all as one, with the light of Your face, for by the light of Your face You have given us, LORD our God, the Torah of life and love of kindness, righteousness, blessing, compassion, life and peace. May it be good in Your eyes to bless Your people Israel at every time, in every hour, with Your peace.

*Between Rosh HaShana & Yom Kippur:* In the book of life, blessing, peace and prosperity,
may we and all Your people the house of Israel
be remembered and written before You for a good life, and for peace.

Blessed are You, LORD, who blesses His people Israel with peace.

*The following verse concludes the Leader's Repetition of the Amida. See law 368.*

May the words of my mouth and the meditation of my heart
find favor before You, LORD, my Rock and Redeemer. *Ps. 19*

# ברכת כהנים בארץ ישראל

*In* ארץ ישראל, *the following is said by the* שליח ציבור *during the* חזרת הש״ץ *when* כהנים *say* ברכת כהנים. *If there is more than one* כהן, *a member of the* קהל *calls:* (*See laws 370–377.*)

## כֹּהֲנִים

*The* כהנים *respond:*

בָּרוּךְ אַתָּה יהוה אֱלֹהֵינוּ מֶלֶךְ הָעוֹלָם, אֲשֶׁר קִדְּשָׁנוּ בִּקְדֻשָּׁתוֹ שֶׁל אַהֲרֹן וְצִוָּנוּ לְבָרֵךְ אֶת עַמּוֹ יִשְׂרָאֵל בְּאַהֲבָה.

*The* שליח ציבור *calls word by word, followed by the* כהנים*:*

במדבר ו
יְבָרֶכְךָ יהוה וְיִשְׁמְרֶךָ: קהל: אָמֵן
יָאֵר יהוה פָּנָיו אֵלֶיךָ וִיחֻנֶּךָּ: קהל: אָמֵן
יִשָּׂא יהוה פָּנָיו אֵלֶיךָ וְיָשֵׂם לְךָ שָׁלוֹם: קהל: אָמֵן

*The* שליח ציבור *continues with* שִׂים שָׁלוֹם *below.*

*The* קהל *says:*

אַדִּיר בַּמָּרוֹם שׁוֹכֵן בִּגְבוּרָה, אַתָּה שָׁלוֹם וְשִׁמְךָ שָׁלוֹם. יְהִי רָצוֹן שֶׁתָּשִׂים עָלֵינוּ וְעַל כָּל עַמְּךָ בֵּית יִשְׂרָאֵל חַיִּים וּבְרָכָה לְמִשְׁמֶרֶת שָׁלוֹם.

*The* כהנים *say:*

רִבּוֹנוֹ שֶׁל עוֹלָם, עָשִׂינוּ מַה שֶּׁגָּזַרְתָּ עָלֵינוּ, אַף אַתָּה עֲשֵׂה עִמָּנוּ כְּמוֹ שֶׁהִבְטַחְתָּנוּ. הַשְׁקִיפָה מִמְּעוֹן דברים כו
קָדְשְׁךָ מִן־הַשָּׁמַיִם, וּבָרֵךְ אֶת־עַמְּךָ אֶת־יִשְׂרָאֵל, וְאֵת הָאֲדָמָה אֲשֶׁר נָתַתָּה לָנוּ, כַּאֲשֶׁר נִשְׁבַּעְתָּ לַאֲבֹתֵינוּ, אֶרֶץ זָבַת חָלָב וּדְבָשׁ:

*The* שליח ציבור *continues:*

שִׂים שָׁלוֹם טוֹבָה וּבְרָכָה, חֵן וָחֶסֶד וְרַחֲמִים עָלֵינוּ וְעַל כָּל יִשְׂרָאֵל עַמֶּךָ. בָּרְכֵנוּ אָבִינוּ כֻּלָּנוּ כְּאֶחָד בְּאוֹר פָּנֶיךָ, כִּי בְאוֹר פָּנֶיךָ נָתַתָּ לָּנוּ יהוה אֱלֹהֵינוּ, תּוֹרַת חַיִּים וְאַהֲבַת חֶסֶד, וּצְדָקָה וּבְרָכָה וְרַחֲמִים וְחַיִּים וְשָׁלוֹם. וְטוֹב בְּעֵינֶיךָ לְבָרֵךְ אֶת עַמְּךָ יִשְׂרָאֵל, בְּכָל עֵת וּבְכָל שָׁעָה בִּשְׁלוֹמֶךָ.

בעשרת ימי תשובה: בְּסֵפֶר חַיִּים, בְּרָכָה וְשָׁלוֹם, וּפַרְנָסָה טוֹבָה, נִזָּכֵר וְנִכָּתֵב לְפָנֶיךָ, אֲנַחְנוּ וְכָל עַמְּךָ בֵּית יִשְׂרָאֵל, לְחַיִּים טוֹבִים וּלְשָׁלוֹם.

בָּרוּךְ אַתָּה יהוה, הַמְבָרֵךְ אֶת עַמּוֹ יִשְׂרָאֵל בַּשָּׁלוֹם.

*The following verse concludes the* חזרת הש״ץ. *See law 368.*

תהלים יט
יִהְיוּ לְרָצוֹן אִמְרֵי־פִי וְהֶגְיוֹן לִבִּי לְפָנֶיךָ, יהוה צוּרִי וְגֹאֲלִי:

# Prayer for Dew

*On the first day of Pesaḥ, the Ark is opened at the Repetition of the Musaf Amida. All stand. In Israel, the Prayer for Dew is said before the silent Amida and starts on the next page.*

When I proclaim the LORD's name, give glory to our God. *Deut. 32*
O LORD, open my lips, so that my mouth may declare Your praise. *Ps. 51*

PATRIARCHS

▾בָּרוּךְ▾ Blessed are You, LORD our God and God of our fathers, God of Abraham, God of Isaac and God of Jacob; the great, mighty and awesome God, God Most High, who bestows acts of loving-kindness and creates all, who remembers the loving-kindness of the fathers and will bring a Redeemer to their children's children for the sake of His name, in love. King, Helper, Savior, Shield:

בְּדַעְתּוֹ With His consent I will speak of hidden things,
that for this people, by this prayer,
there may be joy in dew.
May the valley and its vegetation
be renewed through dew,
springing up under His shade anew.
Sign of regeneration,
shield of future generations – dew.

▾Blessed are You, LORD, Shield of Abraham.

אַתָּה גִּבּוֹר You are eternally mighty, LORD.
You give life to the dead and have great power to save.

תְּהוֹמוֹת The depths of the earth
yearn for drops of dew;
all the green pastures long for them.
The mention of dew adds to His might,
inscribed as we approach in the Musaf prayer.
Dew – to revive those [buried] in the clefts of the rocks.

# תפילת טל

*On the first day of* פסח, *the* ארון קודש *is opened at the* חזרת הש״ץ *of the* מוסף עמידה. *All stand. In* ארץ ישראל, תפילת טל *is said before the silent* עמידה *and starts on the next page.*

כִּי שֵׁם יהוה אֶקְרָא, הָבוּ גֹדֶל לֵאלֹהֵינוּ: דברים לב

אֲדֹנָי, שְׂפָתַי תִּפְתָּח, וּפִי יַגִּיד תְּהִלָּתֶךָ: תהלים נא

אבות

בָּרוּךְ אַתָּה יהוה, אֱלֹהֵינוּ וֵאלֹהֵי אֲבוֹתֵינוּ, אֱלֹהֵי אַבְרָהָם, אֱלֹהֵי יִצְחָק, וֵאלֹהֵי יַעֲקֹב, הָאֵל הַגָּדוֹל הַגִּבּוֹר וְהַנּוֹרָא, אֵל עֶלְיוֹן, גּוֹמֵל חֲסָדִים טוֹבִים, וְקוֹנֵה הַכֹּל, וְזוֹכֵר חַסְדֵי אָבוֹת, וּמֵבִיא גוֹאֵל לִבְנֵי בְנֵיהֶם לְמַעַן שְׁמוֹ בְּאַהֲבָה. מֶלֶךְ עוֹזֵר וּמוֹשִׁיעַ וּמָגֵן.

בְּדַעְתּוֹ אַבִּיעָה חִידוֹת\
בְּעַם זוּ בְּזוּ בְּטַל לְהַחֲדוֹת.\
טַל גַּיא וּדְשָׁאֶיהָ לַחֲדוֹת\
דָּצִים בְּצִלּוֹ לְהֵחָדוֹת.\
אוֹת יַלְדוּת טַל, לְהָגֵן לְתוֹלָדוֹת

בָּרוּךְ אַתָּה יהוה, מָגֵן אַבְרָהָם.

אַתָּה גִּבּוֹר לְעוֹלָם אֲדֹנָי\
מְחַיֵּה מֵתִים אַתָּה, רַב לְהוֹשִׁיעַ

תְּהוֹמוֹת הֲדוֹם לִרְסִיסוֹ כְּסוּפִים\
וְכָל נְאוֹת דֶּשֶׁא לוֹ נִכְסָפִים.\
טַל זִכְרוֹ גְּבוּרוֹת מוֹסִיפִים\
חָקוּק בְּגִישַׁת מוּסָפִים\
טַל, לְהַחֲיוֹת בּוֹ נְקוּקֵי סְעִיפִים.

*In Israel start here:*

Our God and God of our fathers:

טַל Dew – Grant it to favor Your land;
in Your jubilation, set us as a blessing.
Increase for us our corn and wine.
Establish the city in which You delight – With dew.

טַל Dew – Decree it for a good and resplendent year;
may the fruit of the earth be fine and fair.
As for the city now deserted like a hut,
place it in Your hand like a crown – With dew.

טַל Dew – May it drop gently on the blessed land;
satisfy us with a blessing of the rich gifts of heaven.
Send light in the midst of darkness
to the stock [Israel] who are drawn to You – With dew.

טַל Dew – Let it sweeten the mountain streams;
let the chosen ones taste Your magnanimity.
Free Your beloved ones from captivity,
then sweetly we will raise our voices and sing – With dew.

טַל Dew – May it fill our granaries to overflowing.
Would that now You might renew our days.
Beloved! Let our name endure as Yours.
Make us like a well-watered garden – With dew.

טַל Dew – With it bless our food;
in our fertile lands may there be no scarcity.
The nation You once led like a flock,
on her please, we pray, bestow Your favor – With dew.

*Leader:*

For You, Lord our God, make the wind blow and the dew fall.

*Congregation then Leader, responsively:*

For blessing, and not for curse. *Cong:* Amen.
For life, and not for death. *Cong:* Amen.
For plenty, and not for scarcity. *Cong:* Amen.

*The Ark is closed. In the Diaspora, the Leader continues the Repetition with "He sustains the living" on page 868. In Israel, the Leader says Half Kaddish and the Musaf Amida is recited with the addition of "He makes the dew fall."*

*In* ארץ ישראל *start here:*

## אֱלֹהֵינוּ וֵאלֹהֵי אֲבוֹתֵינוּ

טַל תֵּן לִרְצוֹת אַרְצָךְ שִׁיתֵנוּ בְרָכָה בְּדִיצָךְ
רֹב דָּגָן וְתִירוֹשׁ בְּהַפְרִיצָךְ קוֹמֵם עִיר בָּהּ חֶפְצָךְ בְּטָל.

טַל צַוֵּה שָׁנָה טוֹבָה וּמְעֻטֶּרֶת פְּרִי הָאָרֶץ לְגָאוֹן וּלְתִפְאֶרֶת
עִיר כַּסֻּכָּה נוֹתֶרֶת שִׂימָהּ בְּיָדְךָ עֲטֶרֶת בְּטָל.

טַל נֹפֵף עֲלֵי אֶרֶץ בְּרוּכָה מִמֶּגֶד שָׁמַיִם שַׂבְּעֵנוּ בְרָכָה
לְהָאִיר מִתּוֹךְ חֲשֵׁכָה כַּנָּה אַחֲרֶיךָ מְשׁוּכָה בְּטָל.

טַל יַעֲסִיס צוּף הָרִים טְעֵם בִּמְאוֹדֶיךָ מֻבְחָרִים
חֲנוּנֶיךָ חַלֵּץ מִמַּסְגֵּרִים זִמְרָה נַנְעִים וְקוֹל נָרִים בְּטָל.

טַל וְשֹׂבַע מַלֵּא אֲסָמֵינוּ הֲכָעֵת תְּחַדֵּשׁ יָמֵינוּ
דּוֹד, כְּעֶרְכְּךָ הַעֲמֵד שְׁמֵנוּ גַּן רָוֶה שִׂימֵנוּ בְּטָל.

טַל בּוֹ תְּבָרֵךְ מָזוֹן בְּמַשְׁמַנֵּינוּ אַל יְהִי רָזוֹן
אֲיֻמָּה אֲשֶׁר הִסַּעְתָּ כַּצֹּאן אָנָּא תָּפֵק לָהּ רָצוֹן בְּטָל.

שליח ציבור:

## שָׁאַתָּה הוּא יהוה אֱלֹהֵינוּ
## מַשִּׁיב הָרוּחַ וּמוֹרִיד הַטָּל

שליח ציבור *then* קהל*, responsively:*

לִבְרָכָה וְלֹא לִקְלָלָה קהל: אָמֵן
לְחַיִּים וְלֹא לְמָוֶת קהל: אָמֵן
לְשֹׂבַע וְלֹא לְרָזוֹן קהל: אָמֵן

*The* ארון קודש *is closed. In* חוץ לארץ*, the* שליח ציבור *continues the* חזרת הש״ץ *with* מְכַלְכֵּל חַיִּים *on page 869.* *In* ארץ ישראל*, the* שליח ציבור *says* חצי קדיש *and the* מוסף עמידה *is recited with the addition of* מוֹרִיד הַטָּל.

# Prayer for Rain

*On Shemini Atzeret, the Ark is opened at the Repetition of the Musaf Amida. All stand.*
*In Israel, the Prayer for Rain is said before the silent Amida and starts on the next page.*

When I proclaim the LORD's name, give glory to our God. *Deut. 32*
O LORD, open my lips, so that my mouth may declare Your praise. *Ps. 51*

PATRIARCHS

▾בָּרוּךְ Blessed are You, LORD our God and God of our fathers, God of Abraham, God of Isaac and God of Jacob; the great, mighty and awesome God, God Most High, who bestows acts of loving-kindness and creates all, who remembers the loving-kindness of the fathers and will bring a Redeemer to their children's children for the sake of His name, in love. King, Helper, Savior, Shield:

אַף־בְּרִי Af-bri is the name of the angel of rain,
Who overcasts [the sky],
forms clouds and precipitates them, making them rain
Water to crown the valley with green.
May rain not be withheld from us because
  of our unpaid debts.
May the merit of the faithful Patriarchs
protect their offspring who pray for rain.

▾Blessed are You, LORD, Shield of Abraham.

אַתָּה You are eternally mighty, O LORD.
You give life to the dead and have great power to save.

יַטְרִיחַ May He make him apportion due portions of rain,
Moistening the earth with drops pure as opal.
In the Torah You symbolized Your might by water.
Its drops refresh those in whom was breathed
  the breath of life,
Reviving those who make mention of the powers of rain.

# תפילת גשם

*On* שמיני עצרת*, the* ארון קודש *is opened at the* חזרת הש״ץ *of the* מוסף עמידה*. All stand. In* ארץ ישראל*,* תפילת גשם *is said before the silent* עמידה *and starts on the next page.*

כִּי שֵׁם יהוה אֶקְרָא, הָבוּ גֹדֶל לֵאלֹהֵינוּ: דברים לב

אֲדֹנָי, שְׂפָתַי תִּפְתָּח, וּפִי יַגִּיד תְּהִלָּתֶךָ: תהלים נא

אבות

בָּרוּךְ אַתָּה יהוה, אֱלֹהֵינוּ וֵאלֹהֵי אֲבוֹתֵינוּ, אֱלֹהֵי אַבְרָהָם, אֱלֹהֵי יִצְחָק, וֵאלֹהֵי יַעֲקֹב, הָאֵל הַגָּדוֹל הַגִּבּוֹר וְהַנּוֹרָא, אֵל עֶלְיוֹן, גּוֹמֵל חֲסָדִים טוֹבִים, וְקוֹנֵה הַכֹּל, וְזוֹכֵר חַסְדֵי אָבוֹת, וּמֵבִיא גוֹאֵל לִבְנֵי בְנֵיהֶם לְמַעַן שְׁמוֹ בְּאַהֲבָה. מֶלֶךְ עוֹזֵר וּמוֹשִׁיעַ וּמָגֵן.

אַף־בְּרִי אֻתַּת שֵׁם שַׂר מָטָר\
לְהַעֲבִיב וּלְהַעֲנִין לְהָרִיק וּלְהַמְטַר\
מַיִם אִבִּים בָּם גֵּיא לַעֲטַר\
לְבַל יֵעָצֵרוּ בְּנִשְׁיוֹן שְׁטָר\
אֱמוּנִים גְּנוֹן בָּם, שׁוֹאֲלֵי מָטָר.

בָּרוּךְ אַתָּה יהוה, מָגֵן אַבְרָהָם.

אַתָּה גִּבּוֹר לְעוֹלָם אֲדֹנָי, מְחַיֵּה מֵתִים אַתָּה, רַב לְהוֹשִׁיעַ

יַטְרִיחַ לְפַלֵּג מִפֶּלֶג גֶּשֶׁם\
לְמוֹגֵג פְּנֵי נֶשִׁי בְּצַחוּת לֶשֶׁם\
מַיִם לְאַדְּרָךְ כִּנִּיתָ בְּרֶשֶׁם\
לְהַרְגִּיעַ בְּרַעֲפָם לִנְפוּחֵי נֶשֶׁם\
לְהַחֲיוֹת מַזְכִּירִים גְּבוּרוֹת הַגֶּשֶׁם.

*In Israel start here:*

Our God and God of our fathers.

זְכוֹר Remember the Patriarch [Abraham]
who followed You like water.
You blessed him like a tree planted beside streams of water.
You shielded him and rescued him from fire and water.
You sought him because he sowed [righteousness]
by all waters.
*Cong:* For his sake do not withhold water.

זְכוֹר Remember [Isaac] whose birth was foretold
when [Abraham said] "Let there be brought some water." *Gen. 18*
You told his father to offer him,
to shed his blood like water.
[Isaac], too, cared and poured out his soul like water.
When he dug, he discovered wells of water.
*Cong:* For his righteousness' sake grant abundant water.

זְכוֹר Remember [Jacob] who carried his staff
and crossed the Jordan's water.
With steadfast heart he rolled away the stone
from the well of water.
He wrestled with an angel composed of fire and water,
So You promised to be with him through fire and water.
*Cong:* For his sake do not withhold water.

זְכוֹר Remember [Moses] who in a reed basket
was drawn out of the water.
They said: "He drew water for us, and gave the flock water."
When Your treasured people thirsted for water,
He struck the rock and out gushed water.
*Cong:* For his righteousness' sake grant abundant water.

*In* ארץ ישראל *start here:*

## אֱלֹהֵינוּ וֵאלֹהֵי אֲבוֹתֵינוּ

זְכוֹר אָב נִמְשַׁךְ אַחֲרֶיךָ כַּמַּיִם
בֵּרַכְתּוֹ כְּעֵץ שָׁתוּל עַל פַּלְגֵי מַיִם
גְּנַנְתּוֹ, הִצַּלְתּוֹ מֵאֵשׁ וּמִמַּיִם
דְּרַשְׁתּוֹ בְּזָרְעוֹ עַל כָּל מָיִם.
קהל: בַּעֲבוּרוֹ אַל תִּמְנַע מָיִם.

זְכוֹר הַנּוֹלָד בִּבְשׂוֹרַת יֻקַּח־נָא מְעַט־מַיִם בראשית יח
וְשַׂחְתָּ לְהוֹרוֹ לְשָׁחֲטוֹ לִשְׁפֹּךְ דָּמוֹ כַּמַּיִם
זְהֵר גַּם הוּא לִשְׁפֹּךְ לֵב כַּמַּיִם
חָפַר וּמָצָא בְּאֵרוֹת מָיִם.
קהל: בְּצִדְקוֹ חֹן חַשְׁרַת מָיִם.

זְכוֹר טָעַן מַקְלוֹ וְעָבַר יַרְדֵּן מַיִם
יִחַד לֵב וְגָל אֶבֶן מִפִּי בְּאֵר מַיִם
כְּנֶאֱבַק לוֹ שַׂר בָּלוּל מֵאֵשׁ וּמִמַּיִם
לָכֵן הִבְטַחְתּוֹ הֱיוֹת עִמּוֹ בָּאֵשׁ וּבַמָּיִם.
קהל: בַּעֲבוּרוֹ אַל תִּמְנַע מָיִם.

זְכוֹר מָשׁוּי בְּתֵבַת גֹּמֶא מִן הַמַּיִם
נָמוּ דָּלֹה דָלָה וְהִשְׁקָה צֹאן מַיִם
סְגוּלֶיךָ עֵת צָמְאוּ לַמַּיִם
עַל הַסֶּלַע הָךְ, וַיֵּצְאוּ מָיִם.
קהל: בְּצִדְקוֹ חֹן חַשְׁרַת מָיִם.

זְכוֹר Remember [Aaron], chief officer of the Temple,
who immersed five times in water.
He went and washed his hands in the sanctifying water.
He called out and sprinkled blood,
purifying the people as if with water.
He kept apart from the people who were as unruly as water.
*Cong:* For his sake do not withhold water.

זְכוֹר Remember the twelve tribes
You brought through the divided water,
For whom You sweetened the bitterness of the water.
For Your sake their descendants' blood
was spilled like water.
Turn to us, for troubles engulf our souls like water.
*Cong:* For their righteousness' sake grant abundant water.

*Leader:*

For You, LORD our God,
make the wind blow and the rain fall.

*Congregation then Leader, responsively:*

For blessing, and not for curse. *Cong:* Amen.
For life, and not for death. *Cong:* Amen.
For plenty, and not for scarcity. *Cong:* Amen.

*The Ark is closed. The Leader continues the Repetition with "He sustains the living" on page 868. In Israel, the Leader says Half Kaddish, and the Musaf Amida is said with the addition of "He makes the wind blow and the rain fall."*

זְכוֹר פְּקִיד שָׁתוֹת, טוֹבֵל חָמֵשׁ טְבִילוֹת בַּמַּיִם
צוֹעֶה וּמַרְחִיץ כַּפָּיו בְּקִדּוּשׁ מַיִם
קוֹרֵא וּמַזֶּה טָהֳרַת מַיִם
רֻחַק מֵעַם פַּחַז כַּמָּיִם.
קהל: בַּעֲבוּרוֹ אַל תִּמְנַע מָיִם.

זְכוֹר שְׁנֵים עָשָׂר שְׁבָטִים, שֶׁהֶעֱבַרְתָּ בְּגִזְרַת מַיִם
שֶׁהִמְתַּקְתָּ לָמוֹ מְרִירוּת מַיִם
תּוֹלְדוֹתָם נִשְׁפַּךְ דָּמָם עָלֶיךָ כַּמַּיִם
תֵּפֶן, כִּי נַפְשֵׁנוּ אָפְפוּ מָיִם.
קהל: בְּצִדְקָם חֹן חַשְׁרַת מָיִם.

שליח ציבור:

**שָׁאַתָּה הוּא יהוה אֱלֹהֵינוּ**
**מַשִּׁיב הָרְוּחַ וּמוֹרִיד הַגֶּשֶׁם**

*then* קהל *,responsively* שליח ציבור

לִבְרָכָה וְלֹא לִקְלָלָה קהל: אָמֵן
לְחַיִּים וְלֹא לְמָוֶת קהל: אָמֵן
לְשֹׂבַע וְלֹא לְרָזוֹן קהל: אָמֵן

*The* ארון קודש *is closed. The* שליח ציבור *continues the* חזרת הש״ץ *with* מְכַלְכֵּל חַיִּים *on page 869. In* ארץ ישראל*, the* שליח ציבור *says* חצי קדיש*, and the* מוסף עמידה *is said with the addition of* מַשִּׁיב הָרְוּחַ וּמוֹרִיד הַגֶּשֶׁם.

# Hoshanot

*Hoshanot are said after the Leader's Repetition of the Amida of Musaf (and in some congregations after Hallel) on every day of Sukkot.*

*On weekdays, the Ark is opened, and a Torah scroll is taken to the Bima. Members of the congregation who have a Lulav and Etrog make a circuit around the Bima and say Hoshanot. Mourners do not participate in the circuit.*

*At the conclusion of the Hoshanot, the Torah scroll is returned to the Ark, which is then closed.*

*On Shabbat, turn to page 922. On Hoshana Raba, turn to page 928.*

| *If first day of Sukkot falls on* | *On first day* | *On second day* | *On third day* | *On fourth day* | *On fifth day* | *On sixth day* |
|---|---|---|---|---|---|---|
| *Monday* | For the sake of Your truth | The Foundation Stone | I shall lay out my prayer | "I am a wall," said the people | God of all salvation | A people guarded |
| *Tuesday* | For the sake of Your truth | The Foundation Stone | I shall lay out my prayer | God of all salvation | A people guarded | Master who saves |
| *Thursday* | For the sake of Your truth | The Foundation Stone | A people guarded | I shall lay out my prayer | God of all salvation | Master who saves |
| *Shabbat* | A people guarded | For the sake of Your truth | I shall lay out my prayer | The Foundation Stone | God of all salvation | Master who saves |

*Leader then congregation:*

הוֹשַׁעְנָא Save us, please for Your sake, our God, save us please.

*Leader then congregation:*

Save us, please for Your sake, our Creator, save us, please.

*Leader then congregation:*

Save us, please for Your sake, our Redeemer, save us, please.

*Leader then congregation:*

Save us, please for Your sake, You who seek us, save us, please.

# הושענות

*הושענות are said after the* חזרת הש״ץ *of the* מוסף עמידה *(and in some congregations after* הלל*) on every day of* סוכות.

*On weekdays, the* ארון קודש *is opened, and a* ספר תורה *is taken to the* בימה. *Members of the* קהל *who have a* לולב *and* אתרוג *make a circuit around the* בימה *and say* הושענות. *Mourners do not participate in the circuit.*

*At the conclusion of the* הושענות*, the* ספר תורה *is returned to the* ארון קודש*, which is then closed.*

*On* שבת*, turn to page 923. On* הושענא רבה*, turn to page 929.*

| *If first day of* סוכות *falls on* | *On first day* | *On second day* | *On third day* | *On fourth day* | *On fifth day* | *On sixth day* |
|---|---|---|---|---|---|---|
| *Monday* | לְמַעַן אֲמִתָּךְ | אֶבֶן שְׁתִיָּה | אֶעֱרֹךְ שׁוּעִי | אֹם אֲנִי חוֹמָה | אֵל לְמוֹשָׁעוֹת | אֹם נְצוּרָה |
| *Tuesday* | לְמַעַן אֲמִתָּךְ | אֶבֶן שְׁתִיָּה | אֶעֱרֹךְ שׁוּעִי | אֵל לְמוֹשָׁעוֹת | אֹם נְצוּרָה | אָדוֹן הַמּוֹשִׁיעַ |
| *Thursday* | לְמַעַן אֲמִתָּךְ | אֶבֶן שְׁתִיָּה | אֹם נְצוּרָה | אֶעֱרֹךְ שׁוּעִי | אֵל לְמוֹשָׁעוֹת | אָדוֹן הַמּוֹשִׁיעַ |
| שבת | אֹם נְצוּרָה | לְמַעַן אֲמִתָּךְ | אֶעֱרֹךְ שׁוּעִי | אֶבֶן שְׁתִיָּה | אֵל לְמוֹשָׁעוֹת | אָדוֹן הַמּוֹשִׁיעַ |

קהל *then* שליח ציבור:

**הוֹשַׁע נָא לְמַעַנְךָ אֱלֹהֵינוּ הוֹשַׁע נָא.**

קהל *then* שליח ציבור:

**הוֹשַׁע נָא לְמַעַנְךָ בּוֹרְאֵנוּ הוֹשַׁע נָא.**

קהל *then* שליח ציבור:

**הוֹשַׁע נָא לְמַעַנְךָ גּוֹאֲלֵנוּ הוֹשַׁע נָא.**

קהל *then* שליח ציבור:

**הוֹשַׁע נָא לְמַעַנְךָ דּוֹרְשֵׁנוּ הוֹשַׁע נָא.**

## Save us, please –

לְמַעַן אֲמִתָּךְ For the sake of Your truth – for the sake of Your covenant – for the sake of Your greatness and glory – for the sake of Your Law – for the sake of Your majesty – for the sake of Your promise – for the sake of Your remembrance – for the sake of Your love – for the sake of Your goodness – for the sake of Your Oneness – for the sake of Your honor – for the sake of Your wisdom – for the sake of Your kingship – for the sake of Your eternity – for the sake of Your mystery – for the sake of Your might – for the sake of Your splendor – for the sake of Your righteousness – for the sake of Your holiness – for the sake of Your great compassion – for the sake of Your Presence – for the sake of Your praise – Save us, please.

*Continue with "I and HE: save us, please." on the next page.*

## Save us, please –

אֶבֶן שְׁתִיָּה The Foundation Stone – the House You chose – the threshing-floor of Ornan – the hidden Shrine – Mount Moriah – where He shall be seen – Your glorious Sanctuary – where David camped – the best of Lebanon – the Beauty of Heights, Joy of all the earth – the Place of Perfect Beauty – the Lodge of Goodness – the Place of Your dwelling – the Shelter of Shalem – the tribes' Pilgrimage – the precious Cornerstone – shining Zion – the Holy of Holies – [the walls] lined with love – Residence of Your glory – the Hill toward which all mouths pray – Save us, please.

*Continue with "I and HE: save us, please." on the next page.*

## Save us, please –

אֶעֱרֹךְ שׁוּעִי I shall lay out my prayer – in the house of my prayer – I found my sin, fasting – I seek You from there, to save me – heed the sound of my prayer – and rise up to my aid – remember with compassion, my Savior – making life my delight – Beneficent One, hear my groaning – quickly, bring my savior – put an end to my accuser – that he condemn me no more – quickly, God of my salvation – make eternal my salvation – bear the iniquity of my wickedness – pass over my sin – turn to me and save me – righteous Rock, my Savior – receive, please, my prayer – raise the horn of my salvation – Almighty One, my Savior – come, show Yourself and save me – Save us, please.

*Continue with "I and HE: save us, please" on the next page.*

## Save us, please –

אוֹם אֲנִי חוֹמָה "I am a wall," said the people – bright as the sun – exiled and reviled – fair like a date palm – killed on account of You – like sheep to the slaughter – dispersed among tormentors – wrapped in Your embrace, clinging to You – bearing Your yoke – the one to know Your Oneness – beaten down in exile – learning the awe of You – our faces scratched – given over to the violent – weighed

## הוֹשַׁע נָא

לְמַעַן אֲמִתָּךְ. לְמַעַן בְּרִיתָךְ. לְמַעַן גָּדְלָךְ וְתִפְאַרְתָּךְ. לְמַעַן דָּתָךְ. לְמַעַן הוֹדָךְ. לְמַעַן וִעוּדָךְ. לְמַעַן זִכְרָךְ. לְמַעַן חַסְדָּךְ. לְמַעַן טוּבָךְ. לְמַעַן יִחוּדָךְ. לְמַעַן כְּבוֹדָךְ. לְמַעַן לִמּוּדָךְ. לְמַעַן מַלְכוּתָךְ. לְמַעַן נִצְחָךְ. לְמַעַן סוֹדָךְ. לְמַעַן עֻזָּךְ. לְמַעַן פְּאֵרָךְ. לְמַעַן צִדְקָתָךְ. לְמַעַן קְדֻשָּׁתָךְ. לְמַעַן רַחֲמֶיךָ הָרַבִּים. לְמַעַן שְׁכִינָתָךְ. לְמַעַן תְּהִלָּתָךְ. הוֹשַׁע נָא.

*Continue with* אֲנִי וָהוֹ הוֹשִׁיעָה נָּא *on the next page.*

## הוֹשַׁע נָא

אֶבֶן שְׁתִיָּה. בֵּית הַבְּחִירָה. גֹּרֶן אָרְנָן. דְּבִיר הַמֻּצְנָע. הַר הַמּוֹרִיָּה. וְהַר יֵרָאֶה. זְבוּל תִּפְאַרְתֶּךָ. חָנָה דָוִד. טוֹב הַלְּבָנוֹן. יְפֵה נוֹף מְשׂוֹשׂ כָּל הָאָרֶץ. כְּלִילַת יֹפִי. לִינַת הַצֶּדֶק. מָכוֹן לְשִׁבְתֶּךָ. נָוֶה שַׁאֲנָן. סֻכַּת שָׁלֵם. עֲלִיַּת שְׁבָטִים. פִּנַּת יִקְרַת. צִיּוֹן הַמְּצֻיֶּנֶת. קֹדֶשׁ הַקֳּדָשִׁים. רָצוּף אַהֲבָה. שְׁכִינַת כְּבוֹדֶךָ. תֵּל תַּלְפִּיּוֹת. הוֹשַׁע נָא.

*Continue with* אֲנִי וָהוֹ הוֹשִׁיעָה נָּא *on the next page.*

## הוֹשַׁע נָא

אֶעֱרוֹךְ שׁוּעִי. בְּבֵית שַׁוְעִי. גִּלִּיתִי בַצּוֹם פִּשְׁעִי. דְּרַשְׁתִּיךָ בּוֹ לְהוֹשִׁיעִי. הַקְשִׁיבָה לְקוֹל שַׁוְעִי. וְקוּמָה וְהוֹשִׁיעִי. זְכֹר וְרַחֵם מוֹשִׁיעִי. חַי כֵּן תְּשַׁעַשְׁעִי. טוֹב בְּאֶנֶק שְׁעִי. יוּחַשׁ מוֹשִׁיעִי. כַּלֵּה מַרְשִׁיעִי. לְבַל עוֹד יַרְשִׁיעִי. מַהֵר אֱלֹהֵי יִשְׁעִי. נֶצַח לְהוֹשִׁיעִי. שָׂא נָא עֲוֹן רִשְׁעִי. עֲבֹר עַל פִּשְׁעִי. פְּנֵה נָא לְהוֹשִׁיעִי. צוּר צַדִּיק מוֹשִׁיעִי. קַבֵּל נָא שַׁוְעִי. רוֹמֵם קֶרֶן יִשְׁעִי. שַׁדַּי מוֹשִׁיעִי. תּוֹפִיעַ וְתוֹשִׁיעִי. הוֹשַׁע נָא.

*Continue with* אֲנִי וָהוֹ הוֹשִׁיעָה נָּא *on the next page.*

## הוֹשַׁע נָא

אֹם אֲנִי חוֹמָה. בָּרָה כַּחַמָּה. גּוֹלָה וְסוּרָה. דָּמְתָה לְתָמָר. הַהֲרוּגָה עָלֶיךָ. וְנֶחְשֶׁבֶת כְּצֹאן טִבְחָה. זְרוּיָה בֵּין מַכְעִיסֶיהָ. חֲבוּקָה וּדְבוּקָה בָּךְ. טוֹעֶנֶת עֻלָּךְ. יְחִידָה לְיַחֲדָךְ. כְּבוּשָׁה בַגּוֹלָה. לוֹמֶדֶת יִרְאָתָךְ. מְרוּטַת לֶחִי. נְתוּנָה

down beneath Your burden – oppressed and in turmoil – redeemed by [Moses] Toviya – holy flock – the communities of Jacob – marked out with Your name – roaring, "Save us, please!" – leaning on You – Save us, please.

*Continue with "I and HE: save us, please" below.*

Save us, please –

אֵל לְמוֹשָׁעוֹת God of all salvation – for keeping our four vows – we who draw close in prayer – who come knocking to lay out our prayer – who speak Your words of delight – who revel in their questions – crying out to be heard – we who watch for the Redemption – hear those who hold on to You – who understand Your calendar – who bow to You and pray – to comprehend Your message – as it comes from Your mouth – (You who give salvation) – telling their stories – making known Your testament – You who work salvation – bring a righteous [leader] for the saved – bring close our salvations – with noise, amid thundering – in three brief hours – speed us our salvation – Save us, please.

*Continue with "I and HE: save us, please" below.*

Save us, please –

אָדוֹן הַמּוֹשִׁיעַ Master who saves – there is no one else – mighty, with great power to save – when I was brought low, He saved me – God who saves – who delivers and saves – save those who cry out to You – those who yet watch for You – nourish Your young lambs – make the harvest lavish – sprout every growing thing and save us – do not condemn this valley – make the good fruits sweet and save us – carry the clouds to us – shake down the raindrops – do not hold back the clouds – You who open Your hand and satisfy – relieve those who thirst for You – save those who call to You – save those You have loved – rescue those who rise to seek You – save Your innocent ones – Save us, please.

*I* and *HE*: save us, please.

כְּהוֹשַׁעְתָּ As You saved the mighty ones in Lud with You,
coming down for Your people's deliverance – save us, please.

As You saved nation and God together,
[the people] called for God's salvation – save us, please.

As You saved the crowding hosts,
and angelic hosts along with them – save us, please.

לַמַּכִּים. סוֹבֶלֶת סִבְלָךְ. עֲנִיָּה סוֹעֲרָה. פְּדוּיַת טוֹבִיָּה. צֹאן קָדָשִׁים. קְהִלּוֹת יַעֲקֹב. רְשׁוּמִים בִּשְׁמֶךָ. שׁוֹאֲגִים הוֹשַׁע נָא. תְּמוּכִים עָלֶיךָ. הוֹשַׁע נָא.

*Continue with* אֲנִי וָהוֹ הוֹשִׁיעָה נָּא *below.*

## הוֹשַׁע נָא

אֵל לְמוֹשָׁעוֹת. בְּאַרְבַּע שְׁבוּעוֹת. נָּשִׁים בְּשַׁוְעוֹת. דּוֹפְקֵי עֶרֶךְ שׁוּעוֹת. הוֹגֵי שַׁעֲשׁוּעוֹת. וְחִידוֹת מִשְׁתַּעַשְּׁעוֹת. זוֹעֲקִים לְהַשְׁעוֹת. חוֹכֵי יְשׁוּעוֹת. טְפוּלִים בְּךָ שָׁעוֹת. יוֹדְעֵי בֵּין שָׁעוֹת. כּוֹרְעֶיךָ בְּשַׁוְעוֹת. לְהָבִין שְׁמוּעוֹת. מִפִּיךָ נִשְׁמָעוֹת. נוֹתֵן תְּשׁוּעוֹת. סְפוּרוֹת מַשְׁמָעוֹת. עֵדוֹת מַשְׁמִיעוֹת. פּוֹעֵל יְשׁוּעוֹת. צַדִּיק נוֹשָׁעוֹת. קִרְיַת תְּשׁוּעוֹת. רֶגֶשׁ תְּשׁוּאוֹת. שָׁלֹשׁ שָׁעוֹת. תָּחִישׁ לִתְשׁוּעוֹת. הוֹשַׁע נָא.

*Continue with* אֲנִי וָהוֹ הוֹשִׁיעָה נָּא *below.*

## הוֹשַׁע נָא

אָדוֹן הַמּוֹשִׁיעַ. בִּלְתְּךָ אֵין לְהוֹשִׁיעַ. גִּבּוֹר וְרַב לְהוֹשִׁיעַ. דַּלּוֹתִי וְלִי יְהוֹשִׁיעַ. הָאֵל הַמּוֹשִׁיעַ. וּמַצִּיל וּמוֹשִׁיעַ. זוֹעֲקֶיךָ תּוֹשִׁיעַ. חוֹכֶיךָ הוֹשִׁיעַ. טְלָאֶיךָ תַּשְׂבִּיעַ. יְבוּל לְהַשְׁפִּיעַ. כָּל שִׂיחַ תַּדְשֵׁא וְתוֹשִׁיעַ. לְגֵיא בַּל תַּרְשִׁיעַ. מְגָדִים תַּמְתִּיק וְתוֹשִׁיעַ. נְשִׂיאִים לְהַסִּיעַ. שְׂעִירִים לְהָנִיעַ. עֲנָנִים מִלְּהַמְנִיעַ. פּוֹתֵחַ יָד וּמַשְׂבִּיעַ. צְמֵאֶיךָ תַּשְׂבִּיעַ. קוֹרְאֶיךָ תּוֹשִׁיעַ. רְחוּמֶיךָ תּוֹשִׁיעַ. שׁוֹחֲרֶיךָ הוֹשִׁיעַ. תְּמִימֶיךָ תּוֹשִׁיעַ. הוֹשַׁע נָא.

## אֲנִי וָהוֹ הוֹשִׁיעָה נָּא.

כְּהוֹשַׁעְתָּ אֵלִים בְּלוּד עִמָּךְ.
בְּצֵאתְךָ לְיֵשַׁע עַמָּךְ. כֵּן הוֹשַׁע נָא.

כְּהוֹשַׁעְתָּ גּוֹי וֵאלֹהִים.
דְּרוּשִׁים לְיֵשַׁע אֱלֹהִים. כֵּן הוֹשַׁע נָא.

כְּהוֹשַׁעְתָּ הֲמוֹן צְבָאוֹת.
וְעִמָּם מַלְאֲכֵי צְבָאוֹת. כֵּן הוֹשַׁע נָא.

As You saved pure ones from the grip of slavery,
Gracious One; enslaved in cruel hands – save us, please.

As You saved those submerged betwe5en slices of the deep,
and brought Your own glory through it with them –
save us, please.

As You saved the stem as they sang "And God saved" –
but the Deliverer reads it, "God was saved" – save us, please.

As You saved, and You said, "I took you out,"
but let it be pointed, "I was taken out with you" – save us, please.

As You saved those who encompassed the Altar,
bearing their willows to encircle the Altar – save us, please.

As You saved the Ark of wonders that was wronged,
tormenting Philistia with fury, and saving it – save us, please.

As You saved the communities You sent away to Babylon,
being sent too, for them, Your compassionate Self –
save us, please.

As You saved the returning exiles of the tribes of Jacob,
so come back and return the exiles of the tents of Jacob –
and save us, please.

As You saved those who kept Your commandments and waited for
salvation, / God of all salvation – and save us, please.

*I* and *HE*: save us, please.

*The Torah scroll is returned to the Ark.*

הוֹשִׁיעָה Save Your people; bless Your legacy; tend them and carry *Ps. 28*
them forever. Let these words with which I have pleaded with the *1 Kings 8*
Lord be close to the Lord our God day and night, that He may do justice for His servant, and justice for His people Israel, day after day; so that all the peoples of the earth will know that the Lord is God. There is no other.

*The Ark is closed. On Yom Tov the Leader continues the service with Full Kaddish on page 624; on Ḥol HaMo'ed, with Full Kaddish on page 242.*

כְּהוֹשַׁעְתָּ זַכִּים מִבֵּית עֲבָדִים.
חַנּוּן בְּיָדָם מַעֲבִידִים. כֵּן הוֹשַׁע נָא.

כְּהוֹשַׁעְתָּ טְבוּעִים בְּצוּל גְּזָרִים.
יְקָרְךָ עִמָּם מַעֲבִירִים. כֵּן הוֹשַׁע נָא.

כְּהוֹשַׁעְתָּ כַּנָּה מְשׁוֹרֶרֶת וַיּוֹשַׁע.
לְגוֹחָה מְצֻיֶּנֶת וַיִּוָּשַׁע. כֵּן הוֹשַׁע נָא.

כְּהוֹשַׁעְתָּ מַאֲמַר וְהוֹצֵאתִי אֶתְכֶם.
נָקוּב וְהוֹצֵאתִי אִתְּכֶם. כֵּן הוֹשַׁע נָא.

כְּהוֹשַׁעְתָּ סוֹבְבֵי מִזְבֵּחַ.
עוֹמְסֵי עֲרָבָה לְהַקִּיף מִזְבֵּחַ. כֵּן הוֹשַׁע נָא.

כְּהוֹשַׁעְתָּ פִּלְאֵי אָרוֹן כְּהֻפְשַׁע.
צִעֵר פְּלֶשֶׁת בַּחֲרוֹן אַף, וְנוֹשַׁע. כֵּן הוֹשַׁע נָא.

כְּהוֹשַׁעְתָּ קְהִלּוֹת בָּבֶלָה שִׁלַּחְתָּ.
רַחוּם לְמַעֲנָם שֻׁלַּחְתָּ. כֵּן הוֹשַׁע נָא.

כְּהוֹשַׁעְתָּ שְׁבוּת שִׁבְטֵי יַעֲקֹב.
תָּשׁוּב וְתָשִׁיב שְׁבוּת אָהֳלֵי יַעֲקֹב. וְהוֹשִׁיעָה נָּא.

כְּהוֹשַׁעְתָּ שׁוֹמְרֵי מִצְוֹת וְחוֹכֵי יְשׁוּעוֹת.
אֵל לְמוֹשָׁעוֹת. וְהוֹשִׁיעָה נָּא.

## אֲנִי וָהוּ הוֹשִׁיעָה נָּא.

*The* ספר תורה *is returned to the* ארון קודש.

הוֹשִׁיעָה אֶת־עַמֶּךָ, וּבָרֵךְ אֶת־נַחֲלָתֶךָ, וּרְעֵם וְנַשְּׂאֵם עַד־הָעוֹלָם: וְיִהְיוּ תהלים כח מלכים א׳ ח
דְבָרַי אֵלֶּה, אֲשֶׁר הִתְחַנַּנְתִּי לִפְנֵי יהוה, קְרֹבִים אֶל־יהוה אֱלֹהֵינוּ יוֹמָם
וָלָיְלָה, לַעֲשׂוֹת מִשְׁפַּט עַבְדּוֹ וּמִשְׁפַּט עַמּוֹ יִשְׂרָאֵל, דְּבַר־יוֹם בְּיוֹמוֹ:
לְמַעַן דַּעַת כָּל־עַמֵּי הָאָרֶץ כִּי יהוה הוּא הָאֱלֹהִים, אֵין עוֹד:

*The* ארון קודש *is closed. On* יום טוב *the* שליח ציבור *continues the service with* קדיש שלם *on page 625; on* חול המועד, *with* קדיש שלם *on page 243.*

## HOSHANOT FOR SHABBAT

*The Ark is opened but no Torah scrolls are taken out.*
*The congregation does not walk around the Bima.*

*Leader then congregation:*

הוֹשַׁע נָא Save us, please for Your sake, our God, save us please.

*Leader then congregation:*

Save us, please for Your sake, our Creator, save us, please.

*Leader then congregation:*

Save us, please for Your sake, our Redeemer, save us, please.

*Leader then congregation:*

Save us, please for Your sake, You who seek us, save us, please.

Save us, please –

אֹם נְצוּרָה כְּבָבַת A people guarded like the pupil of Your eye – who understand the Law that refreshes the spirit – who learn through all the laws of the Sabbath – who unfold the rules of carrying on the Sabbath – who fix two thousand cubits as our boundary for the Sabbath – and keep our feet from breaking the Sabbath – who remember early and keep hold of the Sabbath – and speed to hasten in the Sabbath – who for six days work hard for the Sabbath – who sit patiently on before ending the Sabbath – who call her an honor, delight, our Sabbath – who change their clothes, and dress for the Sabbath – who prepare themselves feast and drink for the Sabbath – laying a spread of sweet things on the Sabbath – holding three festive meals for the Sabbath – who break bread over two loaves on the Sabbath – distinguishing four domains on the Sabbath – who light the candles for the command, for the Sabbath – who sanctify the day on the Sabbath – who speak seven blessings [in the Amida] of the Sabbath – who read seven portions of Torah on the Sabbath – bring us into what is ours, the day that will be entirely Sabbath – Save us, please.

# הושענות לשבת

*The* ארון קודש *is opened but no* ספרי תורה *are taken out.*
*The* קהל *does not walk around the* בימה*.*

קהל *then* שליח ציבור:

הוֹשַׁע נָא לְמַעַנְךָ אֱלֹהֵינוּ הוֹשַׁע נָא.

קהל *then* שליח ציבור:

הוֹשַׁע נָא לְמַעַנְךָ בּוֹרְאֵנוּ הוֹשַׁע נָא.

קהל *then* שליח ציבור:

הוֹשַׁע נָא לְמַעַנְךָ גּוֹאֲלֵנוּ הוֹשַׁע נָא.

קהל *then* שליח ציבור:

הוֹשַׁע נָא לְמַעַנְךָ דּוֹרְשֵׁנוּ הוֹשַׁע נָא.

## הוֹשַׁע נָא

אֹם נְצוּרָה כְּבָבַת. בּוֹנֶנֶת בְּדָת נֶפֶשׁ מְשִׁיבַת. גּוֹמֶרֶת הִלְכוֹת שַׁבָּת. דּוֹרֶשֶׁת מַשְׂאַת שַׁבָּת. הַקּוֹבַעַת אַלְפַּיִם תְּחוּם שַׁבָּת. וּמְשִׁיבַת רֶגֶל מִשַּׁבָּת. זָכוֹר וְשָׁמוֹר מְקַיֶּמֶת בַּשַּׁבָּת. חָשָׁה לְמַהֵר בִּיאַת שַׁבָּת. טוֹרַחַת כָּל מִשְׁשָׁה לַשַּׁבָּת. יוֹשֶׁבֶת וּמַמְתֶּנֶת עַד כְּלוֹת שַׁבָּת. כָּבוֹד וָעֹנֶג קוֹרְאָה לַשַּׁבָּת. לְבוּשׁ וּכְסוּת מְחַלֶּפֶת בַּשַּׁבָּת. מַאֲכָל וּמִשְׁתֶּה מְכִינָה לַשַּׁבָּת. נֹעַם מְגָדִים מְנַעֶמֶת לַשַּׁבָּת. סְעוּדוֹת שָׁלֹשׁ מְקַיֶּמֶת בַּשַּׁבָּת. עַל שְׁתֵּי כִכָּרוֹת בּוֹצַעַת בַּשַּׁבָּת. פּוֹרֶטֶת אַרְבַּע רְשֻׁיּוֹת שַׁבָּת. צִוּוּי הַדְלָקַת נֵר מַדְלֶקֶת בַּשַּׁבָּת. קִדּוּשׁ הַיּוֹם מְקַדֶּשֶׁת בַּשַּׁבָּת. רֶנֶן שֶׁבַע מְפַלֶּלֶת בַּשַּׁבָּת. שִׁבְעָה בַּדָּת קוֹרְאָה בַּשַּׁבָּת. תַּנְחִילֶנָּה לְיוֹם שֶׁכֻּלּוֹ שַׁבָּת. הוֹשַׁע נָא.

*I* and *HE*: save us, please.

כְּהוֹשַׁעְתָּ As You saved Adam, formed in Your hands, and protected him, making the holy Sabbath his ransom, clemency – so, save us, please.

As You saved the people who remained distinct while longing for freedom – in their thoughts already marking out the seventh day for rest – so, save us, please.

As You saved the people You led and guided as Your flock, and gave a Law at Mara, by the still waters – so, save us, please.

As You saved those who received Your gift in the Wilderness of Sin, the camp, / who were taught and collected two-fold bread on a Friday – so, save us, please.

As You saved those who clung to You, who learned of their own mind to prepare for the Sabbath, / and [Moses] their shepherd blessed their strength and concurred – so, save us, please.

As You saved those who ate [manna] stored up on [their day of] delight, and it looked no different and its scent had not spoiled – so, save us, please.

As You saved those who learned every law of a journey on the Sabbath, who rested, stopped, and kept the boundaries of domain and encampment – so, save us, please.

As You saved those who could hear the fourth commandment at Sinai: both "Remember" and "Keep" to make the seventh day holy – so, save us, please.

As You saved those commanded to march seven times round Jericho, besieging her to strike until she fell on the Sabbath – so, save us, please.

As You saved Kohelet [Solomon] and his people in the eternal House, when they came to please You for seven days and seven – so, save us, please.

As You saved those who returned, rising up from Exile, redeemed, as they read Your Torah on this Festival, each day – so, save us, please.

## אֲנִי וָהוּ הוֹשִׁיעָה נָּא.

כְּהוֹשַׁעְתָּ אָדָם יְצִיר כַּפֶּיךָ לְגוֹנְנָה.
בְּשַׁבַּת קֹדֶשׁ הִמְצֵאתוֹ כֹּפֶר וַחֲנִינָה. כֵּן הוֹשַׁע נָא.

כְּהוֹשַׁעְתָּ גּוֹי מְצֻיָּן מְקַוִּים חֹפֶשׁ.
דֵּעָה כִּוְּנוּ לָבוֹר שְׁבִיעִי לְנֹפֶשׁ. כֵּן הוֹשַׁע נָא.

כְּהוֹשַׁעְתָּ הָעָם נִהַגְתָּ כַּצֹּאן לְהַנְחוֹת.
וְחֹק שַׂמְתָּ בְּמָרָה עַל מֵי מְנוּחוֹת. כֵּן הוֹשַׁע נָא.

כְּהוֹשַׁעְתָּ זְבוּדֶיךָ בְּמִדְבַּר סִין בַּמַּחֲנֶה.
חָכְמוּ וְלָקְטוּ בַשִּׁשִּׁי לֶחֶם מִשְׁנֶה. כֵּן הוֹשַׁע נָא.

כְּהוֹשַׁעְתָּ טְפוּלֶיךָ הוֹרוּ הֲכָנָה בְּמַדָּעָם.
יִשַּׁר כֹּחָם, וְהוֹדָה לָמוֹ רוֹעָם. כֵּן הוֹשַׁע נָא.

כְּהוֹשַׁעְתָּ כָּלְכְּלוּ בְּעֹנֶג מָן הַמִּשְׁמָר.
לֹא הָפַךְ עֵינוֹ וְרֵיחוֹ לֹא נָמָר. כֵּן הוֹשַׁע נָא.

כְּהוֹשַׁעְתָּ מִשְׁפְּטֵי מַשְּׂאוֹת שַׁבָּת גָּמָרוּ.
נָחוּ וְשָׁבְתוּ, רְשֻׁיּוֹת וּתְחוּמִים שָׁמָרוּ. כֵּן הוֹשַׁע נָא.

כְּהוֹשַׁעְתָּ סִינַי הָשְׁמְעוּ בְּדִבּוּר רְבִיעִי.
עִנְיַן זָכוֹר וְשָׁמוֹר לְקַדֵּשׁ שְׁבִיעִי. כֵּן הוֹשַׁע נָא.

כְּהוֹשַׁעְתָּ פְּקָדוּ יְרִיחוֹ שֶׁבַע לְהַקֵּף.
צָרוּ עַד רִדְתָּהּ בַּשַּׁבָּת לְתַקֵּף. כֵּן הוֹשַׁע נָא.

כְּהוֹשַׁעְתָּ קֹהֶלֶת וְעַמּוֹ בְּבֵית עוֹלָמִים.
רִצּוּךָ בְּחָגְגָם שִׁבְעָה וְשִׁבְעָה יָמִים. כֵּן הוֹשַׁע נָא.

כְּהוֹשַׁעְתָּ שָׁבִים עוֹלֵי גוֹלָה לְפִדְיוֹם.
תּוֹרָתְךָ בְּקָרְאָם בֶּחָג יוֹם יוֹם. כֵּן הוֹשַׁע נָא.

As You saved those who rejoiced for You in the second House, renewed,
in the Sanctuary where they took up the lulav all seven days –
so, save us, please.

As You saved those whose willow beating overrode the Sabbath,
who placed branches from Motza at the base of the Altar –
so, save us, please.

As You saved those who rejoiced with supple, long, high willows,
as they parted from the place calling "Praise to you, Altar!" –
so, save us, please.

As You saved those who gave thanks and who prayed and were true to their words, / all of them repeating "We are the Lord's and to Him our eyes are turned" – so, save us, please.

As You saved those circling [the Altar,] the wine-vat You carved out, with luscious willows, / as they sang out, "*I* and *HE*: save us, please" –
so, save us, please.

As You saved the eager legion [of priests], hastening to serve on the day of rest, / bringing a double Sabbath offering, burnt-offering and meal-offering – so, save us, please.

As You saved Your Levites, making them many on their platform,
singing "A psalm. A song for the Sabbath day" – so, save us, please.

As You saved those You comforted, always delighting in Your commands, and desired and delivered them, bringing them safe to respite and peace – so, save us, please.

As You saved the returning exiles of the tribes of Jacob, / so come back
and return the exiles of the tents of Jacob – and save us, please.

As You saved those who kept Your commandments and waited for salvation, / God of all salvation – save us, please.

*I* and *HE*: save us, please.

הוֹשִׁיעָה Save Your people; bless Your legacy; tend them and carry them forever. Let these words with which I have pleaded with the Lord be close to the Lord our God day and night, that He may do justice for His servant, and justice for His people Israel, day after day; so that all the peoples of the earth will know that the Lord is God. There is no other. *Ps. 28* *1 Kings 8*

*The Ark is closed and the Leader continues the service with Full Kaddish on* *page 624.*

כְּהוֹשַׁעְתָּ מְשַׁמְּחֶיךָ בְּבִנְיַן שֵׁנִי הַמְחֻדָּשׁ.
נוֹטְלִין לוּלָב כָּל שִׁבְעָה בַּמִּקְדָּשׁ. כֵּן הוֹשַׁע נָא.

כְּהוֹשַׁעְתָּ חִבּוּט עֲרָבָה שַׁבָּת מַדְחִים.
מְרְבִּיּוֹת מוֹצָא לִיסוֹד מִזְבֵּחַ מַנִּיחִים. כֵּן הוֹשַׁע נָא.

כְּהוֹשַׁעְתָּ בְּרַכּוֹת וַאֲרֻכּוֹת וּגְבוֹהוֹת מְעַלְּסִים.
בִּפְטִירָתָן יֹפִי לְךָ מִזְבֵּחַ מְקַלְּסִים. כֵּן הוֹשַׁע נָא.

כְּהוֹשַׁעְתָּ מוֹדִים וּמְיַחֲלִים וְלֹא מְשַׁנִּים.
כֻּלָּנוּ אָנוּ לְיָהּ וְעֵינֵינוּ לְיָהּ שׁוֹנִים. כֵּן הוֹשַׁע נָא.

כְּהוֹשַׁעְתָּ יֶקֶב מַחֲצָבֶיךָ סוֹבְבִים בְּרַעֲנָנָה.
רוֹנְנִים אֲנִי וָהוּ הוֹשִׁיעָה נָּא. כֵּן הוֹשַׁע נָא.

כְּהוֹשַׁעְתָּ חֵיל זְרִיזִים מְשָׁרְתִים בִּמְנוּחָה.
קָרְבַּן שַׁבָּת כָּפוּל, עוֹלָה וּמִנְחָה. כֵּן הוֹשַׁע נָא.

כְּהוֹשַׁעְתָּ לְוִיֶּיךָ עַל דּוּכָנָם לְהַרְבַּת.
אוֹמְרִים מִזְמוֹר שִׁיר לְיוֹם הַשַּׁבָּת. כֵּן הוֹשַׁע נָא.

כְּהוֹשַׁעְתָּ נְחוּמֶיךָ בְּמִצְוֹתֶיךָ תָּמִיד יִשְׁתַּעַשְׁעוּן.
וּרְצֵם וְהַחֲלִיצֵם בְּשׁוּבָה וָנַחַת יִוָּשֵׁעוּן. כֵּן הוֹשַׁע נָא.

כְּהוֹשַׁעְתָּ שְׁבוּת שִׁבְטֵי יַעֲקֹב.
תָּשׁוּב וְתָשִׁיב שְׁבוּת אָהֳלֵי יַעֲקֹב. וְהוֹשִׁיעָה נָּא.

כְּהוֹשַׁעְתָּ שׁוֹמְרֵי מִצְוֹת וְחוֹכֵי יְשׁוּעוֹת.
אֵל לְמוֹשָׁעוֹת. וְהוֹשִׁיעָה נָּא.

## אֲנִי וָהוּ הוֹשִׁיעָה נָּא.

הוֹשִׁיעָה אֶת־עַמֶּךָ, וּבָרֵךְ אֶת־נַחֲלָתֶךָ, וּרְעֵם וְנַשְּׂאֵם עַד־הָעוֹלָם: וְיִהְיוּ תהלים כח
דְּבָרַי אֵלֶּה, אֲשֶׁר הִתְחַנַּנְתִּי לִפְנֵי יהוה, קְרֹבִים אֶל־יהוה אֱלֹהֵינוּ יוֹמָם מלכים א׳ ח
וָלָיְלָה, לַעֲשׂוֹת מִשְׁפַּט עַבְדּוֹ וּמִשְׁפַּט עַמּוֹ יִשְׂרָאֵל, דְּבַר־יוֹם בְּיוֹמוֹ:
לְמַעַן דַּעַת כָּל־עַמֵּי הָאָרֶץ כִּי יהוה הוּא הָאֱלֹהִים, אֵין עוֹד:

*The* ארון קודש *is closed and the* שליח ציבור *continues the service with* קדיש שלם *on page 625.*

## HOSHANOT FOR HOSHANA RABA

*It is the custom to leave the Ark open until the end of the Hoshanot.*

*All of the Torah scrolls are held on the Bima. Members of the congregation who have a Lulav and Etrog circle the Bima seven times while the Hoshanot are read. After finishing the first circuit, say "For I said" and immediately proceed to make another circuit, saying "The Foundation Stone," etc.*

*Leader then congregation:*

הוֹשַׁע נָא Save us, please for Your sake, our God, save us please.

*Leader then congregation:*

Save us, please for Your sake, our Creator, save us, please.

*Leader then congregation:*

Save us, please for Your sake, our Redeemer, save us, please.

*Leader then congregation:*

Save us, please for Your sake, You who seek us, save us, please.

Save us, please –

*First Hakafa:*

לְמַעַן אֲמִתָּךְ For the sake of Your truth – for the sake of Your covenant – for the sake of Your greatness and glory – for the sake of Your Law – for the sake of Your majesty – for the sake of Your promise – for the sake of Your remembrance – for the sake of Your love – for the sake of Your goodness – for the sake of Your Oneness – for the sake of Your honor – for the sake of Your wisdom – for the sake of Your kingship – for the sake of Your eternity – for the sake of Your mystery – for the sake of Your might – for the sake of Your splendor – for the sake of Your righteousness – for the sake of Your holiness – for the sake of Your great compassion – for the sake of Your Presence – for the sake of Your praise – Save us, please.

*After circling the Bima the first time, say:*

For I said, *Ps. 89*
the world is built by loving-kindness.

# הושענות להושענא רבה

*It is the custom to leave the* ארון קודש *open until the end of the* הושענות.

*All of the* ספרי תורה *are held on the* בימה.
*Members of the* קהל *who have a* לולב *and* אתרוג *circle the* בימה
*seven times while the* הושענות *are read. After finishing the first circuit,*
*say* כִּי־אָמַרְתִּי *and immediately proceed to make another circuit, saying* אֶבֶן שְׁתִיָּה, *etc.*

קהל *then* שליח ציבור:

הוֹשַׁע נָא לְמַעַנְךָ אֱלֹהֵינוּ הוֹשַׁע נָא.

קהל *then* שליח ציבור:

הוֹשַׁע נָא לְמַעַנְךָ בּוֹרְאֵנוּ הוֹשַׁע נָא.

קהל *then* שליח ציבור:

הוֹשַׁע נָא לְמַעַנְךָ גּוֹאֲלֵנוּ הוֹשַׁע נָא.

קהל *then* שליח ציבור:

הוֹשַׁע נָא לְמַעַנְךָ דּוֹרְשֵׁנוּ הוֹשַׁע נָא.

## הוֹשַׁע נָא

*First* הקפה:

לְמַעַן אֲמִתָּךְ. לְמַעַן בְּרִיתָךְ. לְמַעַן גָּדְלָךְ וְתִפְאַרְתָּךְ. לְמַעַן דָּתָךְ. לְמַעַן הוֹדָךְ. לְמַעַן וִעוּדָךְ. לְמַעַן זִכְרָךְ. לְמַעַן חַסְדָּךְ. לְמַעַן טוּבָךְ. לְמַעַן יִחוּדָךְ. לְמַעַן כְּבוֹדָךְ. לְמַעַן לִמּוּדָךְ. לְמַעַן מַלְכוּתָךְ. לְמַעַן נִצְחָךְ. לְמַעַן סוֹדָךְ. לְמַעַן עֻזָּךְ. לְמַעַן פְּאֵרָךְ. לְמַעַן צִדְקָתָךְ. לְמַעַן קְדֻשָּׁתָךְ. לְמַעַן רַחֲמֶיךָ הָרַבִּים. לְמַעַן שְׁכִינָתָךְ. לְמַעַן תְּהִלָּתָךְ. הוֹשַׁע נָא.

*After circling the* בימה *the first time, say:*

כִּי־אָמַרְתִּי עוֹלָם חֶסֶד יִבָּנֶה׃ תהלים פט

Save us, please –

*Second Hakafa:*

אֶבֶן שְׁתִיָּה The Foundation Stone – the House You chose – the threshing-floor of Arnan – the hidden Shrine – Mount Moriah – where He shall be seen – Your glorious Sanctuary – where David camped – the best of Lebanon – the Beauty of Heights, Joy of all the earth – the Place of Perfect Beauty – the Lodge of Goodness – the Place of Your dwelling – the Shelter of Shalem – the tribes' Pilgrimage – the precious Cornerstone – shining Zion – the Holy of Holies – [the walls] lined with love – Residence of Your glory – the Hill toward which all mouths pray – Save us, please.

*After circling the Bima the second time, say:*

A strong arm is Yours, might is Yours; Ps. 89
Your hand holds its power, Your right hand raised.

Save us, please –

*Third Hakafa:*

אֹם אֲנִי חוֹמָה "I am a wall," said the people – bright as the sun – exiled and reviled – fair like a date palm – killed on account of You – like sheep to the slaughter – dispersed among tormentors – wrapped in Your embrace, clinging to You – bearing Your yoke – the one to know Your Oneness – beaten down in exile – learning the awe of You – our faces scratched – given over to the violent – weighed down beneath Your burden – oppressed and in turmoil – redeemed by [Moses] Toviya – holy flock – the communities of Jacob – marked out with Your name – roaring, "Save us, please!" – leaning on You – Save us, please.

*After circling the Bima the third time, say:*

Grant truth to Jacob, loving-kindness to Abraham. Mic. 7

Save us, please –

*Fourth Hakafa:*

אָדוֹן הַמּוֹשִׁיעַ Master who saves – there is no one else – mighty, with great power to save – when I was brought low, He saved me – God who saves – who delivers and saves – save those who cry out to You – those who yet watch for You – nourish Your young lambs – make the harvest lavish – sprout every growing thing and save us – do not condemn this valley – make the good fruits sweet and save us – carry the clouds to us – shake down the

## הוֹשַׁע נָא

*Second* הקפה*:*

אֶבֶן שְׁתִיָּה. בֵּית הַבְּחִירָה. גֹּרֶן אָרְנָן. דְּבִיר הַמֻּצְנָע. הַר הַמּוֹרִיָּה. וְהַר יֵרָאֶה. זְבוּל תִּפְאַרְתֶּךָ. חָנָה דָוִד. טוֹב הַלְּבָנוֹן. יְפֵה נוֹף מְשׂוֹשׂ כָּל הָאָרֶץ. כְּלִילַת יֹפִי. לִינַת הַצֶּדֶק. מָכוֹן לְשִׁבְתֶּךָ. נָוֶה שַׁאֲנָן. סֻכַּת שָׁלֵם. עֲלִיַּת שְׁבָטִים. פִּנַּת יִקְרַת. צִיּוֹן הַמְצֻיֶּנֶת. קֹדֶשׁ הַקֳּדָשִׁים. רָצוּף אַהֲבָה. שְׁכִינַת כְּבוֹדֶךָ. תֵּל תַּלְפִּיּוֹת. הוֹשַׁע נָא.

*After circling the* בימה *the second time, say:*

לְךָ זְרוֹעַ עִם־גְּבוּרָה, תָּעֹז יָדְךָ תָּרוּם יְמִינֶךָ: תהלים פט

## הוֹשַׁע נָא

*Third* הקפה*:*

אֹם אֲנִי חוֹמָה. בָּרָה כַּחַמָּה. גּוֹלָה וְסוּרָה. דָּמְתָה לְתָמָר. הַהֲרוּגָה עָלֶיךָ. וְנֶחְשֶׁבֶת כְּצֹאן טִבְחָה. זְרוּיָה בֵּין מַכְעִיסֶיהָ. חֲבוּקָה וּדְבוּקָה בָּךְ. טוֹעֶנֶת עֻלָּךְ. יְחִידָה לְיַחֲדָךְ. כְּבוּשָׁה בַגּוֹלָה. לוֹמֶדֶת יִרְאָתָךְ. מְרוּטַת לֶחִי. נְתוּנָה לְמַכִּים. סוֹבֶלֶת סִבְלָךְ. עֲנִיָּה סוֹעֲרָה. פְּדוּיַת טוֹבִיָּה. צֹאן קָדָשִׁים. קְהִלּוֹת יַעֲקֹב. רְשׁוּמִים בִּשְׁמֶךָ. שׁוֹאֲגִים הוֹשַׁע נָא. תְּמוּכִים עָלֶיךָ. הוֹשַׁע נָא.

*After circling the* בימה *the third time, say:*

תִּתֵּן אֱמֶת לְיַעֲקֹב, חֶסֶד לְאַבְרָהָם: מיכה ז

## הוֹשַׁע נָא

*Fourth* הקפה*:*

אָדוֹן הַמּוֹשִׁיעַ. בִּלְתְּךָ אֵין לְהוֹשִׁיעַ. גִּבּוֹר וְרַב לְהוֹשִׁיעַ. דַּלּוֹתִי וְלִי יְהוֹשִׁיעַ. הָאֵל הַמּוֹשִׁיעַ. וּמַצִּיל וּמוֹשִׁיעַ. זוֹעֲקֶיךָ תּוֹשִׁיעַ. חוֹכֶיךָ הוֹשִׁיעַ. טְלָאֶיךָ תַּשְׂבִּיעַ. יְבוּל לְהַשְׁפִּיעַ. כָּל שִׂיחַ תַּדְשֵׁא וְתוֹשִׁיעַ. לְגִיא בַּל תַּרְשִׁיעַ. מְגָדִים תַּמְתִּיק וְתוֹשִׁיעַ. נְשִׂיאִים לְהַסִּיעַ. שְׂעִירִים לְהָנִיעַ.

raindrops – do not hold back the clouds – You who open Your hand and satisfy – relieve those who thirst for You – save those who call to You – save those You have loved – rescue those who rise to seek You – save Your innocent ones – Save us, please.

*After circling the Bima the fourth time, say:*

At Your hand, bliss for evermore. *Ps. 16*

Save us, please –

*Fifth Hakafa:*

אָדָם וּבְהֵמָה Man and beast – body, spirit and soul – muscle, bone, skin – likeness and image woven – glory reduced to mere breath – likened to beasts that fall silent – light and beauty and stature – renew the face of the land – planting trees on desolate ground – winepress and bounty of meadows – vineyard and sycamore fig – bring to the land renowned – mighty rain to scent spices – to recover a devastated place – to raise up the shrub – to make the delightful fruits robust – to make the land glorious with flowers – to soak the plants with rain – to make cool waters flow – to fill out the raindrops – to raise up the earth – the earth that is hung over nothingness – Save us, please.

*After circling the Bima the fifth time, say:*

Lord our Master, how majestic is Your name throughout the earth, *Ps. 8*
Your glory over all the heavens.

Save us, please –

*Sixth Hakafa:*

אֲדָמָה מֵאֶרֶר Save earth from cursedness – save cattle from miscarriage – save threshing floor from pest – save grain from burning – save wealth from want – save sustenance from terror – save olive from windfall – save wheat from grasshopper – save food from vermin – save wine-vat from maggot – save vineyard from worm – save late harvest from locust – save bounty from crickets – save souls from horror – save abundance from insects – save herds from infirmity – save fruits from the gales – save flocks from destruction – save crops from the curse – save plenty from poverty – save the wheat-ears from leanness – save produce from pestilence – Save us, please.

*After circling the Bima the sixth time, say:*

The Lord is righteous in all His ways, *Ps. 145*
and kind in all He does.

עֲנָנִים מִלְּהַמְנִיעַ. פּוֹתֵחַ יָד וּמַשְׂבִּיעַ. צְמֵאֶיךָ תַּשְׂבִּיעַ. קוֹרְאֶיךָ תּוֹשִׁיעַ.
רְחוּמֶיךָ תּוֹשִׁיעַ. שׁוֹחֲרֶיךָ הוֹשִׁיעַ. תְּמִימֶיךָ תּוֹשִׁיעַ. הוֹשַׁע נָא.

*After circling the* בימה *the fourth time, say:*

תהלים טז נְעִמוֹת בִּימִינְךָ נֶצַח:

## הוֹשַׁע נָא

*Fifth* הקפה:

אָדָם וּבְהֵמָה. בָּשָׂר וְרוּחַ וּנְשָׁמָה. גִּיד וְעֶצֶם וְקָרְמָה. דְּמוּת וְצֶלֶם וְרִקְמָה.
הוֹד לַהֶבֶל דָּמָה. וְנִמְשַׁל כַּבְּהֵמוֹת נִדְמָה. זִיו וְתֹאַר וְקוֹמָה. חִדּוּשׁ
פְּנֵי אֲדָמָה. טִיעַת עֲצֵי נְשַׁמָּה. יְקָבִים וְקָמָה. כְּרָמִים וְשִׁקְמָה. לְתֵבֵל
הַמְּסֻיָּמָה. מִטְרוֹת עֹז לְסַמְּמָה. נְשִׁיָּה לְקַיְּמָה. שִׂיחִים לְקוֹמְמָה. עֲדָנִים
לְעָצְמָה. פְּרָחִים לְהַעֲצִימָה. צְמָחִים לְגָשְׁמָה. קָרִים לְזָרְמָה. רְבִיבִים
לְשַׁלְּמָה. שְׁתִיָּה לְרוֹמְמָה. תְּלוּיָה עַל בְּלִימָה. הוֹשַׁע נָא.

*After circling the* בימה *the fifth time, say:*

תהלים ח יהוה אֲדֹנֵינוּ מָה־אַדִּיר שִׁמְךָ בְּכָל־הָאָרֶץ
אֲשֶׁר־תְּנָה הוֹדְךָ עַל־הַשָּׁמָיִם:

## הוֹשַׁע נָא

*Sixth* הקפה:

אֲדָמָה מֵאֶרֶר. בְּהֵמָה מִמְּשַׁכֶּלֶת. גֹּרֶן מִגָּזָם. דָּגָן מִדַּלֶּקֶת. הוֹן מִמְּאֵרָה.
וְאֹכֶל מִמְּהוּמָה. זַיִת מִנֶּשֶׁל. חִטָּה מֵחָגָב. טֶרֶף מִגּוֹבַי. יֶקֶב מִיֶּלֶק. כֶּרֶם
מִתּוֹלַעַת. לֶקֶשׁ מֵאַרְבֶּה. מֶגֶד מִצְּלָצַל. נֶפֶשׁ מִבֶּהָלָה. שֹׂבַע מִסָּלְעָם.
עֲדָרִים מִדַּלּוּת. פֵּרוֹת מִשִּׁדָּפוֹן. צֹאן מִצְּמִיתוּת. קָצִיר מִקְּלָלָה. רֹב מֵרָזוֹן.
שִׁבֹּלֶת מִצִּנָּמוֹן. תְּבוּאָה מֵחָסִיל. הוֹשַׁע נָא.

*After circling the* בימה *the sixth time, say:*

תהלים קמה צַדִּיק יהוה בְּכָל־דְּרָכָיו, וְחָסִיד בְּכָל־מַעֲשָׂיו:

## Save us, please –

*Seventh Hakafa:*

לְמַעַן אֵיתָן For the sake of steadfast [Abraham], who was thrown into flames of fire –
for the sake of his son [Isaac] who was bound on the wood of the fire –
for the sake of the mighty [Jacob] who struggled with a prince of fire –
for the sake of the flags [of the tribes] You led in light and a cloud of fire –
for the sake of one who was raised up to the heights and rose, like an angel of fire –
for the sake of one who is to You like a deputy among erelim of fire –
for the sake of the gift of commandments made in fire –
for the sake of the curtained Tent [of Meeting] and its cloud of fire –
for the sake of that scene on the mountain, of Your coming down to it in fire –
for the sake of the loveliness of that House You preferred above heavens of fire –
for the sake of [Moses] who yearned until the dying of the fire –
for the sake of [Aaron] who took a fire pan to quell a rage of fire –
for the sake of [Pinehas] who burned with a great jealousy, Your fire –
for the sake of [Joshua] who raised his hand and brought down stones of fire –
for the sake of [Samuel] who burned a milk lamb wholly in the fire –
for the sake of [David] who stood in the threshing floor and found favor again through fire –
for the sake of [Solomon] who spoke in the Courtyard and down came fire –
for the sake of Your messenger [Elijah] who rose and was raised up in a chariot with horses of fire –
for the sake of [Hananiah, Mishael and Azariah,] the holy ones flung into fire –
for the sake of [Daniel] who saw the thousands of myriad [angels], the rivers of fire –
for the sake of the desolate remains of Your city burnt up by fire –
for the sake of the past of these clans of Judah whom You shall make as a basin of fire – Save us, please.

*After circling the Bima the seventh time, say:*

לְךָ Yours, Lord, are the greatness and the power, *I Chr. 29*
the glory and the majesty and splendor,
for everything in heaven and earth is Yours.
Yours, Lord, is the kingdom; You are exalted as Head over all.
Then the Lord shall be King over all the earth; *Zech. 14*
on that day the Lord shall be One and His name One.
And in Your Torah it is written:
Listen, Israel: the Lord is our God, the Lord is One. *Deut. 6*
Blessed be the name of His glorious kingdom for ever and all time.

# הוֹשַׁע נָא

*Seventh* הקפה:

לְמַעַן אֵיתָן הַנִּזְרָק בְּלַהַב אֵשׁ.
לְמַעַן בֵּן הַנֶּעֱקַד עַל עֵצִים וָאֵשׁ.
לְמַעַן גִּבּוֹר הַנֶּאֱבַק עִם שַׂר אֵשׁ.
לְמַעַן דְּגָלִים נָחִיתָ בְּאוֹר וַעֲנַן אֵשׁ.
לְמַעַן הֹעֲלָה לַמָּרוֹם, וְנִתְעַלָּה כְּמַלְאֲכֵי אֵשׁ.
לְמַעַן וְהוּא לָךְ כְּסֶגֶן בְּאֶרְאֵלֵּי אֵשׁ.
לְמַעַן זֶבֶד דִּבְּרוֹת הַנִּתּוּנוֹת מֵאֵשׁ.
לְמַעַן חִפּוּי יְרִיעוֹת וַעֲנַן אֵשׁ.
לְמַעַן טֶכֶס הַר יָרַדְתָּ עָלָיו בָּאֵשׁ.
לְמַעַן יְדִידוּת בַּיִת אֲשֶׁר אָהַבְתָּ מִשְּׁמֵי אֵשׁ.
לְמַעַן כָּמַהּ עַד שָׁקְעָה הָאֵשׁ.
לְמַעַן לָקַח מַחְתַּת אֵשׁ וְהֵסִיר חֲרוֹן אֵשׁ.
לְמַעַן מְקַנֵּא קִנְאָה גְדוֹלָה בָּאֵשׁ.
לְמַעַן נָף יָדוֹ וַיֵּרְדוּ אַבְנֵי אֵשׁ.
לְמַעַן שָׂם טְלֵה חָלָב כְּלִיל אֵשׁ.
לְמַעַן עָמַד בַּגֹּרֶן וְנִתְרַצָּה בָאֵשׁ.
לְמַעַן פִּלֵּל בָּעֲזָרָה וַיֵּרְדָה הָאֵשׁ.
לְמַעַן צִיר עָלָה וְנִתְעַלָּה בְּרֶכֶב וְסוּסֵי אֵשׁ.
לְמַעַן קְדוֹשִׁים מֻשְׁלָכִים בָּאֵשׁ.
לְמַעַן רִבּוֹ רִבְבָן חָז וְנַהֲרֵי אֵשׁ.
לְמַעַן שְׁמְמוֹת עִירָךְ הַשְּׂרוּפָה בָאֵשׁ.
לְמַעַן תּוֹלְדוֹת אַלּוּפֵי יְהוּדָה, תָּשִׂים כְּכִיּוֹר אֵשׁ. הוֹשַׁע נָא.

*After circling the* בימה *the seventh time, say:*

לְךָ יהוה הַגְּדֻלָּה וְהַגְּבוּרָה וְהַתִּפְאֶרֶת וְהַנֵּצַח וְהַהוֹד, כִּי־כֹל בַּשָּׁמַיִם וּבָאָרֶץ לְךָ יהוה הַמַּמְלָכָה וְהַמִּתְנַשֵּׂא לְכֹל לְרֹאשׁ: דברי הימים א׳ כט

וְהָיָה יהוה לְמֶלֶךְ עַל־כָּל־הָאָרֶץ, בַּיּוֹם הַהוּא יִהְיֶה יהוה אֶחָד וּשְׁמוֹ אֶחָד: זכריה יד

וּבְתוֹרָתְךָ כָּתוּב לֵאמֹר: שְׁמַע יִשְׂרָאֵל, יהוה אֱלֹהֵינוּ, יהוה אֶחָד: דברים ו
בָּרוּךְ שֵׁם כְּבוֹד מַלְכוּתוֹ לְעוֹלָם וָעֶד.

*I* and *HE*: save us, please.

כְּהוֹשַׁעְתָּ As You saved the mighty ones in Lud with You,
coming down for Your people's deliverance – save us, please.

As You saved nation and God together,
[the people] called for God's salvation – save us, please.

As You saved the crowding hosts,
and angelic hosts along with them – save us, please.

As You saved pure ones from the grip of slavery,
Gracious One; enslaved in cruel hands – save us, please.

As You saved those submerged between slices of the deep,
and brought Your own glory through it with them –
save us, please.

As You saved the stem as they sang "And God saved" –
but the Deliverer reads it, "God was saved" – save us, please.

As You saved, and You said, "I took you out,"
but let it be pointed, "I was taken out with you" – save us, please.

As You saved those who encompassed the Altar,
bearing their willows to encircle the Altar – save us, please.

As You saved the Ark of wonders that was wronged,
tormenting Philistia with fury, and saving it – save us, please.

As You saved the communities You sent away to Babylon,
being sent too, for them, Your compassionate Self –
save us, please.

As You saved the returning exiles of the tribes of Jacob,
so come back and return the exiles of the tents of Jacob –
and save us, please.

As You saved those who kept Your commandments and waited for
salvation, / God of all salvation – and save us, please.

# אֲנִי וָהוּ הוֹשִׁיעָה נָּא.

כְּהוֹשַׁעְתָּ אֵלִים בְּלוּד עִמָּךְ.
בְּצֵאתְךָ לְיֵשַׁע עַמָּךְ. כֵּן הוֹשַׁע נָא.

כְּהוֹשַׁעְתָּ גּוֹי וֵאלֹהִים.
דְּרוּשִׁים לְיֵשַׁע אֱלֹהִים. כֵּן הוֹשַׁע נָא.

כְּהוֹשַׁעְתָּ הֲמוֹן צְבָאוֹת.
וְעִמָּם מַלְאֲכֵי צְבָאוֹת. כֵּן הוֹשַׁע נָא.

כְּהוֹשַׁעְתָּ זַכִּים מִבֵּית עֲבָדִים.
חַנּוּן בְּיָדָם מַעֲבִידִים. כֵּן הוֹשַׁע נָא.

כְּהוֹשַׁעְתָּ טְבוּעִים בְּצוּל גְּזָרִים.
יְקָרְךָ עִמָּם מַעֲבִירִים. כֵּן הוֹשַׁע נָא.

כְּהוֹשַׁעְתָּ כַּנָּה מְשׁוֹרֶרֶת וַיּוֹשַׁע.
לְגוֹחָה מְצֻיֶּנֶת וַיִּוָּשַׁע. כֵּן הוֹשַׁע נָא.

כְּהוֹשַׁעְתָּ מַאֲמַר וְהוֹצֵאתִי אֶתְכֶם.
נָקוּב וְהוּצֵאתִי אִתְּכֶם. כֵּן הוֹשַׁע נָא.

כְּהוֹשַׁעְתָּ סוֹבְבֵי מִזְבֵּחַ.
עוֹמְסֵי עֲרָבָה לְהַקִּיף מִזְבֵּחַ. כֵּן הוֹשַׁע נָא.

כְּהוֹשַׁעְתָּ פִּלְאֵי אָרוֹן כְּהֻפְשַׁע.
צִעֵר פְּלֶשֶׁת בַּחֲרוֹן אַף, וְנוֹשַׁע. כֵּן הוֹשַׁע נָא.

כְּהוֹשַׁעְתָּ קְהִלּוֹת בָּבֶלָה שִׁלַּחְתָּ.
רַחוּם לְמַעֲנָם שֻׁלַּחְתָּ. כֵּן הוֹשַׁע נָא.

כְּהוֹשַׁעְתָּ שְׁבוּת שִׁבְטֵי יַעֲקֹב.
תָּשׁוּב וְתָשִׁיב שְׁבוּת אָהֳלֵי יַעֲקֹב. וְהוֹשִׁיעָה נָּא.

כְּהוֹשַׁעְתָּ שׁוֹמְרֵי מִצְוֹת וְחוֹכֵי יְשׁוּעוֹת.
אֵל לְמוֹשָׁעוֹת. וְהוֹשִׁיעָה נָּא.

*I* and *HE*: save us, please.

תְּתְּנֵנוּ לְשֵׁם Grant us name and honor; / return us to our home, our land; / raise us up, up above; / gather us to the House of prayer; / plant us as a tree on streams of water; / redeem us from infection and illness; / crown us with bridal love; / have us rejoice in the House of prayer; / lead us beside the still waters forever; / fill us with wisdom and insight; / clothe us with strength and dignity; / crown us with the finest crown; / guide us straight along a paved avenue; / set us down upon a straight pathway; / grace us with compassion and mercy; / remember us, "Who is this rising?" / save us, to the end, to Redemption; / have us glow with the splendor of the crowd; / bind us about You like a loincloth girt; / make us greater with Your great hand; / bring us to Your House in song, in jubilation; / make us majestic with salvation and joy; / strengthen us in Your relief and rescue; / sweep our hearts up in the building of Your city anew; / awaken us to Zion in her completion; / grant us the honor to see the city rebuilt on its hill; / set us down to pasture in happiness and joy; / strengthen us, God of Jacob, always –

Save us, please.

*Leader then congregation:*

Please: save us, please.

אָנָּא Please – listen to the plea of those who hunger for Your rescue,
as they bring willows of the stream to delight You –
and save us, please.

Please – redeem this stem You planted,
as You sweep away Duma [the regime that rules us]–
and save us, please.

Please – look to the covenant You have sealed in us,
as You destroy the dark places of this earth –
and save us, please.

Please – remember for our sake our father] Abraham [who knew You,
as You make Your love known to [the others] –
and save us, please.

## אֲנִי וָהוּ הוֹשִׁיעָה נָּא.

| | |
|---|---|
| תְּתְּנֵנוּ לְשֵׁם וְלִתְהִלָּה. | תְּחָנֵּנוּ בְּרַחֲמִים וּבְחֶמְלָה. |
| תְּשִׁיבֵנוּ אֶל הַחֶבֶל וְאֶל הַנַּחֲלָה. | תִּזְכִּירֵנוּ בְּמִי זֹאת עוֹלָה. |
| תְּרוֹמְמֵנוּ לְמַעְלָה לְמָעְלָה. | תּוֹשִׁיעֵנוּ לְקֵץ הַגְּאֻלָּה. |
| תְּקַבְּצֵנוּ לְבֵית הַתְּפִלָּה. | תְּהַדְּרֵנוּ בְּזִיו הֲמֻלָּה. |
| תַּצִּיבֵנוּ כְּעֵץ עַל פַּלְגֵי מַיִם שְׁתוּלָה. | תַּדְבִּיקֵנוּ כְּאֵזוֹר חֲתוּלָה. |
| תִּפְדֵּנוּ מִכָּל נֶגַע וּמַחֲלָה. | תְּגַדְּלֵנוּ בְּיָד הַגְּדוֹלָה. |
| תְּעַטְּרֵנוּ בְּאַהֲבָה כְלוּלָה. | תְּבִיאֵנוּ לְבֵיתְךָ בְּרִנָּה וְצָהֳלָה. |
| תְּשַׂמְּחֵנוּ בְּבֵית הַתְּפִלָּה. | תְּאַדְּרֵנוּ בְּיֶשַׁע וְגִילָה. |
| תְּנַהֲלֵנוּ עַל מֵי מְנוּחוֹת סֶלָה. | תְּאַמְּצֵנוּ בְּרֶוַח וְהַצָּלָה. |
| תְּמַלְּאֵנוּ חָכְמָה וְשִׂכְלָה. | תְּלַבְּבֵנוּ בְּבִנְיַן עִירְךָ כְּבַתְּחִלָּה. |
| תַּלְבִּישֵׁנוּ עֹז וּגְדֻלָּה. | תְּעוֹרְרֵנוּ לְצִיּוֹן בְּשִׁכְלוּלָהּ. |
| תַּכְתִּירֵנוּ בְּכֶתֶר כְּלוּלָה. | תְּזַכֵּנוּ בְּנִבְנְתָה הָעִיר עַל תִּלָּהּ. |
| תְּיַשְּׁרֵנוּ בְּאֹרַח סְלוּלָה. | תַּרְבִּיצֵנוּ בְּשָׂשׂוֹן וְגִילָה. |
| תִּטָּעֵנוּ בְּיֹשֶׁר מְסִלָּה. | תְּחַזְּקֵנוּ אֱלֹהֵי יַעֲקֹב סֶלָה. |

הוֹשַׁע נָא.

*קהל then שליח ציבור:*

## אָנָּא, הוֹשִׁיעָה נָּא.

אָנָּא אֱזוֹן חִין תָּאֵבֵי יִשְׁעָךְ.
בַּעֲרָבֵי נַחַל לְשַׁעְשְׁעָךְ. וְהוֹשִׁיעָה נָּא.

אָנָּא גְּאַל כַּנַּת נִטְעָךְ.
דּוּמָה בְּטַאטְאָךְ. וְהוֹשִׁיעָה נָּא.

אָנָּא הַבֵּט לַבְּרִית טִבְעָךְ.
וּמַחֲשַׁכֵּי אֶרֶץ בְּהַטְבִּיעָךְ. וְהוֹשִׁיעָה נָּא.

אָנָּא זְכָר לָנוּ אָב יְדָעָךְ.
חַסְדְּךָ לָמוֹ בְּהוֹדִיעָךְ. וְהוֹשִׁיעָה נָּא.

Please – as You perform miracles for the pure of heart,
make it known that these are Your own wonders –
and save us, please.

Please – You whose strength is immense, grant us Your salvation,
as You swore to our forefathers – and save us, please.

Please – answer the wishes of the people who entreat You,
like the prayer of [Isaac] bound on the Mountain of
Myrrh – and save us, please.

Please – strengthen [Israel,] the tamarisks You planted,
as You push aside oppressors – and save us, please.

Please – open for us Your treasuries of rain,
as from them You water arid land – and save us, please.

Please – when You shake the earth, lead those who call on You
to pasture in the best of Your meadows – and save us, please.

Please – lift the gates of Your [House] from their destruction,
as You raise the ruins each mouth prays towards –
and save us, please.

*Leader then congregation:*

Please; God, please;
save, please; save us, please.

אֵל נָא God, please; we have gone astray like lost sheep;
do not erase our name from Your book – save, please; save us, please.

God, please; tend the flock destined to slaughter,
raged against, killed in Your name – save, please; save us, please.

God, please; Your flock, the flock You tend,
Your creation, Your beloved – save, please; save us, please.

God, please; the poorest of the flock –
answer their prayer at a time of favor – save, please; save us, please.

אָנָּא טְהוֹרֵי לֵב בְּהַפְלִיאָךְ.
יוֹדֵעַ כִּי הוּא פִלְאָךְ. וְהוֹשִׁיעָה נָּא.

אָנָּא כַּבִּיר כֹּחַ תֵּן לָנוּ יִשְׁעָךְ.
לַאֲבוֹתֵינוּ כְּהִשָּׁבְעָךְ. וְהוֹשִׁיעָה נָּא.

אָנָּא מַלֵּא מִשְׁאֲלוֹת עַם מְשַׁוְּעָךְ.
נֶעֱקַד בְּהַר מוֹר כְּמוֹ שׁוֹעָךְ. וְהוֹשִׁיעָה נָּא.

אָנָּא סַגֵּב אֶשְׁלֵי נִטְעָךְ.
עָרִיצִים בְּהַנִיעָךְ. וְהוֹשִׁיעָה נָּא.

אָנָּא פְּתַח לָנוּ אוֹצְרוֹת רִבְעָךְ.
צִיָּה מֵהֶם בְּהַרְבִּיעָךְ. וְהוֹשִׁיעָה נָּא.

אָנָּא קוֹרְאֶיךָ אֶרֶץ בְּרוֹעֲעָךְ.
רְעֵם בְּטוּב מִרְעָךְ. וְהוֹשִׁיעָה נָּא.

אָנָּא שְׁעָרֶיךָ תַּעַל מִמַּשּׁוֹאָךְ.
תֵּל תַּלְפִּיּוֹת בְּהַשִּׂיאָךְ. וְהוֹשִׁיעָה נָּא.

קהל *then* שליח ציבור:

## אָנָּא, אֵל נָא, הוֹשַׁע נָא וְהוֹשִׁיעָה נָּא.

אֵל נָא תָּעִינוּ כְּשֶׂה אוֹבֵד
שְׁמֵנוּ מִסִּפְרְךָ אַל תְּאַבֵּד הוֹשַׁע נָא וְהוֹשִׁיעָה נָּא.

אֵל נָא רְעֵה אֶת צֹאן הַהֲרֵגָה
קְצוּפָה, וְעָלֶיךָ הֲרוּגָה הוֹשַׁע נָא וְהוֹשִׁיעָה נָּא.

אֵל נָא צֹאנְךָ וְצֹאן מַרְעִיתֶךָ
פְּעֻלָּתְךָ וְרַעְיָתֶךָ הוֹשַׁע נָא וְהוֹשִׁיעָה נָּא.

אֵל נָא עֲנִיֵּי הַצֹּאן
שִׂיחָם עֲנֵה בְּעֵת רָצוֹן הוֹשַׁע נָא וְהוֹשִׁיעָה נָּא.

God, please; those who raise their eyes to You –
may those who rise against You be as nothing beside them –
save, please; save us, please.

God, please; those who pour water out before You –
from the wellsprings of salvation, let them draw water –
save, please; save us, please.

God, please; let the redeemers go up to Zion,
leaning upon You, saved in Your name – save, please; save us, please.

God, please; Your clothes red with blood,
rage and shake away all those who betray –
save, please; save us, please.

God, please; surely remember,
those sold away for a letekh of grain, for a kor –
save, please; save us, please.

God, please; those who seek You with stems of willow,
hear their weeping from the highest heaven –
save, please; save us, please.

God, please; crown this year with blessing,
and hear my words as I pray, on the day of Hoshana –
save, please; save us, please.

*Leader then congregation:*

Please; God, please;
save, please; save us, please; You are our Father.

לְמַעַן For the sake of one perfect in his generation,
who escaped in his righteousness,
saved from the flood, when there came down a deluge of water –
the people that says "I am a wall" –
save, please: save us, please: You are our Father.

For the sake of one whole in all his doings, tested with ten trials,
who saw angels and said, "Please, bring a little water" –
the people shining like the sun –
save, please: save us, please: You are our Father.

אֵל נָא נוֹשְׂאֵי לְךָ עַיִן
מִתְקוֹמְמֶיךָ יִהְיוּ כְּאַיִן הוֹשַׁע נָא וְהוֹשִׁיעָה נָּא.

אֵל נָא לִמְנַסְּכֵי לְךָ מַיִם
כְּמִמַּעַיְנֵי הַיְשׁוּעָה
יִשְׁאֲבוּן מַיִם הוֹשַׁע נָא וְהוֹשִׁיעָה נָּא.

אֵל נָא יַעֲלוּ לְצִיּוֹן מוֹשִׁיעִים
טְפוּלִים בְּךָ וּבְשִׁמְךָ נוֹשָׁעִים הוֹשַׁע נָא וְהוֹשִׁיעָה נָּא.

אֵל נָא חֲמוּץ בְּגָדִים
זְעֹם לְנַעֵר כָּל בּוֹגְדִים הוֹשַׁע נָא וְהוֹשִׁיעָה נָּא.

אֵל נָא וְזָכוֹר תִּזְכֹּר
הַנְּכוּרִים בְּלֶתֶךָ וָכֹר הוֹשַׁע נָא וְהוֹשִׁיעָה נָּא.

אֵל נָא דּוֹרְשֶׁיךָ בְּעַנְפֵי עֲרָבוֹת
גַּעְיָם שְׁעֵה מֵעֲרָבוֹת הוֹשַׁע נָא וְהוֹשִׁיעָה נָּא.

אֵל נָא בָּרֵךְ בְּעִטּוּר שָׁנָה
אֲמָרֵי רְצֵה בְּפִלּוּלִי
בְּיוֹם הוֹשַׁעְנָא הוֹשַׁע נָא וְהוֹשִׁיעָה נָּא.

קהל *then* שליח ציבור:

**אָנָּא, אֵל נָא, הוֹשַׁע נָא וְהוֹשִׁיעָה נָּא, אָבִינוּ אָתָּה.**

לְמַעַן תָּמִים בְּדוֹרוֹתָיו, הַנִּמְלָט בְּרֹב צִדְקוֹתָיו
מֻצָּל מִשֶּׁטֶף בְּבוֹא מַבּוּל מַיִם.
לְאֹם אֲנִי חוֹמָה הוֹשַׁע נָא וְהוֹשִׁיעָה נָּא, אָבִינוּ אָתָּה.

לְמַעַן שָׁלֵם בְּכָל מַעֲשִׂים, הַמְנֻסֶּה בַּעֲשָׂרָה נִסִּים
כְּשֶׁר מַלְאָכִים, נָם יֻקַּח נָא מְעַט מַיִם.
לְבָרָה כַּחַמָּה הוֹשַׁע נָא וְהוֹשִׁיעָה נָּא, אָבִינוּ אָתָּה.

For the sake of a tender, only child, young fruit borne to a man of a hundred,
who cried out, "Where is the lamb for the burnt offering?!"
Whose servants brought him news: "We have found water!" –
the people expelled and banished –
save, please: save us, please: You are our Father.

For the sake of one who came in first to bear blessing,
who gained a foe and waited for salvation by Your name;
who made goats fertile with branches, by troughs of water –
the people likened to a date palm –
save, please: save us, please: You are our Father.

For the sake of the one righteous enough to be chosen as Your priest,
serving You like a bridegroom adorned,
tested at Masa, by the Mei Meriva water –
the good mountain – save, please: save us, please: You are our Father.

For the sake of the one raised to be master of his brothers,
Judah who became the most powerful of brothers,
numerous as dust; his pail overflows with water –
not for us, but for Your sake –
save, please: save us, please: You are our Father.

For the sake of the humblest of men, the most faithful,
for whose righteous sake the manna fell,
pulled to be redeemer, drawn forth from the water –
this people, gazing out – save, please: save us, please: You are our Father.

For the sake of one You raised like angels of the heights, clad with the urim
and tumim, commanded to come into the Temple with sanctified
hands and feet, bathed in water –
this people sick with love –
save, please: save us, please: You are our Father.

For the sake of the prophetess who danced between the camps;
to whom the people on their yearning journey raised their eyes [to lead
them]; for her sake it moved, it rose and it rested, the well of water –
the people of the goodly tents –
save, please: save us, please: You are our Father.

For the sake of the servant who never left the Tent, over whom the holy
spirit rested, for whose sake the Jordan parted its water –
the people beautiful and shining –
save, please: save us, please: You are our Father.

לְמַעַן רַךְ וְיָחִיד נֶחֱנַט פְּרִי לְמֵאָה, זָעַק אַיֵּה הַשֶּׂה לְעֹלָה
בִּשְּׂרוּהוּ עֲבָדָיו מָצָאנוּ מָיִם.
לְגוֹלָה וְסוּרָה הוֹשַׁע נָא וְהוֹשִׁיעָה נָּא, אָבִינוּ אָתָּה.

לְמַעַן קִדֵּם שְׂאֵת בְּרָכָה, הַנִּשְׂטָם וּלְשִׁמְךָ חִכָּה
מְיַחֵם בְּמַקְלוֹת בְּשִׁקְתוֹת הַמָּיִם.
לְדָמְתָה לְתָמָר הוֹשַׁע נָא וְהוֹשִׁיעָה נָּא, אָבִינוּ אָתָּה.

לְמַעַן צָדַק הֱיוֹת לְךָ לְכֹהֵן, כְּחָתָן פְּאֵר יְכַהֵן
מְנֻסֶּה בְּמַסָּה בְּמֵי מְרִיבַת מָיִם.
לְהָהָר הַטּוֹב הוֹשַׁע נָא וְהוֹשִׁיעָה נָּא, אָבִינוּ אָתָּה.

לְמַעַן פְּאֵר הֱיוֹת גְּבִיר לְאֶחָיו, יְהוּדָה אֲשֶׁר גָּבַר בְּאֶחָיו
מִסְפַּר רֹבַע מִדָּלְיָו יִזַּל מָיִם.
לֹא לָנוּ כִּי אִם לְמַעַנְךָ הוֹשַׁע נָא וְהוֹשִׁיעָה נָּא, אָבִינוּ אָתָּה.

לְמַעַן עָנָו מִכֹּל וְנֶאֱמָן, אֲשֶׁר בְּצִדְקוֹ כִּלְכֵּל הַמָּן
מָשׁוּךְ לְגוֹאֵל וּמָשׁוּי מִמָּיִם.
לְזֹאת הַנִּשְׁקָפָה הוֹשַׁע נָא וְהוֹשִׁיעָה נָּא, אָבִינוּ אָתָּה.

לְמַעַן שַׂמְתּוֹ כְּמַלְאֲכֵי מְרוֹמִים, הַלּוֹבֵשׁ אוּרִים וְתֻמִּים
מְצֻוֶּה לָבוֹא בַמִּקְדָּשׁ בְּקִדּוּשׁ יָדַיִם וְרַגְלַיִם וּרְחִיצַת מָיִם.
לְחוֹלַת אַהֲבָה הוֹשַׁע נָא וְהוֹשִׁיעָה נָּא, אָבִינוּ אָתָּה.

לְמַעַן נְבִיאָה מְחוֹלַת מַחֲנַיִם, לְכַמְהֵי לֵב הוּשְׂמָה עֵינַיִם
לְרַגְלָהּ רָצָה עֲלוֹת וָרֶדֶת בְּאֵר מָיִם.
לְטוֹבוּ אֹהָלָיו הוֹשַׁע נָא וְהוֹשִׁיעָה נָּא, אָבִינוּ אָתָּה.

לְמַעַן מְשָׁרֵת לֹא מָשׁ מֵאֹהֶל, וְרוּחַ הַקֹּדֶשׁ עָלָיו אָהֵל
בְּעָבְרוֹ בַיַּרְדֵּן נִכְרְתוּ הַמָּיִם.
לְיָפָה וּבָרָה הוֹשַׁע נָא וְהוֹשִׁיעָה נָּא, אָבִינוּ אָתָּה.

For the sake of the one taught to read a sign of good things,
who cried out, "Where are the wonders now?"
But later wrung rain from the wool – a whole bowl full of water –
the bride of Lebanon –
save, please: save us, please: You are our Father.

For the sake of one who ground his enemies alone, dedicated from the womb
a Nazirite, from the hollow of a jawbone You brought him forth water –
for Your holy name's sake –
save, please: save us, please: You are our Father.

For the sake of those included in the army of Your war,
at whose hands You gave Your salvation,
marked out from the people as from their hands they lapped up water –
those who never betrayed –
save, please: save us, please: You are our Father.

For the sake of the good child growing more and more,
who never allowed himself to take from the people;
when the people repented he said, "Draw forth water!" –
the people, lovely as Jerusalem –
save, please: save us, please: You are our Father.

For the sake of one who laughed and danced in song,
who taught the Torah through any instrument of music,
who libated before You, though he longed to drink water –
those who placed their hope in You –
save, please: save us, please: You are our Father.

For the sake of the pure one who went up in a storm cloud,
who was jealous for You and who turned back Your rage,
at whose word down came fire to lick the dust and water –
the people whose eyes are like pools –
save, please: save us, please: You are our Father.

For the sake of one who served his teacher truly,
and was assigned a double measure of his spirit.
When he called the musician to play, the pools were filled with water –
those who said "Who is like You?" –
save, please: save us, please: You are our Father.

לְמַעַן לָמַד רְאוֹת לְטוֹבָה אוֹת, זָעַק אַיֵּה נִפְלָאוֹת
מִצָּה טַל מִגִּזָּה מְלֹא הַסֵּפֶל מָיִם.
לְכַלַּת לְבָנוֹן הוֹשַׁע נָא וְהוֹשִׁיעָה נָּא, אָבִינוּ אָתָּה.

לְמַעַן כְּלוּלֵי עֲשׂוֹת מִלְחַמְתֶּךָ, אֲשֶׁר בְּיָדָם תַּתָּה יְשׁוּעָתֶךָ
צְרוּפֵי מִגּוֹי בְּלָקְקָם בְּיָדָם מָיִם.
לְלֹא בָגְדוּ בָךְ הוֹשַׁע נָא וְהוֹשִׁיעָה נָּא, אָבִינוּ אָתָּה.

לְמַעַן יָחִיד צוֹרְרִים דָּשׁ, אֲשֶׁר מֵרֶחֶם לְנָזִיר הֻקְדָּשׁ
מִמַּכְתֵּשׁ לֶחִי הִבְקַעְתָּ לוֹ מָיִם.
לְמַעַן שֵׁם קָדְשֶׁךָ הוֹשַׁע נָא וְהוֹשִׁיעָה נָּא, אָבִינוּ אָתָּה.

לְמַעַן טוֹב הוֹלֵךְ וְגָדֵל, אֲשֶׁר מֵעֹשֶׁק עֵדָה חִדֵּל
בְּשׁוּב עִם מֵחֵטְא צִוָּה שְׁאֹב מָיִם.
לְנָאוָה כִּירוּשָׁלָיִם הוֹשַׁע נָא וְהוֹשִׁיעָה נָּא, אָבִינוּ אָתָּה.

לְמַעַן חַיָּךְ מְכַרְכֵּר בְּשִׁיר, הַמְלַמֵּד תּוֹרָה בְּכָל כְּלֵי שִׁיר
מְנַסֵּךְ לְפָנֶיךָ כְּתָאַב שְׁתוֹת מָיִם.
לְשָׁמוּ בְּךָ סִבְרָם הוֹשַׁע נָא וְהוֹשִׁיעָה נָּא, אָבִינוּ אָתָּה.

לְמַעַן זָךְ עָלָה בַּסְּעָרָה, הַמְקַנֵּא וּמֵשִׁיב עֶבְרָה
לְפִלּוּלוֹ יָרְדָה אֵשׁ וְלִחֲכָה עָפָר וּמָיִם.
לְעֵינֶיהָ בְּרֵכוֹת הוֹשַׁע נָא וְהוֹשִׁיעָה נָּא, אָבִינוּ אָתָּה.

לְמַעַן וְשֵׁרֵת בֶּאֱמֶת לְרַבּוֹ, פִּי שְׁנַיִם בְּרוּחוֹ נֶאֱצַל בּוֹ
בְּקַחְתּוֹ מְנַגֵּן נִתְמַלְּאוּ גֵּבִים מָיִם.
לְפָצוּ מִי כָמֹכָה הוֹשַׁע נָא וְהוֹשִׁיעָה נָּא, אָבִינוּ אָתָּה.

For the sake of one who thought to do Your will,
who declared repentance to all Your flock;
then, when the blasphemer came, he stopped up all springs of water –
Zion, perfect beauty –
save, please: save us, please: You are our Father.

For the sake of those who sought You from the heart of Exile,
to whom Your secrets were revealed,
and not to be tainted [by meat and wine]
they asked for grains and water –
those who cry out to You from their distress –
save, please: save us, please: You are our Father.

For the sake of one who learned wisdom and insight,
the keen-minded scribe who set forth a pledge,
the one who made us wiser with words deep as oceans of water –
the [city that] flocked with people –
save, please: save us, please: You are our Father.

For the sake of those who come to You today with all their hearts,
who pour out their words without two minds,
who ask of You Your mighty torrents of water –
those who sang at the sea –
save, please: save us, please: You are our Father.

For the sake of those who say "May Your name be declared great" –
and they are Your inheritance, Your people;
who thirst for Your salvation as an arid land thirsts water –
those for whom You sought out a resting place –
save, please: save us, please: You are our Father.

*Leader then congregation:*

Save, please, God, please,
save us, please.

Save, please, please forgive
and grant us success, please.

Save us, God who is our Refuge.

*Put down the Lulav and Etrog and pick up the Hoshanot.*

לְמַעַן הִרְהֵר עֲשׂוֹת רְצוֹנֶךָ, הַמַּכְרִיז תְּשׁוּבָה לְצֹאנֶךָ
אָז בְּבוֹא מְחָרֵף סָתַם עֵינוֹת מָיִם.
לְצִיּוֹן מִכְלַל יֹפִי הוֹשַׁע נָא וְהוֹשִׁיעָה נָא, אָבִינוּ אָתָּה.

לְמַעַן דְּרָשׁוּךָ בְּתוֹךְ הַגּוֹלָה, וְסוֹדְךָ לָמוֹ נִגְלָה
בְּלִי לְהִתְגָּאֵל דָּרְשׁוּ זֵרְעוֹנִים וּמַיִם.
לְקוֹרְאֶיךָ בַּצָּר הוֹשַׁע נָא וְהוֹשִׁיעָה נָא, אָבִינוּ אָתָּה.

לְמַעַן גָּמַר חָכְמָה וּבִינָה, סוֹפֵר מָהִיר מְפַלֵּשׁ אֲמָנָה
מְחַכְּמֵנוּ אֲמָרִים הַמְּשׁוּלִים בְּרַחֲבֵי מָיִם.
לְרַבָּתִי עָם הוֹשַׁע נָא וְהוֹשִׁיעָה נָא, אָבִינוּ אָתָּה.

לְמַעַן בָּאֵי לְךָ הַיּוֹם בְּכָל לֵב, שׁוֹפְכִים לְךָ שִׂיחַ בְּלֹא לֵב וָלֵב
שׁוֹאֲלִים מִמְּךָ עֹז מִטְרוֹת מָיִם.
לְשׁוֹרְרוּ בַיָּם הוֹשַׁע נָא וְהוֹשִׁיעָה נָא, אָבִינוּ אָתָּה.

לְמַעַן אוֹמְרֵי יִגְדַּל שְׁמֶךָ, וְהֵם נַחֲלָתְךָ וְעַמֶּךָ
צְמֵאִים לְיִשְׁעֲךָ כְּאֶרֶץ עֲיֵפָה לַמָּיִם.
לְתַרְתָּ לָמוֹ מְנוּחָה הוֹשַׁע נָא וְהוֹשִׁיעָה נָא, אָבִינוּ אָתָּה.

*קהל then שליח ציבור:*

**הוֹשַׁע נָא, אֵל נָא**
**אָנָּא הוֹשִׁיעָה נָּא.**

**הוֹשַׁע נָא, סְלַח נָא**
**וְהַצְלִיחָה נָא**

**וְהוֹשִׁיעֵנוּ אֵל מָעֻזֵּנוּ.**

*Put down the לולב and אתרוג and pick up the הושענות.*

תַּעֲנֶה Answer the faithful ones who pour out their hearts
to You like water – and save us, please;
for the sake of [Abraham] who came through
fire and water – and grant us success, please;
He gave the order and said, "Please, bring
a little water" – save us, God our Refuge.

Answer the flagged tribes who went swift through the split sea – and save us, please;
for the sake of [Isaac who was] bound at the
gate of heaven – and grant us success, please;
he who yet lived to return and to dig out
wells of water – save us, God our Refuge.

Answer the pure ones encamped on the water – and save us, please;
for the sake of smooth-skinned [Jacob] who
peeled branches by troughs of water – and grant us success, please;
he who heaved and rolled a rock from the
well of water – save us, God our Refuge.

Answer the beloved ones, heirs to a Law likened to water – and save us, please;
for the sake of those [princes in the wilderness]
whose staffs drew forth water – and grant us success, please;
to prepare for them and for their children –
water – save us, God our Refuge.

Answer those who plead as in the wilderness for water – and save us, please;
for the sake of [Moses], trusted in Your household,
who provided the people with water – and grant us success, please;
he hit the rock and out flowed water – save us, God our Refuge.

Answer those who sang in the wilderness, "Spring up, well
of water!" – and save us, please;
for the sake of [Aaron,] commanded at the
Mei Meriva water – and grant us success, please;
commanded to give those who thirsted, water – save us, God our Refuge.

Answer the holy ones who pour before You water – and save us, please;
for the sake of [David] father of song-makers
who longed to drink water – and grant us success, please;
but who held back and poured before You water –
save us, God our Refuge.

Answer those who come to beseech You with four species
grown by water – and save us, please;
for the sake of the Hill of ruins all mouths pray
towards, the source of water – and grant us success, please;
open up the earth and let the heavens rain down water –
and save us, God our Refuge.

תַּעֲנֶה אֱמוּנִים שׁוֹפְכִים לְךָ לֵב כַּמַּיִם וְהוֹשִׁיעָה נָּא.
לְמַעַן בָּא בָאֵשׁ וּבַמַּיִם וְהַצְלִיחָה נָא.
גָּזַר וְנָם יֻקַּח נָא מְעַט מַיִם וְהוֹשִׁיעֵנוּ אֵל מָעֻזֵּנוּ.

תַּעֲנֶה דְּגָלִים גָּזוּ גִּזְרֵי מַיִם וְהוֹשִׁיעָה נָּא.
לְמַעַן הַנֶּעֱקַד בְּשַׁעַר הַשָּׁמַיִם וְהַצְלִיחָה נָא.
וְשָׁב וְחָפַר בְּאֵרוֹת מַיִם וְהוֹשִׁיעֵנוּ אֵל מָעֻזֵּנוּ.

תַּעֲנֶה זַכִּים חוֹנִים עֲלֵי מַיִם וְהוֹשִׁיעָה נָּא.
לְמַעַן חָלָק מְפַצֵּל מַקְלוֹת בְּשִׁקְתוֹת הַמַּיִם וְהַצְלִיחָה נָא.
טָעַן וְגָל אֶבֶן מִבְּאֵר מַיִם וְהוֹשִׁיעֵנוּ אֵל מָעֻזֵּנוּ.

תַּעֲנֶה יְדִידִים נוֹחֲלֵי דָת מְשׁוּלַת מַיִם וְהוֹשִׁיעָה נָּא.
לְמַעַן כָּרוּ בְּמִשְׁעֲנוֹתָם מַיִם וְהַצְלִיחָה נָא.
לְהָכִין לָמוֹ וּלְצֶאֱצָאֵימוֹ מַיִם וְהוֹשִׁיעֵנוּ אֵל מָעֻזֵּנוּ.

תַּעֲנֶה מִתְחַנְּנִים כְּבִישִׁימוֹן עֲלֵי מַיִם וְהוֹשִׁיעָה נָּא.
לְמַעַן נֶאֱמַן בַּיִת מַסְפִּיק לָעָם מַיִם וְהַצְלִיחָה נָא.
סֶלַע הָךְ וַיָּזוּבוּ מַיִם וְהוֹשִׁיעֵנוּ אֵל מָעֻזֵּנוּ.

תַּעֲנֶה עוֹנִים עֲלֵי בְּאֵר מַיִם וְהוֹשִׁיעָה נָּא.
לְמַעַן פָּקַד בְּמֵי מְרִיבַת מַיִם וְהַצְלִיחָה נָא.
צְמֵאִים לְהַשְׁקוֹת מַיִם וְהוֹשִׁיעֵנוּ אֵל מָעֻזֵּנוּ.

תַּעֲנֶה קְדוֹשִׁים מְנַסְּכִים לְךָ מַיִם וְהוֹשִׁיעָה נָּא.
לְמַעַן רֹאשׁ מְשׁוֹרְרִים כְּתָאַב שְׁתוֹת מַיִם וְהַצְלִיחָה נָא.
שָׁב וְנָסַךְ לְךָ מַיִם וְהוֹשִׁיעֵנוּ אֵל מָעֻזֵּנוּ.

תַּעֲנֶה שׁוֹאֲלִים בְּרִבּוּעַ אֶשְׁלֵי מַיִם וְהוֹשִׁיעָה נָּא.
לְמַעַן תֵּל תַּלְפִּיּוֹת מוֹצָא מַיִם וְהַצְלִיחָה נָא.
תִּפְתַּח אֶרֶץ וְתַרְעִיף שָׁמַיִם וְהוֹשִׁיעֵנוּ אֵל מָעֻזֵּנוּ.

*Leader then congregation:*

Have compassion, please,
for the community of the people of Yeshurun;
forgive and pardon their iniquity,
and save us, God of our salvation.

אֹז As the eyes of slaves are raised / to their masters' hands,
we come before You, judged, save us, God of our salvation.

Proud Masters of masters, / they have brought us to conflict;
they have trampled us; other masters have mastered us,
so save us, God of our salvation.

We have come today, pleading – / before You, Compassionate and Gracious One,
telling and repeating Your wondrous acts, now save us, God of our salvation.

Please do not dry up / what flowed with milk and honey;
heal the land's pain with clouds full of water and save us, God of our salvation.

Plant us in luscious land, / at the hand of the seven shepherds, the eight princes,
righteous, upright God of faithfulness, yes, save us, God of our salvation.

You forged a covenant with the land / for as long as the earth will be,
never to break it apart again, so save us, God of our salvation.

Those who plead with You for water / as willows thirst over streams of water –
remember for them the libation of water and save us, God of our salvation.

As they plead they carry with them / plants, held straight as they grow;
answer their prayer, their voice and save us, God of our salvation.

You who work salvations, / turn to hear their prayers,
and vindicate them, God of salvation, to save us, God of our salvation.

Listen to the voice of their crowds who come, / and open the earth, to bear
fruit of salvation, You who are great in saving, who desire no evil,
save us, God of our salvation.

Open the gates of heaven, / and throw open Your treasury of good.
Save us, and do not press Your claims against us
but save us, God of our salvation.

*Leader then congregation:*

Open the gates of heaven,
and Your treasure-house of goodness – open for us.
Save us and do not extend judgment against us –
and save us, God of our salvation.

קהל then שליח ציבור:

**רַחֵם נָא קְהַל עֲדַת יְשׁוּרוּן, סְלַח וּמְחַל עֲוֹנָם**
**וְהוֹשִׁיעֵנוּ אֱלֹהֵי יִשְׁעֵנוּ.**

אָז כְּעֵינֵי עֲבָדִים אֶל יַד אֲדוֹנִים
בָּאנוּ לְפָנֶיךָ נְדוֹנִים. וְהוֹשִׁיעֵנוּ אֱלֹהֵי יִשְׁעֵנוּ.

גֵּאֶה אֲדוֹנֵי הָאֲדוֹנִים, נִתְגָּרוּ בָנוּ מְדָנִים
דְּשׁוּנוּ וּבְעָלוּנוּ זוּלָתְךָ אֲדוֹנִים. וְהוֹשִׁיעֵנוּ אֱלֹהֵי יִשְׁעֵנוּ.

הֵן גַּשְׁנוּ הַיּוֹם בְּתַחֲנוּן, עָדֶיךָ רַחוּם וְחַנּוּן
וְסִפַּרְנוּ נִפְלְאוֹתֶיךָ בְּשִׁנּוּן. וְהוֹשִׁיעֵנוּ אֱלֹהֵי יִשְׁעֵנוּ.

זָבַת חָלָב וּדְבָשׁ, נָא אַל תִּיבָשׁ
חֲשְׂרַת מַיִם כְּאֵבָה תֶּחְבָּשׁ. וְהוֹשִׁיעֵנוּ אֱלֹהֵי יִשְׁעֵנוּ.

טָעֵנוּ בַשְּׁמֵנָה, בְּיַד שִׁבְעָה וּשְׁמוֹנָה
יָשָׁר צַדִּיק אֵל אֱמוּנָה. וְהוֹשִׁיעֵנוּ אֱלֹהֵי יִשְׁעֵנוּ.

כָּרַתָּ בְּרִית לָאָרֶץ, עוֹד כָּל יְמֵי הָאָרֶץ
לְבִלְתִּי פְּרָץ בָּהּ פָּרֶץ. וְהוֹשִׁיעֵנוּ אֱלֹהֵי יִשְׁעֵנוּ.

מִתְחַנְּנִים עֲלֵי מַיִם, כַּעֲרָבִים עַל יִבְלֵי מַיִם
נָא זְכָר לָמוֹ נִסּוּךְ הַמַּיִם. וְהוֹשִׁיעֵנוּ אֱלֹהֵי יִשְׁעֵנוּ.

שִׂיחִים בְּדֶרֶךְ מַטָּעָתָם, עוֹמְסִים בְּשַׁוְעָתָם
עֲנֵם בְּקוֹל פְּגִיעָתָם. וְהוֹשִׁיעֵנוּ אֱלֹהֵי יִשְׁעֵנוּ.

פּוֹעֵל יְשׁוּעוֹת, פְּנֵה לְפִלּוּלָם שְׁעוֹת
צַדְּקֵם אֵל לְמוֹשָׁעוֹת. וְהוֹשִׁיעֵנוּ אֱלֹהֵי יִשְׁעֵנוּ.

קוֹל רִגְשָׁם תֶּשַׁע, תִּפְתַּח אֶרֶץ וְיִפְרוּ יֶשַׁע
רַב לְהוֹשִׁיעַ וְלֹא חָפֵץ רֶשַׁע. וְהוֹשִׁיעֵנוּ אֱלֹהֵי יִשְׁעֵנוּ.

קהל then שליח ציבור:

**שַׁעֲרֵי שָׁמַיִם פְּתַח, וְאוֹצָרְךָ הַטּוֹב לָנוּ תִפְתַּח.**
**תּוֹשִׁיעֵנוּ וְרִיב אַל תִּמְתַּח. וְהוֹשִׁיעֵנוּ אֱלֹהֵי יִשְׁעֵנוּ.**

*Leader then congregation:*

The voice of the herald, he heralds and says –

אֹמֶן Your true salvation is coming; / the voice of my Beloved, here He is
coming – heralding, saying. / A voice: He is coming with myriad [heavenly]
legions, / coming to stand on the Mount of Olives – heralding, saying. /
A voice: He is coming to sound the shofar, / as the mount is broken in half
beneath Him – heralding, saying. / A voice: He knocks, He looks, He shines
out, / and half the mount is moved from the east – heralding, saying. /
A voice: He is fulfilling the words He spoke / and coming, and all His holy
ones with Him – heralding, saying. / A voice: and for all who have come
into this world, / the echo is heard in all the world – heralding, saying. /
A voice: the children borne of His womb, / were born in a day like a child
of his mother – heralding, saying. / A voice: she labored and bore – who is
this? / Who has heard of anything like this? – heralding, saying. / A voice: *Is. 66*
the Pure One who wrought all this – / and who has seen anything like this? – *Ibid.*
heralding, saying. / A voice: salvation, its time already set; / can the land give *Ibid.*
birth all in a day? – heralding, saying. / A voice: the One mighty above and
below, / can a nation be born all in one birth? – heralding, saying. / A voice: *Ibid.*
when the shining One redeems His people, / as evening falls, there shall be *Zech. 14*
light – heralding, saying. / A voice: saviors shall go up to Mount Zion: / for
Zion has labored and has given birth – heralding, saying. / A voice is heard *Is. 66*
throughout your borders: / "Broaden the spread of your tents!" – heralding, *Is. 54*
saying. / A voice: "Let your home extend as far as Damascus; / receive your
sons and your daughters" – heralding, saying. / A voice: "Be joyful, dune
flower of the coast; / for the [forebears] who slept in Hebron are awoken" –
heralding, saying. / A voice: "Turn to Me and be saved; / today, if you heed *Is. 45*
My voice" – heralding, saying. / A voice: a [savior] has grown up, Tzemaḥ
his name, / and he is none other than David himself – heralding, saying. /
A voice: "Rise up, you who lie in the ashes; / awaken and sing, you who sleep *Is. 26*
in the dust" – heralding, saying. / A voice: the city flocking with people for
his crowning: / a tower of salvation, His own king – heralding, saying. / *II Sam. 22*
A voice to silence the names of the wicked; / dealing kindly with his anointed, *Ibid.*
David – heralding, saying. / A voice: grant salvation to an eternal people; / *Ibid.*
to David and his descendants forever – heralding, saying.

*The Leader says three times, then the congregation repeats three times:*

The voice of the herald, he heralds and says –

קהל then שליח ציבור:

## קוֹל מְבַשֵּׂר מְבַשֵּׂר וְאוֹמֵר.

אֹמֶן יֶשְׁעֲךָ בָּא, קוֹל דּוֹדִי הִנֵּה זֶה בָּא. מְבַשֵּׂר וְאוֹמֵר.
בָּא בְּרִבְבוֹת כִּתִּים, לַעֲמֹד עַל הַר הַזֵּיתִים. מְבַשֵּׂר וְאוֹמֵר.
גִּשְׁתּוֹ בַּשּׁוֹפָר לִתְקַע, תַּחְתָּיו הַר יִבָּקַע. מְבַשֵּׂר וְאוֹמֵר.
דָּפַק וְהֵצִיץ וְזָרַח, וּמָשׁ חֲצִי הָהָר מִמִּזְרָח. מְבַשֵּׂר וְאוֹמֵר.
הֵקִים מִלּוּל נְאֻמוֹ, וּבָא הוּא וְכָל קְדוֹשָׁיו עִמּוֹ. מְבַשֵּׂר וְאוֹמֵר.
וּלְכָל בָּאֵי הָעוֹלָם, בַּת קוֹל יִשָּׁמַע בָּעוֹלָם. מְבַשֵּׂר וְאוֹמֵר.
זֶרַע עֲמוּסֵי רַחְמוֹ, נוֹלְדוּ כְּיֶלֶד מִמְּעֵי אִמּוֹ. מְבַשֵּׂר וְאוֹמֵר.
חָלָה וְיָלְדָה מִי זֹאת, מִי־שָׁמַע כָּזֹאת. מְבַשֵּׂר וְאוֹמֵר. ישעיה סו
טָהוֹר פָּעַל כָּל אֵלֶּה, מִי רָאָה כָּאֵלֶּה. מְבַשֵּׂר וְאוֹמֵר. ישעיה סו
יֶשַׁע וּזְמַן הוּחַד, הֲיוּחַל אֶרֶץ בְּיוֹם אֶחָד. מְבַשֵּׂר וְאוֹמֵר. ישעיה סו
כַּבִּיר רוּם וָתַחַת, אִם־יִוָּלֵד גּוֹי פַּעַם אֶחָת. מְבַשֵּׂר וְאוֹמֵר. ישעיה סו
לְעֵת יִגְאַל עַמּוֹ נָאוֹר, וְהָיָה לְעֵת־עֶרֶב יִהְיֶה־אוֹר. מְבַשֵּׂר וְאוֹמֵר. זכריה יד
מוֹשִׁיעִים יַעֲלוּ לְהַר צִיּוֹן, כִּי־חָלָה גַּם־יָלְדָה צִיּוֹן. מְבַשֵּׂר וְאוֹמֵר. ישעיה סו
נִשְׁמַע בְּכָל גְּבוּלֵךְ, הַרְחִיבִי מְקוֹם אָהֳלֵךְ. מְבַשֵּׂר וְאוֹמֵר. ישעיה נד
שִׂימִי עַד דַּמֶּשֶׂק מִשְׁכְּנוֹתַיִךְ, קַבְּלִי בָנַיִךְ וּבְנוֹתַיִךְ. מְבַשֵּׂר וְאוֹמֵר.
עִלְזִי חֲבַצֶּלֶת הַשָּׁרוֹן, כִּי קָמוּ יְשֵׁנֵי חֶבְרוֹן. מְבַשֵּׂר וְאוֹמֵר.
פְּנוּ אֵלַי וְהִוָּשְׁעוּ, הַיּוֹם אִם בְּקוֹלִי תִשְׁמָעוּ. מְבַשֵּׂר וְאוֹמֵר.
צָמַח אִישׁ צֶמַח שְׁמוֹ, הוּא דָוִד בְּעַצְמוֹ. מְבַשֵּׂר וְאוֹמֵר.
קוּמוּ כְּפוּשֵׁי עָפָר, הָקִיצוּ וְרַנְּנוּ שֹׁכְנֵי עָפָר. מְבַשֵּׂר וְאוֹמֵר. ישעיה כו
רַבָּתִי עָם בְּהַמְלִיכוֹ, מִגְדּוֹל יְשׁוּעוֹת מַלְכּוֹ. מְבַשֵּׂר וְאוֹמֵר. שמואל ב׳ כב
שֵׁם רְשָׁעִים לְהַאֲבִיד, עֹשֶׂה־חֶסֶד לִמְשִׁיחוֹ לְדָוִד. מְבַשֵּׂר וְאוֹמֵר. שמואל ב׳ כב
תְּנָה יְשׁוּעוֹת לְעַם עוֹלָם, לְדָוִד וּלְזַרְעוֹ עַד־עוֹלָם. מְבַשֵּׂר וְאוֹמֵר. שמואל ב׳ כב

שליח ציבור *says three times then* קהל *repeats three times:*

## קוֹל מְבַשֵּׂר מְבַשֵּׂר וְאוֹמֵר.

*Beat the Hoshanot against a chair or the floor five times, then say the following (see law 118):*

הוֹשִׁיעָה Save Your people; bless Your legacy; Ps. 28
tend them and carry them forever.
Let these words with which I have pleaded with the Lord 1 Kings 8
be close to the Lord our God day and night,
that they may do justice for His servant,
and justice for His people Israel, day after day;
so that all the peoples of the earth will know
that the Lord is God.
There is no other.

*The Torah scrolls are returned to the Ark, which is then closed.*

May it be Your will, Lord our God, God of our ancestors, who chooses good prophets, and their good customs – to receive our prayers and our circlings with compassion and favor. Remember for us the merit of Your seven perfect ones, and remove the wall of iron that separates us from You, and hear our pleas, and seal us with a good judgment – You who suspends the world over nothingness. And seal us in the book of good life.

On this day, invest Your mighty Presence with the five sweetened powers – by means of the beating of the willows, the custom of Your holy prophets – and let love be awakened among them. Kiss us with the kisses of Your mouth, which sweetens all might and all judgments. Shine light upon Your mighty Presence, by the name *Yod-Heh-Vav*, which is the dew that is a dew of light. And from that place, emanate plenty to Your servant, who prays here before You; lengthen his life and forgive him his sins and iniquities and rebellions. And extend Your hand, Your right hand, to receive him in full repentance before You. Open Your treasury of good, to satisfy the yearning soul with water, as it is written, "The Lord will open His good treasury for You, open the heavens, to grant your land its rain in its right time, and to bless all the work of your hands:" Amen. Deut. 28

*The Leader continues with Full Kaddish on page 242.*

*Beat the* הושענות *against a chair or the floor five times, then say the following (see law 118):*

הוֹשִׁיעָה אֶת־עַמֶּךָ, וּבָרֵךְ אֶת־נַחֲלָתֶךָ תהלים כח
וּרְעֵם וְנַשְּׂאֵם עַד־הָעוֹלָם:
וְיִהְיוּ דְבָרַי אֵלֶּה, אֲשֶׁר הִתְחַנַּנְתִּי לִפְנֵי יהוה מלכים א׳ ח
קְרֹבִים אֶל־יהוה אֱלֹהֵינוּ יוֹמָם וָלָיְלָה
לַעֲשׂוֹת מִשְׁפַּט עַבְדּוֹ וּמִשְׁפַּט עַמּוֹ יִשְׂרָאֵל
דְּבַר־יוֹם בְּיוֹמוֹ:
לְמַעַן דַּעַת כָּל־עַמֵּי הָאָרֶץ כִּי יהוה הוּא הָאֱלֹהִים
אֵין עוֹד:

*The* ספרי תורה *are returned to the* ארון קודש*, which is then closed.*

יְהִי רָצוֹן מִלְּפָנֶיךָ יהוה אֱלֹהֵינוּ וֵאלֹהֵי אֲבוֹתֵינוּ, הַבּוֹחֵר בִּנְבִיאִים טוֹבִים וּבְמִנְהֲגֵיהֶם הַטּוֹבִים, שֶׁתְּקַבֵּל בְּרַחֲמִים וּבְרָצוֹן אֶת תְּפִלָּתֵנוּ וְהַקָּפוֹתֵינוּ. וּזְכָר לָנוּ זְכוּת שִׁבְעַת תְּמִימֶיךָ, וְתָסִיר מְחִצַּת הַבַּרְזֶל הַמַּפְסֶקֶת בֵּינֵינוּ וּבֵינֶיךָ, וְתַאֲזִין שַׁוְעָתֵנוּ, וְתֵיטִיב לָנוּ הַחֲתִימָה, תּוֹלֶה אֶרֶץ עַל בְּלִימָה, וְחָתְמֵנוּ בְּסֵפֶר חַיִּים טוֹבִים.

וְהַיּוֹם הַזֶּה תִּתֵּן בִּשְׁכִינַת עֻזֶּךָ חָמֵשׁ גְּבוּרוֹת מְמֻתָּקוֹת, עַל יְדֵי חֲבִיטַת עֲרָבָה מִנְהַג נְבִיאֶיךָ הַקְּדוֹשִׁים, וְתִתְעוֹרֵר הָאַהֲבָה בֵּינֵיהֶם. וּתְנַשְּׁקֵנוּ מִנְּשִׁיקוֹת פִּיךָ, מְמַתֶּקֶת כָּל הַגְּבוּרוֹת וְכָל הַדִּינִין. וְתָאִיר לִשְׁכִינַת עֻזְּךָ בְּשֵׁם יוּ״ד הֵ״א וָא״ו שֶׁהוּא טַל אוֹרוֹת טַלֶּךָ, וּמִשָּׁם תַּשְׁפִּיעַ שֶׁפַע לְעַבְדְּךָ הַמִּתְפַּלֵּל לְפָנֶיךָ, שֶׁתַּאֲרִיךְ יָמָיו וְתִמְחַל לוֹ חֲטָאָיו וַעֲוֹנוֹתָיו וּפְשָׁעָיו. וְתִפְשֹׁט יְמִינְךָ וְיָדְךָ לְקַבְּלוֹ בִּתְשׁוּבָה שְׁלֵמָה לְפָנֶיךָ. וְאוֹצָרְךָ הַטּוֹב תִּפְתַּח לְהַשְׂבִּיעַ מַיִם נֶפֶשׁ שׁוֹקֵקָה, כְּמוֹ שֶׁכָּתוּב: יִפְתַּח יהוה דברים כח
לְךָ אֶת־אוֹצָרוֹ הַטּוֹב אֶת־הַשָּׁמַיִם לָתֵת מְטַר־אַרְצְךָ בְּעִתּוֹ, וּלְבָרֵךְ אֵת כָּל־מַעֲשֵׂה יָדֶךָ: אָמֵן.

*The* שליח ציבור *continues with* קדיש שלם *on page 243.*

## ANNULMENT OF VOWS

*On the morning before Rosh HaShana, one should annul vows before three men, who sit as judges, saying:*

שִׁמְעוּ נָא Listen, please, my masters (expert judges): every vow or oath or prohibition or restriction or ban that I have vowed or sworn, whether awake or in a dream, or that I swore with one of the holy names that may not be erased, or by the holy four-letter name of God, blessed be He, or any naziriteship that I accepted on myself, even a naziriteship like that of Samson, or any prohibition, even against enjoyment, whether I forbade it to myself or others, by any expression of prohibition, whether using the language of prohibition or restriction or ban, or any positive commitment, even to perform a [non-obligatory] commandment, that I undertook by way of a vow or voluntary undertaking or oath or naziriteship or any other such expression, whether it was done by handshake or vow or voluntary undertaking or commandment-mandated custom I have customarily practiced, or any utterance that I have verbalized, or any non-obligatory commandment or good practice or conduct I have vowed and resolved in my heart to do, and have done three times without specifying that it does not have the force of a vow, whether it relates to myself or others, both those known to me and those I have already forgotten – regarding all of them, I hereby express my retroactive regret, and ask and seek their annulment from you, my eminences. For I fear that I may stumble and be trapped, Heaven forbid, in the sin of vows, oaths, naziriteships, bans, prohibitions, restrictions and agreements. I do not regret, Heaven forbid, the performance of the good deeds I have done. I regret, rather, having accepted them on myself in the language of vow, oath, naziriteship, prohibition, ban, restriction, agreement or acceptance of the heart.

Therefore I request annulment for them all.

# התרת נדרים

*On the morning before* ראש השנה*, one should annul vows before three men, who sit as judges, saying:*

שִׁמְעוּ נָא רַבּוֹתַי (דַּיָּנִים מֻמְחִים), כָּל נֶדֶר אוֹ שְׁבוּעָה אוֹ אִסָּר אוֹ קוֹנָם אוֹ חֵרֶם שֶׁנָּדַרְתִּי אוֹ נִשְׁבַּעְתִּי בְּהָקִיץ אוֹ בַחֲלוֹם, אוֹ נִשְׁבַּעְתִּי בְּשֵׁמוֹת הַקְּדוֹשִׁים שֶׁאֵינָם נִמְחָקִים וּבְשֵׁם הוי״ה בָּרוּךְ הוּא, וְכָל מִינֵי נְזִירוּת שֶׁקִּבַּלְתִּי עָלַי וַאֲפִלּוּ נְזִירוּת שִׁמְשׁוֹן, וְכָל שׁוּם אִסּוּר וַאֲפִלּוּ אִסּוּר הֲנָאָה שֶׁאָסַרְתִּי עָלַי אוֹ עַל אֲחֵרִים בְּכָל לָשׁוֹן שֶׁל אִסּוּר בֵּין בִּלְשׁוֹן אִסּוּר אוֹ חֵרֶם אוֹ קוֹנָם, וְכָל שׁוּם קַבָּלָה אֲפִלּוּ שֶׁל מִצְוָה שֶׁקִּבַּלְתִּי עָלַי בֵּין בִּלְשׁוֹן נֶדֶר בֵּין בִּלְשׁוֹן נְדָבָה בֵּין בִּלְשׁוֹן שְׁבוּעָה בֵּין בִּלְשׁוֹן נְזִירוּת בֵּין בְּכָל לָשׁוֹן, וְגַם הַנַּעֲשֶׂה בִתְקִיעַת כָּף. בֵּין כָּל נֶדֶר וּבֵין כָּל נְדָבָה וּבֵין שׁוּם מִנְהָג שֶׁל מִצְוָה שֶׁנָּהַגְתִּי אֶת עַצְמִי, וְכָל מוֹצָא שְׂפָתַי שֶׁיָּצָא מִפִּי אוֹ שֶׁנָּדַרְתִּי וְגָמַרְתִּי בְלִבִּי לַעֲשׂוֹת שׁוּם מִצְוָה מֵהַמִּצְוֹת אוֹ אֵיזוֹ הַנְהָגָה טוֹבָה אוֹ אֵיזֶה דָבָר טוֹב שֶׁנָּהַגְתִּי שָׁלֹשׁ פְּעָמִים, וְלֹא הִתְנֵיתִי שֶׁיְּהֵא בְּלִי נֶדֶר. הֵן דָּבָר שֶׁעָשִׂיתִי, הֵן עַל עַצְמִי הֵן עַל אֲחֵרִים, הֵן אוֹתָן הַיְדוּעִים לִי הֵן אוֹתָן שֶׁכְּבָר שָׁכַחְתִּי. בְּכֻלְּהוֹן אִתְחֲרַטְנָא בְהוֹן מֵעִקָּרָא, וְשׁוֹאֵל וּמְבַקֵּשׁ אֲנִי מִמַּעֲלַתְכֶם הַתָּרָה עֲלֵיהֶם, כִּי יָרֵאתִי פֶּן אֶכָּשֵׁל וְנִלְכַּדְתִּי, חַס וְשָׁלוֹם, בַּעֲוֹן נְדָרִים וּשְׁבוּעוֹת וּנְזִירוֹת וַחֲרָמוֹת וְאִסּוּרִין וְקוֹנָמוֹת וְהַסְכָּמוֹת. וְאֵין אֲנִי תוֹהֵא, חַס וְשָׁלוֹם, עַל קִיּוּם הַמַּעֲשִׂים הַטּוֹבִים הָהֵם שֶׁעָשִׂיתִי, רַק אֲנִי מִתְחָרֵט עַל קַבָּלַת הָעִנְיָנִים בִּלְשׁוֹן נֶדֶר אוֹ שְׁבוּעָה אוֹ נְזִירוּת אוֹ אִסּוּר אוֹ חֵרֶם אוֹ קוֹנָם אוֹ הַסְכָּמָה אוֹ קַבָּלָה בְלֵב, וּמִתְחָרֵט אֲנִי עַל זֶה שֶׁלֹּא אָמַרְתִּי הִנְנִי עוֹשֶׂה דָבָר זֶה בְּלִי נֶדֶר וּשְׁבוּעָה וּנְזִירוּת וְחֵרֶם וְאִסּוּר וְקוֹנָם וְקַבָּלָה בְלֵב.

לָכֵן אֲנִי שׁוֹאֵל הַתָּרָה בְּכֻלְּהוֹן.

I regret all these things I have mentioned, whether they related to monetary matters, or to the body or to the soul.

In relation to them all, I regret the language of vow, oath, naziriteship, prohibition, ban, penalty, and acceptance of the heart.

To be sure, according to the law, one who regrets and seeks annulment must specify the vow [from which he seeks release]. But please know, my masters, that it is impossible to specify them, for they are many. I do not seek release from vows that cannot be annulled. Therefore, may it be in your eyes as if I had specified them.

*The judges say the following three times:*

May all be permitted to you. May all be forgiven you. May all be allowed to you. There is now no vow, oath, naziriteship, ban, prohibition, penalty, ostracism, excommunication, or curse. There is now pardon, forgiveness and atonement. And just as the earthly court has granted permission, so may the heavenly court grant permission.

*The one seeking annulment of vows says:*

Behold I make a formal declaration before you that I cancel from now onward all vows and all oaths, naziriteships, prohibitions, penalties, bans, agreements and acceptances of the heart that I may accept upon myself, whether awake or in a dream, except a vow to fast that I undertake at the time of the afternoon prayer. If I forget the conditions of this declaration and make a vow from this day onward, as of now I retroactively regret them and declare them to be null and void, without effect or validity, and they shall have no force whatsoever. Regarding them all, I regret them from now and for ever.

אֲנִי מִתְחָרֵט עַל כָּל הַנִּזְכָּר, בֵּין אִם הָיוּ הַמַּעֲשִׂים מִדְּבָרִים הַנּוֹגְעִים בְּמָמוֹן, בֵּין מֵהַדְּבָרִים הַנּוֹגְעִים בְּגוּף, בֵּין מֵהַדְּבָרִים הַנּוֹגְעִים אֶל הַנְּשָׁמָה.

בְּכֻלְּהוֹן אֲנִי מִתְחָרֵט עַל לְשׁוֹן נֶדֶר וּשְׁבוּעָה וּנְזִירוּת וְאִסּוּר וְחֵרֶם וְקוֹנָם וְקַבָּלָה בְלֵב.

וְהִנֵּה מִצַּד הַדִּין הַמִּתְחָרֵט וְהַמְּבַקֵּשׁ הַתָּרָה צָרִיךְ לִפְרֹט הַנֶּדֶר, אַךְ דְּעוּ נָא רַבּוֹתַי, כִּי אִי אֶפְשָׁר לְפָרְטָם, כִּי רַבִּים הֵם. וְאֵין אֲנִי מְבַקֵּשׁ הַתָּרָה עַל אוֹתָם הַנְּדָרִים שֶׁאֵין לְהַתִּיר אוֹתָם, עַל כֵּן יִהְיוּ נָא בְעֵינֵיכֶם כְּאִלּוּ הָיִיתִי פוֹרְטָם.

*The judges say the following three times:*

הַכֹּל יִהְיוּ מֻתָּרִים לָךְ, הַכֹּל מְחוּלִים לָךְ, הַכֹּל שְׁרוּיִים לָךְ. אֵין כָּאן לֹא נֶדֶר וְלֹא שְׁבוּעָה וְלֹא נְזִירוּת וְלֹא חֵרֶם וְלֹא אִסּוּר וְלֹא קוֹנָם וְלֹא נִדּוּי וְלֹא שַׁמְתָּא וְלֹא אָרוּר. אֲבָל יֵשׁ כָּאן מְחִילָה וּסְלִיחָה וְכַפָּרָה. וּכְשֵׁם שֶׁמַּתִּירִים בְּבֵית דִּין שֶׁל מַטָּה, כָּךְ יִהְיוּ מֻתָּרִים מִבֵּית דִּין שֶׁל מַעְלָה.

*The one seeking annulment of vows says:*

הֲרֵי אֲנִי מוֹסֵר מוֹדָעָה לִפְנֵיכֶם, וַאֲנִי מְבַטֵּל מִכָּאן וּלְהַבָּא כָּל הַנְּדָרִים וְכָל שְׁבוּעוֹת וּנְזִירוֹת וְאִסּוּרִין וְקוֹנָמוֹת וַחֲרָמוֹת וְהַסְכָּמוֹת וְקַבָּלָה בְלֵב שֶׁאֲקַבֵּל עָלַי בְּעַצְמִי, הֵן בְּהָקִיץ הֵן בַּחֲלוֹם, חוּץ מִנִּדְרֵי תַעֲנִית בִּשְׁעַת מִנְחָה. וּבְאִם אֶשְׁכַּח לִתְנַאי מוֹדָעָה הַזֹּאת וְאֶדֹּר מֵהַיּוֹם עוֹד, מֵעַתָּה אֲנִי מִתְחָרֵט עֲלֵיהֶם וּמַתְנֶה עֲלֵיהֶם שֶׁיִּהְיוּ כֻּלָּן בְּטֵלִין וּמְבֻטָּלִין, לָא שְׁרִירִין וְלָא קַיָּמִין, וְלָא יְהוֹן חָלִין כְּלָל וּכְלָל. בְּכֻלָּן אִתְחֲרַטְנָא בְּהוֹן מֵעַתָּה וְעַד עוֹלָם.

## KIDDUSH FOR ROSH HASHANA EVENING

*On Shabbat add:*

*quietly:* And it was evening, and it was morning – *Gen. 1*
יוֹם הַשִּׁשִּׁי the sixth day.
Then the heavens and the earth were completed, *Gen. 2*
and all their array.
With the seventh day, God completed the work He had done.
He ceased on the seventh day from all the work He had done.
God blessed the seventh day and declared it holy,
because on it He ceased from all His work He had created to do.

*On other evenings start Kiddush here:*

*When saying Kiddush for others:* Please pay attention, my masters.

Blessed are You, Lord our God, King of the Universe,
who creates the fruit of the vine.

*On Shabbat, add the words in parentheses:*

בָּרוּךְ Blessed are You, Lord our God,
King of the Universe,
who has chosen us from among all peoples,
raised us above all tongues,
and made us holy through His commandments.
You have given us, Lord our God, in love,
this (Sabbath and this) Day of Remembrance,
a day of (remembering) blowing the shofar (in love),
a holy assembly in memory of the exodus from Egypt,
for You have chosen us and sanctified us above all peoples,
and Your word is true and endures for ever.
Blessed are You, Lord,
King over all the earth,
who sanctifies (the Sabbath and)
Israel and the Day of Remembrance.

# קידוש לליל ראש השנה

*On* שבת *add:*

בראשית א

*quietly* וַיְהִי־עֶרֶב וַיְהִי־בֹקֶר

יוֹם הַשִּׁשִּׁי:

בראשית ב

וַיְכֻלּוּ הַשָּׁמַיִם וְהָאָרֶץ וְכָל־צְבָאָם:
וַיְכַל אֱלֹהִים בַּיּוֹם הַשְּׁבִיעִי מְלַאכְתּוֹ אֲשֶׁר עָשָׂה
וַיִּשְׁבֹּת בַּיּוֹם הַשְּׁבִיעִי מִכָּל־מְלַאכְתּוֹ אֲשֶׁר עָשָׂה:
וַיְבָרֶךְ אֱלֹהִים אֶת־יוֹם הַשְּׁבִיעִי, וַיְקַדֵּשׁ אֹתוֹ
כִּי בוֹ שָׁבַת מִכָּל־מְלַאכְתּוֹ, אֲשֶׁר־בָּרָא אֱלֹהִים, לַעֲשׂוֹת:

*On other evenings start* קידוש *here:*

*When saying* קידוש *for others* סַבְרִי מָרָנָן

בָּרוּךְ אַתָּה יהוה אֱלֹהֵינוּ מֶלֶךְ הָעוֹלָם, בּוֹרֵא פְּרִי הַגָּפֶן.

*On* שבת*, add the words in parentheses:*

בָּרוּךְ אַתָּה יהוה אֱלֹהֵינוּ מֶלֶךְ הָעוֹלָם
אֲשֶׁר בָּחַר בָּנוּ מִכָּל עָם
וְרוֹמְמָנוּ מִכָּל לָשׁוֹן, וְקִדְּשָׁנוּ בְּמִצְוֹתָיו
וַתִּתֶּן לָנוּ יהוה אֱלֹהֵינוּ בְּאַהֲבָה
אֶת יוֹם (הַשַּׁבָּת הַזֶּה וְאֶת יוֹם)
הַזִּכָּרוֹן הַזֶּה, יוֹם (זִכְרוֹן) תְּרוּעָה
(בְּאַהֲבָה) מִקְרָא קֹדֶשׁ, זֵכֶר לִיצִיאַת מִצְרָיִם
כִּי בָנוּ בָחַרְתָּ וְאוֹתָנוּ קִדַּשְׁתָּ מִכָּל הָעַמִּים
וּדְבָרְךָ אֱמֶת וְקַיָּם לָעַד.
בָּרוּךְ אַתָּה יהוה, מֶלֶךְ עַל כָּל הָאָרֶץ
מְקַדֵּשׁ (הַשַּׁבָּת וְ) יִשְׂרָאֵל וְיוֹם הַזִּכָּרוֹן.

*On Motza'ei Shabbat, the following Havdala is added:*

בָּרוּךְ Blessed are You, Lord our God, King of the Universe, who creates the lights of fire.

Blessed are You, Lord our God, King of the Universe, who distinguishes between sacred and secular, between light and darkness, between Israel and the nations, between the seventh day and the six days of work. You have made a distinction between the holiness of the Sabbath and the holiness of festivals, and have sanctified the seventh day above the six days of work. You have distinguished and sanctified Your people Israel with Your holiness. Blessed are You, Lord, who distinguishes between sacred and sacred.

*The following blessing is said on both nights of Rosh HaShana. On the second night, new fruit is placed on the table, and one should have in mind that the blessing is also on the new fruit.*

בָּרוּךְ Blessed are You, Lord our God, King of the Universe,
who has given us life, sustained us, and brought us to this time.

*It is customary for all present to drink of the wine.*

*On the first night, following Kiddush and "HaMotzi," an apple is dipped in honey and the following is said:*

בָּרוּךְ Blessed are You, Lord our God, King of the Universe,
who creates the fruit of the tree.

*After eating some of the apple and honey, say:*

יְהִי רָצוֹן May it be Your will, Lord our God and God of our fathers,
that You renew for us a good and sweet year.

## KIDDUSH FOR ROSH HASHANA DAY

*On Shabbat first say "The children of Israel must keep" and "Remember the Sabbath day" on page 650.*

*On a Yom Tov that falls on a weekday, some start here:*

אֵלֶּה These are the appointed times of the Lord, sacred assemblies, which you shall announce in their due season. Thus Moses announced the Lord's appointed seasons to the children of Israel. *Lev. 23*

*On a Yom Tov that falls on a weekday, start here:*

תִּקְעוּ Sound the shofar on the new moon, *Ps. 81*
on our feast day when the moon is hidden.
For it is a statute for Israel, an ordinance of the God of Jacob.

*When saying Kiddush for others:* Please pay attention, my masters.

בָּרוּךְ Blessed are You, Lord our God, King of the Universe,
who creates the fruit of the vine.

*On מוצאי שבת, the following הבדלה is added:*

בָּרוּךְ אַתָּה יהוה אֱלֹהֵינוּ מֶלֶךְ הָעוֹלָם, בּוֹרֵא מְאוֹרֵי הָאֵשׁ.

בָּרוּךְ אַתָּה יהוה אֱלֹהֵינוּ מֶלֶךְ הָעוֹלָם, הַמַּבְדִּיל בֵּין קֹדֶשׁ לְחֹל, בֵּין אוֹר לְחֹשֶׁךְ, בֵּין יִשְׂרָאֵל לָעַמִּים, בֵּין יוֹם הַשְּׁבִיעִי לְשֵׁשֶׁת יְמֵי הַמַּעֲשֶׂה. בֵּין קְדֻשַּׁת שַׁבָּת לִקְדֻשַּׁת יוֹם טוֹב הִבְדַּלְתָּ, וְאֶת יוֹם הַשְּׁבִיעִי מִשֵּׁשֶׁת יְמֵי הַמַּעֲשֶׂה קִדַּשְׁתָּ, הִבְדַּלְתָּ וְקִדַּשְׁתָּ אֶת עַמְּךָ יִשְׂרָאֵל בִּקְדֻשָּׁתֶךָ. בָּרוּךְ אַתָּה יהוה, הַמַּבְדִּיל בֵּין קֹדֶשׁ לְקֹדֶשׁ.

*The following blessing is said on both nights of ראש השנה. On the second night, new fruit is placed on the table, and one should have in mind that the blessing is also on the new fruit.*

**בָּרוּךְ אַתָּה יהוה אֱלֹהֵינוּ מֶלֶךְ הָעוֹלָם**
**שֶׁהֶחֱיָנוּ וְקִיְּמָנוּ וְהִגִּיעָנוּ לַזְּמַן הַזֶּה.**

*It is customary for all present to drink of the wine.*

*On the first night, following קידוש and המוציא,*
*an apple is dipped in honey and the following is said:*

**בָּרוּךְ אַתָּה יהוה אֱלֹהֵינוּ מֶלֶךְ הָעוֹלָם, בּוֹרֵא פְּרִי הָעֵץ.**

*After eating some of the apple and honey, say:*

יְהִי רָצוֹן מִלְּפָנֶיךָ יהוה אֱלֹהֵינוּ וֵאלֹהֵי אֲבוֹתֵינוּ
שֶׁתְּחַדֵּשׁ עָלֵינוּ שָׁנָה טוֹבָה וּמְתוּקָה.

## קידושא רבה לראש השנה

*On שבת first say* וְשָׁמְרוּ *and* זָכוֹר *on page 651.*

*On יום טוב that falls on a weekday, some start here:*

ויקרא כג אֵלֶּה מוֹעֲדֵי יהוה מִקְרָאֵי קֹדֶשׁ אֲשֶׁר־תִּקְרְאוּ אֹתָם בְּמוֹעֲדָם:
וַיְדַבֵּר מֹשֶׁה אֶת־מֹעֲדֵי יהוה אֶל־בְּנֵי יִשְׂרָאֵל:

*On יום טוב that falls on a weekday, start here:*

תהלים פא **תִּקְעוּ בַחֹדֶשׁ שׁוֹפָר, בַּכֶּסֶה לְיוֹם חַגֵּנוּ:**
**כִּי חֹק לְיִשְׂרָאֵל הוּא, מִשְׁפָּט לֵאלֹהֵי יַעֲקֹב:**

*When saying קידוש for others* סַבְרִי מָרָנָן

**בָּרוּךְ אַתָּה יהוה אֱלֹהֵינוּ מֶלֶךְ הָעוֹלָם, בּוֹרֵא פְּרִי הַגָּפֶן.**

# TASHLIKH

*On the first day of Rosh HaShana (or, if that day is Shabbat, on the second day), it is customary, in the afternoon after Minḥa, to go to the banks of a river, or any stretch of flowing water, and say the following (see law 36):*

מִי־אֵל כָּמְוֹךָ Who, God, is like You, *Mic. 7*
who pardons iniquity
and forgives the transgression
of the remnant of His heritage?
He does not stay angry for ever,
but delights in loving-kindness.
He will again have compassion on us,
suppress our iniquities,
and cast into the depths of the sea all their sins.
Grant truth to Jacob, kindness to Abraham,
as You promised our fathers in days long ago.

מִן־הַמֵּצַר In my distress I called on the LORD. *Ps. 118*
The LORD answered me and set me free.
The LORD is with me; I will not be afraid.
What can man do to me? The LORD is with me.
He is my Helper. I will see the downfall of my enemies.
It is better to take refuge in the LORD than to trust in man.
It is better to take refuge in the LORD than to trust in princes.

# סדר תשליך

*On the first day of* ראש השנה *(or, if that day is* שבת*, on the second day), it is customary, in the afternoon after* מנחה*, to go to the banks of a river, or any stretch of flowing water, and say the following (see law 36):*

מִי־אֵל כָּמוֹךָ מיכה ז
נֹשֵׂא עָוֹן וְעֹבֵר עַל־פֶּשַׁע לִשְׁאֵרִית נַחֲלָתוֹ
לֹא־הֶחֱזִיק לָעַד אַפּוֹ
כִּי־חָפֵץ חֶסֶד הוּא:
יָשׁוּב יְרַחֲמֵנוּ, יִכְבֹּשׁ עֲוֹנֹתֵינוּ
וְתַשְׁלִיךְ בִּמְצֻלוֹת יָם כָּל־חַטֹּאתָם:
תִּתֵּן אֱמֶת לְיַעֲקֹב, חֶסֶד לְאַבְרָהָם
אֲשֶׁר־נִשְׁבַּעְתָּ לַאֲבֹתֵינוּ מִימֵי קֶדֶם:

מִן־הַמֵּצַר קָרָאתִי יָּהּ, עָנָנִי בַמֶּרְחָב יָהּ: תהלים קיח
יהוה לִי לֹא אִירָא, מַה־יַּעֲשֶׂה לִי אָדָם:
יהוה לִי בְּעֹזְרָי, וַאֲנִי אֶרְאֶה בְשֹׂנְאָי:
טוֹב לַחֲסוֹת בַּיהוה, מִבְּטֹחַ בָּאָדָם:
טוֹב לַחֲסוֹת בַּיהוה, מִבְּטֹחַ בִּנְדִיבִים:

## KAPAROT

*Taking a rooster (men), or a hen (women) in the right hand (alternatively one may use money), say the following paragraph three times:*

בְּנֵי אָדָם Children of men,
those who sat in darkness and the shadow of death, *Ps. 107*
cruelly bound in iron chains –
He brought them out from darkness
and the shadow of death and broke open their chains.
Some were fools with sinful ways,
and suffered affliction because of their iniquities.
They found all food repulsive, and came close to the gates of death.
Then they cried to the LORD in their trouble,
and He saved them from their distress.
He sent His word and healed them;
He rescued them from their destruction.
Let them thank the LORD for his loving-kindness
and His wondrous deeds for humankind.
If there is one angel out of a thousand in his defense, *Job 33*
to declare his righteousness on his behalf,
He will be gracious to him and say,
"Spare him from going down to the pit; I have found atonement."

*A man revolves the rooster around his head and says:*

זֶה חֲלִיפָתִי Let this be my exchange, let this be my substitute,
let this be my atonement, let this rooster go to death
while I go and enter a good, long life and peace.

*A woman revolves the hen around her head and says:*

זֹאת חֲלִיפָתִי Let this be my exchange, let this be my substitute,
let this be my atonement, let this hen go to death
while I go and enter a good, long life and peace.

*If money is used, then revolve the money around the head and say:*

אֵלּוּ חֲלִיפָתִי Let this be my exchange, let this be my substitute,
let this be my atonement, let this money go to charity
while I go and enter a good, long life and peace.

# סדר כפרות

*Taking a rooster (men), or a hen (women) in the right hand (alternatively one may use money), say the following paragraph three times:*

בְּנֵי אָדָם

יֹשְׁבֵי חֹשֶׁךְ וְצַלְמָוֶת, אֲסִירֵי עֳנִי וּבַרְזֶל: תהלים קז

יוֹצִיאֵם מֵחֹשֶׁךְ וְצַלְמָוֶת, וּמוֹסְרוֹתֵיהֶם יְנַתֵּק:

אֱוִלִים מִדֶּרֶךְ פִּשְׁעָם, וּמֵעֲוֹנֹתֵיהֶם יִתְעַנּוּ:

כָּל־אֹכֶל תְּתַעֵב נַפְשָׁם, וַיַּגִּיעוּ עַד־שַׁעֲרֵי מָוֶת:

וַיִּזְעֲקוּ אֶל־יהוה בַּצַּר לָהֶם, מִמְּצֻקוֹתֵיהֶם יוֹשִׁיעֵם:

יִשְׁלַח דְּבָרוֹ וְיִרְפָּאֵם, וִימַלֵּט מִשְּׁחִיתוֹתָם:

יוֹדוּ לַיהוה חַסְדּוֹ, וְנִפְלְאוֹתָיו לִבְנֵי אָדָם:

אִם־יֵשׁ עָלָיו מַלְאָךְ מֵלִיץ אֶחָד מִנִּי־אָלֶף, לְהַגִּיד לְאָדָם יָשְׁרוֹ: איוב לג

וַיְחֻנֶּנּוּ, וַיֹּאמֶר פְּדָעֵהוּ מֵרֶדֶת שַׁחַת, מָצָאתִי כֹפֶר:

*A man revolves the rooster around his head and says:*

זֶה חֲלִיפָתִי, זֶה תְּמוּרָתִי, זֶה כַּפָּרָתִי.
זֶה הַתַּרְנְגוֹל יֵלֵךְ לְמִיתָה
וַאֲנִי אֵלֵךְ וְאֶכָּנֵס לְחַיִּים טוֹבִים אֲרֻכִּים וּלְשָׁלוֹם.

*A woman revolves the hen around her head and says:*

זֹאת חֲלִיפָתִי, זֹאת תְּמוּרָתִי, זֹאת כַּפָּרָתִי.
זֹאת הַתַּרְנְגֹלֶת תֵּלֵךְ לְמִיתָה
וַאֲנִי אֵלֵךְ וְאֶכָּנֵס לְחַיִּים טוֹבִים אֲרֻכִּים וּלְשָׁלוֹם.

*If money is used, then revolve the money around the head and say:*

אֵלּוּ חֲלִיפָתִי, אֵלּוּ תְּמוּרָתִי, אֵלּוּ כַּפָּרָתִי.
אֵלּוּ הַמָּעוֹת יֵלְכוּ לִצְדָקָה
וַאֲנִי אֵלֵךְ וְאֶכָּנֵס לְחַיִּים טוֹבִים אֲרֻכִּים וּלְשָׁלוֹם.

## VIDUY FOR MINḤA OF EREV YOM KIPPUR

*The following is said on Erev Yom Kippur (and by a bride and groom on the eve of their wedding), in the Amida before "My God, guard":*

אֱלֹהֵינוּ Our God and God of our fathers,
let our prayer come before You,
and do not hide Yourself from our plea,
for we are not so arrogant or obstinate as to say before You,
LORD, our God and God of our fathers,
we are righteous and have not sinned,
for in truth, we and our fathers have sinned.

*Strike the left side of the chest with the right fist while saying each of the sins:*

אָשַׁמְנוּ We have sinned, we have acted treacherously,
we have robbed, we have spoken slander.
We have acted perversely, we have acted wickedly,
we have acted presumptuously, we have been violent, we have framed lies.
We have given bad advice, we have deceived, we have scorned,
we have rebelled, we have provoked, we have turned away,
we have committed iniquity, we have transgressed,
we have persecuted, we have been obstinate.
We have acted wickedly, we have corrupted,
we have acted abominably, we have strayed, we have led others astray.

סַרְנוּ We have turned away from Your commandments and good laws,
to no avail, for You are just in all that has befallen us,
for You have acted faithfully while we have done wickedly.

מַה נֹּאמַר What can we say before You, You who dwell on high?
What can we declare before You, You who abide in heaven?
Do You not know all, the hidden and revealed alike?

אַתָּה יוֹדֵעַ You know every secret since the world began,
and what is hidden deep inside every living thing.
You search each person's inner chambers examining conscience and mind.
Nothing is shrouded from You, and nothing is hidden, before Your eyes.
And so, may it be Your will, LORD our God and God of our ancestors,
that You forgive us all our sins,
pardon all our iniquities
and grant us atonement for all of our transgressions.

# וידוי למנחה בערב יום הכיפורים

*The following is said on* ערב יום הכיפורים *(and by a* חתן *and* כלה *on the eve of their wedding), in the Amida before* אֱלֹהַי, נְצֹר*:*

אֱלֹהֵינוּ וֵאלֹהֵי אֲבוֹתֵינוּ
תָּבוֹא לְפָנֶיךָ תְּפִלָּתֵנוּ, וְאַל תִּתְעַלַּם מִתְּחִנָּתֵנוּ.
שֶׁאֵין אֲנַחְנוּ עַזֵּי פָנִים וּקְשֵׁי עֹרֶף לוֹמַר לְפָנֶיךָ
יהוה אֱלֹהֵינוּ וֵאלֹהֵי אֲבוֹתֵינוּ
צַדִּיקִים אֲנַחְנוּ וְלֹא חָטָאנוּ. אֲבָל אֲנַחְנוּ וַאֲבוֹתֵינוּ חָטָאנוּ.

*Strike the left side of the chest with the right fist while saying each of the sins:*

אָשַׁמְנוּ, בָּגַדְנוּ, גָּזַלְנוּ, דִּבַּרְנוּ דֹפִי
הֶעֱוִינוּ, וְהִרְשַׁעְנוּ, זַדְנוּ, חָמַסְנוּ, טָפַלְנוּ שֶׁקֶר
יָעַצְנוּ רָע, כִּזַּבְנוּ, לַצְנוּ, מָרַדְנוּ, נִאַצְנוּ, סָרַרְנוּ
עָוִינוּ, פָּשַׁעְנוּ, צָרַרְנוּ, קִשִּׁינוּ עֹרֶף
רָשַׁעְנוּ, שִׁחַתְנוּ, תִּעַבְנוּ, תָּעִינוּ, תִּעְתָּעְנוּ.

סַרְנוּ מִמִּצְוֹתֶיךָ וּמִמִּשְׁפָּטֶיךָ הַטּוֹבִים, וְלֹא שָׁוָה לָנוּ.
וְאַתָּה צַדִּיק עַל כָּל הַבָּא עָלֵינוּ
כִּי אֱמֶת עָשִׂיתָ, וַאֲנַחְנוּ הִרְשָׁעְנוּ.

מַה נֹּאמַר לְפָנֶיךָ יוֹשֵׁב מָרוֹם, וּמַה נְּסַפֵּר לְפָנֶיךָ שׁוֹכֵן שְׁחָקִים
הֲלֹא כָּל הַנִּסְתָּרוֹת וְהַנִּגְלוֹת אַתָּה יוֹדֵעַ.

אַתָּה יוֹדֵעַ רָזֵי עוֹלָם וְתַעֲלוּמוֹת סִתְרֵי כָּל חָי.
אַתָּה חוֹפֵשׂ כָּל חַדְרֵי בָטֶן וּבוֹחֵן כְּלָיוֹת וָלֵב.
אֵין דָּבָר נֶעְלָם מִמֶּךָּ וְאֵין נִסְתָּר מִנֶּגֶד עֵינֶיךָ.
וּבְכֵן, יְהִי רָצוֹן מִלְּפָנֶיךָ, יהוה אֱלֹהֵינוּ וֵאלֹהֵי אֲבוֹתֵינוּ
שֶׁתִּסְלַח לָנוּ עַל כָּל חַטֹּאתֵינוּ
וְתִמְחַל לָנוּ עַל כָּל עֲוֹנוֹתֵינוּ
וּתְכַפֵּר לָנוּ עַל כָּל פְּשָׁעֵינוּ.

*Strike the left side of the chest with the right fist while saying each of the sins.*

עַל חֵטְא For the sin we have sinned before You under duress or freewill,
and for the sin we have sinned before You in hardness of heart.

For the sin we have sinned before You unwittingly,
and for the sin we have sinned before You by an utterance of our lips.

For the sin we have sinned before You by unchastity,
and for the sin we have sinned before You openly or secretly.

For the sin we have sinned before You knowingly and deceitfully,
and for the sin we have sinned before You in speech.

For the sin we have sinned before You by wronging a neighbor,
and for the sin we have sinned before You by thoughts of the heart.

For the sin we have sinned before You in a gathering for immorality,
and for the sin we have sinned before You by insincere confession.

For the sin we have sinned before You by contempt for parents and teachers,
and for the sin we have sinned before You willfully or in error.

For the sin we have sinned before You by force,
and for the sin we have sinned before You by desecrating Your name.

For the sin we have sinned before You by impure lips,
and for the sin we have sinned before You by foolish speech.

For the sin we have sinned before You by the evil inclination,
and for the sin we have sinned before You knowingly or unwittingly.

For all these, God of forgiveness,
forgive us, pardon us, grant us atonement.

*Strike the left side of the chest with the right fist while saying each of the sins.*

עַל חֵטְא שֶׁחָטָאנוּ לְפָנֶיךָ בְּאֹנֶס וּבְרָצוֹן
וְעַל חֵטְא שֶׁחָטָאנוּ לְפָנֶיךָ בְּאִמּוּץ הַלֵּב

עַל חֵטְא שֶׁחָטָאנוּ לְפָנֶיךָ בִּבְלִי דָעַת
וְעַל חֵטְא שֶׁחָטָאנוּ לְפָנֶיךָ בְּבִטּוּי שְׂפָתָיִם

עַל חֵטְא שֶׁחָטָאנוּ לְפָנֶיךָ בְּגִלּוּי עֲרָיוֹת
וְעַל חֵטְא שֶׁחָטָאנוּ לְפָנֶיךָ בְּגָלוּי וּבַסָּתֶר

עַל חֵטְא שֶׁחָטָאנוּ לְפָנֶיךָ בְּדַעַת וּבְמִרְמָה
וְעַל חֵטְא שֶׁחָטָאנוּ לְפָנֶיךָ בְּדִבּוּר פֶּה

עַל חֵטְא שֶׁחָטָאנוּ לְפָנֶיךָ בְּהוֹנָאַת רֵעַ
וְעַל חֵטְא שֶׁחָטָאנוּ לְפָנֶיךָ בְּהַרְהוֹר הַלֵּב

עַל חֵטְא שֶׁחָטָאנוּ לְפָנֶיךָ בִּוְעִידַת זְנוּת
וְעַל חֵטְא שֶׁחָטָאנוּ לְפָנֶיךָ בְּוִדּוּי פֶּה

עַל חֵטְא שֶׁחָטָאנוּ לְפָנֶיךָ בְּזִלְזוּל הוֹרִים וּמוֹרִים
וְעַל חֵטְא שֶׁחָטָאנוּ לְפָנֶיךָ בְּזָדוֹן וּבִשְׁגָגָה

עַל חֵטְא שֶׁחָטָאנוּ לְפָנֶיךָ בְּחֹזֶק יָד
וְעַל חֵטְא שֶׁחָטָאנוּ לְפָנֶיךָ בְּחִלּוּל הַשֵּׁם

עַל חֵטְא שֶׁחָטָאנוּ לְפָנֶיךָ בְּטֻמְאַת שְׂפָתָיִם
וְעַל חֵטְא שֶׁחָטָאנוּ לְפָנֶיךָ בְּטִפְּשׁוּת פֶּה

עַל חֵטְא שֶׁחָטָאנוּ לְפָנֶיךָ בְּיֵצֶר הָרָע
וְעַל חֵטְא שֶׁחָטָאנוּ לְפָנֶיךָ בְּיוֹדְעִים וּבְלֹא יוֹדְעִים

וְעַל כֻּלָּם אֱלוֹהַּ סְלִיחוֹת סְלַח לָנוּ, מְחַל לָנוּ, כַּפֶּר לָנוּ.

For the sin we have sinned before You by deceit and lies,
and for the sin we have sinned before You by bribery.

For the sin we have sinned before You by scorn,
and for the sin we have sinned before You by evil speech.

For the sin we have sinned before You in business,
and for the sin we have sinned before You with food and drink.

For the sin we have sinned before You by interest and extortion,
and for the sin we have sinned before You by being haughty.

For the sin we have sinned before You by the idle chatter of our lips,
and for the sin we have sinned before You by prying eyes.

For the sin we have sinned before You by arrogance,
and for the sin we have sinned before You by insolence.

For all these, God of forgiveness,
forgive us, pardon us, grant us atonement.

For the sin we have sinned before You by casting off the yoke,
and for the sin we have sinned before You by perverting judgment.

For the sin we have sinned before You by entrapping a neighbor,
and for the sin we have sinned before You by envy.

For the sin we have sinned before You by lack of seriousness,
and for the sin we have sinned before You by obstinacy.

For the sin we have sinned before You by running to do evil,
and for the sin we have sinned before You by gossip.

עַל חֵטְא שֶׁחָטָאנוּ לְפָנֶיךָ בְּכַחַשׁ וּבְכָזָב
וְעַל חֵטְא שֶׁחָטָאנוּ לְפָנֶיךָ בְּכַפַּת שֹׁחַד

עַל חֵטְא שֶׁחָטָאנוּ לְפָנֶיךָ בְּלָצוֹן
וְעַל חֵטְא שֶׁחָטָאנוּ לְפָנֶיךָ בְּלָשׁוֹן הָרָע

עַל חֵטְא שֶׁחָטָאנוּ לְפָנֶיךָ בְּמַשָּׂא וּבְמַתָּן
וְעַל חֵטְא שֶׁחָטָאנוּ לְפָנֶיךָ בְּמַאֲכָל וּבְמִשְׁתֶּה

עַל חֵטְא שֶׁחָטָאנוּ לְפָנֶיךָ בְּנֶשֶׁךְ וּבְמַרְבִּית
וְעַל חֵטְא שֶׁחָטָאנוּ לְפָנֶיךָ בִּנְטִיַּת גָּרוֹן

עַל חֵטְא שֶׁחָטָאנוּ לְפָנֶיךָ בְּשִׂיחַ שִׂפְתוֹתֵינוּ
וְעַל חֵטְא שֶׁחָטָאנוּ לְפָנֶיךָ בְּשִׂקּוּר עָיִן

עַל חֵטְא שֶׁחָטָאנוּ לְפָנֶיךָ בְּעֵינַיִם רָמוֹת
וְעַל חֵטְא שֶׁחָטָאנוּ לְפָנֶיךָ בְּעַזּוּת מֵצַח

וְעַל כֻּלָּם אֱלוֹהַּ סְלִיחוֹת סְלַח לָנוּ, מְחַל לָנוּ, כַּפֶּר לָנוּ.

עַל חֵטְא שֶׁחָטָאנוּ לְפָנֶיךָ בִּפְרִיקַת עֹל
וְעַל חֵטְא שֶׁחָטָאנוּ לְפָנֶיךָ בִּפְלִילוּת

עַל חֵטְא שֶׁחָטָאנוּ לְפָנֶיךָ בִּצְדִיַּת רֵעַ
וְעַל חֵטְא שֶׁחָטָאנוּ לְפָנֶיךָ בְּצָרוּת עָיִן

עַל חֵטְא שֶׁחָטָאנוּ לְפָנֶיךָ בְּקַלּוּת רֹאשׁ
וְעַל חֵטְא שֶׁחָטָאנוּ לְפָנֶיךָ בְּקַשְׁיוּת עֹרֶף

עַל חֵטְא שֶׁחָטָאנוּ לְפָנֶיךָ בְּרִיצַת רַגְלַיִם לְהָרַע
וְעַל חֵטְא שֶׁחָטָאנוּ לְפָנֶיךָ בִּרְכִילוּת

For the sin we have sinned before You by vain oath,
and for the sin we have sinned before You by baseless hatred.

For the sin we have sinned before You by breach of trust,
and for the sin we have sinned before You by confusion of heart.

For all these, God of forgiveness,
forgive us, pardon us, grant us atonement.

וְעַל חֲטָאִים And for the sins for which we are liable to bring a burnt-offering,
and for the sins for which we are liable to bring a sin-offering,
and for the sins for which we are liable to bring an offering according to our means,
and for the sins for which we are liable to bring a guilt-offering for certain or possible sin,
and for the sins for which we are liable to lashes for rebellion,
and for the sins for which we are liable to forty lashes,
and for the sins for which we are liable to death by the hands of Heaven,
and for the sins for which we are liable to be cut off and childless,
and for the sins for which we are liable to the four death penalties inflicted by the court: stoning, burning, beheading and strangling.

For positive and negative commandments,
whether they can be remedied by an act or not,
for sins known to us and for those that are unknown –
for those that are known,
we have already declared them before You
and confessed them to You;
and for those that are unknown,
before You they are revealed and known,
as it is said,
"The secret things belong to the LORD our God, *Deut. 29*
but the things that are revealed
are for us and our children for ever,
that we may fulfill all the words of this Torah."
For You are He who forgives Israel
and pardons the tribes of Yeshurun in every generation,
and besides You we have no king who pardons and forgives, only You.

עַל חֵטְא שֶׁחָטָאנוּ לְפָנֶיךָ בִּשְׁבוּעַת שָׁוְא
וְעַל חֵטְא שֶׁחָטָאנוּ לְפָנֶיךָ בְּשִׂנְאַת חִנָּם

עַל חֵטְא שֶׁחָטָאנוּ לְפָנֶיךָ בִּתְשׂוּמֶת יָד
וְעַל חֵטְא שֶׁחָטָאנוּ לְפָנֶיךָ בְּתִמְהוֹן לֵבָב

וְעַל כֻּלָּם אֱלוֹהַּ סְלִיחוֹת סְלַח לָנוּ, מְחַל לָנוּ, כַּפֶּר לָנוּ.

וְעַל חֲטָאִים שֶׁאָנוּ חַיָּבִים עֲלֵיהֶם עוֹלָה
וְעַל חֲטָאִים שֶׁאָנוּ חַיָּבִים עֲלֵיהֶם חַטָּאת
וְעַל חֲטָאִים שֶׁאָנוּ חַיָּבִים עֲלֵיהֶם קָרְבָּן עוֹלֶה וְיוֹרֵד
וְעַל חֲטָאִים שֶׁאָנוּ חַיָּבִים עֲלֵיהֶם אָשָׁם וַדַּאי וְתָלוּי
וְעַל חֲטָאִים שֶׁאָנוּ חַיָּבִים עֲלֵיהֶם מַכַּת מַרְדּוּת
וְעַל חֲטָאִים שֶׁאָנוּ חַיָּבִים עֲלֵיהֶם מַלְקוּת אַרְבָּעִים
וְעַל חֲטָאִים שֶׁאָנוּ חַיָּבִים עֲלֵיהֶם מִיתָה בִּידֵי שָׁמָיִם
וְעַל חֲטָאִים שֶׁאָנוּ חַיָּבִים עֲלֵיהֶם כָּרֵת וַעֲרִירִי
וְעַל חֲטָאִים שֶׁאָנוּ חַיָּבִים עֲלֵיהֶם אַרְבַּע מִיתוֹת בֵּית דִּין
סְקִילָה, שְׂרֵפָה, הֶרֶג, וְחֶנֶק.

עַל מִצְוַת עֲשֵׂה וְעַל מִצְוַת לֹא תַעֲשֶׂה.
בֵּין שֶׁיֵּשׁ בָּהּ קוּם עֲשֵׂה וּבֵין שֶׁאֵין בָּהּ קוּם עֲשֵׂה.
אֶת הַגְּלוּיִים לָנוּ וְאֶת שֶׁאֵינָם גְּלוּיִים לָנוּ
אֶת הַגְּלוּיִים לָנוּ, כְּבָר אֲמַרְנוּם לְפָנֶיךָ, וְהוֹדִינוּ לְךָ עֲלֵיהֶם
וְאֶת שֶׁאֵינָם גְּלוּיִים לָנוּ, לְפָנֶיךָ הֵם גְּלוּיִים וִידוּעִים
כַּדָּבָר שֶׁנֶּאֱמַר
הַנִּסְתָּרֹת לַיהוה אֱלֹהֵינוּ דברים כט
וְהַנִּגְלֹת לָנוּ וּלְבָנֵינוּ עַד־עוֹלָם
לַעֲשׂוֹת אֶת־כָּל־דִּבְרֵי הַתּוֹרָה הַזֹּאת:
כִּי אַתָּה סָלְחָן לְיִשְׂרָאֵל וּמָחֳלָן לְשִׁבְטֵי יְשֻׁרוּן בְּכָל דּוֹר וָדוֹר
וּמִבַּלְעָדֶיךָ אֵין לָנוּ מֶלֶךְ מוֹחֵל וְסוֹלֵחַ אֶלָּא אָתָּה.

אֱלֹהַי My God,
before I was formed I was unworthy,
and now that I have been formed it is as if I had not been formed.
I am dust while alive,
how much more so when I am dead.
See, I am before You like a vessel filled with shame and disgrace.
May it be Your will, LORD my God and God of my fathers,
that I may sin no more,
and as for the sins I have committed before You,
erase them in Your great compassion,
but not by suffering or severe illness.

אֱלֹהַי My God, *Berakhot 17a*
guard my tongue from evil
and my lips from deceitful speech.
To those who curse me, let my soul be silent;
may my soul be to all like the dust.
Open my heart to Your Torah
and let my soul pursue Your commandments.
As for all who plan evil against me,
swiftly thwart their counsel and frustrate their plans.
Act for the sake of Your name; act for the sake of Your right hand;
act for the sake of Your holiness; act for the sake of Your Torah.
That Your beloved ones may be delivered, *Ps. 60*
save with Your right hand and answer me.
May the words of my mouth and the meditation of my heart *Ps. 19*
find favor before You, LORD, my Rock and Redeemer.

*Bow, take three steps back, then bow, first left, then right, then center, while saying:*

May He who makes peace in His high places,
make peace for us and all Israel –
and say: Amen.

יְהִי רָצוֹן May it be Your will, LORD our God and God of our ancestors,
that the Temple be rebuilt speedily in our days,
and grant us a share in Your Torah.
And there we will serve You with reverence,
as in the days of old and as in former years.
Then the offering of Judah and Jerusalem *Mal. 3*
will be pleasing to the LORD as in the days of old and as in former years.

אֱלֹהַי
עַד שֶׁלֹּא נוֹצַרְתִּי אֵינִי כְּדַאי
וְעַכְשָׁיו שֶׁנּוֹצַרְתִּי, כְּאִלּוּ לֹא נוֹצַרְתִּי
עָפָר אֲנִי בְּחַיַּי, קַל וָחֹמֶר בְּמִיתָתִי.
הֲרֵי אֲנִי לְפָנֶיךָ כִּכְלִי מָלֵא בּוּשָׁה וּכְלִמָּה.
יְהִי רָצוֹן מִלְּפָנֶיךָ, יהוה אֱלֹהַי וֵאלֹהֵי אֲבוֹתַי
שֶׁלֹּא אֶחֱטָא עוֹד.
וּמַה שֶּׁחָטָאתִי לְפָנֶיךָ, מְחֹק בְּרַחֲמֶיךָ הָרַבִּים
אֲבָל לֹא עַל יְדֵי יִסּוּרִים וָחֳלָיִם רָעִים.

אֱלֹהַי ברכות יז.
נְצֹר לְשׁוֹנִי מֵרָע וּשְׂפָתַי מִדַּבֵּר מִרְמָה
וְלִמְקַלְלַי נַפְשִׁי תִדֹּם, וְנַפְשִׁי כֶּעָפָר לַכֹּל תִּהְיֶה.
פְּתַח לִבִּי בְּתוֹרָתֶךָ, וּבְמִצְוֹתֶיךָ תִּרְדֹּף נַפְשִׁי.
וְכָל הַחוֹשְׁבִים עָלַי רָעָה
מְהֵרָה הָפֵר עֲצָתָם וְקַלְקֵל מַחֲשַׁבְתָּם.
עֲשֵׂה לְמַעַן שְׁמֶךָ, עֲשֵׂה לְמַעַן יְמִינֶךָ
עֲשֵׂה לְמַעַן קְדֻשָּׁתֶךָ, עֲשֵׂה לְמַעַן תּוֹרָתֶךָ.
לְמַעַן יֵחָלְצוּן יְדִידֶיךָ, הוֹשִׁיעָה יְמִינְךָ וַעֲנֵנִי: תהלים ס
יִהְיוּ לְרָצוֹן אִמְרֵי פִי וְהֶגְיוֹן לִבִּי לְפָנֶיךָ, יהוה צוּרִי וְגֹאֲלִי: תהלים יט

*Bow, take three steps back, then bow, first left, then right, then center, while saying:*

עֹשֶׂה שָׁלוֹם / בעשרת ימי תשובה: הַשָּׁלוֹם/ בִּמְרוֹמָיו
הוּא יַעֲשֶׂה שָׁלוֹם עָלֵינוּ וְעַל כָּל יִשְׂרָאֵל וְאִמְרוּ אָמֵן.

יְהִי רָצוֹן מִלְּפָנֶיךָ יהוה אֱלֹהֵינוּ וֵאלֹהֵי אֲבוֹתֵינוּ
שֶׁיִּבָּנֶה בֵּית הַמִּקְדָּשׁ בִּמְהֵרָה בְיָמֵינוּ, וְתֵן חֶלְקֵנוּ בְּתוֹרָתֶךָ
וְשָׁם נַעֲבָדְךָ בְּיִרְאָה כִּימֵי עוֹלָם וּכְשָׁנִים קַדְמֹנִיּוֹת.
וְעָרְבָה לַיהוה מִנְחַת יְהוּדָה וִירוּשָׁלָםִ כִּימֵי עוֹלָם וּכְשָׁנִים קַדְמֹנִיּוֹת: מלאכי ג

## SERVICE FOR ḤANUKKA

*On each of the eight nights of Ḥanukka, the lights of the menora are lit: one on the first night, two on the second, and so on. On the first night, the rightmost branch of the menora is used; on each subsequent night, an additional light is added to the left. Each night, the new light is lit first, then the others, moving rightwards. If possible, the menora should be displayed near a window so that it is visible from the street.*

*The lights are lit using a separate flame known as the shamash. The lighting should be carried out as soon as possible after nightfall. On Friday night, it must be done before the beginning of Shabbat. See laws 151–157. Before lighting the Ḥanukka lights, say:*

בָּרוּךְ Blessed are You, LORD our God, King of the Universe,
who has made us holy through His commandments,
and has commanded us to light the Ḥanukka lights.

בָּרוּךְ Blessed are You, LORD our God, King of the Universe,
who performed miracles for our ancestors
in those days, at this time.

*On the first night, add:*

בָּרוּךְ Blessed are You, LORD our God, King of the Universe,
who has given us life, sustained us,
and brought us to this time.

---

the LORD, God of Israel, and the strong will not to be separated from the "house of life," from faith. This is the inner world of the Israelite, which is exemplified on the macro level by the High Priest who enters into the inner sanctum on the Holy Day. That small cruse deposited with the seal of the High Priest, the Greeks were incapable of polluting. No force can uproot from *Kelal Yisrael* their deep, inner bond with the LORD, God of Israel. "Many waters cannot extinguish the love and rivers cannot wash it away."[3]

But if the cruse remains small; if the faith remains hidden in the heart and does not manifest in actuality, in life, how will it survive? And once life has already taken another direction which is not based on the inner faith, then God forbid, the surviving remnant might be extinguished.

This is the wonderful power of that hidden flame. Even when it finds lifestyles diametrically opposed to it and opinions held by people who

---

3. Song of Songs 8:7.

# סדר הדלקת נרות חנוכה

*On each of the eight nights of* חנוכה, *the lights of the* חנוכיה *are lit: one on the first night, two on the second, and so on. On the first night, the rightmost branch of the* חנוכיה *is used; on each subsequent night, an additional light is added to the left. Each night, the new light is lit first, then the others, moving rightwards. If possible, the* חנוכיה *should be displayed near a window so that it is visible from the street.*

*The lights are lit using a separate flame known as the* שמש. *The lighting should be carried out as soon as possible after nightfall. On Friday night, it must be done before the beginning of* שבת. *See laws 151–157. Before lighting the* חנוכה *lights, say:*

בָּרוּךְ אַתָּה יהוה אֱלֹהֵינוּ מֶלֶךְ הָעוֹלָם
אֲשֶׁר קִדְּשָׁנוּ בְּמִצְוֹתָיו, וְצִוָּנוּ לְהַדְלִיק נֵר שֶׁל חֲנֻכָּה.

בָּרוּךְ אַתָּה יהוה אֱלֹהֵינוּ מֶלֶךְ הָעוֹלָם
שֶׁעָשָׂה נִסִּים לַאֲבוֹתֵינוּ בַּיָּמִים הָהֵם בַּזְּמַן הַזֶּה.

*On the first night, add:*

בָּרוּךְ אַתָּה יהוה אֱלֹהֵינוּ מֶלֶךְ הָעוֹלָם
שֶׁהֶחֱיָנוּ וְקִיְּמָנוּ וְהִגִּיעָנוּ לַזְּמַן הַזֶּה.

---

חנוכה / ḤANUKKAH

When the Greeks entered the Temple, they polluted all the [olive] oil in the Temple. And when the Hasmonean dynasty grew strong and defeated them, they searched and found but a single cruse of oil deposited with the seal of the High Priest. There was in it enough [oil] for but a single day. A miracle occurred and they were able to light from it for eight days.[1]

The pollution of the oil symbolizes the corruption of the character traits and the opinions; the spiritual oppression of the Greeks impacted the very faith of the Jew. In every Jew there is an aspect of priesthood (*kehunah*). "You shall be to me a kingdom of priests and a holy nation."[2]

Deep within the heart, there dwells the light of the Israelite soul. There is tucked away the inner connection of the Israelite with the core belief in

1. *b. Shabbat* 21b.
2. Exodus 19:6.

*After lighting the first light, say:*

הַנֵּרוֹת הַלָּלוּ We light these lights
because of the miracles and wonders,
deliverances and victories
You performed for our ancestors in those days,
at this time, through Your holy priests.

*Sofrim ch. 20*

Throughout the eight days of Ḥanukka
these lights are holy
and we are not permitted to make any other use of them,
except to look at them,
that we may give thanks and praise to Your great name
for Your miracles, Your wonders and Your deliverances.

*After all the lights are lit:*

מָעוֹז צוּר Refuge, Rock of my salvation:
to You it is a delight to give praise.
Restore my House of prayer,
so that there I may offer You thanksgiving.
When You silence the loud-mouthed foe,
then will I complete, with song and psalm,
the altar's dedication.

רָעוֹת Troubles sated my soul;
my strength was spent with sorrow.
They embittered my life with hardship,
when I was enslaved under Egyptian rule.
But God with His great power
brought out His treasured people,
while Pharaoh's host and followers sank
like a stone into the deep.

---

It was but a small cruse and contained enough oil for but a single day, a single hour, an hour of upliftment, whereby a man was lifted above the baseness of life by connecting with faith in the Lord, God of Israel. But

*After lighting the first light, say:*

מסכת סופרים פרק כ

הַנֵּרוֹת הַלָּלוּ אָנוּ מַדְלִיקִים
עַל הַנִּסִּים וְעַל הַנִּפְלָאוֹת
וְעַל הַתְּשׁוּעוֹת וְעַל הַמִּלְחָמוֹת
שֶׁעָשִׂיתָ לַאֲבוֹתֵינוּ בַּיָּמִים הָהֵם בַּזְּמַן הַזֶּה
עַל יְדֵי כֹּהֲנֶיךָ הַקְּדוֹשִׁים.

וְכָל שְׁמוֹנַת יְמֵי חֲנֻכָּה הַנֵּרוֹת הַלָּלוּ קֹדֶשׁ הֵם
וְאֵין לָנוּ רְשׁוּת לְהִשְׁתַּמֵּשׁ בָּהֶם
אֶלָּא לִרְאוֹתָם בִּלְבָד
כְּדֵי לְהוֹדוֹת וּלְהַלֵּל לְשִׁמְךָ הַגָּדוֹל
עַל נִסֶּיךָ וְעַל נִפְלְאוֹתֶיךָ וְעַל יְשׁוּעָתֶךָ.

*After all the lights are lit:*

מָעוֹז צוּר יְשׁוּעָתִי — לְךָ נָאֶה לְשַׁבֵּחַ
תִּכּוֹן בֵּית תְּפִלָּתִי — וְשָׁם תּוֹדָה נְזַבֵּחַ
לְעֵת תָּכִין מַטְבֵּחַ — מִצָּר הַמְנַבֵּחַ
אָז אֶגְמֹר בְּשִׁיר מִזְמוֹר — חֲנֻכַּת הַמִּזְבֵּחַ.

רָעוֹת שָׂבְעָה נַפְשִׁי — בְּיָגוֹן כֹּחִי כָּלָה
חַיַּי מֵרְרוּ בְקֹשִׁי — בְּשִׁעְבּוּד מַלְכוּת עֶגְלָה
וּבְיָדוֹ הַגְּדוֹלָה — הוֹצִיא אֶת הַסְּגֻלָּה
חֵיל פַּרְעֹה וְכָל זַרְעוֹ — יָרְדוּ כְּאֶבֶן מְצוּלָה.

---

don't even realize that they have embarked on a way at odds with the deepest aspect of their soul – that tiny spark can be fanned into a mighty fire, uprooting all the foreign lifestyles and inimical opinions. The spark can extend to all life's avenues, returning Israel to their Father in Heaven.

דְּבִיר He brought me to His holy abode,
but even there I found no rest.
The oppressor came and exiled me,
because I had served strange gods.
I had drunk poisoned wine. I almost perished.
Then Babylon fell, Zerubbabel came:
within seventy years I was saved.

כְּרֹת The Agagite, son of Hammedatha,
sought to cut down the tall fir tree,
but it became a trap to him,
and his arrogance was brought to an end.
You raised the head of the Benjaminite,
and the enemy's name You blotted out.
His many sons and his household
You hanged on the gallows.

יְוָנִים Then the Greeks gathered against me,
in the days of the Hasmoneans.
They broke down the walls of my towers,
and defiled all the oils.
But from the last remaining flask
a miracle was wrought for Your beloved.
Therefore the sages ordained these eight days
for song and praise.

חֲשׂף Bare Your holy arm,
and hasten the time of salvation.
Take retribution against the evil nation
on behalf of Your servants,
for the hour [of deliverance] has been too long delayed;
there seems no end to the evil days.
Thrust the enemy into the darkness of death,
and establish for us the seven Shepherds.

דְּבִיר קָדְשׁוֹ הֱבִיאַנִי וְגַם שָׁם לֹא שָׁקַטְתִּי
וּבָא נוֹגֵשׂ וְהִגְלַנִי כִּי זָרִים עָבַדְתִּי
וְיֵין רַעַל מָסַכְתִּי כִּמְעַט שֶׁעָבַרְתִּי
קֵץ בָּבֶל זְרֻבָּבֶל לְקֵץ שִׁבְעִים נוֹשַׁעְתִּי.

כְּרֹת קוֹמַת בְּרוֹשׁ בִּקֵּשׁ אֲגָגִי בֶּן הַמְּדָתָא
וְנִהְיָתָה לוֹ לְפַח וּלְמוֹקֵשׁ וְגַאֲוָתוֹ נִשְׁבָּתָה
רֹאשׁ יְמִינִי נִשֵּׂאתָ וְאוֹיֵב שְׁמוֹ מָחִיתָ
רֹב בָּנָיו וְקִנְיָנָיו עַל הָעֵץ תָּלִיתָ.

יְוָנִים נִקְבְּצוּ עָלַי אֲזַי בִּימֵי חַשְׁמַנִּים
וּפָרְצוּ חוֹמוֹת מִגְדָּלַי וְטִמְּאוּ כָּל הַשְּׁמָנִים
וּמִנּוֹתַר קַנְקַנִּים נַעֲשָׂה נֵס לַשּׁוֹשַׁנִּים
בְּנֵי בִינָה יְמֵי שְׁמוֹנָה קָבְעוּ שִׁיר וּרְנָנִים.

חֲשׂף זְרוֹעַ קָדְשֶׁךָ וְקָרֵב קֵץ הַיְשׁוּעָה
נְקֹם נִקְמַת עֲבָדֶיךָ מֵאֻמָּה הָרְשָׁעָה
כִּי אָרְכָה לָנוּ הַשָּׁעָה וְאֵין קֵץ לִימֵי הָרָעָה
דְּחֵה אַדְמוֹן בְּצֵל צַלְמוֹן הָקֵם לָנוּ רוֹעִים שִׁבְעָה.

---

without some enduring bond with the Torah lifestyle, a man will quickly come down once again. Yet there occurred a miracle: Though life in general was not prepared for an expansion of the holy light of core belief, this little cruse of oil lasted for eight days, which hints to a stretch of time that will take us beyond the present into the future, mighty in holiness, when "the earth will be full of the knowledge of the Lord as the waters cover the sea."[1]

---

1. Isaiah 11:9. *EA*, vol. 3, *Shabbat*, chap. 2, par. 12 (pp. 65–66) = *Ma'amrei ha-Rayah*, vol. 1 (Jerusalem, 1980), pp. 152–153.

## SERVICE FOR PURIM

*Before the reading of the Megilla, the congregation stands and the Reader says the following three blessings:*

בָּרוּךְ Blessed are You, LORD our God, King of the Universe,
who has made us holy through His commandments,
and has commanded us about reading the Megilla.

בָּרוּךְ Blessed are You, LORD our God, King of the Universe,
who performed miracles for our ancestors in those days at this time.

בָּרוּךְ Blessed are You, LORD our God, King of the Universe,
who has given us life, sustained us, and brought us to this time.

*The Megilla is read. When the reading is completed, the scroll is rolled up and, if a minyan is present, the Reader continues:*

בָּרוּךְ Blessed are You, LORD our God, King of the Universe,
who pleads our cause, judges our claim, avenges our wrong,
brings retribution to our enemies, and punishes our foes.

Blessed are You, LORD, who on behalf of His people Israel,
exacts punishment from all their foes,
the God who brings salvation.

*The following is said after the night reading of the Megilla:*

אֲשֶׁר הֵנִיא [God] frustrated the plan of the nations, thwarted the intentions of the crafty. An evil man rose up against us, An arrogant branch of Amalek's tree, haughty, rich, he dug his own pit. His hubris became his own snare. He was trapped in the trap he set for others. Seeking to destroy, he was destroyed. Haman shared his ancestors' hate, And stirred against children the hostility of brothers. He did not remember

---

This explains our curious practice of drinking "'*ad de-lo yada*'" ("until one does not know") on Purim. Generally, Judaism frowns on intoxication. "A *shikor* (drunk) who prays is considered as if he worships idolatry."[2] But on Purim we do find those who pray in an inebriated state (and perhaps some leniency can be found for that in Halakhah). Under the influence of alcohol,

---

would have left our bodies intact, so there is no requirement on Ḥanukkah to engage in gustatory celebration. Haman, the villain of the *Megillah*, on the other hand, threatened us with physical extermination, so on Purim a banquet is called for. Rabbi Mordechai Jaffe, *Levush ha-Ḥur, OḤ* 670:2.

2. *b. Berakhot* 31b.

# סדר קריאת המגילה בפורים

*Before the reading of the* מגילה*, the* קהל *stands and the* קורא *says the following three blessings:*

בָּרוּךְ אַתָּה יהוה אֱלֹהֵינוּ מֶלֶךְ הָעוֹלָם
אֲשֶׁר קִדְּשָׁנוּ בְּמִצְוֹתָיו, וְצִוָּנוּ עַל מִקְרָא מְגִלָּה.

בָּרוּךְ אַתָּה יהוה אֱלֹהֵינוּ מֶלֶךְ הָעוֹלָם
שֶׁעָשָׂה נִסִּים לַאֲבוֹתֵינוּ בַּיָּמִים הָהֵם בַּזְּמַן הַזֶּה.

בָּרוּךְ אַתָּה יהוה אֱלֹהֵינוּ מֶלֶךְ הָעוֹלָם
שֶׁהֶחֱיָנוּ וְקִיְּמָנוּ וְהִגִּיעָנוּ לַזְּמַן הַזֶּה.

*The* מגילה *is read. When the reading is completed, the scroll is rolled up and, if a* מנין *is present, the* קורא *continues:*

בָּרוּךְ אַתָּה יהוה אֱלֹהֵינוּ מֶלֶךְ הָעוֹלָם
הָרָב אֶת רִיבֵנוּ, וְהַדָּן אֶת דִּינֵנוּ, וְהַנּוֹקֵם אֶת נִקְמָתֵנוּ
וְהַמְשַׁלֵּם גְּמוּל לְכָל אוֹיְבֵי נַפְשֵׁנוּ, וְהַנִּפְרָע לָנוּ מִצָּרֵינוּ.

בָּרוּךְ אַתָּה יהוה, הַנִּפְרָע לְעַמּוֹ יִשְׂרָאֵל מִכָּל צָרֵיהֶם, הָאֵל הַמּוֹשִׁיעַ.

*The following is said after the night reading of the* מגילה*:*

אֲשֶׁר הֵנִיא עֲצַת גּוֹיִם, וַיָּפֶר מַחְשְׁבוֹת עֲרוּמִים.
בְּקוּם עָלֵינוּ אָדָם רָשָׁע, נֵצֶר זָדוֹן מִזֶּרַע עֲמָלֵק.
גָּאָה בְעָשְׁרוֹ וְכָרָה לוֹ בּוֹר, וּגְדֻלָּתוֹ יָקְשָׁה לּוֹ לָכֶד.
דִּמָּה בְנַפְשׁוֹ לִלְכֹּד וְנִלְכַּד, בִּקֵּשׁ לְהַשְׁמִיד וְנִשְׁמַד מְהֵרָה.
הָמָן הוֹדִיעַ אֵיבַת אֲבוֹתָיו, וְעוֹרֵר שִׂנְאַת אַחִים לַבָּנִים.

---

פורים / PURIM

Purim is a celebration of the "holiness of the body" (*kedushat ha-guf*). Haman sought to physically exterminate the Jewish people, and we commemorate our miraculous victory and our survival by singling out the body for praise.[1]

---

1. Rabbi Mordechai Jaffe explains the difference between Ḥanukkah, when a banquet is optional, and Purim, when a banquet is obligatory. At the time of Ḥanukkah, the "Greeks" (actually Hellenized Syrians) threatened us with spiritual annihilation but

Saul's act of mercy, his pity for Agag, through which a new enemy was born. The wicked planned to cut off the righteous, but the impure were defeated by the pure. [Mordekhai's] goodness overcame the father's [Saul's] error, but the evil [Haman] piled sin upon sin. He hid in his heart his cunning schemes, intent on his evildoing. He stretched out his hand against God's holy ones; he spent his wealth to destroy every memory of them. When Mordekhai saw the wrath go forth, and Haman's decrees issued in Shushan, he put on sackcloth, wrapped himself in mourning, decreed a fast and sat on ashes. "Who will arise to atone for error, and find forgiveness for our ancestors' sins?" A flower blossomed from the palm tree; Hadassa arose to wake those who slept. Her servants hastened Haman to come, to serve him wine with the venom of serpents. He had risen by his wealth, but fell by his evil. He made the very gallows by which he was hanged. All the inhabitants of the world were amazed When Haman's ploy (*pur*) became our joy (*Purim*). The righteous was saved from evil hands, the perpetrator suffered the fate of his intended victim. They undertook to celebrate Purim, and to rejoice on it year after year. You heeded the prayer of Mordekhai and Esther; and Haman and his sons were hanged on the gallows.

*The following is said after both night and morning readings of the Megilla:*

שׁוֹשַׁנַּת יַעֲקֹב The lily of Jacob rejoiced and was glad, When, together, they saw Mordekhai robed in royal blue. You have been their eternal salvation, their hope in every generation; To make known that all who hope in You will not be put to shame, All who trust in You will never be humiliated. Cursed be Haman who sought to destroy me. Blessed be Mordekhai the Yehudi. Cursed be Zeresh, wife of him who terrified me. Blessed be Esther [whose actions saved] me. Cursed be all the wicked; blessed be all Israel. And may Ḥarbona, too, be remembered for good.

*After the night reading, Ma'ariv continues with "You are the Holy One" to "great and glorious" on pages 752–754 (on Motza'ei Shabbat, begin with "May the pleasantness" on page 752). The Leader then continues with Full Kaddish on page 756 (omitting the line "May the prayers and pleas"). (On Motza'ei Shabbat, continue with "May God give you" on page 758.) The service continues with Aleinu on page 764, and Mourner's Kaddish on page 766.*

*In the morning, continue with Ashrei on page 234 and "A redeemer will come" on page 236.*

---

Ari, of blessed memory, on Purim there shines in the world a great spiritual illumination the likes of which exists neither on the Sabbath nor on the Festivals.[1] And because of this light, even the most mundane workday affairs come out of their cursed state and are transformed to blessing. For this reason, the Jews did not accept the prohibition of labor on Purim.[2] On this phenomenal day, even in work one finds the light of holiness.[3]

1. Rabbi Ḥayyim Vital, *Peri 'Ets Ḥayyim, Sha'ar ha-Purim*, chap. 5. In Lurianic parlance, the illumination of Purim is referred to as *"he'arat Yesod Abba."*
2. *b. Megillah* 5b. Cf. Rabbi Nathan Sternhartz, *Likkutei Halakhot, Hil. Basar be-Ḥalav* 5:18.
3. *OR*, vol. 1, pp. 439–441.

וְלֹא זָכַר רַחֲמֵי שָׁאוּל, כִּי בְּחֶמְלָתוֹ עַל אֲגָג נוֹלַד אוֹיֵב.
זָמַם רָשָׁע לְהַכְרִית צַדִּיק, וְנִלְכַּד טָמֵא בִּידֵי טָהוֹר.
חֱסֶד גָּבַר עַל שִׁגְגַת אָב, וְרָשָׁע הוֹסִיף חֵטְא עַל חֲטָאָיו.
טָמַן בְּלִבּוֹ מַחְשְׁבוֹת עֲרוּמָיו, וַיִּתְמַכֵּר לַעֲשׂוֹת רָעָה.
יָדוֹ שָׁלַח בִּקְדוֹשֵׁי אֵל, כַּסְפּוֹ נָתַן לְהַכְרִית זִכְרָם.
כִּרְאוֹת מָרְדְּכַי כִּי יָצָא קֶצֶף, וְדָתֵי הָמָן נִתְּנוּ בְשׁוּשָׁן.
לָבַשׁ שַׂק וְקָשַׁר מִסְפֵּד וְגָזַר צוֹם וַיֵּשֶׁב עַל הָאֵפֶר.
מִי זֶה יַעֲמֹד לְכַפֵּר שְׁגָגָה, וְלִמְחֹל חַטַּאת עֲוֹן אֲבוֹתֵינוּ.
נֵץ פָּרַח מִלּוּלָב, הֵן הֲדַסָּה עָמְדָה לְעוֹרֵר יְשֵׁנִים.
סָרִיסֶיהָ הִבְהִילוּ לְהָמָן, לְהַשְׁקוֹתוֹ יֵין חֲמַת תַּנִּינִים.
עָמַד בְּעָשְׁרוֹ וְנָפַל בְּרִשְׁעוֹ, עָשָׂה לוֹ עֵץ וְנִתְלָה עָלָיו.
פִּיהֶם פָּתְחוּ כָּל יוֹשְׁבֵי תֵבֵל, כִּי פוּר הָמָן נֶהְפַּךְ לְפוּרֵנוּ.
צַדִּיק נֶחֱלַץ מִיַּד רָשָׁע, אוֹיֵב נִתַּן תַּחַת נַפְשׁוֹ.
קִיְּמוּ עֲלֵיהֶם לַעֲשׂוֹת פּוּרִים וְלִשְׂמֹחַ בְּכָל שָׁנָה וְשָׁנָה.
רָאִיתָ אֶת תְּפִלַּת מָרְדְּכַי וְאֶסְתֵּר, הָמָן וּבָנָיו עַל הָעֵץ תָּלִיתָ.

*The following is said after both night and morning readings of the* מגילה:

שׁוֹשַׁנַּת יַעֲקֹב צָהֲלָה וְשָׂמֵחָה בִּרְאוֹתָם יַחַד תְּכֵלֶת מָרְדְּכָי.
תְּשׁוּעָתָם הָיִיתָ לָנֶצַח, וְתִקְוָתָם בְּכָל דּוֹר וָדוֹר.
לְהוֹדִיעַ שֶׁכָּל קוֶֹיךָ לֹא יֵבֹשׁוּ, וְלֹא יִכָּלְמוּ לָנֶצַח כָּל הַחוֹסִים בָּךְ.
אָרוּר הָמָן אֲשֶׁר בִּקֵּשׁ לְאַבְּדִי, בָּרוּךְ מָרְדְּכַי הַיְּהוּדִי.
אֲרוּרָה זֶרֶשׁ אֵשֶׁת מַפְחִידִי, בְּרוּכָה אֶסְתֵּר בַּעֲדִי.
אֲרוּרִים כָּל הָרְשָׁעִים, בְּרוּכִים כָּל יִשְׂרָאֵל, וְגַם חַרְבוֹנָה זָכוּר לַטּוֹב.

*After the night reading,* מעריב *continues with* וְאַתָּה קָדוֹשׁ *to* וַיַּאְדִּיר *on pages 753–755 (on* מוצאי שבת*, begin with* וִיהִי נֹעַם *on page 753). The* שליח ציבור *then continues with* קדיש שלם *on page 757 (omitting the line* תִּתְקַבַּל*). (On* מוצאי שבת*, continue with* וְיִתֶּן־לְךָ *on page 759.) The service continues with* עָלֵינוּ *on page 765, and* קדיש יתום *on page 767.*

*In the morning, continue with* אַשְׁרֵי *on page 235 and* וּבָא לְצִיּוֹן *on page 237.*

---

one is divested of one's intellect and reduced to the body, and it is precisely the praises of the body, its sanctity, that we sing on this day. According to the

# Memorial Day

*At the end of Shaḥarit, after Full Kaddish, the Ark is opened and the following is said by some congregations:*

לַמְנַצֵּחַ For the conductor of music. Upon the death of Labben. A psalm of David. *Ps. 9*
I will thank You, LORD, with all my heart; I will tell of all Your wonders.
I will rejoice and exult in You; I will sing praise to Your name, Most High.
My enemies retreat; they stumble and perish before You.
For You have upheld my case and my cause; You have sat enthroned as righteous Judge.
You have rebuked nations and destroyed the wicked, blotting out their name for ever and all time.
The enemy are finished, ruined forever; You have overthrown their cities; even the memory of them is lost.
But the LORD abides forever; He has established His throne for judgment.
He will judge the world with righteousness, and try the cause of peoples with justice.
The LORD is a refuge for the oppressed, a stronghold in times of trouble.
Those who know Your name trust in You, for You, LORD, do not forsake those who seek You.
Sing praise to the LORD who dwells in Zion; tell the peoples of His deeds.
For He who avenges blood remembers; He does not forget the cry of the afflicted.
Have mercy on me, LORD, see how my enemies afflict me. Lift me up from the gates of death,
That in the gates of the Daughter of Zion I may tell all Your praises and rejoice in Your deliverance.
The nations have fallen into the pit they dug; their feet are caught in the net they hid.
The LORD is known by His justice; the wicked is ensnared by the work of his own hands. Reflect on this, Selah.
The wicked return to the grave, all the nations that forget God.
The needy will not be forgotten forever, nor the hope of the afflicted ever be lost.
Arise, LORD, let not man have power; let the nations be judged in Your presence.
Strike them with fear, LORD; let the nations know they are only men. Selah.

*The Ark is closed.*

# סדר תפילת שחרית ליום הזיכרון

*At the end of* שחרית*, after* קדיש שלם*, the* ארון קודש *is opened and the following is said by some congregations:*

לַמְנַצֵּחַ עַל־מוּת לַבֵּן מִזְמוֹר לְדָוִד: תהלים ט
אוֹדֶה יהוה בְּכָל־לִבִּי, אֲסַפְּרָה כָּל־נִפְלְאוֹתֶיךָ:
אֶשְׂמְחָה וְאֶעֶלְצָה בָךְ, אֲזַמְּרָה שִׁמְךָ עֶלְיוֹן:
בְּשׁוּב־אוֹיְבַי אָחוֹר, יִכָּשְׁלוּ וְיֹאבְדוּ מִפָּנֶיךָ:
כִּי־עָשִׂיתָ מִשְׁפָּטִי וְדִינִי, יָשַׁבְתָּ לְכִסֵּא שׁוֹפֵט צֶדֶק:
גָּעַרְתָּ גוֹיִם אִבַּדְתָּ רָשָׁע, שְׁמָם מָחִיתָ לְעוֹלָם וָעֶד:
הָאוֹיֵב תַּמּוּ חֳרָבוֹת לָנֶצַח, וְעָרִים נָתַשְׁתָּ, אָבַד זִכְרָם הֵמָּה:
וַיהוה לְעוֹלָם יֵשֵׁב, כּוֹנֵן לַמִּשְׁפָּט כִּסְאוֹ:
וְהוּא יִשְׁפֹּט־תֵּבֵל בְּצֶדֶק, יָדִין לְאֻמִּים בְּמֵישָׁרִים:
וִיהִי יהוה מִשְׂגָּב לַדָּךְ, מִשְׂגָּב לְעִתּוֹת בַּצָּרָה:
וְיִבְטְחוּ בְךָ יוֹדְעֵי שְׁמֶךָ, כִּי לֹא־עָזַבְתָּ דֹרְשֶׁיךָ, יהוה:
זַמְּרוּ לַיהוה יֹשֵׁב צִיּוֹן, הַגִּידוּ בָעַמִּים עֲלִילוֹתָיו:
כִּי־דֹרֵשׁ דָּמִים אוֹתָם זָכָר, לֹא־שָׁכַח צַעֲקַת עֲנָוִים:
חָנְנֵנִי יהוה רְאֵה עָנְיִי מִשֹּׂנְאָי, מְרוֹמְמִי מִשַּׁעֲרֵי־מָוֶת:
לְמַעַן אֲסַפְּרָה כָּל־תְּהִלָּתֶיךָ, בְּשַׁעֲרֵי בַת־צִיּוֹן אָגִילָה בִּישׁוּעָתֶךָ:
טָבְעוּ גוֹיִם בְּשַׁחַת עָשׂוּ, בְּרֶשֶׁת־זוּ טָמָנוּ נִלְכְּדָה רַגְלָם:
נוֹדַע יהוה מִשְׁפָּט עָשָׂה, בְּפֹעַל כַּפָּיו נוֹקֵשׁ רָשָׁע, הִגָּיוֹן סֶלָה:
יָשׁוּבוּ רְשָׁעִים לִשְׁאוֹלָה, כָּל־גּוֹיִם שְׁכֵחֵי אֱלֹהִים:
כִּי לֹא לָנֶצַח יִשָּׁכַח אֶבְיוֹן, תִּקְוַת עֲנִיִּים תֹּאבַד לָעַד:
קוּמָה יהוה אַל־יָעֹז אֱנוֹשׁ, יִשָּׁפְטוּ גוֹיִם עַל־פָּנֶיךָ:
שִׁיתָה יהוה מוֹרָה לָהֶם, יֵדְעוּ גוֹיִם, אֱנוֹשׁ הֵמָּה סֶּלָה:

*The* ארון קודש *is closed.*

*Memorial Prayer for Fallen Israeli Soldiers*

אָבִינוּ שֶׁבַּשָּׁמַיִם Heavenly Father, God, Source of the spirits of all flesh,
remember, we pray You, the pure souls of our sons and daughters
who heroically gave their lives
in defense of the people and the Land.
Swifter than eagles, stronger than lions,
they fought for the liberation of their people and homeland,
sacrificing their lives for Israel's rebirth in its holy land.
They breathed a spirit of strength and courage
into the whole house of Israel,
in the Land and the Diaspora,
inspiring it to go forward toward its redemption and liberation.
Remember them, our God, for good,
together with the myriad holy ones and heroes of Israel from ancient times.
May their souls be bound in the bonds of everlasting life,
may the Garden of Eden be their resting place,
may they rest in peace
and receive their reward at the End of Days.
Amen.

לְדָוִד Of David. Blessed is the LORD, my Rock, who trains my hands for war, my fingers for battle. He is my Benefactor, my Fortress, my Stronghold and my Refuge, my Shield in whom I trust, He who subdues nations under me. LORD, what is man that You care for him, what are mortals that You think of them? Man is no more than a breath, his days like a fleeting shadow. LORD, part Your heavens and come down; touch the mountains so that they pour forth smoke. Flash forth lightning and scatter them; shoot Your arrows and panic them. Reach out Your hand from on high; deliver me and rescue me from the mighty waters, from the hands of strangers, whose every word is worthless, whose right hands are raised in falsehood. To You, God, I will sing a new song; to You I will play music on a ten-stringed harp. He who gives salvation to kings, who saved His servant David from the cruel sword: may He deliver me and rescue me from the hands of strangers, whose every word is worthless, whose right hands are raised in falsehood. Then our sons will be like saplings, well nurtured in their youth. Our daughters will be like pillars carved for a palace. Our barns will be filled with every kind of provision. Our sheep will increase by thousands, even tens of thousands in our fields. Our oxen will draw heavy loads. There will be no breach in the walls, no going into captivity, no cries of distress in our streets. Happy are the people for whom this is so; happy are the people whose God is the LORD. *Ps. 144*

*Memorial Prayer for Fallen Israeli Soldiers*

אָבִינוּ שֶׁבַּשָּׁמַיִם, אֵל אֱלֹהֵי הָרוּחוֹת לְכָל בָּשָׂר
זְכֹר נָא אֶת הַנְּשָׁמוֹת הַזַּכּוֹת וְהַטְּהוֹרוֹת שֶׁל בָּנֵינוּ וּבְנוֹתֵינוּ
אֲשֶׁר הֶעֱרוּ אֶת נַפְשָׁם לָמוּת מוֹת גִּבּוֹרִים
בְּהֵחָלְצָם לְעֶזְרַת הָעָם וְהָאָרֶץ.
מִנְּשָׁרִים קַלּוּ מֵאֲרָיוֹת גָּבֵרוּ
בְּמִלְחַמְתָּם לְמַעַן שִׁחְרוּר עַמָּם וּמוֹלַדְתָּם.
בַּעֲלוֹתָם עַל מִזְבַּח תְּקוּמַת יִשְׂרָאֵל בְּאֶרֶץ קָדְשׁוֹ
הֵפִיחוּ רוּחַ עֹז וּגְבוּרָה בְּכָל בֵּית יִשְׂרָאֵל בָּאָרֶץ וּבַתְּפוּצוֹת
וַיִּתְעוֹרֵר לִקְרַאת גְּאֻלָּתוֹ וּפְדוּת נַפְשׁוֹ.
יִזְכְּרֵם אֱלֹהֵינוּ לְטוֹבָה
עִם רִבְבוֹת אַלְפֵי קְדוֹשֵׁי יִשְׂרָאֵל וְגִבּוֹרָיו מִימֵי עוֹלָם
בִּצְרוֹר הַחַיִּים יִצְרֹר אֶת נִשְׁמָתָם
בְּגַן עֵדֶן תְּהֵא מְנוּחָתָם
וְיָנוּחוּ בְשָׁלוֹם עַל מִשְׁכְּבָם
וְיַעַמְדוּ לְגוֹרָלָם לְקֵץ הַיָּמִין
אָמֵן.

לְדָוִד בָּרוּךְ יהוה צוּרִי הַמְלַמֵּד יָדַי לַקְרָב, אֶצְבְּעוֹתַי לַמִּלְחָמָה: חַסְדִּי וּמְצוּדָתִי תהלים קמד
מִשְׂגַּבִּי וּמְפַלְטִי לִי מָגִנִּי וּבוֹ חָסִיתִי הָרוֹדֵד עַמִּי תַחְתָּי: יהוה מָה־אָדָם וַתֵּדָעֵהוּ,
בֶּן־אֱנוֹשׁ וַתְּחַשְּׁבֵהוּ: אָדָם לַהֶבֶל דָּמָה יָמָיו כְּצֵל עוֹבֵר: יהוה הַט־שָׁמֶיךָ וְתֵרֵד
גַּע בֶּהָרִים וְיֶעֱשָׁנוּ: בְּרוֹק בָּרָק וּתְפִיצֵם, שְׁלַח חִצֶּיךָ וּתְהֻמֵּם: שְׁלַח יָדֶיךָ מִמָּרוֹם
פְּצֵנִי וְהַצִּילֵנִי מִמַּיִם רַבִּים מִיַּד בְּנֵי נֵכָר: אֲשֶׁר פִּיהֶם דִּבֶּר־שָׁוְא, וִימִינָם יְמִין
שָׁקֶר: אֱלֹהִים שִׁיר חָדָשׁ אָשִׁירָה לָּךְ, בְּנֵבֶל עָשׂוֹר אֲזַמְּרָה־לָּךְ: הַנּוֹתֵן תְּשׁוּעָה
לַמְּלָכִים הַפּוֹצֶה אֶת־דָּוִד עַבְדּוֹ מֵחֶרֶב רָעָה: פְּצֵנִי וְהַצִּילֵנִי מִיַּד בְּנֵי־נֵכָר אֲשֶׁר־
פִּיהֶם דִּבֶּר־שָׁוְא וִימִינָם יְמִין שָׁקֶר: אֲשֶׁר בָּנֵינוּ כִּנְטִעִים מְגֻדָּלִים בִּנְעוּרֵיהֶם
בְּנוֹתֵינוּ כְזָוִיֹּת מְחֻטָּבוֹת תַּבְנִית הֵיכָל: מְזָוֵינוּ מְלֵאִים מְפִיקִים מִזַּן אֶל־זַן צֹאונֵנוּ
מַאֲלִיפוֹת מְרֻבָּבוֹת בְּחוּצוֹתֵינוּ: אַלּוּפֵינוּ מְסֻבָּלִים אֵין פֶּרֶץ וְאֵין יוֹצֵאת וְאֵין
צְוָחָה בִּרְחֹבֹתֵינוּ: אַשְׁרֵי הָעָם שֶׁכָּכָה לּוֹ אַשְׁרֵי הָעָם שֶׁיהוה אֱלֹהָיו:

# Ma'ariv for Yom HaAtzma'ut

*In Israel and some communities outside Israel, the following is said before Ma'ariv. Each community should follow the decision of its own rabbinical authority.*

הדו Thank the LORD for He is good; His loving-kindness is forever. Let those the LORD redeemed say this – those He redeemed from the enemy's hand, those he gathered from the lands, from east and west, from north and south. Some lost their way in desert wastelands, finding no way to a city where they could live. They were hungry and thirsty, and their spirit grew faint. Then they cried out to the LORD in their trouble, and He rescued them from their distress. He led them by a straight path to a city where they could live. Let them thank the LORD for His loving-kindness and His wondrous deeds for humankind, for He satisfies the thirsty and fills the hungry with good. Some sat in darkness and the shadow of death, cruelly bound in iron chains, for they had rebelled against God's words and despised the counsel of the Most High. He humbled their hearts with hard labor; they stumbled, and there was none to help. Then they cried to the LORD in their trouble, and He saved them from their distress. He brought them out from darkness and the shadow of death and broke open their chains. Let them thank the LORD for His loving-kindness and His wondrous deeds for humankind, for He shattered gates of bronze and broke their iron bars. Some were fools with sinful ways, and suffered affliction because of their iniquities. They found all food repulsive, and came close to the gates of death. Then they cried to the LORD in their trouble, and He saved them from their distress. He sent His word and healed them; He rescued them from their destruction. Let them thank the LORD for His loving-kindness and His wondrous deeds for humankind. Let them sacrifice thanksgiving-offerings and tell His deeds with songs of joy. Those who go to sea in ships, plying their trade in the mighty waters, have seen the works of the LORD, His wondrous deeds in the deep. He spoke and stirred up a tempest that lifted high the waves. They rose to the heavens and plunged down to the depths; their souls melted in misery. They reeled and staggered like drunkards; all their skill was to no avail. Then they cried to the LORD in their trouble, and He brought them out of their distress. He stilled the storm to a whisper, and the waves of the sea grew calm. They rejoiced when all was quiet, then He guided them to their destination. Let them thank the LORD for His loving-kindness and His wondrous deeds for humankind. Let them exalt Him in the assembly of the people and praise Him in the council of the elders. He turns rivers into

*Ps. 107*

# מעריב ליום העצמאות

*In* ארץ ישראל *and some communities in* חוץ לארץ *the following is said before* מעריב*.*
*Each community should follow the decision of its own rabbinical authority.*

תהלים קז
הֹדוּ לַיהוה כִּי־טוֹב, כִּי לְעוֹלָם חַסְדּוֹ: יֹאמְרוּ גְּאוּלֵי יהוה, אֲשֶׁר גְּאָלָם מִיַּד־צָר: וּמֵאֲרָצוֹת קִבְּצָם, מִמִּזְרָח וּמִמַּעֲרָב, מִצָּפוֹן וּמִיָּם: תָּעוּ בַמִּדְבָּר, בִּישִׁימוֹן דָּרֶךְ, עִיר מוֹשָׁב לֹא מָצָאוּ: רְעֵבִים גַּם־צְמֵאִים, נַפְשָׁם בָּהֶם תִּתְעַטָּף: וַיִּצְעֲקוּ אֶל־יהוה בַּצַּר לָהֶם, מִמְּצוּקוֹתֵיהֶם יַצִּילֵם: וַיַּדְרִיכֵם בְּדֶרֶךְ יְשָׁרָה, לָלֶכֶת אֶל־עִיר מוֹשָׁב: יוֹדוּ לַיהוה חַסְדּוֹ, וְנִפְלְאוֹתָיו לִבְנֵי אָדָם: כִּי־הִשְׂבִּיעַ נֶפֶשׁ שֹׁקֵקָה, וְנֶפֶשׁ רְעֵבָה מִלֵּא־טוֹב: יֹשְׁבֵי חֹשֶׁךְ וְצַלְמָוֶת, אֲסִירֵי עֳנִי וּבַרְזֶל: כִּי־הִמְרוּ אִמְרֵי־אֵל, וַעֲצַת עֶלְיוֹן נָאָצוּ: וַיַּכְנַע בֶּעָמָל לִבָּם, כָּשְׁלוּ וְאֵין עֹזֵר: וַיִּזְעֲקוּ אֶל־יהוה בַּצַּר לָהֶם, מִמְּצֻקוֹתֵיהֶם יוֹשִׁיעֵם: יוֹצִיאֵם מֵחֹשֶׁךְ וְצַלְמָוֶת, וּמוֹסְרוֹתֵיהֶם יְנַתֵּק: יוֹדוּ לַיהוה חַסְדּוֹ, וְנִפְלְאוֹתָיו לִבְנֵי אָדָם: כִּי־שִׁבַּר דַּלְתוֹת נְחֹשֶׁת, וּבְרִיחֵי בַרְזֶל גִּדֵּעַ: אֱוִלִים מִדֶּרֶךְ פִּשְׁעָם, וּמֵעֲוֺנֹתֵיהֶם יִתְעַנּוּ: כָּל־אֹכֶל תְּתַעֵב נַפְשָׁם, וַיַּגִּיעוּ עַד־שַׁעֲרֵי מָוֶת: וַיִּזְעֲקוּ אֶל־יהוה בַּצַּר לָהֶם, מִמְּצֻקוֹתֵיהֶם יוֹשִׁיעֵם: יִשְׁלַח דְּבָרוֹ וְיִרְפָּאֵם, וִימַלֵּט מִשְּׁחִיתוֹתָם: יוֹדוּ לַיהוה חַסְדּוֹ, וְנִפְלְאוֹתָיו לִבְנֵי אָדָם: וְיִזְבְּחוּ זִבְחֵי תוֹדָה וִיסַפְּרוּ מַעֲשָׂיו בְּרִנָּה: יוֹרְדֵי הַיָּם בָּאֳנִיּוֹת, עֹשֵׂי מְלָאכָה בְּמַיִם רַבִּים: הֵמָּה רָאוּ מַעֲשֵׂי יהוה, וְנִפְלְאוֹתָיו בִּמְצוּלָה: וַיֹּאמֶר, וַיַּעֲמֵד רוּחַ סְעָרָה, וַתְּרוֹמֵם גַּלָּיו: יַעֲלוּ שָׁמַיִם, יֵרְדוּ תְהוֹמוֹת, נַפְשָׁם בְּרָעָה תִתְמוֹגָג: יָחוֹגּוּ וְיָנוּעוּ כַּשִּׁכּוֹר, וְכָל־חָכְמָתָם תִּתְבַּלָּע: וַיִּצְעֲקוּ אֶל־יהוה בַּצַּר לָהֶם, וּמִמְּצוּקֹתֵיהֶם יוֹצִיאֵם: יָקֵם סְעָרָה לִדְמָמָה, וַיֶּחֱשׁוּ גַּלֵּיהֶם: וַיִּשְׂמְחוּ כִי־יִשְׁתֹּקוּ, וַיַּנְחֵם אֶל־מְחוֹז חֶפְצָם: יוֹדוּ לַיהוה חַסְדּוֹ, וְנִפְלְאוֹתָיו לִבְנֵי אָדָם: וִירוֹמְמוּהוּ בִּקְהַל־עָם, וּבְמוֹשַׁב זְקֵנִים יְהַלְלוּהוּ: יָשֵׂם נְהָרוֹת לְמִדְבָּר, וּמֹצָאֵי

a desert, springs of water into parched land, fruitful land into a salt marsh, because of the wickedness of its inhabitants. He turns the desert into pools of water, parched land into flowing springs; He brings the hungry to live there, they build themselves a town in which to live. They sow fields and plant vineyards that yield a fruitful harvest; He blesses them, and they increase greatly, their herds do not decrease, though they had been few and brought low by oppression, adversity and sorrow. He pours contempt on nobles and makes them wander in a pathless waste. ▸ He lifts the destitute from poverty and enlarges their families like flocks. The upright see and rejoice, but the mouth of all wrongdoers is stopped. Whoever is wise, let him lay these things to heart, and reflect on the loving-kindness of the Lord.

יהוה מָלָךְ The Lord reigns, let the earth be glad. Let the many islands rejoice. *Ps. 97*
Clouds and thick darkness surround Him; righteousness and justice are the foundation of His throne. Fire goes ahead of Him, consuming His enemies on every side. His lightning lights up the world; the earth sees and trembles. Mountains melt like wax before the Lord, before the Lord of all the earth. The heavens proclaim His righteousness, and all the peoples see His glory. All who worship images and boast in idols are put to shame. Bow down to Him, all you heavenly powers. Zion hears and rejoices, and the towns of Judah are glad because of Your judgments, Lord. For You, Lord, are supreme over all the earth; You are exalted far above all heavenly powers. ▸ Let those who love the Lord hate evil, for He protects the lives of His devoted ones, delivering them from the hand of the wicked. Light is sown for the righteous, and joy for the upright in heart. Rejoice in the Lord, you who are righteous, and give thanks to His holy name.

מִזְמוֹר A Psalm. Sing a new song to the Lord, for He has done wondrous *Ps. 98*
things; He has saved by His right hand and His holy arm. The Lord has made His salvation known; He has displayed His righteousness in the sight of the nations. He remembered His loving-kindness and faithfulness to the house of Israel; all the ends of the earth have seen the victory of our Lord. Shout for joy to the Lord, all the earth; burst into song, sing with joy, play music. Play music to the Lord on the harp – on the harp with the sound of singing. With trumpets and the sound of the shofar, shout for joy before the Lord, the King. ▸ Let the sea and all that is in it thunder, the world and all who live in it. Let the rivers clap their hands, the mountains sing together for joy – before the Lord, for He is coming to judge the earth. He will judge the world with justice, and the peoples with equity.

מַיִם לְצִמָּאוֹן: אֶרֶץ פְּרִי לִמְלֵחָה, מֵרָעַת יוֹשְׁבֵי בָהּ: יָשֵׂם מִדְבָּר לַאֲגַם־מַיִם, וְאֶרֶץ צִיָּה לְמֹצָאֵי מָיִם: וַיּוֹשֶׁב שָׁם רְעֵבִים, וַיְכוֹנְנוּ עִיר מוֹשָׁב: וַיִּזְרְעוּ שָׂדוֹת, וַיִּטְּעוּ כְרָמִים, וַיַּעֲשׂוּ פְּרִי תְבוּאָה: וַיְבָרְכֵם וַיִּרְבּוּ מְאֹד, וּבְהֶמְתָּם לֹא יַמְעִיט: וַיִּמְעֲטוּ וַיָּשֹׁחוּ, מֵעֹצֶר רָעָה וְיָגוֹן: שֹׁפֵךְ בּוּז עַל־נְדִיבִים, וַיַּתְעֵם בְּתֹהוּ לֹא־דָרֶךְ: › וַיְשַׂגֵּב אֶבְיוֹן מֵעוֹנִי, וַיָּשֶׂם כַּצֹּאן מִשְׁפָּחוֹת: יִרְאוּ יְשָׁרִים וְיִשְׂמָחוּ, וְכָל־עַוְלָה קָפְצָה פִּיהָ: מִי־חָכָם וְיִשְׁמָר־אֵלֶּה, וְיִתְבּוֹנְנוּ חַסְדֵי יהוה:

תהלים צז
יהוה מָלָךְ תָּגֵל הָאָרֶץ, יִשְׂמְחוּ אִיִּים רַבִּים: עָנָן וַעֲרָפֶל סְבִיבָיו, צֶדֶק וּמִשְׁפָּט מְכוֹן כִּסְאוֹ: אֵשׁ לְפָנָיו תֵּלֵךְ, וּתְלַהֵט סָבִיב צָרָיו: הֵאִירוּ בְרָקָיו תֵּבֵל, רָאֲתָה וַתָּחֵל הָאָרֶץ: הָרִים כַּדּוֹנַג נָמַסּוּ מִלִּפְנֵי יהוה, מִלִּפְנֵי אֲדוֹן כָּל־הָאָרֶץ: הִגִּידוּ הַשָּׁמַיִם צִדְקוֹ, וְרָאוּ כָל־הָעַמִּים כְּבוֹדוֹ: יֵבֹשׁוּ כָּל־עֹבְדֵי פֶסֶל הַמִּתְהַלְלִים בָּאֱלִילִים, הִשְׁתַּחֲווּ־לוֹ כָּל־אֱלֹהִים: שָׁמְעָה וַתִּשְׂמַח צִיּוֹן, וַתָּגֵלְנָה בְּנוֹת יְהוּדָה, לְמַעַן מִשְׁפָּטֶיךָ יהוה: כִּי־אַתָּה יהוה עֶלְיוֹן עַל־כָּל־הָאָרֶץ, מְאֹד נַעֲלֵיתָ עַל־כָּל־אֱלֹהִים: אֹהֲבֵי יהוה שִׂנְאוּ רָע, שֹׁמֵר נַפְשׁוֹת חֲסִידָיו, מִיַּד רְשָׁעִים יַצִּילֵם: › אוֹר זָרֻעַ לַצַּדִּיק, וּלְיִשְׁרֵי־לֵב שִׂמְחָה: שִׂמְחוּ צַדִּיקִים בַּיהוה, וְהוֹדוּ לְזֵכֶר קָדְשׁוֹ:

תהלים צח
מִזְמוֹר, שִׁירוּ לַיהוה שִׁיר חָדָשׁ, כִּי־נִפְלָאוֹת עָשָׂה, הוֹשִׁיעָה־לּוֹ יְמִינוֹ וּזְרוֹעַ קָדְשׁוֹ: הוֹדִיעַ יהוה יְשׁוּעָתוֹ, לְעֵינֵי הַגּוֹיִם גִּלָּה צִדְקָתוֹ: זָכַר חַסְדּוֹ וֶאֱמוּנָתוֹ לְבֵית יִשְׂרָאֵל, רָאוּ כָל־אַפְסֵי־אָרֶץ אֵת יְשׁוּעַת אֱלֹהֵינוּ: הָרִיעוּ לַיהוה כָּל־הָאָרֶץ, פִּצְחוּ וְרַנְּנוּ וְזַמֵּרוּ: זַמְּרוּ לַיהוה בְּכִנּוֹר, בְּכִנּוֹר וְקוֹל זִמְרָה: בַּחֲצֹצְרוֹת וְקוֹל שׁוֹפָר, הָרִיעוּ לִפְנֵי הַמֶּלֶךְ יהוה: › יִרְעַם הַיָּם וּמְלֹאוֹ, תֵּבֵל וְיֹשְׁבֵי בָהּ: נְהָרוֹת יִמְחֲאוּ־כָף, יַחַד הָרִים יְרַנֵּנוּ: לִפְנֵי־יהוה כִּי בָא לִשְׁפֹּט הָאָרֶץ, יִשְׁפֹּט־תֵּבֵל בְּצֶדֶק, וְעַמִּים בְּמֵישָׁרִים:

*It is customary to sing:*

הִתְעוֹרְרִי Wake up, wake up,
For your light has come: rise, shine!
Awake, awake, break out in song,
For the LORD's glory is revealed on you.

This is the day the LORD has made; Ps. 118
let us rejoice and be glad in it.

לֹא תֵבֹשִׁי Do not be ashamed, do not be confounded.
Why be downcast? Why do you mourn?
In you the needy of My people find shelter,
And the city shall be rebuilt on its hill.

This is the day the LORD has made;
let us rejoice and be glad in it.

יָמִין Right and left you shall spread out,
And God you will revere.
Through the descendant of Peretz,
We shall rejoice and we shall be glad.

This is the day the LORD has made;
let us rejoice and be glad in it.

*Ma'ariv for Weekdays (page 314) is said at this point, in the Yom Tov melody. After Full Kaddish, the Ark is opened and the following is said responsively by the Leader and congregation.*

Listen, Israel: the LORD is our God, the LORD is One. Deut. 6

*The following is said three times responsively:*

The LORD, He is God.

*The Leader says the following which is repeated by the congregation.*

מִי שֶׁעָשָׂה May He who performed miracles for our ancestors and for us, redeeming us from slavery to freedom, grant us a complete redemption soon, and gather in our dispersed people from the four quarters of the earth, so that all Israel may be united in friendship, and let us say: Amen.

*The Ark is closed.*

*It is customary to sing:*

הִתְעוֹרְרִי הִתְעוֹרְרִי
כִּי בָא אוֹרֵךְ קוּמִי אוֹרִי
עוּרִי עוּרִי, שִׁיר דַּבֵּרִי
כְּבוֹד יהוה עָלַיִךְ נִגְלָה.

זֶה־הַיּוֹם עָשָׂה יהוה, נָגִילָה וְנִשְׂמְחָה בוֹ: תהלים קיח

לֹא תֵבֹשִׁי וְלֹא תִכָּלְמִי
מַה תִּשְׁתּוֹחֲחִי וּמַה תֶּהֱמִי
בָּךְ יֶחֱסוּ עֲנִיֵּי עַמִּי
וְנִבְנְתָה עִיר עַל תִּלָּהּ.

זֶה־הַיּוֹם עָשָׂה יהוה, נָגִילָה וְנִשְׂמְחָה בוֹ:

יָמִין וּשְׂמֹאל תִּפְרֹצִי
וְאֶת יהוה תַּעֲרִיצִי
עַל יַד אִישׁ בֶּן פַּרְצִי
וְנִשְׂמְחָה וְנָגִילָה.

זֶה־הַיּוֹם עָשָׂה יהוה, נָגִילָה וְנִשְׂמְחָה בוֹ:

*מעריב לחול (page 315) is said at this point, in the יום טוב melody. After קדיש שלם, the ארון קודש is opened and the following is said responsively by the שליח ציבור and the קהל.*

# שְׁמַע יִשְׂרָאֵל, יהוה אֱלֹהֵינוּ, יהוה אֶחָד: דברים ו

*The following is said three times responsively:*

## יהוה הוּא הָאֱלֹהִים.

*The שליח ציבור says the following which is repeated by the קהל.*

מִי שֶׁעָשָׂה נִסִּים לַאֲבוֹתֵינוּ וְלָנוּ, וּגְאָלָנוּ מֵעַבְדוּת לְחֵרוּת, הוּא יִגְאָלֵנוּ גְּאֻלָּה שְׁלֵמָה בְּקָרוֹב, וִיקַבֵּץ נִדָּחֵינוּ מֵאַרְבַּע כַּנְפוֹת הָאָרֶץ, חֲבֵרִים כָּל יִשְׂרָאֵל, וְנֹאמַר אָמֵן.

*The ארון קודש is closed.*

*The Leader continues:*

וְכִי־תָבֹאוּ When you go into battle in your land against an enemy who is attacking you, sound a staccato blast on the trumpets. Then you will be remembered by the LORD your God and you will be delivered from your enemies. On your days of rejoicing – your festivals and new moon celebrations – you shall sound a note on the trumpets over your burnt- and peace-offerings, and they will be a remembrance for you before your God. I am the LORD your God. *Num. 10*

*The shofar is sounded with a Tekia Gedola and the following is said aloud:*

Next year in Jerusalem rebuilt.

*All:*

May it be Your will, LORD our God and God of our fathers,
That as we have merited to witness the beginning of redemption,
So may we merit to hear the sound of the shofar
of our righteous anointed one, swiftly in our days.

*All sing:*

שִׁיר הַמַּעֲלוֹת A song of ascents. When the LORD brought back the exiles of Zion we were like people who dream. Then were our mouths filled with laughter, and our tongues with songs of joy. Then was it said among the nations, "The LORD has done great things for them." The LORD did do great things for us and we rejoiced. Bring back our exiles, LORD, like streams in a dry land. May those who sowed in tears, reap in joy. May one who goes out weeping, carrying a bag of seed, come back with songs of joy, carrying his sheaves. *Ps. 126*

*The Omer is counted (page 357), followed by Aleinu (page 350).*

*All sing:*

אֲנִי מַאֲמִין I believe with perfect faith
in the coming of the Messiah,
and though he may delay,
I wait daily for his coming.

*It is customary to greet each other with the following phrase:*

Happy festival; to a complete redemption!

*The* שליח ציבור *continues:*

וְכִי־תָבְאוּ מִלְחָמָה בְּאַרְצְכֶם עַל־הַצַּר הַצֹּרֵר אֶתְכֶם, וַהֲרֵעֹתֶם בַּחֲצֹצְרֹת, וְנִזְכַּרְתֶּם לִפְנֵי יהוה אֱלֹהֵיכֶם, וְנוֹשַׁעְתֶּם מֵאֹיְבֵיכֶם: וּבְיוֹם שִׂמְחַתְכֶם וּבְמוֹעֲדֵיכֶם וּבְרָאשֵׁי חָדְשֵׁכֶם, וּתְקַעְתֶּם בַּחֲצֹצְרֹת עַל עֹלֹתֵיכֶם וְעַל זִבְחֵי שַׁלְמֵיכֶם, וְהָיוּ לָכֶם לְזִכָּרוֹן לִפְנֵי אֱלֹהֵיכֶם, אֲנִי יהוה אֱלֹהֵיכֶם: במדבר י

*The* שופר *is sounded with a* תקיעה גדולה *and the following is said aloud:*

לַשָּׁנָה הַבָּאָה בִּירוּשָׁלַיִם הַבְּנוּיָה.

*All:*

יְהִי רָצוֹן מִלְּפָנֶיךָ יהוה אֱלֹהֵינוּ וֵאלֹהֵי אֲבוֹתֵינוּ
שֶׁכְּשֵׁם שֶׁזָּכִינוּ לְאַתְחַלְתָּא דִגְאֻלָּה
כֵּן נִזְכֶּה לִשְׁמֹעַ קוֹל שׁוֹפָרוֹ שֶׁל מָשִׁיחַ צִדְקֵנוּ בִּמְהֵרָה בְיָמֵינוּ.

*All sing:*

שִׁיר הַמַּעֲלוֹת, בְּשׁוּב יהוה אֶת־שִׁיבַת צִיּוֹן, הָיִינוּ כְּחֹלְמִים: אָז יִמָּלֵא שְׂחוֹק פִּינוּ וּלְשׁוֹנֵנוּ רִנָּה, אָז יֹאמְרוּ בַגּוֹיִם הִגְדִּיל יהוה לַעֲשׂוֹת עִם־אֵלֶּה: הִגְדִּיל יהוה לַעֲשׂוֹת עִמָּנוּ, הָיִינוּ שְׂמֵחִים: שׁוּבָה יהוה אֶת־שְׁבִיתֵנוּ, כַּאֲפִיקִים בַּנֶּגֶב: הַזֹּרְעִים בְּדִמְעָה בְּרִנָּה יִקְצֹרוּ: הָלוֹךְ יֵלֵךְ וּבָכֹה נֹשֵׂא מֶשֶׁךְ־הַזָּרַע, בֹּא־יָבֹא בְרִנָּה נֹשֵׂא אֲלֻמֹּתָיו: תהלים קכו

*The* עומר *is counted (page 357), followed by* עָלֵינוּ *(page 351).*

*All sing:*

אֲנִי מַאֲמִין בֶּאֱמוּנָה שְׁלֵמָה בְּבִיאַת הַמָּשִׁיחַ
וְאַף עַל פִּי שֶׁיִּתְמַהְמֵהַּ
עִם כָּל זֶה אֲחַכֶּה לּוֹ בְּכָל יוֹם שֶׁיָּבוֹא.

*It is customary to greet each other with the following phrase:*

מוֹעֲדִים לְשִׂמְחָה לִגְאֻלָּה שְׁלֵמָה

# Shaḥarit for Yom HaAtzma'ut

*In Israel and many congregations outside Israel, Pesukei DeZimra of Yom Tov on page 474 are said. Shirat HaYam (page 516) is said verse by verse. After the Leader's Repetition, Full Hallel (page 790) is said followed by Half Kaddish (page 222). On Thursdays the Torah is read (page 222). On all days, the following Haftara is read. See law 262.*

עוֹד הַיּוֹם This day he will halt at Nob; he will wave his hand, mountain of the daughter of Zion, hill of Jerusalem. See, the sovereign LORD of hosts will lop off the boughs with an axe. The tall trees will be felled, the lofty ones laid low. He will cut down the forest thickets with an axe. Lebanon will fall before the Mighty One. A shoot will grow from the stump of Jesse; from his roots a branch will bear fruit. The spirit of the LORD will rest on him – a spirit of wisdom and understanding, a spirit of counsel and power, a spirit of knowledge and the fear of the LORD, and he will delight in the fear of the LORD. He will not judge by what his eyes see, or decide by what his ears hear; with justice he will judge the poor, and with equity defend the humble in the land. He will strike the earth with the rod of his mouth; with the breath of his lips he will slay the wicked. Justice will be his belt and faithfulness the sash around his waist. The wolf will live with the lamb, the leopard will lie down with the kid, the calf and the lion and the yearling together; and a little child will lead them. The cow will graze with the bear, their young will lie down together, and the lion will eat straw like the ox. An infant will play near the cobra's hole, and a young child put his hand into the viper's nest. They will neither harm nor destroy on all My holy mountain, for the earth will be full of the knowledge of the LORD as the waters cover the sea. On that day the stock of Jesse will stand as a banner for the peoples; nations will rally to him, and his place of rest will be glorious. On that day the LORD will reach out His hand a second time to reclaim the remnant that is left of His people from Assyria, Lower Egypt, Pathros, Cush, Elam, Shinar, Hamath and the islands of the sea. He will raise a banner for the nations and gather the exiles of Israel; He will assemble the scattered people

*Is. 10:32–12:6*

# שחרית ליום העצמאות

*In* ארץ ישראל *and many congregations in* חוץ לארץ, פסוקי דזמרה *of* יום טוב *on page 475 are said.* שירת הים *(page 517) is said verse by verse. After* חזרת הש״ץ, הלל שלם *(page 791) is said followed by* חצי קדיש *(page 223). On Thursdays the* תורה *is read (page 223). On all days, the following* הפטרה *is read. See law 262.*

ישעיה י:לב–יב:ו

עוֹד הַיּוֹם בְּנֹב לַעֲמֹד יְנֹפֵף יָדוֹ הַר בַּת־צִיּוֹן גִּבְעַת
יְרוּשָׁלָ͏ִם: הִנֵּה הָאָדוֹן יהוה צְבָאוֹת מְסָעֵף פֻּארָה
בְּמַעֲרָצָה וְרָמֵי הַקּוֹמָה גְּדֻעִים וְהַגְּבֹהִים יִשְׁפָּלוּ: וְנִקַּף סִבְכֵי
הַיַּעַר בַּבַּרְזֶל וְהַלְּבָנוֹן בְּאַדִּיר יִפּוֹל: וְיָצָא חֹטֶר
מִגֵּזַע יִשָׁי וְנֵצֶר מִשָּׁרָשָׁיו יִפְרֶה: וְנָחָה עָלָיו רוּחַ יהוה רוּחַ
חָכְמָה וּבִינָה רוּחַ עֵצָה וּגְבוּרָה רוּחַ דַּעַת וְיִרְאַת יהוה:
וַהֲרִיחוֹ בְּיִרְאַת יהוה וְלֹא־לְמַרְאֵה עֵינָיו יִשְׁפּוֹט וְלֹא־
לְמִשְׁמַע אָזְנָיו יוֹכִיחַ: וְשָׁפַט בְּצֶדֶק דַּלִּים וְהוֹכִיחַ בְּמִישׁוֹר
לְעַנְוֵי־אָרֶץ וְהִכָּה־אֶרֶץ בְּשֵׁבֶט פִּיו וּבְרוּחַ שְׂפָתָיו יָמִית
רָשָׁע: וְהָיָה צֶדֶק אֵזוֹר מָתְנָיו וְהָאֱמוּנָה אֵזוֹר חֲלָצָיו: וְגָר
זְאֵב עִם־כֶּבֶשׂ וְנָמֵר עִם־גְּדִי יִרְבָּץ וְעֵגֶל וּכְפִיר וּמְרִיא
יַחְדָּו וְנַעַר קָטֹן נֹהֵג בָּם: וּפָרָה וָדֹב תִּרְעֶינָה יַחְדָּו יִרְבְּצוּ
יַלְדֵיהֶן וְאַרְיֵה כַּבָּקָר יֹאכַל־תֶּבֶן: וְשִׁעֲשַׁע יוֹנֵק עַל־חֻר
פָּתֶן וְעַל מְאוּרַת צִפְעוֹנִי גָּמוּל יָדוֹ הָדָה: לֹא־יָרֵעוּ וְלֹא־
יַשְׁחִיתוּ בְּכָל־הַר קָדְשִׁי כִּי־מָלְאָה הָאָרֶץ דֵּעָה אֶת־יהוה
כַּמַּיִם לַיָּם מְכַסִּים: וְהָיָה בַּיּוֹם הַהוּא שֹׁרֶשׁ יִשַׁי
אֲשֶׁר עֹמֵד לְנֵס עַמִּים אֵלָיו גּוֹיִם יִדְרֹשׁוּ וְהָיְתָה מְנֻחָתוֹ
כָּבוֹד: וְהָיָה ׀ בַּיּוֹם הַהוּא יוֹסִיף אֲדֹנָי ׀ שֵׁנִית
יָדוֹ לִקְנוֹת אֶת־שְׁאָר עַמּוֹ אֲשֶׁר יִשָּׁאֵר מֵאַשּׁוּר וּמִמִּצְרַיִם
וּמִפַּתְרוֹס וּמִכּוּשׁ וּמֵעֵילָם וּמִשִּׁנְעָר וּמֵחֲמָת וּמֵאִיֵּי הַיָּם:
וְנָשָׂא נֵס לַגּוֹיִם וְאָסַף נִדְחֵי יִשְׂרָאֵל וּנְפֻצוֹת יְהוּדָה יְקַבֵּץ

of Judah from the four quarters of the earth. Ephraim's jealousy will vanish, and Judah's harassment will end. Ephraim will not be jealous of Judah, nor will Judah be hostile toward Ephraim. They will swoop down on the slopes of Philistia to the west; together they will plunder the people to the east. Edom and Moab will be subject to them, and the Ammonites shall obey them. The LORD will dry up the gulf of the Egyptian sea; with a scorching wind He will sweep His hand over the Euphrates River. He will break it up into seven streams so that people can cross over in sandals. There will be a highway for the remnant of His people that is left from Assyria, as there was for Israel when they came up from Egypt. In that day you will say: "I will praise You, O LORD. Although You were angry with me, Your anger has turned away and You have comforted me. Surely God is my salvation; I will trust and not be afraid. The LORD, the LORD, is my strength and my song; He has become my salvation." With joy you will draw water from the wells of salvation. In that day you will say: "Give thanks to the LORD, call on His name; make known among the nations what He has done, and proclaim that His name is exalted. Sing to the LORD, for He has done glorious things; let this be known to all the world. Shout aloud and sing for joy, people of Zion, for great is the Holy One of Israel among you."

*After the Haftara, the Prayer for the State of Israel (page 592) followed by the Memorial for Fallen Israeli Soldiers (page 992) is said. The service then continues with Ashrei until the end of Shaharit. At the end of the service, sing:*

אֲנִי מַאֲמִין I believe with perfect faith
in the coming of the Messiah,
and though he may delay, I wait daily for his coming.

## YOM YERUSHALAYIM

*At Minḥa before Yom Yerushalayim, Taḥanun is omitted. (If Shabbat, Tzidkatekha on page 690 is omitted.) In the evening, Ma'ariv for weekdays is said in the Yom Tov melody. The Omer is counted. Many have the custom to add prayers of thanksgiving at the end of Ma'ariv.*

*In Shaḥarit, many communities outside Israel and in Israel say the Pesukei DeZimra of Yom Tov (page 474). After the Leader's Repetition, Full Hallel (page 790) is said and the regular service continues.*

מֵאַרְבַּע כַּנְפוֹת הָאָרֶץ׃ וְסָרָה קִנְאַת אֶפְרַיִם וְצֹרְרֵי יְהוּדָה יִכָּרֵתוּ אֶפְרַיִם לֹא־יְקַנֵּא אֶת־יְהוּדָה וִיהוּדָה לֹא־יָצֹר אֶת־אֶפְרָיִם׃ וְעָפוּ בְכָתֵף פְּלִשְׁתִּים יָמָּה יַחְדָּו יָבֹזּוּ אֶת־בְּנֵי־קֶדֶם אֱדוֹם וּמוֹאָב מִשְׁלוֹחַ יָדָם וּבְנֵי עַמּוֹן מִשְׁמַעְתָּם׃ וְהֶחֱרִים יהוה אֵת לְשׁוֹן יָם־מִצְרַיִם וְהֵנִיף יָדוֹ עַל־הַנָּהָר בַּעְיָם רוּחוֹ וְהִכָּהוּ לְשִׁבְעָה נְחָלִים וְהִדְרִיךְ בַּנְּעָלִים׃ וְהָיְתָה מְסִלָּה לִשְׁאָר עַמּוֹ אֲשֶׁר יִשָּׁאֵר מֵאַשּׁוּר כַּאֲשֶׁר הָיְתָה לְיִשְׂרָאֵל בְּיוֹם עֲלֹתוֹ מֵאֶרֶץ מִצְרָיִם׃ וְאָמַרְתָּ בַּיּוֹם הַהוּא אוֹדְךָ יהוה כִּי אָנַפְתָּ בִּי יָשֹׁב אַפְּךָ וּתְנַחֲמֵנִי׃ הִנֵּה אֵל יְשׁוּעָתִי אֶבְטַח וְלֹא אֶפְחָד כִּי־עָזִּי וְזִמְרָת יָהּ יהוה וַיְהִי־לִי לִישׁוּעָה׃ וּשְׁאַבְתֶּם־מַיִם בְּשָׂשׂוֹן מִמַּעַיְנֵי הַיְשׁוּעָה׃ וַאֲמַרְתֶּם בַּיּוֹם הַהוּא הוֹדוּ לַיהוה קִרְאוּ בִשְׁמוֹ הוֹדִיעוּ בָעַמִּים עֲלִילֹתָיו הַזְכִּירוּ כִּי נִשְׂגָּב שְׁמוֹ׃ זַמְּרוּ יהוה כִּי גֵאוּת עָשָׂה מוּדַעַת זֹאת בְּכָל־הָאָרֶץ׃ צַהֲלִי וָרֹנִּי יוֹשֶׁבֶת צִיּוֹן כִּי־גָדוֹל בְּקִרְבֵּךְ קְדוֹשׁ יִשְׂרָאֵל׃

*After the* הפטרה*, the Prayer for the State of Israel (page 593) followed by the* אזכרה *for Fallen Israeli Soldiers (page 993) is said. The service then continues with* אַשְׁרֵי *and* וּבָא לְצִיּוֹן *until the end of* שחרית*. At the end of the service, sing:*

אֲנִי מַאֲמִין בֶּאֱמוּנָה שְׁלֵמָה, בְּבִיאַת הַמָּשִׁיחַ
וְאַף עַל פִּי שֶׁיִּתְמַהְמֵהַּ
עִם כָּל זֶה אֲחַכֶּה לּוֹ בְּכָל יוֹם שֶׁיָּבוֹא.

## יום חירות ירושלים

*At* מנחה *before* יום ירושלים, תחנון *is omitted. (If* שבת, צִדְקָתְךָ *on page 691 is omitted.) In the evening,* מעריב לחול *is said in the* יום טוב *melody. The* עומר *is counted. Many have the custom to add prayers of thanksgiving at the end of* מעריב*.*

*In* שחרית *many communities in* חוץ לארץ *and in* ארץ ישראל *say the* פסוקי דזמרה *of* יום טוב *(page 475). After* חזרת הש״ץ, הלל שלם *(page 791) is said and the regular service continues.*

# Seliḥot

*Seliḥot are said on Fast Days. On Tisha B'Av, Kinot are said instead. On the Fast of Gedalya, the Seliḥot for the Ten Days of Repentance are said.*

## SELIḤOT FOR THE TENTH OF TEVET

סְלַח לָנוּ Forgive us, our Father, for in our great foolishness we have blundered. Pardon us, our King, for our iniquities are many.

אֵל אֶרֶךְ You are a God slow to anger, You are called the Master of Compassion, and You have taught the way of repentance. May You remember today and every day the greatness of Your compassion and kindness, for the sake of the descendants of Your beloved ones. Turn toward us in compassion, for You are the Master of Compassion. We come before You in plea and prayer, as You in ancient times showed the humble one [Moses]. Turn from Your fierce anger, as is written in Your Torah. In the shadow of Your wings may we shelter and abide, as on the day when the LORD descended in the cloud. ▸ Overlook sin and wipe away guilt, as on the day when "He stood beside him there." Give ear to our pleading and listen to our speech, as on the day when "he called upon the name of the LORD," and in that place is said –

*Congregation then Leader:*

And the LORD passed by before him and proclaimed: *Ex. 34*

*All say aloud:*

**יהוה The LORD, the LORD, compassionate and gracious God, slow to anger, abounding in loving-kindness and truth, extending loving-kindness to a thousand generations, forgiving iniquity, rebellion and sin, and absolving [the guilty who repent]. Forgive us our iniquity and our sin, and take us as Your inheritance.**

*Continue:*

סְלַח לָנוּ Forgive us, our Father, for we have sinned. Pardon us, our King, for we have transgressed. For You, LORD, are good and forgiving, abounding in loving-kindness to all who call on You. *Ps. 86*

For with the LORD there is loving-kindness, and great is His power to redeem. *Ps. 130* LORD, save Israel from all its troubles. *Ps. 25* It is He who will redeem Israel from all its sins. *Ps. 130* The LORD redeems His servants; those who take refuge in Him shall not be condemned. *Ps. 34*

# סליחות

*סליחות are said on Fast Days. On תשעה באב, קינות are said instead.*
*On צום גדליה, the סליחות for the עשרת ימי תשובה are said.*

## סליחות לעשרה בטבת

סְלַח לָנוּ, אָבִינוּ, כִּי בְּרֹב אִוַּלְתֵּנוּ שָׁגִינוּ.
מְחַל לָנוּ, מַלְכֵּנוּ, כִּי רַבּוּ עֲוֹנֵינוּ.

אֵל אֶרֶךְ אַפַּיִם אַתָּה, וּבַעַל הָרַחֲמִים נִקְרֵאתָ, וְדֶרֶךְ תְּשׁוּבָה הוֹרֵיתָ. גְּדֻלַּת רַחֲמֶיךָ וַחֲסָדֶיךָ, תִּזְכֹּר הַיּוֹם וּבְכָל יוֹם לְזֶרַע יְדִידֶיךָ. תֵּפֶן אֵלֵינוּ בְּרַחֲמִים, כִּי אַתָּה הוּא בַּעַל הָרַחֲמִים. בְּתַחֲנוּן וּבִתְפִלָּה פָּנֶיךָ נְקַדֵּם, כְּהוֹדַעְתָּ לֶעָנָו מִקֶּדֶם. מֵחֲרוֹן אַפְּךָ שׁוּב, כְּמוֹ בְּתוֹרָתְךָ כָּתוּב. וּבְצֵל כְּנָפֶיךָ נֶחֱסֶה וְנִתְלוֹנָן, כְּיוֹם וַיֵּרֶד יהוה בֶּעָנָן. ‹ תַּעֲבֹר עַל פֶּשַׁע וְתִמְחֶה אָשָׁם, כְּיוֹם וַיִּתְיַצֵּב עִמּוֹ שָׁם. תַּאֲזִין שַׁוְעָתֵנוּ וְתַקְשִׁיב מֶנּוּ מַאֲמָר, כְּיוֹם וַיִּקְרָא בְשֵׁם יהוה, וְשָׁם נֶאֱמַר

*:שליח ציבור then קהל*

שמות לד וַיַּעֲבֹר יהוה עַל־פָּנָיו וַיִּקְרָא

*All say aloud:*

**יהוה, יהוה, אֵל רַחוּם וְחַנּוּן, אֶרֶךְ אַפַּיִם, וְרַב־חֶסֶד וֶאֱמֶת: נֹצֵר חֶסֶד לָאֲלָפִים, נֹשֵׂא עָוֹן וָפֶשַׁע וְחַטָּאָה, וְנַקֵּה: וְסָלַחְתָּ לַעֲוֹנֵנוּ וּלְחַטָּאתֵנוּ, וּנְחַלְתָּנוּ:**

*Continue:*

תהלים פו סְלַח לָנוּ אָבִינוּ כִּי חָטָאנוּ, מְחַל לָנוּ מַלְכֵּנוּ כִּי פָשָׁעְנוּ. כִּי־אַתָּה אֲדֹנָי טוֹב וְסַלָּח, וְרַב־חֶסֶד לְכָל־קֹרְאֶיךָ:

תהלים קל / תהלים כה / תהלים קל / תהלים לד
כִּי־עִם־יהוה הַחֶסֶד, וְהַרְבֵּה עִמּוֹ פְדוּת: פְּדֵה אֱלֹהִים אֶת־יִשְׂרָאֵל מִכֹּל צָרוֹתָיו: וְהוּא יִפְדֶּה אֶת־יִשְׂרָאֵל מִכֹּל עֲוֹנֹתָיו: פּוֹדֶה יהוה נֶפֶשׁ עֲבָדָיו, וְלֹא יֶאְשְׁמוּ כָּל־הַחֹסִים בּוֹ:

כְּרַחֵם As a father has compassion for his children,
so, LORD, have compassion for us.
Salvation is the LORD's; on Your people is Your blessing, Selah! *Ps. 3*
The LORD of hosts is with us, the God of Jacob is our stronghold, Selah! *Ps. 46*
LORD of hosts, happy is the one who trusts in You. *Ps. 84*
LORD, save! May the King answer us on the day we call. *Ps. 20*

▸ Forgive, please, this people's iniquity, *Num. 14*
in the abundance of Your kindness,
and as You have forgiven this people from the time of Egypt until now,
and there it is written:

*Congregation then Leader:*

And the LORD said, I have forgiven as you asked.

*Continue:*

הַטֵּה Give ear, my God and hear; open Your eyes and see our desolation, and the city that bears Your name, for it is not on the strength of our righteousness that we throw down our pleadings before You, but on the strength of Your great compassion. LORD, hear me; LORD, forgive; LORD, listen and act and do not delay – for Your sake, my God; for Your city and Your people bear Your name. *Dan. 9*

Our God and God of our fathers:

אֶזְכְּרָה I shall recall the anguish that came to me; He inflicted three blows upon me in this month. He cut me off, He veered me aside, He beat me – but now He has finally drained me out. *Job 16* On the eighth of the month He darkened my right and my left; I marked out all three days for fasting. The king of Greece forced me to write the Torah in his tongue. The plowmen have plowed across my back; they made the furrows long. I raged, on the ninth, in shame and disgrace, my mantle of glory and my wreath were taken from me. The man who gave us the words of Heaven was torn from us on that day – that was Ezra the Scribe. On the tenth, Ezekiel the Seer, son of Buzi was commanded, "Write this happening in the scroll, for the remembrance of a people melted away and disgraced; write this very day." *Ezek. 24* The tenth was listed last among the fasts to show the order of the months. My own mouth gapes open with weeping and wailing, and this chronicle of troubles burns within my heart – as the fugitive came to me and said, "The city is crushed." For these things I have scattered dust upon my face. I have spoken now of all four – would that I could shoot an arrow through my heart. For these great torments, I have dug my own grave. "The LORD is righteous; I have rebelled against His word." *Lam. 1* I have called out Your name as I grieve my troubles. Witness my oppression and hear my voice in its entreaty. Hear my pleading, please, hasten my salvation. Do not block Your ears to my sighing, to my cry. *Lam. 3*
▸ In the month of Tevet I was stricken sorely. The world changed its course, from where I stand. I was stubborn, I sinned – yet may He reveal His goodness to me; the One who told the ocean, "Only thus far, come."

כְּרַחֵם אָב עַל בָּנִים, כֵּן תְּרַחֵם יהוה עָלֵינוּ.

לַיהוה הַיְשׁוּעָה, עַל־עַמְּךָ בִרְכָתֶךָ סֶּלָה: תהלים ג

יהוה צְבָאוֹת עִמָּנוּ, מִשְׂגָּב לָנוּ אֱלֹהֵי יַעֲקֹב סֶלָה: תהלים מו

יהוה צְבָאוֹת, אַשְׁרֵי אָדָם בֹּטֵחַ בָּךְ: תהלים פד

יהוה הוֹשִׁיעָה, הַמֶּלֶךְ יַעֲנֵנוּ בְיוֹם־קָרְאֵנוּ: תהלים כ

› סְלַח־נָא לַעֲוֹן הָעָם הַזֶּה כְּגֹדֶל חַסְדֶּךָ במדבר יד
וְכַאֲשֶׁר נָשָׂאתָה לָעָם הַזֶּה מִמִּצְרַיִם וְעַד־הֵנָּה:
וְשָׁם נֶאֱמַר

*then* שליח ציבור *:*קהל

וַיֹּאמֶר יהוה, סָלַחְתִּי כִּדְבָרֶךָ:

*Continue:*

הַטֵּה אֱלֹהַי אָזְנְךָ וּשְׁמָע, פְּקַח עֵינֶיךָ וּרְאֵה שֹׁמְמֹתֵינוּ וְהָעִיר אֲשֶׁר־נִקְרָא שִׁמְךָ עָלֶיהָ, כִּי לֹא עַל־צִדְקֹתֵינוּ אֲנַחְנוּ מַפִּילִים תַּחֲנוּנֵינוּ לְפָנֶיךָ, כִּי עַל־רַחֲמֶיךָ הָרַבִּים: אֲדֹנָי שְׁמָעָה, אֲדֹנָי סְלָחָה, אֲדֹנָי הַקְשִׁיבָה וַעֲשֵׂה אַל־תְּאַחַר, לְמַעַנְךָ אֱלֹהַי, כִּי־שִׁמְךָ נִקְרָא עַל־עִירְךָ וְעַל־עַמֶּךָ: דניאל ט

אֱלֹהֵינוּ וֵאלֹהֵי אֲבוֹתֵינוּ

אֶזְכְּרָה מָצוֹק אֲשֶׁר קְרָאַנִי. בְּשָׁלֹשׁ מַכּוֹת בַּחֹדֶשׁ הַזֶּה הִכַּנִי. גְּדָעַנִי הֱנִיאַנִי
הִכְאַנִי. אַךְ־עַתָּה הֶלְאָנִי: דְּעָכַנִי בִּשְׁמוֹנָה בוֹ שְׂמָאלִית וִימָנִית. הֲלֹא שְׁלָשְׁתָּן איוב טז
קָבַעְתִּי תַּעֲנִית. וּמֶלֶךְ יָוָן אֲנָסַנִי לִכְתֹּב דָּת, יְוָנִית. עַל גַּבִּי חָרְשׁוּ חוֹרְשִׁים,
הֶאֱרִיכוּ מַעֲנִית. זְעַמְתִּי בְּתִשְׁעָה בוֹ בִּכְלִמָּה וָחֵפֶר. חָשַׂךְ מֵעָלַי מְעִיל הוֹד
וָצֶפֶר. טָרֹף טֹרַף בּוֹ הַנּוֹתֵן אִמְרֵי שָׁפֶר. הוּא עֶזְרָא הַסּוֹפֵר. יוֹם עֲשִׂירִי, צֻוָּה
בֶּן בּוּזִי הַחוֹזֶה. כְּתָב לְךָ בְּסֵפֶר הַמַּחֲזֶה. לְזִכָּרוֹן לְעַם נָמֵס וְנִבְזֶה. אֶת־עֶצֶם יחזקאל כד
הַיּוֹם הַזֶּה: מִנְיַן סֵדֶר חֳדָשִׁים בַּעֲשָׂרָה בוֹ הָעִיר. נְהִי וִילֵל בְּמוֹ פִי אַפְעִיר.
סֵדֶר פֻּרְעָנִיּוֹת בְּתוֹךְ לְבָבִי יַבְעִיר. בְּבֹא אֵלַי הַפָּלִיט לֵאמֹר הֻכְּתָה הָעִיר. עַל
אֵלֶּה, עַל פְּנֵי אָבָק זֵרִיתִי. פַּצְתִּי עַל אַרְבַּעְתָּן, לוּ חֵץ בְּלִבִּי יָרִיתִי. צָרוֹת עַל
אֵלֶּה, קֶבֶר לִי כָּרִיתִי. צַדִּיק הוּא יהוה, כִּי פִיהוּ מָרִיתִי: קָרָאתִי שִׁמְךָ, מִתְנַחֵם איכה א
עַל רָעָתִי. רְאֵה עָנְיִי וּשְׁמַע קוֹל פְּגִיעָתִי. שְׁמַע תְּחִנָּתִי, חִישׁ נָא יְשׁוּעָתִי.
אַל־תַּעְלֵם אָזְנְךָ לְרַוְחָתִי לְשַׁוְעָתִי: › יֶרַח טֵבֵת, מְאֹד לָקִיתִי בוֹ. וְנִשְׁתַּנּוּ איכה ג
עָלַי סִדְרֵי נְתִיבוֹ. סָרַרְתִּי, פָּשַׁעְתִּי, יְגַלֶּה לִי טוּבוֹ. הָאוֹמֵר לַיָּם עַד פֹּה תָבוֹא.

אֵל מֶלֶךְ God, King who sits upon a throne of compassion, who acts with loving-kindness, who pardons the iniquities of His people, passing them before Him in order; who forgives sinners and pardons transgressors; who performs righteousness with all flesh and spirit, do not repay their bad actions in kind. ▸ God, You taught us to speak thirteen attributes: recall for us today the covenant of the thirteen attributes, as You in ancient times showed the humble one [Moses], as is written: The LORD descended in the cloud and stood with him there, and proclaimed in the name of the LORD: *Ex. 34*

*Congregation then Leader:*

And the LORD passed by before him and proclaimed: *Ex. 34*

*All say aloud:*

יהוה The LORD, the LORD, compassionate and gracious God, slow to anger, abounding in loving-kindness and truth, extending loving-kindness to a thousand generations, forgiving iniquity, rebellion and sin, and absolving [the guilty who repent]. Forgive us our iniquity and our sin, and take us as Your inheritance.

*Continue:*

סְלַח לָנוּ Forgive us, our Father, for we have sinned. Pardon us, our King, for we have transgressed. For You, LORD, are good and forgiving, abounding in loving-kindness to all who call on You. *Ps. 86*

God, nations came into Your inheritance, they made Your holy Sanctuary impure, they reduced Jerusalem to ruins. God, wanton people came up against us and a gang of oppressors sought out our lives, and did not place You before them. *Ps. 79*

כְּרַחֵם As a father has compassion for his children,
so, LORD, have compassion for us.
Salvation is the LORD's; on Your people is Your blessing, Selah! *Ps. 3*
The LORD of hosts is with us, the God of Jacob is our stronghold, Selah! *Ps. 46*
LORD of hosts, happy is the one who trusts in You. *Ps. 84*
LORD, save! May the King answer us on the day we call. *Ps. 20*

Our God and God of our fathers:

אֶבֶן הָרֹאשָׁה The Temple, Top Stone, is laid to ruin and plowed over, and the Torah's heirs, Israel, a derision among nations. Within me an aching heart, sickened and pained – we are left as if fatherless, become like orphans. Israel, delicate and refined, fenced by lilies of the Law, has now become mournful, given over to assailants. The faithful city has become like a widow, the countless

אֵל מֶלֶךְ יוֹשֵׁב עַל כִּסֵּא רַחֲמִים, מִתְנַהֵג בַּחֲסִידוּת. מוֹחֵל עֲוֹנוֹת עַמּוֹ, מַעֲבִיר רִאשׁוֹן רִאשׁוֹן. מַרְבֶּה מְחִילָה לְחַטָּאִים, וּסְלִיחָה לְפוֹשְׁעִים. עֹשֶׂה צְדָקוֹת עִם כָּל בָּשָׂר וָרוּחַ, לֹא כְרָעָתָם תִּגְמֹל. ‹ אֵל, הוֹרֵיתָ לָּנוּ לוֹמַר שְׁלֹשׁ עֶשְׂרֵה, וּזְכָר לָנוּ הַיּוֹם בְּרִית שְׁלֹשׁ עֶשְׂרֵה, כְּמוֹ שֶׁהוֹדַעְתָּ לֶעָנָו מִקֶּדֶם, כְּמוֹ שֶׁכָּתוּב: וַיֵּרֶד יהוה בֶּעָנָן, וַיִּתְיַצֵּב עִמּוֹ שָׁם, וַיִּקְרָא בְשֵׁם, יהוה: שמות לד

*שליח ציבור then קהל:*

וַיַּעֲבֹר יהוה עַל־פָּנָיו וַיִּקְרָא שמות לד

*All say aloud:*

יהוה, יהוה, אֵל רַחוּם וְחַנּוּן, אֶרֶךְ אַפַּיִם, וְרַב־חֶסֶד וֶאֱמֶת: נֹצֵר חֶסֶד לָאֲלָפִים, נֹשֵׂא עָוֹן וָפֶשַׁע וְחַטָּאָה, וְנַקֵּה: וְסָלַחְתָּ לַעֲוֹנֵנוּ וּלְחַטָּאתֵנוּ, וּנְחַלְתָּנוּ:

*Continue:*

סְלַח לָנוּ אָבִינוּ כִּי חָטָאנוּ, מְחַל לָנוּ מַלְכֵּנוּ כִּי פָשָׁעְנוּ. כִּי־אַתָּה אֲדֹנָי טוֹב וְסַלָּח, וְרַב־חֶסֶד לְכָל־קֹרְאֶיךָ: תהלים פו

אֱלֹהִים בָּאוּ גוֹיִם בְּנַחֲלָתֶךָ, טִמְּאוּ אֶת־הֵיכַל קָדְשֶׁךָ, שָׂמוּ אֶת־יְרוּשָׁלִַם לְעִיִּים: אֱלֹהִים, זֵדִים קָמוּ עָלֵינוּ, וַעֲדַת עָרִיצִים בִּקְשׁוּ נַפְשֵׁנוּ, וְלֹא שָׂמוּךָ לְנֶגְדָּם. תהלים עט

כְּרַחֵם אָב עַל בָּנִים, כֵּן תְּרַחֵם יהוה עָלֵינוּ.
לַיהוה הַיְשׁוּעָה, עַל־עַמְּךָ בִרְכָתֶךָ סֶּלָה: תהלים ג
יהוה צְבָאוֹת עִמָּנוּ, מִשְׂגָּב לָנוּ אֱלֹהֵי יַעֲקֹב סֶלָה: תהלים מו
יהוה צְבָאוֹת, אַשְׁרֵי אָדָם בֹּטֵחַ בָּךְ: תהלים פד
יהוה הוֹשִׁיעָה, הַמֶּלֶךְ יַעֲנֵנוּ בְיוֹם־קָרְאֵנוּ: תהלים כ

אֱלֹהֵינוּ וֵאלֹהֵי אֲבוֹתֵינוּ

אֶבֶן הָרֹאשָׁה, לְעִיִּים וְלַחֲרִישָׁה, וְנוֹחֲלֵי מוֹרָשָׁה, מָנוֹד רֹאשׁ בַּלְאֻמִּים. בְּקִרְבִּי לֵב נִכְאָב, נִדְוֶה וְנִדְאָב, נִשְׁאַרְנוּ כְּאֵין אָב, וְהָיִינוּ כִּיתוֹמִים. רַכָּה וַעֲנֻגָּה, בְּשׁוֹשַׁנִּים סוּגָה, וְעַתָּה הִיא נוּגָה, מְסוּרָה בְּיַד קָמִים. הָיְתָה

descendants of Jacob have been sold for no price. Refined and delicate, worthy of royalty, they have been plowed across in long furrows over many years and days. The house of Jacob is given over to plunder, to jeering and slander, and the joyous city to plantations of vines. Doused in poison by lawless ones, is the people once desired like offerings, like fragrant incense. They have despised and neglected the Torah of Moses Avi-Zanoaḥ, they can find no rest by night or by day. Awesome, highest God, may the desire arise in You to bring a year of recompense for Israel's strife. Renew our days as of old, Dwelling Place who is our God of old. And wash our red guilt white as wool; our stains as snow. ‣ Strengthen us in awe of You, and in the keeping of Your Law. And come to us, in Your salvation, God who is full of compassion.

אֵל מֶלֶךְ God, King who sits upon a throne of compassion, who acts with loving-kindness, who pardons the iniquities of His people, passing them before Him in order; who forgives sinners and pardons transgressors; who performs righteousness with all flesh and spirit, do not repay their bad actions in kind. ‣ God, You taught us to speak thirteen attributes: recall for us today the covenant of the thirteen attributes, as You in ancient times showed the humble one [Moses], as is written: The Lord descended in the cloud and stood with him there, and *Ex. 34*
proclaimed in the name of the Lord:

*Congregation then Leader:*

And the Lord passed by before him and proclaimed: *Ex. 34*

*All say aloud:*

**יהוה The Lord, the Lord, compassionate and gracious God, slow to anger, abounding in loving-kindness and truth, extending loving-kindness to a thousand generations, forgiving iniquity, rebellion and sin, and absolving [the guilty who repent]. Forgive us our iniquity and our sin, and take us as Your inheritance.**

*Continue:*

סְלַח לָנוּ Forgive us, our Father, for we have sinned. Pardon us, our King, for we have transgressed. For You, Lord, are good and forgiving, abounding in *Ps. 86*
loving-kindness to all who call on You.

*The following is said responsively:*

אֲבוֹתַי When my forebears trusted in the name of God, my Rock,
they grew and were successful and also gave forth fruit.
And from the time when they were drawn away to walk with Him in enmity,
they diminished and diminished until the tenth month. *Gen. 8*

כְּאַלְמָנָה, קִרְיָה נֶאֱמָנָה, וְזֶרַע מִי מָנָה, נִמְכְּרוּ בְּלֹא דָמִים. מְעֻנָּגָה וְרַכָּה, צָלְחָה לִמְלוּכָה, וּמַעֲנִיתָהּ אָרְכָה, זֶה כַּמָּה שָׁנִים וְיָמִים. בֵּית יַעֲקֹב לְבִזָּה, לְלַעַג וּלְעִזָּה, וְהָעִיר הָעַלִּיזָה, לְמַטְּעֵי כְרָמִים. רְוּיָה תַרְעֵלָה, בְּיַד בְּנֵי עַוְלָה, הָרְצוּיָה כְּעוֹלָה, וְכִקְטֹרֶת הַסַּמִּים. מְאַסָּה לִזְנֹחַ, תּוֹרַת אֲבִי זָנוֹחַ, וְלֹא מָצְאָה מָנוֹחַ, לֵילוֹת וְגַם יָמִים. נוֹרָא אֵל עֶלְיוֹן, מִמְּךָ יְהִי צִבְיוֹן, לְהָשִׁיב לְרִיב צִיּוֹן, שְׁנַת שִׁלּוּמִים. חַדֵּשׁ יָמֵינוּ כְּקֶדֶם, מְעוֹנָה אֱלֹהֵי קֶדֶם, וְלַבֵּן כַּצֶּמֶר אָדֶם, וְכַשֶּׁלֶג כְּתָמִים. ‹ חַזְּקֵנוּ בְּיִרְאָתֶךָ, וּבְקִיּוּם תּוֹרָתֶךָ, וּפָקְדֵנוּ בִּישׁוּעָתֶךָ, אֵל מָלֵא רַחֲמִים.

אֵל מֶלֶךְ יוֹשֵׁב עַל כִּסֵּא רַחֲמִים, מִתְנַהֵג בַּחֲסִידוּת. מוֹחֵל עֲוֹנוֹת עַמּוֹ, מַעֲבִיר רִאשׁוֹן רִאשׁוֹן. מַרְבֶּה מְחִילָה לְחַטָּאִים, וּסְלִיחָה לְפוֹשְׁעִים. עֹשֶׂה צְדָקוֹת עִם כָּל בָּשָׂר וָרוּחַ, לֹא כְרָעָתָם תִּגְמֹל. ‹ אֵל, הוֹרֵיתָ לָּנוּ לוֹמַר שְׁלֹשׁ עֶשְׂרֵה, וּזְכֹר לָנוּ הַיּוֹם בְּרִית שְׁלֹשׁ עֶשְׂרֵה, כְּמוֹ שֶׁהוֹדַעְתָּ לֶעָנָו מִקֶּדֶם, כְּמוֹ שֶׁכָּתוּב: וַיֵּרֶד יהוה בֶּעָנָן, וַיִּתְיַצֵּב עִמּוֹ שָׁם, וַיִּקְרָא בְשֵׁם, יהוה: שמות לד

*שליח ציבור then קהל:*

וַיַּעֲבֹר יהוה עַל־פָּנָיו וַיִּקְרָא שמות לד

*All say aloud:*

**יהוה, יהוה, אֵל רַחוּם וְחַנּוּן, אֶרֶךְ אַפַּיִם, וְרַב־חֶסֶד וֶאֱמֶת: נֹצֵר חֶסֶד לָאֲלָפִים, נֹשֵׂא עָוֹן וָפֶשַׁע וְחַטָּאָה, וְנַקֵּה: וְסָלַחְתָּ לַעֲוֹנֵנוּ וּלְחַטָּאתֵנוּ, וּנְחַלְתָּנוּ:**

*Continue:*

סְלַח לָנוּ אָבִינוּ כִּי חָטָאנוּ, מְחַל לָנוּ מַלְכֵּנוּ כִּי פָשָׁעְנוּ. כִּי־אַתָּה אֲדֹנָי טוֹב וְסַלָּח, וְרַב־חֶסֶד לְכָל־קֹרְאֶיךָ: תהלים פו

*The following is said responsively:*

אֲבוֹתַי כִּי בָטְחוּ בְּשֵׁם אֱלֹהֵי צוּרִי
גָּדְלוּ וְהִצְלִיחוּ וְגַם עָשׂוּ פֶרִי
וּמֵעֵת הֻדְּחוּ וְהָלְכוּ עִמּוֹ קֶרִי
הָיוּ הָלוֹךְ וְחָסוֹר עַד הַחֹדֶשׁ הָעֲשִׂירִי. בראשית ח

On the tenth, the king of Babylon laid siege on the city,
and beleaguered it. The chief of the army arrived,
and I was yielded to be trampled,
was tormented in fetters,
and from month to month my harp turned to grief.

Once like the first figs of a new tree,
they were the very first to be destroyed.
They spoke the names of others,
and sin closed their destiny.
They did not recognize God's face and were swept off by the flood –
agony like that of a first childbirth, soars up as high as Heaven.

God brought us a day of evil and siege,
ordered enemies about me to harvest my last fruits.
The day my heart was quelled, no strength to resist,
and He said to the prophet,
"Preach this to the rebellious house."

He took the cloak of authority from the judges at the gate.
His rage burned like fire
and He raised the crown away,
and He cast down the splendor of the Temple, Forest of Lebanon,
and rushing wind and storm make my flesh bristle and shiver.

Once you were called most beautiful;
now you are darkened,
for you have stumbled over iniquity
and your heart has turned back.
You have been attacked from behind,
have been weakened, once, then twice,
and even the slightest dressing or balm not offered you.

The Righteous One, perfect Rock,
who forgives iniquity almost too great to bear,
flew from the cherubs to the threshold,
and from there to a corner of the roof,
because of the iniquity marked out; the scream of it rose up,
their evil as abundant as a fruit-tree's crop.

בָּעֲשִׂירִי לַחֹדֶשׁ סָמַךְ מֶלֶךְ בָּבֶל
וְצָר עַל עִיר הַקֹּדֶשׁ, וְנִקְרַב רַב הַחוֹבֵל
נִתַּתִּי הָדֵשׁ וְעֻנֵּיתִי בַּכֶּבֶל
וְהָיָה מִדֵּי חֹדֶשׁ לְאֵבֶל כִּנּוֹרִי.

רֵאשִׁית בִּכּוּרָה לְרֵאשִׁית הַחֵרֶם
שֵׂם אֲחֵרִים הִזְכִּירָה, וְהֶעָוֹן גּוֹרֵם
פְּנֵי אֵל לֹא הִכִּירָה, וְשֻׁטְּפָה בְּזֶרֶם
צָרָה כְּמַבְכִּירָה כָּעֵת בַּמָּרוֹם תַּמְרִיא.

הָאֱלֹהִים הֵבִיא יוֹם רָעָה וּמָצוֹר
צִוָּה צָרַי סְבִיבַי עוֹלָלַי לִבְצֹר
יוֹם הֵרַךְ לְבָבִי וְאֵין כֹּחַ לַעֲצֹר
וְדַבֵּר אֶל נָבִיא, מְשֹׁל אֶל בֵּית הַמֶּרִי.

מִיּוֹשְׁבֵי שַׁעַר הֶעֱבִיר אַדֶּרֶת
חֲמָתוֹ כָּאֵשׁ בָּעַר, וְהֵרִים עֲטֶרֶת
וּמִלְּבָנוֹן יַעַר הִשְׁלִיךְ תִּפְאֶרֶת
וְרוּחַ סוֹעָה וָסַעַר תְּסַמֵּר שַׂעֲרַת בְּשָׂרִי.

יְפֵיפִיָּה נִמְשַׁלְתְּ, וְעַתָּה קְדוֹרַנִּית
בְּעָוֹן כִּי כָשַׁלְתְּ, וְלִבֵּךְ אֲחוֹרַנִּית
זְנַבוּךְ וְנֶחֱשַׁלְתְּ רִאשׁוֹנָה וְשֵׁנִית
וְהָחְתֵּל לֹא חֻתַּלְתְּ מְעַט צֳרִי.

צַדִּיק הַצּוּר תָּם, נְשֹׂא עָוֹן נִלְאָה
מִכְּרוּב לְמִפְתָּן, לְפִנַּת גַּג דָּאָה
מֵעָוֹן הַנִּכְתָּם, וְצַעֲקָתָם בָּאָה
רַבָּה רָעָתָם כְּעֵץ עֹשֶׂה פֶּרִי.

The One who weighs the actions of people,
strengthened all my attackers,
for my days had been filled with malignant deeds,
and in the shamefulness of my youth
I forgot the good granted me,
and the One who gives me my bread and water,
my flax and my wool.

My attackers opened wide their mouths and swallowed up my legacy.
They overcame me utterly, drank my blood and gulped it down.
Strangers became my enemies, they injured my brothers –
strangers who called out, "Destroy, destroy!"
Descendants of Seir the Horite.

They said, "Come, let us finish them off,
and put an end to their memory."
Jealous, vengeful God, grant retribution;
let them load the burden of their own ruin.
Pay them back for their actions
and have their hopes disgrace them,
like the baker who dreamt his dream
of three baskets of white bread.

My wound was not softened, my bruise enough to kill me,
and my eyes have grown dim with watching for my bright-faced Love.
Is His anger even now not forever forgotten?
Why has He done this; why this burning rage?

This God of mine is compassionate; He shall not forever reject.
The days of my grief have grown long and still my heart sighs.
Return, God, to my tent; do not abandon Your place.
Close the days of my grief. Bring my recompense.

Lord who is the portion allotted me,
come to me quickly, help me,
and loosen my sackcloth,
wrap me around in joy,
and dazzle my darkness with Your light – light up
the twilight I once longed for, for it is You who are my lamp.

חִזֵּק כָּל קָמַי, תּוֹכֵן הָעֲלִילוֹת
כִּי מָלְאוּ יָמַי בְּרֹעַ מִפְעָלוֹת
וּמִבֹּשֶׁת עֲלוּמַי שָׁכַחְתִּי גְּמוּלוֹת
נוֹתֵן לַחְמִי וּמֵימַי, פִּשְׁתִּי וְצַמְרִי.

קָמַי פִּיהֶם פָּעֲרוּ וְנַחֲלָתִי בִּלֵּעוּ
מְאֹד עָלַי גָּבְרוּ וְדָמִי שָׁתוּ וְלָעוּ
נָכְרִים עָלַי צָרוּ וְאֶת אַחַי הֵרֵעוּ
הָאוֹמְרִים עָרוּ עָרוּ, בְּנֵי שֵׂעִיר הַחֹרִי.

אָמְרוּ לְכוּ נְכַלֵּם, וְנַשְׁבִּיתָה זִכְרָם
אֵל קַנּוֹא וְנוֹקֵם, גְּמֹלֵם, יִשְׂאוּ אֶת שִׁבְרָם
כְּמַעֲשֵׂיהֶם שַׁלֵּם וְיֵבוֹשׁוּ מִשִּׁבְרָם
כְּאִישׁ חֲלוֹם חוֹלֵם שְׁלֹשָׁה סַלֵּי חֹרִי.

פְּצָעַי לֹא רֻכְּכָה וְחַבּוּרוֹתַי רֶצַח
וְעֵינַי הַכְּהֻתָה, צוֹפָה לְדוֹדִי צַח
הַעוֹד לֹא שֻׁכְּכָה חֲמָתוֹ לָנֶצַח
עַל מֶה עָשָׂה כָּכָה וּמֶה חֳרִי.

רַחוּם זֶה אֵלִי, אַל לָעַד תִּזְנַח
אָרְכוּ יְמֵי אֶבְלִי וְעוֹד לִבִּי נֶאֱנָח
שׁוּבָה אֶל לְאָהֳלִי, מְקוֹמְךָ אַל תַּנַּח
שַׁלֵּם יְמֵי אֶבְלִי כִּי תָבוֹא עַל שְׂכָרִי.

יהוה מְנָת חֶלְקִי, חוּשָׁה לִּי לְעֶזְרָה
וּפִתַּחְתָּ שַׂקִּי, שִׂמְחָה לִי לְאַזְּרָה
וְתַגִּיהַּ אֶת חָשְׁכִּי בְּאוֹרְךָ לְהָאִירָה
אֶת נֶשֶׁף חִשְׁקִי, כִּי אַתָּה נֵרִי.

Redeem my soul from anguish and sighing,
grant Your people remission, my King and my Holy One.
And turn into relief the fast of Av;
into gladness and joy, the fast of Tammuz and the fast of Tevet.

*Continue with "God, King who sits" on page 1040.*

## SELIḤOT FOR THE FAST OF ESTHER

סְלַח לָנוּ Forgive us, our Father, for in our great foolishness we have blundered. Pardon us, our King, for our iniquities are many.

אֵל אֶרֶךְ You are a God slow to anger, You are called the Master of Compassion, and You have taught the way of repentance. May You remember today and every day the greatness of Your compassion and kindness, for the sake of the descendants of Your beloved ones. Turn toward us in compassion, for You are the Master of Compassion. We come before You in plea and prayer, as You in ancient times showed the humble one [Moses]. Turn from Your fierce anger, as is written in Your Torah. In the shadow of Your wings may we shelter and abide, as on the day when the LORD descended in the cloud. ▸ Disregard transgression and erase guilt as on the day You stood with him [Moses] there. Hear our cry and heed our word, as on the day You proclaimed in the name of the LORD, and there it is written:

*Congregation then Leader:*

And the LORD passed by before him and proclaimed: *Ex. 34*

*All say aloud:*

יהוה The LORD, the LORD, compassionate and gracious God, slow to anger, abounding in loving-kindness and truth, extending loving-kindness to a thousand generations, forgiving iniquity, rebellion and sin, and absolving [the guilty who repent]. Forgive us our iniquity and our sin, and take us as Your inheritance.

*Continue:*

סְלַח לָנוּ Forgive us, our Father, for we have sinned. Pardon us, our King, for we have transgressed. For You, LORD, are good and forgiving, abounding in *Ps. 86*
loving-kindness to all who call on You.

מִיָּגוֹן וַאֲנָחָה, פְּדֵה אֵל אֶת נַפְשִׁי
עֲשֵׂה לְעַמְּךָ הֲנָחָה, מַלְכִּי וּקְדוֹשִׁי
תַּהֲפוֹךְ לִרְוָחָה אֶת צוֹם הַחֲמִישִׁי
לְשָׂשׂוֹן וּלְשִׂמְחָה, צוֹם הָרְבִיעִי וְצוֹם הָעֲשִׂירִי.

*Continue with* אֵל מֶלֶךְ יוֹשֵׁב *on page 1041.*

## סליחות לתענית אסתר

סְלַח לָנוּ, אָבִינוּ, כִּי בְּרֹב אִוַּלְתֵּנוּ שָׁגִינוּ.
מְחַל לָנוּ, מַלְכֵּנוּ, כִּי רַבּוּ עֲוֹנֵינוּ.

אֵל אֶרֶךְ אַפַּיִם אַתָּה, וּבַעַל הָרַחֲמִים נִקְרֵאתָ, וְדֶרֶךְ תְּשׁוּבָה הוֹרֵיתָ. גְּדֻלַּת רַחֲמֶיךָ וַחֲסָדֶיךָ, תִּזְכֹּר הַיּוֹם וּבְכָל יוֹם לְזֶרַע יְדִידֶיךָ. תֵּפֶן אֵלֵינוּ בְּרַחֲמִים, כִּי אַתָּה הוּא בַּעַל הָרַחֲמִים. בְּתַחֲנוּן וּבִתְפִלָּה פָּנֶיךָ נְקַדֵּם, כְּהוֹדַעְתָּ לֶעָנָו מִקֶּדֶם. מֵחֲרוֹן אַפְּךָ שׁוּב, כְּמוֹ בְּתוֹרָתְךָ כָּתוּב. וּבְצֵל כְּנָפֶיךָ נֶחֱסֶה וְנִתְלוֹנָן, כְּיוֹם וַיֵּרֶד יהוה בֶּעָנָן. ‹ תַּעֲבֹר עַל פֶּשַׁע וְתִמְחֶה אָשָׁם, כְּיוֹם וַיִּתְיַצֵּב עִמּוֹ שָׁם. תַּאֲזִין שַׁוְעָתֵנוּ וְתַקְשִׁיב מֶנּוּ מַאֲמָר, כְּיוֹם וַיִּקְרָא בְשֵׁם יהוה, וְשָׁם נֶאֱמַר

*then* קהל *:*שליח ציבור

שמות לד וַיַּעֲבֹר יהוה עַל־פָּנָיו וַיִּקְרָא

*All say aloud:*

**יהוה, יהוה, אֵל רַחוּם וְחַנּוּן, אֶרֶךְ אַפַּיִם, וְרַב־חֶסֶד וֶאֱמֶת: נֹצֵר חֶסֶד לָאֲלָפִים, נֹשֵׂא עָוֹן וָפֶשַׁע וְחַטָּאָה, וְנַקֵּה: וְסָלַחְתָּ לַעֲוֹנֵנוּ וּלְחַטָּאתֵנוּ, וּנְחַלְתָּנוּ:**

*Continue:*

תהלים פו סְלַח לָנוּ אָבִינוּ כִּי חָטָאנוּ, מְחַל לָנוּ מַלְכֵּנוּ כִּי פָשָׁעְנוּ. כִּי־אַתָּה אֲדֹנָי טוֹב וְסַלָּח, וְרַב־חֶסֶד לְכָל־קֹרְאֶיךָ:

We have waited patiently for the LORD, and He has turned toward us and heard our cry. And on the path of Your laws, LORD, we have waited for You, for it is Your name and Your memory that are our souls' desire. *Is. 26*

כְּרַחֵם As a father has compassion for his children,
so, LORD, have compassion for us.
Salvation is the LORD's; on Your people is Your blessing, Selah! *Ps. 3*
The LORD of hosts is with us, the God of Jacob is our stronghold, Selah! *Ps. 46*
LORD of hosts, happy is the one who trusts in You. *Ps. 84*
LORD, save! May the King answer us on the day we call. *Ps. 20*

▸ Forgive, please, this people's iniquity, *Num. 14*
in the abundance of Your kindness,
and as You have forgiven this people from the time of Egypt until now,
and there it is written:

*Congregation then Leader:*

And the LORD said, I have forgiven as you asked.

*Continue:*

הַטֵּה Give ear, my God and hear; open Your eyes and see our desolation, and the city that bears Your name, for it is not on the strength of our righteousness that we throw down our pleadings before You, but on the strength of Your great compassion. LORD, hear me; LORD, forgive, LORD, listen and act and do not delay – for Your sake, my God; for Your city and Your people bear Your name. *Dan. 9*

Our God and God of our fathers:

אָדָם When a man rose up against us, convulsions of trembling seized us. When he attached himself to a government of flattery, we almost stumbled and fell. They cheerfully closed an agreement to sell us, as a person with an unwanted mound gives it away quite freely to one with an unwanted pit. There was no defense. They said, "Come, let us annihilate them from among nations: the name of Israel shall be recalled no more." My eyes turned heavenward and I called on You to curse my enemies: "Cut off name and remnant; expunge their name, let it rot. And be Enemy to my enemies; bring them down in the very deceptions with which they deceived the people of Jacob." And they said, "The LORD will not see; the God of Jacob will not comprehend." Yet God tormented the scattered ones and made them mournful – but did not mean to destroy them utterly. They were guilty on the face of things, and so He terrorized them. By the taking off of a ring, He made them tremble. But God fulfilled the good of His word, raising them up in the view of nations. "In their enemies' land He did not reject them, and did not detest them to the point of destruction." He revealed the premonition of events for a nation begrimed and scratched over. He wrote "I shall surely hide (*astir*) Myself" to hint at Esther, and fragrant "pure myrrh," translated "mar-dokh," to hint at Mordekhai; all to put an end to Haman on the *Ps. 83* *Ps. 94* *Lev. 26*

קַוֵּה קִוִּינוּ יהוה, וַיֵּט אֵלֵינוּ וַיִּשְׁמַע שַׁוְעָתֵנוּ. אַף אֹרַח מִשְׁפָּטֶיךָ יהוה ישעיה כו
קִוִּינוּךָ, לְשִׁמְךָ וּלְזִכְרְךָ תַּאֲוַת־נָפֶשׁ:

כְּרַחֵם אָב עַל בָּנִים, כֵּן תְּרַחֵם יהוה עָלֵינוּ.
לַיהוה הַיְשׁוּעָה, עַל־עַמְּךָ בִרְכָתֶךָ סֶּלָה: תהלים ג
יהוה צְבָאוֹת עִמָּנוּ, מִשְׂגָּב לָנוּ אֱלֹהֵי יַעֲקֹב סֶלָה: תהלים מו
יהוה צְבָאוֹת, אַשְׁרֵי אָדָם בֹּטֵחַ בָּךְ: תהלים פד
יהוה הוֹשִׁיעָה, הַמֶּלֶךְ יַעֲנֵנוּ בְיוֹם־קָרְאֵנוּ: תהלים כ

◂ סְלַח־נָא לַעֲוֹן הָעָם הַזֶּה כְּגֹדֶל חַסְדֶּךָ במדבר יד
וְכַאֲשֶׁר נָשָׂאתָה לָעָם הַזֶּה מִמִּצְרַיִם וְעַד־הֵנָּה:
וְשָׁם נֶאֱמַר

*קהל then שליח ציבור:*

וַיֹּאמֶר יהוה, סָלַחְתִּי כִּדְבָרֶךָ:

*Continue:*

הַטֵּה אֱלֹהַי אָזְנְךָ וּשְׁמָע, פְּקַח עֵינֶיךָ וּרְאֵה שֹׁמְמֹתֵינוּ וְהָעִיר אֲשֶׁר־נִקְרָא דניאל ט
שִׁמְךָ עָלֶיהָ, כִּי לֹא עַל־צִדְקֹתֵינוּ אֲנַחְנוּ מַפִּילִים תַּחֲנוּנֵינוּ לְפָנֶיךָ, כִּי עַל־
רַחֲמֶיךָ הָרַבִּים: אֲדֹנָי שְׁמָעָה, אֲדֹנָי סְלָחָה, אֲדֹנָי הַקְשִׁיבָה וַעֲשֵׂה אַל־
תְּאַחַר, לְמַעַנְךָ אֱלֹהַי, כִּי־שִׁמְךָ נִקְרָא עַל־עִירְךָ וְעַל־עַמֶּךָ:

אֱלֹהֵינוּ וֵאלֹהֵי אֲבוֹתֵינוּ

אָדָם בְּקוּם עָלֵינוּ, חִיל אֲחָזַתְנוּ לִרְעֹד. בְּהִסְתַּפְּחוֹ לְמַלְכוּת חָנֵף, כִּמְעַט
כָּשַׁלְנוּ לִמְעֹד. גָּמְרוּ לְמָכְרֵנוּ כְּתֵל וְחָרִיץ בְּלִי מִסְעוֹד. אָמְרוּ לְכוּ וְנַכְחִידֵם תהלים פג
מִגּוֹי, וְלֹא־יִזָּכֵר שֵׁם־יִשְׂרָאֵל עוֹד: דַּלּוּ עֵינַי לַמָּרוֹם, קְרָאתִיךָ אוֹיְבַי לָקֹב.
הַכְרֵת שֵׁם וּשְׁאָר, וּמְחֵה שֵׁם לִרְקֹב. וְצַר צוֹרְרַי בְּנִכְלֵיהֶם אֲשֶׁר נִכְּלוּ לַעֲקֹב.
וַיֹּאמְרוּ, לֹא יִרְאֶה־יָּהּ, וְלֹא־יָבִין אֱלֹהֵי יַעֲקֹב: זְרוּיִים עִנָּה וַיָּגֶה, וְלֹא מִלֵּב תהלים צד
לְכַלּוֹתָם. חָבוּ לְפָנִים, וְרָדָם בַּהֲסָרַת טַבַּעַת לְהַחֲלוֹתָם. טוֹב דְּבָרוֹ הֵקִים
לְעֵינֵי הַגּוֹיִם לְהַעֲלוֹתָם. בְּאֶרֶץ אֹיְבֵיהֶם לֹא־מְאַסְתִּים וְלֹא־גְעַלְתִּים ויקרא כו

morrow, "From (*hamin*) the tree" foreshadowing his gallows. "In place of the thorn *Is. 55*
bush, shall rise up a cypress, and in place of the nettle, shall rise up myrtle." The king
who listened to lies, dictated accusation and sorrow. He wrapped himself in priestly
clothes, Ahasuerus, having mistaken his reckoning of the End. He ordered "other
vessels" to be used, from the Quarry from which the world was hewn; and the devil *Job 2*
too, came and placed himself among them. When the people in Shushan ate of their
destroyer's meat, the king opened his mouth wide to accuse them, to give them over
into the hands of the one who was ready to pay their price. The Rock, meanwhile,
agreed to write a letter to destroy their hope; "I said that I would yield them up, would *Deut. 32*
put an end to their memory among mankind." The angels, messengers of peace, wept
bitterly, crying out, "Compassionate One, look to the covenant and do not break it,
pushing it away!" The Torah, too, heard of it and put on clothes of widowhood and
sorrow; and she laid her hands upon her head and walked along, crying as she went. *II Sam. 13*
[Elijah] The Tishbite wrapped a covering of sackcloth around his waist. He hurried
and told the three fathers who sleep in the Cave of Makhpelah, and then hastened to
the Shepherd, [Moses] – "What do you mean by sleeping? Rouse yourself! Get up *Jonah 1*
and call out to your God – perhaps He may change His mind!" He told [Mordekhai]
Bilshan of the pronouncement that had been sealed in clay – but not in blood. They
learnt from the example of Nineveh how to overturn anger after a decree; the son
of Kish knocked at the door of the school, and covered himself in sackcloth and sat *Jonah 3*
down on the earth. For three days he gathered the children before him – thirsty, hid-
den from by God – so that, in the voice of Jacob, they might weaken the hand of the
bold-faced king. His hands raised steadily to God, Mordekhai prayed, "Save us now
from insult; that he should not come and slaughter us, mothers and children together." *Gen. 32*
Those and those, from all sides, the children of my mighty ones and teachers, all cried
out, and their plea rose up to the LORD. And God, when those plaintive calls reached
Him, asked, "And what is this bleating of sheep that meets My ears?" The shepherd *I Sam. 15*
Moses answered Him, "These are the little ones of the holy offspring. LORD, save
ones condemned to die, from the evil enemy." The compassion of the Gracious One
was stirred, and He was moved to weep for what had happened. And so it was that *II Kings 5*
when the King of Israel read the letter, He tore it to pieces. The Jew suspended sons
below and father above. Each man covered three *amot*; the fourth *amah* above was
space exposed. Mordekhai saw a double revenge, was delighted, and spoke praises:
"I was returned to my post and he was hanged!" Esther wrote with emphasis, that *Gen. 41*
a Hallel of thanks should be read on that day; and what the beloved ones accepted
down below was established above. A banner shall be raised by those who bear wit-
ness, to make the wonder known now, as it was then. And at this time – may relief *Esther 4*
and salvation rise up for the Jews.

אֵל מֶלֶךְ God, King who sits upon a throne of compassion, who acts with loving-kindness, who pardons the iniquities of His people, passing them before Him in order; who forgives sinners and pardons transgressors; who performs righteousness with all

לְכַלֹּתָם: יָדַע רֶמֶז הַקּוֹרוֹת לְעַם מְעֻפָּר וּמְהֻדָּס. כָּתַב הַסֵּתֶר אַסְתִּיר
וּמָר דְּרוֹר מִפְּרְדָּס. לְשִׁבֹּת הָמָן מִמָּחֳרָת, הֲמָן הָעֵץ קְנֶדֶס. תַּחַת הַנַּעֲצוּץ ישעיה נה
יַעֲלֶה בְרוֹשׁ וְתַחַת הַסִּרְפַּד יַעֲלֶה הֲדַס: מַקְשִׁיב דְּבַר שֶׁקֶר כָּתַב שִׂטְנָה
וָעֶצֶב. נִתְעַטֵּף בְּבִגְדֵי שְׂרָד כְּטָעָה בְּמִנְיַן קֶצֶב. סָדַר לְהִשְׁתַּמֵּשׁ בְּשׁוֹנִים
כְּלֵי הַמַּחְצֵב. וַיָּבוֹא גַם־הַשָּׂטָן בְּתֹכָם לְהִתְיַצֵּב: עִם הַנִּמְצָאִים בְּשׁוּשָׁן, איוב ב
בְּאָכְלָם מִזֶּבַח עוֹכְרָם. פָּעַר פִּיו לְהַשְׂטִינָם, וּלְהַסְגִּירָם בְּיַד נוֹתֵן מִכְרָם.
צוּר הִסְכִּים לִכְתֹּב אִגֶּרֶת לְאַבֵּד שִׁבְרָם. אָמַרְתִּי אַפְאֵיהֶם, אַשְׁבִּיתָה דברים לב
מֵאֱנוֹשׁ זִכְרָם: קְדוֹשִׁים מַלְאֲכֵי שָׁלוֹם מַר יִבְכָּיוּן בִּצְעָקָה. רַחוּם הַבֵּט
לַבְּרִית וְאַל תָּפֵר לְהַרְחִיקָה. שָׁמְעָה מוֹרָשָׁה, וַתִּלְבַּשׁ בִּגְדֵי אַלְמְנוּת
וּמוּעָקָה. וַתָּשֶׂם יָדָהּ עַל־רֹאשָׁהּ, וַתֵּלֶךְ הָלוֹךְ וְזָעָקָה: תִּשְׁבִּי שָׂם אֵזוֹר שמואל ב׳ יג
שַׂק בְּמָתְנָיו תַּחְבֹּשֶׁת. מִהֵר וְהוֹדִיעַ יְשֵׁנֵי מַכְפֵּל, אָבוֹת שְׁלֹשֶׁת. נָחַץ
לָרוֹעֶה, מַה לְּךָ נִרְדָּם לְהִתְעַשֵּׁת. קוּם קְרָא אֶל־אֱלֹהֶיךָ, אוּלַי יִתְעַשֵּׁת: יונה א
חוֹתַם טִיט אֲשֶׁר נַעֲשָׂה, לְבַלְשָׁן סִפֵּר. מִנִּינְוֵה לָמְדוּ לְאַחַר גְּזֵרָה כַּעַס
לְהָפֵר. בֶּן קִישׁ הִקִּישׁ דַּלְתוֹת בֵּית הַסֵּפֶר. וַיְכַס שַׂק, וַיֵּשֶׁב עַל־הָאֵפֶר: יונה ג
רִבֵּץ תִּינוֹקוֹת לְפָנָיו יָמִים שְׁלֹשָׁה, צְמֵאִים וּמְכֻפָּנִים. בְּקוֹל יַעֲקֹב לַחֲלֹשׁ
יְדֵי עַז פָּנִים. יָדָיו אֱמוּנָה לָאֵל, הַצִּילֵנִי נָא מֵעֶלְבּוֹנִים. פֶּן־יָבוֹא וְהִכַּנִי בראשית לב
אֵם עַל־בָּנִים: מִזֶּה אֵלֶּה וּמִזֶּה אֵלֶּה, בְּנֵי אֵיתָנַי וְרַבָּנַי. כֻּלָּם צָעֲקוּ, וַתַּעַל
שַׁוְעָתָם אֶל יהוה. יָהּ, לְקוֹל רִנּוּן כְּבוֹא, שָׁאַל לְפָנַי. וּמֶה קוֹל־הַצֹּאן הַזֶּה שמואל א׳ טו
בְּאָזְנָי: רוֹעֶה הֱשִׁיבוֹ, הֵם קְטַנֵּי קֹדֶשׁ זֶרַע. יָהּ, הַצֵּל לְקוּחִים לַמָּוֶת מֵאוֹיֵב
הָרַע. חַנּוּן נִכְמְרוּ רַחֲמָיו וַיְבַקֵּשׁ לִבְכּוֹת הַמְאֹרָע. וַיְהִי כִּקְרֹא מֶלֶךְ־יִשְׂרָאֵל מלכים ב׳ ה
אֶת־הַסֵּפֶר, וַיִּקְרַע: יְהוּדִי הוֹקִיעַ, יְלָדָיו לְמַטָּה וַאֲבִיהֶם לְמַעְלָה. אִישׁ
אִישׁ בְּשָׁלֹשׁ אַמּוֹת, וְהָרְבִיעִית אֲוִיר מְגֻלֶּה. מִשְׁנֶה נָקַם חֲזֶה, וְשָׂמַח וְשָׁח
תְּהִלָּה. אֹתִי הֵשִׁיב עַל־כַּנִּי וְאֹתוֹ תָלָה: ‹ וַתִּכְתֹּב אֶסְתֵּר תְּקֶף, לִקְרֹא בראשית מא
כִּבְהַלֵּל מְהוֹדִים. מִלְמַעְלָה קִיְּמוּ מַה שֶּׁקִּבְּלוּ לְמַטָּה דוֹדִים. נֵס יְנוֹסֵס
לְפַרְסֵם כְּאָז פִּלְאוֹ מַסְהִידִים. בָּעֵת הַזֹּאת רֶוַח וְהַצָּלָה יַעֲמוֹד לַיְּהוּדִים: אסתר ד

אֵל מֶלֶךְ יוֹשֵׁב עַל כִּסֵּא רַחֲמִים, מִתְנַהֵג בַּחֲסִידוּת. מוֹחֵל עֲוֹנוֹת עַמּוֹ,
מַעֲבִיר רִאשׁוֹן רִאשׁוֹן. מַרְבֶּה מְחִילָה לְחַטָּאִים, וּסְלִיחָה לְפוֹשְׁעִים. עֹשֶׂה

flesh and spirit, do not repay their bad actions in kind. God, You taught us to speak thirteen attributes: recall for us today the covenant of the thirteen attributes, as You in ancient times showed the humble one [Moses], as is written: The LORD descended in the cloud and stood with him there, and proclaimed in the name of the LORD:

*Congregation then Leader:*

And the LORD passed by before him and proclaimed: *Ex. 34*

*All say aloud:*

**יהוה The LORD, the LORD, compassionate and gracious God, slow to anger, abounding in loving-kindness and truth, extending loving-kindness to a thousand generations, forgiving iniquity, rebellion and sin, and absolving [the guilty who repent]. Forgive us our iniquity and our sin, and take us as Your inheritance.**

*Continue:*

סְלַח לָנוּ Forgive us, our Father, for we have sinned. Pardon us, our King, for we have transgressed. For You, LORD, are good and forgiving, abounding in loving- *Ps. 86*
kindness to all who call on You.

כִּי־עִמְּךָ For in You there is a wellspring of life; in Your light shall we see light. As *Ps. 36*
we call You, God of our righteousness, answer us. In a narrow place You have
opened out our horizon; be gracious to us and hear our prayer. And now let the *Num. 14*
strength of the LORD be great, as You have said.

כְּרַחֵם As a father has compassion for his children,
so, LORD, have compassion for us.
Salvation is the LORD's; on Your people is Your blessing, Selah! *Ps. 3*
The LORD of hosts is with us, the God of Jacob is our stronghold, Selah! *Ps. 46*
LORD of hosts, happy is the one who trusts in You. *Ps. 84*
LORD, save! May the King answer us on the day we call. *Ps. 20*

Our God and God of our fathers:

אַתָּה הָאֵל It is You who are the God of wonders. You have made known among nations Your terrifying strength. You redeemed Your people by might from torments, suppressed their foes with ignominious death, when the enemy rose to awaken strife, and seemed about to cut down the exquisite flowers, Israel. He plotted to measure out into the masters' treasuries, a hundred times the silver talents of the sockets in the Tabernacle. You warned Your lambs to announce the shekel offering early; You knew what would be. You warned us to be punctual, and to find a way to douse the fire of ones who sought to burn us. And so, those once

צְדָקוֹת עִם כָּל בָּשָׂר וָרוּחַ, לֹא כְרָעָתָם תִּגְמֹל. ◁ אֵל, הוֹרֵיתָ לָּנוּ לוֹמַר שְׁלֹשׁ עֶשְׂרֵה, וּזְכָר לָנוּ הַיּוֹם בְּרִית שְׁלֹשׁ עֶשְׂרֵה, כְּמוֹ שֶׁהוֹדַעְתָּ לֶעָנָו מִקֶּדֶם, כְּמוֹ שֶׁכָּתוּב: וַיֵּרֶד יהוה בֶּעָנָן, וַיִּתְיַצֵּב עִמּוֹ שָׁם, וַיִּקְרָא בְשֵׁם, יהוה:

*קהל then שליח ציבור:*

וַיַּעֲבֹר יהוה עַל־פָּנָיו וַיִּקְרָא שמות לד

*All say aloud:*

**יהוה, יהוה, אֵל רַחוּם וְחַנּוּן, אֶרֶךְ אַפַּיִם, וְרַב־חֶסֶד וֶאֱמֶת: נֹצֵר חֶסֶד לָאֲלָפִים, נֹשֵׂא עָוֹן וָפֶשַׁע וְחַטָּאָה, וְנַקֵּה: וְסָלַחְתָּ לַעֲוֹנֵנוּ וּלְחַטָּאתֵנוּ, וּנְחַלְתָּנוּ:**

*Continue:*

סְלַח לָנוּ אָבִינוּ כִּי חָטָאנוּ, מְחַל לָנוּ מַלְכֵּנוּ כִּי פָשָׁעְנוּ. כִּי־אַתָּה אֲדֹנָי טוֹב תהלים פו
וְסַלָּח, וְרַב־חֶסֶד לְכָל־קֹרְאֶיךָ:

כִּי־עִמְּךָ מְקוֹר חַיִּים, בְּאוֹרְךָ נִרְאֶה־אוֹר: בְּקָרְאֵנוּ עֲנֵנוּ אֱלֹהֵי צִדְקֵנוּ, תהלים לו
בַּצָּר הִרְחַבְתָּ לָּנוּ, חָנֵּנוּ וּשְׁמַע תְּפִלָּתֵנוּ. וְעַתָּה יִגְדַּל־נָא כֹּחַ אֲדֹנָי, כַּאֲשֶׁר במדבר יד
דִּבַּרְתָּ לֵאמֹר:

כְּרַחֵם אָב עַל בָּנִים, כֵּן תְּרַחֵם יהוה עָלֵינוּ.
לַיהוה הַיְשׁוּעָה, עַל־עַמְּךָ בִרְכָתֶךָ סֶּלָה: תהלים ג
יהוה צְבָאוֹת עִמָּנוּ, מִשְׂגָּב לָנוּ אֱלֹהֵי יַעֲקֹב סֶלָה: תהלים מו
יהוה צְבָאוֹת, אַשְׁרֵי אָדָם בֹּטֵחַ בָּךְ: תהלים פד
יהוה הוֹשִׁיעָה, הַמֶּלֶךְ יַעֲנֵנוּ בְיוֹם־קָרְאֵנוּ: תהלים כ

אֱלֹהֵינוּ וֵאלֹהֵי אֲבוֹתֵינוּ

אַתָּה הָאֵל עוֹשֵׂה פְלָאוֹת, בָּעַמִּים הוֹדַעְתָּ עֹז נוֹרָאוֹת, גָּאַלְתָּ בִּזְרוֹעַ עַמְּךָ מִתְּלָאוֹת, דִּכִּיתָ צָרֵיהֶם בְּמוֹתֵי תַחֲלוּאוֹת. הָאוֹיֵב בְּקוּמוֹ לְעוֹרֵר מְדָנִים, וְדִמָּה לְהַכְרִית פִּרְחֵי עֲדָנִים, זָמַם לִשְׁקֹל לְגִנְזֵי אֲדוֹנִים, חֲלִיפֵי

condemned to death – are marked out for resurrection. When (for appearances,) they worshiped a narrow image, they were yielded up to be clipped off: all those offshoots and grapes. Traps surrounded them on all sides; they turned their eyes to You, they were concealed in Your hiddenness. The lots were overturned, they ruled over their enemies, and the gallows was prepared to receive Haman the Agagite. God struck and swallowed the façade of covering that covered, and He entombed His people's enemies in darkness. Peace and truth were written on all sides; power of salvation, steady rock and fortress. The plunderer was plundered, he was caught in his own trap. The one who spoke against me was swept away; destroyed; eyed disdainfully. The people made celebrations, and these were fixed for all generations. Amalek had entered the Scriptures three times – how could there be a fourth? Yet on High it was agreed and here below it was sealed, and the reason for all that had been fixed, was inscribed in the scroll. Your hand is lifted high to forgive sinners. You set Mordekhai the Jew and Hadassah Esther in their place as saviors, and now their righteousness remains forever to delight us, and the study of their honor to recall to You those who were saved. Be zealous for Your name, Awesome and Sanctified One. Witness Your vineyard, destroyed, trampled; gather our scattered ones and their song to You will be renewed. Sustain them and revive them with the building of the Temple. ▸ And as You did awe-inspiring things in those days, so perform with us the wonder of salvation for all time. Find in Your presence our ransom, our appeasement – God, King who sits upon a throne of compassion.

God, King who sits upon a throne of compassion, who acts with loving-kindness, who pardons the iniquities of His people, passing them before Him in order; who forgives sinners and pardons transgressors; who performs righteousness with all flesh and spirit, do not repay their bad actions in kind. ▸ God, You taught us to speak thirteen attributes: recall for us today the covenant of the thirteen attributes, as You in ancient times showed the humble one [Moses], as is written: The Lord descended in the cloud and stood with him there, and proclaimed in the name of the Lord:

*Congregation then Leader:*

And the Lord passed by before him and proclaimed: *Ex. 34*

*All say aloud:*

יהוה The Lord, the Lord, compassionate and gracious God, slow to anger, abounding in loving-kindness and truth, extending loving-kindness to a thousand generations, forgiving iniquity, rebellion and sin, and absolving [the guilty who repent]. Forgive us our iniquity and our sin, and take us as Your inheritance.

מָאַת כִּכְּרֵי אֲדָנִים. טְלָאֶיךָ הַזְּהֻרַת שִׁקְלֵיהֶם לְהַקְדִּים, יָדַעְתָּ הָעֲתִידוֹת וְדָרַשְׁתָּ נִשְׁקָדִים, כִּבּוּי לְהַמְצִיא לְלַהַב יוֹקְדִים, לְקוּחִים לַמָּוֶת לְתֶחִי נִפְקָדִים. מַסֵּכָה צָרָה בְּעָבְדָם לְפָנִים, נִמְסְרוּ לְהָתֵז קְנוּקָנוֹת וּגְפָנִים, סְבָבוּם מוֹקְשִׁים בְּכָל דְּפָנִים, עֵינֵיהֶם לְךָ תוֹלִים וּבְסִתְרְךָ נִצְפָּנִים. פּוּר נֶהְפַּךְ בְּאוֹיְבִים לִשְׁלֹט, צְלִיבָה הוּכַן אֲגָגִי לִקְלֹט, קַלַּע וּבַלַּע פְּנֵי הַלּוֹט הַלּוֹט, רִיבִי עַם בְּאַשְׁמַנִּים לַעֲלֹט. שָׁלוֹם וֶאֱמֶת נִכְתַּב מִכָּל צַד, תְּקֶף יֶשַׁע סֶלַע וּמְצָד, שׁוֹדֵד הֻשְׁדַּד וּבְרִשְׁתּוֹ נוֹצַד, מְלַשְׁנִי נִסְחַף נִצְמַת וְנִרְצַד. עָשׂוּ שְׂמָחוֹת וְלַדּוֹרוֹת קְבָעוּם, וּמִקְרָאוֹת שְׁלֹשׁוּם וְלֹא רִבְּעוּם, נִסְכְּמוּ מִמַּעַל וּלְמַטָּה טְבָעוּם, בְּסֵפֶר נֶחְקַק עַל מָה קְבָעוּם. רָמָה יָדְךָ לִסְלֹחַ לַפּוֹשְׁעִים, יְהוּדִי וַהֲדַסָּה הֵקַמְתָּ מוֹשִׁיעִים, צִדְקָתָם עוֹמֶדֶת לָעַד לְשַׁעֲשׁוּעִים, חֵקֶר כְּבוּדָם לְהִזָּכֵר לְנוֹשָׁעִים. קַנֵּא לְשִׁמְךָ נוֹרָא וְנִקְדָּשׁ, חֲזֵה כַּרְמְךָ נֶהֱרַס וְנִדָּשׁ, זְרוּיֵינוּ קַבֵּץ וְשִׁיר לְךָ יְחֻדָּשׁ, קַיֵּם וְהַחֲיֵם בְּבִנְיַן בֵּית הַמִּקְדָּשׁ. › וְכַעֲשׂוֹתְךָ נוֹרָאוֹת בְּאוֹתָן הַיָּמִים, אִתָּנוּ הַפְלֵא תְּשׁוּעַת עוֹלָמִים, מָצוֹא לְפָנֶיךָ כֹּפֶר וְתַנְחוּמִים, אֵל מֶלֶךְ יוֹשֵׁב עַל כִּסֵּא רַחֲמִים.

אֵל מֶלֶךְ יוֹשֵׁב עַל כִּסֵּא רַחֲמִים, מִתְנַהֵג בַּחֲסִידוּת. מוֹחֵל עֲוֹנוֹת עַמּוֹ, מַעֲבִיר רִאשׁוֹן רִאשׁוֹן. מַרְבֶּה מְחִילָה לְחַטָּאִים, וּסְלִיחָה לְפוֹשְׁעִים. עֹשֶׂה צְדָקוֹת עִם כָּל בָּשָׂר וָרוּחַ, לֹא כְרָעָתָם תִּגְמֹל. › אֵל, הוֹרֵיתָ לָנוּ לוֹמַר שְׁלֹשׁ עֶשְׂרֵה, וּזְכֹר לָנוּ הַיּוֹם בְּרִית שְׁלֹשׁ עֶשְׂרֵה, כְּמוֹ שֶׁהוֹדַעְתָּ לֶעָנָו מִקֶּדֶם, כְּמוֹ שֶׁכָּתוּב: וַיֵּרֶד יהוה בֶּעָנָן, וַיִּתְיַצֵּב עִמּוֹ שָׁם, וַיִּקְרָא בְשֵׁם, יהוה:

*קהל then שליח ציבור:*

וַיַּעֲבֹר יהוה עַל־פָּנָיו וַיִּקְרָא שמות לד

*All say aloud:*

יהוה, יהוה, אֵל רַחוּם וְחַנּוּן, אֶרֶךְ אַפַּיִם, וְרַב־חֶסֶד וֶאֱמֶת: נֹצֵר חֶסֶד לָאֲלָפִים, נֹשֵׂא עָוֹן וָפֶשַׁע וְחַטָּאָה, וְנַקֵּה: וְסָלַחְתָּ לַעֲוֹנֵנוּ וּלְחַטָּאתֵנוּ, וּנְחַלְתָּנוּ:

*Continue:*

סְלַח לָנוּ Forgive us, our Father, for we have sinned. Pardon us, our King, for we have transgressed. For You, LORD, are good and forgiving, abounding in loving-kindness to all who call on You. *Ps. 86*

*The following is said responsively:*

Small of number we stand pleading before You: do not block Your ears to the cry of people crushed. Listen to their entreaty from the Heaven where You dwell, as You saved Your children in the days of Myrrh and Myrtle [Mordekhai and Esther].

On Israel's praises You sit enthroned, hearing their cry, listening to their prayer. Bringing healing even before the blow, counting it out to help the ones You have acquired; to settle their homes again.

A foe and enemy fixed his eyes like knives on Israel; he opened wide his mouth to swallow up the humble man. He deliberated within him to destroy Mordekhai's great community; in the letter, he etched his intent to destroy the treasured people.

You who take revenge upon foes and persist in Your claim against enemies; You measured them out with the very measure they used against Your loved ones. The fighter and his descendants were hanged, suspended; they were strung up together, like fish on a thread.

On the day on which the enemies hoped to lay carnage among the people You harbor, the rule was overturned and bodies fell; they bore the brunt and fury of Your rage – they were trodden underfoot and washed away.

And so may Your name be raised up, exalted. Your glory covers all the highest heavens. As You lift the downtrodden, those yielded up as plunder, Your praise fills up the valleys to their very ends.

Consider our thoughts, now, and witness our suffering. Rise up, in Your rage, against the bitter enemy. Master, we have called You from a narrow place. Please, take us out into the open, and release us from anguish.

Bring us much, abundant pardon. Hear our prayer, and what is crude in us – pass over. Bring down those who press us and fill them with horror. And as for us – do not forever withhold Your compassion.

*Continue with "God, King who sits" on page 1040.*

*Continue:*

סְלַח לָנוּ אָבִינוּ כִּי חָטָאנוּ, מְחַל לָנוּ מַלְכֵּנוּ כִּי פָשָׁעְנוּ. כִּי־אַתָּה אֲדֹנָי טוֹב תהלים פו
וְסַלָּח, וְרַב־חֶסֶד לְכָל־קֹרְאֶיךָ:

*The following is said responsively:*

בִּמְתֵי מִסְפָּר חִלִּינוּ פָנֶיךָ. לְשַׁוְעַת נְכֵאִים אַל תַּעְלֵם אָזְנֶךָ.
הַקְשֵׁב תְּחִנָּתָם מִשְּׁמֵי מְעוֹנֶךָ. כְּבִימֵי מֹר וַהֲדַס הוֹשַׁעְתָּ בָנֶיךָ.

תְּהִלּוֹת יִשְׂרָאֵל אַתָּה יוֹשֵׁב. שַׁוְעָתָם מַאֲזִין וְרִנָּתָם קוֹשֵׁב.
רְפָאוּת לְמַחַץ מַקְדִּים וּמְחַשֵּׁב. קְנוּיֶיךָ לְהֵיטִיב וּנְוֵיהֶם לְיַשֵּׁב.

צַר וְאוֹיֵב הִלְטִישׁ עֵינָיו. פִּיהוּ פָּעַר לִשְׁאֹף עָנָו.
עֲשֵׂת בְּשֶׁלּוֹ לְהַשְׁמִיד קְהַל הֲמוֹנָיו. סֶגֶל לְאַבֵּד חָרַת בְּנִשְׁתְּוָנָיו.

נוֹקֵם לְצָרִים וְנוֹטֵר לְאוֹיְבִים. מָדַדְתָּ מִדָּתָם כְּזָדוּ לַאֲהוּבִים.
לוֹחֵם וְנִינָיו הֻתְלוּ מְצֻלָּבִים. כְּבַחֲרוֹזֶת דָּגִים חֹרְזוּ תְּחוּבִים.

יוֹם אֲשֶׁר שִׁבְּרוּ צוֹרְרִים. טִבְחָה לָשִׁית בְּעַם נְצוּרִים.
חֻלְּפָה הַדָּת וְנָפְלוּ פְּגָרִים. זָלְעֲפוּ זָעֲמוּ מוּבָסִים מְגֻרִים.

וּבְכֵן יִתְעַלֶּה שִׁמְךָ וְיִתְנַשָּׂא. הוֹדְךָ שְׁמֵי שָׁמַיִם כִּסָּה.
דַּכִּים בְּרוֹמִמְךָ נְתוּנִים לִמְשִׁסָּה. גֵּיא וַאֲפָסֶיהָ תְּהִלָּתְךָ מְכַסָּה.

בִּינָה הֲגִיגֵנוּ עַתָּה, וּרְאֵה בַצָּר. בְּאַפְּךָ קוּמָה עַל צוֹרֵר הַצָּר.
אָדוֹן, קְרָאנוּךָ מִן הַמֵּצַר. אָנָּא הוֹצִיאֵנוּ לַמֶּרְחָב וְחַלְּצֵנוּ מִצָּר.

מְאֹד תַּרְבֶּה לָנוּ מְחִילָה. שְׁמַע תְּפִלָּה, וְהַעֲבֵר תִּפְלָה.
לוֹחֲצֵינוּ הַמְעֵד וּמַלְּאֵם חַלְחָלָה. מִמֶּנּוּ רַחֲמֶיךָ לָעַד לֹא תִכְלָא.

*Continue with* אֵל מֶלֶךְ יוֹשֵׁב *on page 1041.*

# SELIḤOT FOR THE SEVENTEENTH OF TAMMUZ

סְלַח לָנוּ Forgive us, our Father, for in our great foolishness we have blundered. Pardon us, our King, for our iniquities are many.

אֵל אֶרֶךְ You are a God slow to anger, You are called the Master of Compassion, and You have taught the way of repentance. May You remember today and every day the greatness of Your compassion and kindness, for the sake of the descendants of Your beloved ones. Turn toward us in compassion, for You are the Master of Compassion. We come before You in plea and prayer, as You in ancient times showed the humble one [Moses]. Turn from Your fierce anger, as is written in Your Torah. In the shadow of Your wings may we shelter and abide, as on the day when the LORD descended in the cloud. ▸ Disregard transgression and erase guilt as on the day You stood with him [Moses] there. Hear our cry and heed our word, as on the day You proclaimed in the name of the LORD, and there it is written:

*Congregation then Leader:*

And the LORD passed by before him and proclaimed: *Ex. 34*

*All say aloud:*

יהוה The LORD, the LORD, compassionate and gracious God, slow to anger, abounding in loving-kindness and truth, extending loving-kindness to a thousand generations, forgiving iniquity, rebellion and sin, and absolving [the guilty who repent]. Forgive us our iniquity and our sin, and take us as Your inheritance.

*Continue:*

סְלַח לָנוּ Forgive us, our Father, for we have sinned. Pardon us, our King, for
we have transgressed. For You, LORD, are good and forgiving, abounding in *Ps. 86*
loving-kindness to all who call on You.

And do not let Him rest, until He establishes, until He makes Jerusalem the *Is. 62*
praise of all the earth. For in You there is a wellspring of life; in Your light shall *Ps. 36*
we see light. Our God, we are ashamed of our actions, distraught at our sins.

כְּרַחֵם As a father has compassion for his children,
so, LORD, have compassion for us.
Salvation is the LORD's; on Your people is Your blessing, Selah! *Ps. 3*
The LORD of hosts is with us, the God of Jacob is our stronghold, Selah! *Ps. 46*

# סליחות לשבעה עשר בתמוז

סְלַח לָנוּ, אָבִינוּ, כִּי בְּרֹב אִוַּלְתֵּנוּ שָׁגִינוּ.
מְחַל לָנוּ, מַלְכֵּנוּ, כִּי רַבּוּ עֲוֹנֵינוּ.

אֵל אֶרֶךְ אַפַּיִם אַתָּה, וּבַעַל הָרַחֲמִים נִקְרֵאתָ, וְדֶרֶךְ תְּשׁוּבָה הוֹרֵיתָ. גְּדֻלַּת רַחֲמֶיךָ וַחֲסָדֶיךָ, תִּזְכֹּר הַיּוֹם וּבְכָל יוֹם לְזֶרַע יְדִידֶיךָ. תֵּפֶן אֵלֵינוּ בְּרַחֲמִים, כִּי אַתָּה הוּא בַּעַל הָרַחֲמִים. בְּתַחֲנוּן וּבִתְפִלָּה פָּנֶיךָ נְקַדֵּם, כְּהוֹדַעְתָּ לֶעָנָו מִקֶּדֶם. מֵחֲרוֹן אַפְּךָ שׁוּב, כְּמוֹ בְּתוֹרָתְךָ כָּתוּב. וּבְצֵל כְּנָפֶיךָ נֶחֱסֶה וְנִתְלוֹנָן, כְּיוֹם וַיֵּרֶד יהוה בֶּעָנָן. ◂ תַּעֲבֹר עַל פֶּשַׁע וְתִמְחֶה אָשָׁם, כְּיוֹם וַיִּתְיַצֵּב עִמּוֹ שָׁם. תַּאֲזִין שַׁוְעָתֵנוּ וְתַקְשִׁיב מֶנּוּ מַאֲמָר, כְּיוֹם וַיִּקְרָא בְשֵׁם יהוה, וְשָׁם נֶאֱמַר

*שליח ציבור then קהל:*

וַיַּעֲבֹר יהוה עַל־פָּנָיו וַיִּקְרָא — שמות לד

*All say aloud:*

**יהוה, יהוה, אֵל רַחוּם וְחַנּוּן, אֶרֶךְ אַפַּיִם, וְרַב־חֶסֶד וֶאֱמֶת: נֹצֵר חֶסֶד לָאֲלָפִים, נֹשֵׂא עָוֹן וָפֶשַׁע וְחַטָּאָה, וְנַקֵּה: וְסָלַחְתָּ לַעֲוֹנֵנוּ וּלְחַטָּאתֵנוּ, וּנְחַלְתָּנוּ:**

*Continue:*

תהלים פו — סְלַח לָנוּ אָבִינוּ כִּי חָטָאנוּ, מְחַל לָנוּ מַלְכֵּנוּ כִּי פָשָׁעְנוּ. כִּי־אַתָּה אֲדֹנָי טוֹב וְסַלָּח, וְרַב־חֶסֶד לְכָל־קֹרְאֶיךָ:

ישעיה סב / תהלים לו — וְאַל־תִּתְּנוּ דֳמִי לוֹ, עַד־יְכוֹנֵן וְעַד־יָשִׂים אֶת־יְרוּשָׁלִַם תְּהִלָּה בָּאָרֶץ: כִּי־עִמְּךָ מְקוֹר חַיִּים, בְּאוֹרְךָ נִרְאֶה־אוֹר: אֱלֹהֵינוּ, בֹּשְׁנוּ בְּמַעֲשֵׂינוּ וְנִכְלַמְנוּ בַּעֲוֹנֵינוּ.

כְּרַחֵם אָב עַל בָּנִים, כֵּן תְּרַחֵם יהוה עָלֵינוּ.
תהלים ג — לַיהוה הַיְשׁוּעָה, עַל־עַמְּךָ בִרְכָתֶךָ סֶּלָה:
תהלים מו — יהוה צְבָאוֹת עִמָּנוּ, מִשְׂגָּב לָנוּ אֱלֹהֵי יַעֲקֹב סֶלָה:

Lord of hosts, happy is the one who trusts in You. *Ps. 84*
Lord, save! May the King answer us on the day we call. *Ps. 20*

▸ Forgive, please, this people's iniquity, *Num. 14*
in the abundance of Your kindness,
and as You have forgiven this people from the time of Egypt until now,
and there it is written:

*Congregation then Leader:*

And the Lord said, I have forgiven as you asked.

*Continue:*

הַטֵּה Give ear, my God and hear; open Your eyes and see our desolation, and the city that bears Your name, for it is not on the strength of our righteousness that we throw down our pleadings before You, but on the strength of Your great compassion. Lord, hear me; Lord, forgive; Lord, listen and act and do not delay – for Your sake, my God; for Your city and Your people bear Your name. *Dan. 9*

Our God and God of our fathers:

אֶתָנוּ We come before You, Former of the winds. In our many iniquities our sighs have grown heavy; the decrees against us powerful and our screams so many – for on the Seventeenth of Tammuz, the Tablets were smashed. We have been exiled from the House of Your choosing; our judgment was sealed, the decree laid down. And the light has darkened over us – for on the Seventeenth of Tammuz, the Torah scroll was burnt. Our enemies destroyed the Sanctuary, the Divine Presence fled from Its corner, and we were yielded up to the hands of the wanton, to be consumed – for on the Seventeenth of Tammuz, an idol was set up in the Temple. We were scattered from city to city, and old and young of us were seized. The place of our delight was destroyed, and fire raged through her – for on the Seventeenth of Tammuz the city was broken through. The lethal foe took hold of our Temple, and the cherubs, bride and bridegroom were deprived of all their ornament. Because we angered You we were given up to destruction – for on the Seventeenth of Tammuz, the daily offering ceased. All glory and praise there ended. The enemy drew his sword and brandished its point against us; small children and babies were prepared for the slaughter – for on the Seventeenth of Tammuz, the offerings and sacrifices ceased. We rebelled against the One who inhabits the Heavens, and so we were dispersed to all the corners of the world. All our dancing was turned to lament – for on the Seventeenth of Tammuz, the Temple service ended. We acted obstinately with You in the discord of tongues, and so our own tongue has learnt lamentation; we have been abandoned in countless numbers – for on the Seventeenth of Tammuz, sin decided our destiny. We have been dispersed and found no relief, and so our sighs have multiplied within us; Rock, see how

יהוה צְבָאוֹת, אַשְׁרֵי אָדָם בֹּטֵחַ בָּךְ: תהלים פד

יהוה הוֹשִֽׁיעָה, הַמֶּלֶךְ יַעֲנֵנוּ בְיוֹם־קָרְאֵנוּ: תהלים כ

‹ סְלַח־נָא לַעֲוֺן הָעָם הַזֶּה כְּגֹדֶל חַסְדֶּךָ במדבר יד

וְכַאֲשֶׁר נָשָֽׂאתָה לָעָם הַזֶּה מִמִּצְרַיִם וְעַד־הֵנָּה:

וְשָׁם נֶאֱמַר

*שליח ציבור then קהל:*

וַיֹּאמֶר יהוה, סָלַחְתִּי כִּדְבָרֶךָ:

*Continue:*

הַטֵּה אֱלֹהַי אָזְנְךָ וּשְׁמָע, פְּקַח עֵינֶיךָ וּרְאֵה שֹׁמְמֹתֵינוּ וְהָעִיר אֲשֶׁר־נִקְרָא שִׁמְךָ עָלֶיהָ, כִּי לֹא עַל־צִדְקֹתֵינוּ אֲנַחְנוּ מַפִּילִים תַּחֲנוּנֵינוּ לְפָנֶיךָ, כִּי עַל־רַחֲמֶיךָ הָרַבִּים: אֲדֹנָי שְׁמָעָה, אֲדֹנָי סְלָחָה, אֲדֹנָי הַקְשִׁיבָה וַעֲשֵׂה אַל־תְּאַחַר, לְמַעַנְךָ אֱלֹהַי, כִּי־שִׁמְךָ נִקְרָא עַל־עִירְךָ וְעַל־עַמֶּךָ: דניאל ט

אֱלֹהֵינוּ וֵאלֹהֵי אֲבוֹתֵינוּ

אָתָֽנוּ לְךָ יוֹצֵר רוּחוֹת, בְּרוֹב עֲוֹנֵינוּ כָּבְדוּ אֲנָחוֹת, גְּזֵרוֹת עָצְמוּ וְרַבּוּ צְרִיחוֹת, כִּי בְּשִׁבְעָה עָשָׂר בְּתַמּוּז נִשְׁתַּבְּרוּ הַלֻּחוֹת. גָּלִֽינוּ מִבֵּית הַבְּחִירָה, דִּינֵֽנוּ נֶחְתַּם וְנִגְזְרָה גְּזֵרָה, וְחָשַׁךְ בַּעֲדֵֽנוּ אוֹרָה, כִּי בְּשִׁבְעָה עָשָׂר בְּתַמּוּז נִשְׂרְפָה הַתּוֹרָה. הָרְסוּ אוֹיְבֵֽינוּ הַהֵיכָל, וּבָרְחָה שְׁכִינָה מִזָּוִית הֵיכָל, וְנִמְסַֽרְנוּ בִּידֵי זֵדִים לְהִתְאַכָּל, כִּי בְּשִׁבְעָה עָשָׂר בְּתַמּוּז הָעֳמַד צֶֽלֶם בַּהֵיכָל. זֹֽרוּנוּ מֵעִיר אֶל עִיר, וְנִלְכַּד מִמֶּֽנּוּ רַב וְצָעִיר, חָרְבָה מְשׂוֹשֵֽׂנוּ וְאֵשׁ בָּהּ הִבְעִיר, כִּי בְּשִׁבְעָה עָשָׂר בְּתַמּוּז הָבְקְעָה הָעִיר. טָפַשׂ מִקְדָּשֵֽׁנוּ צַר הַמַּשְׁמִיד, וְנָטַל מֵחָתָן וְכַלָּה אֶצְעָדָה וְצָמִיד, יַֽעַן כְּעִסְנֽוּךָ נִתַּֽנוּ לְהַשְׁמִיד, כִּי בְּשִׁבְעָה עָשָׂר בְּתַמּוּז בֻּטַּל הַתָּמִיד. כָּלָה מֶֽנּוּ כָּל הוֹד וָשֶֽׁבַח, חָרְבוּ שָׁלַף אוֹיֵב עָלֵֽינוּ לָאֶֽבַח, לִהְיוֹת עוֹלָלִים וְיוֹנְקִים מוּכָנִים לַטֶּֽבַח, כִּי בְּשִׁבְעָה עָשָׂר בְּתַמּוּז בָּטְלוּ עוֹלָה וָזֶֽבַח. מָרַֽדְנוּ לְשׁוֹכֵן מְעוֹנוֹת, לָכֵן נִתְפַּזַּֽרְנוּ בְּכָל פִּנּוֹת, נֶהְפַּךְ מְחוֹלֵֽנוּ לְקִינוֹת, כִּי בְּשִׁבְעָה עָשָׂר בְּתַמּוּז בָּטְלוּ קָרְבָּנוֹת. סָרַֽרְנוּ לְפָנֶֽיךָ מֵרִיב לְשׁוֹנוֹת, לָכֵן לָמְדָה לְשׁוֹנֵֽנוּ לוֹמַר קִינוֹת, עֻזַּֽבְנוּ בְּלִי לְהִמָּנוֹת, כִּי בְּשִׁבְעָה עָשָׂר בְּתַמּוּז גָּרְמוּ לָֽנוּ עֲוֹנוֹת. פֻּזַּֽרְנוּ בְּלִי מְצוֹא רְוָחָה, לָכֵן רָבְתָה

our souls have been bowed low – and turn our Seventeenth of Tammuz into gladness and joy. We have been obstinate and many calamities have met us; and so we have been yielded up to the plunder, have been pushed into the mud. See, LORD, and release us from disaster – and turn our Seventeenth of Tammuz into joy and gladness. ▸ Turn to us, You who reside on High, and gather in our scattered ones from the very ends of the earth. Say to Zion, "Come, get up," – and turn our Seventeenth of Tammuz to a day of salvation and comfort.

אֵל מֶלֶךְ God, King who sits upon a throne of compassion, who acts with loving-kindness, who pardons the iniquities of His people, passing them before Him in order; who forgives sinners and pardons transgressors; who performs righteousness with all flesh and spirit, do not repay their bad actions in kind. ▸ God, You taught us to speak thirteen attributes: recall for us today the covenant of the thirteen attributes, as You in ancient times showed the humble one [Moses], as is written: The LORD descended in the cloud and stood with him there, and proclaimed in the name of the LORD.

*Congregation then Leader:*

And the LORD passed by before him and proclaimed: *Ex. 34*

*All say aloud:*

יהוה The LORD, the LORD, compassionate and gracious God, slow to anger, abounding in loving-kindness and truth, extending loving-kindness to a thousand generations, forgiving iniquity, rebellion and sin, and absolving [the guilty who repent]. Forgive us our iniquity and our sin, and take us as Your inheritance.

*Continue:*

סְלַח לָנוּ Forgive us, our Father, for we have sinned. Pardon us, our King, for we have transgressed. For You, LORD, are good and forgiving, abounding in loving- *Ps. 86*
kindness to all who call on You.

God, do not rest, do not be silent and do not be still, for Your enemies clamor *Ps. 83*
and those who hate You hold their heads high. God of retribution, *Ps. 94*
LORD; God of retribution, appear

כְּרַחֵם As a father has compassion for his children,
so, LORD, have compassion for us.
Salvation is the LORD's; on Your people is Your blessing, Selah! *Ps. 3*
The LORD of hosts is with us, the God of Jacob is our stronghold, Selah! *Ps. 46*
LORD of hosts: happy is the one who trusts in You. *Ps. 84*
LORD, save! May the King answer us on the day we call. *Ps. 20*

בָּנוּ אֲנָחָה, צוּר רְאֵה נַפְשֵׁנוּ כִּי שָׁחָה, וְשִׁבְעָה עָשָׂר בְּתַמּוּז הֲפָךְ לָנוּ לְשָׂשׂוֹן וּלְשִׂמְחָה. קִשִּׁינוּ עֹרֶף וְרָבְתָה בָּנוּ אָסוֹן, לָכֵן נִתַּנּוּ לִמְשִׁסָּה וְרִפְשׂוֹן, רְאֵה יהוה וְחַלְּצֵנוּ מֵאָסוֹן, וְשִׁבְעָה עָשָׂר בְּתַמּוּז הֲפָךְ לָנוּ לְשִׂמְחָה וּלְשָׂשׂוֹן. ‹ שַׁעֲנוּ שׁוֹכֵן רוּמָה, וְקַבֵּץ נְפוּצוֹתֵינוּ מִקַּצְוּוֹת אֲדָמָה, תֹּאמַר לְצִיּוֹן קוּמָה, וְשִׁבְעָה עָשָׂר בְּתַמּוּז הֲפָךְ לָנוּ לְיוֹם יְשׁוּעָה וְנֶחָמָה.

אֵל מֶלֶךְ יוֹשֵׁב עַל כִּסֵּא רַחֲמִים, מִתְנַהֵג בַּחֲסִידוּת. מוֹחֵל עֲוֹנוֹת עַמּוֹ, מַעֲבִיר רִאשׁוֹן רִאשׁוֹן. מַרְבֶּה מְחִילָה לְחַטָּאִים, וּסְלִיחָה לַפּוֹשְׁעִים. עֹשֶׂה צְדָקוֹת עִם כָּל בָּשָׂר וָרוּחַ, לֹא כְרָעָתָם תִּגְמֹל. ‹ אֵל, הוֹרֵיתָ לָנוּ לוֹמַר שְׁלֹשׁ עֶשְׂרֵה, וּזְכָר לָנוּ הַיּוֹם בְּרִית שְׁלֹשׁ עֶשְׂרֵה, כְּמוֹ שֶׁהוֹדַעְתָּ לֶעָנָו מִקֶּדֶם, כְּמוֹ שֶׁכָּתוּב: וַיֵּרֶד יהוה בֶּעָנָן, וַיִּתְיַצֵּב עִמּוֹ שָׁם, וַיִּקְרָא בְשֵׁם, יהוה:

*שליח ציבור then קהל:*

וַיַּעֲבֹר יהוה עַל־פָּנָיו וַיִּקְרָא שמות לד

*All say aloud:*

**יהוה, יהוה, אֵל רַחוּם וְחַנּוּן, אֶרֶךְ אַפַּיִם, וְרַב־חֶסֶד וֶאֱמֶת: נֹצֵר חֶסֶד לָאֲלָפִים, נֹשֵׂא עָוֹן וָפֶשַׁע וְחַטָּאָה, וְנַקֵּה: וְסָלַחְתָּ לַעֲוֹנֵנוּ וּלְחַטָּאתֵנוּ, וּנְחַלְתָּנוּ:**

*Continue:*

סְלַח לָנוּ אָבִינוּ כִּי חָטָאנוּ, מְחַל לָנוּ מַלְכֵּנוּ כִּי פָשָׁעְנוּ. כִּי־אַתָּה אֲדֹנָי טוֹב וְסַלָּח, וְרַב־חֶסֶד לְכָל־קֹרְאֶיךָ: תהלים פו

אֱלֹהִים אַל־דֳּמִי־לָךְ, אַל־תֶּחֱרַשׁ וְאַל־תִּשְׁקֹט אֵל: כִּי־הִנֵּה אוֹיְבֶיךָ יֶהֱמָיוּן, תהלים פג
וּמְשַׂנְאֶיךָ נָשְׂאוּ רֹאשׁ: אֵל־נְקָמוֹת יהוה, אֵל נְקָמוֹת הוֹפִיעַ: תהלים צד

כְּרַחֵם אָב עַל בָּנִים, כֵּן תְּרַחֵם יהוה עָלֵינוּ.
לַיהוה הַיְשׁוּעָה, עַל־עַמְּךָ בִרְכָתֶךָ סֶּלָה: תהלים ג
יהוה צְבָאוֹת עִמָּנוּ, מִשְׂגָּב לָנוּ אֱלֹהֵי יַעֲקֹב סֶלָה: תהלים מו
יהוה צְבָאוֹת, אַשְׁרֵי אָדָם בֹּטֵחַ בָּךְ: תהלים פד
יהוה הוֹשִׁיעָה, הַמֶּלֶךְ יַעֲנֵנוּ בְיוֹם־קָרְאֵנוּ: תהלים כ

Our God and God of our fathers:

אֲמָרֵר It is bitterly that I weep, over the Hand raised against our ruins. I blasphemed Him in His House, in my unfaithfulness and thieving. The Holy Presence broke out and fled, flew ten stretches and rose up to the seventh Heaven. God cut me off, tormented me, burnt me, in the fourth month. He closed the time set for Him to break those young boys, who were like boughs just sprouting. He shot us with His arrows twice, melted and weakened us, as heedless women wept for Tammuz in the Temple. He condemned me and became Enemy to me, then, in the month of Tammuz. Five traps were laid for me, deep in the Scripture of sufferings sent. Those people overcame me for my impurity on the seventeenth of the month. For I was ensnared like a wretched bride, unfaithful beneath a wedding canopy of peace and success. I did not wait for Moses, my shepherd, until the sixth hour, and the Tablets were smashed. From His hand was I ornamented with jewelry of fine gold, brooch and bracelet. They flowed away on the day of His rage, when I corrupted my way, and denounced my faith. I broke off the order of His service and the constant supplies of the altar – from the Chamber of the Lambs, the daily offering is ended. Israel is crumbled to pieces, scattered, storm battered, oppressed. Likened to a ship without a captain, tossed about like a boat. You have taken her by the head for her sins, exposed her twice over to mourning and moaning. Her enemies waged war on her on this day, and the city was broken through again. She fled out like a chased gazelle to hide, when none sought her. They sharpened their tongues, they made her like a lamb, and left her wool and milk for all takers. She cries out for the cherished thing with which she was crowned: the beloved of her eyes eluded her as Apostomus burnt the Torah. A fool cursed those oppressed and broken to vex them; he taunted abject people: "They shall be consumed;" "God shall hide His face from seeing." When idols were placed in the Temple, God avenged one's hand at the hand of the other, a disgusting item consumed. This, at the time when He gathered anguish over us; for an image was set up in the Sanctuary of God. Miserable and plagued are these children, who were once the very first. Their troubles have come close on one another's heels these many years; stricken as if by the stings of bees and scorpions. They think their hope is gone, that as they sit in this darkness they have no more chance. ▸ Zealous God, in Your restraint towards those who incite You they have flourished fat and succulent. Raise up those who still await You; let them stand firm always, like something planted, or carved out with love. It is on fast days that truth and peace are hewn out. May they become forever times of joy and celebration – festive days.

אֵל מֶלֶךְ God, King who sits upon a throne of compassion, who acts with loving-kindness, who pardons the iniquities of His people, passing them before Him in order; who forgives sinners and pardons transgressors; who performs righteousness with all flesh and spirit, do not repay their bad actions in kind. ▸ God, You taught us to speak thirteen attributes: recall for us today the covenant of the thirteen attributes, as You in ancient times showed the humble one [Moses], as is written: The Lord descended in the cloud and stood with him there, and proclaimed in the name of the Lord:

*Congregation then Leader:*

And the Lord passed by before him and proclaimed: *Ex. 34*

### אֱלֹהֵינוּ וֵאלֹהֵי אֲבוֹתֵינוּ

אֱמֹר בִּבְכִי מִפְּנֵי יַד שְׁלוּחָה בִּעִי. בְּנָאֲצִי בְּתוֹךְ בֵּיתוֹ בִּבְגָדִי וְקָבְעִי. גָּח וּבָרַח וְנָסַע עֶשֶׂר וְעָלָה לַשְּׁבִיעִי. דִּמְּנִי הֱצִיקַנִי הִשִּׁיקַנִי בַּחֹדֶשׁ הָרְבִיעִי. הֵבִיא מוֹעֵד בִּמְלֹאתוֹ לִשְׁבֹּר בַּחוּרֵי גִמּוּז. וְרִבָּה בוֹ פְּעָמִים בִּמְסִמּוּס וּמִזְמוּז. זְבוּלוֹ כְּשֶׁר שַׁאֲנַנּוֹת מְבַכּוֹת אֶת הַתַּמּוּז. חִיְּבַנִי וְאִיְּבַנִי אֲזַי בְּיֶרַח תַּמּוּז. טָמְנוּ פַּחִים חֲמִשָּׁה בְּמִקְרָא תְּלָאוֹת מְשֻׁלָּחוֹת. יָכְלוּ לִי בְּשִׁבְעָה עָשָׂר בּוֹ בַּאֲלִיחוֹת. כִּי נוֹקַשְׁתִּי כְּכַלָּה עֲלוּבָה בְּחֻפַּת שַׁלְוָה וְהַצְלָחוֹת. לְרוֹעִי לֹא הִמְתַּנְתִּי שֵׁשׁ, וְנִשְׁתַּבְּרוּ הַלֻּחוֹת. מִיָּדוֹ עָדִיתִי חֲלִי כֶתֶם, אֶצְעָדָה וְצָמִיד. נִגְּרוֹת בְּיוֹם אַפּוֹ, כְּשִׁחַתִּי דְּרָכַי לְהַשְׁמִיד. סֵדֶר עֲבוֹדָתוֹ וְקֵיץ מִזְבְּחוֹ קַצְתִּי לְהַעֲמִיד. עַל כֵּן מִלִּשְׁכַּת הַטְּלָאִים בֻּטַּל הַתָּמִיד. פּוֹר הִתְפּוֹרְרָה וְנִתְפַּזְּרָה סְעָרָה עֲנִיָּה. צִי נִמְשְׁלָה מִבְּלִי חוֹבֵל, וְנִטְרְפָה כָּאֳנִיָּה. קַחְתָּהּ בְּחַטָּאתָהּ בְּרֹאשָׁהּ, וּבְכֶפֶל תַּאֲנִיָּה וַאֲנִיָּה. רִיבוּהָ צָרֶיהָ כְּהַיּוֹם, וְהָבְקְעָה הָעִיר בַּשְּׁנִיָּה. שֻׁלְּחָה כִּצְבִי מֻדָּח מֵאֵין דּוֹרֵשׁ לְהַסְתִּירָה. שָׁנְנוּ לְשׁוֹנָם וּנְתָנוּהָ כְּשֶׂה, צַמְרָהּ וַחֲלָבָהּ לְהַתִּירָה. תִּצְעַק עַל כְּלִי חֶמְדָּה שֶׁבּוֹ נִכְתָּרָה. תַּחְמוּד עֵינֶיהָ נִצַּל כְּשָׂרָף אַפּוֹסְטְמוֹס הַתּוֹרָה. חֵרֵף עֲשׁוּקִים וּרְצוּצִים בַּעֲבוּר הַרְעִימָם סָכָל. יְרוּדִים בּוֹהֲיָה לֶאֱכֹל וּבְהַסְתֵּר פָּנִים מִלְּהִסְתַּכֵּל. יַד הִשְׁלִים מִכְּנַף שִׁקּוּצִים נֶאֱכָל. עֵת צָרָה כְּהִתְכַּנֵּס וְהָעֳמַד צֶלֶם בַּהֵיכָל. דְּוּוִים סְגוּפִים בָּנִים הֱיוּ מִקֶּדֶם רִאשׁוֹנִים. סְמוּכוֹת צָרוֹתֵיהֶם זוֹ לְזוֹ כַּמָּה שָׁנִים. לוֹקִים כַּאֲשֶׁר תַּעֲשֶׂינָה הַדְּבוֹרִים, וְהָעַקְרַבִּים שׁוֹנִים. הוֹגִים אָבַד שִׁבְרָם וּבָטֵל סִכּוּיָם בָּאִישׁוֹנִים. ◂ אֵל קַנָּא, בְּהִתְאַפֵּק בְּמַקְנִיאֶיךָ דְּשֵׁנִים וְטוֹבִים. מְחַכִּים תְּקִים עוֹמְדִים לְעוֹלָמִים, כִּנְטִיעִים מְחֻטָּבִים בַּאֲהָבִים. הָאֱמֶת וְהַשָּׁלוֹם בְּצוֹמוֹת חֲטוּבִים. נֶצַח הֱיוֹתָם לְשִׂמְחָה וּלְשָׂשׂוֹן וּלְמוֹעֲדִים טוֹבִים.

אֵל מֶלֶךְ יוֹשֵׁב עַל כִּסֵּא רַחֲמִים, מִתְנַהֵג בַּחֲסִידוּת. מוֹחֵל עֲוֹנוֹת עַמּוֹ, מַעֲבִיר רִאשׁוֹן רִאשׁוֹן. מַרְבֶּה מְחִילָה לְחַטָּאִים, וּסְלִיחָה לְפוֹשְׁעִים. עֹשֶׂה צְדָקוֹת עִם כָּל בָּשָׂר וָרוּחַ, לֹא כְרָעָתָם תִּגְמֹל. ◂ אֵל, הוֹרֵיתָ לָּנוּ לוֹמַר שְׁלֹשׁ עֶשְׂרֵה, וּזְכָר לָנוּ הַיּוֹם בְּרִית שְׁלֹשׁ עֶשְׂרֵה, כְּמוֹ שֶׁהוֹדַעְתָּ לֶעָנָו מִקֶּדֶם, כְּמוֹ שֶׁכָּתוּב: וַיֵּרֶד יהוה בֶּעָנָן, וַיִּתְיַצֵּב עִמּוֹ שָׁם, וַיִּקְרָא בְשֵׁם, יהוה:

*שליח ציבור then קהל:*

שמות לד

וַיַּעֲבֹר יהוה עַל־פָּנָיו וַיִּקְרָא

*All say aloud:*

יהוה The Lord, the Lord, compassionate and gracious God, slow to anger, abounding in loving-kindness and truth, extending loving-kindness to a thousand generations, forgiving iniquity, rebellion and sin, and absolving [the guilty who repent]. Forgive us our iniquity and our sin, and take us as Your inheritance.

*Continue:*

סְלַח לָנוּ Forgive us, our Father, for we have sinned. Pardon us, our King, for we
have transgressed. For You, Lord, are good and forgiving, abounding in loving- *Ps. 86*
kindness to all who call on You.

*The following is said responsively:*

Turn to this prisoner who has been yielded up,
to the hand of Babylon and then of Seir;
to You he has been calling all these years, and he pleads like a small child,
on the day the enemy prevailed and the city was broken through.

And so I bow myself and strike my hands together,
on this day of five disasters that scattered me about,
for at the time of the golden calf, the Tablets left me.
And the daily offering was annulled, and they brought me away in a cage.
And an idol was placed in the Sanctuary that was my crowning glory,
and I was deprived of His counsel.
The meal-offering was ended, and Your Law – the foe sent it up in flames,
on the day the enemy prevailed and the city was broken through.

I tremble terribly, I stand horrified, on the day the Lord pushed me aside,
And Sennacherib, the Viper of the north, swept me away like a deluge.
My light grew dark, and Sheshakh [Babylon] too, tossed me about like a ball.
And the hunter stretched out his hand, and the goat of Greece,
the hairy one of Rome,
on the day the enemy prevailed and the city was broken through.

The glory of my heart, my Stronghold, will Your rage fume forever?
Will You not see this weary nation, blackened as if by the furnace?
Close, with the descendant of Peretz, the breach in my fence,
and, from among the thorns, pick out the lily.
Build the Temple, and return the borders of the Carmel and of Bashan.
And open Your eyes, exact vengeance from Etzer and Dishan.
Judge a people struck dumb, so that the damages be paid,
by the one who destroys, the one who burns –
on the day the enemy prevailed and the city was broken through.

*All say aloud:*

**יהוה, יהוה, אֵל רַחוּם וְחַנּוּן, אֶרֶךְ אַפַּיִם, וְרַב־חֶסֶד וֶאֱמֶת: נֹצֵר חֶסֶד לָאֲלָפִים, נֹשֵׂא עָוֹן וָפֶשַׁע וְחַטָּאָה, וְנַקֵּה: וְסָלַחְתָּ לַעֲוֹנֵנוּ וּלְחַטָּאתֵנוּ, וּנְחַלְתָּנוּ:**

*Continue:*

סְלַח לָנוּ אָבִינוּ כִּי חָטָאנוּ, מְחַל לָנוּ מַלְכֵּנוּ כִּי פָשָׁעְנוּ. כִּי־אַתָּה אֲדֹנָי טוֹב וְסַלָּח, וְרַב־חֶסֶד לְכָל־קֹרְאֶיךָ: תהלים פו

*The following is said responsively:*

שָׁעָה נֶאֱסַר, אֲשֶׁר נִמְסַר, בְּיַד בָּבֶל וְגַם שֵׂעִיר.
לָךְ יֶהֱמֶה, זֶה כַּמֶּה, וְיִתְחַנֵּן כְּבֵן צָעִיר.
**יוֹם גָּבַר הָאוֹיֵב וַתִּבָּקַע הָעִיר.**

לְזֹאת אִכַּף, וְאֶסְפֹּק כַּף, בְּיוֹם חֲמִשָּׁה פִּזְרוֹנִי.
וְעַל רֶגֶל הָעֵגֶל, הַלֻּחוֹת יְצָאוּנִי.
וְגַם הִשְׁמִיד הַתָּמִיד, וּבַסּוּגַר הֱבִיאָנִי.
וְהוּשַׂם אֱלִיל בְּהֵיכַל כָּלִיל, וּמֵעֲצָתוֹ כְּלָאָנִי.
וְהַמִּנְחָה הוּנָחָה, וְדָתְךָ, צָר בָּאֵשׁ הִבְעִיר.
**יוֹם גָּבַר הָאוֹיֵב וַתִּבָּקַע הָעִיר.**

מְאֹד אֶתְחַל, וְאֶתְחַלְחַל, בְּיוֹם שַׁדַּי דְּחָפַנִי.
וְהַשְּׁפִיפוֹן מִצָּפוֹן, כְּשִׁבֹּלֶת שְׁטָפָנִי.
מְאוֹר חָשַׁךְ, וְגַם שֵׁשַׁךְ, כְּמוֹ כַדּוּר צְנָפָנִי.
וְהַצַּיָּד שָׁלַח יָד, וְהַצָּפִיר וְהַשָּׂעִיר.
**יוֹם גָּבַר הָאוֹיֵב וַתִּבָּקַע הָעִיר.**

הוֹד לִבִּי וּמִשְׂגַּבִּי, הֲלָעַד אַפְּךָ יֶעְשַׁן.
הֲלֹא תִרְאֶה עַם נִלְאֶה, אֲשֶׁר הָשְׁחַר כְּמוֹ כִבְשָׁן.
גְּדֹר פִּרְצִי בְּבֶן פַּרְצִי, וּמְחֶדֶק לְקֹט שׁוֹשָׁן.
בְּנֵה בֵית זְבוּל, וְהָשֵׁב גְּבוּל הַכַּרְמֶל וְהַבָּשָׁן.
וְעַיִן פְּקַח, וְנָקָם קַח מֵאֱצֶר וּמִדִּישָׁן.
שְׁפֹט אִלֵּם, וְאָז יְשַׁלֵּם הַמַּבְעֶה וְהַמַּבְעִיר.
**יוֹם גָּבַר הָאוֹיֵב וַתִּבָּקַע הָעִיר.**

*On all days continue:*

אֵל מֶלֶךְ God, King who sits upon a throne of compassion, who acts with loving-kindness, who pardons the iniquities of His people, passing them before Him in order; who forgives sinners and pardons transgressors; who performs righteousness with all flesh and spirit, do not repay their bad actions in kind. God, You taught us to speak thirteen attributes: recall for us today the covenant of the thirteen attributes, as You in ancient times showed the humble one [Moses], as is written: The LORD descended in the cloud and stood with him there, and proclaimed in the name of the LORD:

*Congregation then Leader:*

And the LORD passed by before him and proclaimed: *Ex. 34*

*All say aloud:*

יהוה The LORD, the LORD, compassionate and gracious God, slow to anger, abounding in loving-kindness and truth, extending loving-kindness to a thousand generations, forgiving iniquity, rebellion and sin, and absolving [the guilty who repent]. Forgive us our iniquity and our sin, and take us as Your inheritance.

*Continue:*

סְלַח לָנוּ Forgive us, our Father, for we have sinned. Pardon us, our King, for we have transgressed. For You, LORD, are good and forgiving, abounding in *Ps. 86*
loving-kindness to all who call on You.

זְכֹר Remember, LORD, Your compassion and loving-kindness, *Ps. 25*
for they are everlasting. Remember us, LORD, in favoring Your people;
redeem us with Your salvation.

זְכֹר Remember Your congregation, the one that You acquired long ago, *Ps. 74*
the tribe of Your inheritance that You redeemed,
this Mount Zion that You have dwelt in.

זְכֹר Remember, LORD, the fondness of Jerusalem; do not forever forget the
love of Zion. You shall rise up and have compassion for Zion, *Ps. 102*
for now it is right to be gracious, for the time has come.

זְכֹר Remember, LORD, what the Edomites did on the day Jerusalem fell. *Ps. 137*
They said, "Tear it down, tear it down to its very foundations!"

זְכֹר Remember Abraham, Isaac and Jacob, to whom You swore by Your *Ex. 32*
own self, when You said to them, "I shall make Your descendants
as numerous as the stars in the sky, and I shall give all this Land that
I spoke of to your descendants, and they shall inherit it forever."

זְכֹר Remember Your servants, Abraham, Isaac and Jacob; do not attend to *Deut. 9*
the stubbornness of this people, to their wickedness or sinfulness.

*On all days continue:*

אֵל מֶלֶךְ יוֹשֵׁב עַל כִּסֵּא רַחֲמִים, מִתְנַהֵג בַּחֲסִידוּת. מוֹחֵל עֲוֹנוֹת עַמּוֹ, מַעֲבִיר רִאשׁוֹן רִאשׁוֹן. מַרְבֶּה מְחִילָה לְחַטָּאִים, וּסְלִיחָה לְפוֹשְׁעִים. עֹשֶׂה צְדָקוֹת עִם כָּל בָּשָׂר וָרוּחַ, לֹא כְרָעָתָם תִּגְמֹל. ◄ אֵל, הוֹרֵיתָ לָּנוּ לוֹמַר שְׁלֹשׁ עֶשְׂרֵה, וּזְכָר לָנוּ הַיּוֹם בְּרִית שְׁלֹשׁ עֶשְׂרֵה, כְּמוֹ שֶׁהוֹדַעְתָּ לֶעָנָו מִקֶּדֶם, כְּמוֹ שֶׁכָּתוּב: וַיֵּרֶד יהוה בֶּעָנָן, וַיִּתְיַצֵּב עִמּוֹ שָׁם, וַיִּקְרָא בְשֵׁם, יהוה:

*שליח ציבור then קהל:*

שמות לד וַיַּעֲבֹר יהוה עַל־פָּנָיו וַיִּקְרָא

*All say aloud:*

**יהוה, יהוה, אֵל רַחוּם וְחַנּוּן, אֶרֶךְ אַפַּיִם, וְרַב־חֶסֶד וֶאֱמֶת: נֹצֵר חֶסֶד לָאֲלָפִים, נֹשֵׂא עָוֹן וָפֶשַׁע וְחַטָּאָה, וְנַקֵּה: וְסָלַחְתָּ לַעֲוֹנֵנוּ וּלְחַטָּאתֵנוּ, וּנְחַלְתָּנוּ:**

*Continue:*

תהלים פו סְלַח לָנוּ אָבִינוּ כִּי חָטָאנוּ, מְחַל לָנוּ מַלְכֵּנוּ כִּי פָשָׁעְנוּ. כִּי־אַתָּה אֲדֹנָי טוֹב וְסַלָּח, וְרַב־חֶסֶד לְכָל־קֹרְאֶיךָ:

תהלים כה זְכֹר־רַחֲמֶיךָ יהוה וַחֲסָדֶיךָ, כִּי מֵעוֹלָם הֵמָּה:
זָכְרֵנוּ יהוה בִּרְצוֹן עַמֶּךָ, פָּקְדֵנוּ בִּישׁוּעָתֶךָ.
תהלים עד זְכֹר עֲדָתְךָ קָנִיתָ קֶּדֶם, גָּאַלְתָּ שֵׁבֶט נַחֲלָתֶךָ
הַר־צִיּוֹן זֶה שָׁכַנְתָּ בּוֹ:
זְכֹר יהוה חִבַּת יְרוּשָׁלָיִם, אַהֲבַת צִיּוֹן אַל תִּשְׁכַּח לָנֶצַח.
תהלים קב אַתָּה תָקוּם תְּרַחֵם צִיּוֹן, כִּי־עֵת לְחֶנְנָהּ, כִּי־בָא מוֹעֵד:
תהלים קלז זְכֹר יהוה לִבְנֵי אֱדוֹם אֵת יוֹם יְרוּשָׁלָיִם
הָאֹמְרִים עָרוּ עָרוּ, עַד הַיְסוֹד בָּהּ:
שמות לב זְכֹר לְאַבְרָהָם לְיִצְחָק וּלְיִשְׂרָאֵל עֲבָדֶיךָ, אֲשֶׁר נִשְׁבַּעְתָּ לָהֶם בָּךְ
וַתְּדַבֵּר אֲלֵהֶם, אַרְבֶּה אֶת־זַרְעֲכֶם כְּכוֹכְבֵי הַשָּׁמָיִם
וְכָל־הָאָרֶץ הַזֹּאת אֲשֶׁר אָמַרְתִּי אֶתֵּן לְזַרְעֲכֶם, וְנָחֲלוּ לְעֹלָם:
דברים ט זְכֹר לַעֲבָדֶיךָ לְאַבְרָהָם לְיִצְחָק וּלְיַעֲקֹב
אַל־תֵּפֶן אֶל־קְשִׁי הָעָם הַזֶּה וְאֶל־רִשְׁעוֹ וְאֶל־חַטָּאתוֹ:

אַל־נָא Please, do not hold against us the sin that we committed so foolishly, that we have sinned. Num. 12
We have sinned, our Rock; forgive us, our Creator.

*Some say responsively (all continue with "Remember the covenant" on the next page):*

אֵל נָא God, please, heal please, the diseases of this fruitful vine,
ashamed, disgraced and miserable are her fruits.
Redeem her from destruction and from the seeping wound;
answer us as You answered our father Abraham on Mount Moriah –
We have sinned, our Rock;
forgive us, our Creator.

Let the flags of the people redeemed by Your revealed arm,
be spared from plague; let them not be cut down,
and answer our call, and desire the creations of Your hands.
Answer us as You answered our fathers at the Reed Sea –
We have sinned, our Rock;
forgive us, our Creator.

Reveal now the merit of Abraham and Sarah,
the rock from which we were hewn.
Spare us from rage and lead us on a straight path.
Clear our impurity, and open our eyes to the light of Your Torah.
Answer us as You answered Joshua at Gilgal –
We have sinned, our Rock;
forgive us, our Creator.

Lord, witness the ashes of bound Isaac; make our cure spring up.
Put an end to plunder and brokenness, tempest and storm.
Teach us and make us wise with Your perfect word.
Answer us as You answered Samuel at Mitzpah –
We have sinned, our Rock;
forgive us, our Creator.

Jacob who emerged perfect from the womb – do not let his roots dry up.
Cleanse us of all stain and blemish, and do not have us wither.
Help us and we shall be saved,
and receive of Your ways of kindness.
Answer us as You answered Elijah on Mount Carmel –
We have sinned, our Rock;
forgive us, our Creator.

אַל־נָא תָשֵׁת עָלֵינוּ חַטָּאת אֲשֶׁר נוֹאַלְנוּ וַאֲשֶׁר חָטָאנוּ׃ במדבר יב
חָטָאנוּ צוּרֵנוּ, סְלַח לָנוּ יוֹצְרֵנוּ.

*Some say responsively (all continue with* זְכֹר לָנוּ בְּרִית *on the next page):*

אֵל נָא, רְפָא נָא תַּחֲלוּאֵי גֶּפֶן פּוֹרִיָּה
בּוֹשָׁה וְחָפְרָה, וְאֻמְלַל פִּרְיָהּ
גְּאָלֶנָּה מִשַּׁחַת וּמִמַּכָּה טְרִיָּה.
עֲנֵנוּ כְּשֶׁעָנִיתָ לְאַבְרָהָם אָבִינוּ בְּהַר הַמּוֹרִיָּה.
חָטָאנוּ צוּרֵנוּ, סְלַח לָנוּ יוֹצְרֵנוּ.

דְּגָלֵי עָם, פְּדוּיֵי בִּזְרוֹעַ חָשׂוּף
הַצֵּל מִנֶּגֶף וְאַל יִהְיוּ לְשִׁסּוּף
וְתַעֲנֶה קְרִיאָתֵנוּ וּלְמַעֲשֵׂה יָדֶיךָ תִּכְסֹף
עֲנֵנוּ כְּשֶׁעָנִיתָ לַאֲבוֹתֵינוּ עַל יַם סוּף.
חָטָאנוּ צוּרֵנוּ, סְלַח לָנוּ יוֹצְרֵנוּ.

זְכוּת צוּר חֻצַּב הַיּוֹם לָנוּ תְּגַל
חָשְׂכֵנוּ מֵאֱנֹף וּנְחֵנוּ בְּיֹשֶׁר מַעְגָּל
טַהֵר טֻמְאָתֵנוּ וּלְמָאוֹר תּוֹרָתְךָ עֵינֵינוּ גַל
עֲנֵנוּ כְּשֶׁעָנִיתָ לִיהוֹשֻׁעַ בַּגִּלְגָּל.
חָטָאנוּ צוּרֵנוּ, סְלַח לָנוּ יוֹצְרֵנוּ.

יָהּ, רְאֵה דֶּשֶׁן עָקוּד, וְהַצְמַח לָנוּ תְּרוּפָה
כַּלֵּה שֹׁד וָשֶׁבֶר, סַעַר וְסוּפָה
לַמְּדֵנוּ וְחַכְּמֵנוּ אִמְרָתְךָ הַצְּרוּפָה
עֲנֵנוּ כְּשֶׁעָנִיתָ לִשְׁמוּאֵל בַּמִּצְפָּה.
חָטָאנוּ צוּרֵנוּ, סְלַח לָנוּ יוֹצְרֵנוּ.

מְתֻמָּם מְרַחֵם, שָׁרָשָׁיו אַל תְּקַמֵּל
נַקֵּנוּ מִכֶּתֶם וְשֶׁמֶץ, וְלֹא נֵאָמֵל
סַעֲדֵנוּ וְנִוָּשֵׁעָה, וְאָרְחוֹת חֲסָדֶיךָ נִגָּמֵל
עֲנֵנוּ כְּשֶׁעָנִיתָ לְאֵלִיָּהוּ בְּהַר הַכַּרְמֶל.
חָטָאנוּ צוּרֵנוּ, סְלַח לָנוּ יוֹצְרֵנוּ.

Strengthen us by the righteousness of Moses, drawn from water,
and atone our crimes, wanton or foolish.
Free us from the terror of death that thrusts us back,
rule for our salvation; do not let us melt away in our sins.
Answer us as You answered Jonah in the belly of the fish –
We have sinned, our Rock;
forgive us, our Creator.

Remember Your devoted Aaron's sanctity,
for the sake of Israel of the pleasing steps.
Awaken Your compassion, for we are doubly stricken.
Return us resolutely to our awe of You, do not expose us.
Answer us as You answered David, and Solomon his son in Jerusalem –
We have sinned, our Rock;
forgive us, our Creator.

*On the Fast of Esther add:*
Answer those who call You; listen out from Your residence.
Hear the cry of those who call out to You, You who listen to the destitute.
Have compassion for Your children, as a father has for his.
Answer us as You answered Mordekhai and Esther:
and on a fifty-cubit gallows they hanged father and sons –
We have sinned, our Rock.
Forgive us, our Creator.

*All continue:*

זְכֹר Remember the covenant of our fathers, as You have said,
"I shall remember My covenant with Jacob, and My covenant *Lev. 26*
with Isaac, and I shall remember My covenant with Abraham,
and I shall remember the Land."

זְכֹר Remember the covenant of the early ones, as You have said,
"I shall remember for them the covenant of the early ones, *Ibid.*
those I took out of the land of Egypt before the eyes of the nations,
in order to be their God: I am the LORD."

עֲשֵׂה Deal kindly with us as You have promised, "Even so, when they are in the *Ibid.* land of their enemies I shall not reject them and shall not detest them to the point of destruction, to the point of breaking My covenant with them, for I am the LORD their God." Restore our fortunes, and have compassion for us as is written, "And God shall restore your fortunes and have compassion for you, *Deut. 30* and shall return and gather you in from all the nations among whom the LORD

עוֹדְדֵנוּ בְּצֶדֶק מָשׁוּי מִמַּיִם, וְכַפֵּר זָדוֹן וּמְשׁוּגָה
פְּדֵנוּ מִמְּהוּמַת מָוֶת, וְאָחוֹר כָּל נְסוֹגָה
צַוֵּה יְשׁוּעָתֵנוּ, וּבַעֲוֹנוֹתֵינוּ אַל נִתְמוֹגְגָה
עֲנֵנוּ כְּשֶׁעָנִיתָ לְיוֹנָה בִּמְעֵי הַדָּגָה.
חָטָאנוּ צוּרֵנוּ, סְלַח לָנוּ יוֹצְרֵנוּ.

קְדֻשַּׁת אִישׁ חֲסִידֶךָ זְכֹר לִיפַת פַּעֲמַיִם
רַחֲמֶיךָ תְּעוֹרֵר כִּי לָקִינוּ בְּכִפְלַיִם
שׁוּבֵנוּ תֹּקֶף לְיִרְאָתֶךָ וְלֹא נֶחְשַׁף שׁוּלַיִם
עֲנֵנוּ כְּשֶׁעָנִיתָ לְדָוִד וְלִשְׁלֹמֹה בְנוֹ בִּירוּשָׁלָיִם.
חָטָאנוּ צוּרֵנוּ, סְלַח לָנוּ יוֹצְרֵנוּ.

*On* תענית אסתר *add:*

תַּעֲנֶה לְקוֹרְאֶיךָ, וְהַסְכֵּת מִמְּעוֹנִים
תִּשְׁמַע שַׁוְעַת צוֹעֲקֶיךָ, שׁוֹמֵעַ אֶל אֶבְיוֹנִים
תְּרַחֵם עַל בָּנֶיךָ כְּרַחֵם אָב עַל בָּנִים
עֲנֵנוּ כְּמוֹ שֶׁעָנִיתָ לְמָרְדְּכַי וְאֶסְתֵּר
וְתָלוּ עַל עֵץ־חֲמִשִּׁים הָאָב עִם בָּנִים.
חָטָאנוּ צוּרֵנוּ, סְלַח לָנוּ יוֹצְרֵנוּ.

*All continue:*

זְכָר לָנוּ בְּרִית אָבוֹת כַּאֲשֶׁר אָמַרְתָּ: וְזָכַרְתִּי אֶת־בְּרִיתִי יַעֲקוֹב ויקרא כו
וְאַף אֶת־בְּרִיתִי יִצְחָק וְאַף אֶת־בְּרִיתִי אַבְרָהָם אֶזְכֹּר
וְהָאָרֶץ אֶזְכֹּר:

זְכָר לָנוּ בְּרִית רִאשׁוֹנִים כַּאֲשֶׁר אָמַרְתָּ: וְזָכַרְתִּי לָהֶם בְּרִית רִאשֹׁנִים שם
אֲשֶׁר הוֹצֵאתִי־אֹתָם מֵאֶרֶץ מִצְרַיִם לְעֵינֵי הַגּוֹיִם
לִהְיוֹת לָהֶם לֵאלֹהִים, אֲנִי יהוה:

עֲשֵׂה עִמָּנוּ כְּמָה שֶׁהִבְטַחְתָּנוּ: וְאַף גַּם־זֹאת בִּהְיוֹתָם בְּאֶרֶץ אֹיְבֵיהֶם, שם
לֹא־מְאַסְתִּים וְלֹא־גְעַלְתִּים לְכַלֹּתָם, לְהָפֵר בְּרִיתִי אִתָּם, כִּי אֲנִי יהוה
אֱלֹהֵיהֶם: הָשֵׁב שְׁבוּתֵנוּ וְרַחֲמֵנוּ כְּמָה שֶׁכָּתוּב: וְשָׁב יהוה אֱלֹהֶיךָ אֶת־ דברים ל

has scattered you." Gather those of us who have been distanced, as is written, "If your distanced ones are at the very ends of the heavens, from there shall the LORD your God gather you; from there shall He bring You." Wipe out our crimes as if they were a cloud, as if they were a haze, as is written, "I have wiped out your crimes like a cloud, and as a haze your sins; come back to Me for I have redeemed you." Wipe out our crimes for Your sake, as You have said, "I, I am the one who shall wipe out your crimes for My sake, and I shall not recall your sins." Whiten our sins as snow and as wool, as is written, "Come now, let us reason together, says the LORD; If your sins are like scarlet, they shall be whitened like snow; should they be as red as crimson, they shall become like wool." Throw over us pure waters and purify us, as is written, "I shall throw pure waters over you and you shall be pure. I shall purify you of all your impurities and of all your idolatry." Have compassion for us and do not destroy us, as is written, "For the LORD your God is a compassionate God; He will not cease to hold you and He will not destroy you, and will not forget the covenant of your fathers that He pledged to them." Circumcise our hearts to love Your name, as is written, "And the LORD will circumcise your heart and the heart of your descendants to love the LORD your God with all your heart and with all your soul, so that you shall live." Let us find You when we seek You, as is written, "And if from there you seek the LORD your God, you shall find Him, when you seek Him out with all your heart and with all your soul." Bring us to Your holy mountain, and let us rejoice in Your house of prayer, as is written, "I shall bring them to My holy mountain, and I shall make them rejoice in My house of prayer; their offerings and their sacrifices will be accepted, desired on My altar, for My House will be called a house of prayer for all peoples."

*Deut. 30* · *Is. 44* · *Is. 43* · *Is. 1* · *Ezek. 36* · *Deut. 4* · *Deut. 30* · *Deut. 4* · *Is. 56*

*The Ark is opened. The following until ◂ is said responsively, verse by verse:*

שְׁמַע קוֹלֵנוּ Listen to our voice, LORD our God. Spare us and have compassion on us, and in compassion and favor accept our prayer. Turn us back, O LORD, to You, and we will return. Renew our days as of old. Do not cast us away from You, and do not take Your holy spirit from us. Do not cast us away in our old age; when our strength is gone do not desert us.◂ Do not desert us, LORD; our God, do not be distant from us. Give us a sign of good things, and those who hate us shall see it and be ashamed, for You, LORD, will help us and console us. Hear our speech, LORD, consider our thoughts. May the words of our mouths and the thoughts within our hearts be pleasing to You, LORD, our Rock and our Redeemer. For it is You, LORD, that we have longed for; You shall answer us, LORD our God.

*Lam. 5*

*The Ark is closed.*

שְׁבוּתְךָ וְרִחֲמֶךָ, וְשָׁב וְקִבֶּצְךָ מִכָּל־הָעַמִּים אֲשֶׁר הֱפִיצְךָ יהוה אֱלֹהֶיךָ
שָׁמָּה: קַבֵּץ נִדָּחֵינוּ כְּמָה שֶׁכָּתוּב: אִם־יִהְיֶה נִדַּחֲךָ בִּקְצֵה הַשָּׁמָיִם, מִשָּׁם דברים ל
יְקַבֶּצְךָ יהוה אֱלֹהֶיךָ וּמִשָּׁם יִקָּחֶךָ: מְחֵה פְשָׁעֵינוּ כָּעָב וְכֶעָנָן כְּמָה שֶׁכָּתוּב:
מָחִיתִי כָעָב פְּשָׁעֶיךָ וְכֶעָנָן חַטֹּאותֶיךָ, שׁוּבָה אֵלַי כִּי גְאַלְתִּיךָ: מְחֵה פְשָׁעֵינוּ ישעיה מד
לְמַעַנְךָ כַּאֲשֶׁר אָמַרְתָּ: אָנֹכִי אָנֹכִי הוּא מֹחֶה פְשָׁעֶיךָ לְמַעֲנִי, וְחַטֹּאתֶיךָ ישעיה מג
לֹא אֶזְכֹּר: הַלְבֵּן חֲטָאֵינוּ כַּשֶּׁלֶג וְכַצֶּמֶר כְּמָה שֶׁכָּתוּב: לְכוּ־נָא וְנִוָּכְחָה ישעיה א
יֹאמַר יהוה, אִם־יִהְיוּ חֲטָאֵיכֶם כַּשָּׁנִים כַּשֶּׁלֶג יַלְבִּינוּ, אִם־יַאְדִּימוּ כַתּוֹלָע
כַּצֶּמֶר יִהְיוּ: זְרֹק עָלֵינוּ מַיִם טְהוֹרִים וְטַהֲרֵנוּ כְּמָה שֶׁכָּתוּב: וְזָרַקְתִּי עֲלֵיכֶם יחזקאל לו
מַיִם טְהוֹרִים וּטְהַרְתֶּם, מִכֹּל טֻמְאוֹתֵיכֶם וּמִכָּל־גִּלּוּלֵיכֶם אֲטַהֵר אֶתְכֶם:
רַחֵם עָלֵינוּ וְאַל תַּשְׁחִיתֵנוּ כְּמָה שֶׁכָּתוּב: כִּי אֵל רַחוּם יהוה אֱלֹהֶיךָ, לֹא דברים ד
יַרְפְּךָ וְלֹא יַשְׁחִיתֶךָ, וְלֹא יִשְׁכַּח אֶת־בְּרִית אֲבֹתֶיךָ אֲשֶׁר נִשְׁבַּע לָהֶם: מוֹל
אֶת לְבָבֵנוּ לְאַהֲבָה אֶת שְׁמֶךָ כְּמָה שֶׁכָּתוּב: וּמָל יהוה אֱלֹהֶיךָ אֶת־לְבָבְךָ דברים ל
וְאֶת־לְבַב זַרְעֶךָ, לְאַהֲבָה אֶת־יהוה אֱלֹהֶיךָ בְּכָל־לְבָבְךָ וּבְכָל־נַפְשְׁךָ,
לְמַעַן חַיֶּיךָ: הִמָּצֵא לָנוּ בְּבַקָּשָׁתֵנוּ כְּמָה שֶׁכָּתוּב: וּבִקַּשְׁתֶּם מִשָּׁם אֶת־ דברים ד
יהוה אֱלֹהֶיךָ וּמָצָאתָ, כִּי תִדְרְשֶׁנּוּ בְּכָל־לְבָבְךָ וּבְכָל־נַפְשֶׁךָ: תְּבִיאֵנוּ אֶל
הַר קָדְשֶׁךָ וְשַׂמְּחֵנוּ בְּבֵית תְּפִלָּתֶךָ כְּמָה שֶׁכָּתוּב: וַהֲבִיאוֹתִים אֶל־הַר ישעיה נו
קָדְשִׁי וְשִׂמַּחְתִּים בְּבֵית תְּפִלָּתִי, עוֹלֹתֵיהֶם וְזִבְחֵיהֶם לְרָצוֹן עַל־מִזְבְּחִי,
כִּי בֵיתִי בֵּית־תְּפִלָּה יִקָּרֵא לְכָל־הָעַמִּים:

*The ארון קודש is opened. The following until ‣ is said responsively, verse by verse:*

שְׁמַע קוֹלֵנוּ, יהוה אֱלֹהֵינוּ, חוּס וְרַחֵם עָלֵינוּ וְקַבֵּל בְּרַחֲמִים וּבְרָצוֹן אֶת
תְּפִלָּתֵנוּ. הֲשִׁיבֵנוּ יהוה אֵלֶיךָ וְנָשׁוּבָה, חַדֵּשׁ יָמֵינוּ כְּקֶדֶם: אַל תַּשְׁלִיכֵנוּ איכה ה
מִלְּפָנֶיךָ, וְרוּחַ קָדְשְׁךָ אַל תִּקַּח מִמֶּנּוּ. אַל תַּשְׁלִיכֵנוּ לְעֵת זִקְנָה, כִּכְלוֹת
כֹּחֵנוּ אַל תַּעַזְבֵנוּ. ‣ אַל תַּעַזְבֵנוּ יהוה, אֱלֹהֵינוּ אַל תִּרְחַק מִמֶּנּוּ. עֲשֵׂה
עִמָּנוּ אוֹת לְטוֹבָה, וְיִרְאוּ שׂוֹנְאֵינוּ וְיֵבֹשׁוּ, כִּי אַתָּה יהוה עֲזַרְתָּנוּ וְנִחַמְתָּנוּ.
אֲמָרֵינוּ הַאֲזִינָה יהוה, בִּינָה הֲגִיגֵנוּ. יִהְיוּ לְרָצוֹן אִמְרֵי פִינוּ וְהֶגְיוֹן לִבֵּנוּ
לְפָנֶיךָ, יהוה צוּרֵנוּ וְגוֹאֲלֵנוּ. כִּי לְךָ יהוה הוֹחָלְנוּ, אַתָּה תַעֲנֶה אֲדֹנָי אֱלֹהֵינוּ.

*The ארון קודש is closed.*

CONFESSION

אֱלֹהֵינוּ Our God and God of our fathers,
let our prayer come before You, and do not hide Yourself from our plea,
for we are not so arrogant or obstinate as to say before You,
LORD, our God and God of our fathers,
we are righteous and have not sinned,
for in truth, we and our fathers have sinned.

*Strike the left side of the chest with the right fist while saying each of the sins.*

אָשַׁמְנוּ We have been guilty, we have acted treacherously, we have robbed, we have spoken slander. We have acted perversely, we have acted wickedly, we have acted presumptuously, we have been violent, we have framed lies. We have given bad advice, we have deceived, we have scorned, we have rebelled, we have provoked, we have turned away, we have committed iniquity, we have transgressed, we have persecuted, we have been obstinate. We have acted wickedly, we have corrupted, we have acted abominably, we have strayed, we have led others astray.

סַרְנוּ We have turned away from Your commandments, and good laws, to no
avail, for You are just in all that has befallen us, for You have acted faithfully *Neh. 9*
while we have done wickedly.

הִרְשַׁעְנוּ We have been wicked and we have done wrong, and so we have not
been saved. Place it in our hearts to abandon the way of wickedness, and
hasten our salvation, as is written by Your prophet, "Let each wicked person *Is. 55*
abandon his ways, each man of iniquity his thoughts, and let him come back
to the LORD and He will have compassion for him; back to our God for He
will forgive abundantly."

מְשִׁיחַ Your righteous anointed one said to You, "Who can discern his own *Ps. 19*
mistakes? Cleanse me of my hidden faults." Cleanse us, LORD our God, of all
our sins, and purify us of all our impurities and throw clear waters over us to
purify us, as was written by Your prophet, "I shall throw clear waters over you *Ezek. 36*
and you shall be pure. I shall purify you of all your impurities and of all your
idolatry." Your people, Your inheritance, famished of Your good, thirsting for
Your loving-kindness, craving Your salvation – they shall recognize and know
that compassion and forgiveness belong to the LORD our God.

*On days when Taḥanun is not said (such as on the morning of a Brit Mila, or when a bridegroom is present), continue with Avinu Malkenu on page 202 followed by Half Kaddish (page 222).*

וידוי

## אֱלֹהֵינוּ וֵאלֹהֵי אֲבוֹתֵינוּ
## תָּבֹא לְפָנֶיךָ תְּפִלָּתֵנוּ, וְאַל תִּתְעַלַּם מִתְּחִנָּתֵנוּ.
## שֶׁאֵין אֲנוּ עַזֵּי פָנִים וּקְשֵׁי עֹרֶף לוֹמַר לְפָנֶיךָ
## יהוה אֱלֹהֵינוּ וֵאלֹהֵי אֲבוֹתֵינוּ, צַדִּיקִים אֲנַחְנוּ וְלֹא חָטָאנוּ.
## אֲבָל אֲנַחְנוּ וַאֲבוֹתֵינוּ חָטָאנוּ.

*Strike the left side of the chest with the right fist while saying each of the sins.*

**אָשַׁמְנוּ, בָּגַדְנוּ, גָּזַלְנוּ, דִּבַּרְנוּ דֹפִי. הֶעֱוִינוּ, וְהִרְשַׁעְנוּ, זַדְנוּ, חָמַסְנוּ, טָפַלְנוּ שֶׁקֶר. יָעַצְנוּ רָע, כִּזַּבְנוּ, לַצְנוּ, מָרַדְנוּ, נִאַצְנוּ, סָרַרְנוּ, עָוִינוּ, פָּשַׁעְנוּ, צָרַרְנוּ, קִשִּׁינוּ עֹרֶף. רָשַׁעְנוּ, שִׁחַתְנוּ, תִּעַבְנוּ, תָּעִינוּ, תִּעְתָּעְנוּ.**

סַרְנוּ מִמִּצְוֹתֶיךָ וּמִמִּשְׁפָּטֶיךָ הַטּוֹבִים, וְלֹא שָׁוָה לָנוּ. וְאַתָּה צַדִּיק עַל נחמיה ט
כָּל־הַבָּא עָלֵינוּ, כִּי־אֱמֶת עָשִׂיתָ וַאֲנַחְנוּ הִרְשָׁעְנוּ.

הִרְשַׁעְנוּ וּפָשַׁעְנוּ לָכֵן לֹא נוֹשָׁעְנוּ. וְתֵן בְּלִבֵּנוּ לַעֲזֹב דֶּרֶךְ רֶשַׁע, וְחִישׁ
לָנוּ יֶשַׁע, כַּכָּתוּב עַל יַד נְבִיאֶךָ: יַעֲזֹב רָשָׁע דַּרְכּוֹ וְאִישׁ אָוֶן מַחְשְׁבֹתָיו, ישעיה נה
וְיָשֹׁב אֶל־יהוה וִירַחֲמֵהוּ וְאֶל־אֱלֹהֵינוּ כִּי־יַרְבֶּה לִסְלוֹחַ:

מְשִׁיחַ צִדְקֶךָ אָמַר לְפָנֶיךָ: שְׁגִיאוֹת מִי־יָבִין, מִנִּסְתָּרוֹת נַקֵּנִי: נַקֵּנוּ יהוה תהלים יט
אֱלֹהֵינוּ מִכָּל פְּשָׁעֵינוּ וְטַהֲרֵנוּ מִכָּל טֻמְאוֹתֵינוּ וּזְרֹק עָלֵינוּ מַיִם טְהוֹרִים
וְטַהֲרֵנוּ, כַּכָּתוּב עַל יַד נְבִיאֶךָ: וְזָרַקְתִּי עֲלֵיכֶם מַיִם טְהוֹרִים וּטְהַרְתֶּם, יחזקאל לו
מִכֹּל טֻמְאוֹתֵיכֶם וּמִכָּל־גִּלּוּלֵיכֶם אֲטַהֵר אֶתְכֶם: עַמְּךָ וְנַחֲלָתְךָ רְעֵבֵי
טוּבְךָ, צְמֵאֵי חַסְדֶּךָ, תְּאֵבֵי יִשְׁעֶךָ. יַכִּירוּ וְיֵדְעוּ, כִּי לַיהוה אֱלֹהֵינוּ
הָרַחֲמִים וְהַסְּלִיחוֹת.

*On days when* תחנון *is not said (such as on the morning of a* ברית מילה*, or when a* חתן *is present), continue with* אבינו מלכנו *on page 203 followed by* חצי קדיש *(page 223).*

אֵל רַחוּם Compassionate God is Your name; Gracious God is Your name. We are called by Your name; LORD, act for the sake of Your name. Act for the sake of Your truth. Act for the sake of Your covenant. Act for the sake of Your greatness and glory. Act for the sake of Your Law. Act for the sake of Your majesty. Act for the sake of Your promise. Act for the sake of Your remembrance. Act for the sake of Your loving-kindness. Act for the sake of Your goodness. Act for the sake of Your Oneness. Act for the sake of Your honor. Act for the sake of Your wisdom. Act for the sake of Your kingship. Act for the sake of Your eternity. Act for the sake of Your mystery. Act for the sake of Your might. Act for the sake of Your splendor. Act for the sake of Your righteousness. Act for the sake of Your holiness. Act for the sake of Your great compassion. Act for the sake of Your Presence. Act for the sake of Your praise. Act for the sake of those who loved You, who now dwell in the dust. Act for the sake of Abraham, Isaac and Jacob. Act for the sake of Moses and Aaron. Act for the sake of David and Solomon. Act for the sake of Jerusalem, Your holy city. Act for the sake of Zion, the dwelling place of Your glory. Act for the sake of the desolate site of Your Temple. Act for the sake of the ruins of Your altar. Act for the sake of those killed in sanctification of Your name. Act for the sake of those slaughtered over Your unity. Act for the sake of those who have gone through fire and water in sanctification of Your name. Act for the sake of suckling infants who have not sinned. Act for the sake of little ones just weaned who have done no wrong. Act for the sake of schoolchildren. Act for Your own sake if not for ours. Act for Your own sake, and save us.

עֲנֵנוּ Answer us, LORD, answer us. Answer us, our God, answer us. Answer us, our Father, answer us. Answer us, our Creator, answer us. Answer us, our Redeemer, answer us. Answer us, You who seek us, answer us. Answer us, God who is faithful, answer us. Answer us, You who are ancient and kind, answer us. Answer us, You who are pure and upright, answer us. Answer us, You who are alive and remain, answer us. Answer us, You who are good and do good, answer us. Answer us, You who know our impulses, answer us. Answer us, You who conquer rage, answer us. Answer us, You who clothe Yourself in righteousness, answer us. Answer us, Supreme King of kings, answer us. Answer us, You who are awesome and elevated, answer us. Answer us, You who forgive and pardon, answer us. Answer us, You who answer in times of trouble, answer us. Answer us, You who redeem and save, answer us. Answer us, You who are righteous and straightforward, answer us. Answer us, You who are close to those who call, answer us. Answer us, You who are compassionate and gracious, answer us. Answer us, You who listen to the destitute, answer us. Answer us, You who support the innocent, answer us. Answer us, God of our fathers, answer us. Answer us, God of Abraham, answer us. Answer us, Terror of Isaac, answer us. Answer us, Champion of Jacob, answer us. Answer us, Help of the tribes, answer us. Answer us, Stronghold of the mothers, answer us. Answer us, You who are slow to anger, answer us. Answer us, You who are lightly appeased, answer us. Answer us, You who answer at times of favor, answer us. Answer us, Father of orphans, answer us. Answer us, Justice of widows, answer us.

אֵל רַחוּם שְׁמֶךָ. אֵל חַנּוּן שְׁמֶךָ. בָּנוּ נִקְרָא שְׁמֶךָ. יהוה עֲשֵׂה לְמַעַן שְׁמֶךָ. עֲשֵׂה לְמַעַן אֲמִתָּךְ. עֲשֵׂה לְמַעַן בְּרִיתָךְ. עֲשֵׂה לְמַעַן גָּדְלָךְ וְתִפְאַרְתָּךְ. עֲשֵׂה לְמַעַן דָּתָךְ. עֲשֵׂה לְמַעַן הוֹדָךְ. עֲשֵׂה לְמַעַן וִעוּדָךְ. עֲשֵׂה לְמַעַן זִכְרָךְ. עֲשֵׂה לְמַעַן חַסְדָּךְ. עֲשֵׂה לְמַעַן טוּבָךְ. עֲשֵׂה לְמַעַן יִחוּדָךְ. עֲשֵׂה לְמַעַן כְּבוֹדָךְ. עֲשֵׂה לְמַעַן לִמּוּדָךְ. עֲשֵׂה לְמַעַן מַלְכוּתָךְ. עֲשֵׂה לְמַעַן נִצְחָךְ. עֲשֵׂה לְמַעַן סוֹדָךְ. עֲשֵׂה לְמַעַן עֻזָּךְ. עֲשֵׂה לְמַעַן פְּאֵרָךְ. עֲשֵׂה לְמַעַן צִדְקָתָךְ. עֲשֵׂה לְמַעַן קְדֻשָּׁתָךְ. עֲשֵׂה לְמַעַן רַחֲמֶיךָ הָרַבִּים. עֲשֵׂה לְמַעַן שְׁכִינָתָךְ. עֲשֵׂה לְמַעַן תְּהִלָּתָךְ. עֲשֵׂה לְמַעַן אוֹהֲבֶיךָ שׁוֹכְנֵי עָפָר. עֲשֵׂה לְמַעַן אַבְרָהָם יִצְחָק וְיַעֲקֹב. עֲשֵׂה לְמַעַן מֹשֶׁה וְאַהֲרֹן. עֲשֵׂה לְמַעַן דָּוִד וּשְׁלֹמֹה. עֲשֵׂה לְמַעַן יְרוּשָׁלַיִם עִיר קָדְשֶׁךָ. עֲשֵׂה לְמַעַן צִיּוֹן מִשְׁכַּן כְּבוֹדֶךָ. עֲשֵׂה לְמַעַן שִׁמְמוֹת הֵיכָלֶךָ. עֲשֵׂה לְמַעַן הֲרִיסוּת מִזְבְּחֶךָ. עֲשֵׂה לְמַעַן הֲרוּגִים עַל שֵׁם קָדְשֶׁךָ. עֲשֵׂה לְמַעַן טְבוּחִים עַל יִחוּדֶךָ. עֲשֵׂה לְמַעַן בָּאֵי בָאֵשׁ וּבַמַּיִם עַל קִדּוּשׁ שְׁמֶךָ. עֲשֵׂה לְמַעַן יוֹנְקֵי שָׁדַיִם שֶׁלֹּא חָטְאוּ. עֲשֵׂה לְמַעַן גְּמוּלֵי חָלָב שֶׁלֹּא פָשְׁעוּ. עֲשֵׂה לְמַעַן תִּינוֹקוֹת שֶׁל בֵּית רַבָּן. עֲשֵׂה לְמַעַנְךָ אִם לֹא לְמַעֲנֵנוּ. עֲשֵׂה לְמַעַנְךָ וְהוֹשִׁיעֵנוּ.

עֲנֵנוּ יהוה עֲנֵנוּ. עֲנֵנוּ אֱלֹהֵינוּ עֲנֵנוּ. עֲנֵנוּ אָבִינוּ עֲנֵנוּ. עֲנֵנוּ בּוֹרְאֵנוּ עֲנֵנוּ. עֲנֵנוּ גּוֹאֲלֵנוּ עֲנֵנוּ. עֲנֵנוּ דּוֹרְשֵׁנוּ עֲנֵנוּ. עֲנֵנוּ הָאֵל הַנֶּאֱמָן עֲנֵנוּ. עֲנֵנוּ וָתִיק וְחָסִיד עֲנֵנוּ. עֲנֵנוּ זַךְ וְיָשָׁר עֲנֵנוּ. עֲנֵנוּ חַי וְקַיָּם עֲנֵנוּ. עֲנֵנוּ טוֹב וּמֵטִיב עֲנֵנוּ. עֲנֵנוּ יוֹדֵעַ יֵצֶר עֲנֵנוּ. עֲנֵנוּ כּוֹבֵשׁ כְּעָסִים עֲנֵנוּ. עֲנֵנוּ לוֹבֵשׁ צְדָקוֹת עֲנֵנוּ. עֲנֵנוּ מֶלֶךְ מַלְכֵי הַמְּלָכִים עֲנֵנוּ. עֲנֵנוּ נוֹרָא וְנִשְׂגָּב עֲנֵנוּ. עֲנֵנוּ סוֹלֵחַ וּמוֹחֵל עֲנֵנוּ. עֲנֵנוּ עוֹנֶה בְּעֵת צָרָה עֲנֵנוּ. עֲנֵנוּ פּוֹדֶה וּמַצִּיל עֲנֵנוּ. עֲנֵנוּ צַדִּיק וְיָשָׁר עֲנֵנוּ. עֲנֵנוּ קָרוֹב לְקוֹרְאָיו עֲנֵנוּ. עֲנֵנוּ רַחוּם וְחַנּוּן עֲנֵנוּ. עֲנֵנוּ שׁוֹמֵעַ אֶל אֶבְיוֹנִים עֲנֵנוּ. עֲנֵנוּ תּוֹמֵךְ תְּמִימִים עֲנֵנוּ. עֲנֵנוּ אֱלֹהֵי אֲבוֹתֵינוּ עֲנֵנוּ. עֲנֵנוּ אֱלֹהֵי אַבְרָהָם עֲנֵנוּ. עֲנֵנוּ פַּחַד יִצְחָק עֲנֵנוּ. עֲנֵנוּ אֲבִיר יַעֲקֹב עֲנֵנוּ. עֲנֵנוּ עֶזְרַת הַשְּׁבָטִים עֲנֵנוּ. עֲנֵנוּ מִשְׂגַּב אִמָּהוֹת עֲנֵנוּ. עֲנֵנוּ קָשֶׁה לִכְעֹס עֲנֵנוּ. עֲנֵנוּ רַךְ לִרְצוֹת עֲנֵנוּ. עֲנֵנוּ עוֹנֶה בְּעֵת רָצוֹן עֲנֵנוּ. עֲנֵנוּ אֲבִי יְתוֹמִים עֲנֵנוּ. עֲנֵנוּ דַּיַּן אַלְמָנוֹת עֲנֵנוּ.

מִי שֶׁעָנָה The One who answered Abraham our father on Mount Moriah – answer us.
The One who answered Isaac his son, when he was bound upon the altar – answer us.
The One who answered Jacob in Beth-El – answer us.
The One who answered Joseph in prison – answer us.
The One who answered our fathers at the Reed Sea – answer us.
The One who answered Moses at Horeb – answer us.
The One who answered Aaron over his firepan – answer us.
The One who answered Pinehas when he stood up from among the congregation – answer us.
The One who answered Joshua at Gilgal – answer us.
The One who answered Samuel at Mitzpah – answer us.
The One who answered David and Solomon his son in Jerusalem – answer us.
The One who answered Elijah on Mount Carmel – answer us.
The One who answered Elisha at Jericho – answer us.
The One who answered Jonah in the belly of the fish – answer us.
The One who answered Hezekiah the king of Judah in his illness – answer us.
The One who answered Hananiah, Mishael and Azariah in the furnace of fire – answer us.
The One who answered Daniel in the lions' den – answer us.
The One who answered Mordekhai and Esther in Shushan the capital city – answer us.
The One who answered Ezra in his exile – answer us.
The One who answered so many righteous, devoted, innocent and upright people – answer us.

רַחֲמָנָא Loving God, who answers the oppressed: answer us.
Loving God, who answers the broken hearted: answer us.
Loving God, who answers those of humbled spirit: answer us.
Loving God, answer us.
Loving God, spare; Loving God, release; Loving God, save us.
Loving God, have compassion for us now, swiftly, at a time soon coming.

*Continue with "Avinu Malkenu" on page 202.*

מִי שֶׁעָנָה לְאַבְרָהָם אָבִינוּ בְּהַר הַמּוֹרִיָּה, הוּא יַעֲנֵנוּ.
מִי שֶׁעָנָה לְיִצְחָק בְּנוֹ כְּשֶׁנֶּעֱקַד עַל גַּבֵּי הַמִּזְבֵּחַ, הוּא יַעֲנֵנוּ.
מִי שֶׁעָנָה לְיַעֲקֹב בְּבֵית אֵל, הוּא יַעֲנֵנוּ.
מִי שֶׁעָנָה לְיוֹסֵף בְּבֵית הָאֲסוּרִים, הוּא יַעֲנֵנוּ.
מִי שֶׁעָנָה לַאֲבוֹתֵינוּ עַל יַם סוּף, הוּא יַעֲנֵנוּ.
מִי שֶׁעָנָה לְמֹשֶׁה בְּחוֹרֵב, הוּא יַעֲנֵנוּ.
מִי שֶׁעָנָה לְאַהֲרֹן בַּמַּחְתָּה, הוּא יַעֲנֵנוּ.
מִי שֶׁעָנָה לְפִינְחָס בְּקוּמוֹ מִתּוֹךְ הָעֵדָה, הוּא יַעֲנֵנוּ.
מִי שֶׁעָנָה לִיהוֹשֻׁעַ בַּגִּלְגָּל, הוּא יַעֲנֵנוּ.
מִי שֶׁעָנָה לִשְׁמוּאֵל בַּמִּצְפָּה, הוּא יַעֲנֵנוּ.
מִי שֶׁעָנָה לְדָוִד וּשְׁלֹמֹה בְנוֹ בִּירוּשָׁלָיִם, הוּא יַעֲנֵנוּ.
מִי שֶׁעָנָה לְאֵלִיָּהוּ בְּהַר הַכַּרְמֶל, הוּא יַעֲנֵנוּ.
מִי שֶׁעָנָה לֶאֱלִישָׁע בִּירִיחוֹ, הוּא יַעֲנֵנוּ.
מִי שֶׁעָנָה לְיוֹנָה בִּמְעֵי הַדָּגָה, הוּא יַעֲנֵנוּ.
מִי שֶׁעָנָה לְחִזְקִיָּהוּ מֶלֶךְ יְהוּדָה בְּחָלְיוֹ, הוּא יַעֲנֵנוּ.
מִי שֶׁעָנָה לַחֲנַנְיָה מִישָׁאֵל וַעֲזַרְיָה בְּתוֹךְ כִּבְשַׁן הָאֵשׁ, הוּא יַעֲנֵנוּ.
מִי שֶׁעָנָה לְדָנִיֵּאל בְּגוֹב הָאֲרָיוֹת, הוּא יַעֲנֵנוּ.
מִי שֶׁעָנָה לְמָרְדְּכַי וְאֶסְתֵּר בְּשׁוּשַׁן הַבִּירָה, הוּא יַעֲנֵנוּ.
מִי שֶׁעָנָה לְעֶזְרָא בַּגּוֹלָה, הוּא יַעֲנֵנוּ.
מִי שֶׁעָנָה לְכָל הַצַּדִּיקִים וְהַחֲסִידִים וְהַתְּמִימִים וְהַיְשָׁרִים, הוּא יַעֲנֵנוּ.

רַחֲמָנָא דְּעָנֵי לַעֲנִיֵּי עֲנֵינָן.
רַחֲמָנָא דְּעָנֵי לִתְבִירֵי לִבָּא עֲנֵינָן.
רַחֲמָנָא דְּעָנֵי לְמַכִּיכֵי רוּחָא עֲנֵינָן.
רַחֲמָנָא עֲנֵינָן.
רַחֲמָנָא חוּס, רַחֲמָנָא פְּרֹק, רַחֲמָנָא שֵׁיזִב.
רַחֲמָנָא רַחֵם עֲלָן, הַשְׁתָּא בַּעֲגָלָא וּבִזְמַן קָרִיב.

*Continue with* אבינו מלכנו *on page 203.*

# ברכות
## GIVING THANKS


| | | |
|---|---|---|
| ברכת המזון | 1057 | BIRKAT HAMAZON |
| ברכות המצוות | 1077 | BLESSINGS ON MITZVOT |
| ברכות הנהנין, הראייה והשמיעה | 1079 | BLESSINGS ON PLEASURES, SIGHTS AND SOUNDS |
| סדר חנוכת הבית | 1089 | CONSECRATION OF A HOME |
| תפילת הדרך | 1089 | THE TRAVELER'S PRAYER |

## THE MEAL AND ITS BLESSINGS

*On washing hands before eating bread (see laws 409–413):*

Blessed are You, LORD our God, King of the Universe,
who has made us holy through His commandments,
and has commanded us about washing hands.

*Before eating bread:*

Blessed are You, LORD our God, King of the Universe,
who brings forth bread from the earth.

## BIRKAT HAMAZON / GRACE AFTER MEALS

*On days when Taḥanun is said:*

עַל־נַהֲרוֹת By the rivers of Babylon we sat and wept as we remembered Zion. *Ps. 137* There on the willow trees we hung up our harps, for there our captors asked us for songs, our tormentors, for amusement, said: "Sing us one of the songs of Zion!" How can we sing the LORD's song on foreign soil? If I forget you, Jerusalem, may my right hand forget its skill. May my tongue cling to the roof of my mouth if I do not remember you, if I do not set Jerusalem above my highest joy. Remember, LORD, what the Edomites did on the day Jerusalem fell. They said, "Tear it down, tear it down to its very foundations!" Daughter of Babylon, doomed to destruction, happy is he who repays you for what you have done to us, who seizes your infants and dashes them against the rocks.

*On days when Taḥanun is omitted (such as Shabbat and Yom Tov, see full list on page 208):*

שִׁיר הַמַּעֲלוֹת A song of ascents. When the LORD brought back the exiles of *Ps. 126* Zion we were like people who dream. Then were our mouths filled with laughter, and our tongues with songs of joy. Then was it said among the nations, "The LORD has done great things for them." The LORD did do great things for us and we rejoiced. Bring back our exiles, LORD, like streams in a dry land. May those who sowed in tears, reap in joy. May one who goes out weeping, carrying a bag of seed, come back with songs of joy, carrying his sheaves.

*Some say:*

תְּהִלַּת My mouth shall speak the praise of God, and all creatures shall bless *Ps. 145*
His holy name for ever and all time. We will bless God now and for ever. *Ps. 115*
Halleluya! Thank the LORD for He is good; His loving-kindness is for ever. *Ps. 136*
Who can tell of the LORD's mighty acts and make all His praise be heard? *Ps. 106*

# סדר סעודה וברכותיה

*On washing hands before eating bread (see laws 409–413):*

בָּרוּךְ אַתָּה יהוה אֱלֹהֵינוּ מֶלֶךְ הָעוֹלָם
אֲשֶׁר קִדְּשָׁנוּ בְּמִצְוֹתָיו, וְצִוָּנוּ עַל נְטִילַת יָדָיִם.

*Before eating bread:*

בָּרוּךְ אַתָּה יהוה אֱלֹהֵינוּ מֶלֶךְ הָעוֹלָם
הַמּוֹצִיא לֶחֶם מִן הָאָרֶץ.

# ברכת המזון

*On days when תחנון is said:*

עַל־נַהֲרוֹת בָּבֶל, שָׁם יָשַׁבְנוּ גַּם־בָּכִינוּ, בְּזָכְרֵנוּ אֶת־צִיּוֹן: עַל־עֲרָבִים בְּתוֹכָהּ תהלים קלז
תָּלִינוּ כִּנֹּרוֹתֵינוּ: כִּי שָׁם שְׁאֵלוּנוּ שׁוֹבֵינוּ דִּבְרֵי־שִׁיר וְתוֹלָלֵינוּ שִׂמְחָה, שִׁירוּ
לָנוּ מִשִּׁיר צִיּוֹן: אֵיךְ נָשִׁיר אֶת־שִׁיר־יהוה עַל אַדְמַת נֵכָר: אִם־אֶשְׁכָּחֵךְ
יְרוּשָׁלָםִ, תִּשְׁכַּח יְמִינִי: תִּדְבַּק לְשׁוֹנִי לְחִכִּי אִם־לֹא אֶזְכְּרֵכִי, אִם־לֹא אַעֲלֶה
אֶת־יְרוּשָׁלַםִ עַל רֹאשׁ שִׂמְחָתִי: זְכֹר יהוה לִבְנֵי אֱדוֹם אֵת יוֹם יְרוּשָׁלָםִ,
הָאֹמְרִים עָרוּ עָרוּ עַד הַיְסוֹד בָּהּ: בַּת־בָּבֶל הַשְּׁדוּדָה, אַשְׁרֵי שֶׁיְשַׁלֶּם־לָךְ
אֶת־גְּמוּלֵךְ שֶׁגָּמַלְתְּ לָנוּ: אַשְׁרֵי שֶׁיֹּאחֵז, וְנִפֵּץ אֶת־עֹלָלַיִךְ אֶל־הַסָּלַע:

*On days when תחנון is omitted (such as שבת and יום טוב, see full list on page 209):*

שִׁיר הַמַּעֲלוֹת, בְּשׁוּב יהוה אֶת־שִׁיבַת צִיּוֹן, הָיִינוּ כְּחֹלְמִים: אָז יִמָּלֵא שְׂחוֹק תהלים קכו
פִּינוּ וּלְשׁוֹנֵנוּ רִנָּה, אָז יֹאמְרוּ בַגּוֹיִם הִגְדִּיל יהוה לַעֲשׂוֹת עִם־אֵלֶּה: הִגְדִּיל
יהוה לַעֲשׂוֹת עִמָּנוּ, הָיִינוּ שְׂמֵחִים: שׁוּבָה יהוה אֶת־שְׁבִיתֵנוּ, כַּאֲפִיקִים
בַּנֶּגֶב: הַזֹּרְעִים בְּדִמְעָה בְּרִנָּה יִקְצֹרוּ: הָלוֹךְ יֵלֵךְ וּבָכֹה נֹשֵׂא מֶשֶׁךְ־הַזָּרַע,
בֹּא־יָבֹא בְרִנָּה נֹשֵׂא אֲלֻמֹּתָיו:

*Some say:*

תְּהִלַּת יהוה יְדַבֶּר פִּי, וִיבָרֵךְ כָּל־בָּשָׂר שֵׁם קָדְשׁוֹ לְעוֹלָם וָעֶד: וַאֲנַחְנוּ נְבָרֵךְ תהלים קמה תהלים קטו
יָהּ מֵעַתָּה וְעַד־עוֹלָם, הַלְלוּיָהּ: הוֹדוּ לַיהוה כִּי־טוֹב, כִּי לְעוֹלָם חַסְדּוֹ: מִי תהלים קלו תהלים קו
יְמַלֵּל גְּבוּרוֹת יהוה, יַשְׁמִיעַ כָּל־תְּהִלָּתוֹ:

## ZIMMUN / INVITATION

*For the zimmun said at a wedding or during the week of Sheva Berakhot,* *see page 1120.* *At a Brit,* *see page 1098.* *In the house of a mourner when there are three or more men,* *see page 1146.*

*When three or more men say Birkat HaMazon together, the following zimmun is said. When three or more women say Birkat HaMazon, substitute "Friends" for "Gentlemen." The leader should ask permission from those with precedence to lead the Birkat HaMazon.*

*Leader* Gentlemen, let us say grace.

*Others* May the name of the LORD be blessed from now and for ever. *Ps. 113*

*Leader* May the name of the LORD be blessed from now and for ever.
With your permission, (my father and teacher / my mother and teacher / the Kohanim present / our teacher the Rabbi / the master of this house / the mistress of this house)
my masters and teachers,
let us bless (*in a minyan:* our God,)
the One from whose food we have eaten.

*Others* Blessed be (*in a minyan:* our God,) the One from whose food we have eaten, and by whose goodness we live.

**People present who have not taken part in the meal say:*
*Blessed be (*in a minyan:* our God,) the One whose name is continually blessed for ever and all time.

*Leader* Blessed be (*in a minyan:* our God,) the One from whose food we have eaten, and by whose goodness we live.
Blessed be He, and blessed be His name.

### BLESSING OF NOURISHMENT

בָּרוּךְ Blessed are You, LORD our God, King of the Universe,
who in His goodness feeds the whole world
with grace, kindness and compassion.
He gives food to all living things, for His kindness is for ever.
Because of His continual great goodness,
we have never lacked food,
nor may we ever lack it, for the sake of His great name.
For He is God who feeds and sustains all, does good to all,
and prepares food for all creatures He has created.
Blessed are You, LORD, who feeds all.

# סדר הזימון

*For the* זימון *said at a wedding or during the week of* שבע ברכות, *see page 1121.*
*At a* ברית, *see page 1099. In a* בית אבל *when there are three or more men, see page 1147.*

*When three or more men say* ברכת המזון *together, the following* זימון *is said.*
*When three or more women say* ברכת המזון, *substitute* חֲבֵרוֹתַי *for* רַבּוֹתַי.
*The leader should ask permission from those with precedence to lead the* ברכת המזון.

*Leader* רַבּוֹתַי, נְבָרֵךְ.

*Others* יְהִי שֵׁם יהוה מְבֹרָךְ מֵעַתָּה וְעַד־עוֹלָם: תהלים קיג

*Leader* יְהִי שֵׁם יהוה מְבֹרָךְ מֵעַתָּה וְעַד־עוֹלָם:
בִּרְשׁוּת (אָבִי מוֹרִי / אִמִּי מוֹרָתִי / כֹּהֲנִים / מוֹרֵנוּ הָרַב /
בַּעַל הַבַּיִת הַזֶּה / בַּעֲלַת הַבַּיִת הַזֶּה)
מָרָנָן וְרַבָּנָן וְרַבּוֹתַי, נְבָרֵךְ (במנין: אֱלֹהֵינוּ) שֶׁאָכַלְנוּ מִשֶּׁלּוֹ.

*Others* בָּרוּךְ (במנין: אֱלֹהֵינוּ) שֶׁאָכַלְנוּ מִשֶּׁלּוֹ וּבְטוּבוֹ חָיִינוּ.

**People present who have not taken part in the meal say:*
*בָּרוּךְ (במנין: אֱלֹהֵינוּ) וּמְבֹרָךְ שְׁמוֹ תָּמִיד לְעוֹלָם וָעֶד.

*Leader* בָּרוּךְ (במנין: אֱלֹהֵינוּ) שֶׁאָכַלְנוּ מִשֶּׁלּוֹ וּבְטוּבוֹ חָיִינוּ.
בָּרוּךְ הוּא וּבָרוּךְ שְׁמוֹ.

ברכת הזן

בָּרוּךְ אַתָּה יהוה אֱלֹהֵינוּ מֶלֶךְ הָעוֹלָם
הַזָּן אֶת הָעוֹלָם כֻּלּוֹ בְּטוּבוֹ
בְּחֵן בְּחֶסֶד וּבְרַחֲמִים
הוּא נוֹתֵן לֶחֶם לְכָל בָּשָׂר כִּי לְעוֹלָם חַסְדּוֹ.
וּבְטוּבוֹ הַגָּדוֹל, תָּמִיד לֹא חָסַר לָנוּ
וְאַל יֶחְסַר לָנוּ מָזוֹן לְעוֹלָם וָעֶד, בַּעֲבוּר שְׁמוֹ הַגָּדוֹל.
כִּי הוּא אֵל זָן וּמְפַרְנֵס לַכֹּל וּמֵטִיב לַכֹּל
וּמֵכִין מָזוֹן לְכָל בְּרִיּוֹתָיו אֲשֶׁר בָּרָא.
בָּרוּךְ אַתָּה יהוה, הַזָּן אֶת הַכֹּל.

BLESSING OF LAND

נוֹדֶה We thank You, LORD our God,
for having granted as a heritage to our ancestors
a desirable, good and spacious land;
for bringing us out, LORD our God, from the land of Egypt,
freeing us from the house of slavery;
for Your covenant which You sealed in our flesh;
for Your Torah which You taught us;
for Your laws which You made known to us;
for the life, grace and kindness You have bestowed on us;
and for the food by which You continually feed and sustain us,
every day, every season, every hour.

---

*On Ḥanukka:*

עַל הַנִּסִּים [We thank You also] for the miracles, the redemption, the mighty deeds, the salvations, and the victories in battle which You performed for our ancestors in those days, at this time.

בִּימֵי מַתִּתְיָהוּ In the days of Mattityahu, son of Yoḥanan, the High Priest, the Hasmonean, and his sons, the wicked Greek kingdom rose up against Your people Israel to make them forget Your Torah and to force them to transgress the statutes of Your will. It was then that You in Your great compassion stood by them in the time of their distress. You championed their cause, judged their claim, and avenged their wrong. You delivered the strong into the hands of the weak, the many into the hands of the few, the impure into the hands of the pure, the wicked into the hands of the righteous, and the arrogant into the hands of those who were engaged in the study of Your Torah. You made for Yourself great and holy renown in Your world, and for Your people Israel You performed a great salvation and redemption as of this very day. Your children then entered the holiest part of Your House, cleansed Your Temple, purified Your Sanctuary, kindled lights in Your holy courts, and designated these eight days of Ḥanukka for giving thanks and praise to Your great name.

*Continue with "For all this."*

*On Purim:*

עַל הַנִּסִּים [We thank You also] for the miracles, the redemption, the mighty deeds, the salvations, and the victories in battle which You performed for our ancestors in those days, at this time.

בִּימֵי מָרְדְּכַי In the days of Mordekhai and Esther, in Shushan the capital, the wicked Haman rose up against them and sought to destroy, slay and *Esther 3*

## ברכת הארץ

**נוֹדֶה לְּךָ, יהוה אֱלֹהֵינוּ**
**עַל שֶׁהִנְחַלְתָּ לַאֲבוֹתֵינוּ אֶרֶץ חֶמְדָּה טוֹבָה וּרְחָבָה**
**וְעַל שֶׁהוֹצֵאתָנוּ יהוה אֱלֹהֵינוּ מֵאֶרֶץ מִצְרַיִם**
**וּפְדִיתָנוּ מִבֵּית עֲבָדִים**
**וְעַל בְּרִיתְךָ שֶׁחָתַמְתָּ בִּבְשָׂרֵנוּ**
**וְעַל תּוֹרָתְךָ שֶׁלִּמַּדְתָּנוּ, וְעַל חֻקֶּיךָ שֶׁהוֹדַעְתָּנוּ**
**וְעַל חַיִּים חֵן וָחֶסֶד שֶׁחוֹנַנְתָּנוּ**
**וְעַל אֲכִילַת מָזוֹן שָׁאַתָּה זָן וּמְפַרְנֵס אוֹתָנוּ תָּמִיד**
**בְּכָל יוֹם וּבְכָל עֵת וּבְכָל שָׁעָה.**

---

בחנוכה:

עַל הַנִּסִּים וְעַל הַפֻּרְקָן וְעַל הַגְּבוּרוֹת וְעַל הַתְּשׁוּעוֹת וְעַל הַמִּלְחָמוֹת שֶׁעָשִׂיתָ לַאֲבוֹתֵינוּ בַּיָּמִים הָהֵם בַּזְּמַן הַזֶּה.

בִּימֵי מַתִּתְיָהוּ בֶּן יוֹחָנָן כֹּהֵן גָּדוֹל חַשְׁמוֹנַאי וּבָנָיו, כְּשֶׁעָמְדָה מַלְכוּת יָוָן הָרְשָׁעָה עַל עַמְּךָ יִשְׂרָאֵל לְהַשְׁכִּיחָם תּוֹרָתֶךָ וּלְהַעֲבִירָם מֵחֻקֵּי רְצוֹנֶךָ, וְאַתָּה בְּרַחֲמֶיךָ הָרַבִּים עָמַדְתָּ לָהֶם בְּעֵת צָרָתָם, רַבְתָּ אֶת רִיבָם, דַּנְתָּ אֶת דִּינָם, נָקַמְתָּ אֶת נִקְמָתָם, מָסַרְתָּ גִּבּוֹרִים בְּיַד חַלָּשִׁים, וְרַבִּים בְּיַד מְעַטִּים, וּטְמֵאִים בְּיַד טְהוֹרִים, וּרְשָׁעִים בְּיַד צַדִּיקִים, וְזֵדִים בְּיַד עוֹסְקֵי תוֹרָתֶךָ, וּלְךָ עָשִׂיתָ שֵׁם גָּדוֹל וְקָדוֹשׁ בְּעוֹלָמֶךָ, וּלְעַמְּךָ יִשְׂרָאֵל עָשִׂיתָ תְּשׁוּעָה גְדוֹלָה וּפֻרְקָן כְּהַיּוֹם הַזֶּה. וְאַחַר כֵּן בָּאוּ בָנֶיךָ לִדְבִיר בֵּיתֶךָ, וּפִנּוּ אֶת הֵיכָלֶךָ, וְטִהֲרוּ אֶת מִקְדָּשֶׁךָ, וְהִדְלִיקוּ נֵרוֹת בְּחַצְרוֹת קָדְשֶׁךָ, וְקָבְעוּ שְׁמוֹנַת יְמֵי חֲנֻכָּה אֵלּוּ, לְהוֹדוֹת וּלְהַלֵּל לְשִׁמְךָ הַגָּדוֹל.

*Continue with* .וְעַל הַכֹּל

בפורים:

עַל הַנִּסִּים וְעַל הַפֻּרְקָן וְעַל הַגְּבוּרוֹת וְעַל הַתְּשׁוּעוֹת וְעַל הַמִּלְחָמוֹת שֶׁעָשִׂיתָ לַאֲבוֹתֵינוּ בַּיָּמִים הָהֵם בַּזְּמַן הַזֶּה.

בִּימֵי מָרְדְּכַי וְאֶסְתֵּר בְּשׁוּשַׁן הַבִּירָה, כְּשֶׁעָמַד עֲלֵיהֶם הָמָן הָרָשָׁע, בִּקֵּשׁ
לְהַשְׁמִיד לַהֲרֹג וּלְאַבֵּד אֶת־כָּל־הַיְּהוּדִים מִנַּעַר וְעַד־זָקֵן טַף וְנָשִׁים בְּיוֹם אסתר ג

exterminate all the Jews, young and old, children and women, on one day, the thirteenth day of the twelfth month, which is the month of Adar, and to plunder their possessions. Then You in Your great compassion thwarted his counsel, frustrated his plans, and caused his scheme to recoil on his own head, so that they hanged him and his sons on the gallows.

*Continue with "For all this."*

---

וְעַל הַכֹּל For all this, LORD our God,
we thank and bless You.
May Your name be blessed continually
by the mouth of all that lives, for ever and all time –
for so it is written: "You will eat and be satisfied, then you shall bless the LORD your God for the good land He has given you." *Deut. 8*
Blessed are You, LORD, for the land and for the food.

BLESSING FOR JERUSALEM

רַחֵם נָא Have compassion,
please, LORD our God,
on Israel Your people,
on Jerusalem Your city,
on Zion the dwelling place of Your glory,
on the royal house of David Your anointed,
and on the great and holy House that bears Your name.
Our God, our Father,
tend us, feed us,
sustain us and support us,
relieve us and send us relief,
LORD our God,
swiftly from all our troubles.
Please, LORD our God,
do not make us dependent
on the gifts or loans of other people,
but only on Your full, open, holy and generous hand
so that we may suffer neither shame nor humiliation
for ever and all time.

אֶחָד, בִּשְׁלוֹשָׁה עָשָׂר לְחֹדֶשׁ שְׁנֵים־עָשָׂר, הוּא־חֹדֶשׁ אֲדָר, וּשְׁלָלָם לָבוֹז: וְאַתָּה בְּרַחֲמֶיךָ הָרַבִּים הֵפַרְתָּ אֶת עֲצָתוֹ, וְקִלְקַלְתָּ אֶת מַחֲשַׁבְתּוֹ, וַהֲשֵׁבוֹתָ לּוֹ גְּמוּלוֹ בְּרֹאשׁוֹ, וְתָלוּ אוֹתוֹ וְאֶת בָּנָיו עַל הָעֵץ.

*Continue with* וְעַל הַכֹּל.

וְעַל הַכֹּל, יהוה אֱלֹהֵינוּ
אֲנַחְנוּ מוֹדִים לָךְ וּמְבָרְכִים אוֹתָךְ
יִתְבָּרַךְ שִׁמְךָ בְּפִי כָּל חַי תָּמִיד לְעוֹלָם וָעֶד
כַּכָּתוּב: וְאָכַלְתָּ וְשָׂבָעְתָּ, וּבֵרַכְתָּ אֶת־יהוה אֱלֹהֶיךָ דברים ח
עַל־הָאָרֶץ הַטֹּבָה אֲשֶׁר נָתַן־לָךְ:
בָּרוּךְ אַתָּה יהוה, עַל הָאָרֶץ וְעַל הַמָּזוֹן.

ברכת ירושלים

רַחֵם נָא, יהוה אֱלֹהֵינוּ
עַל יִשְׂרָאֵל עַמֶּךָ
וְעַל יְרוּשָׁלַיִם עִירֶךָ
וְעַל צִיּוֹן מִשְׁכַּן כְּבוֹדֶךָ
וְעַל מַלְכוּת בֵּית דָּוִד מְשִׁיחֶךָ
וְעַל הַבַּיִת הַגָּדוֹל וְהַקָּדוֹשׁ שֶׁנִּקְרָא שִׁמְךָ עָלָיו.
אֱלֹהֵינוּ, אָבִינוּ
רְעֵנוּ, זוּנֵנוּ, פַּרְנְסֵנוּ וְכַלְכְּלֵנוּ
וְהַרְוִיחֵנוּ, וְהַרְוַח לָנוּ יהוה אֱלֹהֵינוּ מְהֵרָה מִכָּל צָרוֹתֵינוּ.
וְנָא אַל תַּצְרִיכֵנוּ, יהוה אֱלֹהֵינוּ
לֹא לִידֵי מַתְּנַת בָּשָׂר וָדָם
וְלֹא לִידֵי הַלְוָאָתָם
כִּי אִם לְיָדְךָ הַמְּלֵאָה, הַפְּתוּחָה, הַקְּדוֹשָׁה וְהָרְחָבָה
שֶׁלֹּא נֵבוֹשׁ וְלֹא נִכָּלֵם לְעוֹלָם וָעֶד.

*On Shabbat, say:*

רְצֵה Favor and strengthen us, LORD our God,
through Your commandments,
especially through the commandment of the seventh day,
this great and holy Sabbath.
For it is, for You, a great and holy day.
On it we cease work and rest in love
in accord with Your will's commandment.
May it be Your will, LORD our God,
to grant us rest without distress,
grief, or lament on our day of rest.
May You show us the consolation of Zion Your city,
and the rebuilding of Jerusalem Your holy city,
for You are the Master of salvation and consolation.

*On Rosh Ḥodesh and Festivals, say:*

אֱלֹהֵינוּ Our God and God of our ancestors,
may there rise, come, reach, appear, be favored, heard, regarded
and remembered before You, our recollection and remembrance,
as well as the remembrance of our ancestors,
and of the Messiah, son of David Your servant,
and of Jerusalem Your holy city,
and of all Your people the house of Israel –
for deliverance and well-being,
grace, loving-kindness and compassion,
life and peace, on this day of:

*On Rosh Ḥodesh:* Rosh Ḥodesh.
*On Rosh HaShana:* Remembrance.
*On Pesaḥ:* the Festival of Matzot.
*On Shavuot:* the Festival of Shavuot.
*On Sukkot:* the Festival of Sukkot.
*On Shemini Atzeret & Simḥat Torah:* the Festival of Shemini Atzeret.

On it remember us, LORD our God, for good;
recollect us for blessing, and deliver us for life.
In accord with Your promise of salvation and compassion,
spare us and be gracious to us;
have compassion on us and deliver us,
for our eyes are turned to You because You are God,
gracious and compassionate (*on Rosh HaShana:* King).

*On* שבת*, say:*

רְצֵה וְהַחֲלִיצֵנוּ, יהוה אֱלֹהֵינוּ, בְּמִצְוֹתֶיךָ
וּבְמִצְוַת יוֹם הַשְּׁבִיעִי הַשַּׁבָּת הַגָּדוֹל וְהַקָּדוֹשׁ הַזֶּה
כִּי יוֹם זֶה גָּדוֹל וְקָדוֹשׁ הוּא לְפָנֶיךָ
לִשְׁבָּת בּוֹ, וְלָנוּחַ בּוֹ בְּאַהֲבָה כְּמִצְוַת רְצוֹנֶךָ
וּבִרְצוֹנְךָ הָנִיחַ לָנוּ, יהוה אֱלֹהֵינוּ
שֶׁלֹּא תְהֵא צָרָה וְיָגוֹן וַאֲנָחָה בְּיוֹם מְנוּחָתֵנוּ
וְהַרְאֵנוּ, יהוה אֱלֹהֵינוּ, בְּנֶחָמַת צִיּוֹן עִירֶךָ
וּבְבִנְיַן יְרוּשָׁלַיִם עִיר קָדְשֶׁךָ
כִּי אַתָּה הוּא בַּעַל הַיְשׁוּעוֹת וּבַעַל הַנֶּחָמוֹת.

*On* ראש חודש *and* חגים*, say:*

אֱלֹהֵינוּ וֵאלֹהֵי אֲבוֹתֵינוּ
יַעֲלֶה וְיָבוֹא וְיַגִּיעַ, וְיֵרָאֶה וְיֵרָצֶה וְיִשָּׁמַע
וְיִפָּקֵד וְיִזָּכֵר זִכְרוֹנֵנוּ וּפִקְדוֹנֵנוּ, וְזִכְרוֹן אֲבוֹתֵינוּ
וְזִכְרוֹן מָשִׁיחַ בֶּן דָּוִד עַבְדֶּךָ
וְזִכְרוֹן יְרוּשָׁלַיִם עִיר קָדְשֶׁךָ
וְזִכְרוֹן כָּל עַמְּךָ בֵּית יִשְׂרָאֵל
לְפָנֶיךָ, לִפְלֵיטָה לְטוֹבָה, לְחֵן וּלְחֶסֶד וּלְרַחֲמִים
לְחַיִּים וּלְשָׁלוֹם בְּיוֹם

בראש חודש: רֹאשׁ הַחֹדֶשׁ הַזֶּה.

בראש השנה: הַזִּכָּרוֹן הַזֶּה.

בפסח: חַג הַמַּצּוֹת הַזֶּה.

בשבועות: חַג הַשָּׁבוּעוֹת הַזֶּה.

בסוכות: חַג הַסֻּכּוֹת הַזֶּה.

בשמיני עצרת ושמחת תורה: הַשְּׁמִינִי חַג הָעֲצֶרֶת הַזֶּה.

זָכְרֵנוּ יהוה אֱלֹהֵינוּ בּוֹ לְטוֹבָה, וּפָקְדֵנוּ בוֹ לִבְרָכָה
וְהוֹשִׁיעֵנוּ בוֹ לְחַיִּים.

וּבִדְבַר יְשׁוּעָה וְרַחֲמִים, חוּס וְחָנֵּנוּ וְרַחֵם עָלֵינוּ, וְהוֹשִׁיעֵנוּ
כִּי אֵלֶיךָ עֵינֵינוּ, כִּי אֵל (בראש השנה: מֶלֶךְ) חַנּוּן וְרַחוּם אָתָּה.

*In the house of a mourner, "Comfort" on page 1146 is substituted for the next two paragraphs.*

וּבְנֵה And may Jerusalem the holy city be rebuilt soon, in our time.
Blessed are You, LORD, who in His compassion
will rebuild Jerusalem. Amen.

BLESSING OF GOD'S GOODNESS

בָּרוּךְ Blessed are You, LORD our God, King of the Universe –
God our Father, our King, our Sovereign,
our Creator, our Redeemer, our Maker,
our Holy One, the Holy One of Jacob.
He is our Shepherd, Israel's Shepherd,
the good King who does good to all.
Every day He has done, is doing, and will do good to us.
He has acted, is acting, and will always act kindly toward us for ever,
granting us grace, kindness and compassion, relief and rescue,
prosperity, blessing, redemption and comfort,
sustenance and support, compassion, life, peace and all good things,
and of all good things may He never let us lack.

ADDITIONAL REQUESTS

הָרַחֲמָן May the Compassionate One reign over us
for ever and all time.
May the Compassionate One be blessed
in heaven and on earth.
May the Compassionate One be praised from generation to generation,
be glorified by us to all eternity,
and honored among us for ever and all time.
May the Compassionate One
grant us an honorable livelihood.
May the Compassionate One break the yoke from our neck
and lead us upright to our land.
May the Compassionate One send us many blessings to this house
and this table at which we have eaten.
May the Compassionate One send us Elijah the prophet –
may he be remembered for good –
to bring us good tidings of salvation and consolation.

*In the house of a mourner,* נַחֵם *on page 1147 is substituted for the next two paragraphs.*

וּבְנֵה יְרוּשָׁלַיִם עִיר הַקֹּדֶשׁ בִּמְהֵרָה בְיָמֵינוּ.
בָּרוּךְ אַתָּה יהוה, בּוֹנֵה בְרַחֲמָיו יְרוּשָׁלָיִם, אָמֵן.

ברכת הטוב והמטיב

בָּרוּךְ אַתָּה יהוה אֱלֹהֵינוּ מֶלֶךְ הָעוֹלָם
הָאֵל אָבִינוּ, מַלְכֵּנוּ, אַדִּירֵנוּ
בּוֹרְאֵנוּ, גּוֹאֲלֵנוּ, יוֹצְרֵנוּ, קְדוֹשֵׁנוּ, קְדוֹשׁ יַעֲקֹב
רוֹעֵנוּ, רוֹעֵה יִשְׂרָאֵל, הַמֶּלֶךְ הַטּוֹב וְהַמֵּטִיב לַכֹּל, שֶׁבְּכָל יוֹם וָיוֹם
הוּא הֵיטִיב, הוּא מֵיטִיב, הוּא יֵיטִיב לָנוּ
הוּא גְמָלָנוּ, הוּא גוֹמְלֵנוּ, הוּא יִגְמְלֵנוּ לָעַד
לְחֵן וּלְחֶסֶד וּלְרַחֲמִים, וּלְרֶוַח, הַצָּלָה וְהַצְלָחָה
בְּרָכָה וִישׁוּעָה, נֶחָמָה, פַּרְנָסָה וְכַלְכָּלָה
וְרַחֲמִים וְחַיִּים וְשָׁלוֹם וְכָל טוֹב, וּמִכָּל טוּב לְעוֹלָם אַל יְחַסְּרֵנוּ.

בקשות נוספות

הָרַחֲמָן הוּא יִמְלֹךְ עָלֵינוּ לְעוֹלָם וָעֶד.
הָרַחֲמָן הוּא יִתְבָּרַךְ בַּשָּׁמַיִם וּבָאָרֶץ.
הָרַחֲמָן הוּא יִשְׁתַּבַּח לְדוֹר דּוֹרִים, וְיִתְפָּאַר בָּנוּ לָעַד וּלְנֵצַח נְצָחִים
וְיִתְהַדַּר בָּנוּ לָעַד וּלְעוֹלְמֵי עוֹלָמִים.
הָרַחֲמָן הוּא יְפַרְנְסֵנוּ בְּכָבוֹד.
הָרַחֲמָן הוּא יִשְׁבֹּר עֻלֵּנוּ מֵעַל צַוָּארֵנוּ
וְהוּא יוֹלִיכֵנוּ קוֹמְמִיּוּת לְאַרְצֵנוּ.
הָרַחֲמָן הוּא יִשְׁלַח לָנוּ בְּרָכָה מְרֻבָּה בַּבַּיִת הַזֶּה
וְעַל שֻׁלְחָן זֶה שֶׁאָכַלְנוּ עָלָיו.
הָרַחֲמָן הוּא יִשְׁלַח לָנוּ אֶת אֵלִיָּהוּ הַנָּבִיא זָכוּר לַטּוֹב
וִיבַשֶּׂר לָנוּ בְּשׂוֹרוֹת טוֹבוֹת יְשׁוּעוֹת וְנֶחָמוֹת.

May the Compassionate One bless the State of Israel,
first flowering of our redemption.
May the Compassionate One bless
the members of Israel's Defense Forces,
who stand guard over our land.

*A guest says:*

יְהִי רָצוֹן May it be Your will that the master of this house shall not suffer shame in this world, nor humiliation in the World to Come. May all he owns prosper greatly, and may his and our possessions be successful and close to hand. Let not the Accuser hold sway over his deeds or ours, and may no thought of sin, iniquity or transgression enter him or us from now and for evermore.

הָרַחֲמָן May the Compassionate One bless –

*When eating at one's own table, say (include the words in parentheses that apply):*
me, (my wife/husband, / my father, my teacher / my mother, my teacher/ my children,) and all that is mine,

*A guest at someone else's table says (include the words in parentheses that apply):*
the master of this house, him (and his wife, the mistress of this house / and his children,) and all that is his,

*Children at their parents' table say (include the words in parentheses that apply):*
my father, my teacher, (master of this house,) and my mother, my teacher, (mistress of this house,) them, their household, their children, and all that is theirs.

*For all other guests, add:*
and all the diners here,

together with us and all that is ours.
Just as our forefathers Abraham, Isaac and Jacob were blessed
in all, from all, with all, so may He bless all of us together
with a complete blessing, and let us say: Amen.

בַּמָּרוֹם On high, may grace be invoked for them and for us,
as a safeguard of peace.
May we receive a blessing from the Lord
and a just reward from the God of our salvation,
and may we find grace and good favor in the eyes of God and man.

הָרַחֲמָן הוּא יְבָרֵךְ אֶת מְדִינַת יִשְׂרָאֵל, רֵאשִׁית צְמִיחַת גְּאֻלָּתֵנוּ.
הָרַחֲמָן הוּא יְבָרֵךְ אֶת חַיָּלֵי צְבָא הַהֲגָנָה לְיִשְׂרָאֵל
הָעוֹמְדִים עַל מִשְׁמַר אַרְצֵנוּ.

*A guest says:*

יְהִי רָצוֹן שֶׁלֹּא יֵבוֹשׁ בַּעַל הַבַּיִת בָּעוֹלָם הַזֶּה, וְלֹא יִכָּלֵם לָעוֹלָם הַבָּא, וְיִצְלַח מְאֹד בְּכָל נְכָסָיו, וְיִהְיוּ נְכָסָיו וּנְכָסֵינוּ מֻצְלָחִים וּקְרוֹבִים לָעִיר, וְאַל יִשְׁלֹט שָׂטָן לֹא בְּמַעֲשֵׂה יָדָיו וְלֹא בְּמַעֲשֵׂה יָדֵינוּ. וְאַל יִזְדַּקֵּק לֹא לְפָנָיו וְלֹא לְפָנֵינוּ שׁוּם דְּבַר הִרְהוּר חֵטְא, עֲבֵרָה וְעָוֹן, מֵעַתָּה וְעַד עוֹלָם.

הָרַחֲמָן הוּא יְבָרֵךְ

*When eating at one's own table, say (include the words in parentheses that apply):*

אוֹתִי (וְאֶת אִשְׁתִּי / וְאֶת בַּעְלִי / וְאֶת אָבִי מוֹרִי /
וְאֶת אִמִּי מוֹרָתִי / וְאֶת זַרְעִי) וְאֶת כָּל אֲשֶׁר לִי.

*A guest at someone else's table says (include the words in parentheses that apply):*

אֶת בַּעַל הַבַּיִת הַזֶּה, אוֹתוֹ (וְאֶת אִשְׁתּוֹ בַּעֲלַת הַבַּיִת הַזֶּה /
וְאֶת זַרְעוֹ) וְאֶת כָּל אֲשֶׁר לוֹ.

*Children at their parents' table say (include the words in parentheses that apply):*

אֶת אָבִי מוֹרִי (בַּעַל הַבַּיִת הַזֶּה), וְאֶת אִמִּי מוֹרָתִי (בַּעֲלַת הַבַּיִת הַזֶּה), אוֹתָם וְאֶת בֵּיתָם וְאֶת זַרְעָם וְאֶת כָּל אֲשֶׁר לָהֶם

*For all other guests, add:*

וְאֶת כָּל הַמְּסֻבִּין כָּאן

אוֹתָנוּ וְאֶת כָּל אֲשֶׁר לָנוּ, כְּמוֹ שֶׁנִּתְבָּרְכוּ אֲבוֹתֵינוּ
אַבְרָהָם יִצְחָק וְיַעֲקֹב, בַּכֹּל, מִכֹּל, כֹּל
כֵּן יְבָרֵךְ אוֹתָנוּ כֻּלָּנוּ יַחַד בִּבְרָכָה שְׁלֵמָה, וְנֹאמַר אָמֵן.

בַּמָּרוֹם יְלַמְּדוּ עֲלֵיהֶם וְעָלֵינוּ זְכוּת שֶׁתְּהֵא לְמִשְׁמֶרֶת שָׁלוֹם
וְנִשָּׂא בְרָכָה מֵאֵת יהוה וּצְדָקָה מֵאֱלֹהֵי יִשְׁעֵנוּ
וְנִמְצָא חֵן וְשֵׂכֶל טוֹב בְּעֵינֵי אֱלֹהִים וְאָדָם.

*At a circumcision feast add here "May the Compassionate One bless the father" on page 1100.*

*On Shabbat:* May the Compassionate One let us inherit the time,
that will be entirely Shabbat and rest for life everlasting.

*On Rosh Ḥodesh:* May the Compassionate One renew this month for us,
for good and blessing.

*On Rosh HaShana:* May the Compassionate One renew for us this year,
for good and blessing.

*On Yom Tov:* May the Compassionate One let us inherit the day,
that is all good.

*On Sukkot:* May the Compassionate One restore for us,
the fallen Tabernacle of David.

הָרַחֲמָן May the Compassionate One make us worthy
of the Messianic Age and life in the World to Come.
He gives great / *On Shabbat, Festivals, and Rosh Ḥodesh:* He is a tower of / *II Sam. 22*
salvation to His king, showing kindness to His anointed,
to David and his descendants for ever.
He who makes peace in His high places,
may He make peace for us and all Israel, and let us say: Amen.

יְראוּ Fear the Lord, you His holy ones; those who fear Him lack nothing. *Ps. 34*
Young lions may grow weak and hungry,
but those who seek the Lord lack no good thing.
Thank the Lord for He is good; His loving-kindness is for ever. *Ps. 118*
You open Your hand, and satisfy every living thing with favor. *Ps. 145*
Blessed is the person who trusts in the Lord, *Jer. 17*
whose trust is in the Lord alone.
Once I was young, and now I am old, yet I have never watched *Ps. 37*
a righteous man forsaken or his children begging for bread.
The Lord will give His people strength. *Ps. 29*
The Lord will bless His people with peace.

*If Birkat HaMazon was made on a cup of wine, then the blessing over wine is made and the majority of the cup is drunk, after which Al HaMiḥya, on the next page, is said.*

*At a wedding or Sheva Berakhot, the seven blessings on page 1116 are said, beginning with the second blessing, "who has created all," and ending with the first blessing, that over the wine.*

*At a meal after a* ברית *add here* הָרַחֲמָן הוּא יְבָרֵךְ אֲבִי הַיֶּלֶד *on page 1101.*

בשבת: הָרַחֲמָן הוּא יַנְחִילֵנוּ, יוֹם שֶׁכֻּלּוֹ שַׁבָּת וּמְנוּחָה לְחַיֵּי הָעוֹלָמִים.

בראש חודש: הָרַחֲמָן הוּא יְחַדֵּשׁ עָלֵינוּ, אֶת הַחֹדֶשׁ הַזֶּה לְטוֹבָה וְלִבְרָכָה.

בראש השנה: הָרַחֲמָן הוּא יְחַדֵּשׁ עָלֵינוּ, אֶת הַשָּׁנָה הַזֹּאת לְטוֹבָה וְלִבְרָכָה.

ביום טוב: הָרַחֲמָן הוּא יַנְחִילֵנוּ יוֹם שֶׁכֻּלּוֹ טוֹב.

בסוכות: הָרַחֲמָן הוּא יָקִים לָנוּ אֶת סֻכַּת דָּוִד הַנּוֹפֶלֶת.

הָרַחֲמָן הוּא יְזַכֵּנוּ לִימוֹת הַמָּשִׁיחַ וּלְחַיֵּי הָעוֹלָם הַבָּא
מַגְדִּל / *On* שבת, חגים *and* ראש חודש מִגְדּוֹל / יְשׁוּעוֹת מַלְכּוֹ שמואל ב׳ כב
וְעֹשֶׂה־חֶסֶד לִמְשִׁיחוֹ, לְדָוִד וּלְזַרְעוֹ עַד־עוֹלָם:
עֹשֶׂה שָׁלוֹם בִּמְרוֹמָיו
הוּא יַעֲשֶׂה שָׁלוֹם עָלֵינוּ וְעַל כָּל יִשְׂרָאֵל
וְאִמְרוּ אָמֵן.

יְראוּ אֶת־יהוה קְדֹשָׁיו, כִּי־אֵין מַחְסוֹר לִירֵאָיו: תהלים לד
כְּפִירִים רָשׁוּ וְרָעֵבוּ, וְדֹרְשֵׁי יהוה לֹא־יַחְסְרוּ כָל־טוֹב:
הוֹדוּ לַיהוה כִּי־טוֹב, כִּי לְעוֹלָם חַסְדּוֹ: תהלים קיח
פּוֹתֵחַ אֶת־יָדֶךָ, וּמַשְׂבִּיעַ לְכָל־חַי רָצוֹן: תהלים קמה
בָּרוּךְ הַגֶּבֶר אֲשֶׁר יִבְטַח בַּיהוה, וְהָיָה יהוה מִבְטַחוֹ: ירמיה יז
נַעַר הָיִיתִי גַּם־זָקַנְתִּי, וְלֹא־רָאִיתִי צַדִּיק נֶעֱזָב וְזַרְעוֹ מְבַקֶּשׁ־לָחֶם: תהלים לז
יהוה עֹז לְעַמּוֹ יִתֵּן, יהוה יְבָרֵךְ אֶת־עַמּוֹ בַשָּׁלוֹם: תהלים כט

*If* ברכת המזון *was made on a cup of wine, then* בּוֹרֵא פְּרִי הַגָּפֶן *is said and the majority of the cup is drunk, after which* ברכה מעין שלוש*, on the next page, is said.*

*At a wedding or* שבע ברכות*, the seven blessings on page 1117 are said, beginning with the second blessing,* שֶׁהַכֹּל בָּרָא לִכְבוֹדוֹ*, and ending with the first blessing,* בּוֹרֵא פְּרִי הַגָּפֶן*.*

*Before eating food, other than bread or matza, made from the five species of grain (wheat, barley, rye, oats and spelt), or rice:*

Blessed are You, the LORD our God, King of the Universe,
who creates the various kinds of nourishment.

*Before drinking wine or grape juice:*

Blessed are You, LORD our God, King of the Universe,
who creates fruit of the vine.

*Before eating fruit that grows on trees:*

Blessed are You, LORD our God, King of the Universe,
who creates fruit of the tree.

*Before eating vegetables, or fruit that does not grow on trees:*

Blessed are You, LORD our God, King of the Universe,
who creates fruit of the ground.

*Before eating other food or drinking other liquids:*

Blessed are You, LORD our God, King of the Universe,
by whose word all things came to be.

*Before eating fruit for the first time in a season, the following is said. This blessing is also said when buying or wearing a new garment of significant value (e.g. a dress or suit); entering a new home for the first time; or hearing personal good news.*

Blessed are You, LORD our God, King of the Universe,
who has given us life, sustained us, and brought us to this time.

## BLESSING AFTER FOOD – AL HAMIḤYA

*Grace after eating from the "seven species" of produce with which Israel is blessed: food made from the five grains (but not bread); wine or grape juice; grapes, figs, pomegranates, olives, or dates.*

בָּרוּךְ Blessed are You, LORD our God, King of the Universe,

*After grain products (but not bread or matza):*
for the nourishment and sustenance,

*After wine or grape juice:*
for the vine and the fruit of the vine,

*After grapes, figs, olives, pomegranates or dates:*
for the tree and the fruit of the tree,

*After grain products (but not bread or matza), and wine or grape juice:*
for the nourishment and sustenance
and for the vine and the fruit of the vine,

and for the produce of the field; for the desirable, good and spacious land that You willingly gave as heritage to our ancestors, that they might eat of its fruit and be satisfied with its goodness. Have compassion, LORD our

*Before eating food, other than bread or מצה,*
*made from the five species of grain (wheat, barley, rye, oats and spelt), or rice:*

בָּרוּךְ אַתָּה יהוה אֱלֹהֵינוּ מֶלֶךְ הָעוֹלָם, בּוֹרֵא מִינֵי מְזוֹנוֹת.

*Before drinking wine or grape juice:*

בָּרוּךְ אַתָּה יהוה אֱלֹהֵינוּ מֶלֶךְ הָעוֹלָם, בּוֹרֵא פְּרִי הַגָּפֶן.

*Before eating fruit that grows on trees:*

בָּרוּךְ אַתָּה יהוה אֱלֹהֵינוּ מֶלֶךְ הָעוֹלָם, בּוֹרֵא פְּרִי הָעֵץ.

*Before eating vegetables, or fruit that does not grow on trees:*

בָּרוּךְ אַתָּה יהוה אֱלֹהֵינוּ מֶלֶךְ הָעוֹלָם, בּוֹרֵא פְּרִי הָאֲדָמָה.

*Before eating other food or drinking other liquids:*

בָּרוּךְ אַתָּה יהוה אֱלֹהֵינוּ מֶלֶךְ הָעוֹלָם, שֶׁהַכֹּל נִהְיָה בִּדְבָרוֹ.

*Before eating fruit for the first time in a season, the following שֶׁהֶחֱיָנוּ is said.*
*This blessing is also said when buying or wearing a new garment of significant value (e.g. a dress or suit); entering a new home for the first time; or hearing personal good news.*

בָּרוּךְ אַתָּה יהוה אֱלֹהֵינוּ מֶלֶךְ הָעוֹלָם
שֶׁהֶחֱיָנוּ וְקִיְּמָנוּ וְהִגִּיעָנוּ לַזְּמַן הַזֶּה.

# ברכה מעין שלוש

*Grace after eating from the "seven species" of produce with which Israel is blessed: food made from the five grains (but not bread); wine or grape juice; grapes, figs, pomegranates, olives, or dates.*

בָּרוּךְ אַתָּה יהוה אֱלֹהֵינוּ מֶלֶךְ הָעוֹלָם, עַל

| *After grain products (but not bread or מצה):* | *After wine or grape juice:* | *After grapes, figs, olives, pomegranates or dates:* |
|---|---|---|
| הַמִּחְיָה וְעַל הַכַּלְכָּלָה | הַגֶּפֶן וְעַל פְּרִי הַגֶּפֶן | הָעֵץ וְעַל פְּרִי הָעֵץ |

*After grain products (but not bread or מצה), and wine or grape juice:*

הַמִּחְיָה וְעַל הַכַּלְכָּלָה וְעַל הַגֶּפֶן וְעַל פְּרִי הַגֶּפֶן

וְעַל תְּנוּבַת הַשָּׂדֶה וְעַל אֶרֶץ חֶמְדָּה טוֹבָה וּרְחָבָה, שֶׁרָצִיתָ וְהִנְחַלְתָּ לַאֲבוֹתֵינוּ לֶאֱכֹל מִפִּרְיָהּ וְלִשְׂבֹּעַ מִטּוּבָהּ. רַחֶם נָא יהוה אֱלֹהֵינוּ עַל

God, on Israel Your people, on Jerusalem, Your city, on Zion the home of Your glory, on Your altar and Your Temple. May You rebuild Jerusalem, the holy city swiftly in our time, and may You bring us back there, rejoicing in its rebuilding, eating from its fruit, satisfied by its goodness, and blessing You for it in holiness and purity.

| | |
|---|---|
| *On Shabbat:* | Be pleased to refresh us on this Sabbath Day. |
| *On Rosh Ḥodesh:* | Remember us for good on this day of the New Moon. |
| *On Rosh HaShana:* | Remember us for good on this Day of Remembrance. |
| *On Pesaḥ:* | Grant us joy on this Festival of Matzot. |
| *On Shavuot:* | Grant us joy on this Festival of Shavuot. |
| *On Sukkot:* | Grant us joy on this Festival of Sukkot. |
| *On Shemini Atzeret & Simḥat Torah:* | Grant us joy on this Festival of Shemini Atzeret. |

For You, God, are good and do good to all and we thank You for the land

| *After grain products (but not bread or matza):* | *After wine or grape juice:* | *After grapes, figs, olives, pomegranates or dates:* |
|---|---|---|
| and for the nourishment. Blessed are You, LORD, for the land and for the nourishment. | and for the fruit of the vine.* Blessed are You, LORD, for the land and for the fruit of the vine.* | and for the fruit.** Blessed are You, LORD, for the land and for the fruit.** |

*After grain products (but not bread or matza), and wine or grape juice:*

and for the nourishment and for the fruit of the vine.* Blessed are You, LORD, for the land and for the nourishment and the fruit of the vine.*

* *If the wine is from Israel, then substitute "her vine" for "the vine."*
** *If the fruit is from Israel, then substitute "her fruit" for "the fruit."*

## BLESSING AFTER FOOD – BOREH NEFASHOT

*After food or drink that does not require Birkat HaMazon or Al HaMiḥya – such as meat, fish, dairy products, vegetables, beverages, or fruit other than grapes, figs, pomegranates, olives or dates – say:*

בָּרוּךְ Blessed are You, LORD our God, King of the Universe, who creates the many forms of life and their needs. For all You have created to sustain the life of all that lives, blessed be He, Giver of life to the worlds.

יִשְׂרָאֵל עַמֶּךָ וְעַל יְרוּשָׁלַיִם עִירֶךָ וְעַל צִיּוֹן מִשְׁכַּן כְּבוֹדֶךָ וְעַל מִזְבְּחֶךָ וְעַל הֵיכָלֶךָ. וּבְנֵה יְרוּשָׁלַיִם עִיר הַקֹּדֶשׁ בִּמְהֵרָה בְיָמֵינוּ, וְהַעֲלֵנוּ לְתוֹכָהּ וְשַׂמְּחֵנוּ בְּבִנְיָנָהּ וְנֹאכַל מִפִּרְיָהּ וְנִשְׂבַּע מִטּוּבָהּ, וּנְבָרֶכְךָ עָלֶיהָ בִּקְדֻשָּׁה וּבְטָהֳרָה.

בשבת: וּרְצֵה וְהַחֲלִיצֵנוּ בְּיוֹם הַשַּׁבָּת הַזֶּה

בראש חודש: וְזָכְרֵנוּ לְטוֹבָה בְּיוֹם רֹאשׁ הַחֹדֶשׁ הַזֶּה

בראש השנה: וְזָכְרֵנוּ לְטוֹבָה בְּיוֹם הַזִּכָּרוֹן הַזֶּה

בפסח: וְשַׂמְּחֵנוּ בְּיוֹם חַג הַמַּצּוֹת הַזֶּה

בשבועות: וְשַׂמְּחֵנוּ בְּיוֹם חַג הַשָּׁבוּעוֹת הַזֶּה

בסוכות: וְשַׂמְּחֵנוּ בְּיוֹם חַג הַסֻּכּוֹת הַזֶּה

בשמיני עצרת ושמחת תורה: וְשַׂמְּחֵנוּ בְּיוֹם הַשְּׁמִינִי חַג הָעֲצֶרֶת הַזֶּה

כִּי אַתָּה יהוה טוֹב וּמֵטִיב לַכֹּל, וְנוֹדֶה לְּךָ עַל הָאָרֶץ

*After grain products, (but not bread or* מצה*):*

וְעַל הַמִּחְיָה.
בָּרוּךְ אַתָּה יהוה עַל הָאָרֶץ וְעַל הַמִּחְיָה.

*After wine or grape juice:*

וְעַל פְּרִי הַגֶּפֶן.*
בָּרוּךְ אַתָּה יהוה עַל הָאָרֶץ וְעַל פְּרִי הַגֶּפֶן.*

*After grapes, figs, olives, pomegranates or dates:*

וְעַל הַפֵּרוֹת.**
בָּרוּךְ אַתָּה יהוה עַל הָאָרֶץ וְעַל הַפֵּרוֹת.**

*After grain products (but not bread or* מצה*), and wine or grape juice:*

וְעַל הַמִּחְיָה וְעַל פְּרִי הַגֶּפֶן.*
בָּרוּךְ אַתָּה יהוה, עַל הָאָרֶץ וְעַל הַמִּחְיָה וְעַל פְּרִי הַגֶּפֶן.*

**If the wine is from* ארץ ישראל*, then substitute* גַּפְנָהּ *for* הַגֶּפֶן*.*
***If the fruit is from* ארץ ישראל*, then substitute* פֵּרוֹתֶיהָ *for* הַפֵּרוֹת*.*

## בורא נפשות

*After food or drink that does not require* ברכת המזון *or* מעין שלוש *– such as meat, fish, dairy products, vegetables, beverages, or fruit other than grapes, figs, pomegranates, olives or dates – say:*

בָּרוּךְ אַתָּה יהוה אֱלֹהֵינוּ מֶלֶךְ הָעוֹלָם, בּוֹרֵא נְפָשׁוֹת רַבּוֹת וְחֶסְרוֹנָן עַל כָּל מַה שֶּׁבָּרָאתָ לְהַחֲיוֹת בָּהֶם נֶפֶשׁ כָּל חָי. בָּרוּךְ חֵי הָעוֹלָמִים.

# BLESSINGS

## BLESSINGS ON MITZVOT

*In Israel on separating teruma and first tithe (if there is doubt as to whether the teruma and first tithe have been taken, the following blessing is not said, but the subsequent declaration is):*

Blessed are You, LORD our God, King of the Universe,
who has made us holy through His commandments,
and has commanded us to separate *terumot* and tithes.

Whatever [of the allocated portion] is more than one in a hundred of everything here, is hereby declared to be *teruma gedola* [the priestly portion] and is the northern portion. The one in a hundred that remains here, together with nine equal portions on the upper side of this produce are declared to be the first [levitical] tithe. The one in a hundred I have made first tithe is hereby declared to be *terumat maaser* [the tithe-of-the-tithe set aside for the priests]. Nine other equal portions on the lower side of the produce are declared to be second tithe, but if this produce must have the tithe of the poor separated from it, let them be the tithe of the poor.

*In Israel on separating and redeeming the second tithe (if there is doubt as to whether the second tithe has been taken, the following blessing is not said, but the subsequent declaration is):*

Blessed are You, LORD our God, King of the Universe,
who has made us holy through His commandments,
and has commanded us about the redemption of the second tithe.

This second tithe, together with its additional fifth, is hereby redeemed by one *peruta* of the coins I have set aside for the redemption of the second tithe.

*On taking ḥalla:*

Blessed are You, LORD our God, King of the Universe,
who has made us holy through His commandments,
and has commanded us to set aside ḥalla from the dough.

*On redeeming fourth-year fruit:*

Blessed are You, LORD our God, King of the Universe,
who has made us holy through His commandments,
and has commanded us about the redemption of fruit of the fourth year.

*On fixing a mezuza to the doorpost:*

Blessed are You, LORD our God, King of the Universe,
who has made us holy through His commandments,
and has commanded us to affix the mezuza.

*On making a protective railing around one's roof, or a fence around a pit:*

Blessed are You, LORD our God, King of the Universe,
who has made us holy through His commandments,
and has commanded us to to affix a guard-rail.

# ברכות

## ברכות המצוות

*In* ארץ ישראל *on separating* תרומה *and* מעשר ראשון *(if there is doubt as to whether the* תרומה *and* מעשר ראשון *have been taken, the following blessing is not said, but the subsequent declaration is):*

בָּרוּךְ אַתָּה יהוה אֱלֹהֵינוּ מֶלֶךְ הָעוֹלָם, אֲשֶׁר קִדְּשָׁנוּ בְּמִצְוֹתָיו וְצִוָּנוּ לְהַפְרִישׁ תְּרוּמוֹת וּמַעַשְׂרוֹת.

מַה שֶּׁהוּא יוֹתֵר מֵאֶחָד מִמֵּאָה מִן הַכֹּל שֶׁיֵּשׁ כָּאן, הֲרֵי הוּא תְּרוּמָה גְּדוֹלָה בִּצְפוֹנוֹ, וְהָאֶחָד מִמֵּאָה שֶׁנִּשְׁאַר כָּאן עִם תִּשְׁעָה חֲלָקִים כָּמוֹהוּ בְּצַד הָעֶלְיוֹן שֶׁל הַפֵּרוֹת הַלָּלוּ, הֲרֵי הֵם מַעֲשֵׂר רִאשׁוֹן. אוֹתוֹ הָאֶחָד מִמֵּאָה שֶׁעֲשִׂיתִיו מַעֲשֵׂר רִאשׁוֹן הֲרֵי הוּא תְּרוּמַת מַעֲשֵׂר. עוֹד תִּשְׁעָה חֲלָקִים כָּאֵלֶּה בְּצַד הַתַּחְתּוֹן שֶׁל הַפֵּרוֹת הֲרֵי הֵם מַעֲשֵׂר שֵׁנִי, וְאִם הֵם חַיָּבִים בְּמַעֲשַׂר עָנִי, הֲרֵי הֵם מַעֲשַׂר עָנִי.

*In* ארץ ישראל *on separating and redeeming the* מעשר שני *(if there is doubt as to whether the* מעשר שני *has been taken, the following blessing is not said, but the subsequent declaration is):*

בָּרוּךְ אַתָּה יהוה אֱלֹהֵינוּ מֶלֶךְ הָעוֹלָם, אֲשֶׁר קִדְּשָׁנוּ בְּמִצְוֹתָיו וְצִוָּנוּ עַל פִּדְיוֹן מַעֲשֵׂר שֵׁנִי.

מַעֲשֵׂר שֵׁנִי זֶה, הוּא וְחֻמְשׁוֹ, הֲרֵי הוּא מְחֻלָּל עַל פְּרוּטָה אַחַת מִן הַמַּטְבֵּעַ שֶׁיִּחַדְתִּי לְפִדְיוֹן מַעֲשֵׂר שֵׁנִי.

*On taking* חלה*:*

בָּרוּךְ אַתָּה יהוה אֱלֹהֵינוּ מֶלֶךְ הָעוֹלָם, אֲשֶׁר קִדְּשָׁנוּ בְּמִצְוֹתָיו וְצִוָּנוּ לְהַפְרִישׁ חַלָּה מִן הָעִסָּה.

*On redeeming* נטע רבעי*:*

בָּרוּךְ אַתָּה יהוה אֱלֹהֵינוּ מֶלֶךְ הָעוֹלָם, אֲשֶׁר קִדְּשָׁנוּ בְּמִצְוֹתָיו וְצִוָּנוּ עַל פִּדְיוֹן נֶטַע רְבָעִי.

*On fixing a* מזוזה *to the doorpost:*

בָּרוּךְ אַתָּה יהוה אֱלֹהֵינוּ מֶלֶךְ הָעוֹלָם, אֲשֶׁר קִדְּשָׁנוּ בְּמִצְוֹתָיו וְצִוָּנוּ לִקְבֹּעַ מְזוּזָה.

*On making a protective railing around one's roof, or a fence around a pit:*

בָּרוּךְ אַתָּה יהוה אֱלֹהֵינוּ מֶלֶךְ הָעוֹלָם, אֲשֶׁר קִדְּשָׁנוּ בְּמִצְוֹתָיו וְצִוָּנוּ לַעֲשׂוֹת מַעֲקֶה.

*A woman on ritual immersion:*

Blessed are You, Lord our God, King of the Universe,
who has made us holy through His commandments,
and has commanded us about ritual immersion.

*On immersing utensils made by or bought from a gentile:*

Blessed are You, Lord our God, King of the Universe,
who has made us holy through His commandments,
and has commanded us about immersing a vessel (vessels).

## BLESSINGS ON PLEASURES, SIGHTS AND SOUNDS

*On wearing new clothes:*

Blessed are You, Lord our God, King of the Universe, who clothes the naked.

*On smelling fragrant shrubs or trees:*

Blessed are You, Lord our God, King of the Universe,
who creates fragrant trees.

*On smelling fragrant herbs, grasses or flowers:*

Blessed are You, Lord our God, King of the Universe,
who creates fragrant plants.

*On smelling fragrant fruit:*

Blessed are You, Lord our God, King of the Universe,
who gives pleasant fragrance to fruits.

*On smelling balsam oil:*

Blessed are You, Lord our God, King of the Universe,
who creates pleasing perfume.

*On all other scents:*

Blessed are You, Lord our God, King of the Universe,
who creates the various spices.

*On seeing the wonders of nature, such as lightning, and on the 28-year solar cycle:*

Blessed are You, Lord our God, King of the Universe, Author of creation.

*On hearing thunder or experiencing a hurricane:*

Blessed are You, Lord our God, King of the Universe,
whose power and might fill the world.

*On seeing a rainbow:*

Blessed are You, Lord our God, King of the Universe,
who remembers the covenant, is faithful to the covenant, and fulfills His word.

*On seeing the ocean or the Mediterranean Sea for the first time in thirty days:*

Blessed are You, Lord our God, King of the Universe,
who has made the great sea.

*A woman on ritual immersion:*

בָּרוּךְ אַתָּה יהוה אֱלֹהֵינוּ מֶלֶךְ הָעוֹלָם, אֲשֶׁר קִדְּשָׁנוּ בְּמִצְוֹתָיו
וְצִוָּנוּ עַל הַטְּבִילָה.

*On immersing utensils made by or bought from a gentile:*

בָּרוּךְ אַתָּה יהוה אֱלֹהֵינוּ מֶלֶךְ הָעוֹלָם, אֲשֶׁר קִדְּשָׁנוּ בְּמִצְוֹתָיו
וְצִוָּנוּ עַל טְבִילַת כֶּלִי (כֵּלִים).

## ברכות הנהנין, הראייה והשמיעה

*On wearing new clothes:*

בָּרוּךְ אַתָּה יהוה אֱלֹהֵינוּ מֶלֶךְ הָעוֹלָם, מַלְבִּישׁ עֲרֻמִּים.

*On smelling fragrant shrubs or trees:*

בָּרוּךְ אַתָּה יהוה אֱלֹהֵינוּ מֶלֶךְ הָעוֹלָם, בּוֹרֵא עֲצֵי בְשָׂמִים.

*On smelling fragrant herbs, grasses or flowers:*

בָּרוּךְ אַתָּה יהוה אֱלֹהֵינוּ מֶלֶךְ הָעוֹלָם, בּוֹרֵא עִשְׂבֵי בְשָׂמִים.

*On smelling fragrant fruit:*

בָּרוּךְ אַתָּה יהוה אֱלֹהֵינוּ מֶלֶךְ הָעוֹלָם, הַנּוֹתֵן רֵיחַ טוֹב בַּפֵּרוֹת.

*On smelling balsam oil:*

בָּרוּךְ אַתָּה יהוה אֱלֹהֵינוּ מֶלֶךְ הָעוֹלָם, בּוֹרֵא שֶׁמֶן עָרֵב.

*On all other scents:*

בָּרוּךְ אַתָּה יהוה אֱלֹהֵינוּ מֶלֶךְ הָעוֹלָם, בּוֹרֵא מִינֵי בְשָׂמִים.

*On seeing the wonders of nature, such as lightning, and* ברכת החמה:

בָּרוּךְ אַתָּה יהוה אֱלֹהֵינוּ מֶלֶךְ הָעוֹלָם, עוֹשֶׂה מַעֲשֵׂה בְרֵאשִׁית.

*On hearing thunder or experiencing a hurricane:*

בָּרוּךְ אַתָּה יהוה אֱלֹהֵינוּ מֶלֶךְ הָעוֹלָם, שֶׁכֹּחוֹ וּגְבוּרָתוֹ מָלֵא עוֹלָם.

*On seeing a rainbow:*

בָּרוּךְ אַתָּה יהוה אֱלֹהֵינוּ מֶלֶךְ הָעוֹלָם
זוֹכֵר הַבְּרִית וְנֶאֱמָן בִּבְרִיתוֹ וְקַיָּם בְּמַאֲמָרוֹ.

*On seeing the ocean or the Mediterranean Sea for the first time in thirty days:*

בָּרוּךְ אַתָּה יהוה אֱלֹהֵינוּ מֶלֶךְ הָעוֹלָם, שֶׁעָשָׂה אֶת הַיָּם הַגָּדוֹל.

*On seeing trees blossoming for the first time in the year:*
Blessed are You, LORD our God, King of the Universe,
who has withheld nothing from His world,
but has created in it beautiful creatures and trees for human beings to enjoy.

*On seeing beautiful scenes of nature:*
Blessed are You, LORD our God, King of the Universe,
who has [created] such things in His world.

*On seeing unusual people or animals:*
Blessed are You, LORD our God, King of the Universe,
who makes [all] creatures different.

*On hearing good news from which others as well as oneself will benefit:*
Blessed are You, LORD our God, King of the Universe,
who is good and does good.

*On hearing bad news, and said by a mourner before the ritual tearing of the garment:*
Blessed are You, LORD our God, King of the Universe, the true Judge.

*On seeing an outstanding Torah scholar:*
Blessed are You, LORD our God, King of the Universe,
who has shared of His wisdom with those who revere Him.

*On seeing an outstanding secular scholar:*
Blessed are You, LORD our God, King of the Universe,
who has given of His wisdom with human beings.

*On seeing a Monarch or Head of State:*
Blessed are You, LORD our God, King of the Universe,
who has given of His glory to human beings.

*On seeing 600,000 Jews together in Israel:*
Blessed are You, LORD our God, King of the Universe, who knows all secrets.

*On seeing Jewish settlements in Israel:*
Blessed are You, LORD our God, King of the Universe,
who establishes the border of the widow.

*On seeing the place where miracles occurred to the Jewish people:*
Blessed are You, LORD our God, King of the Universe,
who performed miracles for our ancestors in this place.

*On seeing the place where miracles occurred to oneself or one's family (insert the relevant words):*
Blessed are You, LORD our God, King of the Universe,
who performed a miracle for me (my father / my mother / my ancestors)
in this place.

*On seeing trees blossoming for the first time in the year:*

בָּרוּךְ אַתָּה יהוה אֱלֹהֵינוּ מֶלֶךְ הָעוֹלָם, שֶׁלֹּא חִסַּר בְּעוֹלָמוֹ כְּלוּם וּבָרָא בוֹ בְּרִיּוֹת טוֹבוֹת וְאִילָנוֹת טוֹבִים לְהַנּוֹת בָּהֶם בְּנֵי אָדָם.

*On seeing beautiful scenes of nature:*

בָּרוּךְ אַתָּה יהוה אֱלֹהֵינוּ מֶלֶךְ הָעוֹלָם, שֶׁכָּכָה לּוֹ בְּעוֹלָמוֹ.

*On seeing unusual people or animals:*

בָּרוּךְ אַתָּה יהוה אֱלֹהֵינוּ מֶלֶךְ הָעוֹלָם, מְשַׁנֶּה הַבְּרִיּוֹת.

*On hearing good news from which others as well as oneself will benefit:*

בָּרוּךְ אַתָּה יהוה אֱלֹהֵינוּ מֶלֶךְ הָעוֹלָם, הַטּוֹב וְהַמֵּטִיב.

*On hearing bad news, and said by a mourner before the ritual tearing of the garment:*

בָּרוּךְ אַתָּה יהוה אֱלֹהֵינוּ מֶלֶךְ הָעוֹלָם, דַּיַּן הָאֱמֶת.

*On seeing an outstanding Torah scholar:*

בָּרוּךְ אַתָּה יהוה אֱלֹהֵינוּ מֶלֶךְ הָעוֹלָם, שֶׁחָלַק מֵחָכְמָתוֹ לִירֵאָיו.

*On seeing an outstanding secular scholar:*

בָּרוּךְ אַתָּה יהוה אֱלֹהֵינוּ מֶלֶךְ הָעוֹלָם, שֶׁנָּתַן מֵחָכְמָתוֹ לְבָשָׂר וָדָם.

*On seeing a Monarch or Head of State:*

בָּרוּךְ אַתָּה יהוה אֱלֹהֵינוּ מֶלֶךְ הָעוֹלָם, שֶׁנָּתַן מִכְּבוֹדוֹ לְבָשָׂר וָדָם.

*On seeing 600,000 Jews together in* ארץ ישראל*:*

בָּרוּךְ אַתָּה יהוה אֱלֹהֵינוּ מֶלֶךְ הָעוֹלָם, חֲכַם הָרָזִים.

*On seeing Jewish settlements in* ארץ ישראל*:*

בָּרוּךְ אַתָּה יהוה אֱלֹהֵינוּ מֶלֶךְ הָעוֹלָם, מַצִּיב גְּבוּל אַלְמָנָה.

*On seeing the place where miracles occurred to the Jewish people:*

בָּרוּךְ אַתָּה יהוה אֱלֹהֵינוּ מֶלֶךְ הָעוֹלָם
שֶׁעָשָׂה נִסִּים לַאֲבוֹתֵינוּ בַּמָּקוֹם הַזֶּה.

*On seeing the place where miracles occurred to oneself or one's family (insert the relevant words):*

בָּרוּךְ אַתָּה יהוה אֱלֹהֵינוּ מֶלֶךְ הָעוֹלָם
שֶׁעָשָׂה לִּי (לְאָבִי/לְאִמִּי/לַאֲבוֹתַי) נֵס בַּמָּקוֹם הַזֶּה.

## ADDITIONAL BLESSINGS

*On seeing a friend after thirty days:*

Blessed are You, LORD our God, King of the Universe,
who has given us life, sustained us, and brought us to this time.

*On seeing a friend after twelve months:*

Blessed are You, LORD our God, King of the Universe,
who revives the dead.

*After relieving oneself and washing one's hands, say:*

Blessed are You, LORD our God, King of the Universe,
who formed man in wisdom
and created in him many orifices and cavities.
It is revealed and known before the throne of Your glory
that were one of them to be ruptured or blocked,
it would be impossible to survive and stand before You.
Blessed are You, LORD,
Healer of all flesh who does wondrous deeds.

---

to face, are actually enhanced by temporary separation. "Absence makes the heart grow fonder." These separations are one of the conditions for the nurturing of love within the soul. But when the separation goes on for too long, the imprint tends to be erased; there remain but pinpoint memories buried in the depth of the soul. The renewal of the love relationship after such a lengthy lapse is aptly compared to "resurrection of the dead." On the level of soul, this is the difference between the lapse of thirty days and that of twelve months. Thirty days is the natural cycle in family life; it relates to the woman's menstrual cycle. The separation between husband and wife renews the emotional tie between them; it restores the luster, the glow to a light that has dimmed.[2] But a lapse of a full year is no less than a revolution in the life of a human being. The Sages said that after twelve months the deceased is forgotten from the heart.[3] After such a long-term separation what is required is to rebuild a relation almost from scratch; to resuscitate a delicate plant that has already withered and drooped.[4]

---

2. See the saying of Rabbi Meir in the *beraita* in *b. Niddah* 31b.
3. *b. Berakhot* 58b.
4. *OR*, vol. 1, pp. 381–382 = *EA*, vol. 2, *Berakhot*, chap. 9, par. 122 (pp. 303–304).

## ברכות נוספות

*On seeing a friend after thirty days:*

בָּרוּךְ אַתָּה יהוה אֱלֹהֵינוּ מֶלֶךְ הָעוֹלָם
שֶׁהֶחֱיָנוּ וְקִיְּמָנוּ וְהִגִּיעָנוּ לַזְּמַן הַזֶּה.

*On seeing a friend after twelve months:*

בָּרוּךְ אַתָּה יהוה אֱלֹהֵינוּ מֶלֶךְ הָעוֹלָם
מְחַיֵּה הַמֵּתִים.

*After relieving oneself and washing one's hands, say:*

בָּרוּךְ אַתָּה יהוה אֱלֹהֵינוּ מֶלֶךְ הָעוֹלָם
אֲשֶׁר יָצַר אֶת הָאָדָם בְּחָכְמָה
וּבָרָא בוֹ נְקָבִים נְקָבִים, חֲלוּלִים חֲלוּלִים.
גָּלוּי וְיָדוּעַ לִפְנֵי כִסֵּא כְבוֹדֶךָ
שֶׁאִם יִפָּתֵחַ אֶחָד מֵהֶם אוֹ יִסָּתֵם אֶחָד מֵהֶם
אִי אֶפְשָׁר לְהִתְקַיֵּם וְלַעֲמֹד לְפָנֶיךָ.
בָּרוּךְ אַתָּה יהוה, רוֹפֵא כָל בָּשָׂר וּמַפְלִיא לַעֲשׂוֹת.

---

שֶׁהֶחֱיָנוּ *Who has given us life.*
מְחַיֵּה הַמֵּתִים *Who revives the dead.*

One who sees his friend after thirty days, says: "Blessed... who has given us life, sustained us and brought us to this time."

After twelve months, one says: "Blessed... who revives the dead."[1]

The festivals, which are called *"zemanim"* (times), on account of the fact that they come along from time to time, exert their moral influence precisely through the intervening workdays. When the joyous memories of the sacred festivals are becoming blurred by the workdays intervening, just then, the inner, soulful light is rekindled by the approaching festival.

By the same token, the joy and love revealed when two souls come face

---

1. *b. Berakhot* 58b; Rabbi Yitsḥak Nissim, *Yayin ha-Tov* (Jerusalem, 1979), nos. 48–50; Rabbi Zevi Pesaḥ Frank, *Har Zevi*, vol. 1, *OḤ* (Jerusalem, 1968), no. 115.

*On visiting a cemetery, or seeing a Jewish grave, for the first time in thirty days:*

Blessed are You, Lord our God, King of the Universe,
who formed you in judgment,
who nourished and sustained you in judgment,
who brought death on you in judgment,
who knows the number of you all in judgment,
and who in the future will restore you to life in judgment.
Blessed are You, Lord, who revives the dead.

You are eternally mighty, Lord.
You give life to the dead and have great power to save.
He sustains the living with loving-kindness,
and with great compassion revives the dead.
He supports the fallen, heals the sick, sets captives free,
and keeps His faith with those who sleep in the dust.
Who is like You, Master of might,
and who can compare to You,
O King who brings death and gives life,
and makes salvation grow?
Faithful are You to revive the dead.

---

*In special cases of urgency only (see law 363), the following short form of the Amida may be said. First say the first three blessings of the Amida from "O Lord" on page 174 until "the holy God" page 178, then say:*

הֲבִינֵנוּ Grant us understanding, Lord our God, to know Your ways. Sensitize our hearts so that we may revere You, and forgive us so that we may be redeemed. Keep us far from suffering and satisfy us with the pastures of Your land. Gather our scattered people from the four quarters of the earth. May those who go astray be judged according to Your will: raise Your hand against the wicked. May the righteous rejoice in the rebuilding of Your city, the restoration of Your Temple, the flowering of Your servant David's glory, and the radiant light of the son of Jesse, Your anointed. May You answer us even before we call. Blessed are You, Lord, who listens to prayer.

*Continue with the final three blessings from "Find favor" on page 188 until the end.*

---

*In extreme cases where there is no time to say the abbreviated Amida above, one may say the following. However, if prayer is then possible at a later time, one should say the complete Amida.*

צָרְכֵי The needs of Your people Israel are many, and their patience is thin. May it be Your will, Lord our God and God of our ancestors, to give each one of them enough to sustain him, and to every single body, all that it lacks – and perform what is right in Your eyes. Blessed are You, Lord, who listens to prayer.

*On visiting a cemetery, or seeing a Jewish grave, for the first time in thirty days:*

בָּרוּךְ אַתָּה יהוה אֱלֹהֵינוּ מֶלֶךְ הָעוֹלָם
אֲשֶׁר יָצַר אֶתְכֶם בַּדִּין, וְזָן וְכִלְכֵּל אֶתְכֶם בַּדִּין
וְהֵמִית אֶתְכֶם בַּדִּין, וְיוֹדֵעַ מִסְפַּר כֻּלְּכֶם בַּדִּין
וְהוּא עָתִיד לְהַחֲיוֹתְכֶם וּלְקַיֵּם אֶתְכֶם בַּדִּין.
בָּרוּךְ אַתָּה יהוה, מְחַיֵּה הַמֵּתִים.

אַתָּה גִּבּוֹר לְעוֹלָם אֲדֹנָי
מְחַיֵּה מֵתִים אַתָּה, רַב לְהוֹשִׁיעַ
מְכַלְכֵּל חַיִּים בְּחֶסֶד, מְחַיֵּה מֵתִים בְּרַחֲמִים רַבִּים
סוֹמֵךְ נוֹפְלִים, וְרוֹפֵא חוֹלִים, וּמַתִּיר אֲסוּרִים
וּמְקַיֵּם אֱמוּנָתוֹ לִישֵׁנֵי עָפָר.
מִי כָמְוֹךָ בַּעַל גְּבוּרוֹת וּמִי דּוֹמֶה לָּךְ
מֶלֶךְ מֵמִית וּמְחַיֶּה וּמַצְמִיחַ יְשׁוּעָה
וְנֶאֱמָן אַתָּה לְהַחֲיוֹת מֵתִים.

---

*In special cases of urgency only (see law 363), the following short form of the* עמידה *may be said. First say the first three* ברכות *of the* עמידה *from* אֲדֹנָי, שְׂפָתַי תִּפְתָּח *on page 175 until* הָאֵל הַקָּדוֹשׁ *on page 179, then say:*

הֲבִינֵנוּ יהוה אֱלֹהֵינוּ לָדַעַת דְּרָכֶיךָ, וּמוֹל אֶת לְבָבֵנוּ לְיִרְאָתֶךָ, וְתִסְלַח לָנוּ לִהְיוֹת גְּאוּלִים, וְרַחֲקֵנוּ מִמַּכְאוֹב, וְדַשְּׁנֵנוּ בִּנְאוֹת אַרְצֶךָ, וּנְפוּצוֹתֵינוּ מֵאַרְבַּע תְּקַבֵּץ, וְהַתּוֹעִים עַל דַּעְתְּךָ יִשָּׁפֵטוּ, וְעַל הָרְשָׁעִים תָּנִיף יָדֶךָ, וְיִשְׂמְחוּ צַדִּיקִים בְּבִנְיַן עִירֶךָ וּבְתִקּוּן הֵיכָלֶךָ, וּבִצְמִיחַת קֶרֶן לְדָוִד עַבְדֶּךָ וּבַעֲרִיכַת נֵר לְבֶן יִשַׁי מְשִׁיחֶךָ, טֶרֶם נִקְרָא אַתָּה תַעֲנֶה. בָּרוּךְ אַתָּה יהוה, שׁוֹמֵעַ תְּפִלָּה.

*Continue with the final three* ברכות*, from* רְצֵה *on page 189 until the end.*

---

*In extreme cases where there is no time to say the abbreviated* עמידה *above, one may say the following. However, if prayer is then possible at a later time, one should say the complete* עמידה.

צָרְכֵי עַמְּךָ יִשְׂרָאֵל מְרֻבִּים וְדַעְתָּם קְצָרָה. יְהִי רָצוֹן מִלְּפָנֶיךָ יהוה אֱלֹהֵינוּ וֵאלֹהֵי אֲבוֹתֵינוּ, שֶׁתִּתֵּן לְכָל אֶחָד וְאֶחָד כְּדֵי פַרְנָסָתוֹ, וּלְכָל גְּוִיָּה וּגְוִיָּה דֵּי מַחְסוֹרָהּ, וְהַטּוֹב בְּעֵינֶיךָ עֲשֵׂה. בָּרוּךְ אַתָּה יהוה, שׁוֹמֵעַ תְּפִלָּה.

## SERVICE AT THE CONSECRATION OF A HOUSE

מִזְמוֹר A psalm of David. A song for the dedication of the House. I will exalt You, Lord, for You have lifted me up, and not let my enemies rejoice over me. Lord, my God, I cried to You for help and You healed me. Lord, You lifted my soul from the grave; You spared me from going down to the pit. Sing to the Lord, you His devoted ones, and give thanks to His holy name. For His anger is for a moment, but His favor for a lifetime. At night there may be weeping, but in the morning there is joy. When I felt secure, I said, "I shall never be shaken." Lord, when You favored me, You made me stand firm as a mountain, but when You hid Your face, I was terrified. To You, Lord, I called; I pleaded with my Lord: "What gain would there be if I died and went down to the grave? Can dust thank You? Can it declare Your truth? Hear, Lord, and be gracious to me; Lord, be my help." You have turned my sorrow into dancing. You have removed my sackcloth and clothed me with joy, so that my soul may sing to You and not be silent. Lord my God, for ever will I thank You. *Ps. 30*

מִזְמוֹר A Psalm of David. Lord, who may dwell in Your tent? Who may live on Your holy mountain? One who walks in integrity, does what is right, and speaks the truth from his heart; who has no malice on his tongue, does no wrong to his fellow, nor casts a slur on his neighbor; who scorns those who are vile, but honors those who fear the Lord; who keeps his oath even when it hurts; who does not demand interest on his loans and never takes a bribe against the innocent. One who does these things will never be shaken. *Ps. 15*

רִבּוֹן הָעוֹלָם Master of the Universe, look down from Your holy dwelling place, and in compassion and favor accept the prayer and plea of Your children, who are gathered here to consecrate this house, and to offer You their thanksgiving for all the kindness and truth You have shown them. Please do let not Your kindness depart, nor Your covenant of Your peace be removed from them. Shield this their home so that no evil befalls it. May illness and sadness never come near it, nor the sound of sorrow be heard within its walls. May the members of this household live together in this home in fellowship and friendship. May they love and revere You, hold fast to You, meditating in Your Torah, and living faithfully by its commandments.

*Where appropriate, add the words in parentheses:*

הָרֵק Bestow Your blessings on the owner of this house. Lord bless his resources and find favor in the work of his hands. Keep him far from sin and transgression. May Your tender love be upon him, and establish the work of our hands. May Your kindness be with his wife, she who watches over the affairs of her household, knowing that it is the God-fearing woman who deserves praise. (Bestow on their sons and daughters a spirit of wisdom and understanding. Lead them in the path of Your commandments, so that all who see them recognize that they are children blessed by the Lord, knowing Your Torah and revering You.) Protect them from all evil; protect their lives. May this [Your promise] be fulfilled in them: "You will be blessed when you come in, and blessed when you go out." And as we have been able to consecrate the house, so together may we witness the consecration of the great and holy Temple in Jerusalem Your city, city of our sacred assemblies, swiftly in our days. Amen. *Deut. 33* *Prov. 31* *Is. 61* *Deut. 28*

# סדר חנוכת הבית

מִזְמוֹר שִׁיר־חֲנֻכַּת הַבַּיִת לְדָוִד: אֲרוֹמִמְךָ יהוה כִּי דִלִּיתָנִי, וְלֹא־שִׂמַּחְתָּ אֹיְבַי תהלים ל
לִי: יהוה אֱלֹהָי, שִׁוַּעְתִּי אֵלֶיךָ וַתִּרְפָּאֵנִי: יהוה, הֶעֱלִיתָ מִן־שְׁאוֹל נַפְשִׁי, חִיִּיתַנִי
מִיָּרְדִי־בוֹר: זַמְּרוּ לַיהוה חֲסִידָיו, וְהוֹדוּ לְזֵכֶר קָדְשׁוֹ: כִּי רֶגַע בְּאַפּוֹ, חַיִּים
בִּרְצוֹנוֹ, בָּעֶרֶב יָלִין בֶּכִי וְלַבֹּקֶר רִנָּה: וַאֲנִי אָמַרְתִּי בְשַׁלְוִי, בַּל־אֶמּוֹט לְעוֹלָם:
יהוה, בִּרְצוֹנְךָ הֶעֱמַדְתָּה לְהַרְרִי עֹז, הִסְתַּרְתָּ פָנֶיךָ הָיִיתִי נִבְהָל: אֵלֶיךָ יהוה
אֶקְרָא, וְאֶל־אֲדֹנָי אֶתְחַנָּן: מַה־בֶּצַע בְּדָמִי, בְּרִדְתִּי אֶל שָׁחַת, הֲיוֹדְךָ עָפָר, הֲיַגִּיד
אֲמִתֶּךָ: שְׁמַע־יהוה וְחָנֵּנִי, יהוה הֱיֵה־עֹזֵר לִי: הָפַכְתָּ מִסְפְּדִי לְמָחוֹל לִי, פִּתַּחְתָּ
שַׂקִּי, וַתְּאַזְּרֵנִי שִׂמְחָה: לְמַעַן יְזַמֶּרְךָ כָבוֹד וְלֹא יִדֹּם, יהוה אֱלֹהַי, לְעוֹלָם אוֹדֶךָּ:

מִזְמוֹר לְדָוִד, יהוה מִי־יָגוּר בְּאָהֳלֶךָ, מִי־יִשְׁכֹּן בְּהַר קָדְשֶׁךָ: הוֹלֵךְ תָּמִים וּפֹעֵל תהלים טו
צֶדֶק, וְדֹבֵר אֱמֶת בִּלְבָבוֹ: לֹא־רָגַל עַל־לְשֹׁנוֹ, לֹא־עָשָׂה לְרֵעֵהוּ רָעָה, וְחֶרְפָּה
לֹא־נָשָׂא עַל־קְרֹבוֹ: נִבְזֶה בְּעֵינָיו נִמְאָס, וְאֶת־יִרְאֵי יהוה יְכַבֵּד, נִשְׁבַּע לְהָרַע
וְלֹא יָמִר: כַּסְפּוֹ לֹא־נָתַן בְּנֶשֶׁךְ, וְשֹׁחַד עַל־נָקִי לֹא־לָקָח, עֹשֵׂה אֵלֶּה, לֹא יִמּוֹט
לְעוֹלָם:

רִבּוֹן הָעוֹלָם, הַשְׁקִיפָה מִמְּעוֹן קָדְשְׁךָ, וְקַבֵּל בְּרַחֲמִים וּבְרָצוֹן אֶת תְּפִלַּת בָּנֶיךָ וְתַחֲנוּנָם, אֲשֶׁר הִתְאַסְּפוּ פֹּה לַחֲנֹךְ אֶת הַבַּיִת הַזֶּה וּלְהַקְרִיב לְפָנֶיךָ אֶת תּוֹדָתָם עַל כָּל הַחֶסֶד וְהָאֱמֶת אֲשֶׁר עָשִׂיתָ אִתָּם. אָנָּא חַסְדְּךָ מֵאִתָּם אַל יָמוּשׁ, וּבְרִית שְׁלוֹמְךָ אַל תָּמוּט. הָגֵן בְּעַד בֵּית מְגוּרֵיהֶם, לֹא תְאֻנֶּה אֵלָיו רָעָה, וְנֶגַע וְצַעַר לֹא יִקְרְבוּ אֵלָיו, וְלֹא יִשָּׁמַע קוֹל צְוָחָה בְּתוֹכוֹ. זַכֵּה אֶת בְּנֵי הַבַּיִת לָשֶׁבֶת בְּמִשְׁכְּנָם בְּאַחֲוָה וְרֵעוּת, לְאַהֲבָה וּלְיִרְאָה אוֹתְךָ וּלְדָבְקָה בָךְ, לַהֲגוֹת בְּתוֹרָתְךָ וּלְקַיֵּם מִצְוֹתֶיהָ.

*Where appropriate, add the words in parentheses:*

הָרֵק בִּרְכוֹתֶיךָ עַל בַּעַל הַבַּיִת. בָּרֵךְ יהוה חֵילוֹ, וּפֹעַל יָדָיו תִּרְצֶה: הַרְחִיקֵהוּ מִידֵי דברים לג
עֲבֵרָה וְעָוֹן, וִיהִי נֹעַם עָלָיו, וּמַעֲשֵׂה יָדָיו כּוֹנְנֵהוּ. יְהִי נָא חַסְדְּךָ אֶת אִשְׁתּוֹ,
צוֹפִיָּה הֲלִיכוֹת בֵּיתָהּ: וְתֵדַע כִּי, אִשָּׁה יִרְאַת־יהוה הִיא תִתְהַלָּל: (הוֹפַע עַל משלי לא
בְּנֵיהֶם וּבְנוֹתֵיהֶם רוּחַ חָכְמָה וּבִינָה, הַדְרִיכֵם בִּנְתִיב מִצְוֹתֶיךָ, וְכָל־רֹאֵיהֶם ישעיה סא
יַכִּירוּם כִּי הֵם זֶרַע בֵּרַךְ יהוה, בְּרוּכִים בַּתּוֹרָה וּבְיִרְאַת שָׁמַיִם.) שָׁמְרֵם מִכָּל רָע,
שְׁמֹר אֶת נַפְשָׁם, וִיקַיֵּם בָּהֶם: בָּרוּךְ אַתָּה בְּבֹאֶךָ, וּבָרוּךְ אַתָּה בְּצֵאתֶךָ: וְכַאֲשֶׁר דברים כח
זָכִינוּ לַחֲנֹךְ אֶת הַבַּיִת הַזֶּה עַתָּה, כֵּן נִזְכֶּה גַּם יַחַד לִרְאוֹת חֲנֻכַּת הַבַּיִת הַגָּדוֹל
וְהַקָּדוֹשׁ בִּירוּשָׁלַיִם עִירֶךָ, קִרְיַת מוֹעֲדֵינוּ, בִּמְהֵרָה בְיָמֵינוּ, אָמֵן.

# THE TRAVELER'S PRAYER

*If one intends to return home on the same day, add the words in parentheses:*

יְהִי רָצוֹן May it be Your will,
LORD our God and God of our fathers,
to lead us to peace, direct our steps to peace,
guide us to peace, and bring us to our desired destination in life,
joy and peace
(and bring us back to our home in peace).
Rescue us from any enemy or ambush on the way,
and from all afflictions that trouble the world.
Send blessing to the work of our hands,
and let us find grace, kindness and compassion
from You and from all who see us.
Hear our pleas,
for You are a God who listens to prayer and pleas.
Blessed are You, LORD, who listens to prayer.

May the LORD guard your going out and your return, *Ps. 121*
from now and for all time.

*Repeat three times:*

וַיַּעֲקֹב And Jacob went on his way *Gen. 32*
and angels of God met him.
When he saw them, Jacob said, "This is God's camp"
and he named the place Maḥanaim [two camps].

*Repeat three times:*

יְבָרֶכְךָ May the LORD bless you and protect you. *Num. 6*
May the LORD make His face shine on you and be gracious to you.
May the LORD turn His face toward you and grant you peace.

שִׁיר לַמַּעֲלוֹת A song of ascents. I lift my eyes up to the hills; from where will my help come? My help comes from the LORD, Maker of heaven and earth. He will not let your foot stumble; He who guards you does not slumber. See: the Guardian of Israel neither slumbers nor sleeps. The LORD is your Guardian; the LORD is your Shade at your right hand. The sun will not strike you by day, nor the moon by night. The LORD will guard you from all harm; He will guard your life. The LORD will guard your going and coming, now and for evermore. *Ps. 121*

# תפילת הדרך

*If one intends to return home on the same day, add the words in parentheses:*

יְהִי רָצוֹן מִלְּפָנֶיךָ, יהוה אֱלֹהֵינוּ וֵאלֹהֵי אֲבוֹתֵינוּ
שֶׁתּוֹלִיכֵנוּ לְשָׁלוֹם, וְתַצְעִידֵנוּ לְשָׁלוֹם, וְתַדְרִיכֵנוּ לְשָׁלוֹם
וְתַגִּיעֵנוּ לִמְחוֹז חֶפְצֵנוּ לְחַיִּים וּלְשִׂמְחָה וּלְשָׁלוֹם
(וְתַחֲזִירֵנוּ לְבֵיתֵנוּ לְשָׁלוֹם)
וְתַצִּילֵנוּ מִכַּף כָּל אוֹיֵב וְאוֹרֵב בַּדֶּרֶךְ
וּמִכָּל מִינֵי פֻּרְעָנִיּוֹת הַמִּתְרַגְּשׁוֹת לָבוֹא לָעוֹלָם
וְתִשְׁלַח בְּרָכָה בְּמַעֲשֵׂה יָדֵינוּ
וְתִתְּנֵנוּ לְחֵן וּלְחֶסֶד וּלְרַחֲמִים בְּעֵינֶיךָ וּבְעֵינֵי כָל רוֹאֵינוּ
וְתִשְׁמַע קוֹל תַּחֲנוּנֵינוּ
כִּי אֵל שׁוֹמֵעַ תְּפִלָּה וְתַחֲנוּן אָתָּה.
בָּרוּךְ אַתָּה יהוה, שׁוֹמֵעַ תְּפִלָּה.

יהוה יִשְׁמָר־צֵאתְךָ וּבוֹאֶךָ, מֵעַתָּה וְעַד־עוֹלָם: תהלים קכא

*Repeat three times:*

וְיַעֲקֹב הָלַךְ לְדַרְכּוֹ, וַיִּפְגְּעוּ־בוֹ מַלְאֲכֵי אֱלֹהִים: בראשית לב
וַיֹּאמֶר יַעֲקֹב כַּאֲשֶׁר רָאָם, מַחֲנֵה אֱלֹהִים זֶה
וַיִּקְרָא שֵׁם־הַמָּקוֹם הַהוּא מַחֲנָיִם:

*Repeat three times:*

יְבָרֶכְךָ יהוה וְיִשְׁמְרֶךָ: במדבר ו
יָאֵר יהוה פָּנָיו אֵלֶיךָ וִיחֻנֶּךָּ:
יִשָּׂא יהוה פָּנָיו אֵלֶיךָ וְיָשֵׂם לְךָ שָׁלוֹם:

שִׁיר לַמַּעֲלוֹת, אֶשָּׂא עֵינַי אֶל־הֶהָרִים, מֵאַיִן יָבֹא עֶזְרִי: עֶזְרִי מֵעִם יהוה, תהלים קכא
עֹשֵׂה שָׁמַיִם וָאָרֶץ: אַל־יִתֵּן לַמּוֹט רַגְלֶךָ, אַל־יָנוּם שֹׁמְרֶךָ: הִנֵּה לֹא־יָנוּם
וְלֹא יִישָׁן, שׁוֹמֵר יִשְׂרָאֵל: יהוה שֹׁמְרֶךָ, יהוה צִלְּךָ עַל־יַד יְמִינֶךָ: יוֹמָם
הַשֶּׁמֶשׁ לֹא־יַכֶּכָּה, וְיָרֵחַ בַּלָּיְלָה: יהוה יִשְׁמָרְךָ מִכָּל־רָע, יִשְׁמֹר אֶת־נַפְשֶׁךָ:
יהוה יִשְׁמָר־צֵאתְךָ וּבוֹאֶךָ, מֵעַתָּה וְעַד־עוֹלָם:

# מעגל החיים
# THE CYCLE OF LIFE


| | | |
|---|---|---|
| ברית מילה | 1093 | BRIT MILA |
| פדיון הבן | 1105 | PIDYON HABEN |
| תפילה ליולדת | 1109 | PRAYER AFTER CHILDBIRTH |
| זבד הבת | 1113 | ZEVED HABAT |
| קידושין ונישואין | 1117 | MARRIAGE |
| תפילה לחולה | 1123 | PRAYER FOR RECOVERY |
| לווית המת | 1127 | FUNERAL SERVICE |
| תפילה בבית האבל | 1139 | THE HOUSE OF MOURNING |

# BRIT MILA

*When the baby is brought in, all stand and say:*

Blessed is he who comes.

*The mohel (in some congregations, all) say (in Israel omit):*

וַיְדַבֵּר The LORD spoke to Moses, saying: Pinehas the son of Elazar, the son of Aaron the priest, turned back My rage from the children of Israel, when he was zealous for Me among them, and I did not annihilate the children of Israel in My own zeal. And so tell him, that I now give him My covenant for peace. *Num. 25*

*The following verses, through "LORD, please, grant us success," are only said in Israel.*

*Mohel:* Happy are those You choose and bring near to dwell in Your courts. *Ps. 65*

*All:* May we be sated with the goodness of Your House,
Your holy Temple.

*The father takes the baby in his hands and says quietly:*

אִם אֶשְׁכָּחֵךְ If I forget you, O Jerusalem, may my right hand forget its skill. May my tongue cling to the roof of my mouth, if I do not remember you, if I do not set Jerusalem above my highest joy. *Ps. 137*

*The father says aloud, followed by the congregation:*

Listen, Israel: the LORD is our God, the LORD is One. *Deut. 6*

*The Mohel, followed by the congregation,*
*recites each of the following three phrases twice:*

The LORD is King, the LORD was King,
the LORD shall be King for ever and all time.
LORD, please, save us. *Ps. 118*
LORD, please, grant us success.

*The baby is placed on Eliyahu's seat, and the Mohel says:*

This is the throne of Elijah the prophet, may he be remembered for good.

*The Mohel continues:*

לִישׁוּעָתְךָ For Your salvation I wait, O LORD. I await Your deliverance, *Gen. 49* *Ps. 119*
LORD, and I observe Your commandments. Elijah, angel of the covenant, behold: yours is before you. Stand at my right hand and be close to me.
I await Your deliverance, LORD. I rejoice in Your word like one who finds *Ps. 119*
much spoil. Those who love Your Torah have great peace, and there is

# סדר ברית מילה

*When the baby is brought in, all stand and say:*

## בָּרוּךְ הַבָּא.

*The* מוהל *(in some congregations, all) say (in* ארץ ישראל *omit):*

וַיְדַבֵּר יהוה אֶל־מֹשֶׁה לֵּאמֹר: פִּינְחָס בֶּן־אֶלְעָזָר בֶּן־אַהֲרֹן הַכֹּהֵן במדבר כה
הֵשִׁיב אֶת־חֲמָתִי מֵעַל בְּנֵי־יִשְׂרָאֵל, בְּקַנְאוֹ אֶת־קִנְאָתִי בְּתוֹכָם,
וְלֹא־כִלִּיתִי אֶת־בְּנֵי־יִשְׂרָאֵל בְּקִנְאָתִי: לָכֵן אֱמֹר, הִנְנִי נֹתֵן לוֹ אֶת־
בְּרִיתִי שָׁלוֹם:

*The following verses, through* אָנָּא יהוה הַצְלִיחָה נָא *are only said in Israel.*

המוהל: אַשְׁרֵי תִּבְחַר וּתְקָרֵב, יִשְׁכֹּן חֲצֵרֶיךָ תהלים סה

הקהל: נִשְׂבְּעָה בְּטוּב בֵּיתֶךָ, קְדֹשׁ הֵיכָלֶךָ:

*The father takes the baby in his hands and says quietly:*

אִם־אֶשְׁכָּחֵךְ יְרוּשָׁלָםִ, תִּשְׁכַּח יְמִינִי: תִּדְבַּק לְשׁוֹנִי לְחִכִּי אִם־לֹא אֶזְכְּרֵכִי, תהלים קלז
אִם־לֹא אַעֲלֶה אֶת־יְרוּשָׁלַםִ עַל רֹאשׁ שִׂמְחָתִי:

*The father says aloud, followed by the* קהל*:*

שְׁמַע יִשְׂרָאֵל, יהוה אֱלֹהֵינוּ, יהוה אֶחָד: דברים ו

*The* מוהל*, followed by the* קהל*, repeats each of the following three phrases twice:*

יהוה מֶלֶךְ, יהוה מָלָךְ, יהוה יִמְלֹךְ לְעוֹלָם וָעֶד.
אָנָּא יהוה הוֹשִׁיעָה נָּא תהלים קיח
אָנָּא יהוה הַצְלִיחָה נָא:

*The baby is placed on the* כסא של אליהו*, and the* מוהל *says:*

## זֶה הַכִּסֵּא שֶׁל אֵלִיָּהוּ הַנָּבִיא זָכוּר לַטּוֹב.

*The* מוהל *continues:*

לִישׁוּעָתְךָ קִוִּיתִי יהוה: שִׂבַּרְתִּי לִישׁוּעָתְךָ יהוה, וּמִצְוֹתֶיךָ עָשִׂיתִי: בראשית מט / תהלים קיט
אֵלִיָּהוּ מַלְאַךְ הַבְּרִית, הִנֵּה שֶׁלְּךָ לְפָנֶיךָ, עֲמֹד עַל יְמִינִי וְסָמְכֵנִי.
שִׂבַּרְתִּי לִישׁוּעָתְךָ יהוה: שָׂשׂ אָנֹכִי עַל־אִמְרָתֶךָ, כְּמוֹצֵא שָׁלָל רָב: תהלים קיט

no stumbling block before them. Happy are those You choose and bring Ps. 65
near to dwell in Your courts.

*All respond:*

May we be sated with the goodness of Your House, Your holy Temple.

*The baby is placed on the knees of the Sandak, and the Mohel says:*

בָּרוּךְ Blessed are You, Lord our God, King of the Universe,
who has made us holy through His commandments,
and has commanded us concerning circumcision.

*Immediately after the circumcision, the father says:*

בָּרוּךְ Blessed are You, Lord our God, King of the Universe,
who has made us holy through His commandments,
and has commanded us to bring him [our son]
into the covenant of Abraham, our father.

*In Israel the father adds (some in the Diaspora add it as well):*

בָּרוּךְ Blessed are You, Lord our God, King of the Universe,
who has given us life, sustained us,
and brought us to this time.

*All respond:*

אָמֵן Amen. Just as he has entered into the covenant,
so may he enter into Torah, marriage and good deeds.

*After the circumcision has been completed, the Mohel (or another honoree) takes a cup of wine and says:*

בָּרוּךְ Blessed are You, Lord our God, King of the Universe,
who creates the fruit of the vine.

בָּרוּךְ Blessed are You, Lord our God, King of the Universe, who made the beloved one [Isaac] holy from the womb, marked the decree of circumcision in his flesh, and gave his descendants the seal and sign of the holy covenant. As a reward for this, the Living God, our Portion, our Rock, did order deliverance from destruction for the beloved of our flesh, for the sake of His covenant that He set in our flesh. Blessed are You, Lord, who establishes the covenant.

שָׁלוֹם רָב לְאֹהֲבֵי תוֹרָתֶךָ, וְאֵין־לָמוֹ מִכְשׁוֹל: אַשְׁרֵי תִּבְחַר וּתְקָרֵב, יִשְׁכֹּן חֲצֵרֶיךָ תהלים סה

*All respond:*

נִשְׂבְּעָה בְּטוּב בֵּיתֶךָ, קְדֹשׁ הֵיכָלֶךָ:

*The baby is placed on the knees of the* סנדק*, and the* מוהל *says:*

בָּרוּךְ אַתָּה יהוה אֱלֹהֵינוּ מֶלֶךְ הָעוֹלָם
אֲשֶׁר קִדְּשָׁנוּ בְּמִצְוֹתָיו, וְצִוָּנוּ עַל הַמִּילָה.

*Immediately after the circumcision, the father says:*

בָּרוּךְ אַתָּה יהוה אֱלֹהֵינוּ מֶלֶךְ הָעוֹלָם
אֲשֶׁר קִדְּשָׁנוּ בְּמִצְוֹתָיו
וְצִוָּנוּ לְהַכְנִיסוֹ בִּבְרִיתוֹ שֶׁל אַבְרָהָם אָבִינוּ.

*In* ארץ ישראל *the father adds (some in* חוץ לארץ *add it as well):*

בָּרוּךְ אַתָּה יהוה אֱלֹהֵינוּ מֶלֶךְ הָעוֹלָם
שֶׁהֶחֱיָנוּ וְקִיְּמָנוּ וְהִגִּיעָנוּ לַזְּמַן הַזֶּה.

*All respond:*

אָמֵן. כְּשֵׁם שֶׁנִּכְנַס לַבְּרִית
כֵּן יִכָּנֵס לְתוֹרָה וּלְחֻפָּה וּלְמַעֲשִׂים טוֹבִים.

*After the circumcision has been completed, the* מוהל *(or another honoree) takes a cup of wine and says:*

בָּרוּךְ אַתָּה יהוה אֱלֹהֵינוּ מֶלֶךְ הָעוֹלָם, בּוֹרֵא פְּרִי הַגָּפֶן.

בָּרוּךְ אַתָּה יהוה אֱלֹהֵינוּ מֶלֶךְ הָעוֹלָם, אֲשֶׁר קִדַּשׁ יְדִיד מִבֶּטֶן, וְחֹק בִּשְׁאֵרוֹ שָׂם, וְצֶאֱצָאָיו חָתַם בְּאוֹת בְּרִית קֹדֶשׁ. עַל כֵּן בִּשְׂכַר זֹאת, אֵל חַי חֶלְקֵנוּ צוּרֵנוּ צַוֵּה לְהַצִּיל יְדִידוּת שְׁאֵרֵנוּ מִשַּׁחַת, לְמַעַן בְּרִיתוֹ אֲשֶׁר שָׂם בִּבְשָׂרֵנוּ. בָּרוּךְ אַתָּה יהוה, כּוֹרֵת הַבְּרִית.

אֱלֹהֵינוּ Our God and God of our fathers, preserve this child to his father and mother, and let his name be called in Israel (*baby's name* son of *father's name*). May the father rejoice in the issue of his body, and the mother be glad with the fruit of her womb, as is written, "May your father and mother rejoice, and she who bore you be glad." And it is said, "Then I passed by you and saw you downtrodden in your blood, and I said to you: In your blood, live; and I said to you: In your blood, live." *Prov. 23* *Ezek. 16*

וְנֶאֱמַר And it is said, "He remembered His covenant for ever; the word He ordained for a thousand generations; the covenant He made with Abraham and gave on oath to Isaac, confirming it as a statute for Jacob, an everlasting covenant for Israel." And it is said, "And Abraham circumcised his son Isaac at the age of eight days, as God had commanded him." Thank the Lord for He is good; His loving-kindness is for ever. *Ps. 105* *Gen. 21* *Ps. 118*

*All respond:*

Thank the Lord for He is good; His loving-kindness is for ever.

*The Mohel (or honoree) continues:*

May this child (*baby's name* son of *father's name*) become great. Just as he has entered into the covenant, so may he enter into Torah, marriage and good deeds.

*The Sandak also drinks some of the wine; some drops are given to the baby. The cup is then sent to the mother, who also drinks from it.*

*All say Aleinu on page 244, and Mourner's Kaddish on page 246.*

אֱלֹהֵינוּ וֵאלֹהֵי אֲבוֹתֵינוּ, קַיֵּם אֶת הַיֶּלֶד הַזֶּה לְאָבִיו וּלְאִמּוֹ, וְיִקָּרֵא
שְׁמוֹ בְּיִשְׂרָאֵל (פלוני בֶּן פלוני). יִשְׂמַח הָאָב בְּיוֹצֵא חֲלָצָיו וְתָגֵל אִמּוֹ
בִּפְרִי בִטְנָהּ, כַּכָּתוּב: יִשְׂמַח־אָבִיךָ וְאִמֶּךָ, וְתָגֵל יוֹלַדְתֶּךָ: וְנֶאֱמַר: משלי כג
וָאֶעֱבֹר עָלַיִךְ וָאֶרְאֵךְ מִתְבּוֹסֶסֶת בְּדָמָיִךְ, וָאֹמַר לָךְ בְּדָמַיִךְ חֲיִי, יחזקאל טז
וָאֹמַר לָךְ בְּדָמַיִךְ חֲיִי:

וְנֶאֱמַר: זָכַר לְעוֹלָם בְּרִיתוֹ, דָּבָר צִוָּה לְאֶלֶף דּוֹר: אֲשֶׁר כָּרַת אֶת־ תהלים קה
אַבְרָהָם, וּשְׁבוּעָתוֹ לְיִשְׂחָק: וַיַּעֲמִידֶהָ לְיַעֲקֹב לְחֹק, לְיִשְׂרָאֵל בְּרִית
עוֹלָם: וְנֶאֱמַר: וַיָּמָל אַבְרָהָם אֶת־יִצְחָק בְּנוֹ בֶּן־שְׁמֹנַת יָמִים, כַּאֲשֶׁר בראשית כא
צִוָּה אֹתוֹ אֱלֹהִים: הוֹדוּ לַיהוה כִּי־טוֹב, כִּי לְעוֹלָם חַסְדּוֹ: תהלים קיח

*All respond:*

הוֹדוּ לַיהוה כִּי־טוֹב, כִּי לְעוֹלָם חַסְדּוֹ:

*The* מוהל *(or honoree) continues:*

(פלוני בֶּן פלוני) זֶה הַקָּטֹן גָּדוֹל יִהְיֶה, כְּשֵׁם שֶׁנִּכְנַס לַבְּרִית, כֵּן יִכָּנֵס לְתוֹרָה וּלְחֻפָּה וּלְמַעֲשִׂים טוֹבִים.

*The* סנדק *also drinks some of the wine; some drops are given to the baby. The cup is then sent to the mother, who also drinks from it.*

*All say* עָלֵינוּ *on page 245, and* קדיש יתום *on page 247.*

## BIRKAT HAMAZON AT A BRIT MILA

*Leader* Gentlemen, let us say grace.

*Others* May the name of the Lord be blessed from now and for ever. *Ps. 113*

*Leader* May the name of the Lord be blessed
from now and for ever.

*Leader then others* We give thanks to Your name among the faithful.
Blessed are you to the Lord.

*Leader* With permission of the Almighty, awesome and revered,
a refuge in times of trouble,
Almighty, girded with strength –
majestic on high, the Lord.

*Others* We give thanks to Your name among the faithful.
Blessed are you to the Lord.

*Leader* With permission of the holy Torah,
pure and clear,
given to us as a heritage
by Moses the servant of the Lord.

*Others* We give thanks to Your name among the faithful.
Blessed are you to the Lord.

*Leader* With permission of the priests, the Levites,
I call upon the God of the Hebrews,
declaring His glory to the furthest isles,
and offering blessings to the Lord.

*Others* We give thanks to Your name among the faithful.
Blessed are you to the Lord.

# ברכת המזון לברית מילה

*Leader* רַבּוֹתַי, נְבָרֵךְ.

*Others* יְהִי שֵׁם יהוה מְבֹרָךְ מֵעַתָּה וְעַד־עוֹלָם: תהלים קיג

*Leader* יְהִי שֵׁם יהוה מְבֹרָךְ מֵעַתָּה וְעַד־עוֹלָם:

*Leader then others* נוֹדֶה לְשִׁמְךָ בְּתוֹךְ אֱמוּנַי, בְּרוּכִים אַתֶּם לַיהוה.

*Leader* בִּרְשׁוּת אֵל אָיֹם וְנוֹרָא
מִשְׂגָּב לְעִתּוֹת בַּצָּרָה
אֵל נֶאְזָר בִּגְבוּרָה
אַדִּיר בַּמָּרוֹם יהוה.

*Others* נוֹדֶה לְשִׁמְךָ בְּתוֹךְ אֱמוּנַי, בְּרוּכִים אַתֶּם לַיהוה.

*Leader* בִּרְשׁוּת הַתּוֹרָה הַקְּדוֹשָׁה
טְהוֹרָה הִיא וְגַם פְּרוּשָׁה
צִוָּה לָנוּ מוֹרָשָׁה
מֹשֶׁה עֶבֶד יהוה.

*Others* נוֹדֶה לְשִׁמְךָ בְּתוֹךְ אֱמוּנַי, בְּרוּכִים אַתֶּם לַיהוה.

*Leader* בִּרְשׁוּת הַכֹּהֲנִים וְהַלְוִיִּם
אֶקְרָא לֵאלֹהֵי הָעִבְרִיִּים
אֲהוֹדֶנּוּ בְּכָל אִיִּים
אֲבָרְכָה אֶת יהוה.

*Others* נוֹדֶה לְשִׁמְךָ בְּתוֹךְ אֱמוּנַי, בְּרוּכִים אַתֶּם לַיהוה.

*Leader* With the permission of the rabbis, teachers and friends,
I open my lips with song,
saying from my innermost being:
"Blessed is he that comes in the name of the LORD."

*Others* We give thanks to Your name among the faithful.
Blessed are you to the LORD.

*Leader* With your permission, my masters and teachers,
let us bless (*in a minyan:* our God,)
the One from whose food we have eaten.

*Others* Blessed be (*in a minyan:* our God,)
the One from whose food we have eaten,
and by whose goodness we live.

*Leader* Blessed be (*in a minyan:* our God,)
the One from whose food we have eaten,
and by whose goodness we live.
Blessed be He, and blessed be His name.

*Continue with Birkat HaMazon on page 1058 until "in the eyes of God and man" on page 1068. Then continue:*

*Someone other than the father says:*

הָרַחֲמָן May the Compassionate One
bless the father and mother of this child.
May they be worthy to raise him,
educate him, and train him in wisdom.
From this eighth day onward may his blood be accepted,
and may the LORD his God be with him always.

*Someone other than the Sandak says:*

הָרַחֲמָן May the Compassionate One bless him [the Sandak]
who assisted in the covenant of circumcision
and rejoiced to do this pious deed.
May God doubly reward him for his deed,
exalting him ever higher.

*Leader* בִּרְשׁוּת מָרָנָן וְרַבָּנָן וְרַבּוֹתַי
אֶפְתְּחָה בְּשִׁיר פִּי וּשְׂפָתַי
וְתֹאמַרְנָה עַצְמוֹתַי
בָּרוּךְ הַבָּא בְּשֵׁם יהוה.

*Others* נוֹדֶה לְשִׁמְךָ בְּתוֹךְ אֱמוּנַי, בְּרוּכִים אַתֶּם לַיהוה.

*Leader* בִּרְשׁוּת מָרָנָן וְרַבָּנָן וְרַבּוֹתַי
נְבָרֵךְ (במנין: אֱלֹהֵינוּ) שֶׁאָכַלְנוּ מִשֶּׁלּוֹ.

*Others* בָּרוּךְ (במנין: אֱלֹהֵינוּ) שֶׁאָכַלְנוּ מִשֶּׁלּוֹ וּבְטוּבוֹ חָיִינוּ.

*Leader* בָּרוּךְ (במנין: אֱלֹהֵינוּ) שֶׁאָכַלְנוּ מִשֶּׁלּוֹ וּבְטוּבוֹ חָיִינוּ.
בָּרוּךְ הוּא וּבָרוּךְ שְׁמוֹ.

*Continue with* ברכת המזון *on page 1059 until* בְּעֵינֵי אֱלֹהִים וְאָדָם *on page 1069. Then continue:*

*Someone other than the father says:*

הָרַחֲמָן הוּא יְבָרֵךְ אֲבִי הַיֶּלֶד וְאִמּוֹ
וְיִזְכּוּ לְגַדְּלוֹ וּלְחַנְּכוֹ וּלְחַכְּמוֹ
מִיּוֹם הַשְּׁמִינִי וָהָלְאָה יֵרָצֶה דָמוֹ
וִיהִי יהוה אֱלֹהָיו עִמּוֹ.

*Someone other than the* סנדק *says:*

הָרַחֲמָן הוּא יְבָרֵךְ בַּעַל בְּרִית הַמִּילָה
אֲשֶׁר שָׂשׂ לַעֲשׂוֹת צֶדֶק בְּגִילָה
וִישַׁלֵּם פָּעֳלוֹ וּמַשְׂכֻּרְתּוֹ כְּפוּלָה
וְיִתְּנֵהוּ לְמַעְלָה לְמָעְלָה.

הָרַחֲמָן May the Compassionate One
bless the tender child, circumcised on his eighth day.
May his heart and hands be firm with God,
and may he be worthy to witness the Divine Presence
three times a year.

*Someone other than the Mohel says:*

הָרַחֲמָן May the Compassionate One
bless him who performed the circumcision,
and fulfilled every part of the precept.
The service of the faint-hearted would not be acceptable
if he failed to perform the three essentials of the precept.

הָרַחֲמָן May the Compassionate One
send us His anointed, blameless in life,
through the merit of this child
groomed by the blood of circumcision,
to proclaim good news and consolations
to the unique people scattered
and dispersed among the nations.

הָרַחֲמָן May the Compassionate One send us the righteous priest,
who was taken into hiding,
until a throne, bright as the sun, radiant as a diamond,
is prepared for him;
the prophet who covered his face with his mantle
and wrapped himself in it [when God declared]:
My covenant is with him for life and peace.

*Continue with "May the Compassionate One make us worthy of the Messianic Age" on page 1070.*

*On Shabbat, Rosh Ḥodesh or Yom Tov, continue with the appropriate "May the Compassionate One" at the top of page 1070.*

הָרַחֲמָן הוּא יְבָרֵךְ רַךְ הַנִּמּוֹל לִשְׁמוֹנָה
וְיִהְיוּ יָדָיו וְלִבּוֹ לָאֵל אֱמוּנָה
וְיִזְכֶּה לִרְאוֹת פְּנֵי הַשְּׁכִינָה
שָׁלֹשׁ פְּעָמִים בַּשָּׁנָה.

*Someone other than the* מוהל *says:*

הָרַחֲמָן הוּא יְבָרֵךְ הַמָּל בְּשַׂר הָעָרְלָה
וּפָרַע וּמָצַץ דְּמֵי הַמִּילָה
אִישׁ הַיָּרֵא וְרַךְ הַלֵּבָב עֲבוֹדָתוֹ פְּסוּלָה
אִם שְׁלָשׁ אֵלֶּה לֹא יַעֲשֶׂה לָהּ.

הָרַחֲמָן הוּא יִשְׁלַח לָנוּ מְשִׁיחוֹ הוֹלֵךְ תָּמִים
בִּזְכוּת חֲתַן לַמּוּלוֹת דָּמִים
לְבַשֵּׂר בְּשׂוֹרוֹת טוֹבוֹת וְנִחוּמִים
לְעַם אֶחָד מְפֻזָּר וּמְפֹרָד בֵּין הָעַמִּים.

הָרַחֲמָן הוּא יִשְׁלַח לָנוּ כֹּהֵן צֶדֶק אֲשֶׁר לֻקַּח לְעֵילוֹם
עַד הוּכַן כִּסְאוֹ כַּשֶּׁמֶשׁ וְיַהֲלֹם
וַיָּלֶט פָּנָיו בְּאַדַּרְתּוֹ וַיִּגְלֹם
בְּרִיתִי הָיְתָה אִתּוֹ הַחַיִּים וְהַשָּׁלוֹם.

*Continue with* הָרַחֲמָן הוּא יְזַכֵּנוּ לִימוֹת הַמָּשִׁיחַ
*on page 1071.*

*On* שבת*,* ראש חודש *or* יום טוב*,*
*continue with the appropriate* הָרַחֲמָן *at the top of page 1071.*

## REDEMPTION OF THE FIRSTBORN

*A firstborn male child, must be redeemed on the 31st day of his birth – unless the father is a Kohen or Levi, or the mother is a daughter of a Kohen or a Levi. If the 31st day falls on Shabbat or Yom Tov, the ceremony is postponed to the following weekday.*

*The father, presenting his child to the Kohen, declares:*

זֶה This is my firstborn son, the first issue of his mother's womb.
The Holy One, blessed be He, has commanded us to redeem him, as is said,

"Those who are to be redeemed, *Num. 18*
you must redeem from the age of one month,
at the fixed price of five shekels of silver
by the sacred standard,
which is twenty gerahs to the shekel."

And it is also stated,

"Consecrate to Me every firstborn; *Ex. 13*
the first of every womb among the people of Israel,
whether of man or beast,
belongs to Me."

*The Kohen checks with the mother that this is her firstborn, and then asks if she has miscarried before this child. If her answer is no, he asks the father:*

מַאי Which do you prefer:
to give me your firstborn son,
the first birth of his mother,
or to redeem him for five selas
as you are bound to do according to the Torah?

*The father replies:*

חָפֵץ I wish to redeem my son.
I present you with the cost of his redemption
which I am bound to give according to the Torah.

# סדר פדיון הבן

*A firstborn male child, must be redeemed on the 31st day of his birth – unless the father is a כהן or לוי, or the mother is a daughter of a כהן or a לוי. If the 31st day falls on שבת or יום טוב, the ceremony is postponed to the following weekday.*

*The father, presenting his child to the כהן, declares:*

זֶה בְּנִי בְכוֹרִי הוּא פֶּטֶר רֶחֶם לְאִמּוֹ
וְהַקָּדוֹשׁ בָּרוּךְ הוּא צִוָּה לִפְדּוֹתוֹ
שֶׁנֶּאֱמַר
במדבר יח וּפְדוּיָו מִבֶּן־חֹדֶשׁ תִּפְדֶּה
בְּעֶרְכְּךָ כֶּסֶף חֲמֵשֶׁת שְׁקָלִים בְּשֶׁקֶל הַקֹּדֶשׁ
עֶשְׂרִים גֵּרָה הוּא:
וְנֶאֱמַר
שמות יג קַדֶּשׁ־לִי כָל־בְּכוֹר פֶּטֶר כָּל־רֶחֶם
בִּבְנֵי יִשְׂרָאֵל בָּאָדָם וּבַבְּהֵמָה
לִי הוּא:

*The כהן checks with the mother that this is her firstborn, and then asks if she has miscarried before this child. If her answer is no, he asks the father:*

מַאי בָּעֵית טְפֵי
לִתֵּן לִי בִּנְךָ בְכוֹרְךָ שֶׁהוּא פֶּטֶר רֶחֶם לְאִמּוֹ
אוֹ בָּעֵית לִפְדּוֹתוֹ בְּעַד חָמֵשׁ סְלָעִים
כְּדִמְחֻיַּבְתְּ מִדְּאוֹרַיְתָא.

*The father replies:*

חָפֵץ אֲנִי לִפְדּוֹת אֶת בְּנִי
וְהֵילָךְ דְּמֵי פִדְיוֹנוֹ כְּדִמְחֻיַּבְנָא מִדְּאוֹרַיְתָא.

*Holding the redemption money, the father says:*

בָּרוּךְ Blessed are You, LORD our God, King of the Universe,
who has made us holy through His commandments,
and has commanded us concerning the redemption of a son.

בָּרוּךְ Blessed are You, LORD our God, King of the Universe,
who has given us life, sustained us, and brought us to this time.

*The redemption money is given to the Kohen, who then returns the child to his father.*
*The Kohen takes a cup of wine and says:*

בָּרוּךְ Blessed are You, LORD our God, King of the Universe,
who creates the fruit of the vine.

*Placing his right hand on the head of the child, the Kohen blesses him as follows:*

יְשִׂמְךָ May God make you like *Gen. 48*
Ephraim and Manasseh.
May the LORD bless you and protect you. *Num. 6*
May the LORD make His face shine on you
and be gracious to you.
May the LORD turn His face toward you
and grant you peace.
The LORD is your Guardian; *Ps. 121*
the LORD is your protection at your right hand.
The LORD will guard you against all harm.
He will guard your life.
For length of days, years of life, and peace *Prov. 3*
He will increase for you.

*Holding the redemption money, the father says:*

בָּרוּךְ אַתָּה יהוה אֱלֹהֵינוּ מֶלֶךְ הָעוֹלָם
אֲשֶׁר קִדְּשָׁנוּ בְּמִצְוֹתָיו, וְצִוָּנוּ עַל פִּדְיוֹן הַבֵּן.

בָּרוּךְ אַתָּה יהוה אֱלֹהֵינוּ מֶלֶךְ הָעוֹלָם
שֶׁהֶחֱיָנוּ וְקִיְּמָנוּ וְהִגִּיעָנוּ לַזְּמַן הַזֶּה.

*The redemption money is given to the* כהן*, who then returns the child to his father.*
*The* כהן *takes a cup of wine and says:*

בָּרוּךְ אַתָּה יהוה אֱלֹהֵינוּ מֶלֶךְ הָעוֹלָם
בּוֹרֵא פְּרִי הַגָּפֶן.

*Placing his right hand on the head of the child, the* כהן *blesses him as follows:*

יְשִׂמְךָ אֱלֹהִים כְּאֶפְרַיִם וְכִמְנַשֶּׁה: בראשית מח
יְבָרֶכְךָ יהוה וְיִשְׁמְרֶךָ: במדבר ו
יָאֵר יהוה פָּנָיו אֵלֶיךָ וִיחֻנֶּךָּ:
יִשָּׂא יהוה פָּנָיו אֵלֶיךָ וְיָשֵׂם לְךָ שָׁלוֹם:
יהוה שֹׁמְרֶךָ, יהוה צִלְּךָ עַל־יַד יְמִינֶךָ: תהלים קכא
יהוה יִשְׁמָרְךָ מִכָּל־רָע, יִשְׁמֹר אֶת־נַפְשֶׁךָ:
כִּי אֹרֶךְ יָמִים וּשְׁנוֹת חַיִּים וְשָׁלוֹם יוֹסִיפוּ לָךְ: משלי ג

## THANKSGIVING PRAYER AFTER CHILDBIRTH

*On entering the synagogue, say:*

וַאֲנִי As for me, by Your great love, *Ps. 5*
I will come into Your House.
I will bow down toward Your holy Temple in awe of You.

אָהַבְתִּי I love the Lord, for He hears my voice, my pleas. *Ps. 116*
He turns His ear to me whenever I call.
The bonds of death encompassed me,
the anguish of the grave came upon me,
I was overcome by trouble and sorrow.
Then I called on the name of the Lord: "Lord, I pray, save my life."
Gracious is the Lord, and righteous; our God is full of compassion.
The Lord protects the simple-hearted.
When I was brought low, He saved me.
My soul, be at peace once more, for the Lord has been good to you.
For You have rescued me from death,
my eyes from weeping, my feet from stumbling.
I shall walk in the presence of the Lord in the land of the living.
I had faith, even when I said, "I am greatly afflicted,"
even when I said rashly, "All men are liars."

מָה־אָשִׁיב How can I repay the Lord for all His goodness to me? *Ps. 116*
To You I shall bring a thanksgiving-offering
and call on the Lord by name.
I will fulfill my vows to the Lord in the presence of all His people,
in the courts of the House of the Lord,
in your midst, Jerusalem. Halleluya.

*The mother says:*

בָּרוּךְ Blessed are You, Lord our God, King of the Universe,
who bestows good things on the unworthy,
who has bestowed on me much good.

*All respond:*

אָמֵן Amen. May He who bestowed much good on you,
continue to bestow on you much good. Selah.

# סדר תפילה ליולדת

*On entering the* בית כנסת*, say:*

וַאֲנִי בְּרֹב חַסְדְּךָ אָבוֹא בֵיתֶךָ תהלים ה
אֶשְׁתַּחֲוֶה אֶל־הֵיכַל־קָדְשְׁךָ בְּיִרְאָתֶךָ:

אָהַבְתִּי, כִּי־יִשְׁמַע יהוה, אֶת־קוֹלִי תַּחֲנוּנָי: תהלים קטז
כִּי־הִטָּה אָזְנוֹ לִי, וּבְיָמַי אֶקְרָא:
אֲפָפוּנִי חֶבְלֵי־מָוֶת, וּמְצָרֵי שְׁאוֹל מְצָאוּנִי, צָרָה וְיָגוֹן אֶמְצָא:
וּבְשֵׁם־יהוה אֶקְרָא, אָנָּה יהוה מַלְּטָה נַפְשִׁי:
חַנּוּן יהוה וְצַדִּיק, וֵאלֹהֵינוּ מְרַחֵם:
שֹׁמֵר פְּתָאִים יהוה, דַּלּוֹתִי וְלִי יְהוֹשִׁיעַ:
שׁוּבִי נַפְשִׁי לִמְנוּחָיְכִי, כִּי־יהוה גָּמַל עָלָיְכִי:
כִּי חִלַּצְתָּ נַפְשִׁי מִמָּוֶת, אֶת־עֵינִי מִן־דִּמְעָה, אֶת־רַגְלִי מִדֶּחִי:
אֶתְהַלֵּךְ לִפְנֵי יהוה, בְּאַרְצוֹת הַחַיִּים:
הֶאֱמַנְתִּי כִּי אֲדַבֵּר, אֲנִי עָנִיתִי מְאֹד:
אֲנִי אָמַרְתִּי בְחָפְזִי, כָּל־הָאָדָם כֹּזֵב:

מָה־אָשִׁיב לַיהוה, כָּל־תַּגְמוּלוֹהִי עָלָי: תהלים קטז
לְךָ־אֶזְבַּח זֶבַח תּוֹדָה, וּבְשֵׁם יהוה אֶקְרָא:
נְדָרַי לַיהוה אֲשַׁלֵּם, נֶגְדָה־נָּא לְכָל־עַמּוֹ:
בְּחַצְרוֹת בֵּית יהוה, בְּתוֹכֵכִי יְרוּשָׁלָםִ, הַלְלוּיָהּ:

*The mother says:*

בָּרוּךְ אַתָּה יהוה אֱלֹהֵינוּ מֶלֶךְ הָעוֹלָם
הַגּוֹמֵל לְחַיָּבִים טוֹבוֹת, שֶׁגְּמָלַנִי כָּל טוֹב.

*All respond:*

אָמֵן. מִי שֶׁגְּמָלֵךְ כָּל טוֹב, הוּא יִגְמָלֵךְ כָּל טוֹב, סֶלָה.

אָנָּא O great, mighty and revered God. By Your great love I now come into Your House, to offer You a thanksgiving-offering for all the good You have bestowed on me. Travail beset me, pains seized me. In my distress I cried to You, and from Your habitation You heard my voice and helped me. You healed all my sickness, and crowned me with kindness and compassion. Until now Your mercy has helped me. I pray to You, God, never forsake me. Bestow Your blessing upon Your handmaid. Strengthen and support me together with my husband, that we may raise

*For a boy:*

הַיֶּלֶד the boy that has been born to us, to revere You and serve You in truth, and to walk in the path of righteousness. Protect our tender child in all his ways. Favor him with knowledge, understanding and discernment, and let his portion be in Your Torah, so that he may sanctify Your great name, and become a comfort to us as we grow old. As for me, may my prayer come to You, LORD, at a time of favor. *Ps. 69*
O God, in Your great love, answer me with Your faithful salvation.

*For a girl:*

הַיַּלְדָּה the girl that has been born to us, to revere You and serve You in truth, and to walk in the path of righteousness. Protect our tender child in all her ways. Favor her with knowledge, understanding and discernment, and let her portion be in Your Torah, so that she may sanctify Your great name, and become a comfort to us as we grow old. As for me, may my prayer come to You, LORD, at a time of favor. *Ps. 69*
O God, in Your great love, answer me with Your faithful salvation.

*If the baby is brought to the synagogue,*
*the Rabbi says the following blessings over him/her:*

יְבָרֶכְךָ May the LORD bless you and protect you. *Num. 6*
May the LORD make His face shine on you
and be gracious to you.
May the LORD turn His face toward you
and grant you peace.

אָנָּא הָאֵל הַגָּדוֹל הַגִּבּוֹר וְהַנּוֹרָא, בְּרֹב חַסְדְּךָ אָבוֹא בֵיתֶךָ, לִזְבֹּחַ לְךָ זֶבַח תּוֹדָה עַל כָּל הַטּוֹבוֹת אֲשֶׁר גָּמַלְתָּ עָלָי. אֲפָפוּנִי חֲבָלִים וְצִירִים אֲחָזוּנִי, בַּצַּר לִי קָרָאתִי אֵלֶיךָ, וְשָׁמַעְתָּ מֵהֵיכָלְךָ קוֹלִי וְהָיִיתָ בְּעוֹזְרִי, וְרִפֵּאתָ לְכָל תַּחֲלוּאָי, עִטַּרְתַּנִי חֶסֶד וְרַחֲמִים, עַד הֵנָּה עֲזָרוּנִי רַחֲמֶיךָ, אָנָּא אַל תִּטְּשֵׁנִי לָנֶצַח. הוֹאֵל אֱלוֹהַּ, וּבָרֵךְ אֶת אֲמָתֶךָ, חַזְּקֵנִי וְאַמְּצֵנִי, אוֹתִי וְאֶת בַּעְלִי, וּנְגַדֵּל אֶת

*For a boy:*

הַיֶּלֶד אֲשֶׁר יֻלַּד לָנוּ, לְיִרְאָתְךָ וּלְעָבְדְּךָ בֶּאֱמֶת, וְלָלֶכֶת אֹרַח
מֵישָׁרִים. שְׁמֹר אֶת הַיֶּלֶד הָרַךְ בְּכָל דְּרָכָיו, חָנֵּהוּ דֵּעָה בִּינָה
וְהַשְׂכֵּל, וְתֵן חֶלְקוֹ בְּתוֹרָתֶךָ, וִיקַדֵּשׁ אֶת שִׁמְךָ הַגָּדוֹל, וְהָיָה
לָנוּ לְמֵשִׁיב נֶפֶשׁ בִּימֵי שֵׂיבָתֵנוּ. וַאֲנִי תְפִלָּתִי־לְךָ יהוה עֵת רָצוֹן, תהלים סט
אֱלֹהִים בְּרָב־חַסְדֶּךָ, עֲנֵנִי בֶּאֱמֶת יִשְׁעֶךָ:

*For a girl:*

הַיַּלְדָּה אֲשֶׁר יֻלְּדָה לָנוּ, לְיִרְאָתְךָ וּלְעָבְדְּךָ בֶּאֱמֶת, וְלָלֶכֶת אֹרַח
מֵישָׁרִים. שְׁמֹר אֶת הַיַּלְדָּה הָרַכָּה בְּכָל דְּרָכֶיהָ, חָנֶּהָ דֵּעָה בִּינָה
וְהַשְׂכֵּל, וְתֵן חֶלְקָהּ בְּתוֹרָתֶךָ, וּתְקַדֵּשׁ אֶת שִׁמְךָ הַגָּדוֹל, וְהָיְתָה
לָנוּ לִמְשִׁיבַת נֶפֶשׁ בִּימֵי שֵׂיבָתֵנוּ. וַאֲנִי תְפִלָּתִי־לְךָ יהוה עֵת תהלים סט
רָצוֹן, אֱלֹהִים בְּרָב־חַסְדֶּךָ, עֲנֵנִי בֶּאֱמֶת יִשְׁעֶךָ:

*If the baby is brought to the* בית כנסת*,*
*the Rabbi says the following blessings over him/her:*

יְבָרֶכְךָ יהוה וְיִשְׁמְרֶךָ: במדבר ו
יָאֵר יהוה פָּנָיו אֵלֶיךָ וִיחֻנֶּךָּ:
יִשָּׂא יהוה פָּנָיו אֵלֶיךָ, וְיָשֵׂם לְךָ שָׁלוֹם:

# ZEVED HABAT

*Zeved Habat is a centuries-old Sephardic custom, recently adopted by some Ashkenazim, to mark the birth of a daughter with a special naming ceremony.*

*The mother or father says:*

יוֹנָתִי My dove in the clefts of the rock, *Song. 2*
in the hiding places of the mountain side,
show me your face, let me hear your voice;
for your voice is sweet, and your face is lovely.

*If this is their first daughter, they add:*

אַחַת There is one alone, my dove, my perfect one, *Song. 6*
her mother's only child,
the favorite of the one who bore her.
Maidens see her and called her blessed;
queens and concubines praise her.

*The Rabbi says:*

מִי שֶׁבֵּרַךְ He who blessed our ancestors,
Abraham, Isaac and Jacob, Moses and Aaron, David and Solomon,
Sarah, Rebecca, Rachel and Leah –
may He bless (*mother's name* daughter of *her mother's name*),
who has given birth.

*If the baby has already been named in the synagogue:*
and her newborn daughter, (*baby's name* daughter of *father's name*),
born in favor.

*If the baby has not been named in the synagogue:*
and her newborn daughter, born in favor, whose name in Israel
shall be called (*baby's name* daughter of *father's name*).

Bless, we pray to You, her parents
that they may have the merit to raise her to the Torah,
to the marriage canopy and to good deeds;
and let us say: Amen.

# סדר זבד הבת

*זבד הבת is a centuries-old Sephardic custom, recently adopted by some Ashkenazim, to mark the birth of a daughter with a special naming ceremony.*

*The mother or father says:*

יוֹנָתִי בְּחַגְוֵי הַסֶּלַע, בְּסֵתֶר הַמַּדְרֵגָה
הַרְאִינִי אֶת־מַרְאַיִךְ, הַשְׁמִיעִנִי אֶת־קוֹלֵךְ
כִּי־קוֹלֵךְ עָרֵב וּמַרְאֵיךְ נָאוֶה׃

שיר השירים ב

*If this is their first daughter, they add:*

אַחַת הִיא יוֹנָתִי תַמָּתִי
אַחַת הִיא לְאִמָּהּ, בָּרָה הִיא לְיוֹלַדְתָּהּ
רָאוּהָ בָנוֹת וַיְאַשְּׁרוּהָ, מְלָכוֹת וּפִילַגְשִׁים וַיְהַלְלוּהָ׃

שיר השירים ו

*The Rabbi says:*

מִי שֶׁבֵּרַךְ אֲבוֹתֵינוּ אַבְרָהָם יִצְחָק וְיַעֲקֹב
מֹשֶׁה וְאַהֲרֹן דָּוִד וּשְׁלֹמֹה, שָׂרָה רִבְקָה רָחֵל וְלֵאָה
הוּא יְבָרֵךְ אֶת הָאִשָּׁה הַיּוֹלֶדֶת (פלונית בַּת פלונית)

*If the baby has already been named in the בית כנסת:*

וְאֶת בִּתָּהּ (פלונית בַּת פלוני) שֶׁנּוֹלְדָה לָהּ בְּמַזָּל טוֹב.

*If the baby has not been named in the בית כנסת:*

וְאֶת בִּתָּהּ שֶׁנּוֹלְדָה לָהּ בְּמַזָּל טוֹב
וְיִקָּרֵא שְׁמָהּ בְּיִשְׂרָאֵל (פלונית בַּת פלוני).

אָנָּא בָּרֵךְ אֶת אָבִיהָ וְאֶת אִמָּהּ
וְיִזְכּוּ לְגַדְּלָהּ לְתוֹרָה וּלְחֻפָּה וּלְמַעֲשִׂים טוֹבִים
וְנֹאמַר אָמֵן.

*The parents bless the child:*

יְשִׂמֵךְ May God make you like Sarah, Rebecca, Rachel and Leah.
May the Lord bless you and protect you. *Num. 6*
May the Lord make His face shine on you and be gracious to you.
May the Lord turn His face toward you and grant you peace.

וִיהִי רָצוֹן May it be the will of our Father in heaven,
that He set in your heart the love
and awe of Him all your days,
so that you do not come to sin.
May your desire be for the Torah and the commandments.
May your eyes look straight before you;
may your mouth speak wisdom
and your heart meditate in awe;
may your hands be occupied with the commandments
and may your feet run to do the will of your Father in heaven.

*If grandparents are present, they say the following blessing:*

הָאֱלֹהִים May God before whom my fathers *Gen. 48*
Abraham and Isaac walked –
God who has been my Shepherd all my life to this day,
the angel who has rescued me from all harm –
may He bless the children.
May they be called by my name
and the names of my fathers Abraham and Isaac,
and may they increase greatly on earth.

*All say:*

Our sister, *Gen. 24*
may you grow to become thousands of myriads.

*The parents bless the child:*

יְשִׂמֵךְ אֱלֹהִים כְּשָׂרָה רִבְקָה רָחֵל וְלֵאָה.

במדבר ו יְבָרֶכְךָ יהוה וְיִשְׁמְרֶךָ:

יָאֵר יהוה פָּנָיו אֵלֶיךָ וִיחֻנֶּךָּ:

יִשָּׂא יהוה פָּנָיו אֵלֶיךָ, וְיָשֵׂם לְךָ שָׁלוֹם:

וִיהִי רָצוֹן מִלִּפְנֵי אָבִינוּ שֶׁבַּשָּׁמַיִם

שֶׁיִּתֵּן בְּלִבֵּךְ אַהֲבָתוֹ וְיִרְאָתוֹ

וּתְהִיֶה יִרְאַת יהוה עַל פָּנַיִךְ כָּל יָמַיִךְ שֶׁלֹּא תֶחֱטָאִי

וִיהִי חֶשְׁקֵךְ בַּתּוֹרָה וּבַמִּצְוֹת.

עֵינַיִךְ לְנֹכַח יַבִּיטוּ, פִּיךְ יְדַבֵּר חָכְמוֹת וְלִבֵּךְ יֶהְגֶּה אֵימוֹת

יָדַיִךְ יַעַסְקוּ בְּמִצְוֹת

וְרַגְלַיִךְ יָרוּצוּ לַעֲשׂוֹת רְצוֹן אָבִיךְ שֶׁבַּשָּׁמַיִם.

*If grandparents are present, they say the following blessing:*

בראשית מח הָאֱלֹהִים אֲשֶׁר הִתְהַלְּכוּ אֲבֹתַי לְפָנָיו, אַבְרָהָם וְיִצְחָק

הָאֱלֹהִים הָרֹעֶה אֹתִי, מֵעוֹדִי עַד־הַיּוֹם הַזֶּה:

הַמַּלְאָךְ הַגֹּאֵל אֹתִי מִכָּל־רָע, יְבָרֵךְ אֶת־הַנְּעָרִים

וְיִקָּרֵא בָהֶם שְׁמִי, וְשֵׁם אֲבֹתַי אַבְרָהָם וְיִצְחָק

וְיִדְגּוּ לָרֹב בְּקֶרֶב הָאָרֶץ:

*All say:*

בראשית כד אֲחֹתֵנוּ, אַתְּ הֲיִי לְאַלְפֵי רְבָבָה:

# MARRIAGE SERVICE

## BLESSINGS OF BETROTHAL

*The Rabbi performing the ceremony takes a cup of wine and says:*

בָּרוּךְ Blessed are You, LORD our God, King of the Universe, who creates the fruit of the vine.

בָּרוּךְ Blessed are You, LORD our God, King of the Universe, who has made us holy through His commandments, and has commanded us concerning forbidden unions, forbidding us those who are betrothed, permitting us those who are wedded to us through the rite of the canopy and sacred covenant of marriage. Blessed are You, LORD, who sanctifies His people Israel by the rite of the canopy and sacred covenant of marriage.

*The bride and bridegroom both drink from the wine. The bridegroom takes the ring and, holding it ready to be placed on the forefinger of the bride's right hand, says:*

הֲרֵי Behold you are consecrated to me by this ring
in accordance with the law of Moses and of Israel.

*He then places the ring on the forefinger of the bride's right hand. The Ketuba is read and the bridegroom hands it to the bride. A second cup of wine is taken, and over it, the following Sheva Berakhot are said; the same person should preferably say the first two.*

## THE SEVEN BLESSINGS OF MARRIAGE

בָּרוּךְ Blessed are You, LORD our God, King of the Universe,
who creates the fruit of the vine.

בָּרוּךְ Blessed are You, LORD our God, King of the Universe,
who has created all for His glory.

בָּרוּךְ Blessed are You, LORD our God, King of the Universe,
Creator of mankind.

בָּרוּךְ Blessed are You, LORD our God, King of the Universe,
who made humanity in His image, the image of His likeness,
and out of His very self formed a building for eternity.
Blessed are You, LORD, Creator of mankind.

# סדר קידושין ונישואין

## ברכות האירוסין

*The* מסדר קידושין *takes a cup of wine and says:*

בָּרוּךְ אַתָּה יהוה אֱלֹהֵינוּ מֶלֶךְ הָעוֹלָם, בּוֹרֵא פְּרִי הַגָּפֶן.

בָּרוּךְ אַתָּה יהוה אֱלֹהֵינוּ מֶלֶךְ הָעוֹלָם, אֲשֶׁר קִדְּשָׁנוּ בְּמִצְוֹתָיו, וְצִוָּנוּ עַל הָעֲרָיוֹת, וְאָסַר לָנוּ אֶת הָאֲרוּסוֹת, וְהִתִּיר לָנוּ אֶת הַנְּשׂוּאוֹת לָנוּ עַל יְדֵי חֻפָּה וְקִדּוּשִׁין. בָּרוּךְ אַתָּה יהוה, מְקַדֵּשׁ עַמּוֹ יִשְׂרָאֵל עַל יְדֵי חֻפָּה וְקִדּוּשִׁין.

*The* חתן *and* כלה *both drink from the wine. The* חתן *takes the ring and, holding it ready to be placed on the forefinger of the* כלה*'s right hand, says:*

הֲרֵי אַתְּ מְקֻדֶּשֶׁת לִי בְּטַבַּעַת זוֹ כְּדַת מֹשֶׁה וְיִשְׂרָאֵל.

*He then places the ring on the forefinger of the* כלה*'s right hand. The* כתובה *is read and the* חתן *hands it to the* כלה*. A second cup of wine is taken, and over it, the following* שבע ברכות *are said; the same person should preferably say the first two.*

## שבע ברכות הנשואין

בָּרוּךְ אַתָּה יהוה אֱלֹהֵינוּ מֶלֶךְ הָעוֹלָם, בּוֹרֵא פְּרִי הַגָּפֶן.

בָּרוּךְ אַתָּה יהוה אֱלֹהֵינוּ מֶלֶךְ הָעוֹלָם, שֶׁהַכֹּל בָּרָא לִכְבוֹדוֹ.

בָּרוּךְ אַתָּה יהוה אֱלֹהֵינוּ מֶלֶךְ הָעוֹלָם, יוֹצֵר הָאָדָם.

בָּרוּךְ אַתָּה יהוה אֱלֹהֵינוּ מֶלֶךְ הָעוֹלָם
אֲשֶׁר יָצַר אֶת הָאָדָם בְּצַלְמוֹ, בְּצֶלֶם דְּמוּת תַּבְנִיתוֹ
וְהִתְקִין לוֹ מִמֶּנּוּ בִּנְיַן עֲדֵי עַד.
בָּרוּךְ אַתָּה יהוה, יוֹצֵר הָאָדָם.

שׂוֹשׂ Bring great happiness and joy to one who was barren [Zion],
as her children return to her in joy.
Blessed are You, Lord,
who gladdens Zion through her children.

שַׂמֵּחַ Bring great joy to these loving friends,
as You gave joy to Your creations in the Garden of Eden.
Blessed are You, Lord,
who gives joy to the bridegroom and bride.

בָּרוּךְ Blessed are You, Lord our God, King of the Universe,
who created joy and gladness, bridegroom and bride,
happiness and jubilation, cheer and delight,
love, fellowship, peace and friendship.
Soon, Lord our God, may there be heard in the cities of Judah,
and in the streets of Jerusalem, the sounds of joy and gladness,
the sounds of the bridegroom and bride,
the joyous sounds of bridegrooms from their wedding canopy
and of young people at their feasts of song.
Blessed are You, Lord,
who makes the bridegroom rejoice with the bride.

*The bride and bridegroom both drink from the wine.*
*The bridegroom breaks a glass in memory of the destruction of the Temple. Some say the following beforehand:*

אִם־אֶשְׁכָּחֵךְ If I forget you, O Jerusalem, *Ps. 137*
may my right hand forget its skill.
May my tongue cling to the roof of my mouth
if I do not remember you,
if I do not set Jerusalem above my highest joy.

שׂוֹשׂ תָּשִׂישׂ וְתָגֵל הָעֲקָרָה בְּקִבּוּץ בָּנֶיהָ לְתוֹכָהּ בְּשִׂמְחָה.
בָּרוּךְ אַתָּה יהוה, מְשַׂמֵּחַ צִיּוֹן בְּבָנֶיהָ.

שַׂמֵּחַ תְּשַׂמַּח רֵעִים הָאֲהוּבִים כְּשַׂמֵּחֲךָ יְצִירְךָ בְּגַן עֵדֶן מִקֶּדֶם.
בָּרוּךְ אַתָּה יהוה, מְשַׂמֵּחַ חָתָן וְכַלָּה.

בָּרוּךְ אַתָּה יהוה אֱלֹהֵינוּ מֶלֶךְ הָעוֹלָם
אֲשֶׁר בָּרָא שָׂשׂוֹן וְשִׂמְחָה, חָתָן וְכַלָּה
גִּילָה, רִנָּה, דִּיצָה וְחֶדְוָה
אַהֲבָה וְאַחֲוָה וְשָׁלוֹם וְרֵעוּת.
מְהֵרָה יהוה אֱלֹהֵינוּ
יִשָּׁמַע בְּעָרֵי יְהוּדָה וּבְחוּצוֹת יְרוּשָׁלָיִם
קוֹל שָׂשׂוֹן וְקוֹל שִׂמְחָה, קוֹל חָתָן וְקוֹל כַּלָּה
קוֹל מִצְהֲלוֹת חֲתָנִים מֵחֻפָּתָם וּנְעָרִים מִמִּשְׁתֵּה נְגִינָתָם.
בָּרוּךְ אַתָּה יהוה, מְשַׂמֵּחַ הֶחָתָן עִם הַכַּלָּה.

*The* חתן *and* כלה *both drink from the wine.*
*The* חתן *breaks a glass in memory of the destruction of the* בית המקדש*. Some say the following beforehand:*

תהלים קלז
אִם־אֶשְׁכָּחֵךְ יְרוּשָׁלָםִ, תִּשְׁכַּח יְמִינִי:
תִּדְבַּק לְשׁוֹנִי לְחִכִּי אִם־לֹא אֶזְכְּרֵכִי
אִם־לֹא אַעֲלֶה אֶת־יְרוּשָׁלַםִ עַל רֹאשׁ שִׂמְחָתִי:

# ZIMMUN AFTER A WEDDING OR SHEVA BERAKHOT FEAST

*The leader takes a cup of wine in his hand and says:*

*Leader* Gentlemen, let us say grace.

*Others* May the name of the Lord be blessed from now and for ever. *Ps. 113*

*Leader* May the name of the Lord be blessed from now and for ever.

Banish grief and anger.
Let even the mute celebrate in song.
Guide us in the paths of righteousness.
Hear the blessing of the children of Aaron.

*Add the appropriate words in parentheses:*

With your permission,
(my father and teacher / my mother and teacher /
the Kohanim present / our teacher the Rabbi /
the master of this house / the mistress of this house)
my masters and teachers,
let us bless our God, in whose dwelling place is joy,
from whose food we have eaten .

*Others* Blessed be our God in whose dwelling place is joy,
from whose food we have eaten,
and by whose goodness we live.

*Leader* Blessed be our God in whose dwelling place is joy,
from whose food we have eaten,
and by whose goodness we live.
Blessed be He, and blessed be His name.

*Continue with Birkat HaMazon on page 1058, at the end of which say the Sheva Berakhot (on page 1116) over a cup of wine, beginning with the second blessing, "who has created all," and ending with the first blessing, that over the wine.*

# זימון לסעודת שבע ברכות

*The leader takes a cup of wine in his hand and says:*

*Leader* רַבּוֹתַי, נְבָרֵךְ.

*Others* יְהִי שֵׁם יהוה מְבֹרָךְ מֵעַתָּה וְעַד־עוֹלָם: תהלים קיג

*Leader* יְהִי שֵׁם יהוה מְבֹרָךְ מֵעַתָּה וְעַד־עוֹלָם:

דְּוַי הָסֵר וְגַם חָרוֹן וְאָז אִלֵּם בְּשִׁיר יָרֹן.
נְחֵנוּ בְּמַעְגְּלֵי צֶדֶק שְׁעֵה בִּרְכַּת בְּנֵי אַהֲרֹן.

*Add the appropriate words in parentheses:*

בִּרְשׁוּת
(אָבִי מוֹרִי / אִמִּי מוֹרָתִי / כֹּהֲנִים / מוֹרֵנוּ הָרַב / בַּעַל הַבַּיִת הַזֶּה / בַּעֲלַת הַבַּיִת הַזֶּה)
מָרָנָן וְרַבָּנָן וְרַבּוֹתַי
נְבָרֵךְ אֱלֹהֵינוּ שֶׁהַשִּׂמְחָה בִּמְעוֹנוֹ וְשֶׁאָכַלְנוּ מִשֶּׁלּוֹ.

*Others* בָּרוּךְ אֱלֹהֵינוּ שֶׁהַשִּׂמְחָה בִּמְעוֹנוֹ
שֶׁאָכַלְנוּ מִשֶּׁלּוֹ וּבְטוּבוֹ חָיִינוּ.

*Leader* בָּרוּךְ אֱלֹהֵינוּ שֶׁהַשִּׂמְחָה בִּמְעוֹנוֹ
שֶׁאָכַלְנוּ מִשֶּׁלּוֹ וּבְטוּבוֹ חָיִינוּ.
בָּרוּךְ הוּא וּבָרוּךְ שְׁמוֹ.

*Continue with* ברכת המזון *on page 1059, at the end of which say the* שבע ברכות *(on page 1117) over a cup of wine, beginning with the second blessing,* שֶׁהַכֹּל בָּרָא לִכְבוֹדוֹ*, and ending with the first blessing,* בּוֹרֵא פְּרִי הַגָּפֶן.

## PRAYER FOR RECOVERY FROM ILLNESS

מִזְמוֹר לְדָוִד A psalm of David. The LORD is my Shepherd, I shall not want. *Ps. 23*
He makes me lie down in green pastures. He leads me beside the still waters. He refreshes my soul. He guides me in the paths of righteousness for His name's sake. Though I walk through the valley of the shadow of death, I will fear no evil, for You are with me; Your rod and Your staff, they comfort me. You set a table before me in the presence of my enemies; You anoint my head with oil; my cup is filled to overflowing. May goodness and kindness follow me all the days of my life, and may I live in the House of the LORD for evermore.

לְדָוִד By David. Bless the LORD, my soul; with all my being I bless His holy *Ps. 103*
name. Bless the LORD, my soul, and forget none of His benefits. He forgives all your sins. He heals all your ills. He redeems your life from the pit. He crowns you with love and compassion. He satisfies your soul with good things, so that your youth is renewed like the eagle's. The LORD is righteous in all He does; He brings justice to all the oppressed. He made known His ways to Moses, His deeds to the people of Israel. The LORD is compassionate and gracious, slow to anger, abounding in love. He will not always accuse or nurse His anger for ever. He has not treated us as our sins deserve, or repaid us according to our misdeeds. For as high as the heavens are above the earth, so great is His love for those who fear Him. As far as the east is from the west, so far has He removed our transgressions from us. As a father has compassion on his children, so the LORD has compassion on those who fear Him. For He knows how we are formed; He remembers that we are dust. As for man, his days are like grass; like a flower of the field he flourishes. For a wind passes over it and it is gone, and its place knows it no more. But the kindness of the LORD is for all eternity to those who fear Him; His righteousness is with their children's children – with those who keep His covenant, and remember to obey His precepts. The LORD has established His throne in heaven, and His kingdom rules over all. Bless the LORD, you His angels, mighty in power, who do His bidding, who obey His word. Bless the LORD, all you His host, the ministers who do His will. Bless the LORD, all His works, everywhere in His dominion. Bless the LORD, my soul.

# תפילה לחולה

תהלים כג מִזְמוֹר לְדָוִד, יהוה רֹעִי לֹא אֶחְסָר: בִּנְאוֹת דֶּשֶׁא יַרְבִּיצֵנִי, עַל־מֵי מְנֻחוֹת יְנַהֲלֵנִי: נַפְשִׁי יְשׁוֹבֵב, יַנְחֵנִי בְמַעְגְּלֵי־צֶדֶק לְמַעַן שְׁמוֹ: גַּם כִּי־אֵלֵךְ בְּגֵיא צַלְמָוֶת לֹא־אִירָא רָע, כִּי־אַתָּה עִמָּדִי, שִׁבְטְךָ וּמִשְׁעַנְתֶּךָ הֵמָּה יְנַחֲמֻנִי: תַּעֲרֹךְ לְפָנַי שֻׁלְחָן נֶגֶד צֹרְרָי, דִּשַּׁנְתָּ בַשֶּׁמֶן רֹאשִׁי, כּוֹסִי רְוָיָה: אַךְ טוֹב וָחֶסֶד יִרְדְּפוּנִי כָּל־יְמֵי חַיָּי, וְשַׁבְתִּי בְּבֵית־יהוה לְאֹרֶךְ יָמִים:

תהלים קג לְדָוִד, בָּרְכִי נַפְשִׁי אֶת־יהוה, וְכָל־קְרָבַי אֶת־שֵׁם קָדְשׁוֹ: בָּרְכִי נַפְשִׁי אֶת־יהוה, וְאַל־תִּשְׁכְּחִי כָּל־גְּמוּלָיו: הַסֹּלֵחַ לְכָל־עֲוֺנֵכִי, הָרֹפֵא לְכָל־תַּחֲלוּאָיְכִי: הַגּוֹאֵל מִשַּׁחַת חַיָּיְכִי, הַמְעַטְּרֵכִי חֶסֶד וְרַחֲמִים: הַמַּשְׂבִּיעַ בַּטּוֹב עֶדְיֵךְ, תִּתְחַדֵּשׁ כַּנֶּשֶׁר נְעוּרָיְכִי: עֹשֵׂה צְדָקוֹת יהוה, וּמִשְׁפָּטִים לְכָל־עֲשׁוּקִים: יוֹדִיעַ דְּרָכָיו לְמֹשֶׁה, לִבְנֵי יִשְׂרָאֵל עֲלִילוֹתָיו: רַחוּם וְחַנּוּן יהוה, אֶרֶךְ אַפַּיִם וְרַב־חָסֶד: לֹא־לָנֶצַח יָרִיב, וְלֹא לְעוֹלָם יִטּוֹר: לֹא כַחֲטָאֵינוּ עָשָׂה לָנוּ, וְלֹא כַעֲוֺנֹתֵינוּ גָּמַל עָלֵינוּ: כִּי כִגְבֹהַּ שָׁמַיִם עַל־הָאָרֶץ, גָּבַר חַסְדּוֹ עַל־יְרֵאָיו: כִּרְחֹק מִזְרָח מִמַּעֲרָב, הִרְחִיק מִמֶּנּוּ אֶת־פְּשָׁעֵינוּ: כְּרַחֵם אָב עַל־בָּנִים, רִחַם יהוה עַל־יְרֵאָיו: כִּי־הוּא יָדַע יִצְרֵנוּ, זָכוּר כִּי־עָפָר אֲנָחְנוּ: אֱנוֹשׁ כֶּחָצִיר יָמָיו, כְּצִיץ הַשָּׂדֶה כֵּן יָצִיץ: כִּי רוּחַ עָבְרָה־בּוֹ וְאֵינֶנּוּ, וְלֹא־יַכִּירֶנּוּ עוֹד מְקוֹמוֹ: וְחֶסֶד יהוה מֵעוֹלָם וְעַד־עוֹלָם עַל־יְרֵאָיו, וְצִדְקָתוֹ לִבְנֵי בָנִים: לְשֹׁמְרֵי בְרִיתוֹ, וּלְזֹכְרֵי פִקֻּדָיו לַעֲשׂוֹתָם: יהוה בַּשָּׁמַיִם הֵכִין כִּסְאוֹ, וּמַלְכוּתוֹ בַּכֹּל מָשָׁלָה: בָּרְכוּ יהוה מַלְאָכָיו, גִּבֹּרֵי כֹחַ עֹשֵׂי דְבָרוֹ, לִשְׁמֹעַ בְּקוֹל דְּבָרוֹ: בָּרְכוּ יהוה כָּל־צְבָאָיו, מְשָׁרְתָיו עֹשֵׂי רְצוֹנוֹ: בָּרְכוּ יהוה כָּל־מַעֲשָׂיו, בְּכָל־מְקֹמוֹת מֶמְשַׁלְתּוֹ, בָּרְכִי נַפְשִׁי אֶת־יהוה:

לַמְנַצֵּחַ For the conductor of music. A psalm of David. O LORD, You have examined me and You know me. You know when I sit and when I rise; You understand my thoughts from afar. You encompass my going out and lying down. You are familiar with all my ways. Before a word is on my tongue, You, LORD, know it all. You keep close guard behind and before me. You have laid Your hand upon me. Knowledge so wonderful is beyond me; so high, it is above my reach. Where can I escape from Your spirit? Where can I flee from Your presence? If I climb to heaven, You are there; if I make my bed in the underworld, You are there. If I rise on the wings of the dawn, if I settle on the far side of the sea, even there Your hand will guide me, Your right hand will hold me fast. Were I to say, "Surely the darkness will hide me, and light become night around me," to You the darkness would not be dark; night is light as day; to You dark and light are one. For You created my innermost being; You knitted me together in my mother's womb. I praise You because I am awesomely, wondrously made; wonderful are Your works; I know that full well. My frame was not hidden from You when I was formed in the secret place, woven in the depths of the earth. Your eyes saw my unformed body. All the days ordained for me were written in Your book before one of them came to be. How precious to me are Your thoughts, God, how vast in number they are. Were I to count them, they would outnumber the grains of the sand. I awake and I am still with You. God, if only You would slay the wicked – away from me, you bloodthirsty men. They speak of You with evil intent; Your adversaries misuse Your name. Do I not hate those who hate You, LORD, and loathe those who rise up against You? I have nothing but hatred for them; I count them my enemies. Search me, God, and know my heart; test me and know my innermost thoughts. See if there is grief in the way I follow, and lead me in the everlasting way. *Ps. 139*

תְּפִלָּה לְעָנִי A prayer of one who is afflicted, when he is faint, and pours out his anguish before the LORD. LORD, hear my prayer and let my cry come before You. Do not hide Your face from me in my day of distress. Turn Your ear toward me; answer me swiftly on the day I call. *Ps. 102*

אָנָּא Please, LORD, Healer of all flesh, have pity on me, and support me on my sick bed, in Your great love, for I am weak. Send relief and healing to me and to the others of Your children who are sick. Heal my pain and renew my youth as the eagle's. Grant wisdom to the physician that he may cure my illness, so that my healing may spring up swiftly. Hear my prayer, prolong my life, and let me complete my years in happiness, so that I may be able to serve

תהלים קלט
לַמְנַצֵּחַ לְדָוִד מִזְמוֹר, יהוה חֲקַרְתַּנִי וַתֵּדָע: אַתָּה יָדַעְתָּ שִׁבְתִּי וְקוּמִי, בַּנְתָּה לְרֵעִי מֵרָחוֹק: אָרְחִי וְרִבְעִי זֵרִיתָ, וְכָל־דְּרָכַי הִסְכַּנְתָּה: כִּי אֵין מִלָּה בִּלְשׁוֹנִי, הֵן יהוה יָדַעְתָּ כֻלָּהּ: אָחוֹר וָקֶדֶם צַרְתָּנִי, וַתָּשֶׁת עָלַי כַּפֶּכָה: פְּלִיאָה דַעַת מִמֶּנִּי, נִשְׂגְּבָה לֹא־אוּכַל לָהּ: אָנָה אֵלֵךְ מֵרוּחֶךָ, וְאָנָה מִפָּנֶיךָ אֶבְרָח: אִם־אֶסַּק שָׁמַיִם שָׁם אָתָּה, וְאַצִּיעָה שְּׁאוֹל הִנֶּךָּ: אֶשָּׂא כַנְפֵי־שָׁחַר, אֶשְׁכְּנָה בְּאַחֲרִית יָם: גַּם־שָׁם יָדְךָ תַנְחֵנִי, וְתֹאחֲזֵנִי יְמִינֶךָ: וָאֹמַר אַךְ־חֹשֶׁךְ יְשׁוּפֵנִי, וְלַיְלָה אוֹר בַּעֲדֵנִי: גַּם־חֹשֶׁךְ לֹא־יַחְשִׁיךְ מִמֶּךָ, וְלַיְלָה כַּיּוֹם יָאִיר, כַּחֲשֵׁיכָה כָּאוֹרָה: כִּי־אַתָּה קָנִיתָ כִלְיֹתָי, תְּסֻכֵּנִי בְּבֶטֶן אִמִּי: אוֹדְךָ עַל כִּי נוֹרָאוֹת נִפְלֵיתִי, נִפְלָאִים מַעֲשֶׂיךָ, וְנַפְשִׁי יֹדַעַת מְאֹד: לֹא־נִכְחַד עָצְמִי מִמֶּךָּ, אֲשֶׁר־עֻשֵּׂיתִי בַסֵּתֶר, רֻקַּמְתִּי בְּתַחְתִּיּוֹת אָרֶץ: גָּלְמִי רָאוּ עֵינֶיךָ, וְעַל־סִפְרְךָ כֻּלָּם יִכָּתֵבוּ, יָמִים יֻצָּרוּ, וְלוֹ אֶחָד בָּהֶם: וְלִי מַה־יָּקְרוּ רֵעֶיךָ אֵל, מֶה עָצְמוּ רָאשֵׁיהֶם: אֶסְפְּרֵם מֵחוֹל יִרְבּוּן, הֱקִיצֹתִי וְעוֹדִי עִמָּךְ: אִם־תִּקְטֹל אֱלוֹהַּ רָשָׁע, וְאַנְשֵׁי דָמִים סוּרוּ מֶנִּי: אֲשֶׁר יֹמְרוּךָ לִמְזִמָּה, נָשׂוּא לַשָּׁוְא עָרֶיךָ: הֲלוֹא־מְשַׂנְאֶיךָ יהוה אֶשְׂנָא, וּבִתְקוֹמְמֶיךָ אֶתְקוֹטָט: תַּכְלִית שִׂנְאָה שְׂנֵאתִים, לְאוֹיְבִים הָיוּ לִי: חָקְרֵנִי אֵל וְדַע לְבָבִי, בְּחָנֵנִי וְדַע שַׂרְעַפָּי: וּרְאֵה אִם־דֶּרֶךְ־עֹצֶב בִּי, וּנְחֵנִי בְּדֶרֶךְ עוֹלָם:

תהלים קב
תְּפִלָּה לְעָנִי כִי־יַעֲטֹף, וְלִפְנֵי יהוה יִשְׁפֹּךְ שִׂיחוֹ: יהוה שִׁמְעָה תְפִלָּתִי, וְשַׁוְעָתִי אֵלֶיךָ תָבוֹא: אַל־תַּסְתֵּר פָּנֶיךָ מִמֶּנִּי בְּיוֹם צַר לִי, הַטֵּה־אֵלַי אָזְנֶךָ, בְּיוֹם אֶקְרָא מַהֵר עֲנֵנִי:

אָנָּא יהוה רוֹפֵא כָל בָּשָׂר, רַחֵם עָלַי, וּסְעָדֵנִי בְּחַסְדְּךָ הַגָּדוֹל עַל עֶרֶשׂ דְּוָי, כִּי אֻמְלַל אָנִי. שְׁלַח לִי תְּרוּפָה וּתְעָלָה, בְּתוֹךְ שְׁאָר חוֹלֵי יִשְׂרָאֵל. רַפֵּא אֶת מַכְאוֹבִי, וְחַדֵּשׁ כַּנֶּשֶׁר נְעוּרָי. תֵּן בִּינָה לָרוֹפֵא, וְיִגָּהֶה מִמֶּנִּי מְזוֹרִי, וַאֲרוּכָתִי מְהֵרָה תִצְמָח. שְׁמַע תְּפִלָּתִי, וְהוֹסֵף יָמִים עַל יָמַי, וַאֲכַלֶּה שְׁנוֹתַי בַּנְּעִימִים, לְמַעַן אוּכַל לַעֲבֹד אוֹתְךָ, וְלִשְׁמֹר פִּקּוּדֶיךָ

You and keep Your precepts with a perfect heart. Grant me the understanding to know that this bitter trial has come upon me for my welfare. Let me not reject Your discipline or spurn Your rebuke.

אֱלוֹהַּ סְלִיחוֹת God of forgiveness, gracious and compassionate, slow to anger, abounding in love, I acknowledge before You with a broken and contrite heart that I have sinned and done evil in Your sight. I hereby repent of my evil and turn to You in complete repentance. Help me, God of my salvation, that I may not turn to folly again, but instead walk before You in truth and
integrity. Gladden Your servant's heart, for to You, Lord, I lift up my soul. *Ps. 86*
Heal me, Lord, and I will be healed, save me and I will be saved, for You are *Jer. 17*
my glory. Amen and Amen!

## THANKSGIVING PRAYER AFTER RECOVERY FROM ILLNESS

*Say Psalms 23 and 103 on page 1122. Then continue with:*

אָנָּא O great, mighty and awesome God: By Your great love I come before You to offer thanks for all the good You have bestowed on me. In my distress I called to You and You answered me; from my sick bed I cried to You, and You heard my voice and my pleas. You chastened me severely, Lord, but You did not hand me over to death. In Your love and compassion You lifted my soul from the grave. For Your anger is for a moment, Your favor for a lifetime.
At night there may be weeping, but in the morning there is joy. The living, *Is. 38*
only the living, praise You as I do this day. My soul which You have redeemed shall tell of Your wonders to the children of men. Blessed are You, the faithful Healer of all flesh.

אֵל רַחוּם O God, compassionate and gracious, who grants favors to the undeserving: I am not worthy of all the kindness You have shown to me until now. Purify, please, my heart that I may be worthy to walk before You in the way of the upright. Extend Your help to Your servant. Grant me the strength and resolution to overcome my weakness, and bless me with physical health. Keep sorrow and grief far from me; protect me from all harm, and guide me with Your counsel. May the sun of righteousness shine for me, bringing
healing in its wings. May the words of my mouth and the meditation of my *Ps. 19*
heart find favor before You, O Lord, my Rock and my Redeemer. Amen.

בְּלֵב שָׁלֵם. הֲבִינֵנִי וְאֵדְעָה, כִּי לְשָׁלוֹמִי מַר לִי מָר. וְאַל אֶמְאַס אֶת מוּסָרְךָ, וּבְתוֹכַחְתְּךָ אַל אָקוּץ.

אֱלוֹהַּ סְלִיחוֹת, חַנּוּן וְרַחוּם אֶרֶךְ אַפַּיִם וְרַב חֶסֶד, מוֹדֶה אֲנִי לְפָנֶיךָ בְּלֵב נִשְׁבָּר וְנִדְכֶּה כִּי חָטָאתִי, וְהָרַע בְּעֵינֶיךָ עָשִׂיתִי. הִנֵּה נִחַמְתִּי עַל רָעָתִי, וְאָשׁוּב בִּתְשׁוּבָה שְׁלֵמָה לְפָנֶיךָ. עָזְרֵנִי אֱלֹהֵי יִשְׁעִי, וְלֹא אָשׁוּב
לְכִסְלָה, וְאֶתְהַלֵּךְ לְפָנֶיךָ בֶּאֱמֶת וּבְתָמִים. שַׂמֵּחַ נֶפֶשׁ עַבְדֶּךָ, כִּי־אֵלֶיךָ תהלים פו
אֲדֹנָי, נַפְשִׁי אֶשָּׂא: רְפָאֵנִי יהוה וְאֵרָפֵא, הוֹשִׁיעֵנִי וְאִוָּשֵׁעָה, כִּי תְהִלָּתִי ירמיה יז
אָתָּה: אָמֵן וְאָמֵן.

## תפילה לעומד מחליו

*Say* תהלים כג *and* קג *on page 1123. Then continue with:*

אָנָּא הָאֵל הַגָּדוֹל הַגִּבּוֹר וְהַנּוֹרָא, בְּרֹב חַסְדְּךָ אָבוֹא לְפָנֶיךָ לְהוֹדוֹת לְךָ עַל כָּל הַטּוֹבוֹת אֲשֶׁר גְּמַלְתָּ עָלַי. מִן הַמֵּצַר קְרָאתִיךָ וַתַּעֲנֵנִי, מֵעֶרֶשׂ דְּוַי שִׁוַּעְתִּי אֵלֶיךָ, וַתִּשְׁמַע אֶת קוֹלִי תַּחֲנוּנָי. יַסֹּר יִסְּרַנִּי יָהּ, וְלַמָּוֶת לֹא נְתָנָנִי. בְּאַהֲבָתְךָ וּבְחֶמְלָתְךָ הֶעֱלִיתָ מִן שְׁאוֹל נַפְשִׁי. כִּי רֶגַע בְּאַפּוֹ,
חַיִּים בִּרְצוֹנוֹ, בָּעֶרֶב יָלִין בֶּכִי וְלַבֹּקֶר רִנָּה. חַי חַי הוּא יוֹדֶךָ, כָּמוֹנִי ישעיה לח
הַיּוֹם: וְנַפְשִׁי אֲשֶׁר פָּדִיתָ, תְּסַפֵּר נִפְלְאוֹתֶיךָ לִבְנֵי אָדָם. בָּרוּךְ אַתָּה, רוֹפֵא נֶאֱמָן לְכָל בָּשָׂר.

אֵל רַחוּם וְחַנּוּן, הַגּוֹמֵל לְחַיָּבִים טוֹבוֹת, קָטֹנְתִּי מִכֹּל הַחֲסָדִים אֲשֶׁר עָשִׂיתָ עִמָּדִי עַד הֵנָּה. אָנָּא טַהֵר לְבָבִי, וְזַכֵּנִי לָלֶכֶת בְּדֶרֶךְ יְשָׁרִים לְפָנֶיךָ, וּמְשֹׁךְ עֶזְרְךָ לְעַבְדֶּךָ. חַזְּקֵנִי וְאַמְּצֵנִי מֵרִפְיוֹן, וּבְחִלּוּץ עֲצָמוֹת תְּבָרְכֵנִי. הַרְחֵק מֵעָלַי כָּל צָרָה וְתוּגָה, שָׁמְרֵנִי מִכָּל רָע, וּבַעֲצָתְךָ תַנְחֵנִי. וְזָרְחָה לִי
שֶׁמֶשׁ צְדָקָה, וּמַרְפֵּא בִּכְנָפֶיהָ. יִהְיוּ לְרָצוֹן אִמְרֵי־פִי וְהֶגְיוֹן לִבִּי לְפָנֶיךָ, תהלים יט
יהוה צוּרִי וְגֹאֲלִי: אָמֵן.

## CONFESSION BEFORE DEATH

*The following confession is said by one near death.*
*He or she should be told: "Do not fear. Many confessed their sins, and then recovered.*
*Everyone who does confess has reward in the World to Come" (Shabbat 32a).*

מוֹדֶה אֲנִי I acknowledge before You, Lord my God and God of my ancestors, that my cure and my death are in Your hands. May it be Your will to send me a perfect healing. Yet if my death is fully determined by You, I accept it in love at Your hand. May my death be an atonement for all the sins, iniquities and transgressions I have committed before You. Grant me of the great happiness that is stored up for the righteous. Make known to *Ps. 16*
me the path of life, in Your presence is fullness of joy; at Your right hand bliss for evermore.

אֲבִי יְתוֹמִים Father of orphans and Justice of widows, protect my cherished family, whose souls are bound with mine. Into Your hand I entrust my *Ps. 31*
spirit. May You redeem me, Lord, God of truth. Amen and Amen.

*When the end is approaching, the following should be said.*

*Repeat three times:*

The Lord is King, the Lord was King,
and the Lord will be King for ever and ever.

*Repeat three times:*

Blessed be the name of His glorious
kingdom for ever and all time.

*Repeat seven times:*

The Lord, He is God.

*Once:*

Listen, Israel: the Lord is our God, the Lord is One. *Deut. 6*

# וידוי שכיב מרע

*The following confession is said by one near death.*
*He or she should be told: "Do not fear. Many confessed their sins, and then recovered.*
*Everyone who does confess has reward in the World to Come" (Shabbat 32a).*

מוֹדֶה אֲנִי לְפָנֶיךָ, יהוה אֱלֹהַי וֵאלֹהֵי אֲבוֹתַי, שֶׁרְפוּאָתִי וּמִיתָתִי בְּיָדֶךָ. יְהִי רָצוֹן מִלְּפָנֶיךָ, שֶׁתִּרְפָּאֵנִי רְפוּאָה שְׁלֵמָה, וְאִם אָמוּת, תְּהִי מִיתָתִי כַּפָּרָה עַל כָּל חֲטָאִים וַעֲוֹנוֹת וּפְשָׁעִים שֶׁחָטָאתִי וְשֶׁעָוִיתִי וְשֶׁפָּשַׁעְתִּי לְפָנֶיךָ. וְזַכֵּנִי לָעוֹלָם הַבָּא הַצָּפוּן לַצַּדִּיקִים. תּוֹדִיעֵנִי אֹרַח תהלים טז
חַיִּים, שֹׂבַע שְׂמָחוֹת אֶת־פָּנֶיךָ, נְעִימוֹת בִּימִינְךָ נֶצַח:

אֲבִי יְתוֹמִים וְדַיַּן אַלְמָנוֹת, הָגֵן בְּעַד קְרוֹבַי הַיְקָרִים, אֲשֶׁר נַפְשִׁי קְשׁוּרָה בְּנַפְשָׁם. בְּיָדְךָ אַפְקִיד רוּחִי, פָּדִיתָה אוֹתִי יהוה אֵל אֱמֶת: תהלים לא
אָמֵן וְאָמֵן.

*When the end is approaching, the following should be said.*

*Repeat three times:*

יהוה מֶלֶךְ, יהוה מָלָךְ, יהוה יִמְלֹךְ לְעוֹלָם וָעֶד.

*Repeat three times:*

בָּרוּךְ שֵׁם כְּבוֹד מַלְכוּתוֹ לְעוֹלָם וָעֶד.

*Repeat seven times:*

יהוה הוּא הָאֱלֹהִים.

*Once:*

שְׁמַע יִשְׂרָאֵל, יהוה אֱלֹהֵינוּ, יהוה אֶחָד: דברים ו

# FUNERAL SERVICE

עֲקַבְיָא Akavya ben Mahalalel said: Reflect on three things and you will avoid transgression: Know where you came from, where you are going, and before whom you will have to give an account and reckoning. "Where you came from" – from a putrid drop. "Where you are going" – to a place of dust, worms and maggots. "And before whom you will have to give an account and reckoning" – before the Supreme King of kings, the Holy One, blessed be He. *Mishna Avot 3:1*

*While on the way to the grave, say:*

יֹשֵׁב בְּסֵתֶר He who lives in the shelter of the Most High dwells in the shadow of the Almighty. I say of the LORD, my Refuge and Stronghold, my God in whom I trust, that He will save you from the fowler's snare and the deadly pestilence. With His pinions He will cover you, and beneath His wings you will find shelter; His faithfulness is an encircling shield. You need not fear terror by night, nor the arrow that flies by day; not the pestilence that stalks in darkness, nor the plague that ravages at noon. A thousand may fall at your side, ten thousand at your right hand, but it will not come near you. You will only look with your eyes and see the punishment of the wicked. Because you said "The LORD is my Refuge," taking the Most High as your shelter, no harm will befall you, no plague will come near your tent, for He will command His angels about you, to guard you in all your ways. They will lift you in their hands, lest your foot stumble on a stone. You will tread on lions and vipers, you will trample on young lions and snakes. [God says] "Because he loves Me, I will rescue him; I will protect him, because he acknowledges My name. When he calls on Me, I will answer him, I will be with him in distress, I will deliver him and bring him honor. With long life I will satisfy him, and show him My salvation. With long life I will satisfy him, and show him My salvation." *Ps. 91*

# לויית המת

משנה אבות ג:א
עֲקַבְיָא בֶּן מַהֲלַלְאֵל אוֹמֵר: הִסְתַּכֵּל בִּשְׁלֹשָׁה דְבָרִים, וְאֵין אַתָּה בָא לִידֵי עֲבֵרָה. דַּע מֵאַיִן בָּאתָ, וּלְאָן אַתָּה הוֹלֵךְ, וְלִפְנֵי מִי אַתָּה עָתִיד לִתֵּן דִּין וְחֶשְׁבּוֹן. מֵאַיִן בָּאתָ, מִטִּפָּה סְרוּחָה. וּלְאָן אַתָּה הוֹלֵךְ, לִמְקוֹם עָפָר, רִמָּה וְתוֹלֵעָה. וְלִפְנֵי מִי אַתָּה עָתִיד לִתֵּן דִּין וְחֶשְׁבּוֹן, לִפְנֵי מֶלֶךְ מַלְכֵי הַמְּלָכִים, הַקָּדוֹשׁ בָּרוּךְ הוּא.

*While on the way to the grave, say:*

תהלים צא
יֹשֵׁב בְּסֵתֶר עֶלְיוֹן, בְּצֵל שַׁדַּי יִתְלוֹנָן: אֹמַר לַיהוה מַחְסִי וּמְצוּדָתִי, אֱלֹהַי אֶבְטַח־בּוֹ: כִּי הוּא יַצִּילְךָ מִפַּח יָקוּשׁ, מִדֶּבֶר הַוּוֹת: בְּאֶבְרָתוֹ יָסֶךְ לָךְ, וְתַחַת־כְּנָפָיו תֶּחְסֶה, צִנָּה וְסֹחֵרָה אֲמִתּוֹ: לֹא־תִירָא מִפַּחַד לָיְלָה, מֵחֵץ יָעוּף יוֹמָם: מִדֶּבֶר בָּאֹפֶל יַהֲלֹךְ, מִקֶּטֶב יָשׁוּד צָהֳרָיִם: יִפֹּל מִצִּדְּךָ אֶלֶף, וּרְבָבָה מִימִינֶךָ, אֵלֶיךָ לֹא יִגָּשׁ: רַק בְּעֵינֶיךָ תַבִּיט, וְשִׁלֻּמַת רְשָׁעִים תִּרְאֶה: כִּי־אַתָּה יהוה מַחְסִי, עֶלְיוֹן שַׂמְתָּ מְעוֹנֶךָ: לֹא־תְאֻנֶּה אֵלֶיךָ רָעָה, וְנֶגַע לֹא־יִקְרַב בְּאָהֳלֶךָ: כִּי מַלְאָכָיו יְצַוֶּה־לָּךְ, לִשְׁמָרְךָ בְּכָל־דְּרָכֶיךָ: עַל־כַּפַּיִם יִשָּׂאוּנְךָ, פֶּן־תִּגֹּף בָּאֶבֶן רַגְלֶךָ: עַל־שַׁחַל וָפֶתֶן תִּדְרֹךְ, תִּרְמֹס כְּפִיר וְתַנִּין: כִּי בִי חָשַׁק וַאֲפַלְּטֵהוּ, אֲשַׂגְּבֵהוּ כִּי־יָדַע שְׁמִי: יִקְרָאֵנִי וְאֶעֱנֵהוּ, עִמּוֹ אָנֹכִי בְצָרָה, אֲחַלְּצֵהוּ וַאֲכַבְּדֵהוּ:
אֹרֶךְ יָמִים אַשְׂבִּיעֵהוּ, וְאַרְאֵהוּ בִּישׁוּעָתִי:
אֹרֶךְ יָמִים אַשְׂבִּיעֵהוּ, וְאַרְאֵהוּ בִּישׁוּעָתִי:

*After the funeral, the following is said, except on days on which Taḥanun is omitted, or after nightfall. Some say the following before the funeral.*

## THE ACCEPTANCE OF JUDGMENT

הַצּוּר The Rock, His work is perfect, for all His ways are just; *Deut. 32*
A faithful God who does no wrong, righteous and fair is He.

The Rock, perfect in every deed:
Who can say to Him, "What have You done?"
He rules below and above. He brings death and gives life, *1 Sam. 2*
bringing down to the grave and raising up again.

The Rock, perfect in every act:
Who can say to Him, "Why do You so act?"
You who speak and act: show us kindness we do not deserve,
and in the merit of the one who was bound like a lamb, hear us and act.

Righteous in all His ways, the Rock who is perfect,
slow to anger and full of compassion,
please have pity and spare parents and children,
for Yours, Lord, are forgiveness and compassion.

You are righteous, Lord, in bringing death and giving life.
In Your hand is the safekeeping of all spirits.
Far be it from You to erase our remembrance.
May Your eyes be open to us in compassion,
for Yours, Lord, are compassion and forgiveness.

If one lives for a year or a thousand years,
what does it profit him? He shall be as if he had never been.
Blessed is the true Judge who brings death and gives life.

Blessed is He for His judgment is true, and in His sight He surveys all.
He repays man in accord with his account and just desert,
and all must render acknowledgment to His name.

We know, Lord, that Your judgment is just.
You are just when You speak and fair when You judge.
It is not for us to criticize Your manner of judgment.
You are righteous, Lord, and Your judgments are fair. *Ps. 119*

*After the funeral, the following is said, except on days on which* תחנון *is omitted, or after nightfall. Some say the following before the funeral.*

צדוק הדין

הַצּוּר תָּמִים פָּעֳלוֹ, כִּי כָל־דְּרָכָיו מִשְׁפָּט דברים לב
אֵל אֱמוּנָה וְאֵין עָוֶל, צַדִּיק וְיָשָׁר הוּא:

הַצּוּר תָּמִים בְּכָל פֹּעַל, מִי יֹאמַר לוֹ מַה תִּפְעַל
הַשַּׁלִּיט בְּמַטָּה וּבְמַעַל. מֵמִית וּמְחַיֶּה, מוֹרִיד שְׁאוֹל וַיָּעַל: שמואל א׳ ב

הַצּוּר תָּמִים בְּכָל מַעֲשֶׂה, מִי יֹאמַר לוֹ מַה תַּעֲשֶׂה
הָאוֹמֵר וְעוֹשֶׂה, חֶסֶד חִנָּם לָנוּ תַעֲשֶׂה
וּבִזְכוּת הַנֶּעֱקַד כְּשֶׂה, הַקְשִׁיבָה וַעֲשֵׂה.

צַדִּיק בְּכָל דְּרָכָיו הַצּוּר תָּמִים, אֶרֶךְ אַפַּיִם וּמָלֵא רַחֲמִים
חֲמָל נָא וְחוּס נָא עַל אָבוֹת וּבָנִים
כִּי לְךָ אָדוֹן הַסְּלִיחוֹת וְהָרַחֲמִים.

צַדִּיק אַתָּה יהוה לְהָמִית וּלְהַחֲיוֹת
אֲשֶׁר בְּיָדְךָ פִּקְדוֹן כָּל רוּחוֹת, חָלִילָה לְּךָ זִכְרוֹנֵנוּ לִמְחוֹת
וְיִהְיוּ נָא עֵינֶיךָ בְּרַחֲמִים עָלֵינוּ פְּקוּחוֹת
כִּי לְךָ אָדוֹן הָרַחֲמִים וְהַסְּלִיחוֹת.

אָדָם אִם בֶּן שָׁנָה יִהְיֶה, אוֹ אֶלֶף שָׁנִים יִחְיֶה
מַה יִּתְרוֹן לוֹ, כְּלֹא הָיָה יִהְיֶה
בָּרוּךְ דַּיַּן הָאֱמֶת, מֵמִית וּמְחַיֶּה.

בָּרוּךְ הוּא כִּי אֱמֶת דִּינוֹ, וּמְשׁוֹטֵט הַכֹּל בְּעֵינוֹ
וּמְשַׁלֵּם לְאָדָם חֶשְׁבּוֹנוֹ וְדִינוֹ, וְהַכֹּל לִשְׁמוֹ הוֹדָיָה יִתֵּנוּ.

יָדַעְנוּ יהוה כִּי צֶדֶק מִשְׁפָּטֶךָ, תִּצְדַּק בְּדָבְרֶךָ וְתִזְכֶּה בְשָׁפְטֶךָ
וְאֵין לְהַרְהֵר אַחַר מִדַּת שָׁפְטֶךָ. צַדִּיק אַתָּה יהוה, וְיָשָׁר מִשְׁפָּטֶיךָ: תהלים קיט

True Judge, Judge of righteousness and truth:
Blessed is the true Judge for all His judgments are righteous and true.

In Your hand is the soul of every living thing. Your right hand and power are full of righteousness.
Have compassion on the remnant of the flock of those who serve You,
and say to the angel [of death], "Stay your hand."

Great in counsel and mighty in deed, *Jer. 32*
Your eyes are open to all the ways of men,
giving each according to his ways and the fruit of his deeds:

to proclaim that the LORD is upright; *Ps. 92*
He is my Rock, in whom there is no wrong.

The LORD has given and the LORD has taken away: *Job 1*
blessed be the name of the LORD.

He is compassionate; He forgives iniquity and does not destroy. *Ps. 78*
Repeatedly He suppresses His anger, not rousing His full wrath.

*The following Kaddish, said by the mourners, requires the presence of a minyan.*

*Mourner:* Magnified and sanctified may His great name be,
in the world that will in future be renewed,
reviving the dead and raising them up to eternal life.
He will rebuild the city of Jerusalem
and in it reestablish His Temple.
He will remove alien worship from the earth
and restore to its place the worship of Heaven.
Then the Holy One, blessed be He,
will reign in His sovereignty and splendor.
May it be in your lifetime and in your days,
and in the lifetime of all the house of Israel,
swiftly and soon – and say: Amen.

*All:* May His great name be blessed for ever and all time.

דַּיַּן אֱמֶת, שׁוֹפֵט צֶדֶק וֶאֱמֶת
בָּרוּךְ דַּיַּן הָאֱמֶת, שֶׁכָּל מִשְׁפָּטָיו צֶדֶק וֶאֱמֶת.

נֶפֶשׁ כָּל חַי בְּיָדֶךָ, צֶדֶק מָלְאָה יְמִינְךָ וְיָדֶךָ
רַחֵם עַל פְּלֵטַת צֹאן עֲבָדֶיךָ, וְתֹאמַר לַמַּלְאָךְ הֶרֶף יָדֶךָ.

גְּדֹל הָעֵצָה וְרַב הָעֲלִילִיָּה ירמיה לב
אֲשֶׁר־עֵינֶיךָ פְקֻחוֹת עַל־כָּל־דַּרְכֵי בְּנֵי אָדָם
לָתֵת לְאִישׁ כִּדְרָכָיו, וְכִפְרִי מַעֲלָלָיו:

לְהַגִּיד כִּי־יָשָׁר יהוה, צוּרִי וְלֹא־עַוְלָתָה בּוֹ: תהלים צב

יהוה נָתַן וַיהוה לָקָח, יְהִי שֵׁם יהוה מְבֹרָךְ: איוב א

וְהוּא רַחוּם, יְכַפֵּר עָוֹן וְלֹא־יַשְׁחִית תהלים עח
וְהִרְבָּה לְהָשִׁיב אַפּוֹ, וְלֹא־יָעִיר כָּל־חֲמָתוֹ:

*The following* קדיש*, said by the mourners, requires the presence of a* מנין*.*

אבל: יִתְגַּדַּל וְיִתְקַדַּשׁ שְׁמֵהּ רַבָּא (קהל: אָמֵן)
בְּעָלְמָא דְּהוּא עָתִיד לְאִתְחַדָּתָא
וּלְאַחֲיָאָה מֵתַיָּא, וּלְאַסָּקָא יָתְהוֹן לְחַיֵּי עָלְמָא
וּלְמִבְנֵא קַרְתָּא דִּירוּשְׁלֵם, וּלְשַׁכְלָלָא הֵיכְלֵהּ בְּגַוַּהּ
וּלְמֶעְקַר פָּלְחָנָא נֻכְרָאָה מֵאַרְעָא
וְלַאֲתָבָא פָּלְחָנָא דִשְׁמַיָּא לְאַתְרֵהּ
וְיַמְלִיךְ קֻדְשָׁא בְּרִיךְ הוּא בְּמַלְכוּתֵהּ וִיקָרֵהּ
בְּחַיֵּיכוֹן וּבְיוֹמֵיכוֹן וּבְחַיֵּי דְכָל בֵּית יִשְׂרָאֵל
בַּעֲגָלָא וּבִזְמַן קָרִיב, וְאִמְרוּ אָמֵן. (קהל: אָמֵן)

קהל ואבל: יְהֵא שְׁמֵהּ רַבָּא מְבָרַךְ לְעָלַם וּלְעָלְמֵי עָלְמַיָּא.

*Mourner:* Blessed and praised, glorified and exalted,
raised and honored,
uplifted and lauded
be the name of the Holy One,
blessed be He,
beyond any blessing,
song, praise and consolation
uttered in the world –
and say: Amen.

May there be great peace from heaven,
and life for us and all Israel –
and say: Amen.

*Bow, take three steps back, as if taking leave of the Divine Presence, then bow, first left, then right, then center, while saying:*

May He who makes peace in His high places,
make peace for us and all Israel –
and say: Amen.

*After the funeral, those present form two rows, the mourners pass between them, and the following is said to them:*

May the Almighty comfort you among the other mourners of Zion and Jerusalem.

*Some conclude with:*

May you have no further grief.

*Some have the custom to pick blades of grass and throw them over their shoulders, saying:*

May they of the city grow like the grass of the earth. *Ps. 72*

*Or:*

Remember that we are dust. *Ps. 103*

*After leaving the cemetery, it is customary to wash one's hands and say:*

He will destroy death for ever, and the LORD God will wipe away the tears from all faces and remove the reproach of His people from the whole earth, for the LORD has spoken. *Is. 25*

אבל: יִתְבָּרַךְ וְיִשְׁתַּבַּח וְיִתְפָּאַר
וְיִתְרוֹמַם וְיִתְנַשֵּׂא וְיִתְהַדָּר וְיִתְעַלֶּה וְיִתְהַלָּל
שְׁמֵהּ דְּקֻדְשָׁא בְּרִיךְ הוּא (קהל: בְּרִיךְ הוּא)
לְעֵלָּא מִן כָּל בִּרְכָתָא / בעשרת ימי תשובה: לְעֵלָּא לְעֵלָּא מִכָּל בִּרְכָתָא/
וְשִׁירָתָא, תֻּשְׁבְּחָתָא וְנֶחֱמָתָא
דַּאֲמִירָן בְּעָלְמָא, וְאִמְרוּ אָמֵן. (קהל: אָמֵן)

יְהֵא שְׁלָמָא רַבָּא מִן שְׁמַיָּא
וְחַיִּים, עָלֵינוּ וְעַל כָּל יִשְׂרָאֵל, וְאִמְרוּ אָמֵן. (קהל: אָמֵן)

*Bow, take three steps back, as if taking leave of the Divine Presence, then bow, first left, then right, then center, while saying:*

עֹשֶׂה שָׁלוֹם/ בעשרת ימי תשובה: הַשָּׁלוֹם/ בִּמְרוֹמָיו
הוּא יַעֲשֶׂה שָׁלוֹם
עָלֵינוּ וְעַל כָּל יִשְׂרָאֵל וְאִמְרוּ אָמֵן. (קהל: אָמֵן)

*After the funeral, those present form two rows, the mourners pass between them, and the following is said to them:*

הַמָּקוֹם יְנַחֵם אוֹתְךָ/אוֹתָךְ/אֶתְכֶם
בְּתוֹךְ שְׁאָר אֲבֵלֵי צִיּוֹן וִירוּשָׁלַיִם.

*Some conclude with:*

וְלֹא תוֹסִיפוּ לְדַאֲבָה עוֹד.

*Some have the custom to pick blades of grass and throw them over their shoulders, saying:*

וְיָצִיצוּ מֵעִיר כְּעֵשֶׂב הָאָרֶץ: תהלים עב

*Or:*

זָכוּר כִּי־עָפָר אֲנָחְנוּ: תהלים קג

*After leaving the cemetery, it is customary to wash one's hands and say:*

בִּלַּע הַמָּוֶת לָנֶצַח, וּמָחָה אֲדֹנָי יֱהֹוִה דִּמְעָה מֵעַל כָּל־פָּנִים, וְחֶרְפַּת עַמּוֹ יָסִיר מֵעַל כָּל־הָאָרֶץ, כִּי יהוה דִּבֵּר: ישעיה כה

## PRAYER IN A HOUSE OF MOURNING

*After the regular service, the following psalm is read in a house of mourning during the shiva week. On those days on which Taḥanun is not said, Psalm 16 (below) is substituted.*

לַמְנַצֵּחַ For the conductor of music. Of the sons of Koraḥ. A sacred song. Hear this, all you peoples. Listen, all inhabitants of the world, low and high, rich and poor alike. My mouth will speak words of wisdom; the utterance of my heart will give understanding. I listen with care to a parable; I expound my mystery to the music of the harp. Why should I fear when evil days come, when the wickedness of my foes surrounds me, trusting in their wealth, boasting of their great riches? No man can redeem his brother or pay God the price of his release, for the ransom of a life is costly; no payment is ever enough that would let him live for ever, never seeing the grave. For all can see that wise men die, that the foolish and senseless all perish and leave their wealth to others. They think their houses will remain for ever, their dwellings for all generations; they give their names to their estates. But man, despite his splendor, does not endure; he is like the beasts that perish. Such is the fate of the foolish and their followers who approve their words, Selah. Like sheep they are destined for the grave: death will be their shepherd. The upright will rule over them in the morning. Their forms will decay in the grave, far from their mansions. But God will redeem my life from the grave; He will surely take me to Himself, Selah. Do not be overawed when a man grows rich, when the glory of his house increases, for he will take nothing with him when he dies; his wealth will not descend with him. Though while he lived he counted himself blessed – men always praise you when you prosper – he will join the generation of his ancestors who will never again see the light. A man who, despite his splendor, lacks understanding, is like the beasts that perish. *Ps. 49*

*On those days on which Taḥanun is not said, substitute:*

מִכְתָּם לְדָוִד A musical composition of David. Protect me, God, for in You I have found refuge. I have said to the Lord: You are my Lord: from You alone comes the good I enjoy. All my delight is in the holy ones, the mighty in the land. Those who run after other gods multiply their sorrows. I shall never offer them libations of blood, nor will their names pass my lips. The Lord is my allotted portion and my cup: You direct my fate. The lines have fallen for me in pleasant places; I am well content with my inheritance. I will bless the Lord who has guided me; at night my innermost being admonishes me. I have set the Lord before me at all times. He is at my right hand: I shall not be shaken. Therefore my heart is glad, my spirit rejoices, and my body rests secure. For You will not abandon me to the grave, nor let Your faithful one see the pit. You will teach me the path of life. In Your presence is fullness of joy; at Your right hand, bliss for evermore. *Ps. 16*

# אזכרה

*This prayer is recited by those comforting the mourners after learning Torah at the mourners' home.*

אָנָּא יהוה מֶלֶךְ מָלֵא רַחֲמִים, אֱלֹהֵי הָרוּחוֹת לְכָל בָּשָׂר, אֲשֶׁר בְּיָדְךָ נַפְשׁוֹת הַחַיִּים וְהַמֵּתִים, אָנָּא קַבֵּל בְּחַסְדְּךָ הַגָּדוֹל אֶת נִשְׁמַת

*For a man, say:*

(פלוני בֶּן פלוני) אֲשֶׁר נֶאֱסַף אֶל עַמָּיו. חוּס וַחֲמֹל עָלָיו, סְלַח וּמְחַל לְכָל פְּשָׁעָיו. כִּי אָדָם אֵין צַדִּיק בָּאָרֶץ, אֲשֶׁר יַעֲשֶׂה־טּוֹב וְלֹא קהלת ז
יֶחֱטָא: זְכֹר לוֹ צִדְקָתוֹ אֲשֶׁר עָשָׂה, וִיהִי שְׂכָרוֹ אִתּוֹ, וּפְעֻלָּתוֹ לְפָנָיו. אָנָּא הַסְתֵּר אֶת נִשְׁמָתוֹ בְּצֵל כְּנָפֶיךָ, הוֹדִיעֵהוּ אֹרַח חַיִּים, שֹׂבַע שְׂמָחוֹת אֶת פָּנֶיךָ, נְעִימוֹת בִּימִינְךָ נֶצַח, וְתַשְׁפִּיעַ לוֹ מֵרֹב טוּב הַצָּפוּן לַצַּדִּיקִים.

*For a woman, say:*

(פלונית בַּת פלוני) אֲשֶׁר נֶאֶסְפָה אֶל עַמֶּיהָ. חוּס וַחֲמֹל עָלֶיהָ, סְלַח
וּמְחַל לְכָל פְּשָׁעֶיהָ. כִּי אָדָם אֵין צַדִּיק בָּאָרֶץ, אֲשֶׁר יַעֲשֶׂה־טּוֹב וְלֹא קהלת ז
יֶחֱטָא: זְכֹר לָהּ צִדְקָתָהּ אֲשֶׁר עָשְׂתָה, וִיהִי שְׂכָרָהּ אִתָּהּ, וּפְעֻלָּתָהּ לְפָנֶיהָ. אָנָּא הַסְתֵּר אֶת נִשְׁמָתָהּ בְּצֵל כְּנָפֶיךָ, הוֹדִיעֶהָ אֹרַח חַיִּים, שֹׂבַע שְׂמָחוֹת אֶת פָּנֶיךָ, נְעִימוֹת בִּימִינְךָ נֶצַח, וְתַשְׁפִּיעַ לָהּ מֵרֹב טוּב הַצָּפוּן לַצַּדִּיקִים.

*For a boy, say:*

(פלוני בֶּן פלוני) אֲשֶׁר נֶאֱסַף אֶל עַמָּיו. זְכֹר לוֹ צִדְקָתוֹ אֲשֶׁר עָשָׂה, וִיהִי שְׂכָרוֹ אִתּוֹ, וּפְעֻלָּתוֹ לְפָנָיו. אָנָּא הַסְתֵּר אֶת נִשְׁמָתוֹ בְּצֵל כְּנָפֶיךָ, הוֹדִיעֵהוּ אֹרַח חַיִּים, שֹׂבַע שְׂמָחוֹת אֶת פָּנֶיךָ, נְעִימוֹת בִּימִינְךָ נֶצַח, וְתַשְׁפִּיעַ לוֹ מֵרֹב טוּב הַצָּפוּן לַצַּדִּיקִים.

*For a girl, say:*

(פלונית בַּת פלוני) אֲשֶׁר נֶאֶסְפָה אֶל עַמֶּיהָ. זְכוֹר לָהּ צִדְקָתָהּ אֲשֶׁר עָשְׂתָה, וִיהִי שְׂכָרָהּ אִתָּהּ, וּפְעֻלָּתָהּ לְפָנֶיהָ. אָנָּא הַסְתֵּר אֶת נִשְׁמָתָהּ בְּצֵל כְּנָפֶיךָ, הוֹדִיעֶהָ אֹרַח חַיִּים, שֹׂבַע שְׂמָחוֹת אֶת פָּנֶיךָ, נְעִימוֹת בִּימִינְךָ נֶצַח, וְתַשְׁפִּיעַ לָהּ מֵרֹב טוּב הַצָּפוּן לַצַּדִּיקִים.

As it is written,
"How great is Your goodness Ps. 31
which You have stored up for those who revere You,
which You bestow on those that trust in You
before the children of men."

אָנָּא May the LORD who heals the brokenhearted
and binds up their wounds,
grant consolation to the mourners.

*For a young boy, add:*
May the death of this boy
mark the end of all anguish and sorrow for his parents.

*For a young girl, add:*
May the death of this girl
mark the end of all anguish and sorrow for her parents.

*If the mourners have children, add the words in parentheses:*
חַזְּקֵם Strengthen and support them in the day of their sadness and grief;
and remember them (and their children) for a long and good life.
Put into their hearts love and reverence for You,
so that they may serve You with a perfect heart;
and let their end be peace. Amen.

כְּאִישׁ As a mother comforts her son, Is. 66
so will I comfort you;
and in Jerusalem you shall find comfort.
Your sun shall no more set, Is. 60
your moon shall no more withdraw itself,
for the LORD shall be your everlasting light,
and your days of mourning shall be ended.
He will destroy death for ever; Is. 25
and the LORD God will wipe away the tears from all faces,
and remove the reproach of His people from the whole earth;
for the LORD has spoken it.

כְּמוֹ שֶׁכָּתוּב:
מָה רַב טוּבְךָ אֲשֶׁר־צָפַנְתָּ לִּירֵאֶיךָ תהלים לא
פָּעַלְתָּ לַחוֹסִים בָּךְ נֶגֶד בְּנֵי אָדָם:

אָנָּא יהוה, הָרוֹפֵא לִשְׁבוּרֵי לֵב וּמְחַבֵּשׁ לְעַצְּבוֹתָם
שַׁלֵּם נִחוּמִים לָאֲבֵלִים.

*For a young boy, add:*

וּתְהִי פְּטִירַת הַיֶּלֶד הַזֶּה קֵץ לְכָל צָרָה וְצוּקָה לְאָבִיו וּלְאִמּוֹ.

*For a young girl, add:*

וּתְהִי פְּטִירַת הַיַּלְדָּה הַזֹּאת קֵץ לְכָל צָרָה וְצוּקָה לְאָבִיהָ וּלְאִמָּהּ.

*If the mourners have children, add the words in parentheses:*

חַזְּקֵם וְאַמְּצֵם בְּיוֹם אֶבְלָם וִיגוֹנָם
וְזָכְרֵם (וּזְכֹר אֶת בְּנֵי בֵיתָם) לְחַיִּים טוֹבִים וַאֲרֻכִּים.
תֵּן בְּלִבָּם יִרְאָתְךָ וְאַהֲבָתְךָ לְעָבְדְךָ בְּלֵבָב שָׁלֵם
וּתְהִי אַחֲרִיתָם שָׁלוֹם, אָמֵן.

כְּאִישׁ אֲשֶׁר אִמּוֹ תְּנַחֲמֶנּוּ ישעיה סו
כֵּן אָנֹכִי אֲנַחֶמְכֶם
וּבִירוּשָׁלַםִ תְּנֻחָמוּ:
לֹא־יָבוֹא עוֹד שִׁמְשֵׁךְ, וִירֵחֵךְ לֹא יֵאָסֵף ישעיה ס
כִּי יהוה יִהְיֶה־לָּךְ לְאוֹר עוֹלָם
וְשָׁלְמוּ יְמֵי אֶבְלֵךְ:
בִּלַּע הַמָּוֶת לָנֶצַח ישעיה כה
וּמָחָה אֲדֹנָי יֱהֹוִה דִּמְעָה מֵעַל כָּל־פָּנִים
וְחֶרְפַּת עַמּוֹ יָסִיר מֵעַל כָּל־הָאָרֶץ
כִּי יהוה דִּבֵּר:

## MOURNER'S KADDISH

*The following prayer, said by mourners, requires the presence of a minyan. A transliteration can be found on page 1320.*

*Mourner:* יִתְגַּדַּל Magnified and sanctified
may His great name be,
in the world He created by His will.
May He establish His kingdom
in your lifetime and in your days,
and in the lifetime of all the house of Israel,
swiftly and soon –
and say: Amen.

*All:* May His great name be blessed
for ever and all time.

*Mourner:* Blessed and praised,
glorified and exalted,
raised and honored,
uplifted and lauded
be the name of the Holy One,
blessed be He,
beyond any blessing,
song, praise and consolation
uttered in the world –
and say: Amen.

May there be great peace from heaven,
and life for us and all Israel –
and say: Amen.

*Bow, take three steps back, as if taking leave of the Divine Presence, then bow, first left, then right, then center, while saying:*

May He who makes peace in His high places,
make peace for us and all Israel –
and say: Amen.

## קדיש יתום

*The following prayer, said by mourners, requires the presence of a* מנין.
*A transliteration can be found on page 1320.*

אבל: יִתְגַּדַּל וְיִתְקַדַּשׁ שְׁמֵהּ רַבָּא (קהל: אָמֵן)
בְּעָלְמָא דִּי בְרָא כִרְעוּתֵהּ
וְיַמְלִיךְ מַלְכוּתֵהּ
בְּחַיֵּיכוֹן וּבְיוֹמֵיכוֹן וּבְחַיֵּי דְכָל בֵּית יִשְׂרָאֵל
בַּעֲגָלָא וּבִזְמַן קָרִיב
וְאִמְרוּ אָמֵן. (קהל: אָמֵן)

קהל ואבל: יְהֵא שְׁמֵהּ רַבָּא מְבָרַךְ לְעָלַם וּלְעָלְמֵי עָלְמַיָּא.

אבל: יִתְבָּרַךְ וְיִשְׁתַּבַּח וְיִתְפָּאַר
וְיִתְרוֹמַם וְיִתְנַשֵּׂא וְיִתְהַדָּר וְיִתְעַלֶּה וְיִתְהַלָּל
שְׁמֵהּ דְּקֻדְשָׁא בְּרִיךְ הוּא (קהל: בְּרִיךְ הוּא)
לְעֵלָּא מִן כָּל בִּרְכָתָא / בעשרת ימי תשובה: לְעֵלָּא לְעֵלָּא מִכָּל בִּרְכָתָא/
וְשִׁירָתָא, תֻּשְׁבְּחָתָא וְנֶחֱמָתָא
דַּאֲמִירָן בְּעָלְמָא
וְאִמְרוּ אָמֵן. (קהל: אָמֵן)

יְהֵא שְׁלָמָא רַבָּא מִן שְׁמַיָּא
וְחַיִּים, עָלֵינוּ וְעַל כָּל יִשְׂרָאֵל
וְאִמְרוּ אָמֵן. (קהל: אָמֵן)

*Bow, take three steps back, as if taking leave of the Divine Presence, then bow, first left, then right, then center, while saying:*

עֹשֶׂה שָׁלוֹם/ בעשרת ימי תשובה: הַשָּׁלוֹם/ בִּמְרוֹמָיו
הוּא יַעֲשֶׂה שָׁלוֹם עָלֵינוּ וְעַל כָּל יִשְׂרָאֵל
וְאִמְרוּ אָמֵן. (קהל: אָמֵן)

## BIRKAT HAMAZON IN A HOUSE OF MOURNING

*Leader* Gentlemen, let us say grace.

*Others* May the name of the LORD be blessed from now and for ever. *Ps. 113*

*Leader* May the name of the LORD be blessed from now and for ever.
With your permission,
let us bless the One who comforts mourners
from whose food we have eaten.

*Others* Blessed be the One who comforts mourners,
from whose food we have eaten, and by whose goodness we live.

**People present who have not taken part in the meal say:*
*Blessed be the One who comforts mourners,
whose name is continually blessed for ever and all time.

*Leader* Blessed be the One who comforts mourners,
from whose food we have eaten, and by whose goodness we live.
Blessed be He, and blessed be His name.

*Continue with Birkat HaMazon on page 1058 until before "And may Jerusalem" on page 1066. Then say:*

נַחֵם Comfort, O LORD our God, the mourners of Jerusalem and those who mourn here. Grant them consolation in their mourning and gladness in their grief, as it is said, "As a mother comforts her son, so will I comfort you, and in Jerusalem you shall find comfort." Blessed are You, LORD, who brings comfort to Zion through the rebuilding of Jerusalem. Amen. *Is. 66*

בָּרוּךְ Blessed are You, LORD our God, King of the Universe – God our Father, our King, our Sovereign, our Creator, our Redeemer, our Maker, our Holy One, the Holy One of Jacob. He is our Shepherd, Israel's Sheperd, our living King who is good and does good, the true God, the true Judge, who judges righteously and takes back souls in judgment. He rules the world according to His will, for all His ways are just, and we are His people and His servants. For everything, we are duty bound to acknowledge and bless Him. May He who repairs the breaches in Israel, repair this breach in us and grant us life and peace. May He always bestow on us grace, kindness, compassion and all good things. Of all that is good, may He never let us lack.

*Continue with "May the Compassionate One reign" on page 1066.*

# ברכת המזון בבית האבל

*Leader* רַבּוֹתַי, נְבָרֵךְ.

*Others* יְהִי שֵׁם יהוה מְבֹרָךְ מֵעַתָּה וְעַד־עוֹלָם: תהלים קיג

*Leader* יְהִי שֵׁם יהוה מְבֹרָךְ מֵעַתָּה וְעַד־עוֹלָם:
בִּרְשׁוּת רַבּוֹתַי, נְבָרֵךְ מְנַחֵם אֲבֵלִים שֶׁאָכַלְנוּ מִשֶּׁלּוֹ.

*Others* בָּרוּךְ מְנַחֵם אֲבֵלִים, שֶׁאָכַלְנוּ מִשֶּׁלּוֹ וּבְטוּבוֹ חָיִינוּ.

**People present who have not taken part in the meal say:*

*בָּרוּךְ מְנַחֵם אֲבֵלִים, וּמְבֹרָךְ שְׁמוֹ תָּמִיד לְעוֹלָם וָעֶד.

*Leader* בָּרוּךְ מְנַחֵם אֲבֵלִים, שֶׁאָכַלְנוּ מִשֶּׁלּוֹ וּבְטוּבוֹ חָיִינוּ.
בָּרוּךְ הוּא וּבָרוּךְ שְׁמוֹ.

*Continue with* בִּרְכַּת הַמָּזוֹן *on page 1059 until before* וּבְנֵה יְרוּשָׁלַיִם *on page 1067. Then say:*

נַחֵם יהוה אֱלֹהֵינוּ אֶת אֲבֵלֵי יְרוּשָׁלַיִם, וְאֶת הָאֲבֵלִים הַמִּתְאַבְּלִים בָּאֵבֶל הַזֶּה. נַחֲמֵם מֵאֶבְלָם וְשַׂמְּחֵם מִיגוֹנָם, כָּאָמוּר: כְּאִישׁ אֲשֶׁר אִמּוֹ תְּנַחֲמֶנּוּ, כֵּן אָנֹכִי אֲנַחֶמְכֶם וּבִירוּשָׁלַםִ תְּנֻחָמוּ: בָּרוּךְ אַתָּה יהוה, מְנַחֵם צִיּוֹן בְּבִנְיַן יְרוּשָׁלָיִם. אָמֵן. ישעיה סו

בָּרוּךְ אַתָּה יהוה אֱלֹהֵינוּ מֶלֶךְ הָעוֹלָם, הָאֵל אָבִינוּ מַלְכֵּנוּ אַדִּירֵנוּ בּוֹרְאֵנוּ גּוֹאֲלֵנוּ יוֹצְרֵנוּ קְדוֹשֵׁנוּ קְדוֹשׁ יַעֲקֹב, רוֹעֵנוּ רוֹעֵה יִשְׂרָאֵל, הַמֶּלֶךְ הַחַי, הַטּוֹב וְהַמֵּטִיב. אֵל אֱמֶת, דַּיַּן אֱמֶת, שׁוֹפֵט צֶדֶק, לוֹקֵחַ נְפָשׁוֹת בְּמִשְׁפָּט, וְשַׁלִּיט בְּעוֹלָמוֹ לַעֲשׂוֹת בּוֹ כִּרְצוֹנוֹ, כִּי כָל דְּרָכָיו מִשְׁפָּט, וַאֲנַחְנוּ עַמּוֹ וַעֲבָדָיו, וְעַל הַכֹּל אֲנַחְנוּ חַיָּבִים לְהוֹדוֹת לוֹ וּלְבָרְכוֹ. גּוֹדֵר פִּרְצוֹת יִשְׂרָאֵל, הוּא יִגְדֹּר אֶת הַפִּרְצָה הַזֹּאת מֵעָלֵינוּ לְחַיִּים וּלְשָׁלוֹם. הוּא יִגְמְלֵנוּ לָעַד חֵן וָחֶסֶד וְרַחֲמִים וְכָל טוֹב, וּמִכָּל טוּב לְעוֹלָם אַל יְחַסְּרֵנוּ.

*Continue with* הָרַחֲמָן הוּא יִמְלֹךְ *on page 1067.*

# קריאת התורה
## TORAH READINGS


| | | |
|---|---|---|
| לימי שני וחמישי ומנחה בשבת | 1150 | MONDAYS, THURSDAYS AND SHABBAT MINḤA |
| ראש חודש | 1189 | ROSH ḤODESH |
| תענית ציבור | 1190 | FAST DAYS |
| חנוכה ופורים | 1194 | ḤANUKKA & PURIM |
| שלוש רגלים | 1201 | FESTIVALS |

# קריאת התורה לימי שני וחמישי ובמנחה של שבת

# THE READING OF THE TORAH FOR MONDAYS, THURSDAYS, AND SHABBAT MINḤA

## BERESHIT — בראשית

בראשית א: א–כג בְּרֵאשִׁית בָּרָא אֱלֹהִים אֵת הַשָּׁמַיִם וְאֵת הָאָרֶץ׃ וְהָאָרֶץ הָיְתָה תֹהוּ וָבֹהוּ
וְחֹשֶׁךְ עַל־פְּנֵי תְהוֹם וְרוּחַ אֱלֹהִים מְרַחֶפֶת עַל־פְּנֵי הַמָּיִם׃ וַיֹּאמֶר אֱלֹהִים
יְהִי־אוֹר וַיְהִי־אוֹר׃ וַיַּרְא אֱלֹהִים אֶת־הָאוֹר כִּי־טוֹב וַיַּבְדֵּל אֱלֹהִים בֵּין הָאוֹר
וּבֵין הַחֹשֶׁךְ׃ וַיִּקְרָא אֱלֹהִים ׀ לָאוֹר יוֹם וְלַחֹשֶׁךְ קָרָא לָיְלָה וַיְהִי־עֶרֶב וַיְהִי־
בֹקֶר יוֹם אֶחָד׃

לוי וַיֹּאמֶר אֱלֹהִים יְהִי רָקִיעַ בְּתוֹךְ הַמָּיִם וִיהִי מַבְדִּיל בֵּין מַיִם לָמָיִם׃ וַיַּעַשׂ
אֱלֹהִים אֶת־הָרָקִיעַ וַיַּבְדֵּל בֵּין הַמַּיִם אֲשֶׁר מִתַּחַת לָרָקִיעַ וּבֵין הַמַּיִם אֲשֶׁר
מֵעַל לָרָקִיעַ וַיְהִי־כֵן׃ וַיִּקְרָא אֱלֹהִים לָרָקִיעַ שָׁמָיִם וַיְהִי־עֶרֶב וַיְהִי־בֹקֶר
יוֹם שֵׁנִי׃

ישראל וַיֹּאמֶר אֱלֹהִים יִקָּווּ הַמַּיִם מִתַּחַת הַשָּׁמַיִם אֶל־מָקוֹם אֶחָד וְתֵרָאֶה הַיַּבָּשָׁה
וַיְהִי־כֵן׃ וַיִּקְרָא אֱלֹהִים ׀ לַיַּבָּשָׁה אֶרֶץ וּלְמִקְוֵה הַמַּיִם קָרָא יַמִּים וַיַּרְא
אֱלֹהִים כִּי־טוֹב׃ וַיֹּאמֶר אֱלֹהִים תַּדְשֵׁא הָאָרֶץ דֶּשֶׁא עֵשֶׂב מַזְרִיעַ זֶרַע עֵץ
פְּרִי עֹשֶׂה פְּרִי לְמִינוֹ אֲשֶׁר זַרְעוֹ־בוֹ עַל־הָאָרֶץ וַיְהִי־כֵן׃ וַתּוֹצֵא הָאָרֶץ דֶּשֶׁא
עֵשֶׂב מַזְרִיעַ זֶרַע לְמִינֵהוּ וְעֵץ עֹשֶׂה־פְּרִי אֲשֶׁר זַרְעוֹ־בוֹ לְמִינֵהוּ וַיַּרְא אֱלֹהִים
כִּי־טוֹב׃ וַיְהִי־עֶרֶב וַיְהִי־בֹקֶר יוֹם שְׁלִישִׁי׃

*Some extend the* ישראל *portion on the Thursday reading:*

וַיֹּאמֶר אֱלֹהִים יְהִי מְאֹרֹת בִּרְקִיעַ הַשָּׁמַיִם לְהַבְדִּיל בֵּין הַיּוֹם וּבֵין הַלָּיְלָה
וְהָיוּ לְאֹתֹת וּלְמוֹעֲדִים וּלְיָמִים וְשָׁנִים׃ וְהָיוּ לִמְאוֹרֹת בִּרְקִיעַ הַשָּׁמַיִם לְהָאִיר
עַל־הָאָרֶץ וַיְהִי־כֵן׃ וַיַּעַשׂ אֱלֹהִים אֶת־שְׁנֵי הַמְּאֹרֹת הַגְּדֹלִים אֶת־הַמָּאוֹר
הַגָּדֹל לְמֶמְשֶׁלֶת הַיּוֹם וְאֶת־הַמָּאוֹר הַקָּטֹן לְמֶמְשֶׁלֶת הַלַּיְלָה וְאֵת הַכּוֹכָבִים׃
וַיִּתֵּן אֹתָם אֱלֹהִים בִּרְקִיעַ הַשָּׁמָיִם לְהָאִיר עַל־הָאָרֶץ׃ וְלִמְשֹׁל בַּיּוֹם וּבַלַּיְלָה

וּֽלֲהַבְדִּיל בֵּין הָאוֹר וּבֵין הַחֹשֶׁךְ וַיַּרְא אֱלֹהִים כִּי־טוֹב׃ וַיְהִי־עֶרֶב וַיְהִי־בֹקֶר
יוֹם רְבִיעִי׃
וַיֹּאמֶר אֱלֹהִים יִשְׁרְצוּ הַמַּיִם שֶׁרֶץ נֶפֶשׁ חַיָּה וְעוֹף יְעוֹפֵף עַל־הָאָרֶץ עַל־פְּנֵי
רְקִיעַ הַשָּׁמָיִם׃ וַיִּבְרָא אֱלֹהִים אֶת־הַתַּנִּינִם הַגְּדֹלִים וְאֵת כָּל־נֶפֶשׁ הַחַיָּה ׀
הָרֹמֶשֶׂת אֲשֶׁר שָׁרְצוּ הַמַּיִם לְמִינֵהֶם וְאֵת כָּל־עוֹף כָּנָף לְמִינֵהוּ וַיַּרְא אֱלֹהִים
כִּי־טוֹב׃ וַיְבָרֶךְ אֹתָם אֱלֹהִים לֵאמֹר פְּרוּ וּרְבוּ וּמִלְאוּ אֶת־הַמַּיִם בַּיַּמִּים וְהָעוֹף
יִרֶב בָּאָרֶץ׃ וַיְהִי־עֶרֶב וַיְהִי־בֹקֶר יוֹם חֲמִישִׁי׃

## NOAḤ נח

בראשית ו: ט–כב אֵלֶּה תּוֹלְדֹת נֹחַ נֹחַ אִישׁ צַדִּיק תָּמִים הָיָה בְּדֹרֹתָיו אֶת־הָאֱלֹהִים הִתְהַלֶּךְ־
נֹחַ׃ וַיּוֹלֶד נֹחַ שְׁלֹשָׁה בָנִים אֶת־שֵׁם אֶת־חָם וְאֶת־יָפֶת׃ וַתִּשָּׁחֵת הָאָרֶץ
לִפְנֵי הָאֱלֹהִים וַתִּמָּלֵא הָאָרֶץ חָמָס׃ וַיַּרְא אֱלֹהִים אֶת־הָאָרֶץ וְהִנֵּה נִשְׁחָתָה
כִּי־הִשְׁחִית כָּל־בָּשָׂר אֶת־דַּרְכּוֹ עַל־הָאָרֶץ׃ וַיֹּאמֶר אֱלֹהִים
לְנֹחַ קֵץ כָּל־בָּשָׂר בָּא לְפָנַי כִּי־מָלְאָה הָאָרֶץ חָמָס מִפְּנֵיהֶם וְהִנְנִי מַשְׁחִיתָם
אֶת־הָאָרֶץ׃ עֲשֵׂה לְךָ תֵּבַת עֲצֵי־גֹפֶר קִנִּים תַּעֲשֶׂה אֶת־הַתֵּבָה וְכָפַרְתָּ אֹתָהּ
מִבַּיִת וּמִחוּץ בַּכֹּפֶר׃ וְזֶה אֲשֶׁר תַּעֲשֶׂה אֹתָהּ שְׁלֹשׁ מֵאוֹת אַמָּה אֹרֶךְ הַתֵּבָה
חֲמִשִּׁים אַמָּה רָחְבָּהּ וּשְׁלֹשִׁים אַמָּה קוֹמָתָהּ׃ צֹהַר ׀ תַּעֲשֶׂה לַתֵּבָה וְאֶל־אַמָּה
תְּכַלֶּנָּה מִלְמַעְלָה וּפֶתַח הַתֵּבָה בְּצִדָּהּ תָּשִׂים תַּחְתִּיִּם שְׁנִיִּם וּשְׁלִשִׁים תַּעֲשֶׂהָ׃
לוי *וַאֲנִי הִנְנִי מֵבִיא אֶת־הַמַּבּוּל מַיִם עַל־הָאָרֶץ לְשַׁחֵת כָּל־בָּשָׂר אֲשֶׁר־בּוֹ
רוּחַ חַיִּים מִתַּחַת הַשָּׁמָיִם כֹּל אֲשֶׁר־בָּאָרֶץ יִגְוָע׃ וַהֲקִמֹתִי אֶת־בְּרִיתִי אִתָּךְ
וּבָאתָ אֶל־הַתֵּבָה אַתָּה וּבָנֶיךָ וְאִשְׁתְּךָ וּנְשֵׁי־בָנֶיךָ אִתָּךְ׃ וּמִכָּל־הָחַי מִכָּל־
ישראל בָּשָׂר שְׁנַיִם מִכֹּל תָּבִיא אֶל־הַתֵּבָה לְהַחֲיֹת אִתָּךְ זָכָר וּנְקֵבָה יִהְיוּ׃ *מֵהָעוֹף
לְמִינֵהוּ וּמִן־הַבְּהֵמָה לְמִינָהּ מִכֹּל רֶמֶשׂ הָאֲדָמָה לְמִינֵהוּ שְׁנַיִם מִכֹּל יָבֹאוּ
אֵלֶיךָ לְהַחֲיוֹת׃ וְאַתָּה קַח־לְךָ מִכָּל־מַאֲכָל אֲשֶׁר יֵאָכֵל וְאָסַפְתָּ אֵלֶיךָ וְהָיָה
לְךָ וְלָהֶם לְאָכְלָה׃ וַיַּעַשׂ נֹחַ כְּכֹל אֲשֶׁר צִוָּה אֹתוֹ אֱלֹהִים כֵּן עָשָׂה׃

## LEKH LEKHA לך לך

בראשית יב: א–יג וַיֹּאמֶר יהוה אֶל־אַבְרָם לֶךְ־לְךָ מֵאַרְצְךָ וּמִמּוֹלַדְתְּךָ וּמִבֵּית אָבִיךָ אֶל־הָאָרֶץ
אֲשֶׁר אַרְאֶךָּ׃ וְאֶעֶשְׂךָ לְגוֹי גָּדוֹל וַאֲבָרֶכְךָ וַאֲגַדְּלָה שְׁמֶךָ וֶהְיֵה בְּרָכָה׃ וַאֲבָרְכָה

שלוי מְבָרְכֶיךָ וּמְקַלֶּלְךָ אָאֹר וְנִבְרְכוּ בְךָ כֹּל מִשְׁפְּחֹת הָאֲדָמָה׃ *וַיֵּלֶךְ אַבְרָם כַּאֲשֶׁר
דִּבֶּר אֵלָיו יהוה וַיֵּלֶךְ אִתּוֹ לוֹט וְאַבְרָם בֶּן־חָמֵשׁ שָׁנִים וְשִׁבְעִים שָׁנָה בְּצֵאתוֹ
מֵחָרָן׃ וַיִּקַּח אַבְרָם אֶת־שָׂרַי אִשְׁתּוֹ וְאֶת־לוֹט בֶּן־אָחִיו וְאֶת־כָּל־רְכוּשָׁם
אֲשֶׁר רָכָשׁוּ וְאֶת־הַנֶּפֶשׁ אֲשֶׁר־עָשׂוּ בְחָרָן וַיֵּצְאוּ לָלֶכֶת אַרְצָה כְּנַעַן וַיָּבֹאוּ
אַרְצָה כְּנָעַן׃ וַיַּעֲבֹר אַבְרָם בָּאָרֶץ עַד מְקוֹם שְׁכֶם עַד אֵלוֹן מוֹרֶה וְהַכְּנַעֲנִי
אָז בָּאָרֶץ׃ וַיֵּרָא יהוה אֶל־אַבְרָם וַיֹּאמֶר לְזַרְעֲךָ אֶתֵּן אֶת־הָאָרֶץ הַזֹּאת וַיִּבֶן
שָׁם מִזְבֵּחַ לַיהוה הַנִּרְאֶה אֵלָיו׃ וַיַּעְתֵּק מִשָּׁם הָהָרָה מִקֶּדֶם לְבֵית־אֵל וַיֵּט
אָהֳלֹה בֵּית־אֵל מִיָּם וְהָעַי מִקֶּדֶם וַיִּבֶן־שָׁם מִזְבֵּחַ לַיהוה וַיִּקְרָא בְּשֵׁם יהוה׃
וַיִּסַּע אַבְרָם הָלוֹךְ וְנָסוֹעַ הַנֶּגְבָּה׃

ישראל וַיְהִי רָעָב בָּאָרֶץ וַיֵּרֶד אַבְרָם מִצְרַיְמָה לָגוּר שָׁם כִּי־כָבֵד הָרָעָב בָּאָרֶץ׃
וַיְהִי כַּאֲשֶׁר הִקְרִיב לָבוֹא מִצְרָיְמָה וַיֹּאמֶר אֶל־שָׂרַי אִשְׁתּוֹ הִנֵּה־נָא יָדַעְתִּי
כִּי אִשָּׁה יְפַת־מַרְאֶה אָתְּ׃ וְהָיָה כִּי־יִרְאוּ אֹתָךְ הַמִּצְרִים וְאָמְרוּ אִשְׁתּוֹ זֹאת
וְהָרְגוּ אֹתִי וְאֹתָךְ יְחַיּוּ׃ אִמְרִי־נָא אֲחֹתִי אָתְּ לְמַעַן יִיטַב־לִי בַעֲבוּרֵךְ וְחָיְתָה
נַפְשִׁי בִּגְלָלֵךְ׃

## VAYERA וירא

בראשית יח: א–יד וַיֵּרָא אֵלָיו יהוה בְּאֵלֹנֵי מַמְרֵא וְהוּא יֹשֵׁב פֶּתַח־הָאֹהֶל כְּחֹם הַיּוֹם׃ וַיִּשָּׂא
עֵינָיו וַיַּרְא וְהִנֵּה שְׁלֹשָׁה אֲנָשִׁים נִצָּבִים עָלָיו וַיַּרְא וַיָּרָץ לִקְרָאתָם מִפֶּתַח
הָאֹהֶל וַיִּשְׁתַּחוּ אָרְצָה׃ וַיֹּאמַר אֲדֹנָי אִם־נָא מָצָאתִי חֵן בְּעֵינֶיךָ אַל־נָא
תַעֲבֹר מֵעַל עַבְדֶּךָ׃ יֻקַּח־נָא מְעַט־מַיִם וְרַחֲצוּ רַגְלֵיכֶם וְהִשָּׁעֲנוּ תַּחַת הָעֵץ׃
וְאֶקְחָה פַת־לֶחֶם וְסַעֲדוּ לִבְּכֶם אַחַר תַּעֲבֹרוּ כִּי־עַל־כֵּן עֲבַרְתֶּם עַל־עַבְדְּכֶם
לוי וַיֹּאמְרוּ כֵּן תַּעֲשֶׂה כַּאֲשֶׁר דִּבַּרְתָּ׃ *וַיְמַהֵר אַבְרָהָם הָאֹהֱלָה אֶל־שָׂרָה וַיֹּאמֶר
מַהֲרִי שְׁלֹשׁ סְאִים קֶמַח סֹלֶת לוּשִׁי וַעֲשִׂי עֻגוֹת׃ וְאֶל־הַבָּקָר רָץ אַבְרָהָם
וַיִּקַּח בֶּן־בָּקָר רַךְ וָטוֹב וַיִּתֵּן אֶל־הַנַּעַר וַיְמַהֵר לַעֲשׂוֹת אֹתוֹ׃ וַיִּקַּח חֶמְאָה
וְחָלָב וּבֶן־הַבָּקָר אֲשֶׁר עָשָׂה וַיִּתֵּן לִפְנֵיהֶם וְהוּא עֹמֵד עֲלֵיהֶם תַּחַת הָעֵץ
ישראל וַיֹּאכֵלוּ׃ *וַיֹּאמְרוּ אֵלָיו אַיֵּה שָׂרָה אִשְׁתֶּךָ וַיֹּאמֶר הִנֵּה בָאֹהֶל׃ וַיֹּאמֶר שׁוֹב
אָשׁוּב אֵלֶיךָ כָּעֵת חַיָּה וְהִנֵּה־בֵן לְשָׂרָה אִשְׁתֶּךָ וְשָׂרָה שֹׁמַעַת פֶּתַח הָאֹהֶל
וְהוּא אַחֲרָיו׃ וְאַבְרָהָם וְשָׂרָה זְקֵנִים בָּאִים בַּיָּמִים חָדַל לִהְיוֹת לְשָׂרָה אֹרַח
כַּנָּשִׁים׃ וַתִּצְחַק שָׂרָה בְּקִרְבָּהּ לֵאמֹר אַחֲרֵי בְלֹתִי הָיְתָה־לִּי עֶדְנָה וַאדֹנִי

זָקֵן׃ וַיֹּאמֶר יְהוָה אֶל־אַבְרָהָם לָמָּה זֶּה צָחֲקָה שָׂרָה לֵאמֹר הַאַף אֻמְנָם אֵלֵד
וַאֲנִי זָקַנְתִּי׃ הֲיִפָּלֵא מֵיְהוָה דָּבָר לַמּוֹעֵד אָשׁוּב אֵלֶיךָ כָּעֵת חַיָּה וּלְשָׂרָה בֵן׃

## HAYYEI SARA

## חיי שרה

בראשית כג: א–טז וַיִּהְיוּ חַיֵּי שָׂרָה מֵאָה שָׁנָה וְעֶשְׂרִים שָׁנָה וְשֶׁבַע שָׁנִים שְׁנֵי חַיֵּי שָׂרָה׃ וַתָּמָת
שָׂרָה בְּקִרְיַת אַרְבַּע הִוא חֶבְרוֹן בְּאֶרֶץ כְּנָעַן וַיָּבֹא אַבְרָהָם לִסְפֹּד לְשָׂרָה
וְלִבְכֹּתָהּ׃ וַיָּקָם אַבְרָהָם מֵעַל פְּנֵי מֵתוֹ וַיְדַבֵּר אֶל־בְּנֵי־חֵת לֵאמֹר׃ גֵּר־וְתוֹשָׁב
אָנֹכִי עִמָּכֶם תְּנוּ לִי אֲחֻזַּת־קֶבֶר עִמָּכֶם וְאֶקְבְּרָה מֵתִי מִלְּפָנָי׃ וַיַּעֲנוּ בְנֵי־חֵת
אֶת־אַבְרָהָם לֵאמֹר לוֹ׃ שְׁמָעֵנוּ ׀ אֲדֹנִי נְשִׂיא אֱלֹהִים אַתָּה בְּתוֹכֵנוּ בְּמִבְחַר
קְבָרֵינוּ קְבֹר אֶת־מֵתֶךָ אִישׁ מִמֶּנּוּ אֶת־קִבְרוֹ לֹא־יִכְלֶה מִמְּךָ מִקְּבֹר מֵתֶךָ׃
לוי וַיָּקָם אַבְרָהָם וַיִּשְׁתַּחוּ לְעַם־הָאָרֶץ לִבְנֵי־חֵת׃ *וַיְדַבֵּר אִתָּם לֵאמֹר אִם־יֵשׁ
אֶת־נַפְשְׁכֶם לִקְבֹּר אֶת־מֵתִי מִלְּפָנַי שְׁמָעוּנִי וּפִגְעוּ־לִי בְּעֶפְרוֹן בֶּן־צֹחַר׃
וְיִתֶּן־לִי אֶת־מְעָרַת הַמַּכְפֵּלָה אֲשֶׁר־לוֹ אֲשֶׁר בִּקְצֵה שָׂדֵהוּ בְּכֶסֶף מָלֵא יִתְּנֶנָּה
לִּי בְּתוֹכְכֶם לַאֲחֻזַּת־קָבֶר׃ וְעֶפְרוֹן יֹשֵׁב בְּתוֹךְ בְּנֵי־חֵת וַיַּעַן עֶפְרוֹן הַחִתִּי
אֶת־אַבְרָהָם בְּאָזְנֵי בְנֵי־חֵת לְכֹל בָּאֵי שַׁעַר־עִירוֹ לֵאמֹר׃ לֹא־אֲדֹנִי שְׁמָעֵנִי
הַשָּׂדֶה נָתַתִּי לָךְ וְהַמְּעָרָה אֲשֶׁר־בּוֹ לְךָ נְתַתִּיהָ לְעֵינֵי בְנֵי־עַמִּי נְתַתִּיהָ לָּךְ
ישראל קְבֹר מֵתֶךָ׃ וַיִּשְׁתַּחוּ אַבְרָהָם לִפְנֵי עַם־הָאָרֶץ׃ *וַיְדַבֵּר אֶל־עֶפְרוֹן בְּאָזְנֵי עַם־
הָאָרֶץ לֵאמֹר אַךְ אִם־אַתָּה לוּ שְׁמָעֵנִי נָתַתִּי כֶּסֶף הַשָּׂדֶה קַח מִמֶּנִּי וְאֶקְבְּרָה
אֶת־מֵתִי שָׁמָּה׃ וַיַּעַן עֶפְרוֹן אֶת־אַבְרָהָם לֵאמֹר לוֹ׃ אֲדֹנִי שְׁמָעֵנִי אֶרֶץ אַרְבַּע
מֵאֹת שֶׁקֶל־כֶּסֶף בֵּינִי וּבֵינְךָ מַה־הִוא וְאֶת־מֵתְךָ קְבֹר׃ וַיִּשְׁמַע אַבְרָהָם אֶל־
עֶפְרוֹן וַיִּשְׁקֹל אַבְרָהָם לְעֶפְרֹן אֶת־הַכֶּסֶף אֲשֶׁר דִּבֶּר בְּאָזְנֵי בְנֵי־חֵת אַרְבַּע
מֵאוֹת שֶׁקֶל כֶּסֶף עֹבֵר לַסֹּחֵר׃

## TOLEDOT

## תולדות

בראשית כה:יט–כו:ה וְאֵלֶּה תּוֹלְדֹת יִצְחָק בֶּן־אַבְרָהָם אַבְרָהָם הוֹלִיד אֶת־יִצְחָק׃ וַיְהִי יִצְחָק בֶּן־
אַרְבָּעִים שָׁנָה בְּקַחְתּוֹ אֶת־רִבְקָה בַּת־בְּתוּאֵל הָאֲרַמִּי מִפַּדַּן אֲרָם אֲחוֹת לָבָן
הָאֲרַמִּי לוֹ לְאִשָּׁה׃ וַיֶּעְתַּר יִצְחָק לַיהוָה לְנֹכַח אִשְׁתּוֹ כִּי עֲקָרָה הִוא וַיֵּעָתֶר
לוֹ יְהוָה וַתַּהַר רִבְקָה אִשְׁתּוֹ׃ וַיִּתְרֹצְצוּ הַבָּנִים בְּקִרְבָּהּ וַתֹּאמֶר אִם־כֵּן לָמָּה
לוי גוֹיִם זֶּה אָנֹכִי וַתֵּלֶךְ לִדְרֹשׁ אֶת־יְהוָה׃ *וַיֹּאמֶר יְהוָה לָהּ שְׁנֵי גיים בְּבִטְנֵךְ וּשְׁנֵי

לְאֻמִּים מִמֵּעַיִךְ יִפָּרֵדוּ וּלְאֹם מִלְאֹם יֶאֱמָץ וְרַב יַעֲבֹד צָעִיר׃ וַיִּמְלְאוּ יָמֶיהָ
לָלֶדֶת וְהִנֵּה תוֹמִם בְּבִטְנָהּ׃ וַיֵּצֵא הָרִאשׁוֹן אַדְמוֹנִי כֻּלּוֹ כְּאַדֶּרֶת שֵׂעָר וַיִּקְרְאוּ
שְׁמוֹ עֵשָׂו׃ וְאַחֲרֵי־כֵן יָצָא אָחִיו וְיָדוֹ אֹחֶזֶת בַּעֲקֵב עֵשָׂו וַיִּקְרָא שְׁמוֹ יַעֲקֹב
ישראל וְיִצְחָק בֶּן־שִׁשִּׁים שָׁנָה בְּלֶדֶת אֹתָם׃ *וַיִּגְדְּלוּ הַנְּעָרִים וַיְהִי עֵשָׂו אִישׁ יֹדֵעַ צַיִד
אִישׁ שָׂדֶה וְיַעֲקֹב אִישׁ תָּם יֹשֵׁב אֹהָלִים׃ וַיֶּאֱהַב יִצְחָק אֶת־עֵשָׂו כִּי־צַיִד בְּפִיו
וְרִבְקָה אֹהֶבֶת אֶת־יַעֲקֹב׃ וַיָּזֶד יַעֲקֹב נָזִיד וַיָּבֹא עֵשָׂו מִן־הַשָּׂדֶה וְהוּא עָיֵף׃
וַיֹּאמֶר עֵשָׂו אֶל־יַעֲקֹב הַלְעִיטֵנִי נָא מִן־הָאָדֹם הָאָדֹם הַזֶּה כִּי עָיֵף אָנֹכִי עַל־
כֵּן קָרָא־שְׁמוֹ אֱדוֹם׃ וַיֹּאמֶר יַעֲקֹב מִכְרָה כַיּוֹם אֶת־בְּכֹרָתְךָ לִי׃ וַיֹּאמֶר עֵשָׂו
הִנֵּה אָנֹכִי הוֹלֵךְ לָמוּת וְלָמָּה־זֶּה לִי בְּכֹרָה׃ וַיֹּאמֶר יַעֲקֹב הִשָּׁבְעָה לִּי כַּיּוֹם
וַיִּשָּׁבַע לוֹ וַיִּמְכֹּר אֶת־בְּכֹרָתוֹ לְיַעֲקֹב׃ וְיַעֲקֹב נָתַן לְעֵשָׂו לֶחֶם וּנְזִיד עֲדָשִׁים
וַיֹּאכַל וַיֵּשְׁתְּ וַיָּקָם וַיֵּלַךְ וַיִּבֶז עֵשָׂו אֶת־הַבְּכֹרָה׃
וַיְהִי רָעָב בָּאָרֶץ מִלְּבַד הָרָעָב הָרִאשׁוֹן אֲשֶׁר הָיָה בִּימֵי אַבְרָהָם וַיֵּלֶךְ יִצְחָק
אֶל־אֲבִימֶלֶךְ מֶלֶךְ־פְּלִשְׁתִּים גְּרָרָה׃ וַיֵּרָא אֵלָיו יהוה וַיֹּאמֶר אַל־תֵּרֵד מִצְרָיְמָה
שְׁכֹן בָּאָרֶץ אֲשֶׁר אֹמַר אֵלֶיךָ׃ גּוּר בָּאָרֶץ הַזֹּאת וְאֶהְיֶה עִמְּךָ וַאֲבָרְכֶךָּ כִּי־לְךָ
וּלְזַרְעֲךָ אֶתֵּן אֶת־כָּל־הָאֲרָצֹת הָאֵל וַהֲקִמֹתִי אֶת־הַשְּׁבֻעָה אֲשֶׁר נִשְׁבַּעְתִּי
לְאַבְרָהָם אָבִיךָ׃ וְהִרְבֵּיתִי אֶת־זַרְעֲךָ כְּכוֹכְבֵי הַשָּׁמַיִם וְנָתַתִּי לְזַרְעֲךָ אֵת כָּל־
הָאֲרָצֹת הָאֵל וְהִתְבָּרְכוּ בְזַרְעֲךָ כֹּל גּוֹיֵי הָאָרֶץ׃ עֵקֶב אֲשֶׁר־שָׁמַע אַבְרָהָם
בְּקֹלִי וַיִּשְׁמֹר מִשְׁמַרְתִּי מִצְוֺתַי חֻקּוֹתַי וְתוֹרֹתָי׃

## VAYETZE ויצא

בראשית כח:י-כב וַיֵּצֵא יַעֲקֹב מִבְּאֵר שָׁבַע וַיֵּלֶךְ חָרָנָה׃ וַיִּפְגַּע בַּמָּקוֹם וַיָּלֶן שָׁם כִּי־בָא הַשֶּׁמֶשׁ
וַיִּקַּח מֵאַבְנֵי הַמָּקוֹם וַיָּשֶׂם מְרַאֲשֹׁתָיו וַיִּשְׁכַּב בַּמָּקוֹם הַהוּא׃ וַיַּחֲלֹם וְהִנֵּה
סֻלָּם מֻצָּב אַרְצָה וְרֹאשׁוֹ מַגִּיעַ הַשָּׁמָיְמָה וְהִנֵּה מַלְאֲכֵי אֱלֹהִים עֹלִים וְיֹרְדִים
לוי בּוֹ׃ *וְהִנֵּה יהוה נִצָּב עָלָיו וַיֹּאמַר אֲנִי יהוה אֱלֹהֵי אַבְרָהָם אָבִיךָ וֵאלֹהֵי יִצְחָק
הָאָרֶץ אֲשֶׁר אַתָּה שֹׁכֵב עָלֶיהָ לְךָ אֶתְּנֶנָּה וּלְזַרְעֶךָ׃ וְהָיָה זַרְעֲךָ כַּעֲפַר הָאָרֶץ
וּפָרַצְתָּ יָמָּה וָקֵדְמָה וְצָפֹנָה וָנֶגְבָּה וְנִבְרְכוּ בְךָ כָּל־מִשְׁפְּחֹת הָאֲדָמָה וּבְזַרְעֶךָ׃
וְהִנֵּה אָנֹכִי עִמָּךְ וּשְׁמַרְתִּיךָ בְּכֹל אֲשֶׁר־תֵּלֵךְ וַהֲשִׁבֹתִיךָ אֶל־הָאֲדָמָה הַזֹּאת כִּי
לֹא אֶעֱזָבְךָ עַד אֲשֶׁר אִם־עָשִׂיתִי אֵת אֲשֶׁר־דִּבַּרְתִּי לָךְ׃ וַיִּיקַץ יַעֲקֹב מִשְּׁנָתוֹ

וַיֹּאמֶר אָכֵן יֵשׁ יְהוָה בַּמָּקוֹם הַזֶּה וְאָנֹכִי לֹא יָדָעְתִּי: וַיִּירָא וַיֹּאמַר מַה־נּוֹרָא
ישראל הַמָּקוֹם הַזֶּה אֵין זֶה כִּי אִם־בֵּית אֱלֹהִים וְזֶה שַׁעַר הַשָּׁמָיִם: *וַיַּשְׁכֵּם יַעֲקֹב
בַּבֹּקֶר וַיִּקַּח אֶת־הָאֶבֶן אֲשֶׁר־שָׂם מְרַאֲשֹׁתָיו וַיָּשֶׂם אֹתָהּ מַצֵּבָה וַיִּצֹק שֶׁמֶן
עַל־רֹאשָׁהּ: וַיִּקְרָא אֶת־שֵׁם־הַמָּקוֹם הַהוּא בֵּית־אֵל וְאוּלָם לוּז שֵׁם־הָעִיר
לָרִאשֹׁנָה: וַיִּדַּר יַעֲקֹב נֶדֶר לֵאמֹר אִם־יִהְיֶה אֱלֹהִים עִמָּדִי וּשְׁמָרַנִי בַּדֶּרֶךְ הַזֶּה
אֲשֶׁר אָנֹכִי הוֹלֵךְ וְנָתַן־לִי לֶחֶם לֶאֱכֹל וּבֶגֶד לִלְבֹּשׁ: וְשַׁבְתִּי בְשָׁלוֹם אֶל־בֵּית
אָבִי וְהָיָה יְהוָה לִי לֵאלֹהִים: וְהָאֶבֶן הַזֹּאת אֲשֶׁר־שַׂמְתִּי מַצֵּבָה יִהְיֶה בֵּית
אֱלֹהִים וְכֹל אֲשֶׁר תִּתֶּן־לִי עַשֵּׂר אֲעַשְּׂרֶנּוּ לָךְ:

## וישלח VAYISHLAḤ

בראשית לב:ג-יב וַיִּשְׁלַח יַעֲקֹב מַלְאָכִים לְפָנָיו אֶל־עֵשָׂו אָחִיו אַרְצָה שֵׂעִיר שְׂדֵה אֱדוֹם: וַיְצַו
אֹתָם לֵאמֹר כֹּה תֹאמְרוּן לַאדֹנִי לְעֵשָׂו כֹּה אָמַר עַבְדְּךָ יַעֲקֹב עִם־לָבָן גַּרְתִּי
וָאֵחַר עַד־עָתָּה: וַיְהִי־לִי שׁוֹר וַחֲמוֹר צֹאן וְעֶבֶד וְשִׁפְחָה וָאֶשְׁלְחָה לְהַגִּיד
לוי לַאדֹנִי לִמְצֹא־חֵן בְּעֵינֶיךָ: *וַיָּשֻׁבוּ הַמַּלְאָכִים אֶל־יַעֲקֹב לֵאמֹר בָּאנוּ אֶל־
אָחִיךָ אֶל־עֵשָׂו וְגַם הֹלֵךְ לִקְרָאתְךָ וְאַרְבַּע־מֵאוֹת אִישׁ עִמּוֹ: וַיִּירָא יַעֲקֹב
מְאֹד וַיֵּצֶר לוֹ וַיַּחַץ אֶת־הָעָם אֲשֶׁר־אִתּוֹ וְאֶת־הַצֹּאן וְאֶת־הַבָּקָר וְהַגְּמַלִּים
לִשְׁנֵי מַחֲנוֹת: וַיֹּאמֶר אִם־יָבוֹא עֵשָׂו אֶל־הַמַּחֲנֶה הָאַחַת וְהִכָּהוּ וְהָיָה הַמַּחֲנֶה
ישראל הַנִּשְׁאָר לִפְלֵיטָה: *וַיֹּאמֶר יַעֲקֹב אֱלֹהֵי אָבִי אַבְרָהָם וֵאלֹהֵי אָבִי יִצְחָק יְהוָה
הָאֹמֵר אֵלַי שׁוּב לְאַרְצְךָ וּלְמוֹלַדְתְּךָ וְאֵיטִיבָה עִמָּךְ: קָטֹנְתִּי מִכֹּל הַחֲסָדִים
וּמִכָּל־הָאֱמֶת אֲשֶׁר עָשִׂיתָ אֶת־עַבְדֶּךָ כִּי בְמַקְלִי עָבַרְתִּי אֶת־הַיַּרְדֵּן הַזֶּה
וְעַתָּה הָיִיתִי לִשְׁנֵי מַחֲנוֹת: הַצִּילֵנִי נָא מִיַּד אָחִי מִיַּד עֵשָׂו כִּי־יָרֵא אָנֹכִי
אֹתוֹ פֶּן־יָבוֹא וְהִכַּנִי אֵם עַל־בָּנִים: וְאַתָּה אָמַרְתָּ הֵיטֵב אֵיטִיב עִמָּךְ וְשַׂמְתִּי
אֶת־זַרְעֲךָ כְּחוֹל הַיָּם אֲשֶׁר לֹא־יִסָּפֵר מֵרֹב:

## וישב VAYESHEV

בראשית לז:א-יא וַיֵּשֶׁב יַעֲקֹב בְּאֶרֶץ מְגוּרֵי אָבִיו בְּאֶרֶץ כְּנָעַן: אֵלֶּה ׀ תֹּלְדוֹת יַעֲקֹב יוֹסֵף
בֶּן־שְׁבַע־עֶשְׂרֵה שָׁנָה הָיָה רֹעֶה אֶת־אֶחָיו בַּצֹּאן וְהוּא נַעַר אֶת־בְּנֵי בִלְהָה
וְאֶת־בְּנֵי זִלְפָּה נְשֵׁי אָבִיו וַיָּבֵא יוֹסֵף אֶת־דִּבָּתָם רָעָה אֶל־אֲבִיהֶם: וְיִשְׂרָאֵל

לוי אָהַב אֶת־יוֹסֵף מִכָּל־בָּנָיו כִּי־בֶן־זְקֻנִים הוּא לוֹ וְעָשָׂה לוֹ כְּתֹנֶת פַּסִּים׃ *וַיִּרְאוּ
אֶחָיו כִּי־אֹתוֹ אָהַב אֲבִיהֶם מִכָּל־אֶחָיו וַיִּשְׂנְאוּ אֹתוֹ וְלֹא יָכְלוּ דַּבְּרוֹ לְשָׁלֹם׃
וַיַּחֲלֹם יוֹסֵף חֲלוֹם וַיַּגֵּד לְאֶחָיו וַיּוֹסִפוּ עוֹד שְׂנֹא אֹתוֹ׃ וַיֹּאמֶר אֲלֵיהֶם שִׁמְעוּ־
נָא הַחֲלוֹם הַזֶּה אֲשֶׁר חָלָמְתִּי׃ וְהִנֵּה אֲנַחְנוּ מְאַלְּמִים אֲלֻמִּים בְּתוֹךְ הַשָּׂדֶה
וְהִנֵּה קָמָה אֲלֻמָּתִי וְגַם־נִצָּבָה וְהִנֵּה תְסֻבֶּינָה אֲלֻמֹּתֵיכֶם וַתִּשְׁתַּחֲוֶיןָ לַאֲלֻמָּתִי׃
ישראל *וַיֹּאמְרוּ לוֹ אֶחָיו הֲמָלֹךְ תִּמְלֹךְ עָלֵינוּ אִם־מָשׁוֹל תִּמְשֹׁל בָּנוּ וַיּוֹסִפוּ עוֹד
שְׂנֹא אֹתוֹ עַל־חֲלֹמֹתָיו וְעַל־דְּבָרָיו׃ וַיַּחֲלֹם עוֹד חֲלוֹם אַחֵר וַיְסַפֵּר אֹתוֹ
לְאֶחָיו וַיֹּאמֶר הִנֵּה חָלַמְתִּי חֲלוֹם עוֹד וְהִנֵּה הַשֶּׁמֶשׁ וְהַיָּרֵחַ וְאַחַד עָשָׂר
כּוֹכָבִים מִשְׁתַּחֲוִים לִי׃ וַיְסַפֵּר אֶל־אָבִיו וְאֶל־אֶחָיו וַיִּגְעַר־בּוֹ אָבִיו וַיֹּאמֶר לוֹ
מָה הַחֲלוֹם הַזֶּה אֲשֶׁר חָלָמְתָּ הֲבוֹא נָבוֹא אֲנִי וְאִמְּךָ וְאַחֶיךָ לְהִשְׁתַּחֲוֹת לְךָ
אָרְצָה׃ וַיְקַנְאוּ־בוֹ אֶחָיו וְאָבִיו שָׁמַר אֶת־הַדָּבָר׃

## מקץ MIKETZ

בראשית מא:א–יד וַיְהִי מִקֵּץ שְׁנָתַיִם יָמִים וּפַרְעֹה חֹלֵם וְהִנֵּה עֹמֵד עַל־הַיְאֹר׃ וְהִנֵּה מִן־הַיְאֹר
עֹלֹת שֶׁבַע פָּרוֹת יְפוֹת מַרְאֶה וּבְרִיאֹת בָּשָׂר וַתִּרְעֶינָה בָּאָחוּ׃ וְהִנֵּה שֶׁבַע
פָּרוֹת אֲחֵרוֹת עֹלוֹת אַחֲרֵיהֶן מִן־הַיְאֹר רָעוֹת מַרְאֶה וְדַקּוֹת בָּשָׂר וַתַּעֲמֹדְנָה
אֵצֶל הַפָּרוֹת עַל־שְׂפַת הַיְאֹר׃ וַתֹּאכַלְנָה הַפָּרוֹת רָעוֹת הַמַּרְאֶה וְדַקֹּת הַבָּשָׂר
לוי אֵת שֶׁבַע הַפָּרוֹת יְפֹת הַמַּרְאֶה וְהַבְּרִיאֹת וַיִּיקַץ פַּרְעֹה׃ *וַיִּישָׁן וַיַּחֲלֹם שֵׁנִית
וְהִנֵּה ׀ שֶׁבַע שִׁבֳּלִים עֹלוֹת בְּקָנֶה אֶחָד בְּרִיאוֹת וְטֹבוֹת׃ וְהִנֵּה שֶׁבַע שִׁבֳּלִים
דַּקּוֹת וּשְׁדוּפֹת קָדִים צֹמְחוֹת אַחֲרֵיהֶן׃ וַתִּבְלַעְנָה הַשִּׁבֳּלִים הַדַּקּוֹת אֵת
ישראל שֶׁבַע הַשִּׁבֳּלִים הַבְּרִיאוֹת וְהַמְּלֵאוֹת וַיִּיקַץ פַּרְעֹה וְהִנֵּה חֲלוֹם׃ *וַיְהִי בַבֹּקֶר
וַתִּפָּעֶם רוּחוֹ וַיִּשְׁלַח וַיִּקְרָא אֶת־כָּל־חַרְטֻמֵּי מִצְרַיִם וְאֶת־כָּל־חֲכָמֶיהָ וַיְסַפֵּר
פַּרְעֹה לָהֶם אֶת־חֲלֹמוֹ וְאֵין־פּוֹתֵר אוֹתָם לְפַרְעֹה׃ וַיְדַבֵּר שַׂר הַמַּשְׁקִים אֶת־
פַּרְעֹה לֵאמֹר אֶת־חֲטָאַי אֲנִי מַזְכִּיר הַיּוֹם׃ פַּרְעֹה קָצַף עַל־עֲבָדָיו וַיִּתֵּן אֹתִי
בְּמִשְׁמַר בֵּית שַׂר הַטַּבָּחִים אֹתִי וְאֵת שַׂר הָאֹפִים׃ וַנַּחַלְמָה חֲלוֹם בְּלַיְלָה
אֶחָד אֲנִי וָהוּא אִישׁ כְּפִתְרוֹן חֲלֹמוֹ חָלָמְנוּ׃ וְשָׁם אִתָּנוּ נַעַר עִבְרִי עֶבֶד לְשַׂר
הַטַּבָּחִים וַנְּסַפֶּר־לוֹ וַיִּפְתָּר־לָנוּ אֶת־חֲלֹמֹתֵינוּ אִישׁ כַּחֲלֹמוֹ פָּתָר׃ וַיְהִי כַּאֲשֶׁר
פָּתַר־לָנוּ כֵּן הָיָה אֹתִי הֵשִׁיב עַל־כַּנִּי וְאֹתוֹ תָלָה׃ וַיִּשְׁלַח פַּרְעֹה וַיִּקְרָא אֶת־
יוֹסֵף וַיְרִיצֻהוּ מִן־הַבּוֹר וַיְגַלַּח וַיְחַלֵּף שִׂמְלֹתָיו וַיָּבֹא אֶל־פַּרְעֹה׃

## VAYIGASH ויגש

בראשית מד:יח–ל ויגש אליו יהודה ויאמר בי אדני ידבר־נא עבדך דבר באזני אדני ואל־יחר
אפך בעבדך כי כמוך כפרעה: אדני שאל את־עבדיו לאמר היש־לכם אב
או־אח: ונאמר אל־אדני יש־לנו אב זקן וילד זקנים קטן ואחיו מת ויותר הוא
לוי לבדו לאמו ואביו אהבו: *ותאמר אל־עבדיך הורדהו אלי ואשימה עיני
עליו: ונאמר אל־אדני לא־יוכל הנער לעזב את־אביו ועזב את־אביו ומת:
ותאמר אל־עבדיך אם־לא ירד אחיכם הקטן אתכם לא תספון לראות פני:
ישראל ויהי כי עלינו אל־עבדך אבי ונגד־לו את דברי אדני: *ויאמר אבינו שבו
שברו־לנו מעט־אכל: ונאמר לא נוכל לרדת אם־יש אחינו הקטן אתנו
וירדנו כי־לא נוכל לראות פני האיש ואחינו הקטן איננו אתנו: ויאמר
עבדך אבי אלינו אתם ידעתם כי שנים ילדה־לי אשתי: ויצא האחד מאתי
ואמר אך טרף טרף ולא ראיתיו עד־הנה: ולקחתם גם־את־זה מעם פני
וקרהו אסון והורדתם את־שיבתי ברעה שאלה: ועתה כבאי אל־עבדך
אבי והנער איננו אתנו ונפשו קשורה בנפשו:

## VAYHI ויחי

בראשית מז:כח–מח:ט ויחי יעקב בארץ מצרים שבע עשרה שנה ויהי ימי־יעקב שני חייו שבע
שנים וארבעים ומאת שנה: ויקרבו ימי־ישראל למות ויקרא ׀ לבנו ליוסף
ויאמר לו אם־נא מצאתי חן בעיניך שים־נא ידך תחת ירכי ועשית עמדי
חסד ואמת אל־נא תקברני במצרים: ושכבתי עם־אבתי ונשאתני ממצרים
וקברתני בקברתם ויאמר אנכי אעשה כדברך: ויאמר השבעה לי וישבע
לו וישתחו ישראל על־ראש המטה:
לוי ויהי אחרי הדברים האלה ויאמר ליוסף הנה אביך חלה ויקח את־שני בניו
עמו את־מנשה ואת־אפרים: ויגד ליעקב ויאמר הנה בנך יוסף בא אליך
ויתחזק ישראל וישב על־המטה: ויאמר יעקב אל־יוסף אל שדי נראה־אלי
ישראל בלוז בארץ כנען ויברך אתי: *ויאמר אלי הנני מפרך והרביתך ונתתיך
לקהל עמים ונתתי את־הארץ הזאת לזרעך אחריך אחזת עולם: ועתה
שני־בניך הנולדים לך בארץ מצרים עד־באי אליך מצרימה לי־הם אפרים
ומנשה כראובן ושמעון יהיו־לי: ומולדתך אשר־הולדת אחריהם לך יהיו

עַל שֵׁם אֲחֵיהֶם יִקָּרְאוּ בְּנַחֲלָתָם: וַאֲנִי | בְּבֹאִי מִפַּדָּן מֵתָה עָלַי רָחֵל בְּאֶרֶץ
כְּנַעַן בַּדֶּרֶךְ בְּעוֹד כִּבְרַת־אֶרֶץ לָבֹא אֶפְרָתָה וָאֶקְבְּרֶהָ שָּׁם בְּדֶרֶךְ אֶפְרָת
הִוא בֵּית לָחֶם: וַיַּרְא יִשְׂרָאֵל אֶת־בְּנֵי יוֹסֵף וַיֹּאמֶר מִי־אֵלֶּה: וַיֹּאמֶר יוֹסֵף
אֶל־אָבִיו בָּנַי הֵם אֲשֶׁר־נָתַן־לִי אֱלֹהִים בָּזֶה וַיֹּאמַר קָחֶם־נָא אֵלַי וַאֲבָרְכֵם:

## SHEMOT — שמות

שמות א:א–יז וְאֵלֶּה שְׁמוֹת בְּנֵי יִשְׂרָאֵל הַבָּאִים מִצְרָיְמָה אֵת יַעֲקֹב אִישׁ וּבֵיתוֹ בָּאוּ:
רְאוּבֵן שִׁמְעוֹן לֵוִי וִיהוּדָה: יִשָּׂשכָר זְבוּלֻן וּבִנְיָמִן: דָּן וְנַפְתָּלִי גָּד וְאָשֵׁר:
וַיְהִי כָּל־נֶפֶשׁ יֹצְאֵי יֶרֶךְ־יַעֲקֹב שִׁבְעִים נָפֶשׁ וְיוֹסֵף הָיָה בְמִצְרָיִם: וַיָּמָת יוֹסֵף
וְכָל־אֶחָיו וְכֹל הַדּוֹר הַהוּא: וּבְנֵי יִשְׂרָאֵל פָּרוּ וַיִּשְׁרְצוּ וַיִּרְבּוּ וַיַּעַצְמוּ בִּמְאֹד
מְאֹד וַתִּמָּלֵא הָאָרֶץ אֹתָם:

לוי וַיָּקָם מֶלֶךְ־חָדָשׁ עַל־מִצְרָיִם אֲשֶׁר לֹא־יָדַע אֶת־יוֹסֵף: וַיֹּאמֶר אֶל־עַמּוֹ הִנֵּה עַם
בְּנֵי יִשְׂרָאֵל רַב וְעָצוּם מִמֶּנּוּ: הָבָה נִתְחַכְּמָה לוֹ פֶּן־יִרְבֶּה וְהָיָה כִּי־תִקְרֶאנָה
מִלְחָמָה וְנוֹסַף גַּם־הוּא עַל־שֹׂנְאֵינוּ וְנִלְחַם־בָּנוּ וְעָלָה מִן־הָאָרֶץ: וַיָּשִׂימוּ
עָלָיו שָׂרֵי מִסִּים לְמַעַן עַנֹּתוֹ בְּסִבְלֹתָם וַיִּבֶן עָרֵי מִסְכְּנוֹת לְפַרְעֹה אֶת־פִּתֹם
וְאֶת־רַעַמְסֵס: וְכַאֲשֶׁר יְעַנּוּ אֹתוֹ כֵּן יִרְבֶּה וְכֵן יִפְרֹץ וַיָּקֻצוּ מִפְּנֵי בְּנֵי יִשְׂרָאֵל:
ישראל *וַיַּעֲבִדוּ מִצְרַיִם אֶת־בְּנֵי יִשְׂרָאֵל בְּפָרֶךְ: וַיְמָרְרוּ אֶת־חַיֵּיהֶם בַּעֲבֹדָה קָשָׁה
בְּחֹמֶר וּבִלְבֵנִים וּבְכָל־עֲבֹדָה בַּשָּׂדֶה אֵת כָּל־עֲבֹדָתָם אֲשֶׁר־עָבְדוּ בָהֶם
בְּפָרֶךְ: וַיֹּאמֶר מֶלֶךְ מִצְרַיִם לַמְיַלְּדֹת הָעִבְרִיֹּת אֲשֶׁר שֵׁם הָאַחַת שִׁפְרָה וְשֵׁם
הַשֵּׁנִית פּוּעָה: וַיֹּאמֶר בְּיַלֶּדְכֶן אֶת־הָעִבְרִיּוֹת וּרְאִיתֶן עַל־הָאָבְנָיִם אִם־בֵּן
הוּא וַהֲמִתֶּן אֹתוֹ וְאִם־בַּת הִוא וָחָיָה: וַתִּירֶאןָ הַמְיַלְּדֹת אֶת־הָאֱלֹהִים וְלֹא
עָשׂוּ כַּאֲשֶׁר דִּבֶּר אֲלֵיהֶן מֶלֶךְ מִצְרָיִם וַתְּחַיֶּיןָ אֶת־הַיְלָדִים:

## VA'ERA — וארא

שמות ו:ב–יג וַיְדַבֵּר אֱלֹהִים אֶל־מֹשֶׁה וַיֹּאמֶר אֵלָיו אֲנִי יהוה: וָאֵרָא אֶל־אַבְרָהָם אֶל־יִצְחָק
וְאֶל־יַעֲקֹב בְּאֵל שַׁדָּי וּשְׁמִי יהוה לֹא נוֹדַעְתִּי לָהֶם: וְגַם הֲקִמֹתִי אֶת־בְּרִיתִי
אִתָּם לָתֵת לָהֶם אֶת־אֶרֶץ כְּנָעַן אֵת אֶרֶץ מְגֻרֵיהֶם אֲשֶׁר־גָּרוּ בָהּ: וְגַם | אֲנִי
שָׁמַעְתִּי אֶת־נַאֲקַת בְּנֵי יִשְׂרָאֵל אֲשֶׁר מִצְרַיִם מַעֲבִדִים אֹתָם וָאֶזְכֹּר אֶת־

בְּרִיתִי: *לָכֵן אֱמֹר לִבְנֵי־יִשְׂרָאֵל אֲנִי יהוה וְהוֹצֵאתִי אֶתְכֶם מִתַּחַת סִבְלֹת לוי
מִצְרַיִם וְהִצַּלְתִּי אֶתְכֶם מֵעֲבֹדָתָם וְגָאַלְתִּי אֶתְכֶם בִּזְרוֹעַ נְטוּיָה וּבִשְׁפָטִים
גְּדֹלִים: וְלָקַחְתִּי אֶתְכֶם לִי לְעָם וְהָיִיתִי לָכֶם לֵאלֹהִים וִידַעְתֶּם כִּי אֲנִי יהוה
אֱלֹהֵיכֶם הַמּוֹצִיא אֶתְכֶם מִתַּחַת סִבְלוֹת מִצְרָיִם: וְהֵבֵאתִי אֶתְכֶם אֶל־הָאָרֶץ
אֲשֶׁר נָשָׂאתִי אֶת־יָדִי לָתֵת אֹתָהּ לְאַבְרָהָם לְיִצְחָק וּלְיַעֲקֹב וְנָתַתִּי אֹתָהּ לָכֶם
מוֹרָשָׁה אֲנִי יהוה: וַיְדַבֵּר מֹשֶׁה כֵּן אֶל־בְּנֵי יִשְׂרָאֵל וְלֹא שָׁמְעוּ אֶל־מֹשֶׁה
מִקֹּצֶר רוּחַ וּמֵעֲבֹדָה קָשָׁה:
וַיְדַבֵּר יהוה אֶל־מֹשֶׁה לֵּאמֹר: בֹּא דַבֵּר אֶל־פַּרְעֹה מֶלֶךְ מִצְרָיִם וִישַׁלַּח אֶת־ ישראל
בְּנֵי־יִשְׂרָאֵל מֵאַרְצוֹ: וַיְדַבֵּר מֹשֶׁה לִפְנֵי יהוה לֵאמֹר הֵן בְּנֵי־יִשְׂרָאֵל לֹא־שָׁמְעוּ
אֵלַי וְאֵיךְ יִשְׁמָעֵנִי פַרְעֹה וַאֲנִי עֲרַל שְׂפָתָיִם:
וַיְדַבֵּר יהוה אֶל־מֹשֶׁה וְאֶל־אַהֲרֹן וַיְצַוֵּם אֶל־בְּנֵי יִשְׂרָאֵל וְאֶל־פַּרְעֹה מֶלֶךְ
מִצְרָיִם לְהוֹצִיא אֶת־בְּנֵי־יִשְׂרָאֵל מֵאֶרֶץ מִצְרָיִם:

## בא
## BO

וַיֹּאמֶר יהוה אֶל־מֹשֶׁה בֹּא אֶל־פַּרְעֹה כִּי־אֲנִי הִכְבַּדְתִּי אֶת־לִבּוֹ וְאֶת־לֵב שמות י:א–יא
עֲבָדָיו לְמַעַן שִׁתִי אֹתֹתַי אֵלֶּה בְּקִרְבּוֹ: וּלְמַעַן תְּסַפֵּר בְּאָזְנֵי בִנְךָ וּבֶן־בִּנְךָ אֵת
אֲשֶׁר הִתְעַלַּלְתִּי בְּמִצְרַיִם וְאֶת־אֹתֹתַי אֲשֶׁר־שַׂמְתִּי בָם וִידַעְתֶּם כִּי־אֲנִי יהוה:
וַיָּבֹא מֹשֶׁה וְאַהֲרֹן אֶל־פַּרְעֹה וַיֹּאמְרוּ אֵלָיו כֹּה־אָמַר יהוה אֱלֹהֵי הָעִבְרִים
עַד־מָתַי מֵאַנְתָּ לֵעָנֹת מִפָּנָי שַׁלַּח עַמִּי וְיַעַבְדֻנִי: *כִּי אִם־מָאֵן אַתָּה לְשַׁלֵּחַ לוי
אֶת־עַמִּי הִנְנִי מֵבִיא מָחָר אַרְבֶּה בִּגְבֻלֶךָ: וְכִסָּה אֶת־עֵין הָאָרֶץ וְלֹא יוּכַל
לִרְאֹת אֶת־הָאָרֶץ וְאָכַל | אֶת־יֶתֶר הַפְּלֵטָה הַנִּשְׁאֶרֶת לָכֶם מִן־הַבָּרָד וְאָכַל
אֶת־כָּל־הָעֵץ הַצֹּמֵחַ לָכֶם מִן־הַשָּׂדֶה: וּמָלְאוּ בָתֶּיךָ וּבָתֵּי כָל־עֲבָדֶיךָ וּבָתֵּי
כָל־מִצְרַיִם אֲשֶׁר לֹא־רָאוּ אֲבֹתֶיךָ וַאֲבוֹת אֲבֹתֶיךָ מִיּוֹם הֱיוֹתָם עַל־הָאֲדָמָה
עַד הַיּוֹם הַזֶּה וַיִּפֶן וַיֵּצֵא מֵעִם פַּרְעֹה: *וַיֹּאמְרוּ עַבְדֵי פַרְעֹה אֵלָיו עַד־מָתַי ישראל
יִהְיֶה זֶה לָנוּ לְמוֹקֵשׁ שַׁלַּח אֶת־הָאֲנָשִׁים וְיַעַבְדוּ אֶת־יהוה אֱלֹהֵיהֶם הֲטֶרֶם
תֵּדַע כִּי אָבְדָה מִצְרָיִם: וַיּוּשַׁב אֶת־מֹשֶׁה וְאֶת־אַהֲרֹן אֶל־פַּרְעֹה וַיֹּאמֶר
אֲלֵהֶם לְכוּ עִבְדוּ אֶת־יהוה אֱלֹהֵיכֶם מִי וָמִי הַהֹלְכִים: וַיֹּאמֶר מֹשֶׁה בִּנְעָרֵינוּ
וּבִזְקֵנֵינוּ נֵלֵךְ בְּבָנֵינוּ וּבִבְנוֹתֵנוּ בְּצֹאנֵנוּ וּבִבְקָרֵנוּ נֵלֵךְ כִּי חַג־יהוה לָנוּ: וַיֹּאמֶר

אֲלֵהֶם יְהִי כֵן יהוה עִמָּכֶם כַּאֲשֶׁר אֲשַׁלַּח אֶתְכֶם וְאֶת־טַפְּכֶם רְאוּ כִּי רָעָה
נֶגֶד פְּנֵיכֶם׃ לֹא כֵן לְכוּ־נָא הַגְּבָרִים וְעִבְדוּ אֶת־יהוה כִּי אֹתָהּ אַתֶּם מְבַקְשִׁים
וַיְגָרֶשׁ אֹתָם מֵאֵת פְּנֵי פַרְעֹה׃

## BESHALLAH בשלח

שמות יג:יז–יד:ח וַיְהִי בְּשַׁלַּח פַּרְעֹה אֶת־הָעָם וְלֹא־נָחָם אֱלֹהִים דֶּרֶךְ אֶרֶץ פְּלִשְׁתִּים כִּי קָרוֹב
הוּא כִּי ׀ אָמַר אֱלֹהִים פֶּן־יִנָּחֵם הָעָם בִּרְאֹתָם מִלְחָמָה וְשָׁבוּ מִצְרָיְמָה׃ וַיַּסֵּב
אֱלֹהִים ׀ אֶת־הָעָם דֶּרֶךְ הַמִּדְבָּר יַם־סוּף וַחֲמֻשִׁים עָלוּ בְנֵי־יִשְׂרָאֵל מֵאֶרֶץ
מִצְרָיִם׃ וַיִּקַּח מֹשֶׁה אֶת־עַצְמוֹת יוֹסֵף עִמּוֹ כִּי הַשְׁבֵּעַ הִשְׁבִּיעַ אֶת־בְּנֵי יִשְׂרָאֵל
לֵאמֹר פָּקֹד יִפְקֹד אֱלֹהִים אֶתְכֶם וְהַעֲלִיתֶם אֶת־עַצְמֹתַי מִזֶּה אִתְּכֶם׃ וַיִּסְעוּ
מִסֻּכֹּת וַיַּחֲנוּ בְאֵתָם בִּקְצֵה הַמִּדְבָּר׃ וַיהוה הֹלֵךְ לִפְנֵיהֶם יוֹמָם בְּעַמּוּד עָנָן
לַנְחֹתָם הַדֶּרֶךְ וְלַיְלָה בְּעַמּוּד אֵשׁ לְהָאִיר לָהֶם לָלֶכֶת יוֹמָם וָלָיְלָה׃ לֹא־יָמִישׁ
עַמּוּד הֶעָנָן יוֹמָם וְעַמּוּד הָאֵשׁ לָיְלָה לִפְנֵי הָעָם׃
לוי וַיְדַבֵּר יהוה אֶל־מֹשֶׁה לֵּאמֹר׃ דַּבֵּר אֶל־בְּנֵי יִשְׂרָאֵל וְיָשֻׁבוּ וְיַחֲנוּ לִפְנֵי פִּי
הַחִירֹת בֵּין מִגְדֹּל וּבֵין הַיָּם לִפְנֵי בַּעַל צְפֹן נִכְחוֹ תַחֲנוּ עַל־הַיָּם׃ וְאָמַר פַּרְעֹה
לִבְנֵי יִשְׂרָאֵל נְבֻכִים הֵם בָּאָרֶץ סָגַר עֲלֵיהֶם הַמִּדְבָּר׃ וְחִזַּקְתִּי אֶת־לֵב־פַּרְעֹה
וְרָדַף אַחֲרֵיהֶם וְאִכָּבְדָה בְּפַרְעֹה וּבְכָל־חֵילוֹ וְיָדְעוּ מִצְרַיִם כִּי־אֲנִי יהוה וַיַּעֲשׂוּ־
ישראל כֵן׃ *וַיֻּגַּד לְמֶלֶךְ מִצְרַיִם כִּי בָרַח הָעָם וַיֵּהָפֵךְ לְבַב פַּרְעֹה וַעֲבָדָיו אֶל־הָעָם
וַיֹּאמְרוּ מַה־זֹּאת עָשִׂינוּ כִּי־שִׁלַּחְנוּ אֶת־יִשְׂרָאֵל מֵעָבְדֵנוּ׃ וַיֶּאְסֹר אֶת־רִכְבּוֹ
וְאֶת־עַמּוֹ לָקַח עִמּוֹ׃ וַיִּקַּח שֵׁשׁ־מֵאוֹת רֶכֶב בָּחוּר וְכֹל רֶכֶב מִצְרָיִם וְשָׁלִשִׁם
עַל־כֻּלּוֹ׃ וַיְחַזֵּק יהוה אֶת־לֵב פַּרְעֹה מֶלֶךְ מִצְרַיִם וַיִּרְדֹּף אַחֲרֵי בְּנֵי יִשְׂרָאֵל
וּבְנֵי יִשְׂרָאֵל יֹצְאִים בְּיָד רָמָה׃

## YITRO יתרו

שמות יח:א–יב וַיִּשְׁמַע יִתְרוֹ כֹהֵן מִדְיָן חֹתֵן מֹשֶׁה אֵת כָּל־אֲשֶׁר עָשָׂה אֱלֹהִים לְמֹשֶׁה
וּלְיִשְׂרָאֵל עַמּוֹ כִּי־הוֹצִיא יהוה אֶת־יִשְׂרָאֵל מִמִּצְרָיִם׃ וַיִּקַּח יִתְרוֹ חֹתֵן
מֹשֶׁה אֶת־צִפֹּרָה אֵשֶׁת מֹשֶׁה אַחַר שִׁלּוּחֶיהָ׃ וְאֵת שְׁנֵי בָנֶיהָ אֲשֶׁר שֵׁם הָאֶחָד
גֵּרְשֹׁם כִּי אָמַר גֵּר הָיִיתִי בְּאֶרֶץ נָכְרִיָּה׃ וְשֵׁם הָאֶחָד אֱלִיעֶזֶר כִּי־אֱלֹהֵי אָבִי

בעזרי ויצלני מחרב פרעה: *ויבא יתרו חתן משה ובניו ואשתו אל־משה לוי
אל־המדבר אשר־הוא חנה שם הר האלהים: ויאמר אל־משה אני חתנך
יתרו בא אליך ואשתך ושני בניה עמה: ויצא משה לקראת חתנו וישתחו
וישק־לו וישאלו איש־לרעהו לשלום ויבאו האהלה: ויספר משה לחתנו
את כל־אשר עשה יהוה לפרעה ולמצרים על אודת ישראל את כל־התלאה
אשר מצאתם בדרך ויצלם יהוה: *ויחד יתרו על כל־הטובה אשר־עשה ישראל
יהוה לישראל אשר הצילו מיד מצרים: ויאמר יתרו ברוך יהוה אשר הציל
אתכם מיד מצרים ומיד פרעה אשר הציל את־העם מתחת יד־מצרים:
עתה ידעתי כי־גדול יהוה מכל־האלהים כי בדבר אשר זדו עליהם: ויקח
יתרו חתן משה עלה וזבחים לאלהים ויבא אהרן וכל | זקני ישראל לאכל־
לחם עם־חתן משה לפני האלהים:

## משפטים
## MISHPATIM

ואלה המשפטים אשר תשים לפניהם: כי תקנה עבד עברי שש שנים שמות כא:א־יט
יעבד ובשבעת יצא לחפשי חנם: אם־בגפו יבא בגפו יצא אם־בעל אשה
הוא ויצאה אשתו עמו: אם־אדניו יתן־לו אשה וילדה־לו בנים או בנות
האשה וילדיה תהיה לאדניה והוא יצא בגפו: ואם־אמר יאמר העבד
אהבתי את־אדני את־אשתי ואת־בני לא אצא חפשי: והגישו אדניו
אל־האלהים והגישו אל־הדלת או אל־המזוזה ורצע אדניו את־אזנו
במרצע ועבדו לעלם: *וכי־ימכר איש את־בתו לאמה לא לוי
תצא כצאת העבדים: אם־רעה בעיני אדניה אשר־לא יעדה והפדה לעם לו
נכרי לא־ימשל למכרה בבגדו־בה: ואם־לבנו ייעדנה כמשפט הבנות
יעשה־לה: אם־אחרת יקח־לו שארה כסותה וענתה לא יגרע: ואם־שלש־
אלה לא יעשה לה ויצאה חנם אין כסף: *מכה איש ומת מות ישראל
יומת: ואשר לא צדה והאלהים אנה לידו ושמתי לך מקום אשר ינוס
שמה: וכי־יזד איש על־רעהו להרגו בערמה מעם מזבחי
תקחנו למות: ומכה אביו ואמו מות יומת: וגנב
איש ומכרו ונמצא בידו מות יומת: ומקלל אביו ואמו מות

יוּמָת: וְכִי־יְרִיבֻן אֲנָשִׁים וְהִכָּה־אִישׁ אֶת־רֵעֵהוּ בְּאֶבֶן אוֹ בְאֶגְרֹף
וְלֹא יָמוּת וְנָפַל לְמִשְׁכָּב: אִם־יָקוּם וְהִתְהַלֵּךְ בַּחוּץ עַל־מִשְׁעַנְתּוֹ וְנִקָּה הַמַּכֶּה
רַק שִׁבְתּוֹ יִתֵּן וְרַפֹּא יְרַפֵּא:

## TERUMA — תרומה

שמות כה:א–טז וַיְדַבֵּר יהוה אֶל־מֹשֶׁה לֵּאמֹר: דַּבֵּר אֶל־בְּנֵי יִשְׂרָאֵל וְיִקְחוּ־לִי תְּרוּמָה מֵאֵת
כָּל־אִישׁ אֲשֶׁר יִדְּבֶנּוּ לִבּוֹ תִּקְחוּ אֶת־תְּרוּמָתִי: וְזֹאת הַתְּרוּמָה אֲשֶׁר תִּקְחוּ
מֵאִתָּם זָהָב וָכֶסֶף וּנְחֹשֶׁת: וּתְכֵלֶת וְאַרְגָּמָן וְתוֹלַעַת שָׁנִי וְשֵׁשׁ וְעִזִּים: וְעֹרֹת
לוי אֵילִם מְאָדָּמִים וְעֹרֹת תְּחָשִׁים וַעֲצֵי שִׁטִּים: *שֶׁמֶן לַמָּאֹר בְּשָׂמִים לְשֶׁמֶן
הַמִּשְׁחָה וְלִקְטֹרֶת הַסַּמִּים: אַבְנֵי־שֹׁהַם וְאַבְנֵי מִלֻּאִים לָאֵפֹד וְלַחֹשֶׁן: וְעָשׂוּ
לִי מִקְדָּשׁ וְשָׁכַנְתִּי בְּתוֹכָם: כְּכֹל אֲשֶׁר אֲנִי מַרְאֶה אוֹתְךָ אֵת תַּבְנִית הַמִּשְׁכָּן
ישראל וְאֵת תַּבְנִית כָּל־כֵּלָיו וְכֵן תַּעֲשׂוּ: *וְעָשׂוּ אֲרוֹן עֲצֵי שִׁטִּים אַמָּתַיִם
וָחֵצִי אָרְכּוֹ וְאַמָּה וָחֵצִי רָחְבּוֹ וְאַמָּה וָחֵצִי קֹמָתוֹ: וְצִפִּיתָ אֹתוֹ זָהָב טָהוֹר
מִבַּיִת וּמִחוּץ תְּצַפֶּנּוּ וְעָשִׂיתָ עָלָיו זֵר זָהָב סָבִיב: וְיָצַקְתָּ לּוֹ אַרְבַּע טַבְּעֹת
זָהָב וְנָתַתָּה עַל אַרְבַּע פַּעֲמֹתָיו וּשְׁתֵּי טַבָּעֹת עַל־צַלְעוֹ הָאֶחָת וּשְׁתֵּי טַבָּעֹת
עַל־צַלְעוֹ הַשֵּׁנִית: וְעָשִׂיתָ בַדֵּי עֲצֵי שִׁטִּים וְצִפִּיתָ אֹתָם זָהָב: וְהֵבֵאתָ אֶת־
הַבַּדִּים בַּטַּבָּעֹת עַל צַלְעֹת הָאָרֹן לָשֵׂאת אֶת־הָאָרֹן בָּהֶם: בְּטַבְּעֹת הָאָרֹן
יִהְיוּ הַבַּדִּים לֹא יָסֻרוּ מִמֶּנּוּ: וְנָתַתָּ אֶל־הָאָרֹן אֵת הָעֵדֻת אֲשֶׁר אֶתֵּן אֵלֶיךָ:

## TETZAVEH — תצוה

שמות כז:כ–כח:יב וְאַתָּה תְּצַוֶּה ׀ אֶת־בְּנֵי יִשְׂרָאֵל וְיִקְחוּ אֵלֶיךָ שֶׁמֶן זַיִת זָךְ כָּתִית לַמָּאוֹר
לְהַעֲלֹת נֵר תָּמִיד: בְּאֹהֶל מוֹעֵד מִחוּץ לַפָּרֹכֶת אֲשֶׁר עַל־הָעֵדֻת יַעֲרֹךְ
אֹתוֹ אַהֲרֹן וּבָנָיו מֵעֶרֶב עַד־בֹּקֶר לִפְנֵי יהוה חֻקַּת עוֹלָם לְדֹרֹתָם מֵאֵת בְּנֵי
יִשְׂרָאֵל: וְאַתָּה הַקְרֵב אֵלֶיךָ אֶת־אַהֲרֹן אָחִיךָ וְאֶת־בָּנָיו אִתּוֹ מִתּוֹךְ
בְּנֵי יִשְׂרָאֵל לְכַהֲנוֹ־לִי אַהֲרֹן נָדָב וַאֲבִיהוּא אֶלְעָזָר וְאִיתָמָר בְּנֵי אַהֲרֹן: וְעָשִׂיתָ
בִגְדֵי־קֹדֶשׁ לְאַהֲרֹן אָחִיךָ לְכָבוֹד וּלְתִפְאָרֶת: וְאַתָּה תְּדַבֵּר אֶל־כָּל־חַכְמֵי־לֵב
אֲשֶׁר מִלֵּאתִיו רוּחַ חָכְמָה וְעָשׂוּ אֶת־בִּגְדֵי אַהֲרֹן לְקַדְּשׁוֹ לְכַהֲנוֹ־לִי: וְאֵלֶּה
הַבְּגָדִים אֲשֶׁר יַעֲשׂוּ חֹשֶׁן וְאֵפוֹד וּמְעִיל וּכְתֹנֶת תַּשְׁבֵּץ מִצְנֶפֶת וְאַבְנֵט וְעָשׂוּ
בִגְדֵי־קֹדֶשׁ לְאַהֲרֹן אָחִיךָ וּלְבָנָיו לְכַהֲנוֹ־לִי: וְהֵם יִקְחוּ אֶת־הַזָּהָב וְאֶת־הַתְּכֵלֶת

ואת־הארגמן ואת־תולעת השני ואת־השש:
לוי ועשו את־האפד זהב תכלת וארגמן תולעת שני ושש משזר מעשה חשב:
שתי כתפת חברת יהיה־לו אל־שני קצותיו וחבר: וחשב אפדתו אשר עליו
כמעשהו ממנו יהיה זהב תכלת וארגמן ותולעת שני ושש משזר: ולקחת
ישראל את־שתי אבני־שהם ופתחת עליהם שמות בני ישראל: *ששה משמתם על
האבן האחת ואת־שמות הששה הנותרים על־האבן השנית כתולדתם:
מעשה חרש אבן פתוחי חתם תפתח את־שתי האבנים על־שמת בני
ישראל מסבת משבצות זהב תעשה אתם: ושמת את־שתי האבנים על
כתפת האפד אבני זכרן לבני ישראל ונשא אהרן את־שמותם לפני יהוה
על־שתי כתפיו לזכרן:

## כי תשא
KI TISSA

שמות ל:יא-כא וידבר יהוה אל־משה לאמר: כי תשא את־ראש בני־ישראל לפקדיהם
ונתנו איש כפר נפשו ליהוה בפקד אתם ולא־יהיה בהם נגף בפקד אתם:
זה | יתנו כל־העבר על־הפקדים מחצית השקל בשקל הקדש עשרים
לוי גרה השקל מחצית השקל תרומה ליהוה: *כל העבר על־הפקדים מבן
עשרים שנה ומעלה יתן תרומת יהוה: העשיר לא־ירבה והדל לא ימעיט
ממחצית השקל לתת את־תרומת יהוה לכפר על־נפשתיכם: ולקחת
את־כסף הכפרים מאת בני ישראל ונתת אתו על־עבדת אהל מועד והיה
לבני ישראל לזכרון לפני יהוה לכפר על־נפשתיכם:
ישראל וידבר יהוה אל־משה לאמר: ועשית כיור נחשת וכנו נחשת לרחצה ונתת
אתו בין־אהל מועד ובין המזבח ונתת שמה מים: ורחצו אהרן ובניו ממנו
את־ידיהם ואת־רגליהם: בבאם אל־אהל מועד ירחצו־מים ולא ימתו או
בגשתם אל־המזבח לשרת להקטיר אשה ליהוה: ורחצו ידיהם ורגליהם
ולא ימתו והיתה להם חק־עולם לו ולזרעו לדרתם:

## ויקהל
VAYAK-HEL

שמות לה:א-ב ויקהל משה את־כל־עדת בני ישראל ויאמר אלהם אלה הדברים אשר־
צוה יהוה לעשת אתם: ששת ימים תעשה מלאכה וביום השביעי יהיה

לָכֶם קֹדֶשׁ שַׁבַּת שַׁבָּתוֹן לַיהוָה כָּל־הָעֹשֶׂה בוֹ מְלָאכָה יוּמָת: לֹא־תְבַעֲרוּ
אֵשׁ בְּכֹל מֹשְׁבֹתֵיכֶם בְּיוֹם הַשַּׁבָּת:
לוי וַיֹּאמֶר מֹשֶׁה אֶל־כָּל־עֲדַת בְּנֵי־יִשְׂרָאֵל לֵאמֹר זֶה הַדָּבָר אֲשֶׁר־צִוָּה יְהוָה
לֵאמֹר: קְחוּ מֵאִתְּכֶם תְּרוּמָה לַיהוָה כֹּל נְדִיב לִבּוֹ יְבִיאֶהָ אֵת תְּרוּמַת יְהוָה
זָהָב וָכֶסֶף וּנְחֹשֶׁת: וּתְכֵלֶת וְאַרְגָּמָן וְתוֹלַעַת שָׁנִי וְשֵׁשׁ וְעִזִּים: וְעֹרֹת אֵילִם
מְאָדָּמִים וְעֹרֹת תְּחָשִׁים וַעֲצֵי שִׁטִּים: וְשֶׁמֶן לַמָּאוֹר וּבְשָׂמִים לְשֶׁמֶן הַמִּשְׁחָה
וְלִקְטֹרֶת הַסַּמִּים: וְאַבְנֵי־שֹׁהַם וְאַבְנֵי מִלֻּאִים לָאֵפוֹד וְלַחֹשֶׁן: וְכָל־חֲכַם־לֵב
ישראל בָּכֶם יָבֹאוּ וְיַעֲשׂוּ אֵת כָּל־אֲשֶׁר צִוָּה יְהוָה: *אֶת־הַמִּשְׁכָּן אֶת־אָהֳלוֹ וְאֶת־
מִכְסֵהוּ אֶת־קְרָסָיו וְאֶת־קְרָשָׁיו אֶת־בְּרִיחָו אֶת־עַמֻּדָיו וְאֶת־אֲדָנָיו: אֶת־
הָאָרֹן וְאֶת־בַּדָּיו אֶת־הַכַּפֹּרֶת וְאֵת פָּרֹכֶת הַמָּסָךְ: אֶת־הַשֻּׁלְחָן וְאֶת־בַּדָּיו
וְאֶת־כָּל־כֵּלָיו וְאֵת לֶחֶם הַפָּנִים: וְאֶת־מְנֹרַת הַמָּאוֹר וְאֶת־כֵּלֶיהָ וְאֶת־נֵרֹתֶיהָ
וְאֵת שֶׁמֶן הַמָּאוֹר: וְאֶת־מִזְבַּח הַקְּטֹרֶת וְאֶת־בַּדָּיו וְאֵת שֶׁמֶן הַמִּשְׁחָה וְאֵת
קְטֹרֶת הַסַּמִּים וְאֶת־מָסַךְ הַפֶּתַח לְפֶתַח הַמִּשְׁכָּן: אֵת ׀ מִזְבַּח הָעֹלָה וְאֶת־
מִכְבַּר הַנְּחֹשֶׁת אֲשֶׁר־לוֹ אֶת־בַּדָּיו וְאֶת־כָּל־כֵּלָיו אֶת־הַכִּיֹּר וְאֶת־כַּנּוֹ: אֵת
קַלְעֵי הֶחָצֵר אֶת־עַמֻּדָיו וְאֶת־אֲדָנֶיהָ וְאֵת מָסַךְ שַׁעַר הֶחָצֵר: אֶת־יִתְדֹת
הַמִּשְׁכָּן וְאֶת־יִתְדֹת הֶחָצֵר וְאֶת־מֵיתְרֵיהֶם: אֶת־בִּגְדֵי הַשְּׂרָד לְשָׁרֵת בַּקֹּדֶשׁ
אֶת־בִּגְדֵי הַקֹּדֶשׁ לְאַהֲרֹן הַכֹּהֵן וְאֶת־בִּגְדֵי בָנָיו לְכַהֵן: וַיֵּצְאוּ כָּל־עֲדַת בְּנֵי־
יִשְׂרָאֵל מִלִּפְנֵי מֹשֶׁה:

## פקודי PEKUDEI

שמות לח:כא-לט:א אֵלֶּה פְקוּדֵי הַמִּשְׁכָּן מִשְׁכַּן הָעֵדֻת אֲשֶׁר פֻּקַּד עַל־פִּי מֹשֶׁה עֲבֹדַת הַלְוִיִּם בְּיַד
אִיתָמָר בֶּן־אַהֲרֹן הַכֹּהֵן: וּבְצַלְאֵל בֶּן־אוּרִי בֶן־חוּר לְמַטֵּה יְהוּדָה עָשָׂה אֵת
כָּל־אֲשֶׁר־צִוָּה יְהוָה אֶת־מֹשֶׁה: וְאִתּוֹ אָהֳלִיאָב בֶּן־אֲחִיסָמָךְ לְמַטֵּה־דָן חָרָשׁ
לוי וְחֹשֵׁב וְרֹקֵם בַּתְּכֵלֶת וּבָאַרְגָּמָן וּבְתוֹלַעַת הַשָּׁנִי וּבַשֵּׁשׁ: *כָּל־הַזָּהָב
הֶעָשׂוּי לַמְּלָאכָה בְּכֹל מְלֶאכֶת הַקֹּדֶשׁ וַיְהִי ׀ זְהַב הַתְּנוּפָה תֵּשַׁע וְעֶשְׂרִים
כִּכָּר וּשְׁבַע מֵאוֹת וּשְׁלֹשִׁים שֶׁקֶל בְּשֶׁקֶל הַקֹּדֶשׁ: וְכֶסֶף פְּקוּדֵי הָעֵדָה מְאַת
כִּכָּר וְאֶלֶף וּשְׁבַע מֵאוֹת וַחֲמִשָּׁה וְשִׁבְעִים שֶׁקֶל בְּשֶׁקֶל הַקֹּדֶשׁ: בֶּקַע לַגֻּלְגֹּלֶת
מַחֲצִית הַשֶּׁקֶל בְּשֶׁקֶל הַקֹּדֶשׁ לְכֹל הָעֹבֵר עַל־הַפְּקֻדִים מִבֶּן עֶשְׂרִים שָׁנָה

ומעלה לשש־מאות אלף ושלשת אלפים וחמש מאות וחמשים: ויהי
מאת ככר הכסף לצקת את אדני הקדש ואת אדני הפרכת מאת אדנים
למאת הככר ככר לאדן: *ואת־האלף ושבע המאות וחמשה ושבעים ישראל
עשה ווים לעמודים וצפה ראשיהם וחשק אתם: ונחשת התנופה שבעים
ככר ואלפים וארבע־מאות שקל: ויעש בה את־אדני פתח אהל מועד
ואת מזבח הנחשת ואת־מכבר הנחשת אשר־לו ואת כל־כלי המזבח:
ואת־אדני החצר סביב ואת־אדני שער החצר ואת כל־יתדת המשכן
ואת־כל־יתדת החצר סביב: ומן־התכלת והארגמן ותולעת השני עשו
בגדי־שרד לשרת בקדש ויעשו את־בגדי הקדש אשר לאהרן כאשר צוה
יהוה את־משה:

## VAYIKRA ויקרא

ויקרא אל־משה וידבר יהוה אליו מאהל מועד לאמר: דבר אל־בני ישראל ויקרא א:א-יג
ואמרת אלהם אדם כי־יקריב מכם קרבן ליהוה מן־הבהמה מן־הבקר
ומן־הצאן תקריבו את־קרבנכם: אם־עלה קרבנו מן־הבקר זכר תמים
יקריבנו אל־פתח אהל מועד יקריב אתו לרצנו לפני יהוה: וסמך ידו על
ראש העלה ונרצה לו לכפר עליו: *ושחט את־בן הבקר לפני יהוה והקריבו לוי
בני אהרן הכהנים את־הדם וזרקו את־הדם על־המזבח סביב אשר־פתח
אהל מועד: והפשיט את־העלה ונתח אתה לנתחיה: ונתנו בני אהרן
הכהן אש על־המזבח וערכו עצים על־האש: וערכו בני אהרן הכהנים
את הנתחים את־הראש ואת־הפדר על־העצים אשר על־האש אשר על־
המזבח: וקרבו וכרעיו ירחץ במים והקטיר הכהן את־הכל המזבחה עלה
אשה ריח־ניחוח ליהוה: *ואם־מן־הצאן קרבנו מן־הכשבים ישראל
או מן־העזים לעלה זכר תמים יקריבנו: ושחט אתו על ירך המזבח צפנה
לפני יהוה וזרקו בני אהרן הכהנים את־דמו על־המזבח סביב: ונתח אתו
לנתחיו ואת־ראשו ואת־פדרו וערך הכהן אתם על־העצים אשר על־האש
אשר על־המזבח: והקרב והכרעים ירחץ במים והקריב הכהן את־הכל
והקטיר המזבחה עלה הוא אשה ריח ניחח ליהוה:

## TZAV — צו

ויקרא ו:א-יא וַיְדַבֵּר יְהוָה אֶל־מֹשֶׁה לֵּאמֹר: צַו אֶת־אַהֲרֹן וְאֶת־בָּנָיו לֵאמֹר זֹאת תּוֹרַת
הָעֹלָה הִוא הָעֹלָה עַל מוֹקְדָה עַל־הַמִּזְבֵּחַ כָּל־הַלַּיְלָה עַד־הַבֹּקֶר וְאֵשׁ הַמִּזְבֵּחַ
תּוּקַד בּוֹ: וְלָבַשׁ הַכֹּהֵן מִדּוֹ בַד וּמִכְנְסֵי־בַד יִלְבַּשׁ עַל־בְּשָׂרוֹ וְהֵרִים אֶת־הַדֶּשֶׁן
לוי אֲשֶׁר תֹּאכַל הָאֵשׁ אֶת־הָעֹלָה עַל־הַמִּזְבֵּחַ וְשָׂמוֹ אֵצֶל הַמִּזְבֵּחַ: *וּפָשַׁט אֶת־
בְּגָדָיו וְלָבַשׁ בְּגָדִים אֲחֵרִים וְהוֹצִיא אֶת־הַדֶּשֶׁן אֶל־מִחוּץ לַמַּחֲנֶה אֶל־מָקוֹם
טָהוֹר: וְהָאֵשׁ עַל־הַמִּזְבֵּחַ תּוּקַד־בּוֹ לֹא תִכְבֶּה וּבִעֵר עָלֶיהָ הַכֹּהֵן עֵצִים
בַּבֹּקֶר בַּבֹּקֶר וְעָרַךְ עָלֶיהָ הָעֹלָה וְהִקְטִיר עָלֶיהָ חֶלְבֵי הַשְּׁלָמִים: אֵשׁ תָּמִיד
ישראל תּוּקַד עַל־הַמִּזְבֵּחַ לֹא תִכְבֶּה: *וְזֹאת תּוֹרַת הַמִּנְחָה הַקְרֵב אֹתָהּ
בְּנֵי־אַהֲרֹן לִפְנֵי יְהוָה אֶל־פְּנֵי הַמִּזְבֵּחַ: וְהֵרִים מִמֶּנּוּ בְּקֻמְצוֹ מִסֹּלֶת הַמִּנְחָה
וּמִשַּׁמְנָהּ וְאֵת כָּל־הַלְּבֹנָה אֲשֶׁר עַל־הַמִּנְחָה וְהִקְטִיר הַמִּזְבֵּחַ רֵיחַ נִיחֹחַ
אַזְכָּרָתָהּ לַיהוָה: וְהַנּוֹתֶרֶת מִמֶּנָּה יֹאכְלוּ אַהֲרֹן וּבָנָיו מַצּוֹת תֵּאָכֵל בְּמָקוֹם
קָדֹשׁ בַּחֲצַר אֹהֶל־מוֹעֵד יֹאכְלוּהָ: לֹא תֵאָפֶה חָמֵץ חֶלְקָם נָתַתִּי אֹתָהּ מֵאִשָּׁי
קֹדֶשׁ קָדָשִׁים הִוא כַּחַטָּאת וְכָאָשָׁם: כָּל־זָכָר בִּבְנֵי אַהֲרֹן יֹאכְלֶנָּה חָק־עוֹלָם
לְדֹרֹתֵיכֶם מֵאִשֵּׁי יְהוָה כֹּל אֲשֶׁר־יִגַּע בָּהֶם יִקְדָּשׁ:

## SHEMINI — שמיני

ויקרא ט:א-טז וַיְהִי בַּיּוֹם הַשְּׁמִינִי קָרָא מֹשֶׁה לְאַהֲרֹן וּלְבָנָיו וּלְזִקְנֵי יִשְׂרָאֵל: וַיֹּאמֶר אֶל־אַהֲרֹן
קַח־לְךָ עֵגֶל בֶּן־בָּקָר לְחַטָּאת וְאַיִל לְעֹלָה תְּמִימִם וְהַקְרֵב לִפְנֵי יְהוָה: וְאֶל־
בְּנֵי יִשְׂרָאֵל תְּדַבֵּר לֵאמֹר קְחוּ שְׂעִיר־עִזִּים לְחַטָּאת וְעֵגֶל וָכֶבֶשׂ בְּנֵי־שָׁנָה
תְּמִימִם לְעֹלָה: וְשׁוֹר וָאַיִל לִשְׁלָמִים לִזְבֹּחַ לִפְנֵי יְהוָה וּמִנְחָה בְּלוּלָה בַשָּׁמֶן
כִּי הַיּוֹם יְהוָה נִרְאָה אֲלֵיכֶם: וַיִּקְחוּ אֵת אֲשֶׁר צִוָּה מֹשֶׁה אֶל־פְּנֵי אֹהֶל מוֹעֵד
וַיִּקְרְבוּ כָּל־הָעֵדָה וַיַּעַמְדוּ לִפְנֵי יְהוָה: וַיֹּאמֶר מֹשֶׁה זֶה הַדָּבָר אֲשֶׁר־צִוָּה יְהוָה
לוי תַּעֲשׂוּ וְיֵרָא אֲלֵיכֶם כְּבוֹד יְהוָה: *וַיֹּאמֶר מֹשֶׁה אֶל־אַהֲרֹן קְרַב אֶל־הַמִּזְבֵּחַ
וַעֲשֵׂה אֶת־חַטָּאתְךָ וְאֶת־עֹלָתֶךָ וְכַפֵּר בַּעַדְךָ וּבְעַד הָעָם וַעֲשֵׂה אֶת־קָרְבַּן
הָעָם וְכַפֵּר בַּעֲדָם כַּאֲשֶׁר צִוָּה יְהוָה: וַיִּקְרַב אַהֲרֹן אֶל־הַמִּזְבֵּחַ וַיִּשְׁחַט אֶת־
עֵגֶל הַחַטָּאת אֲשֶׁר־לוֹ: וַיַּקְרִבוּ בְּנֵי אַהֲרֹן אֶת־הַדָּם אֵלָיו וַיִּטְבֹּל אֶצְבָּעוֹ
בַּדָּם וַיִּתֵּן עַל־קַרְנוֹת הַמִּזְבֵּחַ וְאֶת־הַדָּם יָצַק אֶל־יְסוֹד הַמִּזְבֵּחַ: וְאֶת־הַחֵלֶב
וְאֶת־הַכְּלָיֹת וְאֶת־הַיֹּתֶרֶת מִן־הַכָּבֵד מִן־הַחַטָּאת הִקְטִיר הַמִּזְבֵּחָה כַּאֲשֶׁר

צִוָּה יְהֹוָה אֶת־מֹשֶׁה: *וְאֶת־הַבָּשָׂר וְאֶת־הָעוֹר שָׂרַף בָּאֵשׁ מִחוּץ לַמַּחֲנֶה: ישראל
וַיִּשְׁחַט אֶת־הָעֹלָה וַיַּמְצִאוּ בְּנֵי אַהֲרֹן אֵלָיו אֶת־הַדָּם וַיִּזְרְקֵהוּ עַל־הַמִּזְבֵּחַ
סָבִיב: וְאֶת־הָעֹלָה הִמְצִיאוּ אֵלָיו לִנְתָחֶיהָ וְאֶת־הָרֹאשׁ וַיַּקְטֵר עַל־הַמִּזְבֵּחַ:
וַיִּרְחַץ אֶת־הַקֶּרֶב וְאֶת־הַכְּרָעָיִם וַיַּקְטֵר עַל־הָעֹלָה הַמִּזְבֵּחָה: וַיַּקְרֵב אֵת קָרְבַּן
הָעָם וַיִּקַּח אֶת־שְׂעִיר הַחַטָּאת אֲשֶׁר לָעָם וַיִּשְׁחָטֵהוּ וַיְחַטְּאֵהוּ כָּרִאשׁוֹן:
וַיַּקְרֵב אֶת־הָעֹלָה וַיַּעֲשֶׂהָ כַּמִּשְׁפָּט:

## תזריע TAZRIA

וַיְדַבֵּר יְהֹוָה אֶל־מֹשֶׁה לֵּאמֹר: דַּבֵּר אֶל־בְּנֵי יִשְׂרָאֵל לֵאמֹר אִשָּׁה כִּי תַזְרִיעַ ויקרא יב:א-יג:ה
וְיָלְדָה זָכָר וְטָמְאָה שִׁבְעַת יָמִים כִּימֵי נִדַּת דְּוֺתָהּ תִּטְמָא: וּבַיּוֹם הַשְּׁמִינִי
יִמּוֹל בְּשַׂר עָרְלָתוֹ: וּשְׁלֹשִׁים יוֹם וּשְׁלֹשֶׁת יָמִים תֵּשֵׁב בִּדְמֵי טָהֳרָה בְּכָל־
קֹדֶשׁ לֹא־תִגָּע וְאֶל־הַמִּקְדָּשׁ לֹא תָבֹא עַד־מְלֹאת יְמֵי טָהֳרָהּ: *וְאִם־נְקֵבָה לוי
תֵלֵד וְטָמְאָה שְׁבֻעַיִם כְּנִדָּתָהּ וְשִׁשִּׁים יוֹם וְשֵׁשֶׁת יָמִים תֵּשֵׁב עַל־דְּמֵי טָהֳרָה:
וּבִמְלֹאת | יְמֵי טָהֳרָהּ לְבֵן אוֹ לְבַת תָּבִיא כֶּבֶשׂ בֶּן־שְׁנָתוֹ לְעֹלָה וּבֶן־יוֹנָה
אוֹ־תֹר לְחַטָּאת אֶל־פֶּתַח אֹהֶל־מוֹעֵד אֶל־הַכֹּהֵן: וְהִקְרִיבוֹ לִפְנֵי יְהֹוָה וְכִפֶּר
עָלֶיהָ וְטָהֲרָה מִמְּקֹר דָּמֶיהָ זֹאת תּוֹרַת הַיֹּלֶדֶת לַזָּכָר אוֹ לַנְּקֵבָה: וְאִם־לֹא
תִמְצָא יָדָהּ דֵּי שֶׂה וְלָקְחָה שְׁתֵּי־תֹרִים אוֹ שְׁנֵי בְּנֵי יוֹנָה אֶחָד לְעֹלָה וְאֶחָד
לְחַטָּאת וְכִפֶּר עָלֶיהָ הַכֹּהֵן וְטָהֵרָה:

וַיְדַבֵּר יְהֹוָה אֶל־מֹשֶׁה וְאֶל־אַהֲרֹן לֵאמֹר: אָדָם כִּי־יִהְיֶה בְעוֹר־בְּשָׂרוֹ שְׂאֵת ישראל
אוֹ־סַפַּחַת אוֹ בַהֶרֶת וְהָיָה בְעוֹר־בְּשָׂרוֹ לְנֶגַע צָרָעַת וְהוּבָא אֶל־אַהֲרֹן הַכֹּהֵן
אוֹ אֶל־אַחַד מִבָּנָיו הַכֹּהֲנִים: וְרָאָה הַכֹּהֵן אֶת־הַנֶּגַע בְּעוֹר־הַבָּשָׂר וְשֵׂעָר בַּנֶּגַע
הָפַךְ | לָבָן וּמַרְאֵה הַנֶּגַע עָמֹק מֵעוֹר בְּשָׂרוֹ נֶגַע צָרַעַת הוּא וְרָאָהוּ הַכֹּהֵן
וְטִמֵּא אֹתוֹ: וְאִם־בַּהֶרֶת לְבָנָה הִוא בְּעוֹר בְּשָׂרוֹ וְעָמֹק אֵין־מַרְאֶהָ מִן־הָעוֹר
וּשְׂעָרָה לֹא־הָפַךְ לָבָן וְהִסְגִּיר הַכֹּהֵן אֶת־הַנֶּגַע שִׁבְעַת יָמִים: וְרָאָהוּ הַכֹּהֵן
בַּיּוֹם הַשְּׁבִיעִי וְהִנֵּה הַנֶּגַע עָמַד בְּעֵינָיו לֹא־פָשָׂה הַנֶּגַע בָּעוֹר וְהִסְגִּירוֹ הַכֹּהֵן
שִׁבְעַת יָמִים שֵׁנִית:

## מצורע METZORA

וַיְדַבֵּר יְהֹוָה אֶל־מֹשֶׁה לֵּאמֹר: זֹאת תִּהְיֶה תּוֹרַת הַמְּצֹרָע בְּיוֹם טָהֳרָתוֹ ויקרא יד:א-יב

וְהוּבָא אֶל־הַכֹּהֵן: וְיָצָא הַכֹּהֵן אֶל־מִחוּץ לַמַּחֲנֶה וְרָאָה הַכֹּהֵן וְהִנֵּה נִרְפָּא
נֶגַע־הַצָּרַעַת מִן־הַצָּרוּעַ: וְצִוָּה הַכֹּהֵן וְלָקַח לַמִּטַּהֵר שְׁתֵּי־צִפֳּרִים חַיּוֹת
טְהֹרוֹת וְעֵץ אֶרֶז וּשְׁנִי תוֹלַעַת וְאֵזֹב: וְצִוָּה הַכֹּהֵן וְשָׁחַט אֶת־הַצִּפּוֹר הָאֶחָת
לוי אֶל־כְּלִי־חֶרֶשׂ עַל־מַיִם חַיִּים: *אֶת־הַצִּפֹּר הַחַיָּה יִקַּח אֹתָהּ וְאֶת־עֵץ הָאֶרֶז
וְאֶת־שְׁנִי הַתּוֹלַעַת וְאֶת־הָאֵזֹב וְטָבַל אוֹתָם וְאֵת ׀ הַצִּפֹּר הַחַיָּה בְּדַם הַצִּפֹּר
הַשְּׁחֻטָה עַל הַמַּיִם הַחַיִּים: וְהִזָּה עַל הַמִּטַּהֵר מִן־הַצָּרַעַת שֶׁבַע פְּעָמִים
וְטִהֲרוֹ וְשִׁלַּח אֶת־הַצִּפֹּר הַחַיָּה עַל־פְּנֵי הַשָּׂדֶה: וְכִבֶּס הַמִּטַּהֵר אֶת־בְּגָדָיו
וְגִלַּח אֶת־כָּל־שְׂעָרוֹ וְרָחַץ בַּמַּיִם וְטָהֵר וְאַחַר יָבוֹא אֶל־הַמַּחֲנֶה וְיָשַׁב מִחוּץ
לְאָהֳלוֹ שִׁבְעַת יָמִים: וְהָיָה בַיּוֹם הַשְּׁבִיעִי יְגַלַּח אֶת־כָּל־שְׂעָרוֹ אֶת־רֹאשׁוֹ
וְאֶת־זְקָנוֹ וְאֵת גַּבֹּת עֵינָיו וְאֶת־כָּל־שְׂעָרוֹ יְגַלֵּחַ וְכִבֶּס אֶת־בְּגָדָיו וְרָחַץ אֶת־
ישראל בְּשָׂרוֹ בַּמַּיִם וְטָהֵר: *וּבַיּוֹם הַשְּׁמִינִי יִקַּח שְׁנֵי־כְבָשִׂים תְּמִימִם וְכַבְשָׂה אַחַת
בַּת־שְׁנָתָהּ תְּמִימָה וּשְׁלֹשָׁה עֶשְׂרֹנִים סֹלֶת מִנְחָה בְּלוּלָה בַשֶּׁמֶן וְלֹג אֶחָד
שָׁמֶן: וְהֶעֱמִיד הַכֹּהֵן הַמְטַהֵר אֵת הָאִישׁ הַמִּטַּהֵר וְאֹתָם לִפְנֵי יהוה פֶּתַח
אֹהֶל מוֹעֵד: וְלָקַח הַכֹּהֵן אֶת־הַכֶּבֶשׂ הָאֶחָד וְהִקְרִיב אֹתוֹ לְאָשָׁם וְאֶת־לֹג
הַשָּׁמֶן וְהֵנִיף אֹתָם תְּנוּפָה לִפְנֵי יהוה:

## AḤAREI MOT אחרי מות

ויקרא טז:א–יז וַיְדַבֵּר יהוה אֶל־מֹשֶׁה אַחֲרֵי מוֹת שְׁנֵי בְּנֵי אַהֲרֹן בְּקָרְבָתָם לִפְנֵי־יהוה וַיָּמֻתוּ:
וַיֹּאמֶר יהוה אֶל־מֹשֶׁה דַּבֵּר אֶל־אַהֲרֹן אָחִיךָ וְאַל־יָבֹא בְכָל־עֵת אֶל־הַקֹּדֶשׁ
מִבֵּית לַפָּרֹכֶת אֶל־פְּנֵי הַכַּפֹּרֶת אֲשֶׁר עַל־הָאָרֹן וְלֹא יָמוּת כִּי בֶּעָנָן אֵרָאֶה
עַל־הַכַּפֹּרֶת: בְּזֹאת יָבֹא אַהֲרֹן אֶל־הַקֹּדֶשׁ בְּפַר בֶּן־בָּקָר לְחַטָּאת וְאַיִל
לְעֹלָה: כְּתֹנֶת־בַּד קֹדֶשׁ יִלְבָּשׁ וּמִכְנְסֵי־בַד יִהְיוּ עַל־בְּשָׂרוֹ וּבְאַבְנֵט בַּד
יַחְגֹּר וּבְמִצְנֶפֶת בַּד יִצְנֹף בִּגְדֵי־קֹדֶשׁ הֵם וְרָחַץ בַּמַּיִם אֶת־בְּשָׂרוֹ וּלְבֵשָׁם:
וּמֵאֵת עֲדַת בְּנֵי יִשְׂרָאֵל יִקַּח שְׁנֵי־שְׂעִירֵי עִזִּים לְחַטָּאת וְאַיִל אֶחָד לְעֹלָה:
לוי וְהִקְרִיב אַהֲרֹן אֶת־פַּר הַחַטָּאת אֲשֶׁר־לוֹ וְכִפֶּר בַּעֲדוֹ וּבְעַד בֵּיתוֹ: *וְלָקַח
אֶת־שְׁנֵי הַשְּׂעִירִם וְהֶעֱמִיד אֹתָם לִפְנֵי יהוה פֶּתַח אֹהֶל מוֹעֵד: וְנָתַן אַהֲרֹן
עַל־שְׁנֵי הַשְּׂעִירִם גֹּרָלוֹת גּוֹרָל אֶחָד לַיהוה וְגוֹרָל אֶחָד לַעֲזָאזֵל: וְהִקְרִיב
אַהֲרֹן אֶת־הַשָּׂעִיר אֲשֶׁר עָלָה עָלָיו הַגּוֹרָל לַיהוה וְעָשָׂהוּ חַטָּאת: וְהַשָּׂעִיר
אֲשֶׁר עָלָה עָלָיו הַגּוֹרָל לַעֲזָאזֵל יָעֳמַד־חַי לִפְנֵי יהוה לְכַפֵּר עָלָיו לְשַׁלַּח

אֹתוֹ לַעֲזָאזֵל הַמִּדְבָּרָה׃ וְהִקְרִיב אַהֲרֹן אֶת־פַּר הַחַטָּאת אֲשֶׁר־לוֹ וְכִפֶּר
בַּעֲדוֹ וּבְעַד בֵּיתוֹ וְשָׁחַט אֶת־פַּר הַחַטָּאת אֲשֶׁר־לוֹ׃ *וְלָקַח מְלֹא־הַמַּחְתָּה ישראל
גַּחֲלֵי־אֵשׁ מֵעַל הַמִּזְבֵּחַ מִלִּפְנֵי יהוה וּמְלֹא חָפְנָיו קְטֹרֶת סַמִּים דַּקָּה וְהֵבִיא
מִבֵּית לַפָּרֹכֶת׃ וְנָתַן אֶת־הַקְּטֹרֶת עַל־הָאֵשׁ לִפְנֵי יהוה וְכִסָּה ׀ עֲנַן הַקְּטֹרֶת
אֶת־הַכַּפֹּרֶת אֲשֶׁר עַל־הָעֵדוּת וְלֹא יָמוּת׃ וְלָקַח מִדַּם הַפָּר וְהִזָּה בְאֶצְבָּעוֹ
עַל־פְּנֵי הַכַּפֹּרֶת קֵדְמָה וְלִפְנֵי הַכַּפֹּרֶת יַזֶּה שֶׁבַע־פְּעָמִים מִן־הַדָּם בְּאֶצְבָּעוֹ׃
וְשָׁחַט אֶת־שְׂעִיר הַחַטָּאת אֲשֶׁר לָעָם וְהֵבִיא אֶת־דָּמוֹ אֶל־מִבֵּית לַפָּרֹכֶת
וְעָשָׂה אֶת־דָּמוֹ כַּאֲשֶׁר עָשָׂה לְדַם הַפָּר וְהִזָּה אֹתוֹ עַל־הַכַּפֹּרֶת וְלִפְנֵי הַכַּפֹּרֶת׃
וְכִפֶּר עַל־הַקֹּדֶשׁ מִטֻּמְאֹת בְּנֵי יִשְׂרָאֵל וּמִפִּשְׁעֵיהֶם לְכָל־חַטֹּאתָם וְכֵן יַעֲשֶׂה
לְאֹהֶל מוֹעֵד הַשֹּׁכֵן אִתָּם בְּתוֹךְ טֻמְאֹתָם׃ וְכָל־אָדָם לֹא־יִהְיֶה ׀ בְּאֹהֶל מוֹעֵד
בְּבֹאוֹ לְכַפֵּר בַּקֹּדֶשׁ עַד־צֵאתוֹ וְכִפֶּר בַּעֲדוֹ וּבְעַד בֵּיתוֹ וּבְעַד כָּל־קְהַל יִשְׂרָאֵל׃

## KEDOSHIM קדושים

וַיְדַבֵּר יהוה אֶל־מֹשֶׁה לֵּאמֹר׃ דַּבֵּר אֶל־כָּל־עֲדַת בְּנֵי־יִשְׂרָאֵל וְאָמַרְתָּ אֲלֵהֶם ויקרא יט:א–יד
קְדֹשִׁים תִּהְיוּ כִּי קָדוֹשׁ אֲנִי יהוה אֱלֹהֵיכֶם׃ אִישׁ אִמּוֹ וְאָבִיו תִּירָאוּ וְאֶת־
שַׁבְּתֹתַי תִּשְׁמֹרוּ אֲנִי יהוה אֱלֹהֵיכֶם׃ אַל־תִּפְנוּ אֶל־הָאֱלִילִם וֵאלֹהֵי מַסֵּכָה
לֹא תַעֲשׂוּ לָכֶם אֲנִי יהוה אֱלֹהֵיכֶם׃ *וְכִי תִזְבְּחוּ זֶבַח שְׁלָמִים לַיהוה לִרְצֹנְכֶם לוי
תִּזְבָּחֻהוּ׃ בְּיוֹם זִבְחֲכֶם יֵאָכֵל וּמִמָּחֳרָת וְהַנּוֹתָר עַד־יוֹם הַשְּׁלִישִׁי בָּאֵשׁ יִשָּׂרֵף׃
וְאִם הֵאָכֹל יֵאָכֵל בַּיּוֹם הַשְּׁלִישִׁי פִּגּוּל הוּא לֹא יֵרָצֶה׃ וְאֹכְלָיו עֲוֺנוֹ יִשָּׂא כִּי־
אֶת־קֹדֶשׁ יהוה חִלֵּל וְנִכְרְתָה הַנֶּפֶשׁ הַהִוא מֵעַמֶּיהָ׃ וּבְקֻצְרְכֶם אֶת־קְצִיר
אַרְצְכֶם לֹא תְכַלֶּה פְּאַת שָׂדְךָ לִקְצֹר וְלֶקֶט קְצִירְךָ לֹא תְלַקֵּט׃ וְכַרְמְךָ לֹא
תְעוֹלֵל וּפֶרֶט כַּרְמְךָ לֹא תְלַקֵּט לֶעָנִי וְלַגֵּר תַּעֲזֹב אֹתָם אֲנִי יהוה אֱלֹהֵיכֶם׃
*לֹא תִּגְנֹבוּ וְלֹא־תְכַחֲשׁוּ וְלֹא־תְשַׁקְּרוּ אִישׁ בַּעֲמִיתוֹ׃ וְלֹא־תִשָּׁבְעוּ בִשְׁמִי ישראל
לַשָּׁקֶר וְחִלַּלְתָּ אֶת־שֵׁם אֱלֹהֶיךָ אֲנִי יהוה׃ לֹא־תַעֲשֹׁק אֶת־רֵעֲךָ וְלֹא תִגְזֹל
לֹא־תָלִין פְּעֻלַּת שָׂכִיר אִתְּךָ עַד־בֹּקֶר׃ לֹא־תְקַלֵּל חֵרֵשׁ וְלִפְנֵי עִוֵּר לֹא תִתֵּן
מִכְשֹׁל וְיָרֵאתָ מֵּאֱלֹהֶיךָ אֲנִי יהוה׃

## EMOR אמור

וַיֹּאמֶר יהוה אֶל־מֹשֶׁה אֱמֹר אֶל־הַכֹּהֲנִים בְּנֵי אַהֲרֹן וְאָמַרְתָּ אֲלֵהֶם לְנֶפֶשׁ ויקרא כא:א–טו

לֹא־יִטַּמָּא בְּעַמָּיו׃ כִּי אִם־לִשְׁאֵרוֹ הַקָּרֹב אֵלָיו לְאִמּוֹ וּלְאָבִיו וְלִבְנוֹ וּלְבִתּוֹ
וּלְאָחִיו׃ וְלַאֲחֹתוֹ הַבְּתוּלָה הַקְּרוֹבָה אֵלָיו אֲשֶׁר לֹא־הָיְתָה לְאִישׁ לָהּ יִטַּמָּא׃
יִקְרְחוּ לֹא יִטַּמָּא בַּעַל בְּעַמָּיו לְהֵחַלּוֹ׃ לֹא־יקרחה קָרְחָה בְּרֹאשָׁם וּפְאַת זְקָנָם
לֹא יְגַלֵּחוּ וּבִבְשָׂרָם לֹא יִשְׂרְטוּ שָׂרָטֶת׃ קְדֹשִׁים יִהְיוּ לֵאלֹהֵיהֶם וְלֹא יְחַלְּלוּ
שֵׁם אֱלֹהֵיהֶם כִּי אֶת־אִשֵּׁי יְהוָה לֶחֶם אֱלֹהֵיהֶם הֵם מַקְרִיבִם וְהָיוּ קֹדֶשׁ׃
לוי *אִשָּׁה זֹנָה וַחֲלָלָה לֹא יִקָּחוּ וְאִשָּׁה גְּרוּשָׁה מֵאִישָׁהּ לֹא יִקָּחוּ כִּי־קָדֹשׁ הוּא
לֵאלֹהָיו׃ וְקִדַּשְׁתּוֹ כִּי־אֶת־לֶחֶם אֱלֹהֶיךָ הוּא מַקְרִיב קָדֹשׁ יִהְיֶה־לָּךְ כִּי קָדוֹשׁ
אֲנִי יְהוָה מְקַדִּשְׁכֶם׃ וּבַת אִישׁ כֹּהֵן כִּי תֵחֵל לִזְנוֹת אֶת־אָבִיהָ הִיא מְחַלֶּלֶת
בָּאֵשׁ תִּשָּׂרֵף׃ וְהַכֹּהֵן הַגָּדוֹל מֵאֶחָיו אֲשֶׁר־יוּצַק עַל־רֹאשׁוֹ ׀ שֶׁמֶן
הַמִּשְׁחָה וּמִלֵּא אֶת־יָדוֹ לִלְבֹּשׁ אֶת־הַבְּגָדִים אֶת־רֹאשׁוֹ לֹא יִפְרָע וּבְגָדָיו לֹא
יִפְרֹם׃ וְעַל כָּל־נַפְשֹׁת מֵת לֹא יָבֹא לְאָבִיו וּלְאִמּוֹ לֹא יִטַּמָּא׃ וּמִן־הַמִּקְדָּשׁ
לֹא יֵצֵא וְלֹא יְחַלֵּל אֵת מִקְדַּשׁ אֱלֹהָיו כִּי נֵזֶר שֶׁמֶן מִשְׁחַת אֱלֹהָיו עָלָיו אֲנִי
ישראל יְהוָה׃ *וְהוּא אִשָּׁה בִבְתוּלֶיהָ יִקָּח׃ אַלְמָנָה וּגְרוּשָׁה וַחֲלָלָה זֹנָה אֶת־אֵלֶּה
לֹא יִקָּח כִּי אִם־בְּתוּלָה מֵעַמָּיו יִקַּח אִשָּׁה׃ וְלֹא־יְחַלֵּל זַרְעוֹ בְּעַמָּיו כִּי אֲנִי
יְהוָה מְקַדְּשׁוֹ׃

## BEHAR בהר

ויקרא כה:א-יג וַיְדַבֵּר יְהוָה אֶל־מֹשֶׁה בְּהַר סִינַי לֵאמֹר׃ דַּבֵּר אֶל־בְּנֵי יִשְׂרָאֵל וְאָמַרְתָּ
אֲלֵהֶם כִּי תָבֹאוּ אֶל־הָאָרֶץ אֲשֶׁר אֲנִי נֹתֵן לָכֶם וְשָׁבְתָה הָאָרֶץ שַׁבָּת לַיהוָה׃
שֵׁשׁ שָׁנִים תִּזְרַע שָׂדֶךָ וְשֵׁשׁ שָׁנִים תִּזְמֹר כַּרְמֶךָ וְאָסַפְתָּ אֶת־תְּבוּאָתָהּ׃
לוי *וּבַשָּׁנָה הַשְּׁבִיעִת שַׁבַּת שַׁבָּתוֹן יִהְיֶה לָאָרֶץ שַׁבָּת לַיהוָה שָׂדְךָ לֹא תִזְרָע
וְכַרְמְךָ לֹא תִזְמֹר׃ אֵת סְפִיחַ קְצִירְךָ לֹא תִקְצוֹר וְאֶת־עִנְּבֵי נְזִירֶךָ לֹא תִבְצֹר
שְׁנַת שַׁבָּתוֹן יִהְיֶה לָאָרֶץ׃ וְהָיְתָה שַׁבַּת הָאָרֶץ לָכֶם לְאָכְלָה לְךָ וּלְעַבְדְּךָ
וְלַאֲמָתֶךָ וְלִשְׂכִירְךָ וּלְתוֹשָׁבְךָ הַגָּרִים עִמָּךְ׃ וְלִבְהֶמְתְּךָ וְלַחַיָּה אֲשֶׁר בְּאַרְצֶךָ
ישראל תִּהְיֶה כָל־תְּבוּאָתָהּ לֶאֱכֹל׃ *וְסָפַרְתָּ לְךָ שֶׁבַע שַׁבְּתֹת שָׁנִים
שֶׁבַע שָׁנִים שֶׁבַע פְּעָמִים וְהָיוּ לְךָ יְמֵי שֶׁבַע שַׁבְּתֹת הַשָּׁנִים תֵּשַׁע וְאַרְבָּעִים
שָׁנָה׃ וְהַעֲבַרְתָּ שׁוֹפַר תְּרוּעָה בַּחֹדֶשׁ הַשְּׁבִעִי בֶּעָשׂוֹר לַחֹדֶשׁ בְּיוֹם הַכִּפֻּרִים
תַּעֲבִירוּ שׁוֹפָר בְּכָל־אַרְצְכֶם׃ וְקִדַּשְׁתֶּם אֵת שְׁנַת הַחֲמִשִּׁים שָׁנָה וּקְרָאתֶם
דְּרוֹר בָּאָרֶץ לְכָל־יֹשְׁבֶיהָ יוֹבֵל הִוא תִּהְיֶה לָכֶם וְשַׁבְתֶּם אִישׁ אֶל־אֲחֻזָּתוֹ

וְאִישׁ אֶל־מִשְׁפַּחְתּוֹ תָּשֻׁבוּ׃ יוֹבֵל הִוא שְׁנַת הַחֲמִשִּׁים שָׁנָה תִּהְיֶה לָכֶם לֹא
תִזְרָעוּ וְלֹא תִקְצְרוּ אֶת־סְפִיחֶיהָ וְלֹא תִבְצְרוּ אֶת־נְזִרֶיהָ׃ כִּי יוֹבֵל הִוא קֹדֶשׁ
תִּהְיֶה לָכֶם מִן־הַשָּׂדֶה תֹּאכְלוּ אֶת־תְּבוּאָתָהּ׃ בִּשְׁנַת הַיּוֹבֵל הַזֹּאת תָּשֻׁבוּ
אִישׁ אֶל־אֲחֻזָּתוֹ׃

## BEḤUKKOTAI בחוקותי

אִם־בְּחֻקֹּתַי תֵּלֵכוּ וְאֶת־מִצְוֹתַי תִּשְׁמְרוּ וַעֲשִׂיתֶם אֹתָם׃ וְנָתַתִּי גִשְׁמֵיכֶם בְּעִתָּם ויקרא כו:ג–יג
וְנָתְנָה הָאָרֶץ יְבוּלָהּ וְעֵץ הַשָּׂדֶה יִתֵּן פִּרְיוֹ׃ וְהִשִּׂיג לָכֶם דַּיִשׁ אֶת־בָּצִיר וּבָצִיר
יַשִּׂיג אֶת־זָרַע וַאֲכַלְתֶּם לַחְמְכֶם לָשֹׂבַע וִישַׁבְתֶּם לָבֶטַח בְּאַרְצְכֶם׃ *וְנָתַתִּי לוי
שָׁלוֹם בָּאָרֶץ וּשְׁכַבְתֶּם וְאֵין מַחֲרִיד וְהִשְׁבַּתִּי חַיָּה רָעָה מִן־הָאָרֶץ וְחֶרֶב
לֹא־תַעֲבֹר בְּאַרְצְכֶם׃ וּרְדַפְתֶּם אֶת־אֹיְבֵיכֶם וְנָפְלוּ לִפְנֵיכֶם לֶחָרֶב׃ וְרָדְפוּ
מִכֶּם חֲמִשָּׁה מֵאָה וּמֵאָה מִכֶּם רְבָבָה יִרְדֹּפוּ וְנָפְלוּ אֹיְבֵיכֶם לִפְנֵיכֶם לֶחָרֶב׃
וּפָנִיתִי אֲלֵיכֶם וְהִפְרֵיתִי אֶתְכֶם וְהִרְבֵּיתִי אֶתְכֶם וַהֲקִימֹתִי אֶת־בְּרִיתִי אִתְּכֶם׃
*וַאֲכַלְתֶּם יָשָׁן נוֹשָׁן וְיָשָׁן מִפְּנֵי חָדָשׁ תּוֹצִיאוּ׃ וְנָתַתִּי מִשְׁכָּנִי בְּתוֹכְכֶם וְלֹא־ ישראל
תִגְעַל נַפְשִׁי אֶתְכֶם׃ וְהִתְהַלַּכְתִּי בְּתוֹכְכֶם וְהָיִיתִי לָכֶם לֵאלֹהִים וְאַתֶּם תִּהְיוּ־לִי
לְעָם׃ אֲנִי יהוה אֱלֹהֵיכֶם אֲשֶׁר הוֹצֵאתִי אֶתְכֶם מֵאֶרֶץ מִצְרַיִם מִהְיֹת לָהֶם
עֲבָדִים וָאֶשְׁבֹּר מֹטֹת עֻלְּכֶם וָאוֹלֵךְ אֶתְכֶם קוֹמְמִיּוּת׃

## BEMIDBAR במדבר

וַיְדַבֵּר יהוה אֶל־מֹשֶׁה בְּמִדְבַּר סִינַי בְּאֹהֶל מוֹעֵד בְּאֶחָד לַחֹדֶשׁ הַשֵּׁנִי בַּשָּׁנָה במדבר א:א–יט
הַשֵּׁנִית לְצֵאתָם מֵאֶרֶץ מִצְרַיִם לֵאמֹר׃ שְׂאוּ אֶת־רֹאשׁ כָּל־עֲדַת בְּנֵי־יִשְׂרָאֵל
לְמִשְׁפְּחֹתָם לְבֵית אֲבֹתָם בְּמִסְפַּר שֵׁמוֹת כָּל־זָכָר לְגֻלְגְּלֹתָם׃ מִבֶּן עֶשְׂרִים
שָׁנָה וָמַעְלָה כָּל־יֹצֵא צָבָא בְּיִשְׂרָאֵל תִּפְקְדוּ אֹתָם לְצִבְאֹתָם אַתָּה וְאַהֲרֹן׃
וְאִתְּכֶם יִהְיוּ אִישׁ אִישׁ לַמַּטֶּה אִישׁ רֹאשׁ לְבֵית־אֲבֹתָיו הוּא׃ *וְאֵלֶּה שְׁמוֹת לוי
הָאֲנָשִׁים אֲשֶׁר יַעַמְדוּ אִתְּכֶם לִרְאוּבֵן אֱלִיצוּר בֶּן־שְׁדֵיאוּר׃ לְשִׁמְעוֹן שְׁלֻמִיאֵל
בֶּן־צוּרִישַׁדָּי׃ לִיהוּדָה נַחְשׁוֹן בֶּן־עַמִּינָדָב׃ לְיִשָּׂשכָר נְתַנְאֵל בֶּן־צוּעָר׃
לִזְבוּלֻן אֱלִיאָב בֶּן־חֵלֹן׃ לִבְנֵי יוֹסֵף לְאֶפְרַיִם אֱלִישָׁמָע בֶּן־עַמִּיהוּד לִמְנַשֶּׁה
גַּמְלִיאֵל בֶּן־פְּדָהצוּר׃ לְבִנְיָמִן אֲבִידָן בֶּן־גִּדְעֹנִי׃ לְדָן אֲחִיעֶזֶר בֶּן־עַמִּישַׁדָּי׃
לְאָשֵׁר פַּגְעִיאֵל בֶּן־עָכְרָן׃ לְגָד אֶלְיָסָף בֶּן־דְּעוּאֵל׃ לְנַפְתָּלִי אֲחִירַע בֶּן־

קְרוּאֵי עֵינָן: אֵלֶּה קריאי הָעֵדָה נְשִׂיאֵי מַטּוֹת אֲבוֹתָם רָאשֵׁי אַלְפֵי יִשְׂרָאֵל הֵם:
ישראל *וַיִּקַּח מֹשֶׁה וְאַהֲרֹן אֵת הָאֲנָשִׁים הָאֵלֶּה אֲשֶׁר נִקְּבוּ בְּשֵׁמוֹת: וְאֵת כָּל־הָעֵדָה
הִקְהִילוּ בְּאֶחָד לַחֹדֶשׁ הַשֵּׁנִי וַיִּתְיַלְדוּ עַל־מִשְׁפְּחֹתָם לְבֵית אֲבֹתָם בְּמִסְפַּר
שֵׁמוֹת מִבֶּן עֶשְׂרִים שָׁנָה וָמַעְלָה לְגֻלְגְּלֹתָם: כַּאֲשֶׁר צִוָּה יְהֹוָה אֶת־מֹשֶׁה
וַיִּפְקְדֵם בְּמִדְבַּר סִינָי:

## NASO נשא

במדבר ד:כא-לז וַיְדַבֵּר יְהֹוָה אֶל־מֹשֶׁה לֵּאמֹר: נָשֹׂא אֶת־רֹאשׁ בְּנֵי גֵרְשׁוֹן גַּם־הֵם לְבֵית אֲבֹתָם
לְמִשְׁפְּחֹתָם: מִבֶּן שְׁלֹשִׁים שָׁנָה וָמַעְלָה עַד בֶּן־חֲמִשִּׁים שָׁנָה תִּפְקֹד אוֹתָם
כָּל־הַבָּא לִצְבֹא צָבָא לַעֲבֹד עֲבֹדָה בְּאֹהֶל מוֹעֵד: זֹאת עֲבֹדַת מִשְׁפְּחֹת
לוי הַגֵּרְשֻׁנִּי לַעֲבֹד וּלְמַשָּׂא: *וְנָשְׂאוּ אֶת־יְרִיעֹת הַמִּשְׁכָּן וְאֶת־אֹהֶל מוֹעֵד מִכְסֵהוּ
וּמִכְסֵה הַתַּחַשׁ אֲשֶׁר־עָלָיו מִלְמָעְלָה וְאֶת־מָסַךְ פֶּתַח אֹהֶל מוֹעֵד: וְאֵת קַלְעֵי
הֶחָצֵר וְאֶת־מָסַךְ ׀ פֶּתַח ׀ שַׁעַר הֶחָצֵר אֲשֶׁר עַל־הַמִּשְׁכָּן וְעַל־הַמִּזְבֵּחַ סָבִיב
וְאֵת מֵיתְרֵיהֶם וְאֶת־כָּל־כְּלֵי עֲבֹדָתָם וְאֵת כָּל־אֲשֶׁר יֵעָשֶׂה לָהֶם וְעָבָדוּ:
עַל־פִּי אַהֲרֹן וּבָנָיו תִּהְיֶה כָּל־עֲבֹדַת בְּנֵי הַגֵּרְשֻׁנִּי לְכָל־מַשָּׂאָם וּלְכֹל עֲבֹדָתָם
וּפְקַדְתֶּם עֲלֵהֶם בְּמִשְׁמֶרֶת אֵת כָּל־מַשָּׂאָם: זֹאת עֲבֹדַת מִשְׁפְּחֹת בְּנֵי הַגֵּרְשֻׁנִּי
ישראל בְּאֹהֶל מוֹעֵד וּמִשְׁמַרְתָּם בְּיַד אִיתָמָר בֶּן־אַהֲרֹן הַכֹּהֵן: *בְּנֵי מְרָרִי
לְמִשְׁפְּחֹתָם לְבֵית־אֲבֹתָם תִּפְקֹד אֹתָם: מִבֶּן שְׁלֹשִׁים שָׁנָה וָמַעְלָה וְעַד בֶּן־
חֲמִשִּׁים שָׁנָה תִּפְקְדֵם כָּל־הַבָּא לַצָּבָא לַעֲבֹד אֶת־עֲבֹדַת אֹהֶל מוֹעֵד: וְזֹאת
מִשְׁמֶרֶת מַשָּׂאָם לְכָל־עֲבֹדָתָם בְּאֹהֶל מוֹעֵד קַרְשֵׁי הַמִּשְׁכָּן וּבְרִיחָיו וְעַמּוּדָיו
וַאֲדָנָיו: וְעַמּוּדֵי הֶחָצֵר סָבִיב וְאַדְנֵיהֶם וִיתֵדֹתָם וּמֵיתְרֵיהֶם לְכָל־כְּלֵיהֶם וּלְכֹל
עֲבֹדָתָם וּבְשֵׁמֹת תִּפְקְדוּ אֶת־כְּלֵי מִשְׁמֶרֶת מַשָּׂאָם: זֹאת עֲבֹדַת מִשְׁפְּחֹת בְּנֵי
מְרָרִי לְכָל־עֲבֹדָתָם בְּאֹהֶל מוֹעֵד בְּיַד אִיתָמָר בֶּן־אַהֲרֹן הַכֹּהֵן:

*Some extend the* ישראל *portion:*

וַיִּפְקֹד מֹשֶׁה וְאַהֲרֹן וּנְשִׂיאֵי הָעֵדָה אֶת־בְּנֵי הַקְּהָתִי לְמִשְׁפְּחֹתָם וּלְבֵית אֲבֹתָם:
מִבֶּן שְׁלֹשִׁים שָׁנָה וָמַעְלָה וְעַד בֶּן־חֲמִשִּׁים שָׁנָה כָּל־הַבָּא לַצָּבָא לַעֲבֹדָה
בְּאֹהֶל מוֹעֵד: וַיִּהְיוּ פְקֻדֵיהֶם לְמִשְׁפְּחֹתָם אַלְפַּיִם שְׁבַע מֵאוֹת וַחֲמִשִּׁים: אֵלֶּה
פְקוּדֵי מִשְׁפְּחֹת הַקְּהָתִי כָּל־הָעֹבֵד בְּאֹהֶל מוֹעֵד אֲשֶׁר פָּקַד מֹשֶׁה וְאַהֲרֹן
עַל־פִּי יְהֹוָה בְּיַד־מֹשֶׁה:

## בהעלותך BEHAʹALOTEKHA

וַיְדַבֵּר יְהוָה אֶל־מֹשֶׁה לֵּאמֹר: דַּבֵּר אֶל־אַהֲרֹן וְאָמַרְתָּ אֵלָיו בְּהַעֲלֹתְךָ אֶת־ במדבר ח:א–יד
הַנֵּרֹת אֶל־מוּל פְּנֵי הַמְּנוֹרָה יָאִירוּ שִׁבְעַת הַנֵּרוֹת: וַיַּעַשׂ כֵּן אַהֲרֹן אֶל־מוּל
פְּנֵי הַמְּנוֹרָה הֶעֱלָה נֵרֹתֶיהָ כַּאֲשֶׁר צִוָּה יְהוָה אֶת־מֹשֶׁה: וְזֶה מַעֲשֵׂה הַמְּנֹרָה
מִקְשָׁה זָהָב עַד־יְרֵכָהּ עַד־פִּרְחָהּ מִקְשָׁה הִוא כַּמַּרְאֶה אֲשֶׁר הֶרְאָה יְהוָה
אֶת־מֹשֶׁה כֵּן עָשָׂה אֶת־הַמְּנֹרָה:
וַיְדַבֵּר יְהוָה אֶל־מֹשֶׁה לֵּאמֹר: קַח אֶת־הַלְוִיִּם מִתּוֹךְ בְּנֵי יִשְׂרָאֵל וְטִהַרְתָּ לוי
אֹתָם: וְכֹה־תַעֲשֶׂה לָהֶם לְטַהֲרָם הַזֵּה עֲלֵיהֶם מֵי חַטָּאת וְהֶעֱבִירוּ תַעַר עַל־
כָּל־בְּשָׂרָם וְכִבְּסוּ בִגְדֵיהֶם וְהִטֶּהָרוּ: וְלָקְחוּ פַּר בֶּן־בָּקָר וּמִנְחָתוֹ סֹלֶת בְּלוּלָה
בַשָּׁמֶן וּפַר־שֵׁנִי בֶן־בָּקָר תִּקַּח לְחַטָּאת: וְהִקְרַבְתָּ אֶת־הַלְוִיִּם לִפְנֵי אֹהֶל
מוֹעֵד וְהִקְהַלְתָּ אֶת־כָּל־עֲדַת בְּנֵי יִשְׂרָאֵל: *וְהִקְרַבְתָּ אֶת־הַלְוִיִּם לִפְנֵי יְהוָה ישראל
וְסָמְכוּ בְנֵי־יִשְׂרָאֵל אֶת־יְדֵיהֶם עַל־הַלְוִיִּם: וְהֵנִיף אַהֲרֹן אֶת־הַלְוִיִּם תְּנוּפָה
לִפְנֵי יְהוָה מֵאֵת בְּנֵי יִשְׂרָאֵל וְהָיוּ לַעֲבֹד אֶת־עֲבֹדַת יְהוָה: וְהַלְוִיִּם יִסְמְכוּ
אֶת־יְדֵיהֶם עַל רֹאשׁ הַפָּרִים וַעֲשֵׂה אֶת־הָאֶחָד חַטָּאת וְאֶת־הָאֶחָד עֹלָה
לַיהוָה לְכַפֵּר עַל־הַלְוִיִּם: וְהַעֲמַדְתָּ אֶת־הַלְוִיִּם לִפְנֵי אַהֲרֹן וְלִפְנֵי בָנָיו וְהֵנַפְתָּ
אֹתָם תְּנוּפָה לַיהוָה: וְהִבְדַּלְתָּ אֶת־הַלְוִיִּם מִתּוֹךְ בְּנֵי יִשְׂרָאֵל וְהָיוּ לִי הַלְוִיִּם:

## שלח SHELAḤ

וַיְדַבֵּר יְהוָה אֶל־מֹשֶׁה לֵּאמֹר: שְׁלַח־לְךָ אֲנָשִׁים וְיָתֻרוּ אֶת־אֶרֶץ כְּנַעַן אֲשֶׁר־ במדבר יג:א–כ
אֲנִי נֹתֵן לִבְנֵי יִשְׂרָאֵל אִישׁ אֶחָד אִישׁ אֶחָד לְמַטֵּה אֲבֹתָיו תִּשְׁלָחוּ כֹּל נָשִׂיא
בָהֶם: וַיִּשְׁלַח אֹתָם מֹשֶׁה מִמִּדְבַּר פָּארָן עַל־פִּי יְהוָה כֻּלָּם אֲנָשִׁים רָאשֵׁי
בְנֵי־יִשְׂרָאֵל הֵמָּה: *וְאֵלֶּה שְׁמוֹתָם לְמַטֵּה רְאוּבֵן שַׁמּוּעַ בֶּן־זַכּוּר: לְמַטֵּה לוי
שִׁמְעוֹן שָׁפָט בֶּן־חוֹרִי: לְמַטֵּה יְהוּדָה כָּלֵב בֶּן־יְפֻנֶּה: לְמַטֵּה יִשָּׂשכָר יִגְאָל
בֶּן־יוֹסֵף: לְמַטֵּה אֶפְרָיִם הוֹשֵׁעַ בִּן־נוּן: לְמַטֵּה בִנְיָמִן פַּלְטִי בֶּן־רָפוּא: לְמַטֵּה
זְבוּלֻן גַּדִּיאֵל בֶּן־סוֹדִי: לְמַטֵּה יוֹסֵף לְמַטֵּה מְנַשֶּׁה גַּדִּי בֶּן־סוּסִי: לְמַטֵּה דָן
עַמִּיאֵל בֶּן־גְּמַלִּי: לְמַטֵּה אָשֵׁר סְתוּר בֶּן־מִיכָאֵל: לְמַטֵּה נַפְתָּלִי נַחְבִּי בֶּן־
וָפְסִי: לְמַטֵּה גָד גְּאוּאֵל בֶּן־מָכִי: אֵלֶּה שְׁמוֹת הָאֲנָשִׁים אֲשֶׁר־שָׁלַח מֹשֶׁה
לָתוּר אֶת־הָאָרֶץ וַיִּקְרָא מֹשֶׁה לְהוֹשֵׁעַ בִּן־נוּן יְהוֹשֻׁעַ: *וַיִּשְׁלַח אֹתָם מֹשֶׁה ישראל
לָתוּר אֶת־אֶרֶץ כְּנָעַן וַיֹּאמֶר אֲלֵהֶם עֲלוּ זֶה בַּנֶּגֶב וַעֲלִיתֶם אֶת־הָהָר: וּרְאִיתֶם

אֶת־הָאָרֶץ מַה־הִוא וְאֶת־הָעָם הַיֹּשֵׁב עָלֶיהָ הֶחָזָק הוּא הֲרָפֶה הַמְעַט הוּא
אִם־רָב׃ וּמָה הָאָרֶץ אֲשֶׁר־הוּא יֹשֵׁב בָּהּ הֲטוֹבָה הִוא אִם־רָעָה וּמָה הֶעָרִים
אֲשֶׁר־הוּא יוֹשֵׁב בָּהֵנָּה הַבְּמַחֲנִים אִם בְּמִבְצָרִים׃ וּמָה הָאָרֶץ הַשְּׁמֵנָה הִוא
אִם־רָזָה הֲיֵשׁ־בָּהּ עֵץ אִם־אַיִן וְהִתְחַזַּקְתֶּם וּלְקַחְתֶּם מִפְּרִי הָאָרֶץ וְהַיָּמִים
יְמֵי בִּכּוּרֵי עֲנָבִים׃

## KORAḤ — קורח

במדבר טז:א–יג וַיִּקַּח קֹרַח בֶּן־יִצְהָר בֶּן־קְהָת בֶּן־לֵוִי וְדָתָן וַאֲבִירָם בְּנֵי אֱלִיאָב וְאוֹן בֶּן־
פֶּלֶת בְּנֵי רְאוּבֵן׃ וַיָּקֻמוּ לִפְנֵי מֹשֶׁה וַאֲנָשִׁים מִבְּנֵי־יִשְׂרָאֵל חֲמִשִּׁים וּמָאתָיִם
נְשִׂיאֵי עֵדָה קְרִאֵי מוֹעֵד אַנְשֵׁי־שֵׁם׃ וַיִּקָּהֲלוּ עַל־מֹשֶׁה וְעַל־אַהֲרֹן וַיֹּאמְרוּ
אֲלֵהֶם רַב־לָכֶם כִּי כָל־הָעֵדָה כֻּלָּם קְדֹשִׁים וּבְתוֹכָם יְהוָה וּמַדּוּעַ תִּתְנַשְּׂאוּ
לוי עַל־קְהַל יְהוָה׃ *וַיִּשְׁמַע מֹשֶׁה וַיִּפֹּל עַל־פָּנָיו׃ וַיְדַבֵּר אֶל־קֹרַח וְאֶל־כָּל־עֲדָתוֹ
לֵאמֹר בֹּקֶר וְיֹדַע יְהוָה אֶת־אֲשֶׁר־לוֹ וְאֶת־הַקָּדוֹשׁ וְהִקְרִיב אֵלָיו וְאֵת אֲשֶׁר
יִבְחַר־בּוֹ יַקְרִיב אֵלָיו׃ זֹאת עֲשׂוּ קְחוּ־לָכֶם מַחְתּוֹת קֹרַח וְכָל־עֲדָתוֹ׃ וּתְנוּ־
בָהֵן ׀ אֵשׁ וְשִׂימוּ עֲלֵיהֶן ׀ קְטֹרֶת לִפְנֵי יְהוָה מָחָר וְהָיָה הָאִישׁ אֲשֶׁר־יִבְחַר
ישראל יְהוָה הוּא הַקָּדוֹשׁ רַב־לָכֶם בְּנֵי לֵוִי׃ *וַיֹּאמֶר מֹשֶׁה אֶל־קֹרַח שִׁמְעוּ־נָא בְּנֵי
לֵוִי׃ הַמְעַט מִכֶּם כִּי־הִבְדִּיל אֱלֹהֵי יִשְׂרָאֵל אֶתְכֶם מֵעֲדַת יִשְׂרָאֵל לְהַקְרִיב
אֶתְכֶם אֵלָיו לַעֲבֹד אֶת־עֲבֹדַת מִשְׁכַּן יְהוָה וְלַעֲמֹד לִפְנֵי הָעֵדָה לְשָׁרְתָם׃
וַיַּקְרֵב אֹתְךָ וְאֶת־כָּל־אַחֶיךָ בְנֵי־לֵוִי אִתָּךְ וּבִקַּשְׁתֶּם גַּם־כְּהֻנָּה׃ לָכֵן אַתָּה
תַּלִּינוּ וְכָל־עֲדָתְךָ הַנֹּעָדִים עַל־יְהוָה וְאַהֲרֹן מַה־הוּא כִּי תלונו עָלָיו׃ וַיִּשְׁלַח מֹשֶׁה
לִקְרֹא לְדָתָן וְלַאֲבִירָם בְּנֵי אֱלִיאָב וַיֹּאמְרוּ לֹא נַעֲלֶה׃ הַמְעַט כִּי הֶעֱלִיתָנוּ
מֵאֶרֶץ זָבַת חָלָב וּדְבַשׁ לַהֲמִיתֵנוּ בַּמִּדְבָּר כִּי־תִשְׂתָּרֵר עָלֵינוּ גַּם־הִשְׂתָּרֵר׃

## ḤUKAT — חוקת

במדבר יט:א–יז וַיְדַבֵּר יְהוָה אֶל־מֹשֶׁה וְאֶל־אַהֲרֹן לֵאמֹר׃ זֹאת חֻקַּת הַתּוֹרָה אֲשֶׁר־צִוָּה יְהוָה
לֵאמֹר דַּבֵּר ׀ אֶל־בְּנֵי יִשְׂרָאֵל וְיִקְחוּ אֵלֶיךָ פָרָה אֲדֻמָּה תְּמִימָה אֲשֶׁר אֵין־בָּהּ
מוּם אֲשֶׁר לֹא־עָלָה עָלֶיהָ עֹל׃ וּנְתַתֶּם אֹתָהּ אֶל־אֶלְעָזָר הַכֹּהֵן וְהוֹצִיא אֹתָהּ
אֶל־מִחוּץ לַמַּחֲנֶה וְשָׁחַט אֹתָהּ לְפָנָיו׃ וְלָקַח אֶלְעָזָר הַכֹּהֵן מִדָּמָהּ בְּאֶצְבָּעוֹ
וְהִזָּה אֶל־נֹכַח פְּנֵי אֹהֶל־מוֹעֵד מִדָּמָהּ שֶׁבַע פְּעָמִים׃ וְשָׂרַף אֶת־הַפָּרָה לְעֵינָיו

את־עורה ואת־בשרה ואת־דמה על־פרשה ישרף: ולקח הכהן עץ ארז
ואזוב ושני תולעת והשליך אל־תוך שרפת הפרה: *וכבס בגדיו הכהן לוי
ורחץ בשרו במים ואחר יבא אל־המחנה וטמא הכהן עד־הערב: והשרף
אתה יכבס בגדיו במים ורחץ בשרו במים וטמא עד־הערב: ואסף | איש
טהור את אפר הפרה והניח מחוץ למחנה במקום טהור והיתה לעדת
בני־ישראל למשמרת למי נדה חטאת הוא: *וכבס האסף את־אפר הפרה ישראל
את־בגדיו וטמא עד־הערב והיתה לבני ישראל ולגר הגר בתוכם לחקת
עולם: הנגע במת לכל־נפש אדם וטמא שבעת ימים: הוא יתחטא־בו
ביום השלישי וביום השביעי יטהר ואם־לא יתחטא ביום השלישי וביום
השביעי לא יטהר: כל־הנגע במת בנפש האדם אשר־ימות ולא יתחטא
את־משכן יהוה טמא ונכרתה הנפש ההוא מישראל כי מי נדה לא־זרק
עליו טמא יהיה עוד טמאתו בו: זאת התורה אדם כי־ימות באהל כל־
הבא אל־האהל וכל־אשר באהל יטמא שבעת ימים: וכל כלי פתוח אשר
אין־צמיד פתיל עליו טמא הוא: וכל אשר־יגע על־פני השדה בחלל־חרב
או במת או־בעצם אדם או בקבר יטמא שבעת ימים: ולקחו לטמא מעפר
שרפת החטאת ונתן עליו מים חיים אל־כלי:

## BALAK בלק

וירא בלק בן־צפור את כל־אשר־עשה ישראל לאמרי: ויגר מואב מפני במדבר כב:ב-יב
העם מאד כי רב־הוא ויקץ מואב מפני בני ישראל: ויאמר מואב אל־זקני
מדין עתה ילחכו הקהל את־כל־סביבתינו כלחך השור את ירק השדה
ובלק בן־צפור מלך למואב בעת ההוא: *וישלח מלאכים אל־בלעם לוי
בן־בעור פתורה אשר על־הנהר ארץ בני־עמו לקרא־לו לאמר הנה עם
יצא ממצרים הנה כסה את־עין הארץ והוא ישב ממלי: ועתה לכה־נא
ארה־לי את־העם הזה כי־עצום הוא ממני אולי אוכל נכה־בו ואגרשנו
מן־הארץ כי ידעתי את אשר־תברך מברך ואשר תאר יואר: וילכו זקני
מואב וזקני מדין וקסמים בידם ויבאו אל־בלעם וידברו אליו דברי בלק:
*ויאמר אליהם לינו פה הלילה והשבתי אתכם דבר כאשר ידבר יהוה אלי ישראל
וישבו שרי־מואב עם־בלעם: ויבא אלהים אל־בלעם ויאמר מי האנשים

הָאֵלֶּה עִמָּךְ: וַיֹּאמֶר בִּלְעָם אֶל־הָאֱלֹהִים בָּלָק בֶּן־צִפֹּר מֶלֶךְ מוֹאָב שָׁלַח
אֵלָי: הִנֵּה הָעָם הַיֹּצֵא מִמִּצְרַיִם וַיְכַס אֶת־עֵין הָאָרֶץ עַתָּה לְכָה קָבָה־לִּי אֹתוֹ
אוּלַי אוּכַל לְהִלָּחֶם בּוֹ וְגֵרַשְׁתִּיו: וַיֹּאמֶר אֱלֹהִים אֶל־בִּלְעָם לֹא תֵלֵךְ עִמָּהֶם
לֹא תָאֹר אֶת־הָעָם כִּי בָרוּךְ הוּא:

## פינחס PINEḤAS

במדבר כה:י–כו:ד וַיְדַבֵּר יהוה אֶל־מֹשֶׁה לֵּאמֹר: פִּינְחָס בֶּן־אֶלְעָזָר בֶּן־אַהֲרֹן הַכֹּהֵן הֵשִׁיב
אֶת־חֲמָתִי מֵעַל בְּנֵי־יִשְׂרָאֵל בְּקַנְאוֹ אֶת־קִנְאָתִי בְּתוֹכָם וְלֹא־כִלִּיתִי אֶת־
לוי בְּנֵי־יִשְׂרָאֵל בְּקִנְאָתִי: לָכֵן אֱמֹר הִנְנִי נֹתֵן לוֹ אֶת־בְּרִיתִי שָׁלוֹם: *וְהָיְתָה לּוֹ
וּלְזַרְעוֹ אַחֲרָיו בְּרִית כְּהֻנַּת עוֹלָם תַּחַת אֲשֶׁר קִנֵּא לֵאלֹהָיו וַיְכַפֵּר עַל־בְּנֵי
יִשְׂרָאֵל: וְשֵׁם אִישׁ יִשְׂרָאֵל הַמֻּכֶּה אֲשֶׁר הֻכָּה אֶת־הַמִּדְיָנִית זִמְרִי בֶּן־סָלוּא
נְשִׂיא בֵית־אָב לַשִּׁמְעֹנִי: וְשֵׁם הָאִשָּׁה הַמֻּכָּה הַמִּדְיָנִית כָּזְבִּי בַת־צוּר רֹאשׁ
אֻמּוֹת בֵּית־אָב בְּמִדְיָן הוּא:
ישראל וַיְדַבֵּר יהוה אֶל־מֹשֶׁה לֵּאמֹר: צָרוֹר אֶת־הַמִּדְיָנִים וְהִכִּיתֶם אוֹתָם: כִּי־
צֹרְרִים הֵם לָכֶם בְּנִכְלֵיהֶם אֲשֶׁר־נִכְּלוּ לָכֶם עַל־דְּבַר פְּעוֹר וְעַל־דְּבַר כָּזְבִּי
בַת־נְשִׂיא מִדְיָן אֲחֹתָם הַמֻּכָּה בְיוֹם־הַמַּגֵּפָה עַל־דְּבַר פְּעוֹר: וַיְהִי אַחֲרֵי
הַמַּגֵּפָה
וַיֹּאמֶר יהוה אֶל־מֹשֶׁה וְאֶל אֶלְעָזָר בֶּן־אַהֲרֹן הַכֹּהֵן לֵאמֹר: שְׂאוּ אֶת־רֹאשׁ
כָּל־עֲדַת בְּנֵי־יִשְׂרָאֵל מִבֶּן עֶשְׂרִים שָׁנָה וָמַעְלָה לְבֵית אֲבֹתָם כָּל־יֹצֵא צָבָא
בְּיִשְׂרָאֵל: וַיְדַבֵּר מֹשֶׁה וְאֶלְעָזָר הַכֹּהֵן אֹתָם בְּעַרְבֹת מוֹאָב עַל־יַרְדֵּן יְרֵחוֹ
לֵאמֹר: מִבֶּן עֶשְׂרִים שָׁנָה וָמָעְלָה כַּאֲשֶׁר צִוָּה יהוה אֶת־מֹשֶׁה וּבְנֵי יִשְׂרָאֵל
הַיֹּצְאִים מֵאֶרֶץ מִצְרָיִם:

## מטות MATOT

במדבר ל:ב–ו וַיְדַבֵּר מֹשֶׁה אֶל־רָאשֵׁי הַמַּטּוֹת לִבְנֵי יִשְׂרָאֵל לֵאמֹר זֶה הַדָּבָר אֲשֶׁר צִוָּה
יהוה: אִישׁ כִּי־יִדֹּר נֶדֶר לַיהוה אוֹ־הִשָּׁבַע שְׁבֻעָה לֶאְסֹר אִסָּר עַל־נַפְשׁוֹ
לֹא יַחֵל דְּבָרוֹ כְּכָל־הַיֹּצֵא מִפִּיו יַעֲשֶׂה: וְאִשָּׁה כִּי־תִדֹּר נֶדֶר לַיהוה וְאָסְרָה
אִסָּר בְּבֵית אָבִיהָ בִּנְעֻרֶיהָ: וְשָׁמַע אָבִיהָ אֶת־נִדְרָהּ וֶאֱסָרָהּ אֲשֶׁר אָסְרָה
עַל־נַפְשָׁהּ וְהֶחֱרִישׁ לָהּ אָבִיהָ וְקָמוּ כָּל־נְדָרֶיהָ וְכָל־אִסָּר אֲשֶׁר־אָסְרָה

עַל־נַפְשָׁהּ יָקוּם: וְאִם־הֵנִיא אָבִיהָ אֹתָהּ בְּיוֹם שָׁמְעוֹ כָּל־נְדָרֶיהָ וֶאֱסָרֶיהָ
אֲשֶׁר־אָסְרָה עַל־נַפְשָׁהּ לֹא יָקוּם וַיהוָה יִסְלַח־לָהּ כִּי־הֵנִיא אָבִיהָ אֹתָהּ:
וְאִם־הָיוֹ תִהְיֶה לְאִישׁ וּנְדָרֶיהָ עָלֶיהָ אוֹ מִבְטָא שְׂפָתֶיהָ אֲשֶׁר אָסְרָה עַל־
נַפְשָׁהּ: וְשָׁמַע אִישָׁהּ בְּיוֹם שָׁמְעוֹ וְהֶחֱרִישׁ לָהּ וְקָמוּ נְדָרֶיהָ וֶאֱסָרֶהָ אֲשֶׁר־
אָסְרָה עַל־נַפְשָׁהּ יָקֻמוּ: וְאִם בְּיוֹם שְׁמֹעַ אִישָׁהּ יָנִיא אוֹתָהּ וְהֵפֵר אֶת־נִדְרָהּ
אֲשֶׁר עָלֶיהָ וְאֵת מִבְטָא שְׂפָתֶיהָ אֲשֶׁר אָסְרָה עַל־נַפְשָׁהּ וַיהוָה יִסְלַח־לָהּ:
*וְנֵדֶר אַלְמָנָה וּגְרוּשָׁה כֹּל אֲשֶׁר־אָסְרָה עַל־נַפְשָׁהּ יָקוּם עָלֶיהָ: וְאִם־בֵּית לוי
אִישָׁהּ נָדָרָה אוֹ־אָסְרָה אִסָּר עַל־נַפְשָׁהּ בִּשְׁבֻעָה: וְשָׁמַע אִישָׁהּ וְהֶחֱרִשׁ לָהּ
לֹא הֵנִיא אֹתָהּ וְקָמוּ כָּל־נְדָרֶיהָ וְכָל־אִסָּר אֲשֶׁר־אָסְרָה עַל־נַפְשָׁהּ יָקוּם:
וְאִם־הָפֵר יָפֵר אֹתָם ׀ אִישָׁהּ בְּיוֹם שָׁמְעוֹ כָּל־מוֹצָא שְׂפָתֶיהָ לִנְדָרֶיהָ וּלְאִסַּר
נַפְשָׁהּ לֹא יָקוּם אִישָׁהּ הֲפֵרָם וַיהוָה יִסְלַח־לָהּ: *כָּל־נֵדֶר וְכָל־שְׁבֻעַת אִסָּר ישראל
לְעַנֹּת נָפֶשׁ אִישָׁהּ יְקִימֶנּוּ וְאִישָׁהּ יְפֵרֶנּוּ: וְאִם־הַחֲרֵשׁ יַחֲרִישׁ לָהּ אִישָׁהּ
מִיּוֹם אֶל־יוֹם וְהֵקִים אֶת־כָּל־נְדָרֶיהָ אוֹ אֶת־כָּל־אֱסָרֶיהָ אֲשֶׁר עָלֶיהָ הֵקִים
אֹתָם כִּי־הֶחֱרִשׁ לָהּ בְּיוֹם שָׁמְעוֹ: וְאִם־הָפֵר יָפֵר אֹתָם אַחֲרֵי שָׁמְעוֹ וְנָשָׂא
אֶת־עֲוֺנָהּ: אֵלֶּה הַחֻקִּים אֲשֶׁר צִוָּה יְהוָה אֶת־מֹשֶׁה בֵּין אִישׁ לְאִשְׁתּוֹ בֵּין־
אָב לְבִתּוֹ בִּנְעֻרֶיהָ בֵּית אָבִיהָ:

## MASEI מסעי

אֵלֶּה מַסְעֵי בְנֵי־יִשְׂרָאֵל אֲשֶׁר יָצְאוּ מֵאֶרֶץ מִצְרַיִם לְצִבְאֹתָם בְּיַד־מֹשֶׁה במדבר לג:א–נג
וְאַהֲרֹן: וַיִּכְתֹּב מֹשֶׁה אֶת־מוֹצָאֵיהֶם לְמַסְעֵיהֶם עַל־פִּי יְהוָה וְאֵלֶּה מַסְעֵיהֶם
לְמוֹצָאֵיהֶם: וַיִּסְעוּ מֵרַעְמְסֵס בַּחֹדֶשׁ הָרִאשׁוֹן בַּחֲמִשָּׁה עָשָׂר יוֹם לַחֹדֶשׁ
הָרִאשׁוֹן מִמָּחֳרַת הַפֶּסַח יָצְאוּ בְנֵי־יִשְׂרָאֵל בְּיָד רָמָה לְעֵינֵי כָּל־מִצְרָיִם:
*וּמִצְרַיִם מְקַבְּרִים אֵת אֲשֶׁר הִכָּה יְהוָה בָּהֶם כָּל־בְּכוֹר וּבֵאלֹהֵיהֶם עָשָׂה לוי
יְהוָה שְׁפָטִים: וַיִּסְעוּ בְנֵי־יִשְׂרָאֵל מֵרַעְמְסֵס וַיַּחֲנוּ בְּסֻכֹּת: וַיִּסְעוּ מִסֻּכֹּת
וַיַּחֲנוּ בְאֵתָם אֲשֶׁר בִּקְצֵה הַמִּדְבָּר: *וַיִּסְעוּ מֵאֵתָם וַיָּשָׁב עַל־פִּי הַחִירֹת אֲשֶׁר ישראל
עַל־פְּנֵי בַּעַל צְפוֹן וַיַּחֲנוּ לִפְנֵי מִגְדֹּל: וַיִּסְעוּ מִפְּנֵי הַחִירֹת וַיַּעַבְרוּ בְתוֹךְ־הַיָּם
הַמִּדְבָּרָה וַיֵּלְכוּ דֶּרֶךְ שְׁלֹשֶׁת יָמִים בְּמִדְבַּר אֵתָם וַיַּחֲנוּ בְּמָרָה: וַיִּסְעוּ מִמָּרָה
וַיָּבֹאוּ אֵילִמָה וּבְאֵילִם שְׁתֵּים עֶשְׂרֵה עֵינֹת מַיִם וְשִׁבְעִים תְּמָרִים וַיַּחֲנוּ־שָׁם:
וַיִּסְעוּ מֵאֵילִם וַיַּחֲנוּ עַל־יַם־סוּף:

*Some extend the לוי portion:*

וַיִּסְעוּ מִיַּם־סוּף וַיַּחֲנוּ בְּמִדְבַּר־סִין׃ וַיִּסְעוּ מִמִּדְבַּר־סִין וַיַּחֲנוּ בְּדָפְקָה׃ וַיִּסְעוּ
מִדָּפְקָה וַיַּחֲנוּ בְּאָלוּשׁ׃ וַיִּסְעוּ מֵאָלוּשׁ וַיַּחֲנוּ בִּרְפִידִם וְלֹא־הָיָה שָׁם מַיִם לָעָם
לִשְׁתּוֹת׃ וַיִּסְעוּ מֵרְפִידִם וַיַּחֲנוּ בְּמִדְבַּר סִינָי׃ וַיִּסְעוּ מִמִּדְבַּר סִינָי וַיַּחֲנוּ בְּקִבְרֹת
הַתַּאֲוָה׃ וַיִּסְעוּ מִקִּבְרֹת הַתַּאֲוָה וַיַּחֲנוּ בַּחֲצֵרֹת׃ וַיִּסְעוּ מֵחֲצֵרֹת וַיַּחֲנוּ בְּרִתְמָה׃
וַיִּסְעוּ מֵרִתְמָה וַיַּחֲנוּ בְּרִמֹּן פָּרֶץ׃ וַיִּסְעוּ מֵרִמֹּן פָּרֶץ וַיַּחֲנוּ בְּלִבְנָה׃ וַיִּסְעוּ
מִלִּבְנָה וַיַּחֲנוּ בְּרִסָּה׃ וַיִּסְעוּ מֵרִסָּה וַיַּחֲנוּ בִּקְהֵלָתָה׃ וַיִּסְעוּ מִקְּהֵלָתָה וַיַּחֲנוּ
בְּהַר־שָׁפֶר׃ וַיִּסְעוּ מֵהַר־שָׁפֶר וַיַּחֲנוּ בַּחֲרָדָה׃ וַיִּסְעוּ מֵחֲרָדָה וַיַּחֲנוּ בְּמַקְהֵלֹת׃
וַיִּסְעוּ מִמַּקְהֵלֹת וַיַּחֲנוּ בְּתָחַת׃ וַיִּסְעוּ מִתָּחַת וַיַּחֲנוּ בְּתָרַח׃ וַיִּסְעוּ מִתָּרַח וַיַּחֲנוּ
בְּמִתְקָה׃ וַיִּסְעוּ מִמִּתְקָה וַיַּחֲנוּ בְּחַשְׁמֹנָה׃ וַיִּסְעוּ מֵחַשְׁמֹנָה וַיַּחֲנוּ בְּמֹסֵרוֹת׃
וַיִּסְעוּ מִמֹּסֵרוֹת וַיַּחֲנוּ בִּבְנֵי יַעֲקָן׃ וַיִּסְעוּ מִבְּנֵי יַעֲקָן וַיַּחֲנוּ בְּחֹר הַגִּדְגָּד׃ וַיִּסְעוּ
מֵחֹר הַגִּדְגָּד וַיַּחֲנוּ בְּיָטְבָתָה׃ וַיִּסְעוּ מִיָּטְבָתָה וַיַּחֲנוּ בְּעַבְרֹנָה׃ וַיִּסְעוּ מֵעַבְרֹנָה
וַיַּחֲנוּ בְּעֶצְיֹן גָּבֶר׃ וַיִּסְעוּ מֵעֶצְיֹן גָּבֶר וַיַּחֲנוּ בְמִדְבַּר־צִן הִוא קָדֵשׁ׃ וַיִּסְעוּ
מִקָּדֵשׁ וַיַּחֲנוּ בְּהֹר הָהָר בִּקְצֵה אֶרֶץ אֱדוֹם׃ וַיַּעַל אַהֲרֹן הַכֹּהֵן אֶל־הֹר הָהָר
עַל־פִּי יְהוָה וַיָּמָת שָׁם בִּשְׁנַת הָאַרְבָּעִים לְצֵאת בְּנֵי־יִשְׂרָאֵל מֵאֶרֶץ מִצְרַיִם
בַּחֹדֶשׁ הַחֲמִישִׁי בְּאֶחָד לַחֹדֶשׁ׃ וְאַהֲרֹן בֶּן־שָׁלֹשׁ וְעֶשְׂרִים וּמְאַת שָׁנָה בְּמֹתוֹ
בְּהֹר הָהָר׃ וַיִּשְׁמַע הַכְּנַעֲנִי מֶלֶךְ עֲרָד וְהוּא־יֹשֵׁב בַּנֶּגֶב בְּאֶרֶץ
כְּנָעַן בְּבֹא בְּנֵי יִשְׂרָאֵל׃ וַיִּסְעוּ מֵהֹר הָהָר וַיַּחֲנוּ בְּצַלְמֹנָה׃ וַיִּסְעוּ מִצַּלְמֹנָה
וַיַּחֲנוּ בְּפוּנֹן׃ וַיִּסְעוּ מִפּוּנֹן וַיַּחֲנוּ בְּאֹבֹת׃ וַיִּסְעוּ מֵאֹבֹת וַיַּחֲנוּ בְּעִיֵּי הָעֲבָרִים
בִּגְבוּל מוֹאָב׃ וַיִּסְעוּ מֵעִיִּים וַיַּחֲנוּ בְּדִיבֹן גָּד׃ וַיִּסְעוּ מִדִּיבֹן גָּד וַיַּחֲנוּ בְּעַלְמֹן
דִּבְלָתָיְמָה׃ וַיִּסְעוּ מֵעַלְמֹן דִּבְלָתָיְמָה וַיַּחֲנוּ בְּהָרֵי הָעֲבָרִים לִפְנֵי נְבוֹ׃ וַיִּסְעוּ
מֵהָרֵי הָעֲבָרִים וַיַּחֲנוּ בְּעַרְבֹת מוֹאָב עַל יַרְדֵּן יְרֵחוֹ׃ וַיַּחֲנוּ עַל־הַיַּרְדֵּן מִבֵּית
הַיְשִׁמֹת עַד אָבֵל הַשִּׁטִּים בְּעַרְבֹת מוֹאָב׃ *וַיְדַבֵּר יְהוָה אֶל־ ישראל
מֹשֶׁה בְּעַרְבֹת מוֹאָב עַל־יַרְדֵּן יְרֵחוֹ לֵאמֹר׃ דַּבֵּר אֶל־בְּנֵי יִשְׂרָאֵל וְאָמַרְתָּ
אֲלֵהֶם כִּי אַתֶּם עֹבְרִים אֶת־הַיַּרְדֵּן אֶל־אֶרֶץ כְּנָעַן׃ וְהוֹרַשְׁתֶּם אֶת־כָּל־יֹשְׁבֵי
הָאָרֶץ מִפְּנֵיכֶם וְאִבַּדְתֶּם אֵת כָּל־מַשְׂכִּיֹּתָם וְאֵת כָּל־צַלְמֵי מַסֵּכֹתָם תְּאַבֵּדוּ
וְאֵת כָּל־בָּמוֹתָם תַּשְׁמִידוּ׃ וְהוֹרַשְׁתֶּם אֶת־הָאָרֶץ וִישַׁבְתֶּם־בָּהּ כִּי לָכֶם נָתַתִּי
אֶת־הָאָרֶץ לָרֶשֶׁת אֹתָהּ׃

## DEVARIM דברים

דברים א:א–יא אֵ֣לֶּה הַדְּבָרִ֗ים אֲשֶׁ֨ר דִּבֶּ֤ר מֹשֶׁה֙ אֶל־כָּל־יִשְׂרָאֵ֔ל בְּעֵ֖בֶר הַיַּרְדֵּ֑ן בַּמִּדְבָּ֡ר בָּֽעֲרָבָה֩
מ֨וֹל ס֜וּף בֵּֽין־פָּארָ֧ן וּבֵֽין־תֹּ֛פֶל וְלָבָ֥ן וַחֲצֵרֹ֖ת וְדִ֥י זָהָֽב׃ אַחַ֨ד עָשָׂ֥ר יוֹם֙ מֵֽחֹרֵ֔ב
דֶּ֖רֶךְ הַר־שֵׂעִ֑יר עַ֖ד קָדֵ֥שׁ בַּרְנֵֽעַ׃ וַיְהִי֙ בְּאַרְבָּעִ֣ים שָׁנָ֔ה בְּעַשְׁתֵּֽי־עָשָׂ֥ר חֹ֖דֶשׁ
בְּאֶחָ֣ד לַחֹ֑דֶשׁ דִּבֶּ֤ר מֹשֶׁה֙ אֶל־בְּנֵ֣י יִשְׂרָאֵ֔ל כְּ֠כֹל אֲשֶׁ֨ר צִוָּ֧ה יְהוָ֛ה אֹת֖וֹ אֲלֵהֶֽם׃
לוי *אַחֲרֵ֣י הַכֹּת֗וֹ אֵ֚ת סִיחֹן֙ מֶ֣לֶךְ הָֽאֱמֹרִ֔י אֲשֶׁ֥ר יוֹשֵׁ֖ב בְּחֶשְׁבּ֑וֹן וְאֵ֗ת ע֚וֹג מֶ֣לֶךְ
הַבָּשָׁ֔ן אֲשֶׁר־יוֹשֵׁ֥ב בְּעַשְׁתָּרֹ֖ת בְּאֶדְרֶֽעִי׃ בְּעֵ֥בֶר הַיַּרְדֵּ֖ן בְּאֶ֣רֶץ מוֹאָ֑ב הוֹאִ֣יל
מֹשֶׁ֔ה בֵּאֵ֛ר אֶת־הַתּוֹרָ֥ה הַזֹּ֖את לֵאמֹֽר׃ יְהוָ֧ה אֱלֹהֵ֛ינוּ דִּבֶּ֥ר אֵלֵ֖ינוּ בְּחֹרֵ֣ב לֵאמֹ֑ר
רַב־לָכֶ֥ם שֶׁ֖בֶת בָּהָ֥ר הַזֶּֽה׃ פְּנ֣וּ ׀ וּסְע֣וּ לָכֶ֗ם וּבֹ֨אוּ הַ֥ר הָֽאֱמֹרִי֮ וְאֶל־כָּל־שְׁכֵנָיו֒
בָּעֲרָבָ֥ה בָהָ֛ר וּבַשְּׁפֵלָ֥ה וּבַנֶּ֖גֶב וּבְח֣וֹף הַיָּ֑ם אֶ֤רֶץ הַֽכְּנַעֲנִי֙ וְהַלְּבָנ֔וֹן עַד־הַנָּהָ֥ר
ישראל הַגָּדֹ֖ל נְהַר־פְּרָֽת׃ *רְאֵ֛ה נָתַ֥תִּי לִפְנֵיכֶ֖ם אֶת־הָאָ֑רֶץ בֹּ֚אוּ וּרְשׁ֣וּ אֶת־הָאָ֔רֶץ
אֲשֶׁ֣ר נִשְׁבַּ֣ע יְהוָ֡ה לַאֲבֹתֵיכֶם֩ לְאַבְרָהָ֨ם לְיִצְחָ֤ק וּֽלְיַעֲקֹב֙ לָתֵ֣ת לָהֶ֔ם וּלְזַרְעָ֖ם
אַחֲרֵיהֶֽם׃ וָאֹמַ֣ר אֲלֵכֶ֔ם בָּעֵ֥ת הַהִ֖וא לֵאמֹ֑ר לֹא־אוּכַ֥ל לְבַדִּ֖י שְׂאֵ֥ת אֶתְכֶֽם׃
יְהוָ֥ה אֱלֹהֵיכֶ֖ם הִרְבָּ֣ה אֶתְכֶ֑ם וְהִנְּכֶ֣ם הַיּ֔וֹם כְּכוֹכְבֵ֥י הַשָּׁמַ֖יִם לָרֹֽב׃ יְהוָ֞ה אֱלֹהֵ֣י
אֲבוֹתֵכֶ֗ם יֹסֵ֧ף עֲלֵיכֶ֛ם כָּכֶ֖ם אֶ֣לֶף פְּעָמִ֑ים וִיבָרֵ֣ךְ אֶתְכֶ֔ם כַּאֲשֶׁ֖ר דִּבֶּ֥ר לָכֶֽם׃

## VA'ET-ḤANAN ואתחנן

דברים ג:כג–ד:ח וָאֶתְחַנַּ֖ן אֶל־יְהוָ֑ה בָּעֵ֥ת הַהִ֖וא לֵאמֹֽר׃ אֲדֹנָ֣י יְהוִ֗ה אַתָּ֤ה הַֽחִלּ֙וֹתָ֙ לְהַרְא֣וֹת
אֶֽת־עַבְדְּךָ֔ אֶ֨ת־גָּדְלְךָ֔ וְאֶת־יָדְךָ֖ הַחֲזָקָ֑ה אֲשֶׁ֤ר מִי־אֵל֙ בַּשָּׁמַ֣יִם וּבָאָ֔רֶץ אֲשֶׁר־
יַעֲשֶׂ֥ה כְמַעֲשֶׂ֖יךָ וְכִגְבוּרֹתֶֽךָ׃ אֶעְבְּרָה־נָּ֗א וְאֶרְאֶה֙ אֶת־הָאָ֣רֶץ הַטּוֹבָ֔ה אֲשֶׁ֖ר
לוי בְּעֵ֣בֶר הַיַּרְדֵּ֑ן הָהָ֥ר הַטּ֛וֹב הַזֶּ֖ה וְהַלְּבָנֹֽן׃ *וַיִּתְעַבֵּ֨ר יְהוָ֥ה בִּי֙ לְמַ֣עַנְכֶ֔ם וְלֹ֥א
שָׁמַ֖ע אֵלָ֑י וַיֹּ֨אמֶר יְהוָ֤ה אֵלַי֙ רַב־לָ֔ךְ אַל־תּ֗וֹסֶף דַּבֵּ֥ר אֵלַ֛י ע֖וֹד בַּדָּבָ֥ר הַזֶּֽה׃
עֲלֵ֣ה ׀ רֹ֣אשׁ הַפִּסְגָּ֗ה וְשָׂ֥א עֵינֶ֛יךָ יָ֧מָּה וְצָפֹ֛נָה וְתֵימָ֥נָה וּמִזְרָ֖חָה וּרְאֵ֣ה בְעֵינֶ֑יךָ
כִּי־לֹ֥א תַעֲבֹ֖ר אֶת־הַיַּרְדֵּ֥ן הַזֶּֽה׃ וְצַ֥ו אֶת־יְהוֹשֻׁ֖עַ וְחַזְּקֵ֣הוּ וְאַמְּצֵ֑הוּ כִּי־ה֣וּא
יַעֲבֹ֗ר לִפְנֵי֙ הָעָ֣ם הַזֶּ֔ה וְה֗וּא יַנְחִ֣יל אוֹתָ֔ם אֶת־הָאָ֖רֶץ אֲשֶׁ֥ר תִּרְאֶֽה׃ וַנֵּ֣שֶׁב
בַּגָּ֔יְא מ֖וּל בֵּ֥ית פְּעֽוֹר׃

וְעַתָּ֣ה יִשְׂרָאֵ֗ל שְׁמַ֤ע אֶל־הַֽחֻקִּים֙ וְאֶל־הַמִּשְׁפָּטִ֔ים אֲשֶׁ֧ר אָנֹכִ֛י מְלַמֵּ֥ד אֶתְכֶ֖ם
לַעֲשׂ֑וֹת לְמַ֣עַן תִּֽחְי֗וּ וּבָאתֶם֙ וִֽירִשְׁתֶּ֣ם אֶת־הָאָ֔רֶץ אֲשֶׁ֧ר יְהוָ֛ה אֱלֹהֵ֥י אֲבֹתֵיכֶ֖ם

נֹתֵן לָכֶם: לֹא תֹסִפוּ עַל־הַדָּבָר אֲשֶׁר אָנֹכִי מְצַוֶּה אֶתְכֶם וְלֹא תִגְרְעוּ מִמֶּנּוּ
לִשְׁמֹר אֶת־מִצְוֹת יהוה אֱלֹהֵיכֶם אֲשֶׁר אָנֹכִי מְצַוֶּה אֶתְכֶם: עֵינֵיכֶם הָרֹאֹת
אֵת אֲשֶׁר־עָשָׂה יהוה בְּבַעַל פְּעוֹר כִּי כָל־הָאִישׁ אֲשֶׁר הָלַךְ אַחֲרֵי בַעַל־
פְּעוֹר הִשְׁמִידוֹ יהוה אֱלֹהֶיךָ מִקִּרְבֶּךָ: וְאַתֶּם הַדְּבֵקִים בַּיהוה אֱלֹהֵיכֶם חַיִּים
כֻּלְּכֶם הַיּוֹם: *רְאֵה ׀ לִמַּדְתִּי אֶתְכֶם חֻקִּים וּמִשְׁפָּטִים כַּאֲשֶׁר צִוַּנִי יהוה ישראל
אֱלֹהָי לַעֲשׂוֹת כֵּן בְּקֶרֶב הָאָרֶץ אֲשֶׁר אַתֶּם בָּאִים שָׁמָּה לְרִשְׁתָּהּ: וּשְׁמַרְתֶּם
וַעֲשִׂיתֶם כִּי הִוא חָכְמַתְכֶם וּבִינַתְכֶם לְעֵינֵי הָעַמִּים אֲשֶׁר יִשְׁמְעוּן אֵת כָּל־
הַחֻקִּים הָאֵלֶּה וְאָמְרוּ רַק עַם־חָכָם וְנָבוֹן הַגּוֹי הַגָּדוֹל הַזֶּה: כִּי מִי־גוֹי גָּדוֹל
אֲשֶׁר־לוֹ אֱלֹהִים קְרֹבִים אֵלָיו כַּיהוה אֱלֹהֵינוּ בְּכָל־קָרְאֵנוּ אֵלָיו: וּמִי גּוֹי גָּדוֹל
אֲשֶׁר־לוֹ חֻקִּים וּמִשְׁפָּטִים צַדִּיקִם כְּכֹל הַתּוֹרָה הַזֹּאת אֲשֶׁר אָנֹכִי נֹתֵן לִפְנֵיכֶם
הַיּוֹם:

## EKEV

## עקב

וְהָיָה ׀ עֵקֶב תִּשְׁמְעוּן אֵת הַמִּשְׁפָּטִים הָאֵלֶּה וּשְׁמַרְתֶּם וַעֲשִׂיתֶם אֹתָם וְשָׁמַר דברים ז:יב–ח:י
יהוה אֱלֹהֶיךָ לְךָ אֶת־הַבְּרִית וְאֶת־הַחֶסֶד אֲשֶׁר נִשְׁבַּע לַאֲבֹתֶיךָ: וַאֲהֵבְךָ
וּבֵרַכְךָ וְהִרְבֶּךָ וּבֵרַךְ פְּרִי־בִטְנְךָ וּפְרִי־אַדְמָתֶךָ דְּגָנְךָ וְתִירֹשְׁךָ וְיִצְהָרֶךָ שְׁגַר־
אֲלָפֶיךָ וְעַשְׁתְּרֹת צֹאנֶךָ עַל הָאֲדָמָה אֲשֶׁר־נִשְׁבַּע לַאֲבֹתֶיךָ לָתֶת לָךְ: בָּרוּךְ
תִּהְיֶה מִכָּל־הָעַמִּים לֹא־יִהְיֶה בְךָ עָקָר וַעֲקָרָה וּבִבְהֶמְתֶּךָ: וְהֵסִיר יהוה
מִמְּךָ כָּל־חֹלִי וְכָל־מַדְוֵי מִצְרַיִם הָרָעִים אֲשֶׁר יָדַעְתָּ לֹא יְשִׂימָם בָּךְ וּנְתָנָם
בְּכָל־שֹׂנְאֶיךָ: וְאָכַלְתָּ אֶת־כָּל־הָעַמִּים אֲשֶׁר יהוה אֱלֹהֶיךָ נֹתֵן לָךְ לֹא־תָחֹס
עֵינְךָ עֲלֵיהֶם וְלֹא תַעֲבֹד אֶת־אֱלֹהֵיהֶם כִּי־מוֹקֵשׁ הוּא לָךְ: כִּי
תֹאמַר בִּלְבָבְךָ רַבִּים הַגּוֹיִם הָאֵלֶּה מִמֶּנִּי אֵיכָה אוּכַל לְהוֹרִישָׁם: לֹא תִירָא
מֵהֶם זָכֹר תִּזְכֹּר אֵת אֲשֶׁר־עָשָׂה יהוה אֱלֹהֶיךָ לְפַרְעֹה וּלְכָל־מִצְרָיִם: הַמַּסֹּת
הַגְּדֹלֹת אֲשֶׁר־רָאוּ עֵינֶיךָ וְהָאֹתֹת וְהַמֹּפְתִים וְהַיָּד הַחֲזָקָה וְהַזְּרֹעַ הַנְּטוּיָה
אֲשֶׁר הוֹצִאֲךָ יהוה אֱלֹהֶיךָ כֵּן־יַעֲשֶׂה יהוה אֱלֹהֶיךָ לְכָל־הָעַמִּים אֲשֶׁר־אַתָּה
יָרֵא מִפְּנֵיהֶם: וְגַם אֶת־הַצִּרְעָה יְשַׁלַּח יהוה אֱלֹהֶיךָ בָּם עַד־אֲבֹד הַנִּשְׁאָרִים
וְהַנִּסְתָּרִים מִפָּנֶיךָ: לֹא תַעֲרֹץ מִפְּנֵיהֶם כִּי־יהוה אֱלֹהֶיךָ בְּקִרְבֶּךָ אֵל גָּדוֹל
וְנוֹרָא: *וְנָשַׁל יהוה אֱלֹהֶיךָ אֶת־הַגּוֹיִם הָאֵל מִפָּנֶיךָ מְעַט מְעָט לֹא תוּכַל לוי
כַּלֹּתָם מַהֵר פֶּן־תִּרְבֶּה עָלֶיךָ חַיַּת הַשָּׂדֶה: וּנְתָנָם יהוה אֱלֹהֶיךָ לְפָנֶיךָ וְהָמָם

מְהוּמָה גְדֹלָה עַד הִשָּׁמְדָם׃ וְנָתַן מַלְכֵיהֶם בְּיָדֶךָ וְהַאֲבַדְתָּ אֶת־שְׁמָם מִתַּחַת
הַשָּׁמָיִם לֹא־יִתְיַצֵּב אִישׁ בְּפָנֶיךָ עַד הִשְׁמִדְךָ אֹתָם׃ פְּסִילֵי אֱלֹהֵיהֶם תִּשְׂרְפוּן
בָּאֵשׁ לֹא־תַחְמֹד כֶּסֶף וְזָהָב עֲלֵיהֶם וְלָקַחְתָּ לָךְ פֶּן תִּוָּקֵשׁ בּוֹ כִּי תוֹעֲבַת
יְהוָה אֱלֹהֶיךָ הוּא׃ וְלֹא־תָבִיא תוֹעֵבָה אֶל־בֵּיתֶךָ וְהָיִיתָ חֵרֶם כָּמֹהוּ שַׁקֵּץ ׀
תְּשַׁקְּצֶנּוּ וְתַעֵב ׀ תְּתַעֲבֶנּוּ כִּי־חֵרֶם הוּא׃
כָּל־הַמִּצְוָה אֲשֶׁר אָנֹכִי מְצַוְּךָ הַיּוֹם תִּשְׁמְרוּן לַעֲשׂוֹת לְמַעַן תִּחְיוּן וּרְבִיתֶם
וּבָאתֶם וִירִשְׁתֶּם אֶת־הָאָרֶץ אֲשֶׁר־נִשְׁבַּע יְהוָה לַאֲבֹתֵיכֶם׃ וְזָכַרְתָּ אֶת־כָּל־
הַדֶּרֶךְ אֲשֶׁר הוֹלִיכְךָ יְהוָה אֱלֹהֶיךָ זֶה אַרְבָּעִים שָׁנָה בַּמִּדְבָּר לְמַעַן עַנֹּתְךָ
לְנַסֹּתְךָ לָדַעַת אֶת־אֲשֶׁר בִּלְבָבְךָ הֲתִשְׁמֹר מִצְוֹתָו אִם־לֹא׃ וַיְעַנְּךָ וַיַּרְעִבֶךָ
וַיַּאֲכִלְךָ אֶת־הַמָּן אֲשֶׁר לֹא־יָדַעְתָּ וְלֹא יָדְעוּן אֲבֹתֶיךָ לְמַעַן הוֹדִיעֲךָ כִּי
לֹא עַל־הַלֶּחֶם לְבַדּוֹ יִחְיֶה הָאָדָם כִּי עַל־כָּל־מוֹצָא פִי־יְהוָה יִחְיֶה הָאָדָם׃
*שִׂמְלָתְךָ לֹא בָלְתָה מֵעָלֶיךָ וְרַגְלְךָ לֹא בָצֵקָה זֶה אַרְבָּעִים שָׁנָה׃ וְיָדַעְתָּ עִם־ ישראל
לְבָבֶךָ כִּי כַּאֲשֶׁר יְיַסֵּר אִישׁ אֶת־בְּנוֹ יְהוָה אֱלֹהֶיךָ מְיַסְּרֶךָּ׃ וְשָׁמַרְתָּ אֶת־מִצְוֹת
יְהוָה אֱלֹהֶיךָ לָלֶכֶת בִּדְרָכָיו וּלְיִרְאָה אֹתוֹ׃ כִּי יְהוָה אֱלֹהֶיךָ מְבִיאֲךָ אֶל־אֶרֶץ
טוֹבָה אֶרֶץ נַחֲלֵי מָיִם עֲיָנֹת וּתְהֹמֹת יֹצְאִים בַּבִּקְעָה וּבָהָר׃ אֶרֶץ חִטָּה
וּשְׂעֹרָה וְגֶפֶן וּתְאֵנָה וְרִמּוֹן אֶרֶץ־זֵית שֶׁמֶן וּדְבָשׁ׃ אֶרֶץ אֲשֶׁר לֹא בְמִסְכֵּנֻת
תֹּאכַל־בָּהּ לֶחֶם לֹא־תֶחְסַר כֹּל בָּהּ אֶרֶץ אֲשֶׁר אֲבָנֶיהָ בַרְזֶל וּמֵהֲרָרֶיהָ תַּחְצֹב
נְחֹשֶׁת׃ וְאָכַלְתָּ וְשָׂבָעְתָּ וּבֵרַכְתָּ אֶת־יְהוָה אֱלֹהֶיךָ עַל־הָאָרֶץ הַטֹּבָה אֲשֶׁר
נָתַן־לָךְ׃

## ראה RE'EH

רְאֵה אָנֹכִי נֹתֵן לִפְנֵיכֶם הַיּוֹם בְּרָכָה וּקְלָלָה׃ אֶת־הַבְּרָכָה אֲשֶׁר תִּשְׁמְעוּ אֶל־ דברים יא:כו–יב:י
מִצְוֹת יְהוָה אֱלֹהֵיכֶם אֲשֶׁר אָנֹכִי מְצַוֶּה אֶתְכֶם הַיּוֹם׃ וְהַקְּלָלָה אִם־לֹא תִשְׁמְעוּ
אֶל־מִצְוֹת יְהוָה אֱלֹהֵיכֶם וְסַרְתֶּם מִן־הַדֶּרֶךְ אֲשֶׁר אָנֹכִי מְצַוֶּה אֶתְכֶם הַיּוֹם
לָלֶכֶת אַחֲרֵי אֱלֹהִים אֲחֵרִים אֲשֶׁר לֹא־יְדַעְתֶּם׃ וְהָיָה כִּי יְבִיאֲךָ
יְהוָה אֱלֹהֶיךָ אֶל־הָאָרֶץ אֲשֶׁר־אַתָּה בָא־שָׁמָּה לְרִשְׁתָּהּ וְנָתַתָּה אֶת־הַבְּרָכָה
עַל־הַר גְּרִזִים וְאֶת־הַקְּלָלָה עַל־הַר עֵיבָל׃ הֲלֹא־הֵמָּה בְּעֵבֶר הַיַּרְדֵּן אַחֲרֵי
דֶּרֶךְ מְבוֹא הַשֶּׁמֶשׁ בְּאֶרֶץ הַכְּנַעֲנִי הַיֹּשֵׁב בָּעֲרָבָה מוּל הַגִּלְגָּל אֵצֶל אֵלוֹנֵי מֹרֶה׃
כִּי אַתֶּם עֹבְרִים אֶת־הַיַּרְדֵּן לָבֹא לָרֶשֶׁת אֶת־הָאָרֶץ אֲשֶׁר־יְהוָה אֱלֹהֵיכֶם

לוי נֹתֵן לָכֶם וִירִשְׁתֶּם אֹתָהּ וִישַׁבְתֶּם־בָּהּ׃ *וּשְׁמַרְתֶּם לַעֲשׂוֹת אֵת כָּל־הַחֻקִּים
וְאֶת־הַמִּשְׁפָּטִים אֲשֶׁר אָנֹכִי נֹתֵן לִפְנֵיכֶם הַיּוֹם׃ אֵלֶּה הַחֻקִּים וְהַמִּשְׁפָּטִים
אֲשֶׁר תִּשְׁמְרוּן לַעֲשׂוֹת בָּאָרֶץ אֲשֶׁר נָתַן יהוה אֱלֹהֵי אֲבֹתֶיךָ לְךָ לְרִשְׁתָּהּ
כָּל־הַיָּמִים אֲשֶׁר־אַתֶּם חַיִּים עַל־הָאֲדָמָה׃ אַבֵּד תְּאַבְּדוּן אֶת־כָּל־הַמְּקֹמוֹת
אֲשֶׁר עָבְדוּ־שָׁם הַגּוֹיִם אֲשֶׁר אַתֶּם יֹרְשִׁים אֹתָם אֶת־אֱלֹהֵיהֶם עַל־הֶהָרִים
הָרָמִים וְעַל־הַגְּבָעוֹת וְתַחַת כָּל־עֵץ רַעֲנָן׃ וְנִתַּצְתֶּם אֶת־מִזְבְּחֹתָם וְשִׁבַּרְתֶּם
אֶת־מַצֵּבֹתָם וַאֲשֵׁרֵיהֶם תִּשְׂרְפוּן בָּאֵשׁ וּפְסִילֵי אֱלֹהֵיהֶם תְּגַדֵּעוּן וְאִבַּדְתֶּם
אֶת־שְׁמָם מִן־הַמָּקוֹם הַהוּא׃ לֹא־תַעֲשׂוּן כֵּן לַיהוה אֱלֹהֵיכֶם׃ כִּי אִם־אֶל־
הַמָּקוֹם אֲשֶׁר־יִבְחַר יהוה אֱלֹהֵיכֶם מִכָּל־שִׁבְטֵיכֶם לָשׂוּם אֶת־שְׁמוֹ שָׁם
ישראל לְשִׁכְנוֹ תִדְרְשׁוּ וּבָאתָ שָׁמָּה׃ *וַהֲבֵאתֶם שָׁמָּה עֹלֹתֵיכֶם וְזִבְחֵיכֶם וְאֵת
מַעְשְׂרֹתֵיכֶם וְאֵת תְּרוּמַת יֶדְכֶם וְנִדְרֵיכֶם וְנִדְבֹתֵיכֶם וּבְכֹרֹת בְּקַרְכֶם וְצֹאנְכֶם׃
וַאֲכַלְתֶּם־שָׁם לִפְנֵי יהוה אֱלֹהֵיכֶם וּשְׂמַחְתֶּם בְּכֹל מִשְׁלַח יֶדְכֶם אַתֶּם וּבָתֵּיכֶם
אֲשֶׁר בֵּרַכְךָ יהוה אֱלֹהֶיךָ׃ לֹא תַעֲשׂוּן כְּכֹל אֲשֶׁר אֲנַחְנוּ עֹשִׂים פֹּה הַיּוֹם
אִישׁ כָּל־הַיָּשָׁר בְּעֵינָיו׃ כִּי לֹא־בָאתֶם עַד־עָתָּה אֶל־הַמְּנוּחָה וְאֶל־הַנַּחֲלָה
אֲשֶׁר־יהוה אֱלֹהֶיךָ נֹתֵן לָךְ׃ וַעֲבַרְתֶּם אֶת־הַיַּרְדֵּן וִישַׁבְתֶּם בָּאָרֶץ אֲשֶׁר־
יהוה אֱלֹהֵיכֶם מַנְחִיל אֶתְכֶם וְהֵנִיחַ לָכֶם מִכָּל־אֹיְבֵיכֶם מִסָּבִיב וִישַׁבְתֶּם־
בֶּטַח׃

## שופטים SHOFETIM

דברים טז:יח–יז:יג שֹׁפְטִים וְשֹׁטְרִים תִּתֶּן־לְךָ בְּכָל־שְׁעָרֶיךָ אֲשֶׁר יהוה אֱלֹהֶיךָ נֹתֵן לְךָ לִשְׁבָטֶיךָ
וְשָׁפְטוּ אֶת־הָעָם מִשְׁפַּט־צֶדֶק׃ לֹא־תַטֶּה מִשְׁפָּט לֹא תַכִּיר פָּנִים וְלֹא־תִקַּח
שֹׁחַד כִּי הַשֹּׁחַד יְעַוֵּר עֵינֵי חֲכָמִים וִיסַלֵּף דִּבְרֵי צַדִּיקִם׃ צֶדֶק צֶדֶק תִּרְדֹּף לְמַעַן
לוי תִּחְיֶה וְיָרַשְׁתָּ אֶת־הָאָרֶץ אֲשֶׁר־יהוה אֱלֹהֶיךָ נֹתֵן לָךְ׃ *לֹא־
תִטַּע לְךָ אֲשֵׁרָה כָּל־עֵץ אֵצֶל מִזְבַּח יהוה אֱלֹהֶיךָ אֲשֶׁר תַּעֲשֶׂה־לָּךְ׃ וְלֹא־
תָקִים לְךָ מַצֵּבָה אֲשֶׁר שָׂנֵא יהוה אֱלֹהֶיךָ׃ לֹא־תִזְבַּח לַיהוה
אֱלֹהֶיךָ שׁוֹר וָשֶׂה אֲשֶׁר יִהְיֶה בוֹ מוּם כֹּל דָּבָר רָע כִּי תוֹעֲבַת יהוה אֱלֹהֶיךָ
הוּא׃ כִּי־יִמָּצֵא בְקִרְבְּךָ בְּאַחַד שְׁעָרֶיךָ אֲשֶׁר־יהוה אֱלֹהֶיךָ נֹתֵן
לָךְ אִישׁ אוֹ־אִשָּׁה אֲשֶׁר יַעֲשֶׂה אֶת־הָרַע בְּעֵינֵי יהוה־אֱלֹהֶיךָ לַעֲבֹר בְּרִיתוֹ׃
וַיֵּלֶךְ וַיַּעֲבֹד אֱלֹהִים אֲחֵרִים וַיִּשְׁתַּחוּ לָהֶם וְלַשֶּׁמֶשׁ ׀ אוֹ לַיָּרֵחַ אוֹ לְכָל־צְבָא

הַשָּׁמַ֖יִם אֲשֶׁ֥ר לֹא־צִוִּֽיתִי׃ וְהֻגַּד־לְךָ֖ וְשָׁמָ֑עְתָּ וְדָרַשְׁתָּ֣ הֵיטֵ֔ב וְהִנֵּ֤ה אֱמֶת֙ נָכ֣וֹן
הַדָּבָ֔ר נֶעֶשְׂתָ֛ה הַתּוֹעֵבָ֥ה הַזֹּ֖את בְּיִשְׂרָאֵֽל׃ וְהוֹצֵאתָ֣ אֶת־הָאִ֣ישׁ הַה֡וּא א֣וֹ
אֶת־הָאִשָּׁ֣ה הַהִ֡וא אֲשֶׁ֣ר עָשׂוּ֩ אֶת־הַדָּבָ֨ר הָרָ֤ע הַזֶּה֙ אֶל־שְׁעָרֶ֔יךָ אֶת־הָאִ֕ישׁ
א֖וֹ אֶת־הָֽאִשָּׁ֑ה וּסְקַלְתָּ֥ם בָּאֲבָנִ֖ים וָמֵֽתוּ׃ עַל־פִּ֣י ׀ שְׁנַ֣יִם עֵדִ֗ים א֛וֹ שְׁלֹשָׁ֥ה
עֵדִ֖ים יוּמַ֣ת הַמֵּ֑ת לֹ֣א יוּמַ֔ת עַל־פִּ֖י עֵ֥ד אֶחָֽד׃ יַ֣ד הָעֵדִ֞ים תִּֽהְיֶה־בּ֤וֹ בָרִאשֹׁנָה֙
לַהֲמִית֔וֹ וְיַ֥ד כָּל־הָעָ֖ם בָּאַחֲרֹנָ֑ה וּבִעַרְתָּ֥ הָרָ֖ע מִקִּרְבֶּֽךָ׃
כִּ֣י יִפָּלֵא֩ מִמְּךָ֨ דָבָ֜ר לַמִּשְׁפָּ֗ט בֵּֽין־דָּ֨ם ׀ לְדָ֜ם בֵּֽין־דִּ֣ין לְדִ֗ין וּבֵ֥ין נֶ֨גַע֙ לָנֶ֔גַע דִּבְרֵ֥י
רִיבֹ֖ת בִּשְׁעָרֶ֑יךָ וְקַמְתָּ֣ וְעָלִ֔יתָ אֶ֨ל־הַמָּק֔וֹם אֲשֶׁ֥ר יִבְחַ֛ר יְהוָ֥ה אֱלֹהֶ֖יךָ בּֽוֹ׃ וּבָאתָ֗
אֶל־הַכֹּהֲנִים֙ הַלְוִיִּ֔ם וְאֶ֨ל־הַשֹּׁפֵ֔ט אֲשֶׁ֥ר יִהְיֶ֖ה בַּיָּמִ֣ים הָהֵ֑ם וְדָרַשְׁתָּ֙ וְהִגִּ֣ידוּ לְךָ֔
אֵ֖ת דְּבַ֥ר הַמִּשְׁפָּֽט׃ וְעָשִׂ֗יתָ עַל־פִּ֤י הַדָּבָר֙ אֲשֶׁ֣ר יַגִּ֣ידֽוּ לְךָ֔ מִן־הַמָּק֣וֹם הַה֔וּא
אֲשֶׁ֖ר יִבְחַ֣ר יְהוָ֑ה וְשָׁמַרְתָּ֣ לַעֲשׂ֔וֹת כְּכֹ֖ל אֲשֶׁ֥ר יוֹרֽוּךָ׃ *עַל־פִּ֨י הַתּוֹרָ֜ה אֲשֶׁ֣ר ישראל
יוֹר֗וּךָ וְעַל־הַמִּשְׁפָּ֛ט אֲשֶׁר־יֹאמְר֥וּ לְךָ֖ תַּעֲשֶׂ֑ה לֹ֣א תָס֗וּר מִן־הַדָּבָ֛ר אֲשֶׁר־יַגִּ֥ידוּ
לְךָ֖ יָמִ֥ין וּשְׂמֹֽאל׃ וְהָאִ֞ישׁ אֲשֶׁר־יַעֲשֶׂ֣ה בְזָד֗וֹן לְבִלְתִּ֨י שְׁמֹ֤עַ אֶל־הַכֹּהֵן֙ הָעֹמֵ֞ד
לְשָׁ֤רֶת שָׁם֙ אֶת־יְהוָ֣ה אֱלֹהֶ֔יךָ א֖וֹ אֶל־הַשֹּׁפֵ֑ט וּמֵת֙ הָאִ֣ישׁ הַה֔וּא וּבִעַרְתָּ֥ הָרָ֖ע
מִיִּשְׂרָאֵֽל׃ וְכָל־הָעָ֖ם יִשְׁמְע֣וּ וְיִרָ֑אוּ וְלֹ֥א יְזִיד֖וּן עֽוֹד׃

## כי תצא
## KI TETZE

כִּֽי־תֵצֵ֥א לַמִּלְחָמָ֖ה עַל־אֹיְבֶ֑יךָ וּנְתָנ֞וֹ יְהוָ֧ה אֱלֹהֶ֛יךָ בְּיָדֶ֖ךָ וְשָׁבִ֥יתָ שִׁבְיֽוֹ׃ וְרָאִ֨יתָ֙ דברים כא:י-כא
בַּשִּׁבְיָ֔ה אֵ֖שֶׁת יְפַת־תֹּ֑אַר וְחָשַׁקְתָּ֣ בָ֔הּ וְלָקַחְתָּ֥ לְךָ֖ לְאִשָּֽׁה׃ וַהֲבֵאתָ֖הּ אֶל־
תּ֣וֹךְ בֵּיתֶ֑ךָ וְגִלְּחָה֙ אֶת־רֹאשָׁ֔הּ וְעָשְׂתָ֖ה אֶת־צִפָּרְנֶֽיהָ׃ וְהֵסִ֩ירָה֩ אֶת־שִׂמְלַ֨ת
שִׁבְיָ֜הּ מֵעָלֶ֗יהָ וְיָֽשְׁבָה֙ בְּבֵיתֶ֔ךָ וּבָֽכְתָ֛ה אֶת־אָבִ֥יהָ וְאֶת־אִמָּ֖הּ יֶ֣רַח יָמִ֑ים
וְאַ֨חַר כֵּ֜ן תָּב֤וֹא אֵלֶ֨יהָ֙ וּבְעַלְתָּ֔הּ וְהָיְתָ֥ה לְךָ֖ לְאִשָּֽׁה׃ וְהָיָ֞ה אִם־לֹ֧א חָפַ֣צְתָּ בָּ֗הּ
וְשִׁלַּחְתָּהּ֙ לְנַפְשָׁ֔הּ וּמָכֹ֥ר לֹא־תִמְכְּרֶ֖נָּה בַּכָּ֑סֶף לֹא־תִתְעַמֵּ֣ר בָּ֔הּ תַּ֖חַת אֲשֶׁ֥ר
עִנִּיתָֽהּ׃ *כִּֽי־תִהְיֶ֨יןָ לְאִ֜ישׁ שְׁתֵּ֣י נָשִׁ֗ים הָאַחַ֤ת אֲהוּבָה֙ וְהָאַחַ֣ת לוי
שְׂנוּאָ֔ה וְיָֽלְדוּ־ל֣וֹ בָנִ֔ים הָאֲהוּבָ֖ה וְהַשְּׂנוּאָ֑ה וְהָיָ֛ה הַבֵּ֥ן הַבְּכֹ֖ר לַשְּׂנִיאָֽה׃ וְהָיָ֗ה
בְּיוֹם֙ הַנְחִיל֣וֹ אֶת־בָּנָ֔יו אֵ֥ת אֲשֶׁר־יִהְיֶ֖ה ל֑וֹ לֹ֣א יוּכַ֗ל לְבַכֵּר֙ אֶת־בֶּן־הָ֣אֲהוּבָ֔ה
עַל־פְּנֵ֥י בֶן־הַשְּׂנוּאָ֖ה הַבְּכֹֽר׃ כִּי֩ אֶת־הַבְּכֹ֨ר בֶּן־הַשְּׂנוּאָ֜ה יַכִּ֗יר לָ֤תֶת לוֹ֙ פִּ֣י שְׁנַ֔יִם
בְּכֹ֖ל אֲשֶׁר־יִמָּצֵ֣א ל֑וֹ כִּי־הוּא֙ רֵאשִׁ֣ית אֹנ֔וֹ ל֖וֹ מִשְׁפַּ֥ט הַבְּכֹרָֽה׃ *כִּֽי־ ישראל
יִהְיֶ֣ה לְאִ֗ישׁ בֵּ֚ן סוֹרֵ֣ר וּמוֹרֶ֔ה אֵינֶ֣נּוּ שֹׁמֵ֔עַ בְּק֥וֹל אָבִ֖יו וּבְק֣וֹל אִמּ֑וֹ וְיִסְּר֣וּ אֹת֔וֹ

וְלֹא יִשְׁמַע אֲלֵיהֶם: וְתָפְשׂוּ בוֹ אָבִיו וְאִמּוֹ וְהוֹצִיאוּ אֹתוֹ אֶל־זִקְנֵי עִירוֹ וְאֶל־
שַׁעַר מְקֹמוֹ: וְאָמְרוּ אֶל־זִקְנֵי עִירוֹ בְּנֵנוּ זֶה סוֹרֵר וּמֹרֶה אֵינֶנּוּ שֹׁמֵעַ בְּקֹלֵנוּ
זוֹלֵל וְסֹבֵא: וּרְגָמֻהוּ כָּל־אַנְשֵׁי עִירוֹ בָאֲבָנִים וָמֵת וּבִעַרְתָּ הָרָע מִקִּרְבֶּךָ
וְכָל־יִשְׂרָאֵל יִשְׁמְעוּ וְיִרָאוּ:

## KI TAVO — כי תבוא

וְהָיָה כִּי־תָבוֹא אֶל־הָאָרֶץ אֲשֶׁר יְהוָה אֱלֹהֶיךָ נֹתֵן לְךָ נַחֲלָה וִירִשְׁתָּהּ דברים כו:א-טו
וְיָשַׁבְתָּ בָּהּ: וְלָקַחְתָּ מֵרֵאשִׁית | כָּל־פְּרִי הָאֲדָמָה אֲשֶׁר תָּבִיא מֵאַרְצְךָ אֲשֶׁר
יְהוָה אֱלֹהֶיךָ נֹתֵן לָךְ וְשַׂמְתָּ בַטֶּנֶא וְהָלַכְתָּ אֶל־הַמָּקוֹם אֲשֶׁר יִבְחַר יְהוָה
אֱלֹהֶיךָ לְשַׁכֵּן שְׁמוֹ שָׁם: וּבָאתָ אֶל־הַכֹּהֵן אֲשֶׁר יִהְיֶה בַּיָּמִים הָהֵם וְאָמַרְתָּ
אֵלָיו הִגַּדְתִּי הַיּוֹם לַיהוָה אֱלֹהֶיךָ כִּי־בָאתִי אֶל־הָאָרֶץ אֲשֶׁר נִשְׁבַּע יְהוָה
לַאֲבֹתֵינוּ לָתֶת לָנוּ: *וְלָקַח הַכֹּהֵן הַטֶּנֶא מִיָּדֶךָ וְהִנִּיחוֹ לִפְנֵי מִזְבַּח יְהוָה לוי
אֱלֹהֶיךָ: וְעָנִיתָ וְאָמַרְתָּ לִפְנֵי | יְהוָה אֱלֹהֶיךָ אֲרַמִּי אֹבֵד אָבִי וַיֵּרֶד מִצְרַיְמָה
וַיָּגָר שָׁם בִּמְתֵי מְעָט וַיְהִי־שָׁם לְגוֹי גָּדוֹל עָצוּם וָרָב: וַיָּרֵעוּ אֹתָנוּ הַמִּצְרִים
וַיְעַנּוּנוּ וַיִּתְּנוּ עָלֵינוּ עֲבֹדָה קָשָׁה: וַנִּצְעַק אֶל־יְהוָה אֱלֹהֵי אֲבֹתֵינוּ וַיִּשְׁמַע
יְהוָה אֶת־קֹלֵנוּ וַיַּרְא אֶת־עָנְיֵנוּ וְאֶת־עֲמָלֵנוּ וְאֶת־לַחֲצֵנוּ: וַיּוֹצִאֵנוּ יְהוָה
מִמִּצְרַיִם בְּיָד חֲזָקָה וּבִזְרֹעַ נְטוּיָה וּבְמֹרָא גָּדֹל וּבְאֹתוֹת וּבְמֹפְתִים: וַיְבִאֵנוּ
אֶל־הַמָּקוֹם הַזֶּה וַיִּתֶּן־לָנוּ אֶת־הָאָרֶץ הַזֹּאת אֶרֶץ זָבַת חָלָב וּדְבָשׁ: וְעַתָּה
הִנֵּה הֵבֵאתִי אֶת־רֵאשִׁית פְּרִי הָאֲדָמָה אֲשֶׁר־נָתַתָּה לִּי יְהוָה וְהִנַּחְתּוֹ לִפְנֵי
יְהוָה אֱלֹהֶיךָ וְהִשְׁתַּחֲוִיתָ לִפְנֵי יְהוָה אֱלֹהֶיךָ: וְשָׂמַחְתָּ בְכָל־הַטּוֹב אֲשֶׁר נָתַן־
לְךָ יְהוָה אֱלֹהֶיךָ וּלְבֵיתֶךָ אַתָּה וְהַלֵּוִי וְהַגֵּר אֲשֶׁר בְּקִרְבֶּךָ: *כִּי ישראל
תְכַלֶּה לַעְשֵׂר אֶת־כָּל־מַעְשַׂר תְּבוּאָתְךָ בַּשָּׁנָה הַשְּׁלִישִׁת שְׁנַת הַמַּעֲשֵׂר
וְנָתַתָּה לַלֵּוִי לַגֵּר לַיָּתוֹם וְלָאַלְמָנָה וְאָכְלוּ בִשְׁעָרֶיךָ וְשָׂבֵעוּ: וְאָמַרְתָּ לִפְנֵי
יְהוָה אֱלֹהֶיךָ בִּעַרְתִּי הַקֹּדֶשׁ מִן־הַבַּיִת וְגַם נְתַתִּיו לַלֵּוִי וְלַגֵּר לַיָּתוֹם וְלָאַלְמָנָה
כְּכָל־מִצְוָתְךָ אֲשֶׁר צִוִּיתָנִי לֹא־עָבַרְתִּי מִמִּצְוֹתֶיךָ וְלֹא שָׁכָחְתִּי: לֹא־אָכַלְתִּי
בְאֹנִי מִמֶּנּוּ וְלֹא־בִעַרְתִּי מִמֶּנּוּ בְּטָמֵא וְלֹא־נָתַתִּי מִמֶּנּוּ לְמֵת שָׁמַעְתִּי בְּקוֹל
יְהוָה אֱלֹהָי עָשִׂיתִי כְּכֹל אֲשֶׁר צִוִּיתָנִי: הַשְׁקִיפָה מִמְּעוֹן קָדְשְׁךָ מִן־הַשָּׁמַיִם
וּבָרֵךְ אֶת־עַמְּךָ אֶת־יִשְׂרָאֵל וְאֵת הָאֲדָמָה אֲשֶׁר נָתַתָּה לָנוּ כַּאֲשֶׁר נִשְׁבַּעְתָּ
לַאֲבֹתֵינוּ אֶרֶץ זָבַת חָלָב וּדְבָשׁ:

# נצבים
# NITZAVIM

אַתֶּם נִצָּבִים הַיּוֹם כֻּלְּכֶם לִפְנֵי יְהוָה אֱלֹהֵיכֶם רָאשֵׁיכֶם שִׁבְטֵיכֶם זִקְנֵיכֶם דברים כט:ט-כח
וְשֹׁטְרֵיכֶם כֹּל אִישׁ יִשְׂרָאֵל: טַפְּכֶם נְשֵׁיכֶם וְגֵרְךָ אֲשֶׁר בְּקֶרֶב מַחֲנֶיךָ מֵחֹטֵב
עֵצֶיךָ עַד שֹׁאֵב מֵימֶיךָ: לְעָבְרְךָ בִּבְרִית יְהוָה אֱלֹהֶיךָ וּבְאָלָתוֹ אֲשֶׁר יְהוָה
אֱלֹהֶיךָ כֹּרֵת עִמְּךָ הַיּוֹם: *לְמַעַן הָקִים־אֹתְךָ הַיּוֹם ׀ לוֹ לְעָם וְהוּא יִהְיֶה־לְּךָ לוי
לֵאלֹהִים כַּאֲשֶׁר דִּבֶּר־לָךְ וְכַאֲשֶׁר נִשְׁבַּע לַאֲבֹתֶיךָ לְאַבְרָהָם לְיִצְחָק וּלְיַעֲקֹב:
וְלֹא אִתְּכֶם לְבַדְּכֶם אָנֹכִי כֹּרֵת אֶת־הַבְּרִית הַזֹּאת וְאֶת־הָאָלָה הַזֹּאת: כִּי
אֶת־אֲשֶׁר יֶשְׁנוֹ פֹּה עִמָּנוּ עֹמֵד הַיּוֹם לִפְנֵי יְהוָה אֱלֹהֵינוּ וְאֵת אֲשֶׁר אֵינֶנּוּ פֹּה
עִמָּנוּ הַיּוֹם: *כִּי־אַתֶּם יְדַעְתֶּם אֵת אֲשֶׁר־יָשַׁבְנוּ בְּאֶרֶץ מִצְרָיִם וְאֵת אֲשֶׁר־ ישראל
עָבַרְנוּ בְּקֶרֶב הַגּוֹיִם אֲשֶׁר עֲבַרְתֶּם: וַתִּרְאוּ אֶת־שִׁקּוּצֵיהֶם וְאֵת גִּלֻּלֵיהֶם
עֵץ וָאֶבֶן כֶּסֶף וְזָהָב אֲשֶׁר עִמָּהֶם: פֶּן־יֵשׁ בָּכֶם אִישׁ אוֹ־אִשָּׁה אוֹ מִשְׁפָּחָה
אוֹ־שֵׁבֶט אֲשֶׁר לְבָבוֹ פֹנֶה הַיּוֹם מֵעִם יְהוָה אֱלֹהֵינוּ לָלֶכֶת לַעֲבֹד אֶת־אֱלֹהֵי
הַגּוֹיִם הָהֵם פֶּן־יֵשׁ בָּכֶם שֹׁרֶשׁ פֹּרֶה רֹאשׁ וְלַעֲנָה: וְהָיָה בְּשָׁמְעוֹ אֶת־דִּבְרֵי
הָאָלָה הַזֹּאת וְהִתְבָּרֵךְ בִּלְבָבוֹ לֵאמֹר שָׁלוֹם יִהְיֶה־לִּי כִּי בִּשְׁרִרוּת לִבִּי אֵלֵךְ
לְמַעַן סְפוֹת הָרָוָה אֶת־הַצְּמֵאָה: לֹא־יֹאבֶה יְהוָה סְלֹחַ לוֹ כִּי אָז יֶעְשַׁן אַף־
יְהוָה וְקִנְאָתוֹ בָּאִישׁ הַהוּא וְרָבְצָה בּוֹ כָּל־הָאָלָה הַכְּתוּבָה בַּסֵּפֶר הַזֶּה וּמָחָה
יְהוָה אֶת־שְׁמוֹ מִתַּחַת הַשָּׁמָיִם: וְהִבְדִּילוֹ יְהוָה לְרָעָה מִכֹּל שִׁבְטֵי יִשְׂרָאֵל
כְּכֹל אָלוֹת הַבְּרִית הַכְּתוּבָה בְּסֵפֶר הַתּוֹרָה הַזֶּה: וְאָמַר הַדּוֹר הָאַחֲרוֹן בְּנֵיכֶם
אֲשֶׁר יָקוּמוּ מֵאַחֲרֵיכֶם וְהַנָּכְרִי אֲשֶׁר יָבֹא מֵאֶרֶץ רְחוֹקָה וְרָאוּ אֶת־מַכּוֹת
הָאָרֶץ הַהִוא וְאֶת־תַּחֲלֻאֶיהָ אֲשֶׁר־חִלָּה יְהוָה בָּהּ: גָּפְרִית וָמֶלַח שְׂרֵפָה כָל־
אַרְצָהּ לֹא תִזָּרַע וְלֹא תַצְמִחַ וְלֹא־יַעֲלֶה בָהּ כָּל־עֵשֶׂב כְּמַהְפֵּכַת סְדֹם וַעֲמֹרָה
אַדְמָה וצביים אֲשֶׁר הָפַךְ יְהוָה בְּאַפּוֹ וּבַחֲמָתוֹ: וְאָמְרוּ כָּל־הַגּוֹיִם עַל־מֶה וּצְבוֹיִם
עָשָׂה יְהוָה כָּכָה לָאָרֶץ הַזֹּאת מֶה חֳרִי הָאַף הַגָּדוֹל הַזֶּה: וְאָמְרוּ עַל אֲשֶׁר
עָזְבוּ אֶת־בְּרִית יְהוָה אֱלֹהֵי אֲבֹתָם אֲשֶׁר כָּרַת עִמָּם בְּהוֹצִיאוֹ אֹתָם מֵאֶרֶץ
מִצְרָיִם: וַיֵּלְכוּ וַיַּעַבְדוּ אֱלֹהִים אֲחֵרִים וַיִּשְׁתַּחֲווּ לָהֶם אֱלֹהִים אֲשֶׁר לֹא־יְדָעוּם
וְלֹא חָלַק לָהֶם: וַיִּחַר־אַף יְהוָה בָּאָרֶץ הַהִוא לְהָבִיא עָלֶיהָ אֶת־כָּל־הַקְּלָלָה
הַכְּתוּבָה בַּסֵּפֶר הַזֶּה: וַיִּתְּשֵׁם יְהוָה מֵעַל אַדְמָתָם בְּאַף וּבְחֵמָה וּבְקֶצֶף גָּדוֹל
וַיַּשְׁלִכֵם אֶל־אֶרֶץ אַחֶרֶת כַּיּוֹם הַזֶּה: הַנִּסְתָּרֹת לַיהוָה אֱלֹהֵינוּ וְהַנִּגְלֹת לָנוּ
וּלְבָנֵינוּ עַד־עוֹלָם לַעֲשׂוֹת אֶת־כָּל־דִּבְרֵי הַתּוֹרָה הַזֹּאת:

## VAYELEKH

## וילך

דברים לא:א–יג

וַיֵּ֖לֶךְ מֹשֶׁ֑ה וַיְדַבֵּ֛ר אֶת־הַדְּבָרִ֥ים הָאֵ֖לֶּה אֶל־כׇּל־יִשְׂרָאֵֽל׃ וַיֹּ֣אמֶר אֲלֵהֶ֗ם בֶּן־
מֵאָ֨ה וְעֶשְׂרִ֤ים שָׁנָה֙ אָנֹכִ֣י הַיּ֔וֹם לֹא־אוּכַ֥ל ע֖וֹד לָצֵ֣את וְלָב֑וֹא וַיהוה֙ אָמַ֣ר אֵלַ֔י
לֹ֥א תַעֲבֹ֖ר אֶת־הַיַּרְדֵּ֥ן הַזֶּֽה׃ יהוה אֱלֹהֶ֜יךָ ה֣וּא ׀ עֹבֵ֣ר לְפָנֶ֗יךָ הֽוּא־יַשְׁמִ֞יד
אֶת־הַגּוֹיִ֥ם הָאֵ֛לֶּה מִלְּפָנֶ֖יךָ וִירִשְׁתָּ֑ם יְהוֹשֻׁ֗עַ ה֚וּא עֹבֵ֣ר לְפָנֶ֔יךָ כַּאֲשֶׁ֖ר דִּבֶּ֥ר
לוי יהוה׃ *וְעָשָׂ֤ה יהוה֙ לָהֶ֔ם כַּאֲשֶׁ֣ר עָשָׂ֗ה לְסִיח֥וֹן וּלְע֛וֹג מַלְכֵ֥י הָאֱמֹרִ֖י וּלְאַרְצָ֑ם
אֲשֶׁ֥ר הִשְׁמִ֖יד אֹתָֽם׃ וּנְתָנָ֥ם יהוה לִפְנֵיכֶ֑ם וַעֲשִׂיתֶ֣ם לָהֶ֔ם כְּכׇל־הַמִּצְוָ֔ה אֲשֶׁ֥ר
צִוִּ֖יתִי אֶתְכֶֽם׃ חִזְק֣וּ וְאִמְצ֔וּ אַל־תִּֽירְא֥וּ וְאַל־תַּעַרְצ֖וּ מִפְּנֵיהֶ֑ם כִּ֣י ׀ יהוה אֱלֹהֶ֗יךָ
ישראל ה֚וּא הַהֹלֵ֣ךְ עִמָּ֔ךְ לֹ֥א יַרְפְּךָ֖ וְלֹ֥א יַעַזְבֶֽךָּ׃ *וַיִּקְרָ֨א מֹשֶׁ֜ה לִיהוֹשֻׁ֗עַ
וַיֹּ֨אמֶר אֵלָ֜יו לְעֵינֵ֣י כׇל־יִשְׂרָאֵל֮ חֲזַ֣ק וֶאֱמָץ֒ כִּ֣י אַתָּ֗ה תָּבוֹא֙ אֶת־הָעָ֣ם הַזֶּ֔ה
אֶל־הָאָ֕רֶץ אֲשֶׁ֨ר נִשְׁבַּ֧ע יהוה לַאֲבֹתָ֖ם לָתֵ֣ת לָהֶ֑ם וְאַתָּ֖ה תַּנְחִילֶ֥נָּה אוֹתָֽם׃
וַיהוה ה֣וּא ׀ הַהֹלֵ֣ךְ לְפָנֶ֗יךָ ה֚וּא יִהְיֶ֣ה עִמָּ֔ךְ לֹ֥א יַרְפְּךָ֖ וְלֹ֣א יַעַזְבֶ֑ךָּ לֹ֥א תִירָ֖א וְלֹ֥א
תֵחָֽת׃ וַיִּכְתֹּ֣ב מֹשֶׁה֮ אֶת־הַתּוֹרָ֣ה הַזֹּאת֒ וַֽיִּתְּנָ֗הּ אֶל־הַכֹּהֲנִים֙ בְּנֵ֣י לֵוִ֔י הַנֹּ֣שְׂאִ֔ים
אֶת־אֲר֖וֹן בְּרִ֣ית יהוה וְאֶל־כׇּל־זִקְנֵ֖י יִשְׂרָאֵֽל׃ וַיְצַ֥ו מֹשֶׁ֖ה אוֹתָ֣ם לֵאמֹ֑ר מִקֵּ֣ץ ׀
שֶׁ֣בַע שָׁנִ֗ים בְּמֹעֵ֛ד שְׁנַ֥ת הַשְּׁמִטָּ֖ה בְּחַ֥ג הַסֻּכּֽוֹת׃ בְּב֣וֹא כׇל־יִשְׂרָאֵ֗ל לֵרָאוֹת֙
אֶת־פְּנֵי֙ יהוה אֱלֹהֶ֔יךָ בַּמָּק֖וֹם אֲשֶׁ֣ר יִבְחָ֑ר תִּקְרָ֞א אֶת־הַתּוֹרָ֥ה הַזֹּ֛את נֶ֥גֶד
כׇּל־יִשְׂרָאֵ֖ל בְּאׇזְנֵיהֶֽם׃ הַקְהֵ֣ל אֶת־הָעָ֗ם הָֽאֲנָשִׁ֤ים וְהַנָּשִׁים֙ וְהַטַּ֔ף וְגֵרְךָ֖ אֲשֶׁ֣ר
בִּשְׁעָרֶ֑יךָ לְמַ֨עַן יִשְׁמְע֜וּ וּלְמַ֣עַן יִלְמְד֗וּ וְיָֽרְאוּ֙ אֶת־יהוה אֱלֹהֵיכֶ֔ם וְשָׁמְר֣וּ
לַעֲשׂ֔וֹת אֶת־כׇּל־דִּבְרֵ֖י הַתּוֹרָ֥ה הַזֹּֽאת׃ וּבְנֵיהֶ֞ם אֲשֶׁ֣ר לֹא־יָדְע֗וּ יִשְׁמְעוּ֙ וְלָ֣מְד֔וּ
לְיִרְאָ֖ה אֶת־יהוה אֱלֹהֵיכֶ֑ם כׇּל־הַיָּמִ֗ים אֲשֶׁ֨ר אַתֶּ֤ם חַיִּים֙ עַל־הָ֣אֲדָמָ֔ה אֲשֶׁ֨ר
אַתֶּ֜ם עֹבְרִ֧ים אֶת־הַיַּרְדֵּ֛ן שָׁ֖מָּה לְרִשְׁתָּֽהּ׃

## HA'AZINU

## האזינו

דברים לב:א–יח

הַאֲזִ֥ינוּ הַשָּׁמַ֖יִם וַאֲדַבֵּ֑רָה   וְתִשְׁמַ֥ע הָאָ֖רֶץ אִמְרֵי־פִֽי׃
יַעֲרֹ֤ף כַּמָּטָר֙ לִקְחִ֔י   תִּזַּ֥ל כַּטַּ֖ל אִמְרָתִ֑י
כִּשְׂעִירִ֣ם עֲלֵי־דֶ֔שֶׁא   וְכִרְבִיבִ֖ים עֲלֵי־עֵֽשֶׂב׃
כִּ֛י שֵׁ֥ם יהוה אֶקְרָ֑א   הָב֥וּ גֹ֖דֶל לֵאלֹהֵֽינוּ׃
לוי *הַצּוּר֙ תָּמִ֣ים פׇּעֳל֔וֹ   כִּ֥י כׇל־דְּרָכָ֖יו מִשְׁפָּ֑ט
אֵ֤ל אֱמוּנָה֙ וְאֵ֣ין עָ֔וֶל   צַדִּ֥יק וְיָשָׁ֖ר הֽוּא׃

שִׁחֵת לוֹ לֹא בָּנָיו מוּמָם   דּוֹר עִקֵּשׁ וּפְתַלְתֹּל׃
הֲ לַיהוָה תִּגְמְלוּ־זֹאת   עַם נָבָל וְלֹא חָכָם
הֲלוֹא־הוּא אָבִיךָ קָּנֶךָ   הוּא עָשְׂךָ וַיְכֹנְנֶךָ׃

*Some start the לוי portion here:*

*זְכֹר יְמוֹת עוֹלָם   בִּינוּ שְׁנוֹת דֹּר־וָדֹר   ישראל
שְׁאַל אָבִיךָ וְיַגֵּדְךָ   זְקֵנֶיךָ וְיֹאמְרוּ לָךְ׃
בְּהַנְחֵל עֶלְיוֹן גּוֹיִם   בְּהַפְרִידוֹ בְּנֵי אָדָם
יַצֵּב גְּבֻלֹת עַמִּים   לְמִסְפַּר בְּנֵי יִשְׂרָאֵל׃
כִּי חֵלֶק יְהוָה עַמּוֹ   יַעֲקֹב חֶבֶל נַחֲלָתוֹ׃
יִמְצָאֵהוּ בְּאֶרֶץ מִדְבָּר   וּבְתֹהוּ יְלֵל יְשִׁמֹן
יְסֹבְבֶנְהוּ יְבוֹנְנֵהוּ   יִצְּרֶנְהוּ כְּאִישׁוֹן עֵינוֹ׃
כְּנֶשֶׁר יָעִיר קִנּוֹ   עַל־גּוֹזָלָיו יְרַחֵף
יִפְרֹשׂ כְּנָפָיו יִקָּחֵהוּ   יִשָּׂאֵהוּ עַל־אֶבְרָתוֹ׃
יְהוָה בָּדָד יַנְחֶנּוּ   וְאֵין עִמּוֹ אֵל נֵכָר׃

*Most finish here; some start the ישראל portion here:*

*יַרְכִּבֵהוּ עַל־בָּמוֹתֵי אָרֶץ   וַיֹּאכַל תְּנוּבֹת שָׂדָי   בָּמֳתֵי
וַיֵּנִקֵהוּ דְבַשׁ מִסֶּלַע   וְשֶׁמֶן מֵחַלְמִישׁ צוּר׃
חֶמְאַת בָּקָר וַחֲלֵב צֹאן   עִם־חֵלֶב כָּרִים
וְאֵילִים בְּנֵי־בָשָׁן וְעַתּוּדִים   עִם־חֵלֶב כִּלְיוֹת חִטָּה
וְדַם־עֵנָב תִּשְׁתֶּה־חָמֶר׃   וַיִּשְׁמַן יְשֻׁרוּן וַיִּבְעָט
שָׁמַנְתָּ עָבִיתָ כָּשִׂיתָ   וַיִּטֹּשׁ אֱלוֹהַ עָשָׂהוּ
וַיְנַבֵּל צוּר יְשֻׁעָתוֹ׃   יַקְנִאֻהוּ בְּזָרִים
בְּתוֹעֵבֹת יַכְעִיסֻהוּ׃   יִזְבְּחוּ לַשֵּׁדִים לֹא אֱלֹהַ
אֱלֹהִים לֹא יְדָעוּם   חֲדָשִׁים מִקָּרֹב בָּאוּ
לֹא שְׂעָרוּם אֲבֹתֵיכֶם׃   צוּר יְלָדְךָ תֶּשִׁי
וַתִּשְׁכַּח אֵל מְחֹלְלֶךָ׃

## וזאת הברכה
## VEZOT HABERAKHA

וְזֹאת הַבְּרָכָה אֲשֶׁר בֵּרַךְ מֹשֶׁה אִישׁ הָאֱלֹהִים אֶת־בְּנֵי יִשְׂרָאֵל לִפְנֵי מוֹתוֹ׃   דברים לג:א–יז

וַיֹּאמַר יְהוָה מִסִּינַי בָּא וְזָרַח מִשֵּׂעִיר לָמוֹ הוֹפִיעַ מֵהַר פָּארָן וְאָתָה מֵרִבְבֹת
אֵשׁ דָּת קֹדֶשׁ מִימִינוֹ אשדת לָמוֹ׃ אַף חֹבֵב עַמִּים כָּל־קְדֹשָׁיו בְּיָדֶךָ וְהֵם תֻּכּוּ לְרַגְלֶךָ
יִשָּׂא מִדַּבְּרֹתֶיךָ׃ תּוֹרָה צִוָּה־לָנוּ מֹשֶׁה מוֹרָשָׁה קְהִלַּת יַעֲקֹב׃ וַיְהִי בִישֻׁרוּן
מֶלֶךְ בְּהִתְאַסֵּף רָאשֵׁי עָם יַחַד שִׁבְטֵי יִשְׂרָאֵל׃ יְחִי רְאוּבֵן וְאַל־יָמֹת וִיהִי מְתָיו
מִסְפָּר׃ וְזֹאת לִיהוּדָה וַיֹּאמַר שְׁמַע יְהוָה קוֹל יְהוּדָה וְאֶל־עַמּוֹ
תְּבִיאֶנּוּ יָדָיו רָב לוֹ וְעֵזֶר מִצָּרָיו תִּהְיֶה׃
לוי וּלְלֵוִי אָמַר תֻּמֶּיךָ וְאוּרֶיךָ לְאִישׁ חֲסִידֶךָ אֲשֶׁר נִסִּיתוֹ בְּמַסָּה תְּרִיבֵהוּ עַל־מֵי
מְרִיבָה׃ הָאֹמֵר לְאָבִיו וּלְאִמּוֹ לֹא רְאִיתִיו וְאֶת־אֶחָיו לֹא הִכִּיר וְאֶת־בָּנָו לֹא
יָדָע כִּי שָׁמְרוּ אִמְרָתֶךָ וּבְרִיתְךָ יִנְצֹרוּ׃ יוֹרוּ מִשְׁפָּטֶיךָ לְיַעֲקֹב וְתוֹרָתְךָ לְיִשְׂרָאֵל
יָשִׂימוּ קְטוֹרָה בְּאַפֶּךָ וְכָלִיל עַל־מִזְבְּחֶךָ׃ בָּרֵךְ יְהוָה חֵילוֹ וּפֹעַל יָדָיו תִּרְצֶה
מְחַץ מָתְנַיִם קָמָיו וּמְשַׂנְאָיו מִן־יְקוּמוּן׃ לְבִנְיָמִן אָמַר יְדִיד יְהוָה
ישראל יִשְׁכֹּן לָבֶטַח עָלָיו חֹפֵף עָלָיו כָּל־הַיּוֹם וּבֵין כְּתֵפָיו שָׁכֵן׃ *וּלְיוֹסֵף
אָמַר מְבֹרֶכֶת יְהוָה אַרְצוֹ מִמֶּגֶד שָׁמַיִם מִטָּל וּמִתְּהוֹם רֹבֶצֶת תָּחַת׃ וּמִמֶּגֶד
תְּבוּאֹת שָׁמֶשׁ וּמִמֶּגֶד גֶּרֶשׁ יְרָחִים׃ וּמֵרֹאשׁ הַרְרֵי־קֶדֶם וּמִמֶּגֶד גִּבְעוֹת עוֹלָם׃
וּמִמֶּגֶד אֶרֶץ וּמְלֹאָהּ וּרְצוֹן שֹׁכְנִי סְנֶה תָּבוֹאתָה לְרֹאשׁ יוֹסֵף וּלְקָדְקֹד נְזִיר
אֶחָיו׃ בְּכוֹר שׁוֹרוֹ הָדָר לוֹ וְקַרְנֵי רְאֵם קַרְנָיו בָּהֶם עַמִּים יְנַגַּח יַחְדָּו אַפְסֵי־
אָרֶץ וְהֵם רִבְבוֹת אֶפְרַיִם וְהֵם אַלְפֵי מְנַשֶּׁה׃

# קריאת התורה לראש חודש,
# לתעניות ציבור, לחנוכה ולפורים

# THE READING OF THE TORAH FOR ROSH ḤODESH, FAST DAYS, ḤANUKKA AND PURIM

## READING FOR ROSH ḤODESH — קריאה לראש חודש

*For the כהן, the first three verses are read up to עֹלָה תָּמִיד. For the לוי, the third verse is repeated and starts with וְאָמַרְתָּ לָהֶם. For שלישי, continue from עֹלַת תָּמִיד up to וְנִסְכָּהּ. For רביעי, read from וּבְרָאשֵׁי חָדְשֵׁיכֶם until the end. In ארץ ישראל, some read as follows: For the כהן read until רְבִיעִת הַהִין, for the לוי read from אֶת־הַכֶּבֶשׂ until רֵיחַ נִיחֹחַ לַה׳, for שלישי, the last verse is repeated and starts at עֹלַת תָּמִיד up to וְנִסְכָּהּ, and for רביעי, from וּבְרָאשֵׁי חָדְשֵׁיכֶם until the end. On ראש חודש טבת, the כהן reads until רְבִיעִת הַהִין, the לוי reads the portion for שלישי and the שלישי the portion of רביעי; the fourth עולה reads the appropriate day of חנוכה on page 1197.*

במדבר כח:א-טו וַיְדַבֵּר יהוה אֶל־מֹשֶׁה לֵּאמֹר: צַו אֶת־בְּנֵי יִשְׂרָאֵל וְאָמַרְתָּ אֲלֵהֶם אֶת־
לוי קָרְבָּנִי לַחְמִי לְאִשַּׁי רֵיחַ נִיחֹחִי תִּשְׁמְרוּ לְהַקְרִיב לִי בְּמוֹעֲדוֹ: *וְאָמַרְתָּ
לָהֶם זֶה הָאִשֶּׁה אֲשֶׁר תַּקְרִיבוּ לַיהוה כְּבָשִׂים בְּנֵי־שָׁנָה תְמִימִם שְׁנַיִם לַיּוֹם
עד כאן לכהן עֹלָה תָמִיד: *אֶת־הַכֶּבֶשׂ אֶחָד תַּעֲשֶׂה בַבֹּקֶר וְאֵת הַכֶּבֶשׂ הַשֵּׁנִי תַּעֲשֶׂה
בֵּין הָעַרְבָּיִם: וַעֲשִׂירִית הָאֵיפָה סֹלֶת לְמִנְחָה בְּלוּלָה בְּשֶׁמֶן כָּתִית רְבִיעִת
שלישי הַהִין: *עֹלַת תָּמִיד הָעֲשֻׂיָה בְּהַר סִינַי לְרֵיחַ נִיחֹחַ אִשֶּׁה לַיהוה: וְנִסְכּוֹ
רְבִיעִת הַהִין לַכֶּבֶשׂ הָאֶחָד בַּקֹּדֶשׁ הַסֵּךְ נֶסֶךְ שֵׁכָר לַיהוה: וְאֵת הַכֶּבֶשׂ
הַשֵּׁנִי תַּעֲשֶׂה בֵּין הָעַרְבָּיִם כְּמִנְחַת הַבֹּקֶר וּכְנִסְכּוֹ תַּעֲשֶׂה אִשֵּׁה רֵיחַ נִיחֹחַ
לַיהוה:

וּבְיוֹם הַשַּׁבָּת שְׁנֵי־כְבָשִׂים בְּנֵי־שָׁנָה תְּמִימִם וּשְׁנֵי עֶשְׂרֹנִים סֹלֶת מִנְחָה בְּלוּלָה
בַשֶּׁמֶן וְנִסְכּוֹ: עֹלַת שַׁבַּת בְּשַׁבַּתּוֹ עַל־עֹלַת הַתָּמִיד וְנִסְכָּהּ:

רביעי וּבְרָאשֵׁי חָדְשֵׁיכֶם תַּקְרִיבוּ עֹלָה לַיהוה פָּרִים בְּנֵי־בָקָר שְׁנַיִם וְאַיִל אֶחָד
כְּבָשִׂים בְּנֵי־שָׁנָה שִׁבְעָה תְּמִימִם: וּשְׁלֹשָׁה עֶשְׂרֹנִים סֹלֶת מִנְחָה בְּלוּלָה
בַשֶּׁמֶן לַפָּר הָאֶחָד וּשְׁנֵי עֶשְׂרֹנִים סֹלֶת מִנְחָה בְּלוּלָה בַשֶּׁמֶן לָאַיִל הָאֶחָד:
וְעִשָּׂרֹן עִשָּׂרוֹן סֹלֶת מִנְחָה בְּלוּלָה בַשֶּׁמֶן לַכֶּבֶשׂ הָאֶחָד עֹלָה רֵיחַ נִיחֹחַ
אִשֶּׁה לַיהוה: וְנִסְכֵּיהֶם חֲצִי הַהִין יִהְיֶה לַפָּר וּשְׁלִישִׁת הַהִין לָאַיִל וּרְבִיעִת
הַהִין לַכֶּבֶשׂ יָיִן זֹאת עֹלַת חֹדֶשׁ בְּחָדְשׁוֹ לְחָדְשֵׁי הַשָּׁנָה: וּשְׂעִיר עִזִּים אֶחָד
לְחַטָּאת לַיהוה עַל־עֹלַת הַתָּמִיד יֵעָשֶׂה וְנִסְכּוֹ:

## READING FOR FAST DAYS — קריאה לתענית ציבור

*The following is read on a* תענית ציבור *(except* תשעה באב*) in both* שחרית *and* מנחה*. At* מנחה*, the person called up for* שלישי *also reads the* הפטרה*. It is customary for the* קהל *to say aloud the passages marked by arrows, followed by the* קורא *(see law 50).*

שמות לב: יא–יד — וַיְחַל מֹשֶׁה אֶת־פְּנֵי יהוה אֱלֹהָיו וַיֹּאמֶר לָמָה יהוה יֶחֱרֶה אַפְּךָ בְּעַמֶּךָ אֲשֶׁר
הוֹצֵאתָ מֵאֶרֶץ מִצְרַיִם בְּכֹחַ גָּדוֹל וּבְיָד חֲזָקָה: לָמָּה יֹאמְרוּ מִצְרַיִם לֵאמֹר
בְּרָעָה הוֹצִיאָם לַהֲרֹג אֹתָם בֶּהָרִים וּלְכַלֹּתָם מֵעַל פְּנֵי הָאֲדָמָה ‹ שׁוּב מֵחֲרוֹן
אַפֶּךָ וְהִנָּחֵם עַל־הָרָעָה לְעַמֶּךָ: ‹ זְכֹר לְאַבְרָהָם לְיִצְחָק וּלְיִשְׂרָאֵל עֲבָדֶיךָ
אֲשֶׁר נִשְׁבַּעְתָּ לָהֶם בָּךְ וַתְּדַבֵּר אֲלֵהֶם אַרְבֶּה אֶת־זַרְעֲכֶם כְּכוֹכְבֵי הַשָּׁמָיִם
וְכָל־הָאָרֶץ הַזֹּאת אֲשֶׁר אָמַרְתִּי אֶתֵּן לְזַרְעֲכֶם וְנָחֲלוּ לְעֹלָם: וַיִּנָּחֶם יהוה
עַל־הָרָעָה אֲשֶׁר דִּבֶּר לַעֲשׂוֹת לְעַמּוֹ:

שמות לד: א–י, לוי — וַיֹּאמֶר יהוה אֶל־מֹשֶׁה פְּסָל־לְךָ שְׁנֵי־לֻחֹת אֲבָנִים כָּרִאשֹׁנִים וְכָתַבְתִּי עַל־
הַלֻּחֹת אֶת־הַדְּבָרִים אֲשֶׁר הָיוּ עַל־הַלֻּחֹת הָרִאשֹׁנִים אֲשֶׁר שִׁבַּרְתָּ: וֶהְיֵה
נָכוֹן לַבֹּקֶר וְעָלִיתָ בַבֹּקֶר אֶל־הַר סִינַי וְנִצַּבְתָּ לִי שָׁם עַל־רֹאשׁ הָהָר: וְאִישׁ
לֹא־יַעֲלֶה עִמָּךְ וְגַם־אִישׁ אַל־יֵרָא בְּכָל־הָהָר גַּם־הַצֹּאן וְהַבָּקָר אַל־יִרְעוּ
ישראל — אֶל־מוּל הָהָר הַהוּא: *וַיִּפְסֹל שְׁנֵי־לֻחֹת אֲבָנִים כָּרִאשֹׁנִים וַיַּשְׁכֵּם מֹשֶׁה
בַבֹּקֶר וַיַּעַל אֶל־הַר סִינַי כַּאֲשֶׁר צִוָּה יהוה אֹתוֹ וַיִּקַּח בְּיָדוֹ שְׁנֵי לֻחֹת אֲבָנִים:
וַיֵּרֶד יהוה בֶּעָנָן וַיִּתְיַצֵּב עִמּוֹ שָׁם וַיִּקְרָא בְשֵׁם יהוה: וַיַּעֲבֹר יהוה ׀ עַל־פָּנָיו
וַיִּקְרָא ‹ יהוה ׀ יהוה אֵל רַחוּם וְחַנּוּן אֶרֶךְ אַפַּיִם וְרַב־חֶסֶד וֶאֱמֶת: נֹצֵר
חֶסֶד לָאֲלָפִים נֹשֵׂא עָוֹן וָפֶשַׁע וְחַטָּאָה וְנַקֵּה לֹא יְנַקֶּה ‹ פֹּקֵד ׀ עֲוֹן אָבוֹת
עַל־בָּנִים וְעַל־בְּנֵי בָנִים עַל־שִׁלֵּשִׁים וְעַל־רִבֵּעִים: וַיְמַהֵר מֹשֶׁה וַיִּקֹּד אַרְצָה
וַיִּשְׁתָּחוּ: וַיֹּאמֶר אִם־נָא מָצָאתִי חֵן בְּעֵינֶיךָ אֲדֹנָי יֵלֶךְ־נָא אֲדֹנָי בְּקִרְבֵּנוּ כִּי
עַם־קְשֵׁה־עֹרֶף הוּא ‹ וְסָלַחְתָּ לַעֲוֹנֵנוּ וּלְחַטָּאתֵנוּ וּנְחַלְתָּנוּ: ‹ וַיֹּאמֶר הִנֵּה
אָנֹכִי כֹּרֵת בְּרִית נֶגֶד כָּל־עַמְּךָ אֶעֱשֶׂה נִפְלָאֹת אֲשֶׁר לֹא־נִבְרְאוּ בְכָל־הָאָרֶץ
וּבְכָל־הַגּוֹיִם וְרָאָה כָל־הָעָם אֲשֶׁר־אַתָּה בְקִרְבּוֹ אֶת־מַעֲשֵׂה יהוה כִּי־נוֹרָא
הוּא אֲשֶׁר אֲנִי עֹשֶׂה עִמָּךְ:

## HAFTARA FOR FAST DAYS — הפטרה לתענית ציבור

*The blessings for the* הפטרה *can be found on page 585.*

ישעיה נה:ו–נו:ח — דִּרְשׁוּ יהוה בְּהִמָּצְאוֹ קְרָאֻהוּ בִּהְיוֹתוֹ קָרוֹב: יַעֲזֹב רָשָׁע דַּרְכּוֹ וְאִישׁ אָוֶן
מַחְשְׁבֹתָיו וְיָשֹׁב אֶל־יהוה וִירַחֲמֵהוּ וְאֶל־אֱלֹהֵינוּ כִּי־יַרְבֶּה לִסְלוֹחַ: כִּי לֹא

מחשבותי מחשבותיכם ולא דרכיכם דרכי נאם יהוה: כי־גבהו שמים מארץ כן גבהו דרכי מדרכיכם ומחשבתי ממחשבתיכם: כי כאשר ירד הגשם והשלג מן־השמים ושמה לא ישוב כי אם־הרוה את־הארץ והולידה והצמיחה ונתן זרע לזרע ולחם לאכל: כן יהיה דברי אשר יצא מפי לא־ישוב אלי ריקם כי אם־עשה את־אשר חפצתי והצליח אשר שלחתיו: כי־בשמחה תצאו ובשלום תובלון ההרים והגבעות יפצחו לפניכם רנה וכל־עצי השדה ימחאו־כף: תחת הנעצוץ יעלה ברוש תחת הסרפד (ותחת) יעלה הדס והיה ליהוה לשם לאות עולם לא יכרת: כה אמר יהוה שמרו משפט ועשו צדקה כי־קרובה ישועתי לבוא וצדקתי להגלות: אשרי אנוש יעשה־זאת ובן־אדם יחזיק בה שמר שבת מחללו ושמר ידו מעשות כל־רע: ואל־יאמר בן־הנכר הנלוה אל־יהוה לאמר הבדל יבדילני יהוה מעל עמו ואל־יאמר הסריס הן אני עץ יבש: כי־כה אמר יהוה לסריסים אשר ישמרו את־שבתותי ובחרו באשר חפצתי ומחזיקים בבריתי: ונתתי להם בביתי ובחומתי יד ושם טוב מבנים ומבנות שם עולם אתן־לו אשר לא יכרת: ובני הנכר הנלוים על־יהוה לשרתו ולאהבה את־שם יהוה להיות לו לעבדים כל־שמר שבת מחללו ומחזיקים בבריתי: והביאותים אל־הר קדשי ושמחתים בבית תפלתי עולתיהם וזבחיהם לרצון על־מזבחי כי ביתי בית־תפלה יקרא לכל־העמים: נאם אדני יהוה מקבץ נדחי ישראל עוד אקבץ עליו לנקבציו:

## READING FOR TISHA B'AV — קריאה לתשעה באב

*The following is read during שחרית of תשעה באב. The person called up for שלישי also reads the הפטרה. At מנחה, the קריאת התורה and הפטרה are those for regular Fast Days.*

דברים ד:כה–מ

כי־תוליד בנים ובני בנים ונושנתם בארץ והשחתם ועשיתם פסל תמונת כל ועשיתם הרע בעיני־יהוה אלהיך להכעיסו: העידתי בכם היום את־השמים ואת־הארץ כי־אבד תאבדון מהר מעל הארץ אשר אתם עברים את־הירדן שמה לרשתה לא־תאריכן ימים עליה כי השמד תשמדון: והפיץ יהוה אתכם בעמים ונשארתם מתי מספר בגוים אשר ינהג יהוה אתכם שמה: ועבדתם־שם אלהים מעשה ידי אדם עץ ואבן אשר לא־יראון ולא

ישמעון ולא יאכלון ולא יריחן: ובקשתם משם את־יהוה אלהיך ומצאת
לוי כי תדרשנו בכל־לבבך ובכל־נפשך: *בצר לך ומצאוך כל הדברים האלה
באחרית הימים ושבת עד־יהוה אלהיך ושמעת בקלו: כי אל רחום יהוה
אלהיך לא ירפך ולא ישחיתך ולא ישכח את־ברית אבתיך אשר נשבע
להם: כי שאל־נא לימים ראשנים אשר־היו לפניך למן־היום אשר ברא
אלהים ׀ אדם על־הארץ ולמקצה השמים ועד־קצה השמים הנהיה כדבר
הגדול הזה או הנשמע כמהו: השמע עם קול אלהים מדבר מתוך־האש
כאשר־שמעת אתה ויחי: או ׀ הנסה אלהים לבוא לקחת לו גוי מקרב גוי
במסת באתת ובמופתים ובמלחמה וביד חזקה ובזרוע נטויה ובמוראים
גדלים ככל אשר־עשה לכם יהוה אלהיכם במצרים לעיניך: אתה הראת
ישראל לדעת כי יהוה הוא האלהים אין עוד מלבדו: *מן־השמים השמיעך את־
קלו ליסרך ועל־הארץ הראך את־אשו הגדולה ודבריו שמעת מתוך
האש: ותחת כי אהב את־אבתיך ויבחר בזרעו אחריו ויוצאך בפניו בכחו
הגדל ממצרים: להוריש גוים גדלים ועצמים ממך מפניך להביאך לתת־לך
את־ארצם נחלה כיום הזה: וידעת היום והשבת אל־לבבך כי יהוה הוא
האלהים בשמים ממעל ועל־הארץ מתחת אין עוד: ושמרת את־חקיו
ואת־מצותיו אשר אנכי מצוך היום אשר ייטב לך ולבניך אחריך ולמען
תאריך ימים על־האדמה אשר יהוה אלהיך נתן לך כל־הימים:

## HAFTARA FOR TISHA B'AV הפטרה לתשעה באב

*The blessings for the* הפטרה *can be found on page 585.*

ירמיהו ח:יג–ט:כג אסף אסיפם נאם־יהוה אין ענבים בגפן ואין תאנים בתאנה והעלה נבל
ואתן להם יעברום: על־מה אנחנו ישבים האספו ונבוא אל־ערי המבצר
ונדמה־שם כי יהוה אלהינו הדמנו וישקנו מי־ראש כי חטאנו ליהוה: קוה
לשלום ואין טוב לעת מרפה והנה בעתה: מדן נשמע נחרת סוסיו מקול
מצהלות אביריו רעשה כל־הארץ ויבואו ויאכלו ארץ ומלואה עיר וישבי
בה: כי הנני משלח בכם נחשים צפענים אשר אין־להם לחש ונשכו אתכם
נאם־יהוה: מבליגיתי עלי יגון עלי לבי דוי: הנה־קול שועת

בת־עמי מארץ מרחקים היהוה אין בציון אם־מלכה אין בה מדוע הכעסוני
בפסליהם בהבלי נכר: עבר קציר כלה קיץ ואנחנו לוא נושענו: על־שבר
בת־עמי השברתי קדרתי שמה החזקתני: הצרי אין בגלעד אם־רפא אין
שם כי מדוע לא עלתה ארכת בת־עמי: מי־יתן ראשי מים ועיני
מקור דמעה ואבכה יומם ולילה את חללי בת־עמי: מי־יתנני במדבר מלון
ארחים ואעזבה את־עמי ואלכה מאתם כי כלם מנאפים עצרת בגדים:
וידרכו את־לשונם קשתם שקר ולא לאמונה גברו בארץ כי מרעה אל־
רעה | יצאו ואתי לא־ידעו נאם־יהוה: איש מרעהו השמרו ועל־כל־אח
אל־תבטחו כי כל־אח עקוב יעקב וכל־רע רכיל יהלך: ואיש ברעהו יהתלו
ואמת לא ידברו למדו לשונם דבר־שקר העוה נלאו: שבתך בתוך מרמה
במרמה מאנו דעת־אותי נאם־יהוה: לכן כה אמר יהוה צבאות
הנני צורפם ובחנתים כי־איך אעשה מפני בת־עמי: חץ שוחט לשונם מרמה שחוט
דבר בפיו שלום את־רעהו ידבר ובקרבו ישים ארבו: העל־אלה לא־אפקד־
בם נאם־יהוה אם בגוי אשר־כזה לא תתנקם נפשי: על־ההרים
אשא בכי ונהי ועל־נאות מדבר קינה כי נצתו מבלי־איש עבר ולא שמעו
קול מקנה מעוף השמים ועד־בהמה נדדו הלכו: ונתתי את־ירושלם
לגלים מעון תנים ואת־ערי יהודה אתן שממה מבלי יושב: מי־
האיש החכם ויבן את־זאת ואשר דבר פי־יהוה אליו ויגדה על־מה אבדה
הארץ נצתה כמדבר מבלי עבר: ויאמר יהוה על־עזבם
את־תורתי אשר נתתי לפניהם ולא־שמעו בקולי ולא־הלכו בה: וילכו
אחרי שררות לבם ואחרי הבעלים אשר למדום אבותם: לכן
כה־אמר יהוה צבאות אלהי ישראל הנני מאכילם את־העם הזה לענה
והשקיתים מי־ראש: והפיצותים בגוים אשר לא ידעו המה ואבותם ושלחתי
אחריהם את־החרב עד כלותי אותם: כה אמר יהוה צבאות
התבוננו וקראו למקוננות ותבואינה ואל־החכמות שלחו ותבואנה:
ותמהרנה ותשנה עלינו נהי ותרדנה עינינו דמעה ועפעפינו יזלו־מים:
כי קול נהי נשמע מציון איך שדדנו בשנו מאד כי־עזבנו ארץ כי השליכו
משכנותינו: כי־שמענה נשים דבר־יהוה ותקח אזנכם דבר־

פִּיו וְלַמֵּדְנָה בְנוֹתֵיכֶם נֶהִי וְאִשָּׁה רְעוּתָהּ קִינָה: כִּי־עָלָה מָוֶת בְּחַלּוֹנֵינוּ בָּא
בְּאַרְמְנוֹתֵינוּ לְהַכְרִית עוֹלָל מִחוּץ בַּחוּרִים מֵרְחֹבוֹת: דַּבֵּר כֹּה נְאֻם־יהוה
וְנָפְלָה נִבְלַת הָאָדָם כְּדֹמֶן עַל־פְּנֵי הַשָּׂדֶה וּכְעָמִיר מֵאַחֲרֵי הַקֹּצֵר וְאֵין
מְאַסֵּף: כֹּה ׀ אָמַר יהוה אַל־יִתְהַלֵּל חָכָם בְּחָכְמָתוֹ וְאַל־יִתְהַלֵּל
הַגִּבּוֹר בִּגְבוּרָתוֹ אַל־יִתְהַלֵּל עָשִׁיר בְּעָשְׁרוֹ: כִּי אִם־בְּזֹאת יִתְהַלֵּל הַמִּתְהַלֵּל
הַשְׂכֵּל וְיָדֹעַ אוֹתִי כִּי אֲנִי יהוה עֹשֶׂה חֶסֶד מִשְׁפָּט וּצְדָקָה בָּאָרֶץ כִּי־בְאֵלֶּה
חָפַצְתִּי נְאֻם־יהוה:

## FIRST DAY OF HANUKKA קריאה ליום הראשון של חנוכה

וַיְהִי בְּיוֹם כַּלּוֹת מֹשֶׁה לְהָקִים אֶת־הַמִּשְׁכָּן וַיִּמְשַׁח אֹתוֹ וַיְקַדֵּשׁ אֹתוֹ וְאֶת־ במדבר ז:א–יז
כָּל־כֵּלָיו וְאֶת־הַמִּזְבֵּחַ וְאֶת־כָּל־כֵּלָיו וַיִּמְשָׁחֵם וַיְקַדֵּשׁ אֹתָם: וַיַּקְרִיבוּ נְשִׂיאֵי
יִשְׂרָאֵל רָאשֵׁי בֵּית אֲבֹתָם הֵם נְשִׂיאֵי הַמַּטֹּת הֵם הָעֹמְדִים עַל־הַפְּקֻדִים:
וַיָּבִיאוּ אֶת־קָרְבָּנָם לִפְנֵי יהוה שֵׁשׁ־עֶגְלֹת צָב וּשְׁנֵי־עָשָׂר בָּקָר עֲגָלָה עַל־שְׁנֵי
הַנְּשִׂאִים וְשׁוֹר לְאֶחָד וַיַּקְרִיבוּ אוֹתָם לִפְנֵי הַמִּשְׁכָּן: וַיֹּאמֶר יהוה אֶל־מֹשֶׁה
לֵּאמֹר: קַח מֵאִתָּם וְהָיוּ לַעֲבֹד אֶת־עֲבֹדַת אֹהֶל מוֹעֵד וְנָתַתָּה אוֹתָם אֶל־
הַלְוִיִּם אִישׁ כְּפִי עֲבֹדָתוֹ: וַיִּקַּח מֹשֶׁה אֶת־הָעֲגָלֹת וְאֶת־הַבָּקָר וַיִּתֵּן אוֹתָם
אֶל־הַלְוִיִּם: אֵת ׀ שְׁתֵּי הָעֲגָלוֹת וְאֵת אַרְבַּעַת הַבָּקָר נָתַן לִבְנֵי גֵרְשׁוֹן כְּפִי
עֲבֹדָתָם: וְאֵת ׀ אַרְבַּע הָעֲגָלֹת וְאֵת שְׁמֹנַת הַבָּקָר נָתַן לִבְנֵי מְרָרִי כְּפִי עֲבֹדָתָם
בְּיַד אִיתָמָר בֶּן־אַהֲרֹן הַכֹּהֵן: וְלִבְנֵי קְהָת לֹא נָתָן כִּי־עֲבֹדַת הַקֹּדֶשׁ עֲלֵהֶם
בַּכָּתֵף יִשָּׂאוּ: וַיַּקְרִיבוּ הַנְּשִׂאִים אֵת חֲנֻכַּת הַמִּזְבֵּחַ בְּיוֹם הִמָּשַׁח אֹתוֹ וַיַּקְרִיבוּ
הַנְּשִׂיאִם אֶת־קָרְבָּנָם לִפְנֵי הַמִּזְבֵּחַ: וַיֹּאמֶר יהוה אֶל־מֹשֶׁה נָשִׂיא אֶחָד לַיּוֹם
נָשִׂיא אֶחָד לַיּוֹם יַקְרִיבוּ אֶת־קָרְבָּנָם לַחֲנֻכַּת הַמִּזְבֵּחַ: *וַיְהִי לוי
הַמַּקְרִיב בַּיּוֹם הָרִאשׁוֹן אֶת־קָרְבָּנוֹ נַחְשׁוֹן בֶּן־עַמִּינָדָב לְמַטֵּה יְהוּדָה: וְקָרְבָּנוֹ
קַעֲרַת־כֶּסֶף אַחַת שְׁלֹשִׁים וּמֵאָה מִשְׁקָלָהּ מִזְרָק אֶחָד כֶּסֶף שִׁבְעִים שֶׁקֶל
בְּשֶׁקֶל הַקֹּדֶשׁ שְׁנֵיהֶם ׀ מְלֵאִים סֹלֶת בְּלוּלָה בַשֶּׁמֶן לְמִנְחָה: כַּף אַחַת
עֲשָׂרָה זָהָב מְלֵאָה קְטֹרֶת: *פַּר אֶחָד בֶּן־בָּקָר אַיִל אֶחָד כֶּבֶשׂ־אֶחָד בֶּן־ ישראל
שְׁנָתוֹ לְעֹלָה: שְׂעִיר־עִזִּים אֶחָד לְחַטָּאת: וּלְזֶבַח הַשְּׁלָמִים בָּקָר שְׁנַיִם
אֵילִם חֲמִשָּׁה עַתּוּדִים חֲמִשָּׁה כְּבָשִׂים בְּנֵי־שָׁנָה חֲמִשָּׁה זֶה קָרְבַּן נַחְשׁוֹן
בֶּן־עַמִּינָדָב:

## SECOND DAY OF ḤANUKKA קריאה ליום השני של חנוכה

*In* ארץ ישראל*, for* שלישי *repeat the first paragraph:* בַּיּוֹם הַשֵּׁנִי *until* נְתַנְאֵל בֶּן־צוּעָר.

במדבר ז:יח–כט בַּיּוֹם הַשֵּׁנִי הִקְרִיב נְתַנְאֵל בֶּן־צוּעָר נְשִׂיא יִשָּׂשכָר: הִקְרִב אֶת־קָרְבָּנוֹ קַעֲרַת־
כֶּסֶף אַחַת שְׁלֹשִׁים וּמֵאָה מִשְׁקָלָהּ מִזְרָק אֶחָד כֶּסֶף שִׁבְעִים שֶׁקֶל בְּשֶׁקֶל
הַקֹּדֶשׁ שְׁנֵיהֶם ׀ מְלֵאִים סֹלֶת בְּלוּלָה בַשֶּׁמֶן לְמִנְחָה: כַּף אַחַת עֲשָׂרָה זָהָב
לוי מְלֵאָה קְטֹרֶת: *פַּר אֶחָד בֶּן־בָּקָר אַיִל אֶחָד כֶּבֶשׂ־אֶחָד בֶּן־שְׁנָתוֹ לְעֹלָה:
שְׂעִיר־עִזִּים אֶחָד לְחַטָּאת: וּלְזֶבַח הַשְּׁלָמִים בָּקָר שְׁנַיִם אֵילִם חֲמִשָּׁה עַתֻּדִים
חֲמִשָּׁה כְּבָשִׂים בְּנֵי־שָׁנָה חֲמִשָּׁה זֶה קָרְבַּן נְתַנְאֵל בֶּן־צוּעָר:
ישראל בַּיּוֹם הַשְּׁלִישִׁי נָשִׂיא לִבְנֵי זְבוּלֻן אֱלִיאָב בֶּן־חֵלֹן: קָרְבָּנוֹ קַעֲרַת־כֶּסֶף אַחַת
שְׁלֹשִׁים וּמֵאָה מִשְׁקָלָהּ מִזְרָק אֶחָד כֶּסֶף שִׁבְעִים שֶׁקֶל בְּשֶׁקֶל הַקֹּדֶשׁ שְׁנֵיהֶם ׀
מְלֵאִים סֹלֶת בְּלוּלָה בַשֶּׁמֶן לְמִנְחָה: כַּף אַחַת עֲשָׂרָה זָהָב מְלֵאָה קְטֹרֶת:
פַּר אֶחָד בֶּן־בָּקָר אַיִל אֶחָד כֶּבֶשׂ־אֶחָד בֶּן־שְׁנָתוֹ לְעֹלָה: שְׂעִיר־עִזִּים אֶחָד
לְחַטָּאת: וּלְזֶבַח הַשְּׁלָמִים בָּקָר שְׁנַיִם אֵילִם חֲמִשָּׁה עַתֻּדִים חֲמִשָּׁה כְּבָשִׂים
בְּנֵי־שָׁנָה חֲמִשָּׁה זֶה קָרְבַּן אֱלִיאָב בֶּן־חֵלֹן:

## THIRD DAY OF ḤANUKKA קריאה ליום השלישי של חנוכה

*In* ארץ ישראל*, for* שלישי *repeat the first paragraph:* בַּיּוֹם הַשְּׁלִישִׁי *until* אֱלִיאָב בֶּן־חֵלֹן.

במדבר ז:כד–לה בַּיּוֹם הַשְּׁלִישִׁי נָשִׂיא לִבְנֵי זְבוּלֻן אֱלִיאָב בֶּן־חֵלֹן: קָרְבָּנוֹ קַעֲרַת־כֶּסֶף אַחַת
שְׁלֹשִׁים וּמֵאָה מִשְׁקָלָהּ מִזְרָק אֶחָד כֶּסֶף שִׁבְעִים שֶׁקֶל בְּשֶׁקֶל הַקֹּדֶשׁ שְׁנֵיהֶם ׀
מְלֵאִים סֹלֶת בְּלוּלָה בַשֶּׁמֶן לְמִנְחָה: כַּף אַחַת עֲשָׂרָה זָהָב מְלֵאָה קְטֹרֶת:
לוי *פַּר אֶחָד בֶּן־בָּקָר אַיִל אֶחָד כֶּבֶשׂ־אֶחָד בֶּן־שְׁנָתוֹ לְעֹלָה: שְׂעִיר־עִזִּים אֶחָד
לְחַטָּאת: וּלְזֶבַח הַשְּׁלָמִים בָּקָר שְׁנַיִם אֵילִם חֲמִשָּׁה עַתֻּדִים חֲמִשָּׁה כְּבָשִׂים
בְּנֵי־שָׁנָה חֲמִשָּׁה זֶה קָרְבַּן אֱלִיאָב בֶּן־חֵלֹן:
ישראל בַּיּוֹם הָרְבִיעִי נָשִׂיא לִבְנֵי רְאוּבֵן אֱלִיצוּר בֶּן־שְׁדֵיאוּר: קָרְבָּנוֹ קַעֲרַת־כֶּסֶף
אַחַת שְׁלֹשִׁים וּמֵאָה מִשְׁקָלָהּ מִזְרָק אֶחָד כֶּסֶף שִׁבְעִים שֶׁקֶל בְּשֶׁקֶל הַקֹּדֶשׁ
שְׁנֵיהֶם ׀ מְלֵאִים סֹלֶת בְּלוּלָה בַשֶּׁמֶן לְמִנְחָה: כַּף אַחַת עֲשָׂרָה זָהָב מְלֵאָה
קְטֹרֶת: פַּר אֶחָד בֶּן־בָּקָר אַיִל אֶחָד כֶּבֶשׂ־אֶחָד בֶּן־שְׁנָתוֹ לְעֹלָה: שְׂעִיר־עִזִּים
אֶחָד לְחַטָּאת: וּלְזֶבַח הַשְּׁלָמִים בָּקָר שְׁנַיִם אֵילִם חֲמִשָּׁה עַתֻּדִים חֲמִשָּׁה
כְּבָשִׂים בְּנֵי־שָׁנָה חֲמִשָּׁה זֶה קָרְבַּן אֱלִיצוּר בֶּן־שְׁדֵיאוּר:

## FOURTH DAY OF ḤANUKKA קריאה ליום הרביעי של חנוכה

*In* ארץ ישראל*, for* שלישי *repeat the first paragraph:* בַּיּוֹם הָרְבִיעִי *until* אֱלִיצוּר בֶּן־שְׁדֵיאוּר.

במדבר ז:ל–מא בַּיּוֹם הָרְבִיעִי נָשִׂיא לִבְנֵי רְאוּבֵן אֱלִיצוּר בֶּן־שְׁדֵיאוּר׃ קָרְבָּנוֹ קַעֲרַת־כֶּסֶף
אַחַת שְׁלֹשִׁים וּמֵאָה מִשְׁקָלָהּ מִזְרָק אֶחָד כֶּסֶף שִׁבְעִים שֶׁקֶל בְּשֶׁקֶל הַקֹּדֶשׁ
שְׁנֵיהֶם ׀ מְלֵאִים סֹלֶת בְּלוּלָה בַשֶּׁמֶן לְמִנְחָה׃ כַּף אַחַת עֲשָׂרָה זָהָב מְלֵאָה
לוי קְטֹרֶת׃ *פַּר אֶחָד בֶּן־בָּקָר אַיִל אֶחָד כֶּבֶשׂ־אֶחָד בֶּן־שְׁנָתוֹ לְעֹלָה׃ שְׂעִיר־
עִזִּים אֶחָד לְחַטָּאת׃ וּלְזֶבַח הַשְּׁלָמִים בָּקָר שְׁנַיִם אֵילִם חֲמִשָּׁה עַתֻּדִים חֲמִשָּׁה
כְּבָשִׂים בְּנֵי־שָׁנָה חֲמִשָּׁה זֶה קָרְבַּן אֱלִיצוּר בֶּן־שְׁדֵיאוּר׃
ישראל בַּיּוֹם הַחֲמִישִׁי נָשִׂיא לִבְנֵי שִׁמְעוֹן שְׁלֻמִיאֵל בֶּן־צוּרִישַׁדָּי׃ קָרְבָּנוֹ קַעֲרַת־כֶּסֶף
אַחַת שְׁלֹשִׁים וּמֵאָה מִשְׁקָלָהּ מִזְרָק אֶחָד כֶּסֶף שִׁבְעִים שֶׁקֶל בְּשֶׁקֶל הַקֹּדֶשׁ
שְׁנֵיהֶם ׀ מְלֵאִים סֹלֶת בְּלוּלָה בַשֶּׁמֶן לְמִנְחָה׃ כַּף אַחַת עֲשָׂרָה זָהָב מְלֵאָה
קְטֹרֶת׃ פַּר אֶחָד בֶּן־בָּקָר אַיִל אֶחָד כֶּבֶשׂ־אֶחָד בֶּן־שְׁנָתוֹ לְעֹלָה׃ שְׂעִיר־עִזִּים
אֶחָד לְחַטָּאת׃ וּלְזֶבַח הַשְּׁלָמִים בָּקָר שְׁנַיִם אֵילִם חֲמִשָּׁה עַתֻּדִים חֲמִשָּׁה
כְּבָשִׂים בְּנֵי־שָׁנָה חֲמִשָּׁה זֶה קָרְבַּן שְׁלֻמִיאֵל בֶּן־צוּרִישַׁדָּי׃

## FIFTH DAY OF ḤANUKKA קריאה ליום החמישי של חנוכה

*In* ארץ ישראל*, for* שלישי *repeat the first paragraph:* בַּיּוֹם הַחֲמִישִׁי *until* שְׁלֻמִיאֵל בֶּן־צוּרִישַׁדָּי.

במדבר ז:לו–מז בַּיּוֹם הַחֲמִישִׁי נָשִׂיא לִבְנֵי שִׁמְעוֹן שְׁלֻמִיאֵל בֶּן־צוּרִישַׁדָּי׃ קָרְבָּנוֹ קַעֲרַת־
כֶּסֶף אַחַת שְׁלֹשִׁים וּמֵאָה מִשְׁקָלָהּ מִזְרָק אֶחָד כֶּסֶף שִׁבְעִים שֶׁקֶל בְּשֶׁקֶל
הַקֹּדֶשׁ שְׁנֵיהֶם ׀ מְלֵאִים סֹלֶת בְּלוּלָה בַשֶּׁמֶן לְמִנְחָה׃ כַּף אַחַת עֲשָׂרָה זָהָב
לוי מְלֵאָה קְטֹרֶת׃ *פַּר אֶחָד בֶּן־בָּקָר אַיִל אֶחָד כֶּבֶשׂ־אֶחָד בֶּן־שְׁנָתוֹ לְעֹלָה׃
שְׂעִיר־עִזִּים אֶחָד לְחַטָּאת׃ וּלְזֶבַח הַשְּׁלָמִים בָּקָר שְׁנַיִם אֵילִם חֲמִשָּׁה עַתֻּדִים
חֲמִשָּׁה כְּבָשִׂים בְּנֵי־שָׁנָה חֲמִשָּׁה זֶה קָרְבַּן שְׁלֻמִיאֵל בֶּן־צוּרִישַׁדָּי׃
ישראל בַּיּוֹם הַשִּׁשִּׁי נָשִׂיא לִבְנֵי גָד אֶלְיָסָף בֶּן־דְּעוּאֵל׃ קָרְבָּנוֹ קַעֲרַת־כֶּסֶף אַחַת
שְׁלֹשִׁים וּמֵאָה מִשְׁקָלָהּ מִזְרָק אֶחָד כֶּסֶף שִׁבְעִים שֶׁקֶל בְּשֶׁקֶל הַקֹּדֶשׁ שְׁנֵיהֶם ׀
מְלֵאִים סֹלֶת בְּלוּלָה בַשֶּׁמֶן לְמִנְחָה׃ כַּף אַחַת עֲשָׂרָה זָהָב מְלֵאָה קְטֹרֶת׃
פַּר אֶחָד בֶּן־בָּקָר אַיִל אֶחָד כֶּבֶשׂ־אֶחָד בֶּן־שְׁנָתוֹ לְעֹלָה׃ שְׂעִיר־עִזִּים אֶחָד
לְחַטָּאת׃ וּלְזֶבַח הַשְּׁלָמִים בָּקָר שְׁנַיִם אֵילִם חֲמִשָּׁה עַתֻּדִים חֲמִשָּׁה כְּבָשִׂים
בְּנֵי־שָׁנָה חֲמִשָּׁה זֶה קָרְבַּן אֶלְיָסָף בֶּן־דְּעוּאֵל׃

## קריאה ליום השישי של חנוכה וראש חודש
## SIXTH DAY OF ḤANUKKA AND ROSH ḤODESH

*The sixth day is* ראש חודש טבת. *Two* ספרי תורה *are taken out of the* ארון קודש. *From the first, read the* קריאת התורה *for* ראש חודש *(page 1189), from the second, read* בַּיּוֹם הַשִּׁשִּׁי:

במדבר ז:מב–מז בַּיּוֹם הַשִּׁשִּׁי נָשִׂיא לִבְנֵי גָד אֶלְיָסָף בֶּן־דְּעוּאֵל: קָרְבָּנוֹ קַעֲרַת־כֶּסֶף אַחַת
שְׁלֹשִׁים וּמֵאָה מִשְׁקָלָהּ מִזְרָק אֶחָד כֶּסֶף שִׁבְעִים שֶׁקֶל בְּשֶׁקֶל הַקֹּדֶשׁ שְׁנֵיהֶם ׀
מְלֵאִים סֹלֶת בְּלוּלָה בַשֶּׁמֶן לְמִנְחָה: כַּף אַחַת עֲשָׂרָה זָהָב מְלֵאָה קְטֹרֶת:
פַּר אֶחָד בֶּן־בָּקָר אַיִל אֶחָד כֶּבֶשׂ־אֶחָד בֶּן־שְׁנָתוֹ לְעֹלָה: שְׂעִיר־עִזִּים אֶחָד
לְחַטָּאת: וּלְזֶבַח הַשְּׁלָמִים בָּקָר שְׁנַיִם אֵילִם חֲמִשָּׁה עַתֻּדִים חֲמִשָּׁה כְּבָשִׂים
בְּנֵי־שָׁנָה חֲמִשָּׁה זֶה קָרְבַּן אֶלְיָסָף בֶּן־דְּעוּאֵל:

## קריאה ליום השביעי של חנוכה וראש חודש
## SEVENTH DAY OF ḤANUKKA AND ROSH ḤODESH

*If the seventh day is also* ראש חודש, *then two* ספרי תורה *are taken out of the* ארון קודש. *From the first, read the* קריאת התורה *for* ראש חודש *(page 1189), from the second, read* בַּיּוֹם הַשְּׁבִיעִי:

במדבר ז:מח–נג בַּיּוֹם הַשְּׁבִיעִי נָשִׂיא לִבְנֵי אֶפְרָיִם אֱלִישָׁמָע בֶּן־עַמִּיהוּד: קָרְבָּנוֹ קַעֲרַת־כֶּסֶף
אַחַת שְׁלֹשִׁים וּמֵאָה מִשְׁקָלָהּ מִזְרָק אֶחָד כֶּסֶף שִׁבְעִים שֶׁקֶל בְּשֶׁקֶל הַקֹּדֶשׁ
שְׁנֵיהֶם ׀ מְלֵאִים סֹלֶת בְּלוּלָה בַשֶּׁמֶן לְמִנְחָה: כַּף אַחַת עֲשָׂרָה זָהָב מְלֵאָה
קְטֹרֶת: פַּר אֶחָד בֶּן־בָּקָר אַיִל אֶחָד כֶּבֶשׂ־אֶחָד בֶּן־שְׁנָתוֹ לְעֹלָה: שְׂעִיר־עִזִּים
אֶחָד לְחַטָּאת: וּלְזֶבַח הַשְּׁלָמִים בָּקָר שְׁנַיִם אֵילִם חֲמִשָּׁה עַתֻּדִים חֲמִשָּׁה
כְּבָשִׂים בְּנֵי־שָׁנָה חֲמִשָּׁה זֶה קָרְבַּן אֱלִישָׁמָע בֶּן־עַמִּיהוּד:

## SEVENTH DAY OF ḤANUKKA — קריאה ליום השביעי של חנוכה

*If the seventh day is not* ראש חודש, *then read as below. In* ארץ ישראל, *for* שלישי *repeat the first paragraph:* בַּיּוֹם הַשְּׁבִיעִי *until* אֱלִישָׁמָע בֶּן־עַמִּיהוּד.

במדבר ז:מח–נט בַּיּוֹם הַשְּׁבִיעִי נָשִׂיא לִבְנֵי אֶפְרָיִם אֱלִישָׁמָע בֶּן־עַמִּיהוּד: קָרְבָּנוֹ קַעֲרַת־כֶּסֶף
אַחַת שְׁלֹשִׁים וּמֵאָה מִשְׁקָלָהּ מִזְרָק אֶחָד כֶּסֶף שִׁבְעִים שֶׁקֶל בְּשֶׁקֶל הַקֹּדֶשׁ
שְׁנֵיהֶם ׀ מְלֵאִים סֹלֶת בְּלוּלָה בַשֶּׁמֶן לְמִנְחָה: כַּף אַחַת עֲשָׂרָה זָהָב מְלֵאָה
לוי קְטֹרֶת: *פַּר אֶחָד בֶּן־בָּקָר אַיִל אֶחָד כֶּבֶשׂ־אֶחָד בֶּן־שְׁנָתוֹ לְעֹלָה: שְׂעִיר־

עִזִּים אֶחָד לְחַטָּאת: וּלְזֶבַח הַשְּׁלָמִים בָּקָר שְׁנַיִם אֵילִם חֲמִשָּׁה עַתֻּדִים
חֲמִשָּׁה כְּבָשִׂים בְּנֵי־שָׁנָה חֲמִשָּׁה זֶה קָרְבַּן אֱלִישָׁמָע בֶּן־עַמִּיהוּד:

ישראל בַּיּוֹם הַשְּׁמִינִי נָשִׂיא לִבְנֵי מְנַשֶּׁה גַּמְלִיאֵל בֶּן־פְּדָהצוּר: קָרְבָּנוֹ קַעֲרַת־כֶּסֶף
אַחַת שְׁלֹשִׁים וּמֵאָה מִשְׁקָלָהּ מִזְרָק אֶחָד כֶּסֶף שִׁבְעִים שֶׁקֶל בְּשֶׁקֶל הַקֹּדֶשׁ
שְׁנֵיהֶם ׀ מְלֵאִים סֹלֶת בְּלוּלָה בַשֶּׁמֶן לְמִנְחָה: כַּף אַחַת עֲשָׂרָה זָהָב מְלֵאָה
קְטֹרֶת: פַּר אֶחָד בֶּן־בָּקָר אַיִל אֶחָד כֶּבֶשׂ־אֶחָד בֶּן־שְׁנָתוֹ לְעֹלָה: שְׂעִיר־עִזִּים
אֶחָד לְחַטָּאת: וּלְזֶבַח הַשְּׁלָמִים בָּקָר שְׁנַיִם אֵילִם חֲמִשָּׁה עַתֻּדִים חֲמִשָּׁה
כְּבָשִׂים בְּנֵי־שָׁנָה חֲמִשָּׁה זֶה קָרְבַּן גַּמְלִיאֵל בֶּן־פְּדָהצוּר:

## קריאה ליום השמיני של חנוכה — EIGHTH DAY OF ḤANUKKA

במדבר ז:נד–ח:ד

בַּיּוֹם הַשְּׁמִינִי נָשִׂיא לִבְנֵי מְנַשֶּׁה גַּמְלִיאֵל בֶּן־פְּדָהצוּר: קָרְבָּנוֹ קַעֲרַת־כֶּסֶף
אַחַת שְׁלֹשִׁים וּמֵאָה מִשְׁקָלָהּ מִזְרָק אֶחָד כֶּסֶף שִׁבְעִים שֶׁקֶל בְּשֶׁקֶל הַקֹּדֶשׁ
שְׁנֵיהֶם ׀ מְלֵאִים סֹלֶת בְּלוּלָה בַשֶּׁמֶן לְמִנְחָה: כַּף אַחַת עֲשָׂרָה זָהָב מְלֵאָה
לוי קְטֹרֶת: *פַּר אֶחָד בֶּן־בָּקָר אַיִל אֶחָד כֶּבֶשׂ־אֶחָד בֶּן־שְׁנָתוֹ לְעֹלָה: שְׂעִיר־עִזִּים
אֶחָד לְחַטָּאת: וּלְזֶבַח הַשְּׁלָמִים בָּקָר שְׁנַיִם אֵילִם חֲמִשָּׁה עַתֻּדִים חֲמִשָּׁה
כְּבָשִׂים בְּנֵי־שָׁנָה חֲמִשָּׁה זֶה קָרְבַּן גַּמְלִיאֵל בֶּן־פְּדָהצוּר:

ישראל בַּיּוֹם הַתְּשִׁיעִי נָשִׂיא לִבְנֵי בִנְיָמִן אֲבִידָן בֶּן־גִּדְעֹנִי: קָרְבָּנוֹ קַעֲרַת־כֶּסֶף אַחַת
שְׁלֹשִׁים וּמֵאָה מִשְׁקָלָהּ מִזְרָק אֶחָד כֶּסֶף שִׁבְעִים שֶׁקֶל בְּשֶׁקֶל הַקֹּדֶשׁ שְׁנֵיהֶם ׀
מְלֵאִים סֹלֶת בְּלוּלָה בַשֶּׁמֶן לְמִנְחָה: כַּף אַחַת עֲשָׂרָה זָהָב מְלֵאָה קְטֹרֶת:
פַּר אֶחָד בֶּן־בָּקָר אַיִל אֶחָד כֶּבֶשׂ־אֶחָד בֶּן־שְׁנָתוֹ לְעֹלָה: שְׂעִיר־עִזִּים אֶחָד
לְחַטָּאת: וּלְזֶבַח הַשְּׁלָמִים בָּקָר שְׁנַיִם אֵילִם חֲמִשָּׁה עַתֻּדִים חֲמִשָּׁה כְּבָשִׂים
בְּנֵי־שָׁנָה חֲמִשָּׁה זֶה קָרְבַּן אֲבִידָן בֶּן־גִּדְעֹנִי:

בַּיּוֹם הָעֲשִׂירִי נָשִׂיא לִבְנֵי דָן אֲחִיעֶזֶר בֶּן־עַמִּישַׁדָּי: קָרְבָּנוֹ קַעֲרַת־כֶּסֶף אַחַת
שְׁלֹשִׁים וּמֵאָה מִשְׁקָלָהּ מִזְרָק אֶחָד כֶּסֶף שִׁבְעִים שֶׁקֶל בְּשֶׁקֶל הַקֹּדֶשׁ שְׁנֵיהֶם ׀
מְלֵאִים סֹלֶת בְּלוּלָה בַשֶּׁמֶן לְמִנְחָה: כַּף אַחַת עֲשָׂרָה זָהָב מְלֵאָה קְטֹרֶת:
פַּר אֶחָד בֶּן־בָּקָר אַיִל אֶחָד כֶּבֶשׂ־אֶחָד בֶּן־שְׁנָתוֹ לְעֹלָה: שְׂעִיר־עִזִּים אֶחָד
לְחַטָּאת: וּלְזֶבַח הַשְּׁלָמִים בָּקָר שְׁנַיִם אֵילִם חֲמִשָּׁה עַתֻּדִים חֲמִשָּׁה כְּבָשִׂים
בְּנֵי־שָׁנָה חֲמִשָּׁה זֶה קָרְבַּן אֲחִיעֶזֶר בֶּן־עַמִּישַׁדָּי:

בְּי֗וֹם עַשְׁתֵּ֤י עָשָׂר֙ י֔וֹם נָשִׂ֖יא לִבְנֵ֣י אָשֵׁ֑ר פַּגְעִיאֵ֖ל בֶּן־עָכְרָֽן׃ קָרְבָּנ֞וֹ קַעֲרַת־כֶּ֣סֶף אַחַ֗ת שְׁלֹשִׁ֣ים וּמֵאָה֮ מִשְׁקָלָהּ֒ מִזְרָ֤ק אֶחָד֙ כֶּ֔סֶף שִׁבְעִ֥ים שֶׁ֖קֶל בְּשֶׁ֣קֶל הַקֹּ֑דֶשׁ שְׁנֵיהֶ֣ם ׀ מְלֵאִ֗ים סֹ֛לֶת בְּלוּלָ֥ה בַשֶּׁ֖מֶן לְמִנְחָֽה׃ כַּ֥ף אַחַ֛ת עֲשָׂרָ֥ה זָהָ֖ב מְלֵאָ֥ה קְטֹֽרֶת׃ פַּ֣ר אֶחָ֞ד בֶּן־בָּקָ֗ר אַ֧יִל אֶחָ֛ד כֶּֽבֶשׂ־אֶחָ֥ד בֶּן־שְׁנָת֖וֹ לְעֹלָֽה׃ שְׂעִיר־עִזִּ֥ים אֶחָ֖ד לְחַטָּֽאת׃ וּלְזֶ֣בַח הַשְּׁלָמִים֮ בָּקָ֣ר שְׁנַ֒יִם֒ אֵילִ֤ם חֲמִשָּׁה֙ עַתֻּדִ֣ים חֲמִשָּׁ֔ה כְּבָשִׂ֥ים בְּנֵֽי־שָׁנָ֖ה חֲמִשָּׁ֑ה זֶ֛ה קָרְבַּ֥ן פַּגְעִיאֵ֖ל בֶּן־עָכְרָֽן׃

בְּיוֹם֙ שְׁנֵ֣ים עָשָׂ֣ר י֔וֹם נָשִׂ֖יא לִבְנֵ֣י נַפְתָּלִ֑י אֲחִירַ֖ע בֶּן־עֵינָֽן׃ קָרְבָּנ֞וֹ קַעֲרַת־כֶּ֣סֶף אַחַ֗ת שְׁלֹשִׁ֣ים וּמֵאָה֮ מִשְׁקָלָהּ֒ מִזְרָ֤ק אֶחָד֙ כֶּ֔סֶף שִׁבְעִ֥ים שֶׁ֖קֶל בְּשֶׁ֣קֶל הַקֹּ֑דֶשׁ שְׁנֵיהֶ֣ם ׀ מְלֵאִ֗ים סֹ֛לֶת בְּלוּלָ֥ה בַשֶּׁ֖מֶן לְמִנְחָֽה׃ כַּ֥ף אַחַ֛ת עֲשָׂרָ֥ה זָהָ֖ב מְלֵאָ֥ה קְטֹֽרֶת׃ פַּ֣ר אֶחָ֞ד בֶּן־בָּקָ֗ר אַ֧יִל אֶחָ֛ד כֶּֽבֶשׂ־אֶחָ֥ד בֶּן־שְׁנָת֖וֹ לְעֹלָֽה׃ שְׂעִיר־עִזִּ֥ים אֶחָ֖ד לְחַטָּֽאת׃ וּלְזֶ֣בַח הַשְּׁלָמִים֮ בָּקָ֣ר שְׁנַ֒יִם֒ אֵילִ֤ם חֲמִשָּׁה֙ עַתֻּדִ֣ים חֲמִשָּׁ֔ה כְּבָשִׂ֥ים בְּנֵֽי־שָׁנָ֖ה חֲמִשָּׁ֑ה זֶ֛ה קָרְבַּ֥ן אֲחִירַ֖ע בֶּן־עֵינָֽן׃

זֹ֣את ׀ חֲנֻכַּ֣ת הַמִּזְבֵּ֗חַ בְּיוֹם֙ הִמָּשַׁ֣ח אֹת֔וֹ מֵאֵ֖ת נְשִׂיאֵ֣י יִשְׂרָאֵ֑ל קַעֲרֹ֨ת כֶּ֜סֶף שְׁתֵּ֣ים עֶשְׂרֵ֗ה מִֽזְרְקֵי־כֶ֙סֶף֙ שְׁנֵ֣ים עָשָׂ֔ר כַּפּ֥וֹת זָהָ֖ב שְׁתֵּ֥ים עֶשְׂרֵֽה׃ שְׁלֹשִׁ֣ים וּמֵאָ֗ה הַקְּעָרָ֤ה הָֽאַחַת֙ כֶּ֔סֶף וְשִׁבְעִ֖ים הַמִּזְרָ֣ק הָאֶחָ֑ד כֹּ֚ל כֶּ֣סֶף הַכֵּלִ֔ים אַלְפַּ֥יִם וְאַרְבַּע־מֵא֖וֹת בְּשֶׁ֥קֶל הַקֹּֽדֶשׁ׃ כַּפּ֨וֹת זָהָ֤ב שְׁתֵּים־עֶשְׂרֵה֙ מְלֵאֹ֣ת קְטֹ֔רֶת עֲשָׂרָ֧ה עֲשָׂרָ֛ה הַכַּ֖ף בְּשֶׁ֣קֶל הַקֹּ֑דֶשׁ כָּל־זְהַ֥ב הַכַּפּ֖וֹת עֶשְׂרִ֥ים וּמֵאָֽה׃ כָּל־הַבָּקָ֨ר לָעֹלָ֜ה שְׁנֵ֧ים עָשָׂ֣ר פָּרִ֗ים אֵילִ֤ם שְׁנֵים־עָשָׂר֙ כְּבָשִׂ֧ים בְּנֵי־שָׁנָ֛ה שְׁנֵ֥ים עָשָׂ֖ר וּמִנְחָתָ֑ם וּשְׂעִירֵ֥י עִזִּ֛ים שְׁנֵ֥ים עָשָׂ֖ר לְחַטָּֽאת׃ וְכֹ֞ל בְּקַ֣ר ׀ זֶ֣בַח הַשְּׁלָמִ֗ים עֶשְׂרִ֣ים וְאַרְבָּעָה֮ פָּרִים֒ אֵילִ֤ם שִׁשִּׁים֙ עַתֻּדִ֣ים שִׁשִּׁ֔ים כְּבָשִׂ֥ים בְּנֵֽי־שָׁנָ֖ה שִׁשִּׁ֑ים זֹ֚את חֲנֻכַּ֣ת הַמִּזְבֵּ֔חַ אַחֲרֵ֖י הִמָּשַׁ֥ח אֹתֽוֹ׃ וּבְבֹ֨א מֹשֶׁ֜ה אֶל־אֹ֣הֶל מוֹעֵד֮ לְדַבֵּ֣ר אִתּוֹ֒ וַיִּשְׁמַ֨ע אֶת־הַקּ֜וֹל מִדַּבֵּ֣ר אֵלָ֗יו מֵעַ֤ל הַכַּפֹּ֙רֶת֙ אֲשֶׁר֙ עַל־אֲרֹ֣ן הָעֵדֻ֔ת מִבֵּ֖ין שְׁנֵ֣י הַכְּרֻבִ֑ים וַיְדַבֵּ֖ר אֵלָֽיו׃

וַיְדַבֵּ֥ר יְהֹוָ֖ה אֶל־מֹשֶׁ֥ה לֵּאמֹֽר׃ דַּבֵּר֙ אֶל־אַהֲרֹ֔ן וְאָמַרְתָּ֖ אֵלָ֑יו בְּהַעֲלֹֽתְךָ֙ אֶת־הַנֵּרֹ֔ת אֶל־מוּל֙ פְּנֵ֣י הַמְּנוֹרָ֔ה יָאִ֖ירוּ שִׁבְעַ֥ת הַנֵּרֽוֹת׃ וַיַּ֤עַשׂ כֵּן֙ אַהֲרֹ֔ן אֶל־מוּל֙ פְּנֵ֣י הַמְּנוֹרָ֔ה הֶעֱלָ֖ה נֵרֹתֶ֑יהָ כַּאֲשֶׁ֛ר צִוָּ֥ה יְהֹוָ֖ה אֶת־מֹשֶֽׁה׃ וְזֶ֨ה מַעֲשֵׂ֤ה הַמְּנֹרָה֙ מִקְשָׁ֣ה זָהָ֔ב עַד־יְרֵכָ֥הּ עַד־פִּרְחָ֖הּ מִקְשָׁ֣ה הִ֑וא כַּמַּרְאֶ֗ה אֲשֶׁ֨ר הֶרְאָ֤ה יְהֹוָה֙ אֶת־מֹשֶׁ֔ה כֵּ֥ן עָשָׂ֖ה אֶת־הַמְּנֹרָֽה׃

## קריאה לפורים PURIM

שמות יז:ח–טז וַיָּבֹא עֲמָלֵק וַיִּלָּחֶם עִם־יִשְׂרָאֵל בִּרְפִידִם: וַיֹּאמֶר מֹשֶׁה אֶל־יְהוֹשֻׁעַ בְּחַר־
לָנוּ אֲנָשִׁים וְצֵא הִלָּחֵם בַּעֲמָלֵק מָחָר אָנֹכִי נִצָּב עַל־רֹאשׁ הַגִּבְעָה וּמַטֵּה
הָאֱלֹהִים בְּיָדִי: וַיַּעַשׂ יְהוֹשֻׁעַ כַּאֲשֶׁר אָמַר־לוֹ מֹשֶׁה לְהִלָּחֵם בַּעֲמָלֵק
לוי וּמֹשֶׁה אַהֲרֹן וְחוּר עָלוּ רֹאשׁ הַגִּבְעָה: *וְהָיָה כַּאֲשֶׁר יָרִים מֹשֶׁה יָדוֹ וְגָבַר
יִשְׂרָאֵל וְכַאֲשֶׁר יָנִיחַ יָדוֹ וְגָבַר עֲמָלֵק: וִידֵי מֹשֶׁה כְּבֵדִים וַיִּקְחוּ־אֶבֶן וַיָּשִׂימוּ
תַחְתָּיו וַיֵּשֶׁב עָלֶיהָ וְאַהֲרֹן וְחוּר תָּמְכוּ בְיָדָיו מִזֶּה אֶחָד וּמִזֶּה אֶחָד וַיְהִי
יָדָיו אֱמוּנָה עַד־בֹּא הַשָּׁמֶשׁ: וַיַּחֲלֹשׁ יְהוֹשֻׁעַ אֶת־עֲמָלֵק וְאֶת־עַמּוֹ לְפִי־
חָרֶב:

ישראל וַיֹּאמֶר יהוה אֶל־מֹשֶׁה כְּתֹב זֹאת זִכָּרוֹן בַּסֵּפֶר וְשִׂים בְּאָזְנֵי יְהוֹשֻׁעַ כִּי־מָחֹה
אֶמְחֶה אֶת־זֵכֶר עֲמָלֵק מִתַּחַת הַשָּׁמָיִם: וַיִּבֶן מֹשֶׁה מִזְבֵּחַ וַיִּקְרָא שְׁמוֹ יהוה ׀
נִסִּי: וַיֹּאמֶר כִּי־יָד עַל־כֵּס יָהּ מִלְחָמָה לַיהוה בַּעֲמָלֵק מִדֹּר דֹּר:

# קריאת התורה לשלוש רגלים:
# פסח, שבועות וסוכות

# THE READING OF THE TORAH FOR PESAḤ, SHAVUOT AND SUKKOT

## FIRST DAY OF PESAḤ

## קריאה ליום הראשון של פסח

שמות יב:כא–נא
וַיִּקְרָא מֹשֶׁה לְכָל־זִקְנֵי יִשְׂרָאֵל וַיֹּאמֶר אֲלֵהֶם מִשְׁכוּ וּקְחוּ לָכֶם צֹאן
לְמִשְׁפְּחֹתֵיכֶם וְשַׁחֲטוּ הַפָּסַח: וּלְקַחְתֶּם אֲגֻדַּת אֵזוֹב וּטְבַלְתֶּם בַּדָּם אֲשֶׁר־בַּסַּף
וְהִגַּעְתֶּם אֶל־הַמַּשְׁקוֹף וְאֶל־שְׁתֵּי הַמְּזוּזֹת מִן־הַדָּם אֲשֶׁר בַּסָּף וְאַתֶּם לֹא תֵצְאוּ
אִישׁ מִפֶּתַח־בֵּיתוֹ עַד־בֹּקֶר: וְעָבַר יהוה לִנְגֹּף אֶת־מִצְרַיִם וְרָאָה אֶת־הַדָּם
עַל־הַמַּשְׁקוֹף וְעַל שְׁתֵּי הַמְּזוּזֹת וּפָסַח יהוה עַל־הַפֶּתַח וְלֹא יִתֵּן הַמַּשְׁחִית
לָבֹא אֶל־בָּתֵּיכֶם לִנְגֹּף: וּשְׁמַרְתֶּם אֶת־הַדָּבָר הַזֶּה לְחָק־לְךָ וּלְבָנֶיךָ עַד־עוֹלָם:
לוי *וְהָיָה כִּי־תָבֹאוּ אֶל־הָאָרֶץ אֲשֶׁר יִתֵּן יהוה לָכֶם כַּאֲשֶׁר דִּבֵּר וּשְׁמַרְתֶּם אֶת־
הָעֲבֹדָה הַזֹּאת: וְהָיָה כִּי־יֹאמְרוּ אֲלֵיכֶם בְּנֵיכֶם מָה הָעֲבֹדָה הַזֹּאת לָכֶם:
וַאֲמַרְתֶּם זֶבַח־פֶּסַח הוּא לַיהוה אֲשֶׁר פָּסַח עַל־בָּתֵּי בְנֵי־יִשְׂרָאֵל בְּמִצְרַיִם
בְּנָגְפּוֹ אֶת־מִצְרַיִם וְאֶת־בָּתֵּינוּ הִצִּיל וַיִּקֹּד הָעָם וַיִּשְׁתַּחֲווּ: וַיֵּלְכוּ וַיַּעֲשׂוּ בְּנֵי
שלישי יִשְׂרָאֵל כַּאֲשֶׁר צִוָּה יהוה אֶת־מֹשֶׁה וְאַהֲרֹן כֵּן עָשׂוּ: *וַיְהִי ׀ בַּחֲצִי
הַלַּיְלָה וַיהוה הִכָּה כָל־בְּכוֹר בְּאֶרֶץ מִצְרַיִם מִבְּכֹר פַּרְעֹה הַיֹּשֵׁב עַל־כִּסְאוֹ
עַד בְּכוֹר הַשְּׁבִי אֲשֶׁר בְּבֵית הַבּוֹר וְכֹל בְּכוֹר בְּהֵמָה: וַיָּקָם פַּרְעֹה לַיְלָה הוּא
וְכָל־עֲבָדָיו וְכָל־מִצְרַיִם וַתְּהִי צְעָקָה גְדֹלָה בְּמִצְרָיִם כִּי־אֵין בַּיִת אֲשֶׁר אֵין־
שָׁם מֵת: וַיִּקְרָא לְמֹשֶׁה וּלְאַהֲרֹן לַיְלָה וַיֹּאמֶר קוּמוּ צְּאוּ מִתּוֹךְ עַמִּי גַּם־אַתֶּם
גַּם־בְּנֵי יִשְׂרָאֵל וּלְכוּ עִבְדוּ אֶת־יהוה כְּדַבֶּרְכֶם: גַּם־צֹאנְכֶם גַּם־בְּקַרְכֶם קְחוּ
(בשבת רביעי) כַּאֲשֶׁר דִּבַּרְתֶּם וָלֵכוּ וּבֵרַכְתֶּם גַּם־אֹתִי: *וַתֶּחֱזַק מִצְרַיִם עַל־הָעָם לְמַהֵר
לְשַׁלְּחָם מִן־הָאָרֶץ כִּי אָמְרוּ כֻּלָּנוּ מֵתִים: וַיִּשָּׂא הָעָם אֶת־בְּצֵקוֹ טֶרֶם יֶחְמָץ
מִשְׁאֲרֹתָם צְרֻרֹת בְּשִׂמְלֹתָם עַל־שִׁכְמָם: וּבְנֵי־יִשְׂרָאֵל עָשׂוּ כִּדְבַר מֹשֶׁה

וישאלו ממצרים כלי־כסף וכלי זהב ושמלת: ויהוה נתן את־חן העם בעיני
מצרים וישאלום וינצלו את־מצרים:

רביעי (בשבת חמישי) ויסעו בני־ישראל מרעמסס סכתה כשש־מאות אלף רגלי הגברים לבד
מטף: וגם־ערב רב עלה אתם וצאן ובקר מקנה כבד מאד: ויאפו את־
הבצק אשר הוציאו ממצרים עגת מצות כי לא חמץ כי־גרשו ממצרים ולא
יכלו להתמהמה וגם־צדה לא־עשו להם: ומושב בני ישראל אשר ישבו
במצרים שלשים שנה וארבע מאות שנה: ויהי מקץ שלשים שנה וארבע
מאות שנה ויהי בעצם היום הזה יצאו כל־צבאות יהוה מארץ מצרים:
ליל שמרים הוא ליהוה להוציאם מארץ מצרים הוא־הלילה הזה ליהוה
שמרים לכל־בני ישראל לדרתם:

חמישי (בשבת ששי) ויאמר יהוה אל־משה ואהרן זאת חקת הפסח כל־בן־נכר לא־יאכל בו:
וכל־עבד איש מקנת־כסף ומלתה אתו אז יאכל בו: תושב ושכיר לא־יאכל
בו: בבית אחד יאכל לא־תוציא מן־הבית מן־הבשר חוצה ועצם לא תשברו־
(בשבת שביעי) בו: כל־עדת ישראל יעשו אתו: *וכי־יגור אתך גר ועשה פסח ליהוה המול
לו כל־זכר ואז יקרב לעשתו והיה כאזרח הארץ וכל־ערל לא־יאכל בו:
תורה אחת יהיה לאזרח ולגר הגר בתוככם: ויעשו כל־בני ישראל כאשר
צוה יהוה את־משה ואת־אהרן כן עשו: ויהי בעצם היום הזה
הוציא יהוה את־בני ישראל מארץ מצרים על־צבאתם:

*חצי קדיש (page 585) is said, and then the following מפטיר is read from the second ספר תורה on both the first and second days of פסח.*

במדבר כח:טז–כה ובחדש הראשון בארבעה עשר יום לחדש פסח ליהוה: ובחמשה עשר
יום לחדש הזה חג שבעת ימים מצות יאכל: ביום הראשון מקרא־קדש
כל־מלאכת עבדה לא תעשו: והקרבתם אשה עלה ליהוה פרים בני־בקר
שנים ואיל אחד ושבעה כבשים בני שנה תמימם יהיו לכם: ומנחתם סלת
בלולה בשמן שלשה עשרנים לפר ושני עשרנים לאיל תעשו: עשרון עשרון
תעשה לכבש האחד לשבעת הכבשים: ושעיר חטאת אחד לכפר עליכם:
מלבד עלת הבקר אשר לעלת התמיד תעשו את־אלה: כאלה תעשו ליום
שבעת ימים לחם אשה ריח־ניחח ליהוה על־עולת התמיד יעשה ונסכו:
וביום השביעי מקרא־קדש יהיה לכם כל־מלאכת עבדה לא תעשו:

# הפטרה ליום הראשון של פסח

# HAFTARA FOR THE FIRST DAY OF PESAḤ

*Some start from the first verse and some start from the fourth verse.*

יהושע ג:ה–ז ויאמר יהושע אל־העם התקדשו כי מחר יעשה יהוה בקרבכם נפלאות:
ויאמר יהושע אל־הכהנים לאמר שאו את־ארון הברית ועברו לפני העם
וישאו את־ארון הברית וילכו לפני העם: ויאמר יהוה אל־
יהושע היום הזה אחל גדלך בעיני כל־ישראל אשר ידעון כי כאשר הייתי
עם־משה אהיה עמך:

יהושע ה:ב–ו:א בעת ההיא אמר יהוה אל־יהושע עשה לך חרבות צרים ושוב מל את־
בני־ישראל שנית: ויעש־לו יהושע חרבות צרים וימל את־בני ישראל
אל־גבעת הערלות: וזה הדבר אשר־מל יהושע כל־העם היצא ממצרים
הזכרים כל ׀ אנשי המלחמה מתו במדבר בדרך בצאתם ממצרים: כי־מלים
היו כל־העם היצאים וכל־העם הילדים במדבר בדרך בצאתם ממצרים
לא־מלו: כי ׀ ארבעים שנה הלכו בני־ישראל במדבר עד־תם כל־הגוי
אנשי המלחמה היצאים ממצרים אשר לא־שמעו בקול יהוה אשר נשבע
יהוה להם לבלתי הראותם את־הארץ אשר נשבע יהוה לאבותם לתת
לנו ארץ זבת חלב ודבש: ואת־בניהם הקים תחתם אתם מל יהושע
כי־ערלים היו כי לא־מלו אותם בדרך: ויהי כאשר־תמו כל־הגוי להמול
וישבו תחתם במחנה עד חיותם: ויאמר יהוה אל־יהושע היום
גלותי את־חרפת מצרים מעליכם ויקרא שם המקום ההוא גלגל עד היום
הזה: ויחנו בני־ישראל בגלגל ויעשו את־הפסח בארבעה עשר יום לחדש
בערב בערבות יריחו: ויאכלו מעבור הארץ ממחרת הפסח מצות וקלוי
בעצם היום הזה: וישבת המן ממחרת באכלם מעבור הארץ ולא־היה עוד
לבני ישראל מן ויאכלו מתבואת ארץ כנען בשנה ההיא: ויהי
בהיות יהושע ביריחו וישא עיניו וירא והנה־איש עמד לנגדו וחרבו שלופה
בידו וילך יהושע אליו ויאמר לו הלנו אתה אם־לצרינו: ויאמר ׀ לא כי אני
שר־צבא־יהוה עתה באתי ויפל יהושע אל־פניו ארצה וישתחו ויאמר לו
מה אדני מדבר אל־עבדו: ויאמר שר־צבא יהוה אל־יהושע של־נעלך מעל

רַגְלֶךָ כִּי הַמָּקוֹם אֲשֶׁר אַתָּה עֹמֵד עָלָיו קֹדֶשׁ הוּא וַיַּעַשׂ יְהוֹשֻׁעַ כֵּן: וִירִיחוֹ
סֹגֶרֶת וּמְסֻגֶּרֶת מִפְּנֵי בְּנֵי יִשְׂרָאֵל אֵין יוֹצֵא וְאֵין בָּא:

*Some add:*

יהושע ו:כז וַיְהִי יהוה אֶת־יְהוֹשֻׁעַ וַיְהִי שָׁמְעוֹ בְּכָל־הָאָרֶץ:

# קריאה ליום השני של פסח, וכן ליום הראשון של סוכות ויום טוב שני בחוץ לארץ

## READING FOR THE SECOND DAY OF PESAḤ; THE FIRST DAY OF SUKKOT AND THE SECOND DAY IN THE DIASPORA

*On the first day of* חול המועד פסח *in* ארץ ישראל*, for* לוי *start where* רביעי *on* שבת *would otherwise start, for* שלישי *read to the end, and for* רביעי *read from the second* ספר תורה*.*

ויקרא כב:כו–כג:מד וַיְדַבֵּר יהוה אֶל־מֹשֶׁה לֵּאמֹר: שׁוֹר אוֹ־כֶשֶׂב אוֹ־עֵז כִּי יִוָּלֵד וְהָיָה שִׁבְעַת יָמִים
תַּחַת אִמּוֹ וּמִיּוֹם הַשְּׁמִינִי וָהָלְאָה יֵרָצֶה לְקָרְבַּן אִשֶּׁה לַיהוה: וְשׁוֹר אוֹ־שֶׂה
אֹתוֹ וְאֶת־בְּנוֹ לֹא תִשְׁחֲטוּ בְּיוֹם אֶחָד: וְכִי־תִזְבְּחוּ זֶבַח־תּוֹדָה לַיהוה לִרְצֹנְכֶם
תִּזְבָּחוּ: בַּיּוֹם הַהוּא יֵאָכֵל לֹא־תוֹתִירוּ מִמֶּנּוּ עַד־בֹּקֶר אֲנִי יהוה: וּשְׁמַרְתֶּם
מִצְוֹתַי וַעֲשִׂיתֶם אֹתָם אֲנִי יהוה: וְלֹא תְחַלְּלוּ אֶת־שֵׁם קָדְשִׁי וְנִקְדַּשְׁתִּי בְּתוֹךְ
בְּנֵי יִשְׂרָאֵל אֲנִי יהוה מְקַדִּשְׁכֶם: הַמּוֹצִיא אֶתְכֶם מֵאֶרֶץ מִצְרַיִם לִהְיוֹת לָכֶם
לֵאלֹהִים אֲנִי יהוה:

(בשבת לוי) וַיְדַבֵּר יהוה אֶל־מֹשֶׁה לֵּאמֹר: דַּבֵּר אֶל־בְּנֵי יִשְׂרָאֵל וְאָמַרְתָּ אֲלֵהֶם מוֹעֲדֵי
יהוה אֲשֶׁר־תִּקְרְאוּ אֹתָם מִקְרָאֵי קֹדֶשׁ אֵלֶּה הֵם מוֹעֲדָי: שֵׁשֶׁת יָמִים תֵּעָשֶׂה
מְלָאכָה וּבַיּוֹם הַשְּׁבִיעִי שַׁבַּת שַׁבָּתוֹן מִקְרָא־קֹדֶשׁ כָּל־מְלָאכָה לֹא תַעֲשׂוּ
שַׁבָּת הִוא לַיהוה בְּכֹל מוֹשְׁבֹתֵיכֶם:

לוי (בשבת שלישי) אֵלֶּה מוֹעֲדֵי יהוה מִקְרָאֵי קֹדֶשׁ אֲשֶׁר־תִּקְרְאוּ אֹתָם בְּמוֹעֲדָם: בַּחֹדֶשׁ הָרִאשׁוֹן
בְּאַרְבָּעָה עָשָׂר לַחֹדֶשׁ בֵּין הָעַרְבָּיִם פֶּסַח לַיהוה: וּבַחֲמִשָּׁה עָשָׂר יוֹם לַחֹדֶשׁ
הַזֶּה חַג הַמַּצּוֹת לַיהוה שִׁבְעַת יָמִים מַצּוֹת תֹּאכֵלוּ: בַּיּוֹם הָרִאשׁוֹן מִקְרָא־
קֹדֶשׁ יִהְיֶה לָכֶם כָּל־מְלֶאכֶת עֲבֹדָה לֹא תַעֲשׂוּ: וְהִקְרַבְתֶּם אִשֶּׁה לַיהוה שִׁבְעַת
יָמִים בַּיּוֹם הַשְּׁבִיעִי מִקְרָא־קֹדֶשׁ כָּל־מְלֶאכֶת עֲבֹדָה לֹא תַעֲשׂוּ:

(בשבת רביעי לוי בחוה"מ פסח) וַיְדַבֵּר יהוה אֶל־מֹשֶׁה לֵּאמֹר: דַּבֵּר אֶל־בְּנֵי יִשְׂרָאֵל וְאָמַרְתָּ אֲלֵהֶם כִּי־תָבֹאוּ
אֶל־הָאָרֶץ אֲשֶׁר אֲנִי נֹתֵן לָכֶם וּקְצַרְתֶּם אֶת־קְצִירָהּ וַהֲבֵאתֶם אֶת־עֹמֶר

רֵאשִׁית קְצִירְכֶם אֶל־הַכֹּהֵן: וְהֵנִיף אֶת־הָעֹמֶר לִפְנֵי יְהוָה לִרְצֹנְכֶם מִמָּחֳרַת
הַשַּׁבָּת יְנִיפֶנּוּ הַכֹּהֵן: וַעֲשִׂיתֶם בְּיוֹם הֲנִיפְכֶם אֶת־הָעֹמֶר כֶּבֶשׂ תָּמִים בֶּן־
שְׁנָתוֹ לְעֹלָה לַיהוָה: וּמִנְחָתוֹ שְׁנֵי עֶשְׂרֹנִים סֹלֶת בְּלוּלָה בַשֶּׁמֶן אִשֶּׁה לַיהוָה
רֵיחַ נִיחֹחַ וְנִסְכֹּה יַיִן רְבִיעִת הַהִין: וְלֶחֶם וְקָלִי וְכַרְמֶל לֹא תֹאכְלוּ עַד־עֶצֶם
הַיּוֹם הַזֶּה עַד הֲבִיאֲכֶם אֶת־קָרְבַּן אֱלֹהֵיכֶם חֻקַּת עוֹלָם לְדֹרֹתֵיכֶם בְּכֹל
מֹשְׁבֹתֵיכֶם: *וּסְפַרְתֶּם לָכֶם מִמָּחֳרַת הַשַּׁבָּת מִיּוֹם הֲבִיאֲכֶם אֶת־ שלישי ביו״ט ובחוה״מ (בשבת חמישי)
עֹמֶר הַתְּנוּפָה שֶׁבַע שַׁבָּתוֹת תְּמִימֹת תִּהְיֶינָה: עַד מִמָּחֳרַת הַשַּׁבָּת הַשְּׁבִיעִת
תִּסְפְּרוּ חֲמִשִּׁים יוֹם וְהִקְרַבְתֶּם מִנְחָה חֲדָשָׁה לַיהוָה: מִמּוֹשְׁבֹתֵיכֶם תָּבִיאוּ ׀
לֶחֶם תְּנוּפָה שְׁתַּיִם שְׁנֵי עֶשְׂרֹנִים סֹלֶת תִּהְיֶינָה חָמֵץ תֵּאָפֶינָה בִּכּוּרִים לַיהוָה:
וְהִקְרַבְתֶּם עַל־הַלֶּחֶם שִׁבְעַת כְּבָשִׂים תְּמִימִם בְּנֵי שָׁנָה וּפַר בֶּן־בָּקָר אֶחָד
וְאֵילִם שְׁנָיִם יִהְיוּ עֹלָה לַיהוָה וּמִנְחָתָם וְנִסְכֵּיהֶם אִשֵּׁה רֵיחַ־נִיחֹחַ לַיהוָה:
וַעֲשִׂיתֶם שְׂעִיר־עִזִּים אֶחָד לְחַטָּאת וּשְׁנֵי כְבָשִׂים בְּנֵי שָׁנָה לְזֶבַח שְׁלָמִים:
וְהֵנִיף הַכֹּהֵן ׀ אֹתָם עַל לֶחֶם הַבִּכֻּרִים תְּנוּפָה לִפְנֵי יְהוָה עַל־שְׁנֵי כְּבָשִׂים
קֹדֶשׁ יִהְיוּ לַיהוָה לַכֹּהֵן: וּקְרָאתֶם בְּעֶצֶם ׀ הַיּוֹם הַזֶּה מִקְרָא־קֹדֶשׁ יִהְיֶה
לָכֶם כָּל־מְלֶאכֶת עֲבֹדָה לֹא תַעֲשׂוּ חֻקַּת עוֹלָם בְּכָל־מוֹשְׁבֹתֵיכֶם לְדֹרֹתֵיכֶם:
וּבְקֻצְרְכֶם אֶת־קְצִיר אַרְצְכֶם לֹא־תְכַלֶּה פְּאַת שָׂדְךָ בְּקֻצְרֶךָ וְלֶקֶט קְצִירְךָ
לֹא תְלַקֵּט לֶעָנִי וְלַגֵּר תַּעֲזֹב אֹתָם אֲנִי יְהוָה אֱלֹהֵיכֶם:
וַיְדַבֵּר יְהוָה אֶל־מֹשֶׁה לֵּאמֹר: דַּבֵּר אֶל־בְּנֵי יִשְׂרָאֵל לֵאמֹר בַּחֹדֶשׁ הַשְּׁבִיעִי רביעי (בשבת ששי)
בְּאֶחָד לַחֹדֶשׁ יִהְיֶה לָכֶם שַׁבָּתוֹן זִכְרוֹן תְּרוּעָה מִקְרָא־קֹדֶשׁ: כָּל־מְלֶאכֶת
עֲבֹדָה לֹא תַעֲשׂוּ וְהִקְרַבְתֶּם אִשֶּׁה לַיהוָה: וַיְדַבֵּר יְהוָה אֶל־
מֹשֶׁה לֵּאמֹר: אַךְ בֶּעָשׂוֹר לַחֹדֶשׁ הַשְּׁבִיעִי הַזֶּה יוֹם הַכִּפֻּרִים הוּא מִקְרָא־קֹדֶשׁ
יִהְיֶה לָכֶם וְעִנִּיתֶם אֶת־נַפְשֹׁתֵיכֶם וְהִקְרַבְתֶּם אִשֶּׁה לַיהוָה: וְכָל־מְלָאכָה לֹא
תַעֲשׂוּ בְּעֶצֶם הַיּוֹם הַזֶּה כִּי יוֹם כִּפֻּרִים הוּא לְכַפֵּר עֲלֵיכֶם לִפְנֵי יְהוָה אֱלֹהֵיכֶם:
כִּי כָל־הַנֶּפֶשׁ אֲשֶׁר לֹא־תְעֻנֶּה בְּעֶצֶם הַיּוֹם הַזֶּה וְנִכְרְתָה מֵעַמֶּיהָ: וְכָל־הַנֶּפֶשׁ
אֲשֶׁר תַּעֲשֶׂה כָּל־מְלָאכָה בְּעֶצֶם הַיּוֹם הַזֶּה וְהַאֲבַדְתִּי אֶת־הַנֶּפֶשׁ הַהִוא
מִקֶּרֶב עַמָּהּ: כָּל־מְלָאכָה לֹא תַעֲשׂוּ חֻקַּת עוֹלָם לְדֹרֹתֵיכֶם בְּכֹל מֹשְׁבֹתֵיכֶם:
שַׁבַּת שַׁבָּתוֹן הוּא לָכֶם וְעִנִּיתֶם אֶת־נַפְשֹׁתֵיכֶם בְּתִשְׁעָה לַחֹדֶשׁ בָּעֶרֶב מֵעֶרֶב
עַד־עֶרֶב תִּשְׁבְּתוּ שַׁבַּתְּכֶם:
וַיְדַבֵּר יְהוָה אֶל־מֹשֶׁה לֵּאמֹר: דַּבֵּר אֶל־בְּנֵי יִשְׂרָאֵל לֵאמֹר בַּחֲמִשָּׁה עָשָׂר חמישי (בשבת שביעי)

יוֹם לַחֹדֶשׁ הַשְּׁבִיעִי הַזֶּה חַג הַסֻּכּוֹת שִׁבְעַת יָמִים לַיהוָה׃ בַּיּוֹם הָרִאשׁוֹן
מִקְרָא־קֹדֶשׁ כָּל־מְלֶאכֶת עֲבֹדָה לֹא תַעֲשׂוּ׃ שִׁבְעַת יָמִים תַּקְרִיבוּ אִשֶּׁה לַיהוָה
בַּיּוֹם הַשְּׁמִינִי מִקְרָא־קֹדֶשׁ יִהְיֶה לָכֶם וְהִקְרַבְתֶּם אִשֶּׁה לַיהוָה עֲצֶרֶת הִוא
כָּל־מְלֶאכֶת עֲבֹדָה לֹא תַעֲשׂוּ׃ אֵלֶּה מוֹעֲדֵי יְהוָה אֲשֶׁר־תִּקְרְאוּ אֹתָם מִקְרָאֵי
קֹדֶשׁ לְהַקְרִיב אִשֶּׁה לַיהוָה עֹלָה וּמִנְחָה זֶבַח וּנְסָכִים דְּבַר־יוֹם בְּיוֹמוֹ׃ מִלְּבַד
שַׁבְּתֹת יְהוָה וּמִלְּבַד מַתְּנוֹתֵיכֶם וּמִלְּבַד כָּל־נִדְרֵיכֶם וּמִלְּבַד כָּל־נִדְבֹתֵיכֶם
אֲשֶׁר תִּתְּנוּ לַיהוָה׃ אַךְ בַּחֲמִשָּׁה עָשָׂר יוֹם לַחֹדֶשׁ הַשְּׁבִיעִי בְּאָסְפְּכֶם אֶת־
תְּבוּאַת הָאָרֶץ תָּחֹגּוּ אֶת־חַג־יְהוָה שִׁבְעַת יָמִים בַּיּוֹם הָרִאשׁוֹן שַׁבָּתוֹן וּבַיּוֹם
הַשְּׁמִינִי שַׁבָּתוֹן׃ וּלְקַחְתֶּם לָכֶם בַּיּוֹם הָרִאשׁוֹן פְּרִי עֵץ הָדָר כַּפֹּת תְּמָרִים
וַעֲנַף עֵץ־עָבֹת וְעַרְבֵי־נָחַל וּשְׂמַחְתֶּם לִפְנֵי יְהוָה אֱלֹהֵיכֶם שִׁבְעַת יָמִים׃
וְחַגֹּתֶם אֹתוֹ חַג לַיהוָה שִׁבְעַת יָמִים בַּשָּׁנָה חֻקַּת עוֹלָם לְדֹרֹתֵיכֶם בַּחֹדֶשׁ
הַשְּׁבִיעִי תָּחֹגּוּ אֹתוֹ׃ בַּסֻּכֹּת תֵּשְׁבוּ שִׁבְעַת יָמִים כָּל־הָאֶזְרָח בְּיִשְׂרָאֵל יֵשְׁבוּ
בַּסֻּכֹּת׃ לְמַעַן יֵדְעוּ דֹרֹתֵיכֶם כִּי בַסֻּכּוֹת הוֹשַׁבְתִּי אֶת־בְּנֵי יִשְׂרָאֵל בְּהוֹצִיאִי
אוֹתָם מֵאֶרֶץ מִצְרָיִם אֲנִי יְהוָה אֱלֹהֵיכֶם׃ וַיְדַבֵּר מֹשֶׁה אֶת־מֹעֲדֵי יְהוָה אֶל־
בְּנֵי יִשְׂרָאֵל׃

*The* מפטיר *for the second day of* פסח *is the same as for the first day (page 1202).*
*The* מפטיר *and* הפטרה *for* סוכות *appear on pages 1230–1232.*

## הפטרה ליום טוב שני של פסח בחוץ לארץ

## HAFTARA FOR SECOND DAY OF PESAḤ IN THE DIASPORA

*Some start with* וַיִּשְׁלַח הַמֶּלֶךְ *and some start with* וַיְצַו הַמֶּלֶךְ.

וַיִּשְׁלַח הַמֶּלֶךְ וַיַּאַסְפוּ אֵלָיו כָּל־זִקְנֵי יְהוּדָה וִירוּשָׁלָםִ׃ וַיַּעַל הַמֶּלֶךְ בֵּית־יְהוָה מלכים ב׳ כג:א–ט
וְכָל־אִישׁ יְהוּדָה וְכָל־יֹשְׁבֵי יְרוּשָׁלַםִ אִתּוֹ וְהַכֹּהֲנִים וְהַנְּבִיאִים וְכָל־הָעָם
לְמִקָּטֹן וְעַד־גָּדוֹל וַיִּקְרָא בְאָזְנֵיהֶם אֶת־כָּל־דִּבְרֵי סֵפֶר הַבְּרִית הַנִּמְצָא בְּבֵית
יְהוָה׃ וַיַּעֲמֹד הַמֶּלֶךְ עַל־הָעַמּוּד וַיִּכְרֹת אֶת־הַבְּרִית ׀ לִפְנֵי יְהוָה לָלֶכֶת אַחַר
יְהוָה וְלִשְׁמֹר מִצְוֹתָיו וְאֶת־עֵדְוֹתָיו וְאֶת־חֻקֹּתָיו בְּכָל־לֵב וּבְכָל־נֶפֶשׁ לְהָקִים
אֶת־דִּבְרֵי הַבְּרִית הַזֹּאת הַכְּתֻבִים עַל־הַסֵּפֶר הַזֶּה וַיַּעֲמֹד כָּל־הָעָם בַּבְּרִית׃
*וַיְצַו הַמֶּלֶךְ אֶת־חִלְקִיָּהוּ הַכֹּהֵן הַגָּדוֹל וְאֶת־כֹּהֲנֵי הַמִּשְׁנֶה וְאֶת־שֹׁמְרֵי הַסַּף

להוציא מהיכל יהוה את כל-הכלים העשוים לבעל ולאשרה ולכל צבא
השמים וישרפם מחוץ לירושלם בשדמות קדרון ונשא את-עפרם בית-
אל: והשבית את-הכמרים אשר נתנו מלכי יהודה ויקטר בבמות בערי
יהודה ומסבי ירושלם ואת-המקטרים לבעל לשמש ולירח ולמזלות ולכל
צבא השמים: ויצא את-האשרה מבית יהוה מחוץ לירושלם אל-נחל
קדרון וישרף אתה בנחל קדרון וידק לעפר וישלך את-עפרה על-קבר
בני העם: ויתץ את-בתי הקדשים אשר בבית יהוה אשר הנשים ארגות
שם בתים לאשרה: ויבא את-כל-הכהנים מערי יהודה ויטמא את-הבמות
אשר קטרו-שמה הכהנים מגבע עד-באר שבע ונתץ את-במות השערים
אשר-פתח שער יהושע שר-העיר אשר-על-שמאול איש בשער העיר:
אך לא יעלו כהני הבמות אל-מזבח יהוה בירושלם כי אם-אכלו מצות
בתוך אחיהם:

מלכים ב׳ כג:כא–כה ויצו המלך את-כל-העם לאמר עשו פסח ליהוה אלהיכם ככתוב על ספר
הברית הזה: כי לא נעשה כפסח הזה מימי השפטים אשר שפטו את-
ישראל וכל ימי מלכי ישראל ומלכי יהודה: כי אם-בשמנה עשרה שנה
למלך יאשיהו נעשה הפסח הזה ליהוה בירושלם: וגם את-האבות ואת-
הידענים ואת-התרפים ואת-הגללים ואת כל-השקצים אשר נראו בארץ
יהודה ובירושלם בער יאשיהו למען הקים את-דברי התורה הכתבים
על-הספר אשר מצא חלקיהו הכהן בית יהוה: וכמהו לא-היה לפניו מלך
אשר-שב אל-יהוה בכל-לבבו ובכל-נפשו ובכל-מאדו ככל תורת משה
ואחריו לא-קם כמהו:

## THIRD DAY OF PESAḤ — קריאה ליום השלישי של פסח

*If the third day of* פסח *falls on* שבת, *the* קריאת התורה *for* שבת חול המועד *is read* (*page 1212*).

שמות יג:א–טז וידבר יהוה אל-משה לאמר: קדש-לי כל-בכור פטר כל-רחם בבני
ישראל באדם ובבהמה לי הוא: ויאמר משה אל-העם זכור את-היום
הזה אשר יצאתם ממצרים מבית עבדים כי בחזק יד הוציא יהוה אתכם
מזה ולא יאכל חמץ: היום אתם יצאים בחדש האביב: *והיה כי-יביאך לוי
יהוה אל-ארץ הכנעני והחתי והאמרי והחוי והיבוסי אשר נשבע לאבתיך

לתת לך ארץ זבת חלב ודבש ועבדת את־העבדה הזאת בחדש הזה: שבעת ימים תאכל מצת וביום השביעי חג ליהוה: מצות יאכל את שבעת הימים ולא־יראה לך חמץ ולא־יראה לך שאר בכל־גבלך: והגדת לבנך ביום ההוא לאמר בעבור זה עשה יהוה לי בצאתי ממצרים: והיה לך לאות על־ידך ולזכרון בין עיניך למען תהיה תורת יהוה בפיך כי ביד חזקה הוצאך יהוה ממצרים: ושמרת את־החקה הזאת למועדה מימים ימימה:

שלישי

והיה כי־יבאך יהוה אל־ארץ הכנעני כאשר נשבע לך ולאבתיך ונתנה לך: והעברת כל־פטר־רחם ליהוה וכל־פטר ׀ שגר בהמה אשר יהיה לך הזכרים ליהוה: וכל־פטר חמר תפדה בשה ואם־לא תפדה וערפתו וכל בכור אדם בבניך תפדה: והיה כי־ישאלך בנך מחר לאמר מה־זאת ואמרת אליו בחזק יד הוציאנו יהוה ממצרים מבית עבדים: ויהי כי־הקשה פרעה לשלחנו ויהרג יהוה כל־בכור בארץ מצרים מבכר אדם ועד־בכור בהמה על־כן אני זבח ליהוה כל־פטר רחם הזכרים וכל־בכור בני אפדה: והיה לאות על־ידכה ולטוטפת בין עיניך כי בחזק יד הוציאנו יהוה ממצרים:

*רביעי is read from the second ספר תורה:*

במדבר כח: יט–כה

והקרבתם אשה עלה ליהוה פרים בני־בקר שנים ואיל אחד ושבעה כבשים בני שנה תמימם יהיו לכם: ומנחתם סלת בלולה בשמן שלשה עשרנים לפר ושני עשרנים לאיל תעשו: עשרון עשרון תעשה לכבש האחד לשבעת הכבשים: ושעיר חטאת אחד לכפר עליכם: מלבד עלת הבקר אשר לעלת התמיד תעשו את־אלה: כאלה תעשו ליום שבעת ימים לחם אשה ריח־ניחח ליהוה על־עולת התמיד יעשה ונסכו: וביום השביעי מקרא־קדש יהיה לכם כל־מלאכת עבדה לא תעשו:

## FOURTH DAY OF PESAḤ — קריאה ליום הרביעי של פסח

*If the fourth day of פסח falls on Sunday, the קריאת התורה for the third day is read (page 1207).*

שמות כב: כד–כג:יט

אם־כסף ׀ תלוה את־עמי את־העני עמך לא־תהיה לו כנשה לא־תשימון עליו נשך: אם־חבל תחבל שלמת רעך עד־בא השמש תשיבנו לו: כי הוא

כסותה לבדה הוא שמלתו לערו במה ישכב והיה כי־יצעק אלי ושמעתי
כי־חנון אני: *אלהים לא תקלל ונשיא בעמך לא תאר: מלאתך לוי
ודמעך לא תאחר בכור בניך תתן־לי: כן־תעשה לשרך לצאנך שבעת ימים
יהיה עם־אמו ביום השמיני תתנו־לי: ואנשי־קדש תהיון לי ובשר בשדה
טרפה לא תאכלו לכלב תשלכון אתו: לא תשא שמע שוא
אל־תשת ידך עם־רשע להית עד חמס: לא־תהיה אחרי־רבים לרעת ולא־
תענה על־רב לנטת אחרי רבים להטת: ודל לא תהדר בריבו: כי
תפגע שור איבך או חמרו תעה השב תשיבנו לו: כי־תראה חמור
שנאך רבץ תחת משאו וחדלת מעזב לו עזב תעזב עמו: *לא שלישי
תטה משפט אבינך בריבו: מדבר־שקר תרחק ונקי וצדיק אל־תהרג
כי לא־אצדיק רשע: ושחד לא תקח כי השחד יעור פקחים ויסלף דברי
צדיקים: וגר לא תלחץ ואתם ידעתם את־נפש הגר כי־גרים הייתם בארץ
מצרים: ושש שנים תזרע את־ארצך ואספת את־תבואתה: והשביעת
תשמטנה ונטשתה ואכלו אביני עמך ויתרם תאכל חית השדה כן־תעשה
לכרמך לזיתך: ששת ימים תעשה מעשיך וביום השביעי תשבת למען
ינוח שורך וחמרך וינפש בן־אמתך והגר: ובכל אשר־אמרתי אליכם
תשמרו ושם אלהים אחרים לא תזכירו לא ישמע על־פיך: שלש רגלים
תחג לי בשנה: את־חג המצות תשמר שבעת ימים תאכל מצות כאשר
צויתך למועד חדש האביב כי־בו יצאת ממצרים ולא־יראו פני ריקם: וחג
הקציר בכורי מעשיך אשר תזרע בשדה וחג האסף בצאת השנה באספך
את־מעשיך מן־השדה: שלש פעמים בשנה יראה כל־זכורך אל־פני
האדן ׀ יהוה: לא־תזבח על־חמץ דם־זבחי ולא־ילין חלב־חגי עד־בקר:
ראשית בכורי אדמתך תביא בית יהוה אלהיך לא־תבשל גדי בחלב
אמו:

*רביעי is read from the second ספר תורה:*

והקרבתם אשה עלה ליהוה פרים בני־בקר שנים ואיל אחד ושבעה כבשים במדבר כח: יט–כה
בני שנה תמימם יהיו לכם: ומנחתם סלת בלולה בשמן שלשה עשרנים
לפר ושני עשרנים לאיל תעשו: עשרון עשרון תעשה לכבש האחד לשבעת
הכבשים: ושעיר חטאת אחד לכפר עליכם: מלבד עלת הבקר אשר לעלת

התמיד תעשו את־אלה: כאלה תעשו ליום שבעת ימים לחם אשה ריח־
ניחח ליהוה על־עולת התמיד יעשה ונסכו: וביום השביעי מקרא־קדש
יהיה לכם כל־מלאכת עבדה לא תעשו:

## FIFTH DAY OF PESAḤ — קריאה ליום החמישי של פסח

*If the fifth day of* פסח *falls on* שבת, *the* קריאת התורה *for* שבת חול המועד *is read (page 1212), if it falls on Monday, the* קריאת התורה *for the fourth day is read (page 1208).*

שמות לד:א-כו ויאמר יהוה אל־משה פסל־לך שני־לחת אבנים כראשנים וכתבתי על־
הלחת את־הדברים אשר היו על־הלחת הראשנים אשר שברת: והיה
נכון לבקר ועלית בבקר אל־הר סיני ונצבת לי שם על־ראש ההר: ואיש
לא־יעלה עמך וגם־איש אל־ירא בכל־ההר גם־הצאן והבקר אל־ירעו אל־
לוי מול ההר ההוא: *ויפסל שני־לחת אבנים כראשנים וישכם משה בבקר
ויעל אל־הר סיני כאשר צוה יהוה אתו ויקח בידו שני לחת אבנים: וירד
יהוה בענן ויתיצב עמו שם ויקרא בשם יהוה: ויעבר יהוה | על־פניו ויקרא
יהוה | יהוה אל רחום וחנון ארך אפים ורב־חסד ואמת: נצר חסד לאלפים
נשא עון ופשע וחטאה ונקה לא ינקה פקד | עון אבות על־בנים ועל־בני
בנים על־שלשים ועל־רבעים: וימהר משה ויקד ארצה וישתחו: ויאמר
אם־נא מצאתי חן בעיניך אדני ילך־נא אדני בקרבנו כי עם־קשה־ערף
הוא וסלחת לעוננו ולחטאתנו ונחלתנו: ויאמר הנה אנכי כרת ברית נגד
כל־עמך אעשה נפלאת אשר לא־נבראו בכל־הארץ ובכל־הגוים וראה
כל־העם אשר־אתה בקרבו את־מעשה יהוה כי־נורא הוא אשר אני עשה
שלישי עמך: *שמר־לך את אשר אנכי מצוך היום הנני גרש מפניך את־האמרי
והכנעני והחתי והפרזי והחוי והיבוסי: השמר לך פן־תכרת ברית ליושב
הארץ אשר אתה בא עליה פן־יהיה למוקש בקרבך: כי את־מזבחתם
תתצון ואת־מצבתם תשברון ואת־אשריו תכרתון: כי לא תשתחוה לאל
אחר כי יהוה קנא שמו אל קנא הוא: פן־תכרת ברית ליושב הארץ וזנו |
אחרי אלהיהם וזבחו לאלהיהם וקרא לך ואכלת מזבחו: ולקחת מבנתיו
לבניך וזנו בנתיו אחרי אלהיהן והזנו את־בניך אחרי אלהיהן: אלהי מסכה
לא תעשה־לך: את־חג המצות תשמר שבעת ימים תאכל מצות אשר

צִוִּיתִךָ לְמוֹעֵד חֹדֶשׁ הָאָבִיב כִּי בְּחֹדֶשׁ הָאָבִיב יָצָאתָ מִמִּצְרָיִם: כָּל־פֶּטֶר
רֶחֶם לִי וְכָל־מִקְנְךָ תִּזָּכָר פֶּטֶר שׁוֹר וָשֶׂה: וּפֶטֶר חֲמוֹר תִּפְדֶּה בְשֶׂה וְאִם־
לֹא תִפְדֶּה וַעֲרַפְתּוֹ כֹּל בְּכוֹר בָּנֶיךָ תִּפְדֶּה וְלֹא־יֵרָאוּ פָנַי רֵיקָם: שֵׁשֶׁת יָמִים
תַּעֲבֹד וּבַיּוֹם הַשְּׁבִיעִי תִּשְׁבֹּת בֶּחָרִישׁ וּבַקָּצִיר תִּשְׁבֹּת: וְחַג שָׁבֻעֹת תַּעֲשֶׂה
לְךָ בִּכּוּרֵי קְצִיר חִטִּים וְחַג הָאָסִיף תְּקוּפַת הַשָּׁנָה: שָׁלֹשׁ פְּעָמִים בַּשָּׁנָה
יֵרָאֶה כָּל־זְכוּרְךָ אֶת־פְּנֵי הָאָדֹן ׀ יְהוָה אֱלֹהֵי יִשְׂרָאֵל: כִּי־אוֹרִישׁ גּוֹיִם מִפָּנֶיךָ
וְהִרְחַבְתִּי אֶת־גְּבֻלֶךָ וְלֹא־יַחְמֹד אִישׁ אֶת־אַרְצְךָ בַּעֲלֹתְךָ לֵרָאוֹת אֶת־פְּנֵי
יְהוָה אֱלֹהֶיךָ שָׁלֹשׁ פְּעָמִים בַּשָּׁנָה: לֹא־תִשְׁחַט עַל־חָמֵץ דַּם־זִבְחִי וְלֹא־יָלִין
לַבֹּקֶר זֶבַח חַג הַפָּסַח: רֵאשִׁית בִּכּוּרֵי אַדְמָתְךָ תָּבִיא בֵּית יְהוָה אֱלֹהֶיךָ
לֹא־תְבַשֵּׁל גְּדִי בַּחֲלֵב אִמּוֹ:

רביעי *is read from the second* ספר תורה:

במדבר כח:יט–כה וְהִקְרַבְתֶּם אִשֶּׁה עֹלָה לַיהוָה פָּרִים בְּנֵי־בָקָר שְׁנַיִם וְאַיִל אֶחָד וְשִׁבְעָה כְבָשִׂים
בְּנֵי שָׁנָה תְּמִימִם יִהְיוּ לָכֶם: וּמִנְחָתָם סֹלֶת בְּלוּלָה בַשָּׁמֶן שְׁלֹשָׁה עֶשְׂרֹנִים
לַפָּר וּשְׁנֵי עֶשְׂרֹנִים לָאַיִל תַּעֲשׂוּ: עִשָּׂרוֹן עִשָּׂרוֹן תַּעֲשֶׂה לַכֶּבֶשׂ הָאֶחָד לְשִׁבְעַת
הַכְּבָשִׂים: וּשְׂעִיר חַטָּאת אֶחָד לְכַפֵּר עֲלֵיכֶם: מִלְּבַד עֹלַת הַבֹּקֶר אֲשֶׁר לְעֹלַת
הַתָּמִיד תַּעֲשׂוּ אֶת־אֵלֶּה: כָּאֵלֶּה תַּעֲשׂוּ לַיּוֹם שִׁבְעַת יָמִים לֶחֶם אִשֵּׁה רֵיחַ־
נִיחֹחַ לַיהוָה עַל־עוֹלַת הַתָּמִיד יֵעָשֶׂה וְנִסְכּוֹ: וּבַיּוֹם הַשְּׁבִיעִי מִקְרָא־קֹדֶשׁ
יִהְיֶה לָכֶם כָּל־מְלֶאכֶת עֲבֹדָה לֹא תַעֲשׂוּ:

## קריאה ליום הששי של פסח
## SIXTH DAY OF PESAḤ

במדבר ט:א–יד וַיְדַבֵּר יְהוָה אֶל־מֹשֶׁה בְמִדְבַּר־סִינַי בַּשָּׁנָה הַשֵּׁנִית לְצֵאתָם מֵאֶרֶץ מִצְרַיִם
בַּחֹדֶשׁ הָרִאשׁוֹן לֵאמֹר: וְיַעֲשׂוּ בְנֵי־יִשְׂרָאֵל אֶת־הַפָּסַח בְּמוֹעֲדוֹ: בְּאַרְבָּעָה
עָשָׂר־יוֹם בַּחֹדֶשׁ הַזֶּה בֵּין הָעַרְבַּיִם תַּעֲשׂוּ אֹתוֹ בְּמֹעֲדוֹ כְּכָל־חֻקֹּתָיו וּכְכָל־
מִשְׁפָּטָיו תַּעֲשׂוּ אֹתוֹ: וַיְדַבֵּר מֹשֶׁה אֶל־בְּנֵי יִשְׂרָאֵל לַעֲשֹׂת הַפָּסַח: וַיַּעֲשׂוּ
אֶת־הַפֶּסַח בָּרִאשׁוֹן בְּאַרְבָּעָה עָשָׂר יוֹם לַחֹדֶשׁ בֵּין הָעַרְבַּיִם בְּמִדְבַּר סִינָי
לוי כְּכֹל אֲשֶׁר צִוָּה יְהוָה אֶת־מֹשֶׁה כֵּן עָשׂוּ בְּנֵי יִשְׂרָאֵל: *וַיְהִי אֲנָשִׁים אֲשֶׁר הָיוּ
טְמֵאִים לְנֶפֶשׁ אָדָם וְלֹא־יָכְלוּ לַעֲשֹׂת־הַפֶּסַח בַּיּוֹם הַהוּא וַיִּקְרְבוּ לִפְנֵי מֹשֶׁה

וְלִפְנֵי אַהֲרֹן בַּיּוֹם הַהוּא׃ וַיֹּאמְרוּ הָאֲנָשִׁים הָהֵמָּה אֵלָיו אֲנַחְנוּ טְמֵאִים לְנֶפֶשׁ
אָדָם לָמָּה נִגָּרַע לְבִלְתִּי הַקְרִב אֶת־קָרְבַּן יהוה בְּמֹעֲדוֹ בְּתוֹךְ בְּנֵי יִשְׂרָאֵל׃
וַיֹּאמֶר אֲלֵהֶם מֹשֶׁה עִמְדוּ וְאֶשְׁמְעָה מַה־יְצַוֶּה יהוה לָכֶם׃

שלישי וַיְדַבֵּר יהוה אֶל־מֹשֶׁה לֵּאמֹר׃ דַּבֵּר אֶל־בְּנֵי יִשְׂרָאֵל לֵאמֹר אִישׁ אִישׁ כִּי־
יִהְיֶה טָמֵא ׀ לָנֶפֶשׁ אוֹ בְדֶרֶךְ רְחֹקָה לָכֶם אוֹ לְדֹרֹתֵיכֶם וְעָשָׂה פֶסַח לַיהוה׃
בַּחֹדֶשׁ הַשֵּׁנִי בְּאַרְבָּעָה עָשָׂר יוֹם בֵּין הָעַרְבַּיִם יַעֲשׂוּ אֹתוֹ עַל־מַצּוֹת וּמְרֹרִים
יֹאכְלֻהוּ׃ לֹא־יַשְׁאִירוּ מִמֶּנּוּ עַד־בֹּקֶר וְעֶצֶם לֹא יִשְׁבְּרוּ־בוֹ כְּכָל־חֻקַּת הַפֶּסַח
יַעֲשׂוּ אֹתוֹ׃ וְהָאִישׁ אֲשֶׁר־הוּא טָהוֹר וּבְדֶרֶךְ לֹא־הָיָה וְחָדַל לַעֲשׂוֹת הַפֶּסַח
וְנִכְרְתָה הַנֶּפֶשׁ הַהִוא מֵעַמֶּיהָ כִּי ׀ קָרְבַּן יהוה לֹא הִקְרִיב בְּמֹעֲדוֹ חֶטְאוֹ יִשָּׂא
הָאִישׁ הַהוּא׃ וְכִי־יָגוּר אִתְּכֶם גֵּר וְעָשָׂה פֶסַח לַיהוה כְּחֻקַּת הַפֶּסַח וּכְמִשְׁפָּטוֹ
כֵּן יַעֲשֶׂה חֻקָּה אַחַת יִהְיֶה לָכֶם וְלַגֵּר וּלְאֶזְרַח הָאָרֶץ׃

רביעי *is read from the second* ספר תורה*:*

במדבר כח: יט–כה וְהִקְרַבְתֶּם אִשֶּׁה עֹלָה לַיהוה פָּרִים בְּנֵי־בָקָר שְׁנַיִם וְאַיִל אֶחָד וְשִׁבְעָה כְבָשִׂים
בְּנֵי שָׁנָה תְּמִימִם יִהְיוּ לָכֶם׃ וּמִנְחָתָם סֹלֶת בְּלוּלָה בַשָּׁמֶן שְׁלֹשָׁה עֶשְׂרֹנִים
לַפָּר וּשְׁנֵי עֶשְׂרֹנִים לָאַיִל תַּעֲשׂוּ׃ עִשָּׂרוֹן עִשָּׂרוֹן תַּעֲשֶׂה לַכֶּבֶשׂ הָאֶחָד לְשִׁבְעַת
הַכְּבָשִׂים׃ וּשְׂעִיר חַטָּאת אֶחָד לְכַפֵּר עֲלֵיכֶם׃ מִלְּבַד עֹלַת הַבֹּקֶר אֲשֶׁר לְעֹלַת
הַתָּמִיד תַּעֲשׂוּ אֶת־אֵלֶּה׃ כָּאֵלֶּה תַּעֲשׂוּ לַיּוֹם שִׁבְעַת יָמִים לֶחֶם אִשֵּׁה רֵיחַ־
נִיחֹחַ לַיהוה עַל־עוֹלַת הַתָּמִיד יֵעָשֶׂה וְנִסְכּוֹ׃ וּבַיּוֹם הַשְּׁבִיעִי מִקְרָא־קֹדֶשׁ
יִהְיֶה לָכֶם כָּל־מְלֶאכֶת עֲבֹדָה לֹא תַעֲשׂוּ׃

## קריאה לשבת חול המועד פסח וסוכות

## SHABBAT ḤOL HAMO'ED PESAḤ AND SUKKOT

שמות לג: יב–לד:כו וַיֹּאמֶר מֹשֶׁה אֶל־יהוה רְאֵה אַתָּה אֹמֵר אֵלַי הַעַל אֶת־הָעָם הַזֶּה וְאַתָּה לֹא
הוֹדַעְתַּנִי אֵת אֲשֶׁר־תִּשְׁלַח עִמִּי וְאַתָּה אָמַרְתָּ יְדַעְתִּיךָ בְשֵׁם וְגַם־מָצָאתָ
חֵן בְּעֵינָי׃ וְעַתָּה אִם־נָא מָצָאתִי חֵן בְּעֵינֶיךָ הוֹדִעֵנִי נָא אֶת־דְּרָכֶךָ וְאֵדָעֲךָ
לְמַעַן אֶמְצָא־חֵן בְּעֵינֶיךָ וּרְאֵה כִּי עַמְּךָ הַגּוֹי הַזֶּה׃ וַיֹּאמַר פָּנַי יֵלֵכוּ וַהֲנִחֹתִי
לָךְ׃ וַיֹּאמֶר אֵלָיו אִם־אֵין פָּנֶיךָ הֹלְכִים אַל־תַּעֲלֵנוּ מִזֶּה׃ וּבַמֶּה ׀ יִוָּדַע אֵפוֹא

כִּי־מָצָאתִי חֵן בְּעֵינֶיךָ אֲנִי וְעַמֶּךָ הֲלוֹא בְּלֶכְתְּךָ עִמָּנוּ וְנִפְלֵינוּ אֲנִי וְעַמְּךָ
מִכָּל־הָעָם אֲשֶׁר עַל־פְּנֵי הָאֲדָמָה׃
וַיֹּאמֶר יְהוָה אֶל־מֹשֶׁה גַּם אֶת־הַדָּבָר הַזֶּה אֲשֶׁר דִּבַּרְתָּ אֶעֱשֶׂה כִּי־מָצָאתָ לוי
חֵן בְּעֵינַי וָאֵדָעֲךָ בְּשֵׁם׃ וַיֹּאמַר הַרְאֵנִי נָא אֶת־כְּבֹדֶךָ׃ וַיֹּאמֶר אֲנִי אַעֲבִיר
כָּל־טוּבִי עַל־פָּנֶיךָ וְקָרָאתִי בְשֵׁם יְהוָה לְפָנֶיךָ וְחַנֹּתִי אֶת־אֲשֶׁר אָחֹן וְרִחַמְתִּי
אֶת־אֲשֶׁר אֲרַחֵם׃ *וַיֹּאמֶר לֹא תוּכַל לִרְאֹת אֶת־פָּנָי כִּי לֹא־יִרְאַנִי הָאָדָם וָחָי׃ שלישי
וַיֹּאמֶר יְהוָה הִנֵּה מָקוֹם אִתִּי וְנִצַּבְתָּ עַל־הַצּוּר׃ וְהָיָה בַּעֲבֹר כְּבֹדִי וְשַׂמְתִּיךָ
בְּנִקְרַת הַצּוּר וְשַׂכֹּתִי כַפִּי עָלֶיךָ עַד־עָבְרִי׃ וַהֲסִרֹתִי אֶת־כַּפִּי וְרָאִיתָ אֶת־
אֲחֹרָי וּפָנַי לֹא יֵרָאוּ׃
וַיֹּאמֶר יְהוָה אֶל־מֹשֶׁה פְּסָל־לְךָ שְׁנֵי־לֻחֹת אֲבָנִים כָּרִאשֹׁנִים וְכָתַבְתִּי עַל־ רביעי
הַלֻּחֹת אֶת־הַדְּבָרִים אֲשֶׁר הָיוּ עַל־הַלֻּחֹת הָרִאשֹׁנִים אֲשֶׁר שִׁבַּרְתָּ׃ וֶהְיֵה
נָכוֹן לַבֹּקֶר וְעָלִיתָ בַבֹּקֶר אֶל־הַר סִינַי וְנִצַּבְתָּ לִי שָׁם עַל־רֹאשׁ הָהָר׃ וְאִישׁ
לֹא־יַעֲלֶה עִמָּךְ וְגַם־אִישׁ אַל־יֵרָא בְּכָל־הָהָר גַּם־הַצֹּאן וְהַבָּקָר אַל־יִרְעוּ אֶל־
מוּל הָהָר הַהוּא׃ *וַיִּפְסֹל שְׁנֵי־לֻחֹת אֲבָנִים כָּרִאשֹׁנִים וַיַּשְׁכֵּם מֹשֶׁה בַבֹּקֶר חמישי
וַיַּעַל אֶל־הַר סִינַי כַּאֲשֶׁר צִוָּה יְהוָה אֹתוֹ וַיִּקַּח בְּיָדוֹ שְׁנֵי לֻחֹת אֲבָנִים׃ וַיֵּרֶד
יְהוָה בֶּעָנָן וַיִּתְיַצֵּב עִמּוֹ שָׁם וַיִּקְרָא בְשֵׁם יְהוָה׃ וַיַּעֲבֹר יְהוָה ׀ עַל־פָּנָיו וַיִּקְרָא
יְהוָה ׀ יְהוָה אֵל רַחוּם וְחַנּוּן אֶרֶךְ אַפַּיִם וְרַב־חֶסֶד וֶאֱמֶת׃ נֹצֵר חֶסֶד לָאֲלָפִים
נֹשֵׂא עָוֺן וָפֶשַׁע וְחַטָּאָה וְנַקֵּה לֹא יְנַקֶּה פֹּקֵד ׀ עֲוֺן אָבוֹת עַל־בָּנִים וְעַל־בְּנֵי
בָנִים עַל־שִׁלֵּשִׁים וְעַל־רִבֵּעִים׃ וַיְמַהֵר מֹשֶׁה וַיִּקֹּד אַרְצָה וַיִּשְׁתָּחוּ׃ וַיֹּאמֶר
אִם־נָא מָצָאתִי חֵן בְּעֵינֶיךָ אֲדֹנָי יֵלֶךְ־נָא אֲדֹנָי בְּקִרְבֵּנוּ כִּי עַם־קְשֵׁה־עֹרֶף
הוּא וְסָלַחְתָּ לַעֲוֺנֵנוּ וּלְחַטָּאתֵנוּ וּנְחַלְתָּנוּ׃ וַיֹּאמֶר הִנֵּה אָנֹכִי כֹּרֵת בְּרִית נֶגֶד
כָּל־עַמְּךָ אֶעֱשֶׂה נִפְלָאֹת אֲשֶׁר לֹא־נִבְרְאוּ בְכָל־הָאָרֶץ וּבְכָל־הַגּוֹיִם וְרָאָה
כָל־הָעָם אֲשֶׁר־אַתָּה בְקִרְבּוֹ אֶת־מַעֲשֵׂה יְהוָה כִּי־נוֹרָא הוּא אֲשֶׁר אֲנִי עֹשֶׂה
עִמָּךְ׃ *שְׁמָר־לְךָ אֵת אֲשֶׁר אָנֹכִי מְצַוְּךָ הַיּוֹם הִנְנִי גֹרֵשׁ מִפָּנֶיךָ אֶת־הָאֱמֹרִי ששי
וְהַכְּנַעֲנִי וְהַחִתִּי וְהַפְּרִזִּי וְהַחִוִּי וְהַיְבוּסִי׃ הִשָּׁמֶר לְךָ פֶּן־תִּכְרֹת בְּרִית לְיוֹשֵׁב
הָאָרֶץ אֲשֶׁר אַתָּה בָּא עָלֶיהָ פֶּן־יִהְיֶה לְמוֹקֵשׁ בְּקִרְבֶּךָ׃ כִּי אֶת־מִזְבְּחֹתָם
תִּתֹּצוּן וְאֶת־מַצֵּבֹתָם תְּשַׁבֵּרוּן וְאֶת־אֲשֵׁרָיו תִּכְרֹתוּן׃ כִּי לֹא תִשְׁתַּחֲוֶה לְאֵל
אַחֵר כִּי יְהוָה קַנָּא שְׁמוֹ אֵל קַנָּא הוּא׃ פֶּן־תִּכְרֹת בְּרִית לְיוֹשֵׁב הָאָרֶץ וְזָנוּ ׀

אַחֲרֵי אֱלֹהֵיהֶם וְזָבְחוּ לֵאלֹהֵיהֶם וְקָרָא לְךָ וְאָכַלְתָּ מִזִּבְחוֹ׃ וְלָקַחְתָּ מִבְּנֹתָיו
לְבָנֶיךָ וְזָנוּ בְנֹתָיו אַחֲרֵי אֱלֹהֵיהֶן וְהִזְנוּ אֶת־בָּנֶיךָ אַחֲרֵי אֱלֹהֵיהֶן׃ אֱלֹהֵי מַסֵּכָה
שביעי לֹא תַעֲשֶׂה־לָּךְ׃ *אֶת־חַג הַמַּצּוֹת תִּשְׁמֹר שִׁבְעַת יָמִים תֹּאכַל מַצּוֹת אֲשֶׁר
צִוִּיתִךָ לְמוֹעֵד חֹדֶשׁ הָאָבִיב כִּי בְּחֹדֶשׁ הָאָבִיב יָצָאתָ מִמִּצְרָיִם׃ כָּל־פֶּטֶר
רֶחֶם לִי וְכָל־מִקְנְךָ תִּזָּכָר פֶּטֶר שׁוֹר וָשֶׂה׃ וּפֶטֶר חֲמוֹר תִּפְדֶּה בְשֶׂה וְאִם־
לֹא תִפְדֶּה וַעֲרַפְתּוֹ כֹּל בְּכוֹר בָּנֶיךָ תִּפְדֶּה וְלֹא־יֵרָאוּ פָנַי רֵיקָם׃ שֵׁשֶׁת יָמִים
תַּעֲבֹד וּבַיּוֹם הַשְּׁבִיעִי תִּשְׁבֹּת בֶּחָרִישׁ וּבַקָּצִיר תִּשְׁבֹּת׃ וְחַג שָׁבֻעֹת תַּעֲשֶׂה
לְךָ בִּכּוּרֵי קְצִיר חִטִּים וְחַג הָאָסִיף תְּקוּפַת הַשָּׁנָה׃ שָׁלֹשׁ פְּעָמִים בַּשָּׁנָה
יֵרָאֶה כָּל־זְכוּרְךָ אֶת־פְּנֵי הָאָדֹן ׀ יהוה אֱלֹהֵי יִשְׂרָאֵל׃ כִּי־אוֹרִישׁ גּוֹיִם מִפָּנֶיךָ
וְהִרְחַבְתִּי אֶת־גְּבֻלֶךָ וְלֹא־יַחְמֹד אִישׁ אֶת־אַרְצְךָ בַּעֲלֹתְךָ לֵרָאוֹת אֶת־פְּנֵי
יהוה אֱלֹהֶיךָ שָׁלֹשׁ פְּעָמִים בַּשָּׁנָה׃ לֹא־תִשְׁחַט עַל־חָמֵץ דַּם־זִבְחִי וְלֹא־יָלִין
לַבֹּקֶר זֶבַח חַג הַפָּסַח׃ רֵאשִׁית בִּכּוּרֵי אַדְמָתְךָ תָּבִיא בֵּית יהוה אֱלֹהֶיךָ
לֹא־תְבַשֵּׁל גְּדִי בַּחֲלֵב אִמּוֹ׃

*The מפטיר for שבת חול המועד פסח is the same as that for the other days of חול המועד פסח, page 1202. The מפטיר for שבת חול המועד סוכות is the קריאת התורה of the day of חול המועד סוכות on which שבת falls (pages 1233–1235).*

## הפטרה לשבת חול המועד פסח

## HAFTARA FOR SHABBAT ḤOL HAMO'ED PESAḤ

יחזקאל לז:א–יד הָיְתָה עָלַי יַד־יהוה וַיּוֹצִאֵנִי בְרוּחַ יהוה וַיְנִיחֵנִי בְּתוֹךְ הַבִּקְעָה וְהִיא מְלֵאָה
עֲצָמוֹת׃ וְהֶעֱבִירַנִי עֲלֵיהֶם סָבִיב ׀ סָבִיב וְהִנֵּה רַבּוֹת מְאֹד עַל־פְּנֵי הַבִּקְעָה
וְהִנֵּה יְבֵשׁוֹת מְאֹד׃ וַיֹּאמֶר אֵלַי בֶּן־אָדָם הֲתִחְיֶינָה הָעֲצָמוֹת הָאֵלֶּה וָאֹמַר
אֲדֹנָי יֱהֹוִה אַתָּה יָדָעְתָּ׃ וַיֹּאמֶר אֵלַי הִנָּבֵא עַל־הָעֲצָמוֹת הָאֵלֶּה וְאָמַרְתָּ
אֲלֵיהֶם הָעֲצָמוֹת הַיְבֵשׁוֹת שִׁמְעוּ דְּבַר־יהוה׃ כֹּה אָמַר אֲדֹנָי יֱהֹוִה לָעֲצָמוֹת
הָאֵלֶּה הִנֵּה אֲנִי מֵבִיא בָכֶם רוּחַ וִחְיִיתֶם׃ וְנָתַתִּי עֲלֵיכֶם גִּידִים וְהַעֲלֵתִי
עֲלֵיכֶם בָּשָׂר וְקָרַמְתִּי עֲלֵיכֶם עוֹר וְנָתַתִּי בָכֶם רוּחַ וִחְיִיתֶם וִידַעְתֶּם כִּי־אֲנִי
יהוה׃ וְנִבֵּאתִי כַּאֲשֶׁר צֻוֵּיתִי וַיְהִי־קוֹל כְּהִנָּבְאִי וְהִנֵּה־רַעַשׁ וַתִּקְרְבוּ עֲצָמוֹת
עֶצֶם אֶל־עַצְמוֹ׃ וְרָאִיתִי וְהִנֵּה־עֲלֵיהֶם גִּדִים וּבָשָׂר עָלָה וַיִּקְרַם עֲלֵיהֶם עוֹר
מִלְמָעְלָה וְרוּחַ אֵין בָּהֶם׃ וַיֹּאמֶר אֵלַי הִנָּבֵא אֶל־הָרוּחַ הִנָּבֵא בֶן־אָדָם

ואמרת אל־הרוח כה־אמר ׀ אדני יהוה מארבע רוחות באי הרוח ופחי
בהרוגים האלה ויחיו: והנבאתי כאשר צוני ותבוא בהם הרוח ויחיו ויעמדו
על־רגליהם חיל גדול מאד מאד: ויאמר אלי בן־אדם העצמות האלה
כל־בית ישראל המה הנה אמרים יבשו עצמותינו ואבדה תקותנו נגזרנו
לנו: לכן הנבא ואמרת אליהם כה־אמר אדני יהוה הנה אני פתח את־
קברותיכם והעליתי אתכם מקברותיכם עמי והבאתי אתכם אל־אדמת
ישראל: וידעתם כי־אני יהוה בפתחי את־קברותיכם ובהעלותי אתכם
מקברותיכם עמי: ונתתי רוחי בכם וחייתם והנחתי אתכם על־אדמתכם
וידעתם כי אני יהוה דברתי ועשיתי נאם־יהוה:

## SEVENTH DAY OF PESAḤ — קריאה לשביעי של פסח

ויהי בשלח פרעה את־העם ולא־נחם אלהים דרך ארץ פלשתים כי קרוב — שמות יג:יז–טו:כו
הוא כי ׀ אמר אלהים פן־ינחם העם בראתם מלחמה ושבו מצרימה: ויסב
אלהים ׀ את־העם דרך המדבר ים־סוף וחמשים עלו בני־ישראל מארץ
מצרים: ויקח משה את־עצמות יוסף עמו כי השבע השביע את־בני ישראל
לאמר פקד יפקד אלהים אתכם והעליתם את־עצמתי מזה אתכם: *ויסעו — (בשבת לוי)
מסכת ויחנו באתם בקצה המדבר: ויהוה הלך לפניהם יומם בעמוד ענן
לנחתם הדרך ולילה בעמוד אש להאיר להם ללכת יומם ולילה: לא־ימיש
עמוד הענן יומם ועמוד האש לילה לפני העם:
וידבר יהוה אל־משה לאמר: דבר אל־בני ישראל וישבו ויחנו לפני פי — לוי
החירת בין מגדל ובין הים לפני בעל צפן נכחו תחנו על־הים: ואמר פרעה — (בשבת שלישי)
לבני ישראל נבכים הם בארץ סגר עליהם המדבר: וחזקתי את־לב־פרעה
ורדף אחריהם ואכבדה בפרעה ובכל־חילו וידעו מצרים כי־אני יהוה ויעשו־
כן: *ויגד למלך מצרים כי ברח העם ויהפך לבב פרעה ועבדיו אל־העם — (בשבת רביעי)
ויאמרו מה־זאת עשינו כי־שלחנו את־ישראל מעבדנו: ויאסר את־רכבו
ואת־עמו לקח עמו: ויקח שש־מאות רכב בחור וכל רכב מצרים ושלשם
על־כלו: ויחזק יהוה את־לב פרעה מלך מצרים וירדף אחרי בני ישראל
ובני ישראל יצאים ביד רמה: *וירדפו מצרים אחריהם וישיגו אותם חנים — שלישי
על־הים כל־סוס רכב פרעה ופרשיו וחילו על־פי החירת לפני בעל צפן: — (בשבת חמישי)

וּפַרְעֹ֖ה הִקְרִ֑יב וַיִּשְׂא֣וּ בְנֵֽי־יִשְׂרָאֵ֣ל אֶת־עֵ֠ינֵיהֶ֠ם וְהִנֵּ֨ה מִצְרַ֤יִם ׀ נֹסֵ֣עַ אַחֲרֵיהֶ֗ם
וַיִּֽירְאוּ֙ מְאֹ֔ד וַיִּצְעֲק֥וּ בְנֵֽי־יִשְׂרָאֵ֖ל אֶל־יהוה׃ וַיֹּאמְרוּ֮ אֶל־מֹשֶׁה֒ הַֽמִבְּלִ֤י אֵין־
קְבָרִים֙ בְּמִצְרַ֔יִם לְקַחְתָּ֖נוּ לָמ֣וּת בַּמִּדְבָּ֑ר מַה־זֹּאת֙ עָשִׂ֣יתָ לָּ֔נוּ לְהוֹצִיאָ֖נוּ
מִמִּצְרָֽיִם׃ הֲלֹא־זֶ֣ה הַדָּבָ֗ר אֲשֶׁר֩ דִּבַּ֨רְנוּ אֵלֶ֤יךָ בְמִצְרַ֙יִם֙ לֵאמֹ֔ר חֲדַ֥ל מִמֶּ֖נּוּ
וְנַעַבְדָ֣ה אֶת־מִצְרָ֑יִם כִּ֣י ט֥וֹב לָ֙נוּ֙ עֲבֹ֣ד אֶת־מִצְרַ֔יִם מִמֻּתֵ֖נוּ בַּמִּדְבָּֽר׃ וַיֹּ֨אמֶר
מֹשֶׁ֣ה אֶל־הָעָם֮ אַל־תִּירָאוּ֒ הִֽתְיַצְּב֗וּ וּרְאוּ֙ אֶת־יְשׁוּעַ֣ת יהוה אֲשֶׁר־יַעֲשֶׂ֥ה לָכֶ֖ם
הַיּ֑וֹם כִּ֗י אֲשֶׁ֨ר רְאִיתֶ֤ם אֶת־מִצְרַ֙יִם֙ הַיּ֔וֹם לֹ֥א תֹסִ֛פוּ לִרְאֹתָ֥ם ע֖וֹד עַד־עוֹלָֽם׃
יהוה יִלָּחֵ֣ם לָכֶ֑ם וְאַתֶּ֖ם תַּחֲרִשֽׁוּן׃

רביעי (בשבת ששי) וַיֹּ֤אמֶר יהוה אֶל־מֹשֶׁ֔ה מַה־תִּצְעַ֖ק אֵלָ֑י דַּבֵּ֥ר אֶל־בְּנֵֽי־יִשְׂרָאֵ֖ל וְיִסָּֽעוּ׃ וְאַתָּ֞ה
הָרֵ֣ם אֶת־מַטְּךָ֗ וּנְטֵ֧ה אֶת־יָדְךָ֛ עַל־הַיָּ֖ם וּבְקָעֵ֑הוּ וְיָבֹ֧אוּ בְנֵֽי־יִשְׂרָאֵ֛ל בְּת֥וֹךְ הַיָּ֖ם
בַּיַּבָּשָֽׁה׃ וַאֲנִ֗י הִנְנִי֙ מְחַזֵּק֙ אֶת־לֵ֣ב מִצְרַ֔יִם וְיָבֹ֖אוּ אַחֲרֵיהֶ֑ם וְאִכָּבְדָ֤ה בְּפַרְעֹה֙
וּבְכָל־חֵיל֔וֹ בְּרִכְבּ֖וֹ וּבְפָרָשָֽׁיו׃ וְיָדְע֥וּ מִצְרַ֖יִם כִּֽי־אֲנִ֣י יהוה בְּהִכָּבְדִ֣י בְּפַרְעֹ֔ה
בְּרִכְבּ֖וֹ וּבְפָרָשָֽׁיו׃ וַיִּסַּ֞ע מַלְאַ֣ךְ הָאֱלֹהִ֗ים הַהֹלֵךְ֙ לִפְנֵי֙ מַחֲנֵ֣ה יִשְׂרָאֵ֔ל וַיֵּ֖לֶךְ
מֵאַחֲרֵיהֶ֑ם וַיִּסַּ֞ע עַמּ֤וּד הֶֽעָנָן֙ מִפְּנֵיהֶ֔ם וַיַּעֲמֹ֖ד מֵאַחֲרֵיהֶֽם׃ וַיָּבֹ֞א בֵּ֣ין ׀ מַחֲנֵ֣ה
מִצְרַ֗יִם וּבֵין֙ מַחֲנֵ֣ה יִשְׂרָאֵ֔ל וַיְהִ֤י הֶֽעָנָן֙ וְהַחֹ֔שֶׁךְ וַיָּ֖אֶר אֶת־הַלָּ֑יְלָה וְלֹא־קָרַ֥ב
זֶ֛ה אֶל־זֶ֖ה כָּל־הַלָּֽיְלָה׃ וַיֵּ֨ט מֹשֶׁ֣ה אֶת־יָדוֹ֮ עַל־הַיָּם֒ וַיּ֣וֹלֶךְ יהוה ׀ אֶת־הַ֠יָּם
בְּר֨וּחַ קָדִ֤ים עַזָּה֙ כָּל־הַלַּ֔יְלָה וַיָּ֥שֶׂם אֶת־הַיָּ֖ם לֶחָרָבָ֑ה וַיִּבָּקְע֖וּ הַמָּֽיִם׃ וַיָּבֹ֧אוּ
בְנֵֽי־יִשְׂרָאֵ֛ל בְּת֥וֹךְ הַיָּ֖ם בַּיַּבָּשָׁ֑ה וְהַמַּ֤יִם לָהֶם֙ חוֹמָ֔ה מִימִינָ֖ם וּמִשְּׂמֹאלָֽם׃
וַיִּרְדְּפ֤וּ מִצְרַ֙יִם֙ וַיָּבֹ֣אוּ אַחֲרֵיהֶ֔ם כֹּ֚ל ס֣וּס פַּרְעֹ֔ה רִכְבּ֖וֹ וּפָרָשָׁ֑יו אֶל־תּ֖וֹךְ הַיָּֽם׃
וַֽיְהִי֙ בְּאַשְׁמֹ֣רֶת הַבֹּ֔קֶר וַיַּשְׁקֵ֤ף יהוה אֶל־מַחֲנֵ֣ה מִצְרַ֔יִם בְּעַמּ֥וּד אֵ֖שׁ וְעָנָ֑ן וַיָּ֕הָם
אֵ֖ת מַחֲנֵ֥ה מִצְרָֽיִם׃ וַיָּ֗סַר אֵ֚ת אֹפַ֣ן מַרְכְּבֹתָ֔יו וַֽיְנַהֲגֵ֖הוּ בִּכְבֵדֻ֑ת וַיֹּ֣אמֶר מִצְרַ֗יִם
אָנ֙וּסָה֙ מִפְּנֵ֣י יִשְׂרָאֵ֔ל כִּ֣י יהוה נִלְחָ֥ם לָהֶ֖ם בְּמִצְרָֽיִם׃

חמישי (בשבת שביעי) וַיֹּ֤אמֶר יהוה אֶל־מֹשֶׁ֔ה נְטֵ֥ה אֶת־יָדְךָ֖ עַל־הַיָּ֑ם וְיָשֻׁ֤בוּ הַמַּ֙יִם֙ עַל־מִצְרַ֔יִם עַל־
רִכְבּ֖וֹ וְעַל־פָּרָשָֽׁיו׃ וַיֵּט֩ מֹשֶׁ֨ה אֶת־יָד֜וֹ עַל־הַיָּ֗ם וַיָּ֨שָׁב הַיָּ֜ם לִפְנ֥וֹת בֹּ֙קֶר֙ לְאֵ֣יתָנ֔וֹ
וּמִצְרַ֖יִם נָסִ֣ים לִקְרָאת֑וֹ וַיְנַעֵ֧ר יהוה אֶת־מִצְרַ֖יִם בְּת֥וֹךְ הַיָּֽם׃ וַיָּשֻׁ֣בוּ הַמַּ֗יִם וַיְכַסּ֤וּ
אֶת־הָרֶ֙כֶב֙ וְאֶת־הַפָּ֣רָשִׁ֔ים לְכֹל֙ חֵ֣יל פַּרְעֹ֔ה הַבָּאִ֥ים אַחֲרֵיהֶ֖ם בַּיָּ֑ם לֹֽא־נִשְׁאַ֥ר
בָּהֶ֖ם עַד־אֶחָֽד׃ וּבְנֵ֧י יִשְׂרָאֵ֛ל הָלְכ֥וּ בַיַּבָּשָׁ֖ה בְּת֣וֹךְ הַיָּ֑ם וְהַמַּ֤יִם לָהֶם֙ חֹמָ֔ה
מִימִינָ֖ם וּמִשְּׂמֹאלָֽם׃ וַיּ֨וֹשַׁע יהוה בַּיּ֥וֹם הַה֛וּא אֶת־יִשְׂרָאֵ֖ל מִיַּ֣ד מִצְרָ֑יִם וַיַּ֤רְא
יִשְׂרָאֵל֙ אֶת־מִצְרַ֔יִם מֵ֖ת עַל־שְׂפַ֥ת הַיָּֽם׃ וַיַּ֨רְא יִשְׂרָאֵ֜ל אֶת־הַיָּ֣ד הַגְּדֹלָ֗ה אֲשֶׁ֨ר
עָשָׂ֤ה יהוה בְּמִצְרַ֔יִם וַיִּֽירְא֥וּ הָעָ֖ם אֶת־יהוה וַיַּֽאֲמִ֙ינוּ֙ בַּֽיהוה וּבְמֹשֶׁ֖ה עַבְדּֽוֹ׃

אָז יָשִׁיר־מֹשֶׁה וּבְנֵי יִשְׂרָאֵל אֶת־הַשִּׁירָה הַזֹּאת לַיהוָה וַיֹּאמְרוּ
לֵאמֹר    אָשִׁירָה לַיהוָה כִּי־גָאֹה גָּאָה    סוּס
וְרֹכְבוֹ רָמָה בַיָּם׃    עָזִּי וְזִמְרָת יָהּ וַיְהִי־לִי
לִישׁוּעָה    זֶה אֵלִי וְאַנְוֵהוּ    אֱלֹהֵי
אָבִי וַאֲרֹמְמֶנְהוּ׃    יְהוָה אִישׁ מִלְחָמָה יְהוָה
שְׁמוֹ׃    מַרְכְּבֹת פַּרְעֹה וְחֵילוֹ יָרָה בַיָּם    וּמִבְחַר
שָׁלִשָׁיו טֻבְּעוּ בְיַם־סוּף׃    תְּהֹמֹת יְכַסְיֻמוּ יָרְדוּ בִמְצוֹלֹת כְּמוֹ־
אָבֶן׃    יְמִינְךָ יְהוָה נֶאְדָּרִי בַּכֹּחַ    יְמִינְךָ
יְהוָה תִּרְעַץ אוֹיֵב׃    וּבְרֹב גְּאוֹנְךָ תַּהֲרֹס
קָמֶיךָ    תְּשַׁלַּח חֲרֹנְךָ יֹאכְלֵמוֹ כַּקַּשׁ׃    וּבְרוּחַ
אַפֶּיךָ נֶעֶרְמוּ מַיִם    נִצְּבוּ כְמוֹ־נֵד
נֹזְלִים    קָפְאוּ תְהֹמֹת בְּלֶב־יָם׃    אָמַר
אוֹיֵב אֶרְדֹּף אַשִּׂיג    אֲחַלֵּק שָׁלָל תִּמְלָאֵמוֹ
נַפְשִׁי    אָרִיק חַרְבִּי תּוֹרִישֵׁמוֹ יָדִי׃    נָשַׁפְתָּ
בְרוּחֲךָ כִּסָּמוֹ יָם    צָלֲלוּ כַּעוֹפֶרֶת בְּמַיִם
אַדִּירִים׃    מִי־כָמֹכָה בָּאֵלִם יְהוָה    מִי
כָּמֹכָה נֶאְדָּר בַּקֹּדֶשׁ    נוֹרָא תְהִלֹּת עֹשֵׂה
פֶלֶא׃    נָטִיתָ יְמִינְךָ תִּבְלָעֵמוֹ אָרֶץ׃    נָחִיתָ
בְחַסְדְּךָ עַם־זוּ גָּאָלְתָּ    נֵהַלְתָּ בְעָזְּךָ אֶל־נְוֵה
קָדְשֶׁךָ׃    שָׁמְעוּ עַמִּים יִרְגָּזוּן    חִיל
אָחַז יֹשְׁבֵי פְּלָשֶׁת׃    אָז נִבְהֲלוּ אַלּוּפֵי
אֱדוֹם    אֵילֵי מוֹאָב יֹאחֲזֵמוֹ רָעַד    נָמֹגוּ
כֹּל יֹשְׁבֵי כְנָעַן׃    תִּפֹּל עֲלֵיהֶם אֵימָתָה
וָפַחַד    בִּגְדֹל זְרוֹעֲךָ יִדְּמוּ כָּאָבֶן    עַד־
יַעֲבֹר עַמְּךָ יְהוָה    עַד־יַעֲבֹר עַם־זוּ
קָנִיתָ׃    תְּבִאֵמוֹ וְתִטָּעֵמוֹ בְּהַר נַחֲלָתְךָ    מָכוֹן
לְשִׁבְתְּךָ פָּעַלְתָּ יְהוָה    מִקְּדָשׁ אֲדֹנָי כּוֹנְנוּ
יָדֶיךָ׃    יְהוָה ׀ יִמְלֹךְ לְעֹלָם וָעֶד׃    כִּי
בָא סוּס פַּרְעֹה בְּרִכְבּוֹ וּבְפָרָשָׁיו בַּיָּם וַיָּשֶׁב יְהוָה עֲלֵהֶם אֶת־מֵי
הַיָּם    וּבְנֵי יִשְׂרָאֵל הָלְכוּ בַיַּבָּשָׁה בְּתוֹךְ    הַיָּם׃

וַתִּקַּח מִרְיָם הַנְּבִיאָה אֲחוֹת אַהֲרֹן אֶת־הַתֹּף בְּיָדָהּ וַתֵּצֶאןָ כָל־הַנָּשִׁים אַחֲרֶיהָ
בְּתֻפִּים וּבִמְחֹלֹת: וַתַּעַן לָהֶם מִרְיָם שִׁירוּ לַיהוה כִּי־גָאֹה גָּאָה סוּס וְרֹכְבוֹ
רָמָה בַיָּם: וַיַּסַּע מֹשֶׁה אֶת־יִשְׂרָאֵל מִיַּם־סוּף וַיֵּצְאוּ אֶל־מִדְבַּר־שׁוּר
וַיֵּלְכוּ שְׁלֹשֶׁת־יָמִים בַּמִּדְבָּר וְלֹא־מָצְאוּ מָיִם: וַיָּבֹאוּ מָרָתָה וְלֹא יָכְלוּ לִשְׁתֹּת
מַיִם מִמָּרָה כִּי מָרִים הֵם עַל־כֵּן קָרָא־שְׁמָהּ מָרָה: וַיִּלֹּנוּ הָעָם עַל־מֹשֶׁה לֵּאמֹר
מַה־נִּשְׁתֶּה: וַיִּצְעַק אֶל־יהוה וַיּוֹרֵהוּ יהוה עֵץ וַיַּשְׁלֵךְ אֶל־הַמַּיִם וַיִּמְתְּקוּ הַמָּיִם
שָׁם שָׂם לוֹ חֹק וּמִשְׁפָּט וְשָׁם נִסָּהוּ: וַיֹּאמֶר אִם־שָׁמוֹעַ תִּשְׁמַע לְקוֹל ׀ יהוה
אֱלֹהֶיךָ וְהַיָּשָׁר בְּעֵינָיו תַּעֲשֶׂה וְהַאֲזַנְתָּ לְמִצְוֺתָיו וְשָׁמַרְתָּ כָּל־חֻקָּיו כָּל־הַמַּחֲלָה
אֲשֶׁר־שַׂמְתִּי בְמִצְרַיִם לֹא־אָשִׂים עָלֶיךָ כִּי אֲנִי יהוה רֹפְאֶךָ:

*The מפטיר is read from the second ספר תורה:*

במדבר כח: יט–כה
וְהִקְרַבְתֶּם אִשֶּׁה עֹלָה לַיהוה פָּרִים בְּנֵי־בָקָר שְׁנַיִם וְאַיִל אֶחָד וְשִׁבְעָה כְבָשִׂים
בְּנֵי שָׁנָה תְּמִימִם יִהְיוּ לָכֶם: וּמִנְחָתָם סֹלֶת בְּלוּלָה בַשָּׁמֶן שְׁלֹשָׁה עֶשְׂרֹנִים
לַפָּר וּשְׁנֵי עֶשְׂרֹנִים לָאַיִל תַּעֲשׂוּ: עִשָּׂרוֹן עִשָּׂרוֹן תַּעֲשֶׂה לַכֶּבֶשׂ הָאֶחָד לְשִׁבְעַת
הַכְּבָשִׂים: וּשְׂעִיר חַטָּאת אֶחָד לְכַפֵּר עֲלֵיכֶם: מִלְּבַד עֹלַת הַבֹּקֶר אֲשֶׁר לְעֹלַת
הַתָּמִיד תַּעֲשׂוּ אֶת־אֵלֶּה: כָּאֵלֶּה תַּעֲשׂוּ לַיּוֹם שִׁבְעַת יָמִים לֶחֶם אִשֵּׁה רֵיחַ־
נִיחֹחַ לַיהוה עַל־עוֹלַת הַתָּמִיד יֵעָשֶׂה וְנִסְכּוֹ: וּבַיּוֹם הַשְּׁבִיעִי מִקְרָא־קֹדֶשׁ
יִהְיֶה לָכֶם כָּל־מְלֶאכֶת עֲבֹדָה לֹא תַעֲשׂוּ:

## הפטרה לשביעי של פסח

## HAFTARA FOR SEVENTH DAY OF PESAḤ

שמואל ב׳ כב:א–נא
וַיְדַבֵּר דָּוִד לַיהוה אֶת־דִּבְרֵי הַשִּׁירָה הַזֹּאת בְּיוֹם
הִצִּיל יהוה אֹתוֹ מִכַּף כָּל־אֹיְבָיו וּמִכַּף שָׁאוּל:
וַיֹּאמַר יהוה סַלְעִי וּמְצֻדָתִי וּמְפַלְטִי־לִי: אֱלֹהֵי
צוּרִי אֶחֱסֶה־בּוֹ מָגִנִּי וְקֶרֶן יִשְׁעִי מִשְׂגַּבִּי
וּמְנוּסִי מֹשִׁעִי מֵחָמָס תֹּשִׁעֵנִי: מְהֻלָּל
אֶקְרָא יהוה וּמֵאֹיְבַי אִוָּשֵׁעַ: כִּי אֲפָפֻנִי מִשְׁבְּרֵי־
מָוֶת נַחֲלֵי בְלִיַּעַל יְבַעֲתֻנִי: חֶבְלֵי
שְׁאוֹל סַבֻּנִי קִדְּמֻנִי מֹקְשֵׁי־

מָוֶת׃ בַּצַּר־לִי אֶקְרָא יְהוָה וְאֶל־
אֱלֹהַי אֶקְרָא וַיִּשְׁמַע מֵהֵיכָלוֹ
קוֹלִי וְשַׁוְעָתִי בְּאָזְנָיו׃ ותגעש וַיִּתְגָּעַשׁ
וַתִּרְעַשׁ הָאָרֶץ מוֹסְדוֹת הַשָּׁמַיִם
יִרְגָּזוּ וַיִּתְגָּעֲשׁוּ כִּי־חָרָה לוֹ׃ עָלָה
עָשָׁן בְּאַפּוֹ וְאֵשׁ מִפִּיו
תֹּאכֵל גֶּחָלִים בָּעֲרוּ מִמֶּנּוּ׃ וַיֵּט
שָׁמַיִם וַיֵּרַד וַעֲרָפֶל תַּחַת
רַגְלָיו׃ וַיִּרְכַּב עַל־כְּרוּב וַיָּעֹף וַיֵּרָא
עַל־כַּנְפֵי־רוּחַ׃ וַיָּשֶׁת חֹשֶׁךְ סְבִיבֹתָיו
סֻכּוֹת חַשְׁרַת־מַיִם עָבֵי שְׁחָקִים׃ מִנֹּגַהּ
נֶגְדּוֹ בָּעֲרוּ גַּחֲלֵי־אֵשׁ׃ יַרְעֵם מִן־שָׁמַיִם
יְהוָה וְעֶלְיוֹן יִתֵּן קוֹלוֹ׃ וַיִּשְׁלַח
חִצִּים וַיְפִיצֵם בָּרָק ויהמם׃ וַיֵּרָאוּ אֲפִקֵי וַיָּהֹם
יָם יִגָּלוּ מֹסְדוֹת תֵּבֵל בְּגַעֲרַת
יְהוָה מִנִּשְׁמַת רוּחַ אַפּוֹ׃ יִשְׁלַח מִמָּרוֹם
יִקָּחֵנִי יַמְשֵׁנִי מִמַּיִם רַבִּים׃ יַצִּילֵנִי
מֵאֹיְבִי עָז מִשֹּׂנְאַי כִּי אָמְצוּ
מִמֶּנִּי׃ יְקַדְּמֻנִי בְּיוֹם אֵידִי וַיְהִי
יְהוָה מִשְׁעָן לִי׃ וַיֹּצֵא לַמֶּרְחָב
אֹתִי יְחַלְּצֵנִי כִּי־חָפֵץ בִּי׃ יִגְמְלֵנִי
יְהוָה כְּצִדְקָתִי כְּבֹר יָדַי יָשִׁיב
לִי׃ כִּי שָׁמַרְתִּי דַּרְכֵי יְהוָה וְלֹא
רָשַׁעְתִּי מֵאֱלֹהָי׃ כִּי כָל־מִשְׁפָּטָו
לְנֶגְדִּי וְחֻקֹּתָיו לֹא־אָסוּר מִמֶּנָּה׃ וָאֶהְיֶה
תָמִים לוֹ וָאֶשְׁתַּמְּרָה מֵעֲוֺנִי׃ וַיָּשֶׁב יְהוָה לִי
כְּצִדְקָתִי כְּבֹרִי לְנֶגֶד עֵינָיו׃ עִם־
חָסִיד תִּתְחַסָּד עִם־גְּבוֹר תָּמִים
תִּתַּמָּם׃ עִם־נָבָר תִּתָּבָר וְעִם־

עִקֵּשׁ תִּתַּפָּל׃ וְאֶת־עַם עָנִי
תּוֹשִׁיעַ וְעֵינֶיךָ עַל־רָמִים תַּשְׁפִּיל׃ כִּי־
אַתָּה נֵירִי יְהֹוָה וַיהֹוָה יַגִּיהַּ
חָשְׁכִּי׃ כִּי בְכָה אָרוּץ גְּדוּד בֵּאלֹהַי
אֲדַלֶּג־שׁוּר׃ הָאֵל תָּמִים
דַּרְכּוֹ אִמְרַת יְהֹוָה צְרוּפָה מָגֵן
הוּא לְכֹל הַחֹסִים בּוֹ׃ כִּי מִי־אֵל מִבַּלְעֲדֵי
יְהֹוָה וּמִי צוּר מִבַּלְעֲדֵי אֱלֹהֵינוּ׃ הָאֵל
מָעוּזִּי חָיִל וַיַּתֵּר תָּמִים
דרכו׃ מְשַׁוֶּה רגליו כָּאַיָּלוֹת וְעַל־ דַּרְכִּי רַגְלַי
בָּמוֹתַי יַעֲמִידֵנִי׃ מְלַמֵּד יָדַי
לַמִּלְחָמָה וְנִחַת קֶשֶׁת־נְחוּשָׁה זְרֹעֹתָי׃ וַתִּתֶּן־
לִי מָגֵן יִשְׁעֶךָ וַעֲנֹתְךָ תַּרְבֵּנִי׃ תַּרְחִיב צַעֲדִי
תַּחְתֵּנִי וְלֹא מָעֲדוּ קַרְסֻלָּי׃ אֶרְדְּפָה
אֹיְבַי וָאַשְׁמִידֵם וְלֹא אָשׁוּב עַד־
כַּלּוֹתָם׃ וָאֲכַלֵּם וָאֶמְחָצֵם וְלֹא יְקוּמוּן וַיִּפְּלוּ
תַּחַת רַגְלָי׃ וַתַּזְרֵנִי חַיִל
לַמִּלְחָמָה תַּכְרִיעַ קָמַי תַּחְתֵּנִי׃ וְאֹיְבַי
תַּתָּה לִּי עֹרֶף מְשַׂנְאַי וָאַצְמִיתֵם׃ יִשְׁעוּ וְאֵין
מֹשִׁיעַ אֶל־יְהֹוָה וְלֹא עָנָם׃ וְאֶשְׁחָקֵם
כַּעֲפַר־אָרֶץ כְּטִיט־חוּצוֹת אֲדִקֵּם
אֶרְקָעֵם׃ וַתְּפַלְּטֵנִי מֵרִיבֵי עַמִּי תִּשְׁמְרֵנִי
לְרֹאשׁ גּוֹיִם עַם לֹא־יָדַעְתִּי
יַעַבְדֻנִי׃ בְּנֵי נֵכָר יִתְכַּחֲשׁוּ־לִי לִשְׁמוֹעַ
אֹזֶן יִשָּׁמְעוּ לִי׃ בְּנֵי נֵכָר יִבֹּלוּ וְיַחְגְּרוּ
מִמִּסְגְּרוֹתָם׃ חַי־יְהֹוָה וּבָרוּךְ צוּרִי וְיָרֻם
אֱלֹהֵי צוּר יִשְׁעִי׃ הָאֵל הַנֹּתֵן נְקָמֹת
לִי וּמוֹרִיד עַמִּים תַּחְתֵּנִי׃ וּמוֹצִיאִי
מֵאֹיְבָי וּמִקָּמַי תְּרוֹמְמֵנִי מֵאִישׁ חֲמָסִים

תַּצִּילֵנִי׃ עַל־כֵּן אוֹדְךָ יְהוָה בַּגּוֹיִם וּלְשִׁמְךָ
אֲזַמֵּר׃ מגדיל יְשׁוּעוֹת מִגְדּוֹל
מַלְכּוֹ וְעֹשֶׂה־חֶסֶד לִמְשִׁיחוֹ
לְדָוִד וּלְזַרְעוֹ עַד־עוֹלָם׃

## קריאה ליום אחרון של פסח או שבועות, ולשמיני עצרת בחוץ לארץ

## LAST DAY OF PESAḤ AND SHAVUOT, AND SHEMINI ATZERET IN THE DIASPORA

*If the eighth day of* פסח *or the second day of* שבועות *falls on* שבת*, start here.*
*If it falls on a weekday, start with* כָּל־הַבְּכוֹר *on the next page. On* שמיני עצרת *start here.*

דברים יד:כב–טז:יז

עַשֵּׂר תְּעַשֵּׂר אֵת כָּל־תְּבוּאַת זַרְעֶךָ הַיֹּצֵא הַשָּׂדֶה שָׁנָה שָׁנָה׃ וְאָכַלְתָּ לִפְנֵי ׀
יְהוָה אֱלֹהֶיךָ בַּמָּקוֹם אֲשֶׁר־יִבְחַר לְשַׁכֵּן שְׁמוֹ שָׁם מַעְשַׂר דְּגָנְךָ תִּירֹשְׁךָ וְיִצְהָרֶךָ
וּבְכֹרֹת בְּקָרְךָ וְצֹאנֶךָ לְמַעַן תִּלְמַד לְיִרְאָה אֶת־יְהוָה אֱלֹהֶיךָ כָּל־הַיָּמִים׃ וְכִי־
יִרְבֶּה מִמְּךָ הַדֶּרֶךְ כִּי לֹא תוּכַל שְׂאֵתוֹ כִּי־יִרְחַק מִמְּךָ הַמָּקוֹם אֲשֶׁר יִבְחַר יְהוָה
אֱלֹהֶיךָ לָשׂוּם שְׁמוֹ שָׁם כִּי יְבָרֶכְךָ יְהוָה אֱלֹהֶיךָ׃ וְנָתַתָּה בַּכָּסֶף וְצַרְתָּ הַכֶּסֶף
בְּיָדְךָ וְהָלַכְתָּ אֶל־הַמָּקוֹם אֲשֶׁר יִבְחַר יְהוָה אֱלֹהֶיךָ בּוֹ׃ וְנָתַתָּה הַכֶּסֶף בְּכֹל
אֲשֶׁר־תְּאַוֶּה נַפְשְׁךָ בַּבָּקָר וּבַצֹּאן וּבַיַּיִן וּבַשֵּׁכָר וּבְכֹל אֲשֶׁר תִּשְׁאָלְךָ נַפְשֶׁךָ
וְאָכַלְתָּ שָּׁם לִפְנֵי יְהוָה אֱלֹהֶיךָ וְשָׂמַחְתָּ אַתָּה וּבֵיתֶךָ׃ וְהַלֵּוִי אֲשֶׁר־בִּשְׁעָרֶיךָ לֹא
תַעַזְבֶנּוּ כִּי אֵין לוֹ חֵלֶק וְנַחֲלָה עִמָּךְ׃ מִקְצֵה ׀ שָׁלֹשׁ שָׁנִים תּוֹצִיא
אֶת־כָּל־מַעְשַׂר תְּבוּאָתְךָ בַּשָּׁנָה הַהִוא וְהִנַּחְתָּ בִּשְׁעָרֶיךָ׃ וּבָא הַלֵּוִי כִּי אֵין־
לוֹ חֵלֶק וְנַחֲלָה עִמָּךְ וְהַגֵּר וְהַיָּתוֹם וְהָאַלְמָנָה אֲשֶׁר בִּשְׁעָרֶיךָ וְאָכְלוּ וְשָׂבֵעוּ
לְמַעַן יְבָרֶכְךָ יְהוָה אֱלֹהֶיךָ בְּכָל־מַעֲשֵׂה יָדְךָ אֲשֶׁר תַּעֲשֶׂה׃ *מִקֵּץ (בשבת לוי)
שֶׁבַע־שָׁנִים תַּעֲשֶׂה שְׁמִטָּה׃ וְזֶה דְּבַר הַשְּׁמִטָּה שָׁמוֹט כָּל־בַּעַל מַשֵּׁה יָדוֹ
אֲשֶׁר יַשֶּׁה בְּרֵעֵהוּ לֹא־יִגֹּשׂ אֶת־רֵעֵהוּ וְאֶת־אָחִיו כִּי־קָרָא שְׁמִטָּה לַיהוָה׃
אֶת־הַנָּכְרִי תִּגֹּשׂ וַאֲשֶׁר יִהְיֶה לְךָ אֶת־אָחִיךָ תַּשְׁמֵט יָדֶךָ׃ אֶפֶס כִּי לֹא יִהְיֶה־
בְּךָ אֶבְיוֹן כִּי־בָרֵךְ יְבָרֶכְךָ יְהוָה בָּאָרֶץ אֲשֶׁר יְהוָה אֱלֹהֶיךָ נֹתֵן־לְךָ נַחֲלָה
לְרִשְׁתָּהּ׃ רַק אִם־שָׁמוֹעַ תִּשְׁמַע בְּקוֹל יְהוָה אֱלֹהֶיךָ לִשְׁמֹר לַעֲשׂוֹת אֶת־
כָּל־הַמִּצְוָה הַזֹּאת אֲשֶׁר אָנֹכִי מְצַוְּךָ הַיּוֹם׃ כִּי־יְהוָה אֱלֹהֶיךָ בֵּרַכְךָ כַּאֲשֶׁר
דִּבֶּר־לָךְ וְהַעֲבַטְתָּ גּוֹיִם רַבִּים וְאַתָּה לֹא תַעֲבֹט וּמָשַׁלְתָּ בְּגוֹיִם רַבִּים וּבְךָ לֹא

יִמְשֹׁלוּ׃ כִּי־יִהְיֶה בְךָ אֶבְיוֹן מֵאַחַד אַחֶיךָ בְּאַחַד שְׁעָרֶיךָ בְּאַרְצְךָ
אֲשֶׁר־יְהוָה אֱלֹהֶיךָ נֹתֵן לָךְ לֹא תְאַמֵּץ אֶת־לְבָבְךָ וְלֹא תִקְפֹּץ אֶת־יָדְךָ מֵאָחִיךָ
הָאֶבְיוֹן׃ כִּי־פָתֹחַ תִּפְתַּח אֶת־יָדְךָ לוֹ וְהַעֲבֵט תַּעֲבִיטֶנּוּ דֵּי מַחְסֹרוֹ אֲשֶׁר
יֶחְסַר לוֹ׃ הִשָּׁמֶר לְךָ פֶּן־יִהְיֶה דָבָר עִם־לְבָבְךָ בְלִיַּעַל לֵאמֹר קָרְבָה שְׁנַת־
הַשֶּׁבַע שְׁנַת הַשְּׁמִטָּה וְרָעָה עֵינְךָ בְּאָחִיךָ הָאֶבְיוֹן וְלֹא תִתֵּן לוֹ וְקָרָא עָלֶיךָ
אֶל־יְהוָה וְהָיָה בְךָ חֵטְא׃ נָתוֹן תִּתֵּן לוֹ וְלֹא־יֵרַע לְבָבְךָ בְּתִתְּךָ לוֹ כִּי בִּגְלַל ׀
הַדָּבָר הַזֶּה יְבָרֶכְךָ יְהוָה אֱלֹהֶיךָ בְּכָל־מַעֲשֶׂךָ וּבְכֹל מִשְׁלַח יָדֶךָ׃ כִּי לֹא־יֶחְדַּל
אֶבְיוֹן מִקֶּרֶב הָאָרֶץ עַל־כֵּן אָנֹכִי מְצַוְּךָ לֵאמֹר פָּתֹחַ תִּפְתַּח אֶת־יָדְךָ לְאָחִיךָ
לַעֲנִיֶּךָ וּלְאֶבְיֹנְךָ בְּאַרְצֶךָ׃ כִּי־יִמָּכֵר לְךָ אָחִיךָ הָעִבְרִי אוֹ הָעִבְרִיָּה
וַעֲבָדְךָ שֵׁשׁ שָׁנִים וּבַשָּׁנָה הַשְּׁבִיעִת תְּשַׁלְּחֶנּוּ חָפְשִׁי מֵעִמָּךְ׃ וְכִי־תְשַׁלְּחֶנּוּ
חָפְשִׁי מֵעִמָּךְ לֹא תְשַׁלְּחֶנּוּ רֵיקָם׃ הַעֲנֵיק תַּעֲנִיק לוֹ מִצֹּאנְךָ וּמִגָּרְנְךָ וּמִיִּקְבֶךָ
אֲשֶׁר בֵּרַכְךָ יְהוָה אֱלֹהֶיךָ תִּתֶּן־לוֹ׃ וְזָכַרְתָּ כִּי עֶבֶד הָיִיתָ בְּאֶרֶץ מִצְרַיִם וַיִּפְדְּךָ
יְהוָה אֱלֹהֶיךָ עַל־כֵּן אָנֹכִי מְצַוְּךָ אֶת־הַדָּבָר הַזֶּה הַיּוֹם׃ וְהָיָה כִּי־יֹאמַר אֵלֶיךָ
לֹא אֵצֵא מֵעִמָּךְ כִּי אֲהֵבְךָ וְאֶת־בֵּיתֶךָ כִּי־טוֹב לוֹ עִמָּךְ׃ וְלָקַחְתָּ אֶת־הַמַּרְצֵעַ
וְנָתַתָּה בְאָזְנוֹ וּבַדֶּלֶת וְהָיָה לְךָ עֶבֶד עוֹלָם וְאַף לַאֲמָתְךָ תַּעֲשֶׂה־כֵּן׃ לֹא־
יִקְשֶׁה בְעֵינֶךָ בְּשַׁלֵּחֲךָ אֹתוֹ חָפְשִׁי מֵעִמָּךְ כִּי מִשְׁנֶה שְׂכַר שָׂכִיר עֲבָדְךָ שֵׁשׁ
שָׁנִים וּבֵרַכְךָ יְהוָה אֱלֹהֶיךָ בְּכֹל אֲשֶׁר תַּעֲשֶׂה׃

*If the eighth day of פסח or the second day of שבועות falls on a weekday, start here:*

(בשבת שלישי) כָּל־הַבְּכוֹר אֲשֶׁר יִוָּלֵד בִּבְקָרְךָ וּבְצֹאנְךָ הַזָּכָר תַּקְדִּישׁ לַיהוָה אֱלֹהֶיךָ לֹא
תַעֲבֹד בִּבְכֹר שׁוֹרֶךָ וְלֹא תָגֹז בְּכוֹר צֹאנֶךָ׃ לִפְנֵי יְהוָה אֱלֹהֶיךָ תֹאכְלֶנּוּ שָׁנָה
בְשָׁנָה בַּמָּקוֹם אֲשֶׁר־יִבְחַר יְהוָה אַתָּה וּבֵיתֶךָ׃ וְכִי־יִהְיֶה בוֹ מוּם פִּסֵּחַ אוֹ
עִוֵּר כֹּל מוּם רָע לֹא תִזְבָּחֶנּוּ לַיהוָה אֱלֹהֶיךָ׃ בִּשְׁעָרֶיךָ תֹּאכְלֶנּוּ הַטָּמֵא
וְהַטָּהוֹר יַחְדָּו כַּצְּבִי וְכָאַיָּל׃ רַק אֶת־דָּמוֹ לֹא תֹאכֵל עַל־הָאָרֶץ תִּשְׁפְּכֶנּוּ
כַּמָּיִם׃

לוי (בשבת רביעי) שָׁמוֹר אֶת־חֹדֶשׁ הָאָבִיב וְעָשִׂיתָ פֶּסַח לַיהוָה אֱלֹהֶיךָ כִּי בְּחֹדֶשׁ הָאָבִיב
הוֹצִיאֲךָ יְהוָה אֱלֹהֶיךָ מִמִּצְרַיִם לָיְלָה׃ וְזָבַחְתָּ פֶּסַח לַיהוָה אֱלֹהֶיךָ צֹאן
וּבָקָר בַּמָּקוֹם אֲשֶׁר יִבְחַר יְהוָה לְשַׁכֵּן שְׁמוֹ שָׁם׃ לֹא־תֹאכַל עָלָיו חָמֵץ
שִׁבְעַת יָמִים תֹּאכַל־עָלָיו מַצּוֹת לֶחֶם עֹנִי כִּי בְחִפָּזוֹן יָצָאתָ מֵאֶרֶץ מִצְרַיִם
שלישי (בשבת חמישי) לְמַעַן תִּזְכֹּר אֶת־יוֹם צֵאתְךָ מֵאֶרֶץ מִצְרַיִם כֹּל יְמֵי חַיֶּיךָ׃ *וְלֹא־יֵרָאֶה לְךָ

שְׂאֹר בְּכָל־גְּבֻלְךָ שִׁבְעַת יָמִים וְלֹא־יָלִין מִן־הַבָּשָׂר אֲשֶׁר תִּזְבַּח בָּעֶרֶב בַּיּוֹם
הָרִאשׁוֹן לַבֹּקֶר: לֹא תוּכַל לִזְבֹּחַ אֶת־הַפָּסַח בְּאַחַד שְׁעָרֶיךָ אֲשֶׁר־יְהוָה
אֱלֹהֶיךָ נֹתֵן לָךְ: כִּי אִם־אֶל־הַמָּקוֹם אֲשֶׁר־יִבְחַר יְהוָה אֱלֹהֶיךָ לְשַׁכֵּן שְׁמוֹ
שָׁם תִּזְבַּח אֶת־הַפֶּסַח בָּעָרֶב כְּבוֹא הַשֶּׁמֶשׁ מוֹעֵד צֵאתְךָ מִמִּצְרָיִם: וּבִשַּׁלְתָּ
וְאָכַלְתָּ בַּמָּקוֹם אֲשֶׁר יִבְחַר יְהוָה אֱלֹהֶיךָ בּוֹ וּפָנִיתָ בַבֹּקֶר וְהָלַכְתָּ לְאֹהָלֶיךָ:
שֵׁשֶׁת יָמִים תֹּאכַל מַצּוֹת וּבַיּוֹם הַשְּׁבִיעִי עֲצֶרֶת לַיהוָה אֱלֹהֶיךָ לֹא תַעֲשֶׂה
רביעי (בשבת ששי) מְלָאכָה: *שִׁבְעָה שָׁבֻעֹת תִּסְפָּר־לָךְ מֵהָחֵל חֶרְמֵשׁ בַּקָּמָה תָּחֵל
לִסְפֹּר שִׁבְעָה שָׁבֻעוֹת: וְעָשִׂיתָ חַג שָׁבֻעוֹת לַיהוָה אֱלֹהֶיךָ מִסַּת נִדְבַת יָדְךָ
אֲשֶׁר תִּתֵּן כַּאֲשֶׁר יְבָרֶכְךָ יְהוָה אֱלֹהֶיךָ: וְשָׂמַחְתָּ לִפְנֵי ׀ יְהוָה אֱלֹהֶיךָ אַתָּה
וּבִנְךָ וּבִתֶּךָ וְעַבְדְּךָ וַאֲמָתֶךָ וְהַלֵּוִי אֲשֶׁר בִּשְׁעָרֶיךָ וְהַגֵּר וְהַיָּתוֹם וְהָאַלְמָנָה
אֲשֶׁר בְּקִרְבֶּךָ בַּמָּקוֹם אֲשֶׁר יִבְחַר יְהוָה אֱלֹהֶיךָ לְשַׁכֵּן שְׁמוֹ שָׁם: וְזָכַרְתָּ כִּי־
עֶבֶד הָיִיתָ בְּמִצְרָיִם וְשָׁמַרְתָּ וְעָשִׂיתָ אֶת־הַחֻקִּים הָאֵלֶּה:
חמישי (בשבת שביעי) חַג הַסֻּכֹּת תַּעֲשֶׂה לְךָ שִׁבְעַת יָמִים בְּאָסְפְּךָ מִגָּרְנְךָ וּמִיִּקְבֶךָ: וְשָׂמַחְתָּ בְּחַגֶּךָ
אַתָּה וּבִנְךָ וּבִתֶּךָ וְעַבְדְּךָ וַאֲמָתֶךָ וְהַלֵּוִי וְהַגֵּר וְהַיָּתוֹם וְהָאַלְמָנָה אֲשֶׁר
בִּשְׁעָרֶיךָ: שִׁבְעַת יָמִים תָּחֹג לַיהוָה אֱלֹהֶיךָ בַּמָּקוֹם אֲשֶׁר־יִבְחַר יְהוָה כִּי
יְבָרֶכְךָ יְהוָה אֱלֹהֶיךָ בְּכֹל תְּבוּאָתְךָ וּבְכֹל מַעֲשֵׂה יָדֶיךָ וְהָיִיתָ אַךְ שָׂמֵחַ:
שָׁלוֹשׁ פְּעָמִים ׀ בַּשָּׁנָה יֵרָאֶה כָל־זְכוּרְךָ אֶת־פְּנֵי ׀ יְהוָה אֱלֹהֶיךָ בַּמָּקוֹם אֲשֶׁר
יִבְחָר בְּחַג הַמַּצּוֹת וּבְחַג הַשָּׁבֻעוֹת וּבְחַג הַסֻּכּוֹת וְלֹא יֵרָאֶה אֶת־פְּנֵי יְהוָה
רֵיקָם: אִישׁ כְּמַתְּנַת יָדוֹ כְּבִרְכַּת יְהוָה אֱלֹהֶיךָ אֲשֶׁר נָתַן־לָךְ:

*The* מפטיר *for* יום שמיני של פסח *is the same as that for the other days of* חול המועד פסח*, page 1218. The* מפטיר *for* יום שני של שבועות *appears on page 1227. The* הפטרה *for* שבועות *appears on page 1229 and that of* שמיני עצרת בחוץ לארץ *on page 1238.*

## הפטרה ליום אחרון של פסח

## HAFTARA FOR LAST DAY OF PESAḤ

בַּת־ ישעיהו י:לב–יב:ו

עוֹד הַיּוֹם בְּנֹב לַעֲמֹד יְנֹפֵף יָדוֹ הַר בֵּית־צִיּוֹן גִּבְעַת יְרוּשָׁלָםִ: הִנֵּה
הָאָדוֹן יְהוָה צְבָאוֹת מְסָעֵף פֻּארָה בְּמַעֲרָצָה וְרָמֵי הַקּוֹמָה גְּדוּעִים וְהַגְּבֹהִים
יִשְׁפָּלוּ: וְנִקַּף סִבְכֵי הַיַּעַר בַּבַּרְזֶל וְהַלְּבָנוֹן בְּאַדִּיר יִפּוֹל: וְיָצָא
חֹטֶר מִגֵּזַע יִשָׁי וְנֵצֶר מִשָּׁרָשָׁיו יִפְרֶה: וְנָחָה עָלָיו רוּחַ יְהוָה רוּחַ חָכְמָה וּבִינָה

רוח עצה וגבורה רוח דעת ויראת יהוה: והריחו ביראת יהוה ולא־למראה
עיניו ישפוט ולא־למשמע אזניו יוכיח: ושפט בצדק דלים והוכיח במישור
לענוי־ארץ והכה־ארץ בשבט פיו וברוח שפתיו ימית רשע: והיה צדק אזור
מתניו והאמונה אזור חלציו: וגר זאב עם־כבש ונמר עם־גדי ירבץ ועגל
וכפיר ומריא יחדו ונער קטן נהג בם: ופרה ודב תרעינה יחדו ירבצו ילדיהן
ואריה כבקר יאכל־תבן: ושעשע יונק על־חר פתן ועל מאורת צפעוני
גמול ידו הדה: לא־ירעו ולא־ישחיתו בכל־הר קדשי כי־מלאה הארץ דעה
את־יהוה כמים לים מכסים: והיה ביום ההוא שרש ישי אשר
עמד לנס עמים אליו גוים ידרשו והיתה מנחתו כבוד: והיה ׀
ביום ההוא יוסיף אדני ׀ שנית ידו לקנות את־שאר עמו אשר ישאר מאשור
וממצרים ומפתרוס ומכוש ומעילם ומשנער ומחמת ומאיי הים: ונשא נס
לגוים ואסף נדחי ישראל ונפצות יהודה יקבץ מארבע כנפות הארץ: וסרה
קנאת אפרים וצררי יהודה יכרתו אפרים לא־יקנא את־יהודה ויהודה לא־
יצר את־אפרים: ועפו בכתף פלשתים ימה יחדו יבזו את־בני־קדם אדום
ומואב משלוח ידם ובני עמון משמעתם: והחרים יהוה את לשון ים־מצרים
והניף ידו על־הנהר בעים רוחו והכהו לשבעה נחלים והדריך בנעלים:
והיתה מסלה לשאר עמו אשר ישאר מאשור כאשר היתה לישראל ביום
עלתו מארץ מצרים: ואמרת ביום ההוא אודך יהוה כי אנפת בי ישב אפך
ותנחמני: הנה אל ישועתי אבטח ולא אפחד כי־עזי וזמרת יה יהוה ויהי־
לי לישועה: ושאבתם־מים בששון ממעיני הישועה: ואמרתם ביום ההוא
הודו ליהוה קראו בשמו הודיעו בעמים עלילתיו הזכירו כי נשגב שמו:
זמרו יהוה כי גאות עשה מידעת זאת בכל־הארץ: צהלי ורני יושבת ציון מודעת
כי־גדול בקרבך קדוש ישראל:

## FIRST DAY OF SHAVUOT קריאה ליום טוב ראשון של שבועות

אקדמות *appears on page 851.*

בחדש השלישי לצאת בני־ישראל מארץ מצרים ביום הזה באו מדבר שמות
סיני: ויסעו מרפידים ויבאו מדבר סיני ויחנו במדבר ויחן־שם ישראל יט:א–כ:כג

נֶגֶד הָהָר: וּמֹשֶׁה עָלָה אֶל־הָאֱלֹהִים וַיִּקְרָא אֵלָיו יהוה מִן־הָהָר לֵאמֹר כֹּה
תֹאמַר לְבֵית יַעֲקֹב וְתַגֵּיד לִבְנֵי יִשְׂרָאֵל: אַתֶּם רְאִיתֶם אֲשֶׁר עָשִׂיתִי לְמִצְרָיִם
וָאֶשָּׂא אֶתְכֶם עַל־כַּנְפֵי נְשָׁרִים וָאָבִא אֶתְכֶם אֵלָי: וְעַתָּה אִם־שָׁמוֹעַ תִּשְׁמְעוּ
בְּקֹלִי וּשְׁמַרְתֶּם אֶת־בְּרִיתִי וִהְיִיתֶם לִי סְגֻלָּה מִכָּל־הָעַמִּים כִּי־לִי כָּל־הָאָרֶץ:
וְאַתֶּם תִּהְיוּ־לִי מַמְלֶכֶת כֹּהֲנִים וְגוֹי קָדוֹשׁ אֵלֶּה הַדְּבָרִים אֲשֶׁר תְּדַבֵּר אֶל־
בְּנֵי יִשְׂרָאֵל: *וַיָּבֹא מֹשֶׁה וַיִּקְרָא לְזִקְנֵי הָעָם וַיָּשֶׂם לִפְנֵיהֶם אֵת כָּל־הַדְּבָרִים לוי
הָאֵלֶּה אֲשֶׁר צִוָּהוּ יהוה: וַיַּעֲנוּ כָל־הָעָם יַחְדָּו וַיֹּאמְרוּ כֹּל אֲשֶׁר־דִּבֶּר יהוה
נַעֲשֶׂה וַיָּשֶׁב מֹשֶׁה אֶת־דִּבְרֵי הָעָם אֶל־יהוה: וַיֹּאמֶר יהוה אֶל־מֹשֶׁה הִנֵּה
אָנֹכִי בָּא אֵלֶיךָ בְּעַב הֶעָנָן בַּעֲבוּר יִשְׁמַע הָעָם בְּדַבְּרִי עִמָּךְ וְגַם־בְּךָ יַאֲמִינוּ
לְעוֹלָם וַיַּגֵּד מֹשֶׁה אֶת־דִּבְרֵי הָעָם אֶל־יהוה: וַיֹּאמֶר יהוה אֶל־מֹשֶׁה לֵךְ
אֶל־הָעָם וְקִדַּשְׁתָּם הַיּוֹם וּמָחָר וְכִבְּסוּ שִׂמְלֹתָם: וְהָיוּ נְכֹנִים לַיּוֹם הַשְּׁלִישִׁי
כִּי ׀ בַּיּוֹם הַשְּׁלִשִׁי יֵרֵד יהוה לְעֵינֵי כָל־הָעָם עַל־הַר סִינָי: וְהִגְבַּלְתָּ אֶת־הָעָם
סָבִיב לֵאמֹר הִשָּׁמְרוּ לָכֶם עֲלוֹת בָּהָר וּנְגֹעַ בְּקָצֵהוּ כָּל־הַנֹּגֵעַ בָּהָר מוֹת יוּמָת:
לֹא־תִגַּע בּוֹ יָד כִּי־סָקוֹל יִסָּקֵל אוֹ־יָרֹה יִיָּרֶה אִם־בְּהֵמָה אִם־אִישׁ לֹא יִחְיֶה
בִּמְשֹׁךְ הַיֹּבֵל הֵמָּה יַעֲלוּ בָהָר: *וַיֵּרֶד מֹשֶׁה מִן־הָהָר אֶל־הָעָם וַיְקַדֵּשׁ אֶת־ שלישי
הָעָם וַיְכַבְּסוּ שִׂמְלֹתָם: וַיֹּאמֶר אֶל־הָעָם הֱיוּ נְכֹנִים לִשְׁלֹשֶׁת יָמִים אַל־תִּגְּשׁוּ
אֶל־אִשָּׁה: וַיְהִי בַיּוֹם הַשְּׁלִישִׁי בִּהְיֹת הַבֹּקֶר וַיְהִי קֹלֹת וּבְרָקִים וְעָנָן כָּבֵד
עַל־הָהָר וְקֹל שֹׁפָר חָזָק מְאֹד וַיֶּחֱרַד כָּל־הָעָם אֲשֶׁר בַּמַּחֲנֶה: וַיּוֹצֵא מֹשֶׁה
אֶת־הָעָם לִקְרַאת הָאֱלֹהִים מִן־הַמַּחֲנֶה וַיִּתְיַצְּבוּ בְּתַחְתִּית הָהָר: וְהַר סִינַי
עָשַׁן כֻּלּוֹ מִפְּנֵי אֲשֶׁר יָרַד עָלָיו יהוה בָּאֵשׁ וַיַּעַל עֲשָׁנוֹ כְּעֶשֶׁן הַכִּבְשָׁן וַיֶּחֱרַד
כָּל־הָהָר מְאֹד: וַיְהִי קוֹל הַשֹּׁפָר הוֹלֵךְ וְחָזֵק מְאֹד מֹשֶׁה יְדַבֵּר וְהָאֱלֹהִים
יַעֲנֶנּוּ בְקוֹל: *וַיֵּרֶד יהוה עַל־הַר סִינַי אֶל־רֹאשׁ הָהָר וַיִּקְרָא יהוה לְמֹשֶׁה רביעי
אֶל־רֹאשׁ הָהָר וַיַּעַל מֹשֶׁה: וַיֹּאמֶר יהוה אֶל־מֹשֶׁה רֵד הָעֵד בָּעָם פֶּן־יֶהֶרְסוּ
אֶל־יהוה לִרְאוֹת וְנָפַל מִמֶּנּוּ רָב: וְגַם הַכֹּהֲנִים הַנִּגָּשִׁים אֶל־יהוה יִתְקַדָּשׁוּ
פֶּן־יִפְרֹץ בָּהֶם יהוה: וַיֹּאמֶר מֹשֶׁה אֶל־יהוה לֹא־יוּכַל הָעָם לַעֲלֹת אֶל־הַר
סִינָי כִּי־אַתָּה הַעֵדֹתָה בָּנוּ לֵאמֹר הַגְבֵּל אֶת־הָהָר וְקִדַּשְׁתּוֹ: וַיֹּאמֶר אֵלָיו
יהוה לֶךְ־רֵד וְעָלִיתָ אַתָּה וְאַהֲרֹן עִמָּךְ וְהַכֹּהֲנִים וְהָעָם אַל־יֶהֶרְסוּ לַעֲלֹת
אֶל־יהוה פֶּן־יִפְרָץ־בָּם: וַיֵּרֶד מֹשֶׁה אֶל־הָעָם וַיֹּאמֶר אֲלֵהֶם:
וַיְדַבֵּר

אֱלֹהִים אֵת כָּל־הַדְּבָרִים הָאֵלֶּה לֵאמֹר: אָנֹכִי יְהוָה אֱלֹהֶיךָ אֲשֶׁר
הוֹצֵאתִיךָ מֵאֶרֶץ מִצְרַיִם מִבֵּית עֲבָדִים: לֹא־יִהְיֶה לְךָ אֱלֹהִים אֲחֵרִים עַל־
פָּנַי לֹא תַעֲשֶׂה־לְּךָ פֶסֶל | וְכָל־תְּמוּנָה אֲשֶׁר בַּשָּׁמַיִם | מִמַּעַל וַאֲשֶׁר בָּאָרֶץ
מִתַּחַת וַאֲשֶׁר בַּמַּיִם | מִתַּחַת לָאָרֶץ לֹא־תִשְׁתַּחְוֶה לָהֶם וְלֹא תָעָבְדֵם כִּי
אָנֹכִי יְהוָה אֱלֹהֶיךָ אֵל קַנָּא פֹּקֵד עֲוֺן אָבֹת עַל־בָּנִים עַל־שִׁלֵּשִׁים וְעַל־רִבֵּעִים
לְשֹׂנְאָי וְעֹשֶׂה חֶסֶד לַאֲלָפִים לְאֹהֲבַי וּלְשֹׁמְרֵי מִצְוֺתָי: לֹא תִשָּׂא
אֶת־שֵׁם־יְהוָה אֱלֹהֶיךָ לַשָּׁוְא כִּי לֹא יְנַקֶּה יְהוָה אֵת אֲשֶׁר־יִשָּׂא אֶת־שְׁמוֹ
לַשָּׁוְא:

זָכוֹר אֶת־יוֹם הַשַּׁבָּת לְקַדְּשׁוֹ שֵׁשֶׁת יָמִים תַּעֲבֹד וְעָשִׂיתָ כָּל־מְלַאכְתֶּךָ
וְיוֹם הַשְּׁבִיעִי שַׁבָּת | לַיהוָה אֱלֹהֶיךָ לֹא תַעֲשֶׂה כָל־מְלָאכָה אַתָּה וּבִנְךָ
וּבִתֶּךָ עַבְדְּךָ וַאֲמָתְךָ וּבְהֶמְתֶּךָ וְגֵרְךָ אֲשֶׁר בִּשְׁעָרֶיךָ כִּי שֵׁשֶׁת־יָמִים עָשָׂה
יְהוָה אֶת־הַשָּׁמַיִם וְאֶת־הָאָרֶץ אֶת־הַיָּם וְאֶת־כָּל־אֲשֶׁר־בָּם וַיָּנַח בַּיּוֹם
הַשְּׁבִיעִי עַל־כֵּן בֵּרַךְ יְהוָה אֶת־יוֹם הַשַּׁבָּת וַיְקַדְּשֵׁהוּ: כַּבֵּד
אֶת־אָבִיךָ וְאֶת־אִמֶּךָ לְמַעַן יַאֲרִכוּן יָמֶיךָ עַל הָאֲדָמָה אֲשֶׁר־יְהוָה אֱלֹהֶיךָ
נֹתֵן לָךְ: לֹא תִּרְצָח: לֹא
תִּנְאָף: לֹא תִּגְנֹב: לֹא־
תַעֲנֶה בְרֵעֲךָ עֵד שָׁקֶר: לֹא
תַחְמֹד בֵּית רֵעֶךָ לֹא־
תַחְמֹד אֵשֶׁת רֵעֶךָ וְעַבְדּוֹ וַאֲמָתוֹ וְשׁוֹרוֹ וַחֲמֹרוֹ וְכֹל אֲשֶׁר
לְרֵעֶךָ:

חמישי וְכָל־הָעָם רֹאִים אֶת־הַקּוֹלֹת וְאֶת־הַלַּפִּידִם וְאֵת קוֹל הַשֹּׁפָר וְאֶת־הָהָר
עָשֵׁן וַיַּרְא הָעָם וַיָּנֻעוּ וַיַּעַמְדוּ מֵרָחֹק: וַיֹּאמְרוּ אֶל־מֹשֶׁה דַּבֵּר־אַתָּה עִמָּנוּ
וְנִשְׁמָעָה וְאַל־יְדַבֵּר עִמָּנוּ אֱלֹהִים פֶּן־נָמוּת: וַיֹּאמֶר מֹשֶׁה אֶל־הָעָם אַל־
תִּירָאוּ כִּי לְבַעֲבוּר נַסּוֹת אֶתְכֶם בָּא הָאֱלֹהִים וּבַעֲבוּר תִּהְיֶה יִרְאָתוֹ עַל־פְּנֵיכֶם
לְבִלְתִּי תֶחֱטָאוּ: וַיַּעֲמֹד הָעָם מֵרָחֹק וּמֹשֶׁה נִגַּשׁ אֶל־הָעֲרָפֶל אֲשֶׁר־שָׁם
הָאֱלֹהִים: וַיֹּאמֶר יְהוָה אֶל־מֹשֶׁה כֹּה תֹאמַר אֶל־בְּנֵי יִשְׂרָאֵל
אַתֶּם רְאִיתֶם כִּי מִן־הַשָּׁמַיִם דִּבַּרְתִּי עִמָּכֶם: לֹא תַעֲשׂוּן אִתִּי אֱלֹהֵי כֶסֶף
וֵאלֹהֵי זָהָב לֹא תַעֲשׂוּ לָכֶם: מִזְבַּח אֲדָמָה תַּעֲשֶׂה־לִּי וְזָבַחְתָּ עָלָיו אֶת־עֹלֹתֶיךָ

וְאֶת־שְׁלָמֶיךָ אֶת־צֹאנְךָ וְאֶת־בְּקָרֶךָ בְּכָל־הַמָּקוֹם אֲשֶׁר אַזְכִּיר אֶת־שְׁמִי
אָבוֹא אֵלֶיךָ וּבֵרַכְתִּיךָ׃ וְאִם־מִזְבַּח אֲבָנִים תַּעֲשֶׂה־לִּי לֹא־תִבְנֶה אֶתְהֶן גָּזִית
כִּי חַרְבְּךָ הֵנַפְתָּ עָלֶיהָ וַתְּחַלְלֶהָ׃ וְלֹא־תַעֲלֶה בְמַעֲלֹת עַל־מִזְבְּחִי אֲשֶׁר לֹא־
תִגָּלֶה עֶרְוָתְךָ עָלָיו׃

*The following* מפטיר *is read from the second* ספר תורה *on both days of* שבועות*:*

וּבְיוֹם הַבִּכּוּרִים בְּהַקְרִיבְכֶם מִנְחָה חֲדָשָׁה לַיהוָה בְּשָׁבֻעֹתֵיכֶם מִקְרָא־ במדבר כח:כו–לא
קֹדֶשׁ יִהְיֶה לָכֶם כָּל־מְלֶאכֶת עֲבֹדָה לֹא תַעֲשׂוּ׃ וְהִקְרַבְתֶּם עוֹלָה לְרֵיחַ
נִיחֹחַ לַיהוָה פָּרִים בְּנֵי־בָקָר שְׁנַיִם אַיִל אֶחָד שִׁבְעָה כְבָשִׂים בְּנֵי שָׁנָה׃
וּמִנְחָתָם סֹלֶת בְּלוּלָה בַשָּׁמֶן שְׁלֹשָׁה עֶשְׂרֹנִים לַפָּר הָאֶחָד שְׁנֵי עֶשְׂרֹנִים
לָאַיִל הָאֶחָד׃ עִשָּׂרוֹן עִשָּׂרוֹן לַכֶּבֶשׂ הָאֶחָד לְשִׁבְעַת הַכְּבָשִׂים׃ שְׂעִיר עִזִּים
אֶחָד לְכַפֵּר עֲלֵיכֶם׃ מִלְּבַד עֹלַת הַתָּמִיד וּמִנְחָתוֹ תַּעֲשׂוּ תְּמִימִם יִהְיוּ־לָכֶם
וְנִסְכֵּיהֶם׃

## הפטרה ליום טוב ראשון של שבועות

## HAFTARA FOR FIRST DAY OF SHAVUOT

וַיְהִי ׀ בִּשְׁלֹשִׁים שָׁנָה בָּרְבִיעִי בַּחֲמִשָּׁה לַחֹדֶשׁ וַאֲנִי בְתוֹךְ־הַגּוֹלָה עַל־נְהַר־ יחזקאל א:א–כח
כְּבָר נִפְתְּחוּ הַשָּׁמַיִם וָאֶרְאֶה מַרְאוֹת אֱלֹהִים׃ בַּחֲמִשָּׁה לַחֹדֶשׁ הִיא הַשָּׁנָה
הַחֲמִישִׁית לְגָלוּת הַמֶּלֶךְ יוֹיָכִין׃ הָיֹה הָיָה דְבַר־יְהוָה אֶל־יְחֶזְקֵאל בֶּן־בּוּזִי
הַכֹּהֵן בְּאֶרֶץ כַּשְׂדִּים עַל־נְהַר־כְּבָר וַתְּהִי עָלָיו שָׁם יַד־יְהוָה׃ וָאֵרֶא וְהִנֵּה רוּחַ
סְעָרָה בָּאָה מִן־הַצָּפוֹן עָנָן גָּדוֹל וְאֵשׁ מִתְלַקַּחַת וְנֹגַהּ לוֹ סָבִיב וּמִתּוֹכָהּ כְּעֵין
הַחַשְׁמַל מִתּוֹךְ הָאֵשׁ׃ וּמִתּוֹכָהּ דְּמוּת אַרְבַּע חַיּוֹת וְזֶה מַרְאֵיהֶן דְּמוּת אָדָם
לָהֵנָּה׃ וְאַרְבָּעָה פָנִים לְאֶחָת וְאַרְבַּע כְּנָפַיִם לְאַחַת לָהֶם׃ וְרַגְלֵיהֶם רֶגֶל יְשָׁרָה
וְכַף רַגְלֵיהֶם כְּכַף רֶגֶל עֵגֶל וְנֹצְצִים כְּעֵין נְחֹשֶׁת קָלָל׃ וידו אָדָם מִתַּחַת כַּנְפֵיהֶם וִידֵי
עַל אַרְבַּעַת רִבְעֵיהֶם וּפְנֵיהֶם וְכַנְפֵיהֶם לְאַרְבַּעְתָּם׃ חֹבְרֹת אִשָּׁה אֶל־אֲחוֹתָהּ
כַּנְפֵיהֶם לֹא־יִסַּבּוּ בְלֶכְתָּן אִישׁ אֶל־עֵבֶר פָּנָיו יֵלֵכוּ׃ וּדְמוּת פְּנֵיהֶם פְּנֵי אָדָם

וּפְנֵי אַרְיֵה אֶל־הַיָּמִין לְאַרְבַּעְתָּם וּפְנֵי־שׁוֹר מֵהַשְּׂמֹאול לְאַרְבַּעְתָּן וּפְנֵי־נֶשֶׁר
לְאַרְבַּעְתָּן׃ וּפְנֵיהֶם וְכַנְפֵיהֶם פְּרֻדוֹת מִלְמָעְלָה לְאִישׁ שְׁתַּיִם חֹבְרוֹת אִישׁ
וּשְׁתַּיִם מְכַסּוֹת אֵת גְּוִיֹּתֵיהֶנָה׃ וְאִישׁ אֶל־עֵבֶר פָּנָיו יֵלֵכוּ אֶל אֲשֶׁר יִהְיֶה־שָׁמָּה
הָרוּחַ לָלֶכֶת יֵלֵכוּ לֹא יִסַּבּוּ בְּלֶכְתָּן׃ וּדְמוּת הַחַיּוֹת מַרְאֵיהֶם כְּגַחֲלֵי־אֵשׁ
בֹּעֲרוֹת כְּמַרְאֵה הַלַּפִּדִים הִיא מִתְהַלֶּכֶת בֵּין הַחַיּוֹת וְנֹגַהּ לָאֵשׁ וּמִן־הָאֵשׁ
יוֹצֵא בָרָק׃ וְהַחַיּוֹת רָצוֹא וָשׁוֹב כְּמַרְאֵה הַבָּזָק׃ וָאֵרֶא הַחַיּוֹת וְהִנֵּה אוֹפַן
אֶחָד בָּאָרֶץ אֵצֶל הַחַיּוֹת לְאַרְבַּעַת פָּנָיו׃ מַרְאֵה הָאוֹפַנִּים וּמַעֲשֵׂיהֶם כְּעֵין
תַּרְשִׁישׁ וּדְמוּת אֶחָד לְאַרְבַּעְתָּן וּמַרְאֵיהֶם וּמַעֲשֵׂיהֶם כַּאֲשֶׁר יִהְיֶה הָאוֹפַן
בְּתוֹךְ הָאוֹפָן׃ עַל־אַרְבַּעַת רִבְעֵיהֶן בְּלֶכְתָּם יֵלֵכוּ לֹא יִסַּבּוּ בְּלֶכְתָּן׃ וְגַבֵּיהֶן
וְגֹבַהּ לָהֶם וְיִרְאָה לָהֶם וְגַבֹּתָם מְלֵאֹת עֵינַיִם סָבִיב לְאַרְבַּעְתָּן׃ וּבְלֶכֶת
הַחַיּוֹת יֵלְכוּ הָאוֹפַנִּים אֶצְלָם וּבְהִנָּשֵׂא הַחַיּוֹת מֵעַל הָאָרֶץ יִנָּשְׂאוּ הָאוֹפַנִּים׃
עַל אֲשֶׁר יִהְיֶה־שָּׁם הָרוּחַ לָלֶכֶת יֵלֵכוּ שָׁמָּה הָרוּחַ לָלֶכֶת וְהָאוֹפַנִּים יִנָּשְׂאוּ
לְעֻמָּתָם כִּי רוּחַ הַחַיָּה בָּאוֹפַנִּים׃ בְּלֶכְתָּם יֵלֵכוּ וּבְעָמְדָם יַעֲמֹדוּ וּבְהִנָּשְׂאָם
מֵעַל הָאָרֶץ יִנָּשְׂאוּ הָאוֹפַנִּים לְעֻמָּתָם כִּי רוּחַ הַחַיָּה בָּאוֹפַנִּים׃ וּדְמוּת עַל־
רָאשֵׁי הַחַיָּה רָקִיעַ כְּעֵין הַקֶּרַח הַנּוֹרָא נָטוּי עַל־רָאשֵׁיהֶם מִלְמָעְלָה׃ וְתַחַת
הָרָקִיעַ כַּנְפֵיהֶם יְשָׁרוֹת אִשָּׁה אֶל־אֲחוֹתָהּ לְאִישׁ שְׁתַּיִם מְכַסּוֹת לָהֵנָּה
וּלְאִישׁ שְׁתַּיִם מְכַסּוֹת לָהֵנָּה אֵת גְּוִיֹּתֵיהֶם׃ וָאֶשְׁמַע אֶת־קוֹל כַּנְפֵיהֶם כְּקוֹל
מַיִם רַבִּים כְּקוֹל־שַׁדַּי בְּלֶכְתָּם קוֹל הֲמֻלָּה כְּקוֹל מַחֲנֶה בְּעָמְדָם תְּרַפֶּינָה
כַנְפֵיהֶן׃ וַיְהִי־קוֹל מֵעַל לָרָקִיעַ אֲשֶׁר עַל־רֹאשָׁם בְּעָמְדָם תְּרַפֶּינָה כַנְפֵיהֶן׃
וּמִמַּעַל לָרָקִיעַ אֲשֶׁר עַל־רֹאשָׁם כְּמַרְאֵה אֶבֶן־סַפִּיר דְּמוּת כִּסֵּא וְעַל דְּמוּת
הַכִּסֵּא דְּמוּת כְּמַרְאֵה אָדָם עָלָיו מִלְמָעְלָה׃ וָאֵרֶא ׀ כְּעֵין חַשְׁמַל כְּמַרְאֵה־
אֵשׁ בֵּית־לָהּ סָבִיב מִמַּרְאֵה מָתְנָיו וּלְמָעְלָה וּמִמַּרְאֵה מָתְנָיו וּלְמַטָּה רָאִיתִי
כְּמַרְאֵה־אֵשׁ וְנֹגַהּ לוֹ סָבִיב׃ כְּמַרְאֵה הַקֶּשֶׁת אֲשֶׁר יִהְיֶה בֶעָנָן בְּיוֹם הַגֶּשֶׁם
כֵּן מַרְאֵה הַנֹּגַהּ סָבִיב הוּא מַרְאֵה דְּמוּת כְּבוֹד־יהוה וָאֶרְאֶה וָאֶפֹּל עַל־פָּנַי
וָאֶשְׁמַע קוֹל מְדַבֵּר׃

וַתִּשָּׂאֵנִי רוּחַ וָאֶשְׁמַע אַחֲרַי קוֹל רַעַשׁ גָּדוֹל בָּרוּךְ כְּבוֹד־יהוה מִמְּקוֹמוֹ׃ יחזקאל ג:יב

*The* קריאת התורה *for the second day of* שבועות *is the same as that of the eighth day of* פסח *on page 1221. The* מפטיר *is the same as that of the first day of* שבועות *(previous page).*

# הפטרה ליום טוב שני של שבועות

## HAFTARA FOR SECOND DAY OF SHAVUOT

וַיהוָה בְּהֵיכַל קָדְשׁוֹ הַס מִפָּנָיו כָּל־הָאָרֶץ׃ תְּפִלָּה לַחֲבַקּוּק הַנָּבִיא עַל שִׁגְיֹנוֹת׃ חבקוק ב:כ–ג:יט

*Many say the following* יַצִּיב פִּתְגָם *in the* הפטרה.

יַצִּיב פִּתְגָם, לְאָת וּדְגַם, בְּרִבּוֹ רִבְבָן עִירִין.
עָנֵה אֲנָא, בְּמִנְיָנָא, דְּפָסְלִין אַרְבְּעָה טוּרִין.
קָדָמוֹהִי, לְגוֹ מוֹהִי, נְגִיד וּנְפִיק נְהַר דִּי נוּרִין.
בְּטוּר תַּלְגָּא, נְהוֹר שְׁרָגָא, וְזִיקִין דִּי נוּר וּבָעוּרִין.
בְּרָא וּסְכָא, מַה בַּחֲשׁוֹכָא, וְעִמֵּהּ שָׁרְיָין נְהוֹרִין.
רְחִיקִין צְפָא, בְּלָא שִׁטְפָא, וּגְלֵין לֵהּ דְּמִטַּמְּרִין.
בְּעֵית מִנֵּהּ, יָת הַרְמָנֵהּ, וּבָתְרוֹהִי עֲדֵי גְבָרִין.
יָדְעֵי הִלְכְּתָא, וּמַתְנִיתָא, וְתוֹסֶפְתָּא סִפְרָא וְסִפְרִין.
מֶלֶךְ חַיָּא, לְעָלְמַיָּא, יִמַּגַּר עַם לְהוֹן מְשַׁחֲרִין.
אֲמִיר עֲלֵיהוֹן, כְּחַלְּא יְהוֹן, וְלָא יִתְמְנוֹן הֵיךְ עַפְרִין.
יְחַוְּרוּן כְּעַן, לְהוֹן בִּקְעָן, יְטוּפוּן נַעֲוֵי חַמְרִין.
רְעוּתְהוֹן הַב, וְאַפֵּיהוֹן צְהַב, יְנַהֲרוּן כִּנְהוֹר צַפְרִין.
לִי הַב תְּקוֹף, וְעֵינָךְ זְקוֹף, חֲזִי עֲרָךְ דְּבָךְ כָּפְרִין.
יְהוֹן כְּתִבְנָא, בְּגוֹ לִבְנָא, כְּאַבְנָא יִשְׁתְּקוּן חָפְרִין.
כְּקָאֶמְנָא, וְתַרְגֵּמְנָא, בְּמִלּוֹי דִּבְחִיר סָפְרִין.
יְהוֹנָתָן, גְּבַר עִנְוְתָן, בְּכֵן נַמְטִין אַפְרִין.

יהוה שָׁמַעְתִּי שִׁמְעֲךָ יָרֵאתִי יהוה פָּעָלְךָ בְּקֶרֶב שָׁנִים חַיֵּיהוּ בְּקֶרֶב שָׁנִים
תּוֹדִיעַ בְּרֹגֶז רַחֵם תִּזְכּוֹר׃ אֱלוֹהַּ מִתֵּימָן יָבוֹא וְקָדוֹשׁ מֵהַר־פָּארָן סֶלָה כִּסָּה
שָׁמַיִם הוֹדוֹ וּתְהִלָּתוֹ מָלְאָה הָאָרֶץ׃ וְנֹגַהּ כָּאוֹר תִּהְיֶה קַרְנַיִם מִיָּדוֹ לוֹ וְשָׁם
חֶבְיוֹן עֻזֹּה׃ לְפָנָיו יֵלֶךְ דָּבֶר וְיֵצֵא רֶשֶׁף לְרַגְלָיו׃ עָמַד ׀ וַיְמֹדֶד אֶרֶץ רָאָה וַיַּתֵּר
גּוֹיִם וַיִּתְפֹּצְצוּ הַרְרֵי־עַד שַׁחוּ גִּבְעוֹת עוֹלָם הֲלִיכוֹת עוֹלָם לוֹ׃ תַּחַת אָוֶן
רָאִיתִי אָהֳלֵי כוּשָׁן יִרְגְּזוּן יְרִיעוֹת אֶרֶץ מִדְיָן׃ הֲבִנְהָרִים חָרָה
יהוה אִם בַּנְּהָרִים אַפֶּךָ אִם־בַּיָּם עֶבְרָתֶךָ כִּי תִרְכַּב עַל־סוּסֶיךָ מַרְכְּבֹתֶיךָ

יְשׁוּעָה: עֶרְיָה תֵעוֹר קַשְׁתֶּךָ שְׁבֻעוֹת מַטּוֹת אֹמֶר סֶלָה נְהָרוֹת תְּבַקַּע־אָרֶץ:
רָאוּךָ יָחִילוּ הָרִים זֶרֶם מַיִם עָבָר נָתַן תְּהוֹם קוֹלוֹ רוֹם יָדֵיהוּ נָשָׂא: שֶׁמֶשׁ יָרֵחַ
עָמַד זְבֻלָה לְאוֹר חִצֶּיךָ יְהַלֵּכוּ לְנֹגַהּ בְּרַק חֲנִיתֶךָ: בְּזַעַם תִּצְעַד־אָרֶץ בְּאַף
תָּדוּשׁ גּוֹיִם: יָצָאתָ לְיֵשַׁע עַמֶּךָ לְיֵשַׁע אֶת־מְשִׁיחֶךָ מָחַצְתָּ רֹּאשׁ מִבֵּית רָשָׁע
עָרוֹת יְסוֹד עַד־צַוָּאר סֶלָה: נָקַבְתָּ בְמַטָּיו רֹאשׁ פְּרָזָו יִסְעֲרוּ
לַהֲפִיצֵנִי עֲלִיצֻתָם כְּמוֹ־לֶאֱכֹל עָנִי בַּמִּסְתָּר: דָּרַכְתָּ בַיָּם סוּסֶיךָ חֹמֶר מַיִם
רַבִּים: שָׁמַעְתִּי ׀ וַתִּרְגַּז בִּטְנִי לְקוֹל צָלְלוּ שְׂפָתַי יָבוֹא רָקָב בַּעֲצָמַי וְתַחְתַּי
אֶרְגָּז אֲשֶׁר אָנוּחַ לְיוֹם צָרָה לַעֲלוֹת לְעַם יְגוּדֶנּוּ: כִּי־תְאֵנָה לֹא־תִפְרָח וְאֵין
יְבוּל בַּגְּפָנִים כִּחֵשׁ מַעֲשֵׂה־זַיִת וּשְׁדֵמוֹת לֹא־עָשָׂה אֹכֶל גָּזַר מִמִּכְלָה צֹאן
וְאֵין בָּקָר בָּרְפָתִים: וַאֲנִי בַּיהוָה אֶעְלוֹזָה אָגִילָה בֵּאלֹהֵי יִשְׁעִי: יֱהוִה אֲדֹנָי
חֵילִי וַיָּשֶׂם רַגְלַי כָּאַיָּלוֹת וְעַל־בָּמוֹתַי יַדְרִכֵנִי לַמְנַצֵּחַ בִּנְגִינוֹתָי:

## מפטיר ליום הראשון של סוכות, ויום טוב שני בחוץ לארץ

## MAFTIR FOR FIRST DAY OF SUKKOT, AND SECOND DAY IN THE DIASPORA

*The* קריאת התורה *for the first two days of* סוכות *is the same as that of the second day of* פסח *(page 1204). The following* מפטיר *is then read from the second* ספר תורה*:*

וּבַחֲמִשָּׁה עָשָׂר יוֹם לַחֹדֶשׁ הַשְּׁבִיעִי מִקְרָא־קֹדֶשׁ יִהְיֶה לָכֶם כָּל־מְלֶאכֶת במדבר
עֲבֹדָה לֹא תַעֲשׂוּ וְחַגֹּתֶם חַג לַיהוָה שִׁבְעַת יָמִים: וְהִקְרַבְתֶּם עֹלָה אִשֵּׁה כט:יב–טז
רֵיחַ נִיחֹחַ לַיהוָה פָּרִים בְּנֵי־בָקָר שְׁלֹשָׁה עָשָׂר אֵילִם שְׁנָיִם כְּבָשִׂים בְּנֵי־שָׁנָה
אַרְבָּעָה עָשָׂר תְּמִימִם יִהְיוּ: וּמִנְחָתָם סֹלֶת בְּלוּלָה בַשָּׁמֶן שְׁלֹשָׁה עֶשְׂרֹנִים
לַפָּר הָאֶחָד לִשְׁלֹשָׁה עָשָׂר פָּרִים שְׁנֵי עֶשְׂרֹנִים לָאַיִל הָאֶחָד לִשְׁנֵי הָאֵילִם:
וְעִשָּׂרוֹן עִשָּׂרוֹן לַכֶּבֶשׂ הָאֶחָד לְאַרְבָּעָה עָשָׂר כְּבָשִׂים: וּשְׂעִיר־עִזִּים אֶחָד
חַטָּאת מִלְּבַד עֹלַת הַתָּמִיד מִנְחָתָהּ וְנִסְכָּהּ:

## הפטרה ליום הראשון של סוכות

## HAFTARA FOR FIRST DAY OF SUKKOT

הִנֵּה יוֹם־בָּא לַיהוָה וְחֻלַּק שְׁלָלֵךְ בְּקִרְבֵּךְ: וְאָסַפְתִּי אֶת־כָּל־הַגּוֹיִם ׀ אֶל־ זכריה יד:א–כא
יְרוּשָׁלִַם לַמִּלְחָמָה וְנִלְכְּדָה הָעִיר וְנָשַׁסּוּ הַבָּתִּים וְהַנָּשִׁים תשגלנה וְיָצָא חֲצִי תִּשָּׁכַבְנָה

הָעִיר בַּגּוֹלָה וְיֶתֶר הָעָם לֹא יִכָּרֵת מִן־הָעִיר׃ וְיָצָא יְהוָה וְנִלְחַם בַּגּוֹיִם הָהֵם כְּיוֹם הִלָּחֲמוֹ בְּיוֹם קְרָב׃ וְעָמְדוּ רַגְלָיו בַּיּוֹם־הַהוּא עַל־הַר הַזֵּיתִים אֲשֶׁר עַל־פְּנֵי יְרוּשָׁלִַם מִקֶּדֶם וְנִבְקַע הַר הַזֵּיתִים מֵחֶצְיוֹ מִזְרָחָה וָיָמָּה גֵּיא גְּדוֹלָה מְאֹד וּמָשׁ חֲצִי הָהָר צָפוֹנָה וְחֶצְיוֹ נֶגְבָּה׃ וְנַסְתֶּם גֵּיא־הָרַי כִּי־יַגִּיעַ גֵּי־הָרִים אֶל־אָצַל וְנַסְתֶּם כַּאֲשֶׁר נַסְתֶּם מִפְּנֵי הָרַעַשׁ בִּימֵי עֻזִּיָּה מֶלֶךְ־יְהוּדָה וּבָא יְהוָה אֱלֹהַי כָּל־קְדֹשִׁים עִמָּךְ׃ וְהָיָה בַּיּוֹם הַהוּא לֹא־יִהְיֶה אוֹר יְקָרוֹת יקפאון׃ וְהָיָה (וְקִפָּאוֹן) יוֹם־אֶחָד הוּא יִוָּדַע לַיהוָה לֹא־יוֹם וְלֹא־לָיְלָה וְהָיָה לְעֵת־עֶרֶב יִהְיֶה־אוֹר׃ וְהָיָה ׀ בַּיּוֹם הַהוּא יֵצְאוּ מַיִם־חַיִּים מִירוּשָׁלִַם חֶצְיָם אֶל־הַיָּם הַקַּדְמוֹנִי וְחֶצְיָם אֶל־הַיָּם הָאַחֲרוֹן בַּקַּיִץ וּבָחֹרֶף יִהְיֶה׃ וְהָיָה יְהוָה לְמֶלֶךְ עַל־כָּל־הָאָרֶץ בַּיּוֹם הַהוּא יִהְיֶה יְהוָה אֶחָד וּשְׁמוֹ אֶחָד׃ יִסּוֹב כָּל־הָאָרֶץ כָּעֲרָבָה מִגֶּבַע לְרִמּוֹן נֶגֶב יְרוּשָׁלִָם וְרָאֲמָה וְיָשְׁבָה תַחְתֶּיהָ לְמִשַּׁעַר בִּנְיָמִן עַד־מְקוֹם שַׁעַר הָרִאשׁוֹן עַד־שַׁעַר הַפִּנִּים וּמִגְדַּל חֲנַנְאֵל עַד יִקְבֵי הַמֶּלֶךְ׃ וְיָשְׁבוּ בָהּ וְחֵרֶם לֹא יִהְיֶה־עוֹד וְיָשְׁבָה יְרוּשָׁלִַם לָבֶטַח׃

וְזֹאת ׀ תִּהְיֶה הַמַּגֵּפָה אֲשֶׁר יִגֹּף יְהוָה אֶת־כָּל־הָעַמִּים אֲשֶׁר צָבְאוּ עַל־יְרוּשָׁלִָם הָמֵק ׀ בְּשָׂרוֹ וְהוּא עֹמֵד עַל־רַגְלָיו וְעֵינָיו תִּמַּקְנָה בְחֹרֵיהֶן וּלְשׁוֹנוֹ תִּמַּק בְּפִיהֶם׃ וְהָיָה בַּיּוֹם הַהוּא תִּהְיֶה מְהוּמַת־יְהוָה רַבָּה בָּהֶם וְהֶחֱזִיקוּ אִישׁ יַד רֵעֵהוּ וְעָלְתָה יָדוֹ עַל־יַד רֵעֵהוּ׃ וְגַם־יְהוּדָה תִּלָּחֵם בִּירוּשָׁלִָם וְאֻסַּף חֵיל כָּל־הַגּוֹיִם סָבִיב זָהָב וָכֶסֶף וּבְגָדִים לָרֹב מְאֹד׃ וְכֵן תִּהְיֶה מַגֵּפַת הַסּוּס הַפֶּרֶד הַגָּמָל וְהַחֲמוֹר וְכָל־הַבְּהֵמָה אֲשֶׁר יִהְיֶה בַּמַּחֲנוֹת הָהֵמָּה כַּמַּגֵּפָה הַזֹּאת׃ וְהָיָה כָּל־הַנּוֹתָר מִכָּל־הַגּוֹיִם הַבָּאִים עַל־יְרוּשָׁלִָם וְעָלוּ מִדֵּי שָׁנָה בְשָׁנָה לְהִשְׁתַּחֲוֺת לְמֶלֶךְ יְהוָה צְבָאוֹת וְלָחֹג אֶת־חַג הַסֻּכּוֹת׃ וְהָיָה אֲשֶׁר לֹא־יַעֲלֶה מֵאֵת מִשְׁפְּחוֹת הָאָרֶץ אֶל־יְרוּשָׁלִַם לְהִשְׁתַּחֲוֺת לְמֶלֶךְ יְהוָה צְבָאוֹת וְלֹא עֲלֵיהֶם יִהְיֶה הַגָּשֶׁם׃ וְאִם־מִשְׁפַּחַת מִצְרַיִם לֹא־תַעֲלֶה וְלֹא בָאָה וְלֹא עֲלֵיהֶם תִּהְיֶה הַמַּגֵּפָה אֲשֶׁר יִגֹּף יְהוָה אֶת־הַגּוֹיִם אֲשֶׁר לֹא יַעֲלוּ לָחֹג אֶת־חַג הַסֻּכּוֹת׃ זֹאת תִּהְיֶה חַטַּאת מִצְרָיִם וְחַטַּאת כָּל־הַגּוֹיִם אֲשֶׁר לֹא יַעֲלוּ לָחֹג אֶת־חַג הַסֻּכּוֹת׃ בַּיּוֹם הַהוּא יִהְיֶה עַל־מְצִלּוֹת הַסּוּס קֹדֶשׁ לַיהוָה וְהָיָה הַסִּירוֹת בְּבֵית יְהוָה כַּמִּזְרָקִים לִפְנֵי הַמִּזְבֵּחַ׃ וְהָיָה כָּל־סִיר בִּירוּשָׁלִַם וּבִיהוּדָה קֹדֶשׁ לַיהוָה צְבָאוֹת וּבָאוּ כָּל־הַזֹּבְחִים וְלָקְחוּ מֵהֶם וּבִשְּׁלוּ בָהֶם וְלֹא־יִהְיֶה כְנַעֲנִי עוֹד בְּבֵית־יְהוָה צְבָאוֹת בַּיּוֹם הַהוּא׃

# הפטרה ליום טוב שני של סוכות בחוץ לארץ

## HAFTARA FOR SECOND DAY OF SUKKOT IN THE DIASPORA

ויקהלו אל־המלך שלמה כל־איש ישראל בירח האתנים בחג הוא החדש מלכים א׳ ח:ב–כא
השביעי: ויבאו כל זקני ישראל וישאו הכהנים את־הארון: ויעלו את־ארון
יהוה ואת־אהל מועד ואת־כל־כלי הקדש אשר באהל ויעלו אתם הכהנים
והלוים: והמלך שלמה וכל־עדת ישראל הנועדים עליו אתו לפני הארון
מזבחים צאן ובקר אשר לא־יספרו ולא ימנו מרב: ויבאו הכהנים את־ארון
ברית־יהוה אל־מקומו אל־דביר הבית אל־קדש הקדשים אל־תחת כנפי
הכרובים: כי הכרובים פרשים כנפים אל־מקום הארון ויסכו הכרבים על־
הארון ועל־בדיו מלמעלה: ויארכו הבדים ויראו ראשי הבדים מן־הקדש
על־פני הדביר ולא יראו החוצה ויהיו שם עד היום הזה: אין בארון רק שני
לחות האבנים אשר הנח שם משה בחרב אשר כרת יהוה עם־בני ישראל
בצאתם מארץ מצרים: ויהי בצאת הכהנים מן־הקדש והענן מלא את־
בית יהוה: ולא־יכלו הכהנים לעמד לשרת מפני הענן כי־מלא כבוד־יהוה
את־בית יהוה: אז אמר שלמה יהוה אמר לשכן בערפל: בנה
בניתי בית זבל לך מכון לשבתך עולמים: ויסב המלך את־פניו ויברך את
כל־קהל ישראל וכל־קהל ישראל עמד: ויאמר ברוך יהוה אלהי ישראל
אשר דבר בפיו את דוד אבי ובידו מלא לאמר: מן־היום אשר הוצאתי
את־עמי את־ישראל ממצרים לא־בחרתי בעיר מכל שבטי ישראל לבנות
בית להיות שמי שם ואבחר בדוד להיות על־עמי ישראל: ויהי עם־לבב
דוד אבי לבנות בית לשם יהוה אלהי ישראל: ויאמר יהוה אל־דוד אבי
יען אשר היה עם־לבבך לבנות בית לשמי הטיבת כי היה עם־לבבך: רק
אתה לא תבנה הבית כי אם־בנך היצא מחלציך הוא־יבנה הבית לשמי:
ויקם יהוה את־דברו אשר דבר ואקם תחת דוד אבי ואשב ׀ על־כסא
ישראל כאשר דבר יהוה ואבנה הבית לשם יהוה אלהי ישראל: ואשם
שם מקום לארון אשר־שם ברית יהוה אשר כרת עם־אבתינו בהוציאו
אתם מארץ מצרים:

# קריאה ליום הראשון דחול המועד סוכות

## FIRST DAY OF ḤOL HAMO'ED SUKKOT

*In* ארץ ישראל*, the first three verses,* וּבַיּ֣וֹם הַשֵּׁנִ֗י *through* וּמִנְחָתָ֖הּ וְנִסְכֵּיהֶֽם*, are read for each of the four* עליות*.*

במדבר כט:יז–כה וּבַיּ֣וֹם הַשֵּׁנִ֗י פָּרִ֧ים בְּנֵי־בָקָ֛ר שְׁנֵ֥ים עָשָׂ֖ר אֵילִ֣ם שְׁנָ֑יִם כְּבָשִׂ֧ים בְּנֵי־שָׁנָ֛ה
אַרְבָּעָ֥ה עָשָׂ֖ר תְּמִימִֽם׃ וּמִנְחָתָ֣ם וְנִסְכֵּיהֶ֡ם לַ֠פָּרִים לָאֵילִ֧ם וְלַכְּבָשִׂ֛ים
בְּמִסְפָּרָ֖ם כַּמִּשְׁפָּֽט׃ וּשְׂעִיר־עִזִּ֥ים אֶחָ֖ד חַטָּ֑את מִלְּבַד֙ עֹלַ֣ת הַתָּמִ֔יד וּמִנְחָתָ֖הּ
לוי וְנִסְכֵּיהֶֽם׃ *וּבַיּ֧וֹם הַשְּׁלִישִׁ֛י פָּרִ֥ים עַשְׁתֵּי־עָשָׂ֖ר אֵילִ֣ם שְׁנָ֑יִם כְּבָשִׂ֧ים
בְּנֵי־שָׁנָ֛ה אַרְבָּעָ֥ה עָשָׂ֖ר תְּמִימִֽם׃ וּמִנְחָתָ֣ם וְנִסְכֵּיהֶ֡ם לַ֠פָּרִים לָאֵילִ֧ם וְלַכְּבָשִׂ֛ים
בְּמִסְפָּרָ֖ם כַּמִּשְׁפָּֽט׃ וּשְׂעִ֥יר חַטָּ֖את אֶחָ֑ד מִלְּבַד֙ עֹלַ֣ת הַתָּמִ֔יד וּמִנְחָתָ֖הּ
שלישי וְנִסְכָּֽהּ׃ *וּבַיּ֧וֹם הָרְבִיעִ֛י פָּרִ֥ים עֲשָׂרָ֖ה אֵילִ֣ם שְׁנָ֑יִם כְּבָשִׂ֧ים בְּנֵי־שָׁנָ֛ה
אַרְבָּעָ֥ה עָשָׂ֖ר תְּמִימִֽם׃ מִנְחָתָ֣ם וְנִסְכֵּיהֶ֡ם לַ֠פָּרִים לָאֵילִ֧ם וְלַכְּבָשִׂ֛ים בְּמִסְפָּרָ֖ם
כַּמִּשְׁפָּֽט׃ וּשְׂעִיר־עִזִּ֥ים אֶחָ֖ד חַטָּ֑את מִלְּבַד֙ עֹלַ֣ת הַתָּמִ֔יד מִנְחָתָ֖הּ וְנִסְכָּֽהּ׃
רביעי וּבַיּ֣וֹם הַשֵּׁנִ֗י פָּרִ֧ים בְּנֵי־בָקָ֛ר שְׁנֵ֥ים עָשָׂ֖ר אֵילִ֣ם שְׁנָ֑יִם כְּבָשִׂ֧ים בְּנֵי־שָׁנָ֛ה
אַרְבָּעָ֥ה עָשָׂ֖ר תְּמִימִֽם׃ וּמִנְחָתָ֣ם וְנִסְכֵּיהֶ֡ם לַ֠פָּרִים לָאֵילִ֧ם וְלַכְּבָשִׂ֛ים
בְּמִסְפָּרָ֖ם כַּמִּשְׁפָּֽט׃ וּשְׂעִיר־עִזִּ֥ים אֶחָ֖ד חַטָּ֑את מִלְּבַד֙ עֹלַ֣ת הַתָּמִ֔יד וּמִנְחָתָ֖הּ
וְנִסְכֵּיהֶֽם׃ וּבַיּ֧וֹם הַשְּׁלִישִׁ֛י פָּרִ֥ים עַשְׁתֵּי־עָשָׂ֖ר אֵילִ֣ם שְׁנָ֑יִם כְּבָשִׂ֧ים
בְּנֵי־שָׁנָ֛ה אַרְבָּעָ֥ה עָשָׂ֖ר תְּמִימִֽם׃ וּמִנְחָתָ֣ם וְנִסְכֵּיהֶ֡ם לַ֠פָּרִים לָאֵילִ֧ם וְלַכְּבָשִׂ֛ים
בְּמִסְפָּרָ֖ם כַּמִּשְׁפָּֽט׃ וּשְׂעִ֥יר חַטָּ֖את אֶחָ֑ד מִלְּבַד֙ עֹלַ֣ת הַתָּמִ֔יד וּמִנְחָתָ֖הּ
וְנִסְכָּֽהּ׃

# קריאה ליום השני דחול המועד סוכות

## SECOND DAY OF ḤOL HAMO'ED SUKKOT

*In* ארץ ישראל*, the first three verses,* וּבַיּ֧וֹם הַשְּׁלִישִׁ֛י *through* וּמִנְחָתָ֖הּ וְנִסְכָּֽהּ*, are read for each of the four* עליות*.*

במדבר כט:כ–כח וּבַיּ֧וֹם הַשְּׁלִישִׁ֛י פָּרִ֥ים עַשְׁתֵּי־עָשָׂ֖ר אֵילִ֣ם שְׁנָ֑יִם כְּבָשִׂ֧ים בְּנֵי־שָׁנָ֛ה אַרְבָּעָ֥ה עָשָׂ֖ר
תְּמִימִֽם׃ וּמִנְחָתָ֣ם וְנִסְכֵּיהֶ֡ם לַ֠פָּרִים לָאֵילִ֧ם וְלַכְּבָשִׂ֛ים בְּמִסְפָּרָ֖ם כַּמִּשְׁפָּֽט׃
לוי וּשְׂעִ֥יר חַטָּ֖את אֶחָ֑ד מִלְּבַד֙ עֹלַ֣ת הַתָּמִ֔יד וּמִנְחָתָ֖הּ וְנִסְכָּֽהּ׃ *וּבַיּ֧וֹם
הָרְבִיעִ֛י פָּרִ֥ים עֲשָׂרָ֖ה אֵילִ֣ם שְׁנָ֑יִם כְּבָשִׂ֧ים בְּנֵי־שָׁנָ֛ה אַרְבָּעָ֥ה עָשָׂ֖ר תְּמִימִֽם׃

מִנְחָתָם וְנִסְכֵּיהֶם לַפָּרִים לָאֵילִם וְלַכְּבָשִׂים בְּמִסְפָּרָם כַּמִּשְׁפָּט: וּשְׂעִיר־
שלישי עִזִּים אֶחָד חַטָּאת מִלְּבַד עֹלַת הַתָּמִיד מִנְחָתָהּ וְנִסְכָּהּ: *וּבַיּוֹם
הַחֲמִישִׁי פָּרִים תִּשְׁעָה אֵילִם שְׁנָיִם כְּבָשִׂים בְּנֵי־שָׁנָה אַרְבָּעָה עָשָׂר תְּמִימִם:
וּמִנְחָתָם וְנִסְכֵּיהֶם לַפָּרִים לָאֵילִם וְלַכְּבָשִׂים בְּמִסְפָּרָם כַּמִּשְׁפָּט: וּשְׂעִיר
חַטָּאת אֶחָד מִלְּבַד עֹלַת הַתָּמִיד וּמִנְחָתָהּ וְנִסְכָּהּ:
רביעי וּבַיּוֹם הַשְּׁלִישִׁי פָּרִים עַשְׁתֵּי־עָשָׂר אֵילִם שְׁנָיִם כְּבָשִׂים בְּנֵי־שָׁנָה אַרְבָּעָה עָשָׂר
תְּמִימִם: וּמִנְחָתָם וְנִסְכֵּיהֶם לַפָּרִים לָאֵילִם וְלַכְּבָשִׂים בְּמִסְפָּרָם כַּמִּשְׁפָּט:
וּשְׂעִיר חַטָּאת אֶחָד מִלְּבַד עֹלַת הַתָּמִיד וּמִנְחָתָהּ וְנִסְכָּהּ: וּבַיּוֹם
הָרְבִיעִי פָּרִים עֲשָׂרָה אֵילִם שְׁנָיִם כְּבָשִׂים בְּנֵי־שָׁנָה אַרְבָּעָה עָשָׂר תְּמִימִם:
מִנְחָתָם וְנִסְכֵּיהֶם לַפָּרִים לָאֵילִם וְלַכְּבָשִׂים בְּמִסְפָּרָם כַּמִּשְׁפָּט: וּשְׂעִיר־עִזִּים
אֶחָד חַטָּאת מִלְּבַד עֹלַת הַתָּמִיד מִנְחָתָהּ וְנִסְכָּהּ:

## קריאה ליום השלישי דחול המועד סוכות

## THIRD DAY OF ḤOL HAMO'ED SUKKOT

*In* ארץ ישראל, *the first three verses,* וּבַיּוֹם הָרְבִיעִי *through* מִנְחָתָהּ וְנִסְכָּהּ, *are read for each of the four* עליות.

במדבר כט:כג–לא וּבַיּוֹם הָרְבִיעִי פָּרִים עֲשָׂרָה אֵילִם שְׁנָיִם כְּבָשִׂים בְּנֵי־שָׁנָה אַרְבָּעָה עָשָׂר תְּמִימִם:
מִנְחָתָם וְנִסְכֵּיהֶם לַפָּרִים לָאֵילִם וְלַכְּבָשִׂים בְּמִסְפָּרָם כַּמִּשְׁפָּט: וּשְׂעִיר־
לוי עִזִּים אֶחָד חַטָּאת מִלְּבַד עֹלַת הַתָּמִיד מִנְחָתָהּ וְנִסְכָּהּ: *וּבַיּוֹם
הַחֲמִישִׁי פָּרִים תִּשְׁעָה אֵילִם שְׁנָיִם כְּבָשִׂים בְּנֵי־שָׁנָה אַרְבָּעָה עָשָׂר תְּמִימִם:
וּמִנְחָתָם וְנִסְכֵּיהֶם לַפָּרִים לָאֵילִם וְלַכְּבָשִׂים בְּמִסְפָּרָם כַּמִּשְׁפָּט: וּשְׂעִיר
שלישי חַטָּאת אֶחָד מִלְּבַד עֹלַת הַתָּמִיד וּמִנְחָתָהּ וְנִסְכָּהּ: *וּבַיּוֹם הַשִּׁשִּׁי
פָּרִים שְׁמֹנָה אֵילִם שְׁנָיִם כְּבָשִׂים בְּנֵי־שָׁנָה אַרְבָּעָה עָשָׂר תְּמִימִם: וּמִנְחָתָם
וְנִסְכֵּיהֶם לַפָּרִים לָאֵילִם וְלַכְּבָשִׂים בְּמִסְפָּרָם כַּמִּשְׁפָּט: וּשְׂעִיר חַטָּאת
אֶחָד מִלְּבַד עֹלַת הַתָּמִיד מִנְחָתָהּ וּנְסָכֶיהָ:
רביעי וּבַיּוֹם הָרְבִיעִי פָּרִים עֲשָׂרָה אֵילִם שְׁנָיִם כְּבָשִׂים בְּנֵי־שָׁנָה אַרְבָּעָה עָשָׂר תְּמִימִם:
מִנְחָתָם וְנִסְכֵּיהֶם לַפָּרִים לָאֵילִם וְלַכְּבָשִׂים בְּמִסְפָּרָם כַּמִּשְׁפָּט: וּשְׂעִיר־עִזִּים
אֶחָד חַטָּאת מִלְּבַד עֹלַת הַתָּמִיד מִנְחָתָהּ וְנִסְכָּהּ: וּבַיּוֹם הַחֲמִישִׁי
פָּרִים תִּשְׁעָה אֵילִם שְׁנָיִם כְּבָשִׂים בְּנֵי־שָׁנָה אַרְבָּעָה עָשָׂר תְּמִימִם: וּמִנְחָתָם

וְנִסְכֵּיהֶם לַפָּרִים לָאֵילִם וְלַכְּבָשִׂים בְּמִסְפָּרָם כַּמִּשְׁפָּט׃ וּשְׂעִיר חַטָּאת אֶחָד
מִלְּבַד עֹלַת הַתָּמִיד וּמִנְחָתָהּ וְנִסְכָּהּ׃

## קריאה ליום הרביעי דחול המועד סוכות

## FOURTH DAY OF ḤOL HAMO'ED SUKKOT

*In* ארץ ישראל*, the first three verses,* וּבַיּוֹם הַחֲמִישִׁי *through* וּמִנְחָתָהּ וְנִסְכָּהּ*, are read for each of the four* עליות*.*

במדבר כט:כו–לד וּבַיּוֹם הַחֲמִישִׁי פָּרִים תִּשְׁעָה אֵילִם שְׁנָיִם כְּבָשִׂים בְּנֵי־שָׁנָה אַרְבָּעָה עָשָׂר
תְּמִימִם׃ וּמִנְחָתָם וְנִסְכֵּיהֶם לַפָּרִים לָאֵילִם וְלַכְּבָשִׂים בְּמִסְפָּרָם כַּמִּשְׁפָּט׃
לוי וּשְׂעִיר חַטָּאת אֶחָד מִלְּבַד עֹלַת הַתָּמִיד וּמִנְחָתָהּ וְנִסְכָּהּ׃ *וּבַיּוֹם
הַשִּׁשִּׁי פָּרִים שְׁמֹנָה אֵילִם שְׁנָיִם כְּבָשִׂים בְּנֵי־שָׁנָה אַרְבָּעָה עָשָׂר תְּמִימִם׃
וּמִנְחָתָם וְנִסְכֵּיהֶם לַפָּרִים לָאֵילִם וְלַכְּבָשִׂים בְּמִסְפָּרָם כַּמִּשְׁפָּט׃ וּשְׂעִיר
שלישי חַטָּאת אֶחָד מִלְּבַד עֹלַת הַתָּמִיד מִנְחָתָהּ וּנְסָכֶיהָ׃ *וּבַיּוֹם הַשְּׁבִיעִי
פָּרִים שִׁבְעָה אֵילִם שְׁנָיִם כְּבָשִׂים בְּנֵי־שָׁנָה אַרְבָּעָה עָשָׂר תְּמִימִם׃ וּמִנְחָתָם
וְנִסְכֵּהֶם לַפָּרִים לָאֵילִם וְלַכְּבָשִׂים בְּמִסְפָּרָם כְּמִשְׁפָּטָם׃ וּשְׂעִיר חַטָּאת אֶחָד
מִלְּבַד עֹלַת הַתָּמִיד מִנְחָתָהּ וְנִסְכָּהּ׃
רביעי וּבַיּוֹם הַחֲמִישִׁי פָּרִים תִּשְׁעָה אֵילִם שְׁנָיִם כְּבָשִׂים בְּנֵי־שָׁנָה אַרְבָּעָה עָשָׂר
תְּמִימִם׃ וּמִנְחָתָם וְנִסְכֵּיהֶם לַפָּרִים לָאֵילִם וְלַכְּבָשִׂים בְּמִסְפָּרָם כַּמִּשְׁפָּט׃
וּשְׂעִיר חַטָּאת אֶחָד מִלְּבַד עֹלַת הַתָּמִיד וּמִנְחָתָהּ וְנִסְכָּהּ׃ וּבַיּוֹם
הַשִּׁשִּׁי פָּרִים שְׁמֹנָה אֵילִם שְׁנָיִם כְּבָשִׂים בְּנֵי־שָׁנָה אַרְבָּעָה עָשָׂר תְּמִימִם׃
וּמִנְחָתָם וְנִסְכֵּיהֶם לַפָּרִים לָאֵילִם וְלַכְּבָשִׂים בְּמִסְפָּרָם כַּמִּשְׁפָּט׃ וּשְׂעִיר
חַטָּאת אֶחָד מִלְּבַד עֹלַת הַתָּמִיד מִנְחָתָהּ וּנְסָכֶיהָ׃

## קריאה ליום החמישי דחול המועד סוכות בארץ ישראל

## FIFTH DAY OF ḤOL HAMO'ED SUKKOT IN ISRAEL

*In* ארץ ישראל*, the following is read for each of the four* עליות*.*

במדבר כט:כט–לא וּבַיּוֹם הַשִּׁשִּׁי פָּרִים שְׁמֹנָה אֵילִם שְׁנָיִם כְּבָשִׂים בְּנֵי־שָׁנָה אַרְבָּעָה עָשָׂר
תְּמִימִם׃ וּמִנְחָתָם וְנִסְכֵּיהֶם לַפָּרִים לָאֵילִם וְלַכְּבָשִׂים בְּמִסְפָּרָם כַּמִּשְׁפָּט׃
וּשְׂעִיר חַטָּאת אֶחָד מִלְּבַד עֹלַת הַתָּמִיד מִנְחָתָהּ וּנְסָכֶיהָ׃

## קריאה להושענא רבה
## HOSHANA RABA

*In* ארץ ישראל*, the three verses from* וביום השביעי *through* מנחתה ונסכה *are read for each of the four* עליות°.

במדבר כט:כו–לד וביום החמישי פרים תשעה אילם שנים כבשים בני־שנה ארבעה עשר
תמימם: ומנחתם ונסכיהם לפרים לאילם ולכבשים במספרם כמשפט:
לוי ושעיר חטאת אחד מלבד עלת התמיד ומנחתה ונסכה: *וביום
הששי פרים שמנה אילם שנים כבשים בני־שנה ארבעה עשר תמימם:
ומנחתם ונסכיהם לפרים לאילם ולכבשים במספרם כמשפט: ושעיר
שלישי חטאת אחד מלבד עלת התמיד מנחתה ונסכיה: *וביום השביעי
פרים שבעה אילם שנים כבשים בני־שנה ארבעה עשר תמימם: ומנחתם
ונסכהם לפרים לאילם ולכבשים במספרם כמשפטם: ושעיר חטאת אחד
מלבד עלת התמיד מנחתה ונסכה:
רביעי וביום הששי פרים שמנה אילם שנים כבשים בני־שנה ארבעה עשר
תמימם: ומנחתם ונסכיהם לפרים לאילם ולכבשים במספרם כמשפט:
ושעיר חטאת אחד מלבד עלת התמיד מנחתה ונסכיה: °ביום
השביעי פרים שבעה אילם שנים כבשים בני־שנה ארבעה עשר תמימם:
ומנחתם ונסכהם לפרים לאילם ולכבשים במספרם כמשפטם: ושעיר
חטאת אחד מלבד עלת התמיד מנחתה ונסכה:

## קריאה לשבת חול המועד סוכות
## SHABBAT ḤOL HAMO'ED SUKKOT

*The* קריאת התורה *for* שבת חול המועד סוכות *is the same as that of* שבת חול המועד פסח *(page 1212). The* מפטיר *is the* קריאת התורה *of the day of* חול המועד סוכות *on which* שבת *falls.*

## הפטרה לשבת חול המועד סוכות
## HAFTARA FOR SHABBAT ḤOL HAMO'ED SUKKOT

יחזקאל לח:יח–לט:טז והיה | ביום ההוא ביום בוא גוג על־אדמת ישראל נאם אדני יהוה תעלה

חֲמָתִי בְּאַפִּי: וּבְקִנְאָתִי בְאֵשׁ־עֶבְרָתִי דִּבַּרְתִּי אִם־לֹא ׀ בַּיּוֹם הַהוּא יִהְיֶה
רַעַשׁ גָּדוֹל עַל אַדְמַת יִשְׂרָאֵל: וְרָעֲשׁוּ מִפָּנַי דְּגֵי הַיָּם וְעוֹף הַשָּׁמַיִם וְחַיַּת
הַשָּׂדֶה וְכָל־הָרֶמֶשׂ הָרֹמֵשׂ עַל־הָאֲדָמָה וְכֹל הָאָדָם אֲשֶׁר עַל־פְּנֵי הָאֲדָמָה
וְנֶהֶרְסוּ הֶהָרִים וְנָפְלוּ הַמַּדְרֵגוֹת וְכָל־חוֹמָה לָאָרֶץ תִּפּוֹל: וְקָרָאתִי עָלָיו
לְכָל־הָרַי חֶרֶב נְאֻם אֲדֹנָי יֱהֹוִה חֶרֶב אִישׁ בְּאָחִיו תִּהְיֶה: וְנִשְׁפַּטְתִּי אִתּוֹ
בְּדֶבֶר וּבְדָם וְגֶשֶׁם שׁוֹטֵף וְאַבְנֵי אֶלְגָּבִישׁ אֵשׁ וְגָפְרִית אַמְטִיר עָלָיו וְעַל־אֲגַפָּיו
וְעַל־עַמִּים רַבִּים אֲשֶׁר אִתּוֹ: וְהִתְגַּדִּלְתִּי וְהִתְקַדִּשְׁתִּי וְנוֹדַעְתִּי לְעֵינֵי גּוֹיִם
רַבִּים וְיָדְעוּ כִּי־אֲנִי יְהוָה: וְאַתָּה בֶן־אָדָם הִנָּבֵא עַל־גּוֹג וְאָמַרְתָּ
כֹּה אָמַר אֲדֹנָי יֱהֹוִה הִנְנִי אֵלֶיךָ גּוֹג נְשִׂיא רֹאשׁ מֶשֶׁךְ וְתֻבָל: וְשֹׁבַבְתִּיךָ
וְשִׁשֵּׁאתִיךָ וְהַעֲלִיתִיךָ מִיַּרְכְּתֵי צָפוֹן וַהֲבִאוֹתִיךָ עַל־הָרֵי יִשְׂרָאֵל: וְהִכֵּיתִי
קַשְׁתְּךָ מִיַּד שְׂמֹאולֶךָ וְחִצֶּיךָ מִיַּד יְמִינְךָ אַפִּיל: עַל־הָרֵי יִשְׂרָאֵל תִּפּוֹל
אַתָּה וְכָל־אֲגַפֶּיךָ וְעַמִּים אֲשֶׁר אִתָּךְ לְעֵיט צִפּוֹר כָּל־כָּנָף וְחַיַּת הַשָּׂדֶה
נְתַתִּיךָ לְאָכְלָה: עַל־פְּנֵי הַשָּׂדֶה תִּפּוֹל כִּי אֲנִי דִבַּרְתִּי נְאֻם אֲדֹנָי יֱהֹוִה:
וְשִׁלַּחְתִּי־אֵשׁ בְּמָגוֹג וּבְיֹשְׁבֵי הָאִיִּים לָבֶטַח וְיָדְעוּ כִּי־אֲנִי יְהוָה: וְאֶת־שֵׁם
קָדְשִׁי אוֹדִיעַ בְּתוֹךְ עַמִּי יִשְׂרָאֵל וְלֹא־אַחֵל אֶת־שֵׁם־קָדְשִׁי עוֹד וְיָדְעוּ
הַגּוֹיִם כִּי־אֲנִי יְהוָה קָדוֹשׁ בְּיִשְׂרָאֵל: הִנֵּה בָאָה וְנִהְיָתָה נְאֻם אֲדֹנָי יֱהֹוִה
הוּא הַיּוֹם אֲשֶׁר דִּבַּרְתִּי: וְיָצְאוּ יֹשְׁבֵי ׀ עָרֵי יִשְׂרָאֵל וּבִעֲרוּ וְהִשִּׂיקוּ בְּנֶשֶׁק
וּמָגֵן וְצִנָּה בְּקֶשֶׁת וּבְחִצִּים וּבְמַקֵּל יָד וּבְרֹמַח וּבִעֲרוּ בָהֶם אֵשׁ שֶׁבַע שָׁנִים:
וְלֹא־יִשְׂאוּ עֵצִים מִן־הַשָּׂדֶה וְלֹא יַחְטְבוּ מִן־הַיְּעָרִים כִּי בַנֶּשֶׁק יְבַעֲרוּ־אֵשׁ
וְשָׁלְלוּ אֶת־שֹׁלְלֵיהֶם וּבָזְזוּ אֶת־בֹּזְזֵיהֶם נְאֻם אֲדֹנָי יֱהֹוִה: וְהָיָה
בַיּוֹם הַהוּא אֶתֵּן לְגוֹג ׀ מְקוֹם־שָׁם קֶבֶר בְּיִשְׂרָאֵל גֵּי הָעֹבְרִים קִדְמַת הַיָּם
וְחֹסֶמֶת הִיא אֶת־הָעֹבְרִים וְקָבְרוּ שָׁם אֶת־גּוֹג וְאֶת־כָּל־הֲמוֹנֹה וְקָרְאוּ גֵּיא
הֲמוֹן גּוֹג: וּקְבָרוּם בֵּית יִשְׂרָאֵל לְמַעַן טַהֵר אֶת־הָאָרֶץ שִׁבְעָה חֳדָשִׁים:
וְקָבְרוּ כָּל־עַם הָאָרֶץ וְהָיָה לָהֶם לְשֵׁם יוֹם הִכָּבְדִי נְאֻם אֲדֹנָי יֱהֹוִה: וְאַנְשֵׁי
תָמִיד יַבְדִּילוּ עֹבְרִים בָּאָרֶץ מְקַבְּרִים אֶת־הָעֹבְרִים אֶת־הַנּוֹתָרִים עַל־פְּנֵי
הָאָרֶץ לְטַהֲרָהּ מִקְצֵה שִׁבְעָה־חֳדָשִׁים יַחְקֹרוּ: וְעָבְרוּ הָעֹבְרִים בָּאָרֶץ וְרָאָה
עֶצֶם אָדָם וּבָנָה אֶצְלוֹ צִיּוּן עַד קָבְרוּ אֹתוֹ הַמְקַבְּרִים אֶל־גֵּיא הֲמוֹן גּוֹג: וְגַם
שֶׁם־עִיר הֲמוֹנָה וְטִהֲרוּ הָאָרֶץ:

## MAFTIR FOR SHEMINI ATZERET מפטיר לשמיני עצרת

*In חוץ לארץ, the קריאת התורה for שמיני עצרת is the same as that of the eighth day of פסח, page 1221. In ארץ ישראל the קריאת התורה for שמיני עצרת is that of שמחת תורה, page 1239. The following מפטיר is then read:*

במדבר כט:לה–ל:א

בַּיּוֹם הַשְּׁמִינִי עֲצֶרֶת תִּהְיֶה לָכֶם כָּל־מְלֶאכֶת עֲבֹדָה לֹא תַעֲשׂוּ: וְהִקְרַבְתֶּם עֹלָה אִשֵּׁה רֵיחַ נִיחֹחַ לַיהוָה פַּר אֶחָד אַיִל אֶחָד כְּבָשִׂים בְּנֵי־שָׁנָה שִׁבְעָה תְּמִימִם: מִנְחָתָם וְנִסְכֵּיהֶם לַפָּר לָאַיִל וְלַכְּבָשִׂים בְּמִסְפָּרָם כַּמִּשְׁפָּט: וּשְׂעִיר חַטָּאת אֶחָד מִלְּבַד עֹלַת הַתָּמִיד וּמִנְחָתָהּ וְנִסְכָּהּ: אֵלֶּה תַּעֲשׂוּ לַיהוָה בְּמוֹעֲדֵיכֶם לְבַד מִנִּדְרֵיכֶם וְנִדְבֹתֵיכֶם לְעֹלֹתֵיכֶם וּלְמִנְחֹתֵיכֶם וּלְנִסְכֵּיכֶם וּלְשַׁלְמֵיכֶם: וַיֹּאמֶר מֹשֶׁה אֶל־בְּנֵי יִשְׂרָאֵל כְּכֹל אֲשֶׁר־צִוָּה יְהוָה אֶת־מֹשֶׁה:

## הפטרה לשמיני עצרת בחוץ לארץ
## HAFTARA FOR SHEMINI ATZERET IN THE DIASPORA

*In ארץ ישראל, the הפטרה for שמיני עצרת is that of שמחת תורה, page 1244.*

מלכים א׳ ח:נד–ט:א

וַיְהִי ׀ כְּכַלּוֹת שְׁלֹמֹה לְהִתְפַּלֵּל אֶל־יְהוָה אֵת כָּל־הַתְּפִלָּה וְהַתְּחִנָּה הַזֹּאת קָם מִלִּפְנֵי מִזְבַּח יְהוָה מִכְּרֹעַ עַל־בִּרְכָּיו וְכַפָּיו פְּרֻשׂוֹת הַשָּׁמָיִם: וַיַּעֲמֹד וַיְבָרֶךְ אֵת כָּל־קְהַל יִשְׂרָאֵל קוֹל גָּדוֹל לֵאמֹר: בָּרוּךְ יְהוָה אֲשֶׁר נָתַן מְנוּחָה לְעַמּוֹ יִשְׂרָאֵל כְּכֹל אֲשֶׁר דִּבֵּר לֹא־נָפַל דָּבָר אֶחָד מִכֹּל דְּבָרוֹ הַטּוֹב אֲשֶׁר דִּבֶּר בְּיַד מֹשֶׁה עַבְדּוֹ: יְהִי יְהוָה אֱלֹהֵינוּ עִמָּנוּ כַּאֲשֶׁר הָיָה עִם־אֲבֹתֵינוּ אַל־יַעַזְבֵנוּ וְאַל־יִטְּשֵׁנוּ: לְהַטּוֹת לְבָבֵנוּ אֵלָיו לָלֶכֶת בְּכָל־דְּרָכָיו וְלִשְׁמֹר מִצְוֹתָיו וְחֻקָּיו וּמִשְׁפָּטָיו אֲשֶׁר צִוָּה אֶת־אֲבֹתֵינוּ: וְיִהְיוּ דְבָרַי אֵלֶּה אֲשֶׁר הִתְחַנַּנְתִּי לִפְנֵי יְהוָה קְרֹבִים אֶל־יְהוָה אֱלֹהֵינוּ יוֹמָם וָלָיְלָה לַעֲשׂוֹת ׀ מִשְׁפַּט עַבְדּוֹ וּמִשְׁפַּט עַמּוֹ יִשְׂרָאֵל דְּבַר־יוֹם בְּיוֹמוֹ: לְמַעַן דַּעַת כָּל־עַמֵּי הָאָרֶץ כִּי יְהוָה הוּא הָאֱלֹהִים אֵין עוֹד: וְהָיָה לְבַבְכֶם שָׁלֵם עִם יְהוָה אֱלֹהֵינוּ לָלֶכֶת בְּחֻקָּיו וְלִשְׁמֹר מִצְוֹתָיו כַּיּוֹם הַזֶּה: וְהַמֶּלֶךְ וְכָל־יִשְׂרָאֵל עִמּוֹ זֹבְחִים זֶבַח לִפְנֵי יְהוָה: וַיִּזְבַּח שְׁלֹמֹה אֵת זֶבַח הַשְּׁלָמִים אֲשֶׁר זָבַח לַיהוָה בָּקָר עֶשְׂרִים וּשְׁנַיִם אֶלֶף וְצֹאן מֵאָה וְעֶשְׂרִים אָלֶף וַיַּחְנְכוּ אֶת־בֵּית יְהוָה הַמֶּלֶךְ וְכָל־בְּנֵי יִשְׂרָאֵל: בַּיּוֹם הַהוּא קִדַּשׁ הַמֶּלֶךְ אֶת־תּוֹךְ הֶחָצֵר אֲשֶׁר לִפְנֵי בֵית־יְהוָה כִּי־עָשָׂה שָׁם אֶת־הָעֹלָה וְאֶת־

הַמִּנְחָה וְאֵת חֶלְבֵי הַשְּׁלָמִים כִּי־מִזְבַּח הַנְּחֹשֶׁת אֲשֶׁר לִפְנֵי יהוה קָטֹן מֵהָכִיל
אֶת־הָעֹלָה וְאֶת־הַמִּנְחָה וְאֵת חֶלְבֵי הַשְּׁלָמִים: וַיַּעַשׂ שְׁלֹמֹה בָעֵת־הַהִיא ׀
אֶת־הֶחָג וְכָל־יִשְׂרָאֵל עִמּוֹ קָהָל גָּדוֹל מִלְּבוֹא חֲמָת ׀ עַד־נַחַל מִצְרַיִם לִפְנֵי
יהוה אֱלֹהֵינוּ שִׁבְעַת יָמִים וְשִׁבְעַת יָמִים אַרְבָּעָה עָשָׂר יוֹם: בַּיּוֹם הַשְּׁמִינִי
שִׁלַּח אֶת־הָעָם וַיְבָרֲכוּ אֶת־הַמֶּלֶךְ וַיֵּלְכוּ לְאׇהֳלֵיהֶם שְׂמֵחִים וְטוֹבֵי לֵב עַל
כׇּל־הַטּוֹבָה אֲשֶׁר עָשָׂה יהוה לְדָוִד עַבְדּוֹ וּלְיִשְׂרָאֵל עַמּוֹ: וַיְהִי
כְּכַלּוֹת שְׁלֹמֹה לִבְנוֹת אֶת־בֵּית־יהוה וְאֶת־בֵּית הַמֶּלֶךְ וְאֵת כׇּל־חֵשֶׁק שְׁלֹמֹה
אֲשֶׁר חָפֵץ לַעֲשׂוֹת:

## קריאה לשמחת תורה SIMḤAT TORAH

*In* ארץ ישראל, *if* שמחת תורה *falls on* שבת, *the first three verses of the* קריאה לחתן תורה *(page 1241) from* מְעֹנָה אֱלֹהֵי קֶדֶם *through* עַל־בָּמוֹתֵימוֹ תִדְרֹךְ *are read for* ששי.

וְזֹאת הַבְּרָכָה אֲשֶׁר בֵּרַךְ מֹשֶׁה אִישׁ הָאֱלֹהִים אֶת־בְּנֵי יִשְׂרָאֵל לִפְנֵי מוֹתוֹ: דברים לג:א-כו
וַיֹּאמַר יהוה מִסִּינַי בָּא וְזָרַח מִשֵּׂעִיר לָמוֹ הוֹפִיעַ מֵהַר פָּארָן וְאָתָה מֵרִבְבֹת
קֹדֶשׁ מִימִינוֹ אשדת לָמוֹ: אַף חֹבֵב עַמִּים כׇּל־קְדֹשָׁיו בְּיָדֶךָ וְהֵם תֻּכּוּ לְרַגְלֶךָ אֵשׁ דָּת
יִשָּׂא מִדַּבְּרֹתֶיךָ: תּוֹרָה צִוָּה־לָנוּ מֹשֶׁה מוֹרָשָׁה קְהִלַּת יַעֲקֹב: וַיְהִי בִישֻׁרוּן
מֶלֶךְ בְּהִתְאַסֵּף רָאשֵׁי עָם יַחַד שִׁבְטֵי יִשְׂרָאֵל: יְחִי רְאוּבֵן וְאַל־יָמֹת וִיהִי מְתָיו
מִסְפָּר: וְזֹאת לִיהוּדָה וַיֹּאמַר שְׁמַע יהוה קוֹל יְהוּדָה וְאֶל־עַמּוֹ
תְּבִיאֶנּוּ יָדָיו רָב לוֹ וְעֵזֶר מִצָּרָיו תִּהְיֶה:
וּלְלֵוִי אָמַר תֻּמֶּיךָ וְאוּרֶיךָ לְאִישׁ חֲסִידֶךָ אֲשֶׁר נִסִּיתוֹ בְּמַסָּה תְּרִיבֵהוּ עַל־מֵי לוי
מְרִיבָה: הָאֹמֵר לְאָבִיו וּלְאִמּוֹ לֹא רְאִיתִיו וְאֶת־אֶחָיו לֹא הִכִּיר וְאֶת־בָּנָו לֹא
יָדָע כִּי שָׁמְרוּ אִמְרָתֶךָ וּבְרִיתְךָ יִנְצֹרוּ: יוֹרוּ מִשְׁפָּטֶיךָ לְיַעֲקֹב וְתוֹרָתְךָ לְיִשְׂרָאֵל
יָשִׂימוּ קְטוֹרָה בְּאַפֶּךָ וְכָלִיל עַל־מִזְבְּחֶךָ: בָּרֵךְ יהוה חֵילוֹ וּפֹעַל יָדָיו תִּרְצֶה
מְחַץ מׇתְנַיִם קָמָיו וּמְשַׂנְאָיו מִן־יְקוּמוּן: לְבִנְיָמִן אָמַר יְדִיד יהוה
יִשְׁכֹּן לָבֶטַח עָלָיו חֹפֵף עָלָיו כׇּל־הַיּוֹם וּבֵין כְּתֵפָיו שָׁכֵן: *וּלְיוֹסֵף שלישי
אָמַר מְבֹרֶכֶת יהוה אַרְצוֹ מִמֶּגֶד שָׁמַיִם מִטָּל וּמִתְּהוֹם רֹבֶצֶת תָּחַת: וּמִמֶּגֶד
תְּבוּאֹת שָׁמֶשׁ וּמִמֶּגֶד גֶּרֶשׁ יְרָחִים: וּמֵרֹאשׁ הַרְרֵי־קֶדֶם וּמִמֶּגֶד גִּבְעוֹת עוֹלָם:
וּמִמֶּגֶד אֶרֶץ וּמְלֹאָהּ וּרְצוֹן שֹׁכְנִי סְנֶה תָּבוֹאתָה לְרֹאשׁ יוֹסֵף וּלְקׇדְקֹד נְזִיר
אֶחָיו: בְּכוֹר שׁוֹרוֹ הָדָר לוֹ וְקַרְנֵי רְאֵם קַרְנָיו בָּהֶם עַמִּים יְנַגַּח יַחְדָּו אַפְסֵי־אָרֶץ

רביעי וְהֵם רִבְבוֹת אֶפְרַיִם וְהֵם אַלְפֵי מְנַשֶּׁה: *וְלִזְבוּלֻן אָמַר שְׂמַח זְבוּלֻן
בְּצֵאתֶךָ וְיִשָּׂשכָר בְּאֹהָלֶיךָ: עַמִּים הַר־יִקְרָאוּ שָׁם יִזְבְּחוּ זִבְחֵי־צֶדֶק כִּי שֶׁפַע
יַמִּים יִינָקוּ וּשְׂפֻנֵי טְמוּנֵי חוֹל: וּלְגָד אָמַר בָּרוּךְ מַרְחִיב גָּד כְּלָבִיא
שָׁכֵן וְטָרַף זְרוֹעַ אַף־קָדְקֹד: וַיַּרְא רֵאשִׁית לוֹ כִּי־שָׁם חֶלְקַת מְחֹקֵק סָפוּן
חמישי וַיֵּתֵא רָאשֵׁי עָם צִדְקַת יהוה עָשָׂה וּמִשְׁפָּטָיו עִם־יִשְׂרָאֵל: *וּלְדָן
אָמַר דָּן גּוּר אַרְיֵה יְזַנֵּק מִן־הַבָּשָׁן: וּלְנַפְתָּלִי אָמַר נַפְתָּלִי שְׂבַע רָצוֹן וּמָלֵא
בִּרְכַּת יהוה יָם וְדָרוֹם יְרָשָׁה: וּלְאָשֵׁר אָמַר בָּרוּךְ מִבָּנִים אָשֵׁר
יְהִי רְצוּי אֶחָיו וְטֹבֵל בַּשֶּׁמֶן רַגְלוֹ: בַּרְזֶל וּנְחֹשֶׁת מִנְעָלֶךָ וּכְיָמֶיךָ דָּבְאֶךָ: אֵין
כָּאֵל יְשֻׁרוּן רֹכֵב שָׁמַיִם בְּעֶזְרֶךָ וּבְגַאֲוָתוֹ שְׁחָקִים:

## CALLING UP THE ḤATAN TORAH — רשות לחתן תורה

*The following is said by the* גבאי *to call up the* חתן תורה *to his* עליה:

מֵרְשׁוּת הָאֵל הַגָּדוֹל הַגִּבּוֹר וְהַנּוֹרָא, וּמֵרְשׁוּת מִפָּז וּמִפְּנִינִים יְקָרָה, וּמֵרְשׁוּת סַנְהֶדְרִין הַקְּדוֹשָׁה וְהַבְּחוּרָה, וּמֵרְשׁוּת רָאשֵׁי יְשִׁיבוֹת וְאַלּוּפֵי תוֹרָה, וּמֵרְשׁוּת זְקֵנִים וּנְעָרִים יוֹשְׁבֵי שׁוּרָה, אֶפְתְּחָה פִּי בְּשִׁיר וּבְזִמְרָה, לְהוֹדוֹת לְהַלֵּל לְדָר בִּנְהוֹרָא, שֶׁהֶחֱיָנוּ וְקִיְּמָנוּ בְּיִרְאָתוֹ הַטְּהוֹרָה, וְהִגִּיעָנוּ לִשְׂמֹחַ בְּשִׂמְחַת הַתּוֹרָה, הַמְשַׂמַּחַת לֵב וְעֵינַיִם מְאִירָה, הַנּוֹתֶנֶת חַיִּים וְעֹשֶׁר וְכָבוֹד וְתִפְאָרָה, הַמְאַשֶּׁרֶת הוֹלְכִים בְּדֶרֶךְ הַטּוֹבָה וְהַיְשָׁרָה, הַמַּאֲרֶכֶת יָמִים וּמוֹסֶפֶת גְּבוּרָה, לְאוֹהֲבֶיהָ וּלְשׁוֹמְרֶיהָ בְּצִוּוּי וְאַזְהָרָה, לְעוֹסְקֶיהָ וּלְנוֹצְרֶיהָ בְּאַהַב וּבְמוֹרָא. וּבְכֵן יְהִי רָצוֹן מִלִּפְנֵי הַגְּבוּרָה, לָתֵת חֵן וָחֶסֶד וְחַיִּים וָנֵזֶר וַעֲטָרָה, לְרַבִּי (פלוני ב״ר פלוני) הַנִּבְחָר לְהַשְׁלִים הַתּוֹרָה, לְאַמְּצוֹ לְבָרְכוֹ לְגַדְּלוֹ בְּתַלְמוּד תּוֹרָה, לְדָרְשׁוֹ לְהַדְּרוֹ לְוַעֲדוֹ בַּחֲבוּרָה, לְזַכּוֹתוֹ לְחַיּוֹתוֹ לְטַכְּסוֹ בְּטֶכֶס אוֹרָה, לְיַשְּׁרוֹ לְכַלְּלוֹ לְלַמְּדוֹ לֶקַח וּסְבָרָה, לְמַלְּטוֹ לְנַשְּׂאוֹ לְסַעֲדוֹ בְּסַעַד בְּרוּרָה, לְעַדְּנוֹ לְפַרְנְסוֹ לְצַדְּקוֹ בְּעַם נִבְרָא, לְקָרְבוֹ לְרַחֲמוֹ לְשָׁמְרוֹ מִכָּל צוּקָה וְצָרָה, לְתַקְּפוֹ לְתָמְכוֹ לְתוֹמְמוֹ בְּרוּחַ נִשְׁבָּרָה. עֲמֹד עֲמֹד רַבִּי (פלוני ב״ר פלוני) חֲתַן הַתּוֹרָה, וְתֵן כָּבוֹד לָאֵל גָּדוֹל וְנוֹרָא, וּבִשְׂכַר זֶה תִּזְכֶּה מֵאֵל נוֹרָא, לִרְאוֹת בָּנִים וּבְנֵי בָנִים עוֹסְקִים בַּתּוֹרָה, וּמְקַיְּמֵי מִצְוֹת בְּתוֹךְ עַם יָפָה וּבָרָה, וְתִזְכֶּה לִשְׂמֹחַ בְּשִׂמְחַת בֵּית הַבְּחִירָה, וּפָנֶיךָ לְהָאִיר בִּצְדָקָה כְּאַסְפַּקְלַרְיָא הַמְּאִירָה, כִּנְבָא יְשַׁעְיָהוּ מָלֵא רוּחַ עֵצָה וּגְבוּרָה, שִׂמְחוּ אֶת יְרוּשָׁלַםִ וְגִילוּ בָהּ מְהֵרָה, שִׂישׂוּ אִתָּהּ מָשׂוֹשׂ כָּל הַמִּתְאַבְּלִים בְּאֵבֶלָה וְצָרָה, עֲמֹד עֲמֹד רַבִּי (פלוני ב״ר פלוני) חֲתַן הַתּוֹרָה, מֵרְשׁוּת כָּל הַקָּהָל הַקָּדוֹשׁ הַזֶּה וְהַשְׁלֵם הַתּוֹרָה. יַעֲמֹד רַבִּי (פלוני ב״ר פלוני) חֲתַן הַתּוֹרָה.

## READING FOR THE HATAN TORAH — קריאה לחתן תורה

דברים לג:כז–לד:יב מְעֹנָה אֱלֹהֵי קֶדֶם וּמִתַּחַת זְרֹעֹת עוֹלָם וַיְגָרֶשׁ מִפָּנֶיךָ אוֹיֵב וַיֹּאמֶר הַשְׁמֵד:
וַיִּשְׁכֹּן יִשְׂרָאֵל בֶּטַח בָּדָד עֵין יַעֲקֹב אֶל־אֶרֶץ דָּגָן וְתִירוֹשׁ אַף־שָׁמָיו יַעַרְפוּ־
טָל: אַשְׁרֶיךָ יִשְׂרָאֵל מִי כָמוֹךָ עַם נוֹשַׁע בַּיהוה מָגֵן עֶזְרֶךָ וַאֲשֶׁר־חֶרֶב גַּאֲוָתֶךָ
וְיִכָּחֲשׁוּ אֹיְבֶיךָ לָךְ וְאַתָּה עַל־בָּמוֹתֵימוֹ תִדְרֹךְ: וַיַּעַל מֹשֶׁה מֵעַרְבֹת
מוֹאָב אֶל־הַר נְבוֹ רֹאשׁ הַפִּסְגָּה אֲשֶׁר עַל־פְּנֵי יְרֵחוֹ וַיַּרְאֵהוּ יהוה אֶת־כָּל־
הָאָרֶץ אֶת־הַגִּלְעָד עַד־דָּן: וְאֵת כָּל־נַפְתָּלִי וְאֶת־אֶרֶץ אֶפְרַיִם וּמְנַשֶּׁה וְאֵת
כָּל־אֶרֶץ יְהוּדָה עַד הַיָּם הָאַחֲרוֹן: וְאֶת־הַנֶּגֶב וְאֶת־הַכִּכָּר בִּקְעַת יְרֵחוֹ עִיר
הַתְּמָרִים עַד־צֹעַר: וַיֹּאמֶר יהוה אֵלָיו זֹאת הָאָרֶץ אֲשֶׁר נִשְׁבַּעְתִּי לְאַבְרָהָם
לְיִצְחָק וּלְיַעֲקֹב לֵאמֹר לְזַרְעֲךָ אֶתְּנֶנָּה הֶרְאִיתִיךָ בְעֵינֶיךָ וְשָׁמָּה לֹא תַעֲבֹר:
וַיָּמָת שָׁם מֹשֶׁה עֶבֶד־יהוה בְּאֶרֶץ מוֹאָב עַל־פִּי יהוה: וַיִּקְבֹּר אֹתוֹ בַגַּי בְּאֶרֶץ
מוֹאָב מוּל בֵּית פְּעוֹר וְלֹא־יָדַע אִישׁ אֶת־קְבֻרָתוֹ עַד הַיּוֹם הַזֶּה: וּמֹשֶׁה בֶּן־
מֵאָה וְעֶשְׂרִים שָׁנָה בְּמֹתוֹ לֹא־כָהֲתָה עֵינוֹ וְלֹא־נָס לֵחֹה: וַיִּבְכּוּ בְנֵי יִשְׂרָאֵל
אֶת־מֹשֶׁה בְּעַרְבֹת מוֹאָב שְׁלֹשִׁים יוֹם וַיִּתְּמוּ יְמֵי בְכִי אֵבֶל מֹשֶׁה: וִיהוֹשֻׁעַ
בִּן־נוּן מָלֵא רוּחַ חָכְמָה כִּי־סָמַךְ מֹשֶׁה אֶת־יָדָיו עָלָיו וַיִּשְׁמְעוּ אֵלָיו בְּנֵי־
יִשְׂרָאֵל וַיַּעֲשׂוּ כַּאֲשֶׁר צִוָּה יהוה אֶת־מֹשֶׁה: וְלֹא־קָם נָבִיא עוֹד בְּיִשְׂרָאֵל
כְּמֹשֶׁה אֲשֶׁר יְדָעוֹ יהוה פָּנִים אֶל־פָּנִים: לְכָל־הָאֹתֹת וְהַמּוֹפְתִים אֲשֶׁר שְׁלָחוֹ
יהוה לַעֲשׂוֹת בְּאֶרֶץ מִצְרָיִם לְפַרְעֹה וּלְכָל־עֲבָדָיו וּלְכָל־אַרְצוֹ: וּלְכֹל הַיָּד
הַחֲזָקָה וּלְכֹל הַמּוֹרָא הַגָּדוֹל אֲשֶׁר עָשָׂה מֹשֶׁה לְעֵינֵי כָּל־יִשְׂרָאֵל:

## CALLING UP THE HATAN BERESHIT — רשות לחתן בראשית

*The following is said by the* גבאי *to call up the* חתן בראשית *to his* עליה*:*

מֵרְשׁוּת מְרוֹמָם עַל כָּל בְּרָכָה וְשִׁירָה, נוֹרָא עַל כָּל תְּהִלָּה וְזִמְרָה, חֲכַם לֵבָב וְאַמִּיץ כֹּחַ וּגְבוּרָה, מוֹשֵׁל עוֹלָם אֲדוֹן כָּל יְצִירָה, וּמֵרְשׁוּת כְּבוּדָּה בַת מֶלֶךְ פְּנִימָה וַעֲצוּרָה, רֵאשִׁית קִנְיָנָהּ אַלְפַּיִם אֲצוּרָה, בָּרָה תְּמִימָה מְשִׁיבַת נֶפֶשׁ וּמַחֲזִירָה, יְשֻׁרוּן נִתְּנָה מוֹרָשָׁה לְעָבְדָהּ וּלְשָׁמְרָהּ, מְלַמְּדֶיהָ גְּאוֹנֵי יַעֲקֹב לְפָתְחָהּ וּלְסָגְרָהּ, כְּלִיל הוֹד נְשִׂיא מַרְבֵּה הַמִּשְׂרָה, יוֹשְׁבֵי מִדִּין מְשִׁיבֵי מִלְחָמָה שַׁעְרָה, רָאשֵׁי יְשִׁיבוֹת רָאשֵׁי גוֹלָה פְּזוּרָה, וּמֵרְשׁוּת חֲבוּרַת צֶדֶק עֵדָה זוֹ הַמְּאֻשָּׁרָה, זְקֵנִים וּנְעָרִים יַחַד בְּכָל שׁוּרָה, קְבוּצִים פֹּה הַיּוֹם לְשִׂמְחַת תּוֹרָה, וְנֶעֱצָרִים לְסַיֵּם וּלְהָחֵל בְּגִיל וּבְמוֹרָא, אוֹתָהּ

מְחַבְּבִים כְּיוֹם נְתִינָתָהּ בַּהֲדָרָה, מְסַלְסְלִים בָּהּ כַּחֲדָשָׁה וְלֹא כִישָׁנָה שֶׁעָבְרָה, צְמֵאִים לָמֹץ וּלְהִתְעַנֵּג מִזִּיו יְקָרָהּ, בְּיַעַן מְשַׂמַּחַת לֵב וְעֶצֶב מְסִירָה, תַּנְחוּמֶיהָ יְשַׁעַשְׁעוּ נַפְשָׁם בָּהּ לְהִתְפָּאֲרָה, וְהוֹגִים בְּמִקְרָא וְהַגָּדָה בְּמִשְׁנָה וּגְמָרָא, רָצִים וּמְבִיאִים טַפָּם לְבֵית הָעֲתִירָה, הוֹלְכִים וְעוֹשִׂים לְהַזְהִירָה, לָכֵן גָּדוֹל שְׂכָרָם מֵאֵת הַגְּבוּרָה, עַל רֹאשָׁם שִׂמְחַת עוֹלָם קְשׁוּרָה, דָּאִים לִרְאוֹת בְּבֵית הַבְּחִירָה, וּבְכֵן נִסְמַכְתִּי דַּעַת כֻּלָּם לְבָרְרָה, בָּחוּר הֲרִימוֹתִי מֵעָם תּוֹךְ הַחֲבוּרָה, מְצָאתִיו לֵב נָבוֹן לְהַסְבִּירָה, צֶדֶק וָחֶסֶד רוֹדֵף בְּאֹרַח יְשָׁרָה, וּנְשָׂאוֹ לִבּוֹ וְנָדְבָה רוּחוֹ לְהִתְעוֹרְרָה, תְּחִלָּה וְרִאשׁוֹן הֱיוֹת לְהַתְחִיל הַתּוֹרָה. וְעַתָּה קוּם רַבִּי (פלוני ב״ר פלוני) עֲמֹד לְהִתְאַזְּרָה, בֹּא וְהִתְיַצֵּב וַעֲמֹד לִימִינִי וּקְרָא, מַעֲשֵׂה בְּרֵאשִׁית לִכְבוֹדוֹ צוּר בָּרָא, עַל זֹאת מַתְכִּיפִין הַתְחָלָה לְהַשְׁלָמָה בִּתְדִירָה, שָׂטָן שֶׁלֹּא יְרַגֵּל בְּעַם זוּ לְשַׁקְּרָה, יַעַן נַעֲשֵׂית רִאשׁוֹן לְמִצְוָה גְּמוּרָה, מָה רַב טוּבְךָ וּמַשְׂכֻּרְתְּךָ יְתֵרָה, טוֹב עַיִן תְּבֹרַךְ בְּנִדְבָתְךָ מִלְּעָצְרָה, וּמִבִּרְכַּת בּוֹרַאֲךָ תִּדּוֹר יָדְךָ מִלְּקַצְּרָה, בַּעֲבוּר שֶׁכָּל הַמְכַבֵּד תּוֹרָה בִּצְפִירָה, יְהֵא גּוּפוֹ מְכֻבָּד לְהִתְאַשְּׁרָה. מַהֵר עֲמֹד עֲמֹד רַבִּי (פלוני ב״ר פלוני) חֲתַן בְּרֵאשִׁית בָּרָא, מֵרְשׁוּת הַקָּהָל הַקָּדוֹשׁ הַזֶּה וּבָרֵךְ אֵל גָּדוֹל וְנוֹרָא, אָמֵן יַעֲנוּ אַחֲרֶיךָ הַכֹּל מְהֵרָה.
יַעֲמֹד רַבִּי (פלוני ב״ר פלוני) חֲתַן בְּרֵאשִׁית.

## קריאה לחתן בראשית

## READING FOR THE ḤATAN BERESHIT

בראשית א:א–ב:ג בְּרֵאשִׁית בָּרָא אֱלֹהִים אֵת הַשָּׁמַיִם וְאֵת הָאָרֶץ: וְהָאָרֶץ הָיְתָה תֹהוּ וָבֹהוּ
וְחֹשֶׁךְ עַל־פְּנֵי תְהוֹם וְרוּחַ אֱלֹהִים מְרַחֶפֶת עַל־פְּנֵי הַמָּיִם: וַיֹּאמֶר אֱלֹהִים
יְהִי־אוֹר וַיְהִי־אוֹר: וַיַּרְא אֱלֹהִים אֶת־הָאוֹר כִּי־טוֹב וַיַּבְדֵּל אֱלֹהִים בֵּין הָאוֹר
וּבֵין הַחֹשֶׁךְ: וַיִּקְרָא אֱלֹהִים ׀ לָאוֹר יוֹם וְלַחֹשֶׁךְ קָרָא לָיְלָה וַיְהִי־עֶרֶב וַיְהִי־
בֹקֶר יוֹם אֶחָד:
וַיֹּאמֶר אֱלֹהִים יְהִי רָקִיעַ בְּתוֹךְ הַמָּיִם וִיהִי מַבְדִּיל בֵּין מַיִם לָמָיִם: וַיַּעַשׂ
אֱלֹהִים אֶת־הָרָקִיעַ וַיַּבְדֵּל בֵּין הַמַּיִם אֲשֶׁר מִתַּחַת לָרָקִיעַ וּבֵין הַמַּיִם אֲשֶׁר
מֵעַל לָרָקִיעַ וַיְהִי־כֵן: וַיִּקְרָא אֱלֹהִים לָרָקִיעַ שָׁמָיִם וַיְהִי־עֶרֶב וַיְהִי־בֹקֶר
יוֹם שֵׁנִי:
וַיֹּאמֶר אֱלֹהִים יִקָּווּ הַמַּיִם מִתַּחַת הַשָּׁמַיִם אֶל־מָקוֹם אֶחָד וְתֵרָאֶה הַיַּבָּשָׁה
וַיְהִי־כֵן: וַיִּקְרָא אֱלֹהִים ׀ לַיַּבָּשָׁה אֶרֶץ וּלְמִקְוֵה הַמַּיִם קָרָא יַמִּים וַיַּרְא

אֱלֹהִ֖ים כִּי־טֽוֹב׃ וַיֹּ֣אמֶר אֱלֹהִ֗ים תַּֽדְשֵׁ֤א הָאָ֙רֶץ֙ דֶּ֔שֶׁא עֵ֚שֶׂב מַזְרִ֣יעַ זֶ֔רַע עֵ֣ץ
פְּרִ֞י עֹ֤שֶׂה פְּרִי֙ לְמִינ֔וֹ אֲשֶׁ֥ר זַרְעוֹ־ב֖וֹ עַל־הָאָ֑רֶץ וַֽיְהִי־כֵֽן׃ וַתּוֹצֵ֨א הָאָ֜רֶץ דֶּ֠שֶׁא
עֵ֣שֶׂב מַזְרִ֤יעַ זֶ֙רַע֙ לְמִינֵ֔הוּ וְעֵ֧ץ עֹֽשֶׂה־פְּרִ֛י אֲשֶׁ֥ר זַרְעוֹ־ב֖וֹ לְמִינֵ֑הוּ וַיַּ֥רְא אֱלֹהִ֖ים
כִּי־טֽוֹב׃ וַֽיְהִי־עֶ֥רֶב וַֽיְהִי־בֹ֖קֶר י֥וֹם שְׁלִישִֽׁי׃
וַיֹּ֣אמֶר אֱלֹהִ֗ים יְהִ֤י מְאֹרֹת֙ בִּרְקִ֣יעַ הַשָּׁמַ֔יִם לְהַבְדִּ֕יל בֵּ֥ין הַיּ֖וֹם וּבֵ֣ין הַלָּ֑יְלָה
וְהָי֤וּ לְאֹתֹת֙ וּלְמ֣וֹעֲדִ֔ים וּלְיָמִ֖ים וְשָׁנִֽים׃ וְהָי֤וּ לִמְאוֹרֹת֙ בִּרְקִ֣יעַ הַשָּׁמַ֔יִם לְהָאִ֖יר
עַל־הָאָ֑רֶץ וַֽיְהִי־כֵֽן׃ וַיַּ֣עַשׂ אֱלֹהִ֔ים אֶת־שְׁנֵ֥י הַמְּאֹרֹ֖ת הַגְּדֹלִ֑ים אֶת־הַמָּא֤וֹר
הַגָּדֹל֙ לְמֶמְשֶׁ֣לֶת הַיּ֔וֹם וְאֶת־הַמָּא֤וֹר הַקָּטֹן֙ לְמֶמְשֶׁ֣לֶת הַלַּ֔יְלָה וְאֵ֖ת הַכּוֹכָבִֽים׃
וַיִּתֵּ֥ן אֹתָ֛ם אֱלֹהִ֖ים בִּרְקִ֣יעַ הַשָּׁמָ֑יִם לְהָאִ֖יר עַל־הָאָֽרֶץ׃ וְלִמְשֹׁל֙ בַּיּ֣וֹם וּבַלַּ֔יְלָה
וּֽלֲהַבְדִּ֔יל בֵּ֥ין הָא֖וֹר וּבֵ֣ין הַחֹ֑שֶׁךְ וַיַּ֥רְא אֱלֹהִ֖ים כִּי־טֽוֹב׃ וַֽיְהִי־עֶ֥רֶב וַֽיְהִי־בֹ֖קֶר
י֥וֹם רְבִיעִֽי׃
וַיֹּ֣אמֶר אֱלֹהִ֔ים יִשְׁרְצ֣וּ הַמַּ֔יִם שֶׁ֖רֶץ נֶ֣פֶשׁ חַיָּ֑ה וְעוֹף֙ יְעוֹפֵ֣ף עַל־הָאָ֔רֶץ עַל־פְּנֵ֖י
רְקִ֥יעַ הַשָּׁמָֽיִם׃ וַיִּבְרָ֣א אֱלֹהִ֔ים אֶת־הַתַּנִּינִ֖ם הַגְּדֹלִ֑ים וְאֵ֣ת כָּל־נֶ֣פֶשׁ הַֽחַיָּ֣ה ׀
הָֽרֹמֶ֡שֶׂת אֲשֶׁר֩ שָׁרְצ֨וּ הַמַּ֜יִם לְמִֽינֵהֶ֗ם וְאֵ֨ת כָּל־ע֤וֹף כָּנָף֙ לְמִינֵ֔הוּ וַיַּ֥רְא אֱלֹהִ֖ים
כִּי־טֽוֹב׃ וַיְבָ֧רֶךְ אֹתָ֛ם אֱלֹהִ֖ים לֵאמֹ֑ר פְּר֣וּ וּרְב֗וּ וּמִלְא֤וּ אֶת־הַמַּ֙יִם֙ בַּיַּמִּ֔ים וְהָע֖וֹף
יִ֥רֶב בָּאָֽרֶץ׃ וַֽיְהִי־עֶ֥רֶב וַֽיְהִי־בֹ֖קֶר י֥וֹם חֲמִישִֽׁי׃
וַיֹּ֣אמֶר אֱלֹהִ֗ים תּוֹצֵ֨א הָאָ֜רֶץ נֶ֤פֶשׁ חַיָּה֙ לְמִינָ֔הּ בְּהֵמָ֥ה וָרֶ֛מֶשׂ וְחַֽיְתוֹ־אֶ֖רֶץ
לְמִינָ֑הּ וַֽיְהִי־כֵֽן׃ וַיַּ֣עַשׂ אֱלֹהִים֩ אֶת־חַיַּ֨ת הָאָ֜רֶץ לְמִינָ֗הּ וְאֶת־הַבְּהֵמָה֙ לְמִינָ֔הּ
וְאֵ֛ת כָּל־רֶ֥מֶשׂ הָֽאֲדָמָ֖ה לְמִינֵ֑הוּ וַיַּ֥רְא אֱלֹהִ֖ים כִּי־טֽוֹב׃ וַיֹּ֣אמֶר אֱלֹהִ֔ים נַֽעֲשֶׂ֥ה
אָדָ֛ם בְּצַלְמֵ֖נוּ כִּדְמוּתֵ֑נוּ וְיִרְדּוּ֩ בִדְגַ֨ת הַיָּ֜ם וּבְע֣וֹף הַשָּׁמַ֗יִם וּבַבְּהֵמָה֙ וּבְכָל־הָאָ֔רֶץ
וּבְכָל־הָרֶ֖מֶשׂ הָֽרֹמֵ֥שׂ עַל־הָאָֽרֶץ׃ וַיִּבְרָ֨א אֱלֹהִ֤ים ׀ אֶת־הָֽאָדָם֙ בְּצַלְמ֔וֹ בְּצֶ֥לֶם
אֱלֹהִ֖ים בָּרָ֣א אֹת֑וֹ זָכָ֥ר וּנְקֵבָ֖ה בָּרָ֥א אֹתָֽם׃ וַיְבָ֣רֶךְ אֹתָם֮ אֱלֹהִים֒ וַיֹּ֨אמֶר לָהֶ֜ם
אֱלֹהִ֗ים פְּר֥וּ וּרְב֛וּ וּמִלְא֥וּ אֶת־הָאָ֖רֶץ וְכִבְשֻׁ֑הָ וּרְד֞וּ בִּדְגַ֤ת הַיָּם֙ וּבְע֣וֹף הַשָּׁמַ֔יִם
וּבְכָל־חַיָּ֖ה הָֽרֹמֶ֥שֶׂת עַל־הָאָֽרֶץ׃ וַיֹּ֣אמֶר אֱלֹהִ֗ים הִנֵּה֩ נָתַ֨תִּי לָכֶ֜ם אֶת־כָּל־
עֵ֣שֶׂב ׀ זֹרֵ֣עַ זֶ֗רַע אֲשֶׁר֙ עַל־פְּנֵ֣י כָל־הָאָ֔רֶץ וְאֶת־כָּל־הָעֵ֛ץ אֲשֶׁר־בּ֥וֹ פְרִי־עֵ֖ץ
זֹרֵ֣עַ זָ֑רַע לָכֶ֥ם יִֽהְיֶ֖ה לְאָכְלָֽה׃ וּֽלְכָל־חַיַּ֣ת הָ֠אָרֶץ וּלְכָל־ע֨וֹף הַשָּׁמַ֜יִם וּלְכֹ֣ל ׀
רוֹמֵ֣שׂ עַל־הָאָ֗רֶץ אֲשֶׁר־בּוֹ֙ נֶ֣פֶשׁ חַיָּ֔ה אֶת־כָּל־יֶ֥רֶק עֵ֖שֶׂב לְאָכְלָ֑ה וַֽיְהִי־כֵֽן׃
וַיַּ֤רְא אֱלֹהִים֙ אֶת־כָּל־אֲשֶׁ֣ר עָשָׂ֔ה וְהִנֵּה־ט֖וֹב מְאֹ֑ד וַֽיְהִי־עֶ֥רֶב וַֽיְהִי־בֹ֖קֶר י֥וֹם
הַשִּׁשִּֽׁי׃

וַיְכֻלּוּ הַשָּׁמַיִם וְהָאָרֶץ וְכָל־צְבָאָם: וַיְכַל אֱלֹהִים בַּיּוֹם הַשְּׁבִיעִי מְלַאכְתּוֹ אֲשֶׁר עָשָׂה וַיִּשְׁבֹּת בַּיּוֹם הַשְּׁבִיעִי מִכָּל־מְלַאכְתּוֹ אֲשֶׁר עָשָׂה: וַיְבָרֶךְ אֱלֹהִים אֶת־יוֹם הַשְּׁבִיעִי וַיְקַדֵּשׁ אֹתוֹ כִּי בוֹ שָׁבַת מִכָּל־מְלַאכְתּוֹ אֲשֶׁר־בָּרָא אֱלֹהִים לַעֲשׂוֹת:

*The* מפטיר *for* שמחת תורה *is the same as that of* שמיני עצרת *on page 1238.*

## HAFTARA FOR SIMḤAT TORAH — הפטרה לשמחת תורה

יהושע א:א–יח

וַיְהִי אַחֲרֵי מוֹת מֹשֶׁה עֶבֶד יְהוָה וַיֹּאמֶר יְהוָה אֶל־יְהוֹשֻׁעַ בִּן־נוּן מְשָׁרֵת מֹשֶׁה לֵאמֹר: מֹשֶׁה עַבְדִּי מֵת וְעַתָּה קוּם עֲבֹר אֶת־הַיַּרְדֵּן הַזֶּה אַתָּה וְכָל־הָעָם הַזֶּה אֶל־הָאָרֶץ אֲשֶׁר אָנֹכִי נֹתֵן לָהֶם לִבְנֵי יִשְׂרָאֵל: כָּל־מָקוֹם אֲשֶׁר תִּדְרֹךְ כַּף־רַגְלְכֶם בּוֹ לָכֶם נְתַתִּיו כַּאֲשֶׁר דִּבַּרְתִּי אֶל־מֹשֶׁה: מֵהַמִּדְבָּר וְהַלְּבָנוֹן הַזֶּה וְעַד־הַנָּהָר הַגָּדוֹל נְהַר־פְּרָת כֹּל אֶרֶץ הַחִתִּים וְעַד־הַיָּם הַגָּדוֹל מְבוֹא הַשָּׁמֶשׁ יִהְיֶה גְּבוּלְכֶם: לֹא־יִתְיַצֵּב אִישׁ לְפָנֶיךָ כֹּל יְמֵי חַיֶּיךָ כַּאֲשֶׁר הָיִיתִי עִם־מֹשֶׁה אֶהְיֶה עִמָּךְ לֹא אַרְפְּךָ וְלֹא אֶעֶזְבֶךָּ: חֲזַק וֶאֱמָץ כִּי אַתָּה תַּנְחִיל אֶת־הָעָם הַזֶּה אֶת־הָאָרֶץ אֲשֶׁר־נִשְׁבַּעְתִּי לַאֲבוֹתָם לָתֵת לָהֶם: רַק חֲזַק וֶאֱמַץ מְאֹד לִשְׁמֹר לַעֲשׂוֹת כְּכָל־הַתּוֹרָה אֲשֶׁר צִוְּךָ מֹשֶׁה עַבְדִּי אַל־תָּסוּר מִמֶּנּוּ יָמִין וּשְׂמֹאול לְמַעַן תַּשְׂכִּיל בְּכֹל אֲשֶׁר תֵּלֵךְ: לֹא־יָמוּשׁ סֵפֶר הַתּוֹרָה הַזֶּה מִפִּיךָ וְהָגִיתָ בּוֹ יוֹמָם וָלַיְלָה לְמַעַן תִּשְׁמֹר לַעֲשׂוֹת כְּכָל־הַכָּתוּב בּוֹ כִּי־אָז תַּצְלִיחַ אֶת־דְּרָכֶךָ וְאָז תַּשְׂכִּיל: הֲלוֹא צִוִּיתִיךָ חֲזַק וֶאֱמָץ אַל־תַּעֲרֹץ וְאַל־תֵּחָת כִּי עִמְּךָ יְהוָה אֱלֹהֶיךָ בְּכֹל אֲשֶׁר תֵּלֵךְ: וַיְצַו יְהוֹשֻׁעַ אֶת־שֹׁטְרֵי הָעָם לֵאמֹר: עִבְרוּ בְּקֶרֶב הַמַּחֲנֶה וְצַוּוּ אֶת־הָעָם לֵאמֹר הָכִינוּ לָכֶם צֵדָה כִּי בְּעוֹד שְׁלֹשֶׁת יָמִים אַתֶּם עֹבְרִים אֶת־הַיַּרְדֵּן הַזֶּה לָבוֹא לָרֶשֶׁת אֶת־הָאָרֶץ אֲשֶׁר יְהוָה אֱלֹהֵיכֶם נֹתֵן לָכֶם לְרִשְׁתָּהּ: וְלָרְאוּבֵנִי וְלַגָּדִי וְלַחֲצִי שֵׁבֶט הַמְנַשֶּׁה אָמַר יְהוֹשֻׁעַ לֵאמֹר: זָכוֹר אֶת־הַדָּבָר אֲשֶׁר צִוָּה אֶתְכֶם מֹשֶׁה עֶבֶד־יְהוָה לֵאמֹר יְהוָה אֱלֹהֵיכֶם מֵנִיחַ לָכֶם וְנָתַן לָכֶם אֶת־הָאָרֶץ הַזֹּאת: נְשֵׁיכֶם טַפְּכֶם וּמִקְנֵיכֶם יֵשְׁבוּ בָּאָרֶץ אֲשֶׁר נָתַן לָכֶם מֹשֶׁה בְּעֵבֶר הַיַּרְדֵּן וְאַתֶּם תַּעַבְרוּ חֲמֻשִׁים לִפְנֵי אֲחֵיכֶם כֹּל גִּבּוֹרֵי הַחַיִל וַעֲזַרְתֶּם אוֹתָם: עַד אֲשֶׁר־יָנִיחַ יְהוָה לַאֲחֵיכֶם כָּכֶם וְיָרְשׁוּ גַם־הֵמָּה אֶת־הָאָרֶץ אֲשֶׁר־יְהוָה אֱלֹהֵיכֶם נֹתֵן לָהֶם וְשַׁבְתֶּם לְאֶרֶץ יְרֻשַּׁתְכֶם וִירִשְׁתֶּם אוֹתָהּ אֲשֶׁר נָתַן לָכֶם

מֹשֶׁה֙ עֶ֣בֶד יְהוָ֔ה בְּעֵ֥בֶר הַיַּרְדֵּ֖ן מִזְרַ֥ח הַשָּֽׁמֶשׁ׃ וַֽיַּעֲנ֔וּ אֶת־יְהוֹשֻׁ֖עַ לֵאמֹ֑ר כֹּ֣ל
אֲשֶׁר־צִוִּיתָ֙נוּ֙ נַעֲשֶׂ֔ה וְאֶל־כָּל־אֲשֶׁ֥ר תִּשְׁלָחֵ֖נוּ נֵלֵֽךְ׃ כְּכֹ֤ל אֲשֶׁר־שָׁמַ֙עְנוּ֙ אֶל־
מֹשֶׁ֔ה כֵּ֖ן נִשְׁמַ֣ע אֵלֶ֑יךָ רַ֠ק יִֽהְיֶ֞ה יְהוָ֤ה אֱלֹהֶ֙יךָ֙ עִמָּ֔ךְ כַּאֲשֶׁ֥ר הָיָ֖ה עִם־מֹשֶֽׁה׃
כָּל־אִ֞ישׁ אֲשֶׁר־יַמְרֶ֣ה אֶת־פִּ֗יךָ וְלֹֽא־יִשְׁמַ֧ע אֶת־דְּבָרֶ֛יךָ לְכֹ֥ל אֲשֶׁר־תְּצַוֶּ֖נּוּ
יוּמָ֑ת רַ֖ק חֲזַ֥ק וֶאֱמָֽץ׃

The text (*nusaḥ*) of the siddur that we use today is based on the siddur of the Geonim, primarily *Seder Rav Amram Gaon* from the ninth century. The *nusaḥ* we call "*Nusaḥ Ashkenaz*" refers to the prayer texts and customs of Ashkenazi Jewry, which included the Jews of Germany and northern France. When Ashkenazi Jews moved eastward, they brought their practices with them to Poland and Russia, as well as Lithuania, Bohemia, Moravia, Austro-Hungary, Romania and the Balkans. Similarly, Ashkenazi Jews moved westward to Switzerland, France, Belgium, Holland, Northern Italy, England and, lastly, to Israel and America.

There is no single, authoritative version of *Nusaḥ Ashkenaz*. Certain differences in *nusaḥ* developed between the Jews of western Germany and eastern Germany (known today as *Minhag Polin*). For the most part, *Minhag Polin* is what Ashkenazi Jews follow today. But not exclusively. In the eighteenth century, Ḥasidic Jews adopted a new *nusaḥ* based on the Ari (R. Isaac Luria, 1534–1572), which strongly resembles the *nusaḥ* of Sephardi Jewry. As a result, many Jews of Ashkenazi descent now follow what is called "*Nusaḥ Sepharad*." Another variation on *Nusaḥ Ashkenaz* was developed by the Vilna Gaon (R. Eliyahu b. Shelomo, 1720–1797) and is called "*Minhag HaGra*." Students of the Vilna Gaon who moved to Israel in the nineteenth century brought *Minhag HaGra* with them, and it is the dominant Ashkenazi practice in Israel today.

In this Siddur we have tried to present *Nusaḥ Ashkenaz* as it is typically practiced in Ashkenazi congregations in the United States and Israel, with the differences noted in the instructions. Some practices referred to as "Israeli" are also followed by select congregations in the United States. In the pages below, we also note certain practices of *Nusaḥ Sepharad* which have become more common in Ashkenazi circles.

Rabbi Eli D. Clark

# GUIDE TO THE JEWISH YEAR

## ELUL

1 Beginning on the first day of Elul (the second day of Rosh Ḥodesh) and for the entire month of Elul, it is customary to say לְדָוִד, יהוה אוֹרִי (page 263) in the evening at the end of Ma'ariv and in the morning after saying the Psalm of the Day [אשי ישראל, פמ״ה:ג].

2 In addition, four shofar blasts are sounded at the end of weekday morning prayers, prior to (or following) recitation of לְדָוִד, יהוה אוֹרִי [רמ״א או״ח, תקפא:א].

### *Pre-Rosh HaShana Customs*

3 On the Motza'ei Shabbat prior to Rosh HaShana, the congregation gathers at midnight to say *Seliḥot*. This is often preceded by a sermon from the rabbi. If Rosh HaShana falls on Monday or Tuesday, the first recitation of *Seliḥot* is moved back to the preceding Motza'ei Shabbat [רמ״א או״ח, תקפא:א].

4 The congregation says *Seliḥot* each weekday thereafter through Erev Yom Kippur. Although the original custom was to say *Seliḥot* every night after midnight and before dawn, most congregations today say them prior to Shaḥarit; some say them during the preceding evening [ערוה״ש שם, ב-ד].

5 The *Shaliaḥ Tzibbur* chosen to lead the *Seliḥot* should preferably be distinguished in Torah scholarship and personal virtue, over the age of thirty and married [רמ״א או״ח, תקפא:א].

6 One who is praying alone is permitted to say *Seliḥot* without a *minyan*, provided one omits the י״ג מידות ("Thirteen Attributes of Mercy") and the Aramaic passages [תקפא:ד]. However, one who is alone may read the י״ג מידות with *ta'amei hamikra* [שו״ע או״ח תקסה:ה].

### *Erev Rosh HaShana (29th of Elul)*

7 The recitation of *Seliḥot* (the longest of the year) precedes regular Shaḥarit for weekdays. The congregation omits *Taḥanun* and shofar blowing [שו״ע ורמ״א או״ח, תקפא: ג].

8 It is customary to say the formula of **התרת נדרים**, the Annulment of Vows (page 959), in front of three adult males after Shaḥarit [חיי אדם, קלח: ח]. The formula may be said at any time of the day [שו״ע יו״ד, רלד: נו] and may be said any day prior to Yom Kippur.

9 Some have the custom to immerse in the mikveh. Other customs include fasting and visiting the graves of departed relatives [שו״ע או״ח, תקפא: ב; רמ״א, שם: ד].

10 When Rosh HaShana falls on Thursday and Friday, each household must prepare an *Eiruv Tavshilin* (page 817); this makes it permissible to prepare food on Friday for the Shabbat meals [שו״ע או״ח, תקכו].

# TISHREI

## *Rosh HaShana (1st–2nd of Tishrei)*

▸ LAWS OF ROSH HASHANA EVE

11 Candle lighting: Two blessings are said: (1) **לְהַדְלִיק נֵר שֶׁל יוֹם טוֹב** ("to light the festival light") and (2) **שֶׁהֶחֱיָנוּ** ("Who has given us life…"). When Rosh HaShana eve falls on Friday night, the conclusion of the first blessing is: **לְהַדְלִיק נֵר שֶׁל שַׁבָּת וְשֶׁל יוֹם טוֹב** ("to light the Shabbat and Festival light") (page 383).

12 Ma'ariv: for Shabbat and Yom Tov. Before saying the Amida for Rosh HaShana, most congregations say **תִּקְעוּ בַחֹדֶשׁ שׁוֹפָר** (Ps. 81:4–5). After the Amida, the Ark is opened and the *Shaliaḥ Tzibbur* and congregation say responsively Psalm 24, **לְדָוִד מִזְמוֹר, לַיהוה הָאָרֶץ וּמְלוֹאָהּ**. This is followed by Full Kaddish (some say Psalm 24 after the Full Kaddish), *Aleinu*, Mourner's Kaddish, Psalm 27 and Mourner's Kaddish. It is customary to conclude with the singing of Adon Olam or Yigdal.

13 Changes to the Kaddish: It is customary to replace the phrase **לְעֵלָּא מִן כָּל** ("beyond any") with **לְעֵלָּא לְעֵלָּא מִכָּל** ("above and beyond any") [משנ״ב, נו: ב] and to change the phrase **עֹשֶׂה שָׁלוֹם** ("He who makes peace") to **עֹשֶׂה הַשָּׁלוֹם** ("He who makes the peace") [ערוה״ש או״ח, תקפב: ח]. One who forgets either of these changes is not required to repeat the Kaddish.

14 Special additions to the Amida: On Rosh HaShana and Yom Kippur, additional phrases are added to the Amida: זָכְרֵנוּ לְחַיִּים is added in the first blessing; מִי כָמוֹךָ in the second; four paragraphs are added to the third, and the ending is changed to הַמֶּלֶךְ הַקָּדוֹשׁ; וּכְתֹב is added in the penultimate blessing; and בְּסֵפֶר חַיִּים is added to the final blessing, and the ending is changed to עוֹשֶׂה הַשָּׁלוֹם (some do not change the ending of the blessing). One who forgets to say any of these passages is not required to repeat the Amida with the forgotten additions [שו״ע ורמ״א או״ח, תקפב: ה]. However, one who forgets to change the ending of the third blessing to הַמֶּלֶךְ הַקָּדוֹשׁ must repeat the Amida from the beginning, unless one corrects the error תוך כדי דיבור (see source in the *Shulḥan Arukh* for a discussion of this rule.) [שו״ע או״ח, תקפא: ג].

15 When Rosh HaShana eve falls on Friday night, Ma'ariv is preceded by the last two psalms of Kabbalat Shabbat: מִזְמוֹר שִׁיר לְיוֹם הַשַּׁבָּת and יהוה מָלָךְ, גֵּאוּת לָבֵשׁ (page 405). בַּמֶּה מַדְלִיקִין is omitted. The Amida is said with additions for Shabbat. After the Amida, before saying Psalm 24 the congregation says וַיְכֻלּוּ הַשָּׁמַיִם, and the *Shaliaḥ Tzibbur* says the abbreviated Repetition of the Amida as is customary on Shabbat eve [שו״ע או״ח, תריט: ג].

16 On the eve of Rosh HaShana, it is customary to greet one another with wishes for inscription for a good new year: "לשנה טובה תיכתב ותחתם" [רמ״א או״ח, תקפב: ט].

17 Upon returning home, one says the Kiddush for Rosh HaShana. When Rosh HaShana eve falls on Friday night, the additions for Shabbat are said (page 963).

18 On the first night of Rosh HaShana, after eating the *ḥalla*, it is customary to say the blessing on fruit, eat a slice of apple dipped in honey, then say a prayer for a sweet new year [רמ״א או״ח, תקפג: א]. יַעֲלֶה וְיָבוֹא is added to *Birkat HaMazon* (page 1065).

19 Shaḥarit: *Pesukei DeZimra* for Shabbat and Yom Tov is said. The *Shaliaḥ Tzibbur* for Shaḥarit begins from the words הַמֶּלֶךְ יוֹשֵׁב. After *Yishtabaḥ*, the Ark is opened and the congregation says Psalm 130 responsively. (Some say Psalm 130 before נִשְׁמַת כָּל חַי.)

20 After *Barekhu*, the congregation says הַמֵּאִיר לָאָרֶץ or, if it is Shabbat, הַכֹּל יוֹדוּךָ. The Amida for Rosh HaShana is said; if also Shabbat, one says the additions for Shabbat. The *Shaliaḥ Tzibbur* repeats the Amida, adding *piyutim* before the *Kedusha*. The congregation says *Avinu Malkenu*, but not on Shabbat [רמ״א או״ח, תקפד: א]. (Some congregations say at this point the Daily Psalm and Psalm 27, followed by the Mourner's Kaddish.) When the Torah is taken from the Ark, most congregations say the "Thirteen Attributes of Mercy" and a special supplication, except on Shabbat.

21 Torah Reading: first day – Gen. 21: 1–34; second day – Gen. 22:1–24. Five men are called up, seven on Shabbat. Maftir (both days): Num. 29:1–6. Haftara: first day – I Sam. 1:1–2:10; second day – Jer. 31:1–19 [שו״ע או״ח, תקפד: ב; שם, תרא: א].

22 The Haftara is followed by (*Yekum Purkan* on Shabbat, then) the prayers for the government and the State of Israel. It is customary for the rabbi to deliver a sermon prior to the sounding of the shofar. If there is a Brit Mila, it takes place before the shofar blowing.

▸ LAWS OF SHOFAR BLOWING

23 Hearing the sound of the shofar is an affirmative mitzva from the Torah. A deaf person is exempt from this mitzva, but a blind person is not; consequently, a blind person may blow the shofar for others, but a deaf person may not. Women are exempt from this mitzva, but a woman is permitted to blow shofar for herself and other women. If a man is blowing shofar for one or more women, the women should say the blessings for themselves [שו״ע ורמ״א או״ח, תקפט: ג].

24 The first thirty shofar blasts sounded prior to Musaf represent the minimum number of shofar sounds that one is required to hear [שו״ע או״ח, תקצ: א]. However, it is customary to blow a hundred blasts. The Ashkenazi custom is to blow thirty before Musaf, thirty during the Repetition of the Amida and forty more in sets of thirty and ten during the Full Kaddish after Musaf [משנ״ב, תקצב: ד]. Some congregations follow the Sephardi custom of blowing the shofar during the silent Amida, rather than the Repetition (see law 34).

25 The person blowing the shofar is required to stand; the congregation is permitted to sit during the first set of shofar sounds, although the custom is to stand [שו״ע או״ח, תקפה: א; משנ״ב, שם: ב].

26 Two blessings are said by the person blowing the shofar: (1) לִשְׁמֹעַ קוֹל שׁוֹפָר, and (2) שֶׁהֶחֱיָנוּ [שו״ע או״ח, תקפה: ב].

27 To prevent distractions while performing the mitzva of hearing the shofar, the congregation is, until completion of the first thirty shofar blasts, forbidden to speak about matters unrelated to shofar and, until completion of the hundredth blast, forbidden to speak about matters unrelated to prayer [שו״ע או״ח, תקצב: ג].

28 The rabbis ruled that we do not blow the shofar when Rosh HaShana falls on Shabbat [ראש השנה, כט.; שו״ע או״ח, תקפח: ה].

29 After the shofar is blown, *Ashrei* is said and the Torah scrolls are returned to the Ark. The *Shaliaḥ Tzibbur* for Musaf says a special prefatory prayer, הִנְנִי הֶעָנִי מִמַּעַשׂ ("Here am I, poor of deeds"), and Half Kaddish.

30 Musaf for Rosh HaShana: Unique among the Amidot said on Shabbat and Yom Tov, the Musaf for Rosh HaShana comprises nine blessings, rather than seven. Instead of one blessing devoted to the Festival, there are three extended blessings dedicated to three separate Rosh HaShana themes: Kingship, Remembrance and the Shofar [שו״ע או״ח, תקצא:א; שם:ד].

31 Before *Kedusha, piyutim* are said, culminating with וּנְתַנֶּה תֹּקֶף.

32 The fourth blessing in the Repetition of the Amida contains *Aleinu*. The Ark is opened, and the *Shaliaḥ Tzibbur* (and, in most communities, the entire congregation) kneels in prostration at the words וַאֲנַחְנוּ כּוֹרְעִים. Because one is forbidden to touch one's head against the bare stone floor when kneeling, one should place a piece of cloth or paper between one's head and the floor [רמ״א או״ח, קלא:ח].

33 Upon completion by the *Shaliaḥ Tzibbur* of each of the three middle blessings of the Amida, ten shofar blasts are sounded, and the congregation says הַיּוֹם הֲרַת עוֹלָם and אֲרֶשֶׁת שְׂפָתֵינוּ. If Rosh HaShana falls on Shabbat, the shofar is not sounded and אֲרֶשֶׁת שְׂפָתֵינוּ is omitted. The Kohanim say *Birkat Kohanim.*

34 After Musaf, the *Shaliaḥ Tzibbur* says Full Kaddish. Forty more shofar blasts are sounded, in sets of thirty and ten [רמ״א או״ח, תקצו:א; פמ״ג, שם]. Some congregations pause during the Full Kaddish to blow the thirty blasts and sound the last ten after the completion of the Full Kaddish; others sound the thirty after the completion of the Full Kaddish and the last ten prior to *Aleinu*. This is followed by *Ein Keloheinu*; the Rabbis' Kaddish; *Aleinu*; Mourner's Kaddish; the Daily Psalm; Psalm 27; Mourner's Kaddish; *Anim Zemirot*; Mourner's Kaddish and Adon Olam.

35 Minḥa: for Shabbat and Yom Tov. When Rosh HaShana falls on Shabbat, the beginning of *Ha'azinu* is read. The Amida is identical to that said during Shaḥarit, except that it is preceded by the verse beginning כִּי שֵׁם יהוה אֶקְרָא (Deut. 32:3), and, for the final blessing, the paragraph שָׁלוֹם רָב ("Great peace") substitutes for the paragraph שִׂים שָׁלוֹם ("Grant peace"). After the *Shaliaḥ Tzibbur* repeats the Amida, the congregation says *Avinu Malkenu*, except when Rosh HaShana falls on Shabbat.

36 After Minḥa, it is customary to say *Tashlikh* (page 967) beside a source of running water. If the first day of Rosh HaShana falls on Shabbat, *Tashlikh* is said on the second day [רמ״א או״ח, תקפג:ב] or on any weekday prior to Yom Kippur.

### *Rosh HaShana – Second Day (2nd of Tishrei)*

37 Eve of second day: Candle lighting and preparations for the meal must be performed after nightfall. If the first day of Rosh HaShana fell on Shabbat, the

congregation adds the paragraph וַתּוֹדִיעֵנוּ in the middle section of the Amida. Similarly, in Kiddush, the two blessings for Havdala are inserted prior to the blessing שֶׁהֶחֱיָנוּ (page 963); thus the order of blessings is: wine, Kiddush, flame, Havdala, שֶׁהֶחֱיָנוּ.

38 On the second night of Rosh HaShana, it is customary to eat a new fruit or wear a new garment. However, one says שֶׁהֶחֱיָנוּ during Kiddush even if there is no new fruit or garment [שו״ע או״ח, תר: ב]. Similarly, שֶׁהֶחֱיָנוּ is said before blowing shofar on the second day, even if the shofar was blown on the first day [שם: ג].

39 Ma'ariv, Shaḥarit and Minḥa: Except as noted above, the prayers for the second day of Rosh HaShana parallel the prayers for the first.

40 Motza'ei Rosh HaShana: Ma'ariv for weekdays is said. In the fourth blessing of the Amida, the paragraph of אַתָּה חוֹנַנְתָּנוּ is said (page 333). Havdala is said over a cup of wine or grape juice; no blessing is made over spices or a flame [שו״ע או״ח, תרא: א].

## *Laws of Aseret Yemei Teshuva (the Ten Days of Repentance)*

41 Changes to the Kaddish: see law 13.

42 During the morning prayers, it is customary, after *Yishtabaḥ*, to open the Ark and say Psalm 130 responsively (page 139) [משנ״ב או״ח, נד: ד]. Some say Psalm 130 before *Yishtabaḥ*.

43 Additions to the Amida: See law 14. One should also change the ending of the eleventh blessing of the Amida from מֶלֶךְ אוֹהֵב צְדָקָה וּמִשְׁפָּט to הַמֶּלֶךְ הַמִּשְׁפָּט [שו״ע או״ח, תקפא: ג], but one who forgets to do so is not required to repeat the Amida [רמ״א או״ח, קיח: א].

44 In Shaḥarit and Minḥa, after the Amida, the Ark is opened and the congregation says *Avinu Malkenu*. This is omitted on Friday afternoon and Shabbat [רמ״א או״ח, תרב: א].

## *Fast of Gedalya (3rd of Tishrei)*

45 This fast commemorates the slaying of Gedalya ben Aḥikam by Yishmael ben Netanya, at the behest of Ba'alis, the king of Amon (circa 586 BCE). Shortly after the Babylonian conquest of Jerusalem, Gedalya was appointed governor of Judea. His assassination just months after the appointment spelled the end of Jewish self-government in the land of Israel in that era and led to the dispersion of the Jews who remained in the land of Israel after the destruction of the First Temple [II Kings 25:22–26; Jer. 40:4–41:18].

46 If the 3rd of Tishrei falls on Shabbat, the fast is postponed to Sunday.

47 The fast begins at dawn [שו״ע או״ח, תקנ:ב]. One is permitted to wake before dawn to eat and drink, but only if one had the intention to do so before going to sleep [שו״ע או״ח, תקסד:א].

48 Eating and drinking are forbidden, but other activities (bathing, wearing leather shoes) are permitted [שו״ע או״ח, תקנ:ב]. Pregnant and nursing women are exempt from fasting [רמ״א, שם:א].

49 Shaḥarit: The recitation of *Seliḥot* precedes Shaḥarit for weekdays. The additions for *Aseret Yemei Teshuva* are said. During the Repetition of the Amida, the *Shaliaḥ Tzibbur* says the paragraph עֲנֵנוּ between the seventh and eighth blessings (page 181) [שו״ע או״ח, תקסו:א]. This is followed by *Avinu Malkenu* and *Taḥanun*.

50 Torah Reading (page 1190): The Torah is read only if at least six people (according to some: three people) are fasting. Only people who are fasting are called up. It is customary for the congregation to say the following passages aloud: the last seven words of Ex. 32:12: שׁוּב מֵחֲרוֹן אַפֶּךָ, וְהִנָּחֵם עַל־הָרָעָה לְעַמֶּךָ, the "Thirteen Attributes of Mercy": יהוה יהוה אֵל רַחוּם וְחַנּוּן אֶרֶךְ אַפַּיִם וְרַב־חֶסֶד וֶאֱמֶת: נֹצֵר חֶסֶד לָאֲלָפִים נֹשֵׂא עָוֹן וָפֶשַׁע וְחַטָּאָה וְנַקֵּה, and the last four words of Ex. 34:9: "וְסָלַחְתָּ לַעֲוֹנֵנוּ וּלְחַטָּאתֵנוּ וּנְחַלְתָּנוּ" [משנ״ב, שם (ג)].

51 Minḥa: After *Ashrei* and Half Kaddish, the Torah is read. The reading is the same as that of the morning. The third *oleh* reads the Haftara (page 1190) [רמ״א, שם]. After the Torah is returned to the Ark, the *Shaliaḥ Tzibbur* says Half Kaddish, and Minḥa Amida for weekdays is said.

52 During the silent recitation of the Amida, those who are fasting say the paragraph עֲנֵנוּ as part of the sixteenth blessing, שׁוֹמֵעַ תְּפִלָּה (page 295); during the Repetition of the Amida, the *Shaliaḥ Tzibbur* says עֲנֵנוּ between the seventh and eighth blessings, as in the morning (page 287). After the blessing הַטּוֹב שִׁמְךָ וּלְךָ נָאֶה לְהוֹדוֹת, the *Shaliaḥ Tzibbur* says the paragraph relating to *Birkat Kohanim* (page 301). For the final blessings of the Amida, שִׂים שָׁלוֹם is said instead of שָׁלוֹם רָב. After the Amida, the congregation says *Avinu Malkenu*. This is followed by *Taḥanun*, Full Kaddish and *Aleinu*.

## *Shabbat Shuva*

53 Shabbat Shuva is named for the first word of the Haftara, *Shuva*. It is sometimes referred to as Shabbat Teshuva, "Shabbat of Repentance."

54 Kabbalat Shabbat: If Shabbat Shuva falls on the 3rd of Tishrei, Ma'ariv is preceded only by the last two psalms of Kabbalat Shabbat: מִזְמוֹר שִׁיר לְיוֹם הַשַּׁבָּת and

יהוה מָלָךְ, גֵּאוּת לָבֵשׁ (page 405). בַּמֶּה מַדְלִיקִין is omitted. Ma'ariv Amida for Shabbat is said with additions for the *Aseret Yemei Teshuva*. Similarly, when the *Shaliaḥ Tzibbur* says the paragraph מָגֵן אָבוֹת, he says הַמֶּלֶךְ הַקָּדוֹשׁ instead of הָאֵל הַקָּדוֹשׁ (page 437) [שו״ע או״ח, תקפב: ג].

55 Shaḥarit: for Shabbat. The congregation says Psalm 130 responsively before *Yishtabaḥ* (some say Psalm 130 before נִשְׁמַת כָּל חַי). Amida for Shabbat is said with additions for *Aseret Yemei Teshuva*. The Haftara is Hosea 14:2–10; Joel 2:15–27.

56 It is customary for the rabbi to deliver a sermon relating to repentance.

57 It is customary not to say *Kiddush Levana* until after Yom Kippur [רמ״א או״ח, תרב: א].

## *Erev Yom Kippur (9th of Tishrei)*

58 It is a mitzva to eat and drink on the day before Yom Kippur [שו״ע או״ח, תרד: א].

59 Every person should ask forgiveness from others, because Yom Kippur atones for sins against one's fellows only if the wronged individual has offered his or her forgiveness [שו״ע או״ח, תרו: א].

60 It is customary to say *Kaparot* (page 969) [רמ״א או״ח, תרה: א], and for males to immerse in the mikveh [שו״ע ורמ״א או״ח, תרו: ד].

61 In the morning, an abbreviated *Seliḥot* is said, followed by Shaḥarit for weekdays. During *Pesukei DeZimra*, the congregation omits Psalm 100. Similarly, *Avinu Malkenu*, *Taḥanun* and לַמְנַצֵּחַ (Psalm 20) are omitted. However, if Erev Yom Kippur falls on Friday, the congregation does not omit *Avinu Malkenu* [שו״ע ורמ״א או״ח, תרד: ב].

62 Minḥa: Most communities schedule an early recitation of Minḥa, to allow time for the congregants to return home and eat a final meal (*Se'uda Mafseket*) prior to the fast. Minḥa for weekdays is said with additions for *Aseret Yemei Teshuva*. Before saying the paragraph אֱלֹהַי, נְצֹר at the conclusion of the Amida, each individual says *Viduy* (page 971) [שו״ע או״ח, תרז: א]. *Viduy* is not said by the *Shaliaḥ Tzibbur* during the Repetition of the Amida. As in the morning, both *Avinu Malkenu* and *Taḥanun* are omitted.

63 The *Se'uda Mafseket* (final meal) must be finished a few minutes before sunset [שו״ע או״ח, תרח: א]. It is customary for parents to say a special blessing for their children after the meal [חיי אדם, קמד: יט].

64 Candle lighting: Two blessings are said: (1) לְהַדְלִיק נֵר שֶׁל יוֹם הַכִּפּוּרִים, and (2) שֶׁהֶחֱיָנוּ. When Yom Kippur eve falls on Friday night, the conclusion of the first blessing is: לְהַדְלִיק נֵר שֶׁל שַׁבָּת וְשֶׁל יוֹם הַכִּפּוּרִים (page 385) [שו״ע ורמ״א או״ח, תרי: א–ב].

65 One should also light a candle that will burn at least 25 hours, such as a *yahrzeit*

candle, from which to light the Havdala candle after the conclusion of Yom Kippur.

## *Yom Kippur (10th of Tishrei)*

**66** Yom Kippur Eve: Many individuals say *Tefilla Zaka* ("Pure Prayer") prior to *Kol Nidrei* [משנ״ב או״ח, תרז:א]. It is customary for married men to put on their tallit before *Kol Nidrei*; many also wear a *kittel* [רמ״א או״ח, תרי: ד]. The Ark is opened, and two leaders of the congregation each bear a Torah scroll to the *bima*, where they stand on either side of the *Shaliaḥ Tzibbur*, while he chants *Kol Nidrei*. At the conclusion, the entire congregation says the blessing שֶׁהֶחֱיָנוּ (except women who said the blessing when lighting candles), and the scrolls are returned to the Ark [שו״ע או״ח, תריט:א].

**67** Ma'ariv: for Shabbat and Yom Tov. When saying Shema, the congregation pronounces בָּרוּךְ שֵׁם כְּבוֹד מַלְכוּתוֹ לְעוֹלָם וָעֶד out loud [שו״ע או״ח, תריט:ב]. Before the Yom Kippur Amida, many say the verse כִּי בַיּוֹם הַזֶּה... (Lev. 16:30). After the Amida (with additions – see law 14), the *Shaliaḥ Tzibbur* leads the congregation in saying *Seliḥot* and *Viduy*. After *Viduy*, the Ark is opened and the congregation says *Avinu Malkenu* (unless Yom Kippur falls on Shabbat) and Psalm 24. This is followed by Full Kaddish, *Aleinu*, Mourner's Kaddish, Psalm 27 and Mourner's Kaddish. It is customary to conclude with the singing of Adon Olam or Yigdal. Some congregations also say Psalms 1–4, *Shir HaYiḥud* and *Anim Zemirot*.

**68** When Yom Kippur eve falls on Friday night, Ma'ariv is preceded by the last two psalms of Kabbalat Shabbat: מִזְמוֹר שִׁיר לְיוֹם הַשַּׁבָּת and יהוה מָלָךְ, גֵּאוּת לָבֵשׁ (page 405). בַּמֶּה מַדְלִיקִין is omitted. The Amida is said with additions for Shabbat. After the Amida, the congregation says וַיְכֻלּוּ הַשָּׁמַיִם, and the *Shaliaḥ Tzibbur* says the abbreviated Repetition of the Amida as is customary on Shabbat eve [שו״ע או״ח, תריט:ג].

**69** Shaḥarit: Many have the custom to wear a *kittel* under their tallit. The Daily Psalm is said after putting on the tallit. *Pesukei DeZimra* for Shabbat and Yom Tov is said. The *Shaliaḥ Tzibbur* for Shaḥarit begins from the words הַמֶּלֶךְ יוֹשֵׁב ("The King – enthroned..."). After *Yishtabaḥ*, the Ark is opened and the congregation says Psalm 130 responsively (some say Psalm 130 before נִשְׁמַת כָּל חַי).

**70** After *Barekhu*, the congregation says הַמֵּאִיר לָאָרֶץ or, if it is also Shabbat, הַכֹּל יוֹדוּךָ. The Amida for Yom Kippur is said; if also Shabbat, one says the additions for Shabbat. The *Shaliaḥ Tzibbur* repeats the Amida, adding *piyutim* before *Kedusha*. In all the services of the day, the *Kedusha* of Musaf (נַעֲרִיצְךָ) is said. In the fourth blessing, the congregation says זְכוֹר רַחֲמֶיךָ and *Viduy*.

**71** The congregation says *Avinu Malkenu*, but not on Shabbat [רמ״א או״ח, תקפד:א].

This is followed by Full Kaddish. When the Torah is taken from the Ark, most congregations say the "Thirteen Attributes of Mercy" and a special supplication, except on Shabbat.

72 Torah reading: Lev. 16:1–34. Six men are called up, seven on Shabbat. Maftir: Num. 29:7–11. Haftara: Is. 57:14–58:14 [שו״ע או״ח, תרכא: א].

73 The Haftara is followed by (*Yekum Purkan* on Shabbat, then) the prayers for the government and the State of Israel and *Yizkor*. It is customary for the rabbi to deliver a sermon prior to *Yizkor*. Some have the custom to leave the synagogue for *Yizkor*, if both their parents are still alive [גשר החיים, לא: ב]. One who is praying alone may still say *Yizkor* [גשר החיים, לב: א].

74 After *Yizkor*, the congregation says **אַב הָרַחֲמִים** and *Ashrei*, and the Torah scrolls are returned to the Ark. The *Shaliaḥ Tzibbur* for Musaf says a special prefatory prayer, הִנְנִי הֶעָנִי מִמַּעַשׂ ("Here am I, poor of deeds") and Half Kaddish.

75 If there is a Brit Mila, it takes place before *Ashrei* [משנ״ב, תרכא: ו], and the cup of wine or grape juice is given to one who need not fast and the infant [רמ״א או״ח, תרכא: ג].

76 Musaf: During the Repetition of the Amida, *piyutim* are said before *Kedusha*, culminating with וּנְתַנֶּה תֹּקֶף.

77 The fourth blessing in the Repetition of the Amida contains *Aleinu*. The Ark is opened, and the *Shaliaḥ Tzibbur* (and, in most communities, the entire congregation) kneels in prostration at the words וַאֲנַחְנוּ כּוֹרְעִים. This is followed by *piyutim* describing the Yom Kippur Temple service (in which the congregation's kneeling is repeated three or four additional times), reenacting the High Priest's public pronunciation of the ineffable name of God. Because one is forbidden to touch one's head against the bare stone floor when kneeling, one should place a piece of cloth or paper between one's head and the floor [רמ״א או״ח, קלא: ח].

78 The Kohanim say *Birkat Kohanim*.

79 After Musaf, the *Shaliaḥ Tzibbur* says Full Kaddish. *Ein Keloheinu* and *Aleinu* are not said.

80 Minḥa: Neither *Ashrei* nor **וּבָא לְצִיּוֹן** is said; rather, Minḥa commences with taking the Torah from the Ark [רמ״א או״ח, תרכב: א]. Torah reading: Lev. 18:1–30. The third *oleh* reads the Haftara – the book of Jonah, and Micah 7:18–20 [שו״ע או״ח, תרכב: ב]. After returning the Torah to the Ark, the *Shaliaḥ Tzibbur* says Half Kaddish. The Amida is identical to that of Shaharit, except that it is preceded by the verse beginning **כִּי שֵׁם יהוה אֶקְרָא** (Deut. 32:3). The Repetition of the Amida by the *Shaliaḥ Tzibbur* includes the *Kedusha* starting with **נַעֲרִיצְךָ**, *Viduy* and the

paragraph relating to *Birkat Kohanim*. *Avinu Malkenu* is said, unless Yom Kippur falls on Shabbat or time is running short, as the *Shaliaḥ Tzibbur*'s Repetition of *Ne'ila* must begin before sunset [משנ״ב, שם: יב].

81 *Ne'ila*: The congregation prays a fifth service on Yom Kippur, called *Ne'ila* ("Closing"), beginning shortly before sunset. The service commences as Minḥa for Shabbat and Yom Tov: *Ashrei*, וּבָא לְצִיּוֹן, Half Kaddish [רמ״א או״ח, תרכג: א]. The congregation says the Amida for *Ne'ila*; in the Amida the term כָּתְבֵנוּ ("inscribe us") in all its conjugations is changed to חָתְמֵנוּ ("seal us") [רמ״א או״ח, תרכג: ב]. In the last blessing, שִׂים שָׁלוֹם is said. In *Viduy*, instead of עַל חֵטְא, a long, heartfelt supplication is said.

82 The Ark is opened for the entire Repetition of the Amida, which includes the *Kedusha* starting with נַעֲרִיצְךָ, *Seliḥot*, an abridged form of *Viduy* and the paragraph relating to *Birkat Kohanim*.

83 *Avinu Malkenu* is said, even when Yom Kippur falls on Shabbat; again the term כָּתְבֵנוּ is changed to חָתְמֵנוּ.

84 At the conclusion of *Ne'ila*, the *Shaliaḥ Tzibbur* leads the congregation in the responsive chanting of several verses, followed by Full Kaddish, and the sounding of the shofar [רמ״א, שם: ו]. It is customary to conclude with the singing of לַשָּׁנָה הַבָּאָה בִּירוּשָׁלָיִם ("Next Year in Jerusalem").

85 Ma'ariv: as for weekdays. In the fourth blessing of the Amida, the paragraph of אַתָּה חוֹנַנְתָּנוּ (page 333) is said [שו״ע או״ח, תרכד: א]. Havdala is said over a cup of wine or grape juice, and the Havdala candle is lit from the flame that was lit before Yom Kippur began. No blessing is made over spices (unless it is also Motza'ei Shabbat) [שו״ע או״ח, תרכד: ד].

86 There is a custom to begin construction of the sukka on the night following Yom Kippur [רמ״א, שם: ה, ותרכה: א].

87 *Taḥanun* is not said between Yom Kippur and Sukkot [שו״ע או״ח, קלא: ז].

## *Erev Sukkot (14th of Tishrei)*

88 The construction and decoration of the sukka should be completed before Sukkot begins. Likewise, the myrtle (*hadasim*) and willow (*aravot*) should be bound to the lulav before the holiday begins [שו״ע או״ח, תרנא: א].

89 When Sukkot falls on Thursday and Friday, each household must prepare an *Eiruv Tavshilin* (page 817); this makes it permissible to prepare food on Friday for the Shabbat meals [שו״ע או״ח, תקכז].

## *First days of Sukkot (15th–16th of Tishrei)*

**90** Candle lighting: Two blessings are said: (1) לְהַדְלִיק נֵר שֶׁל יוֹם טוֹב and (2) שֶׁהֶחֱיָנוּ. When Sukkot eve falls on Friday night, the conclusion of the first blessing is: לְהַדְלִיק נֵר שֶׁל שַׁבָּת וְשֶׁל יוֹם טוֹב (page 383).

**91** Ma'ariv: for Shabbat and Yom Tov (page 415). Many congregations say the special verse for Yom Tov (וַיְדַבֵּר מֹשֶׁה), before saying the Amida for Yom Tov (page 831 This is followed by Full Kaddish, *Aleinu*, Mourner's Kaddish, Psalm 27 and Mourner's Kaddish. It is customary to conclude with the singing of Adon Olam or Yigdal.

**92** When Sukkot eve falls on Friday night, Ma'ariv for Shabbat is preceded by the last two psalms of Kabbalat Shabbat: מִזְמוֹר שִׁיר לְיוֹם הַשַּׁבָּת and יהוה מָלָךְ, גֵּאוּת לָבֵשׁ (page 405). בַּמֶּה מַדְלִיקִין is omitted. וְשָׁמְרוּ (page 423) precedes the Yom Tov Amida, which is said with additions for Shabbat. After the Amida, the congregation says וַיְכֻלּוּ הַשָּׁמַיִם, and the *Shaliaḥ Tzibbur* says the abbreviated Repetition of the Amida as is customary on Shabbat eve [שו״ע או״ח, תרמב: א].

**93** When the eve of the second day falls on Motza'ei Shabbat, the congregation adds the paragraph וַתּוֹדִיעֵנוּ in the middle section of the Amida.

**94** Upon returning home, one enters the sukka. Some say the *Ushpizin* (page 827). When saying the Kiddush for Yom Tov on the first night, the blessing לֵישֵׁב בַּסֻּכָּה ("to dwell in the sukka") precedes the blessing שֶׁהֶחֱיָנוּ. On the second night, the blessing שֶׁהֶחֱיָנוּ is said prior to the blessing לֵישֵׁב בַּסֻּכָּה [שו״ע או״ח, תרסא: א]; some say the blessings in the same order as on the first night. [משנ״ב, שם: ב] When Sukkot eve falls on Friday night, Kiddush is said with additions for Shabbat. When the second night of Sukkot falls on Motza'ei Shabbat, the two blessings for Havdala are inserted prior to the blessing שֶׁהֶחֱיָנוּ; thus the order of blessings is: wine, Kiddush, flame, Havdala, שֶׁהֶחֱיָנוּ, sukka (pages 821–823) [שו״ע או״ח, תרמג: א]. In *Birkat HaMazon*, one adds יַעֲלֶה וְיָבוֹא (page 1065).

**95** Shaḥarit: for Shabbat and Yom Tov (page 475). The *Shaliaḥ Tzibbur* for Shaḥarit begins from the words הָאֵל בְּתַעֲצוּמוֹת עֻזֶּךָ (page 525). After *Barekhu*, the congregation says הַמֵּאִיר לָאָרֶץ or, if it is also Shabbat, הַכֹּל יוֹדְוּךָ. The Amida for Yom Tov is said (page 831); if also Shabbat, one says the additions for Shabbat.

**96** After the *Shaliaḥ Tzibbur* repeats the Amida, the congregation takes the lulav and says the blessing עַל נְטִילַת לוּלָב. On the first day the lulav is taken, the blessing שֶׁהֶחֱיָנוּ is also said (page 789). On Shabbat, one does not take the lulav [שו״ע או״ח, תרמד: א; שם, תרסב: א–ב]. Hallel is said, and some congregations say *Hoshanot* after Hallel. This is followed by Full Kaddish and taking the Torah from the Ark.

Some congregations precede taking the Torah from the Ark with the Daily Psalm and Psalm 27, followed by the Mourner's Kaddish. Most congregations say the "Thirteen Attributes of Mercy" and a special supplication (page 571), except on Shabbat.

97 Torah Reading: first day and second day – page 1204. Maftir and Haftarot – pages 1230–1232 [שו״ע או״ח, תרנט: א, תרסב: ג].

98 The Haftara is followed by (*Yekum Purkan* on Shabbat, then) the prayers for the government and the State of Israel. The *Shaliaḥ Tzibbur* says יָהּ אֵלִי וְגוֹאֲלִי (page 867) (except when Sukkot falls on Shabbat), the congregation says *Ashrei*, and the Torah scrolls are returned to the Ark. The *Shaliaḥ Tzibbur* says Half Kaddish.

99 Musaf: for Festivals (page 869). If also Shabbat, one says the additions for Shabbat. During the Repetition of the Amida, the Kohanim say *Birkat Kohanim*. After the Repetition, the congregation takes the lulav, the Ark is opened and one Torah scroll is taken out. The *Shaliaḥ Tzibbur* leads the congregation in saying the *Hoshanot*, while making a circuit around the *bima* (page 915) [שו״ע או״ח, תרס: א]. On Shabbat, the Ark is opened, and the special *Hoshanot* for Shabbat, אוֹם נְצוּרָה and כְּהוֹשַׁעְתָּ אָדָם (page 923), are said [שו״ע, שם: ג]. The Torah scroll is returned to the Ark, and the *Shaliaḥ Tzibbur* says Full Kaddish. This is followed by *Ein Kelo-heinu*, the Rabbis' Kaddish, *Aleinu*, Mourner's Kaddish, the Daily Psalm, Psalm 27, Mourner's Kaddish, *Anim Zemirot*, Mourner's Kaddish and Adon Olam.

100 Minḥa: for Shabbat and Yom Tov. When Sukkot falls on Shabbat, the Torah is taken from the Ark and the beginning of וְזֹאת הַבְּרָכָה (page 1187) is read. After returning the Torah to the Ark, the *Shaliaḥ Tzibbur* says Half Kaddish, and the congregation says the Amida for Yom Tov (page 831), with additions for Shabbat.

## *Ḥol HaMo'ed Sukkot*

101 During Shaḥarit, Minḥa and Ma'ariv, יַעֲלֶה וְיָבוֹא is added to the seventeenth blessing of the Amida (רְצֵה). It is also added during *Birkat HaMazon* (page 1065) [שו״ע או״ח, תצ: ב]. If one forgets to say יַעֲלֶה וְיָבוֹא in its proper place, see law 422.

102 The traditional Ashkenazi practice is to wear tefillin during Shaḥarit until the recitation of Hallel. However, some congregations follow the Sephardi custom, in which tefillin are not worn on Ḥol HaMo'ed; this is also the practice in Israel [שו״ע ורמ״א או״ח, לא: ב].

103 First Evening of Ḥol HaMo'ed: Ma'ariv for weekdays (page 315). אַתָּה חוֹנַנְתָּנוּ is added in the fourth blessing of the Amida. Havdala is said in the sukka (unless Ḥol HaMo'ed begins on Friday night). No blessing is made over spices or a flame

(unless Ḥol HaMo'ed begins on Saturday night), but one says the blessing לֵישֵׁב בַּסֻּכָּה before drinking (page 783).

104 Shaḥarit: for weekdays. After the *Shaliaḥ Tzibbur* repeats the Amida, the congregation takes the lulav and says the blessing עַל נְטִילַת לוּלָב [שו״ע או״ח, תרסב: א]. Hallel is said, and some congregations say *Hoshanot* after Hallel instead of after Musaf. This is followed by Full Kaddish.

105 Torah Reading: Pages 1233–1236. Four men are called up. Each day's reading is nine verses long. For each of the first three *aliyot*, one reads three verses. The fourth *oleh* goes back to the beginning and reads the first six verses a second time [רמ״א או״ח, תרסג: א].

106 After the Torah reading, Half Kaddish is said, the Torah is returned to the Ark, and *Ashrei* and וּבָא לְצִיּוֹן are said. The *Shaliaḥ Tzibbur* then says Half Kaddish.

107 Musaf: for Festivals (page 869). The *Kedusha* for weekdays is said; no *Birkat Kohanim* is said. After the Repetition of the Amida, the congregation takes the lulav, the Ark is opened and one Torah scroll is taken out. The *Shaliaḥ Tzibbur* leads the congregation in saying the *Hoshanot* of the day (see table on page 915), while making a circuit around the *bima*. The Torah scroll is returned to the Ark, and the *Shaliaḥ Tzibbur* says Full Kaddish. This is followed by *Aleinu* (page 245), and the conclusion of the weekday service.

## *Shabbat Ḥol HaMo'ed Sukkot*

108 Ma'ariv for Shabbat is preceded by Psalms 92 and 93: מִזְמוֹר שִׁיר לְיוֹם הַשַּׁבָּת and יהוה מָלָךְ, גֵּאוּת לָבֵשׁ (page 405). בַּמֶּה מַדְלִיקִין is not said. The Amida for Shabbat is said with the addition of יַעֲלֶה וְיָבוֹא [שו״ע או״ח, תרסג: ב]. The conclusion of Ma'ariv is as for Shabbat (pages 437–449).

109 Shaḥarit: for Shabbat (page 475). The Amida for Shabbat is said with the addition of יַעֲלֶה וְיָבוֹא [שם]. Hallel is said, and some congregations say *Hoshanot* after Hallel instead of after Musaf. This is followed by Full Kaddish, the reading of *Kohelet* and Mourner's Kaddish [רמ״א או״ח, תצ: ט].

110 Torah Reading: page 1212. Maftir: Reading for the fourth *aliya* of the appropriate day (pages 1233–1236). Haftara: page 1236 [שו״ע או״ח, תרסג: ג]. In the concluding blessing after the Haftara, one says מְקַדֵּשׁ הַשַּׁבָּת וְיִשְׂרָאֵל וְהַזְּמַנִּים [משנ״ב, שם: ט].

111 The Haftara is followed by (*Yekum Purkan* on Shabbat, then) the prayers for the government and the State of Israel. *Ashrei* is said and the Torah scrolls are returned to the Ark. The *Shaliaḥ Tzibbur* says Half Kaddish.

112 Musaf: for Festivals, with additions for Shabbat (page 869). However, אַדִּיר אַדִּירֵנוּ

is not added to *Kedusha*, and *Birkat Kohanim* is not said. After the Repetition of the Amida, the Ark is opened, no Torah scroll is taken out, and the special *Hoshanot* for Shabbat, אֹם נְצוּרָה and כְּהוֹשַׁעְתָּ אָדָם (page 923), are said. The Ark is closed, and the *Shaliaḥ Tzibbur* says Full Kaddish. This is followed by *Ein Keloheinu* (page 625) and the conclusion of Musaf, as for Shabbat.

113 Minḥa: for Shabbat (page 665). The Torah is taken from the Ark and the beginning of וְזֹאת הַבְּרָכָה (page 1187) is read. After returning the Torah to the Ark, the *Shaliaḥ Tzibbur* says Half Kaddish, and the congregation says the Amida for Shabbat with the addition of יַעֲלֶה וְיָבוֹא.

114 Motza'ei Shabbat: Ma'ariv for Motza'ei Shabbat is said. After the Amida, וִיהִי נֹעַם is omitted, and the *Shaliaḥ Tzibbur* says Full Kaddish. וְיִתֶּן־לְךָ (page 759) is said [רמ״א או״ח, רצה: ט].

## *Hoshana Raba (21st of Tishrei)*

115 Shaḥarit: It is customary for the *Shaliaḥ Tzibbur* to wear a *kittel*. *Pesukei DeZimra* for Shabbat and Yom Tov is said, including Psalm 100 (מִזְמוֹר לְתוֹדָה, page 483). After אָז יָשִׁיר־מֹשֶׁה (page 517), prayers continue with Shaḥarit for weekdays (page 137) [שו״ע ורמ״א או״ח, תרסד: א]. Some have the custom to open the Ark after *Yishtabaḥ*, and say Psalm 130 responsively (some say Psalm 130 before *Yishtabaḥ*). After the *Shaliaḥ Tzibbur* repeats the Amida, the congregation takes the lulav and says the blessing עַל נְטִילַת לוּלָב. Hallel is said, and some congregations say *Hoshanot* after Hallel instead of after Musaf. This is followed Full Kaddish.

116 While the Torah is taken from the Ark, the congregation says *Ein Kamokha* (page 571) [רמ״א, שם]. Most congregations say the "Thirteen Attributes of Mercy" and a special supplication (page 571). Torah Reading: page 1236. Some have the custom to read in the melody of *Yamim Nora'im*.

117 After the Torah reading, Half Kaddish is said, the Torah is returned to the Ark, and *Ashrei* and וּבָא לְצִיּוֹן are said. The *Shaliaḥ Tzibbur* says Half Kaddish.

118 Musaf: for Festivals (page 869). It is customary for the *Shaliaḥ Tzibbur* to wear a *kittel* [רמ״א, שם]. The *Kedusha* for Yom Tov is said, but *Birkat Kohanim* is not. After the Repetition of the Amida, the congregation takes the lulav, the Ark is opened and seven Torah scrolls are taken out to the *bima*. Many congregations have the custom of taking out all the Torah scrolls [רמ״א או״ח, תרס: א]. The *Shaliaḥ Tzibbur* leads the congregation in saying the *Hoshanot* while making seven circuits around the *bima* (page 929) [רמ״א או״ח, תרסד: א]. These are followed by special *piyutim* asking for rain. Then five willow branches (*aravot*) are taken

and beaten five times before the Torah scrolls are returned to the Ark (page 957). Some have the custom of beating the *aravot* after the *Shaliaḥ Tzibbur* says the Full Kaddish [רמ״א, שם:ו]. This is followed by *Ein Keloheinu*, Rabbis' Kaddish, *Aleinu*, Mourner's Kaddish, the Daily Psalm, Psalm 27 and Mourner's Kaddish.

## *Shemini Atzeret (22nd of Tishrei)*

119 Candle lighting: Two blessings are said: (1) לְהַדְלִיק נֵר שֶׁל יוֹם טוֹב, and (2) שֶׁהֶחֱיָנוּ. When Shemini Atzeret eve falls on Friday night, the conclusion of the first blessing is: לְהַדְלִיק נֵר שֶׁל שַׁבָּת וְשֶׁל יוֹם טוֹב.

120 Ma'ariv: for Shabbat and Yom Tov. Many congregations say the special verse for Yom Tov (וַיְדַבֵּר מֹשֶׁה), before saying the Amida for Yom Tov (page 423). This is followed by Full Kaddish, *Aleinu*, Mourner's Kaddish, Psalm 27 and Mourner's Kaddish. It is customary to conclude with the singing of Adon Olam or Yigdal.

121 When Shemini Atzeret eve falls on Friday night, Ma'ariv is preceded by the last two psalms of Kabbalat Shabbat: מִזְמוֹר שִׁיר לְיוֹם הַשַּׁבָּת and יהוה מָלָךְ, גֵּאוּת לָבֵשׁ (page 405). בַּמֶּה מַדְלִיקִין is omitted. וְשָׁמְרוּ (page 423) precedes the Yom Tov Amida, which is said with additions for Shabbat. After the Amida, the congregation says וַיְכֻלּוּ הַשָּׁמַיִם, and the *Shaliaḥ Tzibbur* says the abbreviated Repetition of the Amida as is customary on Shabbat eve.

122 When Shemini Atzeret eve falls on Friday night, Kiddush for Yom Tov is said with additions for Shabbat.

123 Outside Israel the traditional Ashkenazi practice is to sit in the sukka on Shemini Atzeret, without saying the blessing לֵישֵׁב בַּסֻּכָּה [שו״ע או״ח, תרסח:א]. However, some follow the Ḥasidic custom, according to which Kiddush is said in the sukka on Shemini Atzeret eve, while the rest of the meals are eaten in the house.

124 Shaḥarit: for Shabbat and Yom Tov (page 475). The *Shaliaḥ Tzibbur* for Shaḥarit begins from the words הָאֵל בְּתַעֲצוּמוֹת עֻזֶּךָ (page 525). After *Barekhu*, the congregation says הַמֵּאִיר לָאָרֶץ or, if it is also Shabbat, הַכֹּל יוֹדוּךָ. The Amida for Yom Tov is said (page 831); if also Shabbat, one says the additions for Shabbat. The Repetition of the Amida is followed by Hallel and Full Kaddish. On Shabbat, *Kohelet* is read, followed by the Mourner's Kaddish.

125 While the Torah is taken from the Ark, most congregations say the "Thirteen Attributes of Mercy" and a special supplication (page 571), except on Shabbat.

126 Torah Reading: page 1221. Maftir and Haftara: page 1238 [שו״ע או״ח, תרסח:ב].

127 The Haftara is followed by (*Yekum Purkan* on Shabbat, then) the prayers for the government and the State of Israel, *Yizkor* (page 859), and אַב הָרַחֲמִים [משנ״ב, שם:טו].

The congregation says *Ashrei* (page 601), and the Torah scrolls are returned to the Ark. The *Shaliaḥ Tzibbur* says Half Kaddish.

**128** Musaf for Festivals (page 869) is said. If also Shabbat, one says the additions for Shabbat. It is customary for the *Shaliaḥ Tzibbur* to wear a *kittel*. In most congregations, the announcement to begin saying מַשִּׁיב הָרְוּחַ וּמוֹרִיד הַגֶּשֶׁם precedes the silent recitation of the Amida [רמ״א או״ח, קיד:ב]. The Repetition of the Amida begins with the opening of the Ark, and the *Shaliaḥ Tzibbur* says the Prayer for Rain (page 909). The Kohanim say *Birkat Kohanim*. After the Repetition, the service continues with Full Kaddish, and the conclusion of the service is as for Shabbat and Yom Tov (page 625).

▸ LAWS OF מַשִּׁיב הָרְוּחַ

**129** One begins saying מַשִּׁיב הָרְוּחַ in Musaf of Shemini Atzeret and continues until Musaf of the first day of Pesaḥ [שו״ע או״ח, קיד:א].

**130** If one forgets to say מַשִּׁיב הָרְוּחַ in its proper place but realizes before beginning the words of the blessing מְחַיֵּה הַמֵּתִים, one should immediately say מַשִּׁיב הָרְוּחַ and continue with the rest of the blessing. If one realizes the omission immediately after completing the blessing מְחַיֵּה הַמֵּתִים, one should say מַשִּׁיב הָרְוּחַ and continue with the following blessing. If one realizes the omission after beginning the words אַתָּה קָדוֹשׁ, one must repeat the Amida from the beginning [שו״ע או״ח, קיד:ו].

**131** If one forgets to say מַשִּׁיב הָרְוּחַ but says מוֹרִיד הַטָּל (as is the custom in Israel, and that of *Nusaḥ Sepharad*, in the spring and summer months), one need not repeat the Amida [שו״ע או״ח, קיד:ה]. If there is doubt whether one said מַשִּׁיב הָרְוּחַ, the presumption is as follows: within the first thirty days from *Shemini Atzeret*, one should assume that one forgot to say מַשִּׁיב הָרְוּחַ. After thirty days, one should assume that one said מַשִּׁיב הָרְוּחַ [שו״ע או״ח, קיד:ח].

**132** Minḥa: for Shabbat and Yom Tov. When Shemini Atzeret falls on Shabbat, the Torah is taken from the Ark and the beginning of וְזֹאת הַבְּרָכָה (page 1187) is read. After returning the Torah to the Ark, the *Shaliaḥ Tzibbur* says Half Kaddish, and the congregation says the Amida for Yom Tov (page 831).

## *Simḥat Torah (23rd of Tishrei)*

**133** Candle lighting: Two blessings are said: (1) לְהַדְלִיק נֵר שֶׁל יוֹם טוֹב, and (2) שֶׁהֶחֱיָנוּ.

**134** Ma'ariv: as for Shabbat and Yom Tov. Many congregations say the special verse for Yom Tov (וַיְדַבֵּר מֹשֶׁה), before saying the Amida for Yom Tov (page 423). If Shemini Atzeret fell on Shabbat, the congregation adds the paragraph וַתּוֹדִיעֵנוּ in the middle section of the Amida.

135 After Full Kaddish, the verses of אַתָּה הָרְאֵתָ are said responsively (page 847). The ark is opened, all of the Torah scrolls are taken from the Ark, and the seven *Hakafot* are performed amid joyous singing and dancing. After completion of seven *Hakafot*, all of the Torah scrolls except one are returned to the Ark. The *Shaliaḥ Tzibbur* takes the remaining scroll, and leads the congregation in saying שְׁמַע יִשְׂרָאֵל and the rest of the ceremony for taking the Torah from the Ark (page 575) [רמ״א או״ח, תרסט:א].

136 Torah reading: Customs differ. Most congregations read the beginning of וְזֹאת הַבְּרָכָה (page 1187) and three (in some congregations, five) are called up. It is customary for the Reader to use the melody of *Yamim Nora'im*. After the completion of the reading, the Torah is returned to the Ark (page 603). This is followed by *Aleinu* (page 441), and Mourner's Kaddish. It is customary to conclude with the singing of Adon Olam or Yigdal.

137 Kiddush for Yom Tov (page 821) is said. If Shemini Atzeret fell on Shabbat, the two blessings for Havdala (page 823) are inserted prior to the blessing שֶׁהֶחֱיָנוּ.

138 Shaḥarit: for Shabbat and Yom Tov. The *Shaliaḥ Tzibbur* for Shaḥarit begins from the words הָאֵל בְּתַעֲצוּמוֹת עֻזֶּךָ. After *Barekhu*, the congregation says הַמֵּאִיר לָאָרֶץ. The Amida for Yom Tov is said (page 831). During the Repetition of the Amida, the Kohanim say *Birkat Kohanim*. This is followed by Hallel and Full Kaddish. The Ark is opened and the verses of אַתָּה הָרְאֵתָ (page 847) are said responsively. All of the Torah scrolls are taken from the Ark, and the seven *Hakafot* are performed amid joyous singing and dancing.

139 Torah Reading: pages 1239–1240. The Torah reading is repeated, in cycles of five *aliyot*, until all males over thirteen have received an *aliya* [רמ״א או״ח, תרסט:א]. It is customary for children under 13 years to participate in an *aliya*, known as *Kol HaNe'arim*, in which multiple tallitot are spread to form a canopy over the children and the *oleh*. This is followed by the calling up of the *Ḥatan Torah*, for whom the final verses of the Torah are read. After the completion of the reading, it is customary that *Hagbaha* is performed with arms crossed, so that when the Torah is raised and the arms uncrossed, the lettering on the scroll faces outward toward the congregation. A second scroll is opened; the *Ḥatan Bereshit* is called up and the first verses of *Bereshit* are read [שו״ע ורמ״א או״ח, תרסט:א]. It is customary to pause in the reading for the congregation to read aloud וַיְהִי־עֶרֶב וַיְהִי בֹקֶר for each day of Creation, and to read aloud the last three verses, starting with וַיְכֻלּוּ הַשָּׁמַיִם. This is followed by Half Kaddish. A third scroll is opened for Maftir. The Haftara is the beginning of the book of Joshua (page 1244) [שם].

140 After the Haftara, the prayers for the government and the State of Israel are

said. The congregation says *Ashrei*, and the Torah scrolls are returned to the Ark. The *Shaliaḥ Tzibbur* says Half Kaddish.

141 Musaf: for Festivals (page 869). The Kohanim do not say *Birkat Kohanim*, because they are assumed to have drunk alcohol. The Repetition of the Amida is followed by Full Kaddish, and the conclusion of the service is as for Shabbat and Yom Tov (page 625).

142 Minḥa: for Shabbat and Yom Tov.

### *Motza'ei Sukkot (24th of Tishrei)*

143 Ma'ariv: for weekdays. In the fourth blessing of the Amida, the paragraph of אַתָּה חוֹנַנְתָּנוּ is said (page 333). Havdala is said over a cup of wine or grape juice; no blessing is made over spices or a flame [שו״ע או״ח, תרא: א].

### *Shabbat Bereshit (Mevarkhim Ḥodesh Marḥeshvan)*

144 On the Shabbat preceding Rosh Ḥodesh Marḥeshvan (and each subsequent Rosh Ḥodesh), *Birkat HaḤodesh* (page 597) is said after the prayers for the government and the State of Israel. This is followed immediately by *Ashrei*. אַב הָרַחֲמִים is generally omitted on the Shabbat preceding Rosh Ḥodesh, except those preceding Rosh Ḥodesh Iyar and Sivan.

145 Minḥa: It is customary to say Psalm 104 (בָּרְכִי נַפְשִׁי) and the fifteen Songs of Ascents (page 699) after Minḥa on Shabbat, from *Shabbat Bereshit* until before *Shabbat HaGadol* [רמ״א או״ח, רצב: ב].

## MARḤESHVAN

▸ LAWS OF BAHAB (בה״ב)

146 Some have the custom to say special *Seliḥot* after the Repetition of the Amida of Shaḥarit on the first Monday, the first Thursday and the second Monday of Marḥeshvan. Historically, these days were dedicated to fasting to atone for overstepping halakhic limits during the celebration of the Yom Tov. This custom is also observed on the first Monday, the first Thursday and the second Monday of Iyar [שו״ע ורמ״א או״ח, תצב: א].

# KISLEV

## *4th–5th of December*

147 In most years, during Ma'ariv on the evening of the 4th of December, one begins to say וְתֵן טַל וּמָטָר לִבְרָכָה in the ninth blessing of the Amida. In the year preceding a civil leap year, one begins to say וְתֵן טַל וּמָטָר לִבְרָכָה one day later, on the night of the 5th of December [שו״ע או״ח, קיז: א].

148 If one forgets to say וְתֵן טַל וּמָטָר לִבְרָכָה in its proper place but realizes before saying God's name in the ninth blessing (מְבָרֵךְ הַשָּׁנִים), one should immediately say וְתֵן טַל וּמָטָר לִבְרָכָה and continue with the rest of the blessing. If one realizes the omission after completing the blessing מְבָרֵךְ הַשָּׁנִים, one should say וְתֵן טַל וּמָטָר לִבְרָכָה prior to the words כִּי אַתָּה שׁוֹמֵעַ in the sixteenth blessing (שׁוֹמֵעַ תְּפִלָּה). If one realizes the omission after beginning the seventeenth blessing (רְצֵה), one must repeat the Amida from the beginning of the ninth blessing (מְבָרֵךְ הַשָּׁנִים). If one realizes the omission after completing the Amida, one must repeat the entire Amida [שו״ע או״ח, קיז: ה].

149 If there is doubt whether one properly said וְתֵן טַל וּמָטָר לִבְרָכָה, the presumption is as follows: within the first thirty days from December 4th (or 5th), one should assume that one forgot to say וְתֵן טַל וּמָטָר לִבְרָכָה. After thirty days, one should assume that one said וְתֵן טַל וּמָטָר לִבְרָכָה.

## *Ḥanukka (25th of Kislev–2nd of Tevet)*

150 On Ḥanukka, עַל הַנִּסִּים is added to the Amida in Ma'ariv, Shaḥarit and Minḥa, as well as the second blessing of *Birkat HaMazon*. If one forgets to say עַל הַנִּסִּים, one does not repeat the Amida or *Birkat HaMazon* [שו״ע או״ח, תרפב: א].

151 It is customary to light Ḥanukka lights in the synagogue, either before or after Ma'ariv of each evening of Ḥanukka. The procedure is identical to that of lighting in the home, as described below, except that the lights should be placed along the southern wall of the synagogue.

152 After Ma'ariv, Ḥanukka lights are lit in the home. On the first night, three blessings are said: (1) לְהַדְלִיק נֵר שֶׁל חֲנֻכָּה, (2) שֶׁעָשָׂה נִסִּים ("Who performed miracles") and (3) שֶׁהֶחֱיָנוּ (page 981). On subsequent nights, only the first two blessings are said [שו״ע או״ח, תרעו: א]. When adding lights each night, the new light is always added to the left. The newest candle is lit first, and one then lights the rest of the lights from left to right.

153 The lights must burn for at least half an hour after nightfall [שו״ע או״ח, תרעב:ב; משנ״ב, שם: ד]. If one did not light during this time, one is permitted to light any time before daybreak. In such a case, one says the appropriate blessings when lighting, but only if other household members are awake [שו״ע, שם; משנ״ב, שם: יא].

154 Most have the custom for each member of the household to light separately, but the head of household may light one menora for the entire family [שו״ע ורמ״א או״ח, תרעא: ב].

155 Women are obligated to light Ḥanukka lights [שו״ע או״ח, תרעה: ג]. Hence, a woman can light for herself, on behalf of her household, and on behalf of an adult male [משנ״ב, שם: ט].

156 The menora is generally lit indoors, but near a window, so that the lights are visible to the general public as well [שו״ע או״ח, תרעה: ז].

157 After the lighting, it is customary to sing הַנֵּרוֹת הַלָּלוּ and מָעוֹז צוּר (pages 983–985) [שו״ע או״ח, תרעו: ד].

158 Shaḥarit: It is customary to light the menora in the synagogue without a blessing before the prayers begin. Shaḥarit for weekdays is said. עַל הַנִּסִּים is added to the Amida, as discussed above. After the Repetition of the Amida, *Taḥanun* is omitted and the *Shaliaḥ Tzibbur* leads the congregation in saying Full Hallel (page 791) [שו״ע או״ח, תרפג: א]. This is followed by Half Kaddish and taking the Torah from the Ark (page 223).

159 Torah reading: pages 1194–1199. Three men are called up [שו״ע או״ח, תרפד: א]. The Torah is returned to the Ark, *Ashrei* and וּבָא לְצִיּוֹן are said, but לַמְנַצֵּחַ is omitted, and the *Shaliaḥ Tzibbur* says Full Kaddish. This is followed by *Aleinu*, Mourner's Kaddish, the Daily Psalm, Psalm 30 (page 101), and Mourner's Kaddish.

▸ SHABBAT ḤANUKKA

160 Ḥanukka lights are lit at home prior to lighting the Shabbat candles. Care must be taken that the lights, though lit prior to sunset, will burn for at least half an hour after dark [שו״ע או״ח, תרעט: א]. Ḥanukka lights are lit in the synagogue after Minḥa [משנ״ב, שם: ג].

161 Ma'ariv: for Shabbat and Yom Tov. עַל הַנִּסִּים is added to the Amida (see law 150).

162 Shaḥarit: for Shabbat and Yom Tov. The Repetition of the Amida is followed by Hallel [שו״ע או״ח, תרפג: א]. Two Torah scrolls are taken from the Ark, three if Shabbat falls on Rosh Ḥodesh Tevet.

163 Torah Reading: Seven men are called up for the portion of the week (usually מִקֵּץ). Maftir: The appropriate day's reading from pages 1194–1199. Haftara: Zech.

2:14–4:7. If there are two Shabbatot during Ḥanukka, on the second Shabbat the Haftara is 1 Kings 7:40–50 [שו״ע או״ח, תרפד:ב]. If Shabbat falls on Rosh Ḥodesh Tevet, three Torah scrolls are taken from the Ark. Six men are called up for the portion of the week, and the seventh reads the Musaf offerings for Shabbat and Rosh Ḥodesh (page 1189) from the second scroll [שו״ע, שם:ג]. Half Kaddish is said. For Maftir, the portion for Ḥanukka is read from the third scroll.

164 The rest of the service continues as for Shabbat, except that אַב הָרַחֲמִים is omitted and עַל הַנִּסִּים is added to the Musaf Amida [שו״ע או״ח, תרפב:ב; תרפג:א].

165 Minḥa: עַל הַנִּסִּים is added to the Amida for Minḥa, and צִדְקָתְךָ is omitted [שם].

▸ MOTZA'EI SHABBAT ḤANUKKA

166 Ma'ariv: for weekdays. In the fourth blessing of the Amida, the paragraph of אַתָּה חוֹנַנְתָּנוּ (page 333) is said. עַל הַנִּסִּים is added to the eighteenth blessing of the Amida. In the synagogue, the Ḥanukka lights are lit prior to making Havdala [שו״ע או״ח, תרפא:ב]. In the home, Havdala is made first [ערוה״ש, שם:ב].

# TEVET

## *Rosh Ḥodesh Tevet*

167 On a weekday, Shaharit for weekdays is said. יַעֲלֶה וְיָבוֹא and עַל הַנִּסִּים are added to the Amida. After the Repetition of the Amida, *Taḥanun* is omitted and the *Shaliaḥ Tzibbur* leads the congregation in saying Hallel. This is followed by Full Kaddish.

168 Torah reading: Two scrolls are removed from the Ark. Three men are called up to the first scroll, and Num. 28:1–15 (page 1189) is read. A fourth man is called up to the second scroll, from which the appropriate day's reading from Num. 7:42–53 (page 1197) is read. The *Shaliaḥ Tzibbur* then says Half Kaddish. Prayers continue as on a regular Rosh Ḥodesh, except that עַל הַנִּסִּים is added to the Amida of Musaf.

169 On Shabbat Rosh Ḥodesh Tevet, Shaharit for Shabbat and Yom Tov is said. יַעֲלֶה וְיָבוֹא and עַל הַנִּסִּים are added to the Amida. The recitation of Hallel is followed by Full Kaddish.

170 Torah reading: See law 163. Prayers continue as on a regular Shabbat Rosh Ḥodesh, except that עַל הַנִּסִּים is added to the Amida of Musaf.

### *Asara B'Tevet (10th of Tevet)*

171 This fast commemorates the besieging of Jerusalem by Nebuchadnezzar, which led to the capture of the city and the destruction of the First Temple (Ezek. 24:1–2).

172 The fast begins at dawn (see laws 47–48) [שו״ע או״ח, תקנ: ב].

173 Shaḥarit: for weekdays. During the Repetition of the Amida, the *Shaliaḥ Tzibbur* says עֲנֵנוּ between the seventh and eighth blessings (page 181) [שו״ע או״ח, תקסו: א]. This is followed by *Seliḥot, Avinu Malkenu* and *Taḥanun* [ערוה״ש או״ח, תקסו: ח].

174 Torah Reading: Page 1190 (see law 50) [שו״ע או״ח, תקסו: א].

175 Minḥa: for weekdays, except that after *Ashrei* and Half Kaddish, the Torah is read. The reading is the same as that of the morning. The third *oleh* reads the Haftara (page 1190) [רמ״א, שם]. After the Torah is returned to the Ark, the *Shaliaḥ Tzibbur* says Half Kaddish, and continues with the rest of Minḥa for weekdays.

176 During the silent recitation of the Amida, those who are fasting say עֲנֵנוּ as part of the sixteenth blessing, שׁוֹמֵעַ תְּפִלָּה (page 295). During the Repetition of the Amida, the *Shaliaḥ Tzibbur* says עֲנֵנוּ between the seventh and eighth blessings, as in the morning (page 287). After the eighteenth blessing (מוֹדִים), the *Shaliaḥ Tzibbur* says the paragraph relating to *Birkat Kohanim* (page 301). For the final blessing of the Amida, שִׂים שָׁלוֹם is said instead of שָׁלוֹם רָב. After the Amida, the congregation says *Avinu Malkenu*. This is followed by *Taḥanun*, Full Kaddish and *Aleinu*. If the fast falls on Friday, *Avinu Malkenu* and *Taḥanun* are omitted [משנ״ב, תקנ: יא].

## SHEVAT

### *Tu BiShevat (15th of Shevat)*

177 *Taḥanun* is omitted [שו״ע או״ח, קלא: ו].

178 It is customary to eat many different fruits, especially fruits that are among the Seven Species associated with the land of Israel, namely, grapes, figs, pomegranates, olives and dates [משנ״ב, שם: לא].

### *Shabbat Parashat Shekalim (Mevarkhim Ḥodesh Adar)*

179 Torah reading: On the Shabbat preceding Rosh Ḥodesh Adar (in a leap year,

Rosh Ḥodesh Adar II), a second Torah scroll is taken from the Ark. From it, *Parashat Shekalim*, the first of four special Maftir-Haftara units (ארבע פרשיות), is read. Maftir: Ex. 30:11–16. Haftara: II Kings 12:1–17 [שו״ע או״ח, תרפה: א]. אַב הָרַחֲמִים is omitted.

180 When Rosh Ḥodesh Adar (in a leap year, Rosh Ḥodesh Adar II) falls on Shabbat, three Torah scrolls are taken from the Ark. Six men are called up to the first scroll and the portion of the week is read. A seventh man is called to the second scroll for the reading of Num. 28:9–15. Half Kaddish is said. Maftir (Ex. 30:11–16) is read from the third scroll. Haftara is II Kings 12:1–17 [שם]. אַב הָרַחֲמִים is omitted.

# ADAR

## *Purim Katan (14th–15th of Adar I)*

181 In a leap year, on the dates during Adar I corresponding to Purim and Shushan Purim, both *Taḥanun* and לַמְנַצֵּחַ are omitted [שו״ע או״ח, תרצז: א].

## *Shabbat Parashat Zakhor (Shabbat preceding Purim)*

182 There is an affirmative Torah obligation to recall the actions of Amalek, in attacking the children of Israel after the exodus from Egypt [שו״ע או״ח, קלז: ז]. This mitzva is fulfilled on the Shabbat preceding Purim, when a second Torah scroll is taken from the Ark, from which *Parashat Zakhor* (Deut. 25:17–19), the second of the four special Maftir-Haftara units (ארבע פרשיות), is read. Haftara: I Sam. 15:2–34 [שו״ע או״ח, תרפה: ב]. אַב הָרַחֲמִים is omitted.

183 Because men and women are equally obligated to perform this *mitzva*, many congregations organize an additional reading of *Parashat Zakhor* for those who missed the first reading.

## *Fast of Esther (13th of Adar)*

184 This fast commemorates Esther's fast prior to going to see King Ahasuerus without an invitation (Esther 4:15–16). Unlike other fast days, the fast of Esther is considered a custom, and anyone who experiences serious discomfort is permitted to eat or drink [רמ״א או״ח, תרפו: ב].

185 If the 13th of Adar falls on Shabbat, the fast is observed on the preceding Thursday [שו״ע, שם].

186 The fast begins at dawn (see laws 47–48).

187 Prayers as for the 10th of Tevet (see laws 173–176), except that *Avinu Malkenu* and *Taḥanun* are not said during Minḥa. However, if the 13th of Adar falls on Shabbat and the fast is moved back to Thursday, *Avinu Malkenu* and *Taḥanun* are said.

## *Purim (14th of Adar)*

188 On Purim, עַל הַנִּסִּים is added to the Amida in Ma'ariv, Shaḥarit and Minḥa, as well as the second blessing of *Birkat HaMazon*. If one forgets to say עַל הַנִּסִּים, one does not repeat the Amida or *Birkat HaMazon* [שו״ע או״ח, תרצג: ב].

189 Ma'ariv: for weekdays. After recitation of the Amida, the *Shaliaḥ Tzibbur* says the Full Kaddish. The Reader of the Megilla says three blessings: (1) עַל מִקְרָא מְגִלָּה ("about reading the Megilla"), (2) שֶׁעָשָׂה נִסִּים ("Who performed miracles") and (3) שֶׁהֶחֱיָנוּ (page 987). The Megilla is read and the concluding blessing, הָרָב אֶת רִיבֵנוּ is said. The congregation says אֲשֶׁר הֵנִיא and concludes with a joyous singing of שׁוֹשַׁנַּת יַעֲקֹב. The *Shaliaḥ Tzibbur* leads the congregation in saying וְאַתָּה קָדוֹשׁ (page 753). On Motza'ei Shabbat, this is preceded by וִיהִי נֹעַם (page 753) [שו״ע או״ח, תרצג: א]. This is followed by Full Kaddish (omitting the sentence beginning תִּתְקַבַּל), and *Aleinu* [משנ״ב, שם: א]. On Motza'ei Shabbat, however, וְיִתֶּן־לְךָ (page 759) and Havdala precede *Aleinu* [ערוה״ש, שם: ג].

190 Women are obligated to hear the reading of the Megilla [שו״ע או״ח, תרפט: א].

191 Shaḥarit: for weekdays. After the Repetition of the Amida, the *Shaliaḥ Tzibbur* says Half Kaddish and the Torah is taken from the Ark. The Torah reading (page 1200) is followed by Half Kaddish and returning the Torah to the Ark [שו״ע או״ח, תרצג: ד]. The Megilla reading is repeated, with the introductory blessings and the concluding blessing. אֲשֶׁר הֵנִיא is not said a second time, but שׁוֹשַׁנַּת יַעֲקֹב is. The congregation says *Ashrei* and וּבָא לְצִיּוֹן, followed by Full Kaddish, *Aleinu*, the Daily Psalm and Mourner's Kaddish.

192 On Purim day, one is commanded to fulfill the mitzvot of מתנות לאביונים (gifts to the poor – *tzedaka* given to at least two poor people) [שו״ע או״ח, תרצד: א]; משלוח מנות (sending at least two portions of food to one person) [שם, תרצה: ד]; and סעודת פורים (the Purim feast), at which one should drink "until he cannot distinguish between 'Cursed be Haman' and 'Blessed be Mordekhai'" [שם, תרצה: ב].

## *Shushan Purim (15th of Adar)*

193 Both *Taḥanun* and לַמְנַצֵּחַ are omitted [שו״ע או״ח, תרצו: א].

### *Shabbat Parashat Para*
### (*Shabbat preceding Shabbat Parashat HaḤodesh*)

194 On the penultimate Shabbat of the month of Adar (Adar II in a leap year), a second Torah scroll is taken from the Ark, from which *Parashat Para* (Num. 19:1–22), the third of the four special Maftir-Haftara units, is read. Haftara: Ezek. 36:16–38 [שו״ע או״ח, תרפה: ג]. אַב הָרַחֲמִים is omitted.

### *Shabbat Parashat HaḤodesh* (*Mevarkhim Ḥodesh Nisan*)

195 On the Shabbat preceding Rosh Ḥodesh Nisan, a second Torah scroll is taken from the Ark, from which *Parashat HaḤodesh* (Ex. 12:1–20), the fourth of the four special Maftir-Haftara units, is read. Haftara: Ezek. 45:16–46:18 [שו״ע או״ח, תרפה: ד]. אַב הָרַחֲמִים is omitted.

196 When Rosh Ḥodesh Nisan falls on Shabbat, three Torah scrolls are taken from the Ark. Six men are called up to the first scroll and the portion of the week is read. A seventh man is called to the second scroll for the reading of Num. 28:9–15. Half Kaddish is said. Maftir (Ex. 12:1–20) is read from the third scroll. Haftara is Ezek. 45:16–46:18. אַב הָרַחֲמִים is omitted.

## NISAN

197 During the month of Nisan, *Taḥanun* is omitted on weekdays, and אַב הָרַחֲמִים (page 599) and צִדְקָתְךָ (page 691) are omitted on Shabbat [שו״ע ורמ״א או״ח, תכט: ב].

198 Many have the custom not to eat matza from Rosh Ḥodesh Nisan [משנ״ב, שם: יב]. Some refrain from eating matza from Purim.

199 One may not eat matza on Erev Pesaḥ [רמ״א או״ח, תעא: ב]. On Erev Pesaḥ it is permissible to eat certain kinds of matza which are not considered proper matza, such as matza made with juice instead of water, or which was cooked or fried after it was baked [שו״ע או״ח תעא, ב].

### *Shabbat HaGadol* (*Shabbat preceding Pesaḥ*)

200 The Shabbat preceding Pesaḥ is known as *Shabbat HaGadol* [שו״ע או״ח, תל: א]. A special Haftara is said: Mal. 3:4–24. It is customary for the rabbi to deliver a sermon relating to Pesaḥ.

## *Erev Pesaḥ (14th of Nisan)*

▸ LAWS OF BEDIKAT ḤAMETZ

201 As soon as possible after dark, one is required to do *Bedikat Ḥametz* in one's home (page 817) [שו״ע או״ח, תלא:א]. It is customary for a household member to hide ten pieces of *ḥametz* to be found during the search [רמ״א או״ח, תלב:ב]. Before beginning the search one says the blessing עַל בִּעוּר חָמֵץ [שו״ע או״ח, תלב:א]. The custom is to conduct the search at night by the light of a candle, but use of a flashlight is also permitted. If Pesaḥ falls on Motza'ei Shabbat, the search is made on Thursday night. Those who plan to be away on Pesaḥ should conduct the search the night before their departure, but without making a blessing. After completion of the search, one says כָּל חֲמִירָא (page 817), an Aramaic formula disclaiming one's ownership of any *ḥametz* the whereabouts of which are unknown.

202 Shaḥarit: for weekdays. מִזְמוֹר לְתוֹדָה and לַמְנַצֵּחַ are omitted [רמ״א או״ח, נא:ט].

203 First born males are required to fast (תענית בכורות), unless they attend a *siyum* (celebratory meal to mark the completion of a unit of Torah study), which is traditionally held immediately following Shaḥarit [שו״ע או״ח, תע:א].

204 One is forbidden from eating *ḥametz* from the end of the first third of the day [שו״ע או״ח, תמג:א]. There is a dispute between halakhic authorities whether the day is measured from daybreak to nightfall (Magen Avraham), or from sunrise to sunset (Vilna Gaon). One should follow local communal practice in this regard.

205 One is forbidden from owning *ḥametz* from the end of the first 5/12 of the day, by which time one should burn or otherwise destroy any *ḥametz* remaining in one's possession [שם]. One should say כָּל חֲמִירָא (page 817) a second time before the end of the first 5/12 of the day [שו״ע או״ח, תלד:ב].

206 If the first day of Pesaḥ falls on Thursday, each household must prepare an *Eiruv Tavshilin* (page 817); this makes it permissible to prepare food on Friday for the Shabbat meals [שו״ע או״ח, תקכז].

207 After Minḥa, some have the custom to say the biblical verses describing the sacrifice of the Pesaḥ lamb (Ex. 12:1–13) [משנ״ב או״ח, תעא:כב].

208 If Pesaḥ eve falls on Motza'ei Shabbat, the Fast of the Firstborn is held on the preceding Thursday [שו״ע ורמ״א או״ח, תע:ב]. *Bedikat Ḥametz* is done on Thursday night, and the *ḥametz* is burned (see law 206) on Friday morning without saying כָּל חֲמִירָא, while leaving enough *ḥametz* for Shabbat. On Shabbat morning, after eating the last of one's *ḥametz*, any leftovers must be given to a non-Jew or made inedible (e.g. by flushing it down the toilet), by the end of the first 5/12 of the day [שו״ע או״ח, תמד:ב].

**209** If Erev Pesaḥ falls on Shabbat, for *Se'uda Shelishit* one can eat neither *ḥametz* nor matza (see laws 199, 204). Several solutions have been suggested: to eat matza which is not forbidden (see law 199) [שו״ע או״ח, תמד: א]; to eat the meal without bread [רמ״א, שם]; or to divide the morning meal in two, pausing in the middle and saying *Birkat HaMazon* in between [משנ״ב, שם: ח בשם הגר״א]. Some congregations hold morning services early, in order to allow ample time to eat the morning meal and destroy any *ḥametz* which is left.

## *Pesaḥ (15th–16th of Nisan)*

**210** Candle lighting: Two blessings are said: (1) לְהַדְלִיק נֵר שֶׁל יוֹם טוֹב, and (2) שֶׁהֶחֱיָנוּ. When Pesaḥ eve falls on Friday night, the conclusion of the first blessing is: לְהַדְלִיק נֵר שֶׁל שַׁבָּת וְשֶׁל יוֹם טוֹב.

**211** Ma'ariv: for Shabbat and Yom Tov. The congregation says the special verse for Yom Tov (וַיְדַבֵּר מֹשֶׁה), before saying the Amida for Yom Tov (page 423). In some congregations Hallel is said after the Amida [שו״ע ורמ״א או״ח, תפז: ד]. This is followed by Full Kaddish, *Aleinu*, and Mourner's Kaddish. Kiddush is not said in the synagogue. It is customary to conclude with the singing of Adon Olam or Yigdal.

**212** On the second night of Pesaḥ, one begins counting the Omer (page 357) [שו״ע או״ח, תפט: א]. Some have the custom to count the first night of the Omer at the second Seder. (See laws 221–224.)

**213** When Pesaḥ eve falls on Friday night, Ma'ariv for Shabbat is preceded by the last two psalms of Kabbalat Shabbat: מִזְמוֹר שִׁיר לְיוֹם הַשַּׁבָּת and יהוה מָלָךְ, גֵּאוּת לָבֵשׁ (page 405). בַּמֶּה מַדְלִיקִין is omitted. וְשָׁמְרוּ and the special verse for Yom Tov (וַיְדַבֵּר מֹשֶׁה) (page 423) precede the Yom Tov Amida, which is said with additions for Shabbat. After the Amida, the congregation says וַיְכֻלּוּ הַשָּׁמַיִם, but the *Shaliaḥ Tzibbur* does not say the abbreviated Repetition of the Amida [שו״ע או״ח, תפז: א].

**214** If either of the first two nights of Pesaḥ falls on Motza'ei Shabbat, the congregation adds the paragraph וַתּוֹדִיעֵנוּ in the middle section of the Amida on that night.

**215** Shaḥarit: for Shabbat and Yom Tov (page 475). The *Shaliaḥ Tzibbur* for Shaḥarit begins from the words הָאֵל בְּתַעֲצוּמוֹת עֻזֶּךָ (page 525). After *Barekhu*, the congregation says הַמֵּאִיר לָאָרֶץ or, if it is also Shabbat, הַכֹּל יוֹדוּךָ. The Amida for Yom Tov is said (page 831); if also Shabbat, one says the additions for Shabbat. This is followed by Hallel, Full Kaddish and taking the Torah from the Ark. Most congregations say the "Thirteen Attributes of Mercy" and a special supplication (page 571), except on Shabbat.

**216** Torah Reading: first day – page 1201; second day – page 1204. Five men are called up, seven on Shabbat. Maftir: page 1202. Haftara: first day – page 1203; second day – page 1206 [שו״ע או״ח, תפח: ג; שם, תצ: א].

Hallel, Full Kaddish, the reading of שיר השירים and Mourner's Kaddish [רמ״א או״ח, תצ: ט].

235 Torah Reading: Pages 1212–1214. Seven men are called up. Maftir: page 1212. Haftara: page 1214.

236 After the Haftara, the congregation says *Yekum Purkan*. This is followed by the prayers for the government and the State of Israel. *Ashrei* is said and the Torah scrolls are returned to the Ark. The *Shaliaḥ Tzibbur* says Half Kaddish.

237 Musaf: for Festivals with additions for Shabbat (page 869). However, אַדִּיר אַדִּירֵנוּ is not added to *Kedusha*, and *Birkat Kohanim* is not said. After the Repetition of the Amida, the *Shaliaḥ Tzibbur* says Full Kaddish. This is followed by *Ein Keloheinu* (page 625) and the conclusion of Musaf, as for Shabbat.

238 Minḥa: for Shabbat and Yom Tov (page 665). The Torah is removed from the Ark and the beginning of the portion of the week is read. After returning the Torah to the Ark, the *Shaliaḥ Tzibbur* says Half Kaddish, and the congregation says the Amida for Shabbat with the addition of יַעֲלֶה וְיָבוֹא.

239 Motza'ei Shabbat – Ma'ariv: After the Amida, וִיהִי נֹעַם is omitted, and the *Shaliaḥ Tzibbur* says Full Kaddish. וְיִתֶּן־לְךָ (page 759) is said [רמ״א או״ח, רצה: ט].

## *Seventh and Eighth Days of Pesaḥ (21st–22nd of Nisan)*

240 If the seventh day of Pesaḥ falls on Thursday, each household must prepare an *Eiruv Tavshilin* (page 817); this makes it permissible to prepare food on Friday for the Shabbat meals [שו״ע או״ח, תקכז].

241 Candle lighting: One blessing is said: לְהַדְלִיק נֵר שֶׁל יוֹם טוֹב (שֶׁהֶחֱיָנוּ is not said) [שו״ע או״ח, תצ: ז]. When Pesaḥ eve falls on Friday night, the conclusion of the first blessing is: לְהַדְלִיק נֵר שֶׁל שַׁבָּת וְשֶׁל יוֹם טוֹב.

242 Ma'ariv: for Shabbat and Yom Tov (page 415). The congregation says the special verse for Yom Tov (וַיְדַבֵּר מֹשֶׁה), before saying the Amida for Yom Tov (page 423). This is followed by Full Kaddish, the counting of the Omer, *Aleinu*, and Mourner's Kaddish. It is customary to conclude with the singing of Adon Olam or Yigdal.

243 When the eve of the seventh or eighth day falls on Friday night, Ma'ariv is preceded by the last two psalms of Kabbalat Shabbat: מִזְמוֹר שִׁיר לְיוֹם הַשַּׁבָּת and יהוה מָלָךְ, גֵּאוּת לָבֵשׁ (page 405). בַּמֶּה מַדְלִיקִין is omitted. וְשָׁמְרוּ (page 423) precedes the Yom Tov Amida, which is said with additions for Shabbat. After the Amida, the congregation says וַיְכֻלּוּ הַשָּׁמַיִם, and the *Shaliaḥ Tzibbur* says the abbreviated Repetition of the Amida as is customary on Shabbat eve [שו״ע או״ח, תרמב: א].

## *Yom HaAtzma'ut (5th of Iyar)*

258 If the 5th of Iyar falls on Friday or Shabbat, Yom HaAtzma'ut is moved back to the preceding Thursday. If the 5th of Iyar falls on a Monday, Yom HaAtzma'ut is postponed to Tuesday.

259 On Yom HaAtzma'ut, the mourning customs of *Sefirat HaOmer* are suspended. It is permissible to cut one's hair, shave, attend parties, celebrate weddings and bar/bat mitzvas, and listen to music. The custom is to permit shaving and cutting one's hair before nightfall in honor of the holiday.

260 Ma'ariv: Customs differ (see pages 995–1001). The service adopted by the Israeli Chief Rabbinate is as follows: selections from Psalms and other readings precede Ma'ariv for weekdays. It is customary for the *Shaliaḥ Tzibbur* to lead Ma'ariv using melodies associated with Yom Tov. After the Amida, the *Shaliaḥ Tzibbur* says Full Kaddish. Responsive readings and Psalm 126 to the tune of "*HaTikva*" follow. The service concludes with the counting of the Omer, *Aleinu*, Mourner's Kaddish and communal singing of אֲנִי מַאֲמִין.

261 Shaḥarit: *Pesukei DeZimra* as for Shabbat and Yom Tov, with the addition of מִזְמוֹר לְתוֹדָה (page 483). נִשְׁמַת is not said. After אָז יָשִׁיר (page 517), prayers continue with Shaḥarit for weekdays (page 137). The Repetition of the Amida by the *Shaliaḥ Tzibbur* is followed by Hallel and Half Kaddish. On a Thursday (see law 259,) the Torah is taken from the Ark and the appropriate section of the Torah is read. After the Torah reading, Half Kaddish is said. Haftara is said without blessings (page 1003). The Prayer for the State of Israel (page 593) is said, followed by the Memorial Prayer for fallen soldiers (page 993). Shaḥarit continues as for weekdays (page 235). At the end of the service, the congregation sings אֲנִי מַאֲמִין (page 1005).

262 *Taḥanun* is omitted during Shaḥarit and Minḥa on the 5th of Iyar, even if Yom HaAtzma'ut is celebrated on a different day.

## *Pesaḥ Sheni (14th of Iyar)*

263 *Taḥanun* is omitted during Shaḥarit and Minḥa but not on Minha of the preceding day.

## *Lag BaOmer (18th of Iyar)*

264 The mourning customs of *Sefirat HaOmer* are suspended. It is permissible to cut one's hair, shave, attend parties, celebrate weddings and bar/bat mitzvas, and listen to music [שו״ע ורמ״א או״ח, תצג: ב].

265 For some communites, the mourning period that started at Pesaḥ, ends after Lag BaOmer. For others, it continues until three days before Shavuot [שם] (see law 252).

266 When Lag BaOmer falls on Sunday, shaving and cutting one's hair are permitted on the preceding Friday, in honor of Shabbat.

267 *Taḥanun* is omitted during Shaḥarit and Minḥa [משנ״ב או״ח, תצג:ט].

### *Yom Yerushalayim (28th of Iyar)*

268 The mourning customs of *Sefirat HaOmer* are suspended. It is permissible to cut one's hair, shave, attend parties, celebrate weddings and bar/bat mitzvas, and listen to music.

269 Shaharit: *Pesukei DeZimra* as for Shabbat and Yom Tov, with the addition of מִזְמוֹר לְתוֹדָה (page 483). נִשְׁמַת is not said. After אָז יָשִׁיר (page 517), prayers continue with Shaḥarit as for weekdays (page 137). The Repetition of the Amida is followed by Hallel and Half Kaddish. On Monday or Thursday, the Torah is taken from the Ark and the appropriate section of the Torah is read. After the Torah reading, Half Kaddish is said, followed by the Prayer for the State of Israel. On Monday or Thursday, the Torah is returned to the Ark. *Ashrei* and וּבָא לְצִיּוֹן are said, followed by Full Kaddish, *Aleinu*, Mourner's Kaddish, the Daily Psalm, and Mourner's Kaddish.

270 *Taḥanun* is omitted during Shaḥarit and Minḥa.

271 On the Shabbat preceding Rosh Ḥodesh Sivan, אַב הָרַחֲמִים is said (see law 599).

## SIVAN

272 From Rosh Ḥodesh Sivan until the day after Shavuot, *Taḥanun* is omitted in Shaḥarit and Minḥa [רמ״א או״ח, תצד:ג].

### *Sheloshet Yemei Hagbala (3rd–5th of Sivan)*

273 The three days prior to Shavuot commemorate the three days before the Torah was given at Sinai, when the Jewish people were enjoined to prepare themselves for the Divine Revelation.

274 For those who observe the customs of mourning after Lag BaOmer, the mourning period ends on the 3rd of Sivan.

**291** Torah Reading: Page 1190 (see law 50).

**292** Minḥa: for weekdays, except that after *Ashrei* and Half Kaddish, the Torah is read. The reading is the same as that of the morning. The third *oleh* reads the Haftara (page 1190) [רמ״א, או״ח, תקסו: א]. After the Torah is returned to the Ark, the *Shaliaḥ Tzibbur* says Half Kaddish, and Minḥa continues as for weekdays.

**293** During the silent Amida, those who are fasting say עֲנֵנוּ as part of the sixteenth blessing, שׁוֹמֵעַ תְּפִלָּה (page 295). During the Repetition of the Amida, the *Shaliaḥ Tzibbur* says עֲנֵנוּ between the seventh and eighth blessings, as in the morning (page 287). After the eighteenth blessing (מודים), the *Shaliaḥ Tzibbur* says the paragraph relating to *Birkat Kohanim* (page 301). For the final blessings of the Amida, שִׂים שָׁלוֹם is said instead of שָׁלוֹם רָב. After the Amida, the congregation says *Avinu Malkenu*. This is followed by *Taḥanun*, Full Kaddish and *Aleinu*.

**294** From the 17th of Tammuz until Tisha B'Av (the "Three Weeks"), certain mourning rituals are observed: one does not cut one's hair, shave, listen to music, buy new things, or hold weddings and other parties [שו״ע או״ח תקנא, א]. Some permit shaving during this period.

# AV

**295** From Rosh Ḥodesh Av through Tisha B'Av (the "Nine Days") additional mourning rituals are observed: one abstains from eating meat or drinking wine, clothes are not laundered or pressed, and one generally minimizes joyful activities [שו״ע ורמ״א או״ח, תקנא].

## *Shabbat Ḥazon (Shabbat preceding Tisha B'Av)*

**296** The Shabbat preceding Tisha B'Av is known as *Shabbat Ḥazon*, named for the first word of the Haftara, חֲזוֹן. On Friday night, many congregations sing *Lekha Dodi* to the melody of אֱלִי צִיּוֹן. The special Haftara (Is. 1:1–27) is read to the tune of *Eikha*.

**297** On Motza'ei Shabbat, *Kiddush Levana* is not said [רמ״א או״ח, תקנא: ח].

## *Erev Tisha B'Av (8th of Av)*

**298** *Taḥanun* is omitted from Minḥa.

**299** The *Se'uda Mafseket* (final meal) is eaten after Minḥa. The custom is to eat no more than one cooked item. Three adult males should not eat together, so that no *zimmun* is said. Some have the custom to sit on the floor and eat eggs with ashes [שו״ע ורמ״א או״ח, תקנב].

300 When the final meal is eaten on Shabbat afternoon, these restrictions do not apply; however, the meal must be finished before sunset [שם: י].

## *Tisha B'Av (9th of Av)*

301 According to the Mishna (*Ta'anit* 4:6), the fast of the 9th of Av commemorates five calamities that befell the Jewish people on that date: (1) God decreed that the children of Israel would not be allowed to enter the land of Israel, (2) the First Temple was destroyed, (3) the Second Temple was destroyed, (4) Beitar was captured, and (5) Jerusalem was plowed over.

302 The fast begins at sunset. In addition to eating and drinking, one is prohibited from washing and anointing oneself and from wearing leather shoes. Marital relations are likewise forbidden. One abstains from Torah study, except for topics such as mourning laws, *Eikha*, Job, and the unhappy portions of Jeremiah [שו״ע או״ח, תקנד: א–ב]. One does not greet other people or inquire after their welfare [שם: כ].

303 Ma'ariv: for weekdays. The Amida is followed by Full Kaddish, the reading of *Eikha* and the recitation of *Kinot*. The congregation says וְאַתָּה קָדוֹשׁ (page 753), followed by Full Kaddish (omitting the line beginning תִּתְקַבַּל), *Aleinu* (page 765), and Mourner's Kaddish. When Tisha B'Av falls on Motza'ei Shabbat, וְיִתֶּן־לְךָ is omitted.

304 If the fast falls (or is observed) on Motza'ei Shabbat, וִיהִי נֹעַם is omitted, and Havdala is not said. The blessing בּוֹרֵא מְאוֹרֵי הָאֵשׁ is said on a flame [שו״ע או״ח, תקנו: א].

305 Shaharit: Neither tallit nor tefillin is worn in the morning [שו״ע או״ח, תקנה: א]. During the Repetition of the Amida, the *Shaliah Tzibbur* says עֲנֵנוּ between the seventh and eighth blessings (page 181). *Tahanun* is omitted.

306 Torah Reading: page 1191. Three men are called up. The third *oleh* reads the Haftara: page 1192 [רמ״א או״ח תקנד, ד]. Afterwards, the first three blessings following the Haftara (page 587) are said. After the Torah is returned to the Ark, *Kinot* are said. This is followed by *Ashrei*, וּבָא לְצִיּוֹן (omitting the verse וַאֲנִי זֹאת בְּרִיתִי, see page 237), Full Kaddish (omitting the line beginning תִּתְקַבַּל), *Aleinu*, and Mourner's Kaddish.

307 During Minha both tallit and tefillin are worn.

308 Minha starts with the Daily Psalm (pages 249–261), *Ashrei* and Half Kaddish. The Torah is read: page 1190. Three men are called up; the third reads the

Haftara: page 1190. After the Torah is returned to the Ark, the *Shaliaḥ Tzibbur* says Half Kaddish.

309 During the silent recitation of the Amida (page 283), the congregation says נַחֵם as part of the fourteenth blessing (בּוֹנֵה יְרוּשָׁלָיִם), עֲנֵנוּ as part of the sixteenth blessing (שׁוֹמֵעַ תְּפִלָּה) (unless one is not fasting), and שִׂים שָׁלוֹם in place of שָׁלוֹם רָב (page 301). During the Repetition of the Amida, the *Shaliaḥ Tzibbur* says עֲנֵנוּ between the seventh (גּוֹאֵל יִשְׂרָאֵל) and eighth (רוֹפֵא חוֹלֵי עַמּוֹ יִשְׂרָאֵל) blessings, נַחֵם as part of the fourteenth blessing, the paragraph relating to *Birkat Kohanim* [שו״ע ורמ״א או״ח, תקנו: א], and שִׂים שָׁלוֹם. Minḥa ends with Full Kaddish and *Aleinu*.

310 After Ma'ariv, *Kiddush Levana* is said (page 771). When Tisha B'Av begins on Motza'ei Shabbat, Havdala is said on Sunday night, preferably over a cup of wine or grape juice; no blessing is made over spices or a flame.

311 Although the fast is broken after nightfall, it is customary to continue the other mourning customs until midday of the 10th of Av. However, if the 10th of Av falls on Friday, one is permitted to bathe and otherwise prepare for Shabbat prior to midday [רמ״א או״ח, תקנח: א].

## *Shabbat Naḥamu (Shabbat following Tisha B'Av)*

312 Named for the first word of the Haftara, נַחֲמוּ. The first of the seven Shabbatot (שבע דנחמתא) between Tisha B'Av and Rosh HaShana, on which a Haftara is read from Isaiah containing words of consolation.

## *Tu B'Av (15th of Av)*

313 According to the Mishna (*Ta'anit* 4:8), on the 15th of Av, the young women of Jerusalem would put on borrowed white dresses and dance together in the vineyards. Young men would come out to watch them, and the women would urge the men not to be swayed by beauty, but to be drawn to women of good family.

314 *Taḥanun* is omitted during Shaharit and Minḥa. If it falls on Shabbat, אַב הָרַחֲמִים is omitted during Shaharit, and צִדְקָתְךָ during Minḥa.

# DAILY PRAYER

## ON WAKING

315 The custom is to say מוֹדֶה אֲנִי immediately on waking, even before washing hands [משנ״ב או״ח, א: ח].

### *Laws of Washing Hands;* בִּרְכַּת אֲשֶׁר יָצַר; אֱלֹהַי נְשָׁמָה

316 Upon waking, one is obligated to wash hands [שבת, קח:]. Some hold that one should not walk four *amot* (around six feet) prior to washing hands [משנ״ב או״ח, א: ב (בשם הזוהר)].

317 According to some authorities, there is a separate obligation to wash hands prior to prayer [ערוה״ש או״ח, ד: ה]. One who washes and says the blessing of עַל נְטִילַת יָדָיִם after waking, does not repeat the blessing when washing prior to prayer [רמ״א או״ח, ו: ב].

318 Hands should preferably be washed using a cup, but a cup is not required [שו״ע ורמ״א, או״ח: ד, ז]. The custom is to pour water from the cup onto the right hand, then the left, and repeat a total of three times [משנ״ב, שם: י]. Where water is unavailable, one may clean one's hands using any appropriate material; in that case, the blessing is changed to עַל נְקִיּוּת יָדָיִם [שו״ע או״ח, ד: כב].

319 The blessing of עַל נְטִילַת יָדָיִם may be said before drying one's hands or afterward [משנ״ב, ד: ב].

320 A number of reasons have been offered for washing hands upon waking. The Gemara states that, during the night, hands are enveloped by an "evil vapor," רוח רעה, which is removed by washing one's hands [שבת, קח:]. In addition, there is a concern that, while sleeping, one's hands may have touched an unclean part of

the body [ראש ברכות, פ״ט: כג]. Finally, it is noted that a person who wakes is like a newborn; therefore, one needs to sanctify oneself by washing [שו״ת רשב״א ח״א, קצא].

321 The blessing of אֲשֶׁר יָצַר should be said each time after relieving oneself. It is recommended that one should go to the bathroom immediately after washing hands, then say the blessings of עַל נְטִילַת יָדַיִם followed by אֲשֶׁר יָצַר. However, even if one does not relieve oneself, one is permitted to say אֲשֶׁר יָצַר after washing hands [רמ״א או״ח, ד: א]. One should not postpone going to the bathroom [שו״ע או״ח, ג: יז].

322 According to the Gemara, the blessing of אֱלֹהַי נְשָׁמָה should be said upon waking [ברכות, ס:]. The contemporary custom is to say אֱלֹהַי נְשָׁמָה immediately after אֲשֶׁר יָצַר [משנ״ב, שם: יב]. However, some rule that one who stays up all night should not say אֱלֹהַי נְשָׁמָה and the blessing הַמַּעֲבִיר שֵׁנָה מֵעֵינַי, and should instead hear them from others [משנ״ב, מו: כד].

323 The custom is to say the *Birkhot HaTorah* after אֲשֶׁר יָצַר, because one should not read or recite Torah verses before making the requisite blessings on Torah study [שו״ע ורמ״א, או״ח: מו, ט].

## *Laws of Tzitzit*

324 Putting on a four-cornered garment with tzitzit attached fulfills an affirmative mitzva from the Torah. The obligation applies only during the daytime [מנחות, מג.]. Since wearing tzitzit is a time-bound mitzva, women are exempt [שו״ע או״ח, יז: ב].

325 The accepted practice is to wear a *tallit katan* all day long and to wear a *tallit gadol* during Shaḥarit [שו״ע או״ח, כד: א]. The dominant Ashkenazi custom is to begin wearing a *tallit gadol* when one marries [משנ״ב, יז: י], but Jews of German and Sephardi descent begin wearing the *tallit gadol* at an earlier age. Nevertheless, the custom is to wear a *tallit gadol* – even if unmarried – when acting as *Shaliaḥ Tzibbur*, reading from or being called up to the Torah, opening the Ark or performing *hagbaha* or *gelila*.

326 One should put on the *tallit katan* immediately upon dressing. One should first examine the strings of the tzitzit to ensure that they are not torn [שו״ע או״ח, ח: ט]. Then, while standing [שו״ע או״ח, ח: א], one should say the blessing of עַל מִצְוַת צִיצִית and immediately put on the garment [רמ״א או״ח, ח: ו]. One does not say the blessing if (a) one is about to put on a *tallit gadol*, and (b) one will have in mind the *tallit katan* when saying the blessing on the *tallit gadol*. On the other hand, if there is a substantial interruption between the time one puts on the *tallit katan* and one puts on the *tallit gadol*, one should say the separate blessing on the *tallit katan* [שו״ע או״ח, ח: יג].